CONSTITUTIONAL LAW & JUDICIAL POLICY MAKING

CONSTITUTIONAL LAW & JUDICIAL POLICY MAKING

Second Edition

Edited and Written by

JOEL B. GROSSMAN
University of Wisconsin, Madison

RICHARD S. WELLS
University of Oklahoma

JOHN WILEY & SONS

New York • Chichester • Brisbane • Toronto • Singapore

Copyright © 1972, 1980 by John Wiley & Sons, Inc.

All rights reserved. Published simultaneously in Canada.

Reproduction or translation of any part of
this work beyond that permitted by Sections
107 and 108 of the 1976 United States Copyright
Act without the permission of the copyright
owner is unlawful. Requests for permission
or further information should be addressed to
the Permissions Department, John Wiley & Sons.

Library of Congress Cataloging in Publication Data:

Grossman, Joel B   comp.
  Constitutional law and judicial policy making.

  Includes bibliographical references and indexes.
  1.   United States—Constitutional law.   2.   Judicial
process—United States.   I.   Wells, Richard S., joint
comp.   II.   Title.
KF4550.G76   1980   347'.73'12   79-20206
ISBN 0-471-32849-9

Printed in the United States of America

10 9 8 7 6 5 4 3 2

preface to the second edition

We have been enormously pleased with the reception given the first edition of *Constitutional Law and Judicial Policy Making,* and we hope that in fashioning this second edition we have retained the most popular features of the first. "Improving" a text is hazardous, yet we have attempted just that, stimulated and guided by the criticism of students and teachers who have used the book.

The fundamental conception of the first edition, that the study of constitutional law is best carried out by stressing the social and political context of Supreme Court decisions, remains firm in our thinking. Judicial decisions are events—often central events—in ongoing political processes, and ought to be presented as such. Each chapter, including many chapter subsections as well, is designed to present that context for the cases included in it. In reading a case, and the contextual supporting materials, the student ought to obtain a good understanding of not only the issues, and what the Supreme Court decided, but also the political interests at stake, some elements of litigation strategy, and at least some preliminary appreciation of the impact each case had. Cases are thus seen as the medium through which the Supreme Court acts as a primary maker of public policy, and we have chosen cases which best illustrate the nuances, and the ebb and flow, of judicial policies. Salient policy issues, rather than formal constitutional structures, remain the basis for organizing the chapters in Part II.

A major problem with the first edition, identified by many critics, was an overly selective view of the Court's work. Our deliberate omission of some of the traditional subject matter of constitutional law books left many potential users—and some users—uncomfortable if not downright unhappy. We have responded to this criticism in part by creating a new section dealing with the religion clauses of the First Amendment. And we have included a full treatment of *The Slaughterhouse Cases* (1873), whose omission in the first edition, more than any other case, elicited negative comment. Indeed, our own experience in teaching with the book convinced us that students needed a full treatment of this seminal event in the jurisprudence of the Supreme Court.

Another problem noted by our readers was that our editing of cases and other materials too often presumed that the implicit and tacit meaning of these items would be evident to the student. In this edition we have made strenuous efforts to provide explanatory notes before most cases—and following the more important ones as well—to assist the student in interpreting the meaning of the Court's decision. In this respect, the balance between cases and explanatory notes has shifted toward increased emphasis on the latter.

Constitutional law is a dynamic subject at any time, and it has been particularly so in the eight years since the first edition went to press. The first edition was dominated by decisions of, and our preoccupation with, the Warren Court. The Burger Court, by 1971, had yet to establish a firm and identifiable philosophy, although even some of its early decisions presaged important doctrinal changes. Thus, we could identify a number of potentially critical confrontations between the emerging philosophy of the Burger Court and its predecessor, particularly over such salient criminal justice issues as the "Miranda" rules, and the exclusionary rule. Now, nearly a decade later, the dominant themes of the Burger Court with regard to these doctrines are more clear.

The new policy directions of the Burger Court forced us to re-examine and often reconstruct every policy chapter. Thus, the Court's new hard line on access to the federal courts, its closing off of the inviting avenues of *Flast v. Cohen* (1968), and its tightening of policies toward standing (while loosening the restrictions of "mootness") required substantial changes and some enlargement of the section on doctrines of self-limitation. School busing and affirmative action questions required considerable enlargement of the materials on racial equality. When the first edition went to press, the Supreme Court had decided only one gender classification case, *Reed v. Reed* (1971). But that opened the floodgates and we have selected a half dozen more to illustrate how the Court has grappled with such issues.

As expected, a major focus of the Burger Court, especially after the third and fourth appointments by President Nixon were made in 1971, was criminal justice. Efforts to chip away at *Miranda v. Arizona* (1966) and undermine, if not overrule, *Mapp v. Ohio* (1961), have been among the most visible enterprises of the Court in recent years. So, too, has been its grappling with the complex legal and moral questions of capital punishment. Search and seizure issues have become especially prominent, and there is increased emphasis on such cases. And some account is taken of the Court's involvement in prisoners' rights cases.

Our chapter on the presidency has been substantially changed to include the increased focus of the 1970s on the domestic side of presidential power, particularly as new limits on its exercise were pressed in the wake of the Watergate scandals. But we have also expanded our treatment of treaties and executive agreements, and of various efforts by Congress to restore some of the balance between it and the presidency in foreign policy decision making.

The chapter on personal rights has been almost entirely recast, and substantially expanded. We have added a section on religious freedom cases, and expanded the treatment of issues involving the press—prior restraints, libel, the asserted privilege of confidentiality for reporters, and issues of access to, and by, the media.

In the first edition we concluded with a chapter on "frontiers" which considered newly emerging issues, such as gender equality, and older but not yet resolved issues such as reapportionment and wealth/status equality. None of these issues can still be described as a constitutional frontier. Individual cases in each area continue to come to the Court, but the main policy determinations have been made. All have been incorporated into our enlarged chapter on "equality."

For reasons described more fully in the concluding chapter of this second edition, which we have entitled "The Burger Court and the Old Frontier," we have been unable to identify a current salient frontier issue—at least not one recognized by a majority of the members of the Supreme Court. Of course the Court is constantly challenged by new issues. In some instances, such as affirmative action, it has taken up the challenge; in others, it has not. But in none of these issues do we detect the same sense of "prospect" suggested by our first edition frontier cases. In a very fundamental sense this may simply reflect philosophical differences between the Warren Court's "idea of progress,"[1] and the Burger Court's preference for reducing the role of the Court to somewhat more orthodox dimensions.

This is a much larger book than the first edition. The additional size results both from our efforts to be comprehensive and from design changes intended to make the book more readable. Students should still be able to afford it, especially since it is likely to be used for a two semester or two quarter course. We also *hope* that they can carry it. But as so many of the students who take constitutional law courses plan to attend law school after graduation, they might as well develop their muscles as well as their minds.

Joel B. Grossman
Richard S. Wells
December, 1979

[1]See Alexander M. Bickel, *The Supreme Court and the Idea of Progress* (New York: Harper and Row, 1970).

preface to the first edition

Three recent developments in American political science have provided materials that meet some of the inadequacies inherent in traditional "casebooks." First, the behavioral revolution in political science directed attention to many neglected facets of the judicial process, with a particular emphasis on Supreme Court decision making. Second, political scientists have developed conceptions of the "judiciary" that extend its processes and recognize its impact well beyond the courtroom. The pervasive societal context of the judiciary is readily apparent, and a parochial focus on one narrow arena is clearly inadequate. Third, within the societal context of judicial action, political scientists seem increasingly interested in the contributions of the Supreme Court to the development of public policy in the United States, rather than in Supreme Court decisions for their own sake.

Our view of Supreme Court policy making recognizes that there are both similarities and differences between the Court and other political institutions. Studying the decision-making processes of the court from the perspective of political decision making generally has produced enormous gains in our understanding, but at the same time the unique aspects of the judicial process should be recognized. For the same reasons judicial policy *outputs* may have unique properties, but they also share characteristics with policy decisions made by nonjudicial institutions. We have attempted to show this integration of decision making and policy within the Court and between the Court and other institutions. The Court is not simply an end in itself, to be studied on a presumption of its importance. Instead, it should be viewed as a significant part of a larger and much more complex social system. The Court is important, yet its importance is neither uniform nor self-evident. As some of the succeeding chapters will show, there are some areas in which the Supreme Court has exercised considerable influence and others where it has had little or no impact.

Viewed from this general perspective, particular problems emerge for the writer-editor in explicating the ways of the Supreme Court. First, there is the question of a rationale for inclusion and exclusion of materials. Second, there is the problem of the "case"—how it is to be viewed and what its function is, both for purposes of the Court and for providing an understanding of its actions. Third, what balance should be struck between historical factors, technically legal considerations (the nice points that attract the aspiring Perry Masons in undergraduate classes), and behavioral matters of professional political science.

Developing a "rationale" worthy of that word proved to be a difficult undertaking. Initially we stipulated that certain cases would be included and would not be the highly abbreviated hatchet jobs found in some casebooks. The notion was to allow the student to see the *full* development of judicial policy and craftsmanship in a limited number of areas. We planned to have generous exerpts from the "classical" as well as the contemporary, "cutting-edge", critical literature. We would be interdisciplinary, and draw generously from the range of social sciences, and perhaps even more exotic reaches of academic and other professional endeavors. However, space and cost as well as our own teaching experiences impinged on the grandness of our original notions. We found that shortened editorial versions of cases accompanied by editorial notes were clearer than a series of cases and articles designed to highlight subtle meanings. The generous and dispassionately friendly criticism of colleagues and "readers" helped us even more in transforming grand rationale into practical editorial guides.

Basically, we have tried to minimize case materials in comparison with other textbooks. Our intention has been to demonstrate that the Court deals with ideas in order to shape events and that these ideas have consequences. The introductions to each chapter are intended to provide a setting within which the variety of materials are made to seem coherent; they are also efforts to reduce the sheer amount of materials that we would have had to use in order to show the background against which all policy action is taken. "Policy" chapters are organized around problem areas rather than by constitutional label. Our purpose is not a catalogue of decisions but a selective view of how the Court has contributed to the allocation of power and the determination of important policy issues. No attempt has been made to cover all of the things that the Supreme Court does.

The Supreme Court speaks to a variety of public issues. More often than not, no single case is sufficient to delineate action that one would presume to consider policy making. We have thus tried to use a series of court decisions wherever possible so that we can provide a glimpse of judicial policy in the Court's "own words." Occasionally, however, the Court does not enunciate clearly in a decision, and it is necessary to resort to critical literature to clarify what is important but vague. Where the Court seems ambivalent in its actions we attempt to provide secondary materials that demonstrate the complexities of the issues with which the Court is apparently wrestling. We hope through the use of such secondary materials to show the enormity of the Court's task in a society that is changing rapidly and the implicit limits on its judicial style of policy making.

Our conception of the "case" is that it is a single instance of Court action in a social setting, or context, that is complex and ambiguous. Obviously, a major portion of the context is additional cases, but the social circumstances that represent the problem that the decision speaks to are delineated by a range of social actors other than judges.

In our view the judge cannot be the exclusive focal point of any current textbook on law and the judicial process. The increasing attention to the societal context of the legal process and to questions of compliance and impact makes the judge perhaps more an instrumental presence who conveys ideas. Therefore his policies become the result of many factors of which he and the influence of his background are only a part. Our view has increasingly been that attention should shift from near exclusive concern with the judge to explication of the range of circumstances and situations in which parties seeking particular social results must act. Thus, our materials are selected with an eye to a wider span than that often found in traditional or process-oriented textbooks.

A problem that exists for anyone developing a textbook in constitutional law is the balance to be struck between materials that are traditional and of historic importance and those reflecting current processes of development. Wherever possible we have conveyed traditional conceptions as background. Some notions that have long been abandoned still have relevance in explaining current developments, and these have been included. Others seemed to us to be primarily of historical interest, and these have on the whole been ignored.

For example, we have included such cases as *Gibbons* v. *Ogden* (1824) and the *Cooley* case (1851) because we felt them essential to any treatment of economic policy making by the Supreme Court. Likewise, the *Civil Rights Cases* (1883) and *Plessy* v. *Ferguson* (1896) seemed important enough as examples of how the Court in the past met problems still current, while the *Slaughterhouse Cases* (1873) seemed adequately conveyed by a more concise summary. Older cases were included where it seemed particularly important to convey a sense of doctrinal development or to show the constancy of problems and issues that have confronted the Supreme Court throughout its history. By contrast, we have included many very recent cases which indicate where the Supreme Court is moving now, although we recognize that this may only be concerned speculation and that these cases may never achieve any lasting historical importance. Our experience in teaching has convinced us that, on the whole, students are most interested in the current relevance of the Supreme Court; we share that view and we think, on balance, that this book reflects it as well. In the interest of brevity and readability, footnotes have been omitted from articles and cases included in the book.

The materials finally included in the book represent less than half of those initially compiled. The need to produce a book which the student could both afford *and* carry has forced us not only to cut cases and materials more than we intended but also to delete a few topics of obvious importance. We have done this in the belief that it was more important to be thorough than exhaustive. What remains is, in our view, appropriate for a two-semester or two-quarter course, leaving room for the course instructor to assign a variety of supplementary materials. With some omissions the book should also be suitable for a one-semester course. We have tried to be eclectic, yet it would have been impossible to make the book all things to all teachers. We shall see.

Joel B. Grossman
Richard S. Wells

acknowledgments

Many changes in this edition resulted from comments and suggestions of those who used the first edition, students as well as teachers. In particular we are indebted to our own students. They gave the most direct responses to our efforts with a spirit of helpfulness. Although there are too many students to name individually, we acknowledge their contributions collectively.

Once again we acknowledge the help of our teacher, John R. Schmidhauser, who helped us form ideas of what a good text should be. Although we are by now far from being new arrivals to the study and teaching of constitutional politics, we are still guided by the contextual approach that we first learned under his influence. Kenneth Dolbeare helped us form our conception of a text, and we thank him for his early good counsel.

Many friends, professional colleagues, and student assistants contributed to our thinking about this book and to its execution. Special thanks go to Alan Buckley, Stephen Daniels, Philip Dubois, Ronald Fiscus, Christine Harrington, David Den Hartigh, Don Kash, James Robert Kirk, Lila Klanderman, Stephen McDougal, John Shockley, Pamela Solberg, Paul Tharp, Stanley Vardys, Stephen Wasby, and Jack White. Many hands contributed to typing and preparation of the manuscript. We are grateful to Leslie Byster, Renee Gibson, Shari Graney, Terry Gromala, Judith Lerdahl, Jean Mindel, Elizabeth Pringle, Geri Rowden, Dorothy Shaw, Christine Thornburg, and Edith Wilimovsky. We are particularly grateful for the help of the Barkouras Foundation of Oklahoma City, especially for the counsel and friendship of Dr. George Barkouras and Dr. Robert Phillips.

Stuart Scheingold, William Dunn, and Bradley Canon read the entire manuscript for the publisher and made many helpful suggestions for revision. The editorial staff at John Wiley provided us with the full range of support and encouragement, particularly Malcolm Easterlin, Elaine Miller, Elizabeth Do-ble, Cathy Starnella, and Susan Giniger. These professionals transformed an impossibly large and messy manuscript into a book. Finally, Wayne Anderson, Wiley's political science editor, is hereby designated the godfather of this edition. His subtle blend of prodding and encouragement and of making the best of delays and coming up with offers for redemption that we couldn't refuse kept the project going at times when lesser editors would have merely let out a contract. Bringing this book to print has not been an easy task for him. We hope the results sufficiently justify his labors.

Once again our wives, Mary and Maurine, and our children, Alison, Joanna, and Daniel Grossman, and Caroline and John Wells, have endured and survived our writing. We particularly thank our wives for their patience and forbearance. As for our children, who can now read and perhaps judge our efforts, we thank them for not asking too often why "the book" took that much time and effort.

J.B.G.
R.S.W.

overview of contents

contents

PART TWO

CHAPTER ONE
THE SUPREME COURT AND THE ECONOMY

CHAPTER FOUR
PRESIDENTIAL POWER IN AN AGE OF INTERNATIONALISM

part one

a political view of the supreme court

1. THE SUPREME COURT AS A POLITICAL INSTITUTION

A. *Introductory Essay*

The Supreme Court of the United States is different from all other courts, past and present. It decides fundamental social and political questions that would never be put to judges in other countries—the boundaries between church and state, the relations between the white and Negro races, the powers of the national legislature and executive. One could easily forget that it is a court at all. Its public image seems sometimes to be less that of a court than of an extraordinarily powerful demigod sitting on a remote throne and letting loose constitutional thunderbolts whenever it sees a wrong crying for correction.

But the Supreme Court is not a demigod, nor even a roving inspector general with a conscience. It is a court, and for all its power it must operate in significant respects as courts have always operated. It cannot, like a legislature or governor or President, initiate measures to cure the ills it perceives. It is . . . a substantially passive instrument to be moved only by the initiative of litigants. In short, the Court must sit and wait for issues to be presented to it in lawsuits.

Anthony Lewis, *Gideon's Trumpet*[1]

[1]Anthony Lewis, *Gideon's Trumpet* (New York: Random House, 1964), pp. 11–12.

The Supreme Court of the United States is popularly considered the guardian of our constitutional process, the ultimate repository of legal wisdom, and the institution that has the "final" word on all legal questions. Like most popular views of the political system, this one is part fiction, part fact, and part fancy. Like many myths, however, this view of the Court is extremely functional. Not only does it "explain" the Court to most people in terms satisfactory to them, but in time of crisis it is said to protect the Court from the retributive acts of its enemies.

The difficulty most people have in understanding the Court lies partly in the fact that, as Anthony Lewis has written it is "different from all other courts, past and present," and it does "decide fundamental social and political questions that would never be put to judges in other countries. . . ." And, to complicate matters, Lewis might have added, it performs its functions in a physical setting with appropriate majestic and honorific rituals designed to convey the image of a *court* rather than the image of a quasi-judicial body as much concerned with politics as with law.

In the 1970s it is difficult to deny that the Supreme Court is an important political institution. As Robert Dahl wrote more than two decades ago, "As a political institution, the Court is highly unusual, not least because Americans are not quite willing to accept the fact that it *is* a political institution and not quite capable of denying it." And he observed further that as a result of this confusion, "frequently we take both positions at once. This is confusing to foreigners, amusing to logicians, and rewarding to ordinary Americans who thus manage to retain the best of both worlds."[2]

The Supreme Court's political role is neither new nor newly discovered. Describing the Court's development in his classic work, Charles Haines observed:

From the time of its formation, the Constitution of the United States has been, to a considerable extent at least, a political document designed as the "vehicle of the life of a nation" and not a mere "lawyer's document." As such a political document it has been interpreted and applied in a political manner by all departments of the government, including the Judiciary. There is ample evidence to sustain the view that "Congresses and Senates, and Presidents have used the Supreme Bench as constituting a part of the political machinery of the great parties of the country." Though there are marked evidences of partisanship in the process of constitutional construction, it is also apparent that certain fundamental assumptions or postulates give color and direction to the trend of interpretation; and these assumptions are the results of deepseated personal convictions and attitudes which may have little relation to partisan views or political affiliations.[3]

Recognition of the Court's political role is basic to any understanding of its place in the American political system. The statement does not imply that there are no differences between the Court and nonlegal political institutions. It is a court of law and exhibits properties and performs functions in ways different if not distinct from legislative or administrative bodies. Describing the Court as a political institution implies recognition of the interrelationship and, indeed,

[2]Robert A. Dahl, "Decision-Making in a Democracy: The Supreme Court as National Policy-Maker, **6** *Journal of Public Law* (1967), 279.
[3]Charles G. Haines, *The Role of the Supreme Court in American Government and Politics, 1798–1835* (Berkeley: University of California Press, 1944), p. 45.

integration, of law and politics, not the exclusion of either. It may be, as Philip Kurland has written, that the Supreme Court operates on a continuum between the "political mode" and the "judicial mode."[4] The exact spot on the continuum will be determined by the issue before the Court, its composition and ideological complexion. Although the strength of the pull toward either mode will vary, the Court must inescapably operate with both in mind.

Adopting this political perspective requires the reassessment of theories that have stated, in various forms, that the judge is restricted largely to a mechanical function of "finding" the law and applying it in a detached and neutral manner to cases that pass before him. Judges—and Supreme Court justices in particular—have considerable policy discretion in deciding cases, a discretion that varies with the type of case or issue, with the existence of strength or weaknesses of precedents, and with their own views of appropriate judicial action. Even the late Justice Felix Frankfurter, an ardent advocate of judicial self-restraint, recognized "that judges are not merely expert reporters of pre-existing law. Because of the free play allowed by the Constitution, judges inevitably fashion law. And law is one of the shaping forces of society."[5] But for both practical and nostalgic reasons, the idea that judges have but a mechanical function to perform still has its adherents, among professionals and in the general public. As Daniel Boorstin has noted, Americans "retain an incurable belief that constitutions are born but not made."[6] Yet even such adherents would be hard pressed to defend Justice Robert's famous response to charges that a majority of justices on the Court on which he sat were reading their own policy preferences into the law:

When an act of Congress is appropriately challenged in the Courts as not conforming to the constitutional mandate the judicial branch of the Government has only one duty—to lay the article of the Constitution which is invoked beside the statute which is challenged and to decide whether the latter squares with the former. All the Court does, or can do, is to announce its considered judgment upon the question. This Court neither approves nor condemns any legislative policy.[7]

There are three practical reasons to explain the persistence of the myth of mechanical jurisprudence. First, when the Court has come under attack for its decisions, it has often proved useful to argue in its defense that the judges are not really responsible for the unpopular decisions, that they had little or no choice. Second, given the low esteem in which Americans generally hold their political leaders, and politics in general, it is usually to the advantage of the judiciary to maintain its distinctive character and allegedly distinctive function. And, third, the myth complements and supports the orthodox view of our government as one of separation of powers.

The political utility of the myth should not be discounted. It materially increases the range of choices that the Court may exercise, whether these choices result in positive policy actions or in an avoidance of judicial involvement in a

---

[4]Philip B. Kurland, *Politics, The Constitution and the Warren Court* (Chicago: University of Chicago Press, 1970), p. 2.
[5]Felix Frankfurter, *Mr. Justice Holmes and the Supreme Court* (New York: Atheneum, 1965), pp. 6–8.
[6]Daniel J. Boorstin, "The Perils of Indwelling Law," in Wolff (ed.), *The Rule of Law* (New York: Simon and Schuster, 1971), p. 90.
[7]Opinion of the Court in *United States* v. *Butler* (1936).

particular controversy. When the Court makes a positive policy decision involving, for example, the powers of a coordinate branch of government, it can seek to legitimize this decison by asserting that as a court it had little choice in deciding the matter in a particular way. On the other hand, when the Court chooses for one or another reason to abstain from entering a controversy, it can justify this abstention by claiming that it represents an inappropriate decision for judges to make. The myth thus becomes a source of flexibility and is important to the policy capability of the Supreme Court.

Aside from contributing to an understanding of the utility of the myth, adopting a political perspective performs several additional functions. First, it helps to define the Court's contribution to the determination of important public policy questions. With a special emphasis on defining individual rights and setting limitations on the exercise of governmental power, the Supreme Court decides cases across a broad spectrum of public policy questions. Its decisions contribute to the establishment and enforcement of widely followed norms of behavior (and some not so widely followed, to be sure), to the allocation and occasional redistribution of scarce resources, to the compromise and resolution of political and social conflict, and to the authoritative allocation of values in a democratic society. Traditionally, there have been classes of policy questions which the Supreme Court has been unwilling to decide. But these have been the exception rather than the rule, and the trend of the Warren Court was to consider and decide many issues once thought unsuitable for constitutional adjudication. Questions of reapportionment of legislative bodies, issues of proper police behavior, military draft classifications, challenges to the welfare system, and challenges to federal taxing and spending policies now comprise an important segment of the Court's business.

A second important implication of identifying the Court as a political institution is that it enables us more accurately to construct a picture of its relationship with other institutions of government. Each branch of the government has political functions, some completely separate and others overlapping. Public policy formation is rarely achieved exclusively by one branch; more often it is an amalgam of decisions and compromises reached within and across branch lines. The separation of powers doctrine, to the extent that it suggests the contrary, performs a disservice. In the United States, more political power is shared than is divided, and the constitutional assignment of functions to one or another branch of government is often misleading. It may be that on certain issues the Supreme Court is more concerned—at least formally—with procedure rather than with the substance or content of policy. However, substantive policy conflicts are often fought in procedural terms, and in many policy spheres the Supreme Court is unabashedly concerned with substance as well as with procedure.

It has been suggested, first by Alexander Hamilton in No. 78 of the *Federalist Papers*, and most recently by Professor Alexander Bickel,[8] that the Court is qualitatively different, and less "dangerous" than the other branches because it lacks the powers of sword and purse. It is certainly true that the Court can neither appropriate funds nor raise revenue, and it surely could not raise or direct an army. But these limitations are perhaps not as important as they might have been at one time. In any case, the extent of the Supreme Court's power and influence is an empirical question and not merely a theoretical proposition.

[8]Alexander Bickel, *The Least Dangerous Branch* (Indianapolis: Bobbs-Merrill, 1963).

A third implication of identifying the Court as a political institution is that it enables us to describe and understand recruitment of justices and the Court's decision-making procedures in the same terms used to describe the procedures of other institutions. These procedures are not identical, but there are strong similarities and further evidence of close connections between the Court and the political world. The recruitment of justices is a complex and very political process, bearing little or no resemblance to the accepted popular view that the president chooses for judgeships (or ought to choose) the best qualified lawyers in the country.[9] Patterns of recruitment of both Supreme Court and other federal judges suggest that the heaviest emphasis is placed on political factors including, but not limited to, partisanship, ideology, and patronage. Judicial recruitment decisions exhibit the same basic characteristics as other political decisions. Likewise, the procedures by which the Supreme Court decides a case bear a strong resemblance to political decision-making procedures generally. To be sure, justices wear robes and make their formal appearances and presentations in an august and ritualized setting. But the evidence indicates that, behind the purple curtain, the real decision making involves the same sort of interplay of values and leadership and bargaining processes that are acknowledged to exist in legislative and administrative decision making. Implicit in the myth of mechanical jurisprudence, and in the previously quoted statement of the late Justice Roberts, is the notion that law and politics are distinct phenomena. Alternatively, some also suggest that the role that politics does play in judicial decision making ought to be concealed or defined as an aberration. Much more persuasive is the view, recently advanced by Richardson and Vines, that the courts are best understood in terms of the interaction between and merger of two traditions which they identify as the "legal sub-culture" and the "democratic sub-culture."[10] Whatever formulation is used, both law *and* politics are indispensable ingredients in the judicial process.

Convincing ourselves that the Supreme Court is a political institution is easy. Defining with some precision the precise role that it plays in the American political system is, of course, more difficult. We are interested in understanding how the Court makes its decisions, what sorts of decisions it makes, and what impact these decisions may have (or have had) on our society. The remaining selections in this chapter further define the Court's political role, consider the limits of the law generally, and the Court in particular, as agents of social change, and present a model of the policy-making process to guide the student.

B. Earl Latham, *The Supreme Court, Politics, and Political Theory*

In one sense, all law that gets itself enforced through public secular institutions (policemen and judges) is public law, for enforcement by private institutions would be the rule of the vendetta, lynch law, or the law of the

---

[9]For a summary and reassessment of the recruitment of Supreme Court justices, see Joel B. Grossman and Stephen L. Wasby,"The Senate and Supreme Court Nominations: Some Reflections," 1972 *Duke Law Journal*, 557–591. Also see materials in Chapter Three, *infra*.
[10]Richard Richardson and Kenneth Vines, *The Politics of Federal Courts* (Boston: Little, Brown, 1970), pp. 7–14.

Reprinted from Earl Latham, "The Supreme Court as a Political Institution," **31** *Minnesota Law Review* (1947), 205–208, 210–216, 227–228.

beer barons of the 1920's. In the manner of speaking of lawyers, however, public law is more commonly supposed to concern itself with the activities of public institutions, in their relations with each other and, collectively, as government, in their relations to the people. So considered, public law (including American constitutional law) is concerned with politics in its broadest sense, the subject matter of which is power in human relations—its origin, forms, accumulation, administration, obsolescence, and control within the frame of accepted norms of social ethics. Theories of public law are necessarily, therefore, theories of politics, and American constitutional law is a body of juristic theories of American politics. . . .

The pattern of the public law at any given instant of time is the balance of the relations existing among these various and numerous elements of the society. Where conflict is absent (or slight) relations may be said to be stable, and agreement on common rules prevails. Where serious conflict exists, relations are in turmoil and the rules themselves are exposed to pressure for change. A German writer has remarked that developments in constitutional and administrative law may be looked for precisely when some special interest is seeking to arrogate to itself the signs and seals of the public interest. The life of the law is indeed experience, and not logic, as Holmes once observed, but it is the experience of the society through which the dynamism of social change works as a ferment. Judges are but one of the voices through which this experience finds tongue and expression, yet because of the strategic position in the American political process won for the Supreme Court by John Marshall, the utterances of the justices of the Supreme Court have assumed a disproportionate weight in the shifting balance of these social forces.

Each generation necessarily defines the basic distribution of public powers for itself, and it is the function of the political apparatus of society to give expression to this decision, including the Court as a political institution. What we call the "Constitution of the United States" is the prevailing sense that men now have of the proper distribution of political powers, and of the nature of the forms and methods necessary to achieve the ends for which such powers were distributed. The vigor of this Constitution is not in the minds of men long dead but in the conceptions of the living.

The following pages discuss the role of the Supreme Court as a political institution, not as a trafficker in party votes and electoral stratagems, but as one of the principal holders of public power, responsible to no constituency, and strategically located to slow down or divert those great pivotal movements in American society when the weight of political power shifts from one point and plane to another. As one of the institutional holders of public power, the Court has inevitably been involved with juristic theories of politics in three major areas of doctrine: federalism; the priority of the estates; and the separation of powers. . . .

The use of the power of the Supreme Court as a political institution may be observed in the role it played in interpreting the Federal system in two critical periods: Marshall's time and the years directly after the Civil War. In the first, the Court defined a broad area of Federal competence and put constitutional fences of verbal wire around it; in the second, the Court sought to restate the role of the States as entities of the Federal system and to set metes and bounds to Federal encroachment. In both instances, the Court intervened in a popular struggle, in one case succoring a party fatally defeated at the polls and in the other, frustrating the aims of the victor; and by the shrewd exposition and interpretation of its own doctrines perpetuated its views about the nature of the Federal union and, incidentally, extended its own dominion.

In the early 1800s, there were other views of the nature of the Federal union than the Federalist conception of Chief Justice Marshall equally consistent with the language of the Constitution and, in some cases, better supported by the electorate. The debates of the Federal Convention were secret and not made known through Madison's notes until 1840 so that argument on the basis of what the Framers intended was speculative at best. Nor did Marshall often attempt to use such argument, since there was no particular force in it; those who ratified the Constitution presumed that their understanding of that for which they voted would be equally valid in fixing the meaning of the document. The Framers after all were merely the draftsmen of a document whose meaning could as well (better) be fixed by the common understanding of those who adopted it as by the undisclosed intentions of those who had written the words.

. . . Fundamental questions about the nature of the Federal union were temporarily taken out of the hands of the judges by the war in 1861; national policy was for the time being no longer being shaped by the law of books but of battles. During the carnage, the judges in the main, bided their time. While the war was on the Supreme Court (although sometimes over the protest of minority judges) avoided embarrassing the Federal Government; it waited until after Appomattox for example before declaring military trials unconstitutional when held in a peaceful theater. From time to time the Court had occasion to observe the spoils of Reconstruction but, throughout, managed to avoid direct judicial intervention, although here too the judges were far from unanimous in their course. In sum the Court declined to interfere with the progress of the war or of Reconstruction, but later subjected the Fourteenth Amendment to a special (and probably unintended) interpretation that appropriated the guarantees of freedom designed for former slaves and donated them to men of property.

Although reluctant to meet the issues of the war and Reconstruction frontally, the Court exhibited a strong resolve to restore the Federal union as nearly to its ante-bellum division as possible regardless of the intentions of the framers of the new amendments. Many of the cases after 1865 read lectures upon the need for national unity and although the paramountcy of the Federal Government was not denied, but indeed vigorously asserted, care was taken to reassert the role of the States in the Federal system. . . .

The *Slaughterhouse Cases* were a sign that the post Civil War Court was not disposed to tolerate the argument that the war had wrought any fundamental change in the nature of the Federal union, however disposed individual judges might be to argue the refinements of its division. Despite the evident desires of the Congressional Reconstructionists to retain, by means of the Fourteenth Amendment, the authority to legislate the victory in perpetuity, the Court with appropriate applause for national unity, nevertheless construed the words of grant into vaporous futility in the *Civil Rights Cases* of 1883. The Fourteenth Amendment was construed to have intended no alteration in the historic relationship between the Federal Government and the States (a doubtful conclusion), and the Court offered itself to the States as a repository of the trust that they might not commit to a hostile Congress.

In these dissertations about the nature of the Federal union, the judges were dealing with profound problems of the basic political organization of the Federal society. Chief Justice Marshall's task, as he [had] conceived it, was to mark out the sphere for the Federal Government, to make the master design, the details of which could be filled in later. The post Civil War Court sought to maintain the position of the States as entities of the Federal Union, at a time when an overriding Congress and a victorious army seemed bent upon distorting what the Court considered to be an historic relationship, to be restored and perpetuated. President Lincoln had argued that the Union preceded the States, and indeed was responsible for having brought the latter into being, on the assumption that the people became one in 1776. . . . The contribution of the Supreme Court was to refuse to agree that the war had made any basic change in the position of the States in the American Federal union. In so doing, it exercised political power of considerable influence in a critical moment of American history.

The re-asserted role of the States in the Federal Union scarcely interrupted the expansion of the Federal Government, however, especially when the industrial revolution after the Civil War brought large scale Federal regulation. Someone has remarked that the United States never goes to the right or the left, but always expands in the middle. Something of the sort operated in the field of Federal-State relations; for the

growth of governmental activity after the Civil War was less a matter of encroachment by the Federal Government upon the competences of the States than an increase of both Federal and State activity. If the expansion of Federal activities appeared to dominate, it was because the Federal Government was almost for the first time faced with the necessity of dealing with a variety of problems requiring uniform national treatment, for the new business enterprise knew few State loyalties, and the solicitude of business lawyers for the historic rights of the States was all too frequently a maneuver to defeat the public interest. It was a rare case in which the States themselves, through their public attorneys could assert the need for protection from the Federal Government. In the usual case, it was a debaters' point between lawyers for private clients to assert that the interest of the client was not peculiarly his own, but that of the State of his residence or incorporation.

In the main, the authentication of the exercise of Federal power by the Supreme Court was based upon doctrines of the Federal competence sketched out by Marshall. In this manner did the Court find the words to certify the approval of the Founding Fathers for acts of accommodation to the social change which transformed a sea-board confederation into a world empire, a feat of augury which was accomplished without the addition of any new substantive powers to the Federal Government by formal amendment of the written Constitution. . . .

Now what do these observations on the way in which the Court has dealt with fundamental political questions of the distribution of power amount to? What of it if the Court has pronounced its views about the fundamental nature of the Federal Union;

does it not have to in the adjudication of cases before it? The answer to the first of these points is that the Court by reason of its power to declare acts of legislation unconstitutional does more than express its views about the nature of the Federal Union, a right that judges possess in common with all citizens in a democratic society; because of its position, its views acquire a definitive character from which there is neither recourse nor appeal. The answer to the second is that the fundamental pattern of the Federal union could probably have been quite as well preserved without the Court's power to void State acts unconstitutional, as with it. This view contradicts the opinion once expressed by Mr. Justice Holmes that the Court could well afford to yield its power to review the constitutionality of acts of Congress, but that it would be unfortunate if it lost its power to declare State acts unconstitutional. It is not entirely clear why this should be so, and there are serious considerations which support a contrary conclusion.

It is doubtful that the Court has been uniquely responsible for maintaining the basic structure of the American Federal union. As it has frequently said itself, it has neither the power of the purse or the sword, and in the only real clashes of authority, as in President Jackson's dispute with the nullificationists of South Carolina, or President Washington's enforcement of the revenue laws in the Whiskey Rebellion, and of course the Civil War, the maintenance of Federal authority in the face of State opposition has been the function of the President and Congress. But, it may be said, these are instances of defiance of the Federal authority;

what of the encroachment by the Federal Government into the domain of the States? Has not the Court performed a service to the people in maintaining the integrity of the States as entities of the Federal Union? The answer to this, as to the previous question, is that the elected officials of the Federal Government and the States have probably been more effective in this respect than the Court. . . .

In a democratic society, the basic political questions are for the people to decide, acting directly or through representatives responsible to them. To vest the authority to decide these basic questions of the organization and distribution of political power in other officials than those who owe an immediate responsibility to the electorate, is to take out of popular control the making of the important political decisions. . . .

As one of the principal holders of public power, the Supreme Court in the general areas of political theory commented upon has frequently professed the doctrines and bespoken the interests of minority groups; the Federalists with their gospel of strong central power and liberal interpretation; the defeated States of the South after the Civil War; the acquisitive minorities bred by the industrial revolution; and the judicial bureaucracy. The imputed views of the fictitious multitude of the *Marbury* Case, represented by judges, have found the struggles of the living to move from one precarious social balance to another. One comment has summarized the political activity of the Court in the following words.*

It is at once a judicial and a political body. It is judicial in that its usages are of a court of law. . . . It is political in that its

*Walton Hamilton and G.D. Braden, "The Special Competence of the Supreme Court," **50** *Yale Law Journal* (1941) 1319–1375, @ 1324.

orders extend far beyond the individuals immediately involved; it fixes conditions and sets bounds about the resort to law; it revises the pattern of the separation of powers among the agencies of government; it endows with intent, discovers latent meaning and resolves conflicts between legislative acts; it invokes Constitution, statute, its own decisions to hold Congress, department, administrative body in its place. Even when it imposes self-denial upon itself, politically it extends the frontiers of some other agency of control. Judgments along these lines are political, not legal decisions. Issues of due process, equal protection, privileges and immunities, are questions of the limits of the province of government. . . .

The Court, in short, has exercised a political power of the highest influence; and although subject to the chance of the docket and able only to function interstitially, as Holmes remarked, nevertheless it has been in a strategic position to cast its weight this way and that when the balance could be tipped.

C. The Study of Constitutional Law and the Legal System

Most of the courses in which this textbook is read will be entitled "Constitutional Law." However, this book is not an exhaustive or detailed interpretation of the federal Constitution. It is very much concerned with the modern Supreme Court's interpretation of the Constitution, and as such, it is an introduction to American constitutional law for nonlaw students. But it emphasizes the political dimensions because our approach to the subject is as much political as it is purely legal.

Understanding the technical meaning of the Constitution is still important. But to study the Constitution apart from its political environment wuld be a sterile exercise. The late Professor Thomas Reed Powell once warned his Harvard Law School students against reading the Constitution, "lest it confuse their minds." Surely that is (in today's terms) overkill. But if not taken literally, his statement does warn against excessive formalism. The Constitution's commands should not be equated with life itself. Its meaning is to be found in our political experience as a nation. The Constitution, as a document, is a part of that experience. But as a charter of government it provides a bare skeleton of organization; seven thousand words sketching out some of the basic rules and values— some clear and noncontroversial, others far more abstract and difficult to apply and therefore the subject of continuing reinterpretation and controversy.

The Constitution is an instrument of government. It is also a symbol. As an instrument, it organizes the government, establishes some basic controls, and provides a core statement of national values. As a symbol, its effects are as important if not as well understood. In the minds of many, the American Constitution stands for permanence and stability, "an unchanging foundation from which to face a changing unreckonable world."[1] In a nation without a hereditary ruling class or comparable social institutions, the Constitution may satisfy a human need for symbols of tradition and certainty. At the same time, it must respond to those who seek orderly change. Because a society needs both stability and change, and because we often see our Constitution as the ultimate source of an-

---

[1] Karl Llewellyn, "The Constitution as an Institution," **34** *Columbia Law Review* (1934), 5.

swers to difficult political questions, we often expect contradictory things from it. We expect it to be changeless but also changing, divine but also secular, transcendental but also pragmatic.[2]

Attachment to the Constitution has often bordered on worship. However irrational that may appear at first, it is an important political fact. "Adoration of the Constitution soon became adoration of its guardians, the Justices," observes David Adamany, "despite lingering doubts about the constitutional source of their self-proclaimed power of judicial review."[3] The Supreme Court has recognized how its own legitimacy derives, at least initially, from the Constitution and has often drawn on it for support in time of controversy. If constitutionalism has shaped our judicial process, it has also had an important effect on politics in general—on the ways in which political issues are debated and how policy preferences are expressed.

An understanding of constitutional law also requires some explanation of its relationship to the American legal system generally. In fact, there is not *one* legal system in the United States but several. There is a system of federal courts and a system of courts and a constitution in each state. In many of our largest cities there are also quasi-autonomous courts. In theory, the Supreme Court of the United States sits at the top of the "pyramid," and constitutional policies made at the top are enforced by lower federal and state courts. As the remainder of this book will make clear, however, hierarchy and bureaucracy are inadequate concepts to illustrate the complex functioning and interdependence of our legal institutions. Important constitutional policies are made throughout the system. There are important differences in law and policy in the courts of different states or even in different circuits of the federal court system.

Constitutional law cases constitute only a minute fraction of the business of our courts; obviously, they are more important than their numbers. The Supreme Court itself ultimately decides only a fraction of those constitutional cases that do arise. Most claims of constitutional deprivation are heard initially *and* finally by lower federal courts, federal courts of appeal, and state courts. Nor are all constitutional policies made by courts. Important constitutional policies are made by legislatures and executives at least initially, and very often not reviewed by courts.

The student of constitutional law must also have some understanding of the different *types* of law that are found in our legal systems. Merely to define the term "law" is a problem for which students of jurisprudence have no agreed-upon answer. For this book, law might be defined as "all of the rules of conduct established and enforced by the authority, legislation, or custom of a given community."[4] Defined in this way, law is secular, consisting of man-made rules. This is often called *positive law*.

Sometimes the sources of law are not sought in human experience but in some "higher" law—of nature, or of the creator. This is called *natural law*. It has no authoritative standing

[2]Daniel Boorstin, "The Perils of Indwelling Law," in Wolff (ed.), *The Rule of Law* (New York: Simon & Schuster, 1971), pp. 75–97.
[3]David Adamany, "Legitimacy, Realigning Elections, and the Supreme Court," 1973 *Wisconsin Law Review*, 791.
[4]Stephen D. Ford, *The American Legal System: Its Dynamics and Limits* (St. Paul: West Publishing Co., 1974) p. 3.

in a secular legal system, but it has had a significant influence on the development of American law. One can see "natural law" concepts in the Declaration of Independence, the Bill of Rights, and many Supreme Court decisions. Though without legal force, natural law is often a provocative and effective normative standard by which positive law can be criticized and evaluated.[5]

Common law refers to the system of law that developed in England. It was the law applied by the king's judges throughout the realm before and during the commercial revolution. It was (and, in common law legal systems, *is*) concerned mostly with the resolution of disputes between private parties. A decision in one case stands as a "rule of law" to govern the decisions of courts in similar cases arising in the future. It depends heavily on the rule of precedent—*stare decisis*—and on the use of syllogistic logic and reasoning by analogy.[6] Common law is "unwritten" in that it exists only in the form of judicial decisions. It is also "judge-made" in that it does not depend on legislative statutes to have legal force, although in modern times statutory law superseded common law in many areas. For its time the common law was flexible; changes in technology, circumstance, or social patterns might be accommodated by new rules; old rules, no longer practical, might be "distinguished" and limited in application to the circumstances that produced them. This capacity of the common law to reflect change led to Oliver Wendell Holmes' famous dictum: "The life of the law has not been logic—it has been experience. The felt necessities of the time, prevalent moral and political theories, were more important than syllogism in determining rules."[7]

The common law was used in the colonial courts and in the state court systems that succeeded them, with some changes to reflect the American experience. Even today, common law is used in the resolution of most private disputes that reach the courts. Several state constitutions declare it to be the authoritative law in the absence of any statutory law on a particular subject. There is no federal common law,[8] but many of the concepts, and much of the experience, of the common law are utilized in the federal courts. Indeed, the federal courts, under *Erie Railroad* v. *Tompkins* (1938), are obligated to apply state common law in diversity of citizenship cases. So too, interpretation of various parts of the Constitution often hinges on how a substantive rule developed, or what it meant, under the common law, for example, the function and size of juries.

Equity law also developed in England, as a supplement to the common law. It was often referred to as the "conscience" of the common law: designed to correct injustices with which the common law could not deal effectively. In particular, it was concerned with *preventing* injustices. The common law emphasizes restitution and compensation as remedies for wrongful acts; money damages are the primary remedy. Yet, there are many situations in which money damages are insufficient. Some in-

---

[5]The classic exploration of the subject is Edward Corwin, *The Higher Law Background of American Constitutional Law* (Ithaca, N.Y.: Great Seal Books, 1955). First published in **42** *Harvard Law Review* (1928–1929), 149–185, 365–409.

[6]See Edward Levi, *An Introduction to Legal Reasoning* (Chicago: University of Chicago Press, 1949).

[7]Oliver Wendell Holmes, *The Common Law,* (Little, Brown, 1881).

[8]See *Erie Railroad* v. *Tompkins* (1938).

juries are, by their very nature, *ir-reparable*. Thus, one major function of equity is to prevent wrongful acts that cannot be adequately compensated by money damages. A court of equity may issue an order (known as an *injunction* or *restraining order*), where a showing of irreparable harm has been made *and* where the judge believes that the plaintiff will prevail on the merits of his claim when it is fully heard by a court. In a modern-day example, a property owner may contest state condemnation of a portion of her property to be used for highway construction. If her objection is only that a fair price has not been offered, then she would have no claim to equitable relief; a court of law could, at some later time, determine a fair price. But if the property owner claims that in taking this property, the state will also be cutting down a grove of trees that ought to be saved (conservation interests) or that provide an important wind barrier for her crops or house, she will be asserting a potentially irreparable harm, and an equity court could, if it accepted her contentions, enjoin the government from cutting down the trees.

Equity jurisdiction also gives judges considerable discretion in the fashioning of appropriate remedies. In the second *Brown* case concerning public school desegregation (*Brown* v. *Board of Education* II, 1955), the Supreme Court assigned to the district courts the responsibility, "guided by equitable principles," for carrying into effect the original desegregation ruling of 1954. Federal judges were given a wide range of discretion (subject to the Supreme Court's policy guidelines) in fashioning appropriate remedies to dismantle racially segregated school systems.

In England, equity was handled by a separate system of chancery courts. This is also true in a few states in the United States. But the Constitution extends "the judicial power of the United States to all cases in law and equity," and federal courts handle both types of cases.

Statutory law is law enacted by Congress or by a legislature. It supersedes common law whenever there is any conflict or inconsistency, but it is also different in nature. It is primarily *public law*, designed to regulate relationships of individuals to the government, or institutions of government to each other, rather than private disputes between individuals. It has often supplanted the common law by transforming private disputes into matters of public policy. Thus, much of the common law of negligence that governed claims for damages by employees against employers was, over time, superseded by workmen's compensation statutes.[9] Statutory law is universalistic rather than particularistic; it is designed to govern predictable future situations, whereas common law developed out of the immediate need by judges to solve actual disputes. In the United States, the growth and primacy of statutory law, at both the state and federal levels, roughly paralleled the industrial revolution and the development of the welfare state. Initially, judges greeted statutory law with suspicion and hostility; it was, after all, an intrusion into a domain they had long controlled ("statutes in derogation of the common law are to be strictly construed" was a common rule of judicial interpretation[10]). But today the legitimacy and primacy of statutory law have been well established.

Just as the American legal system

[9]*Op. Cit.*, Note 6.
[10]Karl Llewellyn, *The Common Law Tradition: Deciding Appeals* (Boston: Little, Brown, 1960).

is a mixture of court systems, so too is it a mixture of different types of law. The law of the Constitution is paramount. But its development and significance cannot be understood apart from the legal system as a whole.

2. LAW AND SOCIAL CHANGE

A. E. Adamson Hoebel, The Functions of Law

Law performs certain functions essential to the maintenance of all but the very most simple societies.

The first is to define relationships among the members of a society, to assert what activities are permitted and what are ruled out, so as to maintain at least minimal integration between the activities of individuals and groups within the society.

The second is derived from the necessity of taming naked force and directing force to the maintenance of order. It is the allocation of authority and the determination of who may exercise physical coercion as a socially recognized privilege-right, along with the selection of the most effective forms of physical sanction to achieve the social ends that the law serves.

The third is the disposition of trouble cases as they arise.

The fourth is to redefine relations between individuals and groups as the conditions of life change. It is to maintain adaptability.

Purposive definition of personal relations is the primary law-job. Other aspects of culture likewise work to this end, and, indeed, the law derives its working principles (jural postulates) from postulates previously developed in the nonlegal spheres of action. However, the law's important contribution to the basic organization of society as a whole is that the law specifically and explicitly defines relations. It sets the expectancies of man to man and group to group so that each knows the focus and the limitations of its demand-rights on others, its duties to others, its privilege-rights and powers as against others, and its immunities and liabilities to the contemplated or attempted acts of others. This is the "bare-bones job," as Karl Llewellyn likes to call it. It is the ordering of the fundamentals of living together. . . .

The second function of the law—the allocation of authority to exercise coercive physical force—is something almost peculiar to things legal.

Custom has regularity, and so does law. Custom defines relationships, and so does law. Custom is sanctioned, and so is law. But the sanctions of law may involve physical coercion. Law is distinguished from mere custom in that it endows certain selected individuals with the privilege-right of applying the sanction of physical coercion, if need be. The legal, let it be repeated, has teeth that can bite. But the biting, if it is to be legal and not mere gangsterism, can be done only by those persons to whom the law has allocated the privilege-right for the affair at hand.

We have seen that in primitive law authority is a shifting, temporary

Reprinted from *The Law of Primitive Man* (Cambridge: Harvard University Press, 1954), pp. 275–282, 287.

thing. Authority to enforce a norm resides (for private wrongs) with the wronged individual and his immediate kinsmen—but only for the duration of time necessary to follow through the procedural steps that lead to redress or punishment of the culprit. In primitive law the tendency is to allocate authority to the party who is directly injured. This is done in part out of convenience, for it is easier to let the wronged party assume the responsibility for legal action. It is also done because the primitive kinship group, having a more vital sense of entity, is naturally charged with a heavier emotional effect. In any event, when the community qua community acknowledges the exercise of force by a wronged person or his kinship group as correct and proper in a given situation, and so restrains the wrongdoer from striking back, then law prevails and order triumphs over violence.

We have also found in our studies of primitive societies that in a limited number of situations authority is directly exercised by the community on its own behalf. It takes the form of lynch law in some instances where clear procedures have not been set up in advance, as in the Comanche treatment of excessive sorcery and Shoshone treatment of cannibalism. Lynch law among primitives, however, is not a backsliding from, or detouring around, established formal law as it is with us. It is a first fitful step toward the emergence of criminal law in a situation in which the exercise of legal power has not yet been refined and allocated to specific persons. It is a blunt crude tool wielded by the gang hand of an outraged public.

Yet lynch law is rare among primitives. Even the simplest of them have crystallized standards as to what constitutes criminal behavior, and the exercise of public authority is dele-gated to official functionaries—the chieftain, the council of chiefs, and the council of elders.

Power may sometimes be personal, as is the power of the bully in the society of small boys, and as was to some extent the power of William the Conqueror. But personal tyranny is a rare thing among primitives. Brute force of the individual does not prevail. Chiefs must have followers. Followers always impose limitations on their leaders. Enduring power is always institutionalized power. It is *transpersonalized.* It resides in the office, in the social status, rather than in the man. . . .

The third function of law calls for little additional comment. . . . some trouble cases pose absolutely new problems for solution. In these cases the first and second functions may predominate. Yet this is not the situation in the instance of most legal clashes in which the problem is not the formulation of law to cover a new situation but rather the application of preexisting law. These cases are disposed of in accordance with legal norms already set before the issue in question arises. The job is to clean the case up, to suppress or penalize the illegal behavior and to bring the relations of the disputants back into balance, so that life may resume its normal course. This type of law-work has frequently been compared to work of the medical practitioner. It is family doctor stuff, essential to keeping the social body on its feet. In more homely terms, Llewellyn has called it, "garage-repair work on the general order of the group when that general order misses fire, or grinds gears, or even threatens a total breakdown." It is not ordinarily concerned with grand design, as is the first law-job. Nor is it concerned with redesign as is the fourth. It works to clean up all the little social messes (and the occasional big ones) that recurrently arise between the members of the society from day to day.

Most of the trouble cases do not, in a civilized society, of themselves loom large on the social scene, although in a small community even one can lead directly to a social explosion if not successfully cleaned up. Indeed, in a primitive society the individual case always holds the threat of a little civil war if procedure breaks down, for from its inception it sets kin group against kin group—and if it comes to fighting, the number of kinsmen who will be involved is almost always immediately enlarged. The fight may engulf a large part of the tribe in internecine throat-cutting. Relatively speaking, each run-of-the-mill trouble case in primitive law imposes a more pressing demand for settlement upon the legal system than is the case with us.

While system and integration are essential, flexibility and constant revision are no less so. Law is a dynamic process in which few solutions can be permanent. Hence, the fourth function of law: the redefinition of relations and the reorientation of expectancies.

Initiative with scope to work means new problems for the law. New inventions, new ideas, new behaviors keep creeping in. Especially do new behaviors creep in, nay, sweep in, when two unlike societies come newly into close contact. Then the law is called upon to decide what principles shall be applied to conflicts of claims rooted in disparate cultures. Do the new claims fit comfortably to the old postulates? Must the newly realized ways of behaving be wholly rejected and legally suppressed because they are out of harmony with the old values? Or can they be modified here and altered there to gain legal acceptance? Or can the more difficult operation of altering or even junking old postulates to ac-

commodate a new way be faced? Or can fictions be framed that can lull the mind into acceptance of the disparate new without the wrench of acknowledged junking of the old? What is it that is wanted? The known and habitual, or the promise of the new and untested? Men may neglect to turn the law to the answer of such questions. But they do not for long. Trouble cases generated by the new keep marching in. And the fourth law-job presses for attention. . . .

Work under [the fourth] function represents social planning brought into focus by the case of the instant and with an eye to the future.

The problem of reorienting conduct and redirecting it through the law when new issues emerge is always tied to the bare-bones demand of basic organization and the minimal maintenance of order and regularity. It may also shade over into work colored by a greater or lesser desire to achieve more than a minimum of smoothness in social relations. When this becomes an important aspect of law-work, a special aspect of law-ways activity may be recognized: the creation of techniques that efficiently and effectively solve the problems posed to all the other law-jobs so that the basic values of the society are realized through the law and not frustrated by it.

The doing of it has been called by Llewellyn "Juristic Method." It is the method not only of getting the law-jobs done but doing them with a sure touch for the net effect that results in smoothness in the doing and a harmonious wedding of what is aspired to by men and what is achieved through the law. It is the work not just of the craftsman but of the master craftsman—the kind of man the Polynesians call *Tui Thonga*, Great Adept.

Skill in juristic method may be the

unique quality of a great judge or chief who judges for his people. In which case you may have a single man, or occasional men, cropping up to soften hard-shell legalism. Or it may become an institutional quality of a whole system in which a tradition of method is to keep one eye on the ultimate social goals of men and another on the working machinery to see that it is steering toward those goals. For juristic method, while it works on the immediate grievance to see that "justice" receives its due, also looks beyond to discern as far as possible the ultimate effect of the social policy that the *ratio decidendi* will produce. It weighs and balances the "rights" of the individual in *this particular case* against the need for order per se and the far-running needs of the group as a whole. It recognizes that regularity exists not only for the sake of regularity, which is no *Ding an sich,* but as a means to social and individual existence. But it also knows that absolute regularity is impossible in social physiology. It seeks as best it may to keep the working law flexible enough to allow leeway at the points where leeway will not cause the social fabric to part at the seams, and at the same time it seeks to maintain sufficient stiffness in the fiber of the law so that it will not lose its binding effect. . . .

When the law-jobs get done, these norms inevitably become the common denominator of legal culture. But the functions of law, whatever the norms they may give rise to in any particular society, are what constitute the crucial universal elements of the law. Any one or half-hundred societies may select one rule of law and not another—the range is wide—but none can ignore the law-jobs. In the last analysis, that the law-jobs get done is more important than how they are done. Their minimal doing is an imperative of social existence. Their doing with juristic finesse is an achievement of high skill.

B. *William M. Evan, Law as an Instrument of Social Change*

In imaginary societies, such as some authors of utopias have depicted, there is such a high degree of social harmony and tranquility that no law is necessary—and no lawyers either. Such societies enjoy a perfect state of social equilibrium because there is a perfect degree of congruence between the ideal prescriptions and proscriptions of behavior and actual behavior. The free and frictionless association among all citizens makes the state superfluous as the source of law and as an instrument of social control.

In all real societies, whether "primitive" or "civilized," such an ideal state is not to be found. In fact, we can argue that in principle it is impossible for human beings ever to attain that blissful state of equilibrium which would not require law or some form of legal system. Disequilibrating forces are generated from both outside and inside a society. These pressures for change stem in part from the impossibility of achieving perfect congruence between the ideal cultural blueprint of a society and the actual social reality. A certain amount of social deviance occurs in all societies, if only because the socialization process through childhood as well as through the rest of the life cycle can not possibly be uniform and perfectly successful. As a consequence, in all societies of any appreci-

Reprinted from Gouldner and Miller (eds.), *Applied Sociology* (New York: Free Press, 1965), pp. 285–291.

able size, there is a tendency for law to emerge distinct from "the cake of custom." Law in this context does not necessarily refer to a written statement of a rule of conduct, since in nonliterate societies this cannot occur, but rather to a particular social status—such as that of a tribal chieftain or a judge—the incumbent of which has the authority to assert a norm, resolve conflicts, and bring to bear the coercive power of the community against those guilty of violating a norm.

Contrasting Conceptions of the Function of Law

Law emerges not only to *codify* existing customs, morals, or mores, but also to *modify* the behavior and the values presently existing in a particular society. The conception of law as a codification of existing customs, morals, or mores implies a relatively passive function. On the other hand, the conception of law as a means of social change, i.e., as a potential for modifying behavior and beliefs, implies a relatively active function.

The passive law, namely, that one cannot legislate mores and people's behavior, is rooted in the 19th century philosophies of Social Darwinism and historical jurisprudence. At the turn of the century, William Graham Sumner articulated this conception of the law. It assumes that law is a passive, rather than an active social force, which gradually emerges into a formal or codified state only after it has taken root in the behavior of the members of a society. Whenever an effort is made to enact a law in contradiction to existing folkways and mores, conflicts arise which result in the eventual undoing of the law. Since Sumner claims there is a "strain toward a consistency of the mores," he concludes, in effect, that "state-ways cannot change folkways." An implicit assumption of this view is that the exclusive function of law is to reinforce the mores and to provide a uniform and predictable procedure for the evaluation and punishment of deviance. That is to say, the function of law is social control and the major problem is one of designing legal sanctions to minimize deviance and maintain social stability.

A contrary view is that law is not merely a reflection of existing customs, morals or codes, but also a potentially independent social force which can influence behavior and beliefs. As an instrument of social change, law entails two interrelated processes: the institutionalization and the internalization of patterns of behavior. In this context, institutionalization of a pattern of behavior means the establishment of a norm with provisions for its enforcement, and internalization of a pattern of behavior means the incorporation of the value or values implicit in a law. Law, as has been noted by others, can affect behavior directly only through the process of institutionalization; if, however, the institutionalization process is successful, it, in turn, facilitates the internalization of attitudes or beliefs.

A Continuum of Resistance to Law

These opposing views of the function of law suggest a hypothetical continuum of the amount of potential resistance to the enactment of a new law. When there is likely to be zero percent resistance to a law, one would obviously question the need for it, since complete agreement between the behavior required by the law and the existing customs or morals apparently exists. In this situation, there would be no need to codify the mores into law. At the other extreme, when there is likely to be 100 percent resistance to a law, one would expect the law to be totally ineffective, because nobody would enforce it and the authority of the lawmaker would be undermined.

No law would ever emerge if these two extremes existed at all times. Between these ends of our continuum, there are evidently two important thresholds involved in law-making. Somewhere at the lower end of our hypothetical continuum of resistance, where a certain degree of nonconformity or deviance from existing mores is reached, society acts to control it by codifying mores. What this threshold of nonconformity is for different societies, we do not yet know. Similarly, somewhere at the higher end of our continuum there is a threshold of such massive resistance to a new law that enforcement is impossible. At what point on this continuum a new law provokes the overwhelming majority of the citizenry to violate it so as to nullify it, we also do not know. Civil wars and revolutions approximate this form of massive resistance to law culminating in its "decodification." Thus, in considering the social functions of law, we have to focus on the intermediate portion of our hypothetical continuum of resistance to law.

Whenever a law is enacted in the face of any appreciable resistance, that is to say, whenever it falls somewhere in the middle of our hypothetical continuum, the legal system becomes involved in an educational as well as in a social control task. If the educational task is not accomplished, a situation exists in which individuals are obligated to obey a law at the threat of punishment, while, in fact, not believing in it. This situation produces what Festinger calls "forced compliance," viz., a discrepancy between public behavior and private belief. So long as behavior involves forced compliance, there is no internalization of the values implicit or explicit in a new law. The resulting tension may lead to disobedience of the law, depending on the nature of the sanctions and the consistency and efficiency of enforcement. If law is to perform an educational function, it is necessary to convert *forced* compliance into *voluntary* compliance.

Necessary Conditions for Law Performing an Educational Function

Under what conditions can law succeed, not only in institutionalizing a new pattern of conduct, but also in generating the internalization of new attitudes implicit in the conduct required by the new law? The failure to specify these conditions leaves the theoretical problems of the relation of law to social change unanswered. It also leaves unsolved the administrative problems of the conscious use of law as an agent of social change. As a first approximation to an answer to this problem, we shall consider seven necessary, though perhaps not sufficient, conditions for law to perform an educational function.

The first condition is that the source of the new law be authoritative and prestigeful. This condition may at first appear to be trivial, since law, by definition, connotes an authoritative or legitimate action. There are, in fact, four authoritative lawmaking sources in our society: legislative, executive, administrative, and judicial. It is hypothesized that they differ not only in their reputed authoritativeness and prestige in exercising a law-making function, but also in their effectiveness in performing an educational function. A law enacted by a legislature—rather than issued as a decision by a court or an administrative agency, or as an executive order—probably lends itself more readily to performing an educational function. For, in the minds of the average citizens, legislatures—whether at the local, state or federal level—are probably perceived to be the proper and legitimate forums for the enactment of new laws. This perception may be due to the fact that legislatures are more sensitive to public pressures and sentiments than are the other sources of lawmaking. Second in the perceived rank order of authoritativeness and prestige are probably executive orders, followed by the decisions of administrative agencies; and lastly, in all likelihood, are the decisions of the courts.

This hypothesis about the differential in perceived authoritativeness and prestige of lawmaking sources leads us, in turn, to the hypothesis that the more drastic the social change to be effected by law, i.e., the higher the proportion of potential resistance on our hypothetical scale, the more authoritative and prestigeful the lawmaking agency should be to effect the change. In other words, when there is a low degree of consensus regarding the norms involved in a law, "legislative lawmaking"—the most authoritative and prestigeful source of law—is apt to be more effective than "judicial lawmaking," the least authoritative and prestigeful source of law.

The Supreme Court's decision to desegregate the public school system is generally acknowledged as representing an effort to effect a drastic social change. Consequently, we venture to suggest—in light of the hypothesis stated above—that Congress would have been a more effective lawmaking source in this instance. To be sure, had the Supreme Court in 1954 declined the opportunity to revise its 1896 doctrine of "separate but equal" treatment, enunciated in *Plessy* v. *Ferguson*, it might have taken many years for Congress to enact a desegregation law in view of the monumental resistance of the Southern pressure group.

The second condition is that the rationale of a new law clarify its continuity and compatibility with existing institutionalized values. The fulfillment of this condition helps to overcome possible objections to a new law and establishes its legitimacy in the eyes of the citizenry. Such a rationale is readily imaginable in the desegregation decision. The Thirteenth and Fourteenth Amendments, as well as the Declaration of Independence and various judicial decisions in the preceding decade, clearly establish the rights of all citizens of this country to equal treatment by the law, including agencies of the state, such as the public school system. Thus, a legislative enactment of school desegregation could have drawn on prior legal support, quite apart from general cultural and historical justifications.

The third necessary condition for making law an educational force is the use of models or reference groups for compliance. This could involve several possible actions by a lawmaking body. It might single out a group or a community in which the proposed pattern of behavior already exists without any observable adverse effects. Thus, for instance, it would have been possible to point to any number of communities in this country where desegregation has been in effect for many years without any known untoward effects on either whites or Negroes. Also relevant would have been a reference to the successful desegregation in the armed services in both Northern and Southern installations. The examples cited of models for compliance may not have proved adequate for the law in question. The idea, however, of deliberately upholding a pragmatic model which is visible and the likely object of admiration by potential recalcitrants might contribute to overcoming resistance to a proposed change.

The fourth condition is that law make a conscious use of the element of time in introducing a new pattern of behavior. This is essential for breaking an old pattern and instituting a new one. To be sure, the Supreme Court took the time element into consideration when it resorted to the intentionally ambiguous phrase "with all deliberate speed" in its desegregation decision.

It may be hypothesized that if a significant pattern of social behavior is to be changed, the less the transition time, the easier—rather than the harder—the adaptation to the change. The rationale for this proposition is that the reduction of time delay minimizes the chances for the growth of organized or unorganized resistance to the projected legal change. The possible validity of this hypothesis depends on at least two conditions, to which we now turn.

The first of these, our fifth condition, is that the enforcement agents must themselves be committed to the behavior required by the law, even if not to the values implicit in it. Any evidence of hypocrisy or corruptibility on the part of the personnel of the legal system, whose task it is to implement the law, undermines the chances of its being effectuated. One of the major reasons for the failure of the Prohibition Amendment was the disrespect for the law evidenced by enforcement agents, particularly local police, on whom the major task of enforcement devolved.

The sixth condition, which also bears on the time factor mentioned earlier, is that as resistance to a new law increases, positive sanctions are probably as important as negative ones. Legal sanctions are almost invariably negative in character, e.g., fines and/or imprisonment. As the severity of the punishment increases, compliance does not necessarily increase. Severe punishment often affords people the opportunity to neutralize any guilt experienced for their wrong-doing with what feels like justified resentment against punishment. To encourage the learning of a new pattern of behavior and a new attitude, some positive reinforcement is required, as learning theorists have found experimentally. We would speculate that as the proportion of potential resistance to a new law increases, the need for including some positive sanctions or rewards for compliance also increases. In the case of the school desegregation decision, such rewards might have consisted of a special Federal school subsidy for teachers' salaries and school construction, and possibly even a rebate on Federal income tax for a given length of time for the people in those communities complying with the law. Although the Anglo-Saxon legal system generally does not provide for positive sanctions, there is no reason to doubt their value when law is used as an instrument of social change, particularly of a significant magnitude.

The seventh and final condition under which law performs an educational function is that effective protection be provided for the rights of those persons who would suffer if the law were evaded or violated. If an individual is required, because of the legal doctrine of "standing" in court, to vindicate his rights against those of an organized entity, public or private, whose resources are infinitely greater, his rights are, in fact, unprotected. Only if the law should provide that he have the aid of a public organization, such as an administrative agency charged with the enforcement of the law, or the aid of a private organization of his own choosing, does he stand a chance to obtain justice. . . .

C. Stanley Diamond, The Rule of Law Versus the Order of Custom

We must distinguish the rule of law from the authority of custom. In a recent effort to do so (which I shall critically examine because it is so typical), Paul Bohannan contends, under the imprimateur of the *International Encyclopedia of the Social Sciences,* that laws result from "double institutionalization." He means by this the lending of a specific force, a cutting edge to the functioning of "customary" institutions: marriage, the family, religion. But, he tells us, the laws so emerging assume a character and dynamic of their own. They form a structured legal dimension of society; they do not merely reflect, but interact with given institutions. Therefore, Bohannan is led to maintain that laws are typically out of phase with society and it is this process which is both a symptom and cause of social change. Thus, the laws of marriage, to illustrate Bohannan's argument with the sort of concrete example his definition lacks, are not synonymous with the institution of marriage. They reinforce certain rights and obligations while neglecting others. Moreover, they subject partners defined as truant to intervention by an external, impersonal agency whose decisions are sanctioned by the power of the police.

Bohannan's sociological construction *does* have the virtue of denying the primacy of the legal order, and of implying that law is generic to unstable (or progressive) societies, but it is more or less typical of abstract efforts to define the eternal essence of the law, and it begs the significant questions. Law has no such essence but a definable historical nature. Thus, if we inquire into the structure of the contemporary institutions, which according to Bohannan stand in a primary relation to the law, we find that their customary content has drastically diminished. Paul Radin made the point as follows: "A custom is in no sense a part of our properly functioning culture. It belongs definitely to the past. At best, it is moribund. But customs are an integral part of the life of primitive peoples. There is no compulsive submission to them. They are not followed because the weight of tradition overwhelms a man. . . . A custom is obeyed because it is intimately intertwined with a vast living network of interrelations, arranged in a meticulous and ordered manner. They are tied up with all the mechanisms used in government." And, "What is significant in this condition," as J. G. Peristiany indicates, "it is not that common values should exist, but that they should be expressed although no common political organization corresponds to them." No contemporary institution functions with the kind of autonomy that permits us to postulate a significant dialectic between law and custom. We live in a law-ridden society; law has cannibalized the institutions which it presumably reinforces or with which it interacts.

Accordingly, morality continues to be reduced to or confused with legal-

Reprinted from Wolff (ed.) *The Rule of Law,* (New York: Simon and Schuster, 1971), pp. 116–120, 135–141.

ity. We tend to assume that legal behavior is the measure of moral behavior, and it is a matter of some interest that a former Chief Justice of the Supreme Court proposed, with the best of intentions, that a federal agency be established in order to advise government employees, and those doing business with the government, concerning the legal/ethical propriety of their behavior. Any conflict of interest not legally enjoined would thus become socially or morally acceptable. These efforts to legislate conscience by an external political power are the antithesis of custom: customary behavior comprises precisely those aspects of social behavior which are traditional, moral, and religious, which are, in short, conventional and nonlegal. Put another way, custom *is* social morality. The relation between custom and law is, basically, one of contradiction, not continuity.

The customary and the legal orders are historically, not logically related. They touch coincidentally; one does not imply the other. Custom, as most anthropologists agree, is characteristic of primitive society, and laws of civilization. Robert Redfield's dichotomy between primitive "moral order" and the civilized "legal" or "technical" order remains a classic statement of the case.

"The dispute," writes William Seagle, "whether primitive societies have law or custom, is not merely a dispute over words. Only confusion can result from treating them as interchangeable phenomena. If custom is spontaneous and automatic, law is the product of organized force. Reciprocity is in force in civilized communities too but at least nobody confuses social with formal legal relationships." Parenthetically, one should note that students of primitive society who use the term "customary law" blur the issue semantically, but

nonetheless recognize the distinction.

It is this overall legalization of behavior in modern society which Bohannan slights. In fascist Germany, for example, laws flourished as never before. By 1941, more edicts had been proclaimed than in all the years of the Republic and the Third Reich. At the same time, ignorance of the law inevitably increased. In a sense, the very force of the law depends upon ignorance of its specifications, which is hardly recognized as a mitigating circumstance. As Seagle states, law is not definite and certain while custom is vague and uncertain. Rather, the converse holds. Customary rules must be clearly known; they are not sanctioned by organized political force, hence serious disputes about the nature of custom would destroy the integrity of society. But laws may always be invented, and stand a good chance of being enforced: "Thus, the sanction is far more important than the rule in the legal system . . . but the tendency is to minimize the sanction and to admire the rule."

In fascist Germany, customs did not become laws through a process of "double institutionalization." Rather, repressive laws, conjured up in the interests of the Nazi party and its supporters, cannibalized the institutions of German society. Even the residual customary authority of the family was assaulted: children were encouraged to become police informers, upholding the laws against their kin. "The absolute reign of law has often been synonymous with the absolute reign of lawlessness." Certainly, Germany under Hitler was a changing society, if hardly a progressive one, but it was a special case of the general process in civilization through which the organs of the state have become increasingly irresistible. It will be recalled that Bohannan takes law as opposed to custom to be symptomatic of changing societies. But the historical inadequacy of his argument is exactly here: he does not intimate the overall direction of that change and therefore fails to clarify the actual relation between custom and law. Accordingly, the notion that social change is a function of the law, and vice versa, implies a dialectic that is out of phase with *historical* reality.

Plato understood this well enough when he conceived the problem of civilization as primarily one of *injustice,* which he did not scant by legalistic definition. His remedy was the thorough restructuring of society. Whether we admire his utopia or not, the *Republic* testifies to Plato's recognition that laws follow social change and reflect prevailing social relationships but are the cause of neither.

Curiously, this view of the relationship between law and society accords with the Marxist perspective on the history of culture. Customary societies are said to precede legal societies, an idea which, semantics aside, most students of historical jurisprudence would accept. But Marxists envision the future as being without laws as we know them, as a return to custom, so to speak, on a higher level, since the repressive and punitive functions of law will become superfluous. Conflicts of economic and political interest will be resolved through the equitable reordering of institutions. Law for the Marxists and most classic students of historical jurisprudence is the cutting edge of the state—but the former, insisting on both a historical and normative view of man, define the state as the instrument of the ruling class, anticipating its dissolution with the abolition of classes, and the common ownership of the basic means of production. But whatever our view of the ultimate Marxist dynamic, law is clearly inseparable from the state. Sir Henry

Maine equates the history of individual property with that of civilization: "Nobody is at liberty to attack several property and to say at the same time that he values civilization. The history of the two cannot be disentangled. Civilization is nothing more than the name for the . . . order . . . dissolved but perpetually reconstituting itself under a vast variety of solvent influences, of which infinitely the most powerful have been those which have, slowly, and in some parts of the world much less perfectly than others, substituted several property for collective ownership." In the words of Jeremy Bentham, "Property and law are born together and die together."

Law, thus, is symptomatic of the emergence of the state; the legal sanction is not simply the cutting edge of institutions at all times and in all places. The "double institutionalization" to which Bohannan refers is, where it occurs, primarily a historical process of unusual complexity. And it occurs in several modes. Custom—spontaneous, traditional, personal, commonly known, corporate, relatively unchanging—is the modality of primitive society; law is the instrument of civilization, of political society sanctioned by organized force, presumably above society at large, and buttressing a new set of social interests. Law and custom both involve the regulation of behavior but their characters are entirely distinct; no evolutionary balance has been struck between developing law and custom, traditional—or emergent. . . .

D. A Note on Law and Social Change

Change is a constant in American life, and may be both a cause and effect of political action. People respond to change (or the threat of change) or seek it in part by recourse to the political system. At the same time they may also have to respond to changes that are brought about largely by political action. Politics and change have always been interrelated in these ways. But, at least since the New Deal, political leaders and institutions have sought, and have been largely granted, new and major responsibilities for the management of change. Whether one views the Supreme Court as a legal or a political body, or as a combination of the two, it has played a basic role in the management of change—a role that antedates the more recent large-scale involvement of other political institutions.

The task of coping with or managing change involves four considerations: perception, knowledge, articulation, and instrumentality. Perception is the identification of the need for change, or of the conditions associated with it. Individuals perceive the world in different ways, and conflicting perceptions often form the basis of conflicting political goals or actions. Persons perceive differently because of differential accumulations of knowledge, because of differences in status and role, for various psychological reasons, and because they are differently affected by social, economic, or political forces.

Law and the courts are often a medium of social perception and thus affect the form in which particular knowledge exists. It is possible to hypothesize that at least some problems of change are seen as they are because of the way in which they are treated by legal institutions. For example, when crime is seen mainly as a "law and order" problem, attempts to convert it into a "social problem" by social scientists are usually rejected. Legal institutions may not only affect the ways in which people perceive problems of change, but they may themselves be prisoners of their own conceptions. Thus, courts that articulate a sociological view of crime and its causes, or that emphasize due process rather than crime control values, are perceived as "deviant" legal institutions and frequently subjected to severe criticism. On the other hand, courts may, by articulating different values from those generally accepted, set in motion processes which may ultimately bring about an acceptance of those values; likewise they may impede or obstruct change by reinforcing or legitimizing appropriate antichange values.

There are several ways in which law or legal institutions may act as the instrumentality of social change beyond the functions of perception and articulation already described. They set authoritative rules or norms which define the limits of permissible behavior and prescribe sanctions to be levied against those violating these rules. They may also offer negative inducements or positive rewards to encourage persons to obey the law. For example, financial or other subsidies may be withheld from those not complying with a legal directive. The capacity of the law to compel people to conform to its rules is, of course, imperfect.

A second change-related function of the law is to legitimize or ratify norms or changes in behavior patterns which occur without any initial assistance from the legal system. This ratification may take the form of providing sanctions to induce compliance with the new norm (thus restating it in "legal" terms), or it may take the form of negating or repealing existing laws which obstruct the path of the particular changes. Law may also serve as the means of reallocating whatever scarce resources are needed to accomplish the change.

Generally speaking, law conditions the processes of change. As Willard

Hurst has so cogently observed, law has a stable bias for change. But it is a bias toward slow, deliberate, incremental, and orderly change through established procedures. It has, if anything, a strong bias against the rapid substitution of norms or the bypassing of established procedures. Related to this, law (and politics) in the United States strongly favors compromise, the peaceful resolution of disputes, and the reduction of controversy; proposed changes that do not meet this criterion may be disfavored or, more important, unable to effectively harness the strength of the law in their behalf.

Until now we have spoken of the law in abstract terms, as if it were a monolithic and discrete entity. This is, of course, a convenient oversimplification. Law is a complex network of individual and institutional relationships, an amalgam of many sets of often conflicting or contradictory impulses and values. In the United States it is as heterogeneous and decentralized as the political system and the population generally. It is neither exclusively for or against change, nor is it for or against any particular types of change. This is not meant to imply that particular laws or judicial doctrines do not have specific change-related biases. They do, of course, although the biases may be unintentional. For example, the doctrine that places the burden on those assailing the validity of a particular welfare statute to demonstrate that the statute is unreasonable or serves no compelling state interest obviously mitigates against any change in the statute via the courts. If the burden is shifted so that the state has to prove that its statute is reasonable or that it has a compelling interest in such a regulation, then the prospects of those assailing the regulation would improve materially.

As an institution that reflects both legal and political values, and that operates in some sense in the United States as a link between the legal and political systems, the Supreme Court is an important denominator of change. Its decisions have sometimes led to major changes, although causal relationships are particularly difficult to prove. It frequently acts as an instrument of change by adopting and thus helping to legitimize change values or goals pursued by others.

Whether the Supreme Court *can* have an effect on social change, and whether it *ought* to have are parallel but obviously related questions. There can be little doubt that many members of the Warren Court were committed to the idea of achieving social change and progress through constitutional decisions. Critics have contended that such a commitment was not only impractical, given the adjudicatory nature of the judicial process, but also a serious perversion of the proper judicial role.[1] Chief Justice Warren Burger has given public support to those critics, arguing that social change through law generally, and through the Supreme Court in particular, is slow and painful. In an interview in the *New York Times*, the Chief Justice expressed these views:[2]

Q. Do you feel that at this point in time the Chief Justice can have more effect for

---

[1]See Alexander Bickel, *The Supreme Court and the Idea of Progress* (New York: Harper & Row, 1970), and Philip B. Kurland, *Politics, the Constitution and the Warren Court* (Chicago: University of Chicago Press, 1970). For a more sympathetic view, see Archibald Cox, *The Warren Court* (Cambridge: Harvard University Press, 1968).

[2]*The New York Times,* July 4, 1971, p. 24.

constructive change outside the Court acting through the legal profession and perhaps other institutions, than through the process of deciding cases?

Chief Justice Burger: *Well, I think that is where it ought to be if we are thinking about the same subject. If there is any influence on the part of Justices of the Supreme Court generally for changes in the law, only a few areas are open to change by decisions, at least as I see it. And changes in the law made by judicial decisions ought to be approached with considerable caution. It was never contemplated in our system that judges would make drastic changes by judicial decision. That is what the legislative function and the rule making function is all about.*

In my conception of it, the primary role of the Court is to decide cases. From the decision of cases, of course, some changes develop, but to try to create or substantially change civil or criminal procedure, for example, by judicial decision is the worst possible way to do it. The Supreme Court is simply not equipped to do the job properly.

Contrasting views about the propriety of the Supreme Court assuming an activist role in promoting social change illuminate some basic considerations—and controversies—about the Court's proper role. This debate is continuous. Traditionally, it has been articulated as the contrast between "judicial activism" and "judicial self-restraint." Current critics of the Supreme Court have substituted the term "imperialism" for activism to describe a Court that they believe has overstepped its proper boundaries.

Such terms are of limited utility in describing the Supreme Court's role and the range of limits that conditions its decision making. A more accurate picture might be obtained by recognizing the existence of two models, or "ideal types," that define the polar opposites of a continuum. Neither model adequately describes the Supreme Court, but the continuum that they demarcate does define a range of behaviors and values that describes the Court's modern role. We have seen that the Supreme Court is a hybrid institution in which law and politics mix in a unique way. These two models help us to understand that mix.

The models have been loosely designated the "Model of Law" and the "Model of Politics." The Model of Law is very much the orthodox conception of the Supreme Court's role. It does not deny that the Supreme Court has a political role to play, but it does emphatically reject the claim that "judges are merely politicians in robes." It chooses to emphasize the differences between law and politics, not their convergence or unity. That difference can be appreciated best as a distinction in the justification of legal and political decisions. The justification of legal decisions, so the argument goes, is one of procedure and method, of means and not ends. The strength, and ultimately the legitimacy, of the law and the courts lies in the establishment and application of fair procedures, not in producing any particular result. Law is the application of principles to the solution of human problems, and it is only when judges objectively apply "neutral" principles that they are acting as judges and as such are entitled to legitimacy and respect. Achieving the "right" or socially desirable result (assuming agreement on what that ought to be), or even the most popular result, is not the function of the courts, and it is not the criterion by which they should be, or are, judged.

There are two basic reasons why courts should act in accord with the Model of Law. The first is that by failing to do so they seriously risk compromising their legitimacy. Because courts, especially the non-elected

U.S. Supreme Court, are not democratic institutions, they must not substitute their own values and judgments for those of elected legislatures and executives. The legitimacy of courts rests in their fidelity to the law and its enforcement. If some interstitial policy making is inevitable, at least by appellate courts, then it should be kept at a bare minimum. But laws and the Constitution should be "strictly construed" by judges to give effect to their fair and original meaning, not to what judges think they ought to mean. And the rule of *stare decisis* should be followed. Courts should be more concerned with upholding the values that a society, through its political processes, has adopted than with being in the forefront of social change. In this way, courts can ensure that social change will proceed in an orderly and stable manner. Courts are not the proper institutions to determine what these changes should be or what new values should supplant traditional ones. If courts do not preserve their distinctiveness from other political bodies, if they cease being "courts," then their claim to legitimacy—and their power—will erode.

If the first reason for adherence to the Model of Law focuses on the expected and proper function of courts and views the consequences for not doing so as a loss of legitimacy, the second reason focuses on the *capacity* of the courts to undertake certain tasks. It emphasizes the limitations in policy making through adjudication (which is, after all, the only way that courts can make policy) and the very limited power of the Supreme Court to implement and monitor compliance with its decisions. The nature of the judicial process is such that courts only rarely get a full picture of the social reality on which policy is based. The futility of courts supervising urban school desegregation, or disci-

plinary practices in schools and prisons, or the decennial legislative reapportionment process are but a few examples. Not only are courts often incapable of bringing about the results they seek, but just as often the cost of trying to bring about "socially desirable results" is, arguably, very great. Thus the costs of a system of strict and detailed judicial supervision of the criminal justice process, the "price of perfect justice" as one critic recently put it, may be a proliferation of appeals and a dragging out of cases that helps no one. The requirement of extensive due process procedures in welfare termination hearings may ultimately result in less money being distributed to the poor and more power going to the bureaucrats, clearly not what the Supreme Court majority in *Goldberg* v. *Kelly* (1970) expected. All of this illustrates the limitations of constitutional policy making. Constitutional rules, once made, are difficult to change and often are not responsive to the very problems they were designed to remedy.

The Model of Politics, in our time, is responsive to a different priority of values. It does not deny the values to a society that flow from a more traditional view of the law and the functions of courts, but it places greater weight on an ethic of aspiration that emphasizes the quest for justice, equality, and the good life. As the late Chief Justice Warren said in 1969, "We have no constituency. We serve no majority. We serve no minority. We serve only the public interest as we see it, guided only by the Constitution and our own consciences." The Model of Politics argues that a total emphasis on procedure and judicial craftsmanship is a thinly disguised mask for defending the status quo and that while this undoubtedly legitimizes the courts for some people, it alienates a greater number. Thus, courts ought to have and promote fair procedures, but they also ought to ensure that the substantive rules of law that they apply are fair and just. Courts can, and should, bring about just results. They should be less concerned with maintaining their own legitimacy and bolder in trying to steer the society toward true justice and equality. Courts may not be democratic if the only criterion is whether or not judges are elected. The realities of power in Congress belie any such simplistic notion. But judges play an important role in a democratic system when they are especially responsive to the rights and needs of minorities, those who are unlikely to exert their fair share of political power.

To play this role, the Constitution must be regarded as a dynamic and often flexible charter, capable of growth, and not a document engraved in stone. Constitutional interpretation is, and must continue to be, a major forum for policy making. It is true, as the critics charge, that constitutional rules, once made, are difficult to change. And it is also true that the judicial forum is not always the best forum in which to decide important policy questions. But often, judges, if they are to live up to their oaths to do justice alike to the rich and to the poor, have no choice but to intervene. It is the worst kind of legalism for courts to mindlessly apply the law without paying any attention to its consequences. As Donald Kommers has observed, "A good constitutional ruling is often a combination of sound policy and bad law."[3]

Each of these models has described an ideal conception of the judicial role.[4] In practice, that is, in actual cases that are decided by the Supreme Court, the choices between them are relative rather than absolute, often being differences of degree rather than differences in kind. Thus, in any particular case the Supreme Court may take a position that is more or less restrained or more or less activist. It may be more or less responsive to legal consideration or to political ones. If no court, or no individual justice, is exclusively or adequately described in terms of one model or the other, neither is there any concurrence between these models and a particular political ideology.

It has become customary to speak of self-restraint, or the Model of Law, as a *conservative* position, and to equate judicial activism, or the Model of Politics, with *liberalism*. Certainly at the present time this is an accurate depiction. But at other times in the Court's history, the configuration was reversed. Liberals on the Court favored the self-restraint position, and it was they who accused the conservatives of unconscionable activism. This is illustrated by a now classic exchange of views in 1936 and 1937 between Justice Harlan Fiske Stone, for the liberals, and Justice George Sutherland, for the conservatives. At the time, the Court was dominated by a conservative majority that had invalidated a large number of state and congressional statutes dealing with problems of economic recovery. Dissenting in *United States* v. *Butler* (1936), a case in which the Supreme Court invalidated the Agricultural Adjustment Act, a major New Deal statute, Justice Stone wrote:

The power of courts to declare a statute unconstitutional is subject to two guiding principles of decision which ought never to be absent from judicial consciousness. One is that courts are con-

---

[3]Donald P. Kommers, *Judicial Politics in West Germany* (Beverly Hills: Sage Publications, 1976), p. 303.

[4]On the question of justifying "legal" decisions, see Virginia Held, "Justification and Legal Ethics," **86** *Ethics* (1975), 1–16.

cerned only with the power to enact statutes, not with their wisdom. The other is that while unconstitutional exercise of power by the executive and legislative branches of the government is subject to judicial restraint, the only check upon our own exercise of power is our own sense of self-restraint. For the removal of unwise laws from the statute books appeal lies not to the courts but to the ballot and to the process of democratic governments.

A tortured construction of the Constitution is not to be justified by recourse to extreme examples of reckless congressional spending which might occur if courts could not prevent expenditures which, even if they could be thought to affect any national purpose, would be possible only by action of a legislature lost to all sense of public responsibility. Such suppositions are addressed to the mind accustomed to believe that it is the business of courts to sit in judgment of legislative action. Courts are not the only agency of government that must be assumed to have the capacity to govern.

Stone's dissent was a strong—and personal—attack on the conservative justices, and a reply was not long in coming. Ironically, the reply also came in the form of a dissenting opinion, since the case of *West Coast* v. *Parrish* (1937) *upheld* the power of the state of Washington to fix minimum working hours for women. Justice Sutherland spoke for the conservatives:

Under our form of government, where the written Constitution, by its own terms, is the supreme law, some agency, of necessity, must have the power to say the final word as to the validity of a statute assailed as unconstitutional. The Constitution makes it clear that the power has been entrusted in this court when the question arises in a controversy within its jurisdiction; and so long as the power remains there, its exercise cannot be avoided without betrayal of the trust.

It has been pointed out many times, as in the Adkins *case, that this judicial duty is one of gravity and delicacy; and that rational doubts must be resolved in favor of the constitutionality of the statute. But whose doubts, and by whom resolved? Undoubtedly it is the duty of a member of the court, in the process of reaching a right conclusion, to give due weight to the opposing views of his associates; but in the end, the question which he must answer is not whether such views seem sound to those who entertain them, but whether they convince him that the statute is constitutional or engender in his mind a rational doubt upon that issue. The oath which he takes is not a composite oath, but an individual one. And in passing upon the validity of a statute, he discharges a duty imposed upon him, which cannot be consummated justly by an automatic acceptance of the views of others which have neither convinced, nor created a reasonable doubt in his mind. If upon a question so important he thus surrender his deliberate judgment, he stands foresworn. . . .*

The suggestion that the only check upon the exercise of the judicial power, when properly invoked, to declare a constitutional right superior to an unconstitutional statute is the judge's own faculty of self-restraint, is both ill considered and mischievous. Self-restraint belongs in the domain of will and not of judgment. The check upon the judge is that imposed by his oath of office, by the Constitution and by his own conscientious and informed convictions. . . .

E. A Note on Social Science, the Supreme Court, and Social Change

In reading this book the student ought to be continuously alert to, and concerned about, the use and utility of the social sciences in understanding the Supreme Court and, perhaps more important, the impact of the social sciences on the policy role of the Court.

With increasing frequency, social

scientists have sought to explain the behavior of Supreme Court justices in terms of behavioral models and concepts. Often, these involve the use of quantitative techniques. There has been much resistance to this approach. Some have argued that the Court is unique in that its work cannot be understood by reference to methods and theories devised to study other nonjudicial political actors. Others have decried the demeaning effect of "reducing the justices to numbers"; they fear that the mystique of the law, and consequently the legitimacy of the Supreme Court, will be reduced by treating the Court as just another political body. They attack the social science approach as merely an extension of the Legal Realist movement of an earlier generation.

The use of social science techniques *to study* the Supreme Court will be discussed further in Chapter 3 of this part of the book. The question is raised here only to draw the parallel between it and the increased use of, and reliance on, social science evidence *by* the Supreme Court. That the Court has increasingly relied on the work of social science cannot be doubted: a quick perusal of footnotes and even the text of major Supreme Court opinions will reveal the increasing citation of works in all the social sciences. Questions about the impact of malapportionment, of legislatures, the impact of racial segregation on black and white schoolchildren, the impact of reading pornographic books on deviant sexual behavior, and the deterrent effects of capital punish-

ment are just a few prominent examples in which the influence of social science is clearly discernible. Just recently, the Court, after a thorough canvass of the extensive social science literature on the subject, held that five-person juries were unconstitutional.[1]

Reliance on social science data and interpretation is not a new phenomenon. Supreme Court opinions, going back to the days of John Marshall, have at least sporadically incorporated such observations. In a few cases, these observations have been specific; most often, they have been implicit in the value choices made by the Court. When John Marshall observed in *Gibbons* v. *Ogden* (1824), in interpreting the commerce clause of the Constitution, that "all America understands and has traditionally understood the word commerce to comprehend navigation," he was making an assumption about public opinion. Of course, no data were cited; none existed. An equally dubious empirical proposition formed the basis of the Supreme Court's early views on the constitutional status of women. In *Bradwell* v. *Illinois* (1872), upholding the refusal of a state to permit women to practice law, the Court noted:

The natural and proper timidity and delicacy which belongs to the female sex evidently unfits it for many of the occupations of civil life. The constitution of the family organization, which is founded in the divine ordinance, as well as in the nature of things, indicates the domestic sphere as that which properly belongs to the domain and functions of womanhood. . . .

[1]*Ballew* v. *Georgia* (1978). But see *Craig* v. *Boren* (1976), where the Court rejected Oklahoma's statistical defense of its gender-based drinking age law. In the course of his opinion for the Court, Justice Brennan remarked: "It is unrealistic to expect either members of the judiciary or state officials to be well versed in the rigors of experimental or statistical technique. But this merely illustrates that proving broad sociological propositions by statistics is a dubious business, and one that inevitably is in tension with the normative philosophy that underlies the Equal Protection Clause. . . ."

Perhaps the most pervasive theory of society utilized by the Supreme Court in premodern times was Social Darwinism—the social application of the evolutionary concept of the survival of the fittest. Popularized in the United States by the sociologist William Graham Sumner, the theory found strong expression in Supreme Court decisions opposing regulation of the economy, such as *Lochner* v. *New York* (1905, *infra*) and in decisions such as *Plessy* v. *Ferguson* (1896, *infra*), upholding racial discrimination under the doctrine of "separate but equal," and *Buck* v. *Bell* (1927), upholding the compulsory sterilization of mental defectives.

A major turn toward reliance on more systematic social science findings came in *Muller* v. *Oregon* (1908). In attempting to justify an Oregon statute limiting working hours for women, attorney Louis Brandeis presented to the Court a brief that contained minimal legal arguments and extensive social science data about the impact of long hours of work on women. The Court accepted Brandeis' argument and took special note of this type of advocacy, which became known as the "Brandeis Brief." Debate over the merits and propriety of the Brandeis Brief approach was rekindled in the aftermath of *Brown* v. *Board of Education* (1954). The record in the case included several studies of the impact of segregation on black children. These were footnoted in the Supreme Court's opinion, as was a reference to the now classic work by the Swedish economist, Gunnar Myrdal, *An American Dilemma*. Those who opposed the decision found its reliance on social science, especially its mention of the writings of a foreign scholar (who also happened to

be a socialist), outrageous. But even those who sympathized with the decision found the use of social science findings of some concern. Professor Edmond Cahn argued, for example, that constitutional rights ought not to depend on the vicissitudes of social science, a warning now being recalled in the light of "new thinking" about the efficacy of integration as a device to improve the learning of black schoolchildren.[2] A similar contemporary backlash against Brandeis' substantive arguments in *Muller* v. *Oregon* has also occurred in the wake of the women's rights movement.

It would be easy to say that increased judicial reliance on social science is a response to increasing demands for changes in legal doctrine. One way of challenging venerable rules of law effectively, without suggesting that they were never correct or proper, is to show that the conditions that supported them no longer exist. Social science has also provided a means for challenging old assumptions about the nature of the human condition. As Archibald Cox has noted,

Modern psychology has raised doubts concerning freedom of the will that raise skepticism of the very notion of crime. Sociologists have cast doubt upon the efficacy of punishment and deterrence in the face of the social, economic and psychological causes of criminal conduct. When an issue is nicely balanced between the interests of the public and the claims of individual liberty, the substitution of such doubts for once-accepted verities may be enough to tip the scales against the prosecution.

If this is true in criminal procedure, may not similar forces be partly responsible for the turmoil in other areas of constitutional law? . . . While the social sci-

[2]Edmund Cahn, "A Dangerous Myth in the School Segregation Cases," **30** *New York University Law Review* (1955), 150–169. See also I.A. Newby, *Challenge to the Court* (Baton Rouge: Louisiana State University Press, 1969).

entists [are] changing our understanding of man . . . judges will inevitably be stimulated to reexamine the law's own presuppositions. One wonders, indeed, whether the gulf between the Supreme Court and the Congress is not partly a reflection of the closer kinship the justices have with the intellectual community.[3]

Still, it would be wrong to conclude that social science data are utilized only in challenging the status quo. Social science is not monolithic. It is rarely conclusive. Courts are under no compulsion to follow its dictates.[4] Courts do have an obligation to decide cases; they cannot wait for "perfect" answers or ultimate empirical "truths." Thus, social science is available to be used, and is used, often by opposing sides in the same dispute. Inevitably, the findings of social science must be interpreted normatively as well as empirically. In that sense, its limits are also the basis of its legitimacy in the judicial process. It does not dictate decisions but instead informs judges and is available to support decisions they wish to make.[5]

Increased use of social science is also an indicator of the degree to which judges have moved from the traditional and basic judicial function of deciding concrete disputes between identifiable litigants to an acknowledged broader policy function. Disputes between litigants provide only the structure for consideration of disputes between competing social, political, or economic "interests." The outcome of a particular case may be less important than the issues that it raises. As Martin Shapiro has noted correctly, parties become merely "an example or sample of the social reality."[6] If this is true, then the choice of a particular "sample" of reality as the basis for consideration of major public policy issues is critically important. On the other hand, to combat the limitations inherent in the "social reality" of any particular case, there is a strong current trend among Supreme Court justices to openly consider a broad range of evidence bearing on the operation of a particular policy, including evidence not presented by the parties. As Miller and Barron have observed, "adjudicative facts" become submerged in the Court's consideration of larger social problems,[7] and the proscription against "advi-

---

[3]Quoted in Nathan Glazer, "Towards an Imperial Judiciary?" *The Public Interest* (1975), p. 116.

[4]Compare Justice Frankfurter's opinion in *Goesaert* v. *Cleary* (1948), a case upholding a state law denying bartender's licenses to women except wives and daughters of licensed male bar owners:

Michigan could, beyond question, forbid all women from working behind a bar. This is so despite the vast changes in the social and legal position of women. The fact that women may now have achieved the virtues that men have long claimed as their prerogatives and now indulge in vices that men have long practiced, does not preclude the States from drawing a sharp line between the sexes, certainly in such matters as the regulation of the liquor traffic. [The] Constitution does not require legislatures to reflect sociological insight, or shifting social standards, any more than it requires them to keep abreast of the latest scientific standards.

[5]For a more extended discussion of the role of social science, see Victor G. Rosenblum, "A Place for Social Science Along the Judiciary's Constitutional Law Frontier," **66** *Northwestern University Law Review* (1971), 455–480.

[6]Martin Shapiro, "Courts," in Polsby and Greenstein (eds.), *Handbook of Political Science*, Vol. V (Reading, Massachusetts: Addison-Wesley Publishing Co., 1975), 348.

[7]Arthur Selwyn Miller and Jerome A. Barron, "The Supreme Court, the Adversary System, and the Flow of Information to the Justices: A Preliminary Inquiry," **61** *Virginia Law Review* (1975), 1187–1245.

sory opinions" becomes more difficult to maintain. Whatever the consequences for the purity of the adversary system, at least in this way the Court can protect itself against making pol-

icy on the basis of inadequate information. But it also makes the Court's lawmaking function that much more difficult to disguise.

3. SUPREME COURT POLICY MAKING

A. *A Note on the Definition of "Policy"*

We have assumed from the outset that the Supreme Court is an important national policymaker. But what is meant by "policy"? Policy should be considered as an authoritative and prospective standard of action that is applied to the solution of a perceived problem. Certain features of this definition must be emphasized. First, it is important to distinguish action from the standard by which the taking of action is governed; policy is not equivalent to action, but to the criteria governing a decision to act. Second, policy is by definition prospective, and states, in effect, what *will be done* in response to a particular problem. This is not inconsistent with the concept of judicial retroactivity (see pp. 872–875). Most judicial decisions are retroactively applied in the sense that they are applied to govern the resolution of an existing dispute. However, the application of a particular policy is always prospective.

Third, our definition of policy carries a strong implication of rationality, insofar as the standard of action is directed to a perceived problem. In the judicial context, it is rationality in the form of serial adjudication. A Supreme Court policy may come full blown out of a particular case; more

likely it will evolve out of a series of cases which consider various aspects of a problem. Fourth, and finally, the development and application of a policy is instrumental and secondary to its initial conception. Implementation of Supreme Court decisions is, as we have seen and will continue to emphasize throughout the book, highly decentralized. The Court has primary control over determining the content of legal policies through its authority to interpret the Constitution and the laws. But once a policy has been enunciated—or, as is very often the case with the Supreme Court, suggested or alluded to—it is the wider political environment, and the characteristics and processes of other institutions and actors, which determine the convergence between action and policy.

B. *Herbert Jacob, Policy Making and Norm Enforcement*

. . . Every day, courts in America make "political" decisions. They settle conflicts that otherwise would have to be settled by legislative or executive action. Not only do courts mediate disputes, as other political agencies do, but they also formulate

Reprinted from *Justice in America* (Boston: Little, Brown, 1965), pp. 3–4, 26–33.

policy in the same manner. It makes little difference to those affected whether desegregation is the consequence of a legislative act, an executive order, or a court decision. It is a governmental policy that must be obeyed at the risk of imprisonment. Throughout the Republic's history, courts have engaged in policy-making. When the courts enforced debts after the Revolution, they were making important economic policy. When they decided in the *Dred Scott* case that the provisions concerning slaves in the Missouri Compromise were unconstitutional, they helped set the stage for the Civil War. When they protected corporations under the cloak of the Fourteenth Amendment, they helped create the environment in which American industrialism grew. Each of these decisions and many more affect the agenda of legislators and executive officials throughout the country. Such decisions set policies that necessitate further action from other government agencies.

Courts do not always set policy. Of the thousands of decisions judges make, only a handful can be classified as policy decisions. Most of the time the judiciary enforces community norms. Courts prescribe punishment for thieves, sex deviates, murderers, and other criminals. They enforce contractual relationships and force payment of damages for injuries due to negligence. Decisions of this sort constitute the bulk of the judiciary's business. Most such decisions are routine. Nevertheless, in deciding such cases, judges exercise discretion, for they must fit the law to the particular circumstances. By the gradual accretion of decisions that accommodate the law to the conditions that confront judges, new law is made. It would be misleading to categorize the norm enforcement activities of judges as policy-making, even when judges make new law, for they are not consciously establishing norms to regulate subsequent behavior when they render an enforcement decision. Yet, like judicial policy-making, judicial enforcement of norms may immerse the courts in controversy and politics.

The occasions on which the courts make policy or enforce community norms are determined by the characteristics of the judicial process. In some ways judicial decision-making is like other governmental processes. Courts respond—although less immediately—to societal pressures; they are moved by the same tides of public opinion as are legislatures and executives, although the judiciary is somewhat more resistant to the lesser currents. Many of the same problems that confront legislators and executives find their way to the courtroom. When the nation is enveloped by a "Red Scare," the courts find cases involving national security and civil rights on their dockets. If labor racketeering attracts Congressional attention, it is not long before the alleged racketeers are in court defending their activities. Whenever Congress adopts controversial legislation, opponents of the law soon challenge it in court. . . .

The distinction between law enforcement and policy-making rests on qualitative differences. In enforcing laws, the courts intend each decision to apply only to the present case. Such decisions (usually by trial courts) are not designed to create precedent or set policy. Often they are unaccompanied by an opinion or, if opinions are written, they remain unpublished, so that as a result of their inaccessibility these decisions cannot become precedent. Although a series of norm-enforcement decisions may constitute a trend and change the law slowly through judicial usage, judges who make such decisions are often unaware of the direction or pace of the trend. This is true not only in the administration of criminal justice but also in cases concerning divorce and other familial matters, personal injury litigation, and labor disputes.

When they make policy, the courts do not exercise more discretion than when they enforce community norms. The difference lies in the intended impact of the decision. Policy decisions are intended to be guideposts for future actions; norm-enforcement decisions are aimed at the instant case alone. Policy-making decisions are usually accompanied by published opinions to which other lawyers can refer in other courts. Appellate courts most frequently make policy decisions. Trial courts set policy only occasionally.

Opportunities for judicial policy-making arise less frequently than occasions for enforcing norms. Every case affords the chance to enforce a norm. Only when a norm is itself challenged can the courts engage in policy-making. Such occasions may require the courts to interpret statutes or to interpret constitutional provisions.

In interpreting statutes, American courts determine the effects of legislative decisions. To many judges a legislative enactment is not law until enforced and interpreted by the courts. In most instances the courts interpret statutes routinely, for most cases fall squarely inside or outside the law's provisions. Yet there are cases where the legislature's intent is ambiguous; these provide the courts an opportunity to engage in policy-making. For instance, the courts must determine whether a usury law extends to installment purchases as well as to loans made by small loan companies and banks. Sometimes a legislature intentionally enacts an ambiguous

statute, leaving its detailed interpretation to the courts. Antitrust statutes, for instance, permit much judicial policy-making, for Congress has enacted only the most general guides to policy. . . .

The courts are often called upon to interpret the Constitution. Every controversial statute and many controversial executive actions are challenged in court on grounds of unconstitutionality. The occasion to interpet constitutional provisions arises more often in federal than state courts because the national Constitution is more ambiguous in many of its key provisions. State constitutions, by contrast, are much more detailed documents and leave much less room for judicial interpretation. Both state and federal courts usually ratify the decision of other government officials by finding the challenged legislation or executive action constitutional. Sometimes, however, they declare the law or action unconstitutional. When deciding on the constitutionality of a government action, the courts must choose what meaning they wish to give the Constitution and which social objectives to pursue. . . .

Even though Americans do not usually perceive their courts as policy-makers, they often bring important controversies to them. The power of courts to review the constitutionality of legislative and executive action, commonly called the power of "judicial review," constantly involves American courts in conscious policy-making.

Judicial policy-making is not distinguished from other court actions only by the intent of judges, the form of their decisions, and the impact of their actions. It is also characterized by a different array of participants. Whereas norm-enforcement decisions usually concern only the immediate litigants, policy decisions draw a wider group of participants to the courtroom. They especially attract the concern of organized interest groups. In part this is because it is difficult and expensive to engage in litigation; it requires the commitment of considerable financial resources as well as the willingness to wait patiently until the case has been won. Consequently, litigants who are more interested in changing policy than in correcting a single wrong seldom stand by themselves.

Moreover, not everyone may sue in court. In order to litigate, one must have "standing"—that is, one must be personally involved in the sense that one's own person or property has been threatened. Therefore, those who wish to test a law in court often violate the law's provisions intentionally in order to provide an opportunity to sue in court. . . .

A test case not only requires careful selection of the individual litigant whose name is lent to the suit but also necessitates careful planning of courtroom strategy. The action protested against must be challengeable only on constitutional grounds. If a judge rules that it is wrong because some procedure has not been followed or because the law does not apply to the particular case in question, the group will have won its case without gaining its broader policy objective. Such a victory is a Pyrrhic one, for other officials may still proceed against the group as before. The group's lawyers, therefore, must plan its case so that a decision can only be reached on constitutional grounds. All other avenues of deciding the case must be foreclosed; no gaps may remain open that might allow a court to avoid the issue the group wishes to press on it.

The technique of instituting test cases has been perfected by the National Association for the Advance-ment of Colored People and the Jehovah's Witnesses. It is responsible for their marked success in winning important policy changes for themselves. For the Jehovah's Witnesses it won a new measure of religious freedom; for the N.A.A.C.P. the technique abolished discrimination by state and local governments. Test cases, however, do not guarantee that an appellate court will hear the case or that a court will respond to the challenge presented by the case. Despite whatever skill has been invested in the case, an appellate court may simply refuse to review or may find legal technicalities that allow it to avoid the policy issue that the group wishes to resolve. For instance, for many years most courts stated that reapportionment issues were not justiciable; consequently, cases involving malapportionment were rarely successful. In such instances judges felt that they could provide no legal remedy for what was admitted to be a moral wrong. Not until 1962 in the famous *Baker* v. *Carr* case were litigants successful in convincing the Supreme Court that the issue was justiciable. The earlier failure of groups to convince the Court was not the result of less skillful presentations; it seems more plausible that the Court was prepared in 1962 to decide a matter it was unwilling to decide earlier. Yet the Court would have been unable to render such a decision without the willingness of litigants to press their test case through the courts. . . .

Test cases are not the sole means by which groups participate in the policy-making activities of the courts. Some cases involving policy reach the courts without initial group participation. Appeals by defendants in criminal cases, for instance, are often instigated by the defendant himself, not by a group, even though his appeal may raise policy questions. Moreover, groups other than the one that initiated a test case sometimes want to be heard in court. Under such circumstances groups may participate by submitting an *amicus curiae* (friend of the court) brief to the court. Such briefs are most often filed with an appellate court. . . . To file such a brief, a group must first obtain permission from the litigants in the case or, failing that, from the court.

An *amicus* brief places the group's opinions and attitudes on the record. It gives a court additional information on which it may decide a case.

. . . *Amicus curiae* briefs involve groups more casually than test cases do. They parallel to a striking degree the principal technique of lobbyists before executive agencies and legislatures, for they rely on the utility of information. It is hoped that giving the courts information will incline them to rule in favor of the group's interest. Furthermore, an *amicus curiae* brief is an effective means of showing a group's support for a particular cause that has reached the court through someone else's initiative. It satisfies a group's own members by dramatically demonstrating the organization's activity in behalf of causes about which they are concerned. On the other hand, presenting such a brief to an appellate court involves fewer risks and less cost than making a test case. No member of the group is personally threatened with imprisonment or the other consequences of a lost lawsuit; the group's own interests are usually not so directly involved that a reversal in court would lastingly damage them. However, although the tactic is less dangerous, it is also less effective. *Amicus curiae* briefs on one side of a case often evoke similar briefs on the other side. There is little evidence that judges are particularly influenced by these briefs. Occasionally

an opinion will quote material from an *amicus* brief or follow the logic suggested in it, but the judge might have come to the same conclusions without the brief.

The participation of interest groups in judicial policy-making illustrates one of the similarities between judicial and other governmental policy-making. There are important differences as well. Judicial policies have a narrower scope; they often are directed at government agencies rather than the public at large; and their impact is often more ambiguous than legislative policies.

Some issues are almost never raised in courtrooms, so that the courts rarely formulate policies with regard to them. Foreign affairs, although increasingly important to the American political system, are ordinarily beyond the scope of court action. With very few exceptions (involving cases questioning the validity of treaties), courts have not become involved in foreign affairs. Judicial policy-making is restricted to domestic affairs.

Even in the domestic arena judicial policies do not touch on all matters. The appropriation of funds and the levying of taxes are almost never successfully challenged in court. Moreover, courts rarely demand that funds be appropriated for a particular purpose. Such issues remain the almost exclusive domain of legislative and executive decision-making.

Most judicial policies are concerned with the regulatory activities of government. Judicial concern with government regulation arises from the constitutional guarantees of individual freedom and the right to hold property subject only to government action through the due process of law. All regulatory policies restrict freedom and property. Therefore, courts have often been asked to determine whether such regulations were imposed through due process or not. Such conflicts have required the courts to develop judicial policies restricting government regulation to reasonable acts adopted through lawful procedures.

Judicial policy-making, moreover, is usually directed at other government agencies rather than at private individuals. This is another consequence of the interpretive role that courts play. They interpret statutes and constitutional provisions, and in so doing, they permit or prohibit the action of other government agencies. For instance, they have prohibited racial discrimination by *government* agencies in schools, parks, elections, and similar affairs, but they have not prohibited racial discrimination by private individuals. The latter prohibitions, insofar as they have been enacted, are the consequences of legislative and executive policy making.

A third important characteristic of judicial policies is that their intended scope is often quite ambiguous. This is a consequence of the process by which policies are adopted. Courts make policy in response to the particular factual situations raised by the cases they are considering. Although judges may informally consider a much wider range of facts than those present in a case, the decision itself is based on the facts of the instant case. The judges who write the opinion may intend their decision to apply to many similar situations, but that intention is usually not clear until other cases have been litigated and the new doctrine has been extended to them. In the meantime, there can be much uncertainty about the policy's extent because its phraseology has been necessarily ambiguous. Although it cannot be argued that legislative policy is never ambiguous, its ambiguities

arise from other causes. Legislative policy is not usually adopted because of a single incident, and precedents which are themselves ambiguous do not play as large a role in justifying the policy.

The ambiguity of judicial policy statements leads to a rhythm of action typical in judicial policy-making. A high court will declare a new policy in a case involving one constellation of facts. A series of cases then follows in which the high court or lower ones extend the policy to other fact situations. Over the course of a few years the scope of the policy becomes more certain.

The fact that courts make policy conditions the political process in America. It opens another avenue for seeking favorable decisions for those who are unsuccessful with the legislature or executive. If a group fails to capture or hold a legislative majority, and if it fails to elect its man as chief executive of the state or nation, it may nevertheless seek to alter public policy through litigation. Access to the courts and success before them depend not on electoral victories but on legal skill and sufficient financial resources.

The fact that the courts constitute an additional policy-making arena creates further uncertainty about public policy in the United States. A controversial matter is not settled when Congress enacts a law and the President decides to enforce it. The courts must also approve the policy. At the very least, judicial participation in the process delays decisions by several months. At the most, it stymies Congress and the President and leads to the enactment of policies favored by judges. The increased fragmentation of the policymaking process in the United States has another consequence besides delaying action. It allows certain people

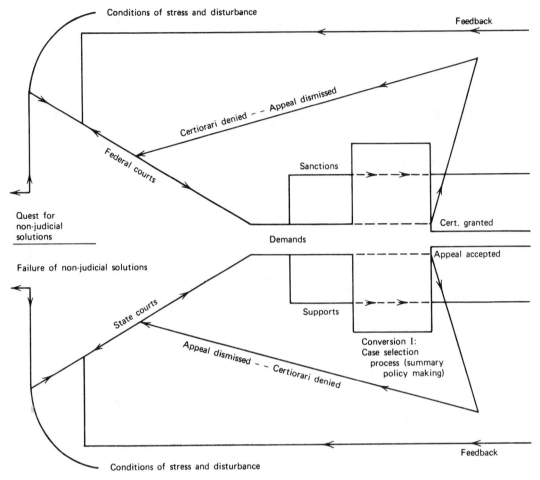

Figure 1.   A model of Supreme Court policy making.

who would otherwise be excluded from politics to have a voice in the making of public decisions. . . .

C. A Model of Supreme Court Policy Making

A course in constitutional law that focuses almost exclusively on a few prominent Supreme Court decisions risks losing sight of the fact that the Court is but a part of a larger political process. An understanding of the Court's policies and their impact requires a systemwide perspective that recognizes the pertinent roles played by other actors, groups, and institutions. A schematic diagram provides this perspective in part (see Figure 1), although it necessarily describes only some of the elements that comprise the policy-making process.

The study of constitutional law is more than the study of Supreme Court decisions. It is also the study of the workings of an institution whose members make decisions affecting the character of the society we live in, and whose decisions, in turn, are the products in part of competing forces in that society. A model can only suggest the nuances and idiosyncrasies that characterize the judicial process, as well as the main actors in that process, who are constantly changing. However, there is stability as well as

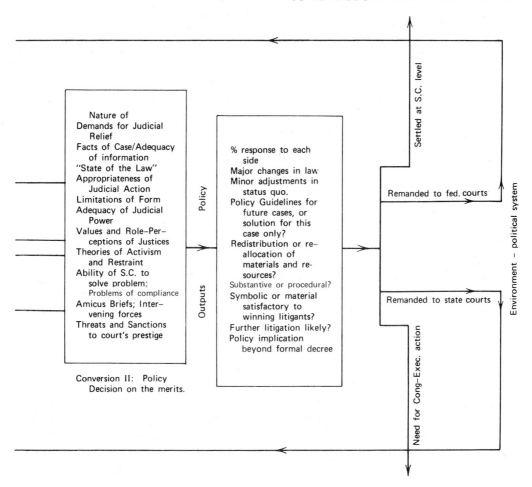

Nature of
Demands for Judicial
Relief
Facts of Case/Adequacy
of information
"State of the Law"
Appropriateness of
Judicial Action
Limitations of Form
Adequacy of Judicial
Power
Values and Role-Per-
ceptions of Justices
Theories of Activism
and Restraint
Ability of S.C. to
solve problem;
Problems of compliance
Amicus Briefs; Inter-
vening forces
Threats and Sanctions
to court's prestige

Conversion II: Policy
Decision on the merits.

Policy

Outputs

% response to each
side
Major changes in law
Minor adjustments in
status quo.
Policy Guidelines for
future cases, or
solution for this
case only?
Redistribution or re-
allocation of
materials and re-
sources?
Substantive or procedural?
Symbolic or material
satisfactory to
winning litigants?
Further litigation likely?
Policy implication
beyond formal decree

Settled at S.C. level

Remanded to fed. courts

Remanded to state courts

Need for Cong-Exec. action

Environment – political system

change in the judicial process, and it is possible for the student to observe certain regularities of behavior and certain patterns of policy development.

The basic assumptions underlying the model shown here have already been suggested. The importance of the Supreme Court in American life is not that it exists, but that it is one of several important policy-making institutions. What the Court does may have a large impact on the values and actions of individuals and groups. The Court, like the law generally, is an important factor in the ways in which our society is governed and in how it responds to the need for change. The Court monitors and helps to preserve the rules by which other institutions operate. It also creates some of those rules. It reminds us of, and to some extent protects, our heritage of individual rights. It umpires the disputes between other institutions in a federal system of government. The Court is, in short, many things to many people. An accurate view of its policy-making function must account for this diversity.

A more traditional view of the Supreme Court would no doubt depict the justices "deciding" great constitutional issues by determining the meaning of various clauses of the Constitution. But this static view, reflecting the school of "mechanical jurisprudence" previously described, fails to comprehend the complexities of the judicial process. It ignores almost entirely the role of the individual judge as a decision maker with considerable autonomy and discretion. It ignores the continuous pressures on the Court to make decisions favoring one or another interest or set of values. And it ignores the limits of the law—and of the Supreme Court. Knowing the "meaning" of the Constitution, therefore, is a necessary but not sufficient guide to the dynamics of constitutional law.

We think the most useful way of viewing Supreme Court policy making is to regard it as a process that includes actors and variables extending beyond the court and what is generally understood as law. Precisely what role the Court may play in this process varies with the problem, but there may be certain elements common to every type of policy problem that enters the judicial arena. These common elements include the need to make conscious choices between competing claims about the validity of a particular governmental or private action, the legal, political, or economic status of an individual or group, or the validity of a particular pattern of behavior. Judicial solutions are not always clearly articulated. In most cases to come to the Supreme Court, there will be no formal decision and thus, inferentially at least, a decision in favor of the status quo and against the interests of the particular litigant who has sought the help of the Court. The Supreme Court rarely has either the first or the last word on a major issue of public policy. Its decisions, like many others in the political process, vary in their impact.

For analytical purposes it is useful to think of the judicial process as a *system* or pattern of human behaviors that relate to each other in various ways. The judicial system consists primarily of five component parts, each of which will be discussed below. Although the judicial system has properties that it shares with related and overlapping systems, it is useful to hypothesize the existence of boundaries which separate one system from another, recognizing the difficulty of precisely defining such boundaries.

The five components of the judicial system are (1) the environment in which it operates; (2) the inputs from other systems; (3) the conversion process, by which inputs are transformed into outputs directed within the system and across system boundaries to other systems; (4) the outcomes of the policy outputs; and (5) the feedback as a result of these outputs and outcomes which returns to the system in the form of new inputs.

1. The environment is both a constant and a variable in the decision-making process. What is meant by environment in this context is the variety of conditions under which judges operate, conditions that range from the relationship between the Court and the Congress to the internal workings of the Court, such as the conference and oral argument, which are determined by precedent and tradition. To a large extent, what we call environmental variables form a conduit that tends to shape the probable judicial response to a particular case or controversy. If the Court has traditionally refused to hear a particular type of case, if the law applicable to a particular case is clear and venerable, and if there is strong public and political support for the continuance of a particular legal policy, then the environment is likely to be hostile to those who would seek change. Likewise, great pressures for change and the

demonstrated unworkability of an existing policy are likely to create a favorable and inviting environment for those who seek change. The concept of environment, as used in this context, is one of perception and communication rather than one of empirical fact.

2. Inputs to the judicial system usually come in two forms: demands for change triggered by dissatisfaction with prevailing conditions, and supports for prevailing policies or supports for the judiciary as a viable institution of government. Those who make demands are not necessarily attacking the judiciary as an institution, and those supporting specific existing policies may not be supporting the judiciary as an institution beyond the need to protect specific interests.

Demands for judicial action often result from the inability of other institutions to provide adequate solutions or policy guidance for important social problems, thus permitting disturbances to the equilibrium of power which require amelioration or readjustment. It is not true today, as de-Tocqueville predicted in 1835, that every question of politics eventually becomes a question of constitutional law. But many such questions do reach the judicial arena, and they seek—if they do not always get—a judicial policy response.

Demands on the Supreme Court usually come as appeals from decisions of lower federal courts or, in fewer instances, from the highest state courts. The parties who bring these cases may be individual citizens, government agencies, social and political groups. They may seek the aid of the Court in enforcing an existing rule of law, in interpreting a statute or ordinance, or in halting a particular action that they deem unconstitutional or illegal. This book provides examples of the wide array of demands on the Court that are made annually.

Regulation of demands is a crucial function of any system. The Supreme Court has developed an intricate series of rules designed to regulate the types of questions it will hear, and when and by whom it will hear them. These rules customarily fall under the heading of jurisdiction (whether the Court has the legal right to hear a case) and justiciability (whether it is appropriate and feasible for the Court to hear a case or decide a particular issue), but they are in fact much more intricate and, indeed, idiosyncratic, than might appear on the surface. Many factors that affect the regulation of demands on the judiciary are not formally articulated by the justices themselves and must be derived from statistical indices or inferred from textual analysis of the Court's opinions. The next two chapters describe the function of demand regulation in greater detail.

3. The heart of the policy-making process is the conversion stage. Not only is this the most visible and dramatic part of the Court's life but also the most studied and written about. What is meant by conversion simply is the transformation of inputs (demands and supports) into outputs (constitutional and statutory policies). Constitutional policies do not just appear, nor are they brought, in Max Lerner's classic quip, by judicial storks. They result from the interaction of the value preferences of the individual justices, the type, feasibility, and potential consequences of demands made on the Court, the "state" of the law in a particular area, the dynamics of the collegial decision-making process, pressures from the environment, and other factors. A fuller description of the conversion process appears in

Chapter Three of this part of the book.

The model divides the conversion process on the Supreme Court into two analytically distinct but overlapping stages; first, the decision whether to grant review to hear a particular case and, second, if review is granted, the decision on the substantive policy issues (e.g. the decision "on the merits"). Most cases coming to the Supreme Court fail to reach the second stage—that is, they are denied review. The decision to hear a case characteristically involves more individual and less collegial decision making, although the formal procedures are nearly identical. The first stage is almost totally invisible to the general public, although vastly more cases are "decided" by denying review than after a full hearing on the merits. Most important policy making takes place at the second stage, although by establishing a particular pattern of denials of review, the Court may indeed exert an important policy impact, for example, by consistently refusing to hear reapportionment cases (as was the practice until 1962) or questions concerning the legality of the war in Indochina.

4. The conversion process produces policies or outputs—decisions by a majority or the justices favoring a particular litigant or set of values and opposing others. Policy decisions have several dimensions. First, and most obviously, they are statements about the law, describing or defining the meaning or development of a particular ordinance, statute, or constitutional provision. They may prescribe certain rights and duties or required behavior by citizens, or proscribe or prohibit other behavior. Beyond this formal level, however, it is useful to conceptualize such decisions as tentative, usually incremental, attempts to provide interim solutions to con-

tinuing problems. It may also be useful to think of Supreme Court decisions in the following terms:

a. Does the decision make major changes in the law, requiring equally large changes in the behavior of persons or institutions, or does a decision represent only a minor adjustment to the status quo?

b. If a decision requires things to be done—that is, if it is not self-executing—what things must be done and, equally important, by whom—other judges, public officials, ordinary citizens, and so forth?

c. What values or ideologies does the decision support? Is the decision likely to offer *more* than symbolic support for those forces in society advancing these values? If so, what types of specific strategic and tactical support does a particular court decision offer? How can a particular decision be used most effectively by those whose interests it supports?

d. In what ways does a decision mandate, support, or deter the reallocation of physical, economic, or social resources?

e. What impact does the decision have on the allocation of power in the various branches and institutions of government? Are these allocations likely to be short run or long range?

f. Is further litigation likely? What impact does the decision have on the legal status of the litigants? To what extent does the decision have implications that extend beyond the immediate litigants or the immediate issue in dispute?

g. What impact will the decision have on the Court's capacity to function effectively in the future, for example, on its power, prestige, and authority? Will the decision encourage or stimulate retributive measures against the Court by the Congress? Will it result in a loss of public support?

5. The mere fact that the Supreme Court makes a decision is no assurance that it will be complied with or that it will have its intended effect. The following essay explores the gap between outputs and outcomes, as well as some other characteristics of Supreme Court policy making.

D. *The Characteristics of Supreme Court Policy Making*

Social change is, for the most part, a long-term phenomenon and very difficult to define with precision.[1] An accurate assessment of the Supreme Court's impact on social change is thus very difficult. When one tries to assess even the Court's proximate impact or attempts to measure compliance with *specific* decisions, the difficulties of measuring the long-term effect on social change can be appreciated.

Measuring the impact of a policy-making institution usually assumes that there are concrete "policies" that require specific compliant acts. Certainly, there are some Supreme Court policies that adhere to this model. But Supreme Court policy making is a much more complex enterprise than merely directing that certain acts be done. Levine and Becker have argued that the primary policy impact of the Supreme Court comes from its ability to manipulate symbols.[2] Others have suggested that the Court's most im-

portant power, and policy function, is to define national issues and priorities and to monitor (and sometimes create) decision rules for other governmental institutions.

Supreme Court policy making is not independent of its adjudicative function, which further complicates efforts to assess its impact. Policy statements (other than those directing action in the particular case) are often not clearly stated, and ambiguity in policy can only breed ambiguity in implementation. Policies that are primarily open-ended, that state general goals or values without specifying the means of attainment, are particularly prone to be read ambiguously and complied with unevenly.

Analysis of policy impact is, of course, just a special case of the problem of determining causality in human behavior. Comparing the terms "compliance" and "impact" demonstrates this difficulty with regard to the Supreme Court. Although frequently used interchangeably, or in conjunction, the terms are conceptually different. Compliance is the narrower term, referring to an action taken in response to and according to the dictates of a particular policy decision. Compliance with a court decision may not result from that decision alone or from that decision directly. It may occur in response to other pressures or forces within the system that a particular Supreme Court decision has generated. One must also differentiate, if possible, between actions that might have occurred in any event, but that happen to conform to

---

[1]Joel B. Grossman, "The Supreme Court and Social Change: A Preliminary Inquiry," 13 *American Behavioral Scientist* (1970), 535–551.

[2]James P. Levine and Theodore L. Becker, "Toward and Beyond a Theory of Supreme Court Impact," in Becker and Feeley (eds.) *The Impact of Supreme Court Decisions* (New York: Oxford University Press, 1973), pp. 230–245.

Supreme Court policies, and actions that occurred primarily in response to a particular policy.

Impact, by contrast, is a broader and more diffuse concept. Compliance is a form of impact and may in some instances constitute all the impact that is important. But a Supreme Court decision may also have a negative impact or unforeseen and unintended consequences. Widespread evasion or noncompliance with a decision may be regarded as part of the impact of a decision. Conversely, a high level of compliance may nevertheless yield only relatively low impact. For example, the relatively high percentage of law enforcement officers who give the *Miranda* warnings suggests high compliance. Yet the *Miranda* warnings are not ends in themselves; they are instruments designed to achieve certain substantive reforms in the criminal interrogation process. And the evidence shows, at least in the first decade, only modest achievement of these reforms.

The *intentions* of policy makers, and the time dimension, are also important and often puzzling ingredients in assessing causality. Few Supreme Court decisions rival *Miranda* in the candor of its expression of desirable goals and initial premises. Thus, it is often asked, "What did the majority intend?" For example, in the *Bakke* decision in 1978, a 5-4 majority of the Court held that it was unconstitutional for a university medical school to set aside a fixed number of places in its entering class for minority students, at least where there was no showing of prior discrimination against minorities at

that university and where such an affirmative action program was not specifically mandated by Congress. But in the same case, a different 5-4 majority held that it was permissible to consider race as a factor in college admissions. Few professional schools in the United States had affirmative action programs quite as rigid as that declared unconstitutional in the *Bakke* case (at the University of California–Davis Medical School). Those schools that had such programs could entertain few doubts that they were unconstitutional. But for the vast majority, the impact of the *Bakke* case, and what they might have to do to comply with it, was at best ambiguous. Quite clearly, the Supreme Court itself was uncertain. Its decision invalidated a few affirmative action programs but provided little guidance for the rest. Further guidance from the Court will come, presumably, in future cases that require it to be more precise in deciding what kinds of affirmative action programs are permitted under the Constitution. Thus, as Wasby has perceptively noted, impact (and causality) is both a long- and a short-term phenomenon. The importance of a decision, and its real impact, may not be understood until a substantial time period has elapsed.[3] All attributions of causality, especially those relating the Supreme Court to social change, carry an element of risk. As Levine has noted, even where decisions appear to have been complied with, the cause-and-effect linkages may be probabilistic and incomplete.[4] As in other social science research, it is always necessary to consider the existence of "rival

---

[3]Wasby uses the term "aftermath" to cover actions which followed, were congruent with, but did not necessarily follow from, Supreme Court decisions. Stephen Wasby, *The Impact of the United States Supreme Court: Some Perspectives* (Homewood, Illinois: Dorsey Press, 1970), Chapter 2.

[4]James P. Levine, "Methodological Concerns in Studying Supreme Court Efficacy," 4 *Law and Society Review* (1970), 583–607.

plausible hypotheses" to explain results tentatively attributed to Supreme Court decisions.[5]

The gap between policy making and implementation is familiar to all students of the law, and indeed of politics generally. Legal rules and doctrines, even assuming that they are clearly stated, are thus very imperfect descriptions of actual behavior. The congruence between a legal rule and actual behavior in society is probably greatest when that rule has developed (or changed) to reflect and enforce existing values of behavioral patterns. On the other hand, the gap is likely to be large, at least initially, where change in the law is designed to promote behavioral change and where a substantial consensus on values is lacking. Sometimes the gap is intended, reflecting a balance of political forces and an accommodation of competing values. This phenomenon is best expressed by Thurman Arnold. Writing about the experience of Prohibition, Arnold observed: "Most unenforced criminal laws survive in order to satisfy moral obligations to establish modes of conduct. They are unenforced because we want to continue our conduct, and unrepealed because we want to preserve our morals."[6]

The gap between policy and implementation is often expressed as the distinction between *outputs* and *outcomes*. Outputs refer to Supreme Court decisions, not only to specific rulings about who wins and who loses in a particular case but also to the broad policy expressed or inherent in a decision. Some cases focus on narrow issues that are of interest primarily to the litigants. Few such cases get to the Supreme Court. The more important cases, and most of those that reach the Supreme Court, will affect not only the litigants but also a wider range of interests in society. Often the allocation of social, economic, or political resources is involved.

Outcomes may be a direct result of a policy decision or may reflect the impact of multiple variables, judicial as well as nonjudicial. The orthodox and "official" view is that Supreme Court decisions, or policies, are enforced by lower court judges or other officials in near perfect bureaucratic harmony. In fact, of course, such harmony of purpose and action is rare. Supreme Court decisions can be described more accurately as tools or resources used by the participants in a controversy to achieve their own ends. The very fact that a particular issue has come to the Supreme Court for decision suggests a lack of consensus. Court decisions are themselves "inputs" to the larger political system. In some situations, what the Supreme Court decides will be controlling; in others, its policies will have to compete in the political arena in order to be fully vindicated.

It is possible to examine the question of outcomes at three levels. First, there is the immediate question of compliance. Are the particular mandates of the Court accepted and carried out by those persons to whom they are directed? If not, what are the variables that affect the rate and degree of compliance? What powers does the Court have to secure compliance with its decisions?

A second level of outcomes consists of the responses to a particular decision, or a set or pattern of decisions, by

---

[5]Richard Lempert, "Strategies of Research Design in the Legal Impact Study: The Control of Rival Plausible Hypotheses," 1 *Law and Society Review* (1966), 111–132.

[6]Thurman Arnold, *The Symbols of Government* (New Haven: Yale University Press, 1935), p. 160.

other political institutions and by the public. These responses may, of course, also have an impact on the rate of formal compliance with a decision. But they are independently significant as outcomes. One possible outcome of a Court decision may be a loss of perceived legitimacy or prestige that negatively affects the Court's powers in future cases. Another outcome may be a retaliatory response of Congress and/or the president designed to deny the Court the formal power to make similar decisions or designed to punish the Court or the individual justices. A third type of outcome may be an increased or decreased use of litigation in future efforts at solving similar problems. Finally, court decisions may produce within groups, publics, or institutions internal responses that affect the goals or procedures of those units. Court decisions may serve to activate a variety of political forces whose mobilization may have important future effects.

A third level of outcomes may be broadly defined as social change fostered or encouraged by political decisions of the Supreme Court. At this level we are talking about broad changes in the social, economic, or political behavior of groups of individuals. For example, Court policies may have an impact on particular institutional or structural arrangements in the political system which in turn, and over time, result in important social change. Court policies may have an impact directly on popular norms or values, and they may have an important effect in supporting or changing aspects of elite behavior.

The gap between Supreme Court policy making and implementation, we have observed, is not unique. It is typical of all policy-making enterprises and endemic to the political system as a whole. However, there are some special characteristics of the Supreme Court that contribute to the difficulties of translating its outputs into responsive outcomes.

The Court's Hybrid Role: Problems of Legitimacy

In the introductory essay we noted that the Supreme Court is a hybrid institution, combining in an often uneasy alliance the cultures of law and politics. The demands that are made on the Supreme Court often require it to reconcile the needs of the law with the wisdom and pragmatism of politics. Good law is not always good politics, and vice versa. Promoting justice and equality, the twin goals of American law, is a difficult and controversial enterprise at best. These factors contribute to a permanent tension; sometimes it is a creative tension that produces strong judicial leadership for change. At other times, it simply boils over into deep-seated division on the Court and withdrawal of public support. Critics accuse the Supreme Court of usurping power, of overstepping its bounds, of being something other than "a court."

Debate over the proper role of the Supreme Court may detract from its legitimacy as an institution and from the legitimacy of particular controversial decisions. Those who opposed the school segregation decision (*Brown* v. *Board of Education*, 1954) attacked the right of the Supreme Court to make such a decision, its lawfulness, as well as its wisdom. By contrast, it is very rare today to find comparable criticism of Congress, no matter how heated the opposition. The right of Congress to legislate, within constitutional limits, on matters of national importance is rarely challenged, at least not in the same way. That members of the Supreme Court are appointed rather than elected, are not politically accountable, and serve for life contributes to the Court's vulnerability to such allegations. So, too, does the perpetual debate over the legitimacy of the power of judicial review first asserted in *Marbury* v. *Madison* (1803).

There seems to be little question that views about the Court's proper role, and the legitimacy of its power, are important operative facts that shape and limit the exercise of judicial power and the public's response to the Supreme Court. Yet, citizen views are hard to interpret. Many citizens do not know enough about the Supreme Court to express any intelligent opinions, although they may have an opinion about current issues particularly salient to them.

Traditionally, citizens have less confidence in the Court than in the presidency or Congress; by a large margin they think it does less important things than the other branches of government.[7] Murphy and Tanenhaus reported that only 27 percent of the respondents in their national survey were aware of the Court and held some opinion about its legitimacy as an institution. Of these, less than half granted the Court "diffuse" support, although this group probably included many of the nation's opinion leaders. Almost no respondents who approved specific decisions refused to give the Court diffuse (institutional) support. But a large number of respondents who supported the Court as an institution failed to support specific decisions. The largest single category of respondents gave the Court neither specific nor diffuse support.[8] There is some evidence, in the aftermath of Watergate, that public confidence in the Supreme Court is increasing, absolutely, and relative to the declining levels of confidence in Congress and the president.[9] It remains to be seen whether or not this is a continuing phenomenon, and if so, what effect it will have on the Supreme Court.

A profile of public attitudes toward the Supreme Court is suggestive but does not establish any direct linkage to behavioral responses to Supreme Court decisions. Many respondents who support the Court generally might oppose it in a particular case (although the mode of their opposition may be tempered). Likewise, many who do not support the Court, or even oppose specific decisions, might nonetheless comply with those decisions or remain passive in their opposition. Americans generally rank high in "law abidingness" and thus might be expected to comply with, or at least not actively oppose, Supreme Court decisions that they dislike. On the other hand, there is also research showing that responses to laws are likely to be "situation specific" and

---

[7]Kenneth M. Dolbeare. "The Public Views the Supreme Court," in Jacob (ed.), *Law, Politics and the Federal Courts* (Boston: Little, Brown, 1967), pp. 194–212, at 196–197. See also Dolbeare and Phillip Hammond, "The Political Party Basis of Attitudes Toward the Supreme Court," 31 *Public Opinion Quarterly* (1967), pp. 16–30, and John H. Kessel, "Public Perceptions of the Supreme Court," 10 *Midwest Journal of Political Science* (1966), 167–191.

[8]Walter F. Murphy and Joseph Tanenhaus, "Public Opinion and the United States Supreme Court: A Preliminary Mapping of Some Prerequisites for Court Legitimation of Regime Changes," in Grossman and Tanenhaus (eds.), *Frontiers of Judicial Research* (New York: John Wiley and Sons. 1969), pp. 273–303.

[9]Jack Dennis, "Mass Public Support for the U.S. Supreme Court," paper delivered at the annual meeting of the American Association for Public Opinion Research, (1976).

not strongly related to general attitudes about legal obedience.

Perceptions of the legitimacy of the Supreme Court undoubtedly vary widely in communities and subcultures throughout the United States. Thus, national attitudes toward the Supreme Court are of limited utility in explaining citizen responses to particular Supreme Court decisions. Evidence also shows that much effective opposition to Supreme Court decisions comes from passive noncompliance, what Dolbeare and Hammond called "the banality of non-compliance." This kind of response is unlikely to be strongly related to abstract views of the legitimacy of the Court.[10]

The Nature of the Court's Policy-Making Function

Supreme Court decisions tend to be incremental, marginal adjustments to existing rules of law rather than broad and comprehensive statements of means and ends. In this respect, they are similar to policy decisions made by nonjudicial political actors. But it may be that policy making by adjudication exaggerates these tendencies. Lacking a stated sense of purpose or goals, Supreme Court decisions are often difficult to translate into behavioral requirements. The adversary context of judicial policy making, the need to decide a specific case or controversy, is not conducive to concrete and coherent policy statements. Indeed, Supreme Court policies are characteristically articulated in negative terms—"thou shalt nots"—rather than as statements of expected specific performance. When policies do not convey a clear sense of

expectation or a measurable standard of behavior, the inherent gap between policy and implementation will increase, particularly where the expected compliant acts are controversial and where they require mobilization of effort and allocation of resources. Conversely, policies that are self-executing, or where specific compliance can be measured, are less subject to those impediments to implementation.

The Competition for Policy Dominion: Other Courts, Elected Officials, Bureaucracies

We have described some of the internal attributes of Supreme Court policy making. But it is equally important to consider the policy role of the Court in relation to competing centers of political power. The first of these is the court system. We have already noted that the orthodox view of the judicial system as a hierarchy, in which policy is made at the top and implemented at the bottom, is at best a textbook formulation. State courts and the lower federal courts must be viewed as competing power centers. All judicial policies are not made at the Supreme Court level, and not all policies made by the Supreme Court are carried out uniformly by lower court judges. Indeed, except in unusual cases, the Supreme Court makes neither the first nor the last decision in a case. Often its decisions are "remanded" to a lower court for disposition "not inconsistent" with the opinion. This vague remand order may, as Murphy suggests, ease tensions in the federal system.[11] But it also facilitates, if it does not invite, noncompliance or less than full com-

[10]Kenneth M. Dolbeare and Phillip Hammond, *The School Prayer Decisions* (Chicago: University of Chicago Press, 1971).

[11]Walter F. Murphy, "Lower Court Checks on Supreme Court Power," **53** *American Political Science Review* (1959), 1017–1031.

pliance.[12] Whatever the verbal formula, it is the lower federal courts and the state courts that control the final disposition of cases. And these courts are not as dependent on the Supreme Court as is widely believed. It is not unusual to find parties or interests that have lost in the Supreme Court claiming victory in the lower courts. As Jack Peltason has observed, most judges "will do what they are told by the United States Supreme Court." But where decisions are ambiguous, lower court judges may resolve doubts in favor of the values and prejudices of "strongly entrenched local institutions."[13] And, as Martin Shapiro has noted, "The less clear and direct the policy communication from the Supreme Court the more likely are the resisting circuit judges to 'misunderstand' it and continue along their own path."[14]

There are no figures to portray the overall levels of compliance with Supreme Court decisions, since most scholarly research has concentrated on a few visible instances of noncompliance. Krislov's study of free speech cases from 1867 to 1958 found that Supreme Court decisions in these areas were not ignored but were rarely followed by the lower federal and state courts.[15] Sanders' study of the lower court response to the *Mallory* ruling found that in 40 percent of the cases in

which it was cited, *Mallory* was distinguished, that is, it was found not to apply to the facts of the particular case. In only three cases was it followed; Sanders' conclusion that the "lower federal courts have not received favorably the *Mallory* precedent" seems a significant understatement.[16]

Partly because of its confusing nature, many lower courts had difficulty in applying the ruling in *Dennis* v. *United States* (1951).[17] Manwaring's study of the impact of *Mapp* v. *Ohio* (1961) suggests some of the factors associated with compliance. First, Manwaring found that the imposition of the exclusionary rule was clear and unambiguous and that state courts could not avoid it. Beyond that, he found much resistance by the states to adopting all or most of the federal precedents on search and seizure accompanying the exclusionary rule. Surprisingly, perhaps, he also found that those states that had anticipated *Mapp* and adopted the exclusionary rule had done so with several variations that state courts were reluctant to discard. "Where a state is forced into a major change of direction, with no indigenous precedents or rules to turn to, it may be much more willing to adopt the federal guidelines as a whole."[18]

There are also examples of outright

---

[12]*Ibid.*

[13]Jack W. Peltason, *Fifty-Eight Lonely Men: Southern Federal Judges and School Desegregation* (New York: Harcourt, Brace & World, 1961), p. 243.

[14]Martin Shapiro, *The Supreme Court and Administrative Agencies* (New York: Free Press, 1968), p. 171.

[15]Samuel Krislov, *The Supreme Court and Political Freedom* (New York: Free Press, 1968), pp. 175–177.

[16]Paul H. Sanders, "The Warren Court and the Lower Federal Courts," in Schmidhauser (ed.), *Constitutional Law in the Political Process* (Chicago: Rand McNally, 1963), pp. 430–431 and passim.

[17]Robert Mallan, "Smith Act Prosecutions: The Effects of the *Dennis* and *Yates* Decisions," **26** *University of Pittsburgh Law Review* (1965), 710–711.

[18]David Manwaring, "The Impact of *Mapp* v. *Ohio*," in Everson (ed.), *The Supreme Court as Policy-Maker: Three Studies on the Impact of Judicial Decisions* (Carbondale, Ill.: Public Affairs Research Bureau, Southern Illinois University, 1968), p. 26.

defiance of Supreme Court decisions. The tradition of defiance by state courts goes back to the Supreme Court's early days, including but not limited to the classic states' rights battles at issue in *Martin* v. *Hunter's Lessee* (1816) and *Cohens* v. *Virginia* (1821). The pre-Civil War period produced in *Ableman* v. *Booth* (1859) a clash between Wisconsin and the federal fugitive slave law. The state courts in Wisconsin several times released, on habeas corpus, a prisoner accused of violating the federal statute, and it was several years after the Supreme Court's decision before the federal courts could enforce the order. Perhaps the most horrifying example of defiance in modern times occurred in 1953, in *Williams* v. *Georgia*. Williams had been sentenced to death. His conviction was appealed, in part because the jury selection process then in effect in Georgia discriminated against Negroes. This was contrary to the ruling of another Supreme Court decision handed down after Williams' trial. Georgia conceded that its jury selection process was now unconstitutional, but the state supreme court denied the appeal because it was not made in a timely fashion (since no objection to the jury selection procedure had been raised during the trial). The Supreme Court sent the case back to the Georgia Supreme Court for reconsideration. The latter reaffirmed the conviction with a strongly worded opinion refusing to "supinely surrender sovereign powers of this state." Inexplicably, in the face of this outright defiance, the Supreme Court denied further review, and Williams was executed.

Most noncompliance does not consist of outright defiance but is more subtle. Intelligent judges can almost always find facts to distinguish the case before them from an applicable precedent that they do not wish to follow. Precedents that are unclear (or where there are conflicting precedents) increase the scope of a judge's discretion. If a Supreme Court decision is ambiguous, a judge can usually proceed in the direction he or she prefers. The decision might be reversed if the Supreme Court ultimately decides the same issue differently. But a bold judge would expect to be reversed some of the time.

The school segregation cases, *Brown* v. *Board of Education* (1954, 1955), provide a classic example of lower court evasion and defiance. Having decided that segregated public schools were unconstitutional under the Fourteenth Amendment, the Supreme Court delegated enforcement of that decision to the lower federal courts. But it provided them only with the ambiguous standard of "with all deliberate speed" and emphasized that lower courts had considerable discretion to fashion remedies that took account of local conditions. This meant that moderate judges, who were at least willing if not eager to enforce the Supreme Court's decision, were deprived of a clear mandate to enforce the decision. This made them especially vulnerable to local criticism and pressure if they seemed to advocate anything more than the bare minimum of compliance. Since the Supreme Court itself did not specify immediate compliance, any southern federal judge who did was announcing his or her own personal convictions on a volatile issue. Few judges had the courage to forcefully implement *Brown* under these conditions. Had the Supreme Court been more specific, lower court judges could have assumed the role of enforcers without also accepting the ideological onus of "agreeing" with *Brown*. A strong Supreme Court order would have helped to liberate federal judges from the constraints of local politics and social pressure.

Lower federal court autonomy is fostered by several political facts. Although nominally chosen by the president, federal judges are most often chosen by senators or political leaders in their state. Their allegiance may be to the local constituency or to those leaders to whom they owe their appointments. They are likely to share the prevailing local views on major social and political issues.

Other factors also contribute to the independence of lower federal court judges. Trial judges have virtually complete control over their courtrooms and calendars. They may use these powers to delay, and in this way, they can often defeat the claims of litigants of which they disapprove. The study of Judge Harold Cox of Mississippi and his handling of voting rights cases (see Part Two, Chapter Two) is a good example. Trial judges have great discretion in their findings of a fact. As Jerome Frank and others have argued, facts are frequently the key to judicial outcomes.[19] Finally, only a fraction of cases decided in the federal district courts are appealed to the courts of appeals, and only a minute fraction of that number are appealed to the Supreme Court. For most litigants, the decision of a federal district court is final.

Against these centrifugal forces the Supreme Court has few effective sanctions. Judges do swear to uphold the federal Constitution, but they take no special oath or affirmation of fealty toward the Supreme Court. Reversal by a higher court—usually the court of appeals and occasionally the Su-

preme Court—is the most effective sanction. Presumably every judge aspires to some level of professional competence and recognition, and too frequent reversal may be evidence of a poor job. But where a judge's decisions are responsive to deeply felt personal values or to strong community pressures, the personal "costs" of reversal diminish.

The Supreme Court has no power to remove, demote, or fine a disobedient lower federal court judge, although in theory the judge may be cited for contempt. The sanction of contempt is so infrequently used as to be of little practical value in enforcing judicial compliance with Supreme Court decisions. A recent action by the Judicial Council of the Tenth Circuit, which refused to assign any more cases to an eccentric and uncooperative judge, suggests an additional disciplinary option. But the work load of the federal courts is so heavy that removing a judge's docket without being able to replace him may preclude frequent employment of that sanction.[20] It should also be noted that the Supreme Court has no positive inducements to offer, such as promotion or a pay raise—the usual bureaucratic rewards.

State judges are even more remote and insulated from Supreme Court control. They are likely to be even more sensitive than lower federal judges to local values and culture. They often take the same judicial oath as federal judges and are also bound by the supremacy clause (Article VI) of the Constitution. But they are frequently elected for short to medium-length terms, and the sanction of the electorate and the vicissitudes of poli-

[19]Jerome Frank, *Courts on Trial* (Princeton, N.J.: Princeton University Press, 1949); and Richard Richardson and Kenneth Vines, *The Politics of Federal Courts* (Boston: Little, Brown, 1970), Chapters 5 and 7.

[20]See *Chandler v. Judicial Council of the Tenth Circuit* (1970).

tics may be more real and immediate to them than the remote displeasure of the U.S. Supreme Court. Thus the psychological, personal, and political costs of compliance with a Supreme Court ruling that is locally unpopular may be greater than any possible costs of evasion. The contempt power is available, but where a judge refuses to obey a Supreme Court decision, it is rarely used. Because the Supreme Court will review only those aspects of state court cases that raise *federal* constitutional or statutory questions, it is frequently possible to dispose of cases on the basis of state constitutions or statutes and defeat the intent of a Supreme Court decision. Furthermore, the Supreme Court will only review cases that have exhausted all state remedies and that come from the highest state court in which a decision could be had. This usually, but not always, means a state's highest court.

Supreme Court review of state court decisions has always been a troublesome, and often an explosive, issue, exposing the most vulnerable strands of our federal system. Unquestionably, there is today considerably more federal court involvement in state judicial proceedings. The nationalizing trends of the Warren Court have not been totally reversed, although surely their forward movement has been halted. More recent decisions of the Supreme Court, such as *Younger* v. *Harris* (1971), have sought to redress the balance in favor of the more traditional view that in the absence of unusual circumstances, state court autonomy should be preserved from federal court interference. Revival of the notion of deference to state court decisions, though not setting the clock back to the days before the Warren Court, is clearly discernible in some

decisions of the Burger Court today.

Just as the Supreme Court's policy-making authority is shared with other, supposedly "inferior" courts, it is also shared with Congress and the president. A good example is the Watergate tapes case, *Nixon* v. *United States* (1974). The Supreme Court decided that a lower court's subpoena for the tapes, known to be relevant to a pending criminal prosecution, took precedence over Nixon's claim of executive privilege. Yet the Court's opinion was the first judicial recognition that the doctrine of executive privilege, asserted by many presidents, had some constitutional legitimacy. The Court did not specify the boundaries of executive privilege other than to note that it was not absolute and must yield on occasion to higher priorities. For the foreseeable future at least, the meaning of executive privilege will continue to be defined by the courts and by presidents, mostly by the latter, within the broad boundaries set by the Supreme Court in the Tapes Cases. One can find many similar examples of shared policy power between Congress and the Court. This might take the form of legislative action followed by judicial review and then some legislative counterreaction or adjustment to bring a particular policy in line with stated judicial objections.

In some policy areas, the Supreme Court is predominant. On questions of reapportionment, school prayers, and interrogation of criminal suspects, the Supreme Court's policies have been sustained and, for the most part, implemented, despite considerable negative response. In some policy areas, the Court's role has been quite secondary and interstitial, though occasionally critical. On questions of environmental protection or the rights of Indians, the Supreme Court has neither sought nor had the opportunity yet to play a major role. Sometimes by tradition, sometimes because of constitutional limitations, and often for prudential reasons, the Supreme Court will actively avoid certain types of policy questions. It rarely decides questions of foreign policy or of peace and war. For the most part (with some exceptions), it has not interfered with the internal workings of Congress.

The boundary line that defines appropriate judicial policy concerns is neither fixed nor entirely clear. It is responsive to a number of factors. In subsequent chapters we will explore in detail how the Supreme Court defines its own policy role and how constitutional rules and the nature of the adjudicative process limit the Court's policy options. The Supreme Court's role as a national policy maker is also related to the political configuration of the nation at any particular time. In a now classic article, Robert Dahl argued that inevitably the Supreme Court is part of a national ruling coalition. Its members are responsive to, and represent, the same values dominant elsewhere in the political system. Except during transitional periods, when an old coalition is disintegrating and a new one forming, the Supreme Court's major policy role, according to Dahl, is to confer legitimacy on the major politics of the coalition—in effect, lending some of the Court's own legitimacy. The Court cannot successfully oppose major policies of the coalition, although it can be an innovative policy maker

within a shared framework of values *or* on policy questions where the coalition is unstable and no effective check on the Supreme Court could be mobilized. Where the Court strikes out on its own, it must depend on the existence of widespread consensus that what it is doing is right, even if those views have not yet been adopted by the coalition.[21]

Dahl's thesis has been criticized by a number of commentators. Adamany argues, persuasively, that it is precisely during times of political realignment that the Court's legitimacy will be at its lowest ebb, since the Court will almost always be representing past values, not those in ascendance.[22] Jonathan Casper has argued, also persuasively, that Dahl's view, and empirical measure, of policy making was too narrow.[23] If viewed not just in terms of decisions for and against particular litigants, or as the prescription of rules, but as part of a process of mobilizing political forces throughout the political system (and not just within the ruling coalition), Supreme Court policy making takes on new significance. Dahl's view of the Court is heavily dependent on a "New Deal" view of the political landscape. In a time of increasing political fragmentation and issue-oriented politics, the basis for Dahl's argument has been eroded seriously. It may be, as Howard and Bushoven have argued, that the most important aspect of Supreme Court policy making is precisely when it goes *outside* of the ruling coalition and decides questions that have not been resolved by

[21]Robert A. Dahl, "Decision Making in a Democracy: The Supreme Court as a National Policy-Maker," **6** *Journal of Public Law* (1957), 279–295.

[22]David Adamany "Legitimacy, Realigning Elections, and the Supreme Court," 1973 *Wisconsin Law Review*, pp. 790–846.

[23]Jonathan Casper "The Supreme Court and National Policy Making," **70** *American Political Science Review* (1976), 50–63.

the political process.[24] Dahl's data were exclusively concerned with the exercise of judicial review over acts of Congress. To the extent that review of national legislation is involved, Dahl was probably correct, and his conclusions retain some validity. But since 1957 the major thrust of Supreme Court policy making has focused on civil rights and civil liberties, issues traditionally decided at the state and local levels. It is on such policy questions that the Court has been most innovative, most controversial, and most successful.

Notwithstanding all the recent criticism of Dahl's thesis, one of his basic points remains undisturbed. As a political institution, the Court must operate in the political process. Being a political institution creates opportunities for the Supreme Court that it would not have as an exclusively legal institution, but it also sets limits on what policies the Court will make, how much compliance can be expected, and what impact those policies will have.

Finally, some brief attention should be paid to the "fourth branch of government," the bureaucracy. We have already suggested how Supreme Court decisions are undermined in the lower courts, in what might loosely be called the judicial bureaucracy. Many Supreme Court decisions, however, either are directed at bureaucratic agencies or require some agency action. What kind of response can be expected? The situation abounds in paradox, for it would appear that bureaucracy is both necessary to the implementation of many Supreme Court

decisions and the major obstacle to others. Dolbeare and Hammond, and other students of the impact of the Supreme Court's prayer decisions, have noted the absence of institutional commitment to enforcing those decisions as a major obstacle.[25] On the other hand, there are numerous studies showing that getting bureaucracies to enforce constitutional rights is a major problem. Bureaucratic decisions are often invisible to the public. Communications of rights to their beneficiaries is rarely effective, beneficiaries often are too dependent on bureaucracies to encourage complaints, and resources for monitoring bureaucratic action simply are inadequate. A number of civil rights lawyers have argued recently that what is needed is not additional "rights" but mobilization of resources to police bureaucratic denial of those rights.

An excellent example of bureaucracy defeating the intent of a Supreme Court decision is the aftermath of *Goldberg* v. *Kelly* (1971), in which the Supreme Court decided that welfare recipients were entitled to hearings and other due process rights *prior* to termination of welfare benefits. A study of the New York welfare agency the following year uncovered substantial failures to provide procedural safeguards: 5 percent of the appellants received no notice of a proposed adverse action; 25 percent of the appellants did not receive timely notice; two-thirds of the notices failed to provide an adequate statement of the action proposed and the reasons for it; 15 percent of the cases had not

---

[24]J. Woodford Howard, Jr., and Cornelius Bushoven, "Discussant's Remarks: Is the Burger Court a Nixon Court?" **23** *Emory Law Journal* (1974), 745.

[25]Dolbeare and Hammond, *op cit.*, note 10; Frank Sorauf, *The Wall of Separation: The Constitutional Politics of Church and State* (Princeton: Princeton University Press, 1976); and William K. Muir Jr., *Prayer in the Public Schools: Law and Attitude Change* (Chicago: University of Chicago Press, 1967).

been continued pending appeals; only 25 percent of the appellants who requested access to relevant agency files prior to appeal received such access; and in only 7 percent of the cases was an opportunity for cross-examination afforded by having the complaining witness present.[26]

4. THE ANATOMY OF SUPREME COURT POLICY MAKING

A. *Two Views of Protest as Political Expression*

A "settled" constitutional policy is rarely the result of a single Supreme Court decision. Instead, as Clement Vose has observed, it is often the end result of decades of litigation.[1] Supreme Court policy making is thus best viewed as a continuous process; even where a doctrine appears to be settled, new challenges and changing conditions may provoke reexamination and further doctrinal change, or outright rejection. Supreme Court cases may express a number of policy judgments. The same case that announces an important substantive point of law may also articulate a procedural policy or make several substantive policy statements of importance. Policy making occurs by inaction as well as by a formal decision. Thus the most crucial aspect of a case may be what was not decided. As the foregoing suggests, Supreme Court policy making is a complex endeavor. Analysis must seek to capture that complexity.

The two cases that follow provide a first exposure to the details of the decision-making process in the context of an actual case, and they raise a number of issues about the Supreme Court's proper role. One case, *Tinker v. Des Moines Independent Community School District* (1969) challenged the authority of school boards to prohibit the wearing of black armbands in school by students protesting the war in Vietnam. The case required the Supreme Court to decide how much of the First Amendment guarantee of free speech applied to schoolchildren and whether or not the wearing of armbands was constitutionally protected political expression. Underlying these issues was the question of whether or not schoolchildren were entitled to any of the constitutional rights ordinarily granted to adults. The other case, *United States v. O'Brien* (1968), was an appeal from a criminal conviction for draft-card burning. Thus, it also raised First Amendment questions: To what extent does constitutional protection extend to nonverbal political protest? Where the *Tinker* case had overtones of federalism, the *O'Brien* case contains the additional problem of judicial deference to Congress.

In both cases, the Supreme Court was asked by the party that lost in the lower courts to set aside a duly consid-

---

[26]D. Kirchheimer, "Community Evaluation of Fair Hearing Procedures Available to Public Assistance Recipients," May 1973, on file at the New York City Human Resource Administration, cited in Jerry Mashaw, "The Management Side of Due Process: Some Theoretical and Litigation Notes on the Assurance of Accuracy, Fairness, and Timeliness in the Adjudication of Social Welfare Claims," **59** *Cornell Law Review* (1974), 785.

[1]Clement Vose, *Constitutional Change* (Lexington, Mass.: D.C. Heath, 1973), p. 336.

ered policy of another political institution and to substitute a judicially fashioned rule. Both cases sought to involve the Court in the controversy over the war in Vietnam. Petitioners sought specific relief and symbolic support for those opposing the war. The cases were decided during a period of national crisis. How do you account for the Supreme Court's response in each case? On what basis can you reconcile the votes of individual justices who voted in favor of the right of the Tinker children to wear black armbands to school and in favor of affirming O'Brien's conviction for burning his draft card? How much discretion did the Supreme Court have in deciding these cases? Why did the Court decide to hear these cases at all?

(1) Tinker v. Des Moines Community School District (1969)

+Fortas, Douglas, Warren, Brennan, Stewart, White, Marshall
−Black, Harlan

[A group of parents and students decided, in early December, 1965, to protest the war in Vietnam by the wearing of black armbands. The protest was scheduled to begin on December 16 and to continue through the Christmas holiday season; it also included two days of fasting, on December 16 and January 1. Reacting to the announced protest, the school principals of Des Moines passed a regulation forbidding the wearing of armbands in the schools. Students who violated this regulation were subject to suspension until they were willing to return to school without the armbands. The expressed view of school officials was that the schools were inappropriate places for political protest and that such activities would have a disturbing effect on the schools' regular curriculum. There was predictable opposition. The school board president argued that "our country's leaders have decided on a course of

action and we should support them"; gym teachers at some schools apparently required their students to chant "Beat the Viet Cong" while performing jumping exercises.

About ten students actually wore armbands to school, and three of these were eventually suspended—John Tinker, aged 15, Christopher Eckhardt, aged 16, both high school students, and John's sister, Mary Beth Tinker, aged 13, a junior high school student. With the support of the Iowa Civil Liberties Union, their parents filed a complaint in the Federal District Court for the Southern District of Iowa, asking for an injunction preventing the school authorities from disciplining their children and also seeking nominal damages. The children remained out of school for several days past the vacation period and then returned without their armbands. Meanwhile the Des Moines School Board met to review the situation and to consider the question of school discipline and the First Amendment rights of students. The school board also sought legal guidance and, on January 4, 1966, voted, 5-2, to uphold the ban on armbands. There seemed to be substantial agreement by all school board members that high school students did not have the same protest rights as college students, but the board members could not agree on where to draw the line.

On September 1, 1966, eight months later, the case was heard by Federal District Court Judge Roy L. Stephenson. In a memorandum opinion, he ruled that the regulations were reasonable and did not deprive the students of their freedom of speech. Judge Stephenson agreed that the First Amendment rights of students were protected against infringement by the state but held that school officials have a right and a duty to prevent anything that may be disruptive provided that their preventive actions were reasonable. He found the regulations reasonable because of possible disruptive actions and hostile comments about the armbands and armband wearers which might detract from a disciplined classroom atmosphere. He specifically refused to follow (and was not required to do so) a decision from another circuit that wearing of armbands cannot be prohibited unless they "materially and substantially interfere with the requirements of appropriate discipline in the operation of the school." The difference between Judge Stephenson's decision and that just quoted lay in the matter of burden of proof: to Judge Stephenson the burden was on the protestors to prove that they were not likely to disrupt normal activities; under the alternative formula, the burden was on the school board to prove that there was actually a substantial interference with appropriate discipline.

On November 3, 1967, the Court of Appeals for the Eighth Circuit, sitting en banc (that is, the entire court rather than the usual panel of three judges) affirmed the judgment of the district court by an equally divided vote. Because there was no majority, there was no opinion for the court and the arguments for each side remain unknown.

Petitioners then sought, and were granted, a writ of certiorari from the United States Supreme Court (that is, they sought review of the decision; for details on how and when certiorari is granted, see Chapter Three in this part of the book). One year later, on November 12, 1968, attorneys for the American Civil Liberties Union and attorneys for the state of Iowa argued the case before the Supreme Court of the United States. The ACLU attorneys argued that the prohibition against wearing armbands was a denial of petitioners' First Amendment rights and that these rights do not end at the school door but in fact should be fostered affirmatively by a school system. They argued that the regulation constituted a forbidden "prior restraint" on the speech of the petitioners, that the wearing of armbands in and of itself was not an activity which should—or did—cause disruption, and that if disruption had occurred, it was the proper duty of the school to punish the disrupters, rather than prohibit the armbands and punish those expressing themselves by this means. The ACLU argued that the First Amendment does not permit suppression of free speech rights merely because a regulation seems "reasonable."

Attorneys for the state of Iowa sought to emphasize the special situation of the schools, the youth of the protesters, and the great need for maintaining discipline. They argued that it was not for the Supreme Court to determine that the regulations were wise or unwise, as long as they were reasonable. They argued that the possible consequences of the demonstration could have been serious if they had not been prevented. Although they did not specifically say so, it seems clear that they were implicitly arguing that full First Amendment rights, clearly protected out of school, were not entitled to the same protections within the schools.]

MR. JUSTICE FORTAS delivered the opinion of the Court.

. . . First Amendment rights, applied in light of the special characteristics of the school environment, are available to teachers and students. It can hardly be argued that either students or teachers shed their constitutional rights to freedom of speech or expression at the schoolhouse gate. This has been the unmistakable holding of this Court for almost 50 years. . . .

In *West Virginia* v. *Barnette* (1943), this Court held that under the First Amendment, the student in public school may not be compelled to salute the flag. Speaking through Mr. Justice Jackson, the Court said:

The Fourteenth Amendment, as now applied to the States, protects the citizen against the State itself and all of its creatures—Boards of Education not excepted. These have, of course, important, delicate, and highly discretionary functions, but none that they may not perform within the limits of the Bill of Rights. That they are educating the young for citizenship is reason for scrupulous protection of Constitutional freedoms of the individual, if we are not to strangle the free mind at its source and teach youth to discount important principles of our government as mere platitudes.

On the other hand, the Court has repeatedly emphasized the need for affirming the comprehensive authority of the States and of school authorities, consistent with fundamental constitutional safeguards, to prescribe and control conduct in the schools. . . . Our problem lies in the area where students in the exercise of First Amendment rights collide with the rules of the school authorities.

The problem presented by the present case does not relate to regulation of the length of skirts or the type of clothing, to hair style or deportment. . . . It does not concern aggressive, disruptive action or even group demonstrations. Our problem involves direct, primary First Amendment rights akin to "pure speech."

The school officials banned and sought to punish petitioners for a silent, passive, expression of opinion, unaccompanied by any disorder or disturbance on the part of petitioners. There is here no evidence whatever of petitioners' interference, actual or nascent, with the school's work or of collision with the rights of other students to be secure and to be let alone. Accordingly, this case does not concern speech or action that intrudes upon the work of the school or the rights of other students.

Only a few of the 18,000 students in the school system wore the black armbands. Only five students were suspended for wearing them. There is no indication that the work of the school or any class was disrupted. Outside the classrooms, a few students made hostile remarks to the children wearing armbands, but there were no threats or acts of violence on school premises.

The District Court concluded that the action of the school authorities was reasonable because it was based upon their fear of a disturbance from the wearing of the armbands. But, in our system, undifferentiated fear or apprehension of disturbance is not enough to overcome the right to freedom of expression. Any departure from absolute regimentation may cause trouble. Any variation from the majority's opinion may inspire fear. Any word spoken, in class, in the lunchroom or on the campus, that deviates from the views of another person, may start an argument or cause a disturbance. But our Constitution says we must take this risk, *Terminiello* v. *Chicago* . . . (1948); and our history says that it is this sort of hazardous freedom—this kind of openness—that is the basis of our national strength and of the independence and vigor of Americans who grow up and live in this relatively permissive, often disputatious society.

In order for the State in the person of school officials to justify prohibition of a particular expression of opinion, it must be able to show that its action was caused by something more than a mere desire to avoid the discomfort and unpleasantness that always accompany an unpopular viewpoint. Certainly where there is no finding and no showing that the exercise of the forbidden right would "materially and substantially interfere with the requirements of appropriate discipline in the operation of the school," the prohibition cannot be sustained. . . .

In the present case, the District Court made no such finding, and our independent examination of the record fails to yield evidence that the school authorities had reason to anticipate that the wearing of the armbands would substantially interfere with the work of the school or impinge upon the rights of other students. Even an official memorandum prepared after the suspension that listed the reasons for the ban on wearing the armbands made no reference to the anticipation of such disruption. On the contrary, the action of the school authorities appears to have been based upon an urgent wish to avoid the controversy which might result from the expression, even by the silent symbol of armbands, of opposition to this Nation's part in the conflagration in Vietnam. It is revealing, in this respect, that the meeting at which the school principals decided to issue the contested regulation was called in response to a student's statement to the journalism teacher in one of the schools that he wanted to write an article on Vietnam and have it published in the school paper. (The student was dissuaded.)

It is also relevant that the school authorities did not purport to prohibit the wearing of all symbols of political or controversial significance. The record shows that students in some of the schools wore buttons relating to national political campaigns, and some even wore the Iron Cross, traditionally a symbol of nazism. The order prohibiting the wearing of armbands did not extend to these. Instead, a particular symbol—black armbands worn to exhibit opposition to this Nation's involvement in Vietnam—was singled out for prohibition. Clearly, the prohibition of expression of one particular opinion, at least without evidence that it is necessary to avoid material and substantial interference with school work or discipline, is not constitutionally permissible.

In our system, state-operated schools may not be enclaves of totalitarianism. School officials do not possess absolute authority over their students. Students in school as well as out of school are "persons" under our Constitution. They are possessed of fundamental rights which the State must respect, just as they themselves must respect their obligations to the State. In our system, students may not be regarded as closed-circuit recipients of only that which the State chooses to communicate. They may not be confined to the expression of those sentiments that are officially approved. In the absence of a specific showing of constitutionally valid reasons to regulate their speech, students are entitled to freedom of expression of their views. . . .

This principle has been repeated by this Court on numerous occasions during the intervening years. In *Keyishian* v. *Board of Regents . . .*, Mr. Justice Brennan, speaking for the Court, said:

The vigilant protection of constitutional freedoms is nowhere more vital than in the community of American schools." . . . The classroom is peculiarly the "market-place of ideas." The Nation's future depends upon leaders trained through wide exposure to that robust exchange of ideas which discovers truth "out of a multitude of tongues, [rather] than through any kind of authoritative selection. . . .

The principle of these cases is not confined to the supervised and ordained discussion which takes place in the classroom. The principal use to which the schools are dedicated is to accommodate students during prescribed hours for the purpose of certain types of activities. Among those activities is personal intercommunication among the students. This is not only an inevitable part of the process of attending school. It is also an important part of the educational process. A student's rights therefore, do not embrace merely the classroom hours. When he is in the cafeteria, or on the playing field, or on the campus during the authorized hours, he may express his opinions, even on controversial subjects like the conflict in Vietnam, if he does so "without materially and substantially interfering with appropriate discipline in the operation of the school" and without colliding with the rights of others. . . . But conduct by the student, in class or out of it, which for any reason—whether it stems from time, place, or type of behavior—materially disrupts classwork or involves substantial disorder or invasion of the rights of others is, of course, not immunized by the constitutional guaranty of freedom of speech. . . .

Under our Constitution, free speech is not a right that is given only to be so circumscribed that it exists in principle but not in fact. Freedom of expression would not truly exist if the right could be exercised only in an area that a benevolent government has provided as a safe haven for crackpots. The Constitution says that Congress (and the States) may not abridge the right to free speech. This provision means what it says. We properly read it to permit reasonable regulation of speech-connected activities in carefully restricted circumstances. But we do not confine the permissible exercise of First Amendment rights to a telephone booth or the four corners of a pamphlet, or to supervised and ordained discussion in a school classroom. . . .

As we have discussed, the record does not demonstrate any facts which might reasonably have led school authorities to forecast substantial disruption of or material interference with school activities, and no disturbances or disorders on the school premises in fact occurred. These petitioners merely went about their ordained rounds in school. Their deviation consisted only in wearing on their sleeve a band of black-cloth, not more than two inches wide. They wore it to exhibit their disapproval of the Vietnam hostilities and their advocacy of a truce, to make their views known, and by their example, to influence others to adopt them. They neither interrupted school activities nor sought to intrude in the school affairs or the lives of others. They caused discussion outside of the class rooms, but no interference with work and no disorder. In the circumstances, our Constitution does not permit officials of the State to deny their form of expression.

We express no opinion as to the form of relief which should be granted, this being a matter for the lower courts to determine. We reverse and remand for further proceedings consistent with this opinion.

Reversed and remanded.

MR. JUSTICE STEWART, CONCURRING.

Although I agree with much of what is said in the Court's opinion, and with its judgment in this case, I cannot share the Court's uncritical assumption that, school discipline aside, the First Amendment rights of children are co-extensive with those of adults. Indeed, I had thought the Court decided otherwise just last Term in *Ginsberg* v. *New York*. . . . I continue to hold the view I expressed in that case: "[A] State may permissibly determine that, at least in some precisely delineated areas, a child—like someone in a captive audience—is not possessed of that full capacity for individual choice which is the presupposition of First Amendment guarantees."

MR. JUSTICE WHITE, CONCURRING.

While I join the Court's opinion, I deem it appropriate to note, first, that the Court continues to recognize a distinction between communicating by words and communicating by acts or conduct which sufficiently impinge on some valid state interest; . . .

MR. JUSTICE HARLAN, DISSENTING (OMITTED).

MR. JUSTICE BLACK, DISSENTING.

. . . Assuming that the Court is correct in holding that the conduct of wearing armbands for the purpose of conveying political ideas is protected by the First Amendment, the crucial remaining questions are whether students and teachers may use the schools at their whim as a platform for the exercise of free speech— "symbolic" or "pure"—and whether the Courts will allocate to themselves the function of deciding how the pupils' school day will be spent. While I have always believed that under the First and Fourteenth Amendments neither the State nor Federal Government has any authority to regulate or censor the content of speech, I have never believed that any person has a right to give speeches or engage in demonstrations where he pleases and when he pleases. This Court has already rejected such a notion. In *Cox* v. *Louisiana* . . . (1965), for example, the Court clearly stated that the rights of free speech and assembly "do not mean that anyone with opinions or beliefs to express may address a group at any public place and at any time." . . .

While the record does not show that any of these armband students shouted, used profane language or were violent in any manner, a detailed report by some of them shows their armbands caused comments, warnings by other students, the poking of fun at them, and a warning by an older football player that other, non-protesting students had better let them alone. There is also evidence that the professor of mathematics had his lesson period practically "wrecked" chiefly by disputes with Beth Tinker, who wore her armband for her "demonstration." Even a casual reading of the record shows that this armband did divert students' minds from their regular lessons, and that talk, comments, etc., made John Tinker "self-conscious" in attending school with his armband. While the absence of obscene or boisterous and loud disorder perhaps justifies the Court's statement that the few armband students did not actually "disrupt" the classwork, I think the record overwhelmingly shows that the armbands did exactly what the elected school officials and principals foresaw it would, that is, took the students' minds off their classwork and diverted them to thoughts about the highly emotional subject of the Vietnam war. And I repeat that if the time has come when pupils of state-supported schools, kindergarten, grammar school or high school, can defy and flaunt orders of school officials to keep their minds on their own school work, it is the beginning of a new revolutionary era of permissiveness in this country fostered by the judiciary. The next logical step, it appears to me, would be to hold unconstitutional laws that bar pupils under 21 or 18 from voting, or from being elected members of the Boards of Education. . . .

The truth is that a teacher of kindergarten, grammar school, or high school pupils no more carries into a school with him a complete right to freedom of speech and expression than an anti-Catholic or anti-Semitic carries with him a complete freedom of speech and religion into a Catholic church or Jewish synagogue. Nor does a person carry with him into the United States Senate or House, or to the Supreme Court, or any other court, a complete constitutional right to go into those places contrary to their rules and speak his mind on any subject he pleases. It is a myth to say that any person has a constitutional right to say what he pleases, where he pleases, and when he pleases. Our Court has decided precisely the opposite. . . .

In my view, teachers, in state-controlled public schools are hired to teach there. . . . [A] teacher is not paid to go into school and teach subjects the State does not hire him to teach as a part of its selected curriculum. Nor are public school students sent to the schools at public expense to broadcast political or any other views to educate and inform the public. The original idea of schools, which I do not believe is yet abandoned as worthless or out of date, was that children had not yet reached the point of experience and wisdom which enabled them to teach all of their elders. It may be that the Nation has outworn the old-fashioned slogan that "children are to be seen not heard," but one may, I hope, be permitted to harbor the thought that taxpayers send children to school on the premise that at their age they need to learn, not teach. . . . And as I have pointed out before, the record amply shows that public protest in the school classes against the Vietnam war "distracted from that singleness of purpose which the State (here Iowa) desired to exist in its public educational institutions." Here the Court should accord Iowa educational institutions the same right to determine for itself what free expression and no more should be allowed in its schools that it accorded Mississippi with reference to freedom of assembly. But even if the record were silent as to protest against the Vietnam war distracting students from their assigned class work, members of this Court, like all other citizens, know, without being told, that the disputes over the wisdom of the Vietnam war have disrupted and divided this country as few other issues ever have. Of course students, like other people, cannot concentrate on lesser issues when black

armbands are being ostentatiously displayed in their presence to call attention to the wounded and dead of the war, some of the wounded and the dead being their friends and neighbors. It was, of course, to distract the attention of other students that some students insisted up to the very point of their own suspension from school that they were determined to sit in school with their symbolic armbands.

Change has been said to be truly the law of life but sometimes the old and the tried and true are worth holding. The schools of this Nation have undoubtedly contributed to giving us tranquility and to making us a more law-abiding people. Uncontrolled and uncontrollable liberty is an enemy to domestic peace. We cannot close our eyes to the fact that some of the country's greatest problems are crimes committed by the youth, too many of school age. School discipline, like parental discipline, is an integral and important part of training our children to be good citizens—to be better citizens. Here a very small number of students have crisply and summarily refused to obey a school order designed to give pupils who want to learn the opportunity to do so. One does not need to be a prophet or the son of a prophet to know that after the Court's holding today some students in Iowa schools and indeed in all schools will be ready, able, and willing to defy their teachers on practically all orders. This is the more unfortunate for the schools since groups of students all over the land are already running loose, conducting break-ins, sit-ins, lie-ins, and smash-ins. Many of these student groups, as is all too familiar to all who read the newspapers and watch the television news programs, have already engaged in rioting, property seizures and destruction. They have picketed schools to force students not to cross their picket lines and have too often violently attacked earnest but frightened students who wanted an education that the picketers did not want them to get. Students engaged in such activities are apparently confident that they know far more about how to operate public school systems than do their parents, teachers, and elected school officials. It is no answer to say that the particular students here have not yet reached such high points in their demands to attend classes in order to exercise their political pressures. Turned loose with lawsuits for damages and injunctions against their teachers like they are here, it is nothing but wishful thinking to imagine that young, immature students will not soon believe it is their right to control the schools rather than the right of the States that collect the taxes to hire the teachers for the benefit of the pupils. This case, therefore, wholly without constitutional reasons in my judgment, subjects all the public schools in the country to the whims and caprices of their loudest-mouthed, but maybe not their brightest, students. I, for one, am not fully persuaded that school pupils are wise enough, even with this Court's expert help from Washington, to run the 23,390 public school systems in our 50 States. I wish, therefore, wholly to disclaim any purpose on my part, to hold that the Federal Constitution compels the teachers, parents, and elected school officials to surrender control of the American public school system to public school students. I dissent.

[By the time the Supreme Court had decided the Tinker case, the older students had already graduated from high school. Mary Beth Tinker, a junior high school student at the time, was now a senior in high school. The order against armbands had been rescinded within four months, three years prior to the Supreme Court's decision. The Tinker family moved from Des Moines in the spring of 1969 and therefore was not personally affected by the decision. The main impact of the decision would be on other school children, throughout the country, who would claim the same or similar rights of political expression.

The vast majority of Americans never have, never will, and probably could not intelligently read a Supreme Court decision. What little information they get about the Court will come from wire service summaries or feature articles in newspapers, magazines, and television. If one looks at the coverage of this decision in the *Des Moines Register,* the newspaper that most Iowans read, it would indeed have been difficult to get an accurate picture of the Court's decision. Greater emphasis was given to the warnings to demonstrators in the opinion of the Court, and in Justice Black's dissenting opinion, than to the more positive aspects of Fortas' opinion. For example, the lead article in the *Register* was entitled "Campus Rioters Warned by Court in D. M. Ruling" (February 28, 1969), and the stress of the article was on the restrictive side of the Court's decision. Another article in the *Register,* entitled "An Angry Dissent on Armbands," featured Black's dissenting opinion to the virtual exclusion of the rights which protesting students had in the light of the majority's decision. Judging from this coverage, few Iowans were likely to understand that the substance of the decision was to extend greater protection to peaceful student demonstrations.

Whatever the limits of its local and immediate impact, *Tinker* has become a landmark decision, a foundation for still-developing doctrines concerning the First Amendment rights of student protesters and the due process rights of students confronted with disciplinary procedures. *Tinker* did not specifically decide related questions of dress codes, long hair regulations, and the like. Justice Fortas was careful to note that these were different problems not controlled by the Supreme Court's decision on the wearing of black armbands. Nonetheless, the *Tinker* case, in its recognition that students have constitutional rights, certainly provided ammunition for those opposing dress or hair codes as infringing upon the personal privacy and other rights of students. The lower federal courts were about evenly divided on the issue: about half the circuits favored extending *Tinker* to dress and hair codes, the rest did not. And the Supreme Court itself has yet to decide these questions. Thus, hair and dress codes are constitutionally permissible in some parts of the country and, at best, constitutionally suspect elsewhere. Justice Black's dissenting opinion has been widely cited with approval. Like many Supreme Court decisions, *Tinker* raised at least as many questions as it answered.]

(2) United States v. O'Brien (1968)

+Warren, Black, Brennan, Harlan, Stewart, White, Clark
  −Douglas
  NP Marshall

[How may citizens protest the policies of their government? Are they limited to voting against those who make the policies or to verbal or written statements of opposition? May they express their dissent in other ways? Beginning in 1964 and 1965, opposition to the war in Vietnam and to the military draft presented in new form for this generation of Americans a question raised often in the past. One means of protest is by symbolic actions, such as the wearing of a black armband. In the *Tinker* case the Supreme Court found this type of protest protected by the First Amendment. Although the decision went against a considerable amount of tradition in America about the need for discipline in our schools, it was not a hard decision for the Court to make. No significant *national* policy was at stake; allowing the wearing of armbands in schools would not likely have much effect beyond local controversy. But the Court is in a much more delicate and exposed position when a particular form of protest violates not just a school board regulation but also an act of Congress. Here the citizen is in direct confrontation with a branch of government, Congress, which is coequal with the Supreme Court. The basic question is the same as in the *Tinker* case, but the circumstances and events are significantly different. Is political protest protected only in its traditional verbal form, or is it an evolving concept that has come—or should come—to embrace peaceful conduct as well?

Protest against the Vietnam war rose markedly in the summer of 1965, when American forces openly entered the conflict. On July 31, 1965, a large demonstration took place in front of the Army Recruiting Center in New York City, where several young men burned their draft cards. The reaction of Congress was as swift as it was predictable.

The existing draft regulations, dating back to the Selective Service Act of 1917, required each registrant to have his card in his possession at all times. Willful violation of this regulation was a criminal offense, and any person who burned his card was clearly incapable of complying with the regulation. Nonetheless, with little discussion and no hearing, Congress, in 1965, overwhelmingly passed a bill introduced by L. Mendel Rivers, chairman of the House Armed Services Committee, which also made it a criminal offense to "knowingly destroy" or "knowingly mutilate" one's registration certificate or classification notice. Maximum punishment was set at five years imprisonment and/or a fine of $10,000.

The Report of the House Armed Services Committee stressed the need to reemphasize the will of Congress that "the acts of destroying or mutilating the cards are offenses which pose such a grave threat to the security of the Nation that no question whatsoever should be left as to the intention of the Congress that such wanton and irresponsible acts should be punished."

On March 31, 1966, David O'Brien, 19 years old, and three other men burned their registration certificates on the steps of a courthouse in Boston. All were arrested and charged with violation of the statute, as amended in 1965. The four men were themselves nonviolent, but their action caused a hostile counterreaction by the large crowd of onlookers, and they had to be led to the safety of the courthouse by FBI agents witnessing the protest.

Trial was held in the federal district court in Boston. There was no dispute as to the facts of the case. O'Brien's defense was that the 1965 amendments to the Selective Service Act infringed on his rights to free speech, that this amendment served no valid legislative purpose, and that the symbolic act of draft-card burning was a form of political expression protected by the First Amendment. The argument was rejected by the district judge, sitting without a jury, and O'Brien was convicted. The court held that the statute did not abridge First Amendment rights on its face and that it was a reasonable exercise of congressional power to raise and support armies. The court refused to delve into the motives that lay behind congressional passage. Because of his youth, O'Brien was sentenced under the Youth Correction Act to a maximum period of six years supervision and treatment.

On appeal, the Court of Appeals for the First Circuit held that the amendment to the statute was unconstitutional as an abridgment of free speech. The court held that since, by virtue of the "nonpossession" part of the statute, burning a draft card was already punishable, the amendment served no valid legislative purpose. Furthermore, the court held that since private destruction was already a crime, the amendment must have been—and obviously was—directed "at public as distinguished from private destruction." By singling out only those persons who committed an act of protest in public, the amendment violated the First Amendment. However, the court then affirmed O'Brien's conviction by ruling that his actions had also violated the already existing nonpossession regulations which it regarded as a lesser, included offense within the draft-card destruction amendment. Both O'Brien and the government petitioned the Supreme Court for certiorari, and it agreed to hear the case.

The case was argued on January 24, 1968, and was decided, in favor of the government, on May 27th. Arguing for the government, Solicitor General Erwin Griswold made three major points. First, he argued that draft card burning is action, not speech, and thus not entitled to the protections of the First Amendment. He conceded that there might be circumstances where greater leeway could be given to actions as expressions protected by the Constitution, but only where traditional means of expression were closed to a particular minority group or where

the action is indispensable to some oral communication. Second, he argued that since action rather than speech was involved, a valid government purpose may outweigh any "incidental" intrusion on First Amendment freedoms. And, third, he argued that the motives of Congress in passing the 1965 amendment were beyond the proper scope of judicial inquiry.

Attorneys for O'Brien argued that the 1965 amendment was a deliberate attempt to limit and intimidate freedom of speech without any rational purpose and that where First Amendment freedoms were involved, the Court had the duty to consider the motives behind the statute. They argued that O'Brien had engaged in "symbolic speech" and that this type of expression was entitled to full constitutional protection, subject to the limitation that the act not constitute a "clear and present danger." Finally, O'Brien's attorneys argued that the substitution by the Court of Appeals of a conviction for an offense for which he was not indicted, nor even charged, also violated his constitutional rights. His six-year sentence was additionally attacked as a violation of the Eighth Amendment's ban on cruel and unusual punishment.]

MR. CHIEF JUSTICE WARREN delivered the opinion of the Court.

. . .

O'Brien first argues that the 1965 Amendment is unconstitutional as applied to him because his act of burning his registration certificate was protected "symbolic speech" within the First Amendment. His argument is that the freedom of expression which the First Amendment guarantees includes all modes of "communication of ideas by conduct," and that his conduct is within this definition because he did it in "demonstration against the war and against the draft."

We cannot accept the view that an apparently limitless variety of conduct can be labelled "speech" whenever the person engaging in the conduct intends thereby to express an idea. However, even on the assumption that the alleged communicative element in O'Brien's conduct in suffi- cient to bring into play the First Amendment, it does not necessarily follow that the destruction of a regis- tration certificate is constitutionally protected activity. This Court has held that when "speech" and "nonspeech" elements are combined in the same course of conduct, a sufficiently im- portant governmental interest in reg- ulating the nonspeech element can justify incidental limitations on First Amendment freedoms. To charac- terize the quality of the governmental interest which must appear, the Court has employed a variety of descriptive terms: compelling; substantial; sub- ordinating; paramount; cogent; strong. Whatever imprecision inheres in these terms, we think it clear that a government regulation is sufficiently justified if it is within the constitu- tional power of the government; if it furthers an important or substantial governmental interest; if the gov- ernmental interest is unrelated to the suppression of free expression; and if the incidental restriction on alleged First Amendment freedom is no greater than is essential to the furth- erance of that interest. We find that the 1965 Amendment to § 462 (b)(3) of the Universal Military Training and Service Act meets all of these re- quirements, and consequently that O'Brien can be constitutionally con- victed for violating it.

The constitutional power of Con- gress to raise and support armies and to make all laws necessary and proper to that end is broad and sweeping. *Lichter* v. *United States* . . . (1948); Selective Draft Law Cases . . . (1918). . . .

The power of Congress to classify and conscript manpower for military service is "beyond question." Pur- suant to this power, Congress may es- tablish a system of registration for in-

dividuals liable for training and ser- vice, and may require such individu- als within reason to cooperate in the registration system. The issuance of certificates indicating the registra- tion and eligibility classification of in- dividuals is a legitimate and substan- tial administrative aid in the function- ing of this system. And legislation to insure the continuing availability of issued certificates serves a legitimate and substantial purpose in the sys- tem's administration.

O'Brien's argument to the contrary is necessarily premised upon his un- realistic characterization of Selective Service certificates. He essentially adopts the position that such certifi- cates are so many pieces of paper de- signed to notify registrants of their registration of classification, to be re- tained or tossed in the wastebasket according to the convenience or taste of the registrant. Once the registrant has received notification, according to this view, there is no reason for him to retain the certificates. O'Brien notes that most of the information on a registration certificate serves no notification purpose at all; the regis- trant hardly needs to be told his ad- dress and physical characteristics. We agree that the registration certifi- cate contains much information of which the registrant needs no notifi- cation. This circumstance, however, leads not to the conclusion that the certificate serves no purpose but that, like the classification certificate, it serves purposes in addition to initial notification. Many of these purposes would be defeated by the certificates' destruction or multilation. Among these are:

1. The registration certificate serves as proof that the individual de- scribed thereon has registered for the draft. The classification certificate

shows the eligibility classification of a named but undescribed individual. Voluntarily displaying the two certificates is an easy and painless way for a young man to dispel a question as to whether he might be delinquent in his Selective Service obligations. Correspondingly, the availability of the certificates for such display relieves the Selective Service System of the administrative burden it would otherwise have in verifying the registration and classification of all suspected delinquents. Further, since both certificates are in the nature of "receipts" attesting that the registrant has done what the law requires, it is in the interest of the just and efficient administration of the system that they be continually available, in the event, for example, of a mix-up in the registrant's file. Additionally, in a time of national crisis, reasonable availability to each registrant of the two small cards assures a rapid and uncomplicated means for determining his fitness for immediate induction, no matter how distant in our mobile society he may be from his local board.

2. The information supplied on the certificates facilitates communication between registrants and local boards, simplifying the system and benefiting all concerned. . . .

3. Both certificates carry continual reminders that the registrant must notify his local board of any change of address, and other specified changes in his status. . . .

4. The regulatory scheme involving Selective Service certificates includes clearly valid prohibitions against the alteration, forgery or similar deceptive misuse of certificates. The destruction or mutilation of certificates obviously increases the difficulty of detecting and tracing abuses such as these. Further, a mutilated certificate might itself be used for deceptive purposes.

The many functions performed by Selective Service certificates establish beyond doubt that Congress has a legitimate and substantial interest in preventing their wanton and unrestrained destruction and assuring their continuing availability by punishing people who knowingly and willfully destroy or multilate them. And we are unpersuaded that the pre-existence of the nonpossession regulations in any way negates this interest. . . .

We think it apparent that the continuing availability to each registrant of his Selective Service certificates substantially furthers the smooth and proper functioning of the system that Congress has established to raise armies. We think it also apparent that the Nation has a vital interest in having a system for raising armies that functions with maximum efficiency and is capable of easily and quickly responding to continually changing circumstances. For these reasons, the Government has a substantial interest in assuring the continuing availability of issued Selective Service certificates. . . .

In conclusion, we find that because of the Government's substantial interest in assuring the continuing availability of issued Selective Service certificates, because amended § 462(b) is an appropriately narrow means of protecting this interest and condemns only the independent noncommunicative impact of conduct within its reach, and because the noncommunicative impact of O'Brien's act of burning his registration certificate frustrated the Government's interest, a sufficient governmental interest has been shown to justify O'Brien's conviction.

O'Brien finally argues that the 1965 Amendment is unconstitutional as enacted because what he calls the "purpose" of Congress was "to suppress freedom of speech." We reject this argument because under settled principles the purpose of Congress, as O'Brien uses that term, is not a basis for declaring this legislation unconstitutional.

It is a familiar principle of constitutional law that this Court will not strike down an otherwise constitutional statute on the basis of an alleged illicit legislative motive. . . .

Inquiries into congressional motives or purposes are a hazardous matter. When the issue is simply the interpretation of legislation, the Court will look to statements by legislators for guidance as to the purpose of the legislature, because the benefit to sound decision-making in this circumstance is thought sufficient to risk the possibility of misreading Congress' purpose. It is entirely a different matter when we are asked to void a statute that is, under well-settled criteria, constitutional on its face, on the basis of what fewer than a handful of Congressmen said about it. What motivates one legislator to make a speech about a statute is not necessarily what motivates scores of others to enact it, and the stakes are sufficiently high for us to eschew guesswork. We decline to void essentially on the ground that it is unwise legislation which Congress had the undoubted power to enact and which could be reenacted in its exact form if the same or another legislator made a "wiser" speech about it. . . .

Since the 1965 Amendment to §12(b)(3) of the Universal Military Training and Service act is constitutional as enacted and as applied, the Court of Appeals should have affirmed the judgment of conviction entered by the District Court. Accordingly, we vacate the judgment of the Court of Appeals, and reinstate the judgement and sentence of the District Court. This disposition makes unnecessary consideration of O'Brien's claim that the Court of Appeals erred in affirming his conviction on the basis of the nonpossession regulation.

It is so ordered.

MR. JUSTICE HARLAN, CONCURRING (OMITTED.)
MR. JUSTICE DOUGLAS, DISSENTING

The Court states that the constitutional power of Congress to raise and support armies is "broad and sweeping" and that Congress' power "to classify and conscript manpower for military service is 'beyond question.' " This is undoubtedly true in times when, by declaration of Congress, the Nation is in a state of war. The underlying and basic problem in this case, however, is whether conscription is permissible in the absence of a declaration of war. That question has not been briefed nor was it presented in oral argument; but it is, I submit, a question upon which the litigants and the country are entitled to a ruling. I have discussed in *Holmes* v. *United States* . . . the nature of the legal issue and it will be seen from my dissenting opinion in that case that this Court has never ruled on the question. It is time that we made a ruling. This case should be put down for reargument. . . .

[For two reasons, the impact of the Court's decision has been limited. First, in the light of O'Brien's conviction, the tactics of war protesters changed. Many began mailing their draft cards back to the draft boards which issued them, thus circumventing the possibility of being charged with mutilation or destruction, though still leaving open the possibility of a charge of nonpossession. As of the time of the Court's decision, only 26 prosecutions had been brought under the 1965 amendment; 16 had resulted in convictions, six were then awaiting trial, and four had been dismissed. The second factor limiting the impact of the decision was the Court's refusal to give full consideration to the concept of symbolic speech, and its consequent failure to define the constitutional protections that might be afforded to those engaging in similar actions. It failed to consider how great the government's interest had to be before an infringement on speech could be considered merely incidental, and it failed to define what constituted a "compelling" government interest. It assumed, and then asserted, that the government's primary interest was in maintaining the viability of the draft, and not in suppressing speech, and that this was sufficient to justify a prohibition of draft-card burning. It accepted at face value the contention of the government that the rules against nonpossession and mutilation of draft cards were administratively necessary, making no serious effort to investigate how, why, or when a public burning interfered with the government's admittedly legitimate interest in assuring the workable operation of the draft. By following this line, the Court also avoided the necessity of confronting the issue which was, after all, at the heart of O'Brien's protest—the legality of the war in Vietnam.]

B. "Briefing" a Supreme Court Decision: The Nuts and Bolts of Constitutional Cases

Students may find it useful to summarize each Supreme Court decision in the form of a "brief," which outlines the major points and significance of the decision. This will serve as a guide to reading and understanding cases. There is no single standard form of a study brief, but the student will want to know at least the following about each case.

(1) Title of Case: *Tinker v. Des Moines Community School District*

Quite simply, the title tells (often in abbreviated fashion) who is opposing whom. Normally, the party who lost in the lower courts and is seeking reversal of that decision in the Supreme Court is listed first. The party seeking certiorari by the Supreme Court is called the "petitioner." In this case, Tinker sought, and was granted, a writ of certiorari by the Supreme Court. He is thus referred to as the petitioner. The party victorious in the lower court (who normally opposes review of that decision by the Supreme Court) is called the respondent. In this case, the Des Moines School District is referred to as the respondent. If the case is brought to the Supreme Court by an appeal, the party bringing the case is known as the appellant; the party opposing the granting of an appeal is known as the appellee.

There is often some confusion between these terms and those used to describe the parties when a case first comes to a court of law. In a criminal prosecution, the government that brings criminal charges is usually referred to simply as "the prosecution," and the person against whom charges are brought, as the "defendant." In a civil case, the party who brings a case is referred to as the "plaintiff," while the party against whom the case is brought is again referred to as the "defendant." Sometimes the party who brings a case to court is also the party who, having lost in the lower courts, seeks review of that decision in the Supreme Court. Thus, Tinker was the plaintiff in the lower court and the petitioner in the Supreme Court. But sometimes it is the defendant in the lower courts who becomes the petitioner or appellant in the Supreme Court; sometimes it is the plaintiff or prosecution in the lower courts who becomes the respondent or appellant in the Supreme Court. And often a Supreme Court opinion may refer to the same party, at various times, by both types of designations.

(2) Citation: 393 U.S. 503; 21 L. Ed.2d 731; 89 S. Ct. 733 (1969)

All decisions of the Supreme Court are reported chronologically in the United States Supreme Court Reports, published by the U.S. Government Printing Office, and additionally in two private reporting systems, the United States Supreme Court Reports, Lawyers' Edition, and the Supreme Court Reporter. The latter reports are cross-indexed with the official United States Reports but have their own citation systems as well. In all three, the first number in the citation is the volume in which the case may be found. This is followed by the abbreviated notation of the system, and then by the first page at which the particular case is located. It is also customary to list in parentheses the year in which the case was decided. Thus the *Tinker* case may be found, as indicated, in volume 393 of the United States Supreme Court Reports at page 503, in volume 21 of the second series of the Lawyers' Edition at page 731, and in volume 89 of the Supreme Court Reporter at page 733. Supreme Court decisions before 1875 were published by authorized reporters whose name, or abbreviation, appears in the citation instead of "U.S." Thus, *Marbury* v. *Madison* is cited as 1 Cranch 137 (1803), indicating that it appears in the first volume, at page 137, of the reports issued by Cranch. Other vintage Supreme Court decisions were reported by Dallas, Wheaton, Peters, Howard, Black, and Wallace, the latter's reports ending in 1874. Citations of cases included in this book are listed in the Index of Cases.

(3) Votes of the Justices

Which justices voted for which party? In this book, those justices voting with the majority are listed as "+"

and those with the minority as "−". A justice who dissents in part is listed as +/−, and justices who did not participate in the case for any reason are listed as "NP".

(4) Opinion of the Court by

When the Court has reached a preliminary decision on a case, the Chief Justice, if he is in the majority, or the senior associate justice in the majority, assigns the writing of the opinion. If this opinion commands a majority of participating justices it becomes the "opinion of the Court." If, as sometimes happens, enough justices who originally voted in the majority decide not to join the main opinion but rather to write their own, leaving four justices or less, then the opinion becomes merely the plurality "opinion of Mr. Justice————" and whatever justices join with him. A plurality opinion, while it is decisive for the litigants in the case, is usually not regarded as being of precedential strength equal to an opinion of the Court. Occasionally justices will write their own concurring opinions *in addition* to joining in the opinion of the Court. A justice not listed as writing either a concurring or disenting opinion, or the opinion of the Court, may be presumed to have joined that opinion. In the *Tinker* case, the opinion of the Court was by Mr. Justice Fortas. Justices White and Stewart filed concurring opinions and Justices Black and Harlan dissented in separate opinions. The final tally of votes in the case was 7-2 in favor of Tinker.

(5) Facts of the Case

A brief ought to contain a summary of the pertinent facts; these are usually summarized in the opinion of the Court, or in the editors' notes which appear in brackets before the opinion of the court in each case presented. Where the facts are not agreed on, it is useful to indicate which are the disputed facts. In the *Tinker* case there was no substantial disagreement as to facts, except insofar as Justices Fortas and Black perceived differently the level of controversy and disruption in the school occasioned by the children wearing armbands. Since the question of disruption was crucial to the case, this difference ought to be noted in the brief. Otherwise the summary might be as follows: "Petitioners and several other children were suspended from school for wearing black armbands to protest the war in Vietnam in contravention of school regulations. Petitioners subsequently returned to school without their armbands, and their parents filed suit in federal court seeking to enjoin the school authorities from disciplining them. The complaint was dismissed by the District Court on the grounds that the action of the school authorities was reasonable and did not deprive petitioners of any constitutional rights. On appeal, the Court of Appeals for the Eighth Circuit was evenly divided and affirmed the District Court's decision without opinion."

(6) Questions to be Decided

What are the precise questions which the Court must decide? In this case they might be stated as follows: (A) Is the wearing of armbands as a means of peaceful protest "symbolic speech" entitled to the protection of the First and Fourteenth Amendments? (B) May such symbolic speech appropriately be exercised in the public schools? if so, under what conditions? (C) Were the Tinker children in this case entitled to wear armbands without interference from the school authorities? This case posed no important question of jurisdiction—that is, no question of whether the Supreme Court might properly decide this case. If such a question were to arise, it would *normally* be the first question to be decided, since a lack of jurisdiction implies a lack of power to decide *any* aspect of the case.

(7) Decision

This can normally be summarized as answers to the questions posed in step 6. In this case, the answer to all three questions would be "Yes." The Court's answer to the subquestion under "B" can be summarized as part of the summary of the Court's opinion.

(8) Opinion of the Court

This should take the form of a summary of the major arguments of the opinion; in this case the following might be appropriate: "First Amendment rights of expression are available to students and teachers. On the other hand, states and school authorities have comprehensive authority to prescribe rules for conduct in the public schools consistent with constitutional safeguards. In order for the state to justify prohibition of a particular expression of opinion, *it must be able to show* that the expression of such opinion would 'materially and substantially interfere with the requirements of appropriate discipline,' and not merely that such opinion might lead to inconvenience or controversy. There was no showing in this case that petitioners' wearing of armbands interfered with school activities, caused a disturbance, or collided with the rights of other students to be secure or to be let alone. Other symbols of political expression were not banned; only the black armbands protesting the war in Vietnam were singled out for prohibition."

(9) Concurring Opinions

In many cases in this book, concurring opinions are omitted. Where they are reprinted they, too, should be summarized. In this case, Justice Stewart's opinion may be summarized as follows: "First Amendment rights of children are not coextensive with those of adults. In some circumstances and under certain limited conditions, a state may determine that children do not have the full capacity for individual choice." Justice Stewart's reliance on the *Ginsberg* case refers to the Court's approval of a state statute prohibiting the sale of pornographic literature to minors (See Part Two, Chapter Five). Justice White's concurring opinion was written to emphasize that the Court's opinion retains the traditional distinction between pure speech and the communication of ideas by acts or conduct which may impinge on a valid state interest, a distinction that Justice White felt was obscured by the Court's opinion. One common function of concurring opinions is to emphasize exactly what the Court did or did not do in a particular case.

(10) Dissenting Opinions

The author of a dissenting opinion is normally less limited in what he may say than is the author of the Court's opinion. The latter must represent the majority, while frequently the former writes only for himself. In this case, Justice Black's dissent expresses his opposition not only to the decision in this case, but also to what he sees as a more general trend of permissiveness both on the Court and in society. He tries to show the possible consequences of decisions such as this. No summary could do complete justice to what amounts to an essay on political and judicial morality: "Neither the state nor the federal government may regulate or censor the content of speech, but no person has a right to give speeches or engage in demonstrations where and when he pleases. While the armbands in this case may not have caused major disruption, there is evidence that students' minds were diverted from their regular lessons. Permitting this sort of behavior merely contributes to the new revolutionary era of permissiveness in this country fostered by the judiciary. The very purpose of wearing the armbands was to distract students and teachers. Decisions such as this contribute to a breakdown of law and order in the schools which has already progressed too far. Students may soon come to believe that they ought to run the schools, but nothing in the Constitution holds that the schools must be surrendered to student control."

the structure of judicial policy making

1. INTRODUCTORY ESSAY

The capacity of the Supreme Court to make important policy determinations rests on a slim and unpretentious sentence in Article III of the Constitution: "The judicial Power of the United States, shall be vested in one supreme Court, and in such inferior Courts as the Congress may from time to time ordain and establish." Amplified only slightly by an additional paragraph defining generally the sorts of cases or controversies to which the judicial power extends, this is the sole constitutional authorization of the Supreme Court. While the terms "the Executive Power" and "the Legislative Power" were used to describe the powers of the other branches of government, it is also true that each of these other branches received further constitutional instructions, and their expected functions were in any case more widely accepted and understood than those of the proposed Supreme Court.

That the Court would become an important policy-making agency was surely not predictable from its origin. Writing in the *Federalist Papers,* No. 78, Alexander Hamilton observed:

Whoever attentively considers the different departments of power must perceive that, in a government in which they are separated from each other, the judiciary, from the nature of its functions, will always be the least dangerous to the political rights of the Constitution; because it will be least in a capacity to annoy or injure them. The Executive not only dispenses the honors, but holds the sword of the community. The legislature not only commands the purse, but prescribes the rules by which the duties and rights of every citizen are to be regulated. The judiciary, on the contrary, has no influence over either sword or the purse; no direction either of the strength or of the wealth of the society; and can take no active action whatever. It may truly be said to have neither FORCE nor WILL, but merely judgment; and must ultimately depend upon the aid of the executive arm even for the efficacy of its judgments.

Hamilton may only have been making a relative observation rather than an absolute judgment, but neither he nor his contemporaries expected the Court to exercise a pervasive influence on American life.

Why, then, was the Court included at all in the new government? Its inclusion was in part a measure of the conservatism of the framers and their distrust of popular democracy. The Court was to be a check on the popular will. But it was included also because the framers, committed to the idea of separation of powers, felt that a check and balance system needed a judicial branch. Precisely how this would fit into the scheme of things and precisely what powers the Court would exercise were questions postponed for the consideration of the Congress and, ultimately, the Court itself. As a result, until the development of the modern presidency, the Supreme Court set the limits of its own powers more than the other branches of government.

The extent and success of judicial policy making depend initially on the kind of power available to the Court and on its effective use of that power. Judicial power is neither consistent nor entirely formal. It is a function not only of constitutional and statutory rules but also of the changing relationship of institutions, the cumulative impact of individual decisions and Court behavior, and the acceptance of these powers by the general public. "Power" is a social and political concept, not strictly a legal one.

One useful way to view power is as a form of influence. Influence can be depicted as a relational concept: "A influences B to the extent that he gets B to do something that B would not otherwise do." The extent of A's influence can be measured by the "extent or amount of change in B's behavior from what it would have been," always assuming that other factors are constant. If A does not wish to exercise his influence over B, he still retains the potential for doing so. If A values something enough to want it accomplished over B's constant objections, A can resort to compulsion or coercion. He may use physical force on B or, more likely, he may deprive B of something B wants or needs, or merely threaten to do so.

If influence can be plotted on a continuum, it becomes clear that some influence will rest entirely on persuasion, some on compulsion or coercion, and in a democratic society, most will fall somewhere in between. Robert Dahl defines "power" as coercive influence "based on the threat or expectation of extremely severe penalties or great losses, particularly physical punishment, torture, imprisonment, and death."[1] But if "power" is to be used in respect to

---

[1]*Modern Political Analysis* (Englewood Cliffs, New Jersey: Prentice Hall, 1963), Chapter 5.

the Supreme Court, it is probably best to define it in terms of negative rather than positive coercion: the withholding of rewards. In either case, power must be seen essentially as an attribute of bargaining in which the parties may have differential resources, varying motivations, and different evaluations of the acceptability of alternate outcomes.

To this point we have considered judicial power in terms of its formal sources and definitional characteristics, but it is necessary to note that power is also a function of practical results. Formal power exercised without effect eventually ceases to be power; conversely, only the effects of a given action may signify the presence of power. This is especially true of the Supreme Court, which has neither of the conventional levers of power: the purse and the sword. Because the Court cannot easily compel obedience to its orders, it must be especially sensitive to the political ramifications of its decisions while at the same time faithful to its mission to interpret the law and the Constitution. It has, and needs, substantial discretion in carrying out this task, but it cannot abuse that discretion without endangering its legitimacy and its power. It is precisely because of the questionable role of judicial review in a democracy that this burden falls heavily on the Supreme Court.

The effective use of judicial power, therefore, implies constant attention to its continued legitimacy and preservation. For the Supreme Court, deciding what cases *not* to decide is a critical policy function. As a practical matter the Court can decide only a small fraction of the cases that actually come to it each year, presently about 4,000 annually. Less than 200 of these cases are chosen for decision on the merits, that is, decision by written opinion after hearing oral argument. Several hundred more are decided in summary fashion with a short memorandum opinion. The vast majority are rejected without explanation. With virtually complete discretion over its docket, therefore, the Supreme Court is able to weed out cases that seem inappropriate for decision on legal grounds, but it can also eliminate those that are politically risky and that might provoke enough opposition to detract from the Court's power and prestige. A number of doctrines have developed that express the Court's policies as to which cases should, or should not, be decided.

The second part of this chapter is primarily concerned with such self-imposed limitations. Some of these limitations are constitutional in nature, others are traditional to common law courts. How these limitations are expressed and when they are invoked are often a function of justices' perceptions of external conditions and threats to the Court's integrity, although they are usually expressed as "norms" rather than openly as responses to outside pressures. These limitations, taken as a whole, exert a substantial influence on the Court's role as a public policy maker. They relate to the types of cases that the Court will hear, the types or qualifications of litigants permitted to bring cases to the Court, and the sorts of solutions that the Court is likely to offer in response to the problems presented to it. They are a major source of judicial discretion.

The debate between those who believe that the Supreme Court ought to play an important and positive policy making role and those who see its legitimate function as being less assertive is often characterized, as we have noted in the previous chapter, as one between "judicial activism" and "judicial self-restraint." These terms mark the parameters of the debate over the Court's proper function which seems to arise periodically in each generation.

The rhetorical and ideological "loading" of these terms has tended to obscure the very fundamental character of judicial style that actually depends heavily on a mixture of activist and restraint policies in the Court's pursuit of its policy goals. Of the two, the activist posture has possibly become the less meaningful in terms of its describing a discrete style of judicial behavior. On the other hand, the concept of self-restraint still retains some meaning and considerable force and vitality. It rests on six basic assumptions, which were described briefly in the previous chapter but which are worth restating in greater detail here:

The first assumption is that the Court is basically undemocratic because it is nonelective and presumably nonresponsive to the popular will. Because of its alleged oligarchic composition, it is said the Court should defer wherever possible to the "more" democratic branches of the government. Second, the doctrine of self-restraint is often premised on the questionable origins of the great power of judicial review, a power not explicitly granted in the Constitution. This only exacerbates the charge that the Court lacks legitimate power to consider the validity of statutes passed by the elected representatives of the people. Third, the doctrine of separation of powers, taken in conjunction with the first two assumptions, is often relied on to counsel limitations on the judicial function. Fourth, it is said that the concept of federalism, dividing power between the nation and the states, requires of the Court deference toward the actions of state governments and officials. Fifth, self-restraint rests on the nonideological but pragmatic assumption that since the Court is dependent on the Congress for its jurisdiction and resources, and dependent on public acceptance for its effectiveness, it ought not to overstep its boundaries without consideration of the risks involved. And, finally, self-restraint rests for a few on the aristocratic notion that, being a court of *law* and inheritor and custodian of the Anglo-American legal tradition, it ought not descend too far to the mere level of politics—law being the process of reason and judgment and politics being concerned only with power and influence.

2. CONSTITUTIONALISM AS A SOURCE AND SYMBOL OF JUDICIAL POWER

[When Richard M. Nixon resigned from the presidency on August 8, 1974, he justified his resignation with the statement, "I no longer have a strong enough political base in the Congress to justify continuing." The Supreme Court played a significant role in the drama that culminated in President Nixon's resignation, a role that serves as an example of judicial power, albeit of a very complex and subtle sort. For those to whom power is an overt act of force or will, grounded in legitimate authority, it may seem strange to select the Nixon resignation as an example of the consequences of judicial power. No one forced Richard Nixon to resign; no other governmental official challenged his right to office; no other institution, least of all the Supreme Court, attempted to usurp the powers of the presidency. Yet, the Court's decision in *United States* v. *Nixon*, announced on July 24, 1974, required the disclosure of taped information about the Watergate "cover-up" which the president had sought to withhold. The release of those tapes led to revelations of presidential misconduct that destroyed Nixon's "political base in Congress." The Judiciary Committee of the House of Representatives voted to recommend impeachment of the president, and rather than wait for that impeachment and almost certain conviction by the Senate, Richard Nixon became the first president ever to resign from office. It is a measure of power that the Supreme Court could make such a decision and that President Nixon felt obliged to comply with it.

It is the idea of "constitutionalism" that makes such power possible in a system like ours. The idea that general political power shall be limited by the criteria of fundamental law, as interpreted and enunciated by a Supreme Court, is the essence of American constitutionalism. That is the basic fact of the matter, and all other considerations—such as the meaning, or propriety, or method of use of judicial review—are theoretically secondary.

Yet an irony of sorts must be noted. Constitutionalism is that which leads to judicial review, but judicial review is that which makes constitutionalism meaningful in practice, something more than an artifact of political theory. Constitutional theory and judicial review may be symbiotic in their relationship; even so, consideration of judicial review in the following pages must proceed from appreciation of the fact that a given institution—the Supreme Court—acts to keep alive "our historic commitment to the rule of law," however frustrating or inconvenient that rule of law may be for some, from time to time. The special prosecutor called on the courts to compel disclosure of the presidential tapes for use as evidence in a criminal trial. Although Nixon's attorneys argued in Court that it was the president, and not the courts, who should determine whether or not such materials would be released, when the Supreme Court decided differently, the president reluctantly obeyed. His action, forestalling almost certain impeachment, was an acknowledgment of the subtle force of constitutionalism in our political system.]

A. *An Excerpt from* United States *v.* Nixon *(1974)*

. . . In the performance of assigned constitutional duties each branch of the Government must initially interpret the Constitution, and the interpretation of its powers by any branch is due great respect from the others. The President's counsel, as we have noted, reads the Constitution as providing an absolute privilege of confidentiality for all presidential communications. Many decisions of this Court, however, have unequivocally reaffirmed the holding of *Marbury* v. *Madison* (1803), that "it is emphatically the province and duty of the judicial department to say what the law is."

. . . [T]his presumptive privilege must be considered in light of our historic commitment to the rule of law. This is nowhere more profoundly manifest than in our view that "the twofold aim [of criminal justice] is that guilt shall not escape or innocence suffer." *Berger* v. *United States* (1935). We have elected to employ an adversary system of criminal justice in which the parties contest all issues before a court of law. The need to develop all relevant facts in the adversary system is both fundamental and comprehensive. The ends of criminal justice would be defeated if judgments were to be founded on a partial or speculative presentation of the facts. The very integrity of the judicial system and public confidence in the system depends on full disclosure of all the facts, within the framework of the rules of evidence. To ensure that justice is done, it is imperative to the function of courts that compulsory process be available for the production of evidence needed either by the prosecution or by the defense. . . .

B. Robert McCloskey, The Genesis and Nature of Judicial Power

. . . The Constitution has comparatively little to say about the Court or the federal judiciary in general. The "judicial power of the United States," whatever it may be, is vested in the Supreme Court and in such other courts as Congress may establish. But the composition of the Court, including the number of its members, is left for congressional decision; and, while federal judges cannot be removed except by impeachment, there is nothing to prevent Congress from creating additional judgeships whenever it chooses. Furthermore, although the judicial power "extends" to a variety of cases described in Article III, section 2, the second paragraph of that section significantly qualifies what the first seems to have granted, and gives Congress power to control the Supreme Court's jurisdiction over appeals from lower courts. Since the cases that reach the Court directly without first being heard in other courts are comparatively minor in quantity or importance, this legislative authority over appeals (over the "appellate jurisdiction") is a license for Congress to decide whether the Supreme Court will be a significant or a peripheral factor in American government.

Most important of all, the Constitution makes no explicit statement about the nature of the Court's power even when a case admittedly falls within its jurisdiction. Some of the uncertainties outlined above were resolved, temporarily at any rate, by the passage of the Judiciary Act. Its famous Section 25 gave the Supreme Court power to reverse or affirm state court decisions which had denied claims based on the federal Constitution, treaties, or laws. This meant that such cases could be reached by the Supreme Court through its appellate jurisdiction. But suppose a state court had denied such a claim under the federal Constitution and the Supreme Court of the United States reversed on the ground that the state court's interpretation of the Constitution was in error. And suppose further that the state court obstinately continued to insist upon its own interpretation. Was there anything in the Constitution to guarantee that the Supreme Court's opinion would prevail, that the Supreme Court's authority was superior to state courts? Or suppose, to carry the matter a step further, that the state court had held a federal law invalid as conflicting with the *national* Constitution and the Supreme Court *agreed* with this holding, thus asserting its authority to overthrow an act of Congress. Does the Constitution make it *clear* that the Court has this final authority of "judicial review" over national legislative enactments?

The answer to both questions is a fairly solid "no." As for state decisions it has been argued that the "supreme law of the land" clause and the clause extending the judicial power to cases arising under the Constitution do make it clear that the Supreme Court was intended to be preeminent on questions of constitutional interpretation. If the Constitution is supreme and the Supreme Court has jurisdiction over cases involving the Constitution, then it follows that the Court's word on such matters is paramount over all others—so the argument runs. But in the first place this reasoning is not

Reprinted from Robert McCloskey, *The American Supreme Court* (Chicago: University of Chicago Press, 1960), pp. 6–17.

unassailable, for as defenders of states' rights were later passionately to insist, the fact that the Constitution is supreme does not settle the question of who decides what the Constitution means. And in the second place enthusiasts for judicial review have never quite been able to explain why so formidable a power was granted by implication rather than by flat statement. As for judicial review of congressional acts, the support in the language of the Constitution was even more suppositious, and arguments for the authority derived solely from the language seem inevitably to beg the question.

None of this is to say that the framers of the Constitution would have been surprised to see the Supreme Court exercising the power of judicial review in some form, both as against the states and as against Congress. Indeed there is ample evidence that most of them who had thought about it expected that the Court would do so, however distressing it is that they failed to make their expectations explicit. But neither the framers nor the ratifying state conventions (whose views are in some ways more relevant to the issue) had any general understanding about the particular form that the judicial review would take and the role that the Supreme Court would therefore assume.

Some, like Alexander Hamilton, certainly hoped that the justices would act as general monitors, broadly supervising the other branches of government and holding them to the path of constitutional duty, though even he seems to have conceived this exalted notion only after the Convention's adjournment. Others, like Robert Yates, also of New York, feared that the Court would so regard its function. But James Madison, the highest possible

authority on the Constitution's intent, though apparently expecting the Supreme Court to disallow laws that *clearly* contravened the Constitution, by no means conceded that the Court could apply its negative judgment to more debatable points or that the judicial pronouncements were intended to be final and binding on the other branches of government. And the evidence of both the Convention and the ratification controversy suggests that other participants were equally doubtful about these questions and that many more had simply not considered the matter at all. . . .

For the Constitution was potentially the convergence point for all the ideas about fundamental law that had been current in America since the colonization period. Of course the notion of a law-above-government, a "higher" law, was well known throughout the Western world, but the colonists had given it a special domestic cast, infusing it with interpretations drawn from their own unique experience. While most Europeans thought of higher law as exercising a moral restraint on government, they did not argue that this moral limit was legally enforceable, that it was positive law, practically binding the governors. Even before the Revolutionary controversy, Americans had found it easy to assume that it was just that, for their own legislatures had long been literally bound by "higher law" in such forms as the colonial charters and decisions of the British Privy Council. But the struggle with England turned assumption into fiery conviction. . . .

Such circumstances might help explain, at least initially, why the Constitution won such ready devotion. But the question remains, it might be said, why the Court should be chosen to share in and perpetuate the Constitution's glory. We have seen that the language of the Constitution is inconclusive on this matter and that the intentions of the framers were ambiguous. Jefferson, Madison and many other almost equally illustrious statesmen were later to argue that the Congress, the President, and even the individual states were, no less than the courts, guardians of the Constitution and co-equal interpreters of its meaning. What warrant then had our four new judges for hoping that history would reject these rival claimants and confirm the Supreme Court's constitutional prerogative? To put the question somewhat differently, what made it likely, though perhaps not certain, that the Court would play the great part it has played in American life?

With the benefit of hindsight, it is not hard to find a number of answers to these questions. The common law traditions deriving from the great seventeenth-century English jurist, Sir Edward Coke, exalted judges above other folk, and that tradition was cherished by Americans with peculiar tenacity. The Federalists, who enjoyed political ascendancy during the first decade of the Republic's history, tried to use their temporary prestige to implant in the popular mind a respect for judges, so that Federalism might find a haven against the adversity of a Jeffersonian political victory. The very fact that the concept of judicial review was, at the outset, imperfectly understood was a point in its favor, for it enabled judges to build up the Court's power gradually and almost imperceptibly and its opponents thus found themselves in the frustrating position of those who fight shadows. . . .

To understand that condition it is necessary to look again at the climate of political opinion in eighteenth-century America and particularly at the quarter-century that preceded the Constitution. We have seen that the old doctrine of fundamental law was stimulated by the events and idea currents of the Revolutionary era. Now it must be observed that the movement for revolution also supplied a vital impetus for another, and in some ways, contradictory, notion—the theory of popular sovereignty. American pamphleteers had insisted on the principle of home rule; the Declaration of Independence had founded just government on the "consent of the governed"; the next and natural step was to regard the people as not only a consenting but a willing entity and to declare, as Jefferson later said, that "the will of the majority is in all cases to prevail." These reasonable and perhaps inevitable deductions from the Spirit of '76 were widely prevalent in America during the Articles of Confederation period. Many of the solid citizens deplored such "mad democracy" and longed to curb it, but they could not evade the fact that the will-of-the-people concept was now firmly planted in American minds as one of the premises of political thinking.

Yet plainly that concept conflicted with the doctrine of fundamental law which was also, and concurrently, treasured by Americans. Popular sovereignty suggests *will*; fundamental law suggests *limit*. The one idea conjures up the vision of an active, positive state; the other idea emphasizes the negative, restrictive side of the political problem. It may be possible to harmonize these seeming opposites by logical sleight of hand, by arguing that the doctrines of popular sovereignty and fundamental law were fused in the Constitution, which was a popularly willed limitation. But it seems unlikely that Americans in general achieved such a synthesis and far more probable, considering our later political history, that most of them retained the two ideas side by side. This propensity to hold contradictory ideas simultaneously is one of the most significant qualities of the American political mind at all stages of national history, and it helps substantially in explaining the rise to power of the United States Supreme Court.

For with their political hearts thus divided between the will of the people and the rule of law, Americans were naturally receptive to the development of institutions that reflected each of these values separately. The legislature with its power to initiate programs and policies, to respond to the expressed interest of the public, embodied the doctrine of popular sovereignty. The courts, generally supposed to be without will as Hamilton said, generally revered as impartial and independent, fell heir almost by default to the guardianship of the fundamental law. It did not avail for Jeffersonian enemies of the judicial power to insist that a single department could exercise *both* the willing and the limiting functions. The bifurcation of the two values in the American mind impellingly suggested that the functions should be similarly separated. And the devotion of Americans to both popular sovereignty and fundamental law insured public support for the institution that represented each of them.

This dualism of the American mind, symbolized on the one hand by "political" institutions like the Congress and the Presidency and on the other hand by the Court and the Constitution, helps account for a good deal that seems baffling in later history. In logical terms it might appear strange that the nation should resoundingly approve the New Deal in 1936 and a few months later stoutly defend against attack the Supreme

Court that had cut the heart from the New Deal program. But the paradox is related as branch to root to the historic dualism between popular sovereignty and the doctrine of fundamental law that developed with the birth throes of the American political system. The separation of the two ideas in the American mind had been emphasized by intervening events: strong-minded judges had added new arguments for the Court's constitutional prerogative; congressmen and presidents, busy with more pressing concerns, had been content except for fitful rebellious impulses to let those arguments go unchallenged; and the cake of custom had hardened over the original disjunction. But it was made possible at the outset by our native tendency to harbor conflicting ideas without trying, or caring, to resolve them.

The United States began its history, then, with a Constitution that posed more questions than it answered and with a Supreme Court whose birthright was most uncertain. The temper of the times and the deep-seated inclinations of the American political character favored the future of both these institutions and at the same time prescribed their limits and helped determine their nature. American devotion to the principle of fundamental law gave the Constitution its odor of sanctity, and the American bent for evading contradictions by assigning values to separate compartments allowed the Supreme Court to assume the priestly mantle. But like most successes, in politics and elsewhere, this one had a price. The failure to resolve the conflict between popular sovereignty and fundamental law perhaps saved the latter principle, but by the same token it left the former intact. And this meant that the fundamental law could be enforced only within delicately defined boundaries, that constitutional law though not simply the creature of the popular will nevertheless had always to reckon with it, that the mandates of the Supreme Court must be shaped with an eye not only to legal right and wrong, but with an eye to what popular opinion would tolerate.

We have seen, then, that the Constitution makers postponed some of the most vital questions confronting them, that the Constitution and the Supreme Court inherited the quasi-religious symbolic quality attached to the doctrine of "higher law," but that the dogmas of popular sovereignty also continued to survive and flourish and therefore influence constitutionalism. The consequences of all this were several. For one thing the Constitution itself could not become the certain and immutable code of governmental conduct that some of its latter-day idolators imagined it to be. Conceived in ambiguity as well as liberty, it could never escape that legacy. The framers had said in effect: with respect to certain questions, some of them very momentous, the Constitution means whatever the circumstances of the future will allow it to mean. But since those circumstances were almost sure to vary, the result was that alterability be-

came the law of the Constitution's being: it might mean one thing in 1855, something else in 1905, and something still different in 1955, depending upon what circumstances, including popular expectations, warranted. . . .

As for the Supreme Court, its nature has also been heavily and permanently influenced by the factors just described. As might be expected, any description of the judicial function in America is shot through with paradoxes. To begin with, the observer confronts the fact that the Court does inherit a responsibility for helping to guide the nation, especially with respect to those long-term "value questions" that are so vital to the maintenance of a just political order. A good many gallons of ink have been spilled over the issue of whether such a heavy assignment should have devolved on the judiciary. John Marshall, "the great Chief Justice," has been accused of seizing the bitter cup all too gladly and thus setting a pattern of usurpation for future judges to follow. Insofar as this indictment rests on the supposed "intent of the framers," it suffers from the weakness already remarked: that so few of the framers had any clear views one way or another about the subject. . . .

3. JUDICIAL REVIEW AND JUDICIAL SUPREMACY

A. *Judicial Review Before Marbury*

In the foregoing pages, Robert McCloskey noted that the "United States began its history with a Constitution that posed more questions than it answered and with a Supreme Court whose birthright was most uncertain." The expected role of the Su-

preme Court and the power of judicial review was but one of several vital questions not answered at the convention.

Judicial review is the power of a court to determine the validity of a governmental act. It can be exercised both with respect to coordinate branches of government (i.e., Congress and the president) and over the acts of state government. In its most exalted sense, judicial review is the power to invalidate a law conflicting with the basic charter of government. But declaring a law to be unconstitutional is only the apex in a continuum of reviewing functions exercised by the Supreme Court.

The Constitution does not mention any power of judicial review, but the framers were conversant with both the abstract concept of judicial review and its reality. The English Privy Council had long exercised review powers over colonial legislatures. Judicial review was exercised sporadically by several state courts between 1776 and 1789. Yet it was hardly an accepted judicial function, at least as exercised by colonial judges. Leonard Levy has observed that on most occasions, its invocation produced outrage. And its use had been limited largely to instances of courts seeking to protect their own prerogatives, rather than exercising any broad policy check on governmental power.[1]

At the Constitutional Convention, a proposal for a Council of Revision, consisting of the executive and several members of the Supreme Court, was rejected three times. A proposal to give the Supreme Court as a whole powers of revision over legislation was also defeated. There was no formal proposal, and no debate, over whether the Supreme Court should, or could, refuse to enforce statutes it believed contrary to the Constitution. Critics differ on whether the absence of explicit language in the Constitu-

tion implied that judicial review was an inherent power of judges, or whether it was to be construed as a rejection of that power.[2]

Debates over ratification of the Constitution seemed to assume the former. Judicial power to enforce the Constitution was asserted in *Federalist Paper* No. 17. Most influential was Hamilton's argument in *Federalist Paper* No. 78 that the power of judicial review was necessary to the workings of a written constitution. In the Virginia Ratifying Convention, a youthful John Marshall asked, rhetorically (and prophetically): "To what quarter will you look for protection from an infringement on the Constitution if you will not give the power to the judiciary?" But in New York, Robert Yates expressed the fears of many: "This power in the judicial branch will enable them to mold the government into any shape they please. . . . Men placed in this position will generally soon feel themselves independent of heaven itself." It was in response to such fears that Hamilton contended, in No. 78 of the *Federalist Papers,* that judicial review did not imply judicial superiority over legislatures: "It only supposes that the power of the people is superior to both."

Prior to the historic case of *Marbury* v. *Madison* (1803), the Supreme Court had in fact exercised judicial review. Two minor state statutes had been invalidated. And in 1851 it was discovered, belatedly, that the Supreme Court in an unreported opinion had declared a federal law unconstitutional in 1794. Finally, in the famous case of *Hylton* v. *United States* (1796), which challenged the

---

[1]Leonard W. Levy, "Judicial Review, History, and Democracy: An Introduction," in Levy (ed.) *Judicial Review and the Supreme Court: Selected Essays* (New York: Harper & Row, 1967), pp. 1–42.
[2]*Ibid.*

validity of a federal carriage tax, the Supreme Court had *upheld* the tax against challenges to its constitutionality. Yet it was not until the *Marbury* case that the Supreme Court's assumption of this *power* was fully articulated.

B. *Marbury v. Madison (1803)*

+Marshall, Paterson, Washington, Chase

NP Cushing, Moore

[John Marshall's opinion in *Marbury* remains to this day the classic argument for the power of judicial review. But the case is also a fascinating example of interaction between the Supreme Court and the elected branches of government. As such, it is a vivid reminder of the Court's political role. The scenario of intrigue in this case is unusual, but the lesson it offers about the practicalities of judicial power are even more instructive today.

The case arose out of the conflict between the Federalist and Jeffersonian parties. Federalist President Adams was defeated for reelection in 1800, and after 36 ballots in the House of Representatives, the tie between Jefferson and Burr was resolved in favor of Jefferson. A Jeffersonian Congress was also elected, and the Federalists feared political extinction. One hope for continued Federalist influence was the Supreme Court, which consisted of six justices—all Federalists. After the elections, but before Jefferson took office on March 4, 1801, Chief Justice Oliver Ellsworth resigned because of ill health and Adams appointed John Marshall to succeed him. Marshall was then secretary of state in the Adams' administration and held both posts from February 4 to March 3, 1801. Marshall was strongly Federalist in his convictions, a veteran politician, and an arch political enemy (as well as a cousin) of Jefferson. Although his nomination was approved by the lame duck Federalist Congress, it was expected to, and did, outrage the Jeffersonians.

The second Federalist strategy was to increase the number of Federalist judges on the lower courts. On February 13, 1801, Congress passed a new Circuit Court Bill with the osten-

sible purpose of eliminating the onerous "circuit riding" chores which each Supreme Court Justice had to undertake. Sixteen new federal judgeships and a new series of intermediate "circuit courts" were established, and all 16 positions were given to Federalists. Adams' appointments were confirmed by the Senate on March 2, signed by the president, sealed by Secretary of State Marshall on March 3, and delivered before Jefferson was inaugurated the next day. These were to be known as the "midnight judges."

On February 27, 1801, just five days before the inauguration, Congress passed the District of Columbia Organic Act, which provided for the appointment by the president of 42 justices of the peace for Washington and Alexandria, Virginia. On March 2, Adams nominated 23 new JPs for Washington and 19 for Alexandria, and these nominations were confirmed by the Senate on March 3. They were signed by Adams and sealed by Marshall before midnight on March 3. Marshall's brother James was given the chore of delivering the commissions, but was unable to complete the task before midnight and returned the remaining commissions to John Marshall. Among those not delivered was one for William Marbury.

On March 4, 1801, Jefferson became president (sworn in by Chief Justice Marshall) and James Madison was sworn in as his secretary of state. Madison refused to deliver Marbury's commission, and the stage for the litigation was set. The Supreme Court was then in recess, and although it met for its August term, the *Marbury* case did not come before it until December, 1801. Represented by Charles Lee, Adams' attorney general, Marbury sought a writ of mandamus compelling Madison to deliver his Commission, and Marshall responded by issuing an order to Madison to "show cause" why the mandamus should not be issued, the order returnable at the June, 1802 term of the Court.

Although they believed the Supreme Court to be without the power to issue the mandamus, the Jeffersonians were outraged at what they considered Marshall's audacity and willingness to rule against them. To forestall the Court, Congress abolished the June term in favor of annual sessions beginning each February. This meant that the Supreme Court was forcibly recessed until February, 1803, when the *Marbury* suit was finally heard—after a 14 months' delay.

If anything, the Jeffersonians were even *more* outraged by the new Federalist circuit judges, and on March 31, 1802 the act of February 13 was repealed and the new judgeships were abolished. Since this returned the old provisions of the Judiciary Act of 1789 to full force, it meant that the Supreme Court justices had to ride circuit again—a physical punishment of major proportions. Even more important was the debate which raged over the possible right of the Supreme Court to review acts of Congress—a power which the Jeffersonians rejected, as they did Marshall's right to issue a mandamus to the secretary of state. Several prominent congressmen asserted that any attempt to enforce such an order would leave the justices open to impeachment. This was not an empty threat, since one federal judge—John Pickering—had been impeached in 1802, and Justice Samuel Chase was to be impeached three years later. In fact, during Chase's impeachment trial, a fearful Marshall suggested that Congress surrender the power of impeachment of judges in return for the power to exercise appellate jurisdiction over decisions of the Court that were deemed objectionable.

Such was the politically charged atmosphere in which the Supreme Court considered Marbury's suit. Since this suit invoked the original jurisdiction of the Court, the case was tried on its facts, and several witnesses were heard. James Marshall submitted an affidavit attesting to the signing of the commission, and Jefferson's attorney general, Levi Lincoln, appeared as a witness. No attorney appeared to represent Secretary of State Madison.

Chief Justice John Marshall participated fully in the trial and, of course, in deciding the case. Yet the propriety of his participation was at least open to question in view of his involvement in the events under scrutiny. Perhaps one reason he chose to participate was that neither Justice Cushing nor Justice Moore was present at the trial and were thus disqualified; if Marshall had also taken himself out of the case, a quorum would have been lacking and no decision could be rendered. For Marshall to lose this opportunity to read Jefferson a lecture on political morality—and incidentally to claim the great power of judicial review for the court—would have been too great a sacrifice.]

CHIEF JUSTICE MARSHALL delivered the opinion of the court.

The first object of inquiry is,

1st. Has the applicant a right to the commission he demands?

. . . It is, therefore, decidedly the opinion of the court, that when a commission has been signed by the president, the appointment is made; and that the commission is complete when the seal of the United States has been affixed to it by the secretary of state.

Where an officer is removable at the will of the executive, the circumstances which complete his appointment is of no concern; because the act is at any time revocable; and the commission may be arrested, if still in the office. But when the officer is not removable at the will of the executive, the appointment is not revocable, and cannot be annulled. It has conferred legal rights which cannot be resumed. . . .

To withhold his commission, therefore, is an act deemed by the court not warranted by law, but violative of a vested legal right.

This bring us to the second inquiry; which is,

If he has a right, and that right has been violated, do the laws of his country afford him a remedy?

The very essence of civil liberty certainly consists in the right of every individual to claim the protection of the laws, whenever he receives an injury. One of the first duties of government is to afford that protection. . . .

The government of the United States has been emphatically termed a government of laws, and not of men. It will certainly cease to deserve this high appellation, if the laws furnish no remedy for the violation of a vested legal right. . . .

By the constitution of the United States, the president is invested with certain important political powers, in the exercise of which he is to use his own discretion, and is accountable only to his country in his political character and to his own conscience. To aid him in the performance of these duties, he is authorized to appoint certain officers, who act by his authority, and in conformity with his orders.

In such cases, their acts are his acts; and whatever opinion may be entertained of the manner in which executive discretion may be used, still there exists, and can exist, no power to control that discretion. . . .

The conclusion from this reasoning is, that where the heads of departments are the political or confidential agents of the executive, merely to execute the will of the president, or rather to act in cases in which the executive possesses a constitutional or legal discretion, nothing can be more perfectly clear than that their acts are only politically examinable. But where a specific duty is assigned by law, and individual rights depend upon the performance of that duty, it seems equally clear that the individual who considers himself injured, has a right to resort to the laws of his country for a remedy.

. . . It is, then, the opinion of the court,

1st. That by signing the commission of Mr. Marbury, the President of the United States appointed him a justice of peace for the county of Washington, in the district of Columbia; and that the seal of the United States, affixed thereto by the secre-

tary of state, is conclusive testimony of the verity of the signature, and of the completion of the appointment; and that the appointment conferred on him a legal right to the office for the space of five years.

2dly. That, having this legal title to the office, he has a consequent right to the commission; a refusal to deliver which is a plain violation of that right, for which the laws of his country afford him a remedy.

It remains to be inquired whether,

He is entitled to the remedy for which he applies. This depends on,

1st. The nature of the writ applied for; and,

2dly. The power of this court. . . .

1st. With respect to the officer to whom it would be directed. The intimate political relation subsisting between the president of the United States and the heads of departments, necessarily renders any legal investigation of the acts of one of those high officers peculiarly irksome, as well as delicate; and excites some hesitation with respect to the propriety of entering into such investigation. Impressions are often received, without much reflection or examination, and it is not wonderful that in such a case as this, the assertion, by an individual, of his legal claims in a court of justice, to which claims it is the duty of that court to attend, should at first view be considered by some, as an attempt to intrude into the cabinet, and to intermeddle with the prerogatives of the executive.

It is scarcely necessary for the court to disclaim all pretensions to such a jurisdiction. An extravagance, so absurd and excessive, could not have been entertained for a moment. The province of the court is, solely, to decide on the rights of individuals, not to inquire how the executive, or executive officers, perform duties in which they have a discretion. Questions in their nature political, or which are, by the constitution and laws, submitted to the executive, can never be made in this court.

If one of the heads of departments commits any illegal act, under colour of his office, by which an individual sustains an injury, it cannot be pretended that his office alone exempts him from being compelled to obey the judgment of the law. How, then, can his office exempt him from this particular mode of deciding on the legality of his conduct, if the case be such a case as would, were any other individual the party complained of, authorize the process?

. . . This, then, is a plain case for a *mandamus*, either to deliver the commission, or a copy of it from the record; and it only remains to be inquired,

Whether it can issue from this court.

The act to establish the judicial courts of the United States authorizes the supreme court "to issue writs of *mandamus*, in cases warranted by the principles and usages of law, to any courts, appointed, or persons holding office, under the authority of the United States." The secretary of state, being a person holding an office under the authority of the United States, is precisely within the letter of the description; and if this court is not authorized to issue a writ of *mandamus* to such an officer, it must be because the law is unconstitutional, and therefore absolutely incapable of conferring the authority, and assigning the duties which its words purport to confer and assign.

The constitution vests the whole judicial power of the United States in one supreme court, and such inferior courts as congress shall, from time to time, ordain and establish. This power is expressly extended to all cases arising under the laws of the United States; and consequently, in some form may be exercised over the present case; because the right claimed is given by a law of the United States.

In the distribution of this power it is declared that "the supreme court shall have original jurisdiction in all cases affecting ambassadors, other public ministers and consuls, and those in which a state shall be a party. In all other cases, the supreme court shall have appellate jurisdiction."

It has been insisted, at the bar, that as the original grant of jurisdiction, to the supreme and inferior courts, is general, and the clause, assigning original jurisdiction to the supreme court, contains no negative or restrictive words, the power remains to the legislature, to assign original jurisdiction to that court in other cases than those specified in the article which has been recited; provided those cases belong to the judicial power of the United States.

If it had been intended to leave it in the discretion of the legislature to apportion the judicial power between the supreme and inferior courts according to the will of that body, it would certainly have been useless to have proceeded further than to have defined the judicial power, and the tribunals in which it should be vested. The subsequent part of the section is mere surplusage, is entirely without meaning, if such is to be the construction. If congress remains at liberty to give this court appellate jurisdiction, where the constitution has declared their jurisdiction shall be original; and original jurisdiction where the constitution has declared it shall be appellate; the distribution of jurisdiction, made in the constitution, is form without substance. . . .

It cannot be presumed that any clause in the constitution is intended to be without effect; and, therefore, such a construction is inadmissible, unless the words require it. . . .

When an instrument organizing fundamentally a judicial system, divides it into one supreme, and so many inferior courts as the legislature may ordain and establish; then enumerates its powers, and proceeds so far to distribute them, as to define the jurisdiction of the supreme court by declaring the cases in which it shall take original jurisdiction, and that in others it shall take appellate jurisdiction; the plain import of the words seems to be, that in one class of cases its jurisdiction is original, and not appellate; in the other it is appellate, and not original. If any other construction would render the clause inoperative, that is an additional reason for rejecting such other construction, and for adhering to their obvious meaning.

To enable this court, then, to issue a *mandamus,* it must be shown to be an exercise of appellate jurisdiction, or to be necessary to enable them to exercise appellate jurisdiction.

It has been stated at the bar that the appellate jurisdiction may be exercised in a variety of forms, and that if it be the will of the legislature that a *mandamus* should be used for that purpose, that will must be obeyed. This is true, yet the jurisdiction must be appellate, not original.

It is the essential criterion of appellate jurisdiction, that it revises and corrects the proceedings in a cause already instituted, and does not create that cause. Although, therefore, a *mandamus* may be directed to courts, yet to issue such a writ to an officer for the delivery of a paper, is in effect the same as to sustain an original action for that paper, and, therefore, seems not to belong to appellate, but to original jurisdiction. Neither is it necessary in such a case as this, to

enable the court to exercise its appellate jurisdiction.

The authority, therefore, given to the supreme court, by the act establishing the judicial courts of the United States, to issue writs of *mandamus* to public officers, appears not to be warranted by the constitution; and it becomes necessary to inquire whether a jurisdiction so conferred can be exercised.

The question, whether an act, repugnant to the constitution, can become the law of the land, is a question deeply interesting to the United States; but, happily, not of an intricacy proportioned to its interest. It seems only necessary to recognise certain principles, supposed to have been long and well established, to decide it.

That the people have an original right to establish, for their future government, such principles as, in their opinion, shall most conduce to their own happiness is the basis on which the whole American fabric has been erected. The exercise of this original right is a very great exertion; nor can it, nor ought it, to be frequently repeated. The principles, therefore, so established, are deemed fundamental. . . .

The original and supreme will organizes the government, and assigns to different departments their respective powers. It may either stop here, or establish certain limits not to be transcended by those departments.

The government of the United States is of the latter description. The powers of the legislature are defined and limited; and that these limits may not be mistaken, or forgotten, the constitution is written. To what purpose are powers limited, and to what purpose is that limitation committed to writing, if these limits may, at any time, be passed by those intended to be restrained? The distinction between a government with limited and unlimited powers is abolished, if those limits do not confine the persons on whom they are imposed, and if acts prohibited and acts allowed, are of equal obligation. . . .

Between these alternatives, there is no middle ground. The constitution is either a superior paramount law, unchangeable by ordinary means, or it is on a level with ordinary legislative acts, and, like other acts, is alterable when the legislature shall please to alter it.

Certainly all those who have framed written constitutions contemplate them as forming the fundamental and paramount law of the nation, and, consequently, the theory of every such government must be, that an act of the legislature, repugnant to the constitution, is void. This theory is essentially attached to a written constitution, and, is consequently, to be considered, by this court, as one of the fundamental principles of our society. . . .

If an act of the legislature, repugnant to the constitution, is void, does it, notwithstanding its invalidity, bind the courts, and oblige them to give it effect? Or, in other words, though it be not law, does it constitute a rule as operative as if it was a law? . . .

It is emphatically the province and duty of the judicial department to say what the law is. Those who apply the rule to particular cases, must of necessity expound and interpret that rule. If two laws conflict with each other, the courts must decide on the operation of each.

So if a law be in opposition to the constitution; if both the law and the constitution apply to a particular case, so that the court must either decide that case conformably to the law, disregarding the constitution; or conformably to the constitution, dis-

regarding the law; the court must determine which of these conflicting rules governs the case. This is of the very essence of judicial duty.

If, then, the courts are to regard the constitution, and the constitution is superior to any ordinary act of the legislature, the constitution, and not such ordinary act, must govern the case to which they both apply.

Those, then, who controvert the principle that the constitution is to be considered, in court, as a paramount law, are reduced to the necessity of maintaining that courts must close their eyes on the constitution, and see only the law.

This doctrine would subvert the very foundation of all written constitutions. It would declare that an act which, according to the principles and theory of our government, is entirely void, is yet, in practice, completely obligatory. It would declare that if the legislature shall do what is expressly forbidden, such act, notwithstanding the express prohibition, is in reality effectual. It would be giving to the legislature a practical and real omnipotence, with the same breath which professes to restrict their powers within narrow limits. It is prescribing limits, and declaring that those limits may be passed at pleasure. . . .

The judicial power of the United States is extended to all cases arising under the constitution.

Could it be the intention of those who gave this power, to say that in using it the constitution should not be looked into? That a case arising under the constitution should be decided without examining the instrument under which it arises?

This is too extravagant to be maintained. . . .

. . . [I]t is apparent, that the framers of the constitution contemplated that instrument as a rule for the government of *courts,* as well as of the legislature.

Why otherwise does it direct the judges to take an oath to support it? This oath certainly applies in an especial manner, to their conduct in their official character. How immoral to impose it on them, if they were to be used as the instruments, and the knowing instruments, for violating what they swear to support! . . .

Why does a judge swear to discharge his duties agreeably to the constitution of the United States, if that constitution forms no rule for his government? if it is closed upon him, and cannot be inspected by him? . . .

It is also not entirely unworthy of observation, that in declaring what shall be the *supreme* law of the land, the *constitution* itself is first mentioned; and not the laws of the United States generally, but those only which shall be made in *pursuance* of the constitution, have that rank.

Thus, the particular phraseology of the constitution of the United States confirms and strengthens the principle, supposed to be essential to all written constitutions, that a law repugnant to the constitution is void; and that *courts,* as well as other departments, are bound by that instrument.

The rule must be discharged.

C. A Note on Eakin v. Raub (1825)

[Part of the majesty and persuasiveness of Marshall's opinion in *Marbury* v. *Madison* comes from the absolute certainty with which he speaks. It is as if no reasonable person could possibly deny the logic of his argument that judicial review is necessary to the operation of a written constitution. That Marshall believed that logic alone could win the day is evident from his omission of even a single case citation—although the omission could also have resulted from Marshall's recognition that there were no strong precedents in favor of judicial review.

But there were, and are, opposing arguments worthy of consideration. Jefferson contended that each of the three branches of government was entitled "to decide on the validity of an act according to its own judgment and uncontrolled by the opinions of any other department." Perhaps Jefferson was suggesting that certain types of questions were peculiarly "political" in scope and not conducive to judicial scrutiny. If so, it was a good prediction, for the Court soon established a doctrine of "Political Questions" which exempted just such cases from judicial scrutiny. On the other hand, Jefferson may also have intended to exempt all acts of Congress or the executive from judicial review, but history has in large part supported Marshall's position.

The decision of the Supreme Court in *Marbury* was unanimous and, reflecting Marshall's influence, there was but a single opinion of the Court announced by the Chief Justice. The former practice of *seriatim* opinions, under which each justice would write an opinion in each case, might have provided an alternative—or opposing—view, but none was forthcoming. Since the Supreme Court did not again invalidate an act of Congress until the *Dred Scott* decision in 1857, there was little opportunity for any discussion of the power of judicial review by succeeding courts. The best contemporary judicial argument against Marshall's claim came instead from the Pennsylvania Supreme Court in 1825 in *Eakin* v. *Raub.*]

MR. JUSTICE GIBSON, DISSENTING.

. . .

The Constitution and the right of the legislature to pass the Act, may be in collision. But is that a legitimate subject for judicial determination? If it be, the judiciary must be a peculiar organ, to revise the proceedings of the legislature, and to correct its mistakes; And in what part of the Constitution are we to look for this proud pre-eminence? Viewing the matter in the opposite direction, what would be thought of an Act of Assembly in which it should be declared that the Supreme Court had, in a particular case, put a wrong construction of the Constitution of the United States, and that the judgment should therefore be reversed? It would doubtless be thought a usurpation of judicial power. But it is by no means clear, that to declare a law void which has been enacted according to the forms prescribed in the Constitution, is not a usurpation of legislative power. It is an act of sovereignty; and sovereignty and legislative power are said by Sir William Blackstone to be convertible terms. It is the business of the judiciary to interpret the laws, not scan the authority of the lawgiver; and without the latter, it cannot take cognizance of a collision between a law and the Constitution. . . .

But it has been said to be emphatically the business of the judiciary, to ascertain and pronounce what the law is; and that this necessarily involves a consideration of the Constitution. It does so: but how far? If the judiciary will inquire into anything beside the form of enactment, where shall it stop? There must be some point of limitation to such an inquiry; for no one will pretend, that a judge would be justifiable in calling for the election returns, or scrutinizing the qualifications of those who composed the legislature. . . .

But the judges are sworn to support the Constitution, and are they not bound by it as the law of the land? In some respects they are. In the very few cases in which the judiciary, and not the legislature, is the immediate organ to execute its provisions, they are bound by it in preference to any Act of Assembly to the contrary. In such cases, the Constitution is a rule to the courts. . . . But what I have in view in this inquiry, is the supposed right of the judiciary to interfere, in cases where the Constitution is to be carried into effect through the instrumentality of the legislature, and where that organ must necessarily first decide on the constitutionality of its own act. The oath to support the Constitution is not peculiar to the judges, but is taken indiscriminately by every officer of the government, and is designed rather as a test of the political principles of the man, than to bind the officer in the discharge of his duty. . . . But granting it to relate to the official conduct of the judge, as well as every other officer, and not to his political principles, still it must be understood in reference to supporting the Constitution, only as far as that may be involved in his official duty; and, consequently, if his official duty does not comprehend an inquiry into the authority of the legislature, neither does his oath. . . . The official oath, then, relates only to the official conduct of the officer, and does not prove that he ought to stray from the path of his ordinary business to search for violations of duty in the business of others; nor does it, as supposed, define the powers of the officer.

But do not the judges do a positive act in violation of the Constitution, when they give effect to an unconstitutional law? Not if the law has been passed according to the forms established in the Constitution. The fallacy of the question is, in supposing that the judiciary adopts the Acts of the Legislature as its own; whereas the enactment of a law and the interpretation of it are not concurrent acts, and as the judiciary is not required to concur in the enactment, neither is it in the breach of the Constitution which may be the consequence of the enactment. The fault is imputable to the legislature, and on it the responsibility exclusively rests. In this respect, the judges are in the predicament of jurors who are bound to serve in capital cases, although unable, under any circumstances, to reconcile it to their duty to deprive a human being of life. To one of these, who applied to be discharged from the panel, I once heard it remarked, by an eminent and humane judge, "You do not deprive a prisoner of life by finding him guilty of a capital crime: you but pronounce his case to be within the law, and it is therefore those who declare the law, and not you, who deprive him of life."

D. *The Legitimacy of Judicial Review*

Judicial review might be said to share the institutional discomfort of the king in Shakespeare's *Henry IV,* who said: "Uneasy lies the head that wears a crown." The power to pass judgment upon the constitutional validity of governmental action has never occupied a comfortable place in the American polity. On a few, but important, occasions, when conflicting claims to power were involved, presidents and the Congress have seriously challenged the Court's authority or capacity to decide the issues of a case and have threatened political retaliation. Furthermore, students of American politics have displayed a persistent discomfort with the seeming inconsistency between representative democracy and an institution operating within that form of government, capable of nullifying acts of popularly elected officials.

Despite this discomfort, and the perennial debate over the legitimacy of the origins of judicial review, its history and long acquiescence have all but settled the issue. Marshall's

position "that it is the province and duty of the Judiciary to say what the law is" has survived; indeed, as noted at the beginning of this chapter, it was restated with approval by the Supreme Court in the Nixon Tapes Case. Judicial review exists; it is an institutionalized aspect of our political system. Even Justice Gibson, the most articulate critic of judicial review in the time of Marshall, conceded twenty years after his dissent in *Eakin* v. *Raub* that American practice had made a tacit choice in favor of review.

Leonard Levy has noted that once the fury of the *Marbury* case had subsided, more pragmatic reasons for the acceptance of judicial review developed almost immediately. The idea of the Supreme Court as a protector of individual rights appealed not only to Federalists but to the Jeffersonians as well. Both parties, when out of office, found it expedient to call upon the Supreme Court to invalidate acts of which they disapproved; the Jeffersonians (Democrat–Republicans), its chief critics at the time of *Marbury*, had sought judicial invalidation of the Alien and Sedition Acts, the carriage tax, and, later, the Bank of the United States.[1] After *Marbury*, no other act of Congress was invalidated until the *Dred Scott* case, decided in 1857.[2] Critics of judicial review of acts of Congress thus had few concrete targets to attack. As we shall see in the next section, the primary focus of discontent in the post-*Marbury* period was over the Supreme Court's review of the decisions of state courts as authorized by Congress in Section 25 of the Judiciary Act of 1789. Here, too, judicial review has also survived as a useful political instrument. In a complex federal system, there is need

---

[1]Leonard Levy (ed.), *Judicial Review and the Supreme Court: Selected Essays* (New York: Harper & Row, 1967).

[2]*Dred Scott* v. *Sandford* (1857).

for an umpire, and the Supreme Court has filled that role acceptably. As Archibald Cox has noted, the institution of judicial review has been responsive to "a deep and continuing American belief in natural law"[3] and to a perennial distrust of unchecked government power.

From 1789 until 1974 the Supreme Court declared an act of Congress invalid on 109 occasions, 115 statutory provisions in all. Only two came before the Civil War, and more than half have come since 1943. Indeed, the Burger Court invalidated twenty-seven statutory provisions in its first seven years.[4] Thus, notwithstanding the "activist-restraint" debate, which often portrays the Burger Court as more restrained than its predecessor, it is, at least by this one measure, the most activist court in history.

The year 1943 is an important dividing line. Before then, the largest number of federal statutes held invalid were economic regulations limiting the rights of private property. Since then, the power of judicial review over Congress has focused primarily on statutes limiting civil rights and civil liberties.

Whether the 109 occasions of judicial review are "excessive" is a relative judgment. Certainly the Supreme Court has been much less deferential toward state legislation, having invalidated more than 900 state laws and judicial decisions for being inconsistent with the Constitution.

The vitality of judicial review as a political force has not dampened debate over the legitimacy of its origins or its compatibility with the democratic character of the American political system. Judicial review is both democratic and undemocratic, vulnerable and yet impregnable, legitimized by use and sanctified by tradition and yet never quite compelling. Combining in a single institution divergent, and often seemingly incompatible, functions is an intriguing quality of judicial policy making.

Among the threshold questions is whether the Constitution anticipated that judicial review would or should be exerted by the Supreme Court. Only one fact is clear—judicial review is not explicitly mentioned in the Constitution. But what is the meaning of such constitutional silence? If it stems from an initial intent to withhold from the Court the *exclusive* exercise of judging the constitutionality of governmental action, then its exercise by the Court is at best incidental to its other powers and not something the Court *must* exercise. On the other hand, if the power of judicial review is interpreted as having been intended as the primary function of the Court, then the Court's choice in its use is narrowed, and those seeking constitutional redress have a "right" to its exercise by the Supreme Court.

The bases for these differing positions have been elaborated in a famous academic exchange between Judge Learned Hand and Professor Herbert Wechsler.[5] Hand contends that even though early judicial prec-

---

[3]Archibald Cox, *The Role of the Supreme Court in American Government* (New York: Oxford University Press, 1976), p. 16.

[4]Henry Abraham, *The Judicial Process* (New York: Oxford University Press, 1975), pp. 279–293.

[5]See Learned Hand, *The Bill of Rights* (Cambridge: Harvard University Press, 1959), and Herbert Wechsler, "Toward Neutral Principles of Constitutional Law," **73** *Harvard Law Review* (1959). These two statements were presented initially in the Holmes Lecture Series at the Harvard Law School, Hand's in 1958 and Wechsler's in 1959, the latter being a response to the former.

edent in this country supports exercise of judicial review, it is doubtful that such a question—that is, whether federal courts should have the power to invalidate acts of Congress—would have received a favorable vote at the Constitutional Convention. The power, then, does not follow from the text of the Constitution but instead is an implied general power of courts to construe statutes, presumably because of their obligation to be consistent with the terms of a written constitution.

In citing Hamilton's *Federalist Paper* No. 78 in support of his view, Hand is careful to note that such a power does not necessarily place the judiciary above any other coordinate branch. Instead, it is placed in a position to heed the long-term will of the people as voiced in a constitution, rather than short-term values expressed in the form of legislation. Hand charges that judicial review as the sole purpose behind the Court's creation would be in violation of the separation of powers principle. But he then proceeds to argue that the power of judicial review is supportable for various reasons insofar as its presence can be *inferred*. As he puts it:

As an approach, let us try to imagine what would have been the result if the power did not exist. There were two alternatives, each prohibitive, I submit. One was that the decision of the first "Department" before which an issue arose should be conclusive, whenever it arose later. That doctrine, coupled with its conceded power over the purse, would have made Congress substantially omnipotent, for by far the greater number of issues that could arise would depend upon its prior action. . . .

*What I have called the first alternative would have meant that the in-*terpretation of the Constitution on a given occasion would be left to that "Department" before which the question happened first to come; and such a system would have been so capricious in operation, and so different from that designed, that it could not have endured. Moreover, the second alternative would have been even worse, for under it each "Department" would have been free to decide constitutional issues as it thought right, regardless of any earlier decision of the others. Thus it would have been the President's privilege, and indeed his duty, to execute only those statutes that seemed to him constitutional, regardless even of a decision of the Supreme Court. The courts would have entered such judgments as seemed to them consonant with the Constitution; but neither the President, nor Congress, would have been bound to enforce them if he or it disagreed, and without their help the judgments would have been waste paper.*[6]

The potential for political stalemate in such a situation is very great and, in Hand's view, requires judicial interpretation "to prevent the defeat of the venture at hand." To this point, Hand's argument has a charming plausibility, but it is just the foundation on which his major contention about judicial review rests:

. . . Since this power is not a logical deduction from the structure of the Constitution but only a practical condition upon its successful operation, it need not be exercised whenever a court sees, or think it sees, an invasion of the Constitution.[7]

In taking issue with Hand's view, Wechsler cites the language of the supremacy clause: *"This Constitution, and the Laws of the United States which shall be made in Pursuance thereof; . . . shall be the su-*

[6]Hand, *op. cit.*, Note 5, pp. 10, 14.
[7]*Ibid.*, p. 15.

preme Law of the Land; and the Judges in every State shall be bound thereby . . ." As Hand interpreted that clause, it

did indeed require state courts to follow federal laws and the federal constitution when the state laws or the state constitution were 'to the contrary'. . . However, the clause was obviously directed against the states alone. . . . Such a grant cannot be stretched into a general authority to pass upon other instances of legislative conflict with the Constitution. . . .[8]

To Wechsler, however, such an interpretation is simply without reason. He asks, rhetorically, "Are you satisfied . . . to view the supremacy clause in this way, as a grant of jurisdiction in state courts, implying a denial of the power and the duty of all others?"[9] In answer, Wechsler cites Article III, Section I, which declares that the federal judicial power shall be vested in *"one supreme Court, and in such inferior Courts as the Congress may from time to time ordain and establish."* Section 2 of the same article delineates the scope of this power, which includes extension to *"Cases, in Law and Equity, arising under this Constitution. . . ."* The section goes on to note the Supreme Court's appellate jurisdiction in such matters, elaborated in Section 25 of the Judiciary Act of 1789, making actions of state courts subject to review by the Supreme Court if a federal constitutional issue is involved.

With such a basis, Wechsler takes "the final step" in his argument:

Is it a possible construction of the Constitution, measured strictly as Judge Hand admonishes by the test of "general purpose," that if Congress opts . . . to create a set of lower courts, those courts in cases falling within their respective jurisdictions and the Supreme Court when it passes upon their judgments are less or differently constrained by the supremacy clause than are the state courts, and the Supreme Court when it reviews their judgments?"[10]

To Wechsler, the actions of Congress, based upon provisions in addition to those in the supremacy clause, make Hand's contention unacceptable. As he puts it: "For me, as for anyone who finds the judicial power anchored in the Constitution, there is no such escape from the judicial obligation; the duty cannot be attenuated in this way."[11]

It is important to note that Wechsler's position rests on a presumed interdependent relationship between the Court's power and the actions of Congress. It has always been an accepted and obvious canon of constitutional politics that Congress has a vast influence upon the capacities of the Supreme Court, given the Article III provision that appellate jurisdiction is to be regulated by Congress. An obvious corollary of this is the considerable influence the other majoritarian institution, the presidency, has on the selection of Supreme Court judges.

If judicial review cannot be fully justified because of its origins, if it is contrary to the democratic principle of majority rule, and if it is not indispensable that the Court preserve and facilitate a written constitution, then how can judicial review be defended? Two major arguments have been advanced in its favor, one old and one of more recent vintage.

[8]*Ibid.,* pp. 5–6.
[9]Wechsler, *op. cit.,* Note 5, p. 3.
[10]*Ibid.,* pp. 4–5.
[11]*Ibid.,* p. 6.

The "old" argument is that the Supreme Court plays an important role in making democracy work. It does this by enforcing the rules of the game, by acting as a stable anchor for the political system, and perhaps most importantly, by acting as protector of the rights of underrepresented minorities. Scholars who argue that judicial review is compatible with democratic principles base their justification for judicial review on the premise that the Supreme Court plays an important representational role. Representation, like politics, is a complex phenomenon, not captured entirely by the electoral process. In order to accommodate a pluralist system, it is important to maintain multiple routes of access to political power to assure that no one group or set of interests is completely dominant or completely excluded. By competing for access, and power, groups act as mutual checks and balances. The Supreme Court, to the extent that it does in fact reflect the interests of certain groups, is an important if not indispensable part of this process.

Empirically the historical record to support this argument is mixed. Until the post-New Deal period the Court's use of judicial review had been to uphold the rights of minorities, not the underrepresented minorities, but rather the privileged minorities who were already holding great economic and political power. Since 1937, and particularly with the advent of the Warren Court in 1953, this argument in support of judicial review gains a little more force. The transformation of the Supreme Court from a defender of property rights to a defender of individual rights became apparent between 1954 and 1974. Set against this shift of representational roles are two claims. One is that the recent liberal activism of the Supreme Court is a "fluke." Inevitably, and probably sooner than later, the Court will follow its natural tendencies toward conservatism. As David Adamany notes, "The minority rights activism of the Warren Court is already fading; that one 15 year period will not counterbalance the whole of the Court's historical record, . . .[12] There is force in this assertion, but it ignores the impact of this period of activism on the political landscape and on the Court itself. One cannot simply turn the clock back to 1937. What the Warren Court has done, including the role it defined for itself which many now regard as legitimate, suggests that there really is no turning back, at least not in the sense of a total reversion to the pre-1937 Court. It is true that there have been cyclical shifts in the past, but never before has there been such a wrenching change in the Supreme Court's philosophy and role.[13] Thus, it is at least premature to assume that, inevitably, the Court will "return" to its reactionary past.

The second attack on the Court's role as defender of minority rights is normative. It holds that the liberal activism of the Warren Court has had its costs, both for the Supreme Court as an institution and for the political system as a whole. To protect minority rights effectively, the Supreme Court has had to shed some of the limiting, but also protecting, maxims of judicial self-restraint. It has acted less like a "court" and more openly as a policy maker. The costs to the system, many have argued, can be found in a lessened political vitality, a sap-

[12]David Adamany, "Legitimacy, Realigning Elections, and the Supreme Court," 1973 *Wisconsin Law Review*, p. 795.
[13]Nathan Glazer, "Toward an Imperial Judiciary?" *The Public Interest* (1975), pp. 104–23.

ping of the strength of the majoritarian institutions that comes (it is said) inevitably with greater reliance on the Court. Nowhere is this argument more potent than with respect to the reapportionment cases. The essence of the argument is captured in Ward Elliott's concept of a "guardian democracy," which maintains that one cannot make democracy work better by judicially "forcing it" to be more democratic.[14]

The "new" argument justifying judicial review focuses on the Supreme Court's relationship to Congress and the president. Robert Dahl, in a provocative and influential article, framed the matter thus:

The main objective of presidential leadership is to build a stable and dominant aggregation of minorities with a high probability of winning the presidency and one or both houses of Congress. The main task of the Court is to confer legitimacy on the fundamental policies of the successful coalition.[15]

Dahl proceeded to show, through analysis of the patterns of presidential appointment to the Supreme Court, that the decisions of the Court were never likely to be very far from the views of the dominant lawmaking majorities. On the average, one new justice is appointed every twenty-two months. In the case of Franklin Roosevelt, the odds were four to one that he would have to wait for four years to make his first appointment, but his first opportunity for a Supreme Court appointment did not come until his fifth year as President. In addition to the fact that appointment patterns resulted in Court personnel who were sensitive to current political concerns, Dahl examined the relationship between judicial declarations of unconstitutionality and congressional response over time. His study showed that the capacity of the Court to resist majoritarian influence was limited. Table I indicates the political timing of such declarations.

Dahl's evidence (through 1958) shows that nearly half of all congressional legislation held unconstitutional met its fate within four years of

Table I Percentage of Cases Held Unconstitutional Arranged by Time Intervals Between Legislation and Decision*

Number of Years	New Deal Legislation (%)	Other (%)	All Legislation (%)
2 or less	92	19	30
3 to 4	8	19	18
5 to 8	0	28	24
9 to 12	0	13	11
13 to 16	0	8	6
17 to 20	0	1	1
21 or more	0	12	10
Total	100	100	100

*From Dahl, "Decision-Making in a Democracy," *loc. cit.,* p. 286.

[14]Ward Elliott, *The Rise of Guardian Democracy: The Supreme Court's Role in Voting Rights Disputes 1845–1969* (Cambridge: Harvard University Press, 1974).

[15]Robert A. Dahl, "Decision-Making in a Democracy: The Supreme Court as a National Policy-Maker," **6** *Journal of Public Law* (1958), 294 (Emphasis added).

enactment. This is a critical period of time because it suggests that the political coalition that established the policy might still be in a position to reaffirm it and reject the Court's contrary view. Over time, as Dahl shows, there are few instances in which the Court had prevailed absolutely over Congress; occasionally, it has succeeded in delaying certain policies. It is clear that congressional deference to the Court's sense of constitutional propriety is often lacking; ultimately a determined Congress will prevail.

Furthermore, Dahl argues that the legitimating function performed by the Court is not merely mindless acquiescence with congressional policies but is relevant to and dependent on those policies and procedures "required for the operation of a democracy." Here Dahl refers to the protection of rights and liberties, and it is clear that, for him, it is the protection of these rights that constitutes the only acceptable basis of Supreme Court legitimacy. One problem with Dahl's analysis, as Adamany has noted, is that in order to protect individual rights and liberties, the Supreme Court must not only affirm government policies that protect liberties but must also strike down as unconstitutional those policies that do not.[16] These normative criteria are at odds with Dahl's original argument that the court functions to legitimate policies of the national majority.

Two recent studies that examine Dahl's thesis shed further light on the "new" justification for judicial review. Both focus on Supreme Court activity during periods of "realigning"

elections.[17] By definition, in a period of realignment, "popular political feeling is so intense that the basic underlying patterns of the electorate's party identifications are changed, and a new party balance is created which endures over several decades."[18] An obvious example would be the period surrounding the election of Franklin Roosevelt in 1932.

In his assessment of executive and legislative interaction with the Supreme Court in these periods of realignment, Adamany notes four political characteristics: (1) the new party coalition took office in a condition of tension with the judiciary; (2) after at least two realigning elections the Court used its power to thwart the policies of the new coalition; (3) after each realigning election there was intense and—most significantly— "highly visible" conflict between the Court and the lawmaking majority; and (4) the clash rose to such a level of intensity that elected officials felt compelled to attack the Court. His conclusion from this assessment is that judicial review may result in a "delegitimizing" influence by the Court:

But it is enough to conclude here that the legitimacy conferring capacity of the Supreme Court is vastly reduced by these battles. When the Court finally comes into line with the new majority, it appears to capitulate to overpowering force rather than freely to legitimize. And those who disagree with the new regime's policies, who must be persuaded of its legitimacy, and who would be attentive enough to comprehend legitimizing action by the justices must certainly also be

[16]Adamany, *op. cit.*, Note 12.

[17]See Richard Funston, "The Supreme Court and Critical Elections," **69** *American Political Science Review* (1975), 795–811, and Adamany, *op. cit.*, Note 12, pp. 790–846.

[18]Funston, *Ibid.*, p. 798. Adamany and Funston differ slightly in their counting of such periods, but this difference is not critical to their interpretations.

counted intelligent enough to draw the common inference that the Court has been taken by storm rather than by persuasive constitutional argument. Little legitimization is likely in such circumstances. [19]

Richard Funston's treatment of judicial activity during realigning periods is similar in its description but different in some of its interpretation and conclusions. After repeating Dahl's essential thesis—that is, when the Court strikes down legislation as unconstitutional, it is seldom successful in the long run in thwarting the majority policy—Funston notes: "The crucial point is that most of the time the Court will not be striking down national legislation."[20] He proposes, therefore, to examine this basic question: When are Supreme Court decisions most likely to conflict with the will of a national majority?

According to Funston, there have been ninety-four cases in the 168-year period that includes the various periods of judicial review and realigning electoral activity. He characterizes these periods of time as "critical" and "noncritical" and notes the cases that belong to each period (see Table II).

The aggregation of cases presents a difficulty because the Court's action may well be counter to a majoritarian influence, but in some particular cases, this could be politically irrelevant. That is, it is possible that a given judicial decision overturns a majority policy that is fifty years old or more. In such an instance, the relationship of the Court to a *current* majority is difficult to ascertain. Funston corrects for this possibility by limiting consideration to judicial declarations of unconstitutionality that take place within four years of legislative enactment. The result is that the index for critical periods is 0.50; for noncritical periods it is 0.16, and the coefficient of counter-majoritarianism jumps to 3.1. In short, during periods of realignment, the Court is three times more likely to declare legislation unconstitutional than during noncritical periods. As Funston succinctly puts it:

. . . [I]t is not merely that during critical periods of partisan realignment the Court is more likely to declare recently enacted federal legislation unconstitutional than at other times, but that during realigning periods this is the very sort of congressional legislation which is most likely to be nullified by the Court. [21]

The difficulty with Funston's analysis, as Canon and Ulmer have

Table II: Incidence of All Supreme Court Cases Declaring Congressional Legislation Unconstitutional*

	Total Years	Number of Cases	Index
Critical periods	32	21	0.66
Noncritical periods	136	73	0.54
Coefficient of counter-majoritarianism		1.2	

*From Funston, *loc. cit.*, p. 804. The index is a ratio of years of the period to the number of cases in the period. The coefficient is obtained by dividing the index for critical periods by that of noncritical periods.

[19]Adamany, *op. cit.*, Note 12, p. 842.
[20]Funston, *op. cit.*, Note 17, p. 796.
[21]*Ibid.*, p. 806.

noted, is that it is skewed by the over-whelming number of judicial nullifi-cations during one time period, the New Deal. If one focuses exclusively on the other critical periods, the ex-pected relationship is reversed. Fur-thermore, if one compares these criti-cal periods with noncritical periods, there are more nullifications during the latter. At best, it can be said that there does not appear to be any "sys-tematic rise and fall of Supreme Court counter-majoritarian behavior in con-junction with critical elections."[22]

With some recent and notable ex-ceptions in the area of race and gender discrimination, the record shows that the Supreme Court has not success-fully acted as a protector of minority interests against *national* policies. Nonetheless, Adamany and Martin Shapiro before him have raised a more general question about the rela-tionship between legitimation and ju-dicial action. What does it mean to "legitimate" a policy? Are policies somehow "incomplete" without a ju-dicial seal of approval?

Writing with particular reference to the policies of administrative agen-cies, Shapiro observes:

The difficulty with the legitimation ar-gument, at least when applied to court-agency relations, is that the administra-tive agencies have been sufficiently rec-ognized as supplementary law-makers in their own right, that their decisions in-dependently have all the legitimacy they need. Litigants do not go to court because they are not sure whether they must obey an agency decision until a court gives it the judicial imprimatur. They go to court precisely because they know they should and must obey the agency unless they

can get the Court to intervene in their behalf. When the court says no or says nothing to the individual litigant, it has simply refused to help him. There is little use dressing this negative up in the posi-tive language of legitimation.[23]

Producing a completely satisfac-tory and consistent defense of judicial review obviously is a difficult task. Both the "old" argument, which points to the Supreme Court's defense of minority rights, and the "new" ar-gument, which justifies judicial re-view because of its legitimating func-tion, are vulnerable to empirical and normative attack. Faced with this di-lemma, Funston revives a traditional defense:

Assuming that we wish to have princi-pled government, some agency must, in the normal operation of the policy pro-cess, be primarily concerned with soci-ety's fundamental, underlying values; and practical, if not philosophic, reasons dictate that this agency be one or another of the branches of the federal govern-ment. Which one? I submit not only that it should be but also that, in the Ameri-can constitutional system, it can only be the Supreme Court.[24]

This is both a normative preference and a recognition of an American be-lief, referred to previously, in some form of natural law or "principled" check on political power. This norma-tive justification loses some force with the observation that the Su-preme Court cannot operate exclu-sively as a "principled" court. Of course, the notion of a "principled" court does little to reduce the anxi-eties of those who reject *any* external judicial check on majority rule.

[22]Bradley Canon and S. Sidney Ulmer, "The Supreme Court and Critical Elections: A Dissent," **70** *American Political Science Review* (1976) 1215–1218.

[23]Martin Shapiro, *The Supreme Court and Administrative Agencies* (New York: Free Press, 1968), p. 265.

[24]Funston, *op. cit.,* Note 17, p. 810.

Ultimately, there is no satisfactory resolution to this problem. Judicial review—indeed, judicial power generally—will remain an enigma in a political system that constantly balances conflicting precepts of democratic theory with the practical needs of governance. The Supreme Court does not serve all the ends that its defenders assert, and it is not in such total contradiction to democratic theory as its detractors maintain. This does not obviate the case for either the continued practice of judicial review or the need for continual questioning of its function.

4. THE SUPREME COURT AND THE DOCTRINE OF NATIONAL (JUDICIAL) SUPREMACY

A. John R. Schmidhauser,
States' Rights and the Origin of
the Supreme Court's Power in
Federal-State Relations

. . . One of the major reasons for holding the Philadelphia Convention had been the necessity to find a remedy for the evils arising from state legislation which hurt or interfered with the interests of other states, infringed treaties made by the Confederation Congress, oppressed individuals, or invaded the sphere of authority of the confederation government. The convention delegates were faced with the task of finding suitable means of restraining such state legislation or action. Despite the fact that the idea of a judicial arbiter was understood and widely discussed before the opening of the Convention, the creation of a high federal court to solve this problem was by no means a foregone conclusion. Years after the close of the Convention, James Madison referred to the situation in the following manner: ". . . [T]he obvious necessity of a control of the laws of the States so far as they might violate the Constitution and laws of the United States left no option, but as to mode . . .," noting as the three possible choices "a veto (executive) on the passage of the State Laws, a Congressional repeal of them, a judicial annulment of them."

Analysis of the record of the Philadelphia Convention underscores the fact that the granting of power to the Federal Supreme Court to arbitrate finally in federal-state relations came about through a complex series of developments. Basically they represented a compromise between the strong nationalists who originally wanted a veto over the states vested in the new national legislature or executive and the states' righters who either opposed such supervision of the states or preferred that such power be vested in what they considered a weaker and more impartial agency, notably the supreme federal court suggested in the original Paterson Plan.

Among the more important of these developments were (a) the repudiation of coercion of the states by force and the adoption of coercion of individuals by law, (b) the readiness of every major bloc in the Convention to set up a federal judiciary, (c) the

Reprinted from **4** *Wayne Law Review* (1958), 101–104.

demands of one powerful group for a system of inferior federal tribunals, (d) the defeat of the congressional negative proposals and the substitution by Luther Martin of a supremacy clause, and (e) the tendency to look upon a federal judiciary as a protector of individual and states' rights which was reflected in the proposals for a Council of Revision. Very often these developments seemed totally unrelated, but their cumulative effect was the granting of final interpretive powers in federal-state relations to a supreme federal tribunal. . . .

Actually, every major plan for union—Randolph's, Hamilton's and Paterson's—had provided for a national judicial system. The essential difference between the nationalistic plans of Randolph and Hamilton and the states' rights of Paterson is that the latter failed to provide a system of inferior federal courts. The nationalists did not actually oppose the adoption of a judicial arbiter, but merely felt, as James Wilson later indicated, that a judicial check on the states would not be sufficient to maintain a strong central government. . . .

On the other hand, the advocates of a strong central government, while favoring the granting of broad judicial powers, had realized that judicial nullification of state laws was possible only when federal questions arose in bona fide cases before the new Supreme Court. Madison's letter to Jefferson after the close of the convention indicated the lack of assurance he shared with other strong government advocates. He wrote:

It may be said that the Judicial authority under our new system will keep the states within their proper limits and supply the place of a negative on their laws. The answer is that it is more con-venient to prevent the passage of a law than to declare it void, after it is passed; that this will be particularly the case, where the law aggrieves individuals who may be unable to support an appeal against a state to the Supreme Judiciary, that a state which would violate the legislative rights of the Union would not be very ready to obey a Judicial decree in support of them, and that a recurrence to force, which in the event of disobedience would be necessary, is an evil which the new Constitution meant to exclude as far as possible. A Constitutional negative on the laws of the states seems equally necessary to secure individuals against encroachments on their rights. The mutability of the laws of the States is found to be a serious evil.

After the final defeat of the congressional negative in the Convention on August 23, the nationalists determined to make the best of an unhappy situation by strengthening the federal arbiter by means of grants of broad constitutional jurisdiction and through institution of a complete system of inferior federal courts. The extension of the Supreme Court's jurisdiction to all cases, state and federal, arising under the Constitution was made without a states' rights argument. But the attempt at creation of a system of inferior federal courts aroused such fierce opposition that the nationalists were compelled to accept a compromise by which the establishment of such courts was left to the discretion of the new Congress. . . .

The Philadelphia Convention record indicates unmistakably that the new Supreme Court had been clearly designated the final judicial arbiter in the Convention which had brought this to pass. The nationalists had not opposed the creation of the judicial arbiter, but had felt strongly that a national judiciary would not, by itself, be strong enough to cope with state encroachments on national authority. . . .

These facts stand out as a result of this analysis of the Philadelphia Convention and the state ratifying conventions. Both the nationalists and the states' righters were in substantial agreement on the need for a supreme judicial arbiter in federal-state relations. By 1789 it was clearly understood that the Supreme Court of the United States was to fulfill that role. Naturally enough, the nationalists tended to emphasize the aspect of judicial arbitership concerned with the protection of national supremacy against state encroachments. However, both nationalists and states' righters explicitly recognized that the Supreme Court's role was that of an impartial arbiter. Thus, it was also anticipated that federal laws violative of states' rights were to be declared unconstitutional. . . .

B. *Martin v. Hunter's Lessee (1816)*

+Story, Todd, Washington, Johnson, Livingston, Duvall
NP Marshall

[Judicial review over acts of Congress was quickly overshadowed by a much more explosive issue: federal review of the decisions of state courts.Current espousal of a states' rights philosophy finds easily identifiable roots in the controversy over early Supreme Court attempts to review the decisions of the highest state courts.

Schmidhauser has noted the compromise by which creation of an inferior federal court system and definition of its jurisdiction was left to Congress. Congress, in turn, acted cautiously. Its first attention was given to establishment of a federal court system, resulting in the Judiciary

Act of 1789. In its famous Section 25, the act gave to the Supreme Court a limited appellate jurisdiction to review state court decisions. Only in those cases in which state courts invalidated a federal statute or treaty or a provision of the federal constitution, or where the validity of a state act was upheld against a federal constitutional challenge, could there be review by the United States Supreme Court. This compromise between what the nationalists wanted and what the states' rights interests would accept was, nonetheless, controversial. By comparison, under present law (to be defined more precisely in the following chapter), the Supreme Court can review any decision from the "highest" state court in which a decision could be made in which a federal question is involved and necessary to the disposition of that case.

The constitutional relationship between the nation and the states hinged on whether the Constitution was merely a compact of the states, a confederation, or whether it was a federal system created by the people. Assuming the latter, who was to umpire the inevitable disputes that would occur along the boundaries of power?

The Constitution does not explicitly authorize Supreme Court review of state court decisions. But the supremacy clause (Article VI) does impose on all state officials the duty of obedience to the Constitution, to laws made in pursuance thereof, and to treaties made under the authority of the United States. And in Article III, the Constitution does authorize the Supreme Court to exercise appellate jurisdiction over certain classes of cases—subject to congressional regulation—which were as likely to arise in state as in federal courts. If no lower federal courts had been created, then such cases would have arisen only in state courts. The textual case for Supreme Court review of state court decisions was much stronger than for judicial review of acts of Congress. Thus, as Archibald Cox has noted, "*Marbury* made inevitable the establishment of a like authority over state courts."[1]

Fletcher v *Peck* (1810) was the first case in

---

[1]Archibald Cox, *The Role of the Supreme Court in American Government* (New York: Oxford University Press, 1976), p. 11.

which a state statute was declared unconstitutional by the Supreme Court. There had been previous cases of state laws invalidated because of conflict with federal statutes or treaties. In this case, the Court held that Georgia could not repeal a statute, passed by a corrupt legislature, which provided for the distribution of land along the Yazoo River to land speculators. Some of the land had been sold to apparently innocent third parties. The original act had been passed in 1795, and the case was extensively debated in Congress and elsewhere. When the case reached the Supreme Court in 1810, John Marshall declared, for a unanimous Court, that the original act could not be rescinded. Courts could not inquire into legislative motives, Marshall argued. Furthermore, the act was an interference with private rights and protected by the general principles of the Constitution. Finally, Marshall argued, the statute violated the constitutional prohibition against impairing the obligation of contract, which included agreements between government and citizens and not just agreements between private citizens.

Perhaps the most explosive challenge to the right of the Supreme Court to review state court decisions came from Virginia. Led by its chief justice, Spencer Roane, an ardent states' rights advocate and a political adversary of John Marshall, the Virginia Court of Appeals openly defied an order of the United States Supreme Court.

The case arose from a dispute over possession of lands formerly held by a British subject and Tory sympathizer, Lord Fairfax. Fairfax was a citizen of Virginia and, on his death in 1781, the land was willed to his nephew, Denny Martin, a British subject. Virginia's law prohibited enemy aliens from inheriting land, and part of the devise was confiscated by the state and gradually sold to a number of purchasers. Among those who received a grant of land was Hunter, who received his in 1785. In a later transaction, John and James Marshall purchased a large portion of the estate from Lord Fairfax's heir, Denny Martin, and the chief justice was thus peripherally involved in the case.

Litigation over ownership of the property began in 1791 and continued in the Virginia courts until 1810, when the Virginia Court of Appeals sustained Hunter's claim. Previously, however, the United States had concluded a Treaty of Peace with Great Britain (1783), and the treaty specifically prohibited "future confiscations" of property formerly held by British subjects who had not supported the Revolution. The same point was reemphasized in the Jay Treaty of 1794.

The Virginia court considered, and rejected, the argument that the confiscation of the Fairfax devise violated these treaties, and the case came to the United States Supreme Court on a writ of error. In 1813, in *Fairfax's Devisee* v. *Hunter's Lessee* (1813), the Court reversed and held that the Jay Treaty of 1794 protected British property from confiscation. Thus, Martin was entitled to sole ownership of the property, and Hunter was out any funds he had advanced. The opinion of the Court was written by Justice Story, with the Chief Justice not participating because of his involvement in the controversy.

The Supreme Court's order to the Virginia Court of Appeals was met with both opposition and excitement, and the stage for this great confrontation was set. The Virginia court held hearings on whether or not to obey the order, appointing eminent lawyers to argue each position, and then announced that:

This court is unanimously of opinion that the appellate power of the Supreme Court of the United States does not extend to this court, under a sound construction of the constitution of the United States; —that so much of the 25th section of the Act of Congress . . . as extends the appellate jurisdiction of the Supreme Court is not in pursuance of the Constitution of the United States; that the writ of error in this case was improvidently allowed under the authority of that act; . . . and that obedience to its mandate be declined by this court.

The Virginia judges had thus declared Section 25 unconstitutional. They conceded that they were bound to observe the Constitution, but insisted that its meaning was for them to decide since they represented a different sovereign than did the Supreme Court of the United States and were not an "inferior" court within the meaning of the Constitution. Martin then filed another writ of error with the United States Supreme Court. Chief Justice Marshall again did not participate.]

MR. JUSTICE STORY delivered the opinion of the Court:

. . . The questions involved in this judgment are of great importance and delicacy. Perhaps it is not too much to affirm that, upon their right decision, rest some of the most solid principles which have hitherto been supposed to sustain and protect the constitution itself. The great respectability, too, of the court whose decisions we are called upon to review, and the entire deference which we entertain for the learning and ability of that court, add much to the difficulty of the task which has so unwelcomely fallen upon us. . . .

The constitution of the United States was ordained and established, not by the states in their sovereign capacities, but emphatically, as the preamble of the constitution declares, by "the People of the United States." There can be no doubt, that it was competent to the people to invest the general government with all the powers which they might deem proper and necessary; to extend or restrain these powers according to their own good pleasure, and to give them a paramount and supreme authority. As little doubt can there be, that the people had a right to prohibit to the states the exercise of any powers which were, in their judgment, incompatible with the objects of the general compact; to make the powers of the state governments, in given cases, subordinate to those of the na-

tion, or to reserve to themselves those sovereign authorities which they might not choose to delegate to either. The constitution was not, therefore, necessarily carved out of existing state sovereignties, nor a surrender of powers already existing in state institutions, for the powers of the states depend upon their own constitutions; and the people of every state had the right to modify and restrain them, according to their own views of policy or principle. On the other hand it is perfectly clear that the sovereign powers vested in the state governments, by their respective constitutions, remained unaltered and unimpaired, except so far as they were granted to the government of the United States.

These deductions do not rest upon general reasoning, plain and obvious as they seem to be. They have been positively recognized by one of the articles in amendment of the constitution, which declares, that "the powers not delegated to the United States by the constitution, nor prohibited by it to the states, are reserved to the states respectively, or to the people."

The government . . . of the United States can claim no powers which are not granted to it by the constitution, and the powers actually granted, must be such as are expressly given, or given by necessary implication. On the other hand, this instrument, like every other grant, is to have a reasonable construction, according to the import of its terms; and where a power is expressly given, in general terms, it is not to be restrained to particular cases, unless that construction grow out of the context, expressly, or by necessary implication. The words are to be taken in their natural and obvious sense, and not in a sense unreasonably restricted or enlarged.

The constitution unavoidably deals in general language. It did not suit the purposes of the people, in framing this great charter of our liberties, to provide for minute specifications of its powers, or to declare the means by which those powers should be carried into execution. It was foreseen, that this would be perilous and difficult, if not an impracticable, task. The instrument was not intended to provide merely for the exigencies of a few years, but was to endure through a long lapse of ages, the events of which were locked up in the inscrutable purposes of Providence. It could not be foreseen, what new changes and modifications of power might be indispensable to effectuate the general objects of the charter; and restrictions and specifications, which, at the present, might seem salutary, might, in the end, prove the overthrow of the system itself. Hence, its powers are expressed in general terms, leaving to the legislature, from time to time, to adopt its own means to effectuate legitimate objects, and to mould and model the exercise of its powers, as its own wisdom, and the public interests, should require. . . .

This leads us to the consideration of the great question, as to the nature and extent of the appellate jurisdiction of the United States. We have already seen, that appellate jurisdiction is given by the constitution to the supreme court, in all cases where it has not original jurisdiction; subject, however, to such exceptions and regulations as congress may prescribe. . . .

As then, by the terms of the constitution, the appellate jurisdiction is not limited as to the supreme court, and as to this court, it may be exercised in all other cases than those of which it has original cognisance,

what is there to restrain its exercise over state tribunals, in the enumerated cases? The appellate power is not limited by the terms of the third article to any particular courts. The words are, "the judicial power (which includes appellate power) shall extend to all cases," &c., and "in all other cases before mentioned the supreme court shall have appellate jurisdiction." It is the case, then, and not the court, that gives the jurisdiction. If the judicial power extends to the case, it will be in vain to search in the letter of the constitution for any qualification as to the tribunal where it depends. . . .

But it is plain, that the framers of the constitution did contemplate that cases within the judicial cognisance of the United States, not only might, but would, arise in the state courts, in the exercise of their ordinary jurisdiction. With this view, the sixth article declares, that "this constitution, and the laws of the United States which shall be made in pursuance thereof, and all treaties made, or which shall be made, under the authority of the United States, shall be the supreme law of the land, and the judges in every state shall be bound thereby, anything in the constitution or laws of any state to the contrary notwithstanding." It is obvious, that this obligation is imperative upon the state judges, in their official, and not merely in their private capacities. From the very nature of their judicial duties, they would be called upon to pronounce the law applicable to the case in judgment. They were not to decide merely according to the laws or constitution of the state, but according to the constitution, laws and treaties of the Supreme Court—"the supreme law of the land." . . .

It must, therefore, be conceded, that the constitution not only contemplated, but meant to provide for cases within the scope of the judicial power of the United States, which might yet depend before the state tribunals. It was foreseen, that in the exercise of their ordinary jurisdiction, state courts would incidentally take cognisance of cases arising under the constitution, the laws and treaties of the United States. Yet, to all these cases, the judicial power, by the very terms of the constitution, is to extend. It cannot extend, by original jurisdiction, if that was already rightfully and exclusively attached in the state courts, which (as has been already shown) may occur; it must, therefore, extend by appellate jurisdiction, or not at all. It would seem to follow, that the appellate power of the United States must, in such cases, extend to state tribunals. . . .

It has been argued, that such an appellate jurisdiction over state courts is inconsistent with the genius of our governments, and the spirit of the constitution. That the latter was never designed to act upon state sovereignties, but only upon the people, and that if the power exists, it will materially impair the sovereignty of the states, and the independence of their courts. We cannot yield to the force of this reasoning; it assumes principles which we cannot admit, and draws conclusions to which we do not yield our assent.

It is a mistake, that the constitution was not designed to operate upon states, in their corporate capacities. It is crowded with provisions which restrain or annul the sovereignty of the states, in some of the highest branches of their prerogatives. The tenth section of the first article contains a long list of disabilities and prohibitions imposed upon the states. Surely, when such essential portions of state sovereignty are taken away,

or prohibited to be exercised, it cannot be correctly asserted, that the constitution does not act upon the states. . . .

This is not all. A motive of another kind, perfectly compatible with the most sincere respect for state tribunals, might induce the grant of appellate power over their decisions. That motive is the importance, and even necessity of uniformity of decisions throughout the whole United States, upon all subjects within the purview of the constitution. Judges of equal learning and integrity, in different states, might differently interpret the statute, or a treaty of the United States, or even the constitution itself: if there were no revising authority to control these jarring and discordant judgments, and harmonize them into uniformity, the laws, the treaties and the constitution of the United States would be different, in different states, and might, perhaps, never have precisely the same construction, obligation or efficiency, in any two states. The public mischiefs that would attend such a state of things would be truly deplorable. . . .

There is an additional consideration, which is entitled to great weight. The constitution of the United States was designed for the common and equal benefit of all the people of the United States. The judicial power was granted for the same benign and salutary purposes. It was not to be exercised exclusively for the benefit of parties who might be plaintiffs, and would elect the national *forum*, but also for the protection of defendants who might be entitled to try their rights, or assert their privileges, before the same forum. . . .

It is the opinion of the whole court, that the judgment of the court of appeals of Virginia, rendered on the mandate in this cause, be reversed, and the judgment of the district court, held at Winchester, be, and the same is hereby affirmed.

MR. JUSTICE JOHNSON, CONCURRING (OMITTED).

C. The Aftermath of Martin v. Hunter's Lessee: John Marshall in Cohens v. Virginia (1821)

Historians dispute whether the Supreme Court's order was ever carried out. To avoid a second confrontation with the Virginia Court of Appeals, the remand order was issued directly to the district court in Virginia that had first heard the case. But there is no agreement on whether or not the order to Hunter to vacate the land was ever issued.

Justice Story's opinion in *Martin* v. *Hunter's Lessee* seemed to dispose of the constitutional issue involved, but it could not prevent continued Jeffersonian attacks on the federal judiciary. The doctrine of federal judicial supremacy was unacceptable to many states—as it has remained unacceptable today to some states in certain critical doctrinal areas such as race relations and Bible readings in public schools. Lacking more forceful instruments to ensure compliance, all the Supreme Court could do at the time was to restate its position. The otherwise obscure case of *Cohens* v. *Virginia* (1821) provided John Marshall with his first personal opportunity to speak to the question. The case involved a criminal prosecution in which two brothers named Cohen were convicted in a Virginia court of selling lottery tickets in violation of a state statute. The Cohens' defense was that since the tickets were issued in the District of Columbia under an act of Congress, they were immune from state prosecution. But it is with the jurisdictional ques-

tion of whether or not the Supreme Court could even hear the case that we are concerned. For the record, it can be noted that the appeal *was heard* and was dismissed on its merits.

To the surprise of no one, Marshall used the occasion to reiterate Story's earlier opinion affirming the validity of Section 25 of the Judiciary Act. More importantly, he gave eloquent testimony to the needs of a united, rather than a divided, country:

That the United States form, for many, and for most important purposes, a single nation, has not yet been denied. In war, we are one people. In making peace, we are one people. In all commercial regulations, we are one and the same people. In many other respects, the American people are one; and the government which is alone capable of controlling and managing their interests in all these respects, is the government of the Union. It is their government, and in that character, they have no other. America has chosen to be, in many respects, and to many purposes, a nation; and for all these purposes, her government is complete; to all these objects it is competent. The people have declared, that in the exercise of all powers given for these objects, it is supreme. It can, then, in effecting these objects, legitimately control all individuals or governments within the American territory. The constitution and the laws of a state, so far as they are repugnant to the constitution and laws of the United States, are absolutely void. These states are constituent parts of the United States; they are members of one great empire—for some purposes sovereign, for some purposes subordinate.

The *Cohens* case is important for its resolution of two other questions. First, since the case involved an appeal to the Supreme Court by individuals against a state, Virginia argued that the suit was precluded by the Eleventh Amendment, forbidding suits against a state without its consent. If Marshall had accepted this argument, a precedent would have been set precluding Supreme Court review of criminal prosecutions in the state courts—an unimportant question in 1821, but a subject which occupies more than one-quarter of the Supreme Court's docket today. Marshall argued, however, that in such cases it is the state which originally brings the individual to court, and by appealing to the United States Supreme Court, the individual is not, in the sense of the Eleventh Amendment, "suing" the state.

Second, one of the options open to Marshall, or suggested to him, was the dismissal of the suit for want of jurisdiction. Rather than merely asserting that he *had* jurisdiction, Marshall offered the opinion that the Court *had no choice* but to decide a case where it had jurisdiction. His dicta to this effect, quoted below, has long been an embarrassment to later generations of judges who have followed the practice of refusing to hear cases even where jurisdiction clearly existed:

It is most true, that this court will not take jurisdiction if it should not; but it is equally true, that it must take jurisdiction, if it should. The judiciary cannot, as the legislature may, avoid a measure, because it approaches the confines of the constitution. We cannot pass it by, because it is doubtful. With whatever doubts, with whatever difficulties, a case may be attended, we must decide it, if it be brought before us. We have no more right to decline the exercise of jurisdiction which is given, than to usurp that which is not given. The one or the other would be treason to the constitution. Questions may occur, which we would gladly avoid; but we cannot avoid them. All we can do is, to exercise our best judgment, and conscientiously to perform our duty. In doing this, on the present occasion, we find this tribunal

invested with appellate jurisdiction in all cases arising under the constitution and laws of the United States. We find no exception to this grant, and we cannot insert one. . . .

[Query: Of what importance is the power of the Supreme Court to review state court decisions? Consider Oliver Wendell Holmes' famous answer: "I do not think the United States would come to an end if we lost our power to declare an Act of Congress void. I do think the Union would be imperiled if we could not make that declaration as to the laws of the several states."]

D. McCulloch v. Maryland (1819)

+Marshall, Story, Livingston, Washington, Duvall, Todd, Johnson

[The question of federal judicial supremacy depended in part on federal supremacy generally. The Supreme Court could not hope to preserve its power and influence while that of Congress and the president dissipated under a states' rights attack. The question decided in the *McCulloch* case was thus important not just because of its concern with the issue of congressional implied powers—for which it is justly and primarily famous—but also because it contributed to the counteroffensive against the compact theory of the Constitution, including immunity from national judicial review, which was urged by many states even after it was rejected by the Court in *Martin* v. *Hunter's Lessee*.

The *McCulloch* case arose out of the seemingly endless controversy over the Bank of the United States. First chartered in 1791, the bank had been strongly opposed by Jefferson and his supporters as an unconstitutional exercise of congressional power. Hostility to the bank also reflected the traditional suspicions of farmers to urban and capitalist institutions. The charter of the bank was allowed to expire in 1811, but the need for a national bank soon became obvious, and a new Bank of the United States was chartered in 1816. Whereas the first bank had been staffed largely by Federalists and had adopted a conservative fiscal policy, the recharted Bank's directors were appointed by Presidents Madison and Monroe and pursued more liberal, speculative policies. These policies were alleged to have brought several state banks to ruin, and a number of states passed laws designed to eliminate local branches of the Bank of the United States. Maryland was one of these states. It sought to tax the bank branch in Baltimore out of existence by placing a $15,000 tax on any bank within the state which issued notes not authorized by the state. A prohibitive alternative tax of $100 per such bank note was also provided. Since there was only one bank in Maryland that issued unauthorized notes, there could be no doubt as to the purpose or object of the statute. McCulloch, the cashier of the branch bank in Baltimore, was ordered to refuse to pay the state tax. Maryland brought suit in the local state court to compel payment, and a judgment in favor of the state was affirmed by the Maryland Court of Appeals. The Supreme Court heard the case on a writ of error following a leisurely nine days of oral argument.]

MR. CHIEF JUSTICE MARSHALL delivered the opinion of the Court.

. . . The first question in the cause is—has congress power to incorporate a bank?

. . . The power now contested was exercised by the first congress elected under the present constitution. The bill for incorporating the Bank of the United States did not steal upon an unsuspecting legislature, and pass unobserved. Its principle was completely understood, and was opposed with equal zeal and ability. . . .

The powers of the general government, it has been said, are delegated by the states, who alone are truly sovereign; and must be exercised in subordination to the states, who alone possess supreme dominion.

It would be difficult to sustain this proposition. The convention which framed the constitution was indeed elected by the state legislatures. But the instrument, when it came from their hands, was a mere proposal, without obligation, or pretensions to it. It was reported to the then existing congress of the United States, with a request that it might "be submitted to a convention of delegates, chosen in each state by the people thereof, under the recommendation of its legislature, for their assent and ratification." This mode of proceeding was adopted and by the convention, by congress, and by the state legislatures, the instrument was submitted to the *people*. They acted upon it in the only manner in which they can act safely, effectively and wisely, on such a subject, by assembling in convention. It is true, they assembled in their several states—and where else should they have assembled? No political dreamer was ever wild enough to think of breaking down the lines which separate the states, and of compounding the American people into one common mass. Of consequence, when they act, they act in their states. But the measures they adopt do not, on that account, cease to be the measures of the people themselves, or become the measures of the state governments.

From these conventions, the constitution derives its whole authority. The government proceeds directly from the people; is "ordained and established," in the name of the people; and is declared to be ordained, "in order to form a more perfect union, establish justice, insure domestic tranquility, and secure the blessings of liberty to themselves and to their posterity." The assent of the states, in their sovereign capacity, is implied, in calling a convention, and thus submitting that instrument to the people. But the people were at perfect liberty to accept or reject it; and their act was final. It required not the affirmance, and could not be nega-tived, by the state governments. The constitution, when thus adopted, was a complete obligation, and bound the state sovereignties.

It has been said, that the people had already surrendered all their powers to the state sovereignties, and had nothing more to give. But, surely, the question whether they may re-sume and modify the powers granted to government, does not remain to be settled in this country. . . .

This government is acknowledged by all, to be one of enumerated pow-ers. . . .

If any one proposition could com-mand the universal assent of man-kind, we might expect it would be this—that the government of the Union, though limited in its powers, is supreme within its sphere of action. This would seem to result, necessar-ily, from its nature. It is the govern-ment of all; its powers are delegated by all; it represents all, and acts for all. Though any one state may be willing to control its operations, no state is willing to allow others to con-trol them. The nation, on those sub-jects on which it can act, must neces-sarily bind its component parts. But this question is not left to mere rea-son: the people have, in express terms, decided it, by saying, "this constitution, and the laws of the United States, which shall be made in pursuance thereof," "shall be the supreme law of the land," and by re-quiring that the members of the state legislatures, and the officers of the executive and judicial departments of the states, shall take the oath of fidelity to it.

The government of the United States, then, though limited in its powers, is supreme; and its laws, when made in pursuance of the con-stitution, form the supreme law of the land, "anything in the constitution or

laws of the state to the contrary not-withstanding."

Among the enumerated powers, we do not find that of establishing a bank or creating a corporation. But there is no phrase in the instrument which, like the articles of confedera-tion, excludes incidental or implied powers; and which requires that ev-erything granted shall be expressly and minutely described. Even the 10th amendment, which was framed for the purpose of quieting the exces-sive jealousies which had been ex-cited, omits the word "expressly," and declares only, that the powers "not delegated to the United States, nor prohibited to the states, are re-served to the states or to the people;" thus leaving the question, whether the particular power which may be-come the subject of contest, has been delegated to the one government, or prohibited to the other, to depend on a fair construction of the whole in-strument. The men who drew and adopted this amendment had experi-enced the embarrassments resulting from the insertion of this word in the articles of confederation, and proba-bly omitted it, to avoid those embar-rassments. A constitution, to contain an accurate detail of all the subdivi-sions of which its great powers will admit, and of all the means by which they may be carried into execution, would partake of the prolixity of a legal code, and could scarcely be em-braced by the human mind. It would, probably, never be understood by the public. . . . In considering this ques-tion, then, we must never forget that it is a *constitution* we are expound-ing.

Although, among the enumerated powers of government, we do not find the word "bank" or "incorporation," we find the great powers, to lay and collect taxes; to borrow money; to regulate commerce; to declare and conduct a war; and to raise and support armies and navies. The sword and the purse, all the external relations, and no inconsiderable portion of the industry of the nation, are intrusted to its government. It can never be pretended, that these vast powers draw after them others of inferior importance, merely because they are inferior. Such an idea can never be advanced. But it may with great reason be contended, that a government, intrusted with such ample powers, on the due execution of which the happiness and prosperity of the nation so vitally depends, must also be intrusted with ample means for their execution. The power being given, it is the interest of the nation to facilitate its execution. It can never be their interest, and cannot be presumed to have been their intention, to clog and embarrass its execution, by withholding the most appropriate means. . . . Is that construction of the constitution to be preferred, which would render these operations difficult, hazardous and expensive? Can we adopt that construction (unless the words imperiously require it), which would impute to the framers of that instrument, when granting these powers for the public good, the intention of impeding their exercise, by withholding a choice of means? . . .

It is not denied, that the powers given to the government imply the ordinary means of execution. That, for example, of raising revenue, and applying it to national purposes, is admitted to imply the power of conveying money from place to place, as the exigencies of the nation may require, and of employing the usual means of conveyance. But it is denied, that the government has its choice of means; or, that it may employ the most convenient means, if, to employ them, it be necessary to erect a corporation. On what foundation does this argument rest? On this alone: the power of creating a corporation, is one appertaining to sovereignty, and is not expressly conferred on congress. This is true. But all legislative powers appertain to sovereignty. . . .

But the constitution of the United States has not left the right of congress to employ the necessary means, for the execution of the powers conferred on the government, to general reasoning. To its enumeration of powers is added, that of making "all laws which shall be necessary and proper, for carrying into execution the foregoing powers, and all other powers vested by this constitution, in the government of the United States, or in any department thereof." The counsel for the state of Maryland have urged various arguments, to prove that this clause, though, in terms, a grant of power, is not so, in effect; but is really restrictive of the general right, which might otherwise be implied, of selecting means for executing the enumerated powers. In support of this proposition, they have found it necessary to contend, that this clause was inserted for the purpose of conferring on congress the power of making laws. That, without it, doubts might be entertained, whether congress could exercise its powers in the form of legislation. . . .

But the argument on which most reliance is placed, is drawn from that peculiar language of this clause. Congress is not empowered by it to make all laws, which may have relation to the powers conferred on the government, but such only as may be *"necessary and proper"* for carrying them into execution. The word *"necessary"* is considered as controlling the whole sentence, and as limiting the right to pass laws for the execution of the granting powers, to such as are indispensable, and without which the power would be nugatory. That it excludes the choice of means, and leaves to congress, in each case, that only which is most direct and simple.

Is it true, that this is the sense in which the word "necessary" is always used? Does it always import an absolute physical necessity, so strong, that one thing to which another may be termed necessary, cannot exist without that other? We think it does not. If reference be had to its use, in the common affairs of the world, or in approved authors, we find that it frequently imports no more than that one thing is convenient, or useful, or essential to another. To employ the means necessary to an end, is generally understood as employing any means calculated to produce the end, and not as being confined to those single means, without which the end would be entirely unattainable. . . .

The subject is the execution of those great powers on which the welfare of a nation essentially depends. It must have been the intention of those who gave these powers, to insure, so far as human prudence could insure, their beneficial execution. This could not be done, by confiding the choice of means to such narrow limits as not to leave it in the power of congress to adopt any which might be appropriate, and which were conducive to that end. This provision is made in a constitution, intended to endure for ages to come, and consequently, to be adapted to the various *crises* of human affairs.

. . . We admit, as all must admit, that the powers of the government are limited, and that its limits are not to be transcended. But we think the sound construction of the constitution must allow to the national legislature that discretion, with respect to

the means by which the powers it confers are to be carried into execution, which will enable that body to perform the high duties assigned to it, in the manner most beneficial to the people. Let the end be legitimate, let it be within the scope of the constitution, and all means which are appropriate, which are plainly adapted to that end, which are not prohibited, but consist with the letter and spirit of the constitution, are constitutional.

. . . After the most deliberate consideration, it is the unanimous and decided opinion of this court, that the act to incorporate the Bank of the United States is a law made in pursuance of the constitution, and is a part of the supreme law of the land.

2. Whether the state of Maryland may, without violating the constitution, tax that branch? That the power of taxation is one of vital importance; that it is retained by the states; that it is not abridged by the grant of a similar power to the government of the union; that it is to be concurrently exercised by the two governments— are truths which have never been denied. But such is the paramount character of the constitution, that its capacity to withdraw any subject from the action of even this power, is admitted. The states are expressly forbidden to lay any duties on imports or exports, except what may be absolutely necessary for executing their inspection laws. If the obligation of this prohibition must be conceded—if it may restrain a state from the exercise of its taxing power on imports and exports—the same paramount character would seem to restrain, as it certainly may restrain, a state from such other exercise of this power, as is in its nature incompatible with, and repugnant to, the constitutional laws of the Union. A law, absolutely repugnant to another, as entirely re-

peals that other as if express terms of repeal were used.

. . . This great principle is, that the constitution and the laws made in pursuance thereof are supreme; that they control the constitution and laws of the respective states, and cannot be controlled by them. From this, which may be almost termed an axiom, other propositions are deduced as corollaries, on the truth or error of which, and on the application to this case, the cause has been supposed to depend. These are, 1st. That a power to create implies a power to preserve: 2d. That a power to destroy, if wielded by a different hand, is hostile to, and incompatible with these powers to create and to preserve: 3d. That where this repugnancy exists, that authority which is supreme must control, not yield to that over which it is supreme.

These propositions, as abstract truths, would, perhaps, never be controverted. Their application to this case, however, has been denied; and both in maintaining the affirmative and the negative, a splendor of eloquence, and strength of argument, seldom, if ever, surpassed, have been displayed. . . .

The argument on the part of the state of Maryland, is, not that the states may directly resist a law of congress, but that they may exercise their acknowledged powers upon it, and that the constitution leaves them this right, in the confidence that they will not abuse it. Before we proceed to examine this argument, and to subject it to the test of the constitution, we must be permitted to bestow a few considerations on the nature and extent of this original right of taxation, which is acknowledged to remain with the states. It is admitted, that the power of taxing the people and their property, is essential to the very existence of government, and may be

legitimately exercised on the objects to which it is applicable, to the utmost extent to which the government may choose to carry it. The only security against the abuse of this power, is found in the structure of the government itself. In imposing a tax, the legislature acts upon its constituents. This is, in general, a sufficient security against erroneous and oppressive taxation. . . .

The sovereignty of a state extends to everything which exists by its own authority, or is introduced by its permission; but does it extend to those means which are employed by congress to carry into execution powers conferred on that body by the people of the United States? We think it demonstrable, that it does not. Those powers are not given by the people of a single state. They are given by the people of the United States, to a government whose laws, made in pursuance of the constitution, are declared to be supreme. Consequently, the people of a single state cannot confer a sovereignty which will extend over them. . . .

Let us resume the inquiry, whether this power can be exercised by the respective states, consistently with a fair construction of the constitution?

That the power to tax involves the power to destory; that the power to destroy may defeat and render useless the power to create; that there is a plain repugnance in conferring on one government a power to control the constitutional measures of another, which other, with respect to those very measures, is declared to be supreme over that which exerts the control, are propositions not to be denied. But all inconsistences are to be reconciled by the magic of the word *confidence*. Taxation, it is said, does not necessarily and unavoidably destroy. To carry it to the excess of destruction, would be an abuse, to presume which, would banish that confidence which is essential to all government.

But is this a case of confidence? Would the people of any one state trust those of another with a power to control the most insignificant operations of their government? We know they would not. Why, then, should we suppose, that the people of any one state should be willing to trust those of another with a power to control the operations of a government to which they have confided their most important and most valuable interests? In the legislature of the Union alone, are all represented. The legislature of the Union alone, therefore, can be trusted by the people with the power of controlling measures which concern all, in the confidence that it will not be abused. This, then, is not a case of confidence, and we must consider it as it really is.

If we apply the principle for which the state of Maryland contends, to the constitution, generally, we shall find it capable of changing totally the character of that instrument. We shall find it capable of arresting all the measures of the government, and of prostrating it at the foot of the states. The American people have declared their constitution and the laws made in pursuance thereof, to be supreme; but this principle would transfer the supremacy, in fact, to the states.

If the states may tax one instrument, employed by the government in the execution of its powers, they may tax any and every other instrument. They may tax the mail; they may tax the mint; they may tax patent-rights; they may tax the papers of the custom-house; they may tax judicial process; they may tax all the means employed by the government, to an excess which would defeat all the ends of government. This

was not intended by the American people. They did not design to make their government dependent on the states.

. . . It has also been insisted, that, as the power of taxation in the general and state governments is acknowledged to be concurrent, every argument which would sustain the right of the general government to tax banks chartered by the states, will equally sustain the right of the states to tax banks chartered by the general government.

But the two cases are not on the same reason. The people of all the states have created the general government, and have conferred upon it the general power of taxation. The people of all the states, and the states themselves, are represented in congress, and, by their representatives, exercise this power. When they tax the chartered institutions of the states, they tax their constituents; and these taxes must be uniform. But when a state taxes the operations of the government of the United States, it acts upon institutions created, not by their own constituents, but by people over whom they claim no control. It acts upon the measures of a government created by others as well as themselves, for the benefit of others in common with themselves. The difference is that which always exists, and always must exist, between the action of the whole on a part, and the action of a part on the whole—between the laws of a government declared to be supreme, and those of a government which, when in opposition to those laws, is not supreme. . . .

The court has bestowed on this subject its most deliberate consideration. The result is a conviction that the states have no power, by taxation or otherwise, to retard, impede, burden, or in any manner control, the operations of the constitutional laws enacted by congress to carry into execution the powers vested in the general government. This is, we think, the unavoidable consequence of that supremacy which the constitution has declared.

We are unanimously of opinion, that the law passed by the legislature of Maryland, imposing a tax on the Bank of the United States, is unconstitutional and void.

[Marshall's opinion in this case, regarded by many scholars as his greatest, did not settle the bank controversy. Like many Supreme Court decisions, it was just a phase in a continuing political controversy. There were bitter attacks on the Supreme Court. Spencer Roane published a series of anonymous newspaper articles condemning the decisions, to which John Marshall replied, also anonymously. The Virginia legislature urged again that the Supreme Court be deprived of its power to review acts of state courts. Ohio, which had a similar law placing a tax of $50,000 on each branch of the Bank of the United States, was not deterred. State officials "collected" the tax by seizing $100,000 from the federal bank in Chilicothe, Ohio. Federal officials responded by obtaining a federal court order barring state officials from depositing the stolen money in the state treasury, a decision ultimately affirmed by the Supreme Court in *Osborn* v. *Bank of the United States* (1824). William McCulloch, who received a measure of lasting fame by refusing to comply with the Maryland law and standing fast for the honor of the United States, turned out to be something less than a selfless patriot. Two months after the decision in *McCulloch* v. *Maryland*, he was dismissed when it was discovered that he had embezzled funds from the bank.

Ultimately the bank went out of existence. But Marshall's expansive view of the implied powers of Congress and his corresponding rejection of the Tenth Amendment as a viable limitation on federal power remain today as im-

portant cornerstones of our constitutional system. Often forgotten is the fact that Marshall, though attacked for his strong support of national power, took an intermediate position. He rejected Jefferson's limiting construction of the necessary and proper clause, but he also declined to adopt an interpretation giving Congress virtually unlimited power. James Wilson, for one, had argued at the Constitutional Convention that Congress ought to have the power to deal with *any* national problem, whether or not the power was delegated or fairly implied.

The doctrine that the nation has powers equal to the magnitude of need, sometimes referred to as the doctrine of "residual powers," was rejected by the Supreme Court in *Kansas* v. *Colorado* (1907), and often thereafter. Nevertheless, the notion that emergency need creates (or should create) power has not been put to rest entirely. Emergencies do occur and one way or another governments have to deal with them. There would probably be little support today for a constitutional amendment permitting the government to "rule by decree" in cases of emergency. In its place, we have a pragmatic tradition which on occasion has sanctioned the bending of rules to deal with real emergencies while rejecting as unconstitutional abstract principles of emergency power. As Chief Justice Hughes once said, in upholding a Minnesota statute that readjusted farm mortgages during the Depression to prohibit foreclosures, "emergencies do not create power, but they may furnish the occasion for the exercise of power."[1] Most claims to the exercise of extraordinary power, especially in the twentieth century, have come from the executive branch. Further consideration of this question, therefore, will be postponed until Part Two, Chapter Four.

McCulloch v. *Maryland*, though not the last word on the subject, provides at least an outline of the boundaries between nation and state in a federal system. There are some powers that belong *exclusively* to the federal government, either by specific constitutional delegation, by implication, or by necessity of function. Examples include the treaty power, the power to

---

[1]See *Home Building & Loan Association* v. *Blaisdell*, (1934).

declare and wage war, and the power to establish a postal system. The theory of the Constitution held that there were some powers exclusively reserved to the state governments because they have not been delegated to the federal government. That is what the Tenth Amendment says. In modern times, we find multiple examples of federal intrusion into what might formerly have been called the domain of the states. The field of education is a prime example; welfare is another. As Marshall notes in the second part of the *McCulloch* case, there are also powers that can be exercised concurrently, although a conflict between assertions of state and federal power, assuming that each is independently legitimate, must be resolved in favor of federal power. Taxation is the best example of a concurrent power. The states, as quasi-sovereign entities, have a strong interest in, and a need for, the power to tax. The power is not immune from constitutional limitations, but judicial scrutiny of the state taxing power is usually deferential. Regulation of aspects of interstate commerce is another area where state power often comes into conflict with federal prerogatives. The difficult questions are not abstract but practical: not *can* the states tax or regulate aspects of commerce, but *how much,* and *when?*[2]]

E. *Cooper v. Aaron (1958)*

+Warren, Black, Douglas, Frankfurter, Burton, Clark, Harlan, Brennan, Whittaker

[Occasional challenges to federal judicial supremacy still occur, notwithstanding the clear and forceful interpretations of the supremacy clause by Story and Marshall and by justices in succeeding generations. Though often rejected as a constitutional nullity, the doctrine of "interposition"[1] still has its adherents. A flagrant example comes out of the southern response to the Supreme Court's landmark decision in *Brown* v. *Board of Education* (1954).

Following the *Brown* decision, the Little Rock School Board adopted a public policy of compliance. It conducted studies to determine the problems of a transition to a desegregated school system, and eventually adopted a plan providing for desegregating the high school grades, followed successively by desegregation at the junior high and elementary school levels. This plan was upheld by the federal courts against challenges by Negro parents desiring more rapid desegregation. In contrast to the actions of the Little Rock board, school systems elsewhere in the state, and throughout the south, were pursuing programs of evasion and noncompliance. Various state statutes were enacted, as part of the state's "massive resistance" program, to facilitate school board noncompliance. Nevertheless, officials in Little Rock maintained their plans to carry out the first stage of desegregation in the fall of 1957.

One day prior to the scheduled opening of school, the governor dispatched troops of the Arkansas National Guard to bar the Negro students. This action served to harden opposition to the plan on the part of those who had reluctantly accepted the inevitability of desegregation. Mobs formed, violence seemed imminent, and the school board, caught in the middle, petitioned the district court for further instructions. That court ordered the original plan to be carried out, but efforts to bring the Negro children to Central High School were thwarted by the troops. After three weeks of this impasse, the district court granted an injunction against the governor and officers of the Arkansas National Guard, prohibiting them from interfering with the school board plan or otherwise obstructing the orders of the court. The Guard was then withdrawn. The next day, the Negro children entered the school under the protection of the local and state police, but the aggregation of a large mob outside the school forced their removal. Several days later President Eisenhower dispatched federal troops and the Negro children remained in school the balance of the school year.

[2]See below, Part II, Chapter One, pp. 328–342.

[1]"Interposition" is the attempt by a state to protect its citizens from the operation of a harmful federal law which it believes to be null and void.

Because of the steadily deteriorating situation, and also because of extreme public hostility and local pressure, the school board petitioned the district court in February 1958 for a two-and-a-half-year postponement of the desegregation program. Finding that the "intolerable" conditions of turmoil had had an adverse effect on the educational program of the school, the district court granted the order. The Negro respondents appealed to the Court of Appeals for the Eighth Circuit, and also filed a petition for certiorari directly with the Supreme Court. The Supreme Court met in special session in late August 1958, and on September 12, unanimously affirmed the stay order which in the meantime had been granted by the Court of Appeals. Because of the extraordinary circumstances, the Court issued its order immediately, with its written opinion being issued at a later date. To emphasize its support of the principles in the *Brown* case, the opinion of the Court listed every judge by name as a co-author. And it took another unusual step in indicating that those justices who had joined the Court in the interim were united in support of those principles.]

Opinion of the Court by the CHIEF JUSTICE, MR. JUSTICE BLACK, MR. JUSTICE FRANKFURTER, MR. JUSTICE DOUGLAS, MR. JUSTICE BURTON, MR. JUSTICE CLARK, MR. JUSTICE HARLAN, MR. JUSTICE BRENNAN, and MR. JUSTICE WHITTAKER.

As this case reaches us it raises questions of the highest importance to the maintenance of our federal system of government. It necessarily involves a claim by the Governor and Legislature of a State that there is no duty on state officials to obey federal court orders resting on this Court's considered interpretation of the United States Constitution. . . . We are urged to uphold a suspension of the Little Rock School Board's plan to do away with segregated public school in Little Rock until state laws and efforts to upset and nullify our holding in *Brown* v. *Board of Educa-*

tion have been further challenged and tested in the courts. We reject these contentions. . . .

In affirming the judgment of the Court of Appeals which reversed the District Court we have accepted without reservation the position of the School Board, the Superintendent of Schools, and their counsel that they displayed entire good faith in the conduct of these proceedings and in dealing with the unfortunate and distressing sequence of events which has been outlined. We likewise have accepted the findings of the District Court as to the conditions at Central High School during the 1957–1958 school year, and also the findings that the educational progress of all the students, white and colored, of that school has suffered and will continue to suffer if the conditions which prevailed last year are permitted to continue.

The significance of these findings, however, is to be considered in light of the fact, indisputably revealed by the record before us, that the conditions they depict are directly traceable to the actions of legislators and executive officials of the State of Arkansas, taken in their official capacities, which reflect their own determination to resist this Court's decision in the *Brown* case and which have brought about violent resistance to that decision in Arkansas. In its petition for certiorari filed in this Court, the School Board itself describes the situation in this language: "The legislative, executive, and judicial departments of the state government opposed the desegregation of Little Rock schools by enacting laws, calling out troops, making statements villifying federal law and federal courts, and failing to utilize state law enforcement agencies and judicial processes to maintain public peace."

One may well sympathize with the position of the Board in the face of the frustrating conditions which have confronted it, but, regardless of the Board's good faith, the actions of the other state agencies responsible for those conditions compel us to reject the Board's legal position. Had Central High School been under the direct management of the State itself, it could hardly be suggested that those immediately in charge of the school should be heard to assert their own good faith as a legal excuse for delay in implementing the constitutional rights of these respondents, when vindication of those rights was rendered difficult or impossible by the actions of other state officials. The situation here is in no different posture because the members of the School Board and the Superintendent of Schools are local officials; from the point of view of the Fourteenth Amendment, they stand in this litigation as the agents of the State.

The constitutional rights of respondents are not to be sacrificed or yielded to the violence and disorder which have followed upon the actions of the Governor and Legislature. As this Court said some 41 years ago in a unanimous opinion in a case involving another aspect of racial segregation: "It is urged that this proposed segregation will promote the public peace by preventing race conflicts. Desirable as this is, and important as is the preservation of the public peace, this aim cannot be accomplished by laws or ordinances which deny rights created or protected by the federal Constitution," *Buchanan* v. *Warley*. . . . Thus law and order are not here to be preserved by depriving the Negro children of their constitutional rights. The record before us clearly establishes that the growth of the Board's difficulties to a magnitude beyond its unaided power

to control is the product of state action. Those difficulties, as counsel for the Board forthrightly conceded on the oral argument in this Court, can also be brought under control by state action.

The controlling legal principles are plain. The command of the Fourteenth Amendment is that no "State" shall deny to any person within its jurisdiction the equal protection of the laws. "A State acts by its legislative, its executive, or its judicial authorities. It can act in no other way. The constitutional provision, therefore, must mean that no agency of the State, or of the officers or agents by whom its powers are exerted, shall deny to any person within its jurisdiction the equal protection of the laws. Whoever, by virtue of public position under a State government . . . denies or takes away the equal protection of the laws, violates the constitutional inhibition; and as he acts in the name and for the State, and is clothed with the State's power, his act is that of the State. This must be so, or the constitutional prohibition has no meaning." . . . Thus the prohibitions of the Fourteenth Amendment extend to all action of the State denying equal protection of the laws; whatever the agency of the State taking the action. . . . In short, the constitutional rights of children not to be discriminated against in school admission on grounds of race or color declared by this Court in the *Brown* case can neither be nullified openly and directly by state legislators or state executive or judicial officers, nor nullified indirectly by them through evasive schemes for segregation whether attempted "ingeniously or ingenuously." . . .

What has been said, in the light of the facts developed, is enough to dispose of the case. However, we should answer the premise of the actions of the Governor and Legislature that they are not bound by our holding in the *Brown* case. It is necessary only to recall some basic constitutional propositions which are settled doctrine.

Article VI of the Constitution makes the Constitution the "supreme Law of the Land." In 1803, Chief Justice Marshall, speaking for a unanimous Court, referring to the Constitution as "the fundamental and paramount law of the nation," declared in the notable case of *Marbury* v. *Madison* . . . that "It is emphatically the province and duty of the judicial department to say what the law is." This decision declared the basic principle that the federal judiciary is supreme in the exposition of the law of the Constitution, and that principle has ever since been respected by this Court and the Country as a permanent and indispensable feature of our constitutional system. It follows that the interpretation of the Fourteenth Amendment enunciated by this Court in the *Brown* case is the supreme law of the land, and Art. VI of the Constitution makes it of binding effect on the States "any Thing in the Constitution or Laws of any State to the Contrary notwithstanding." Every state legislator and executive and judicial officer is solemnly committed by oath taken pursuant to Art. VI, § 3 "to support this Constitution." . . .

No state legislator or executive or judicial officer can war against the Constitution without violating his undertaking to support it. Chief Justice Marshall spoke for a unanimous Court in saying that: "If the legislatures of the several states may, at will, annul the judgments of the courts of the United States, and destroy the rights acquired under those judgments, the constitution itself becomes a solemn mockery. . . ." A Governor who asserts a power to nullify a federal court order is similarly re-

strained. If he had such power, said Chief Justice Hughes, in 1932, also for a unanimous Court, "it is manifest that the fiat of a state Governor, and not the Constitution of the United States, would be the supreme law of the land; that the restrictions of the Federal Constitution upon the exercise of state power would be but impotent phrases. . . ."

It is, of course, quite true that the responsibility for public education is primarily the concern of the States, but it is equally true that such responsibilities, like all other state activity, must be exercised consistently with federal constitutional requirements as they apply to state action. The Constitution created a government dedicated to equal justice under law. The Fourteenth Amendment embodied and emphasized that ideal. State support of segregated schools through any arrangement, management, funds, or property cannot be squared with the Amendment's command that no State shall deny to any person within its jurisdiction the equal protection of the laws. The right of a student not to be segregated on racial grounds in schools so maintained is indeed so fundamental and pervasive that it is embraced in the concept of due process of law. . . . The basic decision in *Brown* was unanimously reached by this Court only after the case had been briefed and twice argued and the issues had been given the most serious consideration. Since the first *Brown* opinion three new Justices have come to the Court. They are at one with the Justices still on the Court who participated in that basic decision as to its correctness, and that decision is now unanimously reaffirmed. The principles announced in that decision and the obedience of the States to them, according to the command of the Constitution, are indispensable for the protection of the freedoms guaranteed by our fundamental charter for all of us. Our constitutional ideal of equal justice under law is thus made a living truth.

MR. JUSTICE FRANKFURTER, CONCURRING (OMITTED).

F. *Edelman v. Jordan (1974)*

+Burger, Stewart, White, Powell, Rehnquist
−Douglas, Brennan, Marshall, Blackmun

[The Eleventh Amendment to the Constitution was enacted in 1798 in response to the Supreme Court's decision in *Chisholm* v. *Georgia* (1793). In *Chisholm* the Supreme Court broadly interpreted Article III as extending the judicial power of the United States to controversies between an individual and a state. The Supreme Court accepted original jurisdiction over a suit by Chisholm, a resident of South Carolina, against the state of Georgia in a land dispute. Indeed, hostility toward the decision was so great that Georgia passed a law providing that anyone attempting to enforce *Chisholm* should be condemned to hang "without benefit of clergy."

Reversing *Chisholm,* the Eleventh Amendment provides that "The judicial power of the United States shall not be construed to extend to any suit in law or equity, commenced or prosecuted against any one of the United States by Citizens of another state, or by Citizens or Subjects of any Foreign State." The concept of state sovereign immunity originally intended by Founding Fathers such as Hamilton (see Federalist Paper No. 81) was thus reaffirmed. However the principle of state sovereign immunity does not apply universally to bar all suits against a state. For example, a state is not immune from a suit by the United States or another State (*United States* v. *Texas* 1892), and municipal corporations do not share the state's immunity (*Chicot County* v. *Sherwood* 1893). A state may also waive its immunity under the Eleventh Amendment by voluntarily submitting to a law-suit, or by a law consenting to be sued in federal courts. The Eleventh Amendment cannot limit a suit for damages brought under congressional legislation pursuant to the enabling powers of the Fourteenth Amendment (*Fitzpatrick* v. *Bitzer* 1976); however such suits must be based on an expressed congressional intent to lift immunity. In *Employees* v. *Department of Public Health and Welfare* (1973) the Supreme Court held that Congress did not intend to override the Eleventh Amendment by allowing employees the right to sue a state under the Wagner Act.

The Eleventh Amendment does not bar individuals from all suits against state officials. In *Ex Parte Young* (1908) the Supreme Court held that a state officer could be sued or enjoined from actions alleged to violate the federal constitutional rights of citizens. However, official immunity such as executive immunity provides a "qualified immunity" which protects certain official actions that are carried out in accordance with duties and responsibilities of the office (*Scheuer* v. *Rhodes* 1974).

Although damages may be sought against state officials, the Supreme Court in *Edelman* v. *Jordan* had to address the issue of whether or not a state could be sued in federal court for recovery of funds from the state treasury. Jordan and other welfare recipients filed a class action suit against state welfare officials in Illinois and against the Comptroller of Cook County (Chicago). They alleged that Illinois was not administering the AABD (Aid to the Aged, Blind and Disabled) program consistent with federal regulations, to the detriment of the recipients. AABD is a categorical aid program, funded equally by state and federal funds. This suit asked for an injunction to require Illinois to administer the grants properly *and* sought back payments for funds alleged to have been wrongfully withheld. Both the District Court and the Court of Appeals held for the plaintiffs. They found that the Illinois rules were inconsistent with the federal regulations, and hence invalid. And they ordered repayment of funds due to the recipients. Illinois' claim that this suit was barred by the Eleventh Amendment was also rejected. The Supreme Court granted certiorari.]

MR. JUSTICE REHNQUIST delivered the opinion of the Court.

The historical basis of the Eleventh Amendment has been oft-stated, and it represents one of the more dramatic examples of this Court's effort to derive meaning from the document given to the Nation by the Framers nearly 200 years ago. A leading historian of the Court tells us:

"The right of the Federal Judiciary to summon a State as defendant and to adjudicate its rights and liabilities had been the subject of deep apprehension and of active debate at the time of the adoption of the Constitution; but the existence of any such right had been disclaimed by many of the most eminent advocates of the new Federal Government, and it was largely owing to their successful dissipation of the fear of the existence of such Federal power that the Constitution was finally adopted." . . .

Despite such disclaimers, the very first suit entered in this Court at its February Term in 1791 was brought against the State of Maryland by a firm of Dutch bankers as creditors. . . .

The issue was squarely presented to the Court in a suit brought at the August 1792 Term by two citizens of South Carolina, executors of a British creditor, against the State of Georgia. After a year's postponement for preparation on the part of the State of Georgia, the Court, after argument, rendered in February 1793, its short-lived decision in *Chisholm* v. *Georgia* . . . (1793). The decision in that case, that a State was liable to suit by a citizen of another State or of a foreign country, literally shocked the Nation. Sentiment for passage of a constitutional amendment to override the decision rapidly gained momentum, and five years after *Chisholm* the Eleventh Amendment was ratified. . . .

While the Amendment by its terms does not bar suits against a State by its own citizens, this Court has consistently held that an unconsenting State is immune from suits brought in federal courts by her own citizens as well as by citizens of another State. . . . It is also well established that even though a State is not named a party to the action, the suit may nonetheless be barred by the Eleventh Amendment. . . . Thus the rule has evolved that a suit by private parties seeking to impose a liability which must be paid from public funds in the state treasury is barred by the Eleventh Amendment. . . .

The Court of Appeals in this case, while recognizing that the . . . line of cases permitted the State to raise the Eleventh Amendment as a defense to suit by its own citizens, nevertheless concluded that the Amendment did not bar the award of retroactive payments of the statutory benefits found to have been wrongfully withheld. The Court of Appeals held that the above cited cases, when read in light of the Court's landmark decision in *Ex Parte Young* . . . (1908), do not preclude the grant of such a monetary award in the nature of equitable restitution.

Petitioner concedes that *Ex Parte Young* is no bar to that part of the District Court's judgment that prospectively enjoined petitioner's predecessors from failing to process applications within the time limits established by the federal regulations. Petitioner argues, however, that *Ex Parte Young* does not extend so far as to permit a suit which seeks the award of an accrued monetary liability which must be met from the general revenues of a State, absent consent or waiver by the State of its Eleventh Amendment immunity, and that therefore the award of retroactive benefits by the District Court was improper.

Ex Parte Young was a watershed

case in which this Court held that the Eleventh Amendment did not bar an action in the federal courts seeking to enjoin the Attorney General of Minnesota from enforcing a statute claimed to violate the Fourteenth Amendment of the United States Constitution. This holding has permitted the Civil War Amendments to the Constitution to serve as a sword, rather than merely as a shield, for those whom they were designed to protect. But the relief awarded in *Ex Parte Young* was prospective only; the Attorney General of Minnesota was enjoined to conform his future conduct of that office to the requirement of the Fourteenth Amendment. Such relief is analogous to that awarded by the District Court in the prospective portion of its order under review in this case.

But the retroactive position of the District Court's order here, which requires the payment of a very substantial amount of money which that court held should have been paid, but was not, stands on quite a different footing. . . .

. . . The funds to satisfy the award in this case must inevitably come from the general revenues of the State of Illinois, and thus the award resembles far more closely the monetary award against the State itself, . . . than it does the prospective injunctive relief awarded in *Ex Parte Young*. . . .

As in most areas of the law, the difference between the type of relief barred by the Eleventh Amendment and that permitted under *Ex Parte Young* will not in many instances be that between day and night. The injunction issued in *Ex Parte Young* was not totally without effect on the State's revenues, since the state law which the Attorney General was enjoined from enforcing provided substantial monetary penalties against railroads which did not conform to its provisions. Later cases from this Court have authorized equitable relief which has probably had greater impact on state treasuries than did that awarded in *Ex Parte Young*. In *Graham* v. *Richardson* . . . (1971), Arizona and Pennsylvania welfare officials were prohibited from denying welfare benefits to otherwise qualified recipients who were aliens. In *Goldberg* v. *Kelly* . . . (1970), New York City welfare officials were enjoined from following New York State procedures which authorized the termination of benefits paid to welfare recipients without prior hearing. But the fiscal consequences to state treasuries in these cases were the necessary result of compliance with decrees which by their terms were prospective in nature. State officials, in order to shape their official conduct to the mandate of the Court's decrees, would more likely have to spend money from the state treasury than if they had been left free to pursue their previous course of conduct. Such an ancillary effect on the state treasury is a permissible and often an inevitable consequence of the principle announced in *Ex Parte Young*, . . .

But that portion of the District Court's decree which petitioners challenge on Eleventh Amendment grounds goes much further than any of the cases cited. It requires payment of state funds, not as a necessary consequence of compliance in the future with a substantive federal question determination, but as a form of compensation to those whose applications were processed on the slower time schedule at a time when petitioners were under no court-imposed obligation to conform to a different standard. While the Court of Appeals described this retroactive award of monetary relief as a form of "equitable restitution," it is in practical effect indistinguishable in many aspects from an award of damages against the State. . . .

Three fairly recent District Court judgments requiring state directors of public aid to make the type of retroactive payment involved here have been summarily affirmed by this Court notwithstanding Eleventh Amendment contentions made by state officers who were appealing from the District Court judgment. *Shapiro* v. *Thompson* . . . (1969), is the only instance in which the Eleventh Amendment objection to such retroactive relief was actually presented to this Court in a case which was orally argued. The three-judge District Court in that case had ordered the retroactive payment of welfare benefits found by that court to have been unlawfully withheld because of residency requirements held violative of equal protection. . . . This Court, while affirming the judgment, did not in its opinion refer to or substantively treat the Eleventh Amendment argument. . . .

This case, therefore, is the first opportunity the Court has taken to fully explore and treat the Eleventh Amendment aspects of such relief in a written opinion. *Shapiro* v. *Thompson* [is] of precedental value in support of the contention that the Eleventh Amendment does not bar the relief awarded by the District Court in this case. Equally obviously [it is] not of the same precedental value as would be an opinion of this Court treating the question on the merits. Since we deal with a constitutional question, we are less constrained by the principle of *stare decisis* than we are in other areas of the law. Having now had an opportunity to more fully consider the Eleventh Amendment issue after briefing and argument, we disapprove the Eleventh Amendment holdings of those cases to the extent that they are inconsistent with our holding today.

The Court of Appeals held in the alternative that even if the Eleventh Amendment be deemed a bar to the retroactive relief awarded respondent in this case, the State of Illinois had waived its Eleventh Amendment immunity and consented to the bringing of such a suit by participating in the federal AABD program. . . .

The Court of Appeals held that as a matter of federal law Illinois had "constructively consented" to this suit by participating in the federal AABD program and agreeing to administer federal and state funds in compliance with federal law. Constructive consent is not a doctrine commonly associated with the surrender of constitutional rights, and we see no place for it here. In deciding whether a State has waived its constitutional protection under the Eleventh Amendment, we will find waiver only where stated "by the most express language or by such overwhelming implications from the text as will leave no room for any other reasonable construction." . . . We see no reason to retreat from the Court's statement in *Great Northern Insurance Co.* v. *Read* . . . (1945) . . . .

[W]hen we are dealing with the sovereign exemption from judicial interference in the vital field of financial administration a clear declaration of the state's intention to submit its fiscal problems to other courts than those of its own creation must be found.

The mere fact that a State participates in a program through which the Federal Government provides assistance for the operation by the State of a system of public aid is not sufficient to establish consent on the part of the State to be sued in the federal courts. . . .

For the foregoing reasons we decide that the Court of Appeals was wrong in holding that the Eleventh

Amendment did not constitute a bar to that portion of the District Court decree which ordered retroactive payments of benefits found to have been wrongfully withheld. The judgment of the Court of Appeals is therefore reversed and the cause remanded for further proceedings consistent with this opinion.

Reversed and remanded.

MR. JUSTICE DOUGLAS, DISSENTING. (OMITTED)
MR. JUSTICE BRENNAN, DISSENTING. (OMITTED)
MR. JUSTICE MARSHALL, WITH WHOM MR. JUSTICE BLACKMUN JOINS, DISSENTING.

The Social Security Act's categorical assistance programs, including the Aid to the Aged, Blind, and Disabled (AABD) program involved here, are fundamentally different from most federal legislation. Unlike the Fair Labor Standards Act . . ., or the FELA . . ., the Social Security Act does not impose federal standards and liability upon all who engage in certain regulated activities, including often-unwilling state agencies. Instead, the Act seeks to induce state participation in the federal welfare programs by offering federal matching funds in exchange for the State's voluntary assumption of the Act's requirements. I find this basic distinction crucial: It leads me to conclude that by participation in the programs, the States waive whatever immunity they might otherwise have from federal court orders requiring retroactive payment of welfare benefits.

In its contacts with the Social Security Act's assistance programs in recent years, the Court has frequently described the Act as a "scheme of cooperative federalism." . . . While this phrase captures a number of unique characteristics of these programs, for present purposes it serves to emphasize that the States' decision to participate in the programs is a voluntary one. In deciding to participate, however, the States necessarily give up their freedom to operate assistance programs for the needy as they see fit, and bind themselves to conform their programs to the requirements of the federal statute and regulations. . . .

In agreeing to comply with the requirements of the Social Security Act and HEW regulations, I believe that Illinois has also agreed to subject itself to suit in the federal courts to enforce these obligations. I recognize, of course, that the Social Security Act does not itself provide for a cause of action to enforce its obligations. As the Court points out, the only sanction expressly provided in the Act for a participating State's failure to comply with federal requirements is the cutoff of federal funding by the Secretary of HEW. . . .

But a cause of action is clearly provided by 42 U.S.C. [Sec.] 1983 (1970), which in terms authorizes suits to redress deprivations of rights secured by the "laws" of the United States. And we have already rejected the argument that Congress intended the funding cutoff to be the sole remedy for noncompliance with federal requirements. In *Rosado* v. *Wyman* . . . (1970), we held that suits in federal court under [Sec.] 1983 were proper to enforce the provisions of the Social Security Act against participating States. Mr. Justice Harlan, writing for the Court, examined the legislative history and found "not the slightest indication" that Congress intended to prohibit suits in federal court to enforce compliance with federal standards. . . .

In particular, I am firmly convinced that Congress intended the restitution of wrongfully withheld assistance payments to be a remedy available to the federal courts in these suits. Benefits under the categorical assistance programs "are a matter of statutory entitlement for persons qualified to receive them." *Goldberg* v. *Kelly* . . . (1970). Retroactive payment of benefits secures for recipients this entitlement which was withheld in violation of federal law. . . .

Absent any remedy which may act with retroactive effect, state welfare officials have everything to gain and nothing to lose by failing to comply with the congressional mandate that assistance be paid with reasonable promptness to all eligible individuals. This is not idle speculation without basis in practical experience. In this very case, for example, Illinois officials have knowingly violated since 1968 a federal regulation on the strength of an argument as to its invalidity which even the majority deems unworthy of discussion. . . . Without a retroactive payment remedy, we are indeed faced with "the spectre of a state, perhaps calculatingly, defying federal law and thereby depriving welfare recipients of the financial assistance Congress thought it was giving them." . . . Like the Court of Appeals, I cannot believe that Congress could possibly have intended any such result. . . .

5. DOCTRINES OF SELF-LIMITATION

A. A Summary Note on Doctrines of Self-limitation

Earlier sections of this chapter have made clear that the Supreme Court's power is subject to a variety of limitations. There are political considerations stemming from presidential powers of appointment, from congressional control of the Court's appellate jurisdiction, from the power of Congress to override an unpopular decision by corrective legislation, and generally from the political climate in which the Court must operate. Analytically, these may be characterized as external limitations.

There is also a set of limitations emanating from the common law tradition that characterizes Anglo-American legal institutions, from specific constitutional provisions, and from the Court's own assessment of its proper role. It is to these limitations that the remainder of this chapter is devoted. We use the term "self-limitation" to differentiate from limits externally imposed. Yet the boundary line between the two sets of limitations is neither clear nor fixed. The development of doctrines of self-limitation cannot be understood apart from the external environment.

The doctrine of *stare decisis* is an important component of the common law tradition. The rule of precedent, as it is commonly known, obliges the court to apply a settled rule of law to subsequent like cases. This infuses the law with an element of predictability and limits the discretion of any individual judge. But the law also must be flexible, and *stare decisis* has never been perceived as an absolute limitation on Supreme Court discretion in matters of constitutional law.

The workings of *stare decisis* characterize a critical relationship between doctrines of self-restraint and the policy-making functions of the Supreme Court, a relationship that supports the capacity of a justice to choose between adherence to precedent and pursuit of other, "unprecedented" options. Thus, while the doctrine of *stare decisis* is a *standard* for choice and a limitation on judicial discretion, it can also operate in a way that controls choice and facilitates discretion. The potential for such diversity is illustrated in a 1969 case following up the Supreme Court's landmark decision in *Miranda* v. *Arizona* (1966). In *Orozco* v. *Texas* (1969), Justice Harlan reluctantly concurred with the majority, but said:

> [D]*espite my strong inclination to join in the dissent of my Brother White, I can find no acceptable avenue of escape from* Miranda v. Arizona *in judging this case.... Therefore, and purely out of respect for* stare decisis, *I reluctantly feel compelled to acquiesce in today's decision....*

But Justice Stewart (who joined in dissent with White) observed in response that "those who dissented [in *Miranda*] remain free not only to express our continuing disagreement with that decision, but also to oppose any broadening of its impact." Needless to say, Harlan had dissented in *Miranda*.

Stare decisis is neither a creation of the Supreme Court nor a constitutional obligation. The extent of its influence upon the outcome of any given decision is clearly within the discretion of the justices. Its force comes from tradition, from respect for the rule of law, and from the recognition that its use may accord Supreme Court decisions an extra measure of legitimacy. The notion that the law should be consistent against powerful currents of change is pervasive and, in many instances, persuasive.

Essentially, the same is true of a set of judicially created rules of self-restraint, which operate not only to regularize the Supreme Court's use of its powers but also to provide avenues of choice in the broaching or resolving of issues framed in constitutional terms. These rules, or "maxims," can be enumerated in various ways. Five rules of self-limitation seem equally important:[1]

1. The Court must be presented with a real (i.e., not hypothetical) *case* or *controversy* between *real* parties, one of whom has suffered or can allege a real injury. This does not preclude what are called "friendly suits," and on rare occasion, an issue will be joined purely for the sake of testing a law. But even in such contrived situations the norm is that there must be an actual case or controversy. The Supreme Court will not render formal advisory opinions.

2. Closely related to the case or controversy rule is the doctrine of *standing to sue*. This involves "whether the party seeking relief has alleged such a personal stake in the outcome of the controversy as to assume that concrete adverseness which sharpens the presentation of issues upon which the Court so largely depends for illumination of difficult constitutional questions." Thus, for example, a doctor normally may not challenge a law on behalf of her patients; even though she is affected, she is not in the class of persons that the questioned law critically affects.

3. The Court will not entertain questions that are rendered *moot* by changing circumstances. For exam-

[1]For a concise and nontechnical discussion of these "maxims," see Henry J. Abraham, *The Judicial Process*, 3rd ed. (New York: Oxford University Press, 1975), pp. 354–376.

ple, it is difficult to challenge state laws on restrictive residence requirements for voting because by the time the issue works its way "up" to the Supreme Court, the person challenging the law has often met the legal requirement and the case is mooted. These rules are flexible, and a notable exception was stated by Justice Blackmun in the first abortion case, *Roe* v. *Wade* (1973):

Pregnancy often comes more than once to the same woman, and in the general population, if man is to survive, it will always be with us. Pregnancy provides a classic justification for a conclusion of nonmootness.

On the other hand, the Supreme Court refused to make such an exception in the law school affirmative action case, *DeFunis* v. *Odegaard* (1974). DeFunis, who originally had been denied admission to the University of Washington Law School, was admitted under court order. By the time the Supreme Court was to decide the case, DeFunis was in his last semester of law school. However the Supreme Court decided the issue, he would have graduated as scheduled (barring illness or some other unforeseen event). A 5–4 majority of the Court voted to dismiss the case as moot and did not decide the important constitutional issues.

4. Issues that are within the province of a coordinate branch of government are usually avoided by the Supreme Court insofar as they are considered to be *political questions*. This doctrine, however, is subject to a wide variety of interpretations, so much so that some students of the judicial process have been led to state that a political question is a label for whatever issue the justices choose to avoid. Although it is thus difficult to define, the doctrine is an important device of judicial avoidance of those issues that could place the Court in political jeopardy.

5. All legal remedies available to parties in lower courts or other governmental units must have been exhausted before the Supreme Court will agree to take a case for consideration. This insistence upon the *ripeness* of an issue is in the interests of protecting the finality of judgment that is considered so essential to a court of last resort.

In addition to these five major rules of self-limitation, a series of related Court practices might also be mentioned. For example, there is a general presumption of constitutionality in the consideration of challenged laws; a challenger cannot benefit from a law that he or she challenges, and whenever possible, the Supreme Court will resort to nonconstitutional grounds for decision.

Doctrines of self-limitation flow from constitutional requirements, from the Supreme Court's perceptions of its role, and from efforts to accommodate judicial power to democratic theory. These sources are somewhat theoretical. But neither the effect nor the workings of these doctrines are exclusively theoretical. They have an important effect on access to a major process of policy making—that is, on *who* gets to the Supreme Court, and *what* issues the Court will decide.

Two matters of consequence are involved in gaining access to the Court: first, in determining just who shall have access, the Court implicitly allocates justice; second, in determining what issues will be decided, the Court manages and protects its capacity to provide time and attention to what the justices consider the most important problems of the society. Obviously, the two matters are closely related. A narrow, constrained view of access, such as might be implied from very strict rules of "standing" or an enlarged view of "political questions," implies a "private rights" view of the judicial function. The loosening of such barriers implies a broader "public action" view.[2] But whether the judicial function should serve the few or the many, judicial actions should be grounded in principles of justice, and these are difficult to achieve without time for the Court to be deliberate and careful in its decisions. The Supreme Court cannot right every wrong; it cannot decide every issue in which an error of law has been made. It must do justice at the broadest levels of policy and not merely by fashioning remedies that suit the needs of individual litigants.

Doctrines of self-limitation contribute to this very necessary gatekeeping function. The Court must have the power to avoid issues that it cannot resolve or that it can resolve only at too great a cost to its power and prestige. In deciding that a particular case is appropriate for decision on the merits, the Supreme Court must recognize the impact of such a decision on future cases. Will it open a Pandora's box? Litigants are quick to recognize signs of judicial receptivity to a particular line of reasoning or set of claims. Thus, manipulation of access doctrines is important to the Supreme Court in defining its policy role and in controlling its work load.

Rules of access, including doctrines of self-limitation, are equally important from the perspective of potential litigants. They define the threshold of success in constitutional litigation. "Getting to the Supreme Court" is, almost, literally, more than half the battle. If citizens have no effective legal forum in which to vindicate constitutional rights, then the substantive importance of these rights is diminished. Not all would favor an expanded function for "private attorneys general,"[3] or Justice Douglas' view that trees should have "standing" in environmental suits.[4] But his view suggest the range of options that the Court must consider, and the important policy consequences of seemingly dry technical rules.

B. A Further Comment on the Case or Controversy Doctrine

Beginning as early as Marshall's landmark opinion in *Marbury* v. *Madison,* it has been accepted that the jurisdiction of the Supreme Court extended only to the "cases or controversies" mentioned in Article III of the Constitution. But what is a case or controversy? The Court has ruled on various occasions that there are three basic requirements. First, the litigation must be one with adverse parties, that is, parties who represent opposing positions or interests. Second, between these adverse parties there must be an actual dispute, as yet unsettled, and not merely a theoretical disagreement. And, third, the issue must be one in which the

[2]See, generally, Louis Jaffe, "Standing to Secure Judicial Review: Public Actions," 74 *Harvard Law Review* (1961), 1265–1314. Jaffee argues that while there is no substitute for judicial review of private wrongs, vindication of public actions would be better performed administratively. The prime argument, thus, for public action would be the absence of administrative and political controls. Public actions, according to Jaffee, "strain the judicial function and distort the political process."

[3]See *Alyeska Pipeline Service Co.* v. *Wilderness Society* (1975).

[4]See his opinion in *Sierra Club* v. *Morton* (1974).

Supreme Court can provide a remedy and have the final decision.

Out of the general case or controversy requirement, several specific applications developed. First, there is the rule against advisory opinions. An advisory opinion is one which is not issued to settle a case or controversy, but only hypothetically or in the abstract. Chief Justice Jay refused to respond to a request by President Washington for an opinion on the legality of a proposed treaty, setting a precedent which has been generally if not uniformly followed. Second, there is the rule against collusive or "friendly," suits between parties who have no real adverse interests. In 1892 the Supreme Court decided that "It was never thought that, by means of a friendly suit, a party beaten in the legislature could transfer to the courts an inquiry as to the constitutionality of the legislative act." But this requirement has often been evaded by the technique of a stockholders' suit. For example, the federal income tax was ruled unconstitutional in *Pollock* v. *Farmers' Loan Company* (1895). Pollock, a stockholder, sued the Farmers' Loan Company to prevent it from paying what he alleged to be an invalid federal tax. The bank defended by arguing that the tax was valid and that it wanted to pay. This was sheer duplicity, but since Pollock's interests and those of the bank were technically adverse, the obvious collusion was overlooked and a bare majority of the Court gleefully ruled that the tax was unconstitutional. A similar device was used successfully to invalidate the Guffey Coal Act of 1935, a major piece of New Deal Legislation, in *Carter* v. *Carter Coal Company* (1936).

On the other hand, there are many instances where the Supreme Court has refused to decide a case which appeared to lack the element of adverseness in the parties. In *Muskrat* v. *United States* (1911) the Court was faced with a question of the legality of redistribution of Indian lands under an act of Congress. Since Congress assumed that many Indians would be dissatisfied with the redistribution, the act itself provided that David Muskrat and others could bring suit in the Court of Claims, with a right of appeal to the Supreme Court, to test the validity of the statute. Congress also mandated that the court give preference to this case, and that Muskrat's attorneys' fees be paid by the government if he lost the decision. This was a bit too obvious, and the Court responded by dismissing the suit.

The third component of the case or controversy requirement is that the controversy between the litigants not be settled by the time it reaches the Court. If a decision can have no practical effect on the controversy, or if the law was changed to eliminate the basis of a complaint, the Court will normally dismiss the case as "moot." Until 1968, the Court interpreted this rule strictly. For example, in *Parker* v. *Ellis* (1960), the Court considered a case involving a claim for a writ of habeas corpus by a prisoner in Texas. By the time the case reached the Supreme Court, Parker had been released on parole, and the Court dismissed the action as moot. But this action ignored the practical fact that the conviction which was being attacked as illegal had consequences for the prisoner which extended beyond the question of his confinement. In 1968, in *Carafas* v. *LaVallee*, the Court ruled that it would hear a habeas corpus action even after the prisoner had been released from custody, if he had in fact been imprisoned when the action reached the

Supreme Court. Of course, this case merely altered the definition of what made a case moot. The previously mentioned decisions in the abortion and law school admission cases suggest the Court's flexibility in defining mootness. A case which is moot is still not a case or controversey under the Constitution.

Stemming from the case or controversy requirement are the concepts of standing to sue and standing to defend. These doctrines require that the litigant have a real, substantial, personal, and immediate interest in the litigation, not merely a general interest in the subject shared with other citizens. The rule in the federal courts until 1968 was that a citizen taxpayer did not have standing to contest the validity of a statute merely because some minute fraction of his tax assessments might be said to support the operation of the law. On the other hand, taxpayers' suits are frequently permitted under the more relaxed rules of state courts. But the fact that citizens can maintain such a suit at the state level is no assurance that they will have standing to pursue an otherwise valid appeal to the Supreme Court, which makes its own independent determination of the standing of the litigants in each case.

Two cases decided together in 1923 were, until 1968, the most authoritative pronouncements on the subject. Both cases challenged the constitutionality of a congressional statute providing for grant-in-aids to states subscribing to the provisions of the Maternity Act designed to reduce maternal and infant mortality and improve the health of mothers and infants. In *Massachusetts* v. *Mellon,* the state filed an original jurisdiction suit in the Supreme Court seeking to enjoin the operation of the act (Mellon, the nominal defendant, was Sec-

retary of the Treasury). In *Frothingham* v. *Mellon* a taxpayer sought a similar action in the courts of the District of Columbia and, on appeal, to the Supreme Court. In both cases it was alleged that the appropriations under the act were for local rather than national purposes, that the grant-in-aid provisions were an unconstitutional inducement to the states to surrender a portion of their sovereign rights, and that the burden of supporting such a statute with taxes fell unequally on the industrial states such as Massachusetts. The act, it was contended, was a usurpation of federal power and an invasion of states rights protected by the Tenth Amendment. Mrs. Frothingham claimed additionally that the statute would deprive her of her property, under the guise of taxation, without due process of law. And Massachusetts claimed on its own behalf and on the behalf of the citizens, *parens patriae,* that its powers as a sovereign state were invaded and the rights of its citizens infringed.

The Supreme Court dismissed both cases for want of jurisdiction. It found that Massachusetts could not sue merely to contest an abstract question of political power, and that the suit constituted a "political question" which was not justiciable. The state may not ordinarily intervene as *parens patriae* to protect its citizens from the actions of the federal government, since its citizens are first and foremost citizens of the United States. In the *Frothingham* case, the Court found that the relation of a taxpayer to federal expenditures is so minute and indeterminable that no court could possibly determine the extent of the taxpayer's interest in the expenditure. By contrast, the Court suggested, the interest of a taxpayer in municipal expenditures is direct and immediate. Furthermore, the Court considered the possible chaos that might result if individual taxpayers could by such suits tie up federal appropriations.

The requirement that an individual must have suffered a substantial and personal injury from the operation of a law in order to acquire the standing to challenge it can work a hardship on those seeking to vindicate their constitutional rights. Such persons are frequently forced to risk the punishment of breaking a law in order to get a legal determination of their rights. These risks can sometimes be circumvented by obtaining a declaratory judgment or legal determination of the rights of the parties in dispute in advance of the actual alleged abridgement of rights. The parties must show that there is an actual controversy, and that the threat of abridgement of rights is real and substantial. Most state courts and the federal courts are empowered to issue declaratory judgments.

Usually, a litigant may only sue to protect his or her own personal rights or, in a class action, the rights of others similarly situated. The converse of this rule is that a *defendant* in a suit may only assert his own constitutional rights. But under certain circumstances he may be able to assert the constitutional rights of a third party as a defense to the charges brought against him. For example, a defendant charged with violating a statute which, on its face, seems to abridge or threaten First Amendment rights, may attack the validity of the statute as a whole and as it applies generally, rather than only as applied to him in the instant case. Likewise, an association may be allowed standing to assert the constitutional rights of its individual members to free speech and association in contesting threats to its or-

ganizational integrity. The NAACP was thus permitted to defend its refusal to provide membership lists demanded by the state of Alabama of all corporations doing business within the state, on the grounds that to do so would be to expose its members in that state to harassment and violence and other deterrents to exercising their constitutional rights, *NAACP* v. *Alabama* (1958). In a related case, the NAACP was permitted to assert the First Amendment rights of its members in defense to a claim by Virginia that the organization had engaged in barratry (the illegal solicitation of legal business) and had otherwise violated the canons of legal ethics, *NAACP* v. *Button* (1963). For another example of the flexibility of the rule of standing to defend, see the Note on *Barrows* v. *Jackson* (1953), (Part Two, Chapter Two, pp. 528–530).

C. O'Shea v. Littleton (1974)

+Burger, Stewart, White, Powell, Rehnquist
+/−Blackmun
−Douglas, Brennan Marshall

[This case stems from a class action by a group of Negro and white residents of Cairo, Illinois, against two local judges. They claimed they were consistently discriminated against, as a result of their racial protest activities, in the criminal justice system. Specifically, they charged that persons who engaged in such activities and were arrested were held under illegal bond, subject to discriminatory sentences and subject to other wrongs that deprived them of their civil rights under the First, Sixth, Eighth, Thirteenth, and Fourteenth Amendments and the civil rights statutes. The federal district court dismissed the case for lack of jurisdiction to issue the injunction sought; the court of appeals reversed, holding that if the plaintiffs could prove what they alleged, they were entitled to injunctive relief.]

MR. JUSTICE WHITE delivered the opinion of the Court:

. . .

We reverse the judgment of the Court of Appeals. The complaint failed to satisfy the threshold requirement imposed by Art. III of the Constitution that those who seek to invoke the power of federal courts must allege an actual case or controversy. . . . Plaintiffs in the federal courts "must allege some threatened or actual injury resulting from the putatively illegal action before a federal court may assume jurisdiction." . . . There must be a "personal stake in the outcome" such as to "assure that concrete adverseness which sharpens the presentation of issues upon which the court so largely depends for illumination of difficult constitutional questions." *Baker* v. *Carr* . . . (1962). Nor is the principle different where statutory issues are raised. . . . Abstract injury is not enough. It must be alleged that the plaintiff "has sustained or is immediately in danger of sustaining some direct injury" as the result of the challenged statute or official conduct. *Massachusetts* v. *Mellon* . . . (1923). The injury or threat of injury must be both "real and immediate," not "conjectural" or "hypothetical." . . . Moreover, if none of the named plaintiffs purporting to represent a class establishes the requisite of a case or controversy with the defendants, none may seek relief on behalf of himself or any other member of the class. . . .

In the complaint that began this action, the sole allegations of injury are that petitioners "have engaged in, and continue to engage in, a pattern and practice of conduct . . . all of which has deprived, and continues to deprive, plaintiffs and members of their class of their constitutional rights" and, again, that petitioners "have denied and continue to deny to plaintiffs and members of their class their constitutional rights" by illegal bond, sentencing, and jury fee practices. None of the named plaintiffs is identified as having himself suffered any injury in the manner specified. In sharp contrast to the claim for relief against the State's Attorney where specific instances of misconduct with respect to particular individuals are alleged, the claim against petitioners alleged injury in only the most general terms. At oral argument, respondents' counsel stated that some of the named plaintiffs-respondents, who could be identified by name if necessary, had actually been defendants in proceedings before petitioners and had suffered from the alleged unconstitutional practices. Past exposure to illegal conduct does not in itself show a present case or controversy regarding injunctive relief, however, if unaccompanied by any continuing, present adverse effects. Neither the complaint nor respondents' counsel suggested that any of the named plaintiffs at the time the complaint was filed was himself serving an allegedly illegal sentence or was on trial or awaiting trial before petitioners. Indeed, if any of the respondents were then serving an assertedly unlawful sentence, the complaint would inappropriately be seeking relief from or modification of current, existing custody. . . . Furthermore, if any were then on trial or awaiting trial in state proceedings, the complaint would be seeking injunctive relief that a federal court should not provide. *Younger* v. *Harris* . . . (1971).

Of course, past wrongs are evidence bearing on whether there is a real and immediate threat of repeated injury. But here the prospect of future injury rests on the likelihood that respondents will again be arrested for and charged with violations of the criminal law and will again be subjected to bond proceedings, trial, or sentencing before petitioners. Important to this assessment is the absence of allegations that any relevant criminal statute of the State of Illinois is unconstitutional on its face or as applied that plaintiffs have been or will be improperly charged with violating criminal law. If the statutes that might possibly be enforced against respondents are valid laws, and if charges under these statutes are not improvidently made or pressed, the question becomes whether any peceived threat to respondents is sufficiently real and immediate to show any existing controversy simply because they anticipate violating lawful criminal statutes and being tried for their offenses, in which event they may appear before petitioners and, if they do, will be affected by the allegedly illegal conduct charged. Apparently, the proposition is that *if* respondents proceed to violate an unchallenged law and *if* they are charged, held to answer, and tried in any proceedings before petitioners, they will be subjected to the discriminatory practices that petitioners are alleged to have followed. But it seems to us that attempting to anticipate whether and when these respondents will be charged with crime and will be made to appear before either petitioner takes us into the area of speculation and conjecture. . . . The nature of the respondents' activities is not described in detail and no specific threats are alleged to

have been made against them. Accepting that they are deeply involved in a program to eliminate racial discrimination in Cairo and that tensions are high, we are nonetheless unable to conclude that the case or controversy requirement is satisfied by general assertions or inferences that in the course of their activities respondents will be prosecuted for violating valid criminal laws. We assume that respondents will conduct their activities within the law and so avoid prosecution and conviction as well as exposure to the challenged course of conduct said to be followed by petitioners.

As in *Golden* v. *Zwickler* . . . (1969), we doubt that there is "sufficient immediacy and reality" to respondents' allegations of future injury to warrant invocation of the jurisdiction of the District Court. There, "it was wholly conjectural that another occasion might arise when Zwickler might be prosecuted for distributing the handbills referred to in the complaint." . . . Here we can only speculate whether respondents will be arrested, either again or for the first time, for violating a municipal ordinance or a state statute, particularly in the absence of any allegations that unconstitutional criminal statutes are being employed to deter constitutionally protected conduct. . . . Even though *Zwickler* attacked a specific statute under which he had previously been prosecuted, the threat of a new prosecution was not sufficiently imminent to satisfy the jurisdictional requirements of the federal courts. Similarly, respondents here have not pointed to any imminent prosecutions contemplated against any of their number and they naturally do not suggest that any one of them expects to violate valid criminal laws. Yet their vulnerability to the alleged threatened injury from which relief is sought is necessarily contingent upon the bringing of prosecutions against one or more of them. Under these circumstances, where respondents do not claim any constitutional right to engage in conduct proscribed by therefore presumably permissible state laws, or that it is otherwise their intention to so conduct themselves, the threat of injury from the alleged course of conduct they attack is simply too remote to satisfy the "case or controversy" requirement and permit adjudication by a federal court. . . .

The foregoing considerations obviously shade into those determining whether the complaint states a sound basis for equitable relief; and even if we were inclined to consider the complaint as presenting an existing case or controversy, we would firmly disagree with the Court of Appeals that an adequate basis for equitable relief against petitioners had been stated. The Court has recently reaffirmed the "basic doctrine of equity jurisprudence that courts of equity should not act, and particularly should not act to restrain a criminal prosecution, when the moving party has an adequate remedy at law and will not suffer irreparable injury if denied equitable relief." *Younger* v. *Harris* . . . (1971). Additionally, recognition of the need for a proper balance in the concurrent operation of federal and state courts counsels restraint against the issuance of injunctions against state officers engaged in the administration of the State's criminal laws in the absence of a showing of irreparable injury which is "both great and immediate." . . .

A federal court should not intervene to establish the basis for future intervention that would be so intrusive and unworkable. In concluding that injunctive relief would be available in this case because it would not interfere with prosecutions to be commenced under challenged statutes, the Court of Appeals misconceived the underlying basis for withholding federal equitable relief when the normal course of criminal proceedings in the state courts would otherwise be disrupted. The objection is to unwarranted anticipatory interference in the state criminal process by means of continuous or piecemeal interruptions of the state proceedings by litigation in the federal courts; the object is to sustain "the special delicacy of the adjustment to be preserved between federal equitable power and State administration of its own law." . . . An injunction of the type contemplated by respondents and the Court of Appeals would disrupt the normal course of proceedings in the state courts via resort to the federal suit for determination of the claim *ab initio*, just as would the request for injunctive relief from an ongoing state prosecution against the federal plaintiff which was found to be unwarranted in *Younger*. Moreover, it would require for its enforcement the continuous supervision by the federal court over the conduct of the petitioners in the course of future criminal trial proceedings involving any of the members of the respondent's broadly-defined class. The Court of Appeals disclaimed any intention of requiring the District Court to sit in constant day-to-day supervision of these judicial officers, but the "periodic reporting" system it thought might be warranted would constitute a form of monitoring of the operation of state court functions that is antipathetic to established principles of comity. . . . Moreover, because an injunction against acts which might occur in the course of future criminal proceedings would necessarily impose continuing obligations of compliance, the question arises of how compliance might be enforced if the beneficiaries of the injunction were to charge that it had been disobeyed. Presumably, any member of respondents' class who appeared as an accused before petitioners could allege and have adjudicated a claim that petitioners were in contempt of the federal court's injunction order, with review of adverse decisions in the Court of Appeals and, perhaps, in this Court. Apart from the inherent difficulties in defining the proper standards against which such claims might be measured, and the significant problems of proving noncompliance in individual cases, such a major continuing intrusion of the equitable power of the federal courts into the daily conduct of state criminal proceedings is in sharp conflict with the principles of equitable restraint which this Court has recognized in the decisions previously noted.

Respondents have failed, moreover, to establish the basic requisites of the issuance of equitable relief in these circumstances—the likelihood of substantial and immediate irreparable injury, and the inadequacy of remedies at law. We have already canvassed the necessarily conjectural nature of the threatened injury to which respondents are allegedly subjected. And if any of the respondents are ever prosecuted and face trial, or if they are illegally sentenced, there are available state and federal procedures which could provide relief from the wrongful conduct alleged. Open to a victim of the discriminatory practices asserted under state law are the right to a substitution of judge or a change of venue, . . . review on direct appeal or on postconviction collateral review, and the opportunity to demonstrate that the conduct of these judicial officers is so prejudicial to the administration of justice that available disciplinary proceedings, including the possibility of suspension or removal, are warranted. . . . In appropriate circumstances, moreover, federal habeas relief would undoubtedly be available.

Nor is it true that unless the injunction sought is available federal law will exercise no deterrent effect in these circumstances. Judges who would willfully discriminate on the grounds of race or otherwise would willfully deprive the citizen of his constitutional rights, as this complaint alleges, must take account of 18 U.S.C. §242. . . . That section provides:

Whoever, under color of any law, statute, ordinance, regulation, or custom willfully subjects any inhabitant of any State . . . to the deprivation of any rights, privileges, or immunities, secured or protected by the Constitution or laws of the United States, or to different punishments, pains or penalties, on account of such inhabitant being an alien, or by reason of his color, or race, than are prescribed for the punishment of citizens, shall be fined . . . or imprisoned. . . .

Considering the availability of other avenues of relief open to respondents for the serious conduct they assert, and the abrasive and unmanageable intercession which the injunctive relief they seek would represent, we conclude that, apart from the absence of an existing case or controversy presented by respondents for adjudication, the Court of Appeals erred in deciding that the District Court should entertain respondents' claim.

Reversed.

MR. JUSTICE BLACKMUN, CONCURRING IN PART (OMITTED).
MR. JUSTICE DOUGLAS, WITH WHOM MR. JUSTICE BRENNAN AND MR. JUSTICE MARSHALL CONCUR, DISSENTING (OMITTED).

D. *Flast v. Cohen* (1968)

+Warren, Black, Douglas, Brennan, Stewart, White, Fortas, Marshall
 −Harlan

[In this suit against the secretary of Health, Education, and Welfare, the appellants as taxpayers sought to enjoin the allegedly unconstitutional expenditure of federal funds for the financing of instruction and purchasing of supplies for the teaching of secular subjects in parochial schools. The government moved to dismiss the suit on the grounds that appellants lacked standing to maintain the suit under the authority of *Frothingham* v. *Mellon* (1922). A three-judge federal court was convened and ruled against the appellants, who then appealed directly to the Supreme Court.]

MR. CHIEF JUSTICE WARREN delivered the opinion of the Court.
. . .
For reasons explained at length below, we hold that appellants do have standing as federal taxpayers to maintain this action, and the judgment below must be reversed. . . .
Although the barrier *Frothingham* erected against federal taxpayer suits has never been breached, the decision has been the source of some confusion and the object of considerable criticism. The confusion has developed as commentators have tried to determine whether *Frothingham* establishes a constitutional bar to taxpayer suits or whether the Court was simply invoking a rule of self-restraint which was not constitutionally compelled. The conflicting view-

points are reflected in the arguments made to this Court by the parties in this case. The Government has pressed upon us the view that *Frothingham* announced a constitutional rule, compelled by the Article III limitations on federal court jurisdiction and grounded in considerations of the doctrine of separation of powers. Appellants, however, insist that *Frothingham* expressed no more than a policy of judicial self-restraint which can be disregarded when compelling reasons for assuming jurisdiction over a taxpayer's suit exist. The opinion delivered in *Frothingham* can be read to support either position. The concluding sentence of the opinion states that, to take jurisdiction of the taxpayer's suit, "would not be to decide a judicial controversy, but to assume a position of authority over the governmental acts of another and co-equal department, an authority which plainly we do not possess." . . .
Yet the concrete reasons given for denying standing to a federal taxpayer suggest that the Court's holding rests on something less than a constitutional foundation. For example, the Court conceded that standing had previously been conferred on municipal taxpayers to sue in that capacity. However, the Court viewed the interest of a federal taxpayer in total federal tax revenues as "comparatively minute and indeterminable" when measured against a municipal taxpayer's interest in a smaller city treasury. . . . This suggests that the petitioner in *Frothingham* was denied standing not because she was a taxpayer but because her tax bill was not large enough. In addition, the Court spoke of the "attendant inconveniences" of entertaining that taxpayer's suit because it might open the door of federal courts to countless such suits "in

respect of every other appropriation act and statute whose administration requires the outlay of public money, and whose validity may be questioned." . . . Such a statement suggests pure policy considerations.

To the extent that *Frothingham* has been viewed as resting on policy considerations, it has been criticized as depending on assumptions not consistent with modern conditions. For example, some commentators have pointed out that a number of corporate taxpayers today have a federal tax liability running into hundreds of millions of dollars, and such taxpayers have a far greater monetary stake in the Federal Treasury than they do in any muncipal treasury. To some degree, the fear expressed in *Frothingham* that allowing one taxpayer to sue would inundate the federal courts with countless similar suits has been mitigated by the ready availability of the devices of class actions and joinder under the Federal Rules of Civil Procedure, adopted subsequent to the decision in *Frothingham*. Whatever the merits of the current debate over *Frothingham*, its very existence suggests that we should undertake a fresh examination of the limitations upon standing to sue in a federal court and the application of those limitations to taxpayer suits.

The jurisdiction of federal courts is defined and limited by Article III of the Constitution. In terms relevant to the question for decision in this case, the judicial power of federal courts is constitutionally restricted to "cases" and "controversies." As is so often the situation in constitutional adjudication, those two words have an iceberg quality, containing beneath their surface simplicity submerged complexities which go to the very heart of our constitutional form of government. Embodied in the words

"cases" and "controversies" are two complementary but somewhat different limitations. In part those words limit the business of federal courts to questions presented in an adversary context and in a form historically viewed as capable of resolution through the judicial process. And in part those words define the role assigned to the judiciary in a tripartite allocation of power to assure that the federal courts will not intrude into areas committed to the other branches of government. Justiciability is the term of art employed to give expression to this dual limitation placed upon federal courts by the case and controversy doctrine.

Justiciability is itself a concept of uncertain meaning and scope. Its reach is illustrated by the various grounds upon which questions sought to be adjudicated in federal courts have been held not to be justiciable. Thus, no justiciable controversy is presented when the parties seek adjudication of only a political question, when the parties are asking for an advisory opinion, when the question sought to be adjudicated has been mooted by subsequent developments, and when there is no standing to maintain the action. Yet it remains true that "[j]usticiability is . . . not a legal concept with a fixed content of susceptible or scientific verification. Its utilization is the resultant of many subtle pressures. . . ." *Poe* v. *Ullman* . . . (1961). . . .

Additional uncertainty exists in the doctrine of justiciability because that doctrine has become a blend of constitutional requirements and policy considerations. And a policy limitation is "not always clearly distinguished from the constitutional limitation." *Barrows* v. *Jackson* . . . (1953). For example, in his concurring opinion in *Ashwander* v. *Tennessee Valley Authority* . . . (1936),

Mr. Justice Brandeis listed seven rules developed by this Court "for its own governance" to avoid passing prematurely on constitutional questions. Because the rules operate in "cases confessedly within [the Court's] jurisdiction" . . . they find their source in policy, rather than purely constitutional, considerations. However, several of the cases cited by Mr. Justice Brandeis in illustrating the rules of self-governance articulated purely constitutional grounds for decision. . . . The many subtle pressures" which cause policy considerations to blend into the constitutional limitations of Article III make the justiciability doctrine one of uncertain and shifting contours.

It is in this context that the standing question presented by this case must be viewed and that the Government's argument on that question must be evaluated. As we understand it, the Government's position is that the constitutional scheme of separation of powers, and the deference owed by the federal judiciary to the other two branches of government within that scheme, presents an absolute bar to taxpayer suits challenging the validity of federal spending programs. The government views such suits as involving no more than the mere disagreement by the taxpayer "with the uses to which tax money is put." According to the Government, the resolution of such disagreements is committed to other branches of the Federal Government and not to the judiciary. Consequently, the Government contends that, under no circumstances, should standing be conferred on federal taxpayers to challenge a federal taxing or spending program. An analysis of the function served by standing limitations compels a rejection of the Government's position. . . .

Despite the complexities and un-

certainties, some meaningful form can be given to the jurisdictional limitations placed on federal court power by the concept of standing. The fundamental aspect of standing is that it focuses on the party seeking to get his complaint before a federal court and not on the issues he wishes to have adjudicated. The "gist of the question of standing" is whether the party seeking relief has "alleged such a personal stake in the outcome of the controversy as to assure that concrete adverseness which sharpens the presentation of issues upon which the court so largely depends for illumination of difficult constitutional questions." . . . In other words, when standing is placed in issue in a case, the question is whether the person whose standing is challenged is a proper party to request an adjudication of a particular issue and not whether the issue itself is justiciable. Thus, a party may have standing in a particular case, but the federal court may nevertheless decline to pass on the merits of the case because, for example, it presents a political question. . . .

When the emphasis in the standing problem is placed on whether the person invoking a federal court's jurisdiction is a proper party to maintain the action, the weakness of the Government's argument in this case becomes apparent. The question whether a particular person is a proper party to maintain the action does not, by its own force, raise separation of powers problems related to improper judicial interference in areas committed to other branches of the Federal Government. Such problems arise, if at all, only from the substantive issues the individual seeks to have adjudicated. Thus, in terms of Article III limitations on Federal court jurisdiction, the question of standing is related only to whether the dispute sought to be adjudicated will be presented in an adversary context and in a form historically viewed as capable of judicial resolution. It is for that reason that the emphasis in standing problems is on whether the party invoking federal court jurisdiction has "a personal stake in the outcome of the controversy," *Baker* v. *Carr* . . ., and whether the dispute touches upon "the legal relations of parties having adverse legal interests." . . . A taxpayer may or may not have the requisite personal stake in the outcome, depending upon the circumstances of the particular case. Therefore, we find no absolute bar in Article III to suits by federal taxpayers challenging allegedly unconstitutional federal taxing and spending programs. There remains, however, the problem of determining the circumstances under which a federal taxpayer will be deemed to have the personal stake and interest that imparts the necessary concrete adverseness to such litigation so that standing can be conferred on the taxpayer qua taxpayer consistent with the constitutional limitations of Article III.

The various rules of standing applied by federal courts have not been developed in the abstract. Rather, they have been fashioned with specific reference to the status asserted by the party whose standing is challenged and to the type of question he wishes to have adjudicated. We have noted that, in deciding the question of standing, it is not relevant that the substantive issues in the litigation might be nonjusticiable. However, our decisions establish that, in ruling on standing, it is both appropriate and necessary to look to the substantive issues for another purpose, namely, to determine whether there is a logical nexus between the status asserted and the claim sought to be adjudicated. For example, standing requirements will vary in First Amendment religion cases depending upon whether the party raises an Establishment Clause claim or a claim under the Free Exercise Clause. See *McGowan* v. *Maryland* . . . (1961). Such inquiries into the nexus between the status asserted by the litigant and the claim he presents are essential to assure that he is a proper and appropriate party to invoke federal judicial power. Thus, our point of reference in this case is the standing of individuals who assert only the status of federal taxpayers and who challenge the constitutionality of a federal spending program. Whether such individuals have standing to maintain that form of action turns on whether they can demonstrate the necessary stake as taxpayers in the outcome of the litigation to satisfy Article III requirements.

The nexus demanded of federal taxpayers has two aspects to it. First, the taxpayer must establish a logical link between that status and the type of legislative enactment attacked. Thus, a taxpayer will be a proper party to allege the unconstitutionality only of exercises of congressional power under the taxing and spending clause of Art. I, §8, of the Constitution. It will not be sufficient to allege an incidental expenditure of tax funds in the administration of an essentially regulatory statute. This requirement is consistent with the limitation imposed upon state taxpayer standing in federal courts in *Doremus* v. *Board of Education* . . . (1952). Secondly the taxpayer must establish a nexus between the status and the precise nature of the constitutional infringement alleged. Under this requirement, the taxpayer must show that the challenged enactment exceeds specific constitutional limitations imposed upon the exercise of the congressional taxing and spending power and not simply that the enactment is generally beyond the powers delegated to Congress by Art. I, §8. When both nexuses are established, the litigant will have shown a taxpayer's stake in the outcome of the controversy and will be a proper and appropriate party to invoke the federal court's jurisdiction.

The taxpayer-appellants in this case have satisfied both nexuses to support their claim of standing under the test we announce today. Their constitutional challenge is made to an exercise by Congress of its power under Art. I, §8, to spend for the general welfare, and the challenged program involves a substantial expenditure of federal tax funds. In addition, appellants have alleged that the challenged expenditures violate the Establishment and Free Exercise Clauses of the First Amendment. Our history vividly illustrates that one of the specific evils feared by those who drafted the Establishment Clause and fought for its adoption was that the taxing and spending power would be used to favor one religion over another or to support religion in general. . . .

The allegations of the taxpayer in *Frothingham* v. *Mellon* . . ., were quite different from those made in this case, and the result in *Frothingham* is consistent with the test of taxpayer standing announced today. The taxpayer in *Frothingham* attacked a federal spending program and she, therefore, established the first nexus required. However, she lacked standing because her constitutional attack was not based on an allegation that Congress, in enacting the Maternity Act of 1921, had breached a specific limitation upon its taxing and spending power. The

taxpayer in *Frothingham* alleged essentially that Congress, by enacting the challenged statute, had exceeded the general powers delegated to it by Art. I, §8, and that Congress had thereby invaded the legislative province reserved to the States by the Tenth Amendment. To be sure, Mrs. Frothingham made the additional allegation that her tax liability would be increased as a result of the allegedly unconstitutional enactment, and she framed that allegation in terms of a deprivation of property without due process of law. However, the Due Process Clause of the Fifth Amendment does not protect taxpayers against increases in tax liability, and the taxpayer in *Frothingham* failed to make any additional claim that the harm she alleged resulted from a breach by Congress of the specific constitutional limitations imposed upon an exercise of the taxing and spending power. In essence, Mrs. Frothingham was attempting to assert the States' interest in their legislative prerogatives and not a federal taxpayer's interest in being free of taxing and spending in contravention of specific constitutional limitations imposed upon Congress' taxing and spending power.

We have noted that the Establishment Clause of the First Amendment does specifically limit the taxing and spending power confered by Art. I, §8. Whether the Constitution contains other specific limitations can be determined only in the context of future cases. However, whenever such specific limitations are found, we believe a taxpayer will have a clear stake as a taxpayer in assuring that they are not breached by Congress. Consequently, we hold that a taxpayer will have standing consistent with Article III to invoke federal judicial power when he alleges that congressional action under the tax-

ing and spending clause is in derogation of those constitutional provisions
which operate to restrict the exercise
of the taxing and spending power. . . .
Under such circumstances, we feel
confident that the questions will be
framed with the necessary specificity, that the issues will be contested
with the necessary adverseness and
that the litigation will be pursued
with the necessary vigor to assure
that the constitutional challenge will
be made in a form traditionally
thought to be capable of judicial resolution. We lack that confidence in
cases such as *Frothingham* where a
taxpayer seeks to employ a federal
court as a forum in which to air his
generalized grievances about the
conduct of government or the allocation of power in the Federal System.
. . .

Reversed.

MR. JUSTICE DOUGLAS, CONCURRING.

While I have joined the opinion of
the Court, I do not think that the test
it lays down is a durable one for the
reasons stated by my Brother Harlan.
I think, therefore, that it will suffer
erosion and in time result in the demise of *Frothingham* v. *Mellon*. . . .
It would therefore be the part of wisdom, as I see the problem, to be rid of
Frothingham here and now.

I do not view with alarm, as does
my Brother Harlan, the consequences of that course. *Frothingham,* decided in 1923, was in the
heyday of substantive due process,
when courts were sitting in judgement on the wisdom or reasonableness of legislation. The claim in
Frothingham was that a federal regulatory Act dealing with maternity
deprived the plaintiff of property
without due process of law. When the
Court used substantive due process to
determine the wisdom or reasonableness of legislation, it was indeed

transforming itself into the Court of
Revision which was rejected by the
Constitutional Convention. It was
that judicial attitude, not the theory
of standing to sue rejected in
Frothingham, that involved "important hazards for the continued effectiveness of the federal judiciary," to
borrow a phrase from my Brother
Harlan. A contrary result in
Frothingham in that setting might
well have accentuated an ominous
trend to judicial supremacy.

But we no longer undertake to
exercise that kind of power. Today's
problem is in a different setting.

. . . I would not be niggardly therefore in giving private attorneys general standing to sue. I would certainly
not wait for Congress to give its blessing to our deciding cases clearly
within our Article III jurisdiction. To
wait for a sign from Congress is to
allow important Constitutional questions to go undecided and personal
liberty unprotected. . . .

I would be as liberal in allowing
taxpayers standing to object to these
violations of the First Amendment as
I would be in granting standing of
people to complain of any invasion of
their rights under the Fourth
Amendment or the Fourteenth or
under any other guarantee in the
Constitution itself or in the Bill of
Rights.

MR. JUSTICE STEWART, CONCURRING
(OMITTED).
MR. JUSTICE FORTAS, CONCURRING
(OMITTED).
MR. JUSTICE HARLAN, DISSENTING.

The problems presented by this
case are narrow and relatively
abstract, but the principles by which
they must be resolved involve
nothing less than the proper functioning of the federal courts, and so run to
the roots of our constitutional system.
The nub of my view is that the end

result of *Frothingham* v. *Mellon* . . ., was correct, even though, like others, I do not subscribe to all of its reasoning and premises. Although I therefore agree with certain of the conclusions reached today by the Court, I cannot accept the standing doctrine that it substitutes for *Frothingham,* for it seems to me that this new doctrine rests on premises that do not withstand analysis. Accordingly, I respectfully dissent.

. . . It seems to me clear that public actions, whatever the constitutional provisions on which they are premised, may involve important hazards for the continued effectiveness of the federal judiciary. Although I believe such actions to be within the jurisdiction conferred upon the federal courts by Article III of the Constitution, there surely can be little doubt that they strain the judicial function and press to the limit of judicial authority. There is every reason to fear that unrestricted public actions might well alter the allocation of authority among the three branches of the Federal Government. It is not, I submit, enough to say that the present members of the Court would not seize these opportunities for abuse, for such actions would, even without conscious abuse, go far toward the final transformation of this Court into the Council of Revision which, despite Madison's support, was rejected by the Constitutional Convention. I do not doubt that there must be "some effectual power in the government to restrain or correct the infractions" of the Constitution's several commands, but neither can I suppose that such power resides only in the federal courts. We must as judges recall that, as Mr. Justice Holmes wisely observed, the other branches of the Government "are ul-

timate guardians of the liberties and welfare of the people in quite as great a degree as the courts." . . . The powers of the federal judiciary will be adequate for the great burdens placed upon them only if they are employed prudently, with recognition of the strengths as well as the hazards that go with our kind of representative government. . . .

E. *United States v. Richardson* *(1974)*

+Burger, White, Blackmun, Powell, Rehnquist

−Douglas, Brennan, Stewart, Marshall

[Read narrowly, *Flast* v. *Cohen* opened but a small loophole in the rule of *Frothingham:* taxpayers had standing to challenge spending under the taxing and spending clause where that spending allegedly violated the establishment clause of the First Amendement. Read more broadly, *Flast* stated that a taxpayer might challenge the constitutionality of any bill, under the taxing and spending clause, which violated a specific constitutional prohibition that could be shown to specifically limit the taxing and spending power. Such taxpayers' suits, the Court said, did not constitute the sort of "generalized grievances" that *Frothingham* barred. Many chose to read *Flast* even more broadly, as an end-run around, if not a repudiation of, *Frothingham.* Certainly it was a common feeling that the doctrine of standing was being liberalized and that this was appropriate at a time when citizens in increasing numbers were going to court to express their grievances against the operation of government.

From 1968 to 1974 the Supreme Court's response to claims for continued expansion of the standing doctrine was mixed. A guiding principle was difficult to discern; indeed the Court itself noted that "generalizations about standing to sue are largely worthless as such."[1] A

---

[1]See *Association of Data Processing Service Organizations* v. *Camp* (1973).

few examples demonstrate the truth of this admission. The Court uniformly rejected efforts by various plaintiffs to challenge the legality of the war in Vietnam. And in *Laird* v. *Tatum* (1972), it refused to hear a complaint about Army surveillance of civilian political activity. Appellants were unable to show any objective "harm," only a subjective "chilling effect" of such surveillance to their constitutional rights. In the abortion case, *Roe* v. *Wade* (1973), a couple without children who claimed future problems if their efforts at contraception failed, were denied standing. The Court felt that their claim was too speculative.

Sierra Club v. *Morton* (1972) challenged a proposed recreational development by Walt Disney Enterprises on federal land in California. The Supreme Court agreed that "aesthetic and environmental well-being" are judicially protectable interests. But, the Court said, the Sierra Club's allegation that the development "would destroy or otherwise affect the scenery, natural and historic objects and wildlife of the park . . ." was insufficient. It did not state or allege any "injury in fact" to the club or to any of its members. Said Justice Stewart for a 4-3 majority:

The Club apparently regarded any allegations of individualized injury as superfluous, on the theory that this was a "public" action involving questions as to the use of natural resources, and that the Club's longstanding concern with and expertise in such matters were sufficient to give it standing as a "representative of the public." This theory reflects a misunderstanding of our cases involving so-called "public actions." . . .

This decision was not a major barrier to environmental suits since it turned on a defect in the pleadings (which was cured in subsequent litigation). In other environmental cases, in which specific allegations of harm were made, the federal courts accepted standing. Justice Douglas' dissent in the *Sierra Club* case suggested a special rule for environmental cases:

The critical question of "standing" would be simplified and also put neatly in focus if we fashioned a federal rule that allowed environmental issues to be litigated before federal agencies or federal courts in the name of the inanimate subject about to be despoiled, defaced, or invaded by roads and bulldozers and where injury is the subject of public outrage. Contemporary public concern for protecting nature's ecological equilibrium should lead to the conferral of standing upon environmental objects to sue for their own preservation. See Stone, Should Trees Have Standing?— Toward Legal Rights for Natural Objects, 45 S. Cal. L. Rev. 450 (1972). This suit would therefore be more properly labeled as "Mineral King v. Morton."

Inanimate objects are sometimes parties in litigation. A ship has a legal personality, a fiction found useful for maritime purposes. The corporation sole—a creature of ecclesiastical law—is an acceptable adversary and large fortunes ride on its cases. The ordinary corporation is a "person" for purposes of the adjudicatory processes, whether it represents propriety, spiritual, aesthetic, or charitable causes.

So it should be as respects valleys, alpine meadows, rivers, lakes, estuaries, beaches, ridges, groves of trees, swampland, or even air that feels the destructive pressures of modern technology and modern life. The river, for example, is the living symbol of all life it sustains or nourishes—fish, aquatic insects, water ouzels, otter, deer, elk, bear, and all other animals, including man, who are dependent on it or who enjoy it for its sight, its sound, or its life. The river as plaintiff speaks for the ecological unit of life that is part of it. Those people who have a meaningful relation to that body of water—whether it be a fisherman, a canoeist, a zoologist, or a logger—must be able to speak for the values which the river represents and which are threatened with destruction. . . .

The Solicitor General takes a wholly different approach. He considers the problem in terms of "government by the Judiciary." With all respect, the problem is to make certain that the inanimate objects, which are the very core of America's beauty, have spokesmen before they are destroyed. It is, of course, true that most of them are under the control of a federal or state agency. The standards given those agencies are usually expressed in terms of the "public interest." Yet "public interest" has so many differing shades of meaning as to be quite meaningless on the environmental front. . . .

Yet the pressures on agencies for favorable action one way or the other are enormous. The suggestion that Congress can stop action which is undesirable is true in theory; yet even Congress is too remote to give meaningful direction and its machinery is too ponderous to use very often. The federal agencies of which I speak are not venal or corrupt. But they are notoriously under the control of powerful interests who manipulate them through advisory committees, or friendly working relations, or who have that natural affinity with the agency which in time develops between the regulator and the regulated. . . .

The voice of the inanimate object, therefore, should not be stilled. That does not mean that the judiciary takes over the managerial functions from the federal agency. It merely means that before these priceless bits of Americana (such as a valley, an alpine meadow, a river, or a lake) are forever lost or are so transformed as to be reduced to the eventual rubble of our urban environment, the voice of the existing beneficiaries of these environmental wonders should be heard.

Perhaps they will not win. Perhaps the bulldozers of "progress" will plow under all the aesthetic wonders of this beautiful land. That is not the present question. The sole question is, who has standing to be heard?

That the defect in standing in *Sierra Club* was technical became clear in a case the following year, *United States* v. *SCRAP* (Students Challenging Regulatory Agency Procedures). Five law students formed an unincorporated association and challenged the failure of the Interstate Commerce Commission to suspend a temporary surcharge on freight rates. The alleged injury, which the Court referred to as an

acceptable if "attenuated line of causation," was as follows: a general rate increase would allegedly cause increased use of nonrecyclable commodities as compared to recyclable goods. Some of these resources might be taken from the Washington area (where the students lived) and might result in more refuse being discarded in national parks in that area. The students alleged that its members breathe the air and use the forest, rivers, streams, and so on in those parks and that they would suffer economic, recreational, and aesthetic harm. The Supreme Court accepted standing, rejecting the argument that the alleged harm was too widespread and diffuse to isolate any individual harm done to the plaintiffs. Three dissenting justices argued that "the alleged injuries are so remote, speculative and insubstantial in fact that they fail to confer standing."

In the past, most rules of standing have been judge-made. Where judicial challenges are provided for by statute, as in the Administrative Procedure Act, the Court has applied a relatively looser standard. Both *Sierra Club* and *SCRAP* involved "statutory" standing. This is not a violation of the *Muskrat* rule. Congress cannot authorize a federal court to decide a case that is not a "case or controversy." But the definition of a case or controversy, as we have seen, is flexible enough to permit some stretching. A case or controversy, it might be said, is what a Court, in fact, decides it is.

The *Richardson* case is particularly important because it signals a turn toward a new restrictive view of standing, a view particularly responsive to the views of Chief Justice Burger that the Supreme Court was overstepping its bounds by meddling in all sorts of public policy issues.]

MR. CHIEF JUSTICE BURGER delivered the opinion of the Court.

We granted certiorari in this case to determine whether the respondent has standing to bring an action as a federal taxpayer alleging that certain provisions concerning public reporting of expenditures under the Central Intelligence Agency Act. . . (1970), violate Art. 1, § 9, cl. 7 of the Constitution which provides:

No Money shall be drawn from the Treasury, but in Consequence of Appropriations made by Law; and a regular Statement of Account of the Receipts and Expenditures of all public money shall be published from time to time.

Respondent brought this suit in the United States District Court on a complaint in which he recites attempts to obtain from the Government information concerning detailed expenditures of the Central Intelligence Agency. According to the complaint, respondent wrote to the Government Printing Office in 1967 and requested that he be provided with the documents "published by the Government in compliance with Article I, section 9, clause (7) of the United States Constitution." The Fiscal Service of the Bureau of Accounts of the Department of the Treasury replied, explaining that it published the document known as the "Combined Statement of Receipts, Expenditures, and Balances of the United States Government." Several copies of the monthly and daily reports of the office were sent with the letter. Respondent then wrote to the same office and, quoting part of the CIA Act, asked whether this statute did not "cast reflection upon the authenticity of the Treasury's statement." He also inquired as to how he could receive further information on the expenditures of the CIA. The Bureau of Accounts replied stating that it had no other available information.

In another letter, respondent asserted that the CIA Act was repugnant to the Constitution and requested that the Treasury Department seek an opinion of the Attorney General. The Department answered declining to seek such an opinion and this suit followed. . . . In essence, the respondent asked the federal court to declare unconstitutional that provision of the Central Intelligence Agency Act which permits the Agency to account for its expenditures "solely on the certificate of the Director. . . ." . . . The only injury alleged by respondent was that he "cannot obtain a document that sets out the expenditures and receipts" of the CIA but on the contrary was "asked to accept a fraudulent document." The District Court granted a motion for dismissal on the ground respondent lacked standing under *Flast* v. *Cohen* . . . (1968), and that the subject matter raised political questions not suited for judicial disposition.

The Court of Appeals sitting *en banc*, with three judges dissenting, reversed, . . . holding that the respondent had standing to bring this action. The majority relied chiefly on *Flast* v. *Cohen* . . . and its two-tier test that taxpayer standing rests on a showing of (a) a "logical link" between the status as a taxpayer and the challenged legislative enactment, *i.e.*, an attack on an enactment under the taxing and spending clause of Art. I, §8 of the Constitution; and (b) a "nexus" between the plaintiff's status and a specific constitutional limitation imposed on the taxing and spending power. . . . While noting that the respondent did not directly attack an appropriations act, as did the plaintiff in *Flast*, the Court of Appeals concluded that the CIA statute challenged by the respondent was "integrally related," . . . to his ability to challenge the appropriations since he could not question an appropriation about which he had no knowledge. The Court of Appeals seemed to rest its holding on an assumption that this case was a prelude to a later case challenging, on the basis of information obtained in this suit, some particular appropriation for or expenditure of the CIA; respondent stated no such an intention in his complaint. The dissenters took a different approach urging denial of standing principally because, in their view, respondent alleged no specific injury but only a general interest common to all members of the public.

We conclude that respondent lacks standing to maintain a suit for the relief sought and we reverse.

As far back as *Marbury* v. *Madison* . . . (1803), this Court held that judicial power may be exercised only in a case properly before it—a "case or controversy" not suffering any of the limitations of the political question doctrine, not then moot or calling for an advisory opinion. . . . Recently in *Association of Data Processing Service Organizations, Inc.* v. *Camp* . . . (1970), the Court, while noting that "[g]eneralizations about standing to sue are largely worthless as such," . . . emphasized that "[o]ne generalization is, however, necessary and that is that the question of standing in the federal courts is to be considered in the framework of Art. III which restricts judicial power to 'cases' and 'controversies.' "

Although the recent holding of the Court in *Flast* v. *Cohen* . . . is a starting point in an examination of respondent's claim to prosecute this suit as a taxpayer, that case must be read with reference to its principal predecessor, *Frothingham* v. *Mellon* . . . (1923). In *Frothingham*, the injury alleged was that the congressional enactment challenged as unconstitutional would, if implemented, increase the complainant's future federal income taxes. Denying standing, the *Frothingham* Court rested on the "comparatively minute . . . remote, fluctuating and uncertain," . . . impact on the taxpayer, and the failure to allege the kind of direct injury required for standing. . . .

When the Court addressed the question of standing in *Flast*, Chief Justice Warren traced what he de-scribed as the "confusion" following *Frothingham* as to whether the Court had announced a constitutional doctrine barring suits by taxpayers challenging federal expenditures as unconstitutional or simply a policy rule of judicial self-restraint. In an effort to clarify the confusion and to take into account intervening developments, of which class actions and joinder under the Federal Rules of Civil Procedure were given as examples, the Court embarked on "a fresh examination of the limitations upon standing to sue in a federal court and the application of those limitations to taxpayer suits." . . . That re-examination led, however, to the holding that a "taxpayer will have standing *consistent with Article III* to invoke federal judicial power when he alleges that congressional action under the taxing and spending clause is in derogation of those constitutional provisions *which operate to restrict the exercise of the taxing and spending power.*" (Emphasis supplied.) . . . The Court then announced a two-pronged standing test which requires allegations: (a) challenging an enactment under the taxing and spending clause of Art. I, §8 of the Constitution; and (b) claiming that the challenged enactment exceeds specific constitutional limitations imposed on the taxing and spending power. . . . While the "impenetrable barrier to suits against Acts of Congress brought by individuals who can assert only the interest of federal taxpayers," . . . had been slightly lowered, the Court made clear it was reaffirming the principle of *Frothingham* precluding a taxpayer's use of "a federal court as a forum in which to air his generalized grievances about the conduct of government or the allocation of power in the Federal System." . . .

Although the Court made it very

explicit in *Flast* that a "fundamental aspect of standing" is that it focuses primarily on the *party* seeking to get his complaint before the federal court rather than "on the issues he wishes to have adjudicated," . . . it made equally clear that

in ruling on [taxpayer] standing, it is both appropriate and necessary to look to the substantive issues for another purpose, namely to determine whether there is a logical nexus between the status asserted and the claim sought to be adjudicated. . . .

We therefore turn to an examination of the issues sought to be raised by respondent's complaint to determine whether he is "a proper and appropriate party to invoke federal judicial power," . . . with respect to those issues.

We need not and do not reach the merits of the constitutional attack on the statute; our inquiry into the "substantive issues" is for the limited purpose indicated above. The mere recital of the respondent's claims and an examination of the statute under attack demonstrates how far he falls short of the standing criteria of *Flast* and how neatly he falls within the *Frothingham* holding left undisturbed. Although the status he rests on is that he is a taxpayer, his challenge is not addressed to the taxing or spending power but to the statutes regulating the CIA, . . . That section provides different accounting and reporting requirements and procedures for the CIA, as is also done with respect to other governmental agencies dealing in confidential areas.

Respondent makes no claim that appropriated funds are being spent in violation of a "specific constitutional limitation upon the . . . taxing and spending power. . . ." . . . Rather, he asks the courts to compel the Government to give him information on

precisely how the CIA spends its funds. Thus there is no "logical nexus" between the asserted status of taxpayer and the claimed failure of the Congress to require the Executive to supply a more detailed report of the expenditures of that agency.

The question presented thus is simply and narrowly whether these claims meet the standards for taxpayer standing set forth in *Flast;* we hold they do not. Respondent is seeking "to employ a federal court as a forum in which to air his generalized grievances about the conduct of the government." . . . Both *Frothingham* and *Flast* . . . reject that basis for standing.

The Court of Appeals held that the basis of taxpayer standing

need not be the appropriation and spending of [Petitioner's] money for an invalid purpose. The personal stake may come from an injury in fact even if it is not directly economic in nature. . . .

The respondent's claim is that without detailed information on CIA expenditures—and hence its activities—he cannot intelligently follow the actions of Congress or the Executive, nor can he properly fulfill his obligations as a member of the electorate in voting for candidates seeking national office.

This is surely the kind of a generalized grievance described in both *Frothingham* and *Flast* since the impact on him is plainly undifferentiated and "common to all members of the public." *Ex parte Levitt* . . . (1938); *Laird* v. *Tatum* . . . (1972). While we can hardly dispute that this respondent has a genuine interest in the use of funds and that his interest may be prompted by his status as a taxpayer, he has not alleged that, as a taxpayer, he is in danger of suffering any particular concrete injury as a result of the operation of this statute. . . .

It can be argued that if respondent is not permitted to litigate this issue, no one can do so. In a very real sense, the absence of any particular individual or class to litigate these claims gives support to the argument that the subject matter is committed to the surveillance of Congress, and ultimately to the political process. Any other conclusion would mean that the Founding Fathers intended to set up something in the nature of an Athenian democracy or a New England town meeting to oversee the conduct of the National Government by means of lawsuits in federal courts. The Constitution created a *representative* Government with the representatives directly responsible to their constituents at stated periods of two, four, and six years; that the Constitution does not afford a judicial remedy does not, of course, completely disable the citizen who is not satisfied with the "ground rules" established by the Congress for reporting expenditures of the Executive Branch. Lack of standing within the narrow confines of Art. III jurisdiction does not impair the right to assert his views in the political forum or at the polls. Slow, cumbersome and unresponsive though the traditional electoral process may be thought at times, our system provides for changing members of the political branches when dissatisfied citizens convince a sufficient number of their fellow electors that elected representatives are delinquent in performing duties committed to them.

As our society has become more complex, our numbers more vast, our lives more varied and our resources more strained, citizens increasingly request the intervention of the courts on a greater variety of issues than at any period of our na-

tional development. The acceptance of new categories of judicially cognizable injury has not eliminated the basic principle that to invoke judicial power the claimant must have a "personal stake in the outcome," *Baker* v. *Carr*, . . . or a "particular concrete injury," *Sierra Club*, . . . in short, something more than "generalized grievances," . . . Respondent has failed to meet these fundamental tests; accordingly, the judgment of the Court of Appeals is reversed.

MR. JUSTICE POWELL, CONCURRING (OMITTED)
MR. JUSTICE DOUGLAS, DISSENTING (OMITTED)
MR. JUSTICE STEWART, WITH WHOM MR. JUSTICE MARSHALL JOINS, DISSENTING.

The Court's decisions in *Flast* v. *Cohen* . . . (1968), and *Frothingham* v. *Mellon* . . . (1923), throw very little light on the question at issue in this case. For, unlike the plaintiffs in those cases, Richardson did not bring this action asking a court to invalidate a federal statute on the ground that it was beyond the delegated power of Congress to enact or that it contravened some constitutional prohibition. Richardson's claim is of an entirely different order. It is that Art. I, § 9, cl. 7 of the Constitution, the Statement and Account Clause, gives him a right to receive, and imposes on the Government a corresponding affirmative duty to supply, a periodic report of the receipts and expenditures "of all public Money." In support of his standing to litigate this claim, he has asserted his status both as a taxpayer and as a citizen-voter. Whether the Statement and Account Clause imposes upon the Government an affirmative duty to supply the information requested and whether that duty runs to every tax-payer or citizen are questions that go to the substantive merits of this litigation. Those questions are not now before us, but I think that the Court is quite wrong in holding that the respondent was without standing to raise them in the trial court. . . .

F. A Note on the Doctrine of Ripeness and the Birth Control Issue

The right of a state to ban or limit the use or conveyance of birth control devices and information was long an explosive political issue. Connecticut was one of several states in which such statutes, enacted during the late nineteenth century, remained on the books but were virtually never enforced. The ethnic and religious composition of the state had changed radically since the law was enacted and a political stalemate ensued. There would have been no possibility of passing such a law anew, but the dominant Catholic forces in the state refused to consent to its repeal. Liberals seeking repeal thus sought the aid of the judiciary.

In 1943 the first birth control case from Connecticut came to the Supreme Court, *Tileston* v. *Ullman*. Tileston was a doctor who sought a declaratory judgment from the Connecticut courts that the law, which prohibited the use of drugs or instruments to prevent conception as well as giving advice or assistance in their use, was unconstitutional as applied to him and his patients. He stated that the statute would prevent him from giving professional advice to three women patients whose lives might be endangered by further childbearing; he further alleged that law enforcement officers intended to prosecute him for giving this advice.

The Connecticut court upheld the validity of the statute and interpreted it as a prohibition against his giving such advice. The Supreme Court of the United States, in a *per curiam* opinion, ruled that Tileston had no standing to assert the constitutional rights of his patients. This ruling followed the doctrine limiting access to the courts to those alleging a personal injury, but the Court might well have exercised another option open to it. In *Pierce* v. *Society of Sisters* (1927), a parochial school was permitted to challenge the constitutionality of an Oregon statute requiring parents to send their children to public schools, and the Court might have found that Dr. Tileston had such a close relationship with his patients as to permit him also to sue in their behalf. But the birth control issue obviously would have been an explosive issue in 1943 and the justices' caution is understandable.

Attempts to repeal or invalidate the Connecticut statute continued, and a second suit was begun under the state declaratory judgment act. Seeking to avoid the pitfalls of the *Tileston* case, the suit was brought by two woman patients and their obstetrician. The women, suing under the fictitious names of Poe and Doe, alleged that they might suffer irreparable damage to their health, and possible death, if they were to become pregnant again. Mrs. Poe also alleged that she had already borne three defective children each of whom died almost immediately after birth. Dr. Buxton, a professor at the Yale Medical School and the women's obstetrician, alleged the same facts and claimed that the statute prohibiting him from giving contraceptive advice to these women deprived him of liberty and property without due process of the law. It was generally known that these test cases were designed to clear the legal path for the opening of a birth control clinic in New Haven. The suits alleged that

Ullman, the state's attorney, "intends to prosecute any offense" against the birth control statute, an allegation confirmed by Ullman. But the attorney for the plaintiffs, Professor Fowler Harper of the Yale Law School, was forced to concede in oral argument before the Supreme Court that there never had been enforcement of the law against *users,* and that contraceptives were notoriously available and sold throughout the state.

By a 5-4 decision the Supreme Court again refused to consider the constitutionality of the Connecticut statute. Justice Frankfurter argued for the majority that the facts showed no real threat of enforcement nor any realistic fear of prosecution of a private physician advising his patients. Thus, Frankfurter found, the case was not yet "ripe" for decision and to decide it would be merely to issue an abstract or advisory opinion. In a brief concurring opinion, Justice Brennan argued that the record did not demonstrate that the plaintiffs were caught in an "inescapable dilemma." He noted that the suit was intended to clear away the legal barriers to opening a birth control clinic in New Haven—a very different proposition than the alleged threat of prosecution of a private physician or user of contraceptives. "It will," he said, "be time enough to decide the constitutional questions urged upon us when, if ever, that real controversy flares up again."

Shortly after *Poe* v. *Ullman* was decided, the Planned Parenthood League of Connecticut opened a clinic in New Haven, "to provide instruction, and medical advice to married persons. . . ." Charges were brought against the director, Mrs. A. Whitney Griswold, widow of the late president of Yale University, and against the medical director, Dr. Buxton, one of the plaintiffs in the *Poe* case. They were convicted of "aiding, abetting, and counselling" married women in violation of the statute and fined $100 each. The convictions were affirmed by the Connecticut Supreme Court of Errors, and an appeal was taken to the Supreme Court of the United States in *Griswold* v. *Connecticut* (1965).

Now there could be no question of "ripeness," since an actual criminal conviction had ensued. There remained still a question of standing to defend, since attorneys for Mrs. Griswold and Dr. Buxton asserted in their behalf that the rights of the married persons whom they had counseled were violated by the statute. Distinguishing both the *Tileston* and *Poe* cases, Justice Douglas argued that whereas it was appropriate to enforce strict standards of standing in declaratory judgment actions, more lenient standards were appropriate in a criminal case. Justice Frankfurter had retired from the Court, and there was no dissent from the proposition that the Court now ought to decide on the validity of the birth control statute. By a 7-2 vote, the statute was found to be unconstitutional. (The *Griswold* case is discussed further in Part Two, Chapter 5.)[1]

In a similar situation the Court

[1]In a later birth control case, *Eisenstadt* v. *Baird* (1972), Baird, a married person, was prosecuted for illegal public display and distribution of birth control devices at a lecture at Boston University. The statute prohibited anyone but registered pharmacists from distributing birth control devices. And such devices could only be sold to married persons. Baird was granted standing to challenge the constitutionality of the statute, as "an advocate of the rights of persons to obtain contraceptives" and also because the statute would "naturally impair the ability of single persons to obtain contraceptives."

applied the "ripeness" doctrine to prevent federal court interference with an allegedly threatened state prosecution. Black residents in Chicago asked for an injunction against the enforcement of several state statutes prohibiting mob action, resisting arrest, and intimidation. Justice Black, for the majority, argued that there was no showing of irreparable harm that might occur if the state were to bring criminal charges under the statutes: "The normal course of state criminal prosecutions cannot be disrupted or blocked on the basis of charges which in the last analysis amount to nothing more than speculation about the future. The policy of a century and a half against interference by the federal courts with state law enforcement is not to be set aside on such flimsy allegations as those relied upon here." The proper duty of the federal court was to abstain until state proceedings were exhausted or there was a clear case of intimidation and harassment, *Boyle* v. *Landry* (1971).

G. *Younger* v. *Harris* (1971)

+Black, Burger, Harlan, Brennan, Stewart, White, Marshall, Blackmun
  −Douglas

[Harris was indicted in a California court for violation of the California Criminal Syndicalism Act, an act held valid in *Whitney* v. *California* (1927). Criminal syndicalism is the crime of advocating or aiding and abetting the commission of crime, sabotage or other unlawful acts of force designed to accomplish "a change in industrial ownership or control or effecting any political change." Harris sought an injunction in the federal courts to prohibit this prosecution on the ground that both the prosecution and the mere existence of the act inhibited him in the exercise of rights guaranteed by the First and Fourteenth Amendments.

A virtually identical statute had been held unconstitutional by the Supreme Court in *Brandenberg* v. *Ohio* (1969); the Court noted in its *per curiam* opinion that *Whitney* had been thoroughly discredited by later decisions. It stated: "Accordingly we are here confronted with a statute which, by its own words, purports to punish mere advocacy and to forbid, on pain of criminal punishment, assembly with others merely to advocate the described type of action. Such a statute falls within the condemnation of the First and Fourteenth Amendments. The contrary teaching of (*Whitney* v. *California*) cannot be supported, and that decision is therefore overruled." A three-judge federal court held the act void for vagueness and overbreadth contrary to the First and Fourteenth Amendments. The state appealed.]

MR. JUSTICE BLACK delivered the opinion of the Court.

Since the beginning of this Country's history Congress has, subject to few exceptions, manifested a desire to permit state courts to try state cases free from interference by federal courts. In 1793 an Act unconditionally provided: ". . . nor shall a writ of injunction be granted to stay proceedings in any court of any state. . . ." A comparison of the 1793 Act with 28 U. S. C. § 2283, its present-day successor, graphically illustrates how few and minor have been the exceptions granted from the flat, prohibitory language of the old Act. During all this lapse of years from 1793 to 1970 the statutory exceptions to the 1793 congressional enactment have been only three: (1) ". . . except as expressly authorized by Act of Congress . . ."; (2) ". . . where necessary in aid of its jurisdiction . . ."; and (3) ". . . to protect or effectuate its judgments . . . ." In addition, a judicial exception to the long-standing policy evidenced by the statute has been made where a person about to be prosecuted in a state court can show that he will, if the proceeding in the state court is not enjoined, suffer irreparable damages. . . .

The precise reasons for this longstanding public policy against federal court interference with state court proceedings have never been specifically identified but the primary sources of the policy are plain. One is the basic doctrine of equity jurisprudence that courts of equity should not act, and particularly should not act to restrain a criminal prosecution, when the moving party has an adequate remedy at law and will not suffer irreparable injury if denied equitable relief. The doctrine may originally have grown out of circumstances peculiar to the English judicial system and not applicable in this country, but its fundamental purpose of restraining equity jurisdiction within narrow limits is equally important under our Constitution, in order to prevent erosion of the role of the jury and avoid a duplication of legal proceedings and legal sanctions where a single suit would be adequate to protect the rights asserted. This underlying reason for restraining courts of equity from interfering with criminal prosecutions is reinforced by an even more vital consideration, the notion of "comity," that is a proper respect for state functions, a recognition of the fact that the entire country is made up of a Union of separate state governments, and a continuance of the belief that the National Government will fare best if the States and their institutions are left free to perform their separate functions in their separate ways. . . . The concept does not mean blind deference to "States' Rights" any more than it means centralization of control over every important issue in our National Government and its courts. The Framers rejected both these courses. What the concept does represent is a system in which there is sensitivity to the legitimate interests of both State and National Governments, and in which the National Government, anxious though it may be to vindicate and protect federal rights and federal interests, always endeavors to do so in ways that will not unduly interfere with the legitimate activities of the States. . . .

This brief discussion should be enough to suggest some of the reasons why it has been perfectly natural for our cases to repeat time and time again that the normal thing to do when federal courts are asked to enjoin pending proceedings in state courts is not to issue such injunctions. . . .

This is where the law stood when the Court decided *Dombrowski* v. *Pfister* . . . (1965), and held that an injunction against the enforcement of certain state criminal statutes could properly issue under the circumstances presented in that case. In *Dombrowski*, . . . the complaint made substantial allegations that:

the threats to enforce the statutes against appellants are not made with any expectation of securing valid convictions, but rather are part of a plan to employ arrests, seizures, and threats of prosecution under color of the statutes to harass appellants and discourage them and their supporters from asserting and attempting to vindicate the constitutional rights of Negro citizens of Louisiana.

The appellants in *Dombrowski* had offered to prove that their offices had been raided and all their files and records seized pursuant to search and arrest warrants that were later summarily vacated by a state judge for lack of probable cause. They also offered to prove that despite the state court order quashing the warrants and suppressing the evidence seized, the prosecutor was continuing to threaten to initiate new prosecutions of appellants under the same statutes, was holding public hearings at which photostatic copies of the illegally seized documents were being used, and was threatening to use other copies of the illegally seized documents to obtain grand jury indictments against the appellants on charges of violating the same statutes. These circumstances, as viewed by the Court sufficiently establish the kind of irreparable injury, above and beyond that associated with the defense of a single prosecution brought in good faith, that had always been considered sufficient to justify federal intervention. . . .

It is against the background of these principles that we must judge the propriety of an injunction under the circumstances of the present case. Here a proceeding was already pending in the state court, affording Harris an opportunity to raise his constitutional claims. There is no suggestion that this single prosecution against Harris is brought in bad faith or is only one of a series of repeated prosecutions to which he will be subjected. In other words, the injury that Harris faces is solely "that incidental to every criminal proceeding brought lawfully and in good faith," . . . and therefore under the settled doctrine we have already described he is not entitled to equitable relief "even if such statutes are unconstitutional."

The District Court, however, thought that the *Dombrowski* decision substantially broadened the availability of injunctions against state criminal prosecutions and that under that decision the federal courts may give equitable relief, without regard to any showing of bad faith or harassment, whenever a state statute is found "on its face" to be vague or overly broad, in violation of the First Amendment. We recognize that there are some statements in the *Dombrowski* opinion that would seem to support this argument. But as we have already seen, such statements were unnecessary to the decision of that case, because the Court found that the plaintiffs had alleged a basis for equitable relief under the long-established standards. In addition, we do not regard the reasons adduced to support this position as sufficient to justify such a substantial departure from the established doctrines regarding the availability of injunctive relief. It is undoubtedly true, as the Court stated in *Dombrowski,* that "A criminal prosecution under a statute regulating expression usually involves imponderables and contingencies that themselves may inhibit the full exercise of First Amendment freedoms." . . . But this sort of "chilling effect," as the Court called it, should not by itself justify federal intervention. In the first place, the chilling effect cannot be satisfactorily eliminated by federal injunctive relief. In *Dombrowski* itself the Court stated that the injunction to be issued there could be lifted if the State obtained an "acceptable limiting construction" from the state courts. The Court then made clear that once this was done, prosecutions could then be brought for conduct occurring before the narrowing construction was made, and proper convictions could stand so long as the defendants were not deprived of fair warning. . . . The kind of relief granted in *Dombrowski* thus does not effectively eliminate uncertainty as to the coverage of the state statute and leaves most citizens with virtually the same doubts as before regarding the danger that their conduct might eventually be subjected to criminal sanctions. The chilling effect can, of course, be eliminated by an injunction that would prohibit any prosecution whatever for conduct occurring prior to a satisfactory rewriting of the statute. But the States would then be stripped of all power to prosecute even the socially dangerous and constitutionally unprotected conduct that had been covered by the statute, until a new statute could be passed by the state legislature and approved by the federal courts in potentially lengthy trial and appellate proceedings. Thus, in *Dombrowski* itself the Court carefully reaffirmed the principle that even in the direct prosecution in the State's own courts, a valid narrowing construction can be applied to conduct occurring prior to the date when the narrowing construction was made, in the absence of fair warning problems.

Moreover, the existence of a "chilling effect," even in the area of First Amendment rights, has never been considered a sufficient basis, in and of itself, for prohibiting state action. Where a statute does not directly abridge free speech, but—while regulating a subject within the State's power—tends to have the incidental effect of inhibiting First Amendment rights, it is well settled that the statute can be upheld if the effect on speech is minor in relation to the need for control of the conduct and the lack of alternative means for doing so. . . . Just as the incidental "chilling effect" of such statutes does not automatically render them unconstitutional, so the chilling effect that admittedly can result from the very existence of certain laws on the statute books does not in itself justify prohibiting the State from carrying out the important and necessary task of enforcing these laws against so-

cially harmful conduct that the State believes in good faith to be punishable under its laws and the Constitution.

Beyond all this is another, more basic consideration. Procedures for testing the constitutionality of a statute "on its face" in the manner apparently contemplated by *Dombrowski,* and for then enjoining all action to enforce the statute until the State can obtain court approval for a modified version, are fundamentally at odds with the function of the federal courts in our constitutional plan. The power and duty of the judiciary to declare laws unconstitutional is in the final analysis derived from its responsibility for resolving concrete disputes brought before the courts for decision; a statute apparently governing a dispute cannot be applied by judges, consistently with their obligations under the Supremacy Clause, when such an application of the statute would conflict with the Constitution, *Marbury* v. *Madison.* . . . But this vital responsibility, broad as it is, does not amount to an unlimited power to survey the statute books and pass judgment on laws before the courts are called upon to enforce them. Ever since the Constitutional Convention rejected a proposal for having members of the Supreme Court render advice concerning pending legislation it has been clear that, even when suits of this kind involve a "case or controversy" sufficient to satisfy the requirements of Article III of the Constitution, the task of analyzing a proposed statute, pinpointing its deficiencies, and requiring correction of these deficiencies before the statute is put into effect, is rarely if ever an appropriate task for the judiciary. The combination of the relative remoteness of the controversy, the impact on the legislative process of the relief sought, and above all the speculative and amorphous nature of the required line-by-line analysis of detailed statutes, . . . ordinarily results in a kind of case that is wholly unsatisfactory for deciding constitutional questions, whichever way they might be decided. In light of this fundamental conception of the Framers as to the proper place of the federal courts in the governmental processes of passing and enforcing laws, it can seldom be appropriate for these courts to exercise any such power of prior approval or veto over the legislative process.

For these reasons, fundamental not only to our federal system but also to the basic functions of the Judicial Branch of the National Government under our Constitution, we hold that the *Dombrowski* decision should not be regarded as having upset the settled doctrines that have always confined very narrowly the availability of injunctive relief against state criminal prosecutions. We do not think that opinion stands for the proposition that a federal court can properly enjoin enforcement of a statute solely on the basis of a showing that the statute "on its face" abridges First Amendment rights. There may, of course, be extraordinary circumstances in which the necessary irreparable injury can be shown even in the absence of the usual prerequisites of bad faith and harassment. . . . It is sufficient for purposes of the present case to hold, as we do, that the possible unconstitutionality of a statute "on its face" does not in itself justify an injunction against good faith attempts to enforce it, and that appellee Harris has failed to make any showing of bad faith, harassment, or any other unusual circumstance that would call for equitable relief. . . .

The judgment of the District Court is reversed, and the case is remanded for further proceedings not inconsistent with this opinion.

Reversed.

MR. JUSTICE BRENNAN, WITH WHOM MR. JUSTICE WHITE AND MR. JUSTICE MARSHALL JOIN, CONCURRING IN THE RESULT(OMITTED).

MR. JUSTICE STEWART, WITH WHOM MR. JUSTICE HARLAN JOINS, CONCURRING (OMITTED).

MR. JUSTICE DOUGLAS DISSENTING (OMITTED).

H. The Doctrine of Political Questions: Reapportionment, Vietnam, Adam Clayton Powell, and Impeachment

[Many observers have contended that when a case within the Court's jurisdiction qualifies for review by constitutional standards (for example, it meets the case or controversy requirements, raises a federal question, etc.), the Supreme Court is obligated to decide the case on its merits and reach a decision. Authority for this position is often traced to John Marshall's opinion in *Cohens* v. *Virginia* (see p. 112, *supra*). But the Court quickly realized the impracticality of so rigid an interpretation of the Constitution. A new category of cases that were "nonjusticiable," that is, inappropriate for judicial decision notwithstanding the presence of jurisdictional power, emerged. Cases referred to as "political questions" are nonjusticiable, although the precise definition of a political question is difficult to discern.

The first major attempt by the Court to define a "political question" came in 1849, in the case of *Luther* v. *Borden*. The case involved a suit by Luther against Borden for an admitted trespass, but the case turned on a much more dramatic and important set of facts. A group of citizens in Rhode Island, long dissatisfied with the existing "Charter" government of that state (so named because it dated back to the original charter granted the colonists by Charles II), sought to replace the Charter government with a more modern one of their own. They called a new convention, held "elections," and proclaimed the formation of a new government with Thomas W. Dorr as its governor. The Charter government rejected the validity of the new government and sought to regain political control of the state by force. Martial law was declared, and many of the leaders of the "Dorr Rebellion" were arrested. Dorr himself was sentenced to life imprisonment. His attempt to challenge his arrest and defend the legitimacy of his government was thwarted when the Supreme Court dismissed his habeas corpus suit for lack of jurisdiction. The trespass case was then used by the Dorr forces in an attempt to have the Charter government declared illegal.

Chief Justice Taney's opinion for the Court outlined a variety of reasons why the Court should not decide the case. He noted the chaos that would follow a judicial replacement of the existing government with a new one. But primarily he found that this was an issue on which the Court had no standards to govern its decision and which was, in any case, committed by the Constitution to the other branches of government. The Constitution's guarantee to each state of a republican form of government was not the sort of guarantee that the Supreme Court could protect; hence it was a "political question." Taney's discussion of what constituted appropriate cases for the judiciary to decide proved to have great impact on the development of the doctrine of political questions.

The irony of this doctrine, largely misnamed to the extent that it suggests that the Court *never* decides political issues, is that its operation demonstrates beyond any reasonable doubt the very political nature of the judicial process. That the justices should consider—implicitly or explicitly—questions of power and influence, questions affecting the Court's prestige and status, the Court's relationship to the other branches of the government, and the very pragmatic question of its ability to effectively decide a particular case is much more revealing and persuasive than any nominal rejection of "political" cases.]

(1) Baker v. Carr (1962)

+Brennan, Warren, Douglas, Black, Clark, Stewart
−Frankfurter, Harlan
NP Whittaker

MR. JUSTICE BRENNAN delivered the opinion of the court.

This civil action was brought . . . to redress the alleged deprivation of federal constitutional rights. The complaint, alleging that by means of a 1901 statute of Tennessee apportioning the members of the General Assembly among the State's 95 counties, "these plaintiffs and others similarly situated, are denied the equal protection of the laws accorded them by the Fourteenth Amendment to the Constitution of the United States by virtue of the debasement of their votes," was dismissed by a three-judge court . . . in the Middle District of Tennessee. The court held that it lacked jurisdiction of the subject matter and also that no claim was stated upon which relief could be granted. . . . We hold that the dismissal was error, and remand the cause to the District Court for trial and further proceedings consistent with this opinion.

. . . Tennessee's standard for allocating legislative representation among her counties is the total number of qualified voters resident in the respective counties, subject only to minor qualifications. . . .

Between 1901 and 1961, Tennessee has experienced substantial growth and redistribution of her population. In 1901 the population was 2,020,616, of whom 487,380 were eligible to vote. The 1960 Federal Census reports the State's population at 3,567,089, of whom 2,092,891 are eligible to vote. The relative standings of the counties in terms of qualified voters have changed significantly. It is primarily the continued application of the 1901 Apportionment Act to this shifted and enlarged voting population which gives rise to the present controversy.

Indeed, the complaint alleges that the 1901 statute, even as of the time of its passage, "made no apportionment of Representatives and Senators in accordance with the constitutional formula . . . , but instead arbitrarily and capriciously apportioned representatives in the Senate and House without reference . . . to any logical or reasonable formula whatever." It is further alleged that "because of the population changes since 1900, and the failure of the Legislature to reapportion itself since 1901," the 1901 statute became "unconstitutional and obsolete." Appellants also argue that, because of the composition of the legislature effected by the 1901 Apportionment Act, redress in the form of a state constitutional amendment to change the entire mechanism for reapportioning, or any other change short of that, is difficult or impossible. The complaint concludes that "these plaintiffs and others similarly situated, are denied the equal protection of the laws accorded them by the Fourteenth Amendment to the Constitution of the United States by virtue of the debasement of their votes." They seek a declaration that the 1901 statute is unconstitutional and an injunction restraining the appellees from acting to conduct any further elections under it. . . .

Jurisdiction of the Subject Matter

The District Court was uncertain whether our cases withholding federal judicial relief rested upon a lack of federal jurisdiction or upon the inappropriateness of the subject matter for judicial consideration—what we have designated "nonjusticiability." The distinction between the two grounds is significant. In the instance of nonjusticiability, consideration of the cause is not wholly and immediately foreclosed; rather, the Court's inquiry necessarily proceeds to the point of deciding whether the duty asserted can be judicially identified and its breach judicially determined, and whether protection for the right asserted can be judicially molded. In the instance of lack of jurisdiction the cause either does not "arise under" the Federal Constitution, laws or treaties (or fall within one of the other enumerated categories of Art. III, § 2), or is not a "case or controversy" within the meaning of that section; or the cause is not one described by any jurisdictional statute. [We] hold only that the matter set forth in the complaint does arise under the Constitution. . . .

An unbroken line of our precedents sustains the federal courts' jurisdiction of the subject matter of federal constitutional claims of this nature. . . .

The appellees refer to *Colegrove* v. *Green* . . . as authority that the District Court lacked jurisdiction of the subject matter. Appellees misconceive the holding of that case. The holding was precisely contrary to their reading of it. Seven members of the Court participated in the decision. Unlike many other cases in this field which have assumed without discussion that there was jurisdiction, all three opinions filed in *Colegrove* discussed the question. Two of the opinions expressing the views of four of the Justices, a majority, flatly held that there was jurisdiction of the subject matter. MR. JUSTICE BLACK joined by MR. JUSTICE DOUGLAS and MR. JUSTICE MURPHY stated: "It is my judgment that the District Court had jurisdiction . . . ," . . .Mr. Justice Rutledge, writing separately, expressed agreement with this conclusion. . . . Indeed, it is even questionable that the opinion of Mr. Justice Frankfurter, joined by Justices Reed and Burton, doubted jurisdiction of the subject matter. . . .

Two cases decided with opinions after *Colegrove* likewise plainly imply that the subject matter of this suit is within District Court jurisdiction.

We hold that the District Court has jurisdiction of the subject matter of the federal constitutional claim asserted in the complaint.

Standing

A federal court cannot "pronounce any statute, either of a State or of the United States, void, because irreconcilable with the Constitution, except as it is called upon to adjudge the legal rights of litigants in actual controversies." . . . Have the appellants alleged such a personal stake in the outcome of the controversy as to assure that concrete adverseness which sharpens the presentation of issues upon which the court so largely depends for illumination of difficult constitutional questions? . . .

We hold that the appellants do have standing to maintain this suit. Our decisions plainly support this conclusion. Many of the cases have assumed rather than articulated the premise in deciding the merits of similar claims. And *Colegrove* v. *Green*. . . squarely held that voters who allege facts showing disadvantage to themselves as individuals have standing to sue. A number of cases decided after *Colegrove* recognized the standing of the voters there involved to bring those actions. . . .

It would not be necessary to decide whether appellants' allegations of impairment of their votes by the 1901 apportionment will, ultimately, entitle them to any relief, in order to hold that they have standing to seek it. If such impairment does produce a legally cognizable injury, they are among those who have sustained it. They are asserting "a plain, direct and adequate interest in maintaining the effectiveness of their votes," *Coleman* v. *Miller* . . . not merely a claim of "the right, possessed by every citizen, to require that the Government be administered according to law. . . ." . . . They are entitled to a hearing and to the District Court's decision on their claims.

Justiciability

. . . Of course the mere fact that the suit seeks protection of a political right does not mean it presents a political question. Such an objection "is little more than a play upon words." . . . Rather, it is argued that apportionment cases, whatever the actual wording of the complaint, can involve no federal constitutional right except one resting on the guaranty of a republican form of government, and that complaints based on that clause have been held to present political questions which are nonjusticiable.

We hold that the claim pleaded here neither rests upon nor implicates the Guaranty Clause and that its justiciability is therefore not foreclosed by our decisions of cases involving that clause. The District Court misinterpreted *Colegrove* v. *Green* and other decisions of this Court on which it relied. Appellants' claim that they are being denied equal protection is justiciable, and if "discrimination is sufficiently shown, the right to relief under the equal protection clause is not diminished by the fact that the discrimination relates to political rights." . . . To show why we reject the argument based on the Guaranty Clause, we must examine the authorities under it. . . .

Our discussion, even at the price of extending this opinion, requires review of a number of political question cases, in order to expose the attributes of the doctrine—attributes which, in various settings, diverge, combine, appear, and disappear, in seeming disorderliness. . . . That review reveals that in the Guaranty Clause cases and in the other "political question" cases, it is the relationship between the judiciary and the coordinate branches of the Federal Government, and not the federal judiciary's relationship to the States, which gives rise to the "political question." . . .

. . . It is apparent that several formulations which vary slightly according to the settings in which the questions arise may describe a political question, although each has one or more elements which identify it as essentially a function of the separation of powers. Prominent on the surface of any case held to involve a political question is found a textually demonstrable commitment of the issue to a coordinate political department; or a lack of judicially discoverable and manageable standards for resolving it; or the impossibility of deciding without an initial policy determination of a kind clearly for nonjudicial discretion; or the impossibility of a court's undertaking independent resolution without expressing lack of the respect due coordinate branches of government; or an unusual need for unquestioning adherence to a political decision already made; or the potentiality of embarassment from multifarious pronouncements by various departments on one question.

. . .

We come, finally, to the ultimate inquiry whether our precedents as to what constitutes a nonjusticiable "political question" bring the case before us under the umbrella of that doctrine. A natural beginning is to note whether any of the common characteristics which we have been able to identify and label descriptively are present. We find none. The question here is the consistency of state action with the Federal Constitution. We have no question decided, or to be decided, by a political branch of government coequal with this Court. Nor do we risk embarrassment of our government abroad, or grave disturbance at home if we take issue with Tennessee as to the constitutionality of her action here challenged. Nor need the appellants, in order to succeed in this action, ask the Court to enter upon policy determinations for which judicially manageable standards are lacking. Judicial standards under the Equal Protection Clause are well developed and familiar, and it has been open to courts since the enactment of the Fourteenth Amendment to determine, if on the particular facts they must, that a discrimination reflects *no* policy, but simply arbitrary and capricious action.

This case does, in one sense, involve the allocation of political power within a State, and the appellants might conceivably have added a claim under the Guaranty Clause. Of course, as we have seen, any reliance on that clause would be futile. But because any reliance on the Guaranty Clause could not have succeeded it does not follow that appellants may not be heard on the equal protection claim which in fact they tender. True, it must be clear that the Fourteenth Amendment claim is not so enmeshed with those political question elements which render Guaranty Clause claims nonjusticiable as actually to present a political question itself. But we have found that not to be the case here.

. . . We conclude then that the nonjusticiability of claims resting on the Guaranty Clause which arises from their embodiment of questions that were thought "political," can have no bearing upon the justiciability of the equal protection claim presented in this case. Finally, we emphasize that it is the involvement in Guaranty Clause claims of the elements thought to define "political questions," and no other feature, which could render them nonjusticiable. Specifically, we have said that such claims are not held nonjusticiable because they touch matters of state governmental organization. Brief examination of a few cases demonstrates this.

When challenges to state action respecting matters of "the administration of the affairs of the State and the officers through whom they are conducted" have rested on claims of constitutional deprivation which are amenable to judicial correction, this Court has acted upon its view of the merits of the claim. . . . And only last Term, in *Gomillion* v. *Lightfoot* . . . we applied the Fifteenth Amendment to strike down a redrafting of municipal boundaries which effected a discriminatory impairment of voting rights, in the face of what a majority of the Court of Appeals thought to be a sweeping commitment to state legislatures of the power to draw and redraw such boundaries.

. . . We conclude that the complaint's allegations of a denial of equal protection present a justiciable constitutional cause of action upon which appellants are entitled to a trial and a decision. The right asserted is within the reach of judicial protection under the Fourteenth Amendment.

The judgment of the District Court is reversed and the cause is remanded for further proceedings consistent with this opinion.

Reversed and remanded.

MR. JUSTICE DOUGLAS, CONCURRING (OMITTED).

MR. JUSTICE CLARK, CONCURRING.

One emerging from the rash of opinions with their accompanying clashing of views may well find himself suffering a mental blindness. The Court holds that the appellants have alleged a cause of action. However, it refuses to award relief here—although the facts are undisputed—and fails to give the District Court any guidance whatever. One dissenting opinion, bursting with words that go through so much and conclude with so little, contemns the majority action as "a massive repudiation of the experience of our whole past." Another describes the complaint as merely asserting conclusory allegations that Tennessee's apportionment is "incorrect," "arbitrary," "obsolete," and "unconstitutional."

. . . Although I find the Tennessee apportionment statute offends the Equal Protection Clause, I would not consider intervention by this Court into so delicate a field if there were any other relief available to the people of Tennessee. But the majority of the people of Tennessee have no "practical opportunities for exerting their political weight at the polls" to correct the existing "invidious discrimination." Tennessee has no initiative and referendum. I have searched diligently for other "practical opportunities" present under the law. I find none other than through the federal courts. The majority of the voters have been caught up in a legislative strait jacket. Tennessee has an "informed, civically militant electorate" and "an aroused popular conscience," but it does not sear "the conscience of the people's representatives." This is because the legislative policy has riveted the present seats in the Assembly to their respective constituencies, and by the votes of their incumbents a reapportionment of any kind is prevented. The people have been rebuffed at the hands of the Assembly; they have tried the constitutional convention route, but since the call must originate in the Assembly it, too, has been fruitless. They have tried Tennessee courts with the same result, and Governors have fought the tide· only to flounder. It is said that there is recourse in Congress and perhaps that may be, but from a practical standpoint this is without substance. To date Congress has never undertaken such a task in any State. We therefore must conclude that the people of Tennessee are stymied and without judicial intervention will be saddled with the present discrimination in the affairs of their state government.

. . . [We] must consider if there are any appropriate modes of effective judicial relief. The federal courts are of course not forums for political debate, nor should they resolve themselves into state constitutional conventions or legislative assemblies. Nor should their jurisdiction be exercised in the hope that such a declaration, as is made today, may have the direct effect of bringing on legislative action and relieving the courts of the problem of fashioning relief. To my mind this would be nothing less than black-jacking the Assembly into reapportioning the State. If judicial competence were lacking to fashion an effective decree, I would dismiss this appeal. However, like the Sol-

icitor General of the United States, I see no such difficulty in the position of this case. One plan might be to start with the existing assembly districts, consolidate some of them, and award the seats thus released to those counties suffering the most egregious discrimination. Other possibilities are present and might be more effective. But the plan here suggested would at least release the strangle hold now on the Assembly and permit it to redistrict itself. . . .

In view of the detailed study that the Court has given this problem, it is unfortunate that a decision is not reached on the merits. The majority appears to hold, at least *sub silentio,* that an invidious discrimination is present, but it remands to the three-judge court for it to make what is certain to be that formal determination. . . .

It is well for this Court to practice self-restraint and discipline in constitutional adjudication, but never in its history have those principles received sanction where the national rights of so many have been so clearly infringed for so long a time. National respect for the courts is more enhanced through the forthright enforcement of those rights rather than by rendering them nugatory through the interposition of subterfuges. In my view the ultimate decision today is in the greatest tradition of this Court.

MR. JUSTICE STEWART, CONCURRING.

The separate writings of my dissenting and concurring Brothers stray so far from the subject of today's decision as to convey, I think, a distressingly inaccurate impression of what the Court decides. For that reason, I think it appropriate, in joining the opinion of the Court, to emphasize in a few words what the opinion does and does not say.

The Court today decides three things and no more: "(a) that the court possessed jurisdiction of the subject matter; (b) that a justiciable cause of action is stated upon which appellants would be entitled to appropriate relief; and (c) . . . that the appellants have standing to challenge the Tennessee apportionment statutes." . . .

MR. JUSTICE FRANKFURTER, WHOM MR. JUSTICE HARLAN JOINS, DISSENTING.

The Court today reverses a uniform course of decision established by a dozen cases, including one by which the very claim now sustained was unanimously rejected only five years ago. The impressive body of rulings thus cast aside reflected the equally uniform course of our political history regarding the relationship between population and legislative representation—a wholly different matter from denial of the franchise to individuals because of race, color, religion or sex. Such a massive repudiation of the experience of our whole past in asserting destructively novel judicial power demands a detailed analysis of the role of this Court in our constitutional scheme. Disregard of inherent limits in the effective exercise of the Court's "judicial Power" not only presages the futility of judicial intervention in the essentially political conflict of forces by which the relation between population and representation has time out of mind been and now is determined. It may well impair the Court's position as the ultimate organ of "the supreme Law of the Land" in that vast range of legal problems, often strongly entangled in popular feeling, on which this Court must pronounce. The Court's authority—possessed neither of the purse nor the sword—ultimately rests on sustained public confidence in its moral sanction.

Such feeling must be nourished by the Court's complete detachment, in fact and in appearance, from political entanglements and by abstention from injecting itself into the clash of political forces in political settlements.

. . . In effect, today's decision empowers the courts to decide the proper composition of the legislatures of the fifty States. If state courts should for one reason or another find themselves unable to discharge this task, the duty of doing so is put on the federal courts or on this Court, if State views do not satisfy this Court's notion of what is proper districting.

We were soothingly told at the bar of this Court that we need not worry about the kind of remedy a court could effectively fashion once the abstract constitutional right to have courts pass on a state-wide system of electoral districting is recognized as a matter of judicial rhetoric, because legislatures would heed the Court's admonition. This is not only an euphoric hope. It implies a sorry confession of judicial impotence in place of a frank acknowledgment that there is not under our Constitution judicial remedy for every political mischief, for every undesirable exercise of legislative power. The Framers carefully and with deliberate forethought refused so to enthrone the judiciary. In this situation, as in others of like nature, appeal for relief does not belong here. Appeal must be to an informed, civically militant electorate. In a democratic society like ours, relief must come through an aroused popular conscience that sears the conscience of the people's representatives. In any event there is nothing judicially more unseemly nor more self-defeating than for this Court to make *in terrorem* pronouncements, to indulge in merely empty rhetoric, sounding a word of promise to the ear, sure to be disappointing to the hope. . . .

What, then, is this question of legislative apportionment? Appellants invoke the right to vote and to have their votes counted. But they are permitted to vote and their votes are counted. They go to the polls, they cast their ballots, they send their representatives to the state councils. Their complaint is simply that the representatives are not sufficiently numerous or powerful—in short, that Tennessee has adopted a basis of representation with which they are dissatisfied. Talk of "debasement" or "dilution" is circular talk. One cannot speak of "debasement" or "dilution" of the value of a vote until there is first defined a standard of reference as to what a vote should be worth. What is actually asked of the Court in this case is to choose among competing bases of representation— ultimately, really, among competing theories of political philosophy—in order to establish an appropriate frame of government for the State of Tennessee and thereby for all States of the Union.

In such a matter, abstract analogies which ignore the facts of history deal in unrealities; they betray reason. This is not a case in which a State has, through a device however oblique and sophisticated, denied Negroes or Jews or redheaded persons a vote, or given them only a third or a sixth of a vote. That was *Gomillion* v. *Lightfoot*, . . . What Tennessee illustrates is an old and still widespread method of representation—representation by local geographical division, only in part respective of population—in preference to others, others, forsooth, more appealing. Appellants contest this choice and seek to make this Court the arbiter of the disagreement. They would make the Equal Protection Clause the charter of adjudication, asserting that the equality which it guarantees comports, if not the assurance of equal weight to every voter's vote, at least the basic conception that representation ought to be proportionate to population, a standard by reference to which the reasonableness of apportionment plans may be judged. . . .

Manifestly, the Equal Protection Clause supplies no clearer guide for judicial examination of apportionment methods than would the Guarantee Clause itself. Apportionment, by its character, is a subject of extraordinary complexity, involving—even after the fundamental theoretical issues concerning what is to be represented in a representative legislature have been fought out or compromised—considerations of geography, demography, electoral convenience, economic and social cohesions or divergencies among particular local groups, communications, the practical effects of political institutions like the lobby and the city machine, ancient traditions and ties of settled usage, respect for proven incumbents of long experience and senior status, mathematical mechanics, censuses compiling relevant data, and a host of others. Legislative responses throughout the country to the reapportionment demands of the 1960 Census have glaringly confirmed that these are not factors that lend themselves to evaluations of a nature that are the staple of judicial determinations or for which judges are equipped to adjudicate by legal training or experience or native wit. And this is the more so true because in every strand of this complicated, intricate web of values meet the contending forces of partisan politics. The practical significance of apportionment is that the next election results may differ because of it. Apportionment battles are overwhelmingly party or inter-party contests. It will add a virulent source of friction and tension in federal-state relations to embroil the federal judiciary in them.

MR. JUSTICE HARLAN, DISSENTING (OMITTED).

[The substantive question of reapportionment is considered in Part Two, Chapter Two.]

(2) Massachusetts v. Laird (1970)

+Burger, Black, Brennan, White, Marshall, Blackmun
  −Douglas, Harlan, Stewart

[In an effort to force the Supreme Court to consider the legality of the war in Indochina, a new strategy was adopted in 1970. In turning down previous challenges to the legality of the war, the Supreme Court had given no reasons. But inferences from the dissenting opinions of Justices Douglas and Stewart in an earlier case, *Mora* v. *McNamara* (1967), suggested that the doctrines of standing to sue and political questions were the barriers to overcome.

The new strategy thus focused on the need to "create" standing. Borrowing in part from the discredited theory of "interposition," Massachusetts was the first of several states to pass a law making it unlawful for any inhabitant of that state inducted into the military forces "to serve outside the territorial limits of the United States in armed hostilities not an emergency nor otherwise authorized by powers granted to the president unless preceded or followed by a congressional declaration of war." The statute provided that the state attorney general should bring an appropriate action under the original jurisdiction of the Supreme Court and, failing that, to initiate an action for a declaratory judgment in a lower federal court. Such an action was filed by the attorney general of Massachusetts asking that the United States' participation in the Indochina War be declared unconstitutional because it was not authorized or

subsequently ratified by congressional declaration. It also sought an injunction preventing the secretary of defense from increasing present troop levels and asked that, if appropriate congressional action was not forthcoming within 90 days of the Court's action, the secretary of defense be enjoined from ordering any inhabitant of Massachusetts to Indochina for the purpose of participating in the war. The Supreme Court denied permission to file the bill of complaint (that is, refused to hear the case); three justices dissented, one short of the number necessary to have the case heard on the merits.]

MR. JUSTICE DOUGLAS, DISSENTING.
. . .

The threshold issues for granting leave to file a complaint in this case are standing and justiciability. I believe that Massachusetts has standing and the controversy is justiciable. At the very least, however, it is apparent that the issues are not so clearly foreclosed as to justify a summary denial of leave to file.

Standing

In *Massachusetts* v. *Mellon* . . . the Court held a State lacked standing to challenge, as parens patriae, a federal grant-in-aid program under which the Federal Government was allegedly usurping powers reserved to the States. . . .

The Solicitor General argues that *Mellon* stands as a bar to this suit.

Yet the ruling of the Court in that case is not dispositive of this one. The opinion states "We need not go so far as to say that a state may never intervene by suit to protect its citizens against any form of enforcement of unconstitutional acts of Congress; but we are clear that the right to do so does not arise here." . . . Thus the case did not announce a per se rule to bar all suits against the Federal Government as parens patriae, and a closer look at the bases of the opinion is necessary to determine the limits on its applicability.

Mellon relates to an Act of Congress signed by the Executive, . . .

Massachusetts attacks no federal statute. In fact, the basis of Massachusetts' complaint is that only one representative of the people, the Executive, has acted and the other representatives of the citizens have not acted, although, it is argued, the Constitution provides that they must act before an overseas "war" can be conducted.

There was a companion case to *Mellon* in which the Court held that a taxpayer lacked standing to challenge the same federal spending statute, *Frothingham* v. *Mellon*. . . . Two years ago we reconsidered Frothingham and found at least part of the ruling could not stand the test of time. Concurring in the result, I stated:

Frothingham, decided in 1923, was in the heyday of substantive due process, when courts were sitting in judgment on the wisdom or reasonableness of legislation. The claim in Frothingham was that a federal regulatory Act dealing with maternity deprived the plaintiff of property without due process of law. When the Court used substantive due process to determine the wisdom or reasonableness of legislation, it was indeed transforming itself into the Council of Revision which was rejected by the Constitutional Convention. It was that judicial attitude, not the theory of standing to sue rejected in Frothingham, *that involved "important hazards for the continued effectiveness of the federal judiciary," to borrow a phrase from my Brother Harlan. A contrary result in* Frothingham *in that setting might have accentuated an ominous trend to judicial supremacy. . . . In* Flast *we held a taxpayer had standing to challenge a federal spending program, if he showed*

that Congress breached a specific limitation on its taxing and spending power. As Mr. Justice Stewart stated in his concurring opinion, "[t]he present case is thus readily distinguishable from Frothingham v. Mellon, . . . *where the taxpayer did not rely on an explicit constitutional prohibition but instead questioned the scope of the powers delegated to the national legislature by Article I of the Constitution. . . .*

The erosion of *Frothingham* does not, of course, necessarily mean that the authority of *Mellon* has been affected. But if the current debate over *Frothingham* ". . . suggests that we should undertake a fresh examination of the limitations upon standing to sue," . . . then surely the erosion of *Frothingham* suggests it is time to reexamine its companion case. *Mellon*, too, has been eroded by time. In the spring of 1963 the Governor of Alabama moved for leave to file a complaint to prevent the President from using troops in Birmingham during civil rights marches there. Under the Solicitor General's reading of *Mellon* Alabama would lack standing to challenge such an exercise of presidential authority. The Court denied Alabama relief, not because of *Mellon*, but because:

"In essence the papers show no more than the President has made ready to exercise the authority conferred upon him by 10 USC § 333 by alerting and stationing military personnel in the Birmingham area. Such purely preparatory measures and their alleged adverse general effects upon the plaintiffs afford no basis for the granting of any relief." *Alabama* v. *United States*. . . .

In *South Carolina* v. *Katzenbach* . . . *Mellon* was further weakened. In that case we denied standing to South Carolina to assert claims under the Bill of Attainder Clause of Article I and the principle of separation of powers which were regarded "only as protections for individual persons and private groups who are particularly vulnerable to nonjudicial determinations of guilt." . . . Yet we went on to allow South Carolina to challenge the Voting Rights Act of 1965 as beyond congressional power under the Fifteenth Amendment.

The main interest of *South Carolina* was in the continuing operation of her election laws. Massachusetts' claim to standing in this case is certainly as strong as *South Carolina's* was in the *Katzenbach* case.

Massachusetts complains, as parens patriae, that her citizens are drafted and sent to fight in an unconstitutional overseas war. Their lives are in jeopardy. Their liberty is impaired. Furthermore, the basis on which *Flast* distinguished *Frothingham* is also present here. The allegation in both *Mellon* and *Frothingham* was that Congress had exceeded the general powers delegated to it by Art I, § 8, and invaded the reserved powers of the States under the Tenth Amendment. The claim was not specific; but, as *Flast* held, if a taxpayer can allege spending violates a specific constitutional limitation, then he has standing. Here Massachusetts points to a specific provision of the Constitution. Congress by Art I, § 8, has the power "To declare War." Does not that make this case comparable to *Flast*?

It has been settled at least since 1901 that "if the health and comfort of the inhabitants of a State are threatened, the State is the proper party to represent and defend them." *Missouri* v. *Illinois*. . . . Those cases involved injury to inhabitants of one State by water or air pollution of another State, by interference with navigation, by economic losses caused by an out-of-state agency, and

the like. The harm to citizens of Massachusetts suffered by being drafted for a war are certainly of no less a magnitude. Massachusetts would clearly seem to have standing as parens patriae to represent as alleged in its complaint, its male citizens being drafted for overseas combat in Indochina.

Justiciability

A question that is "political" is opposed to one that is "justiciable." In reviewing the dimensions of the "political" question we said in *Baker* v. *Carr*. . . .

. . . *Prominent on the surface of any case held to involve a political question is found a textually demonstrable constitutional commitment of the issue to a coordinate political department; or a lack of judicially discoverable and manageable standards for resolving it; or the impossibility of deciding without an initial policy determination of a kind clearly for non-judicial discretion; or the impossibility of a court's undertaking independent resolution without expressing lack of the respect due coordinate branches of government; or an unusual need for unquestioning adherence to a political decision already made; or the potentiality of embarrassment from multifarious pronouncements by various departments on one question.*

1. *A textually demonstrable constitutional commitment of the issue to a coordinate political department.* At issue here is the phrase in Art I, § 8, cl 11: "To declare War." Congress definitely has that power. The Solicitor General argues that only Congress can determine whether it has declared war. He states, " 'To declare War' includes a power to determine, free of judicial interference, the form which its authorization of hostilities will take." This may be correct. But as we stated

in *Powell* v. *McCormack* . . . the question of a textually demonstrable commitment and "what is the scope of such commitment are questions [this Court] . . . must resolve for the first time in this case." . . . It may well be that it is for Congress, and Congress alone, to determine the form of its authorization, but if that is the case we should only make that determination after full briefs on the merits and oral argument.

2. *A lack of judicially discoverable and manageable standards for resolving the issue.* The standards that are applicable are not elusive. The case is not one where the Executive is repelling a sudden attack. The present Indochina "war" has gone on for six years. The question is whether the Gulf of Tonkin Resolution was a declaration of war or whether other Acts of Congress were its equivalent.

3. *The impossibility of deciding without an initial policy determination of a kind clearly for nonjudicial discretion.* In *Ex parte Milligan* . . . (concurring opinion), it was stated that "neither can the President, in war more than in peace, intrude upon the proper authority of Congress. . . ." The issue in this case is not whether we ought to fight a war in Indochina, but whether the Executive can authorize it without congressional authorization. This is not a case where we would have to determine the wisdom of any policy.

4. *The impossibility of a court's undertaking independent resolution without expressing lack of respect due coordinate branches of government.* The Solicitor General argues it would show disrespect of the Executive to go behind his statements and determine his authority to act in these circumstances. Both *Powell* and the *Steel Seizure Case* . . . however, demonstrate that the duty of this Court is to interpret the

Constitution, and in the latter case we did go behind an executive order to determine his authority. As Mr. Justice Frankfurter stated in the *Steel Seizure Case*:

To deny inquiry into the President's power in a case like this, because of the damage to the public interest to be feared from upsetting its exercise by him, would in effect always preclude inquiry into challenged power, which presumably only avowed great public interest brings into action. . . .

It is far more important to be respectful to the Constitution than to a coordinate branch of government.

5. *An unusual need for unquestioning adherence to a political decision already made.* This test is essentially a reference to a commitment of a problem and its solution to a coordinate branch of government, a matter not involved here.

6. *The potentiality of embarrassment from multifarious pronouncements by various departments of government on one question.* Once again this relates back to whether the problem and its solution are committed to a given branch of government.

We have never ruled, I believe, that when the Federal Government takes a person by the neck and submits him to punishment, imprisonment, taxation, or submission to some ordeal, the complaining person may not be heard in court. The rationale in cases such as the present is that government cannot take life, liberty, or property of the individual and escape adjudication by the courts of the legality of its action.

That is the heart of this case. It does not concern the wisdom of fighting in Southeast Asia. Likewise no question of whether the conflict is either just or necessary is present. We are asked instead whether the Executive has power, absent a congressional declaration of war, to commit Massachusetts citizens in armed hostilities on foreign soil. Another way of putting the question is whether under our Constitution presidential wars are permissible? Should that question be answered in the negative we would then have to determine whether Congress has declared war. That question which Massachusetts presents is in my view justiciable.

It is said that "the notion has persisted, despite the results in *Baker* v. *Carr,* and *Powell* v. *McCormack, . . .* that there is a means for the Court to avoid deciding any case or issue upon the basis of a broad, highly general, and almost discretionary principle of nondecision." . . . Yet no such discretionary principle, if germane to our problem, is applicable here.

"The war power of the United States like its other powers . . . is subject to constitutional limitations." *Hamilton* v. *Kentucky Distilleries and Warehouse Co.* . . . No less than the war power—the greatest leveler of them all—is the power of the Commander-in-Chief subject to constitutional limitations. That was the crux of the Steel Seizure Case. Concurring in that case, Mr. Justice Clark stated: "I conclude that where Congress has laid down specific procedures to deal with the type of crisis confronting the President, he must follow those procedures in meeting the crisis. . . . I cannot sustain the seizure in question because . . . Congress had [sic] prescribed methods to be followed by the President. . . ." If the President must follow procedures prescribed by Congress, it follows *a fortiori* that he must follow procedures prescribed by the Constitution.

This Court has previously faced issues of presidential war making. The legality of Lincoln's blockade was considered in the *Prize Cases . . .* and although the Court narrowly split in supporting the President's position, the split was on the merits, not on whether the claim was justiciable. And even though that war was the Civil War and not one involving an overseas expedition, the decision was 5 to 4.

In the *Steel Seizure Case* members of this Court wrote seven opinions and each reached the merits of the Executive's seizure. In that case, as here, the issue related to the President's powers as Commander-in-Chief and the fact that all nine Justices decided the case on the merits and construed the powers of a coordinate branch at a time of extreme emergency should be instructive. . . .

If we determine that the Indochina conflict is unconstitutional because it lacks a congressional declaration of war, the Chief Executive is free to seek one, as was President Truman free to seek congressional approval after our *Steel Seizure* decision.

There is, of course, a difference between this case and the *Prize Cases* and the *Steel Seizure Case.* In those cases a private party was asserting a wrong to him: his *property* was being taken and he demanded a determination of the legality of the taking. Here the *lives* and *liberties* of Massachusetts citizens are in jeopardy. Certainly the Constitution gives no greater protection to *property* than to *life* and *liberty.* It might be argued that the authority in the *Steel Seizure Case* was not textually apparent in the Constitution, while the power of the Commander-in-Chief to commit troops is obvious and therefore a different determination on justiciability is needed. The *Prize Cases,* however, involved Lincoln's exercise of power in ordering a blockade by virtue of his powers as the Commander-in-Chief.

Since private parties—represented by Massachusetts as parens patriae—are involved in this case the teaching of the *Prize Cases* and the *Steel Seizure Case* is that their claims are justiciable.

The Solicitor General urges that no effective remedy can be formulated. He correctly points out enforcing or supervising injunctive relief would involve immense complexities and difficulties. But there is no requirement that we issue an injunction. Massachusetts seeks declaratory relief as well as injunctive relief. . . . It may well be that even declaratory relief would be inappropriate respecting many of the numerous issues involved if the Court held that the war were unconstitutional. I restrict this opinion to the question of the propriety of a declaratory judgment that no Massachusetts man can be taken against his will and made to serve in that war. *Powell* involved just one man while this case involves large numbers of men. But that goes only to the mechanical task of making any remedy granted available to all members of a large class.

Today we deny a hearing to a State which attempts to determine whether it is constitutional to require its citizens to fight in a foreign war absent a congressional declaration of war. Three years ago we refused to hear a case involving draftees who sought to prevent their shipment overseas. *Mora* v. *McNamara.* . . . The question of an unconstitutional war is neither academic nor "political." These cases have raised the question in adversary settings. It should be settled here and now.

I would set the motion for leave to file down for argument and decide the merits only after full argument.

MR. JUSTICE HARLAN AND MR. JUSTICE STEWART DISSENT. They would set this motion for argument on the questions of standing and justiciability.

(3) Powell v. McCormack (1969)

+Warren, Black, Douglas, Harlan, Brennan, White, Marshall
−Stewart

[In November, 1966, Adam Clayton Powell was reelected to Congress by the Harlem constituency he had served since 1942. Because of allegations about improper use of congressional funds and other incidents, Powell was not permitted to take his seat at the beginning of the Ninetieth Congress, in January 1967. Powell and some of his supporters filed suit in federal district court claiming that the House could exclude him only if he failed to meet the requirements of age, citizenship, and residence described in Article I, Section 2, of the Constitution—requirements which he clearly met. The district court dismissed the complaint for lack of jurisdiction over the subject matter, and the court of appeals affirmed. On certiorari the Supreme Court reversed and ruled that Powell had been unlawfully excluded from the Ninetieth Congress.]

CHIEF JUSTICE WARREN delivered the opinion of the Court:
. . . Respondents assert that the Speech or Debate Clause of the Constitution, Art. I, § 6, is an absolute bar to petitioners' action. This Court has on four prior occasions—*Dombrowski* v. *Eastland* . . . (1967); *United States* v. *Johnson* . . . (1966); *Tenney* v. *Brandhove* . . . (1951); and *Kilbourn* v. *Thompson* . . . (1881)—been called upon to determine if allegedly unconstitutional action taken by legislators or legislative employees is insulated from judicial review by the Speech or Debate Clause. . . .

The Speech or Debate Clause, adopted by the Constitutional Convention without debate or opposition, finds its roots in the conflict between

Parliament and the Crown culminating in the Glorious Revolution of 1688 and the English Bill of Rights of 1689. . . . Although the clause sprung from a fear of seditious libel actions instituted by the Crown to punish unfavorable speeches made in Parliament, we have held that it would be a "narrow view" to confine the protection of the Speech or Debate Clause to words spoken in debate. Committee reports, resolutions, and the act of voting are equally covered, as are "things generally done in a session of the House by one of its members in relation to the business before it." . . . Furthermore, the clause provides not only a defense on the merits but also protects a legislator from the burden of defending himself.

Our cases make it clear that the legislative immunity created by the Speech or Debate Clause performs an important function in representative government. It insures that legislators are free to represent the interests of their constituents without fear that they will be later called to task in the courts for that representation. . . .

Legislative immunity does not, of course, bar all judicial review of legislative acts. That issue was settled by implication as early as 1803, see *Marbury* v. *Madison* . . . and expressly in *Kilbourn* v. *Thompson*, the first of this Court's cases interpreting the reach of the Speech or Debate Clause. Challenged in *Kilbourn* was the constitutionality of a House resolution ordering the arrest and imprisonment of a recalcitrant witness who had refused to respond to a subpoena issued by a House investigating committee. While holding that the Speech or Debate Clause barred Kilbourn's action for false imprisonment brought against several members of the House, the Court nevertheless reached the merits of Kilbourn's attack and decided that, since the

House had no power to punish for contempt, Kilbourn's imprisonment pursuant to the resolution was unconstitutional. It therefore allowed Kilbourn to bring his false imprisonment action against Thompson, the House's Sergeant-at-Arms, who had executed the warrant for Kilbourn's arrest.

The Court first articulated in *Kilbourn* and followed in *Dombrowski* v. *Eastland* the doctrine that, although an action against a Congressman may be barred by the Speech or Debate Clause, legislative employees who participated in the unconstitutional activity are responsible for their acts. . . .

That House employees are acting pursuant to express orders of the House does not bar judicial review of the constitutionality of the underlying legislative decision. *Kilbourn* decisively settles this question, since the Sergeant-at-Arms was held liable for false imprisonment even though he did nothing more than execute the House resolution that Kilbourn be arrested and imprisoned. . . .

The purpose of the protection afforded legislators is not to forestall judicial review of legislative action but to insure that legislators are not distracted from or hindered in the performance of their legislative tasks by being called into court to defend their actions. A legislator is no more or no less hindered or distracted by litigation against a legislative employee calling into question the employee's affirmative action than he would be by a lawsuit questioning the employee's failure to act. Nor is the distraction or hindrance increased because the claim is for salary rather than damages, or because the litigation questions action taken by the employee within rather than without the House. Freedom of legislative activity and the purposes of the Speech or Debate Clause are fully protected if legislators are relieved of the burden of defending themselves. . . .

As we pointed out in *Baker* v. *Carr* . . . (1962), there is a significant difference between determining whether a federal court has "jurisidction over the subject matter" and determining whether a cause over which a court has subject matter jurisdiction is "justiciable." The District Court determined that "to decide this case on the merits . . . would constitute a clear violation of the doctrine of separation of powers" and then dismissed the complaint "for want of jurisdiction of the subject matter." . . . However, as the Court of Appeals correctly recognized, the doctrine of separation of powers is more properly considered in determining whether the case is "justiciable." We agree with the unanimous conclusion of the Court of Appeals that the District Court had jurisdiction over the subject matter of this case. However . . . we disagree with the Court of Appeals' conclusion that this case is not justiciable. . . .

Two determinations must be made in this regard. First, we must decide whether the claim presented and the relief sought are of the type which admit of judicial resolution. Second, we must determine whether the structure of the Federal Government renders the issue presented a "political question"—that is, a question which is not justiciable in federal court because of the separation of powers provided by the Constitution.

In deciding generally whether a claim is justiciable, a court must determine whether "the duty asserted can be judicially identified and its breach judicially determined, and whether protection for the right asserted can be judicially molded." . . . Respondents do not seriously contend that the duty asserted and its alleged breach cannot be judicially determined. If petitioners are correct, the House had a duty to seat Powell once it determined he met the standing requirements set forth in the Constitution. It is undisputed that he met those requirements and that he was nevertheless excluded.

Respondents do maintain, however, that this case is not justiciable because, they assert, it is impossible for a federal court to "mold effective relief for resolving this case." Respondents emphasize that petitioners asked for coercive relief against the officers of the House, and, they contend, federal courts cannot issue mandamus or injunctions compelling officers or employees of the House to perform specific official acts. Respondents rely primarily on the Speech or Debate Clause to support this contention.

We need express no opinion about the appropriateness of coercive relief in this case, for petitioners sought a declaratory judgment, a form of relief the District Court could have issued. . . . We thus conclude that in terms of the general criteria of justiciability, this case is justiciable.

Respondents' maintain that even if this case is otherwise justiciable, it presents only a political question. It is well-established that the federal courts will not adjudicate political questions. . . . In *Baker* v. *Carr* . . . we noted that political questions are not justiciable primarily because of the separation of powers within the Federal Government. After reviewing our decisions in this area, we concluded that on the surface of any case held to involve a political question was at least one of the following formulations: "a textually demonstrable constitutional commitment of the issue to a co-ordinate political department; or a lack of judicially discoverable and manageable standards for resolving it; or the impossibility of deciding without an initial policy determination of a kind clearly for nonjudicial discretion; or the impossibility of a court's undertaking independent resolution without expressing lack of the respect due coordinate branches of government; or an unusual need for unquestioning adherence to a political decision already made; or the potentiality of embarrassment from multifarious pronouncements by various departments on one question." . . .

Respondents' first contention is that this case presents a political question because under Art. I, § 5, there has been a "textually demonstrable constitutional commitment" to the House of the "adjudicatory power" to determine Powell's qualifications. Thus it is argued that the House, and the House alone, has power to determine who is qualified to be a member. . . .

Respondents maintain that the House has broad power under § 5, and, they argue, the House may determine which are the qualifications necessary for membership. On the other hand, petitioners allege that the Constitution provides that an elected representative may be denied his seat only if the House finds he does not meet one of the standing qualifications expressly prescribed by the Constitution. . . .

In order to determine the scope of any "textual commitment" under Art. I, § 5, we necessarily must determine the meaning of the phrase to "judge the qualifications of its members." Petitioners argue that the records of the debates during the Constitutional Convention, available commentary from the post-Convention, pre-ratification period, and early congressional applications of Art. I, § 5, support their construction of the section. Respondents in-

sist, however, that a careful examination of the pre-Convention practices of the English Parliament and American colonial assemblies demonstrates that by 1787, a legislature's power to judge the qualifications of its members was generally understood to encompass exclusion or expulsion on the ground that an individual's character or past conduct rendered him unfit to serve. When the Constitution and the debates over its adoption are thus viewed in historical perspective, argue respondents, it becomes clear that the "qualifications" expressly set forth in the Constitution were not meant to limit the long recognized legislative power to exclude or expel at will, but merely to establish "standing incapacities," which could be altered only by a constitutional amendment. Our examination of the relevant historical materials leads us to the conclusion that petitioners are correct and that the Constitution leaves the House without authority to *exclude* any person, duly elected by his constituents, who meets all the requirements for membership expressly prescribed in the Constitution. . . .

Had the intent of the Framers emerged from these materials with less clarity, we would nevertheless have been compelled to resolve any ambiguity in favor of a narrow construction of the scope of Congress' power to exclude members-elect. A fundamental principle of our representative democracy is, in Hamilton's words, "that the people should choose whom they please to govern them." . . .

For these reasons, we have concluded that Art. I, § 5, is at most a "textually demonstrable commitment" to Congress to judge only the qualifications expressly set forth in the Constitution. Therefore, the "textual commitment" formulation of the political question doctrine does not bar federal courts from adjudicating petitioners' claims.

Respondents' alternate contention is that the case presents a political question because judicial resolution of petitioners' claim would produce a "potentially embarrassing confrontation between coordinate branches" of the Federal Government. But, as our interpretation of Art. I, § 5, discloses, a determination of Petitioner Powell's right to sit would require no more than an interpretation of the Constitution. Such a determination falls within the traditional role accorded courts to interpret the law, and does not involve a "lack of respect due [a] coordinate branch of government," nor does it involve an "initial policy determination of a kind clearly for nonjudicial discretion." . . . Our system of government requires that federal courts on occasion interpret the Constitution in a manner at variance with the construction given the document by another branch. The alleged conflict that such an adjudication may cause cannot justify the courts' avoiding their constitutional responsibility.

Nor are any of the other formulations of a political question "inextricable from the case at bar." . . . Petitioners seek a determination that the House was without power to exclude Powell from the 90th Congress, which, we have seen, requires an interpretation of the Constitution—a determination for which clearly there are "judicially manageable standards." Finally, a judicial resolution of petitioners' claim will not result in "multifarious pronouncements by various departments on one question." . . . [I]t is the responsibility of this Court to act as the ultimate interpreter of the Constitution. . . . Thus, we conclude that petitioners' claim is not barred by the political question doctrine, and having determined that the claim is otherwise generally justiciable, we hold that the case is justiciable.

To summarize, we have determined the following: (1) This case has not been mooted by Powell's seating in the 91st Congress. (2) Although this action should be dismissed against respondent Congressmen, it may be sustained against their agents. (3) The 90th Congress' denial of membership to Powell cannot be treated as an expulsion. (4) We have jurisdiction over the subject matter of this controversy. (5) The case is justiciable.

MR. JUSTICE DOUGLAS, CONCURRING (OMITTED).
MR. JUSTICE STEWART, DISSENTING (OMITTED).

[Adam Clayton Powell was reelected to the Ninety-first Congress. He was permitted to take his seat but was fined $25,000 and stripped of his seniority and chairmanship of the House Labor and Education Committee. Thus, when the case reached the Supreme Court, he was again a member of Congress in good standing. The Court rejected claims of mootness by noting that the issue of back pay was still open.

If Powell had been *expelled* for misconduct, could the Supreme Court have reviewed the case? In a concurring opinion, Justice Douglas suggested that *expulsion* of a member of Congress would *not* be reviewable. Another question formally left unanswered was whether or not the Supreme Court could—or would— review a challenge to the factual determinations of Article I, Section 2 standards. Suppose a member of Congress were excluded because of a disputed finding that he or she was not a citizen? A footnote to the Court's opinion suggested that such questions would *not* be reviewable!

In his well-known book *Impeachment,* Raoul Berger has argued forcefully that *Baker* and *Powell* have very seriously undermined the political questions doctrine, so much so that the question of judicial review of Senate conviction on impeachment charges must be reopened.[1] Berger argues that the categories of *exclusion* from the House of Representatives—age, residence, and citizenship—are much clearer than those defining impeachment (treason, bribery, high crimes and misdemeanors). Furthermore, he argues that it is factual questions, such as in *Luther* v. *Borden* (which government was in fact authorized by the voters of Rhode Island?) that implicate the political questions doctrine, not just "constitutional boundaries." *Powell* v. *McCormack*, Berger argues, stands for the proposition that the Supreme Court may inquire into any governmental action in excess of jurisdiction, for example, any alleged usurpation of power. He finds in the Constitution the general principle that all arbitrary power must be condemned and that all constitutional limits are subject to judicial enforcement. The resignation of President Nixon forclosed any immediate opportunity for the Supreme Court to review a presidential conviction on impeachment charges.]

6. THE LIMITS OF SUPREME COURT POWER IN A DEMOCRATIC SOCIETY

[Is the Supreme Court an anomaly in a democratic society? One's response to that simple question will influence a subsequent judgment about the Court's proper role. The selections that follow summarize the main lines of thought on this subject. They are, of course, only samples of a large and diverse literature.]

A. A Note On The Supreme Court's "Special Role": Mr. Justice Stone's "Footnote 4"

In the introductory essay to this chapter, we introduced the concepts of "judicial self-restraint" and "judicial activism." Debate about the Supreme Court's proper role is continuous, but at no time in recent history has it been more visible, and perhaps more bitterly contested, than on the Court itself during the New Deal period. Franklin D. Roosevelt was elected president in 1932, with large majorities in the Senate and the House of Representatives. Congress enacted a number of important bills that sought to relieve the stress and hasten recovery from the Depression. Much of this legislation, however, was anathema to the conservative justices on the Court. A number of important recovery statutes were held to be unconstitutional, and Roosevelt's frustration at these setbacks produced the constitutional crisis of 1937 when he introduced legislation to expand the number of justices on the Supreme Court. (Details about Roosevelt's "court packing plan," as it came to be known by its opponents, are presented in the next chapter.)

On the Court, the three liberal justices, Benjamin Cardozo, Louis Brandeis, and Harlan Stone, protested vigorously at what they believed to be a usurpation of judicial power. Speaking for the liberal dissenters, Stone delivered an unusually sharp criticism of the majority's lack of restraint in *United States* v. *Butler* (1936). An exerpt from this dissent, and Justice Sutherland's response to it in a later case, has already been presented (see pp. 31–32).

In 1937 (in events to be described more fully in the next chapter, see pp. 248–251), the tides of battle on the

---

[1]Raoul Berger, *Impeachment: The Constitutional Problems* (Cambridge: Harvard University Press, 1973), chap. 3.

Court began to turn. A new Supreme Court majority, which included the three liberals and Chief Justice Hughes and Justice Roberts, voted in *West Coast Hotel* v. *Parrish* (1937) to *uphold* the validity of a state law fixing minimum wages and maximum hours for women. Later that year in *National Labor Relations Board* v. *Jones & Loughlin Steel Corp* (1937), the same justices voted in favor of the validity of the National Labor Relations Act, the New Deal's successor to the National Recovery Act, which had been invalidated by the Court in 1935. Several new Supreme Court appointments by President Roosevelt, his first since taking office, gave further support to the liberal repudiation of the doctrine that the Supreme Court could sit as a super legislature and overturn economic regulations by either Congress or the states of which it did not approve. One question that had to be answered, however, was whether or not this new policy of judicial self-restraint applied across the board to *all* types of cases, or whether it was to be restricted only to those that challenged economic regulations.

One answer to that question came from Justice Stone, who wrote the Court's opinion in *United States* v. *Carolene Products Corporation* (1938). In a footnote to that opinion, which otherwise upheld a regulatory statute, Stone sought to distinguish between economic legislation, which was entitled to the strongest presumption of constitutionality, and other legislative acts that restricted noneconomic individual rights. Those rights, Stone said, were deserving of *special* protection from the Court, particularly if they were claimed by individuals or groups otherwise excluded from the political process. "Footnote 4," as it has come to be known, was to become a charter

statement of the philosophy that the Supreme Court had a special "activist" role to play in protecting civil rights and civil liberties:

There may be a narrower scope for operation of the presumption of constitutionality when legislation appears on its face to be within a specific prohibition of the Constitution, such as those of the first ten amendments, which are deemed equally specific when held to be embraced within the Fourteenth.

It is unnecessary to consider now whether legislation which restricts those political processes which can ordinarily be expected to bring about repeal of undesirable legislation, is to be subjected to more exacting judicial scrutiny under the general prohibitions of the Fourteenth Amendment than are most other types of legislation. . . .

Nor need we enquire whether similar considerations enter into the review of statutes directed at particular religious . . . or national . . . or racial minorities . . . whether prejudice against discrete and insular minorities may be a special condition, which tends seriously to curtail the operation of those political processes ordinarily to be relied upon to protect minorities, and which may call for a correspondingly more searching judicial inquiry.

B. Mr. Justice Frankfurter, Dissenting in West Virginia Board of Education v. Barnette (1943)

[Among recent justices, Felix Frankfurter was the most eloquent exponent of judicial self-restraint. Perhaps his most memorable expression of this philosophy came in the second "flag salute" case, *West Virginia Board of Education* v. *Barnette* (1943). In this case the Court overruled its prior decision in *Minersville School District* v. *Gobitis* (1940) and held that a state could not require children of the Jehovah's Witness faith, contrary to their religious beliefs, to salute the American flag.

Frankfurter, author of the *Gobitis* opinion, now found himself in dissent.]

One who belongs to the most vilified and persecuted minority in history is not likely to be insensible to the freedoms guaranteed by our Constitution. Were my purely personal attitude relevant I should wholeheartedly associate myself with the general libertarian views in the Court's opinion, representing as they do the thought and action of a lifetime. But as judges we are neither Jew nor Gentile, neither Catholic nor agnostic. We owe equal attachment to the Constitution and are equally bound by our judicial obligations whether we derive our citizenship from the earliest or the latest immigrants to these shores. As a member of this Court I am not justified in writing my private notions of policy into the Constitution, no matter how deeply I may cherish them or how mischievous I may deem their disregard. The duty of a judge who must decide which of two claims before the Court shall prevail, that of a State to enact and enforce laws within its general competence or that of an individual to refuse obedience because of the demands of his conscience, is not that of the ordinary person. It can never be emphasized too much that one's own opinion about the wisdom or evil of a law should be excluded altogether when one is doing one's duty on the bench. The only opinion of our own even looking in that direction that is material is our opinion whether legislators could in reason have enacted such a law. In the light of all the circumstances, including the history of this question in this Court, it would require more daring than I possess to deny that reasonable legislators could have taken the action which is before us for review. . . .

Not so long ago we were admonished that "the only check upon our own exercise of power is our own sense of self-restraint. For the removal of unwise laws from the statute books appeal lies not to the courts but to the ballot and to the processes of democratic government." . . .

The admonition that judicial self-restraint alone limits arbitrary exercise of our authority is relevant every time we are asked to nullify legislation. The Constitution does not give us greater veto power when dealing with one phase of "liberty" than with another, or when dealing with grade school regulations than with college regulations that offend conscience. . . . In neither situation is our function comparable to that of a legislature or are we free to act as though we were a super-legislature. Judicial self-restraint is equally necessary whenever an exercise of political or legislative power is challenged. There is no warrant in the constitutional basis of this Court's authority for attributing different roles to it depending upon the nature of the challenge to the legislation. Our power does not vary according to the particular provision of the Bill of Rights which is invoked. The right not to have property taken without just compensation has, so far as the scope of judicial power is concerned, the same constitutional dignity as the right to be protected against unreasonable searches and seizures, and the latter has no less claim than freedom of the press or freedom of speech or religious freedom. In no instance is this Court the primary protector of the particular liberty that is invoked. . . .

The reason why from the beginning even the narrow judicial authority to nullify legislation has been viewed with a jealous eye is that it serves to prevent the full play of the democratic process. The fact that it may be an undemocratic aspect of our scheme of government does not call for its rejection or its disuse. But it is the best of reasons, as this Court has frequently recognized, for the greatest caution in its use. . . .

The subjection of dissidents to the general requirement of saluting the flag, as a measure conducive to the training of children in good citizenship, is very far from being the first instance of exacting obedience to general laws that have offended deep religious scruples. Compulsory vaccination . . . food inspection regulations . . . the obligation to bear arms . . . testimonial duties . . . compulsory medical treatment . . . these are but illustrations of conduct that has often been compelled in the enforcement of legislation of general applicability even though the religious consciences of particular individuals rebelled at the exaction.

Law is concerned with external behavior and not with the inner life of man. It rests in large measure upon compulsion. Socrates lives in history partly because he gave his life for the conviction that duty of obedience to secular law does not presuppose consent to its enactment or belief in its virtue. The consent upon which free government rests is the consent that comes from sharing in the process of making and unmaking laws. The state is not shut out from a domain because the individual conscience may deny the state's claim. The individual conscience may profess what faith it chooses. It may affirm and promote that faith—in the language of the Constitution, it may "exercise" it freely—but it cannot thereby restrict community action through political organs in matters of community concern, so long as the action is not asserted in a discriminatory way either openly or by stealth. One

may have the right to practice one's religion and at the same time owe the duty of formal obedience to laws that run counter to one's beliefs. . . .

We are told that symbolism is a dramatic but primitive way of communicating ideas. Symbolism is inescapable. Even the most sophisticated live by symbols. But it is not for this Court to make psychological judgments as to the effectiveness of a particular symbol in inculcating concededly indispensable feelings, particularly if the state happens to see fit to utilize the symbol that represents our heritage and our hopes. . . . The significance of a symbol lies in what it represents. To reject the swastika does not imply rejection of the Cross. And so it bears repetition to say that it mocks reason and denies our whole history to find in the allowance of a requirement to salute our flag on fitting occasions the seeds of sanction for obeisance to a leader. To deny the power to employ educational symbols is to say that the state's educational system may not stimulate the imagination because this may lead to unwise stimulation. . . .

One's conception of the Constitution cannot be severed from one's conception of a judge's function in applying it. The Court has no reason for existence if it merely reflects the pressures of the day. Our system is built on the faith that men set apart for this special function, freed from the influences of immediacy and from the deflections of worldly ambition, will become able to take a view of longer range than the period of responsibility entrusted to Congress and legislatures. We are dealing with matters as to which legislators and voters have conflicting views. Are we as judges to impose our strong convictions on where wisdom lies? . . .

Of course patriotism can not be enforced by the flag salute. But neither can the liberal spirit be enforced by judicial invalidation of illiberal legislation. Our constant preoccupation with the constitutionality of legislation rather than with its wisdom tends to preoccupation of the American mind with a false value. The tendency of focussing attention on constitutionality is to make constitutionality synonymous with wisdom, to regard a law as all right if it is constitutional. Such an attitude is a great enemy of liberalism. Particularly in legislation affecting freedom of thought and freedom of speech much which should offend a free-spirited society is constitutional. Reliance for the most precious interests of civilization, therefore, must be found outside of their vindication in courts of law. Only a persistent positive translation of the faith of a free society into the convictions and habits and actions of a community is the ultimate reliance against unabated temptations to fetter the human spirit.

C. Mr. Justice Blackmun, Dissenting in Furman v. Georgia (1972)

[In a surprising decision, the Supreme Court decided, by a 5-4 majority, that the death penalty, as imposed and carried out in the United States at that time, was cruel and unusual punishment which violated the Eighth and Fourteenth Amendments. Each justice wrote a separate opinion in the case, and the judgment of the Court was announced in a brief *per curiam* opinion. The justices in the majority agreed that the discretionary procedures used to apply the death penalty were selective and arbitrary—wanton and freakish, like being struck by lightning—although at least two justices, Brennan and Marshall, argued that the death penalty was unconstitutional per se. Justice Harry Blackmun, President Nixon's second appointment to the Court and a former judge on the Court of Appeals for the Eighth Circuit, was one of the four dissenters. His opinion did not address these constitutional questions but challenged the propriety of judicial intervention into what had always been left to legislative determination.]

Cases such as these provide for me an excruciating agony of the spirit. I yield to no one in the depth of my distaste, antipathy, and, indeed, abhorrence, for the death penalty, with all its aspects of physical distress and fear and of moral judgment exercised by finite minds. That distaste is buttressed by a belief that capital punishment serves no useful purpose that can be demonstrated. For me, it violates childhood's training and life's experiences, and is not compatible with the philosophical convictions I have been able to develop. It is antagonistic to any sense of "reverence for life." Were I a legislator, I would vote against the death penalty for the policy reasons argued by counsel for the respective petitioners and expressed and adopted in the several opinions filed by the Justices who vote to reverse these judgments.

. . .

The several concurring opinions acknowledge, as they must, that until today capital punishment was accepted and assumed as not unconstitutional *per se* under the Eighth Amendment or the Fourteenth Amendment.

. . .

Suddenly, however, the course of decision is now the opposite way, with the Court evidently persuaded that somehow the passage of time has taken us to a place of greater maturity and outlook. The argument, plausible and high-sounding as it may be, is not persuasive. . . . The Court has just decided that it is time to strike down the death penalty. . . .

The Court has recognized, and I certainly subscribe to the proposition, that the Cruel and Unusual Punishments clause "may acquire meaning as public opinion becomes enlightened by a humane justice.". . .

My problem, however, as I have indicated, is the suddenness of the Court's perception of progress in the human attitude since decisions of only a short while ago. . . .

It is easier to strike the balance in favor of life and against death. It is comforting to relax in the thoughts—perhaps the rationalizations—that this is the compassionate decision for a maturing society; that this is the moral and the "right" thing to do; that thereby we convince ourselves that we are moving down the road toward human decency; that we value life even though that life has taken another or others or has grievously scarred another or others and their families; and that we are less barbaric than we were in 1879, or in 1890, or in 1910, or in 1947, or in 1958, or in 1963, or a year ago, in 1971. . . .

This, for me, is good argument, and it makes some sense. But it is good argument and it makes sense only in a legislative and executive way and not as a judicial expedient. As I have said above, were I a legislator, I would do all I could to sponsor and to vote for legislation abolishing the death penalty. And were I the chief executive of a sovereign State, I would be sorely tempted to exercise executive clemency as Governor Rockefeller of Arkansas did recently just before he departed from office. There—on the Legislative Branch of the State or Federal Government, and secondarily, on the Executive Branch—is where the authority and responsibility for this kind of action lies. The authority should not be taken over by the judiciary in the modern guise of an Eighth Amendment issue.

I do not sit on these cases, however, as a legislator, responsive, at least in part, to the will of constituents. Our task here, as must so frequently be emphasized and re-emphasized, is to pass upon the constitutionality of legislation that has been enacted and that is challenged. This is the sole task for judges. We should not allow our personal preferences as to the wisdom of legislative and congressional action, or our distaste for such action, to guide our judicial decision in cases such as these. The temptations to cross that policy line are very great. In fact, as today's decision reveals, they are almost irresistible.

. . .

I trust the Court fully appreciates what it is doing when it decides these cases the way it does today. Not only are the capital punishment laws of 39 States and the District of Columbia struck down, but also all those provisions of the federal statutory structure that permit the death penalty apparently are voided.

. . .

It is impossible for me to believe that the many lawyer-members of the House and Senate—including, I might add, outstanding leaders and prominent candidates for higher office—were callously unaware and insensitive of constitutional overtones in legislation of this type. The answer, of course, is that in 1961, in 1965, and in 1970 these elected representatives of the people—far more conscious of the temper of the times, of the maturing of society, and of the contemporary demands for man's dignity, than are we who sit cloistered on this Court—took it as settled that the death penalty then, as it always had been, was not in itself unconstitutional. Some of those Members of Congress, I suspect, will be surprised at this Court's giant stride today. . . .

["Activism" and "self-restraint" are relative terms. No member of the Supreme Court has ever (it is reasonable to assume) exhibited complete fidelity to one role or the other. A justice who preaches self-restraint under one set of circumstances may find the activist position compelling under others. Less than a year after the *Furman* case was decided, the Supreme Court struck down the abortion laws of every state on the grounds that such laws constituted an impermissible invasion of privacy. The 7-2 opinion of the Court, *Roe* v. *Wade* (1973), was written by Justice Harry Blackmun and joined in by two other justices who had dissented in *Furman,* Lewis Powell and Chief Justice Warren Burger. Justice William Rehnquist alone dissented in both cases, joined in *Roe* by Justice Byron White, who had voted in *Furman* to invalidate the death penalty and who now claimed that the Supreme Court was usurping the legitimate authority of the states by invalidating state abortion laws.]

D. *Alexander Bickel, The Web of Subjectivity*

. . . The insistence on reason in the judicial process, on analytical coherence, and on principled judgment no matter how narrow its compass, is traditional. Despite the countless lapses, it is an unmistakable thread in the fabric of our law—not alone the law of the Constitution—and of its literature. . . .

The restraints of reason tend to ensure also the independence of the judge, to liberate him from the demands and fears—dogmatic, arbitrary, irrational, self-or group-centered—that so often enchain other public officials. They make it possible for the judge, on some occasions, at any rate, to oppose against the will and faith of others, not merely his own will or deeply-felt faith, but a method of reaching judgments that may command the allegiance, on a second thought, even of those who

find a result disagreeable. The judge is thus buttressed against the world, but what is perhaps more significant and certain, against himself, against his own natural tendency to give way before waves of feeling and opinion that may be as momentary as they are momentarily overwhelming.

The obverse of the assurance of independence in the judge is the justification that his pursuit of the method of reason may provide for his supreme autonomy. Constitutional judgment is a high policy-making function performed in a political democracy by an institution that has to be regarded as deviant. For purposes of its one-man, one-vote doctrine, the Supreme Court has, paradoxically enough, persuaded itself that our government is organized on the populist principle. This is an admission against interest on the part of the Court. Nevertheless, our government is not, and ought not be, strictly majoritarian.

The Madisonian model of a multiplicity of factions vying against each other and checking each other still more nearly fits our system, which retains traces of resemblance even to Calhoun's model of concurrent majorities. It is perfectly clear as well that, aside from the judges, many other elites that are not immediately and not directly controlled by the electoral process wield power in American government. Yet elections do influence, and sometimes they determine, the movement of public policy, the policy of the nonjudicial elites as well as that of the immediately responsive officials. And the prospect of elections that may be so determinative has vast influence in the intervals between, for the electorate puts men in office and deposes them, in-

Reprinted from *The Supreme Court and the Idea of Progress* (New York: Harper & Row, 1970), pp. 81–87, 173–178.

cluding ultimately members of elites.

But elections are the tip of the iceberg; the bulk of the political process is below. The jockeying, the bargaining, the trading, the threatening and the promising, the checking and the balancing, the spurring and the vetoing are continuous. They not only form the environment of government, legislative and executive, elected and elite, they are its engine. The judges are insulated from this environment, and secure against its influence, as well as against the influence of elections. The judges' engine in some aspects of their function is legislative policy, which they must find and execute; in others it is themselves.

The independence of the judges is an absolute requirement if individual justice is to be done, if a society is to ensure that individuals will be dealt with in accordance with duly enacted general policies of the society, not by the whim of officials or of mobs, and dealt with evenhandedly, under rules that would apply also to others similarly situated, no matter who they might be. The methods of reason and the norms of the craft of law bolster this independence. . . . But supreme judicial autonomy, the judge answerable only to his own conscience in making policy for the society, in adjusting, conformably to one or another choice of values, the conflicting interests, desires, and ethical and moral aspirations and preferences of the groups that constitute the society—that is something else again, even though men, using the words in a different sense, may call various choices of policy just or unjust. . . .

Access to political power is not a function solely of the franchise, just as the franchise, even for groups that have and exercise it to the full, does not provide all the access and leverage that intensity of interest, convic-

tion, or grievance may demand and justify. But the franchise is important, and symbolically it is crucial. . . .

The business of the Court is not to become the instrument for attaining the substantive objectives of such an excluded group, but to nullify the exclusion, as in the case of the Negroes the Court has in recent times consistently striven to do, pursuant to the mandate of the Fifteenth Amendment. (The Nineteenth Amendment, guaranteeing the vote to women, has happily proved self-executing.) . . .

Putting aside, then, justice to the individual, and the function, so seldom in issue, of guarding the elemental integrity of a system in which all groups have access to political power, the supreme autonomy that the Court asserts in many matters of substantive policy needs justification in a political democracy. And it can have it, if at all, only in the claim that the function never relinquishes the pursuit of reason, and that ultimately it is principled, that the Court does not discharge its office even by doing what most people may think is right or necessary, unless it does it in principled fashion. The justification must be that constitutional judgment turns on issues of moral philosophy and political theory, which we abstract from the common political process, at least initially, because it would be wrong to decide them merely by a count of noses, or by striking some bargain. . . .

Certainly the Court, like other institutions, is in part the maker of the tradition that influences it, and other institutions are also constrained in some measure by the history they have made. And certainly history is more a storehouse of caveats than of patented remedies for the ills of mankind. But while the other institutions may be, the Court is not the place for the heedless break with the past, not the place for the half loaf that is better than none, for the split difference and other arbitrary choices, or for the action supported by nothing but rhetoric, sentiment, anger, or prejudice. The Court is the place for principled judgment, disciplined by the method of reason familiar to the discourse of moral philosophy, and in constitutional adjudication, the place only for that, or else its insulation from the political process is inexplicable. . . .

If my probe into a near-term future is not wildly off the mark, therefore, the upshot is that the Warren Court's noblest enterprise—school desegregation—and its most popular enterprise—reapportionment—not to speak of school-prayer cases and those concerning aid to parochial schools, are heading toward obsolescence, and in large measure abandonment. And, if this assessment has any validity, it must be read as a lesson.

The future may yet belong to the Warren Court. There is no possible assurance to the contrary. But if the future follows more nearly the scenario I have just reviewed, then we must consider first of all whether the predicament might not have been escaped by a more faithful adherence to the method of analytical reason, and a less confident reliance on the intuitive judicial capacity to identify the course of progress. Pragmatic skepticism is certainly an attitude of its Progressive realist progenitors that the gallant Warren Court emulated all too little. More careful analysis of the realities on which it was imposing its law, and an appreciation of historical truth, with all its uncertainties, in lieu of a recital of selected historical slogans, would long since have rendered the Warren Court wary of its one-man, one-vote

simplicities. The Court might have been inclined to stop shortly after its initial venture into the field, and to be content with striking down obsolete apportionments, with requiring legislatures to act after each census, and with formulating otherwise only the rule that at least one institution of a state government, commonly the executive, must be purely majoritarian. . . .

The judicial process is too principle-prone and principle-bound—it has to be, there is no other justification or explanation for the role it plays. It is also too remote from conditions, and deals, case by case, with too narrow a slice of reality. It is not accessible to all the varied interests that are in play in any decision of great consequence. It is, very properly, independent. It is passive. It has difficulty controlling the stages by which it approaches a problem. It rushes forward too fast, or it lags; its pace hardly ever seems just right. For all these reasons, it is, in a vast, complex, changeable society, a most unsuitable instrument for the formation of policy.

Nothing is more evident in the Supreme Court's past than that most of its prior major enterprises—the better part of Marshall's nationalizing decisions being always a splendid exception—have not worked out. And yet nothing is more easily induced by the Supreme Court's past than complacency about its future. Somehow the Court has always managed to survive its failures. It has endured; hence perhaps it always will.

We wish it to endure—the people, it may be, have wished it to endure—because, aside from its forays into broad social policy, the Court discharges a much narrower, but still reasoned and principled, law-making function. It makes law interstitially, with effects that may be far-reaching and widely felt, if they are at all, only in the aggregate, over time. Someone must do this, whether an administrative elite or a more independent judicial one. Elected legislatures cannot do it prospectively, and no one can do it abstractly, outside the context of a concrete controversy. It might be done by a politically more responsive elite, but in the cases which call for performance of this task, a line between the demands of individual justice and the elements of more general policy is often difficult to draw. . . .

There is a body of opinion—and there has been, throughout our history—which holds that the Court can well apply obvious principles, plainly acceptable to a generality of the population, because they are plainly stated in the constitution (*e.g.*, the right to vote shall not be denied on account of race), or because they are almost universally shared; but the Court should not manufacture principle. However, although the Constitution plainly contains a number of admonitions, it states very few plain principles; and few are universally accepted. Principles that may be thought to have wide, if not universal, acceptance may not have it tomorrow, when the freshly-coined, quite novel principle may, in turn, prove acceptable. The true distinction, therefore, relevant to the bulk of the Court's business, lies not so much between more and less acceptable principles as between principles of different orders of magnitude and complexity in the application. . . .

The society also values the capacity of the judges to draw its attention to issues of the largest principle that may have gone unheeded in the welter of its pragmatic doings. *Brown* v. *Board of Education* and other education cases, as also the reapportion-ment decisions, fulfilled this role of the Court. Having highlighted an issue of principle, however, the Court proceeds with the attempt to make the society live up to its resolution of it, which is another sort of function altogether. But again, since we are unable to formulate a rule that will ensure performance of the one function while guarding against assumption of the other, we tolerate both.

These are all reasons why the Court has endured. Another, perhaps the deepest, is a widely-shared if inarticulate hope that Learned Hand was wrong when he said "that a society so riven that the spirit of moderation is gone, no court *can* save." A society "where that spirit flourishes," Judge Hand added in this deservedly famous passage, "no court *need* save." Here, I believe, he might have said "can," for he was talking about social policy made by judges, and they cannot, as I have just suggested, make it well. But is there not a chance that the judges might recall a riven society to its senses?

E. Raoul Berger, The Imperial Court

The Burger Court's gradual withdrawal from some of the Warren Court's civil liberties decisions is leading dejected liberals to reappraise the role of the Supreme Court. Lamentations fill the air. Because the Warren Court decisions realized liberal aspirations, liberals sang its praises, glossing over the question of constitutional authority and forgetting that for many decades the Court had employed similar techniques for anti-democratic purposes, to block badly needed social and economic reforms.

The shift in liberal thinking is

Reprinted from *The New York Times Magazine*, October 9, 1977.

strikingly exemplified by Yale Law Professor Charles Black, an ardent admirer of the Warren Court. Discontented with a recent death-penalty decision, he asked in late 1976 "whether we do well to entrust the Court with the job of a rational defense of ordered liberty?" And he wondered "whether we liberals . . . may not be in part to blame for a . . . quite evident trend toward the point of view that reason doesn't matter much and can be brushed aside if only the result is thought desirable." That viewpoint was unabashedly expressed in 1966 by Black's colleague, Professor Fred Rodell, who exulted that Chief Justice Earl Warren "brushed off pedantic impediments to the results he felt were right," that he was not a "look-it-up-in-the-library intellectual," and that he was "almost unique" in his "offhand dismissal of legal and historical research from both sides and in pragmatic dependence on present-day results." Rodell only expressed pungently what his fellow result-oriented academicians phrased more obliquely.

Current liberal disorientation illustrates afresh that approval of judicial decisions turns on the accidents of political appointments to the Bench—a Burger for a Warren. My liberal brethren are chagrined because the result-oriented tactics of the Warren Court are now being employed by the Burger Court for goals of which they disapprove. But liberals, I wrote back in 1942, cannot complain if a conservative succession employs techniques which they have sanctified, adding that I like it no better when the "reconstructed" Court reads my predilections into the Constitution than when Justices Pierce Butler, James McReynolds, George Sutherland and Willis Van Devanter read in theirs in order to halt the New Deal. The test of constitutionality is not that we like the result but whether the given power was granted. In the words of Chief Justice John Marshall, "The peculiar circumstances of the moment may render a measure more or less wise, but cannot render it more or less constitutional."

My theme, by no means novel and recently restated by Chicago Law Professor Philip Kurland, is that the Court has usurped "general governmental powers on the pretext that its authority derives from the 14th Amendment." It has taken over the policy-making powers of the state legislatures and substituted government-by-judiciary. By resort to the allegedly vague "equal protection" and "due process" clauses, it has replaced the choices of the framers by personal predilections of the Justices, which vary with the changing of the judicial guard. At the peak of dissatisfaction with the anti-New Deal Court (1937), Professor Felix Frankfurter wrote President Franklin Roosevelt, "People have been taught to believe that when the Supreme Court speaks it is not they [the Justices] who speak but the Constitution, whereas, of course, in so many vital cases, it is *they* who speak and *not* the Constitution. And I verily believe that that is what the country needs most to understand." Whether popular understanding has since advanced may be doubted; when the people are told that "the Constitution requires busing" they take it on trust that is what the *Constitution* truly requires, apparently unaware that the words which fall from the lips of the Delphic oracle are uttered by the priests.

That, an eminent liberal student of the Court, Claremont Professor Leonard Levy, explains is inescapable: "From the beginning . . . the

Court . . . read the Constitution to mean whatever it wanted. Despite pretenses to the contrary, the Court could do no other, for . . . American constitutional law exists in the collective eye of those who happen at any moment to dominate the Court."

If, indeed, constitutional law exists only in the "collective eye" of a dominant Court majority, the Burger Court legitimately may claim, "now it is our turn." The name of the game is "Two Can Play." The Burger Justices were selected by President Nixon precisely because, for example, they viewed the administration of state criminal law quite differently from the Warren Court. And, since the Warren Court had discarded long-standing precedents in wholesale lots, the Burger Court is hardly to be blamed for showing no more respect for the very recent Warren Court precedents. Once it is posited that adjudication inevitably is result-oriented—what is constitutional is just what a majority of the Court desires—we should not complain because a new majority prefers its own policies to those of its predecessor. On that view the Constitution is like a weather vane that turns with shifting political winds. And, as Justice Hugo Black and others have charged, it permits the Court to amend the Constitution under the guise of interpretation, and to take over the legislative function of policy-making for the nation. The result is government-by-judiciary.

One example may suffice. The reapportionment decisions of the early 1960's illustrate how the Warren Court supplanted the unmistakable intention of the framers of the 14th Amendment by its own view of what the national welfare required. The overwhelming weight of the evidence shows that the framers entirely *excluded* suffrage from its scope and left control with the states, where it had resided from the beginning. But the Court, reading the beguiling slogan "one man-one vote" into the - "equal protection" clause of the amendment, assumed control of how votes within the states should be weighted. As a matter of abstract justice the slogan is impeccable—why should the vote of a rural redneck count for five or more times that of a city-dweller? But as Justice John Harlan demonstrated in a dissent which Chief Justice Warren made no attempt to refute—a demonstration generally considered to be irrefutable, which even Justice Black came to accept—the framers plainly excluded suffrage from Federal control. Consequently the "one man-one vote" decisions represent a judicial revision in flat contradiction of the framers' intention, an intention, on traditional canons, that is as good as written into the amendment. . . .

As a palpable revision of the Constitution, the reapportionment cases represent an awesome exercise of power not given to the Court. This is not a matter of "strict construction"; it plainly flouts the unmistakable intention of the framers. In one desegregation case, Chief Justice Warren did not mince words; faced with the unfavorable history of the 14th Amendment, he declared, "we cannot turn back the clock to 1868 when the amendment was adopted." That is to say, what the framers (and the people who ratified it on the strength of their representations) intended is irrelevant; the Court laid claim to power to "adapt" the Constitution to its view of what was required by the contemporary scene. True, malapportionment could be corrected in no other way because the classes it favored could block all attempts at cure by amendment. But one may condemn the practice and yet reject the exercise of unauthorized power to abolish it. The power of amendment is given exclusively to the people by Article V of the Constitution, and then only through the mechanism there provided—approval by two-thirds of the Congress and three-fourths of the states. The Court is not empowered to amend the Constitution even in the noblest of causes; the usurpation of power stands no higher in the hands of a Warren than of a Nixon.

What about the so-called "majestic generalities," the "vague" terms of the Constitution, such as "due process of law," which allegedly set the Court at large? If due process is vague, it is because, as Charles Curtis, a distinguished lawyer and writer, rejoiced, the Court made it so. Professor Robert G. McCloskey, a noted student of the Court, described the development of substantive due process as "the classic example of government-by-judiciary." The development is readily demonstrable. At the adoption of the Constitution, due process meant the service of proper process in due course in order to afford a defendant an opportunity to answer in a *judicial proceeding.* In almost every state constitution as well as the Federal Bill of Rights, due process (or its equivalent, the law of the land) was located alongside of other safeguards of a defendant charged with crime, again indicating that it applied to *judicial procedure.* One thing due process clearly did *not* mean; it did not embrace judicial authority to *override legislation* on substantive or policy grounds, let alone to dictate national policy on the Court's own initiative.

On the very eve of the Constitutional Convention, Alexander Hamilton stated in the New York Assembly: "The words 'due process' have a technical import, and are applicable *only* to the process and proceedings of the courts of justice; they *can never be referred to an act of the legislature.*"

In combing the records of the Constitutional Convention, the Ratification Conventions and the First Congress which framed the due process clause, I found no expression to the contrary. In 1866 the framers of the 14th Amendment reiterated the received connotation—judicial procedure. Deep into the 19th century it was the all but universal view that due process applies only to *judicial* procedure.

It was not until the 1890's that the Court transformed due process into an instrument for the overturn of *legislation* which it deemed "socialistic." In 1905, for example, the Court set aside a statute that sought to protect bakery workers by limiting their toil to 10 hours a day, 6 days a week, on the alleged ground that it violated their "liberty of contract." Not only was this a splendid example of judicial casuistry, but it rested on the untenable premise that "liberty of contract" was a branch of the "liberty" protected by the due process clause, when in fact the liberty thus secured was historically only liberty from physical restraint, i.e. imprisonment by due course of judicial proceedings.

Invoking the protection afforded to "property" by the clause, the Court defeated a whole array of such legislative attempts to deal with pernicious economic practices, a course that came to be known as "economic due process." By 1937, this practice, the Court itself acknowledges, had become discredited and economic due process had become a "dirty phrase." Now the Court ventured into fresh pastures, fashioning a new set of restrictions under the mantle of "liberty" in order to fulfill libertarian aspirations. But the logic which now withholds due process protection for "property" while extending it to favored aspects of the companion term "liberty" has yet to be spelled out. For as Judge Learned Hand pointed out, "life, liberty or property" are on a par in the due process clause; one is nowhere set above the other. In fact the Founders rated property highest because they considered that without property life and liberty were empty promises. Anatole France made the point ironically: The poor are as free as the rich to sleep under a bridge.

Assuming that the Founding Fathers meant due process to pertain exclusively to judicial procedure, why, apologists for the Warren Court's result-oriented decisions ask, should we be bound by the "dead hand of the past," why should the framers "rule us from their graves." Those who would adhere to the "original intention" of the framers are scornfully charged with "filiopietism," "verbal archeology," "antiquarian historicism that would freeze [the] original meaning of the Constitution." Yet the interpretation of all documents—contracts, wills, statutes—seeks to ascertain the intention of the draftsmen and to give it effect. James Wilson, second only to Madison as an architect of the Constitution, observed, "The first and governing maxim in the interpretation of a statute is, to discover the meaning of those who made it." As President, Jefferson pledged to administer the Constitution according to the "meaning to be found in the explanations of those who advocated it."

The reason the "original intention" is so important was stated by Madison long ago: "If the sense in which the Constitution was accepted and ratified by the nation . . . be not the guide in expounding it, there can

be no faithful exercise of its powers." Without adherence to the "original intention," the words employed by the framers are but "empty shells" into which the Court may, and does, pour its own meaning. Then is the Burger no less free than the Warren Court to do so, then are the "chains of the Constitution" with which Jefferson hoped to bind down our delegates "from mischief," reduced to ropes of sand. To thrust aside the "dead hand" of the framers, therefore, is to thrust aside the Constitution.

Ours is a government "founded on the consent of the governed." The people, declared James Iredell of North Carolina, one of the ablest of the founders, "have chosen to be governed under such principles. They have not chosen to be governed or promised to submit upon any other." The Constitution is a charter of delegated powers and, as the Court said, it "limits" the powers of all government officers, judges included. It was no more given to the Court than to President Nixon to rewrite the charter and assume powers not granted by the people. An agent, said Hamilton, "may not new-model his commission"; he may not change an authorization to sell your car into one to sell your house.

The courts, as James Bradley Thayer and Learned Hand pointed out, were empowered to *police* constitutional boundaries, to insure that the departments did not "overleap their bounds." But within those bounds the exercise of discretion was left to the departments, free of judicial interference. Policy-making, for example, was the province of the legislature. The separation of powers excludes the judiciary from intrusion into that domain, as the 1780 Massachusetts Constitution, drafted by John Adams, made explicit: so that "the judiciary shall not exercise the powers of the legislature." "Legislative power" does not become vested in the Court because Congress fails to exercise it.

The exclusion of the courts from legislative policy-making does not rest solely on the argument from principle—it was spelled out by the framers. In the Constitutional Convention it was proposed that the Justices be joined with the President in a Council of Revision for the veto of undesirable legislation, on the ground that the judicial power to declare laws unconstitutional would not stretch to laws that, though constitutional, were "unwise, dangerous, destructive." This was rejected because, in the words of Nathaniel Gorham of Massachusetts, judges were not thought "to possess any peculiar knowledge of the mere policy of public measures," because, as Elbridge Gerry of Massachusetts observed, it was "quite foreign" to the "nature of the judicial office to make them judges of the policy of public measures," to make them "legislators." The framers, in John Dickinson's words, did not want judges to be "law-givers." Like Learned Hand 150 years later, Gerry refused to set judges up as "the guardians of the rights of the people."

Whenever proponents of a judicial policy are at a loss for constitutional authority, they trot out the invocation to a "living Constitution," based on a dictum of Chief Justice Marshall in *McCulloch* v. *Maryland*. The classic appeal was that of Chief Justice Charles Evans Hughes in 1934. Rejecting the argument "that the great clauses of the Constitution must be confined to the interpretation" placed upon them by the framers, he stated, "It was to guard against such a narrow conception that Chief Justice Marshall uttered a memorable warning—'We must never forget that it is a Constitution we are expounding . . . a Constitution intended to endure for ages to come, and consequently to be adapted to the various *crises* of human affairs.' "

No comfort for *judicial* adaptation can be extracted from Marshall's dictum. There he merely pleaded for some leeway in Congress's *choice of means* to effectuate broadly phrased powers. Even so, his decision came under attack, by Madison among others, and he rose to its defense in a series of pseudonymous articles where he emphatically and repeatedly disclaimed "the most distant allusion to *any extension by construction* of the powers of Congress." (Italics mine.) He declared that the exercise of judicial power to decide all questions "arising under the Constitution" "can *not* be the assertion of a *right to change* that instrument." (Italics mine.) Justice Black justly commented that "in recalling that it is a Constitution 'intended to endure for ages to come,' we also remember that the Founders wisely provided for the means of the endurance: Changes in the Constitution . . . are to be proposed by Congress or conventions and ratified by the states."

The Founders foresaw the need for adaptation of the Constitution to future exigencies and provided for it in Article V by a process that enables *the people* to deliberate and decide upon a change, whether the grant of more power is desirable or safe. True, the process is cumbersome, but that does not authorize the Justices to dispense with a referral to the people and to amend the Constitution in their stead, even in the worthiest of causes. This was underscored by Hamilton in Federalist No. 78, his great defense of the judicial power to set aside action not warranted by the Constitution: "Until the people have, by some solemn and authoritative act, annulled or changed the established form, it is binding upon themselves collectively, as well as individually; and no presumption, or even knowledge of their sentiments, can warrant their representatives in a departure from it, prior to such an act."

We must reject the notion that the black-robed Justices are a priesthood to whom was given sole charge of arcane mysteries. The deflation of the "mystique of the Presidency" in Richard Nixon's wake should caution against indulging in a "mystique of the Court." Decisions of the Court, so Justices themselves have stated, are entitled only to so much respect as derives from their reasoning. Repeatedly the Court has confessed error by overruling its prior decisions; it has acknowledged that its resort to "due process" for governance of the nation's economic affairs was wrong. These are not the marks of an infallible priesthood. Justice Robert Jackson reminded the Court in 1953 that "We are not final because we are infallible; we are infallible because we are final." So, too, we must not equate the assertion of power with its letitimacy. No more than Nixon may the Court claim that "when the Court does it, it is legal." A claim to power withheld by the Constitution no more clothes the Court with it than repeated Presidential claims to warmaking power could vest the President with power the Constitution confined to Congress.

At times the administration of law results in injustice, or a desirable amendment may not be obtainable. But it does not follow, for example, because reapportionment was just, that the Court was authorized to require it. The Constitution exalts conformity with it above the demands of justice; judges are not sworn to do justice but "to support this Constitution." Over the lintel of the Supreme Court is inscribed "Equal Justice *Under* Law," not "Justice, cost what it may." Once limits are prescribed, Chief Justice Marshall declared, they may not "be passed at pleasure." Chief Judge Benjamin Cardozo wrote that judges do not have "the right to ignore the mandate of a statute, and render judgment in spite of it." Still less are they authorized to reverse the clearly discernible choice of the people expressed in the 14th Amendment.

The reasons for shrinking from such an exercise of unauthorized power were forcibly expressed in Washington's Farewell Address: "If in the opinion of the people, the distribution or modification of the Constitutional powers be in any particular wrong, let it be corrected by an amendment in the way in which the Constitution designates. But let there be no change by usurpation; for though this, in one instance, may be the instrument of good, it is the customary weapon by which free governments are destroyed. The precedent must always greatly overbalance in permanent evil any partial or transient benefit which the use can at any time yield." And the precedent made on the plea of emergency opens the door to the exercise of power where there is no emergency whatever.

Against this it is often urged that the words of the Constitution have acquired a patina of judicial interpretation for over a century; in other words, the exercise of extra-constitutional judicial power has been legitimized by usage . Judicial arrogation of a power to amend the Constitution in despite of Article V, which entrusts the power to the people alone, subverts the Constitution. Usurpation is no more legitimated by repetition than larceny becomes more lawful the 10th time than the first. It is not hallowed by the passage of time. Justice Oliver Wendell Holmes branded a hundred-year-old judicial doctrine as an "unconstitutional assumption of power by courts . . . which no lapse of time or respectable opinion should make us hesitate to correct."

Some have sought to rationalize the practice by the argument that the people have ratified it by tacit acquiescence. But they were never told that the Court was engaged over the years in amending the Constitution; they are always told that it is the Constitution, not the Court, that speaks. The Justices rebuffed Justice Jackson's plea in the 1954 "desegregation" case to tell the people that "we are making new law for a new day." Without disclosure there can be no ratification; nor can ratification by inertia displace the steps Article V reguires for amendment even by the people themselves.

"Our peculiar security," President Jefferson declared, "is the possession of a written Constitution. Let us not make it a blank paper by construction." As Jefferson indicated, the Founders regarded the Constitution as the bulwark of their liberties, to be cherished, in Hamilton's words, with "sacred reverence." A Constitution that may be rewritten in accordance with the predilections of any given majority of Justices is a "thing of wax," not the bulwark of our liberties. History confirms Justice Black's statement that the struggle for a written Constitution was "to make certain that men in power would be governed by *law* not the arbitrary fiat of the man or men in power," "according to the law of the land," not by the "law of judges." To countenance judicial amendment of the Constitution, even for a benign purpose, is to substitute government-by-judiciary for government by the people, to act upon the discredited principle that the end justifies the means. The essence of democracy is that policy be made by elected representative bodies, not by life-time appointees to the bench who are insulated from responsibility to the people. Better the risk of misgovernment by the people than the prospect of Utopia under the reign of nine—often only five— Platonic Guardians.

the decision-making process

1. INTRODUCTORY ESSAY

In order to understand how judicial policies are made, it is important to know the formal rules and procedures by which the Supreme Court conducts its business. At the same time, attention should also be given to the development of informal norms that give life and substance to the formal structure. Some thought should also be devoted to the policy implications of the Court's procedures and norms. We have already seen how norms regarding judicial self-restraint, or views toward the legitimacy of judicial review, might affect a justice's policy-making perspective. Now we are in a position to ask the same questions about procedures. For example: What are the policy implications of the way in which the Court decides cases, or the ways in which opinions are assigned and written, or the amount of discretion the Court exercises over its docket? In what ways do these and related factors limit or expand the Court's policy-making potential? In what ways do these factors push the Court toward more liberal, or more conservative, policy results?

An observer of the Court in action is immediately struck by the attention to form and ritual, by the precision of the Court's public appearances, and of course, by the majesty of the setting in which it functions. The magnificent marble palace, built in 1935, emphasizes the Court's stature as an independent and coequal branch of the federal government. At the same time, the austerity of the public corridors and the silence imposed on all visitors reinforce the image of isolation; the Court is part of the system, but at the same time, it is somewhat aloof from it and not to be disturbed in its routines. The Court's setting is the symbol of judicial independence and of the separation of powers.

Many of the rituals that have become part of the decision-making process convey important symbolic meaning. The high bench from which the justices, each in a custom-built leather chair, look down on the attorneys arguing cases, the black robes worn by the justices, the opening incantation of the bailiff that begins each session, and the formal discourse liberally sprinkled with archaic words all remind the observer of the long-standing traditions of which the Court is curator. The formal key in which the Court communicates its decisions, through written opinions sometimes laboriously read in open court and with little attention to the needs of the media, serves to emphasize the distinctiveness of the judicial process and the uniqueness of the Supreme Court. Such distinctions of ritual and style are both functional and purposeful: they tend to symbolize and to emphasize the basic orientation of the Court toward conservatism and stability rather than change, toward reasoned rather than subjective decisions, toward certainty rather than doubt and toward legal rather than mere policy considerations. Of course, there is more to the Court than meets the eye. But the manipulation of symbols primarily intended for the public and its image of the Court cannot help but affect the internal workings of the Court.

No institution can be totally impervious to change, and the Supreme Court's procedures have occasionally been altered. But there have been few major changes. One facet of the Court's work that has undergone major change is the practice of opinion writing. Under its first three chief justices—Jay, Rutledge, and Ellsworth—the practice was for each member of the Court to write a separate opinion in each case. This writing of *seriatim* opinions emphasized the internal divisions among the justices and is said to have detracted from the Court's prestige and power in its early days.

Before John Marshall, the Chief Justice was more of a presiding officer than a leader. Under Marshall, a startling reversal of form and procedure took place. The election of Thomas Jefferson as president in 1800 left the Federalists in control only of the Supreme Court, and the need to make the Court a more effective power within the government must have strongly influenced Marshall's actions. His claim to the power of judicial review was one step toward raising the stature of the Court.

Marshall successfully sought to establish himself as *the* leader on the Court. He accomplished this in part by his commanding intellect, his dominating personality, and his dexterity in social leadership. But he also instituted important procedural changes. The practice of *seriatim* opinions was abolished. The Chief Justice, when he voted with the majority, assigned the writing of the Court's opinion and very frequently wrote the opinion himself. Airing of dissident views by way of concurring or dissenting opinions was discouraged, if not altogether prevented. Those justices who publicly presumed to depart from the Court's opinion were subject to varying social pressures, and the number of such opinions during Marshall's reign was very small. Most of the Court's decisions during this period were unanimous. Under succeeding chief justices, more freedom to write dissenting and concurring opinions was permitted, although these were still discouraged. Chief Justices such as William Howard

Taft (1922–1930) and Charles Evans Hughes (1930–1941) placed great emphasis on uniting the Court behind a single opinion, which masked the reservations and disagreements of individual justices and gave the appearance of certainty and unanimity. Today, the frequency of dissent has increased so much that some have called it a virtual return to the practice of *seriatim* opinions.

Another procedural change of importance was the establishment of the practice of hiring law clerks. Today, each justice is entitled to three clerks and the Chief Justice to five. The clerks are all recent graduates of the nation's top law schools, chosen individually by the justices they serve. Normally they serve for a year—two at the most. Their major function is to provide research assistance to the justices, but few doubt that they also provide a source of fresh ideas and intellectual stimulation to the Court.

There have been few important changes in the routines by which the justices decide cases. The time allotted to oral argument before the Court has been drastically curtailed. Few cases get more than an hour equally divided between the opposing parties, and none receive the week or more of leisurely argument that characterized some of the most famous cases before the Marshall Court. Under a change by Chief Justice Warren, opinions, which used to be delivered only on Mondays, are now released any day of the week; most justices merely summarize their opinions rather than reading them verbatim. The change in opinion announcement practice was made ostensibly to help the news media which, under a flood of decisions on Mondays, could only provide brief and frequently inaccurate summaries of what decisions the Court had made. Even so routine a change as this was questioned by some as an unnecessary departure from the traditions of the Court. And most opinions still come down on Mondays.

The annual term of the Supreme Court begins each year on the first Monday in October. Adjournment usually comes at the end of June. During the term, the Court alternates between periods of several weeks allocated to oral arguments and announcement of decisions and several weeks devoted to research and opinion writing. Conferences, at which the justices decide which cases are to be considered and how cases should be decided, are currently held on Wednesday afternoons and Fridays throughout the term. These conferences are private; only the justices are permitted in the conference room. If some books or papers are needed from outside the room, the junior justice in terms of service passes messages to a bailiff at the door and receives whatever items have been requested.

Before each conference, it is customary for each justice to shake hands with each of his colleagues, a tradition, symbolizing internal harmony, that began at the turn of the century. Prior to conference, each justice has received a copy of the certiorari petition and supporting documents. Most justices will have summaries of each case prepared by their law clerks; only Justice Brennan, it is said, personally reads all of the 4000 petitions for review that come to the Supreme Court annually. For each conference there is a list of cases to be considered and a shorter "Discuss List" which consists of those cases thought worthy of discussion by at least one justice. Cases that do not make the "Discuss List," about 70 percent of the total, are automatically and summarily rejected.

The Chief Justice begins the discussion for each case. He presents the facts and his views as to the proper disposition of the case. In descending order of seniority, each member of the Court follows suit. Voting used to be in reverse order of seniority. That procedure has recently been modified slightly under Chief Justice Burger. A justice may indicate his tentative vote when taking his turn discussing a case. However, when a formal vote is taken, the traditional practice of the junior justice voting first and the chief justice last is followed: Any case that receives four or more votes is granted review by certiorari or appeal. Those cases that fail to get four votes for review are dismissed summarily.

The decision to grant review is made solely on the basis of the record, which includes formal written briefs submitted by the litigants and by other interested parties known as *amici curiae* (friends of the Court). About half of the cases in which certiorari or appeal is granted are set down for oral argument; some are decided summarily in short memorandum opinions. For those cases set for argument, new briefs are submitted that emphasize not why the Court should (or should not) hear the case, since that has already been decided, but what should be the Court's decision "on the merits."

Oral argument is usually held several months later. Each party has thirty minutes to present its side of the case and respond to questions from the bench. Often, questions occupy most of the allotted time. The justices have read the briefs, and this is the only opportunity they have to confront the adversaries directly with questions of fact and law. Some justices, like the late Justice Frankfurter, are known for their virtuoso performances and badgering of lawyers. Others are content to simply ask direct questions. Some leading questions seem clearly intended to help an attorney in trouble, while others devastatingly expose the weakness in an attorney's case.

Shortly after the oral argument, each case is discussed at conference for an average of about thirty minutes each. The conference procedures are the same as those for considering certiorari petitions, except of course that it takes a majority of five and not just a minority of four to decide each case (assuming a full complement of nine justices; six constitute a quorum). Several days after conference, the Chief Justice circulates a list of opinion assignments for those cases in which he has voted in the majority. Where the Chief Justice is not in the majority, the senior associate justice in the majority assigns the writing of the opinion for the Court. Dissenting justices may file separate dissents or agree on a common opinion. Each justice is entirely free to write a separate concurring or dissenting opinion in every case.

Opinion drafts are then circulated to all members of the Court. On some, there is initial agreement; for others, considerable bargaining is needed before all members of a majority are in agreement. It is not unusual for justices who voted in the majority initially to end up in dissent nor, reciprocally, for dissenters to emerge as spokesmen for the Court. A justice may change his vote in a case until the decision is publicly announced. Cases that are finally agreed upon are printed in final form by the Court's own printer and announced in open court on the next decision day. Normally, the time from oral argument to announced decision is at least several months. But in exceptional instances, procedures can be expedited. The Nixon tapes case, *United States* v. *Nixon* (1974), was decided just sixteen days after argument, and the Pentagon Papers case, *New York Times* v. *United States* (1971), was decided and announced only four days after it was argued.

It is difficult to relate the Court's procedures to specific decision-making patterns, since these procedures have remained largely constant through periods of both liberalism and conservatism on the court. The frequency and direction of dissenting opinions, for example, is usually a reflection of a current balance of power rather than any long-range phenomenon. Recalling our concern in the first chapter with the question of social change, it is possible to hypothesize that the Court's internal procedures are not conducive to social change policy making. Its size, relatively small staff, limited facilities for acquiring information, and its essentially negative array of powers, limit its capacity to formulate positive policy directives, The Court is relatively insulated from the political environment, and this is said to be necessary to preserve its independence. But insulation also has its negative aspects which, in the case of the Supreme Court, results in poor communication both to and from the outside. One of the Court's major policy weaknesses is its limited capacity to receive and act on feedback information. It makes its decisions but may have little control over, or knowledge about, their implementation and actual impact.

The previous chapters have suggested just how fragile and dependent is the Court's power. It may be that a proliferation of opinions diffuses this power even more. Yet in the long run, it may be in the Court's (and the country's) interest to permit a full and open airing of its internal policy disagreements. Innovation in legal doctrine and a sensitivity to the need for change seem, on the whole, better served by open exposition of differing points of view. Internal dissents that are camouflaged by a unanimous opinion cannot serve as a stimulus to further exploration of the issues and principles involved, nor as a catalyst to those seeking but not yet able to achieve important social and legal change. There is something both unseemly and unreal about justices never disagreeing among themselves over issues that have divided the nation and about which reasonable individuals can and do disagree. There is one final reason for encouragement rather than discouragement of multi-opinion decisions. Majority opinions, which have been criticized as "desperately negotiated documents," may reflect the need to command a majority to the detriment of setting forth clear exposition of policy preferences. Supreme Court opinions are often very poor policy directives. In an attempt to account for all espoused positions, they sometimes adequately account for none.

Our account of the decision-making process is not limited to the formal rules and internal procedures of the Court. The justices themselves provide an important input. Their personal values, the forceful interchange of ideas and personalities, their perceptions of their proper roles and functions are crucial ingredients. Like all political actors, justices are influenced by the institutional norms within which they operate. For some this is extremely confining and in conflict with deeply felt personal values. For other justices, the norms defining their role reinforce existing personal values. What seems clear is that justices of the Supreme Court have substantial discretion in deciding cases.

Explaining and understanding the factors that influence a judicial decision is not at all a new concern. A large amount of jurisprudential thinking has been devoted to both the normative and descriptive aspects of this subject. Likewise, lawyers have learned to take into account in the preparation of a case the judge or judges before whom they will be arguing, in addition to strictly legal questions. The lawyer's concern with the values of the judge may be intuitive, or it may involve some degree of advance calculation and planning. In practice such strategies may be as obvious as those employed by counsel in the trial of the "Chicago 7," or as subtle as arguments contained in a brief to the Supreme Court that are designed to pick up one or more "uncommitted" votes. Few cases can match the preparation of the NAACP Legal Defense Fund in the *Brown* case. Potential arguments to the Court were tried out in mock oral argument with Howard University law students playing the role of each of the sitting Supreme Court justices.

Social science has come relatively late to a recognition of the importance of the judge as an individual in the decision-making process. But social science writing and research can be differentiated from intuitive or jurisprudential concerns only by its emphasis on empirical—and frequently quantitative—evidence to describe the judicial function. The social scientist has been concerned more with general patterns of behavior, and with comparing these decision-making patterns to those exhibited by nonjudicial actors. The primary payoff for the lawyer is winning the case. For the social scientist the payoff may come in the development of descriptive theory or in the testing of new methods of data acquisition and analysis. For both, the payoff converges in increased understanding not only of how judges decide cases, but of how and why particular policy results come about.

2. DEMANDS ON THE SUPREME COURT: THE CASE SELECTION PROCESS

A. *A Note on the Jurisdiction of the Supreme Court*

Article III of the Constitution articulates only a bare set of guidelines for the operation of the judicial system. It provides that "the judicial power of the United States" be vested in one Supreme Court and such inferior federal courts as Congress may establish. Whatever the meaning of the term "judicial power," it is clear that *all* of it is to be exercised by the federal courts. It cannot be allocated by Congress to another branch of government, although Congress may restrict the courts to exercising less than the whole power.

The Constitution provides that this judicial power extends to certain cases because of their *subject matter* and to others because of the nature of the *parties* in dispute. Subject matter jurisdiction includes all cases, in law and equity, arising under the Constitution, federal statutes, and treaties. Jurisdiction also extends to cases where the United States is a party; to all cases involving ambassadors, other public ministers, and consuls; to disputes between two or more states and between citizens of different states; to cases between a state or its citizens and foreign states or citizens; and to controversies between citizens of the same state claiming lands under the grants of different states.

In cases affecting ambassadors, other public ministers, and consuls and in cases in which a state is a party, the Supreme Court has original jurisdiction. In all other cases, it has only appellate jurisdiction, subject to regulation by Congress. Original jurisdiction cases compose a minute fraction of the workload to the Supreme Court. By statute (now Section §1251, Title 28, U.S. Code), Congress has provided that the Supreme Court shall have original *and* exclusive jurisdiction over controversies between two or more states and "all actions or proceedings against ambassadors or other public ministers of foreign states or their domestics or domestic servants, not inconsistent with the law of nations." The Supreme Court has original *but not exclusive* jurisdiction over controversies between the United States and a state, "actions or proceedings by a state against the citizens of another state or against aliens," and "actions or proceedings brought by ambassadors or other public ministers of states or to which consuls or vice consuls of foreign states are parties."

About 150 original jurisdiction cases have been decided since the first term of the Supreme Court in 1789. Most such cases involve suits between two or more states: for example, suits between states over ownership of off-shore oil deposits, territorial disputes, or controversies over water rights where a river flows through or between two or more states. *Massachusetts* v. *Laird* (1971, *supra*) sought to test the validity of the war in Vietnam, but the Supreme Court refused to hear the case. Since the controversy was between a state and the United States, it fell into the category of nonexclusive original jurisdiction, and Massachusetts was free to begin its litigation again in the lower federal courts. *South Carolina* v. *Katzenbach* (1966; see Part Two, Chapter Two) was an original jurisdiction case brought to test the constitutionality of the Voting Rights Act of 1965. The

Supreme Court heard the case and ruled in favor of the act. A larger number of potential suits in original jurisdiction were precluded by passage of the Eleventh Amendment, which barred suits against states by citizens of other states without the consent of the state (see *Edelman* v. *Jordan,* 1974, *supra*). Whatever role the framers may have seen for original jurisdiction suits, they have accounted for a numerically insignificant portion of the work of the Supreme Court, but on occasion they have produced some important decisions.

The vast majority of cases that come to the Supreme Court arise under its appellate jurisdiction, over which Congress has control. Congress can deny to the Court jurisdiction over a subject or category of cases that Congress does not want the Court to decide (*Ex Parte McCardle,* 1869) and can require the Court to decide types of cases that the Court would rather not hear. Thus the jurisdiction of the Supreme Court is less than the full "judicial power" of the United States.

Appellate jurisdiction cases come to the Supreme Court of the United States by three methods: appeal, certiorari, and certification.

Appeal

Appeals may come from three-judge federal courts, from the federal courts of appeals, in limited circumstances directly from a federal district court (e.g., when such a court invalidates an act of Congress), and from the highest state court in which a judgment could be rendered in a particular case. Under the statutes, the Supreme Court has an obligation to decide appeals. In practice, the Court treats them in approximately the same discretionary manner as the writ of certiorari. A party filing an appeal is required first to file a "jurisdictional statement." If, on the basis of that statement, the Supreme Court does not believe a substantial federal question has been raised, the appeal will be dismissed or the decision in a lower court summarily affirmed.

Any party to a case in a federal court that holds an act of Congress unconstitutional may appeal directly to the Supreme Court. There is also a direct right of appeal to the Supreme Court from some decisions of three-judge federal courts. These are special courts set up specifically to consider challenges to the validity of acts of Congress or state legislatures or state judicial proceedings alleged to be in violation of the federal Constitution. In the 1960s and early 1970s, some of the most important constitutional litigation originated in such courts. The right of direct appeal to the Supreme Court made them especially attractive to litigants seeking a fast judicial response to their claims. Congress, however, responding to pressures from conservatives, and from Chief Justice Burger, who argued that such a direct right of appeal helped to clog the Supreme Court's docket, severely limited the jurisdiction of such courts.

A party relying on a state statute held by a court of appeals to be invalid under the federal Constitution, federal laws, or treaties is also entitled to appeal. Final judgments rendered in the highest courts of a state may be appealed where (1) the validity of a treaty or statute of the United States is drawn in question and the decision is against its validity, and (2) where the validity of a state statute is challenged as contrary to the federal Constitution and the decision is in favor of its validity. Most cases on appeal come from state courts and from special three-judge federal courts.

Certiorari

In cases other than those mentioned above, the losing party has no statutory right to Supreme Court review. But discretionary review by a writ of certiorari may be sought. Any party to any decision by a federal court of appeals may seek a writ of certiorari. Likewise, any decision in the Court of Claims or the Court of Customs and Patent Appeals may be reviewed by certiorari. Cases from the highest state courts not eligible for review by appeal that raise a question about the validity of a state or federal statute may be reviewed on a writ of certiorari. Most cases reviewed by the Supreme Court come via the writ of certiorari, and of these, most come from the federal courts of appeals. The following section explores the operation of the writ of certiorari in greater detail.

Certification

This is a procedure by which a court of appeals or the Court of Claims seeks further instructions on a point of law from the Supreme Court. Its occurrence is infrequent, and the Supreme Court rarely decides important constitutional issues in this way.

The preceding chapter has already explored the distinction between *jurisdiction* and *justiciability*, but it seems appropriate to remind the student again of that distinction. To say that the Supreme Court has jurisdiction in a case means that it has the legal or constitutional power to decide the case, assuming satisfaction of other requirements such as the "case or controversy" or "standing" norms. Whether the Court *ought* to decide a case, whether the issue is deemed by the justices to be appropriate and ready for judicial action, or whether pragmatic considerations may foreclose consideration are separate if not always distinct questions.

Normally, the Court should first consider in every case whether or not it has jurisdiction. If it does not, then the Court has no basis to decide the case on its merits. Occasionally, as in *Marbury* v. *Madison,* consideration of the jurisdiction issue will be "postponed" until after the substantive claims have been considered. Questions of jurisdiction may seem excessively technical and dry compared to the substantive controversies before the Court. But they are of crucial strategic importance; they are the foot in the judicial door.

Rules of jurisdiction may also appear neutral when, in fact, they express important value choices. For example, recall the emotional and intense debate over Section 25 of the Judiciary Act of 1789, which gave to the Supreme Court authority to review *some* decisions of the highest courts in each state. But the Supreme Court was not given the full authority that Congress might have extended to it. It was limited to hearing appeals in those cases that raised "federal questions"; it could only hear cases arising from the highest state courts in which a decision was possible; and it could only hear cases where the final state court had decided against the validity of a federal statute or a provision of the federal Constitution or in favor of a state law challenged as repugnant to the federal Constitution or federal law or treaty. This limited grant of jurisdiction was part of a compromise solution worked out be-

tween those in Congress who favored establishment of a system of inferior federal courts and those who opposed it. If no inferior courts had been established, the Supreme Court would have received cases exclusively from the state courts.

Certainly the importance of setting the Supreme Court's jurisdictional boundaries is attested to by the repeated attempts by Congress to regulate, rearrange, and sometimes dilute the Court's appellate jurisdiction for political reasons.

B. *The Supreme Court's Certiorari Jurisdiction*

Of the nearly 4000 cases annually that make up the docket of the Supreme Court, approximately 90 percent are petitions for certiorari. Appeals account for most of the remaining 10 percent. Since the rate of granting appeals (about 18 percent) is higher than that for granting certiorari (about 5 percent), cases on appeal account for about one-third of all cases on the merits which the Court decides with full opinion.

The Supreme Court's present authority to issue the writ of certiorari traces back to the "Judge's Bill" of 1925, so named because of the influence and extensive campaigning of Chief Justice William Howard Taft for the bill's passage. Before 1925, about 75 percent of the Court's cases fell within its obligatory appeals jurisdiction. A steadily rising case load, a lengthening backlog of cases, and Taft's lobbying persuaded Congress to grant the Supreme Court considerably more discretion over its docket. A number of categories of cases that the Court formerly was obliged to decide were made discretionary. Instead of access by right, litigants, for the most part, now have access only by grace of the Court.[1]

Relieving the Supreme Court of a burdensome work load was not the only reason that Congress acted, however. Broader policy considerations were involved. As long as the Court was bound to consider every case within its jurisdiction, at least in theory, it would be forced to consider many cases of little general importance. The emerging view then, and now, is that the Supreme Court should not function as a court of error but should conserve resources for its main responsibility of deciding cases that raise important issues of general policy importance. Said the late Chief Justice Fred Vinson:

The function of the Supreme Court is . . . to resolve conflicts of opinion on federal questions that have arisen among lower courts, to pass upon questions of wide import under the Constitution, laws and treaties of the United States, and to exercise supervisory power over lower federal courts. If we took every case in which an interesting legal question is raised, or our prima facie impression is that the decision below is erroneous, we could not fulfill the Constitutional and statutory responsibilities placed upon the Court. To remain effective, the Supreme Court must continue to decide only those cases which present questions whose resolution will have immediate importance far beyond the particular facts and parties involved.

Those of you whose petitions for certiorari are granted by the Supreme Court will know, therefore, that you are, in a sense, prosecuting or defending class actions; that you represent not only your clients, but tremendously important principles, upon which are based the plans, hopes, and aspirations of a great many people throughout the country.[2]

There are occasions when the Supreme Court departs from this set of priorities. Several times each term it will decide a case of no national policy importance merely to rectify a rank injustice. Likewise, the justices may sometimes decide a case, or a set of cases, that they think have been wrongly decided. Just such a group of cases arose in the 1940s and 1950s concerning questions of the right of railroad workers to recover damages for job-related injuries under the Federal Employer's Liability Act.

When and why does the Supreme Court grant or deny certiorari? Official reasons are almost never revealed. Cases decided on the merits following a grant of certiorari will often allude to some reason for granting review, for example, that the case was of importance, or to resolve a conflict in the law applied by the lower courts. But such references are not very helpful; at best, they appear in a random fashion. The denial of a writ of certiorari is never officially explained. The "opinion" of the Court is only a cryptic "petition for certiorari denied." In rare instances (somewhat less rare in recent years), one or more justices will dissent from a denial of certiorari (or from a summary dismissal of appeal or denial of leave to file in original jurisdiction). In such cases, the dissenting justice's opinion may suggest some reason why the case ought to have been

[1]Steven Halpern and Kenneth Vines, "Dissent, the Judges' Bill and the Role of the U.S. Supreme Court" (1974). Paper delivered at the 1974 Annual Meeting of the American Political Science Association, p. 3.

[2]Quoted in John R. Schmidhauser, *The Supreme Court: Its Politics, Personalities and Procedures* (New York: Holt, Rinehart and Winston, 1960), p. 132.

heard. In *Massachusetts* v. *Laird* (1971, *supra*), for example, one can derive from Justice Douglas' dissenting opinion a good indication of the private reasons advanced by the other justices in refusing to hear the case.

Rule 19, of the Supreme Court's own rules, is the only official statement of policy on why certiorari is or is not granted. It offers little guidance:

A review on writ of certiorari is not a matter of right, but of sound judicial discretion and will be granted only where there are special and important reasons therefor. The following, while neither controlling nor fully measuring the court's discretion, indicate the character of reasons which will be considered:

(a) Where a state court has decided a federal question of substance not theretofore determined by this court, or has decided it in a way probably not in accord with applicable decisions of this court.

(b) Where a court of appeals has rendered a decision in conflict with the decision of another court of appeals on the same matter; or has decided an important state or territorial question in a way in conflict with applicable state or territorial law; or has decided an important question of federal law which has not been, but should be, settled by this court; or has decided a federal question in a way in conflict with applicable decisions of this court; or has so far departed from the accepted and usual course of judicial proceedings, or so far sanctioned such departure by a lower court, as to call for an exercise of this court's power of supervision.

Of course, each of these standards requires some subjective judgments, which can only be made on a case-by-case basis. None is formally binding on the Supreme Court. Observers have hypothesized certain conditions or sets of facts most likely to result in grants of certiorari: where a large number of persons or groups are potentially affected by a decision that clearly transcends the interests of the litigants themselves; where a substantial amount of litigation in the lower courts depends on a ruling by the Supreme Court; where there has been an egregious and obvious miscarriage of justice; where the death penalty is involved; where the case comes from the federal rather than from the state courts; and where certiorari is requested by the solicitor general.

Assuming the presence of one or more of the above factors, the Supreme Court is also likely to prefer cases in which there is an adequate record with issues presented clearly and in which few, if any, problems of standing are present or "political questions" are posed. The Supreme Court is unlikely to want to decide a case where its decision will be ineffectual, counterproductive, or perhaps lead to a political confrontation that jeopardizes the Court's power and prestige. Never to be overlooked are the individual views of each justice on the importance of particular issues coming before the Court.

Several recent empirical studies have been directed to identifying the most important factors accounting for grants or denials of certiorari. Tanenhaus and his colleagues found positive correlations between grants of certiorari and the presence of three factors: a "civil liberties" issue; a conflict in the lower courts or among government agencies; a review sought by the solicitor general.[3] A

---

[3]See Joseph Tanenhaus, et al., "The Supreme Court's Certiorari Jurisdiction: Cue Theory," in Schubert (ed.), *Judicial Decision-Making* (New York: The Free Press, 1963), pp. 111–127.

later study found that only the third factor, petition for review by the federal government, had a significant impact on the grant of certiorari.[4]

None of these variables is precise enough, nor the relationships strong enough, to support any claims of causality. And other studies relating the decision to grant certiorari to the presence or absence of agreement in the lower courts are, at best, inconclusive. It is at least plausible to maintain that the Supreme Court is more likely "to hear reversed decisions more than affirmed decisions, non-unanimous decisions more than unanimous decisions, and en banc decisions more than panel decisions" from the courts of appeals.[5] Another perspective on reasons for certiorari flows from substantive decisions on the merits. Roughly two-thirds of all grants of certiorari result in reversals of lower court decisions. Thus, it is not unreasonable to conclude, as does J. Woodford Howard, that "justices grant certiorari primarily to reverse decisions below."[6] This is consistent with the theory that decisions on certiorari are, and must be considered, an integral part of the judicial policy making process. They are just an early, strategic articulation of the policy views of the justices.

So far, social science research provides us with additional insight but no conclusive answer to the question of when and why certiorari is granted. What seems clear enough is that the decision to grant certiorari is a political (e.g., policy) decision, not an "objective" legal decision, and one that reflects the personal values and attitudes of each justice.

Strategic considerations may also be involved. A justice may vote to grant certiorari in a case merely because of its apparent importance, without regard to its ultimate outcome. But a justice, or group of justices, with a strong interest in a particular outcome must be more careful. Four votes control the grant of certiorari, but five are needed to control disposition of a case on its merits. At least one additional vote must be obtained, assuming that all four justices voting for certiorari agree on how the case ought to be decided once review has been granted. Normally, it is not good strategy for a justice to vote to review a case that is certain to be decided against his policy views. A low-visibility adverse decision in the lower courts does not carry with it the political consequences of a major defeat in the Supreme Court. No unfavorable precedents are created, and the view that a particular justice, or bloc of justices, espouses may prevail at a later day.[7]

What is the legal meaning, or consequence, of a denial of certiorari? For the litigants, of course, it has the effect of affirming the lower court decision for which review had been

[4]S. Sidney Ulmer, et al., "The Decision to Grant or Deny Certiorari: Further Consideration of Cue Theory," 6 *Law and Society Review* (1972), 637–643, and Ulmer, "Revising the Jurisdiction of the Supreme Court: Mere Administrative Reform or Substantive Policy Change?" 58 *Minnesota Law Review* (1973), 121–155.

[5]J. Woodford Howard, Jr., "Litigation Flow in Three United States Courts of Appeals," 8 *Law and Society Review* (1973), 49.

[6]*Ibid.*, p. 42. See also S. Sidney Ulmer, "The Decision to Grant Certiorari as an Indicator to Decision 'On the Merits,' " 4 *Polity* (1972), 429–447.

[7]See Glendon Schubert's famous "Certiorari Game" in *Quantitative Analysis of Judicial Behavior* (Glencoe: The Free Press, 1959), Ch. 4. For a discussion of comparable behavior on state supreme courts, see Lawrence Baum, "Policy Goals in Judicial Gatekeeping: A Proximity Model of Discretionary Jurisdiction," 21 *American Journal of Political Science* (1977), 13–35.

sought. The orthodox view is that denial of the writ of certiorari means nothing with respect to the merits of the case. In an oft-quoted statement, Justice Frankfurter once observed: "[A] denial simply means that fewer than four members of the Court deemed it desirable to review a decision of the lower court as a matter of sound judicial discretion . . ." (*Maryland* v. *Baltimore Radio Show*, 1950). Questions of finality, ripeness, adequacy of the record, or political timeliness may diminish support for reviewing an otherwise "eligible" lower court decision. Despite official support on the Court for Frankfurter's position, there is continuous discussion of the meaning of a denial of certiorari. Attention to the question has been stimulated by an increase in the number of certiorari denials in which a dissenting opinion is filed. After leaving the Court, Chief Justice Earl Warren wrote: "Denials of certiorari can and do have a significant impact on the ordering of constitutional and legal priorities. Many potential and important developments in the law have been frustrated, at least temporarily, by a denial of certiorari."[8] Accepting that denial of certiorari may have no precedential value, one cannot accept the interpretation that such denials are totally without policy significance. Lawyers, and even Supreme Court justices from time to time, *cite* cases in which certiorari has been denied.[9] And the policy significance of certiorari votes is underscored by Ulmer's recent research

suggesting a strong parallel between a justice's initial vote on the question of certiorari and his eventual vote on the merits.[10]

C. A Note on the Business of the Supreme Court

The ways in which the Supreme Court conducts its business, and the business it transacts, often have significant policy implications. We have already suggested the policy implications of jurisdictional rules, of the procedures by which review is granted, and of the Court's choice of cases to decide.

In 1840, 92 new cases were filed in the Supreme Court. By 1860, this had increased to 320. In 1935, less than 1000 new cases were filed, and in the 1977 term, 3980 *new* cases were docketed. That the business of the Supreme Court has increased significantly in almost all categories should not be regarded as the only noteworthy characteristic. Where have the cases come from? How have they been decided? What does this tell us about the role and function of the Court in American society? This section focuses on the sources of the Supreme Court's business, on how its cases are disposed, and on patterns of choice, all evident from an inspection of cases on the dockets. In Section D we will explore the current controversy over the Supreme Court's workload.

Figure 1 shows the sources of

[8]"Retired Chief Justice Warren Attacks, Chief Justice Burger Defends Freund Study Group's Composition and Proposal," **49** *American Bar Association Journal* (1973), 728.

[9]Stephen L. Wasby, "The Supreme Court's Docket, Discretionary Jurisdiction, and Judicial Behavior Studies" (1975), paper delivered at the Midwest Political Science Association Meeting, p. 6. See also Wasby, *Continuity and Change* (Pacific Palisades, Calif.: Goodyear Publishing Company, 1976). Ch. 2.

[10]S. Sidney Ulmer, "Supreme Court Justices as Strict and Not-So-Strict Constructionists: Some Implications," **8** *Law and Society Review* (1973), 27–28.

cases filed with the Supreme Court in the 1971 term. In that term, a total of 4371 cases were docketed: 91.7 percent sought writs of certiorari, 8.3 percent were on appeal, and nearly one-third came from state courts; 41.1 percent were civil cases, 42.6 percent were criminal, and 17.5 percent were habeas corpus actions.

A steadily increasing proportion of cases on the Supreme Court's docket consists of petitions filed *in forma pauperis* (paupers' petitions, or IFP petitions). These are petitions filed by indigents unable to pay the filing costs; most are inmates of state and federal penitentiaries. In the 1971 term, 53.7 percent (2347) of the docketed cases fell into this category. In the 1977 term, the number of IFP cases (2355) dipped to just under 50 percent. By comparison, in 1940, there were 120 such cases; by 1960 the number had risen to 1085. Clearly the growth of IFP petitions since 1940 has constituted a major change in the business of the Supreme Court.

What happens to all of these cases? Table I summarizes the final disposition of cases for the 1972–1977 terms of the Court. The number of cases disposed of by signed written opinion

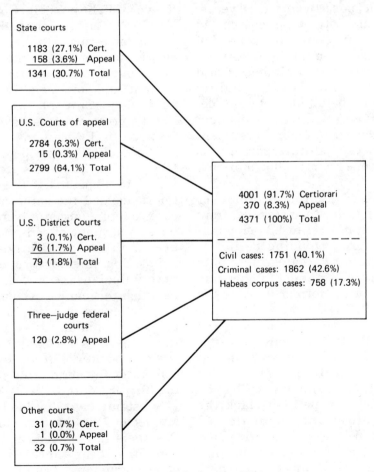

Figure 1. Supreme Court cases docketed—1971 term.

Source. "Report of the Study Group on the Caseload of the Supreme Court," Federal Judicial Center (1972), p. A–11.)

Table I. Final Disposition of Cases, 1972–1977 Terms[a]

By	1972	1973	1974	1975	1976	1977
Written opinion	182	188	159	184	170	159
Per curiam	261	339	177	178	203	119
Denial or dismissal of appeal or petitions for review[b]	3299	3347	3508	3441	3633	3375
Original jurisdiction (Denial of leave to file complaint)	6	2	3	3	0	1
Total	3748	3876	3847	3806	4006	3654

[a] *Source. Harvard Law Review,* annual summaries of the docket of the Supreme Court.

[b] This category primarily includes dismissals of appeals and dispositions of petitions for certiorari. It also includes dispositions of other applications for review, such as petitions for writs of habeas corpus or writs of mandamus.

has fluctuated between 90 and 190 during the past twenty-five years. The vast majority of cases docketed in the Supreme Court are disposed of without a decision on the merits. Of related interest, the number of oral arguments each term is slightly greater than the number of cases decided with a signed written opinion. But the time spent on oral argument of cases has actually decreased. Less time, now one hour, is alloted to each case.

The rate of granting petitions for certiorari has declined steadily, from 17.5 percent in 1941 to 4.3 percent in the 1977 term. Dividing certiorari petitions into two categories, paid and IFP, reveals a much higher rate of review for the former than for the latter. In 1977, 8.0 percent of the paid petitions were granted, but only 0.7 percent of the IFP petitions, the latter well down even from the 3.3 percent granted as recently as 1971.

Most IFP petitions are filed by prisoners. These petitions lack the polished prose and sophisticated legal analysis that characterize paid petitions. The cost constraints that serve to limit the number of paid petitions do not operate here. There is little incentive for indigent prisoners

not to petition for review, even with the very slight possibility of success. Many IFP petitions are plainly frivolous, not in terms of the earnest desire of prisoners to escape their confinement, but in terms of presenting important and new constitutional issues. Yet some of the Supreme Court's greatest cases have come in response to IFP petitions.

The decline in the percentage of IFP petitions granted is greater than would be expected if the Supreme Court decided the same number of cases out of a larger universe of petitions. A strategy of conservative justices on the Burger Court has been to reduce Supreme Court supervision of the criminal justice process. One way in which this can be accomplished is by deciding fewer criminal cases and generally reducing the visibility of the subject as a constitutional "issue." Chapter Three, Part Two, elaborates further on this strategy of the Burger Court.

Substantively, what kinds of cases are decided by the Supreme Court? Observers have noted, and Table II confirms, that there has been a noticeable change from the 1930s to the present, from a jurisprudence of "property" to a jurisprudence of

Table II. The Business of the Supreme Court: A Comparison of the Hughes, Vinson, Warren, and Burger Courts (Full Opinion Cases)

Type of Case	Term of Court					
	1935	1950	1964	1967	1974	1977
Original jurisdiction	4 (3%)	0	2 (2%)	1 (1%)	1 (1%)	1 (1%)
Civil actions from federal courts[a]	74 (59%)	59 (60%)	68 (59%)	63 (50%)	86 (63%)	77 (57%)
Federal criminal cases	6 (5%)	10 (10%)	10 (9%)	16 (13%)	18 (13%)	18 (13%)
Federal habeas corpus from state and federal courts	—	4 (4%)	3 (3%)	8 (6%)	9 (7%)	6 (4%)
State criminal cases	2 (2%)	5 (5%)	22 (19%)	20 (16%)	10 (7%)	12 (9%)
Civil actions from state courts	39 (31%)	20 (20%)	9 (8%)	19 (15%)	13 (9%)	21 (16%)
Total	125	98	114	127	137	135

[a] Includes cases involving state or federal government and private litigation.

"status."[1] The 1935 term was the last full term of the Supreme Court before the election of 1936, the announcement in 1937 of President Roosevelt's "court-packing" plan, and the subsequent liberal reorientation of the Court with Roosevelt appointees. The 1950 term occurred midway through the stewardship of Chief Justice Fred Vinson. The 1964 and 1967 terms have been selected as examples of the Warren Court, and 1974 and 1977 represent the Burger Court.

In 1935, 31 percent of the Court's cases involved civil actions from the state courts. Many of these cases involved tests of the validity of state welfare and economic regulatory statutes. This was the heyday of "substantive due process." By 1964, cases in this category had dropped to just 8 percent. More recent increases in civil actions from the state courts during the Warren Court years reflected attention to civil liberties and civil rights issues.

In 1935, criminal cases from state courts were few in number. By 1967, they accounted for nearly one-quarter of the business of the Supreme Court (including habeas corpus actions). The recent drop in state criminal cases, like the aforementioned reduction in IFP cases, signals a change in attitude of the Burger Court toward the Supreme Court's role in the criminal justice process.

Several additional items complete this statistical picture of the business of the Supreme Court. First, the Supreme Court decides more "non-constitutional" than "constitutional" cases. For example, in the 1977 term, only 44 percent of the cases decided with full opinion formally raised constitutional issues. Students too easily assume that the study of constitutional law defines the business of the Court, whereas in fact the Court spends much of its time interpreting the meaning of federal statutes and administrative rules and a somewhat lesser amount of time settling essentially private disputes. But it is also true that many cases that formally concern only statutory or administra-

[1]C. Herman Pritchett and Alan F. Westin (eds.). *The Third Branch of Government* (New York: Harcourt, Brace & World, 1963), pp. 4–10.

tive law questions have strong constitutional overtones.

Second, to what extent are the federal and state governments successful participants in cases before the Supreme Court? As revealed by Table III, the federal government prevailed, on the average, in 72 percent of the civil cases in which it was a party in four recent terms of the Court. By comparison, the state governments were much less successful, prevailing in only 47 percent of the civil cases in which they were involved. However, state governments seem to be increasingly successful in Supreme Court litigation, while the federal government is not uniformly successful at the high rates of some years. This does not confirm but is certainly consistent with observed trends on the Burger Court of greater indulgence toward state governmental actions.

Even more noteworthy is the increasing success rate of the federal government in criminal cases. In 1967 the federal government prevailed in only 19 percent of the criminal cases in which it was a party; in 1970, 1974, and 1977 combined, it prevailed in 68 percent. A similar re-versal of fortunes with the Burger Court can be observed in habeas corpus actions decided against state governments. These data are consistent with observations that the Burger Court is less inclined to be sympathetic toward the claims of criminal defendants.

D. The Workload of the Supreme Court: Is There a Problem?

There has been much recent attention paid to the workload of the Supreme Court. Pointing to a huge increase in cases on the docket, many critics, including some of the justices, have charged that the Supreme Court will soon be unable to perform its primary function of deciding important policy issues. Instead, it will have to devote an increasing portion of its time to deal with the heavy flow of certiorari petitions.

In a famous article in the *Harvard Law Review* in 1959, well before the current surge in certiorari petitions, Professor Henry Hart argued that the heavy burdens on the Court made it unlikely that any justice could do his

Table III. Governments as Litigants in the Supreme Court (Full Opinion Cases)

	1967	1970	1974	1977
Civil suits				
Decided against federal government	5 (14%)	13 (41%)	8 (19%)	20 (35%)
Decided for federal government	30 (86%)	19 (59%)	35 (81%)	37 (65%)
Decided against state governments	16 (80%)	19 (53%)	12 (39%)	9 (50%)
Decided for state governments	4 (20%)	17 (47%)	19 (61%)	9 (50%)
Criminal cases				
Decided against federal government	13 (81%)	3 (27%)	6 (33%)	7 (39%)
Decided for federal government	3 (19%)	11 (73%)	12 (67%)	11 (61%)
Decided against state governments	14 (74%)	8 (67%)	7 (70%)	9 (75%)
Decided for state governments	5 (26%)	4 (33%)	3 (30%)	3 (25%)
Habeas corpus (state prisoners)				
Decided against state governments	8 (89%)	3 (43%)	4 (57%)	4 (75%)
Decided for state governments	1 (11%)	4 (57%)	3 (43%)	1 (25%)

job properly. Not only were there more cases coming to the Court but also certiorari was granted in too many frivolous cases, and the justices were writing more opinions— dissenting and concurring opinions in particular had proliferated. In Hart's judgment, shared by many, the *quality* of the Court's work, as reflected in its written opinions, had declined.[1]

Since Hart's article, the Court's case load has more than doubled. In 1971, Chief Justice Warren Burger set up a study committee to make recommendations about the problem. The committee was chaired by Professor Paul Freund of the Harvard Law School, and its report, issued in December 1972, became known as the "Freund Committee Report." The report has been widely discussed and is highly controversial. Although most of the reforms that it suggested are unlikely to be adapted at this time, it did serve to place the subject of reform on the agenda of public discussion. Consideration of its recommendations also affords considerable insight into the process of Supreme Court decision making.

The Freund committee and other observers noted the most obvious changes in the Supreme Court's docket over the years. Constitutional litigation (which may be more time-consuming) has increased much faster than nonconstitutional cases (21 percent to 32 percent from 1957 to 1972). Criminal cases now account for about one-third of the current docket of the Supreme Court, nearly

double that in 1957. IFP cases have increased so rapidly that they now make up nearly half of the Court's docket. There have also been significant litigation increases in other subject matter areas of current concern: civil rights, education, reapportionment, labor relations, gender equality, and so forth.

Accounting for these increases is at best speculative. Casper and Posner suggest several factors:[2] (1) generally increasing litigiousness in an already highly litigious population; (2) increases in discretionary as opposed to obligatory jurisdiction (as the Freund committee said, the solution to the work load problem in 1925 had become part of the problem in 1972); (3) changes in substantive rules *and* procedural rules of access; for example, it is simply easier to get to the federal courts, and to the Supreme Court, today than it was twenty years ago, for reasons already explored in the preceding chapter; and (4) population growth; more people inevitably brings more litigation, although there is no necessary direct correlation between the two.[3]

The Freund Committee Report stated a very simple conclusion. The Supreme Court's docket had reached the saturation point. If permitted to grow much larger the function of the Court would necessarily have to change. Implicit in the report, though never stated, was a fear (echoing Professor Hart's earlier charge) that the quality of the Court's work would also (continue to) diminish. The report did suggest that issues decided on the

[1]Henry M. Hart, Jr., "The Time Chart of the Justices," **73** *Harvard Law Review* (1959), 84.

[2]Gerhard Casper and Richard A. Posner, "A Study of the Supreme Court's Caseload," **3** *Journal of Legal Studies* (1974), 339–375. See also Stephen L. Wasby, *Continuity and Change: From the Warren Court to the Burger Court* (Pacific Palisades, Calif.: Goodyear Publishing Co., 1976), Ch. 2.

[3]On the relationship between population and litigation, see Joel B. Grossman and Austin Sarat, "Litigation in the Federal Courts: A Comparative Perspective," **9** *Law and Society Review* (1975), 321–346.

merits a generation ago are passed over today. Also, it suggested that consideration given to cases on the merits is compromised by the pressures of processing an inflated docket. The committee's interpretation of the problem has been every bit as controversial as its proposed solutions. The committee recognized that the reform it was recommending involved some loss of control by the Supreme Court over its docket, but it believed this to be a necessary cost if a runaway case load was to be brought under control.

The Freund committee proposed a number of minor changes that have not been controversial. It suggested that all petitions for review by the Supreme Court come by a discretionary writ of certiorari. The present obligatory appeals jurisdiction would be abolished. The committee noted that, in fact, the Court treats appeals and petitions for certiorari in about the same manner. But appeals are granted at a higher rate and often take up more time. Also proposed was elimination of the special three-judge federal courts whose decisions can be appealed directly to the Supreme Court. Direct review of cases from the Interstate Commerce Commission and of antitrust cases decided in the federal district courts would be eliminated. A nonjudicial body to investigate prisoner complaints would be established. The report did not make clear whether this administrative remedy would have to be "exhausted" before prisoner cases came to the federal courts or whether

it would be merely "advisory." One possibility was that federal judges could refer cases to such an agency before undertaking to consider them.

The committee considered and rejected a number of alternative solutions. One was an increase in the number of law clerks. The committee felt it would be inadvisable to encourage further delegation of the justices' individual responsibilities.[4] Dividing the Supreme Court into panels was also rejected. There are potential constitutional problems in such a plan (the Constitution speaks of "one Supreme Court"). Such a division might also serve to depreciate the authority and legitimacy of the Supreme Court, and it would add the elements of a lottery to petitions for review. The committee also rejected the idea of limiting the Court to deciding only constitutional cases, noting how difficult it is to separate constitutional from statutory issues. One commonly suggested reform has been to exclude certain categories of cases, particularly those coming under the diversity of citizenship jurisdiction of the federal courts. This, too, was rejected by the Freund committee on the grounds that such cases, though mostly concerned with private law questions, *might* occasionally produce a constitutional question of importance. A final solution rejected was the establishment of specialized courts to hear administrative appeals and prisoner petitions.

The major proposal of the Freund committee was the establishment of

---

[4]The role of law clerks to the individual justices, and their influence, has been a contentious issue for some time. There is some evidence that the law clerks, at least in some chambers, play a greater role than any justice is willing to admit. A classic attack on the role of law clerks was made by William Rehnquist, "Who Writes Decisions of the Supreme Court?" **43** *United States News and World Report* (1957), 74–75. The most recent of many statements by justices denying undue influence of the law clerks is in Lewis F. Powell, Jr., "Myths and Misconceptions About the Supreme Court," **61** *American Bar Association Journal* (1975), 1346.

a new National Court of Appeals. Its membership would be drawn, on a rotating basis, from the existing federal courts of appeals. Its function would be to screen all petitions for review, on certiorari or appeal. Those that it regarded as most meritorious, estimated at 400 to 500 annually, would be referred to the Supreme Court. All others would be denied. In addition, the new court would be empowered to decide cases of conflicts between the circuits, although those of special importance would be referred to the Supreme Court. Those cases referred to the Supreme Court would be screened again; in some cases, review would be denied, while in others the Supreme Court would decide the case on the merits. Feeling that relief for the Supreme Court was imperative, the Freund committee believed this to be the solution with the fewest problems.

Reactions to the Freund Committee Report were mixed, on the Court and off. Chief Justice Burger, though never officially endorsing the report, appeared to support the principles of reform embodied in its conclusions. Justice Douglas continued to articulate his long-standing opposition to any workload reform. For instance, in *Warth* v. *Seldin* (1975), he stated that "no justice . . . need work more than four days a week to carry his burden." The late Chief Justice Earl Warren denied that there was evidence "that any member of the Court was distracted from full devotion to the decisional process by having to consider weekly circulations of certiorari petitions."[5] Perhaps the most detailed negative response came

from Justice Brennan, an excerpt of which follows. In response to Douglas' charges, Justice Powell has noted that few justices have Douglas' speed-reading capacity or his photographic memory. There are also differences in experience, capacity, and style that do not lead to any agreement on the time needed to process certiorari petitions.[6] No other justice works only four days a week.

One internal response to the workload problem has been an experiment in clerk sharing by five justices— Burger, Blackmun, Powell, Rehnquist, and White. A rotating pool of three clerks from the office of these justices reviews and summarizes the approximately 100 certiorari petitions that come to the Court each week. The memoranda prepared by these clerks are then circulated to the chambers of the participating justices and reviewed by one of the justice's own clerks and by the justice himself. How much time is saved is not known. But this work-sharing arrangement is novel on a Court where there is virtually no division of labor except in the distribution of opinions.

E. William J. Brennan, Jr., The National Court of Appeals: Another Dissent

. . . In its recently published and widely publicized report, the Study Group on the Caseload of the Supreme Court, often referred to as the Freund Committee, recommends a number of far-reaching changes— changes that would surely rank in importance with the creation of the

[5]"Retired Chief Justice Warren Attacks, Chief Justice Burger Defends Freund Study Group's Composition and Proposal," **59** *American Bar Association Journal* (1973), 727.

[6]Powell, *op. cit.*, Note 4, p. 1345.

Address before the First Circuit Judicial Conference, Portsmouth, New Hampshire, May 23, 1973.

Circuit Court of Appeals in 1891, and with the reduction of the Court's mandatory appellate jurisdiction in 1925. Many of the recommendations seem to me entirely sound. In particular, I share the Study Group's view that the existence of two distinct lines of access to the Supreme Court, appeal and certiorari, can no longer be justified. Direct appeals to the Supreme Court, whether from a one-judge court under the antitrust Expediting Act or from a three-judge court convened to consider the constitutionality of a state or federal statute, are my special candidates for repeal, and it is encouraging that Congress is now considering such legislation. These cases consume a disproportionate amount of the limited time available for oral argument. Yet we are regularly constrained to grant review, not so much because the question presented is especially important or because the District Court may well have erred, but rather because we are reluctant to deprive the losing litigant of any opportunity for appellate review of the trial court's decision. Since the policy considerations that gave rise to the distinction between review by appeal and review by writ of certiorari have long since lost their force, I support most enthusiastically the proposal to abandon the appellate jurisdiction and leave a writ of certiorari as the only means of obtaining review by the Supreme Court. This proposal is not, however, the major focus of the Study Group's report; it is only incidental to a far more important and far more controversial recommendation. Having reviewed the size of our docket and considered the burden of screening out the cases that will be set for plenary review, the Study Group concludes that a fundamental restructuring of the federal judiciary is warranted. Specifically, they pro-

pose the creation of a National Court of Appeals, made up of seven United States circuit judges, who would assume upwards of 90 percent of the screening burden that now falls to the Supreme Court. That proposal seems to me fundamentally unnecessary and ill-advised, and I strongly hope that Congress will reject it.

As envisioned by the Study Group, the National Court of Appeals would have two major functions. First, it would assist the Supreme Court in selecting the cases that will be set for oral argument and plenary review. It is our current practice to hear, in the course of a Term, between 150 and 200 cases, carefully selected from the 3500 to 4000 applications for review that we annually receive. It may interest you that we do not set a quota of 150 to 200 cases: our procedures operate annually to produce that number without regard to the actual number of appeals and petitions that may be docketed in a particular Term. Under the proposed scheme, all applications for review would be channelled through the National Court of Appeals, and that Court would screen out approximately seven-eighths of the cases filed. Thus, each year that Court would pass up to the Supreme Court some 400 to 500 cases, and it is from that group of cases that we would choose the 150 or 200 that would be set for argument. The decision by the National Court of Appeals to deny access to the Supreme Court would be final and unreviewable by the Supreme Court, although it would apparently be possible for the Supreme Court to grant certiorari in any given case prior to the screening decision of the National Court of Appeals. Second, the National Court of Appeals would be charged with the task of resolving on the merits certain conflicts between circuits, except where the conflict concerns a question of substantial importance. The decision of the National Court of Appeals, reached after oral argument and the submission of briefs, would also be unreviewable by the Supreme Court. . . .

. . . [M]y now almost 17 years service as an Associate Justice of the Supreme Court . . . afford me an unusual perspective on the proposal, and I am anxious to describe to you what seem to me two glaring defects in the plan. First, its fundamental premise that "consideration given to the cases actually decided on the merits is compromised by the pressures of processing the inflated docket of petitions and appeals" is entirely unsupportable. Contrary to the Study Group's assumption, the Supreme Court is not overworked. Indeed, my law clerks tell me each year that the burden on the District and Circuit Courts with which they served before coming to me is no less substantial than the burden on the Supreme Court. Our docket has most definitely not swollen to a point where the burden of screening cases has impaired our ability to discharge our other vital responsibilities. Second, the Study Group has regrettably misconceived both the nature and the importance of the screening process. Even if it were as time-consuming and difficult as the Study Group believes, that would underscore, not diminish, its importance. It is a task that should, I am convinced, be performed only by the Members of the Court. . . .

At the outset, I want to examine the Study Group's assumptions concerning the present workload of the Supreme Court. They observe, and I fully agree, that "the indispensable condition for discharge of the Court's responsibility is adequate time and ease of mind for research, reflection, and consultation in reaching a judg-ment, for critical review by colleagues when a draft opinion is prepared, and for clarification and revision in light of all that has gone before." But insofar as that observation implies that the screening function is so time-consuming and onerous that it imperils existence of the "indispensable condition," I emphatically disagree. It is true, of course, that the number of cases docketed has increased greatly over the past 30 or 40 years. There were 3643 cases filed with the Court during the 1971 Term as the Study Group Report itself points out, and the present indication is that the total filings during the present 1972 Term will be within 1% of that figure. This is twice as many as were filed in my first Term 17 years ago, and 3½ times the number filed in 1935, and by itself, those statistics might lead one to believe that the Court is surely in need of help. But to concentrate merely on raw statistics, as the Study Group seems principally to have done, is misleading and I think that is especially true in this situation. As one critic has observed: "Raw statistics as to case filings . . . are but the starting point for identifying and evaluating the real workload of the Court. How much time is actually spent by the nine Justices and their law clerks in screening cases? How many of the cases are easily and quickly disposed of, and how many require more prolonged consideration? If it be true, as various Justices have indicated, that more than 60% of the paid cases and 90% of the *in forma pauperis* cases, are utterly without merit for review purposes, cannot these petitions for review be denied with a minimum of time and effort? How many cases are actually discussed at the Court's conferences? None of these questions or their answers are found in the [Study Group] Report." The answers to these questions are critical to an evaluation of the proposal and I shall undertake to answer them from the vantage point of my service on the Court. For we ought not replace present procedures if there is no pressing problem justifying their replacement. And I do not think that there is such a problem.

Let me begin by explaining briefly the timetable and the procedure used by the Court to screen the 3600 cases submitted for review. As cases are filed with the Court, they are collected by the Clerk's Office and eventually placed on a conference agenda. The agenda, together with the relevant papers as to the cases listed thereon, is circulated to the various chambers approximately two weeks prior to the scheduled conference date. We have about 30 scheduled conferences each Term. Approximately half of the cases are paid filings, with the other half being *in forma pauperis* filings. The ratio of petitions for certiorari to appeals is about 9 to 1, the vast majority of the appeals being among the paid filings.

The method of screening the cases differs among the individual Justices, and thus I will confine myself to my own practice. That practice reflects my view that the screening function is second to none in importance—a point I shall touch upon more fully a little later. I try not to delegate any of the screening function to my law clerks and to do the complete task myself. I make exceptions during the summer recess when their initial screening of petitions is invaluable training for next Term's new law clerks. And I also must make some few exceptions during the Term on occasions when opinion work must take precedence. When law clerks do screening, they prepare a memorandum of not more than a page or two in each case, noting whether the case is properly before the Court, what federal issues are presented, how they were decided by the Courts below, and summarizing the positions of the parties pro and con the grant of the case.

For my own part, I find that I don't need a great amount of time to perform the screening function—certainly not an amount of time that compromises my ability to attend to decisions of argued cases. In a substantial percentage of cases I find that I need read only the "Questions Presented" to decide how I will dispose of the case. This is certainly true in at least two types of cases—those presenting clearly frivolous questions and those that must be held for disposition of pending cases. Because of my familiarity with the issues of pending cases the cases to be held are, for me, easily recognizable. For example, we heard argument early this Term in eight obscenity cases because we decided to undertake a general re-examination of that subject. Every agenda since then has included several cases of conviction or injunction under state obscenity laws and I simply mark those cases "hold." Similarly, with other cases I can conclude from a mere reading of the question presented that for me at least the question is clearly frivolous for review purposes. For example, during recent weeks, I thought wholly frivolous for review purposes questions such as: "Are Negroes in fact Indians and therefore entitled to Indians' exemptions from federal income taxes?" "Are the federal income tax laws unconstitutional insofar as they do not provide a deduction for depletion of the human body?" "Is the 16th Amendment unconstitutional as violative of the 14th Amendment?" and only last week, "Does a ban on drivers turning right on a red light constitute an unreasonable burden on interstate commerce?"

Nor is an unduly extended or

time-consuming examination required of many of the cases that present clearly non-frivolous questions. For very often even non-frivolous questions are simply not of sufficient national importance to warrant Supreme Court review. And after a few years of experience, it is fair to say that a Justice develops a "feel" for such cases. For example, when the question is whether a Court of Appeals in a diversity case correctly applied governing state law, or correctly directed entry of a judgment notwithstanding the verdict, the question of error, if any, ordinarily does not fall within the area of questions warranting Supreme Court review. As to cases where my initial reading of the questions presented suggests to me that the case may merit Supreme Court review—the special "feel" one develops after a few years on the Court enables one to recognize the cases that are candidates for such review. I need not spend much time examining the papers in depth when the questions strike me as worthy of review, or at least as warranting conference discussion.

After examining or having law clerks examine each of the cases on the week's agenda, each Justice advises the Chief Justice of the cases that he wishes to have stricken from the agenda and laid over to a later date so that further views can be requested of the parties or of an interested non-party such as the Solicitor General. Several days before conference, the Chief Justice circulates a "Discuss List" that designates the cases on the agenda that he believes are worthy of discussion at conference. Any Justice who wishes to add cases to the Discuss List can do so simply by making such a request. On the day before conference, the completed Discuss List is circulated to the individual chambers and

the papers and memoranda relating to those cases are collected and taken to the conference room.

The conferences themselves are ordinarily held on Friday and usually last the better part of the day, with much of the time devoted to discussion of motions and of argued cases and the remainder of the time to the discussion of cases seeking plenary review. The initial conference at the beginning of the Term lasts several days and is devoted exclusively to the discussion of appeals and petitions listed on the summer conference agenda. This agenda contains approximately one-fourth, or about 900, of the total cases filed during the Term and thus much of the Term's screening work is completed even before the Term actually begins. Up to 300 cases are discussed over the several days of the initial conference; at a regular Friday conference during the Term, the number of cases discussed may vary from as few as 10 to as many as 30 or 40. Overall, however, approximately only 30% of the docketed cases are discussed at conference. In other words, the Court is unanimously of the view in 70% of all docketed cases, that the questions sought to be reviewed do not even merit conference discussion. That has proved to be true throughout my time on the Court and a check I made two weeks ago shows that it will be true this Term.

I should emphasize here that the longer one works at the screening function, the less onerous and time-consuming it becomes. I can state categorically that I spent no more time screening the 3643 cases of the 1971 term than I did screening half as many in my first Term in 1956. Unquestionably, the equalizer is experience, and for experience there can be no substitute—not even a second court. I subscribe completely to the observation of the late Mr. Justice

Harlan that "Frequently the question whether a case is 'certworthy' is more a matter of 'feel' than of precisely ascertainable rules." . . . I fear that the Study Group gave insufficient weight to this vital fact in assuming that inflated numbers of appeals and petitions must inevitably make the screening function a more onerous and time-consuming burden.

Moreover, the proposal that a National Court of Appeals be created to ease the Supreme Court's workload may properly be challenged, not only with respect to the Study Group's understanding of that workload, but also with regard to its understanding of the nature of the screening process itself. As I have previously indicated, approximately 30% of all cases docketed annually (that means in this Term, 1100 cases) are placed on the "Discuss List" each Term. Under this system, a single Justice may set a case for discussion at conference and, in many instances, that Justice succeeds in persuading three or more of his colleagues that the case is worthy of plenary review. Thus, the existing system provides a forum in which the particular interests or sensitivities of individual Justices may be expressed, and therefore assures a flexibility that is essential to the effective functioning not only of the screening process but also of the decisional process of which it is an inseparable part.

Much of this flexibility would be lost, however, if the scheme advanced by the Study Group were to be adopted. As envisioned by its proponents, the National Court of Appeals could certify a case to the Supreme Court only if three of its seven judges concurred. It is estimated that about 400 cases per Term would be passed on to the Supreme Court in this manner for final consideration. As a result, each year the Justices of the Supreme Court would be denied the opportunity even to consider the merits of approximately 700 cases that presently would be deemed of sufficient importance to warrant full debate at conference. This loss of flexibility in the screening process would necessarily have a substantial and detrimental effect upon the functions and responsibilities of the Court.

Similarly, an artifical limitation of the Supreme Court's docket to only 400 cases per year would seriously undermine the important impact dissents from denial of review frequently have had upon the development of the law. Such dissents often herald the appearance on the horizon of a possible re-examination of what may seem to the judges of the National Court of Appeals to be an established and unimpeachable principle. Indeed, a series of dissents from denials of review played a crucial role in the Court's re-evaluation of the reapportionment question and the question of the application of the Fourth Amendment to electronic searches. Actually, every Justice has strong feelings about some constitutional view that may not yet command the support of a majority of the Court. . . . The creation of a National Court of Appeals that would certify the 400 "most reviewworthy" cases to the Court each Term would inevitably sacrifice this invaluable aid to constitutional adjudication by denying certification in cases that might otherwise afford appropriate vehicles for such dissents.

Moreover, the assumption that the judges of the National Court of Appeals could accurately select the 400 "most review-worthy" cases wholly ignores the inherently subjective nature of the screening process. The cases docketed each Term cannot simply be placed in a computer that will instantaneously identify those that are "most review-worthy." And this is particularly true with respect to distinctions among the 1100 or so cases presently deemed to be of sufficient "review-worthiness" to merit discussion at one of our weekly conferences. . . .

For the more statistically oriented, the subjective nature of the decision whether a particular case is of sufficient "importance" to merit plenary consideration is amply demonstrated by the voting pattern of the Justices in the screening process. Under our rules, a case may be granted review only if at least four of the nine Justices agree that such review is appropriate. It is noteworthy that, of the cases granted review this Term, approximately 60 percent received the votes of only four or five of the Justices. In only 9 percent of the granted cases were the Justices unanimous in the view that plenary considerations are warranted. Thus, insofar as the key determinant is the "substantiality" of the question presented, there can be no doubt that the appraisal is necessarily a subjective one. And I share the concern voiced by Chief Justice Warren who warned, "the delegation of most of the screening process to the National Court of Appeals would mean that the certiorari 'feel' of the rotating panels of that court would begin to play a vital role in the ordering of our legal priorities and in the control of the Supreme Court docket. More than that, this lower court 'feel' would be divorced from any intimate understanding of the concerns and interests and philosophies of the Supreme Court Justices; and that 'feel' could reflect none of the many other intangible factors and trends within the Supreme Court that often play a role in the certiorari processes."

In response to these objections, it might of course be suggested that the National Court of Appeals certify to the Supreme Court, not 400 cases per Term, but, rather, all 1100 or so cases normally placed on the "Discuss List." As I have already indicated, however, by far the greatest portion of the Court's time and energy presently devoted to the screening process is concentrated, not in the selection of cases to be discussed at conference, but, rather, in the selection from that group of cases of the 150 to 200 cases that will be granted plenary review each Term. Thus, even if the judges of the National Court of Appeals could accurately identify all or most of the cases that normally would be placed on the "Discuss List," such a scheme would inevitably prove virtually useless in terms of administrative efficiency.

Finally, it should be noted that the Study Group's recommendation that the breadth of the Court's screening function be curtailed rests in part upon what I consider to be the mistaken assumption that the screening function plays only a minor and separable part in the exercise of the Court's fundamental responsibilities. In my view, the screening function is inextricably linked to the fulfillment of the Court's essential duties and is vital to the effective performance of the Court's unique mission "to define the rights guaranteed by the Constitution, to assure the uniformity of federal law, and to maintain the constitutional distribution of powers in our federal union."

The choice of issues for decision largely determines the image that the American people have of their Supreme Court. The Court's calendar mirrors the ever changing concerns of this society with ever more powerful and smothering government. The calendar is therefore the indispensable source for keeping the Court abreast of these concerns. Our Constitution is a living document and the Court often becomes aware of the necessity for reconsideration of its interpretation only because filed cases reveal the need for new and previously unanticipated applications of constitutional principles. . . .

. . . [T]he evolution of constitutional doctrine is not merely a matter of hearing arguments and writing opinions in cases granted plenary review. The screening function is an inseparable part of the whole responsibility; to turn over seven-eighths of that task to a National Court of Appeals is to rent a seamless web. I expect that only a Justice of the Court can know how inseparably intertwined are all the Court's functions, and how arduous and long is the process of developing the sensitivity to constitutional adjudication that marks the role. . . . The initial confrontation on the United States Supreme Court with the astounding differences in function and character of role, and the necessity for learning entirely new criteria for decisions, can be a traumatic experience for the neophyte. How much more traumatic and difficult must be the task of the National Court of Appeals composed of rotating Circuit Judges required to do major Supreme Court work without ever being afforded the slightest glimpse of the whole picture of a Justice's function. It is not only that constitutional principles evolve over long periods and that one must know the history of each before he feels competent to grapple with their application in new contexts never envisioned by the Framers. It is also that he must acquire an understanding of the extraordinary complex factors that enter into the distribution of judicial power between state and federal courts and other problems of "Our Federalism." The screening function is an indispensable and inseparable

part of this entire process, and it cannot be curtailed without grave risk of impairing the very core of the extraordinary function of the Supreme Court. . . .

F. A Note on Prospects for Workload Reform

The Freund Committee's proposal for a new National Court of Appeals is unlikely to be enacted. In its place, a number of substitutes have been proposed. The most prominent is a recommendation of the Commission on Revision of the Federal Court Appellate System, chaired by Senator Roman Hruska of Nebraska. This commission proposed a National Court of Appeals that would have "reference jurisdiction" from the Supreme Court and "transfer jurisdiction" from existing courts of appeals. In the latter category would be primarily cases of circuit conflict. Presumably (though not defined by the commission), the Supreme Court would refer cases that were of some national importance but not so important as to warrant immediate attention by the Supreme Court. All decisions of the National Court of Appeals would be reviewable by the Supreme Court on a writ of certiorari; the hope and expectation is that in all but a few cases, decisions of the National Court would be final. Various other suggestions have been articulated about which cases might, or ought to, be assigned or referred to such a National Court of Appeals. Tax cases, patent cases, state criminal appeals, and review of administrative agency decisions are among the types of cases most often suggested.

These proposals are as controversial as the original Freund Committee Report. Until some consensus is reached, no major reform is likely. What seems reasonably clear now is that no one can predict precisely the impact of such reforms on the policy role of the Supreme Court. Would the Supreme Court, relieved of the drudgery of countless certiorari petitions, become more creative and innovative?[1] There are many who favor reform who might be appalled at such a result.

One reform that has widespread support is the elimination of the remaining vestiges of the Supreme Court's mandatory (Appeals) jurisdiction. A bill to consolidate the Supreme Court's jurisdiction into a single discretionary writ of certiorari (S. 450) passed the Senate by a vote of 61–30, but only after it had been amended to include a provision barring the federal courts, including the Supreme Court, from passing on the validity of state laws "relating to voluntary prayers in public schools and public buildings." That amendment, sponsored by Senator Jesse Helms (R-North Carolina), was designed to permit the states to evade the ban on school prayers established by the Supreme Court in *Engel* v. *Vitale* (1962) and *Abington Township* v. *Schempp* (1963) [See pp. 1289–1292]. Many liberal senators who favored elimination of the Court's mandatory jurisdiction voted against the bill because of the Helms amendment.

In June of 1978, all nine justices of the Supreme Court took the very unusual step of writing a public letter endorsing the elimination of mandatory jurisdiction. That letter, which follows, was addressed to Senator Dennis DeConcini (D-New Mexico):

Supreme Court of the United States
Washington, D.C., June 22, 1978

Dear Senator DeConcini:

In response to your invitation and inquiries, we write to comment on proposed limitations of the Supreme Court's mandatory jurisdiction, specifically those contained in S. 3100 [an earlier version of S. 450—Ed.]. Various Justices have spoken out publicly on the issue on prior occasions, all stating essentially the view that the Court's mandatory jurisdiction should be severely limited or eliminated altogether. Your invitation, however, enables all of us, after discussions within the Court, to express our common view on the matter.

We endorse S. 3100 without reservation and urge the Congress to enact it promptly.

Our reasons are similar to those so ably presented in hearings before the Senate. . . by Solicitor General McCree, Assistant Attorney General Meador, Professor Gressman and others. First, any provision for mandatory jurisdiction by definition permits litigants to bring cases to this Court as of right and without regard to whether those are of any general public importance or concern. Thus, the Court is required to devote time and other finite resources to deciding on the merits cases which do not, in Chief Justice Taft's words, "involve principles, the application of which are of wide public importance or governmental interest, and which should be authoritatively declared by the final court." To the extent that we are

---

[1]Such a possibility is raised in S. Sidney Ulmer and John Alan Stookey, "How the Ox Is Being Gored: Toward a Theory of Docket Size and Innovation in the U.S. Supreme Court," **7** *University of Toledo Law Review* (1975), 1–28.

obligated by statute to devote our energies to these less important cases, we cannot devote our time and attention to the more important issues and cases constantly pressing for resolution in an increasing volume—as witness the current Term now in its closing weeks.

The problem we describe is substantial. We are attaching to this letter an appendix consisting of statistical tables covering the October 1976 Term. As these tables indicate, during the 1976 Term almost half of the cases decided by this Court on the merits were cases brought here as of right under the Court's mandatory jurisdiction. Although presumably the percentage decreased during the 1977 Term because of Congressional action in 1976 severely limiting the jurisdiction of three-judge federal district courts, the burden posed by appeals as of right remained substantial and unduly expended the Court's resources on cases better left to other courts.

Second, the retention of mandatory jurisdiction at a time when the Court's caseload is heavy and growing requires the Court to resort to the generally unsatisfactory device of summary dispositions of appeals. There is no necessary correlation between the difficulty of the legal questions in a case and its public importance. Accordingly, the Court often is required to call for full briefing and oral argument in difficult cases of no general public importance. The Court cannot, however, accord plenary review to all appeals; to have done so during the October 1976 Term, for example, would have required at least 13 additional weeks of oral argument, almost a doubling of the argument calendar—an utterly impossible assignment. As a consequence, the Court must dispose summarily of a substantial portion of cases within the mandatory jurisdiction, often without written opinion. However, because these summary dispositions are decisions on the merits, they are binding on state courts and other federal courts. See *Mandel* v. *Bradley* . . . (1977); *Hicks* v. *Miranda* . . . (1975). Yet as we know from experience, our summary dispositions often are uncertain guides to the courts bound to follow them and not infrequently create more confusion than clarity. From this dilemma we perceive only one escape consistent with past Congressional decisions defining the Court's mandatory jurisdiction: Congressional action eliminating that jurisdiction. Accordingly, we endorse S. 3100 and urge its adoption.

Cordially and respectfully,

WARREN E. BURGER, WILLIAM J. BRENNAN, POTTER STEWART, BYRON R. WHITE, THURGOOD MARSHALL, HARRY A. BLACKMUN, LEWIS F. POWELL, WILLIAM H. REHNQUIST, JOHN P. STEVENS.

3. DECISION ON THE MERITS

[Each case in which certiorari is granted, or in which an appeal is not dismissed, is scheduled for oral argument. As described previously, new briefs are then submitted that emphasize substantive rather than jurisdictional issues. Several months later, oral argument will be heard. Except in cases of special national importance, oral argument is limited to one hour per case, equally divided between the parties (including any time allotted to amicus curiae on each side). At the first conference following argument, the case is considered by the justices and a tentative decision is reached. The chief justice, if he is in the majority, assigns the opinion, to himself or to another justice.

Oral argument is time-consuming, and yet it plays a useful role in the decision-making process. It is the only opportunity that the Court has to confront attorneys in a case and ask direct questions of them, seek additional interpretations or facts to bolster what has been written in the briefs, and satisfy itself that the issues are what the justices understand them to be. Oral argument serves the additional useful function of giving the justices some public exposure, albeit limited in time and to the relatively few persons who attend the Court's sessions. It adds a human, public dimension to the work of an institution that some feel is already excessively shrouded in mystique and secrecy.]

A. *John P. Frank, Opinion Writing*

Once the opinion is written, its author circulates a print to the other Justices for their reactions. This may result in a clear "I agree" or in an equally clear "I shall dissent." It may also result in suggestions, a Justice agreeing to go along if certain items are changed. Each Justice must face the practical question of how much time he wishes to devote to tinkering with another man's work. A very common attitude is that of Justice Bradley, to whom Chief Justice Waite once sent an opinion with a request for criticism. Bradley's note of response was, "Where I concur in the doctrine I am willing to trust the Chief Justice in the mode of expressing it."

In cases of especially fine work, the responsive notes may be very enthusiastic. On the other hand, a Justice may disagree with major details of an opinion, and the result may be considerable revision or sharpening as the opinion goes through draft after draft to accommodate all of the suggestions. The writing judge may make extensive concessions either to keep his majority or to get as close to unanimity as possible.

The final opinion is thus truly the opinion of the particular judge, but it is also truly an institutional product. By this process of refinement the comparative casualness with which the case was decided in conference is compensated for; indeed, cases are sometimes reversed in this process of circulation and criticism within the Court. This happens in two ways. Sometimes the writing Justice finds, as he digs in, that he is no longer persuaded of the rightness of his own original vote. He then turns the case back to the Chief for reassignment; and frequently the Chief suggests that the newly converted Justice circulate a new draft to see whether the rest of the Justices may also wish to change their minds.

The second type of change occurs when a Justice has circulated an opinion to which a dissent is also circulated. The remaining Justices may find the dissent more persuasive than the majority opinion. The majority may then shift, and what was a dissent may become the opinion of the Court. On rare instances a reader can pick out those cases, because the judges may not change their written opinions much after the conversion, and sometimes an "opinion of the Court" *reads* as though it had originally been a dissent. There are also rare occasions in which the Justice

Reprinted from *Marble Palace* (New York: Knopf, 1958), pp. 119–129.

who has written the majority opinion is persuaded by the dissent, changes his mind, and withdraws his own earlier draft.

When the whole process is over, and each Justice has taken his stand, the opinion is ready to be announced. The time ranges from a week to six months or more, with an average of about six weeks after the argument. In rare instances the case must be reargued; and sometimes a case goes over from year to year. . . .

The opinions are announced orally from the bench. This is a remarkable proceeding; a busy institution interrupts pressing work in order to tell a handful of persons in the courtroom what everyone else in the country necessarily learns by reading. . . .

Nonetheless, this ceremony is deeply gratifying to those who see it. Clearly it is expendable, but in the various adjustments to the pressures of time, it should be among the last to go. The tradition of announcing opinions orally is old, and while the announcements are sometimes a bore when a case is not particularly interesting or the opinion is poorly announced, they are sometimes lively and exciting. The Justices themselves sometimes control tedium by giving extremely short statements summarizing the holdings, but occasionally they respond to the inherent drama of the situation by giving the statements with some verve. Variances between the oral statements and the written statements occasionally provide color, although the variations are of no practical importance. Sometimes a Justice is carried away by his enthusiasm, as when Justice McReynolds is supposed to have said from the bench in a lugubrious dissent: "The Constitution is gone." In an earlier day lengthy oral statements misled the press. Reporters might have the impression that an opinion was going one way while a Justice examined one side of the argument, and then at a later stage he might reverse his field and come out the other way. Where major speculations were involved, this sometimes had unfortunate financial consequences; stocks fluctuated because of different impressions gained in the course of a long opinion. This very practical evil is avoided now by giving printed copies of the opinions to the press as a Justice begins his delivery so that the reporters can at once see how the story comes out. . . .

There remain, however, two other types of opinion, the concurrence and the dissent, which any Justice is free to use at any time he desires. The concurrence is simply a variation of the old series type of opinion of the 1790's. It means that an individual Justice is saying his say separate from the Court.

It is the general, but not the universal, view that concurrences ought to be saved for very substantial occasions and ought not be lightly used. . . .

There are bound to be occasions on which some Justices will get to the end result of "affirm" or "reverse" by pathways wholly different from those followed by other Justices. This sometimes leads to puzzling results. For example, in the *United Mine Workers* case arising from the coal strike immediately after World War II . . . [t]here were five Justices to support one reason for the result, a different alignment of five Justices to support a second reason for the result, and a total of four votes against each reason for the result.

In an even more remarkable case of this kind, involving again a double ground, there was a majority *against* each of the grounds for the result, but as a majority could be counted for the result itself, the case was decided for a party despite the fact that a majority of the Court rejected each individual reason as to why that party should prevail. Of this rare kind of mix-up in connection with the *Insular Cases* after the Spanish-American War, Mr. Dooley, the favorite wiseacre of the time, quipped: "Mr. Justice Brown delivered the opinion of the Court and only eight Justices dissented." . . .

However good the uses of concurrences, they are contrary to the system established by Marshall and conflict directly with achieving as massive as possible an "opinion of the Court." They ought not to be used where differences are either minor or insignificant.

Justice Frankfurter directly challenges the soundness of this view, by concurring extremely frequently. By now there has been sufficient experience with the technique of that Justice to permit serious doubt as to its wisdom. The use of judicial opinions can be analyzed by studying the extent to which they are later referred to and applied in subsequent cases or in scholarly writings. . . . An analysis of the Frankfurter concurrences for a period of two years, made after sufficient time had elapsed to give them an opportunity to be applied, showed that in almost no instance were the concurrences ever used by anyone. The lower courts in subsequent cases frequently applied the majority opinions with which Frankfurter had concurred, but they did not use the concurrences as well, or treat the main opinions as modified in any way by the concurrences. Much the same thing was true of the scholarly literature. . . .

The occasion for dissent is also a highly variable matter of judicial taste. Dissents are always colorful, and Justices Holmes and Brandeis gave the practice a glorious connotation because their dissents were usually so far superior to the majority opinions, and because so many of their dissents subsequently became the law. Stylewise, the dissent has a greater freedom and verve than majority opinions because the majority opinion has been through the institutional process of opinion, agreement, revision, conciliation, and so on, while the dissent need please only its author. . . .

In other days dissents were usually saved for serious business. Hughes described them as "an appeal to the brooding spirit of the law, to the intelligence of a future day, when a later decision may possibly correct the error into which the dissenting judge believes the Court to have been betrayed." It is commonly believed, for example, that if Hughes was outvoted, he usually joined the majority without further argument. Unfortunately, today dissents are as common as the snows of winter. There are functions for dissent, but overliberal dissent tends to cheapen the currency and reduce the value of the dissents that are really worthwhile. Dissent ought to be free always in constitutional cases, because by tradition constitutional decisions may be more freely reexamined by the Court itself than decisions that merely interpret statutes or declare other parts of the law. There is good reason for this: the amendment process is so difficult that in most instances only the Court can correct its own errors, while Congress can easily change mere statutory interpretations. Since constitutional questions are open to reexamination, Justices in disagreement should freely note their differences so that the bar can know whether to raise a topic again. . . .

In the general run of cases, none of these things is true. Where differences are of minor significance, once a case is decided, the Court, including the dissenting Justices, will peacefully abide by the result. In such cases the dissent serves no useful purpose. . . .

These casual dissents do not unsettle the law; it is almost certain that in each of the cases mentioned, the law as declared by the majority will continue for the rest of time. But these dissents do use up judicial energy. In the instances mentioned, the effort may have been slight, but, whatever it was, it could have been given to something else. Of graver consequence, the constancy of dissent on little matters weakens the Court as an institution, robbing it of that oracular quality which it needs on the big cases. The impression that the "Court can't agree on anything" not only helps to drain dissents of their potency where they might matter a great deal, but also robs Supreme-Court-made law itself of much of its dignity. . . .

B. Felix Frankfurter, Justice Holmes and the Pipeline Cases

. . . The case finally came before the Supreme Court. It took some time before the litigation got underway and before it got through the lower courts. In the Supreme Court it hung fire for a whole year. The case was argued for the government by the then Solicitor General, John W. Davis, and for the pipelines by some of the most eminent, towering figures of the bar. Finally, on the last day of Court sitting in 1914, down came the opinion by Holmes with one dissenting voice, Mr. Justice McKenna. Holmes said, in effect, in a very unsatisfactory opinion—on its face an extremely unsatisfactory opinion and

everybody found it unsatisfactory who thought about those things—except that the statute was sustained. . . . But the reasoning by which the statute was sustained was meager and inadequate because Holmes said that these pipelines were in fact common carriers in all but form, and Congress just made them common carriers in form. Some aid was given to the mode of explaining the legislation by the form of the statute which said, "shall be deemed to be common carriers"—in other words as though this was a declaratory statement instead of a creative pronouncement. Instead of saying, "We make them common carriers," this was legislation which said, "We recognize them to be common carriers." And that, in substance, was almost all Holmes said with a hint here and there.

. . . [His opinion raises] the whole problem of the considerations that lead a court to write an opinion one way rather than another, or the considerations that lead a court to have an opinion written for it one way rather than another.

On the face of things the *Pipeline* cases were argued at the very beginning of the term in October, and they weren't decided until the last day of the term on June 22, 1914. It is a matter of common knowledge . . . that Holmes dashes off his opinions within a few days after a case is assigned to him, and for him to take even a week for the writing of an opinion, even the most complicated case, is rare. The *Pipeline* case was an important case, but not complicated on its facts, and it didn't require a vast amount of what we call legal research, certainly not for Holmes. One thing is incontestable, and that

Reprinted from *Felix Frankfurter Reminisces* (New York: Reynal & Co., 1960), pp. 295–299.

is that it took all this time to get the case out not because Holmes took a lot of time to write the opinion. Considering the nature of the legislation and the make-up of the Court, one can be sure that there were differences within the Court. The ground that seems to you and to me obvious on which to sustain the constitutionality of the statute, namely, that under the Commerce Clause Congress has power to deal with the more or less economic monopoly as much as it has in dealing with a legal monopoly such as a franchise implies, that ground which, I have no doubt, would commend itself to Holmes in the light of his past opinions and might commend itself to one or two other people on the Court might be a little frightening to others on the Court to whom "liberty of contract" and the distinction between private carrier and common carrier is almost as deep and immutable as the differences between the sexes. Therefore, the problem was to get out an opinion that is not disturbing for the future, which sustains this legislation, and gives little further encouragement to the underlying economic impulse behind the legislation which some of the boys certainly feared. This is all speculation, . . .

Well, time passes. After Holmes's death there became available to me the volumes in which he year by year collected the opinions he wrote, his original circulation of printed opinions—he didn't keep any working papers. He wrote and then sent it to the printer, and that's all there was to it. But, in the cases in which he wrote, either for the Court, or in dissent or concurring, he did keep and had bound the opinions that he had circulated and the returns he had, the comments from each of the Justices. When I came into possession of the papers, the opinion as originally circulated in the *Pipeline* case and the opinion that finally became the opinion of the Court, the documents revealed that Holmes did go on this essentially economic justification for Congressional interference, but the boys wouldn't stand for it. In all the years Holmes was on the Court, from 1902 to 1932, in no other case did he write and re-write and circulate and re-circulate with a view to getting an agreement on the part of the Court, and the opinion that now appears is an eviscerated document—a castration really, not an evisceration, a castration of his original opinion. And in his own annotation on his copy of the opinion . . . Holmes wrote in his own handwriting, "This is a wholly unsatisfactory opinion," and then stated why it was unsatisfactory. I don't think there's another instance—well, I can't say that, but I should be greatly surprised—yes, I don't believe that there is another instance in which a member of the Supreme Court, or for that matter any court, analyzed and characterized with such naked candor an opinion of his own as "unsatisfactory" and gave the reasons why it was and why he yielded to having his name put to such an opinion; namely, that if he hadn't done that, the case would not have been decided that Term with the risk of being adversely decided later. It would have gone over, and the important point was to get an adjudication which would sustain the statute. The vital fact is that the statute was sustained. When you have at least five people to agree on something, they can't have that comprehensive completeness of candor which is open to a single man, giving his own reasons untrammeled by what anybody else may do or not do if he put that out.

. . . You may be interested in a story I got from John W. Davis on the

Pipeline case, the first case he argued as Solicitor General. As he put it, he jumped into the stream as it flowed by, and he waited all year for the opinion. After it came down, he had occasion to visit Justice Holmes, and he made some comment to the effect that he was glad the government won, but that he was not entirely happy with the opinion. Mr. Davis reported that Holmes said, "Well, that's the trouble. I write out my opinions, and I send them around to my brethren. One of them picks out a plum here, and the other picks out a plum there, and they send it back to me with nothing but a shapeless mass of dough to father!"

C. *Robert H. Jackson, The Uses of Dissent*

. . . Dissent has a popular appeal, for it is an underdog judge pleading for an underdog litigant. Of course, one party or the other must always be an underdog in a lawsuit, the purpose of which really is to determine which one it shall be. But the tradition of great dissents built around such names as Holmes, Brandeis, Cardozo, and Stone is not due to the frequency or multiplicity of their dissents, but to their quality and the importance of the few cases in which they carried their disagreement beyond the conference table. Also, quite contrary to popular notion, relatively few of all the dissents recorded in the Supreme Court have later become law, although some of these are of great importance.

There has been much undiscriminating eulogy of dissenting opinions. It is said they clarify the issues. Often they do the exact opposite. The technique of the dissenter is often to exaggerate the holding of the Court beyond the meaning of the majority and then to blast away at the excess. So the poor lawyer with a similar case does not know whether the majority opinion meant what it seemed to say or what the minority said it meant. Then, too, dissenters frequently force the majority to take positions more extreme than was originally intended. The classic example is the *Dred Scott Case,* in which Chief Justice Taney's extreme statements were absent in his original draft and were inserted only after Mr. Justice McLean, then a more than passive candidate for the presidency, raised the issue in dissent.

The *right of dissent* is a valuable one. Wisely used on well-chosen occasions, it has been of great service to the profession and to the law. But there is nothing good, for either the Court or the dissenter, in dissenting per se. Each dissenting opinion is a confession of failure to convince the writer's colleagues, and the true test of a judge is his influence in leading, not in opposing, his court. . . .

D. *A Note on the Frequency and Causes of Dissent*

Of the justices regarded as "great dissenters," few have actually been the most frequent dissenters on their respective courts. Holmes, Brandeis, and the "first" dissenter, William Johnson, made their reputations because of the provocative, forceful, and sometimes literary qualities of their dissenting opinions. It may be the verdict of history that contributes to a justice's reputation as a dissenter, where the policies or principles expressed first in dissent become at a later date the law of the land. The

Reprinted from *The Supreme Court in the American System of Government* (Cambridge: Harvard University Press, 1955), pp. 18–19.

two premodern justices who dissented most often were Peter Daniel, before the Civil War, and the first John Marshall Harlan. Harlan dissented 380 times in his thirty-four years on the Court, but he is perhaps best remembered today for two opinions in which his appeal to the spirit of equality in American life and law at the end of the nineteenth century finally became the law of the land in the twentieth—the *Civil Rights Cases* (1883) and *Plessy* v. *Ferguson* (1896).

Prior to Marshall's tenure as chief justice, each justice filed an opinion in each case, and in this *seriatim* process there was little to distinguish the dissenting justice from his brethren. In Marshall's time, dissents were rare; certainly they were discouraged by the chief justice, who followed the practice of not announcing his own disagreements with the majority.

From Taney to Taft the pattern varied slightly. The number of dissents increased but not greatly. According to Halpern and Vines, the percentage of written opinions in which there were dissenting votes did not exceed 25 percent from 1800 until about 1940. Indeed, the low point of dissent in the twentieth century seems to have been reached during the Taft period (1921–1930). A steep rise in the curve begins in the mid-1920s, reaching a peak of about 75 percent during the years of the Warren Court. A similar increase is found in the number of dissenting votes filed per written opinion.[1]

In 1930, 11 percent of the Supreme Court's decisions were nonunanimous, and the average number of dissenting votes per case was 0.27. In 1945, 56 percent of the decisions were nonunanimous, and an average of 1.14 dissenting votes were cast in each case. By 1957, 76 percent of the Court's full opinion cases were nonunanimous; the number of dissenting votes per case had risen to 2.11.[2] Current figures continue to show a relatively constant range of 75 to 80 percent nonunanimous cases, and an average of at least two dissents per case.

It is ironic that the modern trend toward virtually unlimited dissent should have begun when Taft was Chief Justice, since he tried so hard to foster a contrary spirit that emphasized the importance of institutional solidarity. Danelski has noted Taft's efforts to indoctrinate new justices in the "no dissent unless absolutely necessary" tradition.[3] It was quite common for justices to suppress threatened or already written dissents to preserve an outward appearance of unity.[4]

Yet, even then, there were exceptions, and no one questioned a justice's *right* to dissent. Cardozo, for example, endorsed the right of dissent while warning his brethren of its potential for misuse. He noted the absence of collegial participation in

[1]Stephen C. Halpern and Kenneth N. Vines, "Dissent, the Judges' Bill and the Role of the U.S. Supreme Court" (1974). Unpublished paper presented at the 1974 Annual Meeting of the American Political Science Association.

[2]These figures are from Karl ZoBell, "Division of Opinion in the Supreme Court: A History of Judicial Disintegration," **44** *Cornell Law Quarterly* (1959), 205.

[3]David J. Danelski, "The Influence of the Chief Justice in the Decisional Process of the Supreme Court," in Murphy and Pritchett (eds.), *Courts, Judges, and Politics* (New York: Random House, 1974), p. 532. Excerpts from Danelski's article are reprinted below.

[4]Alexander Bickel, *The Unpublished Opinions of Mr. Justice Brandeis* (Chicago: University of Chicago Press, 1967).

most dissenting opinions, compared to the institutional nature of majority opinions. He feared that, without such constraints, dissenting opinions might yield to the temptation to be irresponsible.[5] Charles Evans Hughes, who had resigned from the Supreme Court in 1916 to run for president (and who would be reappointed in 1930 to succeed Taft as Chief Justice), wrote in 1928 that the dissenting opinion was "an appeal to the brooding spirit of the law" which someday might vindicate the position now espoused only in dissent.[6]

What accounts for the changing norms of dissent? Halpern and Vines point to the Judiciary Act of 1925, which enlarged the Court's discretionary jurisdiction, as one important factor. Not only were the justices at least temporarily relieved of some of their burdensome work load, but they also were free to decide only cases of national policy importance. By definition, these are the sorts of cases least likely to be decided unanimously. There is no *a priori* reason to expect Supreme Court Justices to be united on politically contentious issues that divide the country. Thus when the universe of cases that the Court faced contained a higher percentage of controversial issues, more dissents were recorded.[7]

The constitutional and political changes of the 1930s further loosened the restraints on dissent. Ferment in legal thinking, spearheaded by the Legal Realists, emphasized the personal and policy dimensions of judicial decisions and

called for a more open and candid revelation of how judges' decisions were made.[8] The myth of mechanical jurisprudence was seriously eroded. The public expression of judicial dissent seemed more appropriate in a period of great political and social change. Judicial dissent was no longer defended as an occasionally unavoidable evil but hailed as a proper and even important judicial function in a democratic and heterogeneous society.[9] The liberal dissenters of the pre-1937 Court, Holmes, Brandeis, Stone, and Cardozo, were praised for their dissents against the conservative majority, not criticized for destroying the Court's solidarity.

The first Justice Harlan dissented an average of 11.2 times per term. Every justice appointed since 1937 has dissented at a more frequent rate. The second Justice Harlan averaged more than forty-two dissents per term; indeed, he dissented more than twice as often in eighteen terms as had his grandfather in his thirty-four years on the bench. Dissenting *opinions* are, of course, far less frequent than dissenting votes. In the 1974 term, Justice Douglas wrote twenty-six dissenting opinions while casting sixty dissents. Justice Blackmun wrote only five dissenting opinions but cast thirteen dissenting votes.

The frequency of dissent by an individual justice can be attributed to several factors. First, the Chief Justice is almost always an infrequent dissenter. If he dissents, he loses the power to assign majority opinions

---

[5]See, generally, Joel B. Grossman, "Dissenting Blocs on the Warren Court: A Study in Judicial Role Behavior," **30** *Journal of Politics* (1968), 1068–1090.

[6]Charles Evans Hughes, *The Supreme Court of the United States* (New York: Garden City Books, 1928), p. 68.

[7]Halpern and Vines, *op cit.*, Note 1.

[8]Jerome Frank, *Law and the Modern Mind* (New York: Brentano, 1930).

[9]See William O. Douglas, "The Dissent: A Safeguard of Democracy," **32** *Journal of the American Judicature Society* (1948), p. 104–107.

which often implies losing control of the content of those opinions. From 1948 to 1969, the two justices with the lowest frequency of dissent opinions were the chief justices, Vinson and Warren; both also ranked very low, if not quite at the bottom of the list, of dissenting votes. In his first two terms as Chief Justice, Warren Burger cast an unusually high number of dissenting votes and wrote a record number of dissenting opinions (not too dissimilar to Earl Warren in *his* early years as Chief Justice). In those early years, Burger was still part of a conservative minority on the Court. Since then, Burger has cast fewer dissenting votes, but he still dissents more frequently than his predecessors.

Another significant factor is the degree of difference between a justice's policy views and those of the majority in a particular case. Even though the role constraints with which a justice must contend no longer discourage dissent in all or most cases, there are undoubtedly still some institutional pressures for unanimity. Moreover, for strategic reasons, a justice must not be too willing to dissent *whenever* he disagrees with his brethren. Thus, dissent not only measures the degree of polarization of policy views but may also reflect the bargaining situation on the Court. Rates of dissent also change as the membership on the Court changes and as a justice finds himself in a different position vis-à-vis other justices on the Court. A new alignment on the Court in 1970 saw Harlan's dissents decreasing, while those of Douglas, Brennan, and Marshall increased. All of the latter three justices cast their personal high number of dissents in the 1970 term

and continued through the 1974 term to be the most frequent dissenters.

Propensity to dissent may also relate to a justice's role perceptions about the utility and propriety of frequent dissent, and to such intangibles as the current state of his health, his ability to do the extra work required of a dissenting justice, and the clash of personalities on a collegial court. One recent observer has suggested that propensity to dissent is, in part, a function of predisposition to dissent and that "the tendency to express dissent is related to psychological need. . . . A judge, like other persons, wants to reduce whatever psychic tensions may trouble his life. These tensions or frustrations are produced by the blocking of an individual's effort to satisfy a need or achieve a goal. . . . Dissent behavior can be interpreted as a form of compensation for those who perform better in the dissenter's role than in the role of the majority judge—a position often calling for an ability to compromise."[10]

Little research has been reported on the policy implications of dissent. However, some criticisms of the practice of dissent have carried strong ideological overtones. These criticisms have often alleged or implied that dissent is a weapon of liberal and progressive forces designed to subvert the foundations of a conservative judiciary. Both the figures reported in this note and other research contradict this assertion. The leading dissenter on the Warren Court, and the justice with the highest dissenting average, Harlan, was quite clearly of conservative leanings. Reporting on a study of the propensity of Supreme Court justices to dissent and to abandon precedent,

---

[10]S. Sidney Ulmer, "Dissent Behavior and the Social Background of Supreme Court Justices," **32** *Journal of Politics* (1970), 588.

John Schmidhauser wrote that rather than being a doctrinal innovator, "the typical dissenter has been a tenacious advocate of traditional legal doctrines which were being abandoned during his tenure; consequently he adhered to precedent with far greater regularity than his non-dissenting colleagues, and his persistent attempts at turning back the doctrinal tides of his era usually met with failure."[11]

Parenthetically, it should be noted that the high frequency of dissent on the U.S. Supreme Court is relatively unique among judicial institutions. Dissent is rarely found in European courts, where opinions are often issued anonymously, although it has been introduced recently in West Germany.[12] It occurs in India[13] and Japan,[14] although the prevailing norm is to seek harmony through compromise. In the lower federal courts in the United States, dissent is infrequent.[15] A few state courts, most notably Michigan, Pennsylvania, and New York, have exhibited dissent rates approaching 50 percent, but they are clearly in the minority.[16] The reasons suggested by Vines and Glick to explain these variations coincide with our own analysis of dissent on the U.S. Supreme Court. They argue that dissent on state supreme courts is linked to the size of the court—the larger the court, the greater the likelihood of dissent—and to the presence of an intermediate appellate court that can decide many of the routine cases, leaving those that are more controversial (and more likely to produce dissents) to the highest state court. They also note the relationship of dissent to urbanism, heterogeneity of population, and strong political party competition. In other words, in a dynamic society with much disagreement on basic values, in the absence of internal constraints, judicial dissent is likely to be high.[17]

E. Internal Dynamics of the Decision-making Process

(1) A Note on Mobilizing a Majority

Assuming that judges have policy preferences[1] that they wish to see enacted, what are the available re-

[11]John R. Schmidhauser, "Stare Decisis, Dissent, and the Background of the Justices of the Supreme Court of the United States," **14** *University of Toronto Law Journal* (1962), 209.

[12]Donald P. Kommers, *Judicial Politics in West Germany: A Study of the Federal Constitutional Court* (Beverly Hills: Sage Publications, 1976).

[13]George Gadbois, "Indian Supreme Court Judges," 3 *Law and Society Review* (1968–1969), 317.

[14]David J. Danelski, "The People and the Court in Japan," in Grossman and Tanenhaus (eds.), *Frontiers of Judicial Research* (New York: Wiley, 1969), pp. 45–72. See also Walter F. Murphy and Joseph Tanenhaus, *The Study of Public Law* (New York: Random House, 1972), pp. 160–161 and passim.

[15]Sheldon Goldman and Thomas P. Jahnige, *The Federal Courts as a Political System,* 2nd ed. (New York: Harper & Row, 1976, 2nd. ed.) p. 205.

[16]Henry Robert Glick and Kenneth N. Vines, *State Court Systems* (Englewood Cliffs, N.J.: Prentice-Hall, 1973), pp. 78–82.

[17]*Ibid.* Some direct evidence on this point is provided by Bradley Canon and Dean Jaros, "Dissent on Supreme Courts: The Differential Impact of the Characteristics of Judges," 15 *Midwest Journal of Political Science* (1971), 322

[1]For example, see Walter Murphy's description of the "policy-oriented" judge, *Elements of Judicial Strategy* (Chicago: University of Chicago Press, 1964), pp. 3–11.

sources and strategies at their disposal? Each justice of the Supreme Court is theoretically equal; each casts one vote. But differences of intellectual capacity, personality, skill in bargaining, and intensity of preference may give any justice disproportionate influence over his brethren. Also, as we shall see in the next selection, the Chief Justice has certain prerogatives that enable him to exercise strong policy and decision-making leadership.

In order to bring about policy results which he favors, a justice must win the support of a least four additional justices (assuming a full complement of nine justices is deciding a case). What tactics are open to a justice who wishes to mobilize a majority of the Court? According to Walter Murphy there are four basic tactics that can be employed.[2] First, there is "persuasion on the merits." Justices do not always begin a case with a fixed position, and frequently will change their minds when confronted with new information or a persuasive argument. For some justices, persuasion may entail the marshaling of precedent. For others it may be an argument on the efficacy of judicial action (or inaction) or the desirability of attaining certain goals. And for some it may involve a moral argument or an abstract evaluation of right and wrong.

Second, Murphy argues that "increasing personal regard" may be a factor. There is evidence that justices have on occasion gone to some length to "charm" or win the friendship of junior colleagues. And within the social structure of the decision-making process there is ample opportunity for bestowing praise, giving advice, and otherwise enhancing one's personal standing with the brethren. In particular, the comments that justices append to slip opinions circulated for approval are an important medium for communicating such messages.

Third, failing intellectual or social persuasion a justice has certain sanctions that he can utilize. Most important is his vote; the threat of withholding it or of writing a strong dissenting or concurring opinion may often lead to a bargaining situation. The value of a vote will differ from case to case and from justice to justice. The threat of dissent from a "great dissenter," from the author of a prior opinion that is purportedly being followed, or from a justice whose vote is needed to make a majority, will be heeded most. Unless there is some special reason to desire a unanimous court, a single dissenter's threat may be ignored; likewise the threat of dissent from a justice who is so rigidly committed to a contrary position that he cannot be persuaded to join the majority under any circumstances is not likely to be an effective sanction. The threat of dissent is likely to be most effective where it is real and where it can affect the outcome. A justice who threatens dissent often, but rarely carries through his threat, is unlikely to be influential.

Murphy's fourth tactic is bargaining. The threat of withholding one's vote or of writing a concurring opinion is only one aspect of bargaining, although perhaps the most important. Bargaining can take place if there is some commodity that can be exchanged, some sanctions, if the participants are not committed to rigid ideological positions, and if the decision-making milieu encourages majority building and accommodation of disparate views. On a small group such as the Supreme Court,

[2]*Ibid.*, pp. 37–90 and passim.

whose members are in constant contact with one another, the accommodation of views is necessary both as a social and an institutional matter. A justice must learn to disagree without being disagreeable. But there is also a high value placed on teamwork, perhaps higher than on virtuoso performances. Without this emphasis on teamwork and institutional solidarity, the sanction of threatened dissent would be much less valuable and bargaining generally would not be as efficacious.

Viewing the Court from a bargaining perspective rests on the assumption that it is likely to exhibit those distinctive properties often associated with small groups. As summarized most recently by Sidney Ulmer, small groups are said to be

> . . . more accurate than individuals in providing objective solutions to certain kinds of problems (groups make fewer errors); that group members are motivated to support group norms; that support of group values by the individual depends on how important the group is to him; that on questions of judgment the individual group member is heavily influenced by the majority, even contrary to objective evidence; and that the interactions among group members vary in quantity and quality with group size.[3]

One approach to the study of the Supreme Court as a small group which has received considerable attention is bloc analysis. Analysis of voting blocs is commonly used in the analysis of legislative behavior, and has been carried over to collegial courts. Whether or not blocs actually exist on the Supreme Court is open to question and largely a matter of definition. A bloc is a group or faction of two or more justices who vote together. But is it more akin to a "clique" or a "coalition?" A clique has been defined as a persistently cohering group whose members share not only short-run objectives, but long-range interests and a basic value consensus as well. A coalition is a more temporary and shifting alliance of justices who are in agreement on some short-run objectives.[4]

Given the way in which the justices of the Supreme Court make decisions, it is improbable, as Murphy has written, that "any Justice could 'form' a bloc among his colleagues. What he could very possibly do is to discover similar outlooks and voting tendencies among his brethren and then use his social and intellectual skills to reinforce ideological affinities and bring about a measure of co-ordination to individual behavior patterns."[5] By contrast, Ulmer has said that decision-making is "nothing more than the process of forming sub-groups which, according to decision-making rules, bind the larger group."[6]

Attempts to measure the existence of voting blocs on the Supreme Court have failed to demonstrate the existence of anything approaching a clique. What evidence there is, taken mostly from indices of agreement or disagreement between each pair of justices, is at best consistent with the existence of coalitional behavior.[7]

---

[3]S. Sidney Ulmer, *Courts as Small and Not so Small Groups* (New York: General Learning Press, 1971), p. 2.

[4]S. Sidney Ulmer, "Toward a Theory of Sub-Group Formation in the United States Supreme Court," **26** *Journal of Politics* (1965), 133–152.

[5]Murphy, *op. cit.,* Note 1, p. 78. Also see Walter F. Murphy, "Courts as Small Groups," **79** *Harvard Law Review* (1966), 1565–1572.

[6]Ulmer, *op cit.,* Note 4, p. 134.

[7]Joel B. Grossman, "Dissenting Blocs on the Warren Court: A Study in Judicial Role Behavior," **30** *Journal of Politics* (1968), 1068–1090

The mere fact that two or more justices vote together in a case is but weak evidence of interaction. It does not reveal how each justice arrived at his position, or who influenced whom.[8] The existence of cliques, and even to some extent of coalitions as well, is likely to produce the sort of tensions and other costs that would make collegial life very difficult for Supreme Court justices. Nevertheless, much of the work on voting blocs is not inconsistent with, and helps explain, collegial decision-making patterns if conceptual limitations are recognized. Decision-making on the Court is not entirely individualistic, nor is it solely a function of bloc membership.

(2) David Danelski, The Influence of the Chief Justice in the Decisional Process

The Chief Justice of the United States has a unique opportunity for leadership in the Supreme Court. He presides in open court and over the secret conferences where he usually presents each case to his associates, giving his opinion first and voting last. He assigns the Court's opinion in virtually all cases when he votes with the majority; and when the Court is divided, he is in a favorable position to seek unity. But his office does not guarantee leadership. His actual influence depends upon his esteem, ability, and personality and how he performs his various roles.

The conference is the matrix of leadership in the Court. The Court member who is able to present his views with force and clarity and defend them successfully is highly esteemed by his associates. When perplexing questions arise, they turn to him for guidance. He usually makes more suggestions than his colleagues, gives more opinions, and orients the discussion more frequently, emerging as the Court's task leader. In terms of personality, he is apt to be somewhat reserved; and, in concentrating on the decision of the Court, his response to the emotional needs of his associates is apt to be secondary.

Court members frequently disagree in conference and argue their positions with enthusiasm, seeking to persuade their opponents and the undecided brethren. And always, when the discussion ends, the vote declares the victor. All of this gives rise to antagonism and tension, which, if allowed to get out of hand, would make intelligent, orderly decision of cases virtually impossible. However, the negative aspects of conference interaction are more or less counterbalanced by activity which relieves tension, shows solidarity, and makes for agreement. One Court member usually performs more such activity than the other. He invites opinions and suggestions. He attends to the emotional needs of his associates by affirming their values as individuals and as Court members, especially when their views are rejected by the majority. Ordinarily he is the best-liked member of the Court and emerges as its social leader. While the task leader concentrates on the Court's decision, the social leader concentrates on keeping the Court socially cohesive. In terms of personality, he is apt to be warm, receptive, and responsive. Being liked by his associates is ordinarily quite important

[8]Murphy, "Courts as Small Groups," *op cit.,* Note 5, p. 1566.

Reprinted from "The Influence of the Chief Justice in the Decisional Process of the Supreme Court," in Murphy and Pritchett (eds.), *Courts Judges and Politics* (New York: Random House, 1974), pp. 525–534.

to him; he is also apt to dislike conflict.

As presiding officer of the conference, the Chief Justice is in a favorable position to assert task and social leadership. His presentation of cases is an important task function. His control of the conference's process makes it easy for him to invite suggestions and opinions, seek compromises, and cut off debate which appears to be getting out of hand, all important social functions.

It is thus possible for the Chief Justice to emerge as both task and social leader of the conference. This, however, requires the possession of a rare combination of qualities plus adroit use of them. Normally, one would expect the functions of task and social leadership to be performed by at least two Court members, one of whom might or might not be the Chief Justice. As far as the Chief Justice is concerned, the following leadership situations are possible:

	Task Leadership	Social Leadership
I	+	+
II	−	+
III	+	−
IV	−	−

In situation I, the Chief Justice is a "great man" leader, performing both leadership functions. The consequences of such leadership, stated as hypotheses, are: (1) conflict tends to be minimal; (2) social cohesion tends to increase; (3) satisfaction with the conference tends to increase; (4) production, in terms of number of decisions for the time spent, tends to increase. The consequences in situations II and III are the same as in I, particularly if the Chief Justice works in coalition with the associate justice performing complementary leadership functions. However, in situation IV, unless the task and social functions are adequately performed by associate justices, consequences opposite to those in situations I, II, and III tend to occur. . . .

Situation II prevailed in the Taft Court (1921–1930): Chief Justice Taft was social leader, and his good friend and appointee, Justice Van Devanter, was task leader. Evidence of Van Devanter's esteem and task leadership is abundant. Taft, for example, frequently asserted that Van Devanter was the ablest member of the Court. If the Court were to vote, he said, that would be its judgment too. The Chief Justice admitted that he did not know how he could get along without Van Devanter in conference, for Van Devanter kept the Court consistent with itself, and "his power of statement and immense memory make him an antagonist in conference who generally wins against all opposition." At times, Van Devanter's ability actually embarrassed the Chief Justice, and he wondered if he might not be better to have Van Devanter run the conference himself. "Still," said Taft, "I must worry along until the end of my ten years, content to aid in the deliberation when there is a difference of opinion." In other words, Taft was content to perform the social functions of leadership. And he did this well. His humor soothed over the rough spots in conference. "We are very happy with the present Chief," said Holmes in 1922. "He is good-humored, laughs readily, not quite rapid enough, but keeps things moving pleasantly."

Situation I prevailed in the Hughes Court (1930–1941): task and social leadership were combined in Chief Justice Hughes. He was the most esteemed member of his Court. This was due primarily to his performance in conference. Blessed with a photographic memory, he would summarize comprehensively and accurately the facts and issues in each case he presented. When he finished, he would look up and say with a smile: "Now I will state where I come out." Then he would outline his views as to how the case should be decided. Sometimes that is all the discussion a case received, and the justices proceeded to vote for the disposition suggested by the Chief. Where there was discussion, the other Court members gave their views in order of seniority without interruption, stating why they concurred or dissented from the views of the Chief Justice. After they had their say, Hughes would review the discussion, pointing out his agreement and disagreement with the views expressed. Then he would call for a vote. . . .

Situation IV prevailed during most of Stone's Chief Justiceship (1941–1946). When Stone was promoted to the center chair, Augustus Hand indicated in a letter to Hughes that Stone did not seem a sure bet as task leader because of "a certain inability to express himself orally and maintain a position in a discussion." Hand proved to be correct. Stone departed from the conference role cut out by Hughes. When he presented cases, he lacked the apparent certitude of his predecessor; and, at times, his statement indicated that he was still groping for a solution. In that posture, cases were passed on to his associates for discussion. Court members spoke out of turn, and Stone did little to control their debate. Instead, according to Justice Reed, he would join in the debate with alacrity, "delighted to take on all comers around the conference table." "Jackson," he would say, "that's damned nonsense." "Douglas, *you* know better than that."

In other words, Stone was still acting like an associate justice. Since he did not assume the Chief Justice's conference role as performed by Hughes, task leadership began to slip from his grasp. Eventually, Justice Black emerged as the leading contender for task leadership. Stone esteemed Black, but distrusted his unorthodox approach; thus no coalition occurred as in the Taft Court. Justices Douglas, Murphy, Rutledge, and, to a lesser degree, Reed, acknowledged Black's leadership which he was able to reinforce by generally speaking before them in conference. Justices Roberts, Frankfurter, and Jackson, however, either looked to Stone for leadership or competed for it themselves.

The constant vying for task leadership in the Stone conference led to serious conflict, ruffled tempers, severe tension, and antagonism. A social leader was badly needed. Stone was well-liked by his associates and could have performed this function well, but he did not. He did not use his control over the conference process to cut off debates leading to irreconcilable conflict. He did not remain neutral when controversies arose so that he could later mediate them. As his biographer, Alpheus T. Mason, wrote: "He was totally unprepared to cope with the petty bickering and personal conflict in which his Court became engulfed." At times, when conference discussion became extremely heated, Justice Murphy suggested that further consideration of certain cases be postponed. Undoubtedly others also performed social functions of leadership, but in this regard, Stone was a failure. . . .

The consequences of the various Court leadership configurations from 1921 to 1946 may be summarized as follows:

	Taft (II)	Hughes (I)	Stone (IV)
Conflict	Present but friendly.	Present but bridled by CJ.	Considerable; unbridled and at times unfriendly.
Cohesion	Good; team-work and compromise.	Fair; surface personal cordiality; less teamwork than in Taft Court.	Poor; least cohesion in 25-year period; personal feuds in the Court.
Satisfaction	Considerable.	Mixed; Stone dissatisfied prior to 1938; Frankfurter, Roberts, and others highly satisfied.	Least in 25-year period; unrelieved tension and antagonism.
Production	Fair; usually one four- to five-hour conference a week with items carried over.	Good; usually one conference a week.	Poor; frequently more than one conference a week; sometimes three and even four.

Except in production, the Taft Court fared better than the Courts under his two successors. The consequences of leadership in the Stone Court were predictable from the hypotheses, but Hughes' "great man" leadership should have produced consequences more closely approximating those in the Taft Court. The difference in conflict, cohesion, and satisfaction in the two Courts can be perhaps attributed to the fact that Taft was a better social leader than Hughes.

The Chief Justice's power to assign opinions is significant because his designation of the Court's spokesman may be instrumental in:

1. Determining the value of a decision as a precedent, for the grounds of a decision frequently depend upon the justice assigned the opinion.
2. Making a decision as acceptable as possible to the public.
3. Holding the Chief Justice's majority together when the conference is close.
4. Persuading dissenting associates to join in the Court's opinion.

The Chief Justice has maximal control over an opinion when he assigns it to himself; undoubtedly Chief Justices have retained many important cases for that reason. The Chief Justice's retention of "big cases" is generally accepted by his associates. In fact, they expect him to speak for the Court in those cases so that he may lend the prestige of his office to the Court's pronouncement.

When the Chief Justice does not speak for the Court, his influence lies primarily in his assignment of important cases to associates who generally agree with him. From 1925 to 1930, Taft designated his fellow conservatives, Sutherland and Butler, to speak for the Court in about half of the important constitutional cases assigned to associate justices. From 1932 to 1937, Hughes, who agreed more with Roberts, Van Devanter, and Sutherland than the rest of his associates during this period, assigned 44 percent of the important constitutional cases to Roberts and Sutherland. From 1943 to 1945, Stone assigned 55.5 percent of those cases to Douglas and Frankfurter. During that period, only Reed agreed more with Stone than Frankfurter, but Douglas agreed with Stone less than any other justice except Black. Stone had high regard for Douglas' ability, and this may have been the Chief Justice's overriding consideration in making these assignments.

It is possible that the Chief Justice might seek to influence dissenting justices to join in the Court's opinion by adhering to one or both of the following assignment rules:

Rule 1: Assign the case to the justice whose views are the closest to the dissenters on the ground that his opinion would take a middle approach upon which both majority and minority could agree.

Rule 2: Where there are blocs on the Court and a bloc splits, assign the opinion to a majority member of the dissenter's bloc on the grounds that (a) he would take a middle approach upon which both majority and minority could agree and (b) the minority justices would be more likely to agree with him because of general mutuality of agreement.

There is some evidence that early in Taft's Chief Justiceship he followed Rule 1 occasionally and assigned himself cases in an effort to win over dissenters. An analysis of his assignments from 1925 to 1930, however, indicates that he apparently did not adhere to either of the rules with any consistency. The same is true for Stone's assignments from 1943 to 1945. In other words, Taft and Stone did not generally use their assignment power to influence their associates to unanimity. However, an analysis of Hughes' assignments from 1932 to 1937 indicates that he probably did. He appears to have followed Rule 1 when either the liberal or conservative blocs dissented intact. When the liberal bloc dissented, Roberts, who was then a center judge, was assigned 46 percent of the opinions. The remaining 54 percent

were divided among the conservatives, apparently according to their degree of conservatism: Sutherland, 25 percent; Butler, 18 percent; McReynolds, 11 percent. When the conservative bloc dissented, Hughes divided 63 percent of those cases between himself and Roberts.

Hughes probably also followed Rule 2. When the left bloc split, Brandeis was assigned 22 percent of the cases he could have received compared with his 10 percent average for unanimous cases. When the right bloc split, Sutherland was assigned 16 percent of the decisions he could have received compared with his 11 percent average for unanimous cases. He received five of the six cases assigned the conservatives when their bloc split.

Of course, there are other considerations underlying opinion assignment by the Chief Justice, such as equality of distribution, ability, and expertise. It should be noted that opinion assignment may also be a function of social leadership.

One of the Chief Justice's most important roles is that of Court unifier. Seldom has a Chief Justice had a more definite conception of that role than Taft. His aim was unanimity, but he was willing to admit that at times dissents were justifiable and perhaps even a duty. Dissents were proper, he thought, in cases where a Court member strongly believed the majority erred in a matter involving improper principle or where a dissent might serve some useful purpose, such as convincing Congress to pass certain legislation. But, in other cases, he believed a justice should be a good member of the team, silently acquiesce in the views of the majority, and not try to make a record for himself by dissenting.

Since Taft's conception of the function of the dissent was shared by most of his associates, his efforts toward unity were well received. Justices joining the Taft Court were indoctrinated in the "no dissent unless absolutely necessary" tradition, most of them learning it well. . . .

Hughes easily assumed the role of Court unifier which Taft cut out for him, for his views as to unanimity and dissent were essentially the same as Taft's. Believing that some cases were not worthy of dissent, he would join in the majority's disposition of them, though he initially voted the other way. For example, in a 1939 case involving statutory construction, he wrote to an associate: "I choke a little at swallowing your analysis, still I do not think it would serve any useful purpose to expose my views."

Like Taft, Hughes mediated differences of opinion between contending factions, and in order to get a unanimous decision, he would try to find a common ground upon which all could stand. He was willing to modify his own decisions to hold or increase his majority; and if this meant he had to put in some disconnected thoughts or sentences, in they went. In cases assigned to others, he would readily suggest the addition or subtraction of a paragraph in order to save a dissent or a concurring opinion.

When Stone was an associate justice, he prized the right to dissent and occasionally rankled under the "no dissent unless absolutely necessary" tradition of the Taft and Hughes Courts. As Chief Justice, he did not believe it appropriate for him to dissuade Court members from dissenting in individual cases by persuasion or otherwise. A Chief Justice, he thought, might admonish his associates generally to exercise restraint in the matter of dissents and seek to find common ground for decision, but beyond that he should not

go. And Stone usually went no further. His activity or lack of it in this regard gave rise to new expectations on the part of his associates as to their role and the role of the Chief Justice regarding unanimity and dissent. In the early 1940's, a new tradition of freedom of individual expression displaced the tradition of the Taft and Hughes Courts. This explains in part the unprecedented number of dissents and separate opinions during Stone's Chief Justiceship.

Nonetheless, Stone recognized that unanimity was desirable in certain cases. He patiently negotiated a unanimous decision in the Nazi Saboteurs case. It should be pointed out, however, that this case was decided early in his Chief Justiceship before the new tradition was firmly established. By 1946, when he sought unanimity in the case of General Yamashita, the new tradition of freedom was so well established that Stone not only failed to unite his Court, but the dissenters, Murphy and Rutledge, apparently resented his attempts to do so.

The unprecedented number of dissents and concurrences during Stone's Chief Justiceship can be only partly attributed to the displacing of the old tradition of loyalty to the Court's opinion. A major source of difficulty appears to have been the free-and-easy expression of views in conference. Whether the justices were sure of their grounds or not, they spoke up and many times took positions from which they could not easily retreat; given the heated debate which sometimes occurred in the Stone conference, the commitment was not simply intellectual. What began in conference frequently ended with elaborate justification as concurring or dissenting opinions in the United States Reports. This, plus

Stone's passiveness in seeking to attain unanimity, is probably the best explanation for what Pritchett characterized as "the multiplication of division" in the Stone Court. . . .

(3) A Note on the Opinion Assignment Process

Professor Danelski has suggested some of the reasons underlying the chief justice's assignment of the majority opinion. Another factor might well be the personal qualities and background characteristics—or lack of them—which make a judge particularly suitable or unsuitable as a spokesman for the majority. Such was the case in *Smith* v. *Allwright* (1944, See pp. 485–488). The Court decided, after a series of prior decisions, that the "white-primary" system of candidate selection was unconstitutional. Chief Justice Stone assigned the opinion to Justice Frankfurter, but changed his mind and gave the case to Stanley Reed, a Kentuckian, after receiving the following letter from Justice Jackson:

I hope you will forgive me for intruding into the matter of assignments, the difficulties of which I feel you generally resolve with wisdom and always with fairness, but I wonder if you have not overlooked some of the ugly factors in our national life which go to the wisdom of having Mr. Justice Frankfurter act as the voice of the Court in the matter of Smith v. Allwright. It is a delicate matter. We must reverse a recent, well-considered, and unanimous decision [Grovey v. Townsend, 1935]. We deny the entire South the right to a white primary, which is one of its most cherished rights. It seems to me very important that the strength which an all but

unanimous decision would have may be greatly weakened if the voice that utters it is one that may grate on Southern sensibilities. Mr. Justice Frankfurter unites in rare degree factors which unhappily excite prejudice. In the first place, he is a Jew. In the second place, he is from New England, the seat of the abolition movement. In the third place, he has not been thought of as a person particularly sympathetic with the Democratic party in the past. I know that every one of these things is a consideration that to you is distasteful and they are things which I mention only with the greatest reluctance and frank fear of being misunderstood. I told Mr. Justice Frankfurter that in my opinion it is best for this Court and for him that he should not be its spokesman in this matter and that I intend to bring my view of it to your attention. With all humility I suggest that the Court's decision, bound to arouse bitter resentment, will be much less apt to stir ugly reactions if the news that the white primary is dead, is broken to it, if possibly, by a southerner who has been a democrat and is not a member of one of the minorities which stir prejudices kindred to those against the Negro.[1]

(4) David Rohde and Harold Spaeth, Opinion Assignments in the Warren Court

. . . The data we will use to examine the predictions of our theory regarding opinion assignments are derived from a set of 616 civil liberties cases decided by the Warren Court between 1953 and 1969. The cases were organized into 34 issue scales and yielded a total of 480 opinions assigned.

Each scale orders the justices from "left" to "right" (or liberal to conservative) on that issue. In each case we

---

[1]Quoted in Alpheus Mason, *Harlan Fiske Stone: Pillar of the Law* (New York: Viking Press, 1956), p. 615.

Reprinted from *Supreme Court Decision Making* (San Francisco: Freeman, 1976), pp. 176–183 (footnotes deleted).

can compare the scale score of the opinion assigner to the score of any other justice, and thereby determine whether the assigner in fact assigned the opinion to the justice who was closest to him on that issue.

It is unlikely that we will find our predictions supported in every case. We will, therefore, need some yardstick against which we can measure our predictions to determine how accurate our theory is. It seems to us that the most appropriate yardstick to employ is to assume that in every case, each justice in the majority is likely to be assigned the majority opinion. This assumption captures the essence of the necessity of equalizing the opinion-writing work load that we discussed previously. Thus, in any set of cases, we can compare the actual proportion of majority opinions assigned to a justice or a group of justices to the proportion we would expect if opinions were simply randomly assigned among justices who were in the majority. In order for us to accept our predictions as supported by the data, we would have to find that the proportion of opinions assigned in accord with our predictions is substantially greater than the proportion that we would expect to result from random assignment.

For convenience we will employ a couple of symbols to describe these proportions. The letter p indicates the proportion (or percent) of opinions in a set of cases that were actually assigned to a justice or a group of justices, and the Greek letter π indicates the proportion that we would expect to result from random assignment. Thus subtracting the second value from the first $(p - \pi)$ will show us whether our predictions have been either more or less accurate than we expected.

We are now able to make an initial assessment of how well the decision rule we derived from our theory predicts opinion assignments. To recapitulate, we predict that in each case the assigner will either write the majority opinion himself or assign it to the justice who is closest to him on that issue. Thus, if an opinion is to be predicted correctly, it must go to one of a specified group of justices numbering two or more. We will refer to such a group of justices as "the closest group."

Table I presents the data on the three major opinion assigners in the Warren Court (Warren, Frankfurter, and Black). We can see that for each of the assigners the prediction of our decision rule is supported. In each instance, about 10 percent more of the majority opinions go to the closest group than we would expect if assignments were made randomly.

Thus the initial hypothesis is supported by the data. However, to be confident about the predicted relationship between ideological closeness and opinion assignment, we

Table I. Majority Opinion Assignment by Warren, Frankfurter, and Black

Assigner	Total Assigned	Number Assigned to Closest Group	Actual Proportion of Opinions Assigned p	Expected Proportion of Opinions Assigned π	Difference $p - \pi$
Warren	393	219	.557	.439	+.118
Frankfurter	48	26	.542	.444	+.098
Black	25	12	.480	.386	+.094

would also want to find the relationship holding across issue areas and across individual assignees. In other words, perfectly consistent support for the theory would be that the closest group is advantaged (in terms of being assigned opinions) in each individual issue area, and each individual justice is advantaged when he is closest to the assigner and disadvantaged when he is not closest.

Table II [omitted—Ed.] presents the data on opinion assignments by Warren controlled for issue area. The hypothesis is supported in 29 of the 34 issue areas. Moreover, in 19 of the issue areas, the magnitude of $p - \pi$ is .10 or more. We may therefore conclude that the decision rule, although not perfectly supported, holds consistently across issues.

Before we proceed further, one interesting point about the issue area data should be noted. There is, unfortunately, no way to measure the saliency of the various issue areas to the assigners. The logic of the theory indicates that we should expect the prediction to hold more strongly as the saliency of the issues increases. We do have, however, one datum that bears on this point. In an interview just after his resignation as Chief Justice, Warren was asked what was the Supreme Court's most important decision during his tenure. He replied:

I think the reapportionment, not only of state legislatures, but of representative government in this country, is perhaps the most important issue we have had before the Supreme Court.

In addition, he cited the pornography issue as the "most difficult" policy question the Court considered. The data on Warren's assignments in these two areas are consistent with our theoretical expectation. The magnitude of $p - \pi$ for the censorship cases is +.42 (ranking second); for the reapportionment cases it is +.34 (ranking fifth).

Table III shows the data on Warren's assignments to individual justices, controlling for when those justices are closest to Warren and when

Table III. Warren's Assignments to Individual Justices, Controlled for Closeness

| Justice | When Closest | | | When Not Closest | | |
	Actual p	Expected π	Difference $p - \pi$	Actual p	Expected π	Difference $p - \pi$
Brennan	.135	.099	+.036	.018	.027	−.009
Douglas	.092	.071	+.021	.028	.054	−.026
Black	.061	.050	+.011	.043	.065	−.022
Clark	.031	.010	+.021	.066	.069	−.003
Fortas	.015	.018	−.003	.018	.021	−.003
Frankfurter	.013	.007	+.006	.025	.034	−.009
Stewart	.013	.003	+.010	.081	.073	+.008
White	.010	.010	.000	.025	.051	−.026
Marshall	.010	.009	+.001	.013	.014	−.001
Goldberg	.010	.010	.000	.028	.025	+.003
Harlan	—	—	—	.056	.074	−.018
Whittaker	—	—	—	.023	.021	+.002
Reed	—	—	—	.003	.009	−.006
Burton	—	—	—	.013	.021	−.008
Minton	—	—	—	.003	.009	−.006
Jackson	—	—	—	.000	.003	−.003

they are not. Again there is systematic support for the primary hypothesis. Of the 26 data points (10 justices who are on some issue closest to Warren, and all 16 justices when they are not closest), 20 are in the predicted direction. Furthermore, if we restrict our consideration to the 8 justices who were present on the Court for 6 or more of the 16 terms (and whose positions as measured by the scales we may have the most confidence in), there are 15 data points, 13 of which are predicted correctly.

Thus the prediction regarding assignments to the closest group is supported not only in the aggregate, but also when considered in relation to individual issues and individual assignees. We may now turn, therefore, to a consideration of other predictions that follow from the theory.

The theory predicts that the closest group should be advantaged in terms of opinion assignments, and includes as a logical corollary the prediction that justices in other positions should be, *as a group,* disadvantaged. What, however, does the theory have to say about the other positions *individually?*

We have already discussed the fact that the opinion writer is constrained in making policy by the need to gain the adherence of a majority of the Court for his opinion. The Court makes no general policy unless an Opinion of the Court is agreed upon. Moreover, once an opinion is accepted by a majority, there is no need for further adherents, at least as far as the actual policy making is concerned. Thus, if we consider the possible positions from position 1 (the opinion assigner) to position 9 (the justice farthest from the assigner in a unanimously decided case), the theory predicts that positions 1 and 2 should be advantaged. In addition, since the assigner is trying to build an opinion coalition whose position will

be as close as possible to his most preferred position, there usually is no reason why he should try to include any justice beyond position 5. We would also, therefore, predict that positions 6 through 9 should be individually disadvantaged. This leaves positions 3 through 5 to be considered. All three of these positions are necessary to the formation of a minimum winning opinion coalition, for the defection of even one justice will make a majority opinion impossible. In terms of the assigner's preferred position, the justice who is most likely to defect is the one who occupies the fifth position. The surest way to hold him in an opinion coalition would be to let him write the majority opinion himself. Therefore, we would expect that if any one of positions 3 through 5 should be advantaged, it would be the fifth (or pivotal) position. We can summarize our predictions about the nine positions as follows: for position 1 and 2, p should be greater than π; for positions 3, 4, and 6 through 9, p should be less than π; and for position 5 we might expect p to be greater than π.

Table IV presents the aggregate data on assignments to positions for all assigners and shows that the predictions just described are supported. For positions 1 through 4 and 6 through 9, the predicted direction of p — π is correct. For position 5, p — π is positive, but the magnitude is small compared with that for positions 1 and 2. . . .

To this point the data have provided considerable support for the predictions of the theory, but the support has been far from perfect; that is, we have not found that the assigner gives 100 percent of the opinions to the closest group. It is in the explanation of this fact that the impact of the equal work load constraint, which we discussed previously, becomes clear. If all justices

Table IV. Assignments to Positions (All Assigners)

| Position | Assigned | Not Assigned | Opinion Assignment | | |
			Actual p	Expected π	Difference $p - \pi$
1	186	819	.388	.314	+.074
2	74	303	.154	.119	+.035
3	29	243	.060	.092	−.032
4	46	364	.096	.132	−.036
5	72	373	.150	.139	+.011
6	28	287	.058	.088	−.030
7	22	190	.046	.054	−.008
8	15	153	.031	.040	−.009
9	8	87	.017	.022	−.005

occupied the closest position in relation to Warren with approximately equal frequency, then Warren could have assigned the majority opinion to the closest justice in every case, and he still would have satisfied the equal work load constraint. However, all justices were not equally likely to be closest to Warren when they were in the majority. Some justices (such as Brennan) were almost always closest to Warren, whereas others (Harlan, for example) were never closest to Warren. It was, therefore, impossible for Warren invariably to assign the majority opinion to the closest justice *and* equalize the work load. If he had always followed the decision rule, Harlan would never have received an opinion assignment, at least not in this set of cases.

Since all justices were not closest to Warren with equal frequency, we may view his decision about whether to assign the majority opinion to the closest group in a given case to be a judgment concerning the allocation of a scarce resource. In other words, the theory predicts that Warren should always have wanted to follow the decision rule, but observance of the equal work load constraint meant that he could not. Since he could not, then whether the decision rule was followed in a particular case should have been governed by various strategic considerations that would have made it more or less desirable to do so in that instance.

Indeed, this consideration, in conjunction with research completed by another student of the Court, sheds further light on the empirical results we have obtained so far. Gregory Rathjen has recently reported the results of a study that attempted to replicate the research we have been describing, by examining the opinion assignments made by Warren in all *economics* cases decided by the Court between 1959 and 1969. Rathjen found that the predictions of our theory were in general *not* supported by the data on economics cases. If, however, we accept an additional factual assumption—that civil liberties cases were more important to Warren, in general, than economics cases—then a plausible interpretation of the failure of our predictions in Rathjen's analysis may be offered.

It should not be surprising to the reader to discover that the justices who were frequently closest to Warren in the economics cases were the same justices who were frequently closest in the civil liberties cases. We saw in our examination of the value systems of the justices . . . that most of the justices can be described as liberals or conservatives. This means that most members of the Court had the same orientation (either positive or negative) on both civil liberties and economics issues. Thus Warren, because of the equal work load constraint, could not follow the decision rule across the board. If civil liberties issues were indeed more salient to Warren, a reasonable strategy for him to follow would have been to follow the decision rule relatively often in civil liberties cases and seldom in economics cases. This would explain why we found the theory's prediction supported and Rathjen did not.

Rathjen's analysis provides some support for this view. . . . [O]ne justice for whom neither the term "liberal" nor the term "conservative" was an accurate description was Justice Clark. Clark was termed a "New Dealer," which meant he was positively oriented on the value of New Dealism (involving economics cases) and negatively oriented on the values of freedom and equality (involving civil liberties cases). Thus we would expect Clark to appear closest to Warren more often in economics cases than in civil liberties cases. This was in fact the situation. Although our data indicate that Clark was closest to Warren in only 11 percent of the civil liberties cases in which he was in the majority, Rathjen's data found Clark to be closest 51 percent of the time—more than any other justice.

Thus Clark was one justice for whom Warren *could not* follow the decision rule in civil liberties cases, but *could* follow it in economics cases. If our previous argument were correct, we would, therefore, expect Clark to be advantaged in terms of opinion assignments in economics cases. And the data do, in fact, show that. . . .

(5) "The Switch in Time That Saved Nine": A Case Study

(a) A Note on the "Hughberts" Game

During the 1936 term of the Court, President Franklin Roosevelt delivered his famous "court-packing" plan to Congress, in which he asked for a reorganization of the Supreme Court and the power to appoint as many as six new justices to augment the nine already sitting. This plan, ostensibly motivated by the Court's inability to keep up with its docket, was only a thinly disguised attempt to prevent the Court from further blocking important New Deal legislation.

Partly because of resentment toward the disingenuousness of the plan, partly because of a general reluctance to tamper with the Supreme Court, and partly because the Court itself seemed to be switching directions, Congress rejected that part of the plan which sought to increase the membership of the Court. Most scholars have accepted the interpretation that it was the ability of Chief Justice Hughes to persuade Justice Roberts to vote to affirm in a state minimum wage law case, *West Coast Hotel* v. *Parrish* (1937), which reduced the pressure to "pack" the Court. The opinion in this case was delivered after Roosevelt's plan had been announced, and it was generally assumed that the decision—a direct reversal of a case decided only the previous term—was a response to that plan.

To examine the influence of the Chief Justice on the behavior of the Court at this time, Glendon Schubert has utilized some game theory propositions.[1] During the period im-

---

[1]Glendon Schubert, *Quantitative Analysis of Judicial Behavior* (Glencoe: Free Press, 1959), pp. 192–210.

mediately preceding this decision, the Court had been divided among right (Sutherland, Van Devanter, Butler, and McReynolds), left (Stone, Brandeis, and Cardozo), and center (Hughes and Roberts) blocs on economic regulation issues. Compilations of dissents and rate of agreement between the justices during this period showed a very high cohesiveness among the members of the left bloc; also noted was Hughes' tendency rarely to associate himself with the right bloc in dissent, while Roberts tended to dissent about equally with left or right. But in terms of overall interagreement, rather than just dissents, Hughes and Roberts seemed to be clearly more associated with right than left.

Schubert assumed that Hughes, in the face of attack on the Court, would adopt a strategy designed to (1) maximize his own authority within the court, (2) maximize the degree of unanimity on the court, and (3) push the Court into a sufficient liberal posture to forestall attacks on it. Schubert posited that Hughes and Roberts form a single "player," *Hughberts,* whose basic strategy would be to achieve the above objectives, particularly the third. According to Schubert, *Hughberts'* pure strategy would be to form a coalition with the left whenever possible, support the right when it had clearly captured a majority and when he could not form a winning coalition with the left, always join with left and right when they were in agreement. Schubert found, in fact, that Hughes and Roberts did vote in a fashion strikingly similar to the game model.

A further analysis of Hughes' leadership during this critical period showed that he often assigned near

unanimous decisions to justices of the left bloc, left-majority decisions to either Roberts or himself, and right-majority decisions to a member of the right bloc. Given these patterns, Schubert found as the most plausible interpretation of the *Parish* case that both Hughes and Roberts switched "in order to protect the institutional integrity and authority" of the Court. He showed that during the 1936 term—as opposed to the five terms preceding—Hughes and Roberts formed majorities primarily with the left bloc, rarely with the right, converting the left into a fairly consistent majority.

Contrast the analysis of the late Justice Frankfurter, based on a memorandum written by Justice Roberts in 1945, after the latter had resigned from the Supreme Court.

(b) Felix Frankfurter, Mr. Justice Roberts

. . . It is one of the most ludicrous illustrations of the power of lazy repetition of uncritical talk that a judge with the character of Roberts should have attributed to him a change of judicial views out of deference to political consideration. One is more saddened than shocked that a high-minded and thoughtful United States Senator should assume it to be an established fact that it was by reason of "the famous switch of Mr. Justice Roberts" that legislation was constitutionally sustained after President Roosevelt's proposal for reconstructing the Court and because of it. The charge specifically relates to the fact that while Roberts was of the majority in *Morehead* v. *New York ex. rel. Tipaldo* . . . decided June 1, 1936, in reaffirming *Adkins* v. *Chil-*

Reprinted from **104** *University of Pennsylvania Law Review* (1955), 313–316.

dren's Hospital . . . and thereby invalidating the New York Minimum Wage Law, he was again with the majority in *West Coast Hotel Co.* v. *Parrish* . . . decided on March 29, 1937, overruling the *Adkins* case and sustaining minimum wage legislation. Intellectual responsibility should, one would suppose, save a thoughtful man from the familiar trap of *post hoc ergo propter hoc.* Even those whose business it is to study the work of the Supreme Court have lent themselves to a charge which is refuted on the face of the Court records. It is refuted, that is, if consideration is given not only to opinions but to appropriate deductions drawn from data pertaining to the time when petitions for certiorari are granted, when cases are argued, when dispositions are, in normal course, made at conference, and when decisions are withheld because of absences and divisions on the Court. . . .

The truth about the so-called "switch" of Roberts in connection with the *Minimum Wage* cases is that when the *Tipaldo* case was before the Court in the spring of 1936, he was prepared to overrule the *Adkins* decision. Since a majority could not be had for overruling it, he silently agreed with the Court in finding the New York statute under attack in the *Tipaldo* case not distinguishable from the statute which had been declared unconstitutional in the *Adkins* case. That such was his position an alert reader could find in the interstices of the United States Reports. It took not a little persuasion—so indifferent was Roberts to misrepresentation—to induce him to set forth what can be extracted from the Reports. Here it is:

A petition for certiorari was filed in

Morehead v. Tipaldo, *on March 16, 1936. When the petiiton came to be acted upon, the Chief Justice spoke in favor of a grant, but several others spoke against it on the ground that the case was ruled by* Adkins v. Children's Hospital, . . . *Justices Brandeis, Cardozo and Stone were in favor of a grant. They, with the Chief Justice, made up four votes for a grant.*

When my turn came to speak I said I saw no reason to grant the writ unless the Court were prepared to re-examine and overrule the Adkins *case. To this remark there was no response around the table, and the case was marked granted.*

Both in the petition for certiorari, in the brief on the merits and in oral argument, counsel for the State of New York took the position that it was unnecessary to overrule the Adkins *case in order to sustain the position of the State of New York. It was urged that further data and experience and additional facts distinguished the case at bar from the* Adkins *case. The argument seemed to me to be disingenuous and born of timidity. I could find nothing in the record to substantiate the alleged distinction. At conference I so stated, and stated further that I was for taking the State of New York at its word. The State had not asked that the* Adkins *case be overruled but that it be distinguished. I said I was unwilling to put a decision on any such ground. The vote was five to four for affirmance, and the case was assigned to Justice Butler.*

I stated to him that I would concur in an opinion which was based on the fact that the State had not asked us to re-examine or overrule Adkins *and that, as we found no material difference in the facts of the two cases, we should therefore follow the* Adkins *case. The case was originally so written by Justice Butler, but after a dissent had been circulated he added matter to his opinion, seeking to sustain the* Adkins *case in principle. My proper course would have been to concur specially on the narrow ground I had taken. I did not do so. But at conference in the Court I said that I did not propose to review and re-examine the* Adkins *case until a case should come to the Court requiring that this should be done.*

August 17, 1936, an appeal was filed in West Coast Hotels (sic) Company v. Parrish. . . . *The Court as usual met to consider application in the week of Monday, October 5, 1936, and concluded its work by Saturday, October 10. During the conferences the jurisdictional statement in the* Parrish *case was considered and the question arose whether the appeal should be dismissed on the authority of* Adkins *and* Morehead. *Four of those who had voted in the majority in the* Morehead *case voted to dismiss the appeal in the* Parrish *case. I stated that I would vote for the notation of probable jurisdiction. I am not sure that I gave my reason, but it was that in the appeal of the* Parrish *case the authority of* Adkins *was definitely assailed and the Court was asked to reconsider and overrule it. Thus, for the first time, I was confronted with the necessity of facing the soundness of the* Adkins *case. Those who were in the majority in the* Morehead *case expressed some surprise at my vote, and I heard one of the brethren ask another, "What is the matter with Roberts?"*

Justice Stone was taken ill about October 14. The case was argued December 16 and 17, 1936, in the absence of Justice Stone, who at that time was lying in a comatose condition at his home. It came on for consideration at the conference on December 19. I voted for an affirmance. There were three other such votes, those of the Chief Justice, Justice Brandeis, and Justice Cardozo. The other four voted for a reversal.

If a decision had then been announced, the case would have been affirmed by a divided Court. It was thought that this would be an unfortunate outcome, as everyone on the Court knew Justice Stone's views. The case was, therefore, laid over for further consideration when Justice Stone should be able to participate. Justice Stone was convalescent during January and re-

turned to the sessions of the Court on February 1, 1937. I believe that the Parrish *case was taken up at the conference on February 6, 1937, and Justice Stone then voted for affirmance. This made it possible to assign the case for an opinion, which was done. The decision affirming the lower court was announced March 29, 1937.*

These facts make it evident that no action taken by the President in the interim had any causal relation to my action in the Parrish *case.*

More needs to be said for Roberts than he cared to say for himself. As a matter of history it is regrettable that Roberts' unconcern for his own record led him to abstain from stating his position. The occasions are not infrequent when the disfavor of separate opinions, on the part of the bar and to the extent that it prevails within the Court, should not be heeded. Such a situation was certainly presented when special circumstances made Roberts agree with a result but basically disagree with the opinion which announced it. . . .

F. Secrecy and the Supreme Court

In an era marked by increased public concern with secrecy in government decision making, the procedures of the Supreme Court seem just a bit quaint. All of the Court's important decisions are made in private—which cases to hear, how cases are decided, who is to write opinions. The Court regularly "appears" in public for oral argument and for announcement of decisions. And, at least for its full opinion cases, there is a written public recounting of the reasons supporting a particular decision. But the tradition of secrecy is very strong. Elaborate security procedures guard against premature disclosures of Supreme Court decisions.[1] The justices virtually never make public statements that attempt to "clarify" the implications of their opinions. Press conferences and other media events are nonexistent.[2]

There have been some efforts to improve the dissemination of information to the public—through the news media—about what the Court is doing and about its decisions.[3] And there has been some ferment on the Court, to the extent at least of more frequent public dissents from denials of certiorari and appeal. There have been several recent instances in which former law clerks have published accounts of the Court during their period of service.[4] Still, the best "inside" information about the internal workings of the Supreme Court has come from the notes and papers of former justices opened long after their deaths, although sometimes these papers have been "sanitized" by the justices or on their behalf. In an unfortunate backlash against

such posthumous revelations, Justice Black instructed his son to destroy all his log books and conference notes after his death. Although breached at the margins, the "Red Velour Curtain" is still tightly drawn.

Arguments against a continuation of the Supreme Court tradition of secrecy are readily mustered.[5] Democracy is a public process of governance. All important government decisions should be made in public, and the reasons for each decision should be available for public scrutiny. There is no *a priori* principle for excepting the Supreme Court from this general principle. Indeed, so the argument goes, it is especially important to eliminate secrecy from the Supreme Court because the justices are appointed rather than elected, serve in office for life, and generally are not subject to the same checks and balances as elected officials.

A different kind of argument is that opening up the decisional process will result in a better judicial product. Somehow, the glare of the

[1]On two consecutive days in April, 1979, an ABC-TV news correspondent, Tim O'Brien, reported essential details about, and forecast the results of, two pending Supreme Court cases. An investigation by Chief Justice Burger led to the dismissal of an employee in the Court's own printing office. Because O'Brien apparently had been seen after hours in areas of the Supreme Court building normally off-limits to reporters, additional security precautions were instituted. New curfew hours were instituted limiting the times reporters could use the "Press Room"; and reporters wishing to use the Supreme Court's library were required to have an escort. A forthcoming book by Washington Post reporters Bob Woodward and Scott Armstrong, reportedly entitled "The Brethren," is expected to widen the breach in the "Red Velour Curtain" by revealing intimate details of how past cases were decided and of the relationships among the justices.

[2]One major exception certainly was Justice Black's television interview on CBS. While the interview itself was unusual, Justice Black did not reveal anything significant about the Court's internal dynamics that was not already public knowledge or that he had not mentioned in a set of lectures which he had recently delivered at the Columbia Law School.

[3]See David L. Gray, *The Supreme Court and the News Media* (Evanston, Ill.: Northwestern University Press, 1968).

[4]J. Harvie Wilkinson, *Serving Justice: A Supreme Court Clerk's View* (New York: Charterhouse, 1974). The Woodward and Armstrong book, referred to in Note 1, is said to be based on extensive interviews with some former law clerks.

[5]Arthur Selwyn Miller and D.S. Sastri, "Secrecy and the Supreme Court: On the Need for Piercing the Red Velour Curtain," **22** *Buffalo Law Review* (1973), 799–823.

public will improve the craftsmanship of the justices, which, admittedly, is occasionally subject to criticism. Related to this is the assertion (and hope) that an open decision-making process will further erode the mystique of judicial omnipotence and expose the human dynamics of legal doctrine.

There are many arguments in favor of preserving the present system of secret deliberations, perhaps with some minor modifications. First, there is no evidence that the judicial product will be improved by less secrecy; if anything, it is likely to deteriorate, since there will be less opportunity for thought and reflection and more incentive to "shoot from the hip." It is more difficult to retreat from publicly announced positions. One's first impression of a difficult case is not always the best. Frank and open discussion of an issue by the Court should be encouraged. Second, there is something to be said for preserving the mystique of the Court, at least at its presently low ebb. Symbols are important, and whatever its particular makeup or cast of mind on a case, the Court as an institution means something to most citizens. Third, a compelling argument against premature disclosure of a Court's decisions is the possible impact on the litigants. It may not make much difference if the litig-

ant is sitting in a penitentiary cell, hoping that the Court will "spring" him. But what of the litigants in an antitrust suit? What of other observers who may have an important, if uncertain, financial stake in how a case is decided?

Of course, *after* a case has been decided, there is much less reason to encourage, or even allow, secrecy. Observers differ on just how long a wait should be necessary before a justice's private papers, revealing intimate details of conference discussions and votes, should be opened to public inspection. (Should they be considered private at all?) Most justices who have left their papers have imposed waiting periods; twenty-five years is common. Admittedly, even such a long wait for the posthumous publication of a justice's papers could have some affect on the decision-making behavior of a justice for whom the judgment of history is important. But it will be a much smaller effect than would be the case with conferences open to the public.[6] And, with some time lag, it will keep the public critically informed of the workings of an important institution.

[Query: Could Congress require disclosure of judicial papers in the same manner as it has required disclosure of presidential papers? Cf. *Nixon* v. *General Services Administrator* (1977), noted on pages 1090–1091.]

4. THE DECISION-MAKING ENVIRONMENT

A. *The "Strategic" Environment*

Supreme Court decisions, like other political decisions, are shaped by the context in which they are made. In the first chapter of this book, we considered, and rejected, the argument that Supreme Court

---

[6]See J. Woodford Howard, "Comment on Secrecy and the Supreme Court," *Ibid.*, pp. 837–843.

decisions were merely mechanical announcements of "the law," unaffected by the time or circumstance in which the decision was made or by who was making the decision. In this section, we focus on some of the major variables likely to account for Supreme Court decisions.

James Eisenstein has coined the term "strategic environment" to describe the "network of recurring social relationships and responsibilities that affect behavior."[1] The term, as used, is broad enough to cover the wide range of factors we must consider. Just as Supreme Court justices are not mere conveyers of "the law," so too they are not entirely free agents, able to translate perfectly their own policy preferences into legal doctrine. They are limited, first of all, by the internal dynamics of a collegial body. Individual compromises often must be made to accomplish an institutional result. Second, the Court is, in many ways, a reactive institution. For reasons already described, it has virtually no control of cases coming to it and is often limited in what it can decide (although it has almost total discretion in deciding what not to decide). But the matter is not that simple. The way that issues are brought, shaped, and argued, as well as the strategy of litigants, also has an important influence on ultimate Supreme Court decisions.

The strategic environment of the Supreme Court consists not only of decisions about which cases or issues to litigate but also of the functions and demands of other institutions and actors with which the Court may have a continuing relationship. The solicitor general, who represents the federal government in the Supreme Court, occupies a very special role. There is also an amorphous, but real, Supreme Court bar—lawyers who appear continuously before the Court. Often these lawyers represent a few interest groups, such as the American Civil Liberties Union or the Legal Defense Fund, which are the most frequent litigants. Congress may have an important impact on the Court, not only in its formal decisions about jurisdiction but more generally as a barometer of national opinion. Public views of the Supreme Court are also important, although the linkages between public opinion and Supreme Court decisions are indirect and speculative. The justices are aware of public opinion, and in several recent cases, they have been particularly concerned with it. For example, in the recent capital punishment cases (see Part Two, Chapter Three), public attitudes toward the death penalty became relevant in determining the current meaning of "cruel and unusual punishment."

The strategic environment of the Court is not only external. It refers also to the collegial setting in which decisions are made and to the accumulated norms and traditions within which the Court operates. For example, we have already discussed the impact of the common law tradition on constitutional law development. The Supreme Court justices, like virtually all American law school graduates, are exposed to the techniques and methods of common law judges. The role of precedent, in somewhat modified form, is a mark of the influence of the common law tradition. Likewise, the key to common law judging is reasoning by analogy—the extension of existing rules to new situations. Constitu-

[1] James Eisenstein, *Politics and the Legal Process* (New York: Harper and Row, 1973), pp. 81ff.

tional interpretation often requires the same sort of reasoning.

Some of the more subtle influences of the "strategic environment" may be understood by attention to the process by which Supreme Court justices are "socialized" into the judicial role. Socialization is a constant process, one that does not end when a new justice is appointed. But the recruitment process is certainly a primary, if not exclusive, agent of socialization.

All members of societies undergo common socialization experiences, differing, of course, with individual family and ethnic orientations. But these experiences do not prepare them for the specialized roles of political leadership inherent in organized societies. It is the recruitment function to draw members of a society out of particular subcultures and "induct them into the specialized roles of the political system, train them in the appropriate skills, provide them with political cognitive maps, values, expectations, and affects."[2] Recruitment is not the only agent of socialization; the appropriate training and learning of "cues" takes place after as well as before selection. Judges learn their roles partly after accession to the bench as well as in preparation for a judicial career. Judicial actions are constantly being reviewed and criticized by legal scholars, by law reviews, by peer groups, by politicians, and even by the general public. To be a judge is, in part, to be engaged in a constant process of reevaluation. But recruitment is a key element because it operates as a monitor on the socialization process.

As used in this chapter, recruitment is a generalized description of a variety of activities that result in the selection of judges with certain types of training, certain sets of values, and certain sets of expectations, or with a particular view of the judge's "role." The socialization process necessarily involves a variety of factors, including such obvious ones as legal training and experience, possible apprenticeship on lower courts, and a constant participation in the world of legal and political affairs. In the course of this "apprenticeship" period, prospective judges are expected to learn the basic values underlying our legal and political system as well as more specialized information relevant to judging, such as the role of precedent in judicial decisions, judicial temperament, and the proper role of the judiciary in society.

Unlike many countries in continental Europe, which provide formal and highly specialized training for judges, and where judging is a career to be chosen early in life, the American political system makes no such provisions. The system for choosing federal judges is governed by constitutional and statutory regulations, but no standards for choice are offered, no formal training is prescribed, and even more important, the selection is entrusted, not to the bench and bar, but to elected political officials whose determinations must necessarily take account of factors other than those deemed strictly relevant by the legal profession. The lack of formal training and of specified standards for prospective judges, when combined with the vagaries of a decentralized and highly politicized selection process, gives the bench a highly uneven character. People are not "made" into judges by formal

---

[2]Gabriel Almond and James Coleman, *The Politics of the Developing Areas* (Princeton, N.J.: Princeton University Press, 1960), pp. 26–31.

schooling, but become judges usually only after they have had successful political and/or legal careers. Thus, they assume their positions at a time when their core values have probably become highly stable and their corresponding capacity for learning new values or adapting to a new role is low. It is these backgrounds that provide major clues to the ways in which prospective judges will interpret their judicial roles; and it is the recruitment process, which operates to favor certain types of backgrounds and ignore others. Recruitment tends to monitor and reinforce the socialization process by choosing those lawyers who have conformed to the established norms and who therefore give promise of fulfilling the judicial role in an expected manner.

Although the act of selection contributes to the socialization of a new judge by rewarding the values that he has espoused, it more importantly provides a visible demonstration to those who aspire to the bench of the types of behavior and the sets of values to which prospective judges ought to conform. If, for example, a particular selection system appeared to favor a high degree of prior political involvement rather than extensive legal experience as a necessary prerequisite, the types of preparatory activities in which prospective judges would engage would vary accordingly. Of course, the recruitment process also rewards religious or ethnic backgrounds which individuals cannot change. But, by and large, it is the patterns of recruitment that prevail over a period of time which determine the general backgrounds and values of judges.

There is no uniform selection process in the United States. Some states provide for partisan or nonpartisan election; others provide for judicial selection by the legislature or the governor. And a few follow the "Missouri Plan" system whereby a nominating panel of lawyers and laymen provide the governor with a panel of two or three names from which to choose; the person chosen as a judge must then be ratified by the electorate in a noncontested election about a year after he or she ascends the bench, and periodically, thereafter. All federal judges, including Supreme Court justices, are chosen formally in the same manner—by the president with the consent of the senate. But except for Supreme Court nominations, which tend to reflect the president's own values, federal judicial appointments tend to be responsive to local or regional considerations. Thus, federal judges come from a wide variety of social backgrounds and are appointed for many partisan and nonpartisan considerations. The federal judiciary may not be a microcosm of the political system, but it is usually broadly representative of the major groups and interests in society (except blacks and, until recently, women).

In the following sections, we focus on five discrete but interrelated types of "environmental" influences, culminating in a look at the behavior of individual justices in a collegial setting.

B. Clement Vose, Litigation as a Form of Pressure Group Activity

Reasons Organizations Go to Court

. . . Organizations support legal action because individuals lack the

Reprinted from **319** *Annals of the American Academy of Political and Social Science* (1958), 22–24, 27–28.

necessary time, money, and skill. With no delays a case takes an average of four years to pass through two lower courts to the Supreme Court of the United States. A series of cases on related questions affecting the permanent interest of a group may extend over two decades or more. The constant attention that litigation demands, especially when new arguments are being advanced, makes the employment of regular counsel economical. This may be supplemented by a legal staff of some size and by volunteer lawyers of distinction. Parties also pay court costs and meet the expense of printing the record and briefs. Organizations are better able to provide the continuity demanded in litigation than individuals. Some individuals do maintain responsibility for their own cases even at the Supreme Court level, but this is difficult under modern conditions.

The form of group participation in court cases is set by such factors as the type of proceeding, standing of the parties, legal or constitutional issues in dispute, the characteristics of the organization, and its interest in the outcome. Perhaps the most direct and open participation has been by organizations which have been obliged to protect their own rights and privileges. Robert A. Horn has shown that a modern constitutional law of association has developed out of Supreme Court cases concerning churches, trade unions, political parties, and other organizations. The cases have sometimes placed organizations as parties, but more often the organization supports a member or an officer in litigation. One example must suffice.

The constitutional concept of religious freedom has been broadened in recent years by the Supreme Court decisions in cases involving members of the sect known as Jehovah's Wit-

nesses. Most of the cases began when a Jehovah's Witness violated a local ordinance or state statute. Since 1938, the Witnesses, incorporated as the Watch Tower Bible and Tract Society and represented by its counsel, Hayden Cooper Covington, have won forty-four of fifty-five cases in the United States Supreme Court. As a result Jehovah's Witnesses now enjoy

The rights to solicit from house to house, to preach in the streets without a license, to canvass apartment buildings regardless of the tenants' or owners' wishes, to be recognized as ministers of an accredited religion and thus be exempt from the draft, to decline to serve on juries, and to refuse to salute or pledge allegiance to the flag.

The NAACP

Since 1909 the National Association for the Advancement of Colored People has improved the legal status of Negroes immeasurably by the victories it has won in more than fifty Supreme Court cases. During its early years, the NAACP relied upon prominent volunteer lawyers like Moorfield Storey, Louis Marshall, and Clarence Darrow to represent Negroes in the courts. Limited success coupled with its failure to win gains from Congress led the NAACP in the 1930's to make court litigation fundamental to its program. A separate organization, the NAACP Legal Defense and Educational Fund, was incorporated for this purpose. The goal of the NAACP was to make Negroes "an integral part of the nation, with the same rights and guarantees that are accorded to other citizens, and on the same terms." This ambition meant that beginning in 1938 Thurgood Marshall as special counsel for the NAACP Legal Defense and Educational Fund held what was "probably the most demanding legal post in the country."

In aiming to establish racial equality before the law on a broad basis, the Legal Defense Fund has not functioned as a legal aid society. Limited resources have prevented the Fund from participating in all cases involving the rights of Negroes. As early as 1935 Charles Houston, an imaginative Negro lawyer who preceded Marshall as special counsel, set the tone of NAACP efforts when he declared that the legal campaign against inequality should be carefully planned "to secure decisions, rulings and public opinion on the broad principle instead of being devoted to merely miscellaneous cases."

By presenting test cases to the Supreme Court, the NAACP has won successive gains protecting the right of Negroes in voting, housing, transportation, education, and service on juries. Each effort has followed the development of new theories of legal interpretation and required the preparation of specific actions in the courts to challenge existing precedent. The NAACP Legal Defense Fund has accomplished these two tasks through the co-operation of associated and allied groups. First, as many as fifty Negro lawyers practicing in all parts of the country have been counsel in significant civil rights cases in the lower courts. Many of these men received their legal education at the Howard University Law School in Washington, D.C., and have shared membership in the National Bar Association since its founding in 1925. These common associations have contributed to the consensus among Negro lawyers on timing their quest for equality through litigation. Second, the NAACP has long benefitted from its official advisory group, the National Legal Committee composed of leading Negro and white lawyers. Today Lloyd Garrison is Chairman of the

National Legal Committee of forty-five attorneys located in twenty-three cities. This is the nucleus of the many volunteers in many fields who have contributed ideas, often at national conferences, to the planning of litigation. Third, other organizations with no direct connection with the Legal Defense Fund have sponsored a few cases. State and local chapters of the NAACP have often aided Negroes who were parties in cases, especially in the lower courts. The St. Louis Association of Real Estate Brokers was the chief sponsor of the important restrictive covenant case of *Shelley* v. *Kraemer*. A Negro national college fraternity, Alpha Phi Alpha, sponsored quite completely the successful attack on discrimination in interstate railway dining cars.

Individual Test Cases

Winning new constitutional protections for Negroes has depended on the development of individual test cases with a Negro as party in each. There is no chronicle of the human interest stories contained in the roles of Negroes in historic Supreme Court cases. But what is known reveals many difficulties to be inherent in improving the legal status of a group of fifteen million persons through individual court cases. In a suit by a single plaintiff, the case may become moot as the passage of time makes the remedy sought inapplicable. This danger, though avoided by the co-operation of state officials, was created in the Missouri Law School case of 1938 when the plaintiff, Lloyd Gaines, disappeared just as the case was completed. Also the concerted efforts of authorities to deny Negroes participation in the Texas white Democratic primary kept Dr. L. A. Nixon from voting even though he was the plaintiff in two Supreme

Court victories. Furthermore there is always the temptation for compromise by the original plaintiff which would accomplish his narrow purpose but stop the litigation before the broad constitutional issue was before the appellate court.

These dangers were largely overcome in the School Segregation Cases when federal court actions were instituted by individual plaintiffs both on their own behalf and on behalf of persons similarly situated. Since 1955, in the expanding litigation over race relations, the class action has become a procedural device of growing importance. Rule 23 (a) of the Federal Rules of Civil Procedure provides under certain circumstances that

if persons constituting a class are so numerous as to make it impracticable to bring them all before the court, such of them, one or more, as will fairly insure the adequate representation of all may, on behalf of all, sue or be sued.

One authority has said that "school segregation is a group phenomenon which is pecularly suited to resolution in a class action." As Negroes enter a new generation of litigation, their cases are apt increasingly to take the form of the class action. . . .

Organizations as "Friends of the Court"

The appearance of organizations as *amici curiae* has been the most noticed form of group representation in Supreme Court cases. This does not concern the technical office of *amicus curiae* for which an attorney is appointed to assist the court in deciding complex and technical problems. Today, the Supreme Court does sometimes, as in formulating its decree in the School Segregation Cases, issue a special invitation to the Solicitor General or to state Attorneys General to act as *amici curiae*. Of interest here is the rule under which individuals, organizations, and government attorneys have been permitted to file briefs and/or make oral argument in the Supreme Court. During the last decade *amici curiae* have submitted an average of sixty-six briefs and seven oral arguments in an average total of forty cases a term.

The frequent entrance of organizations into Supreme Court cases by means of the *amicus curiae* device has often given litigation the distinct flavor of group combat. This may be illustrated by the group representation in quite different cases. In 1943, when a member of the Jehovah's Witnesses challenged the constitutionality of a compulsory flag salute in the schools, his defense by counsel for the Watchtower Bible and Tract Society was supported by separate *amici curiae,* the American Civil Liberties Union and the Committee on the Bill of Rights of the American Bar Association. The appellant state board of education was supported by an *amicus curiae* brief filed by the American Legion. In 1951, in a case testing state resale price maintenance, the United States was an *amicus* against a Louisiana statute while the Commonwealth of Pennsylvania, the Louisiana State Pharmaceutical Association, American Booksellers, Inc., and the National Association of Retail Druggists entered *amici curiae* briefs in support of the statute.

Many *amici curiae* briefs are workmanlike and provide the Court with helpful legal argument and material. Yet writers who favor their use by organizations and recognize that "the *amicus curiae* has had a long and respected role in our own legal system and before that, in the Roman law," believe that many briefs in recent years display a "timewasting character." Another authority has said that after 1947 there were multiplying signs "that the brief *amicus curiae* had become essentially an instrumentality designed to exert extra-judicial pressure on judicial decisions. Concern over this by members of the Supreme Court was shown in 1946 when Justice Robert H. Jackson, in a dissenting opinion, criticized an *amicus curiae* brief by the American Newspaper Publishers Association:

. . . Of course, it does not cite a single authority not available to counsel for the publisher involved, and does not tell us a single new fact except this one: "This membership embraces more than 700 newspaper publishers whose publications represent in excess of eighty per cent of the total daily and Sunday circulation of newspapers published in this country. The Association is vitally interested in the issue presented in this case, namely, the right of newspapers to publish news stories and editorials about cases pending in the courts."

Justice Jackson told his colleagues, "this might be a good occasion to demonstrate the fortitude of the judiciary." . . .*

[Over time, the role of *amicus curiae* has changed, in Samuel Krislov's words, from "friendship to advocacy."[1] Not only private groups, but the federal government as well, have made extensive use of this technique of "judicial lobbying." Krislov reports that the Department of Justice began to use the *amicus curiae* device consistently under President Theodore Roosevelt, as part of a new "public interest" approach to litigation.[2] It was thus at the beginning of the twentieth century when the federal government began to appear as *amicus* in Supreme Court cases involving broad social issues.

Under current practice, the Department of Justice, unlike private parties, may file an *amicus curiae* brief in any case. It need not obtain consent of the parties to a case or even permission from the Court. Moreover, the Justice Department, in filing an *amicus* brief, need not demonstrate that the arguments it makes, or the facts it presents, are not otherwise presented by the parties. The rationale for government sponsored *amicus* briefs is thus considerably different from those applied to other litigants. The government is given free reign to file because it is the government. In important cases the government may also request additional time for oral argument, whereas a private group filing an *amicus* brief can participate in oral argument only if the principal litigant, on whose behalf the brief is filed, releases some of the time allocated to him (only a half hour in most cases).

The government's use of *amicus curiae* briefs increased significantly during the 1960s. From 1955 to 1961, the government appeared as *amicus* from two to nine times a term. From 1961 to 1973, it appeared an average of nineteen times per term.[3] Not only has the govern-

*[Ed. Note: Under the current rules of the Supreme Court, an *amicus curiae* brief on the merits of a case may be filed only upon order of the Court or when consented to by all parties to the case. Where one of the parties refuses consent, the Court may grant leave to file upon appeal of the individual or group asking to file an *amicus* brief. Consent of the parties is not required where an *amicus* brief is presented for the United States sponsored by the Solicitor General, by any federal agency authorized by law to appear in its own behalf, or by the attorney general or chief law officer of any state or political subdivision.]

[1]Samuel Krislov, "The Amicus Curiae Brief: From Friendship to Advocacy," **72** *Yale Law Journal* (1963), 694–721.

[2]Samuel Krislov, "The Role of the Attorney General as Amicus Curiae Before the Supreme Court," in Houston, Miller, Krislov and Dixon (eds.), *Roles of the Attorney General of the United States* (Washington, D.C.: American Enterprise Institute, 1968), pp. 77–80, 88–91.

[3]Figures through 1966 compiled by Krislov, *Ibid.* From 1967 to 1973, figures are taken from the *Annual Report of the Attorney General* (1974).

ment appeared more often as *amicus,* but its percentage of *amicus* appearances has risen to about one-fourth of all cases in which it appeared before the Supreme Court.[4] Robert Scigliano reports that the government is even more successful as *amicus* than as a party to a case. Its *amicus* success ratio averaged 71 percent from 1958 to 1967; in several terms, its winning percentage approached 90 percent.[5] To what can the government's extraordinary success as *amicus* be attributed? Obviously, the close working relationship between the Solicitor General and the Supreme Court is an important factor. The Solicitor General is a "repeat player," whereas most other litigants before the Court are "one shotters."[6] The Solicitor General is an experienced litigant, the quality of his briefs and oral argument is unusually high, and he is better able than private litigants to "pick his shots" and not enter those cases where his chances of success are remote. The Solicitor General's restraint in bringing cases to the Court, and his willingness to "confess error" when the government is shown to be clearly in the wrong, gives him unusual credibility.]

C. Michael Meltsner, The Legal Defense Fund

Only recently have lawyers associated in numbers to bring court cases in a systematic attempt to change the character of American institutions. The ranks of defense funds, public interest law firms, community law offices, and legal centers which now readily challenge corporate and governmental conduct—from air pollution to prison conditions, selective service to exclusionary zoning—were almost empty ten years ago. Two institutions of any size made law reform the or-

ganized and planned objective of a full-time staff of attorneys.

One was the American Civil Liberties Union (ACLU), founded in 1920 by a nonpartisan group, including Clarence Darrow, Eugene V. Debs, Felix Frankfurter, and Roger Baldwin, to defend the Bill of Rights. Today the Union has 170,000 members, 48 state affiliates, and 350 local chapters, but for most of its existence it subsisted on a shoestring with only several thousand dues payers. The Union legal program was primarily defensive, aimed at beating back incursions on personal liberty rather than systematically enlarging the scope of constitutional rights. ACLU's few staff lawyers had their hands full litigating free speech and assembly cases, dealing with the havoc produced by McCarthyism, and coordinating the activities of scattered affiliates, contentious members, and volunteer attorneys; they had little time and money to spend on test cases brought to change the law.

The other organization was the Legal Defense Fund (LDF), a group of lawyers who originally banded together in order to prod Americans to repay an old debt to the black man but who ultimately found that justice was a chain inescapably linking black and white. Structured differently from the ACLU, LDF had a board of directors and a legal staff but no affiliates or members. Unlike the Civil Liberties Union, whose first mission was to protect the citizenry from an intrusive state, the Legal Defense Fund had no great fear of big

[4]*Ibid.*
[5]Robert Scigliano, *The Supreme Court and the Presidency* (New York: Free Press, 1971), p. 180.
[6]Marc Galanter, "Why the 'Haves' Come Out Ahead: Speculations on the Limits of Legal Change," **9** *Law and Society Review* (1974), 107 and passim.
Reprinted from Michael Meltsner, *Cruel and Unusual: The Supreme Court and Capital Punishment* (New York: Random House, 1973), pp. 4–15.

government—so long as it acted in the interests of black people. . . .

In 1939 influential members of the National Association for the Advancement of Colored People had formed a corporation known formally as the NAACP Legal Defense and Educational Fund, Inc., but soon dubbed "the Legal Defense Fund," "the Inc. Fund," or simply "the Fund," in an attempt to distinguish it from the parent NAACP. The Fund quickly obtained approval from New York State courts to provide legal assistance to the poor despite a state law prohibiting the practice of law by a corporation, but its goals were not local but national: to pursue equality for blacks by bringing test cases in the courts challenging the laws and customs on which racial segregation rested. This was a course the NAACP itself had embarked upon some years earlier, under the leadership of a brilliant Washington black lawyer and Howard Law School vice-dean, Charles Houston, and soon to be appointed Law School Dean (later federal judge) William H. Hastie. The proposed legal program was not severed from NAACP for reasons of policy, but rather to attract the tax-deductible donations which the Internal Revenue Code denies to organizations that devote a substantial part of their time, as did the Association, to lobbying and propaganda.

Today, the Fund is a well-known instrument of American liberalism—a professional resource available to the loosely connected efforts of those who seek to forge a powerful tool of institutional reform from the politics of race and poverty. LDF has a yearly income raised entirely from private sources of almost four million dollars; a staff of some twenty civil rights lawyers stationed in New York City; field offices in California and in four Southern states; and a network of about two hundred, mostly black, cooperating lawyers. Attached to the Fund by ties of various lengths and strengths are social scientists, educators, commercial lawyers, law professors, foundation executives, liberal politicians, corporation and government administrators, community workers, a Mexican-American legal defense fund, a law reform unit that specializes in cases involving discrimination against the poor, and a scholarship program.

The Fund, however, like the ACLU, grew to national prominence from humble origins. In 1940, its full-time legal staff consisted of a young Maryland lawyer named Thurgood Marshall. LDF's income of $10,000 paid Marshall's salary as well as expenses; he worked out of the NAACP's modest New York offices. Some twenty years later, the budget had climbed to $500,000; the full-time legal staff to five. After Southern Senators obtained an Internal Revenue Service ruling that the two organizations could not have common directors, the Fund became totally independent of the policies and leadership of the NAACP.

In 1954 it was Fund staff lawyers and their academic consultants who—capping a twenty-year effort—finally broke the iron grip of segregation on the Constitution by persuading the Supreme Court of the United States to reject the "separate but equal" doctrine of an 1896 decision, *Plessy* v. *Ferguson*. . . .

Following decision of The School Desegregation Cases, known as *Brown* v. *Board of Education*, LDF's small New York legal staff devoted its energies to challenging in the federal courts every form of state-required, supported, or sanctioned racial discrimination: in schools, courtrooms, public facilities, employment, hospitals, housing, voting.

Staff lawyers fought a war of attrition against recalcitrant Southern school officials, and defended those who were charged with crime in the early 1960's when they took the civil rights movement to the streets: freedom riders, sit-inners, and protest marchers. Top priority went to protecting workers in Dr. Martin Luther King, Jr.'s campaigns in St. Augustine, Florida; back-country Mississippi; Montgomery, Selma and Birmingham, Alabama.

The Fund paid the legal bill for local protest movements across the South, in places like Danville, Virginia, Americus and Albany, Georgia; Jackson and Belzoni, Mississippi. LDF lawyers represented King, James Meredith, Medgar and Charles Evers, Ralph Abernathy, Stokely Carmichael, Floyd McKissick, James Foreman, Father James Edmund Groppi, James Farmer, Bob Moses, Dick Gregory, as well as hundreds of their followers. They counseled NAACP branches, the Southern Christian Leadership Conference (SCLC), the Student Non-Violent Coordinating Committee (SNCC), and the Congress of Racial Equality (CORE). Those sued by the Fund were as impressive a list—Orvil Faubus, George Wallace, Ross Barnett, "Bull" Conner, Lester Maddox, Jim Clark, and countless rural sheriffs, school boards, and state public officials.

During these years, few Southern lawyers would represent the civil rights movement. They were spread out like frontier outposts, whose presence was the movement's only protection against constant harassment. Although the Department of Justice dispatched more lawyers and FBI agents to the South after its jurisdiction to do so was clarified by the Civil Rights Acts of 1964, 1965, and 1968, Department intervention cannot even now be realistically expected in any but the more serious or violent racial confrontations. In the early 1960's, the Department's civil rights program was a sick joke told by haggard, circuit-riding attorneys and scarred civil rights workers. But even if Justice Department lawyers and FBI agents, almost all of whom were white, had been stationed in every town in the South, there still would have been an enormous gap of trust and communication between them (ultimately responsible to the Administration in power and its concept of political necessity) and the men and women whose civil rights it was their duty to protect.

Other legal organizations—the National Lawyers' Guild, the Lawyers' Constitutional Defense Committee, the Lawyers' Committee for Civil Rights under Law, and the ACLU— were too poor or understaffed on the front lines to account for more than a fraction of the steadily increasing legal needs of the civil rights movement. By choice as well as necessity, all factions in the black community came to the black attorney in times of stress, but there were few available and fewer still who were able to manage significant civil rights litigation by themselves. They were in the right place at the right time, but were helpless without outside money and manpower and new ideas.

The success of the Fund's legal program was in large measure related to its ability to connect these isolated attorneys to the lawyers and institutions which serviced the New York and Washington liberal leadership. Because the Fund linked the two, it looked in both directions: its legal staff and board of directors were interracial and national; its contributors mostly white and Northern; its clients at first Southerners, although eventually blacks from every region. Due to its relationship with Southern black lawyers, LDF maintained a virtual monopoly over civil rights litigation.

At the high-water mark of civil rights activity, lawyering for the Fund was like being a member of one of those highly trained, specially assembled raider groups which are occasionally deployed in wartime but regularly portrayed in films. These were years when each day brought news of another confrontation between peaceful blacks and outraged segregationists in places that most Americans had never heard of—like Gadsden, Alabama, Orangeburg, South Carolina, and Clinton, Louisiana; when many readers greedily opened *The New York Times* to the "race page"—a concentration of civil rights stories usually located somewhere near the middle of the paper's first section—to learn the results of the previous day's protests much as a baseball fan turns to the sports pages to check box scores and batting averages.

Practicing attorneys rarely have worked so close to the front lines. A staff lawyer might be awakened late at night, called upon to travel to a small Southern city, pass through the hostile white section, and establish himself in the often decrepit offices of a local black attorney or, when there were no such offices, in the back room of a local mortuary or the vestry of a church. He would grind out the legal papers, affidavits, complaints for injunction, and briefs of law which often, but certainly not always, sufficiently restrained Southern white communities until cooler heads—usually those that thought of "new industry" and "image"—realized that, unless their cities were to be torn apart, they must reach an accommodation with angry blacks.

Mapping legal strategy under battlefield conditions, the movement lawyer might be arrested, threatened with injury, or forced to watch his clients suffer intolerable perversions of law—phony charges, high bail, perjured testimony, excessive sentences. But following the fateful 1955 arrest of black seamstress Rosa Parks, for failure to give up her seat on a Montgomery, Alabama, bus to a white man, the lawyers stood between the "race-mixers," as they were then called, and the barely suppressed fury of the Southern legal system. If today many lawyers find themselves as closely identified with their clients' causes as their cases, it is only because this Southern experience radicalized a portion of the profession. William Kunstler, for example, had a humdrum commercial practice before he went South.

Whatever glory may attach to those civil rights lawyers must be kept in perspective. Change was largely the work of courageous Southern blacks, SNCC and SCLC community workers, and their student helpers. The lawyers' work was auxiliary. Material deprivations are unworthy of mention when one considers the existence scratched out by civil rights movement organizers. The physical dangers were small compared to those experienced by any black, especially those who challenged the status quo. . . .

Thurgood Marshall presided over the affairs of the Fund with a steady hand until his appointment in 1961 to the United States Court of Appeals for the Second Circuit by John F. Kennedy. A tireless traveler in the days of long-distance trains and erratic air travel, Marshall was not only a sharp reader of the judicial mind, a successful fund raiser for the cause, and a seasoned advocate who had been to the well in many a hostile Southern town, but a folk hero with a reputation that inspired many to hope for a courtroom revolution. Marshall's personal record of success was enviable. He argued scores of cases before the Supreme Court of the United States and won all but a handful. His appointments in 1965 as Solicitor General of the United States—the man who argues before the Supreme Court on behalf of the federal government—and later as the first black Associate Justice of the Court were surely fitting. Marshall was as familiar with the mechanics of constitutional litigation as most lawyers were with drawing up a deed or a will.

The Fund's success in turning around the constitutional law of race relations spoke of more than Marshall's legendary courtroom accomplishments: influential friends, skillful money raising, and a talented staff made possible his personal recognition. When he selected as his successor Jack Greenberg, a white man who had received his law degree from Columbia Law School, Greenberg inherited not only a litigation program regularly blessed by the Supreme Court, but surprising power, good will, and friendships.

On the surface, the two men were very different. The older man was long-limbed, the younger compact. Marshall usually was relaxed, though his temper could sting like fire; Greenberg was a bundle of energy. Marshall spun yarns in a folksy drawl that suggested the amiable country boy, though he was raised in Baltimore. Greenberg was more the abrupt, businesslike, city boy. But both shared a twenty-four-hour-a-day passion for the Fund's work. They were single-minded, tough leaders who knew how to take command and to strike hard, fast, and, where necessary, without traces.

The modest victories of American liberals are easy enough to identify—projects funded, legislation enacted, a case won, a judicial candidate rejected—but the winning combination is often difficult to find. A successful test case, for example, reflects an invisible politics: tedious skull sessions that hammer out strategy, money-raising lunches at the Ford Foundation, calls to mandarin partners at Wall Street law firms, the intervention of bar associations, an ex-Attorney General, a law school dean, a labor union general counsel. Fund lawyers did not always wait for clients to appear at their door, often they planned a case and then sought out those wishing to sue. These were the keys on which first Marshall and then Greenberg played with confidence, enabling the Fund to earn a reputation as an organization consistently able to put together the coalition of lawyers, clients, staff, consultants, and expert advisors required for success in each project.

Greenberg shared direction of the Fund's civil rights program with Constance Baker Motley until her selection in 1965 as borough president of Manhattan and thereafter as the first black woman appointed to the federal bench. Mrs. Motley was a strong woman, built as solid as an oak tree; she knew exactly what she wanted and suffered little nonsense from white Southerners who stood in her way. This daughter of a Yale University chef took upon herself the most demanding of litigation assignments when she began to commute to Mississippi, laying the groundwork for the state's first experience with integration. The other member of the Fund's Mississippi team was Derrick Bell, Jr., a spirited young black lawyer who had quit the Justice Department during the Eisenhower years shortly after a superior suggested that NAACP membership was inconsistent with his duties. As there were only three black lawyers in the entire state, Motley and Bell carried federal law to Mississippi twice a month, via jet.

Another senior lawyer at the Fund was Yale Law School graduate James Madison Nabrit, III, who was appointed the Fund's associate director after Mrs. Motley became borough president. Jim Nabrit had been weaned on the plans that brought The School Desegregation Cases to the Supreme Court. His father had argued one of the cases; later Nabrit Senior became dean of the Howard University Law School and president of the university. Greenberg tended to be unpredictable; Nabrit on the other hand, while a young man, was a cautious lawyer of the old school. He combined an imposing technical skill with great prudence. At freewheeling strategy sessions, Nabrit defined the limits of the possible to often frustrated, angry colleagues who were anxious to thrust the broadest grounds for decision on a reluctant judiciary, and occasionally preferred to lose in order to "expose the system" rather than to win what they thought to be a paper victory. His was the hard head that reminded all that nothing could be accomplished without craft. Scores of young lawyers passed through his hands with the assurance that they might take upon themselves the difficult task of employing the legal system as a political instrument without the added burden of professional ignorance.

The lawyers that Greenberg, Motley, Nabrit, and Bell attracted to the Fund in the 1960's were not always those who had received the highest grades at law school, but as clever manipulators of the judicial system they had few equals. As a group, they showed a special capacity to seize upon new ideas and tenaciously bend them to their uses. Other attorneys may have logged as many hours, but none more imaginatively served their clients' interests or more readily responded to calls for help which came through a switchboard which seemed to be plugged into the sources of American racism.

If my colleagues at the Fund were the first wave of young lawyers who rejected the rewards of commercial law for a new professional ideal, we were not as a group particularly radical in politics or life-style, fitting more than most would admit De Tocqueville's description of lawyers as men with "certain habits of order, a taste for formalities, and a kind of instinctive regard for the regular connection of ideas, which naturally renders them very hostile to the revolutionary spirit . . ." As bourgeoisie, rather than topple the norms of our profession, we sought to change them piecemeal, by example, and without jeopardy to the good life. . . .

D. Jonathan Casper, Lawyers Before the Supreme Court

. . . The traditional image of the lawyer is of a partisan representative of his client's interests, an advocate whose function is to attempt, in every legal and ethical manner, to advance the interests of his client. But, as is obvious, lawyers also have their own personal preferences, moral values,

Reprinted from "Lawyers Before the Supreme Court: Civil Liberties and Civil Rights, 1957–1966," **22** *Stanford Law Review* (1970), 489–496, 504–508.

and notions of what is good public policy. A lawyer may, in his litigation, pursue a number of different goals that may or may not be identical with those of his client. There may be several individuals and groups whom the lawyer perceives as having a stake in the litigation or whom he sees as a source of norms and values governing his behavior; these reference groups include his client, the judges before whom he argues, opposing attorneys, and the bar in general. Some may be more salient than others; a lawyer's most salient reference group or individual is his "clientele." . . .

The Advocate. The Advocate is very close to the paradigm often associated with the legal profession; he uses his training and skill in litigation simply on behalf of his client. He is concerned almost exclusively with winning his case and will use any legal and ethical means, raise any issue, and seek any satisfactory result. He is indifferent about whom he represents, because the characteristics of his client are of little interest. The Advocate regards his own policy preferences as irrelevant to his activity as a lawyer, and the implications of his case for others in society are also of little concern, unless they directly affect his chances for winning. The Advocate has a single, limited goal, and his interest in using litigation as a policy-development process is minimal; his clientele is his client.

The Group Advocate. The Group Advocate perceives himself as the representative of a particular group and uses his skills in litigation to further the aims of that group. This does not mean that the Group Advocate is simply an Advocate with a group as his client. Rather, the Group Advocate has long-term commitments to the group involved, and, importantly, the group itself may not even be a formal party to the litigation. For example, in a civil-rights case a lawyer may have a single formal client, yet he may perceive his clientele as all black people in America; in a reapportionment case in which the lawyer has a few formal clients, his clientele may be a broad political faction whose interests the lawyer believes he is representing. The Group Advocate is serving *his* group in litigation (though he need not be a member of the group, as when a white civil-rights lawyer defends black clients). The goals of the Group Advocate are those of the group, his clientele, with whose aims he identifies.

The Civil Libertarian. The Civil Libertarian is an activist who initiates or intervenes in litigation in an attempt to further general principles he considers basic to a democratic society—"freedom of speech" or "freedom of religion," for example. He is a gadfly who perceives his clientele as all of society. The American Civil Liberties Union, for example, is a Civil-Libertarian organization largely staffed by lawyers and devoted to using litigation to promote general principles.

The Civil Libertarian's goal is usually broader than the Advocate's or the Group Advocate's. His goal is not so much to vindicate the interests of individuals or groups in litigation but rather to vindicate principles. Although the Civil Libertarian wants to win for his client, his interest in principles leads to a concern that the decision vindicate his principles as broadly as possible. An example of the impersonal view of his litigation and stress upon the principles involved is suggested in the following remarks by a Civil Libertarian who argued a criminal case:

I owed no loyalty to Mr. "Smith" [his client]. Never met him in point of fact. I corresponded with him as infrequently as I could get away with. He had nothing to contribute to the issues. Unlike Justice Fortas who thought, I guess probably correctly, that Gideon did have something to do with the issues. . . . But neither the [appeal to the circuit court] nor the appeal to the Supreme Court had anything to do with a desire to spring Mr. Smith—I couldn't care less. . . .

A. The Advocate

As suggested above, the most salient characteristic of the Advocate, and the one that differentiates him from the other clientele types, is his interest in winning, regardless of the ground for decision or the broader social or political ramifications of the case. This is not because he is particularly fond of his client, for many Advocates view their clients with indifference if not antipathy, but because of the Advocate's perception of his role. The Advocate wants to win. As one lawyer said:

No, I am a professional. . . . I have represented guys who I would have locked up in the death house myself, if it were left to me. . . . It is my job to win when I represent a guy. This is the difference between, let's say, an ACLU lawyer and myself. My commitment to civil liberties is the commitment to represent the guy and what represents his cause is of no importance to me, and following that route I am trying to win. . . . That is my job, and if I have to convince the Court to overrule the first amendment, then I have won the case.

Advocates are likely to prefer narrow to broad grounds. This preference, the product of their legal socialization, is based upon a feeling that a case is more likely to be won upon a narrow ground than upon a sweeping one. Also, some Advocates may argue cases before the Court without being aware of, much less concerned with, the broader issues implicit in their litigation.

The obvious question that arises is why Advocates were so prevalent in criminal cases. The answer to this question lies to some extent in the recruitment pattern by which lawyers who argued criminal cases before the Supreme Court became involved in their litigation. Lawyers who argued criminal cases fell into two relatively distinct groups. One was comprised of lawyers, quite often associates in large law firms, who had little experience with criminal law and little expectation that they would continue to be involved in criminal cases. The other group included the "criminal lawyers," lawyers in private practice or with public or quasi-public agencies whose major practices involved criminal law. The appointed lawyers, "casuals" who moved into criminal law only briefly, comprised the bulk of the Advocates. The experienced criminal lawyers were more likely to be Civil Libertarians.

Appointed lawyers were likely to be Advocates for several reasons. First and most important, the stake of his client loomed particularly large to an attorney lacking extensive experience in criminal law; the client stood to lose his freedom for long periods of time, and sometimes his life. In addition, unlike the more experienced criminal lawyers, appointed attorneys from large law firms had little expectation of extensive future involvement in criminal litigation. Finally, the litigants themselves were primarily interested in avoiding jail, not in participating in landmark decisions. Thus, a particular recruitment mechanism—court appointment—tended to bring into criminal litigation many lawyers interested primarily in simply winning their cases—Advocates.

Those lawyers with more experience in criminal law tended to be Civil Libertarians, to view their cases as vehicles by which broader principles might be vindicated. The reasons why the experienced lawyer tended to be interested in the broader aspects of his case seem to lie in his previous experience and his expectations about his future practice. He was not only less impressed by the severity of the sentence, but saw in his case problems he had encountered before and would encounter in the future. He was concerned not simply with the individual client, but with the broader kinds of problems that each case exemplified.

Recruitment patterns and previous experience are not the only determinants of clientele. A lawyer's clientele may also be influenced by the Court itself. In some of the criminal cases, the Court provided cues to attorneys that suggested that their cases might be decided on the basis of broad policy issues. The two most common means of providing cues were in the grant of certiorari and by grouping cases for argument. The former is almost completely unambiguous; the latter suggests somewhat more subtly that the Court will be concerned with the issue common to the cases grouped for argument. Thus, clientele may in some instances be a product of the activity of the Court itself, though most lawyers appear to keep the clientele with which they began.

A majority of the criminal cases before the Supreme Court were argued by Advocates. The outcomes in the cases, often involving sweeping changes in legal and social policy, were to a large extent the unintended byproducts of the activities of the attorneys. There were quite noticeable discontinuities between the kinds of outcomes pursued by the lawyers and those that eventually emerged from judicial decision. Peltason suggests this phenomenon.

Judicial power is frequently invoked by parties for reasons that have nothing to do with the promotion of large values. For example, a man on trial for murder may raise the claim that he was denied his constitutional right to the assistance of counsel and in so doing represent an interest of a much wider scope than he himself is aware. His own reasons for his activity may be unrelated to, and certainly not designed to promote, any wider interest.

My analysis suggests that Peltason's description applies as well to many of the lawyers as to the defendants. This characteristic of judicial policymaking in the area of criminal law differentiates it from the other areas discussed below.

B. The Group Advocate

Group Advocates formed the largest class of lawyers interviewed. The Group Advocate differs from the other lawyers, and particularly from the Civil Libertarian whom he resembles in many ways, by a particular view of his litigation, a stress upon a kind of "we-they" notion in which the lawyer identifies with the "we." The Group Advocate is a lawyer whose clientele is a group to which the lawyer perceives he has long-term commitments. Though his goals may appear similar to those of a Civil Libertarian, it is the degree of circumstances of the social domain of the goal, the emphasis upon a particular group, that differentiates the Group Advocate from the Civil Libertarian.

The Group Advocate's commitment to his clientele may be one or more of several types. It may be a personal commitment derived from social or friendship ties between lawyers and clients and groups. It may be an ideological commitment representing a congruence of preferences between the lawyer and the group he believes has a stake in the litigation. Or, it may be an institutional commitment, a result of the lawyer's participation in an organization devoted to pursuing the fortunes of a particular group. In the illustrations of these types of commitments in the examples discussed below, it should be noted that the distinctive characteristic of the Group Advocate is his identification with a group and with that group's interests. Group Advocates were active in only three of the four areas: loyalty-security cases, reapportionment cases, and civil-rights cases. . . .

Representation of Interests. The process by which public policy is made through litigation is complex, involving not only a myriad of participants within the legal system but also important interactions between the legal system and other parts of the broader political system. Within the judicial system, participants may be pursuing a variety of goals, some directly related to broad social or political issues, some related only to resolution of the particular conflict that brought them to court. In analyzing the activities of the lawyers who argued civil-liberties and civil-rights cases during the 1957-66 period, and in contrasting their activities in various areas of litigation, one of the most striking facts is the diversity of their motives and interests. In the criminal cases, the important policy outcomes were to a large extent unintended by-products of the activities of attorneys concerned with

a greatly different set of issues. In the reapportionment litigation, the outcomes were directly congruent with the kinds of considerations that motivated the initiation and pursuit of the litigation. In the civil-rights and loyalty-security litigation, the congruence was somewhat mixed, not so much because the lawyers were disinterested in policy, but because the Court itself often chose to decide the cases upon rather more narrow grounds than many of the lawyers and litigants might have wished.

In addition to pointing up this differentiation, the concept of clientele adds to the notion of an "interest" in litigation. Group-process theorists have long talked about litigation as being representative of "interests" in society.

It is necessary to see the distinction between the formal parties to a legal controversy and the interests they represent. A litigant represents and is part of an interest, but should never be confused with the whole interest. A decision has consequences for others—sometimes thousands of others—not immediately before the court. Thus the action of the litigants is but one small segment of all the activity which makes up the interest represented.

Though clientele does not relate directly to the perhaps somewhat metaphysical concept of the "interest" within society that a case abstractly represents, it does suggest that lawyers do differ significantly in their perception of the groups they are serving. It suggests that in different areas of litigation, different kinds of "interests" have been represented, and that the lawyer's perception of his interest may affect his decision to bring a case before the Supreme Court.

Clientele and Lawyer-Client Relations. The Group Advocates and

Civil Libertarians do not fit the traditional image of a legal specialist offering his services to any client able to retain him. They are partisans, sometimes ideologues, committed to the use of litigation for the development of broad social policy, often operating out of institutions committed to similar goals. The Supreme Court itself has begun to recognize changes in the relationship of lawyer to client. Though the changes suggested here in the kinds of lawyers arguing before the Supreme Court may affect only a small number of litigants, they raise important issues about the obligations of the attorney and the expectations an individual may reasonably entertain about his lawyer.

Conflicts between the interests of the lawyer and his client are not so likely to occur in the loyalty-security and civil-rights litigation, for the clients themselves are often interested in vindicating the same principles as the lawyers. But if a serious Civil Libertarian or Group Advocate is paired with a client interested simply in winning, some grave conflicts can emerge, both between lawyer and client and for the lawyer himself. In criminal cases, the conflicts are likely to be more severe. One lawyer suggested this dilemma:

I think all of us in the [Jones] cases had a big period of soul-searching—at least some of [the other lawyers] so indicated to me—as to whether we were asking the Court to go too far. In other words, balancing representation of our client against the broader public interest. . . . [W]e all resolved it, all decided we weren't, but obviously it was a big step and that was something of a problem.

The problem may be resolved in criminal cases by the cues provided by the Court, indicating to the lawyer that he should stress the broader issues, or by a lawyer's rationalization that the larger issue is the only hope for victory.

. . .

Trends in Clientele Types: Judicial Policymaking. Assessing the contribution of the lawyer to the outcome of a case presupposes a verified theory of judicial decision making and an ability to hold the other variables constant. Although such a theory does not exist at this time, at least not in sufficiently rigorous form, some useful speculation is still possible.

A prerequisite for any policy to emerge from the legal system is the existence of litigation, for courts cannot place issues on their own agenda as easily as other political institutions can. The argument can be made that the two types of lawyers discussed here, Group Advocates and Civil Libertarians, are likely to provide the Court with occasions for decision on major policy questions in ways in which the Advocates are not. Of course, the Court can use cases appealed on narrow grounds as vehicles for important policy decisions; the criminal litigation demonstrates this possibility. But, and I think this is important, the Advocate does not actively seek out litigation, and he is not attuned to the policy questions implicit in his litigation. Though after he becomes involved in a suit, his arguments for his client may involve important policy innovations, he is not likely to seek out such litigation, and may settle for a compromise victory at an earlier proceeding. It can be at least speculated that an increase in the number of lawyers primarily concerned with policy, not simply clients, might well be important in providing appeals courts with occasions for policymaking.

. . .

The proliferation of Group Advocates and Civil Libertarians in all areas of civil-liberties and civil-rights litigation before the Supreme Court has significant implications for the process of judicial policymaking. The Group Advocates and Civil Libertarians may perform an important lobbying function by being concerned with policy issues in their litigation and by urging these policy considerations on the Court. By avowedly undertaking litigation in pursuit of particular policy outcomes, these lawyers not only provide occasions for decision, but also indicate the breadth of interest in the policy changes they urge. Thus a proliferation of litigation pursued to promote social and political change, with the presentation of evidence to support such change, may be crucial to the process by which courts are induced to engage in such policymaking. Lawyers, their clients, and the groups that support them are crucial "constituencies" for courts, and they mediate between courts and changes occurring in the broader social and political systems.

The intimate relationship between the legal system, the broader political process, and the "politicization" of litigation is of course not a recent development. The defense of *laissez-faire* economic policy through litigation and the activities of interest groups like the NAACP are two salient examples of ties between litigation and the broader political system. But the use of litigation for political ends is on the increase. The notion of "going to court" as a means to gain desired policy goals—whether to end capital punishment, to liberalize abortion laws, to reform the welfare system, to change drug control laws, or to protect the environment—seems to occur to political partisans not only

in a rapidly expanding number of issue areas, but to occur sooner. What in the past was typically last resort—after other political arenas had been tried—is now becoming an early and integral part of the strategy of those trying to get their way in the process of collective decision. We are presently witnessing movement toward institutionalization of the defense of civil liberties and rights of "traditional" minority groups like blacks and, more recently, the poor, and litigation is becoming an integral part of the strategies of the politically dissatisfied who have not been institutionally oppressed by being denied access to political arenas but who simply have consistently lost in other political arenas. . . .

E. Robert L. Stern, *The Solicitor General's Office*

. . . Congress has provided that there shall be an Attorney General who shall be the head of the Department of Justice, and that there shall be a Solicitor General who shall be "learned in the law." The Attorney General is the chief law officer of the Government, but he is primarily an administrator, policy maker and Presidential adviser.

The Solicitor General, on the other hand, may not unfairly be described as the highest Government official who acts primarily as a lawyer. He has few administrative responsibilities; he can devote his time to studying the legal problems which come before him. Moreover, he must stand on his own feet when he is presenting the most important Government cases to the Supreme Court.

The Solicitor General's staff of

Reprinted from "The Solicitor General's Office and Administrative Agency Litigation," 46 *American Bar Association Journal* (February 1960), 154–156.

from seven to nine lawyers, two of whom act as First and Second Assistants, is almost always chosen on the basis of merit after a search within and without the Government for the best possible man who can be attracted, usually regardless of politics. Many have come from other parts of the Department of Justice or the Government where they have proved their competence in working with the Solicitor General's Office. Many have been Supreme Court law clerks who have been chosen by the Justices on the basis of their outstanding ability.

In part because of the standard of selection and in part because of the job it has to do, the Office has had a high *esprit de corps* and a traditional standard of performance of "nothing but the best". This is recognized and respected by those both within and without the Government who deal with the Office, and the Supreme Court has come to expect it.

I will be speaking interchangeably of the Solicitor General and the Solicitor General's Office—really of the Solicitor General as an institution rather than as an individual. . . .

Whether and to what extent the Solicitor General personally reviews the briefs varies with the individual. He will, of course, scrutinize the briefs in important cases and the cases he argues. Some Solicitors General have insisted on reading all the briefs before they go back for final printing. Others have relied on the staff to call their attention to the important ones or those which present special problems.

Although oral arguments get most of the publicity, as in any law office they take the least amount of time. The Government is a party or *amicus* in about 60 per cent of the cases argued in the Supreme Court, and thus participates in sixty-five to ninety-five arguments per year. The Solicitor General assigns all Government arguments in the Supreme Court. He argues a number of the most important cases himself and distributes the rest among members of his staff and the attorneys in the Divisions of the Department or the independent agencies from which the cases came. When an agency is autonomous, like the ICC, the Solicitor General and its General Counsel agree on assignments, which means that the cases are divided between the Commission and the Department of Justice, as they probably would have been anyhow. . . .

A principal function of the Solicitor General's Office is to decide what cases the Government can appeal. The Solicitor General's duties in this respect are not limited to Supreme Court cases. Whenever, in cases handled by the Department of Justice, the Government loses and the case is appealable, a recommendation for or against appeal or certiorari to the intermediate court or the Supreme Court must be made to the Solicitor General. There can thus be no appeal to any court, or for that matter no decision not to appeal, without his approval.

Since the administrative agencies generally handle their own cases in the lower courts, their litigation comes to the attention of the Solicitor General only when it approaches the Supreme Court. When the agency has lost a case, it decides whether it wants to petition for certiorari, or, when appropriate, take a direct appeal. If it decides to go ahead, it requests the Solicitor General to authorize the petition for certiorari or the appeal. Except for a few agencies like the ICC, which operates under special statutes . . . no agency can take a case to the Supreme Court without the Solicitor General's authorization. . . .

The Standards for Granting Certiorari

Most cases go to the Supreme Court by way of certiorari. In determining whether to petition for certiorari the Solicitor General heeds the Supreme Court's frequent pronouncements, in its rules and elsewhere, that it will grant certiorari only when there is a conflict among the lower appellate courts, when the case is of general importance, or sometimes when there is gross error below—or perhaps when those factors are present in some combination. The Solicitor General attempts to apply the Supreme Court's standards. He will not take up every lower court decision which trial counsel in the Department, or the administrative agency, or the Solicitor General himself, believes to be wrong. . . .

The reasons underlying this traditional approach by the Solicitor General are partly self-serving and partly not.

The Solicitor General regards himself—and the Supreme Court regards him—not only as an officer of the Executive Branch but also as an officer of the Court. This is supposed to be true of all lawyers appearing before all courts, but the Solicitor General takes it seriously. As such he is aware of the necessity from the standpoint of the effective administration of the judicial system of restricting the number of cases taken to the Supreme Court to the number that Court can hear. This alone permits the Court to give adequate consideration to the important matters which the highest tribunal of the land should decide. That is the policy underlying the certiorari system which Congress and the Supreme Court found it necessary to establish to permit the Court to do its job.

A heavy additional burden would be imposed on the Court if the Government, with its great volume of litigation, disregarded that policy and acted like the normal litigant who wants to take one more shot at reversing a decision which is obviously wrong because he lost. . . .

The selfish reason for the Solicitor General's self-restraint in petitioning for certiorari is to give the Court confidence in Government petitions. It is hoped and believed—although no one who has not been on the Court can be sure—that the Court will realize that the Solicitor General will not assert that an issue is of general importance unless it is—and that confidence in the Solicitor General's attempt to adhere to the Court's own standards will cause the Court to grant more Government petitions.

Whatever the reason, from 50 percent to 75 percent of all Government petitions are granted, as contrasted with no more than 10 percent of other petitions. . . .

Some . . . think that the Solicitor General holds too tight a rein in passing upon requests for certiorari. They believe that he acts too much as an adjunct of the Supreme Court and not enough as advocate for the United States or its agencies. Not infrequently, and not entirely jocularly, they remind the members of his staff, if not the Solicitor General himself, that they are not members of the judiciary but are part of the Executive Department which is supposed to act as lawyers for the remainder. On the other hand, I know that members of the Supreme Court frequently admonish a new Solicitor General not to be too liberal in authorizing certiorari. . . .

[In the 1967–1968 term of the Supreme Court, the Solicitor General authorized the government to appeal 36 of 379 cases that it had lost in the courts of appeals—less than 10 percent. By contrast, in the same year, the government's adversaries appealed to the Supreme Court in nearly half of the cases in which the government prevailed in the lower courts.[1] And as noted previously, the Supreme Court normally grants a much higher percentage of the Solicitor General's petitions for review than the average for all cases.

Not only does the government have a much better chance of getting to Court, but in the Supreme Court the government fares very well on the merits. Scigliano reports that the federal government won 62 percent of a sample of nineteenth-century cases and that it has prevailed in 64 percent of its cases during this century. To the extent that the government is appealing from an adverse lower court decision, its winning percentages are comparable to those of all litigants. Those litigants whose petitions for review are accepted by the Supreme Court usually prevail about two-thirds of the time. The reason is clear enough. In its almost totally discretionary jurisdiction, the Supreme Court naturally tends to review more of those cases that seem to have been decided wrongly than those cases in which the outcome is perceived to be correct. There are instances, of course, where the Court will review a clearly correct lower court decision to give its own weight to the point of law or the resulting outcome. Scigliano also reports, however, that where the government is appealing from a lower court defeat, it does somewhat better than the average—and thus contributes disproportionately to the "average".]

F. Congress and the Supreme Court

Congress provides an important counterpoint in understanding the strategic environment of the Supreme Court. The relationship is much more subtle than appears from the relatively few formal occasions for interaction. Congress' reaction to Supreme Court decisions is more complex than any list of specific bills would suggest. And the Court's view of Congress is certainly not captured merely from the words of its decisions.

The core of the theory of judicial self-restraint is deference toward legislative—particularly congressional—decisions. The Supreme Court has utilized its power of judicial review over acts of Congress very sparingly. We have noted that only 115 acts of Congress were invalidated through 1974. By contrast, more than 900 state statutes, local ordinances, or provisions of state constitutions had been invalidated by the Court, most since 1870.[1] When the Court does invalidate an act of Congress, as seems to occur now two or three times a year, it usually does so with expressed regret. Deference to Congress is not only responsive to the theory of separation of powers but is also a very practical recognition that Congress wields substantial potential power over the personnel and jurisdiction of the Supreme Court.

Congress has several means available to it for reversing or modifying an unpopular Supreme Court decision. A constitutional amendment, ratified by three-fourths of the states, would completely repudiate the offending decision. But this is a slow and difficult route to take. Although many "reversal" amendments are introduced in Congress each year, most of these are for local political consumption and are not seriously considered in Congress—or out. Only four Supreme Court decisions have ever been reversed by constitutional

[1]Robert Scigliano, *The Supreme Court and the Presidency* (New York: Free Press, 1971), Ch. 6.

[1]Henry Abraham, *The Judicial Process,* 3rd ed. (New York: Oxford University Press, 1975), p. 280–294.

amendment: *Chisholm* v. *Georgia* (1793), by the Eleventh Amendment; *Dred Scott* v. *Sandford* (1857), by the Thirteenth, Fourteenth, and Fifteenth Amendments; *Pollock* v. *Farmers' Loan and Trust Company* (1895), by the Sixteenth Amendment; and part of *Oregon* v. *Mitchell* (1970), by the Twenty-sixth Amendment.

Where the Supreme Court has invalidated an act of Congress or a state statute, normally the only recourse for those in opposition is a constitutional amendment. However, the Supreme Court's recent expansive interpretation of congressional enforcement power under Section 5 of the Fourteenth Amendment suggests that under certain circumstances Congress might ‘be able to reverse the effects of a decision by statute rather than by constitutional amendment. If the Supreme Court failed to outlaw capital punishment, for example, there might be authority for Congress to do so as an enforcement of Fourteenth Amendment rights to due process and equal protection. A more difficult question would be whether Congress could *restore* the rights of states to impose the death penalty if the Supreme Court ruled that it was unconstitutional under the Eighth and Fourteenth Amendments.[2] In the Crime Control Act of 1968, Congress did attempt to reverse the effects of *Miranda* v. *Arizona* (1966) in the federal courts. That provision is almost certainly invalid but probably will never be tested in the courts. There is no Fourteenth Amendment enforcement power under those circumstances.

When an offending Supreme Court decision is merely one of statutory interpretation, Congress can pass a new statute or amend the old one to reiterate or clarify its intentions. If the Court accepts these congressional changes, the issue is closed. Such was the case in *Palermo* v. *United States* (1960), where the court accepted a congressional statute that modified, but did not reverse, its earlier decision in the *Jencks* case.[3] This type of interaction between Congress and the Court is not at all uncommon and can be viewed as a form of "bargaining." The Court is usually reluctant to invalidate an act of Congress, and under the Brandeis "rules" of self-restraint, it should try to save a statute by interpreting it so as to preserve its constitutionality.[4] Occasionally, as in *United States* v. *Seeger* (1965), which involved the Supreme Being clause in the draft law, the Court can only "save" the statute by attributing to it a meaning contrary to the one intended by Congress. But if Congress persists in an interpretation that the Court believes to be unconstitutional, it may have no choice but to invoke its power of judicial review. Statutory reversal of decisions is the largest single category of congressional responses toward the Supreme Court.[5]

On occasion, Congress will remain

[2]For a discussion of Congress' enforcement powers under the Fourteenth Amendment, see Part Two, Chapter Two, pp. 539–564.

[3]*Jencks* v. *United States* (1956), in which the Supreme Court held that a person charged with a federal offense was entitled to see the notes of informers who testified against him, under the Sixth Amendment right of confrontation. If the government did not want to produce those documents, it could cease prosecution.

[4]See his dissent in *Ashwander* v. *T.V.A.* (1936).

[5]"Congressional Reversal of Supreme Court Decisions, 1945–1957," **71** *Harvard Law Review* (1958), 1324–1335; Also see Stephen L. Wasby, *The Impact of the United States Supreme Court* (Homewood, Ill.: Dorsey Press, 1970), pp. 203–213.

silent in the face of a judicial ruling, and this silence may be interpreted as acquiescence. For example, in 1953 the Court was faced with a challenge to organized baseball's "reserve clause," under which a player is bound to the team with which he originally signs, unless traded, sold, or unconditionally released. This modern form of peonage had been upheld in 1922, when Justice Holmes wrote that baseball was a sport, not a business, and therefore not subject to the antitrust laws or other statutes governing interstate commerce (*Federal Baseball Club of Baltimore* v. *National League*). In the meantime, several efforts to bring baseball under the antitrust statutes failed, and when another case presented the same question in 1953, the Court adhered to its earlier opinion: "Congress has had the ruling under consideration but has not seen fit to bring such business under these laws by legislation. . . . We think that if there are evils in this field which now warrant application to it of the anti-trust laws it should be by legislation" (*Toolson* v. *New York Yankees*). In the next few years, however, the Court refused to extend the *Toolson* precedent and brought football, boxing, and theatrical enterprises under the Sherman Act—but not baseball. Explaining the seeming incongruence of different rules for football and baseball (aside from the rules of play), Chief Justice Warren argued that *Toolson* was "a narrow application of the rule of *stare decisis*" and that the responsibility for overruling

it lay with Congress. In 1972, in *Flood* v. *Kuhn,* the Supreme Court again refused to overrule its 1922 decision, saying that Congress would have to undertake the responsibility for including baseball within the antitrust laws.

With some exceptions, the evidence shows that where Congress has persevered in its conflicts with the Supreme Court, it has prevailed. Sometimes Congress has overruled the Court, and sometimes the Court has retreated in the face of threatened congressional retaliation.[6] Justice Jackson's aphorism, that the Court was not final because it was infallible, but infallible because it was final, is not supported by the evidence.[7] Especially if it is willing to wait for personnel changes, Congress is almost always likely to triumph over determined judicial opposition.

Robert Dahl has noted that the longest recorded time Congress has had to "wait" to have its way with the Supreme Court was twenty-five years, and that was an unusually long wait.[8] In 1916, Congress outlawed the transportation in interstate commerce of goods made by child labor. But in 1918, a divided Court (*Hammer* v. *Dagenhart*) ruled that Congress could not validly bar goods from commerce that were not harmful in themselves—a very restrictive (and novel) view of congressional power. Congress tried again to outlaw child labor in the Revenue Act of 1919. It imposed a tax on mine or factory owners who employed children

[6]This is an observation widely if not uniformly expressed. See Walter F. Murphy, *Congress and the Court* (Chicago: University of Chicago Press, 1962), esp. Ch. 11. On interactions between Congress and the Supreme Court, see also John R. Schmidhauser and Larry Berg, *The Supreme Court and Congress: Conflict and Interaction, 1945–1963* (New York: Free Press, 1972).

[7]Robert H. Jackson, *The Supreme Court in the American System of Government* (Cambridge: Harvard University Press, 1954).

[8]Robert A, Dahl, "Decision-making in a Democracy: The Supreme Court as a National Policy-maker," **6** *Journal of Public Law* (1957), 279–295.

below a certain age to work more than eight hours a day or six days a week. Once again the Court responded by declaring the act invalid (*Bailey* v. *Drexel Furniture*, 1922). It was, the Court said, an improper use of Congress' taxing powers, since the tax was not intended to raise revenue but only to achieve a prohibited regulatory end. Since the tax was obviously not designed for revenue purposes, the Court did not have a difficult time, although it had to distinguish a prior decision that had upheld a prohibitive tax on oleomargarine. In 1924, Congress proposed a constitutional amendment forbidding child labor. The amendment failed to secure the necessary ratification from three-fourths of the states; technically it is still pending, since it did not contain an expiration clause.

In 1938, Congress tried again. It passed the Fair Labor Standards Act which, among other things, prohibited child labor in businesses dealing in interstate commerce. By the time the statute was judicially tested in *United States* v. *Darby* (1941), the Supreme Court's membership had undergone wholesale change, and the Court now decided unanimously that Congress had the power to prohibit child labor. *Hammer* v. *Dagenhart* was overruled. It had taken twenty-five years, but changing times and an infusion of new judicial blood had brought the Court around.

A third potential congressional response to Supreme Court decisions lies in congressional control of the appellate jurisdiction of the Supreme Court. Under the Constitution, Congress may prescribe the regulations governing the appellate jurisdiction of the Supreme Court. In 1869, in *Ex Parte McCardle*, the Court was faced with a congressional removal of its jurisdiction in a case already accepted for argument and decided in conference. Congress, fearing that the Supreme Court would invalidate the Reconstruction Acts of 1867 in deciding on the validity of McCardle's conviction for sedition by a military tribunal, passed a statute withdrawing the Court's jurisdiction. The Court, refusing to question the motives of Congress, acquiesced and dismissed the case. Most observers saw this as a meek submission by the Court to congressional domination and a confession of judicial impotence. Later interpretations have stressed the limited facts of the case and have also pointed to other contemporary cases in which the Supreme Court refused to accept limits on its habeas corpus powers.[9] Although Justices Black and Douglas suggested in 1962 that they would not find the *McCardle* precedent controlling, it has never been overruled.[10]

To prevent further attacks on the Supreme Court such as Roosevelt's

[9]Stanley I. Kutler, "Ex Parte McCardle: Judicial Impotency? The Supreme Court and Reconstruction Reconsidered," **72** *American Historical Review* (1967), 835–850.

[10]*Glidden* v. *Zdanok* (1962). In *Congress* v. *The Supreme Court* (Cambridge: Harvard University Press, 1969), Raoul Berger argues that it was not the intention of the framers of the Constitution to give Congress broad power to regulate the appellate jurisdiction of the Supreme Court. Rather, he argues that this was to be a limited power to regulate jurisdiction over "facts." Any broader reading would be inconsistent with the Court's role as a check upon Congress and enforcer of the Bill of Rights. The idea that Congress could prevent enforcement of the Bill of Rights by withdrawing the Court's jurisdiction to hear cases raising such questions is, for Berger, completely unacceptable. The power of Congress to regulate the jurisdiction of the Court must be subject to all the other provisions of the Constitution. Berger's limited view of congressional power to regulate the appellate

"court-packing" plan of 1937, and to overrule the *McCardle* case, the Senate in 1954 passed the "Butler Amendment." The amendment died in the House Judiciary Committee. It would have frozen the number of justices at nine and provided for their mandatory retirement at age 75. More importantly, it would have repealed the second paragraph of Article III, Section 2 of the Constitution and conferred on the Supreme Court exclusive control over its appellate jurisdiction. Had it passed, the amendment would have precluded any repetition of the *McCardle* incident. There was widespread conservative support for the amendment, and many liberal doubts. Conservatives were trying to insulate the Court from another broadside attack; liberals, historically out of sympathy with the Supreme Court, seemed unwilling to relinquish this important congressional power.[11]

The Butler amendment passed the Senate on May 11, 1954. Six days later the Supreme Court announced its landmark decision in *Brown* v. *Board of Education*, assuring that there would be no further southern support for any amendment to *protect* the Court. In the succeeding years, the Supreme Court made a number of decisions equally unpopular with northern Republicans, most

having to do with the powers of the government to punish individuals for conspiracy to overthrow the government by force and violence or with the reversal of convictions flowing from citations for contempt of Congress.[12]

By 1958 the tide against the Court had become so strong that Senator John Marshall Butler, author of the Butler amendment, cosponsored a bill to *remove* the jurisdiction of the Supreme Court in areas where the Court had made "too liberal decisions." The Jenner-Butler bill, as it was called, was amended to delete the removal of jurisdiction in favor of statutory reversals in all but one area, but it still failed of adoption in the Senate 41–49. Analysis of the debates in the Senate showed a strong consensus against tampering with the jurisdiction of the Supreme Court for punitive purposes. Although some doubts were expressed about the validity of a punitive withdrawal of jurisdiction—as opposed to the fairly common adjustments made for reasons of workload—the defeat of the bill did not alter the precedent allowing congressional regulation for any purpose. Passage of the Helms Amendment (See Footnote 10, *supra.*) would almost certainly require the Supreme Court to consider anew the limits of congressional con-

---

jurisdiction of the Supreme Court, at odds with the apparently plain terms of Article III, Section 2, and with the interpretation of eminent constitutional scholars such as Professor Herbert Wechsler, was largely ignored. But in 1979 he announced that, whatever his earlier views, new research led him to conclude that the enforcement clause of the Fourteenth Amendment (Section 5) gave Congress *exclusive* power to confer jurisdiction on the courts to enforce that amendment, at least insofar as the review of the validity of state laws under the Amendment is concerned. Berger's new view came to light in debate over the proposed "Helms Amendment," an effort to protect state laws seeking to reinstate school prayers by withdrawing the Supreme Court's jurisdiction to review such laws. See Raoul Berger, "The Fourteenth Amendment: Light from the Fifteenth," 74 *Northwestern University Law Review* (1979), 353–355, and passim.

[11]John R. Schmidhauser, "The Butler Amendment," **43** *American Bar Association Journal* (1957), 714–717, 761–764.

[12]See C. Herman Pritchett, *The Political Offender and the Warren Court* (Boston: Boston University Press, 1958).

trol of federal court jurisdiction, and reassess the validity of the *McCardle* precedent.

There are other congressional responses that are strictly punitive. Congress controls the size of the Supreme Court, as well as its budget. Prior to the 1870s, the size of the Court was periodically changed—usually to prevent a "hostile" president from making new appointments or to enable a "friendly" president to make additional ones. Since 1869 the size of the Court has remained constant at nine, surviving even the frontal assault of President Roosevelt's Court Reorganization Plan of 1937. The "court-packing" plan would have given the president the opportunity to appoint as many as six new justices, one each to replace sitting justices who had reached the age of 75. Despite the defeat of the Butler amendment, it seems probable that the current number of justices will remain frozen in the forseeable future. To add more would make the Court unwieldy, and to divide a larger court into divisions would probably violate Chief Justice Hughes' "advisory opinion," rendered at the time of the "court-packing" plan, that "the Constitution does not appear to authorize more than one Supreme Court."

Congress sets judicial salaries provided that it does not infringe the constitutional mandate that judicial salaries "not be diminished during their continuance in office." In 1964, senators who were generally unsympathetic to the Court's "liberal" decisions pushed through an amendment that cut proposed pay raises for the justices from $7500 to $4500. While this placed Supreme Court salaries at $39,500 ($500 more for the chief justice) and could hardly be considered economic strangulation, it constituted a very personal rebuke to the justices. The cuts were restored several years later, and the current annual salary of a Supreme Court justice is $72,000; the Chief Justice receives $75,000. In 1976, a group of federal court judges filed suit, claiming that Congress was effectively "diminishing" their salaries by failing to adjust them according to inflation levels. No Supreme Court justice joined the suit.[13] A Congress bent on destroying the Court as an effective institution could theoretically reduce or eliminate funds for staff and administrative costs. Such drastic action is, of course, highly unlikely.

Congress has several other weapons at its disposal. One is impeachment, although this has fallen into disuse since the impeachment—and acquittal—of Justice Samuel Chase in 1805. It is not likely that a justice today would be impeached merely because of political disagreement with his decisions, notwithstanding the efforts of the John Birch Society to promote the impeachment of Chief Justice Earl Warren. Recent attempts to impeach Justice William Douglas, based in part on conflict of interest charges, were also unsuccessful. While one suspects a political motivation on the part of those seeking Douglas' impeachment, the formal charges rested on claims of conflict of interest and other alleged ethical lapses.[14]

Congress can also express its discontent with the Supreme Court by criticism of nominees to the Court by

---

[13]The suit was lost in the lower courts. On January 9, 1978, the Supreme Court left standing that lower court decision. See *Atkins* v. *U.S.*, certiorari denied (1978).

[14]H. Res. 920, House Judiciary Committee, April 15, 1970, requesting impeachment and citing charges. Also see H. Res. 922, House Judiciary Committee, April 16, 1970, creating a select committee to conduct an inves-

subjecting these nominees to grueling interrogation before the Senate Judiciary Committee, and occasionally blocking a nomination entirely. There have been numerous bills introduced in the Congress to set minimum qualifications for appointment to the Supreme Court, on the assumption that sitting justices lack these qualifications and would do a better job if they had them. One of the most common in recent years has been the effort to require a minimum number of years of prior judicial experience for nominees; such experience, it is stated, would make the justices less willing to depart from tradition and precedent. Notwithstanding evidence to the contrary, proposals of this type recur.[15]

When, and how often, does Congress respond negatively to Supreme Court decisions? Statutory reversals are most common. One study showed 50 instances in which Congress revised a much larger number of Court decisions, in the sixteen-year period beginning 1944.[16] Nagel found 165 court-curbing proposals through 1965, excluding constitutional amendments, statutory reversals, and resolutions.[17] Only 9 of these 165 bills passed the Congress. But, as Nagel correctly assumes, the measure of success should not be limited to those bills that passed. In other instances, he recorded Supreme Court "retreats" in the face of very vocal congressional opposition. Of the 165

bills, about 30 percent would have either limited or abolished the power of judicial review, and the same number were concerned with personnel matters. Half of the personnel bills related to judicial qualifications. Twenty-seven percent related to the jurisdiction of the Supreme Court, and 7 percent to questions of procedure and court organization. By Nagel's criteria of relative success (which measured whether or not bills got out of committee and whether or not there was some Supreme Court retreat), about 19 percent of these bills had some measure of success.

These court-curbing efforts were not evenly distributed but tended to occur in a few intense periods of crisis frequently following periods of highly visible or intensive use by the Supreme Court of its power to review acts of Congress and often in periods of political party realignment.[18] Nagel found that, on the whole, "court-curbing bills are more likely to succeed where federal-state relations or separation of powers represent the prime subject matters involved." Intensely held economic interests or civil libertarian interests were less likely to induce successful Court-curbing efforts, although economic issues incited more bills. Nagel also found some positive relationship between intra-Court disagreement and congressional attack; the incidence of Court-curbing bills was also higher where a majority of justices belonged

tigation of certain activities of Justice Douglas to determine if impeachment proceedings were warranted; Gerald R. Ford, "Conduct of Associate Justice Douglas," Speech before House of Representatives calling for Justice Douglas' Impeachment, April 15, 1970.

[15]See John R. Schmidhauser, "Stare Decisis, Dissent and the Background of the Justices of the United States Supreme Court," 14 *University of Toronto Law Journal* (1962), 194–212. Schmidhauser found that prior judicial experience was *inversely* related to a tendency to adhere to precedent.

[16]Cited in Wasby, *op. cit.*, Note 5, pp. 209–210.

[17]Stuart S. Nagel, "Court-Curbing Periods in American History," 18 *Vanderbilt Law Review* (1965), 925–944.

[18]David Adamany, "Legitimacy, Realigning Elections, and the Supreme Court," 1973 *Wisconsin Law Review*, 790–846.

to the minority political party in Congress.[19]

Considering the explosive political, social, and economic issues decided by the Supreme Court, it is surprising to find so few successful efforts by the Congress to curb the Court's powers. Perhaps the relatively greater frequency and success of bills to reverse or modify particular Supreme Court decisions acts as a safety valve that permits the more controversial and punitive anti-Court efforts to be limited largely to relatively harmless rhetoric. The tradition of judicial independence may be one explanation for the relative restraint of Congress, although Stumpf found "no evidence . . . that use of this symbol in debate on bills anti-Court in flavor or content in and of itself inhibits their passage."[20] But he does suggest that the value of judicial independence is so internalized among members of Congress that it needs little overt expression to act as an effective restraint. A more recent study of congressional roll calls between 1945 and 1968 suggested that attitudes toward the Supreme Court were less important than partisan and ideological considerations. Voting on measures affecting the Supreme Court was similar to voting patterns on other legislation. Northern, urban Democrats supported a liberal Court far more often than did southern Democrats or Re-

publicans.[21] The implication of these data is that, in the long run, the Supreme Court's political salvation may depend less on congressional reverance for the Court as an institution than on reducing the ideological disparity between it and congressional majorities.

However, the "reverence" hypothesis should not be discarded merely because congressional voting on measures affecting the Supreme Court follows existing partisan divisions. Legislators are sensitive to constituent views, and there is evidence that the *public* values the independence of the Supreme Court. Cantwell found that there was never a majority of public opinion support for Roosevelt's Court Reorganization Plan in 1937, and what support there was dwindled rapidly when the resignation of Justice Van Devanter, the "Switch in Time that Saved Nine" [see pp. 248–251], and other events raised the possibility that the Supreme Court could or would be "brought around" by less drastic means.[22] Dolbeare found that nearly half of his sample in Wisconsin believed in the myth of mechanical jurisprudence and that this was associated with high support for the Court.[23] Murphy and Tanenhaus found that 37 percent of their national sample extended diffuse support to the Court as an institution (as

[19]Nagel, *op. cit.*, Note 17. Also see Walter Murphy, *Congress and the Court, op. cit.*, Note 6.

[20]Harry P. Stumpf, "The Political Efficacy of Judicial Symbolism," **19** *Western Political Quarterly* (1966), 293–303. Also see C. Herman Pritchett, *Congress Versus the Supreme Court* (Minneapolis: University of Minnesota Press, 1961), pp. 119–120.

[21]Schmidhauser and Berg, *op. cit.*, Note 6, p. 172 and passim.

[22]Frank V. Cantwell, "Public Opinion and the Legislative Process," **40** *American Political Science Review* (1946), 924–935.

[23]Kenneth M. Dolbeare, "The Public Views the Supreme Court," in Jacob (ed.), *Law, Politics and the Federal Courts* (Boston: Little, Brown, 1967), pp. 194–212, at 208–210. See also Dolbeare and Phillip Hammond, "The Political Party Basis of Attitudes Toward the Supreme Court," **31** *Public Opinion Quarterly* (1967), 16–30; and John H. Kessel, "Public Perceptions of the Supreme Court," **10** *Midwest Journal of Political Science* (1966), 167–191.

opposed to only one-fourth that number who supported specific decisions of the Court); only 10 percent were strongly negative toward the Court. If the percentages are recomputed to exclude the 30 percent who could not be classified, then about 53 percent of those who responded supported the Court as an institution.[24]

In the final analysis, one should not fall into the trap of assuming that an attempt to reverse a Supreme Court decision, by whatever means, necessarily implies lack of support for the Court as an institution. It is reasonable to expect that on important public issues, the country, like the Court, will be divided. Those whose views are rejected by the Court, if the views are intensely held, are likely to continue the battle on other grounds. If the Supreme Court is to be regarded as a legitimate policy-making institution, dynamic responses to its decisions are well within normal bounds and not inconsistent with respect for the Court. It is only under a different theory, where the Supreme Court merely expounds the law and does not make it, that attempts to override the Court's decisions might be met with suspicion.

G. The Recruitment of Supreme Court Justices

(1) The Politics of Judicial Selection

The Constitutional Basis of Judicial Selection. . . . Although constitutional rules often fail to tell the whole story about a particular aspect of the political process . . . they do provide the framework within which the political process operates, and usually manage to condition the course and content of that process. Constitutional rules can have the effect of giving an advantage to particular groups or interests in the political process; moreover, at least initially, they may generally structure the nature of political leadership and influence.

The rules for selecting federal judges were the subject of extensive debate at the Constitutional Convention. Although the delegates were certainly concerned with securing as judges men of integrity and ability, they were equally aware that the method of selection would also have to satisfy implicit requirements of political stability and balance. The question of selecting federal judges was discussed in relation to the greater issues of the Convention— large state-small state rivalry, executive-legislative checks and balances, and so on—and was ultimately settled in the light of the compromises which resolved these basic issues. . . .

. . . [T]he Constitution, as it was written in 1787 and as it stands today, made no provision for establishing minimum qualifications of judges as a guide to executive choice.
. . .

In choosing to follow neither the Continental model, in which judges constituted a separate vocation and received separate training, nor even the British model, in which judges were almost always chosen from a select group of barristers, the framers left a void which could have

---

[24]Walter F. Murphy and Joseph Tanenhaus, "Public Opinion and the United States Supreme Court: A Preliminary Mapping of Some Prerequisites for Court Legitimation of Regime Change," in Grossman and Tanenhaus (eds.), *Frontiers of Judicial Research* (New York: John Wiley, 1969), pp. 273–303.

Adapted from Joel B. Grossman, *Lawyers and Judges* (New York, John Wiley, 1965).

been—but was not—filled by either Congress or the executive. It is true that Congress, in the Judiciary Act of 1789, created the principle of geographical distribution of Supreme Court justices by assigning them to circuit duty. But Congress has set no formal qualifications for the federal bench. It is tradition alone which has dictated that district court nominees are usually residents of the state and district area in which they will serve and that all prospective judges are lawyers. . . . [I]t is also true that the framers *assumed* that at least the judges of the Supreme Court would be chosen from among the best trained men available—at that time a very small number. In number 81 of *The Federalist*, Alexander Hamilton predicted that Supreme Court judges would be "selected for their knowledge of the laws, acquired by long and laborious study." . . .

. . . [T]he process of judicial selection came to reflect the political standards and balances of each generation. The process was an "open" one, which was vulnerable at a number of points to a variety of individuals and groups, each of which would strive to have its "own" standards accepted by the appointing agents. The impact of the selection process on the socialization and recruitment of judges was necessarily dynamic. The selection process became an effective conduit of forces seeking to reshape the institutionalized judicial role, and through it, the style, scope, and substance of judicial decisions. . . .

The President, the Attorney General, and the Senate. The constitutional responsibility for selecting justices of the Supreme Court, "by and with the advice and consent of the senate," rests with the president. Inferior federal court judges need not be chosen in this manner. Congress could vest selection of lower court judges in the "Head of a Department"—presumably the Chief Justice or even the entire Supreme Court. But, traditionally, the power to appoint lower-court judges has also rested with the President.

In the exercise of this function, the president could depend on the advice of any person or group. He could—as some have suggested he should—create an independent commission of lawyers and laymen to suggest names; he could delegate the recruitment work to any of his White House staff, or to any cabinet or other officer of the government. . . .

The attorney general theoretically recommends to the president, in a formal letter, that "John Doe be appointed to the United States District Court for the Eastern District of Wisconsin," and the president decides whether or not to accept that recommendation and make the nomination. But in practice the attorney general's letter is a formality. In most cases the choice of a federal judge is the attorney general's to make—provided only that he makes it within the framework of the relevant norms of behavior which operate on the selection process. No president could devote the time needed to personally consider even all *serious* candidates for each vacancy, although presidents do vary in the degree of interest they show in judicial-selection problems. Generally, presidents will control Supreme Court nominations and exhibit some interest in a few of the more important lower-court vacancies.

Depending on his own personal interests, the attorney general may or may not play an active role himself in the judicial-selection process. Traditionally, the deputy attorney general and *his* staff have handled the recruitment chores, and it is they who establish the foundation of information and recommendations, on which the eventual choice is based. The decisions they make, at early stages of the process, in determining which names will be given further consideration and which will be dropped from contention limit the alternatives which the attorney general has in making his formal recommendations to the president. With the exception of those few nominations that are likely to become major public issues, recruiting judges is essentially a staff operation in the name of the attorney general—and ultimately in the name of the president.

In addition to the obvious limitations that a staff operation places on the president's prerogatives, his choices are even more circumscribed by the traditional assertion of senatorial prerogative. In fact, the role of the president in the selection of federal judges is a substantial modification of the plain words of the Constitution. Those of the framers who favored a strong role for the executive in the selection of all public officials appeared to have won their point in the Constitutional Convention. Alexander Hamilton interpreted the Constitution on that point as follows.

. . .It will be the office of the President to NOMINATE, and with the advice and consent of the SENATE to APPOINT. There will, of course, be no exertion of choice on the part of the Senate. They may defeat one choice of the Executive and oblige him to make another; but they cannot themselves CHOOSE– they can only ratify or reject the choice of the President. They might even entertain a preference to some other person at the very moment they were assenting to the one proposed, because there might be no positive ground of opposition to him; and they could not be sure, if they withheld their assent, that the subsequent nomination would fall upon their favorite, or upon any other person in their estimation more meritorious than the one rejected.

. . . [T]he power given to the Senate was intended as a safeguard against bad appointments and a salutary influence on the president—a test of the *fitness* of judicial nominees rather than a significant limitation on executive choice. But in delegating to the Senate the power to advise and consent, the framers opened the door to a perversion of the principle of executive responsibility.

The extent of this senatorial limitation on executive choice has varied with particular administrations. Few presidents in the twentieth century have accorded senators as much leeway as did President Harding, who stated that "he would look to the Republican . . . Senators from the state to give final judgment as to the wisdom of the appointment." If, according to Harding, the senators were to recommend men "who prove to be unworthy or lack the ability to perform the duties of the offices to which they are appointed, the president will place upon them the responsibility for whatever trouble arises through this means." But on the other hand, no president has found it possible—or perhaps even desirable—to ignore the advice of individual senators. . . .

Of the three levels of federal courts, the president's latitude for choice is greatest with regard to nominations to the Supreme Court. . . . With rare exceptions presidents have considered Supreme Court appointments to be their personal prerogative, and senators of the same party as the president have always considered district court appointments to fall within *their* sphere of responsibility. Nominations to the Courts of Appeals and nonconstitutional courts appear to "go either way," depending on the case at hand. The choice more often than not is the president's, but senatorial opposition and prerogative cannot be discounted. Occasionally, the president will circumvent certain opposition and invocation of senatorial courtesy by promoting a controversial district court judge to the Court of Appeals for the District of Columbia. Where there is no senator of the president's party in a particular state, the president may rely on the state party officials to suggest prospective candidates for a judicial vacancy. Although no state party official can exercise the pressure in behalf of a candidate that a senator could, the president usually relies on those who are "close" to the local situation.

Who is Appointed? The reasons why presidents have chosen particular men for the Supreme Court vary. Ideology has often played an important role in determining the nominee, but often other factors appear to have been just as decisive. Political rewards, personal friendships, party service, and even prior judicial experience have been the major justifications for Supreme Court appointments.

Presidents have made most of their Supreme Court selections from among the members of their own political party; at last count, 91 of 101

justices were of the same party as the President who appointed them. But it is also customary to have at least one member of each major political party on the high bench, and to satisfy this "requirement" Presidents have, at least occasionally, chosen "out-party" judges [see Table I].

The principles of religious and geographic balance have also been influential, although no president has considered himself absolutely bound by them. President Truman replaced Catholic Frank Murphy with a non-Catholic in 1949, the first time since 1898 that the Court had no Catholic justice. President Eisenhower's appointment of William Brennan in 1956 brought another Catholic member to the Court. The "Jewish" seat, which began with the appointment of Louis Brandeis in 1916, was never vacant until the resignation of Abe Fortas in 1969. In fact, President Hoover's appointment of Benjamin Cardozo in 1930 to replace Oliver Wendell Holmes temporarily doubled the "Jewish representation" on the Court.

Thurgood Marshall, chosen by Lyndon Johnson in 1967, was the first black to be appointed to the Court. It would be politically difficult for a president in the immediate future to replace Marshall with a Caucasian. Gender is the dominant issue of representation today. No

Table I. Supreme Court Appointments by Political Party, 1933–1976

President	Democrat	Republican	Percent Own Party
Roosevelt (Dem.)	8	1	88.9
Truman (Dem.)	3	1	75.0
Eisenhower (Rep.)	1	4	80.0
Kennedy (Dem.)	2	0	100.0
Johnson (Dem.)	2	0	100.0
Nixon (Rep.)	1	3	75.0
Ford (Rep.)	0	1	100.0

woman has ever been nominated to the Supreme Court, a tradition likely to be broken soon.

Ideology appears to have been a frequently important factor. For example, Grant's two appointments in 1871 were made on the basis of the known views of the appointees on the legal-tender issue then before the Court. All of Franklin Roosevelt's Supreme Court appointees were New Deal supporters. On the other hand, ideology has appeared to be a minor factor in other instances, such as Eisenhower's appointment of Brennan, Wilson's appointment of McReynolds, and Hoover's selection of Cardozo.

Supreme Court "politics" can also be important. In at least one instance in the twentieth century, the selection of a Chief Justice (Vinson) was apparently determined in part by an internal situation on the Court—the feud between Justices Black and Jackson. Vinson, a close personal friend of President Truman and a former Appeals Court judge, was chosen in part for his ability to bring together the warring justices whose battle had brought the Supreme Court into considerable disrepute.

A president's choice for the Court may also reflect political needs of a different order. President Nixon's 1968 campaign promised more conservative appointees to reverse the liberal trend of the Warren Court. In addition, the vicissitudes of electoral politics forced Mr. Nixon to adopt and maintain a "southern strategy" to attract votes from supporters of George Wallace, the third-party candidate. Part of this strategy consisted of the promise to appoint a southern conservative to the Court.

President Nixon's first Supreme Court appointment, Warren Burger as Chief Justice, was responsive to the first promise. His nomination of Clement Haynsworth, and then G. Harrold Carswell to fill the vacancy occasioned by the resignation of Abe Fortas was an attempt to fulfill the second promise. Both the Haynsworth and Carswell nominations were defeated by the Senate, and Nixon appointed a northern conservative to the Court, Harry Blackmun. To replace retiring Justices Black and Harlan, Nixon in 1971 appointed William Rehnquist and Lewis Powell, the latter a southerner and both conservatives.

Presidential nominees to the Supreme Court are chosen for "representational" reasons and for policy or "doctrinal" reasons.[1] But presidents also seek to appoint qualified individuals. What makes a person qualified for the Supreme Court? Clearly, there is no litmus test, no objective criterion. But an exceptional academic record, a broad range of legal and political experience, appropriate judicial temperament, and perhaps some prior judicial experience are relevant. A person may be qualified by reason of intellectual performance and experience but "unqualified" because of defects of personality or character. Presidents have recognized that, on the whole, good appointments are also good politics. And those who wish to be "represented" on the Supreme Court have no desire to be identified with an incompetent. Supreme Court nominations do not always go to the best scholars or the brightest minds. But certainly in recent years, with perhaps one exception, they have

[1]The terms are used by David Rohde and Harold Spaeth, *Supreme Court Decision-Making* (San Francisco: Freeman, 1975) Ch. 5.

gone to men clearly qualified to hold that office.[2]

The Consent of the Senate. Individual senators are free to suggest nominees to the president for his consideration, but the Senate as a whole does not "advise" the president on Supreme Court nominations. Until very recently, it had become the normal expectation of presidents that Supreme Court nominations would be confirmed by the Senate. Opposition might delay such confirmation or provide some embarrassing moments for the nominee as he testified before the Senate Judiciary Committee. Charges of incompetency, disloyalty and the like might be aired, but in the final analysis the nomination would be confirmed. Only one Supreme Court nomination had been defeated in the twentieth century prior to 1968, that of Judge John Parker in 1930.

In 1968, President Johnson announced his nomination of Justice Abe Fortas to succeed Earl Warren as Chief Justice. Initially motivated by partisan opposition and visions of a Republican victory in the 1968 presidential election, some Republican senators announced their opposition to Fortas. Charges that Fortas had improperly acted as an advisor to the president, allegations of unethical behavior, and President Johnson's decision not to run for reelection contributed to the impasse that developed. When Senate action became unlikely, Fortas asked that his nomination be withdrawn. Chief Justice Warren, whose resignation had been contingent on approval of a successor, agreed to serve an additional year. Further investigation of Fortas soon uncovered more serious evidence of impropriety, and he resigned under fire in the spring of 1969.

President Nixon's nomination of Warren Burger to replace Earl Warren as chief justice was easily confirmed. But his nominations, first of Judge Clement Haynsworth, and then of Judge G. Harrold Carswell, to replace Fortas, were defeated in the Senate—only the tenth and eleventh nominees formally rejected by the Senate in the history of the Supreme Court.

These events make it necessary to take a fresh look at the Senate's role in the selection of Supreme Court justices. President Nixon attempted to salvage the Carswell nomination by an eleventh-hour assertion of presidential prerogative. In a letter to Senator William Saxbe of Ohio, obviously meant for public consumption, Nixon wrote:

What is centrally at issue in this nomination is the constitutional responsibility of the President to appoint members of the Court—and whether this responsibility can be frustrated by those who wish to substitute their own philosophy or their own judgment for that of the one person entrusted by the Constitution with the power of appointment. The question arises whether I, as President of the United States, shall be accorded the same right of choice in naming Supreme Court Justices which has been freely accorded to my predecessors of both parties.

If the Senate attempts to substitute

---

[2]President Nixon's nomination of Judge C. Harrold Carswell was widely criticized on the grounds that Carswell was incompetent as a lawyer and as a judge. The allegations were persuasive and were given added currency when Senator Hruska of Nebraska defended the nomination on the ground that mediocrity also needed representation on the Supreme Court. For a full account, see Joel B. Grossman and Stephen L. Wasby, "The Senate and Supreme Court Nominations: Some Reflections," 1972 *Duke Law Journal*, pp. 557–591.

its judgment as to whom should be appointed, the traditional constitutional balance is in jeopardy and the duty of the President under the Constitution impaired.

The Senate's response to this theory was clear enough in the case at hand—Carswell was defeated with votes to spare. It seems equally unlikely that in the future the Senate will acquiesce in this very restricted view of its constitutional function. On the other hand, it also seems unlikely that many Supreme Court nominations will fail of Senate confirmation. Senatorial deference to presidential prerogative will continue as long as this deference is not mistaken for total abdication. President Nixon was quite correct in asserting that the Senate was circumscribing his freedom of choice, but he was wrong in claiming that that freedom of choice was his constitutional right. The president has the exclusive power to "nominate" Supreme Court justices, but the right of "appointment" is shared with the Senate.

In light of the controversy over the Fortas and Haynsworth nominations, involving questions of judicial ethics, the Senate may investigate the past financial affairs of prospective justices more seriously. But there seems little prospect of the Senate as a whole playing a more significant role than determining that a presidential nominee is "qualified" for judicial office.

Most members of the Senate concede to the president the right to nominate an individual who shares his political views, provided that nominee appears otherwise qualified. Parker and Haynsworth were clearly "qualified" by intellect and experience. Haynsworth was defeated partly because of conflict of interest charges. Widely believed allegations of incompetence against Carswell contributed to his defeat. But all three men had records with a taint of racism, and it would appear that nominees with such views must, at present, overcome a special burden before confirmation is assured. Carswell had made a racist speech in his youth; as a lawyer he had helped to convert a public club to a private one to avoid integration. Haynsworth, as a court of appeals judge, did not enthusiastically enforce the Supreme Court's decision in *Brown v. Board of Education* (1954), although he did not denounce it or openly defy its mandate.[3]

Apart from allegations of racism, and in Parker's case, allegations of hostility toward organized labor, no Supreme Court nominee in the twentieth century has been defeated because of his policy views. Rohde and Spaeth found a correlation between liberalism and conservatism and Senate voting on Supreme Court nominations. However, in most contested cases such decisions are controlled by moderates, who tend to emphasize non-policy-related qualifications.[4] Thus, Senator Proxmire, a liberal Democrat, announced that he would support President Nixon's nomination of William Rehnquist. Proxmire argued that the Senate should confirm a Supreme Court

---

[3]*Ibid.* See also Joel B. Grossman and Stephen L. Wasby, "Haynsworth and Parker: History Does Live Again," **23** *South Carolina Law Review* (1971), 345–359; and Henry Abraham, *Justices and Presidents* (New York: Oxford University Press, 1974).

[4]Rohde and Spaeth, *op. cit.*, Note 1, pp. 103–106, 111–113; but for a slightly different view, see Donald Songer, "The Relevance of Policy Values for the Confirmation of Supreme Court Nominees," **13** *Law and Society Review* (1979), 927–948.

nominee of obvious intellectual ability without consideration of any substantive views that he might hold.
The one exception, Proxmire stated,
would be a showing that the nominee
did not understand or would not support the Bill of Rights and other constitutional protections.[5]

Interest Groups. The federal judicial selection process has long been
marked by extensive interest group
activity. A group may suggest candidates of its own, although this is usually done discreetly to prevent too
close an identification between the
group and its candidate. Interest
groups are more likely to work to prevent selection of candidates unsympathetic to the group's ideology. The
opposition of a particular group, or
set of interests, depends on many factors: the occupant of the White
House, the existing composition of
the Court, prior commitments made
by the president, and the group's own
political needs. Groups that have traditionally aligned with the opposition
party will have less influence than
those supporting the incumbent president. Democratic presidents are unlikely to be seriously concerned with
the views of the Chamber of Commerce, and Republican presidents
will not be much persuaded by the
AFL-CIO or the American Civil
Liberties Union. On the other hand,
interest groups opposed to a nominee
of the president may fight against
Senate confirmation, and occasionally they will prevail. Coalitions of
labor and liberal groups were responsible for organizing opposition to and
mobilizing Senate votes against the
three Supreme Court nominees not
confirmed in the twentieth century—Parker, Haynsworth, and
Carswell.

The organized bar has always had
a special interest in the selection of
judges. Since 1946, its Committee on
Federal Judiciary has evaluated
nominees for the lower federal
courts, and since 1956 it has also
provided the president and the Senate with an evaluation of the qualifications of Supreme Court nominees.
The ABA Committee has had considerably less influence on the nomination of Supreme Court justices than
on the nominations of lower-court
judges. President Nixon was the first
president to agree to forego a prospective Supreme Court nomination not
approved in advance by the ABA
Committee. His nomination of
Carswell in 1970 produced only an
unenthusiastic rating of "Qualified."
In 1971, the ABA Committee reported unfavorably on Herschel Friday, an Arkansas lawyer, and
Mildred Lillie, a California state
judge, whose names had been submitted for evaluation and who reportedly were Nixon's top choices to succeed Justices Black and Harlan.
President Nixon then nominated William Rehnquist and Lewis Powell;
Rehnquist was Deputy Attorney General and Powell, a Virginia lawyer,
was a former president of the American Bar Association.

Word of the ABA Committee's
negative evaluation of Friday and Lillie leaked to the press, and an angry
attorney general, John Mitchell, terminated the committee's special relationship to the attorney general's office. That relationship was restored
by Attorney General Edward Levi in
1975, and the committee did evaluate
a number of prospective nominees to
fill the vacancy caused by the retirement of Justice Douglas. Candidates
for nomination to the Supreme Court
are now rated as "Not qualified,"

[5]Quoted in Grossman and Wasby, *op. cit.*, Note 2, p. 562, n. 16.

"Not Opposed," and "Meets high standards of professional competence, judicial temperament and integrity."

The Success of Presidential Predictions. With a few exceptions, presidents tend to nominate to the Supreme Court persons who share their views about some issues of particular importance. President Nixon was more vocal than most presidents in announcing that he was seeking individuals who were "strict constructionists" and who shared his conservative opposition to Warren Court decisions liberalizing the rights of criminal defendants. The record, on the whole, suggests that Nixon's four appointees have vindicated his confidence in them. The Nixon "bloc" has voted together cohesively on most decisions involving criminal procedure.[6] On the other hand, "Nixon's justices" voted against him in several key cases. One was *United States* v. *United States District Court* (1972), which rejected the administration's claim to broad, warrantless authority to conduct electronic surveillance in national security cases. And—the cruelest of ironies—three of the four justices were part of an 8-0 majority that dealt a fatal blow to the Nixon presidency by requiring release of the disputed Watergate tapes, *United States* v. *Nixon* (1974).

Efforts to measure the "success" of presidential appointments to the Supreme Court are difficult at best. Presidents do not always articulate what it is they have in mind in making a particular nomination. They may seek specific policy goals, as Nixon certainly did, or they may simply seek an individual with a general predisposition toward conservatism or liberalism. Sometimes, presidents will make appointments *despite* the known political views of the nominee; such was the case with Hoover's nomination of Cardozo in 1930, and with Eisenhower's selection of Brennan in 1956. Or a president may have unrelated goals, as Wilson reputedly did in 1914 in wanting to remove McReynolds from his Cabinet. Such data as there are suggest that, within broad limits, most Supreme Court justices have voted in approximate congruence with the policy views of the appointing president.[7]

(2) Francis Biddle, An Inside View of Appointing Supreme Court Justices

. . . F.D.R. took his time about appointing judges, and never considered there was any particular hurry about filling a vacancy. While I was in office there was only one on the Supreme Court, caused by the resignation of Justice James Francis Byrnes on October 3, 1942, to become director of Economic Stabilization. For ten months Byrnes had been on leave of absence from the Court, working with the President in the war effort.

Several times I suggested to F.D.R. that the Court was shorthanded, that Byrnes ought to resign and the President should appoint a successor; but he waved me aside impatiently, saying let's keep it open for Jimmy, they can get along. But when the 1943 term opened there were several mildly critical editorials. For nearly

[6]Rohde and Spaeth, *op. cit.,* Note 1, pp. 107–110.
[7]*Ibid.* See also Robert Scigliano, *The Supreme Court and the Presidency* (New York: Free Press, 1971), Ch. 5.
Reprinted from *In Brief Authority* (Garden City: Doubleday, 1962), pp. 192–195.

two years the Court had felt the burden of the extra work, a load that is always great and at times, when each member is not pulling his full weight, may become intolerable. Chief Justice Stone asked me if I would speak to the President, and I took it up with him again, urging him to make the appointment as soon as he could find the right man. He nodded an unwilling assent, he supposed I was right, he would think it over.

Eventually I convinced him that we could not keep the position open for Jimmy Byrnes any longer. Well then, could we not appoint some old boy for two or three years who would agree to retire when he had reached seventy, so that Jimmy could be brought back? I replied that this would not quite fit in with his often avowed intention to put younger men on the high tribunal. I suppose not, he acquiesced without enthusiasm. I suggested that I might talk to Chief Justice Stone again, and he assented. "See if you can't get me a nice, solid Republican," he said as I left, "to balance things a bit, preferably west of the Mississippi, and not a professor."

When I saw Stone early in November, he said at once that he wanted someone who would "stick"—he had in mind, of course, Byrnes' being taken off for the needs of the war. He wanted a man of broad legal training and experience—a judge from one of the Circuit Courts would fit in admirably. I said I thought the Circuits had little material of first-rate caliber. "Nonsense, Biddle!" he replied, and pulled out a volume of the reports containing a list of the judges. This he read carefully, then looked up. "By gum," he said, "you're about right."

But there were a few: Learned Hand, head and shoulders above all the others; John Parker, Samuel Bratton, who had been on the Tenth Circuit since 1933, a good Democrat, he had been Senator from New Mexico; Orie Phillips, if you want a Republican, also from the Tenth; and there was Wiley Rutledge, who had been on the Court of Appeals for the District of Columbia for four years, after teaching law for fifteen— Rutledge was a good man and young, a little pedestrian but sound. And Charley Fahy? I asked him. He considered, his chin in his hand. They had all liked the way Fahy presented his cases—he was objective, clear, scrupulous. But if we put another Catholic on the Court, he suggested, the Church might feel it was always regularly entitled to two. I mentioned Dean Acheson, but it was clear that Stone preferred one of the federal judges.

Outside of Hand, who was far more distinguished than any of the others, Rutledge seemed to me the most promising, and I had Herbert Wechsler make an analysis of his opinions on the Circuit Court. His views were sound, carefully reasoned, and lawyer-like. He was long-winded, suffering from a sense of obligation to answer everything in the case. He was a liberal who would stand up for human rights, particularly during a war when they were apt to be forgotten. But there was nothing extreme or Messianic about his approach. He was certainly not a nice solid Republican.

All of which I reported to the President. Where did Rutledge come from, he asked me. He was born in Kentucky, taught high school in Indiana, New Mexico, and Colorado and law in Colorado and St. Louis. "He'll do," said the President, and then, "what do you think about Hand?" I repeated what the Chief Justice had said— head and shoulders above the others. F.D.R. told me that he had had a great many letters from men whose opinion he valued, saying he must appoint Hand. He thought well of Fahy. If Frank Murphy could be offered a job connected with the Army, the President said, that he considered important enough he would resign, and Fahy would be the obvious man. He would like to think it over a little more. I mentioned Benjamin Cohen, whose judgment I admired, but the President said that Ben, who was assistant to Byrnes in the Office of Economic Stabilization, could not be spared.

When I saw him again he was much cooler when I spoke of Hand; and I heard later that he resented what he called the "organized pressure" in Hand's behalf. The President told me that he had determined to appoint Rutledge, and that I should get the papers ready and send them to Grace Tully. But before he made the announcement he wanted to have a talk with Rutledge, after I had seen him.

Rutledge was a modest man and he was amazed when I told him—he really believed he was not up to it. Ten years later, when a chance ocean-crossing brought Hand and me together in intimacy, I learned to admire his really first-rate qualities of heart and mind, and came to believe that his appointment would have been more suitable, and that I should have urged the President to appoint him in spite of his age. He had the "fire in his belly" that old Holmes used to talk about.

During the discussions and speculation about Byrnes' successor, it was natural that I should have been mentioned. My two predecessors had gone from Attorney General to the Court, and a pattern of precedent seemed to have been established. I was determined, however, not to accept the appointment even if the President

wished me to do so. My brief experience on the Circuit bench had not been satisfactory, and I did not wish to renew the mild level of judicial life on which I had felt cut off from the world and out of things. The members of the Court in Washington seemed to me terribly overworked. I loved arguing cases as Solicitor General; but that was different—I was doing the arguing, not listening to it.

(3) A Note on the Backgrounds of Supreme Court Justices

Studies of the backgrounds of Supreme Court justices leave little room for the myth that any young man can make it to the Court if he is sufficiently bright, dedicated, and ambitious. A recent study of the backgrounds of the first 91 justices (there have been ten additional appointments since then)[1] showed that few came from humble origins; and about 90 percent came from middle- or upper-class families, many socially rated. More than half came from politically active families; indeed several were related to previous justices of the Supreme Court. All but one had prior political experience, and more than half were occupationally involved in politics.

The study also reported that few of the justices were foreign born (compared to a much larger percentage of foreign-born members of Congress), and of the six who were, three from the British Isles were appointed by George Washington. In modern times only two justices were not born in America; George Sutherland was born in England and Felix Frankfurter in Austria. Ethnically, Supreme Court justices have predominantly British or Irish origins (87 percent). The remainder of the justices in the

[1]John R. Schmidhauser, "The Justices of the Supreme Court: A Collective Portrait," 3 *Midwest Journal of Political Science* (1959), 1–49.

study traced their origins to Europe, most from northern Europe and a few from the Germanic countries. None were from Eastern European, Italian or the Slavic backgrounds and none from Africa or Asia. Thurgood Marshall in 1966 was the first of African descent.

Religious affiliations were overwhelmingly Protestant, and a substantial portion of these were from the higher status Protestant denominations—Episcopalian, Presbyterian, Congregational, and Unitarian. Less than 10 percent were Catholic, Jewish, or Quaker. Since 1957 there have been two additional Jewish appointments raising to five the total of that faith. In terms of their relationship to the population as a whole, Jewish "representation" on the Court has been about average and Catholic representation has been low.

All Supreme Court justices have been lawyers and most have practiced law. A few, many appointed by Franklin Roosevelt, were law school professors. Less than a third had prior judicial experience on a state or federal bench. All recent Supreme Court appointees have not only graduated from law school (the last justice who, in the older tradition, "read law" in preparation for his bar examinations was Charles Whittaker) but most have graduated from high status, "nationally oriented" law schools, including quite a few from Ivy League schools.[2]

"The picture that emerges," according to Schmidhauser, "is one which emphasizes the intimacy of judicial and political affairs." Few men have been appointed who have not had substantial political experience. For many this has meant running for—and occasionally winning—partisan political office. For others it has been involvement in party politics and/or the holding of appointive administrative positions.

One cannot understand the workings of the Supreme Court merely by a knowledge of the sorts of men who have comprised it. But recruitment patterns form an important base on which attempts to understand the decision making of the Court must build. Schmidhauser concluded his study as follows:

It is not at all clear that the social and political background factors in themselves may serve as reliable indicators of precise patterns of judicial behavior. Explanations based entirely upon the causal influence of such factors as family, economic and social status, ethnic background or religious affiliation could scarcely take into account such important considerations as the impact upon individual justices of the traditions of the Supreme Court itself, or that interaction of intelligent and frequently forceful personalities which has been an integral part of the internal procedure of the Court. Complete dependence upon background factors would also ignore the complexity and subtlety of intellect and motivation which is part of the collective picture of the ninety-one individuals who sat on the high bench.[3]

(4) Martin Tolchin, Politics and Judicial Selection in the Carter Administration: Old Wine in New Bottles?

[In response to heightening criticism of the recruitment process and the composition of the

---

[2]Chief Justice Burger, departing from this pattern, received his law degree from a proprietary school, the St. Paul College of Law.

[3]Schmidhauser, *op. cit.*, Note 1., p. 48.

Reprinted from Martin Tolchin, "Wide Search Is On for U.S. Judges, with Politics Still a Major Factor," *The New York Times* (April 22, 1979), pp. 1, 34.

federal judiciary, presidential candidate Jimmy Carter promised to broaden representation of minorities and women by implementing a merit selection process for federal judges. Once elected, his efforts to fulfill this promise were articulated in his Executive Orders of February 1977 and November 1978, which established a Circuit Judge Nominating Commission to replace vacancies in the United States Court of Appeals. The Executive Order calls for a nominating commission of thirteen panels, each consisting of no more than eleven members, appointed by the president for the purpose of screening and recommending candidates to the president. In contrast to most state merit selection plans, the Carter plan does not provide for a six-year staggered term for commissioners. Instead, the nominating panels are appointed and convene on an ad hoc basis as vacancies occur. The purpose of a staggered six-year term, according to judicial reform organizations such as the American Judicature Society, is to prevent executive control over the commission by limiting the number of appointments any one executive could make during his or her term of office.

Congress' creation of 152 new federal judgeships in 1978, the largest increase in the size of the federal judiciary in its history, has raised controversy over the selection process at the district court level as well. With only 27 blacks and 13 women (two of the women are black) currently serving among approximately 500 federal judges, proponents of merit selection have argued that representation of minorities and women will increase under their plan. Senators in twenty-four states have established merit commissions to recommend names for federal district judgeships. However, Attorney General Griffin Bell reported to the Senate Judiciary Committee that these commissions are as likely as individual senators, exercising patronage prerogatives under the unwritten custom of senatorial courtesy, to recommend only white males for judgeships. Ironically, the two most vocal senators who refuse to give up their patronage prerogatives have recommended nearly half of all the minorities and women recommended for district judgeships by all senators and merit selection commissions.]

A senator from North Carolina has recommended his former campaign manager for a Federal judgeship. A Texas senator has recommended a prominent supporter of his ill-fated 1976 Presidential campaign. A Georgia Senator has recommended the son-in-law of a key political supporter. And a Montana senator has recommended a former colleague who was defeated in last fall's primary. Such recommendations follow traditional patterns.

But at the same time, the Texas senator has also recommended a Mexican-American and two women, one of whom would be the first black to serve on the Federal bench in the state; a Massachusetts Senator has recommended a black man and a white woman, and in Georgia, Pennsylvania and Michigan, women have been endorsed for Court of Appeals judgeships.

In such diverse ways are Democratic senators and judicial selection commissions—swayed by pleas to include women and members of minority groups but still strongly influenced by traditional political considerations—beginning to fill the 152 new Federal judgeships created last year, the largest influx of new judges in the history of the Federal judiciary.

"It's a very mixed bag," said Attorney General Griffin B. Bell, referring to recommendations submitted for the new judgeships.

Duties of the Judges

Federal district judges try cases that involve the violation of Federal criminal statutes. They also preside over a wide array of civil cases, including immigration, tax, civil rights and patent matters. Judges on the 11 appellate circuits hear appeals from the district courts; they do not preside over trials.

Since these judgeships are lifetime posts, President Carter has the opportunity to alter the face of the judiciary.

Mr. Bell's deadline of April 1 for filling 80 percent of those judgeships passed with little more than a handful confirmed. Of 35 new appeals court judgeships, only one appointment has been confirmed and four more have been nominated. Of 117 new district court judgeships, only six have been confirmed and 18 more have been nominated.

"We're making slow but important progress," said Edward M. Kennedy, Democrat of Massachusetts, chairman of the Senate Judiciary Committee, which has hired a longtime investigator, Carmine Bellino, to scrutinize the nominees.

Despite statements from both the White House and Congress concerning merit selection and the need to remove judgeships from politics, Federal judgeships continue to be used as political patronage—to reward campaign supporters, mend fences, cement political organizations and create future I.O.U.'s.

Key to Arms Treaty

Some senior White House aides say frankly, but privately, that they expect the new judgeships to help President Carter in his fight for Senate approval of a treaty on limiting strategic arms. "It certainly won't hurt," said a senior aide.

Hamilton Jordan, the President's principal political adviser, had the final voice on the makeup of the President's judicial selection panels, approving and changing lists of names submitted by Mr. Bell. Those commissions include such politically connected persons as the Mayor of Detroit, the president of the United Automobile Workers, several former Congressmen and the counsel to the Mayor of Chicago.

Together with Mr. Bell, Mr. Jordan also has a say in the judicial nominations made by the President.

But along with traditional politics, the White House is trying to use the new judgeships to break the sex and color barriers on the Federal bench. The effort has been strongly criticized as inadequate by groups representing women and blacks.

When President Carter took office, only one woman and one black were among the 97 appeals court judges, and there were only 16 blacks, five women and five Hispanic-Americans out of 399 district court judges.

Few Acceptable Candidates

Mr. Bell insists that there are not many minority members and women to choose from because they make up only a small percentage of the total number of lawyers. Moreover, a great number of white female lawyers have been in practice less than eight years, so they are not regarded as qualified for the bench, he said.

The search for qualified women and minority members and the effort to persuade senators and judicial selection commissions to select them are among the reasons cited by Mr. Bell for the delay in filling the judgeships. He said that he had negotiated with several commissions that failed to name a nonwhite or a woman among the five candidates recommended for each judgeship.

Mr. Bell also said that some of the judicial selection commissions had overstepped what he considered to be the bounds of their authority and questioned candidates about political philosophy.

The sole person to be confirmed for one of the new appeals court judgeships is a woman, and so are two of the four remaining nominees. One of those nominees, Cornelia Kennedy, a Federal district judge in Michigan, is regarded with suspicion by some organizations representing women and blacks because of her "staunch conservative positions on civil rights and the rights of criminal defendants," Representative John Conyers Jr., Democrat of Michigan, recently told the House.

District Court Posts

Of the six newly confirmed district court judges, two are black men and one is a white woman. The 18 remaining nominess include three women, of whom one is black, and a Mexican-American.

"The process of selecting Federal judges is a disaster for women," said Mildred Jeffrey, chairman of the National Women's Political Caucus. "At every stage of the selection process we have found well-qualified women excluded or overlooked. The President must take charge immediately to get more women on the bench."

"The system isn't working," said Brent E. Simmons, a staff attorney with the NAACP Legal Defense and Educational Fund Inc. who specializes in judicial selection. "Minorities are not being nominated anywhere near representative figures. We're simply not getting anywhere near what we need."

Of 13 appeals court judicial selection panels appointed by the White House, five recommended neither women nor blacks. Of district court recommendations received from senators or selection panels in 25 states, 13 recommended neither women nor blacks. The Justice Department does not consider those recommendations final, however.

. . .

President Carter, who in his cam-

paign urged merit selection of all Federal judges and prosecutors, obtained control over the selection of appeals court judges. In an arrangement with former Senator James O. Eastland, then chairman of the Senate Judiciary Committee, the senators of the President's party retained control over district court judges and United States Attorneys.

Mr. Carter urged the senators to follow his lead and appoint judicial selection panels, but senators from only 24 states have thus far done so.

Senator Lloyd Bentsen, Democrat of Texas, was among those who spurned the President's suggestion.

"The responsibility is mine under the Constitution," Senator Bentsen said. "There's no accountability for judicial selection committees, but I have to face the electorate."

The Senator has been widely praised, however, for recommendations that included a Mexican-American and two women, including one who would be the first black to serve on the Federal bench in the state. Senator Bentsen also recommended a Federal judgeship for Harold Barefoot Sanders, a Texas politician who was nominated for a judgeship by President Johnson but whose nomination was withdrawn by President Nixon. Mr. Sanders ran on the Bentsen slate in the 1976 Presidential primary and has been a political supporter of the Senator. "He is eminently qualified," Mr. Bentsen said of Mr. Sanders.

Senator Harry F. Byrd Jr., a Virginia independent, established a judicial selection commission that recommended only white males for four district judgeships, to the consternation of President Carter and Attorney General Bell. Mr. Bell has been negotiating with Mr. Byrd for inclusion of a black or a woman.

Mr. Bell has frequently noted that

some of the nation's most highly regarded judges, including former
Chief Justices Earl Warren and William Howard Taft, had extensive
political connections. Similarly,
senators whose candidates appeared
to have political connections lauded
them for judicial temperament and
qualifications.

. . .

In the long run, the Administration
believes that its efforts will be re-
warded. And Senator Kennedy said,
"I believe that when we get through,
we will have a highly qualified,
highly competent addition to the
courts, and the Federal bench will be
much more representative of our society."

5. JUDICIAL POLICY PREFERENCES

A. *The Causes of Supreme Court Decisions*

What are the causes of judicial decisions? There is no single theory, or
variable, that can explain adequately
why judges vote as they do. One crucial variable in Supreme Court decision making is the individual justice.
A justice's views may flow from
deeply rooted personal values, from
subconscious biases or intuitive
judgments, from personality factors,
from the influence exerted by his
brethren and the need to work and
produce decisions collegially, and
from personal notions of the most appropriate role for the Supreme Court
to play. Yet by focusing on the individual justice as a decision maker,
we are not wholly rejecting institutional or structural factors. Rejection
of the theory of mechanical jurisprudence did not imply that the "law," or
legal factors, were unimportant, only
that they were not exclusive. How a
justice's personal preferences and
values are articulated in a particular
case will depend on the facts of the
case and the state of the law. Is there
a strong precedent to be followed—or
overruled? Is there an appropriate
substitute for the constitutional rule
regarded as inadequate? Is this a
case for "going along" and trying to

influence the majority, or for a public
dissent?

Knowing that all these factors may
be important in explaining judicial
performance is the beginning of
analysis, not the end. Indeed, most of
these factors, and others, have long
been utilized by legal commentators
and biographers attempting to explain the result in a single case or interpreting the life and work of a particular justice. The strength—and
test—of the biographer is his ability to
develop a portrait of a judge that allows the reader to understand his decisions. And from a good biography,
one can usually obtain a fair picture
of the entire Court and the milieu in
which it functioned. But the emphasis is on the judge as an individual. Theories adduced to explain
that judge's behavior may have no
wider application and cannot be re-
plicated. Generalization is thus impossible.

By contrast, the focus of most legal
commentators has been the Court as
an institution, and the development
of legal doctrines punctuated by a
few "great" cases. Judges become
the articulators of particular doctrinal positions, rather than the sub-

jects for analysis. The emphasis is on textual interpretation of decisions and the logic of doctrinal development. This is not unimportant, and many of the essays in the substantive chapters of this book follow such a pattern. However, it tends to emphasize product over process, and it is not particularly concerned with the how and why. A full understanding of the process of Supreme Court decision making therefore requires some systematic understanding of the personal factor.

Rohde and Spaeth have observed that Supreme Court decisions are the result of the interaction of three factors or sets of variables: "goals, rules and situations." By goals, they mean the policy objectives of Supreme Court justices.[1] That justices *do* have policy goals, and that they seek to further these goals in choosing between decisional alternatives, is the basic assumption. This does not mean that justices have developed detailed policy positions on many, or all, public issues. On some issues, they may have, but on most, the term "goals" refers to a set of preferences likely to guide decisional choices. These preferences may be relatively vague in detail, for example, sympathy for the "underdog," or they may be more particularized and issue specific, for example, in favor of due process rights for prisoners such as the right to a hearing before imposition of punishment for infraction of prison rules. They may be intensely held or as weak as mere potential goals, for example, "if given the opportunity, and if there are no excessive costs, then achievement of A might be worthwhile."

Goals may reflect long-standing commitments to a particular set of values, or they may arise in particular cases, tapping long dormant values or recognizing the acquisition of new values. Goals may be associated with policy preferences, but they may also reflect personality needs (recall Ulmer's theory of the dissenting justice, p. 233). Goals may also reflect other kinds of personal needs, such as ambition, affection, popularity, and reputation.

Supreme Court justices do not campaign for office (except perhaps privately), and they rarely speak to the general public. When they do, it would be unthinkable for a justice to articulate a specific set of policy goals, (i.e., a "platform"), although general statements of values couched in terms like equality, justice, and judicial integrity are acceptable. Thus, unlike ordinary politicians who may say what they mean (even if they do not always mean what they say), the policy goals of Supreme Court justices must be derived from their behavior—their votes and their written opinions.

By "rules," Rohde and Spaeth refer to the set of decision-making norms within which the Supreme Court operates. They argue that because justices are not elected and have no political accountability, because normally they have no opportunity or ambition for higher office, and because the Supreme Court is the court of last resort, Supreme Court justices have "greater freedom than other political decision makers to base their decisions solely upon personal policy preferences."[2] We would agree that these three factors support a certain independence in the expression of policy preferences by Supreme Court

---

[1]David Rohde and Harold Spaeth, *Supreme Court Decision Making* (San Francisco: Freeman, 1976), Ch. 4.

[2]*Ibid.*, p. 72.

justices. But by no means do they demonstrate, as Rohde and Spaeth seem to argue, that justices have virtually complete freedom to decide cases according to personal notions of right or wrong. There are *other* constraints on Supreme Court decision makers that preclude a total free play of personal values. One such constraint is the notion of the proper judicial "role," of what is appropriate and what is inappropriate for the Supreme Court to do. Justices may differ in their views of the proper judicial role, but there are some shared norms.

Another set of constraints arises out of the political system. Justices are not elected, nor likely candidates for impeachment, but they are quite aware (though, of course, justices may differ with each other) of how far the Court may go in pursuit of a particular goal before the political backlash becomes too strong. Political "rules" may refer to specific threats or to more abstract considerations, such as those arising out of a belief in federalism or the separation of powers.

"Rules" should also be taken to mean the specific decisional structure and rules within which the Court functions. These rules may be established externally, for example, by Congress, or they may be judicially created traditions. The size of the Court is important, and Congress establishes the number of justices. Jurisdictional rules are important, and Congress sets these as well. On the other hand, the internal procedures by which cases are considered and decided are established by the Court itself (although the "rule of four" in certiorari petitions was an implicit premise of the Judges Bill of 1925) and presumably could be modified by the Court without congres-

sional approval. No one can seriously believe that consideration of certiorari petitions by committee or by the law clerks, or even by some sort of preselection computer process, rather than by the entire Court, would have no effect on policy outcomes.

Rohde and Spaeth do not speak of rules of law in this context, but rules of law (substantive rules), and rules "about" law, are of critical importance in shaping the expression of policy preferences. Substantive rules of law is a self-explanatory concept. Obviously, what the law is, *and how it got that way,* is a predicate for further decision. By "rules about law," we refer to various norms as to how the Supreme Court should interpret the Constitution or statutes. Many of the rules of self-restraint, which we have already considered, are expressed as rules about law; for example, the Constitution should always be construed as internally consistent, wherever possible. There are also rules governing, or guiding, statutory construction and constitutional interpretation. How does one determine the true "meaning" of a particular phrase? Does one rely on its literal meaning, on the intent of its authors, on the common assumption of those who voted in its favor, or on its meaning in contemporary context? None of these rules is absolute, but all play a part.

Supreme Court decisions are also dependent on particular situations. The facts and timing of a case are particularly important. Judges are not free simply to make the policies they prefer. Policy making occurs in the course of adjudication and is limited in that way. The timing of a case may determine whether it is decided and how it is decided. We have already noted several instances where the Supreme Court has refused to decide cases where, it would appear, the consequences would have been particularly unfortunate. "Situations" may also refer to conditions *on* the Supreme Court, relations between the justices, the opinion assignment strategies of the chief justice, and so on.

"Goals, rules and situations" exist in constant dynamic interaction. Thus, an individual justice's policy goals may affect, or be affected by, his perception of appropriate decisional rules—what they are, when they should apply, and their perceived legitimacy. Nevertheless, it is often useful and necessary to treat them as analytically distinct. Modern behavioral research has focused on goals, or policy preferences of the justices, as the dominant variable in explaining Supreme Court decision making. Claims vary, but some studies have asserted that the personal values and attitudes of the justices can account for most of the differences among the justices in specific subsets of cases.

Virtually all of these studies rely heavily on quantitative techniques, which add a significant new dimension to the analysis of judicial behavior. Quantitative techniques provide a means both to generate and to analyze vastly greater amounts of data than would be feasible otherwise. They facilitate comparisons among justices over a much wider range of cases and encourage replication and validation of hypotheses derived from nonquantitative observations. Quantitative analysis of judicial behavior is not a substitute for more traditional approaches but a sophisticated supplement to them.

Quantitative techniques have been used in the exploration of the attitudes and values underlying judicial policy preferences, in relating social background characteristics to decision-making patterns, and in demonstrating the existence of voting blocs on the Supreme Court. Brief glimpses of the uses of such techniques have appeared in earlier parts of the book. In the materials that conclude this chapter, they are described in more detail, both as to process and results. The first selection explores the relationship between social backgrounds and judicial decisions. Tanenhaus' article describes and evaluates the technique of Guttman scaling, the basic approach to analysis of judicial attitudes. Finally, Howard's article, relying not on quantitative data but on research into the private papers of several justices, raises some major questions about the accuracy of interpretations based exclusively on quantitative methods.

B. *Joel B. Grossman, Social Backgrounds and Judicial Decision Making*

Both historically and analytically, attempts to relate social backgrounds to judicial decisions have fallen into three distinct categories. The first, primarily descriptive, involves the systematic collection and organization of a variety of background data. Practically speaking, this means gathering such information about each judge in the sample as age, ethnic and religious affiliations, parental occupations, career patterns,

Reprinted from **79** *Harvard Law Review* (1966), 1553–59, 1562–64, and updated.

prior judicial office, party affiliation, education, and so forth—the number of factors being limited only by the availability of data or the imagination of the researcher.

Studies of this kind date back to the 1930's, but the most recent and influential has been John Schmidhauser's "Collective Portrait" of the Justices of the Supreme Court. . . . In addition to identifying patterns of selections shedding considerable light on the judicial selection process, such . . . [studies] also provide the basis for plausible, though unsystematic, inferences about the sorts of values likely to dominate a court in a particular period. Furthermore, such efforts illuminate one way in which power and status are distributed among various groups and interests in society—what Krislov has called the "representational question."

The second category involves attempts to relate these background characteristics to actual decision patterns, measuring the degree to which a particular characteristic is regularly associated with a particular type of decision. . . . Though these studies differ somewhat in research design and results, all share certain basic theoretical assumptions. First, they all accept the "dynamic" view of the judicial function. . . . Second, they all accept the utility—for research purposes—of abstracting a single item, or variable, from a complex process and treating it in isolation. This leads to what may seem to be a contrary and overly simplistic view of the sources and motivations of judicial behavior—almost akin to mechanical jurisprudence. But all these scholars recognize—to differing degrees and in differing weights—the importance of institutional factors in accounting for particular decisions or groups of decisions. None suggests, except in the abstract, that any par-

ticular background variable "accounts" for certain types of decisions. All reject theories of causality which seem to establish a direct dependent relationship between a background variable and a line of cases. Rather, they argue that evidence of a highly significant statistical relationship between a background variable and a decisional pattern is both relative and associational. For example, though . . . [most] treat political party affiliation as a major independent variable, none suggests that for a judge to have been a Republican or a Democrat automatically results in certain types of decisions. They do suggest that, when placed on a continuum, Democratic judges are more likely to vote in certain ways than Republican judges in certain types of cases. Finally . . . all operate solely with aggregates of judges and cases; they are interested in generalized patterns of association, rather than in discrete individual actions.

These studies also share some methodological techniques. Regardless of the type or level of court being studied, unanimous decisions are eliminated from all samples. While this emphasis on intracourt division certainly introduces an element of bias, particularly since the majority of all cases are decided unanimously, there is no way of including unanimous cases when *comparing* judges. The mere fact that most judges on most courts tend to agree most of the time tells us something about the common process of conditioning and socialization that they undergo and further serves to caution us against placing undue emphasis on the differences among them. But whatever correctives are needed can properly be postponed until we have adequately understood the reasons for patterns of division. In addition, all these authors assume, for purposes of analysis, a simplistic stimulus-response model of judicial behavior; the case is pictured as presenting a clear and uniform stimulus to all judges on a particular court, the judges' votes constitute the primary response, and the background characteristic being tested is the major intervening variable. In fact, of course, all of the judges hearing a particular case may perceive it differently, and their responses may be distillations of complex factors. But techniques of analysis are still too crude to permit the more refined models which would properly account for this complexity. . . .

Those who attempt to explain judicial behavior in terms of the backgrounds of the judges share with historians the problem of never knowing precisely how the past has influenced the present. But even allowing for these failings, background studies have made a contribution by systematically exploring an important dimension of judicial behavior. That early and crude efforts have not yet led to a perfect understanding of such behavior is surely not the measure of these efforts. Such a measure should weigh their contributions against present and potential results to be derived from other methods. A brief catalog of general contributions would include the identification of key background variables and some attempt at explaining their relationship to decisional patterns, the facility for handling quantities of data which extend the basis—in breadth and reliability—of inferences about the judicial process, and the ability to test conclusions and observations of traditional observers. Schmidhauser, for example, was able to demonstrate the shallowness of Rodell's claim that virtually all of Chief Justice Taney's decisions could be "traced, directly or indirectly, to his big-plantation birth

and background." On the other hand, Danelski was able to demonstrate the substantial validity of contemporary observers' predictions that Butler's experience as a railroad lawyer would be clearly reflected in his Supreme Court votes on rate and valuation cases. Danelski did not make the unwarranted generalization that all judges who had been railroad lawyers would have acted the same way as Butler; as Paul Freund has emphasized, the lawyer is not always father to the judge. But an examination of all judges with "railroad" backgrounds might support such a generalization. Inferences and generalizations about the judicial process are all too often made on the basis of a very limited sample—the "great" cases or the work of the "great" judges—which ignore the run-of-the-mill business which constitutes the essence of the judicial process. No theory with any claim to significant explanatory power could afford to rely on such incomplete knowledge.

Efforts to isolate particular background variables as causes of judicial decisions have initially and necessarily overlooked the essentially cumulative and often random nature of human experience. And they have slighted the impact of institutional influences on the judicial mind. That judges are (or were) Republicans or Catholics or corporate lawyers or law professors may tell everything about some judges. More likely it will tell only part of the story. Furthermore, not all judges can be easily classified as "liberal" or "conservative." Some categorization is inherent in all scholarship, but the demands of quantitative analysis in this regard may sometimes seem to be fulfilled at too great a cost.

Finally, methods must be developed which measure judges' intensity of preference and which take into account the vast majority of decisions which are decided unanimously. The latter point is particularly crucial at this stage of research development, since it raises in peculiarly dramatic fashion the question of the actual impact of social backgrounds on judicial behavior.

Nagel's study[1] involved an analysis of the decisional propensities of a sample of the justices of the United States Supreme Court and state courts of last resort—the sample consisting of the 298 judges listed in the 1955 *Directory of American Judges* who were still serving at the close of 1955. Limiting himself to those courts on which there was at least one member of each party, Nagel analyzed all the 1955 cases for each court in fifteen areas of law, determining decisional propensities for each court and decisional scores for each judge. Hypothetically, if the Ames Supreme Court decided 10 of 21 criminal cases for the defendant, and Judge A, a Republican, voted 3 times for the defendant, he would have a decisional score of 3/21 or .14, considerably below the court's mean defendant-support score of .48. If the decisional scores of Republicans on that court were generally in the .14−.40 range, while the scores of Democrats were in the .50−.80 range, Nagel would conclude that there was a strong and possibly significant relationship between party affiliation and propensity to decide for the defendant in criminal cases.

Nagel's findings showed that "in all 15 types of cases the Democratic judges were above the average decision scores of their respective courts (in what might be considered a liberal direction) to a greater extent than the Republican judges." Nagel found that Democratic judges were more prone to favor (1) the defense in criminal cases, (2) administrative agencies in business regulation cases, (3) the private party in cases involving regulation of nonbusiness entities, (4) the claimant in unemployment compensation cases, (5) the libertarian position in free speech cases, (6) the finding of a constitutional violation in criminal cases, (7) the government in tax cases, (8) the divorce seeker in divorce cases, (9) the wife in divorce settlement cases, (10) the tenant in landlord-tenant disputes, (11) the labor union in union-management cases, (12) the debtor in debt collection cases, (13) the consumer in sales of goods cases, (14) the injured party in motor vehicle accident cases, and (15) the employee in employee injury cases. Nine of these findings (1, 2, 4, 6, 7, 10, 13, 14, and 15) proved to be statistically significant relationships.

Nagel concluded that, in these areas of decision, Democratic judges were *more likely than* Republican judges to support the designated liberal position, a result consistent with the findings of Schubert, Ulmer, and Vines, . . . Similar policy differences between Democrats and Republicans have been found to exist among Congressmen and the electorate. Nagel did not suggest a "party-line" theory of judicial decision-making but rather that the same factors which resulted in party identification also resulted in more or less liberal decisions with party affiliation operating as a "feedback reinforcement." In parallel studies, Nagel found that Judges who had been public prosecutors, members of the American Bar Association, or Protestants took the "Republican" position more often and were less likely to support the de-

---

[1] Stuart Nagel, "Political Party Affiliation and Judges' Decisions," **55** *American Political Science Review* (1961), 843−850.

fendant in criminal cases than their brethren, findings which are clearly consistent with existing data on the backgrounds of identifiers with each party.

Schmidhauser's studies focus exclusively on United States Supreme Court Justices. In one study, he examined the relationship of regional background to the decision in 52 major cases involving "sectional rivalry" between 1837 and 1860.[2] Did the Justices "consistently split on regional lines despite other possibly compelling factors such as attitudes toward national supremacy, the integrity of the judicial institution, or the position of their political parties?" Relying primarily on the technique of scalogram analysis, Schmidhauser was able to isolate regional divisions in the voting patterns and hypothesize that (1) among Justices who took extreme positions, party and sectional background both seemed to strengthen underlying attitudes toward regionally divisive issues, and (2) among moderate and neutral judges, party frequently proved stronger than regional background.

In a second study, Schmidhauser sought to test the *a priori* assertion that prior judicial experience was positively related to judicial restraint, particularly to a strong adherence to stare decisis.[3] Focusing on the 81 decisions of the Supreme Court in which a valid precedent had been expressly overruled, he established a "propensity to overrule" score for each Justice participating in one or more of these decisions and then compared these scores with the amount of prior experience each Justice had. The finding was that Justices with experience on lower courts had a greater propensity to abandon stare decisis than did Justices without such experience. While the data did not justify a conclusion of such an inverse relationship, it seemed at least to rebut opposite *a priori* assertions. Schmidhauser also found that Justices who most frequently dissented were those with the lowest propensities to overrule, and he concluded from this and other data that contrary to a common impression, the typical dissenter was not a firebreathing doctrinal innovator, but rather a "tenacious advocate of traditional doctrines which were being abandoned." . . .

Subsequent studies have confirmed that political party is the most important background variable. Goldman's study of Courts of Appeals judges reported some correlation between party and economic liberalism and a lesser correlation with political liberalism. Age and religion were of some minor significance. Goldman concluded that background variables were much weaker than attitudinal variables in their ability to explain judicial voting behavior. He argued that the importance of backgrounds lay more in the shaping of attitudes and values of individual judges than in directly influencing decisions.[4] Scholars will—and should—continue to look to the backgrounds of judges to help explain their decisional pre-

[2]John R. Schmidhauser, "Judicial Behavior and the Sectional Crisis of 1837–1860," **23** *Journal of Politics* (1961), 615–640.

[3]John R. Schmidhauser, "Stare Decisis, Dissent, and the Background of the Justices of the Supreme Court of the United States," **14** *University of Toronto Law Journal* (1962), 194–212.

[4]Sheldon Goldman, "Voting Behavior on the United States Courts of Appeals Revisited," **69** *American Political Science Review* (1975), 491–507; Also see Goldman and Thomas Jahnige, *The Federal Courts as a Political System* (New York: Harper & Row, 1976), pp. 174–178, and the sources cited therein.

ferences. But it does not appear, after more than a decade of quantitative studies, that background variables are especially good indicators of aggregate judicial voting behavior. The breakthrough, if any, will come when more refined data, both as to backgrounds and as to decisions, become available.

C. Joseph Tanenhaus, The Cumulative Scaling of Judicial Decisions

What moves an appellate judge to decide a case as he does? To this time-honored query behavioralists are apt to reply that the judge's structure of social, economic, and political values is perhaps the most important single factor. His value structure leads to judicial attitudes, to predispositions toward deciding given types of cases in particular ways. A judge may, for example, be predisposed to support—or to deny—legal claims by labor unions, criminal defendants, racial minorities, federal regulatory agencies, or state and local authorities. If their assumptions are correct, behavioralists should be able to develop methods to identify the judicial attitudes held by various members of the bench—to explain why individual judges decided particular cases in the past, even in the absence of written opinions, and also to predict how these judges will act in the future.

One of the methods employed by some leading behavioralists to determine the attitudes judges hold and the extent to which these attitudes can account for their decisions is commonly referred to as cumulative scaling. Other terms frequently used to describe this analytical tool are

"scalogram analysis" and "Guttman scaling." In this essay three principal tasks have been set: (1) to explain what cumulative scaling is; (2) to indicate the potential utility of cumulative scaling; and (3) to evaluate major efforts to construct such scales.

What Cumulative Scaling Is. The initial objective in cumulative scaling is to determine whether a set of phenomena such as the votes cast by the members of a court in a group of cases can be arranged in an ordinal relationship. The requirements and implications of this process can be most readily grasped if preliminary attention is directed to three clearly distinguishable scales of measurement: nominal scales, ordinal scales, and interval scales.

(a) Nominal scales.—A nominal scale requires only that objects be assigned to classes with regard to a given characteristic. Civil liberties issues furnish an example. Either a case contains a civil liberties issue or it does not. The relationship among all cases in a given class is one of identity and the relationship between classes that of nonidentity. Since *Korematsu* v. *United States* (sustaining the wartime Japanese evacuation) and *Martin* v. *City of Struthers* (invalidating a city ordinance which barred door-to-door distribution of religious literature) both contain a civil liberties issue, nominal scaling assumes that *Korematsu* equals *Struthers*, that *Struthers* equals *Korematsu*, and that each is equal to any other case containing a civil liberties issue. One cannot say that *Korematsu* contains a more or less important civil liberties issue than *Struthers* or *Brown* v. *Board of Education* (invalidating racial segregation in public schools), or *Murdock* v. *Pennsylvania* (invalidating a municipal license tax as applied to religious colporteurs).

Nominal scales are the most primitive and the least powerful level of measurement. In fact, many scholars deny that they involve measurement in any meaningful sense at all. . . .

(b) Ordinal scales.—To be positioned on an ordinal scale, objects must, as with nominal measurement, share the basis for classification with every other object in the class. But in addition it is necessary to be able to specify whether each object (or sub-class of objects) so classified is equal to (=), greater than (>), or less than (<) every other object (or sub-class) in the class. Returning to the Supreme Court decisions referred to above, let us suppose that *Brown* contains a more important civil liberties issue than *Korematsu* (B > K), *Korematsu* a more important civil liberties issue than *Struthers* (K > S), and *Struthers* a civil liberties issue equal in importance to that in *Murdock* (S = M). Then it must follow that B > S, B > M, K > M, M < B, M < K, S < B, and M = S. Technically the relationship between unequal objects is transitive and asymmetrical, while the relationship between equal objects is transitive and symmetrical. Even more than in the case of nominal scales, a useful array of appropriate nonparametric statistics has been developed. . . .

(c) Interval scales.—With the interval scale, a level of measurement is attained which is quantitative in the ordinary sense of the term. The objects (or sub-classes) in a class must, as in nominal measurement, share a given characteristic, and, as in ordinal measurement, they must be subject to ranking in accord with it. In addition, the distances, or intervals, between objects must bear the same relationships as intervals do in a numeric system. Not only is 5 < 10 < 15, but the interval between 5 and 10 is equivalent to the interval between 10 and 15. This does not imply (as does the structure of cardinal numbers) that 10 is twice and 15 three times as large as 5. An absolute zero point would be necessary if this were to be the case. Nevertheless, most of the more powerful standard statistics, means, standard deviations, correlation, regression, variance, and factor analytic techniques are generally appropriate for use with data that form interval scales because these satisfy the assumptions required by the models upon which the statistics under discussion are based.

Beyond doubt it has been a rather common practice to use statistics technically suitable only with interval (or more restricted) types of scales in analyzing data that can at best be ordinally scaled. Many statisticians consider such usage utterly indefensible and irresponsible. Others, however, feel that such practices can be justified under certain circumstances.

This brief review of some aspects of scaling makes apparent why such strenuous efforts have been made by social scientists to develop methods whereby initially qualitative data can be legitimately transposed into ordinal and interval scales. . . .

In cumulative scaling one seeks to arrange respondents (for example, judges) and stimuli (for example, cases) in a matrix in an effort to determine whether persons who respond affirmatively to a weak stimulus do in fact respond affirmatively to all stronger stimuli—and, in addition, whether persons who respond negatively to a strong stimulus will also respond negatively to all weaker ones. If a single well-structured set of attitudes is shared by all or virtually all respondents, a continuum of stimuli representing varying degrees of intensity should reveal an identifiable point at which each respondent ceases to react affirmatively and begins to react negatively. Table I illustrates such a matrix for six classes of respondents and five stimuli. Each class of respondents constitutes a perfect scale type. As the matrix makes clear, scale type *A* respondents react affirmatively to all stimuli to which type *B* respondents react affirmatively and to weaker stimuli as well. Type *B* respondents hold a similar relationship to type *C* respondents and so on. These relationships are clearly transitive and asymmetrical, and so the structure of the scale is unquestionably cumulative, or ordinal.

Should an unexpected response occur (an affirmative where a negative is expected, as in − + − − −, or a negative where an affirmative is expected, as in + − + + +), the response would be considered an inconsistency or error. Perfect consistency is not to be expected in most areas of human endeavor and especially not in adjudication, where competing interests are almost always involved. As Justice Frankfurter observed in the *Dennis* case: "Adjustment of clash of interests which are at once subtle and fundamental is not likely to reveal entire consistency in a series of instances presenting the clash." And so this thorny question necessarily arises: How much inconsistency can be tolerated without destroying the fundamentally cumulative character of a scale? . . .

The Potential Utility of Scalogram Analysis

As already indicated, cumulative scaling is, first of all, a means for determining whether the votes cast by the members of a court in a group of cases can be arranged in the kind of matrix illustrated in Table I. Let us hypothesize that the members of the United States Supreme Court share a set of attitudes toward civil liberties which can be characterized in this way. That is to say, all Justices will vote to upset strong deprivations of civil liberties, some will vote to upset moderate deprivations as well, and one or two Justices will vote to upset not only strong and moderate deprivations of civil liberties but also weak ones. To test this hypothesis it is necessary to arrange the cases containing civil liberties issues on a continuum in such a manner that varying degrees of intensity are represented in ordinal fashion. The strongest deprivations will fall at one end of the continuum and the weakest deprivations at the other. Then one must be able to classify the judges who participated in these

Table I. Model of a Perfect Cumulative Scale

Classes of Respondents (or Scale Types)	Intensity of Stimuli				
	Very Strong	Strong	Moderate	Weak	Very Weak
A	+	+	+	+	+
B	+	+	+	+	−
C	+	+	+	−	−
D	+	+	−	−	−
E	+	−	−	−	−
F	−	−	−	−	−

cases in accordance with perfect, or nearly perfect, scale types. If one cannot set up a matrix of this character, such as the matrix illustrated in the model, then one does not have a cumulative scale, and the behavior of the judges cannot be accounted for in terms of the single hypothesized dimension.

If, on the other hand, a cumulative scale does result, then impressive evidence in support of the hypothesis has been obtained. To be sure, such evidence gives no absolute assurance that the hypothesis is true. There may be alternative explanations for the scale. Should claims by Communist defendants in Smith Act and deportation cases result in a cumulative scale, it would not necessarily follow that the judges decided the cases as they did because Communists as such were involved. Among the alternative possibilities might be that the Communists were treated as criminal defendants, or as individuals asserting free speech deprivations, or as persons claiming that their civil liberties had been violated. Like the blood test for paternity, cumulative scaling can eliminate erroneous hypotheses, but it cannot by itself demonstrate the existence of true ones.

Yet, in another sense, the blood test for paternity is not an entirely apt analogy, for the blood test is not used to demonstrate the existence of the child in question. However, when a set of cases can be made to scale, this very phenomenon constitutes strong evidence that a single well-structured set of attitudes (whatever its proper label) is shared by the members of a court.

Now let us assume that the votes cast by the members of an appellate court in a given set of cases have in fact been arranged so as to constitute a nearly perfect cumulative scale. What then? For one thing, the probable behavior of the justices in cases not yet before the court can be predicted. All that is necessary if one is to do this is to be able to indicate where a pending case falls on the intensity continuum. To return to the model in Table I once again, if a case can be said to fall in the strong intensity category, then judges who belong to scale types A, B, C, and D should respond affirmatively and those in scale types E and F negatively. Or, if a case belongs in the very weak intensity category, only type A should render affirmative responses. . . .

D. J. Woodford Howard, On the Fluidity of Judicial Choice

. . . It has long been known, of course, that judges change their votes and permit their opinions to be conduits for the ideas of others. *Causes célèbres* such as the Legal Tender and Flag Salute Cases, or the *Carolene* footnote, come quickly to mind. So does Chief Justice Hughes' pungent expression of willingness to alter language in the interest of harmony: "Justice Holmes used to say, when we asked him to excise portions of his opinions which he thought pretty good, that he was willing to be 'reasonably raped.' I feel the same way."

. . . The recently opened papers of Justice Murphy, which contain fairly extensive conference notes for the years 1940–49, as well as docket books for the 1947 term, give a much more plastic impression of judicial choice in the making than the rigidly

Reprinted from **62** *American Political Science Review* (1968), 44–49, 51–53, 55.

stratified bloc warfare by which most of us have characterized the Roosevelt and Vinson Courts. Indeed, when meshed with the Stone and Burton papers, which overlap the same period, the Murphy papers tempt one to say that hardly any major decision in this decade was free from significant alteration of vote and language before announcement to the public. Neither was the phenomenon confined to Justices whose overt allegiances were to professional ideologies of law as reason or to philosophies of self-restraint. One of the most striking aspects of the decade is that the most important instances of judicial flux, from the doctrinal standpoint, occurred precisely among those Justices most suspected of ideological automation and in cases that stand as highpoints of their libertarian commitment. From the very human tendency to change one's mind under pressure, no one, and certainly no "libertarian activist," was immune.

Examples of fluctuating options are legion; but for convenience of illustration, certain types of flux may be distinguished from among well-known civil liberties decisions of the day.

. . . First is the "freshman effect"—i.e., unstable attitudes that seem to have resulted from the process of assimilation to the Court. It is not uncommon for a new Justice to undergo a period of adjustment, often about three years in duration, before his voting behavior stabilizes into observable, not to mention predictable, patterns. Biographical materials suggest the generality of this experience, irrespective of prior background and ranging from Justices as dissimilar as Cardozo and Murphy. Justice Cardozo, according to one clerk's recollection of the docket books, registered surprisingly un-

stable opinions as a newcomer. Frequently voting alone in conference before ultimately submerging himself in a group opinion, Cardozo himself confessed discomfort in adjusting from the common law world of the New York Court of Appeals to the public law orientation of the federal Supreme Court. . . . During his freshman years on the high bench, Murphy swung from the wing of Justice Frankfurter, whom he had assumed would be his intellectual mainstay and ally, to substantial agreement with Justice Black, whose views regarding the First Amendment and state criminal procedure, it should be remembered, were also shifting ground at the time. In the process of adjustment, however, Murphy had problems of craftsmanship in the picketing cases and, along with other members of the Court, groped for a coherent position regarding free speech. . . .

However contrary to preconceptions, it was the libertarian Justice Murphy who had to be talked out of publishing a concurrence in *Cantwell* v. *Connecticut* (in return for different language) which criticized Justice Roberts' Court opinion for inadequately protecting state power to preserve the peace from clashing religious sects. . . .

Parallels in other decision-making groups, e.g., the socialization of freshman Senators, also indicate that the Court is not alone in creating assimilation problems for new members. What occurs is a sort of hiatus between the norms of the individual's belief system and new institutional norms which must be internalized as role expectations unfold. Still, the aggregate effects of such freshman transitions are probably more difficult to trace in the judiciary. Using the concept of cliques, Snyder hypothesized that the high court assimilates its new members through a "pivotal clique" in the ideological center, with the implication that uncommitted newcomers on stratified courts are likely to maximize influence at the outset of their judicial careers, before attitudes and bloc alignments jell. The experience of Justices Cardozo and Murphy suggests the need of refining this concept, however, especially the suggestion that fledgling judges with unstable or inchoate attitudes are more influential than senior, committed members. While a pivotal Justice may have a controlling vote in a given five-four situation, the very reasons for the "freshman effect"— inexperience, feelings of inadequacy, hesitation about premature bloc identification, low seniority in assignments, strategies of playing safe, etc.—all point to the opposite direction of freshmen Justices following rather than leading. Further, to the extent that "freshmanness" does cause newcomers to restrain personal preferences and gravitate toward the center, it may retard the absorption of current ideas into the Court's output, which Robert A. Dahl once argued is a prime effect of the appointive system and a means of harmonizing the institution with the outlook of dominant lawmaking majorities. The problem, in brief, is whether the newcomer's influence should be measured in terms of votes or in terms of formulating doctrine and persuading peers. Only a mechanistic view of the judicial process, in my view, would measure influence exclusively in terms of either.

A second cluster of fluctuating choices may be grouped around the familiar strategic variables of massing the Court and of institutional loyalties. Justices frequently compromise personal opinion in order to maximize their collective force and to safeguard the power and legitimacy of the Court among its reference groups. That personal ideology may be qualified or even defined by organizational perspectives is by no means unique to the judiciary. Neither must a judge genuflect at the mere mention of the tribunal. The evidence of the 1940's suggests that all of the Justices, at one time or another, were constrained by group and institutional interests. Not only was it common for them to offer helpful suggestions and advice to adversaries, according to the official theory of collective responsibility, but they also sacrificed deeply felt views. For example, Justice Murphy stifled a powerful lone dissent in the first Japanese Relocation Case under the badgering and patriotic appeals of Justice Frankfurter, and Justice Douglas did the same in the second. After finding himself alone, and probably under advice from Justice Rutledge, Murphy also withheld an elaborate dissent in the case of runaway spy Gerhard Eisler, with the result that he left stillborn the first known assault by a Justice upon the House Un-American Activities Committee for violating the First Amendment. . . .

More difficult to analyze is a third class of fluctuating options, those which appear to have resulted from the changing factual perceptions of a particular judge. In some cases, the reasons for such a shift may be indistinguishable from pressures to coalesce. Thus, Justice Douglas' acquiescence in *Korematsu* v. *United States* probably was made easier by Chief Justice Stone's continuing reminders that opportunity to challenge relocation orders still remained open to petitioners so long as orders to report to control centers and actual detention were separable. Lack of opportunity for individuals to prove their loyalty was what had troubled Douglas all along. In other cases, shifting perspectives appear to have been a function of additional thought and homework, by a clerk or a Justice, into issues that were only partially perceived at first because of inadequate argument, briefs, or time. The Supreme Court does not follow the practice in some state supreme courts of assigning cases by lot and of infrequent dissent. But it is not uncommon for a Justice assigned to express one consensus to reverse field after further analysis, and then persuade his colleagues to follow suit. . . .

The difficulty is that the reasons for changing perceptions are not usually so obvious. One may argue that flux of this sort is inevitable in the cross-pressures of a collegial court of last resort whose main business lies at the frontier of legal development. One may speculate further about the competing values, the strategies of avoidance, the problems of obtaining linguistic consensus, the rush of business, and the just plain difficulties of substance which induce perceptual change. Occasionally, one may even suspect Justices of doing the unexpected just to confound bloc identification. . . .

But no outsider really knows why judges change their minds. Seldom do they admit, as Jackson hinted in *Everson* v. *Board of Education,* to having switched their votes. Even when overruling themselves later, seldom do they write with the candor of the Canadian jurist who blandly confessed: "the matter does not appear to me now as it appears to have appeared to me then." Nor, it must be stressed, should judges be faulted either for changing their minds or for lack of complete candor. A major objective of the adversary system, after all, is prevention of premature clas-

sification and judgment. That judges may shift position between conference and final voting is not only well understood among themselves, but a testament to the limitations of conference and the effectiveness of the argumentation system. And it is hardly "robism" to suggest that a cloak of secrecy may be just as necessary for judges as for diplomats in making such accommodations possible.

Whatever their causes, however, shifting individual perceptions can significantly affect public policy and the ideological complexion of courts. . . . Reading the opinions in *Colegrove* v. *Green,* no one could have fathomed that Justice Black, author of the three-man opinion which viewed congressional reapportionment as a justiciable issue, had initially expressed contrary conclusions in conference, along with every other Justice but one. Who could have guessed that Justice Black had not only echoed the general fears about entering the apportionment thicket, but himself had attempted to express those sentiments for the Court before he once again changed his mind and wrote the powerful minority opinion which structured a fateful enlargement of judicial power as a supervisor of the electoral process? The answer, of course, is that no one could have inferred such flux from votes or opinions. Having resolved his own misgivings, Justice Black simply advanced his conclusions unencumbered by his previous doubts. . . .

These examples may be extreme because the opinions acknowledged none of the doubts which had been resolved. Yet they serve to make the point. Votes can be a crude measure of attitude. So can opinions, and even the lack of them. The ideological commitments seemingly manifest in both may be lower and the basis of choice far more pragmatic than either imply on their face. Certainly that was true of the 1940's. The disparity between the rigid ideological appearances of opinions and the fluid choices behind them was sufficiently widespread as to pose genuine problems for anyone making ideological inferences, whether by analyzing opinions or by aggregating votes. After all, if it is true that even the most libertarian of Justices sweated so hard over their options, what are we to make of interpretations, advanced by both quantitative analysts and their critics, which explain libertarian judicial behavior as simply attitudinal automatism? Plainly, the data point to a deflation of the ideological component in the decision making of this period.

To deflate ideology is not to explain the disparity between choice and opinion on a Court otherwise known for its ideological cleavages. The tough nut is still knowing when individual attitude and action have been proximate. In grouping the evidence of flux around intervening variables of socialization, strategy, and personal perception, the implication is that group variables moderate personal ideologies. Yet the mediation works both ways. Ideology may be inflated as well as deflated. To generalize whether moderation or exaggeration will result from group interaction, it is plain, would tax the middle range theory the discipline so desperately lacks. My hunch is that systematic application of role theory to the appellate process offers the richest potential aid to the problem. Pending that development, however, a number of discrete variables can be identified from the 1940's which may help to account for disparities of both types. . . .

Whatever the reasons for the dis-parity between plastic deeds and hard argument in the 1940's, however, one untoward effect was exaggeration of doctrinal conflict to the point, it is tempting to say, that outside ideologues preferred. For ideology is also in the mind of the beholder, and scholarship did not escape entrapment in its own polar opposites. However useful pedagogically it may have been to depict judicial struggles of the decade as an epic clash between dichotomous ideologies, the fact is that few major issues took so simple a form. Rather, the fluidity of choice on the Roosevelt and Vinson Courts serves as a reminder that judging, like most American decision-making, is situational and that causation is apt to be more complex than the simple mirroring of precedent or principle or personal belief systems.

This observation has particular bearing on the controversy between "quantifiers" and "qualifiers" regarding the accuracy of attitude measurement. All doubtless would agree that attitudes affect action. All probably would agree with Justice Frankfurter's aphorism that general propositions do decide concrete cases if a judge's convictions are strong enough. The main issue is how to determine attitudes and to chart their effects, and that touches again upon the question whether influence should be measured by doctrines or by votes. This question, of course, has close parallels to an older conflict between aggregationists and survey researchers in the study of voting behavior. An inherent problem of voting analysis generally is that votes, of themselves, do not distinguish underlying variations of intensity, issue perception, and certainty of response among voters. Opinion sampling and scaling techniques were designed to unravel these variables in mass electoral behavior, and today few scholars would seriously dispute their efficacy or rich potential. Guttman scaling, content analysis, and other quantitative techniques were adapted to judicial behavior as surrogates for opinion sampling. But while sampling poses problems enough in mass populations, there is little doubt that the surrogate methods of attitude analysis face rougher sledding in the Supreme Court. The principal reason is that the universe is a collegial elite whose members not only make decisions in a highly structured and secret process but also must offer persuasive collective reasons to the public. While scaling of judicial votes in split decisions has the virtue of stressing relationships among the decisionmakers, the method excludes unanimous decisions and the power considerations which help produce them. Further, the unit of analysis itself is under collegial influences. The very reliance on votes to infer attitudes points to the essential problem of identifying the intervening variables which affect those votes.

These difficulties are reflected especially in the conflict over measurement of attitude intensities. Qualifiers . . . resist suggestions in jurimetrics literature that Supreme Court decisions can be explained or predicted in terms of the attitudes of median men on cumulative scales of split decisions; and many scholars balk at some of the headier conclusions reached in the salad days of quantification, e.g., the Schubert-Spaeth assertions that Justice Clark was the most influential Justice in determining the Court's position in the late 1950's. Quantifiers, in turn, object to rebuttals that median men are, by definition, least affected by the values at play; and Schubert has gone so far as to suggest that they may be involved the most. The truth

seems to be that neither side is wholly right or wrong. For one thing, no general proposition yet framed squares with all that we can reconstruct from the real world of the past. For another, quantifiers do not always agree whether median Justices on attitude scales are most or least structured in attitude or are most or least influential. Ambiguity also lurks in the debate because of a tendency to imply that median Justices on scalograms are the swing-men of particular cases. Clearly, there is no necessary connection, just as there is no reason to assume *a priori* that the most intense Justice is the most influential or that either Justice is the swing-man, the tailman, the group spokesman, or anyone else. Relative attitude intensities and influence are separate questions. . . .

Similar reservations hold for variations of issue perception and certitude among Justices. If anything, these aspects of choice are even harder to infer than intensity. The problem for traditional analysis is that opinions seldom reveal the issue perceptions of all the Justices, and those perceptions which are revealed may reflect collegial influences more than individual cognition. In any event, we are dependent upon what the judges say their perceptions are. The problem for behavioral analysis is that quantification can reach a point of diminishing returns when multiple variables are involved. There are forces at work in the appellate process, to be sure, which are designed to narrow the issues; we also may expect that increasing sophistication in regression techniques may make the multiplicity problem more manageable. Still, the collisions of value which fracture customary blocs . . . also tax ideological analysis. When cases turn on clashes *among* multiple libertarian values, problems of classification and quantification increase. . . . The evidence presented has several implications for the empirical and normative concerns of the discipline. First, assuming that the experience of this decade can be projected, the data point to a potential disparity between a highly complex and fluid "input" stage and a relatively simplistic official "output" in the judicial process. This disparity between choice and explanation aggravates a general analytical problem of reliably classifying hard data, votes and opinions, whether classification proceeds by a single observer or risks are cut by panel techniques. The disparity also points to the complexity of conversion processes, since presumably they too are affected by group interaction. The disparity likewise suggests the need of refining popular concepts about blocs, cliques, and attitudinal automatism which sometimes pass for causal explanations in both quantitative analyses and normative critiques of Supreme Court behavior. . . .

Second, the evidence of the 1940's

lends greater support to the lawyer's ideal of the judicial process as a system of reasoning than many legal realists would accept. Clearly, judges of all ideological persuasions pondered, bargained, and argued in the course of reaching their decisions, and they compromised their ideologies, too. No one can plow through the papers of a Stone or a Murphy without coming out with renewed respect for the give-and-take or without appreciation for the multiplicity of variables and constraints, including that old whipping-post, Law, that went into the decision making of the era. On the other hand, several major decisions were neither so collective nor so ideologically opinionated as the Hart-Arnold debate of a few years back would have it. At present levels of knowledge the central issue of that debate, what constitutes *the* judicial process, defies inclusive description and, because it fails to differentiate institutional layers and responsibilities, perhaps asks a meaningless question.

part two

the supreme court and the economy

1. INTRODUCTORY ESSAY

The relationship of the Supreme Court to the economic system has changed significantly since the early days of the Republic. The once dominant role of the Court has been replaced by one at the periphery of the administrative state. Yet this diminution of power cannot detract from the vital role that the Court did play in the maturing of American capitalism. More significantly, current developments within the society that might be termed "economic"—for example, technological growth, environmental concerns, the emergence of new conceptions of property—present a new set of problems that at least invite, if not assure, the assertion of Supreme Court power. There is also some evidence in recent cases that some justices are no longer content with playing the passive economic role that emerged during the New Deal and that has characterized the Court in the intervening years. Thus the Court's potential for resumption of an active economic policymaking role is considerable.

The Declaration of Independence and Adam Smith's *Wealth of Nations* appeared in the same year, and in the 200 years since, capitalism has been entrenched in the American political and legal systems. The basic tenets of capitalism, as interpreted by early American political leaders, called for fundamental divisions between the public and private sectors of the economic system. In theory, the role of the government was passive, being limited largely to creating or protecting the maximum possible freedom for those engaged in entrepreneurial activities. In practice, the government played an active and important role, notwithstanding its theoretical impotence or rhetorical adherence to the norm of laissez-faire.

The Constitution reflected this ambivalence between theory and practice. If there was one overriding catalyst for the Constitutional Convention of 1787, it was the economic chaos that existed under the Articles of Confederation and the need to bring stability to the formerly colonial economy. In particular, the framers recognized the need to have congressional regulation of commerce, to remove internal tariff barriers, to establish a uniform national currency, and to establish central rather than state control of imports from foreign commerce. A quick glance at the Constitution shows a number of other positive concerns with the economy, such as provisions for establishing postal roads and a postal system, and bankruptcy laws. In addition, the Constitution contains a series of prohibitions, on both the federal government and the states, designed to minimize interference with normal commercial intercourse. States could not issue their own currency, could not interfere with the obligations of contracts, and were admonished to give full faith and credit to the public acts, records, and judicial proceedings of other states.

The economic motives of the framers of the Constitution are revealed by a simple reading of the document itself. The extent to which some of the men who attended the convention may have had more personal economic motives remains a subject for scholarly debate. Thus, while the proposed economic role of the government under the Constitution was not entirely clear, the concept that private property and its owners had special rights was set forth with unmistakable clarity.

Notwithstanding the nostalgic history of those who currently criticize the welfare state, the fact remains that even in the pre–Civil War years, both federal and state governments played an extraordinary and important, albeit limited, role in building the national economy. As Sidney Fine has written:

Whatever the theory, in practice the federal government and the state governments of the era before the Civil War did not confine their activities within the limits recommended by the advocates of laissez faire. The federal government became the promoter of a variety of economic enterprises. It constructed the National Road and military roads on the frontiers, purchased stock in four canal companies, provided surveys and land grants for wagon roads, canals, and railroads, assigned land to the states for the general purpose of internal improvements, and itself improved rivers and harbors. It appropriated the money for the first magnetic telegraph line in the United States. It sought to aid manufacturers in general by enacting a protective tariff and to aid manufacturers of small arms by advancing them funds without interest on government contracts. It promoted the nation's merchant marine by imposing tariff duties and tonnage taxes that discriminated in favor of United States shipping engaged in foreign commerce, by excluding foreign vessels from the coastwise trade, and by providing subsidies for steamships. To the codfishery it offered bounties on exports and a cash subsidy to owners and crews of vessels engaged in the industry. Also, it provided the states with land for both common schools and state universities.[1]

[1] *Laissez-Faire and the General Welfare State* (Ann Arbor: University of Michigan Press, 1956), p. vii.

The Contract Clause

The Constitution assigned no specific economic role to the Supreme Court, but there is little doubt that one of its early policies was to curb governmental infringement on the rights of the wealthy minorities. The Court was particularly concerned with property rights, and certainly through the Marshall years the main themes of judicial decision were restrictions on the power of the states to interfere with business expansion or to violate contract rights, along with the corollary theme of expanding the capacity of the national government to regulate the economy. By stressing the negative, restrictive aspects of the commerce clause, which would not be used by Congress to pass a major statute until 1887, the Court encouraged free trade and the breakdown of economic barriers, while at the same time protecting Congress' power to legislate under the commerce clause at such time as it might choose to do so.

The Court's interpretation of the necessary and proper clause (see *McCulloch* v. *Maryland* (1819), Part One, Chapter Two) and its defense of the principle of federal supremacy were proscriptions on claimed state power that would enable Congress, at a later time, to regulate various aspects of economic life without state interference. The contract clause was used to strike down many attempts by states to regulate private business arrangements by statute. In short, Marshall's defense of orthodox capitalism was also a support for the idea of nationalism.

The geographic and economic growth of the country, and the ascendancy of Andrew Jackson and his followers, somewhat altered the Court's economic role. The Taney Court modified several of Marshall's economic doctrines; it took a more liberal view of a state's right to regulate private contractual business arrangements, and in the famous *Cooley* case of 1851, it enlarged the possible scope of state regulation of interstate commerce in the absence of congressional action. In a dismal swan song, the Taney Court refused to permit a congressional attempt to solve the slavery issue.

It was only after the Civil War, coincidental with the industrial revolution in the United States, that legislative bodies made any serious attempt to regulate business and commerce by statute, and it was in response to these attempts that the Court became deeply involved in fundamental economic questions. From the end of the Civil War until 1937, the Court's role was important but largely negative; its most significant decisions were, with few exceptions, those forbidding the states or the Congress from regulating a particular form of economic activity. In those cases in which a particular form of regulation was held judicially permissible, the Court retained the privilege of continued supervision. It was during this period that John R. Commons could refer accurately to the Supreme Court as "the first authoritative faculty of political economy in the world's history."[2]

Substantive Due Process

The ascendancy of the Court as an economic policymaker rested largely on its use of the due process clause of the Fourteenth Amendment and also on its revisionist views of Marshall's treatment of the commerce clause and the

[2]*The Legal Foundations of Capitalism* (Madison: University of Wisconsin Press, 1924), p. 7.

Tenth Amendment. With the demise of the contract clause as an effective obstacle to state regulation of business, a new constitutional approach was required. Efforts were made in the *Slaughterhouse Cases* (1873) to persuade the Supreme Court that the privileges and immunities clause of the Fourteenth Amendment protected business and property from unwarranted state regulation. The Court rejected this approach with the argument that the major, if not sole purpose of that amendment had been to provide constitutional protection for newly freed Negro slaves. Emphasis then was switched to the due process clause. It was argued that the courts had a positive duty to scrutinize legislative pronouncements, not only to determine that no procedural norms had been violated but also to see whether or not, in the opinion of the judges of a particular court, a statute was "unreasonable." Did the statute in question have a "real" or "substantial" relationship to the objective to be obtained? And, furthermore, was that objective a reasonable and proper one for a legislative body to seek? In short, were the ends legitimate, and if so, were the means reasonably accommodated to achieving those ends?

Since this was nothing less than a judicial inquiry into the wisdom and policy goals of a statute, and not the usual judicial review of compliance with *procedural* norms, it became known as *substantive due process*. Unlike procedural due process, which left to the discretion of a legislature judgment over the reasonableness of its actions and assigned to those challenging the validity of a statute the burden of proof of any unreasonableness, substantive due process implicitly shifted to the state the burden of proving that it had acted reasonably and appropriated to the Supreme Court the ultimate *policy* control.

Most scholars who have traced the origins of this novel doctrine agree that it was first enunciated by the New York State Court of Appeals in *Wynhammer* v. *New York* (1856). In that case, the court invalidated a state law providing for the confiscation of liquor already in possession of its owner when the law took effect, even though the *procedures* for confiscation met all due process requirements. The theory that the substance of a law was subject to due process scrutiny first found its way to the Supreme Court of the United States in the *Dred Scott* case (1857). In invalidating the Missouri Compromise, Chief Justice Taney held that "an act of Congress which deprived a citizen of the United States of his liberty or property merely because he came himself or brought his property into a particular Territory of the United States, and who had committed no offense against the laws, could hardly be dignified with the name of due process of law. . . ."

Taney's opinion rested upon the Fifth Amendment, but the inclusion of a due process clause in the Fourteenth Amendment, ratified in 1868, laid the groundwork for application of "substantive due process" to the states. Perhaps its first expression came in Justice Bradley's dissenting opinion in *The Slaughterhouse Cases* (1873), and counsel for businesses challenging state regulations utilized the argument with alacrity. In fact, Justice Miller had to rebuke counsel in *Davidson* v. *New Orleans* (1878) because of his "excessive zeal" in pressing this notion upon the Court.[3]

It is almost certain that every justice of the Supreme Court before 1902

---

[3]For a fascinating account of the efforts of the bar and the newly formed American Bar Association in trying to persuade courts of the utility of substantive due process, see Benjamin Twiss, *Lawyers and the Constitution* (Princeton: Princeton University Press, 1942), and James Willard Hurst, *The Growth of American Law* (Boston: Little, Brown, 1950), Part V.

accepted, to some degree, the premises of the substantive due process doctrine. It was at least implicitly accepted in *Munn* v. *Illinois* (1877), a decision upholding state regulation of fees charged by grain elevator companies. The rationale of Chief Justice Waite's opinion was that businesses "affected with a public interest" could be regulated. It was made very clear, however, that in the final analysis, it was a judicial function to determine whether a business was serving the public interest (or whether it was in the public interest to regulate a business, as the doctrine was conversely applied.) But the presumption of validity of a regulatory statute was still acknowledged.

A decade later, in *Mugler* v. *Kansas*, the Supreme Court again upheld a regulatory statute, this time a prohibition on the sale of liquor. But Justice Harlan stated the Court's policy somewhat differently: "If therefore, a statute purporting to have been enacted to protect the public health, the public morals, or the public safety, has no real or substantial relation to these object . . . it is the duty of the Courts to so adjudge, and thereby give effect to the Constitution." The presumption of validity had clearly shifted, and the states had to assume the responsibility of justifying regulatory statutes on a case-by-case basis.

An implication of the *Mugler* case was that statutes purporting to regulate public health, safety, and morals (the "police power") were entitled to a greater presumption of validity than "mere" economic regulations. Thus the Court had little trouble, in *Jacobsen* v. *Massachusetts* (1903), in upholding compulsory smallpox vaccinations even though there was some difference of medical opinion about their effectiveness. It found that a state could violate an individual's physical integrity if the *public welfare* is sufficiently well served. But even here, where the state had acted in real fear of a smallpox epidemic, the Supreme Court itself determined whether the law served the public interest. Likewise, the justices approved a maximum hours statute for coal miners who were admittedly engaged in a hazardous occupation, and also for women, whose "frail bodies" (it was then thought) needed protection to enable them to better fulfill their chief biological function (*Holden* v. *Hardy,* 1898; *Muller* v. *Oregon*, 1908). Even the famous brief in behalf of the state of Oregon submitted by attorney Louis Brandeis, which departed from legal custom by dwelling almost entirely on the sociological, psychological, and physiological justifications for the Oregon statute, accepted implicitly the right of the Supreme Court to inquire into the reasonableness of the statute.

Regulatory statutes with primarily economic overtones were much less likely to be approved by the Court. As stated in *Lochner* v. *New York* (1905), such statutes were considered "mere meddlesome interferences" with the rights of individual employers and employees to freely contract for goods and services. Attempting to disguise regulatory statutes as health statutes in order to regulate bakers' hours was disingenuous and, to a majority of the Court, unacceptable.

Economics and the Emergence of the Positive State

Judicial opposition hardened in the face of mounting legislative efforts to deal with economic problems. The doctrine of substantive due process was an effective (if not perfect) obstacle to both state and federal legislation. The

Court's negative response to federal regulatory efforts under the commerce clause took several forms. First, the Court decided in 1895 in the *E.C. Knight* case that "commerce" meant only trade and excluded manufacture. The immediate consequences of the decision were to exempt the E.C. Knight sugar trust, which monopolized 95 percent of the sugar industry, from the antitrust laws. But it also severely limited other efforts by Congress to regulate under the commerce clause.

Congress passed the first child labor act in 1916, but in 1918, in *Hammer* v. *Dagenhart*, the Supreme Court declared the law unconstitutional. It cited the *Knight* case in holding that labor in the production of goods was not commerce but instead "preceded" commerce, and thus it could not be regulated by Congress. It also held that Congress could not prohibit articles made by child labor from being shipped in interstate commerce, because these articles were not (or not necessarily) intrinsically harmful. This doctrine was completely at odds with a previous Supreme Court decision, *Champion* v. *Ames* (1903). Finally, the Court held that Congress' power to regulate child labor under the commerce clause was limited by the Tenth Amendment, which reserved to the states the "police power" to protect the health, safety, welfare, and morals of their citizens. Indeed, the Court even misquoted that amendment, saying that the federal government was forbidden to exercise all powers not "expressly" delegated, whereas the amendment merely reserves to the states those powers "not delegated." This use of the Tenth Amendment as a limit on the powers of Congress became known as the doctrine of *dual federalism*.

The limits on Congress' power under the commerce clause, and the substantive due process limits on state regulation, created a twilight zone in which often neither Congress nor the states could regulate effectively. And when Congress sought to regulate by other means, the Supreme Court found additional constitutional barriers. After *Hammer* v. *Dagenhart*, the child labor act was repassed under the taxing and spending clause. All goods made in whole or in part by child labor and shipped in commerce were subject to a tax of 10 percent. In *Bailey* v. *Drexel Furniture* (1922), the act was struck down, the Court observing that the obvious purpose of the tax was not to raise revenue but to discourage child labor by making it unprofitable. The Court ignored a history of decisions that had upheld similar "penalty taxes" in the past.

The onset of the Depression and the unprecedented legislative recovery efforts of Roosevelt's New Deal administration precipitated *the* major constitutional crisis since the Civil War. Within the Supreme Court, an increasing polarization of views divided the conservative justices—Sutherland, Van Devanter, Butler, and McReynolds—from their more liberal brethren—Brandeis, Stone, Holmes, and Holmes' replacement in 1932, Cardozo. The death of Chief Justice Taft in 1930 removed an important conciliatory force on the high bench, and it remained for Taft's successor, Charles Evans Hughes, to steer the Court through the crisis.

Some parts of the recovery program, such as the move away from the gold standard and, in 1937, the institution of the social security program, were accepted by the Court over bitter conservative dissents, epitomized by McReynolds' intonation from the bench in the *Gold Clause Cases* that "the Constitution is gone." But the Agricultural Adjustment Act, the National Recovery Act, and the Guffey Coal Act, designed to revitalize and restore public confidence in the industrial sector, were all invalidated by the Supreme Court.

The president responded with a bitter attack on the Court, but Roosevelt had no opportunity to fill a Supreme Court vacancy during his first term, and the conservative justices continued to reflect views dominating an earlier time.

Following his landslide victory in the 1936 elections, Roosevelt sought to remove judicial obstacles to his New Deal program. Somewhat disingenuously, he asked for congressional authority to appoint an additional justice for each sitting justice over the age of 75, to a maximum of fifteen justices. Although his plan was nominally part of a larger plan to provide an adequate retirement system for the entire federal judiciary, it was clear that the president was asking for authority to "pack" the Court until its political complexion was in step with his own views. But despite his personal popularity and the size of his electoral and congressional majority in the 1936 election, Roosevelt had seriously misjudged response to his plan. It was bitterly attacked by many who supported the New Deal and seemed, at best, to have the support of a bare majority of the Senate. The death of Roosevelt's floor leader in the Senate, Joseph Robinson of Arkansas, and an unusual public statement by Chief Justice Hughes asserting that the justices, contrary to Roosevelt's allegations, were quite capable of keeping up with their work load and further expressing doubts about the wisdom and constitutionality of a Supreme Court as large as fifteen, were key factors in the ultimate defeat of the plan. So, too, was public opinion, which indicated a striking lack of support for this attack on the Court.

Undoubtedly, the key blow to the plan's chance of success was the Supreme Court's own reversal of its opposition to minimum wage legislation for women, a decision handed down after the "court-packing" plan had been unveiled but which, in fact, had been decided earlier in conference. This unexpected action by the Court evoked the famous pun, "the switch in time that saved nine." But the evidence seems reasonably clear that, while the Court's action was taken at a time of political crisis, the decision had been made prior to the introduction of Roosevelt's scheme and was not directly a response to it.

In *West Coast Hotel* v. *Parrish* (1937), a 5-4 majority overruled a prior line of cases and upheld the validity of a minimum wage law for women in the state of Washington that was nearly identical to a statute invalidated the previous year (see pp. 248–251, *supra*.). In subsequent cases over the next few years, the new "Roosevelt Court" repudiated the doctrine of substantive due process in economic cases. Whether the doctrine still lives in other areas of policy is a question discussed subsequently. But insofar as economic regulation cases are concerned, there seems to be no exception. Judicial abdication in this field was formally restated for a unanimous court in *Ferguson* v. *Skrupa* (1963).

As it was rolling back the doctrine of substantive due process, the Supreme Court in 1937 also repudiated the doctrine of dual federalism, the notion that somehow Congress' power under the commerce clause was limited by what Holmes once sarcastically referred to as "invisible radiations from the Tenth Amendment." At the same time, it began to restore the commerce clause to its former scope. In *National Labor Relations Board* v. *Jones and Laughlin Steel Corporation* (1937), a 5-4 decision validated the National Labor Relations Act by recognizing the practical impact of the labor policies of private industry upon interstate commerce. By 1942, in *Wickard* v. *Filburn*, the Court accepted an application of the Agricultural Adjustment Act limiting the acres a farmer could cultivate for his own use. Window washers of buildings in which interstate commerce was being transacted were deemed within the scope of

Congress' power to set minimum wages. So rapid was this reversal of precedent, so breathtaking the widespread use of Congress' "new" powers to regulate the economy, that a revolution could truly be said to have occurred. Having spent most of its time in the past half-century fighting against government power to regulate the economy, the Court, with several new Roosevelt appointees, did a sudden about-face and proclaimed that Congress and the states were free to regulate—provided that their respective efforts did not clash.

The Modern Court and the Economy

Empirical studies of Supreme Court voting support the conclusion of Harold Spaeth that "the Warren Court's decisions were characterized by a strong attachment to the principles of economic liberalism: they were pro-union, antibusiness, pro-competition, pro-employee in personal-injury suits against employers, and pro-small business in a conflict between large and small business not involving antitrust action."[4] And as Glendon Schubert has pointed out, even where the Court has vetoed a state regulation of the economy or interpreted congressional regulatory statutes, it has almost invariably done so in behalf of a more liberal policy posittion.[5] The history of the Supreme Court shows no comparable role reversal—certainly none in the span of such a few years.

From 1936 to 1976, the Supreme Court did not invalidate a single act of Congress under the commerce clause. Its deference to Congress, in contrast to its attitude before 1937, was striking. Congress used the commerce power as a "national police power," regulating activities far removed from the normal subject of that clause. In 1964, Congress passed, and the Court approved, Title II of the Civil Rights Act forbidding discrimination in public accommodations. And in 1971, in *Perez* v. *United States (infra.)*, the Court upheld the validity of a criminal statute prohibiting loansharking activities. But in 1976, in *National League of Cities* v. *Usery (infra.)*, a divided Court invalidated amendments to the Fair Labor Standards Act, which had brought virtually all municipal and state employees under the coverage of the law. The majority opinion cited the Tenth Amendment in holding that Congress had exceeded its powers.

So much for this brief review of the Court's historic role in the making of economic policy. What of its current, and future role? To think along these lines, it may be useful to grasp the distinction between "the economy" and "commercial activities." The modern economy, as an object of national policy, is a highly interrelated and complex system that includes among its functions the promotion and regulation of economic growth as measured by the gross national product, control of the money supply, and responsibility for maximum levels of employment. To some people, the government has, or should have, the added responsibility of providing or ensuring a more equitable distribution of wealth.

On the other hand, there are analytically distinct sets of activities that occur as a necessary and common feature of American capitalism and that can be

[4]Harold J. Spaeth, *The Warren Court: Cases and Commentaries* (San Francisco: Chandler Publishing Company, 1966), pp. 34–35.
[5]Glendon Schubert, *The Constitutional Polity* (Boston: Boston University Press, 1970), pp. 47–48.

conveniently labeled "commercial." These would include the issuing and trading of securities, regulation of business mergers, issuing and protecting patents and copyrights, policing of fair trade practices, advertising and the like. While these commercial activities have an economic impact, they are much more limited in scope and usually only incidentally related to achievement of the "economic" functions described above.

The relationship of the Supreme Court to these distinctive sets of activities is markedly different. Economic policymaking is fundamentally and characteristically an executive or administrative function. It is often based on authorization by congressional statute, but the key decisions are usually made by or in the name of the president or by one of several independent regulatory agencies over which the president has appointive influence if not actual control. The one exception would be basic tax policies, which usually involve Congress to a greater degree. Most of the economic decisions in this category are made by the exercise of constitutional powers long considered proper—or unreviewable—by the Supreme Court. To the extent that decisions of this sort rest on a foundation of prior judicial rulings, the Court may be said to have been a contributor to modern economic policymaking. But one cannot ignore the analytical distinction between broadly interpreting a constitutional provision to legitimate legislative or executive economic planning and actually utilizing that provision to systematically manage the state of the nation's economy. It is instructive that the Employment Act of 1946, the great economic charter of the welfare state, which assigns major functions for planning and stabilizing the economy to the executive branch, has never been considered by the Supreme Court.

The relationship of the Court to commercial activities is different. A diverse range of commercial activity is constantly regulated by bureaucratic agencies of the national government. The federal judiciary hears appeals from these agencies, and the Supreme Court takes a few of these cases for consideration. For the most part, these cases deal with particular commercial activities or with particular applications of economic policy. In the first category would be labor relations cases, statutory interpretation of the securities laws, the permissible limits of regulation of advertising, or the use of the public airwaves. In the second category, one would find a few antitrust cases that, if anything, demonstrate the Court's incapacity to deal with complex questions of economic life. The conduct of American economic policy is largely and inevitably a bureaucratic process. It depends on the constant accumulation and evaluation of huge amounts of quantitative data on the current behavior of the economic system. Accumulation and evaluation of such sophisticated data go far beyond the capacity of the Supreme Court as an institution, at least given its present mode of operation and its current recruitment patterns. The Court possesses neither the time nor the resources to properly evaluate economic variables, and the process of case-by-case adjudication is a particularly unsuitable approach to questions that must be treated at the system level, just as the Court found in an earlier period that it could not effectively and legitimately engage in economic rate making.

This is not to say that the Court has no economic functions or that it could have no impact on the economy of a vast welfare state. Within the limits suggested above, it does exercise two important functions. First, it can exercise some checking or restraining power on agency or congressional decisions regulating "commercial" activities. And, second, it can force the government to publicly justify certain policies, particularly where those policies may have overtones that raise noneconomic constitutional issues. About 20 percent of the Court's docket is given to regulatory functions of the federal government. But the Court rarely opposes substantive decisions of administrative agencies. The relationship of the Supreme Court to specific economic actors is typically one in which the Court either reinforces administrative decisions on constitutional or procedural grounds or makes its own way through the same problems and reaches the same conclusion. The Court is reluctant, for reasons mentioned above, to upset agency decisions on factual matters or agency exercise of statutory direction, limiting its review (and review by lower federal courts) to "questions of law," which have, in turn, been viewed by the Court in increasingly narrow terms. Thus, even in those few important policy areas in which it plays a part, the Court's role seems typically to be one of reinforcement of government policy decisions. For a good example of this role see the excerpt from the *Vermont Yankee* case (pp. 400–407, *infra*.)

One question that emerges from practically any reading of contemporary discussions of the American economic system is, "Where do they talk about the Supreme Court?" There is only the glaring absence of virtually any mention of the third branch of government. One need only scan the index of John Kenneth Galbraith's *The New Industrial State* for confirmation. Structural change in American capitalism rapidly seems to be relegating the Supreme Court to a fringe role in economic policymaking. Our decision to devote an entire chapter to the Court's economic role does not challenge this assumption directly. It does reflect our view that any proper understanding of the Court's current chief policy concerns and any future economic role that it may play must relate in some way to an understanding of its major policy concerns of the past.

2. THE DEVELOPMENT OF AMERICAN CAPITALISM AND THE CHANGING ROLE OF THE SUPREME COURT

A. *The Development of a National Commercial System*

(1) A Note on the Diverse Demands of Policy

The Supreme Court's role in the fashioning of economic policy during the early years of the American Republic reflected a diverse set of circumstances. The United States then was what we might call today a "developing nation." That development was capitalistic, but it was capitalism complicated by the evolution of peculiar political institutions such as federalism. At the same time, there was an explosion of practical technology in transportation, manufacture, agriculture, and production of basic materials. There were significant discontinuities in this development, represented by agrarian-industrial differences between regions and by competing political outlooks. There were the constant pressures of frontier exploration, resulting in rapidly changing demands upon national and state governments. The economic conditions that political institutions were called upon to regulate were so varied as to make the mere choice of an appropriate standard of commercial and economic regulation itself a major problem of public policy.

This complexity of circumstances was seen and appreciated by our earliest makers of economic policy. It emerges quite clearly in Alexander Hamilton's famous *Report on Manufactures*. Hamilton examined these questions in terms of the need to formulate policies for a young and developing nation that would assure continuation of its political autonomy and national security and build the infrastructure for its economy. He recognized the unity of economic and political independence.

Out of this early awareness, one fundamental policy theme emerged: the need for a *national* economic and commercial system. Not only was this the thrust of Hamilton's argument, but it was also the premise of many of the decisions of the Supreme Court over which John Marshall presided and from which Marshall formulated doctrines that still represent the basic outlines of national economic policy.

(2) Gibbons v. Ogden (1824)

+Marshall, Duvall, Johnson, Story, Todd, Washington
NP Thompson

[This case arose out of a dispute over rights to exclusive steamboat navigation between New York and New Jersey. Robert Fulton and his partner, Robert Livingston, had been granted an exclusive right by the state of New York to operate steamboats in New York waters between New York and New Jersey. Aaron Ogden was a licensee of Fulton and Livingston. Thomas Gibbons, originally a partner of Ogden, was a competitor who secured a coasting license from the federal government to operate

a steam-powered ferryboat between New York City and Elizabethtown, New Jersey. Ogden claimed that he had exclusive rights to steamboat navigation and sought an injunction against Gibbons in the New York State courts. Gibbons responded that his federal license took precedence over any state license.

The injunction was granted and was affirmed by the Court for the Trial of Impeachments and Correction of Errors of New York. Chancellor James Kent, one of early America's foremost jurists, wrote an opinion denying that the state act that conveyed the exclusive license to Ogden was unconstitutional. Gibbons then appealed to the United States Supreme Court, where his case was presented by Daniel Webster. Webster argued that federal power under the commerce clause of the Constitution should be interpreted as broadly as possible and that under some circumstances, federal power had to be regarded as *exclusive*. The Supreme Court would have to decide whether certain areas of commerce could be regulated concurrently by the states in the absence of a direct conflict.

All agreed that a direct conflict between state and federal power had to be resolved in favor of the federal government under the supremacy clause, Article VI of the Constitution. The state of New York countered that regulation of commerce should be presumed concurrent in the absence of a direct conflict. The questions raised were, of course, fundamental to the allocation of power between nation and state, for the commerce power was more than a restraint on state action. It was, or so it was claimed, an important potential source of national authority. In this case, the Supreme Court had its first opportunity to consider the scope of the commerce clause.]

MR. CHIEF JUSTICE MARSHALL delivered the opinion of the court:
. . .

As preliminary to the very able discussions of the constitution, which we have heard from the bar, and as having some influence on its construction, reference has been made to the political situation of these states, anterior to its formation. It has been said, that they were sovereign, were completely independent, and were connected with each other only by a league. This is true. But when these allied sovereigns converted their league into a government . . . the whole character in which the states appear, underwent a change, the extent of which must be determined by a fair consideration of the instrument by which that change was effected.

This instrument contains an enumeration of powers expressly granted by the people to their government. It has been said, that these powers ought to be construed strictly. But why ought they be so construed? Is there one sentence in the constitution which gives countenance to this rule? In the last of the enumerated powers, that which grants, expressly, the means for carrying all others into execution, Congress is authorized "to make all laws which shall be necessary and proper" for the purpose. But this limitation on the means which may be used, is not extended to the powers which are conferred; nor is there one sentence in the constitution, which has been pointed out by the gentlemen of the bar, or which we have been able to discern, that prescribes this rule. We do not, therefore, think ourselves justified in adopting it. What do the gentlemen mean, by a strict construction? If they contend only against that enlarged construction, which would extend words beyond their natural and obvious import, we might question the application of the term, but should not controvert the principle. If they contend for that narrow construction which, in support of some theory not to be found in the constitution, would deny to the government those powers which the words of the grant, as usually understood, import, and which are consistent with the general views

and objects of the instrument—for that narrow construction, which would cripple the government, and render it unequal to the objects for which it is declared to be instituted, and to which the powers given, as fairly understood, render it competent—then we cannot perceive the propriety of this strict construction, nor adopt it as the rule by which the constitution is to be expounded. . . .

The words are, "Congress shall have power to regulate commerce with foreign nations, and among the several states, and with the Indian tribes."

The subject to be regulated is commerce; and our constitution being, as was aptly said at the bar, one of enumeration, and not of definition, to ascertain the extent of the power, it becomes necessary to settle the meaning of the word. The counsel for the appellee would limit it to traffic, to buying and selling, or the interchange of commodities, and do not admit that it comprehends navigation. This would restrict a general term, applicable to many objects, to one of its significations. Commerce, undoubtedly, is traffic, but it is something more—it is intercourse. It describes the commercial intercourse between nations, and parts of nations, in all its branches, and is regulated by prescribing rules for carrying on that intercourse. The mind can scarcely conceive a system for regulating commerce between nations, which shall exclude all laws concerning navigation, which shall be silent on the admission of the vessels of the one nation into the ports of the other, and be confined to prescribing rules for the conduct of individuals, in the actual employment of buying and selling, or of barter.

If commerce does not include navigation, the government of the Union has no direct power over that subject, and can make no law prescribing what shall constitute American vessels, or requiring that they shall be navigated by American seamen. Yet this power has been exercised from the commencement of the government, has been exercised with the consent of all, and has been understood by all to be a commercial regulation. All America understands, and has uniformly understood, the word "commerce," to comprehend navigation. It was so understood, and must have been so understood, when the constitution was framed. The power over commerce, including navigation, was one of the primary objects for which the people of America adopted their government, and must have been contemplated in forming it. The convention must have used the word in that sense, because all have understood it in that sense; and the attempt to restrict it comes too late. . . .

The word used in the constitution, then, comprehends, and has been always understood to comprehend, navigation within its meaning; and a power to regulate navigation, is as expressly granted, as if that term had been added to the word "commerce." To what commerce does this power extend? The constitution informs us, to commerce "with foreign nations, and among the several states, and with the Indian tribes." It has, we believe, been universally admitted, that these words comprehend every species of commercial intercourse between the United States and foreign nations. No sort of trade can be carried on between this country and any other, to which this power does not extend. It has been truly said, that commerce, as the word is used in the constitution, is a unit, every part of which is indicated by the term. . . .

The subject to which the power is next applied, is to commerce, "among the several states." The word "among" means intermingled with.

A thing which is among others, is intermingled with them. Commerce among the states, cannot stop at the external boundary line of each state, but may be introduced into the interior. It is not intended to say, that these words comprehend that commerce, which is completely internal, which is carried on between man and man in a state, or between different parts of the same state, and which does not extend to or affect other states. Such a power would be inconvenient, and is certainly unnecessary. Comprehensive as the word "among" is, it may very properly be restricted to that commerce which concerns more states than one. The phrase is not one which would probably have been selected to indicate the completely interior traffic of a state, because it is not an apt phrase for that purpose; and the enumeration of the particular classes of commerce to which the power was to be extended, would not have been made, had the intention been to extend the power to every description. The enumeration presupposes something not enumerated; and that something, if we regard the language or the subject of the sentence, must be the exclusively internal commerce of a state. The genius and character of the whole government seem to be, that its action is to be applied to all the external concerns of the nation, and to those internal concerns which affect the states generally; but not to those which are completely within a particular state, which do not affect other states, and with which it is not necessary to interfere, for the purpose of executing some of the general powers of the government. The completely internal commerce of a state, then, may be considered as reserved for the state itself.

But in regulating commerce with foreign nations, the power of congress does not stop at the jurisdictional lines of the several states. It would be a very useless power, if it could not pass those lines. The commerce of the United States with foreign nations, is that of the whole United States; every district has a right to participate in it. The deep streams which penetrate our country in every direction, pass through the interior of almost every state in the Union, and furnish the means of exercising this right. If Congress has the power to regulate it, that power must be exercised whenever the subject exists. It exists within the states, if a foreign voyage may commence or terminate at a port within a state, then the power of congress may be exercised within a state.

This principle is, if possible, still more clear, when applied to commerce "among the several states." They either join each other, in which case they are separated by a mathematical line, or they are remote from each other, in which case other states lie between them. What is commerce "among" them; and how it is to be conducted? Can a trading expedition between two adjoining states, commence and terminate outside of each? And if the trading intercourse be between two states remote from each other, must it not commence in one, terminate in the other, and probably pass through a third? Commerce among the states must, of necessity, be commerce with the states. . . .

We are now arrived at the inquiry—what is this power? It is the power to regulate; that is, to prescribe the rule by which commerce is to be governed. This power, like all others vested in Congress, is complete in itself, may be exercised to its utmost extent, and acknowledges no limitations, other than are prescribed in the constitution. These are expressed in plain terms, and do not ef-

fect the questions which arise in this case, or which have been discussed at the bar. If, as has always been understood, the sovereignty of Congress, though limited to specific objects, is plenary as to those objects, the power over commerce with foreign nations, and among the several states, is vested in Congress as absolutely as it would be in a single government, having in its constitution the same restrictions on the exercise of the power as are found in the constitution of the United States. The wisdom and the discretion of congress, their identity with the people, and the influence which their constituents possess at elections, are, in this, as in many other instances, as that, for example, of declaring war, the sole restraints on which they have relied, to secure them from its abuse. They are the restraints on which the people must often rely solely, in all representative governments. The power of Congress, then, comprehends navigation, within the limits of every state in the Union; so far as that navigation may be, in any manner, connected with "commerce with foreign nations, or among the several states, or with the Indian tribes." . . .

But it has been urged, with great earnestness, that although the power of Congress to regulate commerce with foreign nations, and among the several states, be co-extensive with the subject itself, and have no other limits than are prescribed in the constitution, yet the states may severally exercise the same power, within their respective jurisdictions. In support of this argument, it is said, that they possessed it as an inseparable attribute of sovereignty, before the formation of the constitution, and still retain it, except so far as they have surrendered it by that instrument; that this principle results from the nature of the government, and is secured by the tenth amendment; that an affirmative grant of power is not exclusive, unless in its own nature it be such that the continued exercise of it by the former possessor is inconsistent with the grant, and that this is not of that description. The appellant, conceding these postulates, except the last, contends, that full power to regulate a particular subject, implies the whole power, and leaves no residuum; that a grant of the whole is incompatible with the existence of a right in another to any part of it. . . .

The grant of the power to lay and collect taxes is, like the power to regulate commerce, made in general terms, and has never been understood to interfere with the exercise of the same power by the states; and hence has been drawn an argument which has been applied to the question under consideration. But the two grants are not, it is conceived, similar in their terms or their nature. Although many of the powers formerly exercised by the states, are transferred to the government of the Union, yet the state governments remain, and constitute a most important part of our system. The power of taxation is indispensable to their existence, and is a power which, in its own nature, is capable of residing in, and being exercised by, different authorities, at the same time. We are accustomed to see it placed, for different purposes, in different hands. Taxation is the simple operation of taking small portions from a perpetually accumulating mass, susceptible of almost infinite division; and a power in one to take what is necessary for certain purposes, is not, in its nature, incompatible with a power in another to take what is necessary for other purposes. Congress is authorized to lay and collect taxes, . . . to pay the debts, and provide for the common defense and general welfare

of the United States. This does not interfere with the power of the states to tax for the support of their own governments; nor is the exercise of that power by the states, an exercise of any portion of the power that is granted to the United States. In imposing taxes for state purposes, they are not doing what Congress is empowered to do. . . .

In discussing the question, whether this power is still in the states, in the case under consideration, we may dismiss from it the inquiry, whether it is surrendered by the mere grant to congress, or is retained until Congress shall exercise the power. We may dismiss that inquiry, because it has been exercised, and the regulations which Congress deemed it proper to make, are now in full operation. The sole question is, can a state regulate commerce with foreign nations and among the states, while Congress is regulating it? . . .

It has been contended by the counsel for the appellant, that, as the word "to regulate" implies in its nature, full power over the thing to be regulated, it excludes, necessarily, the action of all others that would perform the same operation on the same thing. That regulation is designed for the entire result, applying to those parts which remain as they were, as well as to those which are altered. It produces a uniform whole, which is as much disturbed and deranged by changing what the regulating power designs to leave untouched, as that on which it has operated. There is great force in this argument, and the court is not satisfied that it has been refuted.

Since, however, in exercising the power of regulating their own purely internal affairs, whether of trading or police, the states may sometimes enact laws, the validity of which depends on their interfering with, and being contrary to, an act of congress passed in pursuance of the constitution, the court will enter upon the inquiry, whether the laws of New York, as expounded by the highest tribunal of that state, have, in their application to this case, come into collision with an act of congress, and deprived a citizen of a right to which that act entitles him. Should this collision exist, it will be immaterial, whether those laws were passed in virtue of a concurrent power "to regulate commerce with foreign nations and among the several states," or, in virtue of a power to regulate their domestic trade and police. In one case and the other, the acts of New York must yield to the law of Congress; and the decision sustaining the privilege they confer, against a right given by a law of the Union, must be erroneous. . . .

The nullity of an act, inconsistent with the constitution, is produced by the declaration, that the constitution is the supreme law. . . . In every such case, the act of Congress, or the treaty, is supreme; and the law of the state, though enacted in the exercise of powers not controverted, must yield to it. . . .

[T]his court is of opinion, that the several licenses to the steam-boats, to carry on the coasting trade, which are set up by the appellant, Thomas Gibbons, in his answer to the bill of the respondent, Aaron Ogden, filed in the court of chancery for the state of New York, which were granted under an act of Congress, passed in pursuance of the constitution of the United States, gave full authority to those vessels to navigate the waters of the United States, by steam or otherwise, for the purpose of carrying on the coasting trade, any law of the state of New York to the contrary notwithstanding; and that so much of the several laws of the state of New

York, as prohibits vessels, licensed according to the laws of the United States, from navigating the waters of the state of New York, by means of fire or steam, is repugnant to the said constitution, and void.

MR. JUSTICE JOHNSON, CONCURRING (OMITTED).

(3) Cooley v. Board of Wardens of the Port of Philadelphia (1852)

+Curtis, Taney, Catron, McKinley, Nelson, Grier, Daniel
−McLean, Wayne

[On the question of state power to regulate commerce, Marshall chose a statesmanlike middle course. He sidestepped the argument, advanced by Justice Johnson and known as the "dormant power" theory, that the mere grant of power to Congress to regulate interstate commerce precluded any state regulation whatsoever. And he rejected what was known as the "concurrent power" theory, which held that no aspect of commerce was exclusively reserved either to Congress or to the states and that both could regulate commerce at will except in cases of conflict where the congressional regulation would prevail. Unlike the taxing power, which was admittedly a concurrent power to be exercised both by the states and by the Congress, the commerce power could not be so construed. In some parts of his opinion, Marshall appears to adopt a theory of "mutual exclusiveness." Certain aspects of commerce would remain within the province of state regulation. His examples include "inspection laws, quarantine laws, health laws . . . as well as laws for regulating the internal commerce of a state. . . . No direct general power over these objects is granted to Congress; and, consequently, they remain subject to state legislation." Other aspects of commerce, Marshall seemed to be saying, were exclusively reserved to Congress, such as interstate movement or navigation, or that "commerce which concerns more states than one."

But Marshall didn't stop there. He also argued that in exercising its plenary power the federal government might have to regulate objects that otherwise, or concurrently, were reserved for state regulation. But then he stopped short of adopting, or at least articulating, Webster's theory of "selective exclusiveness" under which Congress had the complete, and to some extent exclusive, power to regulate commerce. Such a complete power, Marshall said, would be "inconvenient and unnecessary." Indeed, as Felix Frankfurter later wrote, Marshall's opinion in *Gibbons* v. *Ogden* was "either unconsciously or calculatedly confused."[1]

What can account for Marshall's uncharacteristic indecisiveness? Why did he not openly adopt Webster's theory, which he most probably agreed with? Herman Pritchett, noting that the theory of mutual exclusiveness was "Jeffersonian doctrine," argues that Marshall sought "to restrain this view by appearing to accept it while at the same time smothering its impact in a welter of words." At the time it may have seemed most prudent to assuage the states' rights forces while not yielding anything of consequence to them.[2]

Frankfurter also finds political motives in Marshall's performance. First, Frankfurter says, Marshall was fearful that the very flexibility of the "selective exclusiveness" doctrine left it open to a pro-states rights interpretation. Second, Marshall may have felt that a forthright exposition of selective exclusiveness would appear to give too much power to the judges and might only exacerbate states' rights jealousies. "He must have felt that the time was not ripe for such contraction of state sovereignty in the name of national interest." A "full throated" theory of selective exclusiveness, which left little to the states, would have been regarded as a threat to the autonomy of the states. Thus, Marshall was content to *imply* a theory of national supremacy, with significant limitations on the states, without stating it plainly or claiming the whole of that power at once. Finally, Marshall was sensitive to the po-

tential impact of a selective exclusiveness theory on the slavery issue; if Congress had such broad power over commerce, could it not use that power to prohibit the importation and transportation of slaves?[3]

The *Cooley* case settled the issue of competing theories. The mutual exclusiveness theory was rejected; Marshall's rejection of the dormant power theory was reaffirmed, and Webster's selective exclusiveness became the basis for what has ever since been known as the "Cooley Rule." The case involved a challenge to the constitutionality of local regulations for river pilots in the Port of Philadelphia.]

MR. JUSTICE CURTIS delivered the opinion of the Court.

. . . That the power to regulate commerce includes the regulation of navigation, we consider settled. And when we look to the nature of the service performed by pilots, to the relations which that service and its compensations bear to navigation between the several states, and between the ports of the United States and foreign countries, we are brought to the conclusion, that the regulation of the qualifications of pilots, of the modes and times of offering and rendering their services, of the responsibilities which shall rest upon them, of the powers they shall possess, of the compensation they may demand, and of the penalties by which their rights and duties may be enforced, do constitute regulations of navigation, and consequently of commerce, within the just meaning of this clause of the Constitution.

The power to regulate navigation is the power to prescribe rules in conformity with which navigation must be carried on. It extends to the per-

---

[1]Felix Frankfurter, *The Commerce Clause Under Marshall, Taney and Waite* (Chicago: Quadrangle Books, 1964), p. 17.

[2]C. Herman Pritchett, *The American Constitution, 3rd edition* (New York: McGraw-Hill, 1977), pp. 202–207.

[3]Frankfurter, *op. cit.*, Note 1, pp. 18–27.

sons who conduct it, as well as to the instruments used. Accordingly, the first Congress assembled under the Constitution passed laws, requiring the masters of ships and vessels of the United States to be citizens of the United States, and established many rules for the government and regulation of officers and seamen. These have been from time to time added to and changed, and we are not aware that their validity has been questioned.

Now, a pilot, so far as respects the navigation of the vessel in that part of the voyage which is his pilotage-ground, is the temporary master charged with the safety of the vessel and cargo, and of the lives of those on board, and intrusted with the command of the crew. He is not only one of the persons engaged in navigation, but he occupies a most important and responsible place among those thus engaged. And if Congress has power to regulate the seamen who assist the pilot in the management of the vessel, a power never denied, we can perceive no valid reason why the pilot should be beyond the reach of the same power. It is true that, according to the usages of modern commerce on the ocean, the pilot is on board only during a part of the voyage between ports of different states, or between ports of the United States and foreign countries; but if he is on board for such a purpose and during so much of the voyage as to be engaged in navigation, the power to regulate navigation extends to him while thus engaged, as clearly as it would if he were to remain on board throughout the whole passage, from port to port. For it is a power which extends to every part of the voyage, and may regulate those who conduct or assist in conducting navigation in one part of a voyage as much as in another part, or during the whole voyage.

Nor should it be lost sight of, that this subject of the regulation of pilots and pilotage has an intimate connection with, and an important relation to, the general subject of commerce with foreign nations and among the several states, over which it was one main object of the Constitution to create a national control. . . .

. . . And a majority of the court are of opinion, that a regulation of pilots is a regulation of commerce, within the grant to Congress of the commercial power, contained in the third clause of the eighth section of the first article of the Constitution.

It becomes necessary, therefore, to consider whether this law of Pennsylvania, being a regulation of commerce, is valid.

The Act of Congress of the 7th of August, 1789, is as follows:—

That all pilots in the bays, inlets, rivers, harbors, and ports of the United States shall continue to be regulated in conformity with the existing laws of the states, respectively, wherein such pilots may be, or with such laws as the states may respectively hereafter enact for the purpose, until further legislative provision shall be made by Congress. . . .

. . . We are brought directly and unavoidably to the consideration of the question, whether the grant of the commercial power to Congress did per se deprive the states of all power to regulate pilots. This question has never been decided by this court, nor, in our judgment, has any case depending upon all the considerations which must govern this one, come before this court. The grant of commercial power to Congress does not contain any terms which expressly exclude the states from exercising an authority over its subject-matter. If they are excluded, it must be because the nature of the power thus granted to Congress requires that a similar authority should not exist in the states. If it were conceded on the one side that the nature of this power, like that to legislate for the District of Columbia, is absolutely and totally repugnant to the existence of similar power in the states, probably no one would deny that the grant of the power to Congress, as effectually and perfectly excludes the states from all future legislation on the subject, as if express words had been used to exclude them. And on the other hand, if it were admitted that the existence of this power in Congress, like the power of taxation, is compatible with the existence of a similar power in the states, then it would be in conformity with the contemporary exposition of the Constitution ("Federalist," No. 32), and with the judicial construction given from time to time by this court, after the most deliberate consideration, to hold that the mere grant of such a power to Congress, did not imply a prohibition on the states to exercise the same power; that it is not the mere existence of such a power, but its exercise by Congress, which may be incompatible with the exercise of the same power by the states, and that the states may legislate in the absence of congressional regulations. . . .

Now, the power to regulate commerce, embraces a vast field, containing not only many, but exceedingly various subjects, quite unlike in their nature; some imperatively demanding a single uniform rule, operating equally on the commerce of the United States in every port; and some, like the subject now in question, as imperatively demanding that diversity, which alone can meet the local necessities of navigation.

Either absolutely to affirm, or deny that the nature of this power requires exclusive legislation by Congress, is

to lose sight of the nature of the subjects of this power, and to assert concerning all of them, what is really applicable but to a part. Whatever subjects of this power are in their nature national, or admit only of one uniform system, or plan of regulation, may justly be said to be of such a nature as to require exclusive legislation by Congress. That this cannot be affirmed of laws for the regulation of pilots and pilotage, is plain. The Act of 1789 contains a clear and authoritative declaration by the first Congress, that the nature of this subject is such that until Congress should find it necessary to exert its power, it should be left to the legislation of the states; that it is local and not national; that it is likely to be the best provided for, not by one system, or plan of regulations, but by as many as the legislative discretion of the several states should deem applicable to the local peculiarities of the ports within their limits. . . .

It is the opinion of a majority of the court that the mere grant to Congress of the power to regulate commerce, did not deprive the states of power to regulate pilots, and that although Congress has legislated on this subject, its legislation manifests an intention, with a single exception, not to regulate this subject, but to leave its regulation to the several states. To these precise questions, which are all we are called on to decide, this opinion must be understood to be confined. It does not extend to the question what other subjects, under the commercial power, are within the exclusive control of Congress, or may be regulated by the states in the absence of all congressional legislation; nor to the general question, how far any regulation of a subject by Congress may be deemed to operate as an exclusion of all legislation by the states upon the same subject.

MR. JUSTICE DANIEL, CONCURRING (OMITTED).

MR. JUSTICE McLEAN, WITH MR. JUSTICE WAYNE CONCURRING, DISSENTING (OMITTED).

(4) A note on the *Cooley* Rule and the Regulation of Commerce by the States

Federalism is the division of power between nation and state. Basically, there are two models, or conceptions, of federalism. One views the nation and the states as competing entities. They pursue different, if sometimes parallel, courses of action. Boundaries between them are relatively fixed, and their respective powers often are mutually exclusive. Where the Constitution has delegated power to the federal government, it may use that power fully, provided that its use does not infringe on the reserved powers of the states, as provided in the Tenth Amendment. There is little incentive for cooperation or for any sharing of constitutional power and responsibility beyond that provided for in the Constitution. The metaphor of a "layer cake" has been used to describe this conception of federalism. The term "dual federalism" has also been applied. In the *Gibbons* case, the "concurrent powers" argument expressed much the same conception of federalism.

The foundations of the *Cooley* Rule lie in a different conception of federalism, currently referred to as "cooperative federalism" and symbolized by the metaphor of the "marble cake."[1] The *Cooley* Rule applies only to interstate commerce, but philosophically, it covers the whole range of federal-state relations. Underlying that rule is the premise that government is a joint venture or partnership. The states retain a limited sovereignty, but the federal government is clearly supreme, and national needs take precedence over local preferences. More than anything else, cooperative federalism must be viewed as a pragmatic and political conception of the division of powers and not one that is exclusively legal.

Under the *Cooley* Rule, there are aspects of interstate commerce that may be regulated by the states individually; there are aspects that may be regulated jointly by Congress and the states; and there are aspects that either by their nature or by congressional decision are regulated by, or left to be regulated by, Congress alone. Conflicts between national and state regulation are resolved in favor of the federal government under the supremacy clause of the Constitution. The questions, therefore, are *what* aspects of commerce may the states regulate, *when* may they regulate, *how* may they regulate and, *where* are the lines to be drawn?

The distribution between Congress and the states of regulatory power over interstate commerce has remained a thorny political and legal problem. The *Cooley* case did not settle the issue. It merely established a set of broad principles to guide courts in the future. As a result, generalizations are not easy. The late Professor Thomas Reed Powell characterized the difficulty by declaring that "Congress may regulate interstate commerce. The states may also regulate interstate commerce, but not too much. How much is too much is beyond the scope of this statement."[2]

[1] See Morton Grodzins, *The American System: A New View of Government in the United States* (Chicago: Rand McNally, 1966), pp. 8–9.

[2] Thomas Reed Powell, *Vagaries and Varieties in Constitutional Interpretation* (New York: Columbia University Press, 1956), p. ix.

"How much is too much" is precisely the question the Supreme Court has been continually asked to address in the century and a quarter since the *Cooley* case was decided.

"How much" the states may regulate commerce depends, of course, on whether or not Congress itself has sought to regulate the same activity and on whether, in the absence of congressional regulation, the subject is of such a nature as to lend itself to decentralized regulation or whether it requires uniform national regulation. The Court has long sought to uphold the constitutional objective of a free flow of commerce among the states. In the absence of conflicting federal law, and assuming that the subject is not one requiring uniform national regulation, the states are free to regulate if the following standards are met. First, legitimate state objectives must be pursued; there must be a substantial state interest in regulating the activity in question. Second, whatever case a state can make for regulation, it cannot discriminate against interstate commerce. Discrimination in favor of local commerce places an unconstitutional burden on interstate commerce. Third, even a nondiscriminatory state regulation must not place an undue burden on interstate commerce. But what is an "undue" burden? And what is a "substantial state interest"? There is no set formula. It is a matter of judgment. The following examples illustrate both the problem and the main lines of doctrine that the Supreme Court has developed.

1. State regulation that discriminates against interstate commerce is an undue burden on commerce and hence unconstitutional. In *Baldwin* v. *Seelig* (1935), the Supreme Court invalidated a New York State law that prohibited importation of milk purchased outside the state at prices below the minimum price imposed on milk produced within the state. The states may not use their police powers, said Justice Cardozo, "with the aim and effect of establishing an economic barrier against competition with the produces of another state." But even a nondiscriminatory state law may be held invalid as an undue burden on commerce. Thus, in *Southern Pacific Railroad* v. *Arizona* (1945), a state safety requirement limiting freight trains to seventy cars and passenger trains to fourteen cars was invalidated because it unduly obstructed interstate commerce and adversely affected the uniformity needed in this area.

2. A state may regulate commerce where it has a substantial and legitimate police power concern; where the means of regulation are within the police power of the state; where, contrary to the *Southern Pacific* case, there is no necessity for uniform national regulation; and where the state's legitimate objectives cannot be reached by other means. The Supreme Court upheld a ban on door-to-door soliciting in the case of *Breard* v. *Alexandria* (1951), where the challenged ordinance fell equally upon interstate and intrastate salespersons and protected a valid social interest—the privacy of the citizens of Alexandria. There were no less drastic means to achieve this end, said the Court, and the ordinance did not discriminate against interstate commerce.

In 1938, the Court upheld a South Carolina regulation limiting the weight of trucks on state highways. The regulation applied to all trucks, including those in interstate commerce. The Court saw the highways, built and maintained by the state, as "so particularly of state concern" that weight limitations were valid even though they did materially interfere with interstate commerce. (*South Carolina State Highway Department* v. *Barnwell*). When, in 1945, the Supreme Court invalidated Arizona's railroad regulations in the *Southern Pacific* case, Chief Justice Stone, writing for the majority, felt obliged to rationalize the different results in that case and the *Barnwell* case. The difference was, he said, that a state has a far greater regulatory interest in cars traveling its highways than in interstate railroads. He likened that interest to state quarantine measures, game laws, and the local regulation of rivers and harbors.

In 1959, in *Bibb* v. *Navajo Freight Lines*, the Court struck down an Illinois law requiring fixed mudguards on trucks traveling state roads and outlawing the more common mudflaps found on most trucks. The law applied equally to interstate and intrastate trucking activity, but the Court held nonetheless that it placed an excessive burden on interstate commerce; weighing heavily in the Court's mind were the trial court findings that the safety benefits of mudguards were marginal. Just recently, in *Raymond Motor Transportation* v. *Rice* (1978), the Court invalidated a Wisconsin law prohibiting trucks longer than fifty-five feet from traveling state highways. The Court observed that no clear safety benefits had been shown. Furthermore, a large number of exemptions for local trucks had been selectively issued by the state. Thus the law not only burdened interstate commerce but discriminated against it as well.

3. An otherwise legitimate policy goal may not be obtained by obstructing the free flow of commerce where less drastic means of achieving that goals are available. In *Dean Milk Co.* v. *City of Madison* (1951), the Supreme Court struck down a city ordinance prohibiting the sale of milk coming from a farm more than twenty-five miles or processed more than five miles from the center of town. The rationale for the ordinance was to ensure healthy and wholesome milk, but the five-mile limit conveniently immunized all the local milk processors and was aimed specifically (if not overtly) at competing milk from southern Wisconsin and northern Illinois. The Supreme Court observed that while the ends were within the city's prerogatives, the means were excessive. The same results could be obtained by requiring uniform inspection of all milk to be sold in Madison, regardless of where it had been processed. The burden on commerce was excessive and hence unconstitutional.

It is now well established that the plenary power of Congress to regulate commerce includes the power to *permit* as well as the power to prohibit state regulation. But it was not always so clear. In the *Cooley* case, Pennsylvania's pilotage law for the port of Philadelphia was considered in the light of a federal statute that authorized such laws. But the Court was careful in noting that the federal law guided but did not compel the Court's conclusion that the subject was one for local control in the absence of congressional regulation. Justice Curtis wrote: "If the Constitution excluded the states from making any law regulating commerce, certainly Congress cannot regrant or in any manner reconvey to the states that power." However, subsequent decisions modified that interpretation. In the *Southern Pacific* case, Chief Justice Stone held that Congress had the power to allocate responsibility for regulating interstate commerce, which included the authority "to permit the states to regulate the commerce in a manner which would otherwise not be permissible."

The full meaning of this declaration became apparent the following year. In 1944, in *United States* v. *South-Eastern Underwriters Association*, the Supreme Court had applied the Sherman Anti-Trust Act to the business of insurance, notwithstanding an 1868 decision holding that insurance was not commerce. Congress promptly enacted a bill known as the McCarran Act of 1945, which declared that continued regulation and taxation of insurance by the states was in the public interest and that the silence of Congress on the subject imposed no barrier to state regulation or taxation. In *Prudential Insurance Company* v. *Benjamin* (1946), the Court upheld the act. Prudential was a New Jersey corporation that objected to a 3 percent tax imposed by South Carolina on all its business done in that state. Since no comparable tax was imposed on South Carolina corporations, the tax was discriminatory, and the Court assumed that it would be invalid under a long line of cases interpreting the commerce clause and its "dormant powers." But, the Court held, the McCarran Act made the tax valid. Congress, in other words, could authorize the states to do what they otherwise could not do under the Constitution.

In the absence of clear congressional intent to permit or prohibit state regulation, the question often arises whether Congress has "preempted" a field from state regulation. This is an especially thorny question for the courts, since it involves judicial interpretation of congressional intent from diverse statutory pronouncements, legislative hearings, and so on. And the search for intent is often intertwined with considerations of the "nature" of the economic activity in question and whether or not it requires uniform national regulation. Three recent cases illustrate this interplay.

In 1973, the Supreme Court ruled 5-4 in *Burbank* v. *Lockheed Air Terminal* that considerations of air-traffic safety, by their very nature, require exclusive federal regulation. On that logic, the Court invalidated an anti-jet noise ordinance of the city of Burbank, California, which prohibited "pure" jet aircraft from landing or taking off between the hours of 11 P.M. and 7 A.M. Congress had not specifically preempted the subject, but Justice Douglas, citing the *Cooley* decision, wrote that local noise ordinances were inconsistent with the pervasive objectives of the federal statutory scheme and with the need for maintaining a "delicate balance between safety and efficiency."

The Court recently held that certain laws of the state of Washington regulating the size of oil tankers entering Puget Sound, the design of those tankers, and the use of state-licensed pilots were invalid, being preempted by federal legislation on the same subjects. In *Ray* v. *Atlantic Richfield Co.* (1978), the Court ruled that the Federal Ports and Waterways Safety Act, dealing with the control of harbor traffic and the safety of vessels in U.S. ports and harbors, authorized the secretary of transportation to make administrative rules governing such subjects. Therefore, state action was precluded under the supremacy clause of the Constitution. In the same decision, the Court upheld Washington statutes concerning the use of tug boats in docking oil tankers, ruling that since the subject of tugs had not been legislated on by Congress and since the statute was not otherwise a burden on commerce, these state laws were valid.

A contrasting result was reached in the case of *Goldstein* v. *California* (1973). The state of California had passed a copyright statute prohibiting the "pirating" of commercial recordings. Goldstein was convicted for violating the statute. The Constitution (Article I, Section 8) gives Congress the power to grant copyrights and patents to authors and inventors for limited periods of time. The California law granted copyright protection for an unlimited period of time. Thus, it was inconsistent with the federal law, but not necessarily in conflict with it. By a 5-4 vote, the Supreme Court upheld Goldstein's conviction, finding that the congressional power over copyrights was *not* exclusive and that the state statute did not conflict with the Constitution.

Writing for the majority, Chief Justice Burger set down a test that appears to draw the balance somewhat more in favor of the states than was done in the *Lockheed* case, in which Burger had joined Douglas's majority opinion. In *Goldstein*, however, Burger held that the states retain all rights *not exclusively delegated* to the national government. Exclusivity is measured by (1) whether or not the power was delegated by the Constitution in exclusive terms; (2) whether or not there was some express prohibition on the state power; and (3) whether or not the exercise of state power would be absolutely and totally contradictory and repugnant to the exercise of authority granted to the national government. In Burger's terms, the Supreme Court should not invoke the federal preemption doctrine where there is merely a possibility of conflict, but only where conflict will necessarily arise. "Inconvenience" is not sufficient; only actual constitutional repugnance can justify

striking down a state statute. The majority did not deny the need for national copyright protection, but it did not feel that it had to be exclusive.

Naturally, a state could not legitimately repudiate national copyright laws. But the *Goldstein* case seems to allow a state, in this instance at least, to augment and enhance such laws through state legislation. Questions naturally arise in more important and controversial areas of regulation: highway safety standards, licensing of nuclear power plants, automobile pollution control, and so on.

B. *The Doctrine of Substantive Due Process*

(1) A Note on the Contract Clause and Substantive Due Process: Private Rights and the Public Interest

One of the major initial purposes of the Supreme Court in the new constitutional scheme was to insure the protection of property from "irresponsible" state governments which, under popular pressures, might weaken the rights and immunities of private property. Early attempts to ensure the sanctity of private contracts relied upon the bill of attainder or ex post facto clauses, but these were held by the Supreme Court to apply only to criminal statutes.

The most effective defense of private property during the Marshall period involved the use of the Contract Clause of Article I, Section 10 of the Constitution. In *Fletcher* v. *Peck* (1810), for example, Marshall was able to hold that contract holders had vested rights that could not be legislated out of existence—not even where it was shown that the contracts (involving Tory lands in the state of Georgia) had been fraudulent, and that the legislature that had disposed of the land was corrupt.

The height of Marshall's defense of private property, however, came in the famous *Dartmouth College* case (1819). Following closely the argument and legal strategy advanced by Daniel Webster, who argued for the college, Marshall found that the college's Royal Charter constituted a contract that remained in force after the Revolution, and that the efforts of the state of New Hampshire to take control of the college by changing the board of directors constituted an impairment of the constitutional protections for private contracts.

But as the voting franchise was extended and as the commercial life of the new nation developed, a reaction set in against some of the more intimidating practices of property owners. In particular, strong opposition developed toward the practice of imprisonment for debt and many states passed bankruptcy and debtor laws designed to regulate and ameliorate the sanctions imposed on debtors. While the Court would never allow such laws to be applied retrospectively to contracts already made, it did decide, in *Ogden* v. *Saunders* (1827), that states could pass bankruptcy laws that applied to all *future* contracts. But even this concession was too much for Marshall, and he recorded the only dissent of his long career. The decision in *Ogden* v. *Saunders* proved to be important, for it provided the states with the power to include in all corporate charters the reserved right of the state to repeal or modify the franchise under certain stated conditions.

With Marshall's death and the succession of Roger Taney as Chief Justice, the Court made further inroads against absolute property rights. The *Charles River Bridge* case (1837) provided the opportunity for Taney to explore the limits of private rights and the public interest. The Charles River Bridge Company had been granted a charter by the state of Massachusetts in 1785 to construct a toll bridge across the Charles River, in return for which the company would pay an annual rent to the state and turn the bridge over to the state after forty years. The bridge opened in 1786, and the charter was then extended to seventy years. In 1828, the legislature incorporated "The proprietors of the Warren Bridge" for the purpose of erecting another bridge over the Charles River, near the old Charles River Bridge and directly competitive with it. The new bridge was to be operated without tolls, and of course, it soon took most of the passengers away from the old bridge.

The Charles River Bridge Company sought an injunction to prevent the erection and operation of the Warren Bridge, on the ground that the Warren Bridge Charter impaired the contract between the state of Massachusetts and the proprietors of the Charles River Bridge and was therefore unconstitutional. The state court dismissed the claim and the case was appealed to the Supreme Court. Upholding the dismissal of the suit, Chief Justice Taney ruled that the original contract contained no provision or grant of monopoly to the Charles River Bridge, and therefore the charter must be narrowly construed in favor of the public interest:

It is the grant of certain franchises by the public to a private corporation, and in a matter where the public interest is concerned. . . . This, like many other cases, is a bargain between a company of adventurers and the public, the terms of which are expressed in the statute; and the rule of construction in all such cases, is now fully established to be this—that any ambiguity in the terms of the contract, must operate against the adventurers and in favor of the public, and the plaintiffs can claim nothing that is not clearly given them by the act.

It was of course true that while the new bridge did not physically interfere with the traffic on the Charles River Bridge, it destroyed its income. But, as Taney pointed out with considerable foresight, to read into charters for public conveyances or turnpikes such a monopoly provision would restrict or halt the many improvements in travel then in progress:

Let it once be understood that such charters carry with them these implied contracts, and give this unknown and undefined property in a line of traveling, and you will soon find the old turnpike corporations awakening from their sleep, and calling upon this court to put down the improvements which have since taken their place. The millions of property which have been invested in railroads and canals, upon lines of travel which had been before occupied by turnpike corporations, will be put in jeopardy. We shall be thrown back to the improvements of the last century, and obliged to stand still until the claims of the old turnpike corporations shall be satisfied, and they shall consent to permit these states to avail themselves of the rights of modern science, and to partake of the benefits of those improvements which are now adding to the wealth and prosperity, and the convenience and comfort, of every other part of the civilized world. Nor is this all. This court will find itself compelled to fix, by some arbitrary rule, the width of this new kind of property in a line of travel; . . . This court is not prepared to sanction principles which must lead to such results.

In 1880 the Court ruled that the police power could not be limited by the contract clause (*Stone* v. *Missis-*

sippi), and it was becoming clear that the contract clause was no longer a reliable shield for private property owners. Other clauses— particularly those contained in the Fourteenth Amendment—seemed more promising.

The *Slaughterhouse Cases* (1873) marked the beginning of a new chapter in the constitutional adjudication of economic matters. In that case, a majority of 5-4 rejected attempts to invoke the Fourteenth Amendment as a constitutional shield against regulation of private property. But Justice Bradley's dissent, which held that the due process clause of the Fourteenth Amendment protected private property against unreasonable government regulation, marked the beginnings of the doctrine of substantive due process in the Supreme Court.

(2) The Slaughterhouse Cases (1873)

+Miller, Clifford, Davis, Strong, Hunt
 −Chase, Swayne, Field, Bradley

[The Fourteenth Amendment was the centerpiece of initial efforts by Congress to pursue a policy of reconstruction after the Civil War. Congress' immediate objectives were to validate the Civil Rights Act of 1866 and to establish equal status under law for the newly freed slaves. To accomplish this objective the Fourteenth Amendment declared that all persons born or naturalized in the United States were citizens of the United States and of the state in which they resided. This had the immediate effect of overruling the *Dred Scott* decision of 1857, which had held that each state could determine for itself who was or was not a citizen of that state. The amendment then went on to provide that "No state shall make or enforce any law which shall abridge the privileges or immunities of citizens of the United States; nor shall any state deprive any person of life, liberty or property, without due process of law; nor deny to any person within its jurisdiction the equal protection of the laws."

The Louisiana state legislature, admittedly a corrupt, carpetbag government, had granted a monopoly to a group of butchers to operate the only slaughterhouse in and around the city of New Orleans. All butchering of animals and all stockyard activities generally were to take place at that location, for which users paid a legally set fee. Another group of butchers who had been disenfranchised challenged the act under the Thirteenth and Fourteenth Amendments, claiming they had been denied the "right" to practice their profession. The *Slaughterhouse Cases,* therefore, provided the first opportunity for the Supreme Court to construe the meaning of the Fourteenth Amendment.

Prior to the Civil War, the only recourse of the butchers would have been under the state constitution or state laws, for in 1833 the Supreme Court, in *Barron* v. *Baltimore*, ruled that the Bill of Rights (including the due process clause of the Fifth Amendment) applied only to the federal government. But the Fourteenth Amendment, despite the clear intent of its framers, contained words that were ambiguous and potentially broader in scope. The allegation of the butchers was that the privileges and immunities clause created new substantive rights limiting state power, rights that had not existed prior to the amendment's ratification. They claimed, invoking the common law doctrine of "vested rights," that the privileges and immunities clause protected, as a right of citizenship, the right to carry on a lawful profession.

The case for the butchers was argued by a former justice, John Campbell, and it was supported strongly by the bar. The argument went beyond the butchers, claiming that the broad goal of the Fourteenth Amendment was to protect laissez-faire individualism. Campbell argued that the Fourteenth Amendment had, in fact, revolutionized the constitutional arrangement by bringing property rights under the protection of the federal constitution and the federal courts.]

MR. JUSTICE MILLER delivered the opinion of the Court.

. . . The wisdom of the monopoly granted by the legislature may be open to question, but it is difficult to see a justification for the assertion that the butchers are deprived of the right to labor in their occupation, or the people of their daily service in preparing food, or how this statute, with the duties and guards imposed upon the company, can be said to destroy the business of the butcher, or seriously interfere with its pursuit.

The power here exercised by the legislature of Louisiana is, in its essential nature, one which has been, up to the present period in the constitutional history of this country, always conceded to belong to the States, however it may *now* be questioned in some of its details.

. . . This is called the police power;

. . . This power is, and must be from its very nature, incapable of any very exact definition or limitation. Upon it depends the security of social order, the life and health of the citizen, the comfort of an existence in a thickly populated community, the enjoyment of private and social life, and the beneficial use of property.

. . . The regulation of the place and manner of conducting the slaughtering of animals, and the business of butchering within a city, and the inspection of the animals to be killed for meat, and of the meat afterwards, are among the most necessary and frequent exercises of this power.

. . . It may, therefore, be considered as established, that the authority of the legislature of Louisiana to pass the present statute is ample, unless some restraint in the exercise of that power is found in the constitution of that State or in the amendments to the Constitution of the United States, adopted since the date of the decisions we have already cited.

. . . The plaintiffs in error accepting this issue, allege that the statute is a violation of the Constitution of the United States in these several particulars:

That it creates an involuntary servitude forbidden by the thirteenth article of amendment;

That it abridges the privileges and immunities of citizens of the United States;

That it denies to the plaintiffs the equal protection of the laws; and,

That it deprives them of their property without due process of law; contrary to the provisions of the first section of the fourteenth article of amendment.

This court is thus called upon for the first time to give construction to these articles.

. . . The most cursory glance at these articles discloses a unity of purpose, when taken in connection with the history of the times, which cannot fail to have an important bearing on any question of doubt concerning their true meaning. Nor can such doubts, when any reasonably exist, be safely and rationally solved without a reference to that history; for in it is found the occasion and the necessity for recurring again to the great source of power in this country, the people of the States, for additional guarantees of human rights; additional powers to the Federal government; additional restraints upon those of the States. Fortunately that history is fresh within the memory of us all, and its leading features, as they bear upon the matter before us, free from doubt.

. . .[O]n the most casual examination of the language of these amendments, no one can fail to be impressed with the one pervading pur-

pose found in them all, lying at the foundation of each, and without which none of them would have been even suggested; we mean the freedom of the slave race, the security and firm establishment of that freedom, and the protection of the newly-made freeman and citizen from the oppressions of those who had formerly exercised unlimited dominion over him. . . .

. . .We do not say that no one else but the negro can share in this protection. Both the language and spirit of these articles are to have their fair and just weight in any question of construction. Undoubtedly while negro slavery alone was in the mind of the Congress which proposed the thirteenth article, it forbids any other kind of slavery, now or hereafter. . . . But what we do say, and what we wish to be understood is, that in any fair and just construction of any section or phrase of these amendments, it is necessary to look to the purpose which we have said was the pervading spirit of them all, the evil which they were designed to remedy, and the process of continued addition to the Constitution, until that purpose was supposed to be accomplished, as far as constitutional law can accomplish it.

. . .[T]he distinction between citizenship of the United States and citizenship of a State is clearly recognized and established. Not only may a man be a citizen of the United States without being a citizen of a State, but an important element is necessary to convert the former into the latter. He must reside within the State to make him a citizen of it, but it is only necessary that he should be born or naturalized in the United States to be a citizen of the Union.

It is quite clear, then, that there is a citizenship of the United States, and a citizenship of a State, which are distinct from each other, and which depend upon different characteristics or circumstances in the individual.

We think this distinction and its explicit recognition in this amendment of great weight in this argument, because the next paragraph of this same section, which is the one mainly relied on by the plaintiffs in error, speaks only of privileges and immunities of citizens of the United States, and does not speak of those of citizens of the several States. The argument, however, in favor of the plaintiffs rests wholly on the assumption that the citizenship is the same, and the privileges and immunities guaranteed by the clause are the same.

The language is: "No state shall make or enforce any law which shall abridge the privileges or immunities of citizens of the United States." It is a little remarkable, if this clause was intended as a protection to the citizen of a state against the legislative power of his own state, that the words "citizen of the state" should be left out when it is so carefully used, and used in contradistinction to "citizens of the United States" in the very sentence which precedes it. It is too clear for argument that the change in phraseology was adopted understandingly and with a purpose.

Of the privileges and immunities of the citizens of the United States, and of the privileges and immunities of the citizen of the state, and what they respectively are, we will presently consider; but we wish to state here that it is only the former which are placed by this clause under the protection of the Federal Constitution, and that the latter, whatever they may be, are not intended to have any additional protection by this paragraph of the Amendment.

If, then, there is a difference between the privileges and immunities belonging to a citizen of the United States as such, and those belonging to the citizen of the state as such, the latter must rest for their security and protection where they have heretofore rested; for they are not embraced by this paragraph of the Amendment.

. . .

With the exception of these and a few other restrictions, the entire domain of the privileges and immunities of citizens of the States . . . lay within the constitutional and legislative power of the States, and without that of the federal government. Was it the purpose of the fourteenth amendment, by the simple declaration that no State should make or enforce any law which shall abridge the privileges and immunities of *citizens of the United States,* to transfer the security and protection of all the civil rights which we have mentioned, from the States to the Federal government? And where it is declared that Congress shall have the power to enforce that article, was it intended to bring within the power of Congress the entire domain of civil rights heretofore belonging exclusively to the States?

All this and more must follow, if the proposition of the plaintiffs in error be sound. . . .

We are convinced that no such results were intended by the Congress which proposed these amendments, nor by the legislatures of the States which ratified them.

. . . We are of opinion that the rights claimed by these plaintiffs in error, if they have any existence, are not privileges and immunities of citizens of the United States within the meaning of the clause of the fourteenth amendment under consideration.

It is sufficient to say that under no construction of that provision that we have ever seen, or any that we deem admissible, can the restraint imposed by the State of Louisiana upon the exercise of their trade by the butchers of New Orleans be held to be a deprivation of property within the meaning of that provision.

. . . We doubt very much whether any action of a State not directed by way of discrimination against the negroes as a class, or on account of their race, will ever be held to come within the purview of this provision. It is so clearly a provision for that race and that emergency, that a strong case would be necessary for its application to any other. . . .

The judgments of the Supreme Court of Louisiana in these cases are AFFIRMED.

MR. JUSTICE FIELD, DISSENTING (OMITTED).
MR. JUSTICE BRADLEY, DISSENTING (OMITTED).

[Two of the four dissenting justices in The *Slaughterhouse Cases* wrote opinions. Justice Field argued that a statute that conferred special privileges and limited access to lawful occupations was in violation of the privileges and immunities clause of the Fourteenth Amendment. To him, all pursuits, professions, and avocations should be open to all "of the same sex, age and condition" except where a state, under its police powers, prescribes suitable regulations. The statute in this case did not meet that test, even though it was directed ostensibly toward ending pollution in the Mississippi River and decontaminating the city's drinking water.

Justice Bradley agreed that the ordinance was unconstitutional under the Fourteenth Amendment for the same reasons advanced by Field—it prohibited a large class of citizens from engaging in a lawful occupation. But Bradley relied, not on the privileges and immunities clause, but on the due process and equal protection clauses of the Fourteenth Amendment. Although Field's dissent was more frequently spoken of at the time, it was Bradley's invocation of the due process clause that became the cornerstone of the doctrine of substantive due process.]

(3) Munn v. Illinois (1877)

+ Waite, Clifford, Miller, Bradley, Swayne, Davis, Hunt
−Field, Strong

MR. CHIEF JUSTICE WAITE delivered the opinion of the Court.

The question to be determined in this case is whether the General Assembly of Illinois can . . . fix by law the maximum of charges for the storage of grain in warehouses at Chicago and other places in the State having not less than one hundred thousand inhabitants. . . .

It is claimed that such a law is repugnant:

1. To that part of section 8, article 1, of the Constitution of the United States which confers upon Congress the power "to regulate commerce with foreign nations and among the several States;"
2. To that part of section 9 of the same article which provides that "No preference shall be given by any regulation of commerce or revenue to the ports of one State over those of another;" and,
3. To that part of Amendment XIV, which ordains that no State shall "Deprive any person of life, liberty or property, without due process of law, nor deny to any person within its jurisdiction the equal protection of the laws."

We will consider the last of these objections first.

Every statute is presumed to be constitutional. The courts ought not to declare one to be unconstitutional, unless it is clearly so. If there is doubt, the expressed will of the Legislature should be sustained.

The Constitution contains no definition of the word "deprive," as used in the 14th Amendment. To determine its signification, therefore, it is necessary to ascertain the effect which usage has given it, when employed in the same or a like connection.

While this provision of the Amendment is new in the Constitution of the United States as a limitation upon the powers of the States, it is old as a principle of civilized government. It is found in Magna Charta, and, in substance if not in form, in nearly or quite all the constitutions that have been from time to time adopted by the several States of the Union. By the 5th Amendment, it was introduced into the Constitution of the United States as a limitation upon the powers of the National Government, and by the 14th, as a guaranty against any encroachment upon an acknowledged right of citizenship by the Legislatures of the States.

When the people of the United Colonies separated from Great Britain, they changed the form, but not the substance of their government. They retained for the purposes of government all the powers of the British Parliament and, through their State Constitutions or other forms of social compact, undertook to give practical effect to such as they deemed necessary for the common good and the security of life and property. All the powers which they retained they committed to their respective States, unless in express terms or by implication reserved to themselves. Subsequently, when it was found necessary to establish a national government for national purposes, a part of the powers of the States and of the people of the States was granted to the United States and the people of the United States. This grant operated as a further limitation upon the powers of the States, so that now the governments of the States possess all the powers of the Parliament of England, except such as have been delegated to the United States or reserved by the people. The reservations by the people are shown in the prohibitions of the constitutions.

From this it is apparent that, down to the time of the adoption of the 14th Amendment, it was not supposed that statutes regulating the use, or even the price of the use, of private property necessarily deprived an owner of his property without due process of law. Under some circumstances they may, but not under all. The Amendment does not change the law in this particular; it simply prevents the States from doing that which will operate as such a deprivation.

This brings us to inquire as to the principles upon which this power of regulation rests, in order that we may determine what is within and what without its operative effect. Looking, then, to the common law, from whence came the right which the Constitution protects, we find that when private property is "affected with a public interest, it ceases to be juris privati only." This was said by Lord Chief Justice Hale more than two hundred years ago . . . and has been accepted without objection as an essential element in the law of property ever since. Property does become clothed with a public interest when used in a manner to make it of public consequence, and affect the community at large. When, therefore, one devotes his property to a use in which the public has an interest, he, in effect, grants to the public an interest in that use, and must submit to be controlled by the public for the common good, to the extent of the interest he has thus created. He may withdraw his grant by discontinuing the use; but, so long as he maintains the use, he must submit to the control. . . .

Under such circumstances it is difficult to see why, if the common carrier, or the miller, or the ferryman, or the innkeeper . . . pursues a public employment and exercises "a sort of public office," these plaintiffs in error do not. They stand, to use again the language of their counsel, in the very "gateway of commerce," and take toll from all who pass. Their business most certainly "tends to a common charge, and is become a thing of public interest and use." . . . Certainly, if any business can be clothed "with a public interest, and cease to be juris privati only," this has been. It may not be made so by the operation of the Constitution of Illinois or this statute, but it is by the facts. . . .

It is insisted, however, that the owner of property is entitled to a reasonable compensation for its use, even though it be clothed with a public interest, and that what is reasonable is a judicial and not a legislative question.

As has already been shown, the practice has been otherwise. In countries where the common law prevails, it has been customary from time immemorial for the Legislature to declare what shall be a reasonable compensation under such circumstances, or, perhaps more properly speaking, to fix a maximum beyond which any charge made would be unreasonable. Undoubtedly, in mere private contracts, relating to matters in which the public has no interest, what is reasonable must be ascertained judicially. But this is because the Legislature has no control over such a contract. So, too, in matters which do affect the public interest, and as to which legislative control may be exercised, if there are no statutory regulations upon the subject, the courts must determine what is reasonable. The controlling fact is the power to regulate at all. If that exists, the right to establish the maximum of charge, as one of the means of regulation, is implied. In fact, the common law rule, which requires the charge to be reasonable, is itself a regulation as to price. Without it the owner could make his rates at will, and compel the public to yield to his terms, or forego the use. . . .

We know that this is a power which may be abused; but that is no argument against its existence. For protection against abuses by Legislatures the people must resort to the polls, not to the courts.

After what has already been said, it is unnecessary to refer at length to the effect of the other provision of the Fourteenth Amendment which is relied upon, viz: that no State shall "deny to any person within its jurisdiction the equal protection of the laws." Certainly, it cannot be claimed that this prevents the State from regulating the fares of hackmen or the charges of draymen in Chicago, unless it does the same thing in every other place within its jurisdiction. But, as has been seen, the power to regulate the business of warehouses depends upon the same principle as the power to regulate hackmen and draymen, and what cannot be done in the one case in this particular cannot be done in the other.

We conclude, therefore, that the statute in question is not repugnant to the Constitution of the United States. . . .

The judgment is affirmed.

MR. JUSTICE FIELD, DISSENTING.

. . . The principle upon which the opinion of the majority proceeds is, in my judgment, subversive of the rights of private property, heretofore believed to be protected by constitutional guarantees against legislative interference, and is in conflict with the authorities cited in its support.

The doctrine of the state court, that no one is deprived of his property, within the meaning of the constitutional inhibition, so long as he retains its title and possession, and the doctrine of this court, that, whenever one's property is used in such a manner as to affect the community at large, it becomes by that fact clothed with a public interest, and ceases to be juris privati only, appear to me to destroy, for all useful purposes, the efficacy of the constitutional guaranty. All that is beneficial in property arises from its use, and the fruits of that use; and whatever deprives a person of them deprives him of all that is desirable or valuable in the title and possession. If the constitutional guaranty extends no further than to prevent a deprivation of use and the fruits of that use, it does not merit the encomiums it has received. Unless I have misread the history of the provision now incorporated into all our State Constitutions, and by the 5th and 14th Amendments into our Federal Constitution, and have misunderstood the interpretation it has received, it is not thus limited in its scope, and thus impotent for good. It has a much more extended operation than either court, State or Federal, has given to it. The provision, it is to be observed, places property under the same protection as life and liberty. Except by due process of law, no State can deprive any person of either. . . .

(4) Lochner v. New York (1905)

+Peckham, Brown, White, Fuller, Brewer
−Harlan, Holmes, White, Day

MR. JUSTICE PECKHAM delivered the opinion of the court.

The indictment . . . charges that the plaintiff in error violated . . . the labor law of the State of New York, and in that he wrongfully and unlawfully required and permitted an employé working for him to work more than sixty hours in one week. . . . It is not an act merely fixing the number of hours which shall constitute a legal day's work, but an absolute prohibition upon the employer permitting, under any circumstances, more than ten hours work to be done in his establishment. The employé may desire to earn the extra money, which would arise from his working more than the prescribed time, but this statute forbids the employer from permitting the employé to earn it.

The statute necessarily interferes with the right of contract between the employer and employes, concerning the number of hours in which the latter may labor in the bakery of the employer. The general right to make a contract in relation to his business is part of the liberty of the individual protected by the Fourteenth Amendment of the Federal Constitution. . . . Under that provision no State can deprive any person of life, liberty or property without due process of law. The right to purchase or to sell labor is part of the liberty protected by this amendment, unless there are circumstances which exclude the right. There are, however, certain powers, existing in the sovereignty of each State in the Union, somewhat vaguely termed police powers, the exact description and limitation of which have not been attempted by the courts. Those powers, broadly stated and without, at present, any attempt at a more specific limitation, relate to the safety, health, morals and general welfare of the public. Both property and liberty are held on such reasonable conditions as may be imposed by the governing power of the State in the exercise of those powers, and with such conditions the Fourteenth Amendment was not designed to interfere. . . .

The State, therefore, has power to prevent the individual from making certain kinds of contracts, and in regard to them the Federal Constitution offers no protection. If the contract be one which the State, in the legitimate exercise of its police power, has the right to prohibit, it is not prevented from prohibiting it by the Fourteenth Amendment. Contracts in violation of a statute, either of the Federal or state government, or a contract to let one's property for immoral purposes, or to do any other unlawful act, could obtain no protection from the Federal Constitution, as coming under the liberty of person or of free contract. Therefore, when the State, by its legislature, in the assumed exercise of its police powers, has passed an act which seriously limits the right to labor or the right of contract in regard to their means of livelihood between persons who are *sui juris* (both employer and employé), it becomes of great importance to determine which shall prevail—the right of the individual to labor for such time as he may choose, or the right of the State to prevent the individual from laboring or from entering into any contract to labor, beyond a certain time prescribed by the State.

It must, of course, be conceded that there is a limit to the valid exercise of the police power by the State. There is no dispute concerning this general proposition. Otherwise the Fourteenth Amendment would have no efficacy and the legislatures of the States would have unbounded power, and it would be enough to say that any piece of legislation was enacted to conserve the morals, the health or the safety of the people; such legislation would be valid, no matter how absolutely without foundation the claim might be. The claim of the police power would be a mere pretext—become another and delusive name for the supreme sovereignty of the State to be exercised free from constitutional restraint. This is not contended for. In every case that comes before this court, therefore, where legislation of this character is concerned and where the protection of the Federal Constitution is sought, the question necessarily arises: Is this a fair, reasonable and appropriate exercise of the police power of the State, or is it an unreasonable, unnecessary and arbitrary interference with the right of the individual to his personal liberty or to enter into those contracts in relation to labor which may seem to him appropriate or necessary for the support of himself and his family? Of course the liberty of contract relating to labor includes both parties to it. The one has as much right to purchase as the other to sell labor.

This is not a question of substituting the judgment of the court for that of the legislature. If the act be within the power of the State it is valid, although the judgment of the court might be totally opposed to the enactment of such a law. But the question would still remain: Is it within the police power of the State? and that question must be answered by the court.

The question whether this act is valid as a labor law, pure and simple, may be dismissed in a few words.

There is no reasonable ground for interfering with the liberty of person or the right of free contract, by determining the hours of labor, in the occupation of a baker. There is no contention that bakers as a class are not equal in intelligence and capacity to men in other trades or manual occupations, or that they are not able to assert their rights and care for themselves without the protecting arm of the State, interfering with their independence of judgment and of action. They are in no sense wards of the State. Viewed in the light of a purely labor law, with no reference whatever to the question of health, we think that a law like the one before us involves neither the safety, the morals nor the welfare of the public, and that the interest of the public is not in the slightest degree affected by such an act. The law must be upheld, if at all, as a law pertaining to the health of the individual engaged in the occupation of a baker. It does not affect any other portion of the public than those who are engaged in that occupation. Clean and wholesome bread does not depend upon whether the baker works but ten hours per day or only sixty hours a week. The limitation of the hours of labor does not come within the police power on that ground. . . .

We think the limit of the police power has been reached and passed in this case. There is, in our judgment, no reasonable foundation for holding this to be necessary or appropriate as a health law to safeguard the public health or the health of the individuals who are following the trade of a baker. If this statute be valid . . . there would seem to be no length to which legislation of this nature might not go. . . .

It is also urged, pursuing the same line of argument, that it is to the interest of the State that its popula-

tion should be strong and robust, and therefore any legislation which may be said to tend to make people healthy must be valid as health laws, enacted under the police power. If this be a valid argument and a justification for this kind of legislation, it follows that the protection of the Federal Constitution from undue interference with liberty of person and freedom of contract is visionary, wherever the law is sought to be justified as a valid exercise of the police power. Scarcely any law but might find shelter under such assumptions, and conduct, properly so called, as well as contract, would come under the restrictive sway of the legislature. Not only the hours of the employés, but the hours of employers, could be regulated, and doctors, lawyers, scientists, all professional men, as well as athletes and artisans, could be forbidden to fatigue their brains and bodies by prolonged hours of exercise, lest the fighting strength of the State be impaired. We mention these extreme cases because the contention is extreme. We do not believe in the soundness of the views which uphold this law. On the contrary, we think that such a law as this, although passed in the assumed exercise of the police power, and as relating to the public health, or the health of the employés named, is not within that power, and is invalid. The act is not, within any fair meaning of the term, a health law, but is an illegal interference with the rights of individuals, both employers and employés, to make contracts regarding labor upon such terms as they may think best, or which they may agree upon with the other parties to such contracts. . . .

Statutes of the nature of that under review, limiting the hours in which grown and intelligent men may labor to earn their living, are mere meddlesome interferences with the rights of the individual, and they are not saved from condemnation by the claim that they are passed in the exercise of the police power and upon the subject of the health of the individual whose rights are interfered with, unless there be some fair ground, reasonable in and of itself, to say that there is material danger to the public health or to the health of the employés, if the hours of labor are not curtailed. If this be not clearly the case the individuals, whose rights are thus made the subject of legislative interference, are under the protection of the Federal Constitution regarding their liberty of contract as well as of person; and the legislature of the State has no power to limit their right as proposed in this statute. All that it could properly do has been done by it with regard to the conduct of bakeries, as provided for in the other sections of the act. . . .

This interference on the part of the legislatures of the several States with the ordinary trades and occupations of the people seems to be on the increase. . . .

It is impossible for us to shut our eyes to the fact that many of the laws of this character, while passed under what is claimed to be the police power for the purpose of protecting the public health or welfare, are, in reality, passed from other motives. We are justified in saying so when, from the character of the law and the subject upon which it legislates, it is apparent that the public health or welfare bears but the most remote relation to the law. . . . It seems to us that the real object and purpose were simply to regulate the hours of labor between the master and his employés (all being men, *sui juris*), in a private business, not dangerous in any degree to morals or in any real and substantial degree to the health of the employes. Under such circumstances the freedom of master and employé to contract with each other in relation to their employment, and in defining the same, cannot be prohibited or interfered with, without violating the Federal Constitution.

Reversed.

MR. JUSTICE HARLAN, WITH WHOM MR. JUSTICE WHITE AND MR. JUSTICE DAY CONCURRED, DISSENTING (OMITTED).

MR. JUSTICE HOLMES DISSENTING.

This case is decided upon an economic theory which a large part of the country does not entertain. If it were a question whether I agreed with that theory, I should desire to study it further and long before making up my mind. But I do not conceive that to be my duty, because I strongly believe that my agreement or disagreement has nothing to do with the right of a majority to embody their opinions in law. It is settled by various decisions of this court that state constitutions and state laws may regulate life in many ways which we as legislators might think as injudicious or if you like as tyrannical as this, and which equally with this interfere with the liberty to contract. Sunday laws and usury laws are ancient examples. A more modern one is the prohibition of lotteries. The liberty of the citizen to do as he likes so long as he does not interfere with the liberty of others to do the same, which has been a shibboleth for some well-known writers, is interfered with by school laws, by the Post Office, by every state or municipal institution which takes his money for purposes thought desirable, whether he likes it or not. The Fourteenth Amendment does not enact Mr. Herbert Spencer's Social Statics. The other day we sustained the Massachusetts vaccination law. *Jacobson* v. *Massachusetts*.

. . . United States and state statutes and decisions cutting down the liberty to contract by way of combination are familiar to this court. *Northern Securities Co.* v. *United States.* . . . Two years ago we upheld the prohibition of sales of stock on margins or for future delivery in the constitution of California. *Otis* v. *Parker.* . . . The decision sustaining an eight hour law for miners is still recent. *Holden* v. *Hardy.* . . . Some of these laws embody convictions or prejudices which judges are likely to share. Some may not. But a constitution is not intended to embody a particular economic theory, whether of paternalism and the organic relation of the citizen to the State or of *laissez faire*. It is made for people of fundamentally different views, and the accident of our finding certain opinions natural and familiar or novel and even shocking ought not to conclude our judgment upon the question whether statutes embodying them conflict with the Constitution of the United States.

General propositions do not decide concrete cases. The decision will depend on a judgment or intuition more subtle than any articulate major premise. But I think that the proposition just stated, if it is accepted, will carry us far toward the end. Every opinion tends to become a law. I think that the word liberty in the Fourteenth Amendment is perverted when it is held to prevent the natural outcome of a dominant opinion, unless it can be said that a rational and fair man necessarily would admit that the statute proposed would infringe fundamental principles as they have been understood by the traditions of our people and our law. It does not need research to show that no such sweeping condemnation can be passed upon the statute before us. A reasonable man might think it a

proper measure on the score of health. Men whom I certainly could not pronounce unreasonable would uphold it as a first installment of a general regulation of the hours of work. Whether in the latter aspect it would be open to the charge of inequality I think it unnecessary to discuss.

(5) North Dakota State Board of Pharmacy v. Snyder's Drug Stores, Inc. (1973)

+Burger, Douglas, Brennan, Stewart, White, Marshall, Blackmun, Powell, Rehnquist

[In the decade following *Lochner*, the Supreme Court upheld a maximum hours law for women and a statute regulating work of both men and women. The first of these decisions was *Muller* v. *Oregon* (1908), argued before the Court by attorney Louis Brandeis. *Muller* was the occasion of what became known as the "Brandeis Brief." Instead of asking the Court to overrule *Lochner*, Brandeis devoted most of his brief to a presentation of social science data supporting the reasonableness of the statute. He convinced the Court that women were the "weaker sex" and that their "special reproductive functions" justified state-imposed limitation of the hours they could work. In effect, Brandeis was asking the Court to apply the "health" exception to sustain the statute.

In unanimously upholding the statute, the Court never mentioned the *Lochner* case, leading many observers to think that *Lochner* had been overruled *sub silentio*. However, *Lochner* was revived in *Adkins* v. *Children's Hospital* (1923), when the Supreme Court invalidated a minimum wage law for women in the District of Columbia. Several other state laws regulating economic transactions were also invalidated in this period.

In 1934, the Court again appeared to be on the verge of repudiating substantive due process. In *Nebbia* v. *New York*, it upheld a New York statute regulating milk prices, citing the *Munn* doctrine permitting regulation of businesses affected with a public interest. Justice Roberts wrote: "There is no closed class or category of businesses affected with a public interest, and the function of courts in the application of the 5th and 14th Amendments is to determine in each case whether circumstances vindicate the challenged regulation as a reasonable exertion of governmental authority. . . . The phrase 'affected with a public interest' can . . . mean no more than that an industry, for adequate reason, is subject to control for the public good."

We have already described the case of *West Coast Hotel* v. *Parrish* (1937), in which the doctrine of economic substantive due process was finally repudiated (See Part One, Chapter Three, pp. 248–251). By the 1940s, the Supreme Court appeared to be taking the position that state economic regulation was subject to no constitutional prohibition other than specific constitutional limitations on state power. In *Williamson* v. *Lee Optical Co.* (1955) the Supreme Court unanimously upheld a state statute that prohibited the fitting of eyeglass lenses by any person who was neither an ophthalmologist nor an optometrist, or without a prescription from an ophthalmologist or optometrist. The trial court, finding that there was no rational reason why a trained optician could not fit old glasses to new frames without a prescription, invalidated the law. The U.S. Supreme Court, per Justice Black, agreed that the statute was needless and wasteful. But, it said, such was exclusively a legislative decision: "The day is gone when this Court uses the Due Process Clause of the Fourteenth Amendment to strike down state laws, regulatory of business and industrial conditions, because they may be unwise, improvident, or out of harmony with a particular school of thought." A similar result was reached in 1963 in *Ferguson* v. *Skrupa*, which involved a state statute limiting the practice of debt collection to lawyers. In that case, only Justice Harlan argued that the Supreme Court at least had the obligation to consider whether a statute "bore a rational relation to a constitutionally permissible objective."

As Robert McCloskey has made clear,[1] the activism of substantive due process in economic regulation cases was replaced by an extreme form of abdication. Why did the Court not choose a halfway position, one that would permit it to continue to consider the rationality of economic statutes but use that power sparingly? Justice Black's position was always that the only limits on state regulation were specific constitutional prohibitions. Justice Douglas' position was somewhat more limited. He accepted the need for retaining some judicial control but was unwilling to use it in the economic realm. For Douglas, the problem with substantive due process was more a matter of the wrong subject than, as Black had argued, a fundamental usurpation of judicial power. Writing in *Poe* v. *Ullman* (1961), Douglas said:

> *The error of the old Court, as I see it, was not in entertaining inquiries concerning the constitutionality of social legislation but in applying the standards that it did. . . . Social legislation dealing with business and economic matters touches no particularized prohibition of the Constitution, unless it be the provision of the Fifth Amendment that private property should not be taken for public use without just compensation. If it is free of the latter guarantees, it has a wide scope for application. Some go so far as to suggest that whatever the majority in the legislature say goes. . . . that there is no other standard of constitutionality. That reduces legislative power to sheer voting strength and the judicial function to a matter of statistics. . . . While the legislative judgment on economic and business matters is 'well nigh conclusive'. . . . it is not beyond judicial inquiry.*

McCloskey was probably correct in suggesting that the Court may have followed Black's lead because extremism begets extremism. One way to reinforce the repudiation of economic substantive due process was to allow no exceptions and to permit no inferences that

[1]Robert McCloskey, "Economic Due Process and the Supreme Court," in Philip B. Kurland (ed.), *The Supreme Court Review: 1962* (Chicago: The University of Chicago Press, 1962), pp. 34–62.

what was then believed to be a usurpation of judicial power would ever be revived. Yet the "paradox of substantive due process is that its rise and decline were simultaneous."[2] At the same time the Supreme Court was withdrawing from a supervisory role in the regulation of the economy, it was fashioning doctrines that would permit it to actively intervene in state regulation of individual rights.

The *North Dakota Pharmacy* case, presented in brief, is interesting for two reasons. First, it demonstrates the Supreme Court's continued unwillingness in the modern era to consider the validity of economic regulations. And it also shows that the concept of substantive due process, at least at the state level, has continued resiliency.]

MR. JUSTICE DOUGLAS delivered the opinion of the Court.

North Dakota passed a statute that requires that the applicant for a permit to operate a pharmacy be "a registered pharmacist in good standing" or "a corporation or association, the majority stock in which is owned by registered pharmacists in good standing, actively and regularly employed in and responsible for the management, supervision, and operation of such pharmacy."

Petitioner denied a permit to Snyder's Drug Stores, Inc., because it did not comply with the stock-ownership requirements of the statute, it appearing that all the common stock of Snyder's was owned by Red Owl Stores and it not being shown if any Red Owl shareholders were pharmacists registered and in good standing in North Dakota. On appeal to the state district court summary judgment was granted Snyder's. On appeal to the Supreme Court of North Dakota, that court held that the North Dakota statute was unconstitutional by reason of our

decision in 1928 in *Liggett Co.* v. *Baldridge,* . . . That case involved a Pennsylvania statute that required that 100% of the stock of the corporation be owned by pharmacists. The North Dakota statute, however, requires only that a majority of the stock be owned by pharmacists. But the North Dakota Supreme Court held that the difference did not take this case out from under the *Liggett* case because under both statutes control of the corporation having a pharmacists' license had to be in the hands of pharmacists responsible for the management and operation of the pharmacy. That court therefore remanded the case, so that the Board could conduct "an administrative hearing on the application, *sans the constitutional issue,* pursuant to our Administrative Agencies Practice Act," . . . .[italics added]

The case is here on a petition for certiorari which we granted. . . .

Liggett, decided in 1928, belongs in that vintage of decisions which exalted substantive due process by striking down state legislation which a majority of the Court deemed unwise. *Liggett* has to date not been expressly overruled. We commented on it disparagingly, however, in *Daniel* v. *Family Security Life Ins. Co.* . . . (1949), which concerned the constitutionality of a state statute providing that life insurance companies and their agents may not operate an undertaking business and undertakers may not serve as agents for life insurance companies. We noted that *Liggett* held that it was "clear" that "mere stock ownership in a corporation, owning and operating a drug store, can have no real or substantial relation to the public health; and that the act in question creates an unreasonable and unnecessary re-

---

[2]C. Herman Pritchett, *The American Constitution,* 2nd Edition, (McGraw-Hill, 1968), p. 684.

striction upon private business," . . . In *Daniel*, however, we stated that "a pronounced shift of emphasis since the *Liggett* case," . . . had deprived the words "unreasonable" and "arbitrary" of the meaning which *Liggett* ascribed to them. We had indeed held in *Lincoln Federal Labor Union* v. *Northwestern Iron and Metal Co.* . . . (1949) that a State had power, so far as the Due Process Clause of the Fourteenth Amendment was concerned, to legislate that no person should be denied the opportunity to obtain or retain employment because he was or was not a member of a labor union. After reviewing *Nebbia* v. *New York* . . . (1934), *Adair* v. *United States* . . . (1908), and *Coppage* v. *Kansas* . . . (1915), we said:

This Court beginning at least as early as 1934, when the Nebbia *case was decided, has steadily rejected the due process philosophy enunciated in the* Adair-Coppage *line of cases. In doing so it has consciously returned closer and closer to the earlier constitutional principle that states have power to legislate against what are found to be injurious practices in their internal commercial and business affairs, so long as their laws do not run afoul of some specific federal constitutional prohibition, or of some valid federal law. . . . Under this constitutional doctrine the due process clause is no longer to be so broadly construed that the Congress and state legislatures are put in a straight jacket when they attempt to suppress business and industrial conditions which they regard as offensive to the public welfare.*

We reached the same result in *Ferguson* v. *Skrupa* . . . (1963), where we sustained the constitutionality of a state law prohibiting persons other than lawyers from engaging in the business of debt adjusting and debt pooling. . . .

The majority of the Court in *Liggett* for which Mr. Justice Suther-

land spoke held that business or property rights could be regulated under the Fourteenth Amendment only if the "legislation bears a real and substantial relation to the public health, safety, morals, or some other phase of the general welfare," . . . The majority held the ownership requirements governing pharmacies "creates an unreasonable and unnecessary restriction upon private business." . . . The opposed view stated by Mr. Justice Holmes and concurred in by Mr. Justice Brandeis was:

A standing criticism of the use of corporations in business is that it causes such business to be owned by people who do not know anything about it. Argument has not been supposed to be necessary in order to show that the divorce between the power of control and knowledge is an evil. The selling of drugs and poisons calls for knowledge in a high degree, and Pennsylvania after enacting a series of other safeguards has provided that in that matter the divorce shall not be allowed. . . . The Constitution does not make it a condition of preventive legislation that it should work a perfect cure. It is enough if the questioned act has a manifest tendency to cure or at least to make the evil less.

Those two opposed views of public policy are considerations for the legislative choice. The *Liggett* case was a creation at war with the earlier constitutional view of legislative power. *Munn* v. *Illinois* . . . (1877), and opposed to our more recent decisions. *Williamson* v. *Lee Optical Co.* . . . (1955); as well as the *Daniel, Lincoln Federal Union*, and *Ferguson* cases already discussed. The *Liggett* case, being a derelict in the stream of the law, is hereby overruled. We reverse and remand the judgment below and free the courts and agencies of North Dakota from what the

State Supreme Court deemed to be the mandate of *Liggett*.

So ordered.

Reversed and remanded.

C. *National Regulation of the Economy*

(1) United States v. Butler (1936)

+Roberts, Hughes, Van Devanter, McReynolds, Butler, Sutherland

−Stone, Cardozo, Brandeis

[In 1933 Congress passed the Agricultural Adjustment Act delegating to the secretary of agriculture the power to regulate acreage allotments in order to support market prices of agricultural commodities. These regulations could be effected by voluntary agreement with producers but could also be imposed by the secretary. A processing tax "to obtain revenue for extraordinary expenses incurred by reason of the national economic emergency" was to be levied on particular commodities at the discretion of the secretary of agriculture. On July 14, 1933, the secretary proclaimed that rental and benefit payments should be made to cotton growers, and he instituted a processing tax on the production of cotton. When the United States claimed taxes owed them by the Hoosac Mills Corporation, the receiver of the corporation refused to pay. A district court found the taxes valid and ordered them paid, but the court of appeals reversed the order on the grounds that the statute was invalid.]

MR. JUSTICE ROBERTS delivered the opinion of the Court.

. . . The tax can only be sustained by ignoring the avowed purpose and operation of the act, and holding it a measure merely laying an excise upon processors to raise revenue for the support of government. Beyond cavil the sole object of the legislation is to restore the purchasing power of agricultural products to a parity with that prevailing in an earlier day; to take money from the processor and bestow it upon farmers who will reduce their acreage for the accomplishment of the proposed end, and, meanwhile to aid these farmers during the period required to bring the prices of their crops to the desired level.

The tax plays an indispensable part in the plan of regulation. As stated by the Agricultural Adjustment Administrator, it is "the heart of the law"; a means of "accomplishing one or both of two things intended to help farmers attain parity prices and purchasing power." A tax automatically goes into effect for a commodity when the Secretary of Agriculture determines that rental or benefit payments are to be made for reduction of production of that commodity. The tax is to cease when rental or benefit payments cease. The rate is fixed with the purpose of bringing about crop-reduction and price-raising. It is to equal the difference between the "current average farm price" and "fair exchange value." It may be altered to such amounts as will prevent accumulation of surplus stocks. If the Secretary finds the policy of the act will not be promoted by the levy of the tax for a given commodity, he may exempt it. The whole revenue from the levy is appropriated in aid of crop control; none of it is made available for general governmental use. The entire agricultural adjustment program embodied in Title I of the acts is to become inoperative when, in the judgment of the President, the national economic emergency ends; and as to any commodity he may terminate the provisions of the law, if he finds them no longer requisite to carrying out the declared policy with respect to such commodity. . . .

We conclude that the act is one regulating agricultural production; that the tax is a mere incident of such regulation and that the respondents have standing to challenge the legality of the exaction. . . .

The Government asserts that even if the respondents may question the propriety of the appropriation embodied in the statute their attack must fail because Article I, §8 of the Constitution authorizes the contemplated expenditure of the funds raised by the tax. This contention presents the great and the controlling question in the case. We approach its decision with a sense of our grave responsibility to render judgment in accordance with the principles established for the governance of all three branches of the Government.

There should be no misunderstanding as to the function of this court in such a case. It is sometimes said that the court assumes a power to overrule or control the action of the people's representatives. This is a misconception. The Constitution is the supreme law of the land ordained and established by the people. All legislation must conform to the principles it lays down. When an act of Congress is appropriately challenged in the courts as not conforming to the constitutional mandate the judicial branch of the Government has only one duty—to lay the article of the Constitution which is invoked beside the statute which is challenged and to decide whether the latter squares with the former. All the court does, or can do, is to announce its considered judgment upon the question. The only power it has, if such it may be called, is the power of judgment. This court neither approves nor condemns any legislative policy. Its delicate and difficult office is to ascertain and declare whether the legislation is in accordance with, or in contravention of, the provisions of the Constitution; and, having done that, its duty ends.
. . .

The clause thought to authorize the legislation . . . confers upon the Congress power "to lay and collect Taxes, Duties, Imposts and Excises, to pay the Debts and provide for the common Defence and general Welfare of the United States. . . ." It is not contended that this provision grants power to regulate agricultural production upon the theory that such legislation would promote the general welfare. The Government concedes that the phrase "to provide for the general welfare" qualifies the power "to lay and collect taxes." The view that the clause grants power to provide for the general welfare, independently of the taxing power, has never been authoritatively accepted.
. . .

The true construction undoubtedly is that the only thing granted is the power to tax for the purpose of providing funds for payment of the nation's debts and making provision for the general welfare.

Nevertheless the Government asserts that warrant is found in this clause for the adoption of the Agricultural Adjustment Act. The argument is that Congress may appropriate and authorize the spending of moneys for the "general welfare"; that the phrase should be liberally construed to cover anything conducive to national welfare; that decision as to what will promote such welfare rests with Congress alone, and the courts may not review its determination; and finally that the appropriation under attack was in fact for the general welfare of the United States.

The Congress is expressly empowered to lay taxes to provide for the general welfare. Funds in the Treasury as a result of taxation may be expended only through appropriation. . . . They can never accomplish the objects for which they were collected unless the power to appropriate is as broad as the power to tax. The necessary implication from the terms of the grant is that the public funds may be appropriated "to provide for the general welfare of the United States." These words cannot be meaningless, else they would not have been used. The conclusion must be that they were intended to limit and define the granted power to raise and to expend money. How shall they be construed to effectuate the intent of the instrument?

Since the foundation of the Nation sharp differences of opinion have persisted as to the true interpretation of the phrase. Madison asserted it amounted to no more than a reference to the other powers enumerated in the subsequent clauses of the same section; that, as the United States is a government of limited and enumerated powers, the grant of power to tax and spend for the general national welfare must be confined to the enumerated legislative fields committed to the Congress. In this view the phrase is mere tautology, for taxation and appropriation are or may be necessary incidents of the exercise of any of the enumerated legislative powers. Hamilton, on the other hand, maintained the clause confers a power separate and distinct from these later enumerated, is not restricted in meaning by the grant of them, and Congress consequently has a substantive power to tax and to appropriate, limited only by the requirement that it shall be exercised to provide for the general welfare of the United States. Each contention has had the support of those whose views are entitled to weight. This court has noticed the question, but has never found it necessary to decide which is the true construction. Mr. Justice Story, in his Commentaries, espouses the Hamiltonian position. . . . Study . . . leads us to conclude that the read-

ing advocated by Mr. Justice Story is the correct one. While, therefore, the power to tax is not unlimited, its confines are set in the clause which confers it, and not in those of section 8 which bestow and define the legislative powers of the Congress. It results that the power of Congress to authorize expenditure of public moneys for public purposes is not limited by the direct grants of legislative power found in the Constitution. . . .

As elsewhere throughout the Constitution the section in question lays down principles which control the use of power, and does not attempt meticulous or detailed directions. Every presumption is to be indulged in favor of faithful compliance by Congress with the mandates of the fundamental law. Courts are reluctant to adjudge any statute in contravention of them. But under our frame of government, no other place is provided where the citizen may be heard to urge that the law fails to conform to the limits set upon the use of a granted power. When such a contention comes here we naturally require a showing that by no reasonable possibility can the challenged legislation fall within the wide range of discretion permitted to the Congress. . . .

We are not now required to ascertain the scope of the phrase "general welfare of the United States" or to determine whether an appropriation in aid of agriculture falls within it. Wholly apart from the question, another principle embedded in our Constitution prohibits the enforcement of the Agricultural Adjustment Act. The act invades the reserved rights of the states. It is a statutory plan to regulate and control agricultural production, a matter beyond the powers delegated to the federal government. The tax, the appropriation of the funds raised, and the direction for their disbursement, are but parts of the plan. They are but means to an unconstitutional end.

From the accepted doctrine that the United States is a government of delegated powers, it follows that those not expressly granted, or reasonably to be implied from such as are conferred, are reserved to the states or to the people. To forestall any suggestion to the contrary, the Tenth Amendment was adopted. The same proposition, otherwise stated, is that powers not granted are prohibited. None to regulate agricultural production is given, and therefore legislation by Congress for that purpose is forbidden. . . .

Congress has no power to enforce its commands on the farmer to the ends sought by the Agricultural Adjustment Act. It must follow that it may not indirectly accomplish those ends by taxing and spending to purchase compliance. The Constitution and the entire plan of our government negative any such use of the power to tax and to spend as the act undertakes to authorize. It does not help to declare that local conditions throughout the nation have created a situation of national concern; for this is but to say that whenever there is a widespread similarity of local conditions, Congress may ignore constitutional limitations upon its own powers and usurp those reserved to the states. If, in lieu of compulsory regulation of subjects within the states' reserved jurisdiction, which is prohibited, the Congress could invoke the taxing and spending power as a means to accomplish the same end, clause 1 of § 8 of Article I would become the instrument for total subversion of the governmental powers reserved to the individual states.

If the act before us is a proper exercise of the federal taxing power, evidently the regulation of all industry throughout the United States may be accomplished by similar exercises of the same power. . . .

Until recently no suggestion of the existence of any such power in the Federal Government has been advanced. The expressions of the framers of the Constitution, the decisions of this court interpreting that instrument, and the writings of great commentators will be searched in vain for any suggestion that there exists in the clause under discussion or elsewhere in the Constitution, the authority whereby every provision and every fair implication from that instrument may be subverted, the independence of the individual states obliterated, and the United States converted into a central government exercising uncontrolled police power in every state of the Union, superseding all local control or regulation of the affairs or concerns of the states. . . .

But to this fatal conclusion the doctrine contended for would inevitably lead. And its sole premise is that, though the makers of the Constitution, in erecting the federal government, intended sedulously to limit and define its powers, so as to reserve to the states and the people sovereign power, to be wielded by the states and their citizens and not to be invaded by the United States, they nevertheless by a single clause gave power to the Congress to tear down the barriers, to invade the states' jurisdiction, and to become a parliament of the whole people, subject to no restrictions save such as are self-imposed. The argument when seen in its true character and in the light of its inevitable results must be rejected. . . .

This judgment is affirmed.

MR. JUSTICE STONE, DISSENTING.

I think the judgment should be reversed.

The present stress of widely held and strongly expressed differences of opinion of the wisdom of the Agricultural Adjustment Act makes it important, in the interest of clear thinking and sound result, to emphasize at the outset certain propositions which should have controlling influence in determining the validity of the Act. They are:

1. The power of courts to declare a statute unconstitutional is subject to two guiding principles of decision which ought never to be absent from judicial consciousness. One is that courts are concerned only with the power to enact statutes, not with their wisdom. The other is that while unconstitutional exercise of power by the executive and legislative branches of the government is subject to judicial restraint, the only check upon our own exercise of power is our own sense of self-restraint. For the removal of unwise laws from the statute books appeal lies not to the courts but to the ballot and to the processes of democratic government.

2. The constitutional power of Congress to levy an excise tax upon the processing of agricultural products is not questioned. The present levy is held invalid, not for any want of power in Congress to lay such a tax to defray public expenditures, including those for the general welfare, but because the use to which its proceeds are put is disapproved.

3. As the present depressed state of agriculture is nationwide in its extent and effects, there is no basis for saying that the expenditure of public money in aid of farmers is not within the specifically granted power of Congress to levy taxes to "provide for the . . . general welfare." The opinion of the Court does not declare otherwise. . . .

A tortured construction of the Constitution is not to be justified by recourse to extreme examples of reckless congressional spending which might occur if courts could not prevent expenditures which, even if they could be thought to effect any national purpose, would be possible only by action of a legislature lost to all sense of public responsibility. Such suppositions are addressed to the mind accustomed to believe that it is the business of courts to sit in judgment on the wisdom of legislative action. Courts are not the only agency of government that must be assumed to have capacity to govern. Congress and the courts both unhappily may falter or be mistaken in the performance of their constitutional duty. But interpretation of our great charter of government which proceeds on any assumption that the responsibility for the preservation of our institutions is the exclusive concern of any one of the three branches of government, or that it alone can save them from destruction is far more likely, in the long run, "to obliterate the constituent members" of "an indestructible union of indestructible states" than the frank recognition that language, even of a constitution, may mean what it says: that the power to tax and spend includes the power to relieve a nationwide economic maladjustment by conditional gifts of money.

MR. JUSTICE BRANDEIS AND MR. JUSTICE CARDOZO JOIN IN THIS OPINION.

(2) N.L.R.B. v. Jones and Laughlin Steel Corporation (1937)

+Hughes, Stone, Brandeis, Roberts, Cardozo

−Sutherland, VanDevanter, McReynolds, Butler

MR. CHIEF JUSTICE HUGHES delivered the opinion of the Court.

In a proceeding under the National Labor Relations Act of 1935, the National Labor Relations Board found that the respondent, Jones & Laughlin Steel Corporation, had violated the Act by engaging in unfair labor practices affecting commerce. . . . The unfair labor practices charged were that the corporation was discriminating against members of the union with regard to hire and tenure of employment, and was coercing and intimidating its employees in order to interfere with their self-organization. The discriminatory and coercive action alleged was the discharge of certain employees.

The National Labor Relations Board, sustaining the charge, ordered the corporation to cease and desist from such discrimination and coercion, to offer reinstatement to ten of the employees named, to make good their losses in pay, and to post for thirty days notices that the corporation would not discharge or discriminate against members, or those desiring to become members, of the labor union. As the corporation failed to comply, the Board petitioned the Circuit Court of Appeals to enforce the order. The court denied the petition, holding that the order lay beyond the range of federal power. . . . We granted certiorari.

The Act is challenged in its entirety as an attempt to regulate all industry, thus invading the reserved powers of the States over their local concerns. It is asserted that the references in the Act to interstate and foreign commerce are colorable at best; that the Act is not a true regulation of such commerce or of matters which directly affect it but on the contrary has the fundamental object of placing under the compulsory supervision of the federal government all industrial labor relations within the nation. The argument seeks support in the broad works of the preamble (section one) and in the sweep of the provisions of the Act, and it is further insisted that its legislative history shows an essential universal purpose in the light of which its scope cannot be limited by either construction or by the application of the separability clause.

If this conception of terms, intent and consequent inseparability were sound, the Act would necessarily fall by reason of the limitation upon the federal power which inheres in the constitutional grant, as well as because of the explicit reservation of the Tenth Amendment. *Schechter Corp.* v. *United States.* . . . The authority of the federal government may not be pushed to such an extreme as to destroy the distinction, which the commerce clause itself establishes, between commerce "among the several States" and the internal concerns of a State. That distinction between what is national and what is local in the activities of commerce is vital to the maintenance of our federal system.

But we are not at liberty to deny effect to specific provisions, which Congress has constitutional power to enact, by superimposing upon them inferences from general legislative declarations of an ambiguous character, even if found in the same statute. The cardinal principle of statutory construction is to save and not to destroy. We have repeatedly held that as between two possible interpretations of a statute, by one of which it would be unconstitutional and by the other valid, our plain duty is to adopt that which will save the act. Even to avoid a serious doubt the rule is the same.

We think it clear that the National Labor Relations Act may be construed so as to operate within the sphere of constitutional authority. The jursidiction conferred upon the Board, and invoked in this instance . . . provides:

Sec. 10(a). The Board is empowered, as hereinafter provided, to prevent any person from engaging in any unfair labor practice (listed in section 8) affecting commerce.

The critical words of this provision, prescribing the limits of the Board's authority in dealing with the labor practices, are "affecting commerce." The Act specifically defines the "commerce" to which it refers. . . .

There can be no question that the commerce thus contemplated by the Act . . . is interstate and foreign commerce in the constitutional sense. The Act also defines the term "affecting commerce":

The term "affecting commerce" means in commerce, or burdening or obstructing commerce or the free flow of commerce, or having led or tending to lead to a labor dispute burdening or obstructing commerce or the free flow of commerce.

This definition is one of exclusion as well as inclusion. The grant of authority to the Board does not purport to extend to the relationship between all industrial employees and employers. Its terms do not impose collective bargaining upon all industry regardless of effects upon interstate or foreign commerce. It purports to reach only what may be deemed to burden or obstruct that commerce and, thus qualified, it must be contrued as contemplating the exercise of control within constitutional bounds. It is a familiar principle that acts which directly burden or obstruct interstate or foreign commerce, or its free flow, are within the reach of the congressional power.

Acts having that effect are not rendered immune because they grow out of labor disputes. . . . Whether or not particular action does affect commerce in such a close, and intimate fashion as to be subject to federal control, and hence to lie within the authority conferred upon the Board, is left by the statute to be determined as individual cases arise. We are thus to inquire whether in the instant case the constitutional boundary has been passed. . . .

Thus, in its present application, the statute goes no further than to safeguard the right of employees to self-organization and to select representatives of their own choosing for collective bargaining or other mutual protection without restraint or coercion by their employer. . . .

That is a fundamental right. Employees have as clear a right to organize and select their representatives for lawful purposes as the respondent has to organize its business and select its own officers and agents. Discrimination and coercion to prevent the free exercise of the right of employees to self-organization and representation is a proper subject for condemnation by competent legislative authority. Long ago we stated the reason for labor organizations. We said that they were organized out of the necessities of the situation; that a single employee was helpless in dealing with an employer; that he was dependent ordinarily on his daily wage for the maintenance of himself and family; that if the employer refused to pay him the wages that he thought fair, he was nevertheless unable to leave the employ and resist arbitrary and unfair treatment; that union was essential to give laborers opportunity to deal on an equality with their employer. . . .

Respondent says that whatever may be said of employees engaged in interstate commerce, the industrial relations and activities in the manufacturing department of respondent's enterprise are not subject to federal regulation. The argument rests upon the proposition that manufacturing in itself is not commerce.

The Government distinguishes these cases. The various parts of respondent's enterprise are described as interdependent and as thus involving "a great movement of iron ore, coal and limestone along well-defined paths to the steel mills, thence through them, and thence in the form of steel products into the consuming centers of the country—a definite and well-understood course of business." It is urged that these activities constitute a "stream" or "flow" of commerce, of which the Aliquippa manufacturing plant is the focal point, and that industrial strife at that point would cripple the entire movement. Reference is made to our decision sustaining the Packers and Stockyards Act. *Stafford* v. *Wallace* . . . The Court found that the stockyards were but a "throat" through which the current of commerce flowed and the transactions which there occurred could not be separated from that movement. Hence the sales at the stockyards were not regarded as merely local transactions, for while they created "a local change of title" they did not "stop the flow," but merely changed the private interests in the subject of the current. . . .

The close and intimate effect which brings the subject within the reach of federal power may be due to activities in relation to productive industry although the industry when separately viewed is local. This has been abundantly illustrated in the application of the federal Anti-Trust Act. . . .

It is thus apparent that the fact that the employers here concerned were engaged in production is not determinative. The question remains as to the effect upon interstate commerce of the labor practice involved. In the *Schechter* case . . . we found that the effect there was so remote as to be beyond the federal power. To find "immediacy or directness" there was to find it "almost everywhere," a result inconsistent with the maintenance of our federal system. In the *Carter* case . . . the Court was of the opinion that the provisions of the statute relating to reproduction were invalid upon several grounds—that there was improper delegation of legislative power, and that the requirements not only went beyond any sustainable measure of protection of interstate commerce but were also inconsistent with due process. These cases are not controlling here. . . .

Giving full weight to respondent's contention with respect to a break in the complete continuity of the "stream of commerce" by reason of respondent's manufacturing operations, the fact remains that the stoppage of those operations by industrial strife would have a most serious effect upon interstate commerce. In view of respondent's far-flung activities, it is idle to say that the effect would be indirect or remote. It is obvious that it would be immediate and might be catastrophic. We are asked to shut our eyes to the plainest facts of our national life and to deal with the question of direct and indirect effects in an intellectual vacuum. Because there may be but indirect and remote effects upon interstate commerce in connection with a host of local enterprises throughout the country, it does not follow that other industrial activities do not have such a close and intimate relation to interstate commerce as to make the presence of industrial strife a matter of the most urgent national concern.

When industries organize themselves on a national scale, making their relation to interstate commerce the dominant factor in their activities, how can it be maintained that their industrial labor relations constitute a forbidden field into which Congress may not enter when it is necessary to protect interstate commerce from the paralyzing consequences of industrial war? We have often said that interstate commerce itself is a practical conception. It is equally true that interferences with the commerce must be appraised by a judgment that does not ignore actual experience.

Experience has abundantly demonstrated that the recognition of the right of employees to self-organization and to have representatives of their own choosing for the purpose of collective bargaining is often an essential condition of industrial peace. Refusal to confer and negotiate has been one of the most prolific causes of strife. This is such an outstanding fact in the history of labor disturbances that it is a proper subject of judicial notice and requires no citation of instances. . . .

The steel industry is one of the great basic industries of the United States, with ramifying activities affecting interstate commerce at every point. The Government aptly refers to the steel strike of 1919–1920 with its far-reaching consequences. The fact that there appears to have been no major disturbance in that industry in the more recent period did not dispose of the possibilities of future and like dangers to interstate commerce which Congress was entitled to foresee and to exercise its protective power to forestall. It is not necessary again to detail the facts as to respondent's enterprise. Instead of being beyond the pale, we think that it presents in a most striking way the close and intimate relation which a man-

ufacturing industry may have to interstate commerce and we have no doubt that Congress had constitutional authority to safeguard the right of respondent's employees to self-organization and freedom in the choice of representatives for collective bargaining. . . .

Our conclusion is that the order of the Board was within its competency and that the Act is valid as here applied. The judgment of the Circuit Court of Appeals is reversed and the cause is remanded for further proceedings in conformity with this opinion.

Reversed.

MR. JUSTICE McREYNOLDS, DISSENTING.

MR. JUSTICE VAN DEVANTER, MR. JUSTICE SUTHERLAND, MR. JUSTICE BUTLER AND I are unable to agree with the decisions just announced. . . .

Considering the far-reaching import of these decisions, the departure from what we understand has been consistently ruled here, and the extraordinary power confirmed to a Board of three, the obligation to present our views becomes plain.

The Court, as we think, departs from well-established principles followed in *Schechter Corp.* v. *United States* . . . (May, 1935) and *Carter* v. *Carter Coal Co* . . . (May, 1936). Upon the authority of those decisions, the Circuit Courts of Appeals of the Fifth, Sixth and Second Circuits in the causes now before us have held the power of Congress under the commerce clause does not extend to relations between employers and their employees engaged in manufacture, and therefore the Act conferred upon the National Labor Relations Board no authority in respect of matters covered by the questioned orders. . . . Six district courts, on the authority of *Schechter's* and *Carter's* cases, have held that the Board has no authority to regulate relations between employers and employees engaged in local production. No decision or judicial opinion to the contrary has been cited and we find none. Every consideration brought forward to uphold the Act before us was applicable to support the Acts held unconstitutional in causes decided within two years. And the lower courts rightly deemed them controlling.

(3) United States v. Darby Lumber Company (1941)

+Stone, Hughes, Brandeis, Black, Douglas, Frankfurter, Roberts, Reed, Jackson

MR. JUSTICE STONE delivered the opinion of the Court.

. . .

The two principal questions raised by the record in this case are, *first,* whether Congress has constitutional power to prohibit the shipment in interstate commerce of lumber manufactured by employees whose wages are less than a prescribed minimum or whose weekly hours of labor at that wage are greater than a prescribed maximum, and, *second,* whether it has power to prohibit the employment of workmen in the production of goods "for interstate commerce" at other than prescribed wages and hours. A subsidiary question is whether in connection with such prohibitions Congress can require the employer subject to them to keep records showing the hours worked each day and week by each of his employers including those engaged "in the production and manufacture of goods to-wit, lumber, for 'interstate commerce' " . . .

The Fair Labor Standards Act set up a comprehensive legislative scheme for preventing the shipment in interstate commerce of certain products and commodities produced in the United States under labor conditions as respects wages and hours which fail to conform to standards set up by the Act. Its purpose . . . is to exclude from interstate commerce goods produced for the commerce and to prevent their production for interstate commerce, under conditions detrimental to the maintenance of the minimum standards of living necessary for health and general well-being, and to prevent the use of interstate commerce as the means of competition in the distribution of goods so produced, and as the means of spreading and perpetuating such substandard labor conditions among the workers of the several states. The Act also sets up an administrative procedure whereby those standards may from time to time be modified generally as to industries subject to the Act or within an industry in accordance with specified standards, by an administrator acting in collaboration with "Industry Committees" appointed by him. . . .

The indictment charges that appellee is engaged, in the State of Georgia, in the business of acquiring raw materials, which he manufactures into finished lumber with the intent, when manufactured, to ship it in interstate commerce to customers outside the state, and that he does in fact so ship a large part of the lumber so produced. There are numerous counts charging appellee with the shipment in interstate commerce from Georgia to points outside the state of lumber in the production of which, for interstate commerce, appellee has employed workmen at less than the prescribed minimum wage or more than the prescribed maximum hours without payment to them of any wage for overtime. Other counts charge the employment by appellee of workmen in the production of lumber for interstate commerce at wages at less than 25 cents an hour or for more than the maximum hours per week without payment to them of the prescribed overtime wage. . . .

The demurrer, so far as now relevant to the appeal, challenged the validity of the Fair Labor Standards Act under the Commerce Clause and the Fifth and Tenth Amendments. The district court quashed the indictment in its entirety upon the broad grounds that the Act, which it interpreted as a regulation of manufacture within the states, is unconstitutional. It declared that manufacture is not interstate commerce and that the regulation by the Fair Labor Standards Act of wages and hours of employment of those engaged in the manufacture of goods which it is intended at the time of production "may or will be" after production "sold in interstate commerce in part or in whole" is not within the congressional power to regulate interstate commerce. . . .

While manufacture is not of itself interstate commerce, the shipment of manufactured goods interstate is such commerce and the prohibition of such shipment by Congress is indubitably a regulation of the commerce. The power to regulate commerce is the power "to prescribe the rule by which commerce is governed." *Gibbons* v. *Ogden.* . . . It extends not only to those regulations which aid, foster and protect the commerce, but embraces those which prohibit it. . . . It is conceded that the power of Congress to prohibit transportation in interstate commerce includes noxious articles, . . . stolen articles, . . . kidnapped persons, . . . and articles such as intoxicating liquor or convict made goods, traffic in which is forbidden or restricted by the laws of the state of destination. . . .

But it is said that the present pro-hibition falls within the scope of none of these categories; that while the prohibition is nominally a regulation of the commerce its motive or purpose is regulation of wages and hours of persons engaged in manufacture, the control of which has been reserved to the states and upon which Georgia and some of the states of destination have placed no restriction; that the effect of the present statute is not to exclude the proscribed article from interstate commerce in aid of state regulation . . . but instead, under the guise of a regulation of interstate commerce, it undertakes to regulate wages and hours within the state contrary to the policy of the state which has elected to leave them unregulated.

The power of Congress over interstate commerce "is complete in itself, may be exercised to its utmost extent, and acknowledges no limitations other than are prescribed in the Constitution." . . . That power can neither be enlarged nor diminished by the exercise or non-exercise of state power. . . . Congress, following its own conception of public policy concerning the restrictions which may appropriately be imposed on interstate commerce, is free to exclude from the commerce articles whose use in the states for which they are destined it may conceive to be injurious to the public health, morals or welfare, even though the state has not sought to regulate their use. . . . Whatever their motive and purpose, regulations of commerce which do not infringe some constitutional prohibition are within the plenary power conferred on Congress by the Commerce Clause. Subject only to that limitation, presently to be considered, we conclude that the prohibition of the shipment interstate of goods produced under the forbidden substandard labor conditions is within the constitutional authority of Congress.

In the more than a century which has elapsed since the decision of *Gibbons* v. *Ogden*, these principles of constitutional interpretation have been so long and repeatedly recognized by this Court as applicable to the Commerce Clause, that there would be little occasion for repeating them now were it not for the decision of this Court twenty-two years ago in *Hammer* v. *Dagenhart*. . . . In that case it was held by a bare majority of the Court over the powerful and now classic dissent of Mr. Justice Holmes setting forth the fundamental issues involved, that Congress was without power to exclude the products of child labor from interstate commerce. The reasoning and conclusion of the Court's opinion there cannot be reconciled with the conclusion which we have reached, that the power of Congress under the Commerce Clause is plenary to exclude any article from interstate commerce subject only to the specific prohibitions of the Constitution.

Hammer v. *Dagenhart* has not been followed. The distinction on which the decision was rested that Congressional power to prohibit interstate commerce is limited to articles which in themselves have some harmful or deleterious property—a distinction which was novel when made and unsupported by any provision of the Constitution—has long since been abandoned. . . . The thesis of the opinion that the motive of the prohibition or its effect to control in some measure the use or production within the states of the article thus excluded from the commerce can operate to deprive the regulation of its constitutional authority has long since ceased to have force. . . .

The conclusion is inescapable that *Hammer* v. *Dagenhart* was a departure from the principles which have prevailed in the interpretation of the Commerce Clause both before and

since the decision and that such vitality, as a precedent, as it then had has long since been exhausted. It should be and now is overruled.

Validity of the wage and hour requirements. Section 15(a)(2) and §§ 6 and 7 require employers to conform to the wage and hour provisions with respect to all employees engaged in the production of goods for interstate commerce. As appellee's employees are not alleged to be "engaged in interstate commerce" the validity of the prohibition turns on the question whether the employment, under other than the prescribed labor standards, of employees engaged in the production of goods for interstate commerce is so related to the commerce and so affects it as to be within the reach of the power of Congress to regulate it. . . .

Without attempting to define the precise limits of the phrase, we think the acts alleged in the indictment are within the sweep of the statute. The obvious purpose of the Act was not only to prevent the interstate transportation of the proscribed product, but to stop the initial step toward transportation, production with the purpose of so transporting it. Congress was not unaware that most manufacturing businesses shipping their product in interstate commerce make it in their shops without reference to its ultimate destination and then after manufacture select some of it for shipping interstate and some intrastate according to the daily demands of their business, and that it would be practically impossible, to restrict the prohibited kind of production to the particular pieces of lumber, cloth, furniture or the like which later move in interstate rather than intrastate commerce. . . .

The recognized need of drafting a workable statute and the well known circumstances in which it was to be applied are persuasive of the conclusion. . . . that the "production for commerce" intended includes at least production of goods, which, at the time of production, the employer, according to the normal course of his business, intends or expects to move in interstate commerce although, through the exigencies of the business, all of the goods may not thereafter actually enter interstate commerce.

There remains the question whether such restriction on the production of goods for commerce is a permissible exercise of the commerce power. The power of Congress over interstate commerce is not confined to the regulation of commerce among the states. It extends to those activities intrastate which so affect interstate commerce or the exercise of the power of Congress over it as to make regulation of them appropriate means to the attainment of a legitimate end, the exercise of the granted power of Congress to regulate interstate commerce. . . .

While this Court has many times found state regulation of interstate commerce, when uniformity of its regulation is of national concern, to be incompatible with the Commerce Clause even though Congress has not legislated on the subject, the Court has never implied such restraint on state control over matters intrastate not deemed to be regulations of interstate commerce or its instrumentalities even though they affect the commerce. . . . In the absence of Congressional legislation on the subject state laws which are not regulations of the commerce itself or its instrumentalities are not forbidden even though they affect interstate commerce. . . .

But it does not follow that Congress may not by appropriate legislation regulate intrastate activities where they have a substantial effect on interstate commerce. . . . A recent example is the National Labor Relations Act. . . . But long before the adoption of the National Labor Relations Act this Court had many times held that the power of Congress to regulate interstate commerce extends to the regulation through legislative action of activities intrastate which have a substantial effect on the commerce or the exercise of the Congressional power over it.

. . . Our conclusion is unaffected by the Tenth Amendment. . . . The amendment states but a truism that all is retained which has not been surrendered. There is nothing in the history of its adoption to suggest that it was more than declaratory of the relationship between the national and state governments as it had been established by the Constitution before the amendment or that its purpose was other than to allay fears that the new national government might seek to exercise powers not granted and that the states might not be able to exercise fully their reserved powers. . . .

The Act is sufficiently definite to meet constitutional demands. One who employs persons, without conforming to the prescribed wage and hour conditions, to work on goods which he ships or expects to ship across state lines, is warned that he may be subject to the criminal penalties of the Act. No more is required. . . .

Reversed.

(4) Robert L. Stern, The Commerce Clause and the National Economy, 1933–1946

. . . .

The Constitution empowers Congress to regulate "commerce among

Reprinted from **59** *Harvard Law Review* (May and July, 1946), 645–647, 945–947.

the several states." For exactly one hundred years after that superficially simple phrase first appeared in the proposed national charter in 1787, Congress made no substantial use of the authority granted to it. The nation was growing, geographically and economically, there was adequate opportunity for men with initiative and ability without the assistance of government, and there was little demand by the public for the intrusion of government—state or federal—into the world of business and commerce. The *laissez-faire* philosophy embodied in legislation—or the lack of it—and judicial decision was a reflection rather than the generating source of the popular feeling that the least government was the best government.

Whether or not it be true as to lawyers and judges, philosophy and economic theory succumb to facts in so far as the public is concerned. When the people began to suffer as a result of the unrestrained freedom of enterprise, they called for help from the only peaceful protective organization at their command, their Government. Their call was addressed to the national government rather than to the states, since the problems of an integrated nationwide economy were obviously not remediable by state action. When the protests became sufficiently loud to arouse enough of the people's legislative representatives, Congress acted.

The Interstate Commerce Act in 1887 and the Sherman Act in 1890 were the first manifestations of this demand that business, and particularly big business, be subjected to regulation in the interest of the public. Other statutes were passed to meet specific abuses, including the Federal Trade Commission Act of 1914 and various acts relating to the railroads. But apart from the anti-trust laws and the regulation of public utilities, few of the statutes imposed substantial restraints upon the operation of business enterprises. . . .

The economic depression of the early 1930's produced a popular reaction strong enough. . . . to induce Congress to exercise its authority to the fullest extent. The problems were economic, and the Commerce Clause was the enumerated power most directly concerned with business and economic, or commercial, matters. Consequently, although other powers, particularly the fiscal and appropriative, were brought into play, it was upon the Commerce Clause that the legislation directed at controlling many aspects of the national economic system was principally predicated.

The commerce power had previously been exerted mainly in connection with interstate transportation, although the Sherman Act was exceptional in this respect. The conditions responsible for the business depression, although they had affected the railroads as much as any other industry, were considerably more deep-seated. Unemployment, the purchasing power of workers and farmers, prices in business and agriculture, unsellable surpluses which overhung the markets and the quantity of goods produced and grown— these were the elements with which it was necessary to deal. Could the Commerce Clause bear the load? . . .

The interpretation of the Commerce Clause had come a long way since the *Railroad Retirement* and *Carter* cases in 1935 and 1936. In the latter, Mr. Justice Sutherland had even resurrected the old *Sugar Trust* case, which had been considered buried in 1911. But within a year the *Carter* case had joined the *Sugar Trust* case in repose. By the end of the decade, every decision which had invalidated a congressional exercise of the commerce power had been disapproved, or distinguished to death. The Tenth Amendment had been restored to its proper place in the constitutional scheme; again it meant only what it said. The theory that the mere existence of state governments limits the scope of the enumerated powers of Congress had been abandoned as a constitutional doctrine, though some members of the Court, notably Mr. Justice Frankfurter, now invoked the same principle as a guide to the construction of federal legislation.

The Commerce Clause was now recognized as a grant of authority permitting Congress to allow interstate commerce to take place on whatever terms it may consider in the interest of the national well-being, subject only to other constitutional limitations, such as the Due Process Clause. The constitutional grant of power over commerce was now interpreted as enabling Congress to enact all appropriate laws for the protection and advancement of commerce among the states, whatever measures Congress might reasonably think adapted to that end, without regard for whether particular acts regulated in themselves were interstate or intrastate. No mechanical formula any longer excluded matters which might be called "local" from the application of these principles.

In our present-day economy the interstate and intrastate aspects of American business are inseparable. The sale, shipment, and transportation of commodities across state lines, which constitute interstate commerce, cannot be segregated economically from "production," a term which comprehends the amount of commodity produced, how it is produced, and the employment relations

of those who produce it, or even from the ultimate distribution within the state of destination. Each of these departments of an industry or business enterprise has an immediate and substantial impact upon the others. The power to regulate interstate commerce itself, as well as all subjects the regulation of which Congress may reasonably consider necessary for effective control or protection of such commerce, places every phase of industries organized on a multistate basis within the federal legislative domain. Since such matters cannot be effectively regulated by the states, this is as it should be, for clearly there ought to be some authority through which the people can control all of the interstate economy in which they live.

This expansion of the judicially recognized limits of the commerce power has not produced, or resulted from, any novel doctrine. On the contrary, the *Darby* case speaks in the language of *McCulloch* v. *Maryland*. . . . The trend has been back to the principles originally enunciated by Marshall in those classic opinions, to the language of the Constitution as understood by those who wrote it, and to the spirit in which it was written, as manifested by the thrice-approved resolution at the Constitutional Convention to permit "the national legislature. . . . to legislate in all cases for the general interest of the union, and also in those to which the states are separately incompetent, or in which the harmony of the United States may be interrupted by the exercise of individual legislation."

The reinvigoration of the Commerce Clause only restores to complete potency a legislative power. The capacity to exercise that power is affirmatively vested by the Constitution in the representatives of the people. The opinions of the Court since the judicial revolution of 1937 indicate that any attempt in good faith by Congress to cope with a national economic problem will be respected. But the broader interpretation of the Commerce Clause does not compel Congress to act; it merely places fewer impediments in the way of the democratic process. . . .

(5) Perez v. United States (1971)

+Burger, Douglas, Brennan, White, Marshall, Blackmun, Powell, Rehnquist
 −Stewart

[We have already noted the growing reluctance of the Supreme Court in the post-1937 period to interfere with state or congressional economic regulation. One aspect of this deference was the Supreme Court's acceptance of congressional use of the commerce clause as a "national police power." The *Perez* case illustrates how far this power, not mentioned anywhere in the Constitution, has come since then.

The police power is the power to regulate the health, safety, welfare, and morals of the community. There is no mention of such a power in the Constitution. It falls among those powers not delegated to the federal government and thus reserved to the states by the Tenth Amendment. Yet the line between those legitimate objectives that Congress could reach and those objectives beyond its constitutional power is not easy to draw. The principle that there was such a line, however, that Congress did *not* have unlimited powers, was stated by John Marshall in *McCulloch* v. *Maryland* (1819): Congress could not, "under the pretext of executing its powers, pass laws for the accomplishment of objects not entrusted to the government." This dictum was undoubtedly inserted in the *McCulloch* opinion to quell fears of those who might interpret Marshall's interpretation of the necessary and proper clause too broadly. But it was quite inconsistent with Marshall's later statement in *Gibbons* v. *Ogden* (1824) that Congress' power to regulate under the commerce clause "is complete in itself, may

be exercised to its utmost extent, and acknowledges no limitations, other than are prescribed in the Constitution."

Marshall's dictum in *McCulloch* remained undisturbed for a long time. It was not challenged primarily because Congress itself did not exercise anything like its full powers under the commerce or taxing and spending clauses. Toward the end of the nineteenth century however, Congress began to utlize that power more fully. The Interstate Commerce Act was passed in 1887, and in 1890 the Sherman Anti-Trust Act was passed. These were clearly designed to regulate "commerce." But Congress also began to regulate objects or activities that traditionally had been left to state control. To the extent that such regulation might be justified under the necessary and proper clause, no constitutional problems existed. Congress could—and did—regulate or prohibit counterfeit money, require safety devices on ships, prohibit the carrying of explosives on trains, and even impose a prohibitive tax on state bank notes. Constitutional problems arose when Congress undertook to tax oleomargarine; to prohibit interstate distribution of obscene literature, contraceptives, and prize fight films; and to prohibit the importation of liquor into "dry" states. Opponents of such legislation claimed that it exceeded the powers delegated to Congress by usurping the police powers of the states.

In *Champion* v. *Ames* (1903), the Supreme Court upheld, 5-4, a federal statute that prohibited the transportation of lottery tickets in interstate commerce. The majority held that Congress could use the commerce power to prevent harm to the public morals. Since lotteries were regarded by many as a moral pestilence, this was a legitimate use of the commerce power. Justice Harlan's opinion for the majority restated Marshall's view, expressed in the *Gibbons* case, that "regulation" of commerce might encompass complete prohibition. And it ignored his *McCulloch* dictum.

In the years following, Congress extended the scope of its regulatory efforts. The Pure Food and Drug Act, passed in 1906, prohibited the transportation in interstate commerce of impure food and drugs. The Mann Act (known as the "White Slave Traffic Act") prohibited transporting women in interstate commerce for immoral purposes. And finally, as described in the introductory essay, Congress in 1916 passed the Child Labor Act. But the Supreme Court, having upheld the earlier laws, found this statute to be unconstitutional in *Hammer* v. *Dagenhart* (1918). The *Darby* case (*supra*) overruled *Hammer* v. *Dagenhart* and restored Marshall's broad conception of the powers of Congress under the commerce clause. A unanimous Supreme Court rejected the doctrine that the Tenth Amendment was a measure of the scope of congressional power over commerce. It reaffirmed that Congress' power over commerce is plenary and may include total prohibition. It was not the Court's function to inquire into the motivations of Congress in determining what objects should be regulated. Thus the *Darby* case represents the full flowering in constitutional doctrine of the "national police power."

Perez was a loan shark convicted in federal court of violating the Consumer Credit Protection Act, which prohibited extortionate loan transactions (the use of threats and violence to collect loans made at usurious rates of interest). His conviction was affirmed by the court of appeals, and the Supreme Court granted certiorari.]

MR. JUSTICE DOUGLAS delivered the opinion of the Court.

. . .

The constitutional question is a substantial one.

. . .

"The loan shark . . . , is the indispensable 'money-mover' of the underworld. He takes 'black' money tainted by its derivation from the gambling or narcotics rackets and turns it 'white' by funneling it into channels of legitimate trade. In so doing, he exacts usurious interest that doubles the black-white money in no time; and, by his special decrees, by his imposition of impossible penalties, he greases the way for the underworld takeover of entire businesses."

There were objections in [Congress] on constitutional grounds. Congressman Eckhardt of Texas said:

Should it become law, the amendment would take a long stride by the Federal Government toward occupying the field of general criminal law and toward exercising a general Federal police power; and it would permit prosecution in Federal as well as State courts of a typically State offense. . . .

I believe that Alexander Hamilton, though a federalist, would be astonished that such a deep entrenchment on the rights of the States in performing their most fundamental function should come from the more conservative quarter of the House.

Senator Proxmire presented to the Senate the Conference Report approving essentially the "loan shark" provision suggested by Congressman McDade, saying:

Once again these provisions raised serious questions of Federal-State responsibilities. Nonetheless, because of the importance of the problem, the Senate conferees agreed to the House provision. Organized crime operates on a national scale. One of the principal sources of revenue of organized crime comes from loan sharking. If we are to win the battle against organized crime, we must strike at their source of revenue and give the Justice Department additional tools to deal with the problem. The problem simply cannot be solved by the States alone. We must bring into play the full resources of the Federal Government.

The Commerce Clause reaches in the main three categories of problems. First, the use of channels of interstate or foreign commerce which Congress deems are being misused, as for example, the shipment of stolen goods or of persons who have been kidnapped. Second, protection of the instrumentalities of interstate commerce, as for example, the destruction of an aircraft or persons or things in commerce, as for example, thefts from interstate shipments. Third, those activities affecting commerce. It is with this last category that we are here concerned.

Chief Justice Marshall said in *Gibbons* v. *Ogden*:

The genius and character of the whole government seems to be, that its action is to be applied to all the external concerns of the nation, and to those internal concerns which affect the states generally; but not to those which are completely within a particular state, which do not affect other states, and with which it is not necessary to interfere, for the purpose of executing some of the general powers of the government. The completely internal commerce of a state, then, may be considered as reserved for the state itself.

Decisions which followed departed from that view; but by the time of *United States* v. *Darby*, and *Wickard* v. *Filburn*, the broader view of the Commerce Clause announced by Chief Justice Marshall had been restored. Chief Justice Stone wrote for a unanimous Court in 1942 that Congress could provide for the regulation of the price of intrastate milk, the sale of which, in competition with interstate milk, affects the price structure and federal regulation of the latter. *United States* v. *Wrightwood Dairy Co.* The commerce power, he said, "extends to those activities intrastate which so affect interstate commerce, or the exertion of the power of Congress over it, as to make regulation of them appropriate means to the attainment of a legitimate end, the effective execution of the granted power to regulate interstate commerce."

Wickard v. *Filburn* soon followed in which a unanimous Court held that wheat grown wholly for home consumption was constitutionally within the scope of federal regulation of wheat production because though never marketed interstate, it supplied the need of the grower which otherwise would be satisfied by his purchases in the open market. We said: ". . . even if appellee's activity be local it may still, whatever its nature, be reached by Congress if it exerts a substantial economic effect on interstate commerce, and this irrespective of whether such effect is what might at some earlier time have been defined as 'direct' or 'indirect.' "

In *United States* v. *Darby*, . . . the decision sustaining an Act of Congress which prohibited the employment of workers in the production of goods "for interstate commerce" at other than prescribed wages and hours, a *class of activities* was held properly regulated by Congress without proof that the particular intrastate activity against which a sanction was laid had an effect on commerce. A unanimous Court said:

. . . . Congress has sometimes left it to the courts to determine whether the intrastate activities have the prohibited effect on the commerce, as in the Sherman Act. It has sometimes left it to an administrative board or agency to determine whether the activities sought to be regulated or prohibited have such effect, as in the case of the Interstate Commerce Act, and the National Labor Relations Act, or whether they come within the statutory definition of the prohibited Act, as in the Federal Trade Commission Act. And sometimes Congress itself has said that a particular activity affects the commerce, as it did in the present Act, the Safety Appliance Act and the Railway Labor Act. In passing on the validity of legislation of the class last mentioned the only function of

courts is to determine whether the particular activity regulated or prohibited is within the reach of the federal power.

That case is particularly relevant here because it involved a criminal prosecution, a unanimous Court holding that the Act was "sufficiently definite to meet constitutional demands." Petitioner is clearly a *member of the class* which engages in "extortionate credit transactions" as defined by Congress and the description of that class has the required definiteness.

It was the "class of activities" test which we employed in *Heart of Atlanta Motel* v. *United States*, to sustain an Act of Congress requiring hotel or motel accommodations for Negro guests. The Act declared that " 'any inn, hotel, motel, or other establishments which provides lodging to transient guests' affects commerce per se." That exercise of power under the Commerce Clause was sustained. . . .

In a companion case, *Katzenbach* v. *McClung*, we ruled on the constitutionality of the restaurant provision of the same Civil Rights Act which regulated the restaurant "if . . . it serves or offers to serve interstate travelers or a substantial portion of the food which it serves . . . has moved in commerce." Apart from the effect on the flow of food in commerce to restaurants, we spoke of the restrictive effect of the exclusion of Negroes. ". . . [T]here was an impressive array of testimony that discrimination in restaurants had a direct and highly restrictive effect upon interstate travel by Negroes. This resulted, it was said, because discriminatory practices prevent Negroes from buying prepared food served on the premises while on a trip, except in isolated and unkempt restaurants and under the most un-

satisfactory and often unpleasant conditions. This obviously discourages travel and obstructs interstate commerce for one can hardly travel without eating. Likewise, it was said, that discrimination deterred professional, as well as skilled people from moving into areas where such practices occurred and thereby caused industry to be reluctant to establish there."

In emphasis of our position that it was the *class of activities* regulated that was the measure, we acknowledged that Congress appropriately considered the "total incidence" of the practice on commerce.

Where the *class of activities* is regulated and that *class* is within the reach of federal power, the courts have no power "to excise, as trivial, individual instances" of the class.

Extortionate credit transactions, though purely intrastate, may in the judgment of Congress affect interstate commerce. In an analogous situation, Mr. Justice Holmes, speaking for a unanimous Court, said " . . . when it is necessary in order to prevent an evil to make the law embrace more than the precise thing to be prevented it may do so." In that case an officer of a state bank which was a member of the Federal Reserve System issued a fraudulent certificate of deposit and paid it from the funds of the state bank. It was argued that there was no loss to the Reserve Bank. Mr. Justice Holmes replied, "But every fraud like the one before us weakens the member bank and therefore weakens the system." In the setting of the present case there is a tie-in between local loan sharks and interstate crime.

The findings by Congress are quite adequate on that ground. The McDade Amendment in the House, as already noted, was the one ultimately adopted. As stated by Congressman McDade it grew out of a "profound study of organized crime, its ramifications and its implications" undertaken by some 22 Congressmen in 1966–1967. Congressman McDade also relied on *The Challenge of Crime in a Free Society, A Report by the President's Commission on Law Enforcement and Administration of Justice* (1967) which stated that loan sharking was "the second largest crime," and is one way by which the underworld obtains control of legitimate business.

The Congress also knew about New York's report, *An Investigation of the Loan Shark Racket* (1965). That report shows the loan shark racket is controlled by organized criminal syndicates, either directly or in partnership with independent operators; that in most instances the racket is organized into three echelons, with the top underworld "bosses" providing the money to their principal "lieutenants," who in turn distribute the money to the "operators" who make the actual individual loans; that loan sharks serve as a source of funds to bookmakers, narcotics dealers, and other racketeers; that the victims are often coerced into the commission of criminal acts in order to repay their loans; that through loan sharking the organized underworld has obtained control of legitimate businesses, including securities, brokerages and banks which are then exploited; and that, "Even where extortionate credit transactions are purely intrastate in character, they nevertheless directly affect interstate and foreign commerce."

. . .

The essence of all these reports and hearings was summarized and embodied in formal congressional findings. They supplied Congress with the knowledge that the loan shark racket provides organized

crime with its second most lucrative source of revenue, exacts millions from the pockets of people, coerces its victims into the commission of crimes against property, and causes the takeover by racketeers of legitimate business.

We have mentioned in detail the economic, financial, and social setting of the problem as revealed to Congress. We do so not to infer that Congress need make particularized findings in order to legislate. We relate the history of the Act in detail to answer the impassioned plea of petitioner that all that is involved in loan sharking is a traditionally local activity. It appears, instead, that loan sharking in its national setting is one way organized interstate crime holds its guns to the heads of the poor and the rich alike and syphons funds from numerous localities to finance its national operations.

Affirmed.

MR. JUSTICE STEWART, DISSENTING (OMITTED).

(6) National League of Cities v. Usery (1976)

+Rehnquist, Burger, Blackmun, Stewart, Powell

−Brennan, White, Marshall, Stevens

[In 1938 Congress enacted the Fair Labor Standards Act (FLSA), setting wage and hour regulations for much of the labor force. The Supreme Court unanimously upheld its constitutionality in *United States* v. *Darby* (1941). The original act specifically excluded the states and their political subdivisions from coverage. However, beginning in 1961, in a series of amendments, Congress gradually extended the minimum wage and maximum hour provisions of the act to public employees. In 1966, coverage was extended to employees of state hospitals, institutions, and schools; this extension was upheld by the Supreme Court in *Mary-*

land v. *Wirtz* (1968). In 1974, Congress sought to include virtually all public employees, declaring that

the employees of an enterprise which is a public agency shall for purposes of this subsection be deemed to be employees engaged in commerce, or in the production of goods for commerce. . . .

As of 1974, with only a few exceptions for such services as police and fire protection, public employers were subject to the same requirements under the FLSA as private employers.

A national association of municipal governments challenged the validity of the 1974 amendments in a suit against the secretary of labor. A three-judge district court was convened and, following *Maryland* v. *Wirtz*, dismissed the suit. But it observed that the challenge to the act raised substantial questions about the reach of Congress' power under the commerce clause: ". . . It may well be that the Supreme Court will feel it appropriate to draw back from the far reaching implications of [*Maryland* v. *Wirtz*]; but that is a decision that only the Supreme Court can make, and as a federal district court we feel obliged to apply the *Wirtz* opinion as it stands."

In 1975, the Supreme Court decided *Fry* v. *United States,* a case of considerable importance to the outcome in this litigation. *Fry* centered on the issue of whether Congress could authorize the president to extend emergency wage and price controls to state employees. President Nixon imposed national wage and price controls in 1970, and a Pay Board created by executive order limited wage increases to 5.5 percent for those employees covered. Ohio enacted a law providing a 10.6 percent increase for its employees, and the United States filed suit to enjoin any pay raises that exceeded the 7 percent that the Pay Board had, by that time, approved for 1972. By a 7-2 vote, the Supreme Court upheld the act and its application to public employees. Writing for the majority, Justice Marshall rested the decision on the broad powers of Congress under the commerce clause and the importance to national economic policy of not allowing major exceptions to a wage and price policy. He rejected the state's claim, based on the Tenth Amendment, that this act, as applied, exceeded Congress' power. But in response to a strong dissent from Justice Rehnquist, Marshall added the following footnote:

(7) . . . Petitioners have stated their argument not in terms of the Commerce power, but in terms of the limitations on that power imposed by the Tenth Amendment. While the Tenth Amendment has been characterized as a "truism," stating merely that "all is retained which has not been surrendered," United States v. Darby *(1941), it is not without significance. The Amendment expressly declares the constitutional policy that Congress may not exercise power in a fashion that impairs the States' integrity or their ability to function effectively in a federal system. Despite the extravagant claims on this score made by some amici, we are convinced that the wage restriction regulations constituted no such drastic invasion of state sovereignty.*

Rehnquist conceded that there might be emergency circumstances when Congress would be empowered to regulate activities of the states in the national interest, but he claimed that Congress could not do so under the commerce power alone. As an example, he cited the war power. Rehnquist also noted circumstances under which restrictions might be imposed on state power under the enforcement clauses of the Fourteenth and Fifteenth Amendments. But he argued that the circumstances here did not rise to the magnitude of an emergency in which other powers might augment Congress' power under the commerce clause. He urged that *Maryland* v. *Wirtz* be overruled instead of followed. In *National League of Cities,* his dissent was adopted by a majority of the court.]

MR. JUSTICE REHNQUIST delivered the opinion of the Court.

. . .

It is established beyond peradventure that the Commerce Clause of Art I of the Constitution is a grant of plenary authority to Congress. That authority is, in the words of Chief Justice Marshall in *Gibbons* v. *Ogden*, ". . . the power to regulate; that is to prescribe the rule by which commerce is to be governed."

When considering the validity of asserted applications of this power to wholly private activity, the Court has made it clear that

[e]ven activity that is purely intrastate in character may be regulated by Congress, where the activity, combined with like conduct by others similarly situated, affects commerce among the States or with foreign nations. Fry v. United States . . . (1975).

Congressional power over areas of private endeavor, even when its exercise may pre-empt express state law determinations contrary to the result which has recommended itself to collective wisdom of Congress, has been held to be limited only by the requirement that "the means chosen by [Congress] must be reasonably adapted to the end permitted by the Constitution." *Heart of Atlanta Motel, Inc.* v. *United States* (1964).

Appellants in no way challenge these decisions establishing the breadth of authority granted Congress under the commerce power. Their contention, on the contrary, is that when Congress seeks to regulate directly the activities of States as public employers, it transgresses an affirmative limitation on the exercise of its power akin to other commerce power affirmative limitations contained in the Constitution. Congressional enactments which may be fully within the grant of legislative authority contained in the Commerce Clause may nonetheless be invalid because found to offend against the right to trial by jury contained in the Sixth Amendment, *United States* v. *Jackson* (1968), or the Due Process

Clause of the Fifth Amendment, *Leary* v. *United States* (1969). Appellants' essential contention is that the 1974 amendments to the Act, while undoubtedly within the scope of the Commerce Clause, encounter a similar constitutional barrier because they are to be applied directly to the States and subdivisions of States as employers.

This Court has never doubted that there are limits upon the power of Congress to override state sovereignty, even when exercising its otherwise plenary powers to tax or to regulate commerce which are conferred by Art. I of the Constitution. In *Wirtz*, for example, the Court took care to assure the appellants that it had "ample power to prevent . . . 'the utter destruction of the State as a sovereign political entity,' " which they feared. . . . Appellee Secretary in this case, both in his brief and upon oral argument, has agreed that our federal system of government imposes definite limits upon the authority of Congress to regulate the activities of the States as States by means of the commerce power. In *Fry*, supra, the Court recognized that an express declaration of this limitation is found in the Tenth Amendment:

While the Tenth Amendment has been characterized as a 'truism,' stating merely that 'all is retained which has not been surrendered,' United States v. Darby (1941), it is not without significance. The Amendment expressly declares the constitutional policy that Congress may not exercise power in a fashion that impairs the States' integrity or their ability to function effectively in a federal system. . . .

In *New York* v. *United States* (1946), Chief Justice Stone, speaking for four Members of an eight-Member Court in rejecting the proposition that Congress could impose taxes on the States so long as it did so in a nondiscriminatory manner, observed:

A State may, like a private individual, own real property and receive income. But in view of our former decisions we could hardly say that a general nondiscriminatory real estate tax (apportioned), or an income tax laid upon citizens and States alike could be constitutionally applied to the State's capitol, its State-house, its public school houses, public parks, or its revenues from taxes or school lands, even though all real property and all income of the citizen is taxed.

The expressions in these more recent cases trace back to earlier decisions of this Court recognizing the essential role of the States in our federal system of government. Chief Justice Chase, perhaps because of the particular time at which he occupied that office, had occasion more than once to speak for the Court on this point. In *Texas* v. *White* (1869), he declared that "[t]he Constitution, in all its provisions, looks to an indestructible Union, composed of indestructible States." . . .

Appellee Secretary argues that the cases in which this Court has upheld sweeping exercises of authority by Congress, even though those exercises pre-empted state regulation of the private sector, have already curtailed the sovereignty of the States quite as much as the 1974 amendments to the Fair Labor Standards Act. We do not agree. It is one thing to recognize the authority of Congress to enact laws regulating individual businesses necessarily subject to the dual sovereignty of the government of the Nation and of the State in which they reside. It is quite another to uphold a similar exercise of congressional authority directed not to private citizens, but to the States as

States. We have repeatedly recognized that there are attributes of sovereignty attaching to every state government which may not be impaired by Congress, not because Congress may lack an affirmative grant of legislative authority to reach the matter, but because the Constitution prohibits it from exercising the authority in that manner. . . .

One undoubted attribute of state sovereignty is the States' power to determine the wages which shall be paid to those whom they employ in order to carry out their governmental functions, what hours those persons will work, and what compensation will be provided where these employees may be called upon to work overtime. The question we must resolve in this case, then, is whether these determinations are "functions essential to separate and independent existence," . . . so that Congress may not abrogate the States' otherwise plenary authority to make them. . . .

Judged solely in terms of increased costs in dollars, these allegations [of additional costs] show a significant impact on the functioning of the governmental bodies involved. . . . The State of California, which must devote significant portions of its budget to fire suppression endeavors, estimated that application of the Act to its employment practices will necessitate an increase in its budget of between $8 million and $16 million.

Increased costs are not, of course, the only adverse effects which compliance with the Act will visit upon state and local governments, and in turn upon the citizens who depend upon those governments. In its complaint in intervention, for example, California asserted that it could not comply with the overtime costs (approximately $750,000 per year) which the Act required to be paid to

California Highway Patrol cadets during their academy training program. California reported that it had thus been forced to reduce its academy training program from 2,080 hours to only 960 hours, a compromise undoubtedly of substantial importance to those whose safety and welfare may depend upon the preparedness of the California Highway Patrol.

. . .

Quite apart from the substantial costs imposed upon the States and their political subdivisions, the Act displaces state policies regarding the manner in which they will structure delivery of those governmental services which their citizens require. The Act, speaking directly to the States qua States, requires that they shall pay all but an extremely limited minority of their employees the minimum wage rates currently chosen by Congress. It may well be that as a matter of economic policy it would be desirable that States, just as private employers, comply with these minimum wage requirements. But it cannot be gainsaid that the federal requirement directly supplants the considered policy choices of the States' elected officials and administrators as to how they wish to structure pay scales in state employment. The State might wish to employ persons with little or no training, or those who wish to work on a casual basis, or those who for some other reason do not possess minimum employment requirements, and pay them less than the federally prescribed minimum wage. It may wish to offer part time or summer employment to teenagers at a figure less than the minimum wage, and if unable to do so may decline to offer such employment at all. But the Act would forbid such choices by the States. The only "discretion" left to them under

the Act is either to attempt to increase their revenue to meet the additional financial burden imposed upon them by paying congressionally prescribed wages to their existing complement of employees, or to reduce that complement to a number which can be paid the federal minimum wage without increasing revenue.

This dilemma presented by the minimum wage restrictions may seem not immediately different from that faced by private employers, who have long been covered by the Act and who must find ways to increase their gross income if they are to pay higher wages while maintaining current earnings. The difference, however, is that a State is not merely a factor in the "shifting economic arrangements" of the private sector of the economy, . . . but is itself a coordinate element in the system established by the framers for governing our federal union.

. . .

This congressionally imposed displacement of state decisions may substantially restructure traditional ways in which the local governments have arranged their affairs. Although at this point many of the actual effects under the proposed Amendments remain a matter of some dispute among the parties, enough can be satisfactorily anticipated for an outline discussion of their general import. The requirement imposing premium rates upon any employment in excess of what Congress has decided is appropriate for a governmental employee's workweek, for example, appears likely to have the effect of coercing the States to structure work periods in some employment areas, such as police and fire protection, in a manner substantially different from practices which have long been commonly accepted among local governments of this Nation. In addition, appellee represents that the Act will require that the premium compensation for overtime worked must be paid in cash, rather than with compensatory time off, unless such compensatory time is taken in the same pay period. This too appears likely to be highly disruptive of accepted employment practices in many governmental areas where the demand for a number of employees to perform important jobs for extended periods on short notice can be both unpredictable and critical. . . .

Our examination of the effect of the 1974 amendments, as sought to be extended to the States and their political subdivisions, satisfies us that both the minimum wage and the maximum hour provisions will impermissibly interfere with the integral governmental functions of these bodies. . . . If Congress may withdraw from the States the authority to make those fundamental employment decisions upon which their systems for performance of these functions must rest, we think there would be little left of the States' "separate and independent existence." . . . Thus, even if appellants may have overestimated the effect which the Act will have upon their current levels and patterns of governmental activity, the dispositive factor is that Congress has attempted to exercise its Commerce Clause authority to prescribe minimum wages and maximum hours to be paid by the States in their capacities as sovereign governments. In so doing, Congress has sought to wield its power in a fashion that would impair the States' "ability to function effectively within a federal system." This exercise of congressional authority does not comport with the federal system of government embodied in the Constitution. We hold that insofar as the challenged amendments operate to directly displace the States' freedom to structure integral operations in areas of traditional governmental functions, they are not within the authority granted Congress by Art. I, § 8, cl. 3.

One final matter requires our attention. Appellee has vigorously urged that we cannot, consistently with the Court's decisions in *Wirtz*, supra, and *Fry*, supra, rule against him here. It is important to examine this contention so that it will be clear what we hold today, and what we do not.

With regard to *Fry*, we disagree with appellee. There the Court held that the Economic Stabilization Act of 1970 was constitutional as applied to temporarily freeze the wages of state and local government employees. The Court expressly noted that the degree of intrusion upon the protected area of state sovereignty was in that case even less than that worked by the amendments to the FLSA which were before the Court in *Wirtz*. The Court recognized that the Economic Stabilization Act was "an emergency measure to counter severe inflation that threatened the national economy."

We think our holding today quite consistent with *Fry*. The enactment at issue there was occasioned by an extremely serious problem which endangered the well-being of all the component parts of our federal system and which only collective action by the National Government might forestall. The means selected were carefully drafted so as not to interfere with the States' freedom beyond a very limited, specific period of time. The effect of the across-the-board freeze authorized by that Act, moreover, displaced no state choices as to how governmental operations should be structured nor did it force the States to remake such choices themselves. Instead, it merely required that the wage scales and employment relationships which the States themselves had chosen be maintained during the period of the emergency. Finally, the Economic Stabilization Act operated to reduce the pressures upon state budgets rather than increase them. These factors distinguish the statute in *Fry* from the provisions at issue here. The limits imposed upon the commerce power when Congress seeks to apply it to the States are not so inflexible as to preclude temporary enactments tailored to combat a national emergency. "[A]lthough an emergency may not call into life a power which has never lived, nevertheless emergency may afford a reason for the exertion of a living power already enjoyed." *Wilson* v. *New* (1917).

With respect to the Court's decision in *Wirtz*, we reach a different conclusion. Both appellee and the District Court thought that decision required rejection of appellants' claims. Appellants, in turn, advance several arguments by which they seek to distinguish the facts before the Court in *Wirtz* from those presented by the 1974 amendments to the Act. There are undoubtedly factual distinctions between the two situations, but in view of the conclusions expressed earlier in this opinion we do not believe the reasoning in *Wirtz* may any longer be regarded as authoritative.

Wirtz relied heavily on the Court's decision in *United States* v. *California* (1936). The opinion quotes the following language from that case:

'[We] *look to the activities to which the states have traditionally engaged as marking the boundary of the restriction upon the federal taxing power. But there is no such limitation upon the plenary power to regulate commerce. The*

State can no more deny the power if its exercise has been authorized by Congress than can an individual.' . . .

But we have reaffirmed today that the States as States stand on a quite different footing than an individual or a corporation when challenging the exercise of Congress' power to regulate commerce. We think the dicta from *United States* v. *California*, simply wrong. Congress may not exercise that power so as to force directly upon the States its choices as to how essential decisions regarding the conduct of integral governmental functions are to be made. We agree that such assertions of power, if unchecked, would indeed, as Mr. Justice Douglas cautioned in his dissent in *Wirtz*, allow "the National Government [to] devour the essentials of state sovereignty," and would therefore transgress the bounds of the authority granted Congress under the Commerce Clause. While there are obvious differences between the schools and hospitals involved in *Wirtz* and the fire and police departments affected here, each provides an integral portion of those governmental services which the States and their political subdivisions have traditionally afforded their citizens. We are therefore persuaded that *Wirtz* must be overruled.

The judgment of the District Court is accordingly reversed and the case is remanded for further proceedings consistent with this opinion.

So ordered.

MR. JUSTICE BLACKMUN, CONCURRING.

The Court's opinion and the dissents indicate the importance and significance of this case as it bears upon the relationship between the Federal Government and our States.

Although I am not untroubled by certain possible implications of the Court's opinion—some of them suggested by the dissents—I do not read the opinion so despairingly as does my Brother Brennan. In my view, the result with respect to the statute under challenge here is necessarily correct. I may misinterpret the Court's opinion, but it seems to me that it adopts a balancing approach, and does not outlaw federal power in areas such as environmental protection, where the federal interest is demonstrably greater and where state facility compliance with imposed federal standards would be essential. With this understanding on my part of the Court's opinion, I join it.

MR. JUSTICE BRENNAN, WITH WHOM MR. JUSTICE WHITE AND MR. JUSTICE MARSHALL JOiN, DISSENTING.

The Court concedes, as of course it must, that Congress enacted the 1974 amendments pursuant to its exclusive power under Art. I, § 8, cl. 3, of the Constitution "To regulate Commerce . . . among the several States." It must therefore be surprising that my Brethren should choose this Bicentennial year of our independence to repudiate principles governing judicial interpretation of our Constitution settled since the time of Chief Justice John Marshall, discarding his postulate that the Constitution contemplates that restraints upon exercise by Congress of its plenary commerce power lie in the political process and not in the judicial process. . . . Only 34 years ago, *Wickard* v. *Filburn* (1942), reaffirmed that "[a]t the beginning Chief Justice Marshall . . . made emphatic the embracing and penetrating nature of [Congress' commerce] power by warning that effective restraints on its exercise must proceed from politi-

cal rather than from judicial processes."

. . .

We said in *United States* v. *California*, that "[t]he sovereign power of the states is necessarily diminished to the extent of the grants of power to the federal government in the Constitution. . . . [T]he power of the state is subordinate to the constitutional exercise of the granted federal power."

. . .

My Brethren thus have today manufactured an abstraction without substance, founded neither in the words of the Constitution nor on precedent. An abstraction having such profoundly pernicious consequences is not made less so by characterizing the 1974 amendments as legislation directed against the "States qua States." . . . [There is] no claim that the 1974 amendments are not regulations of "commerce"; rather they overrule *Wirtz* in disagreement with historic principles that *United States* v. *California*, supra, reaffirmed: "[W]hile the commerce power has limits, valid general regulations of commerce do not cease to be regulations of commerce because a State is involved. If a state is engaging in economic activities that are validly regulated by the federal government when engaged in by private persons, the State too may be forced to conform its activities to federal regulation." Clearly, therefore, my Brethren are also repudiating the long line of our precedents holding that a judicial finding that Congress has not unreasonably regulated a subject matter of "commerce" brings to an end the judicial role. "Let the end be legitimate, let it be within the scope of the constitution, and all means which are appropriate, which are plainly adapted to that end, which are not prohibited, but consist with the letter and spirit of the constitution, are constitutional." *M'Culloch* v. *Maryland*. . . .

The reliance of my Brethren upon the Tenth Amendment as "an express declaration of [a state sovereignty] limitation," . . . not only suggests that they overrule governing decisions of this Court that address this question but must astound scholars of the Constitution. For not only early decisions . . . hold that nothing in the Tenth Amendment constitutes a limitation on congressional exercise of powers delegated by the Constitution to Congress. . . . Rather, as the Tenth Amendment's significance was more recently summarized:

The amendment states but a truism that all is retained which has not been surrendered. There is nothing in the history of its adoption to suggest that it was more than declaratory of the relationship between the national and state governments as it had been established by the Constitution before the amendment or that its purpose was other than to allay fears that the new national government might seek to exercise powers not granted, and that the states might not be able to exercise fully their reserved powers . . . .

From the beginning and for many years the amendment has been construed as not depriving the national government of authority to resort to all means for the exercise of a granted power which are appropriate and plainly adapted to the permitted end. United States *v.* Darby.

. . .

Today's repudiation of this unbroken line of precedents that firmly reject my Brethren's ill-conceived abstraction can only be regarded as a transparent cover for invalidating a congressional judgment with which they disagree. The only analysis even remotely resembling that adopted today is found in a line of opinions dealing with the Commerce Clause and the Tenth Amendment that ultimately provoked a constitutional crisis for the Court in the 1930's. E.g. *Carter* v. *Carter Coal Co* . . . (1936); *United States* v. *Butler* . . . (1936); *Hammer* v. *Dagenhart* . . . (1918). We tend to forget that the Court invalidated legislation during the Great Depression, not solely under the Due Process Clause, but also and primarily under the Commerce Clause and the Tenth Amendment. It may have been the eventual abandonment of that overly restrictive construction of the commerce power that spelled defeat for the Court-packing plan, and preserved the integrity of this institution, *United States* v. *Darby; Mulford* v. *Smith* . . . (1939); *NLRB* v. *Jones & Laughlin Steel Corp.* . . . (1937), but my Brethren today are transparently trying to cut back on that recognition of the scope of the commerce power. My Brethren's approach to this case is not far different from the dissenting opinions in the cases that averted the crisis.

. . .

My Brethren do more than turn aside longstanding constitutional jurisprudence that emphatically rejects today's conclusion. More alarming is the startling restructuring of our federal system, and the role they create therein for the federal judiciary. This Court is simply not at liberty to erect a mirror of its own conception of a desirable governmental structure. If the 1974 amendments have any "vice," my Brother Stevens is surely right that it represents "merely . . . a policy issue which has been firmly resolved by the branches of government having power to decide such questions." It bears repeating "that effective restraints on . . . exercise [of the Commerce power] must proceed from political rather than from judicial processes." . . .

It is unacceptable that the judicial process should be thought superior to the political process in this area. Under the Constitution the judiciary has no role to play beyond finding that Congress has not made an unreasonable legislative judgment respecting what is "commerce." My Brother Blackmun suggests that controlling judicial supervision of the relationship between the States and our National Government by use of a balancing approach diminishes the ominous implications of today's decision. Such an approach, however, is a thinly veiled rationalization for judicial supervision of a policy judgment that our system of government reserves to Congress.

Judicial restraint in this area merely recognizes that the political branches of our Government are structured to protect the interests of the States, as well as the Nation as a whole, and that the States are fully able to protect their own interests in the premises.

. . .

We are left then with a catastrophic judicial body blow at Congress' power under the Commerce Clause. Even if Congress may nevertheless accomplish its objectives—for example by conditioning grants of federal funds upon compliance with federal minimum wage and overtime standards, there is an ominous portent of disruption of our constitutional structure implicit in today's mischievous decision. I dissent.

MR. JUSTICE STEVENS, DISSENTING (OMITTED).

3. THE SUPREME COURT IN THE MODERN ECONOMIC STATE

A. A Note on Judicial Policy Making and the Need for a Doctrine of Substance

We have noted how in most respects, the Supreme Court has withdrawn from active involvement in regulation of the economy. This is largely true of its attitude toward congressional regulation, notwithstanding the *Usery* case, and is most certainly true of its rejection of the doctrine of substantive due process as a vehicle for invalidating state laws. Yet, as already noted, the paradox of substantive due process is that its decline in economic regulation cases has been paralleled by its reemergence in cases involving personal and civil rights, especially those cases involving marital and sexual privacy. To underscore the similarity of the line of cases beginning with *Griswold* v. *Connecticut* (1965) to the earlier economic regulation cases, one commentator, David Adamany, has referred to them as "sexual due process" cases.

The fundamental question is the extent to which the Supreme Court should substitute its judgment on such policy matters for the judgment of a legislative body. There is no disagreement that the Court must and should enforce specific constitutional prohibitions. But what of the vague admonitions of the due process and equal protection clauses of the Fourteenth Amendment? The rejection of substantive due process, vindicating Holmes' famous dissent in *Lochner*, certainly establishes the notion that due process does not embody allegiance to a particular economic philosophy. It does not enact a particular version of capitalism or prefer capitalism to socialism. Holmes' concern was based not so much on the question of the propriety of judicial repudiation of a legislative decision as on the act of judicial intervention lacking an adequate constitutional standard. The laissez-faire theories of Herbert Spencer were not, for Holmes, adequate *constitutional* standards. The Fourteenth Amendment requirement of due process prior to deprivation of property was not a sufficient basis on which to sustain a theory of liberty of contract.

The prohibitive language in the Bill of Rights dwells predominantly on personal rights rather than on economic rights (which, to be sure, are also "personal" rights, but in a different sense). Thus, there is at least some constitutional basis for sustaining a policy role for the Supreme Court in matters of personal rights while denying such a role in economic matters. Yet the distinction is neither clear nor wholly persuasive.

The distinction is illustrated by the famous "Footnote Four" in Justice Harlan Stone's opinion for the Court in *United States* v. *Carolene Products Company* (1938) (reprinted earlier in this book on p. 180). The case itself was hardly notable; it concerned an act of Congress that restricted the movement in interstate commerce of certain kinds of milk products. In his footnote, Stone noted that the reasons for extreme judicial deference to economic regulatory statutes did not necessarily apply where the more specific protections of the Bill of Rights were concerned. Where a statute appeared to contravene a specific protection of the Bill of Rights, the normal presumption of

constitutionality might be reversed. In making this distinction, Stone was laying the groundwork for the current distinction between "strict" and "ordinary" scrutiny. However rationalized, this approach amounts to a double standard of protection; some rights are more important than others, or more likely to be violated, and hence require commensurately greater judicial protection. Thus the contemporary constitutional focus on civil liberties and civil rights is very much a child of the Court's earlier economic concerns.

B. Richard Funston, The Double Standard of Constitutional Protection in the Era of the Welfare State

More than a third of a century ago Justice Harlan Fiske Stone labored and brought forth an opinion for the Supreme Court in the case of *United States* v. *Carolene Products Co.* The case was a pedestrian one, dealing with government regulation of adulterated milk, and Stone's opinion was in keeping with its character. Indeed, the decision might have passed into obscurity with the vast bulk of the Court's nonlandmark cases, had Stone not chosen the occasion to announce in a footnote an entirely new doctrine of judicial review. Hidden in the interstices of *Carolene Products* is, as every serious student of constitutional law knows, the famous Footnote Four. In essence what Footnote Four did, or attempted to do, was to postulate a dichotomy between so-called "civil" or "personal" rights and so-called "property" rights and then to suggest that the standard for judicial review of legislation as-

Reprinted from **90** *Political Science Quarterly* (Summer, 1975), 261–292.

sertedly violating these different rights would itself be different. Alleged infringements of economic rights would be subjected to a minimal inquiry, but government actions touching individual civil liberties would receive strict judicial scrutiny. Subsequent cases building upon Footnote Four magnified the difference in judicial approach and protection accorded to "human" as opposed to "property" rights. Questions of commercial and economic regulation were virtually abandoned to the legislatures, while whole new categories of civil liberties were judicially created or discovered and militantly protected against legislative encroachment. But, of late, the confluence of Stone's "double standard" and Professor Charles Reich's "new property" has put the old orthodoxy of judicial liberalism to serious test and apparently shaken the confidence of some of its chief architects. The application of the double standard to the legislation of the welfare state has raised again the problem of the economic bases of individual liberty. . . .

The Supreme Court's juxtaposition of property rights and civil rights is at odds with a legal and philosophic tradition, traceable to the ancients, which insisted upon the equality of the values of property and liberty. Indeed, there is a sort of perverse continuity between the origins in the law of real property of English constitutional law and contemporary Marxism with its insistence that politics and political freedoms are but the mere function of the economic order. Certainly the framers of the American Constitution were sensitive to the proposition that control of a man's property amounted to control of his liberty.

The primary bulwark for the protection of private property in America was to be the Supreme Court. . . .

While one need not endorse Beard's thesis of the origins of the Constitution, there can be no doubt that one of the motive forces behind its adoption was a desire to protect property, and during the first half of the nineteenth century Chief Justices Marshall and Taney successfully endeavored to carry out the framers' mandate. . . . Property was a value to be protected by the Court, but it was not the *only* value. Such was not to be the case in the next era of judicial creativity.

It is possible, in fact, to contend that it was not Stone in *Carolene Products* who introduced the Supreme Court to the notion that property rights were separable from other forms of liberty but rather that it was the justices of the latter half of the nineteenth century who equated due process of law with laissez-faire economics. In the jurisprudence of the age of enterprise, property came to have a mystical, quasi-religious character. It was elevated to a place of primacy in the pantheon of constitutional values and then defended through a substantive reading of the due process clauses of the Fifth and Fourteenth Amendments. . . . Property became an absolute value, superior to all other legal and political values, different from all other values protected by the Constitution, not subject to adjustment or modification in the light of changed social or economic circumstances. . . .

While it was and is not free of ambiguity, Stone's enunciation of the doctrine of the double standard suggests three interrelated propositions. The first would appear to be that the presumption of constitutionality which normally attaches to legislation is to be restricted, perhaps even abandoned, if a statute facially falls within the purview of a Bill of Rights guarantee. When a value protected by one of the first ten amendments is threatened by legislation, it is the value that commands judicial respect; when it is property that is threatened, it is the legislative judgment that commands judicial respect. In his second paragraph, Stone implies that legislation affecting "those political processes" basic to a democratic system are also to be subjected to more rigorous judicial inquiry than is legislation affecting economic processes. Third, Stone leaves open the suggestion that small and often unpopular groups are to be the particular constituency of the judiciary. Unlike economic interests, these "religious . . . national . . . or racial minorities" may expect to enjoy special judicial protection.

Subsequent cases revealed that Stone himself had intended only to elevate the First Amendment's protections to a "preferred position." But Footnote Four's adumbration of the double standard spoke of the entire Bill of Rights; and Stone's "colleagues, Black, Douglas, Murphy, and [most extremely] Rutledge, interpreted the admonition as being all inclusive, and their opinion frequently prevailed during their joint tenure on the Court between 1943 and 1949—sometimes gaining Jackson's vote, occasionally even Frankfurter's or Reed's. Thus at least five votes to carry the day were frequently available, and a series of memorable decisions was made in behalf of the new concept." The Court, not content to stop there, also liberalized its interpretations of the content of the Bill of Rights prohibitions, even to the point of creating new, albeit implicit, constitutional freedoms.

At the same time, with respect to economic regulatory legislation, the Court more than lowered its sights; it gave up the hunt all together. Retreating to a "hands-off" attitude in the field of commercial regulation,

the Court was willing to postulate virtually any set of facts, no matter how improbable, which would satisfy the standard of rationality. . . .

Following *Carolene Products*, then, what the Supreme Court had done was to assume, virtually beyond refutation, the constitutionality of regulatory legislation in the realm of property but to view legislative efforts in the area of "personal" rights with extreme suspicion. "Just why property itself was not a 'personal right,' " observed Judge Learned Hand, "nobody took the time to explain." Nor, in the decade and a half since Hand's observation, have the justices yet taken that time. Instead, they have remained silent as to the underlying rationale for their total surrender of this area of policy making to the legislative and executive branches of government.

A lesson from the Court's history was about to be relearned, however. Just as the "Court that had enshrined economic liberty in the Constitution under the due process rubric found it increasingly difficult to maintain that the Due Process Clause did not protect other liberties that men might deem important," so too the Warren Court discovered it to be ever more difficult to keep property rights separate from personal rights. In real-life regulatory situations, the two kept bumping into each other. One of the earliest expressions of this difficulty came in *Barsky* v. *Board of Regents* (1954), in which the Court's majority sustained the suspension of a physician's license despite fairly strong evidence that the suspension had been motivated by unreasonable and irrelevant political considerations. Labeling the matter "economic," the majority suggested that administrative discretion in such areas was virtually free of any judicially imposed limitation. Mr. Justice Douglas, sounding very much like Stephen J. Field, dissented.

So far as I know, nothing in a man's political beliefs disables him from setting broken bones or removing ruptured appendixes safely and efficiently. A practicing surgeon is unlikely to uncover many state secrets in the course of his professional activities. . . .

The right to work, I had assumed, was the most precious liberty that man possesses. Man has indeed as much right to work as he has to live, to be free, to own property. . . . To work means to eat. It also means to live. For many it would be better to work in jail, than to sit idle on the curb. The great values of freedom are in the opportunities afforded man to press to new horizons, to pit his strength against the forces of nature, to match skills with his fellow man.

Barsky and subsequent cases, then, illustrated the difficulties of maintaining the double standard's distinctions in a modern America characterized by forms of government largess and economic regulation wholly unlike the problems confronted by the New Deal.

This problem became acute, at least for liberally oriented justices, with the advent of the Great Society and its social programs, coupled with the appearance of the influential—if not always persuasive—work of Professor Charles Reich of the Yale Law School. In two seminal essays, Reich postulated a theoretical argument for the entitlement to welfare, based upon the concept of the "new property." Reich's argument, in brief, begins with the empirical observation that many Americans today receive their incomes either from civil service employment or from businesses which are subsidized by the government because they are thought to perform some function contributory to the general economic welfare.

As we move toward a welfare state, [government] largess will be an ever more important form of wealth. And largess is a vital link in the relationship between the government and private sides of society.

Reich then proceeds to argue that similarly "the poor are affirmative contributors to today's society, for we are so organized as virtually to compel this sacrifice [of affluence] by a segment of the population." Poverty being an inevitable product of the existing economic structure, public assistance is in effect a government subsidy to compensate the indigent for their systemically necessary low wages or unemployment. Reich's conclusion, then, is a revolutionary challenge.

If the individual is to survive in a collective society, he must have protection against its ruthless pressures. There must be sanctuaries or enclaves where no majority can reach. To shelter the solitary human spirit does not merely make possible the fulfillment of individuals; it also gives society the power to change, to grow, and to regenerate, and hence to endure. These were the objects which property sought to achieve. . . . Just as the Homestead Act was a deliberate effort to foster individual values at an earlier time, so we must try to build an economic basis for liberty today—a Homestead Act for rootless twentieth-century man. We must create a new property.

. . . Reich's subsidy-entitlement view of welfare has found some judicial converts, and in *Goldberg* v. *Kelly* a five-man majority gave its qualified endorsement to the "new property." It was qualified because the Court did not go so far as to hold that one had a constitutional right to public assistance, although it did assume that welfare was "property" within the meaning of the due process clause. But, even were the Court to accept the most extreme statements of the "new property" theory, it still must confront the problem presented by the double standard. So long as Footnote Four retains its vitality, equating government largess with property affords it scant constitutional protection.

This was convincingly demonstrated only a fortnight after the *Goldberg* decision in *Dandridge* v. *Williams*. Despite *Goldberg's* elevation of statutory entitlements to the level of property for purposes of due process analysis, the Court in *Dandridge* upheld the validity of Maryland's maximum welfare grant regulation. To preserve the fiscal integrity of its welfare program, Maryland limited to $250 per month the total amount which any single family might receive under the Aid to Families with Dependent Children program. As a result, large families received welfare assistance which was less than their computed need. The Supreme Court, however, sustained the limitation against constitutional attack. Speaking for the majority, Mr. Justice Stewart concluded that the constitutionality of the Maryland practice should be subjected only to the minimal standards of judicial review traditionally employed in business regulation cases, because the maximum grant regulation was economic in nature. Justice Stewart conceded a "dramatically real factual difference" between the interest in securing adequate welfare assistance and the interests at stake in business regulation, but he could find no difference of constitutional dimension significant enough to warrant a more rigorous judicial scrutiny. In the area of economic regulation, wrote Stewart, "A statutory discrimination will not be set aside if any state of facts reasonably may be conceived to justify it. " . . .

Thus, the constitutional validity of the regulation was manifest. Ironically, the double standard had worked to the detriment of judicial liberalism. . . .

One need not desire to turn the clock back to the early part of this century in order to suggest that it might be desirable for the Court to play some role in the shaping of public policies touching upon property interests. But that is not the choice which is open to the modern Court. The rational basis of statutes remains a proper subject for judicial scrutiny. Surely the Court should not strike down an arguably rational law, though a majority of the justices may find it unwise or repugnant. But it would not be inappropriate to require that the legislature make some showing that there is a basis for believing the statute to be rational, nor would it be improper for the Court to consider evidence to the contrary.

Whether this reassertion of a limited judicial role in the sphere of social and economic policy would be better carried out through the interpretation of the equal protection clause or under the rubric of due process is a question which can, at this writing, be left open. The judicial distaste for substantive due process may still persist. But the equal protection clause may be used substantively as well to thwart legislative objectives. There is nothing particularly precise or disciplined about the two-level equal protection approach, particularly when untied to constitutional "specifics." The fundamentality of interests or the suspect nature of classifications still turns upon the justices' subjective judgments. . . .

The meaning of property for constitutional purposes is broad, takes many forms, and may overlap with the meaning of liberty. Indeed, the effective enjoyment of civil liberties requires a degree of command over material resources. For a vast segment of the human race, the central reality of freedom lies at the economic level; thus, Franklin Roosevelt included in his Four Freedoms, along with the freedoms of speech and religion, *the freedom from want*. In the more advanced societies, the institution of the welfare state has created an array of forms of property dispensed by government which provides material well-being but which also serves to control the rights and status of the individual. . . .

C. A Note on Economic Change and Policy Making

Earlier portions of the chapter have dealt with the Supreme Court's involvement in the issues reflected by phases of the economic history of the United States. Although it is by now commonplace to maintain that the Court's deep involvement in economic issues may be at an end, many students of economics maintain that economic relationships have changed as well. Thus, perhaps the more interesting questions about the role of the Constitution and the Supreme Court in the economy have to do with the future and with an unprecedented present.

Much of what the Constitution has come to mean regarding economics reflects an era that may be referred to as "industrialism," which roughly may be said to embrace the period from 1860 to very recent times, perhaps 1945 or 1950. This period was marked by the development of industrial capacity to exploit basic resources, such as steel and oil, as well as the growth of national systems of transportation and further extension of the private financial and commercial systems that facilitated such development. The New Deal and the constitutional doctrines that became implicit in what Arthur Miller refers to below as the "positive state" were the last major constitutional developments to recognize the arrival of industrial America.

At the present time there is considerable speculation that there is emerging a new economic order which is "technological" insofar as it stresses organization and planning in the processes of innovation. In short, once mastery over fundamental resources was established, American industry turned to the uses of organizational skills to produce the great variety of materials and goods that typify the commercial market today. In the process, the fundamental relationship of men to their machines altered dramatically.

The Lockean concept of property held that property—an individual's possessions—was an extension of human personality. Today, individuals may well be more an extension of their possessions than is generally imagined. If this alteration of so fundamental a relationship to property is truly in process, then the capacity of a fundamental legal instrument and its associated political institution to help govern within that circumstance is of considerable importance.

The contemporary view of constitutional politics relevant to economic policy is tantamount to viewing economic society through a rearview mirror. From *Gibbons* v. *Ogden* through *United States* v. *Darby Lumber Co.*, the Constitution speaks to circumstances that hold in lessening degrees of importance. A technological era is emerging that calls for newer conceptions of property and new constitutional recognitions similar to those that emerged from the Supreme Court during the

Gilded Age as well as the New Deal.

The concept of property has also undergone alteration in another fashion. The philosophy of the original Constitution was that private property was to be protected against those who would take it "without just compensation" or due process of law. We have seen how, finally, the Supreme Court came to accept the notion of public control over certain kinds of property under certain types of conditions. The property in question was tangible, but it also conferred on its owners certain rights or privileges not generally available.

The rise of the positive state has fostered the concept of a "new" type of property which, it has been argued, should also carry with it certain privileges and assurances.[1] But this new property refers not to tangible assets but to the interest a citizen may have in a particular kind of government subsidy or benefit, such as social security or welfare payments. Traditionally, no citizen could have a vested right in such benefits. They were merely privileges conferred by the government and revocable at its discretion. Citizens had a constitutional right to be treated equally with other citizens in the same classification (e.g., "over 65") but little more. In the last decade, the Supreme Court has refused to apply the notion of vested rights to this new form of property. It has rejected the claim, as we shall see in the next chapter, that citizens have a constitutional *right* to welfare and other subsistence payments. It has refused to hold that the Constitution imposes on government an affirmative duty to provide minimum economic subsistence for all citizens. *But* it has insisted on certain due process procedures for de-termining eligibility for and termination of welfare payments. And it has held that citizens cannot be forced to waive other constitutional rights as a condition for receipt of such payments. It has modified the old rule, which held only that government must follow its own rules, whatever they are, to state that there are certain minimum due process procedures that must be followed by government whenever it elects to redistribute wealth to a certain class or category of citizens (as well as in other types of government programs).

The limitations of Supreme Court policymaking in the economic sphere are apparent. At best, the Court can make a contribution to the rational and fair implementation of economic policies. It can enforce constitutional rules, and it can provide some standards for judging official action. Of necessity, even these policies must be stated at a high level of generality. The core of economic policymaking and implementation in the public sector is made, and will continue to be made, at the administrative level of rule making and enforcement. Policy at this level is remote from, and unlikely to be directly affected by, the Supreme Court.

D. Arthur S. Miller, *Constitutional Revolution Consolidated: The Rise of the Positive State*

In the long constitutional history of the United States, a very few landmarks stand out with particular clarity. One surely is *Marbury* v. *Madison*. . . . Another is the Civil War, an episode which settled in blood that this nation is truly a union and which

---

[1]Charles Reich, "The New Property," **73** *Yale Law Journal* (1964), 733–787.

Reprinted from **35** *George Washington Law Review* (December 1966), 172–184.

settled in law that *raison d'état* is an operative principle of the American constitutional order. When that war was followed by the anti-slavery amendments, a new constitutional order was ushered in, the contours of which are still being traced in judicial and other official decisions. A third is the rise and fall of "economic due process" in the fifty years before 1937, a period in which the Supreme Court became "the first authoritative faculty of political economy in the world's history." Finally, there is the rise of "positive" government—the Positive State—during the past three decades, epitomized by enactment of the Employment Act of 1946. . . .

The Positive State is a shorthand label for the express acceptance by the federal government—and thus by the American people—of an affirmative responsibility for economic well-being. It involves a societal undertaking and duty to create and maintain economic growth, employment opportunities, and general access to the basic necessities of life. The notion of a constitutional duty upon government itself represents a new departure. Exemplified in a broad range of programs, federal and state, it is the American version of the "welfare state."

The Positive State received its charter not by constitutional amendment but by statute: the Employment Act of 1946, surely one of the most important congressional acts in American constitutional history.

With the pronouncement of its preamble, which made constitutional law as surely as it is created by amendment and, more importantly, by the Supreme Court, came the culmination of the "New Deal" and of the "constitutional revolution" of the 1930's; the act capped a series of statutes, upheld by the Supreme Court beginning in the watershed

year of 1937, under which affirmative government sprang, Minerva-like, from the brow of Congress. The "negative, night watchman state" died and was quietly buried, the final obsequies coming in 1953 when the first Republican administration after the birth of the Positive State not only failed to reject it but in fact contributed to its growth. . . .

In a series of legitimizing decisions beginning with *Nebbia* v. *New York* and the *Gold Clause Cases,* the Supreme Court gave constitutional blessing to the Positive State. The change was so complete that by 1946, when the Employment Act became law, no challenge to its validity could be or was made. The consequences of this new posture of government are still in a process of evolutionary development, but enough is known to enable us to trace their contours.

Most fundamental, perhaps, is the change in the economic sphere from a Constitution of limitations to one of powers; or as Edward S. Corwin put it, "a Constitution of powers in a secular state." The American charter of government was drafted by men who feared despotism and fragmented political power to avoid it. Its core principle was that the national government was to be limited to those powers specifically delegated to it. Even when the Supreme Court rewrote the Constitution in 1819 to add the concept of implied powers, the general posture was still one of limitation; the apotheosis of this concept came in the judicial attempt to establish a laissez-faire government in the late 19th and early 20th centuries.

The notion of limitation, viewed retrospectively, has yielded in the past three decades to the idea that the government has the power, even duty, to take action. This transition was not quite so abrupt as it appeared, for the coming of affirmative government in the post-1937 period can only be understood as part of a process grounded on the principle that government in the United States has always been as strong (or positive) as conditions demanded. Chief Justice Hughes expressed the new concept aptly in *West Coast Hotel* v. *Parrish*: "[T]he liberty safeguarded [by the Fourteenth Amendment] is liberty in a social organization which *requires* the protection of law against the evils which menace the health, safety, morals and welfare of the people." With these words, the Chief Justice gave constitutional sanction to the concept within a decade enacted into law in the Employment Act. His next sentence is one of the most pregnant statements in constitutional history: *Liberty under the Constitution is . . . necessarily subject to the restraints of due process, and regulation which is reasonable in relation to its subject and is adopted in the interests of the community is due process.*

With that utterance the nature of liberty under the Constitution was changed; the Positive State received its constitutional underpinnings. The Court expressly recognized that liberty could be infringed by forces other than government and that to counteract them government intervention may be required. Due process became not only liberty *against* government, but a concept to be used *by* government to justify restraining the liberty of some in the interests of the "community." . . .

The second noteworthy feature of the Positive State is the advent of a system of "economic planning" by federal government.

The American system of planning is noncoercive; it is "facilitative." Government persuades rather than commands. Basic reliance upon the private character of business enterprise is accomplished by an insistence that certain decisions of corporate managers and trade union leaders be taken "in the public interest." As such, the American system falls far short of the almost completely directed economies of Communist China and the USSR, and even short of the system of "indicative programming" employed by such nations as France. . . .

Third in this listing of the contours of the Positive State is the change which has occurred and which is continuing to take place in the constitutional framework of government, principally in the doctrines of federalism and the separation of powers. Economic planning may well be "the DDT of federalism." Any large-scale planning by government generates a need for unified and perhaps uniform economic policies throughout the nation. That need runs counter to the diversity inherent in federalism; it is also contrary to the fragmentation of power within the national government itself, and leads toward centralization of official power. Moreover, of at least tangential interest are the trend toward centralization of governmental power within the executive branch itself and the trend toward "multinationalism." . . .

The alteration in American federalism from the "dual" system established in 1787 to the "cooperative" system of the Positive State is an indisputable fact, although it may be deplored by some and political leaders may plump for "creative" federalism. The political, economic, and technological imperatives of the modern era do not now, and probably never again will, permit that diversity which is the glory and *raison d'être* of federalism. The formal structure of American government may remain, for a political organization has a way of surviving, like a vermiform appendix, long after it has ceased to function, but the substance and the content will be elsewhere. The *important* decisions of government today are made in Washington, even though administration may be and often is in state capitals, county seats, and cities.

As with federalism, so too has the separation of powers in the national government given way to centralization of power. The Positive State is the "administrative state" and the locus of power within the national government, if it can be located at all, is within the executive. . . .

The judiciary also has a changed function with the coming of the Positve State. At one time the ultimate decision-maker in economic policy matters, the Supreme Court now has been reduced to interpretation of statutes and review of administrative actions. While this does not leave the High Bench without power, nonetheless its decisions can be (and have been) reviewed by the avowedly political branches of government. . . . A consequence is that one of the considerations of the judicial process in administrative law matters must be the possibility of legislative reversal of a Court decision. . . .

The fourth item in this listing of the contours of the Positive State concerns both the nature of law and the role of the judiciary: the "politicization" of law and the legal process.

The externalization of standards which Holmes asserted was the hallmark of the growth of a legal system is being lost in the onslaught of an all-pervasive system of public law. Public law, that is, the nebulous standards under which executive-administrative action is ostensibly canalized under the Supreme Court statement of the meaning of the Constitution, is a marriage of "politics" and "external command," of necessarily forward-looking policy-making conducted within the pre-existing limits of known law. But the ideal of a "government of laws and not of men" has never been met; the Positive State is "emphatically a government of men and not of laws."

However much administrators and executive officials may use the terminology of law and justify their actions by using legal opinions, probing beneath the surface shows that law is used for policy ends; it is readily apparent that law and the legal process have been politicized. That conclusion is the lesson to be drawn from the statement by Judge Henry J. Friendly "that the basic deficiency, which underlies and accounts for the most serious troubles of the agencies, is the failure to 'make law' within the broad confines of the agencies' charters. . . ." His point was that much of the "justified dissatisfaction" with administration is the failure of administrators and others "to develop standards sufficiently definite to permit decisions to be fairly predictable and the reasons for them to be understood. . . ."

Judge Friendly was talking principally of the regulatory commissions. If his analysis is valid, then the commissions, too, are involved in a system of politicized law. The description is even more apt for other organs of the public administration which make more important public-policy decisions without the semblance of procedural due process through which the commissions ostensibly operate—those which set monetary and fiscal policy, to take but one example. Here again is public law of great importance, created and administered outside the framework of the judiciary and without reference to those procedural safeguards imbedded in the concept of due process. Here, in short, is politicized law. It is difficult to see how government could otherwise operate given the number and complexity of tasks which face it today. Law in the Positive State is being redefined; no longer does it fit the neat classifications of the premodern era—if indeed it ever did. . . .

Fifth and last in this listing of prominent features of the Positive State is a trend toward the progressive blurring of what purportedly is public and what supposedly is private. In many respects this is a corollary of the fourth characteristic, discussed above, about the symbiotic relationship between government and governed in the American polity—particularly when the governed is made up of those in the pluralistic power centers. The development may be seen in several places, including the reciprocal participation by business leaders in government decisions and by government officials in business decisions; the dependency of large segments of the business community upon government for their existence; and the close reciprocating interactions between the professions and government. . . . Through these and similar relationships, bound together at times by the legal instrument of contract, a radically new posture is evolving in the position of government and the individuals, natural and artificial, who make up American society.

The consequences of this process go far beyond the progressive blurring of the line between public and private. To take just one for illustration: The development has had great significance for the nature of American private law. Property is changing from the ownership of "things" to ownership of "rights"—often made up of government largess. Wealth largely consists of promises, whether from government in the form of largess, corporations in the form of

stock, insurance companies in the form of annuities, or from pension funds. Contract, too, is changing, particularly in the growth of contracts of adhesion and other less-than-wholly-free agreements. The principles of contract and property intertwine to produce a "new feudalism." These two core concepts of the historical legal system—the analogues of the private-enterprise, laissez-faire system of economics—are now fundamentally altered, and understandably so, for with the passing of laissez-faire went the need for the legal concepts which supported it. In essence, the change in private law is from a system based on individualistic notions to one which, haltingly and imperfectly, reflects the organizational basis of society and the position of the individual in that society.

The bureaucratization of American society, a consequence of the organizational revolution which has taken place since the Civil War, is itself a development of constitutional importance. Not the individual, but the organization, predominates in this nation, particularly in economic matters. The individual *qua* individual is diminishing in importance; what significance he has derives from his membership in a group (or several groups). The "autonomous man," is becoming an exceedingly rare phenomenon. . . .

E. J. Skelly Wright, The Courts and the Rulemaking Process: The Limits of Judicial Review

Administrative law has entered an age of rulemaking. Administrators who once acted on whim and instinct have been judicially constrained to

Reprinted from **59** *Cornell Law Review* (1974), 375–378.

promulgate and adhere to consistent guidelines. Agencies which once generated policy in a piecemeal fashion through adjudication are now adopting prospective standards of action valid in a number of different settings and against a wide variety of "parties." And the new agencies established by Congress to deal with contemporary environmental, economic, and energy problems have relied heavily on the promulgation of general regulations. These are healthy and welcome developments. Arguably, some areas of the economy should be deregulated to give fuller play to competitive market forces; and one may doubt that Congress is always wise to delegate to the executive branch and to administrative agencies the responsibility for making fundamental decisions about the economy and the environment. But when Congress *has* adopted a regulatory solution, and when the Delegation Doctrine does not bar that solution, the case for making administrative policy through rules, rather than adjudicatory decisions, is overwhelming.

Trial-like adjudication is extremely costly in time, staff, and money. Before an adjudicatory common law can acquire coherence, conditions typically will have overtaken it. As a consequence, industries subject to adjudicatory regulation are left in a state of perpetual uncertainty, and agencies assume the dangerous power to create new law affecting parties selected at random, or in a discriminatory manner. Orderly innovation is difficult, and emergencies often go unmet. To discern basic agency policy, the public must wade through volumes of scarcely relevant testimony and findings. The technicalities of adjudication allow lawyers to minimize the input of experts and to frustrate agency consid-

eration of relevant scientific and economic perspectives. Regulation becomes an advocate's game. Especially in the rapidly expanding realms of economic, environmental, and energy regulation, the policy disputes are too sharp, the technological considerations too complex, the interests affected too numerous, and the missions too urgent for agencies to rely on the ponderous workings of adjudication.

These observations are not novel and judges have not failed to recognize them. A Supreme Court majority recently suggested that agencies may not use an adjudicatory forum to announce new legal standards which will have only prospective effect. A quarter century ago, the Court advised the agencies that "(t)he function of filling in the interstices of (an act) should be performed, as much as possible, through this quasi-legislative promulgation of rules to be applied in the future." Judge Friendly has persuaded the Second Circuit to take the next logical step, requiring that the National Labor Relations Board promulgate standards of general application only by means of proper rulemaking procedures. The converse claim—that regulated parties have some "right" to an adjudicatory promulgation of general policies merely because these policies affect important interests or preexisting licenses—has been decisively rejected. And when agencies have asserted long dormant rulemaking powers, the courts have been quick to sustain the change of heart.

But a general background of judicial applause is not enough. In rulemaking, no less than in adjudication, Congress has fastened the courts and agencies into an intimate partnership, the success of which requires a precarious balance between judicial deference and self-assertion.

In passing on administrative adjudications, the courts over the years have learned to maintain that balance, but judicial review of rulemaking is presenting a new and troublesome question. Some courts have recently shown an inclination to force rulemakers to adopt trial-like procedures—formal hearings, interrogatories, oral argument, cross-examination, and the like—which clearly are not required by the Administrative Procedure Act (APA). Should this tendency become general, rulemaking will lose most of its peculiar advantages as a tool of administrative policymaking, and the merits of the many rulemaking experiments now under way will be denied a fair opportunity to be tested. The trend in agencies toward overproceduralization arose largely because reviewing courts were hostile to regulation and were uncritically fond of adjudicatory methods for resolving social controversies. From the general paralysis of administration which resulted, the agencies are only now emerging. Before throwing history into reverse, we in the judiciary should at least pause for thought.

F. Vermont Yankee Nuclear Power Corp. v. Natural Resources Defense Council (1978)

+Burger, Brennan, Stewart, White, Marshall, Rehnquist, Stevens
 NP Blackmun, Powell

[The growth of the welfare state has fostered the development of administrative agencies whose primary role is to regulate some aspect of economic life. As the preceding selection by Judge Wright has noted, these agencies are designed to regulate primarily by rule making, not by the slower and costlier process of adjudication. However, there are courtlike procedures that the agencies must follow, most of which have been set down in the Administrative Procedure Act, subsequent amendments to that act, and court decisions interpreting the act. The act, first passed in 1946, was a compromise between liberals, who wished to maximize the freedom of the agencies from judicial control, and conservatives who saw the agencies as threats to the hegemony of the courts and, worse, as the epitomy of New Deal radicalism, and who wished to keep as tight a reign as possible on them. Limits on judicial intervention were established. For example, courts could only set aside an agency decision that was "arbitrary, capricious, an abuse of discretion, or otherwise not in accordance with law." In order for a court to set aside an agency finding of fact, it had to determine that the finding was not merely erroneous but actually unreasonable and not supported by substantial evidence. Courts were also limited in the kinds of procedures that they could impose on the agencies, procedures that in almost all cases would promote adjudicatory—courtlike—processes.

The extent to which agencies should be free to regulate without judicial intervention, or the limits of that intervention, is a perennial question. There have been different political configurations in the relationship between the agencies and the courts. But those interests that have "lost" in the agencies, whatever their political viewpoints, have almost always sought redress in the courts. And since the reviewing function of the courts is not one of second-guessing agency decisions but of assuring that those decisions are reasonable and follow correct procedures, there is a constant appeal to the courts to use their powers of procedural review to obstruct or influence substantive agency decisions. Sometimes the long delays inevitably caused by drawn-out litigation on minor technical points is sufficient to undermine, if not ultimately to block, an agency decision.

The Vermont Yankee case is but one example of this constant interchange between courts and agencies in the context of interest group politics. The case focuses on the proper scope of judicial review of the procedures of the Atomic Energy Commission in the licensing of nuclear power plants. After extensive adjudicatory hearings, the commission (now called the Nuclear Regulatory Commission) issued a license to the Vermont Yankee Nuclear Power Corporation. The issue of environmental effects of fuel reprocessing was excluded from the hearings. Subsequently, that issue was considered and decided (in favor of the power company) in rule-making hearings that did not utilize full adjudicatory procedures. The rule was known as the "spent fuel cycle rule." An environmental group, the Natural Resources Defense Council, which had participated in the hearings, appealed the agency's decision. They contended, in essence, that the rule was defective because it was not the product of open adjudicatory hearings. What they really objected to, of course, was the substance of the rule. The Court of Appeals for the District of Columbia overturned the agency's decision, holding that the proceedings by which the rule was formulated were defective.]

MR. JUSTICE REHNQUIST delivered the opinion of the Court.

In 1946, Congress enacted the Administrative Procedure Act, which as we have noted elsewhere was not only "a new, basic and comprehensive regulation of procedures in many agencies" [*Wong Yang Sun* v. *McGrath*] . . . but was also a legislative enactment which settled "long-continued and hard-fought contentions, and enacts a formula upon which opposing social and political forces have come to rest." . . . Section 553 of the Act, dealing with rulemaking, requires that ". . . notice of proposed rulemaking shall be published in the Federal Register. . . ," describes the contents of that notice, and goes on to require in subsection (c) that after the notice the agency "shall give interested persons an opportunity to participate in the rulemaking through submission of written data, views, or arguments

with or without opportunity for oral presentation. After consideration of the relevant matter presented, the agency shall incorporate in the rules adopted a concise general statement of their basis and purpose." . . . Interpreting this provision of the Act . . . we held that generally speaking this section of the Act established the maximum procedural requirements which Congress was willing to have the courts impose upon agencies in conducting rulemaking procedures. Agencies are free to grant additional procedural rights in the exercise of their discretion, but reviewing courts are generally not free to impose them if the agencies have not chosen to grant them. This is not to say necessarily that there are no circumstances which would ever justify a court in overturning agency action because of a failure to employ procedures beyond those required by the statute. But such circumstances, if they exist, are extremely rare.

. . . It is in the light of this background of statutory and decisional law that we granted certiorari to review two judgments of the Court of Appeals for the District of Columbia Circuit because of our concern that they had seriously misread or misapplied this statutory and decisional law cautioning reviewing courts against engrafting their own notions of proper procedures upon agencies entrusted with substantive functions by Congress. We conclude that the Court of Appeals has done just that in these cases, and we therefore remand them to it for further proceedings. We also find it necessary to examine the Court of Appeals' decision with respect to agency action taken after full adjudicatory hearings. We again conclude that the court improperly intruded into the agency's decision-making process, making it necessary for us to reverse and remand with respect to this part of the cases also.

We . . . turn to the invalidation of the spent fuel cycle rule. But before determining whether the Court of Appeals reached a permissible result, we must determine exactly what result it did reach, and in this case that is no mean feat. Vermont Yankee argues that the court invalidated the rule because of the inadequacy of the procedures employed in the proceedings. . . . Respondent NRDC, on the other hand, labeling petitioner's view of the decision a "straw man," argues to this Court that the court merely held that the record was inadequate to enable the reviewing court to determine whether the agency had fulfilled its statutory obligation. . . . But we unfortunately have not found the parties' characterization of the opinion to be entirely reliable; it appears here, as in *Orloff* v. *Willoughby* (1953), that "in this Court the parties changed positions as nimbly as if dancing a quadrille."

After a thorough examination of the opinion itself, we conclude that while the matter is not entirely free from doubt, the majority of the Court of Appeals struck down the rule because of the perceived inadequacies of the procedures employed in the rulemaking proceedings. The court first determined the intervenors' primary argument to be "that the decision to preclude 'discovery or cross-examination' denied them a meaningful opportunity to participate in the proceedings as guaranteed by due process." . . . The court conceded that absent extraordinary circumstances it is improper for a reviewing court to prescribe the procedural format an agency must follow, but it likewise clearly thought it entirely appropriate to "scrutinize the record as a whole to insure that genuine opportunities to participate

in a meaningful way were provided. . . ." The court also refrained from actually ordering the agency to follow any specific procedures, . . . but there is little doubt in our minds that the ineluctable mandate of the court's decision is that the procedures afforded during the hearings were inadequate. . . . The exploration of the record and the statement regarding its insufficiency might initially lead one to conclude that the court was only examining the sufficiency of the evidence, but the remaining portions of the opinion dispel any doubt that this was certainly not the sole or even the principal basis of the decision. Accordingly, we feel compelled to address the opinion on its own terms, and we conclude that it was wrong.

In prior opinions we have intimated that even in a rulemaking proceeding when an agency is making a "quasi-judicial" determination by which a very small number of persons are " 'exceptionally affected, in each case upon individual grounds,' " in some circumstances additional procedures may be required in order to afford the aggrieved individuals due process. . . . It might also be true, although we do not think the issue is presented in this case and accordingly do not decide it, that a totally unjustified departure from well settled agency procedures of long standing might require judicial correction.

But this much is absolutely clear. Absent constitutional constraints or extremely compelling circumstances "the administrative agencies 'should be free to fashion their own rules of procedure and to pursue methods of inquiry capable of permitting them to discharge their multitudinous duties.' " . . . We have continually repeated this theme through the years, most recently in *Federal Power Comm'n* v. *Transcontinental Gas*

Pipe Line Corp. (1976), decided just two Terms ago. In that case, in determining the proper scope of judicial review of agency action under the Natural Gas Act, we held that while a court may have occasion to remand an agency decision because of the adequacy of the record, the agency should normally be allowed to "exercise its administrative discretion in deciding how, in light of internal organization considerations, it may best proceed to develop the needed evidence and how its prior decision should be modified in light of such evidence as develops." . . . We went on to emphasize that:

At least in the absence of substantial justification for doing otherwise, a reviewing court may not, after determining that additional evidence is requisite for adequate review, proceed by dictating to the agency the methods, procedures, and time dimension of the needed inquiry and ordering the results to be reported to the court without opportunity for further consideration on the basis of the new evidence by the agency. Such a procedure clearly runs the risk of "propel(ling) the court into the domain which Congress has set aside exclusively for the administrative agency."
. . .

Respondent NRDC argues that § 553 of the Administrative Procedure Act merely establishes lower procedural bounds and that a court may routinely require more than the minimum when an agency's proposed rule addresses complex or technical factual issues or "issues of great public import." . . . We have, however, previously shown that our decisions reject this view. . . . We also think the legislative history, even the part which it cites, does not bear out its contention. . . . And the Attorney General's Manual on the Administrative Procedure Act (1947), . . . a contemporaneous interpreta-

tion previously given some deference by this Court because of the role played by the Department of Justice in drafting the legislation, further confirms that view. In short, all of this leaves little doubt that Congress intended that the discretion of the *agencies* and not that of the courts be exercised in determining when extraprocedural devices should be employed.

There are compelling reasons for construing § 553 in this manner. In the first place, if courts continually review agency proceedings to determine whether the agency employed procedures which were, in the Court's opinion, perfectly tailored to reach what the court perceives to be the "best" or "correct" result, judicial review would be totally unpredictable. And the agencies, operating under this vague injunction to employ the "best" procedures and facing the threat of reversal if they did not, would undoubtedly adopt full adjudicatory procedures in every instance. Not only would this totally disrupt the statutory scheme, through which Congress enacted "a formula upon which opposing social and political forces have come to rest," . . . but all the inherent advantages of informal rulemaking would be totally lost.

Secondly, it is obvious that the court in this case reviewed the agency's choice of procedures on the basis of the record actually produced at the hearing, . . . and not on the basis of the information available to the agency when it made the decision to structure the proceedings in a certain way. This sort of Monday morning quarterbacking not only encourages but almost compels the agency to conduct all rulemaking proceedings with the full panoply of procedural devices normally associated only with adjudicatory hearings.

Finally, and perhaps most importantly, this sort of review fundamentally misconceives the nature of the standard for judicial review of an agency rule. The court below uncritically assumed that additional procedures will automatically result in a more adequate record because it will give interested parties more of an opportunity to participate and contribute to the proceedings. But informal rulemaking need not be based solely on the transcript of a hearing held before an agency. Indeed, the agency need not even hold a formal hearing. . . . Thus the adequacy of the "record" in this type of proceeding is not correlated directly to the type of procedural devices employed, but rather turns on whether the agency has followed the statutory mandate of the Administrative Procedure Act or other relevant statutes. If the agency is compelled to support the rule which it ultimately adopts with the type of record produced only after a full adjudicatory hearing, it simply will have no choice but to conduct a full adjudicatory prior to promulgating every rule. In sum, this sort of unwarranted judicial examination of perceived procedural shortcomings of a rulemaking proceeding can do nothing but seriously interfere with that process prescribed by Congress.

Respondent NRDC also argues that the fact that the Commission's inquiry was undertaken in the context of NEPA somehow permits a court to require procedures beyond those specified in § 553 when investigating factual issues through rulemaking. The Court of Appeals was apparently also of this view, indicating that agencies may be required to "develop new procedures to accomplish the innovative task of implementing NEPA through rulemaking." . . . But we search in vain for something in NEPA which would mandate such a result. We have before observed the "NEPA does not repeal by implication any other statute." . . . In fact, just last Term, we emphasized that the only procedural requirements imposed by NEPA are those stated in the plain language of the Act. . . . Thus, it is clear NEPA cannot serve as the basis for a substantial revision of the carefully constructed procedural specifications of the APA.

In short, nothing in the APA, NEPA, the circumstances of this case, the nature of the issues being considered, past agency practice, or the statutory mandate under which the Commission operates permitted the court to review and overturn the rulemaking proceeding on the basis of the procedural devices employed (or not employed) by the Commission so long as the Commission employed at least the statutory minima, a matter about which there is no doubt in this case. . . .

We now turn to the Court of Appeals' holding "that rejection of energy conservation on the basis of the 'threshold test' was capricious and arbitrary,". . . and again conclude the court was wrong.

The Court of Appeals ruled that the Commission's "threshold test" for the presentation of energy conservation contentions was inconsistent with NEPA's basic mandate to the Commission. . . . The Commission, the court reasoned, is something more than an umpire who sits back and resolves adversary contentions at the hearing stage. . . . And when an intervenor's comments "bring 'sufficient, attention to the issue to stimulate the Commission's consideration of it,' " the Commission must "undertake its own preliminary investigation of the proffered alternative sufficient to reach a rational judgment whether it is worthy of detailed consideration in the EIS. Moreover, the Commission must explain the basis for each conclusion that further consideration of a suggested alternative is unwarranted." . . .

While the Court's rationale is not entirely unappealing as an abstract proposition, as applied to this case we think it basically misconceives not only the scope of the agency's statutory responsibility, but also the nature of the administrative process, the thrust of the agency's decision, and the type of issues the intervenors were trying to raise.

There is little doubt that under the Atomic Energy Act of 1954, state public utility commissions or similar bodies are empowered to make the initial decisions regarding the need for power. . . . The Commission's prime area of concern in the licensing context, on the other hand, is public health and safety. . . . And it is clear that the need, as that term is conventionally used, for the power was thoroughly explored in the hearings. . . .

NEPA, of course, has altered slightly the statutory balance, requiring "a detailed statement by the responsible official on . . . alternatives to the proposed action." . . . But as should be obvious even upon a moment's reflection, the term "alternatives" is not self-defining. To make an impact statement something more than an exercise in frivolous boilerplate the concept of alternatives must be bounded by some notion of feasibility. . . . Common sense also teaches us that the "detailed statement of alternatives" cannot be found wanting simply because the agency failed to include every alternative device and thought conceivable by the mind of man. Time and resources are simply too limited to hold that an impact statement fails because the agency failed to ferret out every possible alternative, regardless of how uncommon or unknown that alternative may have been at the time the project was approved.

. . . We think these facts amply demonstrate that the concept of "alternatives" is an evolving one, requiring the agency to explore more or fewer alternatives as they become better known and understood. This was well understood by the Commission, which, unlike the Court of Appeals, recognized that the Licensing Board's decision had to be judged by the information then available to it. And judged in that light we have little doubt the Board's actions were well within the proper bounds of its statutory authority. Not only did the record before the agency give every indication that the project was actually needed, but there was nothing before the Board to indicate to the contrary.

. . . Administrative proceedings should not be a game or a forum to engage in unjustified obstructionism by making cryptic and obscure reference to matters that "ought to be" considered and then, after failing to do more to bring the matter to the agency's attention, seeking to have that agency determination vacated on the ground that the agency failed to consider matters "forcefully presented." In fact, here the agency continually invited further clarification of Saginaw's contentions. Even without such clarification it indicated a willingness to receive evidence on the matters. But not only did Saginaw decline to further focus its contentions, it virtually declined to participate, indicating that it had "no conventional findings of fact to set forth" and that it had not "chosen to search the record and respond to this proceeding by submitting citations of matter which we believe were proved or disproved."

. . . In sum to characterize the actions of the Commission as "arbitrary or capricious" in light of the facts then available to it as described at length above, is to deprive those words of any meaning. . . .

. . . We have also made it clear that the role of a court in reviewing the sufficiency of an agency's consideration of environmental factors is a limited one, limited both by the time at which the decision was made and by the statute mandating review.

Neither the statute nor its legislative history contemplates that a court should substitute its judgment for that of an agency as to the environmental consequences of its actions. . . . Kleppe *v.* Sierra Club *(1976).*

We think the Court of Appeals has forgotten that injunction here and accordingly its judgment in this respect must also be reversed.

. . . Finally, we turn to the Court of Appeals holding that the Licensing Board should have returned the ACRS* report to ACRS for further elaboration, understandable to a layman, of the reference to other problems.

The Court of Appeals reasoned that since one function of the report was "that all concerned may be apprised of the safety or possible hazard of the facilities," the report must be in terms understandable to a layman and replete with cross-references to previous reports in which the "other problems" are detailed. Not only that, but if the report is not, and the Licensing Board fails to *sua sponte* return the report to ACRS for further development, the entire agency action, made after exhaustive studies, reviews and 14 days of hearings, must be nullified.

Again the Court of Appeals has un-

justifiably intruded into the administrative process. It is true that Congress thought publication of the ACRS report served an important function. But the legislative history shows that the function of publication was subsidiary to its main function, that of providing technical advice from a body of experts uniquely qualified to provide assistance. . . . The basic information to be conveyed to the public is not necessarily a full technical exposition of every facet of nuclear energy, but rather the ACRS's position, and reasons therefore, with respect to the safety of a proposed nuclear reactor. Accordingly, the report cannot be faulted for not dealing with every facet of nuclear energy in every report it issues.

Of equal significance is the fact that the ACRS was not obfuscating its findings. The reports to which they referred were matters of public record, on file in the Commission's public document room. Indeed, all ACRS reports are on file there. Furthermore, we are informed that shortly after the Licensing Board's initial decision, ACRS prepared a list which identified its "generic safety concerns." In light of all this it is simply inconceivable that a reviewing court should find it necessary or permissible to order the Board to *sua sponte* return the report to ACRS. Our view is confirmed by the fact that the putative reason for the remand was that the public did not understand the report, and yet not *one* member of the supposedly uncomprehending public even asked that the report be remanded. This surely is, as respondent Consumers Power claims, "judicial intervention run riot." . . .

We also think it worth noting that we find absolutely nothing in the relevant statutes to justify what the

---

*Advisory Committee on Reactor Safeguards—Ed.

court did here. The Commission very well might be able to remand a report for further clarification, but there is nothing to support a court's ordering the Commission to take that step or to support a court's requiring the ACRS to give a short explanation, understandable to a layman, of each generic safety concern.

All this leads us to make one further observation of some relevance to this case. To say that the Court of Appeals' final reason for remanding is insubstantial at best is a gross understatement. Consumers Power first applied in 1969 for a construction permit—not even an operating license, just a construction permit. The proposed plant underwent an incredibly extensive review. The reports filed and reviewed literally fill books. The proceedings took years. The actual hearings themselves over two weeks. To then nullify that effort seven years later because one report refers to other problems, which problems admittedly have been discussed at length in other reports available to the public, borders on the Kafkaesque. Nuclear energy may some day be a cheap, safe source of power or it may not. But Congress has made a choice to at least try nuclear energy, establishing a reasonable review process in which courts are to play only a limited role. The fundamental policy questions appropriately resolved in Congress and in the state legislatures are *not* subject to reexamination in the federal courts under the guise of judicial review of agency action. Time may prove wrong the decision to develop nuclear energy, but it is Congress or the States within their appropriate agencies which must eventually make that judgment. In the meantime courts should perform their appointed function. NEPA does set forth significant substantive goals for the Nation, but its mandate to the agencies is essentially procedural. . . . It is to insure a fully informed and well-considered decision, not necessarily a decision the judges of the Court of Appeals or of this Court would have reached had they been members of the decision-making unit of the agency. Administrative decisions should be set aside in this context, as in every other, only for substantial procedural or substantive reasons as mandated by statute, . . . not simply because the court is unhappy with the result reached. And a single alleged oversight on a peripheral issue, urged by parties who never fully cooperated or indeed raised the issue below, must not be made the basis for overturning a decision properly made after an otherwise exhaustive proceeding.

Reversed and remanded.

CHAPTER TWO

equality in american life: race, gender, wealth, and representation

1. INTRODUCTORY ESSAY: EQUALITY AND THE CONSTITUTION

Equality, like justice, is a foundation value of American society. Yet, like justice, equality is not a term that is easily or conveniently defined, however self-explanatory the notion may appear. Equality has both intrinsic and extrinsic properties. It is valued for its own sake, as an attribute of being human. And it is also valued as an instrument to obtain other things of value. Lack of consensus about the meaning of equality is certainly reflected in the ambivalence that many Americans feel about it. Equality for whom? When? At what cost?

Robert Nisbet and others have noted that there are basically two concepts of equality: equality of opportunity and equality of result or condition.[1] Equality of opportunity is the traditional classical liberal view. It is a view that recognizes, and accepts, the fact that individuals have unequal endowments and talents. Its goal is to provide to each individual the maximum opportunity to achieve while recognizing that individuals will achieve unequally. Inevitably, some will have more than others, but this is quite consistent with the laissez-faire

---

[1]Robert Nisbet, "The Pursuit of Equality," 35 *Public Interest* (1974), 103–102; and Nisbet *Twilight of Authority* (London: Heinemann Educational Books, Ltd., 1976), pp. 198–223.

notion of equal opportunity. The role of the law should be, and sometimes is, to ensure that opportunities are truly equal. In fact, more often than not, the law merely assumes that they are equal. How much the law and government should intervene to ensure this equality of opportunity is a matter of continuing debate.

Equality of result is much the more radical formulation and closer to the contemporary liberal creed. In its most extreme forms, it probably would be incompatible with democratic and representative government as we know it in the United States. But even in its less radical forms, it is very much an ascendant philosophy, a philosophy of reform rather than an acceptance of the status quo. Nisbet has described it as follows:

> *Equality of result is committed to . . . a massive and revolutionary distribution not only of income and property, but of status, knowledge, position, reason and learning. It is equality of result or condition that at the moment threatens to be the number one candidate for America's sovereign, redemptive value.*

Many social critics have noted that to achieve true equality of results or outcomes, government is almost *required* to discriminate, to treat people unequally in order to make them equal. Compensatory action may be required to assure equalized outcomes in a population of unequals. Thus, it appears that the two views of equality are antithetical. It is this dilemma that confronts government and the legal system in very large measure today. Typically, both views of equality have support in the political system, and both are represented in public policy. Thus, our progressive system of income taxation, proposals for a negative income tax, and the demise of literacy tests as a condition of voting are responsive to the second formulation. Regressive taxes such as the sales tax and the social security tax are more congenial to equality as opportunity.

There does not seem to be much dispute with the proposition that government and law must treat all citizens equally, but there is obvious disagreement about what "equally" means in a variety of contexts. Defining who it is who is entitled to be treated equally is not easy. Does it foreclose any forms of classifications, or merely those that are arbitrary? What classifications are rational and not merely the embodiment of traditional prejudice? Must a classification have a sound empirical base?

It is a big jump from the proposition that government must treat people as equally as possible to the proposition that government must use its power to assure that people have equal resources in the private sector. For example, what role should government play in assuring that contracts which are enforceable in the courts are truly the product of agreement by "equals?" It was precisely because relations between working people and big business were unequal that government finally intervened to support the establishment of labor unions. The same is true, currently, in the field of insurance, where there is increasing government intervention on behalf of individuals or groups who are not in a position to bargain equally with insurance companies about premiums, exclusions, and limitations on policy coverage.

Apart from the philosophical question of whether government ought ever to intervene to protect equality of opportunity or assure equality of results, there is the continuing question of the choice of means. There are both political and legal constraints. Obviously, the costs of equality may be too high if achievement requires the use of unacceptable methods. Government expropriation of private property or confiscatory taxation of all wealth beyond a certain limit would be politically unacceptable if not necessarily illegal.

The demands of equality frequently compete with other basic values, and some balance must be struck. For example, as we will see in the following pages, government action to eradicate racial discrimination is obstructed by our society's equally strong commitment to freedom of association in private groups and organizations. Recent attempts to foster political equality by limiting campaign contributions and campaign spending collide with important First Amendment protections of speech and expression, and political freedom. Benign quotas designed to increase minority representation in schools and jobs test the principle of racial equality to its very limits. Equality in housing is obstructed by suburban "snob" zoning laws, which in turn are rationalized by aesthetic considerations and the desirability of achieving a sense of community.

The Constitutional Meaning of Equality

There is no formal provision regarding equality in the original Constitution, although the concept of equal treatment is implicit in several clauses of that document. Thus Article IV, Section 2 provides that "Citizens of each state shall be entitled to all privileges and immunities of citizens in the several states." By this provision, states are admonished to treat all persons equally, their own residents and visitors alike. Of course, this admonition was often honored in the breach. It was limited by the existence of slavery, and even today, there are examples of differential treatment by a state between its own citizens and others. But the current trend certainly is toward abolition of most such distinctions. The "full faith and credit" clause of Article IV also depends on a concept of equality, as does the due process clause in the Fifth Amendment. Equality is clearly the guiding principle in provisions for representation in the House of Representatives, as well as for the contradictory notion of equality of representation of the states in the Senate. The framers made some commitments to equality but often hedged their bet somewhere else in the intricate check and balance system that the Constitution provides.

The emphasis on equality in the Declaration of Independence is well known. Not a legally enforceable document, this "first American state paper" was and is nonetheless strongly influential. Many of its signers were instrumental in writing the Constitution, and the idea of equality certainly did not lose force in the period between the two documents. One reason that the original Constitution made no formal commitment to equality was the need to compromise with the slaveholding interests. Another is that the Declaration's emphasis on the equality of men was, in that context, a reference only to the rights of Englishmen, of which the colonists claimed they were being deprived. Another is the political role of the two documents: the Declaration was a militantly revolutionary document that needed to appeal broadly and intensely to aspirations as well as reality. The Constitution, on the other hand, though not without its ideals, was a practical blueprint for governance. Its framers were forced to accept many inequalities already existing in the social fabric of American society.

Passage of the Fourteenth Amendment renewed the Constitution's commitment to equality under circumstances that held some greater promise for progress toward that goal. By its own words, the Fourteenth Amendment prohibited any *state* from denying to any "person within its jurisdiction the equal protection of the laws." And by Section 5, it conferred on Congress the right to act independently to enforce this guarantee (and, of course, the rest of the amendment as well). But what did "equal protection of the laws" mean in 1868? How was it generally understood? What did those who wrote the Fourteenth Amendment intend? It is important to understand the contemporary meaning of the Fourteenth Amendment because its meaning has changed so much, and its scope has increased, in the century that followed.

The primary intent of the framers of the Fourteenth Amendment was that it would protect blacks from discrimination under the law. They were to enjoy the same civil rights as whites. In effect, this was a protection against the continuation of old discriminatory practices and the passage of new laws. The prevailing view, as articulated by the Supreme Court in the case of *Strauder* v. *West Virginia* (1880), recognized that enjoyment of full legal rights was a necessary prerequisite to the achievement of full equality in civil society. But the opinion also referred to the blacks' "abject and ignorant condition" and suggested they were "unfitted to command the respect of those who had superior intelligence"—sentiments strikingly similar to those expressed by Justice Harlan dissenting three years later in the *Civil Rights Cases*. Thus the Supreme Court certainly did not see the Fourteenth Amendment as a full charter of racial equality. Moreover, in the course of its opinion rejecting racial discrimination in the selection of jurors, the Court held that females, noncitizens, nonproperty owners, minors, and persons lacking educational qualifications *could* be excluded from juries.

The bulk of this chapter is devoted to cases interpreting the meaning of the equal protection clause. But it may be useful to set forth here as a guide some general principles about that clause and how it has been interpreted. First, it applies to all *persons*, not just citizens, as is the case with the privileges and immunities clauses of the Fifth and Fourteenth Amendments. Second, it prohibits discriminatory *state* action. It does not directly limit the federal government (although its basic principles apply to the federal government via the due process clause of the Fifth Amendment), and it does not protect against private discrimination. The term "state action" refers not only to state government per se but also to the agencies of state government, to municipalities, and to enterprises over which the state has control or in whose affairs it is implicated. Third, it is not limited to formal legal rules but applies as well to the intent or results of a law. The classic illustration is *Yick Wo* v. *Hopkins*, a case decided by the Supreme Court in 1883. San Francisco passed an ordinance that prohibited laundries from operating in buildings that were not of stone construction, without special permission of the Board of Supervisors. On its face, this was a legitimate police power regulation, since there are good safety reasons for not permitting laundries in combustible buildings. However, since virtually all Chinese laundries were housed in wooden buildings, the law had the (intended) effect of putting all of them out of business. The Supreme Court had little trouble finding that the law merely masked a discriminatory purpose in the name of safety and held it unconstitutional.

Fourth, not all discrimination or classifications are a violation of the equal protection clause. The Supreme Court has held that legislatures have considerable power to make classification but must treat all persons within the same class equally. It is not discriminatory to establish classes of income and levy different rates of taxes, or to establish a dividing line between those who will receive and those who will not receive a particular government benefit. The federal government does not have to have a national pension program (social security) or a welfare program (AFDC), but if it does establish such programs, then its criteria of inclusion and exclusion must meet equal protection standards. Thus, it is said that the equal protection clause creates no new substantive rights, but merely measures the validity of classifications.

Fifth, the equal protection clause no longer tolerates "equal discrimination." The classic example of the equal discrimination argument is a law against miscegenation (racial intermarriage). In 1882, the Supreme Court upheld an Alabama statute that punished interracial fornication more severely than it punished uniracial fornication. Since both the black and white partners were punished equally, the Court held that this did not offend the Fourteenth Amendment. This doctrine was finally overruled in 1967, in *Loving* v. *Virginia*. In declaring unconstitutional a Virginia miscegenation statute, the Court unanimously held that such a racial classification was subversive of the equality that the Fourteenth Amendment was designed to protect, even if it was nominally designed to bear equally on whites as well as blacks.

Sixth, what is the standard for judging whether or not a particular classification is consistent with the Constitution? There are two questions to be asked. Is the classification itself valid? Are those who fall within the classification treated equally? It is the first of these questions that raises the most important constitutional questions. The traditional test of classifications under the equal protection clause is that they must be reasonable and rationally related to a legitimate governmental end. A classification should not be unreasonably underinclusive or overinclusive. It need not be the necessary or indispensable way in which government responds to a particular problem, merely a suitable and reasonable response. It should not be arbitrary, and it should not adversely affect other constitutional rights.

The theme of the traditional test is "reasonableness." In this sense, it is comparable to the normal test of constitutionality applied to legislation challenged under the due process clause. It is a test within the concept of judicial self-restraint, one by which judges show strong deference toward the legislative judgment. The burden of proof rests squarely on those challenging the validity of a statute. In current parlance, this test has come to be known as *ordinary scrutiny*. Few statutes tested under ordinary scrutiny are invalidated, for there are few statutes that are truly unreasonable.

In the previous chapter, we considered the "simultaneous rise and fall" of the doctrine of substantive due process. The concept of ordinary scrutiny is akin to the views expressed by Holmes and Harlan, dissenting in *Lochner* v. *New York* (1905), by Stone's dissent in *United States* v. *Butler* (1936), and by the views of the majority in such cases as *West Coast Hotel* v. *Parrish* (1937) and *United States* v. *Darby Lumber Co.* (1941). But as these views were taking hold in the field of economic regulation, the Court began to identify a new category of cases that, in the Court's judgment, merited more than "ordinary" judicial scrutiny. Justice Stone's famous "Footnote Four" (see pp. 179–180, *supra*) and the subsequent development of the "preferred freedoms" doctrine became the cornerstone for what is today known as *strict scrutiny*.

When strict scrutiny is applied, the burden of proof shifts from those challenging a statute as unconstitutional to those defending its validity. Instead of showing merely that a statute under attack was not unreasonable or arbitrary, government under the strict scrutiny test must demonstrate a *compelling interest*. It is not enough to argue that a statute is administratively convenient or that it was the most cost-efficient way in which government could have acted. Instead, the burden is on the government to show that the statute is neither seriously overinclusive nor underinclusive. It may have to show that there were no less drastic alternatives that would have met the government's interests. Quite clearly, a statute subjected to the test of strict scrutiny is more vulnerable than one to which only ordinary scrutiny is applied.

As an example, consider the case of *Shapiro* v. *Thompson* (1969). The state of Connecticut, like others, had applied a durational residency requirement for eligibility for welfare benefits. A person had to establish residence and live in the state for a year before becoming eligible. The purpose of the requirement was to discourage the migration into Connecticut of indigents attracted by the state's relatively high welfare benefits. The rule was challenged by several indigents who were otherwise eligible for welfare benefits. Connecticut defended the rule on the grounds that it was a reasonable effort to keep costs down and that the determination of residency for welfare eligibility, to prevent fraud, was a difficult administrative task. By the standard of ordinary scrutiny, that would have been a reasonable response. But, in the Supreme Court's judgment, it fell far short of demonstrating a compelling interest, since there were less restrictive ways in which the same legitimate ends might have been accomplished (see pp. 660–666, *infra*).

When should the standard of strict scrutiny be applied? Some justices would reject the appropriateness of such a test under all circumstances, for the same reasons that an earlier Court rejected the doctrine of substantive due process. Indeed, to those justices, the strict scrutiny approach is merely a revival of the pernicious substantive due process, what some call "substantive equal protection."

The Supreme Court has recognized two "triggers" that call for the application of strict scrutiny to legislative classifications. One is activated by a claim of deprivation of a "fundamental right." Among those rights deemed fundamental for purposes of equal protection analysis are the right to travel, the right to marry and to procreate, some aspects of the right to vote, the right of privacy, and the right of association. It was the claim of the indigent welfare applicants in *Shapiro* v. *Thompson* that Connecticut's durational residency requirement abridged their fundamental constitutional right to travel.

The other trigger is activated when the Supreme Court detects the presence of a "suspect classification," that is, a classification regarded as so pernicious and likely to be discriminatory as to be inherently "suspect." Race is certainly the prototype of a suspect classification. Even while upholding the government's position in the Japanese exclusion case, *Korematsu* v. *United States* (1944), a defense of the relocation of Japanese-Americans from their homes as a war security measure, Justice Black argued that a classification by race could be upheld only under the most extreme circumstances and that most such classifications were presumed invalid. Today it is difficult to think of a valid racial classification other than one that explicitly—and actually—served a benign purpose. The Supreme Court has upheld a variety of affirmative action plans but the *Bakke* decision in 1978 and the *Weber* case decided in 1979 (see pp. 600–608) suggest just how difficult it is to arrive at a consensus on that question. If non-benign racial classifications are extremely suspect, so too are religious ones. Indeed it is difficult to conceive of a valid religious classification.

Besides race and religion, the Supreme Court has designated other types of classifications as suspect under certain circumstances. These include alienage, illegitimacy, and indigency. But none are absolutely within that category. Thus, in *Graham* v. *Richardson* (1971), the Court regarded alienage as suspect and ruled that states could not condition welfare benefits on citizenship. In *Nyquist* v. *Mauclet* (1977), the Court invalidated a New York State law that limited higher education benefits to citizens and aliens applying for citizenship. But in *Foley* v. *Connelie* (1978), the Court upheld a Massachusetts statute that made citizenship a requirement for becoming a law enforcement officer. In the course of that opinion, the Court declared that alienage was not to be regarded as "suspect" for all purposes, even though the equal protection clause, applies to "persons" and not only to citizens.

Gender has never been considered a suspect classification by a majority of justices, for reasons discussed in Section 3 of this chapter. Wealth per se is not a suspect classification. There were some early Supreme Court cases in which the Court held that constitutional rights could not be withheld because of indigency. Thus, in *Griffin* v. *Illinois* (1956), the Court held that where the state provides for a criminal appeal, and where it makes a trial transcript necessary to that appeal, it must provide free transcripts to indigents. A similar rationale underlies the Court's requirement of assigned counsel for all nondiscretionary appeals. Indigency was a factor in *Shapiro* v. *Thompson*, since it was the indigency of the plaintiffs in that case that triggered their right-to-travel claim. *Harper* v. *Virginia Board of Elections* (1966), which invalidated the poll tax in state elections, contained language suggesting that wealth was in fact a suspect classification: "Wealth, like race, creed or color is not germane to one's ability to participate intelligently in the electoral process. Lines drawn on the basis of wealth or property, like those of race . . . are traditionally disfavored." In *Boddie* v. *Connecticut* (1970), the Court invalidated a Connecticut statute that prevented an indigent who could not pay the filing fee from obtaining a divorce.

In more recent cases, however, the trend has been in the other direction. *Dandridge* v. *Williams* (1970) held that a challenge to Maryland's maximum family grant welfare law was to be considered under ordinary scrutiny because the statute was merely an economic regulation. In *San Antonio School District* v. *Rodriguez* (1973), a challenge to school financing by the property tax, the Court held, 5-4, that wealth was not a suspect classification requiring strict scrutiny (in the same case, it also held that education was not a fundamental right). In *United States* v. *Kras* (1973), the Court held that a person too poor to pay the filing fee might be prevented from filing for bankruptcy. And in *Maher* v. *Roe* (1977), in upholding the right of a state not to fund nontherapeutic abortions under the Medicaid program, the Court said there was no obligation on a state to "equalize the ability to exercise fundamental rights in the private sector for persons of differing wealth classifications."

There are two discernible differences between the cases in each group. One, obviously, is the span of time and the changes in the composition of the Court that occurred during that span. Second, in the first group of cases, it was claimed that indigency was a barrier to the realization of some other constitutional right; in the second, the Court was being asked to articulate new and enlarged conceptions of rights.

In a number of recent cases, a middle ground has developed to bridge the gap between ordinary and strict scrutiny. Sometimes called *middle level scrutiny,* or, playfully, "ordinary scrutiny with bite," this test, as its name implies, is stricter than ordinary scrutiny but not as devastating as strict scrutiny. In a recent case involving the validity of an Oklahoma statute setting twenty-one as the beer-purchasing age for boys and eighteen for girls, the Court asked whether the law "served important governmental objectives" and whether it was "substantially related to the achievement of those objectives." In *Craig v. Boren* (1976), it invalidated the statute. In dissent, Justice Rehnquist thought the middle level test applied "so diaphanous and elastic as to invite subjective judicial preferences or prejudices relating to particular types of legislation." In *Personnel Administrator* v. *Feeney* (1979), a case challenging the Massachusetts Veterans' Preference Law on grounds of gender discrimination, the majority opinion of Justice Stewart asked whether the statute bore "a close and substantial relationship to important governmental objectives." Justice Marshall, for himself and Justice Brennan, asked whether the statute bore any "substantial relationship to a legitimate governmental objective." But the disposition of the case turned not so much on slight differences in wording of the middle level scrutiny test, but on whether or not the statute purposefully discriminated on the basis of gender. The majority found that it did not establish a gender classification; the dissenters thought it did and would have put the state to the burden of demonstrating a "legitimate governmental objective."

2. THE SUPREME COURT AND RACIAL EQUALITY

A. Essay: The Supreme Court and Racial Equality

In no part of its work has the Court dealt with problems of wider importance or greater emotional impact than in the field of race relations. The ordinary difficulties that the Court faces in every policy area—stemming from complexities in the law, lack of adequate power to achieve desired results, lack of support from other governmental agencies, and insufficient means to implement its decisions—become magnified when deep-rooted patterns of racial prejudice are involved. There is no better illustration of the limits of the law in fostering change in the social and political fabric of the society. And yet, notwithstanding these obstacles, the Supreme Court has made extensive contributions to a reordering of black-white relationships in the United States—contributions and changes now seen by some as inadequate, but recognized by most as vastly greater than anyone thirty years ago had the right to expect.

Attributing change to particular Court decisions is risky, since a variety of political, social, and economic factors are involved. Nonetheless, it is possible to suggest several types of contributions that the Court has made. First, the Court was the first institution of the federal government in modern times not only to recognize but also to attempt to do something about the disparity between the egalitarian ideals of the Constitution and the Declaration of Independence and the stark reality of Negro life. Its decisions in the period after World War II provided strong symbolic support for the need to resolve what Myrdal had appropriately called the "American dilemma."[1] Second, beginning in the 1930s, the Court provided a forum and political outlet for Negroes and other minority groups otherwise unable to effectively utilize the political system for redressing their grievances. The principle underlying this new role was best stated by the late Justice Stone in his famous "Footnote Four," in *United States* v. *Carolene Products Company* (1938, see pp. 179–180). Third, the Court dismantled the legal foundations of racial discrimination. This involved not only the invalidation of laws and practices discriminatory on their face but also the gradual restoration to Congress and to the states of their legal capacity to deal with the discriminatory conditions that remained. Finally, it must be noted that the Supreme Court's rejection of racial discrimination had a profound impact on, and led to the erosion of, other kinds of discrimination as well. In the next chapter, we will observe

the impact of this egalitarian spirit on the criminal justice system. But its influence also extended to gender discrimination, reapportionment, and the rights of other minority groups. The spirit of equality, once loosed, is difficult to contain.

The Supreme Court's decisions have not eliminated racism in American society. Indeed, in the immediate aftermath of the school segregation cases (*Brown* v. *Board of Education*, 1954, 1955), the hostile reaction of southern whites may have exacerbated racial tensions. The introduction of racial issues into national politics had a temporary destabilizing effect. The third-party presidential candidacy in 1968 of Governor George Wallace of Alabama, which epitomized the "white backlash" to growing black demands for equal treatment; the urban ghetto riots of the 1960s;[2] and the "southern strategy" of candiate and then president Richard Nixon marked this process of racial polarization. The conclusion of the Kerner Commission in 1968, that "our Nation is moving toward two societies, one black, one white—separate and unequal" underscores the paradox of race relations. It also suggests some very real limitations to Supreme Court policymaking.

These limitations should not surprise anyone familiar with the history of race relations in the United States. Black slavery in this country, formally ended by the Civil War, was an

[1]Gunnar Myrdal, *An American Dilemma: The Negro Problem and Modern Democracy*, 2 vols. (New York: Harper & Row, 1944), a classic account. As Charles Silberman has more recently observed, the real tragedy of race relations in America is that, for most Americans, the condition of the Negro presented no dilemma at all. See Silberman, *Crisis in Black and White* (New York: Vintage Books, 1964), p. 10.

[2]There is at least one theory that suggests that this gap between actual conditions and rising expectations is responsible for much of the racial violence in the 1960s. See James Davies, "The 'J' Curve of Rising Expectations," in Graham and Gurr (eds.), *The History of Violence in America: A Report to the National Commission on the Causes and Prevention of Violence* (New York: Bantam Books, 1969), pp. 671–710.

especially cruel oppression. As de Tocqueville and others observed, American slaveowners—and American society—sought not only to keep slaves in bondage but repressed in them the desire for freedom and destroyed their self-respect.[3] The scars of that slavery, "its badges and incidents" as the Supreme Court would refer to them, still bear heavily on us. So, too, in more obvious ways, does the heritage of the Jim Crow system of racial segregation that developed in the United States at the end of the nineteenth century. The Supreme Court countenanced these Jim Crow laws for many years and bears some institutional responsibility for them.

Eliminating racial discrimination has been a major policy goal of the government for about twenty years, dating back to the Civil Rights Act of 1957. Indeed, the society's effort to eliminate discrimination has been prodigious. Yet, in important ways, despite the many gains recorded, racism continues to exist, if not to flourish. Blacks are gaining entry to virtually all jobs and professions but, more often than not, in small numbers. Discrimination in housing seems more impervious to change, and its existence makes efforts to eliminate school desegregation very difficult. Blacks are beginning to occupy elected and appointed political positions, a result, in part, of the major gains in black voting since the 1960s. Yet economic indicators show that blacks have not made economic gains relative to whites.

It is useful to distinguish between "overt" and "institutional" racism. Overt racism is, by definition, open and visible discrimination, what Rodgers and Bullock call "white only" racism.[4] The Jim Crow system was its symbol. Blacks, because of their race, were excluded or separated from whites in virtually all aspects of life. Overt racism has all but been eliminated in the United States today. Supreme Court decisions have played a major role in its demise. There are no valid laws that discriminate on account of race. Blacks, in theory, can attend the same schools, eat at the same restaurants, live in the same houses, and work at the same jobs as whites. But overt racism has been replaced by institutional racism, a more subtle and perhaps more insidious form of discrimination.

Institutional racism is a system by which a minority group is kept subordinated in status and opportunities by reliance on discriminatory private attitudes and by the use of substitute institutional mechanisms such as job tests and requirements that bear no relation to the work involved but serve to exclude the unwanted minority. Other, equally insidious mechanisms that accomplish the same purpose include apprenticeship programs in the craft unions, unnecessary job requirements and exclusions (such as minimum education or absence of an arrest record). Such tests or requirements may seem objective and "fair" on their face, but in practice, they often operate to exclude members of culturally disadvantaged minorities.

Efforts to overcome institutional racism have often taken the form of compensatory "affirmative action" programs, especially in school admissions and in employment. Yet whites, who by a large majority oppose all manifestations of "overt" racism and in principle have favored "integration" have been notably un-

[3]Silberman, op. cit., Note 1, p. 79 and *passim*.
[4]Charles S. Bullock III, and Harrell R. Rodgers, Jr., *Racial Equality in America* (Pacific Palisades, Calif.: Goodyear Publishing Co., 1975), p. 3.

supportive of such efforts. A large number of white citizens, probably a majority, believe that the disadvantages that blacks have in education, housing, and jobs are mainly their own fault.[5] Now that formal discrimination has been eliminated, they feel that blacks ought to compete on an equal basis with whites and not be given any special advantages. Equality of opportunity, not equality of result (to use the terms defined in the previous section), is the predominant white response. "We made it, so can they" is a typical rejoinder of members of white ethnic groups. The idea that the black ghetto is the product of white society, and not of black society, is not widely accepted.

In reviewing the involvement of the Supreme Court in race relations, it is useful to consider four separate periods of time: to the Civil War; from the Civil War to World War I; from World War I to about 1954; and from 1954 to the present. Two major issues of race came to the Supreme Court before the Civil War: efforts to support the institution of slavery by enactment of fugitive slave laws, and the legality and extension of slavery. The Supreme Court was sympathetic to the fugitive slave laws and, in a series of decisions, upheld their validity.[6]

In *Dred Scott* v. *Sandford* (1857), a majority of justices held that the Missouri Compromise of 1820 (which restricted the territorial expansion of slavery) was unconstitutional. Scott, a slave, had been taken by his master from Missouri, where slavery was permitted, to Illinois and the northern section of the Louisiana Territory. Slavery was forbidden in Illinois by state law, and in the northern Louisiana Territory by an act of Congress, the Missouri Compromise of 1820. Scott's owner then took him back to Missouri. When the owner died, title to Scott passed to a man named John Sandford, a citizen of New York. In 1846, Scott sought his freedom in a suit in the Missouri courts, but lost. In 1854, Scott's attorney filed suit in the federal court in Missouri, and the case came to the Supreme Court in 1856.

A majority of justices were initially

---

[5]Ibid., pp. 4, 5.

[6]Article IV, Section 2 of the Constitution states that persons "held to Service or Labour" in one state who escape to another must be "delivered up." But the Constitution did not state who was to enforce this provision. A reasonable assumption, considering the entire context of Article IV, is that each state had the obligation to return fugitive slaves. In 1793, Congress enacted a fugitive slave law which authorized any federal or state court to order the return of a fugitive slave to his master. A number of states enacted similar laws. However, with the rise of the abolitionist movement, a number of northern states enacted laws that provided a measure of due process procedures for fugitive slaves. A few states even provided for trial by jury. Pennsylvania went one step further and passed a law that prohibited state judges from assuming jurisdiction in such cases under the federal law, and virtually prohibited seizing of slaves for the purpose of returning them to slavery. This law was in clear conflict with the federal statute, and a case testing it came before the Supreme Court. In *Prigg* v. *Pennsylvania* (1842), the Supreme Court held that most of the Pennsylvania law was unconstitutional because it was in conflict with a valid federal law. Justice Story, writing for the majority, held that the fugitive slave clause in Article IV was a power exclusively reserved to the federal government. Even if the words of the Constitution did not say precisely that, Story wrote, a uniform system for returning fugitive slaves was necessary. The one provision of the Pennsylvania law that *was* valid, Story held, was the ban on enforcement by state judges of the federal law. States had no obligation to enforce federal law.

prepared to dismiss the case on the authority of an earlier case, *Strader v. Graham* (1850), which had held that a slave's status was determined by state law. Since Missouri permitted slavery, the Court could have simply followed this precedent. However, when two abolitionist justices, McLean and Curtis, prepared dissenting opinions in which they discussed the constitutional issue of slavery in the territories, the majority justices determined to respond in kind. Consensus was lost, and nine opinions produced monumental confusion. Chief Justice Taney's individual opinion was cited most often, although it was not in any sense an opinion *of* the Court.

Taney wrote that Scott was not and could not become a citizen of the United States for two reasons: because he was a Negro and because he was a slave. Taney argued that the framers had not intended to permit Negroes—even nonslaves living in free states—to become citizens of the United States. The Negro had, in Taney's words, "No rights which the white man was bound to respect." Scott could also not be a citizen because he was a slave. Congress exceeded its powers in passing the Missouri Compromise, Taney wrote, and therefore Scott's visit to free territory could not change his status as a slave once he returned to Missouri. For these reasons, Scott could not bring suit in the federal courts (the case had been brought under diversity of citizenship), and the case was dismissed.

Historians continue to debate the importance of this decision in hastening the onset of the Civil War. Certainly, it fanned the flames of controversy and made it clear to all that the Supreme Court could not provide a solution to the slavery issue. It was the most infamous decision the Court ever made, and the stigma of it—both to the Court and to Chief Justice Taney—far outlasted the contemporary vilification heaped upon the Court. For our purposes, it is sufficient to note that the considerable revulsion we feel today for the sentiments Taney expressed was not felt strongly by many abolitionists at the time. The decision was widely criticized, but many of the critics condoned practices not inconsistent with those sentiments. Segregation between the races was accepted behavior in the North; many citizens who opposed slavery nonetheless subscribed to Lincoln's doubts that Negroes could ever be accepted as the social equals of whites.

If the Supreme Court was not supportive of Negroes before the Civil War, its attitude following the war was one of relative indifference. The outcome of the Civil War, the Thirteenth, Fourteenth, and Fifteenth Amendments and eleven Civil Rights acts passed between 1866 and 1875 (the first period of Reconstruction), left the *Dred Scott* case in limbo—not formally overruled but clearly discarded. Negroes (and all persons) were given United States citizenship by virtue of their birth on American soil, and state citizenship by virtue of their residence in a particular state. Slavery was abolished. Racial discrimination in voting was proscribed. States were prohibited from infringing the privileges and immunities of citizens of the United States and prohibited from denying to any person due process of law or the equal protection of the laws. A number of statutes passed by Congress attempted to provide more specific protection against the deprivation of rights in housing, public accommodations, and the making and enforcing of contracts; acts or conspiracies to deprive citizens of their civil rights were prohibited and punishable under federal law.[7]

The early promise of these laws and amendments soon evaporated. Morroe Berger reports that of more than 5000 criminal cases brought in the southern states to enforce the Reconstruction laws (between 1870 and 1895), only about 20 percent resulted in convictions. Unsympathetic judges and predominantly white juries obstructed the full protective sweep of these laws.[8] Negroes enjoyed a measure of formal equality in these former slave states, but only for about a decade. After that, white dominance gradually reappeared, and the Jim Crow system soon became entrenched. The strategy of "separate but equal" (but in reality only separate) was pressed on, and accepted by, the Supreme Court as adequate compliance with the law.[9]

The Compromise of 1877, which produced an electoral majority for Rutherford B. Hayes in the presidential election of 1876 in return for a gradual withdrawal of federal troops from the southern states, marked the beginning of this trend. The Supreme Court's decision in The *Slaughterhouse Cases* (1873) eliminated the privileges and immunities clause of the Fourteenth Amendment as a potential barrier against racial discrimination. The *Civil Rights Cases* (1883) invalidated the Civil Rights Act of 1875 and restricted Congress' power to enforce the Fourteenth Amendment. In that same decision, the Court also limited the scope of the Thirteenth Amendment by refusing to consider "mere" racial discrimination in public accommoda-

tions as among the badges and incidents of slavery prohibited. In *United States* v. *Harris* (1883), the Court ruled that the equal protection clause prevented only discriminatory *state action* and afforded no relief against the failure of a state to prevent discrimination.

It is true that most of these, and similar, decisions came at a time when Negroes were not yet the object of the official discrimination that characterized the Jim Crow system. Justice Bradley could, with some evidence, point out in his opinion in the *Civil Rights Cases* that Congress really did not need broad powers to deal with racial discrimination in public accommodations, because in many states, antidiscrimination laws already existed. But by 1896, when *Plessy* v. *Ferguson* was decided, this contention was no longer credible.

The Jim Crow system reversed the post–Civil War trends toward Negro equality. A good example was the effort to disenfranchise Negro voters. Revisions in state constitutions imposed property qualifications, literacy tests, and the poll tax as requirements for voting; these proved to be almost insurmountable barriers. C. Vann Woodward reports that there were 130,000 registered Negro voters in Louisiana in 1896, but only 1300 in 1904. Since the various qualifying devices tended to exclude poor whites as well as Negroes, a way had to be found to allow poor whites to vote. Many state constitutions thus included "grandfather" clauses, under which any citizen whose grandfather had been eligible to vote was excused from meeting other qualifications.

---

[7]For a useful summary of these events, see United States Commission on Civil Rights, *A Report to the President: Freedom to the Free*, 1863-1963, pp. 5–50, and the sources cited on pp. 209-240.

[8]Morroe Berger, *Equality By Statute*, rev. ed. (Garden City, N.Y.: Anchor Books, 1968), Chapter 2.

[9]See C. Vann Woodward, *The Strange Career of Jim Crow*, 2nd ed. (New York: Oxford University Press, 1966); and Louis R. Harlan, *Separate But Unequal* (New York: Atheneum, 1968).

Since the grandfathers of most Negroes had been slaves, this device allowed most white citizens to vote, while only a few Negroes slipped through the net. The Supreme Court declared the grandfather clause to be unconstitutional in 1915, in *Guinn* v. *United States*.

It was at this time that extensive reliance was placed on the "white primary" to exclude blacks from exercising a meaningful voting franchise even where they could no longer be prohibited from voting. In southern states, Democratic candidates almost invariably won in the general election, since there was, in effect, no opposition. Democratic candidates were usually nominated in primary elections that were considered to be private affairs of the Democratic party. If these primaries could be kept "white," then blacks were effectively excluded from the electoral process. The Supreme Court upheld the constitutionality of the white primary, and then in *Smith* v. *Allwright* (1944), declared it to be unconstitutional. *Allwright* was the first of a series of major Supreme Court decisions in the 1940s and 1950s which began to break down the Jim Crow system that existed not only at the polls but also in virtually all aspects of life in the South.[10]

In the light of these events, the *Plessy* decision demonstrated the Court's agreement with prevailing sentiments favoring segregation. Even Justice Harlan, whose dissents in that case and in the earlier *Civil Rights Cases* are remembered as courageous and liberal protests against racial discrimination, did not contest the underlying assumption of the majority regarding the inherent superiority of the white race. Coming as it did when the Jim Crow movement was just beginning, *Plessy* signaled the southern states that they could expect only minimal interference from the Supreme Court.

The Supreme Court's acquiescence in the separate-but-equal formula for racial discrimination, and its corresponding refusal to permit Congress to prohibit racial discrimination directly, or discrimination that did not flow from "state action," thus had an important effect on the course of race relations in the United States. It is not entirely the responsibility of the Court that Congress passed no civil rights statute from 1883 to 1957. But its opinion in the *Civil Rights Cases* furnished to the southern bloc in Congress an important and effective weapon against the passage of any civil rights legislation.

The contrast between *Plessy* and the celebrated decision of *Lochner* v. *New York* (1905) tells us much about the thinking of the Court at the turn of the century. While states were permitted more or less openly to deny Negroes the right to vote, the right to attend integrated or even adequate schools, and the right to purchase property of their choice, these same states were *prohibited* from regulating the working hours of bakers on the grounds that the relationship between a baker and his employer was an entirely private, contractual relationship in which the state could have no legitimate interest. It must be noted that those justices who protested the *Lochner* decision as an infringement of the rights of the states to regulate social and economic practices believed that the states should have the same discretion in racial questions as well. When the Court subsequently sustained the validity of the white primary, it could state accurately that "if the great mass of white population intends to keep the blacks from voting . . . a name on a

[10]Ibid.

piece of paper will not defeat them."[11]

The onset of World War I found the Negro in the South totally disenfranchised and restricted to a segregated and inferior caste by economic pressures and violence. Most Negroes then lived in the South (89 percent in 1910), and most lived in rural areas. Beginning in 1914, a large northern migration began in response to the needs of northern industry for relatively cheap black labor and because of the dislocations of the war and its negative impact on the economy of the rural south. By the 1960s, nearly 40 percent of all blacks lived outside the South, 75 percent in urban areas; today, less than 25 percent live in the rural South.[12] The migration that began in 1914 continues today. In 1971, Washington, D.C. had a 71 percent black population, and a number of other cities had a 25 to 60 percent black population.

With this migration, race relations inescapably became a national instead of a regional problem. Negroes were moving to areas of the country theoretically less hostile to them. As they began to live and work in the industrialized northern cities, more opportunities became available for political action and organization. Negroes shared in the benefits of the New Deal, some received political positions in federal and state governments, and many achieved a status of equal deprivation with working-class white people in the Depression period.

The liberalism of the New Deal did not extend to advocating such "radical" reforms as open housing, desegregation in public schools, or desegregation in public accommodations. But merely by conferring equal benefits upon Negroes the New Deal contributed to their aspirations and enhanced demands on the political system. The greatest advance for Negroes at this time came with the onset of World War II. Under the threat of a divisive and perhaps violent "march on Washington" led by A. Philip Randolph, President Roosevelt issued an executive order desegregating the armed forces.[13] Unlike World War I, when Negroes were totally excluded from the Marines and given only menial jobs in the Army and Navy, in World War II, Negroes were permitted to fight. However, eliminating the last vestiges of military discrimination remained the task of a succeeding president in the postwar era, Harry Truman. Negroes in World War II still fought in segregated units, and the Red Cross continued its practice—with government approval—of keeping separate supplies of "white" and "black" blood.

Pressures for change came not only from mass migration to the North and from the New Deal but also from protest within the Negro ranks, and it was the Negro protest pressures in particular that were directed at the Supreme Court. Despite the portrayal of a generation of historians, Negroes were not happy and contented with their inferior lot. There is substantial evidence of protest among Negro slaves, ranging from noncooperation to escape to the occasional violent but short-lived slave rebellions. In fact, there may have been greater protest by Negro slaves than by succeeding genera-

[11]Quoted in Loren Miller, *The Petitioners* (Cleveland: Meridian Books, 1967), p. 425.

[12]Thomas Pettigrew, "Race Relations in the United States: A Sociological Perspective," in Parsons (ed.), *American Sociology: Perspectives, Problems, Methods* (New York: Basic Books, 1968), pp. 258–271.

[13]Executive Order of the President 8802, **6** *Fed. Reg.* 3109 (1941).

tions of southern Negroes, who suddenly found political power thrust on them in the Reconstruction period, and just as suddenly found it taken away from them in the last decade of the nineteenth century.

There was relatively little protest by southern Negroes against the Jim Crow system. Indeed, in several instances, Negro state legislators even voted for disenfranchisement or segregation statutes. Negroes were counseled to be patient by Booker T. Washington. Although he fought segregation in many ways, Washington's open advice to Negroes was accommodation and "self-help." Negroes were told to improve themselves in education, job skills, and morality in order to earn the respect of the white man. Needless to say, white southerners found Washington a most effective and eloquent leader who "knew his place."

A small group of Negroes protested against Washington's leadership and formed what was known as the Niagara Movement. They counseled protest instead of accommodation and, more importantly, placed the blame for the Negro's condition on the white man instead of on the Negro himself. With the help of white liberals and socialists, these Negro leaders in 1909 formed the National Association for the Advancement of Colored People.[14] For more than fifty years, the NAACP was the most effective organization of Negro protest, and its tactics set the tone for Negro responses in general. Although the organization had radical roots, the NAACP's main strategy was the elimination of discrimination through the courts, and it is not surprising that such an organization would become the most frequent—and most successful—litigant before the Supreme Court of the United States. The issues that it took to the Court were among the most pressing and visible issues of the day—voting discrimination, discrimination in housing by states as well as by private individuals, violence against Negroes, unfair criminal trials of Negro defendants, and finally, segregation in graduate and professional schools. It was not until the 1950s that grade-school segregation, antimiscegenation laws, discrimination in employment, and discrimination in public accommodations were fought before the Supreme Court, reflecting an obvious, if unstated, sense of priorities in the goals of the organization and a sense of those changes most likely to be acceptable to white people.[15]

Much of the early success of the

---

[14]John A. Morsell, "The National Association for the Advancement of Colored People and Its Strategy," **357** *Annals of the American Academy of Political and Social Science* (1965), 97-101.

[15]Myrdal argued that there existed a "rank order of discrimination." For whites, the closer the social contact with Negroes, the stronger the attachment to discrimination. For Negroes, the inverse was true: "The Negro resists least the discrimination on the ranks placed highest in the white man's evaluation and resents most any discrimination on the lowest level. This is in accord with the Negro's immediate interests."

The rank order was as follows: "*Rank 1:* the bar against intermarriage and sexual intercourse involving white women. *Rank 2:* several etiquettes and discriminations, which specifically concern behavior in personal relations. (These are the barriers against dancing, bathing, eating, drinking together, and social intercourse generally.) *Rank 3:* the segregations and discriminations in use of public facilities such as schools, churches and means of conveyance. *Rank 4:* political disenfranchisement. *Rank 5:* discriminations in law courts, by the police, and by other public servants. *Rank 6:* the discriminations in securing land, credit, jobs, or other means of earning a living, and discriminations in public relief and other social welfare activities." Myrdal, op. cit., vol. 1, Note 1, pp. 60–67.

NAACP resulted from pressing for demands "within" the rules of the game (e.g., through the courts) and in a conservative manner, and because it was supported by white liberals. It was thus seen by many as a "legitimate" (and perhaps co-opted) group rather than as a subversive or fringe organization. The organization's style compared favorably in the eyes of many with Marcus Garvey's "Back to Africa" movement or with the aggressive and ideological polemics of the American Communist Party, which at the time, was especially interested in publicizing the condition of the Negro in America.

Other factors external to the NAACP itself also materially aided its success. By the mid-1930s, a new generation of justices was coming on the Court, justices whose progressive and liberal instincts inevitably extended beyond economic questions to civil liberties and civil rights. Also, by 1937, the Court had turned its back on past efforts to interfere with state and federal economic regulations, leaving a gap in its case load that was quickly filled with cases involving personal liberties and civil rights questions.

The Court's response to Negro demands in this third period was only moderately favorable until the late 1930s. The justices struck down a number of laws preventing blacks from gaining political equality or economic parity. Even in these areas the movement toward equality was slow. It took a number of attempts for the Court to finally decide that the white primary was invalid. In a number of cases, racial discrimination in the administration of justice was outlawed. But in disputes involving the possibility of closer social contact between Negroes and whites, the Supreme Court was very hesitant to extend much constitutional protection. It began to examine the "equal" half of the "separate-but-equal" doctrine, but it was unwilling to reconsider the doctrine itself. And although the Court invalidated forced-housing segregation by law (*Buchanan* v. *Warley,* 1917), it refused to act against more subtle forms of housing discrimination. According to Morroe Berger, from 1868 to 1936, "Negroes won only two of fourteen cases in which they claimed the right to use the same facilities as whites in common carriers, public places, and schools or housing."[16] Judicial relief seemed forthcoming primarily in those areas of "nonsocial" discrimination in which white commitment to maintain the status quo was least intense.[17]

With the onset of World War II, a noticeable shift in judicial response occurred. In 1944, in *Smith* v. *Allwright*, the Court reversed itself and ruled that since primary elections were an integral part of the electoral process of a state, the white primary was invalid as a violation of the Fifteenth Amendment. This decision, and the unwillingness of Negro soldiers returning from the war to passively accept disenfranchisement, contributed to a significant increase in Negro voter registration in the South. In *Shelley* v. *Kraemer* (1948), the Court responded to a twenty-five-year effort by the Legal Defense Fund of the NAACP and ruled that private racially restrictive housing covenants, while not invalid,

[16]Berger, op. cit., Note 8, Chap. 2.

[17]Ibid., pp. 85–87. Berger also argues that the net result of the Court's role "was to support laws which enforced the separation of the Negro and white 'castes' and to strike down laws which allowed or encouraged intercaste contact that implied their social equality."

were judicially unenforceable under the equal protection clause of the Fourteenth Amendment. And, in *Sweatt* v. *Painter*, (1950), in a case involving the application of a Negro student to the University of Texas Law School, the Court extended the pattern, initiated before the war, of requiring that facilities be more than nominally equal to satisfy the "separate-but-equal" formula of *Plessy*. One could already forecast the eventual overruling of the *Plessy* decision, but the Supreme Court in 1950 was not yet prepared to take that momentous step. It continued to make it increasingly difficult for the states to comply with the doctrines of earlier segregationist decisions. But, with the exception of *Smith* v. *Allwright*, it seemed notably reluctant to make a major break with segregationist legal doctrine.

The fourth period began, appropriately enough, with the landmark decision in *Brown* v. *Board of Education* (1954), which held that segregation in public schools was unconstitutional and implied that law-imposed segregation in other areas was equally unjustified.[18] Even though the Court in *Brown* did not order immediate desegregation, and even though, twenty-five years later, integration in public schools has not been fully achieved, the *Brown* decision had immense psychological and symbolic impact on Negroes and whites alike. Louis Lomax wrote:

It would be impossible for a white person to understand what happened within black breasts on that Monday. An ardent segregationist has called it "Black Monday." He was so right, but for reasons other than the ones he advances: that was the day we won; the day we took the white man's laws and won our case be-fore an all-white Supreme Court with a Negro lawyer, Thurgood Marshall, as our chief counsel. And we were proud.[19]

Brown may have rekindled the spark of faith in Negroes that they could win with the "white man's laws," but the aftermath of *Brown* showed that faith to be premature or naive. Negroes, white liberals, and nine justices all miscalculated the intensity and vehemence of the white southern reaction to that decision. Far from bringing about any immediate discernible changes in the status of southern Negroes or resolving the question of racial segregation, *Brown* acted as the catalyst for many hostile counterforces. The immediate aftermath of *Brown* indicated, among other things, that the ultimate resolution of the status of the Negro would not be solved exclusively by the courts but would of necessity involve other political institutions as well. Moreover, it became clear that political, social, and economic rights for black Americans could not be acquired merely by declaring that they had these rights under the law but would come about only as the result of the mobilization of political power, bargaining and protest tactics, and legal and financial sanctions applied against those in opposition.

Part of the difficulty with the *Brown* decision was its ambiguity. What it clearly required was an end to officially sanctioned racial segregation in the public schools. But was that all? Did it also stand for the proposition that any and all racial classifications were invidiously discriminatory and hence invalid under the Fourteenth Amendment? Was it concerned solely with the harmful effects of segregation by law or with segregation per se? Was racial inte-

[18]See Richard Kluger, *Simple Justice* (New York: Vintage Books, 1975).
[19]Louis Lomax, *The Negro Revolt* (New York: Signet Books, 1963), p. 84.

gration an instrumental goal sought as a means of improving the education of Negro schoolchildren or was it an end in itself?

The Court did not clarify its intentions as to these points. Instead, in 1955, it issued a second ruling (*Brown II*). This second ruling led only to further confusion and delay. For the Court proposed no guidelines for the pace or scope of desegregation that might have indicated just what it had in mind. The formula of relegating major enforcement responsibility to the federal district courts, but then providing them with no guidance except the admonition of "all deliberate speed," deprived the *Brown* decision of some of the force and effect it might have had.

Despite these problems, the *Brown* decision of 1954 did serve as the catalyst for increased attention and national concern with civil rights problems, including, ten years later, a resumption by Congress of its policymaking leadership in the field of civil rights. The Court's strong approval of later congressional efforts indicated, as much as anything else, the justices' recognition that, having led the way in breaking down the legal underpinnings of the Jim Crow system, they would have to defer to Congress for implementation and policy guidelines for many of the problems that still remained. The most effective advances by blacks after the *Brown* decision have come through protest action, congressional statutes, and administrative sanctions. Thus, no judicial declaration about the equality in voting protected by the Fifteenth Amendment could match the impact of voter registration drives and the Voting Rights Act of 1965. Likewise, it is doubtful if school integration would have risen even to its present level without the strong financial sanctions levied against noncomplying school districts by the Department of Health, Education, and Welfare under the authority of the Civil Rights Act of 1964.

In Chapter One, it was suggested that the Supreme Court was limited as an effective policymaker by its lack of enforcement powers, by the inherent limitations of the adversary or adjudicatory process, and by its lack of power to constantly reexamine and update policy decisions. Nowhere is this better seen than in the current and continuing controversy over school desegregation. The existence of factors that the Court cannot control or could not predict, such as white emigration from the central cities, has led to a paradox in which continued efforts at integration may lead to more rather than less segregation. Moreover, other evidence suggests that integration may not be the only, or the most effective, answer to unequal educational opportunities for black children. Thus the assumed initial premise of *Brown*—that integration was the key goal—has been questioned, not only by white Southerners whose motives might be suspect, but also by white liberals and even some blacks.

Alexander Bickel observed that "the law may be striving to attain conditions in the public schools that serve no known purpose by way of educational benefit to the child, strictly speaking, and do not further performance of the egalitarian, assimilationist mission of the schools."[20] He suggests that, just as the Court said in *Brown* that it could not turn the clock back to 1896 but had to consider public education in the light of present conditions, so too must we now consider the present

[20]Alexander Bickel, *The Supreme Court and the Idea of Progress* (New York: Harper Torchbooks, 1970), pp. 137–138.

condition as significantly different from 1954:

What the Brown *opinion ultimately envisioned seems for the moment unattainable, and is becoming unwanted. Soon it may be impossible to "turn the clock back" to 1954, when* Brown v. Board of Education *was written. This is not to detract from the nobility of the Warren Court's aspiration in* Brown, *nor from the contribution to American life of the rule that the state may not coerce or enforce the separation of the races. But it is to say that* Brown v. Board of Education, *with emphasis on the education part of the title, may be headed for— dread word—irrelevance.*[21]

The problem that concerned Bickel is, of course, not unique to the Supreme Court. All political institutions—indeed all policymaking bodies—face the problem of precedents that have lost their earlier and intended meaning or that have become counterproductive to the very ends they initially sought to attain. It is almost certain that the justices in 1954 had no clear conception of the events that would follow the *Brown* decision, and like other institutions, the Court responded to those events in incremental, "muddling through" fashion, trying to accommodate new demands into an essentially conservative tradition of stability and continuity.

In its mammoth report on federal civil rights enforcement in 1970, the United States Commission on Civil Rights found that the "great promise of the civil rights laws, executive orders, and judicial decisions of the 1950s and 1960s has not been realized." Observing that there were two types of problems—denials of basic legal rights and basic social and economic injustices—the commission noted that, by and large, civil rights laws attack only the first aspect of the problem: "As for the second, we as a nation have barely begun to deal with them. . . . The Federal civil rights effort has been inadequate to redeem fully the promise of true 'equal protection of the laws' for all Americans."[22]

The commission found that federal agencies had failed to effectively enforce applicable policies. Without this enforcement, it said, the actions of Congress and the courts would be, if not totally nullified, of little overall effect. The commission's report for 1977 echoed the same complaint. It called for a total reorganization of the federal government's civil rights enforcement program.[23]

Inadequate enforcement has stemmed in part from conflicting policies and purposes in a vast bureaucracy, in part from policy opposition from those in key bureaucratic positions, and in part from inadequate resources available for enforcing civil rights policies. The latter condition has also been characteristic of state civil rights agencies, which, with few exceptions, have publicly espoused strong and active civil rights enforcement and less visibly followed much weaker and more passive policies of implementation.[24]

Attainment of civil rights goals, such as increased and compensatory hiring of blacks and increased housing integration, is slowed if not stymied by the lack of a clear national

[21]Ibid., pp. 150–151.

[22]U.S. Civil Rights Commission, *Federal Civil Rights Enforcement Effort* (Washington, D.C.: U.S. Government Printing Office, 1970).

[23]U.S. Civil Rights Commission, *The State of Civil Rights: 1977* (Washington, D.C.: U.S. Government Printing Office, 1978), pp. 34–36.

[24]Berger, op. cit., Note 8, Chap. 4; Duane Lockard, *Toward Equal Opportunity* (New York: Macmillan, 1968).

consensus favoring such policies and by the failure of the national administration to enforce them uniformly. Lacking strong popular support, it is unlikely that substantial progress in eliminating racial injustice can be made—particularly where the areas of concern are those in which whites have been traditionally less receptive to racial integration.

There is also the problem, as Duane Lockard has pointed out, that ". . . laws against discrimination, even at their best, will never be able to cope with some of the forces that sustain alienation. Laws cannot undo history, and discrimination is history-based. The laws can not eliminate poverty, and Negroes, as victims of discrimination, are poverty-bound. The laws can do no more than superficially affect the decisions of wealth-controlling institutions of the nation which by their indifference to the racial crisis contribute to its worsening. Antidiscrimination laws in short are precisely the kind of response to be expected from the political systems of American state and local government. . . . When pressed for action politicians [And judges, too!—Ed.] are inclined to deal with the peripheral aspects of a problem, to act as to appear to be dealing with the problem but in reality to leave conditions as near the status quo as possible. To bring calm over conflict is more important to a politician than ultimate resolution of a problem—which he does not expect in any event."[25]

What of the Supreme Court's present and future role in achieving racial equality? The record of the first ten years of the Burger Court is one of consolidation and some erosion rather than innovation. It is a dis-

tinctly mixed record. On the question of school integration, the Burger Court surprised many observers, in *Swann* v. *Charlotte-Mecklenberg* (1971), by endorsing at least a limited use of school busing where other methods were inadequate to achieve a unitary system. And in *Keyes* v. *School District* (1973), it appeared to be taking a sympathetic view of the problems of suitable remedial action in northern cities that had no history of statutory *de jure* segregation. But in *Milliken* v. *Bradley* (1974), the Court, by a 5-4 vote, rejected a plan to integrate the Detroit schools by interdistrict busing to and from adjoining suburban communities. In all of these cases, the Court emphasized that the remedy must be appropriate to the particular constitutional wrong. Integration for its own sake was not a constitutional requirement.

In a major development, in *Washington* v. *Davis* (1976), the Court held that in most civil rights cases, the plaintiff must prove discriminatory intent on the part of officials, or in a challenged law, in order to prevail. It was not enough, the Court said, merely to demonstrate that a particular policy *resulted* in a racially disproportionate impact. In the *Davis* case, the Court held that a verbal skills test given to applicants for the police department in the District of Columbia, which was neutral on its face and which resulted in a disproportionate failure rate among black applicants, was not invalid for that reason alone. Several school integration cases were remanded to the lower courts in light of *Washington* v. *Davis*. It remains to be seen just how strictly the Court will apply the "intent" standard in such cases.[26]

The evidence of other civil rights

---

[25]Lockard, Ibid., pp. 142–143.

[26]But cf. the Court's decisions at the end of its 1978 Term upholding broad school desegregation orders for Columbus and Dayton, Ohio (See pp. 476–480).

cases is consistent with this pattern. In *Moose Lodge* v. *Irvis* (1972), the Court placed a firm lid on expansion of the state action doctrine, thereby making it more difficult to sustain constitutional attacks on private discriminatory action. And in the celebrated affirmative action case, *California Board of Regents* v. *Bakke* (1978), the Court, while ordering Bakke admitted to medical school, rejected racial quotas but endorsed the use of race as *a* factor in professional school admissions. It remains to be seen whether or not *Bakke* will obstruct governmental affirmative action efforts, and what its effect will be on the more difficult problems of affirmative action programs in employment. Without those efforts, the pace of integration in many walks of life will be sharply reduced. On the other hand, the Court's decision seems reasonably reflective of the prevailing public mood *against* special privileges and treatment for members of minority groups, even those with a long history of discrimination.[27]

The one major exception to this "go slow" pattern of the Burger Court has been on the question of congressional power to enforce civil rights. In a series of decisions in the mid-1960s, the Supreme Court indicated that Congress has extensive enforcement powers under the commerce clause and under the enforcement clauses of the Thirteenth, Fourteenth and Fifteenth Amendments. Congress may enforce those amendments even by prohibiting private discrimination that the Fourteenth and Fifteenth Amendments, as self-executing powers, cannot reach. The Voting Rights Act of 1965 permitted an unprecedented level of federal intervention into the electoral process in the states. In *South Carolina* v. *Katzenbach* (1966), the Court upheld the act. And in 1968, in *Jones* v. *Mayer*, the Court held that the Thirteenth Amendment—which has no state action clause—is broad enough to empower Congress to legislate against private discrimination in housing.

The Burger Court has not seriously questioned this concession of broad civil rights enforcement powers to Congress. For example, in deciding *Washington* v. *Davis* (1976), as described above, the Court distinguished that case from an earlier decision, *Griggs* v. *Duke Power Company* (1971). In Griggs it was held that under Title VII of the Civil Rights Act of 1964, employment tests must be job related. The "good intent or absence of discriminatory intent" of a test or program does not redeem employment practices which have a discriminatory *effect* on minority groups. The net result is that in such cases Congress may impose standards which are stricter than those stemming from the Thirteenth and Fourteenth Amendments alone.

B. *Racial Discrimination in the Public Schools*

(1) Plessy v. Ferguson (1896)

+Brown, Field, Fuller, Gray, Shiras, White, Peckham
−Harlan
NP Brewer

[Among the Jim Crow statutes passed in 1890 by the Louisiana legislature was "An Act to Promote the Comfort of Passengers." This new statute required railroads to "provide equal but separate accommodations for the white and colored races," and, ironically, it only passed

---

[27]But cf. the Court's decision in *United Steelworkers of America v. Weber* (1979), in which it upheld a voluntary, private affirmative action hiring plan worked out between the Union and the Kaiser Aluminum and Chemical Corporation (See pp. 600–608).

the legislature with the assent of sixteen Negro senators. Other Negroes opposed the bill and initiated plans to contest its validity in the courts. They hired a lawyer from upstate New York, Albion Tourgee, to represent them. Indeed, the railroads operating in Louisiana that were affected by the statute cooperated in this challenge to the law, since they did not wish to incur the extra expense of providing separate cars and other facilities for Negroes and whites. The cooperation of the railroads and the train conductor was peculiarly necessary to set up this test case, since the chosen protagonist, Homer Plessy, was "seven-eighths Caucasian and one-eighth African" and could easily have passed for white had he so chosen.

By prearrangement, Plessy paid for a first-class ticket on the East Louisiana Railway from New Orleans to Covington, Louisiana on June 7, 1892, and selected a seat in the "white" car. When he refused to obey the conductor's order to move to the car "for persons not of the white race," he was, with the aid of a police officer, ejected from the train and imprisoned in New Orleans Parish Jail. Plessy was charged with violating the statute, but before the trial could proceed, Tourgee sought a writ of prohibition challenging the validity of the statute. The challenge proceeded directly to the Supreme Court of Louisiana, where it became apparent why Plessy had been chosen. Tourgee advanced the novel argument that Plessy had been deprived of his property without due process of law, the property being "the reputation of being white," with the argument hinging on the definition of blood proportions necessary to establish an individual's race for purposes of the act. Tourgee also argued alternatively that the statute violated the equal protection clause of the Fourteenth Amendment. The Louisiana Supreme Court unanimously sustained the statute and denied the writ of prohibition. It found that opposition to the law was "unreasonable," since "even if it were true that the statute was prompted by prejudice on the part of one race to be thrown in contact with the other, one would suppose that to be a sufficient reason why the pride and self-respect of the other race should equally prompt it to avoid such contact."

Appealing to the Supreme Court of the United States, Tourgee invoked the Thirteenth and Fourteenth Amendments, as well as repeating his due process/property argument. To separate the races forcibly, he argued, was to "debase and distinguish against the inferior race," and merely perpetuate the caste system of slavery.]

MR. JUSTICE BROWN delivered the opinion of the Court.

. . . That it does not conflict with the Thirteenth Amendment, which abolished slavery and involuntary servitude, except as a punishment for crime, is too clear for argument. Slavery implies involuntary servitude—a state of bondage; the ownership of mankind as a chattel, or at least the control of the labor and services of one man for the benefit of another, and the absence of a legal right to the disposal of his own person, property and services. This amendment was said in the *Slaughter-house Cases*, to have been intended primarily to abolish slavery, as it had been previously known in this country, and that it equally forbade Mexican peonage or the Chinese coolie trade, when they amounted to slavery or involuntary servitude, and that the use of the word "servitude" was intended to prohibit the use of all forms of involuntary slavery, of whatever class or name. It was intimated, however, in that case that this amendment was regarded by the statesmen of that day as insufficient to protect the colored race from certain laws which had been enacted in the Southern States . . . and that the Fourteenth Amendment was devised to meet this exigency.

So, too, in the *Civil Rights Cases* . . . it was said that the act of a mere individual, the owner of an inn, a public conveyance or place of amusement, refusing accommodations to colored people, cannot be justly regarded as imposing any badge of slavery or servitude upon the applicant. . . . "It would be running the slavery argument into the ground," said Mr. Justice Bradley, "to make it apply to every act of discrimination. . . ."

The object of the [Fourteenth] amendment was undoubtedly to enforce the absolute equality of the two races before the law, but in the nature of things it could not have been intended to abolish distinctions based upon color, or to enforce social, as distinguished from political equality, or a commingling of the two races upon terms unsatisfactory to either. Laws permitting, and even requiring, their separation in places where they are liable to be brought into contact do not necessarily imply the inferiority of either race to the other, and have been generally, if not universally, recognized as within the competency of the state legislatures in the exercise of their police power. The most common instance of this is connected with the establishment of separate schools for white and colored children, which has been held to be a valid exercise of the legislative power even by courts of States where the political rights of the colored race have been longest and most earnestly enforced.

One of the earliest of these cases is that of *Roberts* v. *City of Boston* . . . , in which the Supreme Judicial Court of Massachusetts held that the general school committee of Boston had power to make provision for the instruction of colored children in separate schools established exclusively for them, and to prohibit their attendance upon the other schools. . . .

Laws forbidding the intermarriage of the two races may be said in a technical sense to interfere with the freedom of contract, and yet have

been universally recognized as within the police power of the State. . . .

The distinction between laws interfering with the political equality of the negro and those requiring the separation of the two races in schools, theatres and railway carriages has been frequently drawn by this court. Thus in *Strauder* v. *West Virginia* . . . it was held that a law of West Virginia limiting to white male persons, 21 years of age and citizens of the State, the right to sit upon juries, was a discrimination which implied a legal inferiority in civil society, which lessened the security of the right of the colored race, and was a step toward reducing them to a condition of servility. . . .

[W]here a statute of Louisiana required those engaged in the transportation of passengers among the States to give to all persons travelling within that State, upon vessels employed in that business, equal rights and privileges in all parts of the vessel, without distinction on account of race or color, and subjected to an action for damages the owner of such a vessel, who excluded colored passengers on account of their color from the cabin set aside by him for the use of whites, it was held to be so far as it applied to interstate commerce, unconstitutional and void. *Hall* v. *De Cuir* . . . . The court in this case, however, expressly disclaimed that it had anything whatever to do with the statute as a regulation of internal commerce, or affecting anything else than commerce among the States. . . .

While we think the enforced separation of the races, as applied to the internal commerce of the State, neither abridges the privileges or immunities of the colored man, deprives him of his property without due process of law, nor denies him the equal protection of the laws, within the meaning of the Fourteenth Amendment, we are not prepared to say that the conductor, in assigning passengers to the coaches according to their race, does not act at his peril, or that the provision of the second section of the act, that denies to the passenger compensation in damages for a refusal to receive him into the coach in which he properly belongs, is a valid exercise of the legislative power. Indeed, we understand it to be conceded by the State's attorney, that such part of the act as exempts from liability the railway company and its officers is unconstitutional. . . .

It is claimed by the plaintiff in error that, in any mixed community, the reputation of belonging to the dominant race, in this instance the white race, is *property,* in the same sense that a right of action, or of inheritance, is property. Conceding this to be so, for the purposes of this case, we are unable to see how this statute deprives him of, or in any way affects his right to, such property. If he be a white man and assigned to a colored coach, he may have his action for damages against the company for being deprived of his so-called property. Upon the other hand, if he be a colored man and be so assigned, he has been deprived of no property, since he is not lawfully entitled to the reputation of being a white man.

In this connection, it is also suggested by the learned counsel for the plaintiff in error that the same argument that will justify the state legislature in requiring railways to provide separate accommodations for the two races will also authorize them to require separate cars to be provided for people whose hair is of a certain color, or who are aliens, or who belong to certain nationalities, or to enact laws requiring colored people to walk upon one side of the street, and white people upon the other, or requiring white men's houses to be painted white, and colored men's black, or their vehicles or business signs to be of different colors, upon the theory that one side of the street is as good as the other, or that a house or vehicle of one color is as good as one of another color. The reply to all this is that every exercise of the police power must be reasonable, and extend only to such laws as are enacted in good faith for the promotion for the public good, and not for the annoyance or oppression of a particular class. . . .

So far, then, as a conflict with the Fourteenth Amendment is concerned, the case reduces itself to the question whether the statute of Louisiana is a reasonable regulation, and with respect to this there must necessarily be a large discretion on the part of the legislature. In determining the question of reasonableness it is at liberty to act with reference to the established usages, customs and traditions of the people, and with a view to the promotion of their comfort, and the preservation of the public peace and good order. Gauged by this standard, we cannot say that a law which authorizes or even requires the separation of the two races in public conveyances is unreasonable, or more obnoxious to the Fourteenth Amendment than the acts of Congress requiring separate schools for colored children in the District of Columbia, the constitutionality of which does not seem to have been questioned, or the corresponding acts of state legislatures.

We consider the underlying fallacy of the plaintiff's argument to consist in the assumption that the enforced separation of the two races stamps the colored race with a badge of inferiority. If this be so, it is not by reason of anything found in the act, but solely because the colored race chooses to put that construction upon it. The argument necessarily assumes that if, as has been more than once the case and is not unlikely to be so again, the colored race should become the dominant power in the state legislature, and should enact a law in precisely similar terms it would thereby relegate the white race to an inferior position. We imagine that the white race, at least would not acquiesce in this assumption. The argument also assumes that social prejudices may be overcome by legislation, and that equal rights cannot be secured to the negro except by an enforced commingling of the two races. We cannot accept this proposition. If the two races are to meet upon terms of social equality, it must be the result of natural affinities, a mutual appreciation of each other's merits and a voluntary consent of individuals. . . . Legislation is powerless to eradicate racial instincts or to abolish distinctions based upon physical differences, and the attempt to do so can only result in accentuating the difficulties of the present situation. If the civil and political rights of both races be equal one cannot be inferior to the other civilly or politically. If one race be inferior to the other socially, the Constitution of the United States cannot put them upon the same plane.

It is true that the question of the proportion of colored blood necessary to constitute a colored person, as distinguished from a white person, is one upon which there is a difference of opinion in the different States, some holding that any visible admixture of black blood stamps the person as belonging to the colored race . . . others that it depends upon the preponderance of blood . . . and still others that the predominance of white blood must only be in the pro-

portion of three fourths. . . . But these are questions to be determined under the laws of each State and are not properly put in issue in this case. Under the allegations of his petition it may undoubtedly become a question of importance whether, under the laws of Louisiana, the petitioner belongs to the white or colored race.

The judgment of the court below is therefore, *Affirmed.*

MR. JUSTICE HARLAN DISSENTING.

. . . In respect of civil rights, common to all citizens, the Constitution of the United States does not, I think, permit any public authority to know the race of those entitled to be protected in the enjoyment of such rights. Every true man has pride of race, and under appropriate circumstances when the rights of others, his equals before the law, are not be affected, it is his privilege to express such pride and to take such action based upon it as to him seems proper. But I deny that any legislative body or judicial tribunal may have regard to the race of citizens when the civil rights of those citizens are involved. . . .

These notable additions to the fundamental law [Civil War Amendments] were welcomed by the friends of liberty throughout the world. They removed the race line from our governmental systems. They had, as this court has said, a common purpose, namely, to secure "to a race recently emancipated, a race that through many generations have been held in slavery, all the civil rights that the superior race enjoy." They declared, in legal effect, this court has further said, "that the law in the States shall be the same for the black as for the white; that all persons, whether colored or white, shall stand equal before the laws of the States, and, in regard to the colored race, for whose protection the amendment was primarily designed, that no discrimination shall be made against them by law because of their color." We also said: "The words of the amendment, it is true, are prohibitory, but they contain a necessary implication of a positive immunity, or right, most valuable to the colored race—the right to exemption from unfriendly legislation against them distinctively as colored . . . .

It was said in argument that the statute of Louisiana does not discriminate against either race, but prescribes a rule applicable alike to white and colored citizens. But this argument does not meet the difficulty. Every one knows that the statute in question had its origin in the purpose, not so much to exclude white persons from railroad cars occupied by blacks, as to exclude colored people from coaches occupied by or assigned to white persons. . . .

The white race deems itself to be the dominant race in this country. And so it is, in prestige, in achievements, in education, in wealth and in power. So, I doubt not, it will continue to be for all time, if it remains true to its great heritage and holds fast to the principles of constitutional liberty. But in view of the Constitution, in the eye of the law, there is in this country no superior, dominant, ruling class of citizens. There is no caste here. Our Constitution is color-blind, and neither knows nor tolerates classes among citizens. In respect of civil rights, all citizens are equal before the law. The humblest is the peer of the most powerful. The law regards man as man, and takes no account of his surroundings or of his color when his civil rights as guaranteed by the supreme law of the land are involved. . . .

In my opinion, the judgment this day rendered will, in time, prove to be quite as pernicious as the decision made by this tribunal in the *Dred Scott case*. . . .

The recent amendments of the Constitution, it was supposed, had eradicated these principles from our institutions. But it seems that we have yet, in some of the States, a dominant race—a superior class of citizens, which assumes to regulate the enjoyment of civil rights, common to all citizens, upon the basis of race. The present decision, it may be apprehended, will not only stimulate aggressions, more or less brutal and irritating, upon the admitted rights of colored citizens, but will encourage the belief that it is possible, by means of state enactments, to defeat the beneficent purposes which the people of the United States had in view when they adopted the recent amendments of the Constitution. . . . Sixty millions of whites are in no danger from the presence here of eight millions of blacks. The destinies of the two races, in this country, are indissolubly linked together, and the interests of both require that the common government of all shall not permit the seeds of race hate to be planted under the sanction of law. What can more certainly arouse race hate, what more certainly create and perpetuate a feeling of distrust between these races, than state enactments, which, in fact, proceed on the ground that colored citizens are so inferior and degraded that they cannot be allowed to sit in public coaches occupied by white citizens? . . . State enactments, regulating the enjoyment of civil rights, upon the basis of race, and cunningly devised to defeat legitimate results of the war, under the pretence of recognizing equality of rights, can have no other result than to render permanent peace impossible, and to keep alive a conflict of races, the continuance of which must do harm to all concerned. This question is not met by the suggestion that social equality cannot exist between the white and black races in this country. That argument, if it can be properly regarded as one, is scarcely worthy of consideration; for social equality no more exists between two races when traveling in a passenger coach or a public highway than when members of the same races sit by each other in a street car or in the jury box, or stand or sit with each other in a political assembly, or when they are in the same room for the purpose of having their names placed on the registry of voters, or when they approach the ballot-box in order to exercise the high privilege of voting.

There is a race so different from our own that we do not permit those belonging to it to become citizens of the United States. Persons belonging to it are, with few exceptions, absolutely excluded from our country. I allude to the Chinese race. But by the statute in question, a Chinaman can ride in the same passenger coach with white citizens of the United States, while citizens of the black race in Louisiana, many of whom, perhaps, risked their lives for the preservation of the Union, who are entitled, by law, to participate in the political control of the State and nation, who are not excluded, by law or by reason of their race, from public stations of any kind, and who have all the legal rights that belong to white citizens, are yet declared to be criminals, liable to imprisonment, if they ride in a public coach occupied by citizens of the white race. It is scarcely just to say that a colored citizen should not object to occupying a public coach assigned to his own race. He does not object, nor, perhaps, would he object to separate coaches for his race, if his rights under the law were recognized. But he objects, and ought never to cease objecting to the proposition, that citizens of the white and black races can be adjudged criminals because they sit, or claim the right to sit, in the same public coach on a public highway.

(2) A Note on the Development of Segregation in Public Schools

Although the *Plessy* case technically did not concern schools, it was to become the legal foundation for segregated schools in America. A close reading of the decision shows that its rationale is derived largely from the pre–Civil War case, *Roberts* v. *City of Boston* (1849), which upheld segregated schools in the heart of abolitionist territory. Conveniently overlooked by all the majority justices was the fact that, coming as it did before the passage of the Thirteenth and Fourteenth Amendments, the *Roberts* case should have been entitled to little or no precedential value. Whatever its justification in 1849, it could not serve as an interpretation of the Fourteenth Amendment, passed in 1868. Harlan made this point in dissent, but to no avail.[1]

Reading the *Plessy* opinion in the

---

[1]What has often not been recognized is that Harlan's strong attack on racial segregation *did not* refer to segregated schools. By implication it is possible to argue, as Chief Justice Vinson apparently did in the first hearings on the *Brown* case, that the Fourteenth Amendment, even interpreted by a sympathetic Harlan, did not reach the question of segregated schools. See S. Sidney Ulmer, "Earl Warren and the Brown Decision,"33 *Journal of Politics* (1971), 691.

light of the *Civil Rights Cases* (1883) and the *Slaughterhouse Cases* (1873), both of which interpreted the Fourteenth Amendment very strictly and narrowed the range of civil rights protections available to Negroes, it is clear that the mood of the Court, like the mood of the country generally, had shifted away from any serious concern with the condition of the Negro. One looks in vain for any discussion of the "equal" part of the "separate-but-equal" formula approved in the *Plessy* case. The Court seemed intentionally unconcerned with the operative effects of its decision. It took refuge in stating its helplessness in affecting the course of race relations and, indeed, seemed to rebuke those with the temerity to suggest that Negroes ought even to be upset by the development of the Jim Crow system. Justice Brown, strongly influenced by the contemporary sociologist, William Graham Sumner, argued that it would be hopeless to expect the Supreme Court to overcome the "natural inclination" of the races to a separate existence. Yet, as C. Vann Woodward points out in his book, *The Strange Career of Jim Crow*,[2] much of the structure of racial segregation in the South had not developed fully by 1896, and far from being impotent, the Supreme Court's decision provided an unmatched measure of support for the development of racial segregation. One cannot say with assurance that *Plessy* had the effect of increasing the scope and intensity of white efforts to circumscribe Negro rights. But whites and Negroes alike could hardly have failed to understand that by providing a formula for racial segregation and by failing even to discuss the implications of the term equality in that formula, the Court

was signalling its withdrawal from any serious effort to insure racial equality. The *Civil Rights Cases* had limited the protective scope of the Fourteenth Amendment to "state action"—that is, to discrimination by a state or its subdivisions—and *Plessy* further limited the scope of the Fourteenth Amendment by defining segregation under the separate-but-equal formula as nondiscriminatory.

The public (and private) school systems of the South became—and remained—totally segregated and unequal, and little serious attempt was made to remedy this until the 1930s. Then, the NAACP, through a series of test cases, began to chip away at the foundations of school segregation. In 1937, it won a Supreme Court ruling that a state could not escape its obligations to provide law training for qualified Negroes by providing tuition payments to an out-of-state law school. The case of *Missouri ex. rel. Gaines* v. *Canada* (1937) is also noteworthy because it was the last occasion until 1970 that a Supreme Court justice argued in favor of school segregation.

After World War II, the NAACP renewed its attack. In a case involving a Negro graduate student in education at the University of Oklahoma, the Court ruled that the university could not force its only black student to sit in a hallway adjoining the classroom in which his course was offered. Nor could it require him to sit in a specially marked-off portion of the room, behind a railing marked "Reserved for Colored." *McLaurin* v. *Oklahoma* established the principle that Negroes must be admitted to graduate schools at state universities, and that they must be treated on an equal basis while in attendance.

[2]New York: Oxford University Press, 1968 (2nd ed.).

By 1950 it became clear to most observers that the Court was in the process of considering, as the *Plessy* court had not done, the meaning of *equal* facilities. But the Court had not yet decided that separate could *never* be equal, nor had it extended its attention below the graduate, professional school level. It would not reaffirm, but neither would it deny, the validity of separate-but-equal.

The real break with the past almost came, also in 1950, in *Sweatt* v. *Painter*. Sweatt refused to register at a proposed negro law school in Texas, but instead demanded admission to the University of Texas Law School. The proposed negro law school would have had four part-time faculty members, had *ordered* 10,000 books, had no full-time librarian, and was not yet accredited. The University of Texas Law School then had a faculty of 16, a library of 650,000 books, 850 students, a *Law Review*, and was a major law school. The trial court ruled that the negro law school met the *Plessy* test of substantial equality and denied Sweatt's petition. By the time the trial had ended, the negro law school had opened, and reflecting some hasty improvements stimulated by the embarrassment of the *Sweatt* case, boasted of five full-time faculty members, 16,000 volumes, a moot court, and one alumnus. Before the Supreme Court, the NAACP argued that not only was the negro law school unequal in any measurement of its tangible assets, but that it was inherently unequal in a variety of intangibles such as reputation, quality of education, and standing in the state. The Court accepted this argument and thus further chipped away at the separate-but-equal doctrine. But the justices declined to reach the

question of the constitutionality of the *Plessy* formula since it was not necessary to do so to decide the case at hand. The handwriting was now clearly on the wall, and it was up to the NAACP to devise a strategy and produce the litigation to compel the Court to reconsider the validity of separate-but-equal; could separate *ever* be equal?

(3) Alfred H. Kelly, An Inside View of "Brown v. Board"

One day in early July 1953, I received a letter from Mr. Thurgood Marshall, general counsel of the Legal Defense and Education Fund of the National Association for the Advancement of Colored People. Would I be willing, Mr. Marshall inquired, to prepare a research paper on the intent of the framers of the 14th amendment with respect to the constitutionality of racially segregated schools?

The U.S. Supreme Court, Mr. Marshall explained, had recently heard arguments on a series of school segregation cases, four of them on appeal from the States and one of them from the Supreme Court of the District of Columbia. Instead of deciding the cases within the merits of the longstanding "separate-but-equal" rule, however, the Court had returned the cases to opposing counsel for reargument, posing to the lawyers on both sides the following questions, here somewhat paraphrased:

What had been the intent of the framers of the 14th amendment, the Court had inquired, with respect to school segregation? Had the authors of the amendment presumed that their constitutional handiwork would render

Reprinted from U. S. Senate, Committee on the Judiciary, *Hearings on the Nomination of Thurgood Marshall*, 85th Cong., 1st Sess. (1961), pp. 167–176.

*segregated schools categorically uncon-
stitutional? Or had they, as a possible
alternative, presumed that Congress
and the courts would have a discretionary power under the amendment to
strike down school segregation, either
by statute or court decision? And what
had been the understanding of the several States who ratified the amendment
with respect to its impact upon school
segregation? And assuming that segregated schools violated the 14th amendment, the court continued, was it within
the Court's authority to exercise its
equity powers to effect a gradual desegregation and thereby to reconcile by
degrees formally segregated public
schools with the requirements of the
Constitution?*

. . . It is easy to criticize the *Plessy*
opinion today, and most constitutional writers have not hesitated to do
so. One recent authority, Robert Harris, has castigated [Justice] Brown's
argument as "a compound of bad
logic, bad history, bad sociology, and
bad constitutional law, permeated
with theories of social Darwinism"
and presenting "overtones of white
racial supremacy as scientific truth."
The indictment is adequate enough
on several counts, but it ignores two
important facts: first, the *Plessy*
opinion rested on a powerful body of
specific precedent built up in long
series of cases in the State courts over
a period of more than 25 years. Second, the Court undoubtedly had
merely translated into constitutional
law the prevalent body of social
myth, institutions, and statute law as
it existed in the United States at the
end of the 19th century. The concept
of "separate but equal" had received
official validation, in school segregation alone, in more than 30 cases between 1868 and 1896. . . . Had the
Court contravened the then-pre-
vailing legal myth, it doubtless
would have found its dictum somehow flouted, circumvented and ignored. *Plessy*, in fact, was about as

valid for its time as *Brown* v. *Board* is
for ours. . . .

Plessy stood like a rock of constitutional law for almost half a century,
but by 1950 it had become apparent
that the foundations of the opinion at
long last were crumbling away under
a protracted legal assault which reflected in turn a profound revolution
in the role of the Negro in American
society. . . .

In this long series of cases from
Gaines (1938) to *Sweatt* (1950), the
Court never once hinted that the
separate-but-equal rule was itself inadequate or subject to possible constitutional assault. Technically, instead, the Court merely was now
treating with increasing seriousness
the injunction that separate facilities
must meet severe tests of equality in
order to fall inside the equal protection rule. Not once did the Court
suggest that separation itself was
prima facie evidence of inequality,
although that was undoubtedly the
ultimate implication of the path
along which it was now marching.

It was becoming increasingly apparent, in a pragmatic sense, that if
the Court were to go much further
with the legalized breakdown of
segregation, the "separate but equal"
rule itself would have to fall. And that
meant something like a revolution in
constitutional law. It would entail a
piece of judicial lawmaking which
could be justified only by a
philosophy of extreme judicial activism, and this at the hands of a
Court wherein several of the Justices
had repeatedly expressed their disapproval of judicial activism and lawmaking by Court-made fiat.

Nevertheless, if the revolution in
the Negro's legal status were to proceed much further, the attempt had
to be made. And it was for this reason
that the lawyers for the NAACP, who
had directed the long legal battle in
the courts from *Gaines* to *Sweatt*,

decided sometime after 1950 to hurl a direct legal challenge at the *Plessy* rule itself. It was, Thurgood Marshall later told me, a deliberate policy decision on his part. Certainly it was an epoch-making one. . . .

The new approach—that is, the direct attack on "separate but equal" as incompatible with equal protection—did not get far in the lower courts. When the association's lawyers used the argument in a segregation case in the Nation's Capital, here attacking segregation as inconsistent with the Civil Rights Act of 1866 and the due process clause of the fifth amendment, their analysis met blunt rejection at the hands of the Supreme Court of the District of Columbia. How was it possible, the court inquired somewhat caustically, to attach such a meaning to due process or to the Civil Rights Act when the same Congress which had passed both the Civil Rights Act and the 14th Amendment had also legislated repeatedly for the support of segregated schools in the District? It was a hard question to answer. It is still a hard question to answer, historically, if not legally. . . .

The five cases came up to the Supreme Court early in 1953 and were argued there by counsel along much the same lines as in the lower courts. Instead of handing down a decision, however, the Court handed the cases back to opposing counsel with a request for reargument on the question of the historical intent of the framers of the 14th amendment. It was at once apparent that the NAACP and its lawyers had scored a tremendous breakthrough. What the Justices' request really seemed to say, the lawyers and scholars at work on the case presently were to agree, was something like this: "we would like to dispose of the *Plessy* rule, for once and for all, as constitutionally outmoded and incompatible with the

realities of the Negro's role in contemporary American society. But we are fearfully embarrassed by the apparent historical absurdity of such an interpretation of the 14th amendment, and equally embarrassed by the obvious charge that the Court will be legislating if it simply imposes a new meaning on the amendment without regard to historical intent. Therefore, learned counsel, produce for us in this Court a plausible historical argument that will justify us in pronouncing, in solemn and awful sovereignty, that the 14th amendment properly was intended by its authors to abolish school segregation, or at least to sanction its abolition by judicial fiat. Thus fortified, we will declare segregated schools in the States to be unconstitutional as a violation of the 14th amendment. . . .

As a constitutional historian, I knew of course that the 14th amendment had evolved, in some considerable part, out of the Civil Rights Act of 1866. Accordingly, I went to work on the 1866 volumes of the Congressional Globe, reading anew the story of the debates that winter and spring for clues concerning the intent which Trumbull, Bingham, Stevens, and the congressional radicals might have had with respect to legalized segregation, and school segregation in particular. I did not really expect to find very much of anything. As any reasonably competent historian could have told the Court and the lawyers on both sides, the historical questions they had framed did not necessarily have very much relevance at all to the issues that seemed consequential then to the embattled radicals who had hammered out the Civil Rights Act and the 14th amendment that spring of 1866. . . .

Now note, if you will, the deadly implications of this situation for the NAACP's brief, at least as we have carried the argument thus far. If the Civil Rights Act, as passed, specifically had been amended so as not to abolish legalized State segregation, and if the 1st section of the 14th amendment had been passed merely to constitutionalize the Civil Rights Act, then it could hardly be argued that the intent of Congress, in submitting the 14th amendment to the States, had been to knock out legalized racial segregation in the States—in schools, in transportation, hotels, or anything else. It looked as if John W. Davis would win the historical argument hands down.

To be sure, there was a little more to the matter than the foregoing, fortunately quite a little more. In the Senate, Howard of Michigan, substituting for Fessenden in presenting the amendment to the floor, had asserted categorically that the first section, with its equal protection, privileges, immunities, and due process clauses, was intended to destroy all "class and caste legislation in the United States." Certainly that included school segregation statutes. That was hopeful language, to be seized upon eagerly and exploited for all it was worth. . . .

The paper I prepared for the September conference was not adequate by any standard. I was trying to be both historian and advocate within the same paper, and the combination, as I found out, was not a very good one. I tried to draw conclusions which were at odds with the thing which most impressed me at the time—the damning modification of the civil rights bill in the House and its apparent identity in purpose with the 14th amendment. . . .

This time a still different task awaited me. On a Thursday morning, I met Thurgood Marshall in his office, where we were joined by John Frank of the Yale Law School, a na-

tionally known lawyer and legal historian and author of a number of leading monographs on the 14th amendment. Marshall informed the two of us that . . . it would not do to get too far involved in specific historical detail with respect to framer intent and that the association's case might best be cast in very generalized terms with a deliberate avoidance of the particular. This tactic, Marshall now informed us, might get past two or three of the Justices for whom, it was clear, he entertained no very great professional regard, but it would darn well never get past Frankfurter or Douglas. "I gotta argue these cases," Thurgood said, "and if I try this approach, those fellows will shoot me down in flames." . . .

There was one optimistic element in all this, as Marshall pointed out: it was obvious, as I remarked earlier, that the Court was looking for a plausible historical answer. It needed merely to be convinced that it was possible to say that the idea of segregation might have had something to do with the amendment, that it was not utterly absurd to argue some connection, so that either a new declaration of historical intent or perhaps merely an abandonment of the old affirmation of original intent as set forth by Justice Brown in *Plessy* could be advanced without making the Justices look ridiculous. In other words, Marshall said, we didn't need to win a historical argument hands down, all we needed was a face saving draw. "0 nothin' score," Thurgood put it, "means we win the ball game." I believe, by the way, that this was a correct interpretation of the Court's mood. . . .

It was apparent at once that Marshall's theory of a "draw bout" on the question of 14th amendment history had been altogether correct. Although John W. Davis and his cohorts had counterattacked NAACP history in a brief which shrieked in outraged indignation that opposing counsel had attempted a veritable rape upon Cleo's virtue, the Court obviously had found what it wanted. Chief Justice Warren's opinion noted briefly that there was a general disagreement among opposing counsel and historians about what the amendment as of 1866 had been intended to mean, and thereupon proceeded to junk the historical approach entirely and instead to settle the question of segregation on straightout sociological ground: racial segregation in the schools, in the context of the 20th century, bred social inferiority for the Negro and must therefore be outlawed. . . .

[In order to win the Brown case, the Legal Defense Fund had two obstacles to overcome. The first was the historical meaning of the Fourteenth Amendment. The second, and equally difficult assignment, was to convince the Supreme Court that separate could *never* be equal, that segregation in the public schools, per se, had a harmful effect on Negro children. There was already an existing social science literature to support this proposition, including Gunnar Myrdal's *An American Dilemma,* published in 1944. In a further effort to convince the Court of this proposition, the Negro plaintiffs in the lower courts relied on the testimony of Dr. Kenneth Clark, a social psychologist. Clark described the "black dolls" test, which he had administered to Negro children. This test supported, if it did not independently demonstrate, the proposition that Negro children developed negative self-perceptions at an early age. But it was impossible to separate out the specific adverse of effects of *school* segregation, as opposed to the totality of a racially segregated environment. There is no evidence that the Supreme Court relied on Clark's testimony, although it did cite his work and Myrdal's book in a footnote as supporting evidence for its decision.]

(4) The School Segregation Cases

(a) *Brown* v. *Board of Education of Topeka* (1954) [*Brown I*].

+Warren, Black, Reed, Frankfurter, Douglas, Jackson, Burton, Clark, Minton

MR. CHIEF JUSTICE WARREN delivered the opinion of the Court.

These cases come to us from the States of Kansas, South Carolina, Virginia, and Delaware. They are premised on different facts and different local conditions, but a common legal question justifies their consideration together in this consolidated opinion.

In each of the cases, minors of the Negro race, through their legal representatives, seek the aid of the courts in obtaining admission to the public schools of their community on a nonsegregated basis. In each instance, they had been denied admission to schools attended by white children under laws requiring or permitting segregation according to race. This segregation was alleged to deprive the plaintiffs of the equal protection of the laws under the Fourteenth Amendment. In each of the cases other than the Delaware case, a three-judge federal district court denied relief to the plaintiffs on the so-called "separate-but-equal" doctrine announced by this Court in *Plessy* v. *Ferguson.* Under that doctrine, equality of treatment is accorded when the races are provided substantially equal facilities, even though these facilities be separate. In the Delaware case, the Supreme Court of Delaware adhered to that doctrine, but ordered that the plaintiffs be admitted to the white schools becase of their superiority to the Negro schools.

The plaintiffs contend that segregated public schools are not "equal" and cannot be made "equal," and that hence they are deprived of the equal protection of the laws. Because of the obvious importance of the question presented, the Court took jurisdiction. Argument was heard in the 1952 Term, and reargument was heard this Term on certain questions propounded by the Court.

Reargument was largely devoted to the circumstances surrounding the adoption of the Fourteenth Amendment in 1868. It covered exhaustively consideration of the Amendment in Congress, ratification by the states, then existing practices in racial segregation, and the views of proponents and opponents of the Amendment. This discussion and our own investigation convince us that, although these sources cast some light, it is not enough to resolve the problem with which we are faced. At best, they are inconclusive. The most avid proponents of the post-War Amendments undoubtedly intended them to remove all legal distinctions among "all persons born or naturalized in the United States." Their opponents, just as certainly, were antagonistic to both the letter and the spirit of the Amendments and wished them to have the most limited effect. What others in Congress and the state legislatures had in mind cannot be determined with any degree of certainty.

An additional reason for the inconclusive nature of the Amendment's history, with respect to segregated schools, is the status of public education at that time. In the South, the movement toward free common schools, supported by general taxation, had not yet taken hold. Education of white children was largely in the hands of private groups. Education of Negroes was almost non-existent, and practically all of the race were illiterate. In fact, any education of Negroes was forbidden by law in some states. Today, in contrast, many Negroes have achieved outstanding success in the arts and sciences as well as in the business and professional world. It is true that public school education at the time of the Amendment had advanced further in the North, but the effect of the Amendment on Northern States was generally ignored in the congressional debates. Even in the North, the conditions of public education did not approximate those existing today. The curriculum was usually rudimentary; ungraded schools were common in rural areas; the school term was but three months a year in many states; and compulsory school attendance was virtually unknown. As a consequence, it is not surprising that there should be so little in the history of the Fourteenth Amendment relating to its intended effect on public education.

In the first cases in this Court construing the Fourteenth Amendment, decided shortly after its adoption, the Court interpreted it as proscribing all state-imposed discriminations against the Negro race. The doctrine of "separate but equal" did not make its appearance in this Court until 1896 in the case of *Plessy* v. *Ferguson* involving not education but transportation. American courts have since labored with the doctrine for over half a century. In this Court, there have been six cases involving the "separate but equal" doctrine in the field of public education. In *Cumming* v. *County Board of Education* and *Gong Lum* v. *Rice* the validity of the doctrine itself was not challenged. In more recent cases, all on the graduate school level, inequality was found in that specific benefits enjoyed by white students were denied to Negro students of the same educational qualifications. In none of these cases was it necessary to re-examine the doctrine to grant relief to the Negro plaintiff. And in *Sweatt* v. *Painter* the Court expressly reserved decision on the question whether *Plessy* v. *Ferguson* should be held inapplicable to public education.

In the instant cases, that question is directly presented. Here, unlike *Sweatt* v. *Painter,* there are findings below that the Negro and white schools involved have been equalized, or are being equalized, with respect to buildings, curricula, qualifications and salaries of teachers, and other "tangible" factors. Our decision, therefore, cannot turn on merely a comparison of these tangible factors in the Negro and white schools involved in each of the cases. We must look instead to the effect of segregation itself on public education.

In approaching this problem, we cannot turn the clock back to 1868 when the Amendment was adopted, or even to 1896 when *Plessy* v. *Ferguson* was written. We must consider public education in the light of its full development and its present place in American life throughout the Nation. Only in this way can it be determined if segregation in public schools deprives these plaintiffs of the equal protection of the laws.

Today, education is perhaps the most important function of state and local governments. Compulsory school attendance laws and the great expenditures for education both demonstrate our recognition of the importance of education to our democratic society. It is required in the performance of our most basic public responsibilities, even service in the armed forces. It is the very founda-tion of good citizenship. Today it is a principal instrument in awakening the child to cultural values, in preparing him for later professional training, and in helping him to adjust normally to his environment. In these days, it is doubtful that any child may reasonably be expected to succeed in life if he is denied the opportunity of an education. Such an opportunity, where the state has undertaken to provide it, is a right which must be made available to all on equal terms.

We come then to the question presented: Does segregation of children in public schools solely on the basis of race, even though the physical facilities and other "tangible" factors may be equal, deprive the children of the minority group of equal educational opportunities? We believe that it does.

In *Sweatt* v. *Painter,* in finding that a segregated law school for Negroes could not provide them equal educational opportunities, this Court relied in large part on "those qualities which are incapable of objective measurement but which make for greatness in a law school." In *McLaurin* v. *Oklahoma State Regents* the Court, in requiring that a Negro admitted to a white graduate school be treated like all other students, again resorted to intangible considerations: ". . . his ability to study, to engage in discussions and exchange views with other students, and, in general, to learn his profession." Such considerations apply with added force to children in grade and high schools. To separate them from others of similar age and qualifications solely because of their race generates a feeling of inferiority as to their status in the community that may affect their hearts and minds in a way unlikely ever to be undone. The effect of this separation on their educational opportunities was well stated by a finding in the Kansas case by a court which nevertheless felt compelled to rule against the Negro plaintiffs:

Segregation of white and colored chil̖dren in public schools has a detrimental effect upon the colored children. The impact is greater when it has the sanction of the law; for the policy of separating the races is usually interpreted as denoting the inferiority of the negro group. A sense of inferiority affects the motivation of a child to learn. Segregation with the sanction of law, therefore, has a tendency to [retard] the educational and mental development of negro children and to deprive them of some of the benefits they would receive in a racial[ly] integrated school system.

Whatever may have been the extent of psychological knowledge at the time of *Plessy* v. *Ferguson*, this finding is amply supported by modern authority. Any language in *Plessy* v. *Ferguson* contrary to this finding is rejected.

We conclude that in the field of public education the doctrine of "separate but equal" has no place. Separate educational facilities are inherently unequal. Therefore, we hold that the plaintiffs and others similarly situated for whom the actions have been brought are, by reason of the segregation complained of, deprived of the equal protection of the laws guaranteed by the Fourteenth Amendment. This disposition makes unnecessary any discussion whether such segregation also violates the Due Process Clause of the Fourteenth Amendment.

Because these are class actions, because of the wide applicability of this decision, and because of the great variety of local conditions, the formulation of decrees in these cases presents problems of considerable complexity. On reargument, the consideration of appropriate relief was necessarily subordinated to the primary question—the constitutionality of segregation in public education. We have now announced that such segregation is a denial of the equal protection of the laws. In order that we may have the full assistance of the parties in formulating decrees, the cases will be restored to the docket, and the parties are requested to present further argument on Questions 4 and 5 previously propounded by the Court for the reargument this Term. The Attorney General of the United States is again invited to participate. The Attorneys General of the states requiring or permitting segregation in public education will also be permitted to appear as *amici curiae* upon request to do so by September 15, 1954, and submission of briefs by October 1, 1954.

(b) *Bolling v. Sharpe (1954)*

+Warren, Black, Reed, Frankfurter, Douglas, Jackson, Burton, Clark, Minton

MR. CHIEF JUSTICE WARREN delivered the opinion of the Court.

This case challenges the validity of segregation in the public schools of the District of Columbia. The petitioners, minors of the Negro race, allege that such segregation deprives them of due process of law under the Fifth Amendment. They were refused admission to a public school attended by white children solely because of their race. They sought the aid of the District Court for the District of Columbia in obtaining admission. That court dismissed their complaint. The Court granted a writ of certiorari before judgment in the Court of Appeals because of the importance of the constitutional question presented.

We have this day held that the Equal Protection Clause of the Fourteenth Amendment prohibits the states from maintaining racially segregated public schools. The legal problem in the District of Columbia is somewhat different, however. The Fifth Amendment, which is applicable in the District of Columbia, does not contain an equal protection clause as does the Fourteenth Amendment which applies only to the states. But the concepts of equal protection and due process, both stemming from our American ideal of fairness, are not mutually exclusive. The "equal protection of the laws" is a more explicit safeguard of prohibited unfairness than "due process of law," and, therefore, we do not imply that the two are always interchangeable phrases. But, as this Court has recognized, discrimination may be so unjustifiable as to be violative of due process.

Classifications based solely upon race must be scrutinized with particular care, since they are contrary to our traditions and hence constitutionally suspect. As long ago as 1896, this Court declared the principle "that the Constitution of the United States, in its present form, forbids, so far as civil and political rights are concerned, discrimination by the General Government, or by the States, against any citizen because of his race." And in *Buchanan* v. *Warley* the Court held that a statute which limited the right of a property owner to convey his property to a person of another race was, as an unreasonable discrimination, a denial of due process of law.

Although the Court has not assumed to define "liberty" with any great precision, that term is not confined to mere freedom from bodily restraint. Liberty under law extends to the full range of conduct which the individual is free to pursue, and it cannot be restricted except for a proper governmental objective. Segregation in public education is not reasonably related to any proper governmental objective, and thus it imposes on Negro children of the District of Columbia a burden that constitutes an arbitrary deprivation of their liberty in violation of the Due Process Clause.

In view of our decision that the Constitution prohibits the states from maintaining racially segregated public schools, it would be unthinkable that the same Constitution would impose a lesser duty on the Federal Government. We hold that racial segregation in the public schools of the District of Columbia is a denial of the due process of law guaranteed by the Fifth Amendment to the Constitution.

For the reasons set out in *Brown* v. *Board of Education*, this case will be restored to the docket for reargument on Question 4 and 5 previously propounded by the Court.

(c) *Brown* v. *Board of Education of Topeka (1955)* [*Brown II*].

+Warren, Black, Reed, Frankfurter, Douglas, Burton, Minton, Clark, Harlan

MR. CHIEF JUSTICE WARREN delivered the opinion of the Court.

These cases were decided on May 17, 1954. The opinions of that date, declaring the fundamental principle that racial discrimination in public education is unconstitutional, are incorporated herein by reference. All provisions of federal, state, or local law requiring or permitting such discrimination must yield to this principle. There remains for consideration the manner in which relief is to be accorded.

Because these cases arose under different local conditions and their disposition will involve a variety of local problems, we requested further argument on the question of relief. In view of the nationwide importance of the decision, we invited the Attorney General of the United States and the Attorneys General of all states requiring or permitting racial discrimination in public education to present their views on that question. The parties, the United States, and the States of Florida, North Carolina, Arkansas, Oklahoma, Maryland, and Texas filed briefs and participated in the oral argument.

These presentations were informative and helpful to the Court in its consideration of the complexities arising from the transition to a system of public education freed of racial discrimination. The presentations also demonstrated that substantial steps to eliminate racial discrimination in public schools have already been taken, not only in some of the communities in which these cases arose, but in some of the states appearing as *amici curiae*, and in other states as well. Substantial progress has been made in the District of Columbia and in the communities in Kansas and Delaware involved in this litigation. The defendants in the cases coming to us from South Carolina and Virginia are awaiting the decisions of this Court concerning relief.

Full implementation of these constitutional principles may require solution of varied local school problems. School authorities have the primary responsibility for elucidating, assessing, and solving these problems; courts will have to consider whether the action of school authorities constitutes good faith implementation of the governing constitutional principles. Because of their proximity to local conditions and the possible need for further hearings, the courts which originally heard these cases can best perform this judicial appraisal. Accordingly, we believe it appropriate to remand the cases to those courts.

In fashioning and effectuating the decrees, the courts will be guided by equitable principles. Traditionally, equity has been characterized by a practical flexibility in shaping its remedies and by a facility for adjusting and reconciling public and private needs. These cases call for the exercise of these traditional attributes of equity power. At stake is the personal interest of the plaintiffs in admission to public schools as soon as practicable on a nondiscriminatory basis. To effectuate this interest may call for elimination of a variety of obstacles in making the transition to school systems operated in accordance with the constitutional principles set forth in our May 17, 1954, decision. Courts of equity may properly take into account the public interest in the elimination of such obstacles in a systematic and effective manner. But it should go without saying that the vitality of these constitutional principles cannot be allowed to yield simply because of disagreement with them.

While giving weight to these public and private considerations, the courts will require that the defendants make a prompt and reasonable start toward full compliance with our May 17, 1954 ruling. Once such a start has been made, the courts may find that additional time is necessary to carry out the ruling in an effective manner. The burden rests upon the defendants to establish that such time is necessary in the public interest and is consistent with good faith compliance at the earliest practicable date. To that end, the courts may consider problems related to administration, arising from the physical condition of the school plant, the school transportation system, personnel, revision of school districts and attendance areas into compact units to achieve a system of determining admission to the public schools on a nonracial basis, and revision of local laws and regulations which may be necessary in solving the foregoing problems. They will also consider the adequacy of any plans the defendants may propose to meet these problems and to effectuate a transition to a racially nondiscriminatory school system. During this period of transition, the courts will retain jurisdiction of these cases.

The judgments below, except that in the Delaware case, are accordingly reversed and the cases are remanded to the District Courts to take such proceedings and enter such orders and decrees consistent with this opinion as are necessary and proper to admit to public schools on a racially nondiscriminatory basis with all deliberate speed the parties to these cases. The judgment in the Delaware case—ordering the immediate admission of the plaintiffs to schools previously attended only by white children—is affirmed on the basis of the principles stated in our May 17, 1954, opinion, but the case is remanded to the Supreme Court of Delaware for such further proceedings as the Court may deem necessary in light of this opinion.

[The *Brown I* decision was unanimous, and there was but a single opinion for the entire Court, written by the Chief Justice. The opinion is short and to the point, more of a statement of conclusions than an attempt at logical persuasion. It has frequently been criticized as an inadequate and indeed an opaque document. To Southerners and to many political conservatives, it was an illegal decision, a self-evident piece of "judicial legislation," in which nine justices in Washington were substituting their own views for those of duly elected state legislatures and probably most white citizens in an entire region of the country. Although the decision itself was welcomed elsewhere in the country and hailed as the second Emancipation Proclamation, it was also regarded as a weak decision, one that failed to spell out in sufficient detail what exactly was required. *Brown II,* conversely, was regarded by Southern critics as somewhat more reasonable; it allayed some of their fears that schools would have to be desegregated immediately. To those who supported the principles of *Brown I,* however, *Brown II* seemed to concede too much discretion to southern federal judges and white-dominated school boards.

The most logical explanation of why the opinion in this benchmark case was unsatisfactory to almost everyone is that it was the product of compromise among the justices. In order to secure a unanimous court, Chief Justice Warren, it was believed, had to make concessions on a number of substantive issues. One major concession may have been deferring consideration of the implementation issue, resulting in the weak implementation order that was the product of *Brown II.* Many thought that when Warren assumed the position of Chief Justice, only a minority or, at best, a bare majority of the justices favored outlawing segregation in the public schools.

Recent evidence suggests, in part to the contrary, that Warren inherited a majority of justices who *favored* outlawing racial segregation, at least in principle, but who differed on the intensity of their commitment to that goal and on the best strategy for achieving it. The evidence, much of which comes from the private papers and conference notes of Justice Harold Burton, suggests that whatever the exact breakdown of opinion on the Court when Warren became Chief Justice, his tactics in conference and his straightforward opinion *either* molded or kept a unanimous Court.[1] That Warren believed unanimity to be important was demonstrated in 1958, when each justice was

[1]S. Sidney Ulmer, "Earl Warren and the Brown Decision," **33** *Journal of Politics* (1971), 688–702. See also Richard Kluger, *Simple Justice* (New York: Vintage Books, 1975), pp. 678–699.

named as the coauthor of the opinion in *Cooper* v. *Aaron* (see pp. 121–125, *supra*) and care was taken to note that each justice appointed after 1955 was in agreement with the *Brown I* decision.]

(5) Earl Warren, The Day the Supreme Court Banned School Segregation

. . . In the entire 16 years that I presided as the Chief Justice of the Supreme court, I never heard an unauthorized voice raised during a session.

Rarely, in fact, did there appear to be even an air of tension in the courtroom, regardless of the importance of the case being argued or reported.

It was very different, however, on May 17, 1954.

That was the day when the historic school segregation case of *Brown* v. *Board of Education* was reported to an expectant American public. Seventeen of our states, by their own laws, had racially segregated public schools. A number of others had de facto segregation because of the rapid growth of ghettos which concentrated minority groups in the larger cities. The *Brown* case, when it came before the Supreme Court, challenged such discrimination in public schools as being unconstitutional.

For weeks before the announcement of our decision, the courtroom had been jammed with people; anticipation had been mounting, and political writers had been hazarding all kinds of guesses as to why the opinion had been delayed from Dec. 8, 1953, when the case had been argued, until this momentous day in May of the following year.

Contrary to speculations in the press, there had not been a division of opinion expressed on the Court at any time. At the weekly conference after arguments in the case, the members, conscious of its gravity and far-reaching effects, decided not to put the case to a vote until we had thoroughly explored the implications of any decision. As a result, we discussed all sides dispassionately week after week, testing arguments of counsel, suggesting various approaches, and at time acting as "devil's advocates" in certain phases of the case, but not stating our final decisions until February of 1954.

At that time we voted unanimously among ourselves to declare racially segregated public schools to be unconstitutional. . . .

There was not even vigorous argument. Our decision represented the judgment of every justice independently arrived at in the finest collegiate tradition. In my entire public career, I have never seen a group of men more conscious of the seriousness of a situation, more intent upon resolving it with as little disruption as possible, or with a greater desire for unanimity. To show how desirous we all were to present a united front, Justice Robert Jackson, who had been in the hospital for a month or so as the result of a heart attack, surprised us all by insisting on dressing and coming to the Court for the announcement. . . .

As we justices marched into the courtroom on that day, there was a tenseness that I have not seen equaled before or since. When I announced that I was about to report the judgment and opinion of the Court in *Brown* v. *Board of Education of Topeka, Kan.*, there was a general shifting of positions in the crowded room and a rapt attention to my words. It was not a long opinion, for I had written it so it could be pub-

Reprinted from *The Memoirs of Chief Justice Earl Warren* (Garden City, N.Y.: Doubleday, 1977), pp. 1–4, 287–292.

lished in the daily press throughout the nation without taking too much space. This enabled the public to have our entire reasoning instead of a few excerpts from a lengthier document.

In the middle of the opinion, I read:

"We come then to the question presented: Does segregation of children in public schools solely on the basis of race, even though the physical facilities and other tangible factors may be equal, deprive the children of the minority group of equal educational opportunities? We unanimously believe that it does."

When the word "unanimously" was spoken, a wave of emotion swept the room; no words or intentional movement, yet a distinct emotional manifestation that defies description.

Some of it undoubtedly was occasioned by relief that the case was decided in such a manner; some of it because of disagreement with the result; but I am sure that much of it stemmed from the word "unanimously," which flew in the face of previous news stories about dissension on the Court with regard to this case.

I assume this because for weeks thereafter people would phone the clerk's office and demand to see the dissenting opinion. When informed that the decision was unanimous and, therefore, there could be no dissenting opinion, they would demand to know, "By what right is the dissenting opinion withheld?" or "Who outlawed dissenting opinions?"

Much has been said and written concerning this unanimity. I have been praised by many who favor the opinion for bringing it about, and I have been condemned by others who object to it. . . . But the real credit for achieving unanimity, in my opinion, should go to the three justices who were born and reared in that part of the nation where segregation was a way of life and where everyone knew

the greatest emotional opposition to the decision would be forthcoming. They were Justices Hugo L. Black of Alabama, Stanley F. Reed of Kentucky, and Tom C. Clark of Texas. The others of us, while enthusiastic in our adherence to the decision and fervent in our desire for unanimity, were not in danger of being faced with animosity and harassment in our home states because of centuries-old patterns of life.

Incidentally, this was the genesis of the phrase "The Warren Court." It was coined not as a symbol of achievement or endearment, but as an indication of scorn by those who resented the decision. Since that time, it has been used in various senses. I say this advisedly because, shortly after *Brown*, Southern congressmen signed and introduced into the Congressional Record the so-called "Southern Manifesto," pledging that they would use every means at their command to overcome the *Brown* decision. Several of them told me personally that I had "stabbed them in the back." I know of no reason why they should have thought me ever to have been in favor of segregation in the first place. As far as I am aware, there was nothing in my career that would convey such an impression. I had been born and reared in California where there was no accepted policy of school segregation. I had attended public schools and the University of California, and had sat in classrooms with blacks and members of almost every minority group. I never gave it a second thought.

. . .

In the *Brown* decision, we decided only that the practice of segregating children in public schools solely because of their race was unconstitutional. This left other questions to be answered. For instance, could plaintiffs bring court actions as *class ac-*

tions for all who were similarly situated or should persons actually joining in the action be entitled to relief only for themselves? What court should determine the decree in each case? For what reason could there or could there not be any delay in obeying the Court's mandate and to what extent? . . .

. . .

. . .Recognizing [in *Brown II*] that because full application of these constitutional principles might require solution of a wide variety of local school desegregation problems, school authorities were given the primary responsibility. . . . However it was stipulated that courts would ultimately have to consider whether the action of school authorities constituted implementation in good faith of the governing constitutional principles.

We discussed at great length in conference whether the Supreme Court should make the factual determinations in such cases or whether they should be left to the courts below, deciding finally to leave them to the latter, subject, of course, to our review, because they were getting closer to the problems involved, and were in a better position to engage meaningfully in the fact-finding process. As guidelines for them, we directed that neither local law nor custom should be permitted to interfere with the establishment of an integrated school system, and that the process of achieving it should be carried out with "all deliberate speed"—a phrase which has been much discussed by those who are of the opinion that desegregation has not proceeded with as much celerity as might have been expected. These people argued that the Supreme Court should merely have directed the school districts to admit Brown and the other plaintiffs to the schools

to which they sought admission, in the belief this would have quickly ended the litigation. This theory, however, overlooks the complexity of our federal system, the time it takes controversial litigation to proceed through the hierarchy of courts to the Supreme Court, the fact that the administration of the public school system is a state and local function so long as it does not contravene constitutional principles, that each state has its own system with different relationships between state and local government and that the relationship can be changed at will by the state government if there should be a determination to bypass or defeat the decision of the Supreme Court. Evidence that such evasion would occur came immediately in some of the resolutions and laws initiated by certain states. In this, they were encouraged by the so-called Southern Manifesto, signed by over a hundred Southern representatives and senators in the Congress of the United States. It urged all such states to defy the Supreme Court decision as being against their way of life and their "good" race relations, and to use "all lawful means" to make the decision ineffective. So reinforcing was this Manifesto to Southern defiance that the doctrine of "Nullification"—first advanced by John C. Calhoun of South Carolina, discredited more than a century before and made forever inapplicable by the Civil War Amendments—was revived by Southern governors, legislators, and candidates there for public office. The doctrine, in simple terms, argued that states have the right to declare null and void and to set aside in practice any law of the federal government which violates their voluntary compact embodied in the United States Constitution. The doctrine, of course, did not prevail, but the delay and bitterness occasioned by it caused inestimable damage to the extension of equal rights to citizens of every race, color, or creed as mandated by the Fourteenth Amendment.

With courage drawn from the "Southern Manifesto" together with oft-repeated congressional speeches and statements to the effect that no nine honest men could possibly have come to the conclusion reached by the Court in *Brown* v. *Board of Education*, excited and racist-minded public officials and candidates for office proposed and enacted every obstacle they could devise to thwart the Court's decision. This was aggravated by the fact that no word of support for the decision emanated from the White House. The most that came from high officials in the Administration was to the effect that they could not be blamed for anything done to enforce desegregation in education because it was the Supreme Court, not the Administration, that determined desegregation to be the law, and the executive branch of the government is required to enforce the law as interpreted by the Supreme Court. Bernard Shanley, the personal counsel of the President, in an effort to allay Southern animosity against the Administration, was reported in the press to have said in a speech that the *Brown* case had set race relations in the South back by a quarter of a century. The aphorism (dear to the hearts of those who are insensitive to the rights of minority groups) that discrimination cannot be eliminated by laws, but only by the hearts of people, also emanated from the White House.

A few years later, Gov. George Wallace was emboldened to stand at the entrance to the University of Alabama, and, in the face of the Deputy Attorney General of the United States, who had read to him the order of a United States district judge directing the university to admit a black student, shouted in defiance, "Segregation in the past, segregation today, segregation forever."

The Court expected some resistance from the South. But I doubt if any of us expected as much as we got. Nor did I believe that there would develop in the Republican Party, which freed the slaves through the Civil War and the 13th Amendment and granted them all the attributes of citizenship through the 14th and 15th amendments, a Southern strategy which had for its purpose a restriction of such rights in order to capture the electors of those states and achieve the presidency. . . . And I still believe that much of our racial strife could have been avoided if President Eisenhower had at least observed that our country is dedicated to the principle that . . . "We hold these Truths to be self-evident, that all Men are created equal, that they are endowed by their Creator with certain unalienable Rights, that among these are Life, Liberty and the Pursuit of Happiness."

With his popularity, if Eisenhower had said that black children were still being discriminated against long after the adoption of the 13th, 14th and 15th amendments, that the Supreme Court of the land had now declared it unconstitutional to continue such cruel practices, and that it should be the duty of every good citizen to help rectify more than 80 years of wrong-doing by honoring that decision—if he had said something to this effect, we would have been relieved, in my opinion, of many of the racial problems which have continued to plague us. But he never even stated that he thought the decision was right until after he had left the White House.

I have always believed that President Eisenhower resented our decision in *Brown* v. *Board of Education* and its progeny. Influencing this belief, among other things, is an incident that occurred shortly before the opinion was announced. The President had a program for discussing problems with groups of people at occasional White House dinners. When the *Brown* case was under submission, he invited me to one of them. I wondered why I should be invited because the dinners were political in nature, and there was no place for me in such discussions. But one does not often decline an invitation from the President to the White House, and I accepted. There were several people present at this particular one. I was the ranking guest, and as such sat at the right of the President and within speaking distance of John W. Davis, the counsel for the segregation states. During the dinner, the President went to considerable lengths to tell me what a great man Mr. Davis was. At the conclusion of the meal, in accordance with custom, we filed out of the dining room in another room where coffee and an after dinner drink were served. The President, of course, precedes, and on this occasion he took me by the arm, as we walked along, speaking of the Southern states in the segregation cases, he said, "These are not bad people. All they are concerned about is to see that their sweet little girls are not required to sit in school alongside some big overgrown Negroes."

Fortunately, by that time, others had filed into the room, so it was not necessary for me to reply. Shortly thereafter the *Brown* case was decided, and with it went our cordial relations. While Nina and I were occasionally invited to the White House after the decision for protocol reasons

when some foreign dignitary was being entertained or were invited to some foreign embassy for a reciprocal honoring of the President, I can recall few conversations that went beyond a polite "Good evening, Mr. President" and "Good evening, Mr. Chief Justice."

. . .

(6) Cooper v. Aaron (1958)

[See Part One, Chapter Two, pp 121–125.]

(7) Green v. School Board of New Kent County (1968)

+Warren, Black, Douglas, Harlan, Brennan, Stewart, White, Fortas, Marshall

[The southern response to *Brown* ranged from massive resistance to outright defiance. The decision was condemned as an invasion of states' rights and branded by some as part of a communist conspiracy. The successful gubernatorial candidate in Georgia in the 1954 elections promised that "Come hell or high water, races will not be mixed in Georgia schools."[1] All the senators and congressmen from the southern states signed the "Southern Manifesto" (1956), a declaration of constitutional principles that challenged the right of the Supreme Court to overturn the separate-but-equal doctrine. And the legislature of Alabama passed a nullification ordinance which held that the Supreme Court's decision was not binding on that state and pledged "to take all appropriate measures honorably and constitutionally available to us, to avoid this illegal encroachment upon our rights. . . ."

Beneath the level of rhetoric, a variety of techniques were devised to avoid complying with the Court's desegregation order. These techniques, which were collectively referred to as "massive resistance," included tuition grants to children who transferred out of the public schools, plans to convert some public schools to private schools, and various kinds of pupil placement laws that usually allowed parents of

---

[1]Benjamin Muse, *Ten Years of Prelude: The Story of Integration Since the Supreme Court's 1954 Decision* (New York: Viking, 1964), p. 24.

all children a "free choice" of schools. In some states, the use of public funds to desegregate schools was made a criminal offense, and some states provided that *all* schools would close if even a single school were desegregated in the state. In Prince Edward County, Virginia, federal court orders to desegregate were met with the outright *abolition* of the public schools, along with the payment of tuition grants to all children. In practice, however, the only private schools available were open only to white children. Black children had no such opportunities, and the availability of tuition grants was meaningless; most went without schooling for nearly four years. President Kennedy was prompted to remark that only in North Korea, Cambodia, North Vietnam, and Prince Edward County were children denied the right to attend school. Eventually, a free school was set up for the black children.

Attempts to desegregate schools in the Deep South thus foundered on massive resistance. The first major constitutional crisis occurred in Little Rock, Arkansas, in the case of *Cooper* v. *Aaron* (1958). The next occasion for Supreme Court intervention arose out of the Prince Edward County situation. A federal district court had held, in the course of protracted litigation, that the public schools of the county could not be closed to avoid complying with the *Brown* decision. The Court of Appeals reversed the decision, holding that the district court should have abstained from deciding the case until the state courts could determine the validity of the closing of the schools in one county. This decision was reversed by the Supreme Court in *Griffin* v. *Prince Edward County School Board* (1964). Justice Black's opinion noted that the school desegregation litigation in Prince Edward County had begun in 1951, that indeed it had been one of the cases decided by the Supreme Court in *Brown,* and that all of the original plaintiffs had long passed school age. "There has been entirely too much deliberation and not enough speed," Justice Black wrote. And he continued: "Whatever non-racial grounds might support a state's allowing a

county to abandon public schools, the object must be a constitutional one, and grounds of race and opposition to desegregation do not qualify as constitutional."

By 1964, there had been considerable desegregation in the border states, but still almost none in the Deep South. In the 1963–1964 school year, only 0.05 percent of black children in Georgia were attending white schools.[2] Even the Supreme Court's decision in the *Griffin* case, which inevitably meant further litigation, was unlikely to hasten the pace substantially. Furthermore, as Rodgers and Bullock have noted, the financial burden on black parents and on the Legal Defense Fund and other groups supporting them was extremely heavy. They simply did not have the resources to effectively combat the massive resistance program.[3]

Passage of the Civil Rights Act of 1964 offered the promise of assistance from the federal government. The attorney general was authorized to sue noncomplying school districts directly on behalf of black parents and children if there was cause to believe they were unable to obtain a proper legal remedy. The attorney general was also authorized to join with private plaintiffs in suits alleging deprivation of equal rights.

Most important, as it turned out, was Title VI of the act, which prohibited discrimination in federally funded programs and directed all federal agencies and departments to withhold financial assistance from those programs that practiced racial discrimination. Ironically, amidst the great debates in Congress and throughout the country over the constitutionality of the Civil Rights Act of 1964, there was little debate about, and little expressed opposition to, Title VI. Most of the attention was focused on Title II, which prohibited discrimination in public accommodations. The inattention to Title VI, especially to its implications for school desegregation, was partly the result of the relatively small federal subsidies then going to southern schools. However, the Federal Aid to Education Act of 1965 significantly increased

---

[2]Harrell R. Rodgers, Jr., and Charles S. Bullock III, *Coercion to Compliance* (Lexington, Mass.: Lexington Books, 1976), p. 14.
[3]Ibid., p. 15.

those subsidies and hence the impact and importance of Title VI for school desegregation.

Pursuant to Title VI, the Department of Health, Education and Welfare issued a set of guidelines to determine the continued eligibility of elementary and secondary school systems for federal aid. These became known as the "HEW Guidelines." A school system would satisfy the guidelines if it were under a final federal court desegregation order and gave evidence of complying with that order or if it submitted a plan for desegregation acceptable to the commissioner of education.

Under the guidelines, the "freedom of choice" plan was most frequently selected. An acceptable plan provided for an annual choice to be made by every student regarding the school he or she wished to attend, with adequate notice given to parents before the choice was to be made. Furthermore, the school district had the burden of demonstrating that the plan was actually working, that is, that the dual school system was being eliminated. As further guides to the elimination of dual systems, certain percentage expectations were introduced. If during the first year (1965 to 1966) 8 to 9 percent transferred from segregated schools, then double that amount would be expected the following year; if only 4 to 5 percent transferred, then triple that amount would be expected in 1966 to 1967, and so on. If the commissioner determined that the plan was "not working," he could require either additional steps or that an alternate plan be adopted. The guidelines also required desegregation of faculty and staff and the closing of small and inferior Negro schools.

The first major challenge to the guidelines was rejected by the Court of Appeals for the Fifth Circuit (*United States* v. *Jefferson County Board of Education*, 1966), and certiorari was denied by the Supreme Court. The circuit court upheld the guidelines as substantially comparable to policies being enforced by the federal courts and capable of faster and more efficient enforcement through administrative sanctions. It found that under existing desegregation plans in the districts involved in the case, only 0.019 percent of the Negro children attended formerly white schools, and there was no faculty desegregation at all. In the 1963–1964 school year, in all eleven states of the Confederacy,

only 1.17 percent of the Negro students attended nominally integrated schools. Under the first year of operation under the guidelines, this figure reached 6 percent, although the states of the Deep South still had less than 1 percent of their Negro students attending integrated schools.

In commenting on the reasons for the slow pace, the circuit court took notice of the local pressures on school and elected officials, on the inadequacies and slowness of case-by-case development of school guidelines in the courts, and the lack of effective sanctions open to judges for enforcing desegregation.

The major constitutional attack contended that the guidelines required "integration," whereas the *Brown* decision had only forbidden discrimination. But the court rejected this interpretation, holding instead that the states had an affirmative duty to bring about integrated, unitary school systems. It recognized that "it is not enough for school authorities to offer Negro children the opportunity to attend formerly all-white schools. The necessity of overcoming the effects of the dual school system in this circuit requires integration of faculties, facilities and activities, as well as students. . . . Freedom of choice is not a goal in itself. It is a means to an end."]

MR. JUSTICE BRENNAN delivered the opinion of the Court.

. . . The question for decision is whether, under all the circumstances here, respondent School Board's adoption of a "freedom-of-choice" plan which allows a pupil to choose his own public school constitutes adequate compliance with the Board's responsibility "to achieve a system of determining admission to the public schools on a non-racial basis. . . ."

Petitioners brought this action in March 1965 seeking injunctive relief against respondent's continued maintenance of an alleged racially segregated school system. New Kent County is a rural county in Eastern Virginia. About one-half of its population of some 4,500 are Negroes. There is no residential segregation in

the county; persons of both races reside throughout. . . . [T]he District
Court found that the "school system
serves approximately 1,300 pupils, of
which 740 are Negro and 550 are
white. The School Board operates one
white combined elementary and high
school and one Negro combined
elementary and high school. There
are no attendance zones. Each school
serves the entire county. The record
indicates that 21 school buses . . .
travel overlapping routes throughout
the county to transport pupils to and
from the two schools.

The segregated system was initially established and maintained
under the compulsion of Virginia
constitutional and statutory provisions mandating racial segregation
in public education. . . . These provisions were held to violate the Federal
Constitution in *Davis* v. *County
School Board of Prince Edward
County*, decided with *Brown* v.
Board of Education. . . . The respondent School Board continued the
segregated operation of the system
after the *Brown* decisions, presumably on the authority of several statutes enacted by Virginia in resistance to those decisions. Some of
these statutes were held to be unconstitutional on their face or as applied.
One statute, the Pupil Placement Act
. . . not repealed until 1966, divested
local boards of authority to assign
children to particular schools and
placed that authority in a State Pupil
Placement Board. Under that Act
children were each year automatically reassigned to the school previously attended unless upon their application the State Board assigned
them to another school; students
seeking enrollment for the first time
were also assigned at the discretion
of the State Board. To September,
1964, no Negro pupil had applied for
admission to the [white] school under
this statute and no white pupil had

applied for admission to the [Negro]
school. . . .

The pattern of separate "white"
and "Negro" schools in the New Kent
County school system established
under compulsion of state laws is
precisely the pattern of segregation to
which *Brown I* and *Brown II* were
particularly addressed, and which
Brown I declared unconstitutionally
denied Negro school children equal
protection of the laws. Racial identification of the system's schools was
complete, extending not just to the
composition of student bodies at the
two schools but to every facet of
school operation—faculty, staff,
transportation, extracurricular activities and facilities. In short, the
State, acting through the local school
board and school officials, organized
and operated a dual system, part
"white" and part "Negro." . . .

It is of course true that for the time
immediately after *Brown II* the concern was with making an initial
break in a long-established pattern of
excluding Negro children from
schools attended by white children.
The principal focus was on obtaining
for those Negro children courageous
enough to break with tradition a
place in the "white" schools. . . .
Under *Brown II* that immediate goal
was only the first step, however. The
transition to a unitary, nonracial system of public education was and is
the ultimate end to be brought about;
it was because of the "complexities
arising from the transition to a system of public education freed of racial discrimination" that we provided
for "all deliberate speed" in the implementation of the principles of
Brown I. . . . Thus we recognized the
task would necessarily involve solutions of "varied local school problems." . . .

It is against this background that
13 years after *Brown II* commanded
the abolition of dual systems we must

measure the effectiveness of respondent School Board's "freedom-of-choice" plan to achieve that end. The School Board contends that it has fully discharged its obligation by adopting a plan by which every student, regardless of race, may "freely" choose the school he will attend. The Board attempts to cast the issue in its broadest form by arguing that its "freedom-of-choice" plan may be faulted only by reading the Fourteenth Amendment as universally requiring "compulsory integration," a reading it insists the wording of the Amendment will not support. But that argument ignores the thrust of *Brown II*. In the light of the command of that case, what is involved here is the question whether the Board has achieved the "racially nondiscriminatory school system" *Brown II* held must be effectuated in order to remedy the established unconstitutional deficiencies of its segregated system. In the context of the state-imposed segregated pattern of long standing, the fact that in 1965 the Board opened the doors of the former "white" school to Negro children and of the "Negro" school to white children merely begins, not ends, our inquiry whether the Board has taken steps adequate to abolish its dual, segregated system. . . .

In determining whether respondent School Board met that command by adopting its "freedom-of-choice" plan, it is relevant that this first step did not come until some 11 years after *Brown I* was decided and 10 years after *Brown II* directed the making of a "prompt and reasonable start." This deliberate perpetuation of the unconstitutional dual system can only have compounded the harm of such a system. Such delays are no longer tolerable. . . . The burden on a school board today is to come forward with a plan that promises realisti-

cally to work, and promises realistically to work *now*. . . .

We do not hold that "freedom of choice" can have no place in such a plan. We do not hold that a "freedom-of-choice" plan might of itself be unconstitutional, although that argument has been urged upon us. Rather, all we decide today is that in desegregating a dual system a plan utilizing "freedom of choice" is not an end to itself. . . . Although the general experience under "freedom of choice" to date has been such as to indicate its ineffectiveness as a tool of desegregation, there may well be instances in which it can serve as an effective device. Where it offers real promise of aiding a desegregation program to effectuate conversion of a state-imposed dual system to a unitary, nonracial system there might be no objection to allowing such a device to prove itself in operation. On the other hand, if there are reasonably available other ways, such for illustration as zoning, promising speedier and more effective conversion to a unitary, nonracial school system, "freedom of choice" must be held unacceptable.

The New Kent School Board's "freedom-of-choice" plan cannot be accepted as a sufficient step to "effectuate a transition" to a unitary system. In three years of operation not a single white child has chosen to attend [the Negro] school and although 115 Negro children enrolled in [the white] school in 1967 (up from 35 in 1965 and 111 in 1966) 85% of the Negro children in the system still attend the all-Negro school. In other words, the school system remains a dual system. Rather than further the dismantling of the dual system, the plan has operated simply to burden children and their parents with a responsibility which *Brown II* placed squarely on the School Board. The

Board must be required to formulate a new plan and in light of other courses which appear open to the Board, such as zoning, fashion steps which promise realistically to convert promptly to a system without a "white" school and a "Negro" school, but just schools. . . .

(8) School Busing and De Facto Segregation: The Limits of Remedial Action

(a) Swann v. Charlotte-Mecklenburg Board of Education and North Carolina Board of Education v. Swann (1971)

[Shortly after taking office, President Richard Nixon and Attorney General John Mitchell announced a change in the government's desegregation policy. The new approach allowed a relaxation of guidelines for some school districts. The emphasis was shifted from *administrative* (e.g., the HEW Guidelines) to *judicial* supervision of school desegregation in the South. Only segregated schools that resulted from prior state laws and policies (*de jure* segregation) would be forced to integrate; those resulting only from *de facto* residential segregation would be allowed to remain segregated. School busing was rejected as an appropriate means of bringing about school integration.

A number of freedom-of-choice plans were approved by a federal district court in Mississippi, but there were numerous delays in requiring them to be put into effect. When the matter came to the Supreme Court, lawyers for the federal government argued for delay—this being the new policy of the Nixon administration. In *Alexander* v. *Holmes County Board of Education* (1969), the Supreme Court unanimously rejected that policy. The school districts were ordered immediately to disband existing dual systems and to begin operating as unitary systems without racial discrimination. The

Court's total repudiation of the government's position was underscored by the fact that its short opinion did not even bother to discuss any of the lengthy rationales for postponement offered by the government.

The Nixon administration's opposition to busing to achieve school integration was at issue in the present cases. The school system that includes the city of Charlotte, North Carolina, had about 84,000 students, 24,000 (29 percent) of whom were black. Of the black students, 14,000 attended twenty-one schools that were totally segregated. The remaining black students attended primarily white schools in varying ratios. This modest amount of desegregation had come about as a result of a court order in 1965, when the present litigation began. After the Supreme Court's decision in *Green* v. *New Kent County* (1968, *supra*), further legal proceedings were instituted. All the parties to the case eventually agreed that in 1969 the system failed to meet the test of a unitary system. Various plans to achieve a higher level of integration were devised. The school board itself adopted a plan that would have produced substantial integration in the high schools, somewhat less in the junior high schools, and very little in the elementary schools. A court-appointed expert countered with a plan that, through rezoning, pairing and grouping of schools, and the busing of children, would have resulted in a range of 9 to 38 percent black students in the elementary schools.

The district court adopted most of this revised plan. The Court of Appeals for the Fifth Circuit accepted its provisions except those for elementary school pupils, fearing that the pairing and busing to integrate the elementary schools would create an unreasonable burden on both the pupils and the school board. The Supreme Court intervened and ordered reinstatement of the district court plan in full. After the school board reluctantly acquiesced in this plan, the case came back to the Supreme Court on a writ of certiorari.

At the same time, the Supreme Court agreed to review the validity of a state law, passed in the course of the above controversy, which *prohibited* school busing to achieve integration (see *North Carolina State Board of Education*

v. *Swann, infra*). The "anti-busing" law had been challenged by the plaintiffs in the *Charlotte-Mecklenburg* case to prevent the state board of education from interfering with the school board's acceptance of the zoning and busing plan.]

MR. CHIEF JUSTICE BURGER delivered the opinion of the Court (in both cases).

This case and those argued with it arose in states having a long history of maintaining two sets of schools in a single school system deliberately operated to carry out a governmental policy to separate pupils in schools solely on the basis of race. That was what *Brown* v. *Board of Education* was all about. These cases present us with the problem of defining in more precise terms than heretofore the scope of the duty of school authorities and district courts in implementing *Brown I* and the mandate to eliminate dual systems and establish unitary systems at once. Meanwhile district courts and courts of appeals have struggled in hundreds of cases with a multitude and variety of problems under the Court's general directive. Understandably, in an area of evolving remedies, those courts had to improvise and experiment without detailed or specific guidelines. This Court, in *Brown*, appropriately dealt with the large constitutional principles; other federal courts had to grapple with the flinty, intractable realities of day-to-day implementation of those constitutional commands. Their efforts, of necessity, embraced a process of "trial and error," and our effort to formulate guidelines must take into account their experience.

. . . Nearly 17 years ago this Court held, in explicit terms, that state-imposed segregation by race in public schools denies equal protection of the laws. At no time has the Court de-

viated in the slightest degree from that holding or its constitutional underpinnings. . . .

Over the 15 years since *Brown II*, many difficulties were encountered in implementation of the basic constitutional requirement that the State not discriminate between public school children on the basis of their race. Nothing in our national experience prior to 1955 prepared anyone for dealing with changes and adjustments of the magnitude and complexity encountered since then. Deliberate resistance of some to the Court's mandates has impeded the good-faith efforts of others to bring school systems into compliance.

By the time the Court considered *Green* v. *County School Board*. . . . very little progress had been made in many areas where dual school systems had historically been maintained by operation of state laws. In *Green*, the Court was confronted with a record of a freedom-of-choice program that the District Court had found to operate in fact to preserve a dual system more than a decade after *Brown II*. While acknowledging that a freedom-of-choice concept could be a valid remedial measure in some circumstances, its failure to be effective in *Green* required that

the burden on a school board today is to come forward with a plan that promises realistically to work . . . now . . . until it is clear that state-imposed segregation has been completely removed.

This was plain language, yet the 1969 Term of Court brought fresh evidence of the dilatory tactics of many school authorities. *Alexander* v. *Holmes County Board of Education*. . . .

The objective today remains to eliminate from the public schools all vestiges of state-imposed segregation. Segregation was the evil struck down by *Brown I* as contrary to the equal protection guarantees of the Constitution. That was the violation sought to be corrected by the remedial measures of *Brown II*. . . .

If school authorities fail in their affirmative obligations under these holdings, judicial authority may be invoked. Once a right and a violation have been shown, the scope of a district court's equitable powers to remedy past wrongs is broad, for breadth and flexibility are inherent in equitable remedies. . . .

This allocation of responsibility once made, the Court attempted from time to time to provide some guidelines for the exercise of the district judge's discretion and for the reviewing function of the courts of appeals. However, a school desegregation case does not differ fundamentally from other cases involving the framing of equitable remedies to repair the denial of a constitutional right. The task is to correct, by a balancing of the individual and collective interests, the condition that offends the Constitution.

In seeking to define even in broad and general terms how far this remedial power extends it is important to remember that judicial powers may be exercised only on the basis of a constitutional violation. Remedial judicial authority does not put judges automatically in the shoes of school authorities whose powers are plenary. Judicial authority enters only when local authority defaults.

School authorities are traditionally charged with broad power to formulate and implement educational policy and might well conclude, for example, that in order to prepare students to live in a pluralistic society each school should have a prescribed ratio of Negro to white students reflecting the proportion for the district

as a whole. To do this as an educational policy is within the broad discretionary powers of school authorities; absent a finding of a constitutional violation, however, that would not be within the authority of a federal court. As with any equity case, the nature of the violation determines the scope of the remedy. In default by the school authorities of their obligation to proffer acceptable remedies, a district court has broad power to fashion a remedy that will assure a unitary school system.

The school authorities argue that the equity powers of federal district courts have been limited by Title IV of the Civil Rights Act of 1964. . . . The language and the history of Title IV shows that it was not enacted to limit but to define the role of the Federal Government in the implementation of the *Brown I* decision. It authorizes the Commissioner of Education to provide technical assistance to local boards in the preparation of desegregation plans, to arrange "training institutes" for school personnel involved in desegregation efforts, and to make grants directly to schools to ease the transition to unitary systems. It also authorizes the Attorney General, in specified circumstances, to initiate federal desegregation suits. Section 200c(b) defines "desegregation" as it is used in Title IV:

"Desegregation" means the assignment of students to public schools and within such schools without regard to their race, color, religion, or national origin, but "desegregation" shall not mean the assignment of students to public schools in order to overcome racial imbalance.

Section 200c-6, authorizing the Attorney General to institute federal suits, contains the following proviso:

nothing herein shall empower any official or court of the United States to issue any order seeking to achieve a racial balance in any school by requiring the transportation of pupils or students from one school to another or one school district to another in order to achieve such racial balance, or otherwise enlarge the existing power of the court to insure compliance with constitutional standards.

On their face, the sections quoted purport only to insure that the provisions of Title IV of the Civil Rights Act of 1964 will not be read as granting new powers. The proviso in 200c-6 is in terms designed to foreclose any interpretation of the Act as expanding the *existing* powers of federal courts to enforce the Equal Protection Clause. There is no suggestion of an intention to restrict those powers or withdraw from courts their historic equitable remedial powers. The legislative history of Title IV indicates that Congress was concerned that the Act might be read as creating a right of action under the Fourteenth Amendment in the situation of so-called "de facto segregation," where racial imbalance exists in the schools but with no showing that this was brought about by discriminatory action of state authorities. In short, there is nothing in the Act which provides us material assistance in answering the question of remedy for state-imposed segregation in violation of *Brown I.* . . .

The central issue in this case is that of student assignment, and there are essentially four problem areas:

(1) to what extent racial balance or racial quotas may be used as an implement in a remedial order to correct a previously segregated system;

(2) whether every all-Negro and all-white school must be eliminated as an indispensable part of a remedial process of desegregation;

(3) what are the limits, if any, on the rearrangement of school districts and attendance zones, as a remedial measure; and

(4) what are the limits, if any, on the use of transportation facilities to correct state-enforced racial school segregation.

(1) Racial Balances or Racial Quotas. The constant theme and thrust of every holding from *Brown I* to date is that state-enforced separation of races in public schools is discrimination that violates the Equal Protection Clause. The remedy commanded was to dismantle dual school systems.

We are concerned in these cases with the elimination of the discrimination inherent in the dual school systems, not with myriad factors of human existence which can cause discrimination in a multitude of ways on racial, religious, or ethnic grounds. The target of the cases from *Brown I* to the present was the dual school system. The elimination of racial discrimination in public schools is a large task and one that should not be retarded by efforts to achieve broader purposes lying beyond the jurisdiction of school authorities. One vehicle can carry only a limited amount of baggage. It would not serve the important objective of *Brown I* to seek to use school desegregation cases for purposes beyond their scope, although desegregation of schools ultimately will have impact on other forms of discrimination. . . .

Our objective in dealing with the issues presented by these cases is to see that school authorities exclude no pupil of a racial minority from any school, directly or indirectly, on account of race; it does not and cannot embrace all the problems of racial prejudice, even when those problems contribute to disproportionate racial concentrations in some schools.

In this case it is urged that the District Court has imposed a racial balance requirement of 71%–29% on individual schools. . . . If we were to read the holding of the District Court to require, as a matter of substantive constitutional right, any particular degree of racial balance or mixing, that approach would be disapproved and we would be obliged to reverse. The constitutional command to desegregate schools does not mean that every school in every community must always reflect the racial composition of the school system as a whole.

As the voluminous record in this case shows, the predicate for the District Court's use of the 71%–29% ratio was twofold: first, its express finding, approved by the Court of Appeals and not challenged here, that a dual school system had been maintained by the school authorities at least until 1969; second, its finding, also approved by the Court of Appeals, that the school board had totally defaulted in its acknowledged duty to come forward with an acceptable plan of its own. . . .

We see therefore that the use made of mathematical ratios was no more than a starting point in the process of shaping a remedy, rather than an inflexible requirement. From that starting point the District Court proceeded to frame a decree that was within its discretionary powers, an equitable remedy for the particular circumstances. As we said in *Green,* a school authority's remedial plan or a district court's remedial decree is to be judged by its effectiveness. Awareness of the racial composition of the whole school system is likely to be a useful starting point in shaping a remedy to correct past constitutional violations. In sum, the very limited use made of mathematical ratios was within the equitable remedial discretion of the District Court.

(2) One-Race Schools. The record in this case reveals the familiar phenomenon that in metropolitan areas minority groups are often found concentrated in one part of the city. In some circumstances certain schools may remain all or largely of one race until new schools can be provided or neighborhood patterns change. Schools all or predominately of one race in a district of mixed population will require close scrutiny to determine that school assignments are not part of state-enforced segregation.

In light of the above, it should be clear that the existence of some small number of one-race, or virtually one-race, schools within a district is not in and of itself the mark of a system which still practices segregation by law. The district judge or school authorities should make every effort to achieve the greatest possible degree of actual desegregation and will thus necessarily be concerned with the elimination of one-race schools. No *per se* rule can adequately embrace all the difficulties of reconciling the competing interests involved; but in a system with a history of segregation the need for remedial criteria of sufficient specificity to assure a school authority's compliance with its constitutional duty warrants a presumption against schools that are substantially disproportionate in their racial composition. Where the school authority's proposed plan for conversion from a dual to a unitary system contemplates the continued existence of some schools that are all or predominately of one race, they have the burden of showing that such school assignments are genuinely nondiscriminatory. The court should scrutinize such schools, and the burden upon the school authorities will be to satisfy the court that their racial composition is not the result of present or past discriminatory action on their part. . . .

(3) *Remedial Altering of Attendance Zones.* The maps submitted in these cases graphically demonstrate that one of the principal tools employed by school planners and by courts to break up the dual school system has been a frank—and sometimes drastic—gerrymandering of school districts and attendance zones. An additional step was pairing, "clustering," or "grouping" of schools with attendance assignments made deliberately to accomplish the transfer of Negro students out of formerly segregated Negro schools and transfer of white students to formerly all-Negro schools. More often than not, these zones are neither compact nor contiguous; indeed they may be on opposite ends of the city. As an interim corrective measure, this cannot be said to be beyond the broad remedial powers of a court.

Absent a constitutional violation there would be no basis for judicially ordering assignment of students on a racial basis. All things being equal, with no history of discrimination, it might well be desirable to assign pupils to schools nearest their homes. But all things are not equal in a system that has been deliberately constructed and maintained to enforce racial segregation. The remedy for such segregation may be administratively awkward, inconvenient and even bizarre in some situations and may impose burdens on some; but all awkwardness and inconvenience cannot be avoided in the interim period when remedial adjustments are being made to eliminate the dual school systems.

No fixed or even substantially fixed guidelines can be established as to how far a court can go, but it must be recognized that there are limits. The objective is to dismantle the dual school system. "Racially neutral" assignment plans proposed by school authorities to a district court may be inadequate; such plans may fail to counteract the continuing effects of past school segregation resulting from discriminatory location of school sites or distortion of school size in order to achieve or maintain an artificial racial separation. . . .

We hold that the pairing and grouping of non-contiguous school zones is a permissible tool and such action is to be considered in light of the objectives sought. . . . Maps do not tell the whole story since non-contiguous school zones may be more accessible to each other in terms of the critical travel time, because of traffic patterns and good highways, than schools geographically closer together. Conditions in different localities will vary so widely that no rigid rules can be laid down to govern all situations.

(4) *Transportation of Students.* The scope of permissible transportation of students as an implement of a remedial decree has never been defined by this Court and by the very nature of the problem it cannot be defined with precision. No rigid guidelines as to student transportation can be given for application to the infinite variety of problems presented in thousands of situations. Bus transportation has been an integral part of the public education system for years, and was perhaps

the single most important factor in the transition from the one-room schoolhouse to the consolidated school. Eighteen million of the nation's public school children, approximately 39%, were transported to their schools by bus in 1969–1970 in all parts of the country.

The importance of bus transportation as a normal and accepted tool of educational policy is readily discernible in this and the companion case. The Charlotte school authorities did not purport to assign students on the basis of geographically drawn zones until 1965 and then they allowed almost unlimited transfer privileges. The District Court's conclusion that assignment of children to the school nearest their home serving their grade would not produce an effective dismantling of the dual system is supported by the record.

Thus the remedial techniques used in the District Court's order were within that court's power to provide equitable relief; implementation of the decree is well within the capacity of the school authority.

The decree provided that the buses used to implement the plan would operate on direct routes. Students would be picked up at schools near their homes and transported to the schools they were to attend. The trips for elementary school pupils average about seven miles and the District Court found that they would take "not over 35 minutes at the most." This system compares favorably with the transportation plan previously operated in Charlotte under which each day 23,600 students on all grade levels were transported an average of 15 miles one way for an average trip requiring over an hour. In these circumstances, we find no basis for holding that the local school authorities may not be required to employ bus transportation as one tool of school desegregation. Desegregation plans cannot be limited to the walk-in school.

An objection to transportation of students may have validity when the time or distance of travel is so great as to risk either the health of the children or significantly impinge on the educational process. . . .

The Court of Appeals, searching for a term to define the equitable remedial power of the district courts, used the term "reasonableness." In *Green, supra,* this Court used the term "feasible" and by implication, "workable," "efffective," and "realistic" in the mandate to develop "a plan that promises realistically to work, and . . . to work *now.*" On the facts of this case, we are unable to conclude that the order of the District Court is not reasonable, feasible and workable. However, in seeking to define the scope of remedial power or the limits on remedial power of courts in an area as sensitive as we deal with here, words are poor instruments to convey the sense of basic fairness inherent in equity. Substance, not semantics, must govern, and we have sought to suggest the nature of limitations without frustrating the appropriate scope of equity. . . .

It does not follow that the communities served by such systems will remain demographically stable, for in a growing, mobile society, few will do so. Neither school authorities nor district courts are constitutionally required to make year-by-year adjustments of the racial composition of student bodies once the affirmative duty to desegregate has been accomplished and racial discrimination through official action is eliminated from the system. This does not mean that federal courts are without power to deal with future problems; but in the absence of a showing that either the school authorities or some other agency of the State has deliberately attempted to fix or alter demographic patterns to affect the racial composition of the schools, further intervention by a district court should not be necessary.

For the reasons herein set forth, judgment of the Court of Appeals is affirmed as to those parts in which it affirmed the judgment of the District Court. . . .

It is so ordered.

North Carolina State Board of Education v. Swann (1971)

. . .

This case is here on direct appeal from the judgment of a three-judge court in the United States District Court for the Western District of North Carolina. The District Court declared unconstitutional a portion of the North Carolina General Statutes known as the Anti-Busing Law, and granted an injunction against its enforcement. . . .

When the litigation in the *Swann* case recommenced in the spring of 1969, the District Court specifically directed that the school board consider altering attendance areas, pairing or consolidation of schools, bus transportation of students, and any other method which would effectuate a racially unitary system. That litigation was actively prosecuted. The board submitted a series of proposals, all rejected by the District Court as inadequate. In the midst of this litigation over the remedy to implement the District Court's order, the North Carolina Legislature enacted the anti-busing bill. . . .

We observed in *Swann* . . . that school authorities have wide discretion in formulating school policy, and

that as a matter of educational policy school authorities may well conclude that some kind of racial balance in the schools is desirable quite apart from any constitutional requirements. However, if a state-imposed limitation on a school authority's discretion operates to inhibit or obstruct the operation of a unitary school system or impede the disestablishing of a dual school system, it must fall; state policy must give way when it operates to hinder vindication of federal constitutional guarantees.

The legislation before us flatly forbids assignment of any student on account of race or for the purpose of creating a racial balance or ratio in the schools. The prohibition is absolute, and it would inescapably operate to obstruct the remedies granted by the District Court in the *Swann* case. But more important the statute exploits an apparently neutral form to control school assignment plans by directing that they be "color blind"; that requirement, against the background of segregation, would render illusory the promise of *Brown* v. *Board of Education* . . . (1954). Just as the race of students must be considered in determining whether a constitutional violation has occurred, so also must race be considered in formulating a remedy. To forbid, at this stage, all assignments made on the basis of race would deprive school authorities of the one tool absolutely essential to fulfillment of their constitutional obligation to eliminate existing dual school systems.

Similarly the flat prohibition against assignment of students for the purpose of creating a racial balance must inevitably conflict with the duty of school authorities to disestablish dual school systems. As we have held in *Swann*, the Constitution does not compel any particular degree of racial balance or mixing, but when past and continuing constitutional violations are found, some ratios are likely to be useful starting points in shaping a remedy. An absolute prohibition against use of such a device—even as a starting point—contravenes the implicit command of *Green* v. *County School Board . . .* (1968), that all reasonable methods be available to formulate an effective remedy.

We likewise conclude that an absolute prohibition against transportation of students assigned on the basis of race, "or for the purpose of creating a balance or ratio," will similarly hamper the ability of local authorities to effectively remedy constitutional violations. . . . [B]us transportation has long been an integral part of all public educational systems, and it is unlikely that a truly effective remedy could be devised without continued reliance upon it. . . .

[The *Swann* decision elicited sharp criticism in Congress, and a number of proposals to limit or ban school busing were debated. In 1972, the Senate barely defeated a proposal by Senator Robert Griffin of Michigan, a staunch ally of President Nixon. His bill provided that "No court of the United States shall have jurisdiction to make any decision, enter any judgment or issue any order the effect of which would be to require that pupils be transported to or from school on the basis of their race, color, religion, or national origin." The vote against the Griffin bill was 50–47; a similar bill lost by an even closer margin, 48–47. The Nixon administration made school busing an issue in the 1972 election and continued to press for congressional action, citing Congress' power to enforce the Fourteenth Amendment as the authority to legislate. Congress did adopt a temporary moratorium on school busing in 1972, but this did not prove to be a significant barrier, since it only affected those court orders "for the purpose of achieving a balance among students

with respect to race, sex, religion, or socioeconomic status."

In late August 1974, *after* President Nixon had resigned, Congress did pass an antibusing law (Title II—Equal Educational Opportunities and Transportation of Students) as part of the Educational Amendments of 1974, a major school financing bill. The compromises that made the bill possible also produced a bill with significant contradictions. Thus the bill includes language demanded by the Senate conferees that the bill was "not intended to modify or diminish the authority of the courts of the United States to enforce fully the Fifth and Fourteenth Amendments." On the other hand, other sections of the bill are quite explicit in their condemnation and prohibition of busing.]

(b) Milliken v. Bradley (1974)

+ Burger, Stewart, Blackmun, Powell, Rehnquist
−Douglas, Brennan, White, Marshall

[Until 1973, the Supreme Court's focus was on elimination of dual school systems in the southern states. Since all of those states had, at one time, required school segregation by law, the Supreme Court did not have to consider whether *de facto* segregation was also prohibited by the Constitution.

In order to apply the principles of *Brown, Green,* and *Swann* to northern school districts, the Supreme Court was pressed to eliminate the distinction between *de jure* and *de facto* segregation and hold that wherever a dual segregated system existed, authorities had an affirmative constitutional duty to eliminate it. The argument for this policy was that whether or not school board authorities pursued an explicit policy of segregation (which, if proved, *would* constitute *de jure* segregation), their budget and districting policies were more subtle forms of state action and also subject to Fourteenth Amendment prohibitions. Alternatively, the Court was asked to find that policies of school boards that resulted in, or contributed to, school segregation constituted *de jure* segregation in and of themselves, for example, that a prohibited "dual" system might result from either statutory or nonstatutory causes.

In *Keyes* v. *School District* (1973), the Supreme Court had its first opportunity to consider school segregation in a northern city, Denver. Only two justices, Powell and Douglas, argued that the distinction between *de jure* and *de facto* segregation be abolished. A majority of the Court, following the second option outlined above, held that school board policies had contributed to segregation in at least one part of the city and that this created a presumption that the entire system was unlawfully segregated. Speaking for the majority, Justice Brennan held that the main difference between *de jure* and *de facto* segregation was purpose, or intent, to segregate.

Another contentious issue was the matter of an appropriate remedy where a court found the existence of *de jure* segregation. *Swann* had authorized busing as a possible remedy. But the increasing proportion of nonwhite children in northern school systems (as whites fled to the suburbs) raised the question of a "metropolitan" or "interdistrict" solution. A metropolitan solution implied an effort to "recapture" whites by including both city and suburban schools in a plan of integration. In a previous case involving this issue, the Supreme Court had divided 4–4. Justice Powell had not participated because the case had come from Richmond, Virginia, where, before his appointment to the Supreme Court, he had long been a member of the school board. But in other cases, including *Keyes,* Powell had expressed skepticism for large-scale forced busing and a strong preference for neighborhood schools.

Milliken v. *Bradley* again raised these questions. The case was a class action suit by Ronald Bradley, his mother, and the NAACP challenging segregation in the Detroit public schools. Bradley alleged that the segregation of Detroit's schools was the result of official *policies* of the Detroit school board and other actions of both city and state officials. In 1970, Michigan had enacted a statute prohibiting implementation of an earlier voluntary desegrega-

tion plan in Detroit. The state had refused to provide transportation funds to Detroit while providing funds to its suburban neighbors. The state had also approved school construction plans that perpetuated all-black schools, and in one instance, it even approved the busing of black suburban students through a white district to an inner-city black school. Under Michigan law, education was a state responsibility, although most day-to-day operation of schools was delegated to local school boards.

The case was heard in the United States District Court in Detroit. The judge found that the state was heavily implicated in the segregation of Detroit's schools and that school board officials had followed policies(of action *and* inaction) that resulted in increased segregation. For example, they maintained an optional attendance zone in an area of racial transition which they should have known would result in increased white flight—and it did. Attendance zones were drawn in a way to minimize integration.

That Detroit's schools were racially segregated was not the main issue of the case, however, since it could hardly be denied. The trial judge concluded that because of the racial composition of the school population, a remedy limited only to Detroit would result in less rather than more integration. Indeed, he also found that an *intra*district remedy would entail *more* transportation of students, not less. He therefore decided that the only solution was an interdistrict, or metropolitan, remedy. After further hearings, he found that fifty-three of the eighty-five suburban school districts should be included with the city of Detroit in a metropolitan desegregation plan. A special commission was appointed to work out the details. On the basis of that commission's report, the city of Detroit was ordered to purchase 295 buses for an interim desegregation plan.

An appeal was taken to the court of appeals, which substantially affirmed the order of the district judge. However, because it thought that all eighty-five suburban districts should have been included, it vacated the district court order. The Supreme Court granted certiorari. In oral argument, the attorney general of Michigan argued that the district judge had usurped powers properly belonging to the state and that he was using the law to attain what he happened to think was a desirable social goal. This was a legislative, not a judicial function, the attorney general argued. Solicitor General Bork intervened on behalf of the United States as *amicus curiae.* He argued that the record did not show that the suburbs were either implicated in, or affected by, racial segregation in Detroit, and thus a broad metropolitan remedy was not called for.

Milliken v. *Bradley* was argued in the Supreme Court just two and one-half months before the twentieth anniversary of *Brown* v. *Board of Education* (1954). Ironically, as it was being argued, a new school segregation case had begun in Topeka, Kansas—a new class action suit by another ten-year-old black girl named Evelyn Johnson. She claimed that Topeka was still systematically discriminating against black students.

Outside of Topeka, where it all began, the desegregation picture was mixed. Southern classrooms were considerably more integrated than those in the northern cities. Virtually all the southern school districts had filed a desegregation plan with HEW or were under court orders to desegregate, whereas many northern and western school districts had not been "touched." Much discrimination remains in the South, and white flight to the suburbs threatened to resegregate many southern urban school systems. Many of the "private" academies, which opened in response to the *Brown* decision, have become permanent bastions of segregation.]

MR. CHIEF JUSTICE BURGER delivered the opinion of the Court.

. . .

We granted certiorari in these consolidated cases to determine whether a federal court may impose a multidistrict, areawide remedy to a single district *de jure* segregation problem absent any finding that the other included school districts have failed to operate unitary school systems within their districts, absent any claim or finding that the boundary lines of any affected school district were established with the purpose of fostering racial segregation in public schools, absent any findings that the included districts committed acts which effected segregation within the other districts, and absent a meaningful opportunity for the included neighboring school districts to present evidence or be heard on the propriety of a multidistrict remedy or on the question of constitutional violations by those neighboring districts.

. . .

Ever since *Brown* v. *Board of Education* . . . (1954), judicial consideration of school desegregation cases has begun with the standard that:

[I]*n the field of public education the doctrine of "separate but equal" has no place. Separate educational facilities are inherently unequal. . . .*

This has been reaffirmed time and again as the meaning of the Constitution and the controlling rule of law.

The target of the *Brown* holding was clear and forthright: the elimination of state mandated or deliberately maintained dual school systems with certain schools for Negro pupils and others for White pupils. This duality and racial segregation was held to violate the Constitution in the cases subsequent to 1954, including particularly *Green* v. *County School Board of New Kent County* . . . (1968); *Raney* v. *Board of Education* . . . (1968); *Monroe* v. *Board of Commissioners* . . . (1968); *Swann* v. *Charlotte-Mecklenburg Board of Education* . . . (1971); *Wright* v. *Council of City of Emporia* . . . (1972); *United States* v. *Scotland Neck Board of Education* . . . (1972).

The *Swann* case, of course, dealt

with the problem of defining in more precise terms than heretofore the scope of the duty of school authorities and district courts in implementing Brown I *and the mandate to eliminate dual systems and establish unitary systems at once. . . .*

In further refining the remedial process, *Swann* held, the task is to correct, by a balancing of the individual and collective interests, "the condition that offends the Constitution." A federal remedial power may be exercised "only on the basis of a constitutional violation" and, "[a]s with any equity case, the nature of the violation determines the scope of the remedy." . . .

Proceeding from these basic principles, we first note that in the District Court the complainants sought a remedy aimed at the *condition* alleged to offend the Constitution—the segregation within the Detroit City school district. The court acted on this theory of the case and in its initial ruling on the "Desegregation Area" stated:

The task before this court, therefore, is now, and . . . has always been, how to desegregate the Detroit public schools. . . .

Thereafter, however, the District Court abruptly rejected the proposed Detroit-only plans on the ground that "while it would provide a racial mix more in keeping with the Black-White proportions of the student population, [it] would accentuate the racial identifiability of the [Detroit] district as a Black school system, and would not accomplish desegregation." . . .

Viewing the record as a whole, it seems clear that the District Court and the Court of Appeals shifted the primary focus from a Detroit remedy to the metropolitan area only because of their conclusion that total desegregation of Detroit would not produce the racial balance which they perceived as desirable. Both courts proceeded on an assumption that the Detroit schools could not be truly desegregated—in their view of what constituted desegregation—unless the racial composition of the student body of each school substantially reflected the racial composition of the population of the metropolitan area as a whole. . . .

Here the District Court's approach to what constituted "actual desegregation" raises the fundamental question, not presented in *Swann*, as to the circumstances in which a federal court may order desegregation relief that embraces more than a single school district. The court's analytical starting point was its conclusion that school district lines are no more than arbitrary lines on a map "drawn for political convenience." Boundary lines may be bridged where there has been a constitutional violation calling for inter-district relief, but, the notion that school district lines may be casually ignored or treated as a mere administrative convenience is contrary to the history of public education in our country. No single tradition in public education is more deeply rooted than local control over the operation of schools; local autonomy has long been thought essential both to the maintenance of community concern and support for public schools and the quality of the educational process. . . . Thus, in *San Antonio School District* v. *Rodriguez* . . . (1973) we observed that local control over the educational process affords citizens an opportunity to participate in decision-making, permits the structuring of school programs to fit local needs, and encourages "experimentation, innovation and a healthy competition for educational excellence." . . .

The controlling principle consistently expounded in our holdings is that the scope of the remedy is determined by the nature and extent of the constitutional violation. . . . Before the boundaries of separate and autonomous school districts may be set aside by consolidating the separate units for remedial purposes or by imposing a cross-district remedy, it must first be shown that there has been a constitutional violation within one district that produces a significant segregative effect in another district. Specifically it must be shown that racially discriminatory acts of the state or local school districts, or of a single school district have been a substantial cause of inter-district segregation. Thus an inter-district remedy might be in order where the racially discriminatory acts of one or more school districts caused racial segregation in an adjacent district, or where district lines have been deliberately drawn on the basis of race. In such circumstances an inter-district remedy would be appropriate to eliminate the inter-district segregation directly caused by the constitutional violation. Conversely, without an inter-district violation and inter-district effect, there is no constitutional wrong calling for an inter-district remedy.

The record before us, voluminous as it is, contains evidence of *de jure* segregated conditions only in the Detroit schools; . . . With no showing of significant violation by the 53 outlying school districts and no evidence of any inter-district violation or effect, the court went beyond the origi-

nal theory of the case as framed by the pleadings and mandated a metropolitan area remedy. To approve the remedy ordered by the court would impose on the outlying districts, not shown to have committed any constitutional violation, a wholly impermissible remedy based on a standard not hinted at in *Brown I* and *II* or any holding of this Court. . . .

The constitutional right of the Negro respondents residing in Detroit is to attend a unitary school system in that district. Unless petitioners drew the district lines in a discriminatory fashion, or arranged for White students residing in the Detroit district to attend schools in Oakland and Macomb Counties, they were under no constitutional duty to make provisions for Negro students to do so. The view of the dissenters, that the existence of a dual system in *Detroit* can be made the basis for a decree requiring cross-district transportation of pupils cannot be supported on the grounds that it represents merely the devising of a suitably flexible remedy for the violation of rights already established by our prior decision. It can be supported only by drastic expansion of the constitutional right itself, an expansion without any support in either constitutional principle or precedent. . . .

We conclude that the relief ordered by the District Court and affirmed by the Court of Appeals was based upon an erroneous standard and was unsupported by record evidence that acts of the outlying districts affected the discrimination found to exist in the schools of Detroit. Accordingly, the decision of the Court of Appeals is vacated and the case is remanded for further proceedings consistent with this opinion leading to prompt formulation of a decree directed to eliminating the segregation found to exist in

Detroit city schools, a remedy which has been delayed since 1970.

MR. JUSTICE STEWART, CONCURRING (OMITTED).

MR. JUSTICE DOUGLAS, DISSENTING.

The Court of Appeals has acted responsibly in these cases and we should affirm its judgment. This was the fourth time the case was before it over a span of less than three years. The Court of Appeals affirmed the District Court on the issue of segregation and on the "Detroit-only" plans of desegregation. The Court of Appeals also approved in principle the use of a metropolitan area plan, vacating and remanding only to allow the other affected school districts to be brought in as parties and in other minor respects. . . .

When we rule against the metropolitan area remedy we take a step that will likely put the problems of the Blacks and our society back to the period that antedated the "separate but equal" regime of *Plessy* v. *Ferguson*, . . . The reason is simple.

The inner core of Detroit is now rather solidly black; and the blacks, we know, in many instances are likely to be poorer, just as were the Chicanos in *San Antonio Independent School District* v. *Rodriguez* . . . (1973). By that decision the poorer school districts must pay their own way. It is therefore, a foregone conclusion that we have now given the States a formula whereby the poor must pay their own way.

Today's decision, given *Rodriguez*, means that there is no violation of the Equal Protection Clause though the schools are segregated by race and though the Black schools are not only "separate" but "inferior."

So far as equal protection is concerned we are not in a dramatic re-

treat from the 8-to-1 decision in 1896 that Blacks could be segregated in public facilities provided they receive equal treatment. . . .

MR. JUSTICE WHITE, WITH WHOM MR. JUSTICE DOUGLAS, MR. JUSTICE BRENNAN, AND MR. JUSTICE MARSHALL JOIN, DISSENTING.

Regretfully, and for several reasons, I can join neither the Court's judgment nor its opinion. The core of my disagreement is that deliberate acts of segregation and their consequences will go unremedied, not because a remedy would be infeasible or unreasonable in terms of the usual criteria governing school desegregation cases, but because an effective remedy would cause what the Court considers to be undue administrative inconvenience to the State. The result is that the State of Michigan, the entity at which the Fourteenth Amendment is directed, has successfully insulated itself from its duty to provide effective desegregation remedies by vesting sufficient power over its public schools in its local school districts. If this is the case in Michigan, it will be the case in most States. . . .

I am even more mystified how the Court can ignore the legal reality that the constitutional violations, even if occurring locally, were committed by governmental entitles for which the State is responsible and that it is the State that must respond to the command of the Fourteenth Amendment. An interdistrict remedy for the infringements that occurred in this case is well within the confines and powers of the State, which is the governmental entity ultimately responsible for desegregating its schools.

. . .

Until today, the permissible contours of the equitable authority of the district courts to remedy the unlawful establishment of a dual school system have been extensive, adaptable, and fully responsive to the ultimate goal of achieving "the greatest possible degree of actual desegregation." There are indeed limitations on the equity powers of the federal judiciary, but until now the Court has not accepted the proposition that effective enforcement of the Fourteenth Amendment could be limited by political or administrative boundary lines demarcated by the very State responsible for the constitutional violation and for the disestablishment of the dual system. Until now the Court has instead looked to practical considerations in effectuating a desegregation decree, such as excessive distance, transportation time and hazards to the safety of the school children involved in a proposed plan. That these broad principles have developed in the context of dual school systems compelled or authorized by state statute at the time of *Brown* v. *Board of Education* . . . does not lessen their current applicability to dual systems found to exist in other contexts, like that in Detroit, where the intentional school segregation does not stem from the compulsion of state law, but from deliberate individual actions of local and state school authorities directed at a particular school system. . . .

MR. JUSTICE MARSHALL, WITH WHOM MR. JUSTICE DOUGLAS, MR. JUSTICE BRENNAN, AND MR. JUSTICE WHITE JOIN, DISSENTING.

In *Brown* v. *Board of Education*, . . . this Court held that segregation of children in public schools on the basis of race deprives minority group children of equal educational opportunities and therefore denies them the equal protection of the laws under the Fourteenth Amendment. This Court recognized then that remedying decades of segregation in public education would not be an easy task. Subsequent events, unfortunately, have seen that prediction bear bitter fruit. But however imbedded old ways, however ingrained old prejudices, this Court has not been diverted from its appointed task of making "a living truth" of our constitutional ideal of equal justice under law. *Cooper* v. *Aaron*, . . . (1958).

After 20 years of small, often difficult steps toward that great end, the Court today takes a giant step backwards. Notwithstanding a record showing widespread and pervasive racial segregation in the educational system provided by the State of Michigan for children in Detroit, this Court holds that the District Court was powerless to require the State to remedy its constitutional violation in any meaningful fashion. Ironically purporting to base its result on the principle that the scope of the remedy in a desegregation case should be determined by the nature and the extent of the constitutional violation, the Court's answer is to provide no remedy at all for the violation provided in this case, thereby guaranteeing that Negro children in Detroit will receive the same separate and inherently unequal education in the future as they have been unconstitutionally afforded in the past.

I cannot subscribe to this emasculation of our constitutional guarantee of equal protection of the laws and must respectfully dissent. Our precedents, in my view, firmly establish that where, as here, state-imposed segregation has been demonstrated, it becomes the duty of the State to eliminate root and branch all vestiges of racial discrimination and to achieve the greatest possible degree of actual desegregation. I agree with both the District Court and the Court of Appeals that, under the facts of this case, this duty cannot be fulfilled unless the State of Michigan involves outlying metropolitan area school districts in its desegregation remedy. Furthermore, I perceive no basis either in law or in the practicalities of the situation justifying the State's interposition of school district boundaries as absolute barriers to the implementation of an effective desegregation remedy. Under established and frequently used Michigan procedures, school district lines are both flexible and permeable for a wide variety of purposes, and there is no reason why they must now stand in the way of meaningful desegregation relief.

The rights at issue in this case are too fundamental to be abridged on grounds as superficial as those called on by the majority today. We deal here with the right of all our children, whatever their race, to an equal start in life and to an equal opportunity to reach their full potential as citizens. Those children who have been denied that right in the past deserve better than to see fences thrown up to deny them that right in the future. Our Nation, I fear, will be ill-served by the Court's refusal to remedy separate and unequal education, for unless our children begin to learn together, there is little hope that our people will ever learn to live together. . . .

Desegregation is not and was never expected to be an easy task. Racial attitudes ingrained in our Nation's childhood and adolescence are not quickly thrown aside in its middle years. But just as the inconvenience of some cannot be allowed to stand in the way of the rights of others, so public opposition, no matter how stri-

dent, cannot be permitted to divert this Court from the enforcement of the constitutional principles at issue in this case. Today's holding, I fear, is more a reflection of a perceived public mood that we have gone far enough in enforcing the Constitution's guarantee of equal justice than it is the product of neutral principles of law. In the short run, it may seem to be the easier course to allow our great metropolitan areas to be divided up each into two cities—one white, the other black—but it is a course, I predict, our people will ultimately regret. I dissent.

[The *Milliken* case was remanded to the district court. Judge Roth, who had heard the case originally, died, and a new judge was assigned to the case. He formulated an intradistrict plan that included a modest amount of busing. By this time, the population of Detroit was approximately 50 percent black, while the school population was 72 percent black. With 260,000 students, it was the nation's fifth largest school system.

Judge DeMascio rejected an NAACP plan for massive busing and also rejected the contention that a suitable constitutional remedy required "racial balance." Instead, he accepted the school board's recommendation that a unitary system could be achieved merely by eliminating "white identifiable" schools. The school board proposed to reduce the percentage of whites in any single school to 50 percent; Judge DeMascio ordered that it be reduced only to 70 percent. In addition, he ordered a variety of compensatory educational programs that had been proposed by the school board. These included special training for teachers, special reading programs, and accentuated guidance and counseling efforts.

The case came back to the Supreme Court in 1977 *(Milliken II)*, and two important questions were raised. First, could a district court order such compensatory programs as a remedy for *de jure* segregation? And, second, "consistent with the Eleventh Amendment," could a federal court require "state officials found responsible for constitutional violations to bear part of the costs of these programs"?

The Supreme Court answered both questions in the affirmative. Chief Justice Burger, writing for the Court, held that such remedial programs were properly designed to "restore the victims of discriminatory conduct to the position they would have occupied in the absence of such conduct." The Eleventh Amendment question was more complex. In 1974, in *Edelman* v. *Jordan* (see pp. 125–130, *supra*), the Supreme Court had held, in a suit for damages against Illinois welfare officials who had deliberately underpaid benefits to eligible welfare recipients, that the Eleventh Amendment barred such recovery. But it had also held that a federal court could enjoin state officials to comply with the law in the future, notwithstanding the substantial costs of such compliance to the state treasury. Here, Chief Justice Burger held that Judge DeMascio's order was within this "prospective-compliance exemption" to the Eleventh Amendment. State officials could be ordered to undertake compensatory programs to comply with federal law and to share in their cost.

Milliken did not foreclose the possibility of court-ordered interdistrict desegregation remedies, but the conditions it laid down made such remedies difficult to achieve—some observers thought impossible. In *Hills* v. *Gautreaux* (1976), the Supreme Court approved such remedies in a case involving not schools but public housing. Gautreaux and other blacks in Chicago brought suit against the federal Department of Housing and Urban Development and the Chicago Housing Authority. They charged that the two agencies had deliberately chosen public housing sites that minimized the possibility of integration. A federal district court eventually ordered the defendant agencies to devise a housing plan that would increase the number of housing units available to blacks. But it held that the plan was to be limited to the city of Chicago, since "the wrongs were committed" there. The Court of Appeals for the Seventh Circuit reversed the decision and ordered the district court to come up with a com-

prehensive "metropolitan" plan. The appeals court distinguished *Milliken* on its facts, finding that in this case there was "evidence of suburban discrimination and of the likelihood that there had been an 'extra-city impact' on the . . . intra-city discrimination." It found that for purposes of low-rent housing, the metropolitan Chicago area was a single entity and that "a city-only remedy will not work."

The Supreme Court affirmed the Court of Appeals' decision. It held, in an opinion by Justice Stewart, that "the critical distinction between HUD and the suburban school districts in *Milliken* is that HUD has been found to have violated the Constitution." Once such a violation has been shown, the Court said, quoting from the *Swann* decision, "the scope of a district court's equitable powers to remedy past wrongs is broad. . . ." In this case, unlike *Milliken,* an interdistrict remedy would not coerce "uninvolved governmental units," since both HUD and the Chicago Housing Authority had violated the Constitution and both had authority to operate outside the city limits of Chicago. No consolidation or restructuring of governmental units would be necessary. Even in the absence of the court order, HUD had the discretionary power to provide alternatives outside of Chicago to the racially segregated housing in Chicago which it helped to create and maintain.]

(C) *Pasadena City Board of Education v. Spangler (1976)*

+Rehnquist, Burger, Blackmun, Powell, White, Stewart
−Marshall, Brennan
NP Stevens

[In 1970, the federal Court for the southern district of California found that the public schools in Pasadena were segregated in violation of the Fourteenth Amendment. A plan of desegregation was approved that prohibited any school in the district from having a majority of minority students. The plan went into effect in the fall of 1970, but the district court retained jurisdiction over the case. In 1974, the school board petitioned the court to dissolve its order. It appears that the court's order had not, in fact, been strictly enforced after the first year and that five of the thirty-two schools in the district had acquired a majority of minority students. The district court denied this motion, and the court of appeals affirmed it by a divided vote.]

MR. JUSTICE REHNQUIST delivered the opinion of the Court.

. . .

We do not have before us any issue as to the validity of the District Court's original judgment, since petitioner's predecessors did not appeal from it. The District Court's conclusion that unconstitutional segregation existed in the PUSD; its decision to order a systemwide school reorganization plan based upon the guidelines which it submitted to the defendants; and the inclusion in those guidelines of the requirement that the plan contain provisions insuring that there be no majority of any minority in any Pasadena school, all became embodied in the 1970 decree. All that is now before us are the questions of whether the District Court was correct in denying relief when petitioners in 1974 sought to modify the "no majority" requirement as then interpreted by the District Court.

. . .

When the District Court's order in this case, as interpreted and applied by that court, is measured against what this Court said in its intervening decision in *Swann* v. *Board of Education* . . . (1971), regarding the scope of the judicially created relief which might be available to remedy violations of the Fourteenth Amendment, we think the inconsistency between the two is clear. The District Court's interpretation of the order appears to contemplate the "substantive constitutional right [to a] particu-

lar degree of racial balance or mixing" which the Court in *Swann* expressly disapproved. . . . It became apparent, at least by the time of the 1974 hearing, that the District Court viewed this portion of its order not merely as a "starting point in the process of shaping a remedy," which *Swann* indicated would be appropriate; . . . but instead as an "inflexible requirement," . . . to be applied anew each year to the school population within the attendance zone of each school.

The District Court apparently believed it had authority to impose this requirement even though subsequent changes to the racial mix in the Pasadena schools might be caused by factors for which the defendants could not be considered responsible. Whatever may have been the basis for such a belief in 1970, in *Swann* the Court cautioned that "it must be recognized that there are limits" beyond which a court may not go in seeking to dismantle a dual school system. . . . These limits are in part tied to the necessity of establishing that school authorities have in some manner caused unconstitutional segregation for "[a]bsent a constitutional violation there would be no basis for judicially ordering assignment of students on a racial basis." . . . While the District Court found such a violation in 1970, and while this unappealed finding afforded a basis for its initial requirement that the defendants prepare a plan to remedy such racial segregation, its adoption of the Pasadena Plan in 1970 established a racially neutral system of student assignment in PUSD. Having done that, we think that in enforcing its order so as to require annual readjustment of attendance zones so that there would not be a majority of any minority in any

Pasadena public school, the District Court exceeded its authority.

In so concluding, we think it important to note what this case does not involve. The "no majority of any minority" requirement with respect to attendance zones did not call for defendants to submit "step at a time" plans by definition incomplete at inception. . . . Nor did it call for a plan embodying specific revisions of the attendance zones for particular schools, as well as provisions for later appraisal of whether such discrete individual modifications had achieved the "unitary system" required by *Brown II*, . . . (1955). The plan approved in this case applied in general terms to all Pasadena schools, and no one contests that its implementation did "achieve a system of determining admission to the public schools on a nonracial basis." . . .

There was also no showing in this case that those post-1971 changes in the racial mix of some Pasadena schools which were focused upon by the lower courts were in any manner caused by segregative actions chargeable to the defendants. The District Court rejected petitioner's assertion that the movement was caused by so-called "white flight" traceable to the decree itself. It stated that the "trends evidenced in Pasadena closely approximates the state-wide trend in California schools, both segregated and desegregated." . . . The fact that black student enrollment at five out of 32 of the regular Pasadena schools came to exceed 50% during the four-year period from 1970 to 1974 apparently resulted from people randomly moving into, out of, and around the PUSD area. This quite normal pattern of human migration resulted in some changes in the demographics of Pasadena's residential patterns, with resultant shifts in the racial makeup of some of the schools. But as these shifts were not attributed to any segregative actions on the part of the defendants, we think this case comes squarely within the sort of situation foreseen in *Swann*:

It does not follow that communities served by [unitary] systems will remain demographically stable, for in a growing, mobile society, few will do so. Neither school authorities nor district courts are constitutionally required to make year-by-year adjustments of the racial composition of student bodies once the affirmative duty to desegregate has been accomplished and racial discrimination through official action is eliminated from the system. . . .

It may well be that petitioners have not yet totally achieved the unitary system contemplated by this quotation from *Swann*. There has been, for example, dispute as to the petitioner's compliance with those portions of the plan specifying procedures for hiring and promoting teachers and administrators. . . . But that does not undercut the force of the principle underlying the quoted language from *Swann*. In this case the District Court approved a plan designed to obtain racial neutrality in the attendance of students at Pasadena's public schools. No one disputes that the initial implementation of this plan accomplished *that* objective. That being the case, the district Court was not entitled to require the School District to rearrange its attendance zones each year so as to ensure that the racial mix desired by the court was maintained in perpetuity. For having once implemented a racially neutral attendance pattern in order to remedy the perceived constitutional violations on the part of the defendants, the District Court had fully performed its function of providing the appropriate remedy for previous racially discriminatory attendance patterns.

. . .

MR. JUSTICE MARSHALL, WITH WHOM MR. JUSTICE BRENNAN JOINS, DISSENTING.

I cannot agree with the Court that the District Court's refusal to modify the "no majority of any minority" provision of its order was erroneous. Because at the time of the refusal "racial discrimination through official action," *Swann* v. *Charlotte-Mecklenburg Board of Education*, . . . (1971), had apparently not yet been eliminated from the Pasadena school system, it is my view that the District Court did not abuse its discretion in refusing to dissolve a major part of its order.

In denying petitioners' motion for modification of the 1970 desegregation order, the District Court described a three-year pattern of opposition by a number of the members of the Board of Education to both the spirit and letter of the Pasadena Plan. It found that "the Pasadena Plan has not had the cooperation from the Board that permits a realistic measurement of its educational success or failure." . . . Moreover, the 1974 Board of Education submitted to the District Court an alternative to the Pasadena Plan, which, at least in the mind of one member of the Court of Appeals, "would very likely result in rapid resegregation." . . . I agree with Judge Ely that there is "abundant evidence upon which the district judge, in the reasonable exercise of his discretion, could rightly determine that the 'dangers' which induced the original determination of constitutional infringements in Pasadena have not diminished suffi-

ciently to require modification or dissolution of the original Order." . . .

The Court's conclusion that modification of the District Court's order is mandated is apparently largely founded on the fact that during the Pasadena Plan's first year, its implementation did result in no school having a majority of minority students. According to the Court, it follows from our decision in *Swann,* *supra,* that as soon as the school attendance zone scheme had been successful, even for a very short period, in fulfilling its objectives, the District Court should have relaxed its supervision over that aspect of the desegregation plan. It is irrelevant to the Court that the system may not have achieved " 'unitary' status in all other respects such as the hiring and promoting of teachers and administrators." . . .

In my view, the Court, in so ruling, has unwarrantedly extended our statement in *Swann* that "[n]either school authorities nor district courts are constitutionally required to make year-by-year adjustments of the racial composition of student bodies *once the affirmative duty to desegregate has been accomplished and racial discrimination through official action is eliminated from the system.*" . . . That statement recognizes on the one hand that a fully desegregated school system may not be compelled to adjust to attendance zones to conform to changing demographic patterns. But on the other hand, it also appears to recognize that *until* such a unitary system is established, a district court may act with broad discretion—discretion which includes the adjustment of attendance zones—so that the goal of a wholly unitary system might be sooner achieved.

In insisting that the District Court

largely abandoned its scrutiny of attendance patterns, the Court might well be insuring that a unitary school system in which segregation has been eliminated "root and branch," . . . will never be achieved in Pasadena. For at the point that the Pasadena system is in compliance with the aspects of the plan specifying procedures for hiring and promoting teachers and administrators, it may be that the attendance patterns within the system will be such as to once again manifest substantial aspects of a segregated system. It seems to me singularly unwise for the Court to risk such a result.

. . .

[Of the many problems faced by federal court judges in desegregation suits, two have proved particularly intractable: (1) determining whether or not a particular condition of segregation, if not the result of past laws, was brought about by the purposeful and intentional actions of officials (as required by the Supreme Court in the *Keyes* case, and reiterated in *Washington* v. *Davis,* 1976); and (2) when such a constitutional violation has been found, determining the appropriate scope of the remedy—in particular whether or not a "system-wide" remedy is appropriate. The questions, of course, are not unrelated. Both were addressed again by the Supreme Court in *Columbus Board of Education* v. *Penick* (1979) and a companion case, *Dayton Board of Education* v. *Brinkman* (1979).

The Columbus litigation had begun in 1973. Figures showed that, as of 1976, about 32% of the school population was black; 70% of the students in the district attended schools which were either 80% black or 80% white; and half of the schools were more than 90% uniracial. Following extensive and prolonged hearings, the district court found that the public schools in Columbus were "openly and intentionally segregated on the basis of race" at the time of the *Brown* case, and that following *Brown* the school board failed to take active measures to dismantle the dual system. Even in recent years, the court found, the school board "ap-proved optional attendance zones, discontiguous attendance areas and boundary changes which have maintained and enhanced racial imbalance in the Columbus Public Schools." The court concluded that segregation in the Columbus schools resulted directly from "intentional segregative acts and omissions" in violation of the Equal Protection Clause. And it further found that, even though black students were concentrated in a few schools in one part of the city in 1954, that the subsequent failure by the school board to effect a transition to a unitary school system, and its intentional segregative acts, had a "systemwide impact" which called for a systemwide remedy. The school board was directed to come up with such a plan, and the Court of Appeals for the Sixth Circuit affirmed. The Columbus School Board petitioned the Supreme Court for a writ of certiorari. It disputed the district court's conclusion that the segregated condition of the Columbus schools (which, in itself, was not disputed) was the result of intentional official action and inaction, and it challenged the finding of a systemwide impact and imposition of a systemwide remedy.

A 7-2 majority of the Supreme Court affirmed the order of the District Court. Justice White wrote:

. . .

"Against this background, we cannot fault the conclusion of the District Court and the Court of Appeals that at the time of trial there was systemwide segregation in the Columbus schools that was the result of recent and remote intentionally segregative actions of the Columbus Board. While appearing not to challenge most of the subsidiary findings of historical fact, . . . petitioners dispute many of the factual inferences drawn from these facts by the two courts below. On this record, however, there is no apparent reason to disturb the factual findings and conclusions entered by the District Court and strongly affirmed by the Court of Appeals after its own examination of the record.

Nor do we discern that the judgments entered below rested on any misapprehension of the controlling law. It is urged that the courts below failed to heed the requirements of *Keyes,*

Washington v. *Davis* . . . (1976), and *Village of Arlington Heights* v. *Metropolitan Housing Dev. Corp* . . . (1977), that a plaintiff seeking to make out an equal protection violation on the basis of racial discrimination must show purpose. Both courts, it is argued, considered the requirement satisfied if it were shown that disparate impact would be the natural and foreseeable consequence of the practices and policies of the Board, which, it is said, is nothing more than equating impact with intent, contrary to the controlling precedent.

The District Court, however, was amply cognizant of the controlling cases. It understood that to prevail the plaintiffs were required to " 'prove not only that segregated schooling exists but also that it was brought about or maintained by intentional state action,' " . . . that is, that the school officials had "intended to segregate." . . . The District Court also recognized that under those cases disparate impact and foreseeable consequences, without more, do not establish a constitutional violation. Nevertheless, the District Court correctly noted that actions having foreseeable and anticipated disparate impact are relevant evidence to prove the ultimate fact, forbidden purpose. Those cases do not forbid "the foreseeable effects standard from being utilized as one of the several kinds of proofs from which an inference of segregative intent may be properly drawn." . . . Adherence to a particular policy or practice, "with full knowledge of the predictable effects of such adherence upon racial imbalance in a school system is one factor among many others which may be considered by a court in determining whether an inference of segregative intent should be drawn." The District Court thus stayed well within the requirements of *Washington* v. *Davis* and *Arlington Heights*. . . .

It is also urged that the District Court and the Court of Appeals failed to observe the requirements of our recent decision in *Dayton I,* which reiterated the accepted rule that the remedy imposed by a court of equity should be commensurate with the violation ascertained and held that the remedy for the violations that had then been established in that case should be aimed at rectifying the "incremental segrega-tive effect" of the discriminatory acts identified. In *Dayton I,* only a few apparently isolated discriminatory practices had been found; yet a systemwide remedy had been imposed without proof of a systemwide impact. Here, however, the District Court repeatedly emphasized that it had found purposefully segregative practices with current, systemwide impact. And the Court of Appeals, responding to similar arguments said:

School board policies of systemwide application necessarily have systemwide impact. 1) The pre-1954 policy of creating an enclave of five schools intentionally designed for black students and known as 'black' schools as found by the District Judge, clearly had a 'substantial'—indeed, a systemwide—impact. 2) The post-1954 failure of the Columbus Board to desegregate the school system in spite of many requests and demands to do so, of course, had systemwide impact. 3) So, too, did the Columbus Board's segregative school construction and siting policy as we have detailed it above. 4) So too did its student assignment policy which, as shown above, produced the large majority of racially identifiable schools as of the school year 1975–1976. 5) The practice of assigning black teachers and administrators only or in large majority to black schools likewise represented a systemwide policy of segregation. This policy served until July 1974 to deprive black students of opportunities for contact with and learning from white teachers, and conversely to deprive white students of similar opportunities to meet, know and learn from black teachers. It also served as discriminatory, systemwide racial identification of schools.

Nor do we perceive any misuse of *Keyes,* where we held that purposeful discrimination in a substantial part of a school system furnishes a sufficient basis for an inferential finding of a systemwide discriminatory intent unless otherwise rebutted, and that given the purpose to operate a dual school system one could infer a connection between such a purpose and racial separation in other parts of the school system. There was no undue reliance here on the inferences permitted by *Keyes,* or upon those recognized by *Swann.* Furthermore, the Board was given ample opportunity to counter the evidence of segregative purpose and current, systemwide impact, and the findings of the courts below were against it in both respects."

By a 5-4 vote a similar result was affirmed in the companion case from Dayton. Justice Stewart and Chief Justice Burger concurred only in the result in the Columbus case, and joined the dissenters in the Dayton case. They felt obliged to defer to the district court's findings in the Columbus case; but in Dayton the federal district judge had ruled against the black plaintiffs, only to be reversed by the Court of Appeals, a critical difference for Stewart and Burger.

The cases turned on two findings of fact. First, both systems were segregated, or "dual" systems at the time the *Brown* case was decided in 1954. This finding imposed on the school board in each case the burden of demonstrating good faith effort to effect a transition to a racially neutral system. In the Dayton case, however, the evidence of more recent official acts with discriminatory intent was weak, while in the Columbus case it was quite strong. Stewart and Burger agreed that the black plaintiffs in the Columbus case had made out a prima facie case of a systemwide violation, but that the plaintiffs in Dayton had not. For them, these differences were crucial.

The scope of the remedy was also at issue. The constitutional test for determining the scope of a remedy against systemwide school discrimination was stated by the Court in *Dayton Board of Education* v. *Brinkman* (1977), an earlier version of the Dayton school case known as "Dayton I":

If such violations are found, the District Court in the first instance, subject to review by the Court of Appeals, must determine how much incremental segregative effect these violations had on the *racial distribution of the school population as presently constituted, when that distribution is compared to what it would have been in the absence of such constitutional violations. The remedy must be designed to redress that difference, and only if there has been a systemwide impact may there be a systemwide remedy.*

Stewart and Burger accepted the findings of the trial judges—that the Columbus School Board was guilty of a systemwide violation and the Dayton School Board was not. Stewart's opinion made clear that he thought the Columbus School Board could have done a better job of showing that some of its schools were not implicated in racial discrimination and thus ought not to be included in the remedy. But they did not carry this burden and Stewart and Burger, with visible reluctance, "[could not] say the remedy was improper."

For the two dissenters, Powell and Rehnquist, the decisions were completely unacceptable. Powell wrote: "The opinions also seem remarkably insensitive to the now widely accepted view that a quarter of a century after *Brown* v. *Board of Education . . .* (1954), the federal judiciary should be limiting rather than expanding the extent to which courts are operating the public schools of our country." He argued that school segregation today is largely the result of demographic factors beyond the control of school boards—or courts:

Federal courts, including this Court today, continue to ignore these indisputable facts. Relying upon fictions and presumptions in school cases that are irreconcilable with principles of equal protection law applied in all other cases . . . federal courts prescribe systemwide remedies without relation to the causes of the segregation found to exist, and implement their decrees by requiring extensive transportation of children of all school ages.

The type of state-enforced segregation that Brown *properly condemned no longer exists in this country. This is not*

*to say that school boards—particularly
in the great cities of the North, Midwest,
and West, are taking all reasonable measures to provide integrated educational
opportunities. As I indicated in . . .*
Keyes *. . . de facto segregation has
existed on a large scale in many of these
cities, and often it is indistinguishable
in effect from the type of* de jure *segregation outlawed by* Brown. *Where there is
proof of intentional segregative action
or inaction, the federal courts must act,
but their remedies should not exceed the
scope of the constitutional violation. . . .
Systemwide remedies such as were ordered by the courts below, and today are
approved by this Court, lack any principled basis when the absence of integration in all schools cannot reasonably be
attributed to discriminatory conduct.*

(9) Harrell Rodgers, Jr. and Charles Bullock III, Law and Change in School Segregation

. . .

This study of school desegregation
confirms previous findings that law
can be a powerful agent of social, economic, and political change.
Change did not come easily in school
desegregation but in the course of fifteen to sixteen years a very important
policy goal was achieved. The significance of the policy innovation accomplished is suggested by the initial
resistance to it, the considerable
struggle necessary for its achievement, and its long-term implications.
In the face of acute opposition, recurring efforts led to a policy innovation
that played a significant part in un-
dercutting the superstructure of racism in the South. Few post–World
War II policies are likely to have more
domestic import.

It is important, however, to note
how school desegregation occurred.
Over a twenty-year period the Su-

preme Court first eroded the "separate but equal" doctrine, and then in
Brown completely overruled it. These
decisions placed the Supreme Court's
imprimatur on the right of black
Americans to attend desegregated
schools, and started the process of
legitimizing this new right. The process of legitimizing is one of the most
powerful functions of American
courts. The ability of the courts to
legitimize rights results from Americans being, as Scheingold says, particularly "responsive to legal symbols." From childhood Americans are
taught to believe in the rule of law. As
we have noted, law is no talisman but
when a right is embodied in law, it is
much more likely to be accepted.

The Court's recognition of the right
of blacks to attend desegregated
schools was one of the major stimuli
for the civil rights movement. *Brown
I and II* created considerable political
controversy about the rights of blacks
and eventually served as one of the
catalysts for political mobilization
that produced hundreds of demonstrations and court suits (over a variety of civil rights matters), and finally
led to a series of civil rights laws.
Thus, standing alone, the Court's
early decisions did not produce great
changes in school desegregation or
any other area of civil rights. But in
time the Court's actions were an important catalyst for very important
policy innovations. Additionally, over
the years, when Congress or the
Executive branch has faltered on
school desegregation, the courts have
chastised and prodded them back
toward the goal of racial equality.

The process of change, but certainly not the ultimate magnitude of
it, initiated by the Court's decisions
on school desegregation is rather typical of the role of law in producing

Reprinted from *Coercion to Compliance* (Lexington, Mass.: Lexington
Books, 1976), pp. 123–130.

important policy innovations. Court decisions and other laws frequently provoke political activities which facilitate achievement of policy goals (most frequently through stronger laws and/or more effective administrative actions). A single court decision or law, however, does not generally produce *great* change unless it is part of an advanced incremental process. Thus, as [James] Levine has said, "Law is better understood as a catalyst of change rather than a singular effector of change."

Obviously not all laws stimulate change. Some laws do not provoke the necessary political mobilization for success. Other laws, although fully implemented, are largely symbolic because they demand little or because their directives or standards are vague. Still others, such as decisions banning schoolhouse religion or those extending the rights of individuals accused of crime, have frequently been inadequately designed and too laxly enforced to accomplish their stated goal. This indicates, of course, that the ability of a specific law to evoke policy innovation depends on a number of leverage factors. Understanding the role of law as a policy innovator, therefore, necessitates identification of the factors that determine the efficacy of laws. This and other studies have begun the task of specifying conditions associated with legal efficacy.

Consistently, studies indicate that cost/benefit factors are important in determining compliance behavior. Decision makers and citizens tend to obey laws, especially but not exclusively unpopular laws, when the benefits and costs of obedience outweigh the benefits and costs of disobedience.

In this study we found federal enforcement activities to be particularly critical in desegregating schools. The coercion necessary to eliminate dual schools in a particular community was associated with factors assumed to measure local decision makers' perceptions of the costs of compliance. In communities in which compliance costs were perceived to be high and rewards low, the most severe coercion was required. The factors that influenced decision makers' perceptions of costs were: (1) the extent to which they agreed with desegregation decisions: (2) whether the community had an elected or appointed superintendent; (3) the compliance behavior of neighboring districts; and (4) two measures of local opposition to desegregation—the size of the black population and community income levels. These factors, singularly and cumulatively, affected decision makers' cost/benefit considerations.

. . .

The cumulative evidence seems to indicate that for a wide range of policy areas the following concise factors are worth consideration: (1) whether the regulated acknowledge that a legal standard which requires compliance has been established; (2) whether the regulated agree with the legal standard; (3) whether the regulated feel that they would benefit from the law; (4) whether environmental factors support or mitigate against compliance; (5) whether the law clearly and carefully defines who is responsible for enforcement; (6) whether the law specifies the type and amount of compliance required; (7) whether the regulated perceive that certain and serious sanctions will result from noncompliance; and (8) whether those who are to receive the benefits of the law are cohesive and take strong actions to achieve their rights.

We do not argue that each of these factors will always be important or that the variables exhaust the range of critical items for all policies. In fact, some of the factors were not important in this study. But generally we suspect that these variables, or at least some of them, will account for a significant amount of the outcome variance in a broad range of policy areas. The dynamics of particular compliance situations will determine which variables are elevated to critical roles. Thus, in attempting to predict compliance with a particular law, these variables constitute a reasonable starting point.

. . .

The increasing sophistication of insights into the factors that determine compliance and thus the impact of laws should considerably enhance our ability to use law as an instrument of creative social change. Presently many laws designed to promote positive social change are ineffective. Some of these laws, of course, were never meant to be effective. In other words, the politics of the situation resulted in a purposefully flawed and weak law. Still, there are policy areas in which sincere attempts to use law as an agent of change have failed. These failures frequently result from two factors. First, the impact of specific laws is often unknown. Even members of the United States Supreme Court have admitted concern about the lack of information on the impact of their decisions. For example, information on the consequences of laws dealing with job discrimination varies from limited to nonexistent. Without information on the effect of laws we frequently cannot know who gets what, when, and how in the political process. Additionally, without impact information, adjustments cannot be made to overcome obstacles to effective policy implementation. In many instances policymakers may not even

recognize that the law has not accomplished its goal, and therefore they may perceive no need for policy alterations.

Second, even when a law has clearly not accomplished its specified objectives, information on the factors that influence the efficacy of laws is necessary if causes of failures are to be understood. In many instances officials' claims of dismay over the failure of a law may be cynical since the law may have intentionally been poorly designed or not enforced. However, without a fairly sophisticated understanding of the factors that influence the efficacy of laws, cynicism may be difficult to detect. Successful policy implementation, therefore, may be facilitated considerably by insights into the leverage variables that determine compliance. Regardless of our insights into the efficacy of laws, many would question whether law is a proper and viable agent of social change. Criticisms usually fall into two categories: (1) that law is intrinsically conservative and thus incapable of promoting progressive change; and (2) that law can never really alter deeply felt attitudes. These arguments warrant examination.

[Edgar] Friedenberg is an excellent example of those who argue that the function of law is to preserve and defend the existing system and thus cannot be a vehicle for social change.

It is not customary for law to yield justice; if law is to perform its social function, justice must yield law. . . . [I]n order to maintain the stability and continuity of any society, the law must encode and legitimate its existing status arrangements, defend their institutional sources, and insure the prerogatives on which succession rests.

The policies that evolve in courts and other political institutions temper

Friedenberg's contention that law is always a conservative force and that it cannot yield justice.

Friedenberg is not completely wrong, but he exaggerates seriously. Without denying that power arrangements in our society favor elites and that many of our laws cause great suffering to the poor and suppressed, the evidence indicates that law has frequently been an important agent of progressive policy change in our society.

Since World War II, the Supreme Court's role in promoting positive change has been extremely important. Some of the more obvious areas in which the Court has played a major policymaking role include the reallocation of political power through reapportionment; the extension of civil rights to blacks in a broad range of areas including enfranchisement, school desegregation, public accommodations, and employment; the extension and protection of the rights of welfare recipients and political dissenters (including demonstrators, conscientious objectors, etc.). These decisions have frequently overcome injustices, promoted a more egalitarian society, and occasionally have reallocated scarce economic resources and power. It is fair to say that these decisions have constituted some of the most important political and civil libertarian advances of the last thirty years.

While considerably more sluggish, Congress and the state legislatures have also passed many laws promoting positive social change during this period. Examples include legislation for freedom of information (sunshine laws), campaign reform, civil rights laws, housing subsidies, Medicare, etc. Additionally, the local court system, while far from perfect, dispenses justice in small but potent doses in a steady manner. Thus law is not always conservative and it frequently can be used to promote justice and equality. . . .

The second argument against law is that it can never change deep-rooted attitudes. This argument is simply incorrect. Legal requirements frequently lead people to think differently about an issue, even in sensitive and emotional areas such as race relations, and the rights of women and juveniles. For example, numerous studies show that whites' attitudes toward blacks have mellowed dramatically during the last twenty years. The evidence indicates that these changes have resulted because laws have drastically altered the social and economic relationships between the races. As [William] Muir has pointed out, law has played a similar role in many other policy areas. Law, then, can educate, inculcate, and change the values of society.

[Thomas] Pettigrew has shown that laws do not promote change the way we might anticipate; i.e., laws do not change attitudes which in turn produce behavior changes. Instead, laws which require a different pattern of behavior (such as public accommodation laws) eventually lead to new attitudes toward the issue. In so doing, law plays an extremely important role. This means, of course, that society need not wait for attitudes to change before a law can be instituted. Indeed, in many instances, until the law is passed and enforced, attitudes are unlikely to change.

Thus law can be, and frequently is, a viable agent of positive social change in our society. Indeed, the evidence on the frequent effectiveness of law as an agent of social change suggests the appropriateness of more rather than less faith in it. The evidence indicates that law can work; we only have to make certain that it does. As [Theodore] Lowi has said, "Law is a plan. Positive law guides and moves in known ways."

. . .

The most important and obvious implication of this study for completing school desegregation in the North is that federal coercion will be necessary. Districts that have maintained segregated systems for decades and have ignored the moral mandate of *Brown* for more than twenty years are not likely to now admit their wrongs and voluntarily implement desegregation.

The culpability of many northern districts was recently established in a Supreme Court decision. In *Keyes,* the Supreme Court stripped away the cloak of innocence that northern districts long hid behind. The myth that northern segregation was fortuitous (*de facto*) rather than purposeful (*de jure,* that is, based on legal or official acts) was substantially undermined. The Court ruled that segregation was illegal if there had ever been any efforts to segregate, regardless of whether segregation had been mandated by law. This definition of illegal segregation allows culpability to turn on school board actions such as student assignment patterns, school construction policies, school site selection, housing laws and codes, and even bank lending policies. Investigations of such acts in northern districts have typically revealed them to be a source of school segregation.

Many northern cities, then, are as guilty of illegal behavior as the South was, and the legal mandate has been established. Despite the *Keyes* decision, the federal government retains a less demanding stance vis-à-vis the North.

Should widespread desegregation of northern schools become a serious objective of federal policy, the degree of coercion required to achieve it will depend on how local officials evaluate the cost/benefits of the situation. As in the South, coercion will have to be more intense if school officials perceive desegregation to be particularly costly. Some of the factors that affect school officials' perceptions of costs include the officials' personal attitudes toward desegregation, the number of black students in the district, the degree and intensity of racism and opposition to desegregation in the community (indicated at least partially by the economic and educational status of the local population), and the degree of vulnerability of school officials to local pressures (elected vs. appointed posts). The compliance status of neighboring districts may also affect school officials' assessments of costs and benefits. If neighboring districts have been allowed to avoid desegregation, the cost of compliance may be perceived as higher, and more pressure may be required. However, if neighboring districts have been sternly dealt with for noncompliance, less pressure may suffice. Of course, pressures on school officials from local citizens can be reduced by specific, direct, and unequivocal federal orders that leave them no choice but to comply.

Since most northern blacks live in urban areas, there will be greater logistical problems than were present in much of the South. The great numbers of students and schools, the geographic spread, and the complexities of transportation systems create difficult problems for reducing racial isolation in urban districts. Nonetheless, southern cities, when faced with desegregation imperatives, have often made notable progress. The pattern in recent years has been for southern city districts to become less segregated while the opposite was occurring in other regions. For example, the Duval County (Jacksonville), Florida; Columbus, Ohio; and Boston school systems are roughly comparable in size and percent black. Between 1968 and 1972 the proportion of black pupils in majority white schools rose from 12.6 to 70.4 percent in Jacksonville, while in Columbus it inched up from 28.8 to 29.4 percent, and in Boston it declined from 23.1 to 17.8 percent. Since Jacksonville operates a larger system than do the two northern cities, its progress reveals that size alone is not a barrier to desegregation. The progress of other southern cities such as Tampa, Nashville, and Charlotte also indicates that far more desegregation is attainable in many northern cities, using existing remedies. Additionally, in a recent decision the Supreme Court has ruled that urban and suburban districts can be consolidated for desegregation purposes if it can be shown that the districts involved engaged in or contributed to segregation. This decision could have substantial impact on desegregation since it would eliminate suburban sanctuaries that have contributed to segregation by allowing whites to flee (or avoid) the city, creating more intense segregation, even sometimes resegregation. . . .

C. The Right to Vote

(1) Smith v. Allwright (1944)

+Stone, Black, Reed, Frankfurter, Douglas, Murphy, Jackson, Rutledge
−Roberts

[In Grovey v. Townsend (1935), the Supreme Court upheld the validity of the white primary by accepting the legal fiction that a primary election was the private affair of a political party and thus not subject to the Fourteenth Amendment. In 1941, however, in an election fraud case in Louisiana (United States v. Classic), the Supreme Court found that for purposes of the federal civil rights statute invoked in that case, the Democratic primary was within the coverage of the Fourteenth Amendment. The 1935 white primary case, Grovey v. Townsend, was specifically distinguished. But the contradiction between the two rulings was clear, and another attempt was made to have the Supreme Court consider the constitutionality of the white primary.

Smith, a Negro citizen, sued Allwright, an election official, for damages for failing to allow him to vote in a primary election for statewide and congressional officers.]

MR. JUSTICE REED delivered the opinion of the Court.

. . . The State of Texas by its Constitution and statues provides that every person, if certain other requirements are met which are not here in issue, qualified by residence in the district or county "shall be deemed a qualified elector." . . . Primary elections for United States Senators, Congressmen and state officers are provided. . . . Under these chapters, the Democratic party was required to hold the primary which was the occasion of the alleged wrong to petitioner. . . .

The Democratic party of Texas is held by the Supreme Court of that State to be a "voluntary association," . . . protected by § 27 of the Bill of Rights, Art. 1, Constitution of Texas, from interference by the State except that:

In the interest of fair methods and a fair expression by their members of their preferences in the selection of their nominees, the State may regulate such elections by proper laws.

The Democratic party on May 24, 1932, in a state convention adopted the following resolution, which has not since been "amended, abrogated, annulled or avoided":

Be it resolved that all white citizens of the State of Texas who are qualified to vote under the Constitution and laws of the State shall be eligible to membership in the Democratic party and, as such, entitled to participate in its deliberations.

It was by virtue of this resolution that the respondents refused to permit the petitioner to vote. . . .

The right of a Negro to vote in the Texas primary has been considered heretofore by this Court. The first case was *Nixon* v. *Herndon.* . . . At that time, 1924, the Texas statute . . . declared "in no event shall a Negro be eligible to participate in a Democratic Party primary election in the State of Texas." Nixon was refused the right to vote in a Democratic primary and brought a suit for damages against the election officers. . . . [T]he Court held that the action of Texas in denying the ballot to Negroes by statute was in violation of the equal protection clause of the Fourteenth Amendment and reversed the dismissal of the suit.

The legislature of Texas reenacted the article but gave the State Executive Committee of a party the power to prescribe the qualifications of its members for voting or other participation. This article remains in the statutes. The State Executive Committee of the Democratic party adopted a resolution that white Democrats and none other might participate in the primaries of that party. Nixon was refused again the privilege of voting in a primary and again brought suit for damages. . . . This Court again reversed the dismissal of the suit for the reason that the Committee action was deemed to be state action and invalid as discriminatory under the Fourteenth Amendment, *Nixon* v. *Condon.* . . .

In *Grovey* v. *Townsend* . . . this Court had before it another suit for damages for the refusal in a primary of a county clerk, a Texas officer with only public functions to perform, to furnish petitioner, a Negro, an absentee ballot. The refusal was solely on the ground of race. This case differed from *Nixon* v. *Condon, supra,* in that a state convention of the Democratic party had passed the resolution of May 24, 1932, herein before quoted. It was decided that the determination by the state convention of the membership of the Democratic party made a significant change from a determination by the Executive Committee. The former was party action, voluntary in character. The latter, as had been held in the *Condon* case, was action by authority of the State. The managers of the primary election were therefore declared not to be an organ of the State. This Court went on to announce that to deny a vote in a primary was a mere refusal of party membership with which "the State need have no concern" . . . while for a State to deny a vote in a general election on the ground of race or color violated the Constitution. . . .

Since *Grovey* v. *Townsend* and prior to the present suit, no case from Texas involving primary elections has been before this Court. We did decide, however, *United States* v. *Classic.* . . . We there held that § 4 of Article I of the Constitution authorized Congress to regulate primary as well as general elections . . . "where the primary is by law made an integral part of the election machinery." . . . This decision depended, too, on the determination that under the Louisiana statutes the primary was a part of the procedure for choice of federal officials. By this decision the doubt as to whether or not such primaries were a part of "elections" subject to federal control, which had remained unanswered since *Newberry* v. *United States* . . . was erased. The *Nixon Cases* were decided under the equal protection clause of the Fourteenth Amendment without a determination of the status of the primary as a part of the electoral process. The exclusion of Negroes from the primaries by action of the State was held invalid under that Amendment. The fusing by the *Classic* case of the primary and general elections into a single instrumentality for choice of officers has a definite bearing on the permissibility under the Constitution of excluding Negroes from primaries. This is not to say that the *Classic* case cuts directly into the rationale of *Grovey* v. *Townsend*. This latter case was not mentioned in the opinion. *Classic* bears upon *Grovey* v. *Townsend* not because exclusion of Negroes from primaries is any more or less state action by reason of the unitary character of the electoral process but because the recognition of the place of the primary in the electoral scheme makes clear that state delegation to a party of the power to fix the qualifications of primary elections is delegation of a state function that may make the party's action the action of the State. When *Grovey* v. *Townsend* was written, the Court looked upon the denial of a vote in a primary as a mere refusal by a party of party membership. . . . [O]ur ruling in *Classic* as to the unitary character of the electoral process calls for a reexamination as to whether or not the exclusion of Negroes from a Texas party primary was state action.

It may now be taken as a postulate that the right to vote in such a primary for the nomination of candidates without discrimination by the State, like the right to vote in a general election, is a right secured by the Constitution. . . . By the terms of the Fifteenth Amendment that right may not be abridged by any State on account of race. Under our Constitution the great privilege of the ballot may

not be denied a man by the State because of his color. . . .

Primary elections are conducted by the party under state statutory authority. . . .

We think that this statutory system for the selection of party nominees for inclusion on the general election ballot makes the party which is required to follow these legislative directions an agency of the State in so far as it determines the participants in a primary election. The party takes its character as a state agency from the duties imposed upon it by state statutes; the duties do not become matters of private law because they are performed by a political party. . . . When primaries become a part of the machinery for choosing officials, state and national, as they have here, the same tests to determine the character of discrimination or abridgment should be applied to the primary as are applied to the general election. If the State requires a certain electoral procedure, prescribes a general election ballot made up of party nominees so chosen and limits the choice of the electorate in general elections for state offices, practically speaking, to those whose names appear on such a ballot, it endorses, adopts and enforces the discrimination against Negroes, practiced by a party entrusted by Texas law with the determination of the qualifications of participants in the primary. This is state action within the meaning of the Fifteenth Amendment. . . .

The privilege of membership in a party may be, as this Court said in *Grovey* v. *Townsend* . . . no concern of a State. But when, as here, that privilege is also the essential qualification for voting in a primary to select nominees for a general election, the State makes the action of the party the action of the State. In reaching this conclusion we are not unmindful of the desirability of continuity of decision in constitutional questions. However, when convinced of former error, this Court has never felt constrained to follow precedent. In constitutional questions, where correction depends upon amendment and not upon legislative action this Court throughout its history has freely exercised its power to re-examine the basis of its constitutional decisions. This has long been accepted practice, and this practice has continued to this day. This is particularly true when the decision believed erroneous is the application of a constitutional principle rather than an interpretation of the Constitution to extract the principle itself. Here we are applying, contrary to the recent decision in *Grovey* v. *Townsend*, the well-established principle of the Fifteenth Amendment, forbidding the abridgement by a State of a citizen's right to vote. *Grovey* v. *Townsend* is overruled.

Judgment Reversed.

MR. JUSTICE FRANKFURTER CONCURS IN THE RESULT.

MR. JUSTICE ROBERTS, DISSENTING.

. . . I have expressed my views with respect to the present policy of the court freely to disregard and to overrule considered decisions and the rules of law announced in them. This tendency, it seems to me, indicates an intolerance for what those who have composed this court in the past have conscientiously and deliberately concluded, and involves an assumption that knowledge and wisdom reside in us which was denied to our predecessors. . . .

The reason for my concern is that the instant decision, overruling that announced about nine years ago, tends to bring adjudications of this tribunal into the same class as a re-stricted railroad ticket, good for this day and train only. I have no assurance, in view of current decisions, that the opinion announced today may not shortly be repudiated and overruled by justices who deem they have new light on the subject. . . .

As that court points out, the statutes of Texas have not been altered since *Grovey* v. *Townsend* was decided. The same resolution is involved as was drawn in question in *Grovey* v. *Townsend*. Not a fact differentiates that case from this except the names of the parties.

It is suggested that *Grovey* v. *Townsend* was overruled *sub silentio* in *United States* v. *Classic*. . . . If so, the situation is even worse than that exhibited by the outright repudiation of an earlier decision, for it is the fact that, in the *Classic* case, *Grovey* v. *Townsend* was distinguished in brief and argument by the Government without suggestion that it was wrongly decided, and was relied on by the appellees, not as a controlling decision, but by way of analogy. . . .

It is regrettable that in an era marked by doubt and confusion, an era whose greatest need is steadfastness of thought and purpose, this court, which has been looked to as exhibiting consistency in adjudication, and a steadiness which would hold the balance even in the face of temporary ebbs and flows of opinion, should now itself become the breeder of fresh doubt and confusion in the public mind as to the stability of our institutions.

(2) Gerald M. Stern, Judge
William Harold Cox and the Right to Vote in Clarke County, Mississippi

. . . In 1957 and again in 1960, Civil Rights Bills were passed, au-

Reprinted from Leon Friedman (ed.), *Southern Justice* (Cleveland: Meridian, 1967), pp. 167–176, 179–181.

thorizing the Department of Justice to initiate suits to secure Negroes the right to vote. The Civil Rights Division was set up primarily to enforce this right. . . .

One of the first witnesses interviewed in Clarke County was Sylvester McRee, a 71-year-old plumber, who was a member of the NAACP for 25 years. He told me that the Negro leaders of the county had been trying to register to vote under every registrar for the past thirty years. He said they would try again each time a new registrar would come into office, but they were always turned away. They waited, and prayed that the next registrar would be fair, or that someone would come to lend a hand. He told me, "I'd been reading the '57 and '60 Civil Rights Bills, and I thought you'd soon be coming to find out about us."

On July 6, 1961, the Federal government filed a lawsuit against the registrar of Clarke County, alleging that none of the 3000 Negroes but a substantial majority of the white persons of voting age were registered to vote, that Negroes had been arbitrarily denied the right to register to vote, and that they were not afforded the same opportunities to register as were white persons. . . .

Under the specific provisions of the 1960 Civil Rights Act, the government has the right to inspect public voting records. But Judge Cox refused to let us see them, and it took many months and many appeals before we were permitted to inspect the voting records in Clarke County.

Even without the voting records it would seem that the statistics of Clarke County demonstrate discrimination—almost all the white persons but none of the Negroes were registered to vote, and none of the Negroes in Clarke County had ever heard of a Negro's being permitted to register to vote. Judge Brown of the United States Court of Appeals for the Fifth Circuit has said, "In the problem of racial discrimination, statistics often tell much, and Courts listen." It is true that the Fifth Circuit listens. However, Judge Cox hears such statistics a bit differently. . . .

Our motion to see the voting records was set for a hearing, but first the lawyers for the registrar filed a motion with the court to postpone our hearing and to allow them more time to answer our complaint. With their motion they filed affidavits stating they were heavily burdened with other civil rights cases and did not have time to work on this case—other than to draw up affidavits to state how busy they were. . . .

Five Negroes from Clarke County were there in court to tell the judge they had not been allowed to vote because they were black. But they were not allowed to testify. All day, legal arguments were made in Judge Cox's courtroom in front of a beautiful mural depicting white people dispensing justice and running industry and Negro people picking cotton and singing happily along the banks of the Mississippi River.

Judge Cox finally ended this long first day by refusing to have the case proceed until the government amended its complaint to allege the names of all the Negroes ever denied the right to register and the dates on which this happened, and the names of all white applicants treated better than Negro applicants, and the dates on which they were registered. He ordered the government to give Mississippi this information without letting us first see the county voting records that told the complete story and were already in the hands of the registrar. . . .

The defense, perhaps taking its cue from Judge Cox, immediately filed a motion for a more definite statement of the government's complaint. In October 1961, we filed an amended complaint listing as many names and dates as we knew, and the defendants replied with a motion to strike parts of our amended complaint as prejudicial to the defendant registrar. They asked again for a more definite statement of our claims.

Time drifted on without a hearing on our motion to see the voting records. In February, 1962, we asked Judge Cox for a ruling on our motion. In March, 1962, we filed a motion for a preliminary injunction. Finally the judge set a hearing for April 2, 1962, on both these motions. But he postponed the date, after hearing the defendant's motions to strike part of the amended complaint and to make the complaint more definite. The judge listened patiently to the defendants' motions, took them under advisement, and cancelled our April 2 hearing date.

In May we filed another motion with the court, asking for a hearing date for our discovery motion. Judge Cox then overruled the defendants' motions, and on June 31, 1962—exactly 365 days after we had filed our complaint and asked to see the voting records—the judge gave us a hearing date for our discovery motion. . . .

The trial lasted three days. The defendant registrar, A. L. Ramsey, is a thin, frail, 82-year-old man. He is friendly and kind, called "Judge" because he had once been a local judge. He was not mean or vicious as are some of the registrars, but was merely trying to do his duty as he saw it and to continue a way of life he had always known.

"Judge" Ramsey had been circuit court clerk, and registrar of voters, since 1953 and registered "practically all" of the white persons now on the registration rolls. He testified it had been the practice from "time immemorial" for white people to register for each other—husbands for wives, parents for children, brothers for sisters, politicians for voters, etc. White people could register by proxy and did not have to take any test. Indeed, they did not even have to go to town to sign the registration book. An FBI handwriting expert testified there were 1500 instances where groups of two or more signatures on the registration book were written by one person—in one case one person had registered for fourteen different people. Since there were only about 5000 white persons registered in the county, the testimony of the FBI expert alone proved that at least 30 percent of the white people had registered by proxy, without taking any kind of test. . . .

Samuel Owens is 79 years old. He has been the principal of the Negro school in Clarke County for the past 55 years. When the county decided to comply with the Supreme Court decision declaring separate but equal schools unconstitutional by building a separate and equal school for the Negroes, they named the school after Samuel Owens. Once, more than 40 years ago, he had been registered to vote, but when he went to vote he was told that Clarke County's primary was for white Democrats only. Soon thereafter the county had a reregistration and his name was scratched from the rolls.

The last reregistration in Clarke County was begun in 1953, about the time Ramsey became registrar. Owens tried to register twice in 1958, but both times Ramsey refused to permit him to apply. He tried again around April 18, 1961, at about the time the FBI was in Clark County checking on complaints about voting discrimination. Ramsey told him he was out of application forms and could not register him. Later the registrar testified he did have some forms that day but did not find them until after Owens left. Whether or not Ramsey actually had forms that day is not important. The point is that almost all white persons in the county registered without forms, even white persons who applied after Owens. . . .

Owens tried again, and on June 1, 1961, a month before we filed our lawsuit, he became the first Negro given the chance to make an application for registration since Ramsey took office. But getting the application form is only the first rung of the ladder. Filling out an application form is no simple matter in Mississippi. An applicant has to answer 17 questions giving information about himself, filing in the right lines and checking the right places. Then he must interpret one of the 265 sections of the Mississippi constitution selected by the registrar. And finally, the applicant must write a statement setting forth his understanding of the duties and obligations of citizenship under a constitutional form of government. There are no standard, correct answers. The interpretation and statement must be acceptable to the registrar, according to his whim.

Ramsey gave Owens an application form and required him to interpret Section 112 of the Mississippi constitution, a long and difficult section dealing with taxation by the legislature. . . .

After completing the form, interpreting Section 112, and writing a statement of the duties and obligations of citizenship, Owens was told he would be notified if he passed, though Ramsey admitted Owen's form looked "O.K." In fact, Owens's interpretation of Section 112 was so good that it was apparently copied verbatim by two white applicants who registered a year later.

Owens was not registered the day he completed the form. Only nine white applicants had been required to fill out forms before Owens. These nine were permitted to register the same day they filled out their forms. The next four white applicants who received forms after Owens was given a form were all registered by Ramsey on the same day they completed their forms. In fact, until September 12, 1961, all white applicants were registered the same day they applied. But Owens had to come back again—the fifth time in 1961—the seventh time since 1958, before he became the first Negro registered to vote in Clarke County in at least thirty years. . . .

After the voting trial was over and both sides had filed briefs, Judge Cox made his findings. He found that at least 1500 white persons had been illegally registered to vote, but he found that the registrar also illegally registered Negroes. For this astounding conclusion, Judge Cox cited the example of the five Negroes placed on the rolls for jury service. This evidence which seemed to prove conclusively that the registrar knew that Negroes had systematically been denied the right to register was used to show that they were given the same opportunities that whites received. . . .

At least half of the white witnesses could not read or write and yet had been registered to vote. Judge Cox solved this problem by ordering that the registrar not register any more illiterates, white or Negro. Judge Cox then ruled that the registrar must apply the tough Mississippi voting laws requiring applicants to interpret any section of the Mississippi constitution. However, in order to be fair, the registrar was ordered to place the first fifty sections in a jar and have each applicant draw out a section.

Almost all white people in the county and almost none of the Negroes were now registered to vote. Requiring the registrar to use the interpretation test would keep the illiterate whites on the rolls and the literate Negroes who are unable to interpret the Mississippi constitution off the rolls.

Judge Cox did find that there had been discrimination against Negroes seeking to register in Clarke County. But the key to the Federal voting referee provisions is a finding that Negroes have been denied the right to register to vote pursuant to a "pattern or practice of discrimination." We asked Judge Cox to find that such a pattern existed in Clarke County. The evidence showed no Negro had been registered in thirty years until a week before our case was filed; the registrar admitted telling Negroes to go home when they came in to register; he told them to go home again when they returned; the most respected Negro in the county, the school principal, had to go to the registrar's office seven times and interpret a section of the constitution that even the Mississippi supreme court has trouble with; white people did not have to take tests or even go to the registrar's office to take the trouble of signing their names in the registration books; and white people were registered even if they could not read or write. Judge Cox found there was no pattern of practice of discrimination.

The U.S. Court of Appeals reversed Judge Cox on appeal and said his finding that there had been no pattern or practice of discrimination was "clearly erroneous."

When the case was sent back to Judge Cox, he still refused to find a pattern or practice of discrimination. To avoid the opinion of the Court of Appeals, he withdrew his finding that there had been *no* pattern or practice

and decided in his discretion not to decide whether or not there had been a pattern or practice. The case is again on appeal.

(3) South Carolina v. Katzenbach (1966)

+Warren, Douglas, Clark, Harlan, Brennan, Stewart, White, Fortas
+/−Black

MR. CHIEF JUSTICE WARREN delivered the opinion of the Court.

By leave of the Court, South Carolina has filed a bill of complaint, seeking a declaration that selected provisions of the Voting Rights Act of 1965 violate the Federal Constitution, and asking for an injunction against enforcement of these provisions by the Attorney General. . . .

We hold that the sections of the Act which are properly before us are an appropriate means for carrying out Congress' constitutional responsibilities and are consonant with all other provisions of the Constitution. We therefore deny South Carolina's request that enforcement of these sections of the Act be enjoined.

The constitutional propriety of the Voting Rights Act of 1965 must be judged with reference to the historical experience which it reflects. Before enacting the measure, Congress explored with great care the problem of racial discrimination in voting. . . .

Two points emerge vividly from the voluminous legislative history of the Act contained in the committee hearings and floor debates. First: Congress felt itself confronted by an insidious and pervasive evil which had been perpetuated in certain parts of our country through unremitting and ingenious defiance of the Constitution. Second: Congress concluded that the unsuccessful remedies which it had prescribed in the past would have to be replaced by sterner and more elaborate measures in order to satisfy the clear demands of the Fifteenth Amendment. . . . [The Court here summarizes the systematic efforts of southern states to disenfranchise the Negro.]

According to the results of recent Justice Department voting suits . . . [discriminatory application of voting tests is now the principal] method used to bar Negroes from the polls. Discriminatory administration of voting qualifications has been found in all eight Alabama cases, in all nine Louisiana cases, and in all nine Mississippi cases which have gone to final judgment. Moreover, in almost all of these cases, the courts have held that the discrimination was pursuant to a widespread "pattern or practice." White applicants for registration have often been excused altogether from the literacy and understanding tests or have been given easy versions, have received extensive help from voting officials, and have been registered despite serious errors in their answers. Negroes, on the other hand, have typically been required to pass difficult versions of all the tests, without any outside assistance and without the slightest error. The good morals requirement is so vague and subjective that it has constituted an open invitation to abuse at the hands of voting officials. Negroes obliged to obtain vouchers from registered voters have found it virtually impossible to comply in areas where almost no Negroes are on the rolls.

In recent years, Congress has repeatedly tried to cope with the problem by facilitating case-by-case litigation against voting discrimination. The Civil Rights Act of 1957 authorized the Attorney General to seek injunctions against public and private interference with the right to vote on racial grounds. Perfecting

amendments in the Civil Rights Act of 1960 permitted the joinder of States as party defendants, gave the Attorney General access to local voting records, and authorized courts to register voters in areas of systematic discrimination. Title I of the Civil Rights Act of 1964 expedited the hearing of voting cases before three-judge courts and outlawed some of the tactics used to disqualify Negroes from voting in federal elections.

Despite the earnest efforts of the Justice Department and of many federal judges, these new laws have done little to cure the problem of voting discrimination. According to the estimates by the Attorney General during hearings on the Act, registration of voting age Negroes in Alabama rose only from 10.2% to 19.4% between 1958 and 1964; in Louisiana it barely inched ahead from 31.7% to 31.8% between 1956 and 1965; and in Mississippi it increased only from 4.4% to 6.4% between 1954 and 1964. In each instance, registration of voting age whites ran roughly 50 percentage points or more ahead of Negro registration.

The previous legislation has proved ineffective for a number of reasons. Voting suits are unusually onerous to prepare, sometimes requiring as many as 6,000 man-hours spent combing through registration records in preparation for trial. Litigation has been exceedingly slow, in part because of the ample opportunities for delay afforded voting officials and others involved in the proceedings. Even when favorable decisions have finally been obtained, some of the States affected have merely switched to discriminatory devices not covered by the federal decrees or have enacted difficult new tests designed to prolong the existing disparity between white and Negro registration. Alternatively, certain local officials have defied and evaded court orders or have simply closed their registration offices to freeze the voting rolls. . . .

The remedial sections of the Act assailed by South Carolina automatically apply to any State, or to any separate political subdivision such as a county or parish, for which two findings have been made: (1) the Attorney General has determined that on November 1, 1964, it maintained a "test or device," and (2) the Director of the Census has determined that less than 50% of its voting age residents were registered on November 1, 1964, or voted in the presidential election of November 1964. . . . As used throughout the Act, the phrase "test or device" means any requirement that a registrant or voter must "(1) demonstrate the ability to read, write, understand, or interpret any matter, (2) demonstrate any education achievement or his knowledge of any particular subject, (3) possess good moral character, or (4) prove his qualifications by the voucher of registered voters or members of any class. . . ."

Statutory coverage of a State or political subdivision . . . is terminated if the area obtains a declaratory judgment from the Court for the District of Columbia, determining that tests and devices have not been used during the preceding five years to abridge the franchise on racial grounds. The Attorney General shall consent to entry of the judgment if he has no reason to believe that the facts are otherwise. . . .

South Carolina was brought within the coverage formula of the Act on August 7, 1965 . . . . On the same day, coverage was also extended to Alabama, Alaska, Georgia, Louisiana, Mississippi, Virginia, 26 counties in North Carolina, and one county in Arizona. Two more counties in Arizona, one county in Hawaii, and one county in Idaho were added to the list on November 19, 1965. Thus far, Alaska, the three Arizona counties, and the single county in Idaho have asked the District Court for the District of Columbia to grant a declaratory judgment terminating statutory coverage.

In a State or political subdivision covered by . . . the Act, no person may be denied the right to vote in any election because of his failure to comply with a "test or device."

On account of this provision, South Carolina is temporarily barred from enforcing the portion of its voting laws which requires every applicant for registration to show that he:

Can both read and write any section of [the State] Constitution submitted to [him] by the registration officer or can show that he owns, and has paid all taxes collectable during the previous year on property in this State assessed at three hundred dollars or more. . . .

In a State or political subdivision covered by . . . the Act, no person may be denied the right to vote in any election because of his failure to comply with a voting qualification or procedure different from those in force on November 1, 1964. This suspension of new rules is terminated, however, under either of the following circumstances: (1) if the area has submitted the rules to the Attorney General, and he has not interposed an objection within 60 days, or (2) if the area has obtained a declaratory judgment from the District Court for the District of Columbia, determining that the rules will not abridge the franchise on racial grounds. These declaratory judgment actions are to be heard by a three-judge panel, with direct appeal to this Court.

South Carolina altered its voting

laws in 1965 to extend the closing hour at polling places from 6 P.M. to 7 P.M. The State has not sought judicial review of this change in the District Court for the District of Columbia, nor has it submitted the new rule to the Attorney General for his scrutiny, although at our hearing the Attorney General announced that he does not challenge the amendment. . . .

These provisions of the Voting Rights Act of 1965 are challenged on the fundamental ground that they exceed the powers of Congress and encroach on an area reserved to the States by the Constitution. . . .

The ground rules for resolving this question are clear. The language and purpose of the Fifteenth Amendment, the proper decisions construing its several provisions, and the general doctrines of constitutional interpretation, all point to one fundamental principle. As against the reserved powers of the States, Congress may use any rational means to effectuate the constitutional prohibition of racial discrimination in voting. . . .

This declaration has always been treated as self-executing and has repeatedly been construed, without further legislative specification, to invalidate state voting qualifications or procedures which are discriminatory on their face or in practice. . . . The gist of the matter is that the Fifteenth Amendment supersedes contrary exertions of state power. . . .

South Carolina contends that the cases cited above are precedents only for the authority of the judiciary to strike down state statutes and procedures—that to allow an exercise of this authority by Congress would be to rob the courts of their rightful constitutional role. On the contrary, sec. 2 of the Fifteenth Amendment expressly declares that "Congress shall have the power to enforce this article by appropriate legislation." By adding this authorization, the framers indicated that Congress was to be chiefly responsible for implementing the rights created in sec. 1. . . .

We . . . reject South Carolina's argument that Congress may appropriately do no more than to forbid violations of the Fifteenth Amendment in general terms—that the task of fashioning specific remedies or of applying them to particular localities must necessarily be left entirely to the courts. Congress is not circumscribed by such artificial rules under sec. 2. of the Fifteenth Amendment. . . .

Congress exercised its authority under the Fifteenth Amendment in an inventive manner when it enacted the Voting Rights Act of 1965. First: the measure prescribed remedies for voting discrimination which go into effect without any need for prior adjudication. This was clearly a legitimate response to the problem, for which there is ample precedent under other constitutional provisions. . . . Congress had found that case-by-case litigation was inadequate to combat widespread and persistent discrimination in voting, because of the inordinate amount of time and energy required to overcome the obstructionist tactics invariably encountered in these lawsuits. After enduring nearly a century of systematic resistance to the Fifteenth Amendment, Congress might well decide to shift the advantage of time and inertia from the perpetrators of the evil to its victims. The question remains, of course, whether the specific remedies prescribed in the Act were an appropriate means of combating the evil, and to this question we shall presently address ourselves.

Second: The Act intentionally confines these remedies to a small number of States and political subdivisions which in most instances were familiar to Congress by name. This, too, was a permissible method of dealing with the problem. Congress had learned that substantial voting discrimination presently occurs in certain sections of the country, and it knew no way of accurately forecasting whether the evil might spread elsewhere in the future. In acceptable legislative fashion, Congress chose to limit its attention to the geographic areas where immediate action seemed necessary. . . . The doctrine of the equality of States, invoked by South Carolina, does not bar this approach, for that doctrine applies only to the terms upon which States are admitted to the Union, and not to the remedies for local evils which have subsequently appeared. . . .

Congress began work with reliable evidence of actual voting discrimination in a great majority of the States and political subdivisions affected by the new remedies of the Act. The formula eventually evolved to describe these areas was relevant to the problem of voting discrimination. . . .

Tests and devices are relevant to voting discrimination because of their long history as a tool for perpetrating the evil; a low voting rate is pertinent for the obvious reason that widespread disenfranchisement must inevitably affect the number of actual voters. Accordingly, the coverage formula is rational in both practice and theory. It was therefore permissible to impose the new remedies on the few remaining States and political subdivisions covered by the formula, at least in the absence of proof that they have been free of substantial voting discrimination in recent years. . . .

It is irrelevant that the coverage formula excludes certain localities which do not employ voting tests and devices but for which there is evidence of voting discrimination by other means. . . .

Acknowledging the possibility of overbreadth, the Act provides for termination of special statutory coverage at the behest of States and political subdivisions in which the danger of substantial voting discrimination has not materialized during the preceding five years. . . .

South Carolina contends that these termination procedures are a nullity because they impose an impossible burden of proof upon States and political subdivisions entitled to relief. As the Attorney General pointed out during hearings on the Act, however, an area need do no more than to submit affidavits from voting officials, asserting that they have not been guilty of racial discrimination through the use of tests and devices during the past five years, and then to refute whatever evidence to the contrary may be adduced by the Federal Government. Section 4 (d) further assures that an area need not disprove each isolated instance of voting discrimination in order to obtain relief in the termination proceedings. The burden of proof is therefore quite bearable. . . .

We now arrive at consideration of the specific remedies prescribed by the Act for areas included within the coverage formula. South Carolina assails the temporary suspensions of existing voting qualifications. The record shows that in most of the States covered by the Act, including South Carolina, various tests and devices have been instituted with the purpose of disenfranchising Negroes, have been framed in such a way as to facilitate this aim, and have been administered in a discriminatory fashion for many years. Under these circumstances, the Fifteenth Amendment has clearly been violated. . . .

The Act suspends literacy tests and similar devices for a period of five years from the last occurrence of substantial voting discrimination. This was a legitimate response to the problem, for which there is ample precedent in Fifteenth Amendment cases. . . . Underlying the response was the feeling that States and political subdivisions which had been allowing white illiterates to vote for years could not sincerely complain about "dilution" of their electorates through the registration of Negro illiterates. Congress knew that continuance of the tests and devices in use at the present time, no matter how fairly administered in the future, would freeze the effect of past discrimination in favor of unqualified white registrants. Congress permissibly rejected the alternative of requiring a complete re-registration of all voters, believing that this would be too harsh on many whites who had enjoyed the franchise for their entire adult lives.

The Act suspends new voting regulations pending scrutiny by federal authorities to determine whether their use would violate the Fifteenth Amendment. This may have been an uncommon exercise of congressional power, as South Carolina contends, but the Court has recognized that exceptional conditions can justify legislative measures not otherwise appropriate. . . . Congress knew that some of the States covered by . . . the Act had resorted to the extraordinary strategem of contriving new rules of various kinds for the sole purpose of perpetuating voting discrimination in the face of adverse federal decrees. Congress had reason to suppose that these states might try similar ma-

neuvers in the future, in order to evade the remedies for voting discrimination contained in the Act itself. Under the compulsion of these unique circumstances, Congress responded in a permissibly decisive manner. . . .

After enduring nearly a century of widespread resistance to the Fifteenth Amendment, Congress has marshalled an array of potent weapons against the evil, with authority in the Attorney General to employ them effectively. Many of the areas directly affected by this development have indicated their willingness to abide by any restraints legitimately imposed upon them. We here hold that the portions of the Voting Rights Act properly before us are a valid means for carrying out the commands of the Fifteenth Amendment. Hopefully, millions of nonwhite Americans will now be able to participate for the first time on an equal basis in the government under which they live. We may finally look forward to the day when truly "the right of citizens of the United States to vote shall not be denied or abridged by the United States or by any State on account of race, color, or previous condition of servitude."

The bill of complaint is dismissed.

MR. JUSTICE BLACK CONCURRED except as to the validity of Sec. 5.

[The Voting Rights Act of 1965 also provided that a person who had successfully completed the sixth grade in public or private school in an American Flag school could not be denied the right to vote merely because he or she could not read or write English. The law would have enfranchised a large number of Puerto Rican residents of New York City. To prevent that occurrence, a suit was brought to enjoin enforcement of the statute. In *Katzenbach* v. *Morgan* (1966), the Supreme Court upheld the validity of the statute as a proper exercise of Congress' power to enforce the equal protection clause of the Fourteenth Amendment. In an earlier case, *Lassiter* v. *Northhampton County Board of Election* (1959), the Court had sustained a North Carolina literacy test against Fourteenth and Fifteenth Amendment challenges. But here the Court said that Congress was free to place any reasonable construction it wished on those amendments and enforce them accordingly. Congress might require by statute, through its enforcement powers, what the Supreme Court had not required by virtue of the Fourteenth Amendment alone. Since the statute was a legitimate exercise of Congress' power, it superseded the contrary state law that required literacy in the English language as a condition of voting.]

(4) Harper v. Virginia Board of Elections (1966)

+Warren, Douglas, Clark, Brennan, White, Fortas
−Black, Harlan, Stewart

MR. JUSTICE DOUGLAS delivered the opinion of the Court.

These are suits by Virginia residents to have declared unconstitutional Virginia's poll tax. The three-judge District Court, feeling bound by our decision in *Breedlove* v. *Suttles* . . . dismissed the complaint.

While the right to vote in federal elections is conferred by Art. I, sec. 2, of the Constitution . . . the right to vote in state elections is nowhere expressly mentioned. It is argued that the right to vote in state elections is implicit, particularly by reason of the First Amendment and that it may not constitutionally be conditioned upon the payment of a tax or fee. We do not stop to canvass the relation between voting and political expression. For it is enough to say that once the franchise is granted to the electorate, lines may not be drawn which are inconsistent with the Equal Protection

Clause of the Fourteenth Amendment. . . . We were speaking there of a state literacy test which we sustained, warning that the result would be different if a literacy test, fair on its face, were used to discriminate against a class. But the *Lassiter* case does not govern the result here, because, unlike a poll tax, the "ability to read and write . . . has some relation to standards designed to promote intelligent use of the ballot."

We conclude that a State violates the Equal Protection Clause of the Fourteenth Amendment whenever it makes the affluence of the voter or payment of any fee an electoral standard. Voter qualifications have no relation to wealth nor to paying or not paying this or any other tax. Our cases demonstrate that the Equal Protection Clause of the Fourteenth Amendment restrains the States from fixing voter qualifications which invidiously discriminate. . . .

Long ago in *Yick Wo* v. *Hopkins*, the Court referred to the political franchise of voting as a "fundamental political right, because preservative of all rights." Recently in *Reynolds* v. *Sims*, we said, "Undoubtedly, the right of suffrage is a fundamental matter in a free and democratic society. Especially since the right to exercise the franchise in a free and unimpaired manner is preservative of other basic civil and political rights, any alleged infringement of the right of citizens to vote must be carefully and meticulously scrutinized." . . .

The principle that denies the State the right to dilute a citizen's vote on account of his economic status or other such factors by analogy bars a system which excludes those unable to pay a fee to vote or who fail to pay.

It is argued that a State may exact fees from citizens for many different kinds of expenses; that if it can demand from all an equal fee for a driver's license, it can demand from all an equal poll tax for voting. But we must remember that the interest of the State, when it comes to voting, is limited to the power to fix qualifications. Wealth, like race, creed, or color is not germane to one's ability to participate intelligently in the electoral process. Lines drawn on the basis of wealth or property, like those of race . . . are traditionally disfavored. . . . To introduce wealth or payment of a fee as a measure of a voter's qualifications is to introduce a capricious or irrelevant factor. The degree of the discrimination is irrelevant. In this contest—that is, as a condition of obtaining a ballot—the requirement of fee paying causes an "invidious" discrimination that runs afoul of the Equal Protection Clause. Levy "by the poll," . . . is an old familiar form of taxation; and we say nothing to impair its validity so long as it is not made a condition to the exercise of the franchise. *Breedlove* v. *Suttles* sanctioned its use as "a prerequisite of voting." To that extent the *Breedlove* case is overruled.

We agree, of course, with Mr. Justice Holmes that the Due Process Clause of the Fourteenth Amendment "does not enact Mr. Herbert Spencer's Social Statics" . . . . Likewise, the Equal Protection Clause is not shackled to the political theory of a particular era. In determining what lines are unconstitutionally discriminatory, we have never been confined to historic notions of equality, any more than we have restricted due process to a fixed catalogue of what was at a given time deemed to be the limts of fundamental rights. . . . Notions of what constitutes equal treatment for purposes of the Equal Protection Clause do change. . . .

Our conclusion, like that in *Reynolds* v. *Sims*, is founded not on what we think governmental policy should be, but on what the Equal Protection Clause requires.

We have long been mindful that where fundamental rights and liberties are asserted under the Equal Protection Clause, classifications which might invade or restrain them must be closely scrutinized and carefully confined. . . .

Reversed.

MR. JUSTICE BLACK, DISSENTING.

. . . A study of our cases shows that this Court has refused to use the general language of the Equal Protection Clause as though it provided a handy instrument to strike down laws which the Court feels are based on bad governmental policy. The equal protection cases carefully analyzed boil down to the principle that distinctions drawn and even discriminations imposed by state laws do not violate the Equal Protection Clause so long as these distinctions and discriminations are not "irrational," "irrelevant," "unreasonable," "arbitrary," or "invidious." These vague and indefinite terms do not, of course, provide a precise formula or an automatic mechanism for deciding cases arising under the Equal Protection Clause. The restrictive connotations of these terms, however . . . are a plain recognition of the fact that under a proper interpretation of the Equal Protection Clause States are to have the broadest kind of leeway in areas where they have a general constitutional competence to act. . . . State poll tax legislation can "reasonably," "rationally" and without an "invidious" or evil purpose to injure anyone be found to rest on a number of state policies including (1) the State's desire to collect its revenue, and (2) its belief that voters who pay a poll tax will be interested in furthering the State's welfare when they vote. Certainly it is rational to believe that people may be more likely to pay taxes if payment is a prerequisite to voting. And if history can be a factor in determining the "rationality" of discrimination in a state law . . . then whatever may be our personal opinion, history is on the side of "rationality" of the State's poll tax policy. Property qualifications existed in the Colonies and were continued by many States after the Constitution was adopted. . . .

Another reason for my dissent from the Court's judgment and opinion is that it seems to be using the old "natural-law-due-process formula" to justify striking down state laws as violations of the Equal Protection Clause. . . .

The Court denies that it is using the "natural-law-due-process formula." . . . I find no statement in the Court's opinion, however, which advances even a plausible argument as to why the alleged discriminations which might possibly be affected by Virginia's poll tax law are "irrational," "unreasonable," "arbitrary," or "invidious" or have no relevance to a legitimate policy which the State wishes to adopt. . . . I can only conclude that the primary, controlling, predominate, if not the exclusive reason for declaring the Virginia law unconstitutional is the Court's deepseated hostility and antagonism, which I share, to making payment of a tax a prerequisite to voting. . . .

I have no doubt at all the Congress has the power under sec. 5 to pass legislation to abolish the poll tax in order to protect the citizens of this country if it believes that the poll tax is being used as a device to deny voters equal protection of the law. . . . But this legislative power which was granted to Congress by sec. 5 of the

Fourteenth Amendment is limited to Congress. . . .

MR. JUSTICE HARLAN, WHOM MR. JUSTICE STEWART JOINS, DISSENTING (OMITTED).

(5) Oregon v. Mitchell (1970)

+Black, Douglas, Brennan, White, Marshall

−Burger, Harlan, Stewart, Blackmun

[In 1970, Congress extended the Voting Rights Act for five years, with some amendments. Literacy tests as a qualification for voting in *any* election, state or national, were suspended nationwide for a period of five years. Durational residency requirements for voting in presidential elections were prohibited. The act provided that voters could register to vote for president within thirty days of the election. Finally, the law prohibited the denial to any citizen over the age of eighteen the right to vote "on account of age" in either state or federal elections. Oregon was one of several states to file original jurisdiction complaints challenging the application of the extended voting age to state and federal elections.

The Supreme Court unanimously upheld the ban on literacy tests, and it upheld the prohibition on durational residency requirements in presidential elections by an 8-1 vote. On the question of extending the vote to eighteen-year-olds, however, the Court was badly split. Four justices—Douglas, Brennan, White, and Marshall—believed that Congress had the power to enfranchise 18-year-olds in both state and federal elections. Four justices—Burger, Harlan, Stewart, and Blackmun—thought that Congress did not have the power to enfranchise 18-year-olds in *either* state or federal elections. Justice Black, casting the deciding vote, held that Congress had the power to enfranchise 18-year-olds in federal elections but not in state elections.

One of the key questions at issue in this case was the extent of congressional power to enforce the equal protection clause. *Katzenbach*

v. *Morgan* (1966) was interpreted by proponents of the bill as holding that Congress had whatever power was necessary, subject to explicit constitutional prohibitions, to enforce the equal protection clause. Others were more cautious, and many were unwilling to believe that Congress had the virtually unlimited discretion that some of the words in the *Morgan* case seemed to imply. What exactly did Justice Brennan mean in *Morgan* when he wrote: "It is not for us to review the congressional resolution of these factors. It is enough that we be able to perceive a basis upon which the Congress might resolve the conflict as it did"?]

MR. JUSTICE BLACK announced the judgments of the Court in an opinion expressing his own view.

. . .

In these suits the States resist compliance with the Voting Rights Act Amendments of 1970, . . . because they believe that the Act takes away from them powers reserved to the States by the Constitution to control their own elections. By its terms the Act does three things. First: It lowers the minimum age of voters in both state and federal elections from 21 to 18. Second: Based upon a finding by Congress that literacy tests have been used to discriminate against voters on account of their color, the Act enforces the Fourteenth and Fifteenth Amendments by barring the use of such tests in all elections, state and national. Third: The Act forbids States from disqualifying voters in national elections for presidential and vice presidential electors because they have not met state residency requirements.

For the reasons set out in Part I of this opinion, I believe Congress can fix the age of voters in national elections, such as congressional, senatorial, Vice-Presidential and Presidential elections, but cannot set the voting age in state and local elections.

For reasons expressed in separate opinions, my Brothers Douglas, Brennan, White and Marshall join me in concluding that Congress can enfranchise 18-year-old citizens in national elections, but dissent from the judgment that Congress cannot extend the franchise to 18-year-old citizens in state and local elections. For reasons expressed in separate opinions, my Brothers The Chief Justice, Harlan, Stewart, and Blackmun join me in concluding that Congress cannot interfere with the age for voters set by the States for state and local elections. They, however, dissent from the judgment that Congress can control voter qualifications in federal elections. In summary, it is the judgment of the Court that the 18-year-old vote provisions of the Voting Rights Act Amendments of 1970 are constitutional and enforceable insofar as they pertain to federal elections and unconstitutional and unenforceable insofar as they pertain to state and local elections.

For the reasons set out in Part II of this opinion, I believe that Congress, in the exercise of its power to enforce the Fourteenth and Fifteenth Amendments, can prohibit the use of literacy tests or other devices used to discriminate against voters on account of their race in both state and federal elections. For reasons expressed in separate opinions, all of my Brethren join me in this judgment. Therefore the literacy test provisions of the Act are upheld.

For the reasons set out in Part III of this opinion, I believe Congress can set residency requirements and provide for absentee balloting in elections for presidential and vice presidential electors. For reasons expressed in separate opinions, my Brothers The Chief Justice, Douglas, Brennan, Stewart, White, Marshall, and Blackmun concur in this judgment. My Brother Harlan, for the reasons stated in his separate opinion, considers that the residency provisions of the statute are unconstitutional. Therefore the residency and absentee balloting provisions of the Act are upheld.

I

The Framers of our Constitution provided in Art I, § 2, that members of the House of Representatives should be elected by the people and that the voters for Representatives should have "the Qualifications requisite for Electors of the most numerous Branch of the State Legislature." Senators were originally to be elected by the state legislatures, but under the Seventeenth Amendment Senators are also elected by the people, and voters for Senators have the same qualifications as voters for Representatives. In the very beginning the responsibility of the States for setting the qualifications of voters in congressional elections was made subject to the power of Congress to make or alter such regulations if it deemed advisable. This was done in Art I, § 4 of the Constitution which provides:

The Times, Places and Manner of holding Elections for Senators and Representatives, shall be prescribed in each state by the legislature thereof; but the Congress may at any time by Law make or alter such Regulations, except as to the Place of Chusing Senators. (Emphasis supplied.)

Moreover, the power of Congress to make election regulations in national elections is augmented by the Necessary and Proper Clause. In *United States* v. *Classic* (1941), where the Court upheld congressional power to regulate party primaries, Mr. Justice Stone speaking for the Court construed the interrelation of these clauses of the Constitution, stating:

While, in a loose sense, the right to vote for representatives in Congress is sometimes spoken of as a right derived from the states, . . . this statement is true only in the sense that the states are authorized by the Constitution, to legislate on the subject as provided by § 2 of Art I, to the extent that Congress has not restricted state action by the exercise of its powers, to regulate elections under § 4 and its more general power under Article I, § 8, clause 18 of the Constitution, "to make all laws which shall be necessary and proper for carrying into execution the foregoing powers."

The breadth of power granted to Congress to make or alter election regulations in national elections, including the qualifications of voters, is demonstrated by the fact that the Framers of the Constitution and the state legislatures which ratified it intended to grant to Congress the power to lay out or alter the boundaries of the congressional districts. In the ratifying conventions speakers "argued that the power given Congress in Art I, § 4, was meant to be used to vindicate the people's right to equality of representation in the House," *Wesberry* v. *Sanders . . .* (1964), and that Congress would "most probably . . . lay the state off into districts." And in *Colegrove* v. *Green*, (1946), no Justice of this Court doubted Congress' power to rearrange the congressional districts according to population; the fight in that case revolved about the judicial power to compel redistricting.

Surely no voter *qualification* was more important to the Framers than the *geographical qualification* embodied in the concept of congressional districts. The Framers expected Congress to use this power to eradicate "rotten boroughs," and

Congress has in fact used its power to prevent States from electing all Congressmen at large. There can be no doubt that the power to alter congressional district lines is vastly more significant in its effect than the power to permit 18-year-old citizens to go to the polls and vote in all federal elections.

Any doubt about the powers of Congress to regulate congressional elections, including the age and other qualifications of the voters should be dispelled by the opinion of this Court in *Smiley* v. *Holm*, . . . (1932). There, Chief Justice Hughes writing for a unanimous Court discussed the scope of congressional power under § 4 at some length. He said:

The subject matter is the "times, places and manner of holding elections for Senators and Representatives." It cannot be doubted that these comprehensive words embrace authority to provide a complete code for congressional elections, not only as to times and places, but in relation to notices, registration, supervision of voting, protection of voters, prevention of fraud and corrupt practices, counting of votes, duties of inspectors and canvassers, and making and publication of election returns; in short, to enact the numerous requirements as to procedure and safeguards which experience shows are necessary in order to enforce the fundamental right involved. . . .

This view is confirmed by the second clause of Article I, section 4, which provides that "the Congress may at any time by law make or alter such regulations," with the single exception stated. . . . In exercising this power, the Congress may supplement these state regulations or may substitute its own. . . . It "has a general supervisory power over the whole subject."

In short, the Constitution allotted to the States the power to make laws regarding national elections, but provided that if Congress became dissatisfied with the state laws, Congress could alter them. . . . The Voting Rights Act Amendments of 1970 now before this Court evidence dissatisfaction of Congress with the voting age set by many of the States for national elections. I would hold, as have a long line of decisions in this Court, that Congress has ultimate supervisory power over congressional elections. Similarly, it is the prerogative of Congress to oversee the conduct of presidential and vice presidential elections and to set the qualifications for voters for electors for those offices. It cannot be seriously contended that Congress has less power over the conduct of presidential elections than it has over congressional elections.

On the other hand, the Constitution was also intended to preserve to the States the power that even the Colonies had to establish and maintain their own separate and independent governments, except insofar as the Constitution itself commands otherwise. My Brother Harlan has persuasively demonstrated that the Framers of the Constitution intended the States to keep for themselves, as provided in the Tenth Amendment, the power to regulate elections. My major disagreement with my Brother Harlan is that, while I agree as to the States' power to regulate the elections of their own officials, I believe, contrary to his view, that Congress has the final authority over federal elections. No function is more essential to the separate and independent existence of the States and their governments than the power to determine within the limits of the Constitution the qualifications of their own voters for state, county, and municipal offices and the nature of their own machinery for filling local public offices. . . .

My Brother Brennan's opinion, if carried to its logical conclusion, would, under the guise of insuring equal protection, blot out all state power, leaving the 50 States little more than impotent figureheads. In interpreting what the Fourteenth Amendment means, the Equal Protection Clause should not be stretched to nullify the States' powers over elections which they had before the Constitution was adopted and which they have retained throughout our history.

Of course, the original design of the Founding Fathers was altered by the Civil War Amendments and various other amendments to the Constitution. The Thirteenth, Fourteenth, Fifteenth, and Nineteenth Amendments have expressly authorized Congress to "enforce" the limited prohibitions of those amendments by "appropriate legislation." The Solicitor General contends in these cases that Congress can set the age qualifications for voters in state elections under its power to enforce the Equal Protection Clause of the Fourteenth Amendment.

Above all else, the Framers of the Civil War Amendments intended to deny to the States the power to discriminate against persons on account of their race. While this Court has recognized in some instances that the Equal Protection Clause of the Fourteenth Amendment protects against discriminations other than those on account of race, see *Reynolds* v. *Sims* . . . (1964) . . . it cannot be successfully argued that the Fourteenth Amendment was intended to strip the States of their power, carefully preserved in the original Constitution, to govern themselves. The Fourteenth Amendment was surely not intended to make every discrimination between groups of people a constitutional denial of equal protection. Nor

was the Enforcement Clause of the Fourteenth Amendment intended to permit Congress to prohibit every discrimination between groups of people. On the other hand, the Civil War Amendments were unquestionably designed to condemn and forbid every distinction, however trifling, on account of race.

To fulfill their goal of ending racial discrimination and to prevent direct or indirect state legislative encroachment on the rights guaranteed by the amendments, the Framers gave Congress power to enforce each of the Civil War Amendments. These enforcement powers are broad. In *Jones* v. *Alfred H. Mayer* . . . (1968), the Court held that § 2 of the Thirteenth Amendment "clothed 'Congress with the power to pass *all laws necessary and proper for abolishing all badges and incidents of slavery in the United States.*' "

As broad as the congressional enforcement power is, it is not unlimited. Specifically, there are at least three limitations upon Congress' power to enforce the guarantees of the Civil War Amendments. First, Congress may not by legislation repeal other provisions of the Constitution. Second, the power granted to Congress was not intended to strip the States of their power to govern themselves or to convert our national government of enumerated powers into a central government of unrestrained authority over every inch of the whole Nation. Third, Congress may only "enforce" the provisions of the amendments and may do so only by "appropriate legislation." Congress has no power under the enforcement section to undercut the Amendments' guarantees of personal equality and freedom from discrimination, see *Katzenbach* v. *Morgan* . . . (1966), or to undermine those protections of the Bill of Rights which we have held the Fourteenth Amendment made applicable to the States.

In enacting the 18-year-old vote provisions of the Act now before the Court, Congress made no legislative findings that 21-year-old vote requirements were used by the States to disenfranchise voters on account of race. I seriously doubt that such a finding, if made, could be supported by substantial evidence. Since Congress has attempted to invade an area preserved to the States by the Constitution without a formulation for enforcing the Civil War Amendments' ban on racial discrimination, I would hold that Congress has exceeded its powers in attempting to lower the voting age in state and local elections. On the other hand, where Congress legislates in a domain not exclusively reserved by the Constitution to the States, its enforcement power need not be tied so closely to the goal of eliminating discrimination on account of race.

To invalidate part of the Voting Rights Act Amendments of 1970, however, does not mean that the entire Act must fall or that the constitutional part of the 18-year-old vote provision cannot be given effect. In passing the Voting Rights Act Amendments of 1970, Congress recognized that the limits of its power under the Enforcement Clauses were largely undetermined, and therefore included a broad severability provision:

If any provision of this Act or the application of any provision thereof to any person or circumstance is judicially determined to be invalid, the remainder of this Act or the application of such provision to other persons or circumstances shall not be affected by such determination.

In this case, it is the judgment of the Court that Title III, lowering the voting age to 18, is invalid as applied to voters in state and local elections. It is also the judgment of the Court that Title III is valid with respect to national elections. We would fail to follow the express will of Congress in interpreting its own statute if we refuse to sever these two distinct aspects of Title III. Moreover, it is a longstanding canon of statutory construction that legislative enactments are to be enforced to the extent that they are not inconsistent with the Constitution, particularly where the valid portion of the statute does not depend upon the invalid part. . . . Here, of course, the enforcement of the 18-year-old vote in national elections is in no way dependent upon its enforcement in state and local elections.

II

. . .

In Title II of the Amendments Congress prohibited the use of any test or device resembling a literacy test in any national, state, or local election in any area of the United States where such test is not already proscribed by the Voting Rights Act of 1965. The State of Arizona maintains that Title II cannot be enforced to the extent that it is inconsistent with Arizona's literacy test requirement. I would hold that the literacy test ban of the 1970 Amendments is constitutional under the Enforcement Clause of the Fifteenth Amendment and that it supersedes Arizona's conflicting statutes under the Supremacy Clause of the Federal Constitution.

In enacting the literacy test ban of Title II Congress had before it a long history of the discriminatory use of literacy tests to disfranchise voters on account of their race. Congress could have found that as late as the summer of 1968, the percentage registration of nonwhite voters in seven Southern States was substantially below the percentage registration of white voters. Moreover, Congress had before it striking evidence to show that the provisions of the 1965 Act had in the span of four years had a remarkable impact on minority group voter registration. Congress also had evidence to show that voter registration in areas with large Spanish-American populations was consistently below the state and national averages. Congressional concern over the use of literacy tests to disfranchise Puerto Ricans in New York State is already a matter of record in this Court, *Katzenbach* v. *Morgan, supra.* And as to the Nation as a whole, Congress had before it statistics which demonstrate that voter registration and voter participation are consistently greater in States without literacy tests.

Congress also had before it this country's history of discriminatory educational opportunities in both the North and the South. . . . There is substantial, if not overwhelming, evidence from which Congress could have concluded that it is a denial of equal protection to condition the political participation of children educated in a dual school system upon their educational achievement. Moreover, the history of this legislation suggests that concern with educational inequality was perhaps uppermost in the minds of the congressmen who sponsored the Act. The hearings are filled with references to educational inequality. Faced with this and other evidence that literacy tests reduce voter participation in a discriminatory manner not only in the South but throughout the Nation, Congress was supported by substantial evidence in concluding that a nationwide ban on literacy tests was appropriate to enforce the Civil War Amendments.

Finally, there is yet another reason for upholding the literacy test provisions of this Act. In this legislation Congress has recognized that discrimination on account of color and racial origin is not confined to the South, but exists in various parts of the country. Congress has decided that the way to solve the problems of racial discrimination is to deal with nationwide discrimination with nationwide legislation. . . .

III

In Title II of the Voting Rights Act Amendments Congress also provided that in presidential and vice presidential elections, no voter could be denied his right to cast a ballot because he had not lived in the jurisdiction long enough to meet its residency requirements. Furthermore, Congress provided uniform national rules for absentee voting in presidential and vice presidential elections. In enacting these regulations for national elections Congress was attempting to insure a fully effective voice to all citizens in national elections. What I said in Part I of this opinion applies with equal force here. Acting under its broad authority to create and maintain a national government, Congress unquestionably has power under the Constitution to regulate federal elections.

MR. JUSTICE DOUGLAS, CONCURRING IN PART AND DISSENTING IN PART (OMITTED).

MR. JUSTICE HARLAN, CONCURRING IN PART AND DISSENTING IN PART (OMITTED).

MR. JUSTICE BRENNAN, JOINED BY JUSTICES WHITE AND MARSHALL, CONCURRING IN PART AND DISSENTING IN PART (OMITTED).

MR. JUSTICE STEWART, JOINED BY CHIEF JUSTICE BURGER AND JUSTICE

BLACKMUN, CONCURRING IN PART AND
DISSENTING IN PART (OMITTED).

[Adoption of the Twenty-sixth Amendment
resolved the dispute over Congress' power to
enfranchise eighteen-year-olds in state elections. Section 1 of that amendment provides
that "the right of citizens of the United States,
who are eighteen years of age or older, to vote
shall not be denied or abridged by the United
States or by any State on account of age." Section 2 gives Congress the power to enforce the
amendment by appropriate legislation.]

(6) A Note on Black Voting in the South: The Voting Rights Act Ten Years After

Black voter registration increased
steadily in the eleven southern states
after the demise of the white primary.
According to Matthews and Prothro,
there were an estimated 250,000
Negroes registered to vote in 1940,
about 5 percent of the nonwhite
adults in those states. Three years
after *Smith* v. *Allwright*, in 1947,
that number had more than doubled,
to nearly 600,000. In 1952, it had
doubled again; 20 percent of the
black adult population was registered
to vote. There was little additional
progress during the late 1950s. One
reason may have been the white response to *Brown* and the crisis precipitated by that response. There was
a substantial increase in racial hostility and tension, and "white resistance to Negro advancement stif-
fened in every realm. . . ." On the
other hand, as Matthews and Prothro
note, there is another possible explanation for the slowdown. The first
wave of Negro voters may have represented the "natural" voters—the
better educated middle class. The
remaining potential Negro voters
were politically apathetic and economically disadvantaged, and so unlikely to register to vote without some
external stimulus.[1]

From 1960 to 1964, black voter registration increased by 500,000, a 14
percent jump, attributable in part to
the voter registration drives and the
sit-in movement and the organizational impetus that they provided.
The Civil Rights Acts of 1957 and
1960 helped to clear the way for black
voters, although as Gerald Stern's article demonstrates, that way was still
hazardous and slow.[2]

The United States Civil Rights
Commission estimates that in the
seven southern states "covered" by
the act, 1,148,000 new black voters
registered between 1964 and 1972. In
1964, the commission reports, about
29 percent of the voting-age black
population was registered to vote; in
1972, it was 56 percent. Even allowing for the lack of uniformity and accuracy in voting statistics, this is an
impressive increase. But it is impossible to determine how much is specifically a result of the provisions of
the Voting Rights Act and how much
is a result of other political and legal
factors.

The data show a steady decline in
the gap between black and white registration rates. Just before the Voting Rights Act, the commission estimated that in the seven states, 73.4
percent of potential white voters, but
only 29.2 percent of potential black
voters were actually registered, a gap
of 44.1 percent. By 1972, the percentage of potential white voters registered had declined slightly, to 67.8
percent, while the black voter registration rate had increased to 56.8 percent, reducing the gap to only 11.2

[1]Donald R. Matthews and James W. Prothro, *Negroes and the New Southern Politics* (New York: Harcourt, Brace & World, 1966), pp. 17–20.
[2]Ibid.

percent.[3] The overall figures conceal important differences among the states, however. In South Carolina and Georgia, for example, the gap was less than 3 percent; in Louisiana and Alabama, it exceeded 20 percent.

Voter registration is one thing, but actual voting is another. Have there been substantial increases in black voting? The answer quite clearly is "yes," but because of inadequate data, the conclusion is primarily inferential. Most states do not keep records of voting by race, but analysis of election data and the results of many surveys support an increase in black voting. What the voting data show is that voter turnout increased in all seven states from the 1964 to the 1968 presidential elections, while the national turnout declined slightly. The largest increases came in Alabama and Mississippi. In the 1972 presidential election, voter turnout increased slightly in four of the seven states and declined slightly in the other three. But the decline was not as great as for the United States as a whole.[4]

One final indicator of increases in black voting is the rapid increase in the number of elected black officials. No one knows how many black elected officials there were in the seven southern states prior to 1965, although it is believed there were less than 100. By April 1974, according to the Civil Rights Commission, the number was approaching 1000. There are now black representatives in every southern state legislature, an event not observed since Reconstruction.

A commission report in 1975, while praising the progress made

under the Voting Rights Act, observed that "for the minority citizen, the right to vote is still a precarious right." It noted that the electoral process, for minorities, was still something of an obstacle course, "still controlled by the people (and in many instances the same individuals) who have long sought to exclude them from effective political participation." Minorities must still overcome discrimination and are still vulnerable to economic, physical, and political pressures.[5]

Looking specifically at the Voting Rights Act, the commission noted the importance of the suspension of literacy tests in 1970. It reported that Section 5, which provides for preclearance by the Attorney General or the United States District Court for the District of Columbia of any change in voter qualifications, practices, or procedures, has become the focal point of enforcement of the act in recent years. However, the attorney general does not have a system for monitoring electoral law changes and is therefore dependent on states and counties to submit such changes for approval. Compliance with that provision has therefore been uneven.

The commission also took note of efforts to dilute the effect of new black voting through racial gerrymandering. In particular, the use of at-large elections and multimember districts have often limited the impact of minority voting. So, too, have such apparently neutral devices as annexation and consolidation of voting units. As we will see in the case that follows, *United Jewish Organization of Williamsburg* v. *Carey* (1977), and in Section 5 of this chap-

[3]U.S. Commission on Civil Rights, *The Voting Rights Act: Ten Years After* (Washington, D.C.: U.S. Government Printing Office, 1975), pp. 40–44.
[4]Ibid., p. 45
[5]Ibid, p. 330.

ter, the Supreme Court has not directly confronted all of these practices.

In 1975, Congress extended coverage under the act for seven years and made permanent the nationwide ban on literacy tests and devices. In Title II, "Language minorities," defined as Spanish-Americans, American Indians, Asian-Americans, and Alaskan natives, were brought under the act with the following triggering formula: a language minority exists where more than 5 percent of the population is of a single language minority; where election materials in 1972 were only available in English; and where less than 50 percent of the voting age population registered or voted in the 1972 presidential election. These provisions effectively added Texas and Alaska to the states covered by the act.

In Title III, bilingual election materials were required until 1985 where more than 5 percent of the population is a language minority and where illiteracy exceeded the national rate (defined as failure to complete the fifth grade). A petition for exemption from these requirements could be made to *any* district court. Finally, in Title IV, the statute provided for awarding attorney's fees to the prevailing party in any enforcement suit.

(7) United Jewish Organizations of Williamsburgh, Inc. v. Carey (1977)

+Brennan, Stewart, White, Blackmun, Powell, Rehnquist, Stevens
 −Burger
 NP Marshall

[Three of the five boroughs of New York City—Brooklyn, Manhattan, and the Bronx—became subject to Sections 4 and 5 of the Vot-

ing Rights Act because, in 1968, they employed a literacy test or device and because less than 50 percent of the voting-age residents of the counties voted in the presidential election that year. Efforts to secure exemption from that coverage failed. It was therefore necessary for the state of New York, in accordance with the act, to secure clearance from either the attorney general or a three-judge district court from the District of Columbia for the state legislative and congressional reapportionment statute enacted in 1972.

In 1974, the attorney general objected to portions of the reapportionment statute involving the three counties. He determined that the reapportionment plan had a racially discriminatory purpose or effect in that some districts had an "abnormally high minority concentration while adjoining minority neighborhoods are significantly diffused into surrounding districts." For example, in Brooklyn, there were three state senate districts with nonwhite majorities of 91 percent, 61 percent, and 53 percent. The state responded by amending the act to even out the nonwhite majorities in the districts concerned. Thus, all three senate districts in Brooklyn fell within the range of a 70 to 75 percent nonwhite majority population.

In order to make the required change, however, the new reapportionment plan divided the Hasidic Jewish community in Brooklyn. In the 1972 plan, this community was located entirely within one senate district, which was only 17 percent nonwhite, and one assembly district, which was 61 percent nonwhite. Under the revised plan, it was divided between two senate and two assembly districts. The division of the Hasidic community was done explicitly because state officials believed they had to have a minimum nonwhite population in one district of about 65 percent.

The Hasidic Jews brought suit, contending that this new reapportionment plan would dilute the value of their votes solely for the purpose of achieving a racial quota, in violation of the Fourteenth Amendment. They also alleged that their assignment to a particular voting district was solely on the basis of race and that this violated the Fifteenth Amendment. The district court dismissed their complaint, holding that there was no constitutional right to be recognized as a community for voting purposes and that racial considerations were proper to correct past discrimination. The court of appeals affirmed, holding that racial considerations in reapportionment were proper under these circumstances. It further noted that 70 percent of the senate and assembly districts in Brooklyn had white majorities, consistent with the fact that about 65 percent of the population of the entire borough was white. The Supreme Court granted certiorari.]

MR. JUSTICE WHITE announced the judgment of the Court and filed an opinion joined wholly by MR. JUSTICE STEVENS and joined in part by JUSTICES BRENNAN, BLACKMUN, and REHNQUIST.

. . .

Petitioners argue that the New York Legislature, although seeking to comply with the Voting Rights Act as construed by the Attorney General, has violated the Fourteenth and Fifteenth Amendments by deliberately revising its reapportionment plan along racial lines. In rejecting petitioners' claims, we address four propositions: first, that whatever might be true in other contexts, the use of racial criteria in districting and apportionment is never permissible; second, that even if racial considerations may be used to redraw district lines in order to remedy the residual effects of past unconstitutional reapportionments, there are no findings here of prior discriminations that would require or justify as a remedy that white voters be reassigned in order to increase the size of black majorities in certain districts; third, that the use of a "racial quota" in redistricting is never acceptable; and fourth, that even if the foregoing general propositions are infirm, what New York actually did in this case

was unconstitutional, particularly its use of 65% nonwhite racial quota for certain districts . . .

It is apparent from the fact of the [Voting Rights] Act, from its legislative history, and from our cases that the Act was itself broadly remedial in the sense that it was "designed by Congress to banish the blight of racial discrimination in voting. . . ."

. . . It is also plain, however, that after "repeatedly try[ing] to cope with the problem of facilitating case-by-case litigation against voting discrimination," . . . Congress became dissatisfied with this approach, which required judicial findings of unconstitutional discrimination in specific situations and judicially approved remedies to cure that discrimination. Instead, Congress devised more stringent measures, one of which, § 5, required the covered States to seek the approval of either the Attorney General or of a three-judge court in the District of Columbia whenever they sought to implement new voting procedures. . . .

Given this coverage of the counties involved, it is evident that the Act's prohibition against instituting new voting procedures without the approval of the Attorney General or the three-judge District Court is not dependent upon proving past unconstitutional apportionments and that in operation the Act is aimed at preventing the use of new procedures until their capacity for discrimination has been examined by the Attorney General or by a court. Although recognizing that the "stringent new remedies," including § 5, were "an uncommon exercise of congressional power," we nevertheless sustained the Act as a "permissible decisive" response to "the extraordinary stratagem of contriving new rules of various kinds for the sole purpose of perpetrating voting discrimination in the face of adverse federal court decrees."

It is also clear that under § 5, new or revised reapportionment plans are among those voting procedures, standards or practices that may not be adopted by a covered State without the Attorney General or a three-judge court ruling that the plan "does not have the purpose and will not have the effect of denying or abridging the right to vote on account of race or color." In *Allen* v. *State Board of Education*, on which the Court of Appeals relied below, we held that a change from district to at-large voting for county supervisors had to be submitted for federal approval under § 5, because of the potential for a "dilution" of minority voting power which could "nullify [its] ability to elect the candidate of [its] choice. . . ." . . . When it renewed the Voting Rights Act in 1970 and again in 1975, Congress was well aware of the application of § 5 to redistricting. In its 1970 extension, Congress relied on findings by the United States Commission on Civil Rights that the newly gained voting strength of minorities was in danger of being diluted by redistricting plans that divided minority communities among predominantly white districts. In 1975, Congress was unmistakably cognizant of this new phase in the effort to eliminate voting discrimination. Former Attorney General Katzenbach testified that § 5 "has had its broadest impact . . . in the areas of redistricting and reapportionment," and the Senate and House reports recommending the extension of the Act referred specifically to the Attorney General's role in screening redistricting plans to protect the opportunities for nonwhites to be elected to public office.

. . .

In *Beer* v. *United States*, . . . (1976), the Court considered the question of what criteria a legislature reapportionment must satisfy under § 5 of the Voting Rights Act to demonstrate that it does not have the "effect" of denying or abridging the right to vote on account of race. *Beer* established that the Voting Rights Act does not permit the implementation of a reapportionment that "would lead to a retrogression in the position of racial minorities with respect to their effective exercise of the electoral franchise." . . . This test was satisfied where the reapportionment increased the percentage of districts where members of racial minorities protected by the Act were in the majority, . . . But if this test were not met, clearance by the Attorney General or the District Court for the District of Columbia could not be implemented.

The reapportionment at issue in *Beer* was approved by this Court, because New Orleans had created one councilmanic district with a majority of black voters where none existed before. But had there been districts with black majorities under the previous law and had New Orleans in fact decreased the number of majority black districts, it would have had to modify its plan in order to implement its reapportionment by carving out a large enough black majority in however many additional districts would be necessary to satisfy the *Beer* test. There was division on the Court as to what a State must show to satisfy § 5; but all eight Justices who participated in the decision implicitly accepted the proposition that a State may revise its reapportionment plan to comply with § 5 by increasing the percentage of black voters in a particular district until it has produced a clear majority. . . . Indeed, the plan eventually approved by this Court in *Beer* was drawn with the purpose of avoiding dilution of the black vote by attaining at least a 54 percent majority of black voters in one district while preventing a 90 percent concentration. . . .

The Court has taken a similar approach in applying § 5 to the extension of city boundaries through annexation. Where the annexation has the effect of reducing the percentage of blacks in the city, the proscribed "effect" on voting rights can be avoided by a post-annexation districting plan which "fairly reflects the strength of the Negro community as it exists after the annexation" and which "would afford [it] representation reasonably equivalent to [its] political strength in the enlarged community." *City of Richmond* v. *United States*, . . .

Implicit in *Beer* and *City of Richmond,* then, is the proposition that the Constitution does not prevent a State subject to the Voting Rights Act from deliberately creating or preserving black majorities in particular districts in order to ensure that its reapportionment plan complies with § 5. That proposition must be rejected and § 5 held unconstitutional to that extent if we are to accept petitioners' view that racial criteria may never be used in redistricting or that they may be used, if at all, only as a specific remedy for past unconstitutional apportionments. We are unwilling to overturn our prior cases, however. Section 5, and its authorization for racial redistricting where appropriate to avoid abridging the right to vote on account of race or color, are constitutional. Contrary to petitioners' first argument, neither the Fourteenth nor the Fifteenth Amendment mandates any per se rule against using racial factors in districting and apportionment. . . .

The permissible use of racial criteria is not confined to eliminating the effects of past discriminatory districting or apportionment.

Moreover, in the process of drawing black majority districts in order to comply with § 5, the State must decide how substantial those majorities must be in order to satisfy the Voting Rights Act. The figure used in drawing the *Beer* plan, for example, was 54% of registered voters. At a minimum and by definition, a "black majority district" must be more than 50% black. But whatever the specific percentage, the State will inevitably arrive at it as a necessary means to ensure the opportunity for the election of a black representative and to obtain approval of its reapportionment plan. Unless we adopted an unconstitutional construction of § 5 in *Beer* and *City of Richmond*, a reapportionment cannot violate the Fourteenth or Fifteenth Amendment merely because a State uses specific numerical quotas in establishing a certain number of black majority districts. Our cases under § 5 stand for at least this much.

Having rejected these three broad objections to the use of racial criteria in redistricting under the Voting Rights Act, we turn to the fourth question, which is whether the racial criteria New York used in this case—the revision of the 1972 plan to create 65% nonwhite majorities in two additional senate and two additional assembly districts—were constitutionally infirm. We hold they are not, on two separate grounds. . . .

The first ground is that petitioners have not shown, or offered to prove, that New York did more than the Attorney General was authorized to require it to do under the nonretrogression principle of *Beer* . . .

In the absence of any evidence regarding nonwhite voting strength under the 1966 apportionment, the creation of substantial nonwhite majorities in approximately 30% of the senate and assembly districts in Kings County was reasonably related to the constitutionally valid statutory mandate of maintaining nonwhite voting strength. The percentage of districts with nonwhite majorities was less than the percentage of nonwhites in the county as a whole (35%). The size of the nonwhite majorities in those districts reflected the need to take account of the substantial difference between the nonwhite percentage of the total population in a district and the nonwhite percentage of the voting age population. Because, as the Court said in *Beer*, the inquiry under § 5 focuses ultimately on "the position of racial minorities with respect to their effective exercise of the electoral franchise," . . . the percentage of eligible voters by district is of great importance to that inquiry. . . .

There is a second, and independent ground for sustaining the particulars of the 1974 plan for Kings County. Whether or not the plan was authorized by or was in compliance with § 5 of the Voting Rights Act, New York was free to do what it did as long as it did not violate the Constitution, particularly the Fourteenth and Fifteenth Amendments; and we are convinced that neither Amendment was infringed.

There is no doubt that in preparing the 1974 legislation, the State deliberately used race in a purposeful manner. But its plan represented no racial slur or stigma with respect to whites or any other race, and we discern no discrimination violative of the Fourteenth Amendment nor any abridgment of the right to vote on account of race within the meaning of the Fifteenth Amendment.

It is true that New York deliberately increased the nonwhite majorities in certain districts in order to enhance the opportunity for election of nonwhite representatives from those districts. Nevertheless, there was no fencing out of the white population from participation in the political processes of the county, and the plan did not minimize or unfairly cancel out white voting strength. . . . Petitioners have not objected to the impact of the 1974 plan on the representation of white voters in the county or in the State as a whole. As the Court of Appeals observed, the plan left white majorities in approximately 70% of the assembly and senate districts in Kings County, which had a countywide population that was 65% white. Thus, even if voting in the county occurred strictly according to race, whites would not be underrepresented relative to their share of the population.

In individual districts where nonwhite majorities were increased to approximately 65%, it became more likely, given racial bloc voting, that black candidates would be elected instead of their white opponents, and it became less likely that white voters would be represented by a member of their own race; but as long as whites in Kings County, as a group, were provided with fair representation, we cannot conclude that there was a cognizable discrimination against whites or an abridgement of their right to vote on the grounds of race. Furthermore, the individual voter in the district with a nonwhite majority has no constitutional complaint merely because his candidate has lost out at the polls and his district is represented by a person for whom he did not vote. Some candidate, along with his supporters, always loses. See *Whitcomb* v. *Chavis* . . . (1971).

Where it occurs, voting for or against a candidate because of his race is an unfortunate practice. But it is not rare; and in any district where it regularly happens, it is unlikely that any candidate will be elected who is a member of the race that is in the minority in that district. However disagreeable this result may be, there is no authority for the proposition that the candidates who are found racially unacceptable by the majority, and the minority voters supporting those candidates, have had their Fourteenth or Fifteenth Amendment rights infringed by this process. Their position is similar to that of the Democratic or Republican minority that is submerged year after year by the adherents to the majority party who tend to vote a straight party line.

It does not follow, however, that the State is powerless to minimize the consequences of racial discrimination by voters when it is regularly practiced at the polls. In *Gaffney* v. *Cummings*, the Court upheld a districting plan "drawn with the conscious intent to . . . achieve a rough approximation of the statewide political strengths of the Democratic and Republican Parties." . . . We there recognized that districting plans would be vulnerable under our cases if "racial or political groups have been fenced out of the political process and their voting strength invidiously minimized." . . . But that was not the case there, and no such purpose or effect may be ascribed to New York's 1974 plan. Rather, that plan can be viewed as seeking to alleviate the consequences of racial voting at the polls and to achieve a fair allocation of political power between white and nonwhite voters in Kings County.

In this respect New York's revision of certain district lines is little different in kind from the decision by a State in which a racial minority is unable to elect representatives from multimember districts to change to single-member districting for the purpose of increasing minority representation. This change might sub-stantially increase minority representation at the expense of white voters, who previously elected all of the legislators but with single-member districts could elect no more than their proportional share. If this intentional reduction of white voting power would be constitutionally permissible, as we think it would be, we think it also permissible for a State, employing sound districting principles such as compactness and population equality, to attempt to prevent racial minorities from being repeatedly outvoted by creating districts that will afford fair representation to the members of those racial groups who are sufficiently numerous and whose residential patterns afford the opportunity of creating districts in which they will be in the majority.

. . .

The judgment is affirmed.

MR. JUSTICE BRENNAN, CONCURRING.

. . .

If we were presented here with a classification of voters motivated by racial animus, . . . or with a classification that effectively downgraded minority participation in the franchise, . . . we promptly would characterize the resort to race as "suspect" and prohibit its use. Under such circumstances, the tainted apportionment process would not necessarily be saved by its proportional outcome, for the segregation of voters into "separate but equal" blocs still might well have the intent or effect of diluting the voting power of minority voters. . . . It follows, therefore, that if the racial redistricting involved here, imposed with the avowed intention of clustering together 10 viable nonwhite majorities at the expense of pre-existing white groupings, is not similarly to be prohibited, the distinctiveness that avoids this prohibition must arise from either or both of two considerations: the permissibility of affording preferential treatment to disadvantaged nonwhites generally, or the particularized application of the Voting Rights Act in this instance.

. . .

MR. JUSTICE STEWART, WITH WHOM MR. JUSTICE POWELL JOINS, CONCURRING IN THE JUDGMENT (OMITTED).

. . .

MR. CHIEF JUSTICE BURGER, DISSENTING.

. . .

I begin with this Court's holding in *Gomillion* v. *Lightfoot*, . . . (1960), the first case to strike down a state attempt at racial gerrymandering. If *Gomillion* teaches anything, I had thought it was that drawing of political boundary lines with the sole, explicit objective of reaching a predetermined racial result cannot ordinarily be squared with the Constitution. The record before us reveals—and it is not disputed—that this is precisely what took place here. In drawing up the 1974 reapportionment scheme, the New York Legislature did not consider racial composition as merely *one* of several political characteristics; on the contrary, race appears to have been the one and only criterion applied.

The principle opinion notes that after the 1972 apportionment plan was rejected, New York officials conferred with the Justice Department as to what plan could obtain the Attorney General's approval. One New York official testified that he "got the feeling [from a Justice Department spokesman] . . . that 65 percentage would be probably an approved figure." . . . Further testimony by that same official is revealing:

Q: *So that your reason for dividing the Hassidic community was to effect compliance with the Department of Justice determination, and the minimum standards they impose—they appear to impose?*
A: *That was the sole reason. We spent over a full day right around the clock, attempting to come up with some other type of districting plan that would maintain the Hassidic community as one entity, and I think that is evidenced clearly by the fact that the district is exactly 65 percent, and it's because we went block by block, and didn't go higher or lower than that, in order to maintain as much of the community as possible.*

. . .

This official also testified that apportionment solutions which would have kept the Hassidic community within a single district, but would have resulted in a 63.4% nonwhite concentration, were rejected for fear that, falling short of "exactly 65 percent," they "would not be acceptable" to the Justice Department. . . .

The words "racial quota" are emotionally loaded and must be used with caution. Yet this undisputed testimony shows that the 65% figure was viewed by the legislative reapportionment committee as so firm a criterion that even a fractional deviation was deemed impermissible. I cannot see how this can be characterized otherwise than a strict quota approach and I must therefore view today's holding as casting doubt on the clear-cut principles established in *Gomillion*.

. . .

Faced with the straightforward obligation to redistrict so as to avoid "a retrogression in the position of racial minorities with respect to their effective exercise of the electoral franchise," *Beer* v. *United States*, . . . (1976), the state legislature mechanically adhered to a plan designed to maintain—without tolerance for even a 1.6% deviation—a "nonwhite" population of 65% within several of the new districts. There is no indication whatever that use of this rigid figure was in any way related—much less necessary—to fulfilling the State's obligation under the Voting Rights Act as defined in *Beer*.

. . .

The record is devoid of any evidence that the 65% figure was a reasoned response to the problem of past discrimination. It is, rather, clear that under the time pressure of upcoming elections, and "in an atmosphere of hasty dickering" . . . the New York Legislature simply accepted the standard formula from the Department of Justice and treated it as a mandatory. Moreover, the formula appears to be based upon factually unsupportable assumptions. For example, it would make no sense to assure nonwhites a majority of 65% in a voting district unless it were assumed that nonwhites and whites vote in racial blocs, and that the blocs vote adversely to, or independent of, one another. Not only is the record in this case devoid of any evidence that such bloc voting has taken or will take place in Kings County, but such evidence as there is points in the opposite direction: We are informed that four out of the five "safe" (65%+) nonwhite districts established by the 1974 plan have since elected white representatives. . . .

The assumption that "whites" and "non-whites" in the County form homogeneous entities for voting purposes is entirely without foundation. The "whites" category consists of a veritable galaxy of national origins, ethnic backgrounds, and religious denominations. It simply cannot be assumed that the legislative interests of all "whites" are even substantially identical. In similar fashion, those described as "non-whites" include, in addition to Negroes, a substantial portion of Puerto Ricans. The Puerto Rican population constitutes 10.4% of the entire county population and one-third of the "non-white" population. . . . The Puerto Rican population, for whose protection the Voting Rights Act was "triggered" in Kings County, . . . has expressly disavowed any identity of interest with the Negroes, and, in fact, objected to the 1974 redistricting scheme because it did not establish a Puerto Rican controlled district within the county.

Although reference to racial composition of a political unit, may under certain circumstances, serve as "a starting point in the process of shaping a remedy," *Swann* v. *Charlotte-Mecklenburg Board of Education*, . . . (1971), rigid adherence to quotas, especially in a case like this, deprives citizens such as petitioners of the opportunity to have the legislature make a determination free from unnecessary bias for or against any racial, ethnic or religious group. I do not quarrel with the proposition that the New York Legislature may choose to take ethnic or community union into consideration in drawing its district lines. Indeed, petitioners are members of an ethnic community which, without deliberate purpose so far as shown on this record, has long been within a single Assembly and Senate District. While petitioners certainly have no constitutional right to remain unified within a single political district, they do have, in my view, the constitutional right not to be carved up so as to create a voting bloc composed of some other ethnic or racial group through the kind of racial gerrymandering the Court condemned in *Gomillion* v. *Lightfoot*.

If districts have been drawn in a racially biased manner in the

past(which the record does not show to have been the case here) the proper remedy is to reapportion along neutral lines. Manipulating the racial composition of electoral districts to assure one minority or another its "deserved" representation will not promote the goal of a racially neutral legislature. On the contrary, such racial gerrymandering puts the imprimatur of the State on the concept that race is a proper consideration in the electoral process. "The vice lies in . . . placing . . . the power of the State behind a racial classification that induces racial prejudice at the polls."
. . .

The result reached by the Court today in the name of the Voting Rights Act is ironic. The use of a mathematical formula tends to sustain the existence of ghettos by promoting the notion that political clout is to be gained or maintained by marshalling particular racial, ethnic or religious groups in enclaves. It suggests to the voter that only a candidate of the same race, religion or ethnic origins can properly represent that voter's interests, and that such candidate can be elected only from a district with a sufficient minority concentration. The device employed by the State of New York, and endorsed by the Court today, moves us one step farther away from a truly homogenous society. This retreat from the ideal of the American "melting pot" is curiously out of step with recent political history—and indeed with what the Court has said and done for more than a decade. The notion that Americans vote in firm blocs has been repudiated in the election of minority members as mayors and legislators in numerous American cities and districts overwhelmingly white. Since I cannot square the mechanical racial gerrymandering in this case with the mandate of the Constitution, I respectfully dissent from the affirmance of the judgment of the Court of Appeals.

D. *The State Action Doctrine*

(1) The Civil Rights Cases (1883)

+Bradley, Waite, Field, Woods, Matthews, Gray, Blatchford
−Harlan

[It was widely assumed at the time that the Thirteenth, Fourteenth, and Fifteenth Amendments conferred on the Congress broad powers to protect the rights of Negro citizens, broader even than the self-executing provisions of the amendments themselves (provisions, that is, which were judicially enforceable without congressional action). We have already seen how the Supreme Court, in the *Slaughterhouse Cases* (1873), narrowed the scope of the Fourteenth Amendment. The Court did observe in that case that, although the amendment was of broader scope, its pervading spirit and primary purpose was to protect the rights of Negroes. But it then went on to hold that the privileges and immunities clause of the amendment protected citizens only from a narrow range of deprivations that were held to be privileges and immunities of "citizens of the United States." In dicta, Justice Miller's opinion noted that the equal protection clause was the intended instrument to invalidate *laws* that discriminated against Negroes. This was a very narrow view of the amendment, which prohibits all discriminatory state actions ("No state shall . . .") and not just discriminatory *laws*. Justice Miller also espoused a limited view of Congress' power to enforce the amendment, holding that Section 5 merely empowered Congress to pass suitable legislation "if the States did not conform their laws to its requirements." These statements are important because they foreshadowed the doctrine of the *Civil Rights Cases*.

In the essay introducing this chapter, reference was made to the "state action" doctrine. To understand the meaning and purpose of this doctrine, it is necessary first to reflect on the underlying philosophy of the Constitution as a whole. The Constitution established a government and set down certain limitations on what *government* could do (as well as some imperatives on what it ought to do). The Constitution and the Bill of Rights were written to protect individual liberties *from the tyranny of government.* With a few exceptions, the remaining amendments to the Constitution are also limitations only on government. One exception is the Thirteenth Amendment, which prohibits slavery and involuntary servitude, whether exacted by government or by a private individual. Another is the Eighteenth Amendment, which prohibited the manufacture, sale, and transportation of alcoholic beverages. The Twenty-first Amendment, which repealed the Eighteenth, prohibited the transportation of liquor into any state or territory in violation of state or local laws. Congress was given power to enforce these amendments by appropriate legislation, and it has done so, but each, on its face, appears to be a self-executing prohibition against private conduct. Of course, only Congress can enforce these provisions by criminal statute.

Under various constitutional powers, Congress (and the states, as well) may, of course, prohibit and punish various types of discriminatory private action. But such actions do not "offend the Constitution," although they may violate the laws. For example, it is not a constitutional violation for a private individual to deny to another individual his right of free speech, say by shouting him down from a platform. Such an act may be sanctioned in a private suit for damages. And it may also be punishable, under certain circumstances, by invocation of state or local breach of the peace statutes. A legislature, under its police powers, may prohibit an individual from practicing racial discrimination in the sale or rental of housing. And Congress may, under recent interpretations of its enforcement powers under the Thirteenth Amendment, also prohibit housing discrimination (see *Jones* v. *Mayer,* 1968, *infra*) by private individuals. But there is no provision of the Constitution that, by itself, prohibits private racial discrimination.

The Fourteenth and Fifteenth Amendments were written consistent with this theory. The Fourteenth Amendment prohibits *states* from denying to citizens due process, equal protection, and privileges and immunities; the Fifteenth Amendment prohibits the *states and the federal government* from abridging the right to vote. Quite clearly, these amendments were directed only at discriminatory governmental action insofar as they are self-executing. But Section 5 of the Fourteenth Amendment, and Section 2 of the Fifteenth Amendment (and also Section 2 of the Thirteenth Amendment) grant to Congress the power to enforce the amendments by appropriate legislation. Is Congress, when enforcing these amendments, also limited to prohibiting only discriminatory "state action"? Or is Congress empowered by the amendments to directly prohibit discrimination by private individuals?

Some evidence on this point is the pattern of coverage of the Reconstruction statutes. Indeed, one of the purposes of the Fourteenth Amendment was to clear up doubts about the constitutionality of the Civil Rights Act of 1866. Most of these statutes were directed at private discrimination as well as state action. Since the Congress that passed the Civil Rights Act of 1866 was virtually the same Congress that passed the Thirteenth and Fourteenth Amendments, it is reasonable to assume that its members believed that Section 5 of the Fourteenth Amendment enabled Congress to legislate against private discrimination.

In 1875, Congress passed the first public accommodations statute in its history, after three years of hard-fought and bitter debate. It was to be the last civil rights bill for eighty-two years, and it came just before the disintegration of the egalitarian consensus that marked the Reconstruction period. The Compromise of 1877, electing Rutherford B. Hayes to the presidency in return for the removal of federal troops from the secessionist southern states ensured the defeat of any attempts to strengthen, or indeed even to modify, congressional civil rights protections. When the Civil Rights Act of 1875 finally came to the Supreme Court in 1883, its policies were already contrary to the growing sentiment that the South had been sufficiently punished and that there was a paramount need to return to normalcy. These facts are particularly important in understanding the impact of the *Civil Rights Cases* on the status of the Negro. Had the statute been tested a decade earlier, with the same judicial result, Congress might well have repassed it in different form. It might have taken the hints in Justice Bradley's opinion and passed the same law in pursuance of its interstate commerce power, rather than under its Section 5 power. But it was a different Congress—indeed a different era—and the Court's decision prevailed.]

MR. JUSTICE BRADLEY delivered the opinion of the Court.

. . . The essence of the law is, not to declare broadly that all persons shall be entitled to the full and equal enjoyment of the accommodations, advantages, facilities, and privileges of inns, public conveyances, and theatres; but that such enjoyment shall not be subject to any conditions applicable only to citizens of a particular race or color, or who had been in a previous condition of servitude. . . .

Has Congress constitutional power to make such a law? Of course, no one will contend that the power to pass it was contained in the Constitution before the adoption of the last three amendments. . . .

It is State action of a particular character that is prohibited. Individual invasion of individual rights is not the subject-matter of the amendment. It has a deeper and broader scope. It nullifies and makes void all State legislation, and State action of every kind, which impairs the privileges and immunities of citizens of the United States, or which injures them in life, liberty, or property without due process of law, or which denies to any of them the equal protection of the laws. It not only does this, but . . . invests Congress with power to enforce it by appropriate legislation. To enforce what? To enforce the prohibition. To adopt appro-

priate legislation for correcting the effects of such prohibited State laws and State acts, and thus to render them effectually null, void, and innocuous. This is the legislative power conferred upon Congress, and this is the whole of it. It does not invest Congress with power to legislate upon subjects which are within the domain of State legislation; but to provide modes of relief against State legislation, or State action, of the kind referred to. It does not authorize Congress to create a code of municipal law for the regulation of private rights; but to provide modes of redress against the operation of State laws, and the action of State officers, executive or judicial, when these are subversive of the fundamental rights specified in the amendment. Positive rights and privileges are undoubtedly secured by the Fourteenth Amendment; but they are secured by way of prohibition against State laws and State proceedings affecting those rights and privileges, and by power given to Congress to legislate for the purpose of carrying such prohibition into effect: and such legislation must necessarily be predicated upon such supposed State laws or State proceedings, and be directed to the correction of their operation and effect. . . .

And so in the present case, until some State law has been passed, or some State action through its officers or agents has been taken, adverse to the rights of citizens sought to be protected by the Fourteenth Amendment, no legislation of the United States under said amendment, nor any proceeding under such legislation, can be called into activity: for the prohibitions of the amendment are against State laws and acts done under State authority. Of course, legislation may, and should be, provided in advance to meet the exigency when it arises; but it should be adapted to the mischief and wrong which the amendment was intended to provide against; and that is, State laws, or State action of some kind, adverse to the rights of the citizen secured by the amendment. Such legislation cannot properly cover the whole domain of rights appertaining to life, liberty and property, defining them and providing for their vindication. That would be to establish a code of municipal law regulative of all private rights between man and man in society. It would be to make Congress take the place of the State legislatures and to supersede them. It is absurd to affirm that, because the rights of life, liberty and property (which include all civil rights that men have), are by the amendment sought to be protected against invasion on the part of the State without due process of law, Congress may therefore provide due process of law for their vindication in every case; and that, because the denial by a State to any persons, of the equal protection of the laws, is prohibited by the amendment, therefore Congress may establish laws for their equal protection. In fine, the legislation which Congress is authorized to adopt in this behalf is not general legislation upon the rights of the citizen, but corrective legislation . . . .

An inspection of the law shows that it makes no reference whatever to any supposed or apprehended violation of the Fourteenth Amendment on the part of the States. It is not predicated on any such view. It proceeds *ex directo* to declare that certain acts committed by individuals shall be deemed offences, and shall be prosecuted and punished by proceedings in the courts of the United States. It does not profess to be corrective of any constitutional wrong committed by the States; it does not make its operation to depend upon any such

wrong committed. It applied equally to cases arising in States which have the justest laws respecting the personal rights of citizens, and whose authorities are ever ready to enforce such laws, as to those which arise in States that may have violated the prohibition of the amendment. In other words, it steps into the domain of local jurisprudence, and lays down rules for the conduct of individuals in society toward each other, and imposes sanctions for the enforcement of those rules, without referring in any manner to any supposed action of the State or its authorities.

If this legislation is appropriate for enforcing the prohibitions of the amendment, it is difficult to see where it is to stop. . . . The truth is, that the implication of a power to legislate in this manner is based upon the assumption that if the States are forbidden to legislate or act in a particular way on a particular subject, and power is conferred upon Congress to enforce the prohibition, this gives Congress power to legislate generally upon that subject, and not merely power to provide modes of redress against such State legislation or action. The assumption is certainly unsound. It is repugnant to the Tenth Amendment. . . .

In this connection it is proper to state that civil rights, such as are guaranteed by the Constitution against State aggression, cannot be impaired by the wrongful acts of individuals, unsupported by State authority in the shape of laws, customs, or judicial or executive proceedings. The wrongful act of an individual, unsupported by any such authority, is simply a private wrong, or a crime of that individual . . . . Hence, in all those cases where the Constitution seeks to protect the rights of the citizen against discriminative and unjust laws of the State by prohibiting such laws, it is not individual offences, but abrogation and denial of rights, which it denounces, and for which it clothes the Congress with power to provide a remedy. This abrogation and denial of rights, for which the States alone were or could be responsible, was the great seminal and fundamental wrong which was intended to be remedied. . . .

Of course, these remarks do not apply to those cases in which Congress is clothed with direct and plenary powers of legislation over the whole subject, accompanied with an express or implied denial of such power to the States, as in the regulation of commerce with foreign nations, among the several States . . . .

We have discussed the question presented by the law on the assumption that a right to enjoy equal accommodation and privileges in all inns, public conveyances, and places of public amusement, is one of the essential rights of the citizen which no State can abridge or interfere with. Whether it is such a right, or not, is a different question which, in the view we have taken of the validity of the law on the ground already stated, it is not necessary to examine. . . .

And whether Congress, in the exercise of its power to regulate commerce amongst the several States, might or might not pass a law regulating rights in public conveyances passing from one State to another, is also a question which is not now before us . . . .

But the power of Congress to adopt direct and primary, as distinguished from corrective legislation, on the subject in hand, is sought, in the second place, from the Thirteenth Amendment, which abolishes slavery. . . .

This amendment, as well as the Fourteenth, is undoubtedly self-executing without any ancillary legislation, so far as its terms are applicable to any existing state of circumstances. By its own unaided force and effect it abolished slavery, and established universal freedom. Still, legislation may be necessary and proper to meet all the various cases and circumstances to be affected by it, and to prescribe proper modes of redress for its violation in letter or spirit. And such legislation may be primary and direct in its character; for the amendment is not a mere prohibition of State laws establishing or upholding slavery, but an absolute declaration that slavery or involuntary servitude shall not exist in any part of the United States.

But is there any similarity between such servitudes and a denial by the owner of an inn, a public conveyance, or a theatre, of its accommodations and privileges to an individual, even though the denial be founded on the race or color of that individual? . . .

It would be running the slavery argument into the ground to make it apply to every act of discrimination which a person may see fit to make as to the guests he will entertain, or as to the people he will take into his coach or cab or car, or admit to his concert or theatre, or deal with in other matters of intercourse or business. Innkeepers and public carriers, by the laws of all States, so far as we are aware, are bound, to the extent of their facilities, to furnish proper accommodation to all unobjectionable persons who in good faith apply for them. If the laws themselves make any unjust discrimination, amenable to the prohibitions of the Fourteenth Amendment, Congress has full power to afford a remedy under that amendment and in accordance with it.

When a man has emerged from slavery, and by the aid of beneficent legislation has shaken off the inseparable concomitants of that state, there must be some stage in the progress of his elevation when he takes the rank of a mere citizen, and ceases to be the special favorite of the laws, and when his rights as a citizen, or a man, are to be protected in the ordinary modes by which other men's rights are protected. There were thousands of free colored people in this country before the abolition of slavery, enjoying all the essential rights of life, liberty and property the same as white citizens, yet no one, at that time, thought that it was any invasion of his personal status as a freeman because he was not admitted to all the privileges enjoyed by white citizens, or because he was subjected to discriminations in the enjoyment of accommodation in inns, public conveyances and places of amusement. Mere discriminations on account of race or color were not regarded as badges of slavery. . . .

Mr. JUSTICE HARLAN DISSENTING.

. . . The court adjudges, I think erroneously, that Congress is without power, under either the Thirteenth or Fourteenth Amendment, to establish such regulations. . . .

The Thirteenth Amendment, it is conceded, did something more than to prohibit slavery as an *institution,* resting upon distinctions of race, and upheld by positive law. My brethren admit that it established and decreed universal *civil freedom* throughout the United States. But did the freedom thus established involve nothing more than exemption from actual slavery? Was nothing more intended than to forbid one man from owning another as property? Was it the purpose of the nation simply to destroy the institution, and then remit the race, theretofore held in bondage, to the several States for such protection,

in their civil rights, necessarily growing out of freedom, as those States, in their discretion, might choose to provide? . . .

[T]he power of Congress under the Thirteenth Amendment is not necessarily restricted to legislation against slavery as an institution upheld by positive law, but may be exerted to the extent, at least, of protecting the liberated race against discrimination, in respect of legal rights belonging to freemen, where such discrimination is based upon race. . . .

[A] keeper of an inn is in the exercise of a quasi public employment. The law gives him special privileges and he is charged with certain duties and responsibilities to the public. The public nature of his employment forbids him from discriminating against any person asking admission as a guest on account of the race or color of that person.

As to places of public amusement. It may be argued that the managers of such places have no duties to perform with which the public are, in any legal sense, concerned, or with which the public have any right to interfere; and, that the exclusion of a black man from a place of public amusement, on account of his race, or the denial to him, on that ground, of equal accommodations at such places, violates no legal right for the vindication of which he may invoke the aid of the courts. My answer is, that places of public amusement, within the meaning of the act of 1875, are such as are established and maintained under direct license of the law. The authority to establish and maintain them comes from the public. The colored race is a part of that public. The local government granting the license represents them as well as all other races within its jurisdiction. . . .

I also submit, whether it can be

said—in view of the doctrines of this court as announced in *Munn* v. *State of Illinois* . . . that the management of places of public amusement is a purely private matter, with which government has no rightful concern? . . .

The doctrines of *Munn* v. *Illinois* have never been modified by this court, and I am justified, upon the authority of that case, in saying that places of public amusement, conducted under the authority of the law, are clothed with a public interest, because used in a manner to make them of public consequence and to affect the community at large. The law may therefore regulate, to some extent, the mode in which they shall be conducted, and consequently, the public have rights in respect of such places, which may be vindicated by the law. It is consequently not a matter purely of private concern.

Congress has not, in these matters, entered the domain of State control and supervision. It does not, as I have said, assume to prescribe the general conditions and limitations under which inns, public conveyances, and places of public amusement, shall be conducted or managed. It simply declares, in effect, that since the nation has established universal freedom in this country, for all time, there shall be no discrimination, based merely upon race or color, in respect of the accommodations and advantages of public conveyances, inns, and places of public amusement.

I am of the opinion that such discrimination practised by corporations and individuals in the exercise of their public or quasi-public functions is a badge of servitude the imposition of which Congress may prevent under its power, by appropriate legislation, to enforce the Thirteenth Amendment; and consequently, without reference to its enlarged power under the Fourteenth Amendment, the act of March 1, 1875, is not, in my judgment, repugnant to the Constitution.

It remains now to consider these cases with reference to the power Congress has possessed since the adoption of the Fourteenth Amendment. Much that has been said as to the power of Congress under the Thirteenth Amendment is applicable to this branch of the discussion and will not be repeated.

But when, under what circumstances, and to what extent, may Congress, by means of legislation, exert its power to enforce the provisions of this amendment? . . .

The assumption that this amendment consists wholly of prohibitions upon State laws and State proceedings in hostility to its provisions, is unauthorized by its language. The first clause of the first section . . . is of a distinctly affirmative character. In its application to the colored race, previously liberated, it created and granted, as well citizenship of the United States, as citizenship of the State in which they respectively resided. It introduced all of that race, whose ancestors had been imported and sold as slaves, at once, into the political community known as the "People of the United States." They became, instantly, citizens of the United States, *and* of their respective States. . . .

The citizenship thus acquired, by that race, in virtue of an affirmative grant from the nation, may be protected, not alone by the judicial branch of the government, but by congressional legislation of a primary direct character; this, because the power of Congress is not restricted to the enforcement of prohibitions upon State laws or State action. It is, in terms distinct and positive, to enforce "the *provisions* of *this article*" of amendment; not simply those of a prohibitive character, but the provisions—*all* of the provisions—affirmative and prohibitive, of the amendment. It is, therefore, a grave misconception to suppose that the fifth section of the amendment has reference exclusively to express prohibitions upon State laws or State action. . . .

With all respect for the opinion of others, I insist that the national legislature may, without transcending the limits of the Constitution, do for human liberty and the fundamental rights of American citizenship, what it did, with the sanction of this court, for the protection of slavery and the rights of the masters of fugitive slaves. If fugitive slave laws, providing modes and prescribing penalties, whereby the master could seize and recover his fugitive slave, were legitimate exertions of an implied power to protect and enforce a right recognized by the Constitution, why shall the hands of Congress be tied, so that—under an express power, by appropriate legislation, to enforce a constitutional provision granting citizenship—it may not, by means of direct legislation, bring the whole power of this nation to bear upon States and their officers, and upon such individuals and corporations exercising public functions as assume to abridge, impair, or deny rights confessedly secured by the supreme law of the land? . . .

The court, in its opinion, reserves the question whether Congress, in the exercise of its power to regulate commerce amongst the several States, might or might not pass a law regulating rights in public conveyances passing from one State to another. I beg to suggest that that precise question was substantially presented here in the only one of these cases relating to railroads. . . .

Might not the act of 1875 be maintained in that case, as applicable at least to commerce between the States, notwithstanding it does not, upon its face, profess to have been passed in pursuance of the power of Congress to regulate commerce? Has it ever been held that the judiciary should overturn a statute, because the legislative department did not accurately recite therein the particular provision of the Constitution authorizing its enactment?

My brethren say, that when a man has emerged from slavery, and by the aid of beneficent legislation has shaken off the inseparable concomitants of that state, there must be some stage in the progress of his elevation when he takes the rank of a mere citizen, and ceases to be the special favorite of the laws, and when his rights as a citizen, or a man, are to be protected in the ordinary modes by which other men's rights are protected. It is, I submit, scarcely just to say that the colored race has been the special favorite of the laws. . . .

(2) Shelley v. Kraemer (1948)

+Vinson, Black, Douglas, Frankfurter, Burton, Murphy
NP Reed, Jackson, Rutledge

[The first recorded municipal housing discrimination ordinance in the United States was enacted in San Francisco in 1879. In 1914, Louisville, Kentucky, passed an ordinance "designed to prevent conflict and ill feeling between the white and colored races." It provided that Negroes could not occupy property on blocks in which a majority of the property was owned by whites and, reciprocally, that whites could not occupy property on blocks where a majority of property owners were black.

A trumped-up suit was designed to test the ordinance. Buchanan, a white person, sold property to Warley, a Negro, on a block that was 80 percent white. Warley refused to pay for the property because of the ordinance that would have prohibited him from building a home on it. So Buchanan sued Warley, contending that the ordinance was unconstitutional, while Warley "claimed" it was valid. The Kentucky Court of Appeals upheld the ordinance. Before the United States Supreme Court, Buchanan, the white, was represented by the NAACP. The Court held the ordinance invalid as a violation of the Fourteenth Amendment *and* the Civil Rights Act of 1866. As Loren Miller has observed, that made everybody happy—Buchanan because he had won, and Warley because he had lost.[1]

Although *Buchanan* v. *Warley* (1917) settled the issue of the constitutionality of local housing segregation ordinances, the problem of private discrimination remained. In a case in 1926, *Corrigan* v. *Buckley*, there were dicta which held that private discriminatory agreements were valid and enforceable in the courts. Racial restrictive housing covenants proliferated and became the mainstay of segregated housing in the United States. The Federal Housing Administration furnished model covenants for builders and for a time insisted on their use as a condition for granting mortgage insurance.

Overruling *Corrigan* and putting an end to racial discrimination in housing became the major goal of the NAACP. It developed test cases, stimulated and planted favorable articles in law reviews (to be cited later in briefs), and then was forced into a case that it did not want but that seemed inexorably to be making its way to the Supreme Court, *Shelley* v. *Kraemer*.[2]

Mrs. Shelley, a black woman, was sold property in St. Louis by a Negro real estate dealer named Bishop, who also was minister of the local Evangelical Church. Bishop had bought the property from a white seller under the fictitious name of Josephine Fitzgerald for $4700. He sold it to Mrs. Shelley for $5700 and failed to tell her that the property was located in a restricted neighborhood and was covered by a housing covenant. A group of white "neighbors" who owned adjacent homes formed the Marcus Avenue Improvement Association and sued to divest Mrs. Shelley of title to the property and to prevent her from taking possession of it. Kraemer, an heir to one of the signers of the covenant, was chosen to be the named plaintiff in the case. Thus the case first came to the circuit court in St. Louis as *Kraemer* v. *Shelley.*

The district consisted of fifty-seven parcels of land. Forty-seven parcels, including the Shelley property, were covered by the restrictive deed, and five of the parcels were owned and occupied by Negro families. The circuit court dismissed Kraemer's petition on the technicality that the restrictive covenant had never become final because it had not been agreed to by all the property owners in the district. The Supreme Court of Missouri reversed, holding that the covenant was enforceable as a matter of law and that enforcing it violated no provisions of the federal Constitution. At this time, Mrs. Shelley and her family were occupying the house in question. The United States Supreme Court granted certiorari.]

MR. CHIEF JUSTICE VINSON delivered the opinion of the Court.

. . .

Petitioners urge that they have been denied the equal protection of the laws, deprived of property without due process of law, and have been denied privileges and immunities of citizens of the United States. . . .

Whether the equal protection clause of the Fourteenth Amendment inhibits judicial enforcement by state courts of restrictive covenants based on race or color is a question which this Court has not heretofore been called upon to consider. . . .

It cannot be doubted that among the civil rights intended to be protected from discriminatory state action by the Fourteenth Amendment are the rights to acquire, enjoy, own

[1]Loren Miller, *The Petitioners* (Cleveland: Meridian Press, 1967), ch. 16.
[2]See Clement Vose, *Caucasians Only* (Berkeley: University of California Press, 1959).

and dispose of property. Equality in the enjoyment of property rights was regarded by the framers of that Amendment as an essential precondition to the realization of other basic civil rights and liberties which the Amendment was intended to guarantee. Thus, §1978 of the Revised Statutes, derived from §1 of the Civil Rights Act of 1866 which was enacted by Congress while the Fourteenth Amendment was also under consideration, provides:

All citizens of the United States shall have the same right, in every State and Territory, as is enjoyed by white citizens thereof to inherit, purchase, lease, sell, hold, and convey real and personal property.

This Court has given specific recognition to the same principle. *Buchanan* v. *Warley* . . . (1917).

It is likewise clear that restrictions on the right of occupancy of the sort sought to be created by the private agreements in these cases could not be squared with the requirements of the Fourteenth Amendment if imposed by state statute or local ordinance. We do not understand respondents to urge the contrary. In the case of *Buchanan* v. *Warley* . . . a unanimous Court declared unconstitutional the provisions of a city ordinance which denied to colored persons the right to occupy houses in blocks in which the greater number of houses were occupied by white persons, and imposed similar restrictions on white persons with respect to blocks in which the greater number of houses were occupied by colored persons.

. . . [T]he present cases, unlike those just discussed, do not involve action by state legislatures or city councils. Here the particular patterns of discrimination and the areas in which the restrictions are to operate, are determined, in the first instance, by the terms of agreements among private individuals. Participation of the State consists in the enforcement of the restrictions so defined. The crucial issue with which we are here confronted is whether this distinction removes these cases from the operation of the prohibitory provisions of the Fourteenth Amendment.

Since the decision of this Court in the *Civil Rights Cases* . . . (1883), the principle has become firmly embedded in our constitutional law that the action inhibited by the first section of the Fourteenth Amendment is only such action as may fairly be said to be that of the States. That Amendment erects no shield against merely private conduct, however discriminatory or wrongful.

We conclude, therefore, that the restrictive agreements standing alone cannot be regarded as violative of any rights guaranteed to petitioners by the Fourteenth Amendment. So long as the purposes of those agreements are effectuated by voluntary adherence to their terms, it would appear clear that there has been no action by the State and the provisions of the Amendment have not been violated. . . .

But here there was more. These are cases in which the purposes of the agreements were secured only by judicial enforcement by state courts of the restrictive terms of the agreements. The respondents urge that judicial enforcement of private agreements does not amount to state action; or, in any event, the participation of the State is so attenuated in character as not to amount to state action within the meaning of the Fourteenth Amendment. . . .

That the action of state courts and judicial officers in their official capacities is to be regarded as action of the State within the meaning of the

Fourteenth Amendment, is a proposition which has long been established by decisions of this Court. . . .

One of the earliest applications of the prohibitions contained in the Fourteenth Amendment to action of state judicial officials occurred in cases in which Negroes had been excluded from jury service in criminal prosecutions by reason of their race or color. These cases demonstrate, also, the early recognition by this Court that state action in violation of the Amendment's provisions is equally repugnant to the constitutional commands whether directed by state statute or taken by a judicial official in the absence of statute. Thus, in *Strauder* v. *West Virginia* . . . (1880), this Court declared invalid a state statute restricting jury service to white persons as amounting to a denial of the equal protection of the laws to the colored defendant in that case. In the same volume of the reports, the Court in *Ex parte Virginia* . . . held that a similar discrimination imposed by the action of a state judge denied rights protected by the Amendment, despite the fact that the language of the state statute relating to jury service contained no such restrictions. . . .

But the examples of state judicial action which have been held by this Court to violate the Amendment's commands are not restricted to situations in which the judicial proceedings were found in some manner to be procedurally unfair. It has been recognized that the action of state courts in enforcing a substantive common-law rule formulated by those courts, may result in the denial of rights guaranteed by the Fourteenth Amendment, even though the judicial proceedings in such cases may have been in complete accord with the most rigorous conceptions of procedural due process.

The short of the matter is that from the time of the adoption of the Fourteenth Amendment until the present, it has been the consistent ruling of this Court that the action of the States to which the Amendment has reference includes action of state courts and state judicial officials. . . .

We have no doubt that there has been state action in these cases in the full and complete sense of the phrase. The undisputed facts disclose that petitioners were willing purchasers of properties upon which they desired to establish homes. The owners of the properties were willing sellers; and contracts of sale were accordingly consummated. It is clear that but for the active intervention of the state courts, supported by the full panoply of state power, petitioners would have been free to occupy the properties in question without restraint.

These are not cases, as has been suggested, in which the states have merely abstained from action, leaving private individuals free to impose such discriminations as they see fit. Rather, these are cases in which the States have made available to such individuals the full coercive power of government to deny to petitioners, on the grounds of race or color, the enjoyment of property rights in premises which petitioners are willing and financially able to acquire and which the grantors are willing to sell. The difference between judicial enforcement and non-enforcement of the restrictive covenants is the difference to petitioners between being denied rights of property available to other members of the community and being accorded full enjoyment of those rights on an equal footing. . . .

We hold that in granting judicial enforcement of the restrictive agreements, in these cases, the States have denied petitioners the equal protection of the laws and that, therefore, the action of the state courts cannot stand. . . .

Respondents urge, however, that since the state courts stand ready to enforce restrictive covenants excluding white persons from the ownership or occupancy of property covered by such agreements, enforcement of covenants excluding colored persons may not be deemed a denial of equal protection of the laws to the colored persons who are thereby affected. This contention does not bear scrutiny. The parties have directed our attention to no case in which a court, state or federal, has been called upon to enforce a covenant excluding members of the white majority from ownership or occupancy of real property on grounds of race or color. But there are more fundamental considerations. The rights created by the first section of the Fourteenth Amendment are, by its terms guaranteed to the individual. The rights established are personal rights. It is, therefore, no answer to these petitioners to say that the courts may also be induced to deny white persons rights of ownership and occupancy on grounds of race or color. Equal protection of the laws is not achieved through indiscriminant imposition of inequalities.

Nor do we find merit in the suggestion that property owners who are parties to these agreements are denied equal protection of the laws if denied access to the courts to enforce the terms of restrictive covenants and to assert property rights which the state courts have held to be created by such agreements. The Constitution confers upon no individual the right to demand action by the State which results in the denial of equal protection of the laws to other individuals. . . .

For the reasons stated, the judgment of the Supreme Court of Missouri must be reversed.

(3) Sequel to Shelley: A Note on Barrows v. Jackson (1953)

The decision in the *Shelley* case was an important symbolic victory, but it did not result in immediate desegregation. Restrictive covenants were not illegal. From Vinson's opinion, it is clear that, insofar as the Fourteenth Amendment is concerned, a private individual has the right to refuse to sell to any person of whom he disapproves—for whatever reasons. But the decision did open the door to those blacks wishing to purchase property in restricted white neighborhoods and who were fortunate enough to find a willing white seller. At least, under the *Shelley* doctrine, or so it was thought, no state could prohibit such as transaction. But the *Shelley* decision was, like most Supreme Court decisions, a legal weapon that could be used effectively *if* the victorious litigants possessed the resources to bring about its implementation.

White property owners and realtors responded to the *Shelley* decision by seeking loopholes to prevent white signers from disregarding the terms of the restrictive deeds to their houses. One method tried was suit for damages *against the white seller*. In a case coming to the Supreme Court from California, *Barrows* v. *Jackson*, an attempt was made to sue the white seller rather than the black buyer. Mrs. Jackson, a white, had sold her property to a black and was sued for $16,000 damages by Barrows, a neighbor and party to the convenant. The California courts ruled that a damage suit could not be maintained because this would merely be an indirect way of enforcing a restrictive convenant, contrary to the doctrine of *Shelley*.

The Supreme Court affirmed by an 8-1 vote, with only Chief Justice Vinson dissenting. It rejected the contention that because Mrs. Jackson was white, she could not use as her defense the constitutional rights of blacks to buy, sell, and own property without discrimination. The Court recognized that to allow damage suits against white sellers was a very effective reinforcement of restrictive covenants. To reach this decision, however, the Court had to dispose of the technical objection that, generally, an individual does not have "standing" to assert the constitutional rights of another person. But, the Court said, this was a legitimate exception:

Under the peculiar circumstances of this case, we believe the reasons which underlie our denying standing to raise another's rights, which is only a rule of practice, are outweighed by the need to protect the fundamental rights which would be denied by permitting the damage action to be maintained.

These cases disposed of the legal side of the restrictive covenant issue. It would be another decade before President Kennedy signed an executive order outlawing discrimination in low-cost public housing, and a decade and a half before Congress would pass the first open housing law since 1866. But the *Shelley* and *Barrows* cases had another, and somewhat more immediate, impact. While they did not go so far as to hold that the state had an affirmative obligation to eliminate housing discrimination, they tended to broaden the definition of discriminatory (and thus prohibited) state action. In practical terms, these decisions expanded the meaning of that doctrine to include otherwise nondiscriminatory actions by a state (for example, enforcement

of otherwise valid contracts between private individuals). In so doing, they opened the possibility of holding the state *responsible* for other forms of purely private discrimination which, for legal or practical reasons, could not succeed without the assistance of the state. It marked an important continuation of the process of expanding constitutional rights by broadening the definition of "public" as opposed to "private" discrimination.

Many of those who objected to *Shelley* objected for precisely these reasons—that it seemed to erode the boundary between private and public discrimination. The most eloquent and widely disseminated liberal criticism came from Professor Herbert Wechsler of the Columbia University Law School. In his Oliver Wendell Holmes lecture of 1959, parts of which have been reprinted earlier in this book, Wechsler argued:[1]

The case of the restrictive covenant presents for me an even harder problem. Assuming that the Constitution speaks to state discrimination on the ground of race but not to such discrimination by an individual even in the use or distribution of his property, although his freedom may no doubt be limited by common law or statute, why is the enforcement of the private covenant a state discrimination rather than a legal recognition of the freedom of the individual? That the action of the state court is action of the state, the point Mr. Chief Justice Vinson emphasizes in the Court's opinion is, of course, entirely obvious. What is not obvious, and is the crucial step, is that the state may properly be charged with the discrimination when it does no more than give effect to an agreement that the individual involved is, by hypothesis, entirely free to make. Again, one is obliged to ask: What

---

[1]"Toward Neutral Principles of Constitutional Law," **73** *Harvard Law Review* (1960), 27–35.

is the principle involved? Is the state forbidden to effectuate a will that draws a racial line, a will that can accomplish any disposition only through the aid of law, or is it a sufficient answer there that the discrimination was the testator's and not the state's? May not the state employ its law to vindicate the privacy of property against a trespasser, regardless of the grounds of his exclusion, or does it embrace the owner's reasons for excluding if it buttresses his power by the law? Would a declaratory judgment that a fee is determinable if a racially restrictive limitation should be violated represent discrimination by the state upon the racial ground? Would a judgment of ejectment? . . .

(4) Burton v. Wilmington Parking Authority (1961)

+Warren, Douglas, Black, Clark, Brennan, Stewart
−Frankfurter, Harlan, Whittaker

[It is possible to read *Shelley* v. *Kraemer* in a number of ways. The broadest interpretation is that the prohibitions of the Fourteenth Amendment apply whenever, by action *or inaction,* a state enables racially discriminatory choices to be carried out, regardless of whether or not the discriminatory act is in fact wholly that of the individual. It makes no difference, for those purposes, that state aid to, or enforcement of, a private decision is entirely neutral on its face. This reading of *Shelley* severely blurs, if it does not obliterate, the distinction between state action and private action.

There are good reasons to give *Shelley* a considerably narrower construction. First, if we recall the emphasis given by Chief Justice Vinson in his opinion in *Shelley* to the autonomy of private discriminatory choices, it is clear that the Court in that case did not intend to eliminate the fundamental distinction between state and private action.

There has been no retreat by the Court from the principle that the Fourteenth Amendment does not pertain to private action. But what is private action? The distinction between public and private action is not fixed, and as the growth of the welfare state has blurred the line between the public and private sectors, many activities formerly considered wholly private are now in an enlarged gray area between the two spheres: private for some purposes but also regulated by government to a greater extent than ever before. Should some, or all, of these activities be considered "state action"? The Supreme Court clearly has been unwilling to regard just *any* connection between government and a private activity or enterprise as sufficient to establish the state action nexus.

Second, the quotation from Professor Herbert Wechsler in the preceding note suggests that there are compelling *normative* reasons to give *Shelley* the narrowest possible construction—the need to give adequate consideration to competing constitutional rights and interests, such as privacy, association, and the right to control the disposition of one's property. Certainly, there are occasions when the "competing right" may be assigned a higher priority than the equal protection claim.[1] Third, is it not possible and desirable to limit *Shelley* to the holding, consistent with the facts in that case, that the state is simply prohibited from intervening in a transaction between a willing buyer and a willing seller in a way that promotes racial discrimination?

Exploring the limits of state action occupied a substantial portion of the Supreme Court's time during the 1960s. A number of "sit-in cases" pressed the Court to rule—which it refused to do—that any action by a state that enforces a private discrimination decision, even if that action is as neutral as a trespass prosecution, constitutes state action under the Fourteenth Amendment. In other cases, the Court groped for linkages between the offensive private discrimination and the responsibility of the state in order to overturn the convictions of sit-in demonstrators.

[1]See Louis Henkin, "*Shelley* v. *Kraemer*: Notes for a Revised Opinion,"
110 *University of Pennsylvania Law Review* (1962), 473–505.

In the present case, Burton was denied service, because of his race, at the Eagle Coffee Shoppe, a privately owned restaurant located in a public parking facility in Wilmington, Delaware. He sought injunctive relief in the state courts. The Supreme Court of Delaware ruled that Eagle—which leased the property from the Wilmington Parking Authority—was acting in a "purely private capacity." Its refusal to serve Burton, therefore, was not discriminatory state action. The Court also held that Eagle was a restaurant, not an inn, under Delaware law and hence was under no obligation to serve all persons equally.]

MR. JUSTICE CLARK delivered the opinion of the Court.

. . .

The *Civil Rights Cases* . . . (1883), "embedded in our constitutional law" the principle "that the action inhibited by the first section [equal protection clause] of the Fourteenth Amendment is only such action as may fairly be said to be that of the states. That Amendment erects no shield against merely private conduct, however discriminatory or wrongful" . . . It is clear, as it always has been since the *Civil Rights Cases*, . . . that "Individual invasion of individual rights is not the subject-matter of the amendment," and that private conduct abridging individual rights does no violence to the equal protection clause unless to some significant extent the state in any of its manifestations has been found to have become involved in it. Because the virtue of the right to equal protection of the laws could lie only in the breadth of its application, its constitutional assurance was reserved in terms whose imprecision was necessary if the right were to be enjoyed in the variety of individual-state relationships which the amendment was designed to embrace. For the same reason, to fashion and apply a precise formula for

recognition of state responsibility under the equal protection clause is an "impossible task" which "This Court has never attempted." . . . Only by sifting facts and weighing circumstances can the nonobvious involvement of the state in private conduct be attributed its true significance.

. . .

The land and building were publicly owned. As an entity, the building was dedicated to "public uses" in performance of the authority's "essential governmental functions." . . . Guests of the restaurant are afforded a convenient place to park their automobiles, even if they cannot enter the restaurant directly from the parking area. Similarly, its convenience for diners may well provide additional demand for the authority's parking facilities. Should any improvements effected in the leasehold by Eagle become part of the reality, there is no possibility of increased taxes being passed on to it since the fee is held by a tax-exempt government agency. Neither can it be ignored, especially in view of Eagle's affirmative allegation that for it to serve Negroes would injure its business, that profits earned by discrimination not only contribute to, but also are indispensable elements in, the financial success of a government agency.

Addition of all these activities, obligations and responsibilities of the authority, the benefits mutually conferred, together with the obvious fact that the restaurant is operated as an integral part of a public building devoted to a public parking service, indicates that degree of state participation and involvement in discriminatory action which it was the design of the Fourteenth Amendment to condemn. It is irony amounting to grave injustice that in one part of a single building, erected and maintained with public funds by an agency of the state to serve a public purpose, all persons have equal rights, while in another portion, also serving the public, a Negro is a second-class citizen, offensive because of his race, without rights and unentitled to service, but at the same time fully enjoys equal access to nearby restaurants in wholly private owned buildings. As the chancellor pointed out, in its lease with Eagle the authority could have affirmatively required Eagle to discharge the responsibilities under the Fourteenth Amendment imposed upon the private enterprise as a consequence of state participation. But no state may effectively abdicate its responsibilities by either ignoring them or by merely failing to discharge them whatever the motive may be. It is of no consolation to an individual denied the equal protection of the laws that it was done in good faith. Certainly the conclusions drawn in similar cases by the various courts of appeals do not depend upon such a distinction. By its inaction, the authority, and through it the state, has not only made itself a party to the refusal of service, but has elected to place its power, property and prestige behind the admitted discrimination. The state has so far insinuated itself into a position of interdependence with Eagle that it must be recognized as a joint participant in the challenged activity, which, on that account, cannot be considered to have been so "purely private" as to fall without the scope of the Fourteenth Amendment.

Because readily applicable formulae may not be fashioned, the conclusions drawn from the facts and circumstances of this record are by no means declared as universal truths on the basis of which every state leasing agreement is to be tested. Owing to the very "largeness" of government, a multitude of relationships might appear to some to fall within the amendment's embrace, but that, it must be remembered, can be determined only in the framework of the peculiar facts or circumstances present. Therefore respondents' prophecy of nigh universal application of a constitutional percept so peculiarly dependent for its invocation upon appropriate facts fails to take into account "Differences in circumstances [which] beget appropriate differences in law," . . . Specifically defining the limits of our inquiry, what we hold today is that when a state leases public property in the manner and for the purpose shown to have been the case here, the proscriptions of the Fourteenth Amendment must be complied with by the lessee as certainly as though they were binding covenants written into the agreement itself.

The judgment of the Supreme Court of Delaware is reversed and the cause remanded for further proceedings consistent with this opinion.

Reversed and remanded.

MR. JUSTICE STEWART, CONCURRING.

I agree that the judgment must be reversed, but I reach that conclusion by a route much more direct than the one traveled by the Court. In upholding Eagle's right to deny service to the appellant solely because of his race, the Supreme Court of Delaware relied upon a statute of that state which permits the proprietor of a restaurant to refuse to serve "persons whose reception or entertainment by him would be offensive to the major part of his customers. . . ." There is no suggestion in the record that the appellant as an individual was such a person. The highest court of Delaware has thus construed this legislative enactment as authorizing discriminatory classification based exclusively on color. Such a law seems to me clearly violative of the Fourteenth Amendment. I think, therefore, that the appeal was properly taken, and that the statute, as authoritatively construed by the Supreme Court of Delaware, is constitutionally invalid.

MR. JUSTICE FRANKFURTER, DISSENTING (OMITTED).
MR. JUSTICE HARLAN, WHOM MR. JUSTICE WHITTAKER JOINS, DISSENTING (OMITTED).

[In *Peterson* v. *Greenville* (1963), the Supreme Court set aside the conviction of a group of demonstrators who had been refused service at a South Carolina lunch counter. The demonstrators were convicted of violating a local trespass statute and fined $100 in lieu of a jail sentence of thirty days. The manager had asked the demonstrators to leave "because it was contrary to local customs" and also because integrated lunch counters were prohibited by a Greenville city ordinance. The Supreme Court held that the existence of the ordinance involved the state "to a significant extent" and constituted state action under the Fourteenth Amendment.

In a companion case, *Lombard* v. *Louisiana* (1963), also involving trespass convictions and arising out of a lunch counter sit-in in New Orleans, there was a significant factual difference. New Orleans had no ordinance requiring segregation. But in the weeks prior to the incident, in response to other events, the mayor and other city officials had publicly condemned such demonstrations. Apparently, they had also put private pressure on lunch counter proprietors not to give in to the demands of sit-in demonstrators. The Supreme Court reversed these convictions too, holding that the statements of city officials were state action as much as the Greenville city ordinance.

In these and other sit-in cases, the Supreme Court was careful not to discuss the "basic" constitutional issue: Did *Shelley* prohibit the neutral enforcement of trespass laws against individuals ejected from private property open to the public for seeking racially nondiscriminatory service? In *Bell* v. *Maryland* (1964), six of the nine justices reached this basic constitutional issue, but divided on it 3-3. The remaining three justices voted to reverse the convictions on other grounds.

Three justices would have invoked *Shelley:* Goldberg, Douglas, and Chief Justice Warren. They argued that there was no privacy of property to be protected here. These businesses were open to the public and should be required to serve all persons equally. Justice Goldberg argued that since Maryland had failed to protect the rights of black persons to equal service, its use of the trespass laws to enforce private discrimination could hardly be considered "neutral." A state, he said, is "obligated under the Fourteenth Amendment to maintain a system of law in which Negroes are not denied protection in their claim to be treated as equal members of the community . . ." Nor, he added, "may a State frustrate this right by legitimating a proprietor's attempt at self-help."

Three justices, Black, Harlan, and White, argued that *Shelley* v. *Kraemer* did not apply at all to this case and that the Fourteenth Amendment does not forbid the neutral application of a state's trespass laws. Justice Black stated the matter succinctly:

It seems pretty clear that the reason judicial enforcement of the restrictive covenants in Shelley *was deemed state action was, not merely the fact that a state court had acted, but rather that it had acted to "deny to petitioners, on the grounds of race or color, the enjoyment of property rights in premises which petitioners are willing and financially able to acquire and which the grantors willing to sell."*

In the *Bell* case, Black noted, the petitioners were asking the Court to use *Shelley* as a precedent to *deny to* the owner of Hopper's restaurant in Baltimore, where the demonstrations had taken place, the same right to use *his* property freely. This, Black said, was a "one-sided" interpretation of federal constitutional guarantees. Since there was no state law or local ordinance, no proclamations from officials, and no other obvious linkage of the refusal to serve with state policy, the trespass convictions were valid. Black's opinion also rejected a contention of Justice Douglas, that because all restaurants are regulated by city and state, and all pay license fees enabling them to do business, therefore the state becomes responsible for their discrimination policies. Black's opinion did suggest, however, that the states and the Congress had power to deal with the problem of discrimination in public accommodations. The Fourteenth Amendment, by itself, conferred no such power on the courts.

The remaining three justices, Brennan, Clark, and Stewart, voted to remand the case to the Maryland Supreme Court to consider the effect of passage of a new state civil rights law that made it a right—and not a crime—to seek the service for which Bell and others had been convicted.

The Solicitor General, Archibald Cox, had argued most of the sit-in cases as *amicus curiae.* His position, consistent throughout, was that the convictions be reversed but not by applying the "broad rule" of *Shelley.* In *Bell,* besides making that argument, he also noted that Congress (in the spring of 1964) was about to pass a new public accommodations statute that would, in all likelihood, make it unnecessary for the Court to confront this great issue. Congress did, in fact, pass the Civil Rights Act of 1964. The statute not only made it a right to obtain equal service in most public accommodations but was also applied retroactively to sit-in cases previously decided but not "finalized" on appeal. Further details are recounted at the beginning of the next section of this chapter.]

(5) Moose Lodge #107 v. Irvis (1972)

+Rehnquist, Burger, Stewart, Blackmun, Powell
−Douglas, Brennan, Marshall

[Irvis, a black member of the Pennsylvania legislature, was refused service as the guest of a member of the Moose Lodge of Harrisburg, Pennsylvania. Irvis brought suit in the federal district court under the civil rights statutes and the Fourteenth Amendment. He claimed that because the state had issued a liquor license to the Moose Lodge, the refusal of service constituted discriminatory state action. A three-judge district court upheld Irvis' contention and invalidated the lodge's liquor license "as long as it follows a policy of racial discrimination in its membership or operating policies or practices."]

MR. JUSTICE REHNQUIST delivered the opinion of the Court.

. . .

Moose Lodge is a private club in the ordinary meaning of that term. It is a local chapter of a national fraternal organization having well defined requirements for membership. It conducts all of its activities in a building that is owned by it. It is not publicly funded. Only members and guests are permitted in any lodge of the order; one may become a guest only by invitation of a member upon invitation of the house committee.

Appellee, while conceding the right of private clubs to choose members upon a discriminatory basis, asserts that the licensing of Moose Lodge to serve liquor by the Pennsylvania Liquor Control Board amounts to such State involvement with the club's activities as to make its discriminatory practices forbidden by the Equal Protection Clause of the Fourteenth Amendment. The relief sought and obtained by appellee in the District Court was an injunction forbidding the licensing by the liquor authority of Moose Lodge until it ceased its discriminatory practices. We conclude that Moose Lodge's refusal to serve food and beverages to a guest by reason of the fact that he was a Negro does not, under the circumstances here presented, violate the Fourteenth Amendment.

In 1883, this Court in *The Civil Rights Cases* . . . set forth the essential dichotomy between discriminatory action by the State, which is prohibited by the Equal Protection Clause, and private conduct, "however discriminatory or wrongful," against which that clause "erects no shield," *Shelley* v. *Kraemer* . . . (1948). That dichotomy has been subsequently reaffirmed in *Shelley* v. *Kraemer*, and in *Burton* v. *Wilmington Parking Authority* . . . (1961).

While the principle is easily stated, the question of whether particular discriminatory conduct is private, on the one hand, or amounts to "State action," on the other hand, frequently admits to no easy answer. "Only by sifting facts and weighing circumstances can the non-obvious involvement of the State in private conduct be attributed its true significance." . . .

Our cases make clear that the impetus for the forbidden discrimination need not originate with the State if it is state action that enforces privately originated discrimination. *Shelley* v. *Kraemer*. The Court held in *Burton* v. *Wilmington Parking Authority* that a private restaurant owner who refused service because of a customer's race violated the Fourteenth Amendment, where the restaurant was located in a building owned by a state created parking authority and leased from the authority. The Court, after a comprehensive review of the relationship between the lessee and the parking authority concluded that the latter had "so far insinuated itself into a position of interdependence with Eagle [the restaurant owner] that it must be recognized as a joint participant in the challenged activity, which, on that account, cannot be considered to have been so 'purely private' as to fall without the scope of the Fourteenth Amendment." . . .

The Court has never held, of course, that discrimination by an otherwise private entity would be violative of the Equal Protection Clause if the private entity receives any sort of benefit or service at all from the State, or if it is subject to state regulation in any degree whatever. Since state-furnished services include such necessities of life as electrcity, water, and police and fire protection, such a holding would utterly emasculate the distinction between private as distinguished from State conduct set forth in *The Civil Rights Cases,* and adhered to in subsequent decisions. Our holdings indicate that where the impetus for the discrimination is private, the State must have "significantly involved itself with invidious discriminations," *Reitman* v. *Mulkey* . . . (1967), in order for the discriminatory action to fall within the ambit of the constitutional prohibition.

Our prior decisions dealing with discriminatory refusal of service in public eating places are significantly different factually from the case now before us. *Peterson* v. *City of Greenville* . . . (1963), dealt with trespass prosecution of persons who "sat in" at a restaurant to protest its refusal of service to Negroes. There the Court held that although the ostensible initiative for the trespass prosecution came from the proprietor, the existence of a local ordinance requiring segregation of races in such places was tantamount to the State having "commanded a particular result," . . . With one exception, which is discussed *infra,* . . . there is no suggestion in this record that the Pennsylvania statutes and regulations governing the sale of liquor are intended either overtly or covertly to encourage discrimination. . . .

With the exception hereafter noted, the Pennsylvania Liquor Control Board plays absolutely no part in establishing or enforcing the membership or guest policies of the club which it licenses to serve liquor. There is no suggestion in this record that the Pennsylvania Act, either as written or as applied, discriminates against minority groups either in their right to apply for club licenses themselves or in their right to purchase and be served liquor in places of public accommodation. The only effect that the state licensing of Moose Lodge to serve liquor can be said to have on the right of any other Pennsylvanian to buy or be served liquor on premises other than those of Moose Lodge is that for some purposes club licenses are counted in the maximum number of licenses which may be issued in a given municipality. . . .

The District Court found that the regulations of the Liquor Control Board adopted pursuant to statute affirmatively require that "every club licensee shall adhere to all the provisions of its constitution and by-laws." Appellant argues that the purpose of this provision "is purely and simply and plainly the prevention of subterfuge," pointing out that the *bona fides* of a private club, as opposed to a place of public accommodation masquerading as a private club, is a matter with which the State Liquor Control Board may legitimately concern itself. Appellee concedes this to be the case, and expresses disagreement with the District Court on this point. There can be no doubt that the label "private club" can and has been used to evade both regulations of State and local liquor authorities, and statutes requiring places of public accommodation to serve all persons without regard to race, color, religion, or national origin. . . .

The effect of this particular regulation on Moose Lodge under the provisions of the constitution placed in the record in the court below would be to place State sanctions behind its discriminatory membership rules, but not behind its guest practices, which were not embodied in the constitution of the lodge. Had there been no change in the relevant circumstances since the making of the record in the District Court, our holding in Part I of this opinion that appellee has standing to challenge only the guest practices of Moose Lodge would have a bearing on our disposition of this issue. Appellee stated upon oral argument, though, and Moose Lodge conceded in its Brief that the bylaws of the Supreme Lodge have been altered since the lower court decision to make applicable to guests the same sort of racial restrictions as are presently applicable to members.

Even though the Liquor Control Board regulation in question is neutral in its terms, the result of its application in a case where the constitution and by-laws of a club required racial discrimination would be to invoke the sanctions of the state to enforce a concededly discriminatory private rule. State action, for purposes of the Equal Protection Clause, may emanate from rulings of administrative and regulatory agencies as well as from legislative or judicial action. *Robinson* v. *Florida* . . . (1964). *Shelley* v. *Kraemer* makes it clear that the application of state sanctions to enforce such a rule would violate the Fourteenth Amendment. Although the record before us is not as clear as one would like, appellant has not persuaded us that the District Court should have denied any and all relief.

Appellee was entitled to a decree enjoining the enforcement of Sec. 113.09 of the regulations promulgated by the Pennsylvania Liquor

Control Board insofar as that regulation requires compliance by Moose Lodge with provisions of its constitution and by-laws containing racially discriminatory provisions. He was entitled to no more. The judgment of the District Court is reversed, and the cause remanded with instructions to enter a decree in conformity with this opinion.

Reversed and remanded.

MR. JUSTICE DOUGLAS, WITH WHOM MR. JUSTICE MARSHALL JOINS, DISSENTING.

My view of the First Amendment and the related guarantees of the Bill of Rights is that they create a zone of privacy which precludes government from interfering with private clubs or groups. The associational rights which our system honors permits all white, all black, all brown, and all yellow clubs to be formed. They also permit all Catholic, all Jewish, or all agnostic clubs to be established. Government may not tell a man or woman who his or her associates must be. The individual can be as selective as he desires. So the fact that the Moose Lodge allows only Caucasians to join or come as guests is constitutionally irrelevant, as is the decision of the Black Muslims to admit to their services only members of their race.

The problem is different, however, where the public domain is concerned. I have indicated in *Garner* v. *Louisiana* . . . and *Lombard* v. *Louisiana* . . . that where restaurants or other facilities serving the public are concerned and licenses are obtained from the State for operating the business, the "public" may not be defined by the proprietor to include only people of his choice; nor may a State or municipal service be granted only to some.

Those cases are not precisely apposite, however, for a private club, by definition, is not in the public domain. And the fact that a private club gets some kind of permit from the State or municipality does not make it *ipso facto* a public enterprise or undertaking, any more than the grant to a householder of a permit to operate an incinerator puts the householder in the public domain. We must therefore examine whether there are special circumstances involved in the Pennsylvania scheme which differentiate the liquor license possessed by Moose Lodge from the incinerator permit.

Pennsylvania has a state store system of alcohol distribution. Resale is permitted by hotels, restaurants, and private clubs which all must obtain licenses from the Liquor Control Board. The scheme of regulation is complete and pervasive; and the state courts have sustained many restrictions on the licensees. . . . Once a license is issued the licensee must comply with many detailed requirements or risk suspension or revocation of the license. Among these requirements is Regulation No. 113.09 which says "Every club licensee shall adhere to all the provisions of its Constitution and By-laws." This regulation means, as applied to Moose Lodge, that it must adhere to the racially discriminatory provision of the Constitution of its Supreme Lodge that "The membership of the lodge shall be composed of male persons of the Caucasian or White race above the age of twenty-one years, and not married to someone other than of the Caucasian or White race, who are of good moral character, physically and mentally normal, who shall profess a belief in a Supreme Being."

It is argued that this regulation only aims at the prevention of subterfuge and at enforcing Pennsylvania's differentiation between places of public accommodation and bona fide private clubs. It is also argued that the regulation only gives effect to the constitutionally protected rights of privacy and of association. But I cannot so read the regulation. While those other purposes are embraced in it, so is the restrictive membership clause. And we have held that "a State is responsible for the discriminatory act of a private party when the State, by its law, has compelled the act." ... It is irrelevant whether the law is statutory, or an administrative regulation. ... And it is irrelevant whether the discriminatory act was instigated by the regulation, or was independent of it. ... The result, as I see it, is the same as though Pennsylvania had put into its liquor licenses a provision that the license may not be used to dispense liquor to Blacks, Browns, Yellows—or atheists or agnostics. ...

Were this regulation the only infirmity in Pennsylvania's licensing scheme, I would perhaps agree with the majority that the appropriate relief would be a decree enjoining its enforcement. But there is another flaw in the scheme not so easily cured. Liquor licenses in Pennsylvania, unlike driver's licenses, or marriage licenses, are not freely available to those who meet racially neutral qualifications. There is a complex quota system, which the majority accurately describes. ... What the majority neglects to say is that the Harrisburg quota, where Moose Lodge No. 107 is located, has been full for many years. No more club licenses may be issued in that city.

This state-enforced scarcity of licenses restricts the ability of blacks to obtain liquor, for liquor is commercially available *only* at private clubs for a significant portion of each week. Access by blacks to places that serve liquor is further limited by the fact that the state quota is filled. A group desiring to form a nondiscriminatory club which would serve blacks must purchase a license held by an existing club, which can exact a monopoly price for the transfer. The availability of such a license is speculative at best, however, for, as Moose Lodge itself concedes, without a liquor license a fraternal organization would be hard-pressed to survive.

Thus, the State of Pennsylvania is putting the weight of its liquor license, concededly a valued and important adjunct to a private club, behind racial discrimination. ...

I would affirm the judgment below.

MR. JUSTICE BRENNAN, WITH WHOM MR. JUSTICE MARSHALL JOINS, DISSENTING.

When Moose Lodge obtained its liquor license, the State of Pennsylvania became an active participant in the operation of the Lodge bar. Liquor licensing laws are only incidentally revenue measures; they are primarily pervasive regulatory schemes under which the State dictates and continually supervises virtually every detail of the operation of the licensee's business. Very few, if any, other licensed businesses experience such complete state involvement. Yet the Court holds that that involvement does not constitute "state action" making the Lodge's refusal to serve a guest liquor solely because of his race a violation of the Fourteenth Amendment. The vital flaw in the Court's reasoning is its complete disregard of the fundamental value underlying the "state action" concept. ...

This is ... a case requiring application of the principle that until today has governed our determinations of the existence of "state action": "Our prior decisions leave no doubt that the mere existence of efforts by the State, through legislation or otherwise, to authorize, encourage, or otherwise support racial discrimination in a particular facet of life constitutes illegal state involvement in those pertinent private acts of discrimination that subsequently occur." . . .

I therefore dissent and would affirm the final decree entered by the District Court.

[In *Jackson v. Metropolitan Edison Co.* (1974), the court continued to embrace the state action logic of *Moose Lodge*. The Supreme Court denied Mrs. Jackson injunctive relief against a privately owned utility that had disconnected her electricity without notice, a hearing, or an opportunity to contest alleged default of payments. She claimed that under state law she was entitled to continuous service from the utility and that its termination of service without notice constituted a "state action" deprivation of her due process rights under the Fourteenth Amendment. In the majority opinion, Justice Rehnquist rejected the claim that state action was involved because the utility was a monopoly. Relying on *Public Utilities Commission* v. *Pollak* (1952) and *Moose Lodge,* he held that "there was insufficient relationship between the challenged actions of the entities involved and their monopoly status."

In response to Mrs. Jackson's claim that state action was present because the utility provided an essential public service, the Court held that the utility had not been delegated powers traditionally exercised by the state, and any obligations imposed upon the utility by the Pennsylvania statute were not thereby made a constitutional obligation of the state. Finally, the Court rejected the argument that state regulations imposed on the utility are, in effect, "state actions" because the utility operates under state regulations. The Court held that "approval by a state utility commission of such a request from a regulated utility, where the commission has not put its own weight on the side of the proposed practice by ordering it, does not transmute a practice initiated by the utility and approved by the Commission into 'state action.' "

In dissent, Justice Douglas argued that determination of state action requires an assessment of the *totality* of the state's involvement and not just an analysis of isolated actions by the state. Charging that the majority failed to consider the totality of the state's involvement in regulating and enforcing regulations, Justice Douglas rejected what he termed the Court's "sequential" analysis of state involvement and narrow interpretation of "state action."]

E. Congress, the Federal Courts, and Civil Rights Protection

(1) Heart of Atlanta Motel v. United States (1964)

+Warren, Black, Douglas, Clark, Harlan, Brennan, Stewart, White, Goldberg

MR. JUSTICE CLARK delivered the opinion of the Court.

This is a declaratory judgment action . . . attacking the constitutionality of Title II of the Civil Rights Act of 1964. . . . In addition to declaratory relief the complaint sought an injunction restraining the enforcement of the Act and damages against respondents based on allegedly resulting injury in the event compliance was required. Appellees counterclaimed for enforcement . . . of the Act and asked for a three-judge district court . . . . A three-judge court . . . sustained the validity of the Act . . . . We affirm the judgment.

The case comes here on admissions and stipulated facts. Appellant owns and operates the Heart of Atlanta Motel which has 216 rooms available to transient guests. The motel . . . is readily accessible to interstate highways 75 and 85 and state highways 23 and 41. Appellant solicits patronage from outside the State of Georgia through various national advertising media, including magazines of national circulation; it maintains over 50 billboards and highway signs within the State, soliciting patronage for the motel; it accepts convention trade from outside Georgia and approximately 75% of its registered guests are from out of State. Prior to passage of the Act the motel had followed a practice of refusing to rent rooms to Negroes, and it alleged that it intended to continue to do so. . . .

The appellant contends that Congress in passing this Act exceeded its power to regulate commerce . . . that the Act violates the Fifth Amendment because appellant is deprived of the right to choose its customers and operate its business as it wishes, resulting in a taking of its liberty and property without due process of law and a taking of its property without just compensation; and, finally, that by requiring appellant to rent available rooms to Negroes against its will, Congress is subjecting it to involuntary servitude in contravention of the Thirteenth Amendment.

The appellees counter that the unavailability to Negroes of adequate accommodations interferes significantly with interstate travel, and that Congress, under the Commerce Clause, has power to remove such obstructions and restraints; that the Fifth Amendment does not forbid reasonable regulation and that consequential damage does not constitute a "taking" within the meaning of that amendment; that the Thirteenth Amendment claim fails because it is entirely frivolous to say that an amendment directed to the abolition of human bondage and the removal of widespread disabilities associated with slavery places discrimination in public accommodations beyond the reach of both federal and state law. . . .

It is admitted that the operation of the motel brings it within the provisions of §201 (a) of the Act and that appellant refused to provide lodging for transient Negroes because of their race or color and that it intends to continue that policy unless restrained.

The sole question posed is, therefore, the constitutionality of the Civil Rights Act of 1964 as applied to these facts. The legislative history of the Act indicates that Congress based the Act on §5 and the Equal Protection Clause of the Fourteenth Amendment as well as its power to regulate interstate commerce. . . .

The Senate Commerce Committee made it quite clear that the fundamental object of Title II was to vindicate "the deprivation of personal dignity that surely accompanies denials of equal access to public establishments." At the same time, however, it noted that such an objective has been and could be readily achieved "by congressional action based on the commerce power of the Constitution." . . . Our study of the legislative record, made in the light of prior cases, has brought us to the conclusion that Congress possessed ample power in this regard, and we have therefore not considered the other grounds relied upon. This is not to say that the remaining authority upon which it acted was not adequate, a question upon which we do not pass, but merely that since the commerce power is sufficient for our decision here we have considered it alone. . . .

In light of our ground for decision, it might be well at the outset to discuss the *Civil Rights Cases* . . . which declared provisions of the Civil Rights Act of 1875 unconstitutional. . . . We think that decision inapposite, and without precedential value in determining the constitutionality of the present Act. Unlike Title II of the present legislation, the 1875 Act broadly proscribed discrimination in "inns, public conveyances on land or water, theaters, and other public places of amusement," without limiting the categories of affected businesses to those impinging upon interstate commerce. In contrast, the applicability of Title II is carefully limited to interstate flow of goods and people, except where state action is involved. Further, the fact that certain kinds of businesses may not in 1875 have been sufficiently involved in interstate commerce to warrant bringing them within the ambit of the commerce power is not necessarily dispositive of the same question today. Our populace had not reached its present mobility, nor were facilities, goods and services circulating as readily in interstate commerce as they are today. Although the principles which we apply today are those first formulated by Chief Justice Marshall in *Gibbons* v. *Ogden* . . .(1824), the conditions of transportation and commerce have changed dramatically, and we must apply those principles to the present state of commerce. The sheer increase in volume of interstate traffic alone would give discriminatory practices which inhibit travel a far larger impact upon the nation's commerce than such practices had in the economy of another day. Finally, there is language in the *Civil Rights Cases* which indicates that the Court did not fully consider whether the 1875 Act could be sustained as an exercise of the commerce power. . . .

[I]t is clear that such a limitation renders the opinion devoid of authority for the proposition that the Commerce Clause gives no power to Congress to regulate discriminatory practices now found substantially to affect interstate commerce. . . .

The power of Congress to deal with these obstructions depends on the meaning of the Commerce Clause. Its meaning was first enunciated 140 years ago by the great Chief Justice John Marshall in *Gibbons* v. *Ogden*, in these words:

> *The subject to be regulated is commerce; and . . . to ascertain the extent of the power, it becomes necessary to settle the meaning of the word. The counsel for the appellee would limit it to traffic, to buying and selling, or the interchange of commodities . . . but it is something more: it is intercourse . . . between nations, and parts of nations, in all its branches, and is regulated by prescribing rules for carrying on that intercourse.*

[A summary of the *Gibbons* doctrine is omitted.]

In short, the determinative test of the exercise of power by the Congress under the Commerce Clause is simply whether the activity sought to be regulated is "commerce which concerns more than one state" and has a real and substantial relation to the national interest. . . .

That the "intercourse" of which the Chief Justice spoke included the movement of persons through more States than one was settled as early as 1849, in the *Passenger Cases* . . . where Mr. Justice McLean stated: "That the transportation of passengers is a part of commerce is not now an open question." . . .

Nor does it make any difference whether the transportation is commercial in character. . . .

The same interest in protecting interstate commerce which led Congress to deal with segregation in interstate carriers and the white slave traffic has prompted it to extend the exercise of its power to gambling . . .; to criminal enterprises . . .; to deceptive practices in the sale of products . . . ; to fraudulent security transactions . . . ; to misbranding of drugs . . . ; to wages and hours . . . ; to members of labor unions . . . ; to crop control . . . ; to discrimination against shippers . . . ; to the protection of small business from injurious price cutting . . . ; to resale price maintenance . . . ; to professional football . . . ; and to racial discrimination by owners and managers of terminal restaurants . . . .

That Congress was legislating against moral wrongs in many of these areas rendered its enactments no less valid. In framing Title II of the Act Congress was also dealing with what it considered a moral problem. But that fact does not detract from the overwhelming evidence of the disruptive effect that racial discrimination has had on commercial intercourse. It was this burden which empowered Congress to enact appropriate legislation, and, given this basis for the exercise of its power, Congress was not restricted by the fact that the particular obstruction to interstate commerce with which it was dealing was also deemed a moral and social wrong.

It is said that the operation of the motel here is of a purely local character. But, assuming this to be true, "if it is interstate commerce that feels the pinch, it does not matter how local the operation that applies the squeeze." *United States* v. *Women's Sportswear Mfrs. Assn.* (1949).

Thus the power of Congress to promote interstate commerce also includes the power to regulate the local incidents thereof, including local activities in both the States of origin and destination, which might have a substantial and harmful effect upon that commerce. . . .

Nor does the Act deprive appellant of liberty or property under the Fifth Amendment. The commerce power invoked here by the Congress is a specific and plenary one authorized by the Constitution itself. The only questions are: (1) whether Congress had a rational basis for finding that racial discrimination by motels affected commerce, and (2) if it had such a basis, whether the means it selected to eliminate that evil are reasonable and appropriate. If they are, appellant has no "right" to select its guests as it sees fit, free from governmental regulation.

There is nothing novel about such legislation. Thirty-two States now have it on their books either by statute or executive order and many cities provide such regulation. Some of these Acts go back fourscore years. It has been repeatedly held by this Court that such laws do not violate the Due Process Clause of the Fourteenth Amendment. . . .

It is doubtful if in the long run appellant will suffer economic loss as a result of the Act. Experience is to the contrary where discrimination is completely obliterated as to all public accommodations. But whether this Court has specifically held that the fact that a "member of the class which is regulated may suffer economic losses not shared by others . . . has never been a barrier" to such legislation. . . .

We find no merit in the remainder of appellant's contentions, including that of "involuntary servitude." . . .

We therefore, conclude that the action of the Congress in the adoption of the Act as applied here to a motel which concededly serves interstate travelers is within the power granted it by the Commerce Clause of the Constitution, as interpreted by this Court for 140 years. It may be argued that Congress could have pursued other methods to eliminate the obstructions it found in interstate commerce caused by racial discrimination. But this is a matter of policy that rests entirely with the Congress not with the courts. How obstructions in commerce may be removed—what means are to be employed—is within the sound and exclusive discretion of the Congress. It is subject only to one caveat—that the means chosen by it must be reasonably adapted to the end permitted by the Constitution. We cannot say that its choice here was not so adopted. The Constitution requires no more.

Affirmed.

Appendix to Opinion of the Court

Title II—Injunctive Relief Against Discrimination in Places of Public Accommodation

Sec. 201. (a) All persons shall be entitled to the full and equal enjoyment of the goods, services, facilities, privileges, advantages, and accommodations of any place of public accommodation, as defined in this section, without discrimination or segregation on the ground of race, color, religion, or national origin.

(b) Each of the following establishments which serves the public is a place of public accommodation within the meaning of this title if its operations affect commerce, or if discrimination or segregation by it is supported by State action:

(1) any inn, hotel, motel, or other establishment which provides lodging to transient guests, other than an establishment located within a building which contains not more than five rooms for rent or hire and which is actually occupied by the proprietor of such establishment as his residence;

(2) any restaurant, cafeteria, lunchroom, lunch counter, soda fountain, or other facility principally engaged in selling food for consumption on the premises, including, but not limited to, any such facility located on the premises of any retail establishment; or any gasoline station;

(3) any motion picture house, theater, concert hall, sports arena, stadium or other place of exhibition or entertainment; and

(4) any establishment (A) (i) which is physically located within the premises of any establishment otherwise covered by this subsection, or (ii) within the premises of which is physically located any such covered establishment, and (B) which holds itself out as serving patrons of such covered establishment.

(c) The operations of an establishment affect commerce within the meaning of this title if (1) it is one of the establishments described in paragraph (1) of subsection (b); (2) in the case of an establishment described in paragraph (2) of subsection (b), it serves or offers to serve interstate travelers or a substantial portion of the food which it serves, or gasoline or other products which it sells, has moved in commerce; (3) in the case of an establishment described in paragraph (3) of subsection (b), it customarily presents films, performances, athletic teams, exhibitions, or other sources of entertainment which move in commerce; and (4) in the case of an establishment described in paragraph (4) of subsection (b), it is physically located within the premises of, or there is physically located within its premises, an establishment the operations of which affect commerce within the meaing of this subsection. For purposes of this section, "commerce" means travel, trade, traffic, commerce, transportation, or communication among the several States, or between the District of Columbia and any State, or between any foreign country or any territory or possession and any State or the District of Columbia, or between points in the same State but through any other State or the District of Columbia or a foreign country.

(d) Discrimination or segregation by an establishment is supported by State action within the meaning of this title if such discrimination or segregation (1) is carried on under color of any law, statute, ordinance, or regulation; or (2) is carried on under color of any custom or usage required or enforced by officials of the State or political subdivision thereof; or (3) is required by action of the State or political subdivision thereof.

(e) The provisions of this title shall not apply to a private club or other establishment not in fact open to the public, except to the extent that the facilities of such establishment are made available to the customers or patrons of an establishment within the scope of subsection (b).

Sec. 202. All persons shall be entitled to be free, at any establishment or place, from discrimination or segregation of any kind on the ground of race, color, religion, or national origin, if such discrimination or segregation is or purports to be required by any law, statute, ordinance, regulation, rule, or order of a State or any agency or political subdivision thereof.

. . .

MR. JUSTICE BLACK, CONCURRING (OMITTED).

MR. JUSTICE DOUGLAS, CONCURRING (OMITTED)

MR. JUSTICE GOLDBERG, CONCURRING.

. . . The primary purpose of the Civil Rights Act of 1964 . . . as the Court recognizes, and as I would underscore, is the vindication of human dignity and not mere economics. . . .

[T]hat this is the primary purpose of the Act is emphasized by the fact that while §201 (c) speaks only in terms of establishments which "affect commerce," it is clear that Congress based this section not only on its power under the Commerce Clause but also on §5 of the Fourteenth Amendment. The cases cited in the Court's opinions are conclusive that Congress could exercise its powers under the Commerce Clause to accomplish this purpose. As §§ 201 (b) and (c) are undoubtedly a valid exercise of the Commerce Clause power for the reasons stated in the opinion of the Court, the Court considers that it is unnecessary to consider whether it is additionally supportable by Congress' exertion of its power under §5 of the Fourteenth Amendment.

In my concurring opinion in *Bell* v. *Maryland* . . . however, I expressed my conviction that §1 of the Fourteenth Amendment guarantees to all Americans the constitutional right "to be treated as equal members of the community with respect to public accommodations," and that "Congress [has] authority under §5 of the Fourteenth Amendment, or under the Commerce Clause, Art. I, §8, to implement the rights protected by §1 of the Fourteenth Amendment. In the give-and-take of the legislative process, Congress can fashion a law drawing the guidelines necessary and appropriate to facilitate practical administration and to distinguish between genuinely public and private accommodations." The challenged Act is just such a law and, in my view, Congress clearly had authority both under §5 of the Fourteenth Amendment and the Commerce

Clause to enact the Civil Rights Act of 1964.

[The Civil Rights Act held constitutional in the *Heart of Atlanta Motel* case not only prohibited discrimination in public accommodations covered by the act, but also prohibited the punishment of any person attempting to exercise the rights secured by the act—for example, the right to be served on an equal basis at the public accommodations in question. Did this mean that a person, faced with prohibited discrimination, who did not seek redress under the statutory provisions of the act, but used extra-legal means to secure his rights was not protected if arrested? And if the use of extra-legal means to secure service was protected by the act, was this a protection to be extended retroactively to cases occurring before passage of the bill or before the *Heart of Atlanta* case?

Hamm v. *Rock Hill* was a "typical" sit-in case which coincidentally was before the Court at this time. Petitioners had sat-in at a chain store in Rock Hill, South Carolina, and were convicted of trespass when they refused to leave the premises. Writing for the Court, Justice Clark argued that, although the law generally condemns self-help (that is, taking the law into one's own hands), it is possible to interpret the Civil Rights Act of 1964 as immunizing peaceable attempts to secure service at establishments "covered" by the statute. Clark noted that the legislative history of the statute specifically referred to its use as a defense to charges of criminal trespass, breach-of-the-peace, and similar prosecutions experienced by sit-in demonstrators. "In effect," Clark said, "the Act prohibits the application of state laws in a way that would deprive any person of the rights granted under the Act."

The more difficult question was the retroactivity of the act. Clark held that since, as in *Bell* v. *Maryland*, the legislature was substituting a right for a crime, if these were federal prosecutions they would clearly be abated under the act. As state prosecutions, Clark argued, the same rule would apply under the supremacy clause of the Constitution, Article VI. In order to reach this conclusion Clark had to overcome the presence of a federal statute specifically designed to prevent retroactive application of statutes containing no specific retroactive provision. But Clark held that this referred merely to technical consequences and that the "drastic changes" contemplated by the Civil Rights Act could not be so limited. As in his opinion in the *Heart of Atlanta* case, Clark brushed aside all objections as unworthy:

As we have said, Congress clearly intended to eradicate an unhappy chapter in our history. The peaceful conduct for which petitioners were prosecuted was on behalf of a principle since embodied in the law of the land. The convictions were based on the theory that the rights of a property owner have been violated. However, the supposed right to discriminate on the basis of race, at least in covered establishments, was nullified by the statute. Under such circumstances the actionable nature of the acts in question must be viewed in the light of the statute and its legislative purpose.]

(2) Expanding Federal Protection of Civil Rights: The *Guest* and *Price* Cases

We have seen, in the *Heart of Atlanta Motel* case, that Congress has the full scope of powers of the commerce clause to use in protecting certain aspects of civil rights (e.g., those that by *any* stretch of the imagination can be said to "affect commerce"). But its primary authority to protect civil rights today comes from the Thirteenth, Fourteenth, and Fifteenth Amendments. Unlike Congress' power under the commerce clause, which is plenary, the enforcement clauses of those amendments give Congress the power "to enforce the amendments by appropriate means." Thus they are limited by the avowed purpose of the amendments. Nevertheless, these powers, as currently interpreted by the Supreme Court, are extremely broad.

There are significant differences among the amendments. Of the three amendments, only the Thirteenth has no state action trigger. But the substantive reach of that amendment is also limited. Congress is free to legislate to abolish the "badges and incidents" of slavery, but it is not free to declare anything to be such a badge. In the *Civil Rights Cases* the Supreme Court refused to accept the contention that discrimination in public accommodations was among those badges and incidents, and it therefore held that the Thirteenth Amendment could *not* be the constitutional basis of the Civil Rights Act of 1875. On the other hand, in *Jones* v. *Mayer* (1968), the Court gave a much broader interpretation to those key words (see pp. 549–553, *infra*).

The Fourteenth Amendment, by contrast, is limited by the state action doctrine but has a much greater potential substantive reach. Clearly, the concept of equal protection of the laws applies to racial discrimination, and it also applies to discrimination by gender or against other minority groups. But could Congress declare that the states violate the equal protection clause by regressive or inequitable taxation and by that means regulate state tax policies? Of course, the Tenth Amendment might prevent this, but the words of the Fourteenth Amendment, by themselves, might not. Likewise, under the guise of enforcing due process guarantees, could Congress impose on the states uniform procedures for arrest, trial, and punishment?

We have noted that, contrary to the expectations of the framers of the Civil War amendments, the Supreme Court imposed narrow limits on them. Congress, the Court said, could only prohibit discriminatory state action, and its remedial powers were limited to nullifying offending state laws. The combined effect of a post-Reconstruction malaise, the growth of the Jim Crow system, the power of the southern bloc in Congress, and the hostility of the Supreme Court to federal civil rights legislation kept the federal civil rights effort at a minimum for three-quarters of a century. In the 1920s, Congress repeatedly turned down proposed anti-lynching bills. From 1885 to 1921, statistics revealed an average of more than 100 lynchings per year. The *Scottsboro* cases in the early 1930s brought home to many Americans the brutality of southern justice, but little was done other than by an occasional Supreme Court reversal of a particularly grave injustice. Apprehension and punishment of whites accused of lynching or attacking Negroes were virtually unknown.

The sit-ins and other protest demonstrations of the 1960s forced the federal government to reconsider its position and its role in the protection of blacks generally and of civil rights workers in particular. The brutality of law enforcement officials toward civil rights demonstrators could not be concealed in the age of mass media, and the violence in Selma and Birmingham, Alabama, and the killing of three civil rights workers in Mississippi shocked the world and seared the conscience of the nation.

One reason for the hesitant federal response to these events, as Burke Marshall has pointed out, was the prevailing notion that in a federal system certain responsibilities must be left with the states and not taken over by the federal government. But it was also a fact that the federal government had inadequate legal tools with which to operate. As Marshall noted, "federal courts strongly resist interfering with state court criminal proceedings. An individual suit asking such relief is barred by statute for most purposes."[1]

A massive show of force could desegregate the University of Mississippi or expel Governor Wallace from the "schoolhouse door" of the University of Alabama. But the greatest threat to blacks was systematic intimidation and violence, often carried out by or with the knowledge of local sheriffs, designed to enforce the rigid caste system. Blacks who did not "know their place" often lost their jobs, could not buy on credit, and suffered other economic and social indignities. Blacks who violated the sexual mores of the white community received far harsher sanctions. In those few instances where the federal government prosecuted whites, all-white juries almost never returned convictions.

In response to increased pressure from civil rights groups, the Justice Department tried to revive two long-dormant civil rights statutes that dated back to Reconstruction. Section 241, carrying a fine of $5000 and a maximum prison sentence of ten years, forbade conspiracies to "injure, oppress, threaten or intimidate any "citizen" from exercising rights *secured* to him by the Constitution or laws of the United States." Section 242 levied a maximum $1000 fine and one year in jail against any person, acting under color of law, statute, ordinance, regulation, or cus-

tom, from willfully depriving any inhabitant of the United States of any rights, privileges, or immunities *secured* or *protected* by the Constitution or laws of the United States. As interpreted until 1966, Section 242 was a broader statute: it protected inhabitants, not just citizens; it applied to substantive actions by individuals and was not limited to conspiracies; and it covered not only secured but protected rights as well (the latter being the broader term). But it was limited by the state action requirement, by the need to prove a *willful* civil rights deprivation, and carried the lesser penalty.

In *United States* v. *Price* (1966) and *United States* v. *Guest* (1966), the Supreme Court considerably broadened the scope of these two civil rights statutes and the scope of civil rights deprivations that Congress could reach by legislation. Both cases came to the Court on motions to quash indictments. In *Price,* indictments were returned against a group of eighteen persons in Mississippi, including three police officers, charging them with conspiring to deprive three civil rights workers—Schwerner, Goodman, and Chaney—of their civil rights by killing them (Section 241)—and also charging the same persons under Section 242. The case was heard by Judge Harold Cox in the District Court for the Southern District of Mississippi. He held the indictment under Section 242 valid against the police officers but not against the private citizens, and he dismissed the indictment under Section 241 against all the de-

[1]Burke Marshall, "The Limitations of Federal Power to Protect Civil Rights Workers," in *Federalism and Civil Rights* (New York: Columbia University Press, 1965).

fendants on the grounds that Section 241 did not reach rights protected by the Fourteenth Amendment, but only rights flowing from the exercise of substantive congressional power (i.e., "secured" rights).

A unanimous Supreme Court reversed and reinstated the indictments. Writing for the Court, Justice Fortas held that Section 242 did not apply to law enforcement officers exclusively but that it could be applied, as alleged in the indictment, to a conspiracy of individuals participating in what he called "official lawlessness." With regard to Section 241, Fortas wrote that the participation of the police officers made this state action within the meaning of the Fourteenth Amendment. Furthermore, he held that, contrary to some previous decisions, Section 241 is not limited to violations of substantive rights but that it applied to rights and privileges secured by *all* of the Constitution and *all* of the laws of the United States— including the Fourteenth Amendment—and that it did not apply only to the limited class of rights of national citizenship as Judge Cox had asserted.

The *Guest* case was also an indictment under Section 241; the six defendants were alleged to have shot and killed a Negro, Colonel Lemuel Penn, who was traveling in a car through Georgia. Unlike the *Price* case, there were no law enforcement officials directly involved or indicted, and the first question to be considered was whether or not there was enough state action to invoke the powers of the Fourteenth Amendment. Writing for three justices, Justice Stewart held that there had to be some state action to maintain the indictment and found it in some smatterings of evidence that showed cooperation of the local sheriff in locating Colonel Penn's automobile.

But the other six justices reached the conclusion, by several different routes, that Section 5 of the Fourteenth Amendment empowers Congress to enact laws punishing *all* conspiracies that interfere with Fourteenth Amendment rights, whether or not state action is present.

Justice Clark, joined by Justices Black and Fortas, stated:

The Court's interpretation of the [Guest] *indictment clearly avoids the question whether Congress, by appropriate legislation, has the power to punish private conspiracies that interfere with Fourteenth Amendment rights. . . . Although the Court specifically rejects any such connotation, it is, I believe, both appropriate and necessary under the circumstances here to say that there can be no doubt that the specific language of section 5 empowers Congress to enact laws punishing all conspiracies—with or without state action—that interfere with Fourteenth Amendment rights.*

And Justice Brennan, joined by Justices Douglas and Chief Justice Warren, stated:

Section 241 reaches such a private conspiracy, not because the Fourteenth Amendment of its own force prohibits such a conspiracy, but because section 241, as an exercise of congressional power under section 5 of that Amendment, prohibits all conspiracies to interfere with the exercise of a [constitutionally secured] right.

Exactly how far the Supreme Court intended to expand the limits of Congress' power under the Fourteenth Amendment to reach private action is not clear. The Court has never directly confronted that question again, primarily because *Jones* v. *Mayer* (1968) and *Griffin* v. *Breckenridge* (1971) seemed to give Congress virtually unlimited power to legislate against racial discrimination (but not other kinds of deprivations) under the Thirteenth Amendment. If we recall also that *South Carolina* v. *Katzenbach* (1966) approved Congress' power under the Fifteenth Amendment to legislate directly against voting rights abuses and that *Katzenbach* v. *Morgan* (1966), in approving the ban on literacy tests for Puerto Ricans with a sixth-grade education under the Fourteenth Amendment, stated that *Congress* could define what actions violated the Fourteenth Amendment independent of judicial interpretations, it is clear that some of the principles of the *Civil Rights Cases* (1883) have been seriously eroded.

(3) Jones v. Mayer (1968)

+Warren, Black, Douglas, Brennan, Stewart, Fortas, Marshall

−Harlan, White

MR. JUSTICE STEWART delivered the opinion of the Court.

In this case we are called upon to determine the scope and the constitutionality of an Act of Congress, 42 USC § 1982,[1] which provides that:

All citizens of the United States shall have the same right, in every State and Territory, as is enjoyed by white citizens thereof to inherit, purchase, lease, sell, hold, and convey real and personal property.

On September 2, 1965, the petitioners filed a complaint in the District Court for the Eastern District of Missouri, alleging that the respondents had refused to sell them a home in the Paddock Woods community of St. Louis County for the sole reason that petitioner Joseph Lee Jones is a Negro. Relying in part upon § 1982, the petitioners sought injunctive and other relief. The District Court sustained the respondents' motion to dismiss the complaint, and the Eighth Circuit affirmed, concluding that § 1982 applies only to state action and does not reach private refusals to sell. We granted certiorari to consider the questions thus presented. For the reasons that follow, we reverse the judgment of the Court of Appeals. We hold that § 1982 bars *all* racial discrimination, private as well as public, in the sale or rental of property, and that the statute, thus construed, is a valid exercise of the power of Congress to enforce the Thirteenth Amendment.

At the outset, it is important to make clear precisely what this case does *not* involve. Whatever else it may be 42 USC § 1982 is not a comprehensive open housing law. In sharp contrast to the fair Housing Title (Title VIII) of the Civil Rights Act of 1968 . . . the statute in this case deals only with racial discrimination and does not address itself to discrimination on grounds of religion or national origin. It does not deal specifically with discrimination in the provision of services or facilities in connection with the sale or rental of a dwelling. It does not prohibit advertising or other representations that indicate discriminatory preferences. It does not refer explicitly to discrimination in financing arrangements or in the provision of brokerage services. It does not empower a federal administrative agency to assist aggrieved parties. It makes no provision for intervention by the Attorney General. And, although it can be enforced by injunction, it contains no provision expressly authorizing a federal court to order the payment of damages.

[1] Originally the Civil Rights Act of 1866.—Ed.

Thus, although §1982 contains none of the exemptions that Congress included in the Civil Rights Act of 1968, it would be a serious mistake to suppose that §1982 in any way diminishes the significance of the law recently enacted by Congress. . . .

This Court last had occasion to consider the scope of 42 USC §1982 in 1948, in *Hurd* v. *Hodge*[2]. . . . That case arose when property owners in the District of Columbia sought to enforce racially restrictive covenants against the Negro purchasers of several homes on their block. A federal district court enforced the restrictive agreements by declaring void the deeds of the Negro purchasers. It enjoined further attempts to sell or lease them the properties in question and directed them to "remove themselves and all of their personal belongings" from the premises within 60 days. The Court of Appeals for the District of Columbia affirmed, and this Court granted certiorari to decide whether §1982, then §1978 of the Revised Statutes of 1874, barred enforcement of the racially restrictive agreements in that case.

The agreements in *Hurd* covered only two-thirds of the lots of a single city block, and preventing Negroes from buying or renting homes in that specific area would not have rendered them ineligible to do so elsewhere in the city. Thus, if §1982 had been thought to do no more than grant Negro citizens the legal capacity to buy and rent property free of prohibitions that wholly disabled them because of their race, judicial enforcement of the restrictive covenants at issue would not have violated §1982. But this Court took a broader view of the statute. Although the covenants could have been enforced without denying the general right of Negroes to purchase or lease real estate, the enforcement of those covenants would nonetheless have denied the Negro purchasers "the same right 'as is enjoyed by white citizens . . to inherit, purchase, lease, sell, hold, and convey real and personal property' ". . . That result, this Court concluded, was prohibited by §1982. To suggest otherwise, the Court said, "is to reject the plain meaning of language." . . .

Hurd v. *Hodge* . . . squarely held, therefore, that a Negro citizen who is denied the opportunity to purchase the home he wants "[s]olely because of [his] race and color," . . . has suffered the kind of injury that §1982 was designed to prevent. . . . The basic source of the injury in *Hurd* was, of course, the action of private individuals--white citizens who had agreed to exclude Negroes from a residential area. But an arm of the Government—in that case, a federal court—had assisted in the enforcement of that agreement. Thus *Hurd* v. *Hodge* . . . did not present the question whether *purely* private discrimination, unaided by any action on the part of government, would violate § 1982 if its effect were to deny a citizen the right to rent or buy property solely because of his race or color.

. . . It is true that a dictum in *Hurd* said that §1982 was directed only toward "governmental action" . . . but neither *Hurd* nor any other case before or since has presented that precise issue for adjudication in this Court. Today we face that issue for the first time.

We begin with the language of the statute itself. In plain and unambiguous terms, §1982 grants to all citizens, without regard to race or color, "the same right" to purchase

[2]A companion case to *Shelley* v. *Kraemer.*—Ed.

and lease property "as is enjoyed by white citizens." As the Court of Appeals in this case evidently recognized, that right can be impaired as effectively by "those who place property on the market" as by the State itself. . . . So long as a Negro citizen who wants to buy or rent a home can be turned away simply because he is not white, he cannot be said to enjoy "the *same* right . . . as is enjoyed by white citizens . . . to . . . purchase [and] lease . . . real and personal property."

On its face, therefore, §1982 appears to prohibit *all* discrimination against Negroes in the sale or rental of property—discrimination by private owners as well as discrimination by public authorities. Indeed, even the respondents seem to concede that, if §1982 "means what it says"—to use the words of the respondents' brief—then it must encompass every racially motivated refusal to sell or rent and cannot be confined to officially sanctioned segregation in housing. Stressing what they consider to be the revolutionary implications of so literal a reading of §1982, the respondents argue that Congress cannot possibly have intended any such result. Our examination of the relevant history, however, persuades us that Congress meant exactly what it said. . . .

In attempting to demonstrate the contrary, the respondents rely heavily upon the fact that the Congress which approved the 1866 statute wished to eradicate the recently enacted Black Codes—laws which had saddled Negroes with "onerous disabilities and burdens, and curtailed their rights . . . to such an extent that their freedom was of little value. . . ." The respondents suggest that the only evil Congress sought to eliminate was that of racially discriminatory laws in the former Confederate States. But the Civil Rights Act was drafted to apply throughout the country, and its language was far broader than would have been necessary to strike down discriminatory statutes.

That broad language, we are asked to believe, was a mere slip of the legislative pen. We disagree. For the same Congress that wanted to do away with the Black Codes *also* had before it an imposing body of evidence pointing to the mistreatment of Negroes by private individuals and unofficial groups, mistreatment unrelated to any hostile state legislation. . . .

Indeed, one of the most comprehensive studies then before Congress stressed the prevalence of private hostility toward Negroes and the need to protect them from the resulting persecution and discrimination. The report noted the existence of laws virtually prohibiting Negroes from owning or renting property in certain towns, but described such laws as "mere isolated cases," representing "the local outcroppings of a spirit. . . found to prevail everywhere"—a spirit expressed, for example, by lawless acts of brutality directed against Negroes who traveled to areas where they were not wanted. The report concluded that, even if anti-Negro legislation were "repealed in all the States lately in rebellion," equal treatment for the Negro would not yet be secured. . . .

In light of the concerns that led Congress to adopt it and the contents of the debates that preceded its passage, it is clear that the Act was designed to do just what its terms suggest: to prohibit all racial discrimination, whether or not under color of law, with respect to the rights enumerated therein—including the right to purchase or lease property.

Nor was the scope of the 1866 Act

altered when it was re-enacted in 1870, some two years after the ratification of the Fourteenth Amendment. It is quite true that some members of Congress supported the Fourteenth Amendment "in order to eliminate doubt as to the constitutional validity of the Civil Rights Act as applied to the States." . . . But it certainly does not follow that the adoption of the Fourteenth Amendment or the subsequent readoption of the Civil Rights Act were meant somehow to *limit* its application to state action. The legislative history furnishes not the slightest factual basis for any such speculation, and the conditions prevailing in 1870 make it highly implausible. For by that time most, if not all, of the former Confederate States, then under the control of "reconstructed" legislatures, had formally repudiated racial discrimination, and the focus of congressional concern had clearly shifted from hostile statutes to the activities of groups like the Ku Klux Klan, operating wholly outside the law. . . .

As we said in a somewhat different setting two Terms ago, "We think that history leaves no doubt that, if we are to give [the law] the scope that its origins dictate, we must accord it a sweep as broad as its language." *United States* v. *Price.* . . . And, as the Attorney General of the United States said at the oral argument of this case, "The fact that the statute lay partially dormant for many years cannot be held to diminish its force today."

The remaining question is whether Congress has power under the Constitution to do what §1982 purports to do: to prohibit all racial discrimination, private and public, in the sale and rental of property. Our starting point is the Thirteenth Amendment, for it was pursuant to that constitu-

tional provision that Congress originally enacted what is now §1982. . . .

As its text reveals, the Thirteenth Amendment "is not a mere prohibition of State laws establishing or upholding slavery, but an absolute declaration that slavery or involuntary servitude shall not exist in any part of the United States." . . . It has never been doubted, therefore, "that the power vested in Congress to enforce the article by appropriate legislation," . . . includes the power to enact laws "direct and primary, operating upon the acts of individuals, whether sanctioned by State legislation or not."

Thus, the fact that §1982 operates upon the unofficial acts of private individuals, whether or not sanctioned by state law, presents no constitutional problem. If Congress has power under the Thirteenth Amendment to eradicate conditions that prevent Negroes from buying and renting property because of their race or color, then no federal statute calculated to achieve that objective can be thought to exceed the constitutional power of Congress simply because it reaches beyond state action to regulate the conduct of private individuals. The constitutional question in this case, therefore, comes to this: Does the authority of Congress to enforce the Thirteenth Amendment "by appropriate legislation" include the power to eliminate all racial barriers to the acquisition of real and personal property? We think the answer to that question is plainly yes.

"By its own unaided force and effect," the Thirteenth Amendment "abolished slavery, and established universal freedom." *Civil Rights Cases.* . . . Whether or not the Amendment *itself* did any more than that—a question not involved in this case—it is at least clear that the Enabling Clause of that Amendment empowered Congress to do much more. For that clause clothed "Congress with power to pass *all laws necessary and proper for abolishing all badges and incidents of slavery in the United States.*"[Emphasis added.]

. . . Surely Congress has the power under the Thirteenth Amendment rationally to determine what are the badges and the incidents of slavery, and the authority to translate that determination into effective legislation. Nor can we say that the determination Congress has made is an irrational one. For this Court recognized long ago that, whatever else they may have encompassed, the badges and incidents of slavery—its "burdens and disabilities"—included restraints upon "those fundamental rights which are the essence of civil freedom, namely the same right . . . to inherit, purchase, lease, sell and convey property, as is enjoyed by white citizens." . . . Just as the Black Codes, enacted after the Civil War to restrict the free exercise of those rights, were substitutes for the slave system, so the exclusion of Negroes from white communities became a substitute for the Black Codes. And when racial discrimination herds men into ghettos and makes their ability to buy property turn on the color of their skin, then it too is a relic of slavery.

Negro citizens North and South, who saw in the Thirteenth Amendment a promise of freedom—freedom to "go and come at pleasure" and to "buy and sell when they please"—would be left with "a mere paper guarantee" if Congress were powerless to assure that a dollar in the hands of a Negro will purchase the same thing as a dollar in the hands of a white man. At the very least, the freedom that Congress is empowered to secure under the Thirteenth

Amendment includes the freedom to buy whatever a white man can buy, the right to live wherever a white man can live. If Congress cannot say that being a free man means at least this much, then the Thirteenth Amendment made a promise the Nation cannot keep.

Reversed.

MR. JUSTICE DOUGLAS CONCURRING (OMITTED).
MR. JUSTICE HARLAN, WHOM MR. JUSTICE WHITE JOINS, DISSENTING (OMITTED).

(4) Griffin v. Breckenridge (1971)

+Burger, Black, Douglas, Harlan, Brennan, Stewart, White, Marshall, Blackmun

[In this case, the Court ruled that the enforcement clause of the Thirteenth Amendment authorized Congress to provide for civil damage suits in the federal courts against individuals who deprive others of their constitutional rights. For many years this statute, which was passed in its original form in 1871, was believed to be unconstitutional or so close to it as to be unusable. As the Supreme Court in the 1960s expanded the meaning of the companion criminal statutes, the validity of this civil remedy against civil rights deprivations was again tested in Court. The alleged facts of the case were that the brothers Breckenridge intercepted a car filled with civil rights workers and assaulted them. Griffin and the other victims filed a suit for damages in federal court.]

MR. JUSTICE STEWART delivered the opinion of the Court.
. . .

The jurisdiction of the federal court was invoked under the language of 42 USC §1985(3) that provides:

"If two or more persons in any State or Territory conspire or go in disguise on the highway or on the premises of another, for the purpose of depriving, either directly or indirectly, any person or class of persons of the equal protection of the laws, or of equal privileges and immunities under the laws. . . . [I]n any case of conspiracy set forth in this section, if one or more persons engaged therein do, or cause to be done, any act in furtherance of the object of such conspiracy, whereby another is injured in his person or property, or deprived of having and exercising any right or privilege of a citizen of the United States, the party so injured or deprived may have an action for the recovery of damages, occasioned by such injury or deprivation, against any one or more of the conspirators."

The District Court dismissed the complaint for failure to state a cause of action, relying on the authority of this Court's opinion in *Collins* v. *Hardyman* . . . , which in effect construed the above language of §1985(3) as reaching only conspiracies under color of state law. The Court of Appeals for the Fifth Circuit affirmed the judgment of dismissal. Judge Goldberg's thorough opinion for that court expressed "serious doubts" as to the "continued vitality" of *Collins* v. *Hardyman* . . . , and stated that "it would not surprise us if *Collins* v. *Hardyman* were disapproved and if §1985(3) were held to embrace private conspiracies to interfere with rights of national citizenship," . . . but concluded that "[s]ince we may not adopt what the Supreme Court has expressly rejected, we obediently abide by the mandate in *Collins*," . . . We granted certiorari. . . .

Collins v. *Hardyman* was decided 20 years ago. The complaint in that case alleged that the plaintiffs were members of a political club that had scheduled a meeting to adopt a resolution opposing the Marshall Plan, and to send copies of the resolution to

appropriate federal officials; that the defendants conspired to deprive the plaintiffs of their rights as citizens of the United States peaceably to assemble and to equal privileges and immunities under the laws of the United States; that in furtherance of the conspiracy, the defendants proceeded to the meeting site and, by threats and violence, broke up the meeting, thus interfering with the right of the plaintiffs to petition the Government for the redress of grievances; and that the defendants did not interfere or conspire to interfere with the meetings of other political groups with whose opinions the defendants agreed. The Court held that this complaint did not state a cause of action under §1985(3). . . .

The Court was careful to make clear that it was deciding no constitutional question, but simply construing the language of the statute, or more precisely, determining the applicability of the statute to the facts alleged in the complaint:

"We say nothing of the power of Congress to authorize such civil actions as respondents have commenced or otherwise to redress such grievances as they assert. We think that Congress has not, in the narrow class of conspiracies defined by this statute, included the conspiracy charged here. We therefore reach no constitutional question." . . . Nonetheless, the Court made equally clear that the construction it gave to the statute was influenced by the constitutional problems that it thought would have otherwise been engendered:

"It is apparent that, if this complaint meets the requirements of this Act, it raises constitutional problems of the first magnitude that, in the light of history, are not without difficulty. These would include issues as to congressional power under and apart from the Fourteenth Amend-

ment, the reserved power of the States, the content of rights derived from national as distinguished from state citizenship, and the question of separability of the Act in its application to those two classes of rights."
. . .

Whether or not *Collins* v. *Hardyman* was correctly decided on its own facts is a question with which we need not here be concerned. But it is clear, in the light of the evolution of decisional law in the years that have passed since that case was decided, that many of the constitutional problems there perceived simply do not exist. Little reason remains, therefore, not to accord to the words of the statute their apparent meaning. That meaning is confirmed by judicial construction of related laws, by the structural setting of §1985(3) itself, and by its legislative history. And a fair reading of the allegations of the complaint in this case clearly brings them within the meaning of the statutory language. As so construed, and as applied to this complaint, we have no doubt that the statute was within the constitutional power of Congress to enact.

We turn, then, to an examination of the meaning of §1985(3). On their face, the words of the statute fully encompass the conduct of private persons. The provision speaks simply of "two or more persons in any State or Territory" who "conspire or go in disguise on the highway or on the premises of another." Going in disguise, in particular, is in this context an activity so little associated with official action and so commonly connected with private marauders that this clause could almost never be applicable under the artificially restrictive construction of *Collins*. And since the "going in disguise" aspect must include private action, it is hard to see how the conspiracy aspect, joined by a disjunctive, could be read

to require the involvement of state officers.

The provision continues, specifying the motivation required. ". . . for the purpose of depriving, either directly or indirectly, any person or class of persons of the equal protection of the laws, or of equal privileges and immunities under the laws." This language is, of course, similar to that of §1 of the Fourteenth Amendment, which in terms speaks only to the States, and judicial thinking about what can constitute an equal protection deprivation has, because of the Amendment's wording, focused almost entirely upon identifying the requisite "state action" and defining the offending forms of state law and official conduct. A century of Fourteenth Amendment adjudication has, in other words, made it understandably difficult to conceive of what might constitute a deprivation of the equal protection of the laws by private persons. Yet there is nothing inherent in the phrase that requires the action working the deprivation to come from the State. . . . Indeed, the failure to mention any such requisite can be viewed as an important indication of congressional intent to speak in §1985(3) of *all* deprivations of "equal protection of the laws" and "equal privileges and immunities under the laws," whatever their source.

The approach of this Court to other Reconstruction civil rights statutes in the years since *Collins* has been to "accord [them] a sweep as broad as [their] language. *United States* v. *Price* . . . *Jones* v. *Alfred H. Mayer Co.* Moreover, very similar language in closely related statutes has early and late received an interpretation quite inconsistent with that given in §1985(3) in *Collins*. . . .

It is evident that all indicators—text, companion provisions, and legislative history—point unwaveringly to §1985(3)'s coverage of private conspiracies. That the statute was meant to reach private action does not, however, mean that it was intended to apply to all tortious, conspiratorial interferences with the rights of others. For, though the supporters of the legislation insisted on coverage of private conspiracies, they were equally emphatic that they did not believe, in the words of Representative Cook, "that Congress has a right to punish an assault and battery when committed by two or more persons within a State." . . . The constitutional shoals that would lie in the path of interpreting §1985(3) as a general federal tort law can be avoided by giving full effect to the congressional purpose—by requiring, as an element of the cause of action, the kind of invidiously discriminatory motivation stressed by the sponsors of the limiting amendment. . . . The language requiring intent to deprive of *equal* protection, or *equal* privileges and immunities, means that there must be some racial, or perhaps otherwise class-based, invidiously discriminatory animus behind the conspirators' action. The conspiracy, in other words, must aim at a deprivation of the equal enjoyment of rights secured by the law to all. . . .

The constitutionality of §1985(3) might once have appeared to have been settled adversely by *United States* v. *Harris* . . . which held unconstitutional its criminal counterpart, then §5519 of the Revised Statutes. The Court in those cases, however, followed a severability rule that required invalidation of an entire statute if any part of it was unconstitutionally overbroad, unless its different parts could be read as wholly independent provisions. . . . This Court has long since firmly rejected that rule. . . . Consequently we need not find the language of §1985(3)

now before us constitutional in all its possible applications in order to uphold its facial constitutionality and its application to the complaint in this case.

That §1985(3) reaches private conspiracies to deprive others of legal rights can, of itself, cause no doubts of its constitutionality. It has long been settled that 18 U.S.C. §241, a criminal statute of far broader phrasing . . . reaches wholly private conspiracies and is constitutional. . . . Our inquiry, therefore, need go only to identifying a source of congressional power to reach the private conspiracy alleged by the complaint in this case.

. . . Surely there has never been any doubt of the power of Congress to impose liability on private persons under § 2 of that amendment "for the amendment is not a mere prohibition of State laws establishing or upholding slavery, but an absolute declaration that slavery or involuntary servitude shall not exist in any part of the United States." *Civil Rights Cases* . . . *Jones* v. *Alfred H. Mayer Co.* . . . Not only may Congress impose such liability, but the varieties of private conduct which it may make criminally punishable or civilly remediable extend far beyond the actual imposition of slavery or involuntary servitude. By the Thirteenth Amendment, we committed ourselves as a Nation to the proposition that the former slaves and their descendants should be forever free. To keep that promise, "Congress has the power under the Thirteenth Amendment rationally to determine what are the badges and the incidents of slavery, and the authority to translate that determination into effective legislation. *Jones* v. *Alfred H. Mayer Co.* . . . We can only conclude that Congress was wholly within its powers under §2 of the Thirteenth

Amendment in creating a statutory cause of action for Negro citizens who have been the victims of conspiratorial, racially discriminatory private action aimed at depriving them of the basic rights that the law secures to all free men.

Our cases have firmly established that the right of interstate travel is constitutionally protected, does not necessarily rest on the Fourteenth Amendment, and is assertable against private as well as governmental interference. . . . The "right to pass freely from State to State" has been explicitly recognized as "among the rights and privileges of National citizenship." . . . That right, like other rights of national citizenship is within the power of Congress to protect by appropriate legislation. . . .

The complaint in this case alleged that the petitioners "were travelling upon the federal, state and local highways in and about" DeKalb, Kemper County, Mississippi. Kemper County is on the Mississippi-Alabama border. One of the results of the conspiracy, according to the complaint, was to prevent the petitioners and other Negroes from exercising their "rights to travel the public highways without restraint in the same terms as white citizens in Kemper County, Mississippi." Finally, the conspiracy was alleged to have been inspired by the respondents' erroneous belief that Grady, a Tennessean, was a worker for Negro civil rights. Under these allegations it is open to the petitioners to prove at trial that they had been engaging in interstate travel or intended to do so, that their federal right to travel interstate was one of the rights meant to be discriminatorily impaired by the conspiracy, that the conspirators intended to drive out-of-state civil rights workers from the State, or that they meant to deter

the petitioners from associating with such persons. This and other evidence could make it clear that the petitioner had suffered from conduct which Congress may reach under its power to protect the right of interstate travel.

In identifying these two constitutional sources of congressional power, we do not imply the absence of any other. . . .

The judgment is reversed, and the case is remanded to the United States District Court for the Southern District of Mississippi for further proceedings consistent with this opinion.

It is so ordered.

MR. JUSTICE HARLAN, CONCURRING (OMITTED)

(5) Runyon v. McCrary (1976)

+Stewart, Burger, Brennan, Marshall, Blackmun, Powell, Stevens
−White, Rehnquist

[This suit was brought by several black children and their parents (McCrary) against the proprietors of a private school in Virginia (Runyon). McCrary alleged, and the facts showed, that McCrary and other black children had been denied admission to this and similar schools solely because of their race. The suit was brought under Section 1981 of the federal civil rights statutes. The federal district judge awarded compensatory damages and the court of appeals affirmed. The Supreme Court granted certiorari.]

MR. JUSTICE STEWART delivered the opinion of the Court.

. . .

It is worth noting at the outset some of the questions that these cases do not present. They do not present any question of the right of a private social organization to limit its membership on racial or any other grounds. They do not present any question of the right of a private school to limit its student body to boys, or girls, or to adherents of a particular religious faith, since 42 USC §1981 is in no way addressed to such categories of selectivity. They do not even present the application of §1981 to private sectarian schools that practice *racial* exclusion on religious grounds. Rather, these cases present only two basic questions: whether §1981 prohibits private, commercially operated, non-sectarian schools from denying admission to prospective students because they are Negroes, and, if so, whether that federal law is constitutional as so applied.

It is now well established that §1 of the Civil Rights Act of 1866. . . . 42 USC §1981 (1970) . . . prohibits racial discrimination in the making and enforcements of private contracts. . . .

In *Jones* [v. *Mayer*] the Court held that the portion of §1 of the Civil Rights Act of 1866 presently codified as 42 USC §1982 . . . prohibits private racial discrimination in the sale or rental of real or personal property. Relying on the legislative history of §1, from which both §1981 and §1982 derive, the Court concluded that Congress intended to prohibit "all racial discrimination, private and public, in the sale . . . of property," . . . and that this prohibition was within Congress' power under §2 of the Thirteenth Amendment "rationally to determine what are the badges and the incidents of slavery, and . . . to translate that determination into effective legislation." . . . That holding necessarily implied that the portion of §1 of the 1866 Act presently codified as 42 USC §1981 . . . likewise reaches purely private acts of racial discrimination. The statutory holding in *Jones* was that the "[1866] Act was designed to do just what its terms

suggest: to prohibit all racial discrimination, whether or not under color of law, with respect to the rights enumerated therein–including the right to purchase or lease property." . . . One of the "rights enumerated" in §1 is "the same right . . . to make and enforce contracts . . . as is enjoyed by white citizens. . . ." Just as in *Jones* a Negro's §1 right is to purchase property on equal terms with whites was violated when a private person refused to sell to the prospective purchaser solely because he was a Negro, so also a Negro's §1 right to "make and enforce contracts" is violated if a person offers or refuses to extend to a Negro, solely because he is a Negro, the same opportunity to enter into contracts as he extends to white offerees.

The applicability of the holding in *Jones* to §1981 was confirmed by this Court's decisions in *Tillman* v. *Wheaton-Haven Recreation Assn.*, and *Johnson* v. *Railway Express Agency, Inc* . . . In *Tillman* the petitioners urged that a private swimming club had violated 42 USC §§ 1981, 1982, and 2000a . . . by enforcing a guest policy that discriminated against Negroes. . . . Referring to its earlier rejection of the respondents' contention that Wheaton-Haven was exempt from §1982 under the private club exception of the Civil Rights Act of 1964, the Court concluded that "[i]n light of the historical interrelationship between §1981 and §1982 [there is] no reason to construe these sections differently when applied, on these facts, to the claim of Wheaton-Haven that it is a private club." . . . In *Johnson* v. *Railway Express Agency, Inc.*, the Court noted . . . "that §1981 affords a federal remedy against discrimination in private employment on the basis of race." . . .

It is apparent that the racial exclusion practiced by the Fairfax-Brewster School and Bobbe's Private School amounts to a classic violation of § 1981. Colin Gonzales' parents sought to enter into a similar relationship with the Fairfax-Brewster School. Under those contractual relationships, the schools would have received payments for services rendered, and the prospective students would have received instruction in return for those payments. The educational services of Bobbe's Private School and the Fairfax-Brewster School were advertised and offered to members of the general public. But neither school offered services on an equal basis to white and non-white students. As the Court of Appeals held, "there is ample evidence in the record to support the trial judge's factual determinations . . . [that] Colin [Gonzales] and Michael [McCrary] were denied admission to the schools because of their race." . . .

The petitioning schools and school association argue principally that § 1981 does not reach private acts of racial discrimination. That view is wholly inconsistent with *Jones'* interpretation of the legislative history of § 1 of the Civil Rights Act of 1866, . . . And this consistent interpretation of the law necessarily requires the conclusion that § 1981, like § 1982, reaches private conduct. . . .

It is noteworthy that Congress in enacting the Equal Employment Opportunity Act of 1972, . . . specifically considered and rejected an amendment that would have repealed the Civil Rights Act of 1866, as interpreted by this Court in *Jones,* insofar as it affords private sector employees a right of action based on racial discrimination in employment. . . . There could hardly be a clearer indication of congressional agreement with the view that § 1981 does reach private acts of racial discrimination.

. . . In these circumstances there is no basis for deviating from the well-settled principles of stare decisis applicable to this Court's construction of federal statutes. . . .

The question remains whether § 1981, as applied, violates constitutionally protected rights of free association and privacy, or a parent's right to direct the education of his children.

. . .

In *NAACP* v. *Alabama,* . . . and similar decisions, the Court has recognized a First Amendment right "to engage in association for the advancement of beliefs and ideas. . . ." . . . That right is protected because it promotes and may well be essential to the "[e]ffective advocacy of both public and private points of view, particularly controversial ones" that the First Amendment is designed to foster. . . .

From this principle it may be assumed that parents have a first Amendment right to send their children to educational institutions that promote the belief that racial segregation is desirable, and that the children have an equal right to attend such institutions. But it does not follow that the *practice* of excluding racial minorities from such institutions is also protected by the same principle. As the Court stated in *Norwood* v. *Harrison,* . . . "the Constitution . . . places no value on discrimination," . . . and while "[i]nvidious private discrimination may be characterized as a form of exercising freedom of association protected by the First Amendment . . . it has never been accorded affirmative constitutional protections. And even some private discrimination is subject to special remedial legislation in certain circumstances under §2 of the Thirteenth Amendment; Congress has made such discrimination unlawful in other significant contexts." . . . In any event, as the Court of Appeals noted, "there is no showing that discontinuance of [the] discriminatory admission practices would inhibit in any way the teaching in these schools of any ideas or dogma." . . .

. . .

In *Meyer* v. *Nebraska,* . . . the Court held that the liberty protected by the Due Process Clause of the Fourteenth Amendment includes the right "to acquire useful knowledge, to marry, establish a home and bring up children" . . . and, concomitantly, the right to send one's children to a private school that offers specialized training—in that case, instruction in the German language. In *Pierce* v. *Society of Sisters,* . . . the Court applied "the doctrine of *Meyer* v. *Nebraska*," . . . to hold unconstitutional an Oregon law requiring the parent, guardian, or other person having custody of a child between eight and 16 years of age to send that child to public school on pain of criminal liability. The Court thought it "entirely plain that the [statute] unreasonably interferes with the liberty of parents and guardians to direct the upbringing and education of children under their control." . . . In *Wisconsin* v. *Yoder,* . . . the Court stressed the limited scope of *Pierce,* pointing out that it lent "no support to the contention that parents may replace state educational requirements with their own idiosyncratic views of that knowledge a child needs to be a productive and happy member of society" but rather "held simply that while a State may posit [educational] standards, it may not preempt the educational process by requiring children to attend public schools."

. . .

It is clear that the present application of §1981 infringes no parental right recognized in *Meyer, Pierce, Yoder,* or *Norwood.* No challenge is made to the petitioners' right to operate their private schools or the right of parents to send their children to a particular private school rather than a public school. Nor do these cases involve a challenge to the subject matter which is taught at any private school. Thus, the Fairfax-Brewster School and Bobbe's Private School and members of the intervenor association remain presumptively free to inculcate whatever values and standards they deem desirable, *Meyer* and its progeny entitle them to no more.

. . .

The Court has held that in some situations the Constitution confers a right of privacy. See *Roe* v. *Wade* . . . *Eisenstadt* v. *Baird* . . . *Stanley* v. *Georgia* . . . *Griswold* v. *Connecticut,* . . .

While the application of § 1981 to the conduct at issue here—a private school's adherence to a racially discriminatory admissions policy—does not present governmental intrusion into the privacy of the home or a similarly intimate setting, it does implicate parental interests. These interests are related to the procreative rights protected in *Roe* v. *Wade,* and *Griswold* v. *Connecticut.* A person's decision whether to bear a child and a parent's decision concerning the manner in which his child is to be educated may fairly be characterized as exercises of familial rights and responsibilities. But it does not follow that because government is largely or even entirely precluded from regulating the child-bearing decision, it is similarly restricted by the Constitution from regulating the implementation of parental decisions concerning a child's education.

The Court has repeatedly stressed that while parents have a constitutional right to send their children to private schools and a constitutional right to select private schools that offer specialized instruction, they have no constitutional right to provide their children with private school education unfettered by reasonable government regulation. . . . Indeed, the Court in *Pierce* expressly acknowledged "the power of the State reasonably to regulate all schools to inspect, supervise and examine them, their teachers and pupils. . . ."

For the reasons stated in this opinion, the judgment of the Court of Appeals is in all respects affirmed.

It is so ordered.

MR. JUSTICE POWELL, CONCURRING.

If the slate were clean I might be inclined to agree with Mr. Justice White that §1981 was not intended to restrict private contractual choices. Much of the review of the history and purpose of this statute set forth in his dissenting opinion is quite persuasive. It seems to me, however, that it comes too late. . . .

Although the range of consequences suggested by the dissenting opinion, . . . go far beyond what we hold today, I am concerned that our decision not be construed more broadly than would be justified.

By its terms §1981 necessarily imposes some restrictions on those who would refuse to extend to Negroes "the same right to make and enforce contracts . . . as [is] enjoyed by white citizens." But our holding that this restriction extends to certain actions by private individuals does not imply the intrusive investigation into the motives of every refusal to contract by a private citizen that is suggested by the dissent. As the Court of Appeals suggested, some contracts are so personal "as to have a discernible rule of exclusivity which is inoffensive to §1980."

In *Sullivan* v. *Little Hunting Park*, we were faced with an association in which "[t]here was no plan or purpose of exclusiveness." Participation was "open to every white person within the geographic area, there being no selective element other than race." . . . In certain personal contractual relationships, however, such as those where the offeror selects those with whom he desires to bargain on an individualized basis, or where the contract is the foundation of a close association (such as, for example, that between an employer and a private tutor, babysitter, or housekeeper), there is reason to assume that, although the choice made by the offeror is selective, it reflects "a purpose of exclusiveness" other than the desire to bar members of the Negro race. Such a purpose, certainly in most cases, would invoke associational rights long respected.

The case presented on the record before us does not involve this type of personal contractual relationship. As the Court of Appeals said, the petitioning "schools are private only in the sense that they are managed by private persons and they are not direct recipients of public funds. Their actual and potential constituency, however, is more public than private." . . . The schools extended a public offer open, on its face, to any child meeting certain minimum qualifications who chose to accept. They advertised in the "yellow" pages of the telephone directories and engaged extensively in general mail solicitations to attract students. The schools are operated strictly on a commercial basis, and one fairly could construe their open-end invitations as offers that matured into binding contracts when accepted by those who met the academic, financial, and other racially neutral specified conditions as to qualifications for entrance. There is no reason to assume that the schools had any special reason for exercising an option of personal choice among those who responded to their public offers. A small kindergarten or music class, operated on the basis of personal invitations extended to a limited number of preidentified students, for example, would present a far different case.

. . .

MR. JUSTICE STEVENS, CONCURRING.

For me the problem in these cases is whether to follow a line of authority which I firmly believe to have been incorrectly decided.

Jones v. *Alfred H. Mayer Co.* . . . and its progeny have unequivocally held that §1 of the Civil Rights Act of 1866 prohibits private racial discrimination. There is no doubt in my mind that that construction of the statute would have amazed the legislators who voted for it. Both its language and the historical setting in which it was enacted convince me that Congress intended only to guarantee all citizens the same legal capacity to make and enforce contracts, to obtain, own and convey property, and to litigate and give evidence. Moreover, since the legislative history discloses an intent not to outlaw segregated public schools at that time, it is quite unrealistic to assume that Congress intended the broader result of prohibiting segregated private schools. Were we writing on a clean slate, I would therefore vote to reverse.

But *Jones* has been decided and is now an important part of the fabric of our law. Although I recognize the force of Mr. Justice White's argument that the construction of §1982 does not control §1981, it would be most incongruous to give those two sections a fundamentally different construction. The net result of the enactment of 1866, the re-enactment in 1870, and the codification in 1874 produced, I believe, a statute resting on the constitutional foundations provided by both the Thirteenth and Fourteenth Amendments. An attempt to give a fundamentally different meaning to two similar provisions by ascribing one to the Thirteenth and the other to the Fourteenth Amendment cannot succeed. I am persuaded, therefore, that we must either apply the rationale of *Jones* or overrule that decision.

There are two reasons which favor overruling. First, as I have already stated, my conviction that *Jones* was wrongly decided is firm. Second, it is extremely unlikely that reliance upon *Jones* has been so extensive that this Court is foreclosed from overruling it. . . . There are, however, opposing arguments of greater force.

The first is the interest in stability and orderly development of the law. As Justice Cardozo remarked, with respect to the routine work of the judiciary, "the labor of judges would be increased almost to the breaking point if every past decision could be reopened in every case, and one could not lay one's own course of bricks on the secure foundation of the courses laid by others who had gone before him." Turning to the exceptional case, Justice Cardozo noted "that when a rule, after it has been duly tested by experience, has been found to be inconsistent with the sense of justice or with the social welfare, there should be less hesitation in frank disavowal and full abandonment. . . . If judges have woefully misinterpreted the *mores* of their day, or if the *mores* of their day are no longer those of ours, they ought not to tie, in helpless submission, the hands of their successors." In this case, those admonitions favor adherence to, rather than departure from, precedent. For even if *Jones* did not accurately reflect the sentiments of the Reconstruction Congress, it surely accords with the prevailing sense of justice today.

The policy of the Nation as formulated by the Congress in recent years has moved constantly in the direction of eliminating racial segregation in all sectors of society. This Court has given a sympathetic and liberal construction to such legislation. For the Court now to overrule *Jones* would be a significant step backwards, with effects that would not have arisen from a correct decision in the first instance. Such a step would be so clearly contrary to my understanding of the *mores* of today that I think the Court is entirely correct in adhering to *Jones*.

With this explanation, I join the opinion of the Court.

MR. JUSTICE WHITE, WITH WHOM MR. JUSTICE REHNQUIST JOINS, DISSENTING.

We are urged here to extend the meaning and reach of 42 USC §1981 . . . so as to establish a a general prohibition against a private individual or institution refusing to enter into a contract with another person because of that person's race. Section 1981 has been on the books since 1870 and to so hold for the first time would be contrary to the language of the section, to its legislative history and to the clear dictum of this Court in the *Civil Rights Cases, . . .* (1883), almost contemporaneously with the passage of the statute, that the section reaches only discriminations imposed by state law. The majority's belated discovery of a congressional purpose which escaped this Court only a decade after the statute was passed and which escaped all other federal courts for almost 100 years is singularly unpersuasive. I therefore respectfully dissent.

42 USC §1981, captioned "equal rights under the law," provides in pertinent part:

All persons within the jurisdiction of the United States shall have the same rights to make and enforce contracts, to sue, be parties, give evidence, and to the full and equal protection of the laws and proceedings for the security of persons and property as is enjoyed by white citizens. . . .

On its face the statute gives "all persons" (plainly including Negroes) the *"same rights* to make . . . contracts . . . as is enjoyed by white citizens." (Emphasis added.) The words "rights . . . enjoyed by white citizens" clearly refer to rights existing apart from this statute. Whites had at the time when §1981 was first enacted, and have (with a few exceptions mentioned below), no right to make a contract with an unwilling private person, no matter what that person's motivation for refusing to contract. Indeed it is and always has been central to the very concept of a "contract" that there be "assent by the terms thereof," . . . The right to make contracts, enjoyed by white citizens, was therefor always a right to enter into binding agreements only with willing second parties. Since the statute only gives Negroes the "same rights" to contract as is enjoyed by whites, the language of the statute confers no right on Negroes to enter into a contract with an unwilling person no matter what that person's motivation for refusing to contract. What is conferred by 42 USC §1981 . . . is the *right*— which was enjoyed by whites—"to make contracts" with other willing parties and to "enforce" those contracts in court. Section 1981 would thus invalidate any state statute or court-made rule of law which would have the effect of disabling Negroes or any other class of persons from making contracts or enforcing contractual obligations or otherwise giving less weight to their obligations than is given to contractual obligations running to whites. The statute by its terms does not require any private individual or institution to enter into a contract or perform any other act under any circumstances; and it consequently fails to supply a cause of action by respondent students against petitioner schools based on the latter's racially motivated decision not to contract with them.

The legislative history of 42 USC §1981 confirms that the statute means what it says and no more, i.e., that it outlaws any legal rule disabling any person from making or enforcing a contract, but does not prohibit private racially motivated refusals to contract. . . .

F. *Affirmative Action and Job Qualification Tests: The Limits of Equal Protection.*

(1) Griggs v. Duke Power Company (1971)

+Burger, Black, Douglas, Harlan, Stewart, White, Marshall, Blackmun
NP Brennan

[Title VII of the Civil Rights Act of 1964 prohibited discrimination in employment on account of race, color, religion, sex, or national origin and provided for class action suits to enforce the act. This case was brought by black employees at the Duke Power Company facility in Draper, North Carolina. They challenged the company's use of a high school education requirement and a standardized intelligence test both as conditions of employment and for transfers and promotions to better jobs within the company. The suit alleged that neither standard was significantly related to successful job performance and that both operated to disproportionately exclude blacks from the better jobs.

The federal district court found that prior to 1965, when the Civil Rights Act took effect, the Duke Power Company openly discriminated against blacks in hiring and job assignments. There were five departments at the plant: labor, coal handling, operations, maintenance, laboratory, and test. Blacks were employed only in the first, where the highest rates of pay fell below the lowest pay rate in any other department. In 1955, the company began to require a high school education for employment in any department except labor and for transfer to any of the "inside" departments (operations, maintenance, laboratory).

When the Civil Rights Act went into effect in 1965, the company abandoned its overt discrimination against blacks. But it then made a high school education a prerequisite to transfer from labor to any of the other departments. However, white employees in the other departments, who did not have a high school education, were permitted to retain their jobs. In 1965, the company also instituted a requirement that all new employees had to pass an aptitude test. And later that year, it permitted employees without a high school education to nonetheless transfer to an "inside" department if they passed a general intelligence test and a test of mechanical aptitude. The tests were not job related but were intended to measure high school equivalency. They were prepared by a professional testing service and were widely used throughout the country.

The district court held that the company had ceased to follow its earlier discriminatory practices and that the impact of those practices "was beyond the reach of corrective action authorized by the [Civil Rights Act]." It also found that the education requirement and job tests were not instituted with any invidious intent and that they had been applied equally to blacks and whites. The court of appeals reversed the district court on the first point, but upheld it on the second. It ruled that in the absence of a discriminatory purpose, the act permitted the use of fairly applied job tests and requirements. It rejected the contention that such tests and requirements were unlawful merely because they had a markedly disproportionate adverse impact on black workers and applicants.]

MR. CHIEF JUSTICE BURGER delivered the opinion of the Court.

. . .

The objective of Congress in the enactment of Title VII is plain from the language of the statute. It was to achieve equality of employment opportunities and remove barriers that have operated in the past to favor an identifiable group of white employees over other employees. Under the Act, practices, procedures, or tests neutral on their face, and even neutral in terms of intent, cannot be maintained if they operate to "freeze" the status quo of prior discriminatory employment practices.

The Court of Appeals' opinion, and the partial dissent, agreed that, on the record in the present case, "whites fare far better on the Company's alternative requirements" than Negroes. This consequence would appear to be directly traceable to race. Basic intelligence must have the means of articulation to manifest itself fairly in a testing process. Because they are Negroes, petitioners have long received inferior education in segregated schools. Congress did not intend by Title VII, however, to guarantee a job to every person regardless of qualifications. In short, the Act does not command that any person be hired simply because he was formerly the subject of discrimination, or because he is a member of a minority group. Discriminatory preference for any group, minority or majority, is precisely and only what Congress has proscribed. What is required by Congress is the removal of artificial, arbitrary, and unnecessary barriers to employment when the barriers operate invidiously to discriminate on the basis of racial or other impermissible classification.

Congress has now provided that tests or criteria for employment or promotion may not provide equality of opportunity only in the sense of the fabled offer of milk to the stork and the fox. On the contrary, Congress has now required that the posture and condition of the job seeker be taken into account. It has—to resort again to the fable—provided that the vessel in which the milk is proffered be one all seekers can use. The Act proscribes not only overt discrimination but also practices that are fair in form but discriminatory in operation. The touchstone is business necessity. If an employment practice which operates to exclude Negroes cannot be shown to be related to job performance, the practice is prohibited.

On the record before us, neither the high school completion requirement nor the general intelligence test is shown to bear a demonstrable relationship to successful performance of the jobs for which it was used. Both were adopted, as the Court of Appeals noted, without meaningful study of their relationship to job-performance ability.

The evidence, however, shows that employees who have not completed high school or taken the tests have continued to perform satisfactorily and make progress in departments for which the high school and test criteria are now used. The promotion record of present employees who would not be able to meet the new criteria thus suggests the possibility that the requirements may not be needed even for the limited purpose of preserving the avowed policy of advancement within the Company. In the context of this case, it is unnecessary to reach the question whether testing requirements that take into account capability for the next succeeding position or related future promotion might be utilized upon a showing that such long range requirements fulfill a genuine business need. In the present case the

Company has made no such showing.

The Court of Appeals held that the Company had adopted the diploma and test requirements without any "intention to discriminate against Negro employees." We do not suggest that either the District Court or the Court of Appeals erred in examining the employer's intent; but good intent or absence of discriminatory intent does not redeem employment procedures or testing mechanisms that operate as "built-in headwinds" for minority groups and are unrelated to measuring job capability.

The Company's lack of discriminatory intent is suggested by special efforts to help the undereducated employees through Company financing of two-thirds the cost of tuition for high school training. But Congress directed the thrust of the Act to the consequences of employment practices, not simply the motivation. More than that, Congress has placed on the employer the burden of showing that any given requirement must have a manifest relationship to the employment in question.

The facts of this case demonstrate the adequacy of broad and general testing devices as well as the infirmity of using diplomas or degrees as fixed measures of capability. History is filled with examples of men and women who rendered highly effective performance without the conventional badges of accomplishment in terms of certificates, diplomas, or degrees. Diplomas and tests are useful servants, but Congress had mandated the common-sense proposition that they are not to become masters of reality.

The Company contends that its general intelligence tests are specifically permitted by §702(h) of the Act. That section authorizes the use of "any professionally developed ability test" that is not "designed, intended, or used to discriminate because of race . . ."

The Equal Employment Opportunity Commission, having enforcement responsibility, has issued guidelines interpreting §703(h) to permit only the use of job-related tests. The administrative interpretation of the Act by the enforcing agency is entitled to great deference. Since the Act and its legislative history support the Commission's construction, this affords good reason to treat the Guidelines as expressing the will of Congress.

From the sum of the legislative history relevant in this case, the conclusion is inescapable that the EEOC's construction of §703(h) to require that employment tests be job-related comports with congressional intent.

Nothing in the Act precludes the use of testing or measuring procedures; obviously they are useful. What Congress has forbidden is giving these devices and mechanisms controlling force unless they are demonstrably a reasonable measure of job performance. Congress has not commanded that the less qualified be preferred over the better qualified simply because of minority origins. Far from disparaging job qualifications as such, Congress has made such qualifications the controlling factor, so that race, religion, nationality, and sex become irrelevant. What Congress has commanded is that any tests used must measure the person for the job and not the person in the abstract.

The judgment of the Court of Appeals is, as to that portion of the judgment appealed from, reversed.

[In *Albemarle Paper Company* v. *Moody* (1975), the Supreme Court considered several questions not resolved in *Griggs*. The Court ruled that back pay could not be denied to employees merely because the company's breach of Title VII was not in "bad faith." An employer's bad faith practices in hiring and promotions constitute an obvious case where back pay should be awarded. But since the purpose of awarding back pay is not to punish the moral turpitude of the employer but to "make whole" the injured worker, the absence of bad faith is an insufficient reason for denying compensation. The general rule is that when a wrong has been done, and the law gives a remedy, the compensation shall be equal to the injury. Quoting from *Griggs,* the Court said: "Title VII is not concerned with the employer's 'good intent or absence of discriminatory intent' for Congress directed the thrust of the Act to the consequences of employment practices, not simply the motivation."

Also at issue in the *Albemarle* case was the question of validation of job tests. *Griggs* had stated the rule that the employer has "the burden of showing that any given requirement [has] . . . a manifest relation to the employment in question," *after* the employee has made out a prima facie case of discrimination. *Albermarle* had employed an expert in industrial psychology to validate the job relatedness of its testing program. However, his conclusion that the tests were valid was challenged. The evidence showed that his "validation" was superficial at best, often subjective, and certainly open to question. The court held that the validation failed to meet the guidelines for such tests promulgated by the Equal Employment Opportunities Commission (EEOC): "Tests are impermissible unless shown, by professionally acceptable methods, to be 'predictive of or significantly correlated with important elements of work behavior which comprise or are relevant to the job or jobs for which candidates are being evaluated.' "]

(2) Washington v. Davis (1976)

+White, Burger, Stewart, Blackmun, Rehnquist, Powell, Stevens

−Brennan, Marshall

[This case involved the validity of a qualifying test and other recruitment procedures administered to applicants for positions as police officers in the District of Columbia. Applicants were required to meet certain physical and character standards, and to pass "Test 21," designed by the Civil Service Commission and used throughout the civil service. Test 21 was a test of verbal ability, vocabulary, reading, and comprehension.

There was no claim of intentional discrimination. Instead, it was alleged that Test 21 was unrelated to the job performance of a police officer and that it had a highly discriminatory *impact* in screening out black candidates. About 45 percent of the Metropolitan Police Department was black, and blacks constituted about the same percentage of new recruits. This percentage was also roughly equivalent to the number of age-eligible blacks in the Washington metropolitan areas. There was evidence in the record of substantial affirmative action efforts by the Police Department to recruit black officers.

The district court judge rejected allegations of discrimination, but the court of appeals reversed. It held that Test 21 invidiously discriminated against black applicants in violation of the due process clause of the Fifth Amendment. The court of appeals held that the standard to be applied was that of *Griggs* v. *Duke Power Company* (1971), which had interpreted and applied Title VII of the Civil Rights Act of 1964. Lack of intent to discriminate was not critical, the court of appeals held. Rather, the fact that four times as many blacks as whites failed the test was sufficient to establish a constitutional violation. The Supreme Court granted certiorari.]

MR. JUSTICE WHITE delivered the opinion of the Court.

. . .

Because the Court of Appeals erroneously applied the legal standards applicable to Title VII cases in resolving the constitutional issue before it, we reverse its judgment in respondents' favor. . . .

As the Court of Appeals understood Title VII, employees or applicants proceeding under it need not concern themselves with the employer's possibly discriminatory purpose but instead may focus solely on the racially differential impact of the challenged hiring or promotion practices. This is not the constitutional rule. We have never held that the constitutional standard for adjudicating claims of invidious racial discrimination is identical to the standards applicable under Title VII, and we decline to do so today.

The central purpose of the Equal Protection Clause of the Fourteenth Amendment is the prevention of official conduct discriminating on the basis of race. It is also true that the Due Process Clause of the Fifth Amendment contains an equal protection component prohibiting the United States from invidiously discriminating between individuals or groups. *Bolling* v. *Sharpe* . . . (1954). But our cases have not embraced the proposition that a law or other official act, without regard to whether it reflects a racially discriminatory purpose, is unconstitutional *solely* because it has a racially disproportionate impact.

Almost 100 years ago, *Strauder* v. *West Virginia* . . . (1880) established that the exclusion of Negroes from grand and petit juries in criminal proceedings violated the Equal Protection Clause, but the fact that a particular jury or a series of juries does not statistically reflect the racial composition of the community does not in itself make out an invidious discrimination forbidden by the Clause. "A purpose to discriminate must be present which may be proven by systematic exclusion of eligible jurymen of the proscribed race or by an unequal application of the law to such an extent as to show intentional discrimination." . . . A defendant in a criminal case is entitled "to require that the State not deliber-ately and systematically deny to the members of his race the right to participate as jurors in the administration of justice." . . .

The rule is the same in other contexts. *Wright* v. *Rockefeller* . . . (1964), upheld a New York congressional apportionment statute against claims that district lines had been racially gerrymandered. The challenged districts were made up predominantly of whites or of minority races, and their boundaries were irregularly drawn. The challengers did not prevail because they failed to prove that the New York legislature "was either motivated by racial considerations or in fact drew the districts on racial lines"; the plaintiffs had not shown that the statute "was the product of a state contrivance to segregate on the basis of race or place of origin." . . . The dissenters were in agreement that the issue was whether the "boundaries . . . were purposefully drawn on racial lines." . . .

The school desegregation cases have also adhered to the basic equal protection principle that the invidious quality of a law claimed to be racially discriminatory must ultimately be traced to a racially discriminatory purpose. That there are both predominantly black and predominantly white schools in a community is not alone violative of the Equal Protection Clause. The essential element of de jure segregation is "a current condition of segregation resulting from intentional state action . . . the differentiating factor between de jure segregation and so-called de facto segregation . . . is *purpose* or *intent* to segregate." *Keyes* v. *School District No. 1* . . . (1973). . . . the Court has also recently rejected allegations of racial discrimination based solely on the statistically disproportionate racial impact of various provisions of the Social Security Act because "the acceptance of appellant's constitutional theory would render suspect each difference in treatment among the grant classes, however lacking the racial motivation and however rational the treatment might be." *Jefferson* v. *Hackney.* . . . (1972). . . .

This is not to say that the necessary discriminatory racial purpose must be express or appear on the face of the statute, or that a law's disproportionate impact is irrelevant in cases involving Constitution-based claims of racial discrimination. A statute, otherwise neutral on its face, must not be applied so as invidiously to discriminate on the basis of race. *Yick Wo.* v. *Hopkins* . . . (1886). It is clear from the cases dealing with racial discrimination in the selection of juries that the systematic exclusion of Negroes is itself such an "unequal application of the law . . . as to show intentional discrimination." . . . A prima facie case of discriminatory purpose may be proved as well by the absence of Negroes on a particular jury combined with the failure of the jury commissioners to be informed of eligible Negro jurors in a community, . . . or with racially non-neutral selection procedures, . . . With a prima facie case made out, "the burden of proof shifts to the State to rebut the presumption of unconstitutional action by showing that permissible racially neutral selection criteria and procedures have produced the monochromatic result." . . .

Necessarily, an invidious discriminatory purpose may often be inferred from the totality of the relevant facts, including the fact, if it is true, that the law bears more heavily on one race than another. It is also not infrequently true that the discriminatory impact—in the jury cases for example, the total or seriously disproportionate exclusion of

Negroes from jury venires—may for all practical purposes demonstrate unconstitutionality because in various circumstances the discrimination is very difficult to explain on nonracial grounds. Nevertheless, we have not held that a law, neutral on its face and serving ends otherwise within the power of government to pursue, is invalid under the Equal Protection Clause simply because it may affect a greater proportion of one race than of another. Disproportionate impact is not irrelevant, but it is not the sole touchstone of an invidious racial discrimination forbidden by the Constitution. Standing alone, it does not trigger the rule, . . . that racial classifications are to be subjected to the strictest scrutiny and are justifiable only by the weightiest of considerations.

There are some indications to the contrary in our cases. In *Palmer* v. *Thompson* . . . (1971), the city of Jackson, Miss., following a court decree to this effect, desegregated all of its public facilities save five swimming pools which had been operated by the city and which, following the decree, were closed by ordinance pursuant to a determination by the city council that closure was necessary to preserve peace and order and that integrated pools could not be economically operated. Accepting the finding that the pools were closed to avoid violence and economic loss, this Court rejected the argument that the abandonment of this service was inconsistent with the outstanding desegregation decree and that the otherwise seemingly permissible ends served by the ordinance could be impeached by demonstrating that racially invidious motivations had prompted the city council's action. The holding was that the city was not overtly or covertly operating segregated pools and was extending identical treatment to both whites and Negroes. The opinion warned against grounding decisions on legislative purpose or motivation, thereby lending support for the proposition that the operative effect of the law rather than its purpose is the paramount factor. But the holding of the case was that the legitimate purposes of the ordinance—to preserve peace and avoid deficits—were not open to impeachment by evidence that the councilmen were actually motivated by racial considerations. Whatever dicta the opinion may contain, the decision did not involve, much less invalidate, a statute or ordinance having neutral purposes but disproportionate racial consequences.

. . .

As an initial matter, we have difficulty understanding how a law establishing a racially neutral qualification for employment is nevertheless racially discriminatory and denies "any person equal protection of the laws" simply because a greater proportion of Negroes fail to qualify than members of other racial or ethnic groups. Had respondents, along with all others who had failed Test 21, whether white or black, brought an action claiming that the test denied each of them equal protection of the laws as compared with those who had passed with high enough scores to qualify them as police recruits, it is most unlikely that their challenge would have been sustained. Test 21, which is administered generally to prospective government employees, concededly seeks to ascertain whether those who take it have acquired a particular level of verbal skill; and it is untenable that the Constitution prevents the government from seeking modestly to upgrade the communicative abilities of

its employees rather than to be satisfied with some lower level of competence, particularly where the job requires special ability to communicate orally and in writing. Respondents, as Negroes, could no more successfully claim that the test denied them equal protection than could white applicants who also failed. The conclusion would not be different in the face of proof that more Negroes than whites had been disqualified by Test 21. That other Negroes also failed to score well would, alone, not demonstrate that respondents individually were being denied equal protection of the laws by the application of an otherwise valid qualifying test being administered to prospective police recruits.

Nor on the facts of the case before us would the disproportionate impact of Test 21 warrant the conclusion that it is a purposeful device to discriminate against Negroes and hence an infringement of the constitutional rights of respondents as well as other black applicants. As we have said, the test is neutral on its face and rationally may be said to serve a purpose the government is constitutionally empowered to pursue. Even agreeing with the District Court that the differential racial effect on Test 21 called for further inquiry, we think the District Court correctly held that the affirmative efforts of the Metropolitan Police Department to recruit black officers, the changing racial composition of the recruit classes and of the force in general, and the relationship of the test to the training program negated any inference that the Department discriminated on the basis of race or that "a police officer qualifies on the color of his skin rather than ability."

Under Title VII, Congress provided

that when hiring and promotion practices disqualifying substantially disproportionate numbers of blacks are challenged, discriminatory purpose need not be proved, and that it is an insufficient response to demonstrate some rational basis for the challenged practices. It is necessary, in addition, that they be "validated" in terms of job performance in any one of several ways, perhaps by ascertaining the minimum skill, ability or potential necessary for the position at issue and determining whether the qualifying tests are appropriate for the selection of qualified applicants for the job in question. However this process proceeds, it involves a more probing judicial review of, and less deference to, the seemingly reasonable acts of administrators and executives than is appropriate under the Constitution where special racial impact, without discriminatory purpose, is claimed. We are not disposed to adopt this more rigorous standard for the purposes of applying the Fifth and the Fourteenth Amendments in cases such as this. . . .

The judgment of the Court of Appeals accordingly is reversed.

. . .

MR. JUSTICE STEVENS, CONCURRING (OMITTED).

MR. JUSTICE BRENNAN, WITH WHOM MR. JUSTICE MARSHALL JOINS, DISSENTING (OMITTED).

(3) Furnco Construction Corporation v. Waters (1978)

+Burger, Stewart, White, Blackmun, Powell, Rehnquist, Stevens

+/−Brennan, Marshall

[The Furnco Corporation specialized in relining steel blast furnaces with "firebrick." Because of the specialized nature of the work, the company, which did not maintain a permanent work force, followed the practice of not "hiring at the gate," that is, not hiring at the site of a particular job. Instead, in line with industry practice, the designated job foreman hired bricklayers whom he knew were competent and experienced or who had been recommended to him.

This employment discrimination case was brought against Furnco by three black bricklayers who sought employment on a job in Cook County, Illinois. All three were admittedly qualified for the work. None was hired immediately, but after a number of white bricklayers had been hired, one of the three black bricklayers was also employed. Furnco hired a total of forty-four bricklayers for this job, ten of whom were black. The job took 1,819 man-days, and 13.3 percent of these were worked by black bricklayers. Furnco had established a self-imposed affirmative action hiring goal of 16 percent blacks; 20 percent of the workers on this job were black.

The federal district court that first heard this case found that the respondents had failed to make out a tenable claim under Title VII of the Civil Rights Act of 1964. The court held that Furnco's hiring practices were a matter of "business necessity," required for the safe and efficient operation of the business. It held that Furnco's practice of not hiring at the gate was racially neutral on its face and had not, in any case, resulted in a "disproportionate impact or effect," as required by *Griggs,* or in "disparate treatment," as forbidden by *McDonnell Douglas Corporation* v. *Green* (1973).

The Court of Appeals for the Seventh Circuit reversed, holding that the black bricklayers had made out a prima facie case of discrimination under *McDonnell* that Furnco had not effectively rebutted. Furnco had claimed that a white bricklayer appearing "at the gate" would have fared no better than the black respondents. The appeals court also rejected Furnco's contention, which the district court had accepted, that its hiring practices were necessary for legitimate, nondiscriminatory reasons. The court of appeals held that Furnco was in violation of

Title VII and proceeded to devise a compromise hiring scheme, "a reasonable middle ground," between hiring at the gate and seeking out suitable bricklayers for each job. This middle ground process involved soliciting written applications and then hiring those best qualified from among the applicants. The Supreme Court granted certiorari.]

MR. JUSTICE REHNQUIST delivered the opinion of the Court.

. . .

We agree with the Court of Appeals that the proper approach was the analysis contained in *McDonnell Douglas*, . . . We also think the Court of Appeals was justified in concluding that as a matter of law respondents made out a prima facie case of discrimination under *McDonnell Douglas*. In that case we held that a plaintiff could make out a prima facie claim by showing:

"(i) that he belongs to a racial minority; (ii) that he applied and was qualified for a job for which the employer was seeking applicants; (iii) that, despite his qualifications, he was rejected; and (iv) that, after his rejection, the position remained open and the employer continued to seek applicants from persons of complainant's qualifications." . . .

This, of course, was not intended to be an inflexible rule, as the Court went on to note that "[t]he facts necessarily will vary in Title VII cases, and the specification . . . of the prima facie proof required from respondent is not necessarily applicable in every respect to differing factual situations." . . . But *McDonnell Douglas* did make clear that a Title VII plaintiff carries the initial burden of showing actions taken by the employer from which one can infer, if such actions remain unexplained, that it is more likely than not that such actions were "based on a dis-

criminatory criterion illegal under the Act." . . . And here respondents carried that initial burden by proving they were members of a racial minority; they did everything within their power to apply for employment; Furnco has conceded that they were qualified in every respect for the jobs which were about to be open; they were not offered employment, although Smith later was, and; the employer continued to seek persons of similar qualifications.

We think the Court of Appeals went awry, however, in apparently equating a prima facie showing under *McDonnell Douglas* with an ultimate finding of fact as to discriminatory refusal to hire under Title VII; the two are quite different and that difference has a direct bearing on the proper resolution of this case. The Court of Appeals, as we read its opinion, thought Furnco's hiring procedures not only must be reasonably related to the achievement of some legitimate purpose, but also must be the method which allows the employer to consider the qualifications of the largest number of minority applicants. We think the imposition of that second requirement simply finds no support either in the nature of the prima facie case or the purpose of Title VII.

The central focus of the inquiry in a case such as this is always whether the employer is treating "some people less favorably than others because of their race, color, religion, sex, or national origin." . . . The method suggested in *McDonnell Douglas* for pursuing this inquiry, however, was never intended to be rigid, mechanized, or ritualistic. Rather, it is merely a sensible, orderly way to evaluate the evidence in light of common experience as it bears on the critical question of discrimination. A prima facie case under *McDonnell Douglas* raises an inference of discrimination only because we presume these acts, if otherwise unexplained, are more likely than not based on the consideration of impermissible factors. . . . And we are willing to presume this largely because we know from our experience that more often than not people do not act in a totally arbitrary manner, without any underlying reasons, especially in a business setting. Thus, when all legitimate reasons for rejecting an applicant have been eliminated as possible reasons for the employer's actions, it is more likely than not the employer, whom we generally assume acts only with *some* reason, based his decision on an impermissible consideration such as race.

When the prima facie case is understood in the light of the opinion in *McDonnell Douglas,* it is apparent that the burden which shifts to the employer is merely that of proving that he based his employment decision on a legitimate consideration, and not an illegitimate one such as race. To prove that, he need not prove that he pursued the course which would both enable him to achieve his own business goal and allow him to consider the *most* employment applications. Title VII forbids him from having as a goal a work force selected by any proscribed discriminatory practice, but it does not impose a duty to adopt a hiring procedure that maximizes hiring of minority employees. To dispel the adverse inference from a prima facie showing under *McDonnell Douglas,* the employer need only "articulate some legitimate nondiscriminatory reason for the employee's rejection." . . .

The dangers of embarking on a course such as that charted by the Court of Appeals here, where the court requires businesses to adopt what it perceives to be the "best" hiring procedures, are nowhere more evident than in the record of this very case. Not only does the record not reveal that the court's suggested hiring procedure would work satisfactorily, but there is nothing in the record to indicate that it would be any less "haphazard, arbitrary, and subjective" than Furnco's method, which the Court of Appeals criticized as deficient for exactly those reasons. Courts are generally less competent than employers to restructure business practices, and unless mandated to do so by Congress they should not attempt it.

This is not to say of course that proof of a justification which is reasonably related to the achievement of some legitimate goal necessarily ends the inquiry. . . . [T]he Court of Appeals . . . premised its disagreement [with the District Court] on a view which we have discussed and rejected above. It did not conclude that the practices were a pretext for discrimination, but only that different practices would have enabled the employer to at least consider, and perhaps to hire, more minority employees. But courts may not impose such a remedy on an employer at least until a violation of Title VII has been proven, and here none had been. . . .

. . . The judgment of the Court of Appeals is reversed and remanded for further proceedings consistent with this opinion.

It is so ordered.

MR. JUSTICE MARSHALL, WITH WHOM MR. JUSTICE BRENNAN JOINS, CONCURRING IN PART AND DISSENTING IN PART.

It is well established under Title VII that claims of employment discrimination because of race may arise in two different ways. . . . An individual may allege that he has been subjected to "disparate treatment" because of his race, or that he has been the victim of a facially neutral practice having a "disparate impact" on his racial group. . . .

The Court of Appeals properly held that respondents had made out a prima facie case of employment discrimination under *McDonnell Douglas.* Once respondents had established their prima facie case, the question for the court was then whether petitioner had carried its burden of proving that respondents were rejected on the basis of legitimate nondiscriminatory considerations. The court, however, failed properly to address that question and instead focused on what other hiring practices petitioner might employ. I therefore agree with the Court that we must remand the case to the Court of Appeals so that it can address, under the appropriate standards, whether petitioner had rebutted respondents' prima facie showing of disparate treatment. . . .

Where the Title VII claim is that a facially neutral employment practice actually falls more harshly on one racial group, thus having a disparate impact on that group, our cases establish a different way of proving the claim. . . . As set out by the Court in *Griggs* v *Duke Power Co.,* . . . to establish a prima facie case on a disparate impact claim, a plaintiff need not show that the employer had a discriminatory intent but need only demonstrate that a particular practice in actuality "operates to exclude Negroes." . . .

Once the plaintiff has established the disparate impact of the practice, the burden shifts to the employer to show that the practice has "a manifest relationship to the employment in question." . . . The "touchstone is business necessity." . . . and the practice "must be shown to be necessary to safe and efficient job performance to survive a Title VII challenge." . . . Under this principle, a practice of limiting jobs to those with prior experience working in an industry or for a particular person, or to those who hear about jobs by word of mouth would be invalid if the practice in actuality impacts more harshly on a group protected under Title VII, unless the practice can be justified by business necessity.

There is nothing in today's opinion that is inconsistent with this approach or with our prior decisions. I must dissent, however, from the Court's apparent decision . . . to foreclose on remand further litigation on the *Griggs* question of whether petitioner's hiring practices had a disparate impact. Respondents claim that petitioner's practice of hiring from a list of those who had previously worked for the foreman foreclosed Negroes from consideration for the vast majority of jobs. Although the foreman also hired a considerable number of Negroes through other methods, respondents assert that the use of other methods to augment the representation of Negroes in the work force does not answer whether the primary hiring practice is discriminatory.

It is clear that an employer cannot be relieved of responsibility for past discriminatory practices merely by undertaking affirmative action to obtain proportional representation in his work force. As the Court said in *Teamsters,* and reaffirms today, a "company's later changes in its hiring and promotion policies could be of little comfort to the victims of the earlier . . . discrimination, and could not erase its previous illegal conduct or its obligation to afford relief to those who suffered because of it." . . . Therefore, it is at least an open question whether the hiring of workers primarily from a list of past employees would, under *Griggs*, violate Title VII where the list contains no Negroes but the company uses additional methods of hiring to increase the numbers of Negroes hired.

. . .

(4) Race as a Suspect Classification: Affirmative Action and Benign Quotas

The first Justice John Marshall Harlan, dissenting in *Plessy* v. *Ferguson* (1896), said that "our Constitution is color-blind." Of course Harlan was writing to protest the Court's "separate but equal" pronouncement in that case, and was lamenting the Court's departure from the constitutional standard. In fact, our Constitution and laws have *never* been truly color-blind.

We have seen how the Supreme Court, in the eighty-five years following the Civil War, selectively enforced the Constitution's prohibitions against racial discrimination. It could outlaw formal discrimination in the selection of juries, *Strauder* v. *West Virginia* (1880), while condoning informal practices that prevented blacks from serving. It could uphold the principles of the Fifteenth Amendment while at the same time—for twenty years—upholding the constitutionality of the white primary, which denied to blacks any effective role in the electoral process in the South. It could invalidate municipally enforced racial dis-

crimination in housing but accept organized private efforts, aided and abetted by the federal government, to maintain housing segregation. And for sixty years, it could maintain the legal fiction of "separate but equal" in schools and public accommodations when little semblance of equality existed.

It was altogether fitting, therefore, for Justice Black to announce in *Korematsu* v. *United States* (1944), a case that *upheld* the exclusion and removal of Japanese-American citizens from the West Coast during World War II, that all racial classifications were inherently *suspect* and therefore subject to the most exacting judicial scrutiny. Since then, in the *Brown* case and elsewhere, the Supreme Court has held, with one exception, that race is virtually a prohibited classification. That one exception is the so-called benign classification that singles out a racial (or other) minority for nonstigmatizing remedial or compensatory treatment (e.g., "affirmative action.")

Affirmative action plans are responsive to the concept of "equality of result," but they are not entirely inconsistent with "equality of opportunity." They rest on the premise that members of a disadvantaged minority are not, in fact, afforded an equal opportunity merely by removing overt legal barriers and other formal obstacles and then telling them to compete with their majority group counterparts. The metaphor of the race is often employed. Can you expect a runner who has been shackled to an iron chain for years to run competitively soon after the chain is removed, when other runners have been training and preparing for years for the same race? The answer, quite obviously, is no—or at the very least, not yet. But how long a wait must be endured before formal equality of opportunity approaches true equality of opportunity? Affirmative action plans are designed to remedy the real inequalities that remain even when formal inequality ends. They are also designed to provide real equality of opportunity in the first instance where institutional discrimination is shown to exclude minorities from a particular enterprise or educational or occupational role as effectively as formal legal barriers once did.

If our society's goal is truly to achieve racial equality (and some would doubt that it has made this commitment), then it must also accept the paradox that to be truly color-blind, the Constitution—and the laws—must be supremely color conscious. The Supreme Court has recognized this paradox for some time and has accepted the idea that in the present society, a government that is truly color-blind is simply blind or is not, in fact, committed to egalitarian goals. The Court echoed these sentiments in the *Green* case in 1968 when it said it would look to results, not intent, in judging whether a dual school system had been dismantled and a unitary system established in its place.

In one of the 1971 school busing cases, *North Carolina* v. *Swann*, Chief Justice Burger wrote for the majority: "Just as the race of students must be considered in determining whether a constitutional violation has occurred, so also race must be considered in formulating a remedy." He noted that the state law "exploited an apparently neutral form to control school assignment plans by requiring that they be 'color blind'; that requirement, against the background of segregation, would render illusory the promise of *Brown*. . . . Race must be considered both in

determining whether a constitutional violation exists and in determining a remedy."

Concurring in the racial gerrymandering case, *United Organizations of Williamsburgh* v. *Carey* (1977), Justice Brennan wrote:

I begin with the settled principle that not every remedial use of race is forbidden. For example, we have authorized and even required race conscious remedies in a variety of corrective settings. . . . Once it is established that circumstances exist where race must be taken into account in fashioning affirmative policies, we must identify those circumstances, and, further, determine how substantial a reliance may be placed upon race.

Brennan then considered several objections: whether a race-conscious policy masks a policy that in fact "perpetuates disadvantageous treatment of the plan's supposed beneficiaries"; whether a race-conscious policy serves "to stimulate our society's latent race consciousness" with the consequence, among others, of stigmatizing the recipient group by implying its inferiority; and whether a benign race-conscious policy is viewed as unjust by others, especially, but not limited to, those who are affected adversely by it. Implicit in Brennan's last thought is the concern that no policy of affirmative action is "benign" for everyone. Wherever the line is drawn to determine who is included, and who is excluded, *someone*, some member of the non-recipient group, is correspondingly disadvantaged.

To the extent that there can ever be a "benign" use of race as a classification, it would seem to embrace both intent and impact. If a racial classification is benign in intent, neither stigmatizing nor invidious, and aimed at remedying a disadvantage for which the society accepts responsibility, does this exclude it from the constitutional category of "suspect" classifications? Does the Constitution permit a race-conscious policy that merely seeks to promote a social goal such as racial integration, or can such a policy flow only from the need to remedy a constitutional wrong? Is there a difference between a "quota" and a "goal"?

The first major affirmative action case to reach the Supreme Court was *DeFunis* v. *Odegaard* (1974). Marco DeFunis, a white male, was denied admission to the University of Washington Law School. He had an excellent undergraduate grade point average of 3.71, but his scores on the Law School Admissions Test were no better than average; his mean score on three tries was 582. The law school computed his "predicted first year average" (PFYA) at 76.23, which put him just below the cutoff line of 77. Nearly all students above that line were accepted. Those who fell below 74.5 were rejected except for returning veterans and minority students. Those in between, including DeFunis, were considered on an individual basis. Minority applicants were treated as a separate group; almost all the minority students in the 74.5–77 range were accepted even though most had PFYAs lower than Defunis;

DeFunis brought suit in the state trial court, which ordered him admitted. The University of Washington complied, and he began law school in September 1971. With DeFunis in school, the university appealed to the state supreme court, which reversed the trial court. It held that the Fourteenth Amendment prohibited only "invidious" racial classifications, those that stigmatized a racial group with the badge of inferiority. Since the goal of preferential treatment for minority applicants is not to separate the races but bring them together, the court reasoned, it does not violate the Constitution. It held that racial classifications were appropriate to remedy the evil of racial imbalance in the law schools and the legal profession. This was a necessary predicate for the opinion, since the University of Washington had no history of racial discrimination, and it was therefore under no obligation to remedy a constitutional wrong.

Even though the Washington Supreme Court decision had gone against him, DeFunis was unlikely to be expelled from law school, where he was achieving a satisfactory record. But because the university was then *legally* free to drop him, he filed an appeal with the United States Supreme Court. An order from Justice Douglas assured him that he would not be dropped from school.

More than two dozen amicus curiae briefs were filed, representing more than 100 organizations, arrayed in somewhat strange alliances. For DeFunis were the large Jewish organizations including B'Nai B'rith Anti-Defamation League, the Chamber of Commerce, and the National Association of Manufacturers. Amici for the university included the American Bar Association, a bevy of civil rights groups, sixty law school deans, the Association of American Law Schools, the Association of Medical Colleges, and the McGovern Labor Coalition (UAW, UMW, Farm Workers). Some of the greatest names in constitutional law were retained to argue the case—Professors Alexander Bickel and Philip Kurland for B'Nai B'rith, and Archibald Cox for the law schools.

The solicitor general, Robert Bork, wanted to file a brief supporting DeFunis, but he was overruled by the White House, which considered the case too controversial. The Civil Service Commission wanted the government to support DeFunis, while the EEOC wanted to file against him. The EEOC actually prepared and filed a brief supporting affirmative action, but the Supreme Court refused to accept it when Bork wrote a letter to the Court objecting to its submission. Paradoxically, while the government was not supporting the University of Washington in this case, the Affirmative Action Office of HEW was charging the university with noncompliance with its affirmative action guidelines for faculty and staff hiring.

When the case was argued before the Court in the winter of 1974, there was some discussion of whether or not it had become moot. DeFunis was about to enter his sixth and last semester of law school, and it was inconceivable that the University of Washington would not let him graduate with his class in June. When the Court's decision was finally announced, the justices had, in fact, voted 5-4 to dismiss the case as moot. Only Justice Douglas, who opposed dismissing the case on those grounds, wrote an opinion discussing the substantive issues. And that opinion, while not pronouncing any conclu-

sions, was hostile to the affirmative action program at the University of Washington. He argued that there was no such thing as a "benign" quota. But he suggested that a compensatory program for disadvantaged students might be constitutional if it was racially neutral and focused on the individual attributes—advantages and disadvantages—of each student as an individual, not on attributes of the group to which they belonged. DeFunis graduated from law school, and the constitutionality of affirmative action programs in professional school admissions remained undecided.[1]

(5) Board of Regents of the University of California v. Bakke (1978)

+Burger, Stewart, Powell, Rehnquist, Stevens
−Brennan, White, Marshall, Blackmun*

[Allan Bakke, a civil engineer of Norwegian descent, applied for admission to the University of California, Davis Medical School in 1973, at the age of 32, and again in 1974. He was rejected both times. He claimed that he was qualified for admission and that he would have been admitted except for a special program for minority students to which 16 places out of an

[1]Of the eighteen minority students admitted to the University of Washington Law School in 1971, fourteen remained when the *DeFunis* case was decided. All but one had been expected to be in the bottom quarter of the class. But after two years in law school, six were in the bottom quarter, five in the third quarter, and three in the second quarter. Of those top three students, two had been predicted to achieve high grades, but one was among the lowest.

*This oversimplifies the complexity of the vote. There were three main issues to be decided, and only Justice Powell voted with the majority in each instance. The first issue was simply whether or not Bakke should be admitted to the University of California, Davis Medical School. The second issue was whether or not that school had employed an improper racial "quota" in selecting applicants for admission. Five justices voted yes on both these issues: Powell, Burger, Stewart, Rehnquist, and Stevens. The third issue was whether there are some circumstances under which the race of an applicant to professional school may be taken into account. Five justices voted affirmatively: Powell, Brennan, White, Marshall and Blackmun. The remaining justices—Burger, Stewart, Rehnquist, and Stevens—held that it was unnecessary to answer this question in this case. Thus the vote was 5-4 in favor of Bakke, 5-4 against racial quotas, and 5-0-4 in favor of allowing race to be considered at all.

entering class of 100 had been allotted. Candidates for those 16 minority slots were considered under a separate admissions program; they did not have to meet the minimum grade point average threshold set for all other applicants. By virtue of this program, all nonminority nondisadvantaged candidates were reduced to competing for 84 positions instead of the full 100 available (for 1974, there were 3,737 applications submitted).

Each candidate for a regular admissions slot was rated on the basis of an undergraduate grade point average and score on the Medical College Admissions Test (MCAT). About one in six applicants was then invited for a personal interview, and those candidates were then given an overall rating, by a panel of six interviewers, that covered the results of the interview, grade point average, and MCAT score. On the basis of these overall scores and another review of each file, offers of admission were made to applicants on a "rolling" basis. Some were rejected, some admitted, and some placed on a waiting list. Bakke did not make the waiting list in either year. On the other hand, in each year, minority applicants who had lower scores than Bakke were admitted under the special program.

After his second rejection, Bakke filed suit in the California courts, claiming deprivation of his rights under the Fourteenth Amendment and under Title VI of the Civil Rights Act of 1964. The university countered with the claim that its special admissions program was lawful and should be upheld. The trial court rejected the university's claim that this was a legitimate remedial program, but it refused to order Bakke admitted to medical school because, in the court's judgment, he had failed to carry the burden of proving that he would have been admitted *but* for the special program. Both sides appealed to the Supreme Court of California.

The California Supreme Court, by a 6-1 vote, held the special admissions program invalid. After the university stipulated that Bakke would have been admitted but for the special program, the court also ordered him to be admitted to medical school. The court held that since a racial classification was involved, the appropri-

ate test was strict scrutiny. It rejected the university's claim that a racial classification is "suspect" only where it discriminates *against* a minority and is designed to stigmatize and separate the races. Whites may not be stigmatized by this benign quota system, the court said, but they are disadvantaged.

The court agreed that the university could properly seek to increase the number of physicians from minority groups, but it held that this special program was not the least intrusive means of achieving that goal. It also conceded that the university could take race into account in devising such a program, but it could not allocate a fixed number of places by race in the entering class and treat applications for those slots entirely separate from the rest: "No applicant may be rejected because of his race, in favor of another who is less qualified, as measured by standards applied without regard to race." The Supreme Court of the United States granted certiorari.

Before the Supreme Court, Bakke was represented by a San Francisco attorney named Reynold Colvin. Colvin, a former president of the San Francisco Board of Education, was, at the age of 60, making his first appearance in the Supreme Court. The University of California was represented by Archibald Cox, former solicitor general of the United States, professor at the Harvard Law School, and a veteran of dozens of cases before the Court. Wade McCree, the solicitor general, and the second black to hold that position, argued amicus curiae for the United States in favor of race-conscious special admissions programs. The thrust of Cox's argument was that the case should be decided in the broad context of affirmative action programs. The Supreme Court should, Cox argued, generally approve the principle of taking race into account but should not pass on the details of the particular method involved. Colvin, by contrast, stressed that this was a lawsuit seeking to protecting Allan Bakke's rights as an individual and that race is always an impermissible criterion to use.

The following excerpts[1] from the oral argument before the Court give some insight into the issues to be decided.

[1]Reprinted from *The New York Times* (October 13, 1977).

Arguments of Archibald Cox on Behalf of the University of California:

MR. COX: This case, here on certiorari to the Supreme Court of California, presents a single vital question: whether a state university, which is forced by limited resources to select a relatively small number of students from a much larger number of well-qualified applicants, is free, voluntarily, to take into account the fact that a qualified applicant is black, Chicano, Asian or native American in order to increase the number of qualified members of those minority groups trained for the educated professions and participating in them, professions from which minorities were long excluded because of generations of pervasive racial discrimination.

The answer which the Court gives will determine, perhaps for decades, whether members of those minorities are to have the kind of meaningful access to higher education in the profession, which the universities have accorded them in recent years, or are to be reduced to the trivial numbers which they were prior to the adoption of minority admissions programs.

There is no racially blind method of selection, which will enroll today more than a trickle of minority students in the nation's colleges and professions. These are the realities which the University of California at Davis Medical School faced in 1968, and which, I say, I think the Court must face when it comes to its decision.

Until 1969, the applicants at Davis, as at most other medical schools, were chosen on the basis of scores on the Medical Aptitude Test, their college grades, and other personal experiences and qualifications, as revealed in the application.

In 1969, the faculty at Davis concluded that drawing into the medical college qualified members of minorities—minorities long victimized by racial discrimination—would yield important education, professional and social benefits.

I want to emphasize that the designation of 16 places was not a quota, at least as I would use that word. Certainly it was not a quota in the older sense of an arbitrary limit put on the number of members of a nonpopular group who would be admitted to an institution which was looking down its nose at them.

JUSTICE STEWART: It did put a limit on the number of white people, didn't it?

MR COX: I think that it limited the number of nonminority, and therefore essentially white, yes. But there are two things to be said about that. One is that this was not pointing the finger at a group which had been marked as inferior in any sense, and it was undifferentiated, it operated against a wide variety of people. So I think it was not stigmatizing in the sense of the old quota against Jews was stigmatizing, in any way.

JUSTICE STEWART: It did put a limit on the number of nonminority people to each class?

MR. COX: It did put a limit, no question about that, and I don't mean to infer that.

JUSTICE STEVENS: Do you agree, then, that there was a quota of 84?

MR. COX: Well, I would deny that it was a quota. We agreed that there were 16 places set aside for qualified disadvantaged minority students. Now, if that number—if setting aside a number, if the amount of resources . . .

JUSTICE STEVENS: No, the question is not whether the 16 is a quota; the question is whether the 84 is a quota? And what is your answer to that?

MR. COX: I would say that neither is properly defined as a quota.

JUSTICE STEVENS: And then, why not?

MR. COX: Because, in the first place—because of my understanding of the meaning of "quota." And I think the decisive things are the facts. And the operative facts are: this is not something imposed from outside, as the quotas are in employment or the targets are in employment sometime, today.

It is not a limit on the number of minority students. Other minority students were in fact accepted through the regular admissions program. It was not a guarantee of a minimum number of minority students, because all of them had to be, and the testimony is that all of them were, fully qualified.

JUSTICE POWELL: Mr. Cox, the facts are not in dispute. Does it really matter what we call this program?

MR. COX: No. I quite agree with you, Mr. Justice. I was trying to emphasize that the facts here have none of the aspects, that there are none of the facts that lead us to think of "quota" as a bad word.

But I would emphasize that it doesn't point the finger at any group, it doesn't say to any group, "You are inferior"; it doesn't promise taking people regardless of their qualifications, regardless of what they promise society, promise the school, or what qualities they have.

And I think those things—and that it is not forced but was really a decision by the school as to how much of its assets, what part of its assets it would allocate to the purposes that it felt were being fulfilled by having minorities in the student body, and increasing the number of minorities in the profession.

Justice Stevens, let us suppose that the student was—that the school was much concerned by the lack of qualified general practitioners in northern California, as indeed it was,

but I want to exaggerate for illustration a little bit, and it told the admissions committee: "Get people who come from rural communities, if they are qualified, and who express the intention of going back there." And the dean of admissions might well say: "Well, how much importance do you give this?"

And the members of the faculty might say, by vote or otherwise, "We think it's terribly important. As long as they are qualified, try and get them in that group."

I don't think I would say that it was a "quota" of 90 students for others. And I think this, while it involves race, of course—that's why we're here—or color, really is essentially the same thing. The decision of the university was that there are social purposes, or purposes aimed in the end at eliminating racial injustice in this country and in bringing equality of opportunity, there will be purposes served by including minority students.

JUSTICE BLACKMUN: Mr. Cox, is it the same thing as an athletic scholarship?

MR. COX: Well, I . . .

JUSTICE BLACKMUN: So many places reserved for athletic scholarships?

MR. COX: In the sense—I don't like to liken it to that in terms of its importance, but I think there are a number of places that may be set aside for an institution's different aims, and the aim of some institutions does seem to be to have athletic prowess. So that in that sense this is a choice made to promote the school's, the faculty's choice of educational and professional objectives.

JUSTICE BLACKMUN: It's the aim of most institutions, isn't it, not just some?

MR. COX: Well, I come from Harvard, sir. . . . I don't know whether it's our aim, but we don't do very well.

JUSTICE REHNQUIST: Mr. Cox, what if Davis Medical School had decided that since the population of doctors in the—among the minority population of doctors in California was so small, instead of setting aside 16 seats for minority doctors, they would set aside 50 seats, until that balance were redressed and the minority population of doctors equaled that of the population as a whole. Would that be any more infirm than the program that Davis has?

MR. COX: Well, I think my answer is this—and it's one which I draw upon Judge Hastie for, in an excellent essay he wrote on this subject—that so long as the numbers are chosen, he said, and they are shown to be reasonably adaptable to the social goal—and I'm thinking of the one you mentioned, Justice Rehnquist—then there is no reason to condemn a program because of the particular number chosen.

JUSTICE POWELL: Mr. Cox, along this same line of discussion, would you relate the number in any way to the population, and, if so, the population of the nation, the state, the city or to what standard?

MR. COX: Well, the number 16 here is not in any way linked to population in California.

JUSTICE POWELL: It's 23 percent, I think, for the minorities.

MR. COX: Well, this was 16.

JUSTICE POWELL: Yes.

MR. COX: . . . I think that I would only say as the number gets higher, I think that it's undesirable to have the number linked to population. I'll be quite frank to say that I think one of the things which causes all of us concern about these programs is the danger that they will give rise to some notion of group entitlement to numbers, regardless either of the ability of the individual or of—which is not always related to inability, ability in the narrow sense—or of their potential contribution to society.

And I think that if the program were to begin to slide over in that direction, I would first, as a faculty member, criticize and oppose it; as a constitutional lawyer, the further it went the more doubts I would have. But I think it's quite clear that this program was not of that character, and, in fact, of course, if we're speaking of what's going to happen to education all over the country, in fact the numbers have not come anywhere— the minorities admitted to professional schools—have not come anywhere near their actual percentage of the population.

While it is true that Mr. Bakke and some others, under conventional standards for admission, would be ranked above the minority applicant, I want to emphasize that, in my judgment and I think in fact, that does not justify saying that the better, generally better-qualified people were excluded to make room for generally less-qualified people.

There's nothing that shows that after the first two years at medical school the grade point averages will make the minority students poorer medical students, and still less to show that it makes them poorer doctors or poorer citizens or poorer people.

It's quite clear that for some of the things that a medical school wishes to accomplish, and this medical school wished to accomplish, that the minority applicant may have qualities that are superior to those of his classmate who is not minority. He certainly will be more effective in bringing it home to the young Chicano, that he too may become a doctor, he too may attend graduate school. He may be far more likely to go back to such a community to practice medicine where he's needed.

I would like to direct my attention, if I may, to one important point, and that's again the significance of the number 16. We submit, first, that the Fourteenth Amendment does not outlaw race-conscious programs where there is no invidious purpose or intent, or where they are aimed at offsetting the consequences of our long tragic history of discrimination, and achieving greater racial equality.

JUSTICE STEVENS: Mr. Cox, may I interrupt you with a question that's always troubled me? It's the use of the term "invidious," which I've always had difficulty really understanding. You suggested, in response to Mr. Justice Rehnquist, that if the number were 50 rather than 16, there would be a greater risk of a finding of invidious purpose. How does one—how does a judge decide when to make such a finding?

MR. COX: Well, I think he has to consider all the facts. They were most recently laid out in Justice Powell's opinion in the *Arlington Heights* case, the sort of thing that he thought the Court should consider. If your honor is asking me what do I mean by "invidious," I mean primarily stigmatizing, marking as inferior—

JUSTICE STEVENS: Let me make my—

MR. COX: —shutting out of participation—

JUSTICE STEVENS: Mr. Cox, let me make my question a little more precise. Can you give me a test which would differentiate the case of 50 students from the case of 16 students?

MR. COX: I would have to make this turn on a subjective inquiry, I think, but I would also have to look and see what the significance of the 50 students was in the overall context of the community, its educational system, and the state.

JUSTICE STEVENS: But in Mr. Jus-

tice Rehnquist's example, he was assuming precisely the same motivation that is present in this case: a desire to increase the number of black and minority doctors, and a desire to increase the mixture of the student population. Why would not that justify the 50?

MR. COX: Well, if the finding is that this was reasonably adapted to the purpose of increasing the number of minority doctors, and that it was not an arbitrary, capricious, selfish setting—and that it would have to be decided in the light of the other medical schools in the state and the needs in the state; but if it's solidly based, then I would say 50 was permissible.

Arguments of Reynold H. Colvin on Behalf of Allan Bakke

MR. COLVIN: It seems to me that the first thing that I ought to say to this honorable Court is that I am Allan Bakke's lawyer and Allen Bakke is my client. And I do not say that in any formal or perfunctory way. I say that because this is a lawsuit. It was a lawsuit brought by Allan Bakke up at Woodland in Yolo County, California, in which Allen Bakke from the very beginning of this lawsuit in the first paper we ever filed stated the case.

And he stated the case in terms of his individual rights. He stated the case in terms of the fact that he had twice applied for admission to the medical school at Davis and twice he had been refused, both in the year 1973 and the year 1974. And he stated in that complaint what now, some three-and-a-half years later, proves to be the very heart of the thing that we are talking about at this juncture. He stated that he was excluded from that school because that school had adopted a racial quota which deprived him of the opportunity for admission into the school.

JUSTICE STEWART: You spoke, Mr. Colvin, of the right to admission. You don't seriously submit that he had a right to be admitted.

MR. COLVIN: That is not Allan Bakke's position. Allan Bakke's position is that he has a right, and that right is not to be discriminated against by reason of his race. And that's what brings Allen Bakke to this Court.

We have the deepest difficulty in dealing with this problem of quota, and many, many questions arise. For example, there is a question of numbers. What is the appropriate quota? What is the appropriate quota for a medical school? Sixteen, eight, 32, 64, 100? On what basis, on what basis is that quota determined? And there is a problem, a very serious problem of judicial determination.

Does the Court leave open to the school the right to choose any number it wants in order to satisfy that quota? Would the Court be satisfied to allow an institution such as the University of California to adopt a quota of 100 percent and thus deprive all persons who are not people within selected minority groups.

JUSTICE WHITE: Well, what's your response to the assertion of the university that it was entitled to have a special program and take race into account and that under the 14th Amendment there was no barrier to its doing that because of the interests that were involved? What's your response to that?

MR. COLVIN: Our response to that is fundamentally that race is an improper classification in this situation. As a matter of fact, the Government in its own brief makes that very point.

JUSTICE WHITE: Part of your submission is: Even if these are compelling interests, even if there is no al-

ternative, the use of the racial classification is unconstitutional?

MR. COLVIN: We believe it is unconstitutional. We do.

JUSTICE BURGER: Because it is limited rigidly to 16?

MR. COLVIN: No, not because it is limited to 16, but because the concept of race itself as a classification becomes in our history and in our understanding an unjust and improper basis upon which to judge people. We do not believe that intelligence, that achievement, that ability are measured by skin pigmentation or by the last surname of an individual, whether or not it sounds Spanish or—]

MR. JUSTICE POWELL announced the judgment of the Court.

. . .

In this Court the parties neither briefed nor argued the applicability of Title VI of the Civil Rights Act of 1964. Rather, as had the California court, they focused exclusively upon the validity of the special admissions program under the Equal Protection Clause. Because it was possible, however, that a decision on Title VI might obviate resort to constitutional interpretation, see *Ashwander* v. *TVA* . . . (1936), we requested supplementary briefing on the statutory issue.

. . .

The language of §601, like that of the Equal Protection Clause, is majestic in its sweep:

No person in the United States shall, on the ground of race, color, or national origin, be excluded from participation in, be denied the benefits of, or be subjected to discrimination under any program or activity receiving Federal financial assistance.

The concept of "discrimination," like the phrase "equal protection of the laws," is susceptible to varying interpretations. . . . We must, therefore, seek whatever aid is available in determining the precise meaning of the statute before us. . . . Examination of the voluminous legislative history of Title VI reveals a congressional intent to halt federal funding of entities that violate a prohibition of racial discrimination similar to that of the Constitution. . . .

The problem confronting Congress was discrimination against Negro citizens at the hands of recipients of federal moneys. . . . Over and over again, proponents of the bill detailed the plight of Negroes seeking equal treatment in such programs. There simply was no reason for Congress to consider the validity of hypothetical preferences that might be accorded minority citizens; the legislators were dealing with the real and pressing problem of how to guarantee those citizens equal treatment.

. . .

Further evidence of the incorporation of a constitutional standard into Title VI appears in the repeated refusals of the legislation's supporters precisely to define the term "discrimination." Opponents sharply criticized this failure, but proponents of the bill merely replied that the meaning of "discrimination" would be made clear by reference to the Constitution or other existing law. For example, Senator Humphrey noted the relevance of the Constitution:

As I have said, the bill has a simple purpose. That purpose is to give fellow citizens–Negroes–the same rights and opportunities that white people take for granted. This is no more than what was preached by the prophets, and by Christ Himself. It is no more than what our Constitution guarantees.

In view of the clear legislative intent, Title VI must be held to proscribe only those racial classifications that would violate the Equal Protection Clause or the Fifth Amendment.

Petitioner does not deny that decisions based on race or ethnic origin by faculties and administrations of state universities are reviewable under the Fourteenth Amendment. . . . For his part, respondent does not argue that all racial or ethnic classifications are *per se* invalid. See, *e.g., Hirabayashi* v. *United States* . . . (1943); *Korematsu* v. *United States* . . . (1944); *United Jewish Organizations* v. *Carey* . . . (1977). The parties do disagree as to the level of judicial scrutiny to be applied to the special admissions program. Petitioner argues that the court below erred in applying strict scrutiny, as this inexact term has been applied in our cases. That level of review, petitioner asserts, should be reserved for classifications that disadvantage "discrete and insular minorities." See *United States* v. *Carolene Products Co.* (1938). Respondent, on the other hand, contends that the California court correctly rejected the notion that the degree of judicial scrutiny accorded a particular racial or ethnic classification hinges upon membership in a discrete and insular minority and duly recognized that the "rights established [by the Fourteenth Amendment] are personal rights." *Shelley* v. *Kramer* . . . (1948).

En route to this crucial battle over the scope of judicial review, the parties fight a sharp preliminary action over the proper characterization of the special admissions program. Petitioner prefers to view it as establishing a "goal" of minority representation in the medical school. Respondent, echoing the courts below, labels it a racial quota.

This semantic distinction is beside the point: the special admissions program is undeniably a classification based on race and ethnic background. To the extent that there existed a pool of at least minimally qualified minority applicants to fill the 16 special admissions seats, white applicants could compete only for 84 seats in the entering class, rather than the 100 open to minority applicants. Whether this limitation is described as a quota or a goal, it is a line drawn on the basis of race and ethnic status.

It is settled beyond question that the "rights created by the first section of the Fourteenth Amendment are, by its terms, guaranteed to the individual. ... The guarantee of equal protection cannot mean one thing when applied to one individual and something else when applied to a person of another color. If both are not accorded the same protection, then it is not equal.

Nevertheless, petitioner argues that the court below erred in applying strict scrutiny to the special admissions programs because white males, such as respondent, are not a "discrete and insular minority" requiring extraordinary protection from the majoritarian political process. ... This rationale, however, has never been invoked in our decisions as a prerequisite to subjecting racial or ethnic distinctions to strict scrutiny. Nor has this Court held that discreteness and insularity constitute necessary preconditions to a holding that a particular classification is invidious. See, *e.g., Skinner* v. *Oklahoma* ... (1942); *Carrington* v. *Rash* ... (1965). These characteristics may be relevant in deciding whether or not to add new types of classifications to the list of "suspect" categories or whether a particular classification survives close examination. ... Ra-

cial and ethnic classifications, however, are subject to stringent examination without regard to these additional characteristics. We declared as much in the first cases explicitly to recognize racial distinctions as suspect:

. . . [A]ll legal restrictions which curtail the rights of a single racial group are immediately suspect. That is not to say that all such restrictions are unconstitutional. It is to say that courts must subject them to the most rigid scrutiny. Korematsu . . .

The Court has never questioned the validity of those pronouncements. Racial and ethnic distinctions of any sort are inherently suspect and thus call for the most exacting judicial examination.

This perception of racial and ethnic distinctions is rooted in our Nation's constitutional and demographic history. The Court's initial view of the Fourteenth Amendment was that its "one pervading purpose" was "the freedom of the slave race, the security and firm establishment of that freedom, and the protection of the newly-made freeman and citizen from the oppressions of those who had formerly exercised dominion over him." *Slaughter-House Cases* . . . (1873). The Equal Protection Clause, however, was "[v]irtually strangled in its infancy by post-civil-war judicial reactionism." It was relegated to decades of relative desuetude while the Due Process Clause of the Fourteenth Amendment, after a short germinal period, flourished as a cornerstone in the Court's defense of property and liberty of contract. See, *e. g., Mugler* v. *Kansas* . . . (1887); *Allgeyer* v. *Louisiana* . . . (1897); *Lochner* v. *New York* . . . (1905). In that cause, the Fourteenth Amendment's "one pervading purpose" was displaced. See, *e. g., Plessy* v. *Ferguson* . . .

(1896). It was only as the era of substantive due process came to a close, see, *e. g.*, *Nebbia* v. *New York*, (1934); *West Coast Hotel* v. *Parrish*, . . . (1937) that the Equal Protection Clause began to attain a genuine measure of vitality, . . .

By that time it was no longer possible to peg the guarantees of the Fourteenth Amendment to the struggle for equality of one racial minority. During the dormancy of the Equal Protection Clause, the United States had become a nation of minorities. Each had to struggle—and to some extent struggles still—to overcome the prejudices not of a monolithic majority, but of a "majority" composed of various minority groups of whom it was said—perhaps unfairly in many cases—that a shared characteristic was a willingness to disadvantage other groups. As the Nation filled with the stock of many lands, the reach of the Clause was gradually extended to all ethnic groups seeking protection from official discrimination. See *Strauder* v. *West Virginia* . . . (1880) (Celtic Irishmen) (dictum); *Yick Wo* v. *Hopkins*, . . . (1886) (Chinese); *Truax* v. *Raich* . . . (1915) (Austrian resident aliens); *Korematsu* . . . (1944) (Japanese); *Hernandez* v. *Texas* . . . (1954) (Mexican-Americans).

Although many of the Framers of the Fourteenth Amendment conceived of its primary function as bridging the vast distance between members of the Negro race and the white "majority," . . . the Amendment itself was framed in universal terms, without reference to color, ethnic origin, or condition of prior servitude. As this Court recently remarked in interpreting the 1866 Civil Rights Act to extend to claims of racial discrimination against white persons, "the 39th Congress was intent upon establishing in federal law a broader principle than would have been necessary to meet the particular and immediate plight of the newly freed Negro slaves." *McDonald* v. *Santa Fe Trail Transp. Co.* . . . (1976). And that legislation was specifically broadened in 1870 to ensure that "all persons," not merely "citizens," would enjoy equal rights under the law. See *Runyon* v. *McCrary*, . . . (1976) (WHITE J., Dissenting).

Over the past 30 years, this Court has embarked upon the crucial mission of interpreting the Equal Protection Clause with the view of assuring to all persons "the protection of equal laws," . . . in a Nation confronting a legacy of slavery and racial discrimination. Because the landmark decisions in this area arose in response to the continued exclusion of Negroes from the mainstream of American society, they could be characterized as involving discrimination by the "majority" white race against the Negro minority. But they need not be read as depending upon that characterization for their results. It suffices to say that "[o]ver the years, this Court consistently repudiated '[d]istinctions between citizens solely because of their ancestry' as being 'odious to a free people whose institutions are founded upon the doctrine of equality.' "

Petitioner urges us to adopt for the first time a more restrictive view of the Equal Protection Clause and hold that discrimination against members of the white "majority" cannot be suspect if its purpose can be characterized as "benign." The clock of our liberties, however, cannot be turned back to 1868. It is far too late to argue that the guarantee of equal protection to *all* persons permits the recognition of special wards entitled to a degree of protection greater than that accorded others. The concepts of "majority" and "minority" necessarily reflect temporary arrangements and political judgments. As observed above, the white "majority" itself is composed of various minority groups, most of which can lay claim to a history of prior discrimination at the hands of the state and private individuals. Not all of these groups can receive preferential treatment and corresponding judicial tolerance of distinctions drawn in terms of race and nationality, for then the only "majority" left would be a new minority of White Anglo-Saxon Protestants. There is no principled basis for deciding which groups would merit "heightened judicial solicitude" and which would not.* Courts would be asked to evaluate the extent of the prejudice and consequent harm suffered by various minority groups. Those whose societal injury is thought to exceed some arbitrary level of tolerability then would be entitled to preferential classifications at the expense of individuals belonging to other groups. Those classifications would be free from exacting judicial scrutiny. As these preferences began to have their desired effect, and the consequences of past discrimination were undone, new judicial rankings would be necessary. The kind of variable sociological and political analysis necessary to produce such rankings simply does not lie within the judicial competence—even if they otherwise were politically feasible and socially desirable.

Moreover, there are serious problems of justice connected with the idea of preference itself. First, it may not always be clear that a so-called preference is in fact benign. Courts may be asked to validate burdens imposed upon individual members of particular groups in order to advance the group's general interest. See *United Jewish Organizations* v. *Carey*, . . . Nothing in the Constitu-

*As I am in agreement with the view that race may be taken into account as a factor in an admissions program, I agree with my Brothers Brennan, White, Marshall, and Blackmun that the portion of the judgment that would proscribe all consideration of race must be reversed. But I disagree with much that is said in their opinion.

They would require as a justification for a program such as petitioner's, only two findings: (i) that there has been some form of discrimination against the preferred minority groups "by society at large," (it being conceded that petitioner had no history of discrimination), and (ii) that "there is reason to believe" that the disparate impact sought to be rectified by the program is the "product" of such discrimination:

> If it was reasonable to conclude—as we hold that it was—that the failure of Negroes to qualify for admission at Davis under regular procedures was due principally to the effects of past discrimination, then there is a reasonable likelihood that, but for pervasive racial discrimination, respondent would have failed to qualify for admission even in the absence of Davis's special admission program.

The breadth of this hypothesis is unprecedented in our constitutional system. The first step is easily taken. No one denies the regrettable fact that there has been societal dsicrimination in this country against various racial and ethnic groups. The second step, however, involves a speculative leap: but for this discrimination by society at large, Bakke "would have failed to qualify for admission" because Negro applicants—nothing is said about Asians, . . .—would have made better scores. Not one word in the record supports this conclusion, and the plurality offers no standard for courts to use in applying such a presumption of causation to other racial or ethnic classifications. This failure is a grave one, since if it may be concluded *on this record* that each of the minority groups preferred by the petitioner's special program is entitled to the benefit of the presumption, it would seem difficult to determine that any of the dozens of minority groups that have suffered "societal discrimination" cannot also claim it, in any area of social intercourse.

tion supports the notion that individuals may be asked to suffer otherwise impermissible burdens in order to enhance the societal standing of their ethnic groups. Second, preferential programs may only reinforce common stereotypes holding that certain groups are unable to achieve success without special protection based on a factor having no relationship to individual worth. Third, there is a measure of inequity in forcing innocent persons in respondent's position to bear the burdens of redressing grievances not of their making.

. . . The mutability of a constitutional principle, based upon shifting political and social judgments, undermines the chances for consistent application of the Constitution from one generation to the next, a critical feature of its coherent interpretation. . . . In expounding the Constitution, the Court's role is to discern "principles sufficiently absolute to give them roots throughout the community and continuity over significant periods of time, and to lift them above the level of the pragmatic political judgments of a particular time and place." . . .

If it is the individual who is entitled to judicial protection against classifications based upon his racial or ethnic background because such distinctions impinge upon personal rights, rather than the individual only because of his membership in a particular group, then constitutional standards may be applied consistently. Political judgments regarding the necessity for the particular classification may be weighed in the constitutional balance, *Korematsu* v. *United States* . . . (1944), but the standard of justification will remain constant. This is as it should be, since those political judgments are the product of rough compromise struck by contending groups within the democratic process. When they touch

upon an individual's race or ethnic background, he is entitled to a judicial determination that the burden he is asked to bear on that basis is precisely tailored to serve a compelling governmental interest. The Constitution guarantees that right to every person regardless of his background. . . .

Petitioner contends that on several occasions this Court has approved preferential classifications without applying the most exacting scrutiny. Most of the cases upon which petitioner relies are drawn from three areas: school desegregation, employment discrimination, and sex discrimination. Each of the cases cited presented a situation materially different from the facts of this case.

The school desegregation cases are inapposite. Each involved remedies for clearly determined constitutional violations. *E. g., Swann* v. *Charlotte-Mecklenburg Board of Education* . . . (1971); . . . Racial classifications thus were designed as remedies for the vindication of constitutional entitlement. Moreover, the scope of the remedies was not permitted to exceed the extent of the violations. *E. g., Dayton Board of Education* v. *Brinkman* . . . (1977); *Milliken* v. *Bradley* . . . (1974); see *Pasadena City Board of Education* v. *Spangler* . . . (1976). See also *Austin Indep. School Dist.* v. *United States,* . . . (1976) (POWELL, J., Concurring). Here, there was no judicial determination of constitutional violation as a predicate for the formulation of a remedial classification.

The employment discrimination cases also do not advance petitioner's cause. For example, in *Franks* v. *Bowman Transportation Co.* . . . (1975), we approved a retroactive award of seniority to a class of Negro truck drivers who had been the victims of discrimination—not just by society at large, but by the respondent in that case. While this relief imposed some burdens on other employees, it was held necessary " 'to make [the victims] whole for injuries suffered on account of unlawful employment discrimination.' " . . . The courts of appeals have fashioned various types of racial preferences as remedies for constitutional or statutory violations resulting in identified, race-based injuries to individuals held entitled to the preference. . . . Such preferences also have been upheld where a legislative or administrative body charged with the responsibility made determinations of past discrimination by the industries affected, and fashioned remedies deemed appropriate to rectify the discrimination. . . . But we have never approved preferential classifications in the absence of proven constitutional or statutory violations.

Nor is petitioner's view as to the applicable standard supported by the fact that gender-based classifications are not subjected to this level of scrutiny. *E. g., Califano* v. *Webster* . . . (1977); . . . *Craig* v. *Boren* . . . (1976). . . . Gender-based distinctions are less likely to create the analytical and practical problems present in preferential programs premised on racial or ethnic criteria. With respect to gender there are only two possible classifications. The incidence of the burdens imposed by preferential classifications is clear. There are no rival groups who can claim that they, too, are entitled to preferential treatment. Classwide questions as to the group suffering previous injury and groups which fairly can be burdened are relatively manageable for reviewing courts. . . . The resolution of these same questions in the context of racial and ethnic preferences presents far more complex and intractable problems than gender-based classifications. More importantly, the per-ception of racial classifications as inherently odious stems from a lengthy and tragic history that gender-based classifications do not share. In sum, the Court has never viewed such classification as inherently suspect or as comparable to racial or ethnic classifications for the purpose of equal-protection analysis.

Petitioner also cites *Lau* v. *Nichols* . . . (1974), in support of the proposition that discrimination favoring racial or ethnic minorities has received judicial approval without the exacting inquiry ordinarily accorded "suspect" classifications. In *Lau*, we held that the failure of the San Francisco school system to provide remedial English instruction for some 1,800 students of oriental ancestry who spoke no English amounted to a violation of Title VI of the Civil Rights Act of 1964, . . . and the regulations promulgated thereunder. Those regulations required remedial instruction where inability to understand English excluded children of foreign ancestry from participation in educational programs. . . . Because we found that the students in *Lau* were denied "a meaningful opportunity to participate in the educational program," . . . we remanded for the fashioning of a remedial order.

Lau provides little support for petitioner's argument. The decision rested solely on the statute, which had been construed by the responsible administrative agency to reach educational practices "which have the effect of subjecting individuals to discrimination," . . . We stated: "Under these state-imposed standards there is no equality of treatment merely by providing students with the same facilities, textbooks, teachers and curriculum; for students who do not understand English are effectively foreclosed from any meaningful education." . . .

Moreover, the "preference" approved did not result in the denial of the relevant benefit—"meaningful participation in the educational program"—to anyone else. No other student was deprived by that preference of the ability to participate in San Francisco's school system, and the applicable regulations required similar assistance for all students who suffered similar linguistic deficiencies. . . .

In a similar vein, petitioner contends that our recent decision in *United Jewish Organizations* v. *Carey* . . . (1977), indicates a willingness to approve racial classifications designed to benefit certain minorities, without denominating the classifications as "suspect." . . . *United Jewish Organizations,* like *Lau,* properly is viewed as a case in which the remedy for an administrative finding of discrimination encompassed measures to improve the previously disadvantaged group's ability to participate, without excluding individuals belonging to any other group from enjoyment of the relevant opportunity—meaningful participation in the electoral process.

In this case, unlike *Lau* and *United Jewish Organizations,* there has been no determination by the legislature or a responsible administrative agency that the University engaged in a discriminatory practice requiring remedial efforts. Moreover, the operation of petitioner's special admissions program is quite different from the remedial measures approved in those cases. It prefers the designated minority groups at the expense of other individuals who are totally foreclosed from competition for the 16 special admissions seats in every medical school class. Because of that foreclosure, some individuals are excluded from enjoyment of a state-provided benefit—admission to the medical school—they otherwise would receive. When a classification denies an individual opportunities or benefits enjoyed by others solely because of his race or ethnic background, it must be regarded as suspect. *E. g., McLaurin* v. *Oklahoma State Regents* . . . (1950).

We have held that in "order to justify the use of a suspect classification, a State must show that its purpose or interest is both constitutionally permissible and substantial, and that its use of the classification is 'necessary . . . to the accomplishment' of its purpose or the safeguarding of its interest." . . . The special admissions program purports to serve the purposes of: (i) "reducing the historic deficit of traditionally disfavored minorities in medical schools and the medical profession;" . . . (ii) countering the effects of societal discrimination; (iii) increasing the number of physicians who will practice in communities currently underserved; and (iv) obtaining the educational benefits that flow from an ethnically diverse student body. It is necessary to decide which, if any, of these purposes is substantial enough to support the use of a suspect classification.

If petitioner's purpose is to assure within its student body some specified percentage of a particular group merely because of its race or ethnic origin, such a preferential purpose must be rejected not as insubstantial but as facially invalid. Preferring members of any one group for no reason other than race or ethnic origin is discrimination for its own sake. This the Constitution forbids. *Loving* v. *Virginia* . . .; *McLaughlin* v. *Florida* . . .; *Brown* v. *Board of Education* (1954).

The State certainly has a legitimate and substantial interest in ameliorating, or eliminating where feasible, the disabling effects of identified discrimination. The line of school desegregation cases, commencing with *Brown*, attests to the importance of this state goal and the commitment of the judiciary to affirm all lawful means towards its attainment. In the school cases, the States were required by court order to redress the wrongs worked by specific instances of racial discrimination. That goal was far more focused than the remedying of the effects of "societal discrimination," an amorphous concept of injury that may be ageless in its reach into the past.

We have never approved a classification that aids persons perceived as members of relatively victimized groups at the expense of other innocent individuals in the absence of judicial, legislative, or administrative findings of constitutional or statutory violations. . . . After such findings have been made, the governmental interest in preferring members of the injured groups at the expense of others is substantial, since the legal rights of the victims must be vindicated. In such a case, the extent of the injury and the consequent remedy will have been judicially, legislatively, or administratively defined. Also, the remedial action usually remains subject to continuing oversight to assure that it will work the least harm possible to other innocent persons competing for the benefit. Without such findings of constitutional or statutory violations, it cannot be said that the government has any greater interest in helping one individual than in refraining from harming another. Thus, the government has no compelling justification for inflicting such harm.

Petitioner does not purport to have made, and is in no position to make, such findings. Its broad mission is education, not the formulation of any legislative policy or the adjudication of particular claims of illegality. For reasons similar to those stated in Part III of this opinion, isolated segments of our vast governmental structures are not competent to make those decisions, at least in the absence of legislative mandates and legislatively determined criteria. . . . Before relying upon these sorts of findings in establishing a racial classification, a governmental body must have the authority and capability to establish, in the record, that the classification is responsive to identified discrimination. . . . Lacking this capability, petitioner has not carried its burden of justification on this issue.

Hence, the purpose of helping certain groups whom the faculty of the Davis Medical School perceived as victims of "societal discrimination" does not justify a classification that imposes disadvantages upon persons like respondent, who bear no responsibility for whatever harm the beneficiaries of the special admissions program are thought to have suffered. To hold otherwise would be to convert a remedy heretofore reserved for violations of legal rights into a privilege that all institutions throughout the Nation could grant at their pleasure to whatever groups are perceived as victims of societal discrimination. That is a step we have never approved. . . .

Petitioner identifies, as another purpose of its program, improving the delivery of health care services to communities currently underserved. It may be assumed that in some situations a State's interest in facilitating the health care of its citizens is sufficiently compelling to support the use of a suspect classification. But there is virtually no evidence in the record indicating that petitioner's special admissions program is either needed or geared to promote that goal. . . .

The fourth goal asserted by petitioner is the attainment of a diverse student body. This clearly is a constitutionally permissible goal for an institution of higher education. Academic freedom, though not a specifically enumerated constitutional right, long has been viewed as a special concern of the First Amendment. The freedom of a university to make its own judgments as to education includes the selection of its student body. Mr. Justice Frankfurter summarized the "four essential freedoms" that comprise academic freedom:

. . . It is the business of a university to provide that atmosphere which is most conducive to speculation, experimemt and creation. It is an atmosphere in which there prevail 'the four essential freedoms' of a university—to determine for itself on academic grounds who may teach, what may be taught, how it shall be taught, and who may be admitted to study. Sweezy v. New Hampshire *(1957) (Frankfurter, J., Concurring).*

The atmosphere of "speculation, experiment and creation"—so essential to the quality of higher education—is widely believed to be promoted by a diverse student body. . . .

Thus, in arguing that its universities must be accorded the right to select those students who will contribute the most to the "robust exchange of ideas," petitioner invokes a countervailing constitutional interest, that of the First Amendment. In this light, petitioner must be viewed as seeking to achieve a goal that is of paramount importance in the fulfillment of its mission.

It may be argued that there is greater force to these views at the undergraduate level than in a medical school where the training is centered primarily on professional competency. But even at the graduate level, our tradition and experience lend support to the view that the contribution of diversity is substantial.

In *Sweatt* v. *Painter* . . . (1950), the Court made a similar point with specific reference to legal education:

The law school, the proving ground for legal learning and practice, cannot be effective in isolation from the individuals and institutions with which the law interacts. Few students and no one who has practiced law would choose to study in an academic vacuum, removed from the interplay of ideas and the exchange of views with which the law is concerned.

Physicians serve a heterogeneous population. An otherwise qualified medical student with a particular background—whether it be ethnic, geographic, culturally advantaged or disadvantaged—may bring to a professional school of medicine experiences, outlooks and ideas that enrich the training of its student body and better equip its graduates to render with understanding their vital service to humanity.

Ethnic diversity, however, is only one element in a range of factors a university properly may consider in attaining the goal of a heterogeneous student body. Although a university must have wide discretion in making the sensitive judgments as to who should be admitted, constitutional limitations protecting individuals rights may not be disregarded. Respondent urges—and the courts below have held—that petitioner's dual admissions program is a racial classification that impermissibly infringes his rights under the Fourteenth Amendment. As the interest of diversity is compelling in the context of a university's admissions program, the question remains whether the program's racial classification is necessary to promote this interest. . . .

It may be assumed that the reservation of a specified number of seats in each class for individuals from the preferred ethnic groups would contribute to the attainment of considerable ethnic diversity in the student body. But petitioner's argument that this is the only effective means of serving the interest of diversity is seriously flawed. In a most fundamental sense the argument misconceives the nature of the state interest that would justify consideration of race or ethnic background. It is not an interest in simple ethnic diversity, in which a specified percentage of the student body is in effect guaranteed to be members of selected ethnic groups, with the remaining percentage an undifferentiated aggregation of students. The diversity that furthers a compelling state interest encompasses a far broader array of qualifications and characteristics of which racial or ethnic origin is but a single though important element. Petitioner's special admissions program, focused *solely* on ethnic diversity, would hinder rather than further attainment of genuine diversity.

Nor would the state interest in genuine diversity be served by expanding petitioner's two-track system into a multitrack program with a prescribed number of seats set aside for each identifiable category of applicants. Indeed, it is inconceivable that a university would thus pursue the logic of petitioner's two-track program to the illogical end of insulating each category of applicants with certain desired qualifications from competition with all other applicants.

The experience of other university admissions programs, which take race into account in achieving the educational diversity valued by the First Amendment, demonstrates that the assignment of a fixed number of places to a minority group is not a necessary means toward that end. . . .

In such an admissions program,

race or ethnic background may be deemed a "plus" in a particular applicant's file, yet it does not insulate the individual from comparison with all other candidates for the available seats.

This kind of program treats each applicant as an individual in the admissions proccess. The applicant who loses out on the last available seat to another candidate receiving a "plus" on the basis of ethnic background will not have been foreclosed from all consideration for that seat simply because he was not the right color or had the wrong surname. It would mean only that his combined qualifications, which may have included similar nonobjective factors, did not outweigh those of the other applicant. His qualifications would have been weighed fairly and competitively, and he would have no basis to complain of unequal treatment under the Fourteenth Amendment.

It has been suggested that an admissions program which considers race only as one factor is simply a subtle and more sophisticated—but no less effective—means of according racial preference than the Davis program. A facial intent to discriminate, however, is evident in petitioner's preference program and not denied in this case. No such facial infirmity exists in an admissions program where race or ethnic background is simply one element—to be weighed fairly against other elements—in the selection process. . . . And a Court would not assume that a university, professing to employ a facially nondiscriminatory admissions policy, would operate it as a cover for the functional equivalent of a quota system. In short, good faith would be presumed in the absence of a showing to the contrary in the manner permitted by our cases. . . .

In summary, it is evident that the

Davis special admission program involves the use of an explicit racial classification never before countenanced by this Court. It tells applicants who are not Negro, Asian, or "Chicano" that they are totally excluded from a specific percentage of the seats in an entering class. No matter how strong their qualifications, quantitative and extracurricular, including their own potential for contribution to educational diversity, they are never afforded the chance to compete with applicants from the preferred groups for the special admission seats. At the same time, the preferred applicants have the opportunity to compete for every seat in the class.

The fatal flaw in petitioner's preferential program is its disregard of individual rights as guaranteed by the Fourteenth Amendment. . . . Such rights are not absolute. But when a State's distribution of benefits or imposition of burdens hinges on the color of a person's skin or ancestry, that individual is entitled to a demonstration that the challenged classification is necessary to promote a substantial state interest. Petitioner has failed to carry this burden. For this reason, that portion of the California court's judgment holding petitioner's special admissions program invalid under the Fourteenth Amendment must be affirmed.

In enjoining petitioner from ever considering the race of any applicant, however, the courts below failed to recognize that the State has a substantial interest that legitimately may be served by a properly devised admissions program involving the competitive consideration of race and ethnic origin. For this reason, so much of the California court's judgment as enjoins petitioner from any consideration of the race of any applicant must be reversed.

With respect to respondent's entitlement to an injunction directing his admission to the Medical School, petitioner has conceded that it could not carry its burden of proving that, but for the existence of its unlawful special admissions program, respondent still would not have been admitted. Hence, respondent is entitled to the injunction, and that portion of the judgment must be affirmed.

MR. JUSTICE BRENNAN, MR. JUSTICE WHITE, MR. JUSTICE MARSHALL, AND MR. JUSTICE BLACKMUN, CONCURRING IN THE JUDGMENT IN PART AND DISSENTING.

The Court today, in reversing in part the judgment of the Supreme Court of California, affirms the constitutional power of Federal and State Government to act affirmatively to achieve equal opportunity for all. The difficulty of the issue presented—whether Government may use race-conscious programs to redress the continuing effects of past discrimination—and the mature consideration which each of our Brethren has brought to it have resulted in many opinions, no single one speaking for the Court. But this should not and must not mask the central meaning of today's opinions: Government may take race into account when it acts not to demean or insult any racial group, but to remedy disadvantages cast on minorities by past racial prejudice, at least when appropriate findings have been made by judicial, legislative, or administrative bodies with competence to act in this area.

The Chief Justice and our Brothers Stewart, Rehnquist, and Stevens, have concluded that Title VI of the Civil Rights Act of 1964, . . . prohibits programs such as that at the Davis Medical School. On this statutory theory alone, they would hold that respondent Allan Bakke's rights have been violated and that he must, therefore, be admitted to the Medical School. Our Brother Powell, reaching the Constitution, concluded that, although race may be taken into account in university admissions, the particular special admissions program used by petitioner, which resulted in the exclusion of respondent Bakke, was not shown to be necessary to achieve petitioner's stated goals. Accordingly, these Members of the Court form a majority of five affirming the judgment of the Supreme Court of California insofar as it holds that respondent Bakke "is entitled to an order that he be admitted to the University."

We agree with Mr. Justice Powell that, as applied to the case before us, Title VI goes no further in prohibiting the use of race than the Equal Protection Clause of the Fourteenth Amendment itself. We also agree that the effect of the California Supreme Court's affirmance of the judgment of the Superior Court of California would be to prohibit the University from establishing in the future affirmative action programs that take race into account. . . . Since we conclude that the affirmative admissions program at the Davis Medical School is constitutional, we would reverse the judgment below in all respects. Mr. Justice Powell agrees that some uses of race in university admissions are permissible and, therefore, he joins with us to make five votes reversing the judgment below insofar as it prohibits the University from establishing race-conscious programs in the future.

. . .

SEPARATE OPINION OF MR. JUSTICE WHITE (OMITTED).

SEPARATE OPINION OF MR. JUSTICE MARSHALL.

I agree with the judgment of the Court only insofar as it permits a uni-versity to consider the race of an applicant in making admissions decisions. I do not agree that petitioner's admissions program violates the Constitution. For it must be remembered that, during most of the past 200 years, the Constitution as interpreted by this Court did not prohibit the most ingenious and pervasive forms of discrimination against the Negro. Now, when a State acts to remedy the effects of that legacy of discrimination. I cannot believe that this same Constitution stands as a barrier.

. . .

The position of the Negro today in America is the tragic but inevitable consequence of centuries of unequal treatment. Measured by any benchmark of comfort or achievement, meaningful equality remains a distant dream for the Negro.

A Negro child today has a life expectancy which is shorter by more than five years than that of a white child. The Negro child's mother is over three times more likely to die of complications in childbirth, and the infant mortality rate for Negroes is nearly twice that for whites. The median income of the Negro family is only 60% that of the median of a white family, and the percentage of Negroes who live in families with incomes below the poverty line is nearly four times greater than that of whites.

When the Negro child reaches working age, he finds that America offers him significantly less than it offers his white counterpart. For Negro adults, the unemployment rate is twice that of whites, and the unemployment rate for Negro teenagers is nearly three times that of white teenagers. A Negro male who completes four years of college can expect a median annual income of merely $110 more than a white male who has only a high school diploma. Although Negroes represent 11.5% of the population, they are only 1.2% of the lawyers and judges, 2% of the physicians, 2.3% of the dentists, 1.1% of the engineers and 2.6% of the college and university professors.

The relationship between those figures and the history of unequal treatment afforded to the Negro cannot be denied. At every point from birth to death the impact of the past is reflected in the still disfavored position of the Negro.

In light of the sorry history of discrimination and its devastating impact on the lives of Negroes, bringing the Negro into the mainstream of American life should be a state interest of the highest order. To fail to do so is to ensure that America will forever remain a divided society.

I do not believe that the Fourteenth Amendment requires us to accept that fate. Neither its history nor our past cases lend any support to the conclusion that a University may not remedy the cumulative effects of society's discrimination by giving consideration to race in an effort to increase the number and percentage of Negro doctors.

. . .

[T]his Court's past cases establish the constitutionality of race-conscious remedial measures. Beginning with the school desegregation cases, we recognized that even absent a judicial or legislative finding of constitutional violation, a school board constitutionally could consider the race of students in making school assignment decisions. . . .

Only last Term, in *United Jewish Organizations* v. *Carey* . . . (1977), we upheld a New York reapportionment plan that was deliberately drawn on the basis of race to enhance the electoral power of Negroes and Puerto Ricans; the plan had the effect of diluting the electoral strength of the Hasidic Jewish Community.

We were willing in *UJO* to sanction the remedial use of a racial classification even though it disadvantaged otherwise "innocent" individuals. In another case last Term, *Califano* v. *Webster* . . . (1977), the Court upheld a provision in the Social Security laws that discriminated against men because its purpose was "the permissible one of redressing our society's long standing disparate treatment of women.' " . . . We thus recognized the permissibility of remedying past societal discrimination through the use of otherwise disfavored classifications.

Nothing in those cases suggests that a university cannot similarly act to remedy past discrimination. It is true that in both *UJO* and *Webster* the use of the disfavored classification was predicated on legislative or administrative action, but in neither case had those bodies made findings that there had been constitutional violations or that the specific individuals to be benefited had actually been the victims of discrimination. Rather, the classification in each of those cases was based on a determination that the group was in need of the remedy because of some type of past discrimination. There is thus ample support for the conclusion that a university can employ race-conscious measures to remedy past societal discrimination, without the need for a finding that those benefited were actually victims of that discrimination.

While I applaud the judgment of the Court that a university may consider race in its admissions process, it is more than a little ironic that, after several hundred years of class-based discrimination against Negroes, the Court is unwilling to hold that a class-based remedy for that discrimination is permissible. In declining to so hold, today's judgment ignores the fact that for several hundred years

Negroes have been discriminated against, not as individuals, but rather solely because of the color of their skins. It is unnecessary in 20th century America to have individual Negroes demonstrate that they have been victims of racial discrimination; the racism of our society has been so pervasive that none, regardless of wealth or position, has managed to escape its impact. The experience of Negroes in America has been different in kind, not just in degree, from that of other ethnic groups. It is not merely the history of slavery alone but also that a whole people were marked as inferior by the law. And that mark has endured. The dream of America as the great melting pot has not been realized for the Negro; because of his skin color he never even made it into the pot.

These differences in the experience of the Negro make it difficult for me to accept that Negroes cannot be afforded greater protection under the Fourteenth Amendment where it is necessary to remedy the effects of past discrimination. In the *Civil Rights Cases*, the Court wrote that the Negro emerging from slavery must cease "to be the special favorite of the laws." We cannot in light of the history of the last century yield to that view. Had the Court in that case and others been willing to "do for human liberty and the fundamental rights of American citizenship, what it did . . . for the protection of slavery and the rights of the masters of fugitive slaves," we would not need now to permit the recognition of any "special wards."

Most importantly, had the Court been willing in 1896, in *Plessy* v. *Ferguson*, to hold that the Equal Protection Clause forbids differences in treatment based on race, we would not be faced with this dilemma in 1978. We must remember, however, that the principle that the "Constitution is colorblind" appeared only in the opinion of the lone dissenter. The majority of the Court rejected the principle of color blindness, and for the next 60 years, from *Plessy* to *Brown* v. *Board of Education*, ours was a Nation where, *by law*, an individual could be given "special" treatment based on the color of his skin.

It is because of a legacy of unequal treatment that we now must permit the institutions of this society to give consideration to race in making decisions about who will hold the positions of influence, affluence and prestige in America. For far too long, the doors to those positions have been shut to Negroes. If we are ever to become a fully integrated society, one in which the color of a person's skin will not determine the opportunities available to him or her, we must be willing to take steps to open those doors. I do not believe that anyone can truly look into America's past and still find that a remedy for the effects of that past is impermissible.

It has been said that this case involves only the individual, Bakke, and this University. I doubt, however, that there is a computer capable of determining the number of persons and institutions that may be affected by the decision in this case. For example, we are told by the Attorney General of the United States that at least 27 federal agencies have adopted regulations requiring recipients of federal funds to take "*affirmative action* to overcome the effects of conditions which resulted in limiting participation . . . by persons of a particular race, color, or national origin." I cannot even guess the number of state and local governments that have set up affirmative action programs, which may be affected by today's decision.

I fear that we have come full circle. After the Civil War our government started several "affirmative action" programs. This Court in the *Civil Rights Cases* and *Plessy* v. *Ferguson* destroyed the movement toward complete equality. For almost a century no action was taken, and this nonaction was with the tacit approval of the courts. Then we had *Brown* v. *Board of Education* and the Civil Rights Acts of Congress, followed by numerous affirmative action programs. *Now,* we have this Court again stepping in, this time to stop affirmative action programs of the type used by the University of California.

SEPARATE OPINION OF MR. JUSTICE BLACKMUN (OMITTED).

MR. JUSTICE STEVENS, WITH WHOM THE CHIEF JUSTICE, MR. JUSTICE STEWART, AND MR. JUSTICE REHNQUIST JOIN, CONCURRING IN THE JUDGMENT IN PART AND DISSENTING IN PART.

. . . Both petitioner and respondent have asked us to determine the legality of the University's special admissions program by reference to the Constitution. Our settled practice, however, is to avoid the decision of a constitutional issue if a case can be fairly decided on a statutory ground. . . . The more important the issue, the more force there is to this doctrine. In this case, we are presented with a constitutional question of undoubted and unusual importance. Since, however, a dispositive statutory claim was raised at the very inception of this case, and squarely decided in the portion of the trial court judgment affirmed by the California Supreme Court, it is our plain duty to confront it. Only if petitioner should prevail on the statutory issue would it be necessary to decide whether the University's admissions program violated the Equal Protection Clause of the Fourteenth Amendment.

Section 601 of the Civil Rights Act of 1964 provides:

No person in the United States shall, on the ground of race, color, or national origin, be excluded from participation in, be denied the benefit of, or be subjected to discrimination under any program or activity receiving Federal financial assistance.

The University, through its special admissions policy, excluded Bakke from participation in its program of medical education because of his race. The University also acknowledges that it was, and still is, receiving federal financial assistance. The plain language of the statute therefore requires affirmance of the judgment below. A different result cannot be justified unless that language misstates the actual intent of the Congress that enacted the statute or the statute is not enforceable in a private action. Neither conclusion is warranted.

. . .

Petitioner contends, however, that exclusion of applicants on the basis of race does not violate Title VI if the exclusion carries with it no racial stigma. No such qualification or limitation of §601's categorical prohibition of "exclusion" is justified by the statute or its history. The language of the entire section is perfectly clear; the words that follow "excluded from" do not modify or qualify the explicit outlawing of any exclusion on the stated grounds.

. . .

As with other provisions of the Civil Rights Act, Congress' expression of its policy to end racial discrimination may independently proscribe conduct that the Constitution does not. However, we need not decide the congruence—or lack of congruence—of the controlling statute and the Constitution since the meaning of the Title VI ban on exclusion is crystal clear: Race cannot be the basis of excluding anyone from participation in a federally funded program. . . .

[In the aftermath of *Bakke,* Anthony Lewis, writing in *The New York Times,*[2] noted the contrast between the six opinions and divided vote in *Bakke* and the unanimity of an earlier Court in *Brown* v. *Board of Education* (1954). But, as Lewis notes, in 1954, racial segregation by law was a clear legal and moral issue, if not one on which all Americans were united. What other judgment could the Court have rendered in *Brown*? On the other hand, there is no comparable consensus today as to the wisdom, efficacy, or morality of affirmative action programs. The Supreme Court in *Bakke* was probably no more divided on that issue than the population at large. Justice Powell's opinion is probably as close to a national consensus as possible, a statesmanlike compromise that put Bakke into medical school, rejected rigid racial quotas, but countenanced the use of race conscious admission policies to promote integration even where no specific discriminatory acts had been perpetrated in the past.

Despite the great buildup and public interest in the case, *Bakke* is not likely to be, in Lewis' words, "a transforming legal event." It was not necessary for the justices to decide some other important affirmative action questions. For example, are remedial racial quotas acceptable where the institution has a past history of racial discrimination? Will the "Harvard type" flexible affirmative action admissions policies that Justice Powell found acceptable, and that are almost certainly to be utilized by all professional

schools, likely to work? Or will they work only if, as Justice Powell suggested would *not* be the case, they operate as a cover for the now proscribed racial quota plans? In fact, the admissions programs of most professional schools probably already come closer to the Harvard than to the Davis model.]

(6) United Steelworkers of America v. Weber (1979)

+Brennan, Stewart, White, Marshall, Blackmun
−Burger, Rehnquist
NP Powell, Stevens

[In 1974 the Steelworkers Union entered into a collective bargaining agreement with the Kaiser Aluminum and Chemical Corporation that contained an affirmative action plan designed to eliminate conspicuous racial imbalance in craft positions in the work force. Each of 15 Kaiser plants set goals for hiring blacks equal to the percentage of blacks in their respective local labor markets. Training programs were established for both black and white unskilled production workers, already employed by Kaiser, to enable them to learn the skills to compete for craft positions. Fifty percent of the openings in these job training programs were reserved for blacks.

At the Kaiser plant in Gramercy, Louisiana, blacks filled only 1.83 percent (5 out of 273) of the skilled craft positions, although the local work force was approximately 39 percent black. Kaiser's practice was to hire only those workers with previous craft experience. Since blacks had long been excluded from the craft unions, few were eligible.[1] Following the collective bargaining agreement, the Kaiser plant in Grammercy decided to fill available craft positions exclusively from the new training program. Production workers who wished to learn craft

---

[2]"*Bakke* May Change a Lot While Changing No Law," *The New York Times* (IV, July 2, 1978), p. 1.

[1]Justice Brennan's opinion observed that exclusion of blacks from craft unions was so notorious and had been documented so often in judicial findings that such exclusions were "a proper subject for judicial notice." This relieved the respondents of the necessity of *proving* that such exclusions had taken place.

skills were selected on the basis of seniority, with 50 percent of the positions in the training program reserved for blacks until such time as black craft workers approximated the percentage of blacks in the local labor market.

In 1974, 13 production workers, 7 of whom were black, were selected to undergo the craft training program. Some of the blacks selected had less seniority than several white production workers who were not admitted to the program. Brian Weber, one of those whites excluded, brought a class action suit in the federal district court. He alleged that by showing preference for blacks over whites on account of race, the training plan violated Title VII of the Civil Rights Act of 1964.[2] The district court agreed and enjoined the company and the union from implementing the affirmative action plan. The Court of Appeals for the Fifth Circuit affirmed by a divided vote, holding that all racial preferences in hiring, even those incidental to a bona fide affirmative action plan, violated Title VII. The Supreme Court granted certiorari.]

MR. JUSTICE BRENNAN delivered the opinion of the Court.

. . .

We emphasize at the outset the narrowness of our inquiry. Since the Kaiser-USWA plan does not involve state action, this case does not present an alleged violation of the Equal Protection Clause of the Constitution. Further, since the Kaiser-USWA plan was adopted voluntarily, we are not concerned with what Title VII re-

quires or with what a court might order to remedy a past proven violation of the Act. The only question before us is the narrow statutory issue of whether Title VII *forbids* private employers and unions from voluntarily agreeing upon bona fide affirmative action plans. . . . That question was expressly left open in *McDonald v. Sante Fe Trail Trans. Co.* . . . (1976) which held, in a case not involving affirmative action, that Title VII protects whites as well as blacks from certain forms of racial discrimination.

Respondent argues that Congress intended in Title VII to prohibit all race-conscious affirmative action plans. Respondent's argument rests upon a literal interpretation of §§703 (a) and (d) of the Act. . . . Since, the argument runs, *McDonald* v. *Santa Fe Trans. Co.* . . . settled that Title VII forbids discrimination against whites as well as blacks, and since the Kaiser-USWA affirmative action plan operates to discriminate against white employees solely because they are white, it follows that the Kaiser-USWA plan violates Title VII.

Respondent's argument is not without force. But it overlooks the significance of the fact that the Kaiser-USWA plan is an affirmative action plan voluntarily adopted by private parties to eliminate tradi-

[2]Section 703 (a), 42 U.S.C. §2000e-2 (a), provides:
"(a) It shall be an unlawful employment practice for an employer—
"(1) to fail or refuse to hire or to discharge any individual, or otherwise to discriminate against any individual with respect to his compensation, terms, conditions, or privileges of employment, because of such individual's race, color, religion, sex, or national origin; or
"(2) to limit or classify his employees or applicants for employment in any way which would deprive or tend to deprive any individual of employment opportunities or otherwise adversely affect his status as an employee, because of such individual's race, color, religion, sex, or national origin."
Section 703 (d), 42 U.S.C. §2000e-2 (d), provides:
"It shall be an unlawful employment practice for any employer, labor organization, or joint labor-management committee controlling apprenticeship or other training or retraining, including on-the-job training programs to discriminate against any individual because of his race, color, religion, sex, or national origin in admission to, or employment in, any program established to provide apprenticeship or other training."

tional patterns of racial segregation. In this context respondent's reliance upon a literal construction of §703 (a) and (d) and upon *McDonald* is misplaced. . . . It is a "familiar rule, that a thing may be within the letter of the statute and yet not within the statute, because not within its spirit, nor within the intention of its makers." *Holy Trinity Church* v. *United States* . . . (1892). The prohibition against racial discrimination in §§703 (a) and (d) of Title VII must therefore be read against the background of the legislative history of Title VII and the historical context from which the Act arose. . . . Examination of those sources makes clear than an interpretation of the sections that forbade all race-conscious affirmative action would "bring about an end completely at variance with the purpose of the statute" and must be rejected. . . .

Congress' primary concern in enacting the prohibition against racial discrimination in Title VII of the Civil Rights Act of 1964 was with "the plight of the Negro in our economy." . . . (remarks of Sen. Humphrey). Before 1964, blacks were largely relegated to "unskilled and semi-skilled jobs." (remarks of Sen. Humphrey); . . . (remarks of Sen. Clark); . . . (remarks of Sen. Kennedy). Because of automation the number of such jobs was rapidly decreasing. . . . As a consequence "the relative position of the Negro worker [was] steadily worsening. In 1947 the non-white unemployment rate was only 64 percent higher than the white rate; in 1962 it was 124 percent higher." . . . Congress considered this a serious social problem. As Senator Clark told the Senate:

The rate of Negro unemployment has gone up consistently as compared with white unemployment for the past 15 years. This is a social malaise and a social situation which we should not tolerate. That is one of the principal reasons why this bill should pass. . . .

Congress feared that the goals of the Civil Rights Act—the integration of blacks into the mainstream of American society—could not be achieved unless this trend were reversed. And Congress recognized that that would not be possible unless blacks were able to secure jobs "which have a future." . . . As Senator Humphrey explained to the Senate.

What good does it do a Negro to be able to eat in a fine restaurant if he cannot afford to pay the bill? What good does it do him to be accepted in a hotel that is too expensive for his modest income? How can a Negro child be motivated to take full advantage of integrated educational facilities if he has no hope of getting a job where he can use that education? . . .

. . .

Without a job, one cannot afford public convenience and accommodations. Income from employment may be necessary to further a man's education, or that of his children. If his children have no hope of getting a good job, what will motivate them to take advantage of educational opportunities. . . .

These remarks echoed President Kennedy's original message to Congress upon the introduction of the Civil Rights Act in 1963.

. . .

Accordingly, it was clear to Congress that "the crux of the problem [was] to open employment oportunities for Negroes in occupations which have been traditionally closed to them," . . . (remarks of Sen. Humphrey), and it was to this problem that Title VII's prohibition against racial discrimination in employment was primarily addressed.

It plainly appears from the House Report accompanying the Civil

Rights Act that Congress did not intend wholly to prohibit private and voluntary affirmative action efforts as one method of solving this problem. The Report provides:

No bill can or should lay claim to eliminating all of the causes and consequences of racial and other types of discrimination against minorities. There is reason to believe, however, that national leadership provided by the enactment of Federal legislation dealing with the most troublesome problems will create an atmosphere conducive to voluntary or local resolution of other forms of discrimination. . . .

Given this legislative history, we cannot agree with respondent that Congress intended to prohibit the private sector from taking effective steps to accomplish the goal that Congress designed Title VII to achieve. The very statutory words intended as a spur or catalyst to cause "employers and unions to self-examine and to self-evaluate their employment practices and to endeavor to eliminate, so far as possible, the last vestiges of an unfortunate and ignominious page in this country's history," *Albemarle* v. *Moody* . . . (1975), cannot be interpreted as an absolute prohibition against all private, voluntary, race-conscious affirmative action efforts to hasten the elimination of such vestiges. It would be ironic indeed if a law triggered by a Nation's concern over centuries of racial injustice and intended to improve the lot of those who had "been excluded from the American dream for so long." . . . constituted the first legislative prohibition of all voluntary, private, race-conscious efforts to abolish traditional patterns of racial segregation and hierarchy.

Our conclusion is further reinforced by examination of the language and legislative history of §703 (j) of Title VII.[3] Opponents of Title VII raised two related arguments against the bill. First, they argued that the Act would be interpreted to *require* employers with racially imbalanced work forces to grant preferential treatment to racial minorities in order to integrate. Second, they argued that employers with racially imbalanced work forces would grant preferential treatment to racial minorities, even if not required to do so by the Act. . . . Had Congress meant to prohibit all race-conscious affirmative action, as respondent urges, it easily could have answered both objections by providing that Title VII would not require or *permit* racially preferential integration ef-

---

[3]Section 703 (j) of Title VII, 42 U.S.C. §2000e-2 (j), provides:

"Nothing contained in this subchapter shall be interpreted to require any employer, employment agency, labor organization, or joint labor-management committee subject to this subchapter to grant preferential treatment to any individual or to any group because of the race, color, religion, sex, national origin of such individual or group on account of an imbalance which may exist with respect to the total number or percentage of persons of any race, color, religion, sex, or national origin employed by any employer, referred or classified for employment by any employment agency or labor organization, or admitted to, or employed in, any apprenticeship or other training program, in comparison with the total number or percentage or persons of such race, color, religion, sex, or national origin in any community, State, section, or other area, or in the available work force in any community, State, section, or other area."

Section 703 (j) speaks to substantive liability under Title VII, but it does not preclude courts from considering racial imbalance as evidence of a Title VII violation. See *Teamsters* v. *United States* (1977). Remedies for substantive violations are governed by §706 (g), 42 U.S.C. §2000e-5 (g).

forts. But Congress did not choose such a course. Rather Congress added §703 (j) which addresses only the first objection. The section provides that nothing contained in Title VII "shall be interpreted to *require* any employer . . . to grant preferential treatment . . . to any group because of the race . . . of such . . . group on account of " a defacto racial imbalance in the employer's work force. The section does *not* state that "nothing in Title VII shall be interpreted to *permit*" voluntary affirmative efforts to correct racial imbalances. The natural inference is that Congress chose not to forbid all voluntary race-conscious affirmative action.

The reasons for this choice are evident from the legislative record. Title VII could not have been enacted into law without substantial support from legislators in both Houses who traditionally resisted federal regulation of private business. Those legislators demanded as a price for their support that "management prerogatives and union freedoms . . . be left undisturbed to the greatest extent possible." . . . Section 703 (j) was proposed by Senator Dirksen to allay any fears that the Act might be interpreted in such a way as to upset this compromise. The section was designed to prevent §703 of Title VII from being interpreted in such a way as to lead to undue "Federal Government interference with private businesses be-

cause of some Federal employee's ideas about racial balance or imbalance."[4] . . . Clearly, a prohibition against all voluntary, race-conscious, affirmative action efforts would disserve these ends. Such a prohibition would augment the powers of the Federal Government and diminish traditional management prerogatives while at the same time impeding attainment of the ultimate statutory goals. In view of this legislative history and in view of Congress' desire to avoid undue federal regulation of private businesses, use of the word "require" rather than the phrase "require or permit" in §703 (j) fortifies the conclusion that Congress did not intend to limit traditional business freedom to such a degree as to prohibit all voluntary, race-conscious affirmative action.

We therefore hold that Title VII's prohibition in §§703 (a) and (d) against racial discrimination does not condemn all private, voluntary, race-conscious affirmative action plans.

We need not today define in detail the line of demarcation between permissible and impermissible affirmative action plans. It suffices to hold that the challenged Kaiser-USWA affirmative action plan falls on the permissible side of the line. The purposes of the plan mirror those of the statute. Both were designed to break down old patterns of racial segregation and hierarchy. Both were

---

[4]Title VI of the Civil Rights Act of 1964, considered in *University of California Regents* v. *Bakke*, 438 U.S. 265 (1978), contains no provision comparable to §703 (j). This is because Title VI was an exercise of federal power over a matter in which the Federal Government was already directly involved: the prohibitions against race-based conduct contained in Title VI governed "program[s] or activit[ies] receiving Federal financial assistance." 42 U.S.C. §2000d. Congress was legislating to assure federal funds would not be used in an improper manner. Title VII, by contrast, was enacted pursuant to the Commerce power to regulate purely private decisionmaking and was not intended to incorporate and particularize the commands of the Fifth and Fourteenth Amendments. Title VII and Title VI, therefore, cannot be read *in pari materia*. See 110 Cong. Rec. 8315 (1964) (remarks of Sen. Cooper). See also *id.*, at 11615 (remarks of Sen. Cooper).

structured to "open employment opportunities for Negroes in occupations which have been traditionally closed to them." . . .

At the same time the plan does not unnecessarily trammel the interests of the white employees. The plan does not require the discharge of white workers and their replacement with new black hires. . . . Nor does the plan create an absolute bar to the advancement of white employees; half of those trained in the program will be white. Moreover, the plan is a temporary measure; it is not intended to maintain racial balance, but simply to eliminate a manifest racial imbalance. Preferential selection of craft trainees at the Gramercy plant will end as soon as the percentage of black skilled craft workers in the Gramercy plant approximates the percentage of blacks in the local labor force. . . .

We conclude, therefore, that the adoption of the Kaiser-USWA plan for the Gramercy plant falls within the area of discretion left by Title VII to the private sector voluntarily to adopt affirmative action plans designed to eliminate conspicuous racial imbalance in traditionally segregated job categories. Accordingly, the judgment of the Court of Appeals for the Fifth Circuit is

Reversed.

MR. JUSTICE BLACKMUN, CONCURRING (OMITTED).

MR. CHIEF JUSTICE BURGER, DISSENTING.

The Court reaches a result I would be inclined to vote for were I a Member of Congress considering a proposed amendment of Title VII. I cannot join the Court's judgment, however, because it is contrary to the explicit language of the statute and arrived at by means wholly incompatible with long-established principles of separation of powers. Under the guise of statutory "construction," the Court effectively rewrites Title VII to achieve what it regards as a desirable result. It "amends" the statute to do precisely what both its sponsors and its opponents agreed the statute was *not* intended to do.

. . .

Often we have difficulty interpreting statutes either because of imprecise drafting or because legislative compromises have produced genuine ambiguities. But here there is no lack of clarity, no ambiguity. The quota embodied in the collective-bargaining agreement between Kaiser and the Steelworkers unquestionably discriminates on the basis of race against individual employees seeking admission to on-the-job training programs. And under the plain language of §703 (d), that is "an *unlawful* employment practice."

Oddly, the Court seizes upon the very clarity of the statute almost as a justification for evading the unavoidable impact of its language. The Court blandly tells us that Congress could not really have meant what it said, for a "literal construction" would defeat the "purpose" of the statute—at least the congressional "purpose" as five Justices divine it today. But how are judges supposed to ascertain the *purpose* of a statute except through the words Congress used and the legislative history of the statute's evolution? One need not even resort to the legislative history to recognize what is apparent from the face of Title VII—that it is specious to suggest that §703 (j) contains a negative pregnant that permits employers to do what §§703 (a) and (d) unambiguously and unequivocally *forbid* employers from doing. Moreover, as Mr. Justice Rehnquist's opinion—which I join—conclusively demonstrates, the legislative history makes equally clear that the supporters and opponents of Title VII reached an agreement about the statute's intended effect. That agreement, expressed so clearly in the language of the statute that no one should doubt its meaning, forecloses the reading which the Court gives the statute today.

. . .

It is often observed that hard cases make bad law. I suspect there is some truth to that adage, for the "hard" cases always tempt judges to exceed the limits of their authority, as the Court does today by totally rewriting a crucial part of Title VII to reach a desirable result. Cardozo no doubt had this type of case in mind when he wrote:

The judge, even where he is free, is still not wholly free. He is not to innovate at pleasure. He is not a knight-errant, roaming at will in pursuit of his own ideal of beauty or of goodness. He is to draw his inspiration from consecrated principles. He is not to yield to spasmodic sentiment, to vague and unregulated benevolence. He is to exercise a discretion informed by tradition, methodized by analogy, disciplined by system, and subordinated to "the primordial necessity of order in the social life." Wide enough in all conscience is the field of discretion that remains. B. Cardozo, The Nature of the Judicial Process 141 (1921).

What Cardozo tells us is beware the "good result," achieved by judicially unauthorized or intellectually dishonest means on the appealing notion that the desirable ends justify the improper judicial means. For there is always the danger that the seeds of precedent sown by good men for the best of motives will yield a rich harvest of unprincipled acts of others also aiming at "good ends."

MR. JUSTICE REHNQUIST, WITH WHOM THE CHIEF JUSTICE JOINS, DISSENTING.

In a very real sense, the Court's opinion is ahead of its time: it could more appropriately have been handed down five years from now, in 1984, a year coinciding with the title of a book from which the Court's opinion borrows, perhaps subconsciously, at least one idea. Orwell describes in his book a governmental official of Oceania, one of the three great world powers, denouncing the current, Eurasia, to an assembled crowd:

It was almost impossible to listen to him without being first convinced and then maddened. . . . The speech had been proceeding for perhaps twenty minutes when a messenger hurried onto the platform and a scrap of paper was slipped into the speaker's hand. He unrolled and read it without pausing in his speech. Nothing altered in his voice or manner, or in the content of what he was saying, but suddenly the names were different. Without words said, a wave of understanding rippled through the crowd. Oceania was at war with Eastasia! . . . The banners and posters with which the square was decorated were all wrong!
. . .
[T]he speaker had switched from one line to the other actually in mid-sentence, not only without a pause, but without even breaking the syntax. G. Orwell, Nineteen Eighty-Four, 182–183 (1949).

Today's decision represents an equally dramatic and equally unremarked switch in this Court's interpretation of Title VII.

The operative sections of Title VII prohibit racial discrimination in employment simpliciter. Taken in its normal meaning, and as understood by all Members of Congress who spoke to the issue during the legislative debates, . . . this language prohibits a covered employer from considering race when making an employment decision, whether the race be black or white. . . .

We have never waivered in our understanding that Title VII "prohibits *all* racial discrimination in employment, without exception for any particular employees." . . . In *Griggs* v. *Duke Power Co.* . . . (1971), our first occasion to interpret Title VII, a unanimous court observed that "[d]iscriminatory preference, for any group, minority or majority, is precisely and only what Congress has proscribed." And in our most recent discussion of the issue, we uttered words seemingly dispositive of this case: "It is clear beyond cavil that the obligation imposed by Title VII is to provide an equal opportunity for *each* applicant regardless of race, without regard to whether members of the applicant's race are already proportionately represented in the work force." *Furnco Construction Corp.* v. *Waters* . . . (1978).

Today, however, the Court behaves much like the Orwellian speaker earlier described, as if it had been handed a note indicating that Title VII would lead to a result unacceptable to the Court if interpreted here as it was in our prior decisions. Accordingly, without even a break in syntax, the Court rejects "a literal construction of §703 (a)" in favor of newly discovered "legislative history," which leads it to a conclusion directly contrary to that compelled by the "uncontradicted legislative history" unearthed in *McDonald* and our other prior decisions. Now we are told that the legislative history of Title VII shows that employers are free to discriminate on the basis of race: an employer may, in the Court's words, "trammel the interests of white employees" in favor of black employees in order to eliminate "racial imbal-

ance." . . . Our earlier interpretations of Title VII, like the banners and posters decorating the square in Oceania, were all wrong.

As if this were not enough to make a reasonable observer question this Court's adherence to the oft-stated principle that our duty is to construct rather than rewrite legislation, *United States* v. *Rutherford* (1979) the Court also seizes upon §703 (j) of Title VII as an independent, or at least partially independent, basis for its holding. Totally ignoring the wording of that section, which is obviously addressed to those charged with the responsibility of interpreting the law rather than those who are subject to its proscriptions, and totally ignoring the months of legislative debates preceding the section's introduction and passage, which demonstrate clearly that it was enacted to prevent precisely what occurred in this case, the Court infers from §703 (j) that "Congress chose not to forbid all voluntary race-conscious affirmative action."

Thus, by a *tour de force* reminiscent not of jurists such as Hale, Holmes, and Hughes, but of escape aritsts such as Houdini, the Court eludes clear statutory language, "uncontradicted" legislative history, and uniform precedent in concluding that employers are, after all, permitted to consider race in making employment decisions. It may be that one or more of the principal sponsors of Title VII would have preferred to see a provision allowing preferential treatment of minorities written into the bill. Such a provision, however, would have to have been expressly or impliedly excepted from Title VII's explicit prohibition on all racial discrimination in employment. There is no such exception in the Act. And a reading of the legislative debates concerning Title VII, in which proponents and opponents alike uniformly denounced discrimination in favor of, as well as discrimination against, Negroes, demonstrates clearly that any legislator harboring an unspoken

desire for such a provision could not possibly have succeeded in enacting it into law.

. . .

3. GENDER EQUALITY

A. A Note on Women's Rights Under the Constitution

There is no area of current interest in constitutional law in which the law has changed more rapidly than with regard to women's rights. Although the contemporary movement toward gender equality had already begun when the first edition of this casebook went to press in 1971, not a single Supreme Court case existed to illustrate that trend (*Reed* v. *Reed, infra,* was decided later that year). Since then, there have been dozens of gender equality cases coming to the Supreme Court. An Equal Rights Amendment was passed by Congress in March of 1972. Cases that were good law—if no longer good politics—a decade ago now seem like hoary remnants of a bygone day.

Changes in the role of women in society have been momentous, in some cases prompting the law to catch up and in other cases flowing from changes in the law, in a constantly interdependent relationship. Change in the law and the Constitution must be seen as part of a broader movement toward equalization of sex roles and rights and, indeed, as a symptom of the increasing "rights consciousness" of all Americans. The primary effect of legal and constitutional change has been to invalidate restrictive laws and to promote equality of treatment before the law for men and women.

The enormously powerful and per-

vasive egalitarian spirit unleashed by the civil rights movement has fueled these changes. The law—and the Supreme Court—became much more sensitive to the psychological and political need for equality. On a practical level, civil rights cases were primarily responsible for opening up access to the federal courts. Skills developed by civil rights lawyers, new and inventive forms of legal action, and the revitalization of the post–Civil War civil rights statutes, all contributed to developing concepts of gender equality. This is not to say that race and sex have received identical treatment. The Supreme Court, as Justice Powell noted in *Bakke*, has refused to consider gender equality as on a par with racial equality. But measured from a basemark of the mid-1960s, the changes in the law on gender equality have been breathtaking indeed.

The provisions of the Fourteenth Amendment have always been thought to extend to the rights of women as persons and citizens. But several post–Civil War cases decided by the Supreme Court made it quite clear that the Fourteenth Amendment did not protect women against different and unequal treatment because of their sex. In *Bradwell* v. *Illinois* (1872), the Court upheld the right of a state to deny women the right to practice law. The paternalism of that decision was best expressed by Justice Bradley:

The natural and proper timidity and delicacy which belongs to the female sex evidently unfits it for many of the occupations of civil life. The constitution of the family organization, which is founded in the divine ordinance, as well as in the nature of things, indicates the domestic sphere as that which properly belongs to the domain and functions of womanhood.

. . .

. . . The paramount destiny and mission of women are to fulfill the noble and benign offices of wife and mother. This is the law of the Creator.

The next year, in *Minor* v. *Happersett*, the Court ruled that women had no constitutional right to vote (a decision eventually reversed by the Nineteenth Amendment in 1920).

In *Strauder* v. *West Virginia* (1880), the Court, while invalidating a statute that prohibited Negroes from serving on juries, stated that jury duty could be limited to men. That dictum merely restated the philosophy of the English common law, under which, except for a limited class of cases, women were considered unqualified for jury duty because of a "defect of sex." Parliament adopted this rule in 1870 and then repealed it in 1919. In the United States, Utah, in 1898, was the first state to qualify women for jury duty. Obviously, those who wrote the Sixth Amendment did not believe that it prohibited the exclusion of women from juries. The Judiciary Act of 1789 established that jurors in the federal courts would have the qualifications of jurors in each state, and women were disqualified from jury duty in every state.

During the Progressive era, indeed well into the New Deal, women became the special object of the law's protection. Laws were passed that excluded women from certain "morally polluting" occupations such as bartending. Legislation limited the hours women could work in general and limited them specifically during and immediately following pregnancy. Laws prescribed the conditions under which women could work, such as the weights they could lift and the special need for sanitary working conditions. Women were exempted from the military draft and from compulsory jury duty.

In *Muller* v. *Oregon* (1908), the Supreme Court adopted the argument of the Brandeis Brief and sustained a law that limited the working hours of women to ten hours per day. The statute was sustainable, the Court said, because "woman's physical structure, and the functions she performs in consequence thereof, justify special legislation restricting or qualifying the conditions under which she should be permitted to toil." Such words, coming from a Court that only three years earlier had decided *Lochner* v. *New York* (1905), are testament to a very strong ideology of paternalism. A similar decision, with a similar rationale, was made in *West Coast Hotel* v. *Parrish* (1937). Both decisions were celebrated in their day as being forward-looking and progressive. The force of the *Muller* decision, as Pauli Murray and Mary Eastwood observe in the following article, was not only that it legitimized protective labor legislation but also that it was quoted with approval and cited in support of differential treatment of women in other walks of life.

Besides the laws that were, or were intended to be, "protective," there were others that were openly discriminatory toward women. The customs and the philosophy that accorded with those laws are, of course, more difficult to change.[1]

In two decisions after World War II, the Supreme Court showed little inclination to change. In *Goesaert* v. *Cleary* (1948), it sustained the validity of a Michigan statute that prohibited licensing a woman to be a bartender unless she was the wife or daughter of the male owner of the bar in which she would work. According to Justice Frankfurter:

Michigan could, beyond question, forbid all women from working behind a bar. This is so despite the vast changes in the social and legal position of women. The fact that women may now have achieved the virtues that men have long claimed as their prerogatives and now indulge in vices that men have long practiced, does not preclude the States from drawing a sharp line between the sexes, certainly in such matters as the regulation of the liquor traffic. The Constitution does not require legislatures to reflect sociological insight, or shifting social standards, any more than it requires them to keep abreast of the latest scientific standards. . . .

He went on to observe that the state had a legitimate interest in combating the "moral and social problems" to which bartending by women could give rise. The state can protect against these evils through "the oversight assured through ownership of a bar by a barmaid's husband or father" which "minimized hazards that might confront a barmaid without such protecting oversight."

In *Hoyt* v. *Florida* (1961), the Supreme Court upheld a state law that included men on jury lists unless *they requested* an exemption but that exempted women unless *they*

volunteered. The Court found this classification reasonable because, notwithstanding the recent "enlightened emancipation of women, . . . woman is still regarded as the center of home and family life."

Neither *Goesaert* nor *Hoyt* has survived as precedent. *Goesaert* has never been explicitly overruled, but like *Bradwell*, it is now a vestigial relic of an earlier time. It would almost certainly not survive equal protection analysis under the least demanding test of ordinary scrutiny (see *Reed* v. *Reed, infra*). A similar case arose in 1970, *Seidenberg* v. *McSorley's Old Ale House.* Faith Seidenberg, a well-known attorney, decided to test the validity of the "men only" policy at a fashionable watering spot. She was excluded and brought suit in the federal district court. That court found no merit in the argument that the presence of women in bars gives rise to "moral and social" problems against which McSorley's could protect itself by barring women. "Social mores have not stood still since that argument was used in 1948 to convince a 6-3 majority of the Supreme court," the court said in 1971. The California Supreme Court invalidated a state law similar to that of Michigan's, under the Civil Rights Act of 1964, the Equal Protection clause, and the California Constitution.

Hoyt was effectively overruled in *Taylor* v. *Louisiana* (1975), a case brought by a *male* defendant who was convicted of aggravated kidnapping and sentenced to death. Taylor claimed, and the Supreme Court agreed, that he had a Sixth Amendment right to trial by a jury drawn from a fair cross section of the community. Since women were exempted

[1]For a good summary of the legal status of women through 1970 see Leo Kanowitz, *Women and the Law* (Albuquerque: University of New Mexico Press, 1970).

from jury duty in Louisiana (as in Florida), the jury clearly did not meet that test, and Taylor's conviction was overturned. The fact that Taylor was not a member of the excluded group was held not to bar his claim. The Supreme Court still has not said directly that women have a Fourteenth Amendment right to serve on juries on the same basis as men, but that is certainly the implication of the *Taylor* decision. States remain free to grant exemptions from jury duty, but the exclusion of any class cannot detract substantially from the representativeness of a jury panel.

Essentially, there have been four interrelated strategies to bring about change in the rights of women. First, there have been political efforts to repeal offending state and federal laws. Second, there have been efforts to use the enforcement machinery of state and federal civil rights commissions, especially the federal Equal Employment Opportunities Commission, to eliminate job discrimination against women. Two federal statutes, the Equal Pay Act of 1963, and Title VII (employment) of the Civil Rights Act of 1964, are often involved. The Equal Pay Act added the principle of equal pay for equal work, regardless of sex, to the Fair Labor Standards Act. And Title VII, besides establishing the EEOC, prohibited discrimination in employment on account of sex (as well as race; sex discrimination is not prohibited in the other sections of the act).

Third, efforts have been directed at constitutional change. The Supreme Court has now included sex as a prohibited discrimination under the Fourteenth Amendment (see *Reed* v. *Reed, infra*). But efforts to have sex declared a "suspect classification" under the equal protection clause

have more or less failed. The remainder of this section is devoted largely to the Supreme Court's response to challenges to gender classifications.

Fourth, and finally, there have been continuing efforts to pass federal and state equal rights amendments. An equal rights amendment was introduced into every Congress from 1923 to 1971. Versions of the amendment passed the Senate in 1950 and 1953, but in each case with the "Hayden rider" attached. The amendment, which provided (in its current version) that "Equality of Rights Under the Law Shall not be denied or abridged by the United States or by any state on account of sex," was modified by the rider so as not to "be construed to impair any rights, benefits, or exemptions now or hereafter conferred by law, upon persons of the female sex." That modification would have seriously undercut the purposes of the amendment, since it would have exempted "protective legislation." As such, it was unacceptable to many sponsors of the amendment. The amendment without the rider passed the House of Representatives in October 1971 by a vote of 354-24. It passed the Senate in March 1972 by a vote of 84-8. Ratification is pending (and is further discussed at the end of this section). Similar provisions are contained in the equal rights amendments passed in a number of states.

B. Pauli Murray and Mary O. Eastwood, Jane Crow and the Law

Negroes have successfully invoked the protection of the Constitution against race discrimination; the

Reprinted from **34** *The George Washington Law Review* (1965), 233–241.

enactment of the Civil Rights Act of 1964 was achieved primarily because of the evils of race discrimination. We think that sex discrimination can be better understood if compared with race discrimination and that recognition of the similarities of the two problems can be helpful in improving and clarifying the legal status of women.

Discriminatory attitudes toward women are strikingly parallel to those regarding Negroes. Women have experienced both subtle and explicit forms of discrimination comparable to the inequalities imposed upon minorities. Contemporary scholars have been impressed by the interrelation of these two problems in the United States, whether their point of departure has been a study of women or of racial theories. In *The Second Sex,* Simone de Beauvoir makes frequent reference to the position of American Negroes. In *An American Dilemma,* Gunnar Myrdal noted that the similarity of the two problems was not accidental, but originated in the paternalistic order of society. "From the very beginning," Dr. Myrdal observed, "the fight in America for the liberation of the Negro slaves was closely coordinated with the fight for women's emancipation. . . . The women's movement got much of its public support by reason of its affiliation with the Abolitionist movement."

The myths built up to perpetuate the inferior status of women and of Negroes were almost identical, Dr. Myrdal found:

As in the Negro problem, most men have accepted as self-evident, until recently, the doctrine that women had inferior endowments in most of those respects which carry prestige, power, and advantages in society, but that they were, at the same time, superior in some other respects. The arguments, when argu-

ments were used, have been about the same: smaller brains, scarcity of geniuses and so on. The study of women's intelligence and personality has had broadly the same history as the one we record for Negroes. As in the case of the Negro, women themselves have often been brought to believe in their inferiority of endowment. As the Negro was awarded his "place" in society, so there was a "woman's place." In both cases the rationalization was strongly believed that men, in confining them to this place, did not act against the true interest of the subordinate groups. The myth of the "contented woman," who did not want to have suffrage or other civil rights and equal opportunities, had the same social function as the myth of the "contented Negro."

Similarly, Ashley Montagu, in his study, *Man's Most Dangerous Myth: The Fallacy of Race,* documents the parallel between antifeminism and race prejudice:

In connection with the modern form of race prejudice it is of interest to recall that almost every one of the arguments used by the racists to "prove" the inferiority of one or another so-called "race" was not so long ago used by the antifeminists to "prove" the inferiority of the female as compared with the male. In the case of these sexual prejudices one generation has been sufficient in which to discover how completely spurious and erroneous virtually every one of these arguments and assertions are.

The myths essentially "deny a particular group equality of opportunity and then assert that because that group has not achieved as much as the groups enjoying complete freedom of opportunity it is obviously inferior and can never do as well." Moreover, Dr. Montagu finds the same underlying motives at work in antifeminism as in racism, "namely, fear, jealousy, feelings of insecurity, fear of economic competition, guilt feelings and the like."

These findings indicate that, in matters of discrimination, the problems of women are not as unique as has been generally assumed. That manifestations of racial prejudice have been more brutal than the more subtle manifestations of prejudice by reason of sex in no way diminishes the force of the equally obvious fact that the rights ·of women and the rights of Negroes are only different phases of the fundamental and indivisible issue of human rights.

The United Nations Charter and the Universal Declaration of Human Rights both stress respect for human rights and fundamental freedoms for all persons without distinction as to race, sex, language, or religion. Until the enactment of the Civil Rights Act of 1964, "sex" generally had not been included with "race, color, religion and national origin" in federal laws and regulations designed to eliminate discrimination. As a practical matter, "civil rights" had become equated with Negro rights, which created bitter opposition and divisions. The most serious discrimination against both women and Negroes today is in the field of employment. The addition of "sex" to Title VII of the Civil Rights Act, making it possible for a second large group of the population to invoke its protection against discrimination in employment, represents an important step toward implementation of our commitment to human rights.

. . .

Obviously, society has a legitimate interest in the protection of women's maternal and familial functions. But in discussing the legal status of women, courts generally have been content to parrot the doctrine that sex forms the basis of a reasonable classification and to ignore the fact that women vary widely in their activities and as individuals. What is needed to remove the present ambiguity of women's legal status is a shift of emphasis from women's class attributes (sex per se) to their *functional* attributes. The boundaries between social policies that are genuinely protective of the familial and maternal functions and those that unjustly discriminate against women as individuals must be delineated.

Before attempting to formulate any principle of equal protection of the laws, certain assumptions that have confused the issue must be reexamined. The first is the assumption that equal rights for women is tantamount to seeking identical treatment with men. This is an oversimplification. As individuals, women seek equality of opportunity for education, employment, cultural enrichment, and civic participation without barriers built upon the myth of the stereotyped "woman." As women, they seek freedom of choice: to develop their maternal and familial functions primarily, or to develop different capacities at different stages of life, or to pursue some combination of these choices.

The second assumption confusing the "woman problem" is that, because of inherent differences between the sexes, differential treatment does not imply inequality or inferiority. The inherent differences between the sexes, according to this view, make necessary the application of different principles to women than to minority groups.

To the degree women perform the function of motherhood, they differ from other special groups. But maternity legislation is not sex legislation; its benefits are geared to the performance of a special service much like veterans' legislation. When the law distinguishes between the "two great classes of men and women," gives men a preferred position by accepted social standards, and regulates the conduct of women in a restrictive manner having no bearing on the maternal function, it disregards individuality and relegates an entire class to inferior status.

The doctrine of "classification by sex" extracted from *Muller* is too sweeping. Courts have sanctioned inequalities as "protection" and "privilege"; suggestions of "chivalry" and concern for the "ladies" conceal continued paternalism. Deriving their respectability from a principle of equality, these applications remain anachronisms in the law.

It may not be too far-fetched to suggest that this doctrine as presently applied has implications comparable to those of the now discredited doctrine of "separate but equal." It makes the legal position of women not only ambiguous but untenable. Through unwarranted extension, it has penalized all women for the biological function of motherhood far in excess of precautions justified by the findings of advanced medical science. Through semantic manipulation, it permits a policy originally directed toward the protection of a segment of a woman's life to dominate and inhibit her development as an individual. It reinforces an inferior status by lending governmental prestige to sex distinctions that are carried over into those private discriminations currently beyond the reach of the law.

Although the "classification by sex" doctrine was useful in sustaining the validity of progressive labor legislation in the past, perhaps it should now be shelved alongside the "separate but equal" doctrine. It could be argued that, just as separate schools for Negro and white children

by their very nature cannot be "equal," classification on the basis of sex is today inherently unreasonable and discriminatory.

There are a few laws that refer to women or men or males or females, but that in reality do not classify by sex and accordingly would not be constitutionally objectionable if classification by sex were prohibited. For example, a law that prohibits rape can apply only to men; a law that provides for maternity benefits can apply only to women. If these laws were phrased in terms of "persons" rather than "men" or "women," the meaning or effect could be no different. Thus, the legislature by its choice of terminology has not made any sex classification.

A second category of law or official practice that would not become invalid if the "classification by sex" doctrine were discarded are those that do not treat men and women differently, but only separately: for example, separate dormitory facilities for men and women in a state university or separate toilet facilities in public buildings. Unlike separation of the races, in our culture separation of the sexes in these situations carries no implication of inferiority for either sex.

If this reappraisal of sex discrimination under the fifth and fourteenth amendments were accepted by the courts, one might speculate as to the effect on various other laws. Alimony based on sex would not be permitted, but alimony not based on sex but provided for the non-paid homemaker could be proper, as would be alimony that takes into account the relative income of the two parties. Any equitable division of property between spouses not based on sex would be permitted. Also permissible, because not based on classification by sex, would be equitable arrangements upon dissolution of a marriage that require one parent to furnish all or a major portion of the financial support and the other parent to bear all or a major portion of responsibility for the care, custody, and education of the children. Laws that provide benefits for wives or widows where the same benefits were not provided for husbands or widowers would be inconsistent, unless based on the non-sex factor of dependency.

To be consistent with the principle of equality of rights, different minimum ages for marriage for boys and girls (if different, lower for girls than for boys) and different ages in state child labor laws (if different, higher for girls than for boys) should be equalized. State labor standards legislation would have to apply equally to men and women. Both sexes would be subject to compulsory military service and jury service, but exemptions could be made for activities, such as care of dependent children or other family members, if based on performance of the function rather than sex.

If laws classifying persons by sex were prohibited by the Constitution, and if it were made clear that laws recognizing functions, *if performed,* are not based on sex per se, much of the confusion as to the legal status of women would be eliminated. Moreover, this may be the only way to give adequate recognition to women who are mothers and homemakers and who do not work outside the home—it recognizes the intrinsic value of child care and homemaking. The assumption that financial support of a family by the husband-father is a gift from the male sex to the female sex and, in return, the male is entitled to preference in the outside world is all too common. Underlying this assumption is the unwillingness to acknowledge any value for child

care and homemaking because they have not been ascribed a dollar value. . . .

C. Gender Classifications

(1) Reed v. Reed (1971)

+Burger, Douglas, Brennan, White, Stewart, Blackmun, Marshall

MR. CHIEF JUSTICE BURGER delivered the opinion of the Court.

Richard Lynn Reed, a minor, died intestate in Ada County, Idaho, on March 29, 1967. His adoptive parents, who had separated sometime prior to his death, are the parties to this appeal. Approximately seven months after Richard's death, his mother, appellant Sally Reed, filed a petition in the Probate Court of Ada County, seeking appointment as administratrix of her son's estate. Prior to the date set for a hearing on the mother's petition, appellee Cecil Reed, the father of the decedent, filed a competing petition seeking to have himself appointed administrator of the son's estate. The probate court held a joint hearing on the two petitions and thereafter ordered that letters of administration be issued to appellee Cecil Reed upon his taking the oath and filing the bond required by law. The court treated §15-312 and §15-314 of the Idaho Code as the controlling statutes and read those sections as compelling a preference for Cecil Reed because he was a male.

Section 15-312 designates the persons who are entitled to administer the estate of one who dies intestate. In making these designations, that section lists 11 classes of persons who are so entitled and provides, in substance, that the order in which those classes are listed in the section shall be determinative of the relative rights of competing applicants for letters of administration. One of the 11 classes so enumerated is "[t]he father or mother" of the person dying intestate. Under this section, the appellant and appellee, being members of the same entitlement class, would seem to have been equally entitled to administer their son's estate. Section 15-314 provides, however, that

[o]*f several persons claiming and equally entitled [under §15-312] to administer, males must be preferred to females, and relatives of the whole to those of the half blood.*

In issuing its order, the probate court implicitly recognized the equality of entitlement of the two applicants under §15-312 and noted that neither of the applicants was under any legal disability; the court ruled, however, that appellee, being a male, was to be preferred to the female appellant "by reason of Section 15-314 of the Idaho Code." In stating this conclusion, the probate judge gave no indication that he had attempted to determine the relative capabilities of the competing applicants to perform the functions incident to the administration of an estate. It seems clear the probate judge considered himself bound by statute to give preference to the male candidate over the female, each being otherwise "equally entitled."

Sally Reed appealed from the probate court order, and her appeal was treated by the District Court of the Fourth Judicial District of Idaho as a constitutional attack on §15-314. In dealing with the attack, that court held that the challenged section violated the Equal Protection Clause of the Fourteenth Amendment and was, therefore, void; the matter was ordered "returned to the Probate Court for its determination of which of the

two parties" was better qualified to administer the estate.

This order was never carried out, however, for Cecil Reed took a further appeal to the Idaho Supreme Court, which reversed the District Court and reinstated the original order naming the father administrator of the estate. In reaching this result, the Idaho Supreme Court first dealt with the governing statutory law and held that under §15-312 "a father and mother are 'equally entitled' to letters of administration," but the preference given to males by §15-314 is "mandatory" and leaves no room for the exercise of a probate court's discretion in the appointment of administrators. Having thus definitively and authoritatively interpreted the statutory provisions involved, the Idaho Supreme Court then proceeded to examine, and reject, Sally Reed's contention that §15-314 violates the Equal Protection Clause by giving a mandatory preference to males over females, without regard to their individual qualifications as potential estate administrators. . . .

Sally Reed thereupon appealed for review by this Court . . . and we noted probable jurisdiction. . . . Having examined the record and considered the briefs and oral arguments of the parties, we have concluded that the arbitrary preference established in favor of males by §15-314 of the Idaho Code cannot stand in the face of the Fourteenth Amendment's command that no State deny the equal protection of the laws to any person within its jurisdiction.

Idaho does not, of course, deny letters of administration to women altogether. Indeed, under §15-312, a woman whose spouse dies intestate has a preference over a son, father, brother, or any other male relative of the decedent. Moreover, we can judicially notice that in this country, presumably due to the greater longevity of women, a large proportion of estates, both intestate and under wills of decedents, are administered by surviving widows.

Section 15-314 is restricted in its operation to those situations where competing applications for letters of administration have been filed by both male and female members of the same entitlement class established by §15-312. In such situations, §15-314 provides that different treatment be accorded to the applicants on the basis of their sex; it thus establishes a classification subject to scrutiny under the Equal Protection Clause.

In applying that clause, this Court has consistently recognized that the Fourteenth Amendment does not deny to States the power to treat different classes of persons in different ways. . . . The Equal Protection Clause of that Amendment does, however, deny to States the power to legislate that different treatment be accorded to persons placed by a statute into different classes on the basis of criteria wholly unrelated to the objective of that statute. A classification "must be reasonable, not arbitrary, and must rest upon some ground of difference having a fair and substantial relation to the object of the legislation, so that all persons similarly circumstanced shall be treated alike." *Royster Guano Co.* v. *Virginia* . . . (1920). The question presented by this case, then, is whether a difference in the sex of competing applicants for letters of administration bears a rational relationship to a state objective that is sought to be advanced by the operation of §15-312 and 15-314.

In upholding the latter section, the Idaho Supreme Court concluded that its objective was to eliminate one area of controversy when two or more persons, equally entitled under §15-312, seek letters of administration and thereby present the probate court "with the issue of which one should be named." The court also concluded that where such persons are not of the same sex, the elimination of females from consideration "is neither an illogical nor arbitrary method devised by the legislature to resolve an issue that would otherwise require a hearing as to the relative merits . . . of the two or more petitioning relatives. . . ."

Clearly the objective of reducing the workload on probate courts by eliminating one class of contests is not without some legitimacy. The crucial question, however, is whether §15-314 advances that objective in a manner consistent with the command of the Equal Protection Clause. We hold that it does not. To give a mandatory preference to members of either sex over members of the other, merely to accomplish the elimination of hearings on the merits is to make the very kind of arbitrary legislative choice forbidden by the Equal Protection Clause of the Fourteenth Amendment; and whatever may be said as to the positive values of avoiding intrafamily controversy, the choice in this context may not lawfully be mandated solely on the basis of sex.

We note that if §15-314 is viewed merely as a modifying appendate to §15-312 and as aimed at the same objective, its constitutionality is not thereby saved. The objective of §15-312 clearly is to establish degrees of entitlement of various classes of persons in accordance with their varying degrees and kinds of relationship to the intestate. Regardless of their sex, persons within any one of the enumerated classes of that section are similarly situated with respect to that objective. By providing dissimilar treatment for men and women who are thus similarly situated, the challenged section violates the Equal Protection Clause. . . .

The judgment of the Idaho Supreme Court is reversed and the case remanded for further proceedings not inconsistent with this opinion.

Reversed and remanded.

(2) Frontiero v. Richardson (1973)

+Burger, Douglas, Brennan, Stewart, White, Marshall, Blackmun, Powell

−Rehnquist

[Sharon Frontiero, a married air force officer, sought additional "dependents' benefits" for her husband. The statutes provided that spouses of male personnel were automatically entitled to such benefits, but spouses of female personnel were entitled only if they were in fact dependent on their wives for more than one-half of their support. Frontiero's application was denied, and she brought suit in the federal district court. That court rejected her claim to denial of due process, based on the conclusion that it was reasonable for Congress to assume that the husband is typically the "breadwinner" and the wife typically the dependent spouse. The case was appealed directly to the Supreme Court.]

MR. JUSTICE BRENNAN ANNOUNCED THE JUDGMENT OF THE COURT AND AN OPINION IN WHICH MR. JUSTICE DOUGLAS, MR. JUSTICE WHITE, AND MR. JUSTICE MARSHALL JOIN.

. . .

At the outset, appellants contend that classifications based upon sex, like classifications based upon race, alienage, and national origin, are inherently suspect and must therefore be subjected to close judicial scrutiny. We agree and, indeed, find at least implicit support for such an approach in our unanimous decision only last Term in *Reed* v. *Reed*, . . .

The Court noted that the Idaho stat-

ute "provides that different treatment be accorded to the applicants on the basis of their sex; it thus establishes a classification subject to scrutiny under the Equal Protection Clause." . . . Under "traditional" equal protection analysis, a legislative classification must be sustained unless it is "patently arbitrary" and bears no rational relationship to a legitimate governmental interest. . . .

In an effort to meet this standard, appellee contended that the statutory scheme was a reasonable measure designed to reduce the workload on probate courts by eliminating one class of contests. Moreover, appellee argued that the mandatory preference for male applicants was in itself reasonable since "men [are] as a rule more conversant with business affairs than . . . women." Indeed, appellee maintained that "it is a matter of common knowledge, that women still are not engaged in politics, the professions, business or industry to the extent that men are." And the Idaho Supreme Court, in upholding the constitutionality of this statute, suggested that the Idaho Legislature might reasonably have "concluded that in general men are better qualified to act as an administrator than are women."

Despite these contentions, however, the Court held the statutory preference for male applicants unconstitutional. In reaching this result, the Court implicitly rejected appellee's apparently rational explanation of the statutory scheme, and concluded that, by ignoring the individual qualifications of particular applicants, the challenged statute provided "dissimilar treatment for men and women who are . . . similarly situated." . . . The Court therefore held that, even though the State's interest in achieving administrative efficiency "is not without some legitimacy," "[t]o give a mandatory preference to members of either sex over members of the other merely to accomplish the elimination of hearings on the merits, is to make the very kind of arbitrary legislative choice forbidden by the [Constitution]. . . ." This departure from "traditional" rational basis analysis with respect to sex-based classifications is clearly justified.

There can be no doubt that our Nation has had a long and unfortunate history of sex discrimination. Traditionally, such discrimination was rationalized by an attitude of "romantic paternalism" which, in practical effect, put women not on a pedestal, but in a cage. . . .

. . . Our statute books gradually became laden with gross, stereotypical distinctions between the sexes and, indeed, throughout much of the 19th century the position of women in our society was, in many respects, comparable to that of blacks under the pre–Civil War slave codes. Neither slaves nor women could hold office, serve on juries, or bring suit in their own names, and married women traditionally were denied the legal capacity to hold or convey property or to serve as legal guardians of their own children. . . . And although blacks were guaranteed the right to vote in 1870, women were denied even that right—which is itself "preservative of other basic civil and political rights"—until adoption of the Nineteenth Amendment half a century later.

It is true, of course, that the position of women in America has improved markedly in recent decades. Nevertheless, it can hardly be doubted that, in part because of the high visibility of the sex characteristic, women still face pervasive, although at times more subtle, discrimination in our education institu-tions, on the job market and, perhaps most conspicuously, in the political arena. . . .

Moreover, since sex, like race and national origin, is an immutable characteristic determined solely by the accident of birth, the imposition of special disabilities upon the members of a particular sex because of their sex would seem to violate "the basic concept of our system that legal burdens should bear some relationship to individual responsibility . . . ." *Weber* v. *Aetna Casualty & Surety Co.* . . . (1972). And what differentiates sex from such nonsuspect statuses as intelligence or physical disability, and aligns it with the recognized suspect criteria, is that the sex characteristic frequently bears no relation to ability to perform or contribute to society. As a result, statutory distinctions between the sexes often have the effect of invidiously relegating the entire class of females to inferior legal status without regard to the actual capabilities of its individual members.

We might also note that, over the past decade, Congress has itself manifested an increasing sensitivity to sex-based classifications. In Title VII of the Civil Rights Act of 1964, for example, Congress expressly declared that no employer, labor union, or other organization subject to the provisions of the Act shall discriminate against any individual on the basis of "race, color, religion, *sex*, or national origin." Similarly, the Equal Pay Act of 1963 provides that no employer covered by the Act "shall discriminate . . . between employees on the basis of *sex*." And §1 of the Equal Rights Amendment, passed by Congress on March 22, 1972, and submitted to the legislatures of the States for ratification, declares that "[e]quality of rights under the law shall not be denied or abridged by the

United States or by any State on account of sex." Thus, Congress has itself concluded that classifications based upon sex are inherently invidious, and this conclusion of a coequal branch of Government is not without significance to the question presently under consideration. . . .

With these considerations in mind, we can only conclude that classifications based upon sex, like classifications based upon race, alienage, or national origin, are inherently suspect, and must therefore be subjected to strict judicial scrutiny. Applying the analysis mandated by that stricter standard of review, it is clear that the statutory scheme now before us is constitutionally invalid.

The sole basis of the classification established in the challenged statutes is the sex of the individuals involved. . . .

Moreover, the Government concedes that the differential treatment accorded men and women under these statutes serves no purpose other than mere "administrative convenience." In essence, the Government maintains that, as an empirical matter, wives in our society frequently are dependent upon their husbands, while husbands rarely are dependent upon their wives. Thus, the Government argues that Congress might reasonably have concluded that it would be both cheaper and easier simply conclusively to presume that wives of male members are financially dependent upon their husbands, while burdening female members with the task of establishing dependency in fact.

The Government offers no concrete evidence, however, tending to support its view that such differential treatment in fact saves the Government any money. In order to satisfy the demands of strict judicial scrutiny the Government must dem-

onstrate, for example, that it is actually cheaper to grant increased benefits with respect to *all* male members, than it is to determine which male members are in fact entitled to such benefits and to grant increased benefits only to those members whose wives actually meet the dependency requirement. Here, however, there is substantial evidence that, if put to the test, many of the wives of male members would fail to qualify for benefits. And in light of the fact that the dependency determination with respect to the husbands of female members is presently made solely on the basis of affidavits, rather than through the more costly hearing process, the Government's explanation of the statutory scheme is, to say the least, questionable.

In any case, our prior decisions make clear that, although efficacious administration of governmental programs is not without some importance, "the Constitution recognizes higher values than speed and efficiency." *Stanley* v. *Illinois*, . . . (1972). And when we enter the realm of "strict judicial scrutiny," there can be no doubt that "administrative convenience" is not a shibboleth, the mere recitation of which dictates constitutionality. See *Shapiro* v. *Thompson*. . . . (1969) . . . On the contrary, any statutory scheme which draws a sharp line between the sexes, *solely* for the purpose of achieving administrative convenience, necessarily commands "dissimilar treatment for men and women who are . . . similarly situated," and therefore involves the "very kind of arbitrary legislative choice forbidden by the [Constitution]. . . ." *Reed* v. *Reed*. . . . We therefore conclude that, by according differential treatment to male and female members of the uniformed services for the sole purpose of achieving administrative convenience, the challenged statutes violate the Due Process Clause of the Fifth Amendment insofar as they require a female member to prove the dependency of her husband.

Reversed.

MR. JUSTICE STEWART concurs in the judgment, agreeing that the statutes before us work an invidious discrimination in violation of the Constitution. *Reed* v. *Reed,. . . .*

MR. JUSTICE POWELL, WITH WHOM THE CHIEF JUSTICE AND MR. JUSTICE BLACKMUN JOIN, CONCURRING IN THE JUDGMENT.

I agree that the challenge statutes constitute an unconstitutional discrimination against service women in violation of the Due Process Clause of the Fifth Amendment, but I cannot join the opinion of Mr. Justice Brennan, which would hold that all classifications based upon sex, "like classification based upon race, alienage, and national origin," are "inherently suspect and must therefore be subjected to close judicial scrutiny." It is unnecessary for the Court in this case to characterize sex as a suspect classification, with all of the far-reaching implications of such a holding. *Reed* v. *Reed* (1971), which abundantly supports our decision today, did not add sex to the narrowly limited group of classifications which are inherently suspect. In my view, we can and should decide this case on the authority of *Reed* and reserve for the future any expansion of its rationale.

There is another and I find compelling, reason for deferring a general categorizing of sex classifications as invoking the strictest test of judicial scrutiny. The Equal Rights Amendment, which if adopted will resolve the substance of this precise question, has been approved by the Congress and submitted for ratification by the States. If this Amendment is duly adopted, it will represent the will of the people accomplished in the manner prescribed by the Constitution. By acting prematurely and unnecessarily, as I view it, the Court has assumed a decisional responsibility at the very time when state legislatures, functioning within the traditional democratic process, are debating the proposed Amendment. It seems to me that this reaching out to pre-empt by judicial action a major political decision which is currently in process of resolution does not reflect appropriate respect for duly prescribed legislative processes.

There are times when this Court, under our system, cannot avoid a constitutional decision on issues which normally should be resolved by the elected representatives of the people. But democratic institutions are weakened, and confidence in the restraint of the Court is impaired, when we appear unnecessarily to decide sensitive issues of broad social and political importance at the very time they are under consideration within the prescribed constitutional processes.

(3) Weinberger v. Wiesenfeld (1975)

+Burger, Brennan, Stewart, White, Marshall, Blackmun, Powell, Rehnquist

NP Douglas

[Under the Social Security Act, survivor's benefits are paid to both the widow and children of a husband and father covered by the act. But benefits are payable only to the minor children, and not to the widower, of a wife and mother covered by the act. Wiesenfeld's wife died in childbirth. She had been employed as a teacher for five years before their marriage, and she continued teaching afterwards. Her salary was the principal source of financial support for the couple. Social security contributions were deducted from *her* earnings.

After her death he elected to devote substantial time to child-care duties and worked only sporadically. He applied for, and received, monthly benefits for his son, but his application for survivor's benefits for himself was rejected. He filed suit in the federal district court in New Jersey, claiming that in denying him survivor's benefits the act was unconstitutionally differentiating between men and women. A three-judge court ruled in Wiesenfeld's favor, and the government appealed to the Supreme Court.]

MR. JUSTICE BRENNAN delivered the opinion of the Court.

. . .

The gender-based distinction made by §402(g) is indistinguishable from that invalidated in *Frontiero* v. *Richardson*. . . . (1973). *Frontiero* involved statutes which provided the wife of a male serviceman with dependents' benefits but not the husband of a servicewomen unless she proved that she supplied more than one-half of her husband's support. The Court held that the statutory scheme violated the right to equal protection secured by the Fifth Amendment. . . . In . . . *Frontiero* the challenged [classification] based on sex [was] premised on overbroad generalizations that could not be tolerated under the Constitution. . . . [T]he assumption . . . was that female spouses of servicemen would normally be dependent upon their husbands, while male spouses of servicewomen would not. . . . A virtually identical "archaic and overbroad" generalization, . . . "not . . . tolerated under the Constitution" underlies the distinction drawn by §402(g), namely, that male workers' earnings are vital to the support of their families, while the earnings of female wage-earners do not significantly contribute to their families' support.

Section 402(g) was added to the Social Security Act in 1939 as one of a large number of amendments designed to "afford more adequate protection to the family as a unit." . . . Monthly benefits were provided to wives, children, widows, orphans, and surviving dependent parents of covered workers. However, children of covered women workers were eligible for survivors' benefits only in limited circumstances, . . . and no benefits whatever were made available to husbands or widowers on the basis of their wives' covered employment.

Underlying the 1939 scheme was the principle that "under a social-insurance plan, the primary purpose is to pay benefits in accordance with the probable needs of beneficiaries rather than to make payments to the estate of a deceased person regardless of whether or not he leaves dependents." . . . It was felt that "[t]he payment of these survivorship benefits and supplements for the wife of an annuitant are . . . in keeping with the principle of social insurance. . . ." Thus, the framers of the Act legislated on the "then generally accepted presumption that a man is responsible for the support of his wife and child." . . .

Obviously, the notion that men are more likely than women to be the primary supporters of their spouses and children is not entirely without empirical support. See *Kahn* v. *Shevin* . . . (1974). But such a gender-based generalization cannot suffice to justify the denigration of the efforts of women who do work and whose earnings contribute significantly to their families' support.

Section 402(g) clearly operates, as did the statutes invalidated by our judgment in *Frontiero*, to deprive women of protection for their families which men receive as a result of their employment. Indeed, the classification here is in some ways more pernicious. First, it was open to the servicewomen under the statutes invalidated in *Frontiero* to prove that her husband was in fact dependent upon her. Here, Stephen Wiesenfeld was not given the opportunity to show, as may well have been the case, that he was dependent upon his wife for his support, or that, had his wife lived, she would have remained at work while he took over care of the child. Second, in this case social security taxes were deducted from Paula's salary during the years in which she worked. Thus, she not only failed to receive for her family the same protection which a similarly situated male worker would have received, but she also was deprived of a portion of her own earnings in order to contribute to the fund out of which benefits would be paid to others. Since the Constitution forbids the gender-based differentiation premised upon assumptions as to dependency made in the statutes before us in *Frontiero,* the Constitution also forbids the gender-based differentiation that results in the efforts of women workers required to pay social security taxes producing less protection for their families than is produced by the efforts of men.

The Government seeks to avoid this conclusion with two related arguments. First, it claims that because social security benefits are not compensation for work done. Congress is not obliged to provide a covered female employee with the same benefits as it provides to a male. Second, it contends that §402(g) was "reasonably designed to offset the adverse economic situation of women by providing a widow with financial assistance to supplement or substitute for her own efforts in the marketplace," . . . and therefore does not contravene the equal protection guarantee.

Appellant relies for the first proposition primarily on *Flemming* v. *Nestor . . .* (1960). We held in *Flemming* that the interest of a covered employee in future social security benefits is "noncontractual," because "each worker's benefits, though flowing from the contributions he made to the national economy while actively employed, are not dependent upon the degree to which he was called upon to support the system by taxation." . . . The Government apparently contends that since benefits derived from the social security program do not correlate necessarily with contributions made to the program, a covered employee has no right whatever to be treated equally with other employees as regards the benefits which flow from his or her employment.

We do not see how the fact that social security benefits are "noncontractual" can sanction differential protection for covered employees which is solely gender-based. From the outset, social security old age, disability, and survivors' (OASDI) benefits have been "afforded as a matter of right, related to past participation in the productive processes of the country.". . . It is true that social security benefits are not necessarily related directly to tax contributions, since the OASDI system is structured to provide benefits in part according to presumed need. For this reason, *Flemming* held that the position of a covered employee "cannot be soundly analogized to that of the holder of an annuity, whose right to benefits is bottomed on contractual payments." . . . But the fact remains that the statutory right to benefits is directly related to years worked and amount earned by a covered employee, and not to the need of the beneficiaries directly. Since OASDI benefits do depend significantly upon the participation in the work force of a covered employee, and since only covered employees and not others are required to pay taxes toward the system, benefits must be distributed according to classifications which do not without sufficient justification differentiate among covered employees solely on the basis of sex.

The Government seems to characterize the classification here as one reasonably designed to compensate women beneficiaries as a group for the economic difficulties which still confront women who seek to support themselves and their families. The Court held in *Kahn* v. *Shevin*, . . . that a statute "reasonably designed to further a state policy of cushioning the financial impact of spousal loss upon that sex for which that loss imposes a disproportionately heavy burden" can survive an equal protection attack. . . . But the mere recitation of a benign, compensatory purpose is not an automatic shield which protects against any inquiry into the actual purposes underlying a statutory scheme. Here, it is apparent both from the statutory scheme itself and from the legislative history of §402(g) that Congress' purpose in providing benefits to young widows with children was not to provide an income to women who were, because of economic discrimination, unable to provide for themselves. Rather, §402(g), linked as it is directly to responsibility for minor children, was intended to permit women to elect not to work and to devote themselves to the care of children. Since this purpose in no way is premised upon any special disadvantages of women, it cannot serve to justify a gender-based distinction which diminishes the protection afforded to women who do work.

That the purpose behind §402(g) is to provide children deprived of one parent with the opportunity for the personal attention of the other could not be more clear in the legislative history. . . .

Given the purpose of enabling the surviving parent to remain at home to care for a child, the gender-based distinction of §402(g) is entirely irrational. The classification discriminates among surviving children solely on the basis of the sex of the surviving parent. Even in the typical family hypothesized by the Act, in which the mother is caring for the children, this result makes no sense. The fact that a man is working while there is a wife at home does not mean that he would, or should be required to, continue to work if his wife dies. It is no less important for a child to be cared for by its sole surviving parent when that parent is male rather than female. And a father, no less than a mother, has a constitutionally protected right to the "companionship, care, custody, and management" of "the children he has sired and raised, [which] undeniably warrants deference and, absent a powerful countervailing interest, protection." *Stanley* v. *Illinois* . . . (1972). Further, to the extent that women who work when they have sole responsibility for children encounter special problems, it would seem that men with sole responsibility for children will encounter the same childcare related problems. Stephen Wiesenfeld, for example, found that providing adequate care for his infant son impeded his ability to work, . . .

Since the gender-based classification of §402(g) cannot be explained as an attempt to provide for the special problems of women, it is indistinguishable from the classification held invalid in *Frontiero*. . . .

MR. JUSTICE POWELL, WITH WHOM THE CHIEF JUSTICE JOINS, CONCURRING (OMITTED).
MR. JUSTICE REHNQUIST, CONCURRING IN THE RESULT (OMITTED).

[Out of the *Reed*, *Frontiero*, and *Wiesenfeld* cases emerges a strong judicial antipathy to the perpetuation of gender stereotypes that now seem archaic, in particular the assumption in the latter cases that wives are dependent on their husbands for economic support and that wives have primary responsibilities for child care. In *Califano* v. *Goldfarb* (1977), the Court, by a 5–4 vote, struck down another provision of the Social Security Act premised on the same assumptions. The act provided that widows automatically receive survivor's benefits based on their husband's earnings. But widowers received such benefits only when they had been more than one-half dependent for support on their wives.

However, there have also been some cases in which gender-based distinctions have been upheld, usually because the law in question has attempted to compensate women for past discrimination and hardship. But the line between the two sets of cases is often difficult to perceive. Three cases are illustrative. In *Kahn* v. *Shevin* (1974), the Supreme Court approved the validity of a Florida statute, dating back to 1885, that conferred a $500 property tax exemption on widows but not on widowers.

Justice Douglas, writing for a 6–3 majority, held that this was a reasonable remedial statute to rectify a well-known and documented disparity between the earnings of men and women. Widowers frequently can continue working, Douglas observed, but widows are often forced to enter the job market at a very late date. He distinguished *Frontiero,* in which he had joined the plurality opinion declaring sex to be a suspect classification, because in that case the *sole* reason for governmental denial of equal benefits to the dependents of female military personnel was administrative convenience. In rejecting the test of strict scrutiny, Douglas observed, in a footnote, that

gender has never been rejected as an impermissible classification in all instances. Congress has not so far drafted women into the Armed Services. . . . The famous Brandeis Brief in Muller *v.* Oregon *. . ., on which the court specifically relied . . . emphasized that the special physical organization of women has a bearing on the "conditions under which she should be permitted to toil."*

Douglas also argued that since this was a tax law the Court must show a special solicitude.

The benign classification of this statute was an insufficient basis for judicial intervention in the most basic power of a state.

The three justices who had joined with Douglas in *Frontiero*—Brennan, White, and Marshall—dissented. They argued that all gender-based classifications are suspect and require the government to meet the "compelling interest" test. The objectives of this statute, the dissenters wrote, meet that test. In other words, for them, this was an acceptable "ameliorative" classification. But, they said, the statute is invalid because it is overinclusive. The same legitimate interests could have been served with a more narrowly drawn statute—presumably one that benefited only needy widows. Of course, that would not have satisfied Mr. Kahn, who would not have received the tax exemption.

A second case was *Schlesinger* v. *Ballard* (1975). Ballard was a male naval officer who had been passed over for promotion twice and discharged after nine years of service. In challenging the navy's promotion system, he noted that female officers operated under a different set of rules. They were given a minimum of thirteen years tenure before they could be discharged for lack of promotion. Writing for a 5–4 majority, Justice Stewart, applying an ordinary scrutiny test, held that Congress could rationally conclude that women officers, who were excluded from combat and sea duty [a policy no longer in effect—Ed.] had fewer opportunities for promotion. *Reed* and *Frontiero* were distinguished because this was an attempt to *equalize* the situation between male and female officers. Justices Brennan, Douglas, White, and Marshall dissented. Brennan argued that this was not really a benign statute (which might have been justified). Furthermore, he argued, following his dissent in *Kahn,* even if it was benign, it should be invalidated because the "means" were faulty. Instead of compensating women through the promotional system, it was better to rectify the disadvantages that led to unequal promotional opportunities.

Finally, in *Califano* v. *Webster* (1977), the Court unanimously *upheld* another provision of the Social Security Act which favored retired female wage earners over male wage earners in the computation of monthly old-age benefits. Women were permitted to exclude three more low-income years than men in computing their "average monthly wage." The Court held that this was a permissible remedy for past salary discrimination against women workers.]

(4) Craig v. Boren (1976)

+Brennan, Stewart, White, Marshall, Blackmun, Powell, Stevens
−Burger, Rehnquist

[Oklahoma prohibited the sale of 3.2 percent beer to males under the age of twenty-one and to females under the age of eighteen. Craig, a male between eighteen and twenty-one, and Whitener, a licensed vendor, sought a declaratory judgment and injunctive relief in the federal district court. They argued that this gender-based discrimination constituted invidious discrimination and thus violated the equal protection clause. The three-judge court denied their claim, and they appealed to the Supreme Court. Craig turned twenty-one before the case came to the Supreme Court, and his claim was therefore dismissed as moot. However, a majority of the Court held that Whitener had an independent claim against enforcement of the statute, had suffered real economic injury, and had standing to sue.]

MR. JUSTICE BRENNAN delivered the opinion of the Court.

. . .

Before 1971, Oklahoma defined the commencement of civil majority at age 18 for females and age 21 for males. In contrast, females were held criminally responsible as adults at age 18 and males at age 16. After the Court of Appeals for the Tenth Circuit held in 1972, on the authority of *Reed* v. *Reed,* (1971), that the age distinction was unconstitutional for purposes of establishing criminal responsibility as adults, . . . the Oklahoma Legislature fixed age 18 as applicable to both males and females. . . . In 1972, 18 also was established as the age of majority for males and females in civil matters except that §241 and 245 of the 3.2 beer statute were simultaneously codified to create an exception to the gender-free rule.

Analysis may appropriately begin with the reminder that *Reed* v. *Reed,* emphasized that statutory classifications that distinguish between males and females are "subject to scrutiny under the Equal Protection Clause." . . . To withstand constitutional challenge, previous cases establish that classifications by gender must serve important governmental objectives and must be substantially related to achievement of those objectives. Thus, in *Reed,* the objectives of "reducing the workload on probate courts," . . . and "avoiding intrafamily controversy," . . . were deemed of insufficient importance to sustain use of an overt gender criterion in the appointment of intestate administrators. Decisions following *Reed* similarly have rejected administrative ease and convenience as sufficiently important objectives to justify gender-based classifications. See, e.g., *Stanley* v. *Illinois* . . . (1972); *Frontiero* v. *Richardson* (1973). And only two Terms ago, *Stanton* v. *Stanton* (1975), expressly stating that *Reed* v. *Reed* was "controlling," held that *Reed* required invalidation of a Utah differential age-of-majority statute, notwithstanding the statute's coincidence with and furtherance of the State's purpose of fostering "old notions" of role-typing and preparing boys for their expected performance in the economic and political worlds. . . .

In this case, too, "*Reed* we feel is controlling . . .". We turn then to the question whether, under *Reed,* the difference between males and females with respect to the purchase of 3.2% beer warrants the differential in age drawn by the Oklahoma statute. We conclude that it does not.

We accept for purposes of discussion the District Court's identification of the objective underlying §241 and 245 as the enhancement of traffic safety. Clearly, the protection of public health and safety represents an important function of state and local governments. However, appellees' statistics in our view cannot support the conclusion that the gender-based distinction closely serves to achieve that objective and therefore the distinction cannot under *Reed* withstand equal protection challenge.

The appellees introduced a variety of statistical surveys. First, an analysis of arrest statistics for 1973 demonstrated that 18–20-year-old male arrests for "driving under the influence" and "drunkenness" substantially exceeded female arrests for that same age period. Similarly, youths aged 17–21 were found to be overrepresented among those killed or injured in traffic accidents, with males again numerically exceeding females in this regard. Third, a random roadside survey in Oklahoma City revealed that young males were more inclined to drive and drink beer than were their female counterparts. Fourth, Federal Bureau of Investigation nationwide statistics exhibited a notable increase in arrests for "driving under the influence." Finally, statistical evidence gathered in other jurisdictions, particularly Minnesota and Michigan, was offered to corroborate Oklahoma's experience by indicating the pervasiveness of youthful participation in motor vehicle accidents following the imbibing of alcohol. Conceding that "the case is not free from doubt," the District Court nonetheless concluded that this statistical showing substantiated "a rational basis for the legislative judgment underlying the challenged classification." . . .

Even were this statistical evidence accepted as accurate, it nevertheless offers only a weak answer to the equal protection question presented here. The most focused and relevant of the statistical surveys, arrests of 18–20-year-olds for alcohol-related driving offenses, exemplifies the ultimate unpersuasiveness of this evidentiary record. Viewed in terms of the correlation between sex and the actual activity that Oklahoma seeks to regulate—driving while under the influence of alcohol—the statistics broadly establish that .18% of females and 2% of males in that age group were arrested for that offense. While such a disparity is not trivial in a statistical sense, it hardly can form the basis for employment of a gender line as a classifying device. Certainly if maleness is to serve as a proxy for drinking and driving, a correlation of 2% must be considered an unduly tenuous "fit." Indeed, prior cases have consistently rejected the use of sex as a decision-making factor even though the statutes in question certainly rested on far more predictive empirical relationships than this.

Moreover, the statistics exhibit a variety of other shortcomings that seriously impugn their value to equal protection analysis. Setting aside the obvious methodological problems, the surveys do not adequately justify the salient features of Oklahoma's gender-based traffic-safety law. None purports to measure the use and dangerousness of 3.2% beer as opposed to alcohol generally, a detail that is of particular importance since, in light of its low alcohol level, Oklahoma apparently considers the 3.2% beverage to be "nonintoxicating." . . . Moreover, many of the studies, while graphically documenting the unfortunate increase in driving while under the influence of alcohol, make no effort to relate their findings to age-sex differentials as involved here. Indeed, the only survey that explicitly centered its attention upon young drivers and their use of beer—albeit apparently not of the diluted 3.2% variety—reached results that hardly can be viewed as impressive in justifying either a gender or age classification.

There is no reason to belabor this line of analysis. It is unrealistic to expect either members of the judiciary or state officials to be well versed in the rigors of experimental or statistical technique. But this merely illustrates that proving broad sociological propositions by statistics is a dubious business, and one that inevitably is in tension with the normative philosophy that underlies the Equal Protection Clause. Suffice to say that the showing offered by the appellees does not satisfy us that sex represents a legitimate, accurate proxy for the regulation of drinking and driving. In fact, when it is further recognized that Oklahoma's statute prohibits only the selling of 3.2% beer to young males and not their drinking the beverage once acquired (even after purchase by their 18–20-year-old female companions), the relationship between gender and traffic safety becomes far too tenuous to satisfy *Reed's* requirement that the gender-based difference be substantially related to achievement of the statutory objective.

We hold, therefore, that under *Reed*, Oklahoma's 3.2% beer statute invidiously discriminates against males 18–20 years of age.

Appellees argue, however, that §241 and 245 enforce state policies concerning the sale and distribution of alcohol and by force of the Twenty-first Amendment should therefore be held to withstand the equal protection challenge. The District Court's response to this contention is unclear. The Court assumed that the Twenty-first Amendment "strengthened" the State's police powers with respect to alcohol regulation, but then said that "the stan-

dards of review [that the Equal Protection Clause mandates] are not relaxed." . . . Our view is, and we hold, that the Twenty-first Amendment does not save the invidious gender-based discrimination from invalidation as a denial of Equal Protection of the Laws in violation of the Fourteenth Amendment. . . .

Once passing beyond consideration of the Commerce Clause, the relevance of the Twenty-first Amendment to other constitutional provisions becomes increasingly doubtful. As one commentator has remarked, "[n]either the text nor the history of the Twenty-first Amendment suggests that it qualifies individual rights protected by the Bill of Rights and the Fourteenth Amendment where the sale or use of liquor is concerned." P. Brest, *Processes of Constitutional Decisionmaking* (1975). Any departures from this historical view have been limited and sporadic. Two States successfully relied upon the Twenty-first Amendment to respond to challenges of major liquor importers to state authority to regulate the importation and manufacture of alcoholic beverages on Commerce Clause and Fourteenth Amendment grounds. . . . In fact, however, the arguments in both cases centered upon importation of intoxicants, a regulatory area where the State's authority under the Twenty-first Amendment is transparently clear, *Hostetter* v. *Idlewild Bon Voyage Liquor Corp* . . . and touched upon purely economic matters that traditionally merit only the mildest review under the Fourteenth Amendment, . . . Cases involving individual rights protected by the Due Process Clause have been treated in sharp contrast. For example, when an individual objected to the mandatory "posting" of her name in retail liquor establishments and her characterization as an "excessive drink[er]," the Twenty-first Amendment was held not to qualify the scope of her due process rights. *Wisconsin* v. *Constantineau* . . . (1971).

It is true that *California* v. *LaRue*, (1972), relied upon the Twenty-first Amendment to "strengthen" the State's authority to regulate live entertainment at establishments licensed to dispense liquor, at least when the performances "partake more of gross sexuality than of communication," . . . Nevertheless, the Court has never recognized sufficient "strength" in the Amendment to defeat an otherwise established claim of invidious discrimination in violation of the Equal Protection Clause. Rather, *Moose Lodge No. 107* v. *Irvis* . . . (1972), establishes that state liquor regulatory schemes cannot work invidious discriminations that violate the Equal Protection Clause.
. . .

In sum, the principles embodied in the Equal Protection Clause are not to be rendered inapplicable by statistically measured but loose-fitting generalities concerning the drinking tendencies of aggregate groups. We thus hold that the operation of the Twenty-first Amendment does not alter the application of equal protection standards that otherwise govern this case. . . .

MR. JUSTICE POWELL, CONCURRING. (OMITTED).
MR. JUSTICE STEVENS, CONCURRING (OMITTED).
MR. JUSTICE BLACKMUN, CONCURRING IN PART (OMITTED).
MR. JUSTICE STEWART, CONCURRING IN THE JUDGMENT (OMITTED).
MR. JUSTICE BURGER, DISSENTING (OMITTED).

MR. JUSTICE REHNQUIST, DISSENTING.

The Court's disposition of this case is objectionable on two grounds. First is its conclusion that *men* challeng-

ing a gender-based statute which treats them less favorably than women may invoke a more stringent standard of judicial review than pertains to most other types of classifications. Second is the Court's enunciation of this standard, without citation to any source, as being that "classifications by gender must serve important governmental objectives and must be substantially related to achievement of those objectives." . . . The only redeeming feature of the Court's opinion, to my mind, is that it apparently signals a retreat by those who joined the plurality opinion in *Frontiero* v. *Richardson* . . . (1973), from their view that sex is a "suspect" classification for purposes of equal protection analysis. I think the Oklahoma statute challenged here need pass only the "rational basis" equal protection analysis . . . and I believe that it is constitutional under that analysis.

. . .

The Court's conclusion that a law which treats males less favorably than females "must serve important governmental objectives and must be substantially related to achievement of those objectives" apparently comes out of thin air. The Equal Protection Clause contains no such language, and none of our previous cases adopt that standard. I would think we have had enough difficulty with the two standards of review which our cases have recognized—the norm of "rational basis," and the "compelling state interest" required where a "suspect classification" is involved—so as to counsel weightily against the insertion of still another "standard" between those two. How is this Court to divine what objectives are important? How is it to determine whether a particular law is "substantially" related to the achievement of such objective, rather than related in some other way to its achievement?

Both of the phrases used are so diaphanous and elastic as to invite subjective judicial preferences or prejudices relating to particular types of legislation, masquerading as judgments whether such legislation is directed at "important" objectives or whether the relationship to those objectives is "substantial" enough.

I would have thought that if this Court were to leave anything to decision by the popularly elected branches of the Government, where no constitutional claim other than that of equal protection is invoked, it would be the decision as to what governmental objectives to be achieved by law are "important," and which are not. As for the second part of the Court's new test, the Judicial Branch is probably in no worse position than the Legislative or Executive Branches to determine if there is *any* rational relationship between a classification and the purpose which it might be thought to serve. But the introduction of the adverb "substantially" requires courts to make subjective judgments as to operational effects, for which neither their expertise nor their access to data fits them. And even if we manage to avoid both confusion and the mirroring of our own preferences in the development of this new doctrine, the thousands of judges in other courts who must interpret the Equal Protection Clause may not be so fortunate.

. . .

The Court's criticism of the statistics relied on by the District Court conveys the impression that a legislature in enacting a new law is to be subjected to the judicial equivalent of a doctoral examination in statistics. Legislatures are not held to any rules of evidence such as those which may govern courts or other administrative bodies, and are entitled to draw factual conclusions on the basis of the

determination of probable cause which an arrest by a police officer normally represents. In this situation, they could reasonably infer that the incidence of drunk driving is a good deal higher than the incidence of arrest. . . .

The Oklahoma Legislature could have believed that 18–20-year-old males drive substantially more, and tend more often to be intoxicated than their female counterparts; that they prefer beer and admit to drinking and driving at a higher rate than females; and that they suffer traffic injuries out of proportion to the part they make up of the population. Under the appropriate rational basis test for equal protection, it is neither irrational nor arbitrary to bar them from making purchases of 3.2% beer, which purchases might in many cases be made by a young man who immediately returns to his vehicle with the beverage in his possession. The record does not give any good indication of the true proportion of males in the age group who drink and drive (except that it is no doubt greater than the 2% who are arrested), but whatever it may be I cannot see that the mere purchase right involved could conceivably raise a due process question. There being no violation of either equal protection or due process, the statute should accordingly be upheld.

(5) General Electric Co. v. Gilbert (1976)

+Burger, Stewart, White, Blackmun, Powell, Rehnquist
−Brennan, Marshall, Stevens

[General Electric Company provided to all employees a disability plan that compensated totally disabled workers for nonoccupational sickness and accidents. Disabilities (defined as the inability to work) related to pregnancy were excluded. Payments equaled 60 percent of an employee's normal weekly earnings and, beginning on the eighth day of disability, were in force for a maximum of twenty-six weeks.

Gilbert and others filed a class action suit challenging the exclusion of pregnancy-related disabilities from this program. They claimed that this exclusion violated their rights under Title VII of the Civil Rights Act of 1964. A federal district court ruled that General Electric, by excluding pregnancy-related disabilities, had engaged in sex discrimination. It found that normal pregnancy, while not necessarily either a "disease" or an "accident" was disabling for most women for six to eight weeks. It also found that 10 percent of pregnancies end in miscarriage, which is disabling, and that another 10 percent of pregnancies are complicated by disease, which results in additional disability. The court found that to include pregnancy-related disabilities in the plan would increase the costs of the plan, but it held that this could not excuse the sex discrimination. The Court of Appeals for the Fourth Circuit affirmed, and the Supreme Court granted certiorari.

Between the time of the district court's decision and the court of appeals decision, the Supreme Court decided the related case of *Geduldig* v. *Aiello* (1974). In that case, the Court upheld California's disability insurance plan for private employees that also excluded pregnancy. The Court, applying the test of ordinary scrutiny, found that exclusion of pregnancy was necessary to keep the costs of the program down to a manageable level and that this rationale met constitutional standards. Indeed, Justice Stewart, writing for the majority, held that this was not even a gender classification:

The California insurance program does not exclude anyone from benefit eligibility because of gender, but merely removes one physical condition–pregnancy–from the list of compensable disabilities. The program divides potential recipients into two groups–pregnant women and nonpregnant persons. While the first group is exclusively female, the second includes members of both sexes.]

MR. JUSTICE REHNQUIST delivered the opinion of the Court.

. . .

Section 703(a) (1) [of Title VII] provides in relevant part that it shall be an unlawful employment practice for an employer

. . . *to discriminate against any individual with respect to his compensation, terms, conditions, or privileges of employment, because of such individual's race, color, religion, sex, or national origin.* . . .

While there is no necessary inference that Congress, in choosing this language, intended to incorporate into Title VII the concepts of discrimination which have evolved from court decisions construing the Equal Protection Clause of the Fourteenth Amendment, the similarities between the congressional language and some of those decisions surely indicate that the latter are a useful starting point in interpreting the former. Particularly in the case of defining the term "discrimination," which Congress has nowhere in Title VII defined, those cases afforded an existing body of law analyzing and discussing that term in a legal context now wholly dissimilar from the concerns which Congress manifested in enacting Title VII. We think, therefore, that our decision in *Geduldig* v. *Aiello*, dealing with a strikingly similar disability plan, is quite relevant in determining whether or not the pregnancy exclusion did discriminate on the basis of sex. . . .

The Court of Appeals was therefore wrong in concluding that the reasoning of *Geduldig* was not applicable to an action under Title VII. Since it is a finding of sex-based discrimination that must trigger, in a case such as this, the finding of an unlawful employment practice . . . *Geduldig* is precisely in point in its holding that an exclusion of pregnancy from a disability benefits plan providing general coverage is not a gender-based discrimination at all.

There is no more showing in this case than there was in *Geduldig* that the exclusion of pregnancy benefits is a mere "pretext designed to effect an invidious discrimination against the members of one sex or another." . . . Pregnancy is of course confined to women, but it is in other ways significantly different from the typical covered disease or disability. The District Court found that it is not a "disease" at all, and is often a voluntarily undertaken and desired condition. . . . We do not therefore infer that the exclusion of pregnancy disability benefits from petitioner's plan is a simple pretext for discriminating against women. The contrary arguments adopted by the lower courts and expounded by our dissenting brethren were largely rejected in *Geduldig*.

The instant suit was grounded on Title VII rather than the Equal Protection Clause, and our cases recognized that a prima facie violation of Title VII can be established in some circumstances upon proof that the effect of an otherwise facially neutral plan or classification is to discriminate against members of one class or another. See *Washington* v. *Davis* . . . (1976). For example, in the context of a challenge, . . . to a facially neutral employment test, this Court held that a prima facie case of discrimination would be established if, even absent proof of intent, the consequences of the test were "invidiously to discriminate on the basis of racial or other impermissible classification," *Griggs* v. *Duke Power Co.* . . . (1971). . . .

As in *Geduldig*, respondents have not attempted to meet the burden of demonstrating a gender-based dis-

criminatory effect resulting from the exclusion of pregnancy-related disabilities from coverage. Whatever the ultimate probative value of the evidence introduced before the District Court on this subject in the instant case, at the very least it tended to illustrate that the selection of risks covered by the Plan did not operate, in fact, to discriminate against women. As in *Geduldig*, we start from the indisputable baseline that "[t]he fiscal and actuarial benefits of the program . . . accrue to members of both sexes," . . . We need not disturb the findings of the District Court to note that there is neither a finding, nor was there any evidence which would support a finding, that the financial benefits of the Plan "worked to discriminate against any definable group or class in terms of the aggregate risk protection derived by that group or class from the program." . . . The Plan, in effect (and for all that appears), is nothing more than an insurance package, which covers some risks, but excludes others. . . . The "package" going to relevant identifiable groups we are presently concerned with—General Electric's male and female employees—covers exactly the same categories of risk, and is facially nondiscriminatory in the sense that "[t]here is no risk from which men are protected and women are not. Likewise, there is no risk from which women are protected and men are not". . . . As there is no proof that the package is in fact worth more to men than to women, it is impossible to find any gender-based discriminatory effect in this scheme simply because women disabled as a result of pregnancy do not receive benefits; that is to say, gender-based discrimination does not result simply because an employer's disability benefits plan is less than all inclusive. For all that appears, pregnancy-related disabilities constitute an *additional* risk, unique to women, and the failure to compensate them for this risk does not destroy the presumed parity of the benefits, accruing to men and women alike, which results from the facially evenhanded *inclusion* of risks. To hold otherwise would endanger the common-sense notion that an employer who has no disability benefits program at all does not violate Title VII even though the "underinclusion" of risks impacts, as a result of pregnancy-related disabilities, more heavily upon one gender than upon the other. Just as there is no facial gender-based discrimination in that case, so, too, there is none here.

We are told, however, that this analysis of the congressional purpose underlying Title VII is inconsistent with the guidelines of the EEOC, which, it is asserted, are entitled to "great deference" in the construction of the Act, . . . The guideline upon which respondents rely most heavily was promulgated in 1972, and states in pertinent part:

Disabilities caused or contributed to by pregnancy, miscarriage, abortion, childbirth, and recovery therefrom are, for all job related purposes, temporary disabilities and should be treated as such under any health or temporary disability insurance or sick leave plan available in connection with employment. . . .[Benefits] shall be applied to disability due to pregnancy or childbirth as they are applied to other temporary disabilities.

In evaluating this contention it should first be noted that Congress, in enacting Title VII, did not confer upon the EEOC authority to promulgate rules or regulations pursuant to that Title. *Albemarle Paper Co.* v. *Moody* . . . (1975). This does not mean that EEOC Guidelines are not

entitled to consideration in determining legislative intent, . . . But it does mean that courts properly may accord less weight to such guidelines than to administrative regulations which Congress has declared shall have the force of law, . . . or to regulations which under the enabling statute may themselves supply the basis for imposition of liability, . . .

The EEOC guideline in question does not fare well under these standards. It is not a contemporaneous interpretation of Title VII, since it was first promulgated eight years after the enactment of that Title. More importantly, the 1972 guideline flatly contradicts the position which the agency had enunciated at an earlier date, closer to the enactment of the governing statute. An opinion letter by the General Counsel of EEOC, dated October 17, 1966, states:

You have requested our opinion whether the above exclusion of pregnancy and childbirth as a disability under the long-term salary continuation plan would be in violation of Title VII of the Civil Rights Act of 1964.

In a recent opinion letter regarding pregnancy, we have stated, "The Commission policy in this area does not seek to compare an employer's treatment of illness or injury with his treatment of maternity since maternity is a temporary disability unique to the female sex and more or less to be anticipated during the working life of most women employees. Therefore, it is our opinion that according to the facts stated above, a company's group insurance program which covers hospital and medical expenses for the delivery of employees' children, but excludes from its long-term salary continuation program those disabilities which result from pregnancy and childbirth would not be in violation of Title VII." . . . A few weeks later in an opinion letter . . . the EEOC's position was that "an insurance or the benefit plan may simply exclude mater-

nity as a covered risk, and such an exclusion would not in our view be discriminatory. . . .

We have declined to follow administrative guidelines in the past where they conflicted with earlier pronouncements of the agency. . . . In short, while we do not wholly discount the weight to be given the 1972 guideline, it does not receive high marks. . . There are also persuasive indications that the more recent EEOC guideline sharply conflicts with other indicia of the proper interpretation of the sex-discrimination provisions of Title VII. The legislative history of Title VII's prohibition of sex discrimination is notable primarily for its brevity. Even so, however, Congress paid especial attention to the provisions of the Equal Pay Act, . . . when it amended §703(h) of Title VII by adding the following sentence:

It shall not be an unlawful employment practice under this subchapter for any employer to differentiate upon the basis of sex in determining the amount of the wages or compensation paid or to be paid to employees of such employer if such differentiation is authorized by the provisions of section 206(d) of Title 29. 42 USC § 2000e-2(h) [42 USCS § 2000e-2(h)].

This sentence was proposed as the Bennett Amendment to the Senate Bill, . . . (1964), and Senator Humphrey, the floor manager of the bill, stated that the purpose of the amendment was to make it "unmistakably clear" that "differences of treatment in industrial benefit plans, including earlier retirement options for women, may continue in operation under this bill if it becomes law." . . . Because of this amendment, interpretations of section 6(d) of the Equal Pay Act are applicable to Title VII as well, and an interpretive regu-

lation promulgated by the Wage and Hour Administrator under the Equal Pay Act explicitly states:

If employer contributions to a plan providing insurance or similar benefits to employees are equal for both men and women, no wage differential prohibited by the equal pay provisions will result from such payments, even though the benefits which accrue to the employees in question are greater for one sex than for the other. The mere fact that the employer may make unequal contributions for employees of opposite sexes in such a situation will not, however, be considered to indicate that the employer's payments are in violation of section 6(d), if the resulting benefits are equal for such employees. . . .

Thus even if we were to depend for our construction of the critical language of Title VII solely on the basis of "deference" to interpretive regulations by the appropriate administrative agencies, we would find ourselves pointed in diametrically opposite directions by the conflicting regulations of the EEOC, on the one hand, and the Wage and Hour Administrator, on the other. Petitioner's exclusion of benefits for pregnancy disability would not be declared an unlawful employment practice under §703(a) (1), but would be declared to to be an unlawful employment practice under §703 (h).

We are not reduced to such total abdication in construing the statute. The EEOC guideline of 1972, conflicting as it does with earlier pronouncements of that agency, and containing no suggestion that some new source of legislative history had been discovered in the intervening eight years, stands virtually alone. Contrary to it are the consistent interpretation of the Wage and Hour Administrator, and the quoted language of Senator Humphrey, the floor manager of Title VII in the Senate. They support what seems to us to be the "plain meaning" of the language used by Congress when it enacted §703(a) (1).

The concept of "discrimination," of course, was well known at the time of the enactment of Title VII, having been associated with the Fourteenth Amendment for nearly a century, and carrying with it a long history of judicial construction. When Congress makes it unlawful for an employer to "discriminate . . . on the basis of . . . sex . . .," without further explanation of its meaning, we should not readily infer that it meant something different than what the concept of discrimination has traditionally meant, . . . There is surely no reason for any such inference here,. . . .

We therefore agree with petitioner that its disability benefits plan does not violate Title VII because of its failure to cover pregnancy-related disabilities. The judgment of the Court of Appeals is reversed.

MR. JUSTICE STEWART, CONCURRING (OMITTED).
MR. JUSTICE BLACKMUN, CONCURRING IN PART (OMITTED).
MR. JUSTICE BRENNAN, WITH WHOM MR. JUSTICE MARSHALL CONCURS, DISSENTING (OMITTED).
MR. JUSTICE STEVENS, DISSENTING (OMITTED).

[In October, 1978 Congress passed an amendment to Title VII to prohibit employment discrimination on the basis of pregnancy. The amendment, intended to overturn the effects of the Court's decision in *General Electric* v. *Gilbert*, prohibits employers from discriminating "because of or on the basis of pregnancy, childbirth, or related medical conditions." The amendment requires that employers who provide disability insurance for their employees, provide women with temporary disability coverage in the event of a pregnancy in order to guarantee them equal employment opportunities.]

(6) Personnel Administrator v. Feeney (1979)

+Stewart, Burger, White, Powell, Blackmun, Rehnquist, Stevens
−Brennan, Marshall

[The federal government and nearly all states grant a hiring preferrence to veterans. Massachusetts grants veterans an "absolute preference" for any civil service position. The preference is available to males and females, including nurses, who were honorably discharged from the armed forces after at least 90 days of active service, at least 1 day of which was during "wartime." Unlike the practice in some states, where a veteran's preference may be exercised only at entry level positions, in others where it may be exercised a finite number of times, or still others where the preference takes the form a predetermined number of "points" added to a veterans' job examination score, in Massachusetts the preference is absolute. Veterans are automatically placed at the top of every job eligibility list for which they apply, ranked by score only among themselves. Disabled veterans, veterans, surviving spouses, and surviving parents of veterans are all eligible for such preferential ranking.

Helen Feeney took and passed a number of examinations for state positions; in several examinations she finished at or near the top. But she never obtained the position she was seeking. One year she was outranked by five male veterans in competition for a position as dental examiner, and a lower-scoring veteran received the position. The next year, she was ranked behind 12 veterans for the same position, although scoring higher than 11 of them. In 1975 she brought suit in the federal district court, alleging that the absolute preference formula operated so as to exclude women from the best civil service positions and thus violated the equal protection clause of the 14th Amendment. A three-judge court was convened and upheld her claim. It found that although the law had not been enacted with the intent to discriminate against women, that it had, in fact, a "devastating impact" on public sector employment opportunities for women. The court concluded that a more limited veterans' preference law would further the state's interests in aiding veterans without impacting so severely on women. The case was appealed to the Supreme Court, which vacated the decision and remanded for reconsideration in light of *Washington* v. *Davis* (1976). In *Davis,* the Court had held that an otherwise neutral law does not violate the equal protection clause solely because it results in a racially disproportionate impact. For a constitutional violation to be found, a discriminatory purpose must be evident. The District Court, however, reaffirmed its original decision. It held that a veteran's preference is inherently nonneutral, and that the discriminatory impact of such a law upon women was too inevitable to be unintended. The case was again appealed to the Supreme Court.]

MR. JUSTICE STEWART delivered the opinion of the Court.

. . .

The veterans' hiring preference in Massachusetts, as in other jurisdictions, has traditionally been justified as a measure designed to reward veterans for the sacrifice of military service, to ease the transition from military to civilian life, to encourage patriotic service, and to attract loyal and well disciplined people to civil service occupations. . . . The Massachusetts law dates back to 1884, when the State, as part of its first civil service legislation, gave a statutory preference to civil service applicants who were Civil War veterans if their qualifications were equal to those of nonveterans. . . . This tie-breaking provision blossomed into a truly absolute preference in 1895, when the State enacted its first general veterans preference law and exempted veterans from all merit selection requirements. . . . In response to a challenge brought by a male nonveteran, this statute was declared violative of state constitutional provisions guaranteeing that government should be for the "common good" and prohibiting hereditary titles. *Brown* v. *Russell* . . .

The current veterans' preference law has its origins in an 1896 statute, enacted to meet the state constitutional standards enunciated in *Brown* v. *Russell.* That statute limited the absolute preference to veterans who were otherwise qualified. . . . A closely divided Supreme Judicial Court, in an advisory opinion issued the same year, concluded that the preference embodied in such a statute would be valid. . . . In 1919, when the preference was extended to cover the veterans of World War I, the formula was further limited to provide for a priority in eligibility, in contrast to an absolute preference in hiring. . . .

Since 1919, the preference has been repeatedly amended to cover persons who served in subsequent wars, declared or undeclared. . . . The current preference formula . . . is substantially the same as that settled upon in 1919. This absolute preference—even as modified in 1919 —has never been universally popular. Over the years it has been subjected to repeated legal challenges, criticism by civil service reform groups, . . . and in 1926 to a referendum in which it was reaffirmed by a majority of 51.9% . . . . The present case is apparently the first to challenge the Massachusetts veterans' preference on the simple ground that it discriminates on the basis of sex.

The first Massachusetts veterans' preference statute defined the term "veterans" in gender-neutral language. . . . Women who have served in official United States military units during wartime, then, have always been entitled to the benefit of the preference. In addition, Massachusetts, through a 1943 amendment to the definition of "wartime service," extended the preference to women who served in unofficial auxiliary woman's units. . . .

When the first general veterans' preference statute was adopted in 1896, there were no women veterans. The statute, however, covered only Civil War veterans. Most of them were beyond middle age, and relatively few were actively competing for public employment. Thus, the impact of the preference upon the employment opportunities of nonveterans as a group and women in particular was slight.

. . .

When this litigation was commenced, then, over 98% of the veterans in Massachusetts were male; only 1.8% were female. And over one-quarter of the Massachusetts population were veterans. During the decade between 1963 and 1973 when the appellee was actively participating in the State's merit selection system, 47,005 new permanent appointments were made in the classified official service. Forty-three percent of those hired were women, and, 57% were men. Of the women appointed, 1.8% were veterans, while 54% of the men had veteran status. A large unspecified percentage of the female appointees were serving in lower paying positions for which males traditionally had not applied. On each of 50 sample eligible lists that are part of the record in this case, one or more woman who would have been certified as eligible for appointment on the basis of test results were displaced by veterans whose test scores were lower.

At the outset of this litigation the State conceded that for "many of the permanent positions for which males and females have competed" the vet-

erans' preference has "resulted in a substantially greater proportion of female eligibles than male eligibles" not being certified for consideration. The impact of the veterans' preference law upon the public employment opportunities of women has thus been severe. This impact lies at the heart of the appellee's federal constitutional claim.

The sole question for decision on this appeal is whether Massachusetts, in granting an absolute lifetime preference to veterans, has discriminated against women in violation of the Equal Protection Clause of the Fourteenth Amendment.

The Equal Protection Guarantee of the Fourteenth Amendment does not take from the States all power of classification. *Massachusetts Bd. of Retirement* v. *Murgia,* . . . Most laws classify, and many affect certain groups unevenly, even though the law itself treats them no differently from all other members of the class described by the law. When the basic classification is rationally based, uneven effects upon particular groups within a class are ordinarily of no constitutional concern. . . . The calculus of effects, the manner in which a particular law reverberates in a society, is a legislative and not a judicial responsibility. . . . In assessing an equal protection challenge, a court is called upon only to measure the basic validity of the legislative classification. . . . When some other independent right is not at stake, see, *e. g. Shapiro* v. *Thompson,* . . . and when there is no "reason to infer antipathy," it is presumed that "even improvident decisions will eventually be rectified by the democratic process. . . ."

Certain classifications, however, in themselves supply a reason to infer antipathy. Race is the paradigm. A racial classification, regardless of purported motivation, is presumptively invalid and can be upheld only upon an extraordinary justification. *Brown* v. *Board of Education . . .; McLaughlin* v. *Florida . . .* This rule applies as well to a classification that is ostensibly neutral but is an obvious pretext for racial discrimination. *Yick Wo* v. *Hopkins. . . .* But, as was made clear in *Washington* v. *Davis,* and *Village of Arlington Heights* v. *Metropolitan Housing Development Corp. . . .* even if a neutral law has a disproportionately adverse effect upon a racial minority, it is unconstitutional under the Equal Protection Clause only if that impact can be traced to a discriminatory purpose.

Classifications based upon gender not unlike those based upon race have traditionally been the touchstone for pervasive and often subtle discrimination. . . . This Court's recent cases teach that such classifications must bear a "close and substantial relationship to important governmental objectives." *Craig* v. *Boren,* and are in many settings unconstitutional. *Reed* v. *Reed . . . Frontiero* v. *Richardson . . . Weinberger* v. *Wiesenfield . . . Craig* v. *Boren . . .; Califano* v. *Goldfarb. . . .* Although public employment is not a constitutional right, *Massachusetts Bd. of Retirement* v. *Murgia,* and the States have wide discretion in framing employee qualifications, . . . these precedents dictate that any state law overtly or covertly designed to prefer males over females in public employment would require an exceedingly persuasive justification to withstand a constitutional challenge under the Equal Protection Clause of the Fourteenth Amendment.

The cases of *Washington* v. *Davis,* and *Village of Arlington Heights* v. *Metropolitan Housing Development*

Corp., recognize that when a neutral law has a disparate impact upon a group that has historically been the victim of discrimination, an unconstitutional purpose may still be at work. But those cases signalled no departure from the settled rule that the Fourteenth Amendment guarantees equal laws, not equal results. . . .

When a statute gender-neutral on its face is challenged on the ground that its effects upon women are disproportionably adverse, a two-fold inquiry is thus appropriate. The first question is whether the statutory classification is indeed neutral in the sense that it is not gender-based. If the classification itself, covert or overt, is not based upon gender, the second question is whether the adverse effect reflects invidious gender-based discrimination. . . . In this second inquiry, impact provides an "important starting point," but purposeful discrimination is "the condition that offends the Constitution." *Swann* v. *Board of Education.* . . .

The question whether ch. 31, §23 establishes a classification that is overtly or covertly based upon gender must first be considered. The appellee has conceded that ch. 31, §23 is neutral on its face. She has also acknowledged that state hiring preferences for veterans are not *per se* invalid, for she has limited her challenge to the absolute lifetime preference that Massachusetts provides to veterans. The District Court made two central findings that are relevant here: first, that ch. 31, §23 serves legitimate and worthy purposes; second, that the absolute preference was not established for the purpose of discriminating against women. The appellee has thus acknowledged and the District Court has thus found that the distinction between veterans and nonveterans drawn by ch. 31, §23 is not a pretext for gender discrimination. The appellee's concession and the District Court's finding are clearly correct.

If the impact of this statute could not be plausibly explained on a neutral ground, impact itself would signal that the real classification made by the law was in fact not neutral. . . . But there can be but one answer to the question whether this veteran preference excludes significant numbers of women from preferred state jobs because they are women or because they are nonveterans. Apart from the fact that the definition of "veterans" in the statute has always been neutral as to gender and that Massachusetts has consistently defined veteran status in a way that has been inclusive of women who have served in the military, this is not a law that can plausibly be explained only as a gender-based classification. Indeed, it is not a law that can rationally be explained on that ground. Veteran status is not uniquely male. Although few women benefit from the preference, the nonveteran class is not substantially all-female. To the contrary, significant numbers of nonveterans are men, and all nonveterans—male as well as female—are placed at a disadvantage. Too many men are affected by ch. 31, §23 to permit the inference that the statute is but a pretext for preferring men over women.

Moreover, as the District Court implicitly found, the purposes of the statute provide the surest explanation for its impact. Just as there are cases in which impact alone can unmask an invidious classification, cf. *Yick Wo* v. *Hopkins*, . . . there are others, in which—notwithstanding impact—the legitimate noninvidious purposes of a law cannot be missed. This is one. The distinction made by ch. 31, §23, is, as it seems to be, quite simply between veterans and nonveterans, not between men and women.

The dispositive question, then, is whether the appellee has shown that a gender-based discriminatory purpose has, at least in some measure, shaped the Massachusetts veterans' preference legislation. As did the District Court, she points to two basic factors which in her view distinguish ch. 31, §23 from the neutral rules at issue in the *Washington* v. *Davis* and *Arlington Heights* cases. The first is the nature of the preference, which is said to be demonstrably gender-biased in the sense that it favors a status reserved under federal military policy primarily to men. The second concerns the impact of the absolute lifetime preference upon the employment opportunities of women, an impact claimed to be too inevitable to have been unintended. The appellee contends that these factors, coupled with the fact that the preference itself has little if any relevance to actual job performance, more than suffice to prove the discriminatory intent required to establish a constitutional violation.

The contention that this veterans' preference is "inherently nonneutral" or "gender-biased" presumes that the State, by favoring veterans, intentionally incorporated into its public employment policies the panoply of sex-based and assertedly discriminatory federal laws that have prevented all but a handful of women from becoming veterans. There are two serious difficulties with this argument. First, it is wholly at odds with the District Court's central finding that Massachusetts has not offered a preference to veterans for the purpose of discriminating against women. Second, it cannot be reconciled with the assumption made by both the appellee and the District

Court that a more limited hiring preference for veterans could be sustained. Taken together, these difficulties are fatal.

To the extent that the status of veteran is one that few women have been enabled to achieve, every hiring preference for veterans, however modest or extreme, is inherently gender-biased. If Massachusetts by offering such a preference can be said intentionally to have incorporated into its state employment policies the historical gender-based federal military personnel practices, the degree of the preference would or should make no constitutional difference. Invidious discrimination does not become less so because the discrimination accomplished is of a lesser magnitude. Discriminatory intent is simply not amenable to calibration. It either is a factor that has influenced the legislative choice or it is not. The District Court's conclusion that the absolute veterans' preference was not originally enacted or subsequently reaffirmed for the purpose of giving an advantage to males as such necessarily compels the conclusion that the State intended nothing more than to prefer "veterans." Given this finding, simple logic suggests that an intent to exclude women from significant public jobs was not at work in this law. To reason that it was by describing the preference as "inherently non-neutral" or "gender-biased," is merely to restate the fact of impact, not to answer the question of intent.

To be sure, this case is unusual in that it involves a law that by design is not neutral. The law overtly prefers veterans as such. As opposed to the written test at issue in *Davis*, it does not purport to define a job related characteristic. To the contrary, it confers upon a specifically described group—perceived to be particularly deserving—a competitive head start. But the District Court found, and the appellee has not disputed, that this legislative choice was legitimate. The basic distinction between veterans and nonveterans, having been found not gender-based, and the goals of the preference having been found worthy, ch. 31 must be analyzed as in any other neutral law that casts a greater burden upon women as a group than upon men as a group. The enlistment policies of the armed services may well have discriminated on the basis of sex. See *Frontiero* v. *Richardson* . . . cf. *Schlesinger* v. *Ballard*, . . . But the history of discrimination against women in the military is not on trial in this case.

The appellee's ultimate argument rests upon the presumption, common to the criminal and civil law, that a person intends the natural and foreseeable consequences of his voluntary actions. . . . The decision to grant a preference to veterans was of course "intentional." So, necessarily, did an adverse impact upon nonveterans follow from that decision. And it cannot seriously be argued that the legislature of Massachusetts could have been unaware that most veterans are men. It would thus be disingenuous to say that the adverse consequences of this legislation for women were unintended, in the sense that they were not volitional or in the sense that they were not foreseeable.

"Discriminatory purpose," however, implies more than intent as volition or intent as awareness of consequences. . . . It implies that the decisionmaker, in this case a state legislature, selected or reaffirmed a particular course of action at least in part "because of," not merely "in spite of," its adverse effects upon an identifiable group. Yet nothing in the record demonstrates that this preference for veterans was originally devised or subsequently re-enacted because it would accomplish the collateral goal of keeping women in a stereotypic and predefined place in the Massachusetts Civil Service.

To the contrary, the statutory history shows that the benefit of the preference was consistently offered to "any person" who was a veteran. That benefit has been extended to women under a very broad statutory definition of the term veteran. The preference formula itself, which is the focal point of this challenge, was first adopted—so it appears from this record—out of a perceived need to help a small group of older Civil War veterans. It has since been reaffirmed and extended only to cover new veterans. When the totality of legislative actions establishing and extending the Massachusetts veterans' preference are considered, . . . the law remains what it purports to be: a preference for veterans of either sex over nonveterans of either sex, not for men over women.

Veterans' hiring preferences represent an awkward—and, many argue, unfair—exception to the widely shared view that merit and merit alone should prevail in the employment policies of government. After a war, such laws have been enacted virtually without opposition. During peacetime they inevitably have come to be viewed in many quarters as undemocratic and unwise. Absolute and permanent preferences, as the troubled history of this law demonstrates, have always been subject to the objection that they give the veteran more than a square deal. But the Fourteenth Amendment "cannot be made a refuge from ill-advised . . . laws." . . . The substantial edge granted to veterans by ch. 31, §23 may reflect unwise policy. The appellee, however, has simply failed to demonstrate that the law in any way reflects a purpose to discriminate on the basis of sex.

The judgment is reversed, and the case is remanded for further proceedings consistent with this opinion.

MR. JUSTICE STEVENS, WITH WHOM MR. JUSTICE WHITE JOINS, CONCURRING (OMITTED).

MR. JUSTICE MARSHALL, WITH WHOM MR. JUSTICE BRENNAN JOINS, DISSENTING.

Although acknowledging that in some circumstances, discriminatory intent may be inferred from the inevitable or foreseeable impact of a statute, . . . the Court concludes that no such intent has been established here. I cannot agree. In my judgment, Massachusetts' choice of an absolute veterans' preference system evinces purposeful gender-based discrimination. And because the statutory scheme bears no substantial relationship to a legitimate governmental objective, it cannot withstand scrutiny under the Equal Protection clause.

. . .

To survive challenge under the Equal Protection Clause, statutes reflecting gender-based discrimination must be substantially related to the achievement of important governmental objectives. . . . Appellants here advance three interests in support of the absolute preference system: (1) assisting veterans in their readjustment to civilian life; (2) encouraging military enlistment; and (3) rewarding those who have served their country. . . . Although each of those goals is unquestionably legitimate, the "mere recitation of a benign compensatory purpose" cannot of itself insulate legislative classifications from constitutional scrutiny. . . . And in this case, the Commonwealth has failed to establish a sufficient relationship between its objectives and the means chosen to effectuate them.

With respect to the first interest, facilitating veterans' transition to civilian status, the statute is plainly overinclusive. . . . By conferring a permanent preference, the legislation allows veterans to invoke their advantage repeatedly, without regard to their date of discharge. . . .

Nor is the Commonwealth's second asserted interest, encouraging military service, a plausible justification for this legislative scheme. In its original and subsequent reenactments, the statute extended benefits retroactively to veterans who had served during a prior specified period. . . . If the Commonwealth's "actual purpose" is to induce enlistment this legislative design is hardly well-suited to that end. . . .

Finally, the Commonwealth's third interest, rewarding veterans, does not "adequately justify the salient features" of this preference system. . . . Where a particular statutory scheme visits substantial hardship on a class long subject to discrimination, the legislation cannot be sustained unless "carefully tuned to alternative considerations." . . . Here, there are a wide variety of less discriminatory means by which Massachusetts could effect its compensatory purposes. For example, a point preference system, such as that maintained by many States and the Federal Government, . . . or an absolute preference for a limited duration, would reward veterans without excluding all qualified women from upper level civil service positions. Apart from public employment, the Commonwealth, can, and does, afford assistance to veterans in various ways, including tax abatements, educational subsidies, and special programs for needy veterans. . . . Unlike these and similar benefits, the costs of which are distributed across the taxpaying public generally, the Massachusetts statute exacts a substantial price from a discrete group of individuals who have long been subject to employment discrimination, and who, "because of circumstances totally beyond their control, have [had] little if any chance of becoming members in the preferred class. . . .

D. The Equal Rights Amendment

1. Equality of Rights Under the Law Shall Not be Denied or Abridged by the United States or by any State on Account of Sex.

2. Congress shall have the power to enforce, by appropriate legislation, the provisions of this article.

3. This amendment shall take effect two years after the date of ratification.

(1) What Would it Accomplish?

The proposed Equal Rights Amendment was passed by Congress in the spring of 1972 and submitted to the states for ratification. Within a year, thirty-four states had ratified the amendment, leaving only four to reach the constitutional requirement of thirty-eight. However, for reasons discussed more fully in item (3) below, the drive for ratification stalled. As of the summer of 1978, thirty-five states had ratified the amendment, but four states rescinded their earlier ratifications. The House of Representatives and the Senate passed a resolution extending the seven-year deadline for ratification from March 1979 to June 1982.

The pendency of the amendment leaves its meaning open to speculation. Indeed, uncertainty as to its meaning has been exploited by those forces opposed to it. But one thing is certain. Like all other provisions in the Constitution, this amendment would be interpreted by the Supreme Court.

A natural first question, therefore, would be whether the main constitutional effect of the amendment would be to make sex a "suspect classification." Clearly, it would do *at least* this much. It is inconceivable that the amendment would be interpreted only as requiring a "rational basis" for sex classifications. If the Court interprets the amendment this way, then not all classifications by gender would be prohibited, but only those for which the government could not demonstrate a compelling need. If sex became a suspect classification, it would be up to the Court to determine, in each case, whether or not the government had met its burden of proof. For example, would the outcomes of *Kahn* v. *Shevin* (1974) or *Califano* v. *Webster* (1977) (see pp. 625–626, *supra*) have to be reversed? Clearly, what the amendment would *not* do is give the Court any guidance for judging whether the government had met this burden. It would remain for the justices, in each case, to make that determination.

It is also possible that the Supreme Court would interpret an Equal Rights Amendment (ERA) as going *beyond* the concept of suspect classification and prohibiting *any and all* gender classifications. But even if it were interpreted that way, it would still be open to the Court to decide whether a particular classification was or was not a *gender* classification. Recall the *Geduldig* v. *Aiello* (1974) and *General Electric Co.* v. *Gilbert* (1976) cases, where the Court held that omission of pregnancy from disability plans was not a classification by gender.

What the ERA might allow are nongender classifications that had the effect of falling more heavily on, or aiding, one sex. Thus, property tax exemptions for widows *and* widowers with certain income levels or employment opportunities might well result in a disproportionate share of exemptions going to widows. Exemptions from jury duty or military service based, not on gender, but on child-care responsibilities would also probably result in more exemptions for women than for men. If, borrowing from its Fourteenth Amendment cases (see *Washington* v. *Davis*, 1976), the Supreme Court were to hold that the key to the ERA was *intent* to discriminate on the basis of sex, and not merely a disproportionate outcome, then the mere fact of such outcome would be constitutionally irrelevant without a showing of intent. If, however, the Court followed its interpretation of Title VII (as in *Griggs* v. *Duke Power Co.*, 1971) and held that a disproportionate outcome was sufficient evidence of a violation of the amendment, then such classifications would be more difficult to sustain. The *fact* that more widows than widowers received the exemption, *or the fact* that more men than women were drafted, might jeopardize the validity of those laws.

Writing in 1971, Mary Eastwood offered a "Five-Point guide" to interpreting the Equal Rights Amendment.[1] A summary of that guide offers some insight into how the ERA might work, keeping in mind that many of the legal changes that the ERA would have brought about have

---

[1]Mary Eastwood, "The Double Standard of Justice: Women's Rights Under the Constitution," 5 *Valparaiso Law Review* (1971), 301–317.

already taken place in the intervening years.

First, where laws "confer a benefit, privilege or obligation of citizenship on one sex, those benefits, privileges and obligations would be extended to both sexes" (or the legislature that passed the law would have the option to withdraw them from both sexes). Examples include protective labor laws, social security benefits, alimony, child support and child custody, control over community property, inheritance rights, loss of consortium, and jury and military service.

For example, alimony would have to be made available to either wife *or* husband according to some non-gender-based standard. Labor laws could still limit the size and weight of objects a worker could lift, but the limitation could not be made purely on the basis of gender and, following *Dothard* v. *Rawlinson* (1977), would have to be "job related." Depending on whether or not the Court used *intent* or *impact* as its standard, it might or might not be possible to establish occupational standards that *had the effect* of excluding all or most women.

Second, laws that restrict or deny freedom or opportunities to one sex would be unconstitutional under the ERA. This would include labor laws that prohibit one sex or the other from holding a particular job or that permit employers to impose such limits. Domicile limitations and the last vestiges of the married women's property acts are other examples. Laws that assume that a husband is head of the household for tax purposes would have to be changed. Married women could not be prohibited from borrowing money or running businesses in their own names. Lending institutions regulated by the government could not discriminate against women in the extension of credit (Congress has already prohibited such discrimination by statute).

Third, had the Supreme Court not already done so under the Fourteenth Amendment, *Craig* v. *Boren* (1977), *Stanton* v. *Stanton* (1976), the ERA would eliminate all sex-based age distinctions, such as the age of majority, age of marriage without parental consent, age limits on the jurisdiction of juvenile courts, and child labor laws. If the ERA is interpreted only as mandating sex as a suspect classification, then in all such cases it would be at least open to government to meet the very difficult burden of showing that such distinctions meet a compelling need. However, if the ERA is interpreted as forbidding all sex classifications, then government would have no choice but to equalize the ages between the sexes in each category—either up or down.

A *fourth* category involves laws that reflect differences in sexual preference or reproductive capacity. Laws that provide maternity benefits would be constitutional, even though only women could receive those benefits. Maternity leave or child care options for fathers might be required. Laws that established arbitrary limits on working by pregnant and postpartum women would probably not be affected, but such laws are already constitutionally suspect under recent Supreme Court decisions. Thus the Court, in *Cleveland* v. *LaFleur* (1974), invalidated termination and return rules for pregnant teachers under the due process clause of the Fourteenth Amendment. Laws prohibiting homosexuality, or certain types of sexual practices, would not be affected by the ERA if they applied equally to males and females alike.

On the other hand, under the ERA, it would be necessary either to eliminate certain common crimes or to apply the law equally to both sexes. Rape, statutory rape, and prostitution are the obvious examples. Some states, such as Wisconsin, have already revised their rape statutes to incorporate the principle of equality. Wisconsin, in fact, has technically abolished the crime of "rape" and substituted in its place three degrees of sexual assault. Sexual assault may be committed by a male upon a female, a female upon a male, or by one person upon another person of the same sex. The element of consent and the use of force and violence become the key determinants. Statutory rape statutes will also have to be amended to apply equally whether the victim is male or female. Prostitution statutes (and enforcement practices) probably would have to be amended to punish both the prostitute and the customer, again without distinction as to gender. At the federal level, it seems likely that the Mann Act, which prohibits the transportation of women across state lines for immoral purposes, would have to be amended to include men as well—or repealed entirely. Males and females could not be treated differently under criminal sentencing statutes. And juvenile courts could not impose sanctions or restrictions on girls for activities (usually sexual activities) that boys can indulge in with impunity ("boys will be boys").

Fifth would be questions of separation by sex. One of the "parade of horribles" raised by opponents of the ERA is what is known colloquially as the "potty issue"—would the ERA require unisex public bathrooms and locker rooms? Virtually all constitutional experts answer emphatically "no." Separate facilities for disrobing, sleeping, and performing certain personal bodily functions (eating, after all, is also a "bodily function")

would be protected by the constitutional right of privacy as articulated by the Supreme Court in *Griswold* v. *Connecticut* (1965). But the definition of "privacy" is culturally based, and as mores change, it is possible that what is, or ought to be, constitutionally protected will also change. (Just recently, a federal judge in New York City, Constance Baker Motley, ordered the dressing room of the New York Yankees opened to female reporters, *Ludtke* v. *Kuhn*, 1978.)

More difficult questions will arise in the context of other institutions or practices that have traditionally been carried out on a gender-separated basis. Congress has already legislated to prohibit sex discrimination in school athletics. It is no longer strange to find girls playing on formerly all boys' teams, at least in noncontact sports. Would the ERA require abolition of even this last distinction?

What about "all boys" and "all girls" schools? It seems clear enough, even under existing case law, that such schools are unconstitutional if they promote rigid sex stereotypes and deny opportunities to girls that are extended to boys. Thus, if a community had a girls' school that emphasized music and art and a boys' school that focused on science and math, boys interested in music and art would have to be permitted entrance to the former school, and girls interested in science and math, to the latter. But suppose that a community operates two all-purpose schools, one for boys, the other for girls, and justifies it as providing for each student the least distracting work environment? The argument is made that such separation is benign and "nonstigmatizing." Is this policy of "separate but equal" constitutionally acceptable now? Would it be acceptable under the ERA? There is no authoritative answer to the first question, since the Supreme Court in a recent case divided 4-4 on the issue. As to the second, it probably would be clearly unconstitutional under the ERA only if that amendment were interpreted as banning all gender distinctions. If it merely imposed on the states an obligation to justify each such distinction as meeting a "compelling interest," then the Supreme Court would still have to decide the issue.

Of course, there are some things even the ERA will not do. For one, it will have no direct effect on private discriminatory action (although such action increasingly is being regulated by statute and administrative rule). The ERA would not *require* either the federal or state governments to *do* anything. Finally, there is at least some question as to whether or not the ERA, which directly applies only to state action, will give the federal government additional authority to legislate against private action beyond existing constitutional authority. Since the ERA contains an enforcement clause similar to Section 5 of the Fourteenth Amendment, it would be reasonable to assume that the Supreme Court, in the absence of any drastic changes in its membership or intervening interpretations, would construe that clause in the same way as Section 5 was construed in *Guest, Price,* and other recent cases interpreting the powers of Congress under the Fourteenth Amendment.

(2) Ratification of the ERA: Constitutional Problems

As of March, 1979, the Equal Rights Amendment had been ratified by thirty-five states—all but Nevada, Utah, Arizona, Illinois, Missouri, Oklahoma, Arkansas, Louisiana, Mississippi, Alabama, Georgia, South Carolina, North Carolina, Florida and Virginia. Four of the ratifying states—Idaho, Nebraska, North Dakota, and Tennessee—later voted to rescind their ratifications. The Kentucky legislature also voted to rescind, but that vote was vetoed by the lieutenant governor, a woman, acting as governor when the governor was out of the state. Pro-ERA forces sought to extend the time limit for ratification from what has become the customary seven years to fourteen years. A compromise extension of three years and three months—to June 1982—was approved by a simple majority in the House of Representatives and the Senate. With the passage of time, a number of court challenges will certainly materialize, if the ERA is ratified during the extension period.

First, there is the question of the authority of Congress to extend the period for ratification by a simple majority vote. Opponents of extension argued that to change the conditions of ratification of a constitutional amendment, a two-thirds vote is required, just as the Constitution requires two-thirds for approval of the amendment itself. But proponents of extension countered that the ratification extension is a separate "detail" that is a matter of congressional policy and not governed by Article V requirements. Furthermore, the seven-year ratification period is not officially a part of the amendment but merely a condition set down by congressional resolution.

Second, there are the reciprocal questions: Can a state ratify an amendment after a prior rejection? Can a state rescind a prior ratification? The Constitution provides no clear answer to either question. The interpretation supported by a majority of commentators is that the Constitution creates only a power to ratify and not a power to reject. Applying that theory to the first question, a state may in fact "ratify" an amendment after it has previously rejected ratification because until it ratifies, it has taken no constitutionally cognizable action. Applying the theory to the second question, a state may not rescind a prior ratification. A legislature only has the power to ratify. Once that is accomplished, it can do no more.

The Supreme Court has never formally passed on these questions. When the issue arose in *Coleman* v. *Miller* (1939), in the context of Kansas' attempt to ratify the Child Labor Amendment, the Court held that such questions, and the related issue of whether or not that amendment could still be ratified thirteen years after passage, were non-justiciable political questions. In the course of his plurality opinion, Chief Justice Hughes said that the question of recision after ratification "should be regarded as a political question pertaining to the political departments with the ultimate authority in the Congress in the exercise of its control over the promulgation of the adoption of the amendment." In a concurring opinion for four justices, Justice Black emphasized that the "Constitution grants Congress exclusive power to control submission of constitutional amendments." While not formally deciding the issue, the Court did cite a number of authorities to the effect that ratification cannot be rescinded and recognized that in the past the "government had dealt with the effect of previous rejection and of attempted withdrawal and determined that both were ineffectual in the presence of actual ratification." The action of Congress and the secretary of state in declaring the Fourteenth Amendment ratified in 1868,

notwithstanding efforts by states to withdraw their consent, is the applicable legislative precedent. Finally, it is worth noting that both the Senate and the House of Representatives, in debating the ERA Extension Bill in 1978, rejected recision amendments that would have allowed states to rescind their earlier approval of the ERA during the extension period.

If the ERA is declared to be ratified, and these issues come to the Supreme Court again, it is not entirely clear that the Court would follow the precedent of *Coleman* and again declare them to be nonjusticiable political questions. *Powell* v. *McCormack* (1968) and *Baker* v. *Carr* (1962) restricted the reach of the political questions doctrine, and the present Court might be unwilling to accept Hughes' *Coleman* dictum that these issues were too complex for judges to decide. It would also be up to the Court to determine if, in the light of *Powell*, Article V makes a "textually demonstrable" commitment to Congress to determine, free of judicial interference, whether an amendment has been ratified. A reading of Article V does not permit a presumption of such a commitment.

(3) Looking Past the ERA: Toward a Constitutional Convention?

If the Equal Rights Amendment is not ratified by the requisite thirty-eight states, or if ratification is successfully challenged in the courts, there are two alternatives. First, it is always open to pro-ERA forces to persuade Congress to pass another ERA, one perhaps with a longer time limit for ratification, and hope that a change in political fortunes will bring about ratification. Second, they can reverse the amendment process by invoking the never used provisions of Article V, which provide for the calling of a constitutional convention. It is that prospect which is of central concern in this essay.

Article V of the Constitution provides for two methods of amendment. One is for Congress, by a two-thirds majority in each house, to submit amendments for ratification by three-fourths of the states. All twenty-six amendments to the Constitution were proposed and ratified by this method. The second route is for Congress to call a constitutional convention "upon application of the legislatures of two-thirds of the states." The convention method was proposed as an alternative mode of constitutional amendment during the last moments of the Convention of 1787. Because the motives of the framers in adapting this alternative are unclear, and because, out of disuse, it has never been interpreted judicially, the convention method of amendment is fraught with uncertainty.

What constitutes a valid "call" for such a convention by two-thirds of the state legislatures? And would such a convention be limited to specific subject matters described in the petitions, or would it be free to propose constitutional amendments on any subject whatsoever? Indeed, could it write an entirely new Constitution? A Committee of the American Bar Association concluded in 1974 that a convention called by Congress in response to petitions from two-thirds (34) of the states would be limited to the subject matter specified in those petitions. However, others, including Yale law professor Charles L. Black, Jr., contend that the intention of the framers in adding this language to Article V was to place no limits on the subjects to be considered by such a convention.

Because of these uncertainties, and because of the silence of the Constitution on other related matters, such as time limitations, delegation apportionment, the process of selecting delegates to such a convention, and whether or not a state can rescind an earlier call for a convention, a number of clarifying bills have been introduced in Congress. All of these bills provided that Congress act as the final arbiter of the validity of state petitions initiating an amendment. Further, they prohibited judicial review of such congressional decisions. The American Bar Association, in contrast, has proposed a limited right of judicial review in those cases where Congress' decisions are "clearly erroneous."

The importance of the Article V option to amend the Constitution by convention cannot be measured solely by its lack of utilization. Many such petitions in the past had considerable political impact, and the political forces mobilized in their behalf often were successful ultimately in achieving their desired goals. For example, more than thirty states submitted applications by 1912 calling for a constitutional convention to provide for the direct election of United States Senators. Congress, in response, passed the Seventeenth Amendment. National convention calls were also influential in inducing Congress to repeal Prohibition (the Twenty-First Amendment), to limit the presidential term of office (the Twenty-Second Amendment), and to provide a suitable mechanism for determining presidential disability (the Twenty-Fifth Amendment).

Calls for a constitutional convention have become commonplace in recent years in response to unpopular Supreme Court decisions. Such a convention has been proposed by opponents of the Court's abortion decision (*Roe* v. *Wade*, 1973). Over thirty state legislatures petitioned Congress to call a convention to amend the Constitution to modify the "one man, one vote" principle of the Court's reapportionment decisions. Currently the National Taxpayers Union has organized a drive to call a convention to amend the Constitution to require a balanced federal budget. As of April, 1979 thirty states had submitted such petitions to the Congress.

4. WEALTH

A. *A Note on the Supreme Court and the Legal Needs of the Poor*

The War on Poverty in the United States in the 1960s underscored the fact that millions of citizens live in substandard conditions far different from those generally prevailing throughout the population. Conditions of economic deprivation are frequently accompanied by loss of dignity and privacy and the absence of other constitutional rights taken for granted by most Americans. It has been said that "poverty is at war with the Constitution," but it is not necessarily true that "the Constitution is equally at war with poverty."[1] The extent to which the Constitution and the Supreme Court have entered the battle, and the extent to which they have the capacity to turn the tide, is the subject of this section.

Whatever may be said of the Constitution's current stance against poverty today, it initially exhibited no special concern. The poor, as well as Negroes, were generally excluded from the protections of that docu-ment. Fugitives from justice, vagabonds, and paupers were expressly excepted from the privileges and immunities of citizens under the Articles of Confederation. The Constitution omitted this exception, but did provide that all persons "held to service or Labour" in one state, presumably including those imprisoned for debt or merely for being paupers, should be delivered up on demand of the state from which they were fleeing. Under the common law and many state laws at the time, paupers and others in a comparable "immoral" condition were liable to arrest and imprisonment for that reason alone. In some states paupers were required to wear badges containing the letter "P," and in others could actually be bought at an auction. Some state constitutions still deny paupers the right to vote, although it is almost certainly now unconstitutional to do so.[2] As Bendich has pointed out, it was at best ironic to say that such persons enjoyed the protections of the Bill of Rights, and particularly the rights to privacy under the Fourth Amendment.[3]

In 1837, the Supreme Court was faced for the first time with a statute discriminating against the poor and, without seeming difficulty, affirmed the law. New York's legislature had excluded poor foreign immigrants from entering the state, and the Supreme Court held that this was a reasonable use of the state's police powers over the public health, safety, and morals and therefore not a burden on interstate commerce. The opinion reasoned that the state could protect itself against the "moral pestilence" of the poor in the same way that it

[1]Albert M. Bendich, "Privacy, Poverty and the Constitution," in tenBroek (ed.), *The Law of the Poor* (San Francisco: Chandler Publishing Co., 1966), p. 83.

[2]*Ibid.*, p. 111, Note 78.

[3]*Ibid.*, pp. 91–92.

could exclude convicts or other "infectious articles." *City of New York v. Miln*, for more than 100 years, thus stood for the proposition that the poor were a danger to society and not eligible for many constitutional protections. It reflected the prevailing view that the causes of poverty lay in "individual character defects or the family pathology" of the poor themselves, rather than in the society.[4] Welfare and Relief programs in the nineteenth century sometimes differentiated between poverty and pauperism. According to Handler,

In the public mind, there was a difference between being poor and being a pauper. Paupers were characterized by the extreme state of their moral degeneracy, drunkenness, vice, and corruption. They were outcasts and no different from the criminal class. The dividing line between the poor and the paupers was the ability and willingness to work. Those who were considered capable of supporting themselves but failed to do so, crossed the line from poverty to pauperism.[5]

In 1941, in *Edwards v. California*, the Supreme Court was again faced with the exclusion by a state of persons without means of support. California's "Okie Law" made it a misdemeanor for a person knowingly to bring into the state a nonresident indigent. This time the Court invalidated the statute. But it did so on the grounds that state laws of this type were a burden on interstate commerce and thus not a valid exercise of the police powers of the state. Thus, poor people were given the same rights to free interstate movement as articles of commerce—at least a

modest improvement over treatment as infectious articles. Writing for the Court, Justice Byrnes doubted whether indigent paupers constituted a "moral pestilence," and the *Miln* precedent, though not clearly overruled, was effectively eliminated. The decision was unanimous, but four justices argued in concurring opinions that the right to interstate migration ought to rest on the privileges and immunities clause of the Fourteenth Amendment. Justice Jackson, in an additional separate opinion, went further and argued that poverty should, or could, never be used to determine an individual's constitutional rights.

Does "indigence" . . . constitute a basis for restricting the freedom of a citizen, as crime or contagion warrants its restriction? We should say now, and in no uncertain terms, that a man's mere property status, without more, cannot be used by a state to test, qualify, or limit his rights as a citizen of the United States. "Indigence" in itself is neither a source of rights nor a basis for denying them. The mere state of being without funds is a neutral fact—constitutionally an irrelevance, like race, creed or color.

Recognition of the needs of the poor in criminal cases came very slowly. In 1938 the Supreme Court ruled that counsel must be provided for indigent defendants in the federal courts.[6] But after appearing to suggest a similar course for indigent defendants in state courts in the famous Scottsboro case, *Powell* v. *Alabama* (1932), the Court in 1942 limited the requirement of appointed counsel to capital cases and those

---

[4]Joel F. Handler, "Reforming the Poor: Welfare Policy, Federalism and Morality," Unpublished Manuscript, 1970, p. 2–1.

[5]*Ibid.*, p. 2–2.

[6]*Johnson* v. *Zerbst* (1938).

cases in which the presence of special circumstances mandated the need for legal assistance.[7] In 1956 the Court took a major step in recognizing that formal equality had little meaning to the individual whose poverty barred equal access to the courts. In *Griffin* v. *Illinois* the Court ruled that a state was required to provide a trial transcript at its own expense to an indigent defendant seeking to appeal his conviction where there was a general right of appeal to all who could afford it. The four dissenting justices denied that a state had any obligation to render individuals "economically equal before its bar of justice." There was some dispute among the justices as to whether the right of appeal involved was a fundamental right; they agreed that *if* it were so construed, then the state would have to pay the costs.

Seven years later, in the landmark case of *Gideon* v. *Wainwright* (1963), the Court unanimously found that where the fundamental right to counsel was involved, the ability of the defendant to hire private counsel could not be the determining factor. There is still the difference between the right to counsel and the right to an effective defense in a criminal case. And there remains the problem, which the Court tried to solve in its *Miranda* decision, of rights abrogated by police actions before a suspect is formally charged with a crime. Nonetheless, the principal that the poor man must be treated equally before the law is established and has had a significant impact. There is still no right to counsel in civil cases.

Laws do not create poverty or determine who will be poor. But laws and the attitudes of courts will have a significant impact on the lives of poor people. Law is not a neutral force, but the embodiment of the prevailing values of the community. It is, as Harold Rothwax has observed, "not, basically or primarily, a response to a sense of justice or injustice. It is by and large a manifestation of power. . . . The poor have not been heard, so the substance of the law does not reflect their needs."[8] And, at least until very recently, courts have espoused largely middle-class values. Indeed, law is intimately connected with poverty in that it has enforced and legitimized a variety of rules or norms that clearly, though not necessarily intentionally, disfavor those without means. In almost all jurisdictions, for example, common law rules favor creditors over debtors, landlords over tenants, and merchants over consumers. Divorce laws and other family law provisions, tax laws, selective service rules, and, of course, the criminal law (despite *Gideon*) favor those with means.[9] Not only have the laws disfavored the poor, but access to the courts is costly, time-consuming, and near impossible for those without adequate legal representation. Even where the laws may be favorable, the poor have difficulties in taking advantage of them. Little wonder that poor people have a low sense of efficacy and do not perceive how the law and courts can help them.[10]

---

[7]*Betts* v. *Brady* (1942).

[8]Harold Rothwax, "The Law as an Instrument of Social Change," in Weissman (ed.), *Justice and the Law in the Mobilization for Youth Experience* (New York: Association Press, 1969), p. 139.

[9]Jerome E. Carlin and Jan Howard, "Legal Representation and Class Justice," **12** *UCLA Law Review* (1965), 381–437.

[10]For example, see Gresham M. Sykes, "Legal Needs of the Poor in the City of Denver," **4** *Law and Society Review* (1969), 255–277.

With the War on Poverty, the development of federally supported or stimulated legal services programs, and the rise of mass organizations devoted to welfare reform, the 1960s witnessed a major and unprecedented legal attack on the problems of the poor. It was of necessity an attack that had to begin on the ground floor because the law, by and large, did not reflect the needs of the poor. There were few cases or precedents available by which to measure the treatment meted out to the poor by various government agencies. A very high degree of creative and reform-oriented lawyering was called for to persuade courts to give recognition to rights that had not been thought to exist before. A great experiment in using the law to achieve social change was begun. New doctrines had to be created out of old—or nonexistent—precedents. Courts had to be made to recognize constitutional dimensions in practices and conditions formerly free of constitutional scrutiny. Court action could not alleviate the general conditions of poverty in the United States. But it could, and did, serve two very useful purposes. First, litigation could provide relief from at least the most oppressive practices of welfare and other agencies serving the poor. And second, litigation in massive amounts could, if successful, tie up the welfare system and provoke a crisis of such proportions as to bring about needed congressional reform. Test cases, by and large, would not alter the system of poverty and welfare. But, as had been the pattern of racial cases, litigation might serve to stimulate legislative and executive action.

Constitutional development of poor people's rights took several parallel forms. First, there was the continued effort, following *Griffin* and other criminal cases, to abolish statutory classifications based on wealth. In *Harper* v. *Virginia Board of Elections* (1966), the Court struck down as invidious and hence unconstitutional the poll tax in state elections required by five southern states. Indeed, Justice Douglas' opinion for the majority seemed to suggest that any classification based on wealth was constitutionally impermissible: "Lines drawn on the basis of wealth or property, like those of race, are traditionally disfavored." In so doing, the Court was following an argument first made in 1949 by tenBroek and Tussman in a famous law review article.[11] They had argued then that, just as racial classifications had been deemed invidious and thus forbidden under the equal protection clause of the Fourteenth Amendment, so, too, legislative classifications regarding wealth and status must be considered void. Or, in case the courts did not wish to go this far, at least such classifications should be considered constitutionally suspect and the normal presumption of constitutionality reversed. They coined the term "substantive equal protection" to describe the doctrine to be used by the courts in breaking down barriers encasing the poor.

In most cases legislative classifications did not specifically single out the poor for special treatment. But certain types of laws tended to fall with an unequally heavy hand on the poor. In *Levy* v. *Louisiana* (1968) the Supreme Court invalidated a regulation cutting off aid to needy children whose mothers subsequently bore illegitimate children. And in

[11]Joseph Tussman and Jacobus tenBroek, "The Equal Protection of the Laws," **37** *California Law Review* (1949), 341–381.

Sniadach v. *Family Finance Corporation* (1969), the Supreme Court struck down a Wisconsin wage garnishment statute which allowed the freezing of a garnishee's wages without notice or hearing and in advance of any court judgment. The decision formally rested on the due process clause, but it was clear from the court opinion of Justice Douglas and the bitter dissent by Justice Black that the decision was based on the social view that the garnishment policy was inhumane, that it tended to drive low income families below the poverty level, and that debts collected by such procedures were likely to be fraudulent. Although the law applied to all debtors, rich and poor, it worked a special hardship "on the poor, ignorant person who is trapped in any easy credit nightmare in which he is charged double for something he could not pay for, even if the proper price was called for, and then hounded into giving up his pound of flesh, and being fired besides."

One main thrust of the developing law of the poor has focused on the welfare system. Essentially there are four types of concerns exhibited by litigation in this area. First, there is the question of the conditions frequently attached to the receipt of welfare benefits, many of which have been alleged to be unconstitutional. These range from invasions of privacy exemplified by the notorious midnight searches by welfare workers to less obnoxious intrusions on the privacy of welfare families. Such conditions, most of which would be at best constitutionally suspect if applied to other citizens, find their authority in the prevailing theory that welfare benefits are a privilege and not a right, and that the society which provides these benefits is entitled to an accountability of their use. As Judge Skelly Wright has observed:

Welfare has long been considered the equivalent of charity and its recipients have been subjected to all kinds of dehumanizing experiences in the government's effort to police its welfare payments. In fact, over half a billion dollars are expended annually for administration and policing in connection with the Aid to Families with Dependent Children program. Why such large sums are necessary for administration and policing has never been adequately explained. No such sums are spent policing the government subsidies granted to farmers, airlines, steamship companies, and junk mail dealers, to name but a few. The truth is that in this subsidy area society has simply adopted a double standard, one for aid to business and the farmer and a different one for welfare.[12]

Second, there is the question of who is eligible for welfare benefits. Some welfare programs are financed and completely administered by the federal government. The basic "social security" system (Old Age Survivors and Insurance, or OASI) has always operated this way, and the Supplemental Security Income Program (SSI) instituted by Congress in the early 1970s completely "federalized" all the adult categories concerning the aged, blind and disabled. But the largest and most controversial welfare programs, Aid to Families with Dependent Children (AFDC), Food Stamps, and Medicaid, are administered by the states as part of a federal grant-in-aid scheme. The basic rules of eligibility are set by the Department of Health, Education and Welfare, within the limits of fed-

[12]"Poverty, Minorities and Respect for Law," 1970 *Duke Law Journal*, 425–451.

eral law, and determinations of individual eligibility and other administrative rules are set and enforced by the states. Thus, one set of problems concerns those standards imposed by the federal government, while the second and more important set involves standards *and* practices of the states which may deviate from federal standards.

There have been relatively few challenges to federal welfare standards as such. In *Flemming* v. *Nestor* (1960), the Court upheld the right of Congress to take away accrued social security benefits. Nestor, an alien, had come to the United States in 1913. From 1937 until 1955 both he and his employer contributed to the social security fund and in 1955 he became eligible to draw payments. In 1956 he was deported for having been a member of the Communist party between 1933 and 1939, when it was not illegal to be a member. Under a law passed by Congress in 1954, anyone deported for party membership lost all social security benefits. By a 5-4 vote the Court ruled that Nestor's property had not been taken unconstitutionally because he had no property right in his social security payments, which were "noncontractual." The Court held that Congress could be prohibited from removing social security benefits only where there was an utter lack of rational justification.

By far the greater problem has been the failure of the states to follow applicable federal standards, or, where federal rules permitted state discretion, the adoption by the states of very restrictive rules of eligibility. In *Sherbert* v. *Verner* (1963), unemployment insurance benefits were removed from an otherwise eligible recipient who refused an employment opportunity which required her to work on Saturdays in conflict with

her religion. South Carolina had defended its action on the grounds that these benefits were a privilege and not a right. But in reversing the Court found it unnecessary to consider that distinction; rather it held that "[i]t is too late in the day to doubt that the liberties of religion and expression may be infringed by the denial of or placing of conditions upon a benefit *or* privilege." The Supreme Court's response to challenges to residency requirements for welfare eligibility, and the *substitute father rule,* also fall in this category.

Third, there have been challenges alleging that various welfare procedures do not meet due process constitutional requirements. And, fourth, there have been challenges to limitations on the amounts of welfare grants.

Initial Supreme Court responses to welfare challenges engendered considerable optimism. The Court had little trouble in invalidating the "substitute father" rule utilized by some states to terminate welfare benefits to families where the mother was living with, or having sexual contact with, a man other than her legal husband or the father of her children. The Court, in *King* v. *Smith* (1968), ignored constitutional challenges to this practice and instead invalidated it as conflicting with applicable federal rules. The highwater mark of welfare reform came the following year in *Shapiro* v. *Thompson* when the Court invalidated a state-imposed one-year residency requirement for welfare recipients. The Court applied the strict scrutiny doctrine, which meant that the normal presumption of validity of the statute would be reversed, and the state would have to assume the not inconsiderable burden of proving that it had a compelling interest in the particular regulation. In *Shapiro,* it was the right to travel of welfare recipients, alleged to be abridged by Connecticut's durational residency requirement, that triggered application of the strict scrutiny standard. But there were also words in Justice Brennan's opinion for the majority, about the dependency of welfare families on public assistance for the necessities of life, which suggest that poverty or lack of wealth, and not the right to travel, was at the core of the decision in this case.

In a case decided at the same time, *McDonald* v. *Board of Election Commissioners* (1969), Chief Justice Warren wrote that "a careful examination on our part is especially warranted where lines are drawn on the basis of wealth or race, two factors which independently render a classification highly suspect and thereby demand a more exacting judicial scrutiny." *Shapiro* and *McDonald*, following on the heels of Douglas' dictum in *Harper* v. *Virginia Board of Elections* (1966), and other decisions, suggested that the liberals on the Warren Court were developing a concept of equal protection as a weapon to redress economic inequality—not only to prevent government from discriminating against poor people, but also perhaps even to impose on government some kind of affirmative obligation to redistribute wealth to ensure at least a minimum of economic subsistence for all persons. Yet, in no case had a state law been held unconstitutional exclusively because of its differential impact on poor people. Of course, no state could pass a law that explicitly discriminated against poor people. But as Justice Harlan said in his dissent in *Douglas* v. *California* (1963), ". . . it is a far different thing to suggest that this provision prevents the State from adopting a law of general applicability that may affect the poor more harshly than it does the rich."

If the Warren Court's legacy to its successor was an invitation to enhance the scope of constitutional protection for poor people in the future, the latter's response was, with a few exceptions, clear enough: it rejected the invitation and adopted instead Harlan's skeptical and cautious view. *Dandridge* v. *Williams* (1970) signaled the approach of the Burger Court, *James* v. *Valtierra* (1971) provided the emphasis, and *San Antonio School District* v. *Rodriguez* (1973) appeared to bury the idea of wealth as a suspect classification.

On the other hand, the Burger Court initially seemed to favor Charles Reich's theory that welfare benefits were a right and not a privilege in requiring pretermination hearings before welfare benefits could be cut off, *Goldberg* v. *Kelly* (1970). But that decision was soon watered down in *Matthews* v. *Eldridge* (1976), and the Reich thesis was rejected by the Court in *Wyman* v. *James* (1971).

If the Burger Court has allowed welfare *eligibility* determinations to remain a federal prerogative, it has been correspondingly deferential to the states on the issue of determining the range of benefits. Two recent abortion cases illustrate this policy. In *Burns* v. *Alcala* (1976), the Court upheld a state statute which denied AFDC benefits to unborn children. It ruled that the intent of Congress was to provide benefits to eligible individuals, and birth was a condition of eligibility. The family of an unborn fetus was thus not eligible for benefits.

In *Maher* v. *Roe* (1977), the Supreme Court reversed a three-judge federal court which had held that exclusion of nontherapeutic abortions under a state welfare program violated the equal protection clause of the Fourteenth Amendment. The Court held that states could rationally subsidize costs incident to childbirth instead of paying for nontherapeutic abortions, and that the state had a legitimate interest in encouraging childbirth. The majority decided that indigent pregnant women were not a "suspect class." Applying the test of ordinary scrutiny the Court found that exclusion of nontherapeutic abortions from state welfare subsidies was not a denial of the constitutional right of a woman to choose to terminate her pregnancy in the first trimester (See *Roe* v. *Wade*, pp. 1325–1333).

No case better demonstrates the philosophy of the Burger Court than *Lindsey* v. *Normet* (1972), a challenge to Oregon's statutory procedures for evicting tenants for nonpayment of rent. The tenants had argued that strict scrutiny should be the judicial test applied. It urged the Court to accept the notion that the "need for decent shelter" and the "right to retain peaceful possession of one's home" are fundamental interests that should evoke strict scrutiny. In reply, for a 5-2 majority, Justice White stated:

We do not denigrate the importance of decent, safe, and sanitary housing. But the Constitution does not provide judicial remedies for every social and economic ill. We are unable to perceive in that document any constitutional guarantee of access to dwellings of a particular quality or any recognition of the right of a tenant to occupy the real property of his landlord beyond the terms of his lease, without payment of rent. ... Absent constitutional mandate, the assurance of adequate housing and the definition of landlord-tenant relationships is a legislative and not a judicial function. Nor should we forget that the Constitution expressly protects

against confiscation of private property or the income therefrom.

B. The Welfare System

(1) King v. Smith (1968)

+Warren, Black, Douglas, Harlan, Brennan, Stewart, White, Marshall, Fortas

[Under the provisions of the Aid to Families with Dependent Children Program (AFDC), one of the three major categorical assistance programs established under the Social Security Act of 1935, states grant federally financed aid to families with children who have been deprived of parental support by death, continued absence from the home, or physical or mental incapacity. Alabama instituted a regulation in 1964 providing that an "able-bodied man, married or single is considered a substitute father of *all* the children of the applicant mother" if he lives in the home or frequently visits for purposes of cohabitation, or if he cohabits with the child's natural or adoptive mother elsewhere. Whether or not this substitute father has a legal obligation to support the children of the mother is deemed irrelevant. Cohabitation was defined to mean frequent or continuing sexual relations; administrative officials differed on whether this meant "at least once a week," "once every three months," or "every six months." Pregnancy or a child less than six months of age was considered *prima facie* evidence of the existence of a substitute father.

In the first three years after the regulation was instituted, the number of AFDC recipients in Alabama decreased by 20,000. In this case the regulation terminated assistance to a widow with four minor children. The alleged substitute father, who "visited" on weekends, had a wife and nine children, with whom he lived and all of whom were dependent on him for support. He was not the father of any of Mrs. Smith's children and was not legally obligated (nor able) to support them. A class action was brought in the federal district court, which found the regulation inconsistent with the Social Security Act and the equal protection clause.]

MR. CHIEF JUSTICE WARREN delivered the opinion of the Court.

. . . We think it well to note at the outset what is *not* involved in this case. There is no question that States have considerable latitude in allocating their AFDC resources, since each State is free to set its own standard of need and to determine the level of benefits by the amount of funds it devotes to the program. . . . Further, there is no question that regular and actual contributions to a needy child, including contributions from the kind of person Alabama calls a substitute father, can be taken into account in determining whether the child is needy. In other words, if by reason of such a man's contributions, the child is not in financial need, the child would be ineligible for AFDC assistance without regard to the substitute father rule. The appellees here, however, meet Alabama's need requirements; their alleged substitute father makes no contribution to their support; and they have been denied assistance solely on the basis of the substitute father regulation. Further, the regulation itself is unrelated to need, because the actual financial situation of the family is irrelevant in determining the existence of a substitute father.

Also not involved in this case is the question of Alabama's general power to deal with conduct it regards as immoral and with the problem of illegitimacy. This appeal raises only the question whether the State may deal with these problems in the matter that it has here—by flatly denying AFDC assistance to otherwise eligible dependent children.

Alabama's argument based on its interests in discouraging immorality and illegitimacy would have been quite relevant at one time in the history of the AFDC program. However, subsequent developments clearly establish that these state interests are not presently legitimate justifications for AFDC disqualifications. Insofar as this or any similar regulation is based on the State's asserted interest in discouraging illicit sexual behavior and illegitimacy, it plainly conflicts with federal law and policy.

A significant characteristic of public welfare programs during the last half of the 19th century in this country was their preference for the "worthy" poor. Some poor persons were thought worthy of public assistance, and others were thought unworthy because of their supposed incapacity for "moral regeneration." . . . This worthy-person concept characterized the mothers' pension welfare programs, which were the precursors of AFDC. . . . Benefits under the mothers' pension programs, accordingly, were customarily restricted to widows who were considered morally fit. . . .

In this social context it is not surprising that both the House and Senate Committee Reports on the Social Security Act of 1935 indicate that States participating in AFDC were free to impose eligibility requirements relating to the "moral character" of applicants. . . . During the following years, many state AFDC plans included provisions making ineligible for assistance dependent children not living in "suitable homes." . . .

As applied, these suitable home provisions frequently disqualified children on the basis of the alleged immoral behavior of their mothers. . . .

In the 1940's, suitable home provisions came under increasing attack. Critics argued, for example, that such disqualification provisions undermined a mother's confidence and authority, thereby promoting continued dependency; that they forced destitute mothers into increased immorality as a means of earning money; that they were habitually used to disguise systematic racial discrimination; and that they senselessly punished impoverished children on the basis of their mothers' behavior, while inconsistently permitting them to remain in the allegedly unsuitable homes. . . .

In the 1950's, matters became further complicated by pressures in numerous States to disqualify illegitimate children from AFDC assistance. Attempts were made in at least 18 States to enact laws excluding children on the basis of their own or their siblings' birth status. . . . In 1960, the federal agency strongly disapproved of illegitimacy disqualifications.

Nonetheless, in 1960, Louisiana enacted legislation requiring, as a condition precedent for AFDC eligibility, that the home of a dependent child be "suitable," and specifying that any home in which an illegitimate child had been born subsequent to the receipt of public assistance would be considered unsuitable. . . . In the summer of 1960, approximately 23,000 children were dropped from Louisiana's AFDC rolls. . . . In disapproving this legislation, then Secretary of Health, Education, and Welfare Flemming issued what is now known as the Flemming Ruling, stating that as of July 1, 1961,

A State plan . . . may not impose an eligibility condition that would deny assistance with respect to a needy child on the basis that the home conditions in which the child lives are unsuitable, while the child continues to reside in the home. Assistance will therefore be continued during the time efforts are being made either to improve the home conditions or to make arrangements for the child elsewhere.

Congress quickly approved the Flemming Ruling, while extending until September 1, 1962, the time for state compliance. . . . At the same time, Congress acted to implement the ruling by providing, on a temporary basis, that dependent children could receive AFDC assistance if they were placed in foster homes after a court determination that their former homes were, as the Senate Report stated, "unsuitable because of the immoral or negligent behavior of the parent." . . .

The most recent congressional amendments to the Social Security Act further corroborate that federal public welfare policy now rests on a basis considerably more sophisticated and enlightened than the "worthy-person" concept of earlier times. State plans are now required to provide for a rehabilitative program of improving and correcting unsuitable homes. . . . to provide voluntary family planning services for the purpose of reducing illegitimate births . . . and to provide a program for establishing the paternity of illegitimate children and securing support for them. . . .

In sum, Congress has determined that immorality and illegitimacy should be dealt with through rehabilitative measures rather than measures that punish dependent children, and that protection of such children is the paramount goal of AFDC. In light of the Flemming Ruling and the 1961, 1962, and 1968 amendments to the Social Security Act, it is simply inconceivable, as HEW has recognized, that Alabama is free to discourage immorality and illegitimacy by the device of absolute disqualification of needy children. Alabama may deal with these problems by several different methods under the Social Security Act. But the method it has chosen plainly conflicts with the Act.

Alabama's second justification for its substitute father regulation is that "there is a public interest in a State not undertaking the payment of these funds to families who because of their living arrangements would be in the same situation as if the parents were married, except for the marriage." In other words, the State argues that since in Alabama the needy children of married couples are not eligible for AFDC aid so long as their father is in the home, it is only fair that children of a mother who cohabits with a man not her husband and not their father be treated similarly. The difficulty with this argument is that it fails to take account of the circumstance that children of fathers living in the home are in a very different position from children of mothers who cohabit with men not their fathers: the child's father has a legal duty to support him, while the unrelated substitute father, at least in Alabama, does not. We believe Congress intended the term "parent" . . . to include only those persons with a legal duty of support. . . .

The question for decision here is whether Congress could have intended that a man was to be regarded as a child's parent so as to deprive the child of AFDC eligibility despite the circumstances: (1) that the man did not in fact support the child; and (2) that he was not legally obligated to support the child. . . .

It is clear, as we have noted, that Congress expected "breadwinners" who secured employment would support their children. This congressional expectation is most reasonably explained on the basis that the kind of breadwinner Congress had in mind was one who was legally obligated to support his children. We think it beyond reason to believe that Congress would have considered that providing employment for the paramour of a deserted mother would benefit the mother's children whom he was not obligated to support.

By a parity of reasoning, we think that Congress must have intended that the children in such a situation remain eligible for AFDC assistance notwithstanding their mother's impropriety. AFDC was intended to provide economic security for children whom Congress could not reasonably expect would be provided for by simply securing employment for family breadwinners. We think it apparent that neither Congress nor any reasonable person would believe that providing employment for some man who is under no legal duty to support a child would in any way provide meaningful economic security for that child. . . .

We think that these provisions corroborate the intent of Congress that the only kind of "parent," whose presence in the home would provide adequate economic protection for a dependent child is one who is legally obligated to support him. Consequently, if Alabama believes it necessary that it be able to disqualify a child on the basis of a man who is not under such a duty of support, its arguments should be addressed to Congress and not this Court.

Alabama's substitute father regulation, as written and as applied in this case, requires the disqualification of otherwise eligible dependent children if their mother "cohabits" with a man who is not obligated by Alabama law to support the children. The regulation is therefore invalid because it defines "parent" in a manner that is inconsistent with the Social Security Act. . . . In denying AFDC assistance to appellees on the basis of this invalid regulation, Alabama has breached its federally imposed obligation to furnish "aid to families with dependent children . . . with reasonable promptness to all eligible individuals. . . ." Our conclusion makes unnecessary consideration of appellees' equal-protection claim, upon which we intimate no views.

We think it well, in concluding, to emphasize that no legitimate interest of the State of Alabama is defeated by the decision we announce today. The State's interest in discouraging illicit sexual behavior and illegitimacy may be protected by other means, subject to constitutional limitations, including state participation in AFDC rehabilitative programs. Its interest in economically allocating its limited AFDC resources may be protected by its undisputed power to set the level of benefits and the standard of need, and by its taking into account in determining whether a child is needy all actual and regular contributions to his support. . . .

We hold today that Congress has made at least this one determination: that destitute children who are legally fatherless cannot be flatly denied federally funded assistance on the transparent fiction that they have a substitute father.

Affirmed.

MR. JUSTICE DOUGLAS, CONCURRING (OMITTED).

(2) Shapiro v. Thompson (1969)

+Brennan, Douglas, Stewart, White, Marshall
−Warren, Black, Harlan

[Three cases that were decided together involved a determination of the constitutionality of the one-year residency requirement for welfare assistance imposed by many states and by the District of Columbia. In each case a federal three-judge district court had held the residency statutes unconstitutional under the equal protection clause, because the requirement was deemed to have a "chilling effect" on the right to travel and, in the District of Columbia case, as a violation of the due process clause of the Fifth Amendment.]

MR. JUSTICE BRENNAN delivered the opinion of the Court.

. . . There is no dispute that the effect of the waiting-period requirement in each case is to create two classes of needy resident families indistinguishable from each other except that one is composed of residents who have resided a year or more, and the second of residents who have resided less than a year, in the jurisdiction. On the basis of this sole difference the first class is granted and the second class is denied welfare aid upon which may depend the ability of the families to obtain the very means to subsist—food, shelter, and other necessities of life. . . . The interests which appellants assert are promoted by the classification either may not constitutionally be promoted by government or are not compelling governmental interests.

Primarily, appellants justify the waiting-period requirement as a protective device to preserve the fiscal integrity of state public assistance programs. It is asserted that people who require welfare assistance during their first year of residence in a State are likely to become continuing burdens on state welfare programs. Therefore, the argument runs, if such people can be deterred from entering the jurisdiction by denying them welfare benefits during the first year, state programs to assist long-time residents will not be impaired by a substantial influx of indigent newcomers.

There is weighty evidence that exclusion from the jurisdiction of the poor who need or may need relief was the specific objective of these provisions. In the Congress, sponsors of federal legislation to eliminate all residence requirements have been consistently opposed by representatives of state and local welfare agencies who have stressed the fears of the States that elimination of the requirements would result in a heavy influx of individuals into States providing the most generous benefits. . . . The sponsor of the Connecticut requirement said in its support: "I doubt that Connecticut can and should continue to allow unlimited migration into the State on the basis of offering instant money and permanent income to all who can make their way to the State regardless of their ability to contribute to the economy." . . .

We do not doubt that the one-year waiting period device is well suited to discourage the influx of poor families in need of assistance. An indigent who desires to migrate, resettle, find a new job, start a new life will doubtless hesitate if he knows that he must risk making the move without the possibility of falling back on state welfare assistance during his first year of residence when his need may be most acute. But the purpose of inhibiting migration by needy persons into the State is constitutionally impermissible.

This Court long ago recognized that the nature of our Federal Union and our constitutional concepts of personal liberty unite to require that all citizens be free to travel throughout the length and breadth of our land uninhibited by statutes, rules, or regulations which unreasonably burden or restrict this movement. . . .

We have no occasion to ascribe the source of this right to travel interstate to a particular constitutional provision. It suffices that, as Mr. Justice Stewart said for the Court in *United States* v. *Guest* . . . (1966):

The constitutional right to travel from one State to another . . . occupies a position fundamental to the concept of our Federal Union. It is a right that has been firmly established and repeatedly recognized.

[T]he right finds no explicit mention in the Constitution. The reason, it has been suggested, is that a right so elementary was conceived from the beginning to be a necessary concomitant of the stronger Union the Constitution created. In any event, freedom to travel throughout the United States has long been recognized as a basic right under the Constitution.

Thus, the purpose of deterring the immigration of indigents cannot serve as justification for the classification created by the one-year waiting period, since that purpose is constitutionally impermissible. If a law has "no other purpose . . . than to chill the assertion of constitutional rights by penalizing those who choose to exercise them, then it is patently unconstitutional." . . .

Alternatively, appellants argue that even if it is impermissible for a State to attempt to deter the entry of all indigents, the challenged classification may be justified as a permissible state attempt to discourage those indigents who would enter the State solely to obtain larger benefits. We observe first that none of the statutes before us is tailored to serve that objective. Rather, the class of barred newcomers is all-inclusive, lumping the great majority who come to the State for other purposes with those who come for the sole purpose of collecting higher benefits. In actual operation, therefore, the three statutes enact what in effect are nonrebuttable presumptions that every applicant for assistance in his first year of residence came to the jurisdiction solely to obtain higher benefits. Nothing whatever in any of these records supplies any basis in fact for such a presumption.

More fundamentally, a State may no more try to fence out those indigents who seek higher welfare benefits than it may try to fence out indigents generally. Implicit in any such distinction is the notion that indigents who enter a State with the hope of securing higher welfare benefits are somehow less deserving than indigents who do not take this consideration into account. But we do not perceive why a mother who is seeking to make a new life for herself and her children should be regarded as less deserving because she considers, among other factors, the level of a State's public assistance. Surely such a mother is no less deserving than a mother who moves into a particular State in order to take advantage of its better educational facilities.

Appellants argue further that the challenged classification may be sustained as an attempt to distinguish between new and old residents on the basis of the contribution they have made to the community through the payment of taxes. We have difficulty seeing how long-term residents who qualify for welfare are making a greater present contribution to the State in taxes than indigent residents who have recently arrived. . . .

But we need not rest on the particular facts of these cases. Appellants' reasoning would logically permit the State to bar new residents from schools, parks, and libraries or deprive them of police and fire protection. Indeed it would permit the State to apportion all benefits and services according to the past tax contributions of its citizens. The Equal Protection Clause prohibits such an apportionment of state services.

We recognize that a State has a valid interest in preserving the fiscal integrity of its programs. It may legitimately attempt to limit its expenditures, whether for public assistance, public education, or any other program. But a State may not accomplish such a purpose by invidious distinctions between classes of its citizens. It could not, for example, reduce expenditures for education by barring indigent children from its schools. Similarly, in the cases before us, appellants must do more than show that denying welfare benefits to new residents saves money. The saving of welfare costs cannot be an independent ground for an invidious classification.

In sum, neither deterrence of indigents from migrating to the State nor limitation of welfare benefits to those regarded as contributing to the State is a constitutionally permissible state objective.

Appellants next advance as justification certain administrative and related governmental objectives allegedly served by the waiting-period requirement. They argue that the requirement (1) facilitates the planning of the welfare budget; (2) provides an objective test of residency; (3) minimizes the opportunity for recipients fraudulently to receive payments from more than one jurisdiction; and (4) encourages early entry of new residents into the labor force.

At the outset, we reject appellants' argument that a mere showing of a rational relationship between the waiting period and these four admittedly permissible state objectives will suffice to justify the classification. . . . The waiting-period provision denies welfare benefits to otherwise eligible applicants solely because they have recently moved into the jurisdiction. But in moving from State to State or to the District of Columbia appellees were exercising a constitutional right, and any classification which serves to penalize the exercise of that right, unless shown to be necessary to promote a *compelling* governmental interest, is unconstitutional.

The argument that the waiting-period requirement facilitates budget predictability is wholly unfounded.

The records in all three cases are utterly devoid of evidence that either State or the District of Columbia in fact uses the one-year requirement as a means to predict the number of people who will require assistance in the budget year. . . .

Similarly, there is no need for a State to use the one-year waiting period as a safeguard against fraudulent receipt of benefits; for less drastic means are available, and are employed, to minimize that hazard. Of course, a State has a valid interest in preventing fraud by any applicant, whether a newcomer or a long-time resident.

Pennsylvania suggests that the one-year waiting period is justified as a means of encouraging new residents to join the labor force promptly. But this logic would also require a similar waiting period for long-term residents of the State. A state purpose to encourage employment provides no rational basis for imposing a one-year waiting-period restriction on new residents only.

We conclude therefore that appellants in these cases do not use and have no need to use the one-year requirement for the governmental purposes suggested. Thus, even under traditional equal protection tests a classification of welfare applicants according to whether they have lived in the State for one year would seem irrational and unconstitutional. But, of course, the traditional criteria do not apply in these cases. Since the classification here touches on the fundamental right of interstate movement, its constitutionality must be judged by the stricter standard of whether it promotes a *compelling* state interest. Under this standard, the waiting period requirement clearly violates the Equal Protection Clause.

Connecticut and Pennsylvania argue, however, that the constitutional challenge to the waiting period requirements must fail because Congress expressly approved the imposition of the requirement by the States as part of the jointly funded AFDC program. . . .

But even if we were to assume, arguendo, that Congress did approve the imposition of a one-year waiting period, it is the responsive *state* legislation which infringes constitutional rights. By itself §402(b) has absolutely no restrictive effect. It is therefore not that statute but only the state requirements which pose the constitutional question.

Finally, even if it could be argued that the constitutionality of §402(b) is somehow at issue here, it follows from what we have said that the provision, insofar as it permits the one-year waiting-period requirement, would be unconstitutional. Congress may not authorize the States to violate the Equal Protection Clause. Perhaps Congress could induce wider state participation in school construction if it authorized the use of joint funds for the building of segregated schools. But could it seriously be contended that Congress would be constitutionally justified in such authorization by the need to secure state cooperation? . . .

The waiting-period requirement in the District of Columbia Code involved in No. 33 is also unconstitutional even though it was adopted by Congress as an exercise of federal power. In terms of federal power, the discrimination created by the one-year requirement violates the Due Process Clause of the Fifth Amendment. "[W]hile the Fifth Amendment contains no equal protection clause, it does forbid discrimination that is 'so unjustifiable as to be violative of due process.' " . . . ; *Bolling* v. *Sharpe* (1954). For the reasons we have stated in invalidating the Pennsylvania and Connecticut provisions, the District of Columbia provision is also invalid—the Due Process Clause of the Fifth Amendment forbids Congress from denying public assistance to poor persons otherwise eligible solely on the ground that they have not been residents of the District of Columbia for one year at the time their applications are filed.

Accordingly, the judgments are *Affirmed.*

MR. JUSTICE STEWART, CONCURRING (OMITTED).

MR. CHIEF JUSTICE WARREN, WITH WHOM MR. JUSTICE BLACK JOINS, DISSENTING.

In my opinion the issue before us can be simply stated: may Congress, acting under one of its enumerated powers, impose minimal nationwide residence requirements or authorize the States to do so? Since I believe that Congress does have this power and has constitutionally exercised it in these cases, I must dissent. . . .

MR. JUSTICE HARLAN, DISSENTING.
. . .

In upholding the equal protection argument, the Court has applied an equal protection doctrine of relatively recent vintage: the rule that statutory classifications which either are based upon certain "suspect" criteria or affect "fundamental rights" will be held to deny equal protection unless justified by a "compelling" governmental interest. . . .

The "compelling interest" doctrine, which today is articulated more explicitly than ever before, constitutes an increasingly significant exception to the long-established rule that a statute does not deny equal protection if it is rationally related to a legitimate governmental objective.

The "compelling interest" doctrine has two branches. The branch which requires that classifications based upon "suspect" criteria be supported by a compelling interest apparently had its genesis in cases involving racial classifications, which have at least since *Korematsu* v. *United States* . . . (1944), been regarded as inherently "suspect." The criterion of "wealth" apparently was added to the list of "suspects" as an alternative justification for the relationale in *Harper* v. *Virginia Bd. of Elections* . . . (1966), in which Virginia's poll tax was struck down. The criterion of political allegiance may have been added in *Williams* v. *Rhodes* . . . (1968). Today the list apparently has been further enlarged to include classifications based upon recent interstate movement, and perhaps those based upon the exercise of *any* constitutional right. . . .

I think that this branch of the "compelling interest" doctrine is sound when applied to racial classifications, for historically the Equal Protection Clause was largely a product of the desire to eradicate legal distinctions founded upon race. However, I believe that the more recent extensions have been unwise. . . . I do not consider wealth a "suspect" statutory criterion.

The second branch of the "compelling interest" principle is even more troublesome. For it has been held that a statutory classification is subject to the "compelling interest" test if the result of the classification may be to affect a "fundamental right," regardless of the basis of the classification. This rule was foreshadowed in *Skinner* v. *Oklahoma* . . . (1942), in which an Oklahoma statute providing for compulsory sterilization of "habitual criminals" was held subject to "strict scrutiny" mainly because it affected "one of the basic civil rights." After a long hiatus, the principle re-emerged in *Reynolds* v. *Sims* . . . (1964). The rule appeared again in *Carrington* v. *Rash* . . . (1965), in which, as I now see that case, the Court applied an abnormally severe equal protection standard to a Texas statute denying certain serviceman the right to vote, without indicating that the statutory distinction between servicemen and civilians was generally "suspect." . . .

A legislature might rationally find that the imposition of a welfare residence requirement would aid in the accomplishment of at least four valid governmental objectives. It might also find that residence requirements have advantages not shared by other methods of achieving the same goals. In light of this undeniable relation of residence requirements to valid legislative aims, it cannot be said that the requirements are "arbitrary" or "lacking in rational justification." . . .

I believe that the balance definitely favors constitutionality. In reaching that conclusion, I do not minimize the importance of the right to travel interstate. However, the impact of residence conditions upon that right is indirect and apparently quite insubstantial. On the other hand, the governmental purposes served by the requirements are legitimate and real, and the residence requirements are clearly suited to their accomplishment. To abolish residence requirements might well discourage highly worthwhile experimentation in the welfare field. . . . Residence requirements have advantages, such as administrative simplicity and relative certainty, which are not shared by the alternative solutions proposed by the appellees. . . .

Today's decision, it seems to me, reflects to an unusual degree the current notion that this Court possesses a peculiar wisdom all its own whose capacity to lead this Nation out of its present troubles is contained only by the limits of judicial ingenuity in contriving new constitutional principles to meet each problem as it arises. For anyone who, like myself, believes that it is an essential function of this Court to maintain the constitutional divisions between state and federal authority and among the three branches of the Federal Government, today's decision is a step in the wrong direction.

[*Shapiro* held that *durational* residency requirements, which "penalized" the right of interstate travel, a right that has no specific constitutional source but that all agree is a fundamental right, were subject to the test of strict scrutiny under the equal protection clause. Durational residency requirements are not to be confused with residency requirements. The former usually establish some waiting period of months, or even years, before a new state resident can become eligible for certain privileges or benefits on the same basis as all other residents. A residency requirement, by contrast, requires an individual to be a resident for certain purposes, for example, to vote or to be eligible for "in-state" tuition at a state-supported educational institution. Evidence of residency is normally found in such things as the location of one's principal place of residence, paying state taxes, registering one's automobile in a state, taking out a state driver's license, and so on. It is possible to be a resident of a state while not yet having met the durational requirement of some program.

In *Dunn* v. *Blumstein* (1972) the Supreme Court invalidated a one-year voter residency requirement. Tennessee required a year's residence in the State and three months in the county before a citizen was eligible to vote. The court found this to be excessive and unnecessary "to promote a compelling government interest." Classifications must be tailored to the purpose to be served. Clearly, Tennessee had a substantial interest in preventing voter fraud and in assuring that voters were knowledgeable about the issues. But a durational residency requirement of one year was much more than the state needed to prevent fraud ("30 days appears to be an ample period of time"). And "the conclusive presumptions of durational residence requirements are much too crude" to effectively ensure the knowledgeability of voters.

The *Shapiro* doctrine was also applied in *Memorial Hospital* v. *Maricopa County* (1974). Arizona required a year's residence in a county before an indigent person was eligible for nonemergency public medical care. The case involved claims for payment of medical expenses for an indigent who moved to Phoenix from New Mexico a month earlier. There was no doubt that the individual was a bona fide resident and that he was indigent. Writing for an 8-1 majority, Justice Marshall held that the one-year waiting period denied new residents the same opportunity to benefit from vital government services as other residents, especially where, as in this case, the "basic necessities of life" were involved. To underscore his point, Marshall quoted from Leviticus 24:22: "Ye shall have one manner of law, as well for the stranger as for one of your own country." Medical care is certainly as much a basic necessity of life to a person without means as are welfare payments, Marshall wrote. Against these imperatives, the state's contentions that the requirement was necessary to assure the fiscal integrity of its hospitals, that it served to inhibit the migration of new indigent residents, that it prevented fraud, and that it protected the interests of permanent residents were found inadequate.

In the interim between *Shapiro* and *Memorial Hospital*, the Court decided two cases involving out-of-state tuition rates. Most state educational institutions charge out-of-state residents a higher tuition rate. This is justified on the grounds that residents (or their parents) have paid taxes that subsidize those institutions. In Wisconsin, for example, out-of-state tuition is set to cover 100 percent of the cost of education; in-state tuition covers only 25 percent. Some states impose a durational residency period before an individual can become

eligible for the lower tuition. Other states make that virtually impossible. In *Starns* v. *Malkerson* (1971), the Court upheld Minnesota's one-year waiting period. (A student would, of course, also have to establish proof of residency). But in *Vlandis* v. *Kline* (1972), the Court invalidated the virtual "irrebuttable presumption" in Connecticut law that an out-of-state student who comes to the state for purposes of obtaining an education is not a resident and can never qualify.

Justice Marshall had to deal with these cases in *Memorial Hospital*. He did so, first, by reaffirming that *Shapiro* did not necessarily undermine *all* durational residency requirements. "Special problems are involved in determining the bona fide residence of college students who come from out of state to attend a public university . . . since those students are characteristically transient." He also noted that the impact of residency requirements for tuition is simply not as great as the denial of medical care to indigents. Denial of in-state tuition rates does not normally preclude a student from obtaining a college education.

The Court upheld a durational residency requirement in *Sosna* v. *Iowa* (1975). That state required a one-year waiting period before filing for a divorce. Writing for a 6-3 majority, Justice Rehnquist, who had been the lone dissenter in *Memorial Hospital,* found that Iowa could justify this requirement on more than budgetary and record-keeping grounds. States traditionally have a strong interest in regulating domestic relations, and a special interest in protecting the rights of all parties to a divorce, including minor children. It is also permissible for a state to avoid "officious intermeddling" in matters in which another state has a paramount interest, and in not becoming a divorce mill. The state interest asserted in this case, Rehnquist argued, was substantially stronger than in *Shapiro, Dunn,* and *Memorial Hospital.*]

(3) Goldberg v. Kelly (1970)

+Brennan, Douglas, Harlan, White, Marshall
−Burger, Black, Stewart

[The case involved a challenge by a group of residents of New York City against the termination of the welfare benefits which they were receiving under the AFDC program or the general relief program of the State of New York. It was charged that their benefits were terminated without prior notice or hearing and that these procedures constituted a violation of the due process clause of the Fourteenth Amendment. After the suits were filed in the federal district court, the city and state adopted procedures for notice and hearing, and the plaintiffs then amended their complaint to challenge the constitutional adequacy of these new procedures. It was argued that these new procedures did not allow for a personal appearance by the recipient before the official reviewing the termination recommendation of the case-worker, and that they did not allow oral presentation of evidence or cross-examination of witnesses. The procedures did, however, provide for a post-termination hearing before an independent examiner which would include these rights. A recipient prevailing at this post-termination hearing would be repaid funds withheld. A recipient who did not prevail at this hearing could seek judicial review. The federal district court held in favor of the recipient, and Goldberg, commissioner of Social Services for New York City, appealed.]

MR. JUSTICE BRENNAN delivered the opinion of the Court.

. . . The constitutional issue to be decided is the narrow one whether the Due Process Clause requires that the recipient be afforded an evidentiary hearing *before* the termination of benefits. The District Court held that only a pre-termination evidentiary hearing would satisfy the constitutional command, and rejected the argument of the state and city officials that the combination of the post-termination "fair hearing" with the informal pre-termination review disposed of all due process claims. The Court said: "While post-termination review is relevant, there is one overpowering fact which controls here. By hypothesis, a welfare recipient is destitute, without funds or assets. . . . Suffice it to say that to

cut off a welfare recipient in the face of . . . 'brutal need' without a prior hearing of some sort is unconscionable, unless overwhelming considerations justify it." . . . The Court rejected the argument that the need to protect the public's tax revenues supplied the requisite "overwhelming consideration."

Against the justified desire to protect public funds must be weighed the individual's overpowering need in this unique situation not to be wrongfully deprived of assistance. . . . While the problem of additional expense must be kept in mind, it does not justify denying a hearing meeting the ordinary standards of due process. Under all the circumstances, we hold that due process requires an adequate hearing before termination of welfare benefits, and the fact that there is a later constitutionally fair proceeding does not alter the result. . . .

Appellant does not contend that procedural due process is not applicable to the termination of welfare benefits. Such benefits are a matter of statutory entitlement for persons qualified to receive them. Their termination involves state action that adjudicates important rights. The constitutional challenge cannot be answered by an argument that public assistance benefits are "a 'privilege' and not a 'right.' " . . . Relevant constitutional restraints apply as much to the withdrawal of public assistance benefits as to disqualification for unemployment compensation, *Sherbert* v. *Verner* . . . (1963); or to denial of a tax exemption, *Speiser* v. *Randall* . . . *(1958)*; or to discharge from public employment, *Slochower* v. *Board of Higher Education* . . . (1956). The extent to which procedural due process must be afforded the recipient is influenced by the extent to which he may be "condemned to suffer grievous loss," and depends upon whether the recipient's interest in avoiding that loss outweighs the governmental interest in summary adjudication. . . .

It is true, of course, that some governmental benefits may be administratively terminated without affording the recipient a pre-termination evidentiary hearing. But we agree with the District Court that when welfare is discontinued, only a pre-termination evidentiary hearing provides the recipient with procedural due process. . . . Thus the crucial factor in this context—a factor not present in the case of the blacklisted government contractor, the discharged government employee, the taxpayer denied a tax exemption, or virtually anyone else whose governmental largesse is ended—is that termination of aid pending resolution of a controversy over eligibility may deprive an *eligible* recipient of the very means by which to live while he waits. Since he lacks independent resources, his situation becomes immediately desperate. His need to concentrate upon finding the means for daily subsistence, in turn, adversely affects his ability to seek redress from the welfare bureaucracy.

Moreover, important governmental interests are promoted by affording recipients a pre-termination evidentiary hearing. From its founding the Nation's basic commitment has been to foster the dignity and well-being of all persons within its borders. We have come to recognize that forces not within the control of the poor contribute to their poverty. This perception, against the background of our tradition, has significantly influenced the development of the contemporary public assistance system. Welfare, by meeting the basic demands of subsistence, can help bring within the reach of the poor the same opportunities that are available to others to participate meaningfully in the life of the community. At the same time, welfare guards against the societal malaise that may flow from a widespread sense of unjustified frustration and insecurity. Public assistance, then, is not mere charity, but a means to "promote the general Welfare, and secure the Blessings of Liberty to ourselves and our Posterity." The same governmental interests which counsel the provision of welfare, counsel as well its uninterrupted provision to those eligible to receive it; pre-termination evidentiary hearings are indispensable to that end.

Appellant does not challenge the force of these considerations but argues that they are outweighed by countervailing governmental interests in conserving fiscal and administrative resources. These interests, the argument goes, justify the delay of any evidentiary hearing until after discontinuance of the grants. Summary adjudication protects the public fisc by stopping payments promptly upon discovery of reason to believe that a recipient is no longer eligible. Since most terminations are accepted without challenge, summary adjudication also conserves both the fisc and administrative time and energy by reducing the number of evidentiary hearings actually held.

We agree with the District Court, however, that these governmental interests are not overriding in the welfare context. . . . The interest of the eligible recipient in uninterrupted receipt of public assistance, coupled with the State's interest that his payments not be erroneously terminated, clearly outweighs the State's competing concern to prevent any increase in its fiscal and administrative burdens. As the District Court correctly concluded, "[t]he stakes are simply too high for the welfare recipient, and the possibility for honest error or irritable misjudgment too great, to allow termination of aid without giving the recipient a chance, if he so desires, to be fully informed of the case against him so that he may contest its basis and produce evidence in rebuttal." . . .

We also agree with the District Court, however, that the pre-termination hearing need not take the form of a judicial or quasi-judicial trial. . . . Thus, a complete record and a comprehensive opinion, which would serve primarily to facilitate judicial review and to guide future decisions, need not be provided at the pre-termination stage. We recognize, too, that both welfare authorities and recipients have an interest in relatively speedy resolution of questions of eligibility, that they are used to dealing with one another informally, and that some welfare departments have very burdensome caseloads. These considerations justify the limitation of the pre-termination hearing to minimum procedural safeguards, adapted to the particular characteristics of welfare recipients, and to the limited nature of the controversies to be resolved. . . .

"The fundamental requisite of due process of law is the opportunity to be heard." . . . The hearing must be "at a meaningful time and in a meaningful manner.". . . In the present context these principles require that a recipient have timely and adequate notice detailing the reasons for a proposed termination, and an effective opportunity to defend by confronting any adverse witnesses and by presenting his own arguments and evidence orally. . . .

We are not prepared to say that the seven-days notice currently provided by New York City is constitutionally insufficient per se, although there may be cases where fairness would require that a longer time be given. Nor do we see any constitutional deficiency in the content or form of the notice. New York employs both a letter and a personal conference with a caseworker to inform a recipient of the precise questions raised about his continued eligibility. Evidently the recipient is told the legal and factual bases for the Department's doubts. This combination is probably the most effective method of communicating with recipients.

The city's procedures presently do not permit recipients to appear personally with or without counsel before the official who finally determines continued eligibility. Thus a recipient is not permitted to present evidence to that official orally, or to confront or cross-examine adverse witnesses. These omissions are fatal to the constitutional adequacy of the procedures.

The opportunity to be heard must be tailored to the capacities and circumstances of those who are to be heard. It is not enough that a welfare recipient may present his position to the decision maker in writing or second-hand through his caseworker. Written submissions are an unrealistic option for most recipients, who lack the educational attainment necessary to write effectively and who cannot obtain professional assistance. . . . Welfare recipients must therefore be given an opportunity to confront and cross-examine the witnesses relied on by the department.

"The right to be heard would be, in many cases, of little avail if it did not comprehend the right to be heard by counsel." . . . We do not say that counsel must be provided at the pre-termination hearing, but only that the recipient must be allowed to retain an attorney if he so desires. Counsel can help delineate the issues, present the factual contentions in an orderly manner, conduct cross-examination, and generally safeguard the interests of the recipient. . . .

Finally, the decisionmaker's conclusion as to a recipient's eligibility must rest solely on the legal rules and evidence adduced at the hearing. . . . To demonstrate compliance with this elementary requirement, the decision maker should state the reasons for his determination and indicate the evidence he relied on, though his statement need not amount to a full opinion or even formal findings of fact and conclusions of law. And, of course, an impartial decision maker is essential. . . . We agree with the District Court that prior involvement in some aspects of a case will not necessarily bar a welfare official from acting as a decision maker. He should not, however, have participated in making the determination under review.

Affirmed.

MR. JUSTICE BLACK, DISSENTING.

In the last half century the United States, along with many, perhaps most, other nations of the world, has moved far towards becoming a welfare state, that is, a nation that for one reason or another taxes its most affluent people to help support, feed, clothe and shelter its less fortunate citizens. The result is that today more than nine million men, women, and children in the United States receive some kind of state or federally financed public assistance in the form of allowances or gratuities, generally paid them periodically, usually by the week, month, or quarter. Since these gratuities are paid on the basis of need, the list of recipients is not static, and some people go off the lists and others are added from time to time. These ever-changing lists put a constant administrative burden on the Government and it certainly could not have reasonably anticipated that this burden would include the additional procedural expense imposed by the Court today. . . .

I do not believe there is any provision in our Constitution that should thus paralyze the Government's efforts to protect itself against making payments to people who are not entitled to them.

Particularly do I not think that the Fourteenth Amendment should be given such an unnecessarily broad construction. That Amendment came into being primarily to protect Negroes from discrimination, and while some of its language can and does protect others, all know that the chief purpose behind it was to protect ex-slaves. The Court, however, relies upon the Fourteenth Amendment and in effect says that failure of the Government to pay a promised charitable instalment to an individual deprives that individual of *his own property*, in violation of the Due Process Clause of the Fourteenth Amendment. It somewhat strains credulity to say that a government's promise of charity to an individual is property belonging to that individual when the Government denies that the individual is honestly entitled to receive such a payment.

I would have little, if any, objection to the majority's decision in this case if it were written as the report of the House Committee on Education and Labor, but as an opinion ostensibly resting on the language of the Constitution I find it woefully deficient. . . .

The Court apparently feels that this decision will benefit the poor and needy. In my judgment the eventual result will be just the opposite. While today's decision requires only an administrative, evidentiary hearing, the inevitable logic of the approach taken will lead to constitutionally imposed, time-consuming delays of a full adversary process of administrative and judicial review. In the next case the welfare recipients are bound to argue that cutting off benefits before judicial review of the agency's decision is also a denial of due process. Since, by hypothesis, termination of aid at that point may still "deprive an *eligible* recipient of the very means by which to live while he waits," . . . I would be surprised if the weighing process did not compel the conclusion that termination without full judicial review would be unconscionable. . . . Thus the end result of today's decision may well be that the Government, once it decides to give welfare benefits, cannot reverse that decision until the recipient has had the benefit of full administrative and judicial review, including, of course, the opportunity to present his case to this Court. Since this process will usually entail a delay of several years, the inevitable result of such a constitutionally imposed burden will be that the Government will not put a claimant on the rolls initially until it has made an exhaustive investigation to determine his eligibility. While this Court will perhaps have insured that no needy person will be taken off the rolls without a full "due process" proceeding, it will also have insured that many will never get on the rolls, or at least that they will remain destitute during the lengthy proceedings followed to determine initial eligibility.

MR. CHIEF JUSTICE BURGER, WITH WHOM MR. JUSTICE BLACK JOINS, DISSENTING.

. . . The Court's action today seems another manifestation of the now familiar constitutionalizing syndrome: once some presumed flaw is observed, the Court then eagerly accepts the invitation to find a constitutionally "rooted" remedy. If no provision is explicit on the point, it is then seen as "implicit" or commanded by the vague and nebulous concept of "fairness."

I can share the impatience of all who seek instant solutions; there is a great temptation in this area to frame remedies which seem fair and can be mandated forthwith as against administrative or congressional action which calls for careful and extended study. That is thought too slow. But however cumbersome or glacial, this is the procedure the Constitution contemplated. . . .

MR. JUSTICE STEWART, DISSENTING (OMITTED).

(4) Dandridge v. Williams (1970)

+Stewart, Burger, Black, Harlan, White
−Douglas, Marshall, Brennan

MR. JUSTICE STEWART delivered the opinion of the Court.

This case involves the validity of a method used by Maryland . . . to reconcile the demands of its needy citizens with the finite resources available to meet those demands. Like every other State in the Union, Maryland participates in the federal Aid to Families with Dependent Children (AFDC) program. . . . Under this jointly financed program, a State computes the so-called "standard of need" of each eligible family unit within its borders. . . . Some States provide that every family shall receive grants sufficient to meet fully the determined standard of need. Other States provide that each family unit shall receive a percentage of the determined need. Still others provide grants to most families in full accord with the ascertained standard of need, but impose an upper limit on the total amount of money any one family unit may receive. Maryland, through administrative adoption of a "maximum grant regulation," has followed this last course. This suit was brought by several AFDC recipients to enjoin the application of the Maryland maximum grant regulation on the ground that it is in conflict with the Social Security Act of 1935 and with the Equal Protection Clause of the Fourteenth Amendment. A three-judge District Court. . . . held that the Maryland regulation violates the Equal Protection Clause. . . . This direct appeal followed . . . and we noted probable jurisdiction.

. . . Maryland . . . computes the standard of need for each eligible family based on the number of children in the family and the circumstances under which the family lives. In general, the standard of need increases with each additional person in the household, but the increments become proportionately smaller. The regulation here in issue imposes upon the grant that any single family may receive an upper limit of $250 per month in certain counties including Baltimore City, and of $240 per month elsewhere in the State. The appellees all have large families, so that their standards of need as computed by the State substantially exceed the maximum grants that they actually receive under the regulation. . . .

The appellees contend that the maximum grant system is contrary to the Social Security Act, as amended, which requires that a state plan shall

provide . . . that all individuals wishing to make application for aid to families with dependent children shall have the

opportunity to do so, and that aid to families with dependent children shall be furnished with reasonable promptness to all eligible individuals.

The argument is that the state regulation denies benefits to the younger children in a large family. Thus, the appellees say, the regulation is in patent violation of the Act, since those younger children are just as "dependent" as their older siblings under the definition of "dependent child" fixed by federal law. . . . Moreover, it is argued that the regulation, in limiting the amount of money any single household may receive, contravenes a basic purpose of the federal law by encouraging the parents of large families to "farm out" their children to relatives whose grants are not yet subject to the maximum limitation.

It cannot be gainsaid that the effect of the Maryland maximum grant provision is to reduce the per capita benefits to the children in the largest families. Although the appellees argue that the younger and more recently arrived children in such families are totally deprived of aid, a more realistic view is that the lot of the entire family is diminished because of the presence of additional children without any increase in payments . . . For the reasons that follow, we have concluded that the Maryland regulation is permissible under the federal law. . . .

The starting point of the statutory analysis must be a recognition that the federal law gives each State great latitude in dispensing its available funds. . . .

The States must respond to federal statutory concern for preserving children in a family environment. Given Maryland's finite resources, its choice is either to support some families adequately and others less adequately, or not to give sufficient support to any family. We see nothing in the federal statute that forbids a State to balance the stresses which uniform insufficiency of payments would impose on all families against the greater ability of large families—because of the inherent economies of scale—to accommodate their needs to diminished per capita payments. The strong policy of the statute in favor of preserving family units does not prevent a State from sustaining as many families as it can, and providing the largest families somewhat less than their ascertained per capita standard of need. Nor does the maximum grant system necessitate the dissolution of family bonds. For even if a parent should be inclined to increase his per capita family income by sending a child away, the federal law requires that the child, to be eligible for AFDC payments, must live with one of several enumerated relatives. The kinship tie may be attenuated but it cannot be destroyed. . . .

This is the view that has been taken by the Secretary of Health, Education, and Welfare, who is charged with the administration of the Social Security Act and the approval of state welfare plans. The parties have stipulated that the Secretary has, on numerous occasions, approved the Maryland welfare scheme, including its provision of maximum payments to any one family, a provision which has been in force in various forms since 1947. Moreover, a majority of the States pay less than their determined standard of need, and 20 of these States impose maximums on family grants of the kind here in issue. The Secretary has not disapproved any state plan because of its maximum grant provisions. . . .

Although a State may adopt a maximum grant system in allocating

its funds available for AFDC payments without violating the Act, it may not, of course, impose a regime of invidious discrimination in violation of the Equal Protection Clause of the Fourteenth Amendment. Maryland says that its maximum grant regulation is wholly free of any invidiously discriminatory purpose or effect, and that the regulation is rationally supportable on at least four entirely valid grounds. The regulation can be clearly justified, Maryland argues, in terms of legitimate state interests in encouraging gainful employment, in maintaining an equitable balance in economic status as between welfare families and those supported by a wage-earner, in providing incentives for family planning, and in allocating available public funds in such a way as fully to meet the needs of the largest possible number of families. . . .

If this were a case involving government action claimed to violate the First Amendment guarantee of free speech, a finding of "overreaching" would be significant and might be crucial. For when otherwise valid governmental regulation sweeps so broadly as to impinge upon activity protected by the First Amendment, its very overbreadth may make it unconstitutional. . . . But the concept of "overreaching" has no place in this case. For here we deal with state regulation in the social and economic field, not affecting freedoms guaranteed by the Bill of Rights, and claimed to violate the Fourteenth Amendment only because the regulation results in some disparity in grants of welfare payments to the largest AFDC families. For this Court to approve the invalidation of state economic or social regulations as "overreaching" would be far too reminiscent of an era when the Court thought the Fourteenth Amendment gave it power to strike down state laws "because they may be unwise, improvident, or out of harmony with a particular school of thought." . . . That era long ago passed into history. . . .

In the area of economics and social welfare, a State does not violate the Equal Protection Clause merely because the classification made by its laws are imperfect. If the classification has some "reasonable basis," it does not offend the Constitution simply because the classification "is not made with mathematical nicety or because in practice it results in some inequality." . . . "The problems of government are practical ones and may justify, if they do not require, rough accommodations—illogical, it may be, and unscientific." . . . "A statutory discrimination will not be set aside if any state of facts reasonably may be conceived to justify it." . . .

To be sure, the cases cited, and many others enunciating this fundamental standard under the Equal Protection Clause, have in the main involved state regulation of business or industry. The administration of public welfare assistance, by contrast, involves the most basic economic needs of impoverished human beings. We recognize the dramatically real factual difference between the cited cases and this one, but we can find no basis for applying a different constitutional standard. . . . It is a standard that has consistently been applied to state legislation restricting the availability of employment opportunities. . . . And it is a standard that is true to the principle that the Fourteenth Amendment gives the federal courts no power to impose upon the States their views of wise economic or social policy.

Under this long-established meaning of the Equal Protection Clause, it is clear that the Maryland maximum grant regulation is constitutionally valid. . . . It is enough that a solid foundation for the regulation can be found in the State's legitimate interest in encouraging employment and in avoiding discrimination between welfare families and the families of the working poor. . . . It is enough that the State's action be rationally based and free from invidious discrimination. The regulation before us meets the test.

We do not decide today that the Maryland regulation is wise, that it best fulfills the relevant social and economic objectives that Maryland might ideally espouse, or that a more just and humane system could not be devised. Conflicting claims of morality and intelligence are raised by opponents and proponents of almost every measure, certainly including the one before us. But the intractable economic, social, and even philosophical problems presented by public welfare assistance programs are not the business of this Court. The Constitution may impose certain procedural safeguards upon systems of welfare administration. . . . But the Constitution does not empower this Court to second-guess state officials charged with the difficult responsibility of allocating limited public welfare funds among the myriad of potential recipients. . . .

The judgment is reversed.

MR. JUSTICE BLACK, WITH WHOM THE CHIEF JUSTICE JOINS, CONCURRING (OMITTED).
MR. JUSTICE HARLAN, CONCURRING (OMITTED).
MR. JUSTICE DOUGLAS, DISSENTING (OMITTED).

MR. JUSTICE MARSHALL, WHOM MR. JUSTICE BRENNAN JOINS, DISSENTING.

. . . I believe that the Court has erroneously concluded that Maryland's maximum grant regulation is consistent with the federal statute. In my view, that regulation is fundamentally in conflict with the basic structure and purposes of the Social Security Act.

More important in the long run than this misreading of a federal statute, however, is the Court's emasculation of the Equal Protection Clause as a constitutional principle applicable to the area of social welfare administration. The Court holds today that regardless of the arbitrariness of a classification it must be sustained if any state goal can be imagined which is arguably furthered by its effects. This is so even though the classification's under- or over-inclusiveness clearly demonstrates that its actual basis is something other than that asserted by the State, and even though the relationship between the classification and the state interests which it purports to serve is so tenuous that it could not seriously be maintained that the classification tends to accomplish the ascribed goals.

The Court recognizes, as it must, that this case involves "the most basic economic needs of impoverished human beings," and that there is therefore a "dramatically real factual difference" between the instant case and those decisions upon which the Court relies. The acknowledgment that these dramatic differences exist is a candid recognition that the Court's decision today is wholly without precedent. . . .

In the instant case, the only distinction between those children with respect to whom assistance is granted and those children who are denied such assistance is the size of the family into which the child permits himself to be born. The class of individuals with respect to whom payments are actually made (the first four or five eligible dependent children in a family), is grossly un-derinclusive in terms of the class which the AFDC program was designed to assist, namely *all* needy dependent children. Such under-inclusiveness manifests "a *prima facie* violation of the equal protection requirement of reasonable classification," compelling the State to come forward with a persuasive justification for the classification.

The Court never undertakes to inquire for such a justification; rather it avoids the task by focusing upon the abstract dichotomy between two different approaches to equal protection problems which have been utilized by this Court.

Under the so-called "traditional test," a classification is said to be permissible under the Equal Protection Clause unless it is "without any reasonable basis." . . . On the other hand, if the classification affects a "fundamental right," then the state interest in perpetuating the classification must be "compelling" in order to be sustained.

This case simply defies easy characterization in terms of one or the other of these "tests." The cases relied on by the Court, in which a "mere rationality" test was actually used . . . , are most accurately described as involving the application of equal protection reasoning to the regulation of business interests. The extremes to which the Court has gone in dreaming up rational bases for state regulation in that area may in many instances be ascribed to a healthy revulsion from the Court's earlier excesses in using the Constitution to protect interests which have more than enough power to protect themselves in the legislative halls. This case, involving the literally vital interests of a powerless minority —poor families without breadwinners—is far removed from the area of business regulation, as the Court concedes. Why then is the standard used in those cases imposed here? We are told no more than that this case falls in "the area of economics and social welfare," with the implication that from there the answer is obvious.

In my view, equal protection analysis of this case is not appreciably advanced by the *a priori* definition of a "right," fundamental or otherwise. Rather, concentration must be placed upon the character of the classification in question, the relative importance to individuals in the class discriminated against of the governmental benefits which they do not receive, and the asserted state interests in support of the classification. As we said only recently, "In determining whether or not a state law violates the Equal Protection Clause, we must consider the facts and circumstances behind the law, the interests which the State claims to be protecting, and the interests of those who are disadvantaged by the classification." . . .

It is the individual interests here at stake which, as the Court concedes, most clearly distinguish this case from the "business regulation" equal protection cases. . . . And this Court has already recognized several times that when a benefit, even a "gratuitous" benefit, is necessary to sustain life, stricter constitutional standards, both procedural and substantive, are applied to the deprivation of that benefit. . . .

In my view Maryland's maximum grant regulation is invalid under the Equal Protection Clause of the Fourteenth Amendment.

(5) Wyman v. James (1971)

+Blackmun, Burger, Black, Harlan, Stewart, White
−Douglas, Brennan, Marshall

[Among the worst abuses of the constitutional rights of welfare recipients were the notorious "midnight raids" in which welfare workers would make unannounced visits in the early morning hours to recipients' homes to determine the presence of a "substitute father" or to confirm the existence of the number of dependent children claimed. Most of these abuses had been eliminated prior to 1971, but in many states there still remained the requirement that case workers make periodic "home visits" to insure that welfare funds were being properly expended. These visits are in the daytime, frequently with advance notice. But if they are refused, the recipient's benefits are terminated.

In this case an effort was made to invalidate the provisions of the New York Social Services Law which required the termination of welfare benefits to AFDC mothers who refused a home visit from a caseworker but had offered to meet with the caseworker and supply any information. A three-judge federal court was convened and found in favor of the appellant, Mrs. James. The court found that the home visit was a search within the meaning of the Fourth and Fourteenth Amendments and thus could not be condoned in the absence either of permission or a search warrant based on probable cause.]

MR. JUSTICE BLACKMUN delivered the opinion of the Court.

. . . When a case involves a home and some type of official intrusion into that home, as this case appears to do, an immediate and natural reaction is one of concern about Fourth Amendment rights and the protection which that Amendment is intended to afford. Its emphasis indeed is upon one of the most precious aspects of personal security in the home. "The right of the people to be secure in their persons, houses, papers, and effects . . . ." This Court has characterized that right as "basic to our free society." . . .

This natural and quite proper protective attitude, however, is not a factor in this case, for the seemingly obvious and simple reason that we are not concerned here with any search by the New York social service agency in the Fourth Amendment meaning of that term. It is true that the governing statute and regulations appear to make mandatory the initial home visit and the subsequent periodic "contacts" (which may include home visits) for the inception and continuance of aid. It is also true that the caseworker's posture in the home visit is perhaps, in a sense, both rehabilitative and investigative. But this latter aspect, we think, is given too broad a character and far more emphasis than it deserves if it is equated with a search in the traditional criminal law context. We note, too, that the visitation in itself is not forced or compelled, and that the beneficiary's denial of permission is not a criminal act. If consent to the visitation is withheld, no visitation takes place. The aid then never begins or merely ceases, as the case may be. There is no entry of the home and there is no search.

If however, we were to assume that a caseworker's home visit, before or subsequent to the beneficiary's initial qualification for benefits, somehow (perhaps because the average beneficiary might feel she is in no position to refuse consent to the visit), and despite its interview nature, does possess some of the characteristics of a search in the traditional sense, we nevertheless conclude that the visit does not fall within the Fourth Amendment's proscription. This is because it does not descend to the level of unreasonableness. It is unreasonableness which is the Fourth Amendment's standard. . . .

There are a number of factors which compel us to conclude that the home visit proposed for Mrs. James is not unreasonable:

1. The public's interest in this particular segment of the area of assistance to the unfortunate is protection and aid for the dependent child whose family requires such aid for that child. The focus is on the *child* and, further, it is on the child who is *dependent*. There is no more worthy object of the public's concern. The dependent child's needs are paramount, and only with hesitancy would we relegate those needs, in the scale of comparative values, to a position secondary to what the mother claims as her rights.

2. The agency, with tax funds provided from federal as well as from state sources, is fulfilling a public trust. The State . . . has appropriate and paramount interest and concern in seeing and assuring that the intended and proper objects of that tax-produced assistance are the ones who benefit from the aid it dispenses. Surely it is not unreasonable, in the Fourth Amendment sense or in any other sense of that term, that the State have at its command a gentle means, of limited extent and of practical and considerate application, of achieving that assurance.

3. One who dispenses purely private charity naturally has an interest in and expects to know how his charitable funds are utilized and put to work. The public, when it is the provider, rightly expects the same. It might well expect more, because of the trust aspect of public funds, and the recipient, as well as the caseworker, has not only an interest but an obligation.

4. The emphasis of the New York statutes and regulations is upon the home, upon "close contact" with the beneficiary, upon restoring the aid recipient "to a condition of self-support," and upon the relief of his distress. . . .

5. The home visit it is true, is not required by federal statute or regulation. But it has been noted that the visit is "the heart of welfare administration"; that it affords "a personal,

rehabilitative orientation, unlike that of most federal programs"; and that the "more pronounced service orientation" effected by Congress with the 1956 amendments to the Social Security Act "gave redoubled importance to the practice of home visiting. . . ."

6. The means employed by the New York agency are significant. Mrs. James received written notice several days in advance of the intended home visit. The date was specified. . . . Privacy is emphasized. The applicant-recipient is made the primary source of information as to eligibility. Outside informational source, other than public records, are to be consulted only with the beneficiary's consent. Forcible entry or entry under false pretenses or visitation outside working hours or snooping in the home are forbidden. . . . All this minimizes any "burden" upon the homeowner's right against unreasonable intrusion.

7. Mrs. James, in fact, on this record presents no specific complaint of any unreasonable intrusion of her home and nothing which supports an inference that the desired home visit had as its purpose the obtaining of information as to criminal activity. She complains of no proposed visitation at an awkward or retirement hour. She suggests no forcible entry. She refers to no snooping. She describes no impolite or reprehensible conduct of any kind. She alleges only, in general and nonspecific terms, that on previous visits and, on information and belief, on visitation at the home of other aid recipients, "questions concerning personal relationships, beliefs and behavior are raised and pressed which are unnecessary for a determination of continuing eligibility." Paradoxically, this same complaint could be made of a conference held elsewhere than in the home, and yet this is what is sought by Mrs. James.

The same complaint could be made of the census taker's questions. . . . What Mrs. James appears to want from the agency which provides her and her infant son with the necessities for life is the right to receive those necessities upon her own informational terms, to utilize the Fourth Amendment as a wedge for imposing those terms, and to avoid questions of any kind.

8. We are not persuaded, as Mrs. James would have us be, that all information pertinent to the issue of eligibility can be obtained by the agency through an interview at a place other than the home, or, as the District Court majority suggested, by examining a lease or a birth certificate, or by periodic medical examinations, or by interviews with school personnel. . . .

9. The visit is not one by police or uniformed authority. It is made by a caseworker of some training whose primary objective is, or should be, the welfare, not the prosecution, of the aid recipient for whom the worker has profound responsibility. . . .

10. The home visit is not a criminal investigation, does not equate with a criminal investigation, and despite the announced fears of Mrs. James and those who would join her, is not in aid of any criminal proceeding. If the visitation serves to discourage misrepresentation or fraud, such a byproduct of that visit does not impress upon the visit itself a dominant criminal investigative aspect. And if the visit should, by chance, lead to the discovery of fraud and a criminal prosecution should follow, then, even assuming that the evidence discovered upon the home visitation is admissible, an issue upon which we express no opinion, that is a routine and expected fact of life and a consequence no greater than that which necessarily ensues upon any

other discovery by a citizen of criminal conduct.

11. The warrant procedure, which the plaintiffs appear to claim to be so precious to them, even if civil in nature, is not without its seriously objectionable features in the welfare context. If a warrant could be obtained (the appellees afford us little help as to how it would be obtained), it presumably could be applied for ex parte, its execution would require no notice, it would justify entry by force, and its hours for execution would not be so limited as those prescribed for home visitation. The warrant necessarily would imply conduct either criminal or out of compliance with an asserted government standard. Of course, the force behind the warrant argument, welcome to the one asserting it, is the fact that it would have to rest upon probable cause, and probable cause in the welfare context, as Mrs. James concedes, requires more than the mere need of the caseworker to see the child in the home and to have assurance that the child is there and is receiving the benefit of the aid which has been authorized for it. In this setting the warrant argument is out of place.

It seems to us that the situation is akin to that where an Internal Revenue Service agent, in making a routine civil audit of a taxpayer's income tax return, asks that the taxpayer produce for the agent's review some proof of a deduction the taxpayer has asserted to his benefit in the computation of his tax. If the taxpayer refuses, there is, absent fraud, only a disallowance of the claimed deduction and a consequent additional tax. The taxpayer is fully within his "rights" in refusing to produce the proof, but in maintaining and asserting those rights a tax detriment results and it is a detriment of the taxpayer's own making. So here

Mrs. James has the "right" to refuse the home visit, but a consequence in the form of cessation of aid, similar to the taxpayer's resultant additional tax, flows from that refusal. The choice is entirely hers, and nothing of constitutional magnitude is involved.

Camara v. *Municipal Court* . . . (1967), and its companion case, *See* v. *City of Seattle* . . . (1967), both by a divided Court, are not inconsistent with our result here. Those cases concerned, respectively, a refusal of entry to city housing inspectors checking for a violation of a building's occupancy permit and a refusal of entry to a fire department representative interested in compliance with a city's fire code. In each case a majority of this Court held that the Fourth Amendment barred prosecution for refusal to permit the desired warrantless inspection. *Frank* v. *Maryland* . . . (1959), a case which reached an opposing result and which concerned a request by a health officer for entry in order to check the source of a rat infestation, was pro tanto overruled. Both *Frank* and *Camara* involved dwelling quarters. *See* had to do with a commercial warehouse.

But the facts of the three cases are significantly different from those before us. Each concerned a true search for violations. *Frank* was a criminal prosecution for the owner's refusal to permit entry. So, too, was *See*. *Camara* had to do with a writ of prohibition sought to prevent an already pending criminal prosecution. The community welfare aspects, of course, were highly important, but each case arose in a criminal context where a genuine search was denied and prosecution followed.

In contrast, Mrs. James is not being prosecuted for her refusal to permit the home visit and is not about to be so prosecuted. Her wishes in that respect are fully honored. We have not been told, and have not found, that her refusal is made a criminal act by any applicable New York or federal statute. The only consequence of her refusal is that the payment of benefits ceases. Important and serious as this is, the situation is no different than if she had exercised a similar negative choice initially and refrained from applying for AFDC benefits. If a statute made her refusal a criminal offense, and if this case were one concerning her prosecution under that statute, *Camara* and *See* would have conceivable pertinency.

Our holding today does not mean, of course, that a termination of benefits upon refusal of a home visit is to be upheld against constitutional challenge under all conceivable circumstances. The early morning mass raid upon homes of welfare recipients is not unknown. . . . But that is not this case.

We therefore conclude that the home visitation as structured by the New York statutes and regulations is a reasonable administrative tool; that it serves a valid and proper administrative purpose for the dispensation of the AFDC program; that it is not an unwarranted invasion of personal privacy; and that it violates no right guaranteed by the Fourth Amendment.

Reversed and remanded with directions to enter a judgment of dismissal.

It is so ordered.

. . .

MR. JUSTICE DOUGLAS, DISSENTING.

We are living in a society where one of the most important forms of property is government largesse which some call the "new property." The payrolls of government are but one aspect of that "new property." Defense contracts, highway contracts, and the other multifarious forms of contracts are another part. So are subsidies to air, rail, and other carriers. So are disbursements by government for scientific research. So are TV and radio licenses to use the air space which of course is part of the public domain. Our concern here is not with those subsidies but with grants that directly or indirectly implicate the *home life* of the recipients.

In 1969 roughly 126 billion dollars were spent by the federal, state, and local governments on "social welfare." To farmers alone, over four billion dollars was paid, in part for not growing certain crops. Almost 129,000 farmers received $5,000 or more, their total benefit exceeding $1,450,000,000. Those payments were in some instances very large, a few running a million or more a year. But the majority were payments under $5,000 each.

Yet almost every beneficiary whether rich or poor, rural or urban, has a "house"—one of the places protected by the Fourth Amendment against "unreasonable searches and seizures." The question in this case is whether receipt of largesse from the government makes the *home* of the beneficiary subject to access by an inspector of the agency of oversight, even though the beneficiary objects to the intrusion and even though the Fourth Amendment's procedure for access to one's *house* or *home* is not followed. The penalty here is not, of course, invasion of the privacy of Barbara James, only her loss of federal or state largesse. That, however, is merely rephrasing the problem. Whatever the semantics, the central question is whether the government by force of its largesse has the power to "buy up" rights guaranteed by the

Constitution. But for the assertion of her constitutional right, Barbara James in this case would have received the welfare benefit. . . .

If the welfare recipient was not Barbara James but a prominent, affluent cotton or wheat farmer receiving benefit payments for not growing crops, would not the approach be different? Welfare in aid of dependent children, like social security and unemployment benefits, has an aura of suspicion. There doubtless are frauds in every sector of public welfare whether the recipient be a Barbara James or someone who is prominent or influential. But constitutional rights—here the privacy of the *home*—are obviously not dependent on the poverty or on the affluence of the beneficiary. It is the precincts of the *home* that the Fourth Amendment protects; and their privacy is as important to the lowly as to the mighty. . . .

It may be that in some tenements one baby will do service to several women and call each one "mom." It may be that other frauds, less obvious will be perpetrated. But if inspectors want to enter the precincts of the home against the wishes of the lady of the house, they must get a warrant. The need for exigent action as in cases of "hot pursuit" is not present for the lady will not disappear; nor will the baby.

I would place the same restrictions on inspectors entering the *homes* of welfare beneficiaries as are on inspectors entering the *homes* of those on the payroll of government, or the *homes* of those who contract with the government, or the *homes* of those who work for those having government contracts. The values of the *home* protected by the Fourth Amendment are not peculiar to capitalism as we have known it; they are equally relevant to the new form of socialism which we are entering. Moreover, as the numbers of functionaries and inspectors multiply, the need for protection of the individual becomes indeed more essential if the values of a free society are to remain. . . .

MR. JUSTICE MARSHALL, WHOM MR. JUSTICE BRENNAN JOINS, DISSENTING.

. . . Simply stated, the issue in this case is whether a state welfare agency can require all recipients of AFDC benefits to submit to warrantless "visitations" of their homes. In answering that question, the majority dodges between constitutional issues to reach a result clearly inconsistent with the decisions of this Court. We are told that there is no search involved in this case; that even if there were a search, it would not be unreasonable; and that even if this were an unreasonable search, a welfare recipient waives her right to object by accepting benefits. I emphatically disagree with all three conclusions. . . .

The Court's assertion that this case concerns no search "in the Fourth Amendment meaning of the term" is neither "obvious" nor "simple." I should have thought that the Fourth Amendment governs all intrusions by agents of the public upon personal security . . . .

Even if the Fourth Amendment does not apply to each and every governmental entry into the home, the welfare visit is not some sort of purely benevolent inspection. No one questions the motives of the dedicated welfare caseworker. Of course, caseworkers seek to be friends, but the point is that they are also required to be sleuths. The majority concedes that the "visitation" is partially investigative, but claims that this investigative aspect has been given "too much emphasis." Emphasis has indeed been given. Time and again, in briefs and at oral argument, appellants emphasized the need to enter AFDC homes to guard against welfare fraud and child abuse, both of which are felonies. . . .

Conceding for the sake of argument that someone might view the "visitation" as a search, the majority nonetheless concludes that such a search is not unreasonable. However, their mode of reaching that conclusion departs from the entire history of Fourth Amendment case law. Of course, the Fourth Amendment test is reasonableness, but in determining whether a search is reasonable, this Court is not free merely to balance, in a totally ad hoc fashion, any number of subjective factors. An unbroken line of cases holds that, subject to a few narrowly drawn exceptions, any search without a warrant is constitutionally unreasonable. . . . In this case, no suggestion that evidence will disappear, that a criminal will escape, or that an officer will be injured, justifies the failure to obtain a warrant. Instead, the majority asserts what amounts to three state interests which allegedly render this search reasonable. None of these interests is sufficient to carve out a new exception to the warrant requirement.

First, it is argued that the home visit is justified to protect dependent children from "abuse" and "exploitation." These are heinous crimes, but they are not confined to indigent households. Would the majority sanction, in the absence of probable cause, compulsory visits to all American homes for the purpose of discovering child abuse? Or is this Court prepared to hold as a matter of constitutional law that a mother, merely because she is poor, is substantially more likely to injure or exploit her children? Such a categorial approach to an entire class of citizens would be dangerously at odds with the tenets of our democracy.

Second, the Court contends that caseworkers must enter the homes of AFDC beneficiaries to determine eligibility. Interestingly, federal regulations do not require the home visit. In fact, the regulations specify the recipient himself as the primary source of eligibility information thereby rendering an inspection of the home only one of several alternative secondary sources. The majority's implication that a biannual home visit somehow assures the verification of actual residence or actual physical presence in the home strains credulity in the context of urban poverty. Despite the caseworker's responsibility for dependent children, he is not even required to see the children as a part of the home visit. . . .

We are told that the plight of Mrs. James is no different from that of a taxpayer who is required to document his right to a tax deduction, but this analogy is seriously flawed. The record shows that Mrs. James has offered to be interviewed anywhere other than her home, to answer any questions and to provide any documentation which the welfare agency desires. The agency curtly refused all these offers and insisted on its "right" to pry into appellee's home. Tax exemptions are also governmental "bounty." A true analogy would be an Internal Revenue Service requirement that in order to claim a dependency exemption, a taxpayer *must* allow a specially trained IRS agent to invade the home for the purpose of questioning the occupants and looking for evidence that the exemption is being properly utilized for the benefit of the dependent. If such a system were even proposed, the cries of constitutional outrage would be unanimous. . . .

Although the Court does not agree

with my conclusion that the home visit is an unreasonable search, its opinion suggests that even if the visit were unreasonable, appellee has somehow waived her right to object. Surely the majority cannot believe that valid Fourth Amendment consent can be given under the threat of the loss of one's sole means of support. Nor has Mrs. James waived her rights. Had the Court squarely faced the question of whether the State can condition welfare payments on the waiver of clear constitutional rights, the answer would be plain. The decisions of this Court do not support the notion that a State can use welfare benefits as a wedge to coerce "waiver" of Fourth Amendment rights. . . .

C. Wealth as a "Suspect Classification"

(1) James v. Valtierra (1971)

+Black, Burger, Harlan, Stewart, White
−Marshall, Brennan, Blackmun
NP Douglas

MR. JUSTICE BLACK delivered the opinion of the Court.

These cases raise but a single issue. It grows out of the United States Housing Act of 1937, which established a federal housing agency authorized to make loans and grants to state agencies for slum clearance and low-rent housing projects. In response, the California Legislature created in each county and city a public housing authority to take advantage of the financing made available by the Federal Housing Act. . . . At the time the federal legislation was passed the California Constitution had for many years reserved to the State's people the power to initiate legislation and to reject or approve by referendum any Act passed by the state legislature. . . . The same section reserved to the electors of counties and cities the power of initiative and referendum over acts of local government bodies. In 1950, however, the State Supreme Court held that local authorities' decisions on seeking federal aid for public housing projects were "executive" and "administrative," not "legislative," and therefore the state constitution's referendum provisions did not apply to these actions. Within six months of that decision the California voters adopted Article XXXIV of the state constitution to bring public housing decisions under the State's referendum policy. The Article provided that no low-rent housing project should be developed, constructed or acquired in any manner by a state public body until the project was approved by a majority of those voting at a community election.

The present suits were brought by citizens of San Jose, California, and San Mateo County, localities where housing authorities could not apply for federal funds because low-cost housing proposals had been defeated in referendums. The plaintiffs, who are eligible for low-cost public housing, sought a declaration that Article XXXIV was unconstitutional because its referendum requirement violated (1) the Supremacy Clause of the United States Constitution; (2) the Privileges and Immunities Clause; and (3) the Equal Protection Clause. A three-judge court held that Article XXXIV denied the plaintiffs equal protection of the laws and it enjoined its enforcement. . . . We noted probable jurisdiction. For the reasons that follow, we reverse.

The three-judge court found the Supremacy Clause argument unpersuasive, and we agree. By the Housing Act of 1937 the Federal Government has offered aid to States and local governments for the creation of low-rent public housing. However, the federal legislation does not purport to require the local governments to accept this or to outlaw local referendums on whether the aid should be accepted. We also find the privileges and immunities argument without merit.

While the District Court cited several cases of this Court, its chief reliance plainly rested on *Hunter* v. *Erickson* . . . (1969). The first paragraph in the District Court's decision stated simply: "We hold Article XXXIV to be unconstitutional. *Hunter* v. *Erickson* . . . ." The court below erred in relying on *Hunter* to invalidate Article XXXIV. Unlike the case before us, *Hunter* rested on the conclusion that Akron's referendum law denied equal protection by placing "special burdens on racial minorities within the governmental process." . . . In *Hunter* the citizens of Akron had amended the city charter to require that any ordinance regulating real estate on the basis of race, color, religion, or national origin could not take effect without approval by a majority of those voting in a city election. The Court held that the amendment created a classification based upon race because it required that laws dealing with racial housing matters could take effect only if they survived a mandatory referendum while other housing ordinances took effect without any such special election. The opinion noted:

"Because the core of the Fourteenth Amendment is the prevention of meaningful and unjustifiable official distinctions based on race . . . racial classifications are 'constitutionally suspect' . . . and subject to the 'most rigid scrutiny. . . .' They 'bear a far heavier burden of justification than other classifications. . . .' "

The Court concluded that Akron had advanced no sufficient reasons to justify this racial classification and hence that it was unconstitutional under the Fourteenth Amendment.

Unlike the Akron referendum provision, it cannot be said that California's Article XXXIV rests on "distinctions based on race." . . . The Article requires referendum approval for any low-rent public housing project, not only for projects which will be occupied by a racial minority. And the record here would not support any claim that a law seemingly neutral on its face is in fact aimed at a racial minority. . . . The present case could be affirmed only by extending *Hunter*, and this we decline to do.

California's entire history demonstrates the repeated use of referendums to give citizens a voice on questions of public policy. A referendum provision was included in the first state constitution, *Calif. Const. of 1849*, and referendums have been a commonplace occurrence in the State's active political life. Provisions for referendums demonstrate devotion to democracy, not to bias, discrimination, or prejudice. Nonetheless, appellees contend that Article XXXIV denies them equal protection because it demands a mandatory referendum while many other referendums only take place upon citizen initiative. They suggest that the mandatory nature of the Article XXXIV referendum constitutes unconstitutional discrimination because it hampers persons desiring public housing from achieving their objective when no such roadblock faces other groups seeking to influence other public decisions to their advantage. But of course a lawmaking procedure that "disadvantages" a particular group does not always deny equal protection. Under any such holding, presumably a State would not be able to require referendums on any subject unless referendums were required on all, because they would always disadvantage some group. And this Court would be required to analyze governmental structures to determine whether a gubernatorial veto provision or a filibuster rule is likely to "disadvantage" any of the diverse and shifting groups that make up the American people.

Furthermore, an examination of California law reveals that persons advocating low-income housing have not been singled out for mandatory referendums while no other group must face that obstacle. Mandatory referendums are required for approval of state constitutional amendments, for the instance of general obligation long-term bonds by local governments, and for certain municipal territorial annexations. . . . California statute books contain much legislation first enacted by voter initiative, and no such law can be repealed or amended except by referendum. . . .

The people of California have also decided by their own vote to require referendum approval of low-rent public housing projects. This procedure ensures that all the people of a community will have a voice in a decision which may lead to large expenditures of local governmental funds for increased public services and to lower tax revenues. It gives them a voice in decisions that will affect the future development of their own community. This procedure for democratic decision-making does not violate the constitutional command that no State shall deny to any person "the equal protection of the laws."

The judgment of the three-judge court is reversed and the case is remanded for dismissal of the complaint.

Reversed.

MR. JUSTICE MARSHALL, WHOM MR. JUSTICE BRENNAN AND MR. JUSTICE BLACKMUN JOIN, DISSENTING.

By its very terms, the mandatory prior referendum provision of Article 34 applies solely to "any development composed of urban or rural dwellings, apartments or other living accommodations for persons of low income, financed in whole or in part by the Federal Government or a state public body or to which the Federal Government or a state public body extends assistance by supplying all or part of the labor, by guaranteeing the payment of liens, or otherwise."

Persons of low income are defined as "persons or families who lack the amount of income which is necessary . . . to enable them, without financial assistance to live in decent, safe and sanitary dwellings, without overcrowding."

The article explicitly singles out low-income persons to bear its burden. Publicly assisted housing developments designed to accommodate the aged, veterans, state employees, persons of moderate income, or any class of citizens other than the poor, need not be approved by prior referenda.

In my view, Article 34 on its face constitutes invidious discrimination which the Equal Protection Clause of the Fourteenth Amendment plainly prohibits. "The States, of course, are prohibited by the Equal Protection Clause from discriminating between 'rich' and 'poor' *as such* in the formulation and application of their laws." *Douglas* v. *California* . . . (1963) (Mr. Justice Harlan, dissenting). Article 34 is neither "a law of general applicability that may affect the poor more harshly than it does the rich," nor an "effort to redress economic imbalances,". . . . It is rather an explicit classification on the basis of poverty—a suspect classification which demands exacting judicial scrutiny. . . .

The Court, however, chooses to subject the article to no scrutiny whatsoever and treats the provision as if it contained a totally benign technical economic classification. Both the appellees and the Solicitor

General of the United States as amicus curiae have strenuously argued, and the court below found, that Article 34, by imposing a substantial burden solely on the poor, violates the Fourteenth Amendment. Yet after observing that the article does not discriminate on the basis of race, the Court's only response to the real questions in this case is the unresponsive assertion that "referendums demonstrate devotion to democracy, not to bias, discrimination, or prejudice." It is far too late in the day to contend that the Fourteenth Amendment prohibits only racial discrimination; and to me, singling out the poor to bear a burden not placed on any other class of citizens tramples the values that the Fourteenth Amendment was designed to protect.

I respectfully dissent.

(2) San Antonio Independent School District v. Rodriguez (1973)

+Burger, Stewart, Blackmun, Powell, Rehnquist
−Douglas, Brennan, White, Marshall

[Rodriguez and others filed a class action suit against the San Antonio School District, alleging that the system of school financing in Texas was in violation of the equal protection clause. A substantial portion of school revenues in each school district is raised through a local property tax. Additional revenues come from a state equalization fund, and some funds come from the federal government. There is in Texas—as in most other states—a wide variation in the value of local property, and hence there are significant disparities in per pupil expenditures. These disparities, plaintiffs claimed, resulted in unacceptable variations in the quality of education afforded pupils in the respective districts and in the tax burden, which fell disproportionately heavily on the residents of the poorest districts.

A three-judge federal district court was convened in 1968, and in 1971 issued a *per curiam* opinion holding the Texas school finance system unconstitutional under the equal protection clause. Before that decision, the school district had switched sides and submitted a brief in behalf of the plaintiffs. The suit was maintained against the state board of education and various state officials even though it retained its original title. The state, therefore, appealed the district court's decision to the Supreme Court.]

MR. JUSTICE POWELL delivered the opinion of the Court.

. . .

Until recent times Texas was a predominantly rural State and its population and property wealth were spread relatively evenly across the State. Sizable differences in the value of assessable property between local school districts became increasingly evident as the State became more industrialized and as rural-to-urban population shifts became more pronounced. The location of commercial and industrial property began to play a significant role in determining the amount of tax resources available to each school district. These growing disparities in population and taxable property between districts were responsible in part for increasingly notable differences in levels of local expenditure for education. . . .

Recognizing the need for increased state funding to help offset disparities in local spending and to meet Texas' changing educational requirements, the state legislature in the late 1940's undertook a thorough evaluation of public education with an eye toward major reform. . . . The Committee's efforts led to the passage of the . . . Texas Minimum Foundation School Program. Today this Program accounts for approximately half of the total educational expenditures in Texas.

The Program calls for state and local contributions to a fund earmarked specifically for teacher salaries, operating expenses, and transportation costs. The State, supplying funds from its general revenues, finances approximately 80% of the Program, and the school districts are responsible—as a unit—for providing the remaining 20%. The districts' share, known as the Local Fund Assignment, is apportioned among the school districts under a formula designed to reflect each district's relative taxpaying ability. . . .

The design of this complex system was two-fold. First, it was an attempt to assure that the Foundation Program would have an equalizing influence on expenditure levels between school districts by placing the heaviest burden on the school districts most capable of paying. Second, the Program's architects sought to establish a Local Fund Assignment that would force every school district to contribute to the education of its children but would not by itself exhaust any district's resources. Today every school district does impose a property tax from which it derives locally expendable funds in excess of the amount necessary to satisfy its Local Fund Assignment under the Foundation Program. . . .

The school district in which appellees reside, the Edgewood Independent School District, has been compared throughout this litigation with the Alamo Heights Independent School District. This comparison between the least and most affluent districts in the San Antonio area serves to illustrate the manner in which the dual system of finance operates and to indicate the extent to which substantial disparities exist despite the State's impressive progress in recent years. Edgewood is one of seven public school districts in the metropolitan area. Approximately 22,000 students are enrolled in its 25 elementary and secondary schools. The district is situated in the core-city sector of San Antonio in a residential neighborhood that has little commercial or industrial property. The residents are predominantly of Mexican-American descent: approximately 90% of the student population is Mexican-American and over 6% is Negro. The average assessed property value per pupil is $5,960—the lowest in the metropolitan area—and the median family income ($4,686) is also the lowest. At an equalized tax rate of $1.05 per $100 of assessed property—the highest in the metropolitan area—the district contributed $26 to the education of each child for the 1967-1968 school year above its Local Fund Assignment for the Minimum Foundation Program. The Foundation Program contributed $222 per pupil for a state-local total of $248. Federal funds added another $108 for a total of $356 per pupil.

Alamo Heights is the most affluent school district in San Antonio. Its six schools, housing approximately 5,000 students, are situated in a residential community quite unlike the Edgewood District. The school population is predominantly Anglo, having only 18% Mexican-Americans and less than 1% Negroes. The assessed property value per pupil exceeds $49,000 and the median family income is $8,001. In 1967–1968 the local tax rate of $.85 per $100 of valuation yielded $333 per pupil over and above its contribution to the Foundation Program. Coupled with the $225 provided from that Program, the district was able to supply $558 per student. Supplemented by a $36 per pupil grant from federal sources, Alamo Heights spent $594 per pupil. . . .

. . . [S]ubstantial interdistrict disparities in school expenditure found by the District Court to prevail in San Antonio and in varying degrees throughout the State still exist. And it was these disparities, largely attributable to differences in the amounts of money collected through local property taxation, that led the District Court to conclude that Texas' dual system of public school finance violated the Equal Protection Clause. The District Court held that the Texas system discriminates on the basis of wealth in the manner in which education is provided for its people. . . . Finding that wealth is a "suspect" classification and that education is a "fundamental" interest, the District Court held that the Texas system could be sustained only if the State could show that it was premised upon some compelling state interest. . . . On this issue the court concluded that "[n]ot only are defendants unable to demonstrate compelling state interests . . . they fail even to establish a reasonable basis for these classifications." . . .

Texas virtually concedes that its historically rooted dual system of financing education could not withstand the strict judicial scrutiny that this Court has found appropriate in reviewing legislative judgments that interfere with fundamental constitutional rights or that involve suspect classifications. . . .

This, then, establishes the framework for our analysis. We must decide, first, whether the Texas system of financing public education operates to the disadvantage of some suspect class or impinges upon a fundamental right explicitly or implicitly protected by the Constitution, thereby requiring strict judicial scrutiny. If so, the judgment of the District Court should be affirmed. If not, the Texas scheme must still be examined to determine whether it rationally furthers some legitimate, articulated state purpose and therefore does not constitute an invidious discrimination in violation of the Equal Protection Clause of the Fourteenth Amendment.

. . . In concluding that strict judicial scrutiny was required, that [district] court relied on decisions dealing with the rights of indigents to equal treatment in the criminal trial and appellate processes, and on cases disapproving wealth restrictions on the right to vote. Those cases, the District Court concluded, established wealth as a suspect classification. Finding that the local property tax system discriminated on the basis of wealth, it regarded those precedents as controlling. It then reasoned, based on decisions of this Court affirming the undeniable importance of education, that there is a fundamental right to education and that, absent some compelling state justification, the Texas system could not stand.

We are unable to agree that this case, which in significant aspects is *sui generis*, may be so neatly fitted into the conventional mosaic of constitutional analysis under the Equal Protection Clause. Indeed, for the several reasons that follow, we find neither the suspect classification nor the fundamental interest analysis persuasive.

The wealth discrimination discovered by the District Court in this case, . . . is quite unlike any of the forms of wealth discrimination heretofore reviewed by this Court. Rather than focusing on the unique features of the alleged discrimination, the courts in these cases have virtually assumed their findings of a suspect classification through a simplistic process of analysis: since, under the traditional systems of financing public schools, some poorer people receive less expensive educations than other more affluent people, these systems discriminate on the basis of wealth. This approach largely ignores the hard threshold questions, including whether it makes a difference for purposes of consideration under the Constitution that the class of disadvantaged "poor" cannot be identified or defined in customary equal protection terms, and whether the relative—rather than absolute—nature of the asserted deprivation is of significant consequence. Before a State's laws and the justifications for the classifications they create are subjected to strict judicial scrutiny, we think these threshold considerations must be analyzed more closely than they were in the court below. . . .

[I]n support of their charge that the system discriminates against the "poor," appellees have made no effort to demonstrate that it operates to the peculiar disadvantage of any class fairly definable as indigent, or as composed of persons whose incomes are beneath any designated poverty level. Indeed, there is reason to believe that the poorest families are not necessarily clustered in the poorest property districts.

Second, neither appellees nor the District Court addressed the fact that, unlike each of the foregoing cases, lack of personal resources has not occasioned an absolute deprivation of the desired benefit. The argument here is not that the children in districts having relatively low assessable property values are receiving no public education; rather, it is that they are receiving a poorer quality education than that available to children in districts having more assessable wealth. Apart from the unsettled and disputed question whether the quality of education may be determined by the amount of money expended for it, a sufficient answer to appellees' argument is that at least where wealth is involved the Equal Protection Clause does not require absolute equality or precisely equal advantages. . . .

The system of alleged discrimination and the class it defines have none of the traditional indicia of suspectness: the class is not saddled with such disabilities, or subjected to such a history of purposeful unequal treatment, or relegated to such a position of political powerlessness as to command extraordinary protection from the majoritarian political process.

We thus conclude that the Texas system does not operate to the peculiar disadvantage of any suspect class. But in recognition of the fact that this Court has never heretofore held that wealth discrimination alone provides an adequate basis for invoking strict scrutiny, appellees have not relied solely on this contention. They also assert that the State's system impermissibly interferes with the exercise of a "fundamental" right and that accordingly the prior decisions of this Court require the application of the strict standard of judicial review. . . . It is this question—whether education is a fundamental right, in the sense that it is among the rights and liberties protected by the Constitution—which has so consumed the attention of courts and commentators in recent years.

In *Brown* v. *Board of Education*, . . . (1954), a unanimous Court recognized that "education is perhaps the most important function of state and local governments." . . .

. . . But the importance of a service performed by the State does not determine whether it must be regarded as fundamental for purposes of examination under the Equal Protection Clause. . . .

. . . It is not the province of this Court to create substantive constitutional rights in the name of guaranteeing equal protection of the laws. Thus the key to discovering whether education is "fundamental" is not to be found in comparisons of the relative societal significance of education as opposed to subsistence or housing. Nor is it to be found by weighing whether education is as important as the right to travel. Rather, the answer lies in assessing whether there is a right to education explicitly or implicitly guaranteed by the Constitution. . . .

Education, of course, is not among the rights afforded explicit protection under our Federal Constitution. Nor do we find any basis for saying it is implicitly so protected. . . . It is appellees' contention, however, that education is distinguishable from other services and benefits provided by the State because it bears a peculiarly close relationship to other rights and liberties accorded protection under the Constitution. Specifically, they insist that education is itself a fundamental personal right because it is essential to the effective exercise of First Amendment freedoms and to intelligent utilization of the right to vote. . . .

We need not dispute any of these propositions. The Court has long afforded zealous protection against unjustifiable governmental interference with the individual's rights to speak and to vote. Yet we have never presumed to possess either the ability or the authority to guarantee to the citizenry the most *effective* speech or the most *informed* electoral choice. . . .

It should be clear, for the reasons stated above and in accord with the prior decisions of this Court, that this is not a case in which the challenged state action must be subjected to the searching judicial scrutiny reserved for laws that create suspect classifications or impinge upon constitutionally protected rights.

We need not rest our decision, however, solely on the inappropriateness of the strict scrutiny test. A century of Supreme Court adjudication under the Equal Protection Clause affirmatively supports the applica-

tion of the traditional standard of review, which requires only that the State's system be shown to bear some rational relationship to legitimate state purposes. This case represents far more than a challenge to the manner in which Texas provides for the education of its children. We have here nothing less than a direct attack on the way in which Texas has chosen to raise and disburse state and local tax revenues. We are asked to condemn the State's judgment in conferring on political subdivisions the power to tax local property to supply revenues for local interests. In so doing, appellees would have the Court intrude in an area in which it has traditionally deferred to state legislatures. . . .

Thus we stand on familiar grounds when we continue to acknowledge that the Justices of this Court lack both the expertise and the familiarity with local problems so necessary to the making of wise decisions with respect to the raising and disposition of public revenues. . . . No scheme of taxation, whether the tax is imposed on property, income, or purchases of goods and services, has yet been devised which is free of all discriminatory impact. In such a complex arena in which no perfect alternatives exist, the Court does well not to impose too rigorous a standard of scrutiny lest all local fiscal schemes become subjects of criticism under the Equal Protection Clause.

In addition to matters of fiscal policy, this case also involves the most persistent and difficult questions of educational policy, another area in which this Court's lack of specialized knowledge and experience counsels against premature interference with the informed judgments made at the state and local levels. Education, perhaps even more than welfare assistance, presents a myriad of "intractable economic, social, and even philosophical problems." . . . The judiciary is well advised to refrain from interposing on the States inflexible constitutional restraints that could circumscribe or handicap the continued research and experimentation so vital to finding even partial solutions to educational problems and to keeping abreast of ever changing conditions.

It must be remembered also that every claim arising under the Equal Protection Clause has implications for the relationship between national and state power under our federal system. Questions of federalism are always inherent in the process of determining whether a State's laws are to be accorded the traditional presumption of constitutionality, or are to be subjected instead to rigorous judicial scrutiny. . . .

The foregoing considerations buttress our conclusion that Texas' system of public school finance is an inappropriate candidate for strict judicial scrutiny. These same considerations are relevant to the determination whether that system, with its conceded imperfections, nevertheless bears some rational relationship to a legitimate state purpose. It is to this question that we next turn our attention.

. . . In its reliance on state as well as local resources, the Texas system is comparable to the systems employed in virtually every other State. . . .

[T]o the extent that the Texas system of school finance results in unequal expenditures between children who happen to reside in different districts, we cannot say that such disparities are the product of a system that is so irrational as to be invidiously discriminatory. . . . The Texas plan is not the result of hurried, ill-conceived legislation. It certainly is not the product of purposeful discrimination against any group or class. On the contrary, it is rooted in decades of experience in Texas and elsewhere, and in major part is the product of responsible studies by qualified people. . . .

In light of the considerable attention that has focused on the District Court opinion in this case and on its California predecessor, *Serrano* v. *Priest* . . . (1971), a cautionary postscript seems appropriate. . . . The need is apparent for reform in tax systems which may well have relied too long and too heavily on the local property tax. And certainly innovative new thinking as to public education, its methods and its funding, is necessary to assure both a higher level of quality and greater uniformity of opportunity. These matters merit the continued attention of the scholars who already have contributed much by their challenges. But the ultimate solutions must come from the lawmakers and from the democratic pressures of those who elect them.

Reversed.

MR. JUSTICE STEWART, CONCURRING.

The method of financing public schools in Texas, as in almost every other State, has resulted in a system of public education that can fairly be described as chaotic and unjust. It does not follow, however, and I cannot find, that this system violates the Constitution of the United States. I join the opinion and judgment of the Court because I am convinced that any other course would mark an extraordinary departure from principled adjudication under the Equal Protection Clause of the Fourteenth Amendment. The uncharted directions of such a departure are suggested, I think, by the imaginative dissenting opinion my Brother MARSHALL has filed today.

Unlike other provisions of the Constitution, the Equal Protection Clause confers no substantive rights and creates no substantive liberties. The function of the Equal Protection Clause, rather, is simply to measure the validity of *classifications* created by state laws. . . .

. . .

MR. JUSTICE BRENNAN, DISSENTING.

Although I agree with my Brother WHITE that the Texas statutory scheme is devoid of any rational basis, and for that reason is violative of the Equal Protection Clause, I also record my disagreement with the Court's rather distressing assertion that a right may be deemed "fundamental" for the purposes of equal protection analysis only if it is "explicitly or implicitly guaranteed by the Constitution." . . . As my Brother MARSHALL convincingly demonstrates, our prior cases stand for the proposition that "fundamentality" is, in large measure, a function of the right's importance in terms of the effectuation of those rights which are in fact constitutionally guaranteed. . . .

Here, there can be no doubt that education is inextricably linked to the right to participate in the electoral process and to the rights of free speech and association guaranteed by the First Amendment. . . . This being so, any classification affecting education must be subjected to strict judicial scrutiny, and since even the State concedes that the statutory scheme now before us cannot pass constitutional muster under this stricter standard of review, I can only conclude that the Texas school financing scheme is constitutionally invalid.

MR. JUSTICE WHITE, WITH WHOM MR. JUSTICE DOUGLAS AND MR. JUSTICE BRENNAN JOIN, DISSENTING (OMITTED).

MR. JUSTICE MARSHALL, WITH WHOM MR. JUSTICE DOUGLAS CONCURS, DISSENTING.

The Court today decides, in effect, that a state may constitutionally vary the quality of education which it offers its children in accordance with the amount of taxable wealth located in the school districts within which they reside. The majority's decision represents an abrupt departure from the mainstream of recent state and federal court decisions concerning the unconstitutionality of state educational financing schemes dependent upon taxable local wealth. More unfortunately, though, the majority's holding can only be seen as a retreat from our historic commitment to equality of educational opportunity and as unsupportable acquiescence in a system which deprives children in their earliest years of the chance to reach their full potential as citizens. The Court does this despite the absence of any substantial justification for a scheme which arbitrarily channels educational resources in accordance with the fortuity of the amount of taxable wealth within each district.

In my judgment, the right of every American to an equal start in life, so far as the provision of a state service as important as education is concerned, is far too vital to permit state discrimination on grounds as tenuous as those presented by this record. Nor can I accept the notion that it is sufficient to remit these appellees to the vagaries of the political process which, contrary to the majority's suggestion, has proven singularly unsuited to the task of providing a remedy for this discrimination. I, for one, am unsatisfied with the hope of an ultimate "political" solution sometime in the indefinite future while, in the meantime, countless children unjustifiably receive inferior educations that "may affect their hearts and minds in a way unlikely ever to be undone." *Brown* v. *Board of Education* . . . (1954). I must therefore respectfully dissent.

The Court acknowledges that "substantial interdistrict disparities in school expenditures" exist in Texas, . . . and that these disparities are "largely attributable to differences in the amounts of money collected through local property taxation," . . . . But instead of closely examining the seriousness of these disparities and the invidiousness of the Texas financing scheme, the Court undertakes an elaborate exploration of the efforts Texas has purportedly made to close the gaps between its districts in terms of levels of district wealth and resulting educational funding. Yet, however praiseworthy Texas' equalizing efforts, the issue in this case is not whether Texas is doing its best to ameliorate the worst features of a discriminatory scheme, but rather whether the scheme itself is in fact unconstitutionally discriminatory in the face of the Fourteenth Amendment's guarantee of equal protection of the laws. When the Texas financing scheme is taken as a whole, I do not think it can be doubted that it produces a discriminatory impact on substantial numbers of the school age children of the State of Texas. . . .

In striking down the Texas financing scheme because of the interdistrict variations in taxable property wealth, the District Court determined that it was insufficient for appellants to show merely that the State's scheme was rationally related to some legitimate state purpose; rather, the discrimination inherent in the scheme had to be shown necessary to promote a "compelling state interest" in order to withstand constitutional scrutiny. The basis for this determination was two-fold: First, the financing scheme divides citizens on a wealth basis, a classification which the District Court viewed as highly suspect; and second, the discriminatory scheme directly affects what it considered to be a "fundamental interest," namely, education.

This Court has repeatedly held that state discrimination which either adversely affects a "fundamental interest," see *e. g., Dunn* v. *Blumstein* . . . (1972); *Shapiro* v. *Thompson* . . . (1969), or is based on a distinction of a suspect character, see, *e. g., Graham* v. *Richardson* . . . (1971); *McLaughlin* v. *Florida* . . . (1964), must be carefully scrutinized to insure that the scheme is necessary to promote a substantial, legitimate state interest. . . . The majority today concludes, however, that the Texas scheme is not subject to such a strict standard of review under the Equal Protection Clause. Instead, in its view, the Texas scheme must be tested by nothing more than that lenient standard of rationality which we have traditionally applied to discriminatory state action in the context of economic and commercial matters. . . . By so doing the Court avoids the telling task of searching for a substantial state interest which the Texas financing scheme, with its variations in taxable district property wealth, is necessary to further. I cannot accept such an emasculation of the Equal Protection Clause in the context of this case. . . .

In conclusion it is essential to recognize that an end to the wide variations in taxable district property wealth inherent in the Texas financing scheme would entail none of the untoward consequences suggested by the Court or by the appellants.

First, affirmance of the District Court's decisions would hardly sound the death knell for local control of education. It would mean neither centralized decisionmaking nor federal court intervention in the operation of public schools. Clearly, this suit has nothing to do with local decisionmaking with respect to educational policy or even educational spending. It involves only a narrow aspect of local control—namely, local control over the raising of educational funds. In fact, in striking down interdistrict disparities in taxable local wealth, the District Court took the course which is most likely to make true local control over educational decisionmaking a reality for *all* Texas school districts.

Nor does the District Court's decision even necessarily eliminate local control of educational funding. The District Court struck down nothing more than the continued interdistrict wealth discrimination inherent in the present property tax. Both centralized and decentralized plans for educational funding not involving such interdistrict discrimination have been put forward. The choice among these or other alternatives remains with the State, not with the federal courts. . . .

. . .

The Court seeks solace for its action today in the possibility of legislative reform. The Court's suggestions of legislative redress and experimentation will doubtless be of great comfort to the school children of Texas' disadvantaged districts, but considering the vested interests of wealthy school districts in the preservation of the status quo, they are worth little more. The possibility of legislative action is, in all events, no answer to this Court's duty under the Constitution to eliminate unjustified state discrimination. In this case we have been presented with an instance of such discrimination, in a particularly invidious form, against an individual interest of large constitutional and practical importance. To support the demonstrated discrimination in the provision of educational opportunity the State has offered a justification which, on analysis, takes on at best an ephemeral character. Thus, I believe that the wide disparities in taxable district property wealth inherent in the local property tax element of the Texas financing scheme render that scheme violative of the Equal Protection Clause. . . .

(3) A Note on Problems in Securing Welfare Entitlements—
Edelman v. *Jordan* (1974)

Jordan and other welfare recipients filed a class action suit against Illinois welfare officials, alleging that the officials had not administrated the AABD (Aid to the Aged, Blind, and Disabled) programs consistent with federal regulations. AABD is a categorical aid program, funded equally by state and federal funds. The suit sought injunctive relief and back payments for benefits alleged to have been wrongfully withheld. The Eleventh Amendment issue raised in the case (see pp. 125–130, *supra*) dominated the Court's analysis and was the central argument for denying retroactive payments to welfare recipients. Justice Rehnquist, writing for the majority, avoided the more substantive argument that welfare benefits were entitlements provided for and protected by federal regulations. Instead, he argued that the "mere fact that a State participates in a program through which the Federal Government provides assistance for the operation by the State of a system of public aid is not sufficient to establish consent on the part of the State to be sued in the federal courts. . . ."

The four justices dissenting in this case argued that the state's voluntary participation in the federal welfare programs was, in effect, an immunity waiver to suits, such as this one, requesting retroactive payments. In his dissent, Justice Marshall reiterated the spirit of *Goldberg* v. *Kelly*, which categorized welfare benefits as "statutory entitlement(s) for persons qualified to receive them." Justice Marshall reasoned that "retroactive payment of benefits secured for recipients this entitlement which was withheld in violation of federal law" by Illinois welfare officials. Apart from dissenting opinions, such as those in this case, in *James* v. *Valtierra*, and in *Rodriguez*, the Supreme Court seems unwilling to regard welfare as an entitlement that merits federal protection under either the "suspect classification" or "fundamental rights" tests for applying strict scrutiny under the Fourteenth Amendment.

D. A Note on Some Other Legal Problems of the Poor

The law has traditionally favored those with property. But with the stimulus of the War on Poverty, the widespread (if still quite incomplete) extension of legal services to indigents, and the egalitarian ideology of the Warren Court, some significant changes have occurred. We have presented materials in this section that deal with the welfare system and with the fight to establish wealth as a "suspect classification" under the equal protection clause. *Goldberg* v. *Kelly* (1970) dealt with the need for due process procedures in pretermi-

nation welfare hearings. Two related areas are the subject of this note: the need for due process restraints on the exercise of creditor's rights, and the problems of providing access to the courts for poor people in civil cases.

The introductory essay discussed the *Sniadach* case, in which the Supreme Court invalidated Wisconsin's wage garnishment statute because it permitted garnishment of wages *prior* to notice and a judicial hearing. In 1972, in *Fuentes* v. *Shevin*, the Court invalidated a Florida "replevin" law (replevin is a legal proceeding for return of property) because it did not provide for an adversary due process hearing *before* an individual could be deprived of possession of tangible personal property, "however brief the dispossession and however slight his monetary interest." The procedure that Florida used was to permit the writ of replevin to be issued by the court clerk. In broad language, the Court held that the Constitution required a due process adversary hearing before any person could be deprived of possession of tangible property. But only seven justices heard the case, and the vote was 4-3. Justices Powell and Rehnquist had not yet taken their seats on the Court.

In *Mitchell* v. *Grant* (1974), with a full complement of nine justices, the Supreme Court approved debt recovery procedures that were substantially the same as those disapproved in *Fuentes*. The case came from Louisiana, which permitted a creditor to obtain a writ of *sequestration* to repossess property in which he or she has an interest and where the debtor has defaulted in payment. The writ was obtainable on an *ex parte* basis, without notice to the debtor or a hearing, from the court clerk. But the creditor was required to post a bond. *After* the writ was issued, the debtor could challenge it, and the burden was on the creditor to prove his facts (e.g., in a typical case that the debtor was delinquent in installment payments). If the creditor could not prove his right to repossession, he had not only to return the property but pay damages to the debtor as well.

The vote in the case was 5-4, with Justices Powell and Rehnquist joining the three dissenters from *Fuentes* to constitute a new majority. Justice White wrote that this was a reasonable procedure. It protected the property in dispute and prevented resort to "self-help" that might cause violence. Furthermore, under Louisiana law (not true in most states, however), the debtor was free to sell off the property and the creditor could lose his vendor's lien.

White sought to distinguish both the *Sniadach* and *Fuentes* cases. *Sniadach* was distinguished because of its much more severe impact on the debtor (e.g., substantial loss of wages versus loss of a television set or similar appliance), because the creditor did not have to post bond, and because the creditor had no prior interest in the property that was seized to pay the debt—the debtor's wages. *Fuentes* was distinguished on the grounds that the Florida procedure was less protective of the debtor. But if the result in *Fuentes* was only distinguished, the broad constitutional rule requiring due process procedures before a creditor could repossess property was overruled.

The dissenters argued that the factual differences between *Fuentes* and *Mitchell* were trivial. They accused the majority of eroding the principle of stare decisis: "Unless we respect the constitutional decisions of this Court, we can hardly expect that others will do so." Justice Stewart noted that many states had already

begun to follow the *Fuentes* rule and had experienced no ill effects. "The only perceivable change that has occurred since the *Fuentes* case is in the makeup of this Court. A basic change in the law upon a ground no firmer than a change in our membership invites the popular misconception that this institution is little different from the two political branches of the Government."

The Court exhibited a similar pattern of give and take on the question of access to the civil courts for certain types of procedures. In *Boddie* v. *Connecticut* (1971), the Court held it to be a denial of due process for a state to refuse to waive the $60 filing fee for indigents seeking a divorce. But the Court majority was careful not to articulate a broad rule of access. Instead, taking account of the "special position of marriage in society's hierarchy of values," it noted that divorce proceedings were a monopoly of the state and that there was no other legitimate way of resolving this kind of dispute.

Two years later, in *United States* v. *Kras* (1973), the Court refused to extend *Boddie* to require a state to waive a $50 filing fee to initiate bankruptcy proceedings. Noting that *Boddie* stopped short of a general rule exempting indigents from the payment of all court fees, Justice Blackmun noted that *Boddie* also involved the fundamental human relationship of marriage and implicated constitutional rights of association. The discharge of debts, he argued, does not rise to the same constitutional level. It is true that while one can only go bankrupt with a court order, there are alternate ways of discharging debts. Bankruptcy legislation should be measured as any other economic and social welfare legislation, by the standard of ordinary scrutiny. In dissent, Justice Stewart argued: "The Court holds today that Congress may say that some of the poor are too poor even to go bankrupt. . . ."

By the same 5-4 majority, the Court, in *Ortwein* v. *Schwab* (1973), refused to invalidate an Oregon statute requiring a $25 filing fee to begin judicial review proceedings after an administrative denial of welfare benefits. An individual's interest in welfare benefits, like bankruptcy, the Court said, "has far less constitutional significance than in the case of divorce." Welfare payments implicate no suspect classification.

(5). POLITICAL EQUALITY AND EQUAL REPRESENTATION

A. *A Note on the Antecedents of Baker v. Carr (1962)*

The decision in *Baker* v. *Carr* culminated a long series of attempts to have the Supreme Court break the legislative apportionment impasse. By the middle of the twentieth century, urban areas had become badly underrepresented in state legislatures and in the House of Representatives. Many states had failed to reapportion since 1900, and rural areas which substantially declined in population retained the legislative seats to which they had once been entitled.

In 1930, large-city residents constituted 30 percent of the population and had a "vote value" of 78 (based on an average vote value of 100), while communities under 25,000, which constituted 16 percent of the total population, had a vote value of 141. By 1960, urban areas constituted 37 percent of the population and had a vote value of 76, a relative decrease, while small communities, now having only 13 percent of the population, increased their vote value to 171. Without federal court intervention, there appeared to be no way of providing equal representation for the populous urban areas.

The first major postwar challenge to reapportionment came in 1946. Kenneth Colegrove, a political science professor at Northwestern University, brought suit in the federal district court in Chicago, alleging gross population inequalities in the Illinois congressional districts and asking that the upcoming general election not be held under the existing apportionment. Cook County had the most populous congressional district, with 914,000 residents, while a downstate Illinois district had but 112,000. It was the most extreme apportionment disparity in the nation at that time.

The decision in *Colegrove* v. *Green* (1946) was frequently misinterpreted. The Supreme Court, with only seven justices sitting, voted 4-3 to deny Colegrove's claim. But only three justices agreed that the Court lacked jurisdiction. The fourth and deciding vote came from Justice Rutledge, who felt that considerations of equity such as the imminence of the 1946 elections made it inadvisable for the Supreme Court to intervene. Three justices, whose position would later be vindicated in *Baker* v. *Carr*, argued that the Court should exercise its power and invalidate the congressional apportionment scheme in Illinois.

In the 1950s, the Supreme Court declined to intervene in several cases that raised questions of legislative apportionment. In 1960, however, it did decide the case of *Gomillion* v. *Lightfoot*, to which we referred earlier in this chapter. The boundaries of the city of Tuskegee, Alabama, were redrawn so that practically all black residents suddenly found themselves living outside the city limits and no longer able to vote in city elections. This racial gerrymander had been engineered to prevent blacks in Tuskegee, who were a majority of the population, from obtaining control of the city government. When the case came to the Supreme Court, it decided unanimously that this action constituted a denial of the right to vote on the basis of race, in violation of the Fifteenth Amendment. Although *Gomillion* did not involve legislative districting, many people felt that the decision implied some loosening of the Court's self-imposed restraints on intervening in apportionment controversies.

B. *Baker* v. *Carr* (1962)

(See pp. 161–169)

C. *Martin Landau, Baker v. Carr and the Ghost of Federalism*

Justice Jackson once remarked on one of the distinctive features of American jurisprudence: That every great movement in our history has produced a leading case in the Supreme Court. By the logic of our system it could not be otherwise—a proposition which I hope will be made clear in the course of these comments.

Baker v. *Carr* appears now as a candidate for admission to that class of events commonly known as "turning points." The issues involved are of formidable proportions: They not only have to do with "the composition of those large contests of policy . . . by which governments and the actions of governments are made and unmade," but they have a direct bearing on the structural form of the American governmental system. Indeed, I think it quite clear that the effect of the decision to take jurisdiction over the matter of apportionment is, as Justice Harlan put it, to strike deep into the heart of our federal system. The issue in this case is "federalism," and it is this issue which I wish to discuss.

There are two major viewpoints reflected in discussions of federalism. On the one hand, federalism is taken as an *end* in and of itself. In this context, the problem which emerges is the maintenance of a specified balance of power and jurisdiction between state and nation. To be sure, jurisdictions are subject to modification and the balances to adjustment but as the Commission on Intergovernmental Relations expressed it, "the enduring values of our federal system fully warrant every effort to preserve and strengthen its essence." On the other hand, federalism is deemed to be an *instrument* of social change, a problem-solving device which possesses utility only for a specified set of conditions. It furnishes the means to "achieve some union where unity is an impossibility"; the goal involved is the development of that "more perfect union" which "federalists" despair of today. The logic of this view leads one to the position that federalism is "a case of political lag which urgently deserves our attention." The difference in these positions is the difference to be found between the classical concepts of mechanics and evolutionism as they were transferred into the social domain. . . .

Reprinted from Glendon Schubert (ed.), *Reapportionment* (New York: Scribner's, 1965), pp. 241, 243–247.

The classical concept of American federalism specifies a relatively fixed relationship between two domains of autonomous or sovereign authority in the same territorial unit. Each possesses an exclusive jurisdiction, neither is subordinate to the other, neither can be stripped of its authority by the other. The constitutional formulations of this concept present, in Corwin's phrase, a model of two states locked into a "mutually exclusive, reciprocally limiting" power of relationship.

To remark on the inadequacy of this model today is quite superfluous. We have Wilson's description, in 1895, of the "altered and declining status of the states." A few years later Bryce voiced concern that we are apt to overrate the effects of "mechanical contrivances" in government. The pragmatic Frank Goodnow concludes in 1916 that industrialization has caused the "old distinction" between interstate and intrastate commerce "almost to disappear." And there is Laski's tale of obsolescence and Max Lerner speaking of the ghost of federalism which "haunts a nation in which every force drives toward centralization." . . .

This is the "crisis of the states." They have had to yield to a "system dominated by the pervasiveness of federal power." They have lost status, prestige, and power. They have lost so much, Leonard White stated, "that competent observers at home and abroad have declared that American federalism is approaching its end." Roscoe Drummond put it more directly: "our federal system no longer exists."

Drummond's conclusion is not sensational. A system so dominated by central power cannot, by definition, be classified as federalist. If, analytically, we stop the system at various times—ranging from 1800 to the present—and if we examine the state of the system at each of these times, i.e., if we compare the operations of government with the classical or constitutional models, we are bound to find less and less correspondence. As a matter of fact this is what our researchers have unquestionably demonstrated. Our findings are of such order that it becomes increasingly difficult to represent our governmental system as federalist. It simply does not possess federal characteristics. . . .

I have taken a long way round to *Baker* v. *Carr* only to make clear that the basis for my judgment as to its significance lies within the context of an evolutionary system . . .

[I]t is inconceivable that a government which reflects the properties and needs of an 18th century environment (society) could be functional, without profound alteration, for a 20th century society. The collection of thirteen autonomous communities standing in relative isolation to one another, the differences in economy, the rural habit, the diversity of norms and behaviors, the multicentered system of communication, the existence of sharp local loyalties themselves the product of a "local consciousness," the magnitude of distance—these are some of the characteristics of 18th century society. Any attempt at unification required the establishment of a structure which would not, in Bryce's words "extinguish their separate administrations, legislatures, and local patriotisms." For the America of 1787, federalism was the only resource. It was a device designed to solve a social problem—a problem of political organization. It was, as Livingston noted in a brilliant essay, "a response to a definite set of stimuli; . . . consciously adopted as a means of solving the problems represented by these stimuli." Indeed, it may be viewed as a stroke of social genius; at once it protected the federal qualities of 18th century society and provided the means for meeting "the desperate need for a modicum of union where unity is impossible."

From a collection of loose, uncentralized or decentralized units, the United States as we are prone to speak, has evolved into a highly centralized, integrated community which exhibits symbiotic relationships. It no longer possesses federal characteristics. The history (evolution) of the last century is a striking story of vast changes in the structure of society and the needs it generated. That nation concealed under federalism finally emerged. The United States has been for a long time now becoming the United States. To be sure this has not proceeded without significant resistance—some of which has been quite bloody—but the naturalization process is quite visibly revealed in the transfer of authority to the central government. Moreover, the nature of the efforts which are today designed to stem the growth of national power, interstate compacts, uniform state laws, federal-state cooperative agreements, shared tax fields, and tax credits—are themselves testimony to the integrated character of the society. It now appears virtually impossible to identify a state problem—and thus a state domain. On the contrary, those historically local problems as housing, health, education, juvenile delinquency, etc., have already been admitted to the central jurisdiction—some quite a few years ago. . . .

American society is all the time "becoming." But the pace of change—national and international, technological and social, technical and scientific—is so swift that newly generated needs threaten our ability to design new coping instruments.

Even more important, however, old instruments, once functional but now quite obstructive, possess a capacity for resistance that challenge a necessary freedom to adapt. Nowhere is this more clearly in evidence than in the election process itself. The logic of our system requires that politics center itself nationally, but the lack of a national party system is the most conspicuous anachronism of our time.

This "lag" which political scientists, almost as a group, attribute to federalism was especially noted by the Committee on Political Parties of the American Political Science Association. "The American political party," it stated, "has its roots in the states. Its regulation and control is conducted almost wholly, although not entirely, by the states acting separately." The consequence of this is clear: "The party system is weighted much more heavily toward the state-local side than is true today of the federal system of government in the United States. *The gap produces serious disabilities in government. It needs to be closed.*"

This, in my judgment, is the historic function of *Baker* v. *Carr*: to close this gap. Tendencies in this direction—in the direction of national parties—have long been observed. It would be a curiosity indeed if the party system remained immune to the press of society. For these tendencies to become characteristic features of our political life, however, requires that the constitutional authorizations of another day be laid aside. It is precisely because the Constitution has traditionally secured such powers as apportionment to the states that a fractionized and decentralized party system has been maintained. The historic justification of this has been the value of local representation but the systems of apportionment in practice have sustained only a spurious and, at best, a technical local interest. The rural areas came first, assumed control and yielded, if at all, only very slowly to the urban shift which, most significantly lies at the base of a national politics.

Justice Harlan's dissent sets the sole issue of *Baker* v. *Carr* as "the right of a state to fix the basis of representation in its own legislature." The Court's decision, he adds, means "to turn our backs on the regard which . . . has always been shown for the judgment of state legislatures and courts *on matters of basically local concern.*"

And this is the point. The decision in *Baker* v. *Carr* is quite to the contrary: The basis of representation for a state legislature is no longer a matter of basic local concern. The Court decision may be interpreted as a move to sustain the urban-national requirements of our time. Justice Frankfurter remarks on the battle between forces whose influence is disparate among the various organs of government. "No shift of power but works a corresponding shift in political influence among the groups composing a society." By the nature of the issue involved, the effect of this decision will be to decrease the power and influence of rural interests and increase the power of metropolitan-urban centers and state governments. It will minimize certain types of conflict, allow for more effective planning, and enable a more coordinate attack on pressing urban problems.

The urbanization of state legislatures will be a relatively slow process. It will involve much litigation and conflict. It will involve the courts directly; it will lead to efforts to revamp state constitutions; it will be fought out in the polls as the prime political

issue it promises to become. And it will be accompanied by the urbanization of state politics.

The ultimate effect of this shift will be to weight the party system toward the urban-national side as against the state-local side and this is a necessary condition for the emergence of a national party system. To augment an already developing bypass of the state via direct national-metropolitan relationships with a national party system that is built upon an urban basis must mean a fundamental restructuring of our formal system of government. *Baker* v. *Carr* is a decision on the functional merits of federalism; it does strike deep into its heart.

Is this such a "massive repudiation of our past"? Or is it a development of our past?

D. *The Reapportionment Cases*

(1) **Wesberry v. Sanders (1964)**

+Warren, Black, Douglas, Brennan, White, Goldberg
+/−Clark, Stewart
−Harlan

MR. JUSTICE BLACK delivered the opinion of the Court.

Appellants are citizens and qualified voters of Fulton County, Georgia, and as such are entitled to vote in congressional elections in Georgia's Fifth Congressional District. That district, one of ten created by a 1931 Georgia statute, includes Fulton, DeKalb, and Rockdale Counties and has a population according to the 1960 census of 823,680. The average population of the ten districts is 394,312, less than half that of the Fifth. One district, the Ninth, has only 272,154 people, less than one-third as many as the Fifth. . . .

Claiming that these population

disparities deprive them and voters similarly situated of a right under the Federal Constitution to have their votes for Congressmen given the same weight as the votes of other Georgians, the appellants brought this action . . . asking that the Georgia statute be declared invalid and that the appellees, the Governor and Secretary of State of Georgia, be enjoined from conducting elections under it. The complaint alleged that appellants were deprived of the full benefit of their right to vote in violation of (1) Art I, §2 of the Constitution of the United States, which provides that "The House of Representatives shall be composed of Members chosen every second year by the People of the several States . . ."; (2) the Due Process, Equal Protection, and Privileges and Immunities Clauses of the Fourteenth Amendment; and (3) that part of Section 2 of the Fourteenth Amendment which provides that "Representatives shall be apportioned among the several States according to their respective numbers. . . ."

The case was heard by a three-judge District Court, which found unanimously, from facts not disputed, that:

It is clear by any standard . . . that the population of the Fifth District is grossly out of balance with that of the other nine congressional districts of Georgia and in fact, so much so that the removal of DeKalb and Rockdale Counties from the District, leaving only Fulton with a population of 556,326, would leave it exceeding the average by slightly more than forty per cent.

Notwithstanding these findings, a majority of the court dismissed the complaint, citing as their guide Mr. Justice Frankfurter's minority opin-

ion in *Colegrove* v. *Green* . . ., an opinion stating that challenges to apportionment of congressional districts raised only "political" questions, which are not justiciable. Although the majority below said that the dismissal here was based on "want of equity" and not on nonjusticiability, they relied on no circumstances which were peculiar to the present case; instead, they adopted the language and reasoning of Mr. Justice Frankfurter's *Colegrove* opinion in concluding that the appellant had presented a wholly "political" question. Judge Tuttle, disagreeing with the court's reliance on that opinion, dissented from the dismissal, though he would have denied an injunction at that time in order to give the Georgia Legislature ample opportunity to correct the "abuses" in the apportionment. He relied on *Baker* v. *Carr* . . . , which, after full discussion of *Colegrove* and all the opinions in it, held that allegations of disparities of population in state legislative districts raise justiciable claims on which courts may grant relief. We noted probable jurisdiction. We agree with Judge Tuttle that in debasing the weight of appellants' votes the State has abridged the right to vote for members of Congress guaranteed them by the United States Constitution, that the District Court should have entered a declaratory judgment to that effect, and that it was therefore error to dismiss this suit. The question of what relief should be given we leave for further consideration and decision by the District Court in light of existing circumstances. . . .

We hold that, construed in its historical context, the command of Art I, §2, that Representatives, be chosen "by the People of the several States" means that as nearly as is practicable one man's vote in a congressional election is to be worth as much as another's. This rule is followed automatically, of course, when Representatives are chosen as a group on a statewide basis, as was a widespread practice in the first 50 years of our Nation's history. It would be extraordinary to suggest that in such statewide elections the votes of inhabitants of some parts of a State, for example, Georgia's thinly populated Ninth District, could be weighed at two or three times the value of the votes of people living in more populous parts of the State. . . . We do not believe that the Framers of the Constitution intended to permit the same vote-diluting discrimination to be accomplished through the device of districts containing widely varied numbers of inhabitants. To say that a vote is worth more in one district than another would not only run counter to our fundamental ideas of democratic government, it would cast aside the principle of a House of Representatives elected "by the People," a principle tenaciously fought for and established at the Constitutional Convention. The history of the Constitution, particularly the part of it relating to the adoption of Art I, §2, reveals that those who framed the Constitution meant that, no matter what the mechanics of an election, whether statewide or by districts, it was population which was to be the basis of the House of Representatives. . . .

It is in the light of such history that we must construe Art I, §2, of the Constitution, which, carrying out the ideas of Madison and those of like views, provides that Representatives shall be chosen "by the People of the several States" and shall be "apportioned among the several States . . . according to their respective num-

bers." It is not surprising that our Court has held that this Article gives persons qualified to vote a constitutional right to vote and to have their votes counted. *United States* v. *Mosley* . . . ; *Ex parte Yarbrough.* . . . Not only can this right to vote not be denied outright, it cannot, consistently with Article I, be destroyed by alteration of ballots, see *United States* v. *Classic* . . . , or diluted by stuffing of the ballot box, see *United States* v. *Saylor.* . . . No right is more precious in a free country than that of having a voice in the election of those who make the laws under which, as good citizens, we must live. Other rights, even the most basic, are illusory if the right to vote is undermined. Our Constitution leaves no room for classification of people in a way that unnecessarily abridges this right. In urging the people to adopt the Constitution, Madison said in No. 57 of The Federalist:

Who are to be the electors of the Federal Representatives. Not the rich more than the poor; not the learned more than the ignorant; not the haughty heirs of distinguished names, more than the humble sons of obscure and unpropitious fortune. The electors are to be the great body of the people of the United States. . . .

Readers surely could have fairly taken this to mean, "one person, one vote." . . .

While it may not be possible to draw congressional districts with mathematical precision, that is no excuse for ignoring our Constitution's plain objective of making equal representation for equal numbers of people the fundamental goal for the House of Representatives. That is the high standard of justice and common sense which the Founders set for us.

Reversed and remanded.

MR. JUSTICE CLARK, CONCURRING IN PART AND DISSENTING IN PART (OMITTED).

MR. JUSTICE HARLAN, DISSENTING (OMITTED).

MR. JUSTICE STEWART, DISSENTING IN PART (OMITTED).

(2) Reynolds v. Sims (1964)

+Warren, Black, Douglas, Clark, Brennan, Stewart, White, Goldberg
−Harlan

[The movement to secure reapportionment of state legislatures took on new life and impetus with the Court's decision in *Baker* v. *Carr* (1962). Despite the refusal of the Supreme Court in that case to set forth constitutional guidelines, the clear implication of the several majority opinions was to favor a movement toward a standard of population equality. Reapportionment suits were brought in virtually every state. In some the suits were revivals of older litigation that had been dismissed by the lower courts following the pre-*Baker* doctrine that reapportionment questions were not justiciable. In other states, new litigation was begun. Of these, suits in six states were chosen for full review by the Supreme Court—Maryland, Delaware, Alabama, Virginia, New York, and Colorado. In general these suits were instigated by liberal Democrats and liberal Republicans from urban areas and opposed by rural interests and existing state constitutional officers. Below the surface, of course, the divisions were not so clearly defined. The "rural-urban" split was in many states a "rural-urban-suburban" division. And the suits also provided the opportunity for the continuation of traditional political rivalries within each state.

Arguing as *amicus curiae* in behalf of the plaintiffs seeking reapportionment was the solicitor general of the United States, Archibald Cox. As Robert Dixon has noted, Cox was not so much *amicus* as the coordinator and chief advocate for the proreapportionment forces in these cases. By contrast, the arguments for the defendant states were uncoordinated, often contradictory, and generally well below the quality of presentations made by the insurgent forces and the Solicitor. As summarized by Dixon, Cox argued that all of the apportionment plans in the six states were unconstitutional:

His basic four point list of guiding propositions went as follows:

1. The basic standard of comparison is the representation accorded qualified voters per capita.

2. The equal protection clause is violated by an apportionment that creates gross inequalities in representation without rhyme or reason.

3. The equal protection clause is violated by a discriminatory apportionment based upon criteria which are contrary to express constitutional limitations or otherwise invidious or irrelevant.

4. The equal protection clause is violated by an apportionment which subordinates the principle of popular representation to the representation of political subdivisions to such a degree as to create gross inequalities in the representation of voters and give control of the legislature to small minorities of the people.[1]

The Colorado case differed from the others in that its apportionment scheme had been approved by a large majority in a popular referendum. But to some extent all of the other cases involved deviation from one or more of Cox's "guidelines." The principle of "one man-one vote" was not espoused by the solicitor general. He took the more cautious position that there might be some validity in particular circumstances, to considering factors other than population, and that no across-the-board rule was called for. But he also opposed those who argued for an explicit rejection of the one man-one vote standard.

The Alabama case, *Reynolds* v. *Sims*, be-

---

[1]Robert G. Dixon, *Democratic Representation: Reapportionment in Law and Politics* (New York: Oxford University Press, 1968), p. 252 and passim.

came the vehicle for the Court's major opinion; each of the other five cases received shorter treatment based on the principles set forth in *Reynolds*, and one week later an additional nine cases were decided in summary fashion in the light of the one man-one vote standard. By any standard the existing apportionment scheme in Alabama was unconstitutional. In the Senate population districts varied as much as 41 to 1; in the House as much as 16 to 1. About a quarter of the population of the state could elect majorities in either house. Typically, the large urban centers of the state were grossly underpresented, since electoral districts had remained unchanged since 1901.

Under judicial pressure in the wake of *Baker v. Carr*, the state legislature convened in special session and drew up two provisional reapportionment schemes. These were in turn combined by a three-judge federal district court. This plan was used in the 1962 election, and both plaintiffs, and the defendant state officials appealed. Under the new plan, population disparities were sharply reduced in the Senate but slightly increased in the House. The proportion of voters needed to elect a majority of the Senate remained substantially the same, but rose to 43 percent for the House. The contrast between these two "measures" of apportionment—extent of deviation from a mythical equal population district, and the percentage of voters needed to elect a majority, demonstrated the problems of defining a constitutional standard of fair apportionment, or representation.]

MR. CHIEF JUSTICE WARREN delivered the opinion of the Court.

In *Baker v. Carr* . . . , we held that a claim asserted under the Equal Protection Clause challenging the constitutionality of a state's apportionment of seats in its Legislature, on the ground that the right to vote of certain citizens was effectively impaired since debased and diluted in effect, presented a justiciable controversy subject to adjudication by Federal courts. The spate of similar cases filed and decided by lower courts since our decision in *Baker* amply shows that the problem of state legislative malapportionment is one that is perceived to exist in a large number of the states. In *Baker* . . . we remanded to the District Court, which had dismissed the action, for consideration on the merits. We intimated no view as to the proper constitutional standards for evaluating the validity of a state legislative apportionment scheme. . . .

We indicated in *Baker*, however, that the Equal Protection Clause provides discoverable and manageable standards for use by lower courts in determining the constitutionality of a state legislative apportionment scheme. . . . Subsequent to *Baker*, we remanded several cases to the courts below for reconsideration in light of the decision.

In *Gray v. Sanders* . . ., we held that the Georgia county unit system, applicable in statewide primary elections, was unconstitutional since it resulted in a dilution of the weight of the votes of certain Georgia voters merely because of where they resided. . . .

Gray and *Wesberry* are of course not dispositive of or directly controlling on our decision in these cases involving state legislative apportionment controversies. Admittedly, those decisions, in which we held that, in statewide and in Congressional elections, one person's vote must be counted equally with those of all other voters in a state, were based on different constitutional considerations and were addressed to rather distinct problems. But neither are they wholly inapposite. *Gray*, though not determinative here since involving the weighting of votes in statewide elections, established the basic principle of equality among voters within a state, and held that voters cannot be classified, constitutionally, on the basis of where they live, at least with respect to voting in statewide elections. And our decision in *Wesberry* was of course grounded on that language of the Constitution which prescribes that members of the Federal House of Representatives are to be chosen "by the people," while attacks on state legislative apportionment schemes, such as that involved in the instant cases, are principally based on the Equal Protection Clause of the 14th Amendment. Nevertheless, *Wesberry* clearly established that the fundamental principle of representative government in this country is one of equal representation for equal numbers of people, without regard to race, sex, economic status, or place of residence within a state. Our problem, then, is to ascertain, in the instant cases, whether there are any constitutionally cognizable principles which would justify departures from the basic standard of equality among voters in the apportionment of seats in state Legislatures.

A predominant consideration in determining whether a state's legislative apportionment scheme constitutes an invidious discrimination violative of rights asserted under the Equal Protection Clause is that the rights allegedly impaired are individual and personal in nature. As stated by the Court . . . , "the right to vote is personal. . . ." While the result of a court decision in a state legislative apportionment controversy may be to require the restructuring of the geographical distribution of seats in a state Legislature, the judicial focus must be concentrated upon ascertaining whether there has been any discrimination against certain of the state's citizens which constitutes an impermissible impairment of their constitutionally protected right to vote. . . .

Legislators represent people, not trees or acres. Legislators are elected by voters, not farms or cities or economic interests. As long as ours is a representative form of government, and our legislatures are those instruments of government elected directly by and directly representative of the people, the right to elect legislators in a free and unimpaired fashion is a bedrock of our political system. It could hardly be gainsaid that a constitutional claim had been asserted by an allegation that certain otherwise qualified voters had been entirely prohibited from voting for members of their state Legislature. And, if a state should provide that the votes of citizens in one part of the state should be given two times, or five times, or 10 times the weight of votes of citizens in another part of the state, it could hardly be contended that the right to vote of those residing in the disfavored areas had not been effectively diluted. It would appear extraordinary to suggest that a state could be constitutionally permitted to enact a law providing that certain of the state's voters could vote two, five or 10 times for their legislative representatives, while voters living elsewhere could vote only once. And it is inconceivable that a state law to the effect that, in counting votes for legislators, the votes of citizens in one part of the state would be multiplied by two, five, or 10, while the votes of persons in another area would be counted only at face value, could be constitutionally sustainable. Of course, the effect of state legislative districting schemes which give the same number of Representatives to unequal numbers of constituents is identical. Overweighting and overvaluation of the votes of those living here has the certain effect of dilution and under-valuation of the votes of those living there. The resulting discrimination against those individual voters living in disfavored areas is easily demonstrable mathematically. Their right to vote is simply not the same right to vote as that of those living in a favored part of the state. Two, five, or 10 of them must vote before the effect of their voting is equivalent to that of their favored neighbor. Weighting the votes of citizens differently, by any method or means, merely because of where they happen to reside hardly seems justifiable. . . .

Logically, in a society ostensibly grounded on representative government, it would seem reasonable that a majority of the people of a state could elect a majority of that state's legislators. To conclude differently, and to sanction minority control of state legislative bodies, would appear to deny majority rights in a way that far surpasses any possible denial of minority rights that might otherwise be thought to result. Since Legislatures are responsible for enacting laws by which all citizens are to be governed, they should be bodies which are collectively responsive to the popular will. And the concept of equal protection has been traditionally viewed as requiring the uniform treatment of persons standing in the same relation to the governmental action questioned or challenged. With respect to the allocation of legislative representatives all voters, as citizens of a state, stand in the same relation regardless of where they live. Any suggested criteria for the differentiation of citizens are insufficient to justify any discrimination, as to the weight of their votes, unless relevant to the permissible purposes of legislative apportionment. . . .

We hold that, as a basic constitutional standard, the Equal Protection Clause requires that the seats in both houses of a bicameral state Legislature must be apportioned on a population basis. Simply stated, an individual's right to vote for state legislators is unconstitutionally impaired when its weight is in a substantial fashion diluted when compared with votes of citizens living in other parts of the state. Since, under neither the existing apportionment provisions nor under either of the proposed plans was either of the houses of the Alabama Legislature apportioned on a population basis, the District Court correctly held that all three of these schemes were constitutionally invalid. Furthermore, the existing apportionment, and also to a lesser extent the apportionment under the Crawford-Webb Act, presented little more than crazy quilts, completely lacking in rationality, and could be found invalid on that basis alone. Although the District Court presumably found the apportionment of the Alabama House of Representatives under the 67−Senator amendment to be acceptable, we conclude that the deviations from a strict population basis are too egregious to permit us to find that that body, under this proposed plan, was apportioned sufficiently on a population basis so as to permit the arrangement to be constitutionally sustained. Although about 43 percent of the state's population would be required to comprise districts which could elect a majority in that body, only 39 of the 106 House seats were actually to be distributed on a population basis, as each of Alabama's 67 counties was given at least one representative, and population variance ratios of close to 5-to-1 would have existed. While mathematical nicety is not a constitutional requisite one could hardly conclude that the Alabama House, under the proposed constitutional amendment had been apportioned sufficiently on a population basis to be sustainable under the requirements of the Equal Protection Clause. . . .

Since neither of the houses of the Alabama Legislature, under any of the three plans considered by the District Court was apportioned on a population basis, we would be justified in proceeding no further. However, one of the proposed plans, that contained in the so-called 67-Senator amendment at least superficially resembles the scheme of legislative representation followed in the Federal Congress. Under this plan each of Alabama's 67 counties is allotted one Senator and no counties are given more than one Senate seat. Arguably, this is analogous to the allocation of two Senate seats, in the Federal Congress, to each of the 50 states, regardless of population. Seats in the Alabama House, under the proposed constitutional amendment, are distributed by giving each of the 67 counties at least one, with the remaining 39 seats being allotted among the more populous counties on a population basis. This scheme, at least at first glance, appears to resemble that prescribed for the Federal House of Representatives, where the 435 seats are distributed among the states on a population basis although each state, regardless of its population, is given at least one Congressman. Thus, although there are substantial differences in underlying rationale and result, the 67-Senator amendment, as proposed by the Alabama Legislature, at least arguably presents for consideration a scheme analogous to that used for apportioning seats in Congress.

Much has been written since our decision in *Baker* v. *Carr* about the applicability of the so-called Federal analogy to state Legislature apportionment arrangements. After considering the matter, the court below concluded that no conceivable analogy could be drawn between the Federal scheme and the apportionment of seats in the Alabama Legislature under the proposed constitutional amendment. We agree with the District Court, and find the Federal analogy inapposite and irrelevant to state legislative districting schemes. Attempted reliance on the Federal analogy appears often to be little more than an after-the-fact rationalization offered in defense of maladjusted state apportionment arrangements. The original constitutions of 36 of our states, provided that representation in both houses of the state Legislatures would be based completely, or predominantly, on population. And the Founding Fathers clearly had no intention of establishing a pattern or model for the apportionment of seats in state Legislatures when the system of representation in the Federal Congress was adopted. Demonstrative of this is the fact that the Northwest Ordinance adopted in the same year, 1787, as the Federal Constitution, provided for the apportionment of seats in territorial legislatures solely on the basis of population. . . .

Political subdivisions of states—counties, cities, or whatever—never were and never have been considered as sovereign entities. Rather, they have been traditionally regarded as subordinate government instrumentalities created by the state to assist in the carrying out of state government functions. . . .

Since we find the so-called Federal analogy inapposite to a consideration of the constitutional validity of state legislative apportionment schemes, we necessarily hold that the Equal Protection Clause requires both houses of a state Legislature to be apportioned on a population basis. The right of a citizen to equal representation and to have his vote weighted equally with those of all other citizens in the election of members of one house of a bicameral state Legislature would amount to little if states could effectively submerge the equal-population principle in the apportionment of seats in the other house. If such a scheme were permissible, an individual citizen's ability to exercise an effective voice in the only instrument of state government directly representative of the people might be almost as effectively thwarted as if neither house were apportioned on a population basis. Deadlock between the two bodies might result in compromise and concession on some issues. But in all too many cases the more probable result would be frustration of the majority will through minority veto in the house not apportioned on a population basis, stemming directly from the failure to accord adequate overall legislative representation to all of the state's citizens on a nondiscriminatory basis. In summary, we can perceive no constitutional difference, with respect to the geographical distribution of state legislative representation, between the two houses of a bicameral state Legislature.

We do not believe that the concept of bicameralism is rendered anachronistic and meaningless when the predominant basis of representation in the two state legislative bodies is required to be the same—population. A prime reason for bicameralism, modernly considered, is to insure mature and deliberate consideration of, and to prevent precipitate action on, proposed legislative measures. Simply because the controlling criterion for apportioning representation is required to be the same in both houses does not mean that there will be no differences in the composition and

complexion of the two bodies. Different constituencies can be represented in the two houses. One body could be composed of single-member districts while the other could have at least some multimember districts. The length of terms of the legislators in the separate bodies could differ. The numerical size of the two bodies could be made to differ, even significantly, and the geographical size of districts from which legislators are elected could also be made to differ. And apportionment in one house could be arranged so as to balance off minor inequities in the representation of certain areas in the other house. . . .

By holding that as a Federal constitutional requisite both houses of a state Legislature must be apportioned on a population basis, we mean that the Equal Protection Clause requires that a state make an honest and good faith effort to construct districts, in both houses of its Legislature, as nearly of equal population as is practicable. We realize that it is a practical impossibility to arrange legislative districts so that each one has an identical number of residents, or citizens, or voters. Mathematical exactness of precision is hardly a workable constitutional requirement. . . .

[S]ome distinctions may well be made between Congressional and state legislative representation. Since, almost invariably there is a significantly larger number of seats in state legislative bodies to be distributed within a state than Congressional seats, it may be feasible to use political subdivision lines to a greater extent in establishing state legislative districts than in Congressional districting while still affording adequate representation to all parts of the state. To do so would be constitutionally valid so long as the resulting apportionment was one based substantially on population and the equal-population principle was not diluted in any significant way. Somewhat more flexibility therefore may be constitutionally permissible with respect to state legislative apportionment than in Congressional districting. . . .

A State may legitimately desire to maintain the integrity of various political subdivisions, insofar as possible, and provide for compact districts of contiguous territory in designing a legislative apportionment scheme. Valid considerations may underlie such aims. Indiscriminate districting, without any regard for political subdivision or natural or historical boundary lines, may be little more than an open invitation to partisan gerrymandering. Single-member districts may be the rule in one state, while another state might desire to achieve some flexibility by creating multimember or floterial districts. Whatever the means of accomplishment, the overriding objective must be substantial equality of population among the various districts, so that the vote of any citizen is approximately equal in weight to that of any other citizen in the state.

History indicates, however, that many states have deviated, to a greater or lesser degree, from the equal-population principle in the apportionment of seats in at least one house of their Legislatures. So long as the divergences from a strict population standard are based on legitimate considerations incident to the effectuation of a rational state policy, some deviations from the equal-population principle are constitutionally permissible with respect to the apportionment of seats in either or both of the two houses of a bicameral state Legislature. But neither history alone, nor economic or other sorts of group interests, are permissible factors in attempting to justify disparities from population-based representation. Citizens, not history or economic interests, cast votes. Considerations of area alone provide an insufficient justification for deviations from the equal-population principle. Again, people, not land or trees or pastures, vote. . . .

That the Equal Protection Clause requires that both houses of a state legislature be apportioned on a population basis does not mean that states cannot adopt some reasonable plan for periodic revision of their apportionment schemes. Decennial reapportionment appears to be a rational approach to readjustment of legislative representation in order to take into account population shifts and growth. Reallocation of legislative seats every 10 years coincides with the prescribed practice in 41 of the states, often honored more in the breach than the observance however. . . . In substance, we do not regard the Equal Protection Clause as requiring daily, monthly, annual or biennial reapportionment, so long as a state has a reasonably conceived plan for periodic readjustment of legislative representation. And we do not mean to intimate that more frequent reapportionment would not be constitutionally permissible or practicably desirable. But if reapportionment were accomplished with less frequency, it would assuredly be constitutionally suspect. . . .

We do not consider here the difficult question of the proper remedial devices which Federal courts should utilize in state legislative apportionment cases. Remedial techniques in this new and developing area of the law will probably often differ with the circumstances of the challenged apportionment and a variety of local conditions. It is enough to say now that, once a state's legislative apportionment scheme has been found to be unconstitutional, it would be the unusual case in which a court would be justified in not taking appropriate action to insure that no further elections are conducted under the invalid plan. However, under certain circumstances, such as where an impending election is imminent and a State's election machinery is already in progress, equitable considerations might justify a court in withholding the granting of immediately effective relief in a legislative apportionment case, even though the existing apportionment scheme was found invalid. In awarding or withholding immediate relief, a court is entitled to and should consider the proximity of a forthcoming election and the mechanics and complexities of state election laws, and should act and rely upon general equitable principles. With respect to the timing of relief, a court can reasonably endeavor to avoid a disruption of the election process which might result from requiring precipitate changes that could make unreasonable or embarrassing demands on a State in adjusting to the requirements of the court's decree. . . .

MR. JUSTICE CLARK, CONCURRING (OMITTED).
MR. JUSTICE STEWART DISSENTING IN PART (OMITTED).

MR. JUSTICE HARLAN, DISSENTING.

Today's holding is that the Equal Protection Clause of the 14th Amendment requires every state to structure its Legislature so that all the members of each house represent substantially the same number of people; other factors may be given play only to the extent that they do not significantly encroach on this basic "Population" principle. Whatever may be thought of this holding as a piece of political ideology—and even on that score the political history and practices of this country from its earliest beginnings leave wide room for debate . . . —I think it demonstrable that the 14th Amendment does not impose political tenets on the states or authorize this Court to do so.

The Court's constitutional discussion . . . is remarkable for its failure to address itself at all to the 14th Amendment as a whole or to the legislative history of the amendment pertinent to the matter at hand. Stripped of aphorisms, the Court's argument boils down to the assertion that petitioners' right to vote has been invidiously "debased" or "diluted" by systems of apportionment which entitle them to vote for fewer legislators than other voters, an assertion which is tied to the Equal Protection Clause only by the consitutionally frail tautology that "equal" means "equal."

Had the court paused to probe more deeply into the matter, it would have found that the Equal Protection Clause was never intended to inhibit the states in choosing any democratic method they pleased for the apportionment of their legislatures. This is shown by the language of the 14th Amendment taken as a whole, by the understanding of those who proposed and ratified it, and by the political practices of the states at the time the amendment was adopted. It is confirmed by numerous state and Congressional actions since the adoption of the 15th Amendment, and by the common understanding of the amendment as evidenced by subsequent constitutional amendments and decisions of this Court before *Baker* v. *Carr* . . . made an abrupt break with the past in 1962.

The failure of the court to consider any of these matters cannot be excused or explained by any concept of "developing" constitutionalism. It is meaningless to speak of constitutional "development" when both the language and history of the controlling provisions of the Constitution are wholly ignored. Since it can, I think, be shown beyond doubt that state legislative apportionments, as such, are wholly free of constitutional limitations, save such as may be imposed by the republican form of government clause (Const., Art. IV, Section 4), the court's action now bringing them within the purview of the 14th Amendment amounts to nothing less than an exercise of the amending power of this Court. . . .

In my judgment, today's decisions are refuted by the language of the amendment which they construe and by the inference fairly to be drawn from subsequently enacted amendments. They are unequivocally refuted by history and by consistent theory and practice from the time of the adoption of the 14th Amendment until today.

The Court's elaboration of its new "constitutional" doctrine indicates how far—and how unwisely—it has strayed from the appropriate bounds of its authority. The consequence of today's decision is that in all but the handful of states which may already satisfy the new requirement the local District Court or, it may be, the state courts, are given blanket authority and the constitutional duty to supervise apportionment of the state legislatures. It is difficult to imagine a more intolerable and inappropriate interference by the judiciary with the independent legislatures of the states.

. . . The Court does not establish, or indeed even attempt to make a case for the proposition that conflicting interests within a state can only be adjusted by disregarding them when voters are grouped for purposes of representation.

With these cases the Court approaches the end of the third round set in motion by the complaint filed in *Baker* v. *Carr*. What is done today deepens my conviction that judicial entry into this realm is profoundly ill-advised and constitutionally impermissible. As I have said before . . . I believe that the vitality of our political system, on which in the last analysis all else depends, is weakened by reliance on the judiciary for political reform; in time a complacent body politic may result.

These decisions also cut deeply into the fabric of our federalism. What must follow from them may eventually appear to be the product of state legislatures. Nevertheless, no thinking person can fail to recognize that the aftermath of these cases, however desirable it may be thought in itself, will have been achieved at the cost of a radical alteration in the relationship between the states and the Federal Government, more particularly the Federal Judiciary. Only one who has an overbearing impatience with the Federal system and its political processes will believe that cost was not too high or was inevitable.

Finally, these decisions give support to a current mistaken view of the Constitution and the constitutional function of this Court. This view, in a nutshell, is that every major social ill in this country can find its cure in some constitutional "Principle," and that this Court should "take the lead" in promoting reform when other branches of government fail to act. The Constitution is not a panacea for every blot upon the public welfare, nor should this court, ordained as a judicial body, be thought of as a general haven for reform movements. . . .

(3) Avery v. Midland County (1968)

+Warren, Black, Douglas, Brennan, White
−Harlan, Stewart, Fortas
NP Marshall

[*Reynolds* and its companion cases established the principle of "one person, one vote" for state legislatures and congressional districts. But did that principle of apportionment apply to all elected government bodies? Hank Avery was the mayor of Midland, Texas, a city with a population of 68,000. Midland was the county seat of Midland County, which had a total population (including the city) of about 70,000. The chief governing body of the county was a Commissioner's Court, which was composed of five members. One, the county judge, was selected at large and in practice voted only to break a tie. Each of the other four commissioners was elected from one of four county districts. Virtually the entire city of Midland was in one district. The other districts had populations, respectively, of 852, 414, and 828. Thus, Midland, which contained 97 percent of the population of the county, elected only 25 percent of the county court.

Avery brought suit in the state trial court, which ruled in his favor. The Texas Supreme Court ruled that several factors, such as number of qualified voters, land areas, geography, and so forth, as well as population, might be considered in setting up commissioners' precincts. The Texas Supreme Court also ruled that only the Commissioner's Court could redistrict itself, within the guidelines just described. The Supreme Court granted certiorari.]

MR. JUSTICE WHITE delivered the opinion of the Court.

. . .

Although the forms and functions of local government and the relationships among the various units are matters of state concern, it is now beyond question that a State's political subdivisions must comply with the Fourteenth Amendment. The actions of local government *are* the actions of the State. A city, town, or county may no more deny the equal protection of the laws than it may abridge freedom of speech, establish an official religion, arrest without probable cause, or deny due process of the law.

When the State apportions its legislature, it must have due regard for the Equal Protection Clause. Similarly, when the State delegates lawmaking power to local government and provides for the election of local officials from districts specified by statute, ordinance, or local charter, it must insure that those qualified to vote have the right to an equally effective voice in the election process. If voters residing in oversize districts are denied their constitutional right to participate in the election of state legislators, precisely the same kind of deprivation occurs when the members of a city council, school board, or county governing board are elected from districts of substantially unequal population. If the five senators representing a city in the state legislature may not be elected from districts ranging in size from 50,000 to 500,000, neither is it permissible to elect the members of the city council from those same districts. In either case, the votes of some residents have greater weight than those of others; in both cases the equal protection of the laws has been denied.

That the state legislature may itself be properly apportioned does not exempt municipalities from the Fourteenth Amendment. While state legislatures exercise extensive power over their constituents and over the various units of local government, the States universally leave much policy and decision making to their governmental subdivisions. Legislators enact many laws but do not attempt to reach those countless matters of local concern necessarily left wholly or partly to those who govern at the local level. What is more, in providing for the governments of their cities, counties, towns, and districts, the States characteristically provide for representative government—for decision making at the local level by representatives elected by the people. And, not infrequently, the delegation of power to local units, is contained in constitutional provisions for local home rule which are immune from legislative interference. In a word, institutions of local government have always been a major aspect of our system, and their responsible and responsive operation is today of increasing importance to the quality of life of more and more of our citizens. We therefore see little difference, in terms of the application of the Equal Protection Clause and of the principles of *Reynolds* v. *Sims,* between the exercise of state power through legislatures and its exercise by elected officials in the cities, towns, and counties.

We are urged to permit unequal districts for the Midland County Commissioners Court on the ground that the court's functions are not sufficiently "legislative." The parties have devoted much effort to urging that alternative labels—"administrative" versus "legislative"—be applied to the Commissioners Court. As the brief description of the court's functions above amply demonstrates, this unit of local government cannot easily be classified in the neat categories favored by civics texts. The Texas commissioners courts are assigned some tasks which would normally be thought of as "legislative," others typically assigned to "executive" or "administrative" departments, and still others which are "judicial." In this regard Midland County's Commissioners Court is representative of most of the governing bodies of American cities, counties, towns, and villages. . . .

While the Texas Supreme Court found that the Commissioners Court's legislative functions are "negligible," . . . the court does have power to make a large number of decisions having a broad range of impacts on all the citizens of the county. It sets a tax rate, equalizes assessments, and issues bonds. It then prepares and adopts a budget for allocating the county's funds, and is given by statute a wide range of discretion in choosing the subjects on which to spend. In adopting the budget the court makes both long-term judgments about the way Midland County should develop—whether industry should be solicited, roads improved, recreation facilities built, and land set aside for schools—and immediate choices among competing needs.

The Texas Supreme Court concluded that the work actually done by the Commissioners Court "disproportionately concern[s] the rural areas," . . . . Were the Commissioners Court a special purpose unit of government assigned the performance of functions affecting definable groups of constituents more than other constituents, we would have to confront the question whether such bodies may be apportioned in ways which give greater influence to the citizens most affected by the organizations' functions. That question, however, is not presented by this case, for while Midland County authorities may concentrate their attention on rural roads, the relevant fact is that the powers of the Commissioners Court include the authority to make a substantial number of decisions that affect all citizens, whether they reside inside or outside the city limits of Midland. The Commissioners maintain buildings, administer welfare services, and determine school districts both inside and outside the city. The taxes imposed by the court fall equally on all property in the county. Indeed, it may not be mere coincidence that a body apportioned with three of its four voting members chosen by residents of the rural area surrounding the city devotes most of its attention to the problems of that area, while paying for its expenditures with a tax imposed equally on city residents and those who live outside the city. And we might point out that a decision not to exercise a function within the court's power—a decision, for example, not to build an airport or a library, or not to participate in the federal food stamp program—is just as much a decision affecting all citizens of the county as an affirmative decision.

The Equal Protection Clause does not, of course, require that the State never distinguish between citizens, but only that the distinctions that are made not be arbitrary or invidious. The conclusion of *Reynolds* v. *Sims* was that bases other than population were not acceptable grounds for distinguishing among citizens when determining the size of districts used to elect members of state legislatures. We hold today only that the Constitution permits no substantial variation from equal population in drawing districts for units of local government having general governmental powers over the entire geographic area served by the body.

MR. JUSTICE HARLAN, DISSENTING (OMITTED).

MR. JUSTICE FORTAS, DISSENTING.

. . . I am in fundamental disagreement. I believe, as I shall discuss, that in the circumstances of this case equal protection of the laws may be achieved—and perhaps can only be achieved—by a system which takes into account a complex of values and factors, and not merely the arithmetic simplicity of one equals one. *Dusch* and *Sailors* were wisely and prudently decided. They reflect a reasoned, conservative, empirical approach to the intricate problem of applying constitutional principle to the complexities of local government. I know of no reason why we now abandon this reasonable and moderate approach to the problem of local suffrage and adopt an absolute and inflexible formula which is potentially destructive of important political and social values. There is no reason why we should insist that there is and can be only one rule for voters in local governmental units—that districts for units of local government must be drawn solely on the basis of population. I believe there are powerful reasons why, while insisting upon reasonable regard for the population-suffrage ratio, we should reject a rigid, theoretical, and authoritarian approach to the problems of local government. In this complex and involved area, we should be careful and conservative in our application of constitutional imperatives, for they are powerful.

Constitutional commandments are not surgical instruments. They have a tendency to hack deeply—to amputate. And while I have no doubt that, with the growth of suburbia and exurbia, the problem of allocating local government functions and benefits urgently requires attention, I am persuaded that it does not call for the hatchet of one man-one vote. It is our duty to insist upon due regard for the value of the individual vote but not to ignore realities or to by-pass the alternatives that legislative alteration might provide. . . .

This rule is appropriate to the selection of members of a State Legislature. The people of a State are similarly affected by the action of the State Legislature. Its functions are comprehensive and pervasive. They are not specially concentrated upon the needs of particular parts of the State or any separate group of citizens. . . .

But the same cannot be said of all local governmental units, and certainly not of the unit involved in this case. Midland County's Commissioners Court has special functions—directed primarily to its rural area and rural population. Its powers are limited and specialized, in light of its missions. Residents of Midland County do not by any means have the same rights and interests at stake in the election of the Commissioners. Equal protection of their rights may certainly take into account the reality of the rights and interests of the various segments of the voting population. It does not require that they all be treated alike, regardless of the stark difference in the impact of the Commissioners Court upon them. - "Equal protection" relates to the substance of citizens' rights and interests. It demands protection adapted to substance; it does not insist upon, or even permit, prescription by arbitrary formula which wrongly assumes that the interests of all citizens in the elected body are the same. . . .

In sum, the Commissioners Court's functions and powers are quite limited, and they are defined and restricted so that their primary and preponderant impact is on the rural areas and residents. The extent of its impact on the city is quite limited. To the extent that there is direct impact in the city, the relevant powers, in important respects, are placed in the hands of officials elected on a one man-one vote basis. Indeed, viewed in terms of the realities of rights and powers, it appears that the city residents have the power to elect the officials who are most important to them, and the rural residents have the electoral power with respect to the Commissioners Court which exercises powers in which they are primarily interested.

In face of this, to hold that "no substantial variation" from equal population may be allowed under the Equal Protection Clause is to ignore the substance of the rights and powers involved. It denies—it does not implement—substantive equality of voting rights. . . .

MR. JUSTICE STEWART, DISSENTING (OMITTED).

[There are many thousands of local governments in the United States that are limited to a single purpose such as flood control, sanitation, education, and the like. These are often called "special district governments," and they are often administered by elected boards. In *Hadley* v. *Junior College District* (1970), the Supreme Court considered a challenge to the apportionment of the elected board of trustees of a junior college district in the Kansas City, Missouri, metropolitan area. The trustees were apportioned for election purposes among eight public school districts that lay within the junior college district. Residents of the Kansas City school district, one of the eight component districts, pointed out that their school district had approximately 60 percent of the population of the junior college district but elected only half of the trustees. According to the statutes, a component district that had between half and two-thirds of the population of a junior college district was entitled to three of the six trustee positions. The Kansas City residents claimed that this arrangement diluted the value of their votes in violation of the equal protection clause of the Fourteenth Amendment. The Missouri courts dismissed their suit, holding that that "one man, one vote" principle did not apply to the election of junior college trustees.

The Supreme Court reversed the decision of the Missouri courts and held that the principles of *Reynolds* and *Avery* governed this case. Writing for the majority, Justice Black said:

We therefore hold today that as a general rule, whenever a state or local government decides to select persons by popular election to perform governmental

*functions, the Equal Protection Clause
. . . requires that each qualified voter
must be given an equal opportunity to
participate in that election, and when
members of an elected body are chosen
from separate districts, each district
must be established on a basis that will
insure, as far as practicable, that equal
numbers of voters can vote for propor-
tionally equal numbers of officials. It is
of course possible that there might be
some case in which a state elects certain
functionaries whose duties are so far
removed from normal governmental activities and so disproportionately affect
different groups that a popular election
in compliance with* Reynolds *. . . might
not be required, but certainly we see
nothing in the present case that indicates that the activities of these trustees
fit in that category. . . . these trustees
. . . are governmental officials in every
relevant sense of that term.*]

(4) Kirkpatrick v. Preisler (1969)

+Brennan, Douglas, Warren,
Black, Marshall, Fortas
−Harlan, Stewart, White

MR. JUSTICE BRENNAN delivered the
opinion of the Court.

In *Wesberry* v. *Sanders* . . . , we
held that "[w]hile it may not be possible [for the states] to draw congressional districts with mathematical
precision," . . . the Constitution requires "as nearly as is practicable one
man's vote in a congressional election is to be worth as much as
another's." . . . We are required in
this case to elucidate the "as nearly
as practicable" standard.

The Missouri congressional redistricting statute challenged in this
case resulted from that State's second attempt at congressional redistricting since *Wesberry* was decided.
. . .

Based on the best population data
available to the legislature in 1967,
the 1960 United States census figures, absolute population equality
among Missouri's 10 congressional
districts would mean a population of
431,981 in each district. The districts
created by the 1967 Act, however,
varied from this ideal within a range
of 12,260 below it to 13,542 above it.
The difference between the least and
most populous districts was thus
25,802. In percentage terms, the
most populous district was 3.13%
above the mathematical ideal, and
the least populous was 2.84% below:

The redistricting effected by the 1967 Act, based on a population of 4,319,813 according to the 1960 census, is as follows:

District No.	Population	% Variation from Ideal
One	439,746	+1.8
Two	436,448	+1.03
Three	436,099	− .95
Four	419,721	−2.84
Five	431,178	− .19
Six	422,238	−2.26
Seven	436,769	+1.11
Eight	445,523	+3.13
Nine	428,223	− .87
Ten	423,868	−1.88

Number of districts within 1.88% of ideal	7
Population difference between largest and smallest districts	25,802
Ideal population per district	431,981
Average variation from ideal	1.6%
Ratio of largest to smallest district	1.06 to 1

The District Court found that the General Assembly had not in fact relied on the census figures but instead had based its plan on less accurate data. In addition, the District Court found that the General Assembly had rejected a redistricting plan submitted to it which provided for districts with smaller population variances among them. Finally, the District Court found that the simple device of switching some counties from one district to another would have produced a plan with markedly reduced variances among districts. Based on these findings, the District Court, one judge dissenting, held that the 1967 Act did not meet the constitutional standard of equal representation for equal numbers of people "as nearly as practicable," and that the State had failed to make any acceptable justification for the variances. . . . We affirm.

Missouri's primary argument is that the population variances among the districts created by the 1967 Act are so small that they should be considered de minimis and for that reason to satisfy the "as nearly as practicable" limitation and not to require independent justification. Alternatively, Missouri argues that justification for the variances was established in the evidence: it is contended that the General Assembly provided for variances out of legitimate regard for such factors as the representation of distinct interest groups, the integrity of county lines, the compactness of districts, the population trends within the State, the high proportion of military personnel, college students, and other nonvoters in some districts, and the political realities of "legislative interplay."

We reject Missouri's argument that there is a fixed numerical or percentage population variance small enough to be considered de minimis and to satisfy without question the "as nearly as practicable" standard. The whole thrust of the "as nearly as practicable" approach is inconsistent with adoption of fixed numerical standards which excuse population variances without regard to the circumstances of each particular case. The extent to which equality may practicably be achieved may differ from State to State and from district to district. . . . The "as nearly as practicable" standard requires that the State make a good-faith effort to achieve precise mathematical equality. . . . Unless population variances among congressional districts are shown to have resulted despite such effort, the State must justify each variance, no matter how small.

There are other reasons for rejecting the de minimis approach. We can see no nonarbitrary way to pick a cutoff point at which population variances suddenly become de minimis. Moreover, to consider a certain range of variances de minimis would encourage legislators to strive for that range rather than for equality as nearly as practicable. . . .

Equal representation for equal numbers of people is a principle designed to prevent debasement of voting power and diminution of access to elected representatives. Toleration of even small deviations detracts from these purposes. Therefore, the command of Art I, § 2, that States create congressional districts which provide equal representation for equal numbers of people permits only the limited population variances which are unavoidable despite a good-faith effort to achieve absolute equality, or for which justification is shown.

Clearly, the population variances among the Missouri congressional districts were not unavoidable. Indeed, it is not seriously contended that the Missouri Legislature came as close to equality as it might have come. The District Court found that, to the contrary, in the two reapportionment efforts of the Missouri Legislature since *Wesberry,* "the leadership of both political parties in the Senate and the House were given nothing better to work with than a makeshift bill produced by what has been candidly recognized to be no more than . . . an expedient political compromise." . . . Legislative proponents of the 1967 Act frankly conceded at the District Court hearing that resort to the simple device of transferring entire political subdivisions of known population between contiguous districts would have produced districts much closer to numerical equality. The District Court found, moreover, that the Missouri Legislature relied on inaccurate data in constructing the districts, and that it rejected without consideration a plan which would have reduced markedly population variances among the districts. Finally, it is simply inconceivable that population disparities of the magnitude found in the Missouri plan were unavoidable. . . . In sum, "it seems quite obvious that the State could have come much closer to providing districts of equal population than it did." . . .

Missouri contends that variances were necessary to avoid fragmenting areas with distinct economic and social interests and thereby diluting the effective representation of those interests in Congress. But to accept population variances, large or small, in order to create districts with specific interest orientations is antithetical to the basic premise of the constitutional command to provide equal representation for equal numbers of people. . . .

We also reject Missouri's argument that "[t]he reasonableness of the population differences in the congressional districts under review must . . . be viewed in the context of legislative interplay. The legislative leaders all testified that the act in question was in their opinion a reasonable legislative compromise. . . . It must be remembered . . . that practical political problems are inherent in the enactment of congressional reapportionment legislation." . . . Problems created by partisan politics cannot justify an apportionment which does not otherwise pass constitutional muster.

Similarly, we do not find legally acceptable the argument that variances are justified if they necessarily result from a State's attempt to avoid fragmenting political subdivisions by drawing congressional district lines along existing county, municipal, or other political subdivision boundaries. The State's interest in constructing congressional districts in this manner, it is suggested, is to minimize the opportunities for partisan gerrymandering. But an argument that deviations from equality are justified in order to inhibit legislators from engaging in partisan gerrymandering is no more than a variant of the argument, already rejected, that considerations of practical politics can justify population disparities.

Missouri further contends that certain population variances resulted from the legislature's taking account of the fact that the percentage of eligible voters among the total population differed significantly from district to district—some districts contained disproportionately large numbers of military personnel stationed at bases maintained by the Armed Forces and students in attendance at universities or colleges. There may be a question whether distribution of congressional seats except according to total population can ever be permissible under Art I, § 2. But assuming without deciding that apportionment may be based on eligible voter population rather than total population, the Missouri plan is still unacceptable. Missouri made no attempt to ascertain the number of eligible voters in each district and to apportion accordingly. At best it made haphazard adjustments to a scheme based on total population: overpopulation in the Eighth District was explained away by the presence in that district of a military base and a university; no attempt was made to account for the presence of universities in other districts or the disproportionate numbers of newly arrived and short-term residents in the City of St. Louis. Even as to the Eighth District, there is no indication that the excess population allocated to that district corresponds to the alleged extraordinary additional numbers of noneligible voters there.

Missouri also argues that population disparities between some of its congressional districts result from the legislature's attempt to take into account projected population shifts. We recognize that a congressional districting plan will usually be in effect for at least 10 years and five congressional elections. Situations may arise where substantial population shifts over such a period can be anticipated. Where these shifts can be predicted with a high degree of accuracy, States that are redistricting may properly consider them. By this we mean to open no avenue for subterfuge. Findings as to population trends must be thoroughly documented and applied throughout the State in a systematic, not an ad hoc, manner.

MR. JUSTICE FORTAS, CONCURRING (OMITTED).

MR. JUSTICE HARLAN, WITH WHOM MR. JUSTICE STEWART JOINS, DISSENTING (OMITTED).

MR. JUSTICE WHITE, DISSENTING.

I have consistently joined the Court's opinions which establish as one of the ground rules for legislative districting that single member districts should be substantially equal in population. I would not now dissent if the Court's present judgment represented a measurable contribution to the ends which I had thought the Court was pursuing in this area, or even if I thought the opinion not very useful but not harmful either. With all due respect, however, I am firmly convinced that the Court's new ruling is an unduly rigid and unwarranted application of the Equal Protection Clause which will unnecessarily involve the courts in the abrasive task of drawing district lines. . . .

It also seems arbitrary for the majority to discard the suggestion of *Reynolds* v. *Sims* . . . that if a legislature seeks an apportionment plan which respects the boundaries of political subdivisions, some variations from absolute equality would be constitutionally permissible. Of course, *Reynolds* involved state legislative apportionment and took pains to say that there may be more leeway in that context. But the Court invokes *Reynolds* today and in no way distinguishes federal from state districting. . . .

In reality, of course, districting is itself a gerrymandering in the sense that it represents a complex blend of political, economic, regional, and historical considerations. In terms of gerrymander, the situation will not be much different if equality means what it literally says—a zero variation—rather than only "substantial" equality which would countenance some variations among legislative districts. Either standard will prevent a minority of the population or a minority party from consistently controlling the state legislature or a congressional delegation and both are powerful forces toward equalizing voter influence on legislative performance. In terms of effective representation for all voters there are only miniscule differences between the two standards. But neither rule can alone prevent deliberate partisan gerrymandering if that is considered an evil which the Fourteenth Amendment should attempt to proscribe.

(5) Whitcomb v. Chavis (1971)

+White, Burger, Black, Harlan, Stewart, Blackmun
—Douglas, Brennan, Marshall

[The initial focus of the reapportionment cases was on disparities in the size of electoral districts. The "one person, one vote" principle is primarily responsive to that problem. However, as Justice Frankfurter prophetically noted in his dissent in *Baker* v. *Carr* (1962), fair representation is a much more complex, sophisticated, and elusive concept than mere population equality. It is possible to arrange electoral districts of approximately equal populations and yet undermine the effective representation of individuals or groups *within* those districts. The Hasidic Jews of the Williamsburgh section of Brooklyn would certainly attest to that (see *United Jewish Organizations of Williamsburgh* v. *Carey*, 1977, *supra*). How district lines are drawn, may, in fact, be more important in the long run than the number of voters in a district.

Two major questions have confronted the Supreme Court. First, the Court has been asked to pass on the validity of multimember electoral districts. Second, it has considered the broader question of political gerrymandering. The latter question will be considered in detail in the comments following the *Whitcomb* case.

Most electoral contests in the United States are held in single-member districts, that is, districts in which one or more candidates seek election to a single available office. All members of the House of Representatives are chosen this way (although this was not always so in the past). Most state legislators are chosen this way. A multimember district, by contrast, is one in which all the voters elect two or more officials to the same office within a particular geographic area.

Multimember districts tend to increase the voting power of the district as a whole, but if a district is heterogeneous in population, important differences within it may also be submerged, and minority representation may be adversely affected. The term "minority" is used in this context to refer not only to racial or religious minorities but also to political minorities. For example, there may be just enough Republicans in a given geographic area to elect one of the area's five alloted representatives—if the district lines are drawn so that most Republicans live in one district. However, if the voters of that area elect all five representatives at large, for example, in a single multimember district, it is highly likely that only Democrats will be elected.

The choice between single and multimember districts therefore is often of crucial political significance. *Wesberry* and *Reynolds,* both of which were premised on the theory that the constitutional right to cast a fairly apportioned vote is an *individual* right, not a group right, gave little guidance. The Supreme Court has refused to invalidate multimember districts as such. In *Burns* v. *Richardson* (1966), it rejected a challenge to Hawaii's multimember district system because no invidious *result* could be proved. "The Equal Protection Clause," the Court said, "does not require single member districts." Multimember districts were permissible, the Court said, if they were not "designed to or would not operate to minimize or cancel out the voting strength of racial or political elements of the voting population."]

MR. JUSTICE WHITE delivered the opinion of the Court.

. . . Indiana has a bicameral general assembly consisting of a house of representatives of 100 members and a senate of 50 members. Eight of the 31 senatorial districts and 25 of the 39 house districts are multimember districts, that is, districts which are represented by two or more legislators elected at large by the voters of the district. Under the statutes here challenged, Marion County [which includes the city of Indianapolis] is a multi-member district electing eight senators and 15 members of the house. . . .

The three-judge court . . . concluded that Marion County's multimember district must be disestablished and, because of population disparities not directly related to the phenomena alleged in the complaint, the entire State must be redistricted. . . .

[Plaintiffs'] first charge is that any multimember district bestows on its voters several unconstitutional advantages over voters in single-member districts or smaller multimember districts. . . . The District Court . . . considered [this] sufficiently persuasive to be a substantial factor in prescribing uniform, single-member districts as the basic scheme of the court's own plan.

[Plaintiffs] demonstrate mathematically that in theory voting power does not vary inversely with the size of the district and that to increase legislative seats in proportion to increased population gives undue voting power to the voter in the multi-member district since he has more chances to determine election outcomes than does the voter in the single-member district. This consequence obtains wholly aside from the quality or effectiveness of representation later furnished by the successful candidates. [L]ike the District Court we note that the position remains a theoretical one and, as plaintiffs' witness conceded, knowingly avoids and does "not take into account any political or other factors which might affect the actual voting power of the residents, which might include party affiliation, race, previous voting characteristics or any other factors which go into the entire political voting situation." The real-life impact of multimember districts on individual voting power has not been sufficiently demonstrated, at least on this record, to warrant departure from prior cases.

The District Court was more impressed with the other branch of the claim that multimember districts inherently discriminate against other districts. This was the assertion that whatever the individual voting power of Marion County voters in choosing legislators may be, they nevertheless have more effective representation in the Indiana general assembly for two reasons. First, each voter is represented by more legislators and therefore, in theory at least, has more chances to influence critical legislative votes. Second, since multimember delegations are elected at large and represent the voters of the entire district, they tend to vote as a bloc, which is tantamount to the district having one representative with several votes. . . . The theory that plural representation itself unduly enhances a district's power and the influence of its voters remains to be demonstrated in practice and in the day-to-day operation of the legislature. Neither the findings of the trial court nor the record before us sustains it, even where bloc voting is posited.

. . . Moreover, Marion County would have no less advantage, if advantage there is, if it elected from individual districts and the elected representatives demonstrated the same bloc-voting tendency, which may also develop among legislators representing single-member districts widely scattered throughout the State. Of course it is advantageous to start with more than one vote for a bill. But nothing before us shows or suggests that any legislative skirmish affecting the State of Indiana or Marion County in particular would have come out differently had Marion County been subdistricted and its delegation elected from single-member-districts.

[T]he trial court struck down Marion County's multimember district because it found the scheme worked invidiously against a specific segment of the county's voters as compared with others. The court identified an area of the city [part of Center Township] as a ghetto, found it predominantly inhabited by poor Negroes with distinctive substantive-law interests and thought this group unconstitutionally underrepresented because the proportion of legislators with residences in the ghetto elected from 1960 to 1968 was less than the ghetto's proportion of the population, less than the proportion of legislators elected from Washington Township, a less populous district [which contained a relatively wealthy white suburb and a middle class Negro area], and less than the ghetto would likely have elected had the county consisted of single-member districts [one senator and two representatives]. We find major deficiencies in this approach. [T]here is no suggestion here that Marion County's multimember district, or similar districts throughout the State, were conceived or operated as purposeful devices to further racial or economic discrimination. As plaintiffs concede, "there was no

basis for asserting that the legislative districts in Indiana were designed to dilute the vote of minorities.". . .

Nor does the fact that the number of ghetto residents who were legislators was not in proportion to ghetto population satisfactorily prove invidious discrimination absent evidence and findings that ghetto residents had less opportunity than did other Marion County residents to participate in the political processes and to elect legislators of their choice. We have discovered nothing in the record or in the court's findings indicating that poor Negroes were not allowed to register or vote, to choose the political party they desired to support, to participate in its affairs or to be equally represented on those occasions when legislative candidates were chosen. Nor did the evidence purport to show or the court find that inhabitants of the ghetto were regularly excluded from the slates of both major parties, thus denying them the chance of occupying legislative seats. It appears reasonably clear that the Republican Party won four of the five elections from 1960 to 1968, that Center Township ghetto voted heavily Democratic and that ghetto votes were critical to Democratic Party success. Although we cannot be sure of the facts since the court ignored the question, it seems unlikely that the Democratic Party could afford to overlook the ghetto in slating its candidates. Clearly, in 1964—the one election which the Democrats won— the party slated and elected one senator and one representative from Center Township ghetto as well as one senator and four representatives from other parts of Center Township and two representatives from census tract 220 [the middle class Negro area]. Nor is there any indication that the party failed to slate candidates satisfactory to the ghetto in other years. Absent evidence or findings we are not sure, but it seems reasonable to infer that had the Democrats won all of the elections or even most of them, the ghetto would have had no justifiable complaints about representation. The fact is, however, that four of the five elections were won by Republicans, which was not the party of the ghetto and which would not always slate ghetto candidates—although in 1962 it nominated and elected one representative and in 1968 two representatives from that area. If this is the proper view of this case, the failure of the ghetto to have legislative seats in proportion to its population emerges more as a function of losing elections than of built-in bias against poor Negroes. The voting power of ghetto residents may have been "cancelled out" as the District Court held, but this seems a mere euphemism for political defeat at the polls.

[T]ypical American legislative elections are district-oriented, head-on races between candidates of two or more parties. As our system has it, one candidate wins, the others lose. Arguably the losing candidates' supporters are without representation since the men they voted for have been defeated; arguably they have been denied equal protection of the laws since they have no legislative voice of their own. This is true of both single-member *and* multimember districts. But we have not yet deemed it a denial of equal protection to deny legislative seats to losing candidates, even in those so-called "safe" districts where the same party wins year after year.

. . . Conceding that all Marion County voters could fairly be said to be represented by the entire delegation, just as each voter in a single-member district by the winning candidate, the District Court thought

ghetto voters' claims to the partial allegiance of eight senators and 15 representatives was not equivalent to the undivided allegiance of one senator and two representatives; nor was the ghetto voters' chance of influencing the election of an entire slate as significant as the guarantee of one ghetto senator and two ghetto representatives.

. . . But are poor Negroes of the ghetto any more underrepresented than poor ghetto whites who also voted Democratic and lost, or any more discriminated against than other interest groups or voters in Marion County with allegiance to the Democratic Party, or conversely, any less represented than Republican areas or voters in years of Republican defeat? We think not. . . .

There is another gap in the trial court's reasoning. . . . Plaintiffs' evidence purported to show disregard for the ghetto's distinctive interests; defendants claimed quite the contrary. We see nothing in the findings of the District Court indicating recurring poor performance by Marion County's delegation with respect to Center Township ghetto, nothing to show what the ghetto's interests were in particular legislative situations and nothing to indicate that the outcome would have been any different if the 23 assemblymen had been chosen from single-member districts. Moreover, even assuming bloc voting by the delegation contrary to the wishes of the ghetto majority, it would not follow that the Fourteenth Amendment had been violated unless it is invidiously discriminatory for a county to elect its delegation by majority vote based on party or candidate platforms and so to some extent predetermine legislative votes on particular issues. Such tendencies are inherent in government by elected representatives; and surely elections in single-member districts visit precisely the same consequences on the supporters of losing candidates whose views are rejected at the polls. . . .

We are not insensitive to the objections long voiced to multi-member district plans. Although not as prevalent as they were in our early history, they have been with us since colonial times and were much in evidence both before and after the adoption of the Fourteenth Amendment. Criticism is rooted in their winner-take-all aspects, their tendency to submerge minorities and to overrepresent the winning party as compared with the party's state-wide electoral position, a general preference for legislatures reflecting community interests as closely as possible and disenchantment with political parties and elections as devices to settle policy differences between contending interests. The chance of winning or significantly influencing intraparty fights and issue-oriented elections has seemed to some inadequate protection to minorities, political, racial, or economic; rather, their voice, it is said, should also be heard in the legislative forum where public policy is finally fashioned. In our view, however, experience and insight have not yet demonstrated that multimember districts are inherently invidious and violative of the Fourteenth Amendment. Surely the findings of the District Court do not demonstrate it. Moreover, if the problems of multimember districts are unbearable or even unconstitutional it is not at all clear that the remedy is a single-member district system with its lines carefully drawn to ensure representation to sizable racial, ethnic, economic or religious groups and with its own capacity for over and underrepresenting parties and interests and even for permitting a minority of the voters to control the legislature and government of a State. . . .

Even if the District Court was correct in finding unconstitutional discrimination against poor inhabitants of the ghetto, it did not explain why it was constitutionally compelled to disestablish the entire county district and to intrude upon state policy any more than necessary to ensure representation of ghetto interests. The court entered judgment without expressly putting aside on supportable grounds the alternative of creating single-member districts in the ghetto and leaving the district otherwise intact, as well as the possibility that the Fourteenth Amendment could be satisfied by simple requirement that some of the at-large candidates each year must reside in the ghetto.

We are likewise at a loss to understand how on the court's own findings of fact and conclusions of law it was justified in eliminating every multimember district in the State of Indiana. . . .

We therefore reverse the judgment . . . and remand the case . . . for further proceedings consistent with this opinion.

SEPARATE OPINION OF MR. JUSTICE HARLAN (OMITTED)

MR. JUSTICE DOUGLAS, WITH WHOM MR. JUSTICE BRENNAN AND MR. JUSTICE MARSHALL CONCUR, DISSENTING.

A showing of racial motivation is not necessary when dealing with multimember districts. Although the old apportionment plan which is in full harmony with the State's 1851 constitution, may not be racially motivated, the test for multimember districts is whether there are invidious effects. . . .

In *Burns* v. *Richardson*, . . . we stated that assuming the requirements of *Reynolds* v. *Sims* were

satisfied, multimember districts are unconstitutional "only if it can be shown that 'designedly or otherwise' . . . [such a district would operate] to minimize or cancel out the voting strength of racial or political elements of the voting population." We went on to suggest how the burden of proof could be met. "It may be that this invidious effect can more easily be shown if, in contrast to the facts in *Fortson*, districts are large in relation to the total numbers of legislators, if districts are not appropriately subdistricted to assure distribution of legislators that are resident over the entire district, or if such districts characterize both houses of a bicameral legislature rather than one." These factors are all present in this case.
. . .

It is said that if we prevent racial gerrymandering today, we must prevent gerrymandering of any special interest group tomorrow, whether it be social, economic, or ideological. I do not agree. Our Constitution has a special thrust when it comes to voting; the Fifteenth Amendment . . . . It is asking the impossible for us to demand that the blacks first show that the effect of the scheme was to discourage or prevent poor blacks from voting or joining such party as they chose. On this record, the voting rights of the blacks have been "abridged," as I read the Constitution.
. . .

[In *White* v. *Regester* (1973), the Court finally decided a case by declaring that the use of multimember districts—at least in those districts—was unconstitutional. It found, in one of the cases, from Bexar County, Texas, that two multimember districts established by the state legislature operated so as to "cancel out or minimize the voting strength of racial groups." However, it did not declare multimember districts unconstitutional, per se.

The manipulation of votes through establishment of multimember districts is merely a special case of the great political art of "gerrymandering." Gerrymandering is the age-old practice of drawing electoral district lines for political advantage. The origin of the term traces to Elbridge Gerry, one of the framers of the Constitution but also a well-seasoned Massachusetts politician. Gerry was responsible for drawing up a legislative district which, its opponents complained, looked like a salamander. Not so, one replied, it is a "Gerrymander." While strangely shaped districts often are the product of gerrymandering, however, the term now applies to all kinds of partisan attempts at fashioning electoral districts.

The most notorious gerrymander in recent times occurred in Tuskegee, Alabama, home of the world-famous Tuskegee Institute. When black voters in that city became sufficiently numerous to take political control, the Alabama legislature passed a law that redefined the boundaries of the city, "altering the shape of Tuskegee from a square to an uncouth twenty-eight sided figure." As a result, all but 4 or 5 of the 400 black voters were disenfranchised. They could vote, not "in" Tuskegee, but in the outlying counties where the number of black voters was small and their votes became politically meaningless. The redistricting of the city, which ran in and around city blocks to exclude most black voters, did not remove a single white voter. The Supreme Court, as already noted, unanimously invalidated this racial gerrymander under the Fifteenth Amendment in *Gomillion* v. *Lightfoot* (1960).

Four years later, in *Wright* v. *Rockefeller* (1964), the Court stepped back from what might be called a "benign" gerrymander. Adam Clayton Powell had represented New York City's Harlem congressional district since 1942. He was pastor of the Abyssinian Baptist Church and the unquestioned black political leader in New York. Most blacks in Manhattan lived in his district, and he was the only elected black representative in Congress from New York. As more blacks and Puerto Ricans moved into Manhattan in the 1950s and 1960s, Powell's district was protected. He refused to permit substantial changes in district lines which would have made his political hold more precarious but which would also, almost certainly, have opened up the possibility of additional districts likely to elect nonwhite representatives. While Powell's district had virtually all black voters, the three districts surrounding his had 29 percent, 28 percent, and 5 percent black voters, respectively.

A court challenge was instituted to break Powell's stranglehold, but the Supreme Court turned it back, holding that it had not been proved that race had been taken into account in fashioning district lines. Justice Goldberg and Douglas argued in dissent that this was a prima facie case of de jure segregation. But the Court contented itself with restating the principles of *Gomillion*—that government has no business designing electoral districts along racial or religious lines. But even these words were weakened by *Whitcomb,* which said merely that districting could not *cancel out* or minimize the voting strength of racial groups.

One might wonder, also, how the principles of *Gomillion* square with the decision, reported earlier in this chapter, of *United Jewish Organizations of Williamsburgh* v. *Carey* (1977), or of *Beer* v. *United States* (1976). In the *Williamsburgh* case, state legislative districts were drawn explicitly to achieve certain percentages of black voters in each of several districts in Brooklyn. *Beer* involved a similar redrawing of district lines in New Orleans to assure a certain level of black representation. But in both cases, the Supreme Court held that race could be taken into account in redistricting in order to comply with Section 5 of the Voting Rights Act of 1965. Said Justice Stewart in the *Beer* case: the purpose of Section 5 "has always been to insure that no voting procedure changes would be made that would lead to a retrogression [emphasis added] in the position of racial minorities with respect to their effective exercise of the electoral franchise." It would appear, therefore, that racial gerrymandering to protect or increase the voting power of racial minorities, in compliance with the Voting Rights Act, is valid but probably invalid in other contexts.

In *Gaffney* v. *Cummings* (1973), the Supreme Court declined to overturn one example of political (not racial) gerrymandering. Connecticut had created a bipartisan board to redistrict the state. By law, the board was directed to draw district lines to approximate the statewide

political strengths of the Democratic and Republican parties. The Court unanimously observed that all districting, by its very nature, is unavoidably "political." It referred to the idea of working solely with census data and not political data as a "politically mindless approach." In the words of Justice White:

It is much more plausible to assume that those who redistrict and reapportion work with both political and census data. Within the limits of the population equality standards of the Equal Protection Clause, they seek, through compromise or otherwise, to achieve the political or other ends of the State, its constituents, and its office holders. What is done in so arranging for elections . . . is not wholly exempt from judicial scrutiny under the Fourteenth Amendment. As we have indicated, for example, multimember districts may be vulnerable, if racial or political groups have been fenced out of the political process and their voting strength invidiously minimized. Beyond this, we have not ventured far or attempted the impossible task of extirpating politics from what are the essentially political processes of the sovereign states. Even more plainly, judicial interest should be at its lowest ebb when the parties in accordance with their voting strength and, within quite tolerable limits, succeed in doing so. . . .

No specific mention of the term is found in Justice White's opinion, but in this case the Court comes very close to deciding that, within the limits of population equality and barring evidence of fencing out minority groups, political districting is a nonjusticiable political question.]

(6) Mahan v. Howell (1973)

+Burger, Stewart, White, Blackmun, Rehnquist
+/−Douglas, Brennan, Marshall
NP Powell

[*Reynolds* v. *Sims* (1964) required states to come as close as practicable to population equality in redistricting, but it set no parameters. It recognized the need for some flexibility in state legislative apportionment but reaffirmed the earlier holding of *Wesberry* v. *Sanders*(1964), which required states to make a good-faith effort to achieve precise mathematical equality in congressional districting. *Kirkpatrick* v. *Preisler* (1969) interpreted this strictly by invalidating a Missouri congressional reapportionment scheme in which the difference between the largest and smallest district was only 5.97 percent. It rejected Missouri's argument that there might be *de minimis* variations (too small to matter). As long as a state could reduce the variation, it had an obligation to do so. This was the last reapportionment decision handed down by the Warren Court.

In *White* v. *Weiser* (1973), the Court invalidated an even smaller deviation in congressional apportionment of 4.1 percent. It reaffirmed the tough stance of *Kirkpatrick*, adding that town and county lines were not to be considered inviolate if they stood in the way of achieving true population equality. But three of the new justices on the Court—Powell, Burger, and Rehnquist—concurred only with great reservations. Indeed, they announced that they would not have supported *Kirkpatrick* initially and were prepared, in another case, to "reconsider"—and presumably overrule—it. This was the first step in the Burger Court's relaxation of apportionment standards.

A second step came in the *Mahan* case, which involved reapportionment of the Virginia state legislature. The Virginia State House of Delegates was divided into fifty-two single-member and multimember districts with a total of 100 delegates. On a strict population basis, the ideal size would have been 46, 485 per delegate. The most populous district was 9.6 percent larger than that figure, the least populous was 6.8 percent less, for a total deviation range of 16.4 percent. There was an average percentage variance of − 3.89 percent. A vote of 49.29 percent of the population was needed to elect a majority in the House of Delegates. Two suits were brought challenging the constitutionality of this redistricting plan on the grounds that the population variances were impermissible and that the multimember districts constituted racial gerrymandering. A three-judge federal court found the population variances too high on the basis of *Kirkpatrick* and produced a substitute plan with a maximum total variation of about 10 percent. Even to achieve that 10 percent, the federal court had to cut through established boundary lines.]

MR. JUSTICE REHNQUIST delivered the opinion of the Court.

. . .

Relying on *Kirkpatrick* v. *Preisler* . . . (1969); *Wells* v. *Rockefeller* . . . (1969), and *Reynolds* v. *Sims* . . . (1964), the District Court concluded that the 16.4% variation was sufficient to condemn the House statute under the "one person, one vote" doctrine. While it noted that the variances were traceable to the desire of the General Assembly to maintain the integrity of traditional county and city boundaries, and that it was impossible to draft district lines to overcome unconstitutional disparities and still maintain such integrity, it held that the State proved no governmental necessity for strictly adhering to political subdivision lines. Accordingly, it undertook its own redistricting and devised a plan having a percentage variation of slightly over 10% from the ideal district, a percentage it believes came "within [the] passable constitutional limits as 'a good-faith effort to achieve absolute equality.' *Kirkpatrick* v. *Preisler*. . . ."

Appellants contend that the District Court's reliance on *Kirkpatrick* v. *Preisler* . . . and *Wells* v. *Rockefeller* . . . in striking down the General Assembly's reapportionment plan was erroneous, and that proper application of the standards enunciated in *Reynolds* v. *Sims*, . . . would have resulted in a finding that the statute was constitutional.

In *Kirkpatrick* v. *Preisler* . . . this Court invalidated state reapportionment statutes for federal congressional districts having [a] maximum percentage deviation of 5.97%. . . The express purpose of these cases was to elucidate the standard first announced in the holding of *Wesberry* v. *Sanders* . . . (1964), that "the command of Art. I, §2, that Representatives be chosen 'by the People of the several States' means that as nearly as is practicable one man's vote in a congressional election is to be worth as much as another's." . . . And it was concluded that command "permits only the limited population variances which are unavoidable despite a good-faith effort to achieve absolute equality, or for which justification is shown." . . . The principal question thus presented for review is whether or not the Equal Protection Clause of the Fourteenth Amendment likewise permits only "the limited population variances which are unavoidable despite a good-faith effort to achieve absolute equality" in the context of state legislative reapportionment.

This Court first recognized that the Equal Protection Clause of the Fourteenth Amendment requires both houses of a bicameral state legislature to be apportioned substantially on a population basis in *Reynolds* v. *Sims*. . . In so doing, it suggested that in the implementation of the basic constitutional principle—equality of population among the districts— more flexibility was constitutionally permissible with respect to state legislative reapportionment than in congressional redistricting. . . .

The Court reiterated that the overriding objective in reapportionment must be "substantial equality of population among the various districts, so that the vote of any citizen is approximately equal in weight to that of any other citizen in the State." . . .

By contrast, the Court in *Wesberry* v. *Sanders* recognized no excuse for the failure to meet the objective of equal representation for equal numbers of people in congressional districting other than the practical impossibility of drawing equal districts with mathematical precision. Thus, whereas population alone has been the sole criterion of constitutionality in congressional redistricting under Art. 1, §2, broader latitude has been afforded the States under the Equal Protection Clause in state legislative redistricting . . . The dichotomy between the two lines of cases has consistently been maintained. In *Kirkpatrick* v. *Preisler*, for example, one asserted justification for population variances was that they were necessarily a result of the State's attempt to avoid fragmenting political subdivisions by drawing congressional district lines along existing political subdivision boundaries. This argument was rejected in the congressional context. But in *Abate* v. *Mundt* . . . (1971), an apportionment for a county legislature having a maximum deviation from equality of 11.9% was upheld in the face of an equal protection challenge, in part because New York had a long history of maintaining the integrity of existing local government units within the county.

Application of the "absolute equality" test of *Kirkpatrick* and *Wells* to state legislative redistricting may impair the normal functioning of state and local governments. Such an effect is readily apparent from an analysis of the District Court's plan in this case. . . .

The court's reapportionment, based on its application of *Kirkpatrick* and *Wells*, resulted in a maximum deviation of slightly over 10%, . . . But to achieve even this limit of variation, the court's plan extended single and multimember districts across subdivision lines in 12 instances, substituting population equality for subdivision representation. . . .

We conclude . . . that the constitutionality of Virginia's legislative redistricting plan was not to be judged by the more stringent standards that *Kirkpatrick* and *Wells* make applicable to congressional reapportionment, but instead by the equal protection test enunciated in *Reynolds* v. *Sims*, . . . We affirm its holding that "the Equal Protection Clause requires that a State make an honest and good faith effort to construct districts, in both houses of its legislature, as nearly of equal population as is practicable." We likewise reaffirm its conclusion that "[s]o long as the divergences from a strict population standard are based on legitimate considerations incident to the effectuation of a rational state policy, some deviations from the equal-population principle are constitutionally permissible with respect to the apportionment of seats in either or both of the two houses of a bicameral state legislature." . . .

. . .

We hold that the legislature's plan for apportionment of the House of delegates may reasonably be said to advance the rational state policy of respecting the boundaries of political subdivisions. The remaining inquiry is whether the population disparities among the districts which have resulted from the pursuit of this plan exceed constitutional limits. We conclude that they do not.

. . .

Neither courts nor legislatures are furnished any specialized calipers which enable them to extract from the general language of the Equal Protection Clause of the Fourteenth Amendment the mathematical formula which establishes what range of percentage deviations are permissible, and what are not. The 16-odd percent maximum deviation which the District Court found to exist in the legislative plan for the reapportionment of the House is substantially less than the percentage deviations which have been found invalid in the previous decisions of this Court. While this percentage may well approach tolerable limits, we do not believe it exceeds them. Virginia has not sacrificed substantial equality to justifiable deviations.

. . .

MR. JUSTICE BRENNAN, WITH WHOM MR. JUSTICE DOUGLAS AND MR. JUSTICE MARSHALL JOIN, CONCURRING IN PART AND DISSENTING IN PART. (OMITTED).

[Four months after *Mahan,* the Supreme Court decided *Gaffney* v. *Cummings* (1973), which involved a challenge to a Connecticut redistricting scheme that provided for a total deviation between the largest and smallest district of 7.83 percents, an average deviation of 1.8 percent. In devising this scheme, the state apportionment board considered town lines (towns, not counties, are the basic governmental unit in Connecticut) and incorporated a policy of "political fairness" by maintaining a rough approximation of the relative strengths of the Democratic and Republican parties.

Writing for a 6-3 majority, Justice White reaffirmed *Mahan's* different standards for congressional and state redistricting. He also stated that certain minimum deviations from population equality in state redistricting would be treated as *de minimis*. In such cases, it would not be necessary for the state to justify the deviation: "Minor deviations from population equality among state legislative districts are insufficient to make out a prima facie case of invidious discrimination under the Fourteenth Amendment so as to require justification by the State." Given the margin of error in census statistics, and population mobility, White said, it made no sense to impose any stricter standards on the states. The maximum deviation in *Gaffney* was 7.8 percent, and in a companion case, *White* v. *Regester*, a 9.9 percent deviation was also regarded as *de minimis*. It might be inferred, therefore, that a maximum deviation from population equality of less than 10 percent would generally be regarded as *de minimis*.

Mahan indicated that a population deviation of 16.4 percent "approached tolerable limits" but could be sustained with justification. In *Chapman* v. *Meier* (1975), the Court overturned a redistricting plan from North Dakota, written by the federal district court, which contained a maximum deviation of 20 percent. The Supreme Court held that "a population deviation [of 20 percent] in a court-ordered plan is constitutionally impermissible in the absence of significant state policies or other acceptable considerations. . . ." Even allowing for the fact that court-ordered redistricting plans are subject to more stringent limits, it would appear that a 20 percent total deviation represents the outer limit of state districting variances, even with justification.

A summary of the Court's policy would therefore be as follows. In congressional redistricting, no deviation is *de minimis*. Each plan must come as close as possible to population equality. In state redistricting, a total deviation from equality of up to 10 percent is regarded as *de minimis* in the absence of any evidence of racial bias or egregious political discrimination. A state may justify a total deviation between 10 and 20 percent but under the standards of strict scrutiny.[1] Deviations over 20 percent are unacceptable.

In his opinion, Justice White stated what is certainly the prevailing philosophy of the Burger Court majority:

Fair and effective representation may be destroyed by gross population variations among districts, but it is apparent that such representation does not depend solely on mathematical equality among district populations. There are other relevant factors to be taken into account and other important interests that States may legitimately be mindful of.

He argued further that the goal of fair and effective representation was not furthered by setting such difficult standards as to ensure regularly that the federal courts must intervene:

We doubt that the Fourteenth Amendment requires repeated displacement of otherwise appropriate state decision-making in the name of essentially minor deviations from perfect census population equality that no one, with confidence, can say will deprive any person of fair and effective representation in his state legislature.

That the Court was not deterred by the hazards of the political thicket . . . does not mean that it should become bogged down in a vast, intractable apportionment slough, particularly when there is little, if anything, to be accomplished by doing so.]

E. A Note on the Impact of the Reapportionment Decisions

There is little doubt that a primary concern of the forces seeking legislative reapportionment was the expectation of policy change in the wake of legislatures electorally more responsive to urban voting populations. The malapportionment of state legislatures was, as Ward Elliot has noted, blamed

for the worst problems of government. It was supposed to have reduced city dwellers to second-class citizens, and to have stifled urgently needed reforms like home rule, slum clearance, metropolitan transit, annexation, labor and welfare legislation, civil rights laws, equal tax laws and equal expenditures on schools

---

[1]It is conceivable that this 10 to 20 percent range might contain a maximum or minimum deviation so large as to be unacceptable. For example, a 20 percent total deviation might consist of ±10 percent. Or it might consist of +19 percent/-1 percent. The latter disparity would be of dubious validity, according to our reading of the cases.—Ed.

and roads because of the ignorance and indifferences of rural legislature.[1]

Malapportionment was also charged with weakening the federal system, obstructing government action generally, and "spawning public cynicism, disillusionment and apathy." Several eminent political scientists identified malapportionment as a key factor in the weakness of state government; in particular, it was alleged to be responsible for divided and ineffective government, lack of party competition, and a general rural and retrogressive bias in state legislatures.[2] Reapportionment, it was argued at the time, would provide a certain, if not immediate, cure for these assorted ills of the American polity. These thoughts, if not always the colorful language used to express them, were echoed widely in social science circles, including the 1962 report of the United States Advisory Commission on Intergovernmental Relations.[3]

Yet as a matter of constitutional litigation, the problem was not viewed in wholly political terms. Its focus was more on the abstract concept of equality and how to obtain it in representational terms. While there had been some attempts in pre-*Baker* litigation in the lower courts to make the policy implications of malapportionment a legal issue, the Supreme Court chose to consider whether malapportionment violated some previously "undiscovered" constitutional principle, specifically whether it was prohibited by the equal protection clause of the Fourteenth Amendment. *Reynolds*

made two things about the Court's "discovery" clear: one's equal protection right against malapportionment was a right personally held and hence not alienable by any political process save constitutional amendment; second, in the aggregate, positive compliance was a matter of numbers. The "full and effective participation" idealistically sought by Chief Justice Warren in his *Reynolds* opinion was a *legal* concept based on considerations of numerical equivalence between voters as to the weight or "impact" of their individualized vote upon the election outcome.

What other options did the Supreme Court have in 1964? One was to do nothing and continue the policy of nonintervention that had been upset by *Baker* v. *Carr*. But having decided in *Baker* that federal courts could intervene in apportionment controversies, the Supreme Court was obligated to come up with some standards or principles to guide those courts. Justice Brennan's assurance in *Baker* that "standards under the Equal Protection Clause are well developed and familiar" was disingenuous. Certainly there were no standards that applied to the particular problems of reapportioning state legislatures.

A second option, which the Court actually chose, might be labeled full intervention. By establishing one person, one vote as the measure of acceptable apportionment, the Court was assuring that the judiciary would, for a long time, be intimately involved in such matters. No state at the time met the standard articulated by the Court in *Reynolds*. Of course,

[1]Ward Elliott, "Prometheus, Proteus, Pandora, and Procrustes Unbound: The Political Consequences of Reapportionment," 37 *University of Chicago Law Review* (1970), 476.
[2]For example, V.O. Key, Jr., *American State Politics: An Introduction* (New York: Knopf, 1950), p. 76; Charles R. Adrian, *State and Local Government* (New York: McGraw-Hill, 1967).
[3]"Apportionment of State Legislatures" (1962).

as we have already observed, by choosing that governing principle, the Court was ignoring the complexity of the concept of fair representation. Representative government is, after all, not a wooden concept, but—at least in the pluralist model —a process of shifting interests of diverse and overlapping groups. As Martin Shapiro has observed, "A vision of the political process as no more than the electoral process and of each citizen as exercising his whole political power in the individual act of voting cannot properly serve even the most populistic philosophy. For in the complex politics of group bargaining and shifting temporary majorities that we actually have in the United States, inequalities in voting strength may contribute to the over-all equality of all participants in the political process as a whole."[4] Similar sentiments were expressed by Justice Stewart in *Lucas* v. *44th General Assembly* (1964). But, as Jan Deutsch has written, is it possible, really, for the courts to examine the realities of the distribution of political power so as to assure real political equality?[5]

In one sense, Warren's opinion in *Reynolds* is as naive in its view of political equality as are Frankfurter's dissenting views about the impossibility of court-ordered reapportionment and the power of a militantly aroused electorate to bring about reapportionment by itself. But in another and perhaps more fundamental sense, the Chief Justice, a man with many years of political experience, was quite sensitive to what courts might realistically be expected to do. His judgment, undoubtedly, was that if they did that much (e.g.,

bring about equal apportionment), they would be making a profound contribution to the cause of political equality. The one person, one vote standard was attractive in many ways. It reflected the full flowering of the egalitarian ideology. It was objective on its face, and it was enforceable. A court might have difficulty grappling with the meaning of equality in the broader political process, but it could ascertain relatively easily whether a state had or had not achieved relative equality of population in its electoral units. It is very much to the point to remember that both during and after his tenure on the Court, Warren, who had written for the Court in *Brown*, regarded the reapportionment cases as his most important contribution.

A third option that the Court might have chosen in 1964 might be called selective intervention. It was, in fact, the course of action urged by Solicitor General Cox. He thought that after declaring the principle of population equality, the Court should have applied it only to the grossest inequalities, the most flagrant cases, while leaving some room for the political process in each state to contribute to a viable reapportionment scheme. One way of achieving this would have been to adopt the "federal analogy" and permit considerations other than population equality to be used in apportioning one house of a bicameral legislature. But Warren explicitly rejected the federal analogy in *Reynolds*.

The history of the Court's reapportionment decisions might be characterized as one of high compliance but low impact, recalling, perhaps, the

---

[4]Martin Shapiro, *Law and Politics in the Supreme Court* (New York: The Free Press, 1964), p. 249.

[5]Jan Deutsch, "Neutrality, Legitimacy, and the Supreme Court," **20** *Stanford Law Review* (1968, 1969), 246–247.

prophecy of one Tennessee legislator upon hearing about the *Baker* v. *Carr* decision: "This is the end of good clean rural government in Tennessee."[6]

Despite strong political opposition in the years immediately following *Wesberry* and *Reynolds*, the one-person, one-vote rule has been widely implemented. The contrast with the aftermath of *Brown* v. *Board of Education* (1954) is striking. Congressional efforts to overturn or modify *Reynolds* were unsuccessful. In 1964 the House of Representatives passed a bill removing the Supreme Court's appellate jurisdiction over state legislative apportionment cases, but the bill was defeated in the Senate. That same year the Senate considered the Dirksen-Mansfield Moratorium Resolution designed to "stay" federal court apportionment intervention for two years. Numerous constitutional amendments were introduced, including one by Senator Dirksen that would have allowed the states to apportion one house of a bicameral legislature on a nonpopulation basis. The Amendment failed by seven votes to obtain the necessary two-thirds majority in the Senate. Efforts were made to call a constitutional convention, but that effort, also led by Senator Dirksen, garnered only 33 petitions from the states, one less than needed to require Congress to call such a convention. But despite these efforts, reapportionment was

never as salient an issue for the public as school segregation. There are no current efforts to overturn *Reynolds* or *Wesberry*, and the pragmatic outlook of the Burger Court on reapportionment standards, best expressed in Justice White's opinion in the *Gaffney* case (see pp. 727, 730–731), seems likely to defuse the issue even further.

The impact of *Reynolds* is quite visible in the altered makeup of American state legislatures, all of which were reapportioned after the 1970 census, and which will be reapportioned again after the 1980 census. Ward Elliott noted that legislative majorities changed in nineteen states, largely as a result of the Court's decisions. Robert Erikson found evidence of restored party competition and a more equitable representation of urban areas. Charles Bullock, however, found little impact on the political careers of individual members of Congress, except where redistricting placed two incumbents in the same district.[7]

However, the *policy* impact of reapportionment is much less visible. The optimism of its early proponents seems, in retrospect, to have been excessive. Some early studies uncovered statistically significant relationships between reapportionment and prourban, proliberal policy changes. More recent studies have reported similar findings, but the vague linkage between reapportionment and

[6]Quoted in Bill Kovach "Some Lessons of Reapportionment," *The Reporter* (September 21, 1967), p. 26.

[7]Ward Elliot, *The Rise of Guardian Democracy: The Supreme Court's Role in Voting Rights Disputes*, 1845–1969, (Cambridge: Harvard University Press, 1974). Charles S. Bullock III, "Redistricting and Congressional Stability, 1962–72," **37** *Journal of Politics* (1975), 575; Robert S. Erikson, "The Partisan Impact of State Reapportionment," **15** *Midwest Journal of Political Science* (1971), 70; but see a dissenting view in Edward R. Tufte, "The Relationship between Seats and Votes in Two-Party Systems," **67** *American Political Science Review* (1973), 554.

policy impact makes it necessary to interpret such results with caution.[8] At this time it seems clear enough that the grander designs of the reformers has not been realized. "Those who contended that malapportionment was the source of most state political woes will be disappointed by [the research] results, but so will earlier policy analysts who contended that legislative apportionment bore no relationship to policy variance."[9]

Fifteen years after *Reynolds* the full impact of the reapportionment decisions is unclear, and perhaps has yet to occur. Demographic changes—the growth of suburbia—diluted the expected increased strength of urban representation. And the Court's relaxation of the one-person, one-vote standard is likely to undercut that impact even more. We have already observed the loosening of the standard in the *Mahan* case. The Burger Court also seems bent on not extending the one-person, one-vote doctrine to other governmental units. In the *Avery* and *Hadley* cases, coverage was extended to a county commissioner's court and a junior college district. Each was said to exercise a generalized governmental function. But in *Salyer Land Co. v. Tulare Lake Basin Water Storage District* (1973) and *Toltec Watershed Improvement District*

(1973), the Court sustained statutory limitations on participation in special district elections. In each instance, it determined that the functions of these governmental units was so specialized as not to come under the *Reynolds* rule.

One other potential of the one person, one vote doctrine must be mentioned. In *Gray v. Sanders* (1963), a case preceding *Reynolds,* the Supreme Court ruled unconstitutional the county unit system in Georgia, which utilized a weighted system of voting that often led to election of a minority candidate for governor. The electoral college method of electing a president of the United States is substantially similar to the county unit system, although the population disparities are not as great as under the Georgia system. Under the electoral college system, a state casts a number of electoral votes equal to the total number of its representatives and senators; all of its electoral votes are cast for the candidate who received a plurality of the state's popular vote. The electoral college vote tends to exaggerate the popular vote of the winning candidate and has, on occasion, produced a winner who had received only a minority of the popular vote. In both 1876 and 1888, the candidate with fewer popular votes was chosen as president. In 1960,

[8]Thomas Dye, *Politics, Economics, and the Public: Policy Outcomes in the American States* (New York: Rand McNally, 1966), p. 280. Also see Herbert Jacob, "The Consequences of Reapportionment: A Note of Caution," **43** *Social Forces* (1964), 256–261. Alternatively, see William E. Bicker, "The Effects of Malapportionment in the States—a Mistrial," in Nelson Polsby (ed.), *Reapportionment in the 70s* (Berkeley: University of California Press, 1971), pp. 151–201. More recent research examples are: H. George Frederickson and Yong Hyo Cho, "Legislative Apportionment and Fiscal Policy in American States," **27** *Western Political Quarterly* (1974), 5–37; Roger A. Hanson and Robert E. Crew, Jr., "The Policy Impact of Reapportionment," **8** *Law and Society Review* (1973), 69–93; William R. Cantrall and Stuart S. Nagel, "The Effects of Reapportionment on the Passage of Nonexpenditure Legislation," in Papyanopoulos (ed.), *Democratic Representation and Apportionment* (New York: New York Academy of Sciences, 1973), pp. 269–79.

[9]Frederickson and Yong, *op cit.,* Note 8, p. 35.

John Kennedy received 49.7 percent of the popular vote but 57 percent of the electoral vote; in 1964, Lyndon Johnson received 61 percent of the popular vote and 90 percent of the electoral vote. There are different views on who benefits most from this system, although the consensus seems to be that, in practice, the large industrial states wield disproportionate influence in choosing presidential candidates and in electing a president.

In 1966, an attempt was made to extend the one man, one vote principle to presidential elections when thirteen states banded together to sue the remaining thirty-seven states in *Delaware* v. *New York*. The allocation of electoral college votes to each state is itself a constitutional principle and could not be challenged, so the suit focused on the practice of casting all of a state's electoral votes for the candidate who won a plurality of the popular vote in that state, regardless of the size of his margin of victory. The suit, which was filed under the Court's original jurisdiction, asked that the Court consider ordering a proportional division of a state's electoral votes according to the distribution of popular votes, or that it order electoral votes to be cast by congressional districts (presumably with the winner of a state's popular vote receiving the bonus of the two "Senate" electoral votes). Alternatively, the suit asked the Court to invalidate the existing general ticket system and give Congress the chance to legislate on the matter. Similar attempts at reform of the electoral college system have been made repeatedly, without success, via the constitutional amendment route. The Supreme Court declined to hear the case, perhaps because of problems with Delaware's standing to maintain the suit (as *parens patriae* for its citizens, or representing its own interests). No opinion accompanied the decision.

the supreme court and the criminal justice system

1. INTRODUCTORY ESSAY

The decade of the 1960s witnessed the first attempt by the Supreme Court to exercise strong policy control over the administration of justice in the United States. A major portion of the Court's docket was composed of criminal cases, and they remain among the most politically explosive issues that the Court has dealt with in recent years.

The Supreme Court has direct supervisory jurisdiction over the lower federal courts. Subject to congressional revision, it establishes their rules of criminal and civil procedure. But less than 1 percent of the criminal cases in the United States arise in the federal courts. The vast majority are handled in state courts, whose rules and procedures are determined by state law. State courts are subject to the policy control of the Supreme Court, however, to the extent that federal constitutional issues are involved in state court proceedings. Thus, the Warren Court's criminal justice decisions can be characterized as establishing federal judicial control over the states' criminal justice systems through a process of "constitutionalization"—that is, interpreting the Fourteenth Amendment due process clause (and other constitutional requirements) as imposing federal constitutional standards of procedure in areas formerly left up to the individual states. The Supreme Court literally began to make policy standards of criminal justice procedure for every court in the Republic. This has been appropriately called by Fred Graham the "due process revolution."[1]

The more traditional method of case-by-case adjudication under a standard of "fundamental fairness" left considerable discretion to the states. In the 1950s and 1960s, however, the Supreme Court began to apply to the state courts some of the more specific requirements of the Bill of Rights, by reading them into the commands of the Fourteenth Amendment. And as these provisions of the Bill of Rights were being applied to the states, the Court was updating and expanding their meaning for both federal and state courts. Often, vague standards of "due process" were replaced by more specific prophylactic rules. For example, in place of the standard of "voluntariness" as the test of the admissibility of confessions, the Supreme Court substituted its own "Miranda" rules (see below, pp. 862–875), requiring persons taken into police custody to be given specific warnings of their constitutional rights before interrogation. Whenever possible, the Court's strategy was to protect the rights of criminal defendants by relying heavily on their access to, and representation by, legal counsel. The assumption—one not entirely borne out by later experience—was that the best protection a criminal suspect could have was an attorney assigned to him as early as possible after his arrest.

Unfortunately for the Supreme Court, its attempts to nationalize the criminal justice system came at a time of rising crime (or so it was publicly perceived) and coincidentally, at a time of political violence and assassination.[2] Superficially there *appeared* to be a connection between this new trend of judicial "permissiveness" and the breakdown of law and order. The justices were accused of "coddling criminals" and "handcuffing the police," notwithstanding the lack of any empirical evidence relating judicial decisions to rising crime rates. Public opinion strongly condemned this trend, particularly the *Miranda* decision.[3]

"Law and order" became an important political issue in the 1968 presidential election, as it did again in 1972. Richard Nixon announced his intention, if elected, to make Supreme Court appointments that would redress the balance between what he termed "the forces of peace and the forces of crime." Congress responded with several anti-Court measures, including a law intended to reverse *Miranda* and a preventive detention bill for the District of Columbia.[4]

---

[1]Fred P. Graham, *The Self-Inflicted Wound* (New York: Macmillan, 1970), Chapter 3.

[2]Crime statistics in the United States are notoriously inaccurate, but there seem to be two facts that are generally accepted: First, that the United States is the most violent "civilized" country and, second, that crime had risen in the decade of the 1960s. The National Commission on the Causes and Prevention of Violence ranked the United States first among fourteen nations in the rate of violent crime. On the basis of a criminal homicide rate per 100,000 population, the United States had 5.8; England, 0.7; Germany, 1.6; France, 0.08; and Switzerland, the lowest, at 0.05. Over 800,000 persons have been killed by guns in the United States since 1900, exceeding the total of military deaths in all wars from the American Revolution to Vietnam. In 1966, there were nearly six times as many gun murders in Houston, Texas (pop. 1.5 million) as in England and Wales (pop. about 55 million). On the other hand, the rates of some crimes, such as murder, have actually decreased since the turn of the century. But, allowing for the estimates that barely half of the crimes in the United States are even reported, the figures showing increases during the decade of the 1960s cannot be denied. See Graham, *ibid.*, Chapter 2, and Ramsey Clark, *Crime in America* (New York: Simon and Schuster, 1970), Chapters 3, 7, and *passim*.

[3]The 1965 Gallup Poll reported that 48 percent of the public thought the Courts were excessively lenient with criminal defendants. In 1968, that opposition had increased to nearly two-thirds.

[4]See the Crime Control Act of 1968, *infra*.

What caused the Court to embark on this revolution of the criminal justice system? The justices seemed to be concerned with the sentiments in Judge Walter Schaefer's dictum that "the quality of a nation's civilization can be largely measured by the methods it uses in the enforcement of its criminal laws."[5] That sentiment, to which perhaps all could abstractly subscribe, does not demand that a single standard be applied to all conditions and situations in all jurisdictions. But the Court rejected a decentralized approach in favor of increasing its own supervisory role.

Like most Court policies, this one evolved without being formally stated. One likely reason for the sudden concern with such issues was the justices' perception that mere admonitions of due process (i.e., general expression of what was "fundamentally fair") had been insufficient to eliminate or control criminal justice procedures that they found objectionable. A second reason would surely be the philosophical orientation of the Warren Court's liberal majority, what Archibald Cox characterized as the "egalitarianism that has become a dominant force in the evolution of our constitutional law. The broader egalitarianism stirred by the civil rights revolution has already found expression in criminal law decisions."[6]

For many justices, egalitarian ideas extend beyond expressions of formal equality to the reality of differential treatment of the poor, blacks, and other minorities who are not part of the dominant white middle-class culture. For example, blacks commit a disproportionate share of the reported violent crimes, particularly urban crimes, and they are proportionately more often the object of criminal justice procedures.[7]

There was a strongly held belief that blacks were discriminated against in the criminal justice system, as elsewhere; this concern may have motivated the justices to tighten the rules for all defendants.[8] They may have felt also, as Herbert Packer suggested, that "the plain fact is that the Court is in the business of policing the police because nobody else is and because in a society that likes to think of itself as 'free' and 'open' someone has to do the job."[9]

Supervising the entire criminal justice system entailed a number of risks for the Supreme Court. First, and perhaps most importantly, the justices may have identified a problem for which there is no ready judicial solution and for which the Supreme Court as an institution is peculiarly unsuited. As the materials in the next section of this chapter demonstrate, the criminal justice system is complex, and practices within it vary widely. The Court can only respond to cases that come before it. Since most criminal cases are not disposed of by trial but rather by a negotiated plea of guilty, the Court's only sanction—reversing convictions obtained by means of improper procedures—is available in very few cases. This, in turn, means that occasionally an obviously guilty person must be released as a deterrent to future police misbehavior. The charge is often made, because of these decisions, that the Court is "soft" on crime. Yet the vast majority of police actions are effectively immune from

[5]Walter Schaefer, "Federalism and State Criminal Procedure," **70** *Harvard Law Review* (1956), 26.
[6]Archibald Cox, *The Warren Court: Constitutional Decision as an Instrument of Reform* (Cambridge: Harvard University Press, 1968), p. 7.
[7]Clark, *op. cit.*, Note 2, pp. 50–51.
[8]Graham, *op. cit.*, Note 1, Chapter 5.
[9]See excerpt from Packer, *infra*, pp. 784–787.

Supreme Court scrutiny. Increasingly, the evidence shows that reversing convictions because evidence or a confession was improperly obtained by the police has not been an effective deterrent to unlawful police action.

Second, increased activism by the Court in the area of criminal justice leads to considerable tension between state and federal courts within our federal system of justice. (Of related political importance, the Court's policies may have contributed to the rapid rise of police and law enforcement associations as a major and anti-Court interest group in national politics.) It is not just the Supreme Court, but the entire federal court system that is seen by the states as the culprit. Before 1940, virtually the only way one could get a state criminal conviction reviewed in the federal courts was to exhaust all remedies in the state courts and then seek review by the U.S. Supreme Court. Collateral review via a writ of habeas corpus from a federal district court was available only in those exceptional and, it was thought, isolated cases where the state courts had clearly convicted a criminal defendant improperly. For example, Justice Frankfurter, in *Rochin* v. *California* (1952), could invalidate a conviction on the grounds that obtaining evidence of drug possession by forcefully pumping the stomach of a suspect was "shocking to the conscience."

After 1940, and especially after *Fay* v. *Noia* (1963), federal courts increasingly utilized habeas corpus writs to review the convictions of inmates of state penitentiaries. In 1970, more than 12,000 such petitions were granted, approximately one-sixth of the civil case load of all federal districts and nearly half the number of criminal cases handled by federal courts. So great was the number of cases and the resulting friction that Chief Justice Burger, in his 1970 "State of the Judiciary" message, identified it as a major area for congressional reform. But he tied his recommended elimination of the habeas corpus route of appeal to enactment by the states of adequate postconviction appeal procedures.[10] In so doing, the Chief Justice was conceding the existence of the inadequacies in state criminal procedures to which the Warren Court and the lower federal courts had been responding. Reducing the opportunities for federal collateral review of state court convictions will not necessarily result in alterations in the prevailing rules for treatment of criminal suspects. But it will reduce substantially the opportunities for the federal courts, and ultimately the Supreme Court, to play a supervisory role in the administration of the criminal justice system.

Efforts are pending in Congress to restrict habeas corpus review of state convictions. In the meantime, the four Nixon appointees on the Supreme Court have called for a judicial reinterpretation of the habeas corpus statute which would limit the number of petitions granted in the district courts. Justice Powell, writing in *Schneckloth* v. *Bustamonte* (1972), concluded that at least in Fourth Amendment (search and seizure) cases, the Court should return to the more limited "traditional" understanding of the writ of habeas corpus. In addition, he contended, the federal district courts should consider the probable guilt or innocence of the defendant and only grant relief where a plausible argument for innocence could be made. This, Powell contended, would reduce the strains on our federal system resulting from continuous federal court supervision of the criminal justice process. A further step was taken in *Stone* v. *Powell* (1976), in which the Court ruled that federal courts could not consider

[10]Reprinted in Howard James, *Crisis in the Courts* (New York: David McKay, 1970, paperback edition), pp. iii–xii.

Fourth Amendment search and seizure questions in habeas corpus proceedings as long as these questions received a fair hearing in the state courts.

The Supreme Court runs a third risk in setting policy for the criminal justice system. Its constitutional mandate to do so is weak (see Section 3 of this chapter), and its legitimacy is at stake. The Warren Court seemed willing to run this risk. But on closer inspection, it appears that the Warren Court pursued a more balanced policy than many believed. What appeared as an escalating supervision of all aspects of the criminal justice system turned out to be far less comprehensive. The last major criminal justice opinion written by Chief Justice Warren (*Terry* v. *Ohio*, 1968, *infra*), was notable more for its solicitude for the problems of the police than for those of criminal defendants. The opinion admitted that the Supreme Court could not effectively police the police, and it went on to approve "stop and frisk" procedures as justified for a police officer's self-protection.

As Graham has noted, the Supreme Court's dissatisfaction with station house interrogation methods did not extend to wiretapping and similar "clean" methods of gathering evidence.[11] The Warren Court thus did not uniformly condemn all existing police methods. And, as we will see in detail later in this chapter, the Court diluted the impact of its policies by refusing to apply them retroactively in most instances.

It should come as no surprise that there is a significant gap between Supreme Court policy and actual police behavior. James Q. Wilson, among others, observed the enormous discretion open to a police officer and the lack of effective control within police organizations.[12] A given police department operates in a particular political environment; it is necessarily responsible and responsive to its local constituencies, and the views expressed by these constituencies are likely to have greater salience to the police than intonations from the U.S. Supreme Court. To be sure, major changes in the criminal justice system have taken place, both directly and indirectly, as a result of Supreme Court decisions. But there is still a long way to go before that system approximates the due process ideal that the Supreme Court has articulated.

In summary, then, the Warren Court tried to reform the criminal justice system in several ways. It pursued a policy of nationalization—that is, that criminal justice procedures should be approximately the same throughout the United States in both state and federal courts. States were still allowed some leeway in devising procedures, but the most important rights were to be uniform. Second, recognizing that it could not directly supervise the administration of criminal justice, the Court sought to structure that process and reduce police discretion as much as possible. In place of the traditional case-by-case approach and "totality of the circumstances" test, the court began to prescribe specific "prophylactic" rules. It is easier to determine whether a specific procedural rule has been followed in a given case than it is to determine whether a particular interrogation or trial was "fair." Rules also educate the police on what is expected of them in criminal investigations and can educate the public as to what to expect from law enforcement officers.

In addition, the Warren Court placed great reliance on providing legal coun-

---

[11]Graham, *op. cit.,* Note 1, pp. 22–23.
[12]James Q. Wilson, *Varieties of Police Behavior* (New York: Atheneum, 1968). See also Neal Milner "Supreme Court Effectiveness and the Police Organization," **36** *Law and Contemporary Problems* (1971), 467–487.

sel to criminal defendants, assuming that the presence of a lawyer was the best assurance that a person's rights were being protected. The Court did not make much allowance for quality of legal representation, nor did it recognize how easily lawyers representing criminal defendants might be co-opted by the system. The Court also acted to open up the appeals process. And, finally, it opened up access to the federal courts by relaxing the habeas corpus rules of other entry barriers. More liberal rules, and more judicial supervision (it was thought), would bring about great change.

Certainly, the Warren Court and its advocates were excessively optimistic. They misjudged the willingness of the police to abide by the new rules and badly miscalculated the public's reaction to the Court's efforts to protect the rights of criminal defendants. The present Burger Court, with four justices appointed by former President Nixon and one by President Ford, is certainly more responsive to the views of the police and the general public. Yet the Burger Court has not repudiated any of the major doctrines of the Warren Court. Its strategy has been to chip away at those doctrines, set some new limits, and restrict new advances. It has shown some preference for a return to a "totality of circumstances" approach, in which the impact of police procedures on the fairness of a particular trial or interrogation would be more important than whether one of the "prophylactic" rules was broken. One can also foresee a growing reinforcement of the "harmless error" philosophy. Eventually, some of the Warren Court doctrines probably will be overruled; the exclusionary rule of *Mapp* v. *Ohio* (1961) and the liberalized interpretation of the habeas corpus statute seem like probable first steps. Yet it seems unlikely that the present Supreme Court would return to a pre-1960s position by deconstitutionalizing the criminal justice process.[13]

2. THE CRIMINAL JUSTICE SYSTEM

A. A Note on the "Due Process" and "Crime Control" Models

Any explanation of the role of the Supreme Court in law enforcement must begin with some understanding of the criminal justice system as a whole. At best, this is a difficult undertaking; it may be a distortion even to use the word "system" to describe what is at best an accumulation of activities the functions and linkages of which are frequently overlapping, contradictory, and ill defined. The President's Commission on Law Enforcement and Administration of Justice made this observation:

The system of criminal justice America uses to deal with those crimes it cannot prevent and those criminals it cannot deter is not a monolithic or even a consistent system. Its philosophic core is that a person may be punished by the Government if, and only if, it has been proved by an impartial and deliberate process that he has violated a specific law. Around that core layer upon layer of

---

[13]For a good analysis of the Burger Court and the criminal justice system, see Stephen L. Wasby, *Continuity and Change: From the Warren Court to the Burger Court* (Pacific Palisades: Goodyear Publishing Co., 1976), Chapter 8.

institutions and procedures, some carefully constructed and some improvised, some inspired by principle and some by expedience, have accumulated.[1]

There are four basic functions performed by a criminal justice system: (1) the prohibition of certain types of behavior (the legislative process), (2) the enforcement of those laws and the apprehension of violators (the police process), (3) the determination of guilt or innocence and the application of sanctions (the judicial process), and (4) the carrying out of the punishments meted out by the courts (what is euphemistically called "correction"). While these functions are related in obvious ways, they rarely work as part of a cohesive and integrated process. More often, they are responsive to disparate values and conflicting constituencies, confused by overlapping jurisdictional lines, and staffed by individuals of very different backgrounds and training who have conflicting views of the crime problem and the ways to meet it. Furthermore, all operate under adverse conditions of rapidly increasing crime and inadequate facilities and budgets.

The federal government has a limited criminal jurisdiction, confined largely to criminal penalties for violation of substantive federal statutes and the protection of federal property. This includes a miscellany of efforts to punish acts of particular national importance or to aid state law enforcement activities—crossing state lines to avoid prosecution, bank robbery, kidnapping, assassinating the president, violation of immigration laws and sedition and espionage statutes, enforcement of civil rights, drug laws, and similar offenses. The vast majority of criminal cases in the United States arise in the state courts. Violations of federal law are prosecuted in the federal district courts with an allowable appeal to the intermediate courts of appeals and the possibility of further review at the discretion of the Supreme Court.

Violations of state laws are prosecuted in the state courts with appeals through the state court system. State criminal cases may be considered by the federal courts only if a violation of a federal right is alleged. The normal route is by direct appeal or writ of certiorari to the Supreme Court from the highest state court in which a decision could be handed down—usually, but not always, the state's highest court. In recent years, as described in the Introductory Essay, a second method of appealing state convictions has developed—by a writ of habeas corpus to a federal district court alleging that an individual is being imprisoned in violation of his constitutional rights. The original conception of habeas corpus was that it was reserved for the "great" cases of deprivation. But it has come to be the most frequent method of involving the federal courts in the supervision of state court proceedings. Any effective federal control of the process of criminal justice of necessity involves controls of *state* procedures and risks federalism tensions. The state and federal governments also run parallel and overlapping law enforcement and corrections systems, further contributing to the fragmentation of the criminal justice system.

Another factor contributing to this diversity is the wide variance in per-

[1]President's Commission on Law Enforcement and Administration of Justice, *The Challenge of Crime in a Free Society* (Washington, D.C.: U.S. Government Printing Office, (1967), p. 7.

ceptions of the system and how it *ought* to function. As reported in the study of the National Commission on the Causes and Prevention of Violence:[2]

Each participant sees the commission of crime and the procedures of justice from a different perspective. His daily experience and his set of values as to what effectiveness requires and what fairness requires are therefore likely to be different. As a result, the mission and priorities of a system of criminal justice will in all likelihood be defined differently by a policeman, a trial judge, a prosecutor, a defense attorney, a correctional administrator, an appellate tribunal, a slum dweller and a resident of the suburbs.

For example: The police see crime in the raw. They are exposed firsthand to the agony of the victims, the danger of streets, the violence of lawbreakers. A major task of the police officer is to track down and arrest persons who have committed serious crimes. It is often discouraging for such an officer to see courts promptly release defendants on bail, or prosecutors reduce charges in order to induce pleas of guilty to lesser offenses, or judges exclude incriminating evidence, or parole officers accept supervision of released prisoners but check on them only a few minutes each month.

Yet the police themselves are often seen by others as contributing to the failure of the system. They are the target of charges of ineptness, discourtesy, brutality, sleeping on duty, illegal searches. They are increasingly attacked by large segments of the community as being insensitive to the feelings and needs of the citizens they are employed to serve.

Trial judges tend to see crime from a more remote and neutral position. They see facts in dispute and two sides to each

issue. They may sit long hours on the bench in an effort to adjudicate cases with dignity and dispatch, only to find counsel unprepared, or weak cases presented, or witnesses missing, or warrants unserved, or bail restrictions unenforced. They find sentencing to be the most difficult of their tasks, yet presentence information is scanty and dispositional alternatives are all too often thwarted by the unavailability of adequate facilities.

Yet criminal courts themselves are often poorly managed and severely criticized. They are seriously backlogged. All too many judges are perceived as being inconsiderate of waiting parties, police officers and citizen witnesses. Throughout the country, lower criminal courts tend to be operated more like turnstiles than tribunals.

Correction officials enter the crime picture long after the offense and deal only with defendants. Their job is to maintain secure custody and design programs which prepare individual prisoners for a successful return to society. They are discouraged when they encounter convicted persons whose sentences are either inadequate or excessive. They are frustrated by legislatures which curtail the flexibility of sentences and which fail to appropriate necessary funds. They are dismayed at police officers who harass parolees, or at a community which fails to provide jobs or refuses to build halfway houses for ex-offenders.

Yet jails are notoriously ill-managed. Sadistic guards are not uncommon. Homosexual assaults among inmates are widely tolerated. Prison work usually bears little relationship to employment opportunities outside. Persons jailed to await trial are typically treated worse than sentenced offenders. Correctional administrators are often said to be presiding over schools in crime.

In the mosaic of discontent which pervades the criminal process, public of-

---

[2]James S. Campbell, Joseph R. Sahid, and David P. Stang, *Law and Order Reconsidered: Staff Report to the National Commission on the Causes and Prevention of Violence* (New York: Bantam Books, 1970), pp. 265–266.

ficials and institutions, bound together with private persons in the cause of reducing crime, each sees his own special mission being undercut by the cross-purpose, frailties or malfunctions of others. As they find their place along the spectrum between the intense concern with victims at one end, and total preoccupation with reforming convicted law-breakers at the other, so do they find their daily perceptions of justice varying or in conflict. The conflicts in turn are intensified by the fact that each part of the criminal process in most cities is overloaded and undermanned, and most of its personnel underpaid and inadequately trained.

A third problem in defining and understanding the operation of the criminal justice system is the disparity between theory and practice, between the ideals of due process and the day-to-day operation of the criminal courts, particularly in large urban areas. These disparities are suggested by the conflicting role perceptions of participants within the sytem. But the dissonance between theory and practice is even greater than suggested above.

The "ideal" of American criminal justice is often expressed as a "due process" or "adversary" model. According to this model, the system seeks, in Blumberg's words, "to develop social, legal and organizational structures which will filter out law violators and at the same time provide an avenue of possible freedom to those who are innocent or simply casual law breakers."[3] It is based on the presumption of innocence, the notion that evidence of crime should not be acquired by coercion or other inquisitorial techniques, and that in the search for evidence, due respect should be given to individual rights, privacy and the constitutional guarantee against self-incrimination. Trial is by a jury of one's peers after indictment by a grand jury. The right to a fair trial includes, among others, the right to effective legal assistance, adequate notice and the opportunity to confront one's accuser, and compulsory process to obtain witnesses and other evidence in one's behalf. The basic assumption of the adversary system is an equality of resources between the government which brings criminal charges and the individual who must answer them. The goal of the system is to determine "legal guilt," the emphasis is on fairness and accuracy rather than efficiency. At least one and probably several appeals are possible. Throughout, there is great care taken to prevent the government from infringing on individual rights and overstepping its bounds.

By contrast, the reality of the system in urban courts is much better described by what has been called the "crime control" or "bureaucratic" model of criminal justice. Here the emphasis is on efficiency and finality, and the unofficial presumption is that individuals charged with an offense are probably guilty of it—or of some other offense. The process is more one of screening out the innocent than determining the guilty. Few individuals elect to go to trial; most criminal charges are resolved by guilty pleas. The large majority of jury trials result in convictions, and the "threat" of more severe penalties that most always follow conviction by a jury effectively dissuades most offenders from electing to go to trial. Particularly for relatively minor offenses, courtroom procedures are informal and mechanical. Some

[3]Abraham Blumberg, *Criminal Justice* (Chicago: Quadrangle Books, 1967), p. 21.

"trials" take but a minute or two and are better characterized as administrative rather than judicial procedures. Few cases are appealed, and few appeals result in reversals. The theory that, by reversing convictions, appellate courts can effectively supervise and control the action of lower courts and law enforcement officials is dubious. If the ideal system seems to some an obstacle course, then the bureaucratic model, in theory and practice, is nothing short of an assembly line.[4] In times of crisis, such as the urban civil disorders of the 1960s, the strains on the criminal justice system are even greater and departures from the due process norm more flagrant and more difficult to control.

The due process and crime control models express tendencies within the system, not polar opposites. At no point is one or the other likely to dominate completely. Judges are aware of the pressures from the crime control perspective, and prosecutors do not totally ignore due process norms. Each may have role perceptions and personal values that emphasize one or the other, but essentially there must be a balancing process. The models also imply strong normative commitments to competing philosophies of the purposes and operations of a criminal justice system. The current emphasis on due process is a legacy of the Warren Court. The emerging philosophy of the Burger Court is more supportive of the needs of law enforcement officials and their crime control orientation. But as already indicated, neither Court was—or is—internally consistent.

There seems to be common agreement today that the criminal justice system has reached a point of crisis, that it has become both ineffective *and* unfair. But a brief canvass of opinion suggests why we cannot expect a system that amalgamates competing philosophies in a very uneasy combination to hold much hope for real consensus. In *Michigan* v. *Tucker* (1974), Justice Rehnquist observed:

Just as the law does not require that a defendant receive a perfect trial, only a fair one, it cannot realistically require that policemen investigating serious crimes make no errors whatsoever. The pressures of law enforcement and the vagaries of human nature would make such an expectation unrealistic.

Rehnquist's words give expression to a most fundamental conservative criticism. Judges are seen as having become too prone to "interfere" in the criminal justice process. The quest for "perfect justice"[5] is a cruel delusion, and it is self-defeating. We expend too much effort to ensure procedural fairness and thereby hinder the search for truth. To be effective, justice must be swift and punishment severe. As former Attorney General John Mitchell said, "We face in the United States a situation where the discovery of guilt or innocence is in danger of drowning in a sea of legalisms."[6] Likewise, former Attorney General Nicholas Katzenbach argued that "we cannot and should not use the criminal justice system to repair all of the social and economic inequities of our society." The system may not be entirely fair, it is conceded, but for different reasons. Because so few persons are actually

---

[4]See Blumberg, *ibid.*; and Herbert Packer, *The Limits of the Criminal Sanction* (Stanford: Stanford University Press, 1968).

[5]Macklin Fleming, *The Price of Perfect Justice* (New York: Basic Books, 1974).

[6]*The New York Times* (January 17, 1971).

convicted of crimes they commit, and those who are convicted are given excessively lenient sentences, it is the victims of crime, and society as a whole, who should complain.

From the political left comes an entirely different view of the problem. It is argued that the criminal justice system is ineffective because it tries to do too much. The United States places too much reliance on the criminal law for social control generally and to legislate morality specifically. As Morris and Hawkins have written, the criminal law in the United States is perhaps "the most moralistic since Geneva in the time of John Calvin."[7] The solution is decriminalization, the elimination of "crimes without victims," what are often referred to as "life-style" crimes. Not only do these crimes lead to the worst sorts of police abuses, it is argued, but they also occupy a disproportionate share of the time and resources of the criminal justice system. If the police and the courts were given more limited and manageable tasks, abuses of discretion would be curbed, and they could effectively be governed by procedures fair to all.

Of course, fairness is not just a matter of procedure. Rules that on the surface meet the tests of fairness may, in practice, result in considerable injustice, especially where basic legal resources are unequal. While the law may attempt to overcome such inequality, it more often reflects social and economic inequalities all too accurately. Some would go so far as to argue that law and justice are wholly incompatible.[8] But the more common view is that from arrest to

punishment the criminal justice system produces, at best, random, "crazy-quilt" results and, at worst, rank injustice.

B. Two Graphic Views of the Criminal Justice System

(See Figures 1 and 2 on pages 748–750)

C. Jerome Skolnick, Law and Order: The Source of the Dilemma

. . . If the police could maintain order without regard to legality, their short-run difficulties would be considerably diminished. However, they are inevitably concerned with interpreting legality because of their use of *law* as an instrument of order. The criminal law contains a set of rules for the maintenance of social order. This arsenal comprises the *substantive* part of the criminal law, that is, the elements of crime, the principles under which the accused is to be held accountable for alleged crime, the principles justifying the enactment of specific prohibitions, and the crimes themselves. Sociologists usually concentrate here, asking how well this control system operates, analyzing the conditions under which it achieves intended goals, and the circumstances rendering it least efficient.

Another part of the criminal law, however, regulates the conduct of state officials charged with processing citizens who are suspected, accused or found guilty of crime. Involved here are such matters as the law of search, the law of arrest, the

[7]Norval Morris and Gordon Hawkins, *The Honest Politician's Guide to Crime Control* (Chicago: University of Chicago Press, 1970), p. 15.

[8]Edgar Friedenberg, "The Side Effects of the Legal Process," in Wolff (ed.), *The Rule of Law* (New York: Simon & Schuster, 1971), pp. 37–53.

Reprinted from *Justice Without Trial* (New York: John Wiley and Sons, Inc., 1966), pp. 6–9.

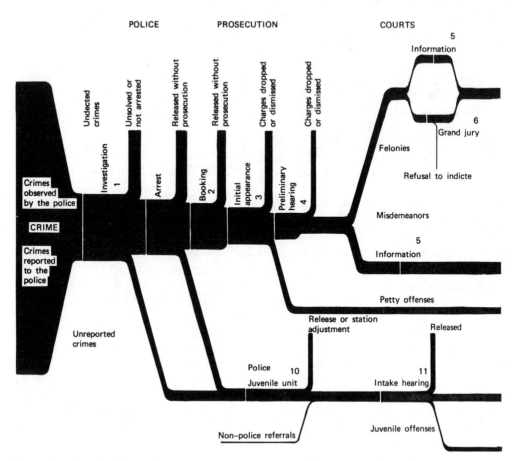

Figure 1. Reprinted from the Report of the President's Commission on Law Enforcement, 1967.

elements and degree of proof, the right to counsel, the nature of a lawful accusation of crime, and the fairness of trial. The procedures of the criminal law, therefore, stress protection of individual liberties, *within* a system of social order.

This dichotomy suggests that the common juxtaposition of "law and order" is an oversimplification. Law is not merely an instrument of order, but may frequently be its adversary. There are communities that appear disorderly to some (such as bohemian communities valuing diversity), but which nevertheless maintain a substantial degree of legality. The con-

trary may also be found: a situation where order is well maintained, but where the policy and practice of legality is not evident. The totalitarian social system, whether in a nation or an institution, is a situation of order without rule of law. Such a situation is probably best illustrated by martial rule, where military authority may claim and exercise the power of amnesty and detention without warrant. If, in addition, the writ of habeas corpus, the right to judicially inquire into these acts, is suspended, as it typically is under martial rule, the executive can exercise arbitrary powers. Such a system of social con-

CORRECTIONS

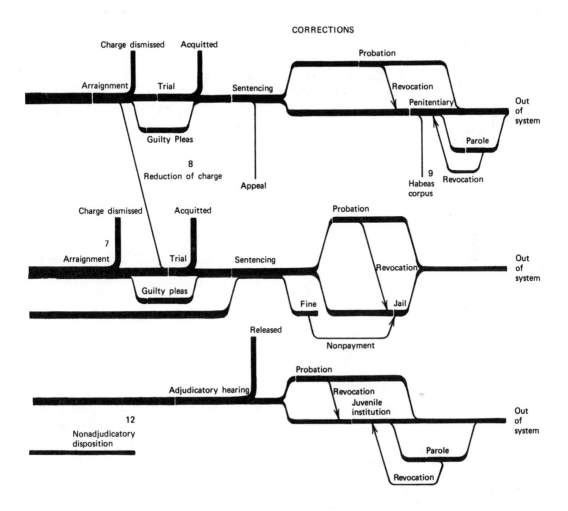

trol is efficient, but does not conform to generally held notions about the "rule of law."

Although there is no precise definition of the rule of law, or its synonym, the principle of legality, its essential element is the reduction of arbitrariness by officials—for example, constraints on the activities of the police—and of arbitrariness in positive law by the application of "rational principles of civic order." A statement expressive of the rule of law is found in a report on police arrests for "investigations." The authors, who are lawyers, write, "Anglo-American law has a tradition of antipathy to the imprisonment of a citizen at the will of executive officers." A more explicit definition of the rule of law in the administration of criminal law has been presented as follows:

The principle of *nulla poena sine lege* imposes formidable restraints upon the definition of criminal conduct. Standards of conduct must meet stringent tests of specificity and clarity, may act only prospectively, and must be strictly construed in favor of the accused. Further, the definition of criminal conduct has largely come to be regarded as a legislative function, thereby precluding

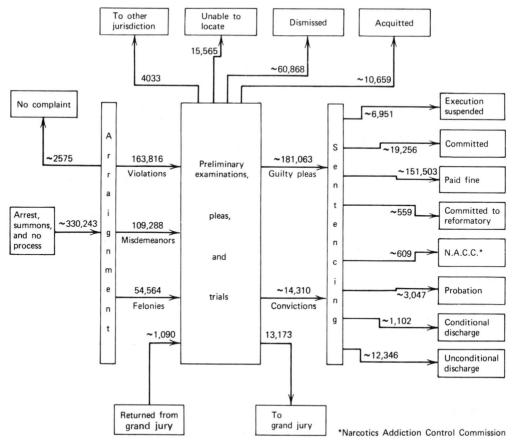

Figure 2. New York City criminal court: Aggregated adjudicatory Flowchart (approximate numbers of defendants charged with nontraffic offenses in 1967). Reprinted from John B. Jennings, "The Flow of Defendants Through the New York City Criminal Court in 1967," Report of the New York City Rand Institute, 1970.

the judiciary from devising new crimes. The public-mischief doctrine and the sometimes over-generalized "ends" of criminal conspiracy are usually regarded as anomalous departures from this main stream. The cognate principle of procedural regularity and fairness, in short, due process of law, commands that the legal standard be applied in the individual case with scrupulous fairness in order to minimize the chances of convicting the innocent, protect against abuse of official power, and generate an atmosphere of impartial justice. As a consequence, a complex network of procedural requirements embodied variously in constitutional,

statutory, or judge-made law is imposed upon the criminal adjudicatory process—public trial, unbiased tribunal, legal representation, open hearing, confrontation, and related concomitants of procedural justice.

Thus, when law is used as the instrument of social order, it necessarily poses a dilemma. The phrase "law and order" is misleading because it draws attention away from the substantial incompatibilities existing between the two ideas. Order under law suggests procedures different from achievement of "social control" through threat of coercion and summary judgment. Order under law is concerned not merely with the achievement of regularized social activity but with the means used to come by peaceable behavior, certainly with procedure, but also with positive law. It would surely be a violation of the rule of law for a legislature to make epilepsy a crime, even though a public "seizure" typically disturbs order in the community. While most law enforcement officials regard drug addicts as menacing to the community, a law making it a crime to *be* an addict has been declared unconstitutional. This example, purposely selected from substantive criminal law, indicates that conceptions of legality apply here as well as in the more traditional realm of criminal procedure. In short, "law" and "order" are frequently found to be in opposition, because law implies rational restraint upon the rules and procedures utilized to achieve order. Order under law, therefore, subordinates the ideal of conformity to the ideal of legality. . . .

D. Plea Bargaining: Negotiated Justice

The question of guilt or innocence is not contested in the overwhelming majority of criminal cases. A recent estimate is that guilty pleas account for 80-90 percent of all convictions; and perhaps as much as 95 percent of misdemeanor convictions. . . . [Taken as a percentage of the total number of criminal cases disposed of, the percentage of guilty pleas is, of course, somewhat smaller, as Figure 3 shows.]

A substantial percentage of guilty pleas are the product of negotiations between the prosecutor and defense counsel or the accused, although again the precise data are unavailable. Commonly known as "plea bargaining," this is a process very much like the pretrial settlement of civil cases. It involves discussions looking toward an agreement under which the accused will enter a plea of guilty in exchange for a reduced charge or a favorable sentence recommendation by the prosecutor. Even when there have been no explicit negotiations, defendants relying on prevailing practices often act on the justifiable assumption that those who plead guilty will be sentenced more leniently.

Few practices in the system of criminal justice create a greater sense of unease and suspicion than the negotiated plea of guilty. The correctional needs of the offender and legislative policies reflected in the criminal law appear to be sacrificed to the need for tactical accommodations between the prosecutor and defense counsel. The offense for which guilt is acknowledged and for which the sentence is imposed often appears almost incidental to keeping the business of the courts moving.

The system usually operates in an informal, invisible manner. There is ordinarily no formal recognition that the defendant has been offered an inducement to plead guilty. Although the participants and frequently the judge know that negotiation has taken place, the prosecutor and defendant must ordinarily go through a courtroom ritual in which they deny that the guilty plea is the result of any threat or promise. As a result there is no judicial review of the propriety of the bargain—no check on the amount of pressure put on the defendant to plead guilty. . . . Moreover, the defendant may not get the benefit he bargained for. There is no guarantee

Reprinted from President's Commission on Law Enforcement and Administration of Justice, *Task Force Report: The Courts* (Washington D.C.: U.S. Government Printing Office, 1967), pp. 9–13.

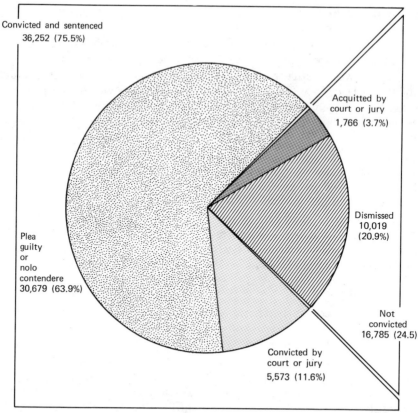

Figure 3. Criminal Defendants Disposed of by Type of Disposition in United States District Courts, twelve-month period ended June 30, 1974. Reprinted from Administrative Office of the United States Courts "Federal Offenders in the U.S. District Courts, 1974," December 1977. p. 3

that the judge will follow the prosecutor's recommendation for lenient sentence. In most instances the defendant does not know what sentence he will receive until he has pleaded guilty and sentence has been imposed. . . .

A more fundamental problem with plea bargaining is the propriety of offering the defendant an inducement to surrender his right to trial. This problem becomes increasingly substantial as the prospective reward increases, because the concessions to the defendant become harder to justify on grounds other than expediency. . . .

Despite the serious questions raised by a system of negotiated pleas, there are important arguments for preserving it. Our system of criminal justice has come to depend upon a steady flow of guilty pleas. There are simply not enough judges, prosecutors, or defense counsel to operate a system in which most defendants go to trial. Many of the Commission's proposals, such as the recommendation to expand appointment of counsel for the indigent, will strain the available resources for many years. If reliance on trial were increased at this time, it would undoubtedly lower the quality of justice throughout the system. Even were the resources available, there is some question whether a just system would require that they be allocated to providing all defendants with a full trial. Trial as we know it is an elaborate mechanism for finding facts. To use this process in cases where the facts are not really in dispute seems wasteful.

The plea agreement, if carried out, eliminates the risk inherent in all adversary litigation. No matter how strong the evidence may appear and how well prepared and conducted a trial may be, each side must realistically consider the possibility of an unfavorable outcome. At its best the trial process is an imperfect method of fact-finding; factors such as the attorney's skill, the availability of witnesses, the judge's attitude, jury vagaries, and luck will influence the result. Each side is interested in limiting these inherent litigation risks. In addition, the concessions of a negotiated plea are also commonly used by prosecutors when a defendant cooperates with law enforcement agencies by furnishing information or testimony against other offenders.

Confining trials to cases involving substantial issues may also help to preserve the significance of the presumption of innocence and the requirement of proof beyond a reasonable doubt. If trial were to become routine even in cases in which there is no substantial issue of guilt, the overwhelming statistical probability of guilt might incline judges and jurors to be more skeptical of the defense than at present. . . .

The plea agreement follows several patterns. In its best known form it is an arrangement between the prosecutor and the defendant or his lawyer whereby the accused pleads guilty to a charge less serious than could be proven at trial. "Less serious" in this context usually means an offense which carries a lower maximum sentence. The defendant's motivation is to confine the upper limits of the judge's sentencing power. Similar results are obtained when the plea is entered in return for the prosecutor's agreement to drop counts in a multicount indictment or not to charge the defendant as a habitual offender. In some situations the benefits obtained by the defendant may be illusory, as when he bargains for a reduction in counts unaware the local judges rarely impose consecutive sentences.

Charge reduction is tied to the exercise of the prosecutor's discretion as to what offenses he will charge originally. Although the charge process is distinct from the plea negotiation, the two are closely related. . . .

Plea negotiations concerning charges provide an opportunity to mitigate the harshness of a criminal code or to rationalize its inconsistencies and to lead to a disposition based on an assessment of the individual factors of each crime. The field over which these negotiations may range is broad; the defendant's conduct on a simple occasion may justify separate charges of robbery, larceny, assault with a deadly weapon, assault, or disorderly conduct. Some of these offenses are felonies, while others are misdemeanors, and the maximum sentences may range from 30 years to less than 1 year. Conviction of a felony may involve serious collateral disabilities, including disqualification from engaging in certain licensed occupations or businesses, while conviction of a misdemeanor may not. . . .

Charge reduction may be used to avoid a mandatory minimum sentence or a restriction on the power to grant probation. In these instances the agreed plea becomes a way of restoring sentencing discretion when it has in part been eliminated from the code. Charge reduction is also used to avoid the community opprobrium that attaches to conviction of certain offenses. Thus to avoid being labeled a child molester . . . the defendant may offer to plead guilty to a charge such as disorderly conduct or assault.

The plea agreement may take forms other than a reduction of charges. A defendant may plead guilty to a charge that accurately describes his conduct in return for the prosecutor's agreement to recommend leniency or for a specific recommendation of probation or of a lesser sentence than would probably be imposed if the defendant insisted upon a trial. Although in theory the judge retains complete discretion as to sentence, in reality the negotiations are conducted by the prosecutor and the defendant or his attorney on the assumption that the recommended sentence will be imposed. The practices of individual judges vary, but they are likely to be known to the parties. . . .

Other forms of plea bargaining may involve judge shopping. In places where there are wide sentencing disparities, a plea of guilty may be entered in exchange for the prosecutor's agreement that the defendant will appear before a particular judge for sentencing. . . .

[In understanding the phenomenon of plea bargaining, we should keep in mind the following: First, not all guilty pleas are the result of explicit plea bargains. Many persons plead guilty for other reasons. Exactly what proportion of guilty pleas are the result of plea *bargains* is not known. Second, there is a substantial variation in the *rate* of guilty pleas between types of crime committed. The highest incidence of guilty pleas is found in misdemeanor cases. Among felonies, the rates fluctuate over time and by type of offense. Thus, one study reported a 34 percent plea rate for homicides, while a more recent study in New York City indicated that in 1973, 80 percent of the homicide charges in that city ended in a guilty plea.[1] Third, the rate of guilty pleas varies dramatically by jurisdiction, within and between states. Some recent studies have reported a 55 percent pretrial dispositional rate in Los Angeles, but a 94 percent rate in San Francisco. Houston, Chicago, and Brooklyn (New York) have very high dispositional rates. Other cities, like Baltimore, Pittsburgh, and Philadelphia, place a much greater reliance on adversarial judicial proceedings.[2] It should also be noted that often there are substantial variations *within* cities, frequently along racial and ethnic geographic boundaries.[3]

What accounts for these variations? The size of a city does not appear to be a factor in the observed differences. Three other, and related, sets of variables have been advanced. The first revolves around the arrest practices of the police, what.types of crimes they perceive as worthy of arrest.[4] The second focuses on the policies of prosecutors; just as there may be different "styles" of policies practice, there are important differences among prosecutors in their view of plea bargaining. Third, with respect to urban areas, the allocation of political power seems important. Those cities that have concentrated political power and strong patronage links to the courts, like Chicago, tend to

---

[1]The *New York Times* (January 27, 1975). This apparent increase in pleas in homicide cases is contrary to the prediction of some observers that the end of capital punishment would produce a decrease in guilty pleas to homicide charges. Compare Michael Meltsner, *Cruel and Unusual* (New York: Random House, 1973), p. 303.

[2]Herbert Jacob, *Urban Justice* (Englewood Cliffs, N.J.: Prentice-Hall, 1973), Chapter 6.

[3]*Ibid.*

[4]See James Q. Wilson, *Varieties of Police Behavior* (New York: Atheneum, 1970). Wilson differentiates between three "styles": watchman, legalistic, and service, each of which produces a different mix of arrests and thus different inputs into the judicial system.

be "disposition oriented," that is, they rely less heavily on criminal trials. In other cities that have much more decentralized government, like Los Angeles, political power is dispersed, and there is a corresponding higher reliance on the formal adversary system.[5]

Plea bargaining, by its very nature, is a low-visibility phenomenon. However, since publication of the President's Crime Commission Report in 1967, it has become increasingly an object of public, political, and judicial concern and criticism. The prosecution of Vice-President Spiro T. Agnew in 1973 ended in history's most famous plea bargain, involving Agnew's resignation from the vice-presidency. It certainly helped to make the public even more aware of its dominance in the criminal justice system. The major justification for plea bargaining has always been economic: it saves the state the cost of a trial. In addition, it was justified by the 1967 Commission as relieving both the defendant and the prosecution of the risks and uncertainties of trial facilitating law enforcement needs by allowing leniency to be exchanged for promises from the suspect for his or her cooperation as witness or informant.

Another presidential commission has recommended abolition of plea bargaining.[6] It argued that, at least under some circumstances, plea bargaining was a threat to the rights of criminal defendants. Defendants may feel compelled to accept a lesser penalty with a plea of guilty rather than risk a more severe sentence by seeking to prove their innocence at trial. The commission admitted that there was "no information available on the extent to which the actual administration of plea negotiation results in conviction of the innocent or in improper distribution of leniency. . . ." But it felt these dangers were inherent in a plea bargaining system. The commission also criticized the adverse effect of plea bargaining on court administration and on society's need for protection from crime. Plea bargaining, it was contended, vitiates the deterrent impact of the law. Assuming what is, at best, a debatable point— that is, that the severity of criminal sanctions is an important deterrent to crime—the commission felt that plea bargaining detracted from the effect of prescribed criminal sanctions.

Guilty pleas and plea bargains have long been part of the criminal justice system, but it is only very recently that the Supreme Court has devoted any significant attention to the subject. Generally the Court has taken a favorable attitude. Chief Justice Burger noted, in *Santobello* v. *New York* (1972), that plea bargaining was "an essential component of the administration of justice," which ought to be encouraged if it is administered fairly and in accordance with constitutional standards.

A negotiated guilty plea is, among other things, a waiver of many constitutional rights. The standards that the Court has applied to plea bargains are essentially the same as those applied to other constitutional waivers: the plea must be voluntary and intelligent and not the result of "actual or threatened physical harm . . . or mental coercion overbearing the will of the defendant." Pleading guilty to a lesser offense in order to avoid a harsher sentence (and in one case, the death penalty) is not coercion, the Court said.[7] Even where the defendant was mistaken about the facts in a case or about the law, or where his attorney gave him erroneous advice about the admissibility of a prior confession, the Supreme Court has refused to invalidate guilty pleas.[8]

Just recently the Court restated the rule that "when a criminal defendant has solemnly admitted in open court that he is in fact guilty of the offense with which he is charged, he may not thereafter raise independent claims relating to the deprivation of constitutional rights" which occurred prior to the plea, *Tollett* v. *Henderson* (1973). On the other hand, in the *Santobello* case, the Court held that prosecutors must live up to whatever bargain has been struck. The

---

[5]See Jacob, *op. cit.*, Note 2; and Isaac Balbus, *The Dialectics of Legal Repression* (New York: Russell Sage Foundation, 1973).

[6]Report of the *National Advisory Commission on Criminal Justice Standards and Goals* (1973), Chapter 3.

[7]*Brady* v. *United States* (1970).

[8]*Ibid.*, and *McCann* v. *Richardson* (1970).

original prosecutor agreed to make no recommendation as to sentence, but his successor recommended that the maximum sentence be imposed, and the judge did, in fact, impose the maximum. Santobello sought to withdraw his plea, but to no avail. Clearly this was unfair. But the justices could not agree on an appropriate remedy—either to permit Santobello to withdraw his plea or to require specific performance of the bargain.]

E. The Problem of "Overcriminalization"

. . . Increasingly in recent years legal scholars have drawn attention to our society's failure to discriminate between appropriate and inappropriate uses of the criminal sanction. According to Herbert L. Packer, one of America's leading students of the criminal law, this failure mars even the monumental work of the President's Commission on Law Enforcement and Administration of Justice: the report of that Commission did not recognize that one major source of crime in the United States is "overcriminalization."

Overcriminalization—the misuse of the criminal sanction—can contribute to disrespect for law, and can damage the ends which law is supposed to serve, by criminalizing conduct regarded as legitimate by substantial segments of the society, by initiating patterns of discriminatory enforcement, and by draining resources away from the effort to control more serious misconduct. Examples of statutes which raise problems of "overcriminalization" are those laws dealing with morals, like sexual conduct and gambling; with illness, like drunkenness and narcotics pos-

session by addicts; and with nuisance, like disorderly conduct, objectionable language, and vagrancy.

The common characteristic of these kinds of conduct is that either there is no "victim" in the usual sense of the word, because the participants in the offense are willing; or the defendant himself is the "victim"; or the interest of the victim is often so insubstantial that it does not justify imposition of the criminal sanction to protect it. Therefore, one of the essential reasons for imposing criminal penalties—to deter conduct that is clearly and significantly harmful to the persons or property of others—is lacking.

Three Categories of Overcriminalization

Morals statutes are of several types. In most U.S. jurisdictions, any sexual activity except "normal" sexual intercourse between married partners is a crime. Probably no laws are broken more often. Indeed, if all violators were prosecuted and punished, a majority of the adult population of the United States would be in prison. Such statutes thus become organized hypocrisy on a national scale. They punish "fornication" between consenting unmarried adults, homosexuality, adultery, and all kinds of "abnormal" sexual conduct even between married persons.

Such laws satisfy public conscience by announcement of strict judgments and public condemnation of "immoral" and "irreligious" behavior, which we, as human beings subject to temptation, regrettably deviate from in private. As Thurman Arnold has written in a much-quoted passage:

Reprinted from *Law and Order Reconsidered: A Staff Report to the National Commission on the Causes and Prevention of Violence* (New York: Bantam Books, 1970), pp. 600–606.

Most unenforced criminal laws survive in order to satisfy moral objections to established modes of conduct. They are unenforced because we want to continue our conduct, and unrepealed because we want to preserve our morals.

Increasingly, however, morals have changed for more and more people, especially for younger people, and the standards embodied in these laws are publicly dissented from by an even larger segment of society. The general failure to enforce these laws is probably the only factor preventing an immediate vocal demand for their appeal.

Akin to the sexual conduct statutes, but with a higher degree of justification, are the morals laws punishing the scale and purchase of prostitutes' services, large-scale gambling, and abortion. These acts have a commercial character and hence a higher degree of repugnance to majority values. Pandering for profit to man's weaknesses seems more abhorrent than mere yielding to temptation. It is also true that these offenses carry other harms in their wake. Thus prostitution, as conducted by streetwalkers and their panderers, often results in making the prospective customer the victim of the "Murphy game" and other fraudulent practices. Prostitution also can spread venereal disease and give offense to respectable persons in neighborhoods frequented by streetwalkers openly purveying their services.

Illness statutes, such as the laws punishing intoxication and possession (as distinguished from sale) of addictive drugs, comprise a second category. The interest of society in preventing these evils and in protecting the offender from himself is much stronger than in the case of the morals statutes. Arrest of alcoholics gets them off the streets where they may come to harm while helplessly intoxicated; in winter it is a charity to provide the often homeless drunk with warmth, shelter, and a meal in jail. Arrest stops the alcoholic from presenting a public spectacle offensive to the sober, particularly when the alcoholic engages in aggressive efforts to obtain handouts from unescorted women and other passers-by. A short jail term keeps him away from the bottle for that period of time and offers, some believe, at least a faint hope of reform.

The narcotics addict is a more serious problem, for his personal destruction is more complete. The correctional system in which he is placed by arrest, prosecution and punishment, recognizes an obligation (albeit ill-fulfilled) to provide rehabilitation. Moreover, the addict, in order to support his habit, often is driven to commit property-related crimes, and his isolation by punishment protects society against them.

Punishment of the possession and sale of non-addictive drugs like marihuana falls somewhere between the morals laws and the illness laws like those dealing with alcoholics and addicts. The use of marihuana is especially popular among the young, although many fear that they may be at least psychologically harmed by frequent use. Moreover, marihuana has become something of a symbol of rebellion against the established order and its two-martini business lunches, and the established order thus finds it particularly difficult to take the step of bringing marihuana-smoking within the pale of legality.

The *nuisance statutes* are the last category of statutes generally considered under the heading of "over-criminalization." These typically penalize disorderly conduct and vagrancy.

Disorderly conduct statutes deal with such matters as "affrays"; with gatherings in public that are "loud and boisterous"; with swearing and profanity in public; with ball games in the street; with indecent proposals; with flying kites; with generally causing a disturbance; and with failure to move on when ordered by a police officer. Related to these areas, but also closely related to the morals laws, are laws punishing the sale or possession of pornographic literature, films, and the like. "Vagrancy" includes the offenses of "leading an immoral or profligate life" without a "lawful means of support"; of frequenting "houses of ill fame" or of "loitering" in gambling establishments, in unlicensed saloons or in places where narcotics are found; and of begging, and "common law vagrancy."

Such laws can serve a clear community interest. They can protect community tranquility and prevent annoyance of the more quiet citizens by the pugnacious, the shiftless, the noisy, and the foulmouthed. The police use such statutes as weapons against prostitutes, gamblers, and others whose apprehension is difficult because of problems of proof, and as legal underpinning for their general peacekeeping and order-maintaining responsibilities.

The Costs of Overcriminalization

Most of the conduct prohibited by the morals, illness and nuisance statutes cited above, is, in some degree, blameworthy or otherwise undesirable. But this observation provides only the beginning of an answer to the question we are concerned with, namely, whether such conduct ought to be prohibited by criminal statute. A single-factor analysis is inadequate. The criminal sanction finds its optimal use only where a number of different kinds of conditions are satis-

fied. In Packer's calculus, for example, the conditions for optimal use of the criminal sanction include the following:

1. The conduct in question is prominent in most people's view of socially threatened behavior, and is not condoned by any significant segment of society.
2. Subjecting it to the criminal sanction is not inconsistent with the goals of punishment.
3. Suppressing it will not inhibit socially desirable conduct.
4. The conduct may be dealt with through evenhanded and non-discriminatory enforcement.
5. Controlling it through the criminal process will not expose that process to severe qualitative or quantitative strains.
6. There are no reasonable alternatives to the criminal sanction for dealing with it.

Application of these criteria to the morals and nuisance statutes raises a number of additional questions concerning the propriety of these laws. Thus laws like those against consensual fornication that are rarely if ever enforced are seen to be prohibitions that are not seriously intended to be generally and even-handedly enforced. In those rare instances where enforcement is sought, the penalties become a discriminatory club against the unwary.

These morals laws that are frequently enforced, like those against homosexuality, have even worse consequences. To make the typical morals squad arrest, a police officer in plain clothes will, in order to elicit an advance, loiter in places like public lavatories that homosexuals are thought to frequent. Such conduct must have a degrading effect on the police officer. Also he has difficulty in making a "good pinch" in such cases and in enforcing the laws against prostitution: if the officer makes the advance, it is "entrapment," which renders a conviction invalid.

Enforcement of laws against crimes without victims also requires the use of a network of informers, who in turn must be compensated; since they themselves are often criminals, the compensation is usually leniency of treatment. Sometimes vice, morals or gambling squads impose arrest "quotas" on officers; often the difficulty in making these cases stick, encourages officers to embellish, if not fabricate, incriminating facts.

Perhaps, also, the evils of prostitution, gambling, and narcotics result more from their illegality than from their inherent harmfulness. Illegality often results in risk for both the seller and the buyer, as in the "Murphy game," in which he who fears exposure becomes the prey, and he who engages in robbery or auto burglary becomes the hunter. And, tragically, it can result in deaths—as from illegal abortions clumsily performed in unclean conditions. The transmission of venereal disease by prostitutes who, if not criminals, would normally (or if licensed could be required to) protect their and their customers' health by periodic medical examinations, is another example. Cheating in illegal gambling, with no lawful redress for the cheated, is a third. The high cost of narcotics because of illegality means that addicts need from $20 to $100 *per day* to support their habit. The only sources of such funds become other crimes, not only prostitution, but violent crimes like burglary, robbery, auto theft, and purse snatching.

The industries of prostitution, gambling, and narcotics require (prostitution to a smaller degree) an organization. The numbers writer and runner is financed by an operator with greater resources who, in turn, must have sources of funds to pay off bets. Narcotics require an immense distribution network. Prostitutes need agents to solicit the diffident and places in which to render their services. Since involvement in any of these activities is unlawful, they are performed and supervised by what is by definition organized crime.

Organized crime as we know it had its birth during prohibition, providing precisely the same kinds of illegal services through a complex industry. Primarily because of the illegality of providing these goods and services, the profits are enormous. To protect these profits, organized crime does not shrink from bribery of public officials and police officers, from coercion, and even from murder.

The moral question cuts more than one way. The need to use the law to enforce a moral code held (even if it were observed in practice) by considerably less than the entire population raises a question of the strength of the moral imperative behind that code. Punishment of the drunk and the narcotics addict for conduct recognized to be a disease, erodes the very foundation of the criminal law, which holds that conduct must be blameworthy in order to deserve punishment. The law degrades its nobility and weakens its moral authority when it punishes as a crime that which is really only an illness.

The laws against disorderly conduct and vagrancy spring from a different set of middle class standards: the quiet, tree-lined street of "Our Town" on a sunny Sunday afternoon in spring. They are enforced, however, in the teeming urban ghetto where life styles—by choice and by necessity—are different. In the heat of summer, people who live in stifling tenements will gather in the public street, to laugh and sing, to talk loudly and use profanity. Youngsters with no parks or playgrounds nearby will play ball in the streets. And city living is by nature public and gregarious; indeed, this is its joy.

Police officers, however, live by the middle class standards that disorderly conduct laws articulate. Enforcement of the suburban or small town life style by arrests for this kind of conduct or by the catchall "move on" order may seriously exacerbate police-community tensions. A "move on" order or arrest for, say, noisiness, can provoke objection from the citizen who feels he is doing nothing wrong, and it can lead to "fighting words" and the escalation of conflict.

The resources devoted to enforcement of laws against immorality, intoxication, narcotics possession and disorderly conduct cannot easily be measured. Arrests for drunkenness, for instance, make up a large percentage of all arrests, but they do not absorb a great deal of patrol time; yet using precincts and jails to house drunks does make space unavailable

for other purposes. Time devoted to harassing patrols of prostitution and to undercover work against . . . narcotics addicts and gambling, probably takes a lot of patrol and detective time. Moreover, when arrests are made, the time of officers in court, and of judges and court personnel and prosecutors, will be taken from other, perhaps more important, matters; then conviction means taking the time of probation personnel and of the already grossly inadequate resources of the correctional system. The result may be assembly-line justice—or worse—for all concerned.

The anomalies and difficulties arising from criminalization of these kinds of conduct implicitly suggest their own solutions, but how can such solutions be implemented, and how can the problems that would arise from "decriminalization" be handled? What are the consequences of legislative repeal of these statutes identified as overcriminalized and what are the alternatives?

3. THE BILL OF RIGHTS, THE FOURTEENTH AMENDMENT, AND THE STATES

A. A Note on the Bill of Rights and the Emerging Notion of Due Process

The Constitution does not expressly grant to the Supreme Court supervisory jurisdiction over the criminal justice process in the states. Indeed, the original Constitution contains only five substantive provisions relating at all to the administration of justice: the law of treason is set forth in narrow terms, with the conditions for conviction purposely made difficult; ex post facto laws and bills of attainder are prohibited both to the

federal and to the state governments; the federal government (the Congress) is prohibited from suspending the writ of habeas corpus "except when in cases of rebellion or invasion the public safety may require it"; and all crimes other than impeachment are to be tried by jury. No criminal penalties are to follow impeachment, but impeachment and removal from office are not barriers to subsequent criminal charges for the same offense. The jury trial provisions of the original Constitution are superseded by the Sixth Amendment.

The Bill of Rights (Amendments 1 through 8) exhibits greater concern with the rights of criminal defendants. It defines twenty-three distinct "rights" and outlines twelve provisions concerned with criminal procedures. When one looks at the simple words of these amendments in the context of the expressed grievances of the American colonists against British rule, however, it becomes apparent that by current standards even the amendments were relatively limited statements of human liberties. The First Amendment was not specifically intended by its authors to overrule the crime of seditious libel. The Fourth Amendment prohibited only *unreasonable* searches and seizures. In an era where lawyers were the exception and not the rule, it would have been hard to argue the Sixth Amendment originally contemplated *assigned counsel* for indigent defendants. The Fifth Amendment's guarantee against self-incrimination was directed primarily at coerced testimony. And the Eighth Amendment did not guarantee the right to bail or define what were proscribed as "cruel and unusual" punishments. But whatever the literal or intended meaning of these provisions, the first major question to arise was whether they applied to the states *at all*. Only two of the amendments, the First and part of the Seventh, referred specifically to the federal government. The others stated general libertarian principles. Did this imply that all *but* the First and Seventh Amendments applied to the states? Such an interpretation would have been inconsistent with the political history of the Amendments. The call for a bill of rights limiting the power of the federal government arose in most state-ratifying conventions in 1787–1788. The move in the First Congress to propose such a bill of rights was a direct response to criticism of its absence made by the Constitution's opponents in the ratifying conventions.

One of the amendments originally drafted by Madison, and passed by the House of Representatives in slightly amended fashion, stated:

Equal rights of conscience, the freedom of speech or of the press, and the right to trial by jury in criminal cases, shall not be infringed by any State.

Madison argued that these rights ought to be protected against infringement by all governments, implying either that without this amendment only the First and Seventh Amendments of the Bill of Rights would *not* apply to the states or that these rights were particularly important and alone should apply. Ultimately, adoption of this proposed amendment failed in the Senate. Thus, whether most or all of the Bill of Rights was intended to apply to the states remained, at best, ambiguous. The question remained: was rejection by the Senate to be interpreted as meaning that this additional amendment was unnecessary, that is, that what became the First and Seventh Amendments and the rest of the Bill of Rights already applied to the states? Or was it intended to signify that all *but* these two amendments applied to the states?

Dispute over the application of the Bill of Rights to the states was settled conclusively by Chief Justice John Marshall in *Barron v. Baltimore* (1833). Barron was the owner of a wharf that became unusable when municipal road construction diverted the streams that led to it. He claimed deprivation of his Fifth Amendment rights to due process and just compensation. Speaking for a unanimous Court, Marshall rejected this claim. He noted that the Bill of Rights was enacted in response to those who feared abuse of federal power. The purpose of the Constitution was to establish a national government. Conceding that the Constitution contained some limitations on the states, he noted that in all such cases, there was separate and specific language. For example, Article I, Section 9 expresses some general limitations on government power, and Article I, Section 10 prohibits the states specifically from engaging in the same practices. Thus, Marshall said, general constitutional limits should be construed as applying only to the national government. Not surprisingly, as a result of Marshall's interpretation, the Supreme Court had no important criminal cases to decide in its early years. Since criminal matters were primarily the responsibility of the states, they could operate free of national constitutional restraints. Most of the guarantees of the Bill of Rights were repeated in the state constitutions. But they could be applied and interpreted only by state judges.

Passage of the Fourteenth Amendment after the Civil War provided an opportunity to reexamine the question of the application of the Bill of Rights to the states. Since the amendment's text says "No State shall . . ." there was no doubt that its provisions were applicable to the states. The states are prohibited from denying (among other things) "due process of law" to all persons within their jurisdictions. What that clause specifically required of the states was, like so much of the Constitution left unclear, and numerous "theories" have been put forth to give the due process clause of the Fourteenth Amendment substantive content. One position was that the due process clause conveniently summarized and applied the first eight amendments to the states. In 1868—as in 1978 to a lesser degree—this was a radical and expansionist position, since its acceptance would have meant an immediate and substantial enlargement of the prevailing rights of individuals in state courts. Initially, a contrary position prevailed: the due process clause merely guaranteed to defendants in state courts the right to a fair trial—that is, trial by lawful procedures.

It could, likewise, be legitimately argued that since the due process clause of the Fourteenth Amendment was a restatement of the due process clause of the Fifth Amendment, it merely articulated Fifth Amendment due process rights, not all the rights enumerated by the other amendments. Why should "due process" mean different things in different amendments? However, this position was rejected as too narrow.

The justices were more willing to use the due process clause of the Fourteenth Amendment as a convenient restatement of the admonition that the government not be arbitrary, capricious, or unreasonable in depriving a citizen of life, liberty, or property. As the late Justice Frankfurter described it:

[D]ue process, unlike some legal rules, is not a technical conception with a fixed content unrelated to time, place, and circumstances. Expressing as it does in its ultimate analysis respect enforced by law for that feeling of just treatment which has been evolved through centuries of Anglo-American constitutional history and civilization, "due process" cannot be imprisoned within the treacherous limits of any formula. Rep-

resenting a profound attitude of fairness between man and man, and more particularly between the individual and government, "due process" is compounded of history, reason, the past course of decisions, and strong confidence in the strength of the democratic faith which we profess. Due process is not a mechanical instrument. It is not a yardstick. It is a process.[1]

Due process could thus be either a limitless weapon against unfairness in government, or it could be a relatively narrow instrument protecting only against those deprivations historically associated with it—intimidation, torture, coercion.

In the years following passage of the Fourteenth Amendment, the Supreme Court rejected periodic attempts to "incorporate" portions of the Bill of Rights into the privileges and immunities and due process clauses of the amendment. The right to indictment by grand jury, the right to trial by a jury of 12 persons, and the right against self-incrimination were among those rejected as not sufficiently "fundamental" to be applied to the states via the Fourteenth Amendment.[2]

In 1925, the Supreme Court announced, in *Gitlow* v. *New York*, that it "assumed" that the First Amendment was applicable to the states via the Fourteenth, a view elaborated and justified by Justice Cardozo in *Palko* v. *Connecticut* (1937). It is a bit ironic that the one amendment of the Bill of Rights that was specifically addressed to Congress became the first of the amendments "incorporated" into the Fourteenth Amendment.

B. *Palko v. Connecticut* (1937)

+Hughes, McReynolds, Brandeis, Sutherland, Stone, Roberts, Cardozo, Black
–Butler

[Frank Palko was accused of killing a Bridgeport, Connecticut policeman. In Fairfield County Court, a jury found him guilty of second-degree murder, and he was sentenced to life imprisonment. Unsatisfied with this outcome, the state appealed the case to the Connecticut Supreme Court of Errors, pursuant to a state statute enacted in 1886. The Connecticut Supreme Court reversed and ordered a new trial. It found that the trial court had erred in (1) excluding testimony as to a confession by the defendant, (2) excluding testimony upon cross-examination of Palko to impeach his credibility, and (3) its instructions to the jury as to the difference between first and second degree murder.

On retrial, a new jury found Palko guilty of first-degree murder, and he was sentenced to death. The state supreme court affirmed this decision. Did Palko's second trial constitute an infringement of his Fourteenth Amendment right to due process of law in state proceedings, a right he claimed included the Fifth Amendment's protection against double jeopardy? Was the Fifth to be absorbed by the Fourteenth? On appeal, the U.S. Supreme Court agreed to review the case.]

MR. JUSTICE CARDOZO delivered the opinion of the Court.

. . .

The argument for appellant is that whatever is forbidden by the Fifth Amendment is forbidden by the Fourteenth also. The Fifth Amendment, which is not directed to the states, but solely to the federal government,

---

[1]*Joint Anti-Fascist Refugee Committee v. McGrath* (1951).
[2]*Hurtado* v. *California* (1884); *Maxwell* v. *Dow* (1900); and *Twining* v. *New Jersey* (1908).

creates immunity from double jeopardy. No person shall be "subject for the same offense to be twice put in jeopardy of life or limb." The Fourteenth Amendment ordains, "nor shall any state deprive any person of life, liberty, or property, without due process of law." To retry a defendant, though under one indictment and only one, subjects him, it is said, to double jeopardy in violation of the Fifth Amendment, if the prosecution is one on behalf of the United States. From this the consequence is said to follow that there is a denial of life or liberty without due process of law, if the prosecution is one on behalf of the people of a state. . . .

We do not find it profitable to mark the precise limits of the prohibition of double jeopardy in federal prosecution. . . . Right-minded men . . . could reasonably, even if mistakenly, believe that a second trial was lawful in prosecutions subject to the Fifth Amendment, if it was all in the same case. Even more plainly, right-minded men could reasonably believe that in espousing that conclusion they were not favoring a practice repugnant to the conscience of mankind. Is double jeopardy in such circumstances, if double jeopardy it must be called, a denial of due process forbidden to the states? The tyranny of labels . . . must not lead us to leap to a conclusion that a word which in one set of facts may stand for oppression or enormity is of like effect in every other.

We have said that in appellant's view the Fourteenth Amendment is to be taken as embodying the prohibitions of the Fifth. His thesis is even broader. Whatever would be a violation of the original bill of rights (Amendments 1 to 8) if done by the federal government is now equally unlawful by force of the Fourteenth Amendment if done by a state. There is no such general rule.

The Fifth Amendment provides, among other things, that no person shall be held to answer for a capital or otherwise infamous crime unless on presentment of indictment of a grand jury. This court has held that, in prosecutions by a state, presentment or indictment by a grand jury may give way to informations at the instance of a public officer. *Hurtado* v. *California.* . . . The Fifth Amendment provides also that no person shall be compelled in any criminal case to be a witness against himself. This court has said that, in prosecutions by a state, the exemption will fail if the state elects to end it. *Twining* v. *New Jersey.* . . . Cf. *Snyder* v. *Massachusetts* . . . ; *Brown* v. *Mississippi.* . . . The Sixth Amendment calls for a jury trial in criminal cases and the Seventh for a jury trial in civil cases at common law where the value in controversy shall exceed twenty dollars. This court has ruled that consistently with those amendments trial by jury may be modified by a state or abolished altogether. . . .

On the other hand, the due process clause of the Fourteenth Amendment may make it unlawful for a state to abridge by its statutes the freedom of speech which the First Amendment safeguards against encroachment by the Congress . . . or the free exercise of religion . . . or the right of peaceable assembly, without which speech would be unduly trammeled . . . or the right of one accused of crime to the benefit of counsel. . . . In these and other situations immunities that are valid as against the federal government by force of the specific pledges of particular amendments have been found to be implicit in the concept of ordered liberty, and thus, through the Fourteenth Amendment, become valid as against the states.

The line of division may seem to be wavering and broken if there is a hasty catalogue of the cases on the one side and the other. Reflection and analysis will induce a different view. There emerges the perception of a rationalizing principle which gives to discrete instances a proper order and coherence. The right to trial by jury and the immunity from prosecution except as the result of an indictment may have value and importance. Even so, they are not of the very essence of a scheme of ordered liberty. To abolish them is not to violate a "principle of justice so rooted in the traditions and conscience of our people as to be ranked as fundamental." . . . Few would be so narrow or provincial as to maintain that a fair and enlightened system of justice would be impossible without them. What is true of jury trials and indictments is true also, as the cases show, of the immunity from compulsory self-incrimination. . . . This too might be lost, and justice still be done. Indeed, today as in the past, there are students of our penal system who look upon the immunity as a mischief rather than a benefit, and who would limit its scope or destroy it altogether. No doubt there would remain the need to give protection against torture, physical or mental. . . . Justice, however, would not perish if the accused were subject to a duty to respond to orderly inquiry. . . .

We reach a different plane of social and moral values when we pass to the privileges and immunities that have been taken over from the earlier articles of the federal bill of rights and brought within the Fourteenth Amendment by a process of absorption. These in their origin were effective against the federal government alone. If the Fourteenth Amendment has absorbed them, the process of absorption has had its source in the belief that neither liberty nor justice would exist if they were sacrificed. . . . This is true, for illustration, of freedom of thought and speech. Of that freedom one may say that it is the matrix, the indispensable condition, of nearly every other form of freedom. . . .

Our survey of the cases serves, we think, to justify the statement that the dividing line between them, if not unfaltering throughout its course, has been true for the most part to a unifying principle. On which side of the line the case made out by the appellant has appropriate location must be the next inquiry and the final one. Is that kind of double jeopardy to which the statute has subjected him a hardship so acute and shocking that our polity will not endure it? Does it violate those "fundamental principles of liberty and justice which lie at the base of all our civil and political institutions?" . . . The answer surely must be "no." What the answer would have to be if the state were permitted after a trial free from error to try the accused over again or to bring another case against him, we have no occasion to consider. We deal with the statute before us and no other. The state is not attempting to wear the accused out by a multitude of cases with accumulated trials. It asks no more than this, that the case against him shall go on until there shall be a trial free from the corrosion of substantial legal error. . . . This is not cruelty at all, nor even vexation in any immoderate degree. If the trial had been infected with error adverse to the accused, there might have been review at his instance, and as often as necessary to purge the vicious taint. A reciprocal privilege, subject at all times to the discretion of the presiding judge . . . has now been granted to the state. There is here no seismic innovation. The edifice of justice stands, in its symmetry, to many, greater than before. . . .

The judgment is affirmed.

MR. JUSTICE BUTLER DISSENTS.

C. A Note on Adamson v. California (1947) and the "Incorporation" Doctrine

Justice Hugo Black, new to the Court at the time, did not dissent from the decision in *Palko*. But he soon emerged as the leader of a minority bloc of justices urging the Court to support the *total incorporation* of the Bill of Rights into the Fourteenth Amendment. The high water mark of this effort came in 1947 in the case of *Adamson v. California*. Admiral Dewey Adamson was convicted of murder and sentenced to death. He did not testify at his own trial.[1] Pursuant to a state statute, the prosecutor commented on this fact in his summation to the jury, implying that failure to testify might be construed as an admission of guilt. Adamson challenged this practice as a violation of his constitutional rights under the Fifth and Fourteenth Amendments.

The U.S. Supreme Court, on appeal, upheld Adamson's conviction by a 5-4 vote. Speaking for the majority, Justice Reed dismissed Adamson's contention that the prosecutor's comments were a violation of his privileges and immunities. And Reed also rejected the argument that the due process clause applied the Fifth Amendment to the states, citing and reaffirming the *Palko* decision. The question then remained of whether there was some independent basis for concluding that the prosecutor's comments had violated Adamson's due process rights. Noting that California was one of only a few states that permitted comment on the failure of the accused to testify, and that the practice was forbidden in the federal courts and prohibited by the Fifth Amendment, Reed could find "no reason why comment should not be made upon his silence. It seems quite natural that . . . the prosecution should bring out the strength of the evidence by commenting upon defendant's failure" to testify.

For the dissenters, Justice Black argued that the Court's use of the due process clause to determine what constituted "civilized decency" or "fundamental principles of liberty and justice" was a usurpation of judicial power. The Court should not have the "boundless power under natural law periodically to expand and contract constitutional standards . . . ," he said, adding:

My study of the historical events that culminated in the Fourteenth Amendment, and the expressions of those who sponsored and favored, as well as those who opposed its submission and passage, persuades me that one of the chief objects that the provisions of the Amendment's first section, separately, and as a whole, were intended to ac-

---

[1]There are a number of reasons why a defendant might not wish to testify in his own behalf in a criminal trial. He may simply not be a credible witness and so might alienate the jury. More importantly, perhaps, by electing to testify, a defendant becomes vulnerable to cross-examination. Details of a prior criminal record may be elicited to impeach his credibility. In those cases where there is a separate penalty trial, a defendant may compromise his ability to plead for mercy (the right of "allocution") where earlier he has denied complicity in the offense charged. And where the jury sentences at the same time as determining guilt, the defendant is forced to choose between proclaiming his innocence *or* taking his Fifth Amendment right to silence and appealing for mercy.

complish was to make the Bill of Rights applicable to the states.² With full knowledge of the import of the Barron decision, the framers and backers of the Fourteenth Amendment proclaimed its purpose to be to overturn the constitutional rule that case had announced. This historical purpose has never received full consideration or exposition in any opinion of this Court interpreting the Amendment.

[O]ur prior decisions, including Twining, do not prevent our carrying out . . . [the] purpose . . . of making applicable to the states, not a mere part, as the Court has, but the full protection of the Fifth Amendment's provision against compelling evidence from an accused to convict him of crime. And I further contend that the "natural law" formula which the Court uses to reach its conclusion in this case should be abandoned as an incongruous excrescence on our Constitution. I believe that formula to be itself a violation of our Constitution, in that it subtly conveys to courts, at the expense of legislatures, ultimate power over public policies in fields where no specific provision of the Constitution limits legislative power. . . .

I cannot consider the Bill of Rights to be an outworn 18th Century "strait jacket" as the Twining opinion did. Its provisions may be thought outdated abstractions by some. And it is true that they were designed to meet ancient evils. But they are the same kind of human evils that have emerged from century to century wherever excessive power is sought by the few at the expense of the many. In my judgment the people of no nation can lose their liberty so long as a Bill of Rights like ours survives and its basic purposes are conscientiously interpreted, enforced and respected so as to afford continuous protection against old, as well as new, devices and practices which might thwart those purposes. I fear to see the consequences of the Court's practice of substituting its own concepts of decency and fundamental justice for the language of the Bill of Rights as its point of departure in interpreting and enforcing that Bill of Rights. If the choice must be between the selective process of the Palko decision applying some of the Bill of Rights to the States, or the Twining rule applying none of them, I would choose the Palko selective process. But rather than accept either of these choices, I would follow what I believe was the original purpose of the Fourteenth Amendment—to extend to all the people of the nation the complete protection of the Bill of Rights. To hold that this Court can determine what, if any, provisions of the Bill of Rights will be enforced, and if so to what degree, is to frustrate the great design of a written Constitution.

In a short, additional dissent, little noted at the time, Justice Murphy, joined by Justice Rutledge, added the following caveat:

. . . But I am not prepared to say that the [14th Amendment] is entirely and necessarily limited by the Bill of Rights. Occasions may arise where a proceeding falls so far short of conforming to fundamental standards or procedures as to warrant constitutional condemnation in terms of a lack of due process despite the absence of a specific provision in the Bill of Rights.

Black's opinion had at least implicitly assumed that the Bill of Rights provided the exclusive meaning for, and thus limited the scope of, the due process clause. Murphy's position, which became known as *incorpora-*

---

²Black argued that the Bill of Rights was incorporated by the entire first section of the Fourteenth Amendment, including the privileges and immunities clause. This was consistent with the views of those framers of the Amendment who favored the incorporation thesis.—Ed.

tion plus, was that the Bill of Rights provided the minimum content of the due process clause but did not define its outer boundaries. As most provisions of the Bill of Rights were incorporated in the 1960s by the Warren Court, the significance of Murphy's argument was recognized. The creation of "new rights," such as the right to privacy, became the defining characteristic of an "activist court".[3] And Black, maintaining his earlier position, became its chief critic (e.g., see *Griswold* v. *Connecticut*, 1965, *infra*), arguing that this was a gross misuse of judicial power, nothing less than a barely concealed return to the discredited doctrine of substantive due process.

The controversy over incorporation of the Bill of Rights can be conveniently summarized by identifying five analytically distinct positions: no incorporation, absorption, selective incorporation, total incorporation, and incorporation plus. The extreme no incorporation position was stated by Justice Matthews in *Hurtado* v. *California* (1884). In rejecting a claim that the Fourteenth Amendment required the application of the Fifth Amendment's grand jury provisions to the states, Matthews held that since due process in the Fifth Amendment did not imply a grand jury requirement, that being stated separately in the amendment, the due process clause of the Fourteenth Amendment could not have a different meaning. But Matthews went even further to suggest that the due process clause of the Fourteenth Amendment *excluded* rights found elsewhere in the Constitution. This extreme position was later to be repudiated.

Palko v. *Connecticut* (1937) illustrates the absorption theory, which is, in fact, a bridge between the no incorporation and selective incorporation positions. It is for the justices to determine whether a particular right is sufficiently fundamental— "implicit in the concept of ordered liberty," as Cardozo put it—to apply it to the states under the due process clause of the Fourteenth Amendment. In making this choice, the Supreme Court may be guided by what is contained in the Bill of Rights, hence the metaphor of "absorption." But the presence of a right in the Bill of Rights is not conclusive. The Court must also be sensitive to the principles of federalism; it must recognize that primary responsibility for enforcement of the criminal laws lies with the states. "Due process" affords the Supreme Court only a limited scrutiny of state criminal justice procedures, as noted at the beginning of this chapter. It is therefore an evolving, open-ended, but limited conception of rights; in 1937, it was a conservative doctrine. It was to become more liberal.

Rochin v. *California* (1952) provides a convenient illustration. Rochin was convicted of a narcotics offense based on evidence forcibly

---

[3] A close reading of Murphy's language, which refers only to "fundamental standards of *procedure*" suggests that he might not have supported some of these later developments. On this point, and on the incorporation controversy generally, see Jacob W. Landynski, "Due Process and the Concept of Ordered Liberty: 'A Screen of Words Expressing Will in the Service of Desire?' " **2** *Hofstra Law Review* (1974), 1–66. In private, Black protested to Murphy: "You imply that my opinion has stated the contrary. I have not intended to say that in the *Adamson* opinion so far as *procedural* due process is concerned—in other words, I have not attempted to tie procedural due process exclusively to the Bill of Rights." (HLB to FM, *Adamson* File, The Papers of Frank Murphy, Michigan Historical Collections).

pumped from his stomach. A unanimous Supreme Court reversed the conviction. At the time, evidence secured illegally in violation of the Fourth Amendment was nonetheless admissible in state courts (*Wolf* v. *Colorado*, 1949). But Justice Frankfurter wrote that this was conduct that "shocks the conscience" and goes beyond acceptable bounds. "They are methods too close to the rack and the screw to permit of constitutional differentiation." Justice Black concurred, but on the basis that Rochin's Fifth Amendment right against self-incrimination had been violated and that this right was guaranteed to him by the Fourteenth Amendment. He repeated his *Adamson* argument against a "natural law" conception of due process; what could be more vague or subjective than a test that requires measurement of how "shocking" conduct is? And why should judges make these choices? Frankfurter responded:

The vague contours of the Due Process Clause do not leave judges at large. We may not draw on our merely personal and private notions and disregard the limits that bind judges in their judicial function. Even though the concept of due process of law is not final and fixed, these limits are derived from considerations that are fused in the whole nature of our judicial process. The Due Process Clause places upon this Court the duty of exercising a judgment, within the narrow confines of judicial power in reviewing State convictions, upon interests of society pushing in opposite directions.

Due process of law thus conceived is not to be derided as resort to a revival of "natural law." To believe that this judicial exercise of judgment could be avoided by freezing "due process of law" at some fixed stage of time or thought is to suggest that the most important aspect of constitutional adjudication is a function for inanimate machines and

not for judges, for whom the independence safe-guarded by Article III of the Constitution was designed and who are presumably guided by established standards of judicial behavior. Even cybernetics has not yet made that haughty claim. To practice the requisite detachment and to achieve sufficient objectivity no doubt demands of judges the habit of self-discipline and self-criticism, incertitude that one's own views are incontestable and alert tolerance toward views not shared. But these are precisely the presuppositions of our judicial process. They are precisely the qualities society has a right to expect from those entrusted with ultimate judicial power.

Restraints on our jurisdiction are self-imposed only in the sense that there is from our decisions no immediate appeal short of impeachment or constitutional amendment. But that does not make due process of law a matter of judicial caprice. The faculties of the Due Process Clause may be indefinite and vague, but the mode of their ascertainment is not self-willed. In each case "due process of law" requires an evaluation based on a disinterested inquiry pursued in the spirit of science, on a balanced order of facts exactly and fairly stated, on the detached consideration of conflicting claims, on a judgment not ad hoc and episodic but duly mindful of reconciling the needs both of continuity and of change in a progressive society.

Selective incorporation can be at least faintly distinguished from absorption by its greater reliance on the specific provisions of the Bill of Rights. It is up to the Court to decide which portions of the Bill of Rights should be applied to the states. But when a right is applied, it is usually because it is part of the Bill of Rights. Moreover, when a provision of the Bill of Rights is incorporated into the Fourteenth Amendment, it is not just the broad governing principle that is applied to the states but also the entire body of supporting case law that had developed when the right was applied only to the federal government (see *Malloy* v. *Hogan, infra*).

A selective incorporation strategy does not eliminate the need for the Court to decide which portions of the Bill of Rights are truly fundamental. Is this any less subjective than determining which rights are truly "fundamental"? Or does it merely appear objective? The main advantage of selective incorporation over the fundamental rights approach is that it encourages consideration of a "total" right guaranteed by the Bill of Rights, not just whatever limited aspect or application of a right is raised in a case. For example, a selective incorporation approach to *Palko* would have considered the entire question of the applicability of the right of double jeopardy to the states, not just the relatively minor component of permitting the state to appeal from a conviction on the basis of legal error. Would Justice Cardozo have been equally willing, in that case, to accept appeal by the state following *acquittal*? A selective incorporation approach would have required full incorporation of the right against double jeopardy, in all its forms.

Total incorporation and incorporation plus have already been defined. Incorporation is justified on historical grounds because it avoids the subjectivity of the fundamental rights approach and because it expresses (in Justice Black's view at least) a literal, limited, and thus more legitimate conception of the proper role of the Supreme Court. Critics note that interpretation of the meaning of most of the provisions of the Bill of Rights is hardly any less subjective than discerning what is "fundamental" at a particular point in time.

D. *Malloy* v. *Hogan* (1964)

+Warren, Black, Douglas, Brennan, Goldberg
−Clark, Harlan, Stewart, White

[The debate between Justices Black and Frankfurter over incorporation tended to conceal an already existing trend toward selective incorporation. By 1950, all the provisions of the First Amendment,[1] the Sixth Amendment rights to a fair trial,[2] counsel in capital cases,[3] and a public trial,[4] and the Fourth Amendment right against unreasonable searches and seizures[5] had been applied to the states. What started gradually became a veritable rush, beginning with *Mapp* v. *Ohio* (1961), in which the exclusionary rule of the Fourth Amendment was also applied to the states. In 1962, the Eighth Amendment right against cruel and unusual punishment was incorporated,[6] followed the next year, in *Gideon* v. *Wainwright*, by the right to appointed counsel in all serious criminal cases. The edifice of *Palko* was crumbling, and *Malloy* v. *Hogan* began the final push.]

MR. JUSTICE BRENNAN delivered the opinion of the Court.

In this case we are asked to reconsider prior decisions holding that the privilege against self-incrimination is not safeguarded against state action by the Fourteenth Amendment. . . .

---

[1]Freedom of speech, *Gitlow* v. *New York* (1925); freedom of the press, *Near* v. *Minnesota* (1931); free exercise of religion, *Hamilton* v. *Board of Regents* (1934); freedom of assembly, *DeJonge* v. *Oregon* (1937); and the right against establishment of religion (separation of church and state), *Everson* v. *Board of Education* (1947).
[2]*Powell* v. *Alabama* (1932).
[3]*Ibid.*, and *Betts* v. *Brady* (1942).
[4]*In re Oliver* (1948).
[5]*Wolf* v. *Colorado* (1949).
[6]*Robinson* v. *California* (1962).

The petitioner was arrested during a gambling raid in 1959 by Hartford, Connecticut, police. He pleaded guilty to the crime of pool-selling, a misdemeanor, and was sentenced to one year in jail and fined $500. . . . About 16 months after his guilty plea, petitioner was ordered to testify before a referee appointed by the Superior Court of Hartford County to conduct an inquiry into alleged gambling and other criminal activities in the county. The petitioner was asked a number of questions related to events surrounding his arrest and conviction. He refused to answer any question "on the grounds it may tend to incriminate me." The Superior Court adjudged him in contempt, and committed him to prison until he was willing to answer the questions. Petitioner's application for a writ of habeas corpus was denied by the Superior Court, and the Connecticut Supreme Court of Errors affirmed. The latter court held that the Fifth Amendment's privilege against self-incrimination was not available to a witness in a state proceeding, that the Fourteenth Amendment extended no privilege to him, and that the petitioner had not properly invoked the privilege available under the Connecticut Constitution. . . . We reverse. We hold that the Fourteenth Amendment guaranteed the petitioner the protection of the Fifth Amendment's privilege against self-incrimination . . . .

We hold today that the Fifth Amendment's exception from compulsory self-incrimination is also protected by the Fourteenth Amendment against abridgment by the States. . . .

. . . [T]he constitutional inquiry is not whether the conduct of state officers in obtaining the confession was shocking, but whether the confession is "free and voluntary; that is, [it] must not be extracted by any sort of threats or violence, nor obtained by any direct or implied promises, however slight, nor by the exertion of any improper influence. . . ." . . . In other words the person must not have been compelled to incriminate himself. We have held inadmissible even a confession secured by so mild a whip as the refusal, under certain circumstances, to allow a suspect to call his wife until he confessed. . . .

Since the Fourteenth Amendment prohibits the States from inducing a person to confess through "sympathy falsely aroused," or other like inducement far short of "compulsion by torture," it follows a fortiori that it also forbids the States to resort to imprisonment, as here, to compel him to answer questions that might incriminate him. The Fourteenth Amendment secures against state invasion the same privilege that the Fifth Amendment guarantees against federal infringement—the right of a person to remain silent unless he chooses to speak in the unfettered exercise of his own will, and to suffer no penalty, as held in *Twining*, for such silence.

This conclusion is fortified by our recent decision in *Mapp* v. *Ohio*, overruling *Wolf* v. *Colorado*, which had held "that in a prosecution in a State court for a State crime the Fourteenth Amendment does not forbid the admission of evidence obtained by a reasonable search and seizure." . . . *Mapp* held that the Fifth Amendment privilege against self-incrimination implemented the Fourth Amendment in such cases, and that the two guarantees of personal security conjoined in the Fourteenth Amendment to make the exclusionary rule obligatory upon the States. . . .

The respondent [State of Connecticut] concedes in its brief that under our decisions, particularly those in-

volving coerced confessions, "the accusatorial system has become a fundamental part of the fabric of our society and, hence, is enforceable against the States." The State urges, however, that the availability of the federal privilege to a witness in a state inquiry is to be determined according to a less stringent standard than is applicable in a federal proceeding. We disagree. We have held that the guarantees of the First Amendment . . . the prohibition of unreasonable searches and seizures of the Fourth Amendment . . . and the right to counsel guaranteed by the Sixth Amendment . . . are all to be enforced against the States under the Fourteenth Amendment according to the same standards that protect those personal rights against federal encroachment. In the coerced confession cases, involving the policies of the privilege itself, there has been no suggestion that a confession might be considered coerced if used in a federal but not a state tribunal. The Court thus has rejected the notion that the Fourteenth Amendment applies to the states only a "watered-down, subjective version of the individual guarantees of the Bill of Rights." If *Cohen* v. *Hurley* . . . and *Adamson* v. *California* . . . suggest such an application of the privilege against self-incrimination that suggestion cannot survive recognition of the degree to which the *Twining* view of the privilege has been eroded. What it accorded is a privilege of refusing to incriminate one's self, and the feared prosecution may be by either federal or state authorities . . . . Therefore, the same standards must determine whether an accused's silence in either a federal or state proceeding is justified.
. . .

Reversed.

MR. JUSTICE HARLAN, WHOM MR. JUSTICE CLARK JOINS, DISSENTING.

Believing that the reasoning behind the Court's decision carries extremely mischievous, if not dangerous consequences for our federal system in the realm of criminal law enforcement, I must dissent. . . .

I can only read the Court's opinion as accepting in fact what it rejects in theory: the application to the States, via the Fourteenth Amendment of the forms of federal criminal procedure embodied within the first eight Amendments to the Constitution. While it is true that the Court deals today with only one aspect of state criminal procedure, and rejects the wholesale "incorporation" of such federal constitutional requirement, the logical gap between the Court's premises and its novel constitutional conclusion can, I submit, be bridged only by the additional premise that the Due Process Clause of the Fourteenth Amendment is a shorthand directive to this Court to pick and choose among the provisions of the first eight Amendments and apply those chosen, freighted with their entire accompanying body of federal doctrine, to law enforcement in the States.

I accept and agree with the proposition that continuing re-examination of the constitutional conception of Fourteenth Amendment "due process" of law is required, and that development of the community's sense of justice may in time lead to expansion of the protection which due process affords. In particular in this case, I agree that principles of justice to which due process gives expression, as reflected in decisions of this Court, prohibit a State, as the Fifth Amendment prohibits the Federal Government, from imprisoning a person solely because he refuses to give evidence which may incriminate him under the laws of the State. I do not understand, however, how this process of re-examination, which must refer always to the guiding standard of due process of law, including, of course, reference to the particular guarantees of the Bill of Rights, can be short-circuited by the simple device of incorporating into due process, without critical examination, the whole body of law which surrounds a specific prohibition directed against the Federal Government. The consequence of such an approach to due process as it pertains to the States is inevitable disregard of all relevant differences which may exist between state and federal criminal law and its enforcement. The ultimate result is compelled uniformity, which is inconsistent with the purpose of our federal system and which is achieved either by encroachment on the States' sovereign powers or by dilution in federal law enforcement of the specific protections found in the Bill of Rights. . . .

It is apparent that Mr. Justice Cardozo's metaphor of "absorption" was not intended to suggest the transplantation of case law surrounding the specifics of the first eight Amendments to the very different soil of the Fourteenth Amendment's Due Process Clause. For, as he made perfectly plain, what the Fourteenth Amendment requires of the States does not basically depend on what the first eight Amendments require of the Federal Government. . . .

The Court's approach in the present case is in fact nothing more or less than "incorporation" in snatches. If, however, the Due Process Clause is something more than a reference to the Bill of Rights and protects only those rights which de-

rive from fundamental principles, as the majority purports to believe, it is just as contrary to precedent and just as illogical to incorporate the provisions of the Bill of Rights one at a time as it is to incorporate them all at once. . . .

The Court concludes, almost without discussion, that "the same standards must determine whether an accused's silence in either a federal or state proceeding is justified." About all that the Court offers in explanation of this conclusion is the observation that it would be "incongruous" if different standards governed the assertion of a privilege to remain silent in state and federal tribunals. Such "incongruity," however, is at the heart of our federal system. The powers and responsibilities of the state and federal governments are not congruent; under our Constitution, they are not intended to be. Why should it be thought, as an a priori matter, that limitations on the investigative power of the States are in all respects identical with limitations on the investigative power of the Federal Government? This certainly does not follow from the fact that we deal here with constitutional requirements; for the provisions of the Constitution which are construed are different.

. . . If the power of the States to deal with local crime is unduly restricted, the likely consequence is a shift of responsibility in this area to the Federal Government, with its vastly greater resources. Such a shift, if it occurs, may in the end serve to weaken the very liberties which the Fourteenth Amendment safeguards by bringing us closer to the monolithic society which our federalism rejects. Equally dangerous to our liberties is the alternative of watering down protections against the Federal

Government embodied in the Bill of Rights so as not unduly to restrict the powers of the States. . . .

MR. JUSTICE WHITE, WITH WHOM MR. JUSTICE STEWART JOINS, DISSENTING (OMITTED).

[The domino effect of *Malloy* was considerable. Not only did it undermine the principles of *Twining* v. *New Jersey* (1908), but it also undercut a number of more recent decisions involving the Fifth Amendment right against self-incrimination. If *Adamson* was not specifically overruled by *Malloy,* it was disposed of the following year in *Griffin* v. *California* (1965), where the Court ruled that a state prosecutor's comment on the failure of a defendant to testify violated the defendant's Fifth and Fourteenth Amendment rights against self-incrimination. Further, by overruling *Cohen* v. *Hurley* (1961), in which the self-incrimination protection had been denied to a lawyer in a state disbarment proceeding, the Supreme Court in *Spevack* v. *Klein* (1967) opened the way for extending the protection. The "two sovereignty" rule in self-incrimination cases was finally abolished.

In *Feldman* v. *United States* (1944), the Supreme Court had ruled, 4-3, that the Fifth Amendment offered no protection from prosecution in the federal courts to a person compelled to testify in a state proceeding under a grant of immunity (as long as there was no evidence of federal complicity). *Feldman* was subsequently overruled in a companion case to *Malloy, Murphy* v. *Waterfront Commission* (1964). In this case, the Court ruled that testimony given at a state proceeding under a grant of immunity could not be used against Murphy in a federal prosecution. It is important to note, however, that while the Court was expanding self-incrimination protections to testimony given under grants of immunity, the Court was also weakening the scope of protection that that immunity offered.

The justification for immunity is that it must be "coextensive" with the privilege against self-incrimination; it must protect an individual as fully as he or she would be protected by refusing to testify. In 1892, in *Counselman* v. *Hitchcock,* the Supreme Court seemed to *require* full *transactional immunity;* that is, a person required to testify could not be prosecuted for any crime related to that evidence. But in *Murphy,* even though the defendant had been granted transactional immunity, the Court implied that only a lesser protection, *use immunity,* was required to give effect to the Fifth Amendment privilege. Under use immunity, only the evidence actually given by a witness under immunity could not be used against him. He might, in fact, be prosecuted at a later date for crimes about which he testified, provided that "other" evidence was used.

In *Kastigar* v. *United States* (1972), the Supreme Court upheld the constitutionality of a 1970 congressional statute that substituted use for transactional immunity. Speaking for a 5-2 majority, Justice Powell held that use immunity satisfied Fifth Amendment requirements as long as the government could demonstrate that the evidence used to secure a conviction was in no way related to the earlier testimony given under a grant of immunity. The dissenters argued that the difficulty of "proving a negative" would lead to acceptance of evidence that might have been suggested inferentially by the earlier testimony of the defendant and would thus dilute the protections allegedly offered by the grant.]

E. Justice Black Reflects on the "Incorporation" Doctrine

[Twenty-one years after he first expressed the view that the first eight amendments were made applicable to the states by the first section of the Fourteenth Amendment (*Adamson* v. *California,*[*]1947), Justice Black was still unwilling to concede anything to the many critics of his position. In a series of lectures at Columbia University, later reprinted in book form, he reiterated his view that the due process clause

Reprinted from Hugo Black, *A Constitutional Faith* (New York: Knopf, 1968), pp. 23–24.

was not intended to allow the Supreme Court to strike down federal or state laws that are found to be "unreasonable, arbitrary, capricious or contrary to a fundamental sense of civilized justice."]

. . . [T]he cornerstone of my constitutional faith is a basic belief that our written Constitution was designed to prevent putting too much uncontrollable power in the hands of any one or more public officials. I cannot subscribe to such a loose interpretation of due process which in effect allows judges, and particularly Justices of the United States Supreme Court, to hold unconstitutional laws they do not like. For what else is the meaning of "unreasonable," "arbitrary," or "capricious"—what sort of limitations or restrictions do these phrases put on the power of judges? What, for example, do the phrases "shock the conscience" or "offend the community's sense of fair play and decency" mean to you? I submit that these expressions impose no limitations or restrictions whatever on judges but leave them completely free to decide constitutional questions on the basis of their own policy judgments. I deeply fear for our constitutional system of government when life appointed judges can strike down a law that passed Congress or a state legislature with no more justification than that the judges believe the law is "unreasonable."

My fear is warranted, I believe, by the decisions of an earlier Supreme Court where a majority of the Justices used their notions of reasonableness, through the instrument of the Due Process Clause, to read their own economic and social philosophy into the Constitution and thwart the power of federal and state governments to enact needed and desired changes in governmental policies.

F. Duncan v. Louisiana (1968)

+Warren, Black, Douglas, Brennan, White, Fortas, Marshall
−Harlan, Stewart

[Gary Duncan, a 19-year-old black from Plaquemines Parish, Louisiana, was charged with simple battery, a misdemeanor punishable by two years imprisonment and a $300 fine. It was alleged that he "pushed or touched" a white youth in a fracas at a newly integrated high school. Duncan requested a jury trial, but his request was denied since the Louisiana Constitution provided for jury trials only in cases where capital punishment or imprisonment at hard labor could be imposed. Duncan was convicted and sentenced to serve sixty days in the Parish prison and pay a fine of $150. He claimed that he had a federal constitutional right to a jury trial. The conviction was affirmed by the Supreme Court of Louisiana. An appeal to the United States Supreme Court was granted.]

MR. JUSTICE WHITE delivered the opinion of the Court.

. . .

The Fourteenth Amendment denies the States the power to "deprive any person of life, liberty, or property, without due process of law." In resolving conflicting claims concerning the meaning of this spacious language, the Court has looked increasingly to the Bill of Rights for guidance; many of the rights guaranteed by the first eight Amendments to the Constitution have been held to be protected against state action by the Due Process Clause of the Fourteenth Amendment. That clause now protects the right to compensation for property taken by the State; the rights of speech, press, and religion covered by the First Amendment; the Fourth Amendment rights to be free from unreasonable searches and seizures and to have excluded from criminal trials any evidence illegally seized; the right guaranteed by the Fifth Amendment to be free of compelled self-incrimination; and the Sixth Amendment rights to counsel, to a speedy and public trial, to confrontation of opposing witnesses, and to compulsory process for obtaining witnesses.

The test for determining whether a right extended by the Fifth and Sixth Amendments with respect to federal criminal proceedings is also protected against state action by the Fourteenth Amendment has been phrased in a variety of ways in the opinions of this Court. The question has been asked whether a right is among those "fundamental principles of liberty and justice which lie at the base of all our civil and political institutions," . . . ; whether it is "basic in our system of jurisprudence," . . . ; and whether it is "a fundamental right essential to a fair trial." . . . The claim before us is that the right to trial by jury guaranteed by the Sixth Amendment meets these tests. The position of Louisiana, on the other hand, is that the Constitution imposes upon the States no duty to give a jury trial in any criminal case, regardless of the seriousness of the crime or the size of the punishment which may be imposed. Because we believe that trial by jury in criminal cases is fundamental to the American scheme of justice, we hold that the Fourteenth Amendment guarantees a right of jury trial in all criminal cases which—were they to be tried in a federal court—would come within the Sixth Amendment's guarantee. Since we consider the appeal before us to be such a case, we hold that the Constitution was violated when appellant's demand for jury trial was refused. . . .

We are aware of prior cases in this Court in which the prevailing opinion contains statements contrary to our holding today that the right to jury trial in serious criminal cases is a fundamental right and hence must be recognized by the States as part of their obligation to extend due process of law to all persons within their jurisdiction. Louisiana relies especially on *Maxwell* v. *Dow* . . . (1900); *Palko* v. *Connecticut* . . . (1937); and *Snyder* v. *Massachusetts* . . . (1934). None of these cases, however, dealt with a State which had purported to dispense entirely with a jury trial in serious criminal cases. *Maxwell* held that no provision of the Bill of Rights applied to the States—a position long since repudiated—and that the Due Process Clause of the Fourteenth Amendment did not prevent a State from trying a defendant for a noncapital offense with fewer than 12 men on the jury. It did not deal with a case in which no jury at all had been provided. In neither *Palko* nor *Snyder* was jury trial actually at issue, although both cases contain important dicta asserting that the right to jury trial is not essential to ordered liberty and may be dispensed with by the States regardless of the Sixth and Fourteenth Amendments. These observations, though weighty and respectable, are nevertheless dicta, unsupported by holdings in this Court that a State may refuse a defendant's demand for a jury trial when he is charged with a serious crime. Perhaps because the right to jury trial was not directly at stake, the Court's remarks about the jury in *Palko* and *Snyder* took no note of past or current developments regarding jury trials, did not consider its purposes and functions, attempted no inquiry into how well it was performing its job, and did not discuss possible distinctions between civil and criminal cases. In *Malloy* v. *Hogan*

. . . the Court rejected *Palko's* discussion of the self-incrimination clause. Respectfully, we reject the prior dicta regarding jury trial in criminal cases.

The guarantees of jury trial in the Federal and State Constitutions reflect a profound judgment about the way in which law should be enforced and justice administered. A right to jury trial is granted to criminal defendants in order to prevent oppression by the Government. Those who wrote our constitutions knew from history and experience that it was necessary to protect against unfounded criminal charges brought to eliminate enemies and against judges too responsive to the voice of higher authority. The framers of the constitutions strove to create an independent judiciary but insisted upon further protection against arbitrary action. Providing an accused with the right to be tried by a jury of his peers gave him an inestimable safeguard against the corrupt or overzealous prosecutor and against the compliant, biased, or eccentric judge. If the defendant preferred the common-sense judgment of a jury to the more tutored but perhaps less sympathetic reaction of the single judge, he was to have it. . . .

. . . We are aware of the long debate, especially in this century, among those who write about the administration of justice, as to the wisdom of permitting untrained laymen to determine the facts in civil and criminal proceedings. Although the debate has been intense, with powerful voices on either side, most of the controversy has centered on the jury in civil cases. Indeed, some of the severest critics of civil juries acknowledge that the arguments for criminal juries are much stronger. In addition, at the heart of the dispute have been express or implicit assertions that juries are incapable of adequately understanding evidence or determining issues of fact, and that they are unpredictable, quixotic, and little better than a roll of dice. Yet, the most recent and exhaustive study of the jury in criminal cases concluded that juries do understand the evidence and come to sound conclusions in most of the cases presented to them and that when juries differ with the result at which the judge would have arrived, it is usually because they are serving some of the very purposes for which they were created and for which they are now employed.

The State of Louisiana urges that holding that the Fourteenth Amendment assures a right to jury trial will cast doubt on the integrity of every trial conducted without a jury. Plainly, this is not the import of our holding. Our conclusion is that in the American States, as in the federal judicial system, a general grant of jury trial for serious offenses is a fundamental right, essential for preventing miscarriages of justice and for assuring that fair trials are provided for all defendants. We would not assert, however, that every criminal trial— or any particular trial—held before a judge alone is unfair or that a defendant may never be as fairly treated by a judge as he would be by a jury. Thus we hold no constitutional doubts about the practices, common in both federal and state courts, of accepting waivers of jury trial and prosecuting petty crimes without extending a right to jury trial. However, the fact is that in most places more trials for serious crimes are to juries than to a court alone; a great many defendants prefer the judgment of a jury to that of a court. Even where defendants are satisfied with bench trials, the right to a jury trial very likely serves its intended purpose of making judicial or prosecutorial unfairness less likely.

Louisiana's final contention is that even if it must grant jury trials in serious criminal cases, the conviction before us is valid and constitutional because here the petitioner was tried for simple battery and was sentenced to only 60 days in the parish prison. We are not persuaded. It is doubtless true that there is a category of petty crimes or offenses which is not subject to the Sixth Amendment jury trial provision and should not be subject to the Fourteenth Amendment jury trial requirement here applied to the States. Crimes carrying possible penalties up to six months do not require a jury trial if they otherwise qualify as petty offenses. . . . But the penalty authorized for a particular crime is of major relevance in determining whether it is serious or not and may in itself, if severe enough, subject the trial to the mandates of the Sixth Amendment. . . . The question, then is whether a crime carrying such a penalty is an offense which Louisiana may insist on trying without a jury.

We think not. So-called petty offenses were tried without juries both in England and in the Colonies and have always been held to be exempt from the otherwise comprehensive language of the Sixth Amendment's jury trial provisions. There is no substantial evidence that the Framers intended to depart from this established common-law practice, and the possible consequences to defendants from convictions for petty offenses have been thought insufficient to outweigh the benefits to efficient law enforcement and simplified judicial administration resulting from the availability of speedy and inexpensive nonjury adjudications. These same considerations compel the same result under the Fourteenth Amendment. Of course the boundaries of the petty offense category have always been ill defined, if not ambulatory. In the absence of an explicit constitutional provision, the definitional task necessarily falls on the courts, which must either pass upon the validity of legislative attempts to identify those petty offenses which are exempt from jury trial or, where the legislature has not addressed itself to the problem, themselves face the question in the first instance. . . .

In determining whether the length of the authorized prison term or the seriousness of other punishment is enough in itself to require a jury trial, we are counseled . . . to refer to objective criteria, chiefly the existing laws and practices in the Nation. In the federal system, petty offenses are defined as those punishable by no more than six months in prison and a $500 fine. In 49 of the 50 States crimes subject to trial without a jury, which occasionally include simple battery, are punishable by no more than one year in jail. Moreover, in the late 18th century in America crimes triable without a jury were for the most part punishable by no more than a six-month prison term, although there appear to have been exceptions to this rule. We need not, however, settle in this case the exact location of the line between petty offenses and serious crimes. It is sufficient for our purposes to hold that a crime punishable by two years in prison is, based on past and contemporary standards in this country, a serious crime and not a petty offense. Consequently, appellant was entitled to a jury trial and it was error to deny it.

The judgment below is reversed and the case is remanded for proceedings not inconsistent with this opinion.

MR. JUSTICE FORTAS, CONCURRING, (OMITTED).
MR. JUSTICE BLACK, WITH WHOM MR. JUSTICE DOUGLAS JOINS, CONCURRING (OMITTED).

MR. JUSTICE HARLAN, WHOM MR. JUSTICE STEWART JOINS, DISSENTING.

Every American jurisdiction provides for trial by jury in criminal cases. The question before us is not whether jury trial is an ancient institution, which it is; nor whether it plays a significant role in the administration of criminal justice, which it does; nor whether it will endure, which it shall. The question in this case is whether the State of Louisiana, which provides trial by jury for all felonies, is prohibited by the Constitution from trying charges of simple battery to the court alone. In my view, the answer to that question, mandated alike by our constitutional history and by the longer history of trial by jury, is clearly "no."

The States have always borne primary responsibility for operating the machinery of criminal justice within their borders, and adopting it to their particular circumstances. In exercising this responsibility, each State is compelled to conform its procedures to the requirements of the Federal Constitution. The Due Process Clause of the Fourteenth Amendment requires that those procedures be fundamentally fair in all respects. It does not, in my view, impose or encourage nationwide uniformity for its own sake; it does not command adherence to forms that happen to be old; and it does not impose on the States the rules that may be in force in the federal courts except where such rules are also found to be essential to basic fairness. . . .

Although I therefore fundamentally disagree with the total incorporation view of the Fourteenth Amendment, it seems to me that such a position does at least have the virtue, lacking in the Court's selective incorporation approach, of internal consistency: we look to the Bill of Rights, word for word, clause for clause, precedent for precedent because, it is said, the men who wrote the Amendment wanted it that way. For those who do not accept this "history," a different source of "intermediate premises" must be found. The Bill of Rights is not necessarily irrelevant to the search for guidance in interpreting the Fourteenth Amendment, but the reason for and the nature of its relevance must be articulated. . . .

G. A Note on the Demise of Palko

By 1968, the verdict on "incorporation" was clear. "Total" incorporation had been rejected in favor of "selective" incorporation. But so many provisions of the Bill of Rights had been selectively incorporated that, in practice there was little difference. Justice Black had lost the battle of labels but came very close to winning the war of doctrine.

Five provisions of the Bill of Rights remained unincorporated into the Fourteenth Amendment:[1] the rights

---

[1]Other than the right to a trial by jury in serious criminal cases, incorporated in *Duncan v. Louisiana (supra)*, the following rights were incorporated from 1964 to 1968: the Sixth Amendment right to confrontation of witnesses, *Pointer v. Texas* (1965); the right to privacy, *Griswold v. Connecticut* (1965); the Sixth Amendment right to a speedy trial, *Klopfer v. North Carolina* (1967); and the right to compulsory process, *Washington v. Texas* (1967). In 1972, the right to appointed counsel for the indigent, established in *Gideon v. Wainwright* (1963) for all serious criminal cases, was extended to all criminal cases resulting in a jail sentence, *Argersinger v. Hamlin*.

to grand jury indictment and against double jeopardy protected by the Fifth Amendment, the Second Amendment's guarantee of the right to bear arms, the Third Amendment's prohibition against quartering of soldiers in private homes, and the right against excessive bail guaranteed by the Eighth Amendment. In addition, the provisions of the Seventh Amendment requiring jury trials in all civil suits involving more than twenty dollars had not been applied to the states.

In 1969, the Supreme Court moved to reduce this list by one. In *Benton* v. *Maryland,* a set of facts similar to, though not identical with, those in *Palko,* developed. Benton was tried in state court on charges of burglary and larceny; he was convicted of the first offense but acquitted of the second. After his appeal had been filed, the Maryland Court of Appeals, in another case, invalidated a portion of the state constitution requiring jurors to swear their belief in the existence of God. Since Benton's jury took this oath, his conviction, along with many others, was reversed and his case scheduled for retrial. Benton was again charged with burglary and larceny. His lawyers argued that he could not constitutionally be retried for larceny since he had already been acquitted on that charge. The trial judge denied the motion, and Benton was convicted on both charges. He was sentenced to five years imprisonment for larceny and fifteen years for burglary, the latter figure representing an increase of five years over his original sentence. Both the conviction and the sentences were upheld by an intermediate appellate court, and the Maryland Court of Appeals denied review. The Supreme Court granted certiorari. By a 6-2 vote, Benton's larceny conviction was invalidated. [The issue of his in-

creased sentence was challenged separately by a habeas corpus proceeding in the federal courts.]

Writing for the majority, Justice Marshall concluded:

In 1937, this Court decided the landmark case of Palko v. Connecticut . . . . *Palko, although indicted for first degree murder, had been convicted of murder in the second degree after a jury trial in a Connecticut state court. The State appealed and won a new trial. Palko argued that the Fourteenth Amendment incorporated, as against the States, the Fifth Amendment requirement that no person "be subject for the same offense to be twice put in jeopardy of life or limb." The Court disagreed. Federal double jeopardy standards were not applicable against the States. Only when a kind of jeopardy subjected a defendant to "a hardship so acute and shocking that our policy will not endure it" did the Fourteenth Amendment apply. . . .*

Recently, however, this Court has "increasingly looked to the specific guarantees of the Bill of Rights to determine whether a state trial was conducted with due process of law. . . ." In an increasing number of cases, the Court "has rejected the notion that the Fourteenth Amendment applies to the States only a 'watered-down, subjective version of the individual guarantees of the Bill of Rights.' " Only last term we found that the right to trial by jury in criminal cases was "fundamental to the American scheme of justice," and held that the Sixth Amendment right to a jury trial was applicable to the States through the Fourteenth Amendment. For the same reasons, we today find that the double jeopardy prohibition of the Fifth Amendment represents a fundamental ideal in our constitutional heritage, and that it should apply to the States through the Fourteenth Amendment. Insofar as it is inconsistent with this holding, Palko v. Connecticut *is overruled.*

Palko represented an approach to basic constitutional rights which this Court's recent decisions have rejected.

. . . Our recent cases have thoroughly rejected the Palko notion that basic constitutional rights can be denied by the States as long as the totality of the circumstances do not disclose a denial of "fundamental fairness." Once it is decided that a particular Bill of Rights guarantee is "fundamental to the American scheme of justice" . . . the same constitutional standards apply against both the State and Federal Governments. Palko's roots had thus been cut away years ago. We today only recognize the inevitable.

As is the case with almost all of the "incorporated" provisions of the Bill of Rights, the act of incorporating does not settle many questions; indeed, in many instances the application of a "right" to the states via the Fourteenth Amendment raises many new and frequently more difficult problems of meaning or interpretation. The double jeopardy clause is a good example. The wording of the clause is not entirely clear: "Nor shall any person be subject for the same offense to be twice put in jeopardy of life or limb." While it seems reasonably certain that a case as bizarre as that of Willie Francis will not occur again,[2] important questions remain about the meaning of "same offense"—about whether and under what circumstances resentencing procedures (where a retrial results in a higher sentence) might constitute double jeopardy, and about whether the "two sovereignties" rule remains in effect.

The double jeopardy provision applies to military as well as to civil-ian courts. It applies to any person who has been either convicted or acquitted of a criminal charge. It also applies to an incompleted trial where the proceedings were halted by the prosecution. It protects against prosecution in adult court of a juvenile convicted of the same offense in juvenile court (*Breed* v. *Jones*, 1975).

Double jeopardy does not apply to a hung jury, to a trial that follows the quashing of an original indictment, or to government appeal of a trial judge's substitution of a verdict of acquittal for a jury finding of guilt (*United States* v. *Wilson*, 1975). A criminal defendant who appeals a conviction and seeks a new trial waives his double jeopardy rights, although he may not be retried on charges for which he was acquitted or, upon retrial, charged with a more serious offense. Double jeopardy does not prohibit prosecution for an offense *and* for conspiracy to commit that offense. Finally, double jeopardy does not bar civil and criminal penalties for the same offense.

The question of multiple prosecutions has been especially perplexing for the Supreme Court. In *Ciucci* v. *Illinois* (1958), the defendant killed his wife and three children. Each was a separate offense. A first prosecution netted a sentence of twenty years, a second forty-five years, and a third finally resulted in the death penalty. In a similar case, *Hoag* v. *New Jersey* (1958), the defendant allegedly robbed five patrons in a tavern. He was acquitted of robbing three of the patrons but was later convicted of

[2]Willie Francis was convicted of murder and sentenced to death. At the time, Louisiana had a portable electric chair that was transported by van from one part of the state to another, as needed. Francis was strapped into the chair, but several attempts to execute him produced only nonlethal electric shocks. His attorneys challenged the state's announced intention to try again. By a 5-4 vote the Supreme Court held that this was neither double jeopardy nor cruel and unusual punishment, and Francis was eventually executed. *Louisiana ex rel. Francis* v. *Resweber* (1947). Justice Black voted with the majority.

robbing a fourth on the basis of testimony of a witness who had testified at the first trial. The Supreme Court upheld the conviction, though stating in dictum that a single trial would be "preferred."

A more recent case produced a different result. In *Ashe* v. *Swenson* (1970), Ashe was acquitted of the robbery of one of the participants in a poker game. Subsequently, he was tried, convicted, and sentenced to thirty-five years imprisonment for the robbery of another player in the same game. The Supreme Court found this second trial to constitute double jeopardy and reversed the conviction. The Court held that an issue already determined in favor of the defendant could not be relitigated. But the Court said that double jeopardy does not bar all multiple prosecutions, only those in which "any crucial element of the second offense was necessarily decided by the first verdict of acquittal." The "same evidence" could not be used again unless the second trial included proof of at least a minor additional fact. Three justices, Brennan, Douglas, and Marshall, concurred in the result but would have established the "same transaction" test as a constitutional rule. Under such a test, all charges against a defendant arising out of a single transaction, episode, or occurrence would have to be tried together unless no single

court had jurisdiction over all the offenses.

In *United States* v. *Lanza* (1922), the Supreme Court articulated what has become known as the "two sovereignties" rule. Both the federal government and the states, or two or more states, may make the same act a criminal offense, since each may have "different interests" to protect. The two sovereignties rule does not apply to prosecutions for the same act by a state and one of its subdivisions.[3]

In two cases in 1959, *Bartkus* v. *Illinois* and *Abbate* v. *United States*, a closely divided Supreme Court upheld the two sovereignties rule. Bartkus was acquitted of bank robbery in a federal court and was then convicted on the same evidence in state court and sentenced to life imprisonment. Abbate and others were convicted both in state court in Illinois and in the federal court in Mississippi of conspiring to sabotage telephone company property in Mississippi. Both convictions were upheld by the Supreme Court. Following this decision, the attorney general of the United States declared, as a matter of policy, that no federal prosecution could be brought without his permission after a state prosecution for the same offense.

Bartkus has never been expressly overruled, although its authority may have been eroded by the demise of

---

[3]In 1970, the Supreme Court held, in *Waller* v. *Florida,* that a person could not be tried for the same criminal act both under a municipal ordinance and on state charges pursuant to a grand jury indictment. The case was remanded to the Florida Supreme Court, which held that these were "different offenses" and thus not subject to the double jeopardy objection. Waller petitioned the Supreme Court again, but certiorari was denied.

A state is *not* prohibited from convicting someone of a crime for which he has also been punished in another state, for example, a conspiracy that took place in two or more states may be punished by each state separately. As a matter of practice, this happens rarely. Some states prohibit such procedures by statute. Wisconsin, for example, bars subsequent prosecutions in its courts where an individual has been either convicted or acquitted of the same act in another state, *unless* the statute requires proof of an additional fact besides those required by the laws of the other state.

Palko. Furthermore, *Bartkus* is, at least in principle, inconsistent with *Murphy* v. *Waterfront Commission* (1964, *supra*), which abolished a comparable "two sovereignties" rule for grants of immunity. However, in a 1978 case, *United States* v. *Wheeler*, the Supreme Court extended the two sovereignties rule to include Indian tribal courts. Wheeler had been convicted of a crime by a Navajo court and was later indicted by a federal grand jury and prosecuted for the same offense in a federal district court. That court dismissed the charges as constituting double jeopardy. Even though there are many federal statutes establishing jurisdiction over crimes committed by Indians, the Supreme Court held that the Navajo tribe had never relinquished its sovereign power to punish tribal offenses and remains an independent sovereign. Tribal and federal prosecutions for the same criminal act were "not for the same offense" and hence do not breech the double jeopardy prohibition.

The question of double jeopardy has also been raised in several cases involving higher sentences on retrial. In *North Carolina* v. *Pearce* (1969), the Supreme Court refused to establish an absolute barrier to higher sentences meted out to a defendant upon retrial.[4] Recognizing that this option might serve to "penalize" defendants who appealed convictions, the Supreme Court held that a judge had to justify an increased penalty with objective reasons, such as the defendant's conduct since the first trial. Any "imposition of a penalty upon the defendant for having successfully pursued a statutory right to appeal or collateral remedy" would violate the due process clause of the Fourteenth Amendment.

In *Chaffin* v. *Stynchcombe* (1973), the Court refused to apply even that limitation where the *jury* did the sentencing. Chaffin was sentenced to fifteen years imprisonment for robbery. He successfully appealed his conviction on the grounds of error in the judge's charge to the jury. Upon retrial, he was again convicted and sentenced to life imprisonment by a different jury. In upholding this higher sentence, the Supreme Court said that there was little possibility of "vindictiveness" where the second trial was held before a different jury that convicted and sentenced the defendant. It rejected allegations that allowing increased sentences would have a "chilling effect" on the exercise of postconviction rights.

The Court, in *Blackledge* v. *Perry* (1974), applied its standard of "vindictiveness" in reversing the conviction of a defendant where the prosecutor had brought more serious charges against him after the defendant had sought a trial *de novo* in appealing a misdemeanor conviction. The Court recognized that, unlike a jury and more so than most judges, prosecutors may have an important stake in discouraging appeals that will require increased utilization of prosecutorial resources. In this case, Perry was convicted of a misdemeanor arising out of a fight with another prison inmate in North Carolina. His notice of appeal and request for a new trial prompted the prosecutor to obtain a felony indictment against Perry for the same conduct. He was convicted of the felony offense and given a sentence of five to seven years to run concurrently

---

[4]This case marked the first attempt by the Supreme Court to set down sentencing standards for trial judges.

with the one he was already serving. There was no evidence that the prosecutor had "acted in bad faith or maliciously." But the Supreme Court said that it was not necessary to prove actual malice. It was enough for the apprehension of retaliation to exist, since such apprehension might deter an individual from pursuing his statutory right to seek a new trial. For technical reasons, the Court's holding was based on the due process clause of the Fourteenth Amendment and not the double jeopardy provision.[5]

Two recent cases illustrate the complexity of double jeopardy law. In *Burks* v. *United States* (1978), the petitioner was tried for armed robbery in a federal court. Burks' defense was insanity. Following conviction, he filed an appeal claiming that the evidence was insufficient to support the verdict. The court of appeals ruled in his favor. However, it remanded the case to trial court "for a determination of whether a directed verdict of acquittal should be entered or a new trial ordered." Burks claimed that the judgment of the court of appeals as to the insufficiency of the evidence was equiva-

lent to a judgment of acquittal and that no further proceedings could be held. The Supreme Court reversed the court of appeals and held that a defendant could not be retried after his conviction was reversed because of insufficient evidence: "Given the requirement for entry of a judgment of acquittal the purpose of the (Double Jeopardy) clause would be negated were we to afford the government an opportunity for the proverbial "second bite at the apple.' "

In the second case, *United States* v. *Scott* (1978), the Court held that where a convicted defendant requested dismissal of the case against him because of a preindictment delay, there was no double jeopardy barrier to a new trial. The defendant's claim, the Court ruled, was merely a technical defense that did not dispute or even reach the issue of culpability. In dissent, Justice Brennan argued that the double jeopardy protection of the Constitution is not based on a showing of innocence but instead is a protection against the "gross unfairness" of undergoing "the strain and agony of more than one trial for any single offense."

4. POLICING THE POLICE

A. *Investigating Criminal Activity*

(1) Herbert L. Packer, The Courts, the Police, and the Rest of Us

. . . [T]he kind of criminal process that we have is profoundly affected by a series of competing value

choices which, consciously or unconsciously, serve to resolve tensions that arise in the system. These values

---

[5]In 1912, the Court held, in *Diaz* v. *United States,* that the jeopardy incident to a trial does not extend to an offense beyond the trial court's jurisdiction.

Reprinted from **57** *Journal of Criminal Law, Criminology, and Police Science* (1966), 238–243.

represent polar extremes which, in real life, are subject to almost infinite modulation and compromise. But the extremes can be identified. The choice, basically, is between what I have termed the Crime Control and the Due Process models. . . .

What we have at work today is a situation in which the criminal process as it actually operates in the large majority of cases probably approximates fairly closely the dictates of the Crime Control model. The real-world criminal process tends to be far more administrative and managerial than it does adversary and judicial. Yet, the officially prescribed norms for the criminal process, as laid down primarily by the Supreme Court, are rapidly providing a view that looks more and more like the Due Process model. This development . . . has been in the direction of "judicializing" each stage of the criminal process, of enhancing the capacity of the accused to challenge the operation of the process, and of equalizing the capacity of all persons to avail themselves of the opportunity for challenge so created.

The nature of the trend is obvious enough. What has brought it about and how durable is it? A definitive answer to this question would comprehend a large slice of the history of our times, but I should like to venture a few tentative and speculative observations on the point. Let us start with the Supreme Court itself. To some extent, the Court's decisions are not simply evidence of the trend but are in themselves a contributor to it. Typically, the Court's intervention in any given phase of the criminal process has started with a highly particularistic decision dealing on a narrow basis with the facts of a particularly flagrant or shocking case brought before it. That was true of the first right to counsel case, *Powell* v. *Alabama,* and it was true also of the first confession case, *Brown* v. *Mississippi.* The confession cases are particularly instructive on this issue. For approximately twenty years following *Brown* v. *Mississippi,* a number of confession cases came before the court. As the standards it sought to lay down emerged, they placed great emphasis on the "special circumstances" of the cases. A given confession was deemed involuntary because of the defendant's personal characteristics—illiterate, of low intelligence, immature, a member of a disadvantaged minority group—or because of coercive forces at work in the interrogation process, or because of some combination of these factors. In those decisions, the Court tried, among other things, to influence police behavior by dealing, in its traditional way, with the facts of the specific case before it. But the gap between aspiration and reality proved too great to bridge in the Court's traditional way. And so, the movement has been to ever increasing generality of statement: from *this* confession was coerced for the following particularistic reasons unique to this case, to *all* confessions are bad when they are obtained from an arrestee who has not been promptly brought before a magistrate, as in the famous *Mallory* rule announced for the federal criminal courts in 1957. . . .

The great criminal procedure decisions of the last few years can all be regarded as exemplifying this movement toward increasingly generalized statement, sparked by the court's despair over the prospect of significantly affecting police practices through its more traditional activity. The court has sensed a lawmaking vacuum into which, rightly or wrongly, it has seen itself as having to rush. *Mapp* v. *Ohio,* in extending the exclusionary rule on unreasonable searches and seizures to the state courts, was explicitly based on the proposition that no other presently available means of control held out any hope for deterring police disregard for the dictates of the Fourth Amendment (which had been held applicable to the states in *Wolf* v. *Colorado,* in 1949). *Gideon* v. *Wainwright* substituted a blanket rule on right to counsel explicitly because the earlier case-by-case approach of *Betts* v. *Brady* had failed to bring about universal compliance with what the court perceived as needed reform in the provision of counsel to indigent defendants.

Moves of this sort by the Supreme Court are, in my view, moves of desperation. Nobody else is exerting control over the law enforcement process, so the justices think that they must. But they can do so, in state cases at any rate, only in the discharge of their duty to construe the Constitution in cases that come before them. And so, the rules of the criminal process, which ought to be the subject of flexible inquiry and adjustment by law-making bodies having the institutional capacity to deal with them are evolved through a process that its warmest defenders recognize as to some extent awkward and inept: the rules become "constitutionalized." The Bill of Rights becomes, as Judge Henry Friendly's gibe has it, a code of criminal procedure.

It is easy enough to poke holes in, not to say fun at, this development. But what it represents is an increased consciousness that our criminal process in its everyday functioning does not live up to minimum standards of fairness or, for that matter, of efficiency. . . .

Perhaps the most powerful propellant of the trend toward the Due Process Model has been provided by the Negro's struggle for his civil rights and the response to that struggle by law enforcement in the Southern states—as well, it needs to be said, by law enforcement in some Northern cities. What we have seen in the South is the perversion of the criminal process into an instrument of official oppression. The discretion which, we are reminded so often, is essential to the healthy operation of law enforcement agencies has been repeatedly abused in the South: by police, by prosecutors, by judges and juries. Police brutality, dragnet arrests, discriminatory official conduct may be debatable issues in the cities of the North; but they have been demonstrated beyond doubt in the streets of Selma and Bogalusa and a dozen other Southern communities. Powers of arrest and prosecution have been repeatedly and flagrantly abused in the interest of maintaining an illegal, not to say unconstitutional, social system. We have had many reminders from abroad that law enforcement may be used for evil as well as for beneficent purposes; but the experience in the South during the last decade has driven home the lesson that law enforcement unchecked by law is tyrannous. . . .

As we all know, the Negro's plight is also, and at least as importantly, a problem of urban poverty in the large cities of the North and West. Our heightened national consciousness about the problems of urban poverty likewise contributes to and sustains the trend in the direction of the Due Process Model. The urban Negro's plight is joined to that of the Puerto Rican, the Mexican-American, and other submerged groups. Law enforcement may not be a cause of social injustice, but it must reckon with the consequences of social injustice. It is broadly recognized that the urban poor, and particularly those who belong to minority groups, provide most of the raw material for the criminal process. As the idea develops and is promoted by governmental programs that the legal rights of the poor require special attention, politically and economically muscular pressure for reforms in the criminal process continues to make itself felt. . . .

(2) A Note on the Law of Arrest, Search and Seizure

The Fourth Amendment protects individuals and "their houses, papers and effects" only from *unreasonable* searches and seizures. Given the exigencies of modern life and the need to accommodate the legitimate needs of law enforcement officials as well as the rights of individuals, defining the standard of reasonableness is no easy task. And defining it in the abstract is considerably easier than applying it to concrete situations. There is no more inscrutable area of constitutional law doctrine, with the possible exception of attempts to provide an operational definition of "obscenity."

The Fourth Amendment does *not* require *arrest* warrants. The constitutional standard for legal arrest is the same as that for obtaining an arrest warrant: *probable cause*. Probable cause is more than mere suspicion, rumor, or even strong suspicion. "Probable cause exists if the facts and circumstances known to the officer warrant a prudent man in believing that the offense has been committed" and that the individual arrested has committed the offense. On the other hand, while probable cause is more than mere suspicion, it does not require evidence sufficient to establish guilt beyond a reasonable doubt (*Henry* v. *United States*, 1959).[1]

In *United States* v. *Watson* (1976), the Supreme Court reaffirmed that arrest warrants were not required to arrest a person in a public place for a previously committed felony. The Court also upheld a warrantless arrest of a felony suspect who was seen by police on the front porch of her house and arrested, after a "hot pursuit," in the vestibule, *United States* v. *Santana* (1976).[2] In both cases, a subsequent search and seizure of incriminating evidence was upheld—in *Watson* under the doctrine of "consent" and in *Santana* as "pursuant to a valid arrest."

[1] In *United States* v. *Harris* (1971), the Supreme Court eliminated the requirement that the police demonstrate that information given by an anonymous informant is credible in order to establish probable cause. The Court has also indirectly upheld unsubstantiated tips by informants in a "stop and frisk" situation. In *Adams* v. *Williams* (1972), the Court ruled that the discovery of evidence during a "stop and frisk" that had been initiated solely on information from an "unknown" informant established probable cause for an arrest.

[2] A recent decision by the United States Court of Appeals for the Second Circuit may now force the Supreme Court to reconsider whether there are some circumstances when an arrest warrant is required. In *Reed* v. *United States* (1978), the appeals court ruled that criminal suspects cannot be arrested in their homes by federal agents without a warrant, except in extreme circumstances. The case involved a narcotics conviction based on evidence seized when the suspect, Reed, was arrested in her apartment without a warrant. It was conceded that the federal agents had both statutory authority and probable cause to make the arrest. But a unanimous court ruled that such arrests could not be made without a warrant where the government could easily have procured one, since the "sanctity of the home" was entitled to the strongest protections under the Fourth Amendment (*New York Times*, April 30, 1978).

Relatively few cases involving the law of arrest have come before the Supreme Court. Questions of search and seizure have been the occasion for much more constitutional litigation, particularly since 1949 (*Wolf* v. *Colorado*), when the Fourth Amendment was applied to the states, and 1961 (*Mapp* v. *Ohio*), when the exclusionary rule to enforce the Fourth Amendment was also applied to the states.

The prevailing rule is. that searches and seizures under the Fourth Amendment are reasonable only if made pursuant to a judicially issued warrant. The constitutional test for obtaining a search warrant is stated in the amendment. It can be issued only on a showing of probable cause, supported by oath or affirmation, and "particularly describing the place to be searched and the persons or things to be seized." The warrant can be issued only by a magistrate or judge, who, alone, is considered to have the requisite detachment and neutrality to perform this function. The affidavit requesting a warrant must allege facts, not merely state conclusions. At the conclusion of the search, a full report to the issuing magistrate must be made. A guiding principle of the law of search and seizure is judicial control.

In *Chimel* v. *California* (1969), the Supreme Court reaffirmed the exis-tence of certain well-recognized ex-ceptions to the search warrant re-quirement while at the same time limiting the scope and occasion of warrantless searches. As a practical matter, it should be recognized that most police searches in the United States are warrantless,[3] although re-liance on warrants differs markedly from one jurisdiction to the next and from one type of criminal offense to another. The necessity for obtaining a warrant may depend on where the expectation of privacy is greatest. The Fourth Amendment "protects people, not places," the Court said in *Katz* v. *United States* (1967). Where expectations of privacy are greatest, for example in one's own home or of-fice, the warrant requirements have been applied more stringently.[4] In the *Katz* case (*infra*), the Court held that a warrant was needed to justify elec-tronic surveillance of a public tele-phone booth in a gambling investiga-tion. Justice Stewart noted that what Katz was seeking to exclude when he entered the booth "was not the in-truding eye—it was the uninvited ear." On the other hand, in the more fluid and dangerous setting of street encounters, where obtaining a war-rant is often impossible, the Court's focus has been on the reasonableness of the search.

There are five recognized excep-tions to the search warrant require-

---

[3]Bradley Canon, "Is the Exclusionary Rule in Failing Health? Some New Data and a Plea Against a Precipitous Conclusion," **62** *Kentucky Law Journal* (1974), 707–716.

[4]Thus, in *United States* v. *Chadwick* (1977), the Supreme Court ruled that federal agents could not make a warrantless search of a footlocker thought to contain narcotics and impounded when the suspects carrying it were arrested. The search was conducted more than an hour after the sus-pects were in custody. Writing for the Court, Chief Justice Burger said: "By placing personal effects inside a double locked footlocker, respondents man-ifested an expectation that the contents would remain free from public examination. No less than one who locks the doors of his home against intruders, one who safeguards his personal possessions in this manner is due the protection of the Fourth Amendment Warrant Clause. There being no exigency, it was unreasonable for the government to conduct this search without the safeguards a judicial warrant provides."

ment. The first is *consent*. A person may waive his Fourth Amendment rights and agree to a warrantless search. Such consent must be granted knowingly (which implies understanding that consent need not be given), voluntarily (free of coercion), and explicitly. It is the government's burden to demonstrate in court that a consensual search was indeed voluntary. That, at least, was the rule until a recent Supreme Court case, *Schneckloth* v. *Bustamonte* (1973). In that case the Supreme Court held that consent *may* be voluntary even though the consenter did not know or was not told that he had a constitutional right to refuse permission. Voluntariness of consent is to be determined by a "totality of circumstances test." The Court said that it would not apply the *Miranda* rule to a noncustodial request for consent; left open was the question of whether a request for consent to a person in custody required an explicit waiver.

A person may consent to a search of *his* person or of property that *he* owns or controls. He may not consent to the search of another person (except a parent or guardian who may consent to the search of or for a dependent child). Under some circumstances, consent may be given to search the belongings of another; a landlord may consent to search of a tenant's apartment only if it has been abandoned; a host may consent to search of premises occupied by a short-term guest; an employer may consent to search of the work area of an employee, but an employee may not consent to search of an employer's premises; a spouse can consent to the search of a residence shared with the other spouse where evidence is sought against the latter; and a tenant may consent to a search of premises jointly held with another.

A second exception to the warrant requirement is a *search pursuant to a lawful arrest*. Prior to *Chimel* v. *California* (1969), the rule was that a lawful arrest justified searching the entire premises where the arrest was made, including other rooms of a house, the garage, and closets, desks, safes, filing cabinets, and drawers. The scope of the search was not limited to places where the defendant could reach to secure a weapon or destroy evidence. Under this rule, the police could, and often did, make "strategic" arrests that would give them an opportunity to search areas for which, independently, a search warrant could not be procured.

In *Chimel*, the Court stated that warrantless searches pursuant to a lawful arrest could be justified only to prevent the arrested person from obtaining a weapon and to prevent the destruction of evidence. The arresting officer may search the person of the arrestee for weapons and evidence; he may also search the immediate area within the arrestee's reach and control to prevent him from grabbing a weapon or destroying evidence. This would include items on a table or in a drawer, provided that the drawer was within reach. An object that comes into view during a proper search incident to a lawful arrest may also be seized. Any further search of the area or premises would require a search warrant. The arrest must precede the search, but they must also be contemporaneous.[5]

The *Chimel* case did not make en-

[5]But compare *United States* v. *Edwards* (1975), where the Court upheld a warrantless seizure of the defendant's clothing ten hours after his arrest. The delay was justified, the Court held, because the defendant was arrested late at night and it took that long to obtain substitute clothing for him.

tirely clear whether it was always permissible to search the area within reach of an arrestee, or whether it is permissible only when the arresting officer has reason to believe that weapons or evidence of the crime is in the immediate area. In *United States* v. *Robinson* (1973), the Supreme Court upheld a full search of a suspect who had been taken into custody following a traffic arrest. The arresting officer had no basis for believing that Robinson carried a weapon or was in possession of contraband. And there was no evidence needed to prove the traffic charge, since the officer already knew that Robinson's driver's license had been suspended. The search (following a frisk of Robinson's outer clothing, which disclosed a "soft bulge" in his jacket pocket) uncovered capsules of heroin. On the basis of this evidence, Robinson was convicted of possession of heroin. For the majority, Justice Rehnquist stated that a broad search power following a custodial arrest was necessary to protect the police (see pp. 799–804, *infra*).

A third exception is the seizure of contraband or evidence within *plain sight* of a police officer, even when not discovered pursuant to a lawful search. An officer is not required to ignore evidence that he or she stumbles on accidentally. Nor does the officer need to refuse to take evidence "volunteered" by an arrestee (provided the *Miranda* warnings have been given if the arrestee is formally interrogated) or provided by a private individual not acting as an agent for law enforcement authorities.

Related to the plain sight rule is the "open fields exception," best illustrated by *Air Pollution Variance Board* v. *Western Alfalfa Corp.* (1974). To perform the required visual tests of smokestack pollution, an official of the Colorado Department of Health entered the outer perimeter of the plant grounds, which were open to the public. He took visual sightings, and that evidence became the basis for a cease and desist order. The company appealed, and the state courts held this "search" unreasonable under the Fourth and Fourteenth Amendments. The Supreme Court unanimously held this to be a permissible procedure, noting that there was no invasion of privacy. The Court distinguished this from a warrantless search of the plant itself, its machinery, or its office files.

A fourth exception is the doctrine of *hot pursuit*. The police need not risk "losing" a suspect to obtain a search warrant. As with the second exception, the justification here is the protection of the officer and the prevention of destruction of evidence. A classic example is the case of *Warden* v. *Hayden* (1967). Hayden robbed a taxicab company, dashed home, peeled off his clothes, and jumped into bed, feigning sleep. Radio cabs following him summoned the police, who entered his apartment and arrested him. The guns and clothing he wore during the robbery were seized and admitted into evidence against him. Clearly, under the hot pursuit rule, the guns were lawfully seized. However, the court of appeals held that the clothing could not be seized because it was neither contraband nor an instrumentality of the crime but "mere evidence." Under that rule, the police were entitled to seize only property that they had a "right" to possess, that is, property that the victim of the search had no right to keep. The Supreme Court reversed, holding that there was no valid reason to distinguish between the clothing and the weapons. The Fourth Amendment protects privacy of persons, not property. Since the clothes were not of testimonial or communicative value (and hence raised no Fifth Amendment questions), they could be seized. The "mere evidence" doctrine was overruled.[6]

The fifth exception is the *automobile exception*. It is based on the need to preserve evidence that otherwise is liable or likely to be moved out of the jurisdiction. It is not limited to automobiles, but they are its major example. The rule has its greatest vitality when applied to moving vehicles. But it has recently been applied to vehicles not capable of being moved. In *Cardwell* v. *Lewis* (1974), the Supreme Court upheld the warrantless search (e.g., to obtain samples of paint and a tire impression) of the exterior of an impounded car, with the murder suspect in custody. Presumably under such circumstances a search of the *interior* of the car, or its trunk, would have necessitated a search warrant. However, in *South Dakota* v. *Opperman* (1976), a 5-4 majority of the Court held that since cars afford less expectation of privacy than do homes, an impounded car can be routinely searched and its contents inventoried to protect valuables inside, especially where some valuables were visible on the dashboard and rear seat.

Apart from these enumerated "exceptions" to the warrant requirement, there are other circumstances in which searches may be warrantless and, in some cases, even conducted without probable cause. The warrant requirement of the Fourth Amendment applies to commercial premises as well as to private homes. But prior to 1967, warrantless searches by health inspectors were permitted. In that year, in *Camara* v. *Municipal Court*, the Supreme Court held that such inspections required warrants. However, the Court stipulated that such warrants did not have to be based on probable cause. They could be issued on a showing that "general characteristics such as the nature of the building or the entire area" indicated the existence of violations of the health and safety laws. The Court held that there was no other way of serving the public interest in eliminating health and safety hazards.

On the other hand, the Court has maintained a long-standing exception to the warrant requirement for "closely regulated" industries "long subject to close supervision and inspection." Liquor and firearms are the best examples of industries that have such a history of government regulation and warrantless inspection that no entrepreneur could have any reasonable expectation of privacy. One who chooses to deal in liquor or guns "has voluntarily chosen to subject himself to a full arsenal of government regulation."

The line of demarcation between "closely regulated" industries, where warrantless searches are permitted, and other businesses, where a warrant is required, is not entirely clear. In *Marshall* v. *Barlow's Inc.* (1978), the Court rejected a claim by the Secretary of Labor that warrantless searches by inspectors of the federal Occupational Health and Safety Administration (OSHA) should be permitted. The Court rejected the contention that businesses in interstate commerce, subject to OSHA's juris-

---

[6]The mere evidence rule was that items having evidential value only are not subject to seizure and must be excluded at trial. "Search warrants may not be used as a means of gaining access to a man's home . . . solely to secure evidence to be used against him in a criminal . . . proceeding" *Gouled* v. *United States* (1921).

diction, were "closely regulated" industries. It noted that in most instances, requests to search for health and safety violations in the "work" or nonpublic areas of a business were granted and that securing a warrant where consent was not forthcoming had not proved to be a significant problem. Under *Camara,* the Court noted, warrants for such searches could be secured under a "less than probable cause" standard. Justice White's opinion for the majority left open the possibility that with stronger evidence some warrantless OSHA searches might be accepted. Barlow's, Inc. was an electrical and plumbing installation business in Pocatello, Idaho, with no history of safety violations or complaints. The search to which it objected was a routine, random inspection.

There are other examples of exceptions to, or modifications of, the warrant requirement. The Court ruled, in *Wyman* v. *James* (1971), that prearranged "home visits" by welfare workers were not covered by the Fourth Amendment. And in *Terry* v. *Ohio* (1968, *infra*), it held that "stop and frisk" procedures, though governed by the Fourth Amendment, could be initiated by police officers on the basis of only reasonable suspicion. The only legitimate purpose of a "stop and frisk" procedure is to search for dangerous weapons; it is justified as a means of protecting police officers. But contraband uncovered during a legitimate "stop and frisk" is admissible as evidence in court.

Customs searches at the country's borders present a different problem. Customs officials may search any person or property entering the country. The entry of persons or property into the United States is a privilege, not a right. Such searches have long been regarded as a sovereign prerogative and "reasonable simply by virtue of the fact that they occur at the border."

It has never been thought that the reasonableness of a border or customs search depends on a showing of probable cause. This constitutional rule was upheld by the Supreme Court in *United States* v. *Ramsey* (1977), in a case that also raised First Amendment questions. The case involved government interception of some bulky letters from Thailand (a known source of narcotics) which were found to contain narcotics. There is a federal statute and also regulations that authorize customs officials to inspect incoming international mail when there is "a reasonable cause to suspect" that it contains contraband. Justice Rehnquist denied the claim of First Amendment violations, holding that the border search exception to the probable cause standards of the Fourth Amendment does not depend on whether the envelopes were carried or mailed.

Additional questions arise when searches occur near the border but not at fixed entry checkpoints. The U.S. Border Patrol has routinely used roving patrols to stop and search cars near the Canadian and Mexican borders to apprehend illegal aliens. In 1973, in *Almeida-Sanchez* v. *United States,* the Supreme Court held 5-4 that such searches were illegal in the absence of either a warrant or probable cause. But Justice Powell, in a concurring opinion, joined the four dissenters in stating that border searches pursuant to a general areawide warrant, based on less than probable cause, would be valid. In this case, Almeida-Sanchez was a Mexican citizen with a U.S. work permit and not an illegal alien. However, a search of the car in which he was riding uncovered a large quantity of marijuana. The Supreme Court held that there was insufficient cause to search the car after Almeida-Sanchez's identity had been established.

In *United States* v. *Brignoni-Ponce* (1975), the court held that stops by *roving patrol cars* required reasonable suspicion that the suspicious automobile contained illegal aliens. Mere identification of the occupants as of Mexican descent, with nothing more, was an inadequate basis for a Fourth Amendment "stop."

In *United States* v. *Ortiz* (1975), the Court held that warrantless vehicle searches at recognized traffic checkpoints must be based on consent or probable cause. However, that decision was distinguished the very next year. In *United States* v. *Martinez-Fuerte* (1976), the Supreme Court held that a vehicle could be *stopped* at a fixed checkpoint (away from the border) and its occupants briefly questioned, even though there is no basis to believe that the car contains illegal aliens. On the basis of such questioning, occupants of a car may be referred to secondary inspection areas "even if it be assumed that such referrals are made largely on the basis of apparent Mexican ancestry." No judicial warrant is required.

A related problem arises out of the common police practice of randomly stopping automobiles to check for driver's licenses and proper auto registration. In *Delaware* v. *Prouse* (1979), the Supreme Court ruled, 8-1, that it is a violation of a motorist's constitutional rights to conduct random stops merely to check for licenses and registration. Police must have an "articulable and reasonable suspicion that a motorist is unlicensed or that an automobile is unregistered, or that either the vehicle or an occupant is otherwise subject to

seizure for violation of law." A stop is a "seizure" in the constitutional sense and must be reasonable under the circumstances. States can develop appropriate methods for conducting spot checks, such as traffic roadblocks, which are less intrusive and "do not involve the unconstrained exercise of discretion." Prouse's car had been stopped randomly. As the police officer approached the car, he detected the odor of marijuana and observed a cellophane bag protruding from under a seat. The bag contained marijuana, and Prouse was indicted for violation of a state statute. However, the trial judge suppressed the evidence on the grounds that it had been illegally obtained. The Supreme Court of Delaware agreed, and the state appealed to the U.S. Supreme Court to reverse the ruling of its own supreme court. Having determined that the stop was unlawful, the Supreme Court agreed that the evidence against Prouse should be suppressed.

Several other points need be made to round out this brief picture of the law of search and seizure. One involves the question of "standing." A person must have standing to object to a search. One cannot object to a search of another's property or of property not lawfully owned or possessed. A person may not object to search of a stolen car in circumstances where the same car, if lawfully owned by the suspect, could not be searched.

Another premise of search and seizure law is the doctrine of emergency. There are some obvious circumstances when a search warrant cannot be obtained, for example, no warrant is needed to search a burning house.[7]

Finally, there is the question of entrapment. A person cannot be en-

---

[7] *Michigan* v. *Tyler* (1978).

trapped by authorities into committing a crime. But what constitutes entrapment? Where is the line to be drawn? In *United States* v. *Russell* (1973), the Supreme Court approved the use of undercover agents in combating crime even where those agents participated in the criminal act. In this case, a narcotics agent had furnished a known supplier with ingredients for manufacturing a drug that was difficult but not otherwise impossible to obtain. The supplier had previously manufactured the same drug without assistance. In upholding his conviction, the Court said that infiltration in narcotics investigations was proper; it was likewise proper, during such undercover activity, to supply "some item of value" needed by a drug ring. Agents could not instigate an illegal act with otherwise innocent persons, but the Court said that the defense of entrapment was not available to those already disposed to commit the crime. For the defense of entrapment to succeed, it must be shown that government agents actually implanted the criminal design.

In all these cases, the question was whether and when to allow exceptions to the search warrant requirement of the Fourth Amendment. In a recent case, *Zurcher* v. *The Stanford Daily* (1978), the Supreme Court was asked to declare that in certain circumstances, an otherwise valid search warrant is an *insufficient* basis on which to conduct a search because of competing constitutional claims, in this instance, the First Amendment.

In 1971, police in Palo Alto, California, obtained a search warrant to search the premises of the student newspaper at Stanford University, seeking photographs of a recent campus demonstration in which nine police officers had been injured. The

editors of the newspaper, who were not suspected of any wrongdoing, charged that their constitutional and civil rights had been violated. A federal district judge ruled that the search was unreasonable and thus violated the Fourth Amendment, declaring that in this case the important First Amendment rights involved took precedence. A search warrant should not have been issued at least until it was shown that a subpoena would not work. With a search warrant, the police can search without prior warning and notice, that is, without an opportunity for the person searched to raise objections. A subpoena can be contested in court; even if the subpoena is upheld, the evidence it seeks can be produced without allowing authorities the opportunity to fully and perhaps indiscriminately search the premises.

The Court of Appeals for the Ninth Circuit upheld this decision. But the Supreme Court reversed by a 5-3 vote. Justice White's majority opinion held that requiring a subpoena prior to authorizing a search warrant would undermine law enforcement efforts. The press is not entitled to any special warning, although White said that a magistrate considering a warrant request should consider the First Amendment implications before issuing it. Opponents feared that the decision would open the way to extensive police searches of media organization files. They noted that there were no such searches recorded for 190 years, but there have been fifteen in the last eight years (all in three states: California, Montana, and Rhode Island). The Supreme Court's decision, they predicted, would open the way for more such searches.

Congress has the power to legislate to curb search warrant abuses. Bills have been introduced that would limit both federal and state search warrants against persons *not* themselves suspected of a crime; some prospective bills would extend this protection only to members of the press not suspected of a crime.

(3) Terry v. Ohio (1968)

+Warren, Black, Harlan, Brennan, Stewart, White, Fortas, Marshall
−Douglas

[John W. Terry and his codefendants were convicted in the Cleveland Court of Common Pleas on charges of carrying concealed weapons. In a pretrial motion, they sought, unsuccessfully, to suppress the evidence because it was illegally obtained in violation of the Fourth Amendment. Their convictions were upheld by the Ohio Supreme Court. The U. S. Supreme Court granted certiorari.

The arresting officer, observing Terry and two companions repeatedly walking back and forth and looking into a store window in the middle of the afternoon, stopped the men, identified himself as a police officer, and asked for their names. When they failed to respond, he "patted them down" to determine if they were carrying any weapons, but he did not search them beneath their outer garments. Terry and one companion were carrying guns and were formally charged with that offense. The judge rejected the prosecution's contention that the guns had been seized following a search incident to a lawful arrest, since the facts demonstrated no probable cause to arrest the men. However, the judge denied the defendant's motion to suppress the evidence on the grounds that the officer had a reasonable basis for believing that the defendants were acting suspiciously and that purely for his own protection he could pat down their outer garments to see if they were armed. The court distinguished between an investigatory "stop" and an arrest, and between a "frisk" of outer clothing searching for weapons and a full search for evidence of a crime. The "frisk" was determined to be essential to the proper performance of the police officer's duties and necessary for his protection.]

MR. CHIEF JUSTICE WARREN delivered the opinion of the Court.
. . . The Fourth Amendment provides that "the right of the people to be secure in their persons, houses, papers, and effects, against unreasonable searches and seizures, shall not be violated. . . ." This inestimable right of personal security belongs as much to the citizen on the streets of our great cities as to the homeowner closeted in his study to dispose of his secret affairs. . . .

We have recently held that "the Fourth Amendment protects people, not places," *Katz* v. *United States* . . . (1967), and wherever an individual may harbor a reasonable "expectation of privacy," . . . he is entitled to be free from unreasonable governmental intrusion. Of course, the specific content and incidents of this right must be shaped by the context in which it is asserted. For "what the Constitution forbids is not all searches and seizures, but unreasonable searches and seizures." . . . Unquestionably petitioner was entitled to the protection of the Fourth Amendment as he walked down the street in Cleveland. . . . The question is whether in all the circumstances of this on-the-street encounter, his right to personal security was violated by an unreasonable search and seizure.

We would be less than candid if we did not acknowledge that this question thrusts to the fore difficult and troublesome issues regarding a sensitive area of police activity—issues which have never before been squarely presented to this Court. Reflective of the tensions involved are the practical and constitutional arguments pressed with great vigor on both sides of the public debate over the power of the police to "stop and frisk"—as it is sometimes euphemistically termed—"suspicious persons."

On the one hand, it is frequently argued that in dealing with the rapidly unfolding and often dangerous situations on city streets the police are in need of an escalating set of flexible responses, graduated in relation to the amount of information they possess. For this purpose it is urged that distinction should be made between a "stop" and an "arrest" (or a "seizure" of a person), and between a "frisk" and a "search." Thus, it is argued, the police should be allowed to "stop" a person and detain him briefly for questioning upon suspicion that he may be connected with criminal activity. Upon suspicion that the person may be armed, the police should have the power to "frisk" him for weapons. If the "stop" and the "frisk" give rise to probable cause to believe that the suspect has committed a crime, then the police should be empowered to make a formal "arrest," and a full incident "search" of the person. This scheme is justified in part upon the notion that a "stop" and a "frisk" amount to mere "minor inconvenience and petty indignity," which can properly be imposed upon the citizen in the interest of effective law enforcement on the basis of a police officer's suspicion.

On the other side the argument is made that the authority of the police must be strictly circumscribed by the law of arrest and search as it has developed to date in the traditional jurisprudence of the Fourth Amendment. . . .

In this context we approach the issues in this case mindful of the limitations of the judicial function in controlling the myriad daily situations in which policemen and citizens confront each other on the street. The State has characterized the issue here as "the right of a police officer . . . to make an on-the-street stop, interrogate and pat down for weapons. . . ." But this is only partly accurate. For the issue is not the abstract propriety of the police conduct, but the admissibility against petitioner of the evidence uncovered by the search and seizure. Ever since its inception, the rule excluding evidence seized in violation of the Fourth Amendment has been recognized as a principal mode of discouraging lawless police conduct. . . . And experience has taught that it is the only effective deterrent to police misconduct in the criminal context, and that without it the constitutional guarantee against unreasonable searches and seizures would be a mere "form of words." . . . The rule also serves another vital function—"the imperative of judicial integrity." . . . Courts which sit under our Constitution cannot and will not be made party to lawless invasions of the constitutional rights of citizens by permitting unhindered governmental use of the fruits of such invasions. Thus in our system evidentiary rulings provide the context in which the judicial process of inclusion and exclusion approves some conduct as comporting with constitutional guarantees and disapproves other actions by state agents. A ruling admitting evidence in a criminal trial, we recognize, has the necessary effect of legitimizing the conduct which produced the evidence, while an application of the exclusionary rule withholds the constitutional imprimatur.

The exclusionary rule has its limitations, however, as a tool of judicial control. It cannot properly be invoked to exclude the products of legitimate police investigative techniques on the ground that much conduct which is closely similar involves unwarranted intrusions upon constitutional protections. . . . Doubtless some police "field interrogation" conduct violates the Fourth Amendment. But a stern refusal by this Court to condone such activity does not necessarily render it responsive to the exclusionary rule. Regardless of how effective the rule may be where obtaining convictions is an important objective of the police, it is powerless to deter invasions of constitutionally guaranteed rights where the police either have no interest in prosecuting or are willing to forgo successful prosecution in the interest of serving some other goal.

Proper adjudication of cases in which the exclusionary rule is invoked demands a constant awareness of these limitations. The wholesale harassment by certain elements of the police community of which minority groups, particularly Negroes, frequently complain, will not be stopped by the exclusion of any evidence from any criminal trial. Yet a rigid and unthinking application of the exclusionary rule, in futile protest against practices which it can never be used effectively to control, may exact a high toll in human injury and frustration of efforts to prevent crime. No judicial opinion can comprehend the protean variety of the street encounter, and we can only judge the facts of the case before us. Nothing we say today is to be taken as indicating approval of police conduct outside the legitimate investigative sphere. Under our decision, courts still retain their traditional responsibility to guard against police conduct which is overbearing or harassing, or which trenches upon personal security without the objective evidentiary justification which the Constitution requires. . . .

Our first task is to establish at what point in this encounter the Fourth Amendment becomes relevant. . . . There is some suggestion in the use of such terms as "stop" and "frisk" that such police conduct is outside the purview of the Fourth Amendment because neither action rises to the level of a "search" or "seizure" within the meaning of the Constitution. We emphatically reject this notion. It is quite plain that the Fourth Amendment governs "seizures" of the person which do not eventuate in a trip to the station house and prosecution for crime—"arrests" in traditional terminology. It must be recognized that whenever a police officer accosts an individual and restrains his freedom to walk away, he has "seized" that person. And it is nothing less than sheer torture of the English language to suggest that a careful exploration of the outer surfaces of a person's clothing all over his or her body in an attempt to find weapons is not a "search." Moreover, it is simply fantastic to urge that such a procedure performed in public by a policeman while the citizen stands helpless, perhaps facing a wall with his hands raised, is a "petty indignity." It is a serious intrusion upon the sanctity of the person, which may inflict great indignity and arouse strong resentment, and it is not to be undertaken lightly. . . .

In this case there can be no question, then, that Officer McFadden "seized" petitioner and subjected him to a "search" when he took hold of him and patted down the outer surfaces of his clothing. We must decide whether at that point it was reasonable for Officer McFadden to have interfered with petitioner's personal security as he did. . . .

[W]e consider first the nature and extent of the governmental interests involved. One general interest is of course that of effective crime prevention and detection; it is this interest which underlies the recognition that a police officer may in appropriate circumstances and in an appropriate manner approach a person for purposes of investigating possible criminal behavior even though there is no probable cause to make an arrest. It was this legitimate investigative function Officer McFadden was discharging when he decided to approach petitioner and his companions. . . . It would have been poor police work indeed for an officer of 30 years' experience in the detection of thievery from stores in this same neighborhood to have failed to investigate this behavior further. . . .

In view of these facts, we cannot blind ourselves to the need for law enforcement officers to protect themselves and other prospective victims of violence in situations where they may lack probable cause for an arrest. When an officer is justified in believing that the individual whose suspicious behavior he is investigating at close range is armed and presently dangerous to the officer or to others, it would appear to be clearly unreasonable to deny the officer the power to take necessary measures to determine whether the person is in fact carrying a weapon and to neutralize the threat of physical harm. . . .

Petitioner does not argue that a police officer should refrain from making any investigation of suspicious circumstances until such time as he has probable cause to make an arrest; nor does he deny that police officers in properly discharging their investigative function may find themselves confronting persons who might well be armed and dangerous. Moreover, he does not say that an officer is always unjustified in searching a suspect to discover weapons. Rather, he says it is unreasonable for the policeman to take that step until

such time as the situation evolves to a point where there is probable cause to make an arrest. . . .

Our evaluation of the proper balance that has to be struck in this type of case leads us to conclude that there must be a narrowly drawn authority to permit a reasonable search for weapons for the protection of the police officer, where he has reason to believe that he is dealing with an armed and dangerous individual, regardless of whether he has probable cause to arrest the individual for a crime. The officer need not be absolutely certain that the individual is armed; the issue is whether a reasonably prudent man in the circumstances would be warranted in the belief that his safety or that of others was in danger. . . . And in determining whether the officer acted reasonably in such circumstances, due weight must be given, not to his inchoate and unparticularized suspicion or "hunch," but to the specific reasonable inferences which he is entitled to draw from the facts in light of his experience. . . .

We need not develop at length in this case, however, the limitations which the Fourth Amendment places upon a protective seizure and search for weapons. These limitations will have to be developed in the concrete factual circumstances of individual cases. . . . Suffice it to note that such a search, unlike a search without a warrant incident to a lawful arrest, is not justified by any need to prevent the disappearance or destruction of evidence of crime. . . . The sole justification is the protection of the police officer and others nearby, and it must therefore be confined in scope to an intrusion reasonably designed to discover guns, knives, clubs, or other hidden instruments for the assault of the police officer. . . .

We merely hold today that where a

police officer observes unusual conduct which leads him reasonably to conclude in light of his experience that criminal activity may be afoot and that the persons with whom he is dealing may be armed and presently dangerous; where in the course of investigating this behavior he identifies himself as a policeman and makes reasonable inquiries; and where nothing in the initial stages of the encounter serves to dispel his reasonable fear for his own or others' safety, he is entitled for the protection of himself and others in the area to conduct a carefully limited search of the outer clothing of such persons in an attempt to discover weapons which might be used to assault him. Such a search is a reasonable search under the Fourth Amendment, and any weapons seized may properly be introduced in evidence against the person from whom they were taken.

Affirmed.

MR. JUSTICE HARLAN, CONCURRING (OMITTED).
MR. JUSTICE BLACK, CONCURRING (OMITTED).
MR. JUSTICE WHITE, CONCURRING (OMITTED).

MR. JUSTICE DOUGLAS, DISSENTING.

I agree that petitioner was "seized" within the meaning of the Fourth Amendment. I also agree that frisking petitioner and his companions for guns was a "search." But it is a mystery how that "search" and that "seizure" can be constitutional by Fourth Amendment standards, unless there was "probable cause" to believe that (1) a crime had been committed or (2) a crime was in the process of being committed or (3) a crime was about to be committed.

The opinion of the Court disclaims the existence of "probable cause." If loitering were an issue and that was

the offense charged, there would be "probable cause" shown. But the crime here is carrying concealed weapons; and there is no basis for concluding that the officer had "probable cause" for believing that crime was being committed. Had a warrant been sought, a magistrate would, therefore, have been unauthorized to issue one, for he can act only if there is a showing of "probable cause." We hold today that the police have greater authority to make a "seizure" and conduct a "search" than a judge has to authorize such action. We have said precisely the opposite over and over again. . . .

To give the police greater power than a magistrate is to take a long step down the totalitarian path. Perhaps such a step is desirable to cope with modern forms of lawlessness. But if it is taken, it should be the deliberate choice of the people through a constitutional amendment. Until the Fourth Amendment, which is closely allied with the Fifth, is rewritten, the person and the effects of the individual are beyond the reach of all government agencies until there are reasonable grounds to believe (probable cause) that a criminal venture has been launched or is about to be launched. . . .

(4) United States v. Robinson (1973)

+Burger, Stewart, White, Blackmun, Powell, Rehnquist
−Douglas, Brennan, Marshall

[On April 12, 1968, at approximately 11 o'clock P.M., Officer Richard Jenks, a 15-year veteran of the District of Columbia Metropolitan Police Department, observed Willie Robinson driving a 1965 Cadillac. As a result of a previous investigation following a check of Robnson's operator's permit four days earlier, Jenks determined that there was reason to believe that Robinson was operating a motor vehicle after revocation of his license. Jenks signaled the respondent to stop the automobile, which Robinson did, and all three occupants emerged from the car. At that point, Jenks informed Robinson that he was under arrest for "operating after revocation and obtaining a permit by misrepresentation." It was subsequently conceded by Robinson, and assumed by the court of appeals, that Jenks had probable cause to arrest Robinson and that he had effected a full custody arrest.

In accordance with prescribed procedures, Jenks began to search Robinson. During the "face-to-face patdown," Jenks felt an object in the left breast pocket of the heavy coat Robinson was wearing. Jenks later testified that he "couldn't tell what it was" and also that he "couldn't actually tell the size of it." Jenks then reached into the pocket and pulled out the object, which turned out to be a "crumpled-up cigarette package." Jenks testified that at that point he still did not know what was in the package: "As I felt the package I could feel objects in the package but I couldn't tell what they were, . . . I knew they weren't cigarettes." Jenks then opened the cigarette pack and found fourteen gelatin capsules of white powder which he thought to be, and which later analysis showed to be, heroin. The heroin was seized and used as evidence in Robinson's conviction for possession and facilitation of concealment of heroin.

Robinson appealed, and the court of appeals remanded the case for an evidentiary hearing on the scope of the search. The district court found that the evidence was admissible, but the court of appeals, sitting *en banc,* reversed. It held that the search that produced the heroin was in violation of the Fourth Amendment. The Supreme Court granted certiorari.]

MR. JUSTICE REHNQUIST delivered the opinion of the Court.

. . .

It is well settled that a search incident to a lawful arrest is a traditional exception to the warrant requirement of the Fourth Amendment. This general exception has historically been formulated into two distinct propositions. The first is that a search may be made of the *person* of the arrestee by virtue of the lawful arrest. The second is that a search may be made of the area within the control of the arrestee.

Examination of this Court's decisions in the area show that these two propositions have been treated quite differently. The validity of the search of a person incident to a lawful arrest has been regarded as settled from its first enunciation, and has remained virtually unchallenged until the present case. The validity of the second proposition, while likewise conceded in principle, has been subject to differing interpretations as to the extent of the area which may be searched.

. . .

The justification or reason for the authority to search incident to a lawful arrest rests quite as much on the need to disarm the suspect in order to take him into custody as it does on the need to preserve evidence on his person for later use at trial. . . . The standards traditionally governing a search incident to lawful arrest are not, therefore, commuted to the stricter *Terry* standards by the absence of probable fruits or further evidence of the particular crime for which the arrest is made.

Nor are we inclined, on the basis of what seems to us to be a rather speculative judgment, to qualify the breadth of the general authority to search incident to a lawful custodial arrest on an assumption that persons arrested for the offense of driving while their license has been revoked are less likely to be possessed of dangerous weapons than are those arrested for other crimes. It is scarcely open to doubt that the danger to an officer is far greater in the case of the extended exposure which follows the taking of a suspect into custody and transporting him to the police station than in the case of the relatively fleeting contact resulting from the typical *Terry*-type stop. This is an adequate basis for treating all custodial arrests alike for purposes of search justification.

But quite apart from these distinctions, our more fundamental disagreement with the Court of Appeals arises from its suggestion that there must be litigated in each case the issue of whether or not there was present one of the reasons supporting the authority for a search of the person incident to a lawful arrest. We do not think the long line of authorities of this Court dating back to *Weeks,* nor what we can glean from the history of practice in this country and in England, requires such a case by case adjudication. A police officer's determination as to how and where to search the person of a suspect whom he has arrested is necessarily a quick *ad hoc* judgment which the Fourth Amendment does not require to be broken down in each instance into an analysis of each step in the search. The authority to search the person incident to a lawful custodial arrest, while based upon the need to disarm and to discover evidence, does not depend on what a court may later decide was the probability in a particular arrest situation that weapons or evidence would in fact be found upon the person of the suspect. A custodial arrest of a suspect based on probable cause is a reasonable intrusion under the Fourth Amendment; that intrusion being lawful, a search incident to the arrest requires no additional justification. It is the fact of the lawful arrest which establishes the authority to search, and we hold that in the case of a lawful custodial arrest a full search of the person is not only an exception to the warrant requirement of the Fourth Amendment, but is also a "reasonable" search under that Amendment.

The search of respondent's person conducted by Officer Jenks in this case and the seizure from him of the heroin, were permissible under established Fourth Amendment law. While thorough, the search partook of none of the extreme or patently abusive characteristics which were held to violate the Due Process Clause of the Fourteenth Amendment in *Rochin* v. *California* . . . (1952). Since it is the fact of custodial arrest which gives rise to the authority to search, it is of no moment that Jenks did not indicate any subjectve fear of the respondent or that he did not himself suspect that respondent was armed. Having in the course of a lawful search come upon the crumpled package of cigarettes, he was entitled to inspect it; and when his inspection revealed the heroin capsules, he was entitled to seize them as "fruits, instrumentalities, or contraband" probative of criminal conduct. . . . The judgment of the Court of Appeals holding otherwise is *Reversed*.

MR. JUSTICE POWELL CONCURRING.

. . .

The Fourth Amendment safeguards the right of "the people to be secure in their persons, houses, papers, and effects, against unreasonable searches and seizures. . . ." These are areas of an individual's life about which he entertains legitimate expectations of privacy. I believe that an individual lawfully subjected to a custodial arrest retains no significant Fourth Amendment interest in the privacy of his person. . . . If the arrest is lawful, the privacy interest guarded by the Fourth Amendment is subordinated to a legitimate and overriding governmental concern. No reason then exists to frustrate law enforcement by requiring some independent justification for a search incident to a lawful custodial arrest. . . .

MR. JUSTICE MARSHALL, WITH WHOM MR. JUSTICE DOUGLAS AND MR. JUSTICE BRENNAN JOIN, DISSENTING.

Certain fundamental principles have characterized this Court's Fourth Amendment jurisprudence over the years. Perhaps the most basic of these was expressed by Mr. Justice Butler, speaking for a unanimous Court in *Go-Bart Co.* v. *United States* . . . (1931): "There is no formula for the determination of reasonableness. Each case is to be decided on its own facts and circumstances." . . .

The majority's approach represents a clear and marked departure from our long tradition of case-by-case adjudication of the reasonableness of searches and seizures under the Fourth Amendment. I continue to believe that "[t]he scheme of the Fourth Amendment becomes meaningful only when it is assured that at some point the conduct of those charged with enforcing the laws can be subjected to the more detached, neutral scrutiny of a judge who must evaluate the reasonableness of a particular search or seizure in light of the particular circumstances." *Terry* v. *Ohio* . . . (1968). Because I find the majority's reasoning to be at odds with these fundamental principles, I must respectfully dissent. . . .

. . .

In the vast majority of cases, the determination of when the right of privacy must reasonably yield to the right of search is required to be made by a neutral judicial officer before the search is conducted. . . . The Constitution requires "that the deliberate, impartial judgment of a judicial officer . . . be interposed between the citizen and the police. . . ." *Wong Sun* v. *United States* . . . (1963).

The requirement that the police seek prior approval of a search from a judicial officer is, no doubt, subject to "a few specifically established and well-delineated exceptions," *Katz* v. *United States* . . . But because an exception is invoked to justify a search without a warrant does not preclude further judicial inquiry into the reasonableness of that search. It is the role of the judiciary, not of police officers, to delimit the scope of exceptions to the warrant requirement. . . . Exceptions to the warrant requirement are not talismans precluding further judicial inquiry whenever they are invoked, . . . but rather are "jealously and carefully drawn." . . .

The majority also suggests that the Court of Appeals reached a novel and unprecedented result by imposing qualifications on the historically recognized authority to conduct a full search incident to a lawful arrest. Nothing could be further from the truth, as the Court of Appeals itself was so careful to point out.

One need not go back to Blackstone's Commentaries, Holmes' Common Law, or Pollock and Maitland in search of precedent for the approach adopted by the Court of Appeals. Indeed, given that mass production of the automobile did not begin until the early decades of the present century, I find it somewhat puzzling that the majority even looks to these sources for guidance on the only question presented in this case:

the permissible scope of a search of the person incident to a lawful arrest for violation of a motor vehicle regulation. The fact is that this question has been considered by several state and federal courts, the vast majority of which have held that absent special circumstances a police officer has no right to conduct a full search to the person incident to a lawful arrest for violation of a motor vehicle regulation.

In *Barnes* v. *State* . . . (1964), for example, police officers stopped a car for a brake light violation. Rather than simply issue a citation, the officers placed the driver under arrest. A full search of the driver's person was then conducted, including shining a flashlight into his overcoat pocket, disclosing a small quantity of marihuana and a package of cigarette papers. The Supreme Court of Wisconsin held the search of the driver's pocket unreasonable. While expressly holding that where a traffic offender is actually arrested, as distinguished from being given a summons, it is reasonable for the arresting officer to search his person for weapons, nevertheless the court held it unreasonable to look inside the driver's overcoat pocket with a flashlight. "We cannot conceive," the court said, "that this aspect of the search was a legitimate search for weapons. . . . We reject the state's contention that any search of the person of one lawfully arrested is a valid search." . . .

The majority's attempt to avoid case-by-case adjudication of Fourth Amendment issues is not only misguided as a matter or principle, but is also doomed to fail as a matter of practical application. As the majority itself is well aware, . . . the powers granted the police in this case are strong ones, subject to potential abuse. Although, in this particular case, Officer Jenks was required by Police Department regulations to make an in-custody arrest rather than to issue a citation, in most jurisdictions and for most traffic offenses the determination of whether to issue a citation or effect a full arrest is discretionary with the officer. There is always the possibility that a police officer, lacking probable cause to obtain a search warrant, will use a traffic arrest as a pretext to conduct a search. . . . I suggest this possibility not to impugn the integrity of our police, but merely to point out that case-by-case adjudication will always be necessary to determine whether a full arrest was effected for purely legitimate reasons or, rather, as a pretext for searching the arrestee. . . .

The majority states that "a police officer's determination as to how and where to search the person of a suspect whom he has arrested is necessarily a quick ad hoc judgment which the Fourth Amendment does not require to be broken down in each instance into an analysis for each step in the search." . . . No precedent is cited for this broad assertion—not surprisingly, since there is none. Indeed, we only recently rejected such "a rigid all-or-nothing model of justification and regulation under the Amendment, [for] it obscures the utility of limitations upon the scope, as well as the initiation, of police action as a means of constitutional regulation. This Court has held in the past that a search which is reasonable at its inception may violate the Fourth Amendment by virtue of its intolerable intensity and scope." *Terry* v. *Ohio* . . . As we there concluded, "in determining whether the seizure and search were 'unreasonable' our inquiry is a dual one—whether the officer's action was justified at its inception, and whether it was reasonably related in scope to the circumstances which justified the interference in the first place." . . .

. . .

The Government does not now contend that the search of respondent's pocket can be justified by any need to find and seize evidence in order to prevent its concealment or destruction, for as the Court of Appeals found, there is no evidence or fruits of the offense with which respondent was charged. The only rationale for a search in this case, then, is the removal of weapons which the arrestee might use to harm the officer and attempt an escape. This rationale, of course, is identical to the rationale of the search permitted in *Terry*. . . . Since the underlying rationale of a *Terry* search and the search of a traffic violator are identical, the Court of Appeals held that the scope of the searches must be the same. And in view of its conclusion that the removal of the object from respondent's coat pocket exceeded the scope of a lawful *Terry* frisk, a conclusion not disputed by the Government nor challenged by the majority here, the plurality of the Court of Appeals held that the removal of the package exceeded the scope of a lawful search incident to arrest of a traffic violator.

. . .

. . . *Terry* did not permit an officer to conduct a weapons frisk of anyone he lawfully stopped on the street, but rather, only where "he has reason to believe that he is dealing with an armed and dangerous individual. . . ." . . . While the policeman who arrests a suspected rapist or robber may well have reason to believe he is dealing with an armed and dangerous

person, certainly this does not hold true with equal force with respect to persons arrested for motor vehicle violations of the sort involved in this case.

. . .

(5) Michigan v. Tyler (1978)

+Burger, Stewart, Blackmun, Powell, Stevens
±White, Marshall
−Rehnquist
NP Brennan

[Tyler and his business partner were convicted of conspiracy to burn the furniture store that they jointly operated. The fire department investigator arrived at the scene of the fire about 2:00 A.M. Two plastic containers of a flammable liquid had been found, and arson was suspected. By 4:00 A.M. the heat and smoke were still too intense to permit a search for further evidence. Investigators returned at 8:00 A.M. to continue their search. Further searches were conducted, off and on, over the next several days. No search warrants were sought or issued. The Michigan Supreme Court reversed the convictions, holding that the warrantless searches were unconstitutional and that the evidence secured by these searches was inadmissible. The Supreme Court granted certiorari.]

MR. JUSTICE STEWART delivered the opinion of the Court.

. . . The decisions of this Court firmly establish that the Fourth Amendment extends beyond the paradigmatic entry into a private dwelling by a law enforcement officer in search of the fruits or instrumentalities of crime. As this Court stated in *Camara* v. *Municipal Court*, . . . the "basic purpose of this Amendment . . . is to safeguard the privacy and security of individuals against arbitrary invasions by government officials." The officials may be health, fire, or building inspectors. Their purpose may be to locate and abate a suspected public nuisance, or simply to perform a routine periodic inspection. The privacy that is invaded may be sheltered by the walls of a warehouse or other commercial establishment not open to the public. . . . These deviations from the typical police search are thus clearly within the protection of the Fourth Amendment.

The petitioner argues, however, that an entry to investigate the cause of a recent fire is outside that protection because no individual privacy interests are threatened. If the occupant of the premises set the blaze, then, in the words of the petitioner's brief, his "actions show that he has no expectation of privacy" because "he has abandoned those premises within the meaning of the Fourth Amendment." And if the fire had other causes, "the occupants of the premises are treated as victims by police and fire officials." In the petitioner's view, "[t]he likelihood that they will be aggrieved by a possible intrusion into what remains of their privacy in badly burned premises is negligible."

This argument is not persuasive. For even if the petitioner's contention that arson establishes abandonment be accepted, its second proposition— that innocent fire victims inevitably have no protectible expectations of privacy in whatever remains of their property—is contrary to common experience. People may go on living in their homes or working in their offices after a fire. Even when it is impossible, private effects often remain on the fire-damaged premises. The petitioner may be correct in the view that most innocent fire victims are treated courteously and welcome inspections of their property to ascertain the origin of the blaze, but "even if true, [this contention] is irrelevant to the question whether the . . . inspection is reasonable within the meaning of the Fourth Amendment." *Camara* . . . Once it is recognized that innocent fire victims retain the protection of the Fourth Amendment, the rest of the petitioner's argument unravels. For it is of course impossible to justify a warrantless search on the ground of abandonment by arson when that arson has not yet been proved, and a conviction cannot be used ex post facto to validate the introduction of evidence used to secure that same conviction.

Thus, there is no diminution in a person's reasonable expectation of privacy nor in the protection of the Fourth Amendment simply because the official conducting the search wears the uniform of a firefighter rather than a policeman, or because his purpose is to ascertain the cause of a fire rather than to look for evidence of a crime, or because the fire might have been started deliberately. Searches for administrative purposes, like searches for evidence of crime, are encompassed by the Fourth Amendment. And under that Amendment, "one governing principle, justified by history and by current experience, has consistently been followed: except in certain carefully defined classes of cases, a search of private property without proper consent is 'unreasonable' unless it has been authorized by a valid search warrant." . . . The showing of probable cause necessary to secure a warrant may vary with the object and intrusiveness of the search, but the necessity for the warrant persists.

The petitioner argues that no purpose would be served by requiring warrants to investigate the cause of a fire. This argument is grounded on the premise that the only fact that need be shown to justify an investigatory search is that a fire of undetermined origin has occurred on those premises. The petitioner contends that his consideration distinguishes this case from *Camara,* which concerned the necessity for warrants to conduct routine building inspections. Whereas the occupant of premises subjected to an unexpected building inspection may have no way of knowing the purpose or lawfulness of the entry, it is argued that the occupant of burned premises can hardly question the factual basis for fire officials wanting access to his property. And whereas a magistrate performs the significant function of assuring that an agency's decision to conduct a routine inspection of a particular dwelling conforms with reasonable legislative or administrative standards, he can do little more than rubber stamp an application to search fire-damaged premises for the cause of the blaze. In short, where the justification for the search is as simple and as obvious to everyone as the fact of a recent fire, a magistrate's review would be a time-consuming formality of negligible protection to the occupant.

The petitioner's argument fails primarily because it is built on a faulty premise. To secure a warrant to investigate the cause of a fire, an official must show more than the bare fact that a fire has occurred. The magistrate's duty is to assure that the proposed search will be reasonable, a determination that requires inquiry into the need for the intrusion on the one hand, and the threat of disruption to the occupant on the other. For routine building inspections, a reasonable balance between these competing concerns is usually achieved by broad legislative or administrative guidelines specifying the purpose, frequency, scope, and manner of conducting the inspections. In the context of investigatory fire searches, which are not programmatic but are responsive to individual events, a more particularized inquiry may be necessary. The number of prior entries, the scope of the search, the time of day when it is proposed to be made, the lapse of time since the fire, the continued use of the building, and the owner's efforts to secure it against intruders might all be relevant factors. Even though a fire victim's privacy must normally yield to the vital social objective of ascertaining the cause of the fire, the magistrate can perform the important function of preventing harassment by keeping that invasion to a minimum. . . .

In addition, even if fire victims can be deeply aware of the factual justification for investigatory searches, it does not follow that they will also recognize the legal authority for such searches. As the Court stated in *Camara,* "when the inspector demands entry [without a warrant], the occupant has no way of knowing whether enforcement of the municipal code involved requires inspection of his premises, no way of knowing the lawful limits of the inspector's power to search, and no way of knowing whether the inspector himself is acting under proper authorization." . . . Thus, a major function of the warrant is to provide the property owner with sufficient information to reassure him of the entry's legality. . . .

In short, the warrant requirement provides significant protection for fire victims in this context, just as it does for property owners faced with routine building inspections. As a general matter, then, official entries to investigate the cause of a fire must adhere to the warrant procedures of the Fourth Amendment. In the words of the Michigan Supreme Court: "Where the cause [of the fire] is undetermined, and the purpose of the investigation is to determine the cause and to prevent such fires from occurring or recurring, a . . . search may be conducted pursuant to a warrant issued in accordance with reasonable legislative or administrative standards or, absent their promulgation, judicially prescribed standards; if evidence of wrongdoing is discovered, it may, of course, be used to establish probable cause for the issuance of a criminal investigative search warrant or in prosecution." But "[i]f the authorities are seeking evidence to be used in a criminal prosecution, the usual standard [of probable cause] will apply." . . . Since all the entries in this case were "without proper consent" and were not "authorized by a valid search warrant," each one is illegal unless it falls within one of the "certain carefully defined classes of cases" for which warrants are not mandatory. . . .

Our decisions have recognized that a warrantless entry by criminal law enforcement officials may be legal when there is compelling need for official action and no time to secure a warrant. *Warden* v. *Hayden* . . . (warrantless entry of house by police in hot pursuit of armed robber); *Ker* v. *California* . . . (warrantless and unannounced entry of dwelling by police to prevent imminent destruction of evidence). Similarly, in the regulatory field, our cases have recognized the importance of "prompt inspections, even without a warrant, . . . in emergency situations." *Camara*, . . .

A burning building clearly presents an exigency of sufficient proportions to render a warrantless entry "reasonable." Indeed, it would defy reason to suppose that firemen must secure a warrant or consent before entering a burning structure to put out the blaze. And once in a building for this purpose, firefighters may seize evidence of arson that is in plain view. . . . Thus, the Fourth and Fourteenth Amendments were not violated by the entry of the firemen to extinguish the fire at Tyler's Auction, nor by Chief See's removal of the two plastic containers of flammable liquid found on the floor of one of the showrooms.

Although the Michigan Supreme Court appears to have accepted this principle, its opinion may be read as holding that the exigency justifying a warrantless entry to fight a fire ends, and the need to get a warrant begins, with the dousing of the last flame. . . . We think this view of the firefighting function is unrealistically narrow, however. Fire officials are charged not only with extinguishing fires, but with finding their causes. Prompt determination of the fire's origin may be necessary to prevent its recurrence, as through the detection of continuing dangers such as faulty wiring or a defective furnace. Immediate investigation may also be necessary to preserve evidence from intentional or accidental destruction. And, of course, the sooner the officials complete their duties, the less will be their subsequent interference with the privacy and the recovery efforts of the victims. For these reasons, officials need no warrant to remain in a building for a reasonable time to investigate the cause of a blaze after it has been extinguished. And if the warrantless entry to put out the fire and determine its cause is constitutional, the warrantless seizure of evidence while inspecting the premises for these purposes also is constitutional.

The respondents argue, however,

that the Michigan Supreme Court was correct in holding that the departure by the fire officials from Tyler's Auction at 4 A.M. ended any license they might have had to conduct a warrantless search. Hence, they say that even if the firemen might have been entitled to remain in the building without a warrant to investigate the cause of the fire, their departure and re-entry four hours later that morning required a warrant.

On the facts of this case, we do not believe that a warrant was necessary for the early morning re-entries on January 22. As the fire was being extinguished, Chief See and his assistants began their investigation, but visibility was severely hindered by darkness, steam, and smoke. Thus they departed at 4 A.M. and returned shortly after daylight to continue their investigation. Little purpose would have been served by their remaining in the building, except to remove any doubt about the legality of the warrantless search and seizure later that same morning. Under these circumstances, we find that the morning entries were no more than an actual continuation of the first, and the lack of a warrant thus did not invalidate the resulting seizure of evidence.

The entries occurring after January 22, however, were clearly detached from the initial exigency and warrantless entry. Since all of these searches were conducted without valid warrants and without consent, they were invalid under the Fourth and Fourteenth Amendments, and any evidence obtained as a result of those entries must, therefore, be excluded at the respondents' retrial.

In summation, we hold than an entry to fight a fire requires no warrant, and that once in the building, officials may remain there for a rea-sonable time to investigate the cause of the blaze. Thereafter, additional entries to investigate the cause of the fire must be made pursuant to the warrant procedures governing administrative searches . . . Evidence of arson discovered in the course of such investigations is admissible at trial, but if the investigating officials find probable cause to believe that arson has occurred and require further access to gather evidence for a possible prosecution, they may obtain a warrant only upon a traditional showing of probable cause applicable to searches for evidence of crime. . . .

These principles require that we affirm the judgment of the Michigan Supreme Court ordering a new trial.

Affirmed.

. . .

MR. JUSTICE BRENNAN TOOK NO PART IN THE CONSIDERATION OR DECISION OF THIS CASE.

MR. JUSTICE STEVENS, CONCURRING IN PART AND CONCURRING IN THE JUDG-MENT (OMITTED).

MR. JUSTICE WHITE WITH WHOM MR. JUSTICE MARSHALL JOINS, CONCUR-RING IN PART AND DISSENTING IN PART.

. . .

The Michigan Supreme Court found that the warrantless searches, at 8 and 9 A.M. were not, in fact, continuations of the earlier entry under exigent circumstances and therefore ruled inadmissible all evidence derived from those searches. The Court offers no sound basis for over-turning this conclusion of the state court that the subsequent re-entries were distinct from the original entry. Even if, under the Court's "reasonable time" criterion, the firemen might have stayed in the building for an additional four hours—a proposition which is by no means clear—the fact remains that the firemen did not choose to remain and continue their search, but instead locked the door and departed from the premises entirely. The fact that the firemen were willing to leave demonstrates that the exigent circumstances justifying their original warrantless entry were no longer present. . . .

. . .

To hold that some subsequent re-entries are "continuations" of earlier ones will not aid firemen, but confuse them for it will be difficult to predict in advance how a court might view a re-entry. In the end, valuable evidence may be excluded for failure to seek a warrant that might have easily been obtained.

Those investigating fires and their causes deserve a clear demarcation of the constitutional limits of their authority. Today's opinion recognizes the need for speed and focuses attention on fighting an ongoing blaze. The fire truck need not stop at the courthouse in rushing to the flames. But once the fire has been extinguished and the firemen have left the premises, the emergency is over. Further intrusion on private property can and should be accompanied by a warrant indicating the authority under which the firemen presumed to enter and search.

. . .

MR. JUSTICE REHNQUIST, DISSENTING.

I agree with my Brother Stevens, for the reasons expressed in his dissenting opinion in *Marshall* v. *Barlow's, Inc.* . . . (1978) . . . that the "Warrant Clause has no application to routine, regulatory inspections of commercial premises." Since in my opinion the searches involved in this case fall within that category, I think the only appropriate inquiry is whether they were reasonable. The Court does not dispute that the en-

tries which occurred at the time of the fire and the next morning were entirely justified, and I see nothing to indicate that the subsequent searches were not also eminently reasonable in light of all the circumstances. . . .

(6) Mapp v. Ohio (1961)

+Warren, Black, Douglas, Clark, Brennan
±Stewart
−Frankfurter, Harlan, Whittaker

[In 1957, three Cleveland police officers forcibly entered the residence of Miss Dollree Mapp, seeking a person wanted in connection with a recent bombing. They also had information that a large amount of gambling equipment was in the house. The officers had no valid search warrant, and when Miss Mapp resisted, she was roughed up and arrested. The officers conducted a full search of the house. No evidence of gambling was discovered, but the officers did uncover some obscene books and pictures. Miss Mapp was tried and convicted of possession of obscene materials and sentenced to one to seven years in prison. The conviction was affirmed by the Ohio Supreme Court. The case came to the Supreme Court on appeal.]

MR. JUSTICE CLARK delivered the opinion of the Court.

. . . The state says that even if the search were made without authority, or otherwise unreasonably, it is not prevented from using the unconstitutionally seized evidence at trial, citing *Wolf* v. *Colorado* (1949) . . . in which this Court did indeed hold "that in a prosecution in a State court for a State crime the Fourteenth Amendment does not forbid the admission of evidence obtained by an unreasonable search and seizure." . . .

In 1949 . . . this Court, in *Wolf* . . .

for the first time, discussed the effect of the Fourth Amendment upon the States through the operation of the Due Process Clause of the Fourteenth Amendment. It said:

> [W]e have no hesitation in saying that were a State affirmatively to sanction such police incursion into privacy it would run counter to the guaranty of the Fourteenth Amendment.

Nevertheless, after declaring that the "security of one's privacy against arbitrary intrusion by the police" is "implicit in the 'concept of ordered liberty' and as such enforceable against the States through the Due Process Clause," cf. *Palko* v. *State of Connecticut* . . . and announcing that it "stoutly adhere[d]" to the *Weeks** decision, the Court decided that the *Weeks* exclusionary rule would not then be imposed upon the States as "an essential ingredient of the right." . . .

The Court in *Wolf* first stated that "[t]he contrariety of views of the States" on the adoption of the exclusionary rule of *Weeks* was "particularly impressive" . . . and, in this connection, that it could not "brush aside the experience of States which deem the incidence of such conduct by the police too slight to call for a deterrent remedy . . . by overriding the [States'] relevant rules of evidence." . . . While in 1949, prior to the *Wolf* case, almost two-thirds of the States were opposed to the use of the exclusionary rule, now, despite the *Wolf* case, more than half of those since passing upon it, by their own legislative or judicial decision. have wholly or partly adopted or adhered to the *Weeks* rule. . . . We note that the second basis elaborated in *Wolf* in support of its failure to enforce the exclusionary doctrine against the States was that "other means of protection" have been afforded "the right to privacy." . . . The experience of California that such other remedies have been worthless and futile is buttressed by the experience of other States. The obvious futility of relegating the Fourth Amendment to the protection of other remedies, has, moreover, been recognized by this Court since *Wolf*. . . .

Likewise, time has set its face against what *Wolf* called the "weighty testimony" of *People* v. *Defore*, 1926. . . . There Justice (then Judge) Cardozo, rejecting adoption of the *Weeks* exclusionary rule in New York, had said that "[t]he Federal rule as it stands is either too strict or too lax." . . . However, the force of that reasoning has been largely vitiated by later decisions of this Court. These include the recent discarding of the "silver platter" doctrine which allowed federal judicial use of evidence seized in violation of the Constitution by state agents, *Elkins* v. *United States* . . . ; the relaxation of the formerly strict requirements as to standing to challenge the use of evidence thus seized, so that now the procedure of exclusion, "ultimately referable to constitutional safeguards," is available to anyone even "legitimately on [the] premises" unlawfully searched . . . ; and finally, the formulation of a method to prevent state use of evidence unconstitutionally seized by federal agents, *Rea* v. *United States* (1956). . . .

It, therefore, plainly appears that the factual considerations supporting

---

Weeks v. *United States* (1914), in which the Supreme Court ruled that evidence illegally obtained in violation of the Fourth Amendment must be excluded from *federal* trials.—Ed.

the failure of the *Wolf* Court to include the *Weeks* exclusionary rule when it recognized the enforceability of the right to privacy against the States in 1949, while not basically relevant to the constitutional consideration, could not . . . now be deemed controlling.

Some five years after *Wolf* in answer to a plea made here Term after Term that we overturn its doctrine on applicability of the *Weeks* exclusionary rule, this Court indicated that such should not be done until the States had "adequate opportunity to adopt or reject the [*Weeks*] rule." . . .

Today, we once again examine *Wolf*'s constitutional documentation of the right to privacy free from unreasonable state intrusion, and, after its dozen years on our books, are led by it to close the only courtroom door remaining open to evidence secured by official lawlessness in flagrant abuse of that basic right, reserved to all persons as a specific guarantee against that very same unlawful conduct. We hold that all evidence obtained by searches and seizures in violation of the Constitution is, by that same authority, inadmissible in a state court.

Since the Fourth Amendment's right of privacy has been declared enforceable against the States through the Due Process Clause of the Fourteenth, it is enforceable against them by the same sanction of exclusion as is used against the Federal Government. Were it otherwise, then just as without the *Weeks* rule the assurance against unreasonable federal searches and seizures would be "a form of words," valueless and undeserving of mention in a perpetual charter of inestimable human liberties, so too, without that rule the freedom from state invasions of privacy would be so ephemeral and so nearly severed from its conceptual nexus with the freedom from all brutish means of coercing evidence as not to merit this Court's high regard as a freedom "implicit in 'the concept of ordered liberty.' " . . . To hold otherwise is to grant the right but in reality to withhold its privilege and enjoyment. Only last year the Court itself recognized that the purpose of the exclusionary rule "is to deter—to compel respect for the constitutional guaranty in the only effectively available way—by removing the incentive to disregard it." . . .

Moreover, our holding that the exclusionary rule is an essential part of both the Fourth and Fourteenth Amendments is not only the logical dictate of prior cases, but it also makes very good sense. There is no war between the Constitution and common sense. Presently, a federal prosecutor may make no use of evidence illegally seized, but a State's attorney across the street may, although he supposedly is operating under the enforceable prohibitions of the same Amendment. Thus, the State, by admitting evidence unlawfully seized, serves to encourage disobedience to the Federal Constitution which it is bound to uphold. Moreover . . . , "[t]he very essence of a healthy federalism depends upon the avoidance of needless conflict between state and federal courts." . . .

Federal-state cooperation in the solution of crime under constitutional standards will be promoted, if only by recognition of their now mutual obligation to respect the same fundamental criteria in their approaches. "However much in a particular case insistence upon such rules may appear as a technicality that inures to the benefit of a guilty person, the history of the criminal law proves that tolerance of shortcut methods in law enforcement impairs its enduring effectiveness." . . .

There are those who say, as did Justice (then Judge) Cardozo, that under our constitutional exclusionary doctrine "[t]he criminal is to go free because the constable has blundered." . . . In some cases this will undoubtedly be the result. But . . . "there is another consideration—the imperative of judicial integrity." . . . The criminal goes free, if he must, but it is the law that sets him free. Nothing can destroy a government more quickly than its failure to observe its own laws, or worse, its disregard of the charter of its own existence. As Mr. Justice Brandeis, dissenting, said in *Olmstead* v. *United States*, (1928) . . . : "Our government is the potent, the omnipresent teacher. For good or for ill, it teaches the whole people by its example. . . . If the government becomes a lawbreaker, it breeds contempt for law; it invites every man to become a law unto himself; it invites anarchy." Nor can it lightly be assumed that, as a practical matter, adoption of the exclusionary rule fetters law enforcement. . . . The Court noted that "The federal courts themselves have operated under the exclusionary rule of *Weeks* for almost half a century; yet it has not been suggested either that the Federal Bureau of Investigation has thereby been rendered ineffective, or that the administration of criminal justice in the federal courts has thereby been disrupted. Moreover, the experience of the states is impressive. . . . The movement toward the rule of exclusion has been halting but seemingly inexorable." . . .

The judgment of the Supreme Court of Ohio is reversed and the cause remanded for further proceedings not inconsistent with this opinion.

MR. JUSTICE BLACK, CONCURRING.

. . .

I am still not persuaded that the Fourth Amendment, standing alone, would be enough to bar the introduction into evidence against an accused of papers and effects seized from him in violation of its commands. For the Fourth Amendment does not itself contain any provision expressly precluding the use of such evidence, and I am extremely doubtful that such a provision could properly be inferred from nothing more than the basic command against unreasonable searches and seizures. Reflection on the problem, however, in the light of cases coming before the Court since *Wolf*, has led me to conclude that when the Fourth Amendment's ban against unreasonable searches and seizures is considered together with the Fifth Amendment's ban against compelled self-incrimination, a constitutional basis emerges which not only justifies but actually requires the exclusionary rule.

MR. JUSTICE DOUGLAS, CONCURRING (OMITTED).

MR. JUSTICE HARLAN, WHOM MR. JUSTICE FRANKFURTER AND MR. JUSTICE WHITTAKER JOIN, DISSENTING.

In overruling the *Wolf* case the Court, in my opinion, has forgotten the sense of judicial restraint which, with due regard for *stare decisis*, is one element that should enter into deciding whether a past decision of this Court should be overruled.

First, it is said that "the factual grounds upon which *Wolf* was based" have since changed, in that more States now follow the *Weeks* exclusionary rule that was so at the time *Wolf* was decided. While that is true, a recent survey indicates that at present one half of the States still adhere to the common-law non-exclusionary rule. . . . But in any case surely all this is beside the point, as the majority itself indeed seems to recognize. Our concern here, as it was in *Wolf,* is not with the desirability of that rule but only with the question whether the States are Constitutionally free to follow it or not as they may themselves determine, and the relevance of the disparity of views among the States on this point lies simply in the fact that the judgment involved is a debatable one. Moreover, the very fact on which the majority relies, instead of lending support to what is now being done, points away from the need of replacing voluntary state action with federal compulsion.

The preservation of a proper balance between state and federal responsibility in the administration of criminal justice demands patience on the part of those who might like to see things move faster among the States in this respect. Problems of criminal law enforcement vary widely from State to State. One State, in considering the totality of its legal picture, may conclude that the need for embracing the *Weeks* rule is pressing because other remedies are unavailable or inadequate to secure compliance with the substantive Constitutional principle involved. Another, though equally solicitous of Constitutional rights, may choose to pursue one purpose at a time, allowing all evidence relevant to guilt to be brought into a criminal trial, and dealing with Constitutional infractions by other means. Still another may consider the exclusionary rule too rough and ready a remedy, in that it reaches only unconstitutional intrusions which eventuate in criminal prosecution of the victims. Further, a State after experimenting with the *Weeks* rule for a time may, because of unsatisfactory experience with it, decide to revert to a nonexclusionary rule. . . .

I regret that I find so unwise in principle and so inexpedient in policy a decision motivated by the high purpose of increasing respect for Constitutional rights . . .

MEMORANDUM OF MR. JUSTICE STEWART

Agreeing fully with Part I of Mr. Justice Harlan's dissenting opinion [in which he noted that the main issue in the case, in briefs and oral argument, was the constitutionality of Ohio's obscenity statute; the exclusionary rule issue was only a subordinate argument.—Ed.], I express no view as to the merits of the constitutional issue which the Court today decides. I would however, reverse the judgment in this case, because I am persuaded the provision of . . . the Ohio Revised Code, upon which the petitioner's conviction was based, is . . . not "consistent with the rights of free thought and expression assured against state action by the Fourteenth Amendment."

[Only a peculiar Ohio Supreme Court procedural rule and a particularly unrestrained majority of the U.S. Supreme Court allowed the exclusionary rule to be extended to the states on the last day of the Court's 1960 term. A majority of less than six members of the Ohio high court were of the opinion that the state's obscenity statute was unconstitutional. It is therefore unlikely that the case would have proceeded to the U.S. Supreme Court had it not been for an Ohio law stipulating that this majority was not sufficient to permit the reversal of a decision of the state's court of appeals.

Even in the U.S. Supreme Court, the case was primarily an obscenity dispute. In oral argument, Mapp's counsel expressly disavowed any attempt to overrule *Wolf.* In Justice Harlan's terms, the majority had to "reach out" in a moment of unusual judicial activism to rule on the admissibility of illegally seized evidence.]

(7) The Exclusionary Rule: Reaffirmation, Revision, or Repudiation?

In *Weeks* v. *United States* (1914), the Supreme Court held that evidence seized in violation of the Fourth Amendment could not be used in criminal trials in the federal courts. The decision departed from the traditional Anglo-American doctrine that the admissibility of evidence was to be determined by its probity and reliability and *not* by how it was obtained. As expressed by Justice Cardozo, "Is the criminal to go free because the constable has blundered?"[1] In *Wolf* v. *Colorado* (1949), the Court considered whether to apply the Fourth Amendment to the states. Colorado officers, without a warrant, had searched the office of Dr. Wolf. On the basis of the medical records that they seized, Dr. Wolf was convicted of performing illegal abortions. The Supreme Court held that the search violated the Fourth and Fourteenth Amendments, the first time the Fourth Amendment had been applied to the states. However, the Court also held that the evidence seized need not be excluded from Dr. Wolf's trial in a state court. The Court's distinction between the recognition of a basic right protected by the Fourth and Fourteenth Amendments, and the enforcement of that right, left the issue of determining how to enforce Fourth Amendment protections to the states.

In *Mapp* v. *Ohio* (1961, *supra*), the Court changed its policy and held that evidence obtained in violation of the Fourth and Fourteenth Amendments was not admissible in state criminal trials, noting that other po-

tential sanctions against illegal police conduct had not worked: internal police department disciplinary procedures were ineffective; civil suits for damages rarely produced enforceable judgments, as juries are often reluctant to award damages against a police officer on the testimony of a convicted criminal; prosecuting attorneys were slow to invoke criminal sanctions; and juries were in any case unlikely to return guilty verdicts against police officers. Additionally, the disparity between procedures in the federal and state courts had produced considerable confusion and inconsistency. The Court, therefore, took the "final" step and in *Mapp* closed "the only courtroom door remaining open to evidence secured by official lawlessness. . . ." Justice Clark cited the need to deter unlawful police behavior and the preservation of judicial integrity as the main reasons for this reversal of policy.

The exclusionary rule was controversial before *Mapp;* virtually half the states had adopted it; and it became even more controversial afterward, though never rising to the level of acrimonious public debate provoked by the *Miranda* decision. Contrary to Clark's prediction, imposition of the exclusionary rule on the states did not result in less federal interference in state criminal processes. To be sure, there was less federal involvement in determining whether evidence in a particular case should or should not have been excluded. But in the aftermath of *Mapp*, the Supreme Court focused considerably greater attention on the substantive meaning of the Fourth Amendment, and of necessity, this involved increased scrutiny of state criminal procedures. As Wasby has noted, the

---

[1]*People* v. *Defore* (1926).

exclusionary rule made it *more* important to be able to distinguish between reasonable and unreasonable searches.[2]

The most salient (and continuing) debate about the exclusionary rule has centered on its effectiveness as a deterrent. The argument for repeal of the rule has shifted. Instead of emphasizing its adverse effect on police (e.g., the Court was "handcuffing the police"), opponents began to claim that the rule is ineffective, that it results in freeing many obvious criminals while not significantly reducing police misconduct. Additionally, opponents point out that the exclusionary rule does not reach police misconduct that does not result in an arrest and charge. It has only a limited effect on that very large proportion of cases that are terminated by a plea of guilty. And it is largely ineffective in controlling police behavior in narcotics, gambling, prostitution, and similar victimless crimes where the testimony of the arrested officer is often, if not always, accepted over claims of entrapment by the alleged offender.

Aside from its ineffectiveness, many argue that the exclusionary rule has more far-reaching negative effects. Necessarily, some criminal offenders whose guilt is not in doubt will go free. Observers have noted also that the rule encourages police perjury and that motions to suppress evidence alleged to have been obtained illegally take up a disproportionate share of judicial time. Even the late Chief Justice Warren, a supporter of the exclusionary rule, noted its limitations in his opinion in *Terry v. Ohio* (1968).[3]

Although criticism of the exclusionary rule often seems overwhelming, there is another side. Some recent evidence suggests that it may be a more effective deterrent than its critics allege.[4] Perhaps, like the Court's decision in *Brown* v. *Board of Education* (1954), the real impact of the exclusionary rule can be seen and appreciated only over the long run. Apart from empirical questions, the exclusionary rule, because it epitomizes the "due process" philosophy of the Warren Court, has become an important symbol both to those who wish to preserve and to those who wish to attack its legacy. Chief Justice Burger has long been an opponent of the exclusionary rule. With Justices Blackmun and Harlan, he mounted a strong attack in two cases in 1971. And he was part of the majority which, in *United States* v. *Calandra* (1974, *infra*), took the first step in limiting the application of *Mapp.*

The 1971 cases were *Coolidge* v. *New Hampshire* and *Bivens* v. *Six Unknown Named Agents of the Federal Bureau of Narcotics.* In Coolidge, the defendant was found guilty of the brutal murder of a young

---

[2]Stephen L. Wasby, *Continuity and Change: From the Warren Court to the Burger Court* (Pacific Palisades, Calif.: Goodyear Pub. Co., 1976).

[3]Certainly the leading academic attack on the exclusionary rule is Dallin Oaks, "Studying the Exclusionary Rule in Search and Seizure," **37** *University of Chicago Law Review* (1970), 665–757. One of the major criticisms of the findings reported by Oaks is that they are primarily from one jurisdiction—Cincinnati—and thus not an adequate basis for generalization. There are important differences among jurisdictions in arrest practices, prosecutorial policies, and search warrant policies—all of which affect police search and seizure policies.

[4]The best statement of caution, and a good critical analysis of the Oaks' findings, is Bradley Canon, "Is the Exclusionary Rule in Failing Health? Some New Data and a Plea Against a Precipitous Conclusion," **62** *Kentucky Law Journal* (1974), 681–730.

girl based on evidence obtained through a warranted search of the defendant's car and house. Defendant claimed that the search warrant was invalid because it had been issued by the state attorney general, who was in charge of investigation of the case, and not by a "neutral and detached magistrate." The state responded that even if the warrant was defective, the evidence was admissible under one of the "exceptions" to the warrant requirement. First, the state said that the search was incident to a valid arrest. Second, it argued that a warrantless search of an automobile was always possible even if, as here, the car was parked in the defendant's driveway and was in no danger of being driven out of the jurisdiction. Third, the state argued that the car itself was an "instrumentality of the crime" and thus might be searched because it was in "plain view." In the *Bivens* case, the plaintiff sought recovery of damages from federal narcotics agents who, without a warrant and allegedly without probable cause, had forcibly searched and stripped the plaintiff. The lower federal courts dismissed the suit but the Supreme Court reversed and held that a person whose Fourth Amendment rights were violated by federal agents could sue for damages. Likewise, the Court reversed Coolidge's conviction. To both of these rulings the Chief Justice dissented, describing the *Coolidge* case as the "monstrous price" of the exclusionary rule.

MR. JUSTICE HARLAN, CONCURRING IN *Coolidge*:

From the several opinions that have been filed in this case it is apparent that the law of search and seizure is due for an overhauling. State and federal law enforcement officers and prosecutorial authorities must find quite intolerable the present state of uncertainty, which extends even to such an everyday operation as the circumstances under which police may enter a man's property to arrest him and seize a vehicle believed to have been used during the commission of a crime.

I would begin this process of reevaluation by overruling *Mapp* v. *Ohio* . . . (1961), and *Ker* v. *California* . . . (1963). The former of these cases made the federal "exclusionary rule" applicable to the States. The latter forced the States to follow all the ins and outs of this Court's Fourth Amendment decisions, handed down in federal cases.

In combination *Mapp* and *Ker* have been primarily responsible for bringing about serious distortions and incongruities in this field of constitutional law. . . . First, the States have been put in a federal mold with respect to this aspect of criminal law enforcement, thus depriving the country of the opportunity to observe the effects of different procedures in similar settings. *See,* e.g. Oaks, "Studying the Exclusionary Rule in Search and Seizure," 37 U. Chi. L. Rev. 665 (1970), suggesting that the assumed "deterrent value" of the exclusionary rule has never been adequately demonstrated or disproved, and pointing out that because of *Mapp* all comparative statistics are 10 years old and no new ones can be obtained. Second, in order to leave some room for the States to cope with their own diverse problems, there has been generated a tendency to relax federal requirements under the Fourth Amendment, which now govern state procedures as well. . . . Until we face up to the basic constitutional mistakes of *Mapp* and *Ker,* no solid progress in setting things straight in search and seizure law will, in my opinion, occur.

But for *Mapp* and *Ker,* I would

have little difficulty in voting to sustain this conviction, for I do not think that anything the State did in this case could be said to offend those values which are "at the core of the Fourth Amendment." . . .

Because of *Mapp* and *Ker*, however, this case must be judged in terms of federal standards, and on that basis I concur, although not without difficulty. It must be recognized that the case is a close one. The reason I am tipped in favor of Mr. Justice Stewart's position is that a contrary result in this case would, I fear, go far towards relegating the warrant requirement of the Fourth Amendment to a position of little consequence in federal search and seizure law, a course which seems to me opposite to the one we took in *Chimel* v. *California* . . . (1969) . . .

Recent scholarship has suggested that in emphasizing the warrant requirement over the reasonableness of the search the Court has "stood the fourth amendment on its head" from a historical standpoint. . . . This issue is perhaps most clearly presented in the case of a warrantless entry into a man's home to arrest him on probable cause.

CHIEF JUSTICE BURGER, DISSENTING IN *Bivens*:

I dissent from today's holding which judicially creates a damage remedy not provided for by the Constitution and not enacted by Congress. We would more surely preserve the important values of the doctrine of separation of powers—and perhaps get a better result—by recommending a solution to the Congress as the branch of government in which the Constitution has vested the legislative power. Legislation is the business of the Congress, and it has the facilities and competence for that task—as we do not. . . .

This case has significance far beyond its facts and its holding. For more than 55 years this Court has enforced a rule under which evidence of undoubted reliability and probative value has been suppressed and excluded from criminal cases whenever it was obtained in violation of the Fourth Amendment. *Weeks* v. *United States* (1914). This rule was extended to the States in *Mapp* v. *Ohio*, . . . (1961). The rule has rested on a theory that suppression of evidence in these circumstances was imperative to deter law enforcement authorities from using improper methods to obtain evidence.

The deterrence theory underlying the Suppression Doctrine, or Exclusionary Rule, has a certain appeal in spite of the high price society pays for such a drastic remedy. Notwithstanding its plausibility many judges and lawyers and some of our most distinguished legal scholars have never quite been able to escape the force of Cardozo's statement of the doctrine's anomalous result:

The criminal is to go free because the constable has blundered.

The plurality opinion in *Irvine* v. *California* . . . (1954), catalogued the doctrine's defects:

Rejection of the evidence does nothing to punish the wrong-doing official, while it may, and likely will release the wrongdoing defendant. It deprives society of its remedy against one lawbreaker because he has been pursued by another. It protects one against whom incriminating evidence is discovered, but does nothing to protect innocent persons who are the victims of illegal and fruitless searches.

From time to time members of the court, recognizing the validity of these protests, have articulated varying alternative justifications for the suppression of important evidence in a criminal trial. Under one of these alternative theories the rule's foundation is shifted to the "sporting contest" thesis that the government must "play the game fairly" and cannot be allowed to benefit from its own illegal acts. *Olmstead* v. *United States* . . . (1928) (dissenting opinions); see *Terry* v. *Ohio* . . . (1968). But the Exclusionary Rule does not ineluctably flow from a desire to ensure that government plays the "game" according to the rules. If an effective alternative remedy is available, concern for official observance of the law does not require adherence to the Exclusionary Rule. Nor is it easy to understand how a court can be thought to endorse a violation of the Fourth Amendment by allowing illegally seized evidence to be introduced against a defendant if an effective remedy is provided against the government.

The Exclusionary Rule has also been justified on the theory that the relationship between the Self-Incrimination Clause of the Fifth Amendment and the Fourth Amendment requires the suppression of evidence seized in violation of the latter. . . .

Even ignoring, however, the decisions of this Court which have held that the Fifth Amendment applies only to "testimonial" disclosures, *United States* v. *Wade* . . . (1967); *Schmerber* v. *California* . . . (1966), it seems clear that the Self-Incrimination Clause does not protect a person from the seizure of evidence that is incriminating. It protects a person only from being the conduit by which the police acquire evidence. Mr. Justice Holmes once put it succinctly, "A party is privileged from producing the evidence but not from its production." . . .

It is clear, however, that neither of these theories undergirds the decided

cases in this Court. Rather, the Exclusionary Rule has rested on the deterrent rationale—the hope that law enforcement officials would be deterred from unlawful searches and seizures if the illegally seized, albeit trustworthy, evidence was suppressed often enough and the courts persistently enough deprived them of any benefits they might have gained from their illegal conduct.

This evidentiary rule is unique to American jurisprudence. Although the English and Canadian legal systems are highly regarded, neither has adopted our rule. . . .

I do not question the need for some remedy to give meaning and teeth to the constitutional guarantees against unlawful conduct by government officials. Without some effective sanction, these protections would constitute little more than rhetoric. Beyond doubt the conduct of some officials requires sanctions as cases like *Irvine* indicate. But the hope that this objective could be accomplished by the exclusion of reliable evidence from criminal trials was hardly more than a wistful dream. Although I would hesitate to abandon it until some meaningful substitute is developed, the history of the Suppression Doctrine demonstrates that it is both conceptually sterile and practically ineffective in accomplishing its stated objective. This is illustrated by the paradox that an unlawful act against a totally innocent person—such as petitioner claims to be—has been left without an effective remedy, and hence the Court finds it necessary now—55 years later—to construct a remedy of its own.

Some clear demonstration of the benefits and effectiveness of the Exclusionary Rule is required to justify it in view of the high price it extracts from society—the release of countless guilty criminals. . . . But there is no empirical evidence to support the claim that the rule actually deters illegal conduct of law enforcement officials. . . .

There are several reasons for this failure. The rule does not apply any direct sanction to the individual official whose illegal conduct results in the exclusion of evidence in a criminal trial. With rare exceptions law enforcement agencies do not impose direct sanctions on the individual officer responsible for a particular judicial application of the Suppression Doctrine. . . . Thus there is virtually nothing done to bring about a change in his practices. The immediate sanction triggered by the application of the rule is visited upon the prosecutor whose case against a criminal is either weakened or destroyed. The doctrine deprives the police in no real sense; except that apprehending wrongdoers is their business, police have no more stake in successful prosecutions than prosecutors or the public.

The Suppression Doctrine vaguely assumes that law enforcement is a monolithic governmental enterprise. . . . But the prosecutor who loses his case because of police misconduct is not an official in the police department; he can rarely set in motion any corrective action or administrative penalties. Moreover, he does not have control or direction over police procedures or police action that lead to the exclusion of evidence. It is the rare exception when a prosecutor takes part in arrests, searches, or seizures so that he can guide police action.

Whatever educational effect the rule conceivably might have in theory is greatly diminished in fact by the realities of law enforcement work. Policemen do not have the time, inclination, or training to read and grasp the nuances of the appellate opinions that ultimately define the standards of conduct they are to follow. The issues which these decisions resolve often admit of neither easy nor obvious answers, as sharply divided courts on what is or is not "reasonable" amply demonstrate. Nor can judges, in all candor, forget that opinions sometimes lack helpful clarity.

The presumed educational effect of judicial opinions is also reduced by the long time lapse—often several years—between the original police action and its final judicial evaluation. Given a policeman's pressing responsibilities, it would be surprising if he ever becomes aware of the final result after such a delay. Finally the Exclusionary Rule's deterrent impact is diluted by the fact that there are large areas of police activity which do not result in criminal prosecutions—hence the rule has virtually no applicability and no effect in such situations. . . .

Today's holding seeks to fill one of the gaps of the Suppression Doctrine—at the price of impinging on the legislative and policy functions which the Constitution vests in Congress. Nevertheless, the holding serves the useful purpose of exposing the fundamental weaknesses of the Suppression Doctrine. Suppressing unchallenged truth has set guilty criminals free but demonstrably has neither deterred deliberate violations of the Fourth Amendment nor decreased those errors in judgment which will inevitably occur given the pressures inherent in police work having to do with serious crimes.

Although unfortunately ineffective, the Exclusionary Rule has increasingly been characterized by a single, monolithic, and drastic judicial response to all official violations of legal norms. Inadvertent errors of judgment that do not work any grave injustice will inevitably occur under the pressure of police work. These honest mistakes have been treated in the same way as deliberate and flagrant *Irvine*-type violations of the Fourth Amendment. . . .

This Court's decision announced today in *Coolidge* v. *New Hampshire* dramatically illustrates the extent to which the doctrine represents a mechanically inflexible response to widely varying degrees of police error and the resulting high price which society pays. I dissented in *Coolidge* primarily because I do not believe the Fourth Amendment had been violated. Even on the Court's contrary premise, however, whatever violation occurred was surely insufficient in nature and extent to justify the drastic result dictated by the Suppression Doctrine. . . .

Freeing either a tiger or a mouse in a schoolroom is an illegal act, but no rational person would suggest that these two acts should be punished in the same way. From time to time judges have occasion to pass on regulations governing police procedures. I wonder what would be the judicial response to a police order authorizing "shoot-to-kill" with respect to every fugitive. It is easy to predict our collective wrath and outrage. We, in common with all rational minds, would say that the police response must relate to the gravity and need; that a "shoot" order might conceivably be tolerable to prevent the escape of a convicted killer but surely not for a car thief, a pickpocket, or a shoplifter.

I submit that society has at least as much right to expect rationally graded responses from judges in place of the universal "capital punishment" we inflict on all evidence when police error is shown in its acquisition. . . . Yet for over 55 years, and with increasing scope and intensity as today's *Coolidge* holding shows, our legal system has treated vastly dissimilar cases as if they were the same. Our adherence to the Exclusionary Rule, our resistance to change, and our refusal even to acknowledge the need for effective enforcement mechanisms brings to mind Holmes' well-known statement:

It is revolting to have no better reason for a rule of law than that it was laid down in the time of Henry IV. It is still more revolting if the grounds upon which it was laid down have vanished long since, and the rule simply persists from blind imitation of the past. . . .

In characterizing the Suppression Doctrine as an anomalous and ineffective mechanism with which to regulate law enforcement, I intend no reflection on the motivation of those members of this Court who hoped it would be a means of enforcing the Fourth Amendment. Judges cannot be faulted for being offended by arrests, searches, and seizures that violate the Bill of Rights or statutes intended to regulate public officials. But we can and should be faulted for clinging to an unworkable and irrational concept of law. My criticism is that we have taken so long to find better ways to accomplish these desired objectives. And there are better ways.

Instead of continuing to enforce the Suppression Doctrine, inflexibly, rigidly, and mechanically, we should view it as one of the experimental steps in the great tradition of the Common Law and acknowledge its shortcomings. But in the same spirit we should be prepared to discontinue what the experience of over half a century has shown neither deters errant officers nor affords a remedy to the totally innocent victims of official misconduct.

I do not propose, however, that we abandon the Suppression Doctrine until some meaningful alternative can be developed. In a sense our legal system has become the captive of its own creation. To overrule *Weeks* and *Mapp*, even assuming the Court was now prepared to take that step, could raise yet new problems. Obviously the public interest would be poorly served if law enforcement officials were suddenly to gain the impression, however erroneous, that all constitutional restraints on police had somehow been removed—that an open season on "criminals" had been declared. I am concerned lest some such mistaken impression might be fostered by a flat overruling of the Suppression Doctrine cases. For years we have relied upon it as the exclusive remedy for unlawful official conduct; in a sense we are in a situation akin to the narcotics addict whose dependence on drugs precludes any intrinsic or immediate withdrawal of the supposed prop, regardless of how futile its continued use may be.

Reasonable and effective substitutes can be formulated if Congress would take the lead. . . . I see no insuperable obstacle to the elimination of the Suppression Doctrine if Congress should provide some meaningful and effective remedy against unlawful conduct by government officials. . . .

I conclude, therefore, that an entirely different remedy is necessary but it is one that in my view is as much beyond judicial power as the step the Court takes today. Congress should develop an administrative or quasi-judicial remedy against the government itself to afford compensation and restitution for persons whose Fourth Amendment rights have been violated. The venerable doctrine of respondent superior in our tort law provides an entirely appropriate conceptual basis for this remedy. If, for example, a security guard privately employed by a department store commits an assault or other tort on a customer such as an improper search, the victim has a simple and obvious remedy—an action for money damages against the guard's employer, the department store. . . . Such a statutory scheme would have the added advantage of providing some remedy to the completely innocent persons who are sometimes the victims of illegal police conduct—something that the Suppression Doctrine, of course, can never accomplish.

A simple structure would suffice. For example, Congress could enact a statute along the following lines:

(a) a waiver of sovereign immunity as to the illegal acts of law enforcement officials committed in the performance of assigned duties;

(b) the creation of a cause of action for damages sustained by any person aggrieved by conduct of governmental agents in violation of the Fourth Amendment or statutes regulating official conduct;

(c) the creation of a tribunal, quasi-judicial in nature or perhaps patterned after the United States Court of Claims, to adjudicate all claims under the statute;

(d) a provision that this statutory remedy is in lieu of the exclusion of evidence secured for use in criminal cases in violation of the Fourth Amendment; and

(e) a provision directing that no evidence, otherwise admissible, shall be excluded from any criminal proceeding because of violation of the Fourth Amendment.

I doubt that lawyers serving on such a tribunal would be swayed either by undue sympathy for officers or by the prejudice against "criminals" that has sometimes moved lay jurors to deny claims. In addition to awarding damages, the record of the police conduct that is condemned would undoubtedly become a relevant part of an officer's personnel file so that the need for additional training or disciplinary action could be identified or his future usefulness as a public official evaluated. Finally, appellate judicial review could be made available on much the same basis that it is now provided as to district courts and regulatory agencies. This would leave to the courts the ultimate responsibility for determining and articulating standards.

Once the constitutional validity of such a statute is established, it can reasonably be assumed that the States would develop their own remedial systems on the federal model. Indeed there is nothing to prevent a State from enacting a comparable statutory scheme without waiting on the Congress. Steps along these lines would move our system toward more responsible law enforcement on the one hand and away from the irrational and drastic results of the Suppression Doctrine on the other. Independent of the alternative embraced in this dissenting opinion, I believe the time has come to reexamine the scope of the Exclusionary Rule and consider at least some narrowing of its thrust so as to eliminate the anomalies it has produced.

In a country that prides itself on innovation, inventive genius, and willingness to experiment, it is a paradox that we should cling for more than a half century to a legal mechanism that was poorly designed and never really worked. I can only hope now that the Congress will manifest a willingness to view realistically the hard evidence of the half-century history of the Suppression Doctrine revealing thousands of cases in which the criminal was set free because the constable blundered and virtually no evidence that innocent victims of police error—such as petitioner claims to be—have been afforded meaningful redress. . . .

(8) United States v. Calandra (1974)

+Burger, Stewart, White, Blackmun, Powell, Rehnquist
−Douglas, Brennan, Marshall

[Federal agents obtained a warrant authorizing a search of Calandra's place of business, the Royal Machine and Tool Company, in Cleveland. The warrant was issued in connection with an extensive investigation of suspected illegal gambling activities and specified the seizure of certain bookmaking records and gambling paraphernalia. No gambling materials were found, but evidence of a loansharking enterprise was discovered and seized. Calandra was then subpoenaed to testify before a grand jury. He refused, citing his Fifth Amendment right against self-incrimination. The government then granted Calandra full transactional immunity. Again he refused to testify and instituted action to suppress the evidence that formed the basis of the subpoena. A federal district court found that the search warrant had been issued without probable cause and that the search had exceeded the scope of the warrant. The evidence was excluded. The court of appeals affirmed, holding explicitly that the grant of immunity to Calandra did not foreclose imposition of the exclusionary rule to bar illegally obtained evidence. The Supreme Court granted certiorari.[1]]

MR. JUSTICE POWELL delivered the opinion of the Court.

. . . The institution of the grand jury is deeply rooted in Anglo-American history. In England, the

---

[1]While not agreeing that the search of Calandra's business was unlawful, the government did not seek review on this issue.

grand jury served for centuries both as a body of accusers sworn to discover and present for trial persons suspected of criminal wrongdoing and as a protector of citizens against arbitrary and oppressive governmental action. In this country the Founders thought the grand jury so essential to basic liberties that they provided in the Fifth Amendment that federal prosecution for serious crimes can only be instituted by "a presentment or indictment of a grand jury." . . . The grand jury's historic functions survive to this day. Its responsibilities continue to include both the determination whether there is probable cause to believe a crime has been committed and the protection of citizens against unfounded criminal prosecutions. . . .

Traditionally the grand jury has been accorded wide latitude to inquire into violations of criminal law. No judge presides to monitor its proceedings. It deliberates in secret and may determine alone the course of its inquiry. The grand jury may compel the production of evidence or the testimony of witnesses as it considers appropriate, and its operation generally is unrestrained by the technical procedural and evidentiary rules governing the conduct of criminal trials. "It is a grand inquest, a body with powers of investigation and inquisition, the scope of whose inquiry is not to be limited by doubts whether any particular individual will be properly subject to an accusation of crime" . . .

The scope of the grand jury's power reflects its special role in insuring fair and effective law enforcement. A grand jury proceeding is not an adversary hearing in which the guilt or innocence of the accused is adjudicated. Rather, it is an *ex parte* investigation to determine whether a crime has been committed and whether criminal proceedings should be instituted against any person. The grand jury's investigative power must be broad if its public responsibility is adequately to be discharged. . . .

The grand jury's sources of information are widely drawn, and the validity of an indictment is not affected by the character of the evidence considered. Thus, an indictment valid on its face is not subject to challenge on the ground that the grand jury acted on the basis of inadequate or incompetent evidence. . . . or even on the basis of information obtained in violation of a defendant's Fifth Amendment privilege against self-incrimination. . . .

The power of a federal court to compel persons to appear and testify before a grand jury is also firmly established. . . . The duty to testify has long been recognized as a basic obligation that every citizen owes his Government. . . . In *Branzburg* v. *Hayes*, the Court noted that "[c]itizens generally are not immune from grand jury subpoenas. . . ." and that "the longstanding principle that 'the public has a right to everyman's evidence' . . . is particularly applicable to grand jury proceedings." . . .

Of course, the grand jury's subpoena power is not unlimited. It may consider incompetent evidence, but it may not itself violate a valid privilege, whether established by the Constitution, statutes, or the common law. . . . Although, for example, an indictment based on evidence obtained in violation of a defendant's Fifth Amendment privilege is nevertheless valid, . . . the grand jury may not force a witness to answer questions in violation of that constitutional guarantee. Rather, the grand jury may override a Fifth Amendment claim only if the witness is granted immunity co-extensive with the privilege against self-incrimination.

In the instant case, the Court of Appeals held that the exclusionary rule of the Fourth Amendment limits the grand jury's power to compel a witness to answer questions based on evidence obtained from a prior unlawful search and seizure. . . .

The purpose of the exclusionary rule is not to redress the injury to the privacy of the search victim . . . Instead, the rule's prime purpose is to deter future unlawful police conduct and thereby effectuate the guarantee of the Fourth Amendment against unreasonable search and seizures. . . .

Despite its broad deterrent purpose, the exclusionary rule has never been interpreted to proscribe the use of illegally seized evidence in all proceedings or against all persons. As with any remedial device, the application of the rule has been restricted to those areas where its remedial objectives are thought most efficaciously served. . . .

In deciding whether to extend the exclusionary rule to grand jury proceedings, we must weigh the potential injury to the historic role and functions of the grand jury against the potential benefits of the rule as applied in this context. It is evident that this extension of the exclusionary rule would seriously impede the grand jury. Because the grand jury does not finally adjudicate guilt or innocence, it has traditionally been allowed to pursue its investigative and accusatorial functions unimpeded by the evidentiary and procedural restrictions applicable to a criminal trial. Permitting witnesses to invoke the exclusionary rule before a grand jury would precipitate adjudication of issues hitherto reserved for the trial on the merits and would delay and disrupt grand jury proceedings. Suppression hearings would halt the orderly progress of an investigation and might necessitate extended litigation of issues only tangentially related to the grand jury's primary objective. The probable result would be "protracted interruptions of grand jury proceedings" . . . effectively transforming them into preliminary trials on the merits. In some cases the delay might be fatal to the enforcement of the criminal law. . . .

. . . In sum, we believe that allowing a grand jury witness to invoke the exclusionary rule would unduly interfere with the effective and expeditious discharge of the grand jury's duties.

Against this potential damage to the role and functions of the grand jury, we must weigh the benefits to be derived from this proposed extension of the exclusionary rule. Suppression of the use of illegally-seized evidence against the search victim in a criminal trial is thought to be an important method of effectuating the Fourth Amendment. But it does not follow that the Fourth Amendment requires adoption of every proposal that might deter police misconduct. . . .

Any incremental deterrent effect which might be achieved by extending the rule to grand jury proceedings is uncertain at best. Whatever deterrence of police misconduct may result from the exclusion of illegally-seized evidence from criminal trials, it is unrealistic to assume that application of the rule to grand jury proceedings would significantly further that goal. Such an extension would deter only police investigation consciously directed toward the discovery of evidence solely for use in a grand jury investigation . . . We therefore decline to embrace a view that would achieve a speculative and undoubtedly minimal advance in the deterrence of police misconduct at the expense of substantially impeding the role of the grand jury.

. . .

The judgment of the Court of Appeals is *Reversed.*

MR. JUSTICE BRENNAN, WITH WHOM MR. JUSTICE DOUGLAS AND MR. JUSTICE MARSHALL, JOIN, DISSENTING.

. . .

[The Court's] downgrading of the exclusionary rule to a determination whether its application in a particular type of proceeding furthers deterrence of future police misconduct reflects a startling misconception, unless it is a purposeful rejection, of the historical objective and purpose of the rule.

. . . The exclusionary rule, if not perfect, accomplished the twin goals of enabling the judiciary to avoid the taint of partnership in official lawlessness and of assuring the people—all potential victims of unlawful government conduct—that the government would not profit from its lawless behavior, thus minimizing the risk of seriously undermining popular trust in government.

That these considerations, not the rule's possible deterrent effect, were uppermost in the minds of the framers of the rule clearly emerges from the decision which fashioned it [citing *Weeks* v. *United States* (1914); *Olmstead* v. *United States* (1928), Holmes and Brandeis dissenting; and *Terry* v. *Ohio* (1968)].

Thus, the Court seriously errs in describing the exclusionary rule as merely "a judicially created remedy designed to safeguard Fourth Amendment rights generally through its deterrent effect. . . . " . . . Rather, the exclusionary rule is "part and parcel of the Fourth Amendment's limitation upon [governmental] encroachment of individual privacy," . . . and "an essential part of both the Fourth and Fourteenth Amendments," . . . that "gives to the individual no more than that which the Constitution guarantees him, to the police officer no less than that to which honest law enforcement is entitled, and, to the courts, that judicial integrity so necessary in the true administration of justice." . . .

. . . For the first time, the Court today discounts to the point of extinction the vital function of the rule to insure that the judiciary avoids even the slightest appearance of sanctioning illegal government conduct . . . When judges appear to become "accomplices in the willful disobedience of a Constitution they are sworn to uphold," . . . we imperil the very foundation of our people's trust in their Government on which our Democracy rests. The exclusionary rule is needed to make the Fourth Amendment something real; a guarantee that does not carry with it the exclusion of evidence obtained by its violation is a chimera.

. . .

It is no answer, as the Court suggests, that the grand jury witnesses' Fourth Amendment rights will be sufficiently protected "by the inadmissibility of the illegally-seized evidence in a subsequent criminal prosecution of the search victim." . . . This, of course, is no alternative for Calandra, since he was granted transactional immunity and cannot be criminally prosecuted. But the fundamental flaw of the alternative is that to compel Calandra to testify in the first place under penalty of contempt necessarily "thwarts" his Fourth Amendment protection and "entangles the courts in the illegal acts of Government agents." . . .

(9) Stone v. Powell (1976)

+Burger, Powell, Stewart, Blackmun, Rehnquist, Stevens
−Brennan, White, Marshall

[Powell was arrested for violation of a vagrancy statute in Henderson, Nevada. A search pursuant to that arrest produced a gun, which turned out to be the weapon in a liquor store robbery and murder in San Bernadino, California about ten hours earlier. Powell was extradited to California and convicted of second-degree murder. His claim to suppress the gun as evidence, on the grounds that the vagrancy statute was unconstitutionally vague, was rejected. His conviction was affirmed by the California District Court of Appeal. That court did not pass upon Powell's challenge to the legality of the search, holding that any error in the testimony of the Henderson police officer about Powell's arrest or in the search that followed it were harmless beyond a reasonable doubt under *Chapman* v. *California* (1967). The Supreme Court of California denied Powell's petition for habeas corpus relief.

Several years later, Powell filed a petition for habeas corpus in the federal district court, repeating his claim that testimony about the weapon should have been excluded as the fruit of an illegal arrest and search. The district court denied Powell's claim, holding that the arresting officer had probable cause to search, and that even if the ordinance was unconstitutional, it would not serve the deterrent purpose of the exclusionary rule to suppress the evidence that the search produced "incident to an otherwise valid arrest."

The court of appeals reversed, holding that since the ordinance was unconstitutional, Powell's arrest was illegal. That made the search illegal and the exclusionary rule was properly invoked as a deterrent, not so much against police officers acting in good faith as against legislatures from passing unconstitutional statutes. The Supreme Court granted certiorari.]

MR. JUSTICE POWELL delivered the opinion of the Court.

. . .

We hold . . . that where the State has provided an opportunity for full and fair litigation of a Fourth Amendment claim, the Constitution does not require that a state prisoner be granted federal habeas corpus relief on the ground that evidence obtained in an unconstitutional search or seizure was introduced at his trial.

The Fourth Amendment assures the "right of the people to be secure in their persons, houses, papers, and effects, against unreasonable searches and seizures." The Amendment was primarily a reaction to the evils associated with the use of the general warrant in England and the writs of assistance in the Colonies . . . and was intended to protect the "sanctity of a man's home and the privacies of life," . . . from searches under unchecked general authority.

The exclusionary rule was a judicially created means of effectuating the rights secured by the Fourth Amendment. . . .

. . .

Although our [past] decisions often have alluded to the "imperative of judicial integrity," . . . the force of this justification becomes minimal where federal habeas corpus relief is sought by a prisoner who previously has been afforded the opportunity for full and fair consideration of his search-and-seizure claim at trial and on direct review.

The primary justification for the exclusionary rule then is the deterrence of police conduct that violates Fourth Amendment rights. Post-*Mapp* decisions have established that the rule is not a personal right. It is not calculated to redress the injury to the privacy of the victim of the search, for any "reparation comes too late." . . . Instead,

the rule is a judicial created remedy designed to safeguard Fourth Amendment rights generally through its deterrent effect. . . . United States v. Calandra (1974)

. . .

But despite the broad deterrent purpose of the exclusionary rule, it has never been interpreted to proscribe the introduction of illegally seized evidence in all proceedings or against all persons. As in the case of any remedial device, "the application of the rule has been restricted to those areas where its remedial objectives are thought most efficaciously served."

. . .

The costs of applying the exclusionary rule even at trial and on direct review are well known: the focus of the trial, and the attention of the participants therein, is diverted from the ultimate question of guilt or innocence that should be the central concern in a criminal proceeding. Moreover, the physical evidence sought to be excluded is typically reliable and often the most probative information bearing on the guilt or innocence of the defendant. . . .

Application of the rule thus deflects the truthfinding process and often frees the guilty. The disparity in particular cases between the error committed by the police officer and the windfall afforded a guilty defendant by application of the rule is contrary to the idea of proportionality that is essential to the concept of justice. Thus, although the rule is thought to deter unlawful police activity in part through the nurturing of respect for Fourth Amendment values, if applied indiscriminately it may well have the opposite effect of generating disrespect for the law and administration of justice. These long-recognized costs of the rule persist when a criminal conviction is sought to be overturned on collateral review on the ground that a search-and-seizure claim was erroneously rejected by two or more tiers of state courts.

Evidence obtained by police officers in violation of the Fourth Amendment is excluded at trial in the hope that the frequency of future violations will decrease. Despite the absence of supportive empirical evidence, we have assumed that the immediate effect of exclusion will be to discourage law enforcement officials from violating the Fourth Amendment by removing the incentive to disregard it. More importantly, over the long term, this demonstration that our society attaches serious consequences to violation of constitutional rights is thought to encourage those who formulate law enforcement policies, and the officers who implement them, to incorporate Fourth Amendment ideals into their value system.

We adhere to the view that these considerations support the implementation of the exclusionary rule at trial and its enforcement on direct appeal of state court convictions. But the additional contribution, if any, of the consideration of search-and-seizure claims of state prisoners on collateral review is small in relation to the costs. To be sure, each case in which such claim is considered may add marginally to an awareness of the values protected by the Fourth Amendment. There is no reason to believe, however, that the overall educative effect of the exclusionary rule would be appreciably diminished if search-and-seizure claims could not be raised in federal habeas corpus review of state convictions. Nor is there reason to assume that any specific disincentive already created by the risk of exclusion of evidence at trial or the reversal of convictions on direct review would be enhanced if there were the further risk that a conviction obtained in state court and affirmed on direct review might be overturned in collateral proceedings often occurring years after the incarceration of the defendant. The view that the deterrence of Fourth Amendment violations would be furthered rests on the dubious assumption that law enforcement authorities would fear that federal habeas review might reveal flaws in a search or seizure that went undetected at trial and on appeal. Even if one rationally could assume that some additional incremental deterrent effect would be present in isolated cases, the resulting advance of the legitimate goal of furthering Fourth Amendment rights would be outweighed by the acknowledged costs to other values vital to a rational system of criminal justice.

. . .

Accordingly, the judgments of the Courts of Appeals are reversed.

MR. CHIEF JUSTICE BURGER, CONCURRING.

. . . [T]he exclusionary rule has been operative long enough to demonstrate its flaws. The time has come to modify its reach, even if it is retained for a small and limited category of cases. . . .

. . .

In evaluating the exclusionary rule, it is important to bear in mind exactly what the rule accomplishes. Its function is simple—the exclusion of truth from the fact-finding process. . . . The operation of the rule is therefore unlike that of the Fifth Amendment's protection against compelled self-incrimination. A confession produced after intimidating or coercive interrogation is inherently dubious. If a suspect's will has been overborne, a cloud hangs over his custodial admissions; the exclusion of such statements is based essentially on their lack of reliability. This is not the case as to *reliable* evidence—a pistol, a packet of heroin, counterfeit money, or the body of a murder victim—which may be judicially declared to be the result of an "unreasonable" search. The reliability of

such evidence is beyond question; its probative value is certain.

. . .

From [its] origin, the exclusionary rule has been changed in focus entirely. It is now used almost exclusively to exclude from evidence articles which are unlawful to be possessed or tools and instruments of crime. . . .

The drastically changed nature of judicial concern—from the protection of personal papers or effects in one's private quarters, to the exclusion of that which the accused had no right to possess—is only one of the more recent anomalies of the rule. The original incongruity was the rule's inconsistency with the general proposition that "our legal system does not attempt to do justice incidentally and to enforce penalties by indirect means." . . . The rule is based on the hope that events in the courtroom or appellate chambers, long after the crucial acts took place, will somehow modify the way in which policemen conduct themselves. A more clumsy, less direct means of imposing sanctions is difficult to imagine, particularly since the issue whether the policeman did indeed run afoul of the Fourth Amendment is often not resolved until years after the event. The "sanction" is particularly indirect when . . . the police go before a magistrate, who issues a warrant. Once the warrant issues, there is literally nothing more the policeman can do in seeking to comply with the law. Imposing an admittedly indirect "sanction" on the police officer in that instance is nothing less than sophisticated nonsense.

Despite this anomaly, the exclusionary rule now rests upon its purported tendency to deter police misconduct, . . . although, as we know, the rule has long been applied to wholly good-faith mistakes and to purely technical deficiencies in warrants. . . .

Despite its avowed deterrent objective, proof is lacking that the exclusionary rule, a purely judge-created device based on "hard cases", serves the purpose of deterrence. Notwithstanding Herculean efforts, no empirical study has been able to demonstrate that the rule does in fact have any deterrent effect.

. . .

In my view, it is an abdication of judicial responsibility to exact such exorbitant costs from society purely on the basis of speculative and unsubstantiated assumptions.

. . .

MR. JUSTICE BRENNAN, WITH WHOM MR. JUSTICE MARSHALL CONCURS, DISSENTING.

The Court today holds "that where the state has provided an opportunity for full and fair litigation of a Fourth Amendment claim, a state prisoner may not be granted federal habeas corpus relief on the ground that evidence obtained in an unconstitutional search or seizure was introduced at his trial." . . . To be sure, my Brethren are hostile to the continued vitality of the exclusionary rule as part and parcel of the Fourth Amendment's prohibition of unreasonable searches and seizures. . . . [D]espite the veil of Fourth Amendment terminology employed by the Court, [the cases] plainly do not involve any question of the right of a defendant to have evidence excluded from use against him in his criminal trial when that evidence was seized in contravention of rights ostensibly secured by the Fourth and Fourteenth Amendments. Rather, they involve the question of the availability of a *federal forum* for vindicating

those federally guaranteed rights. Today's holding portends substantial evisceration of federal habeas corpus jurisdiction, and I dissent.

. . .

[T]he prevailing constitutional *rule* is that unconstitutionally seized evidence *cannot be admitted* in the criminal trial of a person whose federal constitutional rights were violated by the search or seizure. The erroneous admission of such evidence is a violation of the Federal Constitution—*Mapp* inexorably means at least this much, or there would be no basis for applying the exclusionary rule in state criminal proceedings—and an accused against whom such evidence is admitted has been convicted in derogation of rights mandated by, and is "in custody in violation of " the Constitution. . . .

The Court . . . acknowledges that respondents had the right to obtain a reversal of their convictions on appeal in the state courts or on certiorari to this Court. . . . And the basis for reversing those convictions would of course have to be that the states, in rejecting respondent's Fourth Amendment claims, had deprived them of a right in derogation of the Federal Constitution. It is simply inconceivable that that constitutional deprivation suddenly vanishes after the appellate process has been exhausted.

. . .

At least since *Brown* v. *Allen* (1953) detention emanating from judicial proceedings in which constitutional rights were denied has been deemed "contrary to fundamental law," and all constitutional claims have thus been cognizable on federal habeas corpus. There is no foundation in the language or history of the habeas statutes for discriminating between types of constitutional transgressions, and efforts to relegate certain categories of claims to the status of "second-class rights" by excluding them from that jurisdiction have been repulsed. Today's opinion, however, marks the triumph of those who have sought to establish a hierarchy of constitutional rights, and to deny for all practical purposes a federal forum for review of those rights that this Court deems less worthy or important. Without even paying the slightest deference to principles of stare decisis or acknowledging Congress' failure for two decades to alter the habeas statutes in light of our interpretation of congressional intent to render all federal constitutional contentions cognizable on habeas, the Court today rewrites Congress' jurisdiction statutes as heretofore construed and bars access to federal courts by state prisoners with constitutional claims distasteful to a majority of my Brethren. But even ignoring principles of stare decisis dictating that Congress is the appropriate vehicle for embarking on such a fundamental shift in the jurisdiction of the federal courts, I can find no adequate justification elucidated by the Court for concluding that habeas relief for all federal constitutional claims is no longer compelled. . . .

I would address the Court's concerns for effective utilization of scarce judicial resources, finality principles, federal-state friction, and notions of "federalism" only long enough to note that such concerns carry no more force with respect to non-"guilt-related" constitutional claims than they do with respect to claims that affect the accuracy of the fact-finding process. Congressional conferral of federal habeas jurisdiction for the purpose of entertaining petitions from state prisoners necessarily manifested a conclusion that such concerns could not be controlling, and any argument for discriminating among constitutional rights must therefore depend on the nature of the constitutional right involved.

The Court, focusing on Fourth Amendment rights as it must to justify such discrimination, thus argues that habeas relief for non-"guilt-related" constitutional claims do not affect the "basic justice" of a defendant's detention; . . . this is presumably because the "ultimate goal" of the criminal justice system is "truth and justice." . . . This denigration of constitutional guarantees and *constitutionally mandated procedures*, relegated by the Court to the status of mere utilitarian tools, must appall citizens taught to expect judicial respect and support for their constitutional rights. . . . The procedural safeguards mandated in the Framers' Constitution are not admonitions to be tolerated only to the extent they serve functional purposes that ensure that the "guilty" are punished and the "innocent" freed; rather, every guarantee enshrined in the Constitution, our basic charter and the guarantor of our most precious liberties, is by it endowed with an independent vitality and value, and this Court is not free to curtail those constitutional guarantees even to punish the most obviously guilty. Particular constitutional rights that do not affect the fairness of fact-finding procedures cannot for that reason be denied at the trial itself. What possible justification then can there be for denying vindication of such rights on federal habeas when state courts do deny those rights at trial? To sanction disrespect and disregard for the Constitution in the name of protecting society from lawbreakers is to make the government itself lawless and to subvert those values upon which our ultimate freedom and liberty depend.

. . .

Federal courts have the duty to carry out the congressionally assigned responsibility to shoulder the ultimate burden of adjudging whether detentions violate federal law, and today's decision substantially abnegates that duty. The Court does not, because it cannot, dispute that institutional constraints totally preclude any possibility that this Court can adequately oversee whether state courts have properly applied federal law, and does not controvert the fact that federal habeas jurisdiction is partially designed to ameliorate that inadequacy. Thus, although I fully agree that state courts "have a constitutional obligation to safeguard personal liberties and to uphold federal law," and that there is no "general lack of appropriate sensitivity to constitutional rights in the trial and appellate courts of the several States," . . . I cannot agree that it follows that, as the Court today holds, federal court determination of almost all Fourth Amendment claims of state prisoners should be barred and that state court resolution of those issues should be insulated from the federal review Congress intended.

. . .

In summary, while unlike the Court I consider that the exclusionary rule is a constitutional ingredient of the Fourth Amendment, any modification of that rule should at least be accomplished with some modicum of logic and justification not provided today. . . . The Court does not disturb the holding of *Mapp v. Ohio* that, as a matter of federal constitutional law, illegally obtained evidence must be excluded from the trial of a criminal defendant whose rights were transgressed during the search that resulted in acquisition of the evidence. In light of that constitutional rule it is a matter for Congress, not this Court, to prescribe what federal courts are to review state prisoners' claims of constitutional error

committed by state courts. Until this decision, our cases have never departed from the construction of the habeas statutes as embodying a congressional intent that, however substantive constitutional rights are delineated or expanded, those rights may be asserted as a procedural matter under federal habeas jurisdiction. Employing the transparent tactic that today's is a decision construing the Constitution, the Court usurps the authority—vested by the Constitution in the Congress—to reassign federal judicial responsibility for reviewing state prisoners' claims of failure of state courts to redress violations of their Fourth Amendment rights. Our jurisdiction is eminently unsuited for that task, and as a practical matter the only result of today's holding will be that denials by the state courts of claims by state prisoners of violations of their Fourth Amendment rights will go unreviewed by a federal tribunal. I fear that the same treatment ultimately will be accorded state prisoners' claims of violations of other constitutional rights; thus the potential ramifications of this case for federal habeas jurisdiction generally are ominous. The Court, no longer content just to restrict forthrightly the constitutional rights of the citizenry, has embarked on a campaign to water down even such constitutional rights as it purports to acknowledge by the device of foreclosing resort to the federal habeas remedy for their redress.

I would affirm the judgments of the Courts of Appeals.

MR. JUSTICE WHITE, DISSENTING (OMITTED).

[On its face, the Court's decision did not alter the applicability of the exclusionary rule to the states, as Justice Brennan notes in his dissent. Justice Powell's majority decision ostensibly deals only with the question of when federal district courts may take it upon themselves to sit in judgment of the adequacy of state criminal justice procedures. Read narrowly, *Stone* is a statement of deference to the state courts and rests on a view that they are fully capable and willing to apply the law (including the exclusionary rule) without constant supervision by the federal courts. What Powell's decision says, in essence, is that the U.S. Supreme Court trusts the judgment of state courts and that the lower federal courts likewise should assume that state trial procedures are sound and constitutionally acceptable in absence of clear evidence of a *constitutional* violation. When we recall that Powell clearly states that the exclusionary rule is *not* a personal constitutional right, the implication is that failure by state courts to exclude evidence after due consideration of a defendant's motion to suppress evidence is not *in and of itself* reviewable in federal courts.

The issue here is more than the relationship of state and federal courts, although the Court's decision plays upon that theme. At issue is the exclusionary rule itself. By limiting federal review of state court administration of the holding in *Mapp,* the Court has, in effect, limited the impact of the exclusionary rule in state criminal trials without assaulting the *Mapp* decision directly. The Court thus leaves to state courts, many of which are openly hostile to the exclusionary rule, the responsibility of administering the rule. It is a throwback to the situation under *Wolf* v. *Colorado* (1949). The expectation of the conservatives on the Court is clearly that the impact of *Mapp* on state procedures will be weakened. Many of the Burger Court's decisions dealing with the landmark civil liberties decisions of the Warren Court have taken this tactic, as we shall see later in this chapter.

Controversy over the exclusionary rule itself continues. Less than a year after the decision in *Stone* v. *Powell,* Chief Justice Burger renewed his attack on the exclusionary rule in a case involving a coerced confession, *Brewer* v. *Williams* (1977, see p. 888). In a bitter dissent, Burger argued that the exclusionary rule "mechanically and blindly keeps reliable evidence from juries whether the claimed constitu-

tional violation involves gross police misconduct or honest human error." The exclusionary rule should apply only to the former; otherwise it would result in a "knee-jerk" suppression of relevant and reliable evidence.

At the end of its 1978 term, the Supreme Court took part of the step which Burger had been urging. It held, in *Michigan* v. *DeFillippo* (1979), that illegally seized evidence might be used against a criminal suspect if it had been obtained by the police in "good faith." DeFillippo had been arrested by Detroit police who found him at night in an alley with a woman who was undressing. DeFillippo was evasive in response to a police request for identification and was arrested for violating an ordinance which provided that the police may stop and question any individual if there is reasonable cause to believe that individual's behavior "warrants further investigation" for criminal activity. Following DeFillippo's arrest under this ordinance a search uncovered narcotics on his person. He was then charged with a narcotics offense but not with violation of the ordinance.

The trial court denied a motion to suppress the evidence, holding that his arrest had been legal and that the subsequent search was also legal. But the Michigan Supreme Court reversed. It declared the Detroit ordinance unconstitutional as unduly vague. Consequently, both the arrest and the search were invalid, and the evidence was ordered suppressed, even though both the arrest and search had been made "in good faith" under a presumptively valid statute.

The Court, in an opinion by Chief Justice Burger, held that the police had probable cause to make an arrest under a "presumptively valid" ordinance, and that they had probable cause to believe that DeFillippo had violated the ordinance:

Police are charged to enforce laws until and unless they are declared unconstitutional. The enactment of a law forecloses speculation by enforcement officers concerning its constitutionality —with the possible exception of a law so grossly and flagrantly unconstitutional that any person of reasonable prudence would be bound to see its flaws. Society _would be ill served if its police officers took it upon themselves to determine which laws are and which are not constitutionally entitled to enforcement._

Burger noted previous cases, such as *Almeida-Sanchez* v. *United States* (1973), in which the exclusionary rule was held to suppress evidence pursuant to statutes later declared unconstitutional. But, Burger said, those statutes had by their own terms authorized the searches in question without probable cause and without a valid warrant. Thus, in *Almeida-Sanchez* the Court had invalidated a search pursuant to a federal statute authorizing the Border Patrol to search any car "within a reasonable distance" of the border, without a warrant or probable cause. The Detroit ordinance, in this case, did not directly authorize either the arrest or the search. When DeFillippo refused to comply with the police officer's request to identify himself, the officer then had probable cause to believe that DeFillippo was committing an offense in his presence. Michigan's general arrest statute then authorized an arrest, and the incidental search which followed was equally valid. The fact that the ordinance itself was later found to be unconstitutional by the state's own supreme court did not undermine the validity of the arrest.

Writing for himself and Justices Marshall and Stevens, Justice Brennan dissented:

The Court errs, in my view, in focusing on the good faith of the arresting officers and on whether they were entitled to rely on the validity of the Detroit ordinance. For the dispute in this case is not between the arresting officers and respondent. . . . The dispute is between respondent and the State of Michigan. The ultimate issue is whether the State gathered evidence against respondent through unconstitutional means. Since the state is responsible for the actions of _its legislative bodies as well as for the actions of its police, the State can hardly defend against this charge of unconstitutional conduct by arguing that the constitutional defect was the product of legislative action and that the police were merely executing the laws in good faith._

The question, Brennan said, is not whether or not the search was authorized by state law, but whether it was reasonable under the Fourth Amendment. The rights of the police to accost citizens on mere suspicion is a departure from the strict commands of the Fourth Amendment and, as in *Terry* v. *Ohio* (1968), it must be narrowly drawn ". . . [I]ndividuals accosted by police on the basis merely of reasonable suspicion have a right not to be searched, a right to remain silent, and, as a corollary, a right not to be searched if they choose to remain silent."

How far the current Supreme Court majority is willing to stretch this "good faith exception" to the exclusionary rule remains to be seen. If the *DeFillippo* case is a good example of current thinking on the Court, then it does not appear that the Chief Justice can command a majority to directly overturn the exclusionary rule. Instead, the Court may continue to chip away at the scope of its application and perhaps create new and broader exceptions to it. Following the lead of *Stone* v. *Powell* (1976), the Court may also seek other opportunities to limit application of the rule.

The debate between Professor Yale Kamisar and Judge Malcolm Wilkey, excerpts of which follow, captures the essence of current thinking about the exclusionary rule.]

(10) Yale Kamisar, The Exclusionary Rule in Historical Perspective

. . .

Over the years, I have written about the impact of . . . *Mapp* and

Reprinted from Yale Kamisar, "The Exclusionary Rule in Historical Perspective: The Struggle to Make the Fourth Amendment More than 'An Empty Blessing,' " **62** *Judicature* (1979), 340–350. This excerpt and the following response by Judge Malcolm Wilkey (*infra*) were a continuation of an earlier debate between Wilkey and Professor Kamisar, which also appeared in *Judicature*.

other decisions on crime rates and police-prosecution efficiency. . . .

• Long before the exclusionary rule became law in the states—indeed, long before any of the procedural safeguards in the federal Constitution were held applicable to the states—invidious comparisons were made between the rate of crime in our nation and the incidence of crime in others.

Thus, in 1911, the distinguished ex-president of Cornell University, Andrew D. White, pointed out that, although London's population was two million larger than New York's, there were 10 times more murders in New York. And in 1920, Edwin W. Sims, the first head of the Chicago Crime Commission, pointed out that "during 1919 there were more murders in Chicago (with a population of three million) than in the entire British Isles (with a population of forty million). This history ought to raise some doubts about the alleged causal link between the high rate of crime in America and the exclusionary rule.

• England and Wales have not experienced anything like the "revolution" in American criminal procedure which began at least as early as the 1961 *Mapp* case. Nevertheless, from 1955–65 (a decade which happened to be subjected to a most intensive study), the number of indictable offenses against the person in England and Wales increased 162 percent. How do opponents of the exclusionary rule explain such increases in countries which did not suffer from the wounds the Warren Court supposedly inflicted upon America?

• In the decade before *Mapp*, Maryland admitted illegally seized evidence in all felony prosecutions; Virginia, in all cases. District of Columbia police, on the other hand, were subject to both the exclusionary

rule and the *McNabb-Mallory* rule, a rule which "hampered" no other police department during this period. Nevertheless, during this decade the felony rate per 100,000 population increased much more in the three Virginia and Maryland suburbs of the District (69 percent) than in the District itself (a puny one percent).

. . .

The exclusionary rule, to be sure, does free some "guilty criminals" (as would an effective tort remedy that inhibited the police from making illegal searches and seizures in the first place), but very rarely are they robbers or murderers. Rather they are "offenders caught in the everyday world of police initiated vice and narcotics enforcement . . ."

. . .

Judge Wilkey does advance what so far as I know is a new argument: that gun control will be totally ineffective "so long as the exclusionary rule hampers the police in enforcing it." Since [American] criminals know the difficulties of the police in making a valid search," he observes, "the criminals in America do carry guns," unlike criminals in England and other countries.

Why, then, did so many criminals carry guns in New York and more than 20 other states that admitted illegally seized evidence until 1961? New York, for example, passed the Sullivan Act in 1911, making the ownership and carrying of pistols subject to a police permit. But a British gun control expert said recently that, if we compare New York with London in the 10 years after passage of the Sullivan Act, we would probably find

that New York, with its strict controls on the private ownership of pistols, suffered infinitely more from the criminal use of firearms of all types than did Lon-

*don in a period when all firearms were
freely available.*

. . .

The availability of handguns
clearly increases crime rates, but do
changes in the rules of evidence?
Judge Wilkey hints darkly that there
is a "connection" between America's
high crime rate and its "unique"
exclusionary rule. So far as I am
aware, no one has been able to demonstrate such a connection on the
basis of the annual *Uniform Crime
Reports* or any other statistical data.
In Michigan, for example, the rate of
violent crime seems to have fluctuated without regard to the life and
death of the state's "anti-exclusionary" proviso.

From 1960–64, the robbery rate
increased only slightly in the Detroit
Metropolitan Statistical Area but it
quadrupled from 1964 to 1970 (from
152.5 per 100,000 to 648.5). When
the Michigan Supreme Court struck
down the state's "anti-exclusionary"
proviso in 1970, the robbery rate fell
(to 470.3 per 100,000 in 1973),
climbed (to 604.2 in 1975), then
dropped again (to 454.3 in 1977, the
lowest it has been since the 1960's).

From 1960–64, the murder and
nonnegligent manslaughter rate remained almost the same in the Detroit area, but it rose extraordinarily
the next six years (5.0 in 1964 to 14.7
in 1970). In the next four years it continued to climb (but less sharply) to
20.2 in 1974. Then it dropped to 14.1
in 1977, the lowest it has been since
the 1960's.

Finally, I must take issue with
Judge Wilkey's case of the criminal
who "parade[s] in the streets with a
great bulge in his pocket or a submachine gun in a blanket under his
arm," "laugh[ing] in the face of the
officer who might wish to search him
for it." If American criminals "know

the difficulties of the police in making a valid search," as Judge Wilkey
tells us, they know, too, that the exclusionary rule has "virtually no
applicability" in "large areas of police
activity which do not result in criminal prosecutions" and that confiscation of weapons is one of them. (The
criminal might get back his blanket,
but not the submachine gun).

. . . Even if I am wrong, however,
even if the Fourth Amendment does
not permit an officer to make such a
limited search for weapons, *abolishing the exclusionary rule wouldn't
change that.* If an officer now lacks
the lawful authority to conduct a
"frisk" under these circumstances,
he would still lack the lawful authority to do so if the rule were abolished.

. . .

. . .

If we replace the exclusionary rule
with "disciplinary punishment and
civil penalities-directly against the
erring officer involved," as Judge
Wilkey proposes, and if these alternatives "would certainly provide a far
more effective deterrent than . . . the
exclusionary rule," as the judge assures us, the weapon still would not
be brought in as evidence in the case
he poses because the officer would
not *make* the search or frisk if he
lacked the requisite cause to do so.

Judge Wilkey points enviously to
England, where "the criminals know
that the police have a right to search
them *on the slightest suspicion,* and
they know that if a weapon is found
they will be prosecuted" (emphasis
added). But what is the relevance of
this point in an article discussing the
exclusionary rule and its alternatives? Abolishing the rule would not
confer *a right* on our police to search
"on the slightest suspicion"; it would
not affect lawful police practices in
any way. Only a change in the substantive law of search and seizure

can do that. . . . And replacing the exclusionary rule with a statutory remedy against the government would not bring about an increase in unlawful police activity if the alternative were equally effective—and Judge Wilkey expects it to be "a far more effective deterrent."

I venture to say that Judge Wilkey has confused the *content* of the law of search seizure (which proponents of the exclusionary rule need not, and have not always, defended . . .) with the *exclusionary rule*—which "merely states the consequences of a breach of whatever principles might be adopted to control law enforcement officers.". . .

Judge Wilkey makes plain his agreement with Chief Justice Burger that "the continued existence of [the exclusionary rule] . . . inhibits the development of rational alternatives" and that "incentives for developing new procedures or remedies will remain minimal or nonexistent so long as the exclusionary rule is retained in its present form."

Thus, Judge Wilkey warns that "we will never have any alternative in operation until the rule is abolished. So long as we keep the rule, the police are not going to investigate and discipline their men, and thus sabotage prosecutions by invalidating the admissibility of vital evidence . . . ." He argues that *Mapp* "removed from the states both the incentive and the opportunity to deal with illegal search and seizure by means other than suppression." . . .

. . . In light of our history, these comments are simply baffling. First, the fear of "sabotaging" prosecutions has never inhibited law enforcement administrators from disciplining officers for committing the "many unlawful searches of homes and automobiles of innocent people which turn up nothing incriminating, in which no arrest is made, about which

courts do nothing, and about which we never hear."

Second, both defenders of the rule and its critics recognize that

there are large areas of policy activity which do not result in criminal prosecutions [e.g., arrest or confiscation as a punitive sanction, (common in gambling and liquor law violations), illegal detentions which do not result in the acquisition of evidence, unnecessary destruction of property] hence the rule has virtually no applicability and no effect in such situations.

Whatever the reason for the failure to discipline officers for "mistakes" in these "large areas of police activities," it cannot be the existence of the exclusionary rule.

Finally, and most importantly, *for many decades* a majority of the states had no exclusionary rule but *none of them* developed any meaningful alternative. Thirty-five years passed between the time the federal courts adopted the exclusionary rule and the time *Wolf* was decided in 1949, but none of the 31 states which still admitted illegally seized evidence had established an alternative method of controlling the police. Twelve more years passed before *Mapp* imposed the rule on the state courts, but none of the 24 states which still rejected the exclusionary rule had instituted an alternative remedy. This half-century of post-*Weeks* "freedom to experiment" did not produce any meaningful alternative to the exclusionary rule anywhere.

Of course, few critics of the exclusionary rule have failed to suggest alternative remedies that *might be devised or that warranted study.* None of them has become a reality.

In 1922, for example, Dean Wigmore maintained that "the natural way to do justice" would be to enforce the Fourth Amendment directly "by sending for the high-handed, over-zealous marshal who had searched without a warrant, imposing a 30-day imprisonment for his contempt of the Constitution, and then preceeding to affirm the sentence of the convicted criminal." Nothing ever came of that proposal. Another critic of the rule suggested that a civil rights office be established, independent of the regular prosecutor, "charged solely with the responsibility of investigating and prosecuting alleged violations of the Constitution by law-enforcement officials. Nothing came of that proposal either.

Judge Wilkey recognizes that "policemen traditionally are not wealthy," but "[t]he government has a deep purse." Thus, as did Chief Justice Burger in his *Bivens* dissent, Judge Wilkey proposes that in lieu of the exclusion of illegally seized evidence there be a statutory remedy against the government itself to afford meaningful compensation and restitution for the victims of police illegality. Two leading commentators, Caleb Foote and Edward Barrett, Jr. made the same suggestion 20 years ago, but none of the many states that admitted illegally seized evidence at the time seemed interested in experimenting along these lines.

Indeed, the need for, and the desirability of, a statutory remedy against the government itself was pointed out at least as long ago as 1936. In a famous article published that year, Jerome Hall noted that the prospects of satisfying a judgment against a police officer were so poor that the tort remedy in the books "collapses at its initial application to fact."

. . .

This disparity—no longer unnoticed, but still uncorrected—has troubled even the strongest critics of the rule. Thus, more than 35 years ago, J.A.C. Grant suggested "im-plement[ing] the law covering actions for trespass, even going so far as to hold the government liable in damages for the torts of its agents.
. . .

. . .

As I have already indicated, critics of the exclusionary rule have often made proposals for effectuating the Fourth Amendment by means other than the exclusionary rule—but almost always as a *quid pro quo* for rejecting or repealing the rule. Who has ever heard of a police-prosecution spokesman urging—or a law enforcement group supporting—an effective "direct remedy" for illegal searches and seizures in a jurisdiction which *admitted* illegally seized evidence? Abandoning the exclusionary rule without waiting for a meaningful alternative (as Judge Wilkey and Chief Justice Burger would have us do) will not furnish an incentive for devising an alternative, but *relieve* whatever pressure there now exists for doing so. . . .

. . .

Wolf established the "underlying constitutional doctrine" that "the Federal Constitution, by virtue of the Fourteenth Amendment, prohibits unreasonable searches and seizures by state officers" (though it did not require exclusion of the resulting evidence); *Irvine* warned that if the states "defaulted and there were no demonstrably effective deterrents to unreasonable searches and seizures in lieu of the exclusionary rule, the Supreme Court might yet decide that they had not complied with 'minimal standards' of due process." But neither *Wolf* nor *Irvine* stimulated a single state legislature or a single law enforcement agency to demonstrate that the problem could be handled in other ways.

Now Judge Wilkey asks us to believe that the resurrection of *Wolf* (and evidently the overruling of the

65-year-old *Weeks* case as well) will permit "the laboratories of our 51 jurisdictions" to produce meaningful alternatives to the exclusionary rule. His ideological ally, Chief Justice Burger, is even more optimistic. He asks us to believe that a return to the pre-exclusionary rule days "would inspire a surge of activity toward providing some kind of statutory remedy for persons injured by police mistakes or misconduct."

And to think that Judge Wilkey accuses *defenders* of the exclusionary rule of being "stubbornly blind to 65 years of experience"!

(11) Malcolm Richard Wilkey, A Call for Alternatives to the Exclusionary Rule: Let Congress and the Trial Courts Speak

. . . It is obvious, although he does not specifically say so, that Professor Kamisar chooses to defend his position on the second of the two grounds which I posited as his inevitable choices. Thus, he does not claim that the Fourth Amendment necessarily mandates the exclusionary rule; he says only that, under the Constitution, we have a choice of methods to enforce the ban against unreasonable searches and seizures and that the exclusionary rule is the best choice.

If there is to be a choice, however, there must be grounds for a choice. Indisputably valid and convincing evidence cannot be excluded on whim, fancy, or unproven theory. The burden of proof is on those like Professor Kamisar, who would exclude such evidence. No one, not even Professor Kamisar, has come forward with such proof.

Oaks' conclusion of 1970 is still uncontradicted:

[T]oday, more than fifty years after the exclusionary rule was adopted for the federal courts and almost a decade after it was imposed upon the state courts, there is still no convincing evidence to verify the actual premise of deterrence upon which the rule is based or to determine the limits of its effectiveness.

At the same time, however, Oaks did refute Professor Kamisar:

Kamisar is merely saying what the Supreme Court and a considerable number of scholars have said over and over again, that in the absence of any better alternative, we are willing to take the deterrent effect of the exclusionary rule solely on the basis of assumption.

In sum, the rhetoric concerning the factual basis for the exclusionary rule amounts to no more than 'fig-leaf phrases used to cover naked ignorance.'

. . .

It is the downplaying of available alternatives that I find most distressing in Professor Kamisar's position. He argues that "*for many decades a majority of the states had no exclusionary rule but none of them developed any meaningful alternative*" . . . He even dredges up an ancient dilemma—the policeman is liable but financially irresponsible while the state or municipality has financial responsibility but no liability. This ignores the great erosion in the law of sovereign immunity which has occurred, and the capacity of Congress to speak effectively about it.

I do not really know whether any "meaningful" alternative to the exclusionary rule emerged in any of the states prior to *Mapp*, but I do suggest that, wherever we have been and wherever we want to go, we start from where we are now. I propose

Reprinted from **62** *Judicature* (1979), 351–356.

Congressional action to provide meaningful alternatives to the exclusionary rule. Congress could directly provide federal remedies, and indirectly permit and encourage the states to provide the same or alternative remedies. In other words, the exclusionary rule could be abolished now, conditioned on the enactment of acceptable alternatives.

I would prefer to see the exclusionary rule abolished conditionally with alternatives provided simultaneously, but I urge abolition in any case. I do so because the rule is pernicious in its present form, and I am confident that more attractive alternatives would speedily emerge.

At the outset . . . I discussed the question of who should act first, the Supreme Court or Congress. If Congress seizes the initiative, it could simultaneously provide a federal alternative and condition abolition of the rule in the states on their providing an equal remedy. If the Supreme Court acted first, I believe Congress would act speedily to fill the gap with a federal remedy.

Therefore, I respectfully suggest to Professor Kamisar that he has not met the issue squarely: he has given us some history; quotations from almost everyone of prominence who has endorsed the rule; and some crime statistics whose current or past relevance is not immediately apparent. But he has not analyzed the practical working of the present exclusionary rule as compared to the excellent possibilities for logical reform inherent in the proposals I made.

In his discussions of the crime rate and the exclusionary rule and guns and the exclusionary rule, Professor Kamisar generally indicates that I attribute all crime, or all crime with handguns, or all crime rate differences, to the presence or absence of the exclusionary rule. Such a position appears easy to refute by statistics, which necessarily embrace the effect of many factors.

For example, it is no surprise to me that crime did not decrease in Michigan from 1963 to 1970—a period in which the state, in effect, abolished the exclusionary rule. The fact is that crime increased *everywhere* during the turbulent 60s, and no one could expect that abolishing the rule would give Michigan immunity from the nationwide epidemic.

Actually, as Professor Kamisar quoted but failed to recognize, I referred to the "huge social cost . . . of street crimes . . . which flourish *in no small degree* simply because of the exclusionary rule. . . ." . . . I did not rule out other factors here, as I did not rule out other factors in the comparison of the United States and other countries. It may well be, as Chief Justice Burger has suggested, that the effect of the exclusionary rule is not readily susceptible to empirical proof. But I submit that logically we all recognize that the effects of the exclusionary rule, by its presence or absence, must be there in some degree in the various ways that I have described them. The available empirical data tends strongly to support this idea, but obviously selective opposing arguments can be made.

Even if abolishing the rule resulted in minimal effect on the number of illegal searches, and even if the presence or absence of the rule has no discernible effect on the overall crime rate, is this an argument in support of an irrational system of freeing criminals from punishment? This is the most visible, undeniable effect of the exclusionary rule, and one which brings the entire system of justice into disrepute.

[T]here [are] two separate issues: (1) the exclusionary rule as an enforcement tool for the Fourth Amendment, and (2) the standard of probable cause for a valid search and seizure. . . .[E]ven without a change in the standard of probable cause, but after the abolition of the exclusionary rule, we may expect fewer illegal searches but more successful prosecutions.

I made and make no effort to cite literally hundreds of cases in which the standard of probable cause required by the courts, particularly the appellate courts, was so high and unreasonable as to appear absurd, silly, and fatuous to layman and lawyer alike. I do not make that effort because I am firmly convinced that, whatever standard of probable cause is employed, the exclusionary rule is both an ineffective and pernicious remedy for any violation of the constitutional right, no matter how defined.

Having taken the time to make this dichotomy of issues clear, I want to emphasize that the definition of "unreasonable searches and seizures" is nowhere found in the Constitution. It has been a matter for the courts to decide, and it could be a matter for Congress. I go back to former Solicitor General Griswold's principle on seeking certiorari: "If the police officer acted decently, and if he did what you would expect a good, careful, conscientious police officer to do under the circumstances, then he should be supported."

Dean Griswold did not assert, and neither do I, that this would be sufficient for a judicial standard, but it surely is not beyond the realm of possibility for Congress to define a standard of reasonable search and seizure, i.e., the level of probable cause required, in terms which would meet more common sense standards than what we find in many appellate decisions. Such a definition by Congress

of what is a reasonable and an unreasonable search and seizure might be buttressed in the legislative history by a recital of some representative cases which have required utterly absurd levels of probable cause and which no longer could be considered as governing precedent in light of the new statutory standard. In determining such a statutory standard of "reasonableness," which is always Congress's prerogative, Congress might look at our own experience and mores as well as the standards of probable cause for search and seizure used in other civilized nations with cultures similar to our own.

As the Court said only a few years ago, "It is clear, of course, that no Act of Congress can authorize a violation of the Constitution. It is equally apparent that Congress may, in the first instance, describe for purposes of law enforcement such things as what may give rise to "probable cause" and when a warrant may be dispensed with. Statutory characterizations of constitutional provisions will be subject to judicial review, of course, to assure harmony with the judicial understanding of the constitutional requirements, but a prior legislative determination might appropriately inform the content of such open-ended language as "unreasonable" and "probable cause."

Let me emphasize, though, that this review of the standard of reasonableness, i.e., the requisite level of probable cause, should not be made, if at all, until after we have abolished the exclusionary rule and gained some experience with alternative methods of protecting the privacy of individuals and controlling the police. What is "reasonable" is always a function of past experience applied to present time, place, and circumstances. We need to see how the police operate under a new dispensation and how the courts construe "probable cause" without the overhanging distortion of the exclusionary rule threatening to free undeniably guilty criminals. Only then can we, if need be, evaluate the standard of reasonableness and probable cause. . . .

(12) Wiretapping and Electronic Surveillance

(a) *Katz v. United States (1967)*

+Stewart, Warren, Douglas, Harlan, Brennan, White, Fortas
−Black
NP Marshall

[Not very long after the invention of the telephone, the police discovered the utility of wiretapping. But it was not until 1928 that the relationship of wiretapping to the Fourth Amendment was considered by the Supreme Court. In *Olmstead* v. *United States*, a case involving the conviction of some bootleggers based on wiretap evidence, the Supreme Court refused to bring wiretapping within the protections of that amendment. Chief Justice Taft

found that wiretapping lacked the two essentials of searches covered by the Fourth Amendment—it could be obtained without an actual trespass and it involved no physical object. Holmes and Brandeis dissented strongly, but the majority stuck to a literal interpretation. The Court did invite Congress to pass controlling legislation, and the Communications Act of 1934 provided that "no person not being authorized by the sender shall intercept any communication and divulge or publish the contents." In *Nardone* v. *United States* (1937), the Court determined that the statute excluded wiretap evidence in federal trials. In a later case the Court held that the prohibition against wiretap evidence applied to the states, but it declined to apply the exclusionary rule to state trials.

Widespread use of wiretapping by the federal government was justified by several attorneys general on the ground that the statute did not prohibit mere interceptance, but only interceptance *and* divulgence. As long as the government did not seek to use wiretap evidence in court it was free to continue the practice. In 1940, Attorney General Robert Jackson announced that the federal government had completely abandoned wiretapping except in national security cases.[1] In the meantime elec-

---

[1]This was done in response to the following memorandum from President Franklin Roosevelt, dated May 21, 1940:

I have agreed with the broad purpose of the Supreme Court decision relating to wire-tapping in investigations. The Court is undoubtedly sound both in regard to the use of evidence secured over tapped wires in the prosecution of citizens in criminal cases; and is also right in its opinion that under ordinary and normal circumstances wire-tapping by Government should not be carried on for the excellent reason that it is almost bound to lead to abuse of civil rights.

However, I am convinced that the Supreme Court never intended any dictum in the particular case which it decided to apply to grave matters involving the defense of the nation.

It is, of course, well known that certain other nations have been engaged in the organization of propaganda of so-called "fifth columns" in other countries and in preparation for sabotage, as well as in actual sabotage.

It is too late to do anything about it after sabotage, assassinations and "fifth column" activities are completed.

You are, therefore, authorized and directed in such cases as you may approve, after investigation of the need in each case, to authorize the necessary investigation agents that they are at liberty to secure information by listening devices direct to the conversation or other communications of persons suspected of subversive activities against the Government of the United States, including suspect spies. You are requested furthermore to limit these investigations so conducted to a minimum and to limit them insofar as possible to aliens.

tronic eavesdropping entered the technology, and in *Goldman* v. *United States* (1942), in a 6-3 decision, the Supreme Court ruled that eavesdropping was not illegal as long as there was no trespass.

In 1946, at the request of Attorney General Tom Clark, President Truman relaxed government policy to permit wiretapping in the fight against organized crime, and the FBI began to tap openly. Permission of the attorney general was required in writing and in advance, and the number of wiretaps used was reported annually to the House Appropriations Committee. At the same time, the FBI was increasingly resorting to eavesdropping on its own. In 1965 Attorney General Katzenbach found that at least as many "bugs" were being used in Mafia investigations as the total of reported wiretaps.

In 1967, following disclosures of widespread eavesdropping by federal agents, the government "confessed error" in more than a dozen cases pending before the Supreme Court and in each case the conviction under review was reversed. The new attorney general, Ramsey Clark, issued a new set of regulations which forbade all wiretapping and most eavesdropping except in national security cases.[2] In Clark's view, wiretapping and eavesdropping were not very effective means of eradicating crime and involved heavy costs in civil liberties deprivations. His view was that "strike forces" of state, federal, and local law enforcement agents blanketing an area and seeking evidence by conventional means was far more effective. He later reported that in 1967–1968, without the use of electronic surveillance, there were many more organized crime convictions than for any year before 1965.[3]

In 1967 the Supreme Court abandoned the *Olmstead* doctrine and held that wiretapping by the states must conform to Fourth Amendment standards. Under a New York State law, a judge could authorize eavesdropping if a police

officer above the rank of sergeant, a district attorney, or the state attorney general said that there was a reasonable basis to believe that evidence of a crime would be uncovered. Writing his last major opinion, Justice Tom Clark held for a five-man majority that the statute was overly broad and that the two-month time limit was excessive. Some language in the opinion suggested that eavesdropping might never be constitutionally permissible because it would be difficult if not impossible to meet the normal constitutional standards for search warrants (*Berger* v. *New York*).

In the present case, decided six months later, the Court refused to uphold a limited "bug" by which FBI agents uncovered evidence of illegal gambling activities. But the opinion suggested that eavesdropping might be acceptable if carried out under court supervision, thus rejecting the *dicta* of the *Berger* opinion.]

MR. JUSTICE STEWART delivered the opinion of the Court.

The petitioner was convicted in the District Court for the Southern District of California under an eight-count indictment charging him with transmitting wagering information by telephone from Los Angeles to Miami and Boston, in violation of a federal statute. At trial the Government was permitted, over the petitioner's objection, to introduce evidence of the petitioner's end of telephone conversations, overheard by FBI agents who had attached an electronic listening and recording device to the outside of the public telephone booth from which he had placed his calls. In affirming his conviction, the Court of Appeals rejected the contention that the recordings had been obtained in violation of the

---

[2]In 1965, President Johnson sent a memorandum to all department and agency heads ordering the cessation of wiretapping or electronic bugging except in national security cases, and then only with the approval of the attorney general.

[3]Ramsey Clark, *Crime in America* (New York: Simon & Schuster, 1970), Chapter 17. Also see John T. Elliff, *Crime, Dissent and the Attorney-General* (Beverly Hills, Cal.: Sage Publications, 1971), and Victor Navasky, *Kennedy Justice* (New York: Atheneum, 1971).

POLICING THE POLICE ■ 843

Fourth Amendment, because "[t]here was no physical entrance into the area occupied by [the petitioner]." We granted certiorari in order to consider the constitutional questions thus presented.

The petitioner has phrased those questions as follows:

"A. Whether a public telephone booth is a constitutionally protected area so that evidence obtained by attaching an electronic listening recording device to the top of such a booth is obtained in violation of the right to privacy of the user of the booth.

"B. Whether physical penetration of a constitutionally protected area is necessary before a search and seizure can be said to be violative of the Fourth Amendment to the United States Constitution."

We decline to adopt this formulation of the issues. In the first place, the correct solution of Fourth Amendment problems is not necessarily promoted by incantation of the phrase "constitutionally protected area." Secondly, the Fourth Amendment cannot be translated into a general constitutional "right to privacy." That Amendment protects individual privacy against certain kinds of governmental intrusion, but its protections go further, and often have nothing to do with privacy at all. Other provisions of the Constitution protect personal privacy from other forms of governmental invasion. But the protection of a person's *general* right to privacy—his right to be let alone by other people—is, like the protection of his property and of his very life, left largely to the law of the individual States.

Because of the misleading way the issues have been formulated, the parties have attached a great significance to the characterization of the telephone booth from which the petitioner placed his calls. The petitioner has strenuously argued that the booth was a "constitutionally protected area." The Government has maintained with equal vigor that it was not. But this effort to decide whether or not a given "area," viewed in the abstract, is "constitutionally protected" deflects attention from the problem presented by this case. For the Fourth Amendment protects people, not places. What a person knowingly exposes to the public, even in his own home or office, is not a subject of Fourth Amendment protection. . . . But what he seeks to preserve as private, even in an area accessible to the public, may be constitutionally protected. . . .

The Government stresses the fact that the telephone booth from which the petitioner made his calls was constructed partly of glass, so that he was as visible after he entered it as he would have been if he had remained outside. But what he sought to exclude when he entered the booth was not the intruding eye—it was the uninvited ear. He did not shed his right to do so simply because he made his calls from a place where he might be seen. No less than an individual in a business office, in a friend's apartment, or in a taxicab, a person in a telephone booth may rely upon the protection of the Fourth Amendment. One who occupies it, shuts the door behind him, and pays the toll that permits him to place a call, is surely entitled to assume that the words he utters into the mouthpiece will not be broadcast to the world. To read the Constitution more narrowly is to ignore the vital role that the public telephone has come to play in private communication.

The Government contends, however, that the activities of its agents in this case should not be tested by Fourth Amendment requirements, for the surveillance technique they employed involved no physical penetration of the telephone booth from which the petitioner placed his calls. It is true that the absence of such penetration was at one time thought to foreclose further Fourth Amendment inquiry, *Olmstead* v. *United States* . . . for that Amendment was thought to limit only searches and seizures of tangible property. But "[t]he premise that property interests control the right of the Government to search and seize has been discredited." . . . Thus, although a closely divided Court supposed in *Olmstead* that surveillance without any trespass and without the seizure of any material object fell outside the ambit of the Constitution, we have since departed from the narrow view on which that decision rested. Indeed, we have expressly held that the Fourth Amendment governs not only the seizure of tangible items, but extends as well to the recording of oral statements, overheard without any "technical trespass under . . . local property law."

Once this much is acknowledged, and once it is recognized that the Fourth Amendment protects people—and not simply "areas"—against unreasonable searches and seizures, it becomes clear that the reach of that Amendment cannot turn upon the presence or absence of a physical intrusion into any given enclosure.

We conclude that the underpinnings of *Olmstead* and *Goldman* have been so eroded by our subsequent decisions that the "trespass" doctrine there enunciated can no longer be regarded as controlling. The Government's activities in electronically listening to and recording the petitioner's words violated the privacy upon which he justifiably relied while using the telephone booth and thus constituted a "search and sei-

zure" within the meaning of the Fourth Amendment. The fact that the electronic device employed to achieve that end did not happen to penetrate the wall of the booth can have no constitutional significance.

The question remaining for decision, then, is whether the search and seizure conducted in this case complied with constitutional standards. In that regard, the Government's position is that its agents acted in an entirely defensible manner: They did not begin their electronic surveillance until investigation of the petitioner's activities had established a strong probability that he was using the telephone in question to transmit gambling information to persons in other States, in violation of federal law. Moreover, the surveillance was limited, both in scope and in duration, to the specific purpose of establishing the contents of the petitioner's unlawful telephone communications. The agents confined their surveillance to the brief periods during which he used the telephone booth, and they took great care to overhear only the conversations of the petitioner himself.

Accepting this account of the Government's actions as accurate, it is clear that this surveillance was so narrowly circumscribed that a duly authorized magistrate, properly notified of the need for such investigation, specifically informed of the basis on which it was to proceed, and clearly apprised of the precise intrusion it would entail, could constitutionally have authorized, with appropriate safeguards, the very limited search and seizure that the Government asserts in fact took place. . . .

The Government urges that, because its agents relied upon the decision in *Olmstead* and *Goldman*, and because they did no more here than they might properly have done with prior judicial sanction, we should retroactively validate their conduct. That we cannot do. It is apparent that the agents in this case acted with restraint. Yet the inescapable fact is that this restraint was imposed by the agents themselves, not by a judicial officer. They were not required, before commencing the search, to present their estimate of probable cause for detached scrutiny by a neutral magistrate. They were not compelled, during the conduct of the search itself, to observe precise limits established in advance by a specific court order. Nor were they directed, after the search had been completed, to notify the authorizing magistrate in detail of all that had been seized. In the absence of such safeguards, this Court has never sustained a search upon the sole ground that officers reasonably expected to find evidence of a particular crime and voluntarily confined their activities to the least intrusive means consistent with that end. Searches conducted without warrants have been held unlawful "notwithstanding facts unquestionably showing probable cause," . . . for the Constitution requires "that the deliberate, impartial judgment of a judicial officer . . . be interposed between the citizen and the police. . . ." "Over and again this Court has emphasized that the mandate of the [Fourth] Amendment requires adherence to judicial processes," . . . and that searches conducted outside the judicial process, without prior approval by judge or magistrate, are per se unreasonable under the Fourth Amendment—subject only to a few specifically established and well-delineated exceptions.

It is difficult to imagine how any of those exceptions could ever apply to the sort of search and seizure involved in this case. Even electronic surveillance substantially contemporaneous with an individual's arrest could hardly be deemed an "incident" of that arrest. Nor could the use of electronic surveillance without prior authorization be justified on grounds of "hot pursuit." And, of course, the very nature of electronic surveillance precludes its use pursuant to the suspect's consent.

The Government does not question these basic principles. Rather, it urges the creation of a new exception to cover this case. It argues that surveillance of a telephone booth should be exempted from the usual requirement of advance authorization by a magistrate upon a showing of probable cause. We cannot agree. Omission of such authorization "bypasses the safeguards provided by an objective predetermination of probable cause, and substitutes instead the far less reliable procedure of an after-the-event justification for the . . . search, too likely to be subtly influenced by the familiar shortcomings of hindsight judgment." . . . And bypassing a neutral predetermination of the *scope* of a search leaves individuals secure from Fourth Amendment violations "only in the discretion of the police."

These considerations do not vanish when the search in question is transferred from the setting of a home, an office, or a hotel room, to that of a telephone booth. Wherever a man may be, he is entitled to know that he will remain free from unreasonable searches and seizures. The government agents here ignored "the procedure of antecedent justification . . . that is central to the Fourth Amendment," a procedure that we hold to be a constitutional precondition of the kind of electronic surveillance involved in this case. Because the surveillance here failed to meet that condition, and because it led to the petitioner's conviction, the judgment must be reversed.

It is so ordered.

MR. JUSTICE DOUGLAS, WITH WHOM MR. JUSTICE BRENNAN JOINS, CONCURRING.

While I join the opinion of the Court, I feel compelled to reply to the separate concurring opinion of my Brother White, which I view as a wholly unwarranted green light for the Executive Branch to resort to electronic eavesdropping without a warrant in cases which the Executive Branch itself labels "national security" matters.

Neither the President nor the Attorney General is a magistrate. In matters where they believe national security may be involved they are not detached, disinterested, and neutral as a court or magistrate must be. Under the separation of powers created by the Constitution, the Executive Branch is not supposed to be neutral and disinterested. Rather it should vigorously investigate and prevent breaches of national security and prosecute those who violate the pertinent federal laws. The President and Attorney General are properly interested parties, cast in the role of adversary, in national security cases. They may even be the intended victims of subversive action. Since spies and saboteurs are as entitled to the protection of the Fourth Amendment as suspected gamblers like petitioner, I cannot agree that where spies and saboteurs are involved adequate protection of Fourth Amendment rights is assured when the President and Attorney General assume both the position of adversary-and-prosecutor and disinterested, neutral magistrate.

There is, so far as I understand constitutional history, no distinction under the Fourth Amendment between types of crimes. Article III, § 3, gives "treason" a very narrow definition and puts restrictions on its proof. But the Fourth Amendment draws no lines between various substantive offenses. The arrests in cases of "hot pursuit," the arrests on visible or other evidence of probable cause cut across the boards and are not peculiar to any kind of crime.

I would respect the present lines of distinction and not improvise because a particular crime seems particularly heinous. When the Framers took that step, as they did with treason, the worst crime of all, they made their purpose manifest.

MR. JUSTICE HARLAN, CONCURRING (OMITTED).

MR. JUSTICE WHITE, CONCURRING.

I agree that the official surveillance of petitioner's telephone conversations in a public booth must be subjected to the test of reasonableness under the Fourth Amendment and that on the record now before us the particular surveillance undertaken was unreasonable absent a warrant properly authorizing it. This application of the Fourth Amendment need not interfere with legitimate needs of law enforcement.

In joining the Court's opinion, I note the Court's acknowledgment that there are circumstances in which it is reasonable to search without a warrant. In this connection . . . the Court points out that today's decision does not reach national security cases. Wiretapping to protect the security of the Nation has been authorized by successive Presidents. The present Administration would apparently save national security cases from restrictions against wiretapping. . . . We should not require the warrant procedure and the magistrate's judgment if the President of the United States or his chief legal officer, the Attorney General, has considered the requirements of national security and authorized electronic surveillance as reasonable.

MR. JUSTICE BLACK, DISSENTING.

My basic objection is twofold: (1) I do not believe that the words of the Amendment will bear the meaning given them by today's decision, and (2) I do not believe that it is the proper role of this Court to rewrite the Amendment in order "to bring it into harmony with the times" and thus reach a result that many people believe to be desirable.

I do not deny that common sense requires and that this Court often has said that the Bill of Rights' safeguards should be given a liberal construction. This principle, however, does not justify construing the search and seizure amendment as applying to eavesdropping or the "seizure" of conversations. The Fourth Amendment was aimed directly at the abhorred practice of breaking in, ransacking and searching homes and other buildings and seizing people's personal belongings without warrants issued by magistrates. . . .

Since I see no way in which the words of the Fourth Amendment can be construed to apply to eavesdropping, that closes the matter for me. In interpreting the Bill of Rights, I willingly go as far as a liberal construction of the language takes me, but I simply cannot in good conscience give a meaning to words which they have never before been thought to have and which they certainly do not have in common ordinary usage. I will not distort the words of the Amendment in order to "keep the Constitution up to date" or "to bring it into harmony with the times." It was never meant for this Court to have

such power, which in effect would make us a continuously functioning constitutional convention.

With this decision the Court has completed, I hope, its rewriting of the Fourth Amendment, which started only recently when the Court began referring incessantly to the Fourth Amendment not so much as a law against *unreasonable* searches and seizures as one to protect an individual's privacy. By clever word juggling the Court finds it plausible to argue that language aimed specifically at searches and seizures of things that can be searched and seized may, to protect privacy, be applied to eavesdropped evidence of conversations that can neither be searched nor seized. Few things happen to an individual that do not affect his privacy in one way or another. Thus, by arbitrarily substituting the Court's language, designed to protect privacy, for the Constitution's language, designed to protect against unreasonable searches and seizures, the Court has made the Fourth Amendment its vehicle for holding all laws violative of the Constitution which offend the Court's broadest concept of privacy. . . .

(b) A Note on the Wiretapping Controversy and the Omnibus Crime Control Act of 1968, Title III

Responding to the *Berger* and *Katz* cases, Congress authorized court-approved wiretapping and eavesdropping in Title III of the Crime Control Act of 1968. With the exception of surveillance authorized by the president to obtain information about foreign intelligence operations and agents, which does not require prior judicial approval, all other statutory surveillance requires a warrant. A surveillance warrant can be sought in most felony cases, national security offenses, organized crime detection, and in investigating conspiracies to commit these offenses. A warrant can be issued only on the showing of probable cause. No warrant can be for more than thirty days, and extensions can be granted only by reapplication. Any wiretapping or electronic surveillance outside of these narrow boundaries (including all private surveillance) constitutes a criminal offense. The statute authorized the states to establish comparable procedures to permit surveillance by their own law enforcement officials, and it prohibited the admissibility of evidence obtained by illegal electronic surveillance in federal court trials. In addition, any interception in violation of the act was made a federal crime punishable by five years imprisonment, or a $10,000 fine, or both.

In 1969, the new attorney general, John Mitchell, announced that the government would make use of these new powers. And he further announced that the government had the inherent power, *without* court approval, to order surveillance of domestic groups whose activities threatened the political system. In 1969, the Supreme Court decided *Alderman* v. *United States* and ruled that illegal wiretaps must be turned over to the defendants and that such evidence must be excluded from use in court. Lawyers for the defendants in the Chicago Conspiracy Trial filed a motion, before the passage of Title III, asking for disclosure of wiretaps or other illegal surveillance, and asking that evidence obtained by this surveillance be suppressed. The government responded that "any President who takes seriously his oath to 'preserve and protect' and defend the constitution will no doubt determine

that it is not unreasonable to utilize electronic surveillance to gather intelligence information concerning those organizations which are committed to the use of illegal methods to bring about changes in our form of government and which may be seeking to foment disorders." The brief claimed that it was the executive branch, not the courts, that must determine the appropriateness of electronic surveillance. The government admitted that five of the defendants had been subjected to illegal wiretaps, turned over some transcripts to the defense lawyers, and agreed not to use evidence derived from those taps. But the government would not relinquish all the transcripts for national security reasons; Judge Hoffman upheld this position by postponing a hearing until the conclusion of the trial.

(c) *United States v. United States District Court* (1972)

+Burger, Douglas, Brennan, Stewart, White, Marshall, Blackmun, Powell

NP Rehnquist

[Criminal proceedings were begun against several members of the White Panther Party. They were charged with conspiracy to destroy government property, with one defendant accused of bombing the CIA office in Ann Arbor, Michigan. Before trial, the defendants moved to compel the United States to disclose the existence of electronic surveillance and the possible "taint" of evidence used to obtain a grand jury indictment or likely to be used at trial. The government acknowledged that one of the defendants had been overheard lawfully on a wiretap approved by the attorney general. The district court found that in the absence of a judicial warrant, this surveillance violated the Fourth Amendment. Full disclosure to the defendants was ordered. The government then sought a writ of mandamus in the court of appeals, which was denied. The Supreme Court granted certiorari.

The government contended that the president, acting through the attorney general, had the power to authorize electronic surveillance in domestic security cases without prior judicial approval, citing similar actions by presidents dating back to World War II. In the court of appeals, the government had asserted that it was the "inherent power of the President to safeguard the security of the nation" which permitted bypassing of the judicial warrant procedure. Before the Supreme Court, the Solicitor General did not pursue this extreme argument. He asserted that warrantless wiretapping of domestic subversives was "reasonable" within the meaning of the Fourth Amendment; alternatively he argued that warrantless wiretaps of domestic subversives should be regarded as another of the many enumerated "exceptions" to the warrant requirement.]

MR. JUSTICE POWELL delivered the opinion of the Court.

Title III of the Omnibus Crime Control and Safe Streets Act, 18 U.S.C. §§2510–2520, authorizes the use of electronic surveillance for classes of crimes carefully specified in 18 U.S.C. §2516. Such surveillance is subject to prior court order. Section 2518 sets forth the detailed and particularized application necessary to obtain such an order as well as carefully circumscribed conditions for its use. The Act represents a comprehensive attempt by Congress to promote more effective control of crime while protecting the privacy of individual thought and expression. Much of Title III was drawn to meet the constitutional requirements for electronic surveillance enunciated by this Court in *Berger* v. *New York* . . . (1967), and *Katz* v. *United States* . . . (1967).

Together with the elaborate surveillance requirements in Title III, there is the following proviso, . . . §2511(3):

Nothing contained in this chapter or in section 605 of the Communications Act of 1934 . . . shall limit the constitutional power of the President to take such measures as he deems necessary to protect the Nation against actual or potential attack or other hostile acts of a foreign power, to obtain foreign intelligence deemed essential to the security of the United States, or to protect national security information against foreign intelligence activities. Nor shall anything contained in this chapter be deemed to limit the constitutional power of the President to take such measures as he deems necessary to protect the United States against the overthrow of the Government by force or other unlawful means, or against any other clear and present danger to the structure or existence of the Government. *The contents of any wire or oral communication intercepted by authority of the President in the exercise of the foregoing powers may be received in evidence in any trial hearing, or other proceeding only where such interception was reasonable, and shall not be otherwise used or disclosed except as is necessary to implement that power. (Emphasis supplied.)*

The Government relies on §2511(3). It argues that "in excepting national security surveillances from the Act's warrant requirement Congress recognized the President's authority to conduct such surveillance without prior judicial approval." . . . The section thus is viewed as a recognition or affirmance of a constitutional authority in the President to conduct warrantless domestic security surveillance such as that involved in this case.

We think the language of §2511(3), as well as the legislative history of the statute, refutes this interpretation. The relevant language is that:

Nothing contained in this chapter . . . shall limit the constitutional power of the President to take such measures as he deems necessary to protect . . .

against the dangers specified. At most, this is an implicit recognition that the President does not have certain powers in the specified areas. . . .

The language of subsection (3), here involved, is to be contrasted with the language of the exceptions set forth in the preceding section. Rather than stating that warrantless presidential uses of electronic surveillance "shall not be unlawful" and thus employing the standard language of exception, subsection (3) merely disclaims any intention to "limit the constitutional power of the President."

The express grant of authority to conduct surveillance is found in § 2516, which authorizes the Attorney General to make application to a federal judge when surveillance may provide evidence of certain offenses. These offenses are described with meticulous care and specificity. . . .

In view of these and other interrelated provisions delineating permissible interceptions of particular criminal activity upon carefully specified conditions, it would have been incongruous for Congress to have legislated with respect to the important and complex area of national security in a single brief and nebulous paragraph. This would not comport with the sensitivity of the problem involved or with the extraordinary care Congress exercised in drafting other sections of the Act. We therefore think the conclusion inescapable that Congress only intended to make clear that the Act simply did not legislate with respect to national security surveillances. . . .

It is important at the outset to em-phasize the limited nature of the question before the Court. This case raises no constitutional challenge to electronic surveillance as specifically authorized by Title III of the Omnibus Crime Control and Safe Streets Act of 1968. Nor is there any question or doubt as to the necessity of obtaining a warrant in the surveillance of crimes unrelated to the national security interest. *Katz* v. *United States* . . . (1967); *Berger* v. *New York* . . . (1967). Further, the instant case requires no judgment on the scope of the President's surveillance power with respect to the activities of foreign powers, within or without this country. The Attorney General's affidavit in this case states that the surveillances were "deemed necessary to protect the nation from attempts of *domestic organizations* to attack and subvert the existing structure of Government" (emphasis supplied). There is no evidence of any involvement, directly or indirectly, of a foreign power.

Our present inquiry, though important, is therefore a narrow one. It addresses a question left open by *Katz,* . . . .

Whether safeguards other than prior authorization by a magistrate would satisfy the Fourth Amendment in a situation involving the national security. . . .

The determination of this question requires the essential Fourth Amendment inquiry into the "reasonableness" of the search and seizure in question, and the way in which that "reasonableness" derives content and meaning through reference to the warrant clause. *Coolidge* v. *New Hampshire,* . . . (1971).

We begin the inquiry by noting that the President of the United States has the fundamental duty, under Art. II, §1, of the Constitution, to "preserve, protect and defend the Constitution of the United States." Implicit in that duty is the power to protect our Government against those who would subvert or overthrow it by unlawful means. In the discharge of this duty, the President—through the Attorney General—may find it necessary to employ electronic surveillance to obtain intelligence information on the plans of those who plot unlawful acts against the Government. The use of such surveillance in internal security cases has been sanctioned more or less continuously by various Presidents and Attorneys General since July 1946. . . .

Though the Government and respondents debate their seriousness and magnitude, threats and acts of sabotage against the Government exist in sufficient number to justify investigative powers with respect to them. The covertness and complexity of potential unlawful conduct against the Government and the necessary dependency of many conspirators upon the telephone make electronic surveillance an effective investigatory instrument in certain circumstances. The marked acceleration in technological developments and sophistication in their use have resulted in new techniques for the planning, commission and concealment of criminal activities. It would be contrary to the public interest for Government to deny to itself the prudent and lawful employment of those very techniques which are employed against the Government and its law abiding citizens. . . .

But a recognition of these elementary truths does not make the employment by Government of electronic surveillance a welcome development—even when employed with restraint and under judicial supervision. There is, understandably, a deep-seated uneasiness and apprehension that this capability will be used to intrude upon cherished privacy of law-abiding citizens. We look to the Bill of Rights to safeguard this privacy. Though physical entry of the home is the chief evil against which the wording of the Fourth Amendment is directed, its broader spirit now shields private speech from unreasonable surveillance. . . . Our decision in *Katz* refused to lock the Fourth Amendment into instances of actual physical trespass. Rather, the Amendment governs "not only the seizure of tangible items, but extends as well to the recording of oral statements 'without any technical trespass under . . . local property law.'" *Katz, supra,* . . . That decision implicitly recognized that the broad and unsuspected governmental incursions into conversational privacy which electronic surveillance entails necessitate the application of Fourth Amendment safeguards.

National security cases, moreover, often reflect a convergence of First and Fourth Amendment values not present in cases of "ordinary" crime. Though the investigative duty of the executive may be stronger in such cases, so also is there greater jeopardy in constitutionally protected speech. . . . Fourth Amendment protections become the more necessary when the targets of official surveillance may be those suspected of unorthodoxy in their political beliefs. The danger to political dissent is acute where the Government attempts to act under so vague a concept as the power to protect "domestic security." Given the difficulty of defining the domestic security interest, the danger of abuse in acting to protect that interest becomes apparent. . . . The price of lawful public dissent must not be a dread of subjection to an unchecked surveillance power. Nor must the fear of unauthorized official eavesdropping deter vigorous citizen dissent and discussion of Government action in private conversation. For private dissent, no less than open public discourse, is essential to our free society.

As the Fourth Amendment is not absolute in its terms, our task is to examine and balance the basic values at stake in this case: the duty of Government to protect the domestic security, and the potential danger posed by unreasonable surveillance to individual privacy and free expression. If the legitimate need of Government to safeguard domestic security requires the use of electronic surveillance, the question is whether the needs of citizens for privacy and free expression may not be better protected by requiring a warrant before such surveillance is undertaken. We must also ask whether a warrant requirement would unduly frustrate the efforts of Government to protect itself from acts of subversion and overthrow directed against it. . . .

These Fourth Amendment freedoms cannot properly be guaranteed if domestic security surveillances may be conducted solely within the discretion of the executive branch. The Fourth Amendment does not contemplate the executive officers of Government as neutral and disinterested magistrates. Their duty and responsibility is to enforce the laws, to investigate and to prosecute. . . . But those charged with this investigative and prosecutorial duty should not be the sole judges of when to utilize constitutionally sensitive means in pursuing their tasks. The historical judgment, which the Fourth Amendment accepts, is that unreviewed executive discretion may

yield too readily to pressures to obtain incriminating evidence and overlook potential invasions of privacy and protected speech.

It may well be that, in the instant case, the Government's surveillance of Plamondon's [one of the three defendants] conversations was a reasonable one which readily would have gained prior judicial approval. But this Court "has never sustained a search upon the sole ground that officers reasonably expected to find evidence of a particular crime and voluntarily confined their activities to the least intrusive means consistent with that end." *Katz*, . . . The Fourth Amendment contemplates a prior judicial judgment, not the risk that executive discretion may be reasonably exercised. This judicial role accords with our basic constitutional doctrine that individual freedoms will best be preserved through a separation of powers and division of functions among the different branches and levels of government. . . .

It is true that there have been some exceptions to the warrant requirement. . . . But those exceptions are few in number and carefully delineated, *Katz, supra,* . . . ; in general they serve the legitimate needs of law enforcement officers to protect their own well-being and preserve evidence from destruction. . . .

The Government argues that the special circumstances applicable to domestic security surveillances necessitate a further exception to the warrant requirement. It is urged that the requirement of prior judicial review would obstruct the President in the discharge of his constitutional duty to protect domestic security. We are told further that these surveillances are directed primarily to the collecting and maintaining of intelligence with respect to subversive forces, and are not an attempt to gather evidence for specific criminal prosecutions. It is said that this type of surveillance should not be subject to traditional warrant requirements which were established to govern investigation of criminal activity, not on-going intelligence gathering. . . .

The Government further insists that courts "as a practical matter would have neither the knowledge nor the techniques necessary to determine whether there was probable cause to believe that surveillance was necessary to protect national security." These security problems, the Government contends, involve "a large number of complex and subtle factors" beyond the competence of courts to evaluate. . . .

As a final reason for exemption from a warrant requirement, the Government believes that disclosure to a magistrate of all or even a significant portion of the information involved in domestic security surveillances "would create serious potential dangers to the national security and to the lives of informants and agents. . . . Secrecy is the essential ingredient in intelligence gathering; requiring prior judicial authorization would create a greater 'danger of leaks . . . , because in addition to the judge, you have the clerk, the stenographer and some other official like a law assistant or bailiff who may be apprised of the nature' of the surveillance." . . .

These contentions in behalf of a complete exemption from the warrant requirement, when urged on behalf of the President and the national security in its domestic implications, merit the most careful consideration. We certainly do not reject them lightly, especially at a time of worldwide ferment and when civil disorders in this country are more prevalent than in the less turbulent periods of our history. There is, no doubt, pragmatic force to the Government's position.

But we do not think a case has been made for the requested departure from Fourth Amendment standards. The circumstances described do not justify complete exemption of domestic security surveillance from prior judicial scrutiny. Official surveillance, whether its purpose be criminal investigation or on-going intelligence gathering, risks infringement of constitutionally protected privacy of speech. Security surveillances are especially sensitive because of the inherent vagueness of the domestic security concept, the necessarily broad and continuing nature of intelligence gathering, and the temptation to utilize such surveillances to oversee political dissent. We recognize, as we have before, the constitutional basis of the President's domestic security role, but we think it must be exercised in a manner compatible with the Fourth Amendment. In this case we hold that this requires an appropriate prior warrant procedure. . . .

We emphasize, before concluding this opinion, the scope of our decision. . . . We have not addressed, and express no opinion as to, the issues which may be involved with respect to activities of foreign powers or their agents. Nor does our decision rest on the language of §2511(3) or any other section of Title III of the Omnibus Crime Control and Safe Streets Act of 1968. That Act does not attempt to define or delineate the powers of the President to meet domestic threats to the national security.

Moreover, we do not hold that the same type of standards and procedures prescribed by Title III are necessarily applicable to this case. We recognize that domestic security surveillance may involve different policy and practical considerations from the surveillance of "ordinary crime." The gathering of security intelligence is often long range and involves the interrelation of various sources and types of information. The exact targets of such surveillance may be more difficult to identify than in surveillance operations against many types of crime specified in Title III. Often, too, the emphasis of domestic intelligence gathering is on the prevention of unlawful activity or the enhancement of the Government's preparedness for some possible future crisis or emergency. Thus, the focus of domestic surveillance may be less precise than that directed against more conventional types of crime.

It may be that Congress, for example, would judge that the application and affidavit showing probable cause need not follow the exact requirements of §2518 but should allege other circumstances more appropriate to domestic security cases; that the request for prior court authorization could, in sensitive cases, be made to any member of a specially designated court (e.g., the District Court or Court of Appeals for the District of Columbia); and that the time and reporting requirements need not be so strict as those in §2518.

The above paragraph does not, of course, attempt to guide the congressional judgment but rather to delineate the present scope of our own opinion. We do not attempt to detail the precise standards for domestic security warrants any more than our decision in *Katz* sought to set the refined requirements for the specified criminal surveillances which now constitute Title III. We do hold, however, that prior judicial approval is required for the type of domestic security surveillance involved in this case and that such approval may be made in accordance with such reasonable standards as the Congress may prescribe.

. . .

The judgment of the Court of Appeals is hereby affirmed.

THE CHIEF JUSTICE CONCURS IN THE RESULT.
MR. JUSTICE DOUGLAS, CONCURRING [OMITTED].
MR. JUSTICE WHITE, CONCURRING IN THE JUDGMENT [OMITTED].

[The Supreme Court has not ruled directly on the constitutionality of any Title III provisions. In *United States* v. *Kahn* (1974), it expressed general support for the statute and for the practice of electronic surveillance by law enforcement agencies. The Court further held that the statutory language of Title III did not require the government to identify an individual in applying for a surveillance warrant unless it had probable cause to believe that individual was engaged in the criminal activity under investigation and that his conversation would be intercepted. Justices Brennan, Douglas, and Marshall dissented. They argued that if the government was not required to identify all individuals, it was in effect being issued a general warrant to search for evidence.

A further restriction on the rights of defendants to suppress evidence under Title III came in *United States* v. *Donovan* (1977). Clarifying the *Kahn* decision, the Court held that Title III required the government to identify *all* individuals whom it had probable cause to believe were engaged in the criminal activity under investigation and not merely the "principal target[s]" of the investigation. However, the Court also held that the government's failure to comply with the identification requirements did not play a "substantive role" in the regulatory system, and therefore evidence obtained in this case could not be suppressed.

In practice, Title III wiretapping provisions

are used relatively infrequently. As Table I shows, the states are far more active in using electronic surveillance methods than the federal government. The number of convictions obtained solely or primarily from the use of electronic surveillance is unknown. Moreover, merely knowing the number of convictions obtained, without knowing more about *who* was convicted, makes it difficult to assess the impact of electronic surveillance on crime fighting efforts. What is clear from the table is that electronic surveillance is used most frequently in two types of offenses that form the core of organized crime: gambling and narcotics. What the table does *not* show, of course, is the extent of official wiretapping without a warrant, in violation of the statute.

As a result of disclosures in 1975 and 1976 of illegal government surveillance and congressional hostility toward presidential claims of the inherent power to wiretap American citizens within the United States for national security reasons, Congress passed the Foreign Intelligence Surveillance Act of 1978. That act requires the government to demonstrate probable cause in order to place American citizens under surveillance and, for the first time, establishes a judicial warrant procedure for conducting foreign intelligence operations within the United States. The act authorizes seven district court judges to grant warrants, and these decisions are ultimately reviewable by the Supreme Court. The act does not apply to surveillance of United States citizens traveling abroad. In addition, the government may continue warrantless surveillance of communications that it knows are solely between noncitizens of the United States.]

Table I. Authorized Intercepts of Communications—Summary: 1969 to 1976 (Data for jurisdictions with statutes authorizing or approving interception of wire or oral communication)

Item	1969	1970	1971	1972	1973	1974	1975	1976
Jurisdictions reporting interceptions[a]	9	12	14	18	20	19	18	21
Intercept applications authorized, total	301	596	816	855	864	728	701	686
Residence or apartment	202	366	553	569	419	455	435	
Business or other	99	230	263	286	308	309	246	251
Installed	270	582	792	841	812	694	676	635
Average length days	23	22	22	22	24	23	22	23
Tap (telephone wiretap)	250	538	753	779	731	633	620	581
Bug (incl. unspecified)[b]	20	44	39	62	81	61	56	54
Federal	30	179	281	205	130	120	106	137
State	240	403	511	636	682	574	570	549
Avg. number of intercepted communications[c]	544	656	643	600	610	850	654	662
Incriminating	265	296	399	303	304	431	305	272
Persons arrested[d]	625	1,874	2,811	2,861	2,306	2,162	2,234	2,189
Convictions[d]	34	151	322	402	409	179	336	358
Major offense specified in application:								
Gambling	102	326	570	497	446	381	408	378
Drugs	89	127	126	230	229	199	178	190
Homicide and assault	22	20	18	35	47	21	16	10
Larceny and theft	10	31	31	22	36	22	5	9
Bribery	12	16	16	9	25	25	21	24
Other	66	76	55	62	81	80	73	75

Source. Administrative Office of the U.S. Courts, *Reports on Applications for Orders Authorizing or Approving the Interception of Wire or Oral Communications,* 1977.

a Jurisdictions include Federal Government, States, and District of Columbia as of Dec. 31, 1975.

b A listening device, e.g., a microphone. Includes use of a microphone and telephone wiretap simultaneously.

c Per authorized installation.

d Based on information received from intercepts installed in year shown.

(d) Dalia v. United States (1979)

+ Powell, Burger, White, Blackmun, Rehnquist
± Brennan, Stewart
− Marshall, Stevens

[One issue left open by the Supreme Court in *United States* v. *United States District Court* (1972) was whether or not Title III of the Omnibus Crime Control Act of 1968 authorized covert, surreptitious entry to install electronic surveillance equipment, and if it did so, whether or not this was constitutionally permissible.

In March of 1973 federal officials applied to the U.S. District Court in New Jersey for authorization under the statute to intercept conversations on two telephones at Dalia's business office. Evidence was presented showing probable cause to believe that Dalia was a member of a conspiracy to steal goods shipped in interstate commerce, and that his business telephones were used to further the conspiracy. A wiretap order was granted for a period of twenty days, "or until the purpose of the interception was achieved," whichever came first. The order meticulously described the telephones to be tapped, the types of conversations to be monitored, and the care to be used to minimize the number of conversations intercepted. At the government's request the order was extended for an additional twenty days.

In 1975, Dalia was indicted on charges of conspiracy to steal an interstate shipment of fabric. Evidence was introduced, including a number of intercepted conversations, showing that Dalia's warehouse had been used to store the stolen goods. He was convicted of receiving stolen goods and conspiring to transport, receive and possess stolen goods. The District Court twice denied motions to suppress the evidence obtained by electronic surveillance, rejecting Dalia's contention that the court order authorizing the surveillance had not explicitly authorized the covert entry necessary to install it. FBI agents had in fact covertly entered Dalia's office secretly and spent three hours there installing the bug. A second entry was made at the conclusion of the surveillance period to remove the bug. Dalia's conviction was affirmed by the Court of Appeals, although it conceded that it would have been more "prudent" for the government to have stated the need for covert entry at the outset.]

MR. JUSTICE POWELL delivered the opinion of the Court.

. . .

Petitioner first contends that the Fourth Amendment prohibits covert entry of private premises in all cases irrespective of the reasonableness of the entry or the approval of a court. He contends that Title III is unconstitutional insofar as it enables courts to authorize covert entries for the installation of electronic bugging devices.

In several cases this Court has implied that in some circumstances covert entry to install electronic bugging devices would be constitutionally acceptable if done pursuant to a search warrant. Thus, for example, in *Irvine* v. *California* . . . (1954), the plurality stated that in conducting electronic surveillance, state police officers had "flagrantly, deliberately, and persistently violated the fundamental principle declared by the Fourth Amendment as a restriction on the Federal Government." . . . It emphasized that the bugging equipment was installed through a covert entry of the defendant's home "*without a search warrant* or other process." . . . (emphasis added). Similarly, in *Silverman* v. *United States* . . . (1961), it was noted that, "[t]his Court has never held that a federal officer may *without warrant* and without consent physically entrench into a man's office or home, there secretly observe or listen, and relate at the man's subsequent criminal trial what was seen or heard." (Emphasis added.) Implicit in decisions such as *Silverman* and *Irvine* has been the Court's view that covert entries are constitutional in some circumstances, at least if they are made pursuant to warrant.

Moreover, we find no basis for a constitutional rule proscribing all covert entries. It is well established that law officers constitutionally may break and enter to execute a search warrant where such entry is the only means by which the warrant effectively may be executed. . . . Petitioner nonetheless argues that covert entries are unconstitutional for their lack of notice. This argument is frivolous, as was indicated in *Katz* v. *United States* (1967), where the Court stated that "officers need not announce their purpose before conducting an otherwise [duly] authorized search if such an announcement would provoke the escape of the suspect or the destruction of critical evidence." In *United States* v. *Donovan* (1977), we held that Title III provided a constitutionally adequate substitute for advance notice by requiring that once the surveillance operation is completed the authorizing judge must cause notice to be served on those subjected to surveillance. . . . There is no reason why the same notice is not equally sufficient with respect to electronic surveillances requiring covert entry. We make explicit, therefore, what has long been implicit in our decisions dealing with this subject: The Fourth Amendment does not prohibit *per se* a covert entry performed for the purpose of installing otherwise legal electronic bugging equipment.

Petitioner's second contention is that Congress has not given the courts statutory authority to approve covert entries for the purpose of installing electronic surveillance equipment, even if constitutionally it could have done so. Petitioner emphasizes that although Title III sets forth with meticulous care the circumstances in which electronic sur-

veillance is permitted, there is no comparable indication in the statute that covert entry ever may be ordered. . . .

Title III does not refer explicitly to covert entry. The language, structure, and history of the statute, however, demonstrate that Congress meant to authorize courts—in certain specified circumstances—to approve electronic surveillance without limitation on the means necessary to its accomplishment, so long as they are reasonable under the circumstances. Title III provides a comprehensive scheme for the regulation of electronic surveillance, prohibiting all secret interception of communications except as authorized by certain state and federal judges in response to applications from specified federal and state law enforcement officials. See . . . *United States* v. *United States District Court* (1972). Although Congress was fully aware of the distinction between bugging and wiretapping . . . Title III by its terms deals with each form of surveillance in essentially the same manner. . . . Orders authorizing interceptions of either wire or oral communications may be entered only after the court has made specific determinations concerning the likelihood that the interception will disclose evidence of criminal conduct. . . . Moreover, with respect to both wiretapping and bugging, an authorizing court must specify the exact scope of the surveillance undertaken, enumerating the parties whose communications are to be overheard (if they are known), the place to be monitored, and the agency that will do the monitoring. . . .

The plain effect of the detailed restrictions of §2518 is to guarantee that wiretapping or bugging occurs only when there is a genuine need for it and only to the extent that it is needed. Once this need has been demonstrated in accord with the requirements of §2518, the courts have broad authority to "approv[e] interception of wire or oral communications," 18 U.S.C. § 2516 (1), (2), subject of course to constitutional limitations. . . . Nowhere in Title III is there any indication that the authority of courts under §2518 is to be limited to approving those methods of interception that do not require covert entry for installation of the intercepting equipment.

The legislative history of Title III underscores Congress' understanding that courts would authorize electronic surveillance in situations where covert entry of private premises was necessary. Indeed, a close examination of that history reveals that Congress did not explicitly address the question of covert entries in the Act only because it did not perceive surveillance requiring such entries to differ in any important way from that performed without entry. Testimony before subcommittees considering Title III and related bills indicated that covert entries were a necessary part of most electronic bugging operations. . . . Moreover, throughout the Senate report on Title III indiscriminate reference is made to the types of surveillance this Court reviewed in *Berger* v. *New York* . . . (1967), and *Katz* v. *United States* . . . (1967). . . . Apparently committee members did not find it significant that *Berger* involved a covert entry, whereas *Katz* did not. . . .

. . .

Finally, Congress' purpose in enacting the statute would be largely thwarted if we were to accept petitioner's invitation to read into Title III a limitation on the courts' authority under §2518. Congress permitted limited electronic surveillance under Title III because it concluded that both wiretapping and

bugging were necessary to enable law enforcement authorities to combat successfully certain forms of crime. Absent covert entry, however, almost all electronic bugging would be impossible. . . .

In sum, we conclude that Congress clearly understood that it was conferring power upon the courts to authorize covert entries ancillary to their responsibility to review and approve surveillance applications under the statute. To read the statute otherwise would be to deny the "respect for the policy of Congress [that] must save us from imputing to it a self-defeating, if not disingenuous purpose." . . .

Petitioner's final contention is that, if covert entries are to be authorized under Title III, the authorizing court must explicitly set forth its approval of such entries before the fact. . . .

The Fourth Amendment requires that search warrants be issued only "upon probable cause, supported by Oath or affirmation, and particularly describing the place to be searched, and the persons or things to be seized." Finding these words to be "precise and clear," *Stanford* v. *Texas* . . . (1965), this Court has interpreted them to require only three things. First, warrants must be issued by neutral, disinterested magistrates. . . . Second, those seeking the warrant must demonstrate to the magistrate their probable cause to believe that "the evidence sought will aid in a particular apprehension or conviction" for a particular offense. . . . Finally, "warrants must particularly describe the 'things to be seized,' " as well as the place to be searched. . . .

. . .

It would extend the warrant clause to the extreme to require that, whenever it is reasonably likely that

Fourth Amendment rights may be affected in more than one way, the court must set forth precisely the procedures to be followed by the executing officers. Such an interpretation is unnecessary, as we have held—and the Government concedes—that the manner in which a warrant is executed is subject to later judicial review as to its reasonableness. *Zurcher* v. *Stanford Daily . . .* (1978). More important, we would promote empty formalism were we to require magistrates to make explicit what unquestionably is implicit in bugging authorizations: that a covert entry, with its attendant interference with Fourth Amendment interests, may be necessary for the installation of the surveillance equipment. . . . We conclude, therefore, that the Fourth Amendment does not require that a Title III electronic surveillance order include a specific authorization to enter covertly the premises described in the order.

The judgment of the Court of Appeals is *Affirmed.*

MR. JUSTICE BRENNAN, WITH WHOM MR. JUSTICE STEWART JOINS, CONCURRING IN PART AND DISSENTING IN PART. (OMITTED).

MR. JUSTICE STEVENS, WITH WHOM MR. JUSTICE BRENNAN AND MR. JUSTICE MARSHALL JOIN, DISSENTING.
. . .

The perpetrators of these break-ins were agents of the Federal Bureau of Investigation. Their office, however, carries with it no general warrant to trespass on private property. Without legislative or judicial sanction, the conduct of these agents was unquestionably "unreasonable" and therefore prohibited by the Fourth Amendment. Moreover, that conduct violated the Criminal Code of the State of New Jersey unless it was duly authorized.

The only consideration that arguably might legitimate these "otherwise tortious and possibly criminal" invasions of petitioner's private property, is the fact that a federal judge had entered an order authorizing the agents to use electronic equipment to intercept oral communications at petitioner's office. The order, however, did not describe the kind of equipment to be used and made no reference to an entry, covert or otherwise, into private property. Nor does any statute expressly permit such activity or even authorize a federal judge to enter orders granting federal agents a license to commit criminal trespass. The initial question this case raises, therefore, is whether this kind of power should be read into a statute that does not expressly grant it.

In my opinion there are three reasons, each sufficient by itself, for refusing to do so. First, until Congress has stated otherwise, our duty to protect the rights of the individual should hold sway over the interest in more effective law enforcement. Second, the structural detail of this statute precludes a reading that converts silence into thunder. Third, the legislative history affirmatively demonstrates that Congress never contemplated the situation now before the Court.

"Congress, like this Court, has an obligation to obey the mandate of the Fourth Amendment." *Marshall* v. *Barlow's, Inc. . . .* (STEVENS, J., dissenting). But Congress is better equipped than the Judiciary to make the empirical judgment that a previously unauthorized investigative technique represents a "reasonable" accommodation between the privacy interests protected by the Fourth Amendment and effective law enforcement. Throughout our history, therefore, it has been Congress that has taken the lead in granting new authority to invade the citizen's privacy. It is appropriate to accord special deference to Congress whenever it has expressly balanced the need for a new investigatory technique against the undesirable consequences of any intrusion on constitutionally protected interests in privacy. . . .

But no comparable deference should be given federal intrusions on privacy that are not expressly authorized by Congress. In my view, a proper respect for Congress' important role in this area as well as our tradition of interpreting statutes to avoid constitutional issues compels this conclusion.

The Court does not share this view. For this is the third time in as many years that it has condoned a serious intrusion on privacy that was not explicitly authorized by statute and that admittedly raised a substantial constitutional question. In *United States* v. *Ramsey,* . . . the Court upheld an Executive regulation authorizing postal inspectors to open private letters without probable cause to believe they contained contraband. In *United States* v. *New York Telephone Co.,* . . . the Court upheld orders authorizing the surreptitious pen register surveillance of an individual and directing a private company to lend its assistance in that endeavor. Again, no explicit statutory authority existed for either order, despite Congress' otherwise comprehensive treatment of wire surveillance in Title III of the Omnibus Crime Control and Safe Streets Act of 1968. . . .

Today the Court has gone even further in finding an implicit grant of Executive power in Title III. . . . In my judgment, it is most unrealistic to assume that Congress granted such broad and controversial authority to the Executive without making its intention to do so unmistakably plain. This is the paradigm case in which "the exacting words of the statute provide the surest guide to determining Congress' intent." I would not enlarge the coverage of the statute beyond its plain meaning. . . .

Because it is not supported by either the text of the statute or the scraps of relevant legislative history, I fear that the Court's holding may reflect an unarticulated presumption that national police officers have the power to carry out a surveillance order by whatever means may be necessary unless explicitly prohibited by the statute or by the Constitution.

But surely the presumption should run the other way. Congressional silence should not be construed to authorize the Executive to violate state criminal laws or to encroach upon constitutionally protected privacy interests. Before confronting the serious constitutional issues raised by the Court's reading of Title III, we should insist upon an unambiguous statement by Congress that this sort of police conduct may be authorized by a court and that a specific showing of necessity, or at least probable cause, must precede such an authorization. Without a legislative mandate that is both explicit and specific, I would presume that this flagrant invasion of the citizen's privacy is prohibited. . . .

I respectfully dissent.

B. *The Citizen in the Station House*

(1) A Note on Escobedo v. Illinois (1964)

It has often been said that our criminal justice system is "accusatorial" rather than "inquisitorial," meaning, in the words of the late Justice Frankfurter, that when an individual is accused of a crime "society carries the burden of proving its charge against the accused not out of his own mouth but by evidence independently secured through skillful investigation."[1] But it has also been recognized that questioning of witnesses and of the defendant is sometimes indispensable to crime solving. The vast majority of criminal cases in the United States are concluded by an admission of guilt rather than by determination of guilt by a judge or jury.

Until 1964, the standard generally applied to determining whether a confession had been legally obtained was "voluntariness." When the facts showed torture or physical coercion, as in *Brown* v. *Mississippi* (1936), the Supreme Court's job was not difficult. But where the coercion was more subtle, perhaps psychologically induced, the standard was more difficult to apply. Was the defendant of sufficient age, intelligence, and education to have resisted the inherent coerciveness of police questioning? Had he been tricked or given false promises? Was he kept from contact with friends and a lawyer for an extended length of time? Under what conditions of deprivation was he questioned by police officers?

The ambiguity of the voluntariness standard made it an ineffective weapon. Case-by-case adjudication is a difficult enough way to set policies to be followed by officials; where this adjudication did not produce a clear standard (other than the one against outright brutality) it could not be an effective restraint. Efforts by the Supreme Court to set more objective standards in the federal courts proved not much more effective and caused numerous attacks on the Court and its powers by an outraged Congress. In 1957 the Court ruled in *Mallory* v. *United States* that any delay between arrest and arraignment which permitted or facilitated interrogation violated the Federal Rules of Criminal Procedure. Thus even noncoercive confessions were excluded, although in practice few convictions were overturned. The *Mallory* rule was finally reversed by Congress in the Crime Control Act of 1968, which held that no voluntary confession should be excluded unless the delay in arraignment exceeded six hours.

But whatever its merits, the *Mallory* rule did not apply to the state courts which handled the bulk of criminal actions in the United States. Here, as Fred Graham has so perceptively noted, the Supreme Court chose another approach.[2] Instead of further limiting the police directly, the Court decided to extend the right of counsel back from the courtroom to the stationhouse. Since no lawyer would, in theory, permit his client to confess to a crime (at least not in advance of any opportunity for plea bargaining), this would have the same effect as forbidding the police to interrogate prior to arraignment.

Escobedo was arrested in connection with the murder of his brother-in-law. He initially denied any knowledge of the event and was released. When rearrested the police told Escobedo en route to the police station that his alleged partner had identified him as the one who had pulled the trigger and that he might as well confess. Escobedo asked to

[1]*Watts* v. *Indiana* (1949).
[2]Fred P. Graham, *The Self-Inflicted Wound* (New York: Macmillan, 1970), pp. 160, ff.

see his lawyer. Although the lawyer had arrived at the police station shortly after Escobedo, he was not permitted to see his client. Escobedo repeated his wish to see his lawyer and was told that his lawyer "didn't want to see him." As the interrogation wore on, Escobedo claimed that his partner was lying, and when confronted by the partner said, "I didn't shoot Manuel, you did it." Having thus acknowledged his presence at the scene of the crime, Escobedo made additional incriminating statements without being advised of his constitutional rights, and was eventually convicted of murder.

In a 5-4 ruling, the Supreme Court reversed. Justice Goldberg wrote for the Court:

We hold, therefore, that where, as here, the investigation is no longer a general inquiry into an unsolved crime but has begun to focus on a particular suspect, the suspect has been taken into police custody, the police carry out a process of interrogations that lends itself to eliciting incriminating statements, the suspect has requested and been denied an opportunity to consult with his lawyer, and the police have not effectively warned him of his absolute constitutional right to remain silent, the accused has been denied the "Assistance of Counsel" in violation of the Sixth Amendment . . . and that no statement elicited by the police during the interrogation may be used against him at a criminal trial. . . .

Nothing we have said today affects the powers of the police to investigate "an unsolved crime," . . . by gathering information from witnesses and by other "proper investigative efforts." We hold only that where the process shifts from investigatory to accusatory—when its focus is on the accused and its purpose is to elicit a confession—our adversary system begins to operate, and under the circumstances here, the accused must be permitted to consult with his lawyer.

Otherwise, Goldberg wrote, the trial would be nothing more than "an appeal from the interrogation." The opinion questioned the general reliability of confessions, although the actual holding of the case, as quoted above, was much more narrowly drawn. The opinion thus raised more questions than it answered. Was an indigent entitled to a lawyer in the stationhouse as well as the courtroom? Could any questioning be permitted before a lawyer was present, or before the suspect was advised of his rights? The fact that these questions remained unanswered, and the uniqueness of the facts of the case which prevented it from being applied easily to other cases, suggested that sooner or later the Supreme Court would be forced to consider these broader questions of police conduct.

(2) Miranda v. Arizona (1966)

+Warren, Black, Douglas, Brennan, Fortas
−Harlan, Stewart, White
±Clark

[The storm of protest and controversy that greeted the Court's decision in the *Escobedo* case was unusual, in part because of what Justice Goldberg's opinion stated or implied about the standards to be followed in interrogating arrested persons, and in part because the Court had failed to spell out precisely what procedures the police were obligated to follow. Many urged the Court to follow up *Escobedo* with a case-by-case analysis of the circumstances under which a person could remain silent and when counsel would have to be provided. Others urged the Court to establish a rule that defined the procedures with sufficient clarity to allow law enforcement agencies to follow them. The issue inevitably became immersed in, and frequently distorted by, the law-and-order debate in the 1964 presidential election. Denunciations of the decision and the Supreme Court brought a measure of instant popularity to many politicians, and those supporting the Court had to weave a careful path to avoid being labeled "soft on crime."

The most specific suggestion for implementing *Escobedo* came from the American Law Institute (ALI), a prestigious organization of law professors and lawyers. The ALI Model Code of Pre-Arraignment Procedure, first released in late 1965, suggested that the accused should have the right to remain silent and to get a lawyer but that counsel need not be provided to indigent defendants when first taken into custody. It supported the need for carefully defined interrogation procedures.

Supporting this position, Attorney General Katzenbach argued that "the main purpose of police interrogation was not to insure equal treatment but to discover those guilty of crime." Rules governing investigative procedures, Katzenbach argued, could not "remedy all the inequities which may exist in our society." A contrary view was sounded by Ramsey Clark, Katzenbach's eventual successor as attorney general and at the time an assistant attorney general. Clark argued that "Court rules do not cause crime. People do not commit crimes because they know they cannot be questioned."[1]

Not surprisingly, state and federal courts differed in their interpretation of the requirements of the *Escobedo* rule. In November 1965, the Supreme Court, having received and held about 140 appeals raising *Escobedo* questions, granted certiorari in five cases, one of which was *Miranda* v. *Arizona*. Ironically, and yet probably intentionally on the Court's part, the *Miranda* case contained little evidence of coercion or of a confession that was unreliable. Miranda, an emotionally disturbed, 23-year-old truck driver, had been convicted of kidnapping and raping an 18-year-old girl and had been sentenced to twenty to thirty years in prison. He was also convicted on an unrelated charge of robbery and given a sentence of twenty to twenty-five years.

Miranda was not advised of his right to con-

sult an attorney prior to interrogation. There was conflicting testimony as to whether he had been advised of his right to remain silent. Having been identified in a police lineup, he "freely" confessed. (It seems almost certain that under the old standard of voluntariness, his confession would have been valid and his conviction affirmed by the Supreme Court.) The trial court admitted the confession into evidence, and the Arizona Supreme Court upheld that action and affirmed Miranda's conviction.

The Solicitor General had not participated in the *Escobedo* case. *Miranda* was thus the first opportunity for the Justice Department to take a policy position in the confessions controversy. *Amici curiae* briefs were also filed by the American Civil Liberties Union (ACLU) and the National District Attorneys Association (NDAA).

The ACLU asked the Court to broaden the *Escobedo* rule and *require* the presence of counsel at all police interrogations, on the grounds that being in police custody was inherently coercive, and therefore a mere warning to a suspect or witness about his constitutional rights was insufficient. On the other hand, Solicitor General Thurgood Marshall, arguing the government's position, asked the Court to abandon the *Escobedo* rule and hold that there was "no general right to counsel under the 6th Amendment prior to formal proceedings before a magistrate." Marshall urged the Court to return to the pre-*Escobedo* "special circumstances" rule under which failure to warn a suspect of his rights, or denial of counsel, would be factors, but not conclusive, in determining whether a confession or inculpatory statement had been voluntarily made. He proposed the following rule: "Whether the official conduct, taken as a whole, had the effect on the arrested suspect of overriding his free choice to refuse to be a witness against himself within the meaning of the 5th Amendment."

Between these polar positions, various compromises were urged on the Court. Counsel for one of the appellants thought it sufficient for the police to warn a suspect of his rights and offer to secure a lawyer for any person who could not

---

[1]John T. Elliff, *Crime, Dissent, and the Attorney General* (Beverly Hills: Sage Publications, 1971). pp. 54–55.

obtain one. But the suspect had the right to waive his right to counsel in writing. The National District Attorneys Association brief agreed that a suspect who *asked* for a lawyer should have one, appointed by the state if necessary. But it did not think the police had to *offer* to secure counsel. Most importantly, the NDAA, unlike the Justice Department, urged the Court, if it chose to decide these cases at all, to reject the special-circumstances, case-by-case approach and set down clear and specific rules to guide law enforcement agencies.[2]

Knowledge of the arguments and briefs is necessary for understanding the *Miranda* decision in its proper perspective, particularly in light of the strong criticism of the decision as placing unnecessary restrictions on the police and making it impossible to secure confessions. Like most Supreme Court decisions, this one represented a compromise among several policy alternatives.]

MR. CHIEF JUSTICE WARREN delivered the opinion of the Court.

. . . We start here, as we did in *Escobedo,* with the premise that our holding is not an innovation in our jurisprudence, but is an application of principles long recognized and applied in other settings. We have undertaken a thorough re-examination of the *Escobedo* decision and the principles it announced, and we reaffirm it. That case was but an explication of basic rights that are enshrined in our Constitution. . . .

The constitutional issue we decide in each of these cases is the admissibility of statements obtained from a defendant questioned while in custody and deprived of his freedom of action. In each, the defendant was questioned by police officers, detectives, or a prosecuting attorney in a room in which he was cut off from the outside world. In none of these cases was the defendant given a full and effective warning of his rights at the outset of the interrogation process. In all the cases, the questioning elicited oral admissions, and in three of them, signed statements as well which were admitted at their trials. They all thus share salient features—incommunicado interrogation of individuals in a police-dominated atmosphere, resulting in self-incriminating statements without full warnings of constitutional rights.

An understanding of the nature and setting of this in-custody interrogation is essential to our decisions today. The difficulty in depicting what transpires at such interrogations stems from the fact that in this country they have largely taken place incommunicado. From extensive factual studies undertaken in the early 1930's, including the famous Wickersham Report to Congress by a Presidential Commission, it is clear that police violence and the "third degree" flourished at that time. In a series of cases decided by this Court long after these studies, the police resorted to physical brutality—beatings, hanging, whipping—and to sustained and protracted questioning incommunicado in order to extort confessions. The 1961 Commission on Civil Rights found much evidence to indicate that "some policemen still resort to physical force to obtain confessions". . . . The use of physical brutality and violence is not, unfortunately, relegated to the past or to any part of the country. . . .

The examples given above are undoubtedly the exception now, but they are sufficiently widespread to be the object of concern. Unless a proper

[2]This summary of pre-*Miranda* events and arguments is based on John T. Elliff, *Crime, Dissent, and the Attorney General* (Beverly Hills: Sage Publications, 1971).

limitation upon custodial interrogation is achieved—such as these decisions will advance—there can be no assurance that practices of this nature will be eradicated in the foreseeable future. . . .

Again we stress that the modern practice of in-custody interrogation is psychologically rather than physically oriented. . . . "Since *Chambers* v. *Florida* . . . this Court has recognized that coercion can be mental as well as physical, and that the blood of the accused is not the only hallmark of an unconstitutional inquisition." . . . Interrogation still takes place in privacy. Privacy results in secrecy and this in turn results in a gap in our knowledge as to what in fact goes on in the interrogation rooms. A valuable source of information about present police practices, however, may be found in various police manuals and texts which document procedures employed with success in the past, and which recommend various other effective tactics. These texts are used by law enforcement agencies themselves as guides. It should be noted that these texts professedly present the most enlightened and effective means presently used to obtain statements through custodial interrogation. By considering these texts and other data, it is possible to describe procedures observed and noted around the country.

The officers are told by the manuals that the "principal psychological factor contributing to a successful interrogation is *privacy*—being alone with the person under interrogation." . . .

To highlight the isolation and unfamiliar surroundings, the manuals instruct the police to display an air of confidence in the suspect's guilt and from outward appearance to maintain only an interest in confirming certain details. The guilt of the sub-

ject is to be posited as a fact. The interrogator should direct his comments toward the reasons why the subject committed the act, rather than to court failure by asking the subject whether he did it. Like other men, perhaps the subject has had a bad family life, had an unhappy childhood, had too much to drink, had an unrequited attraction to women. The officers are instructed to minimize the moral seriousness of the offense, to cast blame on the victim or on society. These tactics are designed to put the subject in a psychological state where his story is but an elaboration of what the police purport to know already—that he is guilty. Explanations to the contrary are dismissed and discouraged. . . .

From . . . representative samples of interrogation techniques, the setting prescribed by the manuals and observed in practice becomes clear. In essence, it is this: To be alone with the subject is essential to prevent distraction and to deprive him of any outside support. The aura of confidence in his guilt undermines his will to resist. He merely confirms the preconceived story the police seek to have him describe. Patience and persistence, at times relentless questioning, are employed. To obtain a confession, the interrogator must "patiently maneuver himself or his quarry into a position from which the desired object may be obtained." When normal procedures fail to produce the needed result, the police may resort to deceptive stratagems such as giving false legal advice. It is important to keep the subject off balance, for example, by trading on his insecurity about himself or his surroundings. The police then persuade, trick, or cajole him out of exercising his constitutional rights. . . .

In each of the cases, the defendant was thrust into an unfamiliar atmosphere and run through menacing police interrogation procedures. The potentiality for compulsion is forcefully apparent, for example, in *Miranda,* where the indigent Mexican defendant was a seriously disturbed individual with pronounced sexual fantasies, and in *Stewart,* in which the defendant was an indigent Los Angeles Negro who had dropped out of school in the sixth grade. To be sure, the records do not evince overt physical coercion or patent psychological ploys. The fact remains that in none of these cases did the officers undertake to afford appropriate safeguards at the outset of the interrogation to insure that the statements were truly the product of free choice.

It is obvious that such an interrogation environment is created for no purpose other than to subjugate the individual to the will of his examiner. This atmosphere carries its own badge of intimidation. To be sure, this is not physical intimidation, but it is equally destructive of human dignity. The current practice of incommunicado interrogation is at odds with one of our Nation's most cherished principles—that the individual may not be compelled to incriminate himself. Unless adequate protective devices are employed to dispel the compulsion inherent in custodial surroundings, no statement obtained from the defendant can truly be the product of his free choice.
. . .

Today, then, there can be no doubt that the Fifth Amendment privilege is available outside of criminal court proceedings and serves to protect persons in all settings in which their freedom of action is curtailed from being compelled to incriminate themselves. We have concluded that without proper safeguards the process of in-custody interrogation of persons suspected or accused of crime contains inherently compelling pressures which work to undermine the individual's will to resist and to compel him to speak where he would not otherwise do so freely. In order to combat these pressures and to permit a full opportunity to exercise the privilege against self-incrimination, the accused must be adequately and effectively apprised of his rights and the exercise of those rights must be fully honored.

It is impossible for us to foresee the potential alternatives of protecting the privilege which might be devised by Congress or the States in the exercise of their creative rule-making capacities. Therefore we cannot say that the Constitution necessarily requires adherence to any particular solution for the inherent compulsions of the interrogation process as it is presently conducted. Our decision in no way creates a constitutional straitjacket which will handicap sound efforts at reform, nor is it intended to have this effect. We encourage Congress and the States to continue their laudable search for increasingly effective ways of protecting the rights of the individual while promoting efficient enforcement of our criminal laws. However, unless we are shown other procedures which are at least as effective in apprising accused persons of their right of silence and in assuring a continuous opportunity to exercise it, the following safeguards must be observed.

At the outset, if a person in custody is to be subjected to interrogation, he must first be informed in clear and unequivocal terms that he has the right to remain silent. For those unaware of the privilege, the warning is needed simply to make them aware of it—the threshold requirement for an intelligent decision as to its exercise. More important, such a warning is an absolute prerequisite in overcoming the inherent pressures of the interrogation atmosphere. It is not just the subnormal or woefully ignorant who succumb to an interrogator's imprecations, whether implied or expressly stated, that the interrogation will continue until a confession is obtained or that silence in the face of accusation is itself damning and will bode ill when presented to a jury. Further, the warning will show the individual that his interrogators are prepared to recognize his privilege should he choose to exercise it.

The Fifth Amendment privilege is so fundamental to our system of constitutional rule and the expedient of giving an adequate warning as to the availability of the privilege so simple, we will not pause to inquire in individual cases whether the defendant was aware of his rights without a warning being given. . . .

The warning of the right to remain silent must be accompanied by the explanation that anything said can and will be used against the individual in court. This warning is needed in order to make him aware not only of the privilege, but also of the consequences of forgoing it. . . .

The circumstances surrounding in-custody interrogation can operate very quickly to overbear the will of one merely made aware of his privilege by his interrogators. Therefore, the right to have counsel present at the interrogation is indispensable to the protection of the Fifth Amendment privilege under the system we delineate today. Our aim is to assure that the individual's right to choose between silence and speech remains unfettered throughout the interrogation process. A once-stated warning, delivered by those who will conduct the interrogation, cannot itself suffice to that end among those who most require knowledge of their rights. A mere warning given by the

interrogators is not alone sufficient to accomplish that end. Prosecutors themselves claim that the admonishment of the right to remain silent without more "will benefit only the recidivist and the professional." . . . Even preliminary advice given to the accused by his own attorney can be swiftly overcome by the secret interrogation process. . . . Thus, the need for counsel to protect the Fifth Amendment privilege comprehends not merely a right to consult with counsel prior to questioning, but also to have counsel present during any questioning if the defendant so desires.

The presence of counsel at the interrogation may serve several significant subsidiary functions as well. If the accused decides to talk to his interrogators, the assistance of counsel can mitigate the dangers of untrustworthiness. With a lawyer present the likelihood that the police will practice coercion is reduced, and if coercion is nevertheless exercised the lawyer can testify to it in court. The presence of a lawyer can also help to guarantee that the accused gives a fully accurate statement to the police and that the statement is rightly reported by the prosecution at trial. . . .

An individual need not make a preinterrogation request for a lawyer. While such request affirmatively secures his right to have one, his failure to ask for a lawyer does not constitute a waiver. No effective waiver of the right to counsel during interrogation can be recognized unless specifically made after the warnings we here delineate have been given. The accused who does not know his rights and therefore does not make a request may be the person who most needs counsel. . . .

Accordingly we hold that an individual held for interrogation must be clearly informed that he has the right to consult with a lawyer and to have the lawyer with him during interrogation under the system for protecting the privilege we delineate today. As with the warnings of the right to remain silent and that anything stated can be used in evidence against him, this warning is an absolute prerequisite to interrogation. No amount of circumstantial evidence that the person may have been aware of this right will suffice to stand in its stead. . . .

If an individual indicates that he wishes the assistance of counsel before any interrogation occurs, the authorities cannot rationally ignore or deny his request on the basis that the individual does not have or cannot afford a retained attorney. The financial ability of the individual has no relationship to the scope of the rights involved here. The privilege against self-incrimination secured by the Constitution applies to all individuals. The need for counsel in order to protect the privilege exists for the indigent as well as the affluent. In fact, were we to limit these constitutional rights to those who can retain an attorney, our decisions today would be of little significance. The cases before us as well as the vast majority of confession cases with which we have dealt in the past involve those unable to retain counsel. . . .

In order fully to apprise a person interrogated of the extent of his rights under this system then, it is necessary to warn him not only that he has the right to consult with an attorney, but also that if he is indigent a lawyer will be appointed to represent him. . . . As with the warnings of the right to remain silent and of the general right to counsel, only by effective and express explanation to the indigent of this right can there be assurance that he was truly in a position to exercise it.

Once warnings have been given, the subsequent procedure is clear. If the individual indicates in any manner, at any time prior to or during questioning, that he wishes to remain silent, the interrogation must cease. At this point he has shown that he intends to exercise his Fifth Amendment privilege; any statement taken after the person invokes his privilege cannot be other than the product of compulsion, subtle or otherwise. Without the right to cut off questioning, the setting of in-custody interrogation operates on the individual to overcome free choice in producing a statement after the privilege has been once invoked. If the individual states that he wants an attorney, the interrogation must cease until an attorney is present. At that time, the individual must have an opportunity to confer with the attorney and to have him present during any subsequent questioning. If the individual cannot obtain an attorney and he indicates that he wants one before speaking to police, they must respect his decision to remain silent.

This does not mean, as some have suggested, that each police station must have a "station house lawyer" present at all times to advise prisoners. It does mean, however, that if police propose to interrogate a person they must make known to him that he is entitled to a lawyer and that if he cannot afford one, a lawyer will be provided for him prior to any interrogation. If authorities conclude that they will not provide counsel during a reasonable period of time in which investigation in the field is carried out, they may do so without violating the person's Fifth Amendment privilege so long as they do not question him during that time.

If the interrogation continues without the presence of an attorney and a statement is taken, a heavy burden rests on the Government to demonstrate that the defendant knowingly and intelligently waived his privilege against self-incrimination and his right to retained or appointed counsel. . . .

Whatever the testimony of the authorities as to waiver of rights by an accused, the fact of lengthy interrogation or incommunicado incarceration before a statement is made is strong evidence that the accused did not validly waive his rights. In these circumstances the fact that the individual eventually made a statement is consistent with the conclusion that the compelling influence of the interrogation finally forced him to do so. It is inconsistent with any notion of a voluntary relinquishment of the privilege. Moreover, any evidence that the accused was threatened, tricked, or cajoled into a waiver will, of course, show that the defendant did not voluntarily waive his privilege. . . .

The warnings required and the waiver necessary in accordance with our opinion today are, in the absence of a fully effective equivalent, prerequisites to the admissibility of any statement made by a defendant. No distinction can be drawn between statements which are direct confessions and statements which amount to "admissions" of part or all of an offense. The privilege against self-incrimination protects the individual from being compelled to incriminate himself in any manner; it does not distinguish degrees of incrimination. Similarly, for precisely the same reason, no distinction may be drawn between inculpatory statements and statements alleged to be merely "exculpatory." If a statement made were in fact truly exculpatory it would, of course, never be used by the prosecution. In fact, statements merely intended to be exculpatory by the de-

fendant are often used to impeach his testimony at trial or to demonstrate untruths in the statement given under interrogation and thus to prove guilt by implication. These statements are incriminating in any meaningful sense of the word and may not be used without the full warnings and effective waiver required for any other statement. In *Escobedo* itself, the defendant fully intended his accusation of another as the slayer to be exculpatory as to himself. . . .

Our decision is not intended to hamper the traditional function of police officers in investigating crime. . . . When an individual is in custody on probable cause, the police may, of course, seek out evidence in the field to be used at trial against him. Such investigation may include inquiry of persons not under restraint. General on-the-scene questioning as to facts surrounding a crime or other general questioning of citizens in the fact-finding process is not affected by our holding. . . .

In dealing with statements obtained through interrogation, we do not purport to find all confessions inadmissible. Confessions remain a proper element in law enforcement. Any statement given freely and voluntarily without any compelling influences is, of course, admissible in evidence. The fundamental import of the privilege while an individual is in custody is not whether he is allowed to talk to the police without the benefit of warnings and counsel, but whether he can be interrogated. There is no requirement that police stop a person who enters a police station and states that he wishes to confess to a crime, or a person who calls the police to offer a confession or any other statement he desires to make. Volunteered statements of any kind are not barred by the Fifth Amendment and their admissibility is not affected by our holding today. . . .

It is also urged upon us that we withhold decision on this issue until state legislative bodies and advisory groups have had an opportunity to deal with these problems by rule making. We have already pointed out that the Constitution does not require any specific code of procedures for protecting the privilege against self-incrimination during custodial interrogation. Congress and the States are free to develop their own safeguards for the privilege, so long as they are fully as effective as those described above in informing accused persons of their right of silence and in affording a continuous opportunity to exercise it. In any event, however, the issues presented are of constitutional dimensions and must be determined by the courts. . . .

Because of the nature of the problem and because of its recurrent significance in numerous cases, we have to this point discussed the relationship of the Fifth Amendment privilege to police interrogation without specific concentration on the facts of the cases before us. We turn now to these facts to consider the application to these cases of the constitutional principles discussed above. In each instance, we have concluded that statements were obtained from the defendant under circumstances that did not meet constitutional standards for protection of the privilege.

No. 759. *Miranda* v. *Arizona*

On March 13, 1963, petitioner, Ernesto Miranda, was arrested at his home and taken in custody to a Phoenix police station. He was there identified by the complaining wit-

ness. The police then took him to "Interrogation Room No. 2" of the detective bureau. There he was questioned by two police officers. The officers admitted at trial that Miranda was not advised that he had a right to an attorney present. Two hours later, the officers emerged from the interrogation room with a written confession signed by Miranda. At the top of the statement was a typed paragraph stating that the confession was made voluntarily, without threats or promises of immunity and "with full knowledge of my legal rights, understanding any statement I make may be used against me."

At his trial before a jury, the written confession was admitted into evidence over the objection of defense counsel, and the officers testified to the prior oral confession made by Miranda during the interrogation. Miranda was found guilty of kidnapping and rape. He was sentenced to 20 to 30 years' imprisonment on each count, the sentences to run concurrently. On appeal, the Supreme Court of Arizona held that Miranda's constitutional rights were not violated in obtaining the confession and affirmed the conviction. . . .In reaching its decision, the court emphasized heavily the fact that Miranda did not specifically request counsel.

We reverse. From the testimony of the officers and by the admission of respondent, it is clear that Miranda was not in any way apprised of his right to consult with an attorney and to have one present during the interrogation, nor was his right not to be compelled to incriminate himself effectively protected in any other manner. Without these warnings the statements were inadmissible. The mere fact that he signed a statement which contained a typed-in clause stating that he had "full knowledge" of his "legal rights" does not approach the knowing and intelligent waiver required to relinquish constitutional rights. . . .

MR. JUSTICE HARLAN, WHOM MR. JUSTICE STEWART AND MR. JUSTICE WHITE JOIN, DISSENTING.

I believe the decision of the Court represents poor constitutional law and entails harmful consequences for the country at large. How serious these consequences may prove to be only time can tell. But the basic flaws in the Court's justification seem to me readily apparent now once all sides of the problem are considered. . . .

[T]he thrust of the new rules is to negate all pressures, to reinforce the nervous or ignorant suspect, and ultimately to discourage any confession at all. The aim in short is toward "voluntariness" in a utopian sense, or to view it from a different angle, voluntariness with a vengeance.

To incorporate this notion into the Constitution requires a strained reading of history and precedent and a disregard of the very pragmatic concerns that alone may on occasion justify such strains. I believe that reasoned examination will show that the Due Process Clauses provide an adequate tool for coping with confessions and that, even if the Fifth Amendment privilege against self-incrimination be invoked, its precedents taken as a whole do not sustain the present rules. Viewed as a choice based on pure policy, these new rules prove to be a highly debatable if not one-sided appraisal of the competing interests, imposed over widespread objection, at the very time when judicial restraint is most called for by the circumstances. . . .

Examined as an expression of public policy, the Court's new regime proves so dubious that there can be no due compensation for its weakness in constitutional law. Forgoing discussion has shown, I think, how mistaken is the Court in implying that the Constitution has struck the balance in favor of the approach the Court takes. . . . Rather, precedent reveals that the Fourteenth Amendment in practice has been construed to strike a different balance, that the Fifth Amendment gives the Court little solid support in this context, and that the Sixth Amendment should have no bearing at all. Legal history has been stretched before to satisfy deep needs of society. In this instance, however, the Court has not and cannot make the powerful showing that its new rules are plainly desirable in the context of our society, something which is surely demanded before those rules are engrafted onto the Constitution and imposed on every State and county in the land.

Without at all subscribing to the generally black picture of police conduct painted by the Court, I think it must be frankly recognized at the outset that police questioning allowable under due process precedents may inherently entail some pressure on the suspect and may seek advantage in his ignorance and weaknesses. The atmosphere and questioning techniques, proper and fair though they be, can in themselves exert a tug on the suspect to confess, and in this light "[t]o speak of any confessions of crime made after arrest as being 'voluntary' or 'uncoerced' is somewhat inaccurate, although traditional. A confession is wholly and incontestably voluntary only if a guilty person gives himself up to the law and becomes his own accuser." Until today, the role of the Constitution has been only to sift out *undue* pressure, not to assure spontaneous confessions. . . .

What the Court largely ignores is that its rules impair, if they will not eventually serve wholly to frustrate, an instrument of law enforcement that has long and quite reasonably been thought worth the price paid for it. There can be little doubt that the Court's new code would markedly decrease the number of confessions. To warn the suspect that he may remain silent and remind him that his confession may be used in court are minor obstructions. To require also an express waiver by the suspect and an end to questioning whenever he demurs must heavily handicap questioning. And to suggest or provide counsel for the suspect invites the end of the interrogation. . . .

In closing this necessarily truncated discussion of policy considerations attending the new confession rules, some reference must be made to their ironic untimeliness. There is now in progress in this country a massive re-examination of criminal law enforcement procedures on a scale never before witnessed. . . .

It is no secret that concern has been expressed lest long-range and lasting reforms be frustrated by this Court's too rapid departure from existing constitutional standards. Despite the Court's disclaimer, the practical effect of the decision made today must inevitably be to handicap seriously sound efforts at reform, not least by removing options necessary to a just compromise of competing interest. Of course legislative reform is rarely speedy or unanimous, though this Court has been more patient in the past. But the legislative reforms when they came would have

the vast advantage of empirical data and comprehensive study, they would allow experimentation and use of solutions not open to the courts, and they would restore the initiative in criminal law reform to those forums where it truly belongs.

MR. JUSTICE WHITE, WITH WHOM MR. JUSTICE HARLAN AND MR. JUSTICE STEWART, CONCUR, DISSENTING (OMITTED).

MR. JUSTICE CLARK, CONCURRING IN PART AND DISSENTING IN PART (OMITTED).

(3) A Note on *Miranda* and the Problem of Retroactivity

One consequence of the Warren Court's criminal procedure revolution was the necessity to confront again at the constitutional level the question of retroactivity. Under the common law, all judicial decisions were presumed retroactive. A decision overruling a prior precedent was not "new law, but the application of what is, and, therefore had been, the true law."[1] This was the view stated by the English commentator, Blackstone, and it was followed generally by American courts. The rule was not without its critics, who noted the hardships attendant on those who had conducted their affairs on the basis of previously existing law. Modern recognition that judges do, in fact, "make law" and do not merely "discover" it further eroded the basis for automatic retroactivity. In 1932, Justice Cardozo made it clear that the Supreme Court could determine for itself whether "decisions, though later overruled, are law nonetheless for intermediate transactions."[2] A

---

[1]*Linkletter* v. *Walker* (1965).
[2]*Great Northern Railroad Company* v. *Sunburst Oil & Refining Company* (1932).

law, though later overruled, is an operative fact that cannot be ignored. The rule that emerged was that a changed law would be applied to a case not yet finally decided on direct review. Where a case was already finally decided on direct review, but was challenged collaterally, there was no set principle to be applied. Whether the "new" law would be applied retroactively or not would be determined by consideration of the circumstances of the case.

In *Linkletter* v. *Walker* (1965), the Supreme Court, noting that in the past new constitutional rules customarily had been applied retroactively to "finalized" cases,[3] decided that the Constitution neither required nor prohibited such retroactive application. The Court was thus free, in its own discretion, to determine whether a new (or newly announced) constitutional rule should be applied retroactively, in whole or in part.[4]

Linkletter was convicted of burglary in Louisiana on May 28, 1959, over objections about the admissibility of illegally seized evidence. The Supreme Court of Louisiana affirmed the conviction in March 1960. *Mapp* v. *Ohio* was decided on June 19, 1961. Subsequently, Linkletter sought a writ of habeas corpus to have his conviction reversed on the basis of *Mapp;* he noted that the illegal search in his case had occurred after the break-in of Ms. Mapp's house, even though his conviction had been finally affirmed on appeal prior to the *Mapp* decision.

By a 7-2 vote, the Supreme Court declined to apply the *Mapp* rule to Linkletter. But it held that the rule would be applied to all cases still pending on appeal at the time *Mapp* was decided. Justice Clark noted that the states were entitled to rely on the then governing rule of *Wolf* v. *Colorado* (1949). Furthermore, he argued that deterrence of police misconduct was the primary purpose of *Mapp*, and this goal would not be significantly advanced by applying the rule to finalized convictions. To do so would cause disharmony in the "delicate state-federal relationship" which *Mapp* was intended to preserve. He noted that to make *Mapp* fully retroactive would require countless rehearings on the admissibility of evidence and would be extremely disruptive of the administration of justice. And, he noted, in the *Linkletter* case itself neither the reliability of the evidence nor the fairness of the trial was questioned. It would be better judicial policy, the Court concluded, to limit the retroactive application of *Mapp*.

Out of the *Linkletter* case came the three criteria by which the Supreme Court determines retroactivity: (1) the purpose served by the new rules, (2) the extent of law enforcement officials' justifiable reliance on prior standards, and (3) the effect on the administration of justice of a re-

---

[3]For example, *Griffin* v. *Illinois* (1956), involving the right of an indigent to a free transcript necessary for appeal, and *Gideon* v. *Wainwright* (1963), guaranteeing the right to counsel to indigents in serious criminal cases, were both applied retroactively.

[4]There is no record of a fully *prospective* decision, that is, one that applied only to subsequent cases and did not apply even to the litigants in the case in which the rule was changed. Such a rule would, of course, severely discourage litigation of constitutional rights. Justice Douglas continues to argue in dissent, as he and Justice Black did in *Linkletter*, that it is unfair to make a decision fully retroactive to the defendants in that case while excluding all others, expecially when it is often merely a matter of good fortune which of many cases raising the same constitutional issue is decided by the Supreme Court.

troactive application of new rules. Since the Court had opted for a case-by-case determination of retroactivity, the question has to be decided as often as the Supreme Court makes a change in constitutional rules that benefit defendants in criminal cases.

Miranda posed a special problem of retroactivity, since, as noted, the Court had accumulated a backlog of 140 "Escobedo cases" before making its *Miranda* decision. Three of the other cases decided with *Miranda* were covered by the new interrogation rule. But what of the remaining cases? According to Fred Graham, an early draft of the *Miranda* opinion adopted the *Linkletter* formula, rather than full retroactivity. However, all mention of retroactivity was then deleted, and the fourth companion case, *Johnson* v. *New Jersey*, was held over for a week.[5] Using that case as a vehicle to articulate its retroactivity position, the Court then decided that *Miranda* would only apply to *trials* that began after June 13, 1966, the date of the *Miranda* decision. The

remaining "Escobedo cases" that did not make the cutoff would be reconsidered under the old "voluntariness" standard.

This was a more restrictive retroactivity policy than the *Linkletter* standard applied to *Mapp*. As Stephen Wasby has noted, this would set the pattern for many subsequent cases in both the Warren and Burger courts. Subsequent constitutional decisions favorable to criminal defendants were often followed by restrictive and less favorable retroactivity policies.[6] Full retroactivity has been granted only rarely,[7] and the "partial" retroactivity option of *Linkletter* (i.e., retrospective application of a rule to cases not finalized on appeal) has been virtually ignored.[8]

In most instances, a "new" criminal justice policy favorable to defendants has been applied only where the repudiated practice was engaged in after the date of the Supreme Court decision. For example, having decided in *Taylor* v. *Louisiana* (1975)

[5]Fred Graham, *The Self-Inflicted Wound* (New York: Macmillan, 1970), pp. 187–188.

[6]Stephen L. Wasby, *Continuity and Change: From the Warren Court to the Burger Court*, (Pacific Palisades, Calif.: Goodyear Publishing Company, 1976).

[7]See Note 3. *Argersinger* v. *Hamlin* (1972), which extended the *Gideon* rule to all criminal cases in which a jail sentence was imposed, was also made fully retroactive in *Berry* v. *Cincinnati* (1973). *Furman* v. *Georgia* (1972), invalidating capital punishment as then applied and administered in the United States, was applied to all persons then under sentence of death. Later death penalty cases were also applied retroactively. *Barber* v. *Page* (1968), which held that preliminary hearing testimony could not be used at trial without a good faith effort to produce the original witness, was applied retroactively in *Berger* v. *California* (1969). *Waller* v. *Florida* (1970), which held that trials under both a local ordinance and a state law for the same offense violated the constitutional provisions against double jeopardy, was held retroactive in *Robinson* v. *Neil* (1973).

[8]The only other application of the *Linkletter* formula came the next year, in *Tehan* v. *Shott* (1966), which applied *Griffin* v. *California* (prosecutor not permitted to comment on failure of defendant to testify) retroactively to nonfinalized cases. Justice Marshall has subsequently noted that *Linkletter* "is an anomaly . . . and can be explained only by the Court's unfamiliarity with those problems when the case was decided." *Michigan* v. *Payne* (1973). But the *Linkletter* formula was relied upon again in an obscenity case in 1974, *Hamling* v. *United States*, where it was held that the principles of *Miller* v. *California* (1973) would apply to any nonfinal judgment in an obscenity prosecution.

that petit juries must be selected from a panel representative of the community and that women could not be automatically excused from jury duty, the Supreme Court subsequently held, in *Daniel* v. *Louisiana* (1975), that the new rule would apply only to juries *impaneled* after the date of the *Taylor* case. Similar policies governed the retroactivity of the right to trial by jury decision, *Duncan* v. *Louisiana* (1968),[9] and the case limiting higher sentencing on retrial following a successful appeal, *North Carolina* v. *Pearce* (1969). In *Michigan* v. *Payne* (1973), the Supreme Court declined to make *Pearce* retroactive, noting its similarities to *Miranda*. Both cases had established "prophylactic" rules that were designed to protect constitutional guarantees but which were not themselves constitutional rights. And neither case created a "new" constitutional right; defendants not entitled to the benefits of those decisions could still rely on existing constitutional rules to vindicate their constitutional rights. By drawing the line this way, the Court added, it was trying to preclude "windfall benefits" for some defendants who had suffered no constitutional deprivation.

(4) Instructing the Police in the *Miranda* Rules

Interrogation

This Training Bulletin is intended to serve as a guide to police officers on the subject of how interrogation of criminal suspects must be conducted. . . . The June 13, 1966 decision of the Supreme Court of the United States in *Miranda* v. *Arizona* sets forth the procedures that must be complied with if any incriminating statements are to be admissible in evidence at a criminal trial. Other areas of the law of confessions such as voluntariness, promises of lenience or immunity, the effect of failing to take a person who has been arrested before a magistrate without unnecessary delay and the like are not dealt with in this Bulletin.

The Escobedo *Case*

The question of how the privilege against self-incrimination and the right to counsel may combine to restrict traditional police interrogation methods was first considered in a case which began in Chicago in January of 1960 when a man by the name of Manuel Valtierra was murdered. The next morning Danny Escobedo, who was the brother-in-law of the murder victim, was arrested, questioned and released the same day. About 10 days later, he was again arrested and taken to police headquarters for interrogation along with several other suspects.

During the course of the second questioning by the police, Escobedo asked to be allowed to confer with his lawyer. This request was refused. At the same time, the lawyer arrived at headquarters and requested that he be allowed to confer with his client Escobedo. This request was refused. After several hours of questioning, an oral and then a written, confession was obtained.

At his trial, Escobedo argued that his confession should be suppressed as evidence because, before it was taken, the police had violated his

---

[9]*DeStefano* v. *Woods* (1968).
Reprinted from Chicago Police Department, *Law Training Bulletin Series: Interrogation Procedures* (September 23, 1966).

statutory and constitutional rights to consult with his lawyer. The motion to suppress was denied. Escobedo was convicted of murder, largely on the basis of his confession, and sentenced to prison for 20 years.

On appeal the conviction was affirmed by the Supreme Court of Illinois. That court held that, although defendant had a *statutory* right to counsel after arrest, the police had the right to a *reasonable* period for interrogation *before* the defendant conferred with counsel. The court also held that the *constitutional* right to counsel did not begin in the police station.

Thereafter, the Supreme Court of the United States agreed to review the *Escobedo* case and, on June 24, 1964, that Court reversed the decision of the Supreme Court of Illinois, and held, by a vote of 5-4, that Escobedo's confession should not have been admitted into evidence because it was obtained in violation of his constitutional right to counsel.

Although the Court used broad *language* in extending the constitutional right to counsel to police station interrogation after arrest (the Court, in the past had always held that the right to counsel usually began only after indictment), the actual *holding* of the case was seemingly limited to the particular facts.

The murder case against Escobedo was later dropped for lack of sufficient evidence—apart from the confession—to prove his guilt.

After the decision in *Escobedo,* the state supreme courts became divided over the question of what the case meant. . . .

This split between the state supreme courts led the Supreme Court of the United States to take for argument a series of cases which posed the question of how *Escobedo* was to be interpreted. On June 13, 1966, two

years after the *Escobedo* decision, the Supreme Court, in *Miranda* v. *Arizona* held, again by a vote of 5 to 4, that no confessions could thereafter be taken unless the suspect was warned of his right to counsel and privilege against self-incrimination.

What the Miranda Decision Requires

The Court first disposed of the requirement in *Escobedo* that suspicion had to be "focused" upon a suspect before the rule applied. The key element, the Court said, was "custody" or any other "significant deprivation of freedom of action." If a person is in police custody, and the police propose to question him, the warnings must be given.

The first warning to be given is that of the privilege against self-incrimination. This warning cannot be limited simply to a reference to the "Fifth Amendment." It must be given in terms that a prisoner will understand. He must be told that (1) he has a right to remain silent, (2) that he need not answer police questions, and (3) that if he does answer questions his answers may be used as evidence against him.

The second warning to be given is that concerning the right to counsel. Again, this warning must be given in terms which a suspect will understand and the requirement is not satisfied by a simple reference to "a right to counsel." The prisoner must be told (1) that he has the right to consult with an attorney *before or during* police questioning, and (2) that if he decides to exercise that right but does not have funds with which to hire counsel, he is entitled to have a lawyer appointed, without cost, to consult with him *before or during* questioning.

It is important that police officers

make sure that a prisoner *un-derstands* these warnings, for if he is questioned, and a confession is obtained which is later admitted into evidence, the officer who gave the warnings will be required to testify about the manner in which he gave them and the prisoner's response to them. After *each* warning, therefore, the officer should inquire whether the prisoner understands what the officer has told him, and if the prisoner says that he does, the officer should then ask the prisoner whether, understanding these rights, he is nevertheless willing to answer police questions without the presence of an attorney. If the prisoner says that he is willing to answer without an attorney, then, and only then, may the interrogation proceed.

It is not sufficient for an officer simply to give the warnings and then proceed to interrogate. The prisoner must *say* that he understands his rights and is willing to answer questions without counsel. Only then will a court find that a prisoner has *waived* his constitutional rights. A waiver will not be *inferred* simply from the fact that, after being given the warnings, a prisoner answers questions.

Police officers must also use great care to avoid any language which can later be used by defense attorneys to charge that the officer "threatened, tricked or cajoled" the defendant into waiving his rights. The function of the officer is to inform the defendant of his privilege against self-incrimination and right to counsel. He cannot, therefore, tell a prisoner, or even imply, that he "would be better off without a lawyer," or that he "doesn't need a lawyer" or that "all we want is the truth and you don't need a lawyer for that." After being warned, the prisoner must make up his own mind about whether he will claim his right to silence or his right to consult with an attorney. The officer must never say anything which indicates what he thinks the prisoner ought to do.

Sometimes persons who have been warned will ASK the police officer whether he thinks the prisoner should make a statement or talk to a lawyer. The officer cannot properly give an answer to this question. If he says that he thinks the prisoner ought to answer questions, or does not need an attorney, any confession taken thereafter will be inadmissible. If he says that the prisoner should not answer questions, or should consult with an attorney no confession will be forthcoming. If confronted by the situation, the officer should simply tell the prisoner, "Well, I've explained your rights to you and it would not be proper for me to give you any other advice. You must make your own decision."

The TIMING of the warnings is crucial. Under the rule in *Miranda* the warnings must be given before any questioning is begun. It does not make any difference whether the officer intends to take a full, written confession or is merely seeking an oral statement. If the warnings are not given before the prisoner responds to any kind of incriminating questions, any subsequent statement will be inadmissible. This means, therefore, that the warnings should be given between the time the person is taken into custody, or otherwise deprived of his freedom of action in any significant way, and the first questioning.

Police officers should also be aware of the fact that the Supreme Court now looks with disfavor upon "lengthy interrogation or incommunicado detention." If a person has been in police custody for a long period of time, therefore, without talking to outsiders (for example, family or friends), a court may find that a subsequent statement was not voluntary even though the police testify that the prisoner was warned and agreed to make a statement outside the presence of counsel. If a prisoner is to be interrogated, therefore, the warnings should be given before *any* questioning which is likely to produce incriminating answers, and the questioning should begin *as soon as possible* after the person has been taken into custody.

If, BEFORE OR AFTER the warnings, the prisoner indicates, in any manner, that he does not want to be questioned or that he will not give a statement, the questioning must stop. The precise words the prisoner uses are not important. It makes no difference whether he says, "I claim my privilege against self-incrimination" or "I'm not making any statement" or "I won't answer any questions." And once the prisoner has made this choice, it must be respected by the officer. He cannot attempt to "talk the prisoner out of it," or a court will later hold that there was no *voluntary* waiver of rights on the prisoner's part.

Moreover, this rule applies at any time DURING THE QUESTIONING. Suppose that a person has been warned of his rights and he says that he is nevertheless willing to make a statement. After answering a few questions, he then says that he has changed his mind and does not want to answer any *further* questions. If this occurs, the questioning must stop. While the answer given up to this point will be admissible, any subsequent answers could not be used. Or a person, after being warned, may tell the officer that he is willing to answer certain questions but not others. This *limited waiver* of the privilege against self-incrimination must be respected, and

questions outside the area which the prisoner had indicated that he is willing to discuss should not be asked.

The holding by the Court in *Miranda* that a prisoner without funds must be given an appointed attorney to consult with him prior to or during questioning poses problems for the Chicago police officer. If an indigent person is warned of this right and responds by saying that he wants to talk with an attorney before making a statement, the officer has only two choices open to him. *Either he must see to it that a lawyer is found to consult with the prisoner at this point or the questioning must stop altogether.*

Under the present provisions of the Illinois Code of Criminal Procedure, the earliest point at which a public defender or other attorney may be appointed by a court for an indigent person is at the *preliminary hearing.* There is now no provision in our law for the *courts* to appoint counsel at the *interrogation stage* of the proceedings, and there are no police funds available to reimburse such attorneys.

It is unlikely, therefore, that a police officer will be able to fulfill an indigent person's request for counsel. While the Supreme Court held in *Miranda* that they were not requiring "each police station (to) have a 'station house lawyer' present at all times to advise prisoners," they also held that this could be true only as long as the police do not attempt to question a prisoner after he has requested counsel. The rule is, then, that if an indigent person, after being warned of his right to appointed counsel, indicates in any manner that he desires to talk to an attorney, and the police cannot furnish an attorney to consult with him, there can be no interrogation.

Does the *Miranda* rule apply ONLY to "confessions"? The answer is "No." It is important to remember that the Court has applied the new warning rule to all statements made by a prisoner, whether they are called confessions, admissions, or explanations; whether they are labeled inculpatory or exculpatory; whether they are oral or written. The warnings *must* and *should* be given even though the officer expects that the prisoner will deny the crime or offer an alibi, for many times these kinds of statements are as incriminating as full confessions, especially if they differ from the testimony the defendant will offer at his trial, or the prosecutor is able to prove that they are false.

If MORE THAN ONE statement is taken—for example, if there is an oral statement to be followed by a written statement—the warnings should be *repeated* before the second statement, but this time, with reference to the fact that the suspect was also warned at the very beginning. . . .

It is not essential, of course, that the language set forth above be followed exactly. Different police officers have different conversational styles. What is important is that (a) the repeated warning not only protects the second statement, but reinforces the validity of the first by a reference back; (b) the officer should make sure that the *scope* of the warning is essentially the same as set forth above; (c) the officer should train himself to give the *same warning* to *all suspects* that he interrogates. If he does so, it is likely that his latter court testimony concerning the substance and manner in which he gave the warnings will be more consistent and impressive.

If the *Miranda* rule requires that the warnings be given before seeking any kind of statement from a prisoner, are there any occasions in which the police are seeking evidence where the warnings are not required? The answer is "Yes."

FIRST, no warnings are required in the case of persons who volunteer statements. If a person walks into a police station says that he just killed his wife; the body is in the car, and the murder weapon is in his pocket, there is no need for the police officer hearing this to stop the person midway through his statement and give him either of the warnings.

Police officers, however, should remember the difference between a *volunteered statement* and a merely *voluntary* one. A *volunteered statement* is one that is initiated by the suspect, while a *voluntary one* may have been made *in response to questioning*. If the suspect's statements are given by him *without questioning of any kind on the part of the police*, no warnings need be given. If a prisoner's statements follow interrogation, no matter how few questions were asked or even how general they are—for example, "Tell me about it"—*the warnings must come first*.

SECOND, the warnings do not have to be given when the officer is not asking a prisoner for incriminating *testimony*. A police officer may properly ask a prisoner to submit to a blood or breathalyzer test; take his fingerprints or photograph; examine his body, put him in a line-up; ask him to put on a hat or coat; ask him to pick up coins, or put his finger to his nose, and the like *without warning* him first of his privilege against self-incrimination or right to counsel. The difference between these actions, and a statement in response to interrogation, is simply the difference between *non-testimonial* and *testimonial* responses on the part of the prisoner. The first need not be preceded by the warnings; the second must always be.

THIRD, the warnings do not have to be given so long as the person *is not in custody* or has not been deprived of his freedom of action in any significant way. This *does not mean* that the police may interrogate persons who are *actually* in custody but who have not been told that they are "under arrest." Whether a person has been taken into custody, or has been arrested, will be determined *by the facts* of what has happened to him, not by the label the officer attaches to it.

On the other hand, if the police arrive at the scene of an offense and put questions to bystanders who have not been arrested, the warning is not required. The same rule would apply, for example, to motorists involved in an automobile accident who, after telephoning the police, remain at the scene of the collision until the officers arrive.

FOURTH, it is not necessary that the warnings be given to persons who are stopped on the street and questioned because of the suspicious circumstances surrounding their presence—for example, the man in the alley behind a warehouse at 3:00 A.M. On-the-street questioning does not carry with it the possibilities of what the Court called "inherent compulsion" of incommunicado police station interrogation. No warnings are required where motorists or other persons are stopped on the street for the purpose of inquiry. . . .

(5) A Note on the Response to *Miranda*

An irony of the *Miranda* decision was that none of the defendants was freed as a result. Miranda had not appealed his robbery conviction, and thus the 20-year sentence he received on that charge was not affected. The state of Arizona elected to retry him for rape, and even without the now inadmissible confession, Miranda was convicted again. The defendants in the other cases decided with *Miranda* were all also reconvicted and sentenced to long prison terms. None substantially benefited from the Supreme Court's decision.[1]

The political outcry that greeted the *Miranda* decision is well known and documented. Predictions about its disastrous effects on the police and on obtaining confessions were legion. Though roundly condemned, it was not ignored. Police officers were instructed in how to give the *Miranda* warnings, often with the help of printed, wallet-size "*Miranda* cards"; they were also instructed in how to evade the rules as much as possible. Despite the initial resistance, most police today at least give the *Miranda* warnings—on the beat, as well as on serialized television programs.

After much initial resistance, the police have complied with the letter, if not the spirit, of *Miranda*.[2] And there is little evidence to bear out dire predictions of serious handicaps to law enforcement work. Several studies showed that the *Miranda* warnings were not given to suspects in a way designed to encourage utilization.[3] Many suspects did not understand the warnings or believed it

---

[1]Miranda was subsequently released from prison on parole and was killed in a barroom brawl in 1977. Police found a *Miranda* card in his pocket. And the first thing they did when they arrested his killer was to read him his "*Miranda* rights."

[2]For an excellent discussion of the reasons for police hostility to *Miranda*, see Neal Milner, "Supreme Court Effectiveness and the Police Organization," **36** *Law and Contemporary Problems* (1971), 467–487. And see also Jerome Skolnick, *Justice Without Trial* (New York: John Wiley & Sons, 1966).

[3]Richard Medalie, et al., "Custodial Police Interrogation in Our Nation's Capital: The Attempt to Implement Miranda," **66** *Michigan Law Review* (1968), 1347–1422. Michael Wald, et al., "Interrogations in New Haven," **76** *Yale Law Journal* (1967), 1521–1648.

not in their interests to remain silent or request the assistance of counsel. The post-*Miranda* experience also suggested that confessions did not—or need not—play the dominant role in police work that many critics of *Miranda* had asserted.

Indeed, Medalie's study showed that those who obtained the assistance of counsel were *more* likely to make incriminating statements than were those suspects acting on their own.[4] Clearly, this is not what the majority on the Supreme Court had in mind when it spoke of redressing the balance between the police and criminal suspects and ensuring that each suspect would make the most rational decisions in his own behalf. Some police coercion was eliminated. But in its place came the coercive pressures to "plead" from attorneys co-opted by the criminal justice bureaucracy.[5]

The congressional response to *Miranda* was complex but generally hostile. The decision came when Congress already had under consideration major anticrime legislation. A bill was introduced to strip the Supreme Court of appellate jurisdiction over decisions of either state or federal courts on questions of admissibility of confessions. That bill did not pass, but Title II of the Crime Control Act of 1968 did purport to reverse *Miranda*, as well as the earlier decision in *Mallory* v. *United States* (1957):

3501. *Admissibility of Confessions*

(a) *In any criminal prosecution brought by the United States or by the District of Columbia, a confession, as defined in sub-section (e) hereof, shall be admissible in evidence if it is voluntar-*ily *given. Before such confession is received in evidence, the trial judge shall, out of the presence of the jury, determine any issue as to voluntariness. If the trial judge determines that the confession was voluntarily made it shall be admitted in evidence and the trial judge shall permit the jury to hear relevant evidence on the issue of voluntariness and shall instruct the jury to give such weight to the confession as the jury feels it deserves under all the circumstances.*

(b) *The trial judge in determining the issue of voluntariness shall take into consideration all the circumstances surrounding the giving of the confession, including (1) the time elapsing between arrest and arraignment of the defendant making the confession, if it was made after arrest and before arraignment, (2) whether such defendant knew the nature of the offense with which he was charged or of which he was suspected at the time of making the confession, (3) whether or not such defendant was advised or knew that he was not required to make any statement and that any such statement could be used against him, (4) whether or not such defendant had been advised prior to questioning of his right to the assistance of counsel; and (5) whether or not such defendant was without the assistance of counsel when questioned and when giving such confession.*

The presence or absence of any of the above-mentioned factors to be taken into consideration by the judge need not be conclusive on the issue of voluntariness of the confession.

(c) *In any criminal prosecution by the United States or by the District of Columbia, a confession made or given by a person who is a defendant therein, while such person was under arrest or other detention in the custody of any law-enforcement officer or law-enforcement agency, shall not be inadmissible solely because of delay in bringing such person before a commissioner or other officer empowered to commit persons charged with offenses against*

---

[4]Medalie, *Ibid.*, p. 1414.

[5]Abraham Blumberg, "The Practice of Law as a Confidence Game: Organizational Cooptation of a Profession," 1 *Law and Society Review* (1967), 15.

the laws of the United States or of the District of Columbia if such confession is found by the trial judge to have been made voluntarily and if the weight to be given by such person within six hours immediately following his arrest or other detention: Provided, That the time limitation contained in this subsection shall not apply in any case in which the delay in bringing such person before such commission or other officer beyond such six-hour period is found by the trial judge to be reasonable considering the means of transportation and the distance to be traveled to the nearest available such commissioner or other officer.

(d) Nothing contained in this section shall bar the admission in evidence of any confession made or given voluntarily by any person to any other person without interrogation by anyone, or at any time at which the person who made or gave such confession was not under arrest or other detention.

(e) As used in this section, the term "confession" means any confession of guilt of any criminal offense or any self-incriminating statement made or given orally or in writing.

The omnibus bill passed Congress and was signed into law by President Johnson despite his serious misgivings. He declared his opposition to the wiretapping provisions in Title III and instructed federal law enforcement officers to ignore Title II and continue to warn suspects of their constitutional rights. Title II, to the extent that it purports to reverse by statute the constitutional ruling in *Miranda*, is almost certainly unconstitutional. Yet it has not been tested directly in the Supreme Court. If the Burger Court continues to gut the *Miranda* decision (see *Michigan v. Tucker, infra*), the statute will never be tested. Undoubtedly, its greatest effect was political rather than legal. Such an overwhelming and adverse

response by Congress could not help but legitimize widespread criticism and resistance.

There was also a considerable negative reaction to *Miranda* in the state courts. It is there that most questions of guilt or innocence are adjudicated, and there where questions of proper police behavior first arise. State judges are on the firing line and, like the police, often are more vulnerable to, and hence also responsive to, local values and pressures. A recent study found widespread examples of anti-*Miranda* behavior in state supreme courts. But the opposition was uneven; in many states, only token sentiments were expressed. In a few others, more serious, articulate, and effective judicial defiance developed. But the author's conclusion emphasized the relatively high degree of compliance with *Miranda*, at least at the judicial level.[6]

(6) Michigan v. Tucker (1974)

+Rehnquist, Burger, Brennan, Stewart, White, Marshall, Blackmun, Powell
−Douglas

[To conservatives, *Miranda* was the red flag of Warren Court liberalism, the symbol of improper judicial activism and overly solicitous concern with the rights of criminal defendants. Some urged its outright repudiation. Instead, the Burger Court chose to erode *Miranda's* authority without (so far) overruling it in its entirety.

The first step came in *Harris* v. *New York* (1971). Harris was charged with selling heroin to an undercover police officer. Taking the stand in his own defense, he testified that he knew the arresting officer but that he did not make one of the two sales with which he was charged. He admitted making a second "sale"

[6]Bradley C. Canon, "Organizational Contumacy in the Transmission of Judicial Policies: The *Mapp, Escobedo, Miranda* and *Gault* Cases," **20** *Villanova Law Review* (1974), 50–79.

but stated that it was baking powder, not heroin, and merely part of a plot to defraud the purchaser. On cross-examination, he was confronted with a series of contradictory statements he had made immediately following his arrest. The statements were voluntary, but since the *Miranda* warnings had not been given, the prosecution made no effort to use the statements in its case against Harris. However, it was allowed to introduce the statements, in cross-examination, to challenge Harris' credibility. The jury was instructed that the statements, intended to be exculpatory, could be used only to impeach Harris' testimony and could not be considered as evidence of guilt.

The Supreme Court upheld Harris' conviction by a 5-4 vote. It held that while there was language in *Miranda* which suggested that an uncounseled statement could not be used for any purpose, that language was not necessary to the holding of the case (e.g., it was mere *dictum*) and was not controlling. As long as the evidence appeared to be trustworthy, the Court now held, it might be used collaterally to impeach the credibility of the defendant on cross-examination. It found that the prosecutor's ability to impeach a defendant's testimony was important to the fact-finding process and outweighed the "speculative possibility that impermissible police conduct" would be encouraged. Furthermore, the Court said, while a defendant had an absolute right *not* to testify, if he chose to do so, he did not have "the right to commit perjury."

In dissent, Justice Brennan argued that to permit use of a tainted statement "cuts down on the [Fifth Amendment] privilege by making its assertion costly." It was "monstrous," he argued, that courts should thus "aid and abet" a law-breaking police officer. To Brennan, this case clearly was a wedge in the door, the first effort to undermine *Miranda*.

A second challenge to *Miranda* came in the present case. In April 1966, Tucker was arrested for rape and assault. *Miranda* had yet to be decided, but Tucker was given all the warnings that would be incorporated into the *Miranda* rules except the warning that he was entitled to have counsel appointed if he was indigent. Tucker talked freely with the police, saying that he understood his rights. He pre-

sented an alibi, alleging that on most of the evening in which the crime was committed he had been at the home of a friend named Henderson. Henderson was contacted by the police, but his story did not support Tucker, and he provided the police with further damaging evidence.

Prior to trial, which occurred *after Miranda* had been decided by the Supreme Court, Tucker's attorney moved to suppress all of Tucker's own statements and Henderson's as well. The latter contention was based on the fact that Tucker had revealed Henderson's identity to the police without having had the full *Miranda* warnings. The trial judge excluded all of Tucker's own statements, but not Henderson's. Tucker was convicted and sentenced to prison for twenty to forty years. The Michigan Supreme Court affirmed the conviction, but a federal district court granted Tucker's habeas corpus petition. It held that Henderson's testimony also should have been excluded and ordered a new trial. The court of appeals affirmed, and the Supreme Court granted certiorari.]

MR. JUSTICE REHNQUIST delivered the opinion of the Court.

. . .

Although respondent's sole complaint is that the police failed to advise him that he would be given free counsel if unable to afford counsel himself, he did not, and does not now, base his arguments for relief on a right to counsel under the Sixth and Fourteenth Amendments. Nor was the right to counsel, as such, considered to be persuasive by either federal court below. We do not have a situation such as that presented in *Escobedo* v. *Illinois* . . . (1964), where the policemen interrogating the suspect had refused his repeated requests to see his lawyer who was then present at the police station. As we have noted previously, *Escobedo* is not to be broadly extended beyond the facts of that particular case. . . . This case also falls outside the rationale of *Wade* v. *United States* . . . (1967), where the Court held that counsel was needed at a post-indictment lineup in order to protect "the right to a fair trial at which the witnesses against [the defendant] might be meaningfully cross-examined." Henderson was fully available for searching cross-examination at respondent's trial.

Respondent's argument, and the opinions of the District Court and Court of Appeals, instead rely upon the Fifth Amendment right against compulsory self-incrimination and the safeguards designed in *Miranda* to secure that right. In brief, the position urged upon this Court is that proper regard for the privilege against compulsory self-incrimination requires, with limited exceptions not applicable here, that all evidence derived solely from statements made without full *Miranda* warnings be excluded at a subsequent criminal trial. For purposes of analysis in this case we believe that the question thus presented is best examined in two separate parts. We will therefore first consider whether the police conduct complained of directly infringed upon respondent's right against compulsory self-incrimination or whether it instead violated only the prophylactic rules developed to protect that right. We will then consider whether the evidence derived from this interrogation must be excluded.

. . . The importance of a right does not, by itself, determine its scope, and therefore we must continue to hark back to the historical origins of the privilege, particularly the evils at which it was to strike. The privilege against compulsory self-incrimination was developed by painful opposition to a course of ecclesiastical inquisitions and Star Chamber proceedings occurring several centuries ago. . . .

Where there has been genuine compulsion of testimony, the right has been given broad scope. Although the constitutional language in which the privilege is cast might be construed to apply only to situations in which the prosecution seeks to call a defendant to testify against himself at his criminal trial, its application has not been so limited. The right has been held applicable to proceedings before a grand jury, . . . to civil proceedings, . . . to congressional investigations, . . . to juvenile proceedings, . . . and to other statutory inquiries, . . . The privilege has also been applied against the States by virtue of the Fourteenth Amendment. . . .

Although federal cases concerning voluntary confessions often contained references to the privilege against compulsory self-incrimination, . . . it was not until this Court's decision in *Miranda* that the privilege against compulsory self-incrimination was seen as the principal protection for a person facing police interrogation. . . . In *Miranda* the court examined the facts of four separate cases and stated:

In these cases, we might not find the defendants' statements to have been involuntary in traditional terms. Our concern for adequate safeguards to protect precious Fifth Amendment rights is, of course, not lessened in the slightest, . . . To be sure, the records do not evince overt physical coercion or patent psychological ploys. The fact remains that in none of these cases did the officers undertake to afford appropriate safeguards at the outset of the interrogation to insure that the statements were truly the product of free choice. . . .

Thus the Court in *Miranda,* for the first time, expressly declared that the Self-Incrimination Clause was applicable to state interrogations at a police station, and that a defendant's statements might be excluded at trial despite their voluntary character under traditional principles.

To supplement this new doctrine, and to help police officers conduct interrogations without facing a continued risk that valuable evidence would be lost, the Court in *Miranda* established a set of specific protective guidelines, now commonly known as the *Miranda* rules. . . . A series of recommended "procedural safeguards" then followed. . . .

The Court recognized that these procedural safeguards were not themselves rights protected by the Constitution but were instead measures to insure that the right against compulsory self-incrimination was protected. . . . The suggested safeguards were not intended to "create a constitutional straightjacket," . . . but rather to provide practical reinforcement for the right against compulsory self-incrimination.

A comparison of the facts in this case with the historical circumstances underlying the privilege against compulsory self-incrimination strongly indicates that the police conduct here did not deprive respondent of his privilege against compulsory self-incrimination as such, but rather failed to make available to him the full measure of procedural safeguards associated with that right since *Miranda*. Certainly no one could contend that the interrogation faced by respondent bore any resemblance to the historical practices at which the right against compulsory self-incrimination was aimed. The District Court in this case noted that the police had "warned [respondent'] that he had the right to remain silent," . . . and the record in this case clearly shows that respondent was informed that any evidence taken could be used against him. The

record is also clear that respondent was asked whether he wanted an attorney and that he replied that he did not. Thus, his statements could hardly be termed involuntary as that term has been defined in the decisions of this Court. Additionally, there were no legal sanctions, such as the threat of contempt, which could have been applied to respondent had he chosen to remain silent. He was simply not exposed to "the cruel trilemma of self-accusation, perjury, or contempt." *Murphy* v. *Waterfront Commission* . . . (1964).

Our determination that the interrogation in this case involved no compulsion sufficient to breach the right against compulsory self-incrimination does not mean there was not a disregard, albeit an inadvertent disregard, of the procedural rules later established in *Miranda*. The question for decision is how sweeping the judicially imposed consequences of this disregard shall be. This Court said in *Miranda* that statements taken in violation of the *Miranda* principles must not be used to prove the prosecution's case at trial. That requirement was fully complied with by the state court here: respondent's statements, claiming that he was with Henderson and then asleep during the time period of the crime were not admitted against him at trial. This Court has also said, in *Wong Sun* v. *United States* . . . (1963), that the "fruits" of police conduct which actually infringed a defendant's Fourth Amendment rights must be suppressed. But we have already concluded that the police conduct at issue here did not abridge respondent's constitutional privilege against compulsory self-incrimination, but departed only from the prophylactic standards later laid down by this Court in *Miranda* to safeguard that privilege. Thus, in deciding whether Henderson's testimony must be excluded, there is no controlling precedent of this Court to guide us. We must therefore examine the matter as a question of principle.

Just as the law does not require that a defendant receive a perfect trial, only a fair one, it cannot realistically require that policemen investigating serious crimes make no errors whatsoever. The pressures of law enforcement and the vagaries of human nature would make such an expectation unrealistic. Before we penalize police error, therefore, we must consider whether the sanction serves a valid and useful purpose.

We have recently said, in a search and seizure context, that the exclusionary rule's "prime purpose is to deter future unlawful police conduct and thereby to effectuate the guarantee of the Fourth Amendment against unreasonable searches and seizures." *United States* v. *Calandra* . . . (1974). We then continued:

The rule is calculated to prevent, not to repair. Its purpose is to deter—to compel respect for the constitutional guaranty in the only effective available way—by removing the incentive to disregard it. Elkins v. United States, . . . *(1960.)*

When involuntary statements or the right against compulsory self-incrimination are involved, a second justification for the exclusionary rule also has been asserted: protection of the courts from reliance on untrustworthy evidence. Cases which involve the Self-Incrimination Clause must, by definition, involve an element of coercion, since the clause provides only that a person shall not be *compelled* to give evidence against himself. And cases involving statements often depict severe pressures which may override a par-

ticular suspect's insistence on innocence. . . .

. . . The pressures on respondent to accuse himself were hardly comparable even with the least prejudicial of those pressures which have been dealt with in our cases. More important, the respondent did *not* accuse himself. The evidence which the prosecution successfully sought to introduce was not a confession of guilt by respondent, or indeed even an exculpatory statement by respondent, but rather the testimony of a third party who was subjected to no custodial pressures. There is plainly no reason to believe that Henderson's testimony is untrustworthy simply because *respondent* was not advised of *his* right to appointed counsel. Henderson was both available at trial and subject to cross-examination by respondent's counsel, and counsel fully used this opportunity, suggesting in the course of his cross-examination that Henderson's character was less than exemplary and that he had been offered incentives by the police to testify against respondent. Thus the reliability of his testimony was subject to the normal testing process of an adversary trial.

. . .

In summary, we do not think that any single reason supporting exclusion of this witness' testimony, nor all of them together, are very persuasive. By contrast, we find the arguments in favor of admitting the testimony quite strong. For, when balancing the interested involved, we must weigh the strong interest under any system of justice of making available to the trier of fact all concededly relevant and trustworthy evidence which either party seeks to adduce. In this particular case we also "must consider society's interest in the effective prosecution of criminals in light of the protection our pre-*Miranda* standards afford criminal defendants." *Jenkins* v. *Delaware* . . . (1969). . . .

This Court has already recognized that a failure to give interrogated suspects full *Miranda* warnings does not entitle the suspect to insist that statements made by him be excluded in every conceivable context. In *Harris* v. *New York* . . . (1971), the Court was faced with the question of whether the statements of the defendant himself, taken without informing him of his right of access to appointed counsel, could be used to impeach defendant's direct testimony at trial. The Court concluded that they could, . . .

. . . Although *Johnson* enabled respondent to block admission of his own statements, we do not believe that it requires the prosecution to refrain from all use of those statements, and we disagree with the courts below that Henderson's testimony should have been excluded in this case.

Reversed.

MR. JUSTICE BRENNAN, WITH WHOM MR. JUSTICE MARSHALL JOINS, CONCURRING (OMITTED).
MR. JUSTICE STEWART, CONCURRING (OMITTED).
MR. JUSTICE WHITE, CONCURRING (OMITTED).

MR. JUSTICE DOUGLAS, DISSENTING.

. . . I cannot agree when the Court says that the interrogation here "did not abridge respondent's constitutional privilege against self-incrimination, but departed only from the prophylactic standards later laid down by this Court in *Miranda* to safeguard that privilege." . . . The Court is not free to prescribe preferred modes of interrogation absent a constitutional basis. We held the "requirement of warnings and waiver of rights [to be] fundamental with respect to the Fifth Amendment privilege," . . . and without so holding we would have been powerless to reverse Miranda's conviction. While *Miranda* recognized that police need not mouth the precise words contained in the Court's opinion, such warnings were held necessary "unless other fully effective means are adopted to notify the person" of his rights. . . . There is no contention here that other means were adopted. The respondent's statements were thus obtained "under circumstances that did not meet *constitutional* standards for the protection of the privilege [against self-incrimination]." . . .

[Efforts to overrule *Miranda* continue, but the Supreme Court has declined many chances to do so. It has reduced the scope and application of *Miranda* while leaving the basic decision intact. And in a few other cases, it has enforced the principles and policy of *Miranda*.

In *Oregon* v. *Hass* (1975), the Court was presented with a variation of the facts in *Harris* v. *New York* (1971). Hass was charged with burglary and, at the time of his arrest, was given the *Miranda* warnings. En route to the police station, he asked to telephone his lawyer and was told that he could do so when he arrived at the police station. During the ride to the station, however, he made several incriminating statements. During his trial, he told a different story. The police officer then testified to the contrary incriminating statements that Hass had made in the squad car. The judge instructed the jury that these statements could not be used as evidence of guilt but might be used to impeach the truthfulness of Hass' testimony. Hass' conviction was reversed by the intermediate appellate court, and that reversal was affirmed by the Oregon Supreme Court.

The U. S. Supreme Court reversed in a 6-2 decision, holding that *Harris* v. *New York* was controlling: ". . . Here, too, the shield provided by *Miranda* is not to be perverted to a license to testify inconsistently, or even perjuriously, free from the risk of confrontation with prior inconsistent utterances." The Court also rejected Hass' claim that "when state law is more restrictive against the prosecution than federal law this Court has no power to 'compel a state to conform to federal law.' " It is true, Justice Blackmun said, "that a state is free *as a matter of its own law* to impose greater restrictions on policy activity than those this Court holds to be necessary upon federal constitutional standards. . . . But, of course, a state may not impose such greater restrictions as a matter of *federal constitutional law* when this Court specifically refrains from imposing them."

In *United States* v. *Mandujano* (1976) the Court held that a witness testifying before a grand jury was not entitled to the *Miranda* warnings. Mandujano was called to testify before a grand jury and given the following instructions: he was required to answer all questions except those that might be incriminating; he was entitled to consult with a lawyer outside the grand jury room; and he was obliged to answer truthfully or face possible perjury charges. On the basis of his testimony to the grand jury, Mandujano was indicted for attempting to distribute narcotics *and* for perjury. He admitted the latter, but contended that his grand jury testimony was inadmissible because he had not received the *Miranda* warnings. A federal district court granted Mandujano's motion to suppress the testimony, and a federal court of appeals affirmed. The Supreme Court reversed, holding that a witness before a grand jury has an absolute duty to testify absent any Fifth Amendment claims of self-incrimination. A criminal suspect, under *Miranda,* has an absolute right to remain silent, and the Court was unwilling to extend that privilege to grand jury witnesses.

Finally, in *Brewer* v. *Williams* (1976), the Court held that volunteered incriminating statements given by a defendant after arraignment, while he was being transported to another jurisdiction to consult with defense counsel, must be excluded from evidence. Williams was charged with the murder of a 10-year-old girl. He was advised of his rights and requested the assistance of counsel. Police agreed not to question him during the course of transporting him from Davenport to Des Moines, Iowa, the site of the trial. During the ride, one of the officers surreptitiously elicited incriminating testimony that enabled the police to locate the girl's body and that was used in securing Williams' conviction. Against a motion to suppress this testimony, the state argued that Williams waived his right to counsel, since he had been given the *Miranda* warnings in Davenport and understood his rights. While he had initially declined to talk to the police, the state argued, he could change his mind at a later time as long as he was not under any pressures to do so.

The Supreme Court found this to be an invalid waiver, in a bitter 5-4 decision. Chief Justice Burger dissented, calling "the result in this case . . . intolerable in any society which purports to call itself an organized society." He lashed out at the "sporting theory of criminal justice" and noted that the Court, by its decision, had fulfilled "Justice Cardozo's grim prophecy that someday some court might carry the exclusionary rule to the absurd extent that its operative effect would exclude evidence relating to the body of a murder victim because of the means by which it was found." He argued that a truly voluntary and reliable confession, such as he considered Williams' statements to be, should not be suppressed. The exclusionary rule should not be applied to "nonegregious" police conduct. Burger saw little difference between this case and *Stone* v. *Powell* (1976, *supra*).

In *North Carolina* v. *Butler* (1979) the Supreme Court further qualified what constituted a valid waiver of the *Miranda* rights, holding that an explicit statement of waiver is not invariably necessary to support a finding that the defendant waived the right to counsel guaranteed by *Miranda.* Thus, inculpatory statements made to F.B.I. agents following the defendant's refusal to sign a waiver at the end of the Bureau's Advice of Rights form were *not* inadmissible. The Court stated that whereas *Miranda* held that an express written or oral statement *can* constitute a waiver, *Miranda* did not hold that such an express statement is *indispensable* to a finding of waiver, although silence alone after such warnings cannot constitute a waiver.]

5. FAIR TRIAL AND PUNISHMENT

A. *What is a Fair Trial?*

Fairness is a fundamental value in our society. In the context of the law, it is often linked with due process, but the concept of fairness is broader. Equating fairness with due process may encourage excessive attachment to rules, a phenomenon often referred to as "legalism." Undoubtedly, rules are an important element of fairness, and fair rules often produce just results. But too often the contingent impact of rules is overlooked. The fairness of a particular rule is dependent on the fulfillment of certain prerequisites that are often ignored. The most common condition that subverts the formal appearance of fair rules is the lack of equal resources among the parties acting under these rules. The adversary system, a hallmark of American law, is dependent on a real, not just a theoretical or formal, equality between competing parties. To observe the fallacy in this thinking is to belabor the obvious. It is set forth here only to alert the student to think beyond rules and what appears to be formal equality.

To understand what is meant by a fair trial, one might begin by identifying three main components. The first component is the *substance of rules.* These are some things for which a person should not have to stand trial; no amount of procedural fairness could give legitimacy to trials for one's political or religious beliefs. Although other additions to the list might provoke some disagreement, the following might also be included:

thinking "impure" or disloyal thoughts, performing acts of high conscience (whether or not these constitute civil disobedience), or engaging in conduct that is harmless to others.

Legitimate rules must have certain characteristics: they must be clearly defined, in advance. They should be capable of fair enforcement and not demand the unreasonable. One ought not to be liable to punishment for acts that cannot be controlled or for not doing what is clearly beyond one's capacity to perform.[2] While some of these criteria appear to be universalistic, others are bound by historical conditions and cultural values. Conditions change, emergencies arise; rules that were intended to be fair may in practice produce unintended unfair results.

A second component of the fair trial concept raises the question: fairness for whom? when? where? Earlier we referred to the "due process revolution" that characterized the approach of the Warren Court to the criminal justice system. The term "legalization" might also have been used. By legalization, we mean the extension of basic norms of *fair procedure* to individuals, groups, and situations that formerly had operated outside the scope of constitutional guarantees. Or it might imply extension of procedures or rights to some more strategic point in a process, where it might have more effect. Certainly, this was the rationale for extending the right to legal counsel

[1]Judith Shklar, *Legalism* (Cambridge: Harvard University Press, 1964).
[2]For example, the Supreme Court has held that narcotics addiction *per se* cannot constitutionally be made a crime, *Robinson* v. *California* (1962). But compare *Powell* v. *Texas* (1966), where the Supreme Court refused to extend that principle to alcoholism.

from the courtroom to the police station.

A brief canvas of groups that are now, to some extent, "covered" by due process rules formerly denied to them, or by more extensive rules, would include at least the following: criminal defendants; juveniles; prisoners; persons subject to involuntary civil commitment; persons subject to government loyalty and security procedures; immigration, naturalization, and deportation proceedings; officials subject to impeachment; students subject to disciplinary hearings; and public school and university faculty members on questions of tenure, termination, and dismissal. The application of due process guarantees to these groups is discussed at various places in this book. It seems appropriate to mention them here to suggest the wide sweep of the due process revolution.

The third component, of most central concern to us here, is the *nature of those procedures* that set the minimum conditions for a fair trial. In our society generally, and certainly in the context of criminal justice, the emphasis is on determining the rights of individuals. Yet there is a respectable body of opinion that reminds us that fairness expresses a relationship between two or more entities. Justice Cardozo, in his *Palko* opinion, made the argument that the state is also entitled to a fair trial. A similar sentiment finds expression in criticism alleging that the Supreme Court has overlooked the "rights" of society, or the plight of the victim, in its concern for the rights of the criminal defendant. Yet it is understandable that, in the context of a Bill of Rights that expresses the rights of individuals against the government, it

is the individual perspective on fairness that predominates.

What are the essential elements of a constitutionally fair trial? Our society has come a long way from defining due process merely as the right to notice and a hearing. So far in this chapter, we have already considered several important components: the right to trial by jury fairly selected from among one's peers, the rights against self-incrimination and double jeopardy, and some aspects of the right to counsel. It was noted that there are many pretrial events, or conditions surrounding a trial, which, if not controlled, would make a truly fair trial impossible. The Supreme Court has held the constitutional right to confrontation of witnesses[3] and to a speedy trial[4] enforceable against the states.

In the remainder of this section, some additional aspects of a constitutionally fair trial are considered, along with the issues of capital punishment and due process rights for prisoners. Capital punishment is an excellent example of the interplay of substantive and procedural aspects of fairness; it raises the question of whether the death penalty can ever be imposed fairly, but it also considers the fairest way of determining who is to be sentenced to death.

The issue of due process for prisoners is especially relevant for its contrast to those rights deemed essential to a fair trial; one sees the Supreme Court's attempt to balance prisoners' claims of rights and the competing demands of prison administration. It is a reminder that rights cannot exist only in the abstract and that there are other interests that a society may wish—or have—to protect in order to maintain fiscal, administrative, or

[3]*Pointer* v. *Texas* (1965).
[4]*Klopfer* v. *North Carolina* (1967).

social stability. These interests compete with an individual's conception of a fair trial. A recent book by Judge Macklin Fleming, entitled *The Price of Perfect Justice*,[5] argues that our society has gone too far in trying to assure "perfect justice." Not only is perfect justice not achievable, according to the author, but the costs of this futile quest are extraordinarily high. Few innocent persons are aided, many criminals go free, and a seemingly endless process of appeals diminishes the potential deterrent impact and legitimacy of the criminal justice system.

B. The Right to Counsel

(1) Gideon v. Wainwright (1963)

+Black, Warren, Douglas, Clark, Harlan, Brennan, Stewart, White, Goldberg

[It was only in the Scottsboro case, *Powell* v. *Alabama* (1932), that the Supreme Court began to recognize a constitutional right to a fair trial and to associate that right with the availability of effective counsel.[1] In that case the Court, by a 7-2 vote, had reversed the convictions and death sentences of eight young blacks charged with the rape of two white girls in a small Alabama town. The alleged crime had taken place on March 25, 1931. Indictments were handed down on March 31, and the trials were completed a week later. The defendants were not permitted to call friends or secure counsel, although the trial judge at one point did "appoint" all the members of the local bar to act in their behalf. The convictions were affirmed on appeal by the Alabama Supreme Court, and the case became a national cause célebre, exciting the rivalry between the

NAACP and the American Communist Party. Justice Sutherland's opinion spoke expansively of the need for counsel in most criminal cases. But the decision[2] rested on the more narrow ground that "in a capital case, where the defendant is unable to employ counsel, and is incapable adequately of making his own defense because of ignorance, feeblemindedness, illiteracy, or the like, it is the duty of the court, whether requested or not, to assign counsel for him as a necessary requisite of the process of law."

In *Johnson* v. *Zerbst* (1938), the Supreme Court held that counsel had to be provided to indigent defendants in *all* criminal cases in the federal courts. But in *Betts* v. *Brady* (1942), the Court interpreted *Powell* narrowly and refused to hold that counsel had to be appointed for indigents in all state criminal cases. Betts was indicted for robbery, and his request for counsel was denied on the grounds that the state law (Maryland) required appointment of an attorney only in capital cases. Betts was tried by a judge, without a jury, and was convicted. Before the Supreme Court, Betts' counsel argued that *Powell* required the appointment of counsel. Speaking for a 6-3 majority, Justice Roberts agreed that there was a constitutional right to *use* counsel in all cases. But he found that furnishing counsel to all indigent defendants was not a "fundamental right" under the Fourteenth Amendment. Betts, unlike the defendants in the *Powell* case, was not charged with a capital offense. He was of ordinary intelligence, and his alleged crime did not excite the emotions of the community. He was, the Court held, able to protect his own interests. Out of this case emerged what became known as the "special circumstances" rule. Counsel was required in all capital cases[2] and in those other cases in which the circumstances made it difficult for the defendant to defend himself adequately—his own lack of ability or education, the nature of

---

[5]Macklin Fleming, *The Price of Perfect Justice* (New York: Basic Books 1974).

[1]There were, of course, occasional earlier instances where the Supreme Court had reversed a state criminal trial because it lacked due process. Cf. *Tumey* v. *Ohio* (1927) and *Moore* v. *Dempsey* (1923).

[2]Technically, the requirement of counsel in capital cases was not made absolute until 1961.

the crime, or potential prejudice in the community.

Increasingly, and after 1950 invariably, the Supreme Court found one or more "special circumstances" present in the right-to-counsel cases that came before it. Whatever the intent of the rule, it had been swallowed up by its exceptions. The *Betts* case itself, had it been decided in 1960, almost surely would have resulted in a reversal of conviction under the expanding special circumstances rule. Furthermore, other decisions, particularly *Griffin* v. *Illinois* (1956), had undermined the rationale of *Betts*. It was thus not unexpected that the Supreme Court would seek to reconsider the *Betts* rule. That opportunity came when the Court received, in the spring of 1962, a handwritten *in forma pauperis* petition for certiorari from a Florida inmate named Clarence Earl Gideon.[3] Abe Fortas, then one of Washington's leading attorneys, was appointed to represent Gideon.]

MR. JUSTICE BLACK delivered the opinion of the Court.

Petitioner was charged in a Florida state court with having broken and entered a poolroom with intent to commit a misdemeanor. This offense is a felony under Florida law. Appearing in court without funds and without a lawyer, petitioner asked the court to appoint counsel for him, whereupon the following colloquy took place:

The Court: Mr. Gideon, I am sorry, but I cannot appoint Counsel to represent you in this case. Under the laws of the State of Florida, the only time the Court can appoint Counsel to represent a Defendant is when that person is charged with a capital offense. I am sorry, but I will have to deny your request to appoint Counsel to defend you in this case.

The Defendant: The United States Supreme Court says I am entitled to be represented by Counsel.

Put to trial before a jury Gideon conducted his defense about as well as could be expected from a layman. He made an opening statement to the jury, cross-examined the State's witnesses, presented witnesses in his own defense, declined to testify himself, and made a short argument "emphasizing his innocence to the charge contained in the Information filed in this case." The jury returned a verdict of guilty, and petitioner was sentenced to serve five years in the state prison. Later, petitioner filed in the Florida Supreme Court this habeas corpus petition attacking his conviction and sentence on the ground that the trial court's refusal to appoint counsel for him denied him rights "guaranteed by the Constitution and the Bill of Rights by the United States Government." Treating the petition for habeas corpus as properly before it, the State Supreme Court, "upon consideration thereof " but without an opinion, denied all relief. Since 1942, when *Betts* v. *Brady* . . . was decided by a divided Court, the problem of a defendant's federal constitutional right to counsel in a state court has been a continuing source of controversy and litigation in both state and federal courts. To give this problem another review here, we granted certiorari. . . . Since Gideon was proceeding *in forma pauperis*, we appointed counsel to represent him, and requested both sides to discuss in their briefs and oral arguments the following: "Should this Court's holding in *Betts* v. *Brady* . . . be reconsidered?"

The facts upon which Betts claimed that he had been unconstitutionally denied the right to have counsel appointed to assist him are strikingly like the facts upon which

[3]See Anthony Lewis, *Gideon's Trumpet* (New York: Random House, 1963).

Gideon here bases his federal constitutional claim. . . . Betts was denied any relief, and on review this Court affirmed. It was held that a refusal to appoint counsel for an indigent defendant charged with a felony did not necessarily violate the Due Process Clause of the Fourteenth Amendment, which for reasons given the Court deemed to be the only applicable federal constitutional provision. The Court said:

Asserted denial [of due process] is to be tested by an appraisal of the totality of facts in a given case. That which may, in one setting, constitute a denial of fundamental fairness, shocking to the universal sense of justice, may, in other circumstances, and in the light of other considerations, fall short of such denial. . . .

Treating due process as "a concept less rigid and more fluid than those envisaged in other specific and particular provisions of the Bill of Rights," the Court held that refusal to appoint counsel under the particular facts and circumstances in the *Betts* case was not as "offensive to the common and fundamental ideas of fairness" as to amount to a denial of due process. Since the facts and circumstances of the two cases are so nearly indistinguishable, we think the *Betts* v. *Brady* holding if left standing would require us to reject Gideon's claim that the Constitution guarantees him the assistance of counsel. Upon full reconsideration we conclude that *Betts* v. *Brady* should be overruled.

The Sixth Amendment provides, "In all criminal prosecutions, the accused shall enjoy the right . . . to have the Assistance of Counsel for his defense." We have construed this to mean that in federal courts counsel must be provided for defendants unable to employ counsel unless the right is competently and intelligently waived. *Betts* argued that the right is extended to indigent defendants in state courts by the Fourteenth Amendment. In response the Court stated that, while the Sixth Amendment laid down "no rule for the conduct of the States, the question recurs whether the constraint laid by the Amendment upon the national courts expresses a rule so fundamental and essential to a fair trial, and so, to due process of law, that it is made obligatory upon the States by the Fourteenth Amendment." . . . In order to decide whether the Sixth Amendment's guarantee of counsel is of this fundamental nature, the Court in *Betts* set out and considered "[r]elevant data on the subject . . . afforded by constitutional and statutory provisions subsisting in the colonies and the States prior to the inclusion of the Bill of Rights in the national Constitution, and in the constitutional, legislative, and judicial history of the States to the present date." . . . On the basis of this historical data the Court concluded that "appointment of counsel is not a fundamental right, essential to a fair trial." . . . It was for this reason the *Betts* Court refused to accept the contention that the Sixth Amendment's guarantee of counsel for indigent federal defendants was extended to or, in the words of that Court, "made obligatory upon the States by the Fourteenth Amendment." . . .

We think the Court in *Betts* had ample precedent for acknowledging that those guarantees of the Bill of Rights which are fundamental safeguards of liberty immune from federal abridgment are equally protected against state invasion by the Due Process Clause of the Fourteenth Amendment. This same principle was recognized, explained, and applied in *Powell* v. *Alabama* . . .

(1932), a case upholding the right of counsel, where the Court held that despite sweeping language to the contrary in *Hurtado* v. *California* . . . (1884), the Fourteenth Amendment "embraced" those " 'fundamental principles of liberty and justice which lie at the base of all our civil and political institutions,' " even though they had been "specifically dealt with in another part of the federal Constitution." . . . In many cases other than *Powell* and *Betts*, this Court has looked to the fundamental nature of original Bill of Rights guarantees to decide whether the Fourteenth Amendment makes them obligatory on the States. . . .

We accept *Betts* v. *Brady's* assumption, based as it was on our prior cases, that a provision of the Bill of Rights which is "fundamental and essential to a fair trial" is made obligatory upon the States by the Fourteenth Amendment. We think the Court in *Betts* was wrong, however, in concluding that the Sixth Amendment's guarantee of counsel is not one of these fundamental rights. Ten years before *Betts* v. *Brady*, this Court, after full consideration of all the historical data examined in *Betts*, had unequivocally declared that "the right to the aid of counsel is of this fundamental character." *Powell* v. *Alabama* . . . (1932). While the Court at the close of its *Powell* opinion did by its language, as this Court frequently does, limit its holding to the particular facts and circumstances of that case, its conclusions about the fundamental nature of the right to counsel are unmistakable. . . . The fact is that in deciding as it did—that "appointment of counsel is not a fundamental right, essential to a fair trial"—the Court in *Betts* v. *Brady* made an abrupt break with its own well-considered precedents. In returning to these old precedents, sounder we believe than the new, we

but restore constitutional principles established to achieve a fair system of justice. Not only these precedents but also reason and reflection require us to recognize that in our adversary system of criminal justice, any person haled into court, who is too poor to hire a lawyer, cannot be assured a fair trial unless counsel is provided for him. This seems to us to be an obvious truth. . . . The right of one charged with crime to counsel may not be deemed fundamental and essential to fair trials in some countries, but it is in ours. From the very beginning, our state and national constitutions and laws have laid great emphasis on procedural and substantive safeguards designed to assure fair trials before impartial tribunals in which every defendant stands equal before the law. This noble ideal cannot be realized if the poor man charged with crime has to face his accusers without a lawyer to assist him. . . . The Court in *Betts* v. *Brady* departed from the sound wisdom upon which the Court's holding in *Powell* v. *Alabama* rested. Florida, supported by two other States, has asked that *Betts* v. *Brady* be left intact. Twenty-two States, as friends of the Court, argue that *Betts* was "an anachronism when handed down" and that it should now be overruled. We agree.

The judgment is reversed and the cause is remanded to the Supreme Court of Florida for further action not inconsistent with this opinion.

Reversed.

MR. JUSTICE DOUGLAS CONCURRING (OMITTED).

MR. JUSTICE CLARK, CONCURRING IN THE RESULT (OMITTED).

MR. JUSTICE HARLAN, CONCURRING.

I agree that *Betts* v. *Brady* should be overruled, but consider it entitled to a more respectful burial than has been accorded, at least on the part of those of us who were not on the Court when that case was decided.

I cannot subscribe to the view that *Betts* v. *Brady* represented "an abrupt break with its own well-considered precedents." . . . In 1932, in *Powell* v. *Alabama* . . . , this Court declared that under the particular facts there presented—"the ignorance and illiteracy of the defendants, their youth, the circumstances of public hostility . . . and above all that they stood in deadly peril of their lives" . . .—the state court had a duty to assign counsel for the trial as a necessary requisite of due process of law. It is evident that these limiting facts were not added to the opinion as an afterthought; they were clearly regarded as important to the result.

Thus, when this Court, a decade later, decided *Betts* v. *Brady*, it did not more than to admit of the possible existence of special circumstances in noncapital as well as capital trials, while at the same time insisting that such circumstances be shown in order to establish a denial of due process. The right to appointed counsel had been recognized as being considerably broader in federal prosecutions, see *Johnson* v. *Zerbst* . . . , but to have imposed these requirements on the States would indeed have been "an abrupt break" with the almost immediate past. The declaration that the right to appointed counsel in state prosecutions, as established in *Powell* v. *Alabama*, was not limited to capital cases was in truth not a departure from, but an extension of existing precedent.

The principles declared in *Powell* and in *Betts*, however, have had a troubled journey throughout the years that have followed first the one case and then the other. Even by the time of the *Betts* decision, dictum in at least one of the Court's opinions had indicated that there was an absolute right to the services of counsel in the trial of state capital cases. . . .

In noncapital cases, the "special circumstances" rule has continued to exist in form while its substance has been substantially and steadily eroded. In the first decade after *Betts*, there were cases in which the Court found special circumstances to be lacking, but usually by a sharply divided vote. However, no such decision has been cited to us, and I have found none, after . . . 1950. At the same time, there have been not a few cases in which special circumstances were found in little or nothing more than the "complexity" of the legal questions presented, although those questions were often of only routine difficulty. The Court has come to recognize, in other words, that the mere existence of a serious criminal charge constituted in itself special circumstances requiring the services of counsel at trial. In truth the *Betts* v. *Brady* rule is no longer a reality.

This evolution, however, appears not to have been fully recognized by many state courts, in this instance charged with the front-line responsibility for the enforcement of constitutional rights. To continue a rule which is honored by this Court only with lip service is not a healthy thing and in the long run will do disservice to the federal system. . . .

(2) Argersinger v. Hamlin (1972)

+Burger, Douglas, Brennan, Stewart, White, Marshall, Blackmun, Powell, Rehnquist

[Jon Argersinger, an indigent, was charged with carrying a concealed weapon, an offense punishable under Florida law by imprisonment of up to six months and a fine of $1000. Unrepresented by counsel, Argersinger was convicted by a judge, without a jury, and sentenced to ninety days in jail. He instituted a habeas corpus action in the Florida Supreme Court, alleging that as an indigent layman, he was unable to properly prepare and conduct his own defense. The Florida Supreme Court rejected his contention, holding that under the rule of *Duncan* v. *Louisiana* (1968, *supra*) the right to court-appointed counsel extended only to trials "for non-petty offenses punishable by more than six months imprisonment."]

MR. JUSTICE DOUGLAS delivered the opinion of the Court.

. . .

The case is here on a petition for certiorari which we granted. . . . We reverse.

The Sixth Amendment, which in enumerated situations has been made applicable to the States by reason of the Fourteenth Amendment . . . provides specified standards for "all criminal prosecutions." . . .

The right to trial by jury, also guaranteed by the Sixth Amendment by reason of the Fourteenth, was limited by *Duncan* v. *Louisiana*, . . . to trials where the potential punishment was imprisonment of six months or more. But as the various opinions in *Baldwin* v. *New York* . . . [1970] make plain, the right to trial by jury has a different genealogy and is brigaded with a system of trial to a judge alone. . . .

While there is historical support for limiting the "deep commitment" to trial by jury to "serious criminal cases," there is no such support for a similar limitation on the right to assistance of counsel: . . .

The Sixth Amendment thus extended the right to counsel beyond its common-law dimensions. But there is nothing in the language of the Amendment, its history, or in the decisions of this Court, to indicate that it was intended to embody a retraction of the right in petty offenses wherein the common law previously did require that counsel be provided.

. . .

We reject, therefore, the premise that since prosecutions for crimes punishable by imprisonment for less than six months may be tried without a jury, they may always be tried without a lawyer.

The assistance of counsel is often a requisite to the very existence of a fair trial. . . .

In *Gideon* v. *Wainwright*, . . . we dealt with a felony trial. But we did not so limit the need of the accused for a lawyer. . . .

The requirement of counsel, may well be necessary for a fair trial even in a petty offense prosecution. We are by no means convinced that legal and constitutional questions involved in a case that actually leads to imprisonment even for a brief period are any less complex than when a person can be sent off for six months or more. . . .

The trial of vagrancy cases is illustrative. While only brief sentences of imprisonment may be imposed, the cases often bristle with thorny constitutional questions. See *Papachristou* v. *Jacksonville* . . . [1972]. . . .

Beyond the problem of trials and appeals is that of the guilty plea, a problem which looms large in misdemeanor as well as in felony cases. Counsel is needed so that the accused may know precisely what he is doing, so that he is fully aware of the prospect of going to jail or prison, and so that he is treated fairly by the prosecution. . . .

We hold, therefore, that absent a knowing and intelligent waiver, no person may be imprisoned for any offense, whether classified as petty, misdemeanor, or felony, unless he was represented by counsel at his trial. . . .

Under the rule we announce today, every judge will know when the trial of a misdemeanor starts that no imprisonment may be imposed, even though local law permits it, unless the accused is represented by counsel. He will have a measure of the seriousness and gravity of the offense and therefore know when to name a lawyer to represent the accused before the trial starts.

The run of misdemeanors will not be affected by today's ruling. But in those that end up in the actual deprivation of a person's liberty, the accused will receive the benefit of "the guiding hand of counsel" so necessary when one's liberty is in jeopardy.

Reversed.

MR. CHIEF JUSTICE BURGER, CONCURRING IN THE RESULT. . . .

Trial judges sitting in petty and misdemeanor cases—and prosecutors—should recognize exactly what will be required by today's decision. Because no individual can be imprisoned unless he is represented by counsel, the trial judge and the prosecutor will have to engage in a predicative evaluation of each case to determine whether there is a significant likelihood that, if the defendant is convicted, the trial judge will sentence him to a jail term. The judge can preserve the option of a jail sentence only by offering counsel to any defendant unable to retain counsel on his own. This need to predict will place a new load on courts already overburdened and already compelled to deal with far more cases in one day than is reasonable and proper. Yet the prediction is not one beyond the capacity of an experienced judge, aided as he should be by the prosecuting officer. As to jury cases, the latter should be prepared to inform the judge as to any prior record of the accused, the general nature of the case against the accused, including any use of violence, the severity of harm to the victim, and impact on the community and the other factors relevant to the sentencing process.

Since the judge ought to have some degree of such information after judgment of guilt is determined, ways can be found in the more serious misdemeanor cases when jury trial is not waived to make it available to the judge before trial. This will not mean a full "presentence" report on every defendant in every case before the jury passes on guilt, but a prosecutor should know before trial whether he intends to urge a jail sentence and if he does he should be prepared to aid the court with the factual and legal basis for his view on that score. . . .

MR. JUSTICE BRENNAN, WITH WHOM MR. JUSTICE DOUGLAS AND MR. JUSTICE STEWART JOIN, CONCURRING (OMITTED).

MR. JUSTICE POWELL, WITH WHOM MR. JUSTICE REHNQUIST JOINS, CONCURRING IN THE RESULT (OMITTED).

[In *Scott* v. *Illinois* (1979), the Court, in a 5-4 decision, held that the constitutional right to appointed counsel in state criminal proceedings applied only where actual imprisonment occurred, not when the statute merely authorizes a penalty of imprisonment. Scott, an indigent, was convicted of shoplifting under an Illinois statute which set the maximum penalty of $500, one year in jail, or both. He was fined $50 and received no time in jail. Justice Brennan, speaking for the dissenters, argued that the Sixth Amendment right to counsel extended to the trial of any offense for which a convicted defendant is likely to be incarcerated, and the majority's opinion based on a "two-dimensional" test turned the reasoning of *Argersinger* "on its head."]

(3) A Note on the Ubiquity of Counsel

As noted in the introductory essay to this chapter, extension of the right to counsel has been a primary strategy for protecting constitutional rights. *Gideon* and *Argersinger* extended the right to trial counsel for indigents to virtually all criminal proceedings.[1] Each of these cases was made fully retroactive, suggesting special importance in the eyes of the Supreme Court.

But the Supreme Court also recognized that counsel at trial, by itself, would be insufficient to protect constitutional rights. The benefits of the adversary system could easily be lost in pretrial proceedings. Since most criminal cases never reached the trial stage, limiting the right to appointed counsel to trial proceedings would benefit only a small minority of defendants. The *Escobedo* and *Miranda* cases began the extension of counsel back to those critical proceedings between arrest and trial. In *United States* v. *Wade* and *Gilbert* v. *California* (1967), the Court extended the right to counsel to pretrial lineups and other identification procedures. Without the presence of counsel, it was held, a defendant could not effectively vindicate his constitutional right to confront witnesses at trial.

The effect of this rule was seriously diluted, however, when in *Kirby* v. *Illinois* (1972) the Court held that the right to counsel did not apply to *pre*indictment lineups. Nor, the Court said in *United States* v. *Ash,* (1973), did it apply to a "display of pictures" for identification by witnesses. Counsel is generally also required at pretrial hearings or preliminary examinations. There is no right to counsel, appointed or retained, in grand jury proceedings, although in some jurisdictions, a witness may confer with counsel outside the grand jury room.

In *Douglas* v. *California* (1963), the Supreme Court extended the right to counsel to the first appeal. But there is no right to appointed counsel for discretionary appeals, including those to the U. S. Supreme Court itself. Often overlooked is the fact that there is no general right to appeal in American law. But if a state (or the federal government) provides for appeals, then the opportunity must be available equally to all (*Ross* v. *Moffitt*, 1974).

The Supreme Court has also been under pressure to extend the right to counsel (appointed and/or retained) to other legal or quasi-legal proceedings. The right to appointed counsel was extended to juvenile hearings (*In re Gault*, 1967, *infra*) but not to disciplinary hearings for prisoners (*Wolff* v. *McDonnell*, 1974) or to hearings for short-term high school suspensions (*Goss* v. *Lopez*, 1975). It also seems likely that other types of hearings that may result in serious loss of liberty, such as involuntary civil commitment for mental illness, will eventually be brought under the right to counsel rubric. In all of these cases, the Court will be forced to decide whether to impose an adversary cast on proceedings that have traditionally followed (at least in theory) an adjustment or conciliation model.

The Supreme Court has largely ignored two major aspects of the right to counsel question: the meaning of indigency and the adequacy of counsel. On the standards for determining indigency, the Court has said nothing, although it did recently decide

---

[1]With the exception of *Escobedo*, virtually all recent constitutional litigation about the right to counsel has concerned the obligation of the state to *appoint* counsel for indigents. The Sixth Amendment right to employ privately retained counsel at almost any stage of a criminal proceeding is rarely questioned.

the peripheral issue of recoupment. In *Fuller* v. *Oregon* (1974), it upheld the right of a state to obtain reimbursement for the costs of appointed counsel and investigatory expenses where an indigent was later capable of paying.

What constitutes an adequate legal defense? In the legal profession, there is in fact little peer review and few quality controls; the Supreme Court has been reluctant to consider this critical question. In *McMann* v. *Richardson* (1970), it upheld a guilty plea even where the attorney had clearly misjudged the admissibility of a confession and erroneously advised his client to plead guilty. In another case, the Court said that a prisoner in a habeas corpus action had to demonstrate that the legal advice he received was "not within the range of competence demanded in criminal cases" (*Tollett* v. *Henderson,* 1973).

(4) Faretta v. California (1975)

+Douglas, Brennan, Stewart, White, Marshall, Powell

−Burger, Blackmum, Rehnquist

[Anthony Faretta, charged with grand theft, rejected the trial judge's assignment of the public defender to serve as defense counsel. Faretta noted that he had a high school education and had once previously represented himself in a criminal prosecution. He alleged that the public defender "had a very heavy caseload" and could not give his case the attention it deserved. The trial judge advised Faretta not to represent himself but, in a preliminary ruling, accepted his waiver of counsel. Before the trial began, the judge reversed his earlier decision. He held that Faretta had not made an intelligent and knowing waiver and that he had no constitutional right to defend himself. At the judge's insistence, Faretta was not permitted even to act as cocounsel, and his defense was conducted exclusively by a member of the public defender's staff. The jury found Faretta guilty, and he was sentenced to prison. The California Court of Appeals affirmed the conviction and the judge's denial of the right of self-representation. The Supreme Court granted certiorari.]

MR. JUSTICE STEWART delivered the opinion of the Court.

. . .

In the federal courts, the right of self-representation has been protected by statute since the beginnings of our Nation. Section 35 of the Judiciary Act of 1789, . . . 92, enacted by the First Congress and signed by President Washington one day before the Sixth Amendment was proposed, provided that "in all courts of the United States, the parties may plead and manage their own causes personally or by the assistance of counsel. . . ." The right is currently codified in 28 USC §1654. . . .

With few exceptions, each of the several States also accords a defendant the right to represent himself in any criminal case. The constitutions of 36 States explicitly confer that right. Moreover, many state courts have expressed the view that the right is also supported by the Constitution of the United States.

This Court has more than once indicated the same view. In *Adams ex rel. McCann* v. *United States*. . . . the Court recognized that the Sixth Amendment right to the assistance of counsel implicitly embodies a "correlative right to dispense with a lawyer's help." The defendant in that case, indicted for federal mail fraud violations, insisted on conducting his own defense without benefit of counsel. He also requested a bench trial and signed a waiver of his right to trial by jury. The prosecution consented to the waiver of a jury, and the waiver was accepted by the court. The defendant was convicted, but the Court of Appeals reversed the conviction on the ground that a person accused of a felony could not competently waive his right to trial by jury except upon the advice of a lawyer. This Court reversed and reinstated the conviction, holding that "an accused, in the exercise of free and intelligent choice, and with the considered approval of the court, may waive trial by jury, and so likewise may he competently and intelligently waive his Constitutional right to assistance of counsel." . . .

The *Adams* case does not, of course, necessarily resolve the issue before us. It held only that "the Constitution does not force a lawyer upon a defendant." . . . Whether the Constitution forbids a State from forcing a lawyer upon a defendant is a different question. . . .

In other settings as well, the Court has indicated that a defendant has a constitutionally protected right to represent himself in a criminal trial. For example, in *Snyder* v. *Massachusetts* . . . the Court held that the Confrontation Clause of the Sixth Amendment gives the accused a right to be present at all stages of the proceedings where fundamental fairness might be thwarted by his absence. This right to "presence" was based upon the premise that the "defense may be made easier if the accused is permitted to be present at the examination of jurors or the summing up of counsel, *for it will be in his power*, if present, to give advice or suggestion or *even to supercede his lawyers altogether and conduct the trial himself.*" . . .

This Court's past recognition of the right of self-representation, the federal court authority holding the right to be of constitutional dimension, and the state constitutions pointing to the right's fundamental nature form a consensus not easily ignored. "[T]he fact that a path is a beaten one," Mr. Justice Jackson once observed, "is a

persuasive reason for following it." We confront here a nearly universal conviction, on the part of our people as well as our courts, that forcing a lawyer upon an unwilling defendant is contrary to his basic right to defend himself if he truly wants to do so.

. . .

The Sixth Amendment does not provide merely that a defense shall be made for the accused; it grants to the accused personally the right to make his defense. It is the accused, not counsel, who must be "informed of the nature and cause of the accusation," who must be "confronted with witnesses against him," and who must be accorded "compulsory process for obtaining witnesses in his favor." Although not stated in the Amendment in so many words, the right to self-representation—to make one's own defense personally—is thus necessarily implied by the structure of the Amendment. The right to defend is given directly to the accused; for it is he who suffers the consequences if the defense fails.

The counsel provision supplements this design. It speaks of the "assistance" of counsel, and an assistant, however expert, is still an assistant. The language and spirit of the Sixth Amendment contemplate that counsel, like the other defense tools guaranteed by the Amendment, shall be an aid to a willing defendant—not an organ of the State interposed between an unwilling defendant and his right to defend himself personally. To thrust counsel upon the accused, against his considered wish, thus violates the logic of the Amendment. In such a case, counsel is not an assistant, but a master; and the right to make a defense is stripped of the personal character upon which the Amendment insists. It is true that when a defendant chooses to have a lawyer manage and present his case, law and tradition may allocate to the counsel the power to make binding decisions of trial strategy in many areas. . . . This allocation can only be justified, however, by the defendant's consent, at the outset, to accept counsel as his representative. An unwanted counsel "represents" the defendant only through a tenuous and unacceptable legal fiction. Unless the accused has acquiesced in such representation, the defense presented is not the defense guaranteed him by the Constitution, for, in a very real sense, it is not *his* defense.

The Sixth Amendment, when naturally read, thus implies a right of self-representation. This reading is reinforced by the Amendment's roots in English legal history.

. . .

In the American colonies the insistence upon a right of self-representation was, if anything, more fervent than in England.

The colonists brought with them an appreciation of the virtues of self-reliance and a traditional distrust of lawyers. When the Colonies were first settled, "the lawyer was synonomous with the cringing Attorneys-General and Solicitors-General of the Crown and the arbitrary Justices of the King's Court, all bent on the conviction of those who opposed the King's prerogatives, and twisting the law to secure convictions." This prejudice gained strength in the colonies where "distrust of lawyers became an institution." Several Colonies prohibited pleading for hire in the 17th century. The prejudice persisted into the 18th century as "the lower classes came to identify lawyers with the upper class." The years of Revolution and Confederation saw an upsurge of anti-lawyer sentiment, a "sudden revival, after the War of the Revolution of the old dislike and distrust of lawyers as a class." In the

heat of these sentiments the Constitution was forged.

. . .

Here, weeks before trial, Faretta clearly and unequivocally declared to the trial judge that he wanted to represent himself and did not want counsel. The record affirmatively shows that Faretta was literate, competent, and understanding, and that he was voluntarily exercising his informed free will. The trial judge had warned Faretta that he thought it was a mistake not to accept the assistance of counsel, and that Faretta would be required to follow all the "ground rules" of trial procedure. We need make no assessment of how well or poorly Faretta had mastered the intricacies of the hearsay rule and the California code provisions that govern challenges of potential jurors on voir dire. For his technical legal knowledge, as such, was not relevant to an assessment of his knowing exercise of the right to defend himself.

In forcing Faretta, under these circumstances, to accept against his will a state-appointed public defender, the California courts deprived him of his constitutional right to conduct his own defense. Accordingly, the judgment before us is vacated, and the case is remanded for further proceedings not inconsistent with this opinion.

It is so ordered.

MR. CHIEF JUSTICE BURGER, WITH WHOM MR. JUSTICE BLACKMUN AND MR. JUSTICE REHNQUIST JOIN, DISSENTING.

This case, . . . is another example of the judicial tendency to constitutionalize what is thought "good." That effort fails on its own terms here, because there is nothing desirable or useful in permitting every ac-

cused person, even the most unedu-
cated and inexperienced, to insist
upon conducting his own defense to
criminal charges. Moreover, there is
no constitutional basis for the Court's
holding and it can only add to the
problems of an already malfunction-
ing criminal justice system. I therefore dissent.

MR. JUSTICE BLACKMUN, WITH WHOM
THE CHIEF JUSTICE AND MR. JUSTICE
REHNQUIST JOIN, DISSENTING (OMIT-
TED).

C. The Conduct of a Trial

(1) Sheppard v. Maxwell (1966)

+Warren, Douglas, Clark, Harlan,
Brennan, Stewart, White, Fortas
−Black

[A basic component of due process of law is
that decisions about guilt or innocence should
be made according to a predetermined set of
rules and should be made free of outside pressure. A major function of the rules of evidence
(in both civil and criminal cases) is to control the
kind and quality of information that may be
used in arriving at a verdict. Thus, hearsay evidence is inadmissible. Witnesses are cross-
examined by opposing counsel to test the accuracy and veracity of their statements. Confessions and other evidence may be suppressed if
shown to be unreliable. The jury (or judge if
there is no jury) must decide guilt or innocence
only on the basis of what is presented in the
courtroom, not on newspaper reports or because of prejudgments or prior knowledge
about the facts or protagonists in a case. These
are the ideals.

In reality, these ideals occasionally collide
with intense community feelings and outrage,
making the prospect of a fair trial dubious at
best. In the United States, there is also the possibility of collision between the right to a fair trial
and the constitutionally protected rights of a
free press. Where community pressures and/or

adverse pretrial publicity exist, American
courts may respond in several ways. First, a
change of venue may be granted by the judge.
Second, a jury, once chosen, may be sequestered for the entire trial (or at least during deliberations) so that it is not exposed to any outside
information or pressure. Third, the judge will
usually have at least a limited contempt power
to prevent officers of the court, jurors, or witnesses from publicly disclosing potentially prejudicial facts about the case. Fourth, a judge
may limit the size, and may regulate the de-
meanor, of the audience at a trial—within the
constitutional limits set by the defendant's right
to a public trial. Finally, the judge may use the
voir dire to screen out prejudiced jurors.

There are many cases that illustrate the
problem of hostile community pressure.
Perhaps the most famous is the Scottsboro trial,
described previously. Another reached the Supreme Court in *Frank* v. *Mangum* (1915). Leo
Frank, a Jew from New York, managed his un-
cle's factory in Georgia. He was accused of
murdering a female employee and convicted in
a trial that reeked of hatred and anti-semitism.
So inflamed was the atmosphere at trial that the
judge had asked both the defendant and his
lawyer not to be in the courtroom when the verdict was delivered, lest there be violence if the
jury returned a verdict of acquittal. Over the
dissents of Justice Holmes and Hughes, the
Supreme Court upheld the conviction, noting
that the Georgia Supreme Court, in a calmer
atmosphere, had upheld the verdict. Holmes, in
dissent, argued that "mob law does not become due process of law by securing the assent of a terrorized jury." Frank was later ab-
ducted from the state prison farm and lynched.
The principle of *Frank,* that somehow a gross
miscarriage of justice could be rectified by an
orderly appeal, was effectively overruled less
than a decade later (*Moore* v. *Dempsey,* 1923).

There are few such incidents today. The judicial task of ferreting out adverse pretrial publicity and ensuring the requisites of a fair trial is
more subtle, and also more difficult. In 1961
(*Irvin* v. *Doud*), a unanimous Supreme Court,
for the first time, reversed a conviction because
of pretrial publicity. Irvin's confession of six
murders and twenty-four burglaries, his prior

criminal record, and his offer to plead guilty to one count of murder to avoid the death penalty had been given to the press by the police. One change of venue was ordered, but a second was denied. More than half the members of the jury panel asked to be excused because of prejudice. Eight of the jurors finally seated believed the defendant to be guilty but said they would base their decision solely on the facts brought out at trial. The constitutional standard of fairness, the Court said, was "a panel of impartial, indifferent jurors." But a juror did not have to be completely ignorant of the facts or issues in a case or about the defendant. It was open to the defendant's attorney to prove "the actual existence of such an opinion in the mind of the juror as will raise the presumption of partiality."

The intrusion of television into the courtroom was the issue in *Estes* v. *Texas* (1963). Billie Sol Estes, a flamboyant entrepreneur and self-made millionaire, was charged with fraud in a case that received national headlines. The pretrial hearing included television and radio coverage and news photography, and the proceedings resembled a circus more than a court. Some changes were made for the trial itself. The equipment was encased in a booth and live television coverage was prohibited, but televised excerpts from the proceedings were shown regularly on news programs. The Supreme Court reversed, Justice Clark arguing that the practice was inherently prejudicial. Witnesses (who normally are excluded from a trial except when they are testifying themselves) could watch the proceedings and perhaps tailor their testimony accordingly. Clark also noted the temptations for politically elected judges and the potential for harassment of the defendant. "The defendant is entitled to his day in court—not in a stadium or city or nationwide arena," Clark argued. However, Clark did not speak for a majority of justices in holding that a televised trial was inherently prejudicial.

This was the state of the law when the Supreme Court was confronted with probably the most famous nonpolitical murder case of the modern era. In July 1954, Dr. Samuel Sheppard's wife, Marilyn, was bludgeoned to death in the bedroom of their suburban Cleveland home. Sheppard claimed that he had been sleeping on a couch, that his wife had gone to bed, and that he heard his wife cry out in the early hours of the morning. He went upstairs and grappled with an intruder who struck him on the back of the head, causing him to lose consciousness. When he regained his senses, he discovered that his wife was dead. After checking on his son, who had not been harmed, he went downstairs and again encountered the intruder. He pursued the intruder to the lake shore, grappled with him, and again lost consciousness. When he recovered he returned to his house, checked his wife's pulse, and called a neighbor who in turn called the police.

Sheppard was taken to the family medical clinic and treated for his injuries by his brother, also a doctor. While at the clinic, and thereafter, he was repeatedly interrogated by the police. No attorney was present, and although Sheppard talked to the police, he refused a lie detector test. The local press was critical of the handling of the case, including the refusal of his family to permit his immediate questioning by the police. Vivid headlines implied that Sheppard was guilty and alleged that the police were not pressing him hard enough because of friendship and the prominence of the Sheppard family. A front page editorial said that somebody "was getting away with murder." A public inquest was held by the coroner. Sheppard's attorney was present but was not allowed to participate. When the attorney attempted to introduce some documents in the record, he was forcibly ejected to the cheers of the audience. Sheppard was questioned for nearly six hours about his actions the night of the murder, the state of his married life, and a former love affair.

Sheppard repeatedly claimed his innocence, while the press continued to suggest his guilt. Discrepancies in Sheppard's testimony were highlighted in feature articles, and his extramarital love affairs were "pinpointed" as the motive for the crime. Three weeks after the murder an editorial entitled "Why Don't Police Quiz Top Suspect?" demanded Sheppard's arrest, describing him as "Now proved under oath to be a liar, still free to go about his business, shielded by his family, protected by a smart lawyer who has made monkeys of the police and authorities, carrying a gun part of the time, left free to do whatever he pleases . . . ." Other editorials were even more blunt in demanding that he be jailed. Finally, about six weeks after the crime, Sheppard was indicted for the murder of his wife.

The case came to trial shortly before the forthcoming general election in which the prosecutor was running for municipal judge and the judge was a candidate for reelection. The names and addresses of prospective jurors were published in all the Cleveland newspapers, and all received letters and phone calls concerning the trial. The courtroom was overflowing with press and media representatives, and additional rooms in the building were assigned for media use. Private telephone lines and telegraph equipment were installed. A radio station was permitted to broadcast from the room adjoining the jury room, during both the trial and the jury deliberations. The corridors and the sidewalks outside the courthouse were likewise filled with reporters and cameramen who photographed and interviewed the participants as they entered and left the building. Photographs were not permitted during the trial but were allowed in the courtroom when the trial was not in session.

The confusion and noise frequently drowned out the words of the judge and witnesses despite the installation of a loudspeaker. Sheppard was unable to confer privately with his attorneys without leaving the courtroom. The testimony of witnesses was reprinted verbatim in the local press, and pictures of exhibits introduced as evidence were also published. The jurors were allowed to go home during the nine-week trial and were exposed to the incessant barrage of publicity. Further details of the trial are contained in the Court's opinion.

Sheppard was found guilty of murder and spent the next twelve years in jail. Repeated efforts to reverse his conviction failed until, finally, a federal district court in Cleveland ruled that he had not been given a fair trial and ordered his release unless the state wished to retry him. The court of appeals reversed, and the Supreme Court granted certiorari.]

MR. JUSTICE CLARK delivered the opinion of the Court.

. . .

The undeviating rule of this Court was expressed by Mr. Justice Holmes over half a century ago in *Patterson* v. *Colorado* . . . :

The theory of our system is that the conclusions to be reached in a case will be induced only by evidence and argument in open court, and not by any outside influence, whether of private talk or public print.

Moreover, "the burden of showing essential unfairness . . . as a demonstrable reality," . . . need not be undertaken when television has exposed the community "repeatedly and in depth to the spectacle of [the accused] personally confessing in detail to the crimes with which he was later to be charged." . . .

. . .

The court's fundamental error is compounded by the holding that it lacked power to control the publicity about the trial. From the very inception of the proceedings the judge announced that neither he nor anyone else could restrict prejudicial news accounts. . . .

The carnival atmosphere at trial could easily have been avoided since the courtroom and courthouse premises are subject to the control of the court. As we stressed in *Estes,* the presence of the press at judicial proceedings must be limited when it is apparent that the accused might otherwise be prejudiced or disadvantaged. Bearing in mind the massive pretrial publicity, the judge should have adopted stricter rules governing the use of the courtroom by newsmen, as Sheppard's counsel requested. The number of reporters in the courtroom itself could have been limited at the first sign that their presence would disrupt the trial. They certainly should not have been placed inside the bar. Furthermore, the judge should have more closely regulated the conduct of newsmen in the courtroom. For instance, the judge belatedly asked them not to handle and photograph trial exhibits lying on the counsel table during recesses.

Secondly, the court should have insulated the witnesses. All of the newspapers and radio stations apparently interviewed prospective witnesses at will, and in many instances disclosed their testimony. . . .

Thirdly, the court should have made some effort to control the release of leads, information, and gossip to the press by police officers, witnesses, and the counsel for both sides. Much of the information thus disclosed was inaccurate, leading to groundless rumors and confusion. . . .

Defense counsel immediately brought to the court's attention the tremendous amount of publicity in the Cleveland press that "misrepresented entirely the testimony" in the case. Under such circumstances, the judge should have at least warned the newspapers to check the accuracy of their accounts. And it is obvious that the judge should have further sought to alleviate this problem by imposing control over the statements made to the news media by counsel, witnesses, and especially the Coroner and police officers. The prosecution repeatedly made evidence available to the news media which was never offered in the trial. Much of the "evidence" disseminated in this fashion was clearly inadmissible. The exclusion of such evidence in court is rendered meaningless when a news media makes it available to the public. For example, the publicity about Sheppard's refusal to take a lie detector test came direct from police officers and the Coroner. The story that Sheppard had been called a "Jekyll-Hyde" personality by his wife was attributed to a prosecution witness. No such testimony was given. The further report that there was "a 'bombshell witness' on tap who would testify as to Sheppard's fiery temper could only have emanated from the prosecution. Moreover, the newspapers described in detail clues that had been found by the police, but not put into the record.

The fact that many of the prejudicial news items can be traced to the prosecution, as well as the defense, aggravates the judge's failure to take any action. . . .

More specifically, the trial court might well have proscribed extra-judicial statements by any lawyer, party, witness, or court official which divulged prejudicial matters, such as the refusal of Sheppard to submit to interrogation or take any lie detector test; any statement made by Sheppard to officials; the identity of prospective witnesses or their probable testimony; any belief in guilt or innocence; or like statements concerning the merits of the case. [T]he court [has] interpreted Canon 20 of the American Bar Association's Canons of Professional Ethics to prohibit such statements. Being advised of the great public interest in the case, the mass coverage of the press, and the potential prejudicial impact of publicity, the court could also have requested the appropriate city and county officials to promulgate a regulation with respect to dissemination of information about the case by their employees. In addition, reporters who wrote or broadcasted prejudicial stories, could have been warned as to the impropriety of publishing material not introduced in the proceedings. The judge was put on notice of such events by defense counsel's complaint about the WHK broadcast on the second day of trial. . . . In this manner, Sheppard's right to a trial free from outside interference would have been given added protection without corresponding curtailment of the news media. Had the judge, the other officers of the court, and the police placed the interest of justice first, the news media would have soon learned to be content with the task of reporting the case as it unfolded in the courtroom—not pieced together from extra-judicial statements.

From the cases coming here we note that unfair and prejudicial news comment on pending trials has become increasingly prevalent. Due process requires that the accused receive a trial by an impartial jury free from outside influences. Given the pervasiveness of modern communications and the difficulty of effacing prejudicial publicity from the minds of the jurors, the trial courts must take strong measures to ensure that the balance is never weighed against the accused. And appellate tribunals have the duty to make an independent evaluation of the circumstances. Of course, there is nothing that proscribes the press from reporting events that transpire in the courtroom. But where there is a reasonable likelihood that prejudicial news prior to trial will prevent a fair trial, the judge should continue the case until the threat abates, or transfer it to another county not so permeated with publicity. In addition, sequestration of the jury was something the judge should have raised sua sponte with counsel. If publicity during the proceedings threatens the fairness of the trial, a new trial should be ordered. But we must remember that reversals are but palliatives; the cure lies in those remedial measures that

will prevent the prejudice at its inception. The courts must take such steps by rule and regulation that will protect their processes from prejudicial outside interferences. Neither prosecutors, counsel for defense, the accused, witnesses, court staff nor enforcement officers coming under the jurisdiction of the court should be permitted to frustrate its function. Collaboration between counsel and the press as to information affecting the fairness of a criminal trial is not only subject to regulation, but is highly censurable and worthy of disciplinary measures.

Since the state trial judge did not fulfill his duty to protect Sheppard from the inherently prejudicial publicity which saturated the community and to control disruptive influences in the courtroom, we must reverse the denial of the habeas petition. The case is remanded to the District Court with instructions to issue the writ and order that Sheppard be released from custody unless the State puts him to its charges again within a reasonable time.

MR. JUSTICE BLACK DISSENTS (OMITTED).

[Had he not been killed, could Lee Harvey Oswald have received a constitutionally fair trial? The press coverage of the assassination of President Kennedy was so extensive, and Oswald's role as the alleged assassin so prominently displayed in the media, that obtaining an unbiased jury *anywhere* in the United States would have been difficult. Furthermore, there is language in the *Estes* and *Sheppard* opinions, and in the earlier case of *Rideau* v. *Louisiana* (1963), which suggests that in the face of such inflammatory mass publicity, a fair trial is inherently impossible. In none of those three cases did the publicity level reach that surrounding the presidential assassination. Set against that presumption are the Supreme Court's own words in *Irvin* v. *Doud,* quoted earlier, that a fair trial does *not* require jurors who know absolutely nothing about the case or the defendant. The existence of actual prejudice must be determined by examination at the *voir dire.*

In 1975, the Supreme Court reaffirmed that actual prejudice, not mere exposure to information about a defendant, was required to invalidate a state criminal conviction. Moreover, it was the burden of the defendant to demonstrate that the trial setting was inherently prejudicial or that the jury was in fact prejudiced. The case, *Murphy* v. *Florida,* involved the robbery trial of "Murph the Surf" in Miami. Murphy was somewhat famous for his bizarre exploits and flamboyant life-style and for his role in the 1964 theft of the Star of India sapphire from a New York museum. In the two years preceding this trial, he had also been convicted of murder and of transporting stolen securities in interstate commerce. All of these had been "newsworthy" events. Some members of the jury panel were excused for prejudice. Some of the persons chosen to serve on the jury were aware of Murphy's exploits, but all gave assurances of their impartiality.

Murphy's attorney argued that, in this climate, Murphy could not receive a fair trial. He cited the *Estes* and *Sheppard* opinions but relied mainly on a heretofore obscure case, *Marshall* v. *United States* (1959), in which the Supreme Court had held that jurors exposed to information with a high potential for prejudice should be presumed prejudiced. But the *Marshall* case had been decided by the Supreme Court in the exercise of its supervisory power over the federal rules of criminal procedure. The holding of that case, the Court now said in affirming Murphy's conviction, should not be constitutionalized and applied to the state courts.]

(2) Nebraska Press Association v. Stuart (1976)

+Burger, Brennan, Stewart, White, Marshall, Blackmun, Powell, Rehnquist, Stevens

[Charles Simants was accused of murder and sexual assault in the deaths of six members of a neighboring family in their home in a small Nebraska town. Both prosecution and defense attorneys filed motions with the county court alleging that the reasonable likelihood of prejudice would make impaneling of an impartial jury difficult. The court agreed, and after binding Simants over for trial, issued a "protective order" that barred any of the parties, and any person in the courtroom, from releasing information about the preliminary hearing. The news media were specifically prohibited from disseminating anything but factual information about the defendant, the circumstances of his arrest, the nature of the charge, quotations from public records or communications, and the schedule of events. The judge incorporated by reference the Nebraska Press/Bar Guidelines into his order.

The Nebraska Press Association applied to the district court to vacate this gag rule. Judge Stuart terminated the order of the county judge and substituted his own, slightly less restrictive, order that forbade publication or reference to a confession made by the defendant or reference to other statements he had made and forbade publishing the contents of a note he had written, some medical testimony, the identity of the victims who had been sexually assaulted, and the details of the sexual assault. All of these restraints were to apply only until a jury was impaneled (and, presumably, sequestered).

Pending an appeal to the Nebraska Supreme Court, the Press Association sought a stay from Justice Blackmun. Blackmun eliminated the wholesale incorporation of the Press/Bar Guidelines, noting that they were intended to operate as voluntary restraints and were couched in vague language. He also held that there was no persuasive reason for barring publication of the details of the crimes, the identities of the victims, or the testimony of the pathologist at a public hearing. Such testimony, Blackmun said, does not yet implicate a particular defendant, although he conceded that the possibility of prejudice existed. The other restraints were permitted. Prior restraints of this kind, Blackmun said, "are not necessarily and in all cases invalid. . . . The governing principle is that the press, in general, is to be free and unrestrained and that the facts are presumed to be in the public domain. The accused, and the prosecution if it joins him, bears the burden of showing that publicizing the particular facts will irreparably impair the ability of those exposed to them to reach an independent and impartial judgment as to guilt."

Subsequently, the Nebraska Supreme Court considered the case, and it too upheld but limited Judge Stuart's order. Restraints could only be imposed, it said, on reporting the existence or contents of a confession or any statements by the defendant and on reporting other facts "strongly implicative of the accused." The Supreme Court granted certiorari.]

MR. CHIEF JUSTICE BURGER delivered the opinion of the Court.

. . .

The problems presented by this case are almost as old as the Republic. Neither in the Constitution nor in the contemporaneous writings do we find that the conflict between these two important rights was anticipated, yet it is inconceivable that the authors of the Constitution were unaware of the potential conflicts between the right to an unbiased jury and the guarantee of freedom of the press. The unusually able lawyers who helped write the Constitution and later drafted the Bill of Rights were familiar with the historic episode in which John Adams defended British soldiers charged with homicides for firing into a crowd of Boston demonstrators; they were intimately familiar with the clash of the adversary system and the part that passions of the populace sometimes play in influencing potential jurors. They did not address themselves directly to the situation presented by this case; their chief concern was the need for freedom of expression in the political arena and the dialogue in ideas. But they recognized that there were risks to private rights from an unfettered press.

. . .

The Sixth Amendment in terms guarantees "trial by an impartial jury . . ." in federal criminal prosecutions. Because "trial by jury in criminal cases is fundamental to the American scheme of justice," the Due Process Clause of the Fourteenth Amendment guarantees the same right in state criminal prosecutions. *Duncan* v. *Louisiana,* . . . (1968)

. . . .

Taken together, these cases [the cases leading up to *Sheppard* v. *Maxwell* (1966)] demonstrate that pretrial publicity—even pervasive, adverse publicity—does not inevitably lead to an unfair trial. The capacity of the jury eventually impaneled to decide the case fairly is influenced by the tone and extent of the publicity, which is in part, and often in large part, shaped by what attorneys, police, and other officials do to precipitate news coverage. The trial judge has a major responsibility. What the judge says about a case, in or out of the courtroom, is likely to appear in newspapers and broadcasts. More important, the measures a judge takes or fails to take to mitigate the effects of pretrial publicity—the measures described in *Sheppard*—may well determine whether the defendant receives a trial consistent with the requirements of due process. That this responsibility has not always been properly discharged is apparent from the decisions just reviewed. . . .

The state trial judge in the case before us acted responsibly, out of a legitimate concern, in an effort to protect the defendant's right to a fair trial. What we must decide is not simply whether the Nebraska courts erred in seeing the possibility of real danger to the defendant's rights, but whether in the circumstances of this case the means employed were foreclosed by another provision of the Constitution.

The First Amendment provides

that "Congress shall make no law . . . abridging the freedom . . . of the press," and it is "no longer open to doubt that the liberty of the press, and of speech, is within the liberty safeguarded by the due process clause of the Fourteenth Amendment from invasion by state action." *Near* v. *Minnesota* . . . (1931). . . . The Court has interpreted these guarantees to afford special protection against orders that prohibit the publication or broadcast of particular information or commentary—orders that impose a "previous" or "prior" restraint on speech. None of our decided cases on prior restraint involved restrictive orders entered to protect a defendant's right to a fair and impartial jury, but the opinions on prior restraint have a common thread relevant to this case.

In *Near* v. *Minnesota* . . . (1931), the Court held invalid a Minnesota statute providing for the abatement as a public nuisance of any "malicious, scandalous and defamatory newspaper, magazine or other periodical." . . .

Chief Justice Hughes, writing for the Court, noted that freedom of the press is not an absolute right, and the State may punish its abuses. He observed that the statute was "not aimed at the redress of individual or private wrongs." . . . He then focused on the statute:

[T]he operation and effect of the statute in substance is that public authorities may bring the owner or publisher of a newspaper or periodical before a judge upon a charge of conducting a business of publishing scandalous and defamatory matter . . . and unless the owner or publisher is able . . . to satisfy the judge that the [matter is] true and . . . published with good motives . . . his newspaper or periodical is suppressed. . . . This is of the essence of censorship. . . .

A prior restraint, by contract and by definition, has an immediate and irreversible sanction. If it can be said that a threat of criminal or civil sanctions after publication "chills" speech, prior restraint "freezes" it at least for the time.

The damage can be particularly great when the prior restraint falls upon the communication of news and commentary on current events. Truthful reports of public judicial proceedings have been afforded special protection against subsequent punishment. See *Cox Broadcasting Corp.* v. *Cohn* . . . (1975); . . . For the same reasons the protection against prior restraint should have particular force as applied to reporting of criminal proceedings, whether the crime in question is a single isolated act or a pattern of criminal conduct. . . .

The extraordinary protections afforded by the First Amendment carry with them something in the nature of a fiduciary duty to exercise the protected rights responsibly—a duty widely acknowledged but not always observed by editors and publishers. It is not asking too much to suggest that those who exercise First Amendment rights in newspapers or broadcasting enterprises direct some effort to protect the rights of an accused to a fair trial by unbiased jurors.

Of course, the order at issue—like the order requested in *New York Times*—does not prohibit but only postpones publication. Some news can be delayed and most commentary can even more readily be delayed without serious injury, and there often is a self-imposed delay when responsible editors call for verification of information. But such delays are normally slight and they are self-imposed. Delays imposed by governmental authority are a different matter. . . .

The authors of the Bill of Rights did not undertake to assign priorities

as between First Amendment and Sixth Amendment rights, ranking one as superior to the other. In this case, the petitioners would have us declare the right of an accused subordinate to their right to publish in all circumstances. But if the authors of these guarantees, fully aware of the potential conflicts between them, were unwilling or unable to resolve the issue by assigning to one priority over the other, it is not for us to rewrite the Constitution by undertaking what they declined. It is unnecessary, after nearly two centuries, to establish a priority applicable in all circumstances. Yet it is nonetheless clear that the barriers to prior restraint remain high unless we are to abandon what the Court has said for nearly a quarter of our national existence and implied throughout all of it. The history of even wartime suspension of categorical guarantees, such as habeas corpus or the right to trial by civilian courts, see *Ex parte Milligan*, . . . (1866), cautions against suspending explicit guarantees.
. . .

We turn now to the record in this case to determine whether, as Learned Hand put it, "the gravity of the 'evil,' discounted by its improbability, justifies such invasion of free speech as is necessary to avoid the danger." *Dennis* v. *United States*, . . . (1951).

Our review of the pretrial record persuades us that the trial judge was justified in concluding that there would be intense and pervasive pretrial publicity concerning this case. He could also reasonably conclude, based on common human experience, that publicity might impair the defendant's right to a fair trial. He did not purport to say more, for he found only "a clear and present danger that pretrial publicity *could* impinge upon the defendant's right to a fair trial."

[Emphasis added.] His conclusion as to the impact of such publicity on prospective jurors was of necessity speculative, dealing as he was with factors unknown and unknowable.

We find little in the record that goes to another aspect of our task, determining whether measures short of an order restraining all publication would have insured the defendant a fair trial. Although the entry of the order might be read as a judicial determination that other measures would not suffice, the trial courts made no express findings to that effect; the Nebraska Supreme Court referred to the issue only by implication. . . .

We have therefore examined this record to determine the probable efficacy of the measures of prior restraint on the press and speech. There is no finding that alternative measures would not have protected Simants' rights, and the Nebraska Supreme Court did no more than imply that such measures might not be adequate. Moreover, the record is lacking in evidence to support such a finding. . . .

Finally, we note that the events disclosed by the record took place in a community of 850 people. It is reasonable to assume that, without any news accounts being printed or broadcast, rumors would travel swiftly by word of mouth. One can only speculate on the accuracy of such reports, given the generative propensities of rumors; they could well be more damaging than reasonably accurate news accounts. But plainly a whole community cannot be restrained from discussing a subject intimately affecting life within it.

Given these practical problems, it is far from clear that prior restraint on publication would have protected Simants' rights. . . .

Our analysis ends as it began, with

a confrontation between prior restraint imposed to protect one vital constitutional guarantee and the explicit command of another that the freedom to speak and publish shall not be abridged. We reaffirm that the guarantees of freedom of expression are not an absolute prohibition under all circumstances, but the barriers to prior restraint remain high and the presumption against its use continues intact. We hold that, with respect to the order entered in this case prohibiting reporting or commentary on judicial proceedings held in public, the barriers have not been overcome; to the extent that this order restrained publication of such material it is clearly invalid. To the extent that it prohibited publication based on information gained from other sources, we conclude that the heavy burden imposed as a condition to securing a prior restraint was not met and the judgment of the Nebraska Supreme Court is therefore Reversed.

MR. JUSTICE BRENNAN, WITH WHOM MR. JUSTICE STEWART AND MR. JUSTICE MARSHALL CONCUR, CONCURRING IN THE JUDGMENT (OMITTED).
MR. JUSTICE WHITE, CONCURRING (OMITTED).
MR. JUSTICE POWELL, CONCURRING (OMITTED).
MR. JUSTICE STEVENS, CONCURRING IN THE JUDGMENT (OMITTED).

(3) Gannett Co. v. DePasquale (1979)

+Stewart, Burger, Powell, Rehnquist, Stevens
−Blackmun, Brennan, White, Marshall

[While the Supreme Court indicated, in the *Nebraska Press Association* case, that prior restraints upon press reporting in criminal cases would be upheld only in the most extraordinary circumstances, its decision did not necessarily foreclose other types of restraints. In this case, a reporter for the Gannett newspaper chain objected to exclusion of the press from a preliminary hearing in a murder trial in Rochester, New York. The hearing had been scheduled to consider various motions to suppress evidence against two defendants. The murder, efforts to apprehend and extradite the suspects, and the grand jury indictment had already received extensive media coverage. At the suppression hearing defense attorneys argued that continuing buildup of adverse publicity jeopardized the defendants' right to a fair trial and asked that the public and the press be excluded. The district attorney did not object, and Judge DePasquale ordered the hearing closed.

A reporter for the Gannett papers, although present in court at the time, did not object. The following day, however, he wrote a letter to the judge asserting his right to cover the hearing and requesting access to the transcript. The judge replied that the suppression hearing had already ended; decision on release of the transcript was reserved and a hearing on this question was scheduled. At that hearing he acknowledged that the press had a "constitutional right of access," but that it had to be balanced with the defendant's right to a fair trial. In this instance, he ruled, access by the press would "pose a reasonable probability of prejudice," and the transcript was not released.

The newspaper challenged this order in an intermediate appellate court, which ruled that the judge's order was an unlawful prior restraint in violation of the First and Fourteenth Amendments. Meanwhile, both defendants pleaded guilty to lesser included offenses and a copy of the transcript was then made available to the press. The New York Court of Appeals held that the case was now technically moot, but because of its importance considered the substantive issue. It ruled that under state law, trials are presumptively open to the press, but in this case found that the presumption was overcome by excessive and prejudicial publicity endangering the defendants' right to a fair trial.

The Supreme Court granted certiorari. All nine justices agreed that the case was not moot because it was a dispute "capable of repetition, yet evading review." The short duration of pretrial hearings made it unlikely that issues like this could be fully litigated before the end of a hearing. And there was a strong likelihood that the Gannett newspapers would again be subjected to similar closure orders in other criminal trials. On the merits, the Court divided 5-4.]

MR. JUSTICE STEWART delivered the opinion of the Court.

The question presented in this case is whether members of the public have an independent constitutional right to insist upon access to a pretrial judicial proceeding, even though the accused, the prosecutor and the trial judge all have agreed to the closure of that proceeding in order to assure a fair trial.

. . .

This Court has long recognized that adverse publicity can endanger the ability of a defendant to receive a fair trial. . . . To safeguard the due process rights of the accused, a trial judge has an affirmative constitutional duty to minimize the effects of prejudicial pretrial publicity. *Shepard* v. *Maxwell*. . . . And because of the Constitution's pervasive concern for these due process rights, a trial judge may surely take protective measures even when they are not strictly and inescapably necessary.

Publicity concerning pretrial suppression hearings such as the one involved in the present case poses special risks of unfairness. The whole purpose of such hearings is to screen out unreliable or illegally obtained evidence and insure that this evidence does not become known to the jury. . . . Publicity concerning the proceedings at a pretrial hearing, however, could influence public opinion against a defendant and inform potential jurors of inculpatory information wholly inadmissable at the actual trial.

The danger of publicity concerning pretrial suppression hearings is particularly acute, because it may be difficult to measure with any degree of certainty the effects of such publicity on the fairness of the trial. After the commencement of the trial itself, inadmissable prejudicial information about a defendant can be kept from a jury by a variety of means. When such information is publicized during a pretrial proceeding, however, it may never be altogether kept from potential jurors. Closure of pretrial proceedings is often one of the most effective methods that a trial judge can employ to attempt to insure that the fairness of a trial will not be jeopardized by the dissemination of such information throughout the community before the trial itself has even begun. . . .

The Sixth Amendment, applicable to the States through the Fourteenth, surrounds a criminal trial with guarantees such as the rights to notice, confrontation, and compulsory process that have as their overriding purpose the protection of the accused from prosecutorial and judicial abuses. Among the guarantees that the Amendment provides to a person charged with the commission of a criminal offense, and to him alone, is the "right to a speedy and public trial, by an impartial jury." The Constitution nowhere mentions any right of access to a criminal trial on the part of the public; its guarantee, like the others enumerated, is personal to the accused. See *Faretta* v. *California*, . . . ("[T]he specific guarantees of the Sixth Amendment are personal to the accused.") (Blackmun, J., dissenting).

Our cases have uniformly recognized the public trial guarantee as one created for the benefit of the defendant. In *In re Oliver*, . . . this Court held that the secrecy of a criminal contempt trial violated the accused's right to a public trial under the Fourteenth Amendment. The right to a public trial, the Court stated, "has always been recognized as a safeguard against any attempt to employ the courts as instruments of persecution. The knowledge that every criminal trial is subject to contemporaneous review in the forum of public opinion is an effective restraint on possible abuse of judicial power." . . .

Similarly, in *Estes* v. *Texas* . . . the Court held that a defendant was deprived of his right to due process of law under the Fourteenth Amendment by the televising and broadcasting of his trial. In rejecting the claim that the media representatives had a constitutional right to televise the trial, the Court stated that "[T]he purpose of the requirement of a public trial was to guarantee that the accused be fairly dealt with and not unjustly condemned." . . . ("Thus the right of public trial is not one belonging to the public, but one belonging to the accused, and inhering in the institutional process by which justice is administered.") (concurring opinion of Harlan, J.); . . .

Thus both the *Oliver* and *Estes* cases recognized that the constitutional guarantee of a public trial is for the benefit of the defendant. There is not the slightest suggestion in either case that there is any correlative right in members of the public to insist upon a public trial.

While the Sixth Amendment guarantees to a defendant in a criminal case the right to a public trial, it does not guarantee the right to compel a private trial. "The ability to waive a constitutional right does not ordinarily carry with it the right to insist upon the opposite of that right." *Singer* v. *United States*, . . . But the issue here is not whether the defen-

dant can compel a private trial. Rather the issue is whether members of the public have an enforceable right to a public trial that can be asserted independently of the parties in the litigation.

There can be no blinking the fact that there is a strong societal interest in public trials. Openness in court proceedings may improve the quality of testimony, induce unknown witnesses to come forward with relevant testimony, cause all trial participants to perform their duties more conscientiously, and generally give the public an opportunity to observe the judicial system. . . . But there is a strong societal interest in other constitutional guarantees extended to the accused as well. The public, for example, has a definite and concrete interest in seeing that justice is swiftly and fairly administered. . . .

Recognition of an independent public interest in the enforcement of Sixth Amendment guarantees is a far cry, however, from the creation of a constitutional right on the part of the public. In an adversary system of criminal justice, the public interest in the administration of justice is protected by the participants in the litigation. Thus, because of the great public interest in jury trials as the preferred mode of fact-finding in criminal cases, a defendant cannot waive a jury trial without the consent of the prosecutor and judge. . . . But if the defendant waives his right to a jury trial, and the prosecutor and the judge consent, it could hardly be seriously argued that a member of the public could demand a jury trial because of the societal interest in that mode of factfinding. . . . Similarly, while a defendant cannot convert his right to a speedy trial into a right to compel an indefinite postponement, a member of the general public surely has no right to prevent a continuance in order to vindicate the public interest in the efficient administration of justice. In short, our adversary system of criminal justice is premised upon the proposition that the public interest is fully protected by the participants in the litigation.

In arguing that members of the general public have a constitutional right to attend a criminal trial, despite the obvious lack of support for such a right in the structure or text of the Sixth Amendment, the petitioner and amici rely on the history of the public trial guarantee. This history, however, ultimately demonstrates no more than the existence of a common-law rule of open civil and criminal proceedings.

Not many common-law rules have been elevated to the status of constitutional rights. The provisions of our Constitution do reflect an incorporation of certain few common-law rules and a rejection of others. The common-law right to a jury trial, for example, is explicitly embodied in the Sixth and Seventh Amendments. The common-law rule that looked upon jurors as interested parties who could give evidence against a defendant was explicitly rejected by the Sixth Amendment provision that a defendant is entitled to be tried by an "impartial jury." But the vast majority of common-law rules were neither made part of the Constitution nor explicitly rejected by it.

Our judicial duty in this case is to determine whether the common-law rule of open proceedings was incorporated, rejected, or left undisturbed by the Sixth Amendment. In pursuing this inquiry, it is important to distinguish between what the Constitution permits and what it requires. It has never been suggested that by phrasing the public trial guarantee as a right of the accused, the Framers intended to reject the common-law rule of open proceedings. There is no question that the Sixth Amendment permits and even presumes open trials as a norm. But the issue here is whether the Constitution *requires* that a pretrial proceeding such as this one be opened to the public, even though the participants in the litigation agree that it should be closed to protect the defendants' right to a fair trial. The history upon which the petitioner and amici rely totally fails to demonstrate that the Framers of the Sixth Amendment intended to create a constitutional right in strangers to attend a pretrial proceeding, when all that they actually did was to confer upon the accused an explicit right to demand a public trial. In conspicuous contrast with some of the early state constitutions that provided for a public right to open civil and criminal trials, the Sixth Amendment confers the right to a public trial only upon a defendant and only in a criminal case.

But even if the Sixth and Fourteenth Amendments could properly be viewed as embodying the common-law right of the public to attend criminal trials, it would not necessarily follow that the petitioner would have a right of access under the circumstances of this case. For there exists no persuasive evidence that at common law members of the public had any right to attend pretrial proceedings; indeed, there is substantial evidence to the contrary. By the time of the adoption of the Constitution, public trials were clearly associated with the protection of the defendant. And pretrial proceedings, precisely because of the same concern for a fair trial, were never characterized by the same degree of openness as were actual trials.

. . .

For these reasons, we hold that members of the public have no constitutional right under the Sixth and Fourteenth Amendments to attend criminal trials.

The petitioner also argues that members of the press and the public have a right of access to the pretrial hearing by reason of the First and Fourteenth Amendments. In *Pell* v *Procunier,* . . . *Saxbe* v. *Washington Post Co,* . . . and *Houchins* v. *KQED,* Inc, . . . this Court upheld prison regulations that denied to members of the press access to prisons superior to that afforded to the public generally. Some members of the Court, however, took the position in those cases that the First and Fourteenth Amendment do guarantee to the public in general, or the press in particular, a right of access that precludes their complete exclusion in the absence of a significant governmental interest. . . .

The petitioner in this case urges us to narrow our rulings in *Pell, Saxbe,* and *Houchins* at least to the extent of recognizing a First and Fourteenth Amendment right to attend criminal trials. We need not decide in the abstract, however, whether there is any such constitutional right. . . .

Several factors lead to the conclusion that the actions of the trial judge here were consistent with any right of access the petitioner may have had under the First and Fourteenth Amendments. First, none of the spectators present in the courtroom, including the reporter employed by the petitioner, objected when the defendants made the closure motion. Despite this failure to make a contemporaneous objection, counsel for the petitioner was given an opportunity to be heard at a proceeding where he was allowed to voice the petitioner's objections to closure of the pretrial hearing. At this proceeding, which took place after the filing of briefs, the trial court balanced the "constitu-tional rights of the press and the public" against the "defendants' right to a fair trial." The trial judge concluded after making this appraisal that the press and the public could be excluded from the suppression hearing and could be denied immediate access to a transcript, because an open proceeding would pose a "reasonable probability of prejudice to these defendants." Thus the trial court found that the representatives of the press did have a right of access of constitutional dimension, but held, under the circumstances of this case, that this right was outweighed by the defendants right to fair trial. In short, the closure decision was based "on an assessment of the competing societal interests involved . . . rather than on any determination that First Amendment freedoms were not implicated." . . .

Furthermore, any denial of access in this case was not absolute but only temporary. Once the danger of prejudice had dissipated, a transcript of the suppression hearing was made available. The press and the public then had a full opportunity to scrutinize the suppression hearing. Unlike the case of an absolute ban on access, therefore, the press here had the opportunity to inform the public of the details of the pretrial hearing accurately and completely. Under these circumstances, any First and Fourteenth Amendment right of the petitioner to attend criminal trial was not violated.

We certainly do not disparage the general desirability of open judicial proceedings. But we are not asked here to declare whether open proceedings represent beneficial social policy, or whether there would be a constitutional barrier to a state law that imposed a stricter standard of closure than the one here employed by the New York courts. Rather, we are asked to hold that the Constitution itself gave the petitioner an affirmative right of access to this pretrial proceeding, even though all the participants in the litigation agreed that it should be closed to protect the fair trial rights of the defendants.

For all of the reasons discussed in this opinion, we hold that the Constitution provides no such right. Accordingly, the judgment of the New York Court of Appeals is affirmed.

It is so ordered.

MR. CHIEF JUSTICE BURGER, CONCURRING.

I join the opinion of the Court, but I write separately to emphasize my view of the nature of the proceeding involved in today's decision. By definition a hearing on a motion before trial to suppress evidence is not a trial; it is a pretrial hearing.

The Sixth Amendment tells us that "in all criminal prosecutions, the accused shall enjoy the right to . . . public trial." It is the practice in Western societies, and has been part of the common-law tradition for centuries, that trials generally be public. This is an important prophylaxis of the system of justice that constitutes the adhesive element of our society. The public has an interest in observing the performance not only of the litigants and the witnesses, but also of the advocates and the presiding judge. Similarly, if the accused testifies, there is a proper public interest in that testimony. But interest alone does not create a constitutional right.

At common law there was a very different presumption for proceedings which preceded the trial. There was awareness of the untoward effects that could result from the publication of information before an indictment was returned or before a person was bound over for trial. . . .

When the Sixth Amendment was written, and for more than a century after that, no one could have conceived that the Exclusionary Rule and pretrial motions to suppress evidence would be part of our criminal jurisprudence. The authors of the Constitution, imaginative, farsighted, and perceptive as they were, could not conceivably have anticipated the paradox inherent in a judge-made rule of evidence that excludes undoubted truth from the truth-finding processes of the adversary system. Nevertheless, as of now, we are confronted not with a legal theory but with the reality of the unique strictures of the Exclusionary Rule and they must be taken into account in this setting. To make public the evidence developed in a motion to suppress evidence, cf. *Brewer* v. *Williams* . . . (1977), would, so long as the Exclusionary Rule is not modified, introduce a new dimension to the problem of conducting fair trials. . . .

MR. JUSTICE POWELL, CONCURRING (OMITTED).
MR. JUSTICE REHNQUIST, CONCURRING (OMITTED).

MR. JUSTICE BLACKMUN, WITH WHOM MR. JUSTICE BRENNAN, MR. JUSTICE WHITE, AND MR. JUSTICE MARSHALL join, concurring in part and dissenting in part.

. . .

Today's decision, as I view it, is an unfortunate one. I fear that the Court surrenders to the temptation to overstate and overcolor the actual nature of the pre-August 7, 1976 publicity; that it reaches for a strict and flat result; and that in the process it ignores the important antecedents and significant developmental features of the Sixth Amendment. The result is an inflexible per se rule, as Mr. Justice Rehnquist so appropriately observes in his separate concurrence. . . . That rule is to the effect that if the defense and the prosecution merely agree to have the public excluded from a suppression hearing, and the trial judge does not resist—as trial judges may be prone not to do, since nonresistance is easier than resistance—closure shall take place, and there is nothing in the Sixth Amendment that prevents that happily agreed-upon event. The result is that the important interests of the public and the press (as a part of that public) in open judicial proceedings are rejected and cast aside as of little value or significance.

Because I think this easy but wooden approach is without support either in legal history or in the intendment of the Sixth Amendment, I dissent.

. . .

This Court confronts in this case another aspect of the recurring conflict that arises whenever a defendant in a criminal case asserts that his right to a fair trial clashes with the right of the public in general, and of the press in particular, to an open proceeding. It has considered other aspects of the problem in deciding whether publicity was sufficiently prejudicial to have deprived the defendant of a fair trial. Cf. *Murphy* v. *Florida* . . . (1975), with *Sheppard* v. *Maxwell* . . . (1966). And recently it examined the extent to which the First and Fourteenth Amendments protect news organizations' rights to publish, free from prior restraint, information learned in open court during a pretrial suppression hearing. *Nebraska Press Assn.* v. *Stuart* . . . (1976). But the Court has not yet addressed the precise issue raised by this case: whether and to what extent the Constitution prohibits the States from such a hearing.

. . . The issue here, then, is not one of prior restraint on the press but is, rather, one of *access* to a judicial proceeding.

Despite Mr. Justice Powell's concern, this Court heretofore has not found and does not today find, any First Amendment right of access to judicial or other governmental proceedings. . . . One turns then, instead, to that provision of the Constitution that speaks most directly to the question of access to judicial proceedings, namely, the public trial provision of the Sixth Amendment.

The familiar language of the Sixth Amendment . . . reflects the tradition of our system of criminal justice that a trial is a "public event" and that "[w]hat transpires in the court room is public property." *Craig* v. *Harney* . . . (1947). And it reflects, as well, "the notion, deeply rooted in the common law, that "justice must satisfy the appearance of justice.'"

. . .

More importantly, the requirement . . . embodies our belief that secret judicial proceedings would be a menace to liberty. The public trial is rooted in the "principle that justice cannot survive behind walls of silence," *Sheppard* v. *Maxwell* and in the "traditional Anglo-American distrust for secret trials," *In re Oliver* (1948). This Nation's accepted practice of providing open trials in both federal and state courts "has always been recognized as a safeguard against any attempt to employ our courts as instruments of persecution. The knowledge that every criminal trial is subject to contemporaneous review in the forum of public opinion is an effective restraint on possible abuse of judicial power." . . .

The public trial guarantee, moreover, ensures that not only judges but all participants in the criminal justice system are subjected to public scrutiny as they conduct the public's business of prosecuting crime. This publicity "guards against the miscarriage of justice by subjecting the police, prosecutors, and judicial processes to extensive public scrutiny and criticism." . . .

The importance we as a Nation attach to the public trial is reflected both in its deep roots in the English common law and in its seemingly universal recognition in this country since the earliest times. When *In re Oliver* was decided in 1948, the Court was "unable to find a single instance of a criminal trial conducted in camera in any federal, state, or municipal court during the history of this country," . . . with the exception of cases in courts martial and the semi-private conduct of juvenile court proceedings. . . . Nor could it uncover any record "of even one such secret criminal trial in England since abolition of the Court of Star Chamber in 1641." . . .

By its literal terms the Sixth Amendment secures the right to a public trial only to "the accused." And in this case, the accused were the ones who sought to waive that right, and to have the public removed from the pretrial hearing in order to guard against publicity that possibly would be prejudicial to them. . . .

The Court, however, previously has recognized that the Sixth Amendment may implicate interests beyond those of the accused. In *Barker* v. *Wingo* . . . (1972), for example, the Court unanimously found this to be so with respect to the right to a speedy trial. "In addition to the general concern that all accused persons be treated according to decent and fair procedures, there is a societal interest in providing a speedy trial which exists separately from, and at times in opposition to, the interests of the accused." . . . This separate public interest led the Court to reject a rule that would have made the defendant's assertion of his speedy trial right the critical factor in deciding whether the right had been denied, for a rule depending entirely on the defendant's demand failed to take into account that "society has a particular interest in bringing swift prosecutions." . . .

The same is true of other provisions of the Sixth Amendment. In *Singer* v. *United States* . . . (1965), the Court rejected a contention that, since the constitutional right to a jury trial was the right of the accused, he had an absolute right to be tried by a judge alone if he considered a bench trial to be to his advantage. Rejecting a mechanistic waiver approach, the Court reviewed the history of trial by jury at English common law and the practice under the Constitution. The common law did not indicate that the accused had a right to compel a bench trial. Although there were isolated instances where such a right had been recognized in the American colonies, the Court could find no "general recognition of a defendant's right to be tried by the court instead of by a jury. Indeed, if there had been recognition of such a right, it would be difficult to understand why Art III and the Sixth Amendment were not drafted in terms which recognized an option." . . . Noting that practice under the Constitution similarly established no independent right to a bench trial, the Court held that neither the jury trial provision in Art III, § 2, nor the Sixth Amendment empowered an accused to compel the opposite of what he was guaranteed specifically by the Constitution.

. . .

Indeed, in only one case, apparently, *Faretta* v. *California* . . . (1975), has this Court ever inferred from the Sixth Amendment a right that fairly may be termed the "opposite" of an explicit guarantee. . . .

It is thus clear from *Singer*, *Barker*, and *Faretta* that the fact the Sixth Amendment casts the right to a public trial in terms of the right of the accused is not sufficient to permit the inference that the accused may compel a private proceeding simply by waiving that right. Any such right to compel a private proceeding must have some independent basis in the Sixth Amendment. . . .

(4) Illinois v. Allen (1970)

+Black, Burger, Harlan, Brennan, Stewart, White, Marshall
–Douglas

MR. JUSTICE BLACK delivered the opinion of the Court.

The Confrontation Clause of the Sixth Amendment to the United States Constitution provides that "In all criminal prosecutions, the accused shall enjoy the right . . . to be confronted with the witnesses against him. . . ." We have held that the Fourteenth Amendment makes the guarantees of this clause obligatory upon the States. . . . One of the most basic of the rights guaranteed by the Confrontation Clause is the accused's right to be present in the courtroom at every stage of his trial. . . . The question presented in this case is whether an accused can claim the benefit of this constitutional right to remain in the courtroom while at the same time he engages in speech and conduct which is so noisy, disorderly, and disruptive that it is exceedingly difficult or wholly impossible to carry on the trial.

The issue arose in the following way. The respondent, Allen, was convicted by an Illinois jury of armed robbery and was sentenced to serve 10 to 30 years in the Illinois State Penitentiary. . . . The Supreme Court of Illinois affirmed his conviction. . . . Later Allen filed a petition for a writ of habeas corpus in federal court alleging that he had been wrongfully deprived by the Illinois trial judge of his constitutional right to remain present throughout his trial. Finding no constitutional violation, the District Court declined to issue the writ. The Court of Appeals reversed . . . ,

Judge Hastings dissenting. The facts surrounding Allen's expulsion from the courtroom are set out in the Court of Appeals' opinion sustaining Allen's contention:

After his indictment and during the pretrial stage, the petitioner [Allen] refused court-appointed counsel and indicated to the trial court on several occasions that he wished to conduct his own defense. After considerable argument by the petitioner, the trial judge told him, "I'll let you be your own lawyer, but I'll ask Mr. Kelly [court-appointed counsel] [to] sit in and protect the record for you, insofar as possible."

The trial began on September 9, 1956. After the State's Attorney had accepted the first four jurors following their voir dire examination, the petitioner began examining the first juror and continued at great length. Finally, the trial judge interrupted the petitioner, requesting him to confine his questions solely to matters relating to the prospective juror's qualifications. At that point, the petitioner started to argue with the judge in a most abusive and disrespectful manner. At last, and seemingly in desperation, the judge asked appointed counsel to proceed with the examination of the jurors. The petitioner continued to talk, proclaiming that the appointed attorney was not going to act as his lawyer. He terminated his remarks by saying, "When I go out for lunchtime, you're [the judge] going to be a corpse here." At that point he tore the file which his attorney had and threw the papers on the floor. The trial judge thereupon stated to the petitioner, "One more outbreak of that sort and I'll remove you from the courtroom." This warning had no effect on the petitioner. He continued to talk back to the judge, saying, "There's not going to be no trial, either. I'm going to sit here and you're going to talk and you can bring your shackles out and straight jacket and put them on me and tape my mouth, but it will do no good because there's not going to be no trial." After more abusive remarks by the petitioner, the trial judge ordered the trial to proceed in the petitioner's absence. The petitioner was removed from the courtroom. The voir dire examination then continued and the jury was selected in the absence of the petitioner.

After a noon recess and before the jury was brought into the courtroom, the petitioner, appearing before the judge, complained about the fairness of the trial and his appointed attorney. He also said he wanted to be present in the court during his trial. In reply, the judge said that the petitioner would be permitted to remain in the courtroom if he "behaved [himself] and [did] not interfere with the introduction of the case." The jury was brought in and seated. Counsel for the petitioner then moved to exclude the witnesses from the courtroom. The defendant protested this effort on the part of his attorney, saying: "There is going to be no proceeding. I'm going to start talking and I'm going to keep on talking all through the trial. There's not going to be no trial like this. I want my sister and my friends here in court to testify for me." The trial judge thereupon ordered the petitioner removed from the courtroom. . . .

After this second removal, Allen remained out of the courtroom during the presentation of the State's case-in-chief, except that he was brought in on several occasions for purposes of identification. During one of these latter appearances, Allen responded to one of the judge's questions with vile and abusive language. After the prosecution's case had been presented, the trial judge reiterated his promise to Allen that he could return to the courtroom whenever he agreed to conduct himself properly. Allen gave some assurances of proper conduct and was permitted to be present through the remainder of the trial, principally his defense, which was conducted by his appointed counsel.

The Court of Appeals went on to hold that the Supreme Court of Illinois was wrong in ruling that Allen had by his conduct relinquished his constitutional right to be present. . . .

The Court of Appeals felt that the defendant's Sixth Amendment right to be present at his own trial was so "absolute" that, no matter how unruly or disruptive the defendant's conduct might be, he could never be held to have lost that right so long as he continued to insist upon it, as Allen clearly did. Therefore the Court of Appeals concluded that a trial judge could never expel a defendant from his own trial and that the judge's ultimate remedy when faced with an obstreperous defendant like Allen who determines to make his trial impossible is to bind and gag him. We cannot agree that the Sixth Amendment, the cases upon which the Court of Appeals relied, or any other cases of this Court so handicap a trial judge in conducting a criminal trial. . . .

[W]e explicitly hold today that a defendant can lose his right to be present at trial if, after he has been warned by the judge that he will be removed if he continues his disruptive behavior, he nevertheless insists on conducting himself in a manner so disorderly, disruptive, and disrespectful of the court that his trial cannot be carried on with him in the courtroom. Once lost, the right to be present can, of course, be reclaimed as soon as the defendant is willing to conduct himself consistently with the decorum and respect inherent in the concept of courts and judicial proceedings.

It is essential to the proper administration of criminal justice that dignity, order, and decorum be the hallmarks of all court proceedings in our country. The flagrant disregard in the courtroom of the elementary standards of proper conduct should not and cannot be tolerated. We believe trial judges confronted with disruptive, contumacious, stubbornly defiant defendants must be given sufficient discretion to meet the circumstances of each case. No one formula for maintaining the appropriate courtroom atmosphere will be best in all situations. We think there are at least three constitutionally permissible ways for a trial judge to handle an obstreperous defendant like Allen: (1) bind and gag him, thereby keeping him present; (2) cite him for contempt; (3) take him out of the courtroom until he promises to conduct himself properly. . . .

It is not pleasant to hold that the respondent Allen was properly banished from the court for a part of his own trial. But our courts, palladiums of liberty as they are, cannot be treated disrespectfully with impunity. Nor can the accused be permitted by his disruptive conduct indefinitely to avoid being tried on the charges brought against him. It would degrade our country and our judicial system to permit our courts to be bullied, insulted, and humiliated and their orderly progress thwarted and obstructed by defendants brought before them charged with crimes. As guardians of the public welfare, our state and federal judicial systems strive to administer equal justice to the rich and the poor, the good and the bad, the native and foreign born of every race, nationality and religion. Being manned by humans, the courts are not perfect and are bound to make some errors. But, if our courts are to remain what the Founders intended, the citadels of justice, their proceedings cannot and must not be infected with the sort of scurrilous, abusive language and conduct paraded before the Illinois trial judge in this case. The record shows that the Illinois judge at all times conducted himself with that dignity, decorum, and patience that befits a judge. Even in holding that the trial judge had erred, the Court of Appeals praised his "commendable patience under severe provocation."

We do not hold that removing this defendant from his own trial was the only way the Illinois judge could have constitutionally solved the problem

he had. We do hold, however, that there is nothing whatever in this record to show that the judge did not act completely within his discretion. Deplorable as it is to remove a man from his own trial, even for a short time, we hold that the judge did not commit legal error in doing what he did.

The judgment of the Court of Appeals is
Reversed.

MR. JUSTICE BRENNAN, CONCURRING (OMITTED).

MR. JUSTICE DOUGLAS, DISSENTING.
I agree with the Court that a criminal trial, in the constitutional sense, cannot take place where the courtroom is a bedlam and either the accused or the judge is hurling epithets at the other. A courtroom is a hallowed place where trials must proceed with dignity and not become occasions for entertainment by the participants, by extraneous persons, by modern mass media or otherwise.

My difficulty is not with the basic hypothesis of this decision, but with the use of this case to establish the appropriate guidelines for judicial control.

This is a state case, the trial having taken place nearly 13 years ago. That lapse of time is not necessarily a barrier to a challenge of the constitutionality of a criminal conviction. But in this case it should be.

There is more than an intimation in the present record that the defendant was a mental case. The passage of time since 1957, the date of the trial, makes it, however, impossible to determine what the mental condition of the defendant was at that time. The fact that a defendant has been found to understand "the nature and object of the proceedings against him" and thus competent to stand trial does not answer the difficult questions as to what a trial judge should do with an otherwise mentally ill defendant who creates a courtroom disturbance. What a judge should do with a defendant whose courtroom antics may not be volitional is a perplexing problem which we should not reach except on a clear record. This defendant had no lawyer and refused one, though the trial judge properly insisted that a member of the bar be present to represent him. He tried to be his own lawyer and what transpired was pathetic, as well as disgusting and disgraceful.

We should not reach the merits but should reverse the case for staleness of the record and affirm the denial of relief by the District Court. After all, behind the issuance of a writ of habeas corpus is the exercise of an informed discretion. The question, how to proceed in a criminal case against a defendant who is a mental case, should be resolved only on a full and adequate record.

Our real problems of this type lie not with this case but with other kinds of trials. *First* are the political trials. They frequently recur in our history and insofar as they take place in federal courts we have broad supervisory powers over them. That is one setting where the question arises whether the accused has rights of confrontation that the law invades at its peril.

In Anglo-American law, great injustices have at times been done to unpopular minorities by judges, as well as by prosecutors. . . .

Would we tolerate removal of a defendant from the courtroom during a trial because he was insisting on his constitutional rights, albeit vociferously, no matter how obnoxious his philosophy might have been to the bench that tried him? Would we uphold contempt in that situation?

Problems of political indictments and of political judges raise profound questions going to the heart of the social compact. For that compact is two-sided: majorities undertake to press their grievances within limits of the Constitution and in accord with its procedures; minorities agree to abide by constitutional procedures in resisting those claims.

Does the answer to that problem involve defining the procedure for conducting political trials or does it involve the designing of constitutional methods for putting an end to them? This record is singularly inadequate to answer those questions. It will be time enough to resolve those weighty problems when a political trial reaches this Court for review.

Second are trials used by minorities to destroy the existing constitutional system and bring on repressive measures. Radicals on the left historically have used those tactics to incite the extreme right with the calculated design of fostering a regime of repression from which the radicals on the left hope to emerge as the ultimate victor. The left in that role is the provocateur. The Constitution was not designed as an instrument for that form of rough-and-tumble contest. The social compact has room for tolerance, patience, and restraint, but not for sabotage and violence. Trials involving that spectacle strike at the very heart of constitutional government.

I would not try to provide in this case the guidelines for those two strikingly different types of cases. The case presented here is the classical criminal case without any political or subversive overtones. It involves a defendant who was a sick person and who may or may not have been insane in the classical sense but who apparently had a diseased mind. And, as I have said, the record is so stale that it is now much too late to find out what the true facts really were.

(5) A Note on Unruly Defendants and Contumacious Lawyers

It is beyond the scope of this book to explore all the parameters of proper courtroom behavior. Decorum has always been thought necessary to bring about a truly fair and impartial hearing. Yet decorum implies "playing by the rules," and there are situations in which it is not always to the advantage of the defendant to accept some of these rules—or all of them. In some instances, as in *Illinois* v. *Allen* (1970), the defendant's personal hostility to the system, and perhaps his state of mind as well, may contribute to an unwillingness to cooperate. In other cases, unconventional courtroom tactics may symbolize a more coherent political opposition, an effort to "demystify" the law and reduce its legitimacy.[1] Because Ameri-

can law does not recognize a category of "political crimes,"[2] regime opponents may consciously attempt to use the criminal trial as a forum to express their grievances against the system and disdain for its procedures. In such highly explosive and controversial situations, the propriety of conduct by defendants, witnesses, and attorneys is most difficult to define—and to control.

"Contempt of court"[3] is a primary means open to a judge to control courtroom behavior and to compel respect for judicial authority. There are two classes of contempt: civil and criminal. Civil contempt is designed to produce compliance with a judicial order, for example, to testify or produce certain documents. Punishment for civil contempt normally is incarceration. It may be purged by compliance; thus, it is often said that a person imprisoned for civil contempt "has the keys to the jail in his own pocket." Usually, the term of imprisonment is limited by the term of the

---

[1]See, for example, Kenneth M. Dolbeare and Joel B. Grossman, "LeRoi Jones in Newark: A Political Trial?" in Becker (ed.), *Political Trials* (Indianapolis: Bobbs-Merrill, 1971).

[2]B.L. Ingraham and Kazuhiko Tokoro, "Political Crimes in the United States and Japan: A Comparative Study," 4 *Issues in Criminology* (1969), 145–170.

[3]Legislative contempt proceedings are a separate issue. Congress and the state legislatures have the power to punish for contempt. Congress, by statute, has delegated this power to the federal courts. Where a legislature wishes to punish for criminal contempt, and does not act summarily, the defendant must be accorded at least a minimum of due process rights, for example, notice and a hearing. These principles were enunciated in *Groppi* v. *Leslie* (1972). Father James Groppi, a militant Catholic priest, led a demonstration of welfare mothers into the chambers of the Wisconsin State Assembly; from noon to midnight the chamber was "occupied." Groppi was arrested for disorderly conduct. Two days after the demonstration, while Father Groppi was in jail, the assembly passed a resolution citing Groppi for contempt and directing that he be jailed for six months or for the duration of the legislative session, whichever was shorter. There was no opportunity for him to appear and defend his actions. The federal district court granted a writ of habeas corpus, and the Supreme Court affirmed unanimously. The Court noted that since the contempt occurred in the presence of the legislature, summary contempt action was appropriate. But by the time the assembly acted, order had been restored, Father Groppi was safely in jail, and no summary action was needed to permit the legislature to resume its business. As a general rule, the Court said, the legislative contempt power should be limited to the least restrictive alternative adequate to the end desired.

court or grand jury before which the contempt occurred.[4]

Criminal contempt serves a different purpose. Its aim is to vindicate judicial authority by punishment. The contemptuous act has taken place and cannot be "purged." The same course of action may lead, sequentially, to charges of both civil and criminal contempt. But most frequently, criminal contempt charges involve misbehavior in the courtroom.

Historically, judges have had summary power to punish for contempt; trial by jury and other due process protections were not required. As the Warren Court's due process revolution developed, the distinctions between contempt and trials for statutory criminal offenses inevitably became more difficult to justify. The major reason for not applying the Bill of Rights to contempt trials was that any elaborate procedure or delay might compromise the judicial authority that punishment for contempt sought to vindicate. The need to vindicate judicial authority remains an important and operative concept; it still accounts for such differences between contempt and other criminal proceedings as remain.

The Supreme Court has dealt with three major aspects of the law of contempt: first, the circumstances under which a trial judge may personally and summarily punish for contempt; second, the circumstances under which a hearing and a different judge are required; third, the circumstances under which a jury trial is required.

In *Illinois* v. *Allen*, the Supreme Court reaffirmed the right of the judge, as a last resort, to punish summarily for contempt during a trial on the occasion of each contempt. This, along with binding and gagging and exclusion from the courtroom, is the ultimate judicial weapon against disruptive activity. Where multiple instances of contempt occur, the cumulative total sentences may exceed the six-months limit imposed otherwise on nonjury contempt sentences. But summary punishment is to be regarded with disfavor, allowable only under extraordinary circumstances. And even in cases of summary punishment, the contemnor is to be allowed to speak in his own behalf.

If, as most often occurs, the judge warns the defendant or attorney but does not charge him with contempt formally until after the trial has ended, the judge must proceed in a different manner. First, he must decide whether to hear the contempt citation himself. The need for a jury trial also must be considered. The Supreme Court's policy now is that a judge may not try his own *postverdict* contempt citation if he has been the object of personally contemptuous attacks such that he would be presumed to have lost the disin-

---

[4]The potential for abuse of the contempt power by grand juries was recently underscored by the ACLU-funded Center for Studies on National Security. Dissident political organizations seem especially vulnerable. See Morton Halperin, "The FBI Charter Reforming the Basis for Investigation," *First Principles* (June 1978). Recent evidence revealed that Guy Goodwin, head of the Internal Security Division in the Department of Justice during the Nixon administration, supervised over 100 grand juries in thirty-six states from 1970 to 1973. These grand juries called some 2000 witnesses, enforced by subpoena and the threat of contempt, and returned about 400 indictments. Targets of these probes included the Black Panther party, Vietnam Veterans Against the War, the Catholic Left, the Puerto Rican Independence Movement (which is still a principal target today), the American Indian Movement, the Chicano movement, various women's movement organizations, and the National Lawyers Guild. Many witnesses were compelled to testify under grants of use immunity.

terested impartiality that due process requires. For example, a judge who, in the course of a trial, was called a "a dirty sonofabitch," "a dirty tyrannical dog," a "fool," and charged with running a "Spanish Inquisition" should not conduct his own postverdict contempt hearing. The defendant in this case was found to be in contempt on eleven days of the trial and sentenced to a cumulative total of eleven to twenty-two years in prison. The Supreme Court unanimously reversed (*Mayberry* v. *Pennsylvania*, 1971). The rule that emerged depends more on the defendant's conduct than on the judge's response. Even where a judge appears to maintain a veneer of objectivity, the conduct of the defendant may be so outrageous as to warrant the presumption of judicial bias. As stated in a later case (*Taylor* v. *Hayes*, 1974), "in making this ultimate judgment, the inquiry must be not only whether there was actual bias on [the judge's] part, but also whether there was 'such a likelihood of bias or an appearance of bias that the judge was unable to hold the balance between vindicating the interests of the court and the interests of the accused.' "

A person accused of contempt after a trial has ended is entitled to a notice of the charge and a reasonable opportunity to be heard before punishment is imposed. He or she is entitled to a full-scale jury trial if a sentence of more than six months on any single charge, or on all charges cumulatively, is to be imposed. Beginning with *Bloom* v. *Illinois* (1968), the Supreme Court has extended the right to trial by jury to those charged with contempt, distinguishing between serious and petty contempts in the same manner as between serious and petty crimes (cf. *Duncan* v. *Louisiana*, 1968), at least where there was no legislative specification of an appropriate penalty. The only exception to this limitation, as noted above, is where the trial judge punishes summarily during the trial (*Codispoti* v. *Pennsylvania*, 1974).

D. Justice for Juveniles: In Re Gault (1967)

+Warren, Black, Douglas, Clark, Brennan, White, Fortas
−Stewart
±Harlan

[The juvenile court movement in the United States began in the 1890s. By 1905, thirty one states had established some form of juvenile court; by 1928, all but two states had done so. The movement also spread to most of the major nations of the world.[1] Prior to the establishment of juvenile courts, under the common law, children over the age of fourteen were usually treated as adults by the criminal law. Those between the ages of seven and fourteen were presumed incapable of mature reasoning and were not subject to criminal punishment, although the state had the option of rebutting that presumption in individual cases. Children under the age of seven were presumed incapable of criminal intent.

Historians differ on the question of whether the juvenile court movement was a major reform arising out of humanitarian motives, to protect children from the savagery of the criminal law and its institutions, or whether it was merely the culmination of an evolutionary process of developments in penology.[2] Whatever the interpretation, it is clear that the mounting problems of poor urban children had much to do with the search for alternatives. And it is also clear that in creating a "socialized" institution to deal with these problems, the legal doctrine of *parens patriae* played a major role. Under this doctrine, the state became the "ultimate" par-

[1]Frederic L. Faust and Paul J. Brantingham, *Juvenile Justice Philosophy* (St. Paul, Minn.: West Publishing Co., 1974), p. 565.
[2]*Ibid.*, Part VI.

ent. It took over when parents could not, or would not, control their own children. At the same time, it protected the child from the stigma of being convicted of a crime. The juvenile courts were not to deal only with criminality—that is, with acts committed by children which, had they been committed by adults, would have been crimes. Their jurisdiction also covered both the dependent and what might be called the incorrigible child, that is the child who had committed no crime but was in "need of supervision" in order to prevent him from the sort of moral recession that might lead to a life of crime.

As Anthony Platt has noted, the juvenile court movement was very much a middle-class phenomenon:

It was not by accident that the behavior selected for penalizing by the child savers—drinking, begging, roaming the streets, frequenting dance halls and movies, fighting, sexuality, staying out late at night, and incorrigibility—was primarily attributable to the children of lower-class migrant and immigrant families.[3]

The juvenile justice movement also had strong roots in the emerging feminist movement, which accepted the then current notion that women were better than men at raising children. Juvenile justice was a powerful feminist issue, one that provided a legitimate path for women to enter politics.

Thus, the juvenile court emerged to "save children" who were delinquent, dependent, or neglected. Society would be best served by treating each such child individually, apart from the normal criminal process. In return for these "benefits," however, the child gave up all the rights that he or she might have had if treated as an adult. The hallmark of the juvenile court hearing was informality. The adversary system was rejected. There was no formal determination of guilt or innocence, no provision for counsel, and the customary rules of evidence were not followed. A child could be committed for

"care and treatment" until he reached adulthood.

Critics of the juvenile court charged from the very beginning that, whatever the labels, it functioned as a *de facto* criminal court without affording juveniles basic constitutional rights. Moreover, being labeled as a juvenile delinquent was not much better than being labeled a criminal. And, increasingly, reformatories could not be distinguished from penitentiaries. It was not until the 1960s that these charges began to get a responsive hearing in the state courts and legislatures. In *Kent* v. *United States* (1966) the Supreme Court took its first look at the juvenile justice system and recoiled in horror at what is saw.

In 1967, the constitutionalist argument reached its zenith in the case of Gerald Gault. Gault's father sought the release of his son who had been adjudged a juvenile delinquent by a juvenile court in Arizona and committed to the state industrial school. Gault claimed that his son had been committed without the due process of law required by the Fourteenth Amendment. The boy, aged fifteen and already on probation on a previous charge, had been taken into custody and charged with making an obscene phone call to a woman neighbor. He was picked up while his mother and father were both at work. They were not notified directly. When they located their son's whereabouts, they went to the detention home and were told that there would be a hearing the following day.

At the hearing the judge was presented with a petition, not shown to the parents, requesting that Gerald Gault be adjudged a delinquent minor. At the hearing the complainant was not present. No transcript or record of the proceedings was kept. Gerald was questioned by the judge about the telephone call and admitted dialing the number, but said that it was his companion who had actually made the obscene statements. The arresting officer testified that Gerald had admitted making the statements, and the judge corroborated this fact. The hearing ended and another was scheduled several days later. At the second hearing Gerald's mother asked that the complaining witness be present, but the judge ruled

---

[3]Anthony Platt, *The Child Savers: The Intervention of Delinquency* (Chicago: University of Chicago Press, 1969), p. 139.

that this was not necessary. The only communication with the complainant was one phone call between her and the arresting officer. At the conclusion of the hearing the judge committed Gerald to the industrial school until the age of twenty-one.

Under Arizona law no appeal is permitted in juvenile cases. Mr. Gault filed a habeas corpus petition with the Arizona Superior Court. At the habeas corpus hearing, the juvenile judge testified that Gerald had been adjudged a delinquent under a law which defines a delinquent as one who had violated any state law or municipal ordinance. The ordinance Gerald allegedly violated, using vulgar, abusive, or obscene language in the presence or hearing of a woman or child, was a misdemeanor punishable by a maximum $50 fine and two months' imprisonment. The judge also said he had found Gerald to be "habitually involved in immoral matters," basing that determination on a complaint several years before that Gerald had stolen a baseball glove from another boy and lied to the Police Department about the incident. There had been no hearing on this because no charges had been made and as the judge testified, "because of lack of material foundation."

The Court dismissed the writ and the Arizona Supreme Court affirmed]

MR. JUSTICE FORTAS delivered the opinion of the Court.

. . . It is claimed that juveniles obtain benefits from the special procedures applicable to them which more than offset the disadvantages of denial of the substance of normal due process. As we shall discuss, the observance of due process standards, intelligently and not ruthlessly administered, will not compel the States to abandon or displace any of the substantive benefits of the juvenile process. But it is important, we think, that the claimed benefits of the juvenile process should be candidly appraised. Neither sentiment nor folklore should cause us to shut our eyes, for example, to such startling findings as that reported in an exceptionally reliable study of repeaters or recidivism conducted by the Stan-

ford Research Institute for the President's Commission on Crime in the District of Columbia. This Commission's Report states:

In fiscal 1966 approximately 66 percent of the 16- and 17-year-old juveniles referred to the court by the Youth Aid Division had been before the court previously. In 1965, 56 percent of those in the Receiving Home were repeaters. The SRI study revealed that 61 percent of the sample Juvenile Court referrals in 1965 had been previously referred at least once and that 42 percent had been referred at least twice before.

Certainly, these figures and the high crime rates among juveniles to which we have referred . . . could not lead us to conclude that the absence of constitutional inhibitions as it had largely done, is effective to reduce crime or rehabilitate offenders. We do not mean by this to denigrate the juvenile court process or to suggest that there are not aspects of the juvenile system relating to offenders which are valuable. But the features of the juvenile system which its proponents have asserted are of unique benefit will not be impaired by constitutional domestication. For example, the commendable principles relating to the processing and treatment of juveniles separately from adults are in no way involved or affected by the procedural issues under discussion. Further, we are told that one of the important benefits of the special juvenile court procedures is that they avoid classifying the juvenile as a "criminal." The juvenile offender is now classed as a "delinquent." There is, of course, no reason why this should not continue. It is disconcerting, however, that this term has come to involve only slightly less stigma than the term "criminal" applied to adults. It is also emphasized that in practically all jurisdictions, statutes provide that an adjudication of the child as a delinquent shall not operate as a civil disability or disqualify him for civil service appointment. There is no reason why the application of due process requirements should interfere with such provisions. . . .

Ultimately, however, we confront the reality of that portion of the juvenile court process with which we deal in this case. A boy is charged with misconduct. The boy is committed to an institution where he may be restrained of liberty for years. It is of no constitutional consequence—and of limited practical meaning—that the institution to which he is committed is called an Industrial School. The fact of the matter is that, however euphemistic the title, a "receiving home" or an "industrial school" for juveniles is an institution of confinement in which the child is incarcerated for a greater or lesser time. . . .

In view of this, it would be extraordinary if our Constitution did not require the procedural regularity and the exercise of care implied in the phrase "due process." Under our Constitution, the condition of being a boy does not justify a kangaroo court. The traditional ideas of juvenile court procedure, indeed, contemplated that time would be available and care would be used to establish precisely what the juvenile did and why he did it—was it a prank of adolescence or brutal act threatening serious consequences to himself or society unless corrected? Under traditional notions, one would assume that in a case like that of Gerald Gault, where the juvenile appears to have a home, a working mother and father, and an older brother, the Juvenile Judge would have made a careful inquiry and judgment as to the possibility that the boy could be disciplined and dealt with at home, despite his previous transgressions. Indeed, so far as appears in the record before us, ex-

cept for some conversation with Gerald about his school work and his "wanting to go to . . . Grand Canyon with his father," the points to which the judge directed his attention were little different from those that would be involved in determining any charge of violation of a penal statute. The essential difference between Gerald's case and a normal criminal case is that safeguards available to adults were discarded in Gerald's case. The summary procedure as well as the long commitment were possible because Gerald was 15 years of age instead of over 18.

If Gerald had been over 18, he would not have been subject to Juvenile Court proceedings. For the particular offense immediately involved, the maximum punishment would have been a fine of $5 to $50, or imprisonment in jail for not more than two months. Instead, he was committed to custody for a maximum of six years. If he had been over 18 and had committed an offense to which such a sentence might apply, he would have been entitled to substantial rights under the Constitution of the United States as well as under Arizona's laws and constitution. The United States Constitution would guarantee him rights and protections with respect to arrest, search and seizure, and pretrial interrogation. It would assure him of specific notice of the charges and adequate time to decide his course of action and to prepare his defense. He would be entitled to clear advice that he could be represented by counsel, and at least if a felony were involved, the State would be required to provide counsel if his parents were unable to afford it. If the court acted on the basis of his confession, careful procedures would be required to assure its voluntariness. If the case went to trial, confrontation and opportunity for cross-examination would be guaranteed.

So wide a gulf between the State's treatment of the adult and of the child requires a bridge sturdier than mere verbiage, and reasons more persuasive than cliché can provide. As Wheeler and Cottrell have put it, "The rhetoric of the juvenile court movement has developed without any necessarily close correspondence to the realities of court and institutional routines." . . .

Appellants allege that the Arizona Juvenile Code is unconstitutional or alternatively that the proceedings before the Juvenile Court were constitutionally defective because of failure to provide adequate notice of the hearings. . . .

We cannot agree with the court's conclusion that adequate notice was given in this case. Notice, to comply with due process requirements, must be given sufficiently in advance of scheduled court proceedings so that reasonable opportunity to prepare will be afforded, and it must "set forth the alleged misconduct with particularity." . . . Nor, in the circumstances of this case, can it reasonably be said that the requirement of notice was waived.

Appellants charge that Juvenile Court proceedings were fatally defective because the court did not advise Gerald or his parents of their right to counsel, and proceeded with the hearing, the adjudication of delinquency and the order of commitment in the absence of counsel for the child and his parents or an express waiver of the right thereto. . . .

The President's Crime Commission has recently recommended that in order to assure "procedural justice for the child," it is necessary that "Counsel . . . be appointed as a matter of course wherever coercive action is a possibility, without requiring any affirmative choice by child or parent." . . .

We conclude that the Due Process Clause of the Fourteenth Amendment requires that in respect of proceedings to determine delinquency which may result in commitment to an institution in which the juvenile's freedom is curtailed, the child and his parent must be notified of the child's right to be represented by counsel retained by them, or if they are unable to afford counsel, that counsel will be appointed to represent the child. . . .

Appellants urge that the writ of habeas corpus should have been granted because of the denial of the rights of confrontation and cross-examination in the Juvenile Court hearings, and because the privilege against self-incrimination was not observed. The Juvenile Court Judge testified at the habeas corpus hearing that he had proceeded on the basis of Gerald's admissions at the two hearings. Appellants attack this on the ground that the admissions were obtained in disregard of the privilege against self-incrimination. . . .

We conclude that the constitutional privilege against self-incrimination is applicable in the case of juveniles as it is with respect to adults. We appreciate that special problems may arise with respect to waiver of the privilege by or on behalf of children, and that there may well be some differences in technique—but not in principle—depending upon the age of the child and the presence and competence of parents. The participation of counsel will, of course, assist the police, juvenile courts and appellate tribunals in administering the privilege. If counsel is not present for some permissible reason when an admission is obtained, the greatest care must be taken to assure that the admission was voluntary, in the sense not only that it has not been coerced or suggested, but also that it is not the product of ignorance of rights or of adolescent fantasy, fright or despair.

The "confession" of Gerald Gault was first obtained by Officer Flagg, out of the presence of Gerald's parents, without counsel and without advising him of his right to silence, as far as appears. The judgment of the Juvenile Court was stated by the judge to be based on Gerald's admission in court. Neither "admission" was reduced to writing, and, to say the least, the process by which the "admissions" were obtained and received must be characterized as lacking the certainty and order which are required of proceedings of such formidable consequences. Apart from the "admission," there was nothing upon which a judgment or finding might be based. There was no sworn testimony. Mrs. Cook, the complainant, was not present. The Arizona Supreme Court held that "sworn testimony must be required of all witnesses including police officers, probation officers and others who are part of or officially related to the juvenile court structure." We hold that this is not enough. No reason is suggested or appears for a different rule in respect of sworn testimony in juvenile courts than in adult tribunals. Absent a valid confession adequate to support the determination of the Juvenile Court, confrontation and sworn testimony by witnesses available for cross-examination were essential for a finding of "delinquency" and an order committing Gerald to a state institution for a maximum of six years.
. . .

For the reasons stated, the judgment of the Supreme Court of Arizona is reversed and the cause remanded for further proceedings not inconsistent with this opinion.

MR. JUSTICE BLACK, CONCURRING (OMITTED).
MR. JUSTICE WHITE, CONCURRING (OMITTED).
MR. JUSTICE HARLAN, CONCURRING IN PART AND DISSENTING IN PART (OMITTED).
MR. JUSTICE STEWART, DISSENTING (OMITTED).

[In *In Re Winship* (1970), the Supreme Court ruled that proof beyond a reasonable doubt was an essential of due process and was required at the adjudicatory stage of juvenile proceedings where a juvenile was charged with commission of an act which, if committed by an adult, constituted a crime. The lesser standard of "preponderance of the evidence," commonly employed in juvenile proceedings and in civil suits, was not constitutionally adequate. The following year, in *Ivan* v. *City of New York* (1971), this decision was made retroactive. However, in *McKeiver* v. *Pennsylvania* (1971), the Supreme Court rejected efforts to impose a jury trial requirement on juvenile proceedings. It held that the standard of "fundamental fairness" could be met without trial by jury.

Gault did not begin the process of revolutionizing juvenile justice. Efforts to infuse the system with due process protections had already been successful in several states. However, as one major post-*Gault* study has concluded, that decision certainly legitimized and accelerated trends toward reform.[4] On the other hand, changes have come about gradually and inconsistently and not without strong resistance. In many instances, waiver of the right to counsel has negated the spirit, if not the letter, of the *Gault* decision.[5]

Another reason for the limited impact of the decision can be found in the words of the opin-

[4]Norman Lefstein, Vaughan Stapleton, and Lee Teitelbaum, "In Search of Juvenile Justice: *Gault* and Its Implementation," 3 *Law and Society Review* (1969), 558–562.

[5]Donald Horowitz, *The Courts and Social Policy* (Washington, D.C.: Brookings Institute, 1977), pp. 186–187.

ion itself. Justice Fortas' opinion focused only on the adjudicatory stage of proceedings and explicitly ignored "the procedures or constitutional rights applicable to the pre-judicial stages of the judicial process." Thus, a large portion of the work of the juvenile justice system was not affected by *Gault*. Juvenile justice, not unlike the criminal process generally, is more often than not negotiated justice; for any individual, the results of the formal proceedings may be shaped importantly by preadjudicatory events.]

E. Capital Punishment

(1) A Note on the Supreme Court and the Death Penalty

Prior to Gary Gilmore's execution by firing squad in Utah in 1977, and John Spenkelink's execution in Florida in 1979, the last legal execution in the United States took place in Colorado on June 2, 1967. From 1930 to 1967, 3,859 persons were executed by civil authorities—all but 33 under state law.[1] Of this total, 86 percent (3,334) had been convicted of murder, 12 percent (455) had been convicted of rape, and the remainder for offenses such as kidnapping, burglary, robbery, sabotage, aggravated assault, and espionage. Sixty percent of the executions were carried out in the south. Most of the executions took place in five states: Georgia (366), New York (329), Texas (297), California (292), and North Carolina (263). In 1972, forty-one states had laws that permitted capital punishment, but there had been no recent executions in thirty-one of these.

Virtually all executions for rape in this period occurred in the south (there were seven in Missouri), and nearly 90 percent of those executed for rape were black.[2] During this period, blacks accounted for 72 percent of all persons executed in the south, but only 29 percent, 36 percent, and 15 percent in the northeast, north central, and western states, respectively. Overall, 54 percent of the persons executed in the United States were black. Less than 1 percent (32) of those executed were women.

Although the number of executions decreased steadily after 1951 (when there were 105), the number of persons sentenced to death remains high. At the time of the Supreme Court's decision in the case of *Furman* v. *Georgia* (1972), approximately 600 persons were under sentence of death. All of those have now had their sentences commuted to life imprisonment. By 1976, when the Supreme Court again addressed the issue of capital punishment, nearly 400 more persons had been sentenced to death under statutes enacted to comply with the mandate of the *Furman* decision. As of March 1979, nearly 500 men and five women in twenty-five states were under sentence of death.[3] As Willard Lassers had noted,

. . . we have in effect ended one form of barbarity and replaced it by another. We have created colonies of living dead in our state penitentiaries. What has brought us to this? Why do we continue to sentence men to a punishment we are obviously unwilling to carry out?[4]

[1]During this period, the U.S. Army and Air Force executed 160 persons, the last in 1961. One execution was for desertion, the remainder for murder and rape. The navy has not executed anyone since 1849.

[2]In 1972, the death penalty for rape was imposed only in the southern states and in South Africa, Malawi, and Taiwan.

[3]*The New York Times Magazine*, "Will He Be the First?" (March 11, 1979), p. 29.

[4]Willard J. Lassers, "Death Takes a Holiday," *Trans-action* (January 1971), p. 10.

The moratorium on executions in the United States came about for several reasons. Until 1972, public opinion increasingly supported abolition of the death penalty.[5] The issue of capital punishment had been in and out of the Supreme Court almost continuously for a decade, and the Court's refusal to make a firm decision, either positive or negative, created enough uncertainty and doubt to deter those favoring the resumption of capital punishment. Finally, and probably most important, a massive campaign by the Legal Defense Fund to prevent any executions while it was testing the constitutionality of the death penalty in the Supreme Court resulted in hundreds of stays of execution, some literally at the last minute.[6] But even after the Supreme Court upheld the constitutionality of capital punishment in *Gregg* v. *Georgia* (1976), only two executions have been carried out.

Aside from its obvious human consequences, the controversy over its effect as a deterrent, and the fairness of its imposition, capital punishment raises some important constitutional questions. Is the death penalty, per se, a violation of the Eighth Amendment's prohibition against cruel and unusual punishment? The Supreme Court has now rejected that claim, and certainly those who wrote the amendment did not think so. Executions were a common occurrence in the eighteenth century. Furthermore, the Constitution appears to sanction the taking of life in the words of the Fifth Amendment: no person can be deprived of life without due process of law, and no person can be twice put in jeopardy of life (or limb).

The opaque words of the Eighth Amendment, "cruel and unusual punishment" were probably meant only to prohibit barbaric forms of execution and torture. Hanging and whipping were common enough in 1791 so as not to be regarded as either cruel or unusual. When, a century later, the electric chair, firing squads, and then the gas chamber were introduced, they were defended and accepted by the courts as being more humane forms of execution.

The wording "cruel *and* unusual" is also the source of dispute. Does the word "unusual" mean infrequent, or merely exotic? Does it modify "cruel" or is it a separate and distinct constitutional prohibition? Of course, there is no necessary connection between inhumanity and infrequency.

Partly because of its wording, the cruel and unusual punishment clause of the Eighth Amendment was, until recently, constitutionally undeveloped. Prior to *Furman*, the Supreme Court had found only three punishments to be so cruel and unusual as to violate the Constitution.

[5] Cf. these Gallup poll reports:
Question: "Are you in favor of the death penalty for persons convicted of murder?"

	Yes	No	No Opinion
November 1972	57%	32%	11%
March 1972	50	41	9
1971	49	40	11
1969	51	40	9
1966	42	47	11
1965	45	43	12
1960	51	36	13
1953	68	25	7

[6] See Michael Meltsner, *Cruel and Unusual* (New York: Random House, 1973).

In *Trop* v. *Dulles* (1958), it prohibited deprivation of citizenship for wartime desertion by a soldier.[7] In *Robinson* v. *California* (1962), it held that *any* criminal punishment for narcotics *addiction* was prohibited.[8] And in a much earlier case, *Weems* v. *United States* (1910), the Court ruled that a sentence of fifteen years' imprisonment for filing a false statement was so "grossly disproportionate" to the crime as to violate the Eighth Amendment. Thus, the *Weems* and *Trop* cases stand for the proposition that a punishment need not be barbarous or bloody to warrant constitutional condemnation. Punishments cannot be degrading or wantonly imposed. On the other hand, merely because a punishment is proportionate to the crime does not insulate it from the charge that it is cruel and unusual. It seems unlikely in the extreme that the Supreme Court today would approve a punishment of maiming for the crime of mayhem or the cutting off of the hand of a thief.

Perhaps the most important pre-*Furman* doctrinal development was the holding of four members of the Court in *Trop* v. *Dulles* that cruel and unusual punishment is a dynamic concept that expresses "evolving standards of decency." It was not to be imprisoned in its eighteenth-century history and meaning. The Supreme Court could interpret it in response to modern values and in the light of modern conditions.

The Supreme Court confronted the question of capital punishment in the Willie Francis case (*supra,* p. 781, ftn. 2) and refused to prohibit the second—and successful—attempt to execute Francis after an electric chair malfunction. In 1958, a plurality of justices in *Trop* v. *Dulles* observed: "Whatever the arguments may be against capital punishment, both on moral grounds and in terms of accomplishing the purpose of punishment—and they forceful—the death penalty has been employed throughout our history, and, in a day when it is still widely accepted, it cannot be said to violate the constitutional concept of cruelty." But five years later, Justices Goldberg, Black, and Douglas, dissenting from a denial of certiorari in *Rudolph* v. *Alabama* (1963), urged the Court to consider "whether the Eighth and Fourteenth Amendments . . . permit the imposition of the death penalty on a convicted rapist who has neither taken nor endangered human life." Writing for the trio, Justice Goldberg asked: "Is the taking of human life to protect a value other than human life consistent with the constitutional prescription against 'punishments which by their excessive . . . severity are greatly disproportionate to the offenses charged'?"

Changing notions about capital punishment became more evident in the following years. In *Witherspoon* v. *United States* (1968), the Supreme Court overturned a murder conviction where persons opposed to the death penalty were excluded from jury service. This, said Justice Stewart, left a "hanging jury," which, even if it did not decide on the death penalty, was unconstitution-

[7]Arguing that the existence of the death penalty was not a license for government to devise *any* imaginable penalty short of death, Chief Justice Warren wrote: "[Denationalization] is a form of punishment more primitive than torture, for it destroys for the individual the political existence that was centuries in the development. The punishment strips the citizen of his status in the national and international political community. His very existence is at the sufferance of the country in which he happens to find himself."

[8]But compare *Powell* v. *Texas* (1966), in which the Court refused to extend the rationale of *Robinson* to prohibit punishment of alcoholics.

ally impaneled. *Witherspoon* was applied retroactively, and many pending death sentences were commuted as a result.

Yet the Court seemed unwilling to decide squarely whether the death penalty was constitutional. The Legal Defense Fund, which carried the burden of the constitutional attack on capital punishment, sought to litigate other issues that might nullify many existing death sentences. Two such issues, raised in *McGautha* v. *California* and *Crampton* v. *Ohio* (1971), were whether due process was violated when a person was sentenced to death by a jury in the absence of legislatively mandated standards, and whether due process required a bifurcated trial, in which the jury's judgment of guilt or innocence was separate from its imposition of punishment.

McGautha had been convicted of murder and sentenced to death at a separate penalty hearing. Crampton had been sentenced to death by the jury at the same time it found him guilty of first-degree murder. In neither case was the jury given specific standards or guidelines by the presiding judge, although the *McGautha* jury was told it could take into account the defendant's background and any feelings of pity, sympathy, or sentiment it might have for or against the defendant. In a 6-3 decision, the Court held that neither a bifurcated trial nor statutory guidelines were constitutionally required. It agreed that a bifurcated trial, then required in only five states, might be fairer than a single trial in which the defendant was forced to compromise his "right of allocution" in denying that he had committed a crime. But it was not prepared to impose this as a constitutional rule. As for structured guidelines, the Court

seemed unpersuaded that realistic and meaningful standards could be incorporated into any formula.

(2) Furman v. Georgia (1972)

+Douglas, Brennan, Stewart, White, Marshall
−Burger, Blackmun, Powell, Rehnquist

[In January 1972, the Supreme Court heard oral argument in several death penalty cases that raised the fundamental question of its compatibility with the Eighth and Fourteenth Amendments. Attorneys for the plaintiffs emphasized the lack of evidence for the proposition that capital punishment was a deterrent to crime. They argued that the death penalty was imposed in a cruelly random, almost idiosyncratic, fashion and that it fell with discriminatory harshness on those who were poor and black. In recent years, they claimed, only one in every twelve or thirteen homicide convictions resulted in imposition of the death penalty. To support their contention that the death penalty was incompatible with current values, they noted the apparent unwillingness of states to carry it out where it had been imposed. Shortly after oral argument, the California Supreme Court declared that capital punishment in that state was in violation of the state's constitution.[1] This reduced by about 100, to 600, the number of inmates awaiting death who would be affected by the *Furman* decision.

Furman, who was black, had been convicted of felony murder—an accidental shooting death in the course of an attempted nighttime burglary. The jury imposed the death penalty, and the Supreme Court of Georgia affirmed.]

PER CURIAM.

. . . Certiorari was granted limited to the following question: "Does the imposition and carrying out of the death penalty in these cases constitute cruel and unusual punishment in violation of the Eighth and Fourteenth Amendments? . . . The Court holds that the imposition and carry-

---

[1]That decision was subsequently overruled by the voters of California in a referendum that amended the state constitution.

ing out of the death penalty in these cases constitutes cruel and unusual punishment in violation of the Eighth and Fourteenth Amendments. The judgment in each case is therefore reversed insofar as it leaves undisturbed the death sentence imposed, and the cases are remanded for further proceedings. So ordered.

Judgment in each case reversed in part and cases remanded.

MR. JUSTICE DOUGLAS, MR. JUSTICE BRENNAN, MR. JUSTICE STEWART, MR. JUSTICE WHITE, AND MR. JUSTICE MARSHALL have filed separate opinions in support of the judgments.
THE CHIEF JUSTICE, MR. JUSTICE BLACKMUN, MR. JUSTICE POWELL, AND MR. JUSTICE REHNQUIST have filed separate dissenting opinions.

MR. JUSTICE DOUGLAS, CONCURRING.
. . .

That the requirements of due process ban cruel and unusual punishment is now settled. *Louisiana ex rel. Francis* v. *Resweber* (1947) . . . *Robinson* v. *California* . . . It is also settled that the proscription of cruel and unusual punishments forbids the judicial imposition of them as well as their proscription by the legislature. . . .

It has been assumed in our decisions that punishment by death is not cruel, unless the manner of execution can be said to be inhuman and barbarous. *In re Kemmler,* (1890) . . . It is also said in our opinions that the proscription of cruel and unusual punishments "is not fastened to the obsolete, but may acquire meaning as public opinion becomes enlightened by a humane justice." *Weems* v. *United States* (1910) . . . A like statement was made in *Trop* v. *Dulles* (1958) . . . that the Eighth Amendment "must draw its meaning from the evolving standards of decency that mark the progress of a maturing society." . . .

The words "cruel and unusual" certainly include penalties that are barbaric. But the words, at least when read in light of the English proscription against selective and irregular use of penalties, suggest that it is "cruel and unusual" to apply the death penalty—or any other penalty—selectively to minorities whose numbers are few, who are outcasts of society, and who are unpopular, but whom society is willing to see suffer though it would not countenance general application of the same penalty across the boards. . . .

There is increasing recognition of the fact that the basic theme of equal protection is implicit in "cruel and unusual" punishments. "A penalty . . . should be considered 'unusually' imposed if it is administered arbitrarily or discriminatorily." . . . "The extreme rarity with which applicable death penalty provisions are put to use raises a strong inference of arbitrariness."

We cannot say from facts disclosed in these records that these defendants were sentenced to death because they were Black. Yet our task is not restricted to an effort to divine what motives impelled these death penalties. Rather we deal with a system of law and of justice that leaves to the uncontrolled discretion of judges or juries the determination whether defendants committing these crimes should die or be imprisoned. Under these laws no standards govern the selection of the penalty. People live or die, dependent on the whim of one man or of 12. . . .

Those who wrote the Eighth Amendment knew what price their forebears had paid for a system based, not on equal justice, but on discrimination. In those days the target was not the Blacks or the poor, but the dissenters, those who opposed absolutism in government, who struggled for a parliamentary regime, and who opposed governments' recurring efforts to foist a particular religion on the people. . . . But the tool of capital punishment was used with vengeance against the opposition and those unpopular with the regime. One cannot read this history without realizing that the desire for equality was reflected in the ban against "cruel and unusual punishments" contained in the Eighth Amendment.

In a Nation committed to Equal Protection of the laws there is no permissible "caste" aspect of law enforcement. Yet we know that the discretion of judges and juries in imposing the death penalty enables the penalty to be selectively applied, feeding prejudices against the accused if he is poor and despised, poor and lacking political clout, or if he is a member of a suspect or unpopular minority, and saving those who by social position may be in a more protected position. . . .

The high service rendered by the "cruel and unusual" punishment clause of the Eighth Amendment is to require legislatures to write penal laws that are evenhanded, nonselective, and nonarbitrary, and to require judges to see to it that general laws are not applied sparsely, selectively, and spottily to unpopular groups. . . .

MR. JUSTICE BRENNAN, CONCURRING. . . .

We have very little evidence of the Framers' intent in including the Cruel and Unusual Punishments Clause among those restraints upon the new Government enumerated in the Bill of Rights. . . .

We know that the Framers' concern was directed specifically to the exercise of legislative power. They included in the Bill of Rights a prohibition upon "cruel and unusual punishments" precisely because the legislature would otherwise have had the unfettered power to prescribe punishments for crimes. Yet we cannot now know exactly what the

Framers thought "cruel and unusual punishments" were. Certainly they intended to ban torturous punishments, but the available evidence does not support the further conclusion that *only* torturous punishments were to be outlawed. . . . [T]he Framers were well aware that the reach of the Clause was not limited to the proscription of unspeakable atrocities. Nor did they intend simply to forbid punishments considered "cruel and unusual" at the time. The "import" of the Clause is, indeed, "indefinite," and for good reason. A constitutional provision "is enacted, it is true, from an experience of evils, but its general language should not, therefore, be necessarily confined to the form that evil had theretofore taken. Time works changes, brings into existence new conditions and purposes. Therefore a principle, to be vital, must be capable of wider application than the mischief which gave it birth." *Weems* v. *United States*, . . .

Ours would indeed be a simple task were we required merely to measure a challenged punishment against those that history has long condemned. That narrow and unwarranted view of the Clause, however, was left behind with the 19th century. Our task today is more complex. We know "that the words of the [Clause] are not precise, and that their scope is not static." We know, therefore, that the Clause must draw its meaning from the "evolving standards of decency that mark the progress of a maturing society." *Trop* v. *Dulles*, . . . That knowledge, of course, is but the beginning of the inquiry.

In *Trop* v. *Dulles*, . . . it was said that "[t]he question is whether [a] penalty subjects the individual to a fate forbidden by the principle of civilized treatment guaranteed by the [Clause]." It was also said that a challenged punishment must be examined "in light of the basic prohibition against inhuman treatment" embodied in the Clause. . . . It was said, finally, that:

The basic concept underlying the [Clause] is nothing less than the dignity of man. While the State has the power to punish, the [Clause] stands to assure that this power be exercised within the limits of civilized standards.

At bottom, then, the Cruel and Unusual Punishments Clause prohibits the infliction of uncivilized and inhuman punishments. The State, even as it punishes, must treat its members with respect for their intrinsic worth as human beings. A punishment is "cruel and unusual," therefore, if it does not comport with human dignity.

This formulation, of course, does not of itself yield principles for assessing the constitutional validity of particular punishments. Nevertheless, even though "[t]his Court has had little occasion to give precise content to the [Clause]," there are principles recognized in our cases and inherent in the Clause sufficient to permit a judicial determination whether a challenged punishment comports with human dignity.

The primary principle is that a punishment must not be so severe as to be degrading to the dignity of human beings. Pain, certainly, may be a factor in the judgment. The infliction of an extremely severe punishment will often entail physical suffering. . . .

More than the presence of pain, however, is comprehended in the judgment that the extreme severity of a punishment makes it degrading to the dignity of human beings. The barbaric punishments condemned by history, "punishments which inflict torture, such as the rack, the thumbscrew, the iron boot, the stretching of limbs, and the like," are, of course, "attended with acute pain and suffering." *O'Neil* v. *Ver-*

mont . . . (1892) (Field, J., dissenting). When we consider why they have been condemned, however, we realize that the pain involved is not the only reason. The true significance of these punishments is that they treat members of the human race as nonhumans, as objects to be toyed with and discarded. They are thus inconsistent with the fundamental premise of the Clause that even the vilest criminal remains a human being possessed of common human dignity. . . .

In determining whether a punishment comports with human dignity, we are aided also by a second principle inherent in the Clause—that the State must not arbitrarily inflict a severe punishment. This principle derives from the notion that the State does not respect human dignity when, without reason, it inflicts upon some people a severe punishment that it does not inflict upon others. Indeed, the very words "cruel and unusual punishments" imply condemnation of the arbitrary infliction of severe punishments. . . .

A third principle inherent in the Clause is that a severe punishment must not be unacceptable to contemporary society. Rejection by society, of course, is a strong indication that a severe punishment does not comport with human dignity. In applying this principle, however, we must make certain that the judicial determination is as objective as possible.

The question under this principle, . . . is whether there are objective indicators from which a court can conclude that contemporary society considers a severe punishment unacceptable. Accordingly, the judicial task is to review the history of a challenged punishment and to examine society's present practices with respect to its use. . . .

The final principle inherent in the Clause is that a severe punishment must not be excessive. A punishment is excessive under this principle if it is unnecessary: The infliction of a severe punishment by the State cannot comport with human dignity when it is nothing more than the pointless infliction of suffering. . . .

. . .

The question, . . . is whether the deliberate infliction of death is today consistent with the command of the Clause that the State may not inflict punishments that do not comport with human dignity. It is a denial of human dignity for the State arbitrarily to subject a person to an unusually severe punishment that society has indicated it does not regard as acceptable and that cannot be shown to serve any penal purpose more effectively than a significantly less drastic punishment. Under these principles and this test, death is today a "cruel and unusual" punishment.

Death is a unique punishment in the United States. In a society that so strongly affirms the sanctity of life, not surprisingly the common view is that death is the ultimate sanction.

The only explanation for the uniqueness of death is its extreme severity. Death is today an unusually severe punishment, unusual in its pain, in its finality, and in its enormity. No other existing punishment is comparable to death in terms of physical and mental suffering. Although our information is not conclusive, it appears that there is no method available that guarantees an immediate and painless death. . . .

. . .

In comparison to all other punishments today, then, the deliberate extinguishment of human life by the State is uniquely degrading to human dignity. I would not hesitate to hold, on that ground alone, that death is today a "cruel and unusual" punishment, were it not that death is a punishment of long-standing usage and acceptance in this country.

I therefore turn to the second principle—that the State may not arbitrarily inflict an unusually severe punishment.

The outstanding characteristic of our present practice of punishing criminals by death is the infrequency with which we resort to it. The evidence is conclusive that death is not the ordinary punishment for any crime.

. . .

When the punishment of death is inflicted in a trivial number of the cases in which it is legally available, the conclusion is virtually inescapable that it is being inflicted arbitrarily. Indeed, it smacks of little more than a lottery system. . . .

When there is a strong probability that an unusually severe and degrading punishment is being inflicted arbitrarily, we may well expect that society will disapprove of its infliction. I turn, therefore, to the third principle. An examination of the history and present operation of the American practice of punishing criminals by death reveals that this punishment has been almost totally rejected by contemporary society. . . .

Thus, although "the death penalty has been employed throughout our history," *Trop* v. *Dulles*, . . . in fact the history of this punishment is one of successive restriction. What was once a common punishment has become, in the context of a continuing moral debate, increasingly rare. The evolution of this punishment evidences not that it is an inevitable part of the American scene, but that it has proved progressively more troublesome to the national conscience. . . .

The progressive decline in and the current rarity of the infliction of death demonstrate that our society seriously questions the appropriateness of this punishment today. The States point out that many legislatures authorize death as the punishment for certain crimes and that substantial segments of the public, as reflected in opinion polls and referendum votes, continue to support it. Yet the availability of this punishment through statutory authorization, as well as the polls and referenda, which amount simply to approval of that authorization, simply underscores the extent to which our society has in fact rejected this punishment. When an unusually severe punishment is authorized for wide-scale application but not, because of society's refusal, inflicted save in a few instances, the inference is compelling that there is a deep-seated reluctance to inflict it. Indeed, the likelihood is great that the punishment is tolerated only because of its disuse. The objective indicator of society's view of an unusually severe punishment is what society does with it. And today society will inflict death upon only a small sample of the eligible criminals. Rejection could hardly be more complete without becoming absolute. At the very least, I must conclude that contemporary society views this punishment with substantial doubt.

The final principle to be considered is that an unusually severe and degrading punishment may not be excessive in view of the purposes for which it is inflicted. . . .

The more significant argument is that the threat of death prevents the commission of capital crimes because it deters potential criminals who would not be deterred by the threat of imprisonment. The argument is not based upon evidence that the threat of death is a superior deterrent. . . . The States argue, however, that they are entitled to rely upon common human experience, and that experience, they say, supports the conclusion that death must be a more effective deterrent than any less severe punishment. Because people fear death the most, the argument runs, the threat of death must be the greatest deterrent.

It is important to focus upon the precise import of this argument. It is not denied that many, and probably most, capital crimes cannot be deterred by the threat of punishment. Thus the argument can apply only to those who think rationally about the commission of capital crimes. Particularly is that true when the potential criminal, under this argument, must not only consider the risk of punishment, but also distinguish between two possible punishments. The concern, then, is with a particular type of potential criminal, the rational person who will commit a capital crime knowing that the punishment is long-term imprisonment, which may well be for the rest of his life, but will not commit the crime knowing that the punishment is death. On the face of it, the assumption that such persons exist is implausible. . . .

There is, however, another aspect to the argument that the punishment of death is necessary for the protection of society. The infliction of death, the States urge, serves to manifest the community's outrage at the commission of the crime. It is, they say, a concrete public expression of moral indignation that inculcates respect for the law and helps assure a more peaceful community. . . .

There is, then, no substantial reason to believe that the punishment of death, as currently administered, is necessary for the protection of society. The only other purpose suggested, one that is independent of protection for society, is retribution. Shortly stated, retribution in this context means that criminals are put to death because they deserve it.

. . .

. . . Obviously, concepts of justice change; no immutable moral order requires death for murderers and rapists. The claim that death is a just punishment necessarily refers to the existence of certain public beliefs. The claim must be that for capital crimes death alone comports with society's notion of proper punishment. . . . The asserted public belief that murderers and rapists deserve to die is flatly inconsistent with the execution of a random few. . . .

MR. JUSTICE STEWART, CONCURRING.

The penalty of death differs from all other kinds of criminal punishment, not in degree but in kind. It is unique in its total irrevocability. It is unique in its rejection of rehabilitation of the convict as a basic purpose of criminal justice. And it is unique, finally, in its absolute renunciation of all that is embodied in our concept of humanity.

For these and other reasons, at least two of my Brothers have concluded that the infliction of the death penalty is constitutionally impermissible in all circumstances under the Eight and Fourteenth Amendments. Their case is a strong one. But I find it unnecessary to reach the ultimate question they would decide. . . .

These death sentences are cruel and unusual in the same way that being struck by lightning is cruel and unusual. For, of all the people convicted of rapes and murders . . . many just as reprehensible as these, the petitioners are among a capriciously selected random handful upon whom the sentence of death has in fact been imposed. My concurring Brothers have demonstrated that, if any basis can be discerned for the selection of these few to be sentenced to die, it is the constitutionally impermissible basis of race. . . . But racial discrimination has not been proved, and I put it to one side. I simply conclude that the Eighth and Fourteenth Amendments cannot tolerate the infliction of a sentence of death under legal systems that permit this unique penalty to be so wantonly and so freakishly imposed.

. . .

MR. JUSTICE WHITE, CONCURRING.

. . . In joining the Court's judgment, . . . I do not at all intimate that the death penalty is unconstitutional *per se* or that there is no system of capital punishment that would comport with the Eighth Amendment. . . .

The narrower question to which I address myself concerns the constitutionality of capital punishment statutes under which (1) the legislature authorizes the imposition of the death penalty for murder or rape; (2) the legislature does not itself mandate the penalty in any particular class or kind of case (that is, legislative will is not frustrated if the penalty is never imposed) but delegates to judges or juries the decisions as to those cases, if any, in which the penalty will be utilized; and (3) judges and juries have ordered the death penalty with such infrequency that the odds are now very much against imposition and execution of the penalty with respect to any convicted murderer or rapist. It is in this context that we must consider whether the execution of these petitioners violates the Eighth Amendment.

I begin with what I consider a near truism: that the death penalty could so seldom be imposed that it would cease to be a credible deterrent or measurably to contribute to any other kind of punishment in the criminal justice system. . . .

Most important, a major goal of the criminal law—to deter others by punishing the convicted criminal— would not be substantially served where the penalty is so seldom invoked that it ceases to be the credible threat essential to influence the conduct of others. For present purposes I accept the morality and utility of punishing one person to influence another. I accept also the effectiveness of punishment generally and need not reject the death penalty as a more effective deterrent than a lesser punishment. But common sense and experience tell us that seldom-enforced laws become ineffective measures for controlling human conduct and that the death penalty, unless imposed with sufficient frequency, will make little contribution to deterring those crimes for which it may be exacted.

. . .

It is also my judgment that this point has been reached with respect to capital punishment as it is presently administered under the statutes involved in these cases. Concededly, it is difficult to prove as a general proposition that capital punishment, however administered, more effectively serves the ends of the criminal law than does imprisonment. But however that may be, I cannot avoid the conclusion that as the statutes before us are now administered, the penalty is so infrequently imposed that the threat of execution is too attenuated to be of substantial service to criminal justice.

MR. JUSTICE MARSHALL, CONCURRING.
. . .

Perhaps the most important principle in analyzing "cruel and unusual" punishment questions is one that is reiterated again and again in the prior opinions of the Court: i. e., the cruel and unusual language "must draw its meaning from the evolving standards of decency that mark the progress of a maturing society." Thus, a penalty which was permissible at one time in our Nation's history is not necessarily permissible today.

The fact, therefore, that the Court, or individual Justices, may have in the past expressed an opinion that the death penalty is constitutional is not now binding on us. . . .

Faced with an open question, we must establish our standards for decision. The decisions discussed in the previous section imply that a punishment may be deemed cruel and unusual for any one of four distinct reasons.

First, there are certain punishments which inherently involve so much physical pain and suffering that civilized people cannot tolerate them—e. g., use of the rack, the thumbscrew, or other modes of torture.

Second, there are punishments which are unusual, signifying that they were previously unknown as penalties for a given offense. . . .

Third, a penalty may be cruel and unusual because it is excessive and serves no valid legislative purpose. . . . The decisions previously discussed are replete with assertions that one of the primary functions of the cruel and unusual punishments clause is to prevent excessive or unnecessary penalties, . . . these punishments are unconstitutional even though popular sentiment may favor them. . . .

Fourth, where a punishment is not excessive and serves a valid legislative purpose, it still may be invalid if popular sentiment abhors it. For example, if the evidence clearly demonstrated that capital punishment served valid legislative purposes, such punishment would, nevertheless, be unconstitutional if citizens found it to be morally unacceptable. A general abhorrence on the part of the public would, in effect, equate a modern punishment with those barred since the adoption of the Eighth Amendment. There are no prior cases in this Court striking down a penalty on this ground, but the very notion of changing values requires that we recognize its existence.

It is immediately obvious then that since capital punishment is not a recent phenomenon, if it violates the Constitution, it does so because it is excessive or unnecessary, or because it is abhorrent to currently existing moral values.

. . .

There are six purposes conceivably served by capital punishment: retribution, deterrence, prevention of repetitive criminal acts, encouragement of guilty pleas and confessions, eugenics, and economy. . . .

The fact that the State may seek retribution against those who have broken its laws does not mean that retribution may then become the State's sole end in punishing. Our jurisprudence has always accepted deterrence in general, deterrence of individual recidivism, isolation of dangerous persons, and rehabilitation as proper goals of punishment. . . . Retaliation, vengeance, and retribution have been roundly condemned as intolerable aspirations for a government in a free society. . . .

. . . If retribution alone could serve as a justification for any particular penalty, then all penalties selected by the legislature would by definition be acceptable means for designating society's moral approbation of a particular act. The "cruel and unusual" language would thus be read out of the Constitution and the fears of Patrick Henry and the other Founding Fathers would become realities. . . .

. . .

. . . There is but one conclusion that can be drawn from all of this— *i.e.,* the death penalty is an excessive and unnecessary punishment which violates the Eighth Amendment. The statistical evidence is not convincing beyond all doubt, but, it is persuasive. It is not improper at this point to take judicial notice of the fact that for more than 200 years men have labored to demonstrate that capital punishment serves no purpose that life imprisonment could not serve equally as well. And they have done so with great success. . . . We have this evidence before us now. There is no rational basis for concluding that capital punishment is not excessive. It therefore violates the Eighth Amendment. . . .

In striking down capital punishment, this Court does not malign our system of government. On the contrary, it pays homage to it. Only in a free society could right triumph in difficult times, and could civilization record its magnificent advancement. In recognizing the humanity of our fellow beings, we pay ourselves the highest tribute. We achieve "a major milestone in the long road up from barbarism" and join the approximately 70 other jurisdictions in the world which celebrate their regard for civilization and humanity by shunning capital punishment.

I concur in the judgment of the Court.

MR. CHIEF JUSTICE BURGER, WITH WHOM MR. JUSTICE BLACKMUN, MR. JUSTICE POWELL, AND MR. JUSTICE REHNQUIST JOIN, DISSENTING.

At the outset it is important to note that only two members of the Court, Mr. Justice Brennan and Mr. Justice Marshall, have concluded that the Eighth Amendment prohibits capital punishment for all crimes and under all circumstances. Mr. Justice Douglas has also determined that the death penalty contravenes the Eighth Amendment, although I do not read his opinion as necessarily requiring final abolition of the penalty. . . . I conclude that the constitutional prohibition against "cruel and unusual punishments" cannot be construed to bar the imposition of the punishment of death.

Mr. Justice Stewart and Mr. Justice White have concluded that petitioners' death sentences must be set aside because prevailing sentencing practices do not comply with the Eighth Amendment. . . . I believe this approach fundamentally misconceives the nature of the Eighth Amendment guarantee and flies directly in the face of controlling authority of extremely recent vintage. . . .

If we were possessed of legislative power, I would either join with Mr. Justice Brennan and Mr. Justice Marshall or, at the very least, restrict the use of capital punishment to a small category of the most heinous crimes. Our constitutional inquiry, however, must be divorced from personal feelings as to the morality and efficacy of the death penalty and be confined to the meaning and applicability of the uncertain language of the Eighth Amendment. There is no novelty in being called upon to interpret a constitutional provision that is less than self-defining, but of all our fundamental guarantees, the ban on "cruel and unusual punishments" is one of the most difficult to translate into judicially manageable terms. The widely divergent views of the Amendment expressed in today's opinions reveal the haze that surrounds this constitutional command. Yet it is essential to our role as a court that we not seize upon the enigmatic character of the guarantee as an invitation to enact our personal predilections into law. . . .

Today the Court has not ruled that capital punishment is *per se* violative of the Eighth Amendment; nor has it ruled that the punishment is barred for any particular class or classes of crimes. The substantially similar concurring opinions of Mr. Justice Stewart and Mr. Justice White, which are necessary to support the judgment setting aside petitioners' sentences, stop short of reaching the ultimate question. The actual scope of the Court's ruling, which I take to be embodied in these concurring opinions, is not entirely clear. This much, however, seems apparent: if the legislatures are to continue to authorize capital punishment for some crimes, juries and judges can no longer be permitted to make the sentencing determination in the same manner they have in the past. This approach—not urged in oral arguments or briefs—misconceives the nature of the constitutional command against "cruel and unusual punishments," disregards controlling case law, and demands a rigidity in capital cases which, if possible of achievement, cannot be regarded as a welcome change. Indeed the contrary seems to be the case.

As I have earlier stated, the Eighth Amendment forbids the imposition of punishments that are so cruel and inhumane as to violate society's standards of civilized conduct. The Amendment does not prohibit all punishments the States are unable to prove necessary to deter or control crime. The Amendment is not concerned with the process by which a State determines that a particular punishment is to be imposed in a particular case. And the Amendment most assuredly does not speak to the power of legislatures to confer sentencing discretion on juries, rather than to fix all sentences by statute.

. . .

Since there is no majority of the Court on the ultimate issue presented in these cases, the future of capital punishment in this country has been left in an uncertain limbo. Rather than providing a final and unambiguous answer on the basic constitutional question, the collective impact of the majority's ruling is to demand an undetermined measure of change from the various state legislatures and the Congress. . . .

. . .

The highest judicial duty is to recognize the limits on judicial power and to permit the democratic processes to deal with matters falling outside of those limits. . . .

MR. JUSTICE BLACKMUN, DISSENTING (OMITTED). (See pp. 183–185, *supra.*) MR. JUSTICE POWELL, WITH WHOM THE CHIEF JUSTICE, MR. JUSTICE BLACKMUN, AND MR. JUSTICE REHNQUIST JOIN, DISSENTING.

. . .

I now return to the overriding question in these cases: whether this Court, acting in conformity with the Constitution, can justify its judgment to abolish capital punishment as heretofore known in this country. It is important to keep in focus the enormity of the step undertaken by the Court today. Not only does it invalidate hundreds of state and federal laws, it deprives those jurisdictions of the power to legislate with respect to capital punishment in the future, except in a manner consistent with the cloudily outlined views of those Justices who do not purport to undertake total abolition. Nothing short of an amendment to the United States Constitution can reverse the Court's judgment. Meanwhile, all flexibility is foreclosed. The normal democratic process, as well as the opportunities for the several States to respond to the will of their people expressed through ballot referenda (as in Massachusetts, Illinois, and Colorado), is now shut off.

The sobering disadvantage of constitutional adjudication of this magnitude is the universality and permanence of the judgment. The enduring merit of legislative action is its responsiveness to the democratic process, and to revision and change: mistaken judgments may be corrected and refinements perfected. In England and Canada critical choices were made after studies canvassing all competing views, and in those countries revisions may be made in light of experience. . . .

MR. JUSTICE REHNQUIST, WITH WHOM THE CHIEF JUSTICE, MR. JUSTICE BLACKMUN, AND MR. JUSTICE POWELL JOIN, DISSENTING. . . .

The courts in cases properly before them have been entrusted under the Constitution with the last word, short of constitutional amendment, as to whether a law passed by the legislature conforms to the Constitution. But just because courts in general, and this Court in particular, do have the last word, the admonition of Mr. Justice Stone in *United States* v. *Butler* must be constantly borne in mind:

[W]hile *unconstitutional exercise of power by the executive and legislative branches of the government is subject to judicial restraint, the only check upon our own exercise of power is our own sense of self-restraint.* . . .

Rigorous attention to the limits of this Court's authority is likewise enjoined because of the natural desire that beguiles judges along with other human beings into imposing their own views of goodness, truth, and justice upon others. Judges differ only in that they have the power, if not the authority, to enforce their desires. This is doubtless why nearly two centuries of judicial precedent from this Court counsel the sparing use of that power. The most expansive reading of the leading constitutional cases does not remotely suggest that this Court has been granted a roving commission, either by the Founding Fathers or by the framers of the Fourteenth Amendment, to strike down laws that are based upon notions of policy or morality suddenly found unacceptable by a majority of this Court. . . .

(3) Gregg v. Georgia (1976)

+Burger, Stewart, White, Blackmun, Powell, Rehnquist, Stevens
−Brennan, Marshall

[The *Furman* decision was followed by widespread efforts to restore the death penalty by bringing death penalty laws in line with that decision. By the spring of 1976, thirty-five states had reenacted capital punishment in some form.[1] Twenty states imposed a mandatory death penalty for a limited number of crimes. Fifteen states provided for imposition of the death penalty by a jury guided by appropriate standards at a separate penalty trial; in most cases, mandatory appellate review of the sentence was also included. A bill to restore the death penalty in federal law was debated but never enacted, except for the limited category of aircraft piracy. However, the proposed federal bill mirrored actions by the states, and it is helpful to provide some details of it. The federal bill would have provided for imposition of the death penalty for the crimes of murder, treason, and espionage. The death penalty would have been imposed by a jury following a separate penalty trial. The jury could impose the death penalty only if it found present one or more of the "aggravating factors" listed below, and none of the "mitigating factors":

Aggravating Factors
A. Treason and Espionage
  1. Defendant has been convicted of another such offense, for which a sentence of death or life imprisonment was authorized.
  2. Defendant created grave risk of substantial danger to the national security.
  3. Defendant created a grave risk of death to another person.

B. Murder
  1. The death, or injury resulting in death, occurs during the commission, or flight from eight specified offenses: escape, espionage, three explosive offenses involving personal injury or property damage, kidnapping, treason, and aircraft hijacking.
  2. Conviction of another offense, either state or federal, for which the sentence of death or life imprisonment was authorized by statute.
  3. Previous conviction of two or more separate offenses involving serious bodily harm.
  4. Defendant created grave risk of death to another person in addition to the victim.
  5. Crime was committed in an especially heinous, cruel, or depraved manner.
  6. Defendant paid for the crime to be committed.
  7. Defendant was paid to commit the crime.
  8. The victim was the president, vice-president, or another listed government official.

Mitigating Factors—Applicable to All Covered Offenses: Murder, Treason, and Espionage
  1. Defendant was under the age of eighteen at the time of the commission of the offense.
  2. Defendant's mental capacity was significantly impaired.
  3. Defendant acted under unusual and substantial duress.
  4. Defendant had a relatively minor part in the crime in which the killing was committed by another participant.
  5. The defendant could not reasonably have foreseen that his conduct would cause or create a great risk of causing death.

In 1976, the Supreme Court decided five death penalty cases, one of which was *Gregg v. Georgia*. The facts of the case were not seriously disputed. Gregg was convicted of the armed robbery and gruesome murder of the

---

[1]Ten states have formally abolished the death penalty, beginning with Michigan in 1846, Rhode Island in 1852, and Wisconsin in 1853. Five states have neither abolished the death penalty formally nor enacted or reenacted it.

occupants of a car in which he was riding as a hitchhiker. In a separate penalty trial, following conviction, the jury was instructed by the judge *not* to impose the death penalty unless it found at least one of the following: (1) that the murder was committed during the commission of a felony; (2) that the murder was committed for the purpose of receiving the victims' money and the automobile; (3) that the murder was outrageously and wantonly vile, inhuman, and depraved. (Georgia law lists ten possible aggravating circumstances, from which the trial judge selected these three.)

The jury found the first two conditions to be true, found no mitigating circumstances, and imposed the death penalty. The Georgia Supreme Court affirmed both the convictions and the death penalty for murder after reviewing the appropriateness of the penalty in comparison to other capital punishment cases, as provided for by the statute. The death penalty for robbery was reversed because few such sentences had ever been imposed or carried out. Under Georgia law, amended after the *Furman* decision, capital punishment could be imposed for six crimes: murder, kidnapping for ransom or where the victim is harmed, armed robbery, rape, treason, and aircraft hijacking. The Supreme Court granted certiorari.

Two of the five cases heard at the same time involved statutes that imposed a mandatory death penalty upon conviction of certain crimes. Thus, the Court had before it a range of responses to the *Furman* decision. Professor Anthony Amsterdam and Jack Greenberg of the Legal Defense Fund, arguing for the petitioners, claimed that these statutes still violated the *Furman* ruling, that what they established (in the nonmandatory states) was an elaborate winnowing process under which most persons would still avoid the death penalty. Thus, they said, there was still impermissible discretion. Where the death penalty was mandatory for certain crimes, they argued, there was still excessive discretion in the entire criminal process, beginning with the decision to arrest and ending with the sentence and opportunities for executive clemency.[2] They argued

that because death was "unique," special precautions must be taken to prevent arbitrariness, above and beyond the limits that applied to noncapital offenses. The same argument was applied to the deterrence issue. Because death was unique, the state had to meet an extraordinary burden of proof ("strict scrutiny") in demonstrating that capital punishment was an effective deterrent and that there was no equally effective alternative. Life imprisonment, they claimed, was no less effective.

In oral argument before the Court, Justice Powell asked: "Is there any crime that merits the death penalty, e.g. Nazi genocide?" Amsterdam replied: "My first response is to say yes, but applying the 8th Amendment standard my answer is No!" Powell responded: "Suppose a terrorist destroys New York City with a hydrogen bomb?" Amsterdam: "The answer is still no. Such crimes can be better prevented through police methods than through fear of punishment."

It was also argued that the death penalty, per se, violates the Eighth and Fourteenth Amendments because it does not serve the ends of rehabilitation, moral reinforcement, specific deterrence, general deterrence, and retribution. The Legal Defense Fund (LDF) claimed that the death penalty was tolerated only because it was so rarely imposed and that (following Marshall's opinion in *Furman*) if citizens really knew the facts about the way death was imposed, and how randomly it was carried out, they would no longer tolerate its imposition.

Finally, the issue of the Supreme Court's role was addressed. The four dissenters in *Furman* had argued that whether or not to impose the death penalty was primarily a legislative decision, to which the Court should defer. To this, the LDF's response was that the purpose of the Bill of Rights was precisely to "withdraw certain subjects from the vicissitudes of political controversy" and to impose limits on legislative choices. If the mere fact of legislative authorization of a punishment establishes its conformity to the Eighth Amendment, then that amendment would be little more than good advice.

The Solicitor General of the United States,

---

[2]Charles L. Black Jr., *Capital Punishment: The Inevitability of Caprice and Mistake* (New Haven: Yale University Press, 1974).

Robert Bork, appeared as amicus at the invitation of the Court. He argued in favor of the constitutionality of the death penalty. It was clearly anticipated by the words of the Fifth Amendment, he said, and in the 1970s, it was not outside the mainstream of penalties nor contrary to the moral judgment of the people. Nor, he claimed, is it disproportionate to the offense. As to the deterrence argument, Bork interpreted the mountains of evidence as establishing that the death penalty might have some effect. Legislatures were entitled to follow the dictate of common sense that deterrence increases as the costs of committing a crime also increase.

One of the problems confronting the Court was the inconsistency between *Furman* and *McGautha-Crampton*. *McGautha* held that neither standards nor a separate penalty trial were required for imposition of the death penalty and that discretion was permissible and desirable. The common denominator of the five opinions of the justices voting in the majority in *Furman* was randomness and arbitrariness. This could be "cured" either by invariable mandatory imposition of the death penalty *or* by requiring standards and more procedural due process (such as a separate penalty trial). Another cure would be to overrule one of the two decisions, and Bork argued that *Furman* should be overruled.]

MR. JUSTICE STEWART, MR. JUSTICE POWELL, and MR. JUSTICE STEVENS announced the judgment of the Court and filed an opinion delivered by MR. JUSTICE STEWART.

. . .

We address initially the basic contention that the punishment of death for the crime of murder is, under all circumstances, "cruel and unusual" in violation of the Eighth and Fourteenth Amendments of the Constitution. . . .

The Court on a number of occasions has both assumed and asserted the constitutionality of capital punishment. In several cases that assumption provided a necessary foundation for the decision, as the Court was asked to decide whether a particular method of carrying out a capital sentence would be allowed to stand under the Eighth Amendment. But until *Furman* v. *Georgia* . . . (1972), the Court never confronted squarely the fundamental claim that the punishment of death always, regardless of the enormity of the offense or the procedure followed in imposing the sentence, is cruel and unusual punishment in violation of the Constitution. Although this issue was presented and addressed in *Furman,* it was not resolved by the Court. Four Justices would have held that capital punishment is not unconstitutional *per se;* two Justices would have reached the opposite conclusion; and three Justices, while agreeing that the statutes then before the Court were invalid as applied, left open the question whether such punishment may ever be imposed. We now hold that the punishment of death does not invariably violate the Constitution.

. . .

The substantive limits imposed by the Eighth Amendment on what can be made criminal and punished were discussed in *Robinson* v. *California* . . . (1962). The Court found unconstitutional a state statute that made the status of being addicted to a narcotic drug a criminal offense. It held, in effect, that it is "cruel and unusual" to impose any punishment at all for the mere status of addiction. The cruelty in the abstract of the actual sentence imposed was irrelevant: "Even one day in prison would be cruel and unusual punishment for the 'crime' of having a common cold." Most recently, in *Furman* v. *Georgia* (1972), three Justices in separate concurring opinions found the Eighth Amendment applicable to procedures employed to select convicted defendants for the sentence of death.

It is clear from the foregoing precedents that the Eighth Amendment has not been regarded as a static concept. As Chief Justice Warren said, in an oft-quoted phrase, "[t]he Amendment must draw its meaning from the evolving standards of decency that mark the progress of a maturing society." *Trop* v. *Dulles* . . . Thus, an assessment of contemporary values concerning the infliction of a challenged sanction is relevant to the application of the Eighth Amendment. As we develop below more fully, this assessment does not call for a subjective judgment. It requires rather, than we look to objective indicia that reflect the public attitude toward a given sanction.

But our cases also make clear that public perceptions of standards of decency with respect to criminal sanctions was not conclusive. A penalty also must accord with "the dignity of man," which is the "basic concept underlying the Eighth Amendment" (plurality opinion). This means, at least, that the punishment not be "excessive." When a form of punishment in the abstract (in this case, whether capital punishment may ever be imposed as a sanction for murder) rather than in the particular (the propriety of death as a penalty to be applied to a specific defendant for a specific crime) is under consideration, the inquiry into "excessiveness" has two aspects. First the punishment must not involve the unnecessary and wanton infliction of pain. . . . Second, the punishment must not be grossly out of proportion to the severity of the crime. . . .

Of course, the requirements of the Eighth Amendment must be applied with an awareness of the limited role to be played by the courts. This does not mean that judges have no role to play, for the Eighth Amendment is a restraint upon the exercise of legislative power. . . .

But, while we have an obligation to insure that constitutional bounds are not overreached, we may not act as judges as we might as legislators.

Courts are not representative bodies. They are not designed to be a good reflex of a democratic society. Their judgment is best informed, and therefore most dependable, within narrow limits. Their essential quality is detachment, founded on independence. History teaches that the independence of the judiciary is jeopardized when courts become embroiled in the passions of the day and assume primary responsibility in choosing between competing political, economic and social pressures. Dennis v. United States, . . . (1951) (Frankfurter, J., concurring in affirmance).

Therefore in assessing a punishment selected by a democratically elected legislature against the constitutional measure, we presume its validity. We may not require the legislature to select the least severe penalty possible so long as the penalty selected is not cruelly inhumane or disproportionate to the crime involved. And a heavy burden rests on those who would attack the judgment of the representatives of the people.

This is true in part because the constitutional test is intertwined with an assessment of contemporary standards and the legislative judgment weighs heavily in ascertaining such standards. . . .

In the discussion to this point we have sought to identify the principles and considerations that guide a court in addressing an Eighth Amendment claim. We now consider specifically whether the sentence of death for the crime of murder is a *per se* violation of the Eighth and Fourteenth Amendments to the Constitution. We note first that history and precedent strongly support a negative answer to this question. . . .

The petitioners in the capital cases before the Court today renew the "standards of decency" argument, but developments during the four years since *Furman* have undercut substantially the assumptions upon which their argument rested. Despite the continuing debate, dating back to the 19th century, over the morality and utility of capital punishment, it is now evident that a large proportion of American society continues to regard it as an appropriate and necessary criminal sanction.

The most marked indication of society's endorsement of the death penalty for murder is the legislative response to *Furman*. The legislatures of at least 35 states have enacted new statutes that provide for the death penalty for at least some crimes that result in the death of another person. And the Congress of the United States, in 1974, enacted a statute providing the death penalty for aircraft piracy that results in death. These recently adopted statutes have attempted to address the concerns expressed by the Court in *Furman* primarily (i) by specifying the factors to be weighed and the procedures to be followed in deciding when to impose a capital sentence, or (ii) by making the death penalty mandatory for specified crimes. But all of the post-*Furman* statutes make clear that capital punishment itself has not been rejected by the elected representatives of the people.

In the only statewide referendum occurring since *Furman* and brought to our attention, the people of California adopted a constitutional amendment that authorized capital punishment, in effect negating a prior ruling by the Supreme Court of California in *People* v. *Anderson* . . . (1972), that the death penalty violated the California Constitution.

. . . The Court has said that "one of the most important functions any jury can perform is making . . . a selection [between life imprisonment and death for a defendant convicted in a capital case] is to maintain a link between contemporary community values and the penal system." *Witherspoon* v. *Illinois* . . . (1968). It may be true that evolving standards have influenced juries in recent decades to be more discriminating in imposing the sentence of death. But the relative infrequency of jury verdicts imposing the death sentence does not indicate rejection of capital punishment *per se*. Rather, the reluctance of juries in many cases to impose the sentence may well reflect the humane feeling that this most irrevocable of sanctions should be reserved for a small number of extreme cases. . . . Indeed, the actions of juries in many States since *Furman* is fully compatible with the legislative judgments, reflected in the new statutes, as to the continued utility and necessity of capital punishment in appropriate cases. At the close of 1974 at least 254 persons had been sentenced to death since *Furman*, and by the end of March 1976, more than 460 persons were subject to death sentences.

As we have seen, however, the Eighth Amendment demands more than that a challenged punishment be acceptable to contemporary society. The Court also must ask whether it comports with the basic concept of human dignity at the core of the Amendment. Although we cannot "invalidate a category of penalties because we deem less severe penalties adequate to serve the ends of penology," . . . the sanction imposed cannot be so totally without penological justification that it results in the gratuitous infliction of suffering. . . .

The death penalty is said to serve two principal social purposes: retribution and deterrence of capital crimes by prospective offenders.

In part, capital punishment is an expression of society's moral outrage at particularly offensive conduct. This function may be unappealing to many, but it is essential in an ordered society that asks its citizens to rely on legal processes rather than self-help to vindicate their wrongs.

The instinct for retribution is part of the nature of man, and channeling that instinct in the administration of criminal justice serves an important purpose in promoting the stability of a society governed by law. When people begin to believe that organized society is unwilling or unable to impose upon criminal offenders the punishment they "deserve," then there are sown the seeds of anarchy—of self-help, vigilante justice, and lynch law. Furman v. Georgia *(Stewart, J., concurring).*

"Retribution is no longer the dominant objective of the criminal law," *Williams* v. *New York* . . . but neither is it a forbidden objective nor one inconsistent with our respect for the dignity of men. Indeed, the decision that capital punishment may be the appropriate sanction in extreme cases is an expression of the community's belief that certain crimes are themselves so grievous an affront to humanity that the only adequate response may be the penalty of death.

Statistical attempts to evaluate the worth of the death penalty as a deterrent to crimes by potential offenders have occasioned a great deal of debate. The results simply have been inconclusive. As one opponent of capital punishment has said:

". . . after all possible inquiry, including the probing of all possible methods of inquiry, we do not know, and for systematic and easily visible reasons cannot know, what the truth about this 'deterrent' effect may be. . . .

The inescapable flaw is . . . that social conditions in any state are not constant through time, and that social conditions are not the same in any two states. If an effect were observed (and the observed effects, one way or another, are not large) then one could not at all tell whether any of this effect is attributable to the presence or absence of capital

punishment. *A 'scientific'—that is to say, a soundly based—conclusion is simply impossible, and no methodological path out of this tangle suggests itself."* [C. Black, Capital Punishment: The Inevitability of Caprice and Mistake (1974).]

Although some of the studies suggest that the death penalty may not function as a significantly greater deterrent than lesser penalties, there is no convincing empirical evidence either supporting or refuting this view. We may nevertheless assume safely that there are murderers, such as those who act in passion, for whom the threat of death has little or no deterrent effect. But for many others, the death penalty undoubtedly is a significant deterrent. There are carefully contemplated murders, such as murder for hire, where the possible penalty of death may well enter into the cold calculus that precedes the decision to act. And there are some categories of murder, such as murder by a life prisoner, where other sanctions may not be adequate.

The value of capital punishment as a deterrent of crime is a complex factual issue the resolution of which properly rests with the legislatures, which can evaluate the results of statistical studies in terms of their own local conditions and with a flexibility of approach that is not available to the courts. . . . Indeed, many of the post-*Furman* statutes reflect just such a responsible effort to define those crimes and those criminals for which capital punishment is most probably an effective deterrent.

In sum, we cannot say that the judgment of the Georgia legislature that capital punishment may be necessary in some cases is clearly wrong. Considerations of federalism, as well as respect for the ability of a legislature to evaluate, in terms of its particular state, the moral consensus concerning the death penalty and its social utility as a sanction, require us to conclude, in the absence of more convincing evidence, that the infliction of death as a punishment for murder is not without justification and thus is not unconstitutionally severe.

Finally, we must consider whether the punishment of death is disproportionate in relation to the crime for which it is imposed. There is no question that death as a punishment is unique in its severity and irrevocability. . . . When a defendant's life is at stake, the Court has been particularly sensitive to ensure that every safeguard is observed. . . . But we are concerned here only with the imposition of capital punishment for the crime of murder, and when a life has been taken deliberately by the offender, we cannot say that the punishment is invariably disproportionate to the crime. It is an extreme sanction, suitable to the most extreme of crimes.

We hold that the death penalty is not a form of punishment that may never be imposed, regardless of the circumstances of the offense, regardless of the character of the offender, and regardless of the procedure followed in reaching the decision to impose it.

We now consider whether Georgia may impose the death penalty on the petitioner in this case.

While *Furman* did not hold that the infliction of the death penalty *per se* violates the Constitution's ban on cruel and unusual punishments, it did recognize that the penalty of death is different in kind from any other punishment imposed under our system of criminal justice. Because of the uniqueness of the death penalty, *Furman* held that it could not be imposed under sentencing procedures that created a substantial risk that it would be inflicted in an arbitrary and capricious manner.

Mr. Justice White concluded that "the death penalty is exacted with great infrequency even for the most atrocious crimes and . . . there is no meaningful basis for distinguishing the few cases in which it is imposed from the many cases in which it is not." . . . Indeed, the death sentences examined by the Court in *Furman* were "cruel and unusual in the same way that being struck by lightning is cruel and unusual. For, of all the people convicted of [capital crimes], many just as reprehensible as these, the petitioners [in *Furman* were] among a capriciously selected random handful upon which the sentence of death has in fact been imposed. . . . [T]he Eighth and Fourteenth Amendments cannot tolerate the infliction of a sentence of death under legal systems that permit this unique penalty to be so wantonly and so freakishly imposed."

Furman mandates that where discretion is afforded a sentencing body on a matter so grave as the determination of whether a human life should be taken or spared, that discretion must be suitably directed and limited so as to minimize the risk of wholly arbitrary and capricious action. . . .

In summary, the concerns expressed in *Furman* that the penalty of death not be imposed in an arbitrary or capricious manner can be met by a carefully drafted statute that ensures that the sentencing authority is given adequate information and guidance. As a general proposition these concerns are best met by a system that provides for a bifurcated proceeding at which the sentencing authority is apprised of the information relevant to the imposition of sentence and provided with standards to guide its use of the information.

We do not intend to suggest that only the above-described procedures would be permissible under *Furman* or that any sentencing system constructed along these general lines would inevitably satisfy the concerns of *Furman*, for each distinct system must be examined on an individual basis. Rather, we have embarked upon this general exposition to make clear that it is possible to construct capital-sentencing systems capable of meeting *Furman*'s constitutional concerns. . . .

. . . The basic concern of *Furman* centered on those defendants who were being condemned to death capriciously and arbitrarily. Under the procedures before the Court in that case, sentencing authorities were not directed to give attention to the nature or circumstances of the crime committed or to the character or record of the defendant. Left unguided, juries imposed the death sentence in a way that could only be called freakish. The new Georgia sentencing procedures, by contrast, focus the jury's attention on the particularized nature of the crime and the particularized characteristics of the individual defendant. While the jury is permitted to consider any aggravating or mitigating circumstances, it must find and identify at least one statutory aggravating factor before it may impose a penalty of death. In this way the jury's discretion is channeled. No longer can a jury wantonly and freakishly impose the death sentence; it is always circumscribed by the legislative guidelines. In addition, the review function of the Supreme Court of Georgia affords additional assurance that the concerns that prompted our decision in *Furman* are not present to any significant degree in the Georgia procedure applied here.

For the reasons expressed in this opinion, we hold that the statutory system under which Gregg was sentenced to death does not violate the Constitution. Accordingly, the judg-

ment of the Georgia Supreme Court is affirmed.

It is so ordered.

MR. JUSTICE WHITE, WITH WHOM THE CHIEF JUSTICE, AND MR. JUSTICE REHNQUIST JOIN, CONCURRING IN THE JUDGMENT (OMITTED).

MR. JUSTICE BRENNAN, DISSENTING (OMITTED).

MR. JUSTICE MARSHALL, DISSENTING (OMITTED).

[In two of the companion cases, *Proffitt* v. *Florida* and *Jurek* v. *Texas*, the death penalty statutes of those states, similar to the Georgia law, were also upheld by a 7-2 vote. Justices Brennan and Marshall again dissented. However, in the two remaining cases, *Woodson* v. *North Carolina* and *Roberts* v. *Louisiana*, mandatory death penalty statutes were held unconstitutional by a 5-4 vote. In *Woodson* and *Roberts* Justices Brennan and Marshall joined Justices Stewart, Powell, and Stevens to form the majority. Stewart, Powell, and Stevens argued that a mandatory death penalty was unduly harsh and rigid in that it failed to give consideration to any mitigating circumstances as to either the offense or the offender. But Brennan and Marshall did not join in a common opinion. Instead, they merely adhered to their dissents in *Gregg* that the death penalty was unconstitutional *per se*.

A year later, in a case also called *Roberts* v. *Louisiana* (1977), the same five justices held that a mandatory death penalty for the murder of a police officer or fire fighter was unconstitutional, for the same reasons articulated the previous year. The dissenters noted that the state had a special interest in protecting the lives and safety of law enforcement officers. The majority opinion suggested a number of possible mitigating factors, such as absence of a prior criminal record, emotional distress or disturbance, the age of the offender, the influence of alcohol or drugs, and some conceivable moral justification. Justice Rehnquist took special exception to the last factor:

. . . I cannot believe that States are constitutionally required to allow a defense, even at the sentencing stage, which depends on nothing more than the convict's moral belief that he was entitled to kill a peace officer in cold blood. John Wilkes Booth may well have thought he was morally justified in murdering Abraham Lincoln, whom, while fleeing from the stage of Ford's Theater, he characterized as a "tyrant"; I am appalled to believe that the Constitution would have required the government to allow him to argue that as a "mitigating factor" before it could sentence him to death if he were found guilty. I am equally appalled that a State would be required to instruct a jury that such individual beliefs must or should be considered as a possible balancing factor against the admittedly proper aggravating factor.

In another case in 1977, Coker v. Georgia, the Supreme Court held by a 7-2 margin that the Eighth Amendment prohibited imposition of the death penalty for rape of an adult woman. Such a penalty, the Court said, was disproportionate to the crime where no taking of life was involved. The fact that no life was taken was more important in the Court's thinking than was the jury's finding that a prior capital felony conviction and the occurrence of the rape in the course of an armed robbery were aggravating circumstances that justified the death penalty. Georgia was the only state to reenact the death penalty for rape in the post-Furman period, and this was the only case out of ten in which it had been imposed by the Georgia courts. The Supreme Court took note of this lack of public support for the death penalty in rape cases.

A brief synthesis of these cases might be stated as follows: Imposition of the death penalty for a serious crime involving the taking of human life is not unconstitutional, provided that the penalty is not mandatory, provided that the sentencing authority (judge or jury) is guided by explicit standards that take into account the aggravating or mitigating circumstances of the offense and the offender, and provided that there is provision for appellate review of the sentence. The Supreme Court clearly prefers a bifurcated trial and jury sentencing, but these are not constitutionally required. Needless to say, many questions remain unanswered.]

(4) Lockett v. Ohio (1978)

+Burger, Stewart, Marshall, Blackmun, Powell, Stevens
±White, Rehnquist
NP Brennan

[Sandra Lockett was convicted of aggravated murder with specifications and sentenced to death. She had driven the getaway car for a gang that had robbed a pawnshop. In the course of the robbery, a struggle had ensued, and the pawnbroker was killed. The chief witness against Lockett was a coparticipant who had agreed to plead guilty in return for a life sentence. Three times before and during the trial Lockett had refused prosecution offers to plead guilty to a lesser offense: first aggravated manslaughter, which carried a maximum twenty-five-year term, and then aggravated murder, which carried a maximum term of life imprisonment.

Under Ohio law, when a verdict of aggravated murder with specifications is returned, the trial judge must impose the death penalty unless, after considering the nature and circumstances of the offense and Lockett's "history, character and condition," he found by a preponderance of the evidence that (1) the victim had induced or facilitated the offense, (2) it was unlikely that Lockett would have committed the offense but for the fact that she "was under duress, coercion, or strong provocation," or (3) the offense was "primarily the product of [Lockett's] psychosis or mental deficiency." Presentence reports showed Lockett to be of average to low average intelligence and not suffering from mental deficiency. She had no prior major criminal offenses. The trial judge concluded that he "had no alternative, whether he liked the law or not," to imposing the death penalty.

The Supreme Court granted certiorari to consider whether the Ohio death penalty statute violated the Eighth and Fourteenth Amendments by too narrowly limiting the discretion of the sentencing authority to consider the circumstances of the crime and the character of the offender as mitigating circumstances.]

MR. CHIEF JUSTICE BURGER announced the judgment of the Court and delivered an opinion (on the question of the constitutionality of the death penalty statute) in which JUSTICES STEWART, POWELL, and STEVENS joined.

. . .

Lockett challenges the constitutionality of Ohio's death penalty statute on a number of grounds. We find it necessary to consider only her contention that her death sentence is invalid because the statute under which it was imposed did not permit the sentencing judge to consider, as mitigating factors, her character, prior record, age, lack of specific intent to cause death, and her relatively minor part in the crime. . . .

Prior to *Furman* v. *Georgia* . . . (1972), every state that authorized capital punishment had abandoned mandatory death penalties, and instead permitted the jury unguided and unrestrained discretion regarding the imposition of the death penalty in a particular capital case. Mandatory death penalties had proven unsatisfactory, as the plurality noted in *Woodson* v. *North Carolina* (1976), in part because juries "with some regularity disregarded their oaths and refused to convict defendants where a death sentence was the automatic consequence of a guilty verdict."

This Court had never intimated prior to *Furman* that discretion in sentencing offended the Constitution. . . . As recently as *McGautha* v. *California* . . . (1971), the Court had specifically rejected the contention that discretion in imposing the death penalty violated the fundamental standards of fairness embodied in Fourteenth Amendment due process, . . . and had asserted that States were entitled to assume that "jurors confronted with the truly awesome responsibility of decreeing death for a fellow human [would] act with due regard for the consequences of their decision." . . .

The constitutional status of discretionary sentencing in capital cases changed abruptly, however, as a result of the separate opinions supporting the judgment in *Furman*. The question in *Furman* was whether "the imposition and carrying out of the death penalty [in the cases before the Court] constituted cruel and unusual punishment in violation of the Eighth and Fourteenth Amendments." . . . Two Justices concluded that the Eighth Amendment prohibited the death penalty altogether and on that ground voted to reverse the judgments sustaining the death penalties. . . . Three Justices were unwilling to hold the death penalty *per se* unconstitutional under the Eighth and Fourteenth Amendments, but voted to reverse the judgments on other grounds. In separate opinions, the three concluded that discretionary sentencing, unguided by legislatively defined standards, violated the Eighth Amendment because it was "pregnant with discrimination," . . . because it permitted the death penalty to be "wantonly" and "freakishly" imposed, . . . and because it imposed the death penalty with "great infrequency" and afforded "no meaningful basis for distinguishing the few cases in which it [was] imposed from the many cases in which it [was] not," . . . Thus, what had been approved under the Due Process Clause of the Fourteenth Amendment in *McGautha* became impermissible under the Eighth and Fourteenth Amendments by virtue of the judgment in *Furman*. . . .

Four years after *Furman*, we considered Eighth Amendment issues posed by five of the post-*Furman* death penalty statutes. Four Justices took the position that all five statutes complied with the Constitution; two Justices took the position that none of them complied. Hence, the disposition of each case varied according to the votes of a plurality of three Justices who delivered a joint opinion in each of the five cases upholding the constitutionality of the Statutes of Georgia, Florida, and Texas, and holding those of North Carolina and Louisiana unconstitutional.

The plurality reasoned that to comply with *Furman,* sentencing procedures should not create "a substantial risk that the death penalty [will] be inflicted in an arbitrary and capricious manner." In the view of the plurality, however, *Furman* did not require that all sentencing discretion be eliminated, but only that it be "directed and limited," so that the death penalty would be imposed in a more consistent and rational manner and so that there would be a "meaningful basis for distinguishing the . . . cases in which it is imposed from . . . the cases in which it is not." The plurality also concluded, in the course of invalidating North Carolina's mandatory death penalty statute, that the sentencing process must permit consideration of the "character and record of the individual offender and the circumstances of the particular offense as a constitutionally indispensable part of the process of inflicting the penalty of death," *Woodson* v. *North Carolina,* . . . in order to ensure the reliability, under Eighth Amendment standards, of the determination that "death is the appropriate punishment in a specific case." . . .

In the last decade, many of the States have been obliged to revise their death penalty statutes in response to the various opinions supporting the judgments in *Furman, supra,* and *Gregg, supra,* and its companion cases. The signals from this Court have not, however, always been easy to decipher. The States now deserve the clearest guidance that the Court can provide; we have an obligation to reconcile previously differing views in order to provide that guidance.

With that obligation in mind we turn to Lockett's attack on the Ohio statute. Essentially she contends that the Eighth and Fourteenth Amendments require that the sentencer be given a full opportunity to consider mitigating circumstances in capital cases and that the Ohio statute does not comply with that requirement. . . .

We begin by recognizing that the concept of individualized sentencing in criminal cases generally, although not constitutionally required, has long been accepted in this country. . . . Consistent with that concept, sentencing judges traditionally have taken a wide range of factors into account. That States have authority to make aiders and abettors equally responsible, as a matter of law, with principals, or to enact felony murder statutes is beyond constitutional challenge. But the definition of crimes generally has not been thought automatically to dictate what should be the proper penalty. . . . And where sentencing discretion is granted, it generally has been agreed that the sentencing judge's "possession of the fullest information possible concerning the defendant's life and characteristics" is [h]ighly relevant—if *not essential*—[to the] selection of an appropriate sentence. . . ." . . .

Most would agree that "the 19th century movement away from mandatory death sentences marked an enlightened introduction of flexibility into the sentencing process." . . .

Although legislatures remain free

to decide how much discretion in sentencing should be reposed in the judge or jury in noncapital cases, the plurality opinion in *Woodson*, after reviewing the historical repudiation of mandatory sentencing in capital cases. . . . concluded that:

in capital cases the fundamental respect for humanity underlying the Eighth Amendment . . . requires consideration of the character and record of the individual offender and the circumstances of the particular offense as a constitutionally indispensable part of the process of inflicting the penalty of death.

That declaration rested "on the predicate that the penalty of death is qualitatively different" from any other sentence. . . . We are satisfied that this qualitative difference between death and other penalties calls for a greater degree of reliability when the death sentence is imposed. The mandatory death penalty statute in *Woodson* was held invalid because it permitted *no* consideration of "relevant facets of the character and record of the individual offender or the circumstances of the particular offense." The plurality did not attempt to indicate, however, which facets of an offender or his offense it deemed "relevant" in capital sentencing or what degree of consideration of "relevant facets" it would require.

We are now faced with those questions and we conclude that the Eighth and Fourteenth Amendments require that the sentencer, in all but the rarest kind of capital case, [We express no opinion as to whether the need to deter certain kinds of homicide would justify a mandatory death sentence as, for example, when a prisoner—or escapee—under a life sentence is found guilty of murder. See *Roberts* (Harry) v. *Louisiana* . . . (1977).]not be precluded from considering as a *mitigating factor,*

any aspect of a defendant's character or record and any of the circumstances of the offense that the defendant proffers as a basis for a sentence less than death. We recognize that, in noncapital cases, the established practice of individualized sentences rests not on constitutional commands but public policy enacted into statutes. The considerations that account for the wide acceptance of individualization of sentences in noncapital cases surely cannot be thought less important in capital cases. Given that the imposition of death by public authority is so profoundly different from all other penalties, we cannot avoid the conclusion that an individualized decision is essential in capital cases. The need for treating each defendant in a capital case with that degree of respect due the uniqueness of the individual is far more important than in noncapital cases. A variety of flexible techniques—probation, parole, work furloughs, to name a few—and various post conviction remedies, may be available to modify an initial sentence of confinement in noncapital cases. The nonavailability of corrective or modifying mechanisms with respect to an executed capital sentence underscores the need for individualized consideration as a constitutional requirement in imposing the death sentence.

There is no perfect procedure for deciding in which cases governmental authority should be used to impose death. But a statute that prevents the sentencer in all capital cases from giving independent mitigating weight to aspects of the defendant's character and record and to circumstances of the offense proffered in mitigation creates the risk that the death penalty will be imposed in spite of factors which may call for a less severe penalty. When the choice is between life and death, that risk is unacceptable and incompatible with the commands of the Eighth and Fourteenth Amendments.

The Ohio death penalty statute does not permit the type of individualized consideration of mitigating factors we now hold to be required by the Eighth and Fourteenth Amendments in capital cases. Its constitutional infirmities can best be understood by comparing it with the statutes upheld in *Gregg, Proffitt,* and *Zurek.*

In upholding the Georgia statute in *Gregg,* Justices STEWART, POWELL, and STEVENS noted that the statute permitted the jury "to consider any aggravating or mitigating circumstances," . . . and that the Georgia Supreme Court had approved "open and far ranging argument" in presentence hearings. . . . Although the Florida statute approved in *Proffitt* contained a list of mitigating factors, six members of this Court assumed, in approving the statute, that the range of mitigating factors listed in the statute was not exclusive. . . . In this regard the statute now before us is significantly different. Once a defendant is found guilty of aggravated murder with at least one of seven specified aggravating circumstances, the death penalty must be imposed unless, considering "the nature and circumstances of the offense and the history, character, and conditions of the offender," the sentencing judge determines that at least one of the following mitigating circumstances is established by a preponderance of the evidence:

(1) *The victim of the offense induced or facilitated it.*
(2) *It is unlikely that the offense would have been committed but for the fact that the offender was under duress, coercion, or strong provocation.*
(3) *The offense was primarily the product of the offender's psychosis or mental deficiency, though such condition is insufficient to establish the defense of insanity.*

The Ohio Supreme Court has concluded that there is no constitutional distinction between the statute approved in *Proffitt, supra,* and Ohio's statute . . . because the mitigating circumstances in Ohio's statute are "liberally construed in favor of the accused," . . . and because the sentencing judge or judges may consider factors such as the age and criminal record of the defendant in determining whether any of the mitigating circumstances is established. . . . But even under the Ohio court's construction of the statute, only the three factors specified in the statute can be considered in mitigation of the defendant's sentence. . . . We see, therefore, that once it is determined that the victim did not induce or facilitate the offense, that the defendant did not act under duress or coercion, and that the offense was not primarily the product of the defendant's mental deficiency, the Ohio statute mandates the sentence of death. The absence of direct proof that the defendant intended to cause the death of the victim is relevant for mitigating purposes only if it is determined that it sheds some light on one of the three statutory mitigating factors. Similarly, consideration of a defendant's comparatively minor role in the offense, or age, would generally not be permitted, as such, to affect the sentencing decision.

The limited range of mitigating circumstances which may be considered by the sentencer under the Ohio statute is incompatible with the Eighth and Fourteenth Amendments. To meet constitutional requirements, a death penalty statute must not preclude consideration of relevant mitigating factors.

Accordingly, the judgment under

review is reversed to the extent that it sustains the imposition of the death penalty; the case is remanded for further proceedings.

MR. JUSTICE BRENNAN TOOK NO PART IN THE CONSIDERATION OR DECISION OF THIS CASE.
MR. JUSTICE BLACKMUN, CONCURRING (OMITTED).
MR. JUSTICE MARSHALL, CONCURRING (OMITTED).
MR. JUSTICE WHITE, CONCURRING IN PART, DISSENTING IN PART (OMITTED).
MR. JUSTICE REHNQUIST, CONCURRING IN PART, DISSENTING IN PART (OMITTED).

(5) A Note on Public Opinion Toward the Death Penalty

Earlier in this section we reported public opinion data about the death penalty, up to the *Furman* decision (see p. 931). From November 1972 until April 1976 no questions on the death penalty were reported in the Gallup Poll. A Gallup survey in April, 1976 (at a time when there was considerable public attention focused on the forthcoming *Gregg* case) reported 65% in favor of imposing the death penalty on those convicted of murder, 28% opposed, and 7% undecided. This represented a 23 year high total of support for capital punishment. A similar question asked in April, 1978 (after the execution of Gary Gilmore) showed a slight drop to 62% in favor, 27% opposed, and 11% undecided. Those in favor declined slightly from 1976, but opposition reached its lowest level since 1953. In the 1978 survey, men (70%) favored the death penalty more than women (55%), whites (64%) more than nonwhites (42%), and Republicans (72%) more

than Democrats (59%). There were no significant differences between college and high school graduates or between respondents in different age groups.

Murder was, however, the only crime for which the death penalty was supported by a majority. Only 32% supported it for persons convicted of rape, with 56% opposed (and no differences between men and women respondents); 37% supported the death penalty for those convicted of hijacking, and 36% favored capital punishment for those convicted of treason.

(6) Tom Wicker, "Routine of Death"

Gov. Robert Graham of Florida signed warrants last week for the execution of two men convicted of murder in that state. The courts will probably intervene in their cases, but if not, the two will go to the electric chair at 7 A.M. Wednesday, June 27, less than a month after the State of Florida executed John Spenkelink by sending three massive surges of electricity through his body over a period of six minutes.

Governor Graham thus seems determined to make good his plan that executions should become "routine," taking place at the rate of one or two a month during his administration. He has the raw material, since there are 125 people on Death Row in Florida (out of a total of 513 in the nation, 415 of them in the South, with 108 in Texas and 74 in Georgia).

But if the Governor does make executions routine, which he may have the power to do, he will only make a further mockery of another statement he made in sending John Spenkelink to the chair: "There will

Reprinted from The New York Times, June 24, 1979.

be less brutality in our society if it is made clear we value human life."

The brutal spectacle of a six-minute execution carried out while part of the crowd outside Florida State Prison was shouting, "Go, Sparky!" (as some Floridians jovially term the electric chair) exposed this Orwellian reasoning for what it was. The Chicago Tribune, not known for soft-heartedness, pointed out what Governor Graham seemed not to realize, that, "electrocution is a horrible way to die" and that in the Spenkelink case it came at the end of an "inhuman charade" of appeals, stays, hearings, etc., while the condemned man waited to know his fate.

Two more such executions—let alone the one or two a month the Governor wants to make routine—will only add their own brutality to that which is already commonplace in Florida, a state with a high rate of crime and violence.

And taking the lives of those who have taken life can't make clear that "we value life"; under such a policy the state usurps godlike powers to decide when life may be taken legitimately. For one murder, yes, for another murder, no.

In the exercise of such power, there can be no foolproof process, no universal rationality, no escape from caprice, prejudice, accident, error—hence no value placed on life; because whatever procedure may be devised will always be administered by fallible humans miscast as gods. John Spenkelink, for example, died in Sparky's grim embrace; Frank Brumm, who cooperated with the prosecution, confessed to participating in the same murder and went free.

Charles W. Profitt, whose death warrant Governor Graham signed this week, has no criminal record prior to the murder for which he was convicted. An alcoholic who came from a broken home, he was convicted of stabbing a man during a robbery, as the man slept beside his wife. But the wife cannot identify Charles Profitt as the murderer, fingerprints found at the scene were not his, and the wife has asked that he not be executed.

Even if there were a valid case for capital punishment in the abstract, how can death be justified in such ambiguous circumstances? For execution is never abstract. Governor Graham himself has just recommended clemency for two other men convicted of murder; in one of these cases, that of Leo Alford, much evidence has been found, since his conviction, to show that he is innocent. What good would that have done him, had he been executed only a few months ago?

Nor does capital punishment value human life by deterring others from taking it. No evidence has ever been found to justify the deterrent theory; the Burger Court rejected it in 1976 as unprovable; and every serious student of criminal justice agrees that the only real deterrent to crime is swift and certain punishment. But nothing is less swift or certain than legal execution; John Spenkelink was on Death Row for six years.

Capital punishment does not even respond efficiently to the public's justifiable fear of crime. No death penalty law in any state applies to those crimes of which people are most frequently the victim—robbery, burglary, mugging, assault and rape. Many Americans are constantly vulnerable to these outrages, comparatively few need fear murder, the only crime punishable by death.

But if no amount of rhetoric can "make clear" that human life is given value by the death penalty, its racial and economic taint is undeniable.

The clear pattern of capital sentences in America is that those who receive them are nearly all poor; they are overwhelmingly black, when measured against the black percentage of population; and they are almost all convicted of killing whites.

Against such a background, the assertion that electrocuting a John Spenkelink or a Charles Profitt is an act that values life cannot disguise the truth—that execution is a popular sop fed to a fearful public that wants something drastic done about crime. And no prosecutor, judge or governor has to throw a switch that sends 2,000 volts jolting through the body of another human being; if any did, there would be a quick end to execution and to shabby moral pretense.

F. Due Process for Prisoners

(1) Wolff v. McDonnell (1974)

+White, Burger, Stewart, Blackmun, Powell, Rehnquist
±Brennan, Marshall
−Douglas

[The first prison in America was established in Philadelphia in 1790. All inmates were kept in perpetual solitary confinement; they were permitted to communicate only with religious advisors and official visitors. Subsequent reforms permitted prisoners to work with other prisoners, though still under an edict of silence, and return to solitary cells at night. Discipline for violations was harsh, often brutal. The rules and conditions of prison life have been softened over the years. Yet there is, if anything, more criticism today of prison conditions. Things may be better, and yet our expectations have increased regarding what rights prisoners have.

Until very recently, American courts have followed a "hands-off" policy with regard to the administration of penal institutions. Today, that attitude has been replaced by an increasing concern for the legal and constitutional rights of prisoners.

Expressions of this concern can be found in the willingness of most courts to tackle the multitude of "prison" cases now clogging dockets everywhere and in the widespread acceptance of the principle that prisoners, too, have constitutional rights. Perhaps the best symbol of this concern was the 1970 decision of a federal court that the entire prison system of Arkansas was inhumane and thus a violation of the Eighth Amendment.

What is required is a policy that acknowledges the legitimate needs of prison administrators while at the same time according maximum recognition to the constitutional rights of inmates. Just where the line should be drawn, and what these rights are, is the subject of ever-increasing litigation.

This case was brought under the civil rights statutes by inmates of the Nebraska Penal and Correctional Complex. They alleged that prison disciplinary proceedings violated their federal constitutional rights, that the inmate legal assistance program was inadequate, and that mail regulations were too restrictive.]

MR. JUSTICE WHITE delivered the opinion of the Court. . . .

. . .

The State of Nebraska asserts that the procedure for disciplining prison inmates for serious misconduct is a matter of policy raising no constitutional issue. If the position implies that prisoners in state institutions are wholly without the protection of the Constitution and the Due Process Clause, it is plainly untenable. Lawful imprisonment necessarily makes unavailable many rights and privileges of the ordinary citizen, a "retraction justified by the considerations underlying our penal system." *Price* v. *Johnson* . . . (1948). But though his rights may be diminished by the needs and exigencies of the institutional environment, a prisoner is not wholly stripped of constitutional protections when he is imprisoned for crime. There is no iron curtain drawn between the Constitution and the prisons of this country.

Prisoners have been held to enjoy substantial religious freedom under the First and Fourteenth Amendments. . . . He retains his right of access to the courts. . . . Prisoners are protected under the Equal Protection Clause of the Fourteenth Amendment from invidious discrimination based on race. . . . The prisoner may also claim the protections of the Due Process Clause. He may not be deprived of his life, liberty or property without due process of law. . . .

. . . Of course, as we have indicated, that a prisoner retains rights under the Due Process Clause in no way implies that this right is not subject to restrictions imposed by the nature of the regime to which he has been lawfully committed. . . . Prison disciplinary proceedings are not part of a criminal prosecution, and the full panoply of rights due a defendant in such proceedings does not apply. . . . In sum, there must be mutual accommodation between institutional needs and objectives and the provisions of the Constitution that are of general application. . . .

. . . We also reject the assertion of the State that whatever may be true of the Due Process Clause in general or of other rights protected by that clause against state infringement, the interest of prisoners in disciplinary procedures is not included in that "liberty" protected by the Fourteenth Amendment. It is true that the Constitution itself does not guarantee good-time credit for satisfactory behavior while in prison. But here the State itself has not only provided a statutory right to good-time but also specifies that it is to be forfeited only for serious misbehavior. Nebraska may have the authority to create, or not, a right to a shortened prison sentence through the accumulation of credits for good behavior, and it is true that the Due Process Clause does not require a hearing "in every conceivable case of government impairment of private interest." *Cafeteria Workers* v. *McElroy* . . . (1961). But the State having created the right to good time and itself recognizing that its deprivation is a sanction authorized for major misconduct, the prisoner's interest has real substance and is sufficiently embraced within Fourteenth Amendment "liberty" to entitle him to those minimum procedures appropriate under the circumstances and required by the Due Process Clause to insure that the state-created right is not arbitrarily abrogated. . . .

. . . This analysis as to liberty parallels the accepted due-process analysis as to property. The Court has consistently said that some kind of hearing is required at some time before a person is finally deprived of his property interests. *Anti Fascist Committee* v. *McGrath* . . . (1951) (Frankfurther, J., concurring). The requirement for some kind of a hearing applies to the taking of private property, the revocation of licenses, . . . the operation of state dispute settlement mechanisms, when one person seeks to take property from another, or to government-created jobs held absent "cause" for termination, *Board of Regents* v. *Roth* . . . (1972).

We think a person's liberty is equally protected, even when the liberty itself is a statutory creation of the State. The touchstone of due process is protection of the individual against arbitrary action of government, . . . Since prisoners in Nebraska can only lose good-time credits if they are guilty of serious misconduct, the determination of whether such behavior has occurred becomes critical, and the minimum requirements of procedural due process appropriate for the circumstances must be observed.

As found by the District Court, the

Procedures employed are (1) a preliminary conference with the chief corrections supervisor and the charging party, where the prisoner is informed of the misconduct charge and engages in preliminary discussion on its merits; (2) a conduct report is then prepared and a hearing held before the Adjustment Committee, the disciplinary body of the prison, where the report is read to the inmate; and (3) the opportunity at the hearing to ask questions of the charging party. The State contends that the procedures already provided are adequate. The Court of Appeals held them insufficient and ordered the due-process requirements outlined in *Morrissey* and *Scarpelli* be satisfied in serious disciplinary cases at the Prison.

Morrissey [v. *Brewer* (1972)] held that due process imposed certain minimum procedural requirements which must be satisfied before parole could finally be revoked. These procedures were:

(a) written notice of the claimed violations of parole; (b) disclosure to the parolee of evidence against him; (c) opportunity to be heard in person and to present witnesses and documentary evidence; (d) the right to confront and cross-examine adverse witnesses (unless the hearing officer specifically finds good cause for not allowing confrontation); (e) a "neutral and detached" hearing body such as a traditional parole board, members of which need not be judicial officers or lawyers; and (f) a written statement by the factfinders as to the evidence relied on and reasons for revoking parole. . . .

. . . The Court did not reach the question as to whether the parolee is entitled to the assistance of retained counsel or to appointed counsel, if he is indigent. Following the decision in *Morrissey*, in *Gagnon* v. *Scarpelli*

. . . (1973), the Court held the requirements of due process established for parole revocation were applicable to probation revocation proceedings. The Court added to the required minimum procedures of *Morrissey* the right to counsel, where a probationer makes a request, "based on a timely and colorable claim (i) that he has not committed the alleged violation of the conditions upon which he is at liberty; or (ii) that, even if the violation is a matter of public record or is uncontested, there are substantial reasons which justified or mitigated the violations and make revocation inappropriate, and that the reasons are complex or otherwise difficult to develop or present." . . . In doubtful cases, the agency was to consider whether the probationer appeared to be capable of speaking effectively for himself, . . . and a record was to be made of the grounds for refusing to appoint counsel.

We agree with neither the State nor the Court of Appeals: the Nebraska procedures are in some respects constitutionally deficient but the *Morrissey-Scarpelli* procedures need not in all respects be followed in disciplinary cases in state prisons. . . .

. . . We have often repeated that "[t]he very nature of the process negates any concept of inflexible procedures universally applicable to every imaginable situation." [C]onsideration of what procedures due process may require under any given set of circumstances must begin with a determination of the precise nature of the government function involved as well as of the private interest that has been affected by governmental action." . . . Viewed in this light it is immediately apparent that one cannot automatically apply procedural rules designed for free citizens in an open society, or for parolees or probationers under only limited restraints, to the very different situation presented by a disciplinary proceeding in a state prison.

Revocation of parole may deprive the parolee of only conditional liberty, but it nevertheless "inflicts a grievous loss on the parolee and often on others." . . . Simply put, revocation proceedings determine whether the parolee will be free or in prison, a matter of obvious great moment to him. For the prison inmate, the deprivation of good time is not the same immediate disaster that the revocation of the parole is for the parolee. The deprivation, very likely, does not then and there work any change in the conditions of his liberty. It can postpone the data of eligibility for parole and extend the maximum term to be served, but it is not certain to do so, for good time may be restored. Even if not restored, it cannot be said with certainty that the actual date of parole will be affected; and if parole occurs, the extension of the maximum term resulting from loss of good time may affect only the termination of parole, and it may not even do that. The deprivation of good time is unquestionably a matter of considerable importance. The State reserves it as a sanction for serious misconduct, and we should not unrealistically discount its significance. But it is qualitatively and quantitatively different from the revocation of parole or probation.

In striking the balance that the Due Process Clause demands, however, we think the major consideration militating against adopting the full range of procedures suggested by *Morrissey* for alleged parole violators is the very different stake the State has in the structure and content of the prison disciplinary hearing. That the revocation of parole be justified and based on an accurate assessment of the facts is a critical matter to the State as well as the parolee; but the procedures by which it is determined whether the conditions of parole have been breached do not themselves threaten other important state interests, parole officers, the police or witnesses, at least no more so than in the case of the ordinary criminal trial. Prison disciplinary proceedings, on the other hand, take place in a closed, tightly controlled environment peopled by those who have chosen to violate the criminal law and who have been lawfully incarcerated for doing so. Some are first offenders, but many are recidivists who have repeatedly employed illegal and often very violent means to attain their ends. They may have little regard for the safety of others or their property or for the rules designed to provide an orderly and reasonably safe prison life. Although there are very many varieties of prisons with different degrees of security, we must realize that in many of them the inmates are closely supervised and their activities controlled around the clock. Guards and inmates co-exist in direct and intimate contact. Tension between them is unremitting. Frustration, resentment, and despair are commonplace. Relationships among the inmates are varied and complex and perhaps subject to the unwritten code that exhorts inmates not to inform on a fellow prisoner.

It is against this background that disciplinary proceedings must be structured by prison authorities; and it is against this background that we must make our constitutional judgments, realizing that we are dealing with the maximum security institution as well as those where security considerations are not so paramount.

Indeed, it is pressed upon us that the proceedings to ascertain and sanction misconduct themselves play a major role in furthering the institutional goal of modifying the behavior and value systems of prison inmates sufficiently to permit them to live within the law when they are released. Inevitably there is a great range of personality and character among those who have transgressed the criminal law. Some are more amenable to suggestion and persuasion than others. Some may be incorrigible and would merely disrupt and exploit the disciplinary process for their own ends. With some, rehabilitation may be best achieved by simulating procedures of a free society to the maximum possible extent; but with others, it may be essential that discipline be swift·and sure. In any event, it is argued, there would be great unwisdom in encasing the disciplinary procedures in an inflexible constitutional straitjacket that would necessarily call for adversary proceedings typical of the criminal trial, very likely raise the level of confrontation between staff and inmate and make more difficult the utilization of the disciplinary process as a tool to advance the rehabilitative goals of the institution. This consideration, along with the necessity to maintain an acceptable level of personal security in the institution, must be taken into account as we now examine in more detail the Nebraska procedures that the Court of Appeals found wanting.

. . . Two of the procedures that the Court held should be extended to parolees facing revocation proceedings are not, but must be, provided to prisoners in the Nebraska Complex if the minimum requirements of procedural due process are to be satisfied. These are advance written notice of the claimed violation and a written statement of the factfindings as to the evidence relied upon and the reasons for the disciplinary action taken. . . .

. . . We are also of the opinion that the inmate facing disciplinary proceedings should be allowed to call witnesses and present documentary evidence in his defense when permitting him to do so will not be unduly hazardous to institutional safety or correctional goals. Ordinarily, the right to present evidence is basic to a fair hearing; but the unrestricted right to call witnesses from the prison population carries obvious potential for disruption and for interference with the swift punishment that in individual cases may be essential to carrying out the correctional program of the institution. We should not be too ready to exercise oversight and put aside the judgment of prison administrators. . . . Prison officials must have the necessary discretion to keep the hearing within reasonable limits and to refuse to call witnesses that may create a risk of reprisal or undermine authority, as well as to limit access to other inmates to collect statements or to compile other documentary evidence. . . .

. . . Confrontation and cross-examination present greater hazards to institutional interests. If confrontation and cross-examination of those furnishing evidence against the inmate were to be allowed as a matter of course, as in criminal trials, there would be considerable potential for havoc inside the prison walls. Proceedings would inevitably be longer and tend to unmanageability. These procedures are essential in criminal trials where the accused, if found guilty, may be subjected to the most serious deprivations, *Pointer* v. *Texas* . . . (1965), or where a person may lose his job in the society, *Greene* v. *McElroy* . . . (1959). But they are not rights universally applicable to all hearings. . . . Rules of procedure may be shaped by consideration of the risks of error, . . . and should also be shaped by the consequences which will follow their adoption. Although some States do seem to allow cross-examination in disciplinary hearings, we are not apprised of the conditions under which the procedure may be curtailed; and it does not appear that confrontation and crossexamination are generally required. . . .

. . . Our conclusion that some, but not all, of the procedures specified in *Morrissey* and *Scarpelli* must accompany the deprivation of good time by state prison authorities is not graven in stone. As the nature of the prison disciplinary process changes in future years, circumstances may then exist which will require further consideration and reflection of this Court. It is our view, however, that the procedures we have now required in prison disciplinary proceedings represent a reasonable accommodation between the interests of the inmates and the needs of the institution.

. . . The Court of Appeals held that the due process requirements in prison disciplinary proceedings were to apply retroactively so as to require that prison records containing determination of misconduct, not in accord with required procedures, be expunged. We disagree and reverse on this point.

The question of retroactivity of new procedural rules affecting inquiries into infractions of prison discipline is effectively forclosed by this Court's ruling in *Morrissey* that the due process requirements there announced were to be "applicable to "future" revocation of Parole," . . . Despite the fact that procedures are related to the integrity of the fact-finding process, in the context of disciplinary proceedings, where less is generally at stake for an individual than at a criminal trial, great weight should be given to the significant impact a retroactivity ruling would have on the administration of all prisons in the country, and the reliance prison officials placed, in good faith, on prior law not requiring such procedures. During 1973, the Federal Government alone conducted 19,000 misconduct hearings, as compared with 1,173 parole revocation hearings, and 2,023 probation revocation hearings. If *Morrissey-Scarpelli* rules are not retroactive out of consideration for burden on federal and state officials, this case is a fortiori. We also note that a contrary holding would be very troublesome for the parole system since performance in prison is often a relevant criteria for parole. On the whole, we do not think that error was so pervasive in the system under the old procedures to warrant this cost or result.

The issue of the extent to which prison authorities can open and inspect incoming mail from attorneys to inmates, has been considerably narrowed in the course of this litigation. . . .

The State now concedes that it cannot open and read mail from attorneys to inmates, but contends that it may open all letters from attorneys as long as it is done in the presence of the prisoners. The narrow issue thus presented is whether letters determined or found to be from attorneys may be opened by prison authorities in the presence of the inmate or whether such mail must be delivered unopened if normal detection techniques fail to indicate contraband.

. . . Respondent answers that his First, Sixth, and Fourteenth Amendment rights are infringed, under a procedure whereby the State may open mail from his attorney, even though in his presence and even though it may not be read. To begin with, the constitutional status of the rights asserted, as applied in this situation, is far from clear. While First Amendment rights of correspondents with prisoners may protect against the censoring of inmate mail, when not necessary to protect legitimate governmental interests, see *Procunier* v. *Martinez* . . . (1974), this Court has not yet recognized First Amendment rights of prisoners in this context, . . . Furthermore, freedom from censorship is not equivalent to freedom from inspection or perusal. As to the Sixth Amendment, its reach is only to protect the attorney-client relationship from intrusion in the criminal setting, . . . while the claim here would insulate all mail from inspection, whether related to civil or criminal matters. Finally, the Fourteenth Amendment Due Process claim based on access to the courts, . . . has not been extended by this Court to apply further than protecting the ability of an inmate to prepare a petition or complaint. Moreover, even if one were to accept the argument that inspection of incoming mail from an attorney placed an obstacle to access to the court, it is far from clear that this burden is a substantial one. We need not decide, however, which, if any, of the asserted rights are operative here, for the question is whether, assuming some constitutional right is implicated, it is infringed by the procedure now found acceptable by the State. . . .

. . . In our view, . . . none of the above rights is infringed by the procedures the state now accepts. If prison officials had to check in each case whether a communication was from an attorney, before opening it for inspection, a near impossible task of administration would be imposed. We think it entirely appropriate that

the State require any such communications to be specially marked as originated from an attorney, with his name and address being given, if they are to receive special treatment. It would also certainly be permissible that prison authorities require that a lawyer desiring to correspond with a prisoner first identify himself and his client to the prison officials, to assure the letters marked privileged are actually from members of the bar. As to the ability to open the mail in the presence of inmates, this could in no way constitute censorship, since the mail would not be read. Neither could it chill such communications since the inmate's presence insures that prison officials will not read the mail. The possibility that contraband will be enclosed in letters, even those from apparent attorneys, surely warrants prison officials in opening the letters. . . .

The last issue presented is whether the Complex must, and if so has, made available adequate legal assistance, under *Johnson* v. *Avery,* for the preparation of habeas corpus petitions and civil rights actions by inmates. The issue arises in the context of a challenge to a regulation providing, in pertinent part:

A legal advisor has been appointed by the Warden for the benefit of those offenders who are in need of legal assistance. This individual is an offender who has general knowledge of the law procedure. He is not an attorney and can not represent you as such.

No other offender than the legal advisor is permitted to assist you in the preparation of legal documents unless with the specific written permission of the Warden.

Respondent contended that this regulation was invalid because it failed to allow inmates to furnish assistance to one another. The District

Court assumed that the Warden freely gave permission to inmates to give assistance to each other, and that *Johnson* v. *Avery* . . . was thereby satisfied.

In *Johnson* v. *Avery*, an inmate was disciplined for violating a prison regulation which prohibited inmates from assisting other prisoners in preparing habeas corpus petitions. The Court held that "unless and until the State provides some reasonable alternative to assist inmates in the preparation of petitions for postconviction relief," inmates could not be barred from furnishing assistance to each other. . . . The court emphasized that the writ of habeas corpus was of fundamental importance in our constitutional scheme, and since the basic purpose of the writ "is to enable those unlawfully incarcerated to obtain their freedom, it is fundamental that access of prisoners to the courts for the purpose of presenting their complaints may not be denied or obstructed." . . .

. . . Petitioner contends that *Avery* is limited to assistance in the preparation of habeas corpus petitions and disputes the direction of the Court of Appeals to the District Court that the capacity of the inmate advisor be assessed in light of the demand for assistance in civil rights actions as well as in the preparation of habeas writs. Petitioner takes too narrow a view of that decision.

. . . First, the demarcation line between civil rights actions and habeas petitions is not always clear. The Court has already recognized instances where the same constitutional rights must be redressed under either form of relief. . . . Second, while it is true that only in habeas actions may relief be granted which will shorten the term of confinement, it is more pertinent that both actions serve to protect basic constitutional rights. The right of access to the courts, upon which *Avery* was premised, is founded in the Due Process Clause and assures that no person will be denied the opportunity to present to the judiciary allegations concerning violations of fundamental constitutional rights. It is futile to contend that the Civil Rights Act has less importance in our constitutional scheme than does the Great Writ. The recognition by this Court that prisoners have certain constitutional rights which can be protected by civil rights actions would be diluted if inmates, often "totally or functionally illiterate," were unable to articulate their complaints to the courts. Although there may be additional burdens on the Complex, if inmates may seek help from other inmates, or from the inmate adviser if he proves adequate, in both habeas and civil rights actions, this should not prove overwhelming. . . .

MR. JUSTICE DOUGLAS, DISSENTING (OMITTED).
MR. JUSTICE MARSHALL, WITH WHOM MR. JUSTICE BRENNAN JOINS, DISSENTING IN PART (OMITTED).

[In *Meachum* v. *Fano* (1976), the Supreme Court ruled that the due process clause of the Fourteenth Amendment did not require or entitle state prisoners to a hearing when they were transferred from a minimum security prison to a maximum security facility following a rash of arson fires. Each inmate had received both a hearing and a detailed statement of the findings of the prison Classification Board. However, they claimed denial of the right to confront *all* adverse witnesses, inasmuch as the testimony of the prison superintendent had been presented to the board *in camera*. The majority ruled that whatever expectation a prisoner may have about remaining at a particular prison, it is "too ephemeral and insubstantial" to trigger procedural due process protections. To hold otherwise would place the courts "astride the day-to-day functioning of state prisons and involve the judiciary in issues and discretionary decisions that are not the business of federal judges."

Another right secured in part by the due process clause is the right of access to the courts to challenge a conviction. In *Bounds* v. *Smith* (1977), the majority of the Court held that "the fundamental constitutional right to access to the courts requires prison authorities to assist inmates in preparation and filing of meaningful legal papers by providing prisoners with adequate law libraries or adequate assistance from persons trained in the law." However, that same year, the Supreme Court rejected claims by prisoners involving First Amendment rights of association and Fourteenth Amendment rights of equal protection. A North Carolina statute made collective bargaining illegal for prison inmates. In *Jones* v. *North Carolina Prisoner's Labor Union, Inc.*, Justice Rehnquist argued that "associational rights are necessarily curtailed by the realities of confinement. They may be curtailed whenever the institution's officials, in the exercise of their informal discretion, reasonably conclude that such associations . . . possess the likelihood of disruption to prison order or stability, or otherwise interfere with the legitimate penological objectives of the prison environment. . . . When weighted against the First Amendment rights asserted, these institutional reasons are sufficiently weighty to prevail.]

(2) Bell v. Wolfish (1979)

+Rehnquist, Burger, Stewart, White, Blackmun, Powell
−Marshall, Brennan, Stevens

[The Metropolitan Correctional Center (MCC) is a modern detention facility in New York City operated by the federal government. It houses short term prisoners, convicted persons awaiting sentencing and transportation to other facilities, persons detained in custody prior to trial, and witnesses held in protective custody. The facility was constructed in 1975. A series of modular sleeping units, mostly designed for one inmate each, and a commons room replace the traditional jail cells of older

prisons. Prisoners move freely about the facility except for the nighttime hours. An unexpected increase in persons committed to pretrial detention quickly exceeded the planned capacity of the facility, and a practice of "double-bunking" was begun. Despite the relative openness of the interior of the MCC, security precautions against escape and the importation of contraband were extensive, including strip searches and body cavity inspections after every meeting with an outside visitor, including attorneys, and limitations on sources of reading material mailed to the prison.

A group of inmates at the MCC, pretrial detainees and sentenced prisoners alike, filed a class action habeas corpus suit protesting these conditions. A federal district judge enjoined numerous practices of the MCC, particularly but not exclusively as they applied to those persons awaiting trial. These persons, the judge said, were "presumed to be innocent and held only to ensure their presence at trial . . . [therefore] any deprivation or restriction of . . . rights beyond those which are necessary for confinement alone, must be justified by a compelling necessity." The Court of Appeals approved most of the District Court's rulings, especially those applying to pretrial detainees.]

MR. JUSTICE REHNQUIST delivered the opinion of the Court.

Over the past five Terms, this court has in several decisions considered constitutional challenges to prison conditions or practices by convicted prisoners. This case requires us to examine the constitutional rights of pretrial detainees—those persons who have been charged with a crime but who have not yet been tried on the charge. The parties concede that to ensure their presence at trial, these persons legitimately may be incarcerated by the Government prior to a determination of their guilt or innocence, . . . and it is the scope of their rights during this period of confinement prior to trial that is the primary focus of this case.

. . .

The Court of Appeals did not dispute that the Government may permissibly incarcerate a person charged with a crime but not yet convicted to ensure his presence at trial. However, reasoning from the "premise that an individual is to be treated as innocent until proven guilty," the court concluded that pretrial detainees retain the "rights afforded unincarcerated individuals," and that therefore it is not sufficient that the conditions of confinement for pretrial detainees "merely comport with contemporary standards of decency prescribed by the cruel and unusual punishment clause of the eighth amendment." . . . Rather, the court held, the Due Process Clause requires that pretrial detainees "be subjected to only those 'restrictions and privations' which 'inhere in their confinement itself or which are justified by compelling necessities of jail administration.' " . . . Under the Court of Appeals' "compelling necessity" standard, "deprivation of the rights of detainees cannot be justified by the cries of fiscal necessity, . . . administrative convenience, . . . or by the cold comfort that conditions in other jails are worse." . . . The court acknowledged, however, that it could not "ignore" our admonition in *Procunier* v. *Martinez* . . . (1974), that "courts are ill-equipped to deal with the increasingly urgent problems of prison administration," and concluded that it would "not [be] wise for [it] to second-guess the expert administrators on matters on which they are better informed." . . .

Our fundamental disagreement with the Court of Appeals is that we fail to find a source in the Constitution for its compelling necessity standard. Both the Court of Appeals and the District Court seem to have relied on the "presumption of innocence" as the source of the detainee's substan-

tive right to be free from conditions of confinement that are not justified by compelling necessity. . . . But the presumption of innocence provides no support for such a rule.

The presumption of innocence is a doctrine that allocates the burden of proof in criminal trials; it also may serve as an admonishment to the jury to judge an accused's guilt or innocence solely on the evidence adduced at trial and not on the basis of suspicions that may arise from the fact of his arrest, indictment or custody or from other matter not introduced as proof at trial. . . . It is "an inaccurate, shorthand description of the right of the accused to 'remain inactive and secure, until the prosecution has taken up its burden and produced evidence and effected persuasion . . .' [an] 'assumption' that is indulged in the absence of contrary evidence." . . . Without question, the presumption of innocence plays an important role in our criminal justice system. "The principle that there is a presumption of innocence in favor of the accused is the undoubted law, axiomatic and elementary, and its enforcement lies at the foundation of the administration of our criminal law." . . . But it has no application to a determination of the rights of a pretrial detainee during confinement before his trial has even begun.

The Court of Appeals also relied on what it termed the "indisputable rudiments of due process" in fashioning its compelling necessity test. We do not doubt that the Due Process Clause protects a detainee from certain conditions and restrictions of pretrial detainment. Nonetheless, that clause provides no basis for application of a compelling necessity standard to conditions of pretrial confinement that are not alleged to infringe any other, more specific guarantee of the Constitution.

It is important to focus on what is at issue here. We are not concerned with the initial decision to detain an accused and the curtailment of liberty that such a decision necessarily entails. . . . Neither respondents nor the courts below question that the Government may permissibly detain a person suspected of committing a crime prior to a formal adjudication of guilt. . . . Nor do they doubt that the Government has a substantial interest in ensuring that persons accused of crimes are available for trials and, ultimately, for service of their sentences, or that confinement of such persons pending trial is a legitimate means of furthering that interest. . . . Instead, what is at issue when an aspect of pretrial detention that is not alleged to violate any express guarantee of the Constitution is challenged, is the detainee's right to be free from punishment, and his understandable desire to be as comfortable as possible during his confinement, both of which may conceivably coalesce at some point. . . . And to the extent the court relied on the detainee's desire to be free from discomfort, it suffices to say that this desire simply does not rise to the level of those fundamental liberty interests delineated in cases such as *Roe* v. *Wade* . . . (1973); *Eisenstadt* v. *Baird* . . . (1972); *Stanley* v. *Illinois* . . . (1972); *Griswold* v. *Connecticut* . . . (1965). . . .

In evaluating the constitutionality of conditions or restrictions of pretrial detention that implicate only the protection against deprivation of liberty without due process of law, we think that the proper inquiry is whether those conditions amount to punishment of the detainee. For under the Due Process Clause, a detainee may not be punished prior to an adjudication of guilt in accordance with due process of law.. . . A person lawfully committed to pretrial detention has not been adjudged guilty of any crime. He has had only a "judicial determination of probable cause as a prerequisite to [the] extended restraint of [his] liberty following arrest.". . . And, if he is detained for a suspected violation of a federal law, he also has had a bail hearing. . . . Under such circumstances, the Government concededly may detain him to ensure his presence at trial and may subject him to the restrictions and conditions of the detention facility so long as those conditions and restrictions do not amount to punishment, or otherwise violate the Constitution.

Not every disability imposed during pretrial detention amounts to "punishment" in the constitutional sense, however. Once the Government has exercised its conceded authority to detain a person pending trial, it obviously is entitled to employ devices that are calculated to effectuate this detention. Traditionally, this has meant confinement in a facility which, no matter how modern or how antiquated, results in restricting the movement of a detainee in a manner in which he would not be restricted if he simply were free to walk the streets pending trial. Whether it be called a jail, a prison, or custodial center, the purpose of the facility is to detain. Loss of freedom of choice and privacy are inherent incidents of confinement in such a facility. And the fact that such detention interferes with the detainee's understandable desire to live as comfortably as possible and with as little restraint as possible during confinement does not convert the conditions or restrictions of detention into "punishment."
. . .

A court must decide whether the disability is imposed for the purpose of punishment or whether it is but an incident of some other legitimate governmental purpose. . . . Absent a showing of an expressed intent to punish on the part of detention facility officials, that determination generally will turn on "[w]hether an alternative purpose to which [the restriction] may rationally be connected is assignable for it, and whether it appears excessive in relation to the alternative purpose assigned [to it]." . . . Thus, if a particular condition or restriction of pretrial detention is reasonably related to a legitimate governmental objective, it does not, without more, amount to "punishment." Conversely, if a restriction or condition is not reasonably related to a legitimate goal— if it is arbitrary or purposeless—a court permissibly may infer that the purpose of the governmental action is punishment that may not constitutionally be inflicted upon detainees *qua* detainees. . . . Courts must be mindful that these inquiries spring from constitutional requirements and that judicial answers to them must reflect that fact rather than a court's idea of how best to operate a detention facility. . . .

One further point requires discussion. The Government asserts, and respondents concede, that the "essential objective of pretrial confinement is to insure the detainees' presence at trial." . . . While this interest undoubtedly justifies the original decision to confine an individual in some manner, we do not accept respondent's argument that the Government's interest in ensuring a detainee's presence at trial is the *only* objective that may justify restraints and conditions once the decision is lawfully made to confine a person. "If the government could confine or otherwise infringe the liberty of detainees only to the extent necessary to ensure their presence at trial,

house arrest would in the end be the only constitutionally justified form of detention." . . . The Government also has legitimate interests that stem from its need to manage the facility in which the individual is detained. These legitimate operational concerns may require administrative measures that go beyond those that are, strictly speaking, necessary to ensure that the detainee shows up at trial. For example, the Government must be able to take steps to maintain security and order at the institution and make certain no weapons or illicit drugs reach detainees. Restraints that are reasonably related to the institution's interest in maintaining jail security do not, without more, constitute unconstitutional punishment, even if they are discomforting and are restrictions that the detainee would not have experienced had he been released while awaiting trial. . . .

On this record, we are convinced as a matter of law that double-bunking as practiced at the MCC did not amount to punishment and did not, therefore, violate respondents' rights under the Due Process Clause of the Fifth Amendment.

. . .

We disagree with both the District Court and the Court of Appeals that there is some sort of "one man, one cell" principle lurking in the Due Process Clause of the Fifth Amendment. While confining a given number of people in a given amount of space in such a manner as to cause them to endure genuine privations and hardship over an extended period of time might raise serious questions under the Due Process Clause as to whether those conditions amounted to punishment, nothing even approaching such hardship is shown by this record.

Respondents also challenged certain MCC restrictions and practices that were designed to promote security and order at the facility on the ground that these restrictions violated the Due Process Clause of the Fifth Amendment, and certain other constitutional guarantees, such as the First and Fourth Amendments. The Court of Appeals seemed to approach the challenges to security restrictions in a fashion different from the other contested conditions and restrictions. It stated that "once it has been determined that the mere fact of confinement of the detainee justifies the restrictions, the institution must be permitted to use reasonable means to insure that its legitimate interests in security are safeguarded." . . . The court might disagree with the choice of means to effectuate those interests, but it should not "second-guess the expert administrators on matters on which they are better informed. . . . Concern with minutiae of prison administration can only distract the court from detached consideration of the one overriding question presented to it: does the practice or condition violate the Constitution?" . . . Nonetheless, the court affirmed the District Court's injunction against several security restrictions. The Court rejected the arguments of petitioners that these practices served the MCC's interest in security and order and held that the practices were unjustified interferences with the retained constitutional rights of *both* detainees and convicted inmates. In our view, the Court of Appeals failed to heed its own admonition not to "second-guess" prison administrators.

Our cases have established several general principles that inform our evaluation of the constitutionality of the restrictions at issue. First, we have held that convicted prisoners do not forfeit all constitutional protections by reason of their conviction and confinement in prison. . . . "There is no iron curtain drawn between the Constitution and the prisons of this country." *Wolff* v. *McDonnell* (1974). . . . So, for example, our cases have held that sentenced prisoners enjoy freedom of speech and religion under the First and Fourteenth Amendments, . . . that they are protected against invidious discrimination on the basis of race under the Equal Protection Clause of the Fourteenth Amendment, . . . and that they may claim the protection of the Due Process Clause to prevent additional deprivation of life, liberty or property without due process of law, . . . A *fortiori*, pretrial detainees, who have not been convicted of any crimes, retain at least those constitutional rights that we have held are enjoyed by convicted prisoners.

But our cases also have insisted on a second proposition: simply because prison inmates retain certain constitutional rights does not mean that these rights are not subject to restrictions and limitations. "Lawful incarceration brings about the necessary withdrawal or limitation of many privileges and rights, a retraction justified by the considerations underlying our penal system." . . . The fact of confinement as well as the legitimate goals and policies of the penal institution limit these retained constitutional rights. . . . There must be a "mutual accommodation between institutional needs and objectives and the provisions of the Constitution that are of general application." . . . This principle applies equally to pretrial detainees and convicted prisoners. A detainee simply does not possess the full range of freedoms of an unincarcerated individual.

Third, maintaining institutional

security and preserving internal order and discipline are essential goals that may require limitation or retraction of the retained constitutional rights of both convicted prisoners and pretrial detainees. "Central to all other corrections goals is the institutional consideration of internal security within the corrections facilities themselves." . . . Prison officials must be free to take appropriate action to ensure the safety of inmates and corrections personnel and to prevent escape or unauthorized entry. Accordingly, we have held that even when an institutional restriction infringes a specific constitutional guarantee, such as the First Amendment, the practice must be evaluated in the light of the central objective of prison administration, safeguarding institutional security.

Finally, as the Court of Appeals correctly acknowledged, the problems that arise in the day-to-day operation of a corrections facility are not susceptible of easy solutions. Prison administrators therefore should be accorded wide-ranging deference in the adoption and execution of policies and practices that in their judgment are needed to preserve internal order and discipline and to maintain institutional security. . . .

[In sections of the opinion omitted here, the Court approved a policy forbidding inmates to receive books except those mailed directly from publishers or book clubs, while noting with approval that the policy had been modified to include book stores as well and would be modified again to lift all restrictions on paperback books, magazines and newspapers. It approved the prohibition of food packages, except one at Christmas. And it found no constitutional problems with unannounced searches of inmate living areas.]

Inmates at all Bureau of Prisons facilities, including the MCC, are re-quired to expose their body cavities for visual inspection as a part of a strip search conducted after every contact visit with a person from outside the institution. Corrections officials testified that visual cavity searches were necessary not only to discover but also to deter the smuggling of weapons, drugs and other contraband into the institution. . . . The District Court upheld the strip search procedure but prohibited the body cavity searches, absent probable cause to believe that the inmate is concealing contraband. . . . Because petitioners proved only one instance in the MCC's short history where contraband was found during a body cavity search, the Court of Appeals affirmed. In its view, the "gross violation of personal privacy inherent in such a search cannot be outweighed by the government's security interest in maintaining a practice of so little actual utility." . . .

Admittedly, this practice instinctively gives us the most pause. However, assuming for present purposes that inmates, both convicted prisoners and pretrial detainees, retain some Fourth Amendment rights upon commitment to a corrections facility, . . . we nonetheless conclude that these searches do not violate that Amendment. The Fourth Amendment prohibits only unreasonable searches, . . . and under the circumstances, we do not believe that these searches are unreasonable.

The test of reasonableness under the Fourth Amendment is not capable of precise definition or mechanical application. In each case it requires a balancing of the need for the particular search against the invasion of personal rights that the search entails. Courts must consider the scope of the particular intrusion, the manner in which it is conducted, the justification for initiating it and the place in which it is conducted. . . . A detention facility is a unique place fraught with serious security dangers. Smuggling of money, drugs, weapons and other contraband is all too common an occurrence. And inmate attempts to secrete these items into the facility by concealing them in body cavities are documented in this record, . . . That there has been only one instance where an MCC inmate was discovered attempting to smuggle contraband into the institution on his person may be more a testament to the effectiveness of this search technique as a deterrent than to any lack of interest on the part of the inmates to secrete and import such items when the opportunity arises.

We do not underestimate the degree to which these searches may invade the personal privacy of inmates. Nor do we doubt, as the District Court noted, that on occasion a security guard may conduct the search in an abusive fashion. Such abuse cannot be condoned. The searches must be conducted in a reasonable manner. But we deal here with the question whether visual body cavity inspections as contemplated by the MCC rules can *ever* be conducted on less than probable cause. Balancing the significant and legitimate security interests of the institution against the privacy interests of the inmates, we conclude that they can.

. . .

. . . Respondents simply have not met their heavy burden of showing that these officials have exaggerated their response to the genuine security considerations that actuated these restrictions and practices. . . . And as might be expected of restrictions applicable to pretrial detainees, these restrictions were of only limited duration so far as the MCC pretrial detainees were concerned. . . .

There was a time not too long ago when the federal judiciary took a completely "hands-off" approach to the problem of prison administration. In recent years, however, these courts largely have discarded this "hands-off" attitude and have waded into this complex arena. The deplorable conditions and draconian restrictions of some of our Nation's prisons are too well known to require recounting here, and the federal courts rightly have condemned these sordid aspects of our prison systems. But many of these same courts have, in the name of the Constitution, become increasingly enmeshed in the minutiae of prison operations. Judges, after all, are human. They, no less than others in our society, have a natural tendency to believe that their individual solutions to often intractable problems are better and more workable than those of the persons who are actually charged with and trained in the running of the particular institution under examination. But under the Constitution, the first question to be answered is not whose plan is best, but in what branch of the Government is lodged the authority to initially devise the plan. This does not mean that constitutional rights are not to be scrupulously observed. It does mean, however, that the inquiry of federal courts into prison management must be limited to the issue of whether a particular system violates any prohibition of the Constitution, or in the case of a federal prison, a statute. The wide range of "judgment calls" that meet constitutional and statutory requirements are confided to officials outside of the Judicial Branch of Government.

The judgment of the Court of Appeals is, accordingly, reversed and the case is remanded for proceedings consistent with this opinion.

It is so ordered.

MR. JUSTICE POWELL, CONCURRING IN PART AND DISSENTING IN PART (OMITTED).

MR. JUSTICE MARSHALL, DISSENTING.

`. . .

The premise of the Court's analysis is that detainees, unlike prisoners, may not be "punished." . . . Absent from the reformulation is any appraisal of whether the sanction constitutes an affirmative disability or restraint and whether it has historically been regarded as punishment. Moreover, when the Court applies this standard, it loses interest in the inquiry concerning excessiveness, and indeed, eschews consideration of less restrictive alternatives, practices in other detention facilities, and the recommendations of the Justice Department and professional organizations. . . . By this process of elimination, the Court contracts a broad standard, sensitive to the deprivations inposed on detainees, into one that seeks merely to sanitize official motives and prohibit irrational behavior. As thus reformulated, the test lacks any real content.

. . .

Although the Court professes to go beyond the direct inquiry regarding intent and to determine whether a particular imposition is rationally related to a nonpunitive purpose, this exercise is at best a formality. Almost any restriction on detainees, including, as the Court concedes, chains and shackles, . . . can be found to have some rational relation to institutional security, or more broadly, to "the effective management of the detention facility." . . . Yet this toothless standard applies irrespective of the excessiveness of the restraint or the nature of the rights infringed.

Moreover, the Court has not in fact reviewed the rationality of detention officials' decisions, . . . Instead, the majority affords "wide-ranging" deference to those officials "in the adoption of practices that in their judgment are needed to preserve internal order and discipline and to maintain institutional security." . . . Reasoning that security considerations in jails are little different than in prisons, the Court concludes that cases requiring substantial deference to *prison* administrators' determinations on security-related issues are equally applicable in the present context. . . .

Yet as the Court implicitly acknowledges, . . . the rights of detainees, who have not been adjudicated guilty of a crime, are necessarily more extensive than those of prisoners "who have been found to have violated one or more of the criminal laws established by society for its orderly governance." . . . Judicial tolerance of substantial impositions on detainees must be concomitantly less. However, by blindly deferring to administrative judgments on the rational basis for particular restrictions, the Court effectively delegates to detention officials the decision whether pretrial detainees have been punished. This, in my view, is an abdication of a unquestionably judicial function.

Even had the Court properly applied the punishment test, I could not agree to its use in this context. It simply does not advance analysis to determine whether a given deprivation imposed on detainees constitutes "punishment." For in terms of the nature of the imposition and the impact on detainees, pretrial incarceration, although necessary to secure defendants' presence at trial, is essentially indistinguishable from punishment. The detainee is involuntarily confined and deprived of the freedom "to be with his family and friends and to form the other enduring attachments of normal life." . . . Indeed, this Court has previously recognized that incarceration is an "infamous punishment." . . . And if the effect of incarceration itself is inevitably punitive, so too must be the cumulative impact of those restraints incident to that restraint.

A test that balances the deprivations involved against the state interests assertedly served, would be more consistent with the import of the Due Process Clause. Such an approach would be sensitive to the tangible physical and psychological harm that a particular disability inflicts on detainees and to the nature of the less tangible, but significant individual interests at stake. The greater the imposition on detainees, the heavier the burden of justification the Government would bear. . . .

When assessing the restrictions on detainees, we must consider the cumulative impact of restraints imposed during confinement. Incarceration of itself clearly represents a profound infringement of liberty, and each additional imposition increases the severity of that initial deprivation. Since any restraint thus has a serious effect on detainees, I believe the Government must bear a more rigorous burden of justification than the rational basis standard mandates. . . . At a minimum, I would require a showing that a restriction is substantially necessary to jail administration. Where the imposition is of particular gravity, that is, where it implies interests of fundamental importance or inflicts significant harms, the Government should demonstrate that the restriction serves a compelling necessity of jail administration. . . .

In my view, the body cavity searches of MCC inmates represent one of the most grievous offenses against personal dignity and common decency. After every contact visit with someone from outside the facility, including defense attorneys, an inmate must remove all of his or her clothing, bend over, spread the buttocks, and display the anal cavity for inspection by a correctional officer. Women inmates must assume a suitable posture for vaginal inspection, while men must raise their genitals. And, as the Court neglects to note, because of time pressures, this humiliating spectacle is frequently conducted in the presence of other inmates. . . .

The District Court found that the stripping was "unpleasant, embarrassing, and humiliating." . . . A psychiatrist testified that the practice placed inmates in the most degrading position possible, . . . a conclusion amply corroborated by the testimony of the inmates themselves. There was evidence, moreover, that these searches engendered among detainees fears of sexual assault, . . . were the occasion for actual threats of physical abuse by guards, and caused some inmates to forego personal visits. . . .

Not surprisingly, the Government asserts a security justification for such inspections. These searches are necessary, it argues, to prevent inmates from smuggling contraband into the facility. In crediting this justification despite the contrary findings of the two courts below, the Court overlooks the critical facts. As respondents point out, inmates are required to wear one-piece jumpsuits with zippers in the front. To insert an object into the vaginal or anal cavity, an inmate would have to remove the jumpsuit, at least from the upper torso. . . . Since contact visits occur in a glass enclosed room and are continuously monitored by corrections officers, . . . such a feat would seem extraordinarily difficult. There was medical testimony, moreover, that inserting an object into the rectum is painful and "would require time and opportunity which is not available in the visiting areas." . . . and that visual inspection would probably not detect an object once inserted. . . . Additionally, before entering the visiting room, visitors and their packages are searched thoroughly by a metal detector, fluoroscope, and by hand. . . . Correction officers may require that visitors leave packages or handbags with guards until the visit is over. . . . Only by blinding itself to the facts presented on this record can the Court accept the Government's security rationale.

Without question, these searches are an imposition of sufficient gravity to invoke the compelling necessity standard. It is equally indisputable that they cannot meet that standard. Indeed, the procedure is so unnecessarily degrading that it "shocks the conscience." *Rochin* v. *California* . . . (1952). Even in *Rochin*, the police had reason to believe that the petitioner had swallowed contraband. Here, the searches are employed absent any suspicion of wrongdoing. . . .

That the Court can uphold these indiscriminate searches highlights the bankruptcy of its basic analysis. Under the test adopted today, the rights of detainees apparently extend only so far as detention officials decide that cost and security will permit. Such unthinking deference to administrative convenience cannot be justified where the interests at stake are those of presumptively innocent individuals, many of whose only proven offense is the ability to afford bail. I dissent.

MR. JUSTICE STEVENS, WITH WHOM MR. JUSTICE BRENNAN JOINS, DISSENTING. (OMITTED).

[It is rare for a Supreme Court justice to speak out publicly about specific cases decided by the Court, and almost unheard of for a justice to publicly criticize his brethren. Justice Thurgood Marshall's stinging rebuke of some of his colleagues in June, 1979 was thus a noteworthy event. The setting was the annual meeting of the Second Circuit Judicial Conference, and Marshall's comments concerned two recently decided cases, *Bell* v. *Wolfish* and *Herbert* v. *Lando* (see Part II, Chapter Five). In each case the Supreme Court had reversed a decision by the prestigious Court of Appeals for the Second Circuit. Marshall accused the Court of "affording insufficient protection to constitutional rights." He decried the "posture of crippling self-restraint" in the *Bell* case, which had the effect of removing the presumption of innocence from persons not yet convicted of a crime. And he had nothing but scorn for Justice Rehnquist's insensitive attempt at humor, expressed in the homily "There is no one man, one cell principle lurking in the due process clause."

So troubling did Marshall find these decisions that he invited lower court judges "to read the decision narrowly. To read it otherwise would afford pretrial detainees virtually no constitutional protection." And he concluded his remarks by commending the judges of the Second Circuit whose decisions had been reversed by his own court:

This Circuit has done well and must continue to do so. Ill conceived reversals should be considered as no more than temporary interruptions. We must stand fast for the fullest protection of constitutional rights.]

presidential power in an age of internationalism

1. INTRODUCTORY ESSAY

Constitutional politics in the twentieth century has been deeply affected by America's emergence as a dominant international power. The features of domestic politics and economics are etched by the extraordinary technological complexity and consequent expense of maintaining a worldwide system of national defense, and the presidency has grown to such size and power that it has eclipsed the legislative branch as a national policymaker. Recent American experience in Southeast Asia and a so-called imperial president have subjected the constitutional system to stress from a growing skepticism about the propriety of this political relationship, especially with regard to effective popular control of its leaders.

Unlike some other dimensions of policy examined in this book, the constitutional implications of the chief executive's international responsibilities, and the influence of the Supreme Court upon them, are intrinsically unclear. Defense and diplomacy are activities for which the president has definite, if not exclusive, constitutional responsibility. But it is less than clear just what limits the Constitution imposes upon him in meeting those responsibilities. The Supreme Court continually confesses an institutional sense of inadequacy to review many questions falling within this area of policy. Much in the Court's position seems to stem from its reluctance to compromise national interests.

But this situation also reflects a somewhat traditional deferential relationship of the Supreme Court to the presidency.

A plausible historical case can be made for the proposition that both the presidency and the Supreme Court were intended to provide protection against the democratic character of the legislative branch.[1] Such a case has its basis more in the common elitist character of the two institutions than in any indications of an open political alliance. Except for aspects of the episode we call "substantive due process," the judiciary has been least supportive of the legislature in matters where executive and legislative prerogatives have clashed. In such confrontations, the executive branch has never lost significant power by virtue of a judicial decision. Even the Court's badly divided opinion in the *Steel Seizure Case*—holding that the president must be guided by clear legislative preferences in labor matters—contained the views of five justices to the effect that some extraconstitutional or "inherent" presidential power might well exist.

To the extent that history and background bear upon current problems of an expanding presidency, the Supreme Court, by default, is on the side of executive power. Since 1937, the Court has generally been supportive of the centralization of power so fundamental to modern policy. Except in some procedural aspects of administrative law, the growth of bureaucracy has hardly been retarded or discouraged by judicial action. In foreign affairs and clear-cut issues of national security, the Supreme Court has been unwilling to interfere with the actions or power of the president. This judicial passiveness has, in turn, worked to the advantage of the executive branch in its conflicts with other elements of the political system.

Political relationships between the Supreme Court and the presidency include those constitutionally required (e.g., the process of appointing members of the judiciary) as well as informal interactions (e.g., service by justices on special commissions or giving advice to the president based upon prior political association). But it is the common effort to influence constitutional meaning that has defined, and that continues to define, the relationship of Court to president. The clearest example is the persistent historical counterpoint between the hopes of a president for particular policy preferences from his judicial appointees and the subsequent independence of many justices, once appointed.

It has long been customary among students of American politics to assign the "guardianship" of the Constitution to the Supreme Court. For many purposes, this remains a valid conception, primarily because the Court has become the accepted *interpreter* of constitutional meaning. But a useful distinction can be drawn between *interpreting* meaning and *influencing* meaning. It is the latter for which, as stated above, the Supreme Court and the presidency compete. Thus, interpretation can be seen as judicial report on the outcome—that is, who wins the contest.

In this contest for influence, the rise of America's international responsibilities grows proportionately in importance. The fusion of domestic and international concerns in the office of the president has a prominent place among

---

[1]See Robert Scigliano, *The Supreme Court and the Presidency* (New York: Free Press, 1971), especially pp. 7–22.

the many reasons to which one might attribute the seeming desuetude of the Court. Despite the appearances created in such decisions as *United States* v. *Nixon* (1974) or the appealing rhetoric of *United States* v. *Lee* (1882) ("All the officers of the Government, from the highest to the lowest, are creatures of the law and are bound to obey it"), the executive is winning the contest. But this shift in relative position of influence upon constitutional meaning has a great deal to do with the changing institutional character of the presidency. Thus, it is to the concept of the "normal" presidency that attention must now turn.

The "Normal" Presidency–the Faces of Janus

In a trenchant remark made over a decade ago, Aaron Wildavsky observed: "The United States has one President, but it has two presidencies; one presidency is for domestic affairs, and the other is concerned with defense and foreign policy."[2] In the domestic field, the scope of presidential discretion is normally quite limited, mainly as a result of the complex set of mutual institutional relations that are involved in the process of making policy and the political dynamics associated with those relations. But virtually the opposite situation applies to the defense–foreign policy presidency, for in this function lies a range of action over which other political institutions wield little power. Most often, these two presidencies look in different "directions," like the faces of Janus. When they look in the same direction, the political character of the presidency is far different, possessing far wider political power.

No better example of this relationship can be found than the ordeal of Franklin Roosevelt, whose domestic policy was, until Pearl Harbor, faced with an isolationist public mentality, but whose international obligations increasingly compelled the politically daring use of those presidential powers that could be exercised almost unilaterally. Roosevelt waged undeclared and unacknowledged "war" upon Germany and her allies long before Pearl Harbor or Hitler's declaration of war made such actions legitimate in the eyes of the American people.[3] After the formal declaration of war starkly altered his situation, Roosevelt was faced with the other aspect of the "normal" presidency: joining of these "two" presidencies in a tandem use that made them almost indistinguishable. In the situation of modern, declared, total war, these two presidencies cease to be Janus-faced and become one visage. From a constitutional point of view, total war is clearly the most "convenient" kind to wage.[4] But it raised serious normative questions; as Kelly and Harbison note:

The Constitution [after World War II] had met the test of total war; could it also meet the test of survival in a world which lived in a perpetual state of inter-national crisis and half-war lasting not for two or four years but for decades and perhaps genera-

[2]Aaron Wildavsky, "The Two Presidencies," 4, *Trans-Action*, (December 1966). This piece also appeared in Wildavsky (ed.), *The Presidency* (New York: Little, Brown, 1969), pp. 230–243.
[3]Various accounts of this period point to the delicacy of FDR's position. See Dean Acheson, *Present at the Creation* (New York: Norton, 1969), pp. 3–38; and James M. Burns, *Roosevelt: The Soldier of Freedom* (New York: Harcourt, Brace, and Jovanovich, 1976), pp. 3–170.
[4]An immediate postwar appraisal of the effect total war had upon constitutional development can be found in Edward S. Corwin, *Total War and the Constitution* (New York: Alfred A. Knopf, 1947).

tions? Not long after 1945 it became evident that this was perhaps the gravest con-
stitutional question of the twentieth century.[5]

The "normal" aspect of the American presidency, then, is one in which the two presidential functions are distinct and functionally separate until that unique event called "total war" alters this relationship. Then the "wartime presidency" appears to encompass and constitutionally legitimize otherwise extreme forms of executive power. These "new" forms of power, then, are constitutionally consonant with the less striking but parallel avenues of power of the normal domestic presidency.

What had changed in the decades following World War II was that both aspects of the presidency were called into play by the circumstances of modern, *peacetime* international politics. But the obvious and extreme conditions of total war, which make the merging of the two presidencies seem constitutionally proper, do not formally exist in contemporary times, in which matters of "guns and butter" in a situation of neither war nor peace are the country's exigencies.

It has been only recently that presidential prerogatives, informally sanctioned over the years largely by congressional inaction, have become ongoing political issues. Only recently, therefore, have the courts become more than occasionally involved in adjudicating the constitutional limitations of executive power. The scandals of the Nixon administration obviously did not hinder this process—but neither did they begin it. And even here (as with most of the cases in this chapter), the Supreme Court has been generally more deferential to the executive branch than to Congress in the *policy* implications of its decisions, although in all other contexts, the Court—especially the Burger Court—has rarely failed to support congressional policy decisions.

According to the *formal* view of the constitutional relationship that prevails between the executive and legislative branches, there is a distinct separation of function, so that neither branch exercises powers that are clearly those of the other. But what began with attention to distinct separations of power has recently become an issue of legislative independence of the executive on matters of policy. Yet circumstances, especially the informal structures of political power, throw these ostensibly independent institutions together. They are interdependent as a matter of practical politics.

It might appear that the American party system is a cause of this merging of functions, since it is largely through the party system that some degree of common political allegiance between the two branches is maintained. But the party system is more a manifestation than a cause, which is itself rooted in the character of American political power. From the outset of government under the Constitution, the executive exploited its structural advantages over the legislature. For reasons of constitutional propriety, George Washington chose to ignore the situation in his dealings with Congress. Alexander Hamilton, however, was not in a position that called for such scruples:

Hamilton . . . grasped the truth at once . . . that not even the Constitution of the United States could keep apart two such inseparable factors in government as execu-

---

[5]Alfred H. Kelly and Winifred A. Harbison, *The American Constitution*, 3rd ed. (New York: W. W. Norton & Co., 1963), p. 850.

tive and legislature. His official position naturally brought him into close contact with Congress, and enabled him to see that such a loosely organized body was simply waiting for a commander.[6]

For a few brief and exceptional periods of American history, the legislative branch has dealt with the executive branch from a position of relative political strength. But the process has remained one in which the executive takes and maintains the initiative in policymaking, (which, it must be stressed, is not necessarily the same thing as domination of the process).

The rise of the administrative state has only exacerbated this tendency toward executive dominance. Bureaucratic institutions, ostensibly under the ultimate control of Congress, have a unique character in their specialization and coordination of skills needed for government to exert positive regulatory powers, resulting in a distinct decline in legislative capacity to address policy matters on an equal informational base. The few independent legislative sources of data and information, such as the Office of Technological Assessment, are relatively insignificant when compared to the executive's near-monopoly of relevant information, now so vital to the policy process.

Against these tendencies toward the gathering of executive control over the fundamental conditions of policymaking, there exists a formal legislative weapon: the power of the purse. Even after the dramatic changes of the Employment Act of 1946, in which many economic policy functions became the statutory preserve of the executive branch, Congress retained a functional veto in the form of its appropriation decisions. For the domestic presidency, this power of Congress accounts for much of the political motivation for the president to negotiate with Congress on domestic policy decisions. The defense–foreign policy presidency has always been faced with the possibility that congressional power over appropriations might be used to curb executive power, but this had been more a matter of remote speculation than any actual instance of using the appropriations power to deal with presidential authority.

The Vietnam War changed this remote rhetorical possibility into a tangible political issue. With it came tests of how effective Congress' ultimate weapon might be. A major part of the "normal" presidency has consisted largely of the expectation on the part of Congress that executive power was ultimately subject to fiscal limitation, even in areas of foreign policy remote from the political intricacies of domestic policy concerns. Of course, much of the "showdown" potential of this situation was postponed or disguised by the long-standing postwar tradition of bipartisanship in foreign policy, as well as the presence of acutely sensed dangers of an international source. This situation was especially nurtured by such crises as the Post–World War II impression of the imminent fall of Greece and Turkey (with the related declaration of the Truman Doctrine), the Berlin crises of 1947 and 1961, the Korean War, the arms race, the overall cold-war mentality, and the early stages of the Vietnam War. But with growing disenchantment over the guns versus butter problems of the

[6]Ralph V. Harlow, *The History of Legislative Methods in the Period Before 1825* (New Haven: Yale University Press, 1917), p. 140; quoted in Leonard D. White, *The Federalists* (New York: Macmillan Co., 1948), p. 56. White's chapter, "The Executive Impulse," pp. 50–66, is an interesting account of the early circumstances out of which executive power relative to the Congress grew. More generally, see Richard Hofstadter, *The Idea of a Party System* (Berkeley: University of California Press, 1969), on the growth of political parties.

late 1960s and 1970s, consideration of the appropriation decisions as restrictions on the presidency moved from an intellectual posture of "as-a-last-resort-we-could" to a definite movement to finally bring the burgeoning presidency under the constitutional control of the Congress.

The effectiveness of congressional effort to curb the presidency was tested through the "War Powers Resolution"[7] and by subsequent actions connected with that piece of legislation. The resolution itself, enacted over President Nixon's veto, restricts the duration of involvement by the United States in "hostilities," or situations of imminent hostility, in the absence of a formal declaration of war; requires that the president submit a report to Congress within forty-eight hours after the introduction of U.S. forces to a hostile situation; requires that the involvement be terminated within sixty days in the absence of affirmative congressional approval of the president's military action; and calls for presidential consultation with Congress in certain other situations involving executive commitments of armed force. Within the resolution itself, no mention is made of funding restrictions on presidential action by the Congress, although, as noted above, other legislative actions have placed various fiscal restrictions on the president's use of his powers as commander-in-chief.

Since the passage of the War Powers Resolution, four events have called for the president to report to Congress on his military decisions: the *Mayaguez* incident and three other military actions associated with evacuation of American citizens and nationals and friendly foreign nationals from fallen allied countries in Southeast Asia (see pp. 1060–1069, *infra*). All four incidents appear to have involved the reintroduction of American armed forces into situations of hostility in violation of explicit congressional prohibition on the use of funds for such purposes. The Vietnam Contingency Act of 1975 appeared to present an opportunity for Congress to authorize use of public funds for certain evacuation purposes. But political maneuvering concerning the measure caused the chance to be lost; the House leadership withdrew the bill, apparently over the concern that it would have implicitly permitted a political reintroduction of American forces into South Vietnam.

The constitutional issue of the status of such funding prohibitions has developed out of this set of circumstances. Obviously, one argument holds that Congress has the clear authority under the Constitution to place restrictions on the president's powers as commander-in-chief. But the opposing view holds that such limitations are unconstitutional interference with the president's clear authority and duty under the commander-in-chief provisions of the Constitution. It is, of course, the classic constitutional impasse: the effects of one express power upon the exercise of another express power.[8] It is also a classic

---

[7]Joint Resolution of November 7, 1973, P.L. No. 93-148, 87 Stat. 555. Between 1973 and 1975, seven legislative provisions, in various acts, were created, all of which sought to terminate and prevent further military action of Southeast Asia, through fiscal limitations (see below, pp. 1060–1063).

In this section of the essay, we rely heavily upon the partisan but informative article by Michael J. Glennon, "Strengthening the War Powers Resolution: The Case for Purse-String Restrictions," **60** *Minnesota Law Review* (1975), 1–43 (see below, pp. 1064–1069).

[8]For examples of statements representing the contending positions in this issue, see: testimony of Monroe Leigh, the then legal advisor to the State Department, *Hearings on Compliance with the War Powers Resolution Before the Subcommittee on International Relations*, 94th Congress, 1st Session, 90–91 (1975); Glennon, *op cit.* Note 7; and Raoul Berger, *Executive Privilege: A Constitutional Myth* (Cambridge: Harvard University Press, 1974), pp. 108–116.

illustration of the rapidly changing institutional positions of the two branches involved. Congress is now in the ironic position of justifying the very effect that use of its undoubted power would have upon the executive. Resolving the impasse depends as much on politics as on the determination of "right" constitutional principles.

The Emerging Presidency

It should be evident now that the "normal" presidency involves a set of powers formally and informally given the office that are exercised in some relationship to the institutional characteristics of the other branches of government. At best, the president does not have a clearly defined set of powers, especially in the area of international responsibility.

The increased salience of international concerns, especially as they effect domestic policymaking, has led to the emergence of renewed assertions of presidential power and prompted the coining of the phrase "the imperial presidency"[9] as a defining characteristic. What is signified by this seeming hyperbole is that we find the "normal" picture of the presidency inadequate but still desirable. Whether it is possible to restore the "normality" of the office, or whether the institutional course it is on will inexorably take the constitutional system to previously unforeseen lengths of executive authority, one essential fact remains: the enormity of what is emerging under the heading "presidential power" is a fundamental contemporary issue of constitutional government. The emerging presidency has been deviating from the "normal" aspects of that office in unprecedented ways. The Janus-faced office noted by Wildavsky is less and less feasible under modern circumstances of change. Virtually no major problem of public policy can be considered today as addressable solely within the domestic elements of the presidency. This is another way of saying that there is a paramount need for increased authority as a basis of public policy, as noted by most analysts of the American political future.[10]

For the student of constitutional politics, this situation is somewhat difficult to perceive, because the changes that the emerging presidency signify are not at present manifested directly in cases before the courts. There are, of course, some exceptions to this: the impoundment case, *Train* v. *New York* (1975), as well as *United States* v. *Nixon* (1974) deal with issues of asserted executive authority that are new in modern times. But these issues fade in significance when compared with the possibility of a fundamental alteration in the political balance between the executive and the legislature. It is this that the emerging presidency suggests.

---

[9]The term comes, of course, from the book of that title by Arthur Schlesinger, Jr. (Boston: Houghton-Mifflin Co., 1973). As he puts the matter: "The constitutional Presidency . . . has become the imperial Presidency and threatens to be the revolutionary Presidency" (p. viii).
[10]See, for example, Robert Heilbroner, *An Inquiry into The Human Prospect* (New York: Norton, 1974); and Zbigniew Brzezinski, *Between Two Ages* (New York: The Viking Press, 1971).

2. THE CONSTITUTION AS A BASIS FOR EXECUTIVE POWER IN THE CONDUCT OF FOREIGN AFFAIRS

A. A Note on the Constitutional Background of Executive Independence in Foreign Affairs

Legislative-executive struggle over the conduct of foreign relations has long existed in American politics, and the outcome at any given time has depended on a combination of circumstance, including executive "energy" and an occasional judicial decision. As one commentary has put it:

The relations of President and Congress in the diplomatic field have, first and last, presented a varied picture of alternative cooperation and tension, from which emerge two outstanding facts: first, the overwhelming importance of Presidential initiative in this area of power; secondly, the ever increasing dependence of foreign policy on congressional cooperation and support. First one and then the other aspect of the relationship is uppermost.[1]

Early judicial decisions regarding the conduct of American diplomacy reflect this divergence of views on the matter of responsibility for conducting foreign affairs. In 1793, President Washington issued a Proclamation of Neutrality in order to avoid involvement in the outbreak of war between Great Britain and France. Reflecting the dissatisfaction of Jefferson,

James Madison expressed the view that questions of deep import in the international field should be the joint responsibility of the executive and legislative branches; he based this opinion upon the power of Congress to declare war. Alexander Hamilton, rebutting Madison's view, spoke of

... the right of the Executive ... to determine the condition of the nation, though it may, in its consequences, affect the exercise of the power of the legislature to declare war. Nevertheless, the executive cannot thereby control the exercise of that power. The legislature is still free to perform its duties, according to its own sense of them; though the executive, in the exercise of its constitutional powers, may establish an antecedent state of things, which ought to weigh in the legislative decision. The division of the executive power in the Constitution, creates a concurrent authority in the cases to which it relates.[2]

Thus, contrasting views of limited and broad executive powers in foreign relations existed early in our history.[3] Fundamentally, the views of Hamilton have prevailed over time. This has been the case, not so much because of any intrinsic "truth" to his

[1]*The Constitution of the United States of America: Analysis and Interpretation* (Washington, D.C.: U.S. Government Printing Office, 1964), p. 552.

[2]Alexander Hamilton, "Letter of Pacificus, #1" (*Works*, J.C. Hamilton, ed., 1851), Vol. 7, pp. 76, 82–83.

[3]The strict issue in the 1793 debate was the question of neutrality. In 1794, Congress passed a Neutrality Act and thus took the initiative from the executive on this particular issue. However, the general points of view expressed in the Hamilton-Madison debate remain useful, since similar division on related questions has continued.

conception, but because it has been more consistent with governmental needs in an increasingly international world.

In 1795, the Supreme Court, in *Penhallow* v. *Doane,* broached an issue that has persisted in one form or another to the present day and that will continue to characterize congressional-executive competition over the conduct of foreign relations. During the revolutionary war, a British ship was seized by a vessel owned by a citizen of New Hampshire but commissioned by the Continental Congress. A New Hampshire court decided that the ship and cargo were lawful prize, but the British owners sued to recover by appealing to the Continental Congress. Congress referred the matter to a court of appeals, set up under the Articles of Confederation, and this court reversed the decision of the New Hampshire court. Eventually, the federal courts established under the Constitution of 1787 decided in favor of the British claimants, and an appeal was taken to the Supreme Court. Each Justice delivered a separate opinion, as was the practice at the time, but the thrust of judicial suggestion was that conduct of war was a matter of national sovereignty and not specifically dependent on affirmative provisions in the Constitution.

The implications of *Penhallow* were made more explicit in events that developed through President Lincoln's conduct of the early phases of the Civil War. In April 1861, Lincoln issued two blockade proclamations against Southern ports. These proclamations were made while Congress was not in session; in July, Lincoln called a special session of Congress in order to gain approval of his actions and to consider other measures in the prosecution of the

war. In the matter of the blockade, a delicate question of international politics was involved, since an internationally recognizable state of war with the Southern states would have increased the possibilities of British intervention on the side of the Confederacy.

Between May and July 1861, four vessels were seized as prizes by Union ships, acting under the proclamations. The owners brought suit for claims, appealing to the Supreme Court in order to test the validity of blockade proclamations initiated without congressional action. The four instances were argued collectively and were designated the *Prize Cases* (1863). In a 5-4 decision, Justice Grier argued for the majority that the necessity for the blockade and the extent of Southern belligerency were questions for the executive branch to decide. According to Grier, sudden belligerency from the South had created a condition of war necessitating executive action: "The President was bound to meet it in the shape it presented itself, without waiting for Congress to baptize it with a name; and no name given to it by him or them could change the facts."

The extent of presidential initiative in meeting de facto war and the basis in theory upon which the Court supported the president are indicated in the following passages from Justice Grier's opinion:

The law of nations is also called the law of nature; it is founded on the common consent as well as the common sense of the world. It contains no such anomalous doctrine as that which this court are now for the first time desired to pronounce, to wit: That insurgents who have risen in rebellion against their sovereign, expelled her courts, established a revolutionary government, organized armies, and commenced hostilities, are not enemies because they are traitors; and a war levied on the government by traitors, in order to dismember and destroy it, is not a war because it is an "insurrection."

Whether the President in fulfilling his duties, as Commander-in-Chief, in suppressing an insurrection, has met with such armed hostile resistance, and a civil war of such alarming proportions as will compel him to accord to them the character of belligerents, is a question to be decided by him, and this court must be governed by the decisions and acts of the Political Department of the government to which this power was entrusted. "He must determine what degree of force the crisis demands." The proclamation of blockade is, itself, official and conclusive evidence to the court, that a state of war existed which demanded and authorized a recourse to such a measure, under the circumstances peculiar to the case.

What the *Prize Cases* seemed to justify in the peculiar circumstances of the time was also applied to actions later in the Civil War and to actions taken by presidents before and during World Wars I and II. It is apparent that the powers of the president as commander-in-chief are broad in relation to presidentially defined exigencies.[4]

Other events in American political history serve to document the existence of presidential initiative and the unwillingness of the Supreme Court seriously to restrict it. The question is important because it sheds light on the claimed inherent nature of presidential power, especially in regard to international tensions. That inherent executive power, as an attribute of the American constitutional system, it should be suggested, is one of the more fas-cinating aspects of constitutional politics. Presidential prerogative amounting to inherent power is the flying dutchman of our system of government; when it is necessary, its form is seen, but when it is not, its reality is denied. For various presidents, it has been a convenient specter rather vaguely verified by the Court. As one commentator has put it:

There is a paucity of meaningful judicial authority on the inherent power of the Chief Magistrate–i.e., on his power to act, even though the particular act is not comprehended in a specific delegation to him. What authority there is, however, has tended to support the view that the President does possess at least some inherent powers.[5]

The extent of executive power and the associated question of inherent power are unclear primarily because the Constitution leaves the question open for interpretation. Article II mentions the "Executive power," and the duty that "He shall take care that the laws be faithfully executed." Are the "Executive power" and "take care" clauses neutral phrases to be given specific meaning in the context of other specific powers? Or are they phrases that themselves contain independent capacities for executive action aside from other powers given by the Constitution to the executive? The question has long been debated, and two widely differing answers have been given.

As a matter of historical convenience, one may rely on the constitutional views of presidents Theodore Roosevelt and William Howard Taft in order to grasp the fundamental po-

---

[4]For a brief but interesting discussion of this factor, see *The Constitution of the United States of America, op. cit.,* Note 1, pp. 440–445.

[5]Bernard Schwartz, *A Commentary on the Constitution of the United States,* Part I, Vol. II (New York: Macmillan, 1963), p. 61.

sitions on this question. Their theories of presidential power have antecedents going back to Hamilton and Madison and forward to Lyndon Johnson and Richard Nixon. Teddy Roosevelt took the view that as president, he was obliged to take whatever actions were necessary to meet the needs of the nation, unless such action was specifically proscribed by the Constitution. Presidential power was to be used within a "stewardship" role. On the other hand, Taft espoused a considerably more limited view; presidential power existed only in terms of "some specific grant of power or (a power) justly implied and included within such express grant as proper and necessary to its exercise."[6]

Two Supreme Court decisions of the 1890s gave considerable constitutional support to the broader view of presidential prerogative. *In re Neagle* (1890) and *In re Debs* (1895) concerned situations in which no clear statutory or constitutional basis existed for the action taken, but in response to which the Supreme Court stressed the necessity, as a matter of political self-preservation, for such power to exist.

In the *Neagle* case, an extraordinary set of circumstances came together. In order to protect Supreme Court Justice Field from threatened violence while on circuit in California, the president assigned to him a federal marshal (Neagle). When one of the persons who had threatened Field seemed to be carrying out his threat, the marshal shot and killed him. Neagle was arrested by state officers and subsequent habeas corpus proceedings presented to the Supreme Court the question concerning the president's authority to assign

Neagle. In supporting the "take care" duty of the president, the Court asked rhetorically:

Is this duty limited to the enforcement of acts of Congress or of treaties of the United States according to their express terms, or does it include the rights, duties and obligations growing out of the Constitution itself, our international relations, and all the protection implied by the nature of the government under the Constitution?

In the *Debs* case, a similarly broad interpretation by the Court resulted when it upheld the granting of an injunction requested by the government in order to protect the mails against violence in connection with a railway strike. Although there was no statutory authority for the injunction, the Court held that the government's interest in protecting the mails was sufficiently connected with the general welfare to justify the injunction. As Justice Brewer's opinion stated:

Every government, entrusted, by the very terms of its being, with powers and duties to be exercised and discharged for the general welfare, has a right to apply to its own courts for any proper assistance in the exercise of the one and the discharge of the other.

During the Korean War, President Truman's use of his executive power was tested and passed on by the Supreme Court in *Youngstown Sheet and Tube* v. *Sawyer*, known popularly as the *Steel Seizure Case* (1952). *Youngstown* was an unusual opinion insofar as the Court strained to fashion a majority out of a series of different constitutional postures. The decision makes clear only that the president's seizure of the steel mills

---

[6]William Howard Taft, *Our Chief Magistrate and His Powers* (New York: Columbia University Press, 1916), pp. 139–140.

(in order to prevent a halt in the flow of needed war materials) was not upheld. A judicial head count suggested that Congress had implicitly barred seizure by providing by statute a variety of other alternatives. In fact, a majority of five of the justices agreed that, at least under certain circumstances, the president had something called "inherent powers." For present purposes, the *Youngstown* decision was important because it failed to acknowledge the Court's prior supporting decisions on presidential prerogative and yet did not go to the extent of repudiating them. Justice Robert Jackson's concurring opinion, which favored the return of the steel mills but conceded the existence of inherent presidential powers, comes very close to being a compromise between the Taft and Roosevelt theories of presidential power.[7]

Although the previous cases raising questions of inherent presidential power had domestic factual contexts, the Court has held on at least one occasion that extraconstitutional power *does* exist in the field of foreign relations. In *United States* v. *Curtiss-Wright Export Corporation* (1936), a question arose as to the legality of a presidential proclamation prohibiting the sale of arms to countries in conflict in South America. The Curtiss-Wright Corporation had been charged with violating the proclamation. The presidential action was based on a prior Joint Resolution of Congress, and those indicted claimed that the president was acting on the basis of an unlawful delegation of power, since Congress had not specified

under what conditions the suspension of arms could take place. In supporting the government, Justice Sutherland's opinion (*infra*) claims inherent sovereign power for the government (and not just for the president) in the international sphere and treats the joint resolution as virtually unnecessary under the circumstances. The delegation of power argument was rejected although the Court assumed that the delegation would have been invalid in domestic legislation.[8]

A final but major element of the constitutional background concerning capacities to deal with international tensions involves the status of treaties. Constitutionally, treaties are a matter for executive negotiation with approval of the Senate as a condition of ratification; the judiciary has been a very restrained participant in the process. The Supreme Court in 1829 set the precedent for restraint by refusing to rule on an 1804 boundary dispute between Spain and the United States. In this case—*Foster* v. *Neilson* (1829)—the Court referred to the responsibility of the "political departments" in deciding matters of national boundaries. As Chief Justice Marshall put the matter:

In a controversy between two nations concerning a national boundary it is scarcely possible that the courts of either should refuse to abide by the measures adopted by its own government. There being no common tribunal to decide between them, each decides for itself on its own rights, and if they cannot adjust their differences peaceably, the

[7]See excerpt below (pp. 1008–1016) from *Youngstown*. For an elaborately documented and interesting analysis of the case, see Alan Westin, *The Anatomy of a Constitutional Law Case* (New York: Macmillan, 1959).

[8]For a brief criticism of the historical basis of the Sutherland thesis in Curtiss-Wright, see C. Herman Pritchett, *The American Constitution*, 3rd ed. (New York: McGraw-Hill, 1977), pp. 255–256.

right remains with the strongest. The judiciary is not that department of the government to which the assertion of its interests against foreign powers is confided; and its duty commonly is to decide upon individual rights, according to those principles which the political departments of the nation have established.

Foster articulated a rule of judicial restraint based on the concept of political questions; as one commentator has put it, "It is significant that the political questions doctrine has been perhaps most often invoked by the Court to avoid decisions relating to the conduct of American foreign relations."[9]

However, this does not mean that the Supreme Court has been silent in the matter of treaty-making power. The *Head Money Cases* (1884) established that Congress has considerable control in the applicability or modification of treaties and that the Court will extend cognizance to treaties in the context of congressional actions regarding them. In *Missouri* v. *Holland* (1920), the Supreme Court upheld legislation regulating the hunting of migratory game birds on the basis of a treaty with Great Britain. A similar statute, in the absence of a treaty, had earlier been held unconstitutional by a lower federal court on the grounds that Congress had no such power under the Constitution. Writing for the Court in *Missouri* v. *Holland*, Justice Holmes stated in effect that Congress, through a valid treaty, can acquire power that it does not have by direct constitutional delegation. The *Curtiss-Wright* decision of 1936 noted further that the United States, like every sovereign nation, has a

range of powers in foreign relations not necessarily found in the Constitution.

The Court took a more restrictive stand in *Reid* v. *Covert* (1956). The issue was whether dependents of military personnel stationed overseas could be tried by courts-martial. After World War II, many thousands of American servicemen were stationed abroad, often with their families. Ordinarily, dependents of military personnel would be under the local jurisdiction if charged with a crime. However, an executive agreement with Great Britain permitted American courts to exercise exclusive jurisdiction over American military dependents in Great Britain, and a similar situation existed in Japan. An act of Congress provided that military dependents overseas might be tried for crimes by military courts, which would preclude a jury and would not extend all of the protections of the Fifth and Sixth Amendments. *Reid* disposed of several appeals by the wives of military personnel, living on military bases in Great Britain and Japan, who had murdered their husbands and had been convicted by courts-martial.

Of course, in an ordinary criminal trial in the United States it would be constitutionally impossible for Congress to set aside the right of trial by jury or other constitutional protections for defendants. The Supreme Court ruled in *Reid* v. *Covert* that Congress cannot acquire power to do so in the case of military dependents in consequence of an executive agreement with a foreign power. As far as the rights and protections of defendants are concerned, Justice Black wrote for the Court in *Reid* v. *Covert*: "The United States is en-

[9]*Ibid.*, p. 254.

tirely a creature of the Constitution. Its power and authority have no other source. It can only act in accordance with all the limitations imposed by the Constitution." Justice Black went on to point out that *Missouri* v. *Holland* involved a very different situation, for the act of Congress in that case did not conflict with any "limitation imposed by the Constitution."

Thus the full scope of the treaty-making power is considerably broader than its constitutional source, and the president's powers over foreign policy seem to be largely immune to judicial interference. Courts traditionally prefer not to be involved in questions of foreign policy and national defense. If the *Reid* case seems to be an exception, that may be a consequence of the fact that *personal* rights were involved and that there was no broad national interest in need of protection. The accumulated traditions of presidential power in emergency situations seem, in retrospect, far more authoritative and persuasive than occasional reliance upon the reluctant and ever-cautious intervention of the courts.

The reader will have noted that *Reid* v. *Covert* concerned *executive agreements*. The large number of executive agreements in the twentieth century is perhaps the most striking characteristic of the growth of presidential power in foreign affairs. These are diplomatic agreements between the president and other nations which, for most purposes, have the same effect as treaties and which do not require the consent of the Senate. Like treaties, executive agreements can supersede conflicting state laws. Unlike treaties, executive agreements do not supersede prior acts of Congress. The Senate would appear to be far more effective than the Supreme Court in

limiting the president's foreign policymaking power. But as the debate over repeal of the Gulf of Tonkin Resolution and over various resolutions designed to limit the deployment of American troops in Indochina made clear, even an aroused Senate has great difficulty in overcoming its own traditions of deference to presidential leadership and the president's clear advantages of policy leadership and initiative.

The resentment against strong executive power, developing as an outgrowth of postwar isolationism and the Yalta and Potsdam agreements and as a response to the cold war, produced a strong campaign to curb the president's power to make executive agreements and to circumscribe the domestic impact of treaties, the latter being a direct move to reverse Holmes' dictum in *Missouri* v. *Holland*. The most direct expression of this sentiment was the so-called Bricker amendment, an amendment to the Constitution proposed by Senator John Bricker of Ohio in 1952 and 1953 and generally supported by conservatives. It failed of passage in the Senate by only one vote.

General opposition to the growth of presidential power, and a specific reaction against America's first and only four-term president, Franklin Roosevelt, led to passage of the Twenty-second Amendment, limiting tenure in the White House to two elected terms or a maximum of ten years for a president succeeding to that office past the midway point of his predecessor's term. Indeed, the Supreme Court's decision in the *Steel Seizure Case*, coming at the same time as the Twenty-second Amendment and the proposed Bricker amendment, suggests that the Supreme Court at the time was not immune from the prevailing political currents.

B. J. Woodford Howard, A Limited Government as a World Power

Few constitutional problems have produced more discourse, with less result, than the scope of constitutional limitation on foreign policy-making. While challenges to the constitutional capacity of the government have flourished throughout American diplomatic history, we have relied more on Holmes' chief guide, experience, than on the native talent at converting policy distastes into constitutional dogmas. . . .

At the outset, the main argument should be stated. First—and a truism today—it is illusory to expect judges to control foreign policy-makers in any but circumspect ways. Reliance against abuse must be placed largely on political and institutional restraints. Second—and not a truism—even these checks provide no greater assurance of responsible control than do parliamentary governments, and probably less. In an era in which inefficiency itself is unsafe, it is a fair question whether constitutional restrictions have backfired. . . .

What controls did the Constitution actually impose over the conduct of foreign policy? Political life in this country would be simpler were the answer clear; but the range of intended controls, even if now relevant, is not easily discovered under the gloss of interpretation made by successive generations (and the Framers themselves) when facing different problems. Do executive overseas commitments bind the nation? May Congress "direct" the executive to spend appropriated funds against his military judgment as commander-in-chief? Do individual rights limit national authority or vice versa? Are foreign policy powers delegated, resultant, or inherent? One can scan the original handwork *ad infinitum* and find little light on such unforeseen questions. Indeed, one can find little conclusive evidence that the Framers even had an explicit theory of foreign policy making, much less the inherent power and executive primacy principles now favored by the Supreme Court.

. . . When asserting that authority over foreign relations was inherent rather than enumerated, Justice Sutherland argued that *external* sovereignty flowed directly from Great Britain to the Union, whereas *internal* powers lodged in the thirteen states. In fact, the *ad hoc* Continental Congress did not conceive of itself as having received sovereign international capacity from Britain, yet the state governments did. In theory, the division of sovereignty into external and internal compartments conflicts with the basic constitutional postulate that *all* governmental power derived from the "sovereign people" and was subject to the limits imposed by them. The broad phrases of Article VI, distinguishing treaties made "under the authority of the United States" from laws made "in pursuance" of the Constitution, do not support a contrary inference. Quite clearly, that linguistic device aimed at covering existing agreements under the supremacy clause and not at freeing treaties from the principle that power

Reprinted from "Constitutional Limitation and American Foreign Policy," in Dietze (ed.), *Essays on the American Constitution* (Englewood Cliffs, N.J.: Prentice-Hall, 1964), pp. 159–162, 167–170, 172, 177–178.

must be deduced from a written instrument, be it express, implied or, in a pinch, "resultant." While treaty power was considered plenary and intentionally left undefined in scope, no one suggested that it was exempt from constitutional control, even if the enforcement mechanism was far from clear. How foreign policy power thus could be "independent" of the Constitution and yet subject to its prohibitions, Justice Sutherland never explained. The essential difficulty is that governments are considered to be empowered differently in international law and American constitutional thought. Justice Sutherland's undifferentiated conception mixed the two with a contradictory dash of dual sovereignty theory as well. For all its organic realism, his version of inherent power rests on shaky foundations.

Similar hazards face popular myths that the Framers inspired perpetual warfare for congressional-executive relations in foreign affairs. Too much has been read into pragmatic bargains that were not founded in principle at all. Senate participation in treaty-making, for instance, though popularly viewed as part of a grand design to balance authority, resulted only after great flux, if not weariness, in the Convention and was sought to protect sectional commercial interests plainly as much as to guard against Presidents. Modern interpretation may be sound, as a general proposition, that separation of powers was intended to supply an in-built inefficiency for sake of safety against arbitrary government; but in foreign policy, safety against whom? The Framers faced a situation in which foreign relations had been conducted in theory by Congress in the name of the thirteen states, in fact by a cumbersome legislative committee, and occasionally by

states themselves. And in 1787, there the primary focus remained—on the relationship between Congress and runaway state governments, not the potential erosion of power to the Presidency. Even Hamilton, arch proponent of executive authority, dismissed the power to command the armed services as purely military and to receive foreign emissaries as *pro forma*. It took two post-constitutional generations to affirm that the executive was the sole official spokesman of the United States internationally and four to accept the non-military aspects of his power as commander-in-chief. While executive leadership is easily inferred from the Constitution, the notion that checks and balances were designed primarily for legislative protection is a distinctly modern concept. What learning there is suggests that the controls imposed were designed to work at least equally the other way around. Foreign affairs, in fact, may well have been thought of as exempt altogether from the countervailing power principle. . . .

The complex system of power distribution within the national government was assumed to be the major institutional control over foreign policy-making. Although the assumption of easy interbranch collaboration collapsed at its first trial, the crucial nexus has always been the political relations among the Presidency and houses of Congress, and not the courts. The few *cause célèbres* in which the Justices asserted their admitted supervisory function over separation of powers have obscured the small part they have actually played in shaping those relations respecting foreign policy. To be sure, resolution of what was once a great issue—whether the House was legally bound to execute treaties made by President and Senate—was aided by the judicial distinction between self-executing and non-self-executing treaties and by the principle of equality between treaties and statutes, which makes the later in time govern. Both principles enhance the political check by affirming the power of Congress to refuse treaty execution or to repeal the domestic effect of treaties already in force. The result is that international commitments "in no wise diminish Congress' constitutional powers," however infrequently Congress has chosen to use them.

Beyond its impact as an ultimate threat, nonetheless, judicial review has had little to do with the evolution of American foreign policy or the machinery of making it. In no area of public law has judicial self-restraint been more marked. As a matter of history, courts have interpreted treaties in a manner avoiding constitutional conflict; they have refused to subject Congress' "plenary" power over aliens, immigration, and acquisition of territory to more than the barest procedural requirements; they have graced the fusion of Presidential powers with approving references to executive prerogative; and they have explicitly held that the restraints of separation of powers have less force in foreign as distinct from domestic affairs. By recognizing "the very delicate plenary and exclusive power of the President as the sole organ of the federal government in the field of international relations," the Justices have converted a fact of life into constitutional principle.

Perhaps the clearest manifestation of judicial withdrawal is the broad application of the "political question" doctrine to foreign policy issues. No one knows exactly what a political question is or when it will apply. But the Court recently indicated that it is "primarily a function of the separa-tion of powers." Numerous cases have been dismissed as "non-justiciable" when the following elements appeared—the Constitution conferred exclusive discretion on political branches, the issues turned on "standards that defy judicial application," or the situation demanded a "single-voiced statement" and finality of the government's position. Whether or not the doctrine itself is a constitutional command, its fullest coverage has been in foreign affairs. Recognition and non-recognition of states and governments, diplomatic immunities, abrogation of treaties, duration of war, reprisals, the conduct of military government, and the like, all are matters thought to lie within the exclusive domain of the political branches, whose decisions are considered binding on courts. The list doubtless would be longer but for the reinforcing lack of standing of parties to challenge broad classes of executive discretion. Political scientists may quarrel that the legal distinction between discretionary and ministerial duties is unreal, but it, too, has been a useful judicial tool to avoid involvement in delicate matters of statecraft.

Doctrines of deference, of course, have not always been applied consistently nor without judicial discomfort. Supreme Court Justices have not scrapped constitutional distinctions between war and peace, or between military and civil authority, as easily as have other sectors of the government. Obviously, they have been troubled by the legal implications of the nation's far-flung foreign policy activities, especially those which call into question individual liberty or structural distribution of power. Is it still true, as men thought fifty years ago, that all agreements must rest on consent of Congress, express or implied? Is there no specific time limit to domestic regulation under color of delegated war power? Short of specific prohibitions, does the executive possess an inherent aggregate of power to handle emergencies without legislative approval or by means otherwise regulated by Congress? Sufficient doubts have been expressed in court to leave these matters open for future judicial intervention. And intervention is amply precedented. With forceful rhetoric in defense of liberty, Supreme Court Justices have proclaimed again and again that even "the war power . . . is subject to applicable constitutional limitations". Yet the fact remains that with rare exceptions the declaration has been followed by exceptions so wide as to admit the opposite. World War II plainly consolidated a pattern of transferring responsibility from Congress to President, and thence to civilian and military bureaucracies, with full judicial approval. In the Japanese Relocation cases, not only were some Justices eager to join the buck-passing which characterized that sad operation, but the Court affirmed both Charles Evans Hughes' dictum that the war power is "the power to wage war successfully" and Chief Justice Stone's significant addition: "it is not for any Court to sit in review of the wisdom" of action taken by "those branches of the Government on which the Constitution has placed the responsibility of war-making." Despite the return from relativism toward emergency power after the war . . . events have vastly increased national authority and the Presidency's share of it. If judicial supervision of separation of powers means the maintenance of a relatively fixed equilibrium of authority, the force of that principle has long been lost.

. . . Closely associated with the debate over federalism and separation of powers has been the great goal of individual liberty. May foreign policy needs override constitutional rights? Except for occasional aberrations like John Foster Dulles' celebrated Louisville speech, it has been seldom admitted that foreign policy decisions may abridge express constitutional prohibitions; and since Madison's day, a system of expectations has flourished that the defense of liberty is the peculiar province of courts. While few would argue that judges *cannot* review invasions of private guarantees, however, in the twentieth century fears have multiplied that in practice the judiciary *will not* interfere. . . .

If it is a cruel delusion to expect the judiciary to serve as the mainspring of foreign policy control, what judges do is not the end of the matter. Both Constitution and practice entrust the safety of the Republic primarily to the wisdom of the people's representatives, as tempered by elections and by institutional distribution of power. Do these politically enforced precautions of the Constitution achieve their larger purpose of controlling, without weakening, government?

There was a time when the mere recital of the numerous checks available, not to speak of elections and rebellion, supplied a ready answer to that imponderable. Today, unfortunately, the stresses felt by every major government have shaken easy confidence in the capacity of institutional controls to restrain abuse. For one thing, safeguards are hardly available for the kind of situation most likely to be feared. Yalta, Suez, and Cuba have taught us what the Framers already knew—that no constitutional system can prevent rash error without imposing fatal impotence. Experience also suggests that, even when safeguards are available, the Constitution's alternative of restraining authority by dispersing it exacts a heavier price than is commonly assumed. . . . Criticism has mounted because of evidence that division of power encumbers both effective policy formation *and* democratic accountability. . . .

C. The Sources of Inherent Power

(1) Myers v. United States (1926)

+Taft, Van Devanter, Butler, Sutherland, Sanford, Stone
−Holmes, Brandeis, McReynolds

[The Constitution provides four methods of appointment. In Article II, Section 2, the president is given the power, with the "advice and consent of the Senate," to appoint "ambassadors, other public ministers and consuls, Judges of the Supreme Court," and "all other officers of the United States whose appointments are not herein provided for." Congress may, by law, invest the power of appointment over "such inferior officers as they think proper," in the "president alone, in the Courts alone, or in the heads of departments."

What is an "officer of the United States"? Clearly, such an officer has significant executive or administrative powers, but where is the line to be drawn? Reciprocally, what is an "inferior officer"? The suggestion has been made that judges below the level of the Supreme Court constitute "inferior officers" and that Congress could, if it wishes, invest their appointment in the president alone or in the Supreme Court as the head of the judicial department.[1] Congress has not chosen to do this, of course.

Congress has no power of appointment except over employees of the legislative branch. But it can establish an "office" to which appointments must be made, and it can and often does specify qualifications for any particular office such as age, citizenship, political party affiliation, and professional qualifications.

The Constitution does not speak of the power of removal except in the clauses governing impeachments. The absence of any constitutional provision on removal has, from time to time, been the source of heated conflict between the president and Congress. Cases on such questions have often been the occasion for considering the limits of presidential power. Is removal solely an executive function? If so, by what right and what logic? Can the removal power of the president be regulated by Congress?

From 1789 to 1867 the consensus was that the president could remove an officer of the United States without the consent of the Senate, even though the original appointments had been made with Senate consent. The precedent for this view came from the debate in Congress in 1789 over the appointment and removal of the secretary of state. One side contended that a secretary of state appointed with the consent of the Senate could only be removed with Senate approval. Another argument was that Congress could, if it wished, control the removal power under the "necessary and proper" clause. But the prevailing decision was that the president had the sole power to remove a secretary of state and that this power was grounded in the broad concept of "executive power."

In 1867, Congress, locked in a political struggle over Reconstruction with President Andrew Johnson, passed the Tenure of Office Act. The president was forbidden to remove any executive officer appointed with Senate consent without the approval of the Senate. It also provided that executive officers appointed with the consent of the Senate should remain in office during the term of the president who appointed them until a duly qualified successor was appointed and confirmed. Johnson vetoed the bill, but Congress overrode his veto.

In 1868, Johnson summarily dismissed Secretary of War William Stanton, an action seemingly in clear violation of the law. The radical

[1]Harold Chase, *Federal Judges: The Appointing Process* (Minneapolis: University of Minnesota Press, 1972), pp. 204–207.

Republicans in Congress had been waiting for Johnson to commit an "impeachable" act, and two days after Stanton was fired, the House of Representatives voted to impeach the President. Three of the articles of impeachment charged the deliberate violation of the Tenure of Office Act. But the Senate failed to convict the President, the vote of 35 – 19 falling one vote short of the required two-thirds. Seven Republican senators, at great political risk, had joined the Democratic minority to acquit the president. Those seven senators later stated that they believed the Tenure of Office Act was unconstitutional and that Johnson had committed no offense.[2]

The Tenure of Office Act was repealed in 1887 and never tested in the courts. In 1876, Congress enacted a law setting four-year terms for first-, second-, and third-class postmasters and providing that holders of those positions were to be appointed and removed with the advice and consent of the Senate. Myers was appointed postmaster of Portland, Oregon, in 1917. In February 1920, he was removed from office on orders of President Wilson. No effort was made to submit the removal to the Senate for its approval. Myers brought suit in the U.S. Court of Claims for his back salary. The court ruled against Myers, who died shortly thereafter, and the case was taken to the Supreme Court by his widow as administratrix of his estate. The case provided the Court and its Chief Justice, former President William Howard Taft, with the opportunity to consider the broad question of the limits of executive authority. It was also the first occasion when the solicitor general argued against the constitutionality of an act of Congress.]

MR. CHIEF JUSTICE TAFT delivered the opinion of the Court.

This case presents the question whether under the Constitution the President has the exclusive power of removing executive officers of the United States whom he has appointed by and with the advice and consent of the Senate.

. . .

Made responsible under the Constitution for the effective enforcement of the law, the President needs as an indispensable aid to meet it the disciplinary influence upon those who act under him of a reserve power of removal. But it is contended that executive officers appointed by the President with the consent of the Senate are bound by the statutory law, and are not his servants to do his will, and that his obligation to care for the faithful execution of the law does not authorize him to treat them as such. The degree of guidance in the discharge of their duties that the President may exercise over executive officers varies with the character of their service as prescribed in the law under which they act. The highest and most important duties which his subordinates perform are those in which they act for him. In such cases they are exercising not their own but his discretion. This field is a very large one. It is sometimes described as political. *Kendall* v. *United States*. . . . Each head of a department is and must be the President's alter ego in the matters of that department where the President is required by law to exercise authority.

. . .

The duties of the heads of departments and bureaus in which the discretion of the President is exercised and which we have described are the

---

[2]Besides contending that the act was unconstitutional, Johnson's lawyers also argued that it did not apply, since Stanton had been appointed by Lincoln, not Johnson. Opponents contended that Johnson was merely an "acting president" who was serving out the remainder of Lincoln's term. But the principle that a vice-president who succeeds to the office of president is fully the president himself had been *established* by John Tyler's successful claim to that title in the 1840s.

most important in the whole field of executive action of the government. There is nothing in the Constitution which permits a distinction between the removal of the head of a department or a bureau, when he discharges a political duty of the President or exercises his discretion, and the removal of executive officers engaged in the discharge of their other normal duties. The imperative reasons requiring an unrestricted power to remove the most important of his subordinates in their most important duties must therefore control the interpretation of the Constitution as to all appointed by him.

But this is not to say that there are not strong reasons why the President should have a like power to remove his appointees charged with other duties than those above described. The ordinary duties of officers prescribed by statute come under the general administrative control of the President by virtue of the general grant to him of the executive power, and he may properly supervise and guide their construction of the statutes under which they act in order to secure the unitary and uniform execution of the laws which article 2 of the Constitution evidently contemplated in vesting general executive power in the President alone. Laws are often passed with specific provision for the adoption of regulations by a department or bureau head to make the law workable and effective. The ability and judgment manifested by the official thus empowered, as well as his energy and stimulation of his subordinates, are subjects which the President must consider and supervise in his administrative control. Finding such officers to be negligent and inefficient, the President should have the power to remove them. Of course there may be duties so peculiarly and specifically committed to the discretion of a particular officer as to raise a question whether the President may overrule or revise the officer's interpretation of his statutory duty in a particular instance. Then there may be duties of a quasi judicial character imposed on executive officers and members of executive tribunals whose decisions after hearing affect interests of individuals, the discharge of which the President cannot in a particular case properly influence or control. But even in such a case he may consider the decision after its rendition as a reason for removing the officer, on the ground that the discretion regularly entrusted to that officer by statute has not been on the whole intelligently or wisely exercised. Otherwise he does not discharge his own constitutional duty of seeing that the laws be faithfully executed.

We have devoted much space to this discussion and decision of the question of the presidential power of removal in the First Congress, not because a congressional conclusion on a constitutional issue is conclusive, but first because of our agreement with the reasons upon which it was avowedly based, second because this was the decision of the First Congress on a question of primary importance in the organization of the government made within two years after the Constitutional Convention and within a much shorter time after its ratification, and third because that Congress numbered among its leaders those who had been members of the convention. It must necessarily constitute a precedent upon which many future laws supplying the machinery of the new government would be based and, if erroneous, would be likely to evoke dissent and departure in future Congresses. It would come at once before the executive branch of the government for compliance and might well be brought before the judicial branch for a test of its validity. As we shall see, it was soon accepted as a final decision of the question by all branches of the government.

It was, of course, to be expected that the decision would be received by lawyers and jurists with something of the same division of opinion as that manifested in Congress, and doubts were often expressed as to its correctness. But the acquiescence which was promptly accorded it after a few years was universally recognized.

. . .

Summing up, then, the facts as to acquiescence by all branches of the government in the legislative decision of 1789 as to executive officers, whether superior or inferior, we find that from 1789 until 1863, a period of 74 years, there was no act of Congress, no executive act, and no decision of this court at variance with the declaration of the First Congress; but there was, as we have seen, clear affirmative recognition of it by each branch of the government.

Our conclusion on the merits, sustained by the arguments before stated, is that article 2 grants to the President the executive power of the government—i.e., the general administrative control of those executing the laws, including the power of appointment and removal of executive officers—a conclusion confirmed by his obligation to take care that the laws be faithfully executed; that article 2 excludes the exercise of legislative power by Congress to provide for appointments and removals, except only as granted therein to Congress in the matter of inferior offices; that Congress is only given power to provide for appointments and removals of inferior officers after it has vested,

and on condition that it does vest, their appointment in other authority than the President with the Senate's consent; that the provisions of the second section of article 2, which blend action by the legislative branch, or by part of it, in the work of the executive, are limitations to be strictly construed, and not to be extended by implication; that the President's power of removal is further established as an incident to his specifically enumerated function of appointment by and with the advice of the Senate, but that such incident does not by implication extend to removals the Senate's power of checking appointments; and, finally, that to hold otherwise would make it impossible for the President, in case of political or other difference with the Senate or Congress, to take care that the laws be faithfully executed.

. . .

An argument *ab inconvenienti* has been made against our conclusion in favor of the executive power of removal by the President, without the consent of the Senate, that it will open the door to a reintroduction of the spoils system. The evil of the spoils system aimed at in the Civil Service Law and its amendments is in repect to inferior offices. It has never been attempted to extend that law beyond them. Indeed Congress forbids its extension to appointments confirmed by the Senate except with the consent of the Senate. . . . Reform in the federal civil service was begun by the Civil Service Act of 1883. It has been developed from that time, so that the classified service now includes a vast majority of all the civil officers. It may still be enlarged by further legislation. The independent power of removal by the President alone under present conditions works no practical interference with the merit system. Political appointments of inferior officers are still maintained in one important class, that of the first, second and third class postmasters, collectors of internal revenue, marshals, collectors of customs, and other officers of that kind distributed through the country. They are appointed by the President with the consent of the Senate. It is the invention of the Senate in their appointment, and not in their removal, which prevents their classification into the merit system. If such appointments were vested in the heads of departments to which they belong, they could be entirely removed from politics, and that is what a number of Presidents have recommended.

. . .

What then, are the elements that enter into our decision of this case? We have, first, a construction of the Constitution made by a Congress which was to provide by legislation for the organization of the government in accord with the Constitution which had just then been adopted, and in which there were, as Representatives and Senators, a considerable number of those who had been members of the convention that framed the Constitution and presented it for ratification. It was the Congress that launched the government. It was the Congress that rounded out the Constitution itself by the proposing of the first 10 amendments, which had in effect been promised to the people as a consideration for the ratification. It was the Congress in which Mr. Madison, one of the first in the framing of the Constitution, led also in the organization of the government under it. It was a Congress whose constitutional decisions have always been regarded, as they should be regarded, as of the greatest weight in the interpretation of that fundamental instrument. This construction was followed by the

legislative department and the executive department continuously for 73 years, and this, although the matter in the heat of political differences between the executive and the Senate in President Jackson's time, was the subject of bitter controversy, as we have seen. This court has repeatedly laid down the principle that a contemporaneous legislative exposition of the Constitution, when the founders of our government and framers of our Constitution were actively participating in public affairs, acquiesced in for a long term of years, fixes the construction to be given its provisions.

. . .

We are now asked to set aside this construction thus buttressed and adopt an adverse view, because the Congress of the United States did so during a heated political difference of opinion between the then President and the majority leaders of Congress over the reconstruction measures adopted as a means of restoring to their proper status the states which attempted to withdraw from the Union at the time of the Civil War. The extremes to which the majority in both Houses carried legislative measures in that matter are now recognized by all who calmly review the history of that episode in our government leading to articles of impeachment against President Johnson and his acquittal. Without animadverting on the character of the measures taken, we are certainly justified in saying that they should not be given the weight affecting proper constitutional construction to be accorded to that reached by the First Congress of the United States during a political calm and acquiesced in by the whole government for three-quarters of a century, especially when the new construction contended for has never been acquiesced in by either the executive or the judicial departments. While this court has studiously avoided deciding the issue until it was presented in such a way that it could not be avoided, in the references it has made to the history of the question, and in the presumptions it has indulged in favor of a statutory construction not inconsistent with the legislative decision of 1789, it has indicated a trend of view that we should not and cannot ignore. When on the merits we find our conclusion strongly favoring the view which prevailed in the First Congress, we have no hesitation in holding that conclusion to be correct; and it therefore follows that the Tenure of Office Act of 1867, in so far as it attempted to prevent the President from removing executive officers who had been appointed by him by and with the advice and consent of the Senate, was invalid, and that subsequent legislation of the same effect was equally so.

For the reasons given, we must therefore hold that the provision of the law of 1876 by which the unrestricted power of removal of first-class postmasters is denied to the President is in violation of the Constitution and invalid. This leads to an affirmance of the judgment of the Court of Claims.

MR. JUSTICE BRANDEIS, DISSENTING.

. . .

To imply a grant to the President of the uncontrollable power of removal from statutory inferior executive offices involves an unnecessary and indefensible limitation upon the constitutional power of Congress to fix the tenure of the inferior statutory offices. That such a limitation cannot be justified on the ground of necessity is demonstrated by the practice of our governments, state and national. In none of the original 13 states did the chief executive possess such power at the time of the adoption of the federal Constitution. In none of the 48 states has such a power been conferred at any time since by a state Constitution, with a single possible exception. In a few states the Legislature has granted to the Governor, or other appointing power, the absolute power of removal. The legislative practice of most states reveals a decided tendency to limit, rather than to extend, the Governor's power of removal. The practice of the federal government will be set forth in detail.

. . .

From the foundation of the government to the enactment of the Tenure of Office Act, during the period while it remained in force, and from its repeal to this time, the administrative practice in respect to all offices has, so far as appears, been consistent with the existence in Congress of power to make removals subject to the consent of the Senate.

. . .

The practice of Congress to control the exercise of the executive power of removal from inferior offices is evidenced by many statutes which restrict it in many ways besides the removal clause here in question. Each of these restrictive statutes became law with the approval of the President. Every President who has held office since 1861, except President Garfield, approved one or more of such statutes. Some of these statutes, prescribing a fixed term, provide that removal shall be made only for one of several specified causes. Some provide a fixed term, subject generally to removal for cause. Some provide for removal only after hearing. Some provide a fixed term, subject to removal for reasons to be communicated by the President to the Senate. Some impose the restriction in still other ways.

. . .

The historical data submitted present a legislative practice, established by concurrent affirmative action of Congress and the President, to make consent of the Senate a condition of removal from statutory inferior, civil, executive offices to which the appointment is made for a fixed term by the President with such consent. They show that the practice has existed, without interruption, continuously for the last 58 years; that throughout this period, it has governed a great majority of all such offices; that the legislation applying the removal clause specifically to the office of postmaster was enacted more than half a century ago; and that recently the practice has, with the President's approval, been extended to several newly created offices. The data show further that the insertion of the removal clause in acts creating inferior civil offices with fixed tenures is part of the broader legislative practice, which has prevailed since the formation of our government, to restrict or regulate in many ways both removal from and nomination to such offices. A persistent legislative practice which involves a delimitation of the respective powers of Congress and the President, and which has been so established and maintained, should be deemed tantamount to judicial construction, in the absence of any decision by any court to the contrary. . . .

The persuasive effect of this legislative practice is strengthened by the fact that no instance has been found, even in the earlier period of our history, of concurrent affirmative action of Congress and the President which is inconsistent with the legislative practice of the last 58 years to impose the removal clause. Nor has any instance been found of action by Congress which involves recognition in any other way of the alleged uncontrollable executive power to remove an inferior civil officer. The action taken by Congress in 1789 after the great debate does not present such an instance. The vote then taken did not involve a decision that the President had uncontrollable power. It did not involve a decision of the question whether Congress could confer upon the Senate the right and impose upon it the duty, to participate in removals. It involved merely the decision that the Senate does not, in the absence of legislative grant thereof, have the right to share in the removal of an officer appointed with its consent, and that the President has, in the absence of restrictive legislation, the constitutional power of removal without such consent. Moreover, as Chief Justice Marshall recognized, the debate and the decision related to a high political office, not to inferior ones.

. . .

The separation of the powers of government did not make each branch completely autonomous. It left each in some measures, dependent upon the others, as it left to each power to exercise, in some respects, functions in their nature executive, legislative and judicial. Obviously the President cannot secure full execution of the laws, if Congress denies to him adequate means of doing so. Full execution may be defeated because Congress declines to create offices indispensable for that purpose; or because Congress, having created the office, declines to make the indispensable appropriation; or because Congress, having both created the office and made the appropriation, prevents by restrictions which it imposes, the appointment of officials who in quality and character are indispensable to the efficient execution of the law. If, in any such way, adequate means are denied to the President, the fault will lie with Congress. The President performs his full constitutional duty, if, with the means and instruments provided by Congress and within the limitations prescribed by it, he uses his best endeavors to secure the faithful execution of the laws enacted. . . .

Checks and balances were established in order that this should be "a government of laws and not of men." As White said in the House in 1789, an uncontrollable power of removal in the Chief Executive "is a doctrine not to be learned in American governments." Such power had been denied in colonial charters, and even under proprietary grants and royal commissions. It had been denied in the thirteen states before the framing of the federal Constitution. The doctrine of the separation of powers was adopted by the convention of 1787 not to promote efficiency but to preclude the exercise of arbitrary power. The purpose was not to avoid friction but by means of the inevitable friction incident to the distribution of the governmental powers among three departments, to save the people from autocracy. In order to prevent arbitrary executive action, the Constitution provided in terms that presidential appointments be made with the consent of the Senate, unless Congress should otherwise provide; and this clause was construed by Alexander Hamilton in *The Federalist*, No. 77, as requiring like consent to removals. Limiting further executive prerogatives customary in monarchies, the Constitution empowered Congress to vest the appointment of inferior officers, "as we think proper, in the President alone, in the Courts of Law, or in the Heads of Departments." Nothing in support of the claim of uncontrollable power can be inferred from the silence of the convention of 1787 on the subject of removal. For the outstanding fact remains that every specific proposal to confer such uncontrollable power upon the President was rejected. In

America, as in England, the conviction prevailed then that the people must look to the representative assemblies for the protection of their liberties. And protection of the individual, even if he be an official, from the arbitrary or capricious exercise of power was then believed to be an essential of free government.

MR. JUSTICE HOLMES, DISSENTING.

My Brothers McReynolds and Brandeis have discussed the question before us with exhaustive research and I say a few words merely to emphasize my agreement with their conclusion.

We have to deal with an office that owes its existence to Congress and that Congress may abolish tomorrow. Its duration and the pay attached to it while it lasts depend on Congress alone. Congress alone confers on the President the power to appoint to it and at any time may transfer the power to other hands. With such power over its own creation, I have no more trouble in believing that Congress has power to prescribe a term of life for it free from any interference than I have in accepting the undoubted power of Congress to decree its end. I have equally little trouble in accepting its power to prolong the tenure of an incumbent until Congress or the Senate shall have assented to his removal. The duty of the President to see that the laws be executed is a duty that does not go beyond the laws or require him to achieve more than Congress sees fit to leave within his power.

JUSTICE McREYNOLDS, DISSENTING (OMITTED).

[The broad sweep and *dicta* of Taft's opinion in *Myers*, notwithstanding Justice Brandeis' forceful dissent, were regarded as a direct challenge to the power of Congress to limit the removal power of the president. Legislation establishing the early regulatory commissions, such as the Federal Trade Commission, had such limits. But in the wake of the *Myers* decision, Congress backed off, and no removal restrictions were included in the statutes forming the Federal Power Commission in 1930 and the Securities and Exchange Commission in 1934.

The case of *Humphrey's Executor* v. *United States* (1935) gave the Supreme Court another opportunity to consider the question. Humphrey was a member of the Federal Trade Commission who had been appointed to a seven-year term by President Hoover in 1931. His appointment had been confirmed by the Senate. The FTC statute provided that commissioners were removable by the president "for inefficiency, neglect of duty, or malfeasance in office." In 1933, President Roosevelt asked Humphrey to resign on the grounds that he could work better with someone "of his own choosing." Humphrey refused to resign, whereupon Roosevelt dismissed him from office, claiming that he did not have "full confidence" in Humphrey's policies. Although physically barred from his office, Humphrey continued to insist that he was lawfully a member of the commission. Upon Humphrey's death in 1934, his executor maintained his suit in the United States Court of Claims to recover all back salary due him.

Chief Justice Taft and Justice Edward Sanford both died in 1930 and were replaced, respectively, by Charles Evans Hughes and Harlan Fiske Stone. Justice Holmes retired in 1932 and was replaced by Benjamin Cardozo. The three new justices joined the rest of the Court in a unanimous decision in favor of Humphrey. The Court held that Congress had limited the removal power of the president over members of the Federal Trade Commission, and that such limits were constitutionally valid. The *Myers* case was not overruled, but it was distinguished. The Court saw a clear difference between a postmaster, "an executive officer restricted to the performance of executive functions," and a member of an independent regulatory commission who performed discretionary functions of a quasi-judicial, quasi-legislative nature. Such a commissioner is not an extension of the president. Writing for the Court, Justice Sutherland held that the "deci-

sion of 1789" applies only to purely executive officers and those, like postmasters, exercising purely ministerial power. Otherwise, he wrote, Congress could impose whatever removal restrictions it wished.

In *Wiener* v. *United States* (1958), concerning President Eisenhower's removal of a member of the War Claims Commission, the Court extended the logic of *Humphrey's Executor.* The statute establishing the commission provided that members were to serve for the limited life of the commission. Nothing was said about removal. Yet the Court held that *Humphrey's Executor* was controlling. Justice Frankfurter drew a sharp distinction between "purely executive officers" and "members of quasi-judicial bodies" and held the distinction applicable to any official on the basis of his or her *function* within the executive branch. Since the War Claims Commission, like the Federal Trade Commission, was not an executive agency but an independent body, and since its sole function was adjudicatory, like those of a court, the president's power to remove Commissioner Wiener was limited *even in the absence of statutory provisions.*

One other fact must be noted: in neither of these cases was the Supreme Court confronted with the challenge of telling a popular president (Roosevelt and Eisenhower, respectively) to actually reinstate the official who had been illegally removed. In *Humphrey's Executor,* Humphrey had died before the Court decision. All that was at stake substantively, besides the principle of removal, was back pay. Roosevelt's appointee continued to serve on the Federal Trade Commission. In *Wiener,* the War Claims Commission had already ceased to function when the Court ruled; hence, again, all that was tangibly at stake was back pay; reinstatement was not at issue. It is much easier to rule against a president when the impact of the decision will be neither tangible nor immediate. The Court was able to avoid a direct confrontation with the president, while announcing a rule of law inhibiting presidential power. Where a direct confrontation exists, the political dynamics of the situation will be different. Compare, for example, the language of *Humphrey's Executor* with the language in the

Steel Seizure Case or the *Nixon Tapes Case.*

In a recent case, *Buckley* v. *Valeo* (1976), the Supreme Court blocked an effort by Congress to retain some influence in the appointment of members of the Federal Elections Commission. According to the Federal Election Campaign Act of 1974, the commission was to consist of six members, two appointed by the president with the consent of *both* the House of Representatives and the Senate. The remaining four members were to be appointed by the Speaker of the House and the president pro tem of the Senate. The commission had powers of investigation into corrupt election practices, but it also was given substantial rule-making and enforcement powers.

The Court held that if the commission exercised all these powers, then the commissioners were, in fact, at least "officers of the United States" and must be appointed according to Article II, Section 2. Congress has explicit and plenary power to regulate federal elections, but the mode of appointment is controlled by another constitutional provision. Congress' implied powers under the "necessary and proper" clause are insufficient authority to override this principle. Congress is not included in the "Heads of Departments or Courts of Law" exception to presidential appointments. Therefore, the commissioners must be appointed by the president. If Congress wanted to retain the system of appointment, the Court said, then it would have to reduce the powers of the commission so that it was primarily an investigatory arm of Congress. But Congress cannot have it both ways.]

(2) United States v. Curtiss-Wright Export Corporation (1936)

+Sutherland, Hughes, Brandeis, Van Devanter, Burton, Roberts, Cardozo
−McReynolds
NP Stone

MR. JUSTICE SUTHERLAND delivered the opinion of the court.

On January 27, 1936, an indictment was returned ... which charges that appellees, beginning with the 29th day of May, 1934, conspired to sell in the United States certain arms of war, namely fifteen machine guns, to Bolivia, a country then engaged in armed conflict in the Chaco, in violation of the Joint Resolution of Congress approved May 28, 1934, and the provisions of a proclamation issued on the same day by the President of the United States pursuant to authority conferred by § 1 of the resolution. In pursuance of the conspiracy, the commission of certain overt acts was alleged, details of which need not be stated. . . .

First. It is contended that by the Joint Resolution, the going into effect and continued operation of the resolution was conditioned (a) upon the President's judgment as to its beneficial effect upon the reestablishment of peace between the countries engaged in armed conflict in the Chaco; (b) upon the making of a proclamation, which was left to his unfettered discretion, thus constituting an attempted substitution of the President's will for that of Congress; (c) upon the making of a proclamation putting an end to the operation of the resolution, which again was left to the President's unfettered discretion; and (d) further, that the extent of its operation in particular cases was subject to limitation and exception by the President, controlled by no standard. In each of these particulars, appellees urge that Congress abdicated its essential functions and delegated them to the Executive.

Whether, if the Joint Resolution had related solely to internal affairs it would be open to the challenge that it constituted an unlawful delegation of legislative power to the Executive, we find it unnecessary to determine. The whole aim of the resolution is to affect a situation entirely external to the United States and falling within the category of foreign affairs. The determination which we are called to make, therefore, is whether the Joint Resolution, as applied to that situation, is vulnerable to attack under the rule that forbids a delegation of the law-making powers. In other words, assuming (but not deciding) that the challenged delegation, if it were confined to internal affairs, would be invalid, may it nevertheless be sustained on the ground that its exclusive aim is to afford a remedy for a hurtful condition within foreign territory?

It will contribute to the elucidation of the question if we first consider the differences between the powers of the federal government in respect of foreign or external affairs and those in respect of domestic or internal affairs. That there are differences between them, and that these differences are fundamental, may not be doubted.

The two classes of powers are different, both in respect of their origin and their nature. The broad statement that the federal government can exercise no powers except those specifically enumerated in the Constitution, and such implied powers as are necessary and proper to carry into effect the enumerated powers, is categorically true only in respect of our internal affairs. In that field, the primary purpose of the Constitution was to carve from the general mass of legislative powers *then possessed by the states* such portions as it was thought desirable to vest in the federal government, leaving those not included in the enumeration still in the states. *Carter* v. *Carter Coal Co.* . . . That this doctrine applies only to powers which the states had, is self evident. And since the states severally never possessed international powers, such powers could not have been carved from the mass of state powers but obviously were transmitted to the United States from some other source. During the colonial period, those powers were possessed exclusively by and were entirely under the control of the Crown. By the Declaration of Independence, "the Representatives of the United States of America" declared the United [not the several] Colonies to be free and independent states, and as such to have "full Power to levy War, conclude Peace, contract Alliances, establish Commerce and to do all other Acts and Things which Independent States may of right do."

As a result of the separation from Great Britain by the colonies acting as a unit, the powers of external sovereignty passed from the Crown not to the colonies severally, but to the colonies in their collective and corporate capacity as the United States of America. Even before the Declaration, the colonies were a unit in foreign affairs, acting through a common agency—namely the Continental Congress, composed of delegates from the thirteen colonies. That agency exercised the powers of war and peace, raised an army, created a navy, and finally adopted the Declaration of Independence. Rulers come and go; governments end and forms of government change; but sovereignty survives. A political society cannot endure without a supreme will somewhere. Sovereignty is never held in suspense. When, therefore, the external sovereignty of Great Britain in respect of the colonies ceased, it immediately passed to the Union. See *Penhallow* v. *Doane*. . . .

The Union existed before the Constitution, which was ordained and established among other things to form "a more perfect Union." Prior to that event, it is clear that the Union, declared by the Articles of Confederation to be "perpetual," was the sole possessor of external sovereignty and in the Union it remained without change save in so far as the Constitution in express terms qualified its exercise. The Framers' Convention was called and exerted its powers upon the irrefutable postulate that though the states were several their people in respect of foreign affairs were one. . . .

It results that the investment of the federal government with the powers of external sovereignty did not depend upon the affirmative grants of the Constitution. The powers to declare and wage war, to conclude peace, to make treaties, to maintain diplomatic relations with other sovereignties, if they had never been mentioned in the Constitution, would have vested in the federal government as necessary concomitants of nationality. Neither the Constitution nor the laws passed in pursuance of it have any force in foreign territory unless in respect of our own citizens . . . and operations of the nation in such territory must be governed by treaties, international understandings and compacts, and the principles of international law. As a member of the family of nations, the right and power of the United States in that field are equal to the right and power of the other members of the international family. Otherwise, the United States is not completely sovereign. The power to acquire territory by discovery and occupation . . . the power to expel undesirable aliens . . . the power to make such international agreements as do not constitute treaties in the constitutional sense . . . none of which is expressly affirmed by the Constitution, nevertheless exist as inherently inseparable from the conception of nationality. This the court recognized,

and in each of the cases cited found the warrant for its conclusions not in the provisions of the Constitution, but in the law of nations.

It is important to bear in mind that we are here dealing not alone with an authority vested in the President by an exertion of legislative power, but with such an authority plus the very delicate, plenary and exclusive power of the President as the sole organ of the federal government in the field of international relations—a power which does not require as a basis for its exercise an act of Congress, but which, of course, like every other governmental power, must be exercised in subordination to the applicable provisions of the Constitution. It is quite apparent that if, in the maintenance of our international relations, embarrassment—perhaps serious embarrassment—is to be avoided and success for our aims achieved, congressional legislation which is to be made effective through negotiation and inquiry within the international field must often accord to the President a degree of discretion which would not be admissible were domestic affairs alone involved. Moreover, he, not Congress, has the better opportunity of knowing the conditions which prevail in foreign countries, and especially is this true in times of war. . . .

Practically every volume of the United States Statutes contains one or more acts or joint resolutions of Congress authorizing action by the President in respect of subjects affecting foreign relations, which either leave the exercise of the power to his unrestricted judgment, or provide a standard far more general than that which has always been considered requisite with regard to domestic affairs. . . .

The judgment of the court below

must be reversed and the cause remanded for further proceedings in accordance with the foregoing opinion.

Reversed.

MR. JUSTICE McREYNOLDS does not agree. He is of opinion that the court below reached the right conclusion and its judgement ought to be affirmed.

(3) Youngstown Sheet and Tube Company v. Sawyer (1952)

+Black, Douglas, Frankfurter, Jackson, Burton, Clark
−Vinson, Reed, Minton

[In an attempt to forestall a threatened steel strike that might have jeopardized national defense production during the Korean War, President Truman issued an executive order directing the secretary of commerce, Charles Sawyer, to take possession of most of the nation's steel mills and keep them running. Through various maneuvers the strike had already been delayed for four months, and the president was unwilling to invoke the provisions of the Taft-Hartley Act which had been passed by the Congress over his veto. The steel companies challenged the seizure as unlawful, arguing that the president was exercising and usurping lawmaking powers. They initiated a suit for an injunction in the federal district court in Washington, D.C. That court decided in favor of the mill owners and emphatically rejected the government's contention that the executive possessed a broad residuum of "inherent" or emergency powers which flowed from the aggregate of his constitutional powers as chief executive and commander-in-chief and fluctuated with the nature of the emergency involved. It specifically rejected former President Theodore Roosevelt's "stewardship" theory of presidential powers:

That is defendant's [Sawyer's] only support for his "stewardship" theory of the office of President, but with all due deference and respect for that great President of the United States, I am obliged to say that his statements do not comport with our recognized theory of government, but with a theory with which our government of laws and not of men is constantly at war.

The mills were ordered returned to their owners.

When the decision was announced the steel unions called another strike, but this was delayed when the Court of Appeals granted a stay of the district court's order pending a direct appeal by the government to the Supreme Court. Press reaction throughout the country was strongly against the president, but the court of appeals found that there was a serious enough question about the correctness of the district court's decision to warrant the stay. The Supreme Court granted certiorari, continued the stay, and further ordered that the Secretary of Commerce should not, as he had announced, grant a pay increase to the steel workers pending the outcome of the case.]

MR. JUSTICE BLACK delivered the opinion of the Court.

. . . The President's power, if any, to issue the order must stem either from an act of Congress or from the Constitution itself. There is no statute that expressly authorizes the President to take possession of property as he did here. Nor is there any act of Congress to which our attention has been directed from which such a power can fairly be implied. Indeed, we do not understand the Government to rely on statutory authorization for this seizure. There are two statutes which do authorize the President to take both personal and real property under certain conditions. However, the Government admits that these conditions were not met and that the President's order was not rooted in either of the statutes. The Government refers to the seizure provisions of one of these statutes. (§ 201 (b) of the Defence Production Act) as "much too cumbersome, involved, and time-consuming for the crisis which was at hand."

Moreover, the use of the seizure technique to solve labor disputes in order to prevent work stoppages was not only unauthorized by any congressional enactment; prior to this controversy, Congress had refused to adopt that method of settling labor disputes. When the Taft-Hartley Act was under consideration in 1947, Congress rejected an amendment which would have authorized such governmental seizures in cases of emergency. Apparently it was thought that the technique of seizure, like that of compulsory arbitration, would interfere with the process of collective bargaining. Consequently, the plan Congress adopted in that Act did not provide for seizure under any circumstances. Instead, the plan sought to bring about settlements by use of the customary devices of mediation, conciliation, investigation by boards of inquiry, and public reports. In some instances temporary injunctions were authorized to provide cooling-off periods. All this failing, unions were left free to strike after a secret vote by employees as to whether they wished to accept their employers' final settlement offer.

It is clear that if the President had authority to issue the order he did, it must be found in some provision of the Constitution. And it is not claimed that express constitutional language grants this power to the President. The contention is that presidential power should be implied from the aggregate of his powers under the Constitution. Particular reliance is placed on provisions in Article II which say that "The executive Power shall be vested in a President ...."; that "he shall take Care that the Laws be faithfully executed"; and that he "shall be Commander in

Chief of the Army and Navy of the United States."

The order cannot properly be sustained as an exercise of the President's military power as Commander in Chief of the Armed Forces. The Government attempts to do so by citing a number of cases upholding broad powers in military commanders engaged in day-to-day fighting in a theater of war. Such cases need not concern us here. Even though "theater of war" be an expanding concept, we cannot with faithfulness to our constitutional system hold that the Commander in Chief of the Armed Forces has the ultimate power as such to take possession of private property in order to keep labor disputes from stopping production. This is a job for the Nation's lawmakers, not for its military authorities.

Nor can the seizure order be sustained because of the several constitutional provisions that grant executive power to the President. In the framework of our Constitution, the President's power to see that the laws are faithfully executed refutes the idea that he is to be a lawmaker. The Constitution limits his functions in the lawmaking process to the recommending of laws he thinks wise and the vetoing of laws he thinks bad. And the Constitution is neither silent nor equivocal about who shall make laws which the President is to execute. . . .

The President's order does not direct that a congressional policy be executed in a manner prescribed by Congress—it directs that a presidential policy be executed in a manner prescribed by the President. The preamble of the order itself, like that of many statutes, sets out reasons why the President believes certain policies should be adopted, proclaims these policies as rules of conduct to be followed, and again, like a statute, authorizes a government official to promulgate additional rules and regulations consistent with the policy proclaimed and needed to carry that policy into execution. The power of Congress to adopt such public policies as those proclaimed by the order is beyond question. It can authorize the taking of private property for public use. It can make laws regulating the relationships between employers and employees, prescribing rules designed to settle labor disputes, and fixing wages and working conditions in certain fields of our economy. The Constitution does not subject this lawmaking power of Congress to presidential or military supervision or control.

It is said that other Presidents without congressional authority have taken possession of private business enterprises in order to settle labor disputes. But even if this be true, Congress has not thereby lost its exclusive constitutional authority to make laws necessary and proper to carry out the powers vested by the Constitution "in the Government of the United States, or any Department or Officer thereof."

The Founders of this Nation entrusted the lawmaking power to the Congress alone in both good and bad times. It would do no good to recall the historical events, the fears of power and the hopes for freedom that lay behind their choice. Such a review would but confirm our holding that this seizure order cannot stand.

The judgment of the District Court is *Affirmed*.

MR. JUSTICE FRANKFURTER, CONCURRING.

Although the considerations relevant to the legal enforcement of the principle of separation of powers seem to me more complicated and flexible than may appear from what Mr. Justice Black has written, I join his opinion because I thoroughly agree with the application of the principle to the circumstances of this case. Even though such differences in attitude toward this principle may be merely differences in emphasis and nuance, they can hardly be reflected by a single opinion for the Court. Individual expression of views in reaching a common result is therefore important.

The question before the Court comes in this setting. Congress has frequently—at least 16 times since 1916—specifically provided for executive seizure of production, transportation, communications, or storage facilities. In every case it has qualified this grant of power with limitations and safeguards. . . . The power to seize has uniformly been given only for a limited period or for a defined emergency, or has been repealed after a short period. Its exercise has been restricted to particular circumstances such as "time of war or when war is imminent," the needs of "public safety" or of "national security or defense," or "urgent and impending need." The period of governmental operation has been limited, as, for instance, to "sixty days after the restoration of productive efficiency." Seizure statutes usually make executive action dependent on detailed conditions: for example, (a) failure or refusal of the owner of a plant to meet governmental supply needs or (b) failure of voluntary negotiations with the owner for the use of a plant necessary for great public ends. Congress often has specified the particular executive agency which should seize or operate the plants or whose judgments would appropriately test the need for seizure. Congress also has not left to implication that just compensation be paid; it has usually legislated in detail regarding enforcement of this litigation-breeding general requirement. . . . In adopting the provisions, which it did, by the Labor Management Relations Act of 1947, for dealing with a "national emergency" arising out of a breakdown in peaceful industrial relations, Congress was very familiar with Governmental seizure as a protective measure. On a balance of considerations, Congress chose not to lodge this power in the President. It chose not to make available in advance a remedy to which both industry and labor were fiercely hostile. In deciding that authority to seize should be given to the President only after full consideration of the particular situation should show such legislation to be necessary, Congress presumably acted on experience with similar industrial conflicts in the past. . . .

By the Labor Management Relations Act of 1947, Congress said to the President, "You may not seize. Please report to us and ask for seizure power if you think it is needed in a specific situation." This of course calls for a report on the unsuccessful efforts to reach a voluntary settlement, as a basis for discharge by Congress of its responsibility—which it has unequivocally reserved—to fashion further remedies than it provided. But it is now claimed that the President has seizure power by virtue of the Defense Production Act of 1950 and its Amendments. And the claim is based on the occurrence of new events—Korea and the need for stabilization, etc.—although it was well known that seizure power was withheld by the Act of 1947, and although the President, whose specific requests for other authority were in the main granted by Congress, never suggested that in view of the new events he needed the power of seizure

which Congress in its judgment had decided to withhold from him. The utmost that the Korean conflict may imply is that it may have been desirable to have given the President further authority, a freer hand in these matters. Absence of authority in the President to deal with a crisis does not imply want of power in the Government. Conversely the fact that power exists in the Government does not vest it in the President. The need for new legislation does not enact it. Nor does it repeal or amend existing law.

No authority that has since been given to the President can by any fair process of statutory construction be deemed to withdraw the restriction or change the will of Congress as expressed by a body of enactments, culminating in the Labor Management Relations Act of 1947. . . .

MR. JUSTICE DOUGLAS, CONCURRING.

. . . [T]he emergency did not create power; it merely marked an occasion when power should be exercised. And the fact that it was necessary that measures be taken to keep steel in production does not mean that the President, rather than the Congress, had the constitutional authority to act. The Congress, as well as the President, is trustee of the national welfare. The President can act more quickly than the Congress. The President with the armed services at his disposal can move with force as well as with speed. All executive power— from the reign of ancient kings to the rule of modern dictators—has the outward appearance of efficiency. . . .

We could not sanction the seizures and condemnations of the steel plants in this case without reading Article II as giving the President not only the power to execute the laws but to make some. Such a step would most assuredly alter the pattern of the Constitution. . . .

We pay a price for our system of checks and balances, for the distribution of power among the three branches of government. It is a price that today may seem exorbitant to many. Today a kindly President uses the seizure power to effect a wage increase and to keep the steel furnaces in production. Yet tomorrow another President might use the same power to prevent a wage increase, to curb trade unionists, to regiment labor as oppressively as industry thinks it has been regimented by this seizure.

MR. JUSTICE JACKSON, CONCURRING IN THE JUDGMENT AND OPINION OF THE COURT.

. . . While the Constitution diffuses power the better to secure liberty, it also contemplates that practice will integrate the dispersed powers into a workable government. It enjoins upon its branches separateness but interdependence, autonomy but reciprocity. Presidential powers are not fixed but fluctuate, depending upon their disjunction or conjunction with those of Congress. We may well begin by a somewhat over-simplified grouping of practical situations in which a President may doubt, or others may challenge his powers, and by distinguishing roughly the legal consequences of this factor of relativity.

1. When the President acts pursuant to an express or implied authorization of Congress, his authority is at its maximum, for it includes all that he possesses in his own right plus all that Congress can delegate. In these circumstances, and in these only, may he be said (for what it may be worth) to personify the federal sovereignty. If his act is held unconstitutional under these circumstances, it usually means that the Federal Government as an undivided whole lacks power. A seizure executed by the President pursuant to an Act of Congress would be supported by the strongest of presumptions and the widest latitude of judicial interpretation, and the burden of persuasion would rest heavily upon any who might attack it.

2. When the President acts in absence of either a congressional grant or denial of authority, he can only rely upon his own independent powers, but there is a zone of twilight in which he and Congress may have concurrent authority, or in which its distribution is uncertain. Therefore, congressional inertia, indifference or quiescence may sometimes, at least as a practical matter, enable, if not invite, measures on independent presidential responsibility. In this area, any actual test of power is likely to depend on the imperatives of events and contemporary imponderables rather than on abstract theories of law.

3. When the President takes measures incompatible with the expressed or implied will of Congress, his power is at its lowest ebb, for then he can rely only upon his own constitutional powers minus any constitutional powers of Congress over the matter. Courts can sustain exclusive presidential control in such a case only by disabling the Congress from acting upon the subject. Presidential claim to a power at once so conclusive and preclusive must be scrutinized with caution, for what is at stake is the equilibrium established by our constitutional system.

Into which of these classifications does this executive seizure of the steel industry fit? It is eliminated from the first by admission, for it is conceded that no congressional authorization exists for this seizure. That takes away also the support of the many precedents and declarations which were made in relation, and must be confined, to this category.

Can it then be defended under flexible tests available to the second category? It seems clearly eliminated from that class because Congress has not left seizure of private property an open field but has covered it by three statutory policies inconsistent with this seizure. In cases where the purpose is to supply needs of the Government itself, two courses are provided: one, seizure of a plant which fails to comply with obligatory orders placed by the Government; another, condemnation of facilities, including temporary use under the power of eminent domain. The third is applicable where it is the general economy of the country that is to be protected rather than exclusive governmental interests. None of these were invoked. In choosing a different and inconsistent way of his own, the President cannot claim that it is necessitated or invited by failure of Congress to legislate upon the occasions, grounds and methods for seizure of industrial properties.

This leaves the current seizure to be justified only by the severe tests under the third grouping, where it can be supported only by any remainder of executive power after subtraction of such powers as Congress may have over the subject. In short, we can sustain the President only by holding that seizure of such strike-bound industries is within his domain and beyond control by Congress. . . .

In view of the ease, expedition and safety with which Congress can grant and has granted large emergency powers, certainly ample to embrace this crisis, I am quite unim-

pressed with the argument that we should affirm possession of them without statute. Such power either has no beginning or it has no end. If it exists, it need submit to no legal restraint. I am not alarmed that it would plunge us straightway into dictatorship, but it is at least a step in that wrong direction.

MR. JUSTICE BURTON, CONCURRING.

My position may be summarized as follows:

The validity of the President's order of seizure is at issue and ripe for decision. Its validity turns upon its relation to the constitutional division of governmental power between Congress and the President. . . .

The controlling fact here is that Congress, within its constitutionally delegated power, has prescribed for the President specific procedures, exclusive of seizure, for his use in meeting the present type of emergency. Congress has reserved to itself the right to determine where and when to authorize the seizure of property in meeting such an emergency. Under these circumstances, the President's order of April 8 invaded the jurisdiction of Congress. It violated the essence of the principle of the separation of governmental powers. Accordingly, the injunction against its effectiveness should be sustained.

MR. JUSTICE CLARK, CONCURRING.

. . .

The limits of presidential power are obscure. . . . In my view . . . the Constitution does grant to the President extensive authority in times of grave and imperative national emergency. In fact, to my thinking, such a grant may well be necessary to the very existence of the Constitution itself. As Lincoln aptly said, "[is] it possible to lose the nation and yet preserve the Constitution?" In describing this authority I care not whether one calls it "residual," "inherent," "moral," "implied," "aggregate," "emergency," or otherwise. I am of the conviction that those who have had the gratifying experience of being the President's lawyer have used one or more of these adjectives only with the utmost sincerity and the highest of purpose.

I conclude that where Congress has laid down specific procedures to deal with the type of crisis confronting the President, he must follow those procedures in meeting the crisis; but that in the absence of such action by Congress, the President's independent power to act depends upon the gravity of the situation confronting the nation. I cannot sustain the seizure in question because here . . . Congress had prescribed methods to be followed by the President in meeting the emergency at hand.

MR. CHIEF JUSTICE VINSON, WITH WHOM MR. JUSTICE REED AND MR. JUSTICE MINTON JOIN, DISSENTING.

In passing upon the question of Presidential powers in this case, we must first consider the context in which those powers were exercised.

Those who suggest that this is a case involving extraordinary powers should be mindful that these are extraordinary times. A world not yet recovered from the devastation of World War II has been forced to face the threat of another and more terrifying global conflict. . . . [Editors' Note: A long discussion of the United Nations charter, the Korean War, the Marshall Plan, NATO, and other American policies toward preserving the peace is omitted.]

Our treaties represent not merely legal obligations but show congressional recognition that mutual security for the free world is the best security against the threat of aggression on a global scale. The need for mutual security is shown by the very size of the armed forces outside the free world. Defendant's brief informs us that the Soviet Union maintains the largest air force in the world and maintains ground forces much larger than those presently available to the United States and the countries joined with us in mutual security arrangements. Constant international tensions are cited to demonstrate how precarious is the peace.

A review of executive action demonstrates that our Presidents have on many occasions exhibited the leadership contemplated by the Framers when they made the President Commander in Chief, and imposed upon him the trust to "take Care that the Laws be faithfully executed." With or without explicit statutory authorization, Presidents have at such times dealt with national emergencies by acting promptly and resolutely to enforce legislative programs, at least to save those programs until Congress could act. Congress and the courts have responded to such executive initiative with consistent approval.

Our first President displayed at once the leadership contemplated by the Framers. When the national revenue laws were openly flouted in some sections of Pennsylvania, President Washington, without waiting for a call from the state government, summoned the militia and took decisive steps to secure the faithful execution of the laws. When international disputes engendered by the French revolution threatened to involve this country in war, and while congressional policy remained uncertain, Washington issued his Proclamation of Neutrality. Hamilton, whose defense of the Proclamation has endured the test of time, invoked the argument that the Executive has the duty to do that which will preserve peace until Congress acts and, in addition, pointed to the need for keeping the Nation informed of the requirements of existing laws and treaties as part of the faithful execution of the laws.

Without declaration of war, President Lincoln took energetic action with the outbreak of the War Between the States. He summoned troops and paid them out of the Treasury without appropriation therefor. He proclaimed a naval blockade of the Confederacy and seized ships violating that blockade. Congress, far from denying the validity of these acts, gave them express approval. The most striking action of President Lincoln was the Emancipation Proclamation, issued in aid of the successful prosecution of the War Between the States, but wholly without statutory authority.

In an action furnishing a most apt precedent for this case, President Lincoln without statutory authority directed the seizure of rail and telegraph lines leading to Washington. Many months later, Congress recognized and confirmed the power of the President to seize railroads and telegraph lines and provided criminal penalties for interference with Government operation. This Act did not confer on the President any additional powers of seizure. Congress plainly rejected the view that the President's acts had been without legal sanction until ratified by the legislature. Sponsors of the bill declared that its purpose was only to confirm the power which the President already possessed. Opponents insisted a statute authorizing seizure was unnecessary and might even be construed as limiting existing Presidential powers.

Other seizures of private property occurred during the War Between the States, just as they had occurred during previous wars. . . .

In 1909, President Taft was informed that government-owned oil lands were being patented by private parties at such a rate that public oil lands would be depleted in a matter of months. Although Congress had explicitly provided that these lands were open to purchase by United States citizens . . . the President nevertheless ordered the lands withdrawn from sale "[i]n aid of proposed legislation." In *United States* v. *Midwest Oil Co.* . . . (1915), the President's action was sustained as consistent with executive practice throughout our history. . . .

Beginning with the Bank Holiday Proclamation and continuing through World War II, executive leadership and initiative were characteristic of President Franklin D. Roosevelt's administration. In 1939, upon the outbreak of war in Europe, the President proclaimed a limited national emergency for the purpose of strengthening our national defense. In May of 1941, the danger from the Axis belligerents having become clear, the President proclaimed "an unlimited national emergency" calling for mobilization of the Nation's defenses to repel aggression. The President took the initiative in strengthening our defenses by acquiring rights from the British Government to establish air bases in exchange for overage destroyers. . . .

History bears out the genius of the Founding Fathers, who created a Government subject to law but not left subject to inertia when vigor and initiative are required.

When the President acted on April 8, he had exhausted the procedures for settlement available to him. Taft-Hartley was a route parallel to, not connected with, the WSB procedure. The strike had been delayed 99 days as contrasted with the maximum delay of 80 days under Taft-Hartley. There had been a hearing on the issues in dispute and bargaining which promised settlement up to the very hour before seizure had broken down. Faced with immediate national peril through stoppage in steel production on the one hand and faced with destruction of the wage and price legislative programs on the other, the President took temporary possession of the steel mills as the only course open to him consistent with his duty to take care that the laws be faithfully executed.

Plaintiffs' property was taken and placed in the possession of the Secretary of Commerce to prevent any interruption in steel production. It made no difference whether the stoppage was caused by a union-management dispute over terms and conditions of employment, a union-Government dispute over wage stabilization or a management-Government dispute over price stabilization. The President's action has thus far been effective, not in settling the dispute, but in saving the various legislative programs at stake from destruction until Congress could act in the matter.

The diversity of views expressed in the six opinions of the majority, the lack of reference to authoritative precedent, the repeated reliance upon prior dissenting opinions, the complete disregard of the uncontroverted facts showing the gravity of the emergency and the temporary nature of the taking all serve to demonstrate how far afield one must go to affirm the order of the District Court.

The broad executive power granted by Article II to an officer on duty 365 days a year cannot, it is said, be invoked to avert disaster. Instead, the President must confine himself to sending a message to Congress recommending action. Under this messenger-boy concept of the Office, the President cannot even act to preserve legislative programs from destruction so that Congress will have something left to act upon. There is no judicial finding that the executive action was unwarranted because there was in fact no basis for the President's finding of the existence of an emergency for, under this view, the gravity of the emergency and the immediacy of the threatened disaster are considered irrelevant as a matter of law. . . .

(4) A Note on the Implications of the Steel Seizure Case

Despite its obvious rebuke to President Truman, the Supreme Court in the *Steel Seizure Case* did not repudiate the doctrine of inherent powers. A majority of five of the nine justices recognized the existence of such powers. The three dissenters, Chief Justice Vinson and Justices Reed and Minton, believed that the doctrine supported the president in this case. And two justices who voted in the majority against the president, Robert Jackson and Tom Clark, accepted the inevitability of inherent presidential power under other circumstances. Two justices, Felix Frankfurter and Harold Burton, did not discuss the issue, believing that congressional action foreclosed any possible claim of inherent presidential power in this case. Only two justices, Hugo Black and William Douglas, clearly rejected the concept of inherent powers as a matter of principle.

It is unlikely, at least in the foreseeable future, that the Supreme Court will resolve this question with a clear "yes" or "no" answer. It would be inconsistent with the Court's tradition of deference to presidential power, especially in the field of international relations and foreign policy, to say "no." And it would be equally unlikely, in the present political climate of suspicion of presidential power—a climate that developed before Watergate but was exacerbated by it—for the Court to ring forth with an unequivocal "yes." In this respect, in its unwillingness to confront directly the question of the full scope and source of presidential power, the Court's decision in the *Nixon Tapes Case*, to be discussed later in this chapter, is quite similar to the results of the *Steel Seizure Case*.

Problems of the limits of executive discretion abound. We considered them in the previous chapter in the wiretapping case, *United States* v. *United States District Court* (1972). In that case, a unanimous Court repudiated the president's claim to unlimited authority to use electronic surveillance methods in national security cases without securing a judicial warrant. We will see, later in this chapter, the Supreme Court's response to President Nixon's efforts to suppress newspaper publication of the "Pentagon Papers." And we will consider efforts by Congress, such as the War Powers Resolution of 1973, to place statutory limits on presidential power.

D. Treaties and Executive Agreements: Problems of Federalism and the Separation of Powers

(1) A Note on the General Use of Treaties and Executive Agreements

There are three basic types of international agreements: treaties, agreements pursuant to statute or an existing treaty, and "pure" executive agreements. The Constitution provides that treaties between the United States and one or more foreign nations are to be made by the president with the advice and consent of two-thirds of the Senate. In an early draft of the Constitution, the Senate and not the president was given the power to *make* treaties. The president was included only at the last moment, and there is certainly no credible evidence that by the change in wording the president was intended to be the dominant force in the treaty-making process. A limited role for the president, in conjunction with the Senate, was consistent with the existing widespread fear of executive power.

Alexander Hamilton, in No. 75 of the *Federalist Papers,* wrote that the treaty power "partakes more of a legislative than an executive power." And, as Raoul Berger has recently observed, the words of the Constitution belie any intention on the part of the framers to confer on the president the dominant treaty-making role.[1] In Article II, Section 2, Clause 2, the Constitution reads: "He shall have Power, by and with the Advice and Consent of the Senate, to make Treaties, provided two thirds of the Senators present concur." And in the very next clause it adds: "and he shall nominate, and by and with the Advice and Consent of the Senate, shall appoint Ambassadors. . . ." Comparing these two clauses of the same sentence suggests that the "advice and consent" of the Senate is intended to be part of the process of "making" treaties. The Senate's role of concurring in a treaty is covered by a separate clause. On the other hand, the "advice and consent" of the Senate to presidential nominations comes

---

[1]Raoul Berger, *Executive Privilege* (Cambridge: Harvard University Press, 1973), pp. 136–139 and *passim.*

after the president has made his choice and submitted a nomination to the Senate; here "advice and consent" is the functional equivalent of "concurrence" in the previous clause.

Notwithstanding this evidence about the shared role of the president and the Senate in making treaties, the practicalities of treaty negotiation, as well as accumulated traditions, have conceded the dominant role to the president. John Jay, writing in No. 64 of the *Federalist Papers*, observed that the changed words of the treaty clause in Article II were a recognition that only the president could, in fact, "manage the business of intelligence" in a prudent and timely manner. Justice Sutherland's widely quoted opinion in the *Curtiss-Wright* case provided judicial recognition:

. . . In this vast external realm . . . the President alone has the power to speak or listen as a representative of the nation. He makes treaties with the advice and consent of the Senate; but he alone negotiates. Into the field of negotiation the Senate cannot intrude; and Congress itself is powerless to invade it.

For students of judicial policymaking today, the real issue is not whether the framers expected the Senate to play a more active role in making or negotiating treaties. More important are questions of the impact of treaties and executive agreements. Can a properly ratified treaty empower the federal government to act in a manner that would otherwise be precluded in the absence of the treaty? Are executive agreements superior to state law under the principles of the supremacy clause of Article VI? What is the impact of treaties and executive agreements on the constitutional rights of individuals?

Treaties

A treaty that requires no implementing congressional legislation is known as a *self-executing treaty*. A treaty that requires such statutory implementation, such as an appropriation, is known as a *non-self-executing treaty*. Self-executing treaties and non-self-executing treaties that have been implemented are, like laws passed in pursuance of the Constitution, enforceable by the courts under the supremacy clause of Article VI. A non-self-executing treaty that has not been implemented by Congress is not enforceable, and no court may order Congress to implement the treaty.

When a self-executing treaty conflicts with an existing federal statute, the rule is that whichever comes last takes precedence. Since a non-self-executing treaty, by definition, is incomplete without implementing legislation, it cannot prevail over an earlier conflicting act of Congress. Needless to say, treaties "made under the authority of the United States" take precedence over conflicting state laws. Students are often confused by these words of Article VI. What meaning is to be attributed to the difference in wording that makes laws "made in pursuance of the Constitution" and treaties "made under the authority of the United States" both the supreme law of the land? In fact, there is no difference. The different words were merely designed to ensure the supremacy of treaties made *before* the Constitution, under the Articles of Confederation or the Continental Congress after independence from Great Britain was declared.

The great case of *Missouri* v. *Holland* (1920), reprinted after this note, stands as the authority for two propositions. First, treaties take precedence over conflicting state laws, notwithstanding the powers reserved to the states under the Tenth Amendment. Second, Congress may be authorized by a treaty to pass a statute for which no other constitutional authorization exists.

The Constitution makes no provision for terminating a treaty, nor does it prohibit the government from doing so. It is accepted that treaties may be terminated under a number of conditions: informal agreement between the parties, under termination provisions contained in the treaty itself such as a notice of termination provision, or a predetermined time limitation or expiration date. In the first two instances the question arises whether the president has the independent authority to terminate a treaty (either by agreement with the other nation(s), or by giving notice of termination as provided in the treaty itself), or whether he can do so only with the consent of two-thirds of the Senate or a simple majority of both houses of Congress.[2]

The issue arose recently when President Carter announced on December 15, 1978 that our mutual defense treaty with Taiwan, concluded during the Eisenhower Administration (1954), would be terminated at the end of 1979. His action was taken to facilitate normalization of diplomatic relations with the government of the People's Republic of China. The treaty contained a provision permitting either party to give one year's notice of termination. President Carter's action, therefore, did not violate the treaty itself; but many critics—a majority of the Senate as it turned out—believed he had violated the Constitution by taking this action unilaterally. In addition, Carter's action may have contravened a 1978 act of Congress requiring the president to engage in "prior consultation" with the Congress before altering United States' policy toward Taiwan.[3]

Since the Constitution is silent on the procedure for terminating a treaty, supporters of Carter's action have relied on a long history of similar actions by presidents in the past. James Madison, who argued at the time of the Constitution that the President could not terminate a treaty unilaterally any more than he could repeal a statute by himself, was the first President (some twenty-eight years later) to unilaterally terminate a treaty. He annulled a commercial treaty of commerce with The Netherlands dating back to 1782. There are fourteen recorded occasions when presidents have given notice of treaty termination independent of the Senate or the Congress; all but two of these occurred in the twentieth century. The most recent was President Ford's notice in 1975 of termination of United States' participation in the International Labor Organization.

The Supreme Court has never addressed the subject directly. It does appear as if a preponderance of leading constitutional scholars favors the president's position (on the constitutional issue).[4] Nevertheless there is considerable support for the opposing position. On June 6, 1979, the Senate

[2]See pp. 1024–1033.

[3]The International Security Assistance Act of 1978, signed by President Carter on September 26, 1978, provided in Section 26 (known as the Dole-Stone Amendment) that "It is the sense of the Congress that there should be prior consultation between the Congress and the executive branch on any proposed policy changes affecting the continuation in force of the Mutual Defense Treaty of 1954."

[4]For example, see Louis Henkin, *Foreign Affairs and the Constitution* (New York: Norton, 1972), pp. 167–171.

passed the following resolution by a 59-35 vote:

That it is the sense of the Senate that approval of the United States Senate is required to terminate any mutual defense treaty between the United States and another nation.

An excerpt from an article by Senator Barry Goldwater, summarizing the constitutional arguments against unilateral termination of the Taiwan treaty is reprinted below (see pp. 1024–1029).

A group of senators, led by Goldwater, also filed suit in the federal district court for the District of Columbia seeking to block the President's action.[5] They claimed that Carter had acted contrary to the Constitution, that his actions impaired the 1954 Mutual Defense Treaty, and that his termination order violated Section 26 of the International Security Assistance Act of 1978. Judge Oliver Gasch concluded, after reviewing the treaty termination issue, that "the power to terminate treaties is a power shared by the political branches of this government, namely, the President and the Congress." However he declined to intervene in the case at that time because of doubts as to the standing of the plaintiff senators, the ripeness of the issue for adjudication, and problems occasioned by the doctrine of political questions. He did state, however, that if and when the Senate or the Congress had formally disapproved of Carter's action, "then the controversy will be ripe for a judicial decision respecting the President's authority to act unilaterally." He dismissed the plaintiffs' claim under Section 26 of the International Security Assistance Act (quoted in

footnote 3) because the language of the section is general and nonmandatory and therefore does not establish a binding obligation on the President to consult. The President's position was that he and his advisors had consulted with members of Congress before and after the termination proclamation. Judge Gasch specifically refused to decide whether these "contacts" amounted to the consultation described in Section 26. Excerpts from Judge Gasch's opinion appear below (see pp. 1029–1033).

Executive Agreements

Executive agreements are international agreements made at the diplomatic level between the president and foreign nations. They have the same force and effect as self-executing treaties and do not require congressional approval except on questions concerning atomic energy. An executive agreement may not substitute for a peace treaty, and like all treaties, they are subject to the limitations of the Constitution. The legal force of executive agreements was unanimously upheld by the Supreme Court in *United States* v. *Belmont* (1937). In that case, the issue was the precedence of an executive agreement between the United States and the Soviet Union over the laws of the state of New York, but the case afforded the Court an occasion for more general observations about executive agreements.

In 1918, the new Soviet government nationalized the Petrograd Metal Works and confiscated all its property and assets, including assets on deposit in Mr. Belmont's bank in New York City. In 1933, the United States extended diplomatic recogni-

---

[5]*Goldwater* v. *Carter* (1979), U. S. District Court for the District of Columbia, Civil Action 79–2412.

tion to the Soviet Union and, incidental to that recognition, concluded what became known as the "Litvinov Agreements," which were not submitted to the Senate for approval. Under those agreements, nationalized Soviet property in the United States was transferred to the United States. Belmont sought a federal court order to prevent this transfer. A federal district judge upheld his claim that the Soviet "nationalization" of 1918 was mere "confiscation," which was contrary to the public policy of New York and also to that of the United States.

In overruling the lower court, the Supreme Court stated categorically that no state policy could prevail against an international compact. It held further that recognition of the Soviet government by the United States validated all the actions of that government in this country. Since the assets held in Belmont's bank had been taken over by a government recognized by the United States and were, in effect, the property of that government, title to the property could be assigned to the United States, and constitutional limitations against confiscation of private property (in the Fifth Amendment) did not apply. Finally, the Court held that even though agreements of this type did not require the consent of the Senate, they had the same force and effect as a treaty in superceding contrary *state* laws. Executive agreements, however, do *not* supercede conflicting *federal* laws; in this respect, they are analogous to non-self-executing treaties.

Executive agreements are not recent inventions. They go back to the days of George Washington, who was authorized by Congress to make postal agreements. However, they have increased in number and now play a much larger role in the United States' conduct of its foreign relations. From 1789 to 1974, the United States entered into 1254 treaties. In the same period, 7,809 executive agreements were made; 86 percent of all international agreements made by the United States have been executive agreements, whereas only 14 percent have been treaties. It is not known exactly how many of those agreements were "pure" executive agreements and how many were agreements made by the president pursuant to prior authorization by Congress. A recent announcement by the secretary of state stated that only about 3 percent of the executive agreements were of the "pure" type.[6] Table I shows the pattern of treaties and executive agreements concluded through 1974.

Since 1950, the secretary of state has been required by statute to publish the contents of all treaties and international agreements, but many have been withheld for reasons of national security. More serious efforts to control executive agreements, and, more generally, to give Congress a greater check on the foreign policy power of the president, came in 1952 and 1953 with the Bricker Amendment, narrowly defeated in the Senate. Under one version of that amendment, congressional legislation would have been required to make treaties effective as domestic law. Congress would have had the power to regulate all agreements made by the executive with another

[6]See John F. Murphy, "Treaties and International Agreements Other Than Treaties: Constitutional Allocation of Power and Responsibility Among the President, the House of Representatives, and the Senate," **23** *Kansas Law Review* (1975), 221–248.

Table I.   Periodic Use of Treaties and Executive Agreements

Time Period	Treaties	Executive Agreements	Executive Agreements as Percentage of Total
1789–1839	60	27	31.0
1839–1889	215	238	52.5
1889–1929	382	763	66.6
1930–1939	142	154	52.0
1940–1949	116	919	88.8
1950–1959	138	2229	94.2
1960–1969	114	2324	95.3
1970-1974	87	1255	93.0

Source. Congressional Quarterly (August 2, 1975), p. 1714.

nation or an international organization, and all such agreements would be subject to the same limitations as treaties.

The Vietnam War brought new efforts to curb presidential power over foreign affairs, including the authority to negotiate executive agreements. Unlike the Bricker Amendment, which was the product of the political right, efforts to curb presidential authority in the late 1960s and 1970s came from the political left. In 1972, Congress passed the "Case Act" which required the secretary of state to transmit to Congress any international agreement, other than a treaty, within sixty days of its execution; those agreements that were to be kept secret for national security reasons were to be transmitted only to the House and Senate Foreign Relations Committees.

Notwithstanding this law, the Nixon and Ford administrations, it was alleged,[7] failed to transmit as many as 600 agreements in the years following passage of the law. The reason for this was that these administrations did not consider mere "accords" with foreign nations to fall into the category of executive agreements. Perhaps the most controversial "accord" withheld from Congress was a series of letters from President Nixon to President Nguyen Van Thieu of South Vietnam, in which Nixon pledged to use the "full force" of the United States if the government of North Vietnam failed to honor the Paris cease-fire agreement. These letters, the State Department said, were not executive agreements but statements of "personal presidential intent." Direct agreements between United States intelligence agencies and their counterparts in foreign governments have also been withheld from Congress. According to the State Department, these "agency-to-agency" agreements are also not "executive" agreements and thus need not be reported to Congress. In the absence of a more detailed congressional statute that defines the term, then, an executive agreement is whatever the president reports to Congress.

The Nixon and Ford administrations strongly opposed attempts by Congress to interfere with what they regarded as purely executive responsibilities. A number of bills were introduced in Congress that would

[7]*Ibid.*

have limited the president's authority to enter into an executive agreement until Congress had sixty days to consider and reject such agreements before they went into effect. The Ford administration, against whom some of the bills were directed, argued that this would create uncertainty among foreign governments, would interfere with the delicate negotiations often needed to reach agreements, and would generally interfere with the president's powers under the Constitution. Using a separation-of-powers rationale, the contention was that executive agreements made under the president's Article II powers were not subject to congressional limitation. It may be that only a constitutional amendment, or perhaps a definitive Supreme Court ruling on Congress' authority to limit executive agreements by statute, will resolve this continuing and escalating controversy.

(2) Missouri v. Holland (1920)

+Holmes, White, McKenna, Day, McReynolds, Brandeis, Clark
−Pitney, Van Devanter

MR. JUSTICE HOLMES delivered the opinion of the court.

On December 8, 1916, a treaty between the United States and Great Britain was proclaimed by the President. It recited that many species of birds in their annual migrations traversed certain parts of the United States and of Canada, that they were of great value as a source of food and in destroying insects injurious to vegetation, but were in danger of extermination through lack of adequate protection. It therefore provided for specified closed seasons and protection in other forms, and agreed that the two powers would take or propose to their law-making bodies the neces-

sary measures for carrying the treaty out. . . . The above mentioned Act of July 3, 1918, entitled an act to give effect to the convention, prohibited the killing, capturing or selling any of the migratory birds included in the terms of the treaty except as permitted by regulations compatible with those terms, to be made by the Secretary of Agriculture. Regulations were proclaimed on July 31, and October 25, 1918. . . . It is unnecessary to go into any details, because, as we have said, the question raised is the general one whether the treaty and statute are void as an interference with the rights reserved to the States.

To answer this question it is not enough to refer to the Tenth Amendment, reserving the powers not delegated to the United States, because by Article II, § 2, the power to make treaties is delegated expressly and by Article VI treaties made under the authority of the United States, along with the Constitution and laws of the United States made in pursuance thereof, are declared the supreme law of the land. If the treaty is valid there can be no dispute about the validity of the statute under Article I, §8, as a necessary and proper means to execute the powers of the Government. The language of the Constitution as to the supremacy of treaties being general, the question before us is narrowed to an inquiry into the ground upon which the present supposed exception is placed.

It is said that a treaty cannot be valid if it infringes the Constitution, that there are limits, therefore, to the treaty-making power, and that one such limit is that what an act of Congress could not do unaided, in derogation of the powers reserved to the States, a treaty cannot do. An earlier act of Congress that attempted by itself and not in pursuance of a treaty to regulate the killing of migratory birds within the States had been held bad in the District Court. . . . Those decisions were supported by arguments that migratory birds are owned by the States in their sovereign capacity for the benefit of their people, and that . . . this control was one that Congress had no power to displace. The same argument is supposed to apply now with equal force.

Whether the two cases cited were decided rightly or not they cannot be accepted as a test of the treaty power. Acts of Congress are the supreme law of the land only when made in pursuance of the Constitution, while treaties are declared to be so when made under the authority of the United States. It is open to question whether the authority of the United States means more than the formal acts prescribed to make the convention. We do not mean to imply that there are no qualifications to the treaty-making power; but they must be ascertained in a different way. It is obvious that there may be matters of the sharpest exigency for the national well being that an act of Congress could not deal with but that a treaty followed by such an act could, and it is not lightly to be assumed that in matters requiring national action, "a power which must belong to and somewhere reside in every civilized government" is not to be found. . . . The treaty in question does not contravene any prohibitory words to be found in the Constitution. The only question is whether it is forbidden by some invisible radiation from the general terms of the Tenth Amendment. . . .

Here a national interest of very nearly the first magnitude is involved. It can be protected only by national action in concert with that of

another power. The subject matter is only transitorily within the State and has no permanent habitat therein. But for the treaty and the statute there soon might be no birds for any powers to deal with. We see nothing in the Constitution that compels the Government to sit by while a food supply is cut off and the protectors of our forests and our crops are destroyed. It is not sufficient to rely upon the States. The reliance is in vain, and were it otherwise, the question is whether the United States is forbidden to act. We are of opinion that the treaty and statute must be upheld. . . .

Decree affirmed.

(3) Senator Barry Goldwater, Treaty Termination is a Shared Power

On December 15, 1978, while the Congress was out of session, President Carter announced that the United States would recognize the People's Republic of China as the sole legal government of China as of January 1, 1979. At the same time the president also made known, through informal briefings for the media, his unilateral decision to terminate the defense treaty with the Republic of China, claiming authority to act under Article X of that treaty, which states "either party," not "either president," may cancel it after giving one year's notice. Without public announcement, the actual notice of termination of the defense treaty was sent by diplomatic note to the Republic of China on December 23, 1978, to be effective on and as of January 1, 1979.

The president's decisions were shrouded in secrecy and contrary to

Reprinted from U.S. *Congressional Record*, 90th Cong., 1st Sess., 1979, pp. S 7019–7021.

the purpose of Section 26 of the International Security Assistance Act of 1978, a law enacted by Congress just three months preceeding his announcement, which specifically called for prior consultation with the legislative branch.

On December 22 I filed suit in the United States District Court for the District of Columbia, with 15 of my colleagues from both houses of Congress, challenging the validity of the president's attempted termination of the treaty without any supporting legislative authority. We asked the court to declare the president's action unconstitutional and illegal and to set aside his purported notice to cancel the treaty as having no effect.

It is the premise of our case that in acting alone to interpret the defense treaty and to make a self-serving interpretation of the constitutional allotment of powers among the executive and legislative departments, President Carter has not only usurped powers conferred on the Congress, but has attempted to exercise a function the Supreme Court has said is clearly reserved to the judicial branch, the power "to say what the law is," *United States* v. *Nixon* . . . (1974).

The question is not whether any past precedents justify the president's assertion of independent power, although I believe the weight of historical evidence proves that treaties are normally terminated only with legislative approval. The true question is whether his action represents the original intent of the people who drafted the Constitution.

This is a legal and historical question, and the hard fact is that nothing in the records of the federal convention or in the explanations at the state conventions on ratifying the Constitution confirm in any way the president's sweeping claim of unchecked

power. To the contrary, contemporary materials and the text of the Constitution show that the termination of a treaty, involving as it does the sacred honor of the country and serious policy interests, is a decision of such major importance that the framers required the joint participation of both political departments, the executive and legislative, in making that decision.

. . .

However one may feel about the wisdom of independent presidential termination of the defense treaty as a step required to complete full normalization of relations with Peking, we each should remember the admonition of Chief Justice John Marshall: "The peculiar circumstances of the moment may render a measure more or less wise, but cannot render it more or less constitutional." . . .

The Constitution is silent as to how a treaty shall be terminated. It is also silent on how a statute or any other law shall be cancelled. Yet no one makes the argument that the president alone can repeal a statute. In fact, in *The Confiscation Cases* . . . (1874), the Supreme Court expressly said that "no power was ever vested in the president to repeal an act of Congress."

It is my belief that by placing treaties among "the supreme Law of the Land" in Article VI, clause 2, and by requiring in Article II, Section 3, that the president "shall take care that the Laws be faithfully executed," the framers meant, and expected without saying more, that the president would carry out a treaty in good faith. This is exactly the opposite of giving him an implied authority to cancel any treaty at will. It is also well known that the framers were concerned with restoring dependability to treaties made by the United States. They were anxious to gain the respect and confidence of foreign nations by keeping our treaty commitments.

For example, in the preface to his notes on debates in the Constitutional Convention, James Madison singles out the lack of obedience to treaties as one of the conditions the federal Constitution was intended to correct. Our unfaithfulness to treaties, Madison wrote, is among "the defects, the deformities, the diseases and the ominous prospects for which the Convention were to provide a remedy, and which ought never to be overlooked in expounding & appreciating the Constitutional Charter the remedy that was provided."

. . .

Would the framers, who regarded violation of "the sacred faith of treaties" as "wicked," "dishonorable," and contrary to the best interests of the country in acquiring respect in the community of nations, have contradicted these purposes by making it as easy under the new Constitution for a single officer of the government to repeal a treaty as it had been for individual states to nullify a treaty under the Articles of Confederation? . . .

In his landmark work on the subject in 5 *Seton Hall Law Review* 527 (1974) Prof. Arthur Bestor persuasively shows that the doctrine of separation of powers is "prescribed as explicitly for the conduct of foreign relations as for the handling of domestic matters" and explains: "The purpose and effect of any such arrangement is to require the joint participation—the cooperation and concurrence—of the several branches in the making and carrying out of any genuinely critical decision."

Justice Joseph Story, one of the foremost scholars to sit on the Supreme Court, confirms this statement. In his *Commentaries on the*

Constitution, Story writes, in connection with the decision of the framers to allot the treaty authority jointly in the president and the Senate, "his joint possession of the power affords a greater security for its just exercise, than the separate possession of it by either" and that it "is too much to expect, that a free people would confide to a single magistrate, however respectable, the sole authority to act conclusively, as well as exclusively upon treaties."

. . .

In 1917 Prof. Edward Corwin, recognized as one of the leading authorities on the Constitution in this or any other century and generally a defender of broad presidential power, wrote: "[A]ll in all, it appears that legislative precedent, which moreover is generally supported by the attitude of the executive, sanctions the proposition that the power of terminating the international compacts to which the United States is party belongs, as a prerogative of sovereignty, to Congress alone."

Another official admission of the necessity for legislative concurrence in the decision to provide notice in circumstances in which a treaty itself authorizes the giving of notice comes from an attorney general's opinion. In 1941 Francis Biddle, then acting attorney general, was asked to advise President Roosevelt whether, in view of the dislocation of ocean-borne commerce because of war, the International Load Line Convention, which governed ocean tanker tonnage loads, had ceased to be binding. Biddle concluded the convention was inoperative because of the "well-established principle of international law, *rebus sic stantibus*, that a treaty ceases to be binding when the basic conditions upon which it was founded have essentially changed."

But he sharply qualified his opinion. While the president could decide whether the treaty was inoperative or suspended under this principle of international law, the president alone could not terminate the treaty if he acted under a treaty provision allowing withdrawal by giving due notice. Biddle wrote: "It is not proposed that the United States denounce the convention under Article 25 (47 Stat. 2256), nor that it be otherwise abrogated. Consequently, action by the Senate or by the Congress is not required."

Article 25 of that convention provided that it may be denounced by any "contracting government" by notification to the other parties and that the withdrawal should take effect 12 months after the date of notification is received. The article is similar to Article X of the R.O.C. defense treaty, which likewise allows denunciation by the United States after one year's notice. Thus, it is clear that Biddle believed legislative concurrence was needed in order to authorize presidential action pursuant to the terms of a treaty in circumstances identical to those asserted by President Carter as grounds for unilateral action. President Carter's decision to notify the Republic of China on his sole authority is directly in conflict with a 20th century opinion of the country's highest law enforcement officer.

History confirms the denial of an independent treaty termination power of the president, although there are minor exceptions explainable under principles of ordinary contract law. In fact, the first treaty terminations were done by act of Congress in 1798. These were the three treaties of alliance with France, which were cancelled by Congress after repeated French attacks on American shipping.

The second instance of termina-

tion by the United States was in 1846, 57 years after the Constitution was approved. President Polk asked Congress for authority to pull out of a treaty with Britain yielding joint rights to the Oregon Territory. A joint resolution was enacted giving him authority to provide notice of withdrawal, as was authorized in the treaty. This is the first known instance of termination by notice and is impressive historical evidence of what procedure is required to carry out a treaty provision similar to Article X of the R.O.C. defense treaty.

In all, I have identified 48 instances in which treaties have been terminated or suspended by the United States—40 with the clear authorization or ratification of an act of Congress, joint resolution, or Senate resolution. Four others were superseded by a later statute or treaty in conflict with the earlier treaty. The normal practice of treaty termination in the United States has been joint action by the president and Senate or Congress.

Only four treaties have been cancelled by the president entirely independent of any supporting legislative authority. The president may not have acted constitutionally even in these isolated cases, which are abnormal. In fact, Congress may not have been informed, and thus no challenge was made at the time. But if there is any difference in the two groups of cancelled treaties, a logical explanation may be found in contract law.

For in each of the situations of independent presidential action, the other party had first violated the treaty, it was impossible to perform the treaty, or there was a fundamental change of conditions essential to the operation of the treaty and originally assumed as the basis for it. In none of these incidents was the reason for terminating or withdrawing from a treaty the result of a breach or other action on our part inconsistent with the purposes of the treaty concerned.

. . .

The State Department has released a memorandum by Herbert Hansell, its legal adviser, dated December 15, the same day as President Carter's public announcement, claiming the president could do what he did. That paper, actually a legal argument, contains highly selective quotations from authorities (none cited in this article appears in the memo) and sets forth a dubious list of alleged precedents for unilateral presidential action. Although the legal adviser lists 12 precedents for independent treaty termination, he admits on the face of the brief that two were never terminated (notice was withdrawn) and two more were instances in which the other nations first denounced the treaties, which seriously weakens the relevance of the precedents.

. . .

The State Department also omits mentioning in its memo that the early commercial treaty had been concluded with a different state. During the Napoleonic wars the United Netherlands with whom we had signed the treaty in 1782, was absorbed into the French empire, entirely disappearing as a separate nation. After the war it was reformed and joined with other areas. Samuel B. Crandall writes the state thus erected from the ashes of war "differed in name, territory, and form of government from the state which had entered into the treaty. . . ." In other words, if the treaty was annulled, it was because of the disappearance of one of the parties and not because of any broad power held by the president. This is the stuff of which the State Department memo is made.

Of the few alleged precedents that have any plausible basis (three or four at most), all can be explained by invoking the principles of contract law discussed above. None of these exceptions has any application to the R.O.C. defense treaty.

Even as to this handful of precedents, there is no ground for asserting independent presidential power. There is no court decision upholding their legality, and the last precedent is no better than the first. As the Supreme Court said in *Powell* v. *McCormack*, . . . (1969): "That an unconstitutional action has been taken before surely does not render that same action any less unconstitutional at a later date."

It has been suggested that since the president alone has the power to remove executive officers appointed by and with the advice and consent of the Senate, he also has power to remove treaties. The two cases are completely dissimilar. The ability to remove officers clearly under his direction aids in the efficient performance of the president's duties. The removal of treaties violates the president's constitutional duty to see "that the laws be faithfully executed." It is obvious that the president's relation with subordinate officers cannot be equated to his relation with sovereign authorities of other nations.

. . .

The only remaining question is whether, although the president normally cannot terminate a treaty without further legislative action, the Senate has consented to his action in the case of this treaty by having approval language in it that allows termination by notice. The answer is clear that no authority of this type can be inferred from the treaty or legislative history.

. . .

Although it is generally accepted that the president is "the sole organ of the nation in its external relations, and its sole representative with foreign nations," this proves no more than that it is the president who shall act as the official representative of the nation in communicating with the foreign government. His capacity as a diplomatic organ in no way need imply a power of making the critical policy decision required before delivery of the notice.

. . .

(4) *Barry Goldwater et al.* v. *James Earl Carter et al.* (1979) [U.S. District Court for the District of Columbia]

This is a suit by eight members of the United States Senate, a former senator, and sixteen members of the House of Representatives seeking declaratory and injunctive relief against the notice given by defendant President Carter to the Republic of China ("ROC" or "Taiwan") to terminate the 1954 Mutual Defense Treaty Between the United States of America and the Republic of China. Plaintiffs seek to have this Court declare that the termination of the 1954 Treaty cannot be legally accomplished, nor can notice be given of intended termination, without the advice and consent of the United States Senate or the approval of both houses of Congress.

Plaintiffs contend that President Carter's unilateral notice of termination violated their legislative right to be consulted and to vote on the termination and also impaired the effectiveness of prior votes approving the 1954 Mutual Defense Treaty. They also claim that the President's action violated section 26 of the International Security Assistance Act of 1978.

Defendants have moved to dismiss or, in the alternative, for summary judgment contending that this case is nonjusticiable because it presents a political question, plaintiffs lack standing to sue, and the President possesses constitutional authority to give notice of the termination of the Mutual Defense Treaty. . . .

On December 2, 1954, . . . a Mutual Defense Treaty Between the United States of America and the ROC was signed in Washington, D.C. The senate gave its consent to ratification on February 9, 1955 and the treaty was ratified by President Eisenhower on February 11, 1955. The treaty entered into force on March 3, 1955. The Mutual Defense Treaty obligates the United States, upon joint agreement with the ROC and "in accordance with its constitutional processes," to defend Taiwan and the Pescadores from an armed attack. Article X of the treaty contains a termination clause, which states that the treaty "shall remain in force indefinitely," but continues: "Either party may terminate it one year after notice has been given to the other party." The issue posed by this lawsuit is thus not whether the United States has the right to terminate the defense treaty, a right expressly guaranteed by Article X, but the procedure by which that right of termination should be accomplished.

During the past decade, initial steps towards normalizing relations between the United States and the PRC were taken. The PRC has always maintained that recognition of two Chinas was unacceptable and that continuation of the Mutual Defense Treaty with Taiwan was incompatible with normalization of relations with PRC. On December 15, 1978, the leaders of the United States and the PRC announced their agreement to establish diplomatic relations as of January 1, 1979. On December 23, 1978, United States Deputy Secretary of State Warren Christopher, at the direction of the President, gave notice of termination of the Treaty to ROC authorities in Taiwan. According to this notice, the Mutual Defense Treaty will terminate on January 1, 1980.

Perhaps anticipating this change in United States policy, in the latter part of 1978 both houses of Congress passed the International Security Assistance Act of 1978, which was signed by President Carter on September 26, 1978. Section 26 of the Act, popularly known as the Dole-Stone amendment, provides:

"(a) The Congress finds that—

"(1) the continued security and stability of East Asia is a matter of major strategic interest to the United States;

"(2) the United States and the Republic of China have for a period of twenty-four years been linked together by the Mutual Defense Treaty of 1954;

"(3) the Republic of China has during that twenty-four-year period faithfully and continually carried out its duties and obligations under that treaty; and

"(4) it is the responsibility of the senate to give its advice and consent to treaties entered into by the United States.

"(b) It is the sense of the Congress that there should be prior consultation between the Congress and the executive branch on any proposed policy changes affecting the continuation in force of the Mutual Defense Treaty of 1954."

Defendants maintain that consultations with members of both Houses occurred both prior and subsequent to the enactment of this act and that these consultations, which concerned negotiations with the PRC generally and the necessity for terminating the Mutual Defense Treaty, fully complied with the intent of the Dole-Stone amendment. For reasons subsequently set forth, the Court does not reach the question whether the contacts mentioned amount to consultation.

The issue with which the Court is confronted is whether the President has unilateral authority to terminate a mutual defense treaty with a friendly nation which has not violated any of the provisions of the treaty. Reference to the historical precedents since the beginnings of this nation discloses terminations of treaties in more than fifty instances. Some have been terminated by legislative action; some have been terminated by the President with the concurrence of both houses of Congress; some have been terminated by the President with senatorial consent; and some have been terminated by the President acting alone, but these Presidential terminations have been in situations in which it might be inferred that the Congress had no reason to question Presidential action, such as the termination by President Coolidge of the Mexican Smuggling Treaty, which had been found to be completely ineffectual. Based on the Court's consideration of these historical precedents, the Court believes the power to terminate treaties is a power shared by the political branches of this government, namely, the President and the Congress. In this instance, however, since the Congress has not yet acted on the question of treaty termination, a serious question arises concerning the standing of these congressional plaintiffs to seek a judicial injunction or declaration respecting the power of the executive.

An increasing number of senators and congressmen have invoked the jurisdiction of the courts to challenge executive actions and policies. Because of their political overtones, these cases present difficult jurisdictional questions. In a number of cases the United States Court of Appeals for the District of Columbia Circuit has considered the interrelationship between standing to sue and the political question doctrine and expressed its view that the standing issue should be resolved first. Thus, at the outset, the Court must consider whether plaintiffs have standing to obtain a judicial declaration that the President lacks authority unilaterally to terminate the Mutual Defense Treaty with Taiwan.

. . .

Like all plaintiffs, a legislator must show that he has suffered an injury in fact; that the interests he asserts are within the zone protected by the statute or constitutional provision in question; that the injury resulted from the challenged illegal action of defendants; and that the injury be capable of being redressed by a decision in his favor. . . .

Perhaps the most important decision concerning congressional standing is *Kennedy* v. *Sampson* . . . (D.C. Cir. 1974). In that case the Court found that Senator Kennedy had standing to seek a declaratory judgment that a bill for which he had voted had become law despite a presidential pocket veto. The Court held that to the extent the powers of Congress are impaired, so too is the power of each congressman, because his office confers the right to participate in the exercise of the powers of the institution. . . .

Plaintiffs Thurmond and Curtis, who voted to ratify the 1954 Mutual Defense Treaty, rely on *Kennedy* to support their claim that the President's action impaired the effectiveness of their prior votes approving the treaty. In considering the analogous claim of legislators who alleged that they had an interest in ensuring enforcement of laws for which they

voted, however, the United States Court of Appeals for the Fourth Circuit held that once a bill has become law the legislators' interests are indistinguishable from those of any citizen and legislators "cannot claim dilution of their legislative voting power because the legislation they favored became law." *Harrington* v. *Schlesinger* . . . (4th Cir. 1975).

All plaintiffs with the exception of former Senator Curtis claim that the unilateral notice of termination impaired their legislative right to be consulted and to vote on treaty termination. Several courts have suggested that the availability of alternative political remedies to redress executive action, such as impeachment, denial of funds, or a vote on pending legislation, is evidence that there has been no injury in fact to congressional rights or powers. For example, in *Public Citizen* v. *Sampson* . . . (D.C. Cir. 1975), a group of congressmen sued to overturn an agency regulation granting inventors exclusive rights to patents developed under federal research contracts. This regulation was promulgated by the General Services Administration ("GSA") without congressional approval, and the congressmen claimed that it infringed on their right to participate in the disposal of government-owned property. The Court found no injury in fact and denied standing because promulgation of the regulation could not deprive Congress of its uncontested right to dispose of government property by limiting the contractual powers of the GSA, . . .

This analysis of congressional standing is based on a consideration of prudential and functional concerns, similar to those described by the Supreme Court in *Baker* v. *Carr* . . . (1962), the leading statement of the political question doctrine that reflects the deference to be accorded a coordinate branch of government under our system of separation of powers. A suit such as this by a group of individual legislators seeking to vindicate derivative constitutional rights bypasses the political arena which should be the primary and usual forum in which such views are expressed.

At least three resolutions dealing with the treaty termination power and the notice of termination given with respect to the 1954 Mutual Defense Treaty are presently pending before the United States Senate. [One is the Byrd Resolution.] If the Senate as a whole were to take action approving the termination of the Mutual Defense Treaty, the issues raised by this suit would be moot because the President's action would no longer be unilateral. If the Senate or the Congress rejected the President's notice of termination or asserted a right to participate in the treaty termination process, the court would be confronted by a clash of the political branches in a posture suitable for judicial review.

The situation then would be comparable to that presented in *Kennedy v. Sampson*, in which congressional power had been exercised and was about to be frustrated by a pocket veto. Here, however, plaintiffs have not established the necessary injury required for standing. Either the Senate or the Congress as a whole still can utilize the legislative process to assert its right and demonstrate that it possesses a shared power with the President to act in terminating a treaty. Although the Court is inclined to agree with plaintiffs' assertion that the power to terminate the 1954 Mutual Defense Treaty is a shared power to be exercised by the action of both political branches, at the present time there is no indication that

the Congress as a whole intends to assert its prerogative to act. Under these circumstances, the President's notice of termination does not constitute injury. In the absence of any injury to the institution as a whole, the individual legislators here cannot claim a derivative injury.

. . .

Plaintiffs also have alleged that the statutory rights conferred by section 26 of the International Security Assistance Act of 1978, . . . have been violated because there was no prior consultation between the Congress and the executive branch prior to the notice of termination of the Mutual Defense Treaty. Defendants dispute this factual allegation and have submitted an affidavit detailing the consultation that occurred after enactment.

The final language of the Dole-Stone amendment is general and nonmandatory in nature. This was substituted for the apparently mandatory language originally proposed by Senators Dole and Stone. Because section 26 apparently does not set forth a mandatory or binding duty to consult and because the Court could not effectively resolve the question of how much consultation would meet its terms if it were binding, plaintiffs, in alleging injury under this section, have failed to state a claim upon which relief can be granted. . . .

The Court believes that the extraordinary remedy of injunction or the related power of a declaration should be exercised sparingly and only when the legislative branch has been given the opportunity of acting. At least three resolutions are presently pending in the Senate. For these reasons the Court believes that the resolution of the ultimate issue in this case should in the first instance be in the legislative forum. If the Congress approves the President's action, the issue presently before the Court would be moot. If the Senate or the Congress takes action, the result of which falls short of approving the President's termination effort, then the controversy will be ripe for a judicial declaration respecting the President's authority to act unilaterally. Until then, the complaint is dismissed without prejudice.

OLIVER GASCH
Judge.

[In the fall of 1979 Judge Gasch ruled that the President could *not* terminate the Taiwan treaty without congressional consent. That decision was reversed by the Court of Appeals for the District of Columbia on November 30, 1979. Early in December the Supreme Court denied review, thus leaving the decision of the Court of Appeals as final in this case.]

E. *Emergencies and Constitutional Power*

(1) Jacobus Tenbroek, Edward M. Barnhart, and Floyd W. Matson, The Japanese-American Cases

[The "Japanese-American cases" were three decisions of the Supreme Court: *Hirabayashi* v. *United States* (1943), *Ex Parte Endo* (1944), and *Korematsu* v. *United States* (1944), testing the constitutionality of curfew and relocation orders imposed by executive order on Japanese-Americans living on the West Coast in the early days of World War II. Hirabayashi was convicted of failure to observe a curfew and for failure to report for registration leading to evacuation, and the Supreme Court upheld his curfew conviction. Endo was a Japanese-American citizen whose loyalty had been established and who then petitioned for a writ of habeas corpus to secure her release from a relocation center. The Supreme Court upheld her right to the writ, but did not reach the issue of the constitutionality of the detention and relocation program. Korematsu was convicted of violating the detention and evacuation provisions, and the conviction was affirmed by a divided Supreme Court. Writing for the majority, Justice Black argued that racial classifications are constitutionally suspect but not per se unconstitutional—". . . courts must subject them to the most rigid scrutiny. Pressing public necessity may sometimes justify the existence of such restrictions: racial antagonism never can." He found that under the war powers, the government could take action otherwise impermissible, and that in the circumstances of this case the government's action was not invalid. In a bitter dissent, Justice Murphy saw the government's action as going over the "very brink of constitutional power" and falling into the "ugly abyss of racism." He was unpersuaded that the inconvenience and administrative difficulty of holding individual loyalty hearings for the 112,000 persons involved—or even for the 70,000 of those who were native-born citizens—could justify the government's action.]

. . . The Japanese bombs which cascaded upon Pearl Harbor on December 7, 1941, plunging the United States into a global struggle for existence, also plunged the nation into a critical test of its constitutional democracy. If America was to survive, could its Constitution survive with it? Under the conditions of total war, could the constitutional balance be maintained between military and civilian authority, between the executive and the legislative, between all of these and the courts? Could civil liberties, the rights of individuals and of minorities, be tolerated—let alone protected? Could limited government and unlimited war-waging power coexist?

Reprinted from *Prejudice, War, and the Constitution* (Berkeley: University of California Press, 1954), pp. 1–3, 225–229, 259–260.

Nowhere were these questions more clearly defined than in the closely knit series of events which might be called the Japanese-American episode of World War II.

The events that constituted the episode may be briefly summarized. They began the day after Pearl Harbor with the selective apprehension and imprisonment of several hundred enemy aliens—Japanese, German, and Italian. To this precaution were soon added travel restrictions and contraband orders applying to all enemy aliens. Then came curfew, evacuation, and finally detention—the last two applied on a strict racial basis to Japanese Americans only and regardless of citizenship. Accompanying and following these events were incessant demands for the permanent exclusion of the Japanese minority from the West Coast, for a flat prohibition of their entry into agriculture or business, and for their deportation to Japan after the war. Ways and means of stripping American citizens of Japanese ancestry of their citizenship were widely discussed. State legislatures considered memorials urging Congress to propose a constitutional amendment to that end. The Native Sons of the Golden West, flanked by the American Legion, filed suits in federal court for the same purpose. Congress amended the Nationality Act especially to facilitate the renunciation of American citizenship by Japanese Americans. The attorney general of California directed much more vigorous prosecution of Alien Land Law violations than ever before. The legislature of California passed in 1943, repassed in 1945, a law prohibiting first "alien Japanese," then (fearing that this was too specific to be constitutional) "aliens ineligible to citizenship," from commercial fishing in coastal waters. . . .

Can the Japanese-American episode be reconciled with our fundamental constitutional rights and moral ideals? Can it be reconciled with the basic tenets of our democratic system? Or does the unprecedented racism of the episode fade into insignificance before the unprecedented character of the war itself? No doubt traditional views on the limits of military power needed to be reconsidered in World War II. The power to wage war successfully was, in the end, successfully exerted. Does this fact stand as the justification? . . .

The evacuation of American citizens of Japanese ancestry from the Pacific Coast, and their subsequent detention, carried out by the military under a plea or pretext of military necessity, raises the question of the extent of the war powers of the national government. The circumstances in which this question is presented contain at least two complicating factors. The first is the discriminatory character of the action taken. Had that factor not been present—had the question simply been the validity of a universally applied curfew or of the evacuation of all persons from a limited area threatened even remotely by invasion—a basic constitutional issue of fact would still have had to be decided, but it is doubtful that there would have been so much question about the power of the military to impose the restriction. But the curfew, in addition to covering German, Italian, and Japanese aliens, reached citizens of Japanese ancestry, and mass evacuation and detention were applied exclusively to persons of that ancestry.

Second, the problem is complicated by the fact that it involved military control over civilians within the country and thus opens to view the baffling lay and professional chaos surrounding martial law. Had a civilian agency alone handled the evacuation, no martial-law questions would have been raised to confuse the war-powers problem.

"When an area is so beset," said Justice Jackson in his *Korematsu* dissent, "that it must be put under military control at all, the paramount consideration is that its measure be successful, rather than legal. . . . No court can require such a commander in such circumstances to act as a reasonable man"; the general issues orders, "and they may have a certain authority as military commands, although they may be very bad as constitutional law." "But if we cannot confine military expedients by the Constitution," added Justice Jackson, "neither would I distort the Constitution to approve all that the military may deem expedient." "I should hold that a civil court cannot be made to enforce an order which violates constitutional limitations even if it is a reasonable exercise of military authority."

To this, Justice Frankfurter, concurring with the majority, took vigorous exception. "To talk about a military order that expresses an allowable judgment of war needs by those entrusted with the duty of conducting war as 'an unconstitutional order' is to suffuse a part of the Constitution with an atmosphere of unconstitutionality. The Constitution," he said, explicitly granted the war power "for safeguarding the national life by prosecuting war effectively." Hence, "if a military order . . . does not transcend the means appropriate for conducting war, such action by the military is as constitutional as would be any authorized action by the Interstate Commerce Commission."

This Jackson-Frankfurter exchange highlighted and placed in modern context one of the oldest and most crucial problems of constitutional democracy, viz., how to reconcile the conflicting demands of unfettered military power necessary to preserve the state in times of crisis with the system of constitutional limitations and individual rights. Can this sort of military power be brought within the confines of the Constitution, subjected to rule and circumscribed by limitation—or is it governed only by necessity as uninhibited and elemental as national self-preservation? Must we, as Justice Jackson suggests, regard unconstitutionality as an inevitable concomitant of the exercise of military authority even when it is "reasonable?"

The Japanese-American cases required the court to answer the following fundamental questions: (1) In time of war, what are the tests of the war power of the national government, vested by the Constitution in Congress and the Executive as the war-waging branches of government, especially over citizen civilians within the country? (2) How far does the power of the military extend over civilians within the country in time of war? (3) Does such power arise from necessity and exist independently of the Constitution, or is it constitutionally authorized and granted? (4) No matter what its sources, is such power subject to the limitations of the Constitution? (5) To what extent, if at all, is this power dependent upon the concepts of martial law? (6) Is the military judgment of the military necessity for controls over civilians final? Or does the responsibility rest primarily with Congress to determine the existence of the conditions justifying the establishment of partial or total military government and of establishing it? To what extent, and by what tests, if any, are such judgments, by the military or by Congress, subject to judicial review and control? (7) To what degree, if any, do the methods and character of modern warfare require that we relax our democratically indispensable doctrine of the civil control of the military and the responsibility of the latter for its acts?

Merely to mention these questions raises immediately the character and scope of the decision in *Ex parte Milligan*. . . . Decided in 1866 and arising out of an episode of the Civil War, that case has stood in our constitutional history as a landmark of the nature and extent of the wartime power of the military over civilians within the country. It was a "brooding omnipresence" in the Japanese-American cases, albeit undiscussed, unanalyzed, and all but unmentioned. Like many another historical landmark, it has been held to stand for various and often conflicting propositions. In recent years, the majority opinion in the *Milligan* case has been sharply criticized as importing into the Constitution "a mechanical test" which, though a "salutary restraint upon the tyranny of the Stuarts" is not "an appropriate limit on the powers of both executive and legislature in the highly responsible national government." Just as sharply, the majority opinion has been defended as "a monument in the democratic tradition" which "should be the animating force of this branch of our law."

The facts of the *Milligan* case were not exactly like those of the Japanese-American cases. In October, 1864, Milligan was arrested by military order, tried, found guilty and sentenced to hang by a military commission. The offense charged was not disloyalty or suspicion of disloyalty but conspiracy to overthrow the government, a crime under the laws of Congress and therefore punishable in the civil courts, as disloyalty or suspicion of disloyalty is not. In May, 1865, Milligan petitioned the United States circuit court to be discharged from unlawful imprisonment. The two-judge circuit court divided and certified the question to the Supreme Court.

By Act of March 3, 1863, Congress had authorized the President to suspend the privilege of the writ of habeas corpus "whenever, in his judgment, the public safety may require it"; and the President had done so by proclamation. Under the statute, however, the privilege of the writ was not to be suspended if the person "was detained in custody by the order of the President, otherwise than as a prisoner of war; if he was a citizen . . . and had never been in the military or naval service, and the grand jury of the district had met, after he had been arrested, for a period of twenty days, and adjourned without taking any proceedings against him." Milligan was not a prisoner of war and had not been in the military or naval service. Moreover, a federal grand jury had convened in the district and failed to indict him. The privilege of the writ therefore had not been suspended as to him. So the Supreme Court unanimously held. The case being settled on these narrow grounds, here the court might have rested. Unlike their successors eighty years later, however, these judges were not seeking opportunities to evade the underlying grave constitutional issues.

Justice Davis, for a majority of the court, went on to enunciate the doctrine which is the principal heritage of the *Milligan* case. Trial by military commission, he maintained, violated the Third Article of the Constitution, which vests the judicial power in courts ordained and established by Congress and composed of judges appointed "during good behavior." It also violated the jury-trial guarantees in the original Constitution and in the

Fifth and Sixth Amendments and the search and seizure provisions of the Fourth Amendment. The Fathers, said Justice Davis, "secured the inheritance they had fought to maintain, by incorporating in a written constitution the safeguards which *time* had proved were essential to its preservation. Not one of these safeguards can the President, or Congress, or the Judiciary disturb, except the one concerning the writ of habeas corpus." The Fathers "limited the suspension to one great right, and left the rest to remain forever inviolable." "No doctrine, involving more pernicious consequences, was ever invented by the wit of man than that any of its [the Constitution's] provisions can be suspended during any of the great exigencies of government." It did not follow, said Justice Davis, that the nation was helpless in the face of a war crisis, barring the allowance of a theory of power by necessity; "for the government, within the Constitution, has all the powers granted to it, which are necessary to preserve its existence."

This, then, was the system of the *Milligan* majority: that the power to wage war and to wage it successfully, the power to preserve the existence of the nation, is granted by the Constitution; but at no point and in no crisis will its exercise justify the suspension of the constitutional guarantees and limitations, with the single exception of the privilege of the writ of habeas corpus. Moreover, the privilege of the writ of habeas corpus could be suspended only to the extent of warranting detention of individuals, in an hour of emergency, without trial; not to the extent of supplying unconstitutional trials. This aspect of the *Milligan* majority opinion, showing the power of the military to be constitutionally derived and constitutionally limited, is often ignored in

the preoccupation of courts and commentators with Justice Davis' remark about martial law.

This position of the *Milligan* majority is sustained and amplified by the claim that it rejected. That claim was that "in a time of war the commander of an armed force (if in his opinion the exigencies of the country demand it), has the power, within the lines of his military district, to suspend all civil rights and their remedies, and subject citizens as well as soldiers to the rule of his will"; and in the exercise of this authority "cannot be restrained, except by his superior officer or the President of the United States." "If this position is sound to the extent claimed," answered Justice Davis, "then when war exists," the commander of a military district can, "on the plea of necessity, with the approval of the Executive, substitute military force for and to the exclusion of the laws, and punish all persons, as he thinks right and proper, without fixed or certain rules." In that event, "republican government is a failure, and there is an end of liberty regulated by law." This kind of martial law destroys every guarantee of the Constitution, and effectually renders the "military independent of and superior to the civil power"—the attempt to do which by the King of Great Britain was deemed by our fathers such an offense, that they assigned it to the world, as one of the causes which impelled them to declare their independence. . . . Civil liberty and this kind of martial law cannot endure together; the antagonism is irreconcilable, and, in the conflict, one or the other must perish.

The court's opinion in the *Milligan* case thus makes clear that military necessity, even when approved by the Executive, is not a self-justifying plea; that the military judgment that military necessity exists cannot be allowed to stand alone; that the commander is responsible not only to his superiors and the President but to the law and the courts; that the military must act, at least when dealing with citizens within the country, within the confines of the Constitution and subject to civil—that is, judicial—control.

The Japanese-American cases—*Hirabayashi, Korematsu,* and *Endo* —though shrouded in great confusion of rhetoric, and despite the careful statement of doctrine by Chief Justice Stone in *Hirabayashi* (which he himself failed to apply), represent a constitutional yielding to the awe inspired in all men by total war and the new weapons of warfare. They disclose a judicial unwillingness to interfere with—or even to look upon—the actions of the military taken in time of global war, even to the extent of determining whether those actions are substantially or somehow connected with the prosecution of the war. That the actions were directed to and drastically affected citizen civilians within the country and involved decisions, policies, and an administration dominantly civil rather than military, were facts that were hardly noticed, let alone assigned their proper significance. In this context, the Japanese-American cases diminish and render uncertain the public responsibility of the military and relax democratic and judicial controls. In these cases, the historically established balance between the military and the civil—constitutionally sanctified in the United States by the classic majority opinion in *Ex parte Milligan*—has been shifted dangerously to the side of the military by the known and unknown terrors of total war and by a quiescent and irresolute

judiciary. In them, the *Milligan* rule of subordination of the military to the Constitution except in battlefield conditions is abandoned. Instead, the national war powers, though explicitly conferred by the Constitution and not exempted from its limitations, are founded on and circumscribed by a military estimate of military necessity. Citizens, on a mass basis, were allowed to be uprooted, removed and imprisoned by the military without trial, without attribution of guilt, without the institutional or individual procedural guarantees of Article Three and Amendments Five and Six, and without regard to the individual guarantees of Amendments One, Four, Five, and others. The military action was taken upon a mere suspicion of disloyalty arising from racial affinity with the enemy, and was applied discriminatorily to one race only. During most of the period of evacuation and detention there was not even a threat of invasion. The *Milligan* dissenters do not go nearly so far. Can circumstances short of battlefield conditions justify this kind of surrender of the Constitution to the generals? Does the winning of total war require so much—that the military be immune from review in its civil, sociological, and anthropological judgment; that the military be allowed to do militarily irrelevant things; that the military be permitted arbitrarily and unnecessarily to invade individual and civil rights? One may insist with Charles E. Hughes that "the power to wage war is the power to wage war successfully" and that "the power, explicitly conferred and absolutely essential to the safety of the Nation, is not destroyed or impaired by any later provision of the Constitution or by any one of the amendments." One may insist on all that and yet at the same time not deviate from the basic proposition—equally plain if not equally explicit in the Constitution and "absolutely essential" to the perpetuation of the republic—that the war power, when exerted in the military government of citizen civilians within the country, does not exist in the absence of a grave military peril, does not exceed measures reasonably appropriate to cope with that peril, and does not comprehend violations of civil and individual guarantees of the Constitution in the presence of a militarily adequate alternative.

(2) A Note on Emergency Powers and Individual Rights

The preceding selection explored the limits of "extraconstitutional" action by presidents in time of war, with a particular focus on the impact of such power on individual rights. Justice Davis' opinion in *Ex Parte Milligan* (1866) posthumously condemns Lincoln's suspension of the writ of habeas corpus while at the same time acknowledging some flexibility in the Constitution when there is clearly demonstrable military necessity. In the same paragraph in which he denounces the "pernicious" doctrine that there is lodged anywhere in the government the right to suspend provisions of the Constitution in time of war, Davis observes that "the government, within the Constitution, has all the powers granted to it, which are necessary to preserve its existence; as has been happily proved by the result of the great effort to throw off its just authority."

Presidents have followed Lincoln's example more than they have been restrained by Davis' words. And the Supreme Court itself, in the *Korematsu* case, seemed to expand somewhat Davis' conception of what powers the Constitution grants in time of *dire* emergency. For the majority, Justice Black noted that "compulsory exclusion of large groups of citizens from their homes, except under circumstances of direst emergency and peril is inconsistent with our basic governmental institutions." However, he added, "But when under conditions of modern warfare our shores are threatened by hostile forces, *the power to protect must be commensurate with the threatened danger.*" [italics added]. These words have a very different ring to them than his comment the next time a president's claim of emergency powers was considered by the Supreme Court, in 1952 in the *Steel Seizure Case.* Clearly, Black (and a majority of the Court) perceived the dangers of a Japanese invasion of the West Coast in 1942 as much more severe than the dangers to our military action in Korea in 1952 from a prolonged steel strike—severe enough, certainly, to countenance a relocation policy which one of the dissenters in *Korematsu,* Frank Murphy, said bordered on "the ugly abyss of racism."

The fact is that in time of war, or in other extreme emergencies, individual rights have often suffered. Some have argued that this can *never* be tolerated; others have contended that emergency may justify at least the temporary suspension of constitutional rights. Justice Oliver Wendell Holmes, writing in *Schenck v. United States* (1919), expressed it this way: "When a nation is at war, many things that might be said in time of peace are such a hindrance to its effort that their utterance will not be tolerated as long as men fight." An essay in the following chapter explores some of the legal doctrines that developed to rationalize limitations on free speech in time of war or threats to national security.

If there is a consensus "middle position" between these two extremes, it would sound something like this: The guarantees of the Bill of Rights cannot be nullified by actions taken under the war power, but under certain carefully controlled circumstances, abridgements of those rights may, in fact, be countenanced by the courts, particularly so if there is political support for such actions. Times change, and American sensitivity to individual rights is vastly greater today than it was in 1942 and even more than in 1918. Thus, for reasons suggested by the chapters on racial equality and personal freedoms, it seems *inconceivable* today that the Supreme Court would ever approve the sort of racially motivated actions at issue in *Korematsu* or the suppressions of free speech upheld by the Court in *Schenck* and later cases. Whether the Court, under emergency conditions, would openly seek to block any such actions by a future president, or whether it would, following Justice Jackson's dissent in *Korematsu*, neither approve nor disapprove such emergency actions, remains an open question.

In considering the question of emergency power, it is useful to compare emergencies created by war with those of an economic nature. The Great Depression produced a number of cases in which Congress or the states took actions that were contrary to then existing interpretations of constitutional limits. A number of those cases were considered in our chapter on the economy. Eventually, as we saw in that chapter, the Supreme Court came to accept as "normal" the powers of Congress and the states to regulate the economy which were then extraordinary. One case that directly raised the specter of emergency power, that is, power that was clearly "irregular"

and not merely a reasonable extension of existing powers, was *Home Building and Loan Association* v. *Blaisdell* (1934).

That case concerned a challenge by creditor financial institutions to a moratorium on farm mortgage payments enacted by the Minnesota legislature in 1933. Under the moratorium, state courts were empowered to extend the period for payment of mortgage loans in order to prevent foreclosures. The mortgage debts were not forgiven, but it was thought that by extending the period for repayment, many farmers would be able to recover from the worst effects of the Depression. Writing for a 5-4 majority, Chief Justice Hughes approved this "temporary and conditional" relief and held that it did not impair the contract clause of the Constitution. Hughes noted that the contract clause was not only a protection for individuals but also was intended to protect and enhance the integrity of the economic system, to the benefit of all. "The prohibition is not an absolute one and is not to be read with literal exactness like a mathematical formula." Set against the contract clause was the admitted police power of the states, which certainly included the power to impose temporary restraints on contractual obligations when vital public interests would otherwise suffer. Furthermore, this statute did not legislate an across-the-board forgiveness of debts, or even a general extension. In each case, courts had the obligation to review the circumstances and determine whether the moratorium should be applied. Hughes observed that the economic system in the 1930s was considerably more complex than the one that existed in 1787, and the role of government was necessarily different.

At the same time that he was approving this emergency regulation, however, Hughes had to come to terms with *Ex Parte Milligan* and Justice Davis' contention in that case that the Constitution was the same under all conditions. Said Hughes:

Emergency does not create power. Emergency does not increase granted power or remove or diminish the restrictions imposed upon power granted or reserved. The Constitution was adopted in a period of grave emergency. Its grants of power to the federal government and its limitations on the power of the States were determined in the light of emergency, and they are not altered by emergency. . . .

While emergency does not create power, emergency may furnish the occasion for the exercise of power. "Although an emergency may not call into life a power which has never lived, nevertheless emergency may afford a reason for the exertion of a living power already enjoyed." The constitutional question presented in the light of an emergency is whether the power possessed embraces the particular exercise of it in response to particular conditions. Thus, the war power of the federal government is not created by the emergency of war, but it is a power given to meet that emergency.

It is a power to wage war successfully, and thus it permits the harnessing of the entire energies of the people in a supreme co-operative effort to preserve the nation. But even the war power does not remove constitutional limitations safeguarding essential liberties. When the provisions of the Constitution, in grant or restriction, are specific, so particularized as not to admit of construction, no question is presented. Thus, emergency would not permit a state to have more than two senators in the Congress, . . . or permit the States to "coin money" or to "make anything but gold and silver coin a tender in payment of debts." But, where constitutional grants and limitations of power are set forth in general clauses, which afford a broad outline, the process of construction is essential to fill in the details. That is true of the contract clause. . . .

In dissent, Justice Sutherland relied heavily on *Ex Parte Milligan*. He argued that there is no such thing as emergency power or the suspension of ordinary powers or rights in time of emergency: "If the provisions of the Constitution be not upheld when they pinch as well as when they comfort, they may as well be abandoned."

3. THE VIETNAM WAR AND THE CONSTITUTION

A. *The Disputed Legality of the War*

[The United States' extensive military involvement in the Vietnam War is now an appropriate topic for retrospection. Setting aside the debate on the wisdom of that involvement, students of constitutional government recognize that important questions remain to be addressed. A key problem is defining the lawful scope of presidential powers to commit this nation's armed forces to combat. Does the president, as commander-in-chief, have the power to deploy American forces abroad and to enter them into armed conflict solely at his own discretion? Or is his power as commander-in-chief limited, as the words of the Constitution would seem to indicate, by the specific delegation to Congress of the power to declare war?

In No. 69 of the *Federalist Papers*, Alexander Hamilton stated that the commander-in-chief clause of Article II, Section 2, made the president the "First General and Admiral of the Confederacy." There is little debate today that the president occupies such a role. He has the last word on how the armed forces of the United States should be administered, subject, of course, to the constitutional power of Congress to raise armies and navies and to its necessary appropriations power to pay for the establishment of armed forces. Hamilton's metaphor would also seem to grant the president the power that generals and admirals always had, the power to define tactics and strategies and carry out military operations once war has been declared or exists. But does the president's role as commander-in-chief mean more than this?

An early draft of the Constitution gave Congress the power to "make" war. In the final draft, the word "make" was changed to "declare"—presumably to assure the president the power to repel armed attacks on the United States *and* to dispel any doubts that it was the president's power to *conduct* a war. There is some debate among historians, but the consensus seems to be that the framers intended to give to Congress the power to *commence* war, whether or not a formal declaration of war was voted.

Nevertheless, there has always been a shadow of authority supporting the existence of a presidential "war power," either in the commencement of a war or military action or in taking other extraordinary actions such as Roosevelt's Japanese Exclusion Order in 1942 and Truman's seizure of the steel mills to avoid a strike during the Korean War. It was Abraham Lincoln, responding to the secession of the Southern states in 1861, who set the precedent. He fused whatever powers the president had by virtue of the commander-in-chief clause with his powers under the "take care" clause into the dominant "war" role that he and many subsequent presidents exercised. We have already noted some of Lincoln's actions: between the fall of Fort Sumter and the reconvening of the Congress in 1861, he unilaterally added 40,000 men to the Union Army, suspended the writ of habeas corpus, spent more than $2 million in unappropriated funds, and ordered the blockade of Southern ports. The *Prize Cases* (1863), discussed earlier in this chapter, upheld Lincoln's military initiatives, albeit by a divided 5-4 vote.

No president has claimed the power to actually "declare" war, but many presidents after Lincoln took action consistent with his broad theory of presidential power, notwithstanding the Supreme Court's posthumous challenge to that power in *Ex Parte Milligan* (1866). The justification for such action is the necessity and obligation to maintain the security and defense of the United States. Indeed, Assistant Secretary of State Nicholas Katzenbach, testifying before the Senate in August 1967, argued that the very concept of a "declaration of war" was outmoded and not suited to the limited objectives of a military action such as that being conducted in Vietnam.

Congress can, of course, delegate powers to the president. But can it delegate its power to declare war? The Lend-Lease Act of 1941 delegated to the president for two years the power, "whenever he deems it in the interest of national defense," to authorize the production of war materials and to sell *or* transfer title of those articles to a government whose defense the *president* deemed vital to the security of the United States. The transfer of such articles could be on any terms that the president regarded as acceptable. Professor Edward Corwin described this as a "qualified declaration of war," since it permitted the president to convey indispensable assistance to Great Britain without technically violating American neutrality.

The following selections deal with the recurring issue of the "war powers" of the president. The first is an exerpt from a document prepared by the Office of Legal Advisor to the Secretary of State, defending the legality of American participation in Vietnam. The document was released to counter mounting criticism of the war. In parts of the document not reprinted here, it was contended that international law and the United Nations Charter recognized the right of individual and collective self-defense against armed attack, that this right of self-defense applied to South Vietnam even though that country was not a member of the United Nations, and that the United States had a right to assist in the defense of South Vietnam. It noted further that a declaration of war was not required by international law as a prerequisite to taking self-defense measures. The second selection, written by students at the Yale Law School, is a concerted attack on the legality of the war in Vietnam.]

(1) Department of State, Office of the Legal Advisor, The Legality of United States Participation in the Defense of Viet Nam

. . .

The President Has Full Authority to Commit United States Forces in the Collective Defense of South Viet Nam

There can be no question in present circumstances of the President's authority to commit United States forces to the defense of South Viet Nam. The grant of authority to the President in Article II of the Constitution extends to the actions of the United States currently undertaken in Viet Nam. In fact, however, it is unnecessary to determine whether this grant standing alone is sufficient to authorize the actions taken in Viet Nam. These actions rest not only on the exercise of Presidential powers under Article II but on the SEATO Treaty—a treaty advised and consented to by the Senate—and on actions of the Congress, particularly the Joint Resolution of August 10, 1964. When these sources of authority are taken together—Article II of the Constitution, the SEATO Treaty, and actions by the Congress—there can be no question of the legality under domestic law of United States actions in Viet Nam.

A. The President's Power Under Article II of the Constitution Extends to the Actions Currently Undertaken in Viet Nam. Under the Constitution, the President, in addition to being Chief Executive, is Commander-in-Chief of the Army and Navy. He holds the prime responsibility for the conduct of United States foreign relations. These duties carry very broad powers, including the power to deploy American forces abroad and commit them to military operations when the President deems such action necessary to maintain the security and defense of the United States.

At the Federal Constitutional Convention in 1787, it was originally proposed that Congress have the power "to make war." There were objections that legislative proceedings were too slow for this power to be vested in Congress; it was suggested that the Senate might be a better repository. Madison and Gerry then moved to substitute "to declare war" for "to make war," "leaving to the Executive power to repel sudden attacks." It was objected that this might make it too easy for the Executive to involve the nation in war, but the motion carried with but one dissenting vote.

In 1787 the world was a far larger place, and the framers probably had in mind attacks upon the United States. In the 20th century, the world has grown much smaller. An attack on a country far from our shores can impinge directly on the nation's security. In the SEATO Treaty, for example, it is formally declared that an armed attack against Viet Nam would endanger the peace and safety of the United States.

Since the Constitution was adopted there have been at least 125 instances in which the President has ordered the armed forces to take action or maintain positions abroad without obtaining prior Congressional authorization, starting with the "undeclared war" with France (1798–1800). For example, President Truman ordered 250,000 troops to Korea during the Korean War of the early 1950's. President Eisenhower dispatched 14,000 troops to Lebanon in 1958.

The Constitution leaves to the President the judgment to determine whether the circumstances of a particular armed attack are so urgent and the potential consequences so threatening to the security of the United States that he should act without formally consulting the Congress.

B. *The Southeast Asia Collective Defense Treaty Authorizes the President's Actions.* Under Article VI of the United States Constitution, "all Treaties made, or which shall be made, under the Authority of the United States, shall be the supreme Law of the Land." Article IV, paragraph 1 of the SEATO Treaty establishes as a matter of law that a Communist armed attack against South Viet Nam endangers the peace and safety of the United States. In this same provision the United States has undertaken a commitment in the SEATO Treaty to "act to meet the common danger in accordance with its constitutional processes" in the event of such an attack.

Under our Constitution it is the President who must decide when an armed attack has occurred. He has also the constitutional responsibility for determining what measures of defense are required when the peace and safety of the United States are endangered. If he considers that deployment of U.S. forces to South Viet Nam is required, and that military measures against the source of Communist aggression in North Viet Nam are necessary, he is constitutionally empowered to take those measures.

The SEATO Treaty specifies that each party will act "in accordance with its constitutional processes."

It has recently been argued that the use of land forces in Asia is not authorized under the Treaty because their use to deter armed attack was not contemplated at the time the Treaty was considered by the Senate. Secretary Dulles testified at that time that we did not intend to establish (1) a land army in Southeast Asia capable of deterring Communist aggression, or (2) an integrated headquarters and military organization like that of NATO; instead, the United States would rely on "mobile striking power" against the sources of aggression. However, the Treaty obligation in Article IV, paragraph 1, to meet the common danger in the event of armed aggression, is not limited to particular modes of military action. What constitutes an adequate deterrent or an appropriate response, in terms of military strategy, may change; but the essence of our commitment to act to meet the common danger, as necessary at the time of an armed aggression, remains. In 1954 the forecast of military judgment might have been against the use of substantial United States ground forces in Viet Nam. But that does not preclude the President from reaching a different military judgment in different circumstances, twelve years later.

C. *The Joint Resolution of Congress of August 10, 1964 Authorizes United States Participation in the Collective Defense of South Viet Nam.* As stated earlier, the legality of United States participation in the defense of South Viet Nam does not rest only on the constitutional power of the President under Article II—or indeed on that power taken in conjunction with the SEATO Treaty. In addition, the Congress has acted in unmistakable fashion to approve and authorize United States actions in Viet Nam.

Following the North Vietnamese attacks in the Gulf of Tonkin against United States destroyers, Congress adopted, by a Senate vote of 88-2 and a House vote of 416-0, a Joint Resolution containing a series of important declarations and provisions of law.

Section 1 resolved that "the Congress approves and supports the determination of the President, as Commander in Chief, to take all necessary measures to repel any armed attack against the forces of the United States and to prevent further aggression." Thus, the Congress gave its sanction to specific actions by the President to repel attacks against United States naval vessels in the Gulf of Tonkin and elsewhere in the western Pacific. Congress further approved the taking of "all necessary measures . . . to prevent further aggression." This authorization extended to those measures the President might consider necessary to ward off further attacks and to prevent further aggression by North Viet Nam in Southeast Asia.

The Joint Resolution then went on to provide in section 2:

The United States regards as vital to its national interest and to world peace the maintenance of international peace and security in southeast Asia. Consonant with the Constitution of the United States and the Charter of the United Nations and in accordance with its obligations under the Southeast Asia Collective Defense Treaty, the United States is, therefore, prepared, as the President determines, to take all necessary steps, including the use of armed force, to assist any member or protocol state of the Southeast Asia Collective Defense Treaty requesting assistance in defense of its freedom.

Section 2 thus constitutes an authorization to the President, in his discretion, to act—using armed force if he determines that is required—to assist South Viet Nam at its request in defense of its freedom. The identification of South Viet Nam through the reference to "protocol state" in this section is unmistakable, and the grant of authority "as the President determines" is unequivocal.

It has been suggested that the legislative history of the Joint Resolution shows an intention to limit United States assistance to South Viet Nam to aid, advice, and training. This suggestion is based on an amendment offered from the floor by Senator Nelson which would have added the following to the text:

The Congress also approves and supports the efforts of the President to bring the problem of peace in Southeast Asia to the Security Council of the United Nations, and the President's declaration that the United States, seeking no extension of the present military conflict, will respond to provocation in a manner that is "limited and fitting." Our continuing policy is to limit our role to the provision of aid, training assistance, and military advice, and it is the sense of Congress that, except when provoked to a greater response, we should continue to attempt to avoid a direct military involvement in the Southeast Asian conflict.

Senator Fulbright, who had reported the Joint Resolution from the Foreign Relations Committee, spoke on the amendment as follows:

Mr. Fulbright. It states fairly accurately what the President has said would be our policy, and what I stated my understanding was as to our policy; also what other Senators have stated. In other words, it states that our response should be appropriate and limited to the provocation, which the Senator states as "respond to provocation in a manner that is limited and fitting," and so forth. We do not wish any political or military bases there. We are not seeking to gain a colony. We seek to insure the capacity of these people to develop along the lines of their own desires, independent of domination by communism.

The Senator has put into his amendment a statement of policy that is unobjectionable. However, I cannot accept the amendment under the circumstances. I do not believe it is contrary to the joint resolution, but it is an enlargement. I am informed that the House is now voting on this resolution. The House joint resolution is about to be presented to us. I cannot accept the amendment and go to conference with it, and thus take responsibility for delaying matters.

I do not object to it as a statement of policy. I believe it is an accurate reflection of what I believe is the President's policy, judging from his own statements. That does not mean that as a practical matter I can accept the amendment. It would delay matters to do so. It would cause confusion and require a conference, and present us with all the other difficulties that are involved in this kind of legislative action. I regret that I cannot do it, even though I do not at all disagree with the amendment as a general statement of policy.

Senator Nelson's amendment related the degree and kind of U. S. response in Viet Nam to "provocation" on the other side; the response should be "limited and fitting." The greater the provocation, the stronger are the measures that may be characterized as "limited and fitting." Bombing of North Vietnamese naval bases was a "limited and fitting" response to the attacks on U. S. destroyers in August 1964, and the subsequent actions taken by the United States and South Viet Nam have been an appropriate response to the increased war of aggression carried on by North Viet Nam since that date. Moreover, Senator Nelson's proposed amend-

ment did not purport to be a restriction on authority available to the President but merely a statement concerning what should be the continuing policy of the United States.

Congressional realization of the scope of authority being conferred by the Joint Resolution is shown by the legislative history of the measure as a whole. The following exchange between Senators Cooper and Fulbright is illuminating:

Mr. Cooper. . . . The Senator will remember that the SEATO Treaty, in article IV, provides that in the event an armed attack is made upon a party to the Southeast Asia Collective Defense Treaty, or upon one of the protocol states such as South Vietnam, the parties to the treaty, one of whom is the United States, would then take such action as might be appropriate, after resorting to their constitutional processes. I assume that would mean, in the case of the United States, that Congress would be asked to grant the authority to act.

Does the Senator consider that in enacting this resolution we are satisfying that requirement of article IV of the Southeast Asia Collective Defense Treaty? In other words, are we now giving the President advance authority to take whatever action he may deem necessary respecting South Vietnam and its defense, or with respect to the defense of any other country included in the treaty?

Mr. Fulbright. I think that is correct.

Mr. Cooper. Then, looking ahead, if the President decided that it was necessary to use such force as could lead into war, we will give that authority by this resolution?

Mr. Fulbright. That is the way I would interpret it. If a situation later developed in which we thought the approval should be withdrawn it could be withdrawn by concurrent resolution.

The August 1964 Joint Resolution continues in force today.* Section 2 of

*Repealed by Congress on July 10, 1970.

the Resolution provides that it shall expire "when the President shall determine that the peace and security of the area is reasonably assured by international conditions created by action of the United Nations or otherwise, except that it may be terminated earlier by concurrent resolution of the Congress." The President has made no such determination, nor has Congress terminated the Joint Resolution.

Instead, Congress in May 1965 approved an appropriation of $700 million to meet the expense of mounting military requirements in Viet Nam. The President's message asking for this appropriation stated that this was "not a routine request. For each member of Congress who supports this request is also voting to persist in our efforts to halt Communist aggressions in South Viet Nam." The Appropriation Act constitutes a clear Congressional endorsement and approval of the actions taken by the President.

On March 1, 1966 the Congress continued to express its support of the President's policy by approving a $4.8 billion supplemental military authorization by votes of 392-4 and 93-2. An amendment that would have limited the President's authority to commit forces to Viet Nam was rejected in the Senate by a vote of 94-2.

D. *No Declaration of War by the Congress Is Required To Authorize United States Participation in the Collective Defense of South Viet Nam.* No declaration of war is needed to authorize American actions in Viet Nam. As shown in the preceding sections, the President has ample authority to order the participation of United States armed forces in the defense of South Viet Nam.

Over a very long period in our history, practice and precedent have confirmed the constitutional authority to engage United States forces in hostilities without a declaration of war. This history extends from the undeclared war with France and the war against the Barbary Pirates, at the end of the 18th century, to the Korean War of 1950-1953.

James Madison, one of the leading framers of the Constitution, and Presidents John Adams and Jefferson all construed the Constitution, in their official actions during the early years of the Republic, as authorizing the United States to employ its armed forces abroad in hostilities in the absence of any Congressional declaration of war. Their views and actions constitute highly persuasive evidence as to the meaning and effect of the Constitution. History has accepted the interpretation that was placed on the Constitution by the early Presidents and Congresses in regard to the lawfulness of hostilities without a declaration of war. The instances of such action in our history are numerous.

In the Korean conflict, where large-scale hostilities were conducted with an American troop participation of a quarter of a million men, no declaration of war was made by the Congress. The President acted on the basis of his constitutional responsibilities. While the Security Council, under a treaty of this country—the United Nations Charter—recommended assistance to the Republic of Korea against the Communist armed attack, the United States had no treaty commitment at that time obligating us to join in the defense of South Korea. In the case of South Viet Nam we have the obligation of the SEATO Treaty and clear expressions of Congressional support. If the President could act in Korea without a declaration of war, *a fortiori* he is empowered to do so now in Viet Nam.

It may be suggested that a declaration of war is the only available constitutional process by which Congressional support can be made effective for the use of United States armed forces in combat abroad. But the Constitution does not insist on any rigid formalism. It gives Congress a choice of ways in which to exercise its powers. In the case of Viet Nam the Congress has supported the determination of the President by the Senate's approval of the SEATO Treaty, the adoption of the Joint Resolution of August 10, 1964, and the enactment of the necessary authorizations and appropriations.

(2) Indochina: The Constitutional Crisis

. . .

The power to commit American forces to combat was originally entrusted to Congress, which retained it almost unchallenged for over a century. But in the twentieth century, Congress has passively allowed the effective ability to engage the United States in hostile action abroad to be assumed almost entirely by the Presidency. . . .

The Language of the Constitution

The power to commit American troops to battle was allocated by the Constitution between the President and Congress. . . . The President is entrusted with the executive power, made Commander-in-Chief of the Army and Navy, and, with the advice and consent of the Senate, empowered to make treaties and appoint ambassadors. The Congress is empowered to lay taxes to provide for the common defense, to define and punish offenses against the law of nations, to declare war, to raise and support armies (but not to finance them for more than two years at a time), to provide and maintain a navy, to make rules for the land and naval forces, and to provide for calling up and organizing the militia.

The Original Understanding

The Constitution does not say explicitly whether the army may be sent into battle when Congress has not declared war, or if it may, under what circumstances and by whose decision. In interpreting the Constitution on this point, it is helpful to look at the intent of the Framers and to the understanding of the men who first put the Constitution into practice.

The Constitutional Convention debated the clause giving Congress the power to declare war on August 17, 1787. The clause originally empowered Congress "to make war." Some delegates objected that the power should lie with the executive, as it did in England. Most of the Convention seemed firmly of the opinion that the power should lie with Congress, but that the President should have the power to defend against a sudden attack. The Convention decided to "insert 'declare,' striking out 'make' war, leaving to the executive the power to repel sudden attacks." The Framers had in mind a division of functions. The President, as Commander in Chief, was charged with the conduct of hostilities after they are legally begun. He was also expected to take measures to repel any actual attack upon the United States, as an incident of his executive power. But the power to initiate hostilities was clearly meant to be reserved to the Congress, with the President par-

Reprinted from a memorandum prepared by various students and faculty of the Yale Law School and appearing in the *Congressional Record*, S7117–7123, May 13, 1970.

ticipating in that initiative only so far as his signature was necessary to complete an act of Congress. Thus, *the President, unless his veto is overridden, may prevent war, but he cannot constitutionally act alone to begin a war.*

The judicial branch was also quick to conclude that Congress alone can declare war. . . .

Wars and Limited Wars in the Nineteenth Century. If the President's power to engage American forces in hostilities on his own initiative is limited to defensive action by a strict construction of the Constitution, the question of the proper role of Congress arises. Congress clearly has the power to engage the United States in formal war, as it did in 1812 with the President reluctantly assenting. It may declare war at the request of the President. And Congress may also ratify after the fact hostilities begun by the President.

The executive branch very easily recognized the exclusive power of Congress to declare war. In the course of a dispute with Spain in 1805, President Jefferson told Congress:

Considering that Congress alone is constitutionally invested with the power of changing our position from peace to war, I have thought it my duty to await their authority before using force in any degree which could be avoided. . . .

Erosion of the Congressional War-making Power in the 20th Century. In the early part of the twentieth century, the executive began to exercise greater discretion in the use of American armed forces abroad. For instance, without specific congressional approval, President Theodore Roosevelt sent American troops

into Panama in 1903 and President Wilson sent troops into Mexico in 1916 in pursuit of the Pancho Villa bandits.

Since 1945, the executive has regularly used military force abroad as a tool of diplomacy. Aside from Indochina, the greatest use of American force was in Korea, where several hundred thousand troops were committed to combat and major casualties were incurred. There was neither a formal declaration of war, nor any other specific congressional sanction for the Korean conflict. American forces were sent into the Formosan Strait in 1955, into Lebanon in 1958, and into the Dominican Republic in 1965. The Navy was used to blockade Cuba during the missile crisis in 1962. And, most recently, naval vessels were dispatched to the vicinity of Haiti and Trinidad in response to internal conflicts in those countries. Prior congressional resolutions were obtained by the President for the Formosan and Lebanese actions, but both the validity of those resolutions and the degree to which President Eisenhower relied on them has been questioned.

The application of prior historical precedents to unilateral executive use of armed force abroad in the mid-twentieth century can, however, be misleading. For instance, as precedents for the Vietnam War, a State Department Memorandum cites a long series of military actions ordered by the President alone. The majority of the cited military actions undertaken by the executive without congressional approval took place in the nineteenth century. Most of them were not actions that involved conflicts with foreign states; rather, the bulk of them involved the protection of individuals, police actions against pirates or actions against primitive peoples. Furthermore, the United

States did not have a significant standing army during peacetime until after 1945, and the President was limited in the military actions that he could take by the need to approach Congress to ask for any increase in the size of the armed forces. *Today, with a tremendous military machine and modern transport at his immediate disposal, the President is under little practical pressure to seek congressional authorization for his actions, and therefore he is unlikely to seek it unless Congress insists that he do so.*

The Theoretical Bases for Unilateral Presidential Action

The theories on which various Presidents have relied for the use of military force abroad without congressional approval may be divided into three general categories: (1) the sudden attack theory; (2) the neutrality theory; and (3) the collective security theory.

(1) The Sudden Attack Theory. The President as the Chief Executive has the inherent power to defend the sovereignty and integrity of the nation itself and to respond to an armed attack on the territory of the United States without requesting congressional approval. . . . In the absence of an armed attack on American territory proper, the power of the President is more closely circumscribed.

(2) The Neutrality Theory. Also known as "interposition," the neutrality theory was developed during the nineteenth century as a justification for American military involvement abroad to protect American citizens and property. When American armed forces were sent into a foreign nation, their presence was supposed to be "neutral" with respect to any conflicts there. *The executive, in taking such action, was not necessarily "making war" but merely dispatching troops to act as security guards for American citizens and their property. The real difficulty, clearly, was in remaining neutral and avoiding conflict.*

(3) The Collective Security Theory. Since 1945, the United States has entered into many security treaties with foreign nations. Many of these agreements have clauses which indicate that the security of each signatory is vital to the security of each other signatory. Unilateral presidential action under these agreements may be justified as necessary for the protection of American security even though the conflict may arise thousands of miles from American shores, but, *carried to its extreme, the collective security theory would justify almost any unilateral presidential use of armed force abroad, a result contrary to Constitutional standards.*

The Justifications for Unilateral Executive Action in Indochina

The involvement of the United States in Vietnam, the commencement of an air war in Laos, and the expansion of the ground war into Cambodia have resulted almost entirely from executive decisions and actions. The executive branch of the government has justified its action primarily on the grounds of: (1) the presidential prerogative to protect American security interests abroad by whatever means necessary. (2) the SEATO treaty; and (3) the Gulf of Tonkin Resolution. *It cannot be said that the recent actions by the executive in Cambodia or the earlier actions in both Vietnam and Laos are clearly contrary to the Constitution. However, the expansion of the war into Cambodia is the latest in a long series of acts which, taken together, have nearly stripped Congress of its war power.*

(1) The Presidential Prerogative. Undoubtedly, the speed with which crises develop in the modern world necessitate a strong executive who can respond quickly to such crises. The need for a speedy response, the need for secrecy, the need to protect American citizens and property abroad, and the need to protect American security interests in the balance of power are all used to legitimize the use by the executive, without congressional approval, of American armed forces abroad.

However, the real question is whether the balance has shifted too far in favor of the executive. A war, such as the one in Indochina, requires great sacrifices on the part of great numbers of the American people. It is difficult, if not impossible, to predict the ultimate outcome of any American intervention. Consequently, when there is a possibility of large scale American involvement and even a limited risk of war, Congress should pass on the desirability of American military action.

The executive has also placed reliance on the power of the President as chief formulator of foreign policy and as Commander-in-Chief of the armed forces. *Granted that the President does have primary responsibility in the modern world for the handling of foreign policy, he should not have the discretion to initiate war as an instrument of foreign policy.*

Finally, the Commander-in-Chief provision of the Constitution is an expression of civilian control over the military; it does not give the war power to the President.

(2) The SEATO Treaty. The Southeast Asia Treaty Organization is one of the many multilateral collective security treaties which the United States has signed. Neither South Vietnam nor Cambodia is a signatory, but both countries are within "protocol areas" which the signatories consider to be vital to their security interests. The terms of the treaty are ambiguous, and it is at least questionable whether the United States was obligated by the terms of the treaty to come to the aid of South Vietnam.

More importantly, the SEATO agreement cannot help answer the constitutional questions, because it specifically states that action by a signatory in response to an attack on another signatory or a "protocol country" is to be made only after a decision made according to the "constitutional processes" of the signatory.

The more relevant issue is the power of the President to involve American forces in foreign combat on the basis of a treaty. The Constitution requires that the Senate must give its advice and consent to any treaty before it can become effective. Once approved, the treaty is of the same nature as any other duly passed law which the executive is bound to execute faithfully. If, however, the war power is a congressional prerogative, the decisions regarding the initiation of war should be made by both houses of Congress and not just the Senate.

(3) The Tonkin Gulf Resolution. . . . Congressional action which does not amount to a formal declaration of war may be a valid congressional authorization of hostilities, and some commentators think that the Tonkin Gulf Resolution is an adequate congressional authorization for the Vietnamese War.

There are two factors, however, which make the Tonkin Gulf Resolution an invalid basis for continued Congressional inaction. First, it was passed with great speed and in the heat of emotion that resulted from the reported attack on American naval vessels in the Tonkin Gulf. Secondly, there were few American troops in Vietnam in the American ground combat forces there.

It has also been argued that congressional inaction and failure to repeal the Tonkin Gulf Resolution give implicit authorization to the Indochinese War. The logical outcome of such an argument is that the President can do whatever he wishes and the Congress has the affirmative duty to try to stop him. This shifts the presumption of the Framers in favor of congressional control over war-making and gives the initial and continued upper hand to the executive.

B. The Supreme Court and the Vietnam War

(1) A Note on the Legality of the War and the Authority to Conscript: "Inseparable Questions"

The Supreme Court's response to the Vietnam War was indirect and evasive, taking two forms: its refusal to consider in substance the question of the war's legality, and its efforts to deal with legal challenges to military conscription. The constitutional status of the draft, both in principle and in its implementation, does not depend on the legality of the war for which military personnel are recruited. But the Supreme Court's refusal to consider the constitutional validity of the Vietnam War itself certainly left an inference of illegality that fueled the efforts of those persons expressing their opposition to the war by challenging the draft in court and elsewhere.

The Court refused to hear several cases that offered opportunities to consider the legality of the war. As usual, it gave no reason for its action, but in each case, the dissenting opinions of one or more justices (and in every case Justice Douglas) implied reliance on the doctrines of self-limitation considered in Part One, Chapter Two. *Mora* v. *McNamara* (1967) was a challenge to the assignment of draftees to combat duty in Vietnam, based on the contention that military activity in Vietnam was not a "war" within the meaning of Article I, Section 8, Clause 11, of the Constitution. The district court dismissed the suit, and the court of appeals affirmed. The Supreme Court denied certiorari. In dissent, Justices Douglas and Stewart urged that at least the Court openly face preliminary questions of justiciability.

Attempts in *Velvel* v. *Nixon* (1969) and *Massachusetts* v. *Laird* (1970) (both discussed in Part One, Chapter Two) to obtain judicial rulings on the conduct of the war were also rejected. Velvel, a law professor, sought to establish standing to sue on the basis of *Flast* v. *Cohen* (1968), but the Supreme Court concurred in the lower court's dismissal of his case. *Massachusetts* v. *Laird,* an original jurisdiction case, was an explicit effort to "create" an adversarial situation that would overcome the standing barrier. Massachusetts passed a law declaring that "no citizen of the Commonwealth of Massachusetts inducted or serving in the military forces of the United States of America shall be required to serve outside the continental limits of the United States in a combat zone or where actual hostilities have been in existence for more than sixty days . . ." unless preceded or followed by a formal declaration of war by Congress. The law empowered the state's attorney general to bring an original jurisdiction suit in the Supreme Court and, failing that, to seek declaratory relief in a lower federal court. The Supreme Court denied permission to commence the suit. Three justices dissented from that decision, only one short of the four needed to have the case heard on its merits. There is a clear inference in Justice Douglas' dissenting opinion that a majority of the Court believed that Massachusetts had no standing to raise this issue and further believed that the issue constituted a nonjusticiable political question.

The constitutional validity of military conscription was long ago upheld by the Supreme Court.[1] Therefore, challenges to the draft during the Vietnam period focused on the appropriateness of individual selective service classifications (with emphasis on the rules for granting conscientious objector status) and the practice of punitive reclassifications by local draft boards. Congressional policy has long disfavored judicial challenges to draft classifications. All administrative remedies must first be exhausted, and even then, such challenges, according to the law, can only be made as a defense to a criminal prosecution for refusal to report for induction or by a writ of habeas corpus *after* induction.

On the whole, the Supreme Court respected this policy. But in the political cauldron of the Vietnam War, it began to permit exceptions to the rule where draft board actions seemed particularly arbitrary. One such case was *Breen* v. *Selective Service Board* (1970), in which Breen was stripped of his protected II-S classification after turning in his draft card at a public protest rally. The Court found that Congress had not intended to allow draft boards to strip a student of a validly held II-S classification. Since the draft board had acted illegally, Breen was *not* required to wait until he was inducted, or prosecuted for refusing induction, before challenging his reclassification.

Conscientious objection to military service is always a hotly debated issue, involving as it does politics, morality, and religion. The Constitution does not require exemption for conscientious objectors, but Congress has provided for such exemption several times in the twentieth century. In 1917 it permitted exemptions, but only to members of recognized pacifist sects (a distinction certain to arouse constitutional suspicions today). A second conscription act was passed in 1940, and it allowed conscientious objector status to those whose opposition to war in any form was based on "religious training and belief." Conscription lapsed again after World War II but was reinstituted in 1948. In that statute, Congress declared that "religious training and belief" was to be defined as "an individual's belief in relation to a Supreme Being involving duties superior to those arising from any human relation, but [not including] essentially political, sociological, or philosophical views or a merely personal moral code."

In *United States* v. *Seeger* (1965), the Supreme Court interpreted that statute liberally, holding that the term "Supreme Being" was not limited to a belief in God but could encompass any belief that occupied "the same place in the life of the objector as an orthodox belief in God holds in the life of one clearly qualified for exemption." Congress re-

[1]*Selective Draft Law Cases* (1917).

sponded to this decision in 1967 by simply deleting the requirement of belief in a Supreme Being; it left undisturbed the requirement of religious training and belief. In *Welsh* v. *United States* (1970), the Supreme Court reiterated its holding in *Seeger* and applied the test enunciated there to Welsh, even though Welsh himself denied he was making a "religious" claim and stated instead that his opposition to war was based on "reading in the fields of history and sociology."

Within six months of the *Welsh* decision, 57,000 men claimed conscientious objector status, almost as many claims as had been filed in all of World War II. This represented a direct challenge to the integrity of the draft and a not-so-indirect challenge to the legitimacy of the war itself. Many of the claimants went further than either Welsh or Seeger to assert a "selective" objection to the Vietnam War but not necessarily to all wars. At this point, the Supreme Court drew the line and held, in *Gillete* v. *United States* (1971), that Congress' prohibition of selective conscientious objection did not violate the establishment clause of the First Amendment. [See pp. 1311–1315]

(2) Holtzman v. Schlesinger (1973)

[It was pointed out in an earlier section of this book that courts will ordinarily avoid becoming involved in "political questions." There are two basic reasons for this restraint. For one thing, it is viewed as proper under the separation of powers doctrine to leave the resolution of "political" issues to the discretion of the political arms of government—the executive and legislative branches. More importantly, courts place themselves in very risky situations when they engage in head-on confrontations with the political branches, and questions of war and peace are essentially political.

In this case, there is an added complication. Elizabeth Holtzman, a member of Congress from New York City, and others had filed suit to block the continued bombing of Cambodia in the waning days of the Vietnam War. A federal district court had granted an injunction against James Schlesinger, Secretary of Defense, prohibiting him from continuing American air or land military operations in Cambodia. However, the Court of Appeals for the Second Circuit stayed the order of the district court, and the bombing continued. At the time—late July of 1973—the Supreme Court was out of session. Holtzman then sought an order from Justice Thurgood Marshall, who was circuit justice for the Second Circuit, reversing the court of appeals. When Marshall declined to issue such an order, Holtzman was then free to petition any other member of the Court to vacate the stay and reinstate the injunction granted by the district court. The application was made to Justice Douglas, who vacated the stay. Schlesinger then sought an order from Marshall overriding Douglas' decision, since Marshall was the circuit justice to whom the case had originally come. Marshall took the unusual step of polling the remaining seven justices by telephone, presumably to counter the resisting and strident tone of Douglas' opinion, and then issued another order upholding the court of appeals and staying the district court's injunction.]

August 1, 1973

MR. JUSTICE MARSHALL, CIRCUIT JUSTICE.

This case is before me on an application to vacate a stay entered by a three-judge panel of the United States Court of Appeals for the Second Circuit. Petitioners, a Congresswoman from New York and several air force officers serving in Asia, brought this action to enjoin continued United States air operations over Cambodia. They argue that such military activity has not been authorized by Congress and that, absent such authorization, it violates Article I, § 8, cl. 11 of the Constitution. The

United States District Court agreed and, on petitioner's motion for summary judgment, permanently enjoined respondents, the Secretary of Defense, the Acting Secretary of the Air Force, and the Deputy Secretary of Defense, from "participating in any way in military activities in or over Cambodia or releasing any bombs which may fall in Cambodia." However, the effective date of the injunction was delayed until July 27, 1973, in order to give respondents an opportunity to apply to the Court of Appeals for a stay pending appeal. Respondents promptly applied for such a stay, and the application was granted, without opinion, on July 27. Petitioners then filed this motion to vacate the stay. For the reasons stated below, I am unable to say that the Court of Appeals abused its discretion in staying the District Court's order. In view of the complexity and importance of the issues involved and the absence of authoritative precedent, it would be inappropriate for me, acting as a single Circuit Justice, to vacate the order of the Court of Appeals.

Since the facts of this dispute are on the public record and have been exhaustively canvassed in the District Court's opinion, it would serve no purpose to repeat them in detail here. It suffices to note that publicly acknowledged United States involvement in the Cambodian hostilities began with the President's announcement on April 30, 1970, that this country was launching attacks "to clean out major enemy sanctuaries on the Cambodian-Vietnam border," and that American military action in that country has since met with gradually increasing congressional resistance.

Although United States ground troops had been withdrawn from the Cambodian theater by June 30, 1970, in the summer of that year, Congress enacted the so called Fulbright Proviso prohibiting the use of funds for military support to Cambodia. The following winter, Congress reenacted the same limitation with the added proviso that "nothing contained in this section shall be construed to prohibit support of actions required to insure the safe and orderly withdrawal or disengagement of U. S. Forces from Southeast Asia, or to aid in the release of Americans held as prisoners of war." . . . These provisions have been attached to every subsequent military appropriations act. Moreover, in the Special Foreign Assistance Act of 1971, Congress prohibited the use of funds to support American ground combat troops in Cambodia under any circumstances and expressly provided that "[m]ilitary and economic assistance provided by the United States to Cambodia . . . shall not be construed as a commitment by the United States to Cambodia for its defense."

Congressional efforts to end American air activities in Cambodia intensified after the withdrawal of American ground troops from Vietnam and the return of American prisoners of war. On May 10, 1973, the House of Representatives refused an administration request to authorize the transfer of $175 million to cover the costs of the Cambodian bombing. . . . Shortly thereafter, both Houses of Congress adopted the so-called Eagleton Amendment prohibiting the use of any funds for Cambodian combat operations. Although this provision was vetoed by the President, an amendment to the Continuing Appropriations Resolution was ultimately adopted and signed by the President into law which stated:

Notwithstanding any other provision of law, on or after August 15, 1973, no

funds herein or heretofore appropriated may be obligated or expended to finance directly or indirectly combat activities by United States military forces in or over or from off the shores of North Vietnam, South Vietnam, Laos or Cambodia.
. . .

Against this background, petitioners forcefully contend that continued United States military activity in Cambodia is illegal. Specifically, they argue that the President is constitutionally disabled in nonemergency situations from exercising the war-making power in the absence of some affirmative action by Congress. . . . In light of the Fulbright Proviso, petitioners take the position that Congress has never given its assent for military activity in Cambodia once American ground troops and prisoners of war were extricated from Vietnam.

With the case in this posture, however, it is not for me to resolve definitively the validity of petitioners' legal claims. Rather, the only issue now ripe for decision is whether the stay ordered by the Court of Appeals should be vacated. There is, to be sure, no doubt that I have the power, as a single Circuit Justice, to dissolve the stay. . . . But at the same time, the cases make clear that this power should be exercised with the greatest of caution and should be reserved for exceptional circumstances. . . .

. . . There are, of course, many cases suggesting that a Circuit Justice should "balance the equities" when ruling on stay applications and determine on which side the risk of irreparable injury weighs most heavily. . . .

But in this case, the problems inherent in attempting to strike an equitable balance between the parties are virtually insurmountable. On the other hand, petitioners assert that if the stay is not vacated, the lives of thousands of Americans and Cambodians will be endangered by the Executive's arguably unconstitutional conduct. Petitioners argue, not implausibly, that if the stay is not vacated, American pilots will be killed or captured, Cambodian civilians will be made refugees, and the property of innocent bystanders will be destroyed.

Yet on the other hand, respondents argue that if the bombing is summarily halted, important foreign policy goals of our government will be severely hampered. . . .[I]t cannot be denied that the assessment of such injury poses the most sensitive of problems, about which Justices of this Court have little or no information or expertise. While we have undoubted authority to judge the legality of executive action, we are on treacherous ground indeed when we attempt judgments as to its wisdom or necessity. . . .

. . . This case is unusual in that regardless of what action I take, it will likely be impossible to preserve this controversy in its present form for ultimate review by this Court. . . . On August 15, the statutory ban on Southeast Asian military activity will take effect, and the contours of this dispute will then be irrevocably altered. Hence, it is difficult to justify a stay for purpose of preserving the status quo, since no action by this Court can freeze the issues in their present form. . . .

Similarly, as a matter of substantive constitutional law, it seems likely that the President may not wage war without some form of congressional approval—except, perhaps in the case of a pressing emergency or when the President is in the process of extricating himself from a war which Congress once authorized. . . .

A fair reading of Congress' actions concerning the war in Cambodia may well indicate that the legislature has authorized only "partial hostili- ties"—that it has never given its ap- proval to the war except to the extent that it was necessary to extricate American troops and prisoners from Vietnam. Certainly, this seems to be the thrust of the Fulbright Proviso. Moreover, this Court could easily conclude that after the Paris Peace Accords, the Cambodian bombing is no longer justifiable as an extension of the war which Congress did not au- thorize and that the bombing is not required by the type of pressing emergency which necessitates im- mediate presidential response.

Thus, if the decision were mine alone, I might well conclude on the merits that continued American mili- tary operations in Cambodia are un- constitutional. But the Supreme Court is a collegial institution, and its decisions reflect the views of a major- ity of the sitting Justices. It follows that when I sit in my capacity as a Circuit Judge, I act not for myself alone but as a surrogate for the entire Court, from whence my ultimate au- thority in these matters derives. A Circuit Justice therefore bears a heavy responsibility to conscien- tiously reflect the views of his Brethren as best he perceives them, . . . and this responsibility is particularly pressing when, as now, the Court is not in session.

When the problem is viewed from this perspective, it is immeasurably complicated. It must be recognized that we are writing on an almost en- tirely clean slate in this area. The stark fact is that although there have been numerous lower court decisions concerning the legality of the War in Southeast Asia, this Court has never considered the problem, and it cannot be doubted that the issues posed are immensely important and complex. The problem is further complicated by the July 1, 1973, Amendment to the Continuing Appropriations Reso-

lution providing that "on or after Au- gust 15, 1973, no funds herein or heretofore appropriated may be obli- gated or expended to finance directly or indirectly combat activities by United States Military forces in or over or from all the Shores of North Vietnam, South Vietnam, Laos or Cambodia." This, it is urged, is the crux of this case and there is neither precedent nor guidelines toward any definitive conclusion as to whether this is or is not sufficient to order the bombings to be halted prior to August 15.

Lurking in this suit are questions of standing, judicial competence, and substantive constitutional law which go to the roots of the division of power in a constitutional democracy. These are the sort of issues which should not be decided precipitously or with- out the benefit of proper consultation. It should be noted, moreover, that since the stay below was granted in respondents' favor, the issue here is not whether there is some possibility that petitioner will prevail on the merits, but rather whether there is some possibility that respondents will so prevail. In light of the problem, I am unwilling to say that that possibil- ity is nonexistent.

Finally, it is significant that al- though I cannot know with certainty what conclusion my Brethren would reach, I do have the views of a distin- guished panel of the Court of Appeals before me. That panel carefully con- sidered the issues presented and unanimously concluded that a stay was appropriate. Its decision, taken in aid of its own jurisdiction, is enti- tled to great weight. . . . In light of the complexity and importance of the issues posed, I cannot say that the Court of Appeals abused its discre- tion.

When the final history of the Cam- bodian War is written, it is unlikely to make pleasant reading. The decision to send American troops "to distant lands to die of foreign fevers and foreign shot and shell," *New York Times* v. *United States* . . . (1971) (Black, J., concurring), may ultimately be adjudged to have not only been unwise but also unlawful.

But the proper response to an arguably illegal action is not lawlessness by judges charged with interpreting and enforcing the laws. Down that road lies tyranny and repression. We have a government of limited powers, and those limits pertain to the Justices of this Court as well as to Congress and the Executive. Our Constitution assures that the law will ultimately prevail, but it also requires that the law be applied in accordance with lawful procedures. . . .

In my judgment, I would exceed my legal authority were I, acting alone, to grant this application. The application to vacate the stay entered below must therefore be denied.

Application denied.

August 4, 1973

OPINION OF MR. JUSTICE DOUGLAS.

My Brother Marshall, after a hearing, denied this application, . . . which in effect means that the decision of the District Court holding that the bombing of Cambodia is unconstitutional is stayed pending hearing on the merits before the Court of Appeals.

Application for stay denied by one Justice may be made to another. We do not, however, encourage the practice; and when the Term starts, the Justices all being in Washington, D.C., the practice is to refer the second application to the entire Court. That is the desirable practice to discourage "shopping around."

When the Court is in recess that practice cannot be followed, for the Justices are scattered. Yakima, Washington, where I have scheduled the hearing, is nearly 3,000 miles from Washington, D. C. Group action by all Members is therefore impossible.

I approached this decision, however, with a feeling of great deference to the judgment of my Brother Marshall, realizing that while his decision is not binding on me it is one to which I pay the greatest deference.

My Brother Marshall accurately points out that if the foreign policy goals of this Government are to be weighed the Judiciary is probably the least qualified branch to weigh them. He also states that if stays by judicial officers in cases of this kind are to be vacated the circumstances must be "exceptional." I agree with those premises, and I respect the views of those who share my Brother Marshall's predilections.

But this case in its stark realities involves the grim consequences of a capital case. The classic capital case is whether Mr. Lew, Mr. Low, or Mr. Lucas should die. The present case involves whether Mr. X (an unknown person or persons) should die. No one knows who they are. They may be Cambodian farmers whose only "sin" is a desire for socialized medicine to alleviate the suffering of their families and neighbors. Mr. X may be the American pilot or navigator who drops a ton of bombs on a Cambodian village. The upshot is that we know that someone is about to die.

Since that is true I see no reason to balance the equities and consider the harm to our foreign policy if one or a thousand more bombs do not drop. The reason is that we live under the Constitution and in Art. I. § 8, it gives to Congress the power to "declare War." The basic question on the merits is whether Congress within the meaning of Art. I § 8, has "declared war" on Cambodia.

It has become popular to think the President has that power to declare war. But there is not a word in the

Constitution that grants that power to him. It runs only to Congress. . . .

. . . I do not sit today to determine whether the bombing of Cambodia is constitutional. . . . But if the "war" in Vietnam were assumed to be a constitutional one, the Cambodia bombing is quite a different affair. Certainly Congress did not in terms declare war against Cambodia and there is no one so reckless to say that the Cambodian forces are an imminent and perilous threat to our shores. The briefs are replete with references to recent acts of Congress which, to avoid a presidential veto, were passed to make clear—as I read them—that no bombing of Cambodia was to be financed by appropriated funds after August 15, 1973. Arguably that is quite different from saying that Congress has declared war on Cambodia for a limited purpose and only up to and not beyond August 15, 1973. If the acts in question are so construed the result would be, as the District Court said, that the number of votes needed to sustain a presidential veto—one-third plus one—would be all that was needed to bring into operation the new and awesome power of a president to declare war. The merits of the present controversy are therefore, to say the least, substantial, since denial of the application before me would catapult our airmen as well as Cambodian peasants into the death zone. I do what I think any judge would do in a capital case—vacate the stay entered by the Court of Appeals.

It is so ordered.

Stay vacated.

August 4, 1973

MR. JUSTICE MARSHALL, CIRCUIT JUSTICE

On August 1, 1973, I as Circuit Justice for the Second Circuit, denied an application to vacate a stay, . . . entered by the United States Court of Appeals for the Second Circuit on July 27, 1973, staying the order of the District Court for the Eastern District of New York dated July 25, 1973.

On August 2, Elizabeth Holtzman and others, plaintiffs in the original action, presented an application to Mr. Justice Douglas. A hearing was then set in Yakima, Washington, on Friday, August 3. On August 4 an order and opinion were issued by Mr. Justice Douglas . . . vacating the stay entered by the Court of Appeals on July 27, 1973, and thereby reinstating the order of the United States District Court for the Eastern District of New York, . . .

On the same day, August 4, the Solicitor General presented an application for a stay of the order of the United States District Court for the Eastern District of New York.

Since the action of the Court of Appeals in granting a stay is set aside, the only order extant in this case is the order of the District Court dated July 25, 1973. The instant application calls on me to deal directly with that order of the District Court.

In the ordinary course, a Justice acting as a Circuit Justice would defer acting with respect to a District Court order until the Court of Appeals had acted, but in the present circumstances the Court of Appeals has already acted and the consequence of the order of Mr. Justice Douglas is to set aside the Court of Appeals order.

The consequence of the Court of Appeals stay order of August 1, 1973, was to preserve the status quo until it could act on the merits. The Court of Appeals, having originally expedited a hearing on the merits of August 13, 1973, has since further expedited the hearing on the merits of August 8, 1973.

Now, therefore, the order of the District Court dated July 25, 1973, is hereby stayed pending further order by this Court.

I have been in communication with the other Members of the Court, and The Chief Justice, Mr. Justice Brennan, Mr. Justice Stewart, Mr. Justice White, Mr. Justice Blackmun, Mr. Justice Powell, and Mr. Justice Rehnquist agree with this action.

MR. JUSTICE DOUGLAS (DISSENTING) (OMITTED).

C. Congressional Response to the Vietnam War: Limiting the Power of the President

(1) The War Powers Resolution (1973)

JOINT RESOLUTION
Concerning the war powers of Congress and the President.

Resolved by the Senate and House of Representatives of the United States of American in Congress assembled,

. . .

Purpose and Policy

SEC. 2. (a) It is the purpose of this joint resolution to fulfill the intent of the framers of the Constitution of the United States and insure that the collective judgment of both the Congress and the President will apply to the introduction of United States Armed forces into hostilities, or in to situations where imminent involvement in hostilities is clearly indicated by the circumstances, and to the continued use of such forces in hostilities or in such situations.

(b) Under article I, section 8, of the Constitution, it is specifically provided that the Congress shall have the power to make all laws necessary and proper for carrying into execution, not only its own powers but also all other powers vested by the Constitution in the Government of the United States, or in any department or officer thereof.

(c) The constitutional powers of the President as Commander-in-Chief to introduce United States Armed Forces into hostilities, or into situations where imminent involvement in hostilities is clearly indicated by the circumstances, are exercised only pursuant to (1) a declaration of war, (2) specific statutory authorization, or (3) a national emergency created by attack upon the United States, its territories or possessions, or its armed forces.

Consultation

SEC. 3. The President in every possible instance shall consult with Congress before introducing United States Armed Forces into hostilities or into situations where imminent involvement in hostilities is clearly indicated by the circumstances, and after every such introduction shall consult regularly with the Congress until United States Armed Forces are no longer engaged in hostilities or have been removed from such situations.

Reporting

SEC. 4. (a) In the absence of a declaration of war, in any case in which United States Armed Forces are introduced—

(1) into hostilities or into situations where imminent involvement in hostilities is clearly indicated by the circumstances;

(2) into the territory, airspace or waters of a foreign nation, while equipped for combat, except for deployments which relate solely to supply, replacement, repair, or training of such forces; or

(3) in numbers which substantially enlarge United States Armed

Forces equipped for combat already located in a foreign nation;
the President shall submit within 48 hours to the Speaker of the House of Representatives and to the President pro tempore of the Senate a report, in writing, setting forth—

(A) the circumstances necessitating the introduction of United States Armed Forces;

(B) the constitutional and legislative authority under which such introduction took place; and

(C) the estimated scope and duration of the hostilities or involvement.

(b) The President shall provide such other information as the Congress may request in the fulfillment of its constitutional responsibilities with respect to committing the Nation to war and to the use of United States Armed Forces abroad.

(c) Whenever United States Armed Forces are introduced into hostilities or into any situation described in subsection (a) of this section, the President shall, so long as such armed forces continue to be engaged in such hostilities or situation, report to the Congress periodically on the status of such hostilities or situation as well as on the scope and duration of such hostilities or situation, but in no event shall he report to the Congress less often than once every six months.

Congressional Action

SEC. 5. (a) Each report submitted pursuant to section 4(a) (1) shall be transmitted to the Speaker of the House of Representatives and to the President pro tempore of the Senate on the same calendar day. Each report so transmitted shall be referred to the Committee on Foreign Affairs of the House of Representatives and to the Committee on Foreign Relations of the Senate for appropriate action. If, when the report is transmitted, the Congress has adjourned sine die or has adjourned for any period in excess of three calendar days, the Speaker of the House of Representatives and the President pro tempore of the Senate, if they deem it advisable (or if petitioned by at least 30 percent of the membership of their respective Houses) shall jointly request the President to convene Congress in order that it may consider the report and take appropriate action pursuant to this section.

(b) Within sixty calendar days after a report is submitted or is required to be submitted pursuant to section 4(a) (1), whichever is earlier, the President shall terminate any use of United States Armed Forces with respect to which such report was submitted (or required to be submitted), unless the Congress (1) has declared war or has enacted a specific authorization for such use of United States Armed Forces, (2) has extended by law such sixty-day period, or (3) is physically unable to meet as a result of an armed attack upon the United States. Such sixty-day period shall be extended for not more than an additional thirty days if the President determines and certifies to the Congress in writing that unavoidable military necessity respecting the safety of United States Armed Forces requires the continued use of such armed forces in the course of bringing about a prompt removal of such forces.

(c) Notwithstanding subsection (b), at any time that United States Armed Forces are engaged in hostilities outside the territory of the United States, its possessions and territories without a declaration of war or specific statutory authorization, such forces shall be removed by the President if the Congress so directs by concurrent resolution.

*Congressional Priority
Procedures for Joint Resolution
or Bill* (Omitted)

[In this section, provisions are made for prompt congressional action to avoid unnecessary delays. A resolution takes precedence over other legislation pending before the Congress. It must be considered and reported out of committee within a specified period of time, and conference committees to resolve differences between the House and the Senate must act expeditiously.]

*Interpretation of Joint
Resolution*

SEC. 8. (a) Authority to introduce United States Armed Forces into hostilities or into situations wherein involvement in hostilities is clearly indicated by the circumstances shall not be inferred—

(1) from any provision of law (whether or not in effect before the date of the enactment of this joint resolution), including any provision contained in any appropriation Act, unless such provision specifically authorizes the introduction of United States Armed Forces into hostilities or into such situations and states that it is intended to constitute specific statutory authorization within the meaning of this joint resolution; or

(2) from any treaty heretofore or hereafter ratified unless such treaty is implemented by legislation specifically authorizing the introduction of United States Armed Forces into hostilities or into such situations and stating that it is intended to constitute specific statutory authorization within the meaning of this joint resolution.

(b) Nothing in this joint resolution shall be construed to require any further specific statutory authorization to permit members of United States Armed Forces to participate jointly with members of the armed forces of one or more foreign countries in the headquarters operations of high-level military commands which were established prior to the date of enactment of this joint resolution and pursuant to the United Nations Charter or any treaty ratified by the United States prior to such date.

(c) For purposes of this joint resolution, the term "introduction of United States Armed Forces" includes the assignment of members of such armed forces to command, coordinate, participate in the movement of, or accompany the regular or irregular military forces of any foreign country or government when such military forces are engaged, or there exists an imminent threat that such forces will become engaged, in hostilities.

(d) Nothing in this joint resolution—

(1) is intended to alter the constitutional authority of the Congress or of the President, or the provisions of existing treaties; or

(2) shall be construed as granting any authority to the President with respect to the introduction of United States Armed Forces into hostilities or into situations wherein involvement in hostilities is clearly indicated by the circumstances which authority he would not have had in the absence of this joint resolution.

Separability Clause

SEC. 9. If any provision of this joint resolution or the application thereof to any person or circumstance is held invalid, the remainder of the joint resolution and the application of such provision to any other person or circumstance shall not be affected thereby.

Effective Date

SEC. 10. This joint resolution shall take effect on the date of its enactment.

(2) A Note on the Congressional Dilemma

Critics of the War Powers Resolution point out that in the future, all sorts of crises may arise, many beyond the power of Congress to have anticipated in 1973. Congress appears in Section 2, par. (c)(3) to have anticipated no sort of "emergency" except through a direct attack. But there may be an emergency in which the president could effectively defend the country's best interests only by outright violation of the War Powers Resolution; to wait for a direct attack might be disastrously irresponsible.

The *Mayaguez* episode of May 1975 illustrates another flaw in the War Powers Resolution. President Ford's actions in that episode clearly violated the War Powers Resolution, but they were nonetheless widely approved by the public and political leaders. If a president's military initiative is prompt, effective, small in scale, and likely to be politically safe, then the War Powers Resolution will impose little or no restraint. Of course, if the War Powers Resolution in fact limits future presidential military initiatives to those that are prompt, effective, small in scale, and politically safe, then it will have succeeded in curbing the more serious abuses that initiated the resolution in the first place. The resolution was not passed overwhelmingly by a Congress fearful of such minor exercises of presidential power, but by a Congress seared by the experience of a military initiative that was drawn out, ineffective, enormous in scale of effort and in both monetary and human costs, and no longer politically legitimate.

The dilemma of Congress in framing the War Powers Resolution was to limit presidential power, without at the same time limiting congressional power, and to provide for effective enforcement of those limits. As to the first, the question of where to draw the line, Congress understood that if it were to specify the conditions and circumstances under which the president may, in the absence of a declaration of war, commit troops to combat, Congress would have been inviting presidential action right up to that line without regard to what Congress itself believed to be proper at the time. By providing for almost immediate congressional input into a presidential decision to deploy military forces, Congress was assuring for itself sufficient flexibility to approve or disapprove every major presidential war powers action at the time of its occurrence. By structuring its role in this way, Congress was also avoiding—or seeking to avoid—a situation where a president might claim that his acts were in accord with the law, notwithstanding congressional opposition to them. This might produce a political stalemate and/or lengthy litigation in the courts that, inevitably, would foster if not effectively insulate presidential actions from effective interference by Congress.

Congress' most effective weapon against improper or unwise presidential military action, other than the mobilization of adverse public opinion, is the appropriations power. But for that power to be effective, it must be exercised at an early stage. The history of the war in Indochina, and of previous military engagements, is that once American troops are actually engaged in military combat, it is exceedingly difficult politically for

Congress to withhold support for them. It is not difficult for a president to undermine the appropriations power check with appeals to "support our boys" and to the patriotic fervor that accompanies most such military engagements. Congress is especially vulnerable to charges of "weakening national security" if it refuses to support an ongoing military action. In order for the appropriations power to be an effective check on presidential action, therefore, Congress must move quickly to prevent military hostilities of which it does not approve and for which it does not wish to appropriate funds. Nonetheless, there are significant political risks involved.

In the selection that follows, Michael Glennon makes an argument for the need for Congress to run these risks. Glennon's argument is clearly a partisan one favoring Congress. But the constitutional case for presidential discretion is also strong. Much of the argument for that case appeared in previous selections in this chapter, including the State Department memorandum defending the legality of the Vietnam War.[1]

(3) Michael Glennon, Strengthening the War Powers Resolution

. . .

The Resolution, . . . imposes only what may be termed "subsequent limitations" upon the President's use of the armed forces. This contrasts with the Senate version of the Resolution, rejected by the conference committee, which would have also imposed "prior restraints." It would have stated in operative terms, rather than merely as the understanding of Congress, the circumstances in which the armed forces may be introduced into hostilities without a declaration of war. The Senate version differed from the Resolution in two other important respects. It would have explicitly allowed the President to introduce the armed forces to evacuate United States citizens and nationals abroad in certain emergency situations, and, by avoiding reference to the Constitution in defining the circumstances in which the President could independently engage the armed forces in hostilities, it would have avoided indicating that the President has a constitutional right to act independently in those circumstances.

To date, four events—the *Mayaguez* incident and three military actions relating to the evacuation of American and other nationals from South Vietnam and Cambodia—have caused the President to submit a report to Congress under the Resolution. This article suggests that the inability of the Resolution to control the President's use of the armed forces during those and similar crises necessitates amendment of the Resolution to include prior restraints of the sort contained in the Senate bill. The Ford administration, however, has indicated that it considers unconstitutional both the subsequent limitations contained in the Resolution and such prior restraints. At least with respect to the prior restraints, some members of Congress share this view—as is illustrated by the rejection of the Senate version of

[1]A good summary of that argument can be found in J. Terry Emerson, "The War Powers Resolution Tested: The President's Independent Defense Power," **51** *Notre Dame Lawyer* (1975), 187–216.

Reprinted from Michael J. Glennon, "Strengthening the War Powers Resolution: The Case for Purse-Strings Restrictions," **60** *Minnesota Law Review* (1975), 1–38.

the Resolution. These objections create the danger that a President will consider himself justified in ignoring the subsequent limitations and any prior restraints that Congress enacts. Thus the article also proposes that Congress obviate that danger by employing funding prohibitions to enforce both subsequent limitations and prior restraints. Its thesis is that, whatever the constitutional scope of the presidential warmaking power, Congress can and should effectively limit the exercise of that power by means of its exclusive power over the purse. . . .

The scope of the President's power to make war has been the subject of much controversy in recent years. The wide divergence of opinion is illustrated by a comparison of the most recent statement on the matter by Congress, section 2(c) of the War Powers Resolution, with the opinion of Monroe Leigh, Legal Advisor to the State Department. The Resolution states:

(c) The constitutional powers of the President as Commander-in-Chief to introduce United States Armed Forces into hostilities, or into situations where imminent involvement in hostilities is clearly indicated by the circumstances, are exercised only pursuant to (1) a delcaration of war, (2) specific statutory authorization, or (3) a national emergency created by attack upon the United States, its territories or possessions, or its armed forces.

Mr. Leigh, on the other hand, believes:

Besides the three situations listed in subsection 2(c) of the War Powers Resolution, it appears that the President has the constitutional authority to use the Armed Forces to rescue American citizens abroad, to rescue foreign nationals where such action directly facilitates the rescue of U.S. citizens abroad, to

protect U.S. Embassies and Legations abroad, to suppress civil insurrection, to implement and administer the terms of an armistice or cease-fire designed to terminate hostilities involving the United States, and to carry out the terms of security commitments contained in treaties. We do not, however, believe that any such list can be a complete one, just as we do not believe that any single definitional statement can clearly encompass every conceivable situation in which the President's Commander in Chief authority could be exercised.

The Mayaguez Incident

Early in the morning hours of Monday, May 12, 1975, the *Mayaguez*, a merchant vessel of United States registry with a crew of United States citizens, was seized by a Cambodian motor torpedo boat six and one-half miles southeast of Poulo Wai Island and taken to Kho Tang Island. That afternoon, 100 marines were ordered flown from Okinawa and the Philippines to Utapao Air Base in Thailand. . . . [T]he President did not request Congress to "clarify" the statutory funding prohibitions. At 1:00 A.M. Wednesday, May 14, United States aircraft sank a Cambodian patrol craft that had attempted to leave Kho Tang Island. Thereafter two other Cambodian patrol craft were destroyed and four immobilized. Several hours later the *Mayaguez* crew members were put in a fishing vessel and taken to Kompong Som on the Cambodian mainland. At 7:00 P.M. Phnom Penh radio was overheard in Bangkok announcing that the Cambodian government would release the *Mayaguez*. Afterwards, at 7:20 P.M., about 135 marines landed on Koh Tang Island under heavy fire. At 9:00 P.M. marines, boarding from the *U.S.S. Holt*, took possession of the *Mayaguez*. At 10:45 P.M. the destroyer *U.S.S. Wilson* reported a small boat approaching, flying a white flag; at 10:53 P.M. the *Wilson* sent word to the Pentagon that at least 30 Caucasians were aboard the boat. (After the incident, Secretary Schlesinger stated that the crewmen "arrived at the *Wilson* as a result of what is presumed to be the decision of the Cambodians to deliver them up in order to terminate combat activities directed primarily at the mainland.") At 11:00 P.M. United States aircraft struck the airfield at Ream and an oil storage depot on the Cambodian mainland. The Pentagon said that 17 enemy planes had been destroyed on the ground, a hanger smashed, and the runways cratered. By the conclusion of hostilities 41 members of the United States armed forces had been killed. The 39 members of the crew survived unharmed.

The President's report was submitted May 15. Although "taking note of Section 4(a) (1) of the War Powers Resolution," it ignored Section 4(a) (3) in neglecting to mention the enlargement of United States forces in Thailand. Nor did it report any fatalities or refer to the statutory funding prohibitions.

Failure of the Funding Prohibitions

The statements of facts contained in the four reports submitted by the President under Section 4 of the War Powers Resolution leave little doubt that in each case United States forces carried out "military operations" or "combat activities" "in," "over," or "off the shores of" Cambodia or South Vietnam, and thus that in each case the several statutory funding prohibitions were violated. Indeed, in the case of the *Mayaguez* incident this conclusion is implicitly acknowledged by the report's reference to Section 4(a) (1) of the War Powers

Resolution—the section dealing with situations wherein forces are "introduced into hostilities."

Nevertheless, on May 7, just prior to the *Mayaguez* incident, Monroe Leigh expressed to a subcommittee of the House International Relations Committee the view that the statutory funding prohibitions did not apply to the evacuations because "there was . . . a very substantial legislative history that it was not the intent of Congress in the funds limitation statutes to curtail [the] exercise of presidential authority [to evacuate Americans].

Is Mr. Leigh not familiar with the "plain meaning rule"? Moreover, if the statutes were not applicable, why did President Ford request, prior to the Vietnam evacuation, that they be "clarified immediately"? In any event, the legislative history provides almost no support for Mr. Leigh's theory. Only one reasonable inference can be drawn from Mr. Leigh's *ex post facto* claim of executive authority. The failure of Congress to pass the Vietnam Contingency Act and to object to the violation of the funding prohibitions during the evacuations had convinced the administration by the time of the *Mayaguez* incident that most members of Congress would not object to a further violation of the funding prohibitions if the activities constituting the violation were politically acceptable. The law had become a mere inconvenience which—thanks to public support, the legal theories of the State Department, and the acquiescence of Congress—could be ignored.
. . .

Clearly the parade of horribles predicted by President Nixon has not been set to march by enactment of the War Powers Resolution. The evacuations of the *Mayaguez* incident demonstrate that the Resolution

THE VIETNAM WAR AND THE CONSTITUTION ■ 1067

has not diminished the ability of the President to "act decisively and convincingly"—even in the face of statutory funding prohibitions.

On the contrary, events during the spring of 1975 illustrate that the Resolution presents no bar to possible excesses of presidential war-making. . . .

The validity of certain criticism of the Resolution has been vindicated; namely, lacking prior restraints it does not curb unwanted presidential uses of the armed forces. Major military operations can, in modern times, take far less than even 48 hours, let alone 60 or 90 days. The evacuations from Cambodia and Vietnam were completed before the reports required by the Resolution were submitted. Neither during those instances, nor during the *Mayaguez* incident, did the Resolution pose any obstacle to real or potential transgressions of the constitutional limits of the President's warmaking power. . . .

Subsequent Limitations

The effectiveness of the subsequent limitations of the Resolution as a deterrent to congressionally unauthorized use of military force by the President has not yet been tested, but the administration has suggested that it may ignore the subsequent limitations should the question arise. Mr. Leigh indicated, in testifying before the Subcommittee on National Security Policy and Scientific Developments of the House International Relations Committee, that if a President's use of the armed forces is pursuant to a constitutional grant of power—and what President will claim otherwise?—then any statutory provision (such as the 60-day limit of Section 5(b)), to say nothing of a mere concurrent resolution (such as that provided for by Section 5(c)),

purporting to cut short that use is unconstitutional. . . .

One exclusively congressional power—perhaps the most important of congressional powers—is the power over the purse. What is the status of that power? Clearly, congressional acquiescence in its usurpation during the evacuations from Vietnam and Cambodia and the *Mayaguez* incident did not redound to congressional benefit. Those events could conceivably be cited by future Presidents as precedents for military operations for which Congress has denied funds.

The Legal Advisor of the Department of State, in fact, has already entered a two-pronged challenge to the power of Congress to employ funding limitations to restrict presidential military activities. He contends that funding prohibitions are unconstitutional to the extent that they prohibit the exercise of authority granted by the Commander-in-chief clause and, in any event, constitutionally ineffective to limit such authority as long as funds are elsewhere available. Each proposition warrants examination.

General Constitutionality

As previously noted, Mr. Leigh has indicated that he believes that the President possessed the authority to evacuate United States citizens from Cambodia and South Vietnam and to rescue the *Mayaguez* crew, notwithstanding prohibitions against the use of funds for those activities. Although he asserted that the prohibitions were inapplicable because of their legislative history, he also indicated that had they been applicable, he would have considered them unconstitutional:

I do believe personally that such matters [as the Cambodia and Vietnam evacuations] involve the inherent constitutional power of the President and I don't think that every limitation that Congress might enact on an appropriation or otherwise is necessarily a constitutional one. I think there are some that would be plainly unconstitutional.

Which appropriations limitations would be "plainly unconstitutional"? The Constitution provides that "No Money shall be drawn from the Treasury, but in Consequence of Appropriations made by Law." The Supreme Court has never held unconstitutional any use of the appropriations power to limit the exercise of power by the executive branch. The only limitation on an appropriation act that the Court has invalidated exceeded a constitutional limitation on the power of Congress—the prohibition against bills of attainder.

The only prohibitions in the Constitution against the use of the appropriations power to curtail the activities of another branch are the requirements that the Justices of the Supreme Court and the President receive a compensation that may not be diminished. Had the Framers intended further limitations on the appropriations power they would surely have included them. Indeed, in the case of military matters they went to the other extreme. In addition to the power to appropriate funds—and to refuse to do so—they gave Congress the power to "raise and support Armies" and to "provide and maintain a Navy"—and to refuse to do so. Far from giving the President power over the purse so that he could carry out the commander-in-chief clause, as Mr. Leigh suggests, the Framers believed it "particularly dangerous to give the keys of the treasury, and the command of the army, into the same hands." As a result, they transferred the war power, in the words of Jefferson, "from the Executive to the Legislative body, from those who are to spend to those who are to pay." Thus Presidents Jefferson and Jackson, when requesting congressional instructions as to the proper course to pursue in the face of threatened aggression by Spain and marauding by South American pirates, respectively, recognized that control of the "means" necessary to carry out any military effort lies exclusively with Congress. The supremacy of the purse power was recognized by the Nixon administration even as it asserted broad power under the commander-in-chief clause to prosecute the war in Vietnam.

"Conditions Subsequent"?

The second basis for Mr. Leigh's denial that Congress may constitutionally employ funding prohibitions to restrict the President in what he believes to be a constitutional use of armed force is his unexplained theory that such prohibitions are "conditions subsequent." In order to cut off funds for a specific activity, Mr. Leigh argues, Congress must wait for the President to "use up all the money appropriated."

Precisely what type of appropriation Mr. Leigh meant by "all the money appropriated" is not clear. Whether he meant the entire defense budget, something less, or something more, must be guessed, but it is not important, for Mr. Leigh's point is clear. The President can use for one purpose funds that were designated for another until those funds are exhausted, notwithstanding a law prohibiting that use.

This is nonsense. Followed to its logical conclusion, Mr. Leigh's argument would deprive Congress of the power to specify the purpose for which funds are appropriated. The principle is long established that

Congress has the exclusive power to specify how appropriated moneys shall be spent. The only difference between an appropriation for a specified object (a "line-item") and an express prohibition against the use of funds for certain activity is a semantic one, the positive language of the one contrasting with the negative language of the other. Every appropriations act thus contains "conditions subsequent" in the sense that each specifies the purposes for which funds are appropriated—and, by implication, not appropriated. Transfer authority to take funds from one appropriations account and place them in another is a statutorily granted privilege, not a constitutional right. . . .

4. RECENT PRESIDENTIAL ACTIONS AT THE CONSTITUTIONAL LIMITS OF EXECUTIVE POWER

A. The "Pentagon Papers Case": New York Times v. United States (1971)

+Black, Douglas, Brennan, Stewart, White, Marshall
−Burger, Harlan, Blackmun

[As the debate over American involvement in Vietnam became increasingly bitter, the means of resisting the war became more complex. One of the more celebrated resistance efforts was Daniel Ellsberg's leaking to the press of a classified secret government study of the history of American efforts in Southeast Asia. These documents, which became known as the "Pentagon Papers," were an elaborate account of how the United States had become involved in, and had conducted, the Vietnam War. The Nixon administration considered them sensitive national security materials and took action to prevent their publication in the news media.

In mid-June 1971, the *New York Times* began publication of the study. The documents had secretly been in the possession of the newspaper for several months during which time its staff had analyzed and prepared them for publication. The government asked the newspaper to stop publication in the interests of national security, but the *Times* refused. The government then sought an injunction in the federal district court in New York to prohibit further publication of the papers. In the meantime the *Washington Post* also began publica-tion of the documents, followed by several other major urban dailies. The government also sought an injunction against the *Post*. Both district courts denied injunctive relief to the government. The Court of Appeals for the District of Columbia affirmed this denial of relief; the Court of Appeals for the Second Circuit remanded the case to the district court for further hearings. Both the government and the newspapers petitioned the Supreme Court for a writ of certiorari, which was granted. Three days later, on June 26, the Supreme Court held hearings; the written briefs arrived at the Court less than two hours beforehand. Four days after that, the Court handed down a brief per curiam decision, followed by an individual opinion of each justice.]

PER CURIAM.

We granted certiorari in these cases in which the United States seeks to enjoin *The New York Times* and *The Washington Post* from publishing the contents of a classified study entitled "History of U.S. Decision-Making Process on Viet Nam Policy."

"Any system of prior restraints of expression comes to this court bearing a heavy presumption against its constitutional validity." *Bantam Books, Inc.* v. *Sullivan* (1963); see also *Near* v. *Minnesota* (1931). The Government "thus carries a heavy burden of showing justification for the enforcement of such a restraining." . . . The District Court for the Southern District of New York in *The New York Times* case and the District Court and the Court of Appeals for the District of Columbia Circuit in *The Washington Post* case held that the Government had not met that burden.

We agree.

The judgment of the Court of Appeals for the District of Columbia Circuit is therefore affirmed. The order of the Court of Appeals for the Second Circuit is reversed and the case is remanded with directions to enter a judgment affirming the judgment of the District Court for the Southern District of New York. The stays entered June 25, 1971 by the court are vacated. The mandates shall issue forthwith.

So ordered.

Individual Opinions

MR. JUSTICE DOUGLAS, WITH WHOM MR. JUSTICE BLACK JOINS, CONCURRING.

It should be noted at the outset that the First Amendment provides that "Congress shall make no law . . . abridging the freedom of speech or of the press." That leaves, in my view, no room for governmental restraint on the press.

There is, moreover, no statute barring the publication by the press of the material which *The Times* and *Post* seek to use. 18 U.S.C. §793(e)

provides that "whoever having unauthorized possession of, access to, or control over any document, writing, . . . or information relating to the national defense which information the possessor has reason to believe could be used to the injury of the United States or to the advantage of any foreign nation, willfully communicates . . . the same to any person not entitled to receive it . . . shall be fined not more than $10,000 or imprisoned not more than 10 years or both."

The Government suggests that the word "communicates" is broad enought to encompass publication. . . .

The other evidence that Section 793 does not apply to the press is a rejected version of §793. That version read: "During any national emergency resulting from a war to which the U. S. is a party or from threat of such a war, the President may, by proclamation, prohibit the publishing or communicating of, or the attempting to publish or communicate, any information relating to the national defense, which in his judgment is of such character that it is or might be useful to the enemy." During the debates in the Senate the First Amendment was specifically cited and that provision was defeated. . . .

Moreover, the act of Sept. 23, 1950, in amending 18 U. S. C. §793, states in §1 (b) that:

"Nothing in this act shall be construed to authorize, require, or establish military or civilian censorship or in any way to limit or infringe upon freedom of the press or of speech as guaranteed by the Constitution of the United States and no regulation shall be promulgated hereunder having that effect."

Thus Congress has been faithful to the command of the First Amendment in this area.

So any power that the Government

possesses must come from its "inherent power."

The power to wage war is "the power to wage war successfully." . . . But the war power stems from a declaration of war. The Constitution by Article I, Section 8, gives Congress, not the President, power "to declare war." Nowhere are Presidential wars authorized. We need not decide therefore what leveling effect the war power of Congress might have.

These disclosures may have a serious impact. But that is no basis for sanctioning a previous restraint on the press. As stated by Chief Justice Hughes in *Near* v. *Minnesota:*

". . . While reckless assaults upon public men, and efforts to bring obloquy upon those who are endeavoring faithfully to discharge official duties, exert a baleful influence and deserve the severest condemnation in public opinion, it cannot be said that this abuse is greater, and it is believed to be less, than that which characterized the period in which our institutions took shape. Meanwhile, the administration of Government has become more complex, the opportunities for malfeasance and corruption have multiplied, crime has grown to most serious proportions, and the danger of its protection by unfaithful officials and of the impairment of the fundamental security of life and property by criminal alliances and official neglect, emphasizes the primary need of a vigilant and courageous press, especially in great cities. The fact that the liberty of the press may be abused by miscreant purveyors of scandal does not make any the less necessary the immunity of the press from previous restraint in dealing with official misconduct."

The Government says that it has inherent powers to go into court and obtain an injunction to protect that national interest, which in this case is alleged to be national security.

Near v. *Minnesota* repudiated that expansive doctrine in no uncertain terms.

The dominant purpose of the First Amendment was to prohibit the widespread practice of government suppression of embarrassing information. It is common knowledge that the First Amendment was adopted against the widespread use of the common law of seditious libel to punish dissemination of material that is embarrassing to the powers-that-be. . . . The present cases will, I think, go down in history as the most dramatic illustration of that principle. A debate of large proportions goes on in the nation over our posture in Vietnam. That debate antedated the disclosure of the contents of the present documents. The latter are highly relevant to the debate in progress.

Secrecy in government is fundamentally antidemocratic, perpetuating bureaucratic errors. Open debate and discussion of public issues are vital to our national health. On public questions there should be "open and robust debate." . . .

MR. JUSTICE BRENNAN, CONCURRING.

I write separately in these cases only to emphasize what should be apparent: that our judgment in the present cases may not be taken to indicate the propriety, in the future, of issuing temporary stays and restraining orders to block the publication of material sought to be suppressed by the Government. So far as I can determine, never before has the United States sought to enjoin a newspaper from publishing information in its possession. The relative novelty of the question presented, the necessary haste with which decisions were reached, the magnitude of the interests asserted, and the fact that all the parties have concentrated their arguments upon the question whether permanent restraints were proper may have justified at least some of the restraints heretofore imposed in these cases. Certainly it is difficult to fault the several courts below for seeking to assure that the issues here involved were preserved for ultimate review by this Court. But even if it be assumed that some of the interim restraints were proper in the two cases before us, that assumption has no bearing upon the propriety of similar judicial action in the future. To begin with, there has now been ample time for reflection and judgment; whatever values there may be in the preservation of novel questions for appellate review may not support any restraints in the future. More important, the First Amendment stands as an absolute bar to the imposition of judicial restraints in circumstances of the kind presented by these cases. . . .

MR. JUSTICE STEWART, WITH WHOM MR. JUSTICE WHITE JOINS, CONCURRING.

In the governmental structure created by our Constitution, the executive is endowed with enormous power in the two related areas of national defense and international relations. This power, largely unchecked by the legislative and judicial branches, has been pressed to the very hilt since the advent of the nuclear missile age. For better or for worse, the simple fact is that a President of the United States possesses vastly greater constitutional independence in these two vital areas of power than does, say, a prime minister of a country with a parliamentary form of government.

In the absence of the governmental checks and balances present in other areas of our national life, the only effective restraint upon executive policy and power in the areas of national defense and international affairs may lie in an enlightened citizenry—in an informed and critical public opinion which alone can here protect the values of democratic government. For this reason, it is perhaps here that a press that is alert, aware, and free most vitally serves the basic purpose of the First Amendment. For without an informed and free press there cannot be an enlightened people.

Yet is it elementary that the successful conduct of international diplomacy and the maintenance of an effective national defense require both confidentiality and secrecy. Other nations can hardly deal with this nation in an atmosphere of mutual trust unless they can be assured that their confidences will be kept. And within our own executive departments, the development of considered and intelligent international policies would be impossible if those charged with their formulation could not communicate with each other freely, frankly and in confidence. In the area of basic national defense the frequent need for absolute secrecy is, of course, self-evident.

I think there can be but one answer to this dilemma, if dilemma it be. The responsibility must be where the power is. If the Constitution gives the executive a large degree of unshared power in the conduct of foreign affairs and the maintenance of our national defense, then under the Constitution the executive must have the largely unshared duty to determine and preserve the degree of internal security necessary to exercise that power successfully. It is an awesome responsibility, requiring judgment and wisdom of a high order. I should suppose that moral, political, and practical considerations would dictate that a very first principle of that wisdom would be an insistence upon avoiding secrecy for its own sake. For when everything is classified, then nothing is classified, and the system becomes one to be disregarded by the cynical or the careless, and to be manipulated by those intent on self-protection or self-promotion. I should suppose in short, that the hallmark of a truly effective international security system would be the maximum possible disclosure, recognizing that secrecy can best be preserved only when credibility is truly maintained. But be that as it may, it is clear to me that it is the constitutional duty of the Executive—as a matter of sovereign prerogative and not as a matter of law as the courts know law—through the promulgation and enforcement of executive regulations, to protect the confidentiality necessary to carry out its responsibilities in the field of international relations and national defense.

This is not to say that Congress and the courts have no role to play. Undoubtedly Congress has the power to enact specific and appropriate criminal laws to protect Government secrets. Congress has passed such laws, and several of them are of very colorable relevance to the apparent circumstances of these cases, and if a criminal prosecution is instituted, it will be the responsibility of the courts to decide the applicability of the criminal law under which the charge is brought. Moreover, if Congress should pass a specific law authorizing civil proceedings in this field, the courts would likewise have the duty to decide the constitutionality of such a law as well as its applicability to the facts proved.

But in the cases before us we are asked neither to construe specific regulations nor to apply specific laws. We are asked, instead, to perform a function that the Constitution gave to the executive, not the judiciary. We are asked, quite simply, to prevent the publication by two newspapers of material that the executive branch insists should not, in the national interest, be published. I am convinced that the executive is correct with respect to some of the documents involved. But I cannot say that disclosure of any of them will surely result in direct, immediate and irreparable damage to our nation or its people. That being so there can under the First Amendment be but one judicial resolution of the issues before us. I join the judgments of the court.

MR. JUSTICE MARSHALL, CONCURRING.

. . . In this case there is no problem concerning the President's power to classify information as "secret" or "top secret." Congress has specifically recognized Presidential authority, which has been formally exercised in Executive Order 10501, to classify documents and information. . . . Nor is there any issue here regarding the President's power as Chief Executive and Commander in Chief to protect national security by disciplining employees who disclose information and by taking precautions to prevent leaks.

The problem here is whether in this particular case the executive branch has authority to invoke the equity jurisdiction of the courts to protect what it believes to be the national interest. . . . The Government argues that in addition to the inherent power of any government to protect itself, the President's power to conduct foreign affairs and his position as Commander-in-Chief give him authority to impose censorship on the press to protect his ability to deal effectively with foreign nations and to conduct the military affairs of the country. Of course, it is beyond cavil that the President has broad powers by virtue of his primary responsibility for the conduct of our foreign affairs and his position as Commander-in-Chief. . . . And in some situations it may be that under whatever inherent powers the Government may have, as well as the implicit authority derived from the President's mandate to conduct foreign affairs and to act as Commander-in-Chief there is a basis for the invocation of the equity jurisdiction of this Court as an aid to prevent the publication of material damaging to "national security," however, that term may be defined.

It would, however, be utterly inconsistent with the concept of separation of power for this Court to use its power of contempt to prevent behavior that Congress has specifically declined to prohibit. There would be a similar damage to the basic concept of these co-equal branches of government if when the executive has adequate authority granted by Congress to protect "national security," it can choose instead to invoke the contempt power of a court to enjoin the threatened conduct. The Constitution provides that Congress shall make laws, the President execute laws, and courts interpret law. *Youngstown Sheet & Tube Co. v. Sawyer* (1952). It did not provide for government by injunction, in which the courts and the executive can "make law" without regard to the action of Congress. It may be more convenient for the executive if it need only convince a judge to prohibit conduct rather than to ask the Congress to pass a law, and it may be more convenient to enforce a contempt order than seek a criminal conviction in a jury trial. Moreover, it may be considered politically wise to get a court to share the re-

sponsibility for arresting those who the executive has probable cause to believe are violating the law. But convenience and political considerations of the moment do not justify a basic departure from the principles of our system. . . .

MR. JUSTICE BLACK, WITH WHOM MR. JUSTICE DOUGLAS JOINS, CONCURRING.

I adhere to the view that the Government's case against *The Washington Post* should have been dismissed and that the injunction against *The New York Times* should have been vacated without oral argument when the cases were first presented to this Court. I believe that every moment's continuance of the injunctions against these newspapers amounts to a flagrant, indefensible and continuing violation of the First Amendment. Furthermore, after oral agruments, I agree completely that we must affirm the judgment of the Court of Appeals for the District of Columbia and reverse the judgment of the Court of Appeals for the Second Circuit for the reasons stated by my brothers Douglas and Brennan. In my view it is unfortunate that some of my brethren are apparently willing to hold that the publication of news may sometimes be enjoined. Such a holding would make a shambles of the First Amendment. . . .

In seeking injunctions against the newspapers and in its presentation to the court, the executive branch seems to have forgotten the essential purpose and history of the First Amendment. When the Constitution was adopted, many people strongly opposed it because the document contained no bill of rights to safeguard certain basic freedoms. They especially feared that the new powers granted to a central government might be interpreted to permit the government to curtail freedom of religion, press, assembly and speech. In response to an overwhelming public clamor, James Madison offered a series of amendments to satisfy citizens that these great liberties would remain safe and beyond the power of government to abridge. Madison proposed what later became the First Amendment in three parts, two of which are set out below, and one of which proclaimed: "The people shall not be deprived or abridged of their right to speak, to write, or to publish their sentiments; and the freedom of the press, as one of the great bulwarks of liberty, shall be inviolable." The amendments were offered to curtail and restrict the general powers granted to the executive, legislative and judicial branches two years before in the original Constitution. The Bill of Rights changed the original Constitution into a new charter under which no branch of government could abridge the people's freedoms of press, speech, religion and assembly.

Yet the Solicitor General argues and some members of the Court appear to agree that the general powers of the Government adopted in the original Constitution should be interpreted to limit and restrict the specific and emphatic guarantees of the Bill of Rights adopted later. I can imagine no greater perversion of history. . . .

In the First Amendment the Founding Fathers gave the free press the protection it must have to fulfill its essential role in our democracy. The press was to serve the governed, not the governors. The Government's power to censor the press was abolished so that the press would remain forever free to censure the Government. The press was protected so that it could bare the secrets of gov-

ernment and inform the people. Only a free and unrestrained press can effectively expose deception in government. And paramount among the responsibilities of a free press is the duty to prevent any part of the Government from deceiving the people and sending them off to distant lands to die of foreign fevers and foreign shot and shell. In my view, far from deserving condemnation for their courageous reporting, The New York Times, The Washington Post and other newspapers should be commended for serving the purpose that the Founding Fathers saw so clearly. In revealing the workings of government that led to the Vietnam war, the newspapers nobly did precisely that which the founders hoped and trusted they would do.

The Government's case here is based on premises entirely different from those that guided the framers of the First Amendment. The Solicitor General has carefully and emphatically stated:

"Now, Mr. Justice [Black], your construction of . . . [the First Amendment] is well known, and I certainly respect it. You say that no law means no law, and that should be obvious. I can only say, Mr. Justice, that to me it is equally obvious that 'no law' does not mean 'no law', and I would seek to persuade the Court that that is true . . . [t]here are other parts of the Constitution that grant power and responsibilities to the executive end . . . the First Amendment was not intended to make it impossible for the executive to function or to protect the security of the United States."

And the Government argues in its brief that in spite of the First Amendment, "the authority of the executive department to protect the nation against publication of information whose disclosure would endanger the national security stems from two interrelated sources: the constitutional power of the President over the conduct of foreign affairs and his authority as Commander in Chief."

In other words, we are asked to hold that despite the First Amendment's emphatic command, the executive branch, the Congress and the judiciary can make laws enjoining publication of current news and abridging freedom of the press in the name of "national security." The Government does not even attempt to rely on an act of Congress. Instead it makes the bold and dangerously far-reaching contention that the courts should take it upon themselves to "make" a law abridging freedom of the press in the name of equity, Presidential power and national security, even when the representatives of the people in Congress have adhered to the command of the First Amendment and refused to make such a law. . . .

To find that the President has "inherent power" to halt the publication of news by resort to the courts would wipe out the First Amendment and destroy the fundamental liberty and security of the very people the Government hopes to make "secure." No one can read the history of the adoption of the First Amendment without being convinced beyond any doubt that it was injunctions like those sought here that Madison and his collaborators intended to outlaw in this nation for all time.

The word "security" is a broad, vague generality whose contours should not be invoked to abrogate the fundamental law embodied in the First Amendment. The guarding of military and diplomatic secrets at the expense of informed representative government provides no real security for our Republic. . . .

MR. JUSTICE WHITE, WITH WHOM MR. JUSTICE STEWART JOINS, CONCURRING.

I concur in today's judgments, but only because of the concededly extraordinary protection against prior restraints enjoyed by the press under our constitutional system. I do not say that in no circumstances would the First Amendment permit an injunction against publishing information about Government plans or operations. Nor, after examining the materials the Government characterizes as the most sensitive and destructive, can I deny that revelation of these documents will do substantial damage to public interests. Indeed, I am confident that their disclosure will have that result. But I nevertheless agree that the United States has not satisfied the very heavy burden which it must meet to warrant an injunction against publication in these cases, at least in the absence of express and appropriately limited Congressional authorization for prior restraints in circumstances such as these.

The Government's position is simply stated: The responsibility of the executive for the conduct of the foreign affairs and for the security of the nation is so basic that the President is entitled to an injunction against publication of a newspaper story whenever he can convince a court that the information to be revealed threatens "grave and irreparable" injury to the public interest; and the injunction should issue whether or not the material to be published is classified, whether or not publication would be lawful under relevant criminal statutes enacted by Congress and regardless of the circumstances by which the newspaper came into possession of the information.

At least in the absence of legislation by Congress, based on its own investigation and findings, I am quite unable to agree that the inherent powers of the executive and the courts reach so far as to authorize remedies having such sweeping potential for inhibiting publications by the press. Much of the difficulty inheres in the "grave and irreparable danger" standard suggested by the United States. If the United States were to have judgment under such a standard in these cases, our decision would be of little guidance to other courts in other cases, for the material at issue here would not be available from the Court's opinion or from public records, nor would it be published by the press. Indeed, even today where we hold that the United States has not met its burden, the material remains sealed in court records and it is properly not discussed in today's opinions. Moreover, because the material poses substantial dangers to national interests and because of the hazards of criminal sanctions, a responsible press may choose never to publish the more sensitive materials. To sustain the Government in these cases would start the courts down a long and hazardous road that I am not willing to travel, at least without Congressional guidance and direction. . . .

The Criminal Code contains numerous provisions potentially relevant to these cases. Section 797 makes it a crime to publish certain photographs or drawings of military installations. Section 798, also in precise language, proscribes knowing and willful publications of any classified information concerning the cryptographic systems or communication intelligence activities of the United States as well as any information obtained from communication intelligence operations. If any of the material here at issue is of this nature, the newspapers are presumably now on full notice of the position of the United States and must face the consequences if they publish. I would have no difficulty in sustaining convictions under these sections on facts that would not justify the intervention of equity and the imposition of a prior restraint.

The same would be true under those sections of the Criminal Code casting a wider net to protect the national defense. Section 798 (e) makes it a criminal act for any authorized possessor of a document "relating to national defense" either (1) willfully to communicate or cause to be communicated that document to any person not entitled to receive it or (2) willfully to retain the document and fail to deliver it to an officer of the United States entitled to receive it. The subsection was added in 1950 because pre-existing law provided no penalty for the unauthorized possessor unless demand for the documents was made. "The dangers surrounding the unauthorized possession of such items are self-evident, and it is deemed advisable to require their surrender in such a case, regardless of demand, especially since their unauthorized possession may be unknown to the authorities who would otherwise make the demand." . . . Of course, in the cases before us, the unpublished documents have been demanded by the United States and their import has been made known at least to counsel for the newspapers involved. . . .

It is thus clear that Congress has addressed itself to the problem of protecting the security of the country and the national defense from unauthorized disclosure of potentially damaging information. . . . It has not, however, authorized the injunctive remedy against threatened publication. It has apparently been satisfied to rely on criminal sanctions and their deterrent effect on the responsible as well as the irresponsible press. I am not, of course, saying that either of these newspapers has yet committed a crime or that either would commit a crime if they published all the material now in their possession. That matter must await resolution in the context of a criminal proceeding if one is instituted by the United States. In that event, the issue of guilt or innocence would be determined by procedures and standards quite different from those that have purported to govern these injunctive proceedings.

MR. CHIEF JUSTICE BURGER, DISSENTING.

So clear are the constitutional limitations on prior restraint against expression, that from the time of *Near* v. *Minnesota* . . . (1931), until recently . . . we have had little occasion to be concerned with cases involving prior restraints against news reporting on matters of public interest. There is, therefore, little variation among the members of the Court in terms of resistance to prior restraints against publication. Adherence to this basic constitutional principle, however, does not make this case a simple one. In this case, the imperative of a free and unfettered press comes into collision with another imperative, the effective functioning of a complex modern government, and specifically the effective exercise of certain constitutional powers of the executive. Only those who view the First Amendment as an absolute in all circumstances—a view I respect, but reject—can find such a case as this to be simple or easy.

This case is not simple for another and more immediate reason. We do not know the facts of the case. No District Judge knew all the facts. No Court of Appeals Judge knew all the facts. No member of this Court knows all the facts.

Why are we in this posture, in which only those judges to whom the First Amendment is absolute and permits of no restraint in any circumstances or for any reason, are really in a position to act?

I suggest we are in this posture because these cases have been conducted in unseemly haste. . . .

Here, moreover, the frenetic haste is due in large part to the manner in which *The Times* proceeded from the date it obtained the purloined documents. It seems reasonably clear now that the haste precluded reasonable and deliberate judicial treatment of these cases and was not warranted. The precipitous action of this court aborting a trial not yet completed is not the kind of judicial conduct which ought to attend the disposition of a great issue.

The newspapers make a derivative claim under the First Amendment: they denominate this right as the public right to know; by implication, *The Times* asserts a sole trusteeship of that right by virtue of its journalistic "scoop." The right is asserted as an absolute. Of course, the First Amendment right itself is not an absolute, as Justice Holmes so long ago pointed out in his aphorism concerning the right to shout of fire in a crowded theater. There are other exceptions. . . . There are no doubt other exceptions no one has had occasion to describe or discuss. Conceivably such exceptions may be lurking in these cases and would have been flushed had they been properly considered in the trial courts, free from unwarranted deadlines and frenetic pressures.

A great issue of this kind should be tried in a judicial atmosphere conducive to thoughtful, reflective deliberation, especially when haste, in terms of hours, is unwarranted in light of the long period *The Times,* by its own choice, deferred publication.

It is not disputed that *The Times* has had unauthorized possession of the documents for three to four months, during which it has had its expert analysts studying them, presumably digesting them and preparing the material for publication. During all of this time, *The Times,* presumably in its capacity as trustee of the public's "right to know," has held up publication for purposes it considered proper and thus public knowledge was delayed. No doubt this was for a good reason; the analysis of 7,000 pages of complex material drawn from a vastly greater volume of material would inevitably take time and the writing of good news stories takes time.

But why should the United States Government, from whom this information was illegally acquired by someone, along with all the counsel, trial judges, and appellate judges be placed under needless pressure? After these months of deferral, the alleged right to know has somehow and suddenly become a right that must be vindicated instanter.

. . .

Would it have been unreasonable, since the newspaper could anticipate the Government's objections to release of secret material, to give the Government an opportunity to review the entire collection and determine whether agreement could be reached on publication? Stolen or not, if secu-

rity was not in fact jeopardized, much of the material could no doubt have been declassified, since it spans a period ending in 1968.

With such an approach—one that great newspapers have in the past practiced and stated editorially to be the duty of an honorable press—the newspapers and Government might well have narrowed the area of disagreement as to what was and was not publishable, leaving the remainder to be resolved in orderly litigation if necessary. To me it is hardly believable that a newspaper long regarded as a great institution in American life would fail to perform one of the basic and simple duties of every citizen with respect to the discovery or possession of stolen property or secret Government documents. That duty, I had thought —perhaps naively—was to report forthwith, to responsible public officers. This duty rests on taxi drivers, justices and *The New York Times.* The course followed by *The Times,* whether so calculated or not, removed any possibility of orderly litigation of the issues. If the action of the judges up to now has been correct, that result is sheer happenstance. . . .

The consequences of all this melancholy series of events is that we literally do not know what we are acting on. . . . I agree with Mr. Justice Harlan and Mr. Justice Blackmun but I am not prepared to reach the merits.

I would affirm the Court of Appeals for the Second Circuit and allow the District Court to complete the trial aborted by our grant of certiorari, meanwhile preserving the status quo in *The Post* case. I would direct that the District Court on remand give priority to *The Times* case to the exclusion of all other business of that court but I would not set arbitrary deadlines.

I should add that I am in general agreement with much of what Mr. Justice White has expressed with respect to penal sanctions concerning communication or retention of documents or information relating to the national defense. . . .

MR. JUSTICE HARLAN, WITH WHOM THE CHIEF JUSTICE AND MR. JUSTICE BLACKMUN JOIN, DISSENTING.

These cases forcefully call to mind the wise admonition of Mr. Justice Holmes. dissenting in *Northern Securities Co.* v. *United States* (1904):

Great cases like hard cases make bad law. For great cases are called great, not by reason of their real importance in shaping the law of the future, but because of some accident of immediate overwhelming interest which appeals to the feelings and distorts the judgment. These immediate interests exercise a kind of hydraulic pressure which makes what previously was clear seem doubtful, and before which even well settled principles of law will bend.

With all respect, I consider that the Court has been almost irresponsibly feverish in dealing with these cases. . . .

This frenzied train of events took place in the name of the presumption against prior restraints created by the First Amendment. Due regard for the extraordinarily important and difficult questions involved in these litigations should have led the Court to shun such a precipitate timetable. In order to decide the merits of these cases properly, some or all of the following questions should have been faced:

1. Whether the Attorney General is authorized to bring these suits in the name of the United States. Compare *In Re Debs* (1895) with *Youngstown Sheet & Tube Co.* v. *Sawyer* (1952). This question involves as well the construction and validity of a singularly opaque statute—the Espionage Act, 18 U.S.C. §793 (e).

2. Whether the First Amendment permits the Federal Courts to enjoin publication of stories which would present a serious threat to national security. See *Near* v. *Minnesota*, (1931).

3. Whether the threat to publish highly secret documents is of itself a sufficient implication of national security to justify an injunction on the theory that regardless of the contents of the documents harm enough results simply from the demonstration of such a breach of secrecy.

4. Whether the unauthorized disclosure of any of these particular documents would seriously impair the national security.

5. What weight should be given to the opinion of high officers in the executive branch of the Government with respect to questions 3 and 4.

6. Whether the newspapers are entitled to retain and use the documents notwithstanding the seemingly uncontested facts that the documents, or the original of which they are duplicates, were purloined from the Government's possession and that the newspapers received them with the knowledge that they had been feloniously acquired. . . .

7. Whether the threatened harm to the national security or the Government's possessory interest in the documents justifies the issuance of an injunction against publication in light of—

A. The strong First Amendment policy against prior restraints on publication;

B. The doctrine against enjoining

conduct in violation of criminal statutes; and

C. The extent to which the materials at issue have apparently already been otherwise disseminated. . . .

Forced as I am to reach the merits of these cases, I dissent from the opinion and judgments of the Court. Within the severe limitations imposed by the time constraints under which I have been required to operate, I can only state my reasons in telescoped form, even though in different circumstances I would have felt constrained to deal with the cases in the fuller sweep indicated above.

It is a sufficient basis for affirming the Court of Appeals for the Second Circuit in *The Times* litigation to observe that its order must rest on the conclusion that because of the time elements the Government had not been given an adequate opportunity to present its case to the District Court. At the least this conclusion was not an abuse of discretion.

In *The Post* litigation the Government had more time to prepare; this was apparently the basis for the refusal of the Court of Appeals for the District of Columbia Circuit on rehearing to conform its judgment to that of the Second Circuit. But I think there is another and more fundamental reason why this judgment cannot stand—a reason which also furnishes an additional ground for not reinstating the judgment of the District Court in *The Times* litigation, set aside by the Court of Appeals. It is plain to me that the scope of the judicial function in passing upon the activities of the executive branch of the Government in the field of foreign affairs is very narrowly restricted. This view is, I think, dictated by the concept of separation of powers upon which our constitutional system rests.

In a speech on the floor of the House of Representatives, Chief Justice John Marshall, then a member of that body, stated:

"The President is the sole organ of the nation in its external relations and its sole representative with foreign nations." . . .

From that time, shortly after the founding of the nation, to this, there has been no substantial challenge to this description of the scope of executive power. See *United States* v. *Curtiss-Wright Export Corp.* . . . (1936).

From this constitutional primacy in the field of foreign affairs, it seems to me that certain conclusions necessarily follow. Some of these were stated concisely by President Washington, declining the request of the House of Representatives for the papers leading up to the negotiation of the Jay Treaty:

The nature of foreign negotiations requires caution, and their success must often depend on secrecy; and even when brought to a conclusion a full disclosure of all the measures, demands, or eventual concessions which may have been proposed or contemplated would be extremely impolitic; for this might have a pernicious influence on future negotiations, or produce immediate inconveniences, perhaps danger and mischief, in relation to other powers. . . .

The power to evaluate the "pernicious influence" of premature disclosure is not, however, lodged in the executive alone. I agree that, in performance of its duty to protect the values of the First Amendment against political pressures, the judiciary must review the initial executive determination to the point of satisfying itself that the subject matter of the dispute does lie within the proper compass of the President's foreign relations power. Constitutional considerations forbid "a complete abandonment of judicial control." . . . Moreover, the judiciary may properly insist that the determination that disclosure of the subject matter would irreparably impair the national security be made by the head of the executive department concerned—here the Secretary of State or the Secretary of Defense—after actual personal consideration by that office. This safeguard is required in the analogous area of executive claims of privilege for secrets of state. . . .

But in my judgment the judiciary may not properly go beyond these two inquiries and redetermine for itself the probable impact of disclosure on the national security.

The very nature of executive decisions as to foreign policy is political, not judicial. Such decisions are wholly confided by our Constitution to the political departments of the Government, executive and legislative. They are delicate, complex and involve large elements of prophecy. They are and should be undertaken only by those directly responsible to the people whose welfare they advance or imperil. They are decisions of a kind for which the judiciary has neither aptitude, facilities nor responsibility and which has long been held to belong in the domain of political power not subject to judicial intrusion or inquiry, . . .

Even if there is some room for the judiciary to override the executive determination, it is plain that the scope of review must be exceedingly narrow. I can see no indication in the opinions of either the District Court or the Court of Appeals in *The Post* litigation that the conclusions of the executive were given even the deference owing to an administrative agency, much less that owing to a coequal constitutional prerogative. . . .

MR. JUSTICE BLACKMUN, DISSENTING.

I join Mr. Justice Harlan in his dissent. I also am in substantial accord with much that Mr. Justice White says, by way of admonition, in the latter part of his opinion. . . .

The First Amendment, after all, is only one part of an entire Constitution. Article II of the great document vests in the executive branch primary power over the conduct of foreign affairs and places in that branch the responsibility for the nation's safety.

Each provision of the Constitution is important, and I cannot subscribe to a doctrine of unlimited absolutism for the First Amendment at the cost of downgrading other provisions.

First Amendment absolutism has never commanded a majority of this court. See, for example, *Near v. Minnesota* (1931), and *Schenck v. United States* (1919). What is needed here is a weighing, upon properly developed standards, of the broad right of the press to print and of the very narrow right of the Government to prevent. Such standards are not yet developed. The parties here are in disagreement as to what those standards should be. But even the newspapers concede that there are situations where restraint is in order and is constitutional. . . .

The Court, however, decides the cases today the other way. I therefore add one final comment.

I strongly urge, and sincerely hope, that these two newspapers will be fully aware of their ultimate responsibilities to the United States of America. Judge Wilkey, dissenting in the District of Columbia case, after a review of only the affidavits before this Court (the basic papers had not then been made available by either party), concluded that there were a number of examples of documents that, if in the possession of *The Post,* and if published "could clearly result in great harm to the nation," and he defined "harm" to mean "the death of soldiers, and destruction of alliances, the greatly increased difficulty of negotiation with our enemies, the inability of our diplomats to negotiate. . . ." I, for one, have now been able to give at least some cursory study not only to the affidavits, but to the material itself. I regret to say that from this examination I fear that Judge Wilkey's statements have possible foundation. I therefore share his concern. I hope that damage already has not been done.

If, however, damage has been done, and if, with the Court's action today, these newspapers proceed to publish the critical documents and there results therefrom "the death of soldiers, the destruction of alliances, the greatly increased difficulty of negotiation with our enemies, the inability of our diplomats to negotiate," to which list I might add the factors of prolongation of the war and of further delay in the freeing of United States prisoners, then the nation's people will know where the responsibility for these sad consequences rests.

B. *Watergate and the Presidency*

(1) United States v. Nixon (1974)

+Burger, Douglas, Brennan, Stewart, White, Marshall, Blackmun, Powell

NP Rehnquist

[On March 1, 1974, a federal grand jury in Washington D.C. returned an indictment charging seven former members of President Nixon's staff with various offenses in connection with the "Watergate" cover-up, including conspiracy to defraud the United States and conspiracy to obstruct justice. Among the seven were the president's three principal lieutenants: John Mitchell, Bob Haldeman, and John Erlichman. By a vote of 19-0, President Nixon was named in the indictment as an unindicted coconspirator after the Watergate special prosecutor, Leon Jaworski, advised the grand jury that a president in office could not be indicted for a crime.

On April 18, the special prosecutor filed a motion with district judge John Sirica asking that a subpoena *duces tecum* be issued to the president requiring production of certain records, including tape recordings of conversations held with the principal defendants and others in the White House. In support of his request for the subpoena, the special prosecutor described specific conversations, between identified individuals, on specific days that, on the basis of other evidence, were believed to be relevant to the case. These records and tapes were to be produced in advance of September 9, 1974, the date set for trial.

On April 30, President Nixon publicly released *edited transcripts* of a number of White House conversations bearing on Watergate. Some of the twenty subpoenaed conversations were included, but not all. On May 1, the president's attorney, James St. Clair, filed a motion in Judge Sirica's court to quash the subpoena, claiming among other things that these records were protected by the doctrine of "executive privilege."

On May 20, Judge Sirica denied St. Clair's motion and ordered the tapes produced in court by May 31, the originals and not merely transcripts. He also rejected St. Clair's claim that this was a nonjusticiable issue, since it was merely an "intra-executive branch" dispute, and he rejected the claim of executive privilege. The judiciary, not the president, said Sirica, is the final arbiter of a claim of executive privilege. In this case, whatever force that privilege had, it was overcome by the special prosecutor's *prima facie* demonstration of need for the tapes in a criminal case, at least to the point of having them inspected privately by the judge in chambers.

On May 24, St. Clair filed an appeal with the court of appeals. The special prosecutor then petitioned the Supreme Court for certiorari "before judgment," and this was granted. On June 6, St. Clair also filed a petition for certiorari before judgment, and this was also granted. Under an expedited schedule, oral argument was set for July 8, 1974.

There was some question whether or not the Supreme Court had jurisdiction in the case. It is a basic rule of procedure that denial of a motion to quash a subpoena is not a "final" order of a court, and customarily, therefore, it cannot be appealed. But if that rule were applied strictly in this case, it would have forced Judge Sirica to cite the President for contempt of court. An exception should be granted in this case, the Supreme Court said, because it was "peculiarly inappropriate" to follow the contempt route: "To require a President of the United States to place himself in the posture of disobeying an order of a court merely to trigger the procedural mechanism for review of the ruling would be unseemly, and present an unnecessary occasion for constitutional confrontation between two branches of the Government. . . . The issue whether a President can be cited for contempt would itself engender protracted litigation. . . ."]

MR. CHIEF JUSTICE BURGER delivered the opinion of the Court.

. . .

In the District Court, the President's counsel argued that the court lacked jurisdiction to issue the subpoena because the matter was an intrabranch dispute between a subordinate and superior officer of the executive branch and hence not subject to judicial resolution. That argument has been renewed in this Court with emphasis on the contention that the dispute does not present a "case" or "controversy" which can be adjudicated in the Federal courts. The President's counsel argues that the Federal courts should not intrude into areas committed to the other branches of Government.

The mere assertion of a claim of an "intra-branch dispute," without more, has never operated to defeat Federal jurisdiction; justiciability does not depend on such a surface inquiry. In *United States* v. *ICC* . . . (1949), the Court observed, "Courts must look behind names that symbolize the parties to determine whether a justiciable case or controversy is presented," . . .

Our starting point is the nature of the proceeding for which the evidence is sought—here a pending criminal prosecution. It is a judicial proceeding in a Federal court alleging violation of Federal laws and is brought in the name of the United States as sovereign. . . . Under the authority of Art. II, Sec. 2, Congress has vested in the Attorney General the power to conduct the criminal litigation of the United States Government. . . . It has also vested in him the power to appoint subordinate officers to assist him in the discharge of his duties. . . . Acting pursuant to those statutes, the Attorney General has delegated the authority to represent the United States in these particular matters to a special prosecutor with unique authority and tenure. The regulation gives the special prosecutor explicit power to contest the invocation of executive privilege in the process of seeking evidence deemed relevant to the performance of these specially delegated duties. . . .

. . . [It] is theoretically possible for the Attorney General to amend or revoke the regulation defining the special prosecutor's authority. But he has not done so. So long as this regulation remains in force the executive branch is bound by it, and indeed the United States as the sovereign composed of the three branches is bound to respect and to enforce it. Moreover, the delegation of authority to the special prosecutor in this case is not an ordinary delegation by the Attorney General to a subordinate officer. With the authorization of the President, the acting Attorney General provided in the regulation that the special prosecutor was not to be removed without the "consensus" of eight designated leaders of Congress. . . .

The demands of and the resistance to the subpoena present an obvious controversy in the ordinary sense, but that alone is not sufficient to meet Constitutional standards. In the Constitutional sense, controversy means more than disagreement and conflict; rather it means the kind of controversy courts traditionally resolve. Here at issue is the production or nonproduction of specified evidence deemed by the special prosecutor to be relevant and admissible in a pending criminal case. It is sought by one official of the Government within the scope of his express authority; it is resisted by the chief executive on the ground of his duty to preserve the confidentiality of the communications of the President. Whatever the correct answer on the merits, these issues are "of a type which are traditionally justiciable." . . .

In light of the uniqueness of the setting in which the conflict arises, the fact that both parties are officers of the executive branch cannot be viewed as a barrier to justiciability. It would be inconsistent with the applicable law and regulation, and unique facts of this case to conclude other than that the special prosecutor has standing to bring this action and that a justiciable controversy is presented for decision.

. . .

[W]e turn to the claim that the subpoena should be quashed because it demands "confidential conversations between a President and his close advisors that it would be inconsistent with the public interest to produce," . . . The first contention is a broad claim that the separation of powers doctrine precludes judicial review of a president's claim of privilege. The second contention is that if he does not prevail on the claim of absolute privilege, the court should hold as a matter of constitutional law that the privilege prevails over the subpoena duces tecum.

In the performance of assigned constitutional duties each branch of the Government must initially interpret the Constitution, and the interpretation of its powers by any branch is due great respect from the others.

The President's counsel, as we have noted, reads the Constitution as providing an absolute privilege of confidentiality for all Presidential communications. Many decisions of this Court, however, have unequivocally reaffirmed the holding of *Marbury* v. *Madison* . . . (1803), that "it is emphatically the province and duty of the Judicial department to say what the law is." . . .

No holding of the Court has defined the scope of the judicial power specifically relating to the enforcement of a subpoena for confidential Presidential communications for use in a criminal prosecution, but other exercises of powers by the executive branch and the legislative branch have been found invalid as in conflict with the Constitution, . . .

In a series of cases, the Court interpreted the explicit immunity conferred by express provisions of the Constitution on members of the House and Senate by the speech or debate clause, U.S. Const. Art. 1, Sec. 6: *Doe* v. *McMillan* . . . (1973); *Gravel* v. *United States* . . . (1973); *United States* v. *Brewster* . . . (1974); *United States* v. *Johnson* . . . (1966). Since this Court has consistently exercised the power to construe and delineate claims arising under express powers, it must follow that the court has authority to interpret claims with respect to powers alleged to derive from enumerated powers. . . .

Notwithstanding the deference each branch must accord the others, the "judicial power of the United States" vested in the Federal courts by Art. III, Section 1 of the Constitution can no more be shared with the executive branch than the chief executive, for example, can share with the judiciary the veto power, or the Congress share with the judiciary the power to override a Presidential veto. Any other conclusion would be contrary to the basic concept of separation of powers and the checks and balances that flow from the scheme of a tripartite Government. The Federalist, No. 47, . . . We therefore reaffirm that it is "emphatically the province and the duty" of this court "to say what the law is" with respect to the claim of privilege presented in this case.

. . . [N]either the doctrine of separation of powers, nor the need for confidentiality of high level communications, without more, can sustain an absolute unqualified Presidential privilege of immunity from judicial process under all circumstances. The President's need for complete candor and objectivity from advisers calls for great deference from the courts. However, when the privilege depends solely on the broad, undifferentiated claim of public interest in the confidentiality of such conversations, a confrontation with other values arises. Absent a claim of need to protect military, diplomatic or sensitive national security secrets, we find it difficult to accept the argument that even the very important interest in confidentiality of Presi-

dential communications is significantly diminished by production of such material for *in camera* inspection with all the protection that a District Court will be obliged to provide.

The impediment that an absolute, unqualified privilege would place in the way of the primary constitutional duty of the judicial branch to do justice in criminal prosecutions would plainly conflict with the function of the courts under Art. III. In designing the structure of our Government and dividing and allocating the sovereign power among three coequal branches, the framers of the Constitution sought to provide a comprehensive system, but the separate powers were not intended to operate with absolute independence. . . .

To read the Art. II powers of the President as providing an absolute privilege as against a subpoena essential to enforcement of criminal statutes on no more than a generalized claim of the public interest in confidentiality of nonmilitary and nondiplomatic discussions would upset the constitutional balance of "a workable government" and gravely impair the role of the courts under Art. III.

Since we conclude that the legitimate needs of the judicial process may outweigh Presidential privilege, it is necessary to resolve those competing interests in a manner that preserves the essential functions of each branch. The right and indeed the duty to resolve that question does not free the judiciary from according high respect to the representations made on behalf of the President. . . .

The expectation of a President to the confidentiality of his conversations and correspondence, like the claim of confidentiality of judicial deliberations, for example, has all the values to which we accord deference for the privacy of all citizens and added to those values the necessity for protection of the public interest in candid, objective, and even blunt or harsh opinions in Presidential decision-making. A President and those who assist him must be free to explore alternatives in the process of shaping policies and making decisions and to do so in a way many would be unwilling to express except privately. These are the considerations justifying a presumptive privilege for Presidential communications. The privilege is fundamental to the operation of government and inextricably rooted in the separation of powers under the Constitution. . . .

But this presumptive privilege must be considered in light of our historic commitment to the rule of law. This is nowhere more profoundly manifest than in our view that "the twofold aim [of criminal justice] is that the guilty shall not escape or innocent suffer." *Berger* v. *United States* . . . (1935). We have elected to employ an adversary system of criminal justice in which the parties contest all issues before a court of law. The need to develop all relevant facts in the adversary system is both fundamental and comprehensive. The ends of criminal justice would be defeated if judgments were to be founded on a partial or speculative presentation of the facts. The very integrity of the judicial system and public confidence in the system depend on full disclosure of all the facts, within the framework of the rules of evidence.

To ensure that justice is done, it is imperative to the functions of courts that compulsory process be available for the production of evidence needed either by the prosecution or by the defense. . . .

In this case the President challenges a subpoena served on him as a third party requiring the production of materials for use in a criminal prosecution on the claim that he has a privilege against disclosure of confidential communications. He does not place his claim of privilege on the ground they are military or diplomatic secrets. As to these areas of Art. II duties the courts have traditionally shown the utmost deference to Presidential responsibilities. . . .

No case of the Court, however, has extended this high degree of deference to a President's generalized interest in confidentiality. Nowhere in the Constitution, as we have noted earlier, is there any explicit reference to a privilege of confidentiality, yet to the extent this interest relates to the effective discharge of a President's powers, it is constitutionally based.

The right to the production of all evidence at a criminal trial similarly has constitutional dimensions. The Sixth Amendment explicitly confers upon every defendant in a criminal trial the right "to be confronted with the witnesses against him" and "to have compulsory process for obtaining witnesses in his favor." Moreover, the Fifth Amendment also guarantees that no person shall be deprived of liberty without due process of law. It is the manifest duty of the courts to vindicate those guarantees and to accomplish that it is essential that all relevant and admissible evidence be produced.

In this case we must weigh the importance of the general privilege of confidentiality of Presidential communications in performance of his responsibilities against the inroads of such a privilege of the fair administration of criminal justice. The interest in preserving confidentiality is weighty indeed and entitled to great respect. However we cannot conclude that advisers will be moved to temper the candor of their remarks by the infrequent occasions of disclosure because of the possibility that such conversations will be called for in the context of a criminal prosecution.

On the other hand, the allowance of the privilege to withhold evidence that is demonstrably relevant in a criminal trial would cut deeply into the guarantee of due process of law and gravely impair the basic function of the courts. A President's acknowledged need for confidentiality in the communications of his office is general in nature, whereas the constitutional need for production of relevant evidence in a criminal proceeding is specific and central to the fair adjudication of a particular criminal case in the administration of justice.

Without access to specific facts a criminal prosecution may be totally frustrated. The President's broad interest in confidentiality of communications will not be vitiated by disclosure of a limited number of conversations preliminarily shown to have some bearing on the pending criminal cases.

We conclude that when the ground for asserting privilege as to subpoenaed materials sought for use in a criminal trial is based only on the generalized interest in confidentiality, it cannot prevail over the fundamental demands of due process of law in the fair administration of criminal justice. The generalized assertion of privilege must yield to the demonstrated, specific need for evidence in a pending criminal trial. . . .

Enforcement of the subpoena duces tecum was stayed pending this Court's resolution of the issues raised by the petitions for certiorari. Those issues now having been disposed of, the matter of implementation will rest with the District Court. "[T]he guard, furnished to [the President] to protect him from being harassed by vexatious and unnecessary subpoenas, is to be looked for in the con-duct of the [district] Court after the subpoenas have issued; not in any circumstances which is to precede their being issued." *United States* v. *Burr.* Statements that meet the test of admissibility and relevance must be isolated; all other materials must be excised. At this stage, the District Court is not limited to representations of the special prosecutor as to the evidence sought by the subpoena; the material will be available to the District Court. It is elementary that *in camera* inspection of evidence is always a procedure calling for scrupulous protection against any release or publication of material not found by the Court, at that stage, probably admissible in evidence and relevant to the issues of the trial for which it is sought. That being true of an ordinary situation, it is obvious that the District Court has a very heavy responsibility to see to it that Presidential conversations, which are either not relevant or not admissible, are accorded that high degree of respect due the President of the United States. Mr. Chief Justice Marshall sitting as a trial judge in the *Burr* case, supra, was extraordinarily careful to point out that:

[I]n no case of this kind would a court be required to proceed against the President as against an ordinary individual. United States *v.* Burr . . .

Since the matter came before the Court during the pendency of a criminal prosecution, and on representations that time is of the essence, the mandate should issue forthwith.

Affirmed.

[During the tapes controversy, James St. Clair was asked if President Nixon would surrender the tapes if ordered to do so by the Supreme Court. Shortly thereafter, he announced that the President would obey a "definitive order" of the Supreme Court. Whatever the word "definitive" was supposed to mean, a unanimous decision of the Court that included three justices appointed by President Nixon had the ring of "definitiveness" to it. The tapes were publicly released and, it turned out, contained fatally damaging evidence of the president's participation in the cover-up—for example, the "smoking gun."

After the Court's decision was announced on July 25, 1974, but before the tapes were released, the Judiciary Committee of the House of Representatives, following months of testimony and debate, voted to recommend the impeachment of Richard Nixon on three counts relating to the Watergate episode (details are presented in the next section). After the release of the tapes revealed conclusive evidence of the President's participation in an illegal cover-up, the Judiciary Committee voted 38-0 to recommend impeachment to the full House of Representatives. At that point, impeachment and conviction by the Senate seemed certain.

St. Clair's brief for President Nixon in the *Tapes Case* closed by stating that if Judge Sirica's order was upheld, "that decision will alter the nature of the American Presidency profoundly and irreparably." Such a self-serving prophecy of doom was accurate in only one respect. The Court's upholding of Judge Sirica did have a profound and irreparable effect on the presidency of Richard Nixon: it ended it. Nixon resigned on August 9, 1974, stating that he "no longer [had] a strong enough political base in the Congress" to continue in office.

On September 8, 1974, President Gerald Ford granted Nixon a "full, free, and absolute pardon . . . for all of the offenses against the United States which he . . . has committed or may have committed" while serving as president.

As to the "nature of the American presidency," the effect of *United States* v. *Nixon* is, at best uncertain. Very much like the *Steel Seizure Case,* the Supreme Court decided against a particular claim of presidential power while conceding a broad residue of power to the presidency—in that case, a residue of "inherent powers" and in this one of "executive privilege." In fact, *United States* v. *Nixon,* over the

long run, may strengthen the presidency by its recognition of executive privilege. No previous Supreme Court decision had ever formally recognized its existence.

In his book, *The Imperial Presidency,* Arthur Schlesinger writes that the traditional view of presidential privilege with regard to congressional inquiries was "disclosure with exceptions." There were a number of recorded instances—perhaps a dozen—in which presidents had, in fact, withheld information requested by Congress. But no president had ever claimed a general and absolute prerogative to "withhold" information from Congress.

World War II, says Schlesinger, helped to bring forth a different view of the presidency in general, and a different concept of presidential privilege. The Congress and the country acquired an exalted view of what was rapidly becoming, in Schlesinger's terms, an "imperial" presidency. The loyalty–security issue, including the Army-McCarthy hearings in 1954, which focused in part on a demand for information from the Secretary of the Army, put the Eisenhower administration on the "militant defensive."

In responding to Senator Joseph McCarthy's attacks, the Eisenhower administration claimed—with much public sympathy and accord—that there were certain types of information that the president could refuse to disclose at will: ". . . material generated by the internal deliberative processes of government [because] disclosure . . . would inhibit free debate within the executive branch and dry up the flow of candid analysis and recommendations necessary to wise decisions." The privilege was applied to cover everyone in the executive branch. Indeed, the term "executive privilege" was first coined and used by Eisenhower's attorney general (and later Nixon's secretary of state), William Rogers. In Schlesinger's view, the rule that formerly had been "disclosure with exceptions" now became "denial with exceptions."

This was the basis of the Nixon administration's claim to an absolute and unreviewable privilege that applied, at the discretion of the president, to the entire executive branch of government. It was at the core of St. Clair's brief and oral argument in the *Tapes Case*. This claim, coming as it did from an unpopular president charged with serious personal wrongdoing, and coming at a time when presidential power generally was on the defensive, was much less attractive and compelling than when President Eisenhower had made an essentially similar claim to ward off Senator McCarthy in the 1950s. Furthermore, this claim of executive privilege was not in response to a congressional inquest (there was such an inquest, of course, the Senate Watergate Hearings) but to a subpoena issued by a federal judge in the context of a criminal prosecution. All things considered, therefore, the doctrine of executive privilege came out of the *Tapes Case* in better shape than most people would have predicted. It is true that the Supreme Court clearly and specifically rejected the St. Clair-Nixon theory of an absolute and unreviewable executive privilege. But at the same time, it also rejected the counter argument of scholar-advocates like Raoul Berger. In his book *Executive Privilege,* Berger contends that there is no constitutional basis for an assertion of executive privilege under any circumstances.

Thus the net result is that there is now a constitutionally recognized executive privilege of very uncertain boundaries. It applies only to communications "in performance of a [president's] responsibilities . . . of his office" . . . and made "in the process of shaping policies and making decisions." It is not absolute but must be weighed against competing claims, particularly claims arising out of the need for evidence in a criminal prosecution. An asserted privilege that depends on a broad, undifferentiated claim to protect the public interest, and that is not specified as necessary to protect military, diplomatic, or sensitive national security secrets, cannot be accorded much weight. On the other hand, there is at least an implication in Chief Justice Burger's opinion that claims resting on bona fide national security or diplomatic considerations may come close to being entitled to an absolute privilege of nondisclosure. How the privilege would fare against a congressional demand for information remains an open question.

Since the privilege rests on a constitutional basis, there are questions of whether Congress may enact guidelines defining (and presumably limiting) its scope. One partial answer came in the "second" *Nixon Tapes Case, Nixon* v. *Administrator of General Services* (1977). To counteract an agreement that Mr. Nixon—after his resignation—had made with the General Services Administration (GSA) for storage of and limited public access to his presidential papers (42 million documents) and tape recordings (880 tapes), Congress passed the Presidential Recordings and Materials Preservation Act. The act directed the GSA administrator to take custody of all the materials, screen them, return to Nixon all materials that were personal and private in nature, and prepare the rest for eventual public access. The administrator was to ensure the availability of all materials that might be needed in any judicial proceedings.

Nixon filed suit to recover control of the papers. He claimed the act violated his personal privacy and First Amendment rights of freedom of association, the Bill of Attainder clause, the principle of separation of powers, and executive privilege. All claims were rejected by a three-judge federal district court, and Nixon appealed to the Supreme Court. By a 7-2 vote, the Court upheld the validity of the act.

It rejected the separation of powers claim largely because the act was the joint product of Congress and the President (albeit a different president) and because it was not "unduly disruptive" of the executive branch. The Court left open the possibility that, in the future, any particular use of the papers or tapes might be challenged by a *valid* claim of presidential privilege. Nixon had argued that the separation of powers requires that each of the three branches of government must remain "entirely free from the control or coercive influence, direct or indirect, of either of the others." But the Court found this to be an "archaic view of the separation of powers [which required] three airtight departments of government." Instead the Court chose to follow the more flexible concept of separation of powers reflected by Justice Jackson's concurring opinion in the *Steel Seizure Case.*

The claim of presidential privilege was complicated. Whereas such a claim had been made against the judicial branch in the *Tapes Case,* here it was being made "against the very Executive Branch in whose name the privilege is invoked." Because of this, some of the appellees in the case had asserted that the privilege of the claim was available only to an incumbent president. The district court found that at least an incumbent president has a *stronger* claim to invoking presidential privilege, but it did not hold that a former president could never invoke it. The Supreme Court, however, held that the claim is available to a former president:

This Court held in United States v. Nixon *(1974) that the privilege is necessary to provide the confidentiality required for the President's conduct of office. Unless he can give his advisers some assurance of confidentiality, a President could not expect to receive the full and frank submissions of facts and opinions upon which effective discharge of his duties depends. The confidentiality necessary to this exchange cannot be measured by the few months or years between the submission of the information and the end of the President's tenure; the privilege is not for the benefit of the President as an individual, but for the benefit of the Republic. Therefore the privilege survives the individual President's tenure.*

But, the Court said, the fact that neither of Nixon's successors, Ford and Carter, supported his claim certainly detracted from it.

Having granted that Nixon could claim the privilege, however, the Court then declined to apply it in this case. The Court noted that Nixon could only assert the privilege "as to those materials whose contents fall within the scope of the privilege recognized in *United States* v. *Nixon.* . . . In that case the Court held that the privilege is limited to communications 'in performance of [a President's] responsibilities . . . of his office' and made 'in the process of shaping policies and making decisions.' " But the district court concluded that, at most, the claim of privilege would—or could—apply to about 200,000 items with which Nixon was personally familiar. The Supreme Court decided that the

mere screening of these items by the General Services Administration under the procedures of the act—which was all it was called upon to decide in this case—constituted at most a very limited intrusion. Congress was justified in establishing these procedures to protect and preserve these documents for the public good and to aid Congress itself in the performance of its functions. Sufficient safeguards were incorporated to prevent misuse of the papers. Hence, "the claims of Presidential privilege clearly must yield to the important congressional purposes of preserving the materials and maintaining access to them for lawful government and historical purposes."

In closing his opinion for the Court, Justice Brennan wrote:

We, of course, are not blind to appellant's plea that we recognize the social and political realities of 1974. It was a period of political turbulence unprecedented in our history. But this Court is not free to invalidate acts of Congress based upon inferences that we may be asked to draw from our personalized reading of the contemporary scene or recent history. In judging the constitutionality of the Act, we may only look to its terms, to the intent expressed by Members of Congress who voted it passage, and to the existence or nonexistence of legitimate explanations for its apparent effects. We are persuaded that none of these factors is suggestive that the Act is a punitive Bill of Attainder, or otherwise facially unconstitutional.]

(2) A Note on Impeachment as a Limitation on Presidential Power

In 1973, as the political fires of Watergate were building and there was serious talk of impeaching President Nixon, Arthur Schlesinger wrote: "The genius of impeachment lies in the fact that it can punish the man without punishing the office. . . . The trick is to preserve presidential power but to deter Presidents from abusing that power."[1] Schlesinger's distinguished career as a historian of the presidency has often fused into his alternative role as a political actor and advocate. Separating the two roles is not always easy, at least not for his readers. Thus, in the context in which it was written, his statement may be read as partisan advocacy, an effort to give scholarly legitimacy to impeachment efforts still then in the gestation stage. To be sure, it was part of a larger study of the abuse of presidential power later published as *The Imperial Presidency*. But quite clearly, it was an attack on the "runaway" Nixon presidency, one which, Schlesinger charged, "is not an aberration but a culmination. It carries to reckless extremes a compulsion toward presidential power rising out of deep running changes in the foundations of society." And then he added:

Watergate is potentially the best thing to have happened to the presidency in a long time. If the trials are followed to their end, many, many years will pass before another White House staff dares to take the liberties with the Constitution and the laws the Nixon White House has taken. If the nation wants to work its way back to a constitutional presidency, there is only one way to begin. That is by showing Presidents that, when their closest associates place themselves above the law and the Constitution, such transgressions will be not forgiven or forgotten for the sake of the presidency, but exposed and punished for the sake of the presidency.[2]

Whatever Schlesinger's purpose, however self-serving his scholarship,

the question he raises is of fundamental importance. How can the abuse of presidential power be limited without seriously damaging the office? The problem is that whatever the intention of the framers as to how and when the impeachment process should work, it has, in fact, been used only rarely. It is a cumbersome process and a drastic and disruptive remedy to curb presidential abuse. For these reasons, it has not been a deterrent in the past, and it is unlikely to be an important deterrent to presidential action in the future. The impeachment hearings against Richard Nixon showed just how devastating such proceedings could be to the ability of a president to govern, to say nothing of its effect on Congress and the government in general. More than genius is needed, it would seem, to punish the president without punishing the office. Absent a repetition of the pattern of gross misconduct that brought on the Nixon impeachment and ultimately forced him from office, impeachment is likely to remain a last resort.

Impeachment is the sole method of removing a president from office before the expiration of his term.[3] It applies to other officers of the government, including judges, but the principal concern of the framers of the Constitution in writing the impeachment provisions was with curbing presidential power. Impeachment provided some reassurance that the president would never regard himself as infallible or as above the law. It was to be a "constitutional safeguard of the public trust."[4]

[1]Arthur M. Schlesinger, Jr., "The Runaway Presidency," *Atlantic Monthly* (Boston Mass., Atlantic Monthly Co. 1973), p. 54.

[2]*Ibid.*, p. 55.

[3]See generally, Raoul Berger, *Impeachment* (Cambridge: Harvard University Press, 1973); and Charles L. Black, Jr., *Impeachment: A Handbook* (New Haven: Yale University Press, 1974).

[4]Committee on the Judiciary, House of Representatives, *Constitutional Grounds for Presidential Impeachment: Report by the Staff of the Impeachment Inquiry*, 93rd Congress, 2nd Session (1974), p. 8.

The main constitutional provisions for impeachment are set forth in Article I, Sections 2 and 3, and Article II, Section 4. Article I, Section 2, provides that the House of Representatives "shall have the sole power of impeachment." Impeachment by the House is by majority vote. Article I, Section 3, provides that the Senate shall have the sole power to *try* impeachments. It also provides that when the president is tried, the Chief Justice shall preside and that conviction must be by a vote of two-thirds of the members present. Although the Senate is not a traditional "court," when it tries an impeachment it is certainly performing at least a quasi-judicial function. Nevertheless, it is not limited by the due process clause of the Fifth Amendment or by the other portions of the Bill of Rights that govern the functioning of the courts. Nor is it bound to follow the rules of judicial procedure regarding cross-examination, evidence, and the like set down by the Supreme Court. But to ensure that its decision will be regarded politically as legitimate, the Senate is likely to follow very closely the contemporary consensus that defines a "fair trial." This was certainly true with regard to the arrangements made to try President Nixon if he had in fact been impeached.

Article II, Section 4, provides that the president, vice-president, and all civil officers of the United States shall be removed from office on "Impeachment for, and conviction of, Treason, Bribery, or other high Crimes and Misdemeanors." Judges are included but not officers of the military nor members of Congress, who are not regarded as "civil officers of the United States." In fact, Article I, Section 6, provides that "no person holding office under the United States may be a member of Congress." And the Constitution specifically provides that each House is to be the judge of the qualifications and conduct of its own members. These provisions, read together, are strong evidence that members of Congress are not subject to impeachment.

Article III, Section 2, excepts impeachments from the requirement of trial by jury. And Article I, Section 3, states that the only consequence of conviction on impeachment charges is removal from office and disqualification to hold any "office of honor, Trust or Profit under the United States." However, a person convicted on impeachment charges is liable to ordinary criminal laws after removal from office. Since impeachment is not a criminal process and removal from office is not a "punishment," the potential for subsequent criminal prosecution raises no problem of double jeopardy. A person may be impeached *after* resigning from an office, since conviction on impeachment charges also results in disqualification from holding any federal governmental office in the future.

Only thirteen officers of the United States have been impeached by the House of Representatives: President Andrew Johnson in 1868, Secretary of War William Belknap in 1876, Senator William Blount in 1797, and ten federal judges, including Supreme Court justice Samuel Chase in 1804. Four judges were convicted, several were acquitted, including Justice Chase, and a few resigned before or during the proceedings. Blount resigned from the Senate in disgrace before it considered charges against him. The vote against Belknap was insufficient to meet the constitutional requirements, but he resigned before the proceedings were completed. The Senate failed to convict Andrew Johnson by just one vote.

The impeachment proceedings against Richard Nixon raised two troublesome constitutional questions, one crucial to the outcome in that case, the other more speculative and never actually decided. The crucial and immediate question concerned the grounds for impeachment. Treason is defined elsewhere in the Constitution and was not, in any case, at issue in these proceedings. Neither was bribery, which has an established legal definition. If Nixon was to be impeached, it would be because he had been guilty of "other high crimes and misdemeanors." But what does that term mean?

Basically, there are three interpretations, or classes of interpretations. The first was exemplified best by then Representative Gerald Ford who, in 1970, led the fight to impeach Justice William O. Douglas. Ford declared that an impeachable offense is whatever the House and Senate jointly consider it to be: or, as former Attorney General Richard Kleindienst said: "You don't need facts, you don't need evidence to impeach the President, all you need is votes."[5] If this interpretation was correct, then impeachment would be little more than a form of congressional recall. There is no evidence that the framers of the Constitution intended impeachment to be quite so unprincipled. Certainly, it would be most difficult to justify publicly removing a president elected by the voters because a majority of Congress simply did not like him or his policies. In a practical sense, of course, Congressman Ford was correct. But impeachment of a president on such flimsy grounds would make a mockery of the process. The care taken by the House Judiciary Committee in preparing the articles of impeach-

ment against President Nixon, and its hearings on those articles, is the much more likely model for the future.

The second interpretation of the minimum grounds for impeachment, the one advanced by James St. Clair in behalf of President Nixon, is that an indictable criminal offense is required, perhaps only an offense relating to the president's conduct in office. Advocates of this position argue that this is a knowable and reasonably precise standard. If the committee had adopted this formulation, it would have been hard-pressed to formulate charges when it did, because at that time—before the *Nixon Tapes* decision and subsequent revelation of the "smoking gun" evidence of criminal misconduct—it was generally conceded that there was no conclusive evidence that Nixon had, in fact, committed an indictable criminal offense.

The Judiciary Committee staff, after extensive research, recommended to the committee that neither of these interpretations be accepted.[6] Instead, the staff's report contended that while impeachment might proceed only on the basis of an indictable offense, it was primarily concerned with the commission of constitutional wrongs: "grave misconduct that . . . injures or abuses our constitutional institutions and form of government. . . ." They reported that "high crimes and misdemeanors" was a term with a special historical meaning different from the ordinary meaning of the words "crimes" and "misdemeanors." Moreover, the framers apparently were aware that since the fourteenth century the term "high crimes

---

[5]Quoted in Raoul Berger, "Impeachment: An Instrument of Regeneration," *Harper's* (January, 1974), pp. 14–22.
[6]*Constitutional Grounds. . ., op. cit.,* Note 4.

and misdemeanors" was a "term of art" which referred to official abuses of power and attempts to subvert fundamental principles of English government.

There is also direct evidence that the framers intended to use the phrase "high crimes and misdemeanors" in this special way in the Constitution. Originally, the draft Constitution provided that a president could be impeached only for treason and bribery. That was thought to be too limited. George Mason of Virginia then moved to add the word "maladministration," a word used in the impeachment clauses of six of the thirteen state constitutions, including Virginia. James Madison objected that "so vague a term will be equivalent to a tenure during pleasure of the Senate." Mason then withdrew "maladministration" and substituted "high crimes and misdemeanors." This was adopted by a vote of eight states to three, and debate ended. The clear inference is that Mason believed that "high crimes and misdemeanors" would cover the offenses he originally described more graphically as "maladministration."

What the convention and ratification debates show is that impeachment was not intended as a punishment merely for political mistakes or errors of judgment. It was not to be taken lightly. On the other hand, it was a political and not a criminal process, designed to remedy political wrongs committed by the president or other officers of the government. Ten of the thirteen subsequent impeachment cases included one or more counts that did not charge a violation of criminal law. Impeachment is a remedial process. Its primary intent is not to punish a wrongdoing president but to preserve and maintain a constitutional system of government. It is, in the committee staff's words, "a constitutional safety valve." A president can be impeached for committing an ordinary crime, but he can also "be called to account for abusing powers that only a President possesses."[7]

The second issue is the more speculative one. Suppose that President Nixon had been impeached? And if impeached, that he was convicted by a vote of two-thirds of the Senate and ordered removed from office? Would he have had any recourse to the courts to challenge that impeachment and removal? Almost certainly he would have sought relief in the courts, challenging in particular the grounds on which he had been impeached and tried. Can a president be removed who has not committed an indictable criminal offense, or was the House Judiciary Committee correct in interpreting the phrase "high crimes and misdemeanors" to include, besides actual criminal conduct, abuses of constitutional power? Alternatively, could Nixon have challenged some procedural defect in the proceedings against him—perhaps lack of a quorum, or inability to cross-examine witnesses, or the like?

The Constitution does not provide for judicial review of impeachment. The House of Representatives is expressly given the "sole" power to impeach, and the Senate is delegated the power to try impeachments, with the Chief Justice presiding when the president is impeached. In an early draft of the Constitution, the power to try impeachments was originally lodged in the Supreme Court but was then transferred to the Senate. This is often interpreted to mean that the framers decided that they did not

[7]*Ibid.*, p. 25.

want to involve the courts in the impeachment process, and it is one of the strongest arguments against judicial review of impeachment. Moreover, could a Chief Justice who presided over an impeachment trial then participate with the rest of the Court in reviewing that trial? It would seem as if the role of the Chief Justice in presiding over an impeachment trial was intended to be the exclusive judicial input into that procedure.

There are other arguments. One, as Charles Black notes, is the complete lack of a constitutional or statutory base for jurisdiction.[8] Quite clearly, Article III does not comprehend this kind of suit within the Court's *original* jurisdiction. But what about its *appellate* jurisdiction? Article III gives to the Supreme Court appellate jurisdiction "over all cases in law and equity arising under this Constitution." But the terms "law and equity" have a specific historical meaning, and as used in English law, they did *not* include impeachments. Impeachment, it may be argued, is a unique, quasi-legal process, as much political as legal. Article III exempts impeachments from the trial by jury requirement, thereby clearly denoting it as something different from an ordinary trial at law.

Black also argues that the Supreme Court could not hear such a case because Congress has not granted it the power to do so. The words of Article III suggest that Congress merely has the right to regulate the appellate jurisdiction of the Court ("with such exceptions and with such regulations as the Congress shall make"). But, in fact, as noted earlier in this book, the prevailing rule has been that Congress *grants* the Court what appellate jurisdiction it has, and it is assumed that whatever Con-

gress does *not* grant, the Court does *not* have. As a practical matter, Black suggests, it would be impossible to secure an appeal to the Supreme Court from impeachment because there would be no statutory basis of jurisdiction.

It is possible that an impeached president might bring suit in the lower courts, claiming that he had been wrongfully convicted of the charges and that this constituted a violation of his civil rights. Black argues that there is no basis for lower court jurisdiction either, but this is not as convincing an argument. It is true that the framers of the Constitution certainly never comprehended any involvement of the lower federal courts (which, after all, had not even been established yet) in the impeachment process. And it is true that such a case would not fit neatly under any of the jurisdictional categories: suits in admiralty, diversity of citizenship suits, or civil actions arising under the laws and the Constitution "where the amount in controversy exceeds $10,000." However, a suit that sought damages for wrongful removal would certainly exceed the $10,000 jurisdictional floor. And the development of civil rights law is of very recent vintage. Whether or not an incumbent president, duly elected, has a "right" to that office for the *prescribed* term of years, unless removed by the proper constitutional procedures, is a question never answered. Finally, it is at least possible that the *issues* in the case could be tested by a suit for back pay in the Court of Claims, following the precedent of *Humphrey's Executor* v. *United States* (1935). But a victory there would not, alone, entitle a removed president to reclaim that office.

Even if the Supreme Court did

---

[8]Black, *op. cit.*, Note 3, pp. 53–63.

agree to review the impeachment and removal of a president, might it not then decide that it is a nonjusticiable political question? It would seem from the plain words of the Constitution that impeachment and the trial of impeachment are functions exclusively committed to another branch of government by the express words of the Constitution, one of the marks of a political question. Second, what is the remedy the Court would grant if it decided the substantive issues in favor of the president? Could it order him removed from office and enforce that order? Alternatively, suppose the Court agrees with the president's contention and orders him reinstated in office in place of the former vice-president who has been sworn in and assumed the office of president in the meantime? Who would be president? Which, if either, of the "two" presidents would have the legitimacy to govern?[9]

The strength of the case *against* judicial review of impeachments must be tested against the contrary position. And there is a respectable counter argument to be made in favor of judicial review of impeachments.[10] First, the absence of specific mention of judicial review of impeachment in the Constitution is irrelevant, since judicial review itself is not mentioned in the Constitution. Second, the Constitution does not permit the president to be impeached for *any* reason but only for "treason, bribery, and high crimes and misdemeanors." If a president were impeached for some lesser reason, he would have been deprived arbitrarily of his constitutional rights but would be without an appropriate remedy. Suppose, for

example, that the president was impeached for a reason so trivial that it was not even a case of "maladministration"?

The case of *Powell* v. *McCormack* (1968) may be read to stand for the proposition that Congress is obliged to follow constitutional standards and that it is a necessary and proper judicial function to intervene where standards have not been followed. Judicial review in that case was *not* foreclosed by the doctrine of political questions.

There is a constitutional maxim that "there is no place in our system for the exercise of arbitrary power."[11] Raoul Berger argues that because Congress has the "sole" power to legislate, this does not immunize it from accountability for arbitrary actions. Arbitrary action that exceeds those limits would violate the due process clause of the Fifth Amendment.[12] If there are constitutional standards, and if they have not been followed, does it not follow that Congress, by exceeding *its* jurisdiction, has dissolved whatever barriers may have existed to full judicial review?[13] (But compare Chief Justice Burger's opinion in *United States* v. *Richardson* (1974) where, in rejecting a challenge to force Congress to publicly reveal the budget of the CIA, Burger observed that there is not necessarily a judicial remedy for every constitutional wrong.)

The first part of the argument favoring judicial review, made most effectively by Berger, hinges on an interpretation of *Powell* v. *McCormack* that is not universally shared. Many contend that the *Powell* case stands, not for the broad proposition

[9]cf. William Safire, *Full Disclosure* (Garden City, N.Y.: Doubleday, 1977).

[10]Berger, *op. cit.*, Note 3, Chapter 3.

[11]*Yick Wo* v. *Hopkins* (1886).

[12]Berger, *op. cit.*, Note 3, p. 120.

[13]*Ibid.* p. 112.

that the Court may review *any* congressional act that exceeds constitutional limits, but for the more limited proposition that the House of Representatives could not *exclude* a duly elected member, who met all the constitutional qualifications for the office, merely for misconduct. But this was because the Constitution enumerates three standards for exclusion: age, citizenship, and residence, and Powell met all of those standards. The House might have *expelled* Powell for misconduct had it elected to do so, but it could not *exclude* him. Exclusion and expulsion, the Court held, were entirely different, not fungible, procedures. If one compares the "age, citizenship, and residence" standards for exclusion, however, with the "high crimes and misdemeanors" language in the impeachment clause, it is clear that the meaning of the latter is not self-evident, while the meaning of the former is. Therefore, it might be argued, the grounds for impeachment are matters for Congress to decide and therefore are nonjusticiable political questions.

Whether an impeachment/conviction decision violates the *individual* constitutional rights of the president is a question that must also be answered. If removal from the presidency implies the loss of a personal right protected by the Constitution, then the argument for judicial involvement would be strong. As Berger notes, an individual who enters government service does not cease to be a "person" within the meaning of the Fifth Amendment. On the other hand, if impeachment is not punishment in the legal sense (it

is, of course, punishment in the social and political sense) or if it is not the deprivation of a personal constitutional right but merely a remedial action by Congress to protect the integrity of a constitutional office that no one has a "right" to occupy, then there is little justification for judicial intervention. That impeachment is not "punishment" in the constitutional sense is implied by the words of that document. A president who is impeached and convicted is not immunized from subsequent accountability for those same offenses if they also constitute criminal conduct. Yet, if the impeachment and conviction constituted a "punishment," the Constitution would have authorized proceedings in violation of the ban on double jeopardy.

There are some Supreme Court cases holding that whenever the government sets up a procedure to separate its employees, it must follow its own rules.[14] But those were cases involving primarily administrative determinations. And there is certainly an argument to be made that impeachment/conviction and removal of a president is *sui generis*.

Of course, all of this debate is purely speculative. What the Supreme Court might do if confronted with a petition by a president to review his impeachment and/or conviction cannot be predicted (or, alternatively, a petition by the president pro tem of the Senate seeking judicial enforcement of a Senate verdict of conviction and removal that the president has failed to honor). In an interview with the press, Justice Rehnquist was quoted as saying, in this context, that "the Supreme Court has

---

[14]*Vitarelli v. Seaton* (1959).
[15]*Milwaukee Journal*, January 23, 1974, p. 3.

the ability to reverse any conviction it wants to, any conviction that five justices want to reverse."[15]

(3) Articles of Impeachment Against President Richard M. Nixon

[At the end of July 1974, the House Judiciary voted to recommend impeachment of President Nixon on three charges. The votes in favor of impeachment were 27-11, 28-10, and 21-17, respectively. Two additional counts were defeated by a vote of 12-26. One dealt with Mr. Nixon's secret bombing of Cambodia, the other with alleged violations of the income tax laws.]

Resolved, that Richard M. Nixon, President of the United States, is impeached for high crimes and misdemeanors, and that the following articles of impeachment be exhibited to the Senate:

Articles of impeachment exhibited by the House of Representatives of the United States of America in the name of itself and of all the people of the United States of America, against Richard Nixon, President of the United States of America, in maintenance and support of its impeachment against him for high crimes and misdemeanors.

Article I

In his conduct of the office of President of the United States, Richard M. Nixon, in violation of his constitutional oath faithfully to execute the office of President of the United States and, to the best of his ability, preserve, protect, and defend the Constitution of the United States, and in violation of his consitutional duty to take care that the laws be faithfully executed, has prevented, obstructed, and impeded the administration of justice, in that:

On June 17, 1972, and prior thereto, agents of the Committee for the Re-election of the President committed unlawful entry of the headquarters of the Democratic National Committee in Washington, District of Columbia, for the purpose of securing political intelligence. Subsequent thereto, Richard M. Nixon, using the powers of his high office, engaged, personally and through his subordinates and agents, in a course of conduct or plan designed to delay, impede, and obstruct the investigation of such unlawful entry; to cover up, conceal and protect those responsible; and to conceal the existence and scope of other unlawful covert activities.

The means used to implement this course of conduct or plan included one or more of the following:

1. Making or causing to be made false or misleading statements to lawfully authorized investigative officers and employees of the United States;

2. Withholding relevant and material evidence or information from lawfully authorized investigative officers and employees of the United States;

3. Approving, condoning, acquiescing in, and counseling witnesses with respect to the giving of false or misleading statements to lawfully authorized investigative officers and employees of the United States and false or misleading testimony in duly instituted judicial and congressional proceedings;

4. Interfering or endeavoring to interfere with the conduct of investigations by the Department of Justice of the United States, the Federal Bureau of Investigation, the Office of Watergate Special Prosecution Force, and Congressional committees;

5. Approving, condoning, and acquiescing in, the surreptitious payment of substantial sums of money for the purpose of obtaining the silence or influencing the testimony of witnesses, potential witnesses or individuals who participated in such illegal entry and other illegal activities;

6. Endeavoring to misuse the Central Intelligence Agency, an agency of the United States;

7. Disseminating information received from officers of the Department of Justice of the United States to subjects of investigations conducted by lawfully authorized investigative officers and employees of the United States, for the purpose of aiding and assisting such subjects in their attempts to avoid criminal liability;

8. Making false or misleading public statements for the purpose of deceiving the people of the United States into believing that a thorough and complete investigation had been conducted with respect to allegations of misconduct on the part of personnel of the executive branch of the United States and personnel of the Committee for the Re-election of the President, and that there was no involvement of such personnel in such misconduct; or

9. Endeavoring to cause prospective defendants, and individuals duly tried and convicted, to expect favored treatment and consideration in return for their silence or false testimony, or rewarding individuals for their silence or false testimony.

In all of this, Richard M. Nixon has acted in a manner contrary to his trust as President and subversive of constitutional government, to the great prejudice of the cause of law and justice and to the manifest injury of the people of the United States.

Wherefore Richard M. Nixon, by such conduct, warrants impeachment and trial, and removal from office.

Article II

Using the powers of the office of President of the United States, Richard M. Nixon, in violation of his constitutional oath faithfully to execute the office of President of the United States and, to the best of his ability, preserve, protect and defend the Constitution of the United States, and in disregard of his constitutional duty to take care that the laws be faithfully executed, has repeatedly engaged in conduct violating the constitutional rights of citizens, impairing the due and proper administration of justice and the conduct of lawful inquiries, or contravening the laws governing agencies of the executive branch and the purposes of these agencies.

This conduct has included one or more of the following:

1. He has, acting personally and through his subordinates and agents, endeavored to obtain from the International Revenue Service, in violation of the constitutional rights of citizens, confidential information contained in income tax returns for purposes not authorized by law and to cause, in violation of the constitutional rights of citizens, income tax audits or other income tax investigations to be initiated or conducted in a discriminatory manner.

2. He misused the Federal Bureau of Investigation, the Secret Service and other executive personnel in violation or disregard of the constitutional rights of citizens by directing or authorizing such agencies or personnel to conduct or continue electronic surveillance or other investiga-

tions for purposes unrelated to national security, the enforcement of laws or any other lawful function of his office; and he did direct the concealment of certain records made by the Federal Bureau of Investigation of electronic surveillance.

3. He has, acting personally and through his subordinates and agents, in violation or disregard of the constitutional rights of citizens, authorized and permitted to be maintained a secret investigative unit within the office of the president, financed in part with money derived from campaign contributions to him, which unlawfully utilized the resources of the Central Intelligence Agency, engaged in covert and unlawful activities and attempted to prejudice the constitutional right of an accused to a fair trial.

4. He has failed to take care that the laws were faithfully executed by failing to act when he knew or had reason to know that his close subordinates endeavored to impede and frustrate lawful inquiries by duly constituted executive, judicial and legislative entities concerning the unlawful entry into the headquarters of the Democratic National Committee and the cover-up thereof, and concerning other unlawful activities including those relating to the confirmation of Richard Kleindienst as attorney general of the United States, the electronic surveillance of private citizens, the break-in into the office of Dr. Lewis Fielding and the campaign financing practices of the Committee to Re-elect the President.

5. In disregard of the rule of law, he knowingly misused the executive power by interfering with agencies of the executive branch, including the Federal Bureau of Investigation, the Criminal Division and the Office of Watergate Special Prosecution Force, of the Department of Justice and the Central Intelligence Agency, in violation of his duty to take care that the laws be faithfully executed.

In all of this, Richard M. Nixon has acted in a manner contrary to his trust as President and subversive of constitutional government, to the great prejudice of the cause of law and justice and to the manifest injury of the people of the United States.

Wherefore Richard M. Nixon, by such conduct, warrants impeachment and trial and removal from office.

Article III

In his conduct of the office of President of the United States, Richard M. Nixon, contrary to his oath faithfully to execute the office of president of the United States and to the best of his ability, preserve, protect and defend the Constitution of the United States, and in violation of his constitutional duty to take care that the laws be faithfully executed, has failed without lawful cause or excuse to produce papers and things as directed by duly authorized subpoenas issued by the Committee on the Judiciary of the House of Representatives on April 11, 1974; May 15, 1974; May 30, 1974, and June 24, 1974, and willfully disobeyed such subpoenas.

The subpoenaed papers and things were deemed necessary by the Committee in order to resolve by direct evidence fundamental, factual questions relating to presidential direction, knowledge or approval of actions demonstrated by other evidence to be substantial grounds for impeachment of the president.

In refusing to produce these papers and things Richard M. Nixon, substituting his judgment as to what materials were necessary for the inquiry, interposed the powers of the presidency against the lawful subpoenas of the House of Representatives, thereby assuming to himself functions and judgments necessary to the exercise of the sole power of impeachment vested by the Constitution in the House of Representatives.

In all of this, Richard M. Nixon has acted in a manner contrary to his trust as president and subversive of constitutional government, to the great prejudice of the cause of law and justice and to the manifest injury of the people of the United States.

Wherefore, Richard M. Nixon by such conduct, warrants impeachment and trial and removal from office.

C. Executive Impoundment of Funds

(1) Niles Stanton, The Presidency and the Purse

. . . The incident which is commonly recognized as the first recorded instance of impoundment in American history took place in 1803. In his Third Annual Message to Congress, President Jefferson announced that there remained unexpended $50,000 which Congress had appropriated for fifteen gunboats on the Mississippi River. He noted that a "favorable and peaceful turn of affairs . . . rendered . . . immediate [construction] unnecessary" and that more time would be taken to develop the best boat possible. A year and a half later, ten of the boats had been built and more were in progress.

The first truly significant impoundment of funds occurred in 1876, an instance which has heretofore received virtually no attention.

President Grant, upon signing an appropriations law for river and harbor projects, sent a message to the House of Representatives in which he announced that he would not expend all of the funds. The announcement sparked heated remarks in the House, but President Grant refused to alter his position. Pursuant to his instructions, Secretary of War Cameron and the chief of the Army Corps of Engineers spent only $2.3 million of the $5 million which Congress had appropriated.

The House of Representatives responded to the impoundment by passing a resolution which asked the President to state the legal authority for his position. The Secretary of War replied that the President's discretion with regard to spending was not limited except by the public interest and the condition of the treasury and that, in any event, the language of the appropriations act was permissive. In spite of this rather tenuous argument, the House—perhaps because some of the appropriations constituted pork-barrelling—let the matter drop.

Twenty years later, in the 1890's, it was firmly established, through four formal Opinions of United States Attorneys General, that it is the intent of Congress which must control whether the expenditure of appropriated funds is permissive or mandatory in a given situation. In the first Opinion, Attorney General Harmon agreed that permissive language in an appropriations measure gave the executive branch some discretion over expenditures. However, he emphasized that there was a duty to spend funds so long as the condition which Congress wanted corrected

Reprinted from Niles Stanton, "The Presidency and the Purse: Impoundment, 1803–1973," **45** *University of Colorado Law Review* (1973), 26–33.

still existed. The second Opinion indicated that, despite mandatory language in the law, it was not the intent of Congress to require full expenditure if a designated project could be completed for less. The third Attorney General Opinion declared that in the absence of language granting discretionary authority, the executive branch was not to consider the wisdom of congressionally approved projects and was to execute them to the extent that funds allowed. And the final Opinion held that permissive language in appropriations laws was to be read as being mandatory when necessary to effectuate the intent of Congress.

One of the most significant historical developments in the law of impoundment was the passage of the Anti-Deficiency Acts of 1905 and 1906. The Acts provide a method by which excessive expenditures in one portion of a year that can require deficiency or supplemental appropriations may be avoided. Moreover, the Acts stipulate that the expenditure of funds may be waived in the event of extraordinary emergencies which could not have been foreseen when appropriations were made. In essence, the Anti-Deficiency Acts were designed to allow the executive branch to prevent waste and to budget funds over a given period of time. The Acts did not grant any general authority to impound funds.

Impoundments pursuant to the Anti-Deficiency Acts were procedurally formalized during the Harding Administration soon after passage of the Budget and Accounting Act of 1921. However, large-scale exercise of this procedure did not begin on a regular basis until President Roosevelt impounded funds in order to cope with the emergencies of economic depression and war.

In the early 1940's Budget Director Smith ordered the impoundment of millions of dollars which had been appropriated for the surplus labor force of the Civilian Conservation Corps, civilian pilot training projects, the Surplus Marketing Corporation, and numerous civil and military efforts which the War Department could not complete because the projects did not have the requisite priority ratings to obtain scarce resources. These impoundments created a stir in Congress. The public cries and political pressures were greatest, however, when funds impounded were those which had been appropriated for a flood control reservoir at Markham Ferry, Oklahoma, and a flood control levee on the Arkansas River at Tulsa.

. . .

Pressures which mounted at the end of World War II compelled Congress to accept a rider to the Omnibus Appropriations Act of 1951 which amended the Anti-Deficiency Acts by adding a provision which expressly allowed for reserves to be established for various reasons. Although the House of Representatives explicitly declared that the measure was not to be used to thwart congressional intent, the section has subsequently been cited as a prime authority to legally justify executive impoundment of funds.

Major instances of impoundment also occurred during the Truman Administration. Funds were withheld which had been appropriated for a 70-group Air Force and the giant aircraft carriers *U.S.S. United States* and *U.S.S. Forrestal*. President Eisenhower also impounded funds which had been appropriated for defense projects. The most significant impoundments involved funds appropriated for strategic airlift aircraft and initial Nike-Zeus hardware procurements.

The major impoundment controversy during the Kennedy Administration concerned the RS-70, a long-range bomber system. Congress appropriated nearly double the amount the President had sought. Accordingly, Secretary of Defense McNamara refused to release the excess funds, emphasizing that America's missile deterrence capability combined with existing bomber strength was more than adequate. The House Armed Services Committee voted to command full expenditure of funds appropriated for the RS-70 and insisted that if the language directing expenditure "constitutes a test as to whether Congress has the power to so mandate, let the test be made. . . ." Attempting to avoid a constitutional crisis, President Kennedy wrote to Representative Vinson, Chairman of the Armed Services Committee, requesting that the language be made permissive rather than mandatory, and Congress quickly honored the President's request.

Thus while counsel to both President Eisenhower and President Kennedy strongly advised that the impoundment of funds appropriated for domestic programs was legally tenuous, both Presidents made such impoundments on occasion. President Johnson, in contrast, indubitably thought that impoundment relating to domestic projects was legally permissible and accordingly stepped up the pace by impounding agricultural appropriations, highway trust funds, certain education funds, and funds appropriated for low-cost housing and numerous other programs. He was supported in his view by members of his administration. The Acting Attorney General and the Comptroller General concluded, in 1967, that the withholding of highway trust funds was a lawful practice, and

Budget Director Schultze argued that there existed a "general power of the President to operate for the welfare of the economy and the Nation in terms of combating inflationary pressures. . . ." Director Schultze inferred that impounding some of the highway funds would help put the brakes on inflation. Based on these opinions, President Johnson refused to release for obligation billions of dollars which had been appropriated as federal aid to highway construction projects.

Summary. From the earliest years of the Republic through the presidency of Lyndon B. Johnson, the instances of executive impoundment of appropriated funds are generally divisible into three categories. Impoundments were made to (1) prevent the waste of funds, (2) make allowances for defense or foreign policy considerations, and (3) curb inflationary pressures. For obvious pragmatic reasons, Congress did not raise its voice in opposition to impoundments which were made to prevent waste. However, the legislative branch did, without much success and with considerable vicissitude, oppose virtually every refusal to spend which was premised on [any] other rationale. Members of Congress can, at a minimum, be said to have made timely objections. And the objections were made even though no President completely terminated any projects or attempted to reorder domestic priorities via the impoundment of funds.

This history of impoundment is of considerable importance today, for the Nixon Administration lays claim to the support of historical precedent as the touchstone justification for impoundment practices. Additionally, President Nixon has maintained that there inheres in the presidency a constitutional right to refuse to spend appropriated funds.

Does the President have statutory authority to refuse to spend money? Is there constitutional authority for the President to impound funds? If so, from what source is that authority derived and what limitations exist with respect to such authority? As measured against historical precedents, are the Nixon Administration impoundments justifiable? These questions are now answerable.

(2) Train v. City of New York (1975)

+Burger, Douglas, Brennan, Stewart, White, Marshall, Blackmun, Powell, Rehnquist

MR. JUSTICE WHITE delivered the opinion of the Court.

This case poses certain questions concerning the proper construction of the Federal Water Pollution Control Act Amendments of 1972, . . . which provide a comprehensive program for controlling and abating water pollution. Title II of the 1972 Act, . . . makes available federal financial assistance in the amount of 75% of the cost of municipal sewers and sewage treatment works. Under § 207, there is "authorized to be appropriated" for these purposes "not to exceed" $5 billion for fiscal year 1973, "not to exceed" $6 billion for fiscal year 1974, and "not to exceed" $7 billion for fiscal year 1975. Section 205(a) directed that "[s]ums authorized to be appropriated pursuant to § 207" for fiscal year 1973 be allotted "not later than 30 days after October 18, 1972." The "[s]ums authorized" for the later fiscal years, 1973 and 1974, "shall be allotted by the Administrator not later than the January 1st immediately preceding the beginning of the fiscal year for which authorized. . . ." From these allotted sums, § 201(g) authorizes the Administrator "to make grants to

any . . . municipality . . . for the construction of publicly owned treatment works . . . ," pursuant to plans and specifications as required by § 203 and meeting the other requirements of the Act, including those of § 204. Section 203(a) specifies that the Administrator's approval of plans for a project "shall be deemed a contractual obligation of the United States for the payment of its proportional contribution to such project."

The water pollution bill that became the 1972 Act was passed by Congress on October 4, 1972, but was vetoed by the President on October 17. Congress promptly overrode the veto. Thereupon the President, by letter dated November 22, 1972, directed the Administrator "not [to] allot among the States the maximum amounts provided by Section 207" and, instead, to allot "[n]o more than $2 billion of the amount authorized for the fiscal year 1973, and no more than $3 billion of the amount authorized for the fiscal year 1974. . . ." On December 8, the Administrator announced by regulation that in accordance with the President's letter he was allotting for fiscal years 1973 and 1974 sums not to exceed $2 billion and $3 billion respectively."

This litigation, brought by the city of New York and similarly situated municipalities in the State of New York followed immediately. The complaint sought judgment against the Administrator of the Environmental Protection Agency declaring that he was obligated to allot to the States the full amounts authorized by § 207 for fiscal years 1973 and 1974, as well as an order directing him to make those allotments. In May 1973, the District Court denied the Administrator's motion to dismiss and granted the city's motion for summary judgment. The Court of Appeals affirmed, holding that "the Act requires the Administrator to allot the full sums authorized to be appropriated in § 207." . . .

Because of the differing views with respect to the proper construction of the Act between the federal courts in the District of Columbia in this case and those of the Fourth Circuit . . . we granted certiorari. . . . The sole issue before us is whether the 1972 Act permits the Administrator to allot to the States under § 205 less than the entire amounts authorized to be appropriated by § 207. We hold that the Act does not permit such action and affirm the Court of Appeals.

Section 205 provides that the "sums authorized to be appropriated pursuant to § 207 . . . shall be allotted by the Administrator." Section 207 authorizes the appropriation of "not to exceed" specified amounts for each of three fiscal years. The dispute in this case turns principally on the meaning of the foregoing language from the indicated sections of the Act.

The Administrator contends that § 205 directs the allotment of only "sums"—not "all sums"—authorized by § 207 to be appropriated and that the sums that must be allotted are merely sums that do not exceed the amounts specified in § 207 for each of the three fiscal years. In other words, it is argued that there is a maximum, but no minimum, on the amounts that must be allotted under § 205. This is necessarily the case, he insists, because the legislation, after initially passing the House and Senate in somewhat different form, was amended in Conference and the changes, which were adopted by both Houses were intended to provide wide discretion in the Executive to control the rate of spending under the Act. . . .

The Administrator's arguments based on the statutory language and its legislative history are unpersuasive. Section 207 authorized appropriation of "not to exceed" a specified sum for each of the three fiscal years. If the States failed to submit projects sufficient to require obligation, and hence the appropriation, of the entire amounts authorized, or if the Administrator, exercising whatever authority the Act might have given him to deny grants, refused to obligate these total amounts, § 207 would obviously permit appropriation of the lesser amounts. But if, for example, the full amount provided for 1973 was obligated by the Administrator in the course of approving plans and making grants for municipal contracts, § 207, plainly "authorized" the appropriation of the entire $5 billion. If a sum of money is "authorized" to be appropriated in the future by § 207 then § 205 directs that an amount equal to that sum be allotted. Section 207 speaks of sums authorized to be appropriated, not of sums that are required to be appropriated; and as far as § 205's requirement to allot is concerned, we see no difference between the $2 billion the President directed to be allotted for fiscal year 1977 and the $3 billion he ordered withheld. The latter sum is as much authorized to be appropriated by § 207 as is the former. Both must be allotted.

It is insisted that this reading of the Act fails to give any effect to the Conference Committee's changes in the bill. But, as already indicated, the "not to exceed" qualifying language in § 207 has meaning of its own, quite apart from § 205, and reflects the realistic possibility that approved applications for grants from funds already allotted would not total the maximum amount authorized to be appropriated. Surely there is nothing inconsistent between authorizing "not to exceed" $5 billion for 1973 and requiring the full allotment of the $5 billion among the States. Indeed, if the entire amount authorized is *ever* to be appropriated, there must be approved municipal projects in that amount, and grants for those projects may *only* be made from allotted funds.

As for striking the word "all" from § 205, if Congress intended to confer any discretion on the Executive to withhold funds from this program at the allotment stage, it chose quite inadequate means to do so. It appears to us that the word "sums" has no different meaning and can be ascribed no different function in the context of § 205 than would the words "all sums." It is said that the changes were made to give the Executive the discretionary control over the outlay of funds for Title II programs at either stage of the process. But legislative intention, without more, is not legislation. Without something in addition to what is now before us, we cannot accept the addition of the few words to § 207 and the deletion of the one word from § 205 as altering the entire complexion and thrust of the Act. As conceived and passed in both Houses, the legislation was intended to provide a firm commitment of substantial sums within a relatively limited period of time in an effort to achieve an early solution of what was deemed an urgent problem. We cannot believe that Congress at the last minute scuttled the entire effort by providing the Executive with the seemingly limitless power to withhold funds from allotment and obligation. Yet such was the Government's position in the lower courts—combined with the argument that the discretion conferred is unreviewable. . . .

Judgment of Court of Appeals affirmed.

MR. JUSTICE DOUGLAS CONCURS IN THE RESULT.

D. *The Pocket Veto Controversy*

The Constitution affords the President a "qualified" veto over "every bill" and "every order, resolution or vote to which the concurrence of the Senate and the House of Representatives may be necessary." The only exceptions are actions taken by a single house, such as a resolution specifying procedures or policies of that house; constitutional amendments; and so-called concurrent resolutions of Congress. To the extent that such resolutions apply to minor details and legislative housekeeping, the exception is well within the meaning of the Constitution. However, where the resolution is a clear attempt to extend the powers of Congress by imposing a veto-proof oversight on executive action, a clash of constitutional prerogatives between the president and Congress is inevitable. Further discussion of this so-called "legislative veto" is the subject of the next item in this chapter.

The president's veto power is "qualified" in the sense that Congress may override his veto by a two-thirds vote of both houses. A president who wishes to veto a bill returns it unsigned to the House or Senate, wherever the bill originated. If Congress has not overridden the veto before the end of the congressional session, it is sustained and the bill does not become law.

A president may allow a bill to become a law without his signature simply by failing to return it within ten (calendar) days, excluding Sundays. However, if Congress adjourns within the ten-day period the bill does not become law and the president has exercised a "pocket veto." A considerable amount of litigation has explored the meaning of the term "adjournment" in this context. Does it apply only to the end of a Congress, or is Congress in adjournment in the period between its annual sessions? Is an interim recess an adjournment for pocket-veto purposes? Must both houses of Congress be in adjournment at the same time, or need it be only the house in which the bill originated? In *The Pocket Veto Case* (1929), the Supreme Court held that congressional adjournment after the first session of a Congress is adjournment which can activate a pocket veto. It also held that to forestall a pocket veto the house in which the bill originated must be in session so that it can "proceed to reconsider" a bill returned with presidential objections.

The issue took on contemporary importance in *Kennedy* v. *Sampson* (1974). President Nixon refused to sign the Family Practice of Medicine Act, which had passed both houses of Congress and had been submitted to him seven days prior to a five-day House and Senate Christmas recess. Since Congress was in recess prior to the expiration of the ten-day period in which the president had to sign or veto the bill, President Nixon claimed that a pocket veto had taken place. However, Senator Edward Kennedy successfully argued in his lawsuit that Congress was only in a temporary recess, that it had designated its secretary to receive messages from the president during that recess, and that its organization and appropriate officers continued to function without interruption during that recess. A federal district court invalidated Nixon's pocket veto, and that decision was upheld by the Court of Appeals for the District of Columbia. The Department of Justice decided not to take the case to the Supreme Court, thus putting off any immediate resolution of the conflict.

E. The Rise of the Legislative Veto

The legislative veto is a provision in a statute that reserves to the Congress the right to approve or disapprove at a later date actions taken by the president or an administrative agency pursuant to an original congressional delegation of power. In its most common form it retains for Congress the right to approve administrative rules or executive reorganization plans. The agency in question promulgates a set of rules and these rules become law if within a specified period of time—often 60 days—Congress, either house of Congress, or a specified congressional committee have not disapproved of them.

The legislative veto dates back to 1932, and has been utilized with increasing frequency since 1970.[1] For example, in 1976 Congress proposed an amendment to the Administrative Procedure Act (the basic rules governing all agencies), which required that all "substantive rules issued pursuant to the 'notice and comment' procedure" be submitted to Congress for review before taking effect. The amendment was narrowly defeated in the House of Representatives only because, at the time, that body was operating under a special two-thirds rule.[2] Two similar proposals were introduced in 1978, and controversy

---

[1]*Congressional Quarterly Almanac*, Vol. XXXII, 1976, p. 508.
[2]U.S., *Congressional Record*, 94th Cong., 2nd Sess., HR 12048.

about them is intense. President Carter sent a message to Congress denouncing the legislative veto as an unconstitutional infringement on the president's constitutional obligation to execute the laws. He reluctantly approved bills with such provisions in them.[3]

Proponents of the legislative veto argue that it is necessary to restore "an imbalance that has arisen between branches due to broad delegation" of legislative power.[4] Its purpose, they argue, is the valid one of restoring final control over lawmaking back in the hands of Congress. Opponents contend that the legislative veto is merely another method for postponing policy decisions until "a concrete resolution appears in the form of a proposed rule," and hence it does not resolve the problems created by broad delegation but merely extends them.[5] They also argue that the legislative veto usurps the president's role in the legislative process by changing the initial scope of delegated authority. By interfering with presidential and administrative enforcement it intrudes upon presidential prerogatives and further violates the separation of powers doctrine by permitting Congress to participate in the execution of the laws.[6]

Proponents respond to these attacks on the constitutionality of the legislative veto by claiming that "if the power which the legislative veto grants Congress is limited to a power only to *negative* agency action, the legislative veto does not violate the requirement that certain congressional action be submitted to the president for his approval or veto."[7] As to the separation of powers argument, proponents contend that the legislative veto is consistent with that doctrine because it functions to check the exercise of delegated lawmaking powers. They note further that the disapproval procedure has been approved in the initial delegation statute by the methods prescribed in the Constitution—a majority vote in each house and approval by the president, or approval by two-thirds in each house overriding a presidential veto.

A different kind of objection has been lodged against a legislative veto provision, which empowers only one house of Congress, or even a designated congressional committee, to veto a proposed rule. This mode of review, it is said, violates the principle of bicameralism. The principle is further eroded, according to a study by Bruff and Gellhorn, by the less than full legislative consideration that proposed rules often get. They found that floor vetoes on the merits of a particular set of rules, by the entire house, were infrequent. And committee-based review more often than not focused on the concerns of a single committee chairman or member.[8] But the same could be said for the entire legislative process.

It has also been contended that a congressional veto of executive or

[3]*Congressional Quarterly Weekly Report,* March 4, 1978, p. 575, and June 24, 1978, p. 1623.

[4]Geofrey S. Stewart, "Constitutionality of the Legislative Veto," **13** *Harvard Journal of Legislation* (1975), 593–619.

[5]Bruff and Walter Gellhorn, "Congressional Control of Administrative Regulation: A Study of Legislative Vetoes," **90** *Harvard Law Review* (1977), 1373–1440, @ 1379.

[6]William Rehnquist, Administrative Law Section, American Bar Association, Dallas, Texas, August 12, 1969.

[7]Stewart, *op. cit.,* Note 4, p. 619.

[8]Bruff and Gellhorn, *op. cit.,* Note 5, p. 1417.

administrative action pursuant to a prior delegation usurps the judiciary's role in interpreting whether such action was within the statutory delegation of authority.[9] The legislative veto could also effect judicial review of agency action because the courts might well assume that if Congress did not veto a rule it had implicitly ratified it. "If the judiciary defers to agency rule making on this theory, there may be a net loosening of constraints on agency discretion whenever rules have received little direct examination in Congress."[10]

The validity of the legislative veto arose in *Buckley* v. *Valeo* (1976), a case in which the Supreme Court struck down the appointment procedure of the Federal Elections Act (see p. 1005). By doing so the Court prevented existing members of the Commission from exercising rule-making power subject to the congressional veto provided in the act. The issue was technically moot, but Justice White did observe in his concurring opinion that "the provision for congressional disapproval of agency regulations does not appear to transgress the constitutional design, at least where the president has agreed to legislation establishing the disapproval procedure or the legislation has been passed over his veto."

In theory the legislative veto should function to increase administrative accountability as well as congressional responsibility. But the study by Bruff and Gellhorn of five administrative agencies provides evidence which challenges both claims. For example, their study of the Federal Elections Commission reveals that Congress used its veto power to protect its own political interests in setting campaign expenditure limitations, and rejected the Commission's request to remain in session for two additional days so that the rules could take effect before the 1976 elections.[11] The legislative veto provision also increases workloads and encourages delays in the promulgation of administrative rules.

Bruff and Gellhorn also identified several additional problems with the legislative veto procedure, although these problems are of political rather than constitutional concern. Their study of the veto provision in the General Education Provisions Act showed the agency, anticipating the need to compromise with the oversight committee, streamlined its procedures to establish a "substantial administrative bias against changing rules in response to public comment."[12] Thus, a veto provision may "reduce public participation before the agencies by shifting the focus of attention to congressional review procedures."[13] Furthermore, the low visibility of congressional negotiations with the agencies allow Congress to "hide behind" its own statute. While appearing to demand administrative accountability, Bruff and Gellhorn conclude, the legislative veto may be just another political device which fosters congressional irresponsibility.

---

[9]Laurence H. Tribe, *American Constitutional Law* (New York: Foundation Press, 1978), p. 162.
[10]Bruff and Gellhorn, *op. cit.*, Note 5, p. 1380.
[11]*Ibid.*, pp. 1408–1409.
[12]*Ibid.*, pp. 1385–1386.
[13]*Ibid.*, p. 1378.

personal rights in modern society

1. INTRODUCTORY ESSAY

Within broad limits defined by the need for social order, our society has encouraged people to use their inherent capacities to establish themselves as individuals. We make "individualism" a feature of our democracy and assume, as a society, that one's sense of identity is a function of what we are able to know of ourselves and our surroundings. The person who strives to achieve and maintain this level of individuality does so under societally protected conditions that we recognize as matters of right. Such conditions constitute what is meant, in this text, by "personal rights."

Two facets of this definition of "personal rights" must be noted at the outset. First, the combination of societal and personal dimensions is such that the two are inseparable. If dichotomized, they lose their effective meaning. An individual is *simultaneously* a part of society and apart from society; an individual, in any meaningful sense, is never a societal isolate nor ever wholly societal. This results in a difficult problem of conceptual clarity, because we cannot functionally separate that which we can so readily distinguish.

A second consideration is that personal rights are fundamentally different from those rights that were examined in earlier chapters of this text. For example, the right to a fair trial is essentially procedural in its content and civil

1111

in its setting. It is a "civil" right, rather than "personal" right, because its manifestation depends on a particular form of civil action, the result of which is a fair trial. But personal rights are not so oriented to a particular, expected result. For example, freedom of religion calls for no particular civil procedure and, more importantly, does not contain an expectation of some religious result, such as "finding God." The right is a condition under which the person seeks (or does not seek) those profound meanings we associate with religious outlook. Whether or not the seeking results in finding is not a matter encompassed in the meaning of the right.

The fundamental proposition that lies beneath our conception of personal rights can be stated as follows. There is an inner being and an outer being, a personal being and a social being. The organized community facilitates and serves the purposes of each, but primarily those of the social being. In the course of establishing and serving social purposes, conditions for an individual's inner life must be preserved. Milton Konvitz puts the matter well in the course of elaborating the conception of privacy.[1]

Once a civilization has made a distinction between the "outer" and "inner" man, between the life of the soul and the life of the body, between the spiritual and the material, between the sacred and the profane, between the realm of God and the realm of Caesar, between church and state, between rights inherent and inalienable and rights that are in the power of government to give and take away, between public and private, between society and solitude, it becomes impossible to avoid the idea of privacy by whatever name it may be called—the idea of a "private space in which man may become and remain 'himself.' "

The basic method for pursuing such purposes has been to limit the reach of society by "constitutionalizing" those rights that society should not infringe, and it is from this that the notion of the limited state has emerged. But what has happened when limits themselves must be transformed into positive powers of the state to protect the individual from his or her own social inventions and inclinations? That is among the fundamental questions to be considered by any contemporary treatment of personal rights.

Law and the Supreme Court

Law is among those social inventions and calls for conformity, perhaps even more in the United States than in some other societies. Americans resort to the law to accomplish a number of ends that in other societies may be left to private institutions or to individual choice. Law not only protects the values of the majority but also frequently imposes those values on unwilling minorities. But, paradoxically, law can and does also serve as a liberating institution, protecting individuals against at least some of the harshness of demands for conformity and reduction of individuality. It can do this in three ways: (1) by setting limits to the scope of conformity demanded by a society and refusing to enforce, or reinforce, the harsher deprivations imposed on noncomformists; (2) by supporting institutions and practices that contribute to the establishment of

---

[1]Milton Konvitz, "Privacy and the Law: A Philosophical Prelude," 31 *Law and Contemporary Problems* (1966), 272–280. Quotation is from Herbert Marcuse, *One Dimensional Man* (Boston: Beacon Press, 1964), p. 273.

conditions that are necessary to ensure the opportunity for expression of individuality including, where necessary, the reallocation and redistribution of scarce resources; and (3) as Arthur Miller has suggested by the phrase "constitutional duty," protection of rights may depend on the imposition by the Court of positive obligations to create and maintain the protections (and procedures) necessary for individual rights to exist *and to be encouraged.*[2] In some areas it has been argued that this constitutional duty includes the obligation to make up for past deprivations by compensatory treatment. What we have here is the further paradox that effective limitations on governmental intrusion on individual rights may require greater uses of positive governmental power.

The Supreme Court has been a major instrument for the articulation of policies seeking to reduce social and political restraints on individual expression. The notion of privacy—"the right to be let alone,"[3] the acceptability of political expression and political dissent, the right of peaceful protest, and the sanctuaries of religious belief that the state may not invade for its own purpose or convenience are aspects of individuality for which judicial policies have been fashioned. Not all judicial responses have been favorable to the concept of individuality implicit in these types of questions. But certainly the main thrust of recent Supreme Court decisions has been supportive.

As was noted in the first chapter of this book, judicial policies are framed within fairly narrow limits and tend to be limited responses to immediate problems rather than long-term policy statements. The most frequent type of judicial response is a negative one—for example, an order to cease doing something rather than an establishment of those conditions necessary to assure that the offensive action will not be repeated. Thus, judicial policies toward individual expression rarely expound positive conceptions, although such conceptions may be, and often are, implied in judicial opinions.

There are four problems that the Supreme Court must face in adjudicating questions of individual liberties. First, the basic problem in such cases is the necessity to consider and serve community as well as individual interests. One frequently articulated judicial view of this problem is that a viable balance must be struck between the two interests. An opposing judicial point of view argues that merely attempting to strike a balance in this way negates a conception of individual or personal rights to the point of saying that persons have rights until they interfere too much with community needs.

A second problem is the often incompatible character of certain rights: for example, the rights of the press versus the rights of privacy; the principle of a free press versus that of fair trial; and the rights of individual and public expression versus the right of individuals not to have to listen. In such cases, some form of balancing is inevitable unless some rights are accorded a priority position—which in itself is a balancing formula, the difference being in whether the balance is struck in advance of the problem to be resolved or in the application of existing doctrines to the solution of a particular controversy.

A third problem is the difficulty of accommodating traditional conceptions of rights to changing technology and social practices. One of the more glaring

[2]Arthur Miller, "Toward a Concept of Constitutional Duty," in Kurland (ed.), *The Supreme Court Review, 1968* (Chicago: University of Chicago Press, 1968), pp. 199–246, especially pp. 208–215.
[3]Samuel D. Warren and Louis D. Brandeis, "The Right to Privacy," 4 *Harvard Law Review* (1890), 193–220.

examples would be the fact that communication no longer can be thought of solely as an exchange of words; in a society that is increasingly visual and reliant on symbols in its modes of persuasion and communication, a purely "verbal" First Amendment would be inadequate. Likewise, our technology may be propelling us toward a recognition that for many constitutional purposes, action *is*—or ought to be considered as—speech, at least when it is the only available form of persuasive communication. Thus, courts may have to develop standards for determining the appropriateness of certain types of speech substitutes in certain types of communications situations. The two cases reprinted in the first chapter of the book, *Tinker* v. *Des Moines Community School District* (1969) and *United States* v. *O'Brien* (1968) and several cases that follow in this chapter illustrate the problems of determining which symbolic expressions are entitled to constitutional protection. Changing technology has also forced reevaluations of the notion of privacy and the conditions necessary for its protection.

A final major difficulty for the Supreme Court is inherent in the notion of protecting individual and minority rights but needs to be stated separately. Most individuals who claim deprivations of their liberties are, almost by definition, not those who enjoy social status or positions of power and recognition in a majoritarian and conformist society. If the Court is to be the major instrument by which such rights are to be assured, and if it is to be at all effective in this venture, it must take care not to undermine the political structure needed to preserve individual rights. If personal rights were merely an abstract category for judicial consideration, there would be no problem. But they are not. To be effective, rights must be grounded in realistic appraisals of major societal norms. What society may tolerate with respect to the rights claimed by some groups, it may not tolerate with respect to others.

The Problem of Conceptualization

Although the Supreme Court faces particular problems in making policy, there are other, more general problems to be understood by the student of society and politics. Among these is one that takes form as a question: What do we mean by the term "human rights"? In short, conceiving of the general social process, of which the Court's functioning is but a part, is problematic. One of the more perceptive views of human rights that is appropriate to a political scientist's conceptual tasks has been articulated by David Danelski. He poses the question: "What rights do men have simply because they are men?"[4] His response amounts to saying that a three-way series of consecutive behaviors is the basis of the rights people effectively have. First, there is the need to *perceive* individuals as human; this is the basic condition without which human rights would not exist (this is, of course, more than a mere circularity of semantics). The fact is that groups of people throughout history have not been perceived as fully human. Examples have been slaves, blacks, paupers, women, or any ethnic group that one formally or informally singles out as having special characteristics meriting particular (and inferior) treatment. Second, there is the need to *acknowledge* that people, as humans, are

[4]David Danelski, "A Behavioral Conception of Human Rights," 3 *Law in Transition Quarterly* (1966), 63.

entitled to certain forms of treatment simply because they are human. In short, it is the general condition of humanity that is the basis of rights rather than the particulars of status or role. It is when this general condition becomes the basis of treatment of other people that the notion of acknowledgment is meaningful in understanding the idea of rights. Third, it is the action of individuals or groups toward each other that is the basis of effective rights rather than the mere perception of humanness. The ultimate test of human rights is not the expressed norm but, instead, the action that the norm invites or permits. In fact, perception and acknowledgment in the absence of action may well lead to limiting of rights or, at the very least, an irresponsibility that promises but does not fulfill. It is all too easy to fall into the trap of the "myth of rights" by failing to recognize the often very large gap between rights articulated by the Supreme Court and the level of rights that can, in practice, be exercised freely.[5]

Among the major implications of this action-oriented view of rights is that established means of declaring rights often may not have the value and content that tradition and acceptance confer upon them. Consider, for example, the Bill of Rights. Even allowing for its ambiguities, this section of the Constitution calls clearly for perception and acknowledgment, in Danelski's terms, of human relations in the context of limited government. Individuals are to be free of the state for many of the purposes of self-expression, privacy, identity, or freedom from presumptive or coerced guilt for social misbehavior. But as former Justice William O. Douglas suggested, the Bill of Rights "may not be enough."[6]

The inadequacy of the Bill of Rights could stem from a variety of sources. First, although it articulates a broad range of rights, these are for the most part not self-executing; there are no specific means provided for securing these rights. Only those with certain economic resources are likely to have a chance at being effectively protected, even where the law, on its face, treats people equally.[7] Indeed, many of the Supreme Court's major decisions of recent years have been devoted as much to establishing means and/or conditions for redressing grievances as to the demarcation of the rights themselves. Second, rights in practice depend on a multitude of factors over which the law has little or no control. Transient political vicissitudes, public opinion, community norms, and lack of resources may all operate as effective barriers to rights fulfillment. Third, the conceptions of the rights themselves may be inadequate to the times. We have seen, for example, how earlier limited conceptions of the rights of persons accused of crime have been expanded to meet new problems and new technologies of police investigation. We have seen how the prohibitions against discrimination of the Fourteenth Amendment, originally confined by judicial decision to "state action," have been expanded to encompass indirectly some forms of purely private discrimination.

It is in regard to this last problem of inadequate conceptualization that Justice Douglas sees the Bill of Rights as particularly inadequate. He argues that the Bill of Rights fundamentally expresses our notions of liberty by (1) limiting government through the prohibition of certain activities and (2) providing

[5]Stuart Scheingold, *The Politics of Rights* (New Haven: Yale University Press, 1974).

[6]"The Bill of Rights is Not Enough," in Cahn (ed.), *The Great Rights* (New York: Macmillan, 1963), pp. 146–58.

[7]Marc Galanter, "Why The 'Haves' Come Out Ahead: Speculations on the Limits of Legal Change," **9** *Law & Society Review* (1974), 95–159.

some procedures that government must follow in proceedings against the individual. But these devices alone are not adequate to meet all the problems of contemporary society. The main object of the Bill of Rights was to protect the individual by limiting the power of the state. In modern society, rights are as likely to be abridged through the action—or inaction—of other, nongovernmental institutions. The impact on individual rights of what is commonly referred to as the technological-industrial-governmental complex goes far beyond the current limits of Bill of Rights protections. The Bill of Rights presumes one social reality but must aid in the governing of another. Douglas himself puts the matter as follows:[8]

The central problem of the age is the scientific revolution and all the wonders and the damage it brings. The scientific revolution has created new centers of power in those who finance it, viz. federal officials or more particularly, the Pentagon and the Atomic Energy Commission. . . . If the Bill of Rights were being written today, it certainly would provide people with protection against poisoning by insecticides—one of America's acute problems, as Rachel Carson shows in her book Silent Spring.

If the Bill of Rights were being written today, it also would encompass some of the recurring evils arising out of the vast exercise of authority through the administrative agency. Thus in one State an administrative board of three may, on a majority vote, sterilize a person without notice, without an opportunity to be heard, without an application being made to any other tribunal or agency. One State provides that a patient in a state hospital—certified as being "mentally ill" and who has previously committed a crime—may be transferred without any hearing to a hospital for the criminally insane. A business recently was abolished by a Board of Health through an amendment of its Rules that was made without notice or opportunity to be heard even by the business in question. A wilderness area may be destroyed by the fiat of a few men in the Forestry Service through spraying, or logging, or road building. The Bureau of Land Management fences people out of public lands and gets money from Congress to do so—all for the benefit of a few ranchers and to the certain disaster of the antelope who must migrate and yet who cannot jump fences. Here again people lose their inheritance without notice, without hearing, or without the need of the agency to obtain prior approval from another tribunal.

Moreover, traditional ideas of Due Process are not enough to put into harness the modern administrative agency, let alone the modern prosecutor, or the modern legislative committee.

The power of the military to control its posts subjects civilians who work there to unreviewable ideological supervision. Matters that jeopardize a person's job can be adjudicated without the time-honored safeguard of the right of confrontation. The Armed Forces are allowed to downgrade a doctor because of his insistence on his constitutional rights.

Douglas' comments are quite in line with our earlier suggestion that real protection for individual rights may depend on a transformation of the underlying conceptualization from one that emphasizes what government cannot, or should not, do to one that emphasizes what government must do. The Bill of Rights, like the Constitution as a whole, was written by men hostile to any unnecessary extension of governmental power. It was an instrument to protect people from their rulers. To argue that the emphasis must now shift from limit to power is to suggest the need for a fundamental change in the political philosophy of our system. And the basic, if implicit, rationale for many recent

[8]"The Bill of Rights Is Not Enough," *op cit.*, Note 6, pp. 148–50 ff.

Supreme Court decisions has been that only with increased and more creative use of power and control can certain rights be protected.

Rights and Their Activation

This chapter is concerned with three major areas of personal activity that, in varying degrees, are considered to be matters of right. First, we examine the expression of political views in terms of the media available for such expression, the problem of having action serve as the means of expressing one's views, and the difficulties in forming associations to amplify the effects of expressing a political viewpoint. Second, the creative imagination has perennially been a source of expression that is problematic for organized society and its structure of public authority; this too is examined. Third, the growing difficulties of being an individual in the midst of modern society raise questions of constitutional usage, especially in areas of religion, conscience, and privacy.

In each of the three areas of personal rights, there is at work an activating principle that underlies the enormous social complexity of these rights. Political expression, creative imagination, and personal identity are not mere abstractions. They are concepts that describe activities usually pursued in an assertive, often frantic, and sometimes zealous effort to affect events and change behavior; and these activities call for or provoke counter actions and demands.

This relationship of concepts to action is intensified by the capacity of modern technology to project, beyond mere words, into the realm of images. Further, events and actions are communicated almost at first hand, with a minimal delay in time, producing a multiplier effect. The "shot heard round the world" is no longer a mere literary allusion. People often know what others think, hear what they say, and see what they do in rapid-fire order. The products of the creative imagination are more easily produced and more widely disseminated and available than ever before.

Technology is not the only reason for the escalation of "rights consciousness" among Americans, but it is one of the most important. Certainly the courts have made a major contribution to a developing sense of personal identity and entitlement on the part of many citizens. We have already seen examples of this in the chapter on equality. *Tinker* v. *Des Moines Community School District* (1969) is also a good example of how a conception of rights escalates. First, there is a substantive escalation of the meaning of free speech, in this case an extension to communicative actions or "symbolic" speech. Second, there is an escalation or extension to a new "protected" group—children—which can invoke the protection of that right in the courts. And, third, there is an escalation of where such expression, now protected by the Constitution, can be made. In *Tinker*, the Supreme Court held that peaceful, symbolic speech such as the wearing of a black armband by students in school was permissible unless it caused serious disruption of normal school activities.

A final factor of importance is the increased willingness of citizens to articulate their rights and to seek protection for them in the courts. For many, the gap between abstract notions of rights and their existence in practice has narrowed. It is the narrowing of this gap, the loosening of restraints on claiming one's rights that poses a continuing problem for the Supreme Court—and for all courts. The more that rights are claimed, the more they will come into conflict with each other. As long as privacy was defined as the right to be left alone in one's home and in one's thoughts, it needed relatively little judicial protection. It was passive, and thus largely unchallenged. But privacy that embodies the right to seek an abortion free from government interference, quite obviously, is a very different kind of right.

The most common judicial response to such competing claims of rights has been to "balance" recognized or newly acknowledged individual rights with the needs of the society as the judges see them. The "clear and present danger" doctrine is perhaps the best known judicial effort in the twentieth century to strike such a balance. It assumes that expression leads to action and concludes that the validity of certain types of expression must be judged in terms of the actions to which the offending words led, or to which they *might* lead.

The "clear and present danger" doctrine grew out of the need to protect the political expression of dissidents while maintaining a government capacity to protect itself against forcible overthrow. However, when applied, as in *Schenck* v. *United States* (1919), it rarely protected individual expression. And when it was interpreted in such a way as to provide this protection, it was almost always in dissent. The alternative "bad tendency" test enunciated in *Gitlow* v. *New York* (1925) was also a balancing formula but provided even less protection because it did not depend on any showing of imminent danger from the utterance of certain words. In *Gitlow*, the Court also virtually abdicated the field by holding that where a legislature itself had determined that certain types of speech were illegal, that determination carried with it the presumption of validity. This presumption was reversed in *Dennis* v. *United States* (1951), in which it was held to be a *judicial* task to determine if certain utterances were or were not protected by the First Amendment.

Neither the "clear and present danger" and the "bad tendency" tests nor the presumption of legislative reasonableness[9] meets the need for free and protected expression. Balancing under any of these formulas almost always leads to suppression rather than protection of speech. The absolutist approach proposed by Justice Black[10] would eliminate the need for a case-by-case balancing of the needs of the government and the rights of the individual. The government could never punish pure speech. The difficulties of this approach lie in its rigidity. It would bar the inclusion of additional rights and limit the constitutional protection to the narrow context of its meaning at the time of adoption. A similar caveat was expressed by Justice Murphy in concurring with Black's incorporation thesis in *Adamson* v. *California* (1947).

Somewhere in between the absolutist and balancing approaches is the so-called preferred freedoms doctrine, implicitly enunciated by Justice Cardozo in *Palko* v. *Connecticut* (1937), by Justice Stone through his famous Footnote 4 in *United States* v. *Carolene Products Company* (1938), and explicitly stated by Justice Douglas in his majority opinion in *Murdock* v. *Pennsylvania* (1943). The "preferred freedoms" approach placed the burden of proof on legislative

[9]For other descriptions of the Court's approach to these problems, see C. Herman Pritchett, *The American Constitution*, 3rd ed. (New York: McGraw-Hill, 1977), Chapter 19; see also Richard Y. Funston, *Constitutional Counter-Revolution?* (New York: Schenkman, 1977), Chapter 7. And see pp. 1223–1231, *infra*.

[10]For the intellectual architecture of this position, see Alexander Miekeljohn, *Free Speech and Its Relation to Self-Government* (New York: Harper and Row, 1948). Also see Thomas Emerson, *A General Theory of the First Amendment* (New York: Vintage, 1967).

bodies to show the need for the necessity of limitations on free speech. The doctrine by that name has faded from use, but it is the antecedent for two current doctrines that say much the same thing. The first of these is the doctrine of "strict scrutiny" which, in those cases in which it is involved, reverses the normal presumption of constitutionality of a state statute and forces the government to assume the burden of proving its compelling interest in a particular type of restriction.[11]

A second derivative of the "preferred freedoms" doctrine is the doctrine of "overbreadth." It holds that statutes that purport to limit expression or other First Amendment rights must be narrowly and specifically drawn. A statute that may be indiscriminately applied to violate or threaten First Amendment rights is void on its face, even though its application in a particular case may be constitutionally supportable.

A good example of the application of this doctrine occurred in the case of *Aptheker* v. *Secretary of State* (1964). Aptheker, a leading socialist scholar, was editor of the journal *Political Affairs,* the "theoretical organ" of the American Communist Party. His passport was revoked pursuant to an act of Congress that made it unlawful for any member of an organization required to register with the Subversive Activities Control Board to apply for or hold a passport. The Communist Party had been required to register with the board, and that registration order had been upheld by the Supreme Court in 1961. Aptheker brought suit to have the act declared unconstitutional as a violation of his constitutionally protected right to travel. The government admitted that insofar as the act might be applied to persons who were merely supporters or casual members of the Communist Party, it might be difficult to sustain as reasonably related to national security. However, it claimed that no such infirmity existed when the act was applied, as in this case, to Aptheker and other leading members of the Communist Party. By a 6-3 vote, the Supreme Court found that the "act too broadly and indiscriminately restricts the right to travel and thereby abridges the liberty guaranteed by the Fifth Amendment" and was therefore unconstitutional on its face. It refused to accept the government's argument that the act could at least be applied to Aptheker. Where Congress wants to regulate the exercise of important constitutional rights, the Court said, it is required to draft a statute drawn as narrowly as possible to achieve the permissible end.

Along with the doctrine of "overbreadth," the Supreme Court has developed the concept of "chilling effects" to protect the exercise of First Amendment freedoms. Under this doctrine, a statute, investigation, or regulation that does not directly limit First Amendment freedoms may nonetheless be held unconstitutional if its mere existence "chills" or impairs the exercise of such rights. The best example is *Shelton* v. *Tucker* (1963). An Arkansas statute required every schoolteacher, as a condition of employment, to file an annual report of all organizations to which he or she belonged or contributed money. The Supreme Court invalidated the statute by a 5-4 vote. While recognizing the legitimate interest of a state in investigating the competence of its teachers, the Court held that to require disclosure of all memberships impaired teachers' rights to free association, "a right closely allied to freedom of speech and a right which, like free speech, lies at the foundation of a free society." The majority

---

[11]The "strict scrutiny" doctrine was discussed extensively in Chapter Two, Part Two.

opinion by Justice Stewart emphasized that a state was not barred from making *any* inquiry about the organizational—and other outside—activities of teachers, but only from the sort of unlimited and indiscriminate inquiry required by the Arkansas statute. ". . . [T]his Court has held that, even though the governmental purpose be legitimate and substantial, the purpose cannot be pursued by means that broadly stifle fundamental personal liberties when the end can be more narrowly achieved."

The doctrine of "chilling effects" still exists, but recent decisions of the Burger Court have trimmed it somewhat. In *Laird* v. *Tatum* (1972), the Court addressed the issue of whether standing could be conferred when a complainant alleged "that the exercising of his First Amendment rights is being chilled by the mere existence, without more, of governmental investigative and data gathering activities . . . alleged to be broader in scope than is reasonably necessary for the accomplishment of a valid governmental purpose." The complainants were civilians protesting against surveillance carried out against them by the military. The Court dismissed their complaint for lack of standing, holding that allegations of a "subjective chill" were an inadequate substitute for a "claim of specific present objective harm, or a threat of specific future harm." Unlike previous First Amendment cases where "chilling effects" were sufficient to confer standing, in this case no "regulations, proscriptions, or compulsions" were involved. In dissent, Justice Douglas contended that the complainant's injuries were neither remote nor imaginary but the result of "paralyzing governmental surveillance activities."

The above tests were devised to safeguard constitutionally protected speech by narrowing the circumstances in which regulation was permissible. But all accepted the premise that there *might be* circumstances in which speech could be abridged. As Justice Holmes observed in *Schenck* v. *United States* (1919), "the character of every act depends upon the circumstances in which it is done. . . . The most stringent protection of free speech would not protect a man in falsely shouting fire in a theatre and causing a panic."

Traditionally the Court has recognized four exceptions to the First Amendment's protections: commercial speech, libel and slander, "fighting words," and obscenity. The exception for commercial speech has been largely eroded by recent Supreme Court decisions (see pp. 1190–1202). Libel and slander may still be punished without abridging the First Amendment, but the Supreme Court has significantly narrowed the protections of libel and slander law which may be available to "public figures" (see pp. 1143–1170).

The same uncertainties apply to "fighting words" and "obscenity." The Supreme Court continues to maintain that neither is entitled to constitutional protection, but at the same time, it has severely restricted the scope of those concepts. "Fighting words" are words inherently likely to incite immediate physical retaliation; they are thus beyond those words that merely induce unrest or even stir people to anger. In *Chaplinsky* v. *New Hampshire* (1942), the Supreme Court upheld the right of a state to punish the utterance of fighting words. In fact, however, the Court has never upheld sanctions actually imposed for the use of such words. And the Court has recognized that words take on new meanings or become more or less acceptable over time. Thus there is no fixed category of "fighting words." In 1971, the Court, in *Cohen* v. *California* (see pp. 1217–1221), barred criminal punishment of the defendant for wearing a jacket with the words "Fuck the Draft" in a courthouse. And in *Gooding* v.

Wilson (1972), the Court refused to permit application of a "fighting words" statute against a black man who shouted at a police officer, "White son of a bitch, I'll kill you."

The problem of fighting words often implicates the peaceful assembly provisions of the First Amendment. Peaceful assembly can only be regulated under narrowly drawn standards that relate, not to the content of speech or communication, but to the "time, place, and manner" of the assemblage. A public official cannot be given unbridled discretion to grant or withhold a permit or license to hold a public meeting or parade. Assemblies and parades that threaten physical disturbances or serious disorder can be halted by police *if* the risk of imminent violence is clearly demonstrated. The prior obligation of the police, however, is to protect those participating in or attending a meeting against those who might disrupt it. For example, in *Garner* v. *Louisiana* (1961), the Court reversed the breach-of-the-peace convictions of sit-in demonstrators where there was no evidence that they—as opposed to scores of angry onlookers—were disorderly. And in *Edwards* v. *South Carolina* (1963), the Court reversed the convictions of noisy but otherwise peaceful demonstrators on the grounds of the state capitol in Columbia, South Carolina.

Most recently the issue of the hostile audience has arisen in the context of planned demonstrations by the American Nazi party in Skokie, Illinois, a predominantly Jewish suburb of Chicago with a large number of concentration camp survivors and their relatives. A state court injunction prohibiting Nazi party members from parading in uniforms and displaying the swastika was held unconstitutional by the Illinois Supreme Court. It ruled that the mere anticipation of a hostile audience could not justify this prior restraint and that display of the Nazi emblem could not be halted under the "fighting words" doctrine. Initially, the Illinois Supreme Court had refused to disturb the trial court's injunction, but that decision had been reversed by the U.S. Supreme Court in *National Socialist Party* v. *Skokie* (1977).

We have noted that reasonable restraints on the "time, place, and manner" of exercising First Amendment freedoms have been upheld by the Supreme Court. A number of such cases involve "involuntary audiences" who claim First Amendment protections for what they do *not* want to hear or see. The Court has upheld local ordinances making it a misdemeanor to solicit business at a private residence without obtaining the owner's prior consent. In *Breard* v. *Alexandria* (1951), such an ordinance, as applied to a magazine salesman, was upheld. But in *Martin* v. *Struthers* (1943), the Court invalidated an ordinance prohibiting all door-to-door solicitations including those by religious groups. A narrowly drawn law prohibiting loud sound trucks on the streets was upheld in *Kovacs* v. *Cooper* (1949), but in *Pollak* v. *Public Utilities Commission of the District of Columbia* (1952), the Court rejected the claims of passengers that radio receivers installed in privately owned buses and trolleys interfered with their freedom of conversation.

In all of these cases, the Court has been required to make close judgments of controversial facts. What is a "fighting" word as opposed to one that is merely offensive? When can the police stop a demonstration that has incited serious violence? Where is the line between commercial and religious solicitation to be drawn? Similar kinds of questions, only more difficult, have plagued the Court in obscenity cases. In *Roth* v. *United States* (1957), the Court reaffirmed the doctrine that obscenity was not entitled to constitutional protection. But as we will see later in this chapter, the Court spent the better part of the next eighteen years wrestling with definitions of what was, and what was not, constitutionally obscene. No one can say exactly where the line has been drawn, but it is clear beyond any doubt that a vast array of sexually explicit materials that would have been suppressed in 1957 is now purveyed virtually without restraint and with little danger of prosecution. To say that the Court has consistently maintained that obscenity is not protected by the First Amendment is virtually meaningless, for it is only the most extreme hard-core pornography, and sexually explicit materials purveyed to minors, that is in any danger of criminal sanction.

Professor Louis Henkin once said that constitutional interpretation is essentially a process of "drawing lines"—between what is prohibited and what is protected. But often the lines are vague and tend to conceal what is essentially a balancing approach to determining the limits of First Amendment rights. The symbolic word juggling that the Court has engaged in has been called, somewhat pretentiously, a "two level" theory of the First Amendment. But what that means is that under a comforting doctrinal cover, the Court has attempted to recognize and apply the changing limits of societal tolerance for particular types of expression.

Summary

The purpose of this essay has been to introduce the idea that the distinctive aspect of personal rights lies in the intersecting of its societal and personal components. One implication of this idea is that the customary intellectual separation of the two, so characteristic of traditional liberal theory, does not always afford a clear view of how politics and the person relate. A sharp distinction between "political rights" and "personal rights" is somewhat misleading, and we thus avoid that distinction.

We have also contended that the law, in the hands of a policymaking institution like the Supreme Court, has a potential for restriction as well as liberation. This leads to rather particular problems for the Court, and we have attempted to delineate them. An additional problematic matter is the fact that whatever particular issues the Court addresses, the context of these issues involves a general conception of rights, and the student of constitutional politics must grasp this *as a problem*. Our society's general conception is one oriented to action more than abstraction.

Finally, we have attempted to show that judicial policymaking in this area of rights involves not merely espousing certain values but shaping the facts of everyday life around these values. In this sense, we speak of the "activation" of rights. This activation process involves very difficult decisions and choices for the Court, and we have thus felt it necessary as an introductory matter to speak of the ways in which the Supreme Court approaches this matter.

Personal rights present the most difficult problems of judicial policymaking. Not only are the actual choices hard but change in judicial policy is often short term, and the conceptual problems associated with this distinctive area of rights are often especially difficult. The reason for this is, to repeat, that in personal rights, we try to use the political process in order to be free of political and social restrictions. Anything this paradoxical is bound to be difficult.

2. A GENERAL THEORY OF PERSONAL FREEDOM

A. *Thomas I. Emerson, The System of Freedom of Expression*

A system of freedom of expression, operating in a modern democratic society, is a complex mechanism. At its core is a group of rights assured to individual members of the society. This set of rights, which makes up our present-day concept of free expression, includes the right to form and hold beliefs and opinions on any subject, and to communicate ideas, opinions, and information through any medium—in speech, writing, music, art, or in other ways. To some extent it involves the right to remain silent. From the obverse side it includes the right to hear the views of others and to listen to their version of the facts. It encompasses the right to inquire and, to a degree, the right of access to information. As a necessary corollary, it embraces the right to assemble and to form associations, that is, to combine with others in joint expression.

Any system of freedom of expression must also embody principles through which exercise of these rights by one person or group may be reconciled with equal opportunity for other persons or groups to enjoy them. At the same time, the rights of all in freedom of expression must be reconciled with other individual and social interests. It is this process of reconciliation that has given rise to most of the controversial issues in the past and continues to be the major focus of attention today.

Assurance of these rights to freedom of expression involves limitations upon the power of the state to interfere with or abridge them. But the state also has a more affirmative role to play in the maintenance of a system of free expression in modern society. It must protect persons and groups seeking to exercise their rights from private or non-governmental interference either by way of force or to some extent by other methods. It must also undertake positively to promote and encourage freedom of expression, as by furnishing facilities, eliminating distortions in the media of communication, or making information available. Moreover, the increasing role of large organizations in our society now presents the question whether the government should take action to assure individuals in these private centers of power rights to freedom of expression similar to those guaranteed against the public power of government. In addition, the government itself participates extensively in the process of expression, through publication of official statements and reports, by its control over the educational system, and in other ways. Many of these problems are new to our time and are not readily answered on the basis of past theory or experience.

Finally, an effective system of freedom of expression requires a realistic administrative structure. It is not enough merely to formulate the broad principles or simply to incorporate them in general rules of law. It is necessary to develop a framework of doctrines, practices, and institutions

Reprinted from *The System of Freedom of Expression* (New York: Random House, 1970), pp. 3–19.

which will take into account the actual forces at work and make possible the realistic achievement of the objectives sought. Although we have had long experience with these aspects of the problem we have done little to explore the dynamics of operating a system of free expression. . . .

Obviously, the success of any society in maintaining freedom of expression hinges upon many different considerations. Some degree of fundamental consensus—some minimum area of agreement or acquiescence—is essential for a community to operate on any basis other than one of sheer force or terror. Economic institutions and economic conditions, the degree of security or insecurity from external threats, political traditions and institutions, systems of education, methods and media for forming public opinion, public attitudes and philosophy, and many other factors play a vital part. Those who warn us not to rely too much on legal forms are entirely correct that excessive emphasis can easily be placed upon the role of law. Yet in the United States today we have come to depend upon legal institutions and legal doctrines as a major technique for maintaining our system of free expression. We have developed and refined this technique more than has any other country. . . .

In recent years much uncertainty and controversy have marked the effort to formulate the legal doctrines pertaining to freedom of expression and to fix the role of legal institutions in maintaining them. This is due not only to the inherent complexities of the problem. It arises also out of the changes wrought in our society by shifting economic, political, and social forces. The basic theory underlying the legal framework has remained substantially unchanged since its development in the seventeenth and eighteenth centuries. But the conditions under which it must now be applied have greatly altered. There has been little effort to reappraise legal doctrines and institutions in light of the new situation. And even less consideration has been given to the extension of legal theory to new problems posed by modern conditions. . . .

The system of freedom of expression in a democratic society rests upon four main premises. . . .

First, freedom of expression is essential as a means of assuring individual self-fulfillment. The proper end of man is the realization of his character and potentialities as a human being. For the achievement of this self-realization the mind must be free. . . . Moreover, man in his capacity as a member of society has a right to share in the common decisions that affect him. To cut off his search for truth, or his expression of it, is to elevate society and the state to a despotic command over him and to place him under the arbitrary control of others.

Second, freedom of expression is an essential process for advancing knowledge and discovering truth. . . .

Third, freedom of expression is essential to provide for participation in decision making by all members of society. This is particularly significant for political decisions. Once one accepts the premise of the Declaration of Independence—that governments "derive their just powers from the consent of the governed"—it follows that the governed must, in order to exercise their right of consent, have full freedom of expression both in forming individual judgments and in forming the common judgment. The principle also carries beyond the political realm. It embraces the right to participate in the building of the whole culture, and includes freedom of expression in religion, literature, art, science, and all areas of human learning and knowledge.

Finally, freedom of expression is a method of achieving a more adaptable and hence a more stable community, of maintaining the precarious balance between healthy cleavage and necessary consensus. This follows because suppression of discussion makes a rational judgment impossible, substituting force for reason; because suppression promotes inflexibility and stultification, preventing society from adjusting to changing circumstances or developing new ideas; and because suppression conceals the real problems confronting a society, diverting public attention from the critical issues. At the same time the process of open discussion promotes greater cohesion in a society because people are more ready to accept decisions that go against them if they have a part in the decision-making process. Moreover, the state at all times retains adequate powers to promote unity and to suppress resort to force. Freedom of expression thus provides a framework in which the conflict necessary to the progress of a society can take place without destroying the society. It is an essential mechanism for maintaining the balance between stability and change. . . .

Two basic implications of the theory underlying our system of freedom of expression need to be emphasized. The first is that it is not a general measure of the individual's right to freedom of expression that any particular exercise of that right may be thought to promote or retard other goals of the society. The theory asserts that freedom of expression, while not the sole or sufficient end of society, is a good in itself, or at least an essential element in a good society. The society may seek to achieve other or more inclusive ends—such as virtue, justice, equality, or the maximum realization of the potentialities of its members. These are not necessarily gained by accepting the rules for freedom of expression. But, as a general proposition, the society may not seek them by suppressing the beliefs or opinions of individual members. To achieve these other goals it must rely upon other methods: the use of counter-expression and the regulation or control of conduct which is not expression. Hence the right to control individual expression, on the ground that it is judged to promote good or evil, justice or injustice, equality or inequality, is not, speaking generally, within the competence of the good society.

The second implication, in a sense a corollary of the first, is that the theory rests upon a fundamental distinction between belief, opinion, and communication of ideas on the one hand, and different forms of conduct on the other. For shorthand purposes we refer to this distinction hereafter as one between "expression" and "action." As just observed, in order to achieve its desired goals, a society or the state is entitled to exercise control over action—whether by prohibiting or compelling it—on an entirely different and vastly more extensive basis. But expression occupies an especially protected position. In this sector of human conduct, the social right of suppression or compulsion is at its lowest point, in most respects nonexistent. A majority of one has the right to control action, but a minority of . . . one has the right to talk. . . .

. . .

The legal system is, of course, one of the most effective instruments available to a society for controlling the behavior of its members so as to realize the values and goals sought by that society. Because of certain characteristics of a system of free expression, the role of law is of peculiar significance in any social effort to maintain such a system.

First, a system of free expression is designed to encourage a necessary degree of conflict within a society. To be sure, it attempts to avoid resort to force or violence by channeling this conflict into the area of expression and persuasion. And it contemplates that a longer-range consensus will ultimately be achieved. Yet, because it recognizes the right of the citizen to disagree with, arouse, antagonize, and shock his fellow citizens and the government, such an arrangement of human affairs is hardly likely to be automatically achieved. In its short-term effects it may indeed be highly volatile. Hence the system needs the legitimizing and harmonizing influence of the legal process to keep it in successful equilibrium.

Other features of a system of free expression likewise demonstrate the need for buttressing it through law and legal institutions. The full benefits of the system can be realized only when the individual knows the extent of his rights and has some assurance of protection in exercising them. Thus the governing principles of such a system need to be articulated with some precision and clarity. Doubt or uncertainty negates the process. Furthermore, the theory rests upon subordination of immediate interests in favor of long-term benefits. This can be achieved only through the application of principle, not by ad hoc resolution of individual cases. And it requires procedures adequate to relieve immediate pressures and facilitate objective consideration. All these elements a legal system is equipped to supply.

Further, as already observed, the theory of freedom of expression is a sophisticated and even complex one. It does not come naturally to the ordinary citizen, but needs to be learned. It must be restated and reiterated not only for each generation but for each new situation. It leans heavily upon understanding and education, both for the individual and the community as a whole. The legal process is one of the most effective methods for providing the kind of social comprehension essential for the attainment of society's higher and more remote ideals.

Finally, the principles of the system must be constantly reshaped and expanded to meet new conditions and new threats to its existence. This requires the deliberate attention of an institution entrusted with that specific obligation and possessing the expertise to perform such a task.

The function of the legal process is not only to provide a means whereby a society shapes and controls the behavior of its individual members in the interests of the whole. It also supplies one of the principal methods by which a society controls itself, limiting its own powers in the interests of the individual. The role of law here is to mark and guard the line between the sphere of social power, organized in the form of the state, and the area of private right. Judicial institutions function as a mediator between the government and the people. The legal problems involved in maintaining a system of free expression fall largely into these realms. Indeed the use of law to achieve this kind of control has been one of the central concerns of freedom-seeking societies over the ages. Legal recognition of individual rights, enforced through the legal process, has become the core of free society. . . .

In considering the role of the judiciary in a system of freedom of expression it is essential to narrow the issues and establish a fundamental distinction. We are not dealing here with any general function of our judicial institutions to foster the whole range of freedoms in a democratic society. Nor are we dealing with any broad power to supervise or review all major actions of the legislative and executive branches. We are concerned with the specific function of the judiciary in supporting a system of freedom of expression. This involves the application of general principles of law to assure that the basic mechanisms of the democratic process will be respected. It does not involve supervision over the decisions reached or measures adopted as a consequence of employing democratic procedures. Responsibility for this is primarily that of the legislature. In other words, the judicial institutions are here dealing essentially with the methods of conducting the democratic process, not with the substantive results of that process. In this differentiation of function lies a generic distinction between the role of the judiciary and the role of the legislature.

Within this narrower context the courts must play a crucial part in maintaining and extending our system of freedom of expression. Their competence to do so rests upon their independence from the other branches of government, their relative immunity to immediate political and popular pressures, the training and quality of their personnel, their utilization of legal procedures, and their powers of judicial review. The need of the courts to perform this function has become more imperative as the nation has moved from nineteenth-century economic liberalism to twentieth-century mass democracy. In our society today it has become necessary to develop methods for maintaining the system

of freedom of expression, not as a self-adjusting by-product of laissez-faire, but as a positive and deliberate function of the social process. What is required is a consciously formulated structure of protection, embracing legal doctrines that are operationally workable and utilizing legal institutions that are equipped to handle the problem. . . .

The major source of legal doctrine supporting the system of freedom of expression is the First Amendment. The precise meaning of the First Amendment at the time of its adoption is a matter of some dispute. In the broadest terms, however, the provision was plainly intended to assure the new nation the basic elements of a system of free expression as then conceived. As our constitutional law has developed over the years the First Amendment has come to have the same broad significance for our present, more complex, society. The fundamental meaning of the First Amendment, then, is to guarantee an effective system of freedom of expression suitable for the present times.

Other constitutional provisions also have an important bearing upon the system of freedom of expression. The Fourth Amendment's protection against unreasonable searches and seizures, the Fifth Amendment's privilege against self-incrimination, and the due process rules against vagueness and overbreadth in legislation all play a significant role in maintaining the system. In fact, the courts have come to give these constitutional guarantees a substantially different meaning when invoked in behalf of First Amendment rights. Thus the First Amendment has an umbrella effect, drawing within its shelter doctrines from many other areas of the law. . . .

The outstanding fact about the

First Amendment today is that the Supreme Court has never developed any comprehensive theory of what that constitutional guarantee means and how it should be applied in concrete cases. At various times the Court has employed the bad tendency test, the clear and present danger test, an incitement test, and different forms of the ad hoc balancing test. Sometimes it has not clearly enunciated the theory upon which it proceeds. Frequently it has avoided decision on basic First Amendment issues by invoking doctrines of vagueness, overbreadth, or the use of less drastic alternatives. Justice Black, at times supported by Justice Douglas, arrived at an "absolute" test, but subsequently reverted to the balancing test in certain types of cases. The Supreme Court has also utilized other doctrines, such as the preferred position of the First Amendment and prior restraint. Recently it has begun to address itself to problems of "symbolic speech" and the place in which First Amendment activities can be carried on. But it has totally failed to settle on any coherent approach or to bring together its various doctrines into a consistent whole. Moreover, it has done little to deal with some of the newer problems, where the issue is not pure restraint on government interference, but rather the use of governmental power to encourage freedom of expression or actual participation by government itself in the system of expression.

It is not surprising that this chaotic state of First Amendment theory has produced some unhappy results. The major doctrines applied by the Supreme Court have proved inadequate, particularly in periods of tension, to support a vigorous system of freedom of expression. Thus the bad tendency test offers virtually no protection to freedom of expression. The clear and present danger test is not only inapplicable in many situations but permits the government to cut off expression as soon as it comes close to being effective. The incitement test is open to much the same objections. The ad hoc balancing test is so unstructured that it can hardly be described as a rule of law at all. All the tests are excessively vague, little more than exercises in semantics. Efforts of the courts to deal with the more complex theoretical problems, such as "symbolic speech," have only made the situation worse. All in all doctrinal support for the system of freedom of expression is in a sad state of disarray. And this has had a most unfortunate effect upon the work of the lower Federal and State courts, upon the performance of government officials, and upon the understanding of the public.

B. A Note On the Limits of the Constitutional Order in Achieving Personal Rights

We have seen that Emerson's "system" of expressive freedom rests on four premises that systematically relate to each other. Individual self-fulfillment is a necessary precondition of advancement in knowledge and discovery of truth. The latter are presumed in the elements of effective decision making, and adaptability and stability in the community presume a capacity to arrive at good decisions. Thus seen, it is significant that Emerson seeks to unite the extremes of this scale within a single conceptual framework. His effort relates to the sometimes open conflict between the *theory* of personal rights and its *practice,* a conflict that stems from the fact that acutely *personal* dimensions of freedom of expression are realized in, but are not dependent upon, the political community.

It is also important that so elementary a relationship as that of the individual to the community be put in a respectable theoretical framework. The actual relationship is so complex and subtle, so elusive of capture by raw and unassisted observation, that we are initially called upon to conceive of it in ideal terms. It is almost like modern physics; we must first conceive of that which we would point to as being there. Even then, we must use instruments.

On the societal level, our "instrument" is the judiciary, and our conception is still a liberal ideology. To those of us socialized in a liberal tradition of politics, the close linkage of society and the individual seems almost natural. To speak of personal rights is not to speak of persons apart from society but rather of a notion that "rights" presumes the mediation or coercion of social institutions. In the liberal political world, a person has no conceivable meaning apart from society; man as presented in the classic state-of-nature is in a condition that necessitates a social order for the sake of his own individuality. Emerson does not depart from this conception, but he does in theory sharpen distinctions that are blurred in practice.

The liberal conception of rights is starkly outlined in such a procedural right as that to a speedy trial. Obviously, no such right can be said to exist apart from the social mechanism that is the essential ingredient of the right. Seen in this light, the "right" stipulates a particular way in which the state is expected to behave toward the individual in jeopardy of his liberty. Fourth Amendment rights involving search and seizure reflect the same relationship, although the societal instrumentalities—the prob-

able cause and warrant requirement and the availability of courts—are somewhat less tangible. It must be understood, however, that some of this relationship between right and social instrumentality lies in the dual characteristics of the government's being simultaneously a threat to the liberty of the individual and a remedy to that threat. As we have seen in earlier sections of the text (see Chapter Three on criminal justice), this duality underlies such devices as are represented in the *Miranda* doctrine.

In the case of procedural rights, almost all of their meaning and applicability lie within the constitutional order and its major instrumentality, the judiciary. But in the area of personal rights, there are unique limits to the reach of the constitutional order, and it must be understood that such rights are no more than a societally recognized latitude to seek, and perhaps find, a measure of personal meaning and significance. In this sense, personal rights are less tangible and subject to procedure and definition than are other kinds of rights.

It is important to recognize that personal freedom, *in a society like ours,* is a personal achievement, not a result of having a status conferred by public authority. Unless one only conceives of freedom negatively— that is, freedom *from* a host of strictures that might be imposed by public authority—then there are limits within which freedom is directly a result of the activities of public authority. Although many people do think of freedom in terms of what does *not* happen to them, the kind of personal rights of which we speak in this chapter embrace both conceptions.

The First Amendment's provisions concerning religious freedom serve as an example. In speaking to the matter of what the government may *not* do by way of establishment or interference with free exercise, the "right" embraced in these provisions does not suggest a particular result, as is the case in many procedural rights. When one has a right to a fair trial, then a fair trial is the result for which the right calls. But in religious freedom, religious sentiment may or may not result from exercise of the right. This is so because the stimulation of religious sentiment or feeling—for example, the sense of awe in the face of life itself—is intensely personal and does not follow from the presence of conditions permitting or even encouraging the pursuit of meaning in religious terms. In other words, the right is *about* the impulse and in no way constitutes the impulse.

The same is true of other areas of personal right, such as freedom of expression, access to the products of creative imagination, and the right to one's privacy. In none of these cases is any particular result *for the person* presumed. What is presumed is a set of possibilities for the person, and subsequently the society, if the conditions are present within which she or he may pursue questions of personal meaning. What makes personal rights unique and of particular fascination is the fact that their worth lies in what individuals make of themselves by virtue of having the rights. Personal rights are a latitude to seek, and perhaps find; but no result that is particularly a success or a failure is presumed.

Thus seen, there are inherent limits to the scope and effectiveness of the constitutional order in the degree to which personal rights result in human freedom and real senses of individuality. In an age when the state and society are increasingly looked to as a means of gratifying many needs or wants, one must contend with the fact that the ends served by rights that we term "personal" cannot be achieved by societal means. This alone makes them unique in terms of appreciating the limits of our constitutional order.

In the modern world, certain special problems in defining the parameters of freedom of the press have emerged. Government has proclaimed the need for secrecy in dealing with sensitive matters of state, particularly where national security is involved. Although the United States does not have an "official secrets" act comparable to that in the United Kingdom, there are rules governing the classification and release of government documents, and it is a criminal act to divulge a classified document. *The Pentagon Papers* case, presented in the previous chapter, illustrates the clash between the interests of government secrecy and the "norm" of the free press. The student will remember that in that case, although the Supreme Court ruled against the government, it did suggest that a stronger showing by government of the need for secrecy might have been sufficient to justify efforts to halt publication.

Another problem that has emerged is the reporter's claim of confidentiality of sources, a privilege usually extended in American law to doctors, lawyers, and priests. Claims of reporter's privilege have escalated with the growth of investigative reporting, particularly when the subjects are organized crime or political corruption. Most courts, including the Supreme Court, have rejected such claims unless they have been legislatively granted.

A third problem—pretrial publicity—poses important and immediate threats to the integrity of the judicial process. It was not until 1961, in *Irwin* v. *Doud*, that the Supreme Court took steps to deal with what is often called the "free press–fair trial" dilemma.

Finally, the status of "commercial speech" has become an issue. For many years, commercial speech was regarded, along with libel, fighting words, and obscenity, as not protected by the First Amendment. However, as an increasing number of businesses and professions have sought release from the strictures of state regulations proscribing advertising of services and products, the Supreme Court has taken a new look at the commercial speech exception.

3. DIMENSIONS OF POLITICAL EXPRESSION

A. *A Note on Freedom of the Press*

At one time, the "press" was the primary means of public communication about political and social activities. Today, of course, newspapers are but one among many media, and probably not the most important. Still, "freedom of the press" remains the shorthand phrase describing those freedoms associated with the public media, including television, radio, handbills, propaganda newsletters, and newspapers.

Two concepts underlie this freedom. The first is the rule against any prior restraints on publication. This prohibition, which stems from the English law commentator, Blackstone, is in practice far from an unbreachable shield. Yet as the Supreme Court stated in the *Pentagon Papers* case (see pp. 1069–1083), it is the prevailing rule of law to be supplanted only in exceptional circumstances. Prior restraint is prepublication censorship by government. It does not prevent a newspaper or television station from exercising some self-restraint in deciding what is to be published or aired. Nor does prior restraint prevent government from applying its laws to what has already been published or prevent an individual from seeking tort damages in a court of law. Government may prosecute the publisher of an obscene magazine, and a private individual may sue for libel. But neither government nor a private individual may restrain initial publication of the obscene or libelous material.

The second concept is often referred to as the "marketplace of ideas." This metaphor suggests that open access to the media, and to ideas in general, benefits society. It does this by fostering a competition of ideas that, it is assumed, will separate truth from falsehood. It is only by testing ideas against countervailing thoughts that truth—or at least the best ideas—can be known. Censorship robs society of this chance. Since truth cannot be "known" in advance, publication in the media is not conditioned on some prior consensus about what is true, or right, or decent. It is for that reason that not merely falsehood but malicious falsehood is the test for libel of "public" persons, and the libel test for private individuals is the establishment of defendant's negligence, which must show "reckless disregard." And as so defined, libel is not entitled to First Amendment protection.

We have observed that "rights" are complex and often defy neat and ready classification. A case may have meaning for more than one constitutional concept or arrangement of power. The *Pentagon Papers* case is a good example. In the previous chapter, it was presented in the context of restraints on presidential power. But it is also the leading post-New Deal case on the question of prior restraints on the press. The *Pentagon Papers* case turned on the absence of any law that directly empowered the government to enjoin publication of a newspaper. The main thrust of the government's argument, however, an argument rejected by a majority of justices, was that the president's broad powers under Article II to protect the national security were sufficient to justify an injunction against the *New York Times*.

While the decision in the *Pentagon Papers* case was a strong reaffirmation of the rule against prior restraints, it did not go so far as to say that prior restraint of publication of a book or magazine was never possible, only that the government had not met its very strong burden of proof in that case. In the spring of 1979, a federal judge in Milwaukee issued an injunction blocking publication of an article on the hydrogen bomb in *The Progressive* magazine, a liberal journal of opinion. This was the first time in history that a federal court had enjoined publication of a book or magazine for national security reasons.

(1) Prior Restraint

(a) New York Times v. United States (1971)

(See pp. 1069–1083)

(b) United States v. The Progressive, Inc. (1979)

[On March 9, 1979 a federal judge in Milwaukee, at the behest of the government, issued a temporary restraining order against *The Progressive* magazine barring it from publishing an article which would have been entitled "The H-Bomb Secret: How We Got It, Why We're Telling It." The article, written by a freelance writer named Howard Morland and compiled exclusively from public sources and nonclassified materials, included rough sketches and directions on how to build a hydrogen bomb. Its main purpose, however, was to demonstrate both that the veil of secrecy which encapsulates nuclear weapons productions is indeed quite porous, and also that such secrecy is unnecessary and improper in a democratic society.

In seeking a restraining order, the government alleged that publication of the article "will result in grave, direct, immediate and irreparable harm to the security of the United States and its people." In making this claim it exploited a loophole left in the Supreme Court's decision in the *Pentagon Papers* case. In arguing that case for *The New York Times* in 1971, the late Professor Alexander Bickel conceded that there was a single loophole to the general proposition that courts could not restrain a publication. That loophole, in his words, was if publication would "lead directly and unavoidably to a disastrous result." In his concurring opinion in the case, Justice Stewart rephrased the rule as follows: the courts could stop a publication which would "surely result in direct, immediate, and irreparable damage to our nation or its people."

Unlike the *Pentagon Papers* case, in which

no statute was directly invoked in support of the government's request for an injunction, in this case the claim was made under the Atomic Energy Act of 1954. Morland's article, the government contended, was "restricted data." According to the statute, "restricted data" is any information about the design or manufacture of nuclear weapons. Restricted data, according to the government's brief, is "classified at birth." It includes, as in this case, the author's own work product and original ideas. There was no contention by the government that any purloined documents were involved, nor any espionage or even efforts to build an atomic weapon without a permit. Morland was given access to some formerly classified data, but most of what he wrote in the article was obtained from public—though hard to locate—sources. The government's case would have been the same if Morland had merely awakened one morning, inspired by divine revelation, and had written out a description of the essentials of the Hydrogen bomb.

The Atomic Energy Act makes it a crime to "communicate, transmit or disclose" restricted data, and courts are given authority to enjoin publication or transmission of such data. The constitutionality and meaning of this portion of the Atomic Energy Act has never been considered by the Supreme Court. What, for example, is meant by "communicates, transmits or discloses?" Similar words were used in the Espionage Act of 1917, and the Supreme Court refused to enjoin publication of the Pentagon Papers on the basis of those words. Indeed, the federal district judge who first heard that case found that omission of the word "publishes" was deliberate. Those words, Judge Gurfein said, as used in the Espionage Act, were aimed not at open, general disclosure to the public, but at secret or clandestine communication to a person not entitled to such information. Should the words "communicates, transmits, or discloses" be interpreted differently when used in the Atomic Energy Act?

On March 26, 1979 Judge Robert Warren issued a preliminary injunction, based on his finding that the government had a reasonable likelihood of success when the case was considered on its merits, and that the government would suffer irreparable harm if the injunction was not issued. Excerpts from that opinion, and from *amicus* briefs filed in behalf of *The Progressive* in the Court of Appeals, are reprinted below.]

. . .

In its argument and briefs, plaintiff relies on national security, as enunciated by Congress in the Atomic Energy Act of 1954, as the basis for classification of certain documents. Plaintiff contends that, in certain areas, national preservation and self-interest permit the retention and classification of government secrets. The government argues that its national security interest also permits it to impress classification and censorship upon information originating in the public domain, if when drawn together, synthesized and collated, such information acquires the character of presenting immediate, direct and irreparable harm to the interests of the United States.

Defendants argue that freedom of expression as embodied in the First Amendment is so central to the heart of liberty that prior restraint in any form becomes anathema. They contend that this is particularly true when a nation is not at war and where the prior restraint is based on surmise or conjecture. While acknowledging that freedom of the press is not absolute, they maintain that the publication of the projected article does not rise to the level of immediate, direct and irreparable harm which could justify incursion into First Amendment freedoms. . . .

From the founding days of this nation, the rights to freedom of speech and of the press have held an honored place in our constitutional scheme. The establishment and nurturing of these rights is one of the true achievements of our form of government.

Because of the importance of these rights, any prior restraint on publication comes into court under a heavy presumption against its constitutional validity. *New York Times* v. *United States* . . . (1971).

However, First Amendment rights are not absolute. They are not boundless.

Justice Frankfurter dissenting in *Bridges* v. *California* . . . (1941), stated it in this fashion: "Free speech is not so absolute or irrational a conception as to imply paralysis of the means for effective protection of all the freedoms secured by the Bill of Rights." In the *Schenck* case, Justice Holmes recognized: "The character of every act depends upon the circumstances in which it is done." *Schenck* v. *United States*. . . (1931).

In *Near* v. *Minnesota*. . . (1931), the Supreme Court specifically recognized an extremely narrow area, involving national security, in which interference with First Amendment rights might be tolerated and a prior restraint on publication might be appropriate. The Court stated:

When a nation is at war many things that might be said in time of peace are such a hindrance to its effort that their utterance will not be endured so long as men fight and that no Court could regard them as protected by any constitutional right. No one would question but that a government might prevent actual obstruction to its recruiting service or the publication of the sailing dates of transports or the number and location of troops. . . .

Thus, it is clear that few things, save grave national security concerns, are sufficient to override First Amendment interests. A court is well admonished to approach any re-quested prior restraint with a great deal of skepticism.

. . .

The Court is convinced that the government has a right to classify certain sensitive documents to protect its national security. The problem is with the scope of the classification system.

Defendants contend that the projected article merely contains data already in the public domain and readily available to any diligent seeker. They say other nations already have the same information or the opportunity to obtain it. How then, they argue, can they be in violation of 42 U.S.C. §§ 2274(b) and 2280 which purport to authorize injunctive relief against one who would disclose restricted data "with reason to believe such data will be utilized to injure the United States or to secure an advantage to any foreign nation . . ."?

Although the government states that some of the information is in the public domain, it contends that much of the data is not, and that the Morland article contains a core of information that has never before been published.

Furthermore, the government's position is that whether or not specific information is "in the public domain" or has been "declassified" at some point is not determinative. The government states that a court must look at the nature and context of prior disclosures and analyze what the practical impact of the prior disclosures are as contrasted to that of the present revelation. The government feels that the mere fact that Morland could prepare an article explaining the technical processes of thermonuclear weapons does not mean that those processes are available to everyone. They lay heavy emphasis on the argument that the danger lies in the exposition of certain concepts never heretofore disclosed in conjunction with one another.

. . .

The Court has grappled with this difficult problem and has read and studied the affidavits and other documents on file. After all this, the Court finds concepts within the article that it does not find in the public realm—concepts that are vital to the operation of the bomb.

Even if some of the information is in the public domain, due recognition must be given to the human skills and expertise involved in writing this article. The author needed sufficient expertise to recognize relevant, as opposed to irrelevant, information and to assimilate the information obtained. The right questions had to be asked or the correct educated guesses had to be made.

. . .

Does the article provide a "do-it yourself" guide for the hydrogen bomb? Probably not. A number of affidavits make quite clear that a *sine qua non* to thermonuclear capability is a large, sophisticated industrial capability coupled with a coterie of imaginative, resourceful scientists and technicians. One does not build a hydrogen bomb in the basement. However, the article could possibly provide sufficient information to allow a medium size nation to move faster in developing a hydrogen weapon. It could provide a ticket to by-pass blind alleys.

The Morland piece could accelerate the membership of a candidate nation in the thermonuclear club. Pursuit of blind alleys or failure to grasp seemingly basic concepts have been the cause of many inventive failures.

. . . Although the defendants state that the information contained in the article is relatively easy to obtain, only five countries now have a hydro-

gen bomb. Yet the United States first successfully exploded the hydrogen bomb some twenty-six years ago.

The point has also been made that it is only a question of time before other countries will have the hydrogen bomb. That may be true. However, there are times in the course of human history when time itself may be very important. This time factor becomes critical when considering mass annihilation weaponry—witness the failure of Hitler to get his V-1 and V-2 bombs operational quickly enough to materially affect the outcome of World War II.

Defendants have stated that publication of the article will alert the people of this country to the false illusion of security created by the government's futile efforts at secrecy. They believe publication will provide the people with needed information to make informed decisions on an urgent issue of public concern.

However, this Court can find no plausible reason why the public needs to know the technical details about hydrogen bomb construction to carry on an informed debate on this issue. Furthermore, the Court believes that the defendants' position in favor of nuclear non-proliferation would be harmed, not aided, by the publication of this article.

The defendants have also relied on the decision in the *New York Times* case. In that case, the Supreme Court refused to enjoin the *New York Times* and the *Washington Post* from publishing the contents of a classified historical study of United States decision-making in Viet Nam, the so-called "Pentagon Papers."

This case is different in several important respects. In the first place, the study involved in the *New York Times* case contained historical data relating to events some three to twenty years previously. Secondly, the Supreme Court agreed with the lower court that no cogent reasons were advanced by the government as to why the article affected national security except that publication might cause some embarrassment to the United States.

A final and most vital difference between these two cases is the fact that a specific statute is involved here. Section 2274 of the Atomic Energy Act prohibits anyone from communicating, transmitting or disclosing any restricted data to any person "with reason to believe such data will be utilized to injure the United States or to secure an advantage to any foreign nation."

Section 2014 of the Act defines restricted data. " 'Restricted Data' means all data concerning 1) design, manufacture, or utilization of atomic weapons; 2) the production of special nuclear material; or 3) the use of special nuclear material in the production of energy, but shall not include data declassified or removed from the Restricted Data category pursuant to §2162 of this title."

As applied to this case, the Court finds that the statute in question is not vague or overbroad. The Court is convinced that the terms used in the statute—"communicates, transmits or discloses"—include publishing in a magazine.

The Court is of the opinion that the government has shown that the defendants had reason to believe that the data in the article, if published, would injure the United States or give an advantage to a foreign nation. Furthermore, extensive reading and studying of the documents on file lead to the conclusion that not all the data is available in the public realm in the same fashion, if it is available at all.

What is involved here is information dealing with the most destruc-

tive weapon in the history of mankind, information of sufficient destructive potential to nullify the right to free speech and to endanger the right to life itself.

Stripped to its essence then, the question before the Court is a basic confrontation between the First Amendment right to freedom of the press and national security.

. . .

Faced with a stark choice between upholding the right to continued life and the right to freedom of the press, most jurists would have no difficulty in opting for the chance to continue to breathe and function as they work to achieve perfect freedom of expression.

Is the choice here so stark? Only time can give us a definitive answer. But considering another aspect of this panoply of rights we all have is helpful in answering the question now before us. This aspect is the disparity of the risk involved.

The destruction of various human rights can come about in differing ways and at varying speeds. Freedom of the press can be obliterated overnight by some dictator's imposition of censorship or by the slow nibbling away at a free press through successive bits of repressive legislation enacted by a nation's lawmakers. Yet, even in the most drastic of such situations, it is always possible for a dictator to be overthrown, for a bad law to be repealed or for a judge's error to be subsequently rectified. Only when human life is at stake are such corrections impossible.

The case at bar is so difficult precisely because the consequences of error involve human life itself and on such an awesome scale.

. . .

A mistake in ruling against the United States could pave the way for thermonuclear annihilation for us all. In that event, our right to life is extinguished and the right to publish becomes moot.

In the *Near* case, the Supreme Court recognized that publication of troop movements in time of war would threaten national security and could therefore be restrained. Times have changed significantly since 1931 when *Near* was decided. Now war by foot soldiers has been replaced in large part by war by machines and bombs. No longer need there be any advance warning or any preparation time before a nuclear war could be commenced.

In light of these factors, this Court concludes that publication of the technical information on the hydrogen bomb contained in the article is analogous to publication of troop movements or locations in time of war and falls within the extremely narrow exception to the rule against prior restraint.

Because of this "disparity of risk," because the government has met its heavy burden of showing justification for the imposition of a prior restraint on publication of the objected-to technical portions of the Morland article, and because the Court is unconvinced that suppression of the objected-to technical portions of the Morland article would in any plausible fashion impede the defendants in their laudable crusade to stimulate public knowledge of nuclear armament and bring about enlightened debate on national policy questions, the Court finds that the objected-to portions of the article fall within the narrow area recognized by the Court in *Near* v. *Minnesota* in which a prior restraint on publication is appropriate.

. . .

[The following passages are taken from *amicus curiae* briefs submitted to the Court of Appeals for the Seventh Circuit in behalf of *The Progressive*]

From the brief prepared by Professors Thomas I. Emerson and Lee Bollinger in behalf of Scientific American *magazine:*

There has been a tendency to present this case as if the sole issue was whether or not this country should run the risk of a nuclear holocaust by allowing public dissemination of the secret of making a hydrogen bomb. Thus the court below, while not fully adopting that position, did talk about "a stark choice between upholding the right to continued life and the right to freedom of the press." It should be obvious that no one concerned with this case favors such an outcome or would engage in any conduct likely to bring it about. The issues are not that simple. They need to be seen in a broader and more rational context, as viewed by responsible people concerned with the best interests of this nation and the rest of the world.

The case does not involve the theft or purloining of information in the possession of the Government. It does not concern the right of the Government to protect information in its possession by adopting a classification system or other security measures to prohibit Government employes or Government contractors from disclosing such information. It does not relate to any right the Government may have to punish persons, by criminal prosecution or otherwise, *after* the communication has been made. And it does not even involve materials that the Government has classified.

. . .

The rule against prior restraint is certainly one of the most remarkable legal principles in our jurisprudence. Few doctrines in any field of law can boast of such an extraordinary record of adherence and success. . . . The fact that every shade of judicial philosophy has accepted the doctrine, and that the Government has rarely sought to make exceptions to it, bespeaks a national commitment to a legal principle that serves a vital function in maintaining our system of freedom of expression. . . .

The principal objections to the use of advance censorship, or prior restraint, are well known. A prior restraint, which cuts off communication in advance, is the most effective in its results, and the easiest to apply, of any method ever invented by Government to control expression. It is achieved by a stroke of the pen. It can be applied to a vast area of expression with a minimum of manpower. It does not require any originality or imagination, and is usually administered by bureaucrats possessed of limited vision. It forces upon the person desiring to communicate the burden of justification. It leaves that person with the sole option of complying with the censor's demand or being found in violation of the law. It is unaccompanied by the procedural protections built into our law for the enforcement of Government mandates by criminal punishment. The process frequently, as here, takes place in secrecy and is not open to public scrutiny. And the dynamics of the process inevitably press toward an excess of suppression. . . .

The mere willingness of the judiciary to entertain Government requests for injunctive relief against speech has built into it the dysfunction of delay. Ideas and information that otherwise would have seen the light of day now become entangled in the judicial process, which may take weeks or even months to sort everything out. Even clearly protected speech can be forced to wait on the back burner by this process.

. . .

Not only do prior restraints place serious impositions on the system of expression, but they are almost invariably unnecessary. The lesson of the *Pentagon Papers* case was surely that the Government can be expected to indulge in substantial hyperbole when it comes to assessing the likely harm of a free press to our national security. Given the fact that the Pentagon Papers were an historical document, concerned with the actions of *prior,* Democratic administrations, the Nixon Administration's extreme and unwarranted prediction of harm from publication is surely good evidence of the likelihood of Government exaggeration on these matters. That is not to suggest that the Government was then, or is generally, disingenuous; again, it is simply in the nature of government to behave in this manner. It is not to be ignored that the country has survived again and again in the face of the most serious predictions of doom, without having to resort to the method of prior restraints as a means of assuring national security. . . .

Although there is well-nigh universal agreement that a system of prior restraint imposes a disastrous and unacceptable barrier to freedom of expression, there has been disagreement over whether any exceptions should be made to the rule against prior restraint and, if so, what ones. It is our contention (1) that no exceptions to the doctrine of prior restraint should be permitted; (2) that the damage test accepted by the court below is especially restrictive of expression; (3) but that the rule against prior restraint does not apply to communication of information exclusively within the military sector; and (4) that the decisions of the Supreme Court, while not accepting this position as a matter of theory, have not deviated from it in practice.

All the reasons given above for not

tolerating prior restraint also lead to the conclusion that no exceptions should be made to the basic rule. The Government has other methods for controlling unprotected communications and enormous resources for making them effective. It does not need to invoke a device which violates a central purpose, historically and currently, of the First Amendment. There are, however, additional and more specific reasons for not making exceptions to the rule.

First, and most important, the rule against prior restraint is inherently incapable of accommodating exceptions; to impose exceptions upon the rule is in effect to destroy it. This is true because of the way an exception to the rule operates in practical administration. Once an exception has been recognized, all the Government has to do is to allege that a certain contemplated publication falls within the exception. The court then issues a restraining order so as to allow the Government to present its case. A hearing is held and the court decides whether the matter falls within the exception. Appeals to higher courts follow. *This process is itself a system of prior restraint.* It involves an examination of the material by Government officials, an order to withhold publication, and a Governmental decision as to whether the material may be published or not. The scope of the exception is thus determined by the government's claim and the exception has swallowed up the rule. . . .

Second, even if one could solve this dilemma, the nature of public expression is such that it is exceedingly difficult, if not impossible, to formulate an exception that embodies any definite stopping point. If the exception is not wide-open from the beginning it quickly becomes so as Government officials and lower courts continue to invoke it. As Justice [William O.] Douglas has observed, "Sooner or later, any test which provides less than blanket protection . . . will be twisted and relaxed so as to provide virtually no protection at all."

Third, exceptions to the prior restraint rule place an inappropriate burden on the judicial system. As already noted, the court is called upon to make a highly speculative judgment about future and uncertain events. Moreover, in the national security area much of the proceeding—certainly the critical parts—takes place *in camera*. Again, the very nature of the Government's claim requires secrecy in its assertion and proof. Thus no one is entitled to know what the case is really about unless he or she obtains security clearance, a privilege conferred by one of the parties to the case. There is little in this procedure to recommend it in a democratic society.

The dangers of permitting exceptions to the rule against prior restraint are well illustrated by the proposed exception urged by the Government and accepted by the lower court in this case. As formulated in the Findings of Fact and Conclusions of Law, the test is whether the material "will result in direct, immediate and irreparable damage to the United States." And this standard applies not only to classified information possessed by the Government, but to all information discovered by any citizen and "classified at birth."

If this standard were ever accepted, it could be used to stifle freedom of scientific inquiry in the United States. The methods of science are based upon open interchange of ideas and information, open discussion of results obtained, and putting together bits and pieces of available knowledge in order to produce a new concept. Publication of information constitutes the very essence of the scientific method, and is imperative for scientific progress. Yet much of the information and many of the ideas exchanged by scientists—in physics, chemistry, biology, perhaps even in psychology and sociology—could be alleged to be of a character that might result in "direct, immediate and irreparable damage." The formula which defines the exception proposed for this case could thus be used as a basis for Governmental supervision of vast areas of the scientific community and Government control over much scientific activity.

The effect on the right of the public to know could be equally devastating. The solutions to all of the pressing problems of this technological society depend upon access to information. Much of this information involves knowledge that could affect our national security. . . .

From the brief prepared by Floyd Abrams and Dean Ringell in behalf of The New York Times, *the American Society of Newspaper Editors, the Association of American Publishers, the National Association of Broadcasters, the Association of American University Presses, and* The Boston Globe:

The sections of the [Atomic Energy] Act relied upon, as interpreted by the Government and the court below are over-broad and vague. . . .

This definition merits a moment's pause. If the Government's interpretation [of the term "restricted data"] is to be accepted, it means that *any* information whatever about atomic weapons or special nuclear material, whatever its origin, is classified—and that its disclosure provides a basis for criminal sanctions—unless and until the Government sanctions it. A journalist's idle musings about the nature

or use of nuclear weapons or the operation and development of nuclear power facilities—for the crime is not limited to information about nuclear weaponry—thus fits the category. One would have thought this an absurd result until this case was brought.

The flaws inherent in using such a definition as the basis of an actual or potential criminal violation . . . are evident. Such a definition is hopelessly vague. Can one describe the blast at Hiroshima and studies of its victims? Presumably one can and surely many have. But the mere fact that others have published the information in some form is apparently no guarantee that the information has been declassified—*i.e.* is no longer "restricted data."

How is an individual to receive "fair notice" that his conduct will violate the criminal laws? Is he obliged to inquire of the Government each time he wishes to comment on matters affecting nuclear policy whether his insight has been declassified? The literal interpretation of the statute gives rise to such absurd results as to be unthinkable—except that the Government has explicitly urged such an interpretation of the statute and that the court below has apparently adopted it. The power of the Government to pick and choose among those who write about issues of atomic energy, subjecting them to prosecution on the basis of their failure to comply with an unascertainable standard, is precisely the evil the vagueness doctrine seeks to avoid.

Even if it could be said that appellants had been put on sufficient notice here, the overbreadth doctrine gives them standing to challenge the improper reach of the statute to others. The potential for inhibition of speech on the part of those from whom we should most wish to hear—those who are informed about our nation's nuclear policies but are outside the Governmental and professional structure which sets those policies—is enormous.

The application of the Atomic Energy Act in the fashion involved here has the potential to sweep within it and render potentially criminal the words of any critic, in academe or elsewhere, who, *without* access to classified information, happens upon—or creates—a bit of information which some Government official believes harmful to the national interest. At a time when debate over nuclear power daily grows more heated and when the Government's reputation for candor has increasingly been called into question by disclosures of past concealment, the inhibition such interpretation of the statute poses for free expression simply cannot be tolerated. . . .

The district court's analysis departed from the principles of analysis long applied in considering Governmental restrictions—let alone Governmental requests for prior restraints—in two other unusual respects, departures which, while sufficient to support reversal in themselves, also point up deeper misconceptions on the part of the district court. Thus, the court emphasized that it "can find no plausible reason why the public needs to know the technical details about hydrogen bomb construction to carry on an informed debate on this issue. Furthermore, the court believes that the defendants' position in favor of nuclear non-proliferation would be harmed, not aided, by the publication of this article."

Whatever the accuracy of the court's assessment of the wisdom of *The Progressive*'s decision or of the public's "need to know" the information in question, one thing is clear:

these are *not* factors upon which the court may base a decision to issue a prior restraint. As Chief Justice [Warren] Burger said in *Columbia Broadcasting System, Inc.,* v. *Democratic National Committee,* "For better or worse, editing is what editors are for; and editing is selection and choice of material. That editors—newspapers or broadcast—can and do abuse this power is beyond doubt, but that is no reason to deny the discretion Congress provided. Calculated risks of abuse are taken in order to preserve higher values. The presence of these risks is nothing new; the authors of the Bill of Rights accepted the reality that these risks were evils for which there was no acceptable remedy other than a spirit of moderation and a sense of responsibility—and civility—on the part of those who exercise the guaranteed freedoms of expression."

The Chief Justice's observations as to the "risks" accepted by the framers in adopting the Bill of Rights point up another and perhaps even more fundamental flaw in the district court's analysis. Throughout the latter portion of its opinion the court refers to a "disparity of risk." It contrasts the effect of "[a] mistake in ruling against the United States [which] could pave the way for thermonuclear annihilation for us all." In the latter event, the Court continued, "our right to life is extinguished and the right to publish becomes moot."

This "disparity of risk" is explicitly relied upon by the court as a basis for its decision. But any such analysis is a perilous one. In every case in which national security is asserted as a basis for a prior restraint, the consequences of mistakenly denying the restraint may, by definition, be grave. But the consequence of mistake cannot lessen the burden on the Government to demonstrate with the requisite certainty that immediate and direct damage to the nation or its people is at stake. To focus on the danger of a *mistake* is to assure that the asserted national security interest must prevail in virtually all cases because of the greater weight the court assigns—by hypothesis—to such interest, whether or not that interest has been shown to be present.

This flawed logic only underscores the need for rigorous adherence to the stern requirements of proof. . . . It is one thing to say that it is necessary, on rare occasions, for the courts to assess the consequences of a publication upon national security and in so doing, to consider the risks which may attend such publication. But, consistent with the needs of a free and democratic society, they must do so limited by rules requiring proof of fact, not speculation, of sure, direct, immediate and irreparable injury. And they must do so informed by our historic conviction that censorship does not well serve either the interests of free expression or those of national security.

As phrased by Judge [Murray L.] Gurfein in the district court opinion in *The New York Times* case itself, "The security of the nation is not at the ramparts alone. Security also lies in the value of our free institutions. A cantankerous press, an obstinate press, an ubiquitous press must be suffered by those in authority in order to preserve the even greater values of freedom of expression and the right of the people to know. In this case there has been no attempt by the Government at political suppression. There has been no attempt to stifle criticism. Yet in the last analysis it is not merely the opinion of the editorial writer or of the columnist which is protected by the First Amendment. It is the free flow of information so that the public will be informed about the Government and its actions."

[Throughout the course of the litigation, a heavy lid of secrecy was imposed by the government. Legal briefs and exhibits submitted by *The Progressive* were censored and not released to the public. Lawyers for the magazine had to be "cleared" to examine materials filed in their own behalf, and were forbidden to communicate any restricted information to the editors. On June 15, 1979, *The Progressive* filed a motion asking Judge Warren to lift the injunction. In declining to do so, he issued a secret opinion that was not even shown to the defendants.

Early in the proceedings the government lawyers argued that information about the hydrogen bomb was "data restricted at birth," that is, data that became classified as soon as it came into existence. When *The Progressive* appealed the prior restraint order to the Court of Appeals for the Seventh Circuit, the government began to argue that "technical information"—not just technical information about nuclear arms—was speech not protected by the First Amendment.

Oral arguments were held before a three-judge panel on September 13, 1979. However, before the Court of Appeals could decide the case, on September 15th, several newspapers around the country, led by the *The Press Connection* of Madison, Wisconsin, published a letter by another writer, which disclosed almost all of the technical information in the Morland article. On September 17th, the government announced that it would seek dismisal of the case. And, on September 28th, the Court of Appeals vacated Judge Warren's prior restraint injunction. However, it had not, as this book goes to press, decided on the government's motion that the case should be dismissed because it had become "moot," and that all of the legal documents and exhibits that had been suppressed should not be revealed. No authoritative decision has been made on the validity of the government's interpretation of the Atomic Energy Act. The Morland article appeared, in its original form, in the November, 1979 issue of *The Progressive.*]

(2) The Press and Public Figures

(a) *New York Times v. Sullivan* (1964)

+Brennan, Warren, Black, Douglas, Clark, Harlan, Stewart, White, Goldberg

[Among the general purposes of the First Amendment is the protection of open political debate, including the criticism of public officials. The importance of robust political debate to the maintenance of democratic institutions hardly needs to be stated. Yet, at least insofar as the criticism of public officials is concerned, there have always been some limits.

In 1798, a Federalist-controlled Congress, smarting under bitter criticism from its political opposition—the Jeffersonians—over its deteriorating relations with France, sought to stifle that criticism with passage of the infamous Alien and Sedition Acts. Under the Alien Act, the president was empowered to deport any alien whom he believed to be dangerous to the peace and safety of the country. The Sedition Act made it a crime to conspire to oppose any law of the United States and unlawful to write, print, or publish "any false, scandalous and malicious writing . . . against the government of the United States, or either house of the Congress . . . , or the President . . . , with intent to defame . . . , or to bring them, or either of them, into contempt or disrepute; or to excite against them, or either or any of them, the hatred of the good people of the United States."

The Sedition Act was enforced vigorously by the Adams administration and by Federalist judges. Fifteen indictments were obtained, resulting in ten convictions. Indeed, the conduct of some Federalist judges was so inflammatory and prejudicial that several were impeached after the Jeffersonians came to power in 1801. The defendants were not permitted to challenge the constitutionality of the act. Technically, truth was a defense to charges to seditious libel under the Act. But in their zeal to punish their critics, the Federalist judges often charged juries to ignore claims of truth.

Passage of the Sedition Act went to the central meaning of the First Amendment. The Federalists intended to reenact the English common law of seditious libel. They argued that the First Amendment had *not* been meant to abolish that crime but only to incorporate the English rule against prior restraints. Under the English common law, it was virtually impossible to censor a publication, but the government had wide latitude after publication to prosecute those that were hostile to it. Truth was no defense, and convictions were common.

The Jeffersonians opposed passage of the act and argued strenuously that it was unconstitutional. They believed that the First Amendment had been intended to abolish the crime of seditious libel. Indeed, James Madison and Albert Gallatin went even further to contend that the First Amendment prohibited passage of any sedition laws.

The Sedition Act was never tested in the Supreme Court. After the Jeffersonians took control of the government, Congress passed a law providing for repayment of all fines levied on those convicted, on the grounds that the act was unconstitutional. President Jefferson pardoned all those convicted. A broad consensus developed that the act was invalid, and this consensus was, and is, shared by justices of the Supreme Court.

Congress passed sedition acts in 1918 and 1940 (Smith Act), but neither sought to punish mere criticism of government officials or government policy. The 1918 statute punished efforts to obstruct the war, while the Smith Act prohibited conspiracies to advocate the overthrow of the government by force and violence. The Supreme Court held the Smith Act constitutional in *Dennis* v. *United States* (1951), but then in *Yates* v. *United States* (1957), the Court established an evidentiary distinction between direct and abstract advocacy that rendered the act virtually unenforceable. No prosecution was ever again brought under the Smith Act.

The First Amendment prohibits the crime of *seditious* libel (mere criticism of the government), but it is also recognized that there is need for some protection of public officials against libel and slander. Libel is any written or oral statement that is defamatory (i.e., that tends to expose another person to public hatred, ridicule, or contempt). Slander is a false report, uttered with malice, that tends to injure the reputation of another person. Balancing the need for this protection against the need for a free press is no easy task. Under what conditions is the press protected from libel suits by public officials? The *Sullivan* case was the first of a continuing series of contemporary cases to address this issue.]

MR. JUSTICE BRENNAN delivered the opinion of the Court.

We are required in this case to determine for the first time the extent to which the constitutional protections for speech and press limit a State's power to award damages in a libel action brought by a public official against critics of his official conduct.

Respondent L. B. Sullivan is one of the three elected Commissioners of the City of Montgomery, Alabama. He testified that he was "Commissioner of Public Affairs and the duties are supervision of the Police Department, Fire Department, Department of Cemetery and Department of Scales." He brought this civil libel action against the four individual petitioners, who are Negroes and Alabama clergymen, and against petitioner the New York Times Company, a New York corporation which publishes the *New York Times*, a daily newspaper. A jury in the Circuit Court of Montgomery County awarded him damages of $500,000, the full amount claimed, against all the petitioners, and the Supreme Court of Alabama affirmed. . . .

Respondent's complaint alleged that he had been libeled by statements in a full-page advertisement that was carried in the *New York Times* on March 29, 1960. Entitled "Heed Their Rising Voices," the advertisement began by stating that

"As the whole world knows by now, thousands of Southern Negro students are engaged in widespread non-violent demonstrations in positive affirmation of the right to live in human dignity as guaranteed by the U. S. Constitution and the Bill of Rights." It went on to charge that "in their efforts to uphold these guarantees, they are being met by an unprecedented wave of terror by those who would deny and negate that document which the whole world looks upon as setting the pattern for modern freedom. . . ." Succeeding paragraphs purported to illustrate the "wave of terror" by describing certain alleged events. The text concluded with an appeal for funds for three purposes: support of the student movement, "the struggle for the right-to-vote," and the legal defense of Dr. Martin Luther King, Jr., leader of the movement, against a perjury indictment then pending in Montgomery. . . .

Of the 10 paragraphs of text in the advertisement, the third and a portion of the sixth were the basis of respondent's claim of libel. They read as follows:

Third paragraph:

In Montgomery, Alabama, after students sang "My Country, 'Tis of Thee" on the State Capitol steps, their leaders were expelled from school, and truckloads of police armed with shotguns and tear-gas ringed the Alabama State College Campus. When the entire student body protested to state authorities by refusing to re-register, their dining hall was padlocked in an attempt to starve them into submission.

Sixth paragraph:

Again and again the Southern violators have answered Dr. King's peaceful protests with intimidation and violence.

They have bombed his home almost killing his wife and child. They have assaulted his person. They have arrested him seven times—for "speeding," "loitering" and similar "offenses." And now they have charged him with "perjury"—a felony under which they could imprison him for ten years. . . .

Although neither of these statements mentions respondent by name, he contended that the word "police" in the third paragraph referred to him as the Montgomery Commissioner who supervised the Police Department, so that he was being accused of "ringing" the campus with police. He further claimed that the paragraph would be read as imputing to the police, and hence to him, the padlocking of the dining hall in order to starve the students into submission. . . .

It is uncontroverted that some of the statements contained in the two paragraphs were not accurate descriptions of events which occurred in Montgomery. . . .

We hold that the rule of law applied by the Alabama courts is constitutionally deficient for failure to provide the safeguards for freedom of speech and of the press that are required by the First and Fourteenth Amendments in a libel action brought by a public official against critics of his official conduct. We further hold that under the proper safeguards the evidence presented in this case is constitutionally insufficient to support the judgment for respondent.

We may dispose at the outset of two grounds asserted to insulate the judgment of the Alabama courts from constitutional scrutiny. The first is the proposition relied on by the State Supreme Court—that "The Fourteenth Amendment is directed against State action and not private

action." That proposition has no application to this case. . . .

The second contention is that the constitutional guarantees of freedom of speech and of the press are inapplicable here, at least so far as the *Times* is concerned, because the allegedly libelous statements were published as part of a paid, "commercial" advertisement. The argument relies on *Valentine* v. *Chrestensen*. . . .

The reliance is wholly misplaced. . . .

The publication here was not a "commercial" advertisement in the sense in which the word was used in *Chrestensen*. It communicated information, expressed opinion, recited grievances, protested claimed abuses, and sought financial support on behalf of a movement whose existence and objectives are matters of the highest public interest and concern. See *N.A.A.C.P* v. *Button*. . . . That the *Times* was paid for publishing the advertisement is as immaterial in this connection as is the fact that newspapers and books are sold. . . . Any other conclusion would discourage newspapers from carrying "editorial advertisements" of this type, and so might shut off an important outlet for the promulgation of information and ideas by persons who do not themselves have access to publishing facilities—who wish to exercise their freedom of speech even though they are not members of the press. . . . The effect would be to shackle the First Amendment in its attempt to secure "the widest possible dissemination of information from diverse and antagonistic sources." . . . To avoid placing such a handicap upon the freedoms of expression, we hold that if the allegedly libelous statements would otherwise be constitutionally protected from the present judgment, they do not forfeit that protection because they were published in the form of a paid advertisement.

The general proposition that freedom of expression upon public questions is secured by the First Amendment has long been settled by our decisions. The constitutional safeguard, we have said, "was fashioned to assure unfettered interchange of ideas for the bringing about of political and social changes desired by the people." *Roth* v. *United States* . . . . "The maintenance of the opportunity for free political discussion to the end that government may be responsive to the will of the people and that changes may be obtained by lawful means, an opportunity essential to the security of the Republic, is a fundamental principle of our constitutional system." *Stromberg* v. *California* . . . . "[I]t is a prized American privilege to speak one's mind, although not always with perfect good taste, on all public institutions," *Bridges* v. *California* . . . and this opportunity is to be afforded for "vigorous advocacy" no less than "abstract discussions." *N.A.A.C.P.* v. *Button* . . . . The First Amendment, said Judge Learned Hand, "presupposes that right conclusions are more likely to be gathered out of a multitude of tongues, than through any kind of authoritative selection. To many this is, and always will be, folly; but we have staked upon it our all." . . . Mr. Justice Brandeis, in his concurring opinion in *Whitney* v. *California* . . . gave the principle its classic formulation:

Those who won our independence believed . . . that public discussion is a political duty; and that this should be a fundamental principle of the American government. They recognized the risks to which all human institutions are subject. But they knew that order cannot be secured merely through fear of punishment for its infraction; that it is hazardous to discourage thought, hope and imagination; that fear breeds repression; that repression breeds hate; that hate menaces stable government; that the path of safety lies in the opportunity to discuss freely supposed grievances and proposed remedies; and that the fitting remedy for evil counsels is good ones. Believing in the power of reason as applied through public discussion, they eschewed silence coerced by law—the argument of force in its own worst form. Recognizing the occasional tyrannies of governing majorities, they amended the Constitution so that free speech and assembly should be guaranteed.

Thus we consider this case against the background of a profound national commitment to the principle that debate on public issues should be uninhibited, robust, and wide-open, and that it may well include vehement, caustic, and sometimes unpleasantly sharp attacks on government and public officials. . . . The present advertisement, as an expression of grievance and protest on one of the major public issues of our time, would seem clearly to qualify for the constitutional protection. The question is whether it forfeits that protection by the falsity of some of its factual statements and by its alleged defamation of respondent.

Authoritative interpretations of the First Amendment guarantees have consistently refused to recognize an exception for any test of truth, whether administered by judges, juries, or administrative officials— and especially not one that puts the burden of proving truth on the speaker. . . . The constitutional protection does not turn upon "the truth, popularity, or social utility of the ideas and beliefs which are offered,"

Just as factual error affords no warrant for repressing speech that would otherwise be free, the same is true of injury to official reputation. . . .

If neither factual error nor defamatory content suffices to remove the constitutional shield from criticism of official conduct, the combination of the two elements is no less inadequate. . . .

What a State may not constitutionally bring about by means of a criminal statute is likewise beyond the reach of its civil law of libel. The fear of damage awards under a rule such as that invoked by the Alabama courts here may be markedly more inhibiting than the fear of prosecution under a criminal statute. . . . A rule compelling the critic of official conduct to guarantee the truth of all his factual assertions—and to do so on pain of libel judgments virtually unlimited in amount—leads to a comparable "self-censorship." Allowance of the defense of truth, with the burden of proving it on the defendant, does not mean that only false speech will be deterred. Even courts accepting this defense as an adequate safeguard have recognized the difficulties of adducing legal proofs that the alleged libel was true in all its factual particulars. . . . Under such a rule, would-be critics of official conduct may be deterred from voicing their criticism, even though it is believed to be true and even though it is in fact true, because of doubt whether it can be proved in court or fear of the expense of having to do so. . . . The rule thus dampens the vigor and limits the variety of public debate. It is inconsistent with the First and Fourteenth Amendments.

The constitutional guarantees require, we think, a federal rule that prohibits a public official from recovering damages for a defamatory falsehood relating to his official conduct unless he proves that the statement was made with "actual malice"—that is, with knowledge that it was false or with reckless disregard of whether it was false or not. . . .

We hold today that the Constitution delimits a State's power to award damages for libel in actions brought by public officials against critics of their official conduct. Since this is such an action, the rule requiring proof of actual malice is applicable. While Alabama law apparently requires proof of actual malice for an award of punitive damages, where general damages are concerned malice is "presumed." Such a presumption is inconsistent with the federal rule. . . .

The judgment of the Supreme Court of Alabama is reversed and the case is remanded to that court for further proceedings not inconsistent with this opinion.

Reversed and remanded.

MR. JUSTICE BLACK, WITH WHOM MR. JUSTICE DOUGLAS JOINS, CONCURRING. . . .

I base my vote to reverse on the belief that the First and Fourteenth Amendments not merely "delimit" a State's power to award damages to "public officials against critics of their official conduct" but completely prohibit a State from exercising such a power. The Court goes on to hold that a State can subject such critics to damages if "actual malice" can be proved against them. "Malice," even as defined by the Court, is an elusive, abstract concept hard to prove and hard to disprove. The requirement that malice be proved provides at best an evanescent protection for the right critically to discuss public affairs and certainly does not measure up to the sturdy safeguard embodied in the

First Amendment. Unlike the Court, therefore, I vote to reverse exclusively on the ground that the *Times* and the individual defendants had an absolute, unconditional constitutional right to publish in the *Times* advertisement their criticisms of the Montgomery agencies and officials.

. . .

MR. JUSTICE GOLDBERG, WHOM MR. JUSTICE DOUGLAS JOINS, CONCURRING (OMITTED).

[In 1967, the Supreme Court decided *Associated Press* v. *Walker.* General Walker, an outspoken retired army officer had been active in campus rioting at the University of Mississippi in the early 1960s and was an outspoken and prominent opponent of the Kennedy-Johnson administration's efforts to desegregate southern universities. Press coverage of his activities did contain some errors, and under the normal rules of evidence in a libel case, he should have prevailed. However, the Supreme Court accepted the argument that while General Walker was not a "public official," he was a "public figure" involved in an issue in which the public has a justified interest. Therefore, the test to be applied was that articulated in the *Sullivan* case. Unless Walker could demonstrate that the libelous statements were malicious, he could not prevail.

In a companion case, however, *Curtis Publishing Company* v. *Butts*, the Court supported a libel judgment in favor of a retired football coach who sued the publisher of the *Saturday Evening Post.* The magazine story alleged that former Georgia football coach Wally Butts had conspired to fix a football game with the University of Alabama. The Court's judgment appeared to turn on the magazine's lack of reasonable precautions in checking the accuracy of its story and thus did not undercut the rationale of the *Walker* case that the *Sullivan* rule be extended to "public figures."

In *Greenbelt Cooperative Publishing Co.* v. *Bresler* (1970), a person who had applied for a zoning variation was denied libel damages under its "public figure" doctrine. And the fol-

lowing year, in *Monitor Patriot Co.* v. *Roy*, a candidate for public office who had been described as a former bootlegger was also regarded as a public figure and not permitted to collect damages for libel.

The *Gertz* and *Firestone* cases that follow explore the limits of the "public figure" doctrine. In these cases, two standards are considered: the newsworthiness of events, and whether or not the individual claiming libel damages was a seeker of public attention. In an earlier case, *Rosenbloom* v. *Metromedia* (1971), the Supreme Court had emphasized newsworthiness over "seeking" the public arena. *Gertz* overruled *Rosenbloom* and held that whether or not a person sought public attention was to be the primary factor in determining whether the *Sullivan* rule of libel would apply.]

(b) Gertz v. Robert Welch, Inc. (1974)

+Stewart, Marshall, Blackmun, Powell, Rehnquist

−Burger, Douglas, Brennan, White

[Elmer Gertz, a Chicago lawyer, was retained to represent the family of a Chicago youth killed by a policeman named Richard Nuccio in a civil suit for damages against the policeman (who had been convicted of second-degree murder for the killing). *American Opinion,* the magazine of the John Birch Society, commissioned an article about the murder trial and subsequent events as part of its campaign to warn the American public about an alleged conspiracy to discredit law enforcement agencies. The article, entitled "Frame-Up: Richard Nuccio and the War on Police," alleged that the testimony against Nuccio was false and part of a Communist conspiracy. Claiming that he was libeled by the article, Gertz filed suit in federal court against Robert Welch, founder of the John Birch Society.

Welch's lawyers claimed a constitutional privilege against liability based on *New York Times* v. *Sullivan* (1964). They argued that Gertz was a public figure or a public official and that the article concerned an issue of public interest and concern. Therefore, Gertz would have the stiff burden of proving publication of a defamatory falsehood "with actual malice"—that is, in the knowledge that it was false or with reckless disregard for whether it was true or not. They claimed that Gertz could not meet the test because the editor of *American Opinion* did not know that the article contained falsehoods and that he relied on the author's prior record of accuracy and authenticity.

Before the case was submitted to the jury, the court ruled that Gertz was neither a public official nor a public figure. Because some statements in the article were libelous per se under Illinois law, the judge determined that Welch was liable and directed the jury to confine its deliberations only to appropriate damages. The jury awarded the sum of $50,000 to Gertz. After the jury had acted, however, the judge, correctly anticipating a new Supreme Court decision called *Rosenbloom* v. *Metromedia* (1971), decided that Welch was, in fact, protected by *New York Times* v. *Sullivan*. He therefore entered judgment in favor of Welch notwithstanding the jury's verdict. The Court of Appeals affirmed this judgment because there was no evidence that the editor of *American Opinion* had acted with actual malice. The Supreme Court granted certiorari.]

MR. JUSTICE POWELL delivered the opinion of the Court.

. . .

The principal issue in this case is whether a newspaper or broadcaster that publishes defamatory falsehoods about an individual who is neither a public official nor a public figure may claim a constitutional privilege against liability for the injury inflicted by those statements. The Court considered this question on the rather different set of facts presented in *Rosenbloom* v. *Metromedia, Inc.* . . . (1971). . . .

. . . The eight Justices who participated in *Rosenbloom* announced their views in five separate opinions, none of which commanded more than three votes. The several statements not only reveal disagreement about the appropriate result in that case; they also reflect divergent traditions of thought about the general problem of reconciling the law of defamation with the First Amendment. One approach has been to extend the *New York Times* test to an expanding variety of situations. Another has been to vary the level of constitutional privilege for defamatory falsehood with the status of the person defamed. And a third view would grant to the press and broadcast media absolute immunity from liability for defamation. . . .

. . .

Three years after *New York Times*, a majority of the Court agreed to extend the constitutional privilege to defamatory criticism of "public figures." This extension was announced in *Curtis Publishing Co.* v. *Butts* and its companion, *Associated Press* v. *Walker* . . . (1967). The first case involved the *Saturday Evening Post's* charge that Coach Wally Butts of the University of Georgia had conspired with Coach Bear Bryant of the University of Alabama to fix a football game between their respective schools. *Walker* involved an erroneous Associated Press account of Brigadier General Edwin Walker's participation in a University of Mississippi campus riot. Because Butts was paid by a private alumni association and Walker had retired from the Army, neither could be classified as a "public official" under *New York Times*. Although Mr. Justice Harlan announced the result in both cases, a majority of the Court agreed with Mr. Chief Justice Warren's conclusion that the *New York Times* test should apply to criticism of "public figures" as well as "public officials." The Court extended the constitutional privilege announced in that case to protect defamatory criticism of non-

public officials who "are nevertheless intimately involved in the resolution of important public questions, or, by reason of their fame, shape events in areas of concern to society at large."
. . .

In his opinion for the plurality in *Rosenbloom* v. *Metromedia, Inc.* . . (1971), Mr. Justice Brennan took the *New York Times* privilege one step further. He concluded that its protection should extend to defamatory falsehoods relating to private persons if the statements concerned matters of general or public interest. He abjured the suggested distinction between public officials and public figures on the one hand and private individuals on the other. He focused instead on society's interest in learning about certain issues: "If a matter is a subject of public or general interest, it cannot suddenly become less so merely because a private individual is involved or because in some sense the individual did not choose to become involved." . . . Thus, under the plurality opinion, a private citizen involuntarily associated with a matter of general interest has no recourse for injury to his reputation unless he can satisfy the demanding requirements of the *New York Times* test.
. . .

. . . Under the First Amendment there is no such thing as a false idea. However pernicious an opinion may seem, we depend for its correction not on the conscience of judges and juries but on the competition of other ideas. But there is no constitutional value in false statements of fact. Neither the intentional lie nor the careless error materially advanced society's interest in "uninhibited, robust, and wide-open" debate on public issues. *New York Times Co.* v. *Sullivan,* . . . They belong to that category of utterances which "are no essential part of any exposition of ideas, and are of such slight social value as a step to truth that any benefit that may be derived from them is clearly outweighed by the social interest in order and morality." *Chaplinsky* v. *New Hampshire.* . . (1942).

Although the erroneous statement of fact is not worthy of constitutional protection, it is nevertheless inevitable in free debate. . . . And punishment of error runs the risk of inducing a cautious and restrictive exercise of the constitutionally guaranteed freedoms of speech and press. Our decisions recognize that a rule of strict liability that compels a publisher or broadcaster to guarantee the accuracy of his factual assertions may lead to intolerable self-censorship. Allowing the media to avoid liability only by proving the truth of all injurious statements does not accord adequate protection to First Amendment liberties. . . . The First Amendment requires that we protect some falsehood in order to protect speech that matters.

The need to avoid self-censorship by the news media is, however, not the only societal value at issue. If it were, this Court would have embraced long ago the view that publishers and broadcasters enjoy an unconditional and indefeasible immunity from liability for defamation. . . . Such a rule would indeed obviate the fear that the prospect of civil liability for injurious falsehood might dissuade a timorous press from the effective exercise of First Amendment freedoms. Yet absolute protection for the communications media requires a total sacrifice of the competing value served by the law of defamation.

The legitimate state interest underlying the law of libel is the compensation of individuals for the harm inflicted on them by defamatory falsehoods. We would not lightly require the State to abandon this purpose, for, as Mr. Justice Stewart has reminded us, the individual's right to the protection of his own good name

reflects no more than our basic concept of the essential dignity and worth of every human being—a concept at the root of any decent system of ordered liberty. The protection of private personality, like the protection of life itself, is left primarily to the individual states under the Ninth and Tenth Amendments.

The *New York Times* standard defines the level of constitutional protection appropriate to the context of defamation of a public person. Those who, by reason of the notoriety of their achievements or the vigor and success with which they seek the public's attention, are properly classed as public figures and those who hold governmental office may recover for injury to reputation only on clear and convincing proof that the defamatory falsehood was made with knowledge of its falsity or with reckless disregard for the truth. This standard administers an extremely powerful antidote to the inducement to media self-censorship of the common law rule of strict liability for libel and slander. And it exacts a correspondingly high price from the victims of defamatory falsehood. Plainly many deserving plaintiffs, including some intentionally subjected to injury, will be unable to surmount the barrier of the *New York Times* test. Despite this substantial abridgement of the state law right to compensation for wrongful hurt to one's reputation, the Court has concluded that the protection of the *New York Times* privilege should be available to publishers and broadcasters of defamatory falsehoods concerning public officials and public figures. *New York Times Co.* v. *Sullivan. . .* (1964); *Curtis Publishing Co.* v. *Butts. . .*

(1967). We think that these decisions are correct, but we do not find their holdings justified solely by reference to the interest of the press and broadcast media in immunity from liability. Rather, we believe that the *New York Times* rule states an accommodation between this concern and the limited state interest present in the context of libel actions brought by public persons. For the reasons stated below, we conclude that the state interest in compensating injury to the reputation of private individuals requires that a different rule should obtain with respect to them.

Theoretically, of course, the balance between the needs of the press and the individual's claim to compensation for wrongful injury might be struck on a case-by-case basis. . . . But this approach would lead to unpredictable results and uncertain expectations, and it could render our duty to supervise the lower courts unmanageable. Because an *ad hoc* resolution of the competing interests at stake in each particular case is not feasible, we must lay down broad rules of general application. Such rules necessarily treat alike various cases involving differences as well as similarities. Thus it is often true that not all of the considerations which justify adoption of a given rule will obtain in each particular case decided under its authority.

With that caveat we have no difficulty in distinguishing among defamation plaintiffs. The first remedy of any victim of defamation is self-help—using available opportunities to contradict the lie or correct the error and thereby to minimize its adverse impact on reputation. Public officials and public figures usually enjoy significantly greater access to the channels of effective communication and hence have a more realistic opportunity to counteract false statements than private individuals normally enjoy. Private individuals are therefore more vulnerable to injury, and the state interest in protecting them is correspondingly greater.

More important than the likelihood that private individuals will lack effective opportunities for rebuttal, there is a compelling normative consideration underlying the distinction between public and private defamation plaintiffs. An individual who decides to seek governmental office must accept certain necessary consequences of that involvement in public affairs. He runs the risk of closer public scrutiny than might otherwise be the case. And society's interest in the officers of government is not strictly limited to the formal discharge of official duties. As the Court pointed out in *Garrison* v. *Louisiana*. . . (1964), the public's interest extends to "anything that might touch on an official's fitness for office . . . . Few personal attributes are more germane to fitness for office than dishonesty, malfeasance, or improper motivation, even though these characteristics may also affect the official's private character."

Those classed as public figures stand in a similar position. Hypothetically, it may be possible for someone to become a public figure through no purposeful action of his own, but the instances of truly involuntary public figures must be exceedingly rare. For the most part those who attain this status have assumed roles of especial prominence in the affairs of society. Some occupy positions of such persuasive power and influence that they are deemed public figures for all purposes. More commonly, those classed as public figures have thrust themselves to the forefront of particular public controversies in order to influence the resolution of the issues involved. In either event, they invite attention and comment.

Even if the foregoing generalities do not obtain in every instance, the communications media are entitled to act on the assumption that public officials and public figures have voluntarily exposed themselves to increased risk of injury from defamatory falsehoods concerning them. No such assumption is justified with respect to a private individual. He has not accepted public office nor assumed an "influential role in ordering society." . . . He has relinquished no part of his interest in the protection of his own good name, and consequently he has a more compelling call on the courts for redress of injury inflicted by defamatory falsehood. Thus, private individuals are not only more vulnerable to injury than public officials and public figures; they are also more deserving of recovery.

For these reasons we conclude that the States should retain substantial latitude in their efforts to enforce a legal remedy for defamatory falsehood injurious to the reputation of a private individual. The extension of the *New York Times* test proposed by the *Rosenbloom* plurality would abridge this legitimate state interest to a degree that we find unacceptable. And it would occasion the additional difficulty of forcing state and federal judges to decide on an *ad hoc* basis which publications address issues of "general or public interest" and which do not—to determine, in the words of Mr. Justice Marshall, "what information is relevant to self-government." *Rosenbloom* v. *Metromedia, Inc.*. . . We doubt the wisdom of committing this task to the conscience of judges. Nor does the Constitution require us to draw so thin a line between the drastic alternatives of the *New York Times* privilege and the common law of strict liability for defamatory error. The "public or general interest" test for determining the applicability of the

New York Times standard to private defamation actions inadequately serves both of the competing values at stake. On the one hand, a private individual whose reputation is injured by defamatory falsehood that does concern an issue of public or general interest has no recourse unless he can meet the rigorous requirements of *New York Times*. This is true despite the factors that distinguish the state interest in compensating private individuals from the analogous interest involved in the context of public persons. On the other hand, a publisher or broadcaster of a defamatory error which a court deems unrelated to an issue of public or general interest may be held liable in damages even if it took every reasonable precaution to ensure the accuracy of its assertions. And liability may far exceed compensation for any actual injury to the plaintiff, for the jury may be permitted to presume damages without proof of loss and even to award punitive damages.

We hold that, so long as they do not impose liability without fault, the States may define for themselves the appropriate standard of liability for a publisher or broadcaster of defamatory falsehood injurious to a private individual. This approach provides a more equitable boundary between the competing concerns involved here. It recognizes the strength of the legitimate state interest in compensating private individuals for wrongful injury to reputation, yet shields the press and broadcast media from the rigors of strict liability for defamation. At least this conclusion obtains where, as here, the substance of the defamatory statement "makes substantial danger to reputation apparent." . . .

Our accommodation of the competing values at stake in defamation suits by private individuals allows the States to impose liability on the publisher or broadcaster of defamatory falsehoods on a less demanding showing than that required by *New York Times*. This conclusion is not based on a belief that the considerations which prompted the adoption of the *New York Times* privilege for defamation of public officials and its extension to public figures are wholly inapplicable to the context of private individuals. Rather, we endorse this approach in recognition of the strong and legitimate state interest in compensating private individuals for injury to reputation. But this countervailing state interest extends no further than compensation for actual injury. For the reasons stated below, we hold that the States may not permit recovery of presumed or punitive damages, at least when liability is not based on a showing of knowledge of falsity or reckless disregard for the truth. . . .

Notwithstanding our refusal to extend the *New York Times* privilege to defamation of private individuals, respondent contends that we should affirm the judgment below on the ground that petitioner is either a public official or a public figure. There is little basis for the former assertion. Several years prior to the present incident, petitioner had served briefly on housing committees appointed by the mayor of Chicago, but at the time of publication he had never held any remunerative governmental position. Respondent admits this but argues that petitioner's appearance at the coroner's inquest rendered him a "de facto public official." Our cases recognize no such concept. Respondent's suggestion would sweep all lawyers under the *New York Times* rule as officers of the court and distort the plain meaning of the "public official" category beyond all recognition. We decline to follow it.

Respondent's characterization of petitioner as a public figure raises a different question. That designation may rest on either of two alternative bases. In some instances an individual may achieve such pervasive fame or notoriety that he becomes a public figure for all purposes and in all contexts. More commonly, an individual voluntary injects himself or is drawn into a particular public controversy and thereby becomes a public figure for a limited range of issues. In either case such persons assume special prominence in the resolution of public questions.

Petitioner has long been active in community and professional affairs. He has served as an officer of local civic groups and of various professional organizations, and he has published several books and articles on legal subjects. Although petitioner was consequently well-known in some circles, he had achieved no general fame or notoriety in the community. None of the prospective jurors called at the trial had ever heard of petitioner prior to this litigation, and respondent offered no proof that this response was atypical of the local population. We would not lightly assume that a citizen's participation in community and professional affairs rendered him a public figure for all purposes. Absent clear evidence of general fame or notoriety in the community, and pervasive involvement in the affairs of society, an individual should not be deemed a public personality for all aspects of his life. It is preferable to reduce the public figure question to a more meaningful context by looking to the nature and extent of an individual's participation in the particular controversy giving rise to the defamation.

In this context it is plain that petitioner was not a public figure. He played a minimal role at the coroner's inquest, and his participation related solely to his representation of a private client. He took no part in the criminal prosecution of officer Nuccio. Moreover, he never discussed either the criminal or civil litigation with the press and was never quoted as having done so. He plainly did not thrust himself into the vortex of this public issue, nor did he engage the public's attention in an attempt to influence its outcome. We are persuaded that the trial court did not err in refusing to characterize petitioner as a public figure for the purpose of this litigation.

We therefore conclude that the *New York Times* standard is inapplicable to this case and that the trial court erred in entering judgment for respondent. Because the jury was allowed to impose liability without fault and was permitted to presume damages without proof of injury, a new trial is necessary. We reverse and remand for further proceedings in accord with this opinion.

It is so ordered.

MR. JUSTICE BLACKMUN, CONCURRING (OMITTED).

MR. CHIEF JUSTICE BURGER, DISSENTING (OMITTED).

MR. JUSTICE DOUGLAS, DISSENTING.

The Court describes this case as a return to the struggle of "defin[ing] the proper accommodation between the law of defamation and the freedoms of speech and press protected by the First Amendment." It is indeed a struggle, once described by Mr. Justice Black as "the same quagmire" in which the Court "is helplessly struggling in the field of obscenity." *Curtis Publishing Co.* v. *Butts.* . . . I would suggest that the struggle is a quite hopeless one, for, in light of the command of the First Amendment, no "accommodation" of its freedoms can be "proper" except those made by the Framers themselves. . . .

With the First Amendment made applicable to the States through the Fourteenth, I do not see how States have any more ability to "accommodate" freedoms of speech or of the press than does Congress. This is true whether the form of the accommodation is civil or criminal since "[w]hat a State may not constitutionally bring about by means of a criminal statute is likewise beyond the reach of its civil law of libel." *New York Times Co.* v. *Sullivan* . . . Like Congress, States are without power "to use a civil libel law or any other law to impose damages for merely discussing public affairs." . . .

MR. JUSTICE BRENNAN, DISSENTING (OMITTED).
MR. JUSTICE WHITE, DISSENTING (OMITTED).

(c) Time, Inc. v. Firestone (1976)

+Burger, Stewart, Blackmun, Powell, Rehnquist
−Brennan, White, Marshall
NP Stevens

[Time, Inc., publisher of a weekly newsmagazine, was sued for libel by Mary Alice Firestone, former wife of Russell Firestone, heir to his family's tire fortune. *Time* printed the following account of the couple's divorce:

DIVORCED. *By Russell A. Firestone, Jr., 41, heir to the tire fortune; Mary Alice Sullivan Firestone, 32, his third wife; a onetime Palm Beach schoolteacher; on grounds of extreme cruelty and adultery; after six years of marriage, one son; in West Palm Beach, Fla. The 17 month intermittent trial produced enough testimony of extramarital adventures on both sides, said the judge, "to make Dr. Freud's hair curl."*

This account was misleading in a number of respects. The divorce judgment was not granted on a finding that Mrs. Firestone had committed adultery, although that was alleged by her husband. Further, the trial court expressly discounted much of the testimony regarding the sexual adventures of both sides, finding instead "that neither party is domesticated, within the meaning of that term as used by the Supreme Court of Florida." The marriage was dissolved on that basis, although, balancing the equities, the judge granted Mr. Firestone's counterclaim for divorce against his wife's initial complaint for separate maintenance.

Time refused to issue a retraction and a jury in Florida entered a libel verdict for Mrs. Firestone of $100,000. The Florida Supreme Court affirmed, and the Supreme Court granted certiorari.]

MR. JUSTICE REHNQUIST delivered the opinion of the Court.

. . .

Petitioner initially contends that it cannot be liable for publishing any falsehood defaming respondent unless it is established that the publication was made "with actual malice," as that term is defined in *New York Times Co.* v. *Sullivan.* . . (1964). Petitioner advances two arguments in support of this contention: that respondent is a "public figure" within this Court's decisions extending *New York Times* to defamation suits brought by such individuals, See, e.g., *Curtis Publishing Co.* v. *Butts* . . .(1967); and that the *Time* item constituted a report of a judicial proceeding, a class of subject matter which petitioner claims deserves the protection of the "actual malice" standard even if the story is proven to be defamatorily false or inaccurate. We reject both arguments.

In *Gertz* v. *Robert Welch, Inc.* . . .(1974), we have recently further defined the meaning of "public figure" for the purposes of the First and Fourteenth Amendments.

For the most part those who attain this status have assumed roles of especial prominence in the affairs of society. Some occupy positions of such persuasive power and influence that they are deemed public figures for all purposes. More commonly, those classed as public figures have thrust themselves to the forefront of particular public controversies in order to influence the resolution of the issues involved.

Respondent did not assume any role of especial prominence in the affairs of society, other than perhaps Palm Beach society, and she did not thrust herself to the forefront of any particular public controversy in order to influence the resolution of the issues involved in it.

Petitioner contends that because the Firestone divorce was characterized by the Florida Supreme Court as a "cause célèbre," it must have been a public controversy and respondent must be considered a public figure. But in so doing petitioner seeks to equate "public controversy" with all controversies of interest to the public. Were we to accept this reasoning, we would reinstate the doctrine advanced in the plurality opinion in *Rosenbloom* v. *Metromedia, Inc.* . . .(1971), which concluded that the *New York Times* privilege should be extended to falsehoods defamatory of private persons whenever the statements concern matters of general or public interest. In *Gertz*, however, the Court repudiated this position, stating that "extension of the *New York Times* test proposed by the *Rosenbloom* plurality would abridge [a] legitimate state interest to a degree that we find unacceptable." . . .

Dissolution of a marriage through judicial proceedings is not the sort of "public controversy" referred to in *Gertz*, even though the marital difficulties of extremely wealthy individuals may be of interest to some portion of the reading public. Nor did respondent freely choose to publicize issues as to the propriety of her married life. She was compelled to go to court by the State in order to obtain legal release from the bonds of matrimony. . . . Her actions, both in instituting the litigation and in its conduct, were quite different from those of General Walker. . . She assumed no "special prominence in the resolution of public questions." *Gertz* . . . We hold respondent was not a "public figure" for the purpose of determining the constitutional protection afforded petitioner's report of the factual and legal basis for her divorce.

For similar reasons we likewise reject petitioner's claim for automatic extension of the *New York Times* privilege to all reports of judicial proceedings. It is argued that information concerning proceedings in our Nation's courts may have such importance to all citizens as to justify extending special First Amendment protection to the press when reporting on such events. We have recently accepted a significantly more confined version of this argument by holding that the Constitution precludes States from imposing civil liability based upon the publication of truthful information contained in official court records open to public inspection. *Cox Broadcasting Corp.* v. *Cohn* . . . (1975). . . .

Presumptively erecting the *New York Times* barrier against all plaintiffs seeking to recover for injuries from defamatory falsehoods published in what are alleged to be reports of judicial proceedings would effect substantial depreciation of the individual's interest in protection from such harm, without any convincing assurance that such a sacrifice is required under the First Amendment. And in some instances such an undiscriminating approach might achieve results directly at odds with the constitutional balance intended. Indeed, the article upon which the *Gertz* libel action was based purported to be a report on the murder trial of a Chicago police officer. . . . Our decision in that case should make it clear that no such blanket privilege for reports of judicial proceedings is to be found in the Constitution.

It may be argued that there is still room for application of the *New York Times* protections to more narrowly focused reports of what actually transpires in the courtroom. But even so narrowed, the suggested privilege is simply too broad. Imposing upon the law of private defamation the rather drastic limitations worked by *New York Times* cannot be justified by generalized references to the public interest in reports of judicial proceedings. The details of many, if not most, courtroom battles would add almost nothing towards advancing the uninhibited debate on public issues thought to provide principal support for the decision in *New York Times*. . . . And while participants in some litigation may be legitimate "public figures," either generally or for the limited purpose of that litigation, the majority will more likely resemble respondent, drawn into a public forum largely against their will in order to attempt to obtain the only redress available to them or to defend themselves against actions brought by the State or by others. There appears little reason why these individuals should substantially forfeit that degree of protection which the law of defamation would otherwise afford them simply by virtue of their being drawn into a courtroom. The public interest in accurate reports of judicial proceedings is substantially protected by *Cox Broadcasting Co.*

. . . As to inaccurate and defamatory reports of facts, matters deserving no First Amendment protection, . . . we think *Gertz* provides an adequate safeguard for the constitutionally protected interests of the press and affords it a tolerable margin for error by requiring some type of fault. . . .

[The *Gertz* case imposed two constitutional conditions on such liability judgments: first, that no liability be imposed without a finding of fault; second, that compensatory awards "be supported by competent evidence concerning the injury." Finding that nowhere in the proceedings had the element of "fault" against Time, Inc., been proved, the Supreme Court, in a portion of the opinion omitted here, vacated the judgment of the Florida Supreme Court.]

MR. JUSTICE POWELL, WITH WHOM MR. JUSTICE STEWART JOINS, CONCURRING (OMITTED).
MR. JUSTICE BRENNAN, DISSENTING (OMITTED).
MR. JUSTICE MARSHALL, DISSENTING (OMITTED).

[There is an inherent conflict between the activities of the press in some cases and the personal right to privacy. It should be evident that many of the cases that we classify as "privacy" cases (see "Note on the Constitutional Right to Privacy," pp. 1315–1325), such as *Time, Inc.* v. *Hill* (1967), also implicate the rights of the press, and judicial policymaking often amounts to difficult choices between the two.]

(d) Herbert v. Lando (1979)

+White, Burger, Blackmun, Powell, Rehnquist, Stevens
±Brennan
−Stewart, Marshall

[Colonel Anthony Herbert, a retired army officer, had served in Vietnam and while on duty had accused his superiors of covering up reports of atrocities and war crimes. These allegations received widespread media attention.

Some years later, in 1973, CBS broadcast a critical report on the incident. The program was produced by Barry Lando and narrated by Mike Wallace. Lando also published an article about the incident in *Atlantic Monthly* magazine. Herbert filed a defamation suit against Lando, Wallace, CBS, and *Atlantic Monthly* in the federal district court in New York, with jurisdiction based on diversity of citizenship. It was alleged that the program and the article had falsely and maliciously portrayed Herbert as a liar who made the charges of covering up atrocities to cover his own relief from command duty. Herbert conceded that he was a "public figure" who could not recover damages without proof that the defendants had published a damaging falsehood with "actual malice—that is, with knowledge that it was false or with reckless disregard of whether it was false or not."

In preparation of his case, Herbert deposed Lando at great length. Lando refused to answer certain questions about his "state of mind" and intentions in producing the show and writing the article. He claimed protection from the First Amendment against such inquiries of those who edit, produce, or publish. The district court ruled that because Lando's "state of mind" was of central importance to the issue of malice, the questions were relevant and "entirely appropriate to Herbert's efforts to discover whether Lando had any reason to doubt the veracity of certain of his sources, or, equally significant, to prefer the veracity of one of his sources over another." The judge ruled that there was nothing in the First Amendment that required an increase in the already heavy burden that a public figure plaintiff has to meet in such cases.

The Court of Appeals for the Second Circuit reversed by a divided vote. Two judges concluded that the First Amendment protected Lando from inquiry into his thoughts, opinions, and conclusions with respect to these materials. They held that Lando had an absolute privilege not to answer these questions. The Supreme Court granted certiorari.]

MR. JUSTICE WHITE delivered the opinion of the Court.

. . .

Civil and criminal liability for defamation was well established in the common law when the First Amendment was adopted, and there is no indication that the Framers intended to abolish such liability. Until *New York Times* the prevailing jurisprudence was that "[l]ibelous utterances [are not] within the area of constitutionally protected speech. . . ." *Beauharnais* v. *Illinois* . . . (1952) . . . The accepted view was that neither civil nor criminal liability for defamatory publications abridge freedom of speech or freedom of the press, and a majority of jurisdictions made publishers liable civilly for their defamatory publications regardless of their intent. *New York Times* and *Butts* effected major changes in the standards applicable to civil libel actions. Under these cases public officials and public figures who sue for defamation must prove knowing or reckless falsehood in order to establish liability. Later, in *Gertz* v. *Robert Welch, Inc.,* . . . the Court held that nonpublic figures must demonstrate some fault on the defendant's part and, at least where knowing or reckless untruth is not shown, some proof of actual injury to the plaintiff before liability may be imposed and damages awarded.

These cases rested primarily on the conviction that the common law of libel gave insufficient protection to the First Amendment guarantees of freedom of speech and freedom of press and that to avoid self-censorship it was essential that liability for damages be conditioned on the specified showing of culpable conduct by those who publish damaging falsehood. Given the required proof, however, damages liability for defamation abridges neither freedom of speech nor freedom of the press.

Nor did these cases suggest any First Amendment restriction on the sources from which the plaintiff could obtain the necessary evidence to prove the critical elements of his cause of action. On the contrary, *New York Times* and its progeny made it essential to proving liability that plaintiffs focus on the conduct and state of mind of the defendant. To be liable, the alleged defamer of public officials or of public figures must know or have reason to suspect that his publication is false. In other cases proof of some kind of fault, negligence perhaps, is essential to recovery. Inevitably, unless liability is to be completely foreclosed, the thoughts and editorial processes of the alleged defamer would be open to examination.

It is also untenable to conclude from our cases that, although proof of the necessary state of mind could be in the form of objective circumstances from which the ultimate fact could be inferred, plaintiffs may not inquire directly from the defendants whether they knew or had reason to suspect that their damaging publication was in error. In *Butts*, for example, it is evident from the record that the editorial process had been subjected to close examination and that direct as well as indirect evidence was relied on to prove that the defendant magazine had acted with actual malice. The damages verdict was sustained without any suggestion that plaintiff's proof had trenched upon forbidden areas.

Reliance upon such state-of-mind evidence is by no means a recent development arising from *New York Times* and similar cases. Rather, it is deeply rooted in the common-law rule, predating the First Amendment, that a showing of malice on the part of the defendant permitted plaintiffs to recover punitive or enhanced damages. In *Butts*, the Court affirmed the substantial award of punitive damages which in Georgia were conditioned upon a showing of "wanton or reckless indifference or culpable negligence" or "ill will, spite,

hatred and an intent to injure. . . ." . . .

Furthermore, long before *New York Times* was decided, certain qualified privileges had developed to protect a publisher from liability for libel unless the publication was made with malice. Malice was defined in numerous ways, but in general depended upon a showing that the defendant acted with improper motive. This showing in turn hinged upon the intent or purpose with which the publication was made, the belief of the defendant in the truth of his statement, or upon the ill will which the defendant might have borne towards the defendant.

Courts have traditionally admitted any direct or indirect evidence relevant to the state of mind of the defendant and necessary to defeat a conditional privilege or enhance damages. The rules are applicable to the press and to other defendants alike, and it is evident that the courts across the country have long been accepting evidence going to the editorial processes of the media without encountering constitutional objections.

In the face of this history, old and new, the Court of Appeals nevertheless declared that two of this Court's cases had announced unequivocal protection for the editorial process. In each of these cases, *Miami Herald Publishing Co. v. Tornillo* . . . (1974), and *Columbia Broadcasting System v. Democratic National Committee* . . . (1973), we invalidated governmental efforts to preempt editorial decision by requiring the publication of specified material. In *Columbia Broadcasting System*, it was the requirement that a television network air paid political advertisements and in *Tornillo*, a newspaper's obligation to print a political candidate's reply to press criticism. Insofar as the laws at issue in *Tornillo* and *Columbia Broadcasting System* sought to control in advance the content of the publication, they were deemed as invalid as were prior efforts to enjoin publication of specified materials. But holdings that neither a State nor the Federal Government may dictate what must or must not be printed neither expressly nor impliedly suggest that the editorial process is immune from any inquiry whatsoever.

It is incredible to believe that the Court in *Columbia Broadcasting System* or in *Tornillo* silently effected a substantial contraction of the rights preserved to defamation plaintiffs in *Sullivan, Butts,* and like cases. *Tornillo* and *Gertz* v. *Robert Welch, Inc.,* were announced on the same day; and although the Court's opinion in *Gertz* contained an overview of recent developments in the relationship between the First Amendment and the law of libel, there was no hint that a companion case had narrowed the evidence available to a defamation plaintiff. Quite the opposite inference is to be drawn from the *Gertz* opinion, since it, like prior First Amendment libel cases, recited without criticism the facts of record indicating that the state of mind of the editor had been placed at issue. Nor did the *Gertz* opinion, in requiring proof of some degree of fault on the part of the defendant editor and in forbidding punitive damages absent at least reckless disregard of truth or falsity, suggest that the First Amendment also foreclosed direct inquiry into these critical elements.

In sum, contrary to the views of the Court of Appeals, according an absolute privilege to the editorial process of a media defendant in a libel case is not required, authorized or presaged by our prior cases, and would substantially enhance the burden of proving actual malice, contrary to the expectations of *New York Times, Butts* and similar cases.

It is nevertheless urged by respon-

dents that the balance struck in *New York Times* should now be modified to provide further protections for the press when sued for circulating erroneous information damaging to individual reputation. It is not uncommon or improper, of course, to suggest the abandonment, modification or refinement of existing constitutional interpretation, and notable developments in First Amendment jurisprudence have evolved from just such submissions. But in the 15 years since *New York Times,* the doctrine announced by that case, which represented a major development and which was widely perceived as essentially protective of press freedoms, has been repeatedly affirmed as the appropriate First Amendment standard applicable in libel actions brought by public officials and public figures. . . .

We are thus being asked to modify firmly established constitutional doctrine by placing beyond the plaintiff's reach a range of direct evidence relevant to proving knowing or reckless falsehood by the publisher of an alleged libel, elements that are critical to plaintiffs such as Herbert. The case for making this modification is by no means clear and convincing, and we decline to accept it.

. . .

It is also urged that frank discussion among reporters and editors will be dampened and sound editorial judgment endangered if such exchanges, oral or written, are subject to inquiry by defamation plaintiffs. We do not doubt the direct relationship between consultation and discussion on the one hand and sound decisions on the other; but whether or not there is liability for the injury, the press has an obvious interest in avoiding the infliction of harm by the publication of false information, and it is not unreasonable to expect the media to invoke whatever procedures that may be practicable and useful to that end. Moreover, given exposure to liability when there is knowing or reckless error, there is even more reason to resort to prepublication precautions, such as a frank interchange of fact and opinion. Accordingly, we find it difficult to believe that error-avoiding procedures will be terminated or stifled simply because there is liability for culpable error and because the editorial process will itself by examined in the tiny percentage of instances in which error is claimed and litigation ensues. . . .

This is not to say that the editorial discussions or exchanges have no constitutional protection from casual inquiry. There is no law that subjects the editorial process to private or official examination merely to satisfy curiosity or to serve some general end such as the public interest; and if there were, it would not survive constitutional scrutiny as the First Amendment is presently construed. . . .

Evidentiary privileges in litigation are not favored, and even those rooted in the Constitution must give way in proper circumstances. The President, for example, does not have an absolute privilege against disclosure of materials subpoenaed for a judicial proceeding. *United States* v. *Nixon* . . . (1974). In so holding, we found that although the President has a powerful interest in confidentiality of communications between himself and his advisers, that interest must yield to a demonstrated specific need for evidence. As we stated, in referring to existing limited privileges against disclosure, "[w]hatever their origins, these exceptions to the demand for every man's evidence are not lightly created nor expansively construed, for they are in derogation of the search for truth."

With these considerations in mind, we conclude that the present construction of the First Amendment should not be modified by creating the evidentiary privilege which the respondents now urge. . . .

MR. JUSTICE POWELL, CONCURRING (OMITTED).
MR. JUSTICE BRENNAN, DISSENTING IN PART (OMITTED).

MR. JUSTICE STEWART, DISSENTING.
It seems to me that both the Court of Appeals and this Court have addressed a question that is not presented by the case before us. As I understand the constitutional rule of *New York Times* v. *Sullivan*, . . . inquiry into the broad "editorial process" is simply not relevant in a libel suit brought by a public figure against a publisher. And if such an inquiry is not relevant, it is not permissible. . . .

Although I joined the Court's opinion in *New York Times*, I have come greatly to regret the use in that opinion of the phrase "actual malice." For the fact of the matter is that "malice" as used in the *New York Times* opinion simply does not mean malice as that word is commonly understood. In common understanding, malice means ill will or hostility, and the most relevant question in determining whether a person's action was motivated by actual malice is to ask "why." As part of the constitutional standard enunciated in the *New York Times* case, however, "actual malice" has nothing to do with hostility or ill will, and the question "why" is totally irrelevant.

Under the constitutional restrictions imposed by *New York Times* and its progeny, a plaintiff who is a public official or public figure can recover from a publisher for a defamatory statement upon convincingly clear proof of the following elements:

1. the statement was published by the defendant,

2. the statement defamed the plaintiff,

3. the defamation was untrue,

4. and the defendant knew the defamatory statement was untrue, or published it in reckless disregard of its truth or falsity. . . .

The gravamen of such a lawsuit thus concerns that which was in fact published. What was *not* published has nothing to do with the case. And liability ultimately depends upon the publisher's state of knowledge of the falsity of what he published, not at all upon his motivation in publishing it—not at all, in other words, upon actual malice as those words are ordinarily understood.

This is not the first time that judges and lawyers have been led astray by the phrase "actual malice" in the *New York Times* opinion. In *Greenbelt Coop. Pub. Assn.* v. *Bresler,* . . . another defamation suit brought by a public figure against a publisher, the trial judge instructed the jury that the plaintiff could recover if the defendant's publication had been made with malice, and that malice means "spite, hostility, or deliberate intention to harm." In reversing the judgment for the plaintiff, we said that this jury instruction constituted "error of constitutional magnitude." . . .

In the present case, of course, neither the Court of Appeals nor this Court has overtly committed the egregious error manifested in *Bresler*. Both courts have carefully enunciated the correct *New York Times* test. But each has then followed a false trail, explainable only by an unstated misapprehension of the meaning of *New York Times* "actual malice," to arrive at the issue of "editorial process" privilege. This misapprehension is reflected by numerous phrases in the prevailing Court of Appeals opinions: "a journalist's exercise of editorial control and judgment," "how a journalist formulated his judgments," "the editorial selection process of the press," "the heart of the editorial process," "reasons for the inclusion or exclusion of certain material." . . . Similar misapprehension is reflected in this Court's opinion by such phrases as "improper motive," "intent or purpose with which the publication is made," "ill will," and by lengthy footnote discussion about the spite or hostility required to constitute malice at common law. . . .

Once our correct bearings are taken, however, and it is firmly recognized that a publisher's motivation in a case such as this is irrelevant, there is clearly no occasion for inquiry into the editorial process as conceptualized in this case. I shall not burden this opinion with a list of the 84 discovery questions at issue.* Suffice it to say that few if any of them seem

---

*The following are some random samples:

"Did you ever come to a conclusion that it was unnecessary to talk to Capt. Laurence Potter prior to the presentation of the program on February 4th?

"Did you ever come to the conclusion that you did not want to have a filmed interview with Sgt. Carmon for the program?

"When you prepared the final draft of the program to be aired, did you form any conclusion as to whether one of the matters presented by that program was Col. Herbert's view of the treatment of the Vietnamese?

"Do you have any recollection of discussing with anybody at CBS whether that sequence should be excluded from the program as broadcast?

"Prior to the publication of the Atlantic Monthly article, Mr. Lando, did you discuss that article or the preparation of that article with any representative of CBS?"

to me to come within even the most liberal cnstruction of Rule 26(b), Fed. Rule Civ. Proc.†

By the time this case went to the Court of Appeals, the deposition of the respondent Lando alone had lasted intermittently for over a year and had filled 2,903 pages of transcript, with an additional 240 exhibits. The plaintiff had, in Chief Judge Kaufman's words, "already discovered what Lando knew, saw, said and wrote during his investigation." That, it seems to me, was already more than sufficient. . . .

MR. JUSTICE MARSHALL, DISSENTING.

Although professing to maintain the accommodation of interests struck in *New York Times Co.* v. *Sullivan,* . . . (1964), the Court today is unresponsive to the constitutional considerations underlying that opinion. Because I believe that some constraints on pretrial discovery are essential to ensure the "uninhibited [and] robust" debate on public issues which *Sullivan* contemplated, I respectfully dissent.

At issue in this case are competing interests of familiar dimension. States undeniably have an interest in affording individuals some measure of protection from unwarranted defamatory attacks. Libel actions serve that end, not only by assuring a forum in which reputations can be publicly vindicated and dignitary injuries compensated, but also by creating incentives for the press to exercise considered judgment before publishing material that compromises personal integrity. . . .

Against these objectives must be balanced society's interest in promoting unfettered debate on matters of public importance. As this Court recognized in *Sullivan,* error is inevitable in such debate, and if forced to guarantee the truth of all assertions, potential critics might suppress statements believed to be accurate "because of doubt whether [truthfulness] can be proved in court or fear of the expense of having to do so." . . . Such self-censorship would be incompatible with the tenets on which the First Amendment and our democratic institutions are founded. . . .

Yet this standard of liability cannot of itself accomplish the ends for which it was conceived. Insulating the press from ultimate liability is unlikely to avert self-censorship so long as any plaintiff with a deep pocket and a facially sufficient complaint is afforded unconstrained discovery of the editorial process. If the substantive balance of interests struck in *Sullivan* is to remain viable, it must be reassessed in light of the procedural realities under which libel actions are conducted.

The potential for abuse of liberal discovery procedures is of particular concern in the defamation context. As members of the bench and bar have increasingly noted, rules designed to facilitate expeditious resolution of civil disputes have too often proved tools for harassment and delay. . . .

Not only is the risk of *in terrorem* discovery more pronounced in the defamation context, but the societal consequences attending such abuse are of special magnitude. Rather

---

†Rule 26(b) provides in relevant part:
"Parties may obtain discovery regarding any matter, not privileged, which is relevant to the subject matter involved in the pending action. . . . It is not ground for objection that the information sought will be inadmissible at the trial if the information sought appears to be reasonably calculated to lead to the discovery of admissible evidence."

than submit to the intrusiveness and expense of protracted discovery, even editors confident of their ability to prevail at trial or on a motion for summary judgment may find it prudent to " 'steer far wid[e] of the unlawful zone' thereby keeping protected discussion from public cognizance." . . .

Although acknowledging a problem of discovery abuse, the Court suggests that the remedy lies elsewhere, in "major changes in the present rules of civil procedure." And somewhat inconsistently, the Court asserts further that district judges already have "in fact and in law . . . ample powers . . . to prevent abuse." . . . I cannot agree. Where First Amendment rights are critically implicated, it is incumbent on this Court to safeguard their effective exercise. . . .

Accordingly, I would foreclose discovery in defamation cases as to the substance of editorial conversation. Shielding this limited category of evidence from disclosure would be unlikely to preclude recovery by plaintiffs with valid defamation claims. For there are a variety of other means to establish deliberate or reckless disregard for the truth, such as absence of verification, inherent implausibility, obvious reasons to doubt the veracity or accuracy of information, and concessions or inconsistent statements by the defendants. . . .

(e) Hutchinson v. Proxmire (1979)

+Burger, White, Marshall, Blackmun, Powell, Rehnquist, Stevens

±Stewart

−Brennan

[In March, 1975 Senator William Proxmire initiated a "Golden Fleece of the Month" award

to publicize wasteful government spending. The second award went to the National Science Foundation, the National Aeronautics and Space Administration, and the Office of Naval Research for funding research on aggression in animals, often exhibited by kicking, screaming and the clenching of jaws. Proxmire announced this award in a speech on the floor of the Senate (or, recollections vary, by inserting copies of the speech in the Congressional Record without actually delivering it, a common practice), by the distribution of a press release to the media, and by a mass mailing to the Senator's Wisconsin constituents and others. Proxmire's speech concluded as follows:

The funding of this nonsense makes me almost angry enough to scream and kick or even clench my jaws. It seems to me it is outrageous.

Dr. Hutchinson's studies should make the taxpayers as well as his monkeys grind their teeth. In fact, the good doctor has made a fortune from his monkeys and in the process made a monkey out of the American taxpayer.

It is time for the Federal Government to get out of this "monkey business." In view of the transparent worthlessness of Hutchinson's study of jaw-grinding and biting by angry or hard-drinking monkeys, it is time we put a stop to the bite Hutchinson and the bureaucrats who fund him have been taking of the taxpayer.

Proxmire's legislative assistant, Morton Schwartz, a codefendant in this case, subsequently contacted the sponsoring agencies "to discuss the subject," although he denied he attempted to dissuade them from continuing to fund this research. The effect of this pressure, however, was that the funding was terminated.

Unable to get Proxmire or Schwartz to print a retraction for certain erroneous statements, Hutchinson filed suit in a federal district court in Wisconsin, alleging that as a result of actions by Proxmire and Schwartz, including defamatory statements, he had suffered "a loss of respect in his profession, has suffered injury to his feelings, has been humiliated, held up to public scorn, suffered extreme mental anguish and physical illness and pain to his person." He further alleged loss of income and ability to earn income in the future, and infringement of his rights of privacy.

The district court granted Proxmire's motion for summary judgment. It held that the "Speech and Debate Clause" of the Constitution (Article I, Section 6) immunized Proxmire's investigations, his speech in the Senate, and the press release covering the speech. The latter was protected partly because it fell within the "informing" function of Congress and partly because the court felt it was no different than if Proxmire's speech had been televised.

Insofar as the newsletter and various television interviews in which Proxmire repeated his allegations were concerned, the court held that while these were not immunized by the Speech and Debate Clause, that Hutchinson was a "public figure" for purposes of determining Proxmire's liability:

Given Dr. Hutchinson's long involvement with publicly-funded federal research, his active solicitation of federal and state grants, the local press coverage of his research, and the public interest in the expenditure of public funds on the precise activities in which he voluntarily participated, the court concludes that he is a public figure for the purposes of this suit. As he acknowledged in his deposition, "Certainly, any expenditure of public funds is a matter of public interest."

The court then determined that there was no evidence of "actual malice." The Court of Appeals affirmed and the Supreme Court granted certiorari.]

MR. CHIEF JUSTICE BURGER delivered the opinion of the Court.

In support of the Court of Appeals holding that newsletters and press releases are protected by the Speech or Debate Clause, respondents rely upon both historical precedent and present-day congressional practices. They contend that impetus for the Speech or Debate Clause privilege in our Constitution came from the history of parliamentary efforts to protect the right of members to criticize the spending of the Crown and from the prosecution of a Speaker of the House of Commons for publication of a report outside of Parliament. Respondents also contend that in the modern day very little speech or debate occurs on the floor of either House; from this they argue that press releases and newsletters are necessary for Members of Congress to communicate with other Members. For example, in his deposition Proxmire testified:

"I have found in 19 years in the Senate that very often a statement on the floor of the Senate or something that appears in the Congressional Record misses the attention of most members of the Senate, and virtually all members of the House, because they don't read the Congressional Record. If they are handed a news release, or something, that is going to call it to their attention. . . ."

Respondents also argue that an essential part of the duties of a Member of Congress is to inform constituents, as well as other Members, of the issues being considered.

The Speech or Debate Clause has been directly passed on by this Court relatively few times in 190 years. *Eastland* v. *United Servicemen's Fund* (1975); *Doe* v. *McMillan* . . . (1973); *Gravel* v. *United States* . . . (1972); *United States* v. *Brewster* . . . (1972) . . . Literal reading of the Clause would, of course, confine its protection narrowly to a "Speech or Debate *in* either House." But the Court has given the Clause a practical rather than a strictly literal reading which would limit the protection to utterances made within the four walls of either Chamber. Thus, we have held that committee hearings are protected, even if held outside the

Chambers; committee reports are also protected. . . .

The gloss going beyond a strictly literal reading of the Clause has not, however, departed from the objective of protecting only legislative activities. In Thomas Jefferson's view,

[The privilege] is restrained to things done in the House in a Parliamentary course. . . . For [the Member] is not to have privilege contra morem parliamentarium to exceed the bounds and limits of his place and duty. . . .

. . .

In *United States* v. *Brewster* . . . (1971), we acknowledged the historical roots of the Clause going back to the long struggle between the English House of Commons and the Tudor and Stuart monarchs when both criminal and civil processes were employed by crown authority to intimidate legislators. Yet we cautioned that the Clause

must be interpreted in light of the American experience, and in the context of the American constitutional scheme of government rather than the English parliamentary system. . . . [T]heir Parliament is the supreme authority, not a coordinate branch. Our speech or debate privilege was designed to preserve legislative independence, not supremacy.

Nearly a century ago, in *Kilbourn* v. *Thompson* . . . (1881), this Court held that the Clause extended "to things generally done *in a session* of the House by one of its members *in relation to the business before it.*" (Emphasis added.) More recently we expressed a similar definition of the scope of the Clause:

Legislative acts are not all-encompassing. The heart of the Clause is speech or debate in either House. Insofar as the Clause is construed to reach other matters, they must be an integral part of the deliberative and communicative processes by which Members participate in committee and House proceedings with respect to the consideration and passage or rejection of proposed legislation or with respect to other matters which the Constitution places within the jurisdiction of either House. As the Court of Appeals put it, the courts have extended the privilege to matters beyond pure speech or debate in either House, but 'only when necessary to prevent indirect impairment of such deliberations,' Gravel v. United States, . . .

Whatever imprecision there may be in the term "legislative activities," it is clear that nothing in history or in the explicit language of the Clause suggests any intention to create an absolute privilege from liability or suit for defamatory statements made outside the Chamber. . . .

The immunities of the Speech or Debate Clause were not written into the Constitution simply for the personal or private benefit of Members of Congress, but to protect the integrity of the legislative process by insuring the independence of individual legislators.

Claims under the Clause going beyond what is needed to protect legislative independence are to be closely scrutinized. In *Brewster* we took note of this:

The authors of our Constitution were well aware of both the need for the privilege and the abuses that could flow from too sweeping safeguards. In order to preserve other values, they wrote the privilege so that it tolerates and protects behavior on the part of Members not tolerated and protected when done by other citizens, but the shield does not extend beyond what is necessary to preserve the integrity of the legislative process. . . . (Emphasis added).

Indeed, the precedents abundantly support the conclusion that a

Member may be held liable for republishing defamatory statements originally made in either House. We perceive no basis for departing from that long-established rule.

. . .

We reaffirmed that principle in *Doe* v. *McMillan* . . . (1973):

A Member of Congress may not with impunity publish a libel from the speaker's stand in his home district, and clearly the Speech or Debate Clause would not protect such an act even though the libel was read from an official committee report. The reason is that republishing a libel under such circumstances is not an essential part of the legislative process and is not part of that deliberative process 'by which Members participate in committee and House proceedings.'

We reach a similar conclusion here. A speech by Proxmire in the Senate would be wholly immune and would be available to other Members of Congress and the public in the Congressional Record. But neither the newsletters nor the press release was "essential to the deliberations of the Senate" and neither was part of the deliberative process.

Respondents, however, argue that newsletters and press releases are essential to the functioning of the Senate; without them, they assert, a Senator cannot have a significant impact on the other Senators. We may assume that a Member's published statements exert some influence on other votes in the Congress and therefore have a relationship to the legislative and deliberative process. But in *Brewster*, we rejected respondents' expansive reading of the Clause:

It is well known, of course, that Members of the Congress engage in many activities other than the purely legislative activities protected by the Speech or Debate Clause. These include . . . preparing so-called 'news letters' to constituents, news releases, and speeches delivered outside the Congress.

There we went on to note that *Johnson* had carefully distinguished between what is only "related to the due functioning of the legislative process," and what constitutes the legislative process entitled to immunity under the Clause:

In stating that those things [Johnson's attempts to influence the Department of Justice] 'in no wise related to the due functioning of the legislative process' were not *covered by the privilege, the Court did not in any sense imply as a corollary that everything that 'related' to the office of a Member was shielded by the Clause. Quite the contrary, in Johnson we held, citing Kilbourn v. Thompson, supra, that only acts generally done in the course of the process of enacting legislation were protected.*

In no case has this Court ever treated the Clause as protecting all conduct relating to the legislative process.

In its narrowest scope, the Clause is a very large, albeit essential, grant of privilege. It has enabled reckless men to slander [by speech or debate] and even destroy others with impunity, but that was the conscious choice of the Framers.

. . .

We are unable to discern any "conscious choice" to grant immunity for defamatory statements scattered far and wide by mail, press, and the electronic media.

Respondents also argue that newsletters and press releases are privileged as part of the "informing function" of Congress. Advocates of a broad reading of the "informing function" sometimes tend to confuse two uses of the term "informing." In one sense, Congress informs itself collectively by way of hearings of its committees. It was in that sense that Woodrow Wilson used "informing" in a statement quoted by respondents. In reality, Wilson's statement related to congressional efforts to learn of the activities of the Executive Branch and administrative agencies; he did not include wide-ranging inquiries by individual Members on subjects of their choice. Moreover, Wilson's statement itself clearly implies a distinction between the *informing* function and the *legislative* function:

> *Unless Congress have and use every means of acquainting itself with the acts and the disposition of the administrative agents of the government, the country must be helpless to learn how it is being served; and unless Congress both scrutinize these things and sift them by every form of discussion, the country must remain in embarrassing, crippling ignorance of the very affairs which it is most important that it should understand and direct. The informing function of Congress should be preferred even to its legislative function. . . . [T]he only really self-governing people is that people which discusses and interrogates its administration. W. Wilson, Congressional Government 303 (1885).*

It is in this narrower Wilsonian sense that this Court has employed "informing" in previous cases holding that congressional efforts to inform itself through committee hearings are part of the legislative function.

The other sense of the term, and the one relied upon by respondents, perceives it to be the duty of Members to tell the public about their activities. Valuable and desirable as it may be in broad terms, the transmittal of such information by individual Members in order to inform the public and other Members is not a part of the legislative function or the deliberations that make up the legislative process. As a result, transmittal of such information by press releases and newsletters is not protected by the Speech or Debate Clause.

. . .

Since *New York Times* v. *Sullivan* . . . (1964), this Court has sought to define the accommodation required to assure the vigorous debate on public issues that the First Amendment was designed to protect while at the same time affording protection to the reputations of individuals. . . . In *Gertz* v. *Robert Welch, Inc.*, the Court offered a general definition of "public figures":

> *For the most part those who attain this status [of public figure] have assumed roles of especial prominence in the affairs of society. Some occupy positions of such persuasive power and influence that they are deemed public figures for all purposes. More commonly, those classed as public figures have thrust themselves to the forefront of particular public controversies in order to influence the resolution of the issues involved. In either event, they invite attention and comment.*

It is not contended that Hutchinson attained such prominence that he is a public figure for all purposes. Instead, respondents have argued that the District Court and the Court of Appeals were correct in holding that Hutchinson is a public figure for the limited purpose of comment on his receipt of federal funds for research projects. That conclusion was based upon two factors: first, Hutchinson's successful application for federal funds and the reports in local newspapers of the federal grants; second, Hutchinson's access to the media, as demonstrated by the fact that some newspapers and wire services reported his response to the announcement of the Golden Fleece Award. Neither of those factors demonstrates that Hutchinson was a public figure prior to the controversy engendered by the Golden Fleece Award; his access, such as it was, came after the alleged libel.

On this record Hutchinson's activities and public profile are much like those of countless members of his profession. His published writings reach a relatively small category of professionals concerned with research in human behavior. To the extent the subject of his published writings became a matter of controversy it was a consequence of the Golden Fleece Award. Clearly those charged with defamation cannot, by their own conduct, create their own defense by making the claimant a public figure. See *Wolston* v. *Reader's Digest, Inc.* (1979).

Hutchinson did not thrust himself or his views into public controversy to influence others. Respondents have not identified such a particular controversy; at most, they point to concern about general public expenditures. But that concern is shared by most and relates to most public expenditures; it is not sufficient to make Hutchinson a public figure. If it were, everyone who received or benefited from the myriad public grants for research could be classified as a public figure—a conclusion that our previous opinions have rejected. The "use of such subject-matter classifications to determine the extent of constitutional protection afforded defamatory falsehoods may too often result in an improper balance between the competing interests in this area." *Time, Inc.* v. *Firestone* . . .

Moreover, Hutchinson at no time assumed any role of public prominence in the broad question of concern about expenditures. Neither his applications for federal grants nor his publications in professional journals can be said to have invited that degree of public attention and comment

on his receipt of federal grants essential to meet the public figure level. The petitioner in *Gertz* v. *Robert Welch, Inc.*, had published books and articles on legal issues; he had been active in local community affairs. Nevertheless, the Court concluded that his activities did not make him a public figure.

Finally, we cannot agree that Hutchinson had such access to the media that he should be classified as a public figure. Hutchinson's access was limited to responding to the announcement of the Golden Fleece Award. He did not have the regular and continuing access to the media that is one of the accouterments of having become a public figure.

We therefore reverse the judgment of the Court of Appeals and remand the case to the Court of Appeals for further proceedings consistent with this opinion.

Reversed and remanded.

MR. JUSTICE STEWART, CONCURRING.

MR. JUSTICE BRENNAN, DISSENTING.

I disagree with the Court's conclusion that Senator Proxmire's newsletters and press releases fall outside the protection of the speech or debate immunity. In my view, the public criticism by legislators of unnecessary governmental expenditures, whatever its form, is a legislative act shielded by the Speech or Debate Clause. I would affirm the judgment below for the reasons expressed in my dissent in *Gravel* v. *United States* . . . (1972).

[The practical effect of *The New York Times* v. *Sullivan* (1964) ruling is that it is virtually impossible for a "public figure" to win a libel suit. The decision in that case, protecting *The New York Times* from a libel suit by the police commissioner of Montgomery, Alabama, expanded the license of the media to report fully and boldly on public affairs. The *Sullivan* doctrine is still controlling, but in recent years the Court has chipped away at it by substantially narrowing the definition of public figure. The *Proxmire* case was one of two decided in 1979, which held that an otherwise private individual does not become a public figure if he or she is dragged "involuntarily" into the limelight.

The other case was *Wolston* v. *Reader's Digest Association* (1979). In some respects it was even more threatening to media interests. A book published by the Reader's Digest Association in 1974, *KGB, The Secret Work of Soviet Agents* identified Wolston as having been identified as a Soviet agent in the United States. Wolston's suit alleged that passages in the book stating that he had been indicted for espionage and had been a Soviet agent were false and defamatory. He argued, and the facts showed, that while he was the subject of a federal grand jury investigation in 1957 and 1958 into Soviet intelligence activities, he was not, in fact, indicted. He was held in contempt of court for failing to respond to a grand jury subpoena on July 1, 1958 and given a one-year suspended sentence. His pregnant wife's hysterical outburst at the contempt hearing occasioned considerable media coverage of the hearing and the sentence. However this flurry of newspaper reporting subsided shortly thereafter and he returned to private life.

The district court granted the request by the Reader's Digest Association for summary judgment. It held that Wolston was a "public figure" because, by not responding to the grand jury subpoena and "subjecting himself to a citation for contempt," he "became involved in a controversy of a decidedly public nature in a way that invited attention and comment, and thereby created in the public an interest in knowing about his connection with espionage." The Court of Appeals affirmed.

In an opinion by Justice Rehnquist, the Supreme Court reversed by an 8-1 vote. Rehnquist noted that the Court in *Gertz* v. *Robert Welch* (1974) had declined to expand the protections of that doctrine to defamation suits by private individuals. It reasoned that private individuals have fewer opportunities than public figures to respond effectively to defamations and thus are more vulnerable, and that public figures are less deserving of constitutional protection than private individuals because they, like public officials, have "voluntarily exposed themselves to increased risk of injury from defamatory falsehoods concerning them." Wolston led a thoroughly private existence before and after the grand jury proceeding; "he assumed no general fame or notoriety and assumed no role of special prominence in the affairs of society as a result of his contempt citation. . . ."

The district court and the Reader's Digest Association had acknowledged this much. What they claimed was that Wolston was a "limited purpose" public figure. But Rehnquist noted that it was not fair to say that Wolston had voluntarily thrust himself into a public controversy. Rather he was dragged unwillingly into it by the government's investigation and the grand jury subpoena. No doubt his case was newsworthy, but "A private individual is not automatically transformed into a public figure just by becoming involved in or associated with a matter that attracts public attention. To accept this would be to repudiate the doctrine of *Gertz* and *Firestone* that the *Sullivan* doctrine should not extend to *any* private person involved in a matter of public concern. Nor should the Court accept the theory, Rehnquist said, that "any person who engages in criminal conduct automatically becomes a public figure."]

(3) The Media and the Problem of Access—*to* the Press and *by* the Press

[The relationship between the media and society is a two-way street. The effectiveness of social action often depends upon the access people have to the media, but the media must also have access to the processes and institutions of a society. Both aspects of this matter have become problematic. The declining competitiveness of the newspaper industry and the narrowly distributed control and ownership of the electronic media make access to the media highly competitive and often indispensable for certain purposes. On the other hand, a growing societal recognition of the need to protect individual privacy and, in the criminal justice area, the conflicting values of a free press and a fair trial give rise to efforts to restrict the reach of the media. It is for these, and other, reasons that access *to* the mass media *as a matter of right* has become as salient a legal issue as the more traditional dilemma of access *by* the media.

Is the freedom of the press infringed if, in the name of access, it is obliged to present certain views, events, or ideas? If so, is the increase of access—albeit forced access—worth the curtailment of the rights of the press *not to present* certain ideas or cover certain events? What technological factors in the development of the media affect the concept of rightful access? Do the prevailing monopolistic conditions of media ownership alter the assumptions on which traditional interpretations of the First Amendment have been based?

The two cases immediately following this note illustrate the difficulties inherent in the problem of access *to* the media. *Miami Herald v. Tornillo* (1974) deals with a state law that created a "right to reply" for political candidates attacked in the editorial columns of a newspaper. The Supreme Court unanimously declared the law unconstitutional. But in an earlier case, *Red Lion Broadcasting Co.* v. *FCC* (1969), the Court seemed to feel differently. In upholding of the FCC's "fairness" doctrine, which requires the electronic media to present both sides of controversial issues, the Court was in effect recognizing a right analogous to the "right of reply." Another major difference between the two cases was that radio and television can only operate under public license.

Thus, if one is asked the question, "Is there a right of access to the media?" the answer is "It depends." Cases decided after *Red Lion* have not been uniform, and it may be that the right of access to broadcast media is narrower than the *Red Lion* case suggests. For example, in *CBS v. Democratic National Committee* (1973), the network refused to sell advertising time to the Democratic National Committee and to an

antiwar group, citing its uniform ban against paid editorial advertisements. The FCC upheld the network's position, but the court of appeals reversed, holding that a "flat ban on paid public issue announcements is in violation of the First Amendment, at least where other sorts of paid announcements are accepted." The Supreme Court reversed by a 7-2 vote, the majority opinion by Chief Justice Burger emphasizing the constitutional right of broadcasters to determine the content of their programs. Indeed, Burger's opinion denied that the *Red Lion* case created a broad right of access when it upheld the constitutionality of the fairness doctrine.

Access *by* the media often involves collisions with the right of privacy and similar personal rights. Thus, in *Cox Broadcasting Corporation* v. *Cohn* (1975), the Supreme Court refused to allow a damage judgment against a television station that had accurately reported a rape incident and was sued by the father of the rape victim. The information was contained in court records that were open to the public.

In *Smith* v. *Daily Mail Publishing Co.* (1979), a newspaper was indicted for violating a West Virginia statute making it a crime for a newspaper to publish, without consent of the juvenile court, the name of any youth charged with a juvenile offense. The newspaper had discovered the name of the alleged 14-year-old murderer by monitoring the police radio frequency and questioning eye witnesses to the killing. The West Virginia Supreme Court barred the prosecution on the grounds that the state law was unconstitutional under the First and Fourteenth Amendments. The U.S. Supreme Court affirmed in a unanimous decision. The Court's opinion emphasized that it was not disapproving of a state's effort to preserve the anonymity of juvenile offenders. Rather, it held, "The Magnitude of the State's interest in this statute is not sufficient to justify application of a criminal penalty." It also found equal protection defects in the statute, since no comparable restrictions were placed on electronic media or other publications "except newspapers."

If these decisions seemed to draw the balance in favor of newspapers threatened with civil or criminal sanctions for publishing truthful information lawfully obtained, the Court has leaned the other way in a series of recent cases dealing with the *right* of access by the media to restricted sources. Thus, in *Nixon* v. *Warner Communications, Inc.* (1978), the Court held that the common law right of access to judicial records, in this instance the famous White House tapes used in the trials of the Watergate defendants, was limited by the Presidential Recording Act of 1974, which prohibited television networks and others from copying the tapes for public broadcast. The First Amendment right of the press to access to judicial records, the Court said, was no greater than that of the general public. A similar result was reached in *Houchins* v. *KQED* (1978), where the Court held that the press had no special right of access to film prison life. And as we have already seen, in *Gannett* v. *DePasquale* (1979), the Court upheld the right of a judge in a criminal case to exclude the press from a pretrial hearing. The reasoning of the majority opinion was that the Sixth Amendment right to a public trial belongs to the defendant and not to the public.

The precise boundary lines between individual rights of privacy and the right of the media to obtain and disseminate information remains unclear. With respect to criminal proceedings, perhaps it is worthy of note that in our parent democracy—Great Britain—access by the press to trial proceedings is quite limited. The power of the English courts to punish newspapers with contempt charges is extensive and certainly draws the balance differently than has been done in the United States by the Supreme Court.]

(a) Miami Herald Publishing Company v. Tornillo (1974)

+Burger, Douglas, Brennan, Stewart, White, Marshall, Blackmun, Powell, Rehnquist

[Tornillo, executive director of the Classroom Teachers Association in Florida, was a candidate for the state legislature. The *Miami Herald* printed two editorials critical of his candidacy, and Tornillo demanded that the newspaper

print verbatim his replies to these editorials. The newspaper refused, and Tornillo brought suit under a "right to reply" statute—dating back to 1913—which required a newspaper that had assailed the personal character or official record of a candidate to print a reply commensurate in size and location in the paper to the original charges. The circuit court in Florida held the statute unconstitutional, but the Florida Supreme Court reversed. It held that the statute enhanced free speech, rather than curbing it, and that it promoted a strong societal interest in the free flow of information.]

MR. CHIEF JUSTICE BURGER delivered the opinion of the Court.

. . .

Appellant contends the statute is void on its face because it purports to regulate the content of a newspaper in violation of the First Amendment. Alternatively it is urged that the statute is void for vagueness since no editor could know exactly what words would call the statute into operation. It is also contended that the statute fails to distinguish between critical comment which is and is not defamatory.

The appellee and supporting advocates of an enforceable right of access to the press vigorously argue that Government has no obligation to ensure that a wide variety of views reach the public. . . . It is urged that at the time the First Amendment to the Constitution was enacted in 1791 as part of our Bill of Rights the press was broadly representative of the people it was serving. While many of the newspapers were intensely partisan and narrow in their views, the press collectively presented a broad range of opinions to readers. Entry into publishing was inexpensive; pamphlets and books provided meaningful alternatives to the organized press for the expression of unpopular ideas and often treated events and expressed views not covered by conventional newspapers. A true marketplace of ideas existed in which there was relatively easy access to the channels of communication.

Access advocates submit that although newspapers of the present are superficially similar to those of 1791 the press of today is in reality very different from that known in the early years of our national existence. In the past half century a communications revolution has seen the introduction of radio and television into our lives, the promise of a global community through the use of communications satellites, and the spectre of a "wired" nation by means of an expanding cable television network with two-way capabilities. The printed press, it is said, has not escaped the effects of this revolution. Newspapers have become big business and there are far fewer of them to serve a larger literate population. Chains of newspapers, national newspapers, national wire and news services, and one-newspaper towns, are the dominant features of a press that has become noncompetitive and enormously powerful and influential in its capacity to manipulate popular opinion and change the course of events. Major metropolitan newspapers have collaborated to establish news services national in scope. Such national news organizations provide syndicated "interpretative reporting" as well as syndicated features and commentary, all of which can serve as part of the new school of "advocacy journalism."

The elimination of competing newspapers in most of our large cities, and the concentration of control of media that results from the only newspaper being owned by the same interests which own a television station and a radio station, are important components of this trend toward concentration of control of outlets to inform the public.

The result of these vast changes has been to place in a few hands the power to inform the American people and shape public opinion. Much of the editorial opinion and commentary that is printed is that of syndicated columnists distributed nationwide and, as a result, we are told, on national and world issues there tends to be a homogeneity of editorial opinion, commentary, and interpretative analysis. The abuses of bias and manipulative reportage are, likewise, said to be the result of the vast accumulation of unreviewable power in the modern media empires. In effect, it is claimed, the public has lost any ability to respond or to contribute in a meaningful way to the debate on issues. The monopoly of the means of communication allows for little or no critical analysis of the media except in professional journals of very limited readership. . . .

The obvious solution, which was available to dissidents at an earlier time when entry into publishing was relatively inexpensive, today would be to have additional newspapers. But the same economic factors which have caused the disappearance of vast numbers of metropolitan newspapers, have made entry into the marketplace of ideas served by the print media almost impossible. It is urged that the claim of newspapers to be "surrogates for the public" carries with it a concomitant fiduciary obligation to account for that stewardship. From this premise it is reasoned that the only effective way to insure fairness and accuracy and to provide for some accountability is for government to take affirmative action. The First Amendment interest of the public in being informed is said to be in peril because the "marketplace of ideas" is today a monopoly controlled by the owners of the market. . . .

However much validity may be found in these arguments, at each point the implementation of a remedy such as an enforceable right of access necessarily calls for some mechanism, either governmental or consensual. If it is governmental coercion, this at once brings about a confrontation with the express provisions of the First Amendment and the judicial gloss on that amendment developed over the years.

The Court foresaw the problems relating to government enforced access as early as its decision in *Associated Press* v. *United States* . . . (1945). There it carefully contrasted the private "compulsion to print" called for by the Association's Bylaws with the provisions of the District Court decree against appellants which "does not compel AP or its members to permit publication of anything which their 'reason' tells them should not be published." . . . In *Branzburg* v. *Hayes*, . . . (1972), we emphasized that the cases then before us "involve no intrusions upon speech and assembly, no prior restraint or restriction on what the press may publish, and no express or implied command that the press publish what it prefers to withhold." In *Columbia Broadcasting System, Inc.* v. *Democratic National Committee* . . . (1973), the plurality opinion noted:

The power of a privately owned newspaper to advance its own political, social, and economic views is bounded by only two factors: first, the acceptance of a sufficient number of readers—and hence advertisers—to assure financial success; and, second, the journalistic integrity of its editors and publishers.

An attitude strongly adverse to any attempt to extend a right of access to newspapers was echoed by several Members of this Court in their separate opinions in that case. . . .

We see that beginning with *Associated Press* . . . (1945), the Court has expressed sensitivity as to whether a restriction or requirement constituted the compulsion exerted by government on a newspaper to print that which it would not otherwise print. The clear implication has been that any such compulsion to publish that which " 'reason' tells them should not be published" is unconstitutional. A responsible press is an undoubtedly desirable goal, but press responsibility is not mandated by the Constitution and like many other virtues it cannot be legislated.

Appellee's argument that the Florida statute does not amount to a restriction of appellant's right to speak because "the statute in question here has not prevented the *Miami Herald* from saying anything it wished" begs the core question. Compelling editors or publishers to publish that which " 'reason' tells them should not be published" is what is at issue in this case. The Florida statute operates as a command in the same sense as a statute or regulation forbidding appellant from publishing specified matter. Governmental restraint on publishing need not fall into familiar or traditional patterns to be subject to constitutional limitations on governmental powers. . . . The Florida statute exacts a penalty on the basis of the content of a newspaper. The first phase of the penalty resulting from the compelled printing of a reply is exacted in terms of the cost in printing and composing time and materials and in taking up space that could be devoted to other material the newspaper may have preferred to print. It is correct, as appellee contends, that a newspaper is not subject to the finite technological limitations of time that confront a broadcaster but it is not correct to say that, as an economic reality, a newspaper can proceed to infinite expansion of its column space to accommodate the replies that a government agency determines or a statute commands the readers should have available.

Faced with the penalties that would accrue to any newspaper that published news or commentary arguably within the reach of the right of access statute, editors might well conclude that the safe course is to avoid controversy and that, under the operation of the Florida statute, political and electoral coverage would be blunted or reduced. Government enforced right of access inescapably "dampens the vigor and limits the variety of public debate," *New York Times Co.* v. *Sullivan* . . .

Even if a newspaper would face no additional costs to comply with a compulsory access law and would not be forced to forego publication of news or opinion by the inclusion of a reply, the Florida statute fails to clear the barriers of the First Amendment because of its intrusion into the function of editors. A newspaper is more than a passive receptacle or conduit for news, comment, and advertising. The choice of material to go into a newspaper, and the decisions made as to limitations on the size of the paper, content, and treatment of public issues and public officials—whether fair or unfair—constitutes the exercise of editorial control and judgment. It has yet to be demonstrated how governmental regulation of this crucial process can be exercised consistent with First Amendment guarantees of a free press as they have evolved to this time. Accord-ingly, the judgment of the Supreme Court of Florida is reversed.

It is so ordered.

MR. JUSTICE BRENNAN, WITH WHOM MR. JUSTICE REHNQUIST JOINS, CONCURRING (OMITTED).
MR. JUSTICE WHITE, CONCURRING (OMITTED).

(b) Red Lion Broadcasting Co. v. Federal Communications Commission (1969)

+White, Warren, Black, Clark, Harlan, Brennan, Stewart, Marshall
NP Douglas

[The Red Lion Broadcasting Co. carried a 15-minute broadcast by the Reverend Billy James Hargis as part of its "Christian Crusade" series. Hargis discussed a book by Fred J. Cook entitled *Goldwater—Extremist on the Right,* and he claimed that Cook had been fired by a newspaper for making false charges against government officials and that Cook had attacked J. Edgar Hoover and the Central Intelligence Agency. Hargis also stated that Cook had worked with a Communist-affiliated publication and had defended Alger Hiss. Hargis charged that Cook's book on Goldwater was a "book to smear and destroy Barry Goldwater." Cook demanded free time to reply to Hargis' allegations under the personal attack provisions of the FCC's fairness doctrine. The radio station refused to give Cook free time to reply and failed to meet another provision under that fairness doctrine requiring that it send a tape, transcript, or summary of the Hargis broadcast to Cook. Two separate proceedings were initiated to review FCC provisions. In one proceeding, the Court of Appeals for the District of Columbia affirmed the FCC order requiring the station to provide free time for response to such personal attacks. In a separate proceeding, the Court of Appeals for the Seventh Circuit held that the regulations promulgated under the fairness doctrine were invalid and thus reversed the FCC order. Certiorari was granted by the Supreme Court in both cases to resolve the conflict between the Circuits.]

MR. JUSTICE WHITE delivered the opinion of the Court.

The Federal Communications Commission has for many years imposed on radio and television broadcasters the requirement that discussion of public issues be presented on broadcast stations, and that each side of those issues must be given fair coverage. This is known as the fairness doctrine, which originated very early in the history of broadcasting and has maintained its present outlines for some time. It is an obligation whose content has been defined in a long series of FCC rulings in particular cases, and which is distinct from the statutory requirement of § 315 of the Communications Act that equal time be allotted all qualified candidates for public office. Two aspects of the fairness doctrine, relating to personal attacks in the context of controversial public issues and to political editorializing, were codified more precisely in the form of FCC regulations in 1967. The two cases before us now, which were decided separately below, challenge the constitutional and statutory bases of the doctrine and component rules. . . .

. . .

Not long after the *Red Lion* litigation was begun, the FCC issued a Notice of Proposed Rule Making, . . . with an eye to making the personal attack aspect of the fairness doctrine more precise and more readily enforceable, and to specifying its rules relating to political editorials. . . .

As they now stand amended, the regulations read as follows:

Personal attacks; political editorials.
(a) When, during the presentation of
views on a controversial issue of public importance, an attack is made upon the honesty, character, integrity or like personal qualities of an identified person or group, the licensee shall, within a reasonable time and in no event later than 1 week after the attack, transmit to the person or group attacked (1) notification of the date, time and identification of the broadcast; (2) a script or tape (or an accurate summary if a script or tape is not available) of the attack; and (3) an offer of a reasonable opportunity to respond over the licensee's facilities.

(b) The provisions of paragraph (a) of this section shall not be applicable (1) to attacks on foreign groups or foreign public figures; (2) to personal attacks which are made by legally qualified candidates, their authorized spokesmen, or those associated with them in the campaign, on other such candidates, their authorized spokesmen, or persons associated with the candidates in the campaign; and (3) to bona fide newscasts, bona fide news interviews, and on-the-spot coverage of a bona fide news event (including commentary or analysis contained in the foregoing programs, but the provisions of paragraph (a) of this section shall be applicable to editorials of the licensee). . . .

(c) Where a licensee, in an editorial, (i) endorses or (ii) opposes a legally qualified candidate or candidates, the licensee shall, within 24 hours after the editorial, transmit to respectively (i) the other qualified candidate or candidates for the same office or (ii) the candidate opposed in the editorial (1) notification of the date and the time of the editorial; (2) a script or tape of the editorial; and (3) an offer of a reasonable opportunity for a candidate or a spokesman of the candidate to respond over the licensee's facilities: Provided, however, that where such editorials are broadcast within 72 hours prior to the day of the election, the licensee shall comply with the provisions of this paragraph sufficiently far in advance of the broadcast to enable the candidate or candidates to have a reasonable opportunity to prepare a response and to present it in a timely fashion. . . .

Believing that the specific application of the fairness doctrine in *Red Lion,* and the promulgation of the regulations in *RTNDA* [the companion case] are both authorized by Congress and enhance rather than abridge the freedoms of speech and press protected by the First Amendment, we hold them valid and constitutional. . . .

The history of the emergence of the fairness doctrine and of the related legislation shows that the Commission's action in the *Red Lion* case did not exceed its authority, and that in adopting the new regulations the Commission was implementing congressional policy rather than embarking on a frolic of its own.

Before 1927, the allocation of frequencies was left entirely to the private sector, and the result was chaos. It quickly became apparent that broadcast frequencies constituted a scarce resource whose use could be regulated and rationalized only by the Government. Without government control, the medium would be of little use because of the cacaphony of competing voices, none of which could be clearly and predictably heard. Consequently, the Federal Radio Commission was established to allocate frequencies among competing applicants in a manner responsive to the public "convenience, interest, or necessity."

Very shortly thereafter the Commission expressed its view that the "public interest requires ample play for the free and fair competition of opposing views, and the commission believes that the principle applies . . . to all discussions of issues of importance to the public." . . . This doctrine was applied through denial of license renewals or construction permits, both by the FRC, . . . and its successor FCC . . . After an extended period during which the licensee was

obliged not only to cover and to cover fairly the views of others, but also to refrain from expressing his own personal views, . . . the latter limitation on the licensee was abandoned and the doctrine developed into its present form.

There is a twofold duty laid down by the FCC's decisions and described by the 1949 Report on Editorializing by Broadcast Licensees, . . . The broadcaster must give adequate coverage to public issues, . . . and coverage must be fair in that it accurately reflects the opposing views . . . This must be done at the broadcaster's own expense if sponsorship is unavailable. . . .

Moreover, the duty must be met by programming obtained at the licensee's own initiative if available from no other source, . . . The Federal Radio Commission had imposed these two basic duties on broadcasters since the outset, . . . and in particular respects the personal attack rules and regulations at issue here have spelled them out in greater detail. . . .

The statutory authority of the FCC to promulgate these regulations derives from the mandate to the "Commission from time to time, as public convenience, interest, or necessity requires" to promulgate "such rules and regulations and prescribe restrictions and conditions . . . as may be necessary to carry out the provisions of this chapter . . ." . . .

The Commission is specifically directed to consider the demands of the public interest in the course of granting licenses. . . .

Moreover, the FCC has included among the conditions of the Red Lion license itself the requirement that operation of the station be carried out in the public interest, . . . This mandate to the FCC to assure that broadcasters operate in the public interest is a broad one, a power "not niggardly but expansive," *National Broadcasting Co.* v. *United States* . . . *(1943)*, whose validity we have long upheld. . . . It is broad enough to encompass these regulations.

. . .

The broadcasters challenge the fairness doctrine and its specific manifestations in the personal attack and political editorial rules on conventional First Amendment grounds, alleging that the rules abridge their freedom of speech and press. Their contention is that the First Amendment protects their desire to use their alloted frequencies continuously to broadcast whatever they choose and to exclude whomever they choose from ever using that frequency. No man may be prevented from saying or publishing what he thinks, or from refusing in his speech or other utterances to give equal weight to the views of his opponents. This right, they say, applies equally to broadcasters.

Although broadcasting is clearly a medium affected by a First Amendment interest, *United States* v. *Paramount Pictures, Inc.* . . . (1948), differences in the characteristics of new [sic] media justify differences in the First Amendment standards applied to them. *Joseph Burstyn, Inc.* v. *Wilson* . . . (1952). For example, the ability of new technology to produce sounds more raucous than those of the human voice justifies restrictions on the sound level, and on the hours and places of use, of sound trucks so long as the restrictions are reasonable and applied without discrimination. *Kovacs* v. *Cooper* . . .

Just as the Government may limit the use of sound-amplifying equipment potentially so noisy that it drowns out civilized private speech, so may the Government limit the use of broadcast equipment. The right of free speech of a broadcaster, the user of a sound truck, or any other individual does not embrace a right to snuff out the free speech of others. *Associated Press* v. *United States* . . . (1945).

. . .

Where there are substantially more individuals who want to broadcast than there are frequencies to allocate, it is idle to posit an unabridgeable First Amendment right to broadcast comparable to the right of every individual to speak, write, or publish . . . It would be strange if the First Amendment, aimed at protecting and furthering communications, prevented the Government from making radio communication possible by requiring licenses to broadcast and by limiting the number of licenses so as not to overcrowd the spectrum. . . .

This is not to say that the First Amendment is irrelevant to public broadcasting. On the contrary, it has a major role to play as the Congress itself recognized in §326, which forbids FCC interference with "the right of free speech by means of radio communication." Because of the scarcity of radio frequencies, the Government is permitted to put restraints on licensees in favor of others whose views should be expressed on this unique medium. But the people as a whole retain their interest in free speech by radio and their collective right to have the medium function consistently with the ends and purposes of the First Amendment. It is the right of the viewers and listeners, not the right of the broadcasters, which is paramount. . . . It is the purpose of the First Amendment to preserve an uninhibited marketplace of ideas in which truth will ultimately prevail, rather than to countenance monopolization of that market, whether it be by the Government itself or a private licensee. . . .

In view of the scarcity of broadcast frequencies, the Government's role in allocating those frequencies, and the legitimate claims of those unable without governmental assistance to gain access to those frequencies for expression of their views, we hold the regulations and ruling at issue here are both authorized by statute and constitutional. The judgment of the Court of Appeals in *Red Lion* is affirmed and that in *RTNDA* reversed and the causes remanded for proceedings consistent with this opinion.

It is so ordered.

(c) Nebraska Press Association v. Stuart (1976) (See pp. 907–911)

(d) Gannett Co. v. *De Pasquale* (1979) (See pp. 911–918)

(4) The Special Status of the Press

[Professor Thomas Emerson's approach puts great weight upon the general societal benefits to be gained from freedom of expression. It is reasonable, therefore, to assume that those institutions that facilitate the operation of the First Amendment might enjoy a special status. Since the operation of the press depends heavily on the willingness of people to talk with reporters, it follows that this willingness is itself dependent upon the confidence placed in a news reporter that sources of information will be protected. If the confidentiality of sources cannot be relied upon, either because of the personal character of the reporter or as a result of legal compulsions to reveal those sources, then the public's right to know is indirectly, but in an important way, limited.

The *Branzburg* case is the most significant effort by the Supreme Court to address this question. In the recent case of *New York Times*

reporter Myron Farber, *New York Times* v. *New Jersey* (1978), the Court's denial of certiorari sustained a ruling by the Supreme Court of New Jersey that neither Farber nor the newspaper had a First Amendment privilege to refuse compliance, in a murder prosecution, with the defendant's subpoena duces tecum. That subpoena sought *in camera* inspection of Farber's notes and other materials gathered in his investigation of the murders with which the defendant was charged (and later acquitted). Farber claimed that disclosure of these materials would reveal his confidential sources and would impair news gathering. The New Jersey Supreme Court, citing *Branzburg*, held that there was no reporter's privilege of confidentiality protected by the First Amendment.

Since the thrust of *Branzburg* is to deny news reporters' claims to special constitutional status, the critical response following the case is almost as important as the case itself. Indeed, the state of New Jersey passed a "shield" statute for news reporters, but then did not follow it in the *Farber* case. The excerpts from an article by Mark Neubauer, which follow the *Branzburg* case, suggests that the direction of public policy is toward providing some legal protection for news reporters and media organizations.]

(a) Branzburg v. *Hayes* *United States* v. *Caldwell* *In re Pappas* (1972)

+Burger, White, Blackmun, Powell, Rehnquist

−Douglas, Brennan, Stewart, Marshall

[Each of these three companion cases involved efforts to compel testimony from reporters as to the sources of their reports on activities under investigation by grand juries. Branzburg was a reporter for a newspaper in Louisville, Kentucky; he had published accounts of events concerning the manufacture, sale, and use of drugs. In two instances, he was issued a subpoena to appear before a grand jury. He appeared in response to one but refused to answer questions that would identify his sources; in the other instance, he moved to quash the summons to appear. Branzburg claimed that the First Amendment supported his claimed privilege not to answer such questions. The Kentucky Court of Appeals construed a state statute to provide protection in the revelation of news sources but held that the statute did not protect a reporter from a requirement to testify about criminal events observed personally. Branzburg sought a writ of certiorari to review both judgments.

Pappas was a television newsman-photographer assigned to cover civil disorders in New Bedford, Massachusetts. In the course of this assignment he was allowed entrance to a Black Panthers' news conference at their headquarters on the condition that he not reveal what he observed there. Subsequently, he was summoned by a grand jury to testify, and he answered all questions except those pertaining to activities inside Panther headquarters. He claimed a First Amendment privilege not to reveal confidential information and its source. He was issued a second summons, which he moved to quash; his motion was denied by the trial court, which was supported by the Supreme Judicial Court. Pappas petitioned for a writ of certiorari.

Caldwell was a *New York Times* reporter assigned to cover Black Panther activity. He was summoned to testify before a federal grand jury in California and was asked to bring notes and tape recordings of interviews. Although a second summons was issued after negotiations established that he would not be required to produce reportorial materials, Caldwell moved to quash it on First Amendment grounds. The district court denied the motion on the ground that every person is bound to testify if properly summoned. However, the court extended a modified privilege, based on the First Amendment, which required testimony about information given for publication but exempted confidential sources until the government had made a case for an overriding national interest. In a second-term of the grand jury, Caldwell was once again called to testify, and he refused after a motion to quash was refused, with the same exceptions; he was committed for contempt. He appealed the contempt order, which was reversed by the court of appeals in a decision that found the First Amendment to provide a basis for Caldwell's claimed privilege. The government petitioned for certiorari.]

Opinion of the Court by MR. JUSTICE WHITE, **announced by** THE CHIEF JUSTICE.

The issue in these cases is whether requiring newsmen to appear and testify before State or federal grand juries abridges the freedom of speech and press guaranteed by the First Amendment. We hold that it does not.

. . .

Petitioners Branzburg and Pappas and respondent Caldwell press First Amendment claims that may be simply put: that to gather news it is often necessary to agree either not to identify the source of information published or to publish only part of the facts revealed, or both; that if the reporter is nevertheless forced to reveal these confidences to a grand jury, the source so identified and other confidential sources of other reporters will be measurably deterred from furnishing publishable information, all to the detriment of the free flow of information protected by the First Amendment. Although petitioners do not claim an absolute privilege against official interrogation in all circumstances, they assert that the reporter should not be forced either to appear or to testify before a grand jury or at trial until and unless sufficient grounds are shown for believing that the reporter possesses information relevant to a crime the grand jury is investigating, that the information the reporter has is unavailable from other sources, and that the need for the information is sufficiently compelling to override the claimed invasion of First Amendment interests occasioned by the disclosure. . . .

We do not question the significance of free speech, press or assembly to the country's welfare. Nor is it suggested that news gathering does not qualify for First Amendment protection; without some protection for seeking out the news, freedom of the press could be eviscerated. But this case involves no intrusions upon speech or assembly, no prior restraint or restriction on what the press may publish, and no express or implied command that the press publish what it prefers to withhold. No exaction or tax for the privilege of publishing, and no penalty, civil or criminal, related to the content of published material is at issue here. The use of confidential sources by the press is not forbidden or restricted; reporters remain free to seek news from any source by means within the law. No attempt is made to require the press to publish its sources of information or indiscriminately to disclose them on request.

The sole issue before us is the obligation of reporters to respond to grand jury subpoenas as other citizens do and to answer questions relevant to an investigation into the commission of crime. Citizens generally are not constitutionally immune from grand jury subpoenas; and neither the First Amendment nor other constitutional provision protects the average citizen from disclosing to a grand jury information that he has received in confidence. The claim is, however, that reporters are exempt from these obligations because if forced to respond to subpoenas and identify their sources or disclose other confidences, their informants will refuse or be reluctant to furnish newsworthy information in the future. This asserted burden on news gathering is said to make compelled testimony from newsmen constitutionally suspect and to require a privileged position for them.

It is clear that the First Amendment does not invalidate every incidental burdening of the press that may result from the enforcement of civil or criminal statutes of general applicability. . . .

It has generally been held that the First Amendment does not guarantee the press a constitutional right of special access to information not available to the public generally. *Zemel v. Rusk* . . . (1965); *New York Times Co. v. United States* . . . (1971), . . .

It is thus not surprising that the great weight of authority is that newsmen are not exempt from the normal duty of appearing before a grand jury and answering questions relevant to a criminal investigation. At common law, courts consistently refused to recognize the existence of any privilege authorizing a newsman to refuse to reveal confidential information to a grand jury. . . . In 1958, a newsgatherer asserted for the first time that the First Amendment exempted confidential information from public disclosure pursuant to a subpoena issued in a civil suit, . . . but the claim was denied, and this argument has been almost uniformly rejected since then although there are occasional dicta that, in circumstances not presented, a newsman might be excused. . . . The opinions of the state courts in *Branzburg* and *Pappas* are typical of the prevailing view, although a few recent cases, such as *Caldwell*, have recognized and given effect to some form of constitutional newsman's privilege. . . .

The prevailing constitutional view of the newsman's privilege is very much rooted in the ancient role of the grand jury which has the dual function of determining if there is probable cause to believe that a crime has been committed and of protecting citizens against unfounded criminal prosecutions. Grand jury proceedings are constitutionally mandated for the institution of federal criminal prosecutions for capital or other serious crimes, and "its constitutional prerogatives are rooted in long centuries of Anglo-American history." . . . Although the powers of the grand jury are not unlimited and are subject to the supervision of a judge, the long standing principle that "the public has a right to every man's evidence," except for those persons protected by a constitutional, common law, or statutory privilege, . . . is particularly applicable to grand jury proceedings.

A number of States have provided newsmen a statutory privilege of varying breadth, but the majority have not done so, and none has been provided by federal statute. Until now the only testimonial privilege for unofficial witnesses that is rooted in the Federal Constitution is the Fifth Amendment privilege against compelled self-incrimination. We are asked to create another by interpreting the First Amendment to grant newsmen a testimonial privilege that other citizens do not enjoy. This we decline to do. Fair and effective law enforcement aimed at providing security for the person and property of the individual is a fundamental function of government, and the grand jury plays an important, constitutionally mandated role in this process. On the records now before us, we perceive no basis for holding that the public interest in law enforcement and in ensuring effective grand jury proceedings is insufficient to override the consequential, but uncertain, burden on news gathering

which is said to result from insisting that reporters, like other citizens, respond to relevant questions put to them in the course of a valid grand jury investigation of criminal trial.

This conclusion itself involves no restraint on what newspapers may publish or on the type or quality of information reporters may seek to acquire, nor does it threaten the vast bulk of confidential relationships between reporters and their sources. Grand juries address themselves to the issues of whether crimes have been committed and who committed them. Only where news sources themselves are implicated in crime or possess information relevant to the grand jury's task need they or the reporter be concerned about grand jury subpoenas. Nothing before us indicates that a large number or percentage of *all* confidential news sources fall into either category and would in any way be deterred by our holding that the Constitution does not, as it never has, exempt the newsman from performing the citizen's normal duty of appearing and furnishing information relevant to the grand jury's task.

The preference for anonymity of those confidential informants involved in actual criminal conduct is presumably a product of their desire to escape criminal prosecution, and this preference, while understandable, is hardly deserving of constitutional protection. . . .

. . . [W]e cannot accept the argument that the public interest in possible future news about crime from undisclosed, unverified sources must take precedence over the public interest in pursuing and prosecuting those crimes reported to the press by informants and in thus deterring the commission of such crimes in the future. . . .

We are admonished that refusal to

provide a First Amendment reporter's privilege will undermine the freedom of the press to collect and disseminate news. But this is not the lesson history teaches us. . . .

It is said that currently press subpoenas have multiplied, that mutual distrust and tension between press and officialdom have increased, that reporting styles have changed, and that there is now more need for confidential sources, particularly where the press seeks news about minority cultural and political groups or dissident organizations suspicious of the law and public officials. These developments, even if true, are treacherous grounds for a far-reaching interpretation of the First Amendment fastening a nationwide role on courts, grand juries, and prosecuting officials everywhere. . . .

The privilege claimed here is conditional, not absolute; given the suggested preliminary showings and compelling need, the reporter would be required to testify. Presumably, such a rule would reduce the instances in which reporters could be required to appear, but predicting in advance when and in what circumstances they could be compelled to do so would be difficult. Such a rule would also have implications for the issuance of compulsory process to reporters at civil and criminal trials and at legislative hearings. If newsmen's confidential sources are as sensitive as they are claimed to be, the prospect of being unmasked whenever a judge determines the situation justifies it is hardly a satisfactory solution to the problem. For them, it would appear that only an absolute privilege would suffice.

We are unwilling to embark the judiciary on a long and difficult journey to such an uncertain destination. The administration of a constitutional newsman's privilege would present practical and conceptual difficulties of a high order. Sooner or later, it would be necessary to define those categories of newsmen who qualified for the privilege, a questionable procedure in light of the traditional doctrine that liberty of the press is the right of the lonely pamphleteer who uses carbon paper or a mimeograph just as much as of the large metropolitan publisher who utilizes the latest photocomposition methods. . . . Freedom of the press is a "fundamental personal right" which "is not confined to newspapers and periodicals. It necessarily embraces pamphlets and leaflets. . . . The press in its historic connotation comprehends every sort of publication which affords a vehicle of information and opinion." . . . The informative function asserted by representatives of the organized press in the present cases is also performed by lecturers, political pollsters, novelists, academic researchers, and dramatists. Almost any author may quite accurately assert that he is contributing to the flow of information to the public, that he relies on confidential sources of information and that these sources will be silenced if he is forced to make disclosures before a grand jury.

. . .

Thus, in the end, by considering whether enforcement of a particular law served a "compelling" governmental interest, the courts would be inextricably involved in distinguishing between the value of enforcing different criminal laws. By requiring testimony from a reporter in investigations involving some crimes but not in others, they would be making a value judgment which a legislature had declined to make, since in each case the criminal law involved would represent a considered legislative judgment, not constitutionally suspect, of what conduct is liable to criminal prosecution. The task of judges, like other officials outside the legislative branch, is not to make the law but to uphold it in accordance with their oaths. . . .

Finally, as we have earlier indicated, news gathering is not without its First Amendment protections, and grand jury investigations if instituted or conducted other than in good faith, would pose wholly different issues for resolution under the First Amendment. Official harassment of the press undertaken not for purposes of law enforcement but to disrupt a reporter's relationship with his news sources would have no justification. Grand juries are subject to judicial control and subpoenas to motions to quash. We do not expect courts will forget that grand juries must operate within the limits of the First Amendment as well as the Fifth. . . .

. . . From what we have said, it necessarily follows that the decision in *United States* v. *Caldwell*, . . . must be reversed. . . .

The decision in . . . *Branzburg* v. *Hayes* . . . must be affirmed. . . .

MR. JUSTICE POWELL, CONCURRING.

I add this brief statement to emphasize what seems to me to be the limited nature of the Court's holding. The Court does not hold that newsmen, subpoenaed to testify before a grand jury, are without constitutional rights with respect to the gathering of news or in safeguarding their sources. Certainly, we do not hold, as suggested in the dissenting opinion, that state and federal authorities are free to "annex" the news media as "an investigative arm of government." The solicitude repeatedly shown by this Court for First Amendment freedoms should be sufficient assurance against any such

effort, even if one seriously believed that the media—properly free and untrammeled in the fullest sense of these terms—were not able to protect themselves.

. . .

MR. JUSTICE STEWART, WITH WHOM MR. JUSTICE BRENNAN AND MR. JUSTICE MARSHALL JOIN, DISSENTING.

The Court's crabbed view of the First Amendment reflects a disturbing insensitivity to the critical role of an independent press in our society. The question whether a reporter has a constitutional right to a confidential relationship with his source is of first impression here, but the principles which should guide our decision are as basic as any to be found in the Constitution. While MR. JUSTICE POWELL's enigmatic concurring opinion gives some hope of a more flexible view in the future, the Court in these cases holds that a newsman has no First Amendment right to protect his sources when called before a grand jury. The Court thus invites state and federal authorities to undermine the historic independence of the press by attempting to annex the journalistic profession as an investigative arm of government. Not only will this decision impair performance of the press' constitutionally protected functions, but it will, I am convinced, in the long run, harm rather than help the administration of justice.

. . .

The reporter's constitutional right to a confidential relationship with his source stems from the broad societal interest in a full and free flow of information to the public. It is this basic concern that underlies the Constitution's protection of a free press, . . . because the guarantee is "not for the benefit of the press so much as for the benefit of all of us." . . .

Enlightened choice by an informed citizenry is the basic ideal upon which an open society is premised, and a free press is thus indispensable to a free society. . . .

In keeping with this tradition, we have held that the right to publish is central to the First Amendment and basic to the existence of constitutional democracy. . . .

A corollary of the right to publish must be the right to gather news. The full flow of information to the public protected by the free press guarantee would be severely curtailed if no protection whatever were afforded to the process by which news is assembled and disseminated. We have, therefore, recognized that there is a right to publish without prior governmental approval, *Near* v. *Minnesota* . . . (1931), a right to distribute information, see, e.g., *Lovell* v. *Griffin* . . . (1938), . . . and a right to receive printed matter, *Lamont* v. *Postmaster General* . . . (1965).

No less important to the news dissemination process is the gathering of information. News must not be unnecessarily cut off at its source, for without freedom to acquire information the right to publish would be impermissibly compromised. Accordingly, a right to gather news, of some dimensions, must exist. . . . As Madison wrote: "A popular government without popular information or the means of acquiring it is but a prologue to a farce or tragedy or perhaps both." . . .

The right to gather news implies, in turn, a right to a confidential relationship between a reporter and his source. This proposition follows as a matter of simple logic once three factual predicates are recognized: (1) newsmen require informants to gather news; (2) confidentiality—the promise or understanding that names or certain aspects of communications will be kept off-the-record—is essential to the creation and maintenance of a news-gathering relationship with informants; and (3) the existence of an unbridled subpoena power—the absence of a constitutional right protecting in *any* way, a confidential relationship from compulsory process—will either deter sources from divulging information or deter reporters from gathering and publishing information.

It is obvious that informants are necessary to the news-gathering process as we know it today. If it is to perform its constitutional mission, the press must do far more than merely print public statements or publish prepared handouts. Familiarity with the people and circumstances involved in the myriad background activities that result in the final product called "news" is vital to complete and responsible journalism, unless the press is to be a captive mouthpiece of "newsmakers."

. . .

The impairment of the flow of news cannot, of course, be proven with scientific precision, as the Court seems to demand. Obviously, not every news-gathering relationship requires confidentiality. And it is difficult to pinpoint precisely how many relationships do require a promise or understanding of nondisclosure. But we have never before demanded that First Amendment rights rest on elaborate empirical studies demonstrating beyond any conceivable doubt that deterrent effects exist; we have never before required proof of the exact number of people potentially affected by governmental action, who would actually be dissuaded from engaging in First Amendment activity. . . .

MR. JUSTICE DOUGLAS, DISSENTING (OMITTED).

(b) Mark Neubauer, The Aftermath of Branzburg: Newsman's Privilege and the Case for a Federal Shield Law

It has been four years since the Supreme Court ruled in *Branzburg* v. *Hayes* that newsmen did not have an absolute first amendment privilege against subpoenas which sought information regarding newsmen's confidential sources. Against a backdrop of extensive and social and political change which has characterized the ensuing years, the courts and the press have remained locked in a bitter battle over the right of newsmen to protect their confidential source relationships. . . .

Journalists have tried almost every approach to gain a shield against subpoena—common law, state statutes, constitutional law—but each time they have failed to secure the protection desired permanently. Unlike any other group claiming a privilege against giving evidence, newsmen are fighting what is essentially a political battle. Journalists are generally not subpoenaed for information regarding "hard core" crime such as murder, rape and robbery; rather, they become the objects of subpoenas seeking information regarding what might be termed "political" crimes, primarily radical activity and political corruption. The answer to the problem is in a shield derived from a combination of the first amendment protections developed since *Branzburg* and a federal shield statute that would overcome any first amendment failings.

The fight in American courts over a newsman's privilege is a long one. In 1848, reporter John Nugent of the *New York Herald* had the dubious distinction of becoming the subject of the first reported newsman's shield case in the United States. The United States Senate was in secret session to debate the proposed treaty to end the Mexican-American War, when Nugent—in a tradition to be followed by Jack Anderson and Daniel Ellsberg—sent to his editor a copy of the confidential draft of the treaty and other secret documents. Angered, the Senate subpoenaed Nugent and demanded that he reveal his source. The reporter refused and was jailed for contempt of Congress after failing to secure a writ of habeas corpus. Whether Nugent ever relented is unclear, but the battle for a newsman's privilege to protect confidential information and sources had begun.

For the next 110 years, the controversy was an isolated occurrence at best. Claims of privilege to protect a source occasionally arose from stories dealing with political corruption, stories that resulted in a libel suit, or reports of supposedly secret grand jury proceedings.

The accession of the Nixon administration in the late 1960's marked a sharp increase in the frequency of claims. The first sign of the growing use of subpoenas against reporters came in the 1969 trial of the "Chicago Seven," the anti-war activists charged with inciting a riot at the 1968 Democratic National Convention. The Government served subpoenas on all four major Chicago daily newspapers, the three major television networks and *Newsweek*, *Time* and *Life* magazines, calling for all their notes, film footage, stories, rough drafts and anything else in

Reprinted from Mark Neubauer, "The Newsman's Privilege After *Branzburg:* The Case for a Federal Shield Law," **24** *U.C.L.A. Law Review* (1976), 160–192.

their possession that might be connected with the Democratic Convention.

A marked shift in policy on the subpoenaing of reporters and the media to produce evidence was noted by lawyer-journalist Fred Graham:

Before the Nixon administration began to investigate militant activists and to subpoena newsmen who had contacts among them, the Government's efforts to obtain information from journalists had never caused a row. Usually the Government wanted data on Klan-type elements that the reporters had observed, but not from a position of confidence.

The reporters had little sympathy for the suspects, and information was passed along to the Justice Department—sometimes with subpoenas and sometimes without but almost always in a casual, amiable spirit.

But that was changed by Vice President Agnew's attacks on the press and Mr. Mitchell's reputation as a stern prosecutor of left-wing militants who many newsmen felt were justified in some of their militancy.

. . .

The Common Law. The first legal approach considered by newsmen was urging recognition of a privilege at common law. Other common law privileges, such as those protecting the attorney-client and husband-wife relationships, protect only the substance of the communications and not the sources. Newsmen, on the other hand, seek to guard both the source and the message. For this reason, the government informer privilege which shields the source's identity is closest to the type of common law protection that reporters desire. The United States Supreme Court has preserved the confidential identity of government informers because of the public interest in the flow of

information from these sources. Journalists have argued unsuccessfully that this "flow of information" which the Court praises so highly occurs with newsmen as well as the police, and that the flow to the press is also in the public interest. But in *Branzburg,* Justice White's opinion for the majority rejected the theory that "it is better to write about crime than to do something about it." Indeed, the fight for a common law privilege has been almost universally futile. . . .

The Fifth Amendment. Another theory propounded by newsmen in an effort to protect their sources is based upon the fifth amendment protection against self-incrimination. If a newsman-source relationship resulted in a reporter aiding criminals by withholding information or personally observing a crime without reporting it to the police, the newsman could be subject to a charge of misprision or obstruction of justice. Such potential liability would provide sufficient reason for a legitimate invocation of the reporter's fifth amendment rights. Nevertheless, newsmen have been denied fifth amendment protection in cases where the court has found that there is no danger of the newsman having committed any crime and where the reporter has refused to give the court sufficient information to determine whether the right against self-incrimination has been properly invoked. It is evident, therefore, that since the confidential relationships do not always involve criminal activity, the fifth amendment cannot always protect a newsman from divulging sources or information.

State Statutes. Having failed to persuade the courts to recognize a common law right and finding fifth amendment protection rarely adequate, the advocates of a newsman's privilege turned to the state legislatures. Beginning with Maryland in 1896, 26 states have enacted newsmen's privilege statutes. Reporters have found, however, that even this statutory approach has its problems.

Defining the term "newsman" has been a major source of difficulty in drafting and interpreting the shield statutes. Unlike lawyers or doctors who are covered by other privilege statutes, newsmen are not licensed by the state, so there is no easy method of determining who qualifies for the privilege. The statute must be framed to include all those participants in the flow of information that the privilege is meant to protect. Is a newsman merely a newspaper or broadcast reporter, or do freelancers, legmen and stringers also qualify? . . .

Another problem with the state shield laws has been the often limited degree of protection they offer. Such statutes may, as in California, protect newsmen only against contempt citations, but not against obstruction of justice charges or directed libel verdicts. Ohio's statute has been held to protect only the identity of the source, not the communication involved, thus failing to protect off-the-record information. In New York, personal observations by newsmen were held not to be within the confidential relationships protected by that state's shield law.

Waiver provisions have also limited the effectiveness of newsman shield laws. Some statutes, such as New Jersey's, have specific waiver sections which provide that the reporter's right to the privilege is forfeited once he or she discloses any part of the privileged material. . . . Voluntary disclosure of a source has also been held to constitute a waiver in states which do not have a specific statutory waiver. This rule often operates to prevent newsmen from protecting the information as well as the identity of the source.

. . .

The First Amendment. Unable to secure a common law privilege and finding the fifth amendment and state statutory strategies inadequate, journalists have turned to the cornerstone of their profession, the first amendment. Newsmen argue that by forcing them to divulge their sources, subpoenas would close off information and thus deny not only their freedom to publish but also the public's right to receive news.

The first test of this argument occurred when actress Judy Garland sought to discover the source of allegedly defamatory statements about her printed in an article by columnist Marie Torre. Torre refused to identify her source, claiming that disclosure would limit the availability of news and thereby deny her freedom of the press. Justice Potter Stewart, then a judge on the Second Circuit Court of Appeals, partially agreed with this interpretation of the first amendment. He also noted, however, that freedom of the press is not absolute and must be balanced against the duty to testify. Consequently, he ruled that since in this particular situation the identity of the source "went to the heart of the plaintiff's claim," the first amendment protection did not apply. Justice Stewart qualified his refusal to grant the privilege by observing that the *Torre* case did not deal with the wholesale disclosure of a newsman's confidential sources, nor with a news source whose identity was of doubtful relevance or materiality.

Over the next decade, several cases endorsed the *Torre* recognition of a first amendment privilege, but a majority of courts refused to grant newsmen such a privilege in any form. . . .

When the Court ruled [in the *Branzburg* case] that the newsmen in these cases did not have a first amendment privilege, some journalists and civil libertarians saw the Court's opinion as ending any hope of establishing a strong constitutional shield. However, a close examination of Mr. Justice White's majority opinion in *Branzburg* shows that the Court effectively laid the foundation for the recognition of a qualified first amendment shield; although it held that privilege did not apply in the four cases before it, the Court did not define the precise parameters of whatever protection the first amendment affords confidential newsman-source relationships.

Recognition of a qualified first amendment privilege is a logical result of the majority's concession that the news gathering process did merit at least limited first amendment protection. Acknowledgment of the existence of such a right forced the Court to take a balancing approach to the first amendment, weighing the public interest in the news gathering potential of confidential source relationships against the public interest in apprehending criminals. Yet despite a desire to avoid ad hoc rulemaking, the majority's decision in *Branzburg* is so riddled with qualifications that it provides little definitional guidance as to the application of a first amendment privilege. . . .

Despite the initial pessimism generated by the Supreme Court's holding in *Branzburg*, . . . the concept of a constitutional privilege for newsmen is not dead. The Court did not unequivocally reject the notion that newsmen should be allowed to protect confidential relationships. The majority opinion can be read merely

to hold that while disclosing these confidential relationships may infringe on first amendment rights of news gathering, under the specific facts before the Court, the public need for controlling crime outweighed the injury to first amendment interests.

. . .

The Federal Statutory Solution. . . . Currently there exists an ersatz federal shield law in the form of the Attorney General's guidelines for the subpoenaing of news media. The guidelines were issued by John Mitchell in 1970 as part of his campaign to dampen the subpoena controversy and are now codified in the *Code of Federal Regulations*. Although Justice White in the *Branzburg* opinion praised the guidelines as controlling potential abuse of the subpoena power, the protection that they afford is tenuous. Their major thrust is to require negotiation with the news media prior to seeking any subpoena in an effort to keep the intrusion as limited as possible:

(c) Negotiations with the media shall be pursued in all cases in which a subpoena is contemplated. These negotiations should attempt to accommodate the interests of the trial or grand jury with the interests of the media. Where the nature of the investigation permits, the government should make clear what its needs are in a particular case as well as its willingness to respond to particular problems of the media.

. . .

To curb any overly zealous United States Attorney, clearance from the Attorney General is required before any Justice Department official may seek a subpoena:

If negotiations fail, no Justice Department official shall request or make ar-

rangements for, a subpoena to any member of the news media without the express authorization of the Attorney General.

Despite these checks, the guidelines do not provide adequate safeguards to protect the press from unwarranted subpoenas. The guidelines govern only Justice Department personnel; they are not binding on state or local officials or on private parties. The most disturbing aspect of the guidelines is the ease with which they have been ignored. Of eleven subpoenas requested by the Justice Department from August 1970 to October 1972, five were never approved by the Attorney General. Of 76 subpoenas requested by the Justice Department against news personnel from March 1973 to May 1975, 22 were never approved by the Attorney General. . . .

(5) Ideas, Expression, and the Marketplace

(a) Virginia State Board of Pharmacy v. Virginia Citizens Consumer Council, Inc. (1976)

+Blackmun, Burger, Brennan, Stewart, White, Marshall, Powell
−Rehnquist
NP Stevens

[Recent developments in the constitutional meaning of the First Amendment represent somewhat of a twist in the meaning of that liberal phrase "the marketplace of ideas." Within the last three years, the Supreme Court has come to recognize a First Amendment right of "commercial speech," giving constitutional sanction to the ideas of the marketplace.

The leading early case that raised the question of constitutional protections for commercial speech was *Valentine* v. *Chrestensen* (1942). In that case circulation of handbills advertising a submarine exhibition was restricted by a city ordinance. The owner/exhibitor of the sub-

marine altered the content of the handbill so that it contained information as well as outright advertisement, and when the combination was rejected by city authorities, he brought suit claiming infringement of First Amendment rights. The Supreme Court rejected his contention in language suggesting that the First Amendment supposed a use of the streets for dissemination of information and opinion, not the hawking of wares:

This Court has unequivocally held that the streets are proper places for the exercise of the freedom of communicating information and disseminating opinion and that, though the states and municipalities may appropriately regulate the privilege in the public interest, they may not unduly burden or proscribe its employment in these public thoroughfares. We are equally clear that the Constitution imposes no such restraint on government as respects purely commercial advertising.

Following this case, and until 1975, it was generally assumed that commercial content removed material from the protections of the First Amendment.

In *Virginia State Board,* the Court developed a basis for qualifying *Valentine.* In this case, the Virginia State Board of Pharmacy, which by law regulates the practice of pharmacists, licenses them, and maintains disciplinary control over their conduct, promulgated a rule that prohibited advertising of prescription drug prices, even with regard to those drugs (about 95 percent of all prescriptions) that are supplied to the customer in dosage forms prepared by the pharmaceutical manufacturer. The Virginia Citizens Consumer Council and an individual Virginia resident challenged the validity of this restriction as repugnant to the First and Fourteenth Amendments. They claimed that the First Amendment entitles the user of prescription drugs to receive information about drug prices that pharmacists wish to communicate to them through advertising. A three-judge federal district court invalidated the statute and the Pharmacy Board appealed to the Supreme Court.]

MR. JUSTICE BLACKMUN delivered the opinion of the Court.

. . .

The appellants contend that the advertisement of prescription drug prices is outside the protection of the First Amendment because it is "commercial speech." There can be no question that in past decisions the Court has given some indication that commercial speech is unprotected. In *Valentine* v. *Chrestensen* (1942), the Court upheld a New York statute that prohibited the distribution of any "handbill, circular . . . or other advertising matter whatsoever in or upon any street." The Court concluded that, although the First Amendment would forbid the banning of all communication by handbill in the public thoroughfares, it imposed "no such restraint on government as respects purely commercial advertising." Further support for a "commercial speech" exception to the First Amendment may perhaps be found in *Breard* v. *Alexandria* . . . (1951), where the Court upheld a conviction for violation of an ordinance prohibiting door-to-door solicitation of magazine subscriptions. . . .

Since the decision in *Breard,* however, the Court has never *denied* protection on the ground that the speech in issue was "commercial speech." That simplistic approach, which by then had come under criticism or was regarded as of doubtful validity by members of the Court, was avoided in *Pittsburgh Press Co.* v. *Pittsburgh Comm'n on Human Relations* . . .(1973). There the Court upheld an ordinance prohibiting newspapers from listing employment advertisements in columns according to whether male or female employees were sought to be hired. The Court, to be sure, characterized the advertisements as "classic examples of Commercial speech," . . . and a newspaper's printing of the advertisements as of the same character. The Court, however, upheld the ordinance on the ground that the restriction it imposed was permissible because the discriminatory hirings proposed by the advertisements, and by their newspaper layout, were themselves illegal.

Last Term, in *Bigelow* v. *Virginia* . . . (1975), the notion of unprotected "commercial speech" all but passed from the scene. We reversed a conviction for violation of a Virginia statute that made the circulation of any publication to encourage or promote the processing of an abortion in Virginia a misdemeanor. . . . We rejected the contention that the publication was unprotected because it was commercial. *Chrestensen's* continued validity was questioned, and its holding was described as "distinctly a limited one" that merely upheld "a reasonable regulation of the manner in which commercial advertising could be distributed." . . . We concluded that "the Virginia courts erred in their assumptions that advertising, as such, was entitled to no First Amendment protection," and we observed that the "relationship of speech to the marketplace of products or of services does not make it valueless in the marketplace of ideas." . . .

Here, . . . the questions whether there is a First Amendment exception for "commercial speech" is squarely before us. Our pharmacist does not wish to editorialize on any subject, cultural, philosophical, or political. He does not wish to report any particularly newsworthy fact, or to make generalized observations even about commercial matters. The "idea" he wishes to communicate is simply this: "I will sell you the X prescription drug at the Y price." Our question, then, is whether this communication is wholly outside the protection of the First Amendment.

We begin with several propositions that already are settled or beyond serious dispute. It is clear, for example, that speech does not lose its First Amendment protection because money is spent to protect it, as in a paid advertisement of one form or another. . . . *Buckley* v. *Valeo* (1976); . . . Speech likewise is protected even though it is carried in a form that is "sold" for profit, *Smith* v. *California* . . . (books); *Joseph Burstyn, Inc.* v. *Wilson* . . . (1952) (motion pictures); *Murdock* v. *Pennsylvania* . . . (religious literature), and even though it may involve a solicitation to purchase or otherwise pay or contribute money. . . .

If there is a kind of commercial speech that lacks all First Amendment protection, therefore, it must be distinguished by its content. Yet the speech whose content deprives it of protection cannot simply be speech on a commercial subject. No one would contend that our pharmacist may be prevented from being heard on the subject of whether, in general, pharmaceutical prices should be regulated, or their advertisement forbidden. Nor can it be dispositive that a commercial advertisement is uneditorial, and merely reports a fact. Purely factual matter of public interest may claim protection. . . .

Our question is whether speech which does "no more than propose a commercial transaction," *Pittsburgh Press Co.* v. *Pittsburgh Comm'n on Human Relations* . . . is so removed from any "exposition of ideas," *Chaplinsky* v. *New Hampshire*, . . . and from " 'truth, science, morality, and arts in general, in its diffusion of liberal sentiments on the administration of Government,' " *Roth* v. *United States* . . . (1957), that it

lacks all protection. Our answer is that it is not.

Focusing first on the individual parties to the transaction that is proposed in the commercial advertisement, we may assume that the advertiser's interest is a purely economic one. That hardly disqualifies him for protection under the First Amendment. The interests of the contestants in a labor dispute are primarily economic, but it has long been settled that both the employee and the employer are protected by the First Amendment where they express themselves on the merits of the dispute in order to influence its outcome. . . . It was observed in *Thornhill* v. *Alabama* that "the practices in a single factory may have economic repercussions upon a whole region and affect widespread systems of marketing." . . .

As to the particular consumer's interest in the free flow of commercial information, that interest may be as keen, if not keener by far, than his interest in the day's most urgent political debate. Appellees' case in this respect is a convincing one. Those whom the suppression of prescription drug price information hits the hardest are the poor, the sick, and particularly the aged. A disproportionate amount of their income tends to be spent on prescription drugs; yet they are the least able to learn, by shopping from pharmacist to pharmacist, where their scarce dollars are best spent. When drug prices vary as strikingly as they do, information as to who is charging what becomes more than a convenience. It could mean the alleviation of physical pain or the enjoyment of basic necessities.

Generalizing, society also may have a strong interest in the free flow of commercial information. Even an individual advertisement, though entirely "commercial," may be of general public interest. . . . Obviously, not all commercial messages contain the same or even a very great public interest element. There are few to which such an element, however could not be added. Our pharmacist, for example, could cast himself as a commentator on store-to-store disparities in drug prices, giving his own and those of competitor as proof. We see little point in requiring him to do so, and little difference if he does not.

Moreover, there is another consideration that suggests that no line between publicly "interesting" or "important" commercial advertising and the opposite kind could ever be drawn. Advertising, however tasteless and excessive it sometimes may seem, is nonetheless dissemination of information as to who is producing and selling what product, for what reason, and at what price. So long as we preserve a predominantly free enterprise economy, the allocation of our resources in large measure will be made through numerous private economic decisions. It is a matter of public interest that those decisions, in the aggregate, be intelligent and well informed. To this end, the free flow of commercial information is indispensable. . . . And if it is indispensable to the proper allocation of resources in a free enterprise system, it is also indispensable to the formation of intelligent opinions as to how that system ought to be regulated or altered. Therefore, even if the First Amendment were thought to be primarily an instrument to enlighten public decisionmaking in a democracy, we could not say that the free flow of information does not serve that goal.

Arrayed against these substantial individual and societal interests are a number of justifications for the ad-vertising ban. These have to do principally with maintaining a high degree of professionalism on the part of licensed pharmacists. Indisputably, the State has a strong interest in maintaining that professionalism. It is exercised in a number of ways for the consumer's benefit. . . .

Price advertising, it is argued, will place in jeopardy the pharmacist's expertise and, with it, the customer's health. It is claimed that the aggressive price competition that will result from unlimited advertising will make it impossible for the pharmacist to supply professional services in the compounding, handling, and dispensing of prescription drugs. Such services are time-consuming and expensive; if competitors who economize by eliminating them are permitted to advertise their resulting lower prices, the more painstaking and conscientious pharmacist will be forced either to follow suit or to go out of business. It is also claimed that prices might not necessarily fall as a result of advertising. If one pharmacist advertises, others must, and the resulting expense will inflate the cost of drugs. It is further claimed that advertising will lead people to shop for their prescription drugs among the various pharmacists who offer the lowest prices, and the loss of stable pharmacist-customer relationships will make individual attention—and certainly the practice of monitoring—impossible. Finally, it is argued that damage will be done to the professional image of the pharmacist. This image, that of a skilled and specialized craftsman, attracts talent to the profession and reinforces the better habits of those who are in it. Price advertising, it is said, will reduce the pharmacist's status to that of a mere retailer.

The strength of these proffered justifications is greatly undermined by the fact that high professional standards, to a substantial extent, are guaranteed by the close regulation to which pharmacists in Virginia are subject. And this case concerns the retail sale by the pharmacist more than it does his professional standards. . . .

The challenge now made, however, is based on the First Amendment. This casts the Board's justifications in a different light, for on close inspection it is seen that the State's protectiveness of the citizens rests in large measure on the advantages of their being kept in ignorance. The advertising ban does not directly affect professional standards one way or the other. . . .

There is, of course, an alternative to this highly paternalistic approach. That alternative is to assume that this information is not in itself harmful, that people will perceive their own best interests if only they are well enough informed, and that the best means to that end is to open the channels of communication rather than to close them. If they are truly open, nothing prevents the "professional" pharmacist from marketing his own assertedly superior product, and contrasting it with that of the low-cost, high-volume prescription drug retailer. But the choice among these alternative approaches is not ours to make or the Virginia General Assembly's. It is precisely this kind of choice, between the dangers of suppressing information, and the dangers of its misuse if it is freely available, that the First Amendment makes for us. Virginia is free to require whatever professional standards it wishes of its pharmacists; it may subsidize them or protect them

from competition in other ways. . . . But it may not do so by keeping the public in ignorance of the entirely lawful terms that competing pharmacists are offering. In this sense, the justifications Virginia has offered for suppressing the flow of prescription drug price information, far from persuading us that the flow is not protected by the First Amendment, have re-enforced our view that it is. We so hold.

In concluding that commercial speech, like other varieties, is protected, we of course do not hold that it can never be regulated in any way. Some forms of commercial speech regulation are surely permissible. We mention a few only to make clear that they are not before us and therefore are not foreclosed by this case.

There is no claim, for example, that the prohibition on prescription drug price advertising is a mere time, place, and manner restriction. We have often approved restrictions of that kind provided that they are justified without reference to the content of the regulated speech, that they serve a significant governmental interest, and that in so doing they leave open ample alternative channels for communication of the information. . . . Whatever may be the proper bounds of time, place, and manner restrictions on commercial speech, they are plainly exceeded by this Virginia statute, which singles out speech of a particular content and seeks to prevent its dissemination completely. . . .

What is at issue is whether a State may completely suppress the dissemination of concededly truthful information about entirely lawful activity; fearful of that information's effect upon its disseminators and its recipients. Reserving other questions, we conclude that the answer to this one is in the negative.

The judgment of the District Court is affirmed.

It is so ordered.

MR. CHIEF JUSTICE BURGER, CONCURRING (OMITTED).

MR. JUSTICE REHNQUIST, DISSENTING.

The logical consequences of the Court's decision in this case, a decision which elevates commercial intercourse between a seller hawking his wares and a buyer seeking to strike a bargain to the same place as has been previously reserved for the free marketplace of ideas, are far reaching indeed. Under the Court's opinion the way will be open not only for dissemination of price information but for active promotion of prescription drugs, liquor, cigarettes and other products the use of which it has previously been thought desirable to discourage. Now, however, such promotion is protected by the First Amendment so long as it is not misleading or does not promote an illegal product or enterprise. In coming to this conclusion, the Court has overruled a legislative determination that such advertising should not be allowed and has done so on behalf of a consumer group which is not directly disadvantaged by the statute in question. This effort to reach a result which the Court obviously considers desirable is a troublesome one, for two reasons. It extends standing to raise First Amendment claims beyond the previous decisions of this Court. It also extends the protection of that Amendment to purely commercial endeavors which it most vig-

orous champions on this Court had thought to be beyond its pale. . . .

(b) Bates v. State Bar of Arizona (1977)

+Blackmun, Brennan, White, Marshall, Stevens
±Burger, Stewart, Powell
—Rehnquist

[In the previous case, *Virginia State Board of Pharmacy* v. *Virginia Citizens Council*, it is evident that the Supreme Court is embarking on a new policy direction. Justice Blackmun's opinion in that case takes special care to review the fundamentals of the meaning of the First Amendment in the context of "commercial speech." During the 1976–1977 term, three decisions based on the *Pharmacy Board* case were handed down, the most important of which was the *Bates* case. But the others deserve brief mention. In *Carey* v. *Population Services International*, a New York law that included a ban on the advertising of contraceptives was declared unconstitutional on First Amendment grounds and because it infringed on privacy rights recognized in *Griswold* v. *Connecticut* (1965). The doctrine of protected commercial speech was also the basis for striking down an ordinance prohibiting the display of "For Sale" and "Sold" signs in the real estate business. The purpose of the ordinance was to discourage the flight of white homeowners from a racially integrated community. But in *Linmark Associates, Inc.* v. *Township of Willingboro* (1977), the Supreme Court held that this was an impermissible infringement on First Amendment rights.

Bates and his associates, licensed members of the bar of Arizona, operated a legal clinic and advertised the fees for routine services they would charge to persons of moderate means who could not afford full legal costs but were ineligible for free legal services. Advertising was necessary because profits depended on attracting a high volume of clients. The advertisement, placed in the *Arizona Republic,* stated in part: "Do you need a lawyer? Legal Services at Very Reasonable Fees." It listed the fees for uncontested divorces, adoptions, bankruptcies, and changes of name, all under the symbol of the scales of justice. A complaint was filed against Bates by the Arizona State Bar Association, since the advertisement violated the Bar's rules against advertising. A disciplinary committee recommended that Bates and his partner each be suspended from law practice for six months; upon review by the Board of Governors of the Bar, a reduced penalty of one week suspension each was recommended to the Arizona Supreme Court, which affirmed the decision. Appeal to the Supreme Court of the United States was granted.]

MR. JUSTICE BLACKMUN delivered the opinion of the Court.

. . .

In *Parker* v. *Brown,* . . . (1943), this Court held that the Sherman Act was not intended to apply against certain state action. . . . In *Parker* a raisin producer-packer brought suit against California officials challenging a state program designed to restrict competition among growers and thereby to maintain prices in the raisin market. The Court held that the State, "as sovereign, imposed the restraint as an act of government, which the Sherman Act did not undertake to prohibit." . . . Appellee argues, and the Arizona Supreme Court held, that the *Parker* exemption also bars the instant Sherman Act claim. We agree. . . .

Last Term, in *Virginia Pharmacy Board* v. *Virginia Consumer Council,* . . . the Court considered the validity under the First Amendment of a Virginia statute declaring that a pharmacist was guilty of "unprofessional conduct" if he advertised prescription drug prices. The pharmacist would then be subject to a monetary penalty or the suspension or revoca-

tion of his license. The statute thus effectively prevented the advertising of prescription drug price information. We recognized that the pharmacist who desired to advertise did not wish to report any particularly newsworthy fact or to comment on any cultural, philosophical, or political subject; his desired communication was characterized simply: " 'I will sell you the X prescription drug at the Y price.' " Nonetheless, we held that commercial speech of that kind was entitled to the protection of the First Amendment.

Our analysis began, *ibid,* with the observation that our cases long have protected speech even though it is in the form of a paid advertisement, *Buckley* v. *Valeo* . . . (1976); *New York Times Co.* v. *Sullivan* . . . (1964); in a form that is sold for profit, . . . ; or in the form of a solicitation to pay or contribute money. . . . If commercial speech is to be distinguished, it "must be distinguished by its content." . . . But a consideration of competing interests reinforced our view that such speech should not be withdrawn from protection merely because it proposed a mundane commercial transaction. Even though the speaker's interest is largely economic, the Court has protected such speech in certain contexts. . . . The listener's interest is substantial; the consumer's concern for the free flow of commercial speech often may be far keener than his concern for urgent political dialogue. Moreover, significant societal interests are served by such speech. Advertising, though entirely commercial, may often carry information of import to significant issues of the day. . . . And commercial speech serves to inform the public of the availability, nature, and prices of products and services, and thus performs an indispensable role in the allocation of resources in a free enterprise system. . . . In short, such speech serves individual and societal interests in assuring informed and reliable decisionmaking. . . .

We have set out this detailed summary of the *Pharmacy* opinion because the conclusion that Arizona's disciplinary rule is violative of the First Amendment might be said to flow *a fortiori* from it. Like the Virginia statutes, the disciplinary rule serves to inhibit the free flow of commercial information and to keep the public in ignorance. Because of the possibility, however, that the differences among professions might bring different constitutional considerations into play, we specifically reserved judgment as to the other professions.

In the instant case we are confronted with the arguments directed explicitly toward the regulation of advertising by licensed attorneys.

The issue presently before us is a narrow one. First, we need not address the peculiar problems associated with advertising claims relating to the *quality* of legal services. Such claims probably are not susceptible to precise measurement or verification and, under some circumstances, might well be deceptive or misleading to the public, or even false. Appellee does not suggest, nor do we perceive, that appellant's advertisement contained claims, extravagant or otherwise, as to the quality of services. Accordingly, we leave that issue for another day. Second, we also need not resolve the problems associated with in-person solicitation of clients—at the hospital room or the accident site, or in any other situation that breeds undue influence—by attorneys or their agents or "runners." Activity of that

kind might well pose dangers of overreaching and misrepresentation not encountered in newspaper announcement advertising. Hence, this issue also is not before us. Third, we note that appellee's criticism of advertising by attorneys does not apply with much force to some of the basic factual content of advertising: information as to the attorney's name, address, and telephone number, office hours, and the like. The American Bar Association itself has a provision in its current Code of Professional Responsibility that would allow the disclosure of such information, and more, in the classified section of the telephone directory. . . . We recognize, however, that an advertising diet limited to such spartan fare would provide scant nourishment.

The heart of the dispute before us today is whether lawyers also may constitutionally advertise the *prices* at which certain routine services will be performed. Numerous justifications are proffered for the restriction of such price advertising. We consider each in turn:

1. *The Adverse Effect on Professionalism.* Appellee places particular emphasis on the adverse effects that it feels price advertising will have on the legal profession. The key to professionalism, it is argued, is the sense of pride that involvement in the discipline generates. It is claimed that price advertising will bring about commercialization, which will undermine the attorney's sense of dignity and self-worth. . . .

We recognize, of course, and commend the spirit of public service with which the profession of law is practiced and to which it is dedicated. The present Members of this Court, licensed attorneys all, could not feel otherwise. And we would have reason to pause if we felt that our decision today would undercut that spirit. But we find the postulated connection between advertising and the erosion of true professionalism to be severely strained. At its core, the argument presumes that attorneys must conceal from themselves and from their clients the real-life fact that lawyers earn their livelihood at the bar. We suspect that few attorneys engage in such self-deception. And rare is the client, moreover, even one of modest means, who enlists the aid of an attorney with the expectation that his services will be rendered free of charge. . . .

Moreover, the assertion that advertising will diminish the attorney's reputation in the community is open to question. Bankers and engineers advertise, and yet these professions are not regarded as undignified. In fact, it has been suggested that the failure of lawyers to advertise creates public disillusionment with the profession. The absence of advertising may be seen to reflect the profession's failure to reach out and serve the community: studies reveal that many persons do not obtain counsel even when they perceive a need because of the feared prices of services or because of an inability to locate a competent attorney. Indeed, cynicism with regard to the profession may be created by the fact that it long has publicly eschewed advertising, while condoning the actions of the attorney who structures his social or civic associations so as to provide contacts with potential clients. . . .

2. *The Inherently Misleading Nature of Attorney Advertising.* It is argued that advertising of legal services inevitably will be misleading (a) because such services are so individualized with regard to content and quality as to prevent informed comparison on the basis of an advertisement, (b) because the consumer of legal services is unable to determine in advance just what services he needs, and (c) because advertising by attorneys will highlight irrelevant factors and fail to show the relevant factor of skill.

We are not persuaded that restrained professional advertising by lawyers inevitably will be misleading. Although many services performed by the attorneys are indeed unique, it is doubtful that any attorney would or could advertise fixed prices for services of that type. The only services that lend themselves to advertising are the routine ones: the uncontested divorce, the simple adoption, the uncontested personal bankruptcy, the change of name, and the like—the very services advertised by appellants. . . .

The second component of the argument—that advertising ignores the diagnostic role—fares little better. It is unlikely that many people go to an attorney merely to ascertain if they have a clean bill of legal health. Rather, attorneys are likely to be employed to perform specific tasks. Although the client may not know the detail involved in performing the task, he no doubt is able to identify the service he desires at the level of generality to which advertising lends itself.

The third component is not without merit: advertising does not provide a complete foundation on which to select an attorney. But it seems peculiar to deny the consumer, on the ground that the information is incomplete, at least some of the relevant information needed to reach an informed decision. The alternative—the prohibition of advertising—serves only to restrict the information that flows to consumers. . . .

3. The Adverse Effect on the Administration of Justice. Advertising is said to have the undesirable effect of stirring up litigation. The judicial machinery is designed to serve those who feel sufficiently aggrieved to bring forward their claims. Advertising, it is argued, serves to encourage the assertion of legal rights in the courts, thereby undesirably unsettling societal repose. There is even a suggestion of barratry. . . .

But advertising by attorneys is not an unmitigated source of harm to the administration of justice. It may offer great benefits. Although advertising might increase the use of the judicial machinery, we cannot accept the notion that it is always better for a person to suffer a wrong silently than to redress it by legal action. . . .

4. The Undesirable Economic Effects of Advertising. It is claimed that advertising will increase the overhead costs of the profession, and that these costs then will be passed along to consumers in the form of increased fees. Moreover, it is claimed that the additional cost of practice will create a substantial entry barrier, deterring or preventing young attorneys from penetrating the market and entrenching the position of the bar's established members.

These two arguments seem dubious at best. Neither distinguishes lawyers from others, see *Virginia Pharmacy Board* v. *Virginia Consumer Council,* . . . and neither appears relevant to the First Amendment. The ban on advertising serves to increase the difficulty of discovering the lowest-cost seller of acceptable ability. As a result, to this extent attorneys are isolated from competition, and the incentive to price competitively is reduced. Although it is true that the effect of advertising on the price of services has not been

demonstrated, there is revealing evidence with regard to products; where consumers have the benefit of price advertising, retail prices often are dramatically lower than they would be without advertising. It is entirely possible that advertising will serve to reduce, not advance, the cost of legal services to the consumer. . . .

5. The Adverse Effect of Advertising on the Quality of Service. It is argued that the attorney may advertise a given "package" of service at a set price, and will be inclined to provide, by indiscriminate use, the standard package regardless of whether it fits the client's needs.

Restraints on advertising, however, are an ineffective way of deterring shoddy work. An attorney who is inclined to cut quality will do so regardless of the rule on advertising. And the advertisement of a standardized fee does not necessarily mean that the services offered are undesirably standardized. Indeed, the assertion that an attorney who advertises a standard fee will cut quality is substantially undermined by the fixed fee schedule of appellee's own prepaid Legal Services Program. Even if advertising leads to the creation of "legal clinics" like that of appellants'—clinics that emphasize standardized procedures for routine problems—it is possible that such clinics will improve service by reducing the likelihood of error.

6. The Difficulties of Enforcement. Finally, it is argued that the wholesale restriction is justified by the problems of enforcement if any other course is taken. Because the public lacks sophistication in legal matters, it may be particularly susceptible to misleading or deceptive advertising by lawyers. After-the-fact action by the consumer lured by such advertising may not provide a realistic restraint because of the inability of the layman to assess whether the service he has received meets professional standards. Thus, the vigilance of a regulatory agency will be required. But because of the numerous purveyors of services, the overseeing of advertising will be burdensome.

It is at least somewhat incongruous for the opponents of advertising to extol the virtues and altruism of the legal profession at one point, and, at another, to assert that its members will seize the opportunity to mislead and distort. We suspect that, with advertising, most lawyers will behave as they always have: they will abide by their solemn oaths to uphold the integrity and honor of their profession and of the legal system. For every attorney who overreaches through advertising, there will be thousands of others who will be candid and honest and straightforward. And, of course, it will be in the latters' interest, as in other cases of misconduct at the bar, to assist in weeding out those few who abuse their trust.

In sum, we are not persuaded that any of the proffered justifications rises to the level of an acceptable reason for the suppression of all advertising by attorneys.

In the usual case involving a restraint on speech, a showing that the challenged rule served unconstitutionally to suppress speech would end our analysis. In the First Amendment context, the Court has permitted attacks on overly broad statutes without requiring that the person making the attack demonstrate that in fact his specific conduct was protected. . . . Having shown that the disciplinary rule interferes with protected speech, appellants ordinarily could expect to benefit regardless of the nature of their acts.

The First Amendment overbreadth doctrine, however, represents a departure from the traditional rule that a person may not challenge a statute on the ground that it might be applied unconstitutionally in circumstances other than those before the court. . . . The reason for the special rule in First Amendment cases is apparent: an overbroad statute might serve to chill protected speech. First Amendment interests are fragile interests, and a person who contemplates protected activity might be discouraged by the *in terrorem* effect of the statute. . . . Indeed, such a person might choose not to speak because of uncertainty whether his claim of privilege would prevail if challenged. The use of overbreadth analysis reflects the conclusion that the possible harm to society from allowing unprotected speech to go unpunished is outweighed by the possibility that protected speech will be muted.

But the justification for the application of overbreadth analysis applies weakly, if at all, in the ordinary commercial context. As was acknowledged in *Virginia Pharmacy Board* v. *Virgina Consumer Council,* . . . there are "common sense differences" between commercial speech and other varieties. . . . Since advertising is linked to commercial well-being, it seems unlikely that such speech is particularly susceptible to being crushed by overbroad regulation. . . . Moreover, concerns for uncertainty in determining the scope of protection are reduced; the advertiser seeks to disseminate information about a product or service that he provides, and presumably he can determine more readily than others whether his speech is truthful and protected. . . . Since overbreadth has been described by this Court as "strong medicine," which "has been employed . . . sparingly and only as a last resort," . . . we decline to apply it to professional advertising, a context where it is not necessary to further its intended objective. . . .

Is, then, appellants' advertisement outside the scope of basic First Amendment protection? Aside from general claims as to the undesirability of any advertising by attorneys, a matter considered above, appellee argues that appellants' advertisement is misleading, and hence unprotected, in three particulars: (a) the advertisement makes reference to a "legal clinic," an allegedly undefined term; (b) the advertisement claims that appellants offer services at "very reasonable" prices, and, at least with regard to an uncontested divorce, the advertised price is not a bargain; and (c) the advertisement does not inform the consumer that he may obtain a name change without the services of an attorney. . . . On this record, these assertions are unpersuasive. We suspect that the public would readily understand the term "legal clinic"— if, indeed, it focused on the term at all—to refer to an operation like that of appellants' that is geared to provide standardized and multiple services. In fact, in his deposition the President of the State Bar of Arizona observed that there was a committee of the Bar "exploring the ways in which the legal clinic concept can be properly developed." . . . And the clinical concept in the sister profession of medicine surely by now is publicly acknowledged and understood.

As to the cost of an uncontested divorce, appellee stated at oral argument that this runs from $150 to $300 in the area. . . . Appellants advertised a fee of $175 plus a $20 court filing fee, a rate that seems "very reasonable" in light of the customary charge. Appellee's own Legal Service Program sets the rate for an uncontested divorce at $250. . . . Of course, advertising will permit the comparison of rates among competitors, thus exposing if the rates are reasonable.

As to the final argument—the failure to disclose that a name change might be accomplished by the client without the aid of an attorney—we need only note that most legal services may be performed legally by the citizen for himself. See *Faretta* v. *California* . . . (1975); . . . The record does not unambiguously reveal some of the relevant facts in determining whether the nondisclosure is misleading, such as how complicated the procedure is and whether the State provides assistance for laymen. The deposition of one appellant, however, reflects that when he ascertained that a name change required only the correction of a record or the like, he frequently would send the client to effect the change himself. . . .

We conclude that it has not been demonstrated that the advertisement at issue could be suppressed.

In holding that advertising by attorneys may not be subjected to blanket suppression, and that the advertisement at issue is protected, we, of course, do not hold that advertising by attorneys may not be regulated in any way. We mention some of the clearly permissible limitations on advertising not foreclosed by our holding.

Advertising that is false, deceptive, or misleading of course is subject to restraint. . . . Since the advertiser knows his product and has a commercial interest in its dissemination, we have little worry that regulation to assure truthfulness will discourage protected speech. . . . And any concern that strict requirements for truthfulness will undesirably inhibit spontaneity seems inapplicable because commercial speech generally is calculated. Indeed, the public and private benefits from commercial speech derive from confidence in its accuracy and reliability. Thus, the leeway for untruthful or misleading expression that has been allowed in other contexts has little force in the commercial arena. . . . In fact, because the public lacks sophistication concerning legal services, misstatements that might be overlooked or deemed unimportant by other advertising may be found quite inappropriate in legal advertising. For example, advertising claims as to the quality of services—a matter we do not address today—are not susceptible to measurement or verification, accordingly, such claims may be so likely to be misleading as to warrant restriction. Similar objections might justify restraints on in-person solicitation. We do not foreclose the possibility that some limited supplementation, by way of warning or disclaimer or the like, might be required of even an advertisement of the kind ruled upon today so as to assure that the consumer is not misled. In sum, we recognize that many of the problems in defining the boundary between deceptive and nondeceptive advertising remain to be resolved, and we expect that the bar will have a special role to play in assuring that advertising by attorneys flows both freely and cleanly.

As with other varieties of speech, it follows as well that there may be reasonable restrictions on the time, place, and manner of advertising. . . . Advertising concerning transactions that are themselves illegal obviously may be suppressed. . . . And the special problems of advertising on the electronic broadcast media will warrant special consideration. . . .

The constitutional issue in this case is only whether the State may prevent the publication in a newspaper of appellants' truthful advertisement concerning the availability and

terms of routine legal services. We rule simply that the flow of such information may not be restrained, and we therefore hold the present application of the disciplinary rule against appellants to be violative of the First Amendment.

The judgement of the Supreme Court of Arizona is therefore affirmed in part and reversed in part.

It is so ordered.

MR. CHIEF JUSTICE BURGER, CONCURRING IN PART AND DISSENTING IN PART (OMITTED).
MR. JUSTICE POWELL, WITH WHOM MR. JUSTICE STEWART JOINS, CONCURRING IN PART AND DISSENTING IN PART (OMITTED).
MR. JUSTICE REHNQUIST, DISSENTING (OMITTED).

B. *Expression and Action*

(1) A Note on Expression and Action

Thomas Emerson's theory of freedom of expression, reprinted in part at the beginning of this chapter, implies that expression and action are separate and distinct elements. In general, what one *does* is subject to regulation and sanction, while what one says or writes is, with but a few exceptions, protected by the First Amendment. Traditionally, this protection was extended to verbal expression, although it has long been understood that the communicative potential of action or conduct is enormous.

The increasing importance of nonverbal communication reflects the impact of new media technology. In our age, the spoken or written word seems to carry less weight than the image. Certainly in television the spoken word often does little more than supplement visual images portrayed on the screen. We are not merely told about a police chief in Saigon who shoots a captured Vietcong guerrilla in the head—we see it in its full force and horror, in a way that no words could capture. There is an immediacy to actions that words may lack. In our time, the eye is challenging the ear for the mind, and it is winning.

The changing technological circumstances and opportunities for communication have posed difficult problems for the Supreme Court. It has attempted to meet those problems in part by developing three conceptions of communication, each weighed somewhat differently on the scales of the First Amendment: pure speech, speech plus (conduct), and symbolic speech.

The notion of pure speech appears to have stemmed from the recognition, in *Thornhill* v. *Alabama* (1940), that labor union picketing was entitled to qualified protection under the First Amendment, even though it obviously was more than pure speech. To some extent, "pure" speech is an abstraction, since the medium of expression is an inextricable component of any speech. Nevertheless, for constitutional purposes, pure speech represents the "ideal" of face-to-face communication and exchange of ideas and opinions. It assumes a willing listener, open to the persuasive power of words and argument, and a nondisruptive setting. But there are certain limits to this relatively idyllic notion. It does not distinguish between words that are constitutionally protected and those that are not. We have already noted that "fighting words," obscenity, and defamatory statements are generally not entitled to constitutional protection. Moreover, even speech that is constitutionally protected may lose that protection because of the way in which it

is uttered or the circumstances in which it is expressed. There is no constitutional protection to one who falsely shouts "fire" in a theater nor to one whose discussion of the relative merits of capitalism and socialism crosses the line into direct advocacy of the forceful overthrow of the government. It is certainly constitutionally protected speech to discuss the merits of political candidates and to campaign in behalf of them, but in *United Public Workers* v. *Mitchell* (1947), the Supreme Court approved a federal law (the Hatch Act) that severely limited the involvement in politics of government employees.

The concept of "speech plus" recognizes that conduct may at times be an effective supplement to and reinforcement of ordinary expression. Indeed, the "speech plus" doctrine demonstrates the relatively limited utility of the conception of pure speech for constitutional analysis. The "speech plus" category usually includes questions about the use of public places to assemble, picket, march, or patrol (e.g. the use of a "public forum").

For example, in *Hague* v. *Committee for Industrial Organization* (1939), the Court overturned a city ordinance forbidding distribution of printed matter without permits in streets, parks, and other public places. The ordinance in question enabled the director of public safety to refuse a permit if in the director's opinion a riot or disturbance might occur if certain printed material was distributed in public places. The Court held that this was an "instrument of arbitrary suppression of free expression of views on national affairs. . . ." But in *Feiner* v. *New York* (1951), the Court held that where a speaker on public streets encourages the audience to become divided into hostile camps, interferes with traffic, and refuses to obey police officers, a resulting conviction for disorderly conduct is not a violation of the speaker's First Amendment rights. However, in *Edwards* v. *South Carolina* (1963), the Supreme Court held that the arrest and conviction of a group of black protestors for breach of the peace by marching peacefully on sidewalks around the state capital to publicize their opposition to racial discrimination infringed their constitutional rights of free speech, free assembly, and freedom to petition for redress of their grievances. The Court has sustained the right of privately owned shopping centers to prohibit the distribution of handbills on its property when the handbills are unrelated to the shopping center's operations, *Lloyd Corp.* v. *Tanner* (1972).

The fact is that speech is more effective if the most advantageous place, time, audience, and circumstances are also chosen—in most cases, because they improve access to the public. Access to the public forum for purposes of communication has been the source of countless First Amendment cases; in almost all, it is because such access conflicts with other, equally legitimate uses of those places. It may also conflict with the reasonable expectations of privacy of individual members of the public. The intrusiveness of speech is an issue that continually appears in constitutional litigation. Whether it is door-to-door proselytizing for a church, or the use of sound amplification equipment, or the use of a public recreation facility where a certain level of relative tranquility is expected, "speech plus" may conflict with other constitutional guarantees.

Symbolic speech is not entirely distinct from "speech plus," but its emphasis is upon the use of action *as* communication rather than merely as reinforcement for verbal communication. In this conception, action stands in the place of speech and claims the same constitutional protections. In so doing, it inevitably forces recognition of the fact that totally "pure" speech is an abstraction. In real life, speech invariably implicates action in some forms. In the *Tinker* and *O'Brien* cases, discussed in the first chapter of this book, we have seen two examples of symbolic speech seeking constitutional protection. The civil rights movement of the 1960s raised many questions about the constitutional status of protest demonstrations, sit-ins, and similar activities. And a 1974 case, *Smith* v. *Goguen*, required the Supreme Court to decide if the Constitution barred prosecution of a young man who had sewn an American flag on the seat of his pants.

There is no easy solution for the speech/action dilemma. The Supreme Court's approach has been to treat each case individually without attempting to formulate a coherent doctrine. Yet to form such a doctrine, there would have to be a standard sufficiently capable of distinguishing various kinds of action in association with speech. At present, there is no such standard.

(2) Picketing, Demonstrations, and Public Order

(a) Cox v. Louisiana (1965)

+Warren, Douglas, Brennan, Stewart, Goldberg
±Black, Harlan, Clark, White

[About 2000 students, led by the Reverend Elton Cox, a CORE organizer, were protesting the arrest of 23 students from Southern University in Baton Rouge who had been picketing local stores that maintained segregated lunch counters. The demonstration began at the state capitol and culminated in front of the court-house where the 23 students were jailed. The police asked the demonstrators to disperse, and they refused. After several conversations between Cox and the police chief, the demonstrators were directed to the sidewalk opposite the courthouse where they began a program including speeches and the singing of hymns—to which the jailed students responded in kind. About noon, Cox urged the demonstrators to seek lunch service at the stores whose discriminatory practices were being protested. At this point, white onlookers began to "mutter" and "grumble" and the sheriff, believing these instructions to be "inflammatory," ordered the demonstrators to disperse. The demonstrators refused to comply with this order; the police resorted to tear gas, and the area was quickly cleared. No participants were arrested that day. The following day Cox was arrested and charged with four offenses—criminal conspiracy, disturbing the peace, obstructing public passages, and picketing before a courthouse. In a trial before a judge without a jury he was acquitted of the conspiracy charge and convicted of the other three. He was sentenced to a cumulative total of twenty-one months in jail and a fine of $5700.]

MR. JUSTICE GOLDBERG delivered the opinion of the Court.
The Breach of the Peace Conviction. . . . It is clear to us that on the facts of this case, which are strikingly similar to those present in *Edwards* v. *South Carolina* . . . and *Fields* v. *South Carolina* . . . Louisiana infringed appellant's rights of free speech and free assembly by convicting him under this statute. As in *Edwards*, we do not find it necessary to pass upon appellant's contention that there was a complete absence of evidence so that his conviction deprived him of liberty without due process of law. Cf. *Thompson* v. *Louisville* . . . . We hold that Louisiana may not constitutionally punish appellant under this statute for engaging in the type of conduct

which this record reveals, and also that the statute as authoritatively interpreted by the Louisiana Supreme Court is unconstitutionally broad in scope. . . .

The State argues, however, that while the demonstrators started out to be orderly, the loud cheering and clapping by the students in response to the singing from the jail converted the peaceful assembly into a riotous one. The record, however, does not support this assertion. It is true that the students, in response to the singing of their fellows who were in custody, cheered and applauded. However, the meeting was an outdoor meeting and a key state witness testified that while the singing was loud, it was not disorderly. There is, moreover, no indication that the mood of the students was ever hostile, aggressive, or unfriendly. Our conclusion that the entire meeting from the beginning until its dispersal by tear gas was orderly and not riotous is confirmed by a film of the events taken by a television news photographer, which was offered in evidence as a state exhibit. We have viewed the film, and it reveals that the students, though they undoubtedly cheered and clapped, were well-behaved throughout. . . . The singing and cheering does not seem to us to differ significantly from the constitutionally protected activity of the demonstrators in *Edwards*, who loudly sang "while stamping their feet and clapping their hands." . . .

Our conclusion that the record does not support the contention that the students' cheering, clapping and singing constituted a breach of the peace is confirmed by the fact that these were not relied on as a basis for conviction by the trial judge, who, rather, stated as his reason for convicting Cox of disturbing the peace that "[i]t must be recognized to be inherently dangerous and a breach of the peace to bring 1,500 people, colored people, down in the predominantly white business district in the City of Baton Rouge and congregate across the street from the courthouse and sing songs as described to me by the defendant as the CORE national anthem carrying lines such as 'black and white together' and to urge those 1,500 people to descend upon our lunch counters and sit there until they are served. That has to be an inherent breach of the peace, and our statute . . . has made it so."

Finally, the State contends that the conviction should be sustained because of fear expressed by some of the state witnesses that "violence was about to erupt" because of the demonstration. It is virtually undisputed, however, that the students themselves were not violent and threatened no violence. The fear of violence seems to have been based upon the reaction of the group of white citizens looking on from across the street. . . .

This situation, like that in *Edwards*, is a far cry from the situation in *Feiner* v. *New York* . . . . Nor is there any evidence here of "fighting words." See *Chaplinsky* v. *New Hampshire* . . . . Here again, as in *Edwards*, this evidence "showed no more than that the opinions which . . . [the students] were peaceably expressing were sufficiently opposed to the views of the majority of the community to attract a crowd and necessitate police protection." . . . Conceding this was so, the "compelling answer . . . is that constitutional rights may not be denied simply because of hostility to their assertion or exercise." . . .

There is an additional reason why this conviction cannot be sustained. The statute at issue in this case, as authoritatively interpreted by the Louisiana Supreme Court, is unconstitutionally vague in its overly broad scope. . . .

For all these reasons we hold that appellant's freedoms of speech and assembly, secured to him by the First Amendment, as applied to the States by the Fourteenth Amendment, were denied by his conviction for disturbing the peace. The conviction on this charge cannot stand.

The Obstructing Public Passages Conviction. Appellant was convicted under this statute, not for leading the march to the vicinity of the courthouse, which the Louisiana Supreme Court states to have been "orderly" . . . but for leading the meeting on the sidewalk across the street from the courthouse. . . . There is no doubt from the record in this case that this far sidewalk was obstructed, and thus, as so construed, appellant violated the statute.

Appellant, however, contends that as so construed and so applied in this case, the statute is an unconstitutional infringement on freedom of speech and assembly. This contention on the facts here presented raises an issue with which this Court has dealt in many decisions. That is, the right of a State or municipality to regulate the use of city streets and other facilities to assure the safety and convenience of the people in their use and the concomitant right of the people of free speech and assembly.

From these decisions certain clear principles emerge. The rights of free speech and assembly, while fundamental in our democratic society, still do not mean that everyone with opinions or beliefs to express may address a group at any public place and at any time. The constitutional guarantee of liberty implies the existence of an organized society maintaining public order, without which liberty itself would be lost in the excesses of anarchy. The control of travel on the streets is a clear example of governmental responsibility to insure this necessary order. . . . Governmental authorities have the duty and responsibility to keep their streets open and available for movement. A group of demonstrators could not insist upon the right to cordon off a street, or entrance to a public or private building, and allow no one to pass who did not agree to listen to their exhortations.

We emphatically reject the notion urged by appellant that the First and Fourteenth Amendments afford the same kind of freedom to those who would communicate ideas by conduct such as patrolling, marching, and picketing on streets and highways, as these amendments afford to those who communciate ideas by pure speech. . . . We reaffirm the statement of the Court in *Giboney* v. *Empire Storage & Ice Co* . . . that "it has never been deemed an abridgment of freedom of speech or press to make a course of conduct illegal merely because the conduct was in part initiated, evidenced, or carried out by means of language, either spoken, written, or printed."

We have no occasion in this case to consider the constitutionality of the uniform, consistent, and nondiscriminatory application of a statute forbidding all access to streets and other public facilities for parades and meetings. Although the statute here involved on its face precludes all street assemblies and parades, it has not been so applied and enforced by the Baton Rouge authorities. . . .

This Court has recognized that the lodging of such broad discretion in a public official allows him to determine which expressions of view will be permitted and which will not. This thus sanctions a device for the suppression of the communication of ideas and permits the official to act as a censor. . . . Also inherent in such a system allowing parades or meetings only with the prior permission of an official is the obvious danger to the right of a person or a group not to be denied equal protection of the laws. . . . It is clearly unconstitutional to enable a public official to determine which expressions of view will be permitted and which will not or to engage in invidious discrimination among persons or groups either by use of a statute providing a system of broad discretionary licensing power or, as in this case, the equivalent of such a system by selective enforcement of an extremely broad prohibitory statute.

. . .

Reversed.

The Picketing Before a Courthouse Conviction. Appellant was convicted of violating a Louisiana statute which provides:

Whoever, with the intent of interfering with, obstructing, or impeding the administration of justice, or with the intent of influencing any judge, juror, witness, or court officer, in the discharge of his duty pickets or parades in or near a building housing a court of the State of Louisiana . . . shall be fined not more than five thousand dollars or imprisoned not more than one year, or both.

. . . This statute was passed by Louisiana in 1950 and was modeled after a bill pertaining to the federal judiciary, which Congress enacted later in 1950. . . . Since that time, Massachusetts and Pennsylvania have passed similar statutes. . . . The federal statute resulted from the picketing of federal courthouses by partisans of the defendants during trials involving leaders of the Communist Party. This picketing prompted an adverse reaction from both the bar and the general public. A number of groups urged legislation to prohibit it.

This statute, unlike the two previously considered, is a precise, narrowly drawn regulatory statute which proscribes certain specific behavior. . . . It prohibits a particular type of conduct, namely, picketing and parading, in a few specified locations, in or near courthouses.

There can be no question that a State has a legitimate interest in protecting its judicial system from the pressures which picketing near a courthouse might create. Since we are committed to a government of laws and not of men, it is of the utmost importance that the administration of justice be absolutely fair and orderly. This Court has recognized that the unhindered and untrammeled functioning of our courts is part of the very foundation of our constitutional democracy. . . . The Constitutional safeguards relating to the integrity of the criminal process attend every stage of a criminal proceeding, starting with arrest and culminating with a trial "in a courtroom presided over by a judge." . . . There can be no doubt that they embrace the fundamental conception of a fair trial, and that they exclude influence or domination by either a hostile or friendly mob. There is no room at any stage of judicial proceedings for such intervention; mob law is the very antithesis of due process. . . . A State may adopt safeguards necessary and appropriate to assure that the administration of justice at all stages is free from outside control and influence. A narrowly drawn statute such as the one under review is obviously a safeguard both necessary and appropriate to vindicate the State's interest in assuring justice under law.

Nor does such a statute infringe upon the constitutionally protected rights of free speech and free assembly. The conduct which is the subject of this statute—picketing and parading—is subject to regulation even though intertwined with expression and association. . . .

It is, of course, true that most judges will be influenced only by what they see and hear in court. However, judges are human; and the legislature has the right to recognize the danger that some judges, jurors, and other court officials, will be consciously or unconsciously influenced by demonstrations in or near their courtrooms both prior to and at the time of the trial. A State may also properly protect the judicial process from being misjudged in the minds of the public. . . .

Appellant additionally argues that his conviction violated due process as there was no evidence of intent to obstruct justice or influence any judicial offical as required by the statute. . . .

While this case contains direct evidence taking it out of the *Thompson* v. *Louisville* doctrine, even without this evidence, we would be compelled to reject the contention that there was no proof of intent. Louisiana surely has the right to infer the appropriate intent from circumstantial evidence. At the very least, a group of demonstrators parading and picketing before a courthouse where a criminal charge is pending, in protest against the arrest of those charged, may be presumed to intend to influence judges, jurors, witnesses or court officials. . . .

There are, however, more substantial constitutional objections arising from appellant's conviction on the particular facts of this case. Appellant was convicted for demonstrating not "in," but "near" the courthouse. . . . The question is raised as to whether the failure of the statute to define the word "near" renders it unconstitutionally vague. . . . It is clear that there is some lack of specificity in a word such as "near." While this lack of specificity may not render the statute unconstitutionally vague, at least as applied to a demonstration within the sight and hearing of those in the courthouse, it is clear that the statute, with respect to the determination of how near the courthouse a particular demonstration can be, foresees a degree of on-the-spot administrative interpretation by officials charged with responsibility for administering and enforcing it. It is apparent that demonstrators, such as those involved here, would justifiably tend to rely on this administrative interpretation of how "near" the courthouse a particular demonstration might take place. . . .

The record here clearly shows that the officials present gave permission for the demonstration to take place across the street from the courthouse. . . .

The record shows that at no time did the police recommend, or even suggest, that the demonstration be held further from the courthouse than it actually was. . . .

. . . Appellant was led to believe that his demonstration on the far side of the street violated no statute. He was expressly ordered to leave, not because he was peacefully demonstrating too near the courthouse, nor because a time limit originally set had expired, but because officials erroneously concluded that what he said threatened a breach of the peace. . . . Appellant correctly conceived, as we have held . . . that this was not a valid reason for the dispersal order. He therefore was still justified in his continued belief that because of the original official grant of permission he had a right to stay where he was for the few additional

minutes required to conclude the meeting. . . .

Nothing we have said here . . . is to be interpreted as sanctioning riotous conduct in any form of demonstrations, however peaceful their conduct or commendable their motives, which conflict with properly drawn statutes and ordinances designed to promote law and order, protect the community against disorder, regulate traffic, safeguard legitimate interests in private and public property, or protect the administration of justice and other essential governmental functions.

Liberty can only be exercised in a system of law which safeguards order. We reaffirm the repeated holdings of this Court that our constitutional command of free speech and assembly is basic and fundamental and encompasses peaceful social protest, so important to the preservation of the freedoms treasured in a democratic society. We also reaffirm the repeated decisions of this Court that there is no place for violence in a democratic society dedicated to liberty under law, and that the right of peaceful protest does not mean that everyone with opinions or beliefs to express may do so at any time and at any place. There is a proper time and place for even the most peaceful protest and a plain duty and responsibility on the part of all citizens to obey all valid laws and regulations. There is an equally plain requirement for laws and regulations to be drawn so as to give citizens fair warning as to what is illegal; for regulation of conduct that involves freedom of speech and assembly not to be so broad in scope as to stifle First Amendment freedoms, which "need breathing space to survive" . . . for appropriate limitations on the discretion of public officials where speech and assembly are intertwined with regulated conduct; and for all such laws and regulations to be applied with an equal hand. . . .

The application of these principles requires us to reverse the judgment of the Supreme Court of Louisiana.

Reversed.

MR. JUSTICE BLACK, CONCURRING IN THE "BREACH OF THE PEACE" AND "OBSTRUCTING PUBLIC PASSAGES" CONVICTIONS (OMITTED).

MR. JUSTICE BLACK, DISSENTING.

The Conviction for Picketing Near a Courthouse. I fail to understand how the Court can justify the reversal of this conviction because of a permission which testimony in the record denies was given, which could not have been authoritatively given anyway, and which even if given was soon afterwards revoked. While I agree that the record does not show boisterous or violent conduct or indecent language on the part of the "demonstrators," the ample evidence that this group planned the march on the courthouse and carried it out for the express purpose of influencing the courthouse officials in the performance of their official duties brings this case squarely within the prohibitions of the Lousiana statute and I think leaves us with no alternative but to sustain the conviction unless the statute itself is unconstitutional, and I do not believe that this statute is unconstitutional, either on its face or as applied. . . .

The very purpose of a court system is to adjudicate controversies, both criminal and civil, in the calmness and solemnity of the courtroom according to legal procedures. Justice cannot be rightly administered, nor are the lives and safety of prisoners secure, where throngs of people clamor against the processes of justice right outside the courthouse or jailhouse doors. The streets are not now and never have been the proper place to administer justice. Use of the streets for such purposes has always proved disastrous to individual liberty in the long run, whatever fleeting benefits may have appeared to have been achieved. And minority groups, I venture to suggest, are the ones who always have suffered and always will suffer most when street multitudes are allowed to substitute their pressures for the less glamorous but more dependable and temperate processes of the law. Experience demonstrates that it is not a far step from what to many seems the earnest, honest, patriotic, kind-spirited multitude of today, to the fanatical threatening, lawless mob of tomorrow. And the crowds that press in the streets for noble goals today can be supplanted tomorrow by street mobs pressuring the courts for precisely opposite ends.

Minority groups in particular need always to bear in mind that the Constitution, while it requires States to treat all citizens equally and protect them in the exercise of rights granted by the Federal Constitution and laws, does not take away the State's power, indeed its duty, to keep order and to do justice according to law. Those who encourage minority groups to believe that the United States Constitution and federal laws give them a right to patrol and picket in the streets whenever they choose, in order to advance what they think to be a just and noble end, do no service to those minority groups, their cause, or their country. I am confident from this record that this appellant violated the Louisiana statute because of a mistaken belief that he and his followers had a constitutional right to do so, because of what they believed were just grievances. But the history of the past 25 years if it shows nothing else shows that his group's constitutional and statutory rights have to be protected by the courts, which must be kept free from intimidation and coercive pressures of any kind. Government under law as ordained by our Constitution is too precious, too sacred, to be jeopardized by subjecting the courts to intimidatory practices that have been fatal to individual liberty and minority rights wherever and whenever such practices have been allowed to poison the streams of justice. I would be wholly unwilling to join in moving this country a single step in that direction.

MR. JUSTICE CLARK, CONCURRING IN PART AND DISSENTING IN PART (OMITTED).
MR. JUSTICE WHITE, WITH MR. JUSTICE HARLAN, CONCURRING IN PART AND DISSENTING IN PART (OMITTED).

(b) *Walker v. Birmingham (1967)*

+Black, Clark, Stewart, Harlan, White

−Warren, Douglas, Brennan, Fortas

[Passage of the Civil Rights Act of 1964, its validation by the Supreme Court in *Heart-of-Atlanta Motel* v. *Katzenbach* (1964), and its retroactive application to void the nonfinalized convictions of sit-in demonstrators in *Hamm* v. *Rock Hill* (1964), made it unnecessary for the Supreme Court to decide whether the Fourteenth Amendment, by itself, prohibited state enforcement of private discriminatory decisions. A number of southern sit-in cases, however, raised other issues and were decided by the Court in subsequent years. The *Cox* case focused directly on the constitutional linkage between expression and action and the limits, if any, that laws and official policies could impose on protest demonstrations. *Adderley* v. *Florida* (1966) marked the apparent limits of the Supreme Court's indulgence of protest demonstrators. The case was very much like *Cox* in its facts, except for the crucial difference that the picketing took place not before a courthouse but in and around a jail. For the first time, in a 5-4 decision, the Supreme Court affirmed the conviction of a group of sit-in demonstrators.

By the time the *Walker* case had reached the Supreme Court, protest activities had spread from civil rights in the South to antiwar rallies nationwide and, in a more violent form, to racial riots in some northern cities. Underlying the specific legal issues in these sit-in cases was the more general, philosophical question of the constitutional status of civil disobedience. The justices expressed no opinion on the subject in any formal sense, but it could not have been far removed from their thoughts. Particularly as the intensity of protest against the war escalated in the second half of the 1960s, the Court was forced to consider the limits of dissent in American society. Both Justice Goldberg, writing for the Court in the *Cox* case, and Justice Black, dissenting, explored these issues at length. Justice Brennan's dissenting opinion in *Walker* alludes to what must have been a classic debate among the justices in conference over the implications for American society of continuing social and political unrest.

One justice, Abe Fortas, found the subject important enough to write a widely read book outlining what, to him, were the lawful limits of civil disobedience.[1] Supreme Court justices rarely write for public consumption on matters quite as close to the Court's current business as this. Perhaps Fortas was motivated to "go public" by the increasingly strident and bitter attacks on all protest activity by his senior colleague, Hugo Black.

Put in these terms, Fortas' book was radical indeed. But from the perspective of many others, the book was but a skillful defense of the status quo. At some points in the book, Fortas seems to extol the virtues of civil disobedi-

---

[1]Abe Fortas, *Concerning Dissent and Civil Disobedience* (New York: Signet Books, 1968). Also see Howard Zinn's "answer" to Fortas, *Disobedience and Democracy* (New York: Vintage Books, 1968).

ence, using examples from the experience of the Jews in Nazi Germany. But the ultimate message of the book comes through clearly as *not* all that different from Black's position as stated in *Cox:* disadvantaged groups must have faith in the rule of law, in the political system, and in the Supreme Court, to bring about needed reforms without violence. Fortas' definition of permissible civil disobedience is quite limited. It is proper only where the law that is violated is itself the target of protest and is basically offensive to fundamental societal values or to the Constitution. Furthermore, civil disobedience must be peaceful, and the protestors must be willing to accept the legal consequences of their actions.

By Fortas' definition, most of the sit-in demonstrations were unlawful and improper. Few were directed specifically at an offensive "law." Most were directed, more generally, at offensive and discriminatory social conditions and private decisions that may have been the outgrowth of past laws but that presently existed without formal legal sanction. For reasons unknown, and not easily divined, the views that Fortas expressed in his book are probably more consistent with the views of the majority in the *Walker* case than with his own dissent.

The *Walker* case involved a protest demonstration led by the late Dr. Martin Luther King in April 1963. City officials sought an injunction barring King and his followers from participating in or encouraging mass parades or processions without a permit as required by the Birmingham City Code. A local judge issued the injunction, and the protestors announced their intention to disobey it. Two days later, on Good Friday, and again on Easter Sunday, mass marches and meetings were held. Some violence occurred as angry onlookers threw rocks that injured a news reporter and damaged a police vehicle.

The following day, city officials asked the state court to issue a contempt citation against the petitioners for violating the injunction. The latter argued that it was unconstitutional because it was vague and overbroad and a violation of their First Amendment rights. A similar attack was lodged against the parade permit ordinance, with the additional claim that it had in the past been administered arbitrarily and in a discriminatory manner. The state court re-

jected these arguments, noting that there had been no attempt either to contest the injunction or to apply for the permit required by it and by the city ordinance. Petitioners were convicted and sentenced to five days in jail and a $50 fine.]

MR. JUSTICE STEWART delivered the opinion of the Court.

. . .

Howat v. *State of Kansas,* was decided by this Court almost 50 years ago. That was a case in which people had been punished by a Kansas trial court for refusing to obey an anti-strike injunction issued under the state industrial relations act. They had claimed a right to disobey the court's order upon the ground that the state statute and the injunction based upon it were invalid under the Federal Constitution. The Supreme Court of Kansas had affirmed the judgment, holding that the trial court "had general power to issue injunctions in equity, and that even if its exercise of the power was erroneous, the injunction was not void, and the defendants were precluded from attacking it in this collateral proceeding . . . that, if the injunction was erroneous, jurisdiction was not thereby forfeited, that the error was subject to correction only by the ordinary method of appeal, and disobedience to the order constituted contempt."

. . .

This Court, in dismissing the writ of error, not only unanimously accepted but fully approved the validity of the rule of state law upon which the judgment of the Kansas court was grounded: . . .

In the present case, however, we are asked to hold that this rule of law, upon which the Alabama courts relied, was constitutionally impermissible. We are asked to say that the Constitution compelled Alabama to allow the petitioners to violate this injunction, to organize and engage in these mass street parades and demonstrations, without any previous effort on their part to have the injunction dissolved or modified, or any attempt to secure a parade permit in accordance with its terms. Whatever the limits of *Howat* v. *State of Kansas,* we cannot accept the petitioners' contentions in the circumstances of this case. . . .

The generality of the language contained in the Birmingham parade ordinance upon which the injunction was based would unquestionably raise substantial constitutional issues concerning some of its provisions. . . .

The petitioners, however, did not even attempt to apply to the Alabama courts for an authoritative construction of the ordinance. Had they done so, those courts might have given the licensing authority granted in the ordinance a narrow and precise scope.
. . .

The breadth and vagueness of the injunction itself would also unquestionably be subject to substantial constitutional question. But the way to raise that question was to apply to the Alabama courts to have the injunction modified or dissolved. The injunction in all events clearly prohibited mass parading without a permit, and the evidence shows that the petitioners fully understood that prohibition when they violated it.

The petitioners also claim that they were free to disobey the injunction because the parade ordinance on which it was based had been administered in the past in an arbitrary and discriminatory fashion. . . .

This case would arise in quite a different constitutional posture if the petitioners, before disobeying the injunction, had challenged it in the Alabama courts, and had been met with delay or frustration of their constitutional claims. . . .

It cannot be presumed that the Alabama courts would have ignored the petitioners' constitutional claims. Indeed, these contentions were accepted in another case by an Alabama appellate court that struck down on direct review the conviction under this very ordinance of one of these same petitioners. . . .

The rule of law that Alabama followed in this case reflects a belief that in the fair administration of justice no man can be judge in his own case, however exalted his station, however righteous his motives, and irrespective of his race, color, politics, or religion. This Court cannot hold that the petitioners were constitutionally free to ignore all the procedures of the law and carry their battle to the streets. One may sympathize with the petitioners' impatient commitment to their cause. But respect for judicial process is a small price to pay for the civilizing hand of law, which alone can give abiding meaning to constitutional freedom.

Affirmed.

MR. CHIEF JUSTICE WARREN, WHOM MR. JUSTICE BRENNAN AND MR. JUSTICE FORTAS JOIN, DISSENTING.

Petitioners in this case contend that they were convicted under an ordinance that is unconstitutional on its face because it submits their First and Fourteenth Amendment rights to free speech and peaceful assembly to the unfettered discretion of local officials. They further contend that the ordinance was unconstitutionally applied to them because the local officials used their discretion to prohibit peaceful demonstrations by a group whose political viewpoint the officials opposed. The Court does not dispute these contentions, but holds that petitioners may nonetheless be convicted and sent to jail because the patently unconstitutional ordinance was copied into an injunction— issued *ex parte* without prior notice or hearing on the request of the Commissioner of Public Safety—forbidding all persons having notice of the injunction to violate the ordinance without any limitation of time. I dissent because I do not believe that the fundamental protections of the Constitution were meant to be so easily evaded, or that "the civilizing hand of law" would be hampered in the slightest by enforcing the First Amendment in this case. . . .

The Court concedes that "[t]he generality of the language contained in the Birmingham parade ordinance upon which the injunction was based would unquestionably raise substantial constitutional issues concerning some of its provisions." . . . That concession is well founded but minimal. I believe it is patently unconstitutional on its face. Our decisions have consistently held that picketing and parading are means of expression protected by the First Amendment, and that the right to picket or parade may not be subjected to the unfettered discretion of local officials. . . . Although a city may regulate the manner of use of its streets and sidewalks in the interest of keeping them open for the movement of traffic, it may not allow local officials unbridled discretion to decide who shall be allowed to parade or picket and who shall not. . . .

MR. JUSTICE DOUGLAS, WITH WHOM THE CHIEF JUSTICE, MR. JUSTICE BRENNAN, AND MR. JUSTICE FORTAS CONCUR, DISSENTING (OMITTED).

MR. JUSTICE BRENNAN, WITH WHOM THE CHIEF JUSTICE, MR. JUSTICE DOUGLAS, AND MR. JUSTICE FORTAS JOIN, DISSENTING.

Under cover of exhortation that the Negro exercise "respect for judicial process," the Court empties the Supremacy Clause of its primacy by elevating a state rule of judicial administration above the right of free expression guaranteed by the Federal Constitution. And the Court does so by letting loose a devastatingly destructive weapon for suppression of cherished freedoms heretofore believed indispensable to maintenance of our free society. I cannot believe that this distortion in the hierarchy of values upon which our society has been and must be ordered can have any significance beyond its function as a vehicle to affirm these contempt convictions. . . .

We cannot permit fears of "riots" and "civil disobedience" generated by slogans like "Black Power" to divert our attention from what is here at stake—not violence or the right of the State to control its streets and sidewalks, but the insulation from attack of *ex parte* orders and legislation upon which they are based even when patently impermissible prior restraints on the exercise of First Amendment rights, thus arming the state courts with the power to punish as a "contempt" what they otherwise could not punish at all. Constitutional restrictions against abridgments of First Amendment freedoms limit judicial equally with legislative and executive power. Convictions for contempt of court orders which invalidly abridge First Amendment freedoms must be condemned equally with convictions for violation of statutes which do the same thing. I respectfully dissent.

(c) *Greer v. Spock* (1976)

+Stewart, Burger, White, Blackmun, Powell, Rehnquist
−Brennan, Marshall
NP Stevens

[Long-standing regulations prohibited partisan speeches and demonstrations on the Fort

Dix Military Reservation in New Jersey. The distribution or posting of flyers, newspapers, handbills, pamphlets, and the like was also prohibited without prior written approval of the military authorities. Dr. Benjamin Spock, candidate for president on the People's party ticket, and others notified the commanding officer at Fort Dix of their intention to enter the reservation in September 1972 to hold a meeting to discuss the issues of the forthcoming presidential election. Upon denial of their request, suit was filed in the federal district court in New Jersey, asking for an injunction against enforcement of the Fort Dix regulations as contrary to the First and Fifth Amendments.

The district court denied a preliminary injunction, but this decision was reversed by the court of appeals. Pursuant to this judgment, Spock conducted a campaign rally at a Fort Dix parking lot on November 4, 1972. Subsequently, the district court granted a permanent injunction that prohibited the military authorities from interfering with political activities in those areas of the reservation open to the general public. The court of appeals affirmed this decision, and the Supreme Court granted certiorari.]

MR. JUSTICE STEWART delivered the opinion of the Court.

. . . In reaching the conclusion that the respondents could not be prevented from entering Fort Dix for the purpose of making political speeches or distributing leaflets, the Court of Appeals relied primarily on this Court's *per curiam* opinion in *Flower v. United States.* . . . In the *Flower* case the Court summarily reversed the conviction of a civilian for entering a military reservation after having been ordered not to do so. At the time of his arrest the petitioner in that case had been "quietly distributing leaflets on New Braunfels Avenue at a point within the limits of Fort Sam Houston, San Antonio, Texas." . . . The Court's decision reversing the conviction, made without the benefit of briefing or oral argument, rested upon the premise that

"New Braunfels Avenue . . . was a completely open street," and the military had "abandoned any claim that it has special interests in who walks, talks, or distributes leaflets on the avenue." . . . Under those circumstances, the "base commandant" could "no more order petitioner off this public street because he was distributing leaflets than could the city police order any leafleter off any public street." . . .

The decision in *Flower* was thus based upon the Court's understanding that New Braunfels Avenue was a public thoroughfare in San Antonio no different from all the other public thoroughfares in that city, and that the military had not only abandoned any right to exclude civilian vehicular and pedestrian traffic from the avenue, but also any right to exclude leafleters—"any claim [of] special interests in who walks, talks, or distributes leaflets on the avenue."

That being so, the Court perceived the *Flower* case as one simply falling under the long established constitutional rule that there cannot be a blanket exclusion of First Amendment activity from a municipality's open streets, sidewalks, and parks for the reasons stated in the familiar words of Mr. Justice Roberts in *Hague* v. *CIO.* . . .

Wherever the title of streets and parks may rest, they have immemorially been held in trust for the use of the public and, time out of mind, have been used for purposes of assembly, communicating thoughts between citizens, and discussing public questions. Such use of the streets and public places has, from ancient times, been a part of the privileges, immunities, rights, and liberties of citizens. The privilege of a citizen of the United States to use the streets and parks for communication of views on national questions may be regulated in the interest of all, it is not absolute, but rel-

ative, and must be exercised in subordination to the general comfort and convenience, and in consonance with peace and good order; but it must not, in the guise of regulation, be abridged or denied.

The Court of Appeals was mistaken, therefore, in thinking that the *Flower* case is to be understood as announcing a new principle of constitutional law, and mistaken specifically in thinking that *Flower* stands for the principle that whenever members of the public are permitted freely to visit a place owned or operated by the Government, then that place becomes a "public forum for purposes of the First Amendment. Such a principle of constitutional law has never existed, and does not exist now. The guarantees of the First Amendment have never meant "that people who want to propagandize protests or views have a constitutional right to do so whenever and however and wherever they please." *Adderley* v. *Florida, . . .* "The State, no less than a private owner of property, has power to preserve the property under its control for the use to which it is lawfully dedicated." . . . See also *Cox* v. *Louisiana, . . .*

The Court of Appeals in the present case did not find, and the respondents do not contend, that the Fort Dix authorities had abandoned any claim of special interest in regulating the distribution of unauthorized leaflets or the delivery of campaign speeches for political candidates within the confines of the military reservation. The record is, in fact, indisputably to the contrary." The *Flower* decision thus does not support the judgment of the Court of Appeals in this case.

Indeed, the Flower decision looks in precisely the opposite direction. For if the *Flower* case was decided the way it was because the military

authorities had "abandoned any claim [of] special interests in who walks, talks, or distributes leaflets on the avenue," then the implication surely is that a different result must obtain on a military reservation where the *authorities have not* abandoned such a claim. And if that is not the conclusion clearly to be drawn from *Flower,* it most assuredly is the conclusion to be drawn from almost 200 years of American constitutional history.

One of the very purposes for which the Constitution was ordained and established was to "provide for the common defence," and this Court over the years has on countless occasions recognized the special constitutional function of the military in our national life, a function both explicit and indispensable. . . .

A necessary concommitant of the basic function of a military installation has been "the historically unquestioned power of [its] commanding officer summarily to exclude civilians from the area of his command." *Cafeteria Workers* v. *McElroy, . . .* The notion that federal military reservations, like municipal streets and parks, have traditionally served as a place for free public assembly and communication of thoughts by private citizens is thus historically and constitutionally false.

The respondents, therefore, had no generalized constitutional right to make political speeches or distribute leaflets at Fort Dix, and it follows that Fort Dix Regulations 210-26 and 210-27 are not constitutionally invalid on their face. These Regulations, moreover, were not unconstitutionally applied in the circumstances disclosed by the record in the present case. . . .

Such a policy is wholly consistent with the American constitutional tradition of a politically neutral military establishment under civilian control. It is a policy that has been reflected in numerous laws and military regulations throughout our history. And it is a policy that the military authorities at Fort Dix were constitutionally free to pursue. . . .

For the reasons set out in this opinion the judgment is reversed. *It is so ordered.*

MR. JUSTICE STEVENS TOOK NO PART IN THE CONSIDERATION OR DECISION OF THIS CASE.
MR. CHIEF JUSTICE BURGER, CONCURRING (OMITTED).
MR. JUSTICE POWELL, CONCURRING (OMITTED).
MR. JUSTICE BRENNAN, WITH WHOM MR. JUSTICE MARSHALL JOINS, DISSENTING (OMITTED).
MR. JUSTICE MARSHALL, DISSENTING (OMITTED).

(3) Symbolic Speech/Action

(a) Tinker v. Des Moines Community School District (1969)

(See pp. 60–68.)

(b) United States v. O'Brien (1968)

(See pp. 68–73.)

(4) Words and Slogans as Objects

(a) Cohen v. California (1971)

+Harlan, Douglas, Brennan, Stewart, Marshall
−Burger, Black, White, Blackmun

[As a protest against the military draft, Cohen entered the Los Angeles County Courthouse wearing a jacket bearing the words "Fuck the Draft." Otherwise, he conducted himself with decorum. He was convicted of willfully disturbing the peace. The U. S. Supreme Court heard the case on appeal.]

MR. JUSTICE HARLAN delivered the opinion of the Court.

This case may seem at first blush too inconsequential to find its way into our books, but the issue it presents is of no small constitutional significance.

. . .

In order to lay hands on the precise issue which this case involves, it is useful first to canvass various matters which this record does *not* present.

The conviction quite clearly rests upon the asserted offensiveness of the *words* Cohen used to convey his message to the public. The only "conduct" which the State sought to punish is the fact of communication. Thus, we deal here with a conviction resting solely upon "speech," . . . not upon any separately identifiable conduct which allegedly was intended by Cohen to be perceived by others as expressive of particular views but which, on its face, does not necessarily convey any message and hence arguably could be regulated without effectively repressing Cohen's ability to express himself. . . . Further, the State certainly lacks power to punish Cohen for the underlying content of the message the inscriptive conveyed. At least so long as there is no showing of an intent to incite disobedience to or disruption of the draft, Cohen could not, consistently with the First and Fourteenth Amendments, be punished for asserting the evident position on the inutility or immorality of the draft his jacket reflected. . . .

Appellant's conviction, then, rests squarely upon his exercise of the "freedom of speech" protected from arbitrary governmental interference by the Constitution and can be justified, if at all, only as a valid regulation of the manner in which he exercised that freedom, not as a permissible prohibition on the substantive message it conveys. This does not end the inquiry, of course, for the First and Fourteenth Amendments have never been thought to give absolute protection to every individual to speak whenever or wherever he pleases, or to use any form of address in any circumstances that he chooses. In this vein, too, however, we think it important to note that several issues typically associated with such problems are not presented here.

In the first place, Cohen was tried under a statute applicable throughout the entire State. Any attempt to support this conviction on the ground that the statute seeks to preserve an appropriately decorous atmosphere in the courthouse where Cohen was arrested must fail in the absence of any language in the statute that would have put appellant on notice that certain kinds of otherwise permissible speech or conduct would nevertheless, under California law, not be tolerated in certain places. . . . No fair reading of the phrase "offensive conduct" can be said sufficiently to inform the ordinary person that distinctions between certain locations are thereby created.

In the second place, as it comes to us, this case cannot be said to fall within those relatively few categories of instances where prior decisions have established the power of government to deal more comprehensively with certain forms of individual expression simply upon a showing that such a form was employed. This is not, for example, an obscenity case. Whatever else may be necessary to give rise to the States' broader power to prohibit obscene expression, such expression must be,

in some significant way, erotic. . . . It cannot plausibly be maintained that this vulgar allusion to the Selective Service System would conjure up such psychic stimulation in anyone likely to be confronted with Cohen's crudely defaced jacket.

This Court has also held that the States are free to ban the simple use, without a demonstration of additional justifying circumstances, of so-called "fighting words," those personally abusive epithets which, when addressed to the ordinary citizens, are, as a matter of common knowledge, inherently likely to provoke violent reaction. *Chaplinsky* v. *New Hampshire*. . . . While the four-letter word displayed by Cohen in relation to the draft is not uncommonly employed in a personally provocative fashion, in this instance it was clearly not "directed to the person of the hearer." . . . No individual actually or likely to be present could reasonably have regarded the words on appellant's jacket as a direct personal insult. Nor do we have here an instance of the exercise of the State's police power to prevent a speaker from intentionally provoking a given group to hostile action. *Feiner* v. *New York* . . . (1951); *Terminiello* v. *Chicago* . . . (1949). There is, as noted above, no showing that anyone who saw Cohen was in fact violently aroused or that appellant intended such a result.

Finally, in arguments before this Court much has been made of the claim that Cohen's distasteful mode of expression was thrust upon unwilling or unsuspecting viewers, and that the State might therefore legitimately act as it did in order to protect the sensitive from otherwise unavoidable exposure to appellant's crude form of protest. Of course, the mere presumed presence of unwitting listeners or viewers does not serve automatically to justify curtailing all speech capable of giving offense. . . . While this Court has recognized that government may properly act in many situations to prohibit intrusion into the privacy of the home of unwelcome views and ideas which cannot be totally banned from the public dialogue, *Rowan* v. *Postmaster General* . . . (1970), we have at the same time consistently stressed that "we are often 'captives' outside the sanctuary of the home and subject to objectionable speech." . . . The ability of government, consonant with the Constitution, to shut off discourse solely to protect others from hearing it is, in other words, dependent upon a showing that substantial privacy interests are being invaded in an essentially intolerable manner. Any broader view of this authority would effectively empower a majority to silence dissidents simply as a matter of personal predilections.

In this regard, persons confronted with Cohen's jacket were in a quite different posture than, say, those subjected to the raucous emissions of sound trucks blaring outside their residences. Those in the Los Angeles courthouse could effectively avoid further bombardment of their sensibilities simply by averting their eyes. And, while it may be that one has a more substantial claim to a recognizable privacy interest when walking through a courthouse corridor than, for example, strolling through Central Park, surely it is nothing like the interest in being free from unwanted expression in the confines of one's own home. Given the subtlety and complexity of the factors involved, if Cohen's "speech" was otherwise entitled to constitutional protection, we do not think the fact that some unwilling "listeners" in a public building may have been briefly exposed to it can serve to justify this breach of the peace conviction where, as here, there was no evi-

dence that persons powerless to avoid appellant's conduct did in fact object to it, and where that portion of the statute upon which Cohen's conviction rests evinces no concern, either on its face or as construed by the California courts, with the special plight of the captive auditor, but, instead, indiscriminately sweeps within its prohibitions all "offensive conduct" that disturbs "any neighborhood or person." . . .

Against this background, the issue flushed by this case stands out in bold relief. It is whether California can excise, as "offensive conduct," one particular scurrilous epithet from the public discourse, either upon the theory of the court below that its use is inherently likely to cause violent reaction or upon a more general assertion that the States, acting as guardians of public morality, may properly remove this offensive word from the public vocabulary.

The rationale of the California court is plainly untenable. At most it reflects an "undifferentiated fear or apprehension of disturbance [which] is not enough to overcome the right to freedom of expression." *Tinker* v. *Des Moines Indep. Community School Dist* . . . (1969). We have been shown no evidence that substantial numbers of citizens are standing ready to strike out physically at whoever may assault their sensibilities with execrations like that uttered by Cohen. There may be some persons about with such lawless and violent proclivities, but that is an insufficient base upon which to erect, consistently with constitutional values, a governmental power to force persons who wish to ventilate their dissident views into avoiding particular forms of expression. The argument amounts to little more than the self-defeating proposition that to avoid physical censorship of one who has not sought to provoke such a response by a hypothetical coterie of the violent and lawless, the States may more appropriately effectuate that censorship themselves . . . [W]e cannot overemphasize that, in our judgment, most situations where the State has a justifiable interest in regulating speech will fall within one or more of the various established exceptions, discussed above but not applicable here, to the usual rule that governmental bodies may not prescribe the form or content of individual expression. Equally important to our conclusion is the constitutional backdrop against which our decision must be made. The constitutional right of free expression is powerful medicine in a society as diverse and populous as ours. It is designed and intended to remove governmental restraints from the arena of public discussion, putting the decision as to what views shall be voiced largely into the hands of each of us, in the hope that use of such freedom will ultimately produce a more capable citizenry and more perfect polity and in the belief that no other approach would comport with the premise of individual dignity and choice upon which our political system rests. . . .

To many, the immediate consequences of this freedom may often appear to be only verbal tumult, discord, and even offensive utterance. These are, however, within established limits, in truth necessary side effects of the broader enduring values which the process of open debate permits us to achieve. That the air may at times seem filled with verbal cacophony is, in this sense not a sign of weakness but of strength. We cannot lose sight of the fact that, in what otherwise might seem a trifling and annoying instance of individual distasteful abuse of a privilege, these fundamental societal values are truly implicated. That is why "[w]holly neutral futilities . . . come under the protection of free speech as fully as do

Keats' poems or Donne's sermons," . . . and why "so long as the means are peaceful, the communication need not meet standards of acceptability," . . . .

Against this perception of the constitutional policies involved, we discern certain more particularized considerations that peculiarly call for reversal of this conviction. First, the principle contended for by the State seems inherently boundless. How is one to distinguish this from any other offensive word? Surely the State has no right to cleanse public debate to the point where it is grammatically palatable to the most squeamish among us. Yet no readily ascertainable general principle exists for stopping short of that result were we to affirm the judgment below. For, while the particular four-letter word being litigated here is perhaps more distasteful than most others of its genre, it is nevertheless often true that one man's vulgarity is another's lyric. Indeed, we think it is largely because governmental officials cannot make principled distinctions in this area that the Constitution leaves matters of taste and style so largely to the individual.

Additionally, we cannot overlook the fact, because it is well illustrated by the episode involved here, that much linguistic expression serves a dual communicative function: it conveys not only ideas capable of relatively precise, detached explication, but otherwise inexpressible emotions as well. In fact, words are often chosen as much for their emotive as their cognitive force. We cannot sanction the view that the Constitution, while solicitous of the cognitive content of individual speech, has little or no regard for that emotive function which, practically speaking, may often be the more important element of the overall message sought to be communicated. Indeed, as Mr. Justice Frankfurter has said, "[o]ne of the prerogatives of American citizenship is the right to criticize public men and measures—and that means not only informed and responsible criticism but the freedom to speak foolishly and without moderation." . . .

Finally, and in the same vein, we cannot indulge the facile assumption that one can forbid particular words without running a substantial risk of suppressing ideas in the process. Indeed, governments might soon seize upon the censorship of particular words as a convenient guise for banning the expression of unpopular views. We have been able, as noted above, to discern little social benefit that might result from running the risk of opening the door to such grave results.

It is, in sum, our judgment that, absent a more particularized and compelling reason for its actions, the State may not, consistently with the First and Fourteenth Amendments, make the simple public display here involved of this single four-letter expletive a criminal offense. Because that is the only arguably sustainable rationale for the conviction here at issue, the judgment below must be

Reversed.

MR. JUSTICE BLACKMUN, WITH WHOM THE CHIEF JUSTICE AND MR. JUSTICE BLACK JOIN, DISSENTING.

I dissent . . . .

Cohen's absurd and immature antic, in my view, was mainly conduct and little speech. . . . The California Court of Appeal appears so to have described it, and I cannot characterize it otherwise. Further, the case appears to me to be well within the sphere of *Chaplinsky* v. *New Hampshire* . . . (1942), where Mr. Justice Murphy, a known champion of First Amendment freedoms, wrote for a unanimous bench. As a consequence, this Court's agonizing over First Amendment values seems misplaced and unnecessary. . . .

(b) Wooley v. Maynard (1977)

+Burger, Brennan, Stewart, Marshall, Powell, Stevens
−White, Blackmun, Rehnquist

[The Court has held that the denial of First Amendment freedoms can only be permitted where there is grave and immediate danger to interests that the state can lawfully protect. In *West Virginia State Board of Education* v. *Barnette* (1943), the Court overturned a state statute requiring all students to salute and say the pledge of allegiance to the flag. According to the statute, failure to conform was insubordination and would result in expulsion. The plaintiffs in this case were Jehovah's Witnesses, who sought to restrain the enforcement of the statute. Similarly, in *Wooley* v. *Maynard,* Jehovah's Witnesses challenged that state's interest in requiring noncommercial vehicular license plates to bear the state motto, "Live Free or Die." George Maynard and his wife, followers of the Jehovah's Witnesses faith, considered that motto repugnant to their moral, religious, and political beliefs and covered up the motto on their automobiles. Mr. Maynard was twice convicted of a misdemeanor for violating the statute and served fifteen days in jail when he refused to pay an accumulated total of $75 in fines.

After serving the jail sentence, Maynard brought suit in the federal district court to enjoin the state from further enforcement of the statute. A three-judge court was convened, and it issued an order prohibiting the state of New Hampshire "from arresting and prosecuting [the Maynards] at any time in the future for covering over that portion of their license plates that contains the motto 'Live Free or Die.' " Appeal was directly to the Supreme Court.]

MR. CHIEF JUSTICE BURGER delivered the opinion of the Court.

. . . The District Court held that by covering up the state motto "Live Free or Die" on his automobile license plate, Mr. Maynard was engaging in symbolic speech and that

"New Hampshire's interest in the enforcement of its defacement statute is not sufficient to justify the restriction on [appellees'] constitutionally protected expression." . . . We find it unnecessary to pass on the "symbolic speech" issue, since we find more appropriate First Amendment grounds to affirm the judgment of the District Court. We turn instead to what in our view is the essence of appellees' objection to the requirement that they display the motto "Live Free or Die" on their automobile license plates. This is succinctly summarized in the statement made by Mr. Maynard in his affidavit filed with the District Court.

I refuse to be coerced by the State into advertising a slogan which I find morally, ethically, religiously and politically abhorrent. . . .

We are thus faced with the question of whether the State may constitutionally require an individual to participate in the dissemination of an ideological message by displaying it on his private property in a manner and for the express purpose that it be observed and read by the public. We hold that the State may not do so.

We begin with the proposition that the right of freedom of thought protected by the First Amendment against state action includes both the right to speak freely and the right to refrain from speaking at all. . . . A system which secures the right to proselytize religious, political, and ideological causes must also guarantee the concomitant right to decline to foster such concepts. The right to speak and the right to refrain from speaking are complementary components of the broader concept of "individual freedom of mind." . . .

New Hampshire's statute in effect requires that appellees use their private property as a "mobile billboard" for the State's ideological message—

or suffer a penalty, as Maynard already has. As a condition to driving an automobile—a virtual necessity for most Americans—the Maynards must display "Live Free or Die" to hundreds of people each day. The fact that most individuals agree with the thrust of New Hampshire's motto is not the test; most Americans also find the flag salute acceptable. The First Amendment protects the right of individuals to hold a point of view different from the majority and to refuse to foster, in the way New Hampshire commands, an idea they find morally objectionable.

Identifying the Maynards' interests as implicating First Amendment protections does not end our inquiry however. We must also determine whether the State's countervailing interest is sufficiently compelling to justify requiring appellees to display the state motto on their license plates. . . . The two interests advanced by the state are that display of the motto (1) facilitates the identification of passenger vehicles, and (2) promotes appreciation of history, individualism and state pride.

The State first points out that only passenger vehicles, but not commercial, trailer, or other vehicles are required to display the state motto. Thus, the argument proceeds, officers of the law are more easily able to determine whether passenger vehicles are carrying the proper plates. However the record here reveals that New Hampshire passenger license plates normally consist of a specific configuration of letters and numbers, which makes them readily distinguishable from other types of plates, even without reference to state motto. Even were we to credit the State's reasons and "even though the governmental purpose be legitimate and substantial, that purpose cannot be pursued by means that broadly stifle fundamental personal liberties when the end can be more narrowly achieved. The breadth of legislative abridgment must be viewed in the light of less drastic means for achieving the same basic purpose." *Shelton* v. *Tucker* . . . (1960) . . . .

The State's second claimed interest is not ideologically neutral. The State is seeking to communicate to others an official view as to proper "appreciation of history, state pride, [and] individualism." Of course, the State may legitimately pursue such interests in any number of ways. However, where the State's interest is to disseminate an ideology, no matter how acceptable to some, such interest cannot outweigh an individual's First Amendment right to avoid becoming the courier for such message.

We conclude that the State of New Hampshire may not require appellees to display the state motto upon their vehicle license plates, and accordingly, we affirm the judgment of the District Court.

Affirmed.

MR. JUSTICE WHITE, WITH WHOM MR. JUSTICE BLACKMUN AND MR. JUSTICE REHNQUIST JOIN, DISSENTING IN PART (OMITTED).

MR. JUSTICE REHNQUIST, DISSENTING (OMITTED).

C. Rights of Political Association

(1) A Note on the Status of Political Rights in an Era of International Tension

The twentieth century has been marked by periodic armed hostilities and by an almost continuous ideological warfare. With the exception of our early experience with the Sedition Act of 1798, American politics had not been characterized by significant government efforts to limit the speech or association of political dissidents or unpopular minorities. But the rise of international socialism and the appearance of a number of radical organizations, as well as the Russian Revolution of 1917, raised the specter of unwelcome and "unwholesome" influences that might infect the American system. These fears, and the reaction to them, raised constitutional questions of the first magnitude.

Attempts to enforce the Espionage Act of 1917 and the Sedition Act of 1918 confronted the Supreme Court with the necessity of defining the limits of political speech. If one rejects the "absolutist" interpretation of the First Amendment, that Congress may make *no* law respecting freedom of speech, then it becomes necessary for the courts to devise a standard for determining when, how, and under what circumstances a statute may limit speech that, in the absence of the statute, would be constitutionally protected.

The first important judicial response came in *Schenck* v. *United States* (1919). The Alien and Sedition acts of 1798, which raised similar questions, had never been tested in the Supreme Court. And the one major free speech case in the intervening 120 years provided little guidance. In *Robertson* v. *Baldwin* (1897), the Supreme Court had interpreted the First Amendment in the narrowest possible terms, saying: "The law is perfectly well settled that the first ten amendments to the Constitution, commonly known as the Bill of Rights, were not intended to lay down any novel principles of government, but simply to embody certain guarantees and immunities which we had inherited from our English ancestors." If this was the law, then the First Amendment prohibited only prior restraint, and following Blackstone, it would have permitted criminal convictions for uttering words which were "improper," mischievous," or illegal—in other words, whatever the government did not wish to hear.

Under English law in force at the time the First Amendment was written, citizens could be prosecuted for the crime of "seditious libel"—criticism of the government or of public officials. Was it possible that the First Amendment had *not* intended to prohibit seditious libel prosecutions? In his classic book *Free Speech in the United States* (1941), Professor Zechariah Chafee argued that the First Amendment *did* abolish seditious libel, and Justice Holmes, writing the majority opinion in the *Schenck* case, took the same position. More recently, however, Professor Leonard Levy, in his book *Legacy of Suppression* (1960), contended that the Congress that passed the First Amendment did *not* intend to abolish seditious libel. Historical evidence seems to support Professor Levy's contention about the intention of those who wrote the First Amendment. But events have supported Holmes and Chafee's view. A later Congress rescinded the fines levied against those convicted under the 1798 act, suggesting at least the belief that it was unconstitutional. And in 1964, in *New York Times* v. *Sullivan,* the Supreme Court declared in *dictum* that the Sedition Act of 1798 had been unconstitutional.

Schenck had been convicted of conspiracy to violate the Espionage Act of 1917 by printing and distributing circulars calling on citizens who had been drafted to refuse induction into the armed forces and by sending such materials through the mails. In reviewing Schenck's conviction, the Supreme Court assumed that the Espionage Act was constitutional. The problem was whether or not the particular acts committed by Schenck—the mailing of antidraft circulars to draft-eligible men, attacking the draft as unconstitutional, and urging them to assert their constitutional rights—violated the provisions of the act that punished obstruction of the draft, causing insubordination in the armed forces, or issuing false statements that might interfere with the prosecution of the war. Finding that Schenck's circulars were not protected by the First Amendment, a unanimous Court affirmed the conviction. Writing for the Court, Justice Holmes drew the line between protected and nonprotected utterances:

The character of every act depends upon the circumstances in which it is done. . . . The most stringent protection of free speech would not protect a man in falsely shouting fire in a theatre and causing a panic. . . . The question in every case is whether the words used are used in circumstances and are of such a nature as to create a clear and present danger that they will bring about the substantive evils that Congress has a right to prevent. It is a question of proximity and degree. . . . When a nation is at war many things that might be said in time of peace are such a hindrance to its effort that their utterance will not be endured so long as men fight and that no Court could regard them as protected by any constitutional right.

At first blush, what Holmes provided here was a fairly simple test designed to *protect* free speech wherever possible. But on closer scrutiny, and read in the context of the result of the case, the test was far less liberal. On its surface, the "clear and present danger test" (as it came to be known) provides that speech is no longer protected when it *results in illegal action.* Holmes' example of falsely shouting fire in a theater is unfortunate, because it raises the questions of whether or not a *true* assertion that results in an illegal act is also punishable. Clearly, to shout fire in a theater and cause a panic where there was actually a fire, or where the warning was honestly shouted but later proved ill-founded, would not constitute a punishable act under Holmes' test. Thus the truth of the assertion (or the honest belief of the person making it) would seem to be crucial. Yet it would be difficult to prove in court the *falsity* of Schenck's statement that conscription was unconstitutional despotism or that Karl Marx's prediction of a revolution of the proletariat was *false*—unwise perhaps, unwelcome to many, yes, but false, no.

Under this test the protections of the First Amendment are withdrawn only when it can be shown that some illegal action has resulted that can be directly attributed to the speech in question. It is only in the simplest sort of street-corner speech cases that one could even venture an assessment of the relationship of the words of the speaker to the actions of the crowd. Yet what substantive evil was Congress trying to prevent, or could it constitutionally try to prevent, with the Espionage Act of 1917? Clearly, it could legislate against obstructions to the draft; but was Holmes suggesting that it could also punish the mere accusation of unconstitutionality without any effort on the government's part to establish a relationship between the speech and actual disruptions? That this may have been the case is supported by the last quoted sentence, where Holmes talks not of substantive evils but of "hindrances" to the war effort. Surely there is a difference between a "hindrance" and an "obstruction." As Holmes said, it is a question of proximity and degree, and read in the context of the facts of the *Schenck* case, the words had to be neither very prox-

imate nor very related to an alleged substantive evil for a conviction to be sustained. The first case in which Holmes sought to use the test to *reverse* a conviction was in *Abrams* v. *United States* (1919). Dissenting with Brandeis, Holmes argued that printing of pamphlets attacking the policy of the government to send military forces to Vladivostok and Murmansk was protected speech. His opinion seemed to add a new element to the test—that the purported illegal result of the speech be so immediate and imminent that it could not be checked by the counterforce of opposing speech. But the rest of the Court remained unconvinced, and the "clear and present danger" test remained more a rationalization for conviction than a protection of First Amendment rights.

The "clear and present danger" test was further limited in *Gitlow* v. *New York* (1925). Here, the situation was somewhat different; a state law rather than a federal statute was involved, and unlike the Espionage Act, the criminal syndicalism statute of New York specifically proscribed certain types of speech, rather than merely certain actions that might be brought about by speech. The majority argued that such a statute was presumptively valid and that the court's sole responsibility was to determine whether the statute was reasonable. Writing for the Court, Justice Sanford argued, "The State cannot reasonably be required to measure the danger from every . . . utterance in the nice balance of a jeweler's scale. A single revolutionary spark may kindle a fire that, smouldering for a time, may burst into a sweeping and destructive conflagration." Thus the question became whether a particular utterance indicated a tendency to bring about a certain evil, hence the label the "bad tendency" test. Whatever the label, punishing speech that *tended* to bring about an evil was certainly different from punishing speech that *will* bring about an evil. This not so subtle shift was unacceptable to Holmes and Brandeis, who dissented bitterly. Parenthetically, it may be noted that it was in the *Gitlow* case that a unanimous Court announced that the First Amendment was applicable to the states via the Fourteenth Amendment.

In *Gitlow*, Holmes and Brandeis appeared to use the "clear and present danger" test as a standard testing the validity of the statute itself and not merely as a rule of evidence to judge the acceptability of a particular speech in a particular set of circumstances. They took a similar position in 1927, in *Whitney* v. *California*, a case involving California's Criminal Syndicalism Act. Anita Whitney had participated in the formation of the Communist party in California but had never espoused nor participated in any illegal acts. Membership alone seems to have been the basis of her conviction, affirmed by the Supreme Court.

The Supreme Court's attitude toward First Amendment freedoms became more positive in the 1930s. But as tensions rose in the years before World War II, political tolerance declined. It was in this period that the House Un-American Activities Committee was formed. In 1940, Congress passed the Alien Registration Act, more commonly known as the "Smith Act." It was the first peacetime sedition act passed since 1798. Under its terms, advocacy of the overthrow of any government in the United States by force or violence was prohibited. The printing and distribution of such materials was outlawed, as was the organization of, or membership in, any group that advo-

cated such goals. Conspiracy to violate any of the substantive provisions of the act was also declared illegal. Thus, it was a crime merely to belong to an organization that advocated the violent overthrow of government, regardless of whether the member actually knew of, or contributed to, that advocacy. The Communist Party was not mentioned by name, but its extinction was the obvious purpose of the act.

In 1948, the government charged eleven leaders of the American Communist Party with conspiring to organize the Communist Party and to advocate the duty and necessity of overthrowing the government. No overt illegal acts such as sabotage or violence were charged, only that the Communist Party had been organized to advocate the overthrow of the government.

After a long and tumultuous trial in New York City, the leaders were convicted (and their attorneys sent to jail on a variety of contempt of court charges). The court of appeals affirmed their convictions, and the Supreme Court agreed to consider the constitutionality of the Smith Act. One of the issues before the Court was the applicability of the "clear and present danger" test, which had been reinterpreted by the court of appeals as a determination of whether the "gravity of the evil discounted by its improbability" justified restrictions on political speech.

The case was known as *Dennis* v. *United States* (1951). The obvious dilemma for the justices was that if they applied the "clear and present danger" test literally, they would have to vote to reverse the convictions, since there was no demonstrable danger from the defendant's activities that was either clear or present. It was the same dilemma that Holmes had faced in the *Schenck* case, and the 6-3 majority of the Court, speaking through Chief Justice Vinson, responded by adopting the substitute formula proposed by the Court of Appeals. Vinson noted that there was a distinction between discussion and advocacy and that it was the latter that was charged in this case. However, he did not effectively distinguish between immediate and theoretical advocacy. Thus, when the trial court judge had charged the jury to return a guilty verdict if it found that the defendants advocated the overthrow of the government "as speedily as circumstances permit," he was not requiring evidence of advocacy of specific acts but merely a theoretical statement of the desirability of overthrowing the government at some time in the future.

The "gravity of the evil" test neatly bridged this gap. Where the evil was great (as, it was contended, was the case here), the threat did not have to be very imminent or probable in order to justify restrictions on First Amendment rights. If the Court's reasoning was not entirely clear, its intent was. The decision provided a constitutional umbrella for the prosecution of Communist Party leaders. In place of the "clear and present danger" test, the Supreme Court undertook to balance individual rights against the needs of the society as a whole.

A second major case involving the prosecution of Communist party leaders reached the Supreme Court in 1957. The results were markedly different. In *Yates* v. *United States,* a somewhat revamped Supreme Court held that the statute of limitations had run on the prohibition of organizing the Communist party and that further prosecutions for that offense were forbidden. Furthermore, the Court held, there was a distinction

between advocacy of abstract doctrine and direct advocacy of unlawful acts. Only the latter was punishable under the law. Five of the fourteen defendants in the case had their convictions reversed outright. New trials were ordered for the remainder, but eventually indictments against them were dismissed, the government having determined that under the doctrine of the *Yates* case, the prosecutions could not be sustained. The case virtually gutted large portions of the Smith Act, and no further convictions under those provisions were ever obtained.

The sole exception came in the case of *Scales* v. *United States* (1961), but even in that case, the Supreme Court read the act very narrowly. Scales was convicted of membership in the Communist Party, but the Court said that his conviction was sustained only because he was a "knowing" member. The evidence showed that Scales had directed a school for members of the Communist Party at which techniques of sabotage and subversion were taught. Ironically, he also left the party in 1957 after being disillusioned by revelations of Stalin's repressive policies and by Soviet repression of the Hungarian uprising in 1956. He was the only person ever to serve a prison term for *membership* in the Communist party.

If the *Yates* and *Scales* cases hastened the demise of the Smith Act, they also showed a renewed willingness on the part of the Supreme Court to distinguish between individual responsibility and guilt by association. Perhaps the final episode in the entire line of cases, from *Schenck* to *Scales*, came in *Brandenburg* v. *Ohio* (1969), where the Supreme Court struck down the Ohio version of the criminal syndicalism act upheld in the *Whitney* case in 1927.

In *Watkins* v. *United States* (1957), the authority of the House Committee on Un-American Activities to compel testimony concerning the past political activities of others in the Communist Party was challenged as a violation of Watkins' First Amendment rights. Watkins, an active labor leader, was subpoenaed by the committee but refused to answer questions concerning the activities of others in the Communist movement. The Court held that such questioning was "justified solely as an adjunct to the legislative process" and that the First Amendment "may be invoked against infringement of the protected freedoms. . . ." "There is no right to expose for the sake of exposure," the Court said in overturning Watkins' contempt citation.

Two years later, in *Barenblatt* v. *United States*, the Court narrowed its holding in *Watkins* and held that the House Committee on Un-American Activities did have statutory authority to question witnesses about the activities of the Communist movement as long as the questions were "pertinent" to the purpose and within the jurisdiction of the committee charter. Distinguishing *Barenblatt* from *Watkins*, Justice Harlan, writing for the majority, ruled that in *Watkins*, the questions under inquiry had not been disclosed in an illuminating manner, in contrast to *Barenblatt*, where the petitioner raised no objection on the ground of pertinency at the time he was questioned. Justice Black, speaking for the four dissenters in *Barenblatt*, stated: "Ultimately all the questions in this case really boil down to one—whether we as a people will try fearfully and futilely to preserve democracy by adopting totalitarian methods, or whether in accordance with our traditions and our Constitution we will have the confidence and courage to be free."

Another response to the concern over the threat of international communism was the Internal Security Act of 1950, which required all Communist organizations to register with the attorney general. The mechanism was the Subversive Activities Control Board (SACB), and the results of registration were severe for the organizations involved: their mail and media items had to be identified as Communist propaganda, nonelective positions with the federal government were precluded, it was a crime for members of such organizations to apply for a passport, and their access to work in plants with defense contracts was severely limited. In 1961, the status of the SACB was upheld in *Communist Party* v. *SACB*, and prosecutions were brought by the board. But in *Aptheker* v. *Secretary of State* (1964), the passport provisions were declared unconstitutional, and the registration provisions met the same fate the following year in *Albertson* v. *SACB*. The work provision was effectively nullified when, in *United States* v. *Robel* (1967), a similar provision in the McCarran Act was declared invalid on the basis of the *Aptheker* decision.

With the erosion of the cold war, public concern over the immediate threat of international communism has largely faded. But the era of such concerns is vividly recounted today in literature and in the media—Woody Allen's film about the Hollywood blacklist, *The Front;* the recent television documentary about Senator Joseph McCarthy of Wisconsin, "Tail-Gunner Joe"; and publication of such books as Lillian Hellman's *Scoundrel Time.* But perhaps what has touched the public's interest most are the repeated efforts to reopen two of the most famous trials of the time—those of Alger Hiss and the Rosenbergs, the latter executed in 1953 after conviction under the Espionage Act. Loyalty oaths in public employment and the struggle of the legal profession to prevent admission to the bar of those with suspect political views are but two vestiges of a very troubled time in American political—and constitutional—history. It remains to be seen whether that experience will preclude a repetition of the same events when confronted by another threatening ideology.

(2) A Note on Political Organizations and the First Amendment

It has been noted often that American politics is especially dependent on the freedom of individuals to organize in pursuit of their common goals and purposes. With the exception of a few organizations, such as the Communist Party, that were outlawed for a time because of the threatening ideologies they espoused, the organizational process has been largely open. Certainly there is general agreement on the principle of free association. Yet in practice, there are many examples of groups seeking to outlaw or seriously constrain the activities of their opposing numbers. And from time to time, both the national and state governments have sought to restrict or penalize group activities. Quite often, government intervention has been indirect, not by attempts to "outlaw" a group, but by imposing severe political and often personal costs on group membership. Thus the loyalty oaths that came into widespread use after World War II were an effort to penalize membership in certain groups by restricting access to various privileges and professions regulated by government. Legislative investigations were another common tool used to "expose" the activities of certain groups and their members, and by that process often subjecting

them to severe social and political reprisals.

Freedom of association is not specifically protected by the First Amendment, but it is recognized as a derivative right flowing from the amendment's protections of assembly, speech, the press, and religion. Despite its solid foundations in American constitutional theory and practice, freedom of association has never been regarded as absolute. There is no freedom to associate for an illegal purpose. Traditionally, the law has punished conspiracies to violate the law as a separate and distinct crime. Indeed, it is often easier to prove a conspiracy than to prove the commission of a substantive crime. Conspiracy statutes are exceptionally vulnerable to prosecutorial abuse, but they remain a key weapon of law enforcement officials.

Conspiracy charges are vulnerable to constitutional challenge. Because they rely on the getting together of two or more persons who agree to commit an illegal act, they immediately implicate the First Amendment freedoms of speech and association. It is the agreement that is the heart of the conspiracy; indeed, no illegal act need be committed so long as intent to do so is established and some overt—but not necessarily illegal—act has been committed. In the *Dennis* case (*supra,* pp. 1226 –1227), the eleven leaders of the Communist Party were convicted of conspiring to organize a group that in turn would advocate the illegal overthrow of the government. Their conviction implied that it was illegal to organize a group to advocate what any of them individually might advocate. Indeed, in a conspiracy, it is possible to obtain a conviction where only one member of the group has committed an overt act in furtherance of the conspiracy.

The Smith Act of 1940 not only

punished the knowing advocacy of the forcible overthrow of government and any conspiracy to accomplish those ends, but it also made it a criminal offense to belong to any organization eventually determined to have advocated that overthrow. If the *Dennis* and *Yates* cases in accepted the idea of guilt by association, at least insofar as it applied to members of the Communist Party, the Court backtracked from this position in *Scales* v. *United States* (1961). In that case, the Court held that Section 2 of the Smith Act, which punished membership in an organization advocating forcible overthrow of the government, only applied to "knowing" and "active" members who could be shown to have had, on an individual basis, a specific intent to overthrow the government.

The idea that mere membership in an association that advocated illegal acts was sufficient to justify criminal conviction dated back to *Whitney* v. *California* (1927). In that case Whitney had been convicted under the California Criminal Syndicalism Act, even though the only overt "act" that she had committed was to join the Communist Labor Party and become a member of its executive committee. She testified that she had personally opposed terrorism and violence even though the party was found to have advocated such tactics. The Supreme Court affirmed her conviction. Although the *Whitney* case was often ignored by the Supreme Court in the following decade, its principles were embodied in the Smith Act and related efforts to outlaw the American Communist Party. It was finally and specifically overruled in *Brandenburg* v. *Ohio* (1969).

If the Smith Act and its progeny were a direct assault on the principle of freedom of association, efforts by the southern states in the 1950s to outlaw the NAACP undermined that principle by indirection. Alabama sought to prevent that organization from doing business in the state. The NAACP is a New York corporation that refused to comply with Alabama laws requiring disclosure of its membership lists, for fear of reprisals against its members. The NAACP did finally comply with Alabama laws requiring out-of-state corporations to register and to provide a list of their officers. For failure to provide the membership lists, the NAACP was held in contempt, fined $100,000, and ordered to stop doing business in the state. The Supreme Court reversed, holding that compelled disclosure of the lists would unconstitutionally limit the rights of members to engage in collective and lawful activities. The Court took notice of past episodes in which disclosure of membership lists had in fact subject NAACP members to coercion, loss of employment, and other reprisals.

In support of its right to compel disclosure of membership lists, Alabama had relied on an earlier Supreme Court case, *Bryant* v. *Zimmerman* (1928), which had upheld New York's compelled disclosure of the membership lists of the Ku Klux Klan. But the Court distinguished between the Klan's violent and often unlawful activities and those of the NAACP.

In a related effort, Virginia moved against the NAACP by charging it with violation of the state's laws against barratry—the solicitation of legal business and "stirring up" of litigation. Of course, the NAACP was not involved in "ambulance chasing," the traditional object of such laws. But admittedly it did solicit litigants for "test cases" as part of its strategy of combating racial discrimination through the courts. The Supreme Court, in *NAACP* v. *Button*

(1963), upheld the NAACP. It distinguished between litigation for the mere resolution of private grievances, against which barratry statutes were traditionally directed, and litigation "for achieving the lawful objectives of equality of treatment . . . for the members of the Negro community in this country. . . . [F]or such a group association for litigation may be the most effective form of political association."

4. CREATIVE EXPRESSION AND PUBLIC AUTHORITY

A. *A Note on the Poet, the State and their Relationship to the Constitutional Problem of Obscenity*

In considering the importance and meaning of the First Amendment, it is essential to assess the relationship between the poet and the state. By "poet," we mean one who gives expression to creative imagination. More often than not that expression is critical of the state or offensive to the values of the community that the state seeks to enforce.

The objectives and values of the state and the poet are often at odds because they flow from different premises. To the state and its rulers, order, stability, and predictability are primary goals. Sudden change, if not anathema, is often dangerous because it is unpredictable. Extreme individuality may threaten values perceived to be important to the common good. The poet, by contrast, does not fear contradiction and disharmony but often celebrates it. There are few great novels about bureaucratic regularity or the "ordinary" lives of ordinary people. But there are many that delve deeply into the tensions among people or explore the contradictions of the psyche and the soul. The poet celebrates the unusual and the unique and has license to distort otherwise accepted reality for the sake of artistry. The poet need not portray people as they think they are but rather as they really are, or might be. The ruler seeks constancy, the poet may revel in disharmony.

It is hardly surprising to find a perennial antagonism between the poet and the state, one that transcends the political experience of many societies. It is well known that Plato, in *The Republic*, sought to banish the poet, presumably on the ground that the people would have their emotions stirred enough to be less susceptible to the influence of those who know the Good. For Plato, the matter is philosophic and involves disputed claims to knowledge of the truth. But the dynamics of the difference between ruler and poet remain. In more contemporary times, the abuses of a highly restrictive order in Russia were subjected to a critique by Dostoevsky that was all the more penetrating because he could elevate real circumstances to the level of universal truth and realization. The recent expulsion of Alexander Solzhenitsen from the Soviet Union is but the latest stark reminder of the power of creative imagination in the face of political repression.

The relevance of these thoughts about the poet and the state as an introduction to the constitutional problems of obscenity may at first seem to be obscure. But we think it important for the student to consider the broad context in which the Supreme Court has attempted to deal with the problem of obscenity. Of course, we do *not* claim that today's purveyor of pornography is an equivalent of the great—or even minor—poets. In fact, as the student will readily observe in the cases reprinted below, the issue of the use of explicit sexual references in serious literature and other works of art has long been resolved in favor of artistic license.

What is still unresolved, and may never be resolved satisfactorily, is the constitutional and legal status of hard-core pornography, the depicting in film, writing, or live performance, of explicit "normal" and "abnormal" sexual acts. Such depictions, most would agree, have little or no artistic value, using that term in its broadest sense, and yet they may have some redeeming social value. Sex as a subject or as a means of expression has characterized every known culture. There is little evidence to support the thesis, once widely assumed, that exposure to such materials directly or indirectly causes antisocial sexual behavior. And it is inescapably true that sexual expression in the form of pornography is a form of social and political criticism in its rejection of prevailing sexual mores. Like Plato's poet, it diverts people from what others think should be higher concerns, and it rejects a set of attitudes and values heretofore regarded as right and proper. The pervasiveness and staying power of pornography, to say nothing directly about its astounding commercial success in the face of concerted political and legal opposition, is impressive evidence that it appeals not only to the deviant and deviate but also to many quite "ordinary" persons.

Until the Supreme Court decided

the *Roth* case in 1957, the constitutional status of obscenity was clear enough: it was *not* regarded as protected speech under the First Amendment. Chief Justice Hughes wrote in *Near* v. *Minnesota* (1931) that it was an exception to the doctrine of no prior restraint (on speech). And Justice Frank Murphy, writing in *Chaplinsky* v. *New Hampshire* (1942), referred to the "lewd and obscene" as a class of speech "the prevention and punishment of which has never been thought to raise any constitutional questions."

Nevertheless, American courts were taking a progressively more sympathetic view toward sexual expression. Until 1934, most courts followed a rule announced in an English case decided in 1868, known as *Regina* v. *Hicklin*. Under the *Hicklin* rule, a book could be declared obscene if it tended to "deprave and corrupt those whose minds are open to such immoral influences, and into whose hands a publication of this sort might fall." Thus, a book could be banned because of a few salacious passages, even if the *tendency* to corrupt was only speculative and applied only to those *most* vulnerable to such corruption.

In 1934, the *Hicklin* rule was repudiated by Judge Augustus Hand of the Court of Appeals for the Second Circuit. Writing in the case *United States* v. *One Book Entitled "Ulysses,"* Hand wrote:

. . . *the proper test of whether a given book is obscene is its dominant effect. In applying this test, relevancy of the objectionable parts of the theme, the established reputation of the work in the estimation of approved critics, if the book is modern, and the verdict of the past, if it is ancient, are persuasive pieces of evidence; for works of art are not likely to sustain a high position with no better warrant for their existence than their obscene content.*

This test, though still quite restrictive, loosened the reins of *Hicklin* considerably. It was an entire work, its dominant effect, and not merely a few dirty words or paragraphs that determined whether or not a book was obscene. The new test was sufficient to permit importation of James Joyce's great book, but how far it would extend beyond the "great books" category remained to be seen.

The Supreme Court first grappled with the constitutional definition of obsenity in two cases decided together in 1957, *Roth* v. *United States* and *Alberts* v. *California*. Roth had been convicted in federal court of sending obscene circulars through the mails to solicit sales of books, photographs, and magazines. Alberts, who ran a mail-order business in Los Angeles, was convicted in a state court of keeping for sale and advertising books that were obscene and indecent.

The Court's approach (as detailed in the opinion, *infra*) was to deal with the problem on two levels. First, it decided that obscenity was *not* protected by the First Amendment, because it was "utterly without redeeming social importance." This was consistent with the law as it had developed over time, but it did not answer the vital question, merely postponed it. That question was, in the broadest sense, what is obscenity? Are all sexual themes and depictions of sexual behavior obscene? If so, then they are not constitutionally protected and are subject to criminal penalties. If not, then where is the line to be drawn between depiction of sexual matters that are permissible and depiction that can be prohibited?

Speaking for a divided Court, Justice Brennan adopted a test that ex-

panded on the *Ulysses* rule in a number of important ways: "whether to the average person, applying contemporary community standards, the dominant theme of the material taken as a whole appeals to prurient interests." It was now the "average person," not the most vulnerable, on whom a book's demonstrable effects must be shown. It was a broad-based "community standard" that was to be applied (presumably, but not necessarily, by a jury), and it was the dominant theme, not a part of the work, that must be shown to appeal to "prurient interests."

The convictions of both Roth and Alberts were affirmed, and although Justice Brennan had stressed that he did not believe sex and obscenity to be identical, many observers predicted that the *Roth* test, as it came to be known, would facilitate and indeed encourage a wave of obscenity prosecutions. Many prosecutions did ensue, but as some of those cases made their way to the Supreme Court, it gave the Court an opportunity to tighten up the *Roth* standards. In *Kingsley International Pictures Corporation* v. *Regents* (1959), it was held that a motion picture that advocates an idea, however unacceptable it may be to some or even to many, is not obscene merely on the basis of that idea. In *Manual Enterprises* v. *Day* (1962), the Supreme Court held that mere appeal to prurient interest did not constitute obscenity unless it was also "patently offensive." And in *Jacobellis* v. *Ohio* (1964), the Court held first that only material that was *utterly* lacking in social importance could be deemed obscene and, furthermore, that the "community standard" mentioned in *Roth* was a national, not a local standard. This progressive tightening of the *Roth* rule was reaffirmed by the Court in the *Fanny Hill* case,

Memoirs of a Woman of Pleasure v. *Massachusetts* (1966). A plurality of justices held that for a book or film to be declared obscene, all three components of the new test had to coalesce: prurient interest, patent offensiveness, and total lack of redeeming social value.

Unlike the original *Roth* test, this new composite standard imposed on prosecutors an extremely difficult burden of proof, so much so that the prevailing view was that only "hardcore pornography" was now to be regarded as obscene within the meaning of the First Amendment. As Justice Stewart remarked in the *Jacobellis* case, he could not define hard-core pornography, but he "knew it when he saw it." His aphorism, widely quoted, showed the great difficulty confronting the Court and also suggested the justices' weariness at having to view a lot of pornographic movies in order to determine, on a case-by-case basis, what was, and what was not, constitutionally obscene.

Political pressure on the Court to contain the spread of pornography certainly did not make its task any easier. Yet when the Court, seemingly in response to this pressure, took a step back from *Roth*, it merely compounded the difficulty of everyone in fathoming what was and what was not to be allowed. Ralph Ginsburg, taking advantage of the new permissive rules, had commenced publication of the magazines *Eros, Liaison,* and a book, *The Housewife's Handbook on Selective Promiscuity.* Their contents, quite mild by today's standards, appeared to fall within the protected area defined by the *Roth* rules. But the offense charged in the federal district court had included the way in which the magazines were advertised.

Mailing privileges had been sought from the small post offices in Intercourse and Blue Ball, Pennsylvania, and when these were rejected, the magazines were mailed from Middlesex, New Jersey. Ginsburg was convicted and sentenced to a five-year prison term; by a 5-4 vote, the Supreme Court affirmed his conviction. The Court agreed with a finding of the lower court that the magazines, standing alone, might not be obscene. But because of the element of pandering, because, in the Court's judgment, the entire enterprise was permeated by the "leer of the sensualist," and because Ginsburg was exploiting people's prurient interest in sex, his conviction was affirmed. Thus, whether or not a publication was obscene was to be determined by the context of its promotion and publication as much as by its contents.

If the public, and even close observers of the Court, could no longer effectively explain what was and what was not constitutionally obscene, the Court itself seemed equally at a loss. In *Redrup* v. *New York* (1967), acknowledging the failure of (but not rejecting) the *Roth* test, the Court announced that it would consider obscenity convictions on an individual basis and would uphold only those that met one of the following conditions: (1) where the statute reflected a particular concern for juveniles in being exposed to supposedly obscene materials; (2) where individuals had been unwillingly exposed to obscene materials in violation of their privacy, and (3) where pandering was involved.

With the advent of the Burger Court, a new attempt was made to deal with the obscenity problem. *Miller* v. *California* (1973, *infra*) and its companion cases were a major effort to reinterpret the *Roth* standard. Not surprisingly, the author of the *Roth* test, Justice Brennan, used his dissent in the *Miller* case to subject that test to rigorous criticism. But unlike the majority, his solution was to abandon the test altogether.

B. *Obscenity and the Constitution*

(1) **Roth v. United States/Alberts v. California (1957)**

+Brennan, Warren, Frankfurter, Burton, Clark, Whittaker
−Douglas, Black
±Harlan

MR. JUSTICE BRENNAN delivered the opinion of the Court.

The constitutionality of a criminal obscenity statute is the question in each of these cases. In *Roth*, the primary constitutional question is whether the federal obscenity statute violates the provision of the First Amendment that "Congress shall make no law . . . abridging the freedom of speech, or of the press." In *Alberts*, the primary constitutional question is whether the obscenity provisions of the California Penal Code invade the freedoms of speech and press as they may be incorporated in the liberty protected from state action by the Due Process Clause of the Fourteenth Amendment. . . .

Roth conducted a business in New York in the publication and sale of books, photographs and magazines. He used circulars and advertising matter to solicit sales. He was convicted by a jury in the District Court for the Southern District of New York upon 4 counts of a 26-count indictment charging him with mailing obscene circulars and advertising, and an obscene book, in violation of the federal obscenity statute. His conviction was affirmed by the Court of Appeals for the Second Circuit. We granted Certiorari.

Alberts conducted a mail-order business from Los Angeles. He was convicted by the Judge of the Municipal Court of the Beverly Hills Judicial District (having waived a jury trial) under a misdemeanor complaint which charged him with lewdly keeping for sale obscene and indecent books, and with writing, composing and publishing an obscene advertisement of them, in violation of the California Penal Code. The conviction was affirmed by the Appellate Department of the Superior Court of the State of California in and for the County of Los Angeles. We noted probable jurisdiction.

The dispositive question is whether obscenity is utterance within the area of protected speech and press. Although this is the first time the question has been squarely presented to this Court, either under the First Amendment or under the Fourteenth Amendment, expressions found in numerous opinions indicate that this Court has always assumed that obscenity is not protected by the freedoms of speech and press. . . .

The guaranties of freedom of expression in effect in 10 of the 14 States which by 1792 had ratified the Constitution, gave no absolute protection for every utterance. Thirteen of the 14 States provided for the prosecution of libel, and all of those States made either blasphemy or profanity, or both, statutory crimes. As early as 1712, Massachusetts made it criminal to publish "any filthy, obscene, or profane song, pamphlet, libel or mock sermon" in imitation or mimicking of religious services. Acts and Laws of the Province of Mass. Bay. . . . Thus, profanity and obscenity were related offenses.

In light of this history, it is apparent that the unconditional phrasing of the First Amendment was not intended to protect every utterance. . . . At the time of the adoption of the First Amendment, obscenity law was not as fully developed as libel law, but there is sufficiently contemporaneous evidence to show that obscenity, too, was outside the protection intended for speech and press.

The protection given speech and press was fashioned to assure unfettered interchange of ideas for the bringing about of political and social changes desired by the people. . . .

All ideas having even the slightest redeeming social importance—unorthodox ideas, controversial ideas, even ideas hateful to the prevailing climate of opinion—have the full protection of the guaranties, unless excludable because they encroach upon the limited area of more important interests. But implicit in the history of the First Amendment is the rejection of obscenity as utterly without redeeming social importance. This rejection for that reason is mirrored in the universal judgment that obscenity should be restrained, reflected in the international agreement of over 50 nations, in the obscenity laws of all of the 48 States, and in the 20 obscenity laws enacted by the Congress from 1842 to 1956. . . . We hold that obscenity is not within the area of constitutionally protected speech or press. . . .

[S]ex and obscenity are not synonymous. Obscene material is material which deals with sex in a manner appealing to prurient interests. The portrayal of sex, e.g., in art, literature and scientific works, is not sufficient reason to deny material the constitutional protection of freedom of speech and press. Sex, a great and mysterious motive force in human life, has indisputably been a subject of absorbing interest to mankind through the ages; it is one of the vital problems of human interest and public concern. . . .

The fundamental freedoms of speech and press have contributed greatly to the development and well-being of our free society and are indispensable to its continued growth. Ceaseless vigilance is the watchword to prevent their erosion by Congress or by the States. The door barring federal and state intrusion into this area cannot be left ajar; it must be kept tightly closed and opened only the slightest crack necessary to prevent encroachment upon more important interests. It is therefore vital that the standards for judging obscenity safeguard the protection of speech and press for material which does not treat sex in a manner appealing to prurient interest.

The early leading standard of obscenity allowed material to be judged merely by the effect of an isolated excerpt upon particularly susceptible persons. *Regina* v. *Hicklin,* (1898). Some American courts adopted this standard but later decisions have rejected it and substituted this test: whether to the average person, applying contemporary community standards, the dominant theme of the material taken as a whole appeals to prurient interest. The *Hicklin* test, judging obscenity by the effect of isolated passages upon the most susceptible persons, might well encompass material legitimately treating with sex, and so it must be rejected as unconstitutionally restrictive of the freedoms of speech and press. On the other hand, the substituted standard provides safeguards adequate to withstand the charge of constitutional infirmity.

Both trial courts below sufficiently followed the proper standard. Both courts used the proper definition of obscenity. In addition, in the *Alberts* case, in ruling on a motion to dismiss, the trial judge indicated that, as the trier of facts, he was judging each item as a whole as it would affect the normal person, and in *Roth,* the trial judge instructed the jury as follows: . . .

The test in each case is the effect of the book, picture or publication considered as a whole, not upon any particular class, but upon all those whom it is likely to reach. . . .

In summary, then, we hold that these statutes, applied according to the proper standard for judging obscenity, do not offend constitutional safeguards against convictions based upon protected material, or fail to give men in acting adequate notice of what is prohibited. . . .

The judgments are affirmed.

MR. CHIEF JUSTICE WARREN, CONCURRING IN THE RESULT (OMITTED).

MR. JUSTICE HARLAN CONCURRING IN PART AND DISSENTING IN PART.

I concur in the judgment of the Court in . . . *Alberts* v. *People of State of California.*

The question in this case is whether the defendant was deprived of liberty without due process of law when he was convicted for selling certain materials found by the judge to be obscene because they would have a "tendency to deprave or corrupt its readers by exciting lascivious thoughts or arousing lustful desire."

In judging the constitutionality of this conviction, we should remember that our function in reviewing state judgments under the Fourteenth Amendment is a narrow one. We do not decide whether the policy of the State is wise, or whether it is based on assumptions scientifically substantiated. We can inquire only whether the state action so subverts the fundamental liberties implicit in

the Due Process Clause that it cannot be sustained as a rational exercise of power. . . .

What, then, is the purpose of this California statute? Clearly the state legislature has made the judgment that printed words *can* "deprave or corrupt" the reader—that words can incite to antisocial or immoral action. The assumption seems to be that the distribution of certain types of literature will induce criminal or immoral sexual conduct. It is well known, of course, that the validity of this assumption is a matter of dispute among critics, sociologists, psychiatrists, and penologists. . . . It seems to be that nothing in the broad and flexible command of the Due Process Clause forbids California to prosecute one who sells books whose dominant tendency might be to "deprave or corrupt" a reader. I agree with the Court, of course, that the books must be judged as a whole and in relation to the normal adult reader.

I dissent in . . . *Roth* v. *United States.*

We are faced here with the question whether the federal obscenity statute, as construed and applied in this case, violates the First Amendment to the Constitution. To me, this question is of quite a different order than the one where we are dealing with state legislation under the Fourteenth Amendment. I do not think it follows that state and federal powers in this area are the same, and that just because the State may suppress a particular utterance, it is automatically permissible for the Federal Government to do the same. . . .

The Constitution differentiates between those areas of human conduct subject to the regulation of the States and those subject to the powers of the Federal Government. The substantive powers of the two governments, in many instances, are distinct. And in every case where we are called upon to balance the interest in free expression against other interests, it seems to me important that we should keep in the forefront the question of whether those other interests are state or federal. . . .

Not only is the federal interest in protecting the Nation against pornography attenuated, but the dangers of federal censorship in this field are far greater than anything the States may do. . . .

MR. JUSTICE DOUGLAS, WITH WHOM MR. JUSTICE BLACK CONCURS, DISSENTING.

When we sustain these convictions, we make the legality of a publication turn on the purity of thought which a book or tract instills in the mind of the reader. I do not think we can approve that standard and be faithful to the command of the First Amendment, which by its terms is a restraint on Congress and which by the Fourteenth is a restraint on the States. . . .

The absence of dependable information on the effect of obscene literature on human conduct should make us wary. It should put us on the side of protecting society's interest in literature, except and unless it can be said that the particular publication has an impact on action that the government can control.

(2) The Constitutional Basis for Prohibitions upon the Dissemination of Explicit Sexual Materials

For many years the Supreme Court assumed, without deciding, that laws generally prohibiting dissemination of obscenity were consistent with the free speech guarantees of the Constitution. . . .

In upholding the constitutionality of obscenity prohibitions, the *Roth* decision did not rely upon findings or conclusions regarding the effect of sexual materials upon persons who are exposed to them. Rather, the fundamental premise of *Roth* was that "obscene" materials are not entitled to the protections accorded to "speech" by the First and Fourteenth Amendments to the Constitution. The Court based this conclusion upon its findings (1) that the Framers of the Bill of Rights did not intend the free speech guarantee of the First Amendment to apply to all utterances and writings, (2) that "obscene" speech—like libel, profanity and blasphemy—was not intended to be protected by the Amendment, and (3) that a universal consensus had existed for many years that the distribution of obscenity should be legally prohibited.

In 1969, in *Stanley* v. *Georgia*, the Supreme Court modified the premise of the *Roth* decision to some extent by holding that the constitutional guarantee of free speech protects the right of the individual to read or view concededly "obscene" material in his own home. Some lower federal courts have held that the *Stanley* decision gives constitutional protection to some distributions of obscenity, as well as to its private possession. Specifically, courts have held unconstitutional the federal importation prohibition as applied to the importation of obscene material for private use, the federal mail prohibition as applied to the mailing of obscene material to persons who request it, and a

Reprinted from *The Report of the Commission on Obscenity and Pornography* (New York: Bantam Books, 1970), pp. 43–48, 57–61.

state prohibition applied to films exhibited to adults at theaters to which minors were not admitted. These courts have held that the constitutional right to possess obscene materials established in *Stanley* implies a correlative right for adults to acquire such materials for their own use or to view them without forcing them upon others. . . .

Constitutional Limitations upon the Definition of "Obscene"

Adult Obscenity Statutes. Although upholding the constitutionality of broad prohibitions upon the dissemination of obscene materials, the *Roth* decision imposed a narrow standard for defining what is "obscene" under such prohibitions. Subsequent decisions have narrowed the permissible test even further.

The prevailing view today in the Supreme Court of the United States, the lower federal courts, and the courts of the States is that three criteria must all be met before the distribution of material may be generally prohibited for all persons, including adults, on the ground that it is "obscene." These criteria are: (1) the dominant theme of the material, taken as a whole, must appeal to a "prurient" interest in sex; (2) the material must be "patently offensive" because it affronts "contemporary community standards" regarding the depiction of sexual matters; and (3) the material must lack "redeeming social value." All three criteria must coalesce before material may be deemed "obscene" for adults.

The requirement that the material appeal to a "prurient" interest in sex is not clear in meaning but appears to refer primarily to material which is sexually arousing in dominant part. Material must appeal to the prurient

interest of the "average" person, unless it is designed for and distributed to a particular group, in which case it is the interests of the members of that group which are relevant. The Supreme Court has never settled the question whether the "community" by whose standards "offensiveness" is to be determined is a "national" community or whether it is the State or locality where the distribution occurs. Whatever the relevant community, a substantial consensus that particular material is offensive is apparently required to violate the community's "standard." There is some disagreement in the Supreme Court over the precise role played by the "social value" criterion. All the Justices have agreed that social value is relevant to obscenity determinations. A plurality (not a majority) has held that unless material is "utterly" without redeeming social value it may not be held to be obscene; a minority of Justices would permit a small degree of social value to be outweighed by prurience and offensiveness. Nor has the Court authoritatively defined what values are redeeming "social" values, although it has suggested that these may include entertainment values as well as the more firmly established scientific, literary, artistic and educational values. Finally, the Court permits the manner of distribution of material to be taken into account in determining the application of the three criteria, at least where the material itself is close to the line of legality.

The application of these three *Roth* criteria to specific materials requires a great deal of subjective judgment because the criteria refer to emotional, aesthetic and intellectual responses to the material rather than to descriptions of its content. As noted above, the precise meaning of the

criteria is also unclear. This subjectivity and vagueness produces enormous uncertainty about what is
"obscene" among law enforcement
officials, courts, juries and the general public. It is impossible for a publisher, distributor, retailer or
exhibitor to know in advance
whether he will be charged with a
criminal offense for distributing a
particular work, since his understanding of the three tests and
their application to his work may differ from that of the police, prosecutor,
court or jury. This uncertainty and
consequent fear of prosecution may
strongly influence persons not to distribute new works which are entitled
to constitutional protection and thus
have a damaging effect upon free
speech. These definitional problems
are also cited by law enforcement officials at all levels as their chief difficulty in enforcing existing obscenity
laws. There is, therefore, almost universal dissatisfaction with present
law.

A series of decisions of the Supreme Court, generally rendered
without opinion, has given an exceedingly narrow scope of actual application to the constitutionally required three-part standard for adult
legislation. These decisions leave it
questionable whether any verbal or
textual materials whatever may
presently be deemed "obscene" for
adults under the constitutional standard and suggest that only the most
graphic pictorial depictions of actual
sexual activity may fall within it.
Present law for adults is therefore
largely ineffective.

The results of empirical research
regarding the application of the three
constitutional criteria confirm the
difficulties of application as well as
their exceedingly narrow scope. Several studies have found that "arousingness" and "offensiveness" are in-

dependent dimensions when applied
to sexual materials; that is, material
that is offensive may or may not be
arousing, and material that is arousing may or may not be offensive. Only
a very restricted range of material
seems to be capable of meeting both
of these criteria for most people.
Further, there is very little consensus
among people regarding either the
"arousingness" or the "offensiveness" of a given sexual depiction. A
wide distribution of judgments in
these two areas occurs, for example,
for depictions of female nudity with
genitals exposed, for explicit depictions of heterosexual sexual intercourse, and for graphic depictions of
oral-genital intercourse. In addition,
judgments differ among different
groups: Males as a group differ from
females as a group in their judgments of both "offensiveness" and
"arousingness"; the young differ
from the old; the college-educated
differ from those with only a high
school education; frequent church attenders differ from less frequent
church attenders.

An additional and very significant
limiting factor is introduced by the
criterion of social value. In the national survey of American public
opinion sponsored by the Commission, substantial portions of the population reported effects which might
be deemed socially valuable from
even the most explicit sexual materials. For example, about 60% of a representative sample of adult American
men felt that looking or reading such
materials would provide information
about sex and about 40% of the sample reported that such an effect had
occurred for himself or someone he
personally knew. About 60% of these
men felt that looking at or reading
explicit sexual materials provided entertainment and almost 50% reported
this effect upon himself or someone

he personally knew. Half of these men felt that looking at or reading explicit sexual materials can improve sex relations of some married couples, and about a quarter of the sample reported such an effect on themselves or on someone they knew personally. Fewer women reported such effects, but 35%, 24% and 21% reported, respectively, information, entertainment, and improved sexual relations in themselves or someone they personally knew as a result of looking at or reading very explicit sexual materials. As previously indicated, two experimental studies found that a substantial number of married couples reported more agreeable and enhanced marital communication and an increased willingness to discuss sexual matters with each other after exposure to erotic stimuli.

In pursuit of its mandate from Congress to recommend definitions of obscenity which are consistent with constitutional rights, the Commission considered drafting a more satisfactory definition of "obscene" for inclusion in adult obscenity prohibitions, should such prohibitions appear socially warranted. To be satisfactory from the point of view of its enforcement and application, such a definition would have to describe the material to be proscribed with a high degree of objectivity and specificity, so that those subject to the law could know in advance what materials were prohibited and so that judicial decisions would not be based upon the subjective reactions of particular judges or jurors. In light of the empirical data, described above, showing both the lack of consensus among adults as to what is both arousing and offensive and the values attributed by substantial numbers of adults to even the most explicit sexual materials, the construction of

such a definition for adults within constitutional limits would be extremely difficult. In any event, the Commission, as developed in its legislative recommendations set forth later in this Report, does not believe that a sufficient social justification exists for the retention or enactment of broad legislation prohibiting the consensual distribution of sexual materials to adults. We, therefore, do not recommend any definition of what is "obscene" for adults. . . .

Legislative Recommendations. . . . The Commission recommends that federal, state, and local legislation should not seek to interfere with the rights of adults who wish to do so to read, obtain, or view explicit sexual materials. On the other hand, we recommend legislative regulations upon the sale of sexual materials to young persons who do not have the consent of their parents, and we also recommend legislation to protect persons from having sexual materials thrust upon them without their consent through the mails or through open public display. . . .

The Commission believes that there is no warrant for continued governmental interference with the full freedom of adults to read, obtain or view whatever such material they wish. Our conclusion is based upon the following considerations:

1. Extensive empirical investigation . . . provides no evidence that exposure to or use of explicit sexual materials play a significant role in the causation of social or individual harms such as crime, delinquency, sexual or nonsexual deviancy or severe emotional disturbances. . . .
2. On the positive side, explicit sexual materials are sought as a source of entertainment and informa-

tion by substantial numbers of American adults. At times, these materials also appear to serve to increase and facilitate constructive communication about sexual matters within marriages. . . .

3. Society's attempts to legislate for adults in the area of obscenity have not been successful. . . . These vague and highly subjective aesthetic, psychological and moral tests do not provide meaningful guidance for law enforcement officials, juries or courts. As a result, law is inconsistently and sometimes erroneously applied and the distinctions made by courts between prohibited and permissible materials often appear indefensible. . . .

4. Public opinion in America does not support the imposition of legal prohibitions upon the right of adults to read or see explicit sexual materials. . . .

5. The lack of consensus among Americans concerning whether explicit sexual materials should be available to adults in our society, and the significant number of adults who wish to have access to such materials, pose serious problems regarding the enforcement of legal prohibitions upon adults, even aside from the vagueness and subjectivity of present law. Consistent enforcement of even the clearest prohibitions upon consensual adult exposure to explicit sexual materials would require the expenditure of considerable law enforcement resources. . . . Inconsistent enforcement of prohibitions . . . invites discriminatory action based upon considerations not directly relevant to the policy of the law. The latter alternative also breeds public disrespect for the legal process.

. . .

9. The Commission has also taken cognizance of the concern of many people that the lawful distribution of explicit sexual materials to adults may have a deleterious effect upon the individual morality of American citizens and upon the moral climate in America as a whole. This concern appears to flow from a belief that exposure to explicit materials may cause moral confusion which, in turn, may induce antisocial or criminal behavior. . . . The Commission has found no evidence to support such a contention. Nor is there evidence that exposure to explicit sexual materials adversely affects character or moral attitudes regarding sex and sexual conduct. . . .

The Commission is of the view that it is exceedingly unwise for government to attempt to legislate individual moral values and standards independent of behavior, especially by restrictions upon consensual communication. . . .

(3) Stanley v. Georgia (1969)

+Warren, Black, Douglas, Harlan, Brennan, Stewart, White, Fortas, Marshall

MR. JUSTICE MARSHALL delivered the opinion of the Court.

An investigation of appellant's alleged bookmaking activities led to the issuance of a search warrant for appellant's home. Under authority of this warrant, federal and state agents secured entrance. They found very little evidence of bookmaking activity, but while looking through a desk drawer in an upstairs bedroom, one of the federal agents, accompanied by a state officer, found three reels of eight-millimeter film. Using a projector and screen found in an upstairs living room, they viewed the films. The state officer concluded that they were obscene and seized them. Since a further examination of the bedroom indicated that appellant occupied it, he was charged with possession of obscene matter and placed under arrest. He was later indicted for "knowingly hav[ing] possession of obscene matter" in violation of Georgia law. Appellant was tried before a jury and convicted. The Supreme Court of Georgia affirmed. . . .

Appellant raises several challenges to the validity of his conviction. We find it necessary to consider only one. Appellant argues here, and argued below, that the Georgia obscenity statute, insofar as it punishes mere private possession of obscene matter, violates the First Amendment, as made applicable to the States by the Fourteenth Amendment. For reasons set forth below, we agree that the mere private possession of obscene matter cannot constitutionally be made a crime. . . .

It is true that *Roth* does declare, seemingly without qualification, that obscenity is not protected by the First Amendment. . . . However, neither *Roth* nor any subsequent decision of this Court dealt with the precise problem involved in the present case. *Roth* was convicted of mailing obscene circulars and advertising, and an obscene book, in violation of a federal obscenity statute. The defendant in a companion case, *Alberts* v. *California* . . . was convicted of "lewdly keeping for sale obscene and indecent books, and [of] writing, composing and publishing an obscene advertisement of them. . . ." . . . None of the statements cited by the Court in *Roth* for the proposition that "this Court has always assumed that obscenity is not protected by the freedoms of speech and press" were made in the context of a statute punishing mere private possession of obscene material; the cases cited deal for the most part with use of the mails to distribute objectionable ma-

terial or with some form of public distribution or dissemination. Moreover, none of this Court's decisions subsequent to *Roth* involved prosecution for private possession of obscene materials. Those cases dealt with the power of the State and Federal Governments to prohibit or regulate certain public actions taken or intended to be taken with respect to obscene matter. Indeed, with one exception, we have been unable to discover any case in which the issue in the present case has been fully considered.

In this context, we do not believe that this case can be decided simply by citing *Roth*. *Roth* and its progeny certainly do mean that the First and Fourteenth Amendments recognize a valid governmental interest in dealing with the problem of obscenity. But the assertion of that interest cannot, in every context, be insulated from all constitutional protections. Neither *Roth* nor any other decision of this Court reaches that far. . . .

Roth and the cases following it discerned such an "important interest" in the regulation of commercial distribution of obscene material. That holding cannot foreclose an examination of the constitutional implications of a statute forbidding mere private possession of such material. . . .

Appellant . . . is asserting the right to read or observe what he pleases— the right to satisfy his intellectual and emotional needs in the privacy of his own home. He is asserting the right to be free from state inquiry into the contents of his library. Georgia contends that appellant does not have these rights, that there are certain types of materials that the individual may not read or even possess. Georgia justifies this assertion by arguing that the films in the present case are obscene. But we think that mere categorization of these films as "obscene" is insufficient justification for such a drastic invasion of personal liberties guaranteed by the First and Fourteenth Amendments. Whatever may be the justifications for other statutes regulating obscenity, we do not think they reach into the privacy of one's own home. If the First Amendment means anything, it means that a State has no business telling a man, sitting alone in his own house, what books he may read or what films he may watch. Our whole constitutional heritage rebels at the thought of giving government the power to control men's minds.

And yet, in the face of these traditional notions of individual liberty, Georgia asserts the right to protect the individual's mind from the effects of obscenity. We are not certain that this argument amounts to anything more than the assertion that the State has the right to control the moral content of a person's thoughts. To some, this may be a noble purpose, but it is wholly inconsistent with the philosophy of the First Amendment. . . .

Whatever the power of the state to control public dissemination of ideas inimical to the public morality, it cannot constitutionally premise legislation on the desirability of controlling a person's private thoughts. . . .

Judgment reversed and case remanded.

MR. JUSTICE BLACK, CONCURRING (OMITTED.)

MR. JUSTICE STEWART, WITH WHOM MR. JUSTICE BRENNAN AND MR. JUSTICE WHITE JOIN, CONCURRING IN THE RESULT.

Before the commencement of the trial in this case, the appellant filed a motion to suppress the films as evidence upon the ground that they had been seized in violation of the Fourth and Fourteenth Amendments. The motion was denied, and the films were admitted in evidence at the trial. In affirming the appellant's conviction, the Georgia Supreme Court specifically determined that the films had been lawfully seized. The appellant correctly contends that this determination was clearly wrong under established principles of constitutional law. But the Court today disregards this preliminary issue in its hurry to move on to newer constitutional frontiers. I cannot so readily overlook the serious inroads upon Fourth Amendment guarantees countenanced in this case by the Georgia courts. . . .

[Implicit in *Stanley* is the rejection of the *Roth* argument that obscenity may lead to antisocial behavior. Instead, there is the suggestion that the proper constitutional control should be limited to minors and "intrusion upon the sensibilities and privacy of the general public." But in 1971, the Burger Court held that *Stanley* did not give one the right to send obscene materials through the mail, *United States* v. *Reidel*. In *Reidel*, the Court, distinguishing *Stanley* as a privacy case, held that the "right to possess is not the same as the right to receive" obscene material. Similarly, in 1973, the Court ruled in *United States* v. *Twelve 200-Foot Reels* that an importer could not import pornographic films for his own personal use; *Stanley* was again held to stand for privacy within the home and not for the right to receive pornographic material to view in the home. The effect of *Reidel* and *Twelve 200-Foot Reels* is to establish a situation where in order to exercise the constitutionally guaranteed right protected by *Stanley*, a citizen must violate other laws.]

(4) Miller v. California (1973)

+Burger, White, Blackmun, Powell, Rehnquist

−Douglas, Brennan, Stewart, Marshall

[On June 21, 1973, the Supreme Court announced seven decisions that collectively modified the *Roth* approach to obscenity. The main cases are *Miller* v. *California* and *Paris Adult Theater* v. *Slaton,* both of which follow. The other decisions, not reprinted here, made the following contributions: *Kaplan* v. *California* held that "contemporary community standards" meant local, California standards. *Heller* v. *New York* upheld a New York Court of Appeals decision that an adversary hearing prior to seizure of an allegedly obscene film was not constitutionally necessary. *Roaden* v. *Kentucky* repudiated a warrantless seizure of allegedly obscene film. *United States* v. *Twelve 200-Foot Reels of Super 8 mm. Film* upheld a ban on the importation of obscene matter, albeit for private use and possession, and held that *Miller* applied to federal law as well as state law. And *United States* v. *Orito* held that Congress has the power to prevent unprotected obscene matter from entering the stream of commerce.

In *Miller* v. *California,* Miller was convicted of knowingly distributing through the mails brochures advertising four books entitled *Intercourse, Man-Woman, Sex-Orgies Illustrated,* and *An Illustrated History of Pornography,* and a film entitled *Marital Intercourse.* The brochures contained pictures of men and women engaged in explicit sexual activity. One unsolicited copy of Miller's brochure was mailed to, and opened by, a restaurant manager and his mother; their complaint to the police initiated the criminal prosecution that followed.]

MR. CHIEF JUSTICE BURGER delivered the opinion of the Court.

This is one of a group of "obscenity-pornography" cases being reviewed by the Court in a re-examination of standards enunciated in earlier cases involving what Mr. Justice Harlan called "the intractable obscenity problem." . . .

This case involves the application of a State's criminal obscenity statute to a situation in which sexually explicit materials have been thrust by aggressive sales action upon unwilling recipients who had in no way indicated any desire to receive such materials. This Court has recognized that the States have a legitimate interest in prohibiting dissemination or exhibition of obscene material when the mode of dissemination carries with it a significant danger of offending the sensibilities of unwilling recipients or of exposure to juveniles. *Stanley* v. *Georgia* . . . (1969) . . . . It is in this context that we are called on to define the standards which must be used to identify obscene material that a State may regulate without infringing the First Amendment as applicable to the States through the Fourteenth Amendment.

. . . [S]ince the Court now undertakes to formulate standards more concrete than those in the past, it is useful for us to focus on two of the landmark cases in the somewhat tortured history of the Court's obscenity decisions. In *Roth* v. *United States* . . . (1957), the Court sustained a conviction under a federal statute punishing the mailing of "obscene, lewd, lascivious or filthy . . ." materials. The key to that holding was the Court's rejection of the claim that obscene materials were protected by the First Amendment. . . .

Nine years later in *Memoirs* v. *Massachusetts* . . . (1966), the Court veered sharply away from the *Roth* concept and, with only three Justices in the plurality opinion, articulated a new test of obscenity. The plurality held that under the *Roth* definition:

. . . *as elaborated in subsequent cases, three elements must coalesce: it must be established that (a) the dominant theme of the material taken as a whole appeals to a prurient interest in sex; (b) the material is patently offensive because it affronts contemporary community standards relating to the description or representation of sexual matters; and (c) the material is utterly without redeeming social value. . . .*

The sharpness of the break with *Roth,* represented by the third element of the *Memoirs* test . . . ,was further underscored when the *Memoirs* plurality went on to state:

The Supreme Judicial Court erred in holding that a book need not be "unqualifiedly worthless before it can be deemed obscene." A book cannot be proscribed unless it is found to be utterly *without redeeming social value. (Emphasis in original.)* . . .

While *Roth* presumed "obscenity" to be "utterly without redeeming social value," *Memoirs* required that to prove obscenity it must be affirmatively established that the material is *"utterly* without redeeming social value." Thus, even as they repeated the words of *Roth,* the *Memoirs* plurality produced a drastically altered test that called on the prosecution to prove a negative, *i. e.,* that the material was *"utterly* without redeeming social value"—a burden virtually impossible to discharge under our criminal standards of proof. . . .

Apart from the initial formulation in the *Roth* case, no majority of the Court has at any time been able to agree on a standard to determine what constitutes obscene, pornographic material subject to regulation under the States' police power. . . . We have seen "a variety of views among the members of the Court unmatched in any other course of constitutional adjudication". . . . This is remarkable, for in the area of freedom of speech and press the courts must always remain sensitive to any infringement on genuinely serious literary, artistic, political, or scientific expression. This is an area in which there are few eternal verities.

The case we now review was tried on the theory that the California Penal Code . . . approximately incorporates the three-stage *Memoirs* test.

. . . But now the *Memoirs* test has been abandoned as unworkable by its author and no member of the Court today supports the *Memoirs* formulation.

This much has been categorically settled by the Court, that obscene material is unprotected by the First Amendment. . . . We acknowledge, however, the inherent dangers of undertaking to regulate any form of expression. State statutes designed to regulate obscene materials must be carefully limited. . . . As a result, we now confine the permissible scope of such regulation to works which depict or describe sexual conduct. That conduct must be specifically defined by the applicable state law, as written or authoritatively construed. A state offense must also be limited to works which, taken as a whole, appeal to the prurient interest in sex, which portray sexual conduct in a patently offensive way, and which, taken as a whole, do not have serious literary, artistic, political, or scientific value.

The basic guidelines for the trier of fact must be: (a) whether "the average person, applying contemporary community standards" would find that the work, taken as a whole, appeals to the prurient interest. . . . (b) whether the work depicts or describes, in a patently offensive way, sexual conduct specifically defined by the applicable state law, and (c) whether the work, taken as a whole, lacks serious literary, artistic, political, or scientific value. We do not adopt as a constitutional standard the *"utterly* without redeeming social value" test of *Memoirs* v. *Massachusetts* . . . (1966); that concept has never commanded the adherence of more than three Justices at one time. . . . If a state law that regulates obscene material is thus limited, as written or construed, the First

Amendment values applicable to the States through the Fourteenth Amendment are adequately protected by the ultimate power of appellate courts to conduct an independent review of constitutional claims when necessary. . . .

Under the holdings announced today, no one will be subject to prosecution for the sales or exposure of obscene materials unless these materials depict or describe patently offensive "hard core" sexual conduct specifically defined by the regulating state law, as written or construed. We are satisfied that these specific prerequisites will provide fair notice to a dealer in such materials that his public and commercial activities may bring prosecution. . . . If the inability to define regulated materials with ultimate, god-like precision altogether removes the power of the States or the Congress to regulate, then "hard core" pornography may be exposed without limit to the juvenile, the passerby, and the consenting adult alike, as, indeed, Mr. Justice Douglas contends. . . . In this belief, however, Mr. Justice Douglas now stands alone.

Mr. Justice Brennan also emphasizes "institutional stress" in justification of his change of view. Noting that "the number of obscenity cases on our docket gives ample testimony to the burden that has been placed upon this Court," he quite rightly remarks that the examination of contested materials "is hardly a source of edification to members of this Court." . . . He also notes, and we agree, that "uncertainty of the standards creates a continuing source of tension between state and federal courts . . . ." "The problem is . . . that one cannot say with certainty that material is obscene until at least five members of this Court, applying inevitably obscure standards, have pronounced it so." . . .

It is certainly true that the absence, since *Roth,* of a single majority view of this Court as to proper standards for testing obscenity has placed a strain on both state and federal courts. But today, for the first time since *Roth* was decided in 1957, a majority of this Court has agreed on concrete guidelines to isolate "hard core" pornography from expression protected by the First Amendment. . . .

This may not be an easy road, free from difficulty. But no amount of "fatigue" should lead us to adopt a convenient "institutional" rationale—an absolutist, "anything goes" view of the First Amendment— because it will lighten our burdens. . . . Nor should we remedy "tension between state and federal courts" by arbitrarily depriving the States of a power reserved to them under the Constitution, a power which they have enjoyed and exercised continuously from before the adoption of the First Amendment to this day. . . .

Under a national Constitution, fundamental First Amendment limitations on the powers of the States do not vary from community to community, but this does not mean that there are, or should or can be, fixed, uniform national standards of precisely what appeals to the "prurient interest" or is "patently offensive." These are essentially questions of fact, and our nation is simply too big and too diverse for this Court to reasonably expect that such standards could be articulated for all 50 States in a single formulation, even assuming the prerequisite consensus exists. When triers of fact are asked to decide whether "the average person, applying contemporary community standards" would consider certain materials "prurient," it would be unrealistic to require that the answer be based on some abstract formulation.

The adversary system, with lay jurors as the usual ultimate factfinders, in criminal prosecutions, has historically permitted triers-of-fact to draw on the standards of their community, guided always by limiting instructions on the law. To require a State to structure obscenity proceedings around evidence of a *national* "community standard" would be an exercise in futility.

As noted before, this case was tried on the theory that the California obscenity statute sought to incorporate the tripartite test of *Memoirs*. This, a "national" standard of First Amendment protection enumerated by a plurality of this Court, was correctly regarded at the time of trial as limiting state prosecution under the controlling case law. The jury, however, was explicitly instructed that, in determining whether the "dominant theme of the material as a whole . . . appeals to the prurient interest" and in determining whether the material "goes substantially beyond customary limits of candor and affronts contemporary community standards of decency" it was to apply "contemporary community standards of the State of California." . . .

We conclude that neither the State's alleged failure to offer evidence of "national standards," nor the trial court's charge that the jury consider state community standards, were constitutional errors. Nothing in the First Amendment requires that a jury must consider hypothetical and unascertainable "national standards" when attempting to determine whether certain materials are obscene as a matter of fact. . . .

It is neither realistic nor constitutionally sound to read the First Amendment as requiring that the people of Maine or Mississippi accept public depiction of conduct found tolerable in Las Vegas, or New York City. . . . People in different States vary in their tastes and attitudes, and this diversity is not to be strangled by the absolutism of imposed uniformity. As the Court made clear in *Mishkin* v. *New York* . . . (1966), the primary concern with requiring a jury to apply the standard of "the average person, applying contemporary community standards" is to be certain that, so far as material is not aimed at a deviant group, it will be judged by its impact on an average person, rather than a particularly susceptible or sensitive person—or indeed a totally insensitive one. . . . We hold the requirement that the jury evaluate the materials with reference to "contemporary standards of the State of California" serves this protective purpose and is constitutionally adequate.

The dissenting Justices sound the alarm of repression. But, in our view, to equate the free and robust exchange of ideas and political debate with commercial exploitation of obscene material demeans the grand conception of the First Amendment and its high purposes in the historic struggle for freedom. . . . The First Amendment protects works which taken as a whole, have serious literary, artistic, political or scientific value, regardless of whether the government or a majority of the people approve of the ideas these works represent. . . . But the public portrayal of hard core sexual conduct for its own sake, and for the ensuing commercial gain, is a different matter.

There is no evidence, empirical or historical, that the stern 19th century American censorship of public distribution and display of material relating to sex, . . . in anyway limited or affected expression of serious literary, artistic, political, or scientific ideas. On the contrary, it is beyond any question that the era following

Thomas Jefferson to Theodore Roosevelt was an "extraordinarily vigorous period" not just in economics and politics, but in *belles lettres* and in "the outlying fields of social and political philosophies." We do not see the harsh hand of censorship of ideas—good or bad, sound or unsound—and "repression" of political liberty lurking in every state regulation of commercial exploitation of human interest in sex.

Mr. Justice Brennan finds "it is hard to see how state-ordered regimentation of our minds can ever be forestalled." . . . These doleful anticipations assume that courts cannot distinguish commerce in ideas, protected by the First Amendment, from commercial exploitation of obscene material. Moreover, state regulation of hard core pornography so as to make it unavailable to nonadults, a regulation which Mr. Justice Brennan finds constitutionally permissible, had all the elements of "censorship" for adults; indeed even more rigid enforcement techniques may be called for with such dichotomy of regulation. . . . One can concede that the "sexual revolution" of recent years may have had useful by-products in striking layers of prudery from a subject long irrationally kept from needed ventilation. But it does not follow that no regulation of patently offensive "hard-core" materials is needed or permissible; civilized people do not allow unregulated access to heroin because it is a derivative of medicinal morphine.

In sum we (a) reaffirm the *Roth* holding that obscene material is not protected by the First Amendment, (b) hold that such material can be regulated by the States, subject to the specific safeguards enunciated above, without a showing that the material is *"utterly* without redeeming social value," and (c) hold that

obscenity is to be determined by applying "contemporary community standards," . . .

Vacated and remanded for further proceedings.

MR. JUSTICE DOUGLAS, DISSENTING.

Today we leave open the way for California to send a man to prison for distributing brochures that advertise books and a movie under freshly written standards defining obscenity which until today's decision were never the part of any law.

The Court has worked hard to define obscenity and concededly has failed. . . .

. . . [E]ven those members of this Court who had created the new and changing standards of "obscenity" could not agree on their application. And so we adopted a *per curiam* treatment of so-called obscene publications that seemed to pass constitutional muster under the several constitutional tests which had been formulated. See *Redrup* v. *New York* . . . [1967]. . . .

Today the Court retreats from the earlier formulations of the constitutional test and undertakes to make new definitions. This effort, like the earlier ones, is earnest and well-intentioned. The difficulty is that we do not deal with constitutional terms, since "obscenity" is not mentioned in the Constitution or Bill of Rights. And the First Amendment makes no such exception from "the press" which it undertakes to protect nor, as I have said on other occasions, is an exception necessarily implied, for there was no recognized exception to the free press at the time the Bill of Rights was adopted which treated "obscene" publications differently from other types of papers, magazines, and books. So there are no constitutional guidelines for deciding what is and what is not "obscene." The Court is at large because we deal with tastes and standards of literature. What shocks me may be sustenance for my neighbor. What causes one person to boil up in rage over one pamphlet or movie may reflect only his neurosis, not shared by others. We deal here with problems of censorship which, if adopted, should be done by constitutional amendment after full debate by the people.

Obscenity cases usually generate tremendous emotional outbursts. They have no business being in the courts. If a constitutional amendment authorized censorship, the censor would probably be an administrative agency. Then criminal prosecutions could follow as if and when publishers defied the censor and sold their literature. Under that regime a publisher would know when he was on dangerous ground. Under the present regime—whether the old standards or the new ones are used—the criminal law becomes a trap.

My contention is that until a civil proceeding has placed a tract beyond the pale, no criminal prosecution should be sustained. . . .

MR. JUSTICE BRENNAN, WITH WHOM MR. JUSTICE STEWART AND MR. JUSTICE MARSHALL JOIN, DISSENTING (OMITTED).

[See Justice Brennan's dissent in *Paris Adult Theatre* v. *Slaton*, below.]

(5) Paris Adult Theatre v. Slaton (1973)

+Burger, White, Blackmun, Powell, Rehnquist
−Douglas, Brennan, Stewart, Marshall

[Petitioners are theaters in Atlanta, Georgia, against whom civil actions were filed by local law enforcement officials. The action maintained that the theaters were exhibiting allegedly obscene films, in violation of state statutes. The local trial court did not, as requested in the state's action, enjoin their exhibition, but it did restrain petitioners from destroying the films. During the trial, it was made clear that the films were shown to the public with ample warning as to their nature. The trial judge dismissed the state's request on the grounds that even though obscenity had been established, exhibition of the films with adequate notice of their nature, and with reasonable precautions against their exposure to minors, was constitutionally permissible. The Georgia Supreme Court reversed unanimously, holding that the films were without constitutional protection, and their exhibition should have been enjoined.

In an opinion by Chief Justice Burger, the case was remanded for reconsideration in light of *Miller, supra.* The fundamental thrust of the opinion is to "hold that there are legitimate state interests at stake in stemming the tide of commercialized obscenity." Thus, the *Miller* redefinition of the guidelines emanating from the *Roth* line of precedents is to be used in an apparent widening of state authority to regulate traffic in obscene material.]

MR. JUSTICE DOUGLAS, DISSENTING (OMITTED).
MR. JUSTICE BRENNAN, WITH WHOM MR. JUSTICE STEWART AND MR. JUSTICE MARSHALL JOIN, DISSENTING.

This case requires the Court to confront once again the vexing problem of reconciling state efforts to suppress sexually oriented expression with the protections of the First Amendment, as applied to the States through the Fourteenth Amendment. No other aspect of the First Amendment has, in recent years, demanded so substantial a commitment of our time, generated such disharmony of views, and remained so resistant to the formulation of stable and manageable standards. I am convinced that the approach initiated 15 years ago in *Roth* v. *United States* (1957), and culminating in the Court's decision today, cannot bring stablity to this area of the law without jeopardizing fundamental First Amendment values, and I have concluded that the time has come to make a significant departure from that approach. . . .

. . . The decision of the Georgia Supreme Court rested squarely on its conclusion that the State could constitutionally suppress these films even if they were displayed only to persons over the age of 21 who were aware of the nature of their contents and who had consented to viewing them. For the reasons set forth in this opinion, I am convinced of the invalidity of the conclusion of law, and I would therefore vacate the judgment of the Georgia Supreme Court. I have no occasion to consider the extent of state power to regulate the distribution of sexually oriented materials to juveniles or to unconsenting adults. Nor am I required, for the purposes of this appeal, to consider whether or not these petitioners had, in fact, taken precautions to avoid exposure of films to minors or unconsenting adults.

. . . The essence of our problem in the obscenity area is that we have been unable to provide "sensitive tools" to separate obscenity from other sexually oriented but constitutionally protected speech, so that efforts to suppress the former do not spill over into the suppression of the latter. The attempt, as the late Mr. Justice Harlan observed, has only "produced a variety of views among the members of the Court unmatched in any other course of constitutional adjudication." . . .

To be sure, five members of the Court did agree in *Roth* that obscenity could be determined by asking "whether to the average person, applying contemporary community standards, the dominant theme of the material taken as a whole appeals to prurient interest." . . . But agreement on that test—achieved in the abstract and without reference to the particular material before the Court, . . . was, to say the least, short lived. By 1967 the following views had emerged: Mr. Justice Black and Mr. Justice Douglas consistently maintained that government is wholly powerless to regulate any sexually oriented matter on the ground of its obscenity. See, *e.g.*, *Ginzburg* v. *United States* . . . (1966) (dissenting opinions); . . . Mr. Justice Harlan, on the other hand, believed that the Federal Government in the exercise of its enumerated powers could control the distribution of "hard-core" pornography, while the States were afforded more latitude to "[ban] any material which, taken as a whole, has been reasonably found in state judicial proceedings to treat with sex in a fundamentally offensive manner, under rationally established criteria for judging such material." *Jacobellis* v. *Ohio* . . . (1973); Mr. Justice Stewart regarded "hard-core" pornography as the limit of both federal and state power. See, *e.g.*, *Ginzburg* v. *United States* . . . (dissenting opinion); . . .

The view that, until today, enjoyed the most, but not majority, support was an interpretation of *Roth* (and not, as the Court suggests, a veering "sharply away from the *Roth* concept" and the articulation of "a new test of obscenity," . . .) adopted by Mr. Chief Justice Warren, Mr. Justice Fortas, and the author of this opinion in *Memoirs* v. *Massachusetts* . . . (1966). We expressed the view that Federal or State Governments could control the distribution of material where "three elements . . . coalesce. It must be established that (a) the dominant theme of the material taken as a whole appeals to a prurient interest in sex; (b) the material is patently offensive because it affronts contemporary community standards relating to the description or representation of sexual matters; and (c) the material is utterly without redeeming social value." . . .

In the face of this divergence of opinion the Court began the practice in 1967 in *Redrup* v. *New York*, . . . of *per curiam* reversals of convictions for the dissemination of materials that at least five members of the Court, applying their separate tests, deemed not to be obscene. This approach capped the attempt in *Roth* to separate all forms of sexually oriented expression into two categories—the one subject to full governmental suppression and the other beyond the reach of governmental regulation to the same extent as any other protected form of speech or press. Today a majority of the Court offers a slightly altered formulation of the basic *Roth* test, while leaving entirely unchanged the underlying approach.

Our experience with the *Roth* approach has certainly taught us that the outright suppression of obscenity cannot be reconciled with the fundamental principles of the First and Fourteenth Amendments. For we have failed to formulate a standard that sharply distinguishes protected from unprotected speech, and out of necessity, we have resorted to the *Redrup* approach, which resolves cases as between the parties, but offers only the most obscure guidance to legislation, adjudication by other courts, and primary conduct. By disposing of cases through summary reversal or denial of certiorari we have deliberately and effectively obscured the rationale underlying the decision. It comes as no surprise that judicial attempts to follow our lead conscientiously have often ended in hopeless confusion.

Of course, the vagueness problem would be largely of our own creation if it stemmed primarily from our failure to reach a consensus on any one standard. But after 15 years of experimentation and debate I am reluctantly forced to the conclusion that none of the available formulas, including the one announced today, can reduce the vagueness to a tolerable level while at the same time striking an acceptable balance between the protections of the First and Fourteenth Amendments, on the one hand, and on the other the asserted state interest in regulating the dissemination of certain sexually oriented materials. Any effort to draw a constitutionally acceptable boundary on state power must resort to such indefinite concepts as "prurient interest," "patent offensiveness," "serious literary value," and the like. The meaning of these concepts necessarily varies with the experience, outlook, and even idiosyncrasies of the person defining them. Although we have assumed that obscenity does exist and that we "know it when [we] see it," *Jacobellis* v. *Ohio* . . . (1964) (Stewart, J., concurring), we are manifestly unable to describe it in advance except by reference to concepts so elusive that they fail to distinguish clearly between protected and unprotected speech. . . .

The vagueness of the standards in the obscenity area produces a number of separate problems, and any improvement must rest on an understanding that the problems are to some extent distinct. First, a vague statute fails to provide adequate notice to persons who are engaged in the type of conduct that the statute could be thought to proscribe. The Due Process Clause of the Fourteenth

Amendment requires that all criminal law provide fair notice of "what the State commands or forbids." . . .

In addition to problems that arise when any criminal statute fails to afford fair notice of what it forbids, a vague statute in the areas of speech and press creates a second level of difficulty. We have indicated that "stricter standards of permissible statutory vagueness may be applied to a statute having a potentially inhibiting effect on speech; a man may the less be required to act at his peril here, because the free dissemination of ideas may be the loser." *Smith* v. *California* (1959). . . .

To implement this general principle, and recognizing the inherent vagueness of any definition of obscenity, we have held that the definition of obscenity must be drawn as narrowly as possible so as to minimize the interference with protected expression. . . .

The problems of fair notice and chilling protected speech are very grave standing alone. But it does not detract from their importance to recognize that a vague statute in this area creates a third, although admittedly more subtle, set of problems. These problems concern the institutional stress that inevitably results where the line separating protected from unprotected speech is excessively vague. In *Roth* we conceded that "there may be marginal cases in which it is difficult to determine the side of the line on which a particular fact situation falls. . . ." . . . Our subsequent experience demonstrates that almost every case is "marginal." And since the "margin" marks the point of separation between protected and unprotected speech, we are left with a system in which almost every obscenity case presents a constitutional question of exceptional difficulty.

As a result of our failure to define standards with predictable application to any given piece of material, there is no probability of regularity in obscenity decisions by state and lower federal courts. That is not to say that these courts have performed badly in the area or paid insufficient attention to the principles we have established. The problem is, rather, that one cannot say with certainty that material is obscene until at least five members of this Court, applying inevitably obscure standards, have pronounced it so. The number of obscenity cases on our docket gives ample testimony to the burden that has been placed upon this Court.

But the sheer number of the cases does not define the full extent of the institutional problem. For quite apart from the number of cases involved and the need to make a fresh constitutional determination in each case, we are tied to the "absurd business of perusing and viewing the miserable stuff that pours into the Court. . . ." *Interstate Circuit, Inc.* v. *Dallas* . . . (1968) (Harlan, J., dissenting). While the material may have varying degrees of social importance, it is hardly a source of edification to the members of this Court who are compelled to view it before passing on its obscenity. . . .

Moreover, we have managed the burden of deciding scores of obscenity cases by relying on *per curiam* reversals or denials of certiorari—a practice which conceals the rationale of decision and gives at least the appearance of arbitrary action by this Court. . . . More important, . . . the practice effectively censors protected expression by leaving lower court determinations of obscenity intact even though the status of the allegedly obscene material is entirely unsettled until final review here. In addition, the uncertainty of the standards creates a continuing source of tension between state and federal courts, since the need for an independent determination by this Court seems to render superfluous even the most conscientious analysis by state tribunals. And our inability to justify our decisions with a persuasive rationale—or indeed, any rationale at all—necessarily creates the impression that we are merely second-guessing state court judges.

The severe problems arising from the lack of fair notice, from the chill on protected expression, and from the stress imposed on the state and federal judicial machinery persuade me that a significant change in direction is urgently required. I turn, therefore, to the alternatives that are now open.

1. The approach requiring the smallest deviation from our present course would be to draw a new line between protected and unprotected speech, still permitting the States to suppress all material on the unprotected side of the line. In my view, clarity cannot be obtained pursuant to this approach except by drawing a line that resolves all doubts in favor of state power and against the guarantees of the First Amendment. We could hold, for example, that any depiction or description of human sexual organs, irrespective of the manner or purpose of the portrayal, is outside the protection of the First Amendment and therefore open to suppression by the States. That formula would, no doubt, offer much fairer notice of the reach of any state statute drawn at the boundary of the State's constitutional power. And it would also, in all likelihood, give rise to a substantial probability of regularity in most judicial determinations under the standard. But such a standard would be appallingly overbroad, permitting the suppression of a vast range of literary, scientific, and artistic masterpieces. Neither the First Amendment nor any free community could possibly tolerate such a standard. Yet short of that extreme it is hard to see how any choice of words could reduce the vagueness problem to tolerable proportions, so long as we remain committed to the view that some class of materials is subject to outright suppression by the State.

2. The alternative adopted by the Court today recognizes that a prohibition against any depiction or description of human sexual organs could not be reconciled with the guarantees of the First Amendment. But the Court does retain the view that certain sexually oriented material can be considered obscene and therefore unprotected by the First and Fourteenth Amendments. To describe that unprotected class of expression, the Court adopts a restatement of the *Roth-Memoirs* definition of obscenity: "The basic guidelines for the trier of fact must be: (a) whether 'the average person, applying contemporary community standards' would find that the work, taken as a whole, appeals to the prurient interest. . . . (b) whether the work depicts or describes, in a patently offensive way, sexual conduct specifically defined by the applicable state law, and (c) whether the work, taken as a whole, lacks serious literary, artistic, political or scientific value."

The Court evidently recognizes that difficulties with the *Roth* approach necessitate a significant change of direction. But the Court does not describe its understanding of those difficulties, nor does it indicate how the restatement of the *Memoirs* test is in any way responsive to the problems that have arisen. In my view, the restatement leaves unresolved the very difficulties that com-

CREATIVE EXPRESSION AND PUBLIC AUTHORITY ■ **1255**

pel our rejection of the underlying *Roth* approach, while at the same time contributing substantial difficulties of its own. The modification of the *Memoirs* test may prove sufficient to jeopardize the analytic underpinnings of the entire scheme. And today's restatement will likely have the effect, whether or not intended, of permitting far more sweeping suppression of sexually oriented expression, including expression that would almost surely be held protected under our current formulation.

Although the Court's restatement substantially tracks the three-part test announced in *Memoirs* v. *Massachusetts, supra,* it does purport to modify the "social value" component of the text. Instead of requiring, as did *Roth* and *Memoirs* that state suppression be limited to material utterly lacking in social value, the Court today permits suppression if the government can prove that the materials lack "*serious* literary, artistic, political or scientific value." But the definition of "obscenity" as expression utterly lacking in social importance is the key to the conceptual basis of *Roth* and our subsequent opinions. In *Roth* we held that certain expression is obscene, and thus outside the protection of the First Amendment, precisely *because* it lacks even the slightest redeeming social value. . . . The Court's approach necessarily assumes that some works will be deemed obscene—even though they clearly have *some* social value— because the State was able to prove that the value, measured by some unspecified standard, was not sufficiently "serious" to warrant constitutional protection. That result is not merely inconsistent with our holding in *Roth;* it is nothing less than a rejection of the fundamental First Amendment premises and rationale of the *Roth* opinion and an invitation

to widespread suppression of sexually oriented speech. Before today, the protections of the First Amendment have never been thought limited to expressions of *serious* literary or political value. . . .

3. I have also considered the possibility of reducing our own role, and the role of appellate courts generally, in determining whether particular matter is obscene. Thus, we might conclude that juries are best suited to determine obscenity *vel non* and that jury verdicts in this area should not be set aside except in cases of extreme departure from prevailing standards. Or, more generally, we might adopt the position that where a lower federal or state court has conscientiously applied the constitutional standard, its finding of obscenity will be no more vulnerable to reversal by this Court than any finding of fact. . . .

4. Finally, I have considered the view, urged so forcefully since 1957 by our Brothers Black and Douglas, that the First Amendment bars the suppression of any sexually oriented expression. That position would effect a sharp reduction, although perhaps not a total elimination, of the uncertainty that surrounds our current approach. Nevertheless, I am convinced that it would achieve that desirable goal only by stripping the States of power to an extent that cannot be justified by the commands of the Constitution, at least so long as there is available an alternative approach that strikes a better balance between the guarantee of free expression and the State's legitimate interests.

Our experience since *Roth* requires us not only to abandon the effort to pick out obscene materials on a case-by-case basis, but also to reconsider a fundamental postulate of

Roth: that there exists a definable class of sexually oriented expression that may be totally suppressed by the Federal and State Governments. Assuming that such a class of expression does in fact exist, I am forced to conclude that the concept of "obscenity" cannot be defined with sufficient specificity and clarity to provide fair notice to persons who create and distribute sexually oriented materials, to prevent substantial erosion of protected speech as a by-product of the attempt to suppress unprotected speech, and to avoid very costly institutional harms. Given these inevitable side-effects of state efforts to suppress what is assumed to be *unprotected* speech, we must scrutinize with care the state interest that is asserted to justify the suppression. For in the absence of some very substantial interest in suppressing such speech, we can hardly condone the ill-effects that seem to flow inevitably from the effort. . . .

[W]hile I cannot say that the interests of the States—apart from the question of juveniles and unconsenting adults—are trivial or nonexistent, I am compelled to conclude that these interests cannot justify the substantial damage to constitutional rights and to this Nation's judicial machinery that inevitably results from state efforts to bar the distribution even of unprotected material to consenting adults. . . . I would hold, therefore, that at least in the absence of distribution to juveniles or obtrusive exposure to unconsenting adults, the First and Fourteenth Amendments prohibit the state and federal governments from attempting wholly to suppress sexually oriented materials on the basis of their allegedly "obscene" contents. Nothing in this approach precludes those governments from taking action to serve what may be strong and legitimate interests through regulation of the manner of distribution of sexually oriented material.

. . . It is surely the duty of this Court, as expounder of the Constitution, to provide a remedy for the present unsatisfactory state of affairs. . . . Difficult questions must still be faced, notably in the areas of distribution to juveniles and offensive exposure to unconsenting adults. Whatever the extent of state power to regulate in those areas, it should be clear that the view I espouse today would introduce a large measure of clarity to this troubled area, would reduce the institutional pressure on this Court and the rest of the State and Federal judiciary, and would guarantee fuller freedom of expression while leaving room for the protection of legitimate governmental interests. Since the Supreme Court of Georgia erroneously concluded that the State has power to suppress sexually oriented material even in the absence of distribution to juveniles or exposure to unconsenting adults, I would reverse that judgment and remand the case to that court for further proceedings not inconsistent with this opinion.

(6) Jenkins v. Georgia (1974)

+Burger, Douglas, Brennan, Stewart, White, Marshall, Blackmun, Powell, Rehnquist

[Jenkins, manager of a theater, was convicted and fined $750 for showing the film *Carnal Knowledge.* He was convicted under a Georgia statute that defined obscenity in conformity with the plurality opinion in *Memoirs* v. *Massachusetts* (1966). His conviction was affirmed by the Supreme Court of Georgia on a divided vote, and he appealed to the U.S. Supreme Court.]

MR. JUSTICE REHNQUIST delivered the opinion of the Court.

. . .

We conclude here that the film "Carnal Knowledge" is not obscene under the constitutional standards announced in *Miller* v. *California*, . . . and that the First and Fourteenth Amendments therefore require that the judgment of the Supreme Court of Georgia affirming appellant's conviction be reversed.

. . .

We agree with the Supreme Court of Georgia's implicit ruling that the Constitution does not require that juries be instructed in state obscenity cases to apply the standards of a hypothetical statewide community. *Miller* approved the use of such instructions; it did not mandate their use. What *Miller* makes clear is that state juries need not be instructed to apply "national standards." We also agree with the Supreme Court of Georgia's implicit approval of the trial court's instructions directing jurors to apply "community standards" without specifying what "community." *Miller* held that it was constitutionally permissible to permit juries to rely on the understanding of the community from which they came as to contemporary community standards, and the States have considerable latitude in framing statutes under this element of the *Miller* decision. A State may choose to define an obscenity offense in terms of "contemporary community standards" as defined in *Miller* without further specification, as was done here, or it may choose to define the standards in more precise geographic terms, as was done by California in *Miller*.

We now turn to the question of whether appellant's exhibition of the film was protected by the First and Fourteenth Amendments, . . .

Appellee contends essentially that under *Miller* the obscenity *vel non* of the film "Carnal Knowledge" was a question for the jury, and that the jury having resolved the question against appellant, and there being some evidence to support its findings, the judgment of conviction should be affirmed. We turn to the language of *Miller* to evaluate appellee's contention.

Miller states that the question of what appeals to the "prurient interest" and what is "patently offensive" under the obscenity test which it formulates are "essentially questions of fact." . . . "When triers of fact are asked to decide whether 'the average person, applying community standards' would consider certain materials 'prurient' it would be unrealistic to require that the answer be based on some abstract formulation. . . . To require a State to structure obscenity proceedings around evidence of a *national* 'community standard' would be an exercise in futility." . . . We held in *Paris Adult Theater I* v. *Slaton* . . . (1973), decided on the same day, that expert testimony as to obscenity is not necessary when the films at issue are themselves placed in evidence. . . .

But all of this does not lead us to agree with the Supreme Court of Georgia's apparent conclusion that the jury's verdict against appellant virtually precluded all further appellate review of appellant's assertion that his exhibition of the film was protected by the First and Fourteenth Amendments. Even though questions of appeal to the "prurient interest" or of patent offensiveness are "essentially questions of fact," it would be serious misreading of *Miller* to conclude that juries have unbridled discretion in determining what is "patently offensive." Not only did we there say that "the First Amendment values applicable to the States through the Fourteenth Amendment are adequately protected by the ultimate power of appellate courts to conduct an independent review of constitutional claims when necessary," . . . but we made it plain that under that holding "no one will be subject to prosecution for the sale or exposure of obscene materials unless these materials depict or describe patently offensive 'hard core' sexual conduct. . . ." . . .

We also took pains in *Miller* to "give a few plain examples of what a state could define for regulation under part (b) of the standard announced," that is, the requirement of patent offensiveness, . . . These examples included "representation or descriptions of ultimate sexual acts, normal or perverted, actual or simulated," and "representation or descriptions of masturbation, excretory functions, and lewd exhibition of the genitals." . . . While this did not purport to be an exhaustive catalog of what juries might find patently offensive, it was certainly intended to fix substantive constitutional limitations, deriving from the First Amendment, on the type of material subject to such a determination. It would be wholly at odds with this aspect of *Miller* to uphold an obscenity conviction based upon a defendant's depiction of a woman with a bare midriff, even though a properly charged jury unanimously agreed on a verdict of guilty.

Our own view of the film satisfies us that "Carnal Knowledge" could not be found under the *Miller* standards to depict sexual conduct in a patently offensive way. Nothing in the movie falls within either of the two examples given in *Miller* of material which may constitutionally be found to meet the "patently offensive" element of those standards, nor is there anything sufficiently similar to such material to justify similar treatment. While the subject matter of the picture is, in a broader sense, sex, and there are scenes in which sexual conduct including "ultimate sexual acts" is to be understood to be

taking place, the camera does not focus on the bodies of the actors at such times. There is no exhibition whatever of the actors' genitals, lewd or otherwise, during these scenes. There are occasional scenes of nudity, but nudity alone is not enough to make material legally obscene under the *Miller* standards.

Appellant's showing of the film "Carnal Knowledge" is simply not the "public portrayal of hard core sexual conduct for its own sake, and for ensuing commercial gain" which we said was punishable in *Miller*. We hold that the film could not, as a matter of constitutional law, be found to depict sexual conduct in a patently offensive way, and that it is therefore not outside the protection of the First and Fourteenth Amendments because it is obscene. No other basis appearing in the record upon which the judgment of conviction can be sustained, we reverse the judgment of the Supreme Court of Georgia.

Reversed.

MR. JUSTICE BRENNAN, WITH WHOM MR. JUSTICE STEWART AND MR. JUSTICE MARSHALL JOIN, CONCURRING IN THE RESULT.

. . . Today's decision confirms my observation in *Paris Adult Theater I.* v. *Slaton* . . . (1973), that the Court's new formulation does not extricate us from the mire of case-by-case determinations of obscenity. . . .

After the Court's decision today, there can be no doubt that *Miller* requires appellate courts—including this Court—to review independently the constitutional fact of obscenity. Moreover, the Court's task is not limited to reviewing a jury finding under part (c) of the *Miller* test that "the work, taken as a whole, lack[ed] serious literary, artistic, political, or scientific value." *Miller* also requires independent review of a jury's determination under part (b) of the *Miller* test that "the work depicts or describes, in a patently offensive way, sexual conduct specifically defined by the applicable state law." . . .

Thus, it is clear that as long as the *Miller* test remains in effect "one cannot say with certainty that material is obscene until at least five members of this Court, applying inevitably obscure standards, have pronounced it so." *Paris Adult Theater I* v. *Slaton* . . . (Brennan, J., dissenting). Because of the attendant uncertainty of such a process and its inevitable institutional stress upon the judiciary, I continue to adhere to my view that, "at least in the absence of distribution to juveniles or obtrusive exposure to unconsenting adults, the First and Fourteenth Amendments prohibit the State and Federal Governments from attempting wholly to suppress sexually oriented materials on the basis of their allegedly 'obscene' contents." . . . It is clear that, tested by that constitutional standard, the Georgia obscenity statutes under which appellant Jenkins was convicted are constitutionally overbroad and therefore facially invalid. I therefore concur in the Court's judgment reversing Jenkins' conviction.

MR. JUSTICE DOUGLAS, being of the view that any ban on obscenity is prohibited by the First Amendment, made applicable to the States through the Fourteenth, CONCURS IN THE REVERSAL OF THIS CONVICTION. . . .

(7) Erznoznik v. Jacksonville (1975)

+Powell, Douglas, Brennan, Stewart, Marshall, Blackmun'
−Burger, White, Rehnquist

[Erznoznik, the manager of a drive-in theater in Florida, was charged with violating a munici-

pal ordinance by showing an "R" rated movie entitled *Class of '74,* in which "female buttocks and bare breasts" were shown. The ordinance prohibited drive-in theaters from showing of any film that portrayed human nudity if the film could be seen "from any public street or public place." Prosecution was stayed while the validity of the ordinance was tested in a separate lawsuit.]

MR. JUSTICE POWELL delivered the opinion of the Court.

. . .

Appellee concedes that its ordinance sweeps far beyond the permissible restraints on obscenity, see *Miller* v. *California* . . . (1973), and thus applies to films that are protected by the First Amendment. See *Joseph Burstyn, Inc.* v. *Wilson* . . . (1952) *Jenkins* v. *Georgia* . . . (1974). Nevertheless, it maintains that any movie containing nudity which is visible from a public place may be suppressed as a nuisance. Several theories are advanced to justify this contention.

Appellee's primary argument is that it may protect its citizens against unwilling exposure to materials that may be offensive. Jacksonville's ordinance, however, does not protect citizens from all movies that might offend; rather it singles out films containing nudity, presumably because the lawmakers considered them especially offensive to passersby.

This Court has considered analogous issues—pitting the First Amendment rights of speakers against the privacy rights of those who may be unwilling viewers or auditors—in a variety of contexts. . . .

Although each case ultimately must depend on its own specific facts, some general principles have emerged. A State or municipality may protect individual privacy by enacting reasonable time, place, and manner regulations applicable to all speech irrespective of content. . . .

But when the government, acting as censor, undertakes selectively to shield the public from some kinds of speech on the ground that they are more offensive than others, the First Amendment strictly limits its power. . . . Such selective restrictions have been upheld only when the speaker intrudes on the privacy of the home, . . . or the degree of captivity makes it impractical for the unwilling viewer or auditor to avoid exposure. . . .

The plain, if at times disquieting, truth is that in our pluralistic society, constantly proliferating new and ingenious forms of expression, "we are inescapably captive audiences for many purposes." . . . Much that we encounter offends our esthetic, if not our political and moral, sensibilities. Nevertheless, the Constitution does not permit the government to decide which types of otherwise protected speech are sufficiently offensive to require protection for the unwilling listener or viewer. Rather, absent the narrow circumstances described above, the burden normally falls upon the viewer to "avoid further bombardment of [his] sensibilities simply by averting [his] eyes." . . .

The Jacksonville ordinance discriminates among movies solely on the basis of content. Its effect is to deter drive-in theaters from showing movies containing any nudity, however innocent or even educational. This discrimination cannot be justified as a means of preventing significant intrusions on privacy. The ordinance seeks only to keep these films from being seen from public streets and places where the offended viewer readily can avert his eyes. In short, the screen of a drive-in theater is not "so obtrusive as to make it impossible for an unwilling individual to avoid exposure to it." . . . Thus, we conclude that the limited privacy interest of persons on the public streets can-

not justify this censorship of otherwise protected speech on the basis of its content.

Appellee also attempts to support the ordinance as an exercise of the city's undoubted police power to protect children. Appellee maintains that even though it cannot prohibit the display of films containing nudity to adults, the present ordinance is a reasonable means of protecting minors from this type of visual influence.

It is well settled that a State or municipality can adopt more stringent controls on communicative materials available to youths than on those available to adults. . . . Nevertheless, minors are entitled to a significant measure of First Amendment protection . . . and only in relatively narrow and well-defined circumstances may government bar public dissemination of protected materials to them. . . .

In this case, assuming the ordinance is aimed at prohibiting youths from viewing the films, the restriction is broader than permissible. The ordinance is not directed against sexually explicit nudity, nor it is otherwise limited. Rather, its sweeping forbids display of all films containing any uncovered buttocks or breasts, irrespective of context or pervasiveness. Thus it would bar a film containing a picture of a baby's buttocks, the nude body of a war victim, or scenes from a culture in which nudity is indigenous. The ordinance also might prohibit newsreel scenes of the opening of an art exhibit as well as shots of bathers on a beach. Clearly all nudity cannot be deemed obscene even as to minors. . . . Nor can such a broad restriction be justified by any other governmental interest pertaining to minors. Speech that is neither obscene as to youths nor subject to some other legitimate proscription cannot be suppressed solely to protect the young from ideas or images that a legislative body thinks unsuitable for them. In most circumstances, the values protected by the First Amendment are no less applicable when government seeks to control the flow of information to minors . . . Thus, if Jacksonville's ordinance is intended to regulate expression accessible to minors it is overbroad in its proscription.

At oral argument appellee, for the first time, sought to justify its ordinance as a traffic regulation. It claimed that nudity on a drive-in movie screen distracts passing motorists, thus slowing the flow of traffic and increasing the likelihood of accidents.

Nothing in the record or in the text of the ordinance suggests that it is aimed at traffic regulation. Indeed, the ordinance applies to movie screens visible from public places as well as public streets, thus indicating that it is not a traffic regulation. But even if this were the purpose of the ordinance, it nonetheless would be invalid. By singling out movies containing even the most fleeting and innocent glimpses of nudity the legislative classification is strikingly underinclusive. There is no reason to think that a wide variety of other scenes in the customary screen diet, ranging from soap opera to violence, would be any less distracting to the passing motorist. . . .

Even though none of the reasons advanced by appellee will sustain the Jacksonville ordinance, it remains for us to decide whether the ordinance should be invalidated on its face. This Court has long recognized that a demonstrably overbroad statute or ordinance may deter the legitimate exercise of First Amendment rights. Nonetheless, when considering a facial challenge it is necessary to proceed with caution and restraint, as invalidation may result in unnecessary interference with a state regulatory program. In accommodating these competing interests the Court had held that a state statute should not be deemed facially invalid unless it is not readily subject to a narrowing construction by the state courts ... . and its deterrent effect on legitimate expression is both real and substantial. . . .

In the present case the possibility of a limiting construction appears remote. Appellee explicitly joined in this test of the facial validity of its ordinance by agreeing to stay appellants' prosecution. Moreover, the ordinance by its plain terms is not easily susceptible to a narrowing construction. Indeed, when the state courts were presented with this overbreadth challenge they made no effort to restrict its application . . . In these circumstances, particularly where as here appellee offers several distinct justifications for the ordinance in its broadest terms, there is no reason to assume that the ordinance can or will be decisively narrowed. . . .

Moreover, the deterrent effect of this ordinance is both real and substantial. Since it applies specifically to all persons employed by or connected with drive-in theaters, the owners and operators of these theaters are faced with an unwelcome choice: to avoid prosecution of themselves and their employees they must either restrict their movie offerings or construct adequate protective fencing which may be extremely expensive or even physically impracticable. . . .

In concluding that this ordinance is invalid we do not deprecate the legitimate interests asserted by the city of Jacksonville. We hold only that the present ordinance does not satisfy the rigorous constitutional standards that apply when government attempts to regulate expression. Where First Amendment freedoms are at stake we have repeatedly emphasized that precision of drafting and clarity of purpose are essential. These prerequisites are absent here. Accordingly the judgment below is

Reversed.

MR. JUSTICE DOUGLAS, CONCURRING (OMITTED).
MR. CHIEF JUSTICE BURGER, WITH WHOM MR. JUSTICE REHNQUIST JOINS, DISSENTING (OMITTED).
MR. JUSTICE WHITE, DISSENTING (OMITTED).

(8) Young v. American Mini Theaters, Inc. (1976)

+Stevens, Burger, White, Rehnquist
±Powell
−Brennan, Stewart, Marshall, Blackmun

[In November 1972, Detroit adopted ordinances that provided for the dispersal of adult theaters and bookstores. An "adult" theater or bookstore is one that presents "material" distinguished or characterized by an emphasis on matter describing or relating to "specified sexual activities" or "specified anatomical areas." Any such theater or bookstore could not be located within 1000 feet of any two other "regulated uses" (cabarets, bars, hotels, pawnshops, billiard or pool halls, etc.), nor closer than 500 feet to a residential area. The purpose of the ordinances was to prevent the proliferation of such establishments and the inevitable urban decay that their presence fosters.

Respondents operated two theaters, one an established motion picture house that began to exhibit adult films in 1973, the other a "mini-theater" (a converted corner gas station) known as the "Pussy Cat." The latter was denied a certificate of occupancy, and both thea-

ters were in fact in violation of the ordinance. Respondents sought a declaratory judgment that the ordinances were unconstitutional and an injunction preventing their enforcement. A federal district court denied the request, holding that the ordinances represented a rational attempt by the city to preserve its neighborhoods. But the court of appeals reversed, holding that the ordinances constituted a prior restraint on constitutionally protected communication. One judge, dissenting, thought the ordinances to be a valid "times, place, and manner" regulation and *not* a regulation of speech on the basis of its content. The Supreme Court granted certiorari and considered three claims: (1) that the ordinances were unconstitutionally vague; (2) that they were invalid as prior restraints, and (3) that the classification of theaters on the basis of the content of films violated the equal protection clause of the Fourteenth Amendment.]

MR. JUSTICE STEVENS delivered the opinion of the Court.

. . .

There are two parts to respondent's claim that the ordinances are too vague. They do not attack the specificity of the definition of "Specified Sexual Activities" or "Specified Anatomical Areas." They argue, however, that they cannot determine how much of the described activity may be permissible before the exhibition is "characterized by an emphasis" on such matter. In addition, they argue that the ordinances are vague because they do not specify adequate procedures or standards for obtaining a waiver of the 1,000-foot restriction.

We find it unnecessary to consider the validity of either of these arguments in the abstract. For even if there may be more uncertainty about the effect of the ordinances on other litigants, they are unquestionably applicable to these respondents. The record indicates that both theaters propose to offer adult fare on a regular basis. Neither respondent has alleged any basis for claiming or anticipating any waiver of the restriction as applied to its theater. It is clear, therefore, that any element of vagueness in these ordinances has not affected these respondents. To the extent that their challenge is predicated on inadequate notice resulting in a denial of procedural due process under the Fourteenth Amendment, it must be rejected. . . .

Because the ordinances affect communication protected by the First Amendment, respondents argue that they may raise the vagueness issue even though there is no uncertainty about the impact of the ordinances on their own rights. On several occasions we have determined that a defendant whose own speech was unprotected had standing to challenge the constitutionality of a statute which purported to prohibit protected speech, or even speech arguably protected. This exception from traditional rules of standing to raise constitutional issues has reflected the Court's judgment that the very existence of some statutes may cause persons not before the Court to refrain from engaging in constitutionally protected speech or expression. . . . The exception is justified by the overriding importance of maintaining a free and open market for the interchange of ideas. Nevertheless, if the statute's deterrent effect on "legitimate expression is not both real and substantive," and if the statute is "readily subject to a narrowing construction by the state courts," . . . the litigant is not permitted to assert the rights of third parties.

We are not persuaded that the Detroit Zoning Ordinances will have a significant deterrent effect on the exhibition of films protected by the First Amendment. As already noted, the only vagueness of the ordinances relates to the amount of sexually explicit activity that may be portrayed before the material can be said to be "characterized by an emphasis" on such matter. For most films the question will be readily answerable; to the extent that an area of doubt exists, we see no reason why the statute is not "readily subject to a narrowing construction by the state courts." Since there is surely a less vital interest in the uninhibited exhibition of material that is on the border line between pornography and artistic expression than in the free dissemination of ideas of social and political significance, and since the limited amount of uncertainty in the statute is easily susceptible of a narrowing construction, we think this is an inappropriate case in which to adjudicate the hypothetical claims of persons not before the Court.

The only area of protected communication that may be deterred by these ordinances comprises films containing material falling within the specific definitions of "Specified Sexual Activities" or "Specified Anatomical Areas." The fact that the First Amendment protects some, though not necessarily all of that material from total suppression does not warrant the further conclusion that an exhibitor's doubts as to whether a border line film may be shown in his theater, as well as in theaters licensed for adult presentations, involves the kind of threat to the free market in ideas and expression that justifies the exceptional approach to constitutional adjudication recognized in cases like *Dombrowski* v. *Pfister* . . .

Petitioners acknowledge that the ordinances prohibit theaters which are not licensed as "adult motion picture theaters" from exhibiting films which are protected by the First Amendment. Respondents argue that the ordinances are therefore invalid as prior restraints on free speech. . . .

It is true . . . that the adult films may only be exhibited commercially in licensed theaters. But that is also true of all motion pictures. The city's general zoning laws require all motion picture theaters to satisfy certain locational as well as other requirements; we have no doubt that the municipality may control the location of theaters as well as the location of other commercial establishments, either by confining them to certain specified commercial areas or by requiring that they be dispersed throughout the city. The mere fact that the commercial exploitation of material protected by the First Amendment is subject to zoning and other licensing requirements is not a sufficient reason for invalidating these ordinances. . . .

A remark attributed to Voltaire characterizes our zealous adherence to the principle that the Government may not tell the citizen what he may or may not say. Referring to a suggestion that the violent overthrow of tyranny might be legitimate, he said, "I disapprove of what you say, but I will defend to the death your right to say it." The essence of that comment has been repeated time after time in our decisions invalidating attempts by the Government to impose selective controls upon the dissemination of ideas.

Thus, the use of streets and parks for the free expression of views on national affairs may not be conditioned upon the sovereign's agreement with what a speaker may intend to say. Nor may speech be curtailed because it invites dispute, creates dissatisfaction with conditions the way they are, or even stirs people to anger. The sovereign's agreement or disagreement with the content of what a speaker has to say may not affect the regulation of the time, place, or manner of presenting the speech. . . .

The question whether speech is, or is not, protected by the First Amendment often depends on the content of the speech. Thus, the line between permissible advocacy and impermissible incitement to crime or violence depends, not merely on the setting in which the speech occurs, but also on exactly what the speaker had to say. Similarly, it is the content of the utterance that determines whether it is a protected epithet or an unprotected "fighting comment." And in time of war "the publication of the sailing of transports or the number and regulation of troops may unquestionably be restrained, . . . although publication of news stories with a different content would be protected."

Even within the area of protected speech, a difference in content may require a different governmental response. In *New York Times Co.* v. *Sullivan*, . . . we have recognized that the First Amendment places limitations on the States' power to enforce their libel laws. We held that a public official may not recover damages from a critic of his official conduct without proof of "malice" as specially defined in that opinion. Implicit in the opinion is the assumption that if the content of the newspaper article had been different—that is, if its subject matter had not been a public official—a lesser standard of proof would have been adequate. . . .

We have recently held that the First Amendment affords some protection to commercial speech. We have also made it clear, however, that the content of a particular advertisement may determine the extent of its protection. A public rapid transit system may accept some advertisements and reject others. A state statute may permit highway billboards to advertise businesses located in the neighborhood but not elsewhere, and regulatory commissions may prohibit businessmen from making statements which, though literally true, are potentially deceptive. The measure of constitutional protection to be afforded commercial speech will surely be governed largely by the content of the communication.

More directly in point are opinions dealing with the question whether the First Amendment prohibits the state and federal governments from wholly suppressing sexually oriented materials on the basis of their "obscene character." In *Ginsberg* v. *New York*, . . . the Court upheld a conviction for selling to a minor magazines which were concededly not "obscene" if shown to adults. Indeed, the Members of the Court who would accord the greatest protection to such materials have repeatedly indicated that the State could prohibit the distribution or exhibition of such materials to juveniles and consenting adults. Surely the First Amendment does not foreclose such a prohibition; yet it is equally clear that any such prohibition must rest squarely on an appraisal of the content of material otherwise within a constitutionally protected area.

Such a line may be drawn on the basis of content without violating the Government's paramount obligation of neutrality in its regulation of protected communication. For the regulation of the places where sexually explicit films may be exhibited is unaffected by whatever social, political, or philosophical message the film may be intended to communicate; whether the motion picture ridicules or characterizes one point of view or another, the effect of the ordinances is exactly the same.

Moreover, even though we recognize that the First Amendment will not tolerate the total suppression of erotic materials that have some arguably artistic value, it is manifest that society's interest in protecting this type of expression is of a wholly different, and lesser, magnitude than the interest in untrammeled political debate that inspired Voltaire's immortal comment. Whether political oratory or philosophical discussion moves us to applaud or to despise what is said, every schoolchild can understand why our duty to defend the right to speak remains the same. But few of us would march our sons and daughters off to war to preserve the citizen's right to see "Specified Sexual Activities" exhibited in the theaters of our choice. Even though the First Amendment protects communication in this area from total suppression, we hold that the State may legitimately use the content of these materials as the basis for placing them in a different classification from other motion pictures.

The remaining question is whether the line drawn by these ordinances is justified by the city's interest in preserving the character of its neighborhoods. On this question we agree with the views expressed by District Judges Kennedy and Gubow. The record discloses a factual basis for the Common Council's conclusion that this kind of restriction will have the desired effect. It is not our function to appraise the wisdom of its decision to require adult theaters to be separated rather than concentrated in the same areas. In either event, the city's interest in attempting to preserve the quality of urban life is one that must be accorded high respect. Moreover, the city must be allowed a reasonable opportunity to experiment with solutions to admittedly serious problems.

Since what is ultimately at stake is nothing more than a limitation on the place where adult films may be exhibited, even though the determination of whether a particular film fits that characterization turns on the nature of its content, we conclude that the city's interest in the present and future character of its neighborhoods adequately supports its classification of motion pictures. We hold that the zoning ordinances requiring that adult motion picture theaters not be located within 1,000 feet of two other regulated uses does not violate the Equal Protection Clause of the Fourteenth Amendment.

The judgment of the Court of Appeals is

Reversed.

MR. JUSTICE POWELL, CONCURRING IN THE JUDGMENT AND PORTIONS OF THE OPINION.

Although I agree with much of what is said in the plurality opinion, and concur in Parts I and II, my approach to the resolution of this case is sufficiently different to prompt me to write separately. I view the case as presenting an example of innovative land-use regulations, implicating First Amendment concerns only incidentally and to a limited extent. . . .

MR. JUSTICE STEWART, WITH WHOM MR. JUSTICE BRENNAN, MR. JUSTICE MARSHALL AND MR. JUSTICE BLACKMUN JOIN, DISSENTING.

The Court today holds that the First and Fourteenth Amendments do not prevent the city of Detroit from using a system of prior restraints and criminal sanctions to enforce content-based restrictions on the geographic location of motion picture theaters that exhibit nonobscene but sexually oriented films. I dissent from this drastic departure from established principles of First Amendment law. . . .

What this case does involve is the constitutional permissibility of selective interference with protected speech whose content is thought to produce distasteful effects. It is elementary that a prime function of the First Amendment is to guard against just such interference. By refusing to invalidate Detroit's ordinance the Court rides roughshod over cardinal principles of First Amendment law which require that time, place and manner regulations that affect protected expression be content-neutral except in the limited context of a captive or juvenile audience. In place of these principles the Court invokes a concept wholly alien to the First Amendment. Since few of us would march our sons and daughters off to war to preserve the citizen's right to see "Specified Sexual Activities" exhibited in the theaters of our choice," . . . the Court implies that these films are not entitled to the full protection of the Constitution. This stands "Voltaire's immortal comment," . . . on its head. For if the guarantees of the First Amendment were reserved for expression that more than a "few of us" would take up arms to defend, then the right of free expression would be defined and circumscribed by current popular opinion. The guarantees of the Bill of Rights were designed to protect against precisely such majoritarian limitations on individual liberty.

The fact that the "offensive" speech here may not address "important" topics—"ideas of social and political significance," in the Court's terminology, . . . does not mean that it is less worthy of constitutional protection. "Wholly neutral futilities . . . come under the protection of free speech as fully as do Keats' poems or Donne's sermons." *Winters* v. *New York* . . . (Frankfurter, J., dissenting). . . . Moreover, in the absence of a judicial determination of obscenity, it is by no means clear that the speech is not "important" even on the Court's terms. "[S]ex and obscenity are not synonymous. . . .

MR. JUSTICE BLACKMUN, WITH WHOM MR. JUSTICE BRENNAN, MR. JUSTICE STEWART, AND MR. JUSTICE MARSHALL JOIN, DISSENTING (OMITTED).

(9) Smith v. United States (1977)

+Burger, White, Blackmun, Powell, Rehnquist

−Brennan, Stewart, Marshall, Stevens

[Smith was convicted of violating federal law prohibiting the mailing of obscene materials. During the trial, in Des Moines, Iowa, and in petitioning for a new trial, Smith alleged that the materials he had mailed—some explicit pornographic magazines and two films entitled *Lovelace* and *Terrorized Virgin*—were not obscene under *Miller* v. *California* (1973).

In *Miller,* the Supreme Court had held that the determination of what is patently offensive and what appeals to a prurient interest were essentially questions of fact to be determined according to *community* standards, not a national standard. In 1973, the Supreme Court of Iowa had held portions of the state's obscenity law unconstitutional under the standards set down in the *Miller* case. The following year, the Iowa legislature repealed virtually all the state's obscenity laws except those prohibiting dissemination of obscene materials to minors (under 18). Thus, what Smith did was clearly not a violation of state law at the time he acted.[1] These events, Miller claimed, were evidence that such publications were not regarded as obscene by local standards. He also pointed to the comparable "explicit sexual materials" sold openly in Des Moines and Davenport, Iowa, in "adult" bookstores.

The federal district court denied Smith's motion for a new trial, holding that the statute under which he was convicted was "a federal law which neither incorporates nor depends upon the laws of the states." Furthermore, the court ruled, the mere fact that such acts had been decriminalized did not mean that the people of Iowa necessarily approved of such conduct. The Court of Appeals for the Eight Circuit affirmed, holding that in a federal prosecution, contemporary community standards were to be determined by a jury. The Supreme Court granted certiorari.]

MR. JUSTICE BLACKMUN delivered the opinion of the Court.

. . .

The phrasing of the *Miller* test makes clear that contemporary community standards take on meaning only when they are considered with reference to the underlying questions of fact that must be resolved in an obscenity case. The test itself shows that appeal to the prurient interest is one such question of fact for the jury to resolve. The *Miller* opinion indicates that patent offensiveness is to be treated in the same way. . . . The fact that the jury must measure patent offensiveness against contemporary community standards does not mean, however, that juror discretion in this area is to go unchecked. . . . In *Jenkins* v. *Georgia* . . . (1974), the Court noted that part (b) of the *Miller* test contained a substantive component as well. The kinds of conduct that a jury would be permitted to label as "patently offensive" . . . are the "hard core" types of conduct suggested by the examples given in *Miller*. . . . Literary, artistic, political, or scientific value, on the other hand, is not discussed in *Miller* in terms of contemporary community standards. . . .

. . . [W]e must decide whether the jury is entitled to rely on its own

[1]In 1976, Iowa reinstated its prohibition on the dissemination of hard-core obscene materials to adults, but classified the offense as a misdemeanor.

knowledge of community standards, or whether a state legislature (or a smaller legislative body) may declare what the community standards shall be, . . .

Obviously, a state legislature would not be able to define contemporary community standards in a vacuum. Rather, community standards simply provide the measure against which the jury decides the questions of appeal to prurient interest and patent offensiveness. . . . It would be just as inappropriate for a legislature to attempt to freeze a jury to one definition of reasonableness as it would be for a legislature to try to define the contemporary standard of appeal to prurient interest or patent offensiveness, if it were even possible for such a definition to be formulated.

This is not to say that state legislatures are completely foreclosed from enacting laws setting substantive limitations for obscenity cases. On the contrary, we have indicated on several occasions that legislation of this kind is permissible. . . . State legislation must still define the kinds of conduct that will be regulated by the State. . . .

If a State wished to adopt a slightly different approach to obscenity regulation, it might impose a geographic limit on the determination of community standards by defining the area from which the jury could be selected in an obscenity case, or by legislating with respect to the instructions that must be given to the jurors in such cases. In addition, the State might add a geographic dimension to its regulation of obscenity through the device of zoning laws. Cf. *Young* v. *American Mini Theaters, Inc.* . . . (1976). It is evident that ample room is left for state legislation even though the question of the community standard to apply, when appeal to prurient interest and patent offensiveness are considered, is not one that can be defined legislatively.

An even stronger reason for holding that a state law regulating distribution of obscene material cannot define contemporary community standards in the case before us is the simple fact that this is a *federal* prosecution. . . . The Court already has held, . . . that the substantive conduct encompassed by [this statute] is confined to "the sort of 'patently offensive representations or descriptions of that specific "hard core" sexual conduct given as examples in *Miller* v. *California*.' " . . . The community standards aspects of [the statute] likewise present issues of federal law, upon which a state statute such as Iowa's cannot have conclusive effect. The kinds of instructions that should be given to the jury are likewise a federal question. . . .

Our decision that contemporary community standards must be applied by juries in accordance with their own understanding of the tolerance of the average person in their community does not mean, as has been suggested, that obscenity convictions will be virtually unreviewable. We have stressed before that juries must be instructed properly, so that they consider the entire community and not simply their own subjective reactions, or the reactions of a sensitive or of a callous minority. . . . The type of conduct depicted must fall within the substantive limitations suggested in *Miller*. . . . The work also must lack serious literary, artistic, political, or scientific value before a conviction will be upheld; this determination is particularly amenable to appellate review. Finally, it is always appropriate for the appellate court to review the sufficiency of the evidence. . . .

Since the Iowa law on obscenity was introduced into evidence, and the jurors were told that they could consider it as evidence of the community standard, petitioner received everything to which he was entitled. To go further, and to make the state law conclusive on the issues of appeal to prurient interest and patent offensiveness, in a federal prosecution . . . would be inconsistent with our prior cases. We hold that those issues are fact questions for the jury, to be judged in light of the jurors' understanding of contemporary community standards. . . .

The judgment of the Court of Appeals is affirmed.

It is so ordered.

MR. JUSTICE POWELL, CONCURRING (OMITTED).

MR. JUSTICE BRENNAN, WITH WHOM MR. JUSTICE STEWART AND MR. JUSTICE MARSHALL JOIN, DISSENTING (OMITTED).

MR. JUSTICE STEVENS, DISSENTING (OMITTED).

(10) Federal Communications Commission v. Pacifica Foundation (1978)

+Stevens, Burger, Rehnquist, Powell, Blackmun

−Brennan, Marshall, Stewart, White

MR. JUSTICE STEVENS delivered the opinion of the Court . . . and an opinion in which the CHIEF JUSTICE and MR. JUSTICE REHNQUIST joined. . . .

This case requires that we decide whether the Federal Communications Commission has any power to regulate a radio broadcast that is indecent but not obscene.

A satiric humorist named George Carlin recorded a 12-minute monologue entitled "Filthy Words" before a live audience in a California theater. He began by referring to his thoughts about "the words you couldn't say on the public, ah, airwaves, um, the ones you definitely wouldn't say, ever." He proceeded to list those words and repeat them over and over again in a variety of colloquialisms. . . .

At about 2 o'clock in the afternoon on Tuesday, October 30, 1973, a New York radio station owned by respondent, Pacifica Foundation, broadcast the "Filthy Words" monologue. A few weeks later a man, who stated that he had heard the broadcast while driving with his young son, wrote a letter complaining to the Commission. . . .

The complaint was forwarded to the station for comment. In its response, Pacifica explained that the monologue had been played during a program about contemporary society's attitude toward language and that immediately before its broadcast listeners had been advised that it included "sensitive language which might be regarded as offensive to some." Pacifica characterized George Carlin as "a significant social satirist" who "like Twain and Sahl before him, examines the language of ordinary people . . . Carlin is not mouthing obscenities, he is merely using words to satirize as harmless and essentially silly our attitudes toward those words." Pacifica stated that it was not aware of any other complaints about the broadcast.

On February 21, 1975, the Commission issued a Declaratory Order granting the complaint and holding that Pacifica "could have been the subject of administrative sanctions." . . . The Commission did not impose formal sanctions, but it did state that the order would be "associated with the station's license file, and in the event that subsequent complaints are received, the Commission will then decide whether it should utilize any

1270 ■ PERSONAL RIGHTS IN MODERN SOCIETY

of the available sanctions it has been granted by Congress." . . .

After the order issued, the Commission was asked to clarify its opinion by ruling that the broadcast of indecent words as part of a live newscast, would not be prohibited. The Commission issued another opinion in which it pointed out that it "never intended to place an absolute prohibition on the broadcast of this type of language, but rather sought to channel it to times of day when children most likely would not be exposed to it." . . .

Having granted the Commission's petition for certiorari, . . . we must decide . . . (2) whether the Commission's order was a form of censorship forbidden by §326; (3) whether the broadcast was indecent within the meaning of §1464; and (4) whether the order violates the First Amendment of the United States Constitution. . . .

The relevant statutory questions are whether the Commission's action is forbidden "censorship" within the meaning of 47 U.S.C. §326 and whether speech that concededly is not obscene may be restricted as "indecent" under the authority of 18 U.S.C. §1464. . . .

Section 29 of the Radio Act of 1927 provided:

Nothing in this Act shall be understood or construed to give the licensing authority the power of censorship over the radio communications or signals transmitted by any radio station, and no regulation or condition shall be promulgated or fixed by the licensing authority which shall interfere with the right of free speech by means of radio communications. No person within the jurisdiction of the United States shall utter any obscene, indecent, or profane language by means of radio communication. . . .

The prohibition against censorship unequivocally denies the Commis-

sion any power to edit proposed broadcasts in advance and to excise material considered inappropriate for the airwaves. The prohibition, however, has never been construed to deny the Commission the power to review the content of completed broadcasts in the performance of its regulatory duties. . . .

Entirely apart from the fact that the subsequent review of program content is not the sort of censorship at which the statute was directed, its history makes it perfectly clear that it was not intended to limit the Commission's power to regulate the broadcast of obscene, indecent, or profane language. A single section of the 1927 Act is the source of both the anticensorship provision and the Commission's authority to impose sanctions for the broadcast of indecent or obscene language. Quite plainly, Congress intended to give meaning to both provisions. Respect for that intent requires that the censorship language be read as inapplicable to the prohibition on broadcasting obscene, indecent, or profane language. . . .

We conclude, therefore, that §326 does not limit the Commission's authority to impose sanctions on licensees who engage in obscene, indecent, or profane broadcasting.

The only other statutory question presented by this case is whether the afternoon broadcast of the "Filthy Words" monologue was indecent within the meaning of §1464. Even that question is narrowly confined by the arguments of the parties.

The Commission identified several words that referred to excretory or sexual activities or organs, stated that the repetitive, deliberate use of those words in an afternoon broadcast when children are in the audience was patently offensive, and held that the broadcast was indecent. Pacifica takes issue with the Commission's definition of indecency, but does not dispute the Commission's preliminary determination that each of the components of its definition was present. Specifically, Pacifica does not quarrel with the conclusion that this afternoon broadcast was patently offensive. Pacifica's claim that the broadcast was not indecent within the meaning of the statute rests entirely on the absence of prurient appeal.

The plain language of the statute does not support Pacifica's argument. The words "obscene, indecent, or profane" are written in the disjunctive, implying that each has a separate meaning. Prurient appeal is an element of the obscene, but the normal definition of "indecent" merely refers to nonconformance with accepted standards of morality.

Pacifica argues, however, that this Court has construed the term "indecent" in related statutes to mean "obscene," as that term was defined in *Miller* v. *California*. . . .

Because neither our prior decisions nor the language or history of §1464 supports the conclusion that prurient appeal is an essential component of indecent language, we reject Pacifica's construction of the statute. When that construction is put to one side, there is no basis for disagreeing with the Commission's conclusion that indecent language was used in this broadcast.

Pacifica makes two constitutional attacks on the Commission's order. First, it argues that the Commission's construction of the statutory language broadly encompasses so much constitutionally protected speech that reversal is required even if Pacifica's broadcast of the "Filthy Words" monologue is not itself protected by the First Amendment. Second, Pacifica argues that inasmuch as the recording is not obscene, the Constitution forbids any abridgement

of the right to broadcast it on the radio.

The first argument fails because our review is limited to the question whether the Commission has the authority to proscribe this particular broadcast. As the Commission itself emphasized, its order was "issued in a specific factual context." . . . That approach is appropriate for courts as well as the Commission when regulation of indecency is at stake, for indecency is largely a function of context—it cannot be adequately judged in the abstract. . . .

When the issue is narrowed to the facts of this case, the question is whether the First Amendment denies government any power to restrict the public broadcast of indecent language in any circumstances. For if the government has any such power, this was an appropriate occasion for its exercise.

The words of the Carlin monologue are unquestionably "speech" within the meaning of the First Amendment. It is equally clear that the Commission's objections to the broadcast were based in part on its content. The order must therefore fall if, as Pacifica argues, the First Amendment prohibits all governmental regulation that depends on the content of speech. Our past cases demonstrate, however, that no such absolute rule is mandated by the Constitution.

The classic exposition of the proposition that both the content and the context of speech are critical elements of First Amendment analysis is Mr. Justice Holmes' statement for the Court in *Schenck* v. *United States:*

We admit that in many places and in ordinary times the defendants in saying all that was said in the circular would have been within their constitutional rights. But the character of every act depends upon the circumstances in which it is done. . . . The most stringent protection of free speech would not protect a man in falsely shouting fire in a theatre and causing a panic. It does not even protect a man from an injunction against uttering words that may have all the effect of force. . . . The question in every case is whether the words used are used in such circumstances and are of such a nature as to create a clear and present danger that they will bring about the substantive evils that Congress has a right to prevent. . . .

Other distinctions based on content have been approved in the years since *Schenck*. The government may forbid speech calculated to provoke a fight. See *Chaplinsky* v. *New Hampshire* . . . It may pay heed to the " 'commonsense differences' between commercial speech and other varieties." *Bates* v. *State Bar* . . . It may treat libels against private citizens more severely than libels against public officials. See *Gertz* v. *Robert Welch, Inc.* . . . Obscenity may be wholly prohibited. *Miller* v. *California* . . . And only two Terms ago we refused to hold that a "statutory classification is unconstitutional because it is based on the content of communication protected by the First Amendment." *Young* v. *American Mini Theaters* . . . .

The question in this case is whether a broadcast of patently offensive words dealing with sex and excretion may be regulated because of its content. Obscene materials have been denied the protection of the First Amendment because their content is so offensive to contemporary moral standards. . . . But the fact that society may find speech offensive is not a sufficient reason for suppressing it. Indeed, if it is the speaker's opinion that gives offense, that consequence is a reason for according it constitutional protection.

For it is a central tenet of the First Amendment that the government must remain neutral in the marketplace of ideas. If there were any reason to believe that the Commission's characterization of the Carlin monologue as offensive could be traced to its political content—or even to the fact that it satirized contemporary attitudes about four letter words—First Amendment protection might be required. But that is simply not this case. These words offend for the same reasons that obscenity offends. Their place in the hierarchy of First Amendment values was aptly sketched by Mr. Justice Murphy when he said, "such utterances are no essential part of any exposition of ideas, and are of such slight social value as a step to truth that any benefit that may be derived from them is clearly outweighed by the social interest in order and morality." *Chaplinsky* v. *New Hampshire* . . . .

Although these words ordinarily lack literary, political, or scientific value, they are not entirely outside the protection of the First Amendment. Some uses of even the most offensive words are unquestionably protected. . . .

Indeed, we may assume . . . that this monologue would be protected in other contexts. Nonetheless, the constitutional protection accorded to a communication containing such patently offensive sexual and excretory language need not be the same in every context. It is a characteristic of speech such as this that both its capacity to offend and its "social value," to use Mr. Justice Murphy's term, vary with the circumstances. Words that are commonplace in one setting are shocking in another. To paraphrase Mr. Justice Harlan, one occasion's lyric is another's vulgarity. . . .

We have long recognized that each

medium of expression presents special First Amendment problems. . . . And of all forms of communication, it is broadcasting that has received the most limited First Amendment protection. Thus, although other speakers cannot be licensed except under laws that carefully define and narrow official discretion, a broadcaster may be deprived of his license and his forum if the Commission decides that such an action would serve "the public interest, convenience, and necessity." Similarly, although the First Amendment protects newspaper publishers from being required to print the replies of those whom they criticize, *Miami Herald Publishing Co. v. Tornillo,* . . . it affords no such protection to broadcasters; on the contrary, they must give free time to the victim of their criticism. . . .

The reasons for these distinctions are complex, but two have relevance to the present case. First, the broadcast media have established a uniquely pervasive presence in the lives of all Americans. Patently offensive, indecent material presented over the airwaves confronts the citizen, not only in public, but also in the privacy of the home, where the individual's right to be let alone plainly outweighs the First Amendment rights of an intruder. . . . Because the broadcast audience is constantly tuning in and out, prior warnings cannot completely protect the listener or viewer from unexpected program content. To say that one may avoid further offense by turning off the radio when he hears indecent language is like saying that the remedy for an assault is to run away after the first blow. One may hang up on an indecent phone call, but that option does not give the caller a constitutional immunity or avoid a harm that has already taken place.

Second, broadcasting is uniquely accessible to children, even those too young to read. Although Cohen's written message might have been incomprehensible to a first grader, Pacifica's broadcast could have enlarged a child's vocabulary in an instant. Other forms of offensive expression may be withheld from the young without restricting the expression at its source. Bookstores and motion picture theaters, for example, may be prohibited from making indecent material available to children. We held in *Ginsberg* v. *New York* . . . that the government's interest in the "well being of its youth" and in supporting "parents' claim to authority in their own household" justified the regulation of otherwise protected expression. . . . The ease with which children may obtain access to broadcast material, coupled with the concerns recognized in *Ginsberg*, amply justify special treatment of indecent broadcasting.

It is appropriate, in conclusion, to emphasize the narrowness of our holding. This case does not involve a two-way radio conversation between a cab driver and dispatcher, or a telecast of an Elizabethan comedy. We have not decided that an occasional expletive in either setting would justify any sanction or, indeed, that this broadcast would justify a criminal prosecution. The Commission's decision rested entirely on a nuisance rationale under which context is all-important. The concept requires consideration of a host of variables. The time of day was emphasized by the Commission. The content of the program in which the language is used will also affect the composition of the audience, and differences between radio, television, and perhaps closed-circuit transmissions, may also be relevant. As Mr. Justice Sutherland wrote, a "nuisance may be merely a right thing in the wrong place—like a pig in the parlor instead of the barnyard." . . . We simply hold that when the Commission finds that a pig has entered the parlor, the exercise of its regulatory power does not depend on proof that the pig is obscene.

The judgment of the Court of Appeals is reversed.

MR. JUSTICE POWELL, WITH WHOM MR. JUSTICE BLACKMUN JOINS, CONCURRING (OMITTED).

MR. JUSTICE BRENNAN, WITH WHOM MR. JUSTICE MARSHALL JOINS, DISSENTING.
. . .

For the second time in two years, see *Young* v. *American Mini Theaters* . . . (1976), the Court refuses to embrace the notion, completely antithetical to basic First Amendment values, that the degree of protection the First Amendment affords protected speech varies with the social value ascribed to that speech by five Members of this Court. . . . Moreover, as do all parties, all Members of the Court agree that the Carlin monologue aired by Station WBAI does not fall within one of the categories of speech, such as "fighting words" . . . or obscenity . . . that is totally without First Amendment protection. This conclusion, of course, is compelled by our cases expressly holding that communications containing some of the words found condemnable here are fully protected by the First Amendment in other contexts. . . . Yet despite the Court's refusal to create a sliding scale of First Amendment protection calibrated to this Court's perception of the worth of a communication's content, and despite our unanimous agreement that the Carlin monologue is protected speech, a majority of the Court nevertheless finds that, on the facts of this case, the FCC is not constitu-

tionally barred from imposing sanctions on Pacifica for its airing of the Carlin monologue. The majority apparently believes that the FCC's disapproval of Pacifica's afternoon broadcast of Carlin's "Dirty Words" recording is a permissible time, place and manner regulation.

. . .

The Court apparently believes that the FCC's actions here can be analogized to the zoning ordinances upheld in *Young* v. *American Mini Theaters* (1976). For two reasons it is wrong. First, the zoning ordinances found to pass constitutional muster in *Young* had valid goals other than the channeling of protected speech. . . . No such goals are present here. Second . . . the ordinances did not restrict the access of distributors or exhibitors to the market or impair the viewing public's access to the regulated material. . . . Again this is not the situation here. Both those desiring to receive Carlin's message over the radio and those wishing to send it to them are prevented from doing so by the Commission's actions. Although . . . Carlin's message may be disseminated or received by other means, this is of little consolation to those broadcasters and listeners who, for a host of reasons, not least among them financial, do not have access to, or cannot take advantage of, these other means.

. . .

It is quite evident that I find the Court's attempt to unstitch the warp and woof of First Amendment law in an effort to reshape its fabric to cover the patently wrong result the Court reaches in this case dangerous as well as lamentable. Yet there runs throughout the opinions . . . another vein I find equally disturbing: a depressing inability to appreciate that in our land of cultural pluralism, there are many who think, act, and talk differently from the Members of this Court, and who do not share their fragile sensibilities. It is only an acute ethnocentric myopia that enables the Court to approve the censorship of communications solely because of the words they contain.

"A word is not a crystal, transparent and unchanged, it is the skin of a living thought and may vary greatly in color and content according to the circumstances and the time in which it is used." *Towne* v. *Eisner* . . . (1918) (Holmes, J.). The words that the Court and the Commission find so unpalatable may be the stuff of everyday conversations in some, if not many, of the innumerable subcultures that comprise this Nation. Academic research indicates that this is indeed the case. See B. Jackson, *Get Your Ass in the Water and Swim Like Me* (1974); J. Dillard, *Black English* (1972); W. Labov,

Language in the Inner City: Studies in the Black English Vernacular (1972). As one researcher concluded, "[W]ords generally considered obscene like 'bullshit' and 'fuck' are considered neither obscene nor derogatory in the [black] vernacular except in particular contextual situations and when used with certain intonations." C. Bins, "Toward an Ethnography of Contemporary African American Oral Poetry," *Language and Linguistics Working Papers* No. 5, at 82 (Georgetown University Press 1972). Cf. *Keefe* v. *Geanakos* (CA1 1969) (finding the use of the word "motherfucker" commonplace among young radicals and protestors). . . .

MR. JUSTICE STEWART, WITH WHOM MR. JUSTICE BRENNAN, MR. JUSTICE WHITE, AND MR. JUSTICE MARSHALL JOIN, DISSENTING (OMITTED).

5. THE PERSON IN SOCIETY

A. *Religious Freedom*

(1) A Note on the Constitutional Background of Religious Freedom

The constitutional language that underlies religious freedom in America is simple and direct: "Congress shall make no law respecting an establishment of religion, or prohibiting the free exercise thereof; . . ." But this constitutional command does not mean exactly what it

says: reference to "Congress" also includes the states, by virtue of the Fourteenth Amendment;[1] reference to "no law" has come practically to mean only those laws that in the judgment of the Supreme Court do not *unduly* involve the government in the affairs of religion, or the re-

---

[1]*Cantwell* v. *Connecticut* (1940) federalized the free exercise provision of the First Amendment. *Everson* v. *Board of Education* (1947) presumptively included the establishment provision in the First and Fourteenth linkage.

verse.[2] The critical language of the amendment is thus in the two phrases "establishment of religion" and "free exercise." Their bearing on constitutional meaning involves the impact of historical factors upon the practical exigencies of policy and outlook.

The historical tradition that underlies the First Amendment is reinforced by the views of no less than Jefferson and Madison. These figures, in their own time, were obliged to strike a balance between the ideal and the practical, and the problem of maintaining that balance has not diminished since. However, both have become ideological apostles and are used to symbolize ideals that in contemporary times must be balanced against policy needs. It is thus useful to understand the resultant historical and constitutional background that effects policymaking under the authority of the First Amendment.

Background

As one of the major by-products of the Enlightenment, America in the late eighteenth century manifested a measure of suspicion—even hostility—toward organized religion. Thomas Jefferson epitomized this rationalist mentality, and his anticlerical views found full expression in his famous letter of 1802 to the Danbury Baptist Association.

Believing with you that religion is a matter which lies solely between a man and his God; that he owes account to none other for his faith or his worship; that the Legislative powers of the Government reach actions only, and not opinions, I contemplate with sovereign reverence that act of the whole American people which declared that their Legislature should "make no law respecting an establishment of religion or prohibiting the free exercise thereof," thus building a wall of separation between Church and State.

The "wall" metaphor came to dominate First Amendment rhetoric, and as an image, it is true to the principle of separation embodied in that amendment. But, like a wall, the idea of separation poses its own questions: Where does protection lie? Jefferson's anticlerical bias provides an answer, which becomes but one of several strands in the fabric of American constitutional interpretation.

Another view is found in the writing of Roger Williams, who established the colony of Rhode Island early in the seventeenth century. Williams, like Jefferson, embraced the image of a wall that separated church from state, but unlike Jefferson, who sought to protect state from church, Williams' view would protect church from state. The church was a "garden," to be separated from the "wilderness" of the world, with its potential for corruption of those values so necessary to religious commitment. But Williams' wall had been breached—his church was *in* the world—and its remaining purpose was to safeguard religious liberty.

---

[2]This is no more than the political common sense of the matter. "No law" is binding and meaningful terminology only in the face of a direct and explicit effort on the part of Congress (or a state) to interfere with free exercise or create a religious establishment. But incidental effects of law or policy upon religion are unavoidable, and it is thus undue effects in the reciprocal relations between the political and religious systems that are to be avoided. As long as religions remain a part of the American pluralistic pattern, this must be the case.

His conception of separation seems not to have been total.[3]

The difference between the Jefferson and Williams views of the separation principle carries certain implications for constitutional meaning. The former, in its hostility, would seem to allow no interaction; the latter is strict only in regard to those actions of government that would threaten the integrity of religious commitment. The Jeffersonian view has tended to prevail, but the Williams view has become part of the basis on which certain interactions, dictated by apparent necessity or practicality, have been permitted.[4]

Within this historical framework, there is a third view, one that modifies the either-or tone of the Jefferson-Williams "dialogue." James Madison, in his famous "Memorial and Remonstrance" (1785), refers to the destruction of "that moderation and harmony which the forbearance of our laws to intermeddle with Religion, has produced amongst its several sects." This reference, and the general purpose of the piece, is the source of a viewpoint to which the label "strife-avoidance" has been attached[5]. The fact that Madison acted and wrote in the shadow of Jefferson should not obscure the fact that

"strife-avoidance" is a rationale underlying First Amendment theory that serves the purposes of general social policy and that even was conceded by Madison to allow government to interfere in conflicts between sects in order to preserve public order.[6] In short, there are secular purposes to be served within the scope of the religion clause of the First Amendment, and a doctrine of strict separation will not always serve such purposes.

Given the importance of religion in the United States, it is surprising that so few early Supreme Court cases dealt with it. During the nineteenth century, there were only seven cases, and between 1900 and 1938 there were also only seven. From 1940, the number of such cases increased, a trend consistent with the libertarian atmosphere of the modern period. The early cases not only reflect the background already discussed but also to some extent establish the pattern by which contemporary cases have been decided. It is thus useful to consider that part of the constitutional background represented by the Court's early cases.

It was not until 1845 that the Supreme Court was asked to decide a case raising issues of religious lib-

---

[3]See Mark Dewolfe Howe, *The Garden and the Wilderness: Religion and Government in American Constitutional History* (Chicago: University of Chicago Press, 1965), for a detailed analysis of this view.

[4]See James C. Kirby, Jr., "*Everson* to *Meek* and *Roemer*: From Separation to Detente in Church-State Relations," 55 *North Carolina Law Review* (April 1977), 563–75.

[5]*Ibid.*, p. 568. "The Memorial and Remonstrance" was written by Madison as part of his efforts in the Virginia General Assembly to defeat passage of a measure entitled "A Bill establishing a provision for Teachers of the Christian Religion." The bill would have established a tax to provide funds in support of Christian teachers. Madison's efforts were successful; after defeat of the Assessment Bill, the Assembly passed the Bill for Establishing Religious Freedom, which had been introduced by Thomas Jefferson in 1779 as a part of his general program of political reform.

[6]The reference is in a private letter, written after the First Amendment was adopted, as cited in Justice Rutledge's dissent, *Everson* v. *Board of Education* (1947).

erty. In *Permoli* v. *New Orleans*, a Roman Catholic priest was convicted under an ordinance that gave a monopoly on funerals to one chapel, which forbade the exposing of corpses in Roman Catholic churches (except for the specified chapel), and which imposed a fine on priests who conducted funerals other than in the approved chapel. The Supreme Court denied Permoli's appeal by noting that the First Amendment did not apply to the states, and thus cities within them. Obviously, *Permoli* is significant only as a first case.

The second issue to come to the Court, in 1872, had more significant effects. *Watson* v. *Jones* involved a dispute between two factions of a Louisville church, and the Court was asked to decide which represented the "true Walnut Street Presbyterian Church." The Court held that it had not power to decide the matter, which was subject to the appropriate ecclesiastical authority. It is important to note that the factions in the church had resorted to the civil courts in order to have a question about control of church property settled. More specifically, the Supreme Court in effect said that even the disposition of church property must, under the circumstances, be subject to the institutional means by which people associate with one another for religious purposes.

Watson seemed to establish the principle that it was not the business of civil courts to examine and pass judgment on religious doctrine, but six years later, a case involving polygamy caused the Court to distinguish between faith and practice—or belief and behavior. The Mormon church considered plural marriage to be a tenet of its faith, but Congress had passed laws against the practice in the territories. In *Reynolds* v. *United States* (1878), the law was challenged as an infringement of a Mormon's rights under the First Amendment. In deciding the case, the Supreme Court cited the Madison-Jefferson views as contained in "The Memorial and Remonstrance" and the Virginia Statute of Religious Liberty. The line between church and state was drawn precisely where action based on faith threatens peace and order.

In 1897, Congress appropriated money for constructing a hospital addition that was to be incorporated and operated by the Roman Catholic church so as to provide a hospital facility for residents of the District of Columbia. A taxpayers' suit resulted, and in *Bradfield* v. *Roberts* (1899), the Supreme Court upheld the contract made between the Commissioners of the District of Columbia and the incorporated addition. In doing so, the Court emphasized the fact that the contract was with the hospital *as a corporation* and not as a religious entity. The distinction between secular and religious characteristics controlled the outcome, and it is this distinction that has provided much of the foundation for subsequent judicial policy toward public activities with religious overtones.

Cochran v. *Louisiana State Board of Education* (1930) stands as the clearest early example. A state statute provided for the purchase of secular textbooks for use in public, private, and parochial schools. Although the statute was attacked on Fourteenth Amendment property/due process grounds (*Cantwell* was still ten years in the future), the Court upheld the law on the basis of its purpose to benefit the child and not private schools, religious or not. As a corollary of the secular/religion distinction, this "child benefit" theory, as it came to be called, had enormous effect in subsequent cases as the need for public funding of education increased.

Contemporary Issues

The early religion cases established two constitutional principles of contemporary significance. First, the principle of separation was paramount in determining the Court's willingness to involve itself in questions of religious belief; but practice and behavior motivated by such belief were not included in the meaning of the principle. Second, religious and secular objectives were distinguishable for purposes of policymaking, even though the activity under constitutional scrutiny might be conducted by institutions of religion.

Everson v. *Board of Education* (1947) marks the first modern effort by the Supreme Court to articulate and develop these principles as instruments of policy. The case also reflects the inherent contradictions in this area of constitutional policymaking. On the one hand, it constitutionalized Jefferson's characterization of the First Amendment as erecting a "wall of separation"; Justice Black's majority opinion articulates that idea in perhaps the most trenchant language ever used in a Court opinion. But Black then proceeded to apply the principle in a startling way. Instead of placing the wall between the state's desire to provide transportation for students and the efforts of denominational schools to educate, the opinion upholds New Jersey's law providing tax-supported transportation for students, including those in denominational schools.[7]

The seeming inconsistency of Black's opinion in *Everson* stems from its implicit adherence to a "child benefit" theory, combined with a doctrine of state neutrality. The idea is that a wall of separation should not exclude persons from benefits offered to all by the state simply because religion is involved. Thus the neutrality of the state in regard to religion becomes of considerable importance in judging the distribution of benefits. Ostensibly, the purpose of the wall is to protect, but not to exclude, at least where general social gains from governmental activity are involved. This theory of benefit was subsequently applied in *Board of Education* v. *Allen* (1968) to a New York law that required school districts to purchase and then lend textbooks to students in private/parochial schools. Although this application of the doctrine was excessive in the eyes of Justice Black, who thought books were far less religiously neutral than buses, the principle was reiterated by the Court as late as 1977, in *Wolman* v. *Walter*.

Everson was a precursor of those situations that the Court faced during the mid-1970s. An ingenious array of doctrines has been fashioned to deal with one basic problem—the extension of social and economic benefits to include religious organizations in light of the increased emphasis upon education and the attendant problem of financing it. One year after *Everson*, the Court examined a program in Illinois schools by which religious instruction was conducted on school premises and during school hours through "released time." In *McCollum* v. *Board of Education* (1948), the Court struck down the Illinois plan, primarily on the basis of its supervisory involvement of public school officials. The resultant protest from church organizations seems to have caused some reconsideration on

---

[7]An edited version of the *Everson* case follows.

the Court. In 1952, a New York plan was approved in *Zorach* v. *Clausen*; its major point of difference from Illinois was that released time for religious instruction was used in facilities other than those of the public school system.

The most politically volatile issue faced by the Court has involved the issue of prayer and Bible reading in the daily routine of public school. New York officials had composed a nonsectarian prayer to be used in schools as a part of moral and spiritual training; in *Engle* v. *Vitale* (1962), it was struck down. Similarly, in *Abington Township* v. *Schempp* (1963), a program of Bible reading as part of normal school exercises in Pennsylvania and Maryland was invalidated on the rationale that it did not meet a test of neutrality that the establishment clause was thought to require. Response to those decisions tended to spearhead negative reaction to the activism of the Warren Court in the 1960s. Politicians tended to act as if the Court had excommunicated God from the schools, but more thoughtful reaction gradually came to prevail, and the prayer issue has assumed only momentary importance compared to issues that involve the needs for tangible support of denominational institutions of education.

The problem of financial aid to parochial schools became primarily the burden of the Burger Court as a result of two cases: *Flast* v. *Cohen* (1968, see pp. 141–147, *supra*) had facilitated legal challenges to parochial school aid under the Education Act of 1965 by relaxing the requirements of "standing." In *Walz* v. *Tax Commission* (1970), the Court reaffirmed the validity of tax exemptions for church organizations. In each instance, the implicit concern was to distinguish secular from religious purpose so as to demonstrate general public benefit from aid to parochial institutions. In 1971, a Rhode Island program that extended salary supplements to teachers of secular subjects in parochial schools was reviewed in *Lemon* v. *Kurtzman* and found unconstitutional on a rationale of *excessive* entanglement. But almost simultaneously, the Court, in *Tilton* v. *Richardson*, found that construction grants for facilities with secular educational purposes did not constitute excessive entanglement.

In 1973, the Court struck down plans for the financing of parochial school repair, reimbursement for parochial school tuition, and tax relief for parents who sent their children to parochial schools. The impermissible advancement of religion under these schemes proved fatal in *Committee for Public Education and Religious Liberty* v. *Nyquist* (1973). These issues returned to the Court in 1975, when in *Meek* v. *Pittinger*, only textbook loan programs were approved out of a package of benefits that would have included testing, counseling, speech and hearing therapy, and other secular services.

Out of the recent cases, there has emerged a three-part test for determining the status of a program under the establishment clause of the Constitution. First, the statute must have a secular purpose. Second, its primary effect must neither advance nor inhibit religion. Third, the statute/ program must avoid excessive entanglement of church and state. The most comprehensive judicial statement of this tripartite test is in *Roemer* v. *Board of Public Works of Maryland* (1976), in which a state program of grants paid to private institutions of higher learning was upheld. The elaboration of the three-pronged test is extensive and stands to date as the definitive opinion in regard to the constitutional test of establishment.

At the outset of this note, we observed that use of the First Amendment's provisions about religion reflected a combination of historical and policy elements. It is evident that the immediate concerns of the Founding Fathers are no longer justified by the current status of religion in the United States. In a sense, there is a vestigial aspect to the First Amendment. But it is also clear that a policy question of considerable importance is posed by the situation in which those espousing particular views as the ultimate meaning of life seek tangible assistance from the general public. However vestigial certain elements of the First Amendment may be, the means of regulating the access certain religious groups have to public support and benefits lies within the religion provisions of the First Amendment. Its policy significance thus emanates from its history and our use of that history.

(2) Everson v. Board of Education (1947)

+Black, Vinson, Douglas, Murphy, Reed

−Jackson, Frankfurter, Rutledge, Burton

[The school district of Ewing, Pennsylvania, authorized reimbursement to parents for the cost of transporting their children to school on buses operated by the public transportation system. Some of these payments were to parents of children who attended parochial schools, which were implicitly included in the state statute that legalized such payments. A district taxpayer brought suit in state court on the grounds that payments for transportation to parochial school violated the First and Four-

teenth Amendments of the federal Constitution, as well as provisions of the state constitution; the court agreed with her. On appeal to the state appellate court, the decision was reversed, and further appeal was taken to the U. S. Supreme Court.

Although the contention that the statute violates the establishment clause is not the only constitutional question presented to the Court, it is the primary point from which the opinion develops. As indicated in the introductory note to this section, *Everson* is the first contemporary judicial effort to use the developed principles of First Amendment meaning as instruments of public policy.]

MR. JUSTICE BLACK delivered the opinion of the Court.

. . . The New Jersey statute is challenged as a "law respecting an establishment of religion." The First Amendment, as made applicable to the states by the Fourteenth, *Murdock* v. *Pennsylvania,* . . . commands that a state "shall make no law respecting an establishment of religion, or prohibiting the free exercise thereof. . . ." These words of the First Amendment reflected in the minds of early Americans a vivid mental picture of conditions and practices which they fervently wished to stamp out in order to preserve liberty for themselves and for their posterity. Doubtless their goal has not been entirely reached; but so far has the Nation moved toward it that the expression "law respecting an establishment of religion," probably does not so vividly remind present-day Americans of the evils, fears, and political problems that caused that expression to be written into our Bill of Rights. Whether this New Jersey law is one respecting an "establishment of religion" requires an understanding of the meaning of that language, particularly with respect to the imposition of taxes. Once again, therefore, it is not inappropriate briefly to review the background and environment of the period in which that constitutional language was fashioned and adopted.

A large proportion of the early settlers of this country came here from Europe to escape the bondage of laws which compelled them to support and attend government-favored churches. The centuries immediately before and contemporaneous with the colonization of America had been filled with turmoil, civil strife, and persecutions, generated in large part by established sects determined to maintain their absolute political and religious supremacy. With the power of government supporting them, at various times and places, Catholics had persecuted Protestants, Protestants had persecuted Catholics, Protestant sects had persecuted other Protestant sects, Catholics of one shade of belief had persecuted Catholics of another shade of belief, and all of these had from time to time persecuted Jews. In efforts to force loyalty to whatever religious group happened to be on top and in league with the government of a particular time and place, men and women had been fined, cast in jail, cruelly tortured, and killed. Among the offenses for which these punishments had been inflicted were such things as speaking disrespectfully of the views of ministers of government-established churches, non-attendance at those churches, expressions of non-belief in their doctrines, and failure to pay taxes and tithes to support them.

These practices of the old world were transplanted to and began to thrive in the soil of the new America. The very charters granted by the English Crown to the individuals and companies designated to make the laws which would control the destinies of the colonials authorized these individuals and companies to erect religious establishments which all, whether believers or non-believers, would be required to support and attend. An exercise of this authority was accompanied by a repetition of many of the old-world practices and persecutions. Catholics found themselves hounded and proscribed because of their faith; Quakers who followed their conscience went to jail; Baptists were peculiarly obnoxious to certain dominant Protestant sects; men and women of varied faiths who happened to be in a minority in a particular locality were persecuted because they steadfastly persisted in worshipping God only as their own consciences dictated. And all of these dissenters were compelled to pay tithes and taxes to support government-sponsored churches whose ministers preached inflammatory sermons designed to strengthen and consolidate the established faith by generating a burning hatred against dissenters.

These practices became so commonplace as to shock the freedom-loving colonials into a feeling of abhorrence. The imposition of taxes to pay ministers' salaries and to build and maintain churches and church property aroused their indignation. It was these feelings which found expression in the First Amendment. No one locality and no one group throughout the Colonies can rightly be given entire credit for having aroused the sentiment that culminated in adoption of the Bill of Rights' provisions embracing religious liberty. But Virginia, where the established church had achieved a dominant influence in political affairs and where many excesses attracted wide public attention, provided a great stimulus and able leadership for the movement. The people there, as elsewhere, reached the conviction that individual religious liberty could be achieved best under a government which was stripped of all power to tax, to support, or otherwise to assist any or all religions, or to interfere with the beliefs of any religious individual or group.

The movement toward this end reached its dramatic climax in Virginia in 1785–86 when the Virginia legislative body was about to renew Virginia's tax levy for the support of the established church. Thomas Jefferson and James Madison led the fight against this tax. Madison wrote his great Memorial and Remonstrance against the law. In it, he eloquently argued that a true religion did not need the support of law; that no person, either believer or nonbeliever, should be taxed to support a religious institution of any kind; that the best interest of a society required that the minds of men always be wholly free; and that cruel persecutions were the inevitable result of government-established religions. Madison's Remonstrance received strong support throughout Virginia, and the Assembly postponed consideration of the proposed tax measure until its next session. When the proposal came up for consideration at that session, it not only died in committee, but the Assembly enacted the famous "Virginia Bill for Religious Liberty" originally written by Thomas Jefferson. . . .

This Court has previously recognized that the provisions of the First Amendment, in the drafting and adoption of which Madison and Jefferson played such leading roles, had the same objective and were intended to provide the same protection against governmental intrusion on religious liberty as the Virginia statute. . . . Prior to the adoption of Fourteenth Amendment, the First Amendment did not apply as a restraint against the states. Most of them did soon provide similar constitutional protections for religious liberty. But some states persisted for about half a century in imposing restraints upon the free exercise of religion and in discriminating against particular religious groups. In recent years, so far as the provision against the establishment of a religion is concerned, the question has most frequently arisen in connection with proposed state aid to church schools and efforts to carry on religious teachings in the public schools in accordance with the tenets of a particular sect. Some churches have either sought or accepted state financial support for their schools. Here again the efforts to obtain state aid or acceptance of it have not been limited to any one particular faith. The state courts, in the main, have remained faithful to the language of their own constitutional provisions designed to protect religious freedom and to separate religions and governments. Their decisions, however, show the difficulty in drawing the line between tax legislation which provides funds for the welfare of the general public and that which is designed to support institutions which teach religion.

The meaning and scope of the First Amendment, preventing establishment of religion or prohibiting the free exercise thereof, in the light of its history and the evils it was designed forever to suppress, have been several times elaborated by the decisions of this Court prior to the application of the First Amendment to the states by the Fourteenth. The broad meaning given the Amendment by these earlier cases has been accepted by this Court in its decisions concerning an individual's religious freedom rendered since the Fourteenth Amendment was interpreted to make the prohibitions of the First applicable to state action abridging religious freedom. There is every reason to give the same application and broad interpretation to the "establishment of religion" clause. . . .

The "establishment of religion" clause of the First Amendment means at least this: Neither a state nor the Federal Government can set up a church. Neither can pass laws which aid one religion, aid all religions, or prefer one religion over another. Neither can force nor influence a person to go to or to remain away from church against his will or force him to profess a belief or disbelief in any religion. No person can be punished for entertaining or professing religious beliefs or disbeliefs, for church attendance or non-attendance. No tax in any amount, large or small, can be levied to support any religious activities or institutions, whatever they may be called, or whatever form they may adopt to teach or practice religion. Neither a state nor the Federal Government can, openly or secretly, participate in the affairs of any religious organizations or groups and *vice versa*. In the words of Jefferson, the clause against establishment of religion by law was intended to erect "a wall of separation between church and State." . . .

We must consider the New Jersey statute in accordance with the foregoing limitations imposed by the First Amendment. But we must not strike that state statute down if it is within the State's constitutional power even though it approaches the verge of that power. . . . New Jersey cannot consistently with the "establishment of religion" clause of the First Amendment contribute tax-raised funds to the support of an institution which teaches the tenets and faith of any church. On the other hand, other language of the amendment commands that New Jersey cannot hamper its citizens in the free exercise of their own religion. Consequently, it cannot exclude individual Catholics, Lutherans, Mohammedans, Baptists, Jews, Methodists, Non-believers, Presbyterians, or the members of any other faith, *because of their faith, or lack of it*, from receiving the benefits of public welfare legislation. While we do not mean to intimate that a state could not provide transportation only to children attending public schools, we must be careful, in protecting the citizens of New Jersey against state-established churches, to be sure that we do not inadvertently prohibit New Jersey from extending its general state law benefits to all its citizens without regard to their religious belief.

Measured by these standards, we cannot say that the First Amendment prohibits New Jersey from spending tax-raised funds to pay the bus fares of parochial school pupils as a part of a general program under which it pays the fares of pupils attending public and other schools. It is undoubtedly true that children are helped to get to church schools. There is even a possibility that some of the children might not be sent to the church schools if the parents were compelled to pay their children's bus fares out of their own pockets when transportation to a public school would have been paid for by the State. The same possibility exists where the state requires a local transit company to provide reduced fares to school children including those attending parochial schools, or where a municipally owned transportation system undertakes to carry all school children free of charge. Moreover, state-paid policemen, detailed to protect children going to and from church schools from the very real hazards of traffic, would serve much the same purpose and accomplish much the same result as state provisions intended to guarantee free transportation of a kind which the state deems to be best for the school children's welfare. And parents might refuse to risk their children to the serious danger of traffic accidents going to and from parochial schools, the approaches to which were not protected by policemen. Similarly, parents might be reluctant to permit their children to attend schools which the state had cut off from such general government services as ordinary police and fire protection, connections for sewage disposal, public highways and sidewalks. Of course, cutting off church schools from these services, so separate and so indisputably marked off from the religious function, would make it far more difficult for the schools to operate. But such is obviously not the purpose of the First Amendment. That Amendment requires the state to be a neutral in its relations with groups of religious believers and non-believers; it does not require the state to be their adversary. State power is no more to be used so as to handicap religions than it is to favor them.

This Court has said that parents may, in the discharge of their duty under state compulsory education laws, send their children to a religious rather than a public school if the school meets the secular educational requirements which the state has power to impose. . . . It appears that these parochial schools meet New Jersey's requirements. The State contributes no money to the schools. It does not support them. Its legislation, as applied, does no more than provide a general program to help parents get their children, regardless of their religion, safely and expeditiously to and from accredited schools.

The First Amendment has erected a wall between church and state.

That wall must be kept high and impregnable. We could not approve the slightest breach. New Jersey has not breached it here.

Affirmed.

MR. JUSTICE JACKSON, DISSENTING.

I find myself, contrary to first impressions unable to join in this decision. I have a sympathy, though it is not ideological, with Catholic citizens who are compelled by law to pay taxes for public schools, and also feel constrained by conscience and discipline to support other schools for their own children. Such relief to them as this case involves is not in itself a serious burden to taxpayers and I had assumed it to be as little serious in principle. Study of this case convinces me otherwise. The Court's opinion marshals every argument in favor of state aid and puts the case in its most favorable light, but much of its reasoning confirms my conclusions that there are no good grounds upon which to support the present legislation. In fact, the undertones of the opinion, advocating complete and uncompromising separation of Church from State, seem utterly discordant with its conclusion yielding support to their commingling in educational matters. The case which irresistibly comes to mind as the most fitting precedent is that of Julia who, according to Byron's reports, "whispering 'I will ne'er consent,'—consented."

The Court sustains this legislation by assuming two deviations from the facts of this particular case; first, it assumes a state of facts the record does not support, and secondly, it refuses to consider facts which are inescapable on the record.

The Court concludes that this "legislation, as applied, does no more than provide a general program to help parents get their children, regardless of their religion, safely and expeditiously to and from accredited schools," and it draws a comparison between "state provisions intended to guarantee free transportation" for school children with services such as police and fire protection, and implies that we are here dealing with "laws authorizing new types of public services. . . ." . . .

The Township of Ewing is not furnishing transportation to the children in any form; it is not operating school buses itself or contracting for their operation; and it is not performing any public service of any kind with this taxpayer's money. All school children are left to ride as ordinary paying passengers on the regular busses operated by the public transportation system. What the Township does, and what the taxpayer complains of, is at stated intervals to reimburse parents for the fares paid, provided the children attend either public schools or Catholic Church schools. This expenditure of tax funds has no possible effect on the child's safety or expedition in transit. As passengers on the public busses they travel as fast and no faster, and are as safe and no safer, since their parents are reimbursed as before.

In addition to thus assuming a type of service that does not exist, the Court also insists that we must close our eyes to a discrimination which does exist. The resolution which authorizes disbursement of this taxpayer's money limits reimbursement to those who attend public schools and Catholic schools. That is the way the Act is applied to this taxpayer.

The New Jersey Act in question makes the character of the school, not the needs of the children, determine the eligibility of parents to reimbursement. The Act permits payment for transportation to parochial schools or public schools but prohibits it to private schools operated in whole or in part for profit. Children often are sent to private schools because their parents feel that they require more individual instruction than public schools can provide, or because they are backward or defective and need special attention. If all children of the state were objects of impartial solicitude, no reason is obvious for denying transportation reimbursement to students of this class, for these often are as needy and as worthy as those who go to public or parochial schools. Refusal to reimburse those who attend such schools is understandable only in the light of a purpose to aid the schools, because the state might well abstain from aiding a profit-making private enterprise. Thus, under the Act and resolution brought to us by this case, children are classified according to the schools they attend and are to be aided if they attend the public schools or private Catholic schools, and they are not allowed to be aided if they attend private secular schools or private religious schools of other faiths.

Of course, this case is not one of a Baptist or a Jew or an Episcopalian or a pupil of a private school complaining of discrimination. It is one of a taxpayer urging that he is being taxed for an unconstitutional purpose. I think he is entitled to have us consider the Act just as it is written. . . . As applied to this taxpayer by the action he complains of, certainly the Act does not authorize reimbursement to those who choose any alternative to the public school except Catholic Church schools.

If we are to decide this case on the facts before us, our question is simply this: Is it constitutional to tax this complainant to pay the cost of carrying pupils to Church schools of one specified denomination?

Whether the taxpayer constitutionally can be made to contribute aid to parents of students because of their attendance at parochial schools depends upon the nature of those schools and their relation to the Church. The Constitution says nothing of education. It lays no obligation on the states to provide schools and does not undertake to regulate state systems of education if they see fit to maintain them. But they cannot, through school policy any more than through other means, invade rights secured to citizens by the Constitution of the United States. . . . One of our basic rights is to be free of taxation to support a transgression of the constitutional command that the authorities "shall make no law respecting an establishment of religion, or prohibiting the free exercise thereof. . . ." . . .

The function of the Church school is a subject on which this record is meager. It shows only that the schools are under superintendence of a priest and that "religion is taught as part of the curriculum." But we know that such schools are parochial only in name—they, in fact, represent a world-wide and age-old policy of the Roman Catholic Church. . . .

It is no exaggeration to say that the whole historic conflict in temporal policy between the Catholic Church and non-Catholics comes to a focus in their respective school policies. The Roman Catholic Church, counseled by experience in many ages and many lands and with all sorts and conditions of men, takes what, from the viewpoint of its own progress and the success of its mission, is a wise estimate of the importance of education to religion. It does not leave the individual to pick up religion by chance. It relies on early and indelible indoctrination in the faith and order of the Church by the word and example of persons consecrated to the task.

Our public school, if not a product of Protestantism, at least is more consistent with it than with the Catholic culture and scheme of values. It is a relatively recent development dating from about 1840. It is organized on the premise that secular education can be isolated from all religious teaching so that the school can inculcate all needed temporal knowledge and also maintain a strict and lofty neutrality as to religion. The assumption is that after the individual has been instructed in worldly wisdom he will be better fitted to choose his religion. Whether such a disjunction is possible, and if possible whether it is wise, are questions I need not try to answer.

I should be surprised if any Catholic would deny that the parochial school is a vital, if not the most vital, part of the Roman Catholic Church. If put to choice, that venerable institution, I should expect, would forego its whole service for mature persons before it would give up education of the young, and it would be a wise choice. Its growth and cohesion, discipline and loyalty, spring from its schools. Catholic education is the rock on which the whole structure rests, and to render tax aid to its Church school is indistinguishable to me from rendering the same aid to the Church itself.

It is of no importance in this situation whether the beneficiary of this expenditure of tax-raised funds is primarily the parochial school and incidentally the pupil, or whether the aid is directly bestowed on the pupil with indirect benefits to the school. The state cannot maintain a Church and it can no more tax its citizens to furnish free carriage to those who attend a Church. The prohibition against establishment of religion cannot be circumvented by a subsidy, bonus or reimbursement of expense to individuals for receiving religious instruction and indoctrination. . . .

It seems to me that the basic fallacy in the Court's reasoning, which accounts for its failure to apply the principles it avows, is in ignoring the essentially religious test by which beneficiaries of this expenditure are selected. A policeman protects a Catholic, of course—but not because he is a Catholic; it is because he is a man and a member of our society. The fireman protects the Church school—but not because it is a Church school; it is because it is property, part of the assets of our society. Neither the fireman nor the policeman has to ask before he renders aid "Is this man or building identified with the Catholic Church?" But before these school authorities draw a check to reimburse for a student's fare they must ask just that question, and if the school is a Catholic one they may render aid because it is such, while if it is of any other faith or is run for profit, the help must be withheld. To consider the converse of the Court's reasoning will best disclose its fallacy. . . .

The Court's holding is that this taxpayer has no grievance because the state has decided to make the reimbursement a public purpose and therefore we are bound to regard it as such. I agree that this Court has left, and always should leave to each state, great latitude in deciding for itself, in the light of its own conditions, what shall be public purposes in its scheme of things. It may socialize utilities and economic enterprises and make taxpayers' business out of what conventionally had been private business. It may make public business of individual welfare, health, education, entertainment or security. But it cannot make public business of religious worship or in-struction, or of attendance at religious institutions of any character. There is no answer to the proposition, more fully expounded by Mr. Justice Rutledge, that the effect of the religious freedom Amendment to our Constitution was to take every form of propagation of religion out of the realm of things which could directly or indirectly be made public business and thereby be supported in whole or in part at taxpayers' expense. That is a difference which the Constitution sets up between religion and almost every other subject matter of legislation, a difference which goes to the very root of religious freedom and which the Court is overlooking today. This freedom was first in the Bill of Rights because it was first in the forefathers' minds; it was set forth in absolute terms, and its strength is its rigidity. It was intended not only to keep the states' hands out of religion, but to keep religion's hands off the state, and, above all, to keep bitter religious controversy out of public life by denying to every denomination any advantage from getting control of public policy or the public purse. Those great ends I cannot but think are immeasurably compromised by today's decision.

This policy of our Federal Constitution has never been wholly pleasing to most religious groups. They all are quick to invoke its protections; they all are irked when they feel its restraints. This Court has gone a long way, if not an unreasonable way, to hold that public business of such paramount importance as maintenance of public order, protection of the privacy of the home, and taxation may not be pursued by a state in a way that even indirectly will interfere with religious proselyting. . . .

But we cannot have it both ways. Religious teaching cannot be a private affair when the state seeks to impose regulations which infringe on it indirectly, and a public affair when it comes to taxing citizens of one faith to aid another, or those of no faith to aid all. If these principles seem harsh in prohibiting aid to Catholic education, it must not be forgotten that it is the same Constitution that alone assures Catholics the right to maintain these schools at all when predominant local sentiment would forbid them. . . . Nor should I think that those who have done so well without this aid would want to see this separation between Church and State broken down. If the state may aid these religious schools, it may therefore regulate them. Many groups have sought aid from tax funds only to find that it carried political controls with it. Indeed this Court has declared that "It is hardly lack of due process for the Government to regulate that which it subsidizes." . . .

But in any event, the great purposes of the Constitution do not depend on the approval or convenience of those they restrain. I cannot read the history of the struggle to separate political from ecclesiastical affairs, well summarized in the opinion of Mr. Justice Rutledge in which I generally concur, without conviction that the Court today is unconsciously giving the clock's hands a backward turn.

MR. JUSTICE RUTLEDGE, WITH WHOM MR. JUSTICE FRANKFURTER, MR. JUSTICE JACKSON AND MR. JUSTICE BURTON AGREE, DISSENTING (OMITTED).

(3) Engel v. Vitale (1962)

+Black, Warren, Douglas, Clark, Harlan, Brennan
  −Stewart
  NP Frankfurter, White

[The Board of Education directed the principal of Union Free School District No. 9, New Hyde Park, New York, to require that the following prayer be said aloud by each class, in the presence of a teacher, at the beginning of each school day:

Almighty God, we acknowledge our dependence upon Thee, and we beg Thy blessings upon us, our parents, our teachers and our Country.

The prayer had been composed by the New York State Board of Regents, which had then recommended that it be used as part of a moral and spiritual training program.

Parents of ten pupils brought suit in a New York State court on grounds that the prayer was contrary to their religious beliefs and that the prayer and its use in the district violated the establishment clause. Use of the prayer was sustained by both the lower state courts as well as by the New York Court of Appeals. The U.S. Supreme Court granted certiorari.

This case and *Abington Township* v. *Schempp*, decided the following year, form what came to be known as the "Prayer Cases." They were among the many politically sensitive decisions made by the Warren Court in the early 1960s and led to efforts at state and national levels to overturn them. All were ultimately unsuccessful]

MR. JUSTICE BLACK delivered the opinion of the Court.

. . .

We think that by using its public school system to encourage recitation of the Regents' prayer, the State of New York has adopted a practice wholly inconsistent with the Establishment Clause. There can, of course, be no doubt that New York's program of daily classroom invocation of God's blessings as prescribed in the Regent's prayer is a religious activity. It is a solemn avowal of divine faith and supplication for the blessings of the Almighty. . . .

The petitioners contend among other things that the state laws requiring or permitting use of the Regents' prayer must be struck down as a violation of the Establishment

Clause because that prayer was composed by governmental officials as a part of a governmental program to further religious beliefs. For this reason, petitioners argue, the State's use of the Regents' prayer in its public school system breaches the constitutional wall of separation between Church and State. We agree with that contention since we think that the constitutional prohibition against laws respecting an establishment of religion must at least mean that in this country it is no part of the business of government to compose official prayers for any group of the American people to recite as a part of a religious program carried on by government.

It is a matter of history that this very practice of establishing governmentally composed prayers for religious services was one of the reasons which caused many of our early colonists to leave England and seek religious freedom in America. . . .

There can be no doubt that New York's state prayer program officially establishes the religious beliefs embodied in the Regents' prayer. The respondents' argument to the contrary, which is largely based upon the contention that the Regents' prayer is "nondenominational" and the fact that the program, as modified and approved by state courts, does not require all pupils to recite the prayer but permits those who wish to do so to remain silent or be excused from the room, ignores the essential nature of the program's constitutional defects. Neither the fact that the prayer may be denominationally neutral nor the fact that its observance on the part of the students is voluntary can serve to free it from the limitations of the Establishment Clause, as it might from the Free Exercise Clause, of the First Amendment, both of which are operative against the States by virtue of the Fourteenth Amendment. Although these two clauses may in certain instances overlap, they forbid two quite different kinds of governmental encroachment upon religious freedom. The Establishment Clause, unlike the Free Exercise Clause, does not depend upon any showing of direct governmental compulsion and is violated by the enactment of laws which establish an official religion whether those laws operate directly to coerce nonobserving individuals or not. This is not to say, of course, that laws officially prescribing a particular form of religious worship do not involve coercion of such individuals. When the power, prestige and financial support of government is placed behind a particular religious belief, the indirect coercive pressure upon religious minorities to conform to the prevailing officially approved religion is plain. But the purposes underlying the Establishment Clause go much further than that. Its first and most immediate purpose rested on the belief that a union of government and religion tends to destroy government and to degrade religion. The history of governmentally established religion, both in England and in this country, showed that whenever government had allied itself with one particular form of religion, the inevitable result had been that it had incurred the hatred, disrespect and even contempt of those who held contrary beliefs. That same history showed that many people had lost their respect for any religion that had relied upon the support of government to spread its faith. The Establishment Clause thus stands as an expression of principle on the part of the Founders of our Constitution that religion is too personal, too sacred, too holy, to permit its "unhallowed perversion" by a civil magistrate. Another purpose of the Establishment Clause rested upon an awareness of the historical fact that governmentally established religions and religious persecutions go hand in hand. . . .

It has been argued that to apply the Constitution in such a way as to prohibit state laws respecting an establishment of religious services in public schools is to indicate a hostility toward religion or toward prayer. Nothing, of course, could be more wrong. The history of man is inseparable from the history of religion. And perhaps it is not too much to say that since the beginning of that history many people have devoutly believed that "More things are wrought by prayer than this world dreams of." It was doubtless largely due to men who believed this that there grew up a sentiment that caused men to leave the cross-currents of officially established state religions and religious persecution in Europe and come to this country filled with the hope that they could find a place in which they could pray when they pleased to the God of their faith in the language they chose. And there were men of this same faith in the power of prayer who led the fight for adoption of our Constitution and also for our Bill of Rights with the very guarantees of religious freedom that forbid the sort of governmental activity which New York has attempted here. These men knew that the First Amendment, which tried to put an end to governmental control of religion and of prayer, was not written to destroy either. They knew rather that it was written to quiet well-justified fears which nearly all of them felt arising out of an awareness that governments of the past had shackled men's tongues to make them speak only the religious thoughts that government wanted them to speak and to pray only to the God that government wanted them to pray to. It is neither sacrilegious nor antireligious to say

that each separate government in this country should stay out of the business of writing or sanctioning official prayers and leave that purely religious function to the people themselves and to those the people choose to look to for religious guidance.

It is true that New York's establishment of its Regents' prayer as an officially approved religious doctrine of that State does not amount to a total establishment of one particular religious sect to the exclusion of all others—that, indeed, the governmental endorsement of that prayer seems relatively insignificant when compared to the governmental encroachments upon religion which were commonplace 200 years ago. To those who may subscribe to the view that because the Regents' official prayer is so brief and general there can be no danger to religious freedom in its governmental establishment, however, it may be appropriate to say in the words of James Madison, the author of the First Amendment:

[I]t is proper to take alarm at the first experiment on our liberties. . . . Who does not see that the same authority which can establish Christianity, in exclusion of all other Religions, may establish with the same ease any particular sect of Christians, in exclusion of all other Sects? That the same authority which can force a citizen to contribute three pence only of his property for the support of any one establishment, may force him to conform to any other establishment in all cases whatsoever?

The judgment of the Court of Appeals of New York is reversed and the cause remanded for further proceedings not inconsistent with this opinion.

MR. JUSTICE DOUGLAS, CONCURRING (OMITTED).

MR. JUSTICE STEWART, DISSENTING.

. . . I think that the Court's task, in this as in all areas of constitutional adjudication, is not responsibly aided by the uncritical invocation of metaphors like "wall of separation," a phrase nowhere to be found in the Constitution. What is relevant here is not the history of an established church in sixteenth century England or in eighteenth century America, but the history of the religious traditions of our people, reflected in countless practices of the institutions and officials of our government.

At the opening of each day's Session of this Court we stand, while one of our officials invokes the protection of God. Since the days of John Marshall our Crier has said, "God save the United States and this Honorable Court." Both the Senate and the House of Representatives open their daily sessions with prayer. Each of our Presidents, from George Washington to John F. Kennedy, has upon assuming his office, asked the protection and help of God.

. . .

Countless similar examples could be listed, but there is no need to belabor the obvious. It was all summed up by this Court just ten years ago [in *Zorach* v. *Clauson*] in a single sentence: "We are a religious people whose institutions presuppose a Supreme Being." . . .

[In *Abington School District* v. *Schempp* and *Murray* v. *Curlett* (1963), the Supreme Court ruled that the establishment clause forbids "requiring the selection and reading at the opening of the school day of verses from the Holy Bible and the recitation of the Lord's Prayer by the students in unison." The Pennsylvania law challenged in *Schempp* provided that ten verses of the Bible be read each day, without comment. The Baltimore school regulation challenged in *Murray* prescribed the daily read-

ing, also without comment, of a chapter from the Bible or the Lord's Prayer. In both cases, children could be excused upon parental request.

For the majority, Justice Clark noted that the establishment clause does more than forbid governmental preference of one religion over another. It also requires government neutrality between organized religion and lack of religious belief. The free exercise clause also supports the principle of government neutrality, but in these cases, primary reliance was placed on the establishment clause for a very practical reason. ". . . [I]t is necessary in a free exercise case for one to show the coercive effect of the enactment as it operates against him in the practice of his religion. The distinction between the two clauses is apparent—a violation of the Free Exercise Clause is predicated on coercion while the Establishment Clause violation need not be so attended."

Clark also rejected the contention of the school districts that these were exercises in pursuit of a secular purpose—"the promotion of moral values, the contradiction to the materialistic trends of our times, the perpetuation of our institutions and the teaching of literature." These purposes may well have been sought, Clark said, but they could not be sought through a religious ceremony. This was not merely an academic study of the Bible, "presented objectively as part of a secular program of education." Rather these were "religious exercises, required by the State in violation of the command of the First Amendment that the Government maintain strict neutrality, neither aiding nor opposing religion." That students could be excused from participating in these exercises was no defense, Clark added.]

(4) Wisconsin v. Yoder (1972)

+Burger, Stewart, Brennan, White, Marshall, Blackmun
±Douglas
NP Powell, Rehnquist

[Members of the Amish religious order refused to permit their children to attend public school after the eighth grade and were accordingly convicted of violating the compulsory school attendance laws of Wisconsin. Yoder, and the other defendants, contended that the law was in violation of their rights under the First and Fourteenth Amendments. Their contention was based upon typical Old Order Amish beliefs that life should be lived in a simple, agrarian fashion apart from the world and "wordly" influences and that to violate this tenet of their faith by undue exposure to these influences through attendance of public schools beyond the elementary grades would jeopardize their salvation and that of their children. The state of Wisconsin stipulated that the beliefs of the defendants were sincere.

The Wisconsin circuit court affirmed the convictions, but the Supreme Court of the state reversed on the basis of the free exercise clause of the First Amendment. The state of Wisconsin petitioned the U.S. Supreme Court for certiorari, and this was granted.

Perhaps more than any case in the history of the Supreme Court, *Yoder* exemplifies the situation out of which the "wall" theory of the First Amendment has come. The uniqueness of the situation in *Yoder* is that tension between the sixteenth-century values of the Amish and those of modern, technological, interdependent society has grown as the two styles of life have diverged. The Amish are vastly more rigorous than was Roger Williams; to them the "garden" can and must be separate from the "wilderness." It is probable, however, that the result in the case is partly explained by the great distance between the two positions.]

MR. CHIEF JUSTICE BURGER delivered the opinion of the Court.

There is no doubt as to the power of a State, having a high responsibility for education of its citizens, to impose reasonable regulations for the control and duration of basic education. . . . *Pierce* v. *Society of Sisters* . . . (1925). Providing public schools ranks at the very apex of the function of the State. Yet even this paramount responsibility was, in *Pierce*, made to yield to the right of parents to provide an equivalent education in a privately operated system. There the Court held that Oregon's statute compelling attendance in a public school from age eight to age 16 unreasonably interfered with the interest of parents in directing the rearing of their offspring including their education in church-operated schools. As that case suggests, the values of parental direction of the religious upbringing and education of their children in their early and formative years have a high place in our society. . . .

It follows that in order for Wisconsin to compel school attendance beyond the eighth grade against a claim that such attendance interferes with the practice of a legitimate religious belief, it must appear either that the State does not deny the free exercise of religious belief by its requirement, or that there is a state interest of sufficient magnitude to override the interest claiming protection under the Free Exercise Clause. . . .

. . . In evaluating [respondents'] claims we must be careful to determine whether the Amish religious faith and their mode of life are, as they claim, inseparable and interdependent. A way of life, however virtuous and admirable, may not be interposed as a barrier to reasonable state regulation of education if it is based on purely secular considerations; to have the protection of the Religion Clauses, the claims must be rooted in religious belief. Although a determination of what is a "religious" belief or practice entitled to constitutional protection may present a most delicate question, the very concept of ordered liberty precludes allowing every person to make his own standards on matters of conduct in which society as a whole has important interests. Thus, if the Amish asserted their claims because of their subjective evaluation and rejection of the contemporary secular values accepted by the majority, much as Thoreau rejected the social values of his time and isolated himself at Walden Pond, their claim would not rest on a religious basis. Thoreau's choice was philosophical and personal rather than religious, and such belief does not rise to the demands of the Religion Clause.

Giving no weight to such secular considerations, however, we see that the record in this case abundantly supports the claim that the traditional way of life of the Amish is not merely a matter of personal preference, but one of deep religious conviction, shared by an organized group, and intimately related to daily living. That the Old Order of Amish daily life and religious practice stems from their faith is shown by the fact that it is in response to their literal interpretation of the Biblical injunction from the Epistle of Paul to the Romans, "Be not conformed to this world. . . ." This command is fundamental to the Amish faith. Moreover, for the Old Order Amish, religion is not simply a matter of theocratic belief. . . .

As the society around the Amish has become more populous, urban, industrialized, and complex, particularly in this century, government regulation of human affairs has correspondingly become more detailed and pervasive. The Amish mode of life has thus come into conflict increasingly with requirements of contemporary society exerting a hydraulic insistence on conformity to majoritarian standards. So long as compulsory education laws were confined to eight grades of elementary basic education imparted in a nearby rural schoolhouse, with a large proportion of students of the Amish faith, the Old Order Amish had little basis to fear that school attendance

would expose their children to the worldly influence they reject. But modern compulsory secondary education in rural areas is now largely carried on in a consolidated school, often remote from the student's home and alien to his daily home life. As the record so strongly shows, the values and programs of the modern secondary school are in sharp conflict with the fundamental mode of life mandated by the Amish religion; modern laws requiring compulsory secondary education have accordingly engendered great concern and conflict. The conclusion is inescapable that secondary schooling, by exposing Amish children to worldly influences in terms of attitudes, goals and values contrary to beliefs, and by substantially interfering with the religious development of the Amish child and his integration into the way of life of the Amish faith community at the crucial adolescent state of development, contravenes the basic religious tenets and practice of the Amish faith, both as to the parent and the child.

The impact of the compulsory attendance law on respondents' practice of the Amish religion is not only severe, but inescapable, for the Wisconsin law affirmatively compels them, under threat of criminal sanction, to perform acts undeniably at odds with fundamental tenets of their religious beliefs. . . . Nor is the impact of the compulsory attendance law confined to grave interference with important Amish religious tenets from a subjective point of view. It carries with it precisely the kind of objective danger to the free exercise of religion which the First Amendment was designed to prevent. As the record shows, compulsory school attendance to age 16 for Amish children carries with it a very real threat of undermining the Amish community and religious practice as it exists today; they must either abandon belief and be assimilated into society at large, or be forced to migrate to some other and more tolerant region. . . .

Wisconsin concedes that under the Religion Clauses religious beliefs are absolutely free from the State's control, but it argues that "actions," even though religiously grounded, are outside the protection of the First Amendment. But our decisions have rejected the idea that religiously grounded conduct is always outside the protection of the Free Exercise Clause. It is true that activities of individuals, even when religiously based, are often subject to regulation by the States in the exercise of their undoubted power to promote the health, safety, and general welfare, or the Federal Government in the exercise of its delegated powers. . . . But to agree that religiously grounded conduct must often be subject to the broad police power of the State is not to deny that there are areas of conduct protected by the Free Exercise Clause of the First Amendment and thus beyond the power of the State to control, even under regulations of general applicability. . . . This case, therefore, does not become easier because respondents were convicted for their "actions" in refusing to send their children to the public high school; in this context belief and action cannot be neatly confined in logic-tight compartments. . . .

We turn . . . to the State's broader contention that its interest in its system of compulsory education is so compelling that even the established religious practices of the Amish must give way. Where fundamental claims of religious freedom are at stake, however, we cannot accept such a sweeping claim; . . .

The State advances two primary arguments in support of its system of compulsory education. It notes, as Thomas Jefferson pointed out early in our history, that some degree of education is necessary to prepare citizens to participate effectively and intelligently in our open political system if we are to preserve freedom and independence. Further, education prepares individuals to be self-reliant and self-sufficient participants in society. We accept these propositions.

However, the evidence adduced by the Amish in this case is persuasively to the effect that an additional one or two years of formal high school for Amish children in place of their long established program of informal vocational education would do little to serve those interests. . . .

The State attacks respondents' position as one fostering "ignorance" from which the child must be protected by the State. No one can question the State's duty to protect children from ignorance but this argument does not square with the facts disclosed in the record. Whatever their idiosyncrasies as seen by the majority, this record strongly shows that the Amish community has been a highly successful social unit within our society even if apart from the conventional "mainstream." Its members are productive and very law-abiding members of society; they reject public welfare in any of its usual modern forms. The Congress itself recognized their self-sufficiency by authorizing exemption of such groups as the Amish from the obligation to pay social security taxes.

It is neither fair nor correct to suggest that the Amish are opposed to education beyond the eighth grade level. What this record shows is that they are opposed to conventional formal education of the type provided by a certified high school because it comes at the child's crucial adolescent period of religious development. . . .

The requirement for compulsory education beyond the eighth grade is a relatively recent development in our history. Less than 60 years ago, the educational requirements of almost all of the States were satisfied by completion of the elementary grades, at least where the child was regularly and lawfully employed. The independence and successful social functioning of the Amish community for a period approaching almost three centuries and more than 200 years in this country is strong evidence that there is at best a speculative gain, in terms of meeting the duties of citizenship, from an additional one or two years of compulsory formal education. Against this background it would require a more particularized showing from the State on this point to justify the severe interference with religious freedom such additional compulsory attendance would entail.

Finally, the State, . . . argues that a decision exempting Amish children from the State's requirement fails to recognize the substantive right of the Amish child to a secondary education, and fails to give due regard to the power of the State as *parens patriae* to extend the benefit of secondary education to children regardless of the wishes of their parents. . . .

This case, of course, is not one in which any harm to the physical or mental health of the child or to the public safety, peace, order, or welfare has been demonstrated or may be properly inferred. The record is to the contrary, and any reliance on that theory would find no support in the evidence. . . .

For the reasons stated we hold, with the Supreme Court of Wisconsin, that the First and Fourteenth Amendments prevent the State from compelling respondents to cause their children to attend formal high school to age 16. . . .

Aided by a history of three centuries as an identifiable religious sect and a long history as a successful and self-sufficient segment of American society, the Amish in this case have convincingly demonstrated the sincerity of their religious beliefs, the interrelationship of belief with their mode of life, and vital role which belief and daily conduct play in the continued survival of Old Order Amish communities and their religious organization, and the hazards presented by the State's enforcement of a statute generally valid as to others. Beyond this, they have carried the even more difficult burden of demonstrating the adequacy of their alternative mode of continuing informal vocational education in their terms of precisely those overall interests that the State advanced in support of its program of compulsory high school education. In light of this convincing showing, one which probably few other religious groups or sects could make, and weighing the minimal difference between what the State would require and what the Amish already accept, it was incumbent in the State to show with more particularity how its admittedly strong interest in compulsory education would be adversely affected by granting an exemption to the Amish. . . .

Affirmed.

MR. JUSTICE STEWART, WITH WHOM MR. JUSTICE BRENNAN JOINS, CONCURRING.

Wisconsin has sought to brand these parents as criminals for following *their* religious beliefs, and the Court today rightly holds that Wisconsin cannot constitutionally do so.

This case in no way involves any questions regarding the right of the children of Amish parents to attend public high schools, or any other institutions of learning, if they wish to do so. As the Court points out, there is no suggestion whatever in the record that the religious beliefs of the children here concerned differ in any way from those of their parents. . . .

It is clear to me, therefore, that this record simply does not present the interesting and important issue discussed in . . . the dissenting opinion of Mr. Justice Douglas. With this observation, I join the opinion and the judgment of the Court.

MR. JUSTICE WHITE, WITH WHOM MR. JUSTICE BRENNAN AND MR. JUSTICE STEWART JOIN, CONCURRING (OMITTED).

MR. JUSTICE DOUGLAS, DISSENTING IN PART.

I agree with the Court that the religious scruples of the Amish are opposed to the education of their children beyond the grade schools, yet I disagree with the Court's conclusion that the matter is within the dispensation of parents alone. The Court's analysis assumes that the only interests at stake in the case are those of the Amish parents on the one hand, and those of the State on the other. The difficulty with this approach is that, despite the Court's claim, the parents are seeking to vindicate not only their own free exercise claims, but also those of their high-school-age children.

First, respondents' motion to dismiss in the trial court expressly asserts, not only the religious liberty of the adults, but also that of the children, as a defense to the prosecutions. It is, of course, beyond question that the parents have standing as defendants in a criminal prosecution to assert the religious interests of their children as a defense. Although the lower courts and the majority in this Court assume an identity of interest between parent and child, it is clear that they have treated the religious interest of the child as a factor in the analysis.

Second, it is essential to reach the question to decide the case not only because the question was squarely raised in the motion to dismiss, but also because no analysis of religious liberty claims can take place in a vacuum. If the parents in this case are allowed a religious exemption, the inevitable effect is to impose the parents' notions of religious duty upon their children. Where the child is mature enough to express potentially conflicting desires, it would be an invasion of the child's rights to permit such an imposition without canvassing his views. . . .

(5) Lemon v. Kurtzman (1971)

+Burger, Marshall, Douglas, Black, Brennan, Harlan, Blackmun, Stewart
±White

[With the *Lemon* and *Meek* cases, attention returns to the problem that was broached in *Everson*—that is, the kind and degree of support that the state may extend to private parochial schools. The "child benefit" approach in combination with "neutrality" largely explained the result in *Everson,* as we noted in the introductory note of this section. But *Lemon* presents a situation in which the increased salience and expense of education create the need for unprecedented public support of private schools.

The *Lemon* set of cases involves the laws of two states: Rhode Island and Pennsylvania. The Rhode Island Salary Supplement Act provided for a 15 percent supplement to be paid to teachers in nonpublic schools at which the per-pupil expenditure for secular subjects was below the average in public schools. Teachers were eligible for this supplement only if they taught courses offered in the public schools, did not teach religious courses, and used the same materials as in public school courses. About 250 teachers at Roman Catholic schools were the beneficiaries of this policy.

Pennsylvania's Nonpublic Elementary and Secondary Education Act authorized the state superintendent of public instruction to "purchase" certain educational services from nonpublic schools and accordingly to reimburse the nonpublic schools for teacher salaries, materials, and textbooks. Restrictions on this reimbursement call for the courses to be secular and the texts to be approved by the superintendent. Challenges to both acts were grounded in the religion clauses of the First Amendment. A three-judge federal court found Rhode Island's law to violate the establishment clause, and the decision was appealed to the U.S. Supreme Court. In Pennsylvania a three-judge federal court held that the act violated neither of the religion clauses of the First Amendment.]

MR. CHIEF JUSTICE BURGER delivered the opinion of the Court.
. . .

In *Everson* v. *Board of Education* . . . (1947), this Court upheld a state statute that reimbursed the parents of parochial school children for bus transportation expenses. There Mr. Justice Black, writing for the majority, suggested that the decision carried to "the verge" of forbidden territory under the Religion Clauses. . . . Candor compels acknowledgment, moreover, that we can only dimly perceive the lines of demarcation in this extraordinarily sensitive area of constitutional law.

The language of the Religion Clauses of the First Amendment is at best opaque, particularly when compared with other portions of the Amendment. Its authors did not simply prohibit the establishment of a state church or a state religion, an area history shows they regarded as very important and fraught with great dangers. Instead they commanded that there should be "no law *respecting* an establishment of reli-

gion." A law may be one "respecting" the forbidden objective while falling short of its total realization. A law "respecting" the proscribed result, that is, the establishment of religion, is not always easily identifiable as one violative of the Clause. A given law might not *establish* a state religion but nevertheless be one "respecting" that end in the sense of being a step that could lead to such establishment and hence offend the First Amendment.

In the absence of precisely stated constitutional prohibitions, we must draw lines with reference to the three main evils against which the Establishment Clause was intended to afford protection: "sponsorship, financial support, and active involvement of the sovereign in religious activity." *Walz* v. *Tax Commission* . . . (1970).

Every analysis in this area must begin with consideration of the cumulative criteria developed by the Court over many years. Three such tests may be gleaned from our cases. First, the statute must have a secular legislative purpose; second, its principal or primary effect must be one that neither advances nor inhibits religion, *Board of Education* v. *Allen* . . . (1968); finally, the statute must not foster "an excessive government entanglement with religion." *Walz, supra.* . . .

Inquiry into the legislative purposes of the Pennsylvania and Rhode Island statutes affords no basis for a conclusion that the legislative intent was to advance religion. On the contrary, the statutes themselves clearly state that they are intended to enhance the quality of the secular education in all schools covered by the compulsory attendance laws. There is no reason to believe the legislatures meant anything else. A State always has a legitimate concern for maintaining minimum standards in all schools it allows to operate. As in *Allen,* we find nothing here that undermines the stated legislative intent; it must therefore be accorded appropriate deference.

In *Allen* the Court acknowledged that secular and religious teachings were not necessarily so intertwined that secular textbooks furnished to students by the State were in fact instrumental in the teaching of religion. . . . The legislatures of Rhode Island and Pennsylvania have concluded that secular and religious education are identifiable and separable. In the abstract we have no quarrel with this conclusion.

The two legislatures, however, have also recognized that church-related elementary and secondary schools have a significant religious mission and that a substantial portion of their activities is religiously oriented. They have therefore sought to create statutory restrictions designed to guarantee the separation between secular and religious educational functions and to ensure that State financial aid supports only the former. All these provisions are precautions taken in candid recognition that these programs approached, even if they did not intrude upon, the forbidden areas under the Religion Clauses. We need not decide whether these legislative precautions restrict the principal or primary effect of the programs to the point where they do not offend the Religion Clause, for we conclude that the cumulative impact of the entire relationship arising under the statutes in each State involves excessive entanglement between government and religion.

In *Walz* v. *Tax Commission, supra,* the Court upheld state tax exemptions for real property owned by religious organizations and used for religious worship. That holding, however, tended to confine rather than enlarge the area of permissible state involvement with religious institutions by calling for close scrutiny of the degree of entanglement involved in the relationship. The objective is to prevent, as far as possible, the intrusion of either into the precincts of the other. . . .

In order to determine whether the government entanglement with religion is excessive, we must examine the character and purposes of the institutions that are benefited, the nature of the aid that the State provides, and the resulting relationship between the government and the religious authority. Mr. Justice Harlan, in a separate opinion in *Walz, supra,* echoed the classic warning as to "programs, whose very nature is apt to entangle the state in details of administration. . . ." . . . Here we find that both statutes foster an impermissible degree of entanglement.

(a) Rhode Island Program

The District Court made extensive findings on the grave potential for excessive entanglement that inheres in the religious character and purpose of the Roman Catholic elementary schools of Rhode Island, to date the sole beneficiaries of the Rhode Island Salary Supplement Act.

The church schools involved in the program are located close to parish churches. This understandably permits convenient access for religious exercises since instruction in faith and morals is part of the total educational process. The school buildings contain identifying religious symbols such as crosses on the exterior and crucifixes, and religious paintings and statues either in the classrooms or hallways. Although only approximately 30 minutes a day are devoted to direct religious instruction, there are religiously oriented extracurricular activities. Approximately two-thirds of the teachers in these schools are nuns of various religious orders. Their dedicated efforts provide an atmosphere in which religious instruction and religious vocations are natural and proper parts of life in such schools. Indeed, as the District Court found, the role of teaching nuns in enhancing the religious atmosphere has led the parochial school authorities to attempt to maintain a one-to-one ratio between nuns and lay teachers in all schools rather than to permit some to be staffed almost entirely by lay teachers. . . .

The substantial religious character of these church-related schools gives rise to entangling church-state relationships of the kind the Religion Clauses sought to avoid. Although the District Court found that concern for religious values did not inevitably or necessarily intrude into the content of secular subjects, the considerable religious activities of these schools led the legislature to provide for careful governmental controls and surveillance by state authorities in order to ensure that state aid supports only secular education. . . .

There is another area of entanglement in the Rhode Island program that gives concern. The statute excludes teachers employed by non-public schools whose average per-pupil expenditures on secular education equal or exceed the comparable figures for public schools. In the event that the total expenditures of an otherwise eligible school exceed this norm, the program requires the government to examine the school's records in order to determine how much of the total expenditures is attributable to secular education and how much to religious activity. This kind of state inspection and evaluation of the religious content of a religious organization is fraught with the sort of entanglement that the Constitution forbids. It is a relationship pregnant with dangers of excessive government direction of church schools and hence of churches. The Court noted "the hazards of government supporting churches" in *Walz v. Tax Commission, supra,* . . . and we cannot ignore here the danger that pervasive modern governmental power will ultimately intrude on religion and thus conflict with the Religion Clauses.

(b) Pennsylvania Program

The Pennsylvania statute also provides state aid to church-related schools for teachers' salaries. The complaint describes an educational system that is very similar to the one existing in Rhode Island. According to the allegations, the church-related elementary and secondary schools are controlled by religious organizations, have the purpose of propagating and promoting a particular religious faith, and conduct their operations to fulfill that purpose. Since this complaint was dismissed for failure to state a claim for relief, we must accept these allegations as true for purposes of our review.

As we noted earlier, the very restrictions and surveillance necessary to ensure that teachers play a strictly nonideological role give rise to entanglements between church and state. The Pennsylvania statute, like that of Rhode Island, fosters this kind of relationship. Reimbursement is not only limited to courses offered in the public schools and materials approved by state officials, but the statute excludes "any subject matter expressing religious teaching, or the morals or forms of worship of any sect." In addition, schools seeking reimbursement must maintain accounting procedures that require the State to establish the cost of the secular as distinguished from the religious instruction.

The Pennsylvania statute, moreover, has the further defect of providing state financial aid directly to the church-related schools. This factor distinguishes both *Everson* and *Allen*, for in both those cases the Court was careful to point out that state aid was provided to the student and his parents—not to the church-related school. . . .

A broader base of entanglement of yet a different character is presented by the divisive political potential of these state programs. In a community where such a large number of pupils are served by church-related schools, it can be assumed that state assistance will entail considerable political activity. Partisans of parochial schools, understandably concerned with rising costs and sincerely dedicated to both the religious and secular educational missions of their schools, will inevitably champion this cause and promote political action to achieve their goals. Those who oppose state aid, whether for constitutional, religious, or fiscal reasons, will inevitably respond and employ all of the usual political campaign techniques to prevail. Candidates will be forced to declare and voters to choose. It would be unrealistic to ignore the fact that many people confronted with issues of this kind will find their votes aligned with their faith. . . .

In *Walz* it was argued that a tax exemption for places of religious worship would prove to be the first step in an inevitable progression leading to the establishment of state churches and state religion. That claim could not stand up against more than 200 years of virtually universal practice imbedded in our colonial experience and continuing into the present.

The progression argument, however, is more persuasive here. We have no long history of state aid to church-related educational institutions comparable to 200 years of tax exemption for churches. Indeed, the state programs before us today represent something of an innovation. We have already noted that modern governmental programs have self-perpetuating and self-expanding propensities. These internal pressures are only enhanced when the schemes involve institutions whose legitimate needs are growing and whose interests have substantial political support. Nor can we fail to see that in constitutional adjudication some steps, which when taken were thought to approach "the verge," have become the platform for yet further steps. A certain momentum develops in constitutional theory and it can be a "downhill thrust" easily set in motion but difficult to retard or stop. Development by momentum is not invariably bad; indeed, it is the way the common law has grown, but it is a force to be recognized and reckoned with. The dangers are increased by the difficulty of perceiving in advance exactly where the "verge" of the precipice lies. As well as constituting an independent evil against which the Religion Clauses were intended to protect, involvement or entanglement between government and religion serves as a warning signal.

Finally, nothing we have said can be construed to disparage the role of church-related elementary and secondary schools in our national life. Their contribution has been and is enormous. Nor do we ignore their economic plight in a period of rising costs and expanding need. Taxpayers generally have been spared vast sums by the maintenance of these educational institutions by religious organizations, largely by the gifts of faithful adherents.

The merit and benefits of these schools, however, are not the issue before us in these cases. The sole question is whether state aid to these schools can be squared with the dictates of the Religion Clauses. Under our system the choice has been made that government is to be entirely excluded from the area of religious instruction and churches excluded from the affairs of government. The Constitution decrees that religion must be a private matter for the individual, the family, and the institutions of private choice, and that while some involvement and entanglement are inevitable, lines must be drawn.

The judgment of the Rhode Island District Court . . . is affirmed. The judgment of the Pennsylvania District Court . . . is reversed, and the case is remanded for further proceedings consistent with this opinion.

MR. JUSTICE DOUGLAS, WHOM MR. JUSTICE BLACK JOINS, CONCURRING (OMITTED).
MR. JUSTICE WHITE, CONCURRING IN PART AND DISSENTING IN PART (OMITTED).

(6) Meek v. Pittinger (1975)

−Stewart, Blackmun, Powell
±Brennan, Douglas, Marshall, Burger, Rehnquist, White

[Two acts of the Commonwealth of Pennsylvania called for supplying to nonpublic schools "auxiliary services" and the lending of materials and equipment. The acts also called for the direct loan of textbooks to children enrolled in these schools. Services included the usual range available to public schools: counseling, testing, psychological and therapeutic services, and special education programs. A suit was brought in the federal district court charging that the statutes violated the First and Fourteenth Amendments. A three-judge panel held that the textbook loan, auxiliary services, and materials loan programs were constitutional but

that the equipment loan programs were unconstitutional. The decision was appealed to the Supreme Court.

The somewhat unusual array of votes indicated above shows the difficulty of this case and others like it. These situations call for the justices to make very fine distinctions between direct aids to pupils and those that go beyond that to "excessive entanglement" or "furthering" of religion. It is clear that making such distinctions has become more rather than less difficult.]

MR. JUSTICE STEWART announced the judgment of the Court and delivered the opinion of the Court, together with an opinion in which MR. JUSTICE BLACKMUN and MR. JUSTICE POWELL, joined.

. . .

In judging the constitutionality of the various forms of assistance authorized by Acts 194 and 195, the District Court applied the three-part test that has been clearly stated, if not easily applied by this Court in recent Establishment Clause cases. . . .

These tests constitute a convenient, accurate distillation of this Court's efforts over the past decades to evaluate a wide range of governmental action challenged as violative of the constitutional prohibition against laws "respecting an establishment of religion," and thus provide the proper framework of analysis for the issues presented in the case before us. It is well to emphasize, however, that the tests must not be viewed as setting the precise limits to the necessary constitutional inquiry, but serve only as guidelines with which to identify instances in which the objectives of the Establishment Clause have been impaired.
. . .

The District Court held that the textbook loan provisions of Act 195 are constitutionally indistinguishable from the New York textbook loan program upheld in *Board of Education* v. *Allen*. . . . We agree.

Approval of New York's textbook loan program in the *Allen* case was based primarily on this Court's earlier decision in *Everson* v. *Board of Education, supra,* holding that the constitutional prohibition against laws "respecting an establishment of religion" did not prevent "New Jersey from spending tax-raised funds to pay the bus fares of parochial school pupils as a part of a general program under with it pays the fares of pupils attending public and other schools." . . . Similarly, the Court in *Allen* found that the New York textbook law "merely makes available to all children the benefits of a general· program to lend school books free of charge. Books are furnished at the request of the pupil and ownership remains, at least technically, in the State. Thus no funds or books are furnished to parochial schools, and the financial benefit is to parents and children, not to schools." . . . The Court conceded that provision of free textbooks might make it "more likely that some children chose to attend a sectarian school, but that was true of the state-paid bus fares in *Everson* and does not alone demonstrate an unconstitutional degree of support for a religious institution. . . .

Like the New York program, the textbook provisions of Act 195 extend to all schoolchildren the benefits of Pennsylvania's well-established policy of lending textbooks free of charge to elementary and secondary school students. As in *Allen,* Act 195 provides that the textbooks are to be lent directly to the student, not to the nonpublic school itself, although, again as in *Allen,* the administrative practice is to have student requests for the books filed initially with the nonpublic school and to have the school authorities prepare collective

summaries of these requests which they forward to the appropriate public officials. . . . Thus, the financial benefit of Pennsylvania's textbook program, like New York's, is to parents and children, not to the nonpublic schools. . . .

Although textbooks are lent only to students, Act 195 authorizes the loan of instructional material and equipment directly to qualifying nonpublic elementary and secondary schools in the Commonwealth. The appellants assert that such direct aid to Pennsylvania's nonpublic schools, including church-related institutions, constitutes an impermissible establishment of religion.

Act 195 is accompanied by legislative findings that the welfare of the Commonwealth requires that present and future generations of schoolchildren be assured ample opportunity to develop their intellectual capacities. Act 195 is intended to further that objective by extending the benefits of free educational aids to every schoolchild in the Commonwealth, including nonpublic school students who comprise approximately one quarter of the school children in Pennsylvania. . . . We accept the legitimacy of this secular legislative purpose. . . . But we agree with the appellants that the direct loan of instructional material and equipment has the unconstitutional primary effect of advancing religion because of the predominantly religious character of the schools benefiting from the Act. . . .

It is, of course, true that as part of general legislation made available to all students, a State may include church-related schools in programs providing bus transportation, school lunches, and public health facilities—secular and nonideological services unrelated to the primary, religious-oriented educational function of the sectarian school. The indirect and incidental benefits to church-related schools from those programs do not offend the constitutional prohibition against establishment of religion . . . But the massive aid provided the church-related nonpublic schools of Pennsylvania by Act 195 is neither indirect nor incidental.

For the 1972-1973 school year the Commonwealth authorized just under $12 million of direct aid to the predominantly church-related nonpublic schools of Pennsylvania through the loan of instructional material and equipment pursuant to Act 195. To be sure, the material and equipment that are the subjects of the loan—maps, charts, and laboratory equipment, for example—are "self-polic(ing), in that starting as secular, nonideological and neutral, they will not change in use. . . . But faced with the substantial amounts of direct support authorized by Act 195, it would simply ignore reality to attempt to separate secular educational functions from the predominantly religious role performed by any of Pennsylvania's church-related elementary and secondary schools and to then characterize Act 195 as channeling aid to the secular without providing direct aid to the sectarian. Even though earmarked for secular purposes, "when it flows to an institution in which religion is so pervasive that a substantial portion of its functions are subsumed in the religious mission," state aid has the impermissible primary effect of advancing religion. . . .

Unlike Act 195, which provides only for the loan of teaching material and equipment, Act 194 authorizes the Secretary of Education, through the intermediate units, to supply professional staff, as well as supportive materials, equipment, and personnel, to the nonpublic schools of the commonwealth. The "auxiliary services"

authorized by Act 194—remedial and accelerated instruction, guidance counseling and testing, speech and hearing services—are provided directly to nonpublic schoolchildren with the appropriate special need. But the services are provided only on the nonpublic school premises, and only when "requested by nonpublic school representatives." . . .

The legislative findings accompanying Act 194 are virtually identical to those in Act 195: Act 194 is intended to assure full development of the intellectual capacities of the children of Pennsylvania by extending the benefits of free auxiliary services to all students in the Commonwealth. . . . The appellants concede the validity of this secular legislative purpose. Nonetheless, they argue that Act 194 constitutes an impermissible establishment of religion because the auxiliary services are provided on the premises of predominantly church-related schools.

In rejecting the appellants' argument, the District Court emphasized that "auxiliary services" are provided directly to the children involved and are expressly limited to those services which are secular, neutral, and nonideological. The court also noted that the instruction and counseling in question served only to supplement the basic, normal educational offerings of the qualifying non-public schools. Any benefits to church-related schools that may result from the provision of such services, the District Court concluded, are merely incidental and indirect, and thus not impermissible. . . . The court also held that no continuing supervision of the personnel providing auxiliary services would be necessary to establish that Act 194's secular limitations were observed or to guarantee that a member of the auxiliary services staff had not "succumb(ed) to sectarianization of his or her professional work."

We need not decide whether substantial state expenditures to enrich the curricula of church-related elementary and secondary schools, like the expenditure of state funds to support the basic educational program of those schools, necessarily results in the direct and substantial advancement of religious activity. For decisions of this Court make clear that the District Court erred in relying entirely on the good faith and professionalism of the secular teachers and counselors functioning in church-related schools to ensure that a strictly nonideological posture is maintained. . . .

The fact that the teachers and counselors providing auxiliary services are employees of the public intermediate unit, rather than of the church-related schools in which they work, does not substantially eliminate the need for continuing surveillance. To be sure, auxiliary services personnel, because not employed by the non-public schools, are not directly subject to the discipline of a religious authority. . . . But they are performing important educational services in schools in which education is an integral part of the dominant sectarian mission and in which an atmosphere dedicated to the advancement of religious belief is constantly maintained. . . . The potential for impermissible fostering of religion under these circumstances, although somewhat reduced, is nonetheless present. To be certain that auxiliary teachers remain religiously neutral, as the Constitution demands, the State would have to impose limitations on the activities of auxiliary personnel and then engage in some form of continuing surveillance to ensure that those restrictions were being followed.

In addition, Act 194, like the statutes considered in *Lemon* v. *Kurtzman, supra,* . . . creates a serious potential for divisive conflict over the issue of aid to religion—"entanglement in the broader sense of continuing political strife." . . . The recurrent nature of the appropriation process guarantees annual reconsideration of Act 194 and the prospect of repeated confrontation between proponents and opponents of the auxiliary services program. The Act thus provides successive opportunities for political fragmentation and division along religious lines, one of the principal evils against which the Establishment Clause was intended to protect. . . . This potential for political entanglement, together with the administrative entanglement which would be necessary to ensure that auxiliary services personnel remain strictly neutral and nonideological when functioning in church-related schools, compels the conclusion that Act 194 violates the constitutional prohibition against laws "respecting an establishment of religion."

The judgment of the District Court as to Act 194 is reversed; its judgment as to the textbook provisions of Act 195 is affirmed, but as to that Act's other provisions now before us its judgment is reversed.

MR. CHIEF JUSTICE BURGER, CONCURRING IN THE JUDGMENT IN PART AND DISSENTING IN PART (OMITTED).

MR. JUSTICE BRENNAN, WITH WHOM MR. JUSTICE DOUGLAS AND MR. JUSTICE MARSHALL JOIN, CONCURRING AND DISSENTING.

I join in the reversal of the District Court's judgment insofar as that judgment upheld the constitutionality of Act 194 and the provisions of Act 195 respecting instructional materials and equipment, but dissent from . . . the affirmance of the judgment upholding the constitutionality of the textbook provisions of Act 195. . . .

MR. JUSTICE REHNQUIST, WITH WHOM MR. JUSTICE WHITE JOINS, CONCURRING IN THE JUDGMENT IN PART AND DISSENTING IN PART, (OMITTED).

[In *Wolman* v. *Walter* (1977), the Court considered the constitutionality of an Ohio statute specifically passed in response to *Meek* v. *Pittinger*. Generally, the law authorized the state to provide pupils in nonpublic schools with books, instructional materials and equipment, testing and scoring, diagnostic services, therapeutic services, and field trip transportation. Funds were to be provided directly to the school districts for direct purchase of the equipment and services. All services were performed off the premises of nonpublic schools. No equipment or services that were not also available to the public schools could be purchased, and the per-pupil costs of these expenditures for nonpublic schools could not exceed the per-pupil cost for public schools.

In another badly split decision, the Court upheld the validity of provisions for textbooks, testing and scoring, diagnostic services, and therapeutic services. Expenditures for instructional materials and equipment and field trip transportation were held invalid. In *Meek* the provision of instruction materials and equipment was held invalid because it involved a program of direct loans to nonpublic schools. Ohio contended that its statute was valid because the loans were made directly to the pupils or parents. But the Court said this was merely a technical change, a distinction without a difference. The equipment could still be stored in nonpublic schools and could be used for sectarian purposes. The field trips provision was held invalid because it contained no restrictions on the purpose of such trips or their destinations. Since the nonpublic schools, not the children, control the timing and destination of the trips, they are, the Court said, truly "the recipients of the service." This fact alone was sufficient to invalidate that portion of the stat- ute. Additionally, they would be led by nonpublic school teachers and would be an integrated part of the educational experience fostered by that school.]

B. *Conscientious Objection*

(1) A Note on Conscientious Objection

At the fringes of the constitutional question of religion is the status of the conscientious objector. Every conscription law has provided for exemption based on religious principles, but as our society has moved in more secular directions, this exemption became more broadly based on beliefs that are *equivalent* to institutionalized religious values. The problem for the Supreme Court has been to give effective meaning to the changes in the law that Congress had made and yet to honor the role of conscience in service to the nation.

The 1917 Draft Act permitted exemptions only to persons affiliated with well-recognized religious organizations espousing pacifist beliefs. The 1940 conscription law permitted conscientious objector status to those whose opposition to war in any form was rooted in "religious training and belief." And in 1948, Congress defined "religious training and belief" as "an individual's belief in a relation to a Supreme Being involving duties superior to those arising from any human relation, but [not including] essentially political, sociological, or philosophical views or a merely personal moral code."

In *United States* v. *Seeger* (1965), the Supreme Court interpreted this language to mean:

. . . *the test of belief "in relation to a Supreme Being" is whether a given belief that is sincere and meaningful occupies a place in the life of its possessor parallel to that filled by the orthodox belief in*

God of one who clearly qualifies for the exemption. Where such beliefs have parallel positions in the lives of their respective holders we cannot say that one is "in relation to a Supreme Being" and the other is not.

The Court's upholding of Seeger's claim to conscientious objector status and its very loose interpretation of the statute were extremely controversial in the already overheated political environment of the Vietnam War. Congress responded by deleting the "Supreme Being" language in an attempt to strengthen the theistic requirements for conscientious objection. The *Welsh* case, which follows, was the Court's first response to that change. The dilemma for the Court was that to accede to congressional pressures to limit conscientious objector status to "orthodox" pacifists, for example, by interpreting the statute literally, meant facing the probability of deciding that the statute was inconsistent with the religion clauses of the First Amendment, as well as perhaps being an unconstitutionally unequal classification prohibited to the federal government by the due process clause of the Fifth Amendment. Faced with the same dilemma in *Seeger*, the Court had chosen, in effect, to rewrite the statute to bring it within constitutional boundaries. But its decision in *Seeger* opened it to the charge of "judicial legislating."

(2) Welsh v. United States (1970)

+Black, Douglas, Brennan, Harlan, Marshall
−Burger, Stewart, White

[Elliott Welsh II was convicted of refusing to submit to induction into the armed forces and sentenced to three years imprisonment. His claim to exemption as a conscientious objector was denied because the court found it was not based on "religious training and belief" as required by the statute. A divided court of appeals affirmed his conviction, and the Supreme Court granted certiorari.]

MR. JUSTICE BLACK announced the judgment of the Court and delivered an opinion in which MR. JUSTICE DOUGLAS, MR. JUSTICE BRENNAN, and MR. JUSTICE MARSHALL join.

The controlling facts in this case are strikingly similar to those in *Seeger*. Both Seeger and Welsh were brought up in religious homes and attended church in their childhood, but in neither case was this church one which taught its members not to engage in war at any time for any reason. Neither Seeger nor Welsh continued his childhood religious ties into his young manhood, and neither belonged to any religious group or adhered to the teachings of any organized religion during the period of his involvement with the Selective Service System. At the time of their registration for the draft, neither had yet come to accept pacifist principles. Their views on war developed only in subsequent years, but when their ideas did truly mature both made application with their local draft boards for conscientious objector exemptions from military service under § 6(j) of the Universal Military Training and Service Act. That section then provided, in part:

Nothing contained in this title shall be construed to require any person to be subject to combatant training and service in the armed forces of the United States who, by reason of religious training and belief, is conscientiously opposed to participation in war in any form. Religious training and belief in this connection means an individual's belief in a relation to a Supreme Being involving duties superior to those arising from any human relation, but does not include essentially political, socio-logical, or philosophical views or a merely personal moral code.

In filling out their exemption applications both Seeger and Welsh were unable to sign the statement which, as printed in the Selective Service form, stated "I am, by reason of my religious training and belief, conscientiously opposed to participation in war in any form." Seeger could sign only after striking the words "training and" and putting quotation marks around the word "religious." Welsh could only sign after striking the words "religious training and." On those same applications, neither could definitely affirm or deny that he believed in a "Supreme Being," both stating that they preferred to leave the question open. But both Seeger and Welsh affirmed on those applications that they held deep conscientious scruples against taking part in wars where people were killed. Both strongly believed that killing in war was wrong, unethical, and immoral, and their consciences forbade them to take part in such an evil practice. Their objections to participating in war in any form could not be said to come from a "still, soft voice of conscience"; rather, for them that voice was so loud and insistent that both men preferred to go to jail rather than serve in the Armed Forces. There was never any question about the sincerity and depth of Seeger's convictions as a conscientious objector, and the same is true of Welsh. . . . But to both cases the Selective Service System concluded that the beliefs of these men were in some sense insufficiently "religious" to qualify them for conscientious objector exemptions under the terms of §6(j). Seeger's conscientious objector claim was denied "solely because it was not based upon a belief in a relation to a Su-

preme Being, as required by §6(j) of the Act," . . . while Welsh was denied the exemption because his Appeal Board and the Department of Justice hearing officer "could find no religious basis for the registrant's belief, opinions, and convictions." . . . Both Seeger and Welsh subsequently refused to submit to induction into the military and both were convicted of that offense. . . .

The Court made it clear [in the *Seeger* case] that these sincere and meaningful beliefs which prompt the registrant's objection to all wars need not be confined in either source or content to traditional or parochial concepts of religion. It held that §6(j) "does not distinguish between externally and internally derived beliefs," . . . and also held that "intensely personal" convictions which some might find "incomprehensible" or "incorrect" come within the meaning of "religious belief" in the Act. . . . What is necessary under *Seeger* for a registrant's conscientious objection to all war to be "religious" within the meaning of §6(j) is that this opposition to war stem from the registrant's moral, ethical, or religious beliefs about what is right and wrong and that these beliefs be held with the strength of traditional religious convictions. Most of the great religions of today and of the past have embodied the idea of a Supreme Being or a Supreme Reality—a God—who communicates to man in some way a consciousness of what is right and should be done, of what is wrong and therefore should be shunned. If an individual deeply and sincerely holds beliefs which are purely ethical or moral in source and content but which nevertheless impose upon him a duty of conscience to refrain from participating in any war at any time, those beliefs certainly occupy in the life of that individual "a place parallel to that filled by . . . God" in traditionally religious persons. Because his beliefs function as a religion in his life, such an individual is as much entitled to a "religious" conscientious objector exemption under §6(j) as is someone who derives his conscientious opposition to war from traditional religious convictions. . . .

In the case before us the Government seeks to distinguish our holding in *Seeger* on basically two grounds, both of which were relied upon by the Court of Appeals in affirming Welsh's conviction. First, it is stressed that Welsh was far more insistent and explicit than Seeger in denying that his views were religious. For example, in filling out their conscientious objector applications, Seeger put quotation marks around the word "religious," but Welsh struck the word "religious" entirely and later characterized his beliefs as having been formed "by reading in the fields of history and sociology." . . . The Court of Appeals found that Welsh had "denied that his objection to war was premised on religious belief" and concluded that "the Appeal Board was entitled to take him at his word." . . . We think this attempt to distinguish *Seeger* fails for the reason that it places undue emphasis on the registrant's interpretation of his own beliefs. The Court's statement in *Seeger* that a registrant's characterization of his own belief as "religious" should carry great weight . . . does not imply that his declaration that his views are nonreligious should be created similarly. When a registrant states that his objections to war are "religious," that information is highly relevant to the question of the function his beliefs have in his life. But very few registrants are fully aware of the broad scope of the word "religious" as used in §6(j), and accordingly a registrant's statement

that his beliefs are nonreligious is a highly unreliable guide for those charged with administering the exemption. Welsh himself presents a case in point. Although he originally characterized his beliefs as nonreligious, he later upon reflection wrote a long and thoughtful letter to his Appeal Board in which he declared that his beliefs were "certainly religious in the ethical sense of that word." . . .

The Government also seeks to distinguish *Seeger* on the ground that Welsh's views, unlike Seeger's, were "essentially political, sociological, or philosophical or a merely personal moral code." As previously noted, the Government made the same argument about Seeger, and not without reason, for Seeger's views had a substantial political dimension. . . . In this case, Welsh's conscientious objection to war was undeniably based in part on his perception of world politics. . . . We certainly do not think that §6(j)'s exclusion of those persons with "essentially political, sociological, or philosophical views or a merely personal moral code" should be read to exclude those who hold strong beliefs about our domestic and foreign affairs or even those whose conscientious objection to participation in all wars is founded to a substantial extent upon considerations of public policy. The two groups of registrants which obviously do fall within these exclusions from the exemption are those whose beliefs are not deeply held and those whose objection to war does not rest at all upon moral, ethical, or religious principle but instead rests solely upon considerations of policy, pragmatism, or expediency. In applying §6(j)'s exclusion to those whose views are "essentially political, etc." it should be remembered that these exclusions are definitional and do not therefore restrict the category of persons who are conscientious objectors "by religious training and belief." Once the Selective Service System has taken the first step and determined under the standards set out here and in *Seeger* that the registrant is a "religious" conscientious objector, it follows that his views cannot be "essentially political, sociological or philosophical." Nor can they be a "merely personal moral code." . . .

Welsh stated that he "believe[d] the taking of life—anyone's life—to be morally wrong." . . .

On the basis of these beliefs and the conclusion of the Court of Appeals that he held them "with the strength of more traditional religious convictions" . . . we think Welsh was clearly entitled to a conscientious objector exemption. Section 6(j) requires no more. That section exempts from military service all those whose consciences, spurred by deeply held moral, ethical, or religious beliefs, would give them no rest or peace if they allowed themselves to become a part of an instrument of war.

The judgment is reversed.

MR. JUSTICE HARLAN, CONCURRING IN THE RESULT (OMITTED).

MR. JUSTICE WHITE, WITH WHOM THE CHIEF JUSTICE AND MR. JUSTICE STEWART JOIN, DISSENTING.

Whether or not Seeger . . . accurately reflected the intent of Congress in providing draft exemptions for religious conscientious objectors to war, I cannot join today's construction of §6(j) extending draft exemption to those who disclaim religious objections to war and whose views about war represent a purely personal code arising not from religious training and belief as the statute requires but from readings in philos-

ophy, history, and sociology. Our obligation in statutory construction cases is to enforce the will of Congress, not our own; and . . . construing §6(j) to include Welsh exempts from the draft a class of persons to whom Congress has expressly denied an exemption.

For me that conclusion should end this case. Even if Welsh is quite right in asserting that exempting religious believers is an establishment of religion forbidden by the First Amendment, he nevertheless remains one of those persons whom Congress took pains not to relieve from military duty. Whether or not §6 (j) is constitutional, Welsh had no First Amendment excuse for refusing to report for induction. If it is contrary to the express will of Congress to exempt Welsh, as I think it is, then there is no warrant for saving the religious exemption and the statute by redrafting it in this Court to include Welsh and all others like him.

If the Constitution expressly provided that aliens should not be exempt from the draft, but Congress purported to exempt them and no others, Welsh, a citizen, could hardly qualify for exemption by demonstrating that exempting aliens is unconstitutional. By the same token, if the Constitution prohibits Congress from exempting them anyway, why should the invalidity of the exemption create a draft immunity for Welsh? Surely not just because he would otherwise go without a remedy along with all those others not qualifying for exemption under the statute. And not as a reward for seeking a declaration of the invalidity of §6(j); for as long as Welsh is among those from whom Congress expressly withheld the exemption, he has no standing to raise the establishment issue even if §6(j) would present no First Amendment problems if it had included Welsh and others like him. "[O]ne to whom application of a statute is constitutional will not be heard to attack the statute on the ground that impliedly it might also be taken as applying to other persons or other situations in which its application might be unconstitutional. . . . Nothing in the First Amendment prohibits drafting Welsh and other nonreligious objectors to war. Saving §6(j) by extending it to include Welsh cannot be done in the name of a presumed congressional will but only by the Court's taking upon itself the power to make draft-exemption policy. . . .

(3) Gillette v. United States (1971)

+Marshall, Burger, Black, Harlan, Brennan, Stewart, White, Blackmun —Douglas

[The increase in conscientious objector claims which followed *Welsh* represented a serious challenge to the integrity of the draft system and, of course, to the war itself. Potentially more disruptive were claims to "selective" conscientious objection to a particular war rather than to war in any form. The statutes provided no exemption for such claimants and, unlike the *Seeger* and *Welsh* cases, the statutory language left little or no room for Supreme Court interpretation.

The major challenge to the exclusion of selective conscientious objectors therefore was on constitutional grounds. In this case Gillette was convicted for failure to report for induction. He claimed exemption because of conscientious objections to the war in Vietnam as an "unjust" war, and claimed that if the statute could not be construed to cover such objections then it was unconstitutional as a violation of the free exercise and establishment clauses of the First Amendment. Gillette stated that he was willing to participate in a war of national defense or a war sponsored by the United Nations as a peacekeeping measure, but that "based on a humanistic approach to religion" guided by fundamental principles of conscience he could not enter or serve in the military forces during the Vietnam conflict. There was no question as to the sincerity of his beliefs. In a companion case, *Negre* v. *Larsen*, Negre sought release from the Army as a conscientious objector by a writ of habeas corpus after he had received orders for duty in Vietnam. His claim was the same as Gillette's, but his basis for opposing the war was different; Negre argued that it was his duty as a devout Catholic to distinguish between just and unjust wars and to refuse participation in the latter.]

MR. JUSTICE MARSHALL delivered the opinion of the Court.

. . .

For purposes of determining the statutory status of conscientious objection to a particular war, the focal language of §6(j) is the phrase, "conscientiously opposed to participation in war in any form." This language, on a straightforward reading, can bear but one meaning; that conscientious scruples relating to war and military service must amount to conscientious opposition to participating personally in any war and all war. . . . It matters little for present purposes whether the words, "in any form," are read to modify "war" or "participation." On the first reading, conscientious scruples must implicate "war in any form," and an objection involving a particular war rather than all war would plainly not be covered by §6(j). On the other reading, an objector must oppose "participation in war." It would strain good sense to read this phrase otherwise than to mean "participation in all war." For the word "war" would still be used in an unqualified generic sense, meaning war as such. Thus, however the statutory clause be parsed, it remains that conscientious objection must run to war in any form. . . .

It should be emphasized that our cases explicating the "religious training and belief" clause of §6(j), or cognate clauses of predecessor provisions, are not relevant to the present issue. The question here is not whether these petitioners' beliefs concerning war are "religious" in nature. Thus petitioners' reliance on *United States* v. *Seeger* . . . (1965), and *Welsh* v. *United States* . . . (1970), is misplaced. Nor do we decide that conscientious objection to a particular war necessarily falls within §6(j)'s expressly excluded class of "essentially political, sociological, or philosophical views, or a merely personal moral code." Rather we hold that Congress intended to exempt persons who oppose participating in all war—"participation in war in any form"—and that persons who object solely to participation in a particular war are not within the purview of the exempting section, even though the latter objection may have such roots in a claimant's conscience and personality that it is "religious" in character.

A further word may be said to clarify our statutory holding. Apart from abstract theological reservations, two other sorts of reservations concerning the use of force have been thought by lower courts not to defeat a conscientious objector claim. Willingness to use force in self-defense, in defense of home and family, or in defense against immediate acts of aggressive violence toward other persons in the community, has not been regarded as inconsistent with a claim of conscientious objection to war as such. . . . But surely willingness to use force defensively in the personal situations mentioned is quite different from willingness to fight in some wars but not in others. . . . Somewhat more apposite to the instant situation are cases dealing with persons who oppose participating in all wars, but cannot say with complete certainty that their present conviction and existing state of mind are unalterable. . . . Unwillingness to deny the possibility of a change of mind, in some hypothetical future circumstances, may be no more than humble good sense, casting no doubt on the claimant's present sincerity of belief. At any rate there is an obvious difference between present sincere objection to all war, and present opposition to participation in a particular conflict only.

Both petitioners argue that §6(j), construed to cover only objectors to all war, violates the religious clauses of the First Amendment. The First Amendment provides that "Congress shall make no law respecting an establishment of religion, or prohibiting the free exercise thereof. . . ." Petitioners contend that Congress interferes with free exercise of religion by failing to relieve objectors to a particular war from military service, when the objection is religious or conscientious in manner. While the two religious clauses—pertaining to "free exercise" and "establishment" of religion—overlap and interact in many ways, see *Abington* v. *Schempp* . . . (1963), . . . it is best to focus first on petitioners' other contention, that §6(j) is a law respecting the establishment of religion. For despite free exercise overtones, the gist of the constitutional complaint is that §6(j) impermissibly discriminates among types of religious belief and affiliations.

On the assumption that these petitioners' beliefs concerning war have roots that are "religious" in nature, within the meaning of the Amendment as well as this Court's decision construing §6(j), petitioners ask how their claims to relief from military service can be permitted to fail, while other "religious" claims are upheld by the Act. It is a fact that §6(j), properly construed, has this effect. Yet we cannot conclude in mechanical fashion, or at all, that the section works an establishment of religion.

An attack founded on disparate treatment of "religious" claims invokes what is perhaps the central purpose of the Establishment Clause—the purpose of ensuring governmental neutrality in matters of religion. . . . The metaphor of a "wall" or impassable barrier between Church and State, taken too literally, may mislead constitutional analysis, . . . but the Establishment Clause stands at least for the proposition that when government activities touch on the religious sphere, they must be secular in purpose, evenhanded in operation, and neutral in primary impact. . . .

The critical weakness of petitioner's establishment claim arises from the fact that §6(j), on its face, simply does not discriminate on the basis of religious affiliation or religious belief, apart of course from beliefs concerning war. The section says that anyone who is conscien-tiously opposed to all war shall be relieved of military service. The specified objection must have a grounding in "religious training and belief," but no particular sectarian affiliation or theological position is required. . . .

We conclude not only that the affirmative purposes underlying §6(j) are neutral and secular, but also that valid neutral reasons exist for limiting the exemption to objectors to all war, and that the section therefore cannot be said to reflect a religious preference.

Apart from the Government's need for manpower, perhaps the central interest involved in the administration of conscription laws is the interest in maintaining a fair system for determining "who serves when not all serve." When the Government exacts so much, the importance of fair, evenhanded, and uniform decisionmaking is obviously intensified. The Government argues that the interest in fairness would be jeopardized by expansion of §6(j) to include conscientious objections to a particular war. The contention is that the claim to relief on account of such objection is intrinsically a claim of uncertain dimensions, and that granting the claim in theory would involve a real danger of erratic, or even discriminatory decisionmaking in administrative purpose. . . .

For their part, petitioners make no attempt to provide a careful definition of the claim to exemptions which they ask the courts to carve out and protect. They do not explain why objection to a particular conflict—much less an objection that focuses on a particular facet of a conflict—should excuse the objector from all military service whatever, even from military operations that are connected with the conflict at hand in remote or tenuous ways. They suggest no solution to the problems arising from the fact that altered circumstances may quickly render the objection to military service moot. . . .

Ours is a Nation of enormous heterogeneity in respect of political views, moral codes, and religious persuasions. It does not bespeak an establishing of religion for Congress to forgo the enterprise of distinguishing those whose dissent has some conscientious basis from those who simply dissent. There is a danger that as between two would-be objectors, both having the same complaint against a war, that objector would succeed who is more articulate, better educated, or better counseled. There is even a danger of unintended religious discrimination—a danger that a claim's chances of success would be greater the more familiar or salient the claim's connection with conventional religiosity could be made to appear. At any rate, it is true that "the more discriminating and complicated the basis of classification for an exemption—even a neutral one—the greater the potential for state involvement" in determining the character of personal beliefs and affiliations, thus "entangl[ing] government in difficult classifications of what is or is not religious," or what is or is not conscientious. . . .

[S]ome have perceived a danger that exempting persons who dissent from a particular war, albeit on grounds of conscience and religion in part, would "open the doors to a general theory of selective disobedience to law" and jeopardize the binding quality of democratic decisions. Report of the National Advisory Commission on Selective Service. In Pursuit of Equity: Who Serves When Not All Serve? . . . (1967). . . . Other fields of legal obligation aside, it is undoubted that the nature of conscription, much less war itself, requires the personal desires and perhaps the dissenting views of those who must serve to be subordinated in some degree to the pursuit of public purposes. It is also true that opposition to a particular war does depend *inter alia* upon particularistic factual beliefs and policy assessments, beliefs and assessments which presumably were overridden by the government that decides to commit lives and resources to a trial of arms. Further, it is not unreasonable to suppose that some persons who are not prepared to assert a conscientious objection, and instead accept the hardships and risks of military service, may well agree at all points with the objector, yet conclude, as a matter of conscience, that they are personally bound by the decision of the democratic process. The fear of the

National Advisory Commission on Selective Service, apparently, is that exemption of objectors to particular wars would weaken the resolve of those who otherwise would feel themselves bound to serve despite personal cost, uneasiness at the prospect of violence, or even serious moral reservations or policy objections concerning the particular conflict.

We need not and do not adopt the view that a categorical global "interest" in stifling individualistic claims to noncompliance, in respect of duties generally exacted, is the neutral and secular basis of §6(j). As is shown by the long history of the very provision under discussion, it is not inconsistent with orderly democratic government for individuals to be exempted by law, on account of special characteristics, from general duties of a burdensome nature. But real danger—dangers of the kind feared by the Commission—might arise if an exemption were made available that in its nature could not be administered fairly and uniformly over the run of relevant fact situations. Should it be thought that those who go to war are chosen unfairly or capriciously, then a mood of bitterness and cynicism might corrode the spirit of public service and the values of willing performance of a citizen's duties that are the very heart of free government. In short, the considerations mentioned in the previous paragraph, when seen in conjunction with the central problem of fairness, are without question properly cognizable by Congress. In light of these valid concerns, we conclude that it is supportable for Congress to have decided that the objector to all war—to all killing in war—has a claim that is distinct enough and intense enough to justify special status, while the objector to a particular war does not.

Of course we do not suggest that

Congress would have acted irrationally or unreasonably had it decided to exempt those who object to particular wars. Our analysis of the policies of §6(j) is undertaken in order to determine the existence *vel non* of a neutral, secular justification for the lines Congress has drawn. We find that justifying reasons exist and therefore hold that the Establishment Clause is not violated. . . .

Since petitioner's statutory and constitutional claims to relief from military service are without merit, it follows that in Gillette's case there was a basis in fact to support administrative denial of exemption, and that in Negre's case there was a basis in fact to support the Army's denial of a discharge. Accordingly, the judgments below are

Affirmed.

MR. JUSTICE BLACK CONCURS IN THE COURT'S JUDGMENT. . . .
MR. JUSTICE DOUGLAS, DISSENTING (OMITTED).

[In *Johnson* v. *Robison* (1974), the Supreme Court held, also by an 8-1 vote, that the government could constitutionally deny veterans' education benefits to conscientious objectors who had performed required alternative civilian service in lieu of their military obligation. Writing for the majority, Justice Brennan first rejected an equal protection claim that the statute had unconstitutionally distinguished between "those who served their country and those who did not." Applying the test of ordinary scrutiny, Brennan said that the government's permissible purpose had been "to compensate for the disruption that military service causes." Justice Douglas, the lone dissenter, argued that this was "an invidious discrimination and a penalty on those who served their religious scruples." The majority opinion also rejected a free exercise claim, stating that the withholding of educational benefits involved only an "incidental burden . . . if, indeed, any burden exists at all." The substantial interest of the government in relating and supporting an army gave great weight to its judgment on this matter. Douglas, citing *Wisconsin* v. *Yoder,* argued that government "may not place a penalty on anyone for asserting his religious scruples." Unlike the majority, he thought that *Gillette* was not controlling, since here the claim to conscientious objection was valid, and the burden on religious belief not merely "incidental."]

C. *Privacy*

(1) A Note on the Constitutional Right to Privacy

The concept of privacy in English and American law predates the Constitution by hundreds of years. But the Constitution mentions no right of privacy as such. Nevertheless, the framers of the Constitution and the Bill of Rights were acutely sensitive to the importance of privacy, and implicit references to it are found in the document. The First Amendment protects religious privacy and privacy of thought and association. The Third Amendment prohibits the nonconsensual quartering of soldiers in private homes in time of peace. The Fourth Amendment protects the right of the people "to be secure in their persons, houses, papers, and effects" from unreasonable searches and seizures. The Fifth Amendment is concerned with privacy in several ways. Most obvious is its prohibition against self-incrimination, but it also commands that liberty and property not be taken away without due process of law. Indeed, at law, privacy was for many years linked to the notion of property. But what is perhaps most striking about the above enumeration is that, despite the framer's concern with privacy and with protecting the individual from the intrusions of government, the Constitution contains no "general right to privacy," perhaps because this was regarded, like the regulation of property generally, to be within the police power jurisdiction of the individual states.

In 1890, two Boston lawyers, Samuel Warren and Louis D. Brandeis, wrote an article in the *Harvard Law Review* entitled "The Right of Privacy." They argued that privacy ought not to be dependent on private property entirely. Instead, they wrote, it should be grounded on the concept of the "inviolate personality—the right to be let alone." Privacy was first and foremost a "human" or personal right, and it had to be conceptualized that way in order to be effective as a protection against the increasing intrusions of a technological society.

Brandeis, appointed to the Supreme Court in 1916 by President Woodrow Wilson, gave eloquent expression to those views in *Olmstead* v. *United States* (1928), a case in which he dissented from the majority's approval of police wiretapping without a warrant:

> ... *The protection guaranteed by the [Fourth and Fifth] Amendments is much broader in scope. The makers of our constitution undertook to secure conditions favorable to the pursuit of happiness. They recognized the significance of man's spiritual nature, of his feelings and of his intellect. They knew that only a part of the pain, pleasure, and satisfactions of life are to be found in material things. They sought to protect Americans in their beliefs, their thoughts, their emotions, and their sensations. They conferred as against the government the right to be let alone— the most comprehensive of rights and the right most valued by civilized men.*

Until 1965, the Supreme Court considered the right of privacy explicitly only in two contexts—libel and Fourth Amendment questions regarding searches and seizures by police officers. In that year, in *Gris-*

wold v. *Connecticut*, a general constitutional right to privacy was articulated for the first time.

The Griswold Case

The setting of the case was the birth control controversy in Connecticut, aspects of which have already been discussed in Part One, Chapter Two. Mrs. Griswold, widow of the late president of Yale University, was executive director of the Planned Parenthood League of Connecticut. Connecticut had an old statute that made it an offense to *use* birth control devices or to instruct anyone in their use. The Supreme Court had refused to consider the validity of the law in *Tileston* v. *Ullman* (1943). Efforts to pave the way for a birth control clinic sponsored by the League resulted in a second attack on the validity of the law. But again the Supreme Court, in *Poe* v. *Ullman* (1961), refused to hear the case on its merits, citing its lack of "ripeness and immediacy." Despite testimony by Ullman, the state's attorney, that the law would be enforced if the clinic opened, the majority emphasized the total lack of enforcement of the statute and the "notorious" availability of contraceptives throughout the state. The clinic then opened its doors and was promptly shut down by the police. Mrs. Griswold, along with Dr. C. Lee Buxton, a world famous gynecologist, professor at Yale Medical School, and medical director of the clinic, were arrested and charged with "aiding and abetting" violations of the law. They were convicted and fined $100. The Connecticut Supreme Court affirmed their convictions.

The Supreme Court reversed by a 7-2 vote, but six opinions were written as the justices struggled with the lack of explicit constitutional recognition for a right of privacy. Justice

Douglas, writing the opinion of the Court, quickly disposed of the preliminary issue of standing—a problem that had obstructed initial attempts (see *Poe* v. *Ullman, supra*) to litigate the birth control issue. Whereas *Poe* was a suit to enjoin state officials from enforcing a law that until then had virtually never been enforced anyway, *Griswold* was a criminal prosecution; no justice thought Mrs. Griswold lacked standing to challenge her conviction. In response to Justice Black's bitter dissent, which charged the majority with resurrecting the discredited doctrine of "substantive due process," Douglas responded that "we do not sit as a super legislature to determine the wisdom, need, and propriety of laws that touch economic problems, business affairs, or social conditions. This law, however, operates directly on an intimate relation of husband and wife and their physician's role in one aspect of that relation."

Emphasis upon the intimacy of marital relations involved in *Griswold* is the opening wedge in Douglas' opinion. The next step is to show that what is not mentioned in the Constitution is nonetheless capable of being declared a right. The catalog of examples is extensive; education of the child in a school of the parents' choice, the right to study a particular subject or foreign language, academic freedom, rights of association. "Without those peripheral rights the specific rights would be less secure," Douglas wrote.

A layer of cases, fortified by an assertion as to their function, thus becomes the basis upon which "new" rights are to be found in the recesses of the Constitution.

The foregoing cases suggest that specific guarantees in the Bill of Rights have penumbras, formed by emanations from those guarantees that help give them life and substance. . . . Various guarantees create zones of privacy. The right of association contained in the penumbra of the First Amendment is one, as we have seen. The Third Amendment in its prohibition against the quartering of soldiers "in any house" in time of peace without the consent of the owner is another facet of that privacy. The Fourth Amendment explicitly affirms the "right of the people to be secure in their persons, houses, papers, and effects, against unreasonable searches and seizures." The Fifth Amendment in its Self-Incrimination Clause enables the citizen to create a zone of privacy which government may not force him to surrender to his detriment. The Ninth Amendment provides: "The enumeration in the Constitution, of certain rights, shall not be construed to deny or disparage other retained by the people."

Since a number of specific guarantees point in common to privacy, and since the Ninth Amendment is explicit in saying that there are rights not enumerated in the Constitution, the foundation for the right of privacy is established. After listing six cases showing that "we have had many controversies over these penumbral rights of 'privacy and repose,' " Douglas drives the final nail in, completing the edifice: "These cases bear witness that the right of privacy which presses for recognition here is a legitimate one." It is anticlimactic to add, as Douglas does, that marriage is within the right of privacy.

It is not surprising that this relatively brief seven-page opinion is accompanied by a number of separate opinions, responsive not only to the opinion of the Court but also to each other. No fully satisfactory constitutional argument could be fashioned that was agreeable to more than three justices. The concurring opinion by Goldberg, in which the Chief Justice and Brennan join, is not at serious odds with Douglas' views, but it does stress the importance of the Ninth Amendment. In doing so, Goldberg's opinion displays other problems of clarity in fashioning a basis on which the personal value of privacy is transformed into a constitutional obligation that binds the states.

After repeating the familiar argument that the due process clause of the Fourteenth Amendment protects those liberties in the Bill of Rights that are deemed fundamental, Goldberg adds:

The language and history of the Ninth Amendment reveal the Framers of the Constitution believed that there are additional fundamental rights, protected from governmental infringements, which exist alongside those fundamental rights specifically mentioned in the first eight constitutional amendments.
. . .
The Ninth Amendment to the Constitution may be regarded by some as a recent discovery but since 1791 it has been a basic part of the Constitution which we are sworn to uphold. To hold that a right so basic and fundamental and so deep-rooted in our society as the right of privacy in marriage may be infringed because that right is not guaranteed in so many words by the first eight amendments to the Constitution is to ignore the Ninth Amendment and to give it no effect whatsoever.

From this it is difficult to say whether the Ninth Amendment is important because it is being used to activate a right that has independently been established as fundamental, or whether the right becomes fundamental because the Ninth Amendment indicates that it may be. If it can be shown that a right is fundamental on some other acceptable basis, even if it is not explicitly mentioned in the Constitution, then the language of the Ninth Amendment would at least support the elevation of that right to constitutional status. But it would not effectively counteract the charge that "finding rights" in the "penumbras" of other rights is little more than a subterfuge for the justices' writing their own views into the Constitution. Furthermore, since the Ninth Amendment does not apply to the states, it can by itself have no legal force in applying such "derivative" rights as the right of privacy to the states. Both of these propositions are noted in the dissenting opinions of Justices Black and Stewart.

Goldberg, of course, recognized that the Ninth Amendment does not apply to the states via the Fourteenth Amendment. But if not, of what use is it?

While the Ninth Amendment—and indeed the entire Bill of Rights—originally concerned restrictions upon federal *power, the subsequently enacted Fourteenth Amendment prohibits the states as well from abridging fundamental personal liberties. And, the Ninth Amendment, in indicating that not all such liberties are specifically mentioned in the first eight amendments, is surely relevant to showing the existence of other fundamental personal rights, now protected from state, as well as federal infringement. In sum, the Ninth Amendment simply lends strong support to the view that the "liberty" protected by the Fifth and Fourteenth Amendments from infringement by the Federal Government or the States is not restricted to rights specifically mentioned in the first eight amendments.*

Thus, in the last analysis, Goldberg agrees that the source of the right to privacy is the totality of the constitutional scheme. The Ninth Amendment simply makes it easier to say that.

The remaining opinions in *Griswold* are more familiar, but combined with Goldberg's, they serve to illustrate the uncertain constitutional basis of the right to privacy. Justice Harlan concurs, citing *Palko* v. *Connecticut* (1937), because the Connecticut law "violates basic values 'implicit in the concept of ordered liberty.' " What disturbs Harlan most is the use to which the incorporation doctrine is put in the opinion of the Court.

I fully agree with the judgment of reversal, but find myself unable to join the Court's opinion. The reason is that it seems to me to evince an approach in this case very much like that taken by my Brothers Black and Stewart in dissent, namely: the Due Process Clause of the Fourteenth Amendment does not touch this Connecticut statute unless the enactment is found to violate some right assured by the letter or penumbra of the Bill of Rights.

In other words, what I find implicit in the Court's opinion is that the "incorporation" doctrine may be used to restrict *the reach of Fourteenth Amendment Due Process. For me this is just as unacceptable constitutional doctrine as is the use of the "incorporation" approach to* impose *upon the States all the requirements of the Bill of Rights as found in the provisions of the first eight amendments and in the decisions of this Court interpreting them.*

Justice White's concurrence is simple and direct. "In my view this Connecticut law as applied to married couples deprives them of 'liberty' without due process of law, as that concept is used in the Fourteenth Amendment." The rest of his opinion examines the relationship between the state's declared objectives in having the law and the means for achieving these objectives, and finds it lacking. This relationship, balanced against the sweeping deprivation of liberty that the law represents, is insufficient and the law is thus invalid. Thus, while accepting the force of a privacy right *in this case*, both Harlan and White stop well short of endorsing a general right of privacy. Marital privacy is an important component of "liberty" and is thus adequately protected by the due process guarantees of the Fourteenth Amendment.

Both Black and Stewart take pains to announce their personal opposition to the birth control statute. Black says it is "every bit as offensive to me as it is to my Brethren." And Stewart regards it as "an uncommonly silly law," unwise or even asinine. But both justices argue that their personal views are not relevant—and not determinative of whether or not the law is unconstitutional.

For Black this is a disguised form of substantive due process:

I realize that many good and able men have eloquently spoken and written, sometimes in rhapsodical strains, about the duty of this Court to keep the Constitution in tune with the times. The idea is that the Constitution must be changed from time to time and this Court is charged with a duty to make those changes. For myself, I must with all deference reject that philosophy. The Constitution makers knew the need for change and provided for it. Amendments suggested by the people's elected representatives can be submitted to the people or their selected agents for ratification. That method of change was good for our Fathers, and being somewhat old-fashioned I must add it is good enough for me. And so, I cannot rely on the Due Process Clause or the Ninth Amendment or any mysterious and uncertain natural law concept as a reason for striking down this state law. The Due Process Clause with an "arbitrary and capricious" or "shocking to the conscience" formula was liberally used by this Court to strike down economic legis-

lation in the early decades of this century, threatening, many people thought, the tranquility and stability of the Nation. See, e.g., Lochner v. New York . . . . *That formula, based on subjective considerations of "natural justice" is no less dangerous when used to enforce this Court's views about personal rights than those about economic rights. I had thought that we had laid that formula, as a means for striking down state legislation, to rest once and for all in cases like* West Coast Hotel v. Parrish . . .

Stewart echoes Black's protest that there is no general right to privacy in the Constitution or the Bill of Rights and that it is improper, by any means, for a majority of the Court to find the right where none exists.

The Expanded Meaning of Privacy

In general, the pattern of doctrinal innovation by the Supreme Court is to establish a doctrine, or right, based on a limited factual situation and then to expand that right based on analogous fact situations in cases subsequently decided. This has been the case with privacy. In *Griswold* the right was exemplified by the sexual intimacy interest in marriage. Few could reasonably doubt the importance of marital privacy, but to what else would this newly articulated right apply? There was little in Douglas' opinion that suggested any special concern with keeping the new right within such confining boundaries. In *Eisenstadt* v. *Baird* (1972), a Massachusetts law making it illegal for *single* persons to obtain contraceptives was overturned. Although the thrust of the opinion was the violation of the equal protection clause of the Fourteenth Amendment, the right of privacy was involved in such a way as to expand its scope.

If under Griswold *the distribution of contraceptives to married persons cannot be prohibited, a ban on distribution to unmarried persons would be equally impermissible. It is true that in* Griswold *the right of privacy in question inhered in the marital relationship. Yet the marital couple is not an independent entity with a mind and heart of its own, but an association of two individuals each with a separate intellectual and emotional makeup. If the right of privacy means anything, it is the right of the individual, married or single, to be free from unwarranted governmental intrusion into matters so fundamentally affecting a person as the decision to bear or beget a child.*

The step from married to single is, as a matter of circumstance, small, but as a step in the expansion of constitutional meaning, it was enormous.

If privacy as a right can protect decisions by married couples or single persons to prevent pregnancy, then a subsequent and obvious question raised is whether postconception decisions such as abortion are to any extent also protected by the right of privacy. In the year following *Eisenstadt*, the Court decided *Roe* v. *Wade*, by far the most important right-of-privacy decision taken by the Supreme Court to date (see pp. 1325–1333). In *Roe*, the Court held that the right, whatever its derivation, "is broad enough to encompass a woman's decision whether or not to terminate her pregnancy." However, the Court also held that the state has important interests in regulating the matter and that these interests had to be balanced against the rights of the woman. Thus the right of privacy, although fundamental and entitled to the strongest judicial protection, is not absolute.

Roe had great significance for the direction of personal rights litigation testing the boundaries of permissible sexual activity. The value of personal autonomy in sex and related activities was enhanced by the *Roe* decision. But in other cases the Court has also placed tacit limits upon this autonomy when "abberrant" sexual behavior is involved. In *Doe* v. *Commonwealth's Attorney* (1976), the Court, without opinion, affirmed a lower court ruling that upheld Virginia's law against sodomy between consenting male adults. In the following term, the same law was involved in a request to the Court to grant a writ of certiorari. The Court denied the request in *Lovisi* v. *Slayton* (1976). Its action leaves certain aspects of the right of privacy in some question in light of the peculiar circumstances of the case and the views of the lower courts. Briefly, *Lovisi* involved a married couple who engaged in fellatio in their own bedroom, but in the presence of a third party who ultimately participated and who took pictures to commemorate the event. The Lovisis were convicted; their contentions at trial and appeal included a right to privacy, which the courts declared had been lost by virtue of the dissemination of pictures and the invited presence of a third party to an otherwise private activity.[1]

The Court similarly denied certiorari in two cases that involved the discharge and disciplining of schoolteachers because of their sexual preference. In *Gaylord* v. *Tacoma School District* (1977), the U. S. Supreme Court's denial of certiorari left standing a Washington Supreme Court decision that upheld the firing of a gay teacher on the grounds that his fellow workers were uncomfortable working with him because he was a homosexual. In *Gish* v. *Board of Education of Paramus* (1977), a New Jersey court had held that a teacher's association with gay rights organizations was "evidence of deviation from . . . mental health" and sufficient grounds for directing the teacher to undergo psychiatric examination. Certiorari was also denied in that case.

To the extent that the denial of certiorari carries any policy significance, it can be said that the Supreme Court has drawn a thin and probably permeable line between the constitutional right of privacy and deviant sexual practices, which leaves the states free to maintain and enforce their laws against such practices. Indeed, gay rights, or what we might broadly term "life-style privacy rights," have recently been attacked by fundamentalist religious groups. The repeal of a Dade County, Florida, ordinance prohibiting discrimination in employment, housing, and public accommodations on the basis of sexual preferences developed into a national anti-gay rights movement lead by actress and religious figure Anita Bryant. Subsequently in 1978, similar ordinances protecting gay people from discrimination were repealed in Eugene, Oregon, St. Paul, Minnesota, and Wichita, Kansas.

The constitutionality of restrictive housing ordinances brought the issue of "life-style privacy rights" before the Court in *Village of Belle Terre* v. *Borass* (1974). The Court upheld the family-based definition of a city zoning ordinance over challenges that it invaded the life-style privacy of students and unmarried couples. The Court held that "the police power

[1]See Carleton H. Taber, "Consent, Not Morality, as the Proper Limitation on Sexual Privacy," 4 *Hastings Constitutional Law Quarterly* (1977), 637–664, for a discussion of the *Lovisi* case in terms of its significance for the concept of privacy.

[exercised under this ordinance] is not confined to elimination of filth, stench, and unhealthy places. It is ample to lay out zones where family values, youth values, and the blessings of quiet seclusion and clean air make the areas a sanctuary for people." The Court failed to recognize any violation of the privacy rights of students or unmarried couples.

The approach in *Lovisi* is that one's otherwise protected right of privacy might be lost by placing one's activities in a setting that makes the expectation of privacy unreasonable. This "expectation of privacy" doctrine was exemplified in *United States* v. *Miller* (1976), which upheld a conviction based upon bank records obtained under provision of the Bank Secrecy Act of 1970.[2] The Court stated that "no Fourteenth Amendment interests of the depositor are implicated here" since there was no expectation of privacy.

Even if we direct our attention to the original checks and deposit slips, . . . we perceive no legitimate "expectation of privacy" in their contents. The checks are not confidential communications but negotiable instruments to be used in commercial transactions. All of the documents obtained, including financial statements and deposit slips, contain only information voluntarily conveyed to the banks and exposed to their employees in the ordinary course of business.

This "expectation" theory of the Fourteenth Amendment is another of the important corollaries to be drawn from the initial emphasis upon privacy in *Griswold*. The definitive effort to identify privacy with the Fourth Amendment came in *Katz* v. *United States* (1967), in which evidence used to convict Katz of gambling offenses had been obtained by attaching listening devices to a public telephone booth. In place of the conventional test of physical penetration of "a constitutionally protected area," the Court innovatively substituted a test by which the amendment protected "people instead of places":

What a person knowingly exposes to the public, even in his own home or office, is not a subject of Fourth Amendment protection . . . But what he seeks to preserve as private, even in an area accessible to the public, may be constitutionally protected.

The uncertain origin of the right of privacy has implications for determining its ultimate scope. For purposes of "clear-cut" Fourth Amendment cases involving such conventional activities as eavesdropping and evidence gathering, it is adequate. But in those instances that implicate competing constitutional values, privacy is less clear. Expression tends to further cloud its meaning. The best example of this is the clash between personal privacy and the news media, which is armed with established First Amendment protections.

In *Time, Inc.* v. *Hill* (1967), a family sued the publisher of *Life* magazine under the provisions of a state right to privacy statute. The family had been held hostage in their home by some prison escapees. *Life* magazine had publicized the event and by doing so, it was alleged, had destroyed the privacy of their home.

---

[2]The act was reviewed by the Court in *California Bankers Association* v. *Schultz* (1974) and declared constitutional. In that case, the issue of whether parties whose records were examined by the government under provisions of the act could invoke First Amendment protections was called "premature."

A lower court had found for the Hill family, but the Supreme Court reversed by applying the standards of libel in *New York Times* v. *Sullivan* (1964). In this case, the rights of the press outweighed those of privacy. Only Justice Fortas drew the balance in favor of privacy rights that had been jeopardized by what he interpreted as irresponsible journalism. Technically, what is at stake in a case such as *Time, Inc.* is the proper test a court may use in awarding damages associated with civil liability. The *New York Times* v. *Sullivan* test of malicious libel is particularly burdensome for those seeking to impose liability upon a newspaper. In contrast, "knowing and reckless disregard of the truth" is a less stringent test used by many states (e.g., a test less protective of the media).

The Supreme Court took a step in the direction of this less exacting standard in *Cantrell* v. *Forest City Publishing Company* (1974). The case is complex, but its constitutional significance is that *Time, Inc.* was distinguished—that is, limited to its own set of facts—and the knowing and reckless disregard of the truth that was found to characterize the action of the newspaper was established as the basis for liability in the case. The *Time, Inc.* decision was again distinguished in a fascinating case decided in 1977. *Zacchini* v. *Scripps-Howard Broadcasting* involved Zacchini's "human cannonball" act, which was filmed (contrary to Zacchini's request) in its entirety (fifteen seconds) and broadcast on a local television station. Zacchini claimed a "right of publicity," and the Supreme Court, in reversing the state appellate court, which had relied upon *Time, Inc.* v. *Hill*, agreed.

The computerized collection and use of personal information such as medical records, for public purposes may place an additional constraint on individual privacy. In *Whalen* v. *Roe* (1977), the Supreme Court unanimously upheld a New York State statute requiring identification of the prescribing physician, dispensing pharmacy, drug and dosage, and the patient's name, address, and age. All this information is recorded on computer tapes and retained by the state health department for a five-year period. The doctors who challenged this statute claimed that it invaded the constitutionally protected "zone of privacy " of doctors and patients. Two-types of privacy interests are involved: (1) an individual's interest in avoiding disclosure of personal matters and (2) an individual's interest in making certain kinds of important decisions independently; for example, an individual may be reluctant to use drugs even when medically necessary because of a fear of public exposure and damage to his reputation. The Court, recognizing that these were protected privacy interests, held that "the right to collect and use such data for public purposes is typically accompanied by a concomitant statutory or regulatory duty to avoid unwarranted disclosures," and the New York legislature had provided sufficient individual protections.

The Concept of Privacy

In the course of expanding the right of privacy on a case-by-case basis, the Supreme Court has raised various conceptual questions. For example, in 1969, the right was invoked to protect possession and viewing of obscene films in the privacy of one's home (*Stanley* v. *Georgia, supra*). But in *Paris Adult Theater* v. *Slaton* (1973), the Court held that the right to privacy did *not* protect the right to view a comparable film in a public motion picture theater, at least

not when that right had been asserted by the manager of the theater
as a defense to a criminal prosecution. The point, of course, is not that
one must see the two places as the
same—they clearly are not—but that
the conceptual basis on which the
meaning of the right rests must, at
some point, be independent of the
circumstances in any particular case.
It is to the problem of knowing just
what privacy *is* that post-*Griswold*
decisions have directed the attention
of legal scholars. As one writer has
put it, "One of the major failings of
the Court has been its treatment of
privacy as a self-explanatory, unitary
concept, when in fact one or more of a
number of distinct meanings may lie
behind a claim to privacy protection."[3]

Whether privacy is seemingly located in the person (as in *Roe* and the
decision to abort a pregnancy), or in a
place (as in *Katz* and the expectations one has by being in a public
telephone booth), or in a relationship
(as in *Lovisi* and the decision as to
the way one is sexually intimate),
what is suggested is the need to understand just what these situations
exemplify. Thus seen, the *conceptual* clarity of privacy is the objective
of legal philosophy, not the result of
case analysis.

Among the most influential efforts
to clarify the concept of privacy is
that of Charles Fried.[4] His work demonstrates how far this right has been
expanded, in comparison to the notion of privacy as simply "the right to
be let alone."

The initial point in Fried's analysis
is that privacy is not properly understood if it is seen as being instrumental. That is, privacy is not simply

a means for achieving something.
While it may be invoked to prevent
the use of such technological resources as remote listening devices,
its *meaning* is more profound than its
being a possible social technique.
"Such analyses of the value of privacy often lead to the conclusion that
the various substantive interests may
after all be protected as well by some
other means, or that if they cannot be
protected as well by some other
means, or that if they cannot be protected quite as well, still those other
means will do, given the importance
of our reasons for violating privacy."[5]
Rather than being instrumental, privacy is the ground upon which our integrity as individuals rests.

*It is my thesis that privacy is not just
one possible means among others to insure some other values, but that it is
necessarily related to ends and relations
of the most fundamental sort: respect,
love, friendship and trust. Privacy is not
merely a good technique for furthering
these fundamental relations; rather
without privacy they are simply inconceivable. They require a context of privacy or the possibility of privacy for
their existence. To make clear the
necessity of privacy as a context for respect, love, friendship and trust is to
bring out also why a threat to privacy
seems to threaten our very integrity as
persons. To respect, love, trust, feel affection for others and to regard ourselves as the objects of love, trust and
affection is at the heart of our notion of
ourselves as persons among persons,
and privacy is the necessary atmosphere
for these attitudes and actions, as oxy-
gen is for combustion.[6]*

One must recognize that to love or
to be friends in any profound sense

[3]Tyler Baker, "*Roe* and *Paris*: Does Privacy Have a Principle?" **26** *Stanford Law Review* (1974), 1161–1189.

[4]Charles Fried, "Privacy, **77** *Yale Law Review* (1968), 475–493.

[5]*Ibid.*, p. 477.

[6]*Ibid.*, pp. 477–478.

involves a free relinquishing to one's friend or beloved of certain entitlements. For example, a person may relinquish the right to be conventionally free of inquiry by other persons about his or her feelings—she welcomes the inquiry from her friend or lover rather than rebuffing it with a none-of-your-business attitude. Relinquishing logically depends upon secure possession of that which is relinquished, and it is herein that privacy is essential, since it is the source of that secure possession. Respect and trust have similar, if not such extreme, characteristics, since they too are relational.

The function of privacy in these relations can be elaborated somewhat. Love, trust, friendship, and the like obviously depend upon privacy as the basis on which we bestow such gifts. But these relations must be seen as being in a social or societal context and are thus possible only if persons accord each other a certain measure of privacy. This, in turn, suggests that privacy cannot be dependent merely upon how limited the knowledge is that others have about oneself. Rather, privacy must inhere in the *control* one has over what the other person may know. Thus, privacy depends upon one's being a part of, rather than apart from, a society or community. In social settings, people usually relate in less emotionally intense ways than love or friendship, but privacy has a vital function in these relations as well. It "grants the control over information which enables us to maintain degrees of intimacy."[7] We thus can add to the list of relationships that have privacy as their basis and note one that is of especial significance for politics—civility. Without control of the range of relationships that form the societal context, civility is not a free choice;

without privacy, such control is not possible.

What remains in understanding the concept of privacy *as a right* is to note that the key element of the concept—control—cannot be simply a personal characteristic, even though it is exerted by persons for reasons that are personal. Rather, this control must be the result of legal title to it. Privacy, as a matter of right, is entitlement to control of what people may know of you.

In his concurring opinion in *Roe* v. *Wade* (1973), Justice Douglas defined privacy in a similar way. According to Douglas, it embodies (1) the autonomous control over the development and expression of one's intellect, interest, tastes, and personality; (2) freedom of choice in the basic decisions of one's life respecting marriage, divorce, procreation, contraception, and the education and upbringing of children; and (3) freedom to care for one's health and person, freedom from bodily restraint or compulsion, freedom to walk, stroll, or loaf.

(2) Roe v. Wade (1973)

+Blackmun, Burger, Douglas, Stewart, Brennan, Marshall, Powell
−White, Rehnquist

[Texas law provided that attempting or procuring an abortion, except to save the life of the mother, was a criminal act. The law was challenged by three different parties, each claiming a different basis for challenging the validity of the state's law. Jane Roe, unmarried and pregnant, was unable to obtain a legal abortion and claimed that the law unconstitutionally abridged her rights of personal privacy held under the First, Fourth, Fifth, Ninth, and Fourteenth Amendments. James H. Hallford was a physician with two prosecutions for abortion pending against him. Hallford challenged the law on the

[7]*Ibid.* p. 485.

basis that it was vague and violated his rights, as well as those of his patients, regarding the privacy of the doctor–patient relationship and also infringed on his rights to practice medicine. The third challenger was a married couple, John and Mary Doe, who desired, for medical and personal reasons, to avoid having children of their own. Mrs. Doe's physician had advised against the use of birth control pills, and she wished to terminate any pregnancy that might occur in the future. Henry Wade was the district attorney of Dallas, against whom the suits were brought.

All three actions were consolidated and heard by a three-judge district court. That court held that Roe and Hallford had standing and presented justiciable controversies but that the Does did not. On the question of the statutes themselves, the court declared them void on constitutional grounds but denied injunctive relief as part of its order. Both sides therefore appealed to the Supreme Court.

The initial sections of the Supreme Court's opinion dealt with the matters of justiciability and standing by declaring that Roe satisfied these requirements, even though she had already given birth to a son and her case, theoretically, was "moot." But Justice Blackmun observed that pregnancy would rarely outlast the litigation process. "Our laws should not be that rigid," he said. "Pregnancy often comes more than once to the same woman, and in the general population, if man is to survive, it will always be with us. Pregnancy provides a classic justification for a conclusion of nonmootness." The Court dismissed the complaints of Hallford and the Does. Since there was a pending state prosecution against Dr. Hallford, the Court said, *Younger* v. *Harris* (1971) prohibited federal court intervention. He could pursue his constitutional claims as a defense to that prosecution. As for the Does, the Court said that their claim was simply too speculative to satisfy the requirements for standing and justiciability.]

MR. JUSTICE BLACKMUN delivered the opinion of the Court.

. . .

The principal thrust of appellant's attack on the Texas statutes is that they improperly invade a right, said to be possessed by the pregnant woman, to choose to terminate her pregnancy. Appellant would discover this right in the concept of personal "liberty" embodied in the Fourteenth Amendment's Due Process Clause; or in personal, marital, familial, and sexual privacy said to be protected by the Bill of Rights or its penumbras, see *Griswold* v. *Connecticut* . . . (1965) . . . Before addressing this claim, we feel it desirable briefly to survey, in several aspects, the history of abortion, for such insight as that history may afford us, and then to examine the state's purposes and interests behind the criminal abortion laws.

. . .

It perhaps is not generally appreciated that the restrictive criminal abortion laws in effect in a majority of States today are of relatively recent vintage. Those laws, generally proscribing abortion or its attempt at any time during pregnancy except when necessary to preserve the pregnant woman's life, are not of ancient or even of common law origin. Instead, they derive from statutory changes effected, for the most part, in the latter half of the 19th century. . . .

It is thus apparent that at common law, at the time of the adoption of our Constitution, and throughout the major portion of the 19th century, abortion was viewed with less disfavor than under most American statutes currently in effect. Phrasing it another way, a woman enjoyed a substantially broader right to terminate a pregnancy than she does in most States today. At least with respect to the early stage of pregnancy, and very possibly without such a limitation, the opportunity to make this choice was present in this country well into the 19th century. Even later, the law continued for some time to treat less punitively an abortion procured in early pregnancy. . . .

[There follows an extensive section setting out the positions of the American Medical Association, the American Public Health Association, and the American Bar Association. In all three instances, a pattern of recent movement toward relaxing the stringent standards of nineteenth-century policy toward abortion appeared evident.]

Three reasons have been advanced to explain historically the enactment of criminal abortion laws in the 19th century and to justify their continued existence.

It has been argued occasionally that these laws were the product of a Victorian social concern to discourage illicit sexual conduct. Texas, however, does not advance this justification in the present case, and it appears that no court or commentator has taken the argument seriously. . . . Thus it has been argued that a State's real concern in enacting a criminal abortion law was to protect the pregnant woman, that is, to restrain her from submitting to a procedure that placed her life in serious jeopardy.

Modern medical techniques have altered this situation. Appellants and various *amici* refer to medical data indicating that abortion in early pregnancy, that is, prior to the end of the first trimester, although not without its risk, is now relatively safe. Mortality rates for women undergoing early abortions, where the procedure is legal, appear to be as low or lower than the rates for normal childbirth. Consequently, any interest of the State in protecting the woman from an inherently hazardous procedure, except when it would be equally dangerous for her to forgo it, has largely disappeared. Of course, important state interests in the area

of health and medical standards do remain. The State has a legitimate interest in seeing to it that abortion, like any other medical procedure, is performed under circumstances that insure maximum safety for the patient. This interest obviously extends at least to the performing physician and his staff, to the facilities involved, to the availability of aftercare, and to adequate provision for any complication or emergency that might arise. The prevalence of high mortality rates at illegal "abortion mills" strengthens, rather than weakens, the State's interest in regulating the conditions under which abortions are performed. Moreover, the risk to the woman increases as her pregnancy continues. Thus the State retains a definite interest in protecting the woman's own health and safety when an abortion is proposed at a late stage of pregnancy.

The third reason is the State's interest—some phrase it in terms of duty—in protecting prenatal life. Some of the argument for this justification rests on the theory that a new human life is present from the moment of conception. The State's interest and general obligation to protect life then extends, it is argued, to prenatal life. Only when the life of the pregnant mother itself is at stake, balanced against the life she carries within her, should the interest of the embryo or fetus not prevail. Logically, of course, a legitimate state interest in this area need not stand or fall on acceptance of the belief that life begins at conception or at some other point prior to live birth. In assessing the State's interest, recognition may be given to the less rigid claim that as long as at least *potential* life is involved, the State may assert interests beyond the protection of the pregnant woman alone. . . .

The Constitution does not explicitly mention any right of privacy. In a line of decisions, however, going back perhaps as far as *Union Pacific R. Co.* v. *Botsford* . . . (1891), the Court has recognized that a right of personal privacy, or a guarantee of certain areas or zones of privacy, does exist under the Constitution. In varying contexts the Court or individual Justices have indeed found at least the roots of that right in the First Amendment, *Stanley* v. *Georgia* . . . (1969); in the Fourth and Fifth Amendments, *Terry* v. *Ohio* . . . (1968), *Katz* v. *United States* . . . (1967); *Boyd* v. *United States* . . . (1886); . . . in the penumbras of the Bill of Rights, *Griswold* v. *Connecticut* . . . (1965); in the Ninth Amendment, . . . or in the concept of liberty guaranteed by the first section of the Fourteenth Amendment, see *Meyer* v. *Nebraska* . . . (1923). These decisions make it clear that only personal rights that can be deemed "fundamental" or "implicit in the concept of ordered liberty," *Palko* v. *Connecticut* . . . (1937), are included in this guarantee of personal privacy. They also make it clear that the right has some extension to activities relating to marriage, *Loving* v. *Virginia* . . . (1967), procreation, *Skinner* v. *Oklahoma* . . . (1942), contraception, *Eisenstadt* v. *Baird* . . . (1972); . . . family relationships, *Prince* v. *Massachusetts* . . . (1944), and child rearing and education, *Pierce* v. *Society of Sisters* . . . (1925), . . .

This right of privacy, whether it be founded in the Fourteenth Amendment's concept of personal liberty and restrictions upon state action, as we feel it is, or, as the District Court determined, in the Ninth Amendment's reservation of rights to the people, is broad enough to encompass a woman's decision whether or not to terminate her pregnancy. The detri-

ment that the State would impose upon the pregnant woman by denying this choice altogether is apparent. Specific and direct harm medically diagnosable even in early pregnancy may be involved. Maternity, or additional offspring, may force upon the woman a distressful life and future. Psychological harm may be imminent. Mental and physical health may be taxed by child care. There is also the distress, for all concerned, associated with the unwanted child, and there is the problem of bringing a child into a family already unable, psychologically and otherwise, to care for it. In other cases, as in this one, the additional difficulties and continuing stigma of unwed motherhood may be involved. All these factors the woman and her responsible physician necessarily will consider in consultation.

On the basis of elements such as these, appellants and some *amici* argue that the woman's right is absolute and that she is entitled to terminate her pregnancy at whatever time, in whatever way, and for whatever reason she alone chooses. With this we do not agree. Appellant's arguments that Texas either has no valid interest at all in regulating the abortion decision, or no interest strong enough to support any limitation upon the woman's sole determination, is unpersuasive. The Court's decisions recognizing a right of privacy also acknowledge that some state regulation in areas protected by that right is appropriate. As noted above, a state may properly assert important interests in safeguarding health, in maintaining medical standards, and in protecting potential life. At some point in pregnancy, these respective interests become sufficiently compelling to sustain regulation of the factors that govern the abortion decision. The privacy right involved, therefore, cannot be said to be absolute. In fact, it is not clear to us that the claim asserted by some *amici* that one has an unlimited right to do with one's body as one pleases bears a close relationship to the right of privacy previously articulated in the Court's decisions. The Court has refused to recognize an unlimited right of this kind in the past. *Jacobsen* v. *Massachusetts* . . . (1905) (vaccination); *Buck* v. *Bell* . . . (1927) (sterilization).

We therefore conclude that the right of personal privacy includes the abortion decision, but that this right is not unqualified and must be considered against important state interests in regulation. . . .

Where certain "fundamental rights" are involved, the Court has held that regulation limiting these rights may be justified only by a "compelling state interest," . . . *Shapiro* v. *Thompson* . . . (1969); . . . and that legislative enactments must be narrowly drawn to express only the legitimate state interests at stake. . . .

The District Court held that the appellee failed to meet his burden of demonstrating that the Texas statute's infringement upon Roe's rights was necessary to support a compelling state interest, and that, although the defendant presented "several compelling justifications for state presence in the area of abortions," the statutes outstripped these justifications and swept "far beyond any areas of compelling state interest." . . . Appellant and appellee both contest that holding. Appellant, as has been indicated, claims an absolute right that bars any state imposition of criminal penalties in the area. Appellee argues that the State's determination to recognize and protect prenatal life from and after conception constitutes a compelling state interest. As noted above, we do not agree with either formulation.

The appellee and certain *amici* argue that the fetus is a "person" within the language and meaning of the Fourteenth Amendment. In support of this they outline at length and in detail the well-known facts of fetal development. If this suggestion of personhood is established, the appellant's case, of course, collapses, for the fetus' right to life is then guaranteed specifically by the Amendment. The appellant conceded as much on reargument. On the other hand, the appellee conceded on reargument that no case could be cited that holds that a fetus is a person within the meaning of the Fourteenth Amendment.

The Constitution does not define "person" in so many words. Section 1 of the Fourteenth Amendment contains three references to "person." The first, in defining "citizens," speaks of "persons born or naturalized in the United States." The word also appears both in the Due Process Clause and in the Equal Protection Clause. "Person" is used in other places in the Constitution: . . . But in nearly all these instances, the use of the word is such that it has application only post-natally. None indicates, with any assurance, that it has any possible pre-natal application.

All this, together with our observation, *supra,* that throughout the major portion of the 19th century prevailing legal abortion practices were far freer than they are today, persuades us that the word "person," as used in the Fourteenth Amendment, does not include the unborn. . . .

The pregnant woman cannot be

isolated in her privacy. She carries an embryo and, later, a fetus, if one accepts the medical definitions of the developing young in the human uterus. . . . The situation therefore is inherently different from marital intimacy, or bedroom possession of obscene material, or marriage, or procreation, or education, with which *Eisenstadt, Griswold, Stanley, Loving, Skinner, Pierce,* and *Meyer* were respectively concerned. As we have intimated above, it is reasonable and appropriate for a State to decide that at some point in time another interest, that of health of the mother or that of potential human life, becomes significantly involved. The woman's privacy is no longer sole and any right of privacy she possesses must be measured accordingly.

Texas urges that, apart from the Fourteenth Amendment, life begins at conception and is present throughout pregnancy, and that, therefore, the State has a compelling interest in protecting that life from and after conception. We need not resolve the difficult question of when life begins. When those trained in the respective disciplines of medicine, philosophy, and theology are unable to arrive at any consensus, the judiciary, at this point in the development of man's knowledge, is not in a position to speculate as to the answer.

It should be sufficient to note briefly the wide divergence of thinking on this most sensitive and difficult question. There has always been strong support for the view that life does not begin until live birth. This was the belief of the Stoics. It appears to be the predominant, though not the unanimous, attitude of the Jewish faith. It may be taken to represent also the position of a large segment of the Protestant community, insofar as that can be ascertained; organized groups that have taken a formal position on the abortion issue have generally regarded abortion as a matter for the conscience of the individual and her family. As we have noted, the common law found greater significance in quickening. Physicians and their scientific colleagues have regarded that event with less interest and have tended to focus either upon conception or upon live birth or upon the interim point at which the fetus becomes "viable," that is, potentially able to live outside the mother's womb, albeit with artificial aid. Viability is usually placed at about seven months (28 weeks) but may occur earlier, even at 24 weeks. The Aristotelian theory of "mediate animation," that held sway throughout the Middle Ages and the Renaissance in Europe, continued to be official Roman Catholic dogma until the 19th century, despite opposition to this "ensoulment" theory from those in the Church who would recognize the existence of life from the moment of conception. The latter is now, of course, the official belief of the Catholic Church. As one of the briefs *amicus* discloses, this is a view strongly held by many non-Catholics as well, and by many physicians. Substantial problems for precise definition of this view are posed, however, by new embryological data that purport to indicate that conception is a "process" over time, rather than an event, and by new medical techniques such as menstrual extraction, the "morning-after" pill, implantation of embryos, artificial insemination, and even artificial wombs.

In areas other than criminal abortion the law has been reluctant to endorse any theory that life, as we recognize it, begins before live birth or to accord legal rights to the unborn except in narrowly defined situations and except when the rights are contingent upon live birth. For example, the traditional rule of tort law had denied recovery for prenatal injuries even though the child was born alive. That rule has been changed in almost every jurisdiction. In most States recovery is said to be permitted only if the fetus was viable, or at least quick, when the injuries were sustained, though few courts have squarely so held. In a recent development, generally opposed by the commentators, some States permit the parents of a stillborn child to maintain an action for wrongful death because of prenatal injuries. Such an action, however, would appear to be one to vindicate the parents' interest and is thus consistent with the view that the fetus, at most, represents only the potentiality of life. Similarly, unborn children have been recognized as acquiring rights or interests by way of inheritance or other devolution of property, and have been represented by guardians *ad litem*. Perfection of the interests involved, again, has generally been contingent upon live birth. In short, the unborn have never been recognized in the law as persons in the whole sense.

In view of all this, we do not agree that, by adopting one theory of life, Texas may override the rights of the pregnant woman that are at stake. We repeat, however, that the State does have an important and legitimate interest in preserving and protecting the health of the pregnant woman, whether she be a resident of the State or a non-resident who seeks medical consultation and treatment there, and that it has still *another* important and legitimate interest in protecting the potentiality of human life. These interests are separate and distinct. Each grows in substantiality as the woman approaches term and, at a point during pregnancy, each becomes "compelling."

With respect to the State's important and legitimate interest in the health of the mother, the "compelling" point, in the light of present medical knowledge, is at approximately the end of the first trimester. This is so because of the now established medical fact, . . . that until the end of the first trimester mortality in abortion is less than mortality in normal childbirth. It follows that, from and after this point, a State may regulate the abortion procedure to the extent that the regulation reasonably relates to the preservation and protection of maternal health. Examples of permissible state regulation in this area are requirements as to the qualifications of the person who is to perform the abortion; as to the licensure of that person; as to the facility in which the procedure is to be performed, that is, whether it must be a hospital or may be a clinic or some other place of less-than-hospital status; as to the licensing of the facility; and the like.

This means, on the other hand, that, for the period of pregnancy prior to this "compelling" point, the attending physician, in consultation with his patient, is free to determine, without regulation by the State, that in his medical judgment the patient's pregnancy should be terminated. If that decision is reached, the judgment may be effectuated by an abortion free of interference by the State.

With respect to the State's important and legitimate interest in potential life, the "compelling" point is at viability. This is so because the fetus then presumably has the capability of meaningful life outside the mother's womb. State regulation protective of fetal life after viability thus has both logical and biological justifications. If the State is interested in protecting fetal life after viability, it may go so far as to proscribe abortion during that period except when it is necessary to preserve the life or health of the mother.

Measured against these standards, Art. 1196 of the Texas Penal Code, in restricting legal abortions to those "procured or attempted by medical advice for the purpose of saving the life of the mother," sweeps too broadly. The statute makes no distinction between abortions performed early in pregnancy and those performed later, and it limits to a single reason, "saving" the mother's life, the legal justification for the procedure. The statute, therefore, cannot survive the consitutional attack made upon it here.

To summarize and to repeat:

1. A state criminal abortion statute of the current Texas type, that excepts from criminality only a *life saving* procedure on behalf of the mother, without regard to pregnancy stage and without recognition of the other interests involved, is violative of the Due Process Clause of the Fourteenth Amendment.

(a) For the stage prior to approximately the end of the first trimester, the abortion decision and its effectuation must be left to the medical judgment of the pregnant woman's attending physician.

(b) For the stage subsequent to approximately the end of the first trimester, the State, in promoting its interest in the health of the mother, may, if it chooses, regulate the abortion procedure in ways that are reasonably related to maternal health.

(c) For the stage subsequent to viability the State, in promoting its interest in the potentiality of human life, may, if it chooses, regulate, and even proscribe, abortion except where it is necessary, in appropriate medical judgment, for the preservation of the life or health of the mother.
. . .

Affirmed in part and reversed in part.

MR. JUSTICE STEWART, CONCURRING (OMITTED).
MR. CHIEF JUSTICE BURGER, CONCURRING (OMITTED).
MR. JUSTICE DOUGLAS, CONCURRING (OMITTED).

MR. JUSTICE REHNQUIST, DISSENTING.

The Court's opinion brings to the decision of this troubling question both extensive historical fact and a wealth of legal scholarship. While its opinion thus commands my respect, I find myself nonetheless in fundamental disagreement with those parts of it which invalidate the Texas statute in question, and therefore dissent. . . .

The fact that a majority of the States, reflecting after all the majority sentiment in those States, have had restrictions on abortions for at least a century seems to me as strong an indication there is that the asserted right to an abortion is not "so rooted in the traditions and conscience of our people as to be ranked as fundamental," . . . Even today, when society's views on abortion are changing, the very existence of the debate is evidence that the "right" to an abortion is not so universally accepted as the appellants would have us believe.

. . .

[L]iberty is not guaranteed absolutely against deprivation, but only against deprivation without due process of law. The test traditionally applied in the area of social and economic legislation is whether or not a law such as that challenged has a rational relation to a valid objective. . . . If the Texas statute were to prohibit an abortion even where the mother's life is in jeopardy, I have little doubt that such a statute would lack a rational relation to a valid state objective. . . . But the Court's sweeping invalidation of any restrictions on abortion during the first trimester is impossible to justify under that standard, and the conscious weighing of competing factors which the Court's opinion apparently substitutes for the established test is far more appropriate to a legislative judgment than to a judicial one.

MR. JUSTICE WHITE, WITH WHOM MR. JUSTICE REHNQUIST JOINS, DISSENTING (OMITTED).

[In a companion case, *Doe* v. *Bolton* (1973), the Supreme Court also invalidated a recently enacted Georgia statute that was considerably more permissive than the old Texas law. An abortion was permitted in Georgia to preserve the life of the mother, when the pregnancy occurred as a result of rape, or when the child would be born with a severe and permanent defect. However, Georgia law required that an abortion be performed in a hospital specially accredited for that purpose, and it further required the approval of two physicians besides the patient's own physician. These requirements, the Court said, infringed the rights of patients and obstructed the right of physicians to practice medicine.

The Supreme Court's decision in these two cases took most people by surprise. Groups that had fought for liberalization of abortion laws—without much prior success—were elated. But those not favoring abortion were poorly organized, and their immediate response, though very critical, was diffuse. Few would have predicted how quickly such groups would organize and how effective they would become politically.

Following Congress' failure to pass what "right-to-life" groups called the "human life" amendment after the *Roe* decision, antiabortion groups began organizing a constitutional convention drive in the states to propose an antiabortion amendment to the Constitution. "Pro-choice" supporters launched a counterattack, opposing a constitutional convention. A constitutional amendment to ban abortions is still pending in the Congress. Congress and the state legislatures have been under intense pressure to cut off funding for abortions in public hospitals and to pass other laws designed to thwart the Supreme Court's decisions; Congress has, in fact, cut off federal funding for most abortions.

Notwithstanding these efforts, which continue today at, if anything, a stepped-up pace, the number of legal abortions in the United States has risen dramatically. According to figures released recently, there is now one reported abortion for every 2.8 live births. In 1972, there were approximately 550,000 abortions. The estimate for 1977 is 1,270,000, of which about 275,000 were funded under the Medicaid program. The vast majority of abortions, 89 percent, are performed during the first trimester of pregnancy. About 10.5 percent are performed during the second trimester, and just a few after that.

Public opinion continues to support abortions under certain circumstances. According to a Gallup poll taken in December 1977, 22 percent of a national sample thought abortions should be legal under any circumstance, 55 percent supported them only under certain circumstances, and only 19 percent thought abortion should be illegal under all circumstances. These figures were almost identical with responses to a similar question asked by Gallup in 1975.

Challenges to state and federal limitations on abortion soon reached the Supreme Court. Missouri, like some other states, passed a comprehensive statute to govern post-*Roe* abortion procedures. While upholding some provisions of the law, including a statutory definition of fetal viability and a requirement that a woman consent in writing to an abortion, the

Supreme Court in *Planned Parenthood of Central Missouri* v. *Danforth* (1976) invalidated the following provisions: (1) a provision requiring written consent from the woman's spouse if she was married and if the abortion was not necessary to save her life; (2) a provision requiring that consent be obtained from the woman's parents if she was under eighteen and unmarried; (3) a blanket prohibition on the method of saline amniocentesis, the most common method used in first trimester abortions; (4) making it a criminal offense for the *physician* to fail to exercise due care to save the life of the fetus. However, in a more recent case, *Colautti* v. *Franklin* (1979), the Court invalidated the viability determination provisions of the Pennsylvania Abortion Control Act. The Court ruled that what "is a viable" and what "may be a viable" fetus are ambiguous determination standards. And the Court held that the statutory standard of care, resting on the "experience, judgment, or professional competence" of the attending physician at an abortion, compounded by the fact that physicians performing abortions were also subjected by the act to criminal liability without regard to fault, were unconstitutionally vague and hence void.

In *Carey* v. *Population Services International* (1977), the Court invalidated a New York State statute that prohibited anyone but a licensed pharmacist from selling or distributing contraceptives to a person over sixteen years of age; prohibited *anyone* from selling or giving contraceptives to a person under sixteen; and prohibited the display of contraceptives. In Justice Brennan's plurality opinion, the ban on sales to minors was linked to the *Danforth* case: "Since the state may not impose a blanket prohibition, or even a blanket requirement of parental consent, on the choice of a minor to terminate her pregnancy, the constitutionality of a blanket prohibition of the distribution of contraceptives to minors is a *fortiori* foreclosed." He went on to state that "read in the light of its progeny, the teaching of *Griswold* is that the Constitution protects individual decisions in matters of childbearing from unjustified intrusion by the State. . . . The right to privacy in connection with decisions affecting procreation extends to minors as well as adults."

These cases suggest that the Court is unwilling to accept any significant direct limitations on its holding in *Roe* v. *Wade.* However, the balance of votes on the Court shifted quite radically when the validity of cutoffs of public funding for abortions became the issue. In *Maher* v. *Roe* (1977), it held that the equal protection clause did not require states to subsidize elective abortions where they did subsidize therapeutic abortions. The Court's opinion, by Justice Powell, denied that this was discrimination against indigent women that violated the Fourteenth Amendment:

This case involves no discrimination against a suspect class. An indigent woman desiring an abortion does not come within the limited category of disadvantaged classes so recognized by our cases. Nor does the fact that the impact of the regulation falls upon those who cannot pay lead to a different conclusion. In a sense, every denial of welfare to an indigent creates a wealth classification as compared to nonindigents who are able to pay for the desired goods or services. But this Court has never held that finanacial need alone identifies a suspect class for purposes of equal protection analysis.

In a companion case, *Poelker* v. *Doe* (1977), the Court, in a per curiam opinion, decided that a city could prohibit elective abortions in municipal hospitals even though it made those facilities available to women carrying to full term. Justices Brennan, Marshall and Blackmun dissented. Wrote Blackmun:

The Court . . . allows the States . . . to accomplish indirectly what the Court in Roe v. Wade . . . *and* Doe v. Bolton . . . *by a substantial majority and with some emphasis, I had thought—said they could not do directly. The Court concedes the existence of a constitutional right but denies the realization and enjoyment of that right on the ground that existence and realization are separate and distinct. For the individual woman concerned, indigent and financially helpless, . . . the result is punitive and* tragic. Implicit in the Court's holdings is the condescension that she may go elsewhere for her abortion. I find that disingenuous and alarming, almost reminiscent of "let them eat cake."

The result the Court reaches is particularly distressing in Poelker v. Doe, where a presumed majority, in electing as mayor one whom the record shows campaigned on the issue of closing public hospitals to non-therapeutic abortions, punitively impresses upon a needy minority its own concepts of the socially desirable, the publicly acceptable, and morally sound, with a touch of the devil-take-the-hindmost. This is not the kind of thing for which our Constitution stands.

The Court's financial argument, of course, is specious. . . . the cost of a non-therapeutic abortion is far less than the cost of maternity care and delivery, and holds no comparison whatsoever with the welfare costs that will burden the State for the new indigents and their support in the long, long years ahead.

. . .

There is another world "out there," the existence of which the Court, I suspect, either chooses to ignore or fears to recognize. And so the cancer of poverty will continue to grow. This is a sad day for those who regard the Constitution as a force that would serve justice to all evenhandedly and, in so doing, would better the lot of the poorest among us.]

the burger court and the old frontier

In the first edition of this book we concluded with a chapter on three "frontier" issues, which, in our judgment, were still in early or incomplete stages of doctrinal development. All of these issues—reapportionment, poverty and welfare, and gender equality—have now been absorbed into the mainstream of constitutional law. They appear in this edition as part of our new umbrella chapter on equality.

Of the three issues only one, gender equality, fulfilled at least some of its developmental promise. The Court's tentative flirtation with an unorthodox and liberalized view of the rights of those without means, best expressed in *Goldberg* v. *Kelly* (1970), began its downward slide to constitutional oblivion that same year in *Dandridge* v. *Williams*, and reached rock bottom with the Supreme Court's decision in the Texas school financing case, *San Antonio Independent School District* v. *Rodriguez* (1973).

In 1971, when the first edition was completed, reapportionment looked like at least a weak frontier issue for several reasons. First, *Kirkpatrick* v. *Preissler* (1969), in rejecting even a de minimis deviation from population equality in congressional districting, suggested that this standard, tougher than expressed in the landmark case of *Reynolds* v. *Sims* (1964), might well be applied to state legislative districting as well. Second, the Court was just beginning to grapple seriously with problems of electoral districting other than population equality, particularly with questions of the constitutionality of multimember districts at the interface of reapportionment and racial equality. Third, it was becoming clear that reapportionment by the numbers, with little more, was an insufficient reflection of the myriad and complex problems of electoral representation in a democratic society. Fourth, no one knew for sure what the policy impact of reapportionment would be.

The Burger Court's response to these problems was to quash the expansive tendency of earlier decisions like *Kirkpatrick*, offer little to settle the problems of multimember districting, and indicate, in *Gaffney* v. *Cummings* (1973), that it was adopting a hands-off policy in all but the most egregious instances of malapportionment. By relieving the court-directed pressure for meeting the one-person, one vote standard, the Court was returning to the state legislatures some of the reapportionment discretion that formerly had been entirely their own. Reapportionment following the 1980 census will reveal just how much discretion the states have in fact recovered.

The rapid constitutional development of gender equality was another story altogether. The constitutional edifice of sex discrimination was swept away in incredibly swift fashion. The Court recognized, in the equal protection clause of the 14th Amendment (and the due process clause of the 5th Amendment), a right against discrimination on account of gender. Most state and congressional statutory provisions that differentiated according to sex were held unconstitutional. Yet a majority of the Supreme Court refused to identify gender as a "suspect classification," and thus bring it within the orbit of strict constitutional scrutiny. And the Court's decisions in *General Electric Company* v. *Gilbert* (1976) and *Personnel Administrator* v. *Feeney* (1979), read in the context of the apparent failure of the proposed Equal Rights Amendment to gain ratification, suggests that neither the Court nor the country is quite ready to abolish all gender based (or gender impacting) public policies.

The fate of these three "frontier" issues in the hands of the Burger Court, along with its handling of major criminal justice issues, suggests that it has assumed an identity that discourages if it does not entirely preclude the establishment of new frontiers in judicial policy making. Like most "courts" in the recent past, the Burger Court spent some time reacting to the judicial legacy of its predecessor. But, so far at least, the Burger Court does not seem to have assumed an identity of its own. We know what it disfavors, but not much about its constitutional vision. In this respect it resembles much more an orthodox and reactive "court" than the proactive Warren Court, which seemed so often to be creating opportunities to respond to concerns of social policy and ideas of "progress".

Many factors contribute to the institutional role that the Supreme Court adopts at any particular time. Some are part of the institution itself—a general sense of self-restraint including, but not limited to, a sensitivity to the force of precedent, a commitment to incremental decision making, and a keen appreciation of the Court's public image and its power relationship with the coequal branches of government. But other factors are situational—a reflection of the attitudes and ideologies of the justices, the interaction of those attitudes with the major issues facing the court, and key changes in the court's membership.

Earl Warren was appointed Chief Justice in 1953. The Court was then an institution beset by internal feuds and factions that had developed in the 12 years the Court had been without effective leadership from the Chief Justice. The Court in 1953 had no discernible philosophy or role concept other than what could be called a post-New Deal malaise. There were signs of emergence of a coherent liberal philosophy. And the Court had made important, although incomplete, strides to break down racial discrimination in the South. But these events, exceptions to the general trend as they were, only emphasized the need for leadership to a new social and political role.

Earl Warren provided that leadership, beginning with his mobilization of the justices toward a unanimous decision in *Brown* v. *Board of Education* (1954). His initial task was made easier because he did not meet the backlash of a great or autocratic leader—a problem Stone had faced when succeeding Charles Evans Hughes in 1941. Hughes was a great judge and a strong chief, but efficiency was often achieved at the expense of full expression of ideas. Stone's easygoing tolerance provided immediate relief from this suffocation, but also encouraged the rise of factions and resulted in an important diminution of espirit d'court. Warren also benefited from the indifference of the president who appointed him. Eisenhower had little familiarity with Warren's politics, and was certainly unprepared for Warren's strong leadership in the school cases. Even in these most favorable of circumstances, it was some time before Warren could mobilize a consistent liberal and activist majority, not really until President Kennedy's appointment of Arthur Goldberg in 1962 to replace Felix Frankfurter. It was only then that the Supreme Court under Earl Warren really became the "Warren Court."

The situation facing Warren Burger, appointed to the chief justiceship by President Richard Nixon in 1969, was quite different. He was replacing a strong and popular leader, many of whose closest associates remained on the Court. His own constitutional views, articulated in many opinions as a judge of the Court of Appeals for the District of Columbia, were well known but quite at variance with those of his predecessor *and* the majority of the Court he now headed. His appointment followed closely a presidential election campaign in which the winning candidate promised to remake the Court in his own conservative image. Thus, unlike Warren, Burger was chosen *because* he had strong views on salient constitutional issues. He was not chosen, as Warren had been, to repay a political debt, but because the President thought he could lead the Supreme Court in a new direction. His appointment, like that of the three Nixon appointees who followed him—Blackmun, Powell, and Rehnquist—was a political signal that the President had kept his campaign promises, including the "southern strategy" that may have been decisive in the 1968 election.

No president since Franklin Roosevelt had made the Supreme Court more of an election issue and announced more specifically his criteria for judicial appointments than Richard Nixon. Nixon sought to create the image of a Court "moving to the right," and of one favoring the "peace forces over the criminal forces." The process by which Nixon filled four vacancies on the high bench, including the losing confirmation battles over Haynsworth and Carswell, created public expectations that were not entirely realistic in terms of how the Supreme Court operates. A president can influence the course of constitutional development by appointing justices who share his philosophy. But justices often turn out to be unpredictable and independent. And the institutional setting in which they function often obstructs the sort of radical policy changes which Nixon sought. It is unfair to newly appointed justices to impose on them the same "mission" as that of the president who appointed them. There was also the irony that justices appointed by a conservative president to foster conservative policy goals and to adopt a "strict constructionist" view of the

Constitution often had to choose between the two. To be a true strict constructionist in the early 1970s implied acceptance of major decisions of the Warren
Court that were, for better or for worse, the "law of the land." To bring about
radical changes in constitution interpretation required the Nixon justices to
be, not at all strict constructionists, but genuine activists.

At the beginning of this essay we noted the existence of certain institutional
factors that help define the role a particular Court may adopt. These factors,
which we now describe in detail, help to explain why the Burger Court has
done little more than modify some of the major doctrines of the Warren Court.
No one would mistake one for the other; but the Burger Court may well be, as
many have observed, the "second most liberal court" in American history.

The Supreme Court is a continuing institution.[1] The addition of a new justice to a group that has been working together is rarely decisive unless the
remaining justices are evenly divided on a particular issue. Most freshman
justices take time to develop coherent judicial philosophies; it is rare for a new
justice to become identified immediately with either the right or left blocs on a
court (if such blocs exist). Warren Burger himself did not follow this pattern.
His outspoken and conservative views, well known to observers of his record on
the Court of Appeals, surfaced almost immediately, but mostly in dissent. Indeed, as we noted in an earlier chapter, he dissented much more frequently in
his early terms on the Court than is customary for a Chief Justice. It was only
with the addition of Blackmun, Powell, and Rehnquist that his views emerged
regularly in opinions of the court.

Added to the constraints of personalities and institutional relationships are
the limits of received traditions and norms about the appropriate judicial role.
No court can afford to ignore the precedents, concepts, framework of thought,
and dominant paradigms that it inherits. The pull toward incrementalism, the
necessity of assimilating past to present are very strong centripetal forces.

Adjudication within the adversary system does not permit the same freedom
to innovate (or even restore the past) as would be possible under nonadjudica-
tive policy making. There may be new justices, but it is very old Court with
a very strong sense of institutional tradition and a commitment to ideas as well
as to procedures. Of course change is also part of the Court's tradition. It has
never been restrained—ultimately—from ignoring prior precedent when convinced that errors had been made, or that changing circumstances dictated
new policies. But rarely is the past repudiated as completely and swiftly as in
the "constitutional revolution" of 1937–1941. (Note that during those four
years, virtually an entire new Court had been appointed by President
Roosevelt.)

Change on the Court is also restrained by the political environment. The
Court chooses the cases it will hear, but litigants have a substantial voice in
setting the Court's agenda. One of the legacies of the Warren Court was a
loosening of the restrictions on the rules of access, and the Burger Court increasingly had to deal not only with a generation of "activist lawyers," but with
a generation of lawyers—and, indeed, citizens generally—more sensitive to
human rights issues and expecting those rights to be judicially protected. Finally, even for a "conservative" court, general social and economic conditions
produce new issues that the Court must eventually confront. Nixon's appoin-

---

[1]Harry Kalven, Jr., "Even When a Nation is at War—, 85 *Harvard Law Review* (1971), 3–36.

tees may have come to the Court with well-developed views on reversing the liberal trend of decisions on the rights of criminal defendants, but it is doubtful if any had as well-structured views on environmental issues, the constitutional rights of Indians, gender equality, and the power of the president to commit American troops to combat without a declaration of war.

If all of these factors coalesce into a coherent explanation of why the Burger Court has dealt so uncertainly with some of the most controversial doctrines of the Warren Court, they also say something about the difficulty of identifying "frontier" issues for the Court of the 1980s. A brief look at the internal mechanics of the Court under the leadership of Warren Burger provides some additional insight. A recent study reports two patterns of opinion assignment by the Chief Justice.[2] First, it appears that disproportionate shares of significant cases went to "nonliberal" justices. Second, the Chief Justice assigned to himself a disproportionate share of the liberal decisions in which he remained in the majority. These patterns (with a major exception in the abortion case, *Roe* v. *Wade*, 1973) may serve to produce language in opinions that is narrow and minimal in its liberal reach and significance. Thus, even where policy changes are made that, in their liberal makeup, would suggest the potential of new frontiers of judicial policy, the scope of the opinion inhibits such inferences. Certainly it is true that part of the liberal image and reputation of the Warren Court was not so much the decisions it made as its willingness—indeed often its obvious delight—to open new doors and suggest new paths to follow in the future.

There is also some evidence of deterioration in the cohesiveness of the Court's conservative bloc. The 1977 term of the Court produced a rather marked tendency of the other Nixon appointees to depart from the cues of the Chief Justice. In that term, Justices Blackmun, Powell, and Rehnquist voted against the position taken by Burger twice as often as in previous terms.[3] If singlemindedness of purpose and cohesiveness are critical to uncovering new frontiers, then the Burger Court may currently lack that critical attribute. The disintegration of consensus on the Burger Court, as evidenced by a proliferation of concurring and dissenting opinions in key cases, some in which no majority opinion was possible, has been widely observed.

If the Burger Court has shown a marked dislike for the "great" decision which announces new constitutional frontiers, it has done little to reduce its own discretion to intervene in many important policy areas. In this respect it may be an even more activist court than its predecessor, which often was content to announce fundamental principles and allow other courts to fill in the details. The limits on this kind of low visibility activism, as Martin Shapiro has correctly noted, are essentially political.[4] As long as the Court's intervention

[2]We rely heavily upon the detailed examination of Chief Justice Burger's opinion assignment practices in Dennis Haines, "Rolling Back the Top on Chief Justice Burger's Opinion Assignment Desk," **38** *University of Pittsburgh Law Review* (1977), 631–693.

[3]See "Nixon's Appointees to High Court Voting Less as a Bloc with Burger," *The New York Times,* July 5, 1978. The article, by Warren Weaver, Jr., indicates that the conservative tenor of the Court has been largely untouched, despite the seeming disaffection of the Nixon appointees from Burger's leadership. The difference appears to have been made up by alignments with other Justices, notably Stewart, White and Stevens. cf. Bob Woodward and Scott Armstrong *The Brethren* (New York: Simon and Schuster, 1979).

[4]Martin Shapiro, "The Supreme Court: From Warren to Burger," in King (ed.), *The New American Political System* (Washington, D.C.: American Enterprise Institute, 1978), pp. 179–211.

looses no red flags, or irritates no especially strong and well-organized interest, its course of action may continue undisturbed for some time. The Burger Court's most notable departure from this strategy in a major case, *Roe* v. *Wade* (1973), continues to be the single most explosive and emotional issue in politics today—notwithstanding the majority's own retreat in later cases. But its hand-ling of school busing, capital punishment, and affirmative action cases—all of which retained for the Court a dominant role in future decisions—gave no opening to those who would attack the Court. Those who oppose busing, capital punishment, and affirmative action continue to fight for those principles, but none has unleashed a campaign that threatens judicial prerogative.

We have tried to suggest some reasons for our inability to identify new fron-tier issues facing the Court in the 1980s. In one sense, however, there is an "old" frontier that the Burger Court majority seems determined to resurrect: a balanced federalism.[5] How the states relate to the national government is a continuing tension built into our constitutional fabric that no Supreme Court can wish away. If the framers of the Constitution feared centralization of power, federalism—the division of powers between the nation and the states—was one of the antidotes prescribed. Federalism diffused power, and thus made its usurpation more difficult. Federalism also increased political participation by dispersing political power and bringing it closer to the people. Finally, it was often claimed, federalism fostered "innovation, experimenta-tion, and self-determination."[6]

The Civil War brought about the realization that the correlation between federalism and protection of civil liberties was not inevitable. States were rec-ognized as potential—and in the case of slavery very real—sources of depriva-tions of human rights. Increasingly, citizens turned to the federal government for protection of their rights. The 14th Amendment became the focus of these efforts. Where federalism—often expressed as "states' rights"—stood in the way of these rights, it was often cast aside abruptly. That federalism was an obstacle to the effective protection of rights, and not a protector of those rights, was the guiding principle of those justices who supported incorporation of the Bill of Rights into the 14th Amendment.

The Burger Court majority has moved inexorably toward this "old" frontier. Of course it cannot today recapture the purity of the doctrine envisioned by Jefferson and Madison in their Virginia and Kentucky Resolutions, or by John Calhoun's doctrine of the concurrent majority. Few would counsel such a course of action. But wherever possible the Court has allowed power federalized under the Warren Court to slip back to the states (again, with *Roe* v. *Wade,* 1973, and *Furman* v. *Georgia,* 1972, as major exceptions). It would have been impossible, in the 1970s, to completely roll back the federal role in the administration of criminal justice in the states. But decisions such as *Stone* v. *Powell* (1976) and *Gregg* v. *Georgia* (1976) take steps in that direc-tion. *Miller* v. *California* (1973) made a similar attempt with regard to obscen-ity and pornography, but not, so it appears, a very successful attempt.

Of all the Burger Court decisions, the one which most embodied—and perhaps most effectively advanced—this newly revived theory of federalism in

[5]Neil D. McFeeley, "The Supreme Court and the Federal System: Federalism from Warren to Burger," 8 *Publius* Fall, 1978), 5–36.
[6]Paul Freund, quoted in McFeeley, *Ibid.,* p. 8.

cases involving individual liberties was *Younger* v. *Harris* (1971). As Justice Black wrote in his opinion for the Court in that case, "Our federalism embodies the belief that the National Government will fare best if the States and their institutions are left free to perform their separate functions in their separate ways." Perhaps it is not surprising that Black would couch his reasons for reaffirming federalism values in terms of what was best for the federal government. But other, continuing, members of the Burger Court have made their view clear that protecting the prerogatives of the states is also in the interest—ultimately—of human liberty.

Justice Brennan has been outspoken in his criticism of the conservative majority for favoring this more traditional conception of federalism at the expense of individual rights. "Federalism need not be a mean spirited doctrine that serves only to limit the scope of human liberty . . . ," he has noted. "One of the strengths of our federal system is that it provides a double source of protection for the rights of our citizens. Federalism is not served when the federal half of that protection is crippled."[7] But however attractive Brennan's reformulation of the doctrine is to civil libertarians, it is *not* the federalism of textbooks or, more importantly, of the Constitution. Whatever the benefits to society of a Supreme Court which protects human liberties against *both* state and national governments, as the Warren Court endeavored to do, the arrangement cannot persuasively be subsumed under the name of federalism.

There is, however, an important irony to be noted. As the Supreme Court has become more restrained and conservative in its definition of individual rights, the liberal initiative has, in very large measure, passed back to state courts and legislatures. A number of states have established *more* restrictive rules on police interrogation than called for by what is left of the *Miranda* rules. And, as Anthony Lewis has recently noted, a number of states have restricted police searches of newsrooms permitted under *Zurcher* v. *Stanford Daily* (1979).[8] Justice Stevens' dissent in that case, calling for limitations on third-party searches, has been enacted into law by the Wisconsin legislature. That law, perhaps the first of its kind in the nation, obliges state officials to issue a subpoena (which, unlike a search warrant, may be challenged in court) when it wants to obtain "documents which may constitute evidence of a crime" unless the documents are in the possession of an individual "reasonably suspected to be concerned in the comission of that crime." The Supreme Court of Minnesota, relying on the provisions against unreasonable searches and seizures in its own Constitution, has taken a similar position: "the states may afford their citizens greater protection than the safeguards guaranteed in the Federal Constitution." Similar efforts to limit the anti-libertarian effects of a Supreme Court decision are underway in many states following *Gannett* v. *DePasquale* (1979). Thus, the Burger Court's efforts to erode some federally guaranteed constitutional protections may result, in a true revival of the federalism doctrine, in greater protection for those liberties.

If the main battleground in the revival of federalism consists of cases raising questions of individual liberties and civil rights, the bugle call to the old fron-

[7]William J. Brennan, Jr., "State Constitutions and the Protection of Individual Rights," **90** *Harvard Law Review* (1977), 489, 503.
[8]Anthony Lewis, "Local Initiative Takes Over in Press-Freedom Cases," *The New York Times* (December 16, 1979).

tier has come in an entirely different kind of case: *National League of Cities* v. *Usery* (1976). In that case, for the first time since 1937, the Court declared unconstitutional a federal regulatory statute otherwise authorized by the commerce clause. The issue was whether Congress could regulate wages and working conditions of state and local government employees. A 5-4 majority, speaking through Justice Rehnquist, said Congress could not do so without violating the 10th Amendment. While Rehnquist's opinion did not directly challenge the dictum of *United States* v. *Darby* (1941), that the 10th Amendment "is but a truism that all is retained which has not been surrendered," it was certainly intended to undermine that dictum and the corollary doctrine that the 10th Amendment is not a yardstick by which the extent of legitimate federal power can be measured. *National League of Cities* may turn out to be nothing more than an isolated exception to the post New Deal practice of extreme judicial deference to congressional economic regulation. Or, depending on the fortunes of presidential appointments to the Supreme Court, it may be just the first of continued efforts to exhume the 10th Amendment and create a new federal balance. A leading scholar of American federalism, Professor Harry N. Scheiber, has stated that "it is clear . . . that currently a new phase in the history of federalism may be taking shape."[9]

---

[9]"American Federalism and the Diffusion of Power: Historical and Contemporary Perspectives," **9** *University of Toledo Law Review* (1978), 676.

CONSTITUTION OF THE UNITED STATES

We the People of the United States, in Order to form a more perfect Union, establish Justice, insure domestic Tranquility, provide for the common defence, promote the general Welfare, and secure the Blessings of Liberty to ourselves and our Posterity, do ordain and establish this Constitution for the United States of America.

ARTICLE I.

SECTION. 1. All legislative Powers herein granted shall be vested in a Congress of the United States, which shall consist of a Senate and House of Representatives.

SECTION. 2. [1] The House of Representatives shall be composed of Members chosen every second Year by the People of the several States, and the Electors in each State shall have the Qualifications requisite for Electors of the most numerous Branch of the State Legislature.

[2] No person shall be a Representative who shall not have attained to the Age of twenty five Years, and been seven Years a Citizen of the United States, and who shall not, when elected, be an Inhabitant of that State in which he shall be chosen.

[3] [Representatives and direct Taxes shall be apportioned among the several States which may be included within this Union, according to their respective Numbers, which shall be determined by adding to the whole Number of free Persons, including those bound to Service for a Term of Years, and excluding Indians not taxed, three fifths of all other Persons.].* The actual Enumeration shall be made within three Years after the first Meeting of the Congress of the United States, and within every subsequent Term of ten Years, in such Manner as they shall by Law direct. The Number of Representatives shall not exceed one for every thirty Thousand, but each State shall have at Least one Representative; and until such enumeration shall be made, the State of New Hampshire shall be entitled to chuse three, Massachusetts eight, Rhode-Island and Providence Plantations one, Connecticut five, New-York six, New Jersey four, Pennsylvania eight, Delaware one, Maryland six, Virginia ten, North Carolina five, South Carolina five, and Georgia three.

[4] When vacancies happen in the Representation from any State, the Executive Authority thereof shall issue Writs of Election to fill such Vacancies.

[5] The House of Representatives shall chuse their Speaker and other Officers; and shall have the sole Power of Impeachment.

SECTION. 3. [1] The Senate of the United States shall be composed of two Senators from each State, [chosen by the Legislature thereof,]† for six Years; and each Senator shall have one Vote.

[2] Immediately after they shall be assembled in Consequence of the first Election, they shall be divided as equally as may be into three Classes. The Seats of the Senators of the first Class shall be vacated at the Expiration of the second Year, of the second Class at the Expiration of the fourth Year, and of the third Class at the Expiration of the sixth Year, so that one third may be chosen every second Year; [and if Vacancies happen by Resignation, or otherwise, during the Recess of the Legislature of any State, the Executive thereof may make temporary Appointments until the next Meeting of the Legislature, which shall then fill such Vacancies.].‡.

[3] No Person shall be a Senator who shall not have attained to the Age of thirty Years, and been nine Years a Citizen of the United States, and who shall not, when elected, be an Inhabitant of that State for which he shall be chosen.

---

*Changed by Section 2 of the Fourteenth Amendment.
†Changed by Section 1 of the Seventeenth Amendment.
‡Changed by Clause 2 of the Seventeenth Amendment.

⁴ The Vice President of the United States shall be President of the Senate, but shall have no Vote, unless they be equally divided.

⁵ The Senate shall chuse their other Officers, and also a President pro tempore, in the Absence of the Vice President, or when he shall exercise the Office of President of the United States.

⁶ The Senate shall have the sole Power to try all Impeachments. When sitting for that Purpose, they shall be on Oath or Affirmation. When the President of the United States is tried, the Chief Justice shall preside: And no Person shall be convicted without the Concurrence of two thirds of the Members present.

⁷ Judgment in Cases of Impeachment shall not extend further than to removal from Office, and disqualification to hold and enjoy any Office of honor, Trust or Profit under the United States: but the Party convicted shall nevertheless be liable and subject to Indictment, Trial, Judgment and Punishment, according to Law.

SECTION. 4. ¹ The Times, Places and Manner of holding Elections for Senators and Representatives, shall be prescribed in each State by the Legislature thereof; but the Congress may at any time by Law make or alter such Regulations, except as to the Places of chusing Senators.

² The Congress shall assemble at least once in every Year, and such Meeting shall [be on the first Monday in December,]* unless they shall by Law appoint a different Day.

SECTION. 5. ¹ Each House shall be the Judge of the Elections, Returns and Qualifications of its own Members, and a Majority of each shall constitute a Quorum to do Business; but a smaller Number may adjourn from day to day, and may be authorized to compel the Attendance of absent Members, in such Manner, and under such Penalties as each House may provide.

² Each House may determine the Rules of its Proceedings, punish its Members for disorderly Behavior, and, with the Concurrence of two thirds, expel a Member.

³ Each House shall keep a Journal of its Proceedings, and from time to time publish the same, excepting such Parts as may in their Judgment require Secrecy; and the Yeas and Nays of the Members of either House on any question shall, at the Desire of one fifth of those Present, be entered on the Journal.

⁴ Neither House, during the Session of Congress, shall, without the Consent of the other, adjourn for more than three days, nor to any other Place than that in which the two Houses shall be sitting.

SECTION. 6. ¹ The Senators and Representatives shall receive a Compensation for their Services to be ascertained by Law, and paid out of the Treasury of the United States. They shall in all Cases, except Treason, Felony and Breach of the Peace, be privileged from Arrest during their Attendance at the Session of their respective Houses, and in going to and returning from the same; and for any Speech or Debate in either House, they shall not be questioned in any other Place.

² No Senator or Representative shall, during the Time for which he was elected, be appointed to any civil Office under the Authority of the United States, which shall have been created, or the Emoluments whereof shall have been encreased during such time; and no Person holding any Office under the United States, shall be a Member of either House during his Continuance in Office.

SECTION. 7. ¹ All Bills for raising Revenue shall originate in the House of Representatives; but the Senate may propose or concur with Amendments as on other Bills.

² Every Bill which shall have passed the House of Representatives and the Senate, shall, before it becomes a Law, be presented to the President of the United States; If he approve he

*Changed by Section 2 of the Twentieth Amendment.

shall sign it, but if not he shall return it, with his Objections to that house in which it shall have originated, who shall enter the Objections at large on their Journal, and proceed to reconsider it. If after such Reconsideration two thirds of that House shall agree to pass the Bill, it shall be sent, together with the Objections, to the other House, by which it shall likewise be reconsidered, and if approved by two thirds of that House, it shall become a Law. But in all such Cases the Votes of both Houses shall be determined by yeas and Nays, and the Names of the Persons voting for and against the Bill shall be entered on the Journal of each House respectively. If any Bill shall not be returned by the President within ten Days (Sundays excepted) after it shall have been presented to him, the Same shall be a Law, in like Manner as if he had signed it, unless the Congress by their Adjournment prevent its Return, in which Case it shall not be a Law.

³ Every Order, Resolution, or Vote to which the Concurrence of the Senate and House of Representatives may be necessary (except on a question of Adjournment) shall be presented to the President of the United States; and before the Same shall take Effect, shall be approved by him, or being disapproved by him, shall be repassed by two thirds of the Senate and House of Representatives, according to the Rules and Limitations prescribed in the Case of a Bill.

SECTION. 8. ¹ The Congress shall have Power To lay and collect Taxes, Duties, Imposts and Excises, to pay the Debts and provide for the common Defence and general Welfare of the United States; but all Duties, Imposts and Excises shall be uniform throughout the United States;

² To borrow Money on the credit of the United States;

³ To regulate Commerce with foreign Nations, and among the several States, and with the Indian Tribes;

⁴ To establish an uniform Rule of Naturalization, and uniform Laws on the subject of Bankruptcies throughout the United States;

⁵ To coin Money, regulate the Value thereof, and of foreign Coin, and fix the Standard of Weights and Measures;

⁶ To provide for the Punishment of counterfeiting the Securities and current Coin of the United States;

⁷ To establish Post Offices and post Roads;

⁸ To promote the Progress of Science and useful Arts, by securing for limited Times to Authors and Inventors the exclusive Right to their respective Writings and Discoveries;

⁹ To constitute Tribunals inferior to the supreme Court;

¹⁰ To define and punish Piracies and Felonies committed on the high Seas, and Offences against the Law of Nations;

¹¹ To declare War, grant Letters of Marque and Reprisal, and make Rules concerning Captures on Land and Water;

¹² To raise and support Armies, but no Appropriation of Money to that Use shall be for a longer Term than two Years;

¹³ To provide and maintain a Navy;

¹⁴ To make Rules for the Government and Regulation of the land and naval Forces;

¹⁵ To provide for calling forth the Militia to execute the Laws of the Union, suppress Insurrections and repel Invasions;

¹⁶ To provide for organizing, arming, and disciplining, the Militia, and for governing such Part of them as may be employed in the Service of the United States, reserving to the States respectively, the Appointment of the Officers, and the Authority of training the Militia according to the discipline prescribed by Congress;

¹⁷ To exercise exclusive Legislation in all Cases whatsoever, over such District (not exceeding ten Miles square) as may, by Cession of particular States, and the Acceptance of Congress, become the Seat of the Government of the United States, and to exercise like

Authority over all Places purchased by the Consent of the Legislature of the State in which the Same shall be, for the Erection of Forts, Magazines, Arsenals, dock-Yards, and other needful Buildings;—And

[18] To make all Laws which shall be necessary and proper for carrying into Execution the foregoing Powers, and all other Powers vested by this Constitution in the Government of the United States, or in any Department or Officer thereof.

SECTION. 9. [1] The Migration or Importation of such Persons as any of the States now existing shall think proper to admit, shall not be prohibited by the Congress prior to the Year one thousand eight hundred and eight, but a Tax or duty may be imposed on such Importation, not exceeding ten dollars for each Person.

[2] The Privilege of the Writ of Habeas Corpus shall not be suspended, unless when in Cases of Rebellion or Invasion the public Safety may require it.

[3] No Bill of Attainder or ex post facto Law shall be passed.

[4] No Capitation, or other direct, Tax shall be laid, unless in Proportion to the Census or Enumeration herein before directed to be taken.*

[5] No Tax or Duty shall be laid on Articles exported from any State.

[6] No Preference shall be given by any Regulation of Commerce or Revenue to the Ports of one State over those of another; nor shall Vessels bound to, or from, one State, be obliged to enter, clear, or pay Duties in another.

[7] No Money shall be drawn from the Treasury, but in Consequence of Appropriations made by Law; and a regular Statement and Account of the Receipts and Expenditures of all public Money shall be published from time to time.

[8] No Title of Nobility shall be granted by the United States: And no Person holding any Office of Profit or Trust under them, shall, without the Consent of the Congress, accept of any present, Emolument, Office, or Title, of any kind whatever, from any King, Prince, or foreign State.

SECTION. 10. [1] No State shall enter into any Treaty, Alliance, or Confederation; grant Letters of Marque and Reprisal; coin Money; emit Bills of Credit; make any Thing but gold and silver Coin a Tender in Payment of Debts; pass any Bill of Attainder, ex post facto Law, or Law impairing the Obligation of the Contracts, or grant any Title of Nobility.

[2] No State shall, without the Consent of the Congress, lay any Imposts or Duties on Imports or Exports, except what may be absolutely necessary for executing it's inspection Laws: and the net Produce of all Duties and Imposts, laid by any State on Imports or Exports, shall be for the Use of the Treasury of the United States; and all such Laws shall be subject to the Revision and Controul of the Congress.

[3] No State shall, without the Consent of Congress, lay any Duty of Tonnage, keep Troops, or Ships of War in time of Peace, enter into any Agreement or Compact with another State, or with a foreign Power, or engage in War, unless actually invaded, or in such imminent Danger as will not admit of delay.

ARTICLE. II.

SECTION. 1. [1] The Executive Power shall be vested in a President of the United States of America. He shall hold his Office during the Term of four Years, and, together with the Vice President, chosen for the same Term, be elected, as follows

[2] Each State shall appoint, in such Manner as the Legislature thereof may direct, a Number of Electors, equal to the whole Number of Senators and Representatives to which the State may be entitled in the Congress: but no Senator or Representative, or Person holding an Office of Trust or Profit under the United States, shall be appointed an Elector.

*See also the Sixteenth Amendment

[The Electors shall meet in their respective States, and vote by Ballot for two Persons, of whom one at least shall not be an Inhabitant of the same State with themselves. And they shall make a List of all the Persons voted for, and of the Number of Votes for each; which List they shall sign and certify, and transmit sealed to the Seat of the Government of the United States, directed to the President of the Senate. The President of the Senate shall, in the Presence of the Senate and House of Representatives, open all the Certificates, and the Votes shall then be counted. The Person having the greatest Number of Votes shall be the President, if such Number be a Majority of the whole Number of Electors appointed; and if there be more than one who have such Majority, and have an equal Number of Votes, then the House of Representatives shall immediately chuse by Ballot one of them for President; and if no Person have a Majority, then from the five highest on the List the said House shall in like Manner chuse the President. But in chusing the President, the Votes shall be taken by States, the Representation from each State having one Vote; A quorum for this Purpose shall consist of a Member or Members from two thirds of the States, and a Majority of all the States shall be necessary to a Choice. In every Case, after the Choice of the President, the Person having the greatest Number of Votes of the Electors shall be the Vice President. But if there should remain two or more who have equal Votes, the Senate shall chuse from them by Ballot the Vice President.]*

³ The Congress may determine the Time of chusing the Electors, and the Day on which they shall give their Votes; which Day shall be the same throughout the United States.

⁴ No person except a natural born Citizen, or a Citizen of the United States, at the time of the Adoption of this Constitution, shall be eligible to the Office of President; neither shall any Person be eligible to that Office who shall not have attained to the Age of thirty five Years, and been fourteen Years a Resident within the United States.

⁵ In case of the Removal of the President from Office, or of his Death, Resignation, or Inability to discharge the Powers and Duties of the said Office,† the Same shall devolve on the Vice President, and the Congress may by Law provide for the Case of Removal, Death, Resignation or Inability, both of the President and Vice President, declaring what Officer shall then act as President, and such Officer shall act accordingly, until the Disability be removed, or a President shall be elected.

⁶ The President shall, at stated Times, receive for his Services, a Compensation, which shall neither be encreased nor diminished during the Period for which he shall have been elected, and he shall not receive within that Period any other Emolument from the United States, or any of them.

⁷ Before he enter on the Execution of his Office, he shall take the following Oath or Affirmation:—"I do solemnly swear (or affirm) that I will faithfully execute the Office of President of the United States, and will to the best of my Ability, preserve, protect and defend the Constitution of the United States."

SECTION. 2. ¹ The President shall be Commander in Chief of the Army and Navy of the United States, and of the Militia of the several States, when called into the actual Service of the United States; he may require the Opinion, in writing, of the principal Officer in each of the executive Departments, upon any Subject relating to the Duties of their respective Offices, and he shall have Power to grant Reprieves and Pardons for Offences against the United States, except in Cases of Impeachment.

² He shall have Power, by and with the Advice and Consent of the Senate, to make Treaties, provided two thirds of the Senators present concur; and he shall nominate, and by and with the Advice and Consent of the Senate, shall appoint Ambassadors, other public Ministers and Consuls, Judges of the supreme Court, and all other Officers of the United

*Superseded by the Twelfth Amendment.
†Affected by the Twenty-fifth Amendment.

States, whose Appointments are not herein otherwise provided for, and which shall be established by Law; but the Congress may by Law vest the Appointment of such inferior Officers, as they think proper, in the President alone, in the Courts of Law, or in the Heads of Departments.

[3] The President shall have Power to fill up all Vacancies that may happen during the Recess of the Senate, by granting Commissions which shall expire at the End of their next Session.

SECTION. 3. He shall from time to time give to the Congress Information of the State of the Union, and recommend to their Consideration such Measures as he shall judge necessary and expedient; he may, on extraordinary Occasions, convene both Houses, or either of them, and in Case of Disagreement between them, with Respect to the Time of Adjournment, he may adjourn them to such Time as he shall think proper; he shall receive Ambassadors and other public Ministers; he shall take Care that the Laws be faithfully executed, and shall Commission all the Officers of the United States.

SECTION. 4. The President, Vice President and all civil Officers of the United States, shall be removed from Office on Impeachment for, and Conviction of, Treason, Bribery, or other high Crimes and Misdemeanors.

ARTICLE. III.

SECTION. 1. The judicial Power of the United States, shall be vested in one supreme Court, and in such inferior Courts as the Congress may from time to time ordain and establish. The Judges, both of the supreme and inferior Courts, shall hold their Offices during good Behaviour, and shall, at stated Times, receive for their Services, a Compensation, which shall not be diminished during their Continuance in Office.

SECTION. 2. [1] The judicial Power shall extend to all Cases, in Law and Equity, arising under this Constitution, the Laws of the United States, and Treaties made, or which shall be made, under their Authority;—to all Cases affecting Ambassadors, other public Ministers and Consuls;—to all Cases of admiralty and maritime Jurisdiction;—to Controversies to which the United States shall be a Party;—to Controversies between two or more States;—between a State and Citizens of another State;*—between Citizens of different States;—between citizens of the same State claiming lands under Grants of different States, and between a State, or the Citizens thereof, and foreign States, Citizens or Subjects.

[2] In all Cases affecting Ambassadors, other public Ministers and Consuls, and those in which a State shall be Party, the supreme Court shall have original Jurisdiction. In all the other Cases before mentioned, the supreme Court shall have appellate Jurisdiction, both as to Law and Fact, with such Exceptions, and under such Regulations as the Congress shall make.

[3] The Trial of all Crimes, except in Cases of Impeachment, shall be by Jury; and such Trial shall be held in the State where the said Crimes shall have been committed; but when not committed within any State, the Trial shall be at such Place or Places as the Congress may by Law have directed.

SECTION. 3. [1] Treason against the United States, shall consist only in levying War against them, or in adhering to their Enemies, giving them Aid and Comfort. No person shall be convicted of Treason unless on the Testimony of two Witnesses to the same overt Act, or on Confession in open Court.

[2] The Congress shall have Power to declare the Punishment of Treason, but no Attainder of Treason shall work Corruption of Blood, or Forfeiture except during the Life of the Person attainted.

---

*Affected by the Eleventh Amendment.

ARTICLE. IV

SECTION. 1. Full Faith and Credit shall be given in each State to the public Acts, Records, and judicial Proceedings of every other State. And the Congress may by general Laws prescribe the Manner in which such Acts, Records and Proceedings shall be proved, and the Effect thereof.

SECTION. 2. [1] The Citizens of each State shall be entitled to all Privileges and Immunities of Citizens in the several States.

[2] A Person charged in any State with Treason, Felony, or other Crime, who shall flee from Justice, and be found in another State, shall on Demand of the executive Authority of the State from which he fled, be delivered up, to be removed to the State having Jurisdiction of the Crime.

[3] [No Person held to Service or Labour in one State, under the Laws thereof, escaping into another, shall, in Consequence of any Law or Regulation therein, be discharged from such Service or Labour, but shall be delivered up on Claim of the Party to whom such Service or Labour may be due.]†

SECTION. 3. [1] New States may be admitted by the Congress into this Union; but no new State shall be formed or erected within the Jurisdiction of any other State; nor any State be formed by the Junction of two or more States, or Parts of States, without the Consent of the Legislatures of the States concerned as well as of the Congress.

[2] The Congress shall have Power to dispose of and make all needful Rules and Regulations respecting the Territory or other Property belonging to the United States; and nothing in this Constitution shall be so construed as to Prejudice any Claims of the United States, or of any particular State.

SECTION. 4. The United States shall guarantee to every State in this Union a Republican Form of Government, and shall protect each of them against Invasion; and on Application of the Legislature, or of the Executive (when the Legislature cannot be convened) against domestic Violence.

ARTICLE. V.

The Congress, whenever two thirds of both Houses shall deem it necessary, shall propose Amendments to this Constitution, or, on the Application of the Legislatures of two thirds of the several States, shall call a Convention for proposing Amendments, which, in either Case, shall be valid to all Intents and Purposes, as Part of this Constitution, when ratified by the Legislatures of three fourths of the several States, or by Conventions in three fourths thereof, as the one or the other Mode of Ratification may be proposed by the Congress; Provided that no Amendment which may be made prior to the Year One thousand eight hundred and eight shall in any Manner affect the first and fourth Clauses in the Ninth Section of the first Article; and that no State, without its Consent, shall be deprived of its equal Suffrage in the Senate.

ARTICLE. VI

[1] All Debts contracted and Engagements entered into, before the Adoption of this Constitution, shall be as valid against the United States under this Constitution, as under the Confederation.

[2] This Constitution, and the Laws of the United States which shall be made in Pursuance thereof; and all Treaties made, or which shall be made, under the Authority of the United States, shall be the supreme Law of the Land; and the Judges in every State shall be bound thereby, any Thing in the Constitution or Laws of any State to the Contrary notwithstanding.

[3] The Senators and Representatives before mentioned, and the Members of the several

†Superseded by the Thirteenth Amendment.

State Legislatures, and all executive and judicial Officers, both of the United States and of the several States, shall be bound by Oath or Affirmation, to support this Constitution; but no religious Test shall ever be required as a Qualification to any Office or public Trust under the United States.

ARTICLE. VII

The Ratification of the Conventions of nine States, shall be sufficient for the Establishment of this Constitution between the States so ratifying the Same.

ARTICLES IN ADDITION TO, AND AMENDMENT OF, THE CONSTITUTION OF THE UNITED STATES OF AMERICA, PROPOSED BY CONGRESS, AND RATIFIED BY THE LEGISLATURES OF THE SEVERAL STATES PURSUANT TO THE FIFTH ARTICLE OF THE ORIGINAL CONSTITUTION.

ARTICLE I

Congress shall make no law respecting an establishment of religion, or prohibiting the free exercise thereof; or abridging the freedom of speech, or of the press; or of the right of the people peaceably to assemble, and to petition the Government for a redress of grievances.

ARTICLE II

A well regulated Militia, being necessary to the security of a free State, the right of the people to keep and bear Arms, shall not be infringed.

ARTICLE III

No Soldier shall, in time of peace be quartered in any house, without the consent of the Owner, nor in time of war, but in a manner to be prescribed by law.

ARTICLE IV

The right of the people to be secure in their persons, houses, papers, and effects, against unreasonable searches and seizures, shall not be violated, and no Warrants shall issue, but upon probable cause, supported by Oath or affirmation, and particularly describing the place to be searched, and the persons or things to be seized.

ARTICLE V

No person shall be held to answer for a capital, or otherwise infamous crime, unless on a presentment or indictment of a Grand Jury, except in cases arising in the land or naval forces, or in the Militia, when in actual service in time of War or public danger; nor shall any person be subject for the same offence to be twice put in jeopardy of life or limb; nor shall be compelled in any criminal case to be a witness against himself, nor be deprived of life, liberty, or property, without due process of law; nor shall private property be taken for public use without just compensation.

ARTICLE VI

In all criminal prosecutions, the accused shall enjoy the right to a speedy and public trial, by an impartial jury of the State and district wherein the crime shall have been committed, which district shall have been previously ascertained by law, and to be informed of the nature and cause of the accusation; to be confronted with the witnesses against him; to have compulsory process for obtaining Witnesses in his favor, and to have the assistance of counsel for his defence.

ARTICLE VII

In Suits at common law, where the value in controversy shall exceed twenty dollars, the right of trial by jury shall be preserved, and no fact tried by a jury, shall be otherwise reexamined in any Court of the United States, than according to the rules of the common law.

ARTICLE VIII

Excessive bail shall not be required, nor excessive fines imposed, nor cruel and unusual punishments inflicted.

ARTICLE IX

The enumeration in the Constitution, of certain rights, shall not be construed to deny or disparage others retained by the people.

ARTICLE X

The powers not delegated to the United States by the Constitution, nor prohibited by it to the States, are reserved to the States respectively, or to the people.

[The first ten amendments to the Constitution, and two others that failed of ratification, were proposed by the Congress on *September 25, 1789*. Ratification was completed on *December 15, 1791*.]

ARTICLE XI

The Judicial power of the United States shall not be construed to extend to any suit in law or equity, commenced or prosecuted against one of the United States by Citizens of another State, or by Citizens or Subjects of any Foreign State.

[The Eleventh amendment to the Constitution was proposed by the Congress on *March 4, 1794*. Ratification was completed on *February 7, 1795*.]

ARTICLE XII

The electors shall meet in their respective states and vote by ballot for President and Vice-President, one of whom, at least, shall not be an inhabitant of the same state with themselves; they shall name in their ballots the person voted for as President, and in distinct ballots the person voted for as Vice-President, and they shall make distinct lists of all persons voted for as President, and of all persons voted for as Vice-President, and of the number of votes for each, which lists they shall sign and certify, and transmit sealed to the seat of the government of the United States, directed to the President of the Senate;—The President of the Senate shall, in the presence of the Senate and House of Representatives, open all the certificates and the votes shall then be counted;—The person having the greatest number of votes for President, shall be the President, if such a number be a majority of the whole number of Electors appointed; and if no person have such majority, then from the persons having the highest numbers not exceeding three on the list of those voted for as President, the House of Representatives shall choose immediately, by ballot, the President. But in choosing the President, the votes shall be taken by states, the representation from each state having one vote; a quorum for this purpose shall consist of a member or members from two-thirds of the states, and a majority of all the states shall be necessary to a choice. [And if the House of Representatives shall not choose a President whenever the right of choice shall devolve upon them, before the fourth day of March next, following, then the Vice-President shall act as President, as in the case of death or other constitutional disability of the President.]* The person having the greatest number of votes as Vice-President, shall be the Vice-President, if such number be a majority of the whole number of Electors appointed, and if no person have a majority, then from the two highest numbers on the list, the Senate shall choose the Vice-President; a quorum for the purpose shall consist of two-thirds of the whole number of Senators, and a majority of the whole number shall be necessary to a choice. But no person constitutionally ineligible to the office of President shall be eligible to that of Vice-President of the United States.

[The Twelfth Amendment to the Constitution was proposed by the Congress on *December 9, 1803*. Ratification was completed on *June 15, 1804*.]

ARTICLE XIII

SECTION 1. Neither slavery nor involuntary servitude, except as a punishment for crime whereof the party shall have been duly convicted, shall exist within the United States, or any place subject to their jurisdiction.

SECTION 2. Congress shall have power to enforce this article by appropriate legislation.

[The Thirteenth Amendment to the Constitution was proposed by the Congress on *January 31, 1865*. Ratification was completed on *December 6, 1865*.]

ARTICLE XIV

SECTION 1. All persons born or naturalized in the United States, and subject to the jurisdiction thereof, are citizens of the United States and of the State wherein they reside. No State shall make or enforce any law which shall abridge the privileges or immunities of citizens of the United States; nor shall any State deprive any person of life, liberty, or property, without due process of law; nor deny to any person within its jurisdiction the equal protection of the laws.

SECTION 2. Representatives shall be apportioned among the several States according to their respective numbers, counting the whole number of persons in each State, excluding Indians not taxed. But when the right to vote at any election for the choice of electors for President and Vice President of the United States, Representatives in Congress, the Executive and Judicial officers of a State, or the members of the Legislature thereof, is denied to any of the male inhabitants of such State, being twenty-one years of age, and citizens of the United States, or in any way abridged, except for participation in rebellion, or other crime, the basis of representation therein shall be reduced in the proportion which the number of such male citizens shall bear to the whole number of male citizens twenty-one years of age in such State.

SECTION 3. No person shall be a Senator or Representative in Congress, or elector of President and Vice President, or hold any office, civil or military, under the United States, or under any State, who, having previously taken an oath, as a member of Congress, or as an officer of the United States, or as a member of any State legislature, or as an executive or judicial officer of any State, to support the Constitution of the United States, shall have engaged in insurrection or rebellion against the same, or given aid or comfort to the enemies thereof. But Congress may by a vote of two-thirds of each House, remove such disability.

SECTION 4. The validity of the public debt of the United States, authorized by law, including debts incurred for payment of pensions and bounties for services in suppressing insurrection or rebellion, shall not be questioned. But neither the United States nor any State

*Superseded by Section 3 of the Twentieth Amendment.

shall assume or pay any debt or obligation incurred in aid of insurrection or rebellion against the United States, or any claim for the loss or emancipation of any slave; but all such debts, obligations and claims shall be held illegal and void.

SECTION 5. The Congress shall have power to enforce, by appropriate legislation, the provisions of this article.

[The Fourteenth Amendment to the Constitution was proposed by the Congress on *June 13, 1866*. Ratification was completed on *July 9, 1868*.]

ARTICLE XV

SECTION 1. The right of citizens of the United States to vote shall not be denied or abridged by the United States or by any State on account of race, color, or previous condition of servitude.

SECTION 2. The Congress shall have power to enforce this article by appropriate legislation.

[The Fifteenth Amendment to the Constitution was proposed by the Congress on *February 26, 1869*. Ratification was completed on *February 3, 1870*, unless the withdrawal of ratification by New York was effective; in which event ratification was completed on *February 17, 1870*, when Nebraska ratified.]

ARTICLE XVI

The Congress shall have power to lay and collect taxes on incomes, from whatever source derived, without apportionment among the several States, and without regard to any census or enumeration.

[The Sixteenth Amendment to the Constitution was proposed by the Congress on *July 12, 1909*. Ratification was completed on *February 3, 1913*.]

ARTICLE XVII

The Senate of the United States shall be composed of two Senators from each State, elected by the people thereof, for six years; and each Senator shall have one vote. The electors in each State shall have the qualifications requisite for electors of the most numerous branch of the State legislatures.

When vacancies happen in the representation of any State in the Senate, the executive authority of such State shall issue writs of election to fill such vacancies: *Provided,* That the legislature of any State may empower the executive thereof to make temporary appointments until the people fill the vacancies by election as the legislature may direct.

This amendment shall not be so construed as to affect the election or term of any Senator chosen before it becomes valid as part of the Constitution.

[The Seventeenth Amendment to the Constitution was proposed by the Congress on *May 13, 1912*. Ratification was completed on *April 8, 1913*.]

ARTICLE XVIII

[SECTION 1. After one year from the ratification of this article the manufacture, sale, or transportation of intoxicating liquors within, the importation thereof into, or the exportation thereof from the United States and all territory subject to the jurisdiction thereof for beverage purposes is hereby prohibited.

[SECTION 2. The Congress and the several States shall have concurrent power to enforce this article by appropriate legislation.

[SECTION 3. This article shall be inoperative unless it shall have been ratified as an amendment to the Constitution by the legislatures of the several States, as provided in the Constitution, within seven years from the date of the submission hereof to the States by the Congress]*

[The Eighteenth Amendment to the Constitution was proposed by the Congress on *December 18, 1917*. Ratification was completed on *January 16, 1919*.]

ARTICLE XIX

The right of citizens of the United States to vote shall not be denied or abridged by the United States or by any State on account of sex.

Congress shall have power to enforce this article by appropriate legislation.

[The Nineteenth Amendment to the Constitution was proposed by the Congress on *June 4, 1919*. Ratification was completed on *August 20, 1920*.]

ARTICLE XX

SECTION 1. The terms of the President and Vice President shall end at noon on the 20th day of January, and the terms of Senators and Representatives at noon on the 3d day of January, of the years in which such terms would have ended if this article had not been ratified; and the terms of their successors shall then begin.

SECTION 2. The Congress shall assemble at least once in every year, and such meeting shall begin at noon on the 3d day of January, unless they shall by law appoint a different day.

SECTION 3. If, at the time fixed for the beginning of the term of the President, the President elect shall have died, the Vice President elect shall become President. If a President shall not have been chosen before the time fixed for the beginning of his term, or if the President elect shall have failed to qualify, then the Vice President elect shall act as President until a President shall have qualified; and the Congress may by law provide for the case wherein neither a President elect nor a Vice President elect shall have qualified, declaring who shall then act as President, or the manner in which one who is to act shall be elected, and such person shall act accordingly until a President or Vice President shall have qualified.

SECTION 4. The Congress may by law provide for the case of the death of any of the persons from whom the House of Representatives may choose a President whenever the right of choice shall have devolved upon them, and for the case of the death of any of the persons from whom the Senate may choose a Vice President whenever the right of choice shall have devolved upon them.

SECTION 5. Sections 1 and 2 shall take effect on the 15th day of October following the ratification of this article.

SECTION 6. This article shall be inoperative unless it shall have been ratified as an amendment to the Constitution by the legislatures of three-fourths of the several States seven years from the date of its submission.

[The Twentieth Amendment to the Constitution was proposed by the Congress on *March 2, 1932*. Ratification was completed on *January 23, 1933*.]

ARTICLE XXI

SECTION 1. The eighteenth article of amendment to the Constitution of the United States is hereby repealed.

SECTION 2. The transportation or importation into any State, Territory, or possession of

*Repealed by Section 1 of the Twenty-first Amendment.

the United States for delivery or use therein of intoxicating liquors, in violation of the laws thereof, is hereby prohibited.

SECTION 3. This article shall be inoperative unless it shall have been ratified as an amendment to the Constitution by conventions in the several States, as provided in the Constitution, within seven years from the date of the submission hereof to the States by the Congress.

[The Twenty-first Amendment to the Constitution was proposed by the Congress on *February 20, 1933*. Ratification was completed on *December 5, 1933*.]

ARTICLE XXII

SECTION 1. No person shall be elected to the office of the President more than twice, and no person who has held the office of President, or acted as President, for more than two years of a term to which some other person was elected President shall be elected to the office of the President more than once. But this Article shall not apply to any person holding the office of President when this Article was proposed by the Congress, and shall not prevent any person who may be holding the office of President, or acting as President, during the term within which this Article becomes operative from holding the office of President or acting as President during the remainder of such term.

SECTION 2. This article shall be inoperative unless it shall have been ratified as an amendment to the Constitution by the legislatures of three-fourths of the several States within seven years from the date of its submission to the States by the Congress.

[The Twenty-second Amendment to the Constitution was proposed by the Congress on *March 21, 1947*. Ratification was completed on *February 27, 1951*.]

ARTICLE XXIII

SECTION 1. The District constituting the seat of Government of the United States shall appoint in such manner as the Congress may direct:

A number of electors of President and Vice President equal to the whole number of Senators and Representatives in Congress to which the District would be entitled if it were a State, but in no event more than the least populous State; they shall be in addition to those appointed by the States, but they shall be considered, for the purposes of the election of President and Vice President, to be electors appointed by a State; and they shall meet in the District and perform such duties as provided by the twelfth article of amendment.

SECTION 2. The Congress shall have power to enforce this article by appropriate legislation.

[The Twenty-third Amendment to the Constitution was proposed by the Congress on *June 17, 1960*. Ratification was completed on *March 29, 1961*.]

ARTICLE XXIV

SECTION 1. The right of citizens of the United States to vote in any primary or other election for President or Vice President, for electors for President or Vice President, or for Senator or Representative in Congress, shall not be denied or abridged by the United States or any State by reason of failure to pay any poll tax or other tax.

SECTION 2. The Congress shall have power to enforce this article by appropriate legislation.

[The Twenty-fourth Amendment to the Constitution was proposed by the Congress on *August 27, 1962*. Ratification was completed on *January 23, 1964*.]

ARTICLE XXV

SECTION 1. In case of the removal of the President from office or of his death or resignation, the Vice President shall become President.

SECTION 2. Whenever there is a vacancy in the office of the Vice President, the President shall nominate a Vice President who shall take office upon confirmation by a majority vote of both Houses of Congress.

SECTION 3. Whenever the President transmits to the President pro tempore of the Senate and the Speaker of the House of Representatives his written declaration that he is unable to discharge the powers and duties of his office, and until he transmits to them a written declaration to the contrary, such powers and duties shall be discharged by the Vice President as Acting President.

SECTION. 4. Whenever the Vice President and a majority of either the principal officers of the executive departments or of such other body as Congress may by law provide, transmit to the President pro tempore of the Senate and the Speaker of the House of Representatives their written declaration that the President is unable to discharge the powers and duties of his office, the Vice President shall immediately assume the powers and duties of the office as Acting President.

Thereafter, when the President transmits to the President pro tempore of the Senate and the Speaker of the House of Representatives his written declaration that no inability exists, he shall resume the powers and duties of his office unless the Vice President and a majority of either the principal officers of the executive department or of such other body as Congress may by law provide, transmit within four days to the President pro tempore of the Senate and the Speaker of the House of Representatives their written declaration that the President is unable to discharge the powers and duties of his office. Thereupon Congress shall decide the issue, assembling within forty-eight hours for that purpose if not in session. If the Congress, within twenty-one days after receipt of the latter written declaration, or, if Congress is not in session, within twenty-one days after Congress is required to assemble, determines by two-thirds vote of both Houses that the President is unable to discharge the powers and duties of his office, the Vice President shall continue to discharge the same as Acting President; otherwise. the President shall resume the powers and duties of his office.

[The Twenty-fifth Amendment to the Constitution was proposed by the Congress on *July 6, 1965*. Ratification was completed on *February 10, 1967*.]

ARTICLE XXVI

SECTION 1. The right of citizens of the United States, who are eighteen years of age or older, to vote shall not be denied or abridged by the United States or by any State on account of age.

SECTION 2. The Congress shall have power to enforce this article by appropriate legislation.

[The Twenty-sixth Amendment was proposed by the Congress on *March 23, 1971*. Ratification was completed on *July 5, 1971*.]

Index of Cases